# DATE DUE

|  |  |  |  |
|---|---|---|---|
|  |  |  |  |
|  |  |  |  |
|  |  |  |  |
|  |  |  |  |
|  |  |  |  |
|  |  |  |  |
|  |  |  |  |
|  |  |  |  |
|  |  |  |  |
|  |  |  |  |
|  |  |  |  |
|  |  |  |  |
|  |  |  |  |
|  |  |  |  |
|  |  |  |  |
|  |  |  |  |
|  |  |  |  |
|  |  |  |  |
|  |  |  |  |
|  |  |  | PRINTED IN U.S.A. |

# LITERARY HISTORY
OF THE
# UNITED STATES:

*BIBLIOGRAPHY*

# LITERARY HISTORY
## OF THE
# UNITED STATES:

*BIBLIOGRAPHY*

*Editors*
ROBERT E. SPILLER · WILLARD THORP
THOMAS H. JOHNSON · HENRY SEIDEL CANBY
RICHARD M. LUDWIG · WILLIAM M. GIBSON

**FOURTH EDITION: REVISED**

MACMILLAN PUBLISHING CO., INC.
NEW YORK

COLLIER MACMILLAN PUBLISHERS
LONDON

First Printing 1974

Published in Two Volumes

Macmillan Publishing Co., Inc.
866 Third Avenue, New York, N.Y. 10022
Collier-Macmillan Canada Ltd.

Printed in the United States of America

Library of Congress Catalog Card Number 73–14014

# PREFACE

The selective bibliographies herein assembled are an integral part of the text of the History, and their organization has been determined by its form and content. At the same time, their scope is not limited by that fact. They are intended as a guide to the present state of resources and scholarship in American literary culture. Though descriptive in nature, they constitute a factual history in which a theory of criticism is implicit in the arrangement.

The essays are organized in four main sections, and the Table of Contents indicates the details of treatment. The three sections which follow the first, the Guide to Resources, are dependent upon it, for the Guide is a basic reference tool without which the other sections cannot be used to full advantage.

The bibliographies on literary history and criticism, movements and influences, parallel themes developed in the text, and suggest sources for studies which lie ahead. Some essays, such as those on the American language and on Indian lore, follow given chapters very closely. Others, notably the extended essays on the frontier, on regionalism, and on cultural background, incorporate material pertinent to several chapters, and have been constructed with the aid of many collaborators. The selection of authors and titles, and the criticism implied in the arrangement of such compilations, however arbitrary, is based on the judgment of experts. The essays on mingling of tongues and on American books abroad gather such material as at present is recommended for study in fields that still await full exploitation. The dependence here on the aid of specialists was especially necessary. The themes of romanticism, realism, puritanism, and democracy, often singled out in histories of American literature, are not here treated separately. The material on these topics cuts through many essays, and has been drawn out under appropriate headings in the index.

The bibliographies by period and type serve as guides to the literary forms, social criticism, cultural history, and the instruments peculiar to various eras. They suffer some distortion in that they depend more heavily than other sections upon cross-reference.

The two hundred and seven individual author bibliographies furnish information on separate and collected works, edited texts and reprints, biography and criticism, primary sources (including manuscript location), and bibliographies. No attempt is made to arrange them in major and minor groups. The listing is alphabetical, and the length of the entries, though chiefly determined by the importance of the authors, reflects in part the quality of critical studies that deal with them. The citing of an author's own works is pointed toward the more important productions, and does not attempt to be definitive with respect to separates, magazine pieces, and ephemera.

Although entries in the several essays are sometimes repeated in the interest of logic and clarity, the duplication is kept to a minimum by the cross-reference already alluded to, and by the index, which serves as an author and subject guide. Since topical bibliographies on fiction, poetry, and drama are not assembled in single essays, the index together with the table of contents will reveal their many ramifications.

The citation herein of critical books and articles, and the comment upon them, constitute acknowledgment of indebtedness, and take the place of reference notes in the text.

The coverage, within the limits of selectivity, attempts to be complete through 1946. In general, unpublished theses have not been included, though some are entered because they have been specifically recommended. The listing of manuscript collections includes only those in public depositories, since collections in private hands are subject to change and often are not available to scholars.

The compilation of the bibliographies was made possible by the advice of the scholars and critics who collaborated in writing the History, and whose names are recorded elsewhere. Further aid was generously given by Charles R. Anderson, Paul M. Angle, Julian P. Boyd, Henry W. Bragdon, James T. Farrell, Charles Shaw, Carl G. Stroven, and Lawrence C. Wroth. The report of its Committee on Materials for Research in American Literary History was made available by the American Literature Group of the Modern Language Association. The published bibliographies and reference texts of Jacob Blanck, James D. Hart, Harry Hartwick, and Fred B. Millett proved constantly useful. The entire volume was checked in manuscript by Gerrish Thurber and Howard Gibson.

December, 1947

# THE THIRD EDITION

In 1948, the first 790 pages of this volume were published as the third (Bibliography) volume of *Literary History of the United States*. In 1959, a supplement of 268 pages was published as a separate volume. These two books are here combined into one to form the second volume of this third edition of the total work.

Except for a few corrections and the omission of the index, the 1948 volume is reprinted here as it appeared originally. It is followed by the 1959 Supplement, with its original Preface and no change in pagination. A new index incorporates references to both parts, those to the original Bibliography in lightface and those to the Supplement in boldface.

Although all bibliographies in the *Literary History* are, like the text, the responsibility of the Editorial Board as a whole rather than of any individual, Thomas H. Johnson undertook the principal work of compilation and editing of the original Bibliography and Richard M. Ludwig of the Supplement. Willard Thorp undertook a similar responsibility for the text of the *History* and Robert E. Spiller was Chairman of the Editorial Board throughout. Henry S. Canby was senior adviser.

February, 1963

# THE FOURTH EDITION

I<small>N</small> 1963, the first 790 pages of this volume were combined with a bibliographical supplement of 268 pages that had been published as a separate volume in 1959. At that time, no attempt was made to repage the whole book or to remake the index. In 1972, a second bibliography supplement appeared, again as a separate volume of 366 pages.

For this fourth edition, we have corrected errors in all three texts, combined the three tables of contents, repaged both supplements, and prepared an entirely new and enlarged index for the convenience of the users of this book. Thomas H. Johnson compiled and edited the original Bibliography, and Richard M. Ludwig the first and second Supplements; but as with the first volume of this *Literary History*, the Editorial Board as a whole bears responsibility for this new edition.

May, 1973

# CONTENTS

## GUIDE TO RESOURCES

CONTENTS xvii

## BIBLIOGRAPHIES: MOVEMENTS AND INFLUENCES

# BIBLIOGRAPHIES: INDIVIDUAL AUTHORS

# BIBLIOGRAPHIES: ADDITIONAL
# INDIVIDUAL AUTHORS

# KEY TO ABBREVIATIONS

| | |
|---|---|
| *AAUP* | American Association of University Professors Bulletin |
| *ABC* | American Book Collector |
| *ABR* | American Benedictine Review |
| *AER* | American Ecclesiastical Review |
| *AH* | American Heritage |
| *AHeb* | American Hebrew |
| *AHR* | American Historical Review |
| *AI* | American Imago |
| *AION-SG* | Annali Istituto Universitario Orientale, Napoli, Sezione Germanica |
| *AJA* | American Jewish Archives |
| *AJES* | American Journal of Economics and Sociology |
| *AKG* | Archiv für Kulturgeschichte (Marburg) |
| *AL* | American Literature |
| *AlaR* | Alabama Review |
| *ALR* | American Literary Realism, 1870–1910 |
| *AmF* | The Americas (Academy of American Franciscan History, Washington, D.C.) |
| *AmMerc* | American Mercury |
| *AmPol SciRev* | American Political Science Review |
| *AN* | Acta Neophilologica (Ljubljana) |
| *AN&Q* | American Notes and Queries |
| *AQ* | American Quarterly |
| *AR* | Antioch Review |
| *ArHQ* | Arkansas Historical Quarterly |
| *ArlQ* | Arlington Quarterly |
| *ArQ* | Arizona Quarterly |
| *AS* | American Speech |
| *ASch* | American Scholar |
| *ASEER* | American Slavic and East European Review |
| *ASR* | American-Scandinavian Review |
| *Atl* | Atlantic Monthly |
| *AUMLA* | Journal of the Australasian Universities Modern Language and Literature Association |

| | |
|---|---|
| *BA* | Books Abroad |
| *BAASB* | British Association for American Studies Bulletin |
| *BaR* | Bard Review |
| *BB* | Bulletin of Bibliography |
| *BBr* | Books at Brown |
| *BCMVASA* | Bulletin of the Central Mississippi Valley American Studies Association |
| *BFHA* | Bulletin of the Friends Historical Association |
| *BHPSO* | Bulletin of the Historical and Philosophical Society of Ohio |
| *BNYPL* | Bulletin of the New York Public Library |
| *BPLQ* | Boston Public Library Quarterly |
| *BSTCF* | Ball State Teachers College Forum |
| *BSUF* | Ball State University Forum |
| *BuR* | Bucknell Review |
| *BUSE* | Boston University Studies in English |
| *BYUS* | Brigham Young University Studies |
| | |
| *CaQ* | Carolina Quarterly |
| *CathHR* | Catholic Historical Review |
| *CathW* | Catholic World |
| *CCC* | College Composition and Communication |
| *CE* | College English |
| *CEAAN* | Center for Editions of American Authors Newsletter (MLA) |
| *CentR* | Centennial Review |
| *CH* | Church History |
| *ChiR* | Chicago Review |
| *Chri Century* | Christian Century |
| *CHSQ* | California Historical Society Quarterly |
| *CJ* | Classical Journal |
| *CJF* | Chicago Jewish Forum |
| *CL* | Comparative Literature |
| *CLAJ* | College Language Association Journal |
| *ClareQ* | Claremont Quarterly |
| *CLC* | Columbia Library Columns |
| *CLQ* | Colby Library Quarterly |
| *CLS* | Comparative Literature Studies |
| *CM* | Cornhill Magazine |
| *ColQ* | Colorado Quarterly |

| | |
|---|---|
| *Com* | Commentary |
| *CompD* | Comparative Drama |
| *ConL* | Contemporary Literature |
| *ConnR* | Connecticut Review |
| *ConR* | Contemporary Review |
| *CP* | Concerning Poetry |
| *CRB* | Cahiers de la Compagnie Madeleine Renaud-Jean-Louis Barrault (Paris) |
| *Crit* | Critique: Studies in Modern Fiction |
| *CritQ* | Critical Quarterly |
| *CRL* | College and Research Libraries |
| *CUF* | Columbia University Forum |
| *Cweal* | Commonweal |
| | |
| *DM* | Dublin Magazine |
| *DownR* | Downside Review |
| *DR* | Dalhousie Review |
| *DramS* | Drama Survey |
| *DULN* | Duke University Library Notes |
| | |
| *EA* | Études Anglaises (Paris) |
| *EAL* | Early American Literature |
| *EALN* | Early American Literature Newsletter |
| *ECS* | Eighteenth-Century Studies |
| *EDH* | Essays by Divers Hands |
| *EIC* | Essays in Criticism (Oxford) |
| *EIHC* | Essex Institute Historical Collections |
| *EJ* | English Journal |
| *EL* | Educational Leader |
| *ELH* | Journal of English Literary History |
| *ELN* | English Language Notes |
| *EM* | English Miscellany |
| *ES* | English Studies (Groningen) |
| *ESA* | English Studies in Africa (Johannesburg) |
| *ESQ* | Emerson Society Quarterly |
| *ESRS* | Emporia State Research Studies |
| *ETJ* | Educational Theatre Journal |
| *EUQ* | Emory University Quarterly |
| *EWR* | East-West Review (Kyoto) |
| | |
| *FAR* | French-American Review |
| *FCHQ* | Filson Club Historical Quarterly |

| | |
|---|---|
| *FeL* | Filologia e Letteratura (Naples) |
| *FH* | Frankfurter Hefte |
| *FHA* | Fitzgerald-Hemingway Annual |
| *FHS* | French Historical Studies |
| *ForumH* | Forum (Houston) |
| *FurmS* | Furman Studies |
| | |
| *GaR* | Georgia Review |
| *GHQ* | Georgia Historical Quarterly |
| *GMHC* | General Magazine and Historical Chronicle |
| *GR* | Germanic Review |
| | |
| *HAB* | Humanities Association Bulletin (Canada) |
| *HAHR* | Hispanic American Historical Review |
| *HC* | Hollins Critic |
| *HJ* | Hibbert Journal |
| *HJAS* | Harvard Journal of Asiatic Studies |
| *HLB* | Harvard Library Bulletin |
| *HLQ* | Huntington Library Quarterly |
| *HR* | Hispanic Review |
| *HTR* | Harvard Theological Review |
| *HudR* | Hudson Review |
| *HumB* | Humanitas (Brescia) |
| | |
| *IAC* | Indo-Asian Culture |
| *IEY* | Iowa English Yearbook |
| *IMH* | Indiana Magazine of History |
| *ISHSJ* | Illinois State Historical Society Journal |
| *Ital* | Italica |
| *IUB* | Indiana University Bookman |
| | |
| *JA* | Jahrbuch für Amerikastudien (Heidelberg) |
| *JAAC* | Journal of Aesthetics and Art Criticism |
| *JAH* | Journal of American History |
| *JAmS* | Journal of American Studies |
| *JEGP* | Journal of English and Germanic Philology |
| *JFI* | Journal of the Franklin Institute |
| *JGE* | Journal of General Education |
| *JHI* | Journal of the History of Ideas |
| *JHS* | Journal of Historical Studies |
| *JISHS* | Journal of the Illinois State Historical Society |
| *JML* | Journal of Modern Literature |

| | |
|---|---|
| *JNE* | Journal of Negro Education |
| *JNH* | Journal of Negro History |
| *JP* | Journal of Philosophy |
| *JPC* | Journal of Popular Culture |
| *JPol* | Journal of Politics |
| *JQ* | Journalism Quarterly |
| *JR* | Journal of Religion |
| *JRUL* | Journal of Rutgers University Library |
| *JSH* | Journal of Southern History |
| | |
| *KAL* | Kyushu American Literature (Fukuoka) |
| *KFLQ* | Kentucky Foreign Language Quarterly |
| *KFQ* | Keystone Folklore Quarterly |
| *KR* | Kenyon Review |
| *KSHSR* | Kentucky State Historical Society Register |
| *KyR* | Kentucky Review |
| | |
| *L&P* | Literature and Psychology |
| *LangQ* | Language Quarterly |
| *LanM* | Les Langues Modernes (Paris) |
| *LaS* | Louisiana Studies |
| *LauR* | Laurel Review |
| *LCrit* | Literary Criterion (Mysore) |
| *LCQJ* | Library of Congress Quarterly Journal |
| *LCUT* | Library Chronicle of the University of Texas |
| *LE&W* | Literature East and West |
| *LetN* | Lettres Nouvelles (Paris) |
| *LH* | Lincoln Herald |
| *LHQ* | Louisiana Historical Quarterly |
| *LHR* | Lock Haven Review |
| *Lit* | Literature |
| *LitR* | Literary Review |
| *LJ* | Library Journal |
| *LonM* | London Magazine |
| *LP* | Literature and Psychology |
| *LQ* | Library Quarterly |
| | |
| *M-A* | Mid-America |
| *MAQR* | Michigan Alumnus Quarterly Review |
| *MAR* | Manitoba Arts Review |
| *MASJ* | Midcontinent American Studies Journal |

| | |
|---|---|
| McNR | McNeese Review |
| MCR | Melbourne Critical Review |
| MD | Modern Drama |
| MdF | Mercure de France (Paris) |
| MF | Midwest Folklore |
| MFS | Modern Fiction Studies |
| Mid | Midstream |
| MidR | Midwest Review |
| MH | Minnesota History |
| MHM | Maryland Historical Magazine |
| MHSB | Missouri Historical Society Bulletin |
| MinnR | Minnesota Review |
| MissQ | Mississippi Quarterly |
| MJ | Midwest Journal |
| MLN | Modern Language Notes |
| MLQ | Modern Language Quarterly |
| MLR | Modern Language Review |
| MM | Masses and Mainstream |
| ModA | Modern Age |
| MP | Modern Philology |
| MQ | Midwest Quarterly |
| MQR | Michigan Quarterly Review |
| MR | Massachusetts Review |
| MSE | Massachusetts Studies in English |
| MSpr | Moderna Språk (Stockholm) |
| MSS | Manuscripts |
| MTJ | Mark Twain Journal |
| MTQ | Mark Twain Quarterly |
| MuK | Maske und Kothurn (Graz-Vienna) |
| MVHR | Mississippi Valley Historical Review |
| | |
| NALF | Negro American Literature Forum |
| N&Q | Notes and Queries |
| NAR | North American Review |
| NAS | Norwegian-American Studies |
| NC | Nuova Corrente (Genoa) |
| NCF | Nineteenth-Century Fiction |
| NCHR | North Carolina Historical Review |
| NDQ | North Dakota Quarterly |
| NEGHR | New England Genealogical and Historical Register |
| NegroD | Negro Digest |

| | |
|---|---|
| *NEQ* | New England Quarterly |
| *NewCol* | New Colophon |
| *NLB* | Newberry Library Bulletin |
| *NMQ* | New Mexico Quarterly |
| *NOQ* | Northwest Ohio Quarterly |
| *NR* | New Republic |
| *NRF* | Nouvelle Revue Française (Paris) |
| *NS* | Die Neueren Sprachen (Marburg) |
| *NSammlung* | Neue Sammlung (Göttingen) |
| *NSch* | New Scholasticism |
| *NwMSCS* | Northwest Missouri State College Studies |
| *NY* | New Yorker |
| *NYFQ* | New York Folklore Quarterly |
| *NYH* | New York History |
| *NYHSQB* | New York Historical Society Quarterly Bulletin |
| *NYTBR* | New York Times Book Review |
| *NYTM* | New York Times Magazine |
| | |
| *OHQ* | Ohio Historical Quarterly |
| *OPL* | Osservatore Politico Letterario (Rome) |
| *OSAHQ* | Ohio State Archaeological and Historical Quarterly |
| *OUR* | Ohio University Review |
| *OW* | Orient/West (Tokyo) |
| | |
| *PAAS* | Proceedings of the American Antiquarian Society |
| *PAPS* | Proceedings of the American Philosophical Society |
| *ParR* | Paris Review |
| *PBSA* | Papers of the Bibliographical Society of America |
| *PELL* | Papers in English Language and Literature |
| *Per* | Perspective |
| *Person* | The Personalist |
| *PF* | Pennsylvania Folklife |
| *PH* | Pennsylvania History |
| *PHR* | Pacific Historical Review |
| *PhR* | Philosophical Review |
| *PL* | Poet Lore |
| *PLL* | Papers on Language and Literature |
| *PMASAL* | Papers of the Michigan Academy of Science, Arts, and Letters |
| *PMHB* | Pennsylvania Magazine of History and Biography |
| *PMHS* | Proceedings of the Massachusetts Historical Society |

| | |
|---|---|
| *PMLA* | Publications of the Modern Language Association of America |
| *PNJHS* | Proceedings of the New Jersey Historical Society |
| *Ponte* | Il Ponte (Florence) |
| *PPR* | Philosophy and Phenomenological Research |
| *PQ* | Philological Quarterly |
| *PR* | Partisan Review |
| *PrS* | Prairie Schooner |
| *PS* | Pacific Spectator |
| *PSQ* | Political Science Quarterly |
| *PULC* | Princeton University Library Chronicle |
| | |
| *QH* | Quaker History: Bulletin of the Friends Historical Association |
| *QJCA* | Quarterly Journal of Current Acquisitions |
| *QJLC* | Quarterly Journal of the Library of Congress |
| *QJS* | Quarterly Journal of Speech |
| *QNL* | Quarterly News Letter (Book Club of California) |
| *QQ* | Queen's Quarterly |
| *QRL* | Quarterly Review of Literature |
| | |
| *RACHSP* | Records of the American Catholic Historical Society of Philadelphia |
| *RdE* | Rivista di Estetica (Padua) |
| *RDM* | Revue des Deux Mondes (Paris) |
| *RdP* | Revue de Paris |
| *REL* | Review of English Literature (Leeds) |
| *Ren* | Renascence |
| *Rep* | Reporter |
| *RES* | Review of English Studies |
| *RGB* | Revue Générale Belge (Brussels) |
| *RIB* | Revista Interamericana di Bibliografía (Washington, D.C.) |
| *RIH* | Rhode Island History |
| *RIP* | Rice Institute Pamphlets |
| *RIPh* | Revue Internationale de Philosophie (Brussels) |
| *RLC* | Revue de Littérature Comparée (Paris) |
| *RLMC* | Rivista di Letterature Moderne e Comparate (Florence) |
| *RLV* | Revue des Langes Vivantes (Brussels) |
| *RMR* | Rocky Mountain Review |
| *RMS* | Renaissance and Modern Studies (Nottingham) |

| | |
|---|---|
| *RPol* | Review of Politics |
| *RS* | Research Studies |
| *RSSCW* | Research Studies of the State College of Washington |
| *RusR* | Russian Review |
| | |
| *SA* | Studi Americani (Rome) |
| *SAB* | South Atlantic Bulletin |
| *SAQ* | South Atlantic Quarterly |
| *SatR* | Saturday Review |
| *SB* | Studies in Bibliography: Papers of the Bibliographical Society of the University of Virginia |
| *SCB* | South Central Bulletin |
| *SCHM* | South Carolina Historical Magazine |
| *SchS* | School and Society |
| *SciMo* | Scientific Monthly |
| *SciS* | Science and Society |
| *SDR* | South Dakota Review |
| *SFQ* | Southern Folklore Quarterly |
| *ShawR* | Shaw Review |
| *Shen* | Shenandoah |
| *SHR* | Southern Humanities Review |
| *SIR* | Studies in Romanticism |
| *SLitI* | Studies in the Literary Imagination |
| *SLJ* | Southern Literary Journal |
| *SLQ* | Saint Louis Quarterly |
| *SM* | Speech Monographs |
| *SN* | Studia Neophilologica (Uppsala) |
| *SNL* | Satire Newsletter |
| *SoQ* | Southern Quarterly |
| *SoR* | Southern Review |
| *SoRA* | Southern Review: An Australian Journal of Literary Studies (Adelaide) |
| *SovL* | Soviet Literature |
| *SP* | Studies in Philology |
| *SQ* | Shakespeare Quarterly |
| *SR* | Sewanee Review |
| *SRL* | Saturday Review of Literature |
| *SS* | Scandinavian Studies |
| *SSF* | Studies in Short Fiction |
| *SSL* | Studies in Scottish Literature |
| *SuF* | Sinn und Form (Potsdam) |
| *SUS* | Susquehanna University Studies |

| | |
|---|---|
| *SWR* | Southwest Review |
| *Sym* | Symposium |
| | |
| *TA* | Theater Annual |
| *TArts* | Theatre Arts |
| *TC* | Twentieth Century |
| *TCL* | Twentieth Century Literature |
| *TDR* | The Drama Review [formerly Tulane Drama Review] |
| *TFSB* | Tennessee Folklore Society Bulletin |
| *THQ* | Tennessee Historical Quarterly |
| *TJ* | Today's Japan |
| *TQ* | Texas Quarterly |
| *TR* | Table Ronde (Paris) |
| *TransR* | Transatlantic Review |
| *TriQ* | Tri-Quarterly |
| *TSE* | Tulane Studies in English |
| *TSL* | Tennessee Studies in Literature |
| *TSLL* | Texas Studies in Literature and Language |
| *TWASAL* | Transactions of the Wisconsin Academy of Sciences, Arts, and Letters |
| *TxSE* | Texas Studies in English |
| | |
| *UCQ* | University College Quarterly |
| *UDQ* | University of Denver Quarterly |
| *UKCR* | University of Kansas City Review |
| *UMSE* | University of Mississippi Studies in English |
| *Univ* | Universitas (Stuttgart) |
| *UPLC* | University of Pennsylvania Library Chronicle |
| *UR* | University Review |
| *UTLC* | University of Texas Library Chronicle |
| *UTQ* | University of Toronto Quarterly |
| *UTSE* | University of Texas Studies in English |
| *UWR* | University of Windsor Review |
| | |
| *VC* | Virginia Cavalcade |
| *VMHB* | Virginia Magazine of History and Biography |
| *VN* | Victorian Newsletter |
| *VQR* | Virginia Quarterly Review |
| | |
| *WAL* | Western American Literature |
| *WF* | Western Folklore |
| *WHR* | Western Humanities Review |

| WLB | Wilson Library Bulletin |
| WMH | Wisconsin Magazine of History |
| WMQ | William and Mary Quarterly |
| WPHM | Western Pennsylvania Historical Magazine |
| WoR | World Review |
| WR | Western Review |
| WSCL | Wisconsin Studies in Contemporary Literature |
| WVH | West Virginia History |
| XR | X, a Quarterly Review |
| XUS | Xavier University Studies |
| YCGL | Yearbook of Comparative and General Literature |
| YLM | Yale Literary Magazine |
| YR | Yale Review |
| YULG | Yale University Library Gazette |
| ZAA | Zeitschrift für Anglistik und Amerikanistik (East Berlin) |

# GUIDE TO RESOURCES

# BIBLIOGRAPHICAL CENTERS

CENTRAL:
*The Washington Area*

The Library of Congress, established in 1800 by Act of Congress as ː Congressional library, has in fact become national. Its holdings of books in a wide variety of fields, its collections of manuscripts, prints and views, maps, recorded and sheet music, and reproductions of historical material are very ex-tensive. Its unrivaled facilities for research, together with its services to other institutions and to individuals, make it the chief bibliographical center in the United States. A law enacted in 1846 required that one copy of every book copyrighted in the United States be deposited in the Library; since 1870, two copies.

Its "National Union Catalog" now being assembled, though not yet national in coverage, is of superlative importance. It is an attempt to gather in one place information indicating the location of any given book. The list now makes such information available for upward of 12,000,000 items, with location in some 700 libraries. A request for information about any item receives prompt attention.

From time to time the Library has published handbooks or checklists dealing with its special holdings or its facilities for research. Such, for example, is Allan B. Slauson, *A Check List of American Newspapers in the Library of Congress* (1901), especially useful for material after 1820; and John V. N. Ingram and Henry S. Parsons, *A Check List of American Eighteenth Cen-tury Newspapers in the Library of Congress* (1936). The *Handbook of Manuscripts in the Library of Congress* (1918) is fully indexed. It was supplemented by "List of Manuscript Collections Received," in the *Annual Report* of the Librarian until 1943, in which year was first published *Library of Congress Quarterly Journal of Current Acquisitions,* Washington, 1943– current. It supplies information about acquisitions of both printed and manu-script material in the Library, with frequent bibliographies. The Modern Language Association of America has prepared a checklist of *Reproductions of Manuscripts and Rare Printed Books* (1942)—a short-title list, with annual supplements, of the rotographs or microfilms on deposit in the Library. Two recent handbooks of special use to the student are Martin A. Roberts, *The*

3

*Library of Congress in Relation to Research* (1939), and William A. Slade, *Some Notes on the Library of Congress as a Center of Research* (1939).

As aids to research, sets of the Library of Congress "Depository Catalog of Printed Cards" have been placed in various large libraries in bibliographical centers. They are usually an author index only. These standard Library of Congress cards are also reproduced by photomechanical process as *A Catalog of Books Represented by Library of Congress Printed Cards.* This compilation (1942–1946) is supplemented by a *Cumulative Catalog . . .,* for the benefit of all libraries desiring bibliographical and reference material. It makes a list of Library of Congress holdings available in instances where the cards themselves are not obtainable. Such are among the important services rendered by the Library as a national institution.

In the same area there are many other libraries whose special collections make the national capital a primary bibliographical center. In a separate building, under the supervision of an expert staff, have recently been gathered the National Archives. These documents are described in a *Guide to the Material in the National Archives,* Washington, 1940. Important for its files of federal government issues is the Documents Office Library, in the Government Printing Office. There are further the special libraries in the various government departments: War, Navy, Justice, Labor, Commerce, Interior, Agriculture, and others. Most of these libraries make their books available for interlibrary loan. The most notable of them is the Army Medical Library (formerly called the Surgeon General's Office) in the War Department Library. It is the national medical library of the United States, and its holdings are the most extensive in its field. Its published *Index-Catalogue of the Library of the Surgeon General's Office* is kept up to date by supplemental series.

In addition to the government department libraries there are the special collections in the libraries of the National Gallery of Art, the Smithsonian Institution, and the Folger Shakespeare Memorial Library in the field of dramatic production and drama literature. There are further the libraries of Georgetown University and Catholic University of America, both rich in holdings of Catholic Americana. In the latter is a collection of early Americana dealing with New England. Others are George Washington University; Howard University, with its special collections of literature dealing with Negro life; and the American University. The Public Library of Washington is a circulating library with good holdings in the general field.

Washington is of further importance as the headquarters of learned societies. The center there for inquiries about research projects in all fields is the American Council of Learned Societies. The main office of the American Historical Association is also in Washington. Its organ, the *American Historical Review*, established in 1895, publishes special reports on research in neglected fields of American civilization, and annual bibliographies. Its cooperative *Guide to Historical Literature* (1931) is brought up to date by later supplements. The Carnegie Institution of Washington maintains facilities for advancing studies in many fields, and publishes its reports annually.

Facilities for study and research in the Washington area are greatly increased by resources in and near the city of Baltimore. Here are located the important libraries of Johns Hopkins University, and of the Peabody Institute, whose published *Catalogue of the Library*, 1888–1905, is notable among dictionary catalogs for the author and subject analyses of its items. The Baltimore Public Library (the Enoch Pratt Free Library) specializes in regional collections, as do the libraries of the University of Maryland and the Maryland Historical Society.

NORTHEAST:
## The New York Area

The extensive resources of special libraries and collections in the greater New York area make it, like that of Washington, a primary center for research. The principal difference, however, is that in general the resources do not include services rendered as a national obligation. No library in the United States, with the possible exception of the Library of Congress, can equal the New York Public Library in the strength of its holdings generally. In the field of American history and literature, with its recent acquisition of the Berg Collection of Americana, it is unrivaled. Though it maintains all facilities for research, it is a reference library solely, and items from its great collections are not available for interlibrary loan. Among its extensive manuscript holdings in the field of Americana, the Griswold and Duyckinck Papers, and the John Jacob Astor Papers, rich in material dealing with the fur trade and the opening up of the West, deserve mention. Its published *Bulletins*, issued for the past fifty years, describe its collections, list its acquisitions, and are indexed.

Among universities in the city of New York, the facilities and the holdings of Columbia University are excellent in the field of American studies. The McAlpin Collection of seventeenth century history and theology at Union Theological Seminary is substantial, and a list of its holdings is made available in the published *Catalogue* of the Collection. At New York University is located a card index to early American periodicals, 1728–1870, compiled by the WPA under competent supervision. The index files the contents of 339 periodicals on some one million cards. Publication of some of the material, particularly articles relating to Emerson and Poe, has been undertaken, and further publication is under way. The scope and resources of the project are described in *Index to Early American Periodical Literature, 1728–1870,* New York, 1941, reprinted from *Pamphleteer Monthly,* I (1940), Nos. 7 and 8. The library of Manhattan College has a notable collection of Irish-American literature.

Important among special libraries is the Pierpont Morgan Library. Its facilities for research and its holdings of rare books and manuscripts are outstanding. Substantial holdings of Americana are in the New York Historical Society. Its collection of American poetry is large, and its extensive manuscript holdings are listed in Susan E. Lyman, *Survey of the Manuscript Collections in the New-York Historical Society,* New York, 1941. The little known New York Society Library, in existence since 1754, has an important collection of early American fiction.

Among published guides, Robert B. Downs, *Resources of New York City Libraries,* Chicago, 1940, is fully indexed, with an extensive bibliography, pp. 309–403. Others are Special Libraries Association, New York Chapter, *Special Libraries Directory of Greater New York . . . ,* New York, 1937; Evarts B. Greene and Richard B. Morris, *A Guide to the Principal Sources for Early American History (1600–1800) in the City of New York,* New York, 1929; Historical Records Survey, *Guide to Manuscript Depositories in New York City,* New York, 1941—a mimeographed descriptive checklist, well indexed; and Ruth Savord and Pearl M. Keefer, *Union List of Periodicals in Special Libraries of the New York Metropolitan District,* New York, 1931. A guide to manuscripts outside the city is George W. Roach, *Guide to Depositories of Manuscript Collections in New York State, Exclusive of New York City* (1941), with supplemental material in *New York Hist.,* XXIV (1943), 265–270, 417–422, 560–564; XXV (1944), 64–68, 226–227.

If the greater New York area may be thought to include central and southwestern Connecticut as part of the bibliographical center, it must add the very extensive resources of the Sterling Memorial Library of Yale University, one of the great university libraries in the United States, with important collections of American and English literature. A published guide to its journalistic collections is *List of Newspapers in the Yale University Library,* New Haven, 1916. There is also within this area the Watkinson Library at Hartford, with special holdings dealing with American Indian language and literature, early American schoolbooks, and books on the Civil War; and the Connecticut Historical Library, with much early regional material. Wesleyan University Library at Middletown contains special collections in Connecticut history and American literature.

*The Philadelphia Area*

Greater Philadelphia is one of the library centers of the United States. Its diversified and very extensive holdings, scattered through many scores of libraries, some of them accumulated over a period extending back to the middle and late eighteenth century, are notably rich in Americana and have been little exploited. Outstanding collections are in the libraries of the University of Pennsylvania, the Historical Society of Pennsylvania, the American Philosophical Society, the Presbyterian Historical Society, the Library Company of Philadelphia, and the Free Library of Philadelphia, including its branch formerly known independently as the Mercantile Library. Further facilities for study are offered by Temple University, and by the near-by colleges of Swarthmore, Haverford, and Bryn Mawr. The Crozer Theological Seminary at Chester includes special collections in Baptist and Shaker church history. An important aid to research, undertaken and completed during the past decade, is the "Union Library Catalogue," a card index in the Philadelphia Bibliographical Center, filed at the University of Pennsylvania, which makes available in one alphabetical list a guide to the library resources of the great number of depositories throughout the metropolitan area. Published guides to special resources are Dorothy H. Litchfield, *Classified List of 4800 Serials Currently Received in the Libraries of the University of Pennsylvania, and of Bryn Mawr, Haverford, and Swarthmore Colleges,* Philadelphia, 1936; Nathan E. Hause, "Annotated Catalogue of Newspaper Files in the Pennsylvania State Library," in *Report of the State Librarian of Pennsylvania,* 1900, pp. 185–308; and Paul Bleyden, *Guide to the Manuscript Collections in the Historical Society of Pennsylvania,* Philadelphia, 1940. Helpful references are included in *Philadelphia Libraries: A Survey of Facilities, Needs, and Opportunities . . . ,* Philadelphia, 1942.

Important regional collections in libraries throughout the state of Pennsylvania may be located in such compilations as Historical Records Survey, *Guide to Depositories of Manuscript Collections in Pennsylvania,* Harrisburg, 1939, ed. by Margaret S. Eliot and Sylvester K. Stevens, and fully indexed; Western Pennsylvania Historical Survey, *Inventory of the Manuscript and Miscellaneous Collections of the Historical Society of Western Pennsylvania,* Pittsburgh, 1933; and *idem, Inventory of Files of American Newspapers in Pittsburgh and Allegheny County, Pennsylvania,* Pittsburgh, 1933.

Within the area are the facilities and resources of the Princeton University Library, with rapidly increasing holdings in the field of American history and literature; the Princeton Theological Seminary Library; the Rutgers University Library (New Brunswick), specializing in early Americana; the New Jersey Historical Society (Newark); and the New Jersey State Library

(Trenton). A published guide to material in the last named library is the Historical Records Survey, *Calendar of the New Jersey State Library Manuscript Collection in the Cataloguing Room, State Library, Trenton, New Jersey,* Newark, 1939. Helpful references are contained in New Jersey Library Association, *Survey of Special Collections in New Jersey Libraries,* New York, 1940.

*The Boston Area*

The library resources of the Boston area, when combined with those of New York and Philadelphia, make the Northeastern section of the United States one of unparalleled bibliographical facilities. The special collections of manuscripts and notable editions of the works of American authors in the Houghton Library of Harvard University are unexcelled. Near by, the Boston Public Library has long been established as a leading institution, and its many important special collections are constantly being increased. Its organ, *More Books,* is published monthly and includes scholarly articles as well as checklists and descriptions of new accessions. The Massachusetts Historical Society, the first American organization of its kind, was founded by Jeremy Belknap in 1791, and his gifts of books and manuscripts together with those of other historical scholars are the nucleus of its present great collection. It began in the eighteenth century to publish volumes of its *Collections,* and its series of *Publications,* appearing at intervals, now total some 70 volumes. It has issued a *Handbook of the Publications and Photostats, 1792–1933,* Boston, 1934. The Boston Athenaeum, founded in 1805 as a private association of literary men, has continued to function as a privately maintained organization, open to scholars. Its holdings of American nineteenth century poetry and fiction are extensive. Its dictionary catalog, *Boston Athenaeum Catalogue, 1807–1871,* Boston, 1874–82, 5 vols., includes some analysis. It has not been brought up to date. Other special libraries, important for their holdings in intellectual history, are the Congregational Library (Boston), and the Andover-Harvard Theological Library (Cambridge). The manuscript material assembled in the library of the New England Historic Genealogical Society (Boston) is important.

The American Antiquarian Society, founded at Worcester by Isaiah Thomas in 1812, is distinguished for its great collection of American historical materials, including newspapers, and some 500,000 manuscript items. Its series of *Proceedings* make available much rare Americana. A description of its collections is Clifford K. Shipton, "The American Antiquarian Society," *William and Mary Quar.,* 3rd ser., II (1945), 164–172. Robert W. G. Vail compiled *A Guide to the Resources of the American Antiquarian Society, a National Library of American History,* Worcester, 1937.

Within the same area are the notable collections in Providence, R.I. The John Carter Brown Library on the campus of Brown University has built up an unexcelled collection of colonial Americana. See Lawrence C. Wroth, *The First Century of the John Carter Brown Library: A History with a Guide to the Collections,* Providence, 1946. Three other collections of Americana at Brown are distinguished: the Harris Collection of American poetry and plays, described in John C. Stockton, *The Anthony Memorial: A Catalogue of the Harris Collection of American Poetry,* Providence, 1886; the McClellan Collection of Lincolniana; and the collections of the Linguistic Atlas of the United States. Regional collections are in the Library of the Rhode Island Historical Society, and in the Providence Athenaeum.

The college and university libraries of northern New England specialize in regional material. In Maine the best collections of such items are at the University of Maine and at Bowdoin and Colby colleges. Dorothy Smith has compiled a *Union List of Serials in Maine Libraries,* Orono, Me., 1937. The best resources in New Hampshire are at Dartmouth College. In Vermont, Middlebury College has specialized in a collection of American literature, listed by Viola C. White in a *Check List of the Abernethy Library of American Literature, Middlebury College,* Middlebury, Vt., 1940. In central and western Massachusetts, the best resources are at Williams College, with its notable collection of rare editions in the Chapin Library, described in Lucy E. Osborne, *The Chapin Library, Williams College: A Short-Title List,* Portland, Me., 1939; at Amherst and at Smith colleges; and in the Forbes Library at Northampton.

Not only are there the regional holdings of state libraries and state historical societies in New England, but the local historical societies are depositories for manuscript diaries, journals, commonplace books, and for books and newspapers issued by local printers. For reference to published data covering such organizations, see pp. 14–16, below.

THE SOUTH

Bibliographical centers in the South are more scattered than in the Northeast. The major manuscript collections relating to the South are at Duke University and the University of North Carolina, described in the Historical Records Survey, *A Guide to the Manuscript Collections in the Duke University Library, Durham, N.C.,* Raleigh, N.C., 1939; and *idem, Guide to the Manuscripts in the Southern Historical Collection of the University of North Carolina,* Chapel Hill, N.C., 1941. Other resources in North Carolina are surveyed in Charles E. Rush, ed., *Library Resources of the University of North Carolina: A Summary of Facilities for Study and Research,* Chapel Hill, N.C., 1945; and in the Historical Records Survey: *Guide to Depositories of Manu-*

*script Collections in North Carolina,* Raleigh, N.C., 1940; and *Guide to the Manuscript Collections in the Archives of the North Carolina Historical Commission,* Raleigh, N.C., 1942. The library of the University of Virginia is steadily increasing its holdings of material relating to the ante-bellum South. Its Tracy William McGregor Collection of rare American imprints now includes the large collection of the Increase and Cotton Mather family items assembled by William Gwinn Mather.

The various state libraries, state university libraries, and state and local historical society libraries are depositories of material dealing with the South which is essential for study and research. A carefully prepared guide is that of Robert B. Downs, *Resources of Southern Libraries: A Survey of Facilities for Research,* Chicago, 1938, covering all states from Virginia south, and west to Texas, Oklahoma, and Arkansas. Published guides to special collections include:

For Virginia: Virginia Historical Society, *Catalogue of the Manuscripts in the Collection of the Virginia Historical Society, and Also of Some Printed Papers,* Richmond, 1901; Harry Clemons, *Survey of Research Materials in Virginia Libraries, 1936–37,* Charlottesville, 1941.

For Tennessee: Laura Luttrell and Mary U. Rothrock, comps., *Calvin Morgan McClung Historical Collection of Books, Pamphlets, Manuscripts, Pictures and Maps Relating to Early Western Travel and the History and Genealogy of Tennessee and Other Southern States,* Knoxville, 1921—items in the Lawson McGhee Library; Mary E. Baker, *Tennessee Serials, Together with the Holdings of Tennessee Libraries: A Tentative List . . . ,* Knoxville, 1937.

For Louisiana: Historical Records Survey, *Louisiana Newspapers, 1794–1940: A Union List of Louisiana Newspaper Files Available . . . in Louisiana,* University, La., 1941.

For Mississippi: Historical Records Survey, *Mississippi Newspapers, 1805–1940: A Preliminary Checklist of Mississippi Newspaper Files Available in the Mississippi Department of Archives and History,* Jackson, Miss., 1942; *idem, Mississippi Newspapers, 1805–1940: A Preliminary Union List of Mississippi Newspaper Files Available in Mississippi,* Jackson, Miss., 1942.

MIDDLE WEST:
*The Chicago Area*

The resources of Chicago make it the chief research center between the Atlantic and Pacific seaboards. One of the important university libraries in the United States is that of the University of Chicago. Its facilities for research work are extensive, and its collections of material relating to the West are increasing. Among special libraries in Chicago, the Newberry Library is out-standing for its holdings of rare books and manuscripts relating to America. Its Edward E. Ayer Collection of narratives of captivities among the Indians of North America is a notable grouping of source material for frontier history. Ruth L. Butler has compiled *A Check List of Manuscripts in the Edward E. Ayer Collection,* Chicago, 1937. Though not primarily concerned with Ameri-cana, the collections of the John Crerar Library deserve mention as among the great assemblies anywhere of material dealing with pure and applied science, technology, and social sciences. There are collections of source mate-rial relating to the Old Northwest in the Northwestern University Library. Newspaper holdings of seven large public and private collections are described in University of Chicago Library, *Newspapers in Libraries of Chicago: A Joint Check List,* Chicago, 1936. The Chicago Historical Society was organized to preserve regional archives, and much material in its files is rare or unique.

Probably no single collection is stronger in holdings of material relating to the early development of the Ohio Valley than that in the Western Reserve Historical Society Library, at Cleveland. A guide to regional serials has been compiled by the Ohio Library Association: *Regional List of Serials in the College and University Libraries in Ohio,* Ann Arbor, Mich., 1936—holdings of 42 Ohio libraries, not recorded in the standard *Union List of Serials.*

One of the leading libraries of the country specializing in Americana is the William L. Clements Library on the campus of the University of Michigan at Ann Arbor. Its manuscript collections relating to the American Revolution are unexcelled. It is equipped for research. In the Detroit Public Library is the Burton Historical Collection, rich in manuscripts, and important for its accumulation of material relating to Michigan and the Old Northwest. A guide to some Indiana regional material has been compiled by Fava E. Goan, *Union List of Serials in Indiana Libraries: Recording the Holdings of Forty-six Public, College, University, Institutional and Special Libraries of the State,* Lafayette, Ind., 1940.

Though all state and historical libraries throughout the region specialize in regional holdings, the Missouri Historical Society Library, at St. Louis, is outstanding as a repository for manuscripts dealing with the early fur trade of the trans-Mississippi, and for collections of books relating to the early Far West.

A notable collection relating to the development of the Mississippi Valley is in the State Historical Society of Wisconsin Library, at Madison. Other of its holdings are described in Ada T. Griswold, *Annotated Catalogue of News-paper Files in the Library of the State Historical Society of Wisconsin,* Madi-son, 1911; and in Alice E. Smith, *Guide to the Manuscripts of the Wisconsin*

*Historical Society,* Madison, 1944. The University of Wisconsin specializes in regional material. Its collection of early American newspapers is substantial.

Other published guides to holdings in depositories in the Middle West are Historical Records Survey, *Guide to Depositories of Manuscript Collections in the United States: Iowa,* Des Moines, 1940; and Grace L. Nute and Gertrude W. Ackermann, *Guide to the Personal Papers in the Manuscript Collections of the Minnesota Historical Society,* St. Paul, 1935.

FAR WEST:
*The Denver Area*

In the Far West a bibliographical center cannot be thought to include so compact an area as it does in the East. The Denver Public Library has compiled a union catalog coded to show the holdings in the principal libraries of the Rocky Mountain area, and is therefore the bibliographical center for research dealing with the region. Its own collections specialize in Far West materials. Other significant regional collections are those dealing with Mormon life, assembled at Salt Lake City principally at the University of Utah —important and little used; and the source material gathered by the Parmly Billings Memorial Library, in Billings, Montana, relating to pioneer life. Three published guides furnish important information about collections in Idaho, Montana, Oregon, Washington, and British Columbia: John Van Male, *Resources of Pacific Northwest Libraries: A Survey of Facilities for Study and Research,* Seattle, 1943—the holdings of 100 libraries; Charles W. Smith, *Special Collections in Libraries of the Pacific Northwest,* Seattle, 1927; and *idem, A Union List of Manuscripts in Libraries in the Pacific Northwest,* Seattle, 1931. There is also the Historical Records Survey, *Guide to the Manuscript Collections of the Oregon Historical Society,* Portland, 1940.

*The San Francisco Area*

The University of California at Berkeley is the largest university west of the Mississippi, and the collections of Californiana and western Americana, particularly fiction, in its Bancroft Library are unsurpassed. Here too are the H. H. Bancroft papers, together with Bancroft's library. It is therefore a leading center for research in the history of the Far West. Stanford University, with excellent facilities, is located at Palo Alto. In the same area are Mills College, at Oakland, specializing in American studies, and the College of the Pacific, at Stockton, both with growing accumulations of Americana.

## The Los Angeles Area

The Henry E. Huntington Library in San Marino is an endowed public library and research institution, unique in the combination of its facilities for research and its extensive collections of incunabula, rare books and manuscripts of English and American literature, Americana, and Spanish-American history. It specializes in material dealing with the history of California and the Far West in general. Among its holdings are the Fort Sutter Papers and the Henry R. Wagner collection of western Americana. In 1931 it began publication of a *Bulletin* (since 1937 published as a *Quarterly*) devoted to articles which are the product of research. Its collections are described in *Hunt. Lib. Bul.*, I (1931), 33–106.

In the same immediate area are large and rapidly increasing collections, especially of western Americana, in the William Andrews Clark Library of the University of California at Los Angeles; and in the Doheny Library of the University of Southern California. Here also is the Southwest Museum, a private library devoted to assembling material relating to the history of the Southwest, built upon the nucleus of the Munk Library of Southwestern Americana.

The private libraries maintained by many of the motion picture studios in Hollywood are repositories for material useful in filming historical sequences. Collections of historic photographs here assembled are very large.

The University of New Mexico Library specializes in the collection of southwestern chronicles, diaries, and travel literature.

A further guide to the resources of the Southwest will be found in Mabel Major and others, *Southwest Heritage: A Literary History with Bibliography*, Albuquerque, N.M., 1938.

## PUBLISHED CATALOGS AND DIRECTORIES

As aids to research, sets of the Library of Congress "Depository Catalog of Printed Cards" have been placed in various large libraries in bibliographical centers. These standard Library of Congress cards are also reproduced, by photomechanical process, as *A Catalog of Books Represented by Library of Congress Printed Cards,* in book form with cumulative supplements to date. The British Museum *Catalogue of Printed Books,* London, 1881–1905, 108 vols., including supplements, is an invaluable tool for research. It is gradually being superseded by the British Museum's issue of *General Catalogue of Printed Books,* a new edition of the first *Catalogue,* brought up to date. Undertaken in 1931, this listing has continuously proceeded. To date, some 160 volumes of the Bibliothèque Nationale, *Catalogue Général des Livres Imprimés,* Paris, 1900–current, have been published. The cataloging is excellent, and it is especially rich in holdings and description of American items. These three published catalogs are the most extensive listings of published books. They may be supplemented by such works as the Peabody Institute's *Catalogue of the Library . . . ,* Baltimore, 1883–1892, 5 vols., together with a *Second Catalogue . . . ,* including the additions made since 1892, Baltimore, 1896–1905, 8 vols. It is a dictionary catalog, notable for the author and subject analysis of its items. The *Boston Athenaeum Catalogue, 1807–1871,* Boston, 1874–1882, 5 vols., is a dictionary catalog, with some analysis. The Carnegie Library of Pittsburgh has issued a *Classified Catalogue . . . , 1895–1916 . . . ,* Pittsburgh, 1907–1926, 11 vols. in 10. Still useful is the Princeton University Library, *Classed List,* Princeton, 1920, 6 vols., a published shelf list indexed by authors in *idem, Alphabetical Finding List,* Princeton, 1921, 5 vols. Special libraries sometimes print catalogs of their collections. Such, for example, is *The Chapin Library, Williams College: A Short-Title List,* comp. by Lucy E. Osborne, Portland, Me., 1939. Similarly, catalogs of special collections in larger libraries are sometimes separately published, as Boston Athenaeum, *Confederate Literature: A List of Books and Newspapers, Maps, Music, and Miscellaneous Matter Printed in the South During the Confederacy, and Now in the Boston Athenaeum,* Boston, 1917.

## UNION LISTS AND SPECIAL COLLECTIONS

Of primary use in indicating bibliographical centers, regional libraries, and the location of special holdings in *Union Catalogs in the United States,* Chicago, 1942, comp. by Robert B. Downs. It includes (pp. 351–391) a "Directory of Union Catalogs in the United States," prepared by Arthur B. Berthold.

Serial publications are easily located by *Union List of Serials in Libraries of the United States and Canada,* first published in 1927, and continually supplemented. The second edition, New York, 1943, lists over 70,000 separate periodicals, with data regarding complete or partly complete sets. For newspapers there is the equally essential compilation of Winifred Gregory, *American Newspapers, 1821–1936: A Union List of Files Available in the United States and Canada,* New York, 1937.* A valuable guide for the location of copies of early English books which have long been held by American libraries is William Warner Bishop, *A Checklist of American Copies of "Short-Title Catalogue" Books,* Ann Arbor, Mich., 1944.

---

* Files of newspapers published before 1820 are located in the compilation by Clarence S Brigham (see p. 26).

Two recent developments of the greatest aid to research students are the process of microfilming and the growth of interlibrary loans. The Philadelphia Bibliographical Center has prepared a *Union List of Microfilms: A Basic List of Holdings in the United States and Canada,* Philadelphia, 1942, with later supplements to date. It is indispensable as a guide for interlibrary loan, that is, a loan from one library to another for the use of students and scholars. *A Union Catalog of Photo Facsimiles in North American Libraries: Material So Far Received by the Library of Congress,* Yardley, Pa., 1929, lists some 1,000 titles. The student should consult Constance M. Winchell, *Locating Books for Interlibrary Loan: With a Bibliography of Printed Aids Which Show Location of Books in American Libraries,* New York, 1930.

Special collections have been gathered, deposited, and cataloged in many hundreds of institutions throughout the country. They are described in such handbooks as W. Dawson Johnston and Isadore G. Mudge, *Special Collections in Libraries in the United States,* Washington, 1912—supplemented by "Additions to Special Collections," *Lib. Jour.,* XXXVIII (1913), 331-333; Library of Congress, *Check List of Collections of Personal Papers in Historical Societies, University and Public Libraries, and Other Learned Institutions in the United States,* Washington, 1918; *idem, Manuscripts in Public and Private Collections in the United States,* Washington, 1924; Special Libraries Association, *Special Libraries Directory of the United States and Canada,* New York, 1935; Rose L. Vormelker, *Special Library Resources,* Vol. I, *United States and Canada,* New York, 1941; Ernest C. Richardson, *An Index Directory to Special Collections in North American Libraries,* Yardley, Pa., 1927; Karl Brown, comp., *The American Library Directory, 1945: A Classified List of 12,140 Libraries with Names of Librarians and Statistical Data,* New York, 1945—with index to special collections, special subjects, and special libraries, periodically revised; and Henry P. Beers, *Bibliographies in American History: Guide to Materials for Research,* New York, 1942.

During the years 1936–1943, under sponsorship of the Works Progress (Work Projects) Administration, inventories were taken of books, manuscripts, and other items in depositories throughout the United States. The work is uneven, but the codifications provided are of great usefulness in locating the immense resources of the country. A checklist of pertinent material is provided by Sargent B. Child and others, *Check List of Historical Records Survey Publications,* Washington, 1943.

In addition to the resources of university libraries, and of public and special libraries, there are important collections in the libraries of learned societies and institutions. Many of these societies issue publications. Handbooks and guides to these resources are contained in Appleton P. C. Griffin, "Bibliography of American Historical Societies: The United States and the

Dominion of Canada," *Amer. Hist. Assn. Annual Report 1905,* Vol. II; Carnegie Institution, *Handbook of Learned Societies and Institutions: American,* Washington, 1908; Christopher Crittenden and Doris Godard, *Historical Societies in the United States and Canada: A Handbook,* Washington, 1944. Leslie W. Dunlap's *American Historical Societies, 1790–1860,* Madison, Wis., 1944, is the most recent compilation and provides descriptions of their establishment, membership and publications. Inventories of collections owned by such institutions have been taken in many instances by the Historical Records Survey, and the student is referred to the Child *Check List,* mentioned in the paragraph above. State and local societies are of course especially well provided with regional material, and the student interested in localized problems might profitably identify and consult such institutions.

## GUIDES TO PROFESSIONAL STUDIES AND BIBLIOGRAPHIES

### GUIDES TO REFERENCE BOOKS AND THESES

At present there is no guide directed toward professional studies in American literature. Tom P. Cross, *Bibliographical Guide to English Studies,* 8th ed., Chicago, 1943, was first published in 1919, and has been frequently brought up to date. It is important for general bibliographical guidance in the field, and complements John W. Spargo, *A Bibliographical Manual for Students of the Language and Literature of England and the United States: A Short-Title List,* Chicago, 2nd ed., rev. and enl., 1941; and Arthur G. Kennedy, *A Concise Bibliography for Students of English, Systematically Arranged,* Stanford Univ., Calif., 2nd ed., 1945. *The Annual Bibliography of English Language and Literature . . . ,* Cambridge, Eng., compiled by members of the Modern Humanities Research Association since 1921, is an annotated list of books and articles, covering particularly the work of scholars in England. Vol. XIX (for 1938) was issued in 1940. Publication has been temporarily discontinued.

Guides to theses and work in progress will be found in *A List of American Doctoral Dissertations . . . ,* Washington, compiled annually by members of the Catalog Division of the Library of Congress since 1913; *Doctoral Dissertations Accepted by American Universities,* compiled annually since 1934 for the National Research Council and the American Council of Learned Societies; *Microfilm Abstracts: A Collection of Abstracts of Doctoral Dissertations Which Are Available in Complete Form on Microfilm,* Ann Arbor, Mich., 1938—with frequent supplements to date; James M. Osborn, comp., *Work in Progress in the Modern Humanities,* annual from 1938 to 1941; and Curtis W.

Garrison and others, *The United States, 1865–1900: A Survey of Current Literature with Abstracts of Unpublished Dissertations,* Fremont, Ohio, 1945. A bibliographical guide, especially to institutional lists of published and unpublished theses, is Thomas R. Palfrey and Henry E. Coleman, Jr., *Guide to Bibliographies of Theses: United States and Canada,* 2nd ed., Chicago, 1940.

SOURCES SPECIFIC TO AMERICAN LITERATURE AND HISTORY:
*General Studies*

Specifically in the field of American literature and history are the following: Ernest E. Leisy, "Materials for Investigation in American Literature: A Bibliography of Dissertations, Articles, Research in Progress, and Collections of Americana . . . ," *Stud. Philol.,* XXIII (1926), 90–115, supplemented with additions and corrections, *ibid.,* XXIV (1927), 480–483; and Ernest E. Leisy and Jay B. Hubbell, "Doctoral Dissertations in American Literature,' *Amer. Lit.,* IV (1933), 419–465. "Research in Progress" has been a regular feature in *American Literature* since the journal was founded in 1929, and continues the "List of Dissertations," comp. by Ernest E. Leisy, which first appeared in *The Reinterpretation of American Literature* (ed. Norman Foerster), New York, 1928. See also Ralph P. Rosenberg, "Bibliographies of Theses in America," *Bul. Bibl.,* XVIII (1945), 181–182.

The first annual bibliography for American literature, still current, appeared as "American Bibliography for 1922," in the March supplement of *PMLA,* XXXVIII (1923), compiled by Norman Foerster.

Extensive listings of "Articles on American Literature Appearing in Current Periodicals" have appeared in each issue of *American Literature* since November, 1929—material gathered by a large staff of compilers.* Other serial bibliographies current, listing works of scholarship on themes concerned with American literature, are those on folklore, appearing in *Southern Folklore Quarterly;* on Anglo-French and Franco-American studies, in *Romanic Review;* on literary theory and criticism, in *American Bookman;* on journalistic subjects, in *Journalism Quarterly;* on German-American studies, in *American-German Review.* "A Bibliography of New England" appears annually in the March issue of the *New England Quarterly;* "A Bibliography of Outstanding American Essays Published in American Periodicals" is featured in each issue of *Essay Annual: A Yearly Collection of Significant Essays, Personal, Critical, Controversial, and Humorous,* Chicago, current since 1933. "A Pacific Northwest Bibliography" is compiled for the *Pacific Northwest Quar-*

* These have been supplemented, corrected, and edited by Lewis Leary as a separate publication, covering the years 1920–1945, issued by the Duke University Press, 1947.

*terly;* and a "North Carolina Bibliography," for the *North Carolina Historical Review.*

### Fiction

The most useful listing of "American editions of novels, novelettes, tales, romances, short stories, and allegories in prose, written by Americans," is Lyle H. Wright, *American Fiction, 1774–1850: A Contribution Toward a Bibliography,* San Marino, Calif., 1939. It includes finding lists. Also standard is Oscar Wegelin, *Early American Fiction, 1774–1830: A Compilation of the Titles of Works of Fiction,* rev. ed., New York, 1929. Useful material will be found in Otis W. Coan and Richard G. Lillard, *America in Fiction: An Annotated List of Novels That Interpret Aspects of Life in the United States,* Stanford Univ., Calif., rev. ed., 1945.

The standard registry for publication of short stories, published annually since 1915, and still current, was established by Edward J. O'Brien: *The Best American Short Stories . . . and The Yearbook of the American Short Story,* Boston. Two short-story indexes are Ina Ten Eyck Firkins, *Index to Short Stories,* New York, 1923, with supplements publ. in 1929, and 1936; and Francis J. Hannigan, *The Standard Index of Short Stories, 1900–1914,* Boston, 1918. For a checklist of material dealing with the short story to 1918 see Fred L. Pattee, "The Short Story," *Camb. Hist. Amer. Lit.,* II (1918), 616–631.

Guides to the field of fiction in general, with some reference to American novels and tales, are Dorothy E. Cook and others, *Fiction Catalog: 1941 Edition. A Subject, Author and Title List of 5050 Works of Fiction in the English Language with Annotations,* New York, 1942, with annual supplements; Ernest A. Baker and James Packman, *A Guide to the Best Fiction, English and American, Including Translations from Foreign Languages,* 3rd ed., New York, 1932—a dictionary of plot summaries; Ernest A. Baker, *A Guide to Historical Fiction,* New York, 1914; Thomas Aldred, *Sequel Stories, English and American,* London, 1928—an author list of stories which have been followed by sequels; Mary R. Lingenfelter, *Vocations in Fiction: An Annotated Bibliography,* 2nd ed., Chicago, 1938; and Jonathan Nield, *A Guide to the Best Historical Novels and Tales,* 5th ed., rev. and enl., London, 1929.

Five descriptive compilations by William M. Griswold are *A Descriptive List of Novels and Tales Dealing with American City Life,* Cambridge, 1891; *A Descriptive List of Novels and Tales Dealing with American Country Life,* Cambridge, 1890; *A Descriptive List of Novels and Tales Dealing with the History of North America,* Cambridge, 1895; *Descriptive List of Romantic*

*Novels,* Cambridge, 1890; and *A Descriptive List of International Novels,* Cambridge, 1891.

An early checklist is Nathaniel L. Goodrich, "Prose Fiction: A Bibliography," *Bul. Bibl.,* IV (1906), 118–121, 133–136, 153–155; V (1907), 11–13, 38–39, 54–55, 78–79.

## Poetry

Few guides to American poetry have been published. The most useful bibliographical compilation dealing with early poetry is Oscar Wegelin, *Early American Poetry: A Compilation of the Titles of Verse and Broadsides,* rev. ed., New York, 1930. See also John C. Frank, comp., *Early American Poetry, 1610–1820: A List of Works in the New York Public Library,* New York, 1917. For the twentieth century there is Allen Tate, *Recent American Poetry and Poetic Criticism: A Selected List of References,* Washington, 1943, an annotated guide; and *idem, Sixty American Poets, 1896–1944 . . . ,* Washington, 1945, with bibls. comp. by Frances Cheney.

## Drama

The most useful drama bibliographies and play lists, covering the American field from the earliest times to 1936, are in Arthur H. Quinn, *A History of the American Drama from the Beginning to the Civil War,* rev. ed., New York, 1943, pp. 395–462; and *A History of the American Drama from the Civil War to the Present Day,* rev. ed., New York, 1936, pp. 305–402. These play lists and bibliographies are frequently annotated.

A checklist of "Anthologies of American Plays" is in Allan G. Halline, *American Plays,* New York, 1935, pp. 774–776, with an analysis of the contents of the most important collections.

The pioneer bibliography of American drama to 1830, first published in 1900, is Oscar Wegelin, *Early American Plays, 1714–1830: A Compilation of the Titles of Plays and Dramatic Poems Written by Authors Born or Residing in North America Previous to 1830,* New York, 1905. Less trustworthy is the list compiled by Robert F. Roden, *Later American Plays, 1831–1900: Being a Compilation of the Titles of Plays by American Authors . . . ,* New York, 1900. A valuable record of early printed plays is Frank P. Hill, *American Plays Printed 1714–1830: A Bibliographical Record,* Stanford Univ., Calif., 1934. A checklist dealing with American drama during the years 1860–1918 is that compiled by Montrose J. Moses in *Camb. Hist. Amer. Lit.,* IV (1921), 760–774.

A checklist of *Dramatic Compositions Copyrighted in the United States* has been published annually by the Copyright Office, Washington, 1870–current.

An index to plays from 1800 to 1935 is that compiled by Ina Ten Eyck Firkins: *Index to Plays, 1800–1926,* New York, 1927. It is indexed by author, title, and subject, and lists nearly 8,000 plays by 2,200 authors. A *Supplement* to 1935 adds some 3,200 titles by 1,300 authors. The *Dramatic Index . . . ,* Boston, 1910–current, is Part II of *Annual Magazine Subject-Index.* It covers articles and illustrations concerning the stage and players in American and English periodicals.

An author and title index to plays appearing in collections published during 1900–1942 is John H. Ottemiller, *Index to Plays in Collections,* New York, 1943. For one-act plays, see Hannah Logasa and Winifred Ver Nooy, *An Index to One-Act Plays,* Boston, 1924—with two supplements, Boston, 1932, and 1941, which complete the index through 1940.

Further reference material is in Bernard Sobel, *The Theatre Handbook and Digest of Plays,* New York, 1940; Blanch M. Baker, *Dramatic Bibliography: An Annotated List of Books on the History and Criticism of the Drama and Stage and on the Allied Arts of the Theatre,* New York, 1933; Frank Shay, *A Guide to Longer Plays: A List of Fifteen Hundred Plays for Little Theatres, Professional and Stock Companies, Art Theatres, Schools, Amateurs and Readers,* New York, 1925; and William D. Adams, *A Dictionary of the Drama: A Guide to the Plays, Playwrights, Players, and Playhouses of the United Kingdom and America, from the Earliest Times to the Present,* Philadelphia, 1904, Vol. I, A–G (no more published).

Special studies are Hilda J. Lawson, "The Negro in American Drama: Bibliography of Contemporary Negro Drama," *Bul. Bibl.,* XVII (1940), 7–8, 27–30; and Edward D. Coleman, *The Jew in English Drama: An Annotated Bibliography,* New York, 1943.

## SOURCES INCIDENTAL TO AMERICAN LITERATURE

The standard bibliography of bibliographies in the field is Clark S. Northup, *A Register of Bibliographies of the English Language and Literature,* New Haven, 1925; it includes contributions by Joseph Q. Adams and Andrew Keogh. Very comprehensive is Nathan Van Patten, *An Index to Bibliographies and Bibliographical Contributions Relating to the Work of American and British Authors, 1923–1932,* Stanford Univ., Calif., 1934. Important checklists will be found in Margaret B. Stillwell, *Incunabula and Americana, 1450–1800: A Key to Bibliographical Study,* New York, 1931. Published annually since 1938 by the H. W. Wilson Co. is *The Bibliographic Index: A Cumulative Bibliography of Bibliographies,* New York. Standard also are Isadore G. Mudge, *Guide to Reference Books,* 6th ed., Chicago, 1936 —with three supplements through 1943; and Norma O. Ireland, *An Index to Indexes: A Subject Bibliography of Published Indexes,* Boston, 1942.

## REGISTRIES OF PUBLICATION

### BOOKS

The monumental compilation of books relating to America is Joseph Sabin, *Bibliotheca Americana: A Dictionary of Books Relating to America, from Its Discovery to the Present Time,* New York, 1868–1936, 29 vols. The work was conceived and begun by Sabin, continued after an interval of 46 years by Wilberforce Eames, and completed by Robert W. G. Vail. It lists some 100,000 numbered entries, alphabetically by author, and is distinguished for its important bibliographical notes, its high degree of accuracy, especially in the later volumes, and its extensive coverage.

Charles Evans, *American Bibliography: A Chronological Dictionary of All Books, Pamphlets, and Periodical Publications Printed in the United States of America from the Genesis of Printing in 1639 Down to and Including the Year 1820, with Bibliographical and Biographical Notes,* Chicago, 1903–[1934], is constantly useful, though it must be checked occasionally for accuracy. Supplementary entries are supplied in Willard O. Waters, "American Imprints, 1648–1797, in the Huntington Library, Supplementing Evans' 'American Bibliography,'" *Huntington Lib. Bul.,* No. 3 (1933), 1–95. The 12 volumes of Evans published to 1934 carry the listings through the year 1799.

There is no registry of publication for the years 1800–1819.

For the years 1820–1862 there is Orville A. Roorbach, *Bibliotheca Americana: Catalogue of American Publications, Including Reprints and Original Works, from 1820 to 1852, Inclusive; Together with a List of Periodicals Published in the United States,* New York, 1939, 4 vols. Originally published in 1849, this valuable compilation was recently reprinted from the edition of 1852, incorporating the supplements of 1850, 1852, 1855, 1858, and 1861. Nicholas Trübner covered the same period as Roorbach in *Trübner's Bibliographical Guide to American Literature: A Classified List of Books Published in the United States of America During the Last Forty Years, with Bibliographical Introduction, Notes, and Alphabetical Index,* London, 1859.

The work of James Kelly picks up where Roorbach leaves off, and covers the years 1861–1871: *The American Catalogue of Books, Original and Reprints, Published in the United States from Jan., 1861, to . . . 1871 . . . ,* New York, 1866–1871, 2 vols. It is notable for its lists of Civil War pamphlets, sermons, and addresses. It is available in reprint, New York, 1938. Both Roorbach and Kelly are incomplete and sometimes inaccurate, but they furnish the most comprehensive listing for the years 1820–1870.

In 1868 appeared the first issue of *The American Booksellers' Guide,* New York; and its seven volumes continuously list issues to Dec. 1, 1875, when it is superseded by *The American Bookseller,* New York, 1876–1893, 32 vols.

The standard listing for the years 1876–1910 is *The American Catalogue of Books . . . 1876–1910,* New York, 1876–1911. It aims to include all books, except local directories, etc., published in the United States. Entries are made under author, title, and subject. It was absorbed into *The United States Catalogue: Books in Print,* New York, 1899–current. This invaluable register is augmented monthly by *The Cumulative Book Index.* The several editions, with respective supplements, constitute the authoritative publication record from 1898 to date. It has undertaken, since 1928, to list all publications in English, wherever issued in the English-speaking world, and its entries are very accurate.

The standard trade journal, listing the week's new publications, carrying announcements, news notes, advertisements for books wanted, and other data of interest to the book trade, is *Publishers' Weekly: The American Book Trade Journal . . .,* New York, 1872–current. Its contents are indexed in the *Readers' Guide to Periodical Literature* (see below). *The Publishers' Trade List Annual . . .,* New York, 1873–current, is an alphabetical gathering of American publishers' trade catalogs. An index was issued in 1902, with supplements for the years 1903–1904 only. An annual listing of prices, auction or trade, of books, manuscripts, autographs, etc., has been issued since 1895 in *American Book-Prices Current . . .,* New York, 1895–current. For data on book auctions and auction catalogs, there is George L. McKay, *American Book Auction Catalogues, 1713–1934: A Union List,* New York, 1937, including some 9,000 entries, fully indexed. See also Clarence S. Brigham, "History of Book Auctions in America," *Bul. N.Y. Pub. Lib.,* XXXIX (1935), 55–90.

Publication of books in England, for the years 1874–1940, is recorded in *The Reference Catalogue of Current Literature, Containing the Full Titles of Books Now in Print and on Sale . . .,* London. It has been issued at irregular intervals, and at present there are none later than 1940.

The United States Copyright Office in Washington has issued annually since 1891 a *Catalogue of Copyright Entries . . .,* a compilation which supplies additional and very accurate data.

Preceding *Publishers' Weekly* as a trade journal was *Norton's Literary Gazette and Publishers' Circular,* issued in New York from May, 1851, through August, 1855. From May to December, 1851, it was called *Norton's Literary Advertiser.* According to *Union List of Serials,* few issues of this interesting *Circular* are extant and no files are complete. Commencing in

September, 1855, the journal was called *American Literary Gazette and Publishers' Circular*. It was issued annually (with slight title variation) until
January, 1872, when it was merged with *Weekly Trade Circular,* soon called
*Publishers' Weekly*. Files of this issue of the *Circular* are more numerous than
of the first, but none is complete.

A rare publication of prime importance as source material for the period
it covers is *Norton's Literary Register,* New York, 1852–1856, an annual register (except for the year 1855, when none was published) containing literary
information, accounts of American libraries, literary necrologies, biographical
sketches, and statistical compilations. Few issues are extant and no files are
complete.

One further approach to the history of publishing in the United States
should not be overlooked. The Historical Records Survey, functioning under
the Works Progress Administration, during the 1930's undertook an inventory
of American imprints on a very extensive scale throughout the country. The
compilation, carried forward under direction by many hundreds of workers,
is uneven, and many of the data require rechecking; but the accumulation
of material and identification of items is an accomplishment of importance.
A survey of the undertaking, with checklists of all items issued, during 1937–
1942, is Douglas C. McMurtrie, "The Bibliography of American Imprints,"
*Pub. Weekly,* CXLIV (1943), 1939–1944.

Miscellaneous items, which occasionally give clues to data on the subject
of publishing, will be found in Earl L. Bradsher, "Book Publishers and Publishing," *Camb. Hist. Amer. Lit.,* New York, IV (1921), 533–553; Henry W.
Boynton, *Annals of American Bookselling, 1638–1850,* London, 1932—a brief
historical review, with essential information difficult to assemble elsewhere;
Winslow L. Webber, *Books About Books: A Bio-Bibliography for Collectors,*
Boston, 1937; Adolf Growoll, *Book-Trade Bibliography in the United States
in the XIXth Century,* New York, 1939—a reprint from the original edition
of 1898, and the best treatment of the subject; Whitman Bennett, *A Practical
Guide to American Book Collecting, 1663–1940 . . . ,* New York, 1941—a
collector's manual; and Carl L. Cannon, *American Book Collectors and Collecting from Colonial Times to the Present,* New York, 1941—listing some 100
collections from Thomas Prince to H. H. Bancroft. A list valuable for references to American bibliography, printing and publishing, book collecting, and
libraries is found in Hellmut Lehmann-Haupt and others, *The Book in
America: A History of the Making, the Selling, and the Collecting of Books
in the United States,* New York, 1939, pp. 385–422.

Information about first editions is assembled in *Merle Johnson's American
First Editions,* 4th ed., rev. and enl. by Jacob Blanck, New York, 1942. First
published by Merle Johnson in 1929, this fourth edition lists nearly 200

authors, some 10,000 titles from Freneau to Steinbeck, and has been rechecked against new data and items. Bradford M. Fullerton, *Selective Bibliography of American Literature, 1775–1900: A Brief Estimate of the More Important American Authors and a Description of Their Representative Works*, New York, 1932, lists some lesser known material not easily available. Patrick K. Foley's *American Authors, 1795–1895: A Bibliography of First and Notable Editions Chronologically Arranged with Notes*, Boston, 1897, is still standard and useful. An admirable sales catalog useful for bibliography is *The Stephen H. Wakeman Collection of Books of Nineteenth Century American Writers: First Editions, Inscribed Presentation and Personal Copies, Original Manuscripts and Letters of Nine American Authors: Bryant, Emerson, Hawthorne, Holmes, Longfellow, Lowell, Poe, Thoreau, Whittier*, New York, 1924. Another useful sales list is *Catalogue of the American Library of the Late Mr. George Brinley . . .*, Hartford, Conn., 1878–1897, 5 vols.—extensive, and meticulously compiled. See George L. McKay, "American Book Auction Catalogues, 1713–1934," *Bul. N.Y. Pub. Lib.*, L (1946), 177–184. Isidore R. Brussel has assembled further data in two books: *Anglo-American First Editions, 1826–1900, East to West, Describing First Editions of English Authors Whose Books Were Published in America Before Their Publication in England . . .*, New York, 1935; and its companion volume, *Anglo-American First Editions, West to East, 1786–1930, . . . of American Authors Whose Books Were Published in England Before Their Publication in America . . .*, New York, 1936.

Information about reprint editions which appear in inexpensive publishers' series is in the *Catalog of Reprints in Series*, New York, 1940–current.

Two outstanding indexes of material in composite books are: *A.L.A. Index . . . to General Literature*, Boston, 1901 (2nd ed.) and 1914 (supplement, chiefly to nineteenth century publications); and *Essay and General Literature Index, 1900–1933*, New York, 1934, with supplements which make it a current index to twentieth century publications. The latter work analyzes books by authors, titles, and subjects, and supplies information about bibliographical material. A highly selective and authoritative book-reviewing medium of current studies in all branches of American culture is the *United States Quarterly Book List*, Washington, 1945–current. The annals of popular literature in the United States may be followed in Alice Payne Hackett, *Fifty Years of Best Sellers, 1895–1945*, New York, 1945, a listing that should be checked for accuracy.

A survey is George P. Winship, "The Literature of the History of Printing in the United States: A Survey," *Library* (1923), 4th ser., III, No. 4, pp. 288–303.

Other information can be gleaned from Charles F. Heartman, *Checklist of Printers in the United States* . . ., New York, 1915; George T. Watkins, *American. Typographical Bibliography* . . ., Indianapolis, 1898; *idem, Bibliography of Printing in America* . . ., Boston, 1906; and Irvin Haas, *Bibliography of Modern American Presses*, Chicago, 1935.

PERIODICALS AND NEWSPAPERS

For the years 1802–1907, *Poole's Index to Periodical Literature,* rev. ed., Boston, 1891, with 6 supplements to 1907, is the primary published guide. It is a subject index only, but it is basic, and the pioneer work of its kind. The card file at New York University, of early American periodicals to 1870, is invaluable as an analytic index. The *Review of Reviews,* London and New York, 1891–1903, 13 vols., indexes periodicals within its span of publication. It also is primarily a subject index, but it covers many periodicals not indexed by *Poole.*

*Annual Literary Index,* New York, 1893–1905, 13 vols., is a composite annual author and subject index to periodicals, general literature, necrology, and bibliographies, published weekly—and succeeded by the *Annual Library Index,* New York, 1905–1910. Both were superseded by the *Readers' Guide,* and by the *International Index.*

The present standard index to general American periodicals is the *Readers' Guide to Periodical Literature,* New York, 1900–current. It is a cumulative index to articles, stories, verse, and (in its early issues) reviews. Issued semi-monthly and cumulated into annual and biennial volumes, it is the basic index in its field. The *Nineteenth Century Readers' Guide to Periodical Literature, 1890–1899: With Supplementary Indexing, 1900–1922,* New York, 1944, 2 vols., was compiled by Helen G. Cushing and Adah V. Morris. It furnishes a standard modern approach by author and subject to material formerly covered by *Poole,* with additions. Fifty-one American and British periodicals are indexed, and book reviews are brought out. *International Index to Periodicals,* New York, 1907–current, is devoted chiefly to the humanities and science. It is a cumulative author and subject index to selected lists of the periodicals of many nations.

The *Annual Magazine Subject-Index* . . ., ed. by Frederick W. Faxon, Boston, 1908–current, is a subject index only, of selected American and English periodicals, in general of those not indexed elsewhere, and therefore a supplement to other indexes. A digest and index of selected book reviews in some 80 American periodicals, principally general in character, is *Book Review Digest,* New York, 1905–current.

Other specialized indexes to and bibliographies of American periodicals are Frederick W. Faxon, "Ephemeral Bibelots: A Bibliography of the Modern Chap-Books and Their Imitators, Including the Short-Story Magazines, from Their First Issue to April 1, 1903," *Bul. Bibl.*, III (1903), 72–74, 92, 106–107, 124–126; William Beer, "Checklist of American Periodicals," *Proc. Amer. Antiq. Soc.*, n.s. XXXII (1922), 330–345—titles of all magazines and periodicals published in the United States, 1741–1800 inclusive; Gertrude C. Gilmer, *Checklist of Southern Periodicals to 1861*, Boston, 1934; Sidney Ditzion, "The History of Periodical Literature in the United States: A Bibliography," *Bul. Bibl.*, XV (1935), 110, 129–133; William B. Cairns, "Magazines and Annuals," *Camb. Hist. Amer. Lit.*, II (1918), 511–518; "Later Magazines," *ibid.*, IV (1921), 774–779—checklists, with items not listed by Faxon; Frederick W. Faxon, "Literary Annuals and Gift Books, American and English: A Bibliography," *Bul. Bibl.*, V (1908), 70–72, 87–90, 105–107, 127–129, 145–149, 171–175, 203–206, VI (1909–1912), 7, 43–44, 77–81, [followed by English items:] 110–113, 147–149, 180, 208–211, 243–245; Ralph Thompson, *American Literary Annuals and Gift Books: 1825–1865*, New York, 1936— supplemented by further titles or variants in Alan E. James, "Literary Annuals and Gift Books," *Jour. Rutgers Univ. Libr.*, I (June, 1938), No. 2, 14–21; Ethel Stephens, "American Popular Magazines: A Bibliography," *Bul. Bibl.*, IX (1916), 7–10, 41–43, 69–70, 95–98; Harriet L. Matthews, "Magazines for Children," *Bul. Bibl.*, I (1899), 133–136; and Ethelyn D. Tucker, "List of Books First Published in Periodicals," *Bul. Bibl.*, I (1897), 11–12, 24–27, 41–43, 60–61, 77–79, 94–95, 108–110, 124–126, 141–142, 154–155.

The standard annual catalog of newspapers since 1880 is *Directory of Newspapers and Periodicals*. Published in Philadelphia by N. W. Ayer & Son, Inc., it was known before 1930 by the title *American Newspaper Annual . . .* Its tabulations and lists are authoritative. George P. Rowell & Co. published *American Newspaper Directory* annually from 1869 to 1908, when it merged with Ayer. It is important for the decade of the seventies. The definitive checklist of newspapers before 1820, arranged by states, has been published by Clarence S. Brigham, *History and Bibliography of American Newspapers, 1690–1820*, Worcester, Mass., 1947, 2 vols. It is indexed by both titles and printers. Useful for reference is Herbert O. Brayer, "Preliminary Guide to Indexed Newspapers in the United States, 1850–1900," *Miss. Valley Hist. Rev.*, XXXIII (1946), 237–258.

Other checklists are Edwin H. Ford, *History of Journalism in the United States: A Bibliography of Books and Annotated Articles*, Minneapolis, 1938; *idem, A Bibliography of Literary Journalism in America*, Minneapolis, 1937— a student manual; and Carl L. Cannon, *Journalism: A Bibliography*, New York, 1924—a comprehensive checklist of material in the New York Public Library. Since 1937 each issue of *Journalism Quarterly* has included an annotated bibliography of journalistic subjects in American magazines currently published.

A most important newspaper index is the *New York Times Index*, begun in 1913. By virtue of its scope, it is a current key to material in other newspapers as well. The *Index* to the *New York Daily Tribune* covers the years 1875–1906.

## DICTIONARIES AND DIGESTS

### BIOGRAPHICAL

The most authoritative biographical dictionary yet published is *Dictionary of American Biography*, New York, 1928–1936, 21 vols., including index. "Supplement One" was issued in 1944. Compiled under the auspices of the American Council of Learned Societies, it was edited by Allen Johnson and (later) Dumas Malone. Persons living are excluded. Biographical sketches of Americans born in Great Britain are included in *Dictionary of National Biography*, ed. by Leslie Stephen and Sidney Lee, 1885–1900, and later supplements.

Biographical facilities are greatly extended by a number of other cyclopedias and dictionaries. *The National Cyclopaedia of American Biography . . .*, New York, 1892–1945, 32 vols., extends to living Americans in vols. publ. after 1926. *Appleton's Cyclopedia of American Biography,* New York, 1887–1900, 7 vols., ed. by James G. Wilson and John Fiske, includes many names not in *DAB*; an enlarged edition was issued 1915, with supplementary volumes to 1931. Still useful is *The Twentieth Century Biographical Dictionary of Notable Americans*, Boston, 1904, 10 vols., ed. by Rossiter Johnson and others. The 7 vols. publ. 1897–1903 appeared under the title *Cyclopaedia of American Biographies*. Other collections that may be consulted are *Lamb's Biographical Dictionary of the United States*, Boston, 1900–1903, 7 vols., ed. by John H. Brown; Francis S. Drake, *Dictionary of American Biography . . .*, Boston, 1872. The most comprehensive one-volume compilation to date—persons living excluded—is Wheeler Preston, *American Biographies*, New York, 1940, which contains brief bibliographies.

Among biographical dictionaries of persons living, the most authoritative is *Who's Who in America*, Chicago, issued biennially since 1899. Its counterpart in England—including a few Americans—is *Who's Who*. A cumulative dictionary is *Encyclopedia of American Biography: New Series*, New York, 1934–current, ed. by Winfield S. Downs and others. *Current Biography: Who's News and Why*, New York, has been issued monthly since 1940 with annual cumulations, ed. by Maxine Block.

For authors, still indispensable is the 5-vol. compilation of Samuel A. Allibone, *A Critical Dictionary of English Literature and British and American Authors Living and Deceased, from the Earliest Accounts to the Latter Half of the Nineteenth Century* . . ., Philadelpha, 1854–1871, 3 vols.; *Supplement,* 1891, 2 vols. There is also Oscar F. Adams, *A Dictionary of American Authors,* 5th ed., rev. and enl., Boston, 1904. The best recent compilations are James D. Hart, *The Oxford Companion to American Literature,* New York, 1941; and Stanley J. Kunitz and Howard Haycraft, *American Authors, 1600– 1900: A Biographical Dictionary of American Literature,* New York, 1938 —incl. some 1,300 sketches. W. J. Burke and Will D. Howe, *American Authors and Books, 1640–1940,* New York, 1943, assemble many data on "the writing, illustrating, editing, publishing, reviewing, collecting, selling, and preservation of American books," but it must be constantly checked for accuracy. A "Biographical Dictionary of [Southern] Authors" constitutes Vol. XV of *Library of Southern Literature* . . ., Atlanta, 1907–1923, 17 vols., ed. by Edwin A. Alderman and others.

For contemporary authors there are Fred B. Millett, *Contemporary American Authors: A Critical Survey and 219 Bio-Bibliographies,* New York, 1940—which supersedes Millett's revision of the Manly-Rickert *Contemporary American Literature*; Stanley J. Kunitz and Howard Haycraft, *Twentieth Century Authors: A Biographical Dictionary of Modern Literature,* New York, 1942—with some 1,850 biographies and 1,700 illustrations, superseding Kunitz's *Living Authors* (1931), and Kunitz and Haycraft's *Authors Today and Yesterday* (1933). The *Directory of American Scholars: A Biographical Directory,* Lancaster, Pa., 1942, ed. by Jaques Cattell, lists some 12,000 living scholars. From time to time, since 1921, have appeared issues of *Who's Who Among North American Authors,* Los Angeles; and many others.

A few colleges have published biographical sketches of their graduates, similar to the sketches made of graduates of the universities of Oxford and Cambridge. Outstanding in this respect, amounting in fact to studies in cultural history, is *Sibley's Harvard Graduates: Biographical Sketches of Graduates of Harvard University* . . ., Cambridge (later Boston), 1873–1945, 7 vols. Vols. I–III (1873–1885), comp. by John L. Sibley, cover the years 1642–1689; vols. IV–VII (1933–1945), comp. by Clifford K. Shipton, brings the work down to 1725. Later volumes are in preparation. Other such works are Franklin B. Dexter, *Biographical Sketches of the Graduates of Yale College, with Annals of the College History,* New York, 1885–1911; New Haven, 1912, 6 vols.—covering the period 1701–1815; and Robert S. Fletcher and Malcolm O. Young, *Amherst College: Biographical Record of the Graduates and Non-Graduates,* Amherst, Mass., rev. ed., 1939—for the years 1821– 1939.

Information not elsewhere available can be found in Lorenzo Sabine, *Biographical Sketches of Loyalists of the American Revolution, with an Historical Essay,* Boston, 1864, 2 vols.; William B. Sprague, *Annals of the*

*American Pulpit; or, Commemorative Notices of Distinguished American Clergymen of Various Denominations, from the Early Settlement of the Country to the Close of the Year Eighteen Hundred and Fifty-five,* New York, 1857–1869, 9 vols.—indexed, and important as source material; Francis C. Wemyss, *The Chronology of the American Stage from 1752 to 1852,* New York, 1852, 4 vols.; and Thomas A. Brown, *History of the American Stage, Containing Biographical Sketches of Nearly Every Member of the Profession That Has Appeared on the American Stage, from 1733 to 1870,* New York, 1870.

Bibliographies and checklists of diaries are Harriette M. Forbes, *New England Diaries, 1602–1800: A Descriptive Catalogue of Diaries, Orderly Books and Sea Journals,* Topsfield, Mass., 1923—its many thousands of entries make it an important bibliographical source book and guide to the study of early American culture; William Matthews, *American Diaries: An Annotated Bibliography of American Diaries Written Prior to the Year 1861,* Berkeley, Calif., 1945—published and unpublished diaries in English including those of immigrants and foreign visitors; and E. F. MacPike, "American and Canadian Diaries, Journals and Note-Books: A Short List," *Bul. Bibl.,* XVIII (1944–1945), 91–92, 107–115, 133–135, 156–158.

Bibliographies directed toward biographical material are Edward H. O'Neill, *Biography by Americans, 1658–1936: A Subject Bibliography,* Philadelphia, 1939—some 7,000 items, excluding autobiographies, diaries, and journals; Helen Hefling and Jessie W. Dyde, *Hefling and Richards' Index to Contemporary Biography and Criticism,* 2nd ed., Boston, 1934; Janet M. Agnew, *A Southern Bibliography: Biography, 1929–1941,* University, La., 1942; Minnie E. Sears, *Standard Catalog: Biography Section,* New York, 1927; Claude E. Jones, "Collected Biographies to 1825," *Bul. Bibl.,* XVII (1941), 90–92, 113–116. Daniel S. Durrie compiled *Index to American Genealogies, and to Genealogical Material Contained in All Works . . .* The 5th ed. (Albany, 1900) lists about 50,000 items with a supplement to 1908. Very comprehensive is Phyllis M. Riches, *An Analytical Bibliography of Universal Collected Biography, Comprising Books Published in the English Tongue in Great Britain and Ireland, America and the British Dominions,* London, 1934.

A useful factual survey is Edward H. O'Neill, *A History of American Biography, 1800–1935,* Philadelphia, 1935, with bibliography, pp. 369–417.

REFERENCE

Standard reference compendiums and digests are James D. Hart, comp., *The Oxford Companion to American Literature,* New York, 1941; and Sir

Paul Harvey, comp., *The Oxford Companion to English Literature*, Oxford, Eng., rev. and enl., 1937. They include bio-bibliographies, summaries of notable plays, novels, poems, and other works of literature, and information on allied topics. *Annals of English Literature, 1475-1925: The Principal Publications of Each Year, Together with an Alphabetical Index of Authors with Their Works*, comp. by J. C. Ghosh and E. G. Withycombe, Oxford, Eng., 1935, includes American publications.

Newspaper indexes are especially serviceable. In addition to the *New York Times Index* and the *Index* to the *New York Daily Tribune*, noted previously, there is the important *Palmer's Index to the Times Newspaper* (of London), 1790-current. It is useful because of the importance of the newspaper and the long period covered. The index to obituary notices frequently supplies biographical material difficult to find elsewhere.

*The American Annual Cyclopedia and Register of Important Events* (Appleton's) was published annually throughout the period 1876-1896. Like the present *World Almanac,* it supplies convenient statistical tables, summaries of historical events, texts of important public documents, and other annals. There is an index to the volumes for 1876-1893 in the 1893 volume, pp 777-875.

Useful current summaries of literary as well as general events are found in such annuals as *American Year Book*, New York, 1911-current; *Americana Annual*, New York, 1923-current; *New International Year Book*, New York, 1908-current; and the *Britannica Book of the Year,* Chicago, 1938-current.

A reference guide to a more extensive period is George W. Douglas, *The American Book of Days: A Compendium of Information About Holidays, Festivals, Notable Anniversaries . . .*, New York, 1937.

The *American Guide Series,* compiled by members of the Writers' Program of the Work Projects Administration, were prepared and published (1937-1941), in various localities, for each state in the Union, and for several of the larger cities. They are illustrated, indexed, and contain brief chapters on folklore and folkways, the arts, newspapers, education, religion, resources, agriculture, industry, labor, and history, together with descriptions of the chief cities, towns, and roads. They conclude with a bibliography. Though they vary in fullness and are not uniformly competent as guides, they are on the whole significant contributions to social history, and are indispensable.

*Notes and Queries* has been continuously published in London since 1850, and runs to some 185 volumes. As a medium of communication for literary antiquarians and genealogists, it often supplies valuable information on out-of-the-way questions in very broad cultural fields. *American Notes and Queries,* modeled on its English counterpart, has been established during the past decade.

## SOURCES FOR CULTURAL HISTORY

*The Dictionary of American History,* New York, 1940, 5 vols., is a collaborative undertaking, compiled by many hundreds of scholars under the general editorship of James T. Adams. Josephus N. Larned, *The Literature of American History: A Bibliographical Guide* . . ., Boston, 1902, with two supplements in the same year, is still valuable for its critical notes. Important also is the previously mentioned compilation of H. P. Beers, *Bibliographies in American History,* rev. ed., New York, 1942, and "Writings on American History" (1902–current; edited 1906–1917 by Grace L. Griffin). Since 1918 the compilation has been issued as a supplement to the *Annual Report* of the American Historical Society. Especially useful for data regarding state and county histories is Thomas L. Bradford and Stanley V. Henkels, *The Bibliographer's Manual of American History* . . ., Philadelphia, 1907–1910, 5 vols. Two other standard guides are Peter G. Mode, *Source Book and Bibliographical Guide for American Church History,* Menasha, Wis., 1921; and Milton Waldman, *Americana: The Literature of American History,* New York, 1925. The compilation of Harriet S. Tapley, *Salem Imprints, 1768–1825: A History of the First Fifty Years of Printing in Salem, Massachusetts,* Salem, 1928, is intentionally limited in scope and coverage, but like Justin Winsor's *The Memorial History of Boston, 1630–1880,* Boston, 1880–1881, 2 vols., it is important, beyond the indication of the title, for the extensive critical notes.

Peter Force compiled *American Archives* . . ., Washington, 1837–1853, 9 vols., consisting of proceedings, state papers, debates, letters, and other public documents providing source material for the early Revolutionary years, 1774–1776. Force also compiled *The National Calendar and Annals of the United States,* Washington, 1820–1836, 14 vols. It is a statistical yearbook based upon official government sources, with historical summaries. Data for the years 1825–1827 are missing.

Hezekiah Niles published *Niles' Weekly Register,* Baltimore, 1811–1849. It is an annual record of current events, of great value to the historiographer, and is notable for the generally unbiased presentation of material. During the years 1836–1839 it was entitled *Niles' National Register.* Other guides to special aspects of social culture are Wilberforce Eames, *Early New England Catechisms: A Bibliographical Account of Some Catechisms Published Before the Year 1800, for Use in New England,* Worcester, 1898; Charles F. Heartman, *The New-England Primer Issued Prior to 1830: A Bibliographical Checklist* . . ., New York, 1934; Robert W. G. Vail, "A Check List of New England Election Sermons," *Proc. Amer. Antiquarian Soc.,* XLV (1935), 233–266—listing copies in over 30 libraries, from the seventeenth into the nineteenth century; Harry B. Weiss, "American Letter-Writers, 1698–1943,"

*Bul. N.Y. Pub. Lib.*, XLVIII (1944), 959–981; XLIX (1945), 33–61; Richard B. Harwell, *Confederate Belles-Lettres: A Bibliography and a Finding List of the Fiction, Poetry, Drama, Songsters, and Miscellaneous Literature Published in the Confederate States of America*, Hattiesburg, Miss., 1941—omitting newspapers and magazines; Dorothy B. Porter, "Early American Negro Writings: A Bibliographical Study," *Papers Bibl. Soc. Amer.*, XXXIX (1945), 192–268—with preliminary checklist for the years 1760–1835, and finding lists; John S. Bassett, "Writers on American History, 1783–1850," *Camb. Hist. Amer. Lit.*, II (1918), 488–499, a checklist; Henry R. Hitchcock, *American Architectural Books: A List of Books . . . Published in America Before 1895 on Architecture and Related Subjects . . .*, Middletown, Conn., 1938–1939; Historical Records Survey, *Bio-Bibliographical Index of Musicians in the United States of America Since Colonial Times*, Washington, 1941; Minnie E. Sears, *Song Index: An Index to More than 12,000 Songs in 177 Song Collections Comprising 262 Volumes*, New York, 1926—a supplement (New York, 1934) lists 7,000 additional songs, items which number many American poets; Oscar George Theodore Sonneck, *A Bibliography of Early Secular American Music (18th Century)*, rev. and enlarged by William Treat Upton, Washington, 1945—well indexed; Harwood L. Childs, *A Reference Guide to the Study of Public Opinion*, Princeton, N.J., 1934; Harold D. Lasswell and others, *Propaganda and Promotional Activities: An Annotated Bibliography*, Minneapolis, 1935; Wilfred Parsons, *Early Catholic Americana: A List of Books and Other Works by Catholic Authors in the United States, 1729–1830*, New York, 1939; George L. McKay, *A Register of Artists, Engravers, Booksellers, Bookbinders, Printers & Publishers in New York City, 1633–1820*, New York, 1942; Mantle Fielding, *Dictionary of American Painters, Sculptors, and Engravers*, Philadelphia, 1925; Elizabeth McCausland, "A Selected Bibliography on American Painting and Sculpture from Colonial Times to the Present," *Mag. of Art*, XXXIX (1946), 329–349—with chronological general section and an alphabetical section on individuals; Hannah Logasa, *Regional United States: A Subject List*, Boston, 1942; Edith J. R. Hawley, "Bibliography of Literary Geography," *Bul. Bibl.*, X (1918), 34–38, 58–60, 76, 93–94, 104–105; and Everett E. Edwards, "A List of American Economic Histories," *U.S. Dept. Agric., Bibliog. Contrib.*, No. 27, 1935.

# BIBLIOGRAPHIES: LITERATURE
AND CULTURE

## DEFINITION, HISTORY, AND CRITICISM

A discussion of primary and secondary sources dealing with American literature before the Revolution will be found in the period bibliography following: The Colonial Period to 1760.

Fiction, poetry, and drama are treated topically in each of the period essays. General bibliographies of all three topics are drawn out in the Guide to Resources. For discussion of fiction elsewhere among the subject bibliographies, see the Table of Contents.

### THE "PENNSYLVANIA MAGAZINE" TO THE "NORTH AMERICAN REVIEW": 1775–1815

The demands for literary independence were a very early part of the national self-consciousness, and magazines were the instruments which effectively gave expression to such interests. The *Pennsylvania Magazine; or, American Monthly Museum*, published at Philadelphia from January, 1775, to July, 1776, by Robert Aitken, was edited by Aitken and Thomas Paine. It was the first of early magazines to devote a large proportion of its space to original material. Hugh Henry Brackenridge edited the *United States Magazine* (Philadelphia, Jan.–Dec., 1779), and introduced Freneau to the public; the short span of publication was compensated for by the excellence of the material which Brackenridge selected. Two other Philadelphia magazines of the period are noteworthy. The *Columbian Magazine; or, Monthly Miscellany, Containing a View of the History, Literature, Manners and Characters of the Year* (1786–1792) was published by a literary group including Mathew Carey and Francis Hopkinson, and featured an unusual amount of native fiction. The *American Museum* (1787–1792), edited by Carey, maintained a notable standard for literary excellence, and among its contributors were Hopkinson, Franklin, and the Connecticut Wits.

During these years the editorial motive of selection was a conscious desire to achieve literary as well as political independence. Writers decried the imitation of foreign themes and models, and the neglect of native sources.

35

Royall Tyler voiced the prevailing aspiration in the prologue to *The Contrast* (first performed in 1787; publ. in 1790), in which the speaker notes the neglect of native material

> Whilst all, which aims at splendour and parade,
> Must come from Europe, and be ready made.

Indeed, the creation of a truly national literature was the main purpose of the Connecticut Wits, chief among whom were Joel Barlow, Timothy Dwight, David Humphreys, and John Trumbull. Their intent was to celebrate and encourage American literary independence.

Among important spokesmen, Philip Freneau made one of the earliest pleas for a native literature in his "Advice to Authors," collected in *The Miscellaneous Works of Mr. Philip Freneau* (1788), though he believed the accomplishment of it would not be effected for several centuries.

In the same decade Noah Webster directed his attention toward a national language. "Customs, habits, and *language*, as well as government should be national," he states in *Dissertations on the English Language* (1789). See the bibliography herein on "The American Language."

By the end of the eighteenth century implementation of the frequently voiced plea had materialized in the form of critical reviews of American publications, most notably in Charles Brockden Brown's *Monthly Magazine, and American Review* (New York, 1799-1800), the periodical which became a quarterly under the title *American Review, and Literary Journal* (1801-1802).

No literary publication of the early national period achieved greater distinction or maintained it longer than the *Port Folio* (Philadelphia, 1801-1827), founded by Joseph Dennie and published weekly during the first eight years that constituted its most productive period. It featured departments of original and selected poetry, and among its contributors were Nicholas Biddle, John Quincy Adams, Joseph Dennie, Charles Brockden Brown, Thomas Green Fessenden, and Royall Tyler. A history of the magazine and checklist of contributors has recently been published by Randolph C. Randall, "Authors of the *Port Folio* Revealed by the Hall Files," *Amer. Lit.*, XI (1940), 379-416. During these years Brown edited the *Literary Magazine, and American Register* (1803-1807), a Philadelphia monthly.

Standard studies of early magazines and magazine publications are (Harold) Milton Ellis, *Joseph Dennie and His Circle: A Study in American Literature from 1792 to 1812*, Austin, Tex., 1915; Lyon N. Richardson, *A History of Early American Magazines, 1741-1789*, New York, 1931; and Frank L. Mott, *A History of American Magazines*, Cambridge, 1938, Vol. I. Useful material is in Howard L. Flewelling's unpublished dissertation, "Literary Criticism in American Periodicals, 1783-1820," Univ. of Michigan, 1931.

A very early attempt to sketch the history of American letters is Samuel Miller, *A Brief Retrospect of the Eighteenth Century . . . Containing a Sketch of the Revolutions and Improvements in Science, Arts, and Literature During That Period*, New York, 1803, 2 vols. Two chapters especially devoted to the subject are entitled "Nations Lately Become Literary: United States of America," and "Novels and Novelists."

Literary clubs have been significant instruments in the history of American cultural development, and are discussed in Robert F. Almy's unpublished dissertation, "The Role of the Club in American Literary History, 1700–1812," Harvard Univ., 1934. One of the earliest was the Tuesday Club of Annapolis (1745–1756), founded by Dr. Alexander Hamilton and by Jonas Green, editor of the *Maryland Gazette*. It was a typical colonial literary coffeehouse. The Friendly Club of New York was an outgrowth (*ca.* 1790) of the Philological Society of New York. It aimed to further the literature of the new nation, and among its members were C. B. Brown and William Dunlap. The Tuesday Club of Philadelphia (1800–1804?) was founded by Joseph Dennie and the group that supported the *Port Folio*. It was Federalist, aristocratic, and intensely pro-English in its political sympathies. Its members included Joseph Hopkinson and Nicholas Biddle. The Anthology Club of Boston was founded *ca.* 1804 by William Tudor, George Ticknor, Joseph Stevens Buckminster, and others, and has had a continuing influence to the present day. It devoted itself to raising the standards of American literature, and selected the *Monthly Anthology; or, Magazine of Polite Literature* (1803–1811) as its organ. Edited by David P. Adams, William Emerson, and others, the periodical numbered among its contributors Daniel Webster, Washington Allston, Joseph Story, and W. C. Bryant. It was scholarly and conservative in its interests, distrustful of democratic "vulgarity," fought provincialism, and was condemned for its pro-English cultural sympathies by such men as Noah Webster, who were outspoken in their desire to establish a native literature, however vague or confused they might be regarding the method of such achievement. The Anthology Club flourished until 1811, and its reading room was the foundation of the Boston Athenaeum, modeled on the Liverpool Athenaeum in England. Buckminster's own library was the nucleus for the library of the Boston Athenaeum, built up during its nearly a century and a half of continuous existence, and it is today distinguished for its files of nineteenth century American periodicals and fiction.

An important informal literary association, the Bread and Cheese Club, was established in New York during the twenties, under the acknowledged leadership of Cooper, and with such members as Bryant, William Dunlap, and Samuel F. B. Morse. In 1827 it divided, one part becoming the Sketch Club. The Century Association, founded 1847, was an outgrowth of the Sketch Club.

At the close of the first decade of the nineteenth century, complaints about the state of American letters were vigorously and repeatedly expressed in public addresses and orations, as well as in newspapers and periodicals. Daniel Webster, delivering the annual Phi Beta Kappa address at Dartmouth College in 1809, chose as subject "The State of Our Literature," expressing skepticism about its merit as an indigenous culture. (See *The Writings and Speeches of Daniel Webster*, Boston, 1903, XV, 575–582.) In the same year Fisher Ames expressed similar doubts in his essay on "American Literature" (*Works*, ed. by Seth Ames, Boston, 1854, II, 428–442).

At the same time, defenses of a growing native literature were cogently expressed and received due attention. Charles Jared Ingersoll, the Philadelphia lawyer soon to become a member of Congress, issued *Inchiquin, The Jesuit's Letters . . .*, New York, 1810, an anonymous novel defending American culture as observed by a supposed Jesuit traveler in the States. The book, written indirectly as an answer to criticism of America by British travelers, was attacked with some violence in the English *Quarterly Review*. The defense of *Inchiquin* was undertaken by James Kirke Paulding, who directed his entire literary effort singleheartedly to championing things American; but most notably by Timothy Dwight, whose *Remarks on the Review of Inchiquin's Letters . . .*, Boston, 1815, is a key document in the beginnings of American literary criticism and the development of a national literature. Thus Paulding, as spokesman for the Knickerbocker Group, and Dwight, as spokesman for the Connecticut Wits, became the established champions of the enraged stay-at-home Americans against the systematic detraction of British critics.

The paper war which followed the naval War of 1812 demonstrated a literary bumptiousness which was first treated at length by William B. Cairns, "On the Development of American Literature from 1815 to 1833, with Especial Reference to Periodicals," *Bul. Univ. Wis. Philol. and Lit.*, ser. 1 (1898), 1–87. Other useful studies are William Charvat, *The Origins of American Critical Thought: 1810–1835*, Philadelphia, 1936; Robert E. Spiller, "Brother Jonathan to John Bull," *So. Atl. Quar.*, XXVI (1927), 346–358—a study of mutual antagonisms; Harry H. Clark, "Nationalism in American Literature," *Univ. Toronto Quar.*, II (1933), 492–519; William E. Sedgwick, "The Materials for an American Literature: A Critical Problem of the Early Nineteenth Century," *Harv. Stud. and Notes in Philol. and Lit.*, XVII (1935), 141–162; John C. McCloskey, "The Campaign of Periodicals After the War of 1812 for National American Literature," *PMLA*, L (1935), 262–273; E. K. Brown, "The National Idea in American Criticism," *Dalhousie Rev.*, XIV (1934), 133–147; Robert W. Bolwell, "Concerning the Study of Nationalism in American Literature," *Amer. Lit.*, X (1939), 405–416. Three recent studies are Jay B. Hubbell, "Literary Nationalism in the Old South," in *American*

*Studies in Honor of William Kenneth Boyd,* Durham, N.C., 1940, pp. 175–220; Earl Bradsher, "The Rise of Nationalism in American Literature," in *Studies for William A. Read,* University, La., 1940, pp. 269–287; and Gregory Paine, "American Literature a Hundred and Fifty Years Ago," *Stud. Philol.,* XLII (1945), 385–402.

The year 1815 is notable in American literary history, not because it marked a high point in chauvinistic self-consciousness, but because it witnessed the establishment of the *North American Review* (1815–1940). Founded in Boston as an outgrowth of the *Monthly Anthology* by Edward T. Channing, William Tudor, R. H. Dana, Sr., and others, it aimed to achieve a greater national scope than any previous American magazine. It began as a quarterly literary, critical, and historical review, modeled on its English contemporaries. During its long and distinguished career it numbered among its editors (besides Tudor and Channing) Edward Everett, Jared Sparks, J. G. Palfrey, C. E. Norton, J. R. Lowell, and Henry Adams. Its contributors are a roster of the most influential literary spokesmen of the nineteenth century, and no single magazine can claim a more widespread or influential place in the history of American letters. Two useful published studies are Harry H. Clark, "Literary Criticism in the *North American Review,* 1815–1835," *Trans. Wis. Acad. Sci., Arts, and Letters,* XXXII (1940), 299–350—including summaries of 231 critical reviews; and Robert E. Streeter, "Association Psychology and Literary Nationalism in the *North American Review,*" *Amer. Lit.,* XVII (1945), 243–254. Further material is in Streeter's unpublished dissertation, "Critical Ideas in the *North American Review,* 1815–1865," Northwestern Univ., 1943.

A general background study is Hans Kohn, *The Idea of Nationalism* . . . , New York, 1944, especially Chap. VI. See also John B. Henneman, "The National Element in Southern Literature," *Sewanee Rev.,* XI (1903), 345–366.

EARLY AMERICAN MISCELLANIES: TO 1829

The miscellany or anthology, like the periodical, was an instrument during the formative period which gave expression to an increasing interest in a national literature. One of the very earliest to include the work of native writers on patriotic grounds was *The American Museum; or, Repository of Ancient and Modern Fugitive Pieces, Prose and Poetical,* published in Philadelphia by Mathew Carey. Twelve volumes were issued between 1787 and 1792, including essays written by Franklin and Paine and poetry by Barlow, Humphreys, Freneau, Ladd, and others. "Several late American productions, when published in Europe, have been received with merited eclat," says the editor (I, 236). "Poets, like prophets, are not without honour, except in their own country and among their own kindred."

Several earlier miscellanies had been devoted to publishing native material, with the implied, though not expressed, desire to show that the colonies could cultivate polite letters. The earliest known seems to have been *Select Essays, with Some Few Miscellaneous Copies of Verses Drawn by Ingenious Hands,* Boston, 1714, a group of undistinguished poems and prose essays evidently the work of Harvard undergraduates who wished to emulate the collections issued by undergraduates at Oxford and Cambridge. The unique copy of the volume is in the library of the Massachusetts Historical Society. Mather Byles undertook to bring out *A Collection of Poems, by Several Hands,* Boston, 1744 (actually 1745), a gathering made up largely of selections from Byles's own writings. Similar in intent to *Select Essays* was *Pietas et Gratulatio Collegii Cantabrigiensis apud Novanglos,* Boston, 1761, addressed to His Majesty King George III on his accession to the throne, by the President and Fellows of Harvard College. A Philadelphia schoolmaster, John Beveridge, evidently with similar intent, published the last pre-Revolutionary miscellany in Philadelphia, 1765: *Epistolae Familiares . . . Familiar Epistles and Other Miscellaneous Pieces, Wrote Originally in Latin Verse . . . To Which are added several Translations into English Verse, by Different Hands.*

Two other collections undertaken in the same year that *The American Museum* first appeared were *Miscellanies, Moral and Instructive, in Prose and Verse; Collected from Various Authors for the Use of Schools, and Improvement of Young Persons of Both Sexes,* Philadelphia, 1787 (and later reprints elsewhere); and *Select Poems on Various Occasions, Chiefly American, among which are several wrote by the celebrated Doctor Ladd,* Boston, 1787.

One of the most interesting of Mathew Carey's collections is *The Beauties of Poetry, British and American . . . ,* Philadelphia, 1791, including verses of Barlow, Dwight, Freneau, Humphreys, Livingston, Ladd, Hopkinson, Markoe, and others. "He hopes," says the editor of his labors, "that to the Americans this work will be more acceptable than those on the same plan from Great Britain." At Litchfield, Conn., in 1793, Elihu Hubbard Smith brought out a volume solely devoted to native poetry: *American Poems, Selected and Original.* In the following year appeared *The Columbian Muse: A Selection of American Poetry from Various Authors of Established Reputation,* New York, 1794. Mathew Carey reprinted selections from newspapers and periodicals in *Miscellaneous Trifles in Prose,* Philadelphia, 1796. Abiel Holmes edited *A Family Tablet: Containing a Selection of Original Poetry,* Boston, 1796—contributions mostly from the family of the Reverend Ezra Stiles, President of Yale.

Imitations of English songsters, with material chosen often for its patriotic interest, may be represented by *The Columbian Songster, or Jovial Companion: being a collection of two hundred and twenty Choice Songs . . . of which near Fifty are American productions*, New York, 1797; and *The American Musical Miscellany: A Collection of the Newest and Most Approved Songs, Set to Music*, Northampton, Mass., 1798. George Bourne selected and edited *The Spirit of the Public Journals; or, Beauties of the American Newspapers, For 1805*, Baltimore, 1806.

The preface of *The Echo, With other Poems* (1807), verse satire by the Connecticut Wits, had first been published in 20 numbers in the *American Mercury* (1791–1805). Their national self-consciousness is explicitly indicated in the preface, which remarks: "Willing to lend their aid to check the progress of false taste in American literature, the authors conceived that ridicule would prove a powerful corrective." *The Cabinet of Momus: A Choice Selection of Humorous Poems*, Philadelphia, 1809, includes poetry written by Americans, and *The American Poetical Miscellany: Original and Selected*, Philadelphia, 1809, remarks in the preface (p. 10), "It cannot escape the attention of the discerning reader, that we have published a much greater portion of *American* productions than are to be found in any other publication of this kind in the English language."

At the beginning of the second quarter of the century miscellanies made up from selections originally published in periodicals were commonplace. One of the best is *Miscellaneous Poems Selected from the United States Literary Gazette*, Boston, 1826, including liberal selections from the poetry of Bryant and Longfellow. John H. A. Frost edited *The Class Book of American Literature . . .*, Boston, 1826, compiled entirely "from the works of our native writers," including selections from the stories of C. B. Brown, Cooper, Irving, and the poetry of Bryant, Longfellow, and George Bancroft.

By far the most significant collection is that edited by Samuel Kettell, *Specimens of American Poetry, with Critical and Biographical Notices*, Boston, 1829, 3 vols. It incorporates selections from Cotton Mather to Whittier and concludes with a "Catalogue of American Poetry," III, 379–407. The critical and bibliographical notes make this compilation a literary history of great importance. In the same decade, American poetry abroad had been recognized by the publication of such miscellanies as *Specimens of the American Poets: With Critical Notices, and a Preface*, London, 1822, and *The Columbian Lyre: Specimens of Transatlantic Poetry*, Glasgow, 1828; for identification of the compiler as Israel Keech Tefft, see Jay B. Hubbell, *Ga. Hist. Quar.*, XXVI (1942), 288.

A discussion of early miscellanies is Richard C. Boys, "The Beginnings of the American Poetical Miscellany, 1714–1800," *Amer. Lit.*, XVII (1945),

127–139. See also Fred L. Pattee, "Anthologies of American Literature Before 1861," *Colophon*, pt. 16 (1934)—an 8-page checklist.

## THE "NORTH AMERICAN REVIEW" TO EMERSON'S "THE AMERICAN SCHOLAR": 1815–1837

De Witt Clinton's observations on the intellectual life of the period are published in *An Introductory Discourse Delivered Before the Literary and Philosophical Society of New York,* New York, 1815, and are especially useful as a survey of literary stirrings in New York City. A brief summary of "The Progress of the United States in Literature" was published in *Niles' Weekly Register,* XI (Sept. 28, 1816), 66–69. In Baltimore, the Delphian Club (founded 1816) was a literary association whose members included John Neal, Francis Scott Key, and Samuel Woodworth. Their literary organ, the *Portico* (1816–1818), issued monthly, was under Neal's editorship. It was chauvinistic in outlook, and unrestrained in criticism of foreign authors. Rhapsodic and uncritical adulation of native writers was epitomized by Solyman Brown's *An Essay on American Poetry,* New Haven, 1818, written in rhymed couplets. It was mercilessly ridiculed by William Cullen Bryant in a review which appeared in the *North American Review,* VII (1818), 198–207, wherein Bryant took occasion to state his own critical values and estimate the accomplishment of American poets, whom he criticized in general for their "sickly and affected imitation" of English popular poets.

One of the most explicit pleas for the use of native material to be published in the first quarter of the century was that of John Knapp in an essay on "National Poetry," written for the *North American Review,* VIII (1819), 169–176, in which he concludes: "A country is undeniably the more endeared by the multitude for its tender and heroical tales and memoirs, fabulous as well as authentic. Let us then not slight even its barbaric annals. Let us not only revisit the dwellings of the European settler exposed to savage incursions, and every variety of affecting vicissitude; but let us hasten to acquaint ourselves with the earlier native."

Though social and literary criticism by Americans was frequently voiced during this period (effectively represented by William Tudor's *Letters on the Eastern States,* 1820), no estimate was more bitterly resented than that of Sydney Smith, the editor of the *Edinburgh Review.* Smith took occasion in reviewing Seybert's *Annals of the United States* in the January, 1820, issue of his magazine to query: "In the four quarters of the globe, who reads an American book? or goes to an American play? or looks at an American picture or statue?" The effect of this well known comment is studied in Robert E. Spiller, "The Verdict of Sydney Smith," *Amer. Lit.,* I (1929), 3–13.

Such British criticism was answered by James K. Paulding, among others, in *A Sketch of Old England by a New England Man* (1822).

Of the great number of speeches and articles on the subject of a national literature published between 1820 and 1830, a few are noteworthy. Charles J. Ingersoll chose as subject for the annual oration before the American Philosophical Society in Philadelphia, 1823, *A Discourse Concerning the Influence of America on the Mind,* advocating a literature that would satisfy the practical and utilitarian American character. Edward Everett, delivering the Phi Beta Kappa address at Harvard in 1824, elected to discuss "The Circumstances Favorable to the Progress of Literature in America," as conceived by one who was at the time Professor of Greek in the College, and an editor of the *North American Review.* (See his *Orations and Speeches* . . . , Boston, 1850, I, 9–44.) An ambitious attempt to write a history of American literature was that of John Neal, who set out to interpret America as favorably as possible to the British by publishing a series of five anonymous essays on "American Writers" in *Blackwood's Magazine,* XVI (1824), 304–311, 415–428, 560–571; XVII (1825), 48–69, 186–207. It took the form of critical reviews of 135 American authors, arranged alphabetically by name, with much the longest essay devoted to himself. The essays are reprinted, ed. with introd., notes, and bibl. by Fred L. Pattee, as *John Neal's American Writers* . . . , Durham, N.C., 1937. A second vigorous defense by Bryant of American themes is his review of Catharine M. Sedgwick's *Redwood* (1824), in *No. Amer. Rev.,* XX (1825), 246–256. The first expression of Longfellow's later fight for the poet's place in American life was given utterance in his Commencement oration at Bowdoin in 1825. He addressed himself to the subject of "Our Native Writers," and observed, "Poetry with us has never yet been anything but a pastime." He returned to the theme later in the dialogue (chapter XX) of his novel *Kavanagh: A Tale* (1849); and he exemplified his belief that writers should use native material in his narrative poems *Evangeline* (1847) and *The Song of Hiawatha* (1855). It was in his later years that Longfellow moved from the nationalist position to the cosmopolitan.

Of central importance in the history of American literary criticism during the period are the four lectures on poetry delivered by Bryant in 1826 on the invitation of the New York Athenaeum. They express not only his own critical theory and that of many of his lesser contemporaries, but also to some degree that of Longfellow and the Cambridge group.

It was also in this era that Cooper published his first extended defense of American literature and institutions, in *Notions of the Americans* (1828), Letter XXIII, concluding: "Notwithstanding the overwhelming influence of British publications, and all the difficulties I have named, original books are getting to be numerous in the United States."

By the end of the decade Samuel L. Knapp had published the first and most ambitious attempt at a history of American literature in book form: *Lectures on American Literature, with Remarks on Some Passages of American History,* New York, 1829.

Among magazines founded during the decade and largely devoted to literature a few are especially significant. The *New York Mirror* (1823-1857) was edited by Samuel Woodworth, and later by N. P. Willis, C. F. Hoffman, Epes Sargent, and others. Poe was engaged by the journal during 1844-1845. The *United States Literary Gazette,* Boston, 1824-1826, was notable for its poetry contributed, among others, by Bryant and Longfellow. Charles Folsom and Bryant edited the *United States Review and Literary Gazette* during its brief career both in Boston and in New York, 1826-1827. The most distinguished periodical established at this time was *Graham's Magazine,* Philadelphia, 1826-1858, which numbered among its editors George R. Graham, Poe, Rufus Griswold, and Bayard Taylor. Its contributors are a roster of the most prominent writers of the time.

An important indication that the West was developing literary consciousness was the founding of the *Western Monthly Review,* Cincinnati, 1827-1830, by Timothy Flint. Flint's purpose in this venture was to interpret the West to the East, and his criticism of American dependence on Europe and of a lack of cultural centers is frequently voiced. The most successful western magazine of its time, and the earliest literary periodical west of Ohio, was James Hall's *Western Monthly Magazine,* Cincinnati and Louisville, 1830-1837, published during its first two years as the *Illinois Monthly Magazine.*

In the South, Stephen Elliott and Hugh S. Legaré founded the *Southern Review,* Charleston, 1828-1832, one of the earliest southern periodicals of distinction. Highly significant, both in the history of southern literature and in the study of the development of many literary figures, was the *Southern Literary Messenger* (1834-1864), founded in Richmond by Thomas W. White. Poe first contributed "Berenice" to it in March, 1835, and in December of that year became its editor. His tales, critical essays, and reviews made the periodical famous, and it achieved its greatest and most merited success during the two years of his editorship. For an account of it, see David K. Jackson, *The Contributors and Contributions to the Southern Literary Messenger, 1834-1864,* Charlottesville, Va., 1936, supplemented by *idem,* "An Estimate of the Influence of *The Southern Literary Messenger,* 1834-1864," *So. Lit. Mes.,* I (1939), 508-514.

An important early general magazine in the East was the *New-England Magazine,* Boston, 1831-1835, edited by Joseph T. Buckingham and others. It was in the thirties also that the *Knickerbocker Magazine* (1833-1865) was established in New York as a monthly literary magazine. Under the editorship (1834–1861) of Lewis Gaylord Clark and his twin brother Willis Gaylord Clark it became, especially during the forties, the most distinguished literary periodical of its day. Its contributors included the best known writers in the country. A third important (western) magazine was founded at about the same time: the *Western Messenger,* Cincinnati and Louisville, 1835–1841, under the editorship of James Freeman Clarke, William H. Channing, and others, who devoted it, as the subtitle at one time specified, to religion and literature.

The great popularity of George B. Cheever's anthology of American poetry gives it some claim to notice. His compilation, *The American Common-place Book of Poetry, with Occasional Notes,* Boston, 1831, was later issued as *The Poets of America, with Occasional Notes,* and by 1876 had gone through 24 printings and many revisions.

The most important evidence of critical maturity manifested itself at this time. William E. Channing published an essay in the *Christian Examiner* for January, 1830, on "The Importance and Means of a National Literature." Ostensibly a review of Ingersoll's *A Discourse Concerning the Influence of America on the Mind,* it was in fact Channing's literary testament. He felt it intolerable that a literature should do no more than reflect the utilitarian mind of a nation. It must do more than accept and express material circumstances. He thus advanced beyond the narrower interpretations of Freneau, Webster, and Cooper, and prepared the way for the most challenging document in the early history of American letters, Emerson's essay on "The American Scholar." Emerson's address was delivered at the invitation of the Phi Beta Kappa Society of Harvard College on August 31, 1837, and the memorable occasion is vividly reconstructed by Bliss Perry in "Emerson's Most Famous Speech" (*The Praise of Folly and Other Papers,* Boston, 1923). The final paragraph epitomizes Emerson's ideas on a national literature: "The scholar is that man who must take up into himself all the ability of the time, all the contributions of the past, all the hopes of the future. . . . We have listened too long to the courtly muses of Europe. . . . We will walk on our own feet; we will work with our own hands; we will speak our own minds. The study of letters shall be no longer a name for pity, for doubt, and for sensual indulgence. . . ."

## "THE AMERICAN SCHOLAR" TO "LEAVES OF GRASS": 1837–1855

The eighteen years which intervened between the delivery of Emerson's address on "The American Scholar" and the publication of the first issue of Whitman's *Leaves of Grass* gave evidence of continuing interest in American letters through the establishment of significant literary periodicals, the com-

pilation of anthologies exclusively devoted to American writers, and the publication of important critical studies.

The *Dial: A Magazine for Literature, Philosophy, and Religion*, Boston,
1840–1844, was edited first by Margaret Fuller, and later (1842–1844) by Emerson. It was the most important of transcendental journals and offered encouragement to writers like Thoreau, whose works did not attract a public
primarily interested in entertainment. Its services to the cause of letters were
proportionately greater than its relatively small and brief circulation would
indicate. In New York, Cornelius Mathews and Evert A. Duyckinck founded
the critical magazine *Arcturus: A Journal of Books and Opinion* (1840–1842),
and secured for it very distinguished American contributors. The *Southern
Quarterly Review* (1842–1857), a proslavery journal issued mainly from
Charleston, never achieved the reputation of the *Southern Review,* though it
published some notable material, especially under the editorship of James
D. B. De Bow (1844–1845) and of William G. Simms (1856–1857). *Brownson's Quarterly Review* (1844–1875), founded and edited by Orestes A.
Brownson, long remained the organ for Brownson's versatile and combative
mind, reflecting at times an influential, if chauvinistic, concern for American
civilization. Much material of literary importance appeared in the *Literary
World* (New York, 1847–1853), a weekly journal of society, literature, and
art, edited by Evert A. Duyckinck and others. After the demise of the *Dial,* a
Boston group including Emerson, Theodore Parker, and J. E. Cabot founded
the *Massachusetts Quarterly Review,* Boston, 1847–1850, a literary philosophical, and humanitarian journal that reflected a more vigorous editorial
policy than had been supported by the *Dial. Harper's Monthly Magazine,*
founded in New York as an eclectic literary periodical by Harper and Brothers
in 1850 (and known since 1925 simply as *Harper's Magazine*), in its early
years drew most heavily upon well known British authors. *Putnam's Monthly
Magazine* (1853–1910) was established as a distinctively American periodical,
with contributions during its early years by leading writers. Suspended in
1857, it was revived briefly in 1868–1870, and again in 1906–1910.

Several notable anthologies were issued in these years. Bryant, by now
established as one of the leading American critics, compiled *Selections from
the American Poets,* New York, 1840, with a brief foreword "To the Reader"
which set forth the principles of selection. John Keese issued *The Poets of
America,* New York, 1840. Much more significant is William D. Gallagher's
*Selections from the Poetical Literature of the West,* Cincinnati, 1841, a compilation of 109 poems written by 38 Ohio Valley poets. In part inspired by
regional pride, it intended to demonstrate that the West as well as the East
might claim some share of recognition in the cultural development of a nation,
as the brief prefatory apology hints.

Undoubtedly the most famous compilations of the period were the three collections published by Rufus W. Griswold. *The Poets and Poetry of America, to the Middle of the Nineteenth Century,* Philadelphia, 1842, however unreliable as text, is still useful for reference. It soon became a standard collection, and was frequently revised and enlarged. Richard H. Stoddard added his name to the title page when he issued it with new material in 1873. Griswold's success with *The Poets* gave him warrant for publishing a companion volume, *The Prose Writers of America: with a Survey of the Intellectual History, Condition, and Prospects of the Country,* Philadelphia, 1847. Similarly unreliable as text, it still remains especially useful for its selections from minor authors. In its later editions it also incorporated new material. Griswold's *The Female Poets of America,* Philadelphia, 1848 (rev. and enl. by R. H. Stoddard, New York, 1874), is also valuable for the student, and the critical judgments therein expressed, together with those in the earlier compilations, are historically significant, however faulty in critical acumen.

An anthology of selections from Anne Bradstreet to Alice and Phoebe Cary is Caroline May, ed., *The American Female Poets,* Philadelphia, 1848. Some material not easily found elsewhere is in John S. Hart's *The Female Prose Writers of America, with Portraits, Biographical Notices, and Specimens of Their Writings,* Philadelphia, 1852 (rev. ed., 1855).

Cooper's *The American Democrat* (1838) is a statement of his social and political aims in terms of principles, and is historically significant during this period as the creed of a very influential literary spokesman for America. An early survey, with some attention to native elements, is Samuel L. Knapp, *Advice in the Pursuits of Literature,* Middletown, N.J., 1837 (also New York, 1841).

By far the most judicious and searching literary history published during these years is Eugène A. Vail's *De la Littérature et des Hommes de Lettres des Etats-Unis d'Amérique,* Paris, 1841, with observations on C. B. Brown, Cooper, Paulding, Bryant, Emerson, Longfellow, and others. The study, undertaken by an American living in France, was written to demonstrate to Europeans a native American literary culture. It indicates furthermore that American literature was the subject of historical study abroad at a very early period. Philarète Chasles, a professor of the Collège de France, published his *Etudes sur la Littérature et les Mœurs des Anglo-Américains au XIX<sup>e</sup> Siècle,* Paris, 1851. Much is derived from Vail, though the chapter on Melville is a recognition which Melville's own countrymen were much slower in giving. The volume appeared in New York in the following year translated by Donald MacLeod as *Anglo-American Literature and Manners.*

Not all believed that America could or should have a national literature, and a strong opposition to it was frequently voiced. Edward Sherman Gould

(1805-1885) delivered a series of lectures published as *American Criticism of American Literature* (1836), extolling British writing, and decrying the native accomplishment. George Tucker opposed the idea in an "Address on American Literature," *So. Lit. Mess.*, IV (1838). Joseph Rocchietti wrote *Why a National Literature Cannot Flourish in the United States* . . ., New York, 1845, 84 pp. E. W. Johnson ridiculed the idea in "American Letters: Their Character and Advancement," *Amer. Whig Rev.*, I (1845), 575-580; and James Russell Lowell wrote an unfavorable review of Longfellow's *Kavanagh*: "Nationality in Literature," *No. Amer. Rev.*, LXIX (1849), 196-215.

One of the very earliest discussions of American drama is James Rees, *The Dramatic Authors of America*, Philadelphia, 1845. It is not a history, and is somewhat inaccurate in detail, but it is valuable as source material.

Poe's sketches of the Knickerbocker Group and other New York authors were published in six installments in *Godey's Lady's Book* during 1846. Though often unsympathetic, their critical discrimination gives them an intrinsic value which posterity recognizes, however odious the judgments seemed at the time to friend or foe. They were published in book form as *The Literati: Some Honest Opinions About Autorial Merits and Demerits* . . ., New York, 1850. Poe's interest in the problem of nationality in American letters, and his growing breadth of comprehension of the question, can be traced in his review of Drake's *The Culprit Fay*, in *So. Lit. Mess.*, April, 1836; "Letter to Mr. ———," *ibid.*, July, 1836; "Marginalia," *ibid.*, July, 1849. His most important utterance on the subject, written in 1842 for *Graham's Magazine*, is his "Exordium"—see *The Complete Works* . . . (ed. Harrison, 1902), XI, 1-8.

Melville's discussion of nationalism is in his essay "Hawthorne and His Mosses," published in the *Literary World*, Aug. 17 and 24, 1850. "Believe me, my friends," he comments, "that men, not very much inferior to Shakespeare, are this day being born on the banks of the Ohio."

In the same year appeared a review of Griswold's *Prose Writers*, attacking the "Bay" school for strain and frigidity, and defending the "Knickerbocker" school, especially Irving, under the title, "Schools in American Literature," *Church Rev.*, III (1850), 329-348.

Undoubtedly the most impressive literary testament of the period is Walt Whitman's preface to the first edition of *Leaves of Grass* (1855). It may properly stand as a synthesis of all the earlier pleas for an American literature, and is remarkable in that Whitman knew so little of the country at first hand. "The proof of a poet," he concludes, "is that his country absorbs him as affectionately as he has absorbed it."

The extent to which ten major writers—Irving, Bryant, Cooper, Poe, Hawthorne, Emerson, Longfellow, Whittier, Holmes, and Lowell—were interested in or affiliated with national problems and parties is the subject of Arthur H. Quinn, "American Literature and American Politics," *Proc. Amer. Antiq. Soc.,* LIX (1944), 59–112. Also useful is Benjamin T. Spencer, "A National Literature, 1837–1855," *Amer. Lit.,* VIII (1936), 125–159.

### DUYCKINCK'S "CYCLOPAEDIA" TO STEDMAN'S "ANTHOLOGY": 1855–1900

One of the earliest and most inclusive collections still valuable for material (especially of minor writers) not otherwise easily available is Evert A. and George L. Duyckinck, *Cyclopaedia of American Literature: Embracing Personal and Critical Notices of Authors, and Selections from Their Writings, from the Earliest Period to the Present Day,* New York, 1855 (and later editions), 2 vols. *The Supplement* (1866) supplies continuations and omitted notices. In 1857 James Russell Lowell established the *Atlantic Monthly;* and he served as its editor until 1861. Since its founding, the *Atlantic Monthly* has continuously maintained rank as one of the leading literary periodicals in the United States. See Mark A. De Wolfe Howe, *The Atlantic Monthly and Its Makers,* Boston, 1919.

In the West William T. Coggeshall made his plea for regional recognition in *The Protective Policy in Literature,* Columbus, Ohio, 1859. *The Poets and Poetry of the West: With Biographical and Critical Notices,* Columbus, 1860, which he edited, was intended to correct the neglect of western writers by Griswold and the Duyckincks.

Holmes was aware of an excessive self-consciousness among American writers of the period, as was Lowell. Both writers turned to European models for style and theme. Nevertheless they recognized the great importance of self-dependence and the value of native material. Lowell's essay in praise of Thoreau, published in *No. Amer. Rev.,* Oct., 1865, and collected in *My Study Windows* (1871), says of Thoreau: ". . . his metaphors and images are always fresh from the soil." In the same essay he takes occasion to extol Emerson: "There is no man to whom our aesthetic culture owes so much."

The New York monthly, the *Galaxy* (1866–1878), was published with the intent of counteracting the alleged provincialism of the *Atlantic Monthly.* Its interest in wider nationalism is demonstrated in the fact that Mark Twain served as an editor, and among contributors were Whitman, John W. De Forest, and H. H. Boyesen. *Lippincott's Magazine* (1868–1916) was a Philadelphia literary monthly of distinction, especially to the 1890's, aiming to be more national in scope than the *Atlantic Monthly.*

Important critical studies of American writers by the leading French critics of the day appeared frequently in the *Revue des Deux Mondes* during the mid-nineteenth century. Among Americans especially singled out for discussion, and occasionally for translation, were Poe, Emerson, Melville, Sealsfield, Longfellow, Hawthorne, Margaret Fuller, Harriet Beecher Stowe, Whitman, Mark Twain, and Bret Harte. An index of articles on American literature was published in *Revue des Deux Mondes: Table Générale, 1831–1874,* Paris, 1875, pp. 471–472.

Critics were now beginning to discuss what the Great American Novel should be. John W. De Forest in his brief essay on "The Great American Novel," *Nation,* VI (1868), 27–29, concludes: "We fear that the wonder will not soon be wrought unless more talent can be enlisted in the work, and we are sure that this sufficient talent can hardly be obtained without the encouragement of an international copyright. And, even then, is it time?" Thomas S. Perry in a review of "American Novels" in the *No. Amer. Rev.,* CXV (1872), 366–378, commented on the American writer, "The less conscious he is of trying to be American, the more truly will he succeed in being so. . . . He must idealize. The idealizing novelist will be the real novelist." A scathing review of Lew Wallace's *The Fair God,* in *Old and New,* IX (1874), 259–261, condemned it on the ground that it was unsuccessfully trying to be the Great American Novel. For discussion of the ideas of mid-nineteenth century critics concerning what the novel should be, see Herbert R. Brown, "The Great American Novel," *Amer. Lit.,* VII (1935), 1–14.

Textbooks and manuals of American literature were slowly introduced into college curriculums. An early text with interestingly fresh judgments, especially on Melville and Whitman, is John Seely Hart, *A Manual of American Literature,* Philadelphia, 1873. A landmark in American literary historical scholarship was established in 1878 with the publication of Moses C. Tyler, *A History of American Literature, 1607–1765,* New York, 1878 (rev. ed., 1897), 2 vols. It was followed by *The Literary History of the American Revolution, 1763–1783,* New York, 1897, 2 vols. (issued, with introd., by Randolph G. Adams, for Facsimile Library, New York, 1941, 2 vols.). These two works by Tyler constitute still the fullest treatment of the periods covered. Indeed, their virtue has been a disadvantage in that Tyler's labors were so careful and detailed that later scholars have been slow in re-evaluating the literature of the colonial period in the light of more recent research. Howard M. Jones' *The Life of Moses Coit Tyler,* Ann Arbor, Mich., 1933, is based on an unpublished dissertation by Thomas E. Casady. See also Richard M. Dorson, "Moses Coit Tyler, Historian of the American Genesis," *Southwest Rev.,* XXVI (1941), 416–427.

John Nichol's *American Literature: An Historical Sketch, 1620–1880,* Edinburgh, 1882, is interesting as a brief historical essay by a Briton.

*Scribner's Monthly,* important from 1870 to 1881 for its serials and short stories often dealing with American themes, became the *Century Illustrated Monthly Magazine* (1881–1930). Richard Watson Gilder edited the *Century Magazine* from 1881 till his death in 1909, and his influence in the tradition of delicacy as a leader of New York literary life was of great importance.

Edwin P. Whipple's *American Literature and Other Papers,* Boston, 1887, devotes the first 138 pages to "American Literature" and concludes with two extensive essays on Emerson and one on Webster as stylists. Charles F. Richardson's *American Literature, 1607–1885,* New York, 1887–1888, 2 vols., an early and inclusive survey, is still useful, though it neglects historical inquiry. The 11-volume collection of Edmund C. Stedman and Ellen M. Hutchinson, *A Library of American Literature from the Earliest Settlement to the Present Time,* New York, 1888–1890, is still useful for its inclusiveness, though it contains no critical or bibliographical matter. Charles Dudley Warner, who edited the "American Men of Letters" series—a task undertaken in the late seventies—brought out the extensive *Library of the World's Best Literature* (30 vols., 1896–1897). Likewise inclusive is Edwin A. Alderman and others, *Library of Southern Literature . . . ,* Atlanta, 1907–1923, 17 vols.

Karl Knortz taught courses in American literature in Germany before coming to the United States late in the century, and published his *Geschichte der Nordamerikanischen Literatur,* Berlin, 1891, 2 vols. See Horst Frenz, "Karl Knortz, Interpreter of American Literature and Culture," *Amer.-Ger. Rev.,* XIII (Dec., 1946), 27–30.

Other studies and surveys published during the last decade of the century include Greenough White, *A Sketch of the Philosophy of American Literature,* Boston, 1891, 66 pp.; Hjalmar H. Boyesen, *Literary and Social Silhouettes,* New York, 1894—with chapters on the American novel; Brander Matthews, *An Introduction to the Study of American Literature,* New York, 1896—a brief survey with chapters largely devoted to major nineteenth century figures; Katharine Lee Bates, *American Literature,* New York, 1898; and Donald G. Mitchell ("Ik Marvel"), *American Lands and Letters,* New York, 1898–1899, 2 vols.—still useful for its illustrations.

In 1900 Lewis E. Gates published *Studies and Appreciations*—impressionistic estimates of a few major nineteenth century writers. It was also in 1900 that Barrett Wendell published *A Literary History of America* (latest printing, New York, 1928), a study heavily biased in favor of the New England tradition.

The most distinguished compilation at the turn of the century was that of Edmund C. Stedman, *An American Anthology, 1787–1900: Selections Illustrating the Editor's Critical Review of American Poetry in the Nineteenth Century,* Boston, 1900. It is prefaced with a critical introduction, pp. xv–xxxiv, and includes selections reaching from Freneau to E. A. Robinson.

For a discussion of the period, see Benjamin T. Spencer, "The New Realism and a National Literature," *PMLA*, LVI (1941), 1116–1132.

### STEDMAN TO "THE CAMBRIDGE HISTORY OF AMERICAN LITERATURE": 1900–1917

The American Academy of Arts and Letters was founded in 1904 as an honorary group of 50 members within the National Institute of Arts and Letters (founded 1898). Its intent was to honor accomplishment in American literature and the arts. The first decade of the twentieth century also witnessed a greatly increased number of studies devoted to American literature and literary history. Among them were James L. Onderdonk, *History of American Verse, 1610–1897,* Chicago, 1901; Charles W. Moulton, *The Library of Literary Criticism of English and American Authors,* Buffalo, 1901–1905, 8 vols.—selected excerpts of periodical and other criticism containing material not easily available elsewhere; Lorenzo Sears, *American Literature in the Colonial and National Periods,* Boston, 1902; William P. Trent, *A History of American Literature, 1607–1865,* New York, 1903—still useful for its critical estimates; George E. Woodberry, *America in Literature,* New York, 1903—marred by its failure to give recognition to Whitman and Mark Twain; Lillie D. Loshe, *The Early American Novel,* New York, 1907, repr. 1930—a pioneer study still valuable for the period before 1830; John (Albert) Macy, *The Spirit of American Literature,* Garden City, N.Y., 1908, rev. ed. 1913—a pioneering contribution to the newer aesthetic and social liberalism, with 16 critical estimates of major authors from Irving to Henry James; William B. Otis, *American Verse, 1625–1807: A History,* New York, 1909—inclusive rather than critical, with a useful bibliography, pp. 277–293; Percival Pollard, *Their Day in Court,* New York, 1909—one of the very earliest critical surveys of twentieth century American writings; William C. Brownell, *American Prose Masters,* New York, 1909—an attempt at a systematic analysis of the cultural past; William B. Cairns, *Selections from Early American Writers, 1607–1800,* New York, 1909; and John Erskine, *Leading American Novelists,* New York, 1910—essays on C. B. Brown, Cooper, Simms, Hawthorne, Stowe, and Bret Harte.

Still valuable for its temperate, balanced critical judgments and for its inclusiveness is William B. Cairns, *A History of American Literature,* New York, 1912 (rev. ed., 1930).

*Poetry: A Magazine of Verse* (1912–current) was founded in Chicago by Harriet Monroe. Devoted exclusively to poetry, it has been the precursor of many "little magazines," and has been one of the most stimulating influences on American literature. It never confined itself to any school or type, and has published the works of such diverse authors as Sandburg, Amy Lowell, T. S. Eliot, Frost, "H. D.," Pound, Lindsay, and Hart Crane—poets whose achievements in many instances it has been first to recognize.

In 1913, William S. Braithwaite published the first *Anthology of Magazine Verse . . . and Yearbook of American Poetry.* Braithwaite edited the volumes annually through 1929. Sporadic issues undertaken by succeeding editors were published till 1942.

Important among later discussions of literary nationalism is Van Wyck Brooks, *America's Coming-of-Age,* New York, 1915. Others during the period who sought to define the shape which they believed American literature should take include Theodore Dreiser, Thomas Beer, Ernest Boyd, Ludwig Lewisohn, V. F. Calverton, Robert Morss Lovett, and J. E. Spingarn.

Fred L. Pattee published *A History of American Literature Since 1870,* New York, 1915, with useful discussions of minor writers and schools, particularly the "local color" group. In the same year, Edward J. O'Brien published the first of his anthologies of *The Best Short Stories . . .* (American), issued annually with checklists till 1942.

Still one of the best balanced anthologies is that edited by Norman Foerster in 1916: *The Chief American Prose Writers* (rev. ed., Boston, 1931).

Ever since 1913, Amy Lowell had served as critic, poet, and adviser to the infant Imagist movement. Her best known critical work, *Tendencies in Modern American Poetry,* was published in Boston in 1917.

A landmark in the study and history of American letters is *The Cambridge History of American Literature,* New York, 1917–1921, 4 vols. Edited by William P. Trent, John Erskine, Stuart P. Sherman, and Carl Van Doren, with articles written by collaborating specialists, it is the first comprehensive history of American literature, and includes extensive bibliographies.

## "THE CAMBRIDGE HISTORY" TO FOERSTER'S "REINTERPRETATION": 1917–1928

The fourth and final volume of *The Cambridge History* was issued in 1921. In the annual March supplement of *PMLA* of 1923 appeared the first systematic current bibliography of American literature (for 1922), compiled by Norman Foerster. Foerster concluded the listing with this comment, significant of the state of scholarship devoted to American letters a quarter of a century ago: "The foregoing record is clearly an indication of the rapidly growing interest in American letters, although it must be admitted that this interest is more popular than scholarly. Substantial studies of American subjects are still rare."

The most significant event during this decade, and one which may properly indicate that the study of American letters had been established on a national basis, was the founding of the American Literature Group as a part of the Modern Language Association of America, in 1921. *American Literature: A Journal of Literary History, Criticism, and Bibliography,* published **quarterly, was founded in 1929, and has served as official organ of the Group.** Two early pleas for a recognition of American literature as a subject for college and graduate study are Arthur H. Quinn, "American Literature as a Subject for Graduate Study," *Educ. Rev.,* LXIV (1922), 7–15; and Fred L. Pattee, "American Literature in the College Curriculum," *ibid.,* LXVII (1924), 266–272.

Historically important is *The Reinterpretation of American Literature: Some Contributions Toward the Understanding of Its Historical Development,* New York, 1928, a collaborative book edited by Norman Foerster for the American Literature Group. It was the first critical inquiry by a group of American scholars into the state of American scholarship, designed to indicate the vast untouched resources, and the pressing need for re-evaluations. It concluded with a selective bibliography of guides to literary and cultural material, and a list of dissertations and articles which had first been published in *Studies in Philology* in 1926 and 1927, here brought up to date. The impetus thus given to American studies by official recognition of a national literature has been profound.

## THE TWENTIETH CENTURY: STUDIES OF
### CRITICAL MOVEMENTS

American criticism in the twentieth century has been divided between the claims of tradition and of revolt. General surveys are Fred B. Millett, "A Critical Survey," in his bio-bibliography of *Contemporary American Authors . . . ,* New York, 1940, pp. 3–204; Morton D. Zabel's introduction to his anthology, *Literary Opinion in America . . . ,* New York, 1937, pp. xv–liv; and Bernard Smith, *Forces in American Criticism . . . ,* New York, 1939. Alfred Kazin's *On Native Grounds . . . ,* New York, 1942, deals with the critical movements and the history of criticism. Henri Peyre's *Writers and Their Critics . . . ,* Ithaca, N.Y., 1944, is a survey of modern literary criticism; chapter II deals with America.

Sketches of the contemporary critical scene include Ernest A. Boyd, *Portraits: Real and Imaginary* (1924); Paul Rosenfeld, *Port of New York: Essays on Fourteen American Moderns* (1924), and *Men Seen* (1925); Elizabeth S. Sergeant, *Fire Under the Andes: A Group of North American Portraits* (1927); Gorham B. Munson, *Destinations: A Canvass of American Literature Since 1900* (1928), and *The Dilemma of the Liberated . . .* (1930); Dorothy

Dudley, *Forgotten Frontiers: Dreiser and the Land of the Free,* New York, 1932; Halford E. Luccock, *Contemporary American Literature and Religion* (1934); and L. Robert Lind, "The Crisis in Literature," *Sewanee Rev.,* XLVII (1939), 35–62, 184–203, 345–364, 524–551; XLVIII (1940), 66–85, 198–203. Halford E. Luccock's *American Mirror: Social, Ethical and Religious Aspects of American Literature, 1930–1940,* New York, 1940, is a reference survey of America's reaction to the depression.

Brief studies include Ronald S. Crane, "History Versus Criticism in the University Study of Literature," *Eng. Jour.,* XXIV (1935), 645–667; Charles I. Glicksberg, "Two Decades of American Criticism," *Dalhousie Rev.,* XVI (1936), 229–242; Edmund Wilson, "Thoughts on Being Bibliographed," *Princeton Univ. Lib. Chron.,* V (1944), 51–61; and Randall Stewart, "The Social School of American Criticism," *So. Atl. Quar.,* XLIII (1944), 22–26. Other estimates are Stanton A. Coblentz, *The Literary Revolution* (1927); and Vernon Loggins, *I Hear America: Literature in the United States Since 1900* (1937).

## Collections

The best of the early collections of criticism is Joel E. Spingarn, ed., *Criticism in America: Its Function and Status* (1924). It deals with material published during the years 1910–1923, and includes essays by Babbitt, Brooks, Brownell, Boyd, Eliot, Mencken, Sherman, Spingarn, and Woodberry. Morton D. Zabel edited *Literary Opinion in America: Essays Illustrating the Status, Methods, and Problems of Criticism in the United States Since the War,* New York, 1937, with selections from T. S. Eliot to R. P. Blackmur, and with a critical introduction. Good selections also are in James C. Bowman, ed., *Contemporary American Criticism* (1926)—twenty-three eclectic selections, mainly contemporary. William A. Drake edited *American Criticism: 1926* (1926). Ludwig Lewisohn edited *A Modern Book of Criticism* (1919), defining and illustrating the impressionist and liberal viewpoints of European and American critics. Harold E. Stearns, in *America and the Young Intellectual* (1921), states the credo of the post-war generation as "revolt." He edited *Civilization in the United States: An Enquiry by Thirty Americans,* New York, 1922, with contributions on the literary scene by Van Wyck Brooks, Joel E. Spingarn, and Conrad Aiken. A companion volume by the same editor is *America Now: An Inquiry into Civilization in the United States by Thirty-six Americans,* New York, 1938. The collection edited by Edwin B. Burgum, *The New Criticism* (1930), is devoted chiefly to aesthetic theory, and among Americans includes Buermeyer, Eliot, Santayana, and Spingarn. An anthology of fifteen authors, from Poe to Van Wyck Brooks, illustrating the development of criticism in America, is Norman Foerster, ed., *American Critical Essays, XIXth and XXth Centuries,* London, 1930. The selection edited by Malcolm Cowley, *After the Genteel Tradition: American Writers Since 1910* (1937), includes critical estimates of recent American writers. Donald Stauffer's collection, *The Intent of the Critic* (1941), includes essays by Auden, Foerster, Ransom, and Wilson. The collection by Allen Tate and John Peale Bishop, eds., *American Harvest: Twenty Years of Creative Writing in the United States,* New York, 1942, supplies introductions and bibliographical notes and covers the period between the world wars. Edmund Wilson's *The Shock of Recognition: Development of Literature in the United States Recorded by the Men Who Made It,* New York, 1943, is a collection of the opinions which notable American writers expressed of one another, from Lowell on Poe to contemporary writers, and is documented. Brief critical estimates by forty contemporary authors are in Donald O. Stewart, ed., *Fighting Words,* New York, 1940.

### Critical Movements: The First Decade

Nineteenth century critics were widely influential at the turn of the century. Among the younger of them was Hamilton Wright Mabie (1845–1916), who is represented in such volumes as *My Study Fire* (1890), *Books and Culture* (1896), and *The Life of the Spirit* (1899). The point of view of Brander Matthews (1852–1929) is expressed in *Aspects of Fiction and Other Ventures in Criticism* (1896), *The Development of the Drama* (1903), and *The American of the Future and Other Essays* (1909). Barrett Wendell (1855–1921) published his historical survey, *A Literary History of America* (1900); and Lewis E. Gates (1860–1924) set forth his doctrine of criticism based on scholarship in *Studies and Appreciations* (1900). George E. Woodberry (1855–1930) gathered his critical opinions in such works as *America in Literature* (1903), *The Torch* (1905), *The Appreciation of Literature* (1907), and *Two Phases of Criticism* (1914). The critical point of view of Charles Eliot Norton (1827–1908) may be seen in his collection of *Letters* (2 vols., 1913). The writings of Henry van Dyke (1852–1933) are gathered as *The Works of Henry van Dyke* (18 vols., 1920–1927); a biography by his son Tertius van Dyke is *Henry van Dyke: A Biography,* New York, 1935.

### Critical Movements: After 1910

At no period has American critical theory achieved greater distinction than during the period since 1910. New trends in criticism are to be found in James

Gibbons Huneker (1860–1921), whose point of view is represented in *Melomaniacs* (1902), and *Promenades of an Impressionist* (1910); the poetic criticism of Ezra Pound; and the dramatic criticism of George Jean Nathan. The viewpoint of H. L. Mencken received expression in his *The Philosophy of Friedrich Nietzsche* (1908). His later criticism was published in *A Book of Prefaces* (1917), and in the six series of *Prejudices,* published in 1919, '20, '22, '24, '26, and '27.

The revival of interest in aesthetic, or "pure," criticism begins with Joel E. Spingarn (1875–1939), whose exposition of Benedetto Croce's aesthetic was published as *The New Criticism* (1911), and continued in *Creative Criticism: Essays on the Unity of Genius and Taste* (1917). He summarized his estimates of the state of American criticism in *Scholarship and Criticism in the United States* (1922).

## Critical Analysis: Literature and American Life

The demand of Brooks, Bourne, Mencken, and others that our writers deal more honestly with American life was met by many criticisms of literature and society based on social and psychological premises. Substantial historical studies of the modern writer and the contemporary scene include John Macy, *The Spirit of American Literature* (1908, rev. ed. 1913)—an early plea for regionalism and the use of indigenous material—and *The Critical Game* (1922); Carl Van Doren, *Many Minds* (1924); Percy H. Boynton, *Some Contemporary Americans: The Personal Equation in Literature* (1924), continued in *More Contemporary Americans* (1927); Thomas K. Whipple, *Spokesmen: Modern Writers and American Life* (1928), supplemented by *Study Out the Land* (1943); Henry S. Canby, *American Estimates* (1929); Joseph Wood Krutch, *The Modern Temper: A Study and Confession* (1929), and *Experience and Art: Some Aspects of the Esthetics of Literature* (1932); Van Wyck Brooks, *Sketches in Criticism* (1932); Kenneth Burke, *Counter-Statement* (1931), and *Permanence and Change: An Anatomy of Purpose* (1935)—investigations of the evolution of ethical ideas. See also Robert E. Spiller, "What Became of the Literary Radicals," *New Repub.,* CXIV (1946), 664–666.

Somewhat more specific in their acceptance of sociological and psychological systems are Upton Sinclair and Max Eastman (b. 1883). Eastman first edited the New York weekly journal of social criticism, the *Masses* (1911). His critical theories are expressed in *The Literary Mind: Its Place in an Age of Science* (1931), and *Artists in Uniform: A Study of Literature and Bureaucratism* (1934). For two studies of Eastman, see Van Wyck Brooks, *Sketches in Criticism,* New York, 1932, pp. 279–290; and Charles I. Glicksberg,

"Max Eastman: Literary Insurgent," *Sewanee Rev.,* XLIV (1936), 323–337. For data on Sinclair, see the individual bibliography herein.

The social criticism of Waldo Frank (b. 1889), an editor of the *Seven Arts* (1916–1917), is represented in such studies as *Our America* (1919), and *The Re-discovery of America: An Introduction to a Philosophy of American Life* (1929). Studies of Frank as a critic include Gorham B. Munson, *Waldo Frank: A Study,* New York, 1923; Paul Rosenfeld, "Waldo Frank," in *Men Seen . . .,* New York, 1925, pp. 89–109; John Jocelyn, "Getting at Waldo Frank," *Sewanee Rev.,* XL (1932), 405–414; Donald Davidson, "Waldo Frank," *Amer. Rev.,* IV (1934), 233–238; and Charles I. Glicksberg, "Waldo Frank: Critic of America," *So. Atl. Quar.,* XXXV (1936), 13–26.

V[ictor] F. Calverton (1900–1940) made his plea for literature as a function of the social order in *The Newer Spirit: A Sociological Criticism of Literature* (1925), with chapters on Stuart P. Sherman, H. L. Mencken, and others, and an introduction by Ernest Boyd; it was followed in 1932 by his Marxian literary history, *The Liberation of American Literature.* See Charles I. Glicksberg, "V. F. Calverton: Marxism Without Dogma," *Sewanee Rev.,* XLVI (1938), 338–351.

Granville Hicks (b. 1901) published his Marxist interpretation as *The Great Tradition: An Interpretation of American Literature Since the Civil War* (1933; rev. ed., 1935).

A collection of some 30 essays on the American proletarian scene is Henry Hart, ed., *American Writers' Congress,* New York, 1935. After the second congress, Hart edited *The Writer in a Changing World,* New York, 1937. A further collection, edited by Granville Hicks and others, is *Proletarian Literature in the United States: An Anthology* (1935)—an attempt to define the proletarian doctrine in literature, with essays by Burgum, Cowley, Hicks, Smith, and others. An autobiographical account by an influential proletarian critic is Joseph Freeman, *An American Testament: A Narrative of Rebels and Romantics,* New York, 1936. In the same year James T. Farrell made his plea for moderation in emphasis on economic values in *A Note on Literary Criticism* (1936). A later volume to define American criticism in Marxist terms is Bernard Smith, *Forces in American Criticism: A Study in the History of American Literary Thought* (1939).

Freudian criticism is to be found in Brooks, Frank, and others, but is best represented in Ludwig Lewisohn, *Expression in America* (1932).

## Neo-humanism

The neo-humanist movement, which fostered an interest in European writers and attempted to establish an aesthetic by means of classic standards, had its foundation in William C. Brownell's *Victorian Prose Masters* (1901), and in his *American Prose Masters* (1909). Brownell recommended an understanding of past cultures in *Criticism* (1914), and *Standards* (1917); and a similar desire for critical standards based on ethical criteria is expressed in the eleven volumes of *Shelburne Essays,* by Paul Elmer More, New York, 1904–1921, supplemented by the three volumes of *New Shelburne Essays* (1928–1936). He reprinted the best among them in *Selected Shelburne Essays* (1935). Stuart P. Sherman undertook his critical estimates of Franklin, Emerson, Hawthorne, and others in *Americans* (1922), in the tradition of Brownell and More, and further elucidated his position in *The Genius of America: Studies in Behalf of the Younger Generation* (1923), and in *The Main Stream* (1927).

The movement became articulate with the publication of Irving Babbitt's *The New Laokoon* (1910), *Rousseau and Romanticism* (1919), and *Democracy and Leadership* (1924). It was further advanced by the publication of Paul Elmer More's *The Drift of Romanticism* (1913), and *Aristocracy and Justice* (1915). For data on Brownell, Babbitt, More, and Sherman, see the individual bibliographies herein. The chief statement of the humanist movement is in Norman Foerster, ed., *Humanism and America: Essays on the Outlook of Modern Civilisation,* New York, 1930, with essays by T. S. Eliot, Babbitt, More, G. R. Elliott, and others. For further sympathetic discussions, see Norman Foerster, *Toward Standards: A Study of the Present Critical Movement in American Letters,* New York, 1930; Seward Collins, "Criticism in America," *Bookman,* LXXI (1930), 241–256, 400–415; LXXII (1930), 145–164, 209–228; Robert Shafer, *Paul Elmer More and American Criticism,* New Haven, 1935; and G. R. Elliott, *Humanism and Imagination,* Chapel Hill, N.C., 1938. See T. S. Eliot's *Selected Essays* (1934) for discussions of Babbitt and humanism. Though the movement did not survive the decade, other defenses of the neo-humanist position are Louis J. A. Mercier, *The Challenge of Humanism: An Essay in Comparative Criticism* (1933); Gorham B. Munson, *The Dilemma of the Liberated: An Interpretation of Twentieth-Century Humanism,* New York, 1930; and Yvor Winters, *Primitivism and Decadence: A Study of American Experimental Poetry* (1937). An attack on the humanist position is C. Hartley Grattan, ed., *The Critique of Humanism: A Symposium* (1930).

### Critical Analysis: Literature and the American Past

For history and criticism of American literature published before 1927, see the sections above, pp. 52–57. Still one of the most stimulating attempts to reorient American literary criticism and open the way to a reinterpretation of literary history by way of social forces is Vernon L. Parrington, *Main Currents in American Thought: An Interpretation of American Literature from the Beginnings to 1920,* New York, 1927–1930, 3 vols. It makes no attempt at aesthetic criticism. The survey of American literature by Van Wyck Brooks began in 1936 with publication of *The Flowering of New England: 1815–1865,* and was continued in *New England: Indian Summer, 1865–1915* (1940), and in *The World of Washington Irving* (1944). Further volumes, planned as a chronological survey, are in progress. Norman Foerster's *American Criticism: A Study in Literary Theory from Poe to the Present,* Boston, 1928, though undertaken as elucidation for the "humanist" position, is a serious, systematic treatment of *criteria* and critical methods, and evaluates cultural traditions by way of an analysis of major figures. Constance Rourke's *The Roots of American Culture and Other Essays* was posthumously published, New York, 1942, edited by Van Wyck Brooks. It constitutes essays toward an unwritten history. An impressionistic interpretation is Thomas Beer, *The Mauve Decade: American Life at the End of the Nineteenth Century* (1926). Lewis Mumford's *The Golden Day: A Study in American Experience and Culture,* New York, 1926, is a critical survey of American society and literature emphasizing the thesis that American culture was the product of the "dispersion" of Europe in the Renaissance. Matthew Josephson in *Portrait of the Artist as American* (1930) champions the Brooks thesis that industrial America frustrates artistic creation.

Useful studies are Henry S. Canby, *Definitions* (2nd ser., 1922–1924), and *Classic Americans: A Study of Eminent American Writers from Irving to Whitman, with an Introductory Survey of the Colonial Background of Our National Literature,* New York, 1931—estimates of Irving, Cooper, Emerson, Thoreau, Hawthorne, Melville, Poe, Whitman; R[ichard] P. Blackmur, *The Expense of Greatness* (1940)—essays on Emily Dickinson, Melville, Henry Adams, and others; F[rancis] O. Matthiessen, *American Renaissance: Art and Expression in the Age of Emerson and Whitman,* New York, 1941—a contribution to American literary and intellectual history, with emphasis on the American tradition of Emerson, Thoreau, Hawthorne, Melville, and Whitman; Ferner Nuhn, *The Wind Blew from the East: A Study in the Orientation of American Culture,* New York, 1942—estimates of Henry James, Henry Adams, T. S. Eliot, and others; and Floyd Stovall, *American Idealism,* Norman, Okla., 1943—a historical survey, with chapters especially devoted to Emerson, Whitman, Robinson, and Frost.

A useful brief survey is that of Stanley T. Williams, *The American Spirit in Letters,* New Haven, 1926—Vol. XI of *The Pageant of America: A Pictorial History of the United States,* edited by Ralph H. Gabriel. A survey text is Walter F. Taylor, *A History of American Letters,* New York, 1936—with full selective bibliographies, pp. 447–664, prepared by Harry Hartwick. An elementary survey, worked out in terms of cultural patterns, is Ernest E. Leisy, *American Literature: An Interpretive Survey*, New York, 1929. Fred L. Pattee began his history of American literature with *A History of American Literature Since 1870* (1915), and completed it with the publication of *The New American Literature, 1890–1930* (1930), and *The First Century of American Literature, 1770–1870* (1935). George E. De Mille surveys nine critics from Lowell to S. P. Sherman in *Literary Criticism in America: A Preliminary Survey*, New York, 1931. An analysis of the theory and practice of eleven nineteenth century major poets from Freneau to Dickinson is Gay W. Allen, *American Prosody*, New York, 1935. A study of the American Negro's consciously produced literature is Jay Saunders Redding, *To Make a Poet Black*, Chapel Hill, N.C., 1939.

A recent examination of the literature of American social history in terms of its varied interpretations of patriotism is Merle Curti, *The Roots of American Loyalty*, New York, 1946. Ralph H. Gabriel touches upon literature in *The Course of American Democratic Thought*, New York, 1940.

## The Analytical and Aesthetic Movement

The revival of interest in aesthetic criticism began with Joel E. Spingarn, whose writings are mentioned above.

T. S. Eliot's *The Sacred Wood* (1920) was a defense of aesthetic values which at the same time emphasized the importance of tradition. His *Selected Essays, 1917–1932*, first published, New York, 1932, was issued in a 2nd ed., rev. and enl., London, 1934.

Recent critics who have continued to lay emphasis on aesthetic values include Edmund Wilson, R. P. Blackmur, Allen Tate, and John Crowe Ransom. Wilson's *Axel's Castle: A Study in the Imaginative Literature of 1870–1930* (1931), and *The Triple Thinkers* (1938) combine aesthetic and social values. See Charles I. Glicksberg, "Edmund Wilson: Radicalism at the Crossroads," *So. Atl. Quar.*, XXXVI (1937), 466–477; and Arthur Mizener, "Edmund Wilson: A Checklist," *Princeton Univ. Lib. Chron.*, V (1944), 62–78. Blackmur may be represented by his two volumes of criticism, *The Double Agent: Essays in Craft and Elucidation* (1935), and *The Expense of Greatness* (1940). Tate's *Reactionary Essays on Poetry and Ideas* appeared in 1936, and *Reason in Madness: Critical Essays,* in 1941. Ransom's criticism includes *The World's Body* (1938), and *The New Criticism* (1941). Later volumes concerned with the theory of aesthetics include Laurence Buermeyer, *The Aesthetic Experience* (1924); and Mortimer J. Adler, *Art and Prudence: A Study in Practical Philosophy* (1937). Analysis of form and style has been undertaken by Joseph Warren Beach in *The Outlook for American Prose* (1926), and by Gorham B. Munson in *Style and Form in American Prose* (1929).

## Magazines of Criticism

One of the most distinguished literary and critical journals during the first quarter of the twentieth century was the *Bookman* (1895–1933). Though it was modeled on the English *Bookman,* it featured criticism of American literature. Its standards were conservative until the editorship of Burton Rascoe (1928–1929). From 1930 to 1933 it was edited by Seward Collins in the interest of the neo-humanist movement; it was discontinued with the founding of the *American Review. Harper's Magazine* (1850–current) undertook after 1900 to deal chiefly with contemporary politics and social problems. Its literary department, "Editor's Easy Chair," was occupied successively by William Dean Howells (1901–1921), E. S. Martin (1921–1935), and Bernard De Voto (1935–current). The *Atlantic Monthly* (1857–current) under the editorship of Bliss Perry (1899–1909), though expressing interest in social problems, preserved its tradition as a conservative literary journal. Its later editors were Ellery Sedgwick (1909–1938) and Edward A. Weeks, Jr. (1938–current). The *Century Illustrated Monthly Magazine* (1881–1930), a continuation of *Scribner's Monthly,* was edited by R. W. Gilder (1881–1909) and Robert Underwood Johnson (1909–1913). With a shortened name its literary editor (1922–1925) was Carl Van Doren. It later declined and merged with the *Forum.* During the early years of the century it serialized novels by Howells, James, Hay, and London. *Scribner's Magazine* (1887–1939) maintained a distinguished list of contributors during the first quarter of the century, including among Americans the Jameses, Bret Harte, Cable, Mrs. Wharton, Stephen Crane, and Huneker. It published the early work of Hemingway and Wolfe. After 1936 it declined.

One of the oldest literary and critical journals still current is the *Sewanee Review,* founded by William P. Trent in 1892, and published at Sewanee, Tennessee. Until recently its contributors have been mainly from the South, and its emphasis has been upon southern culture. The *Yale Review,* also founded in 1892, gained distinction after its reorganization in 1911 under the editorship of Wilbur L. Cross. Its essays and reviews, on subjects concerned with literature, politics, and the arts, have frequently been notable.

The *New Republic* (1914–current) was founded as a weekly journal of liberal opinion by Herbert Croly. Its editorial staff included Walter Lippmann, Robert M. Lovett, Stark Young, Randolph Bourne, and Malcolm Cowley. It has continued its original interest in contemporary literature.

Under Paul Elmer More (1909–1914), the *Nation* was distinguished for its interest in literature. During the editorship of Oswald Garrison Villard (1918–1933), its policies were liberalized and its literary associates included John Macy, Ludwig Lewisohn, Joseph Wood Krutch, and Mark and Carl Van Doren.

The *Freeman* (1920–1924), founded by Van Wyck Brooks, Albert Jay Nock, Francis Nielson, and others, was a liberal weekly magazine of political and literary criticism which achieved great distinction. *The Freeman Book* . . . , New York, 1924, is made up of selections from the 8 volumes. Some account of the *Freeman* will be found in Albert Jay Nock's autobiography, *Memoirs of a Superfluous Man,* New York, 1943.

An important journal of social criticism with strong proletarian bias was the *Masses* (1911–1918), a New York weekly founded by Piet Vlag and edited by Max Eastman. Among the editorial associates were Floyd Dell and John Reed. It drew upon European authors for its literary discussions and was suppressed during the First World War for its pacificism. Revived in 1918 as the *Liberator,* it became a radical journal affiliated with the Communist party, and was suspended in 1924. Again revived in 1926 as the *New Masses,* it was under the editorship of Joseph Freeman, Michael Gold, and others, and renewed its literary interests. An interesting account of literary life in Chicago and New York, dealing especially with Eastman's ten years as editor of the *Masses* and the *Liberator,* is Floyd Dell, *Homecoming: An Autobiography,* New York, 1933.

Victor F. Calverton and others founded the *Modern Quarterly: A Magazine of the Newer Spirit* (1923–1940). After 1929 its title became *Modern Monthly.*

Widely known under the editorship of H. L. Mencken (1924–1934) was the *American Mercury,* a monthly magazine founded by Mencken and George Jean Nathan to present the American scene with vigorous skepticism. During the ten years of Mencken's editorship it published contributions of distinction.

The *Saturday Review of Literature* (1924–current) has been and continues to be the only independent weekly solely devoted to a review of letters. It was founded by Henry Seidel Canby. He edited it 1924–1936, Bernard De Voto 1936–1938; and it is at present edited by Norman Cousins with Christopher Morley, William Rose Benét, and others, as contributing associates. The New York *Evening Post,* edited from 1903 to 1920 by Rollo Ogden, was purchased in 1923 by Cyrus H. K. Curtis, and its literary standards were changed. It was out of the earlier *Evening Post* that the *Saturday Review* developed. The literary supplement of the New York *Herald Tribune* achieved its greatest distinction during the years 1924–1926 when Stuart P. Sherman took over the editorship. The literary supplements of both the *Herald Tribune* and the New York *Times* have continued to be regular features.

The year 1924, which saw the founding of the *American Mercury* and the *Saturday Review of Literature,* was also the year in which the *Commonweal* was established, a weekly review of politics and letters, presenting in the main the Catholic lay viewpoint.

In the following year the *Virginia Quarterly Review* first appeared, issued at the University of Virginia. Its point of view has been and continues to be liberal, and its contributions have been drawn from many sources both here and abroad.

Interest in European literature has been fostered by *Books Abroad: A Quarterly Publication Devoted to Comment on Foreign Books* (1927–current).

*Midland* (1915–1933), established in Iowa City, Iowa, and *Frontier,* founded in 1920, Missoula, Mont., gave attention to material especially from the West. In 1933 the magazines were merged as a regional publication, *Frontier and Midland,* which ceased publication in 1939.

Short-lived but critically important in their time were the *Symposium* (1930–1934), edited by James Burnham and Philip E. Wheelwright, and *American Spectator* (1932–1937), edited till 1935 by George Jean Nathan, Ernest Boyd, Van Wyck Brooks, Dreiser, and O'Neill, under whom it had continued the manner and the tone of the *American Mercury;* it declined after 1935.

Important among recently founded journals and reviews are the *Partisan Review* (1934–current), *Southern Review* (1935–1942), *Science and Society: A Marxian Quarterly* (1936–current), and *Kenyon Review* (1938–current). *Partisan Review,* originally a Marxian journal, has become increasingly literary in its interests, and its contributors include John Dos Passos, T. S. Eliot, James T. Farrell, Archibald MacLeish, and Edmund Wilson. The *Southern Review,* issued at University, La., was more regional in interest. Among its editors were Cleanth Brooks and Robert Penn Warren. It was especially concerned with criticism and critical movements. *Science and Society,* edited by Edwin B. Burgum and others, includes book reviews. The most recent of literary journals, the *Kenyon Review,* is under the editorship of John Crowe Ransom. *The Partisan Reader, 1934–44: An Anthology,* New York, 1946, is edited by William Phillips and Philip Rahv.

## Experimental Magazines

Magazines have customarily been the means by which experimentation in literary forms and styles has taken place. Such magazines, usually short-lived, are known variously as "little magazines," "small magazines," or "advance guard," and in common they have shared in promoting the literary work of the young, new, or little known writers of their day. Though earlier magazines, most notably the *Dial* (1840–1844) under the editorship of Margaret Fuller and of Emerson, and the *Saturday Press* (1858–1866), the New York weekly miscellany edited by Henry Clapp, may be said to foreshadow those which later were designed to be experimental, the era of such magazines did not in fact begin until the last decade of the nineteenth century. Many of the distinguished writers of our own time were thus given their start. The first to achieve note was the *Chap-Book; Semi-Monthly: A Miscellany and Review of Belles Lettres* (1894–1898), published in Chicago. Among its contributors were T. B. Aldrich, G. W. Cable, Stephen Crane, Eugene Field, Hamlin Garland, Henry James, and William Vaughn Moody. Such magazines often cease publication through lack of financial support, and in 1898 the *Chap-Book* was merged into the Chicago *Dial*.

Important also in the same period are the *Lark* and *M'lle New York*. The *Lark* (1895–1897), with gaiety its only policy, was published in San Francisco, and is the most famous of Bohemian magazines. Frank Norris contributed to it. The final issue, edited by Gelett Burgess and others, is entitled the *Epi-Lark*. *M'lle New York* (1895–1899), as an urbane biweekly edited by Vance Thompson and by James Gibbons Huneker, introduced to America such writers as Hamsun, Ibsen, Maeterlinck, Strindberg, and Verlaine.

The second period was introduced in 1912 with the founding in Chicago of *Poetry: A Magazine of Verse,* under the editorship of Harriet Monroe, and its importance among magazines which sought and sponsored the talent of young, obscure writers is great. Its long and continuous publication is unique among magazines of verse. Its policy has been eclectic, and its distinction as an "advance guard" was greatest in the earlier years, when it championed the poetry of T. S. Eliot, Robert Frost, Vachel Lindsay, Amy Lowell, Edgar Lee Masters, Ezra Pound, and Carl Sandburg. It also gave early recognition to Hart Crane.

The years since 1912, under the impetus first supplied by *Poetry,* are notable for the number of authors introduced through such mediums. As a name, the *Dial* has continually had literary association. Revived in 1880 in Chicago as a conservative literary monthly review, its most notable era commenced in 1916 when it was moved to New York under a new group of editors including Conrad Aiken, Randolph Bourne, and Van Wyck Brooks. By 1920, under the editorship of Scofield Thayer, it was regarded as the foremost literary publication in the country. It championed new media in art as well as in literature and drew contributions from many nations. Among its associates were T. S. Eliot, Thomas Mann, Paul Morand, and James Stephens, and its contributors are a roster of virtually all the distinguished writers of the period. In 1925 Marianne Moore succeeded Thayer as editor. The *Dial* ceased publication in 1929.

During these years the number of such magazines is estimated at some six hundred. The editorial policies of many were as irresponsible as their financial backing was unstable. Yet of that large number several achieved a permanent reputation. The Missouri journalist William Marion Reedy (1862–1920) established *Reedy's Mirror* (1913–1920) as a liberal magazine, and sponsored such new writers as Sara Teasdale, J. G. Fletcher, and Julia Peterkin. It was in the *Mirror* that E. L. Masters' *Spoon River Anthology* first appeared.

Deservedly well known is the *Little Review* (1914–1929), founded in Chicago by Margaret C. Anderson, and published sporadically as an eclectic—and finally expatriate—literary "advance guard," in Chicago, San Francisco, New York, and Paris. Here was first serialized James Joyce's *Ulysses* for three years beginning in 1918. Among American contributors it numbered Sherwood Anderson, Malcolm Cowley, Hart Crane, T. S. Eliot, Ernest Hemingway, Ezra Pound, and Carl Sandburg. Valuable memoirs, dealing with many contemporary literary figures and events, especially the founding of the *Little Review,* are contained in Margaret C. Anderson's *My Thirty Years' War: An Autobiography,* New York, 1930.

Likewise distinguished by the list of its contributors was the short-lived *Seven Arts* (1916–1917), with Van Wyck Brooks as one of its editors and Sherwood Anderson, Randolph Bourne, Theodore Dreiser, Vachel Lindsay, Amy Lowell, and H. L. Mencken among its contributors.

No more spectacular magazine was published than *Broom: An International Magazine of the Arts* (1921–1924), which flourished briefly in Rome, Berlin, and finally New York, where it was killed by censorship. Among Americans it produced some of the best writings of Conrad Aiken, Amy Lowell, Edgar Lee Masters, and Gertrude Stein. *Secession* (1922–1924), likewise eclectic and expatriate, was edited by Gorham B. Munson and others in Vienna, Berlin, and New York, and published the writings of Hart Crane, Malcolm Cowley, and others. Two other important magazines belonging to this class are *This Quarter* (1925–1932), published in Paris, with contributions from James T. Farrell, Ernest Hemingway, Joseph Wood Krutch, Ezra Pound, Carl Sandburg, Gertrude Stein, and Allen Tate; and *transition,* founded in Paris in 1927 under the editorship of Eugene Jolas and Elliot Paul. Hart Crane, E. E. Cummings, Ernest Hemingway, and Gertrude Stein have published in it. In 1940 it was moved to Mount Vernon, Iowa.

Lincoln Kirstein founded and edited *Hound and Horn* (1927–1934) in

Cambridge. Varian Fry and R. P. Blackmur were also associated with the editorship before it ceased publication in New York. It was preeminently a magazine of literary criticism, and its contributors included Kenneth Burke, T. S. Eliot, Katherine Anne Porter, Ezra Pound, Gertrude Stein, and Allen Tate.

Other magazines during this period were founded for similar ends but with less eclectic and international points of view; their aim rather was to encourage regionalism and to draw upon the talent of young writers who might wish to exploit the material to be found in their own sections. Among the more successful have been *Midland* (1915–1933), Iowa City, which published Paul Engle's early work; *Frontier* (1920–1939), founded by Prof. H. G. Merriam of Montana State University; the *Reviewer* (1921–1925), edited by Emily Clark, James Branch Cabell, and others in Richmond, Va., and elsewhere, with contributions notably from Paul Green, Du Bose Heyward, and Julia Peterkin; and the *Double Dealer* (1921–1926), published in New Orleans.

Probably the most notable of the regional magazines is the *Fugitive* (1922–1925), a monthly—and later bimonthly—magazine, published in Nashville, Tenn. It is best known as the only magazine in the South during those years devoted to poetry, and it numbered among its contributors Donald Davidson, Merrill Moore, John Crowe Ransom, Allen Tate, and Robert Penn Warren. A collection of material from its issues was published as *Fugitive Anthology* (1928).

A full-length study has recently been made by Frederick J. Hoffman, Charles Allen, and Carolyn F. Ulrich, *The Little Magazine: A History and a Bibliography*, Princeton, 1946. Earlier studies still occasionally useful are René Taupin, *L'Influence du Symbolisme Français sur la Poésie Américaine de 1910 à 1920*, Paris, 1929—the earliest history of experimental literature in America; Ezra Pound, "Small Magazines," *Eng. Jour.*, XIX (1930), 689–704; Albert Parry, *Garrets and Pretenders: A History of Bohemianism in America*, New York, 1933—containing the story of the rise and progress of several such magazines, with a bibliography, pp. 359–369; Lawrence Heyl, "Little Magazines," *Princeton Univ. Lib. Chron.*, II (1940), 21–26; Charles Allen, "The Advance Guard," *Sewanee Rev.*, LI (1943), 410–429; *idem*, "Regionalism and the Little Magazines," *Coll. Eng.*, VII (1945), 10–16; and Frederick J. Hoffman, "Research Value of the 'Little Magazine,'" *Coll. and Research Libraries*, VI (1945), 311–316.

See also Margaret Anderson, *My Thirty Years' War*, New York, 1930; Malcolm Cowley, *Exile's Return: A Narrative of Ideas*, New York, 1934; *idem*, "The Generation That Wasn't Lost," *Coll. Eng.*, V (1944), 233–239; Harriet Monroe, *A Poet's Life*, New York, 1937; and Louis Untermeyer,

*From Another World: The Autobiography of Louis Untermeyer,* New York, 1939. Data are included in Alfred Kreymborg, *Troubadour,* New York, 1925.

## Outlines

G[eorge] Harrison Orians, *A Short History of American Literature: Analyzed by Decades,* New York, 1940, is a chronological outline, with supplementary chapters by M. L. Williams and W. L. Werner, useful for facts, but should be checked. Bartholow V. Crawford, and others, have compiled *An Outline-History of American Literature,* New York, 1946, with bibliographies.

## Anthologies:
## General Surveys

For anthologies dealing specifically with poetry, fiction, drama, and criticism, see the topical and period bibliographies herein.

A balanced one-volume selection is Norman Foerster, ed., *American Poetry and Prose: A Book of Readings, 1607–1916,* Boston, 1925 (rev. 1934, 1947). The compilation by Milton Ellis, Louise Pound, and George W. Spohn, *A College Book of American Literature,* New York, 1940, 2 vols., is eclectic. A convenient anthology of social documents, poetry, and prose, with critical introductions and extensive notes, is Willard Thorp, Merle Curti, and Carlos Baker, eds., *American Issues,* Philadelphia, 1941, 2 vols. (Vol. I, *The Social Record;* Vol. II, *The Literary Record*). Arthur H. Quinn, Albert C. Baugh, and Will D. Howe edited *The Literature of America: An Anthology of Prose and Verse,* New York, 1929.

Oscar Cargill is general editor of the five-volume series, *American Literature: A Period Anthology,* New York, 1933, the most inclusive general anthology. The separate volumes are edited with bibliographical notes as follows: Robert E. Spiller, *The Roots of National Culture, to 1830;* Tremaine McDowell, *The Romantic Triumph, 1830–1860;* Louis Wann, *The Rise of Realism, 1860–1888;* Oscar Cargill, *The Social Revolt, 1888–1914*; and John H. Nelson, *Contemporary Trends, Since 1914.* A revision is in preparation.

Volumes of representative selections from the works of major writers are published as the "American Writers Series" (1934–current), prepared by American scholars under the general editorship of Harry Hayden Clark. Some twenty-five volumes of the series have been issued, each with introduction, bibliography, and notes.

Howard Mumford Jones and Ernest E. Leisy edited *Major American*

*Writers,* New York, 1935 (rev. and enl., 1945), with bibliographies. Jay B. Hubbell's *American Life in Literature,* New York, 1936, 2 vols., is inclusive, with selections from European writers on America. The extensive anthology compiled by Harry R. Warfel, Ralph H. Gabriel, and Stanley T. Williams, *The American Mind: Selections from the Literature of the United States,* New York, 1937, with critical introds. and bibl. notes, emphasizes political and social material. William R. Benét and Norman H. Pearson stress imaginative literature in their compilation, *The Oxford Anthology of American Literature,* New York, 1938.

### Special Surveys and Collections

Van Wyck Brooks, Lewis Mumford, and others compiled *American Caravan: A Yearbook of American Literature.* First published in 1927, it gives special attention to young writers. The fifth volume (1936) is entitled *The New Caravan.* New Directions carries on the Caravan idea. Perry Miller and Thomas H. Johnson, *The Puritans,* New York, 1938, is an anthology principally of seventeenth century New England literature, with introduction and extensive bibliographies.

Representative prose selections from colonial times to the present are in Mark Van Doren, *The Oxford Book of American Prose,* New York, 1932. Victor F. Calverton, ed., *Anthology of American Negro Literature,* New York, 1929, includes drama, poetry, folklore, fiction, and biography. Sterling Brown compiled *The Negro Caravan: Writings by American Negroes,* New York, 1941. Selections descriptive of American life and thought are in Tremaine McDowell, ed., *America in Literature,* New York, 1944.

### INSTRUMENTS OF LITERARY PRODUCTION

Each of the period bibliographies immediately following is provided with a section: Instruments of Culture and Literary Production, which discusses the means by which writers in successive periods became known to the public.

### Magazines

The standard history of the magazine (to 1885) is Frank L. Mott, *A History of American Magazines,* Cambridge, 1938, 3 vols. It furnishes foundation studies and analyses for both general and special reference. Later volumes are in preparation. An account of the relationship of the periodical to general literature during the nineteenth century is Henry M. Alden, *Maga-*

*zine Writing and the New Literature,* New York, 1908. For further studies of periodical literature, see the sections on magazines in the various topical and period bibliographies, and in the Guide to Resources, *ante,* p. 25.

## The Press

An excellent one-volume survey of journalism is Frank L. Mott, *American Journalism: A History of Newspapers in the United States Through 250 Years, 1690–1940,* New York, 1941—a chronological account indicating trends and fashions.* Other studies include Alfred M. Lee, *The Daily Newspaper in America: The Evolution of a Social Instrument,* New York, 1937—solidly factual, with bibl., pp. 754–765; Willard G. Bleyer, *Main Currents in the History of American Journalism,* Boston, 1927—sketches of leading editors and journals, with a history. Earlier accounts are James M. Lee, *History of American Journalism,* rev. ed., Boston, 1923; George H. Payne, *History of Journalism in the United States,* New York, 1920; and Frederic Hudson, *Journalism in the United States, from 1690 to 1872,* New York, 1873.

Special studies include Lucy M. Salmon, *The Newspaper and the Historian,* New York, 1923—characteristics of newspapers as they affect the historian; Allan Nevins, *American Press Opinion, Washington to Coolidge: A Documentary Record of Editorial Leadership and Criticism, 1785–1927,* New York, 1928; George Seldes, *Freedom of the Press,* Indianapolis, 1935—survey of the press as an agent of public liberties; Elmo S. Watson, *A History of Newspaper Syndicates in the United States, 1865–1935,* Chicago, 1936; and John P. Young, *Journalism in California,* San Francisco, 1915—with information not elsewhere easily found.

Several histories of individual newspapers have been published. Those dealing with New York City include Frank M. O'Brien, *The Story of 'The Sun,' New York, 1833–1918,* New York, 1918; Elmer Davis, *History of the New York Times, 1851–1921,* New York, 1921; Allan Nevins, *The Evening Post: A Century of Journalism,* New York, 1922—including a valuable study of Bryant as editor; and James W. Barrett, *Joseph Pulitzer and His 'World,'* New York, 1941.

Histories of journalism in other cities are Joseph E. Chamberlin, *The Boston Transcript: A History of Its First Hundred Years,* Boston, 1930; Gerald Johnson and others, *The Sunpapers of Baltimore,* New York, 1937; Archer H. Shaw, *The Plain Dealer: One Hundred Years in Cleveland,* New York, 1942; Thomas S. Dabney, *One Hundred Great Years: The Story of the Times-Picayune from Its Founding* [1837] *to 1940,* Baton Rouge, La.,

---

* See also Robert W. Jones, *Journalism in the United States,* New York, 1947—from 1704 ʳo date.

1944; and Philip Kinsley, *The Chicago Tribune: Its First Hundred Years,* Chicago, Vol. I, 1847–1865 (1943); Vol. II, 1865–1880 (1945).

## BIBLIOGRAPHIES

General bibliographies are those in *The Cambridge History of American Literature* (4 vols., 1917–1921); Harry Hartwick, in Walter F. Taylor, *A History of American Letters* (1936); Fred B. Millett, *Contemporary American Authors: A Critical Survey and 219 Bio-Bibliographies* (1940); and Jacob Blanck, *Merle Johnson's American First Editions* (4th ed., 1942). Special bibliographies, devoted solely to single writers—such as those in the "American Writers Series"—will be found herein drawn out under individual authors. For special bibliographies, see Guide to Resources, *ante,* p. 27.

# BIBLIOGRAPHIES BY PERIOD
# AND TYPE

## THE COLONIAL PERIOD TO 1760

CULTURAL HISTORY:
*General Studies*

Among the founders who did much in the way of establishing settlements in the colonies, individual bibliographical essays will be found herein on William Bradford. Francis Daniel Pastorius, William Penn, John Smith, and John Winthrop. Individually treated also among leaders who contributed significantly to cultural development are John Bartram, William Byrd II, John Cotton, John Eliot, Benjamin Franklin, Thomas Hooker, Cotton and Increase Mather, Samuel Sewall, Thomas Shepard, Nathaniel Ward, Roger Williams, John Wise, and John Woolman. For early narratives of travel and data on contemporary historians, see the section: Chronicles of the Frontier, *post,* p. 245.

Anthologies of colonial writing, selective and critical rather than inclusive, are William B. Cairns, *Selections from Early American Writers, 1607–1800,* New York, 1909, 1917; Robert E. Spiller, *The Roots of National Culture: American Literature to 1830,* New York, 1933; and Perry Miller and Thomas H. Johnson, *The Puritans,* New York, 1938—with annotated bibliography, pp. 785–834.

A recent study of the influence of environment on cultural life during the colonial era is Curtis P. Nettels, *The Roots of American Civilization: A History of American Colonial Life,* New York, 1938. A useful survey is Max Savelle, *The Foundations of American Civilization,* New York, 1942. Standard studies of political and economic development are Charles M. Andrews, *The Colonial Period of American History,* New Haven, 1934–1938, 4 vols.; Herbert L. Osgood, *The American Colonies in the Seventeenth Century,* New York, 1904–1907, 3 vols.; and *idem, The American Colonies in the Eighteenth Century,* New York, 1924, 3 vols. Two studies by Marcus W. Jernegan deal with political, economic, and social aspects: *The American Colonies, 1492–1750: A Study of Their Political, Economic and Social Development,* New York, 1929; and *Laboring and Dependent Classes in Colonial America, 1607–1783: Studies of the Economic, Educational, and Social Significance of Slaves, Servants, Apprentices, and Poor Folk,* Chicago, 1931. See also Charles A. Beard, *Economic Origins of Jeffersonian Democracy,* New

York, 1915; and Richard B. Morris, *Government and Labor in Early America,* New York, 1946. A useful introduction to legal relationships is *idem, Studies in the History of American Law with Special Reference to the Seventeenth and Eighteenth Centuries,* New York, 1930. The intellectual life in colonial towns is presented in Carl Bridenbaugh, *Cities in the Wilderness: The First Century of Urban Life in America, 1625-1744,* New York, 1938, with bibl., pp. 483-486. One of the earliest works to show an interest in intercultural relations is Edward Eggleston, *The Transit of Civilization from England to America in the Seventeenth Century,* New York, 1901. A recent study of the subject is Harry Bernstein, *Origins of Inter-American Interest, 1700-1812,* Philadelphia, 1945.

A survey primarily concerned with social aspects is James T. Adams, *Provincial Society, 1690-1763,* New York, 1927, with crit. bibl., pp. 324-356. Useful material appears in Elizabeth A. Dexter, *Colonial Women of Affairs: Women in Business and the Professions in America Before 1776,* 2nd ed., Boston, 1931. A recent documented study is Mary S. Benson, *Women in Eighteenth-Century America: A Study of Opinion and Social Usage,* New York, 1935, with crit. bibl., pp. 317-333. Earlier studies, still useful, are Sydney G. Fisher, *Men, Women, and Manners in Colonial Times,* Philadelphia, 1897, 2 vols.; Alice M. Earle, *Home Life in Colonial Days,* New York, 1898; and *idem, Stage-Coach and Tavern Days,* New York, 1900.

## New England

*The Journal of Madam Knight,* first published by Theodore Dwight in 1825, is a sprightly and graphic narrative of rural manners in the early eighteenth century. It is a record of a journey made by Sarah Kemble Knight (1666-1727) from Boston to New York in 1704. It was published with an introduction by George P. Winship, Boston, 1920 (facsimile reprint, 1935). See Anson Titus, "Madam Sarah Knight: Her Diary and Her Times," *Bostonian Soc. Pub.,* IX (1912), 99-126.

The English bookseller John Dunton (1659-1733) came to Boston in 1686, and published the impressions of his visit in *The Life and Errors of John Dunton* (1705), and in his fictional *Letters from New England* (1867).

A detailed and authoritative study of New England intellectual history is Perry Miller, *The New England Mind: The Seventeenth Century,* New York, 1939. Useful introductions to the subject are in Samuel E. Morison, *The Puritan Pronaos: Studies in the Intellectual Life of New England in the Seventeenth Century,* New York, 1936; and *idem, Builders of the Bay Colony,* Boston, 1930. A sympathetic philosophical interpretation is Herbert W. Schneider, *The Puritan Mind,* New York, 1930. See also the introduction in

Perry Miller and Thomas H. Johnson, *The Puritans,* New York, 1938, pp. 1–79. On French cultural influences, especially after 1740, see Mary Ellen Loughrey, *France and Rhode Island, 1686–1800,* New York, 1944.

For the German influence, see Harold S. Jantz, "German Thought and Literature in New England, 1620–1820," *Jour. Eng. and Ger. Philol.,* XLI (1942), 1–45.

Recent studies of domestic relations are George F. Dow, *Domestic Life in New England in the Seventeenth Century,* Topsfield, Mass., 1925; *idem, Everyday Life in the Massachusetts Bay Colony,* Boston, 1935; Edmund S. Morgan, *The Puritan Family: Essays on Religion and Domestic Relations in Seventeenth-Century New England,* Boston, 1944; and Alice M. Earle, *Customs and Fashions in Old New England,* New York, 1893.

## The Middle Colonies

The leading eighteenth century New York historian was Cadwallader Colden (1688–1776). He published the first careful and well documented study of the Iroquois confederacy in *The History of the Five Indian Nations Depending on the Province of New-York in America,* New York, 1727. *The Letters and Papers of Cadwallader Colden, 1711–1775* were published in the *N.Y. Hist. Soc. Coll.,* III–VII (1917–1923), 7 vols. A biography, largely concerned with Colden as a politician, is Alice M. Keys, *Cadwallader Colden: A Representative Eighteenth Century Official,* New York, 1906. A primary source dealing with the French and English strife in the middle colonies, especially in Pennsylvania, is Lewis Evans (*ca.* 1700–1756), *Geographical, Historical, Political, Philosophical, and Mechanical Essays* (1755). A recent biographical sketch is that of Lawrence Henry Gipson, *Lewis Evans,* Philadelphia, 1939. It contains Evans's *Brief Account of Pennsylvania,* and facsimile reprints of his *Geographical Essays.* An authoritative study is Thomas J. Wertenbaker, *The Founding of American Civilization: The Middle Colonies,* New York, 1938. Interesting also is Charles Thomson (1729–1824), *An Enquiry into the Causes of the Alienation of the Delaware and Shawanese Indians from the British Interest* (1759). A documented study of Dutch colonial life and culture is Ellis L. Raesly, *Portrait of New Netherland,* New York, 1945. A glimpse of colonial manners is given by Alice M. Earle's *Colonial Days in Old New York,* New York, 1896. See also Jarvis M. Morse, "Colonial Historians of New York," *N.Y. Hist.,* XXIII (1942), 395–409.

## The South

Important as primary material is *An Essay upon the Government of the English Plantation on the Continent of America* (1701). It is an early proposal for liberty under the British Crown, recently reprinted with two memoranda by William Byrd, ed. by Louis B. Wright, San Marino, Calif., 1945. For studies of the intellectual interests of the planters, see Louis B. Wright and Marion Tinling, eds., *The Secret Diary of William Byrd of Westover, 1709–1712,* Richmond, Va., 1941; and Louis B. Wright, *The First Gentlemen of Virginia: Intellectual Qualities of the Early Colonial Ruling Class,* San Marino, Calif., 1940. A brief study of early Charleston is Frederick P. Bowes, *The Culture of Early Charleston,* Chapel Hill, N.C., 1942, with bibl., pp. 137–145. See also Philip A. Bruce, *Social Life of Virginia in the Seventeenth Century,* Richmond, 1907; and Matthew P. Andrews, *Virginia: The Old Dominion,* New York, 1937.

## THE RELIGIOUS IMPACT

Data on John Cotton, John Eliot, Thomas Hooker, Cotton and Increase Mather, Thomas Shepard, Roger Williams, John Woolman, and on Jonathan Edwards—the most significant philosopher and religious leader during the colonial period—appear in the individual bibliographical essays herein.

Richard Mather (1596–1669) was the first of the Mather dynasty. For a full description of the writings of Richard Mather and twelve of his descendants, exclusive of Increase and Cotton Mather, see Thomas J. Holmes, comp., *The Minor Mathers: A List of Their Works,* Cambridge, 1940. John Norton (1606–1663), a vigorous persecutor of the Quakers and one of the earliest New England leaders, is remembered for two important works: *The Orthodox Evangelist* (1654), and *Heart of New England Rent at the Blasphemies of the Present Generation* (1659). The *summa* of New England theology is gathered in *A Compleat Body of Divinity* (1726)—a posthumously published collection of sermons by Samuel Willard (1640–1707). The work, the largest volume ever issued by the colonial press, remains the authoritative statement of New England orthodoxy. Among early writers widely admired by the Quakers was the sea captain Thomas Chalkley (1675–1741), who preached the Quaker gospel on his many trading and missionary voyages. *A Collection of the Works of Thomas Chalkley, in Two Parts* was issued in Philadelphia, 1749. His *Journal* (1747) was separately issued, London, 1751. In Virginia an early outstanding religious leader was the brilliant pulpit-orator Samuel Davies (1723–1761), who briefly succeeded Jonathan Edwards as president of the College of New Jersey (Princeton University). His *Sermons* are best edited by William B. Sprague (3 vols., 1864).

A recent authoritative survey of the religious impact is William W. Sweet, *Religion in Colonial America,* New York, 1942, with bibl., pp. 341–356. Two other standard studies are Perry Miller, *Orthodoxy in Massachusetts, 1630–1650: A Genetic Study,* Cambridge, 1933; and Rufus M. Jones, *The Quakers in the American Colonies,* London, 1911. Still useful on colonial denominations and sects is the "American Church History Series," edited by Philip Schaff and others (13 vols., 1893–1897). A popular survey is Ernest S. Bates, *American Faith: Its Religious, Political, and Economic Foundations,* New York, 1940. Special studies include Arthur L. Cross, *The Anglican Episcopate and the American Colonies,* New York, 1902; Sister Mary A. Ray, *American Opinion of Roman Catholicism in the Eighteenth Century,* New York, 1936; Sanford H. Cobb, *The Rise of Religious Liberty in America: A History,* New York, 1902; Richard H. Tawney, *Religion and the Rise of Capitalism,* New York, 1926—a presentation of the economic background of Protestantism; Charles H. Maxson, *The Great Awakening in the Middle Colonies,* Chicago, 1920; Wesley M. Gewehr, *The Great Awakening in Virginia, 1740–1790,* Durham, N.C., 1930; and Herbert M. Morais, *Deism in Eighteenth Century America,* New York, 1934.

One of the few comparative studies of the contents of Quaker journals is Howard Brinton, "Stages in Spiritual Development as Recorded in Quaker Journals," in *Children of Light,* New York, 1938, pp. 383–406. See also Mary L. Gambrell, *Ministerial Training in Eighteenth-Century New England,* New York, 1937; Babette M. Levy, *Preaching in the First Half Century of New England History,* Hartford, Conn., 1945; and Lindsay Swift, "The Massachusetts Election Sermons," *Pub. Col. Soc. Mass.,* I (1895), 388–451. Edwin A. R. Rumball-Petre has compiled *America's First Bibles: With a Census of 555 Extant Bibles,* Portland, Me., 1940.

EDUCATION AND SCIENCE

For data on the leading colonial educator and scientist, Benjamin Franklin, see the individual bibliography herein. The first colonial elected a Fellow of the Royal Society was John Winthrop, Jr. (1606–1676). An account of his activities is that of Samuel E. Morison, "John Winthrop, Jr., Industrial Pioneer," in *Builders of the Bay Colony,* Boston, 1930, pp. 269–288, with bibl., p. 354. The founder and first president of the College of William and Mary was James Blair (1655–1743). With Henry Hartwell and Edward Chilton he wrote *The Present State of Virginia and the College,* London, 1727. Important also is his *Our Savior's Divine Sermon on the Mount,* London, 1722–1723, 5 vols. No adequate biography of Blair has been published. Jonathan Dickinson (1688–1747) was the founder and first president of the College of New Jersey (Princeton University). His dialectical skill may be represented by *Familiar Letters to a Gentleman, upon a Variety of Seasonable and Important Subjects in Religion,* Boston, 1745. The proposal made by William Smith (1727–1803) in *A General Idea of the College of Mirania* (1753) won for him the provostship, 1755-1779, of the College of Philadelphia, which became the University of Pennsylvania in 1791. His attack on the Quaker majority in the Pennsylvania Assembly for failing to defend the frontiers against French and Indians was published as *A Brief State of the Province of Pennsylvania,* London, 1755; and was followed by a sequel, *A Brief View of the Conduct of Pennsylvania for the Year 1755,* London, 1756. He edited the *American Magazine, or Monthly Chronicle* (1752–1758) as a journal in which to give vent to his conservative beliefs. His *Discourses on Public Occasions in America* were issued, 2nd ed., London, 1762. H. W. Smith published *The Life and Correspondence of the Rev. William Smith, D.D.,* Philadelphia, 1879–1880, 2 vols. The sketch by Albert Frank Gegenheimer, *William Smith: Educator and Churchman,* Philadelphia, 1943, is a brief study of the central figure in the self-conscious literary life of colonial Philadelphia, and contains a chapter on "Smith and His Group," dealing with the coterie of writers around him.

The acknowledged Anglican leader of his day and the first president of King's College (1754–1763) was Samuel Johnson (1696–1772). He was the chief American exponent of the idealism of his friend the English philosopher Berkeley. His *Ethices Elementa* (1746) was enlarged as *Elementa Philosophica* (1752) and was used as a philosophical text. Significant material on Johnson and the later colonial period has been gathered and edited by Herbert and Carol Schneider in *Samuel Johnson, President of King's College: His Career and Writings,* New York, 1929, 4 vols. See also I[saac] Woodbridge Riley, "Samuel Johnson," in *American Philosophy: The Early Schools,* New York, 1907, pp. 63–125; and Theodore Hornberger, "Samuel Johnson of Yale and King's College: A Note on the Relation of Science and Religion in Provincial America," *New Eng. Quar.,* VIII (1935), 378–397.

Recent studies of American scientific thought and education include Theodore Hornberger, *Scientific Thought in the American Colleges, 1638–1800,* Austin, Tex., 1946; Frederick E. Brasch, "The Newtonian Epoch in the American Colonies (1680–1783)," *Proc. Amer. Antiq. Soc.,* n.s. XLIX (1939), 314–332; and Michael Kraus, "Scientific Relations Between Europe and America in the Eighteenth Century," *Scientific Mo.,* LV (1942), 259–272. Fifteen papers read before the American Philosophical Society have been gathered as "The Early History of Science and Learning in America," *Proc. Amer. Phil. Soc.,* LXXXVI, No. 1 (1942). Other useful studies include Frederick E. Brasch, "The Royal Society of London and Its Influence upon Scientific Thought in the American Colonies," *Scientific Mo.,* XXXIII (1931), 337–355, 448–469; Chester E. Jorgenson, "The New Science in the

Almanacs of Ames and Franklin," *New Eng. Quar.*, VIII (1935), 555–561; Allen O. Hansen, *Liberalism and American Education in the Eighteenth Century*, New York, 1926; and Martha (Ornstein) Bronfenbrenner, *The Rôle of the Scientific Societies in the Seventeenth Century*, New York, 1913— with bibl., pp. 314–322. A pioneer investigation, still standard, is I[saac] Woodbridge Riley, *American Philosophy: The Early Schools*, New York, 1907.

Special studies include William Haynes, *Chemical Pioneers: The Founders of the American Chemical Industry*, New York, 1939—beginning with the work of John Winthrop, Jr.; George L. Kittredge, *Witchcraft in Old and New England*, Cambridge, 1929—the definitive analysis of American aspects; James J. Walsh, *Education of the Founding Fathers of the Republic: Scholasticism in the Colonial Colleges . . .*, New York, 1935—pro-scholastic in emphasis; and Lao G. Simons, *Introduction of Algebra into American Schools in the Eighteenth Century*, Washington, 1924. A document in the history of education is *Charles Morton's "Compendium Physicae,"* ed., by Theodore Hornberger, *Pub. Col. Soc. Mass.*, XXXIII (1940). It was used as a manuscript text in natural science at Harvard College from 1687 to 1720. Invaluable as studies of higher learning in the colonies are the histories by Samuel E. Morison: *The Founding of Harvard College*, Cambridge, 1935; and *Harvard College in the Seventeenth Century*, Cambridge, 1936, 2 vols. Detailed information appears in Arthur O. Norton, "Harvard Textbooks and Reference Books of the Seventeenth Century," *Pub. Col. Soc. Mass.*, XXVIII (1935), 361–438. See also the studies by Robert F. Seybolt: *The Private Schools of Colonial Boston*, Cambridge, 1935; and *The Public Schools of Colonial Boston, 1635–1775*, Cambridge, 1935; and Clifford K. Shipton, "Secondary Education in the Puritan Colonies," *New Eng. Quar.*, VII (1934), 646–661.

For data concerning the middle colonies and Virginia, see William H. Kilpatrick, *The Dutch Schools of New Netherland and Colonial New York*, Washington, 1912; Robert F. Seybolt, *The Evening Schools of Colonial New York City*, Albany, 1921; Philip Alexander Bruce, *Institutional History of Virginia in the Seventeenth Century*, New York, 1910, 2 vols.; and Mrs. P. H. Hiden, "Education and the Classics in the Life of Colonial Virginia," *Va. Mag. of Hist. and Biog.*, XLIX (1941), 20–28.

Two studies by Thomas Woody are *Early Quaker Education in Pennsylvania*, New York, 1920; and *Quaker Education in the Colony and State of New Jersey: A Source Book*, Philadelphia, 1923. Important data on the traditional learning of English schools transmitted by way of English-trained tutors and governesses appear in the letters and journals of Philip Vickers Fithian, mentioned under Memoirs and Journals, *post*, p. 93. See also Allen

O. Hansen, *Liberalism and American Education in the Eighteenth Century,* New York, 1926; and Colyer Meriwether, *Our Colonial Curriculum, 1607–1776,* Washington, 1907.

LITERARY CULTURE:
*General Studies*

Still standard as a general study is Moses Coit Tyler, *A History of American Literature During the Colonial Period,* rev. ed., New York, 1897, 2 vols. A pioneer study in the field of intercultural belles-lettres is Thomas G. Wright, *Literary Culture in Early New England, 1620–1730,* New Haven, Conn., 1920. A recent and authoritative account is Howard M. Jones, "The Literature of Virginia in the Seventeenth Century," in *Memoirs Amer. Acad. Arts and Sciences,* Boston, 1946, pp. 1–47. Elizabeth G. Cook's *Literary Influences in Colonial Newspapers, 1704–1750,* New York, 1912, is a documented monograph with emphasis on interest in English essayists, poets, and dramatists. An attempt to discuss the essay and other forms is Josephine K. Piercy, *Studies in Literary Types in Seventeenth-Century America, 1607–1710,* New Haven, Conn., 1939. Two chapters in Howard M. Jones, *Ideas in America,* Cambridge, 1944, are primarily concerned with colonial literature: "Desiderata in Colonial Literary History," pp. 12–27; and "American Prose Style: 1700–1770," pp. 70–106. Other studies include Charles Francis Adams, "Milton's Impress on the Provincial Literature of New England," *Proc. Mass. Hist. Soc.,* XLII (1909), 154–170; William R. Thayer, "Pen Portraiture in Seventeenth Century Colonial Historians," *Proc. Amer. Antiq. Soc.,* n.s. XXXI (1921), 61–69; E. F. Bradford, "Conscious Art in Bradford's *History of Plymouth Plantation,*" *New Eng. Quar.,* I (1928), 133–157; Clifford K. Shipton, "Literary Leaven in Provincial New England," *ibid.,* IX (1936), 203–217; Perry Miller and Thomas H. Johnson, "The Puritans as Literary Artists," in *The Puritans,* New York, 1938, pp. 64–79; Randall Stewart, "Puritan Literature and the Flowering of New England," *Wm. and Mary Quar.,* III (1946), 319–342; and Robert M. Myers, "The Old Dominion Looks to London: A Study of English Literary Influences upon the *Virginia Gazette,*" *Va. Mag. Hist. and Biog.,* LIV (1946), 195–217. An unpublished thesis is Evan A. Evans, "Literary References in New England Diaries, 1700–1730," Harvard Univ., 1935. Luella M. Wright's *The Literary Life of the Early Friends, 1650–1725,* New York, 1932, is annotated, with bibl., pp. 274–294. An early attempt at a comprehensive survey of colonial Pennsylvania literature is M. Katherine Jackson, *Outlines of the Literary History of Colonial Pennsylvania,* Lancaster, Pa., 1906. Chap. I (pp.1–60) in Arthur H Quinn, *A History of the American Drama from the Beginning to the Civil*

*War,* 2nd ed., New York 1943, discusses "The Drama and the Theatre in the Colonies."

## Poetry

For data on the three best known colonial poets, Edward Taylor, Anne Bradstreet, and Michael Wigglesworth, see the individual bibliographies herein. The first translation of a classic in America was undertaken by George Sandys (1578–1644), while he served in Virginia as treasurer of the London Company: *Ovid's Metamorphosis Englished by G. S.* (1626). John Wilson (*ca.* 1588–1667) published *A Song or, Story, For the Lasting Remembrance of divers famous works . . .,* London, 1626, reissued in Boston, 1680, as *A Song of Deliverance . . .* The first book issued in the American colonies is *The Whole Booke of Psalmes Faithfully Translated into English Metre,* Cambridge, 1640. Generally known as the *Bay Psalm Book,* it was written by John Eliot, Richard Mather, and Thomas Weld. It was reproduced in facsimile with an introduction by Wilberforce Eames, New York, 1903. The early narrative *History* written by Edward Johnson (1598–1672), generally referred to as *Wonder-Working Providence of Sions Savior in New England,* London, 1654, is interspersed with many short verse tributes celebrating men and events.

The verses of Jacob Steendam (*fl.* 1616–1672) were written to attract colonists to America, and were first published 1659, 1661, 1662. They were reprinted in a biography of Steendam (1861) by Henry Cruse Murphy, who also published them in his *Anthology of New Netherland* (1865). Usually considered the best of early elegies is that of Urian Oakes (1631–1681), *An Elegy upon the Death of the Reverend Mr. Thomas Shepard,* Cambridge, 1677. It has been frequently reprinted. A poetic narrative of King Philip's War is the work of Benjamin Tompson (1642–1714), published as *New England Crisis . . . ,* Boston, 1676. The best edition of his works is that of Howard J. Hall, *Benjamin Tompson . . . His Poems,* collected with an introduction, Boston, 1924. Minor corrections and two additions are made in Kenneth B. Murdock, *Handkerchiefs from Paul,* Cambridge, 1927. The earliest blank verse in America was published by Richard Steere (1643–1721), *The Daniel Catcher: The Life of the Prophet Daniel, in a Poem . . .,* Boston, 1713. The Connecticut poet Roger Wolcott (1679–1767) was admired in his time for *Poetical Meditations: Being the Improvement of Some Vacant Hours,* New London, 1725 (repr. Boston, 1898). The polite verses "by a Gentleman of Virginia," William Dawson (1704–1752), were anonymously published as *Poems on Several Occasions* (1736). Mather Byles (1707–1788) first issued much of his poetry in the *New England Weekly Journal.* Most of his verses were collected in *Poems on Several Occasions,* Boston, 1744 (repr.

New York, 1940, ed. by C. L. Carlson), and *The Conflagration* (1755). A biography is that by Arthur W. H. Eaton, *The Famous Mather Byles,* Boston, 1914. A recent authoritative account is that by Clifton K. Shipton in *Sibley's Harvard Graduates,* VII (1946), pp. 464–493, with a checklist of his writings. For a discussion of Byles's letters to Alexander Pope, see Austin Warren, "To Mr. Pope: Epistles from America," *PMLA,* XLVIII (1933), 61–73. The Loyalist poet, Joseph Green (1706–1780), achieved some notice for his collected verses, *Entertainment for a Winter's Evening,* Boston, 1750, and *The Grand Arcanum Debated,* Boston, 1755. A little known work is James Sterling's *An Epistle to the Hon. Arthur Dobbs, Esq. in Europe, From a Clergyman in America,* London, 1752. See Lawrence C. Wroth, "James Sterling: Poet, Priest, and Prophet of Empire," *Proc. Amer. Antiq. Soc.,* n.s. XLI (1931), 25–76.

For the colonial miscellany, see the section above on Early American Miscellanies: to 1829, p. 39.

The early almanacs often served as instruments for the publication of verse. (See the section Almanacs herein, p. 239.) Two modern anthologies which publish seventeenth century Puritan poetry are Kenneth B. Murdock, *Handkerchiefs from Paul . . . ,* Cambridge, 1927—with an introduction on poetry; and Perry Miller and Thomas H. Johnson, *The Puritans,* New York, 1938, pp. 545–663—with introduction, pp. 545–553. An early discussion of poetic theory is that of Michael Wigglesworth, "The prayse of Eloquence," first published in Samuel E. Morison, *Harvard College in the Seventeenth Century,* Cambridge, 1936, pp. 180–183.

A little known but important anthology of New Netherland verse is that edited by Henry Cruse Murphy, *Anthology of New Netherland; or, Translations from the Early Dutch Poets of New York, with Memoirs of Their Lives,* New York, 1865.

An essay, together with a collection of newly discovered verses, most of which are from previously unpublished manuscripts, is Harold S. Jantz, *The First Century of New England Verse,* Worcester, Mass., 1944, with full bibliography, pp. 175–292.

A facsimile reproduction of 101 early broadsides is compiled by Ola E. Winslow, *American Broadside Verse from Imprints of the 17th and 18th Centuries,* New Haven, 1930. It is supplemented by Harold S. Jantz, "Unrecorded Verse Broadsides of Seventeenth-Century New England," *Papers Bibl. Soc. Amer.,* XXXIX (1945), 1–19. James F. Hunnewell edited *Elegies and Epitaphs, 1677–1717,* Boston, 1896. Other recent studies include Hamilton C. Macdougall, *Early New England Psalmody: An Historical Appreciation, 1620–1820,* Brattleboro, Vt., 1940; and Richard C. Boys, "The English Poetical Miscellany in Colonial America," *Stud. Philol.,* XLII (1945), 114–130. Two studies on Milton's early impress are by Leon Howard: "Early American

Copies of Milton," *Huntington Lib. Bul.,* No. 7, pp. 169–179 (1935); and "The Influence of Milton on Colonial American Poetry," *Huntington Lib. Bul.,* No. 9, pp. 63–89 (1936).

For further secondary data, see the section Poetry (p. 19) in Pt. I, Guide to Resources.

### Literary Use of Colonial Folkways

During the mid-nineteenth century several writers turned to the American past for settings of their tales and stories. Most notable use was made by Hawthorne in *Twice-Told Tales* (1837), and *The Scarlet Letter* (1850). Other such writers were Lydia Maria Child, *Hobomok* (1824); Catharine M. Sedgwick, *Hope Leslie* (1827); Delia Bacon, *Tales of the Puritans* (1831); Eliza Lee, *Naomi* (1848); John Lothrop Motley, *Merry Mount* (1849); J. K. Paulding, *The Puritan and His Daughter* (1849); and J. G. Holland, *The Bay Path* (1857). Recently Esther Forbes has made authentic use of seven teenth century Puritan background in her novel *Paradise* (1937).

INSTRUMENTS OF CULTURE AND LITERARY PRODUCTION

### Libraries and Reading:
General Studies

Important for references to early libraries and donations is Louis Shores, *Origins of the American College Library, 1638–1800,* Nashville, Tenn., 1934. The first three chapters in Carl L. Cannon's *American Book Collectors and Collecting from Colonial Times to the Present,* New York, 1941, analyzes the collections of Thomas Prince, William Byrd II, and James Logan. A reliable concise discussion of library development is Ruth S. Granniss, "American Book Collecting and the Growth of Libraries," in Hellmut Lehmann-Haupt and others, *The Book in America* . . . , New York, 1939, pp. 295–318, 355–365, with bibl. footnotes. Other recent studies include Louis B. Wright, "The Purposeful Reading of Our Colonial Ancestors," *Jour. Eng. Lit. Hist.,* IV (1937), 85–111; Thomas E. Keys, "The Colonial Library and the Development of Sectional Differences in the American Colonies," *Lib. Quar.,* VIII (1938), 373–390; Esther C. Dunn, *Shakespeare in America,* New York, 1939; and Mary-Margaret H. Barr, *Voltaire in America, 1744–1800,* Baltimore, 1941.

### New England

Examinations of reading interests in colonial New England will be found in such studies as Franklin B. Dexter, "Early Private Libraries in New England," *Proc. Amer. Antiq. Soc.,* n.s. XVII (1907), 135–147; Charles F. and Robin Robinson, "Three Early Massachusetts Libraries," *Pub. Col. Soc. Mass.,* XXVIII (1935), 107–175—a list of 565 items from three seventeenth century libraries; and George L. Kittredge, "A Harvard Salutatory Oration of 1662," *Pub. Col. Soc. Mass.,* XXVIII (1935), 1–24—a record of taste in reading and poetry. Two studies by Thomas H. Johnson are "Jonathan Edwards' Background of Reading," *ibid.,* 193–222, and *The Poetical Works of Edward Taylor,* New York, 1939—including an annotated inventory of Taylor's library, pp. 201–220. See also the bibliography of "Puritan Libraries, Books, and Reading," pp. 829–831, in Perry Miller and Thomas H. Johnson, *The Puritans,* New York, 1938. An account of early reading taste is George E. Littlefield, *Early Boston Booksellers, 1642–1711,* Boston, 1900. One of the early library companies was the Redwood Library of Newport, founded in 1747.

## The Middle Colonies and the South

Culturally important was the Junto Club (The Junto), founded at Philadelphia in 1727 by Benjamin Franklin. It lasted some 40 years, and its subscription library, established in 1731, is said to be the earliest American public library. Later known as the Library Company of Philadelphia, its published catalog was first issued in 1807. The New York Society Library, founded in 1754, soon published a catalog of its accessions. The catalog of 1850 lists the books which came into its possession from the library collected by John Winthrop, Jr. (1638–1707), of Connecticut. The Library Society of Charleston was founded in 1748.

An early study of the parochial libraries in the 1690's and early 1700's is Bernard C. Steiner, "Thomas Bray and His American Libraries," *Amer. Hist. Rev.,* II (1896), 59–75. Useful material on libraries and reading in colonial New York is in two works by Austin B. Keep: *The Library in Colonial New York,* New York, 1909, and *History of the New York Society Library . . . ,* New York, 1908. An essay, with a descriptive bibliography, on the reading of a Philadelphia gentleman during the mid-eighteenth century is Lawrence C. Wroth, *An American Bookshelf, 1755,* Philadelphia, 1934. The general reading of an agricultural community near Philadelphia during the pre-revolutionary years, with a list of books read, is Chester T. Hallenbeck, "A Colonial Reading List from the Union Library of Hatboro, Pennsylvania," *Pa. Mag. Hist. and Biog.,* LVI (1932), 289–340. Four studies by Joseph T. Wheeler on libraries and reading interests in Maryland are: "Booksellers and Circulating Libraries in Colonial Maryland," *Md. Hist. Mag.,* XXXIV (1939), 111–137; "Thomas Bray and the Maryland Parochial Libraries," *ibid.,* XXXIV (1939), 246–265; "Reading Interests of the Professional Classes in

Colonial Maryland, 1700-1776," *ibid.*, XXXVI (1941), 184-201; and "Reading Interests of Maryland Planters and Merchants, 1700-1776," *ibid.*, XXXVII (1942), 26-41, 291-310. Accounts of Virginia libraries and reading are in R. G. Marsden, "A Virginian Minister's Library, 1635," *Amer. Hist. Rev.*, XI (1905-1906), 328-332; Louis B. Wright, "The 'Gentleman's Library' in Early Virginia," *Hunt. Lib. Quar.*, I (1937), 3-61; *idem*, "The Classical Tradition in Colonial Virginia," *Papers Bibl. Soc. Amer.*, XXXIII (1939), 85-97; and George K. Smart, "Private Libraries in Colonial Virginia," *Amer. Lit.*, X (1938), 24-52. Louis B. Wright edited *Letters of Robert Carter, 1720-1727*, San Marino, Calif., 1940—interesting for the light they shed on literary interests. Other studies of the reading interests of the South include Stephen B. Weeks, "Libraries and Literature in North Carolina in the Eighteenth Century," *Annual Report* of the Amer. Hist. Assn. for 1895; Julia C. Spruill, "The Southern Lady's Library, 1700-1776," *So. Atl. Quar.*, XXXIV (1935), 23-41; and Frederick P. Bowes, *The Culture of Early Charleston*, Chapel Hill, N.C., 1942. See also Joseph T. Wheeler, "The Layman's Libraries and the Provincial Library," *Md. Hist. Mag.*, XXXV (1940), 60-73; *idem*, "Reading and Other Recreations of Marylanders," *ibid.*, XXXVIII (1943), 37-55, 167-180; and Louis B. Wright, "Pious Reading in Colonial Virginia," *Jour. So. Hist.*, VI (1940), 383-392.

### Journals and Magazines

The first newspapers in America were published in Boston. The earliest appears to have been *Publick Occurrences, Both Forreign and Domestick,* which was suppressed after the appearance of one issue, Sept. 25, 1690. The first continuously published American newspaper was the *Boston News-Letter* (1704-1776). James Franklin founded the second newspaper in America, the *Boston Gazette* (1719-1741). He also edited the *New England Courant* (1721-1726), notable for its lively journalism in the manner of the *Spectator*, and for the fact that Benjamin Franklin contributed to it his "Do-Good Papers" (1722).

The earliest newspaper in New York City was the *New York Gazette* (1725-1744), edited by William Bradford. John Peter Zenger (1697-1746) established the *New-York Weekly Journal* (1733-1752) and edited it until 1746 as a rival to the *Gazette*. A study of Zenger and his importance in the development of a free press is Livingston Rutherfurd, *John Peter Zenger: His Press, His Trial and a Bibliography of Zenger Imprints*, New York, 1904.

The earliest among the Philadelphia newspapers was the *Pennsylvania Gazette* (1728-1815), founded by Samuel Keimer and bought and managed by Franklin (1729-1766). The *Virginia Gazette* (1736-1773), printed at Williamsburg, was the first Virginia newspaper, and was significant in the early years for its literary essays, imitative of those produced by London writers of the Queen Anne era.

John Webbe edited the first magazine published in America, the *American Magazine, or A Monthly View of the Political State of the British Colonies,* published by Andrew Bradford in Philadelphia, 1741. It was a monthly which ran for three issues, from January to March. In the same year and month Benjamin Franklin edited and published the *General Magazine, and Historical Chronicle, for all the British Plantations in America,* which continued for six issues, through June. For data on the New York lawyer and political journalist, William Livingston, see the individual bibliography herein. The *Independent Reflector* (1752–1753) was established in New York by Livingston, William Smith, Jr., and John Morin Scott. In 1753 the same writers brought out the short-lived *Occasional Reverberator;* and two years later they launched their third periodical, *John Englishman* (1755). These journals were printed by James Parker (*ca.* 1714–1770), who served as public printer of New York, 1743–1760. For a study of the three New York magazines, see Lyon N. Richardson, *A History of Early American Magazines, 1741–1789,* New York, 1931, pp. 75–94.

The only magazine before the Revolution to meet with any measure of success was the *American Magazine, or Monthly Chronicle for the British Colonies* (Philadelphia, 1757–1758). It was edited by Provost William Smith and contained much of the best work of the colonial Philadelphia writers, including Francis Hopkinson and Thomas Godfrey. For data on the magazine and on Smith, see Richardson, *op. cit.,* pp. 98–123.

The most detailed study of early magazines is Richardson's, mentioned above, with bibl., pp. 362–375. Also standard, though less detailed on the period, is Frank L. Mott, *A History of American Magazines, 1741–1850,* Cambridge, 1938 (Vol. I). The authoritative history of journalism is Frank L. Mott, *American Journalism . . . 1690–1940,* New York, 1941. Still standard is Clyde M. Dunniway, *The Development of Freedom of the Press in Massachusetts,* New York, 1906. An early study of Philadelphia magazines is Albert H. Smyth, *The Philadelphia Magazines and Their Contributors,* Philadelphia, 1892. Special studies include Philip D. Jordan, "The Funeral Sermon: A Phase of American Journalism," *Amer. Book Collector,* IV (1933), 177–188; and Sister Mary M. Redden, *The Gothic Fiction in the American Magazines, 1765–1800,* Washington, 1939.

*Printing and Publishing*

The earliest printer in New England was Stephen Day (*ca.* 1594–1668), who set up his press at Cambridge. Later New England printers of distinction ınclude Marmaduke Johnson—the first American to found a printing house as a private business enterprise (at Boston, 1674)—Thomas Fleet, Samuel Kneeland, Benjamin Edes, and Isaiah Thomas (1749–1831) of Worcester, Mass., the leading publisher of his day, whose *History of Printing in America* (2 vols., 1810) is still an authoritative contribution to the subject.

In the South, William Nuthead established a press in the 1680's, first in Virginia, then in Maryland. William Bradford (1663–1752) established the first press in Philadelphia, and in 1693 became the official Royal Printer at New York. Probably the best known printing family in the colonies were the Franklins: the brothers James and Benjamin, and James, Jr. The last named founded the *Newport Mercury* (1758–current), and edited it until his death (1762). A standard history is Lawrence C. Wroth, *The Colonial Printer*, rev. ed., Portland, Me., 1938. A brief historical review, with essential information difficult to assemble elsewhere, is Henry W. Boynton, *Annals of American Bookselling, 1638–1850*, New York, 1932. Other studies include Worthington C. Ford, *The Boston Book Market, 1679–1700*, Boston, 1917; George P. Winship, *The Cambridge Press, 1638–1692 . . .*, Philadelphia, 1945; Paul L. Ford, ed., *The Journals of Hugh Gaine, Printer*, New York, 1902, 2 vols.—a history of printing in colonial New York City; Gerald McDonald, "Early Printing in the United States," *Pub. Weekly*, CXXXVII (1940), 54–58; and John K. Reeves, "Jeremy Gridley, Editor," *New Eng. Quar.*, XVII (1944), 265–281—his importance as an editor in the 1730's. A manual on certain printed rarities is John T. Winterich, *Early American Books and Printing*, Boston, 1935.

## THE FORMING OF THE REPUBLIC: 1760–1820

CULTURAL HISTORY:
*General Studies*

A survey of critical thought in the early national period is William Charvat, *The Origins of American Critical Thought, 1810–1835*, Philadelphia, 1936. Intellectual life in colonial towns is the subject of Michael Kraus, *Intercolonial Aspects of American Culture on the Eve of the Revolution, with Special Reference to the Northern Towns*, New York, 1928. See also Harry H. Clark, "The Influence of Science on American Ideas, from 1775 to 1809," *Trans. Wis. Acad. Sci., Arts, and Letters*, XXXV (1944), 305–349.

Essays on life in Boston, New York, Philadelphia, Annapolis, Williamsburg, and Charleston are in Thomas J. Wertenbaker, *The Golden Age of Colonial Culture*, New York, 1942. Useful also as social history, especially to

1783, is Carl and Jessica Bridenbaugh, *Rebels and Gentlemen: Philadelphia in the Age of Franklin*, New York, 1942.

Useful background studies in the development of ideas are Adam L. Jones, *Early American Philosophers*, New York, 1898; Herbert M. Morais, *Deism in Eighteenth Century America*, New York, 1934; Vernon Stauffer, *New England and the Bavarian Illuminati*, New York, 1918; and Howard M. Jones, "The Drift to Liberalism in the American Eighteenth Century," in *Ideas in America*, Cambridge, 1944, pp. 107–124. Carl L. Becker, *The Heavenly City of the Eighteenth-Century Philosophers*, New Haven, 1932, is a brilliant analysis of eighteenth century rationalism. Still standard as a study of the history of eighteenth century ideas is Leslie Stephen, *History of English Thought in the Eighteenth Century*, 3rd ed., London, 1902, 2 vols.

For studies of liberalism and nativism in American thought, see Ray A. Billington, *The Protestant Crusade, 1800–1860: A Study of the Origins of American Nativism*, New York, 1938, with bibl., pp. 445–504. Useful as studies of the free-thought movement are Dumas Malone, *The Public Life of Thomas Cooper, 1783–1839*, New Haven, 1926; Niels H. Sonne, *Liberal Kentucky, 1780–1828*, New York, 1939; and Clement Eaton, *Freedom of Thought in the Old South*, Durham, N.C., 1940. See also Patrick F. Quinn, "Agrarianism and the Jeffersonian Philosophy," *Rev. Pol.*, II (1940), 87–104.

Standard studies of early music are Oscar G. T. Sonneck, *Early Opera in America*, New York, 1915; and *idem, Early Concert Life in America (1731–1800)*, Leipzig, 1907. Jennie Holliman has published *American Sports, 1785–1835*, Durham, N.C., 1931, with bibl., pp. 193–211. Indispensable both as history and as source material is William Dunlap, *A History of . . . the Arts of Design in the United States* (1834), rev. ed., Boston, 1918, 3 vols.

An account of the work of Charles Bulfinch (1763–1844), the distinguished architect, is C. A. Place, *Charles Bulfinch: Architect and Citizen* (1925).

## Historical and Political Writing, Including Propaganda and Debate

Extended treatment of the works by and about the major American statesmen (John Adams, Franklin, Hamilton, Jefferson, Madison, and Washington) will be found in the individual bibliographies of those men herein included. Other publicists and men of letters for whom individual bibliographies are provided are St. Jean de Crèvecœur, John Dickinson, William Livingston, James Otis, and Thomas Paine.

Among other spokesmen for the cause of American liberty, the works of a few deserve notice in a literary history. The deistic essay reputedly by

Ethan Allen (1738–1789), *Reason the Only Oracle of Man* (1784), is repr. for the Scholars' Facsimiles and Reprints, New York, 1940, ed. by John Pell. Allen's frequently reprinted *A Narrative of Colonel Ethan Allen's Captivity* . . . (1779), was reproduced from the original Philadelphia edition, with an introductory note by John Pell, Westport, Conn., 1930. The best account of Allen's early, obscure years is John Pell, *Ethan Allen,* Boston, 1929, with a bibl., pp. 271–279. A picturesque life is Stewart H. Holbrook, *Ethan Allen,* New York, 1940. See also Clarence Gohdes, "Ethan Allen and His *Magnum Opus,*" *Open Court,* XLIII (1929), 129–151; and B. T. Schantz, "Ethan Allen's Religious Ideas," *Jour. Rel.,* XVII (1938), 183–217.

The writings of Hannah Adams (1755–1832), considered the first professional woman author in America, were popular in their day, and include *A Summary History of New England* (1799), and *The History of the Jews* . . . (2 vols., 1812).

A vigorous essay on the origin and nature of law is Stephen Hopkins (1707–1785), *The Rights of Colonies Examined,* Providence, 1765. The Maryland lawyer Daniel Dulany (1721–1797) presented legal arguments in opposition to the Stamp Act in *Considerations on the Propriety of Imposing Taxes in the British Colonies* . . ., Annapolis, 1765. The famous oratory of Patrick Henry (1736–1799) is published in William W. Henry, *Patrick Henry: Life, Correspondence and Speeches,* New York, 1891, 3 vols. Moses C. Tyler published an authoritative biography, *Patrick Henry,* Boston, 1887 (Amer. Statesmen Ser.). A life is that of George Morgan, *The True Patrick Henry,* Philadelphia, 1907.

One of the earliest important advocacies of political freedom is that of William Henry Drayton (1742–1779) of South Carolina, *The Letters of Freeman, Etc.,* London, 1771. Josiah Quincy (1744–1775) contributed an important patriotic tract, *Observations on the Act of Parliamen[t] Commonly Called the Boston Port-Bill With Thoughts on Civil Society and Standing Armies,* Philadelphia, 1774. *The Federalist* (1787–1788) constitutes the most impressive series of essays in support of the Constitution, and has been important as authority on the principles of American government. The 85 essays, in the form of letters, appeared in three New York journals: the *Independent Journal,* the *Packet,* and the *Daily Advertiser,* written by Hamilton (who contributed more than half), Madison, and Jay. They were collected and revised by Hamilton (2 vols., 1788). For further details, see the individual bibliography of Hamilton herein. Two well known pamphlets written in opposition to *The Federalist* are "Letters of the Federal Farmer" (1787–1788), written by the Virginian, Richard Henry Lee (1732–1794). Hamilton's *Report on Manufactures* (1791) is a classic statement of American conservatism in business. John Quincy Adams is alleged to have won his appointment as

Minister to the Netherlands (1794) through the publication of *Observations on Paine's Rights of Man, in a Series of Letters, by Publicola,* Edinburgh, 1791—eight of the eleven letters originally published in the *Columbian Centinel,* June–July, 1791. The *Political Essays* (1799) of Thomas Cooper (1759–1839) were directed against the Federalist administration. John Taylor of Caroline (1753–1824) defended agrarianism in two tracts, *Arator: Being a Series of Agricultural Essays, Practical and Political,* Columbia, S.C., 1813; and *An Inquiry into the Principles and Policy of the Government of the United States,* Fredericksburg, Va., 1814. The most recent and authentic study of the Revolutionary agitator Samuel Adams (1722–1803) is John C. Miller, *Sam Adams, Pioneer in Propaganda,* Boston, 1936.

Two important contemporary histories of the Revolution are David Ramsay (1749–1815), *The History of the American Revolution,* London, 1791; and Mercy Otis Warren, *History of the . . . American Revolution,* Boston, 1805, 3 vols. An account written by a loyalist is contained in Robert Proud, *The History of Pennsylvania . . . ,* Philadelphia, 1797–1798, 2 vols.

American histories and state papers were known and admired abroad before 1812. An early significant collection of source material for United States history is Ebenezer Hazard's *Historical Collections, State Papers, and Other Authentic Documents* (2 vols., 1792–1794). Jonathan Elliott edited *The Debates in the Several State Conventions on the Adoption of the Federal Constitution . . . ,* Washington, 1836–1845, 5 vols.—an important body of source material, often reprinted, most recently at Philadelphia, 1937. Well known also as a documentary history of the British colonies in America is Peter Force, *American Archives: Consisting of a Collection of Authentick Records . . .* (1837–1853), 9 vols. Chief Justice Marshall's decision in the case of Marbury vs. Madison (1803) was the first decision to annul an act of Congress as unconstitutional, and as a consequence the judiciary power was increased.

A brilliant portrayal of politics and diplomacy during the early national period is Henry Adams, *History of the United States* (during the administrations of Jefferson and Madison), New York, 1884–1889, 9 vols., repr., New York, 1930, 4 vols., with an introduction by Henry S. Commager. One of the first histories to devote attention to intellectual developments and interests was John B. McMaster, *A History of the People of the United States from the Revolution to the Civil War,* New York, 1883–1913, 8 vols.

Other important studies of the intellectual history of the Revolutionary period are Randolph G. Adams, *Political Ideas of the American Revolution: Britannic-American Contributions to the Problem of Imperial Organization, 1765 to 1775,* Durham, N.C., 1922; John A. Krout and Dixon Ryan Fox, *The Completion of Independence, 1790–1830,* New York, 1944; and Charles F.

Mullett, *Fundamental Law and the American Revolution, 1760–1776,* New York, 1933. A useful survey is G. Adolph Koch, *Republican Religion: The American Revolution and the Cult of Reason,* New York, 1933, with information on the clubs, lectureships, and other instruments by which the deists functioned, and a bibl., pp. 299–328. A documented study is Philip Davidson, *Propaganda and the American Revolution, 1763–1783,* Chapel Hill, N.C., 1941 —with chapters on songs, plays, newspapers, and pulpit oratory, and with bibl., pp. 413–442. A recent standard treatment is Evarts B. Greene, *The Revolutionary Generation, 1763–1790,* New York, 1943.

Special studies include Eugene P. Link, *Democratic-Republican Societies, 1790–1800,* New York, 1942; Jacob N. Beam, *The American Whig Society of Princeton University,* Princeton, 1933; Herbert D. Foster, "International Calvinism Through Locke and the Revolution of 1688," *Amer. Hist. Rev.,* XXXII (1927), 475–499; Michael Kraus, "America and the Utopian Ideal in the Eighteenth Century," *Miss. Valley Hist. Rev.,* XXII (1936), 487–504; Merle Curti, "The Great Mr. Locke: America's Philosopher, 1783–1861," *Hunt. Lib. Bul.,* XI (1937), 107–155; and Lyle H. Wright, "Propaganda in Early American Fiction," *Papers Bibl. Soc. Amer.,* XXXIII (1939), 98–106. See also Chester E. Eisinger, "The Freehold Concept in Eighteenth-Century American Letters," *Wm. and Mary Quar.,* 3rd ser., IV (1947), 42–59.

Important primary source material is in Alexis de Tocqueville, *De la Démocratie en Amérique,* Paris, 1835—most conveniently available in the latest edition, *Democracy in America,* New York, 1945, ed. by Phillips Bradley.

### The Religious Impact

Though the writings of the best known eighteenth century theologians of the Middle Colonies have been published, authoritative biographies and critical estimates are generally lacking. On the Quaker preacher and humanitarian, John Woolman, see the individual bibliography herein.

Among loyalists, the most significant contributions were made by Jonathan Boucher (1738–1804), Jonathan Odell (1737–1818), Myles Cooper (1735–1785), and Samuel Seabury (1729–1796). Boucher's primary contribution was *A View of the Causes and Consequences of the American Revolution* (1797). For an account of Boucher as a man of letters see Moses C. Tyler, *The Literary History of the American Revolution, 1763–1783,* New York, 1897, I, 316–328. Odell denounced the American leaders in "The American Times" (1780). On Odell as a writer, see Moses C. Tyler, *op. cit.,* II, 97–129; and Vernon L. Parrington, *Main Currents in American Thought . . . ,* New York, 1927, I, 255–259. Cooper, who had served as president of King's College, 1763–1775, fled to England in the latter year and there published *National*

*Humiliation and Repentance Recommended,* Oxford, 1777. For a biography see Clarence H. Vance, *Myles Cooper . . . Second President of King's College,* New York, 1930. By virtue of Seabury's position as the first bishop of Connecticut and of the Episcopal Church in the United States, his pamphlets received wide notice. *Letters of a Westchester Farmer, 1774-1775* have been edited with introduction by Clarence H. Vance, White Plains, N.Y., 1930. The most recent life is Walter Chambers, *Samuel Seabury: A Challenge,* New York, 1932. The most significant loyalist contributions made by a layman are those of Joseph Galloway (1731-1803), *Historical and Political Reflections on the Rise and Progress of the American Rebellion,* London, 1780. See Ernest H. Baldwin, *Joseph Galloway, the Loyalist Politician: A Biography,* Philadelphia, 1902. A standard study of the loyalists is Claude H. Van Tyne, *The Loyalists in the American Revolution,* New York, 1902, reprinted 1929. Still useful is Lorenzo Sabine, *The American Loyalists . . . ,* Boston, 1847.

Two important accounts are Daniel Stanton, *A Journal of the Life, Travels, and Gospel Labours of a Faithful Minister of Jesus Christ, Daniel Stanton,* Philadelphia, 1772; and John Churchman, *An Account of the Gospel Labors and Christian Experiences of . . . John Churchman, Late of Nottingham, in Pennsylvania . . . ,* Philadelphia, 1779. Of considerable importance as a religious, educational, and political thinker was John Witherspoon (1723-1794), the Scottish-born Presbyterian who accepted the call to the presidency of the College of New Jersey (Princeton) in 1768. *The Works of John Witherspoon,* first issued 1800-1801, 4 vols., were issued more completely at Edinburgh, 1815, 9 vols. An authoritative life is Varnum L. Collins, *President Witherspoon: A Biography,* Princeton, 1925, 2 vols.

A useful analysis of the clerical impact on political theory is Alice M. Baldwin, *The New England Clergy and the American Revolution,* Durham, N.C., 1928. See also Edward F. Humphrey, *Nationalism and Religion in America, 1774-1789,* Boston, 1924. Other background studies include Oliver W. Elsbree, *The Rise of the Missionary Spirit in America, 1790-1815,* Williamsport, Pa., 1928; Charles H. Maxson, *The Great Awakening in the Middle Colonies,* Chicago, 1920; Wesley M. Gewehr, *The Great Awakening in Virginia, 1740-1790,* Durham, N.C., 1930; and Catharine C. Cleveland, *The Great Revival in the West, 1797-1805,* Chicago, 1916. See also Howard W. Hintz, *The Quaker Influence in American Literature,* New York, 1940.

## Education and Science

Convenient summaries of educational plans proposed during the post-Revolutionary period are in Allen O. Hansen, *Liberalism and American Edu-*

*cation in the Eighteenth Century,* New York, 1926—with stress upon the influence of European and American educational philosophers, and with bibl., pp. 265–296. Other useful background studies are Richard B. Davis, *Francis Walker Gilmer: Life and Learning in Jefferson's Virginia: A Study in Virginia Literary Culture in the First Quarter of the Nineteenth Century,* Richmond, Va., 1939—with bibl., pp. 389–398; and Edward A. Fitzpatrick, *The Educational Views and Influence of De Witt Clinton,* New York, 1911. For a contemporary estimate, written as a reply to an article in *Blackwood's Edinburgh Magazine,* entitled "On the State of Learning in the United States of America, 1819," see Willard Sidney, "On the Means of Education and the State of Learning in the United States," *North Amer. Rev.,* IX (1819), 240–259.

Franklin had founded the American Philosophical Society at Philadelphia in 1743 to promote learning. Jeremy Belknap and other scholars founded the Massachusetts Historical Society at Boston in 1791, the first organization of its kind. Isaiah Thomas founded the American Antiquarian Society at Worcester in 1812. These three organizations have continued in growth and constitute today three of the most important learned societies in America.

The first part of *A Grammatical Institute of the English Language* (1783–1785), by Noah Webster (1758–1843), became his famous *Spelling Book,* which sold some fifteen million copies before 1840 and four times that number by the end of the century. Its importance in standardizing spelling, and to some degree pronunciation, in the United States was very great. For further data on Webster, see also the section American Language, *post,* p. 187. The first geography published in the United States was that compiled by Jedidiah Morse (1761–1826), *Geography Made Easy* (1784), later enlarged as *The American Universal Geography.* Though it was for the most part derivative, it did include material supplied by correspondents who contributed first-hand data. In 1797 Morse published *The American Gazetteer.* All these works were reprinted many times. Among other popular elementary texts were *The American Preceptor* (1794), and *The Columbian Orator* (1797), compiled by Caleb Bingham (1757–1817), and in constant use for many years in New England schools. An early biographical dictionary was that compiled by William Allen (1784–1868): *An American Biographical and Historical Dictionary* (1809). For the significance of *The Old Farmer's Almanack* (1792–current) in supplying education in the rural parts of the country, see the section Almanacs, *post,* p. 239.

The Edinburgh-trained Philadelphia physician John Morgan (1735–1789) founded the medical school of the University of Pennsylvania (1765), and in the same year published *A Discourse upon the Institution of Medical Schools in America.* Humphry Marshall (1722–1801), the Pennsylvania botanist, published *Arbustrum Americanum: The American Grove* (1785), considered the earliest botanical essay written and published by an American. Though the views of Samuel Stanhope Smith (1750–1819), president of the College of New Jersey (1795–1819), were unpopular in their day to the extent that they contradicted the theory of separate creation of the different races of man, his *An Essay on the Causes of the Variety of Complexion and Figure in the Human Species* (1787) is an early and significant defense of the genetic unity of man. The cotton industry was revolutionized by the invention, in 1794, of the cotton gin by Eli Whitney (1765–1825). The Salem mathematician Nathaniel Bowditch (1773–1838) compiled *The New American Practical Navigator* (1802), a work which has gone through some sixty editions and is still standard, known as *Bowditch's Navigator*. The first government-sponsored voyage of exploration to the Southern hemisphere was that described by Henry Marie Brackenridge (1786–1871) in his *Voyage to South America, Performed by Order of the American Government in the Years 1817 and 1818, in the Frigate Congress* (2 vols., 1819).

For a brief discussion of the impetus to scientific thought in the eighteenth century, see Michael Kraus, "Scientific Relations Between Europe and America in the Eighteenth Century," *Scientific Mo.*, LV (1942), 259–272; and Edward Ford, *David Rittenhouse: Astronomer-Patriot, 1732–1796*, Philadelphia, 1946.

### Memoirs and Journals

Useful data concerning the literary and cultural development of America may be found in the posthumously published writings of Ezra Stiles (1727–1795), who during the last seventeen years of his life was president of Yale College. Franklin B. Dexter edited *The Literary Diary of Ezra Stiles*, New York, 1901, 3 vols., covering the years 1769–1795; as well as *Extracts from the Itineraries and Other Miscellanies of Ezra Stiles . . . 1755–1794 . . .*, New Haven, 1916. The painter John Trumbull (1756–1843) was a friend of many leading Revolutionary figures. His *Autobiography, Reminiscences, and Letters . . . from 1756 to 1841* was published, New York, 1841. The loyalist rector of Annapolis, Jonathan Boucher, left an autobiography, published as *Reminiscences of an American Loyalist, 1738–1789*, Boston, 1925. Useful sidelights are in the letters of a Brookline, Mass., loyalist, Ann Hulton (died 1779), addressed to an English correspondent: *Letters of a Loyalist Lady . . .*, Cambridge, 1927. Cultural interests in the middle colonies are recorded in *Philip Vickers Fithian: Journal and Letters, 1767–1774; Student at Princeton College, 1770–72, Tutor at Nomini Hall in Virginia, 1773–74*, ed. by John R. Williams, Princeton, 1900. More recently Robert G. Albion and Leonidas

Dodson edited *Philip Vickers Fithian: Journal, 1775-1776, Written on the Virginia-Pennsylvania Frontier and in the Army Around New York,* Princeton, 1934. Benjamin Rush (1745-1813) published his *Essays: Literary, Moral, and Philosophical,* Philadelphia, 1798. For a recent study of this important Philadelphia scientist, see Nathan G. Goodman, *Benjamin Rush, Physician and Citizen,* Philadelphia, 1934. Samuel Miller (1769-1850) recorded impressions of the intellectual life in Europe and America in *A Brief Retrospect of the Eighteenth Century,* New York, 1803, 2 vols. His *Letters from a Father to His Sons in College,* Philadelphia, 1843—written to five sons in Princeton— are useful source material on the early decades of the nineteenth century. No adequate study of Miller has been published.

Abigail Adams (1744-1818), wife of John Adams, deserves to be remembered for the charming letters, written between 1761 and 1816, which were edited by her grandson Charles Francis Adams: *Letters of Mrs. Adams . . . ,* Boston, 1840, 2 vols. Further letters have been published by Allyn B. Forbes, ed., "Abigail Adams, Commentator," *Proc. Mass. Hist. Soc.,* LXVI (1942), 126-153. See Gamaliel Bradford, "Abigail Adams," in *Portraits of American Women,* Boston, 1919, pp. 3-31.

Significant material on events and characters during the formative period are in *Memoirs of John Quincy Adams, Comprising Portions of His Diary from 1795 to 1848,* ed. by Charles Francis Adams, Philadelphia, 1874-1877, 12 vols. A storehouse of observations on the intellectual life of the Revolutionary period is *The Diary of William Bentley, D.D.* [1759-1819], *Pastor of the East Church, Salem, Massachusetts . . . ,* published at Salem, 1905-1914, 4 vols., from manuscripts in the Essex Institute. Further useful data are in Edward L. Morse, ed., *Samuel F. B. Morse: His Letters and Journals,* Boston, 1914, 2 vols. Ida G. Everson's *George Henry Calvert: American Literary Pioneer,* New York, 1944, gives useful background data. Primary source material on contemporary manners is in *Memoirs of an American Lady* (1808), the anonymously published recollections of Anne McVickar Grant (1755-1838), who was born in Scotland and lived for several years near Albany, New York.

*Foreign Influences*

Among the writings of English and continental thinkers who helped give shape to American culture, none have been more pivotal than those of Sir Isaac Newton, John Locke, Charles de Secondat de Montesquieu, Sir William Blackstone, and Adam Smith. Newton's *Philosophiae Naturalis Principia Mathematica* (1687), a landmark in the development of science, immediately became a cornerstone in the philosophical structure of higher education in

America. Locke's influence was paramount for over a century, and his *Two Treatises of Government* (1690) shaped the thinking of the Revolutionary generation, as did Montesquieu's *L'Esprit des Lois* (1748), which was immediately translated and frequently reprinted. Blackstone's *Commentaries on the Laws of England* (1765–1769) nourished American lawyers throughout the formative period of the Republic; and Smith's *An Enquiry into the Nature and Causes of the Wealth of Nations* (1776) revolutionized economic thinking at a most crucial moment in American history.

Keen interest abroad was expressed in America as a Utopian ideal. Franklin's English friend Richard Price (1723–1791) set forth his ideas in *Observations on the Nature of Civil Liberty, the Principles of Government, and the Justice and Policy of the War with America* (1776), and again in *Observations on the Importance of the American Revolution, and the Means of Making It a Benefit to the World* (1784). The English journalist William Cobbett (1763–1835), who was interested in "causes" and outspoken in his judgments, gave graphic sidelights in *The Life and Adventures of Peter Porcupine* (1796), and in *A Journal of a Year's Residence in the United States* (1818–1819). William Winterbotham saw the United States as a commonwealth of nations, and described it in *A Historical, Geographical, Commercial, and Philosophical View of the European Settlements in America and the West Indies* (4 vols., 1796). John Bristed's *America and Her Resources . . .* (1818) became known in France, where it was translated (2 vols., 1826). Frances Wright (1795–1852) visited the United States in 1818, and returned to England to publish her enthusiastic *Views of Society and Manners in America . . .* (1821). Studies of British interest and influence include William B. Cairns, *British Criticisms of American Writings, 1783–1815,* Madison, Wis., 1918— still a standard treatment, as is Robert E. Spiller, *The American in England During the First Half Century of Independence,* New York, 1926. Other useful studies are Benjamin H. Bissell, *The American Indian in English Literature of the Eighteenth Century,* New Haven, 1925; Annabel Newton, *Wordsworth in Early American Criticism,* Chicago, 1928; Reginald Coupland, *The American Revolution and the British Empire,* London, 1930; Lois Whitney, *Primitivism and the Idea of Progress in English Popular Literature of the Eighteenth Century,* Baltimore, 1934; and Robert B. Heilman, *America in English Fiction, 1760–1800,* University, La., 1937. See also William Ellery Leonard, *Byron and Byronism in America,* Boston, 1905; and Van R. Westfall, *American Shakespearean Criticism, 1607–1865,* New York, 1939. Briefer contributions include Frederic I. Carpenter, "The Vogue of Ossian in America," *Amer. Lit.,* II (1931), 405–417; Leon Howard, "Wordsworth in America," *Mod. Lang. Notes,* XLVIII (1933), 359–365; Chester N. Greenough, "Defoe in Boston," *Pub. Col. Soc. Mass.,* XXVIII (1935), 461–493; and

Guy A. Cardwell, "The Influence of Addison on Charleston Periodicals, 1795–1860," *Stud. Philol.*, XXXV (1938), 456–470.

Three significant French accounts are Charles Pictet, *Tableau de la Situation Actuelle des Etats-Unis d'Amérique, d'après J[edidiah] Morse et les Meilleurs Auteurs Américains* (2 vols., 1795); Ferdinand M. Bayard, *Voyage dans l'Intérieur des Etats-Unis . . .* (1797); and Pierre-Joseph Proudhon, *Du Principe Fédératif et de la Nécessité de Reconstituer le Parti de la Révolution* (1863). An authoritative account is David Baillie Warden (1778–1845), *Description Statistique, Historique, et Politique des Etats-Unis de l'Amérique Septentrionale . . .*, Paris, 1820. The standard treatment of French and other European influence is Howard M. Jones, *America and French Culture, 1750–1848*, Chapel Hill, N.C., 1927. See also Harold E. Mantz, *French Criticism of American Literature Before 1850*, New York, 1917; Lucy M. Gidney, *L'Influence des Etats-Unis d'Amérique sur Brissot, Condorcet, et Mme Roland*, Paris, 1930; Paul M. Spurlin, *Montesquieu in America, 1760–1801*, University, La., 1940; and Gilbert Malcolm Fess, *The American Revolution in Creative French Literature, 1775–1937*, Columbia, Mo., 1941. Two brief studies by Howard M. Jones are "The Importance of French Literature in New York City, 1750–1800," *Stud. Philol.*, XXVIII (1931), 235–251; and "The Importation of French Books in Philadelphia, 1750–1800," *Mod. Philol.*, XXXII (1934), 157–177. An extensive listing of French travelers is Frank Monaghan, *French Travellers in the United States, 1765–1932: A Bibliography*, New York, 1933—a listing of some 1,500 items. For the earlier period there is Bernard Faÿ, *Bibliographie Critique des Ouvrages Français Relatifs aux Etats-Unis, 1770–1800*, Paris, 1925.

German interest in America is shown by such works as Cornelius de Pauw's *Recherches Philosophiques sur les Américains . . .*, first published in Berlin, 1768–1769, 2 vols. Christoph Daniel Ebeling (1741–1817) published *Erdbeschreibung und Geschichte von Amerika*, Hamburg and Bohn, 1787–1816, 5 vols. It was part of an enormous repertory compiled by Anton Friedrich Buesching, and remained a source book for several generations. Ebeling's library was bought for Harvard College in 1818. A brief study is F. H. Wilkens, "Early Influence of German Literature in America," *Americana Germanica*, III (1900–1901), 110–136. More recent studies include Paul C. Weber, *America in Imaginative German Literature in the First Half of the Nineteenth Century*, New York, 1926—with a selected bibliography; Otto Vossler, *Die Amerikanischen Revolutionsideale in ihrem Verhältnis zu den Europäischen*, Berlin, 1929; and Henry Safford King, "Echoes of the American Revolution in German Literature," *Univ. Calif. Pub. in Mod. Philol.*, XIV (1929), 23–193. Paul B. Baginsky, *German Works Relating to America, 1493–1800*, New York, 1942, lists some 1,600 items and includes reviews and translations. See also Harold S. Jantz, "German Thought and Literature in New England, 1620–1820," *Jour. Eng. and Ger. Philol.*, XLI (1942), 1–45; and L. E. Wagner, "The Reserved Attitude of the Early German Romanticists Toward America," *Germanic Rev.*, XVI (1943), 8–12.

Two important Italian works appeared in the early decades of American independence. Carlo Botta's *Storia della Guerra dell' Independenza* . . . (4 vols., 1809), was translated by George Alexander Otis as *History of the War of the Independence of the United States of America*, Philadelphia, 1820–1821, 3 vols. Giuseppe Compagnoni's *Storia dell' America* . . . was issued at Milan, 1820–1822, in 4 vols. A recent study is Giovanni Schiavo, *The Italians in America Before the Civil War*, New York, 1934. See also H. R. Marraro, "Italian Culture in Eighteenth-Century American Magazines," *Italica*, XXII (1945), 21–31; C. R. D. Miller, "Alfieri and America," *Philol. Quar.*, XI (1932), 163–166; Joseph G. Fucilla, "Echoes of the American Revolution in an Italian Poet," *Italica*, XI (1934), 85–87; and Emilio Goggio, "First Personal Contacts Between American and Italian Leaders of Thought," *Romanic Rev.*, XXVII (1936), 1–8.

The Swedish botanist and traveler Peter Kalm (1716–1779) was sent to America in 1748–1751 by the Swedish Academy of Sciences. His naïve observations on manners appear in his authentic botanical study, published in Sweden (3 vols., 1753–1761), translated as *Travels into North America . . .* (2 vols., 1770–1771). The best edition is that of Adolph B. Benson, *The America of 1750: Peter Kalm's Travels in North America* (2 vols., 1937). A useful study is Adolph B. Benson, "Cultural Relations Between Sweden and America to 1830," *German Rev.*, XII (1938), 83–101.

Three general studies by Michael Kraus are "America and the Utopian Ideal in the Eighteenth Century," *Miss. Valley Hist. Rev.*, XXII (1936), 487–504; "Eighteenth Century Humanitarianism: Collaboration Between Europe and America," *Pa. Mag. Hist. and Biog.*, LX (1936), 270–286; and "Literary Relations Between Europe and America in the Eighteenth Century," *Wm. and Mary Quar.*, 3rd ser., I (1944), 210–234. See also Harry Bernstein, *Origins of Inter-American Interest, 1700–1812*, Philadelphia, 1945.

For further details of travelers and observers in America, see the sections dealing with them in the bibliography: Chronicles of the Frontier, *post*, p. 245. See also the bibliographies for Cooper and Irving.

*Literary Studies Specific to the Period*

The fullest and most authoritative history for the early years still remains Moses C. Tyler, *The Literary History of the American Revolution, 1763–1783*, New York, 1897, 2 vols. Standard also for the period are the first two volumes of Vernon L. Parrington's *Main Currents in American Thought,* New York, 1927. Suggestive material is in Fred L. Pattee, *The First Century of American Literature,* New York, 1935; William B. Cairns, *A History of American Literature,* rev. ed., New York, 1930; and Annie R. Marble, *Heralds of American Literature,* Chicago, 1907.

Suggestions regarding possible lines of research are noted in Harry H. Clark, "American Literature, 1787–1800," *Eng. Jour.* XXIII (1934), 481–487.

## Fiction

Francis Hopkinson (1737–1791) published *A Pretty Story . . .* (1774), sometimes alleged to be the first novel written and printed in America, though in fact it ran to but twenty-nine pages. The earliest full-length American novel may perhaps have been that of Thomas Atwood Digges (*fl.* 1741–1821), *Adventures of Alonso: Containing Some Striking Anecdotes of the Present Prime Minister of Portugal,* London, 1775, 2 vols., reproduced in facsimile, New York, 1943, with introd., "The First American Novel," by Robert H. Elias, from *Amer. Lit.,* XII (1941), 419–434.

William Hill Brown's *The Power of Sympathy; or, The Triumph of Nature* (1789), printed by Isaiah Thomas, was published at Boston in two volumes. See Milton Ellis, "The Author of the First American Novel," *Amer. Lit.,* IV (1933), 356–368. In 1792 Hugh Henry Brackenridge published the first two parts of his satirical picaresque novel, *Modern Chivalry . . . ,* and the Massachusetts clergyman and historian, Jeremy Belknap, brought out his historical novel *The Foresters: An American Tale . . .* (1792). Recent studies of Belknap are Charles W. Cole, "Jeremy Belknap: Pioneer Nationalist," *New Eng. Quar.,* X (1937), 743–751; and Oscar Zeichner, ed., "Jeremy Belknap and the William Samuel Johnson Correspondence," *New Eng. Quar.,* XIV (1941), 362–374. *The Emigrants . . .* (3 vols., 1793), a sentimental romance of the Pittsburgh frontier by Gilbert Imlay (*ca.* 1754 to *ca.* 1828) is one of the earliest western novels. See Oliver F. Emerson, "Notes on Gilbert Imlay: Early American Writer," *PMLA,* XXXIX (1924), 406–439; and Edith F. Wyatt, "The First American Novel," *Atl. Mo.,* CXLIV (1929), 466–475. One of the most popular novels ever written is Susanna Haswell Rowson, *Charlotte: A Tale of Truth* (1791), later known as *Charlotte Temple.* It went through some 161 editions by 1933. A study of this early "best seller" is Robert W. G. Vail, "Susanna Haswell Rowson, the Author of *Charlotte Temple:* A Bibliographical Study," *Proc. Amer. Antiq. Soc.,* n.s. XLII (1932), 47–160. What is often considered the most finished of early novels is that by Hannah Webster Foster (1759–1840), *The Coquette; or, The History of Eliza Wharton . . .* (1797). Some thirteen editions had been published by 1833. It was issued in facsimile, ed. by H. R. Brown, from the 1797 ed., New York, 1939. See Robert L. Shurter, "Mrs. Hannah Webster Foster and the Early American Novel," *Amer. Lit.*. IV (1933), 306–308. One of the earliest works to treat a foreign theme is *The Algerine Captive* (1797) by Royall Tyler (1757–1826). Charles Brockden Brown's first novel, *Wieland*, was published in 1798. An early satire of sentimental fiction is *Female Quixotism* (1801), by Tabitha Tenney (1762–1837).

Before 1810, Irving's reputation was established with *Salmagundi* . . . , and *A History of New York* . . . ; and in 1820 Cooper published his first novel, *Precaution*.

An authoritative general study of the early novel is Arthur H. Quinn, *American Fiction*, New York, 1936, pp. 1–39. Special studies include Lillie D. Loshe, *The Early American Novel*, New York, 1907 (and 1930); Mildred D. Doyle, *Sentimentalism in American Periodicals, 1741–1800*, New York, 1944; Lyle H. Wright, "Propaganda in Early American Fiction," *Papers Bibl. Soc. Amer.*, XXXIII (1939), 98–106; G. Harrison Orians, "Censure of Fiction in American Romances and Magazines, 1789–1810," *PMLA*, LII (1937), 195–214; Sister Mary M. Redden, *The Gothic Fiction in the American Magazines, 1765–1800*, Washington, 1939; and Lyon N. Richardson, *A History of Early American Magazines, 1741–1789*, New York, 1931—a detailed study, with bibl., pp. 362–375. An unpublished dissertation is E. D. Finch, "American Prose Fiction, 1789–1800," Yale Univ., 1933. See also Benjamin Brawley, comp., *Early Negro American Writers: Selections with Biographical and Critical Introductions*, Chapel Hill, N.C., 1935.

A valuable bibliographical study is Lyle H. Wright, *American Fiction, 1774–1850: A Contribution Toward a Bibliography*, San Marino, Calif., 1939. It is supplemented by *idem*, "A Statistical Survey of American Fiction, 1774–1850," *Huntington Lib. Quar.*, II (1939), 309–318, which lists best sellers of the period, with a tabular interpretation of 1,400 titles in the author's *American Fiction*. See also Oscar Wegelin, *Early American Fiction, 1774–1830: A Compilation of the Titles of Works of Fiction*, rev. ed., New York, 1929.

## Poetry

One of the best remembered of pre-Revolutionary verse writers is the Philadelphia poet, Thomas Godfrey (1736–1763), who acknowledged that his volume *The Court of Fancy* (1762) was strongly influenced by Chaucer. After his death a collection of his verses was issued under the title *Juvenile Poems on Various Subjects* (1765). On Godfrey, see the individual bibliography herein. Another Philadelphia versifier, Nathaniel Evans (1742–1767), is represented by a posthumous collection, *Poems on Several Occasions with*

*Some Other Compositions* (1772). See Burton A. Milligan, "An Early American Imitator of Milton," *Amer. Lit.,* XI (1939), 200–206. The satirical verses of the loyalist poets Jonathan Odell (1737–1818), and Joseph Stansbury (1742–1809) were first collected as *The Loyal Verses of Joseph Stansbury and Doctor Jonathan Odell* (1860). The Negro poetaster Phillis Wheatley (*ca.* 1753–1784) achieved something of a vogue with the publication of her *Poems on Various Subjects* (1773), though it received little critical notice.

For writings by and about Philip Freneau, generally regarded as the leading poet of the early national period, see the individual bibliography herein. *The Poems of Philip Freneau,* his first collection, was issued in 1786. The romantic verses of the Rhode Island physician, Joseph Brown Ladd (1764–1786), were collected and published in the year of his death as *The Poems of Arouet.* His sister Elizabeth L. Haskins edited *The Literary Remains of Joseph Brown Ladd, M.D.,* New York, 1832. For a checklist of his writings see Lewis Leary, "The Writings of Joseph Brown Ladd, 1764–1786," *Bul. Bibl.,* XVIII (1945), 131–133. Mathew Carey (1760–1839), the Philadelphia publisher, is represented by two verse satires, *The Plagi-Scurilliad: A Hudibrastic Poem* (1786), and *The Porcupiniad: A Hudibrastic Poem* (1799). For a recent study of Carey, principally as an economic pamphleteer, see Kenneth W. Rowe, *Mathew Carey: A Study in American Economic Development,* Baltimore, 1933. On Carey as publisher, see the section below, "Instruments of Culture and Literary Production," p. 103. A collection of the verses of the little known Philadelphia poet and dramatist, Peter Markoe (*ca.* 1752–1792), was issued as *Miscellaneous Poems* (1787). A recent study of Markoe is Sister Mary C. Diebels, *Peter Markoe . . . A Philadelphia Writer,* Washington, 1944, with a bibl., pp. 102–113.

The best known group of writers at the turn of the century was the Connecticut Wits (sometimes known as the Hartford Wits), who set out to quicken interest in native history and literature by declaring America's literary independence. For material by and about the principal figures, John Trumbull, Timothy Dwight, David Humphreys, and Joel Barlow, see the individual bibliographies herein. One of the lesser members of the group, Elihu Hubbard Smith, may be represented by his ballad opera, *Edwin and Angelina; or, The Banditti* (1796). See Marcia E. Bailey, *A Lesser Hartford Wit: Dr. Elihu Hubbard Smith,* Orono, Me., 1928. The gifted and wealthy Richard Alsop (1761–1815) published his satirical verses, *American Poems,* in 1793. See Karl P. Harrington, *Richard Alsop: "A Hartford Wit,"* Middletown, Conn., 1939—a factual biography with selections. The most detailed study of the group is Leon Howard, *The Connecticut Wits,* Chicago, 1943. Vernon L. Parrington edited *The Connecticut Wits,* New York, 1926—an anthology with a critical introduction and bibliography.

The Boston writer, Sarah Wentworth (Apthorp) Morton (1759-1846) extolled the "noble savage" in *Ouâbi; or, The Virtues of Nature: An Indian Tale in Four Cantos,* Boston, 1790. For a critical study see Emily Pendleton and Milton Ellis, *Philenia: The Life and Works of Sarah Wentworth Morton, 1759-1846,* Orono, Me., 1931, with bibl., pp. 113-115. Francis Hopkinson's *Poems on Various Subjects* was issued at Philadelphia, 1792. Thomas Odiorne (1769-1851) published *The Progress of Refinement,* 1792—an early nature poem. See Leon Howard, "Thomas Odiorne: An American Predecessor of Wordsworth," *Amer. Lit.,* X (1939), 417-436. Most of the literary output of John Quincy Adams, who became the sixth President of the United States in 1825, was published during his youth in literary periodicals. His translation from the German of Wieland (1799-1801) was first published as *Oberon: A Poetical Romance in Twelve Books,* New York, 1940, ed. with introd. and notes by Albert B. Faust. William Cliffton (1772-1799) was a voluminous writer of light verse and satire. *The Group; or, An Elegant Representation* (1796) was a verse defense of Jay's treaty. A posthumous collection was issued as *Poems, Chiefly Occasional* (1800). The Pennsylvania poet John Blair Linn (1777-1804) published *Miscellaneous Works, Prose and Poetical* (1795). The verses of Paul Allen (1775-1826), well known as a Philadelphia magazine contributor, were collected in *Original Poems, Serious and Entertaining* (1801). See Lewis Leary, "John Blair Linn, 1777-1804," *Wm. and Mary Quar.,* 3rd ser., IV (1947), 148-176; and *idem,* "The Writings of John Blair Linn, 1777-1804," *Bul. Bibl.,* XIX (1946), 18-19; Tremaine MacDowell, "Last Words of a Sentimental Heroine," *Amer. Lit.,* IV (1932), 174-177; and *idem,* "The First American Novel," *Amer. Rev.,* II (1933), 73-81.

Thomas Green Fessenden (1771-1837), one of the best satirists between John Trumbull and James Russell Lowell, published under his pseudonym "Christopher Caustic." His attack on Jefferson was entitled *Democracy Unveiled; or, Tyranny Stripped of the Garb of Patriotism* (1805). See Porter G. Perrin, *The Life and Works of Thomas Green Fessenden . . . ,* Orono, Me., 1925, with bibl., pp. 178-185. The nature poems of the ornithologist Alexander Wilson (1766-1813) were issued in *The Foresters . . .* (1805). Acclaimed in his day as a leading poet was Robert Treat Paine, Jr. (1773-1811). He established his reputation with his patriotic outburst "Adams and Liberty" (1798). A more ambitious undertaking is *The Hasty-Pudding: A Poem in Three Cantos* (1815). His writings were posthumously collected as *The Works in Prose and Verse of the late Robert Treat Paine . . . ,* Boston, 1812. On Paine, see Vernon L. Parrington, *Main Currents in American Thought,* New York, 1927, I, 288-295; and Philip Hale, "A Boston Dramatic Critic of a Century Ago," *Proc. Mass. Hist. Soc.,* LIX (1926), 312-324. Washington Allston (1779-1843) won notice especially through the praise bestowed by Coleridge upon his writings as a nature poet, represented by *The Sylphs of the Seasons* . . . (1813). "The Star Spangled Banner," adopted as the National Anthem by Act of Congress in 1931, was first issued as a broadside, entitled "The Bombardment of Fort McHenry" (1814). Key's collected *Poems* were posthumously issued in New York, 1857. A recent biography is V. Weybright, *Spangled Banner: The Story of Francis Scott Key,* New York, 1935. Widely praised in his own day was the Baltimore poet John Pierpont (1785-1866). His *Airs of Palestine and Other Poems* (1816) were written in praise of sacred music.

For bibliography of early poetry see Oscar Wegelin, *Early American Poetry: A Compilation of the Titles of Verse and Broadsides,* rev. ed., New York, 1930.

## Songs and Broadsides

Studies of early American songs are Harry Dichter and Elliott Shapiro, *Early American Sheet Music: Its Lure and Its Lore, 1768–1889,* New York, 1942—a description of over 600 pieces, with extensive bibliography; and Margaret and Travis Johnson, *Early American Songs,* New York, 1943. *Series of Old American Songs: Reproduced in Facsimile from Original or Early Editions in the Harris Collection of American Poetry and Plays, Brown University,* Providence, 1936, includes brief annotations supplied by S. Foster Damon and covers the period 1759-1858. A very extensive collection of early broadsides is in the Library of Congress. For a bibliography see Oscar G. T. Sonneck, *A Bibliography of Early Secular American Music,* rev. and enl. by William T. Upton, Washington, 1945. See also S. Foster Damon, "The Negro in Early American Songsters," *Papers Bibl. Soc. Amer.,* XXVIII (1934), 132-163—with bibl., pp. 154-163, of songsters published before 1830.

## Drama

Drama as a literary form received little or no encouragement in America until late in the colonial period. Best known among early American plays is Thomas Godfrey's *The Prince of Parthia,* written in 1759, and published in 1767. Mercy Otis Warren (1728-1814) is represented by *The Adulateur: A Tragedy* (1773), and *The Group* (1775)—a satire. A collection of her *Poems Dramatic and Miscellaneous* was issued in 1790. The best biography is Alice Brown, *Mercy Warren,* New York, 1896. See also Moses C. Tyler, *The Literary History of the American Revolution,* New York, 1897, II, 193-198. Royall Tyler's *The Contrast* (1787) inspired William Dunlap's *The Father; or, American Shandyism* (1789), as well as James Nelson Barker's *Tears and*

*Smiles* (1807). John Howard Payne's first play was *Julia; or, The Wanderer* (1806), though his best known works came several years later: *Charles the Second* (1824), and *Richelieu* (1826)—both written in collaboration with Irving. For writings by and about Godfrey, Tyler, Dunlap, Barker, and Payne, see the individual bibliographies herein. Among minor dramatists, the politician and journalist Mordecai Manuel Noah (1785–1851) achieved some success. His earliest play, *Paul and Alexis* (1812), was a melodrama, later retitled *The Wandering Boys* (1821). Other plays include *She Would Be a Soldier* (1819), and *The Grecian Captive* (1822).

The most authoritative study of early American drama is Arthur H. Quinn, *A History of the American Drama from the Beginning to the Civil War,* rev. ed., New York, 1943, pp. 1–198. William Dunlap's *A History of the American Theatre* (1832) is source material of great value, though it deals principally with the New York stage and must be checked for accuracy. More recent, though less readable, is George O. Seilhamer, *History of the American Theatre* [*1749–1797*], Philadelphia, 1888–1891, 3 vols. See also Paul L. Ford, "The Beginnings of American Dramatic Literature," *New Eng. Mag.,* n.s. IX (1894) 673–687.

The best bibliographies of both primary and secondary sources are those compiled by Arthur H. Quinn in his *History* (1943), pp. 403–411, 425–497. See also Oscar Wegelin, *Early American Plays, 1714–1830: A Compilation of the Titles of Plays and Other Dramatic Poems,* rev. ed., New York, 1905.

INSTRUMENTS OF CULTURE AND LITERARY PRODUCTION
## The Publishing Scene

The leading printer and publisher of the day was the Worcester editor and historian, Isaiah Thomas (1749–1831). The influential *Massachusetts Spy* (1770–1904) was edited by Thomas until 1814. He also edited the *Royal American Magazine* (1774–1775). His *The History of Printing in America . . . ,* Worcester, 1810, 2 vols. (republ., Albany, 1874), is still authoritative as history and is an invaluable source book. For a biography, see Annie R. Marble, *From 'Prentice to Patron . . . ,* New York, 1935. William Bradford (1722–1791) was the grandson of William Bradford (1663–1752), the first Philadelphia printer. The grandson was himself a successful publisher. He put out the *Pennsylvania Journal and Weekly Advertiser* (1743–1797), and was the official printer for the first Continental Congress. The Philadelphia editor Mathew Carey was a literary figure in his own right. A life of Carey, which is also a study of the beginnings of publishing in America, is Earl L. Bradsher, *Mathew Carey: Editor, Author and Publisher: A Study in American Literary Development,* New York, 1912. Employed by Carey as a book agent and peddler of chapbooks was the itinerant preacher Mason Locke Weems (1759–1825). See Lawrence C. Wroth, *Parson Weems: A Biographical and Critical Study,* Baltimore, 1911; and Harold Kellock, *Parson Weems of the Cherry-Tree,* New York, 1928. Noah Webster founded and edited for ten years the New York *American Minerva* (1793–1905), a daily Federalist journal. Less well known is William Goddard (1740–1817), who maintained presses in the East in New York, Philadelphia, Baltimore, New Haven, and Providence, and helped establish printing in the Midwest at Cincinnati in 1793, and Detroit in 1797. He is in addition credited with founding the United States postal system.

Five other newspapers achieved success at the turn of the century. The *Massachusetts Centinel and the Republican Journal* (1784–1840), published in Boston, was distinguished for its coverage, its literary interests, and its cartoons. The *Gazette of the United States* (1789–1847) was a New York weekly founded by John Fenno (1751–1798); it was financed by Hamilton as a Federalist organ. To oppose it, Jefferson financed the Philadelphia *National Gazette* (1791–1793), edited by Freneau, as a mouthpiece of the Democratic-Republican party. Isaiah Thomas founded in Walpole, New Hampshire, the *Farmer's Weekly Museum* (1793–1810), a distinguished journal that numbered among its contributors T. G. Fessenden, Royall Tyler, and Joseph Dennie. It was here that Dennie's "Lay Preacher" essays appeared. Interest attaches to the New York *Time-Piece* (1797–1799) in that it was edited by Freneau. Of special significance was the *National Intelligencer and Washington Advertiser* (1800–1870), which was the organ of the Jefferson, Madison, and Monroe administrations, and before 1825 the only printed record of the official proceedings of Congress.

Among literary periodicals established at the turn of the century, C. B. Brown's *Monthly Magazine and American Review* (1799–1802) is principally remembered for the fact that to it Brown contributed part of *Edgar Huntly.* Chief among literary magazines of the period was the *Port Folio* (1801–1827), edited by Joseph Dennie during its most successful years, 1801–1809. The Delphian Club of Baltimore issued the monthly literary magazine, the *Portico* (1816–1818), of which John Neal was an editor. The Philadelphia *Literary Gazette* (1809–1821) was edited by Irving (1813–1814) under the title, *The Analectic Magazine.* Though it survived but a year, the *American Magazine: A Monthly Miscellany* . . . (1815) deserves to be known. It was founded and edited by Horatio Gates Spafford (1778–1832), and its literary and scientific essays were well selected. For a discussion of Spafford, see Julian P. Boyd, "Horatio Gates Spafford: Inventor, Author, Promoter of Democracy," *Proc. Amer. Antiq. Soc.,* LI (1941), 279–350. What later became the most distinguished and long-lived of American magazines, the *North American Review,* was founded in 1815.

For secondary treatment, see Lyon N. Richardson, *A History of Early American Magazines, 1741-1789,* New York, 1931; Frank L. Mott, *A History of American Magazines,* Cambridge, 1938, 3 vols. (vol. I); and Lawrence C. Wroth, "Book Production and Distribution from the Beginning to the War Between the States," in Hellmut Lehmann-Haupt and others, *The Book in America* . . . , New York, 1939, pp. 3-111.

Special studies include Arthur M. Schlesinger, "Propaganda and the Boston Newspaper Press, 1767-1770," *Pub. Col. Soc. Mass.,* XXXII (1937), 396-416; Sidney Kobre, *The Development of the Colonial Newspaper,* Pittsburgh, 1944, with bibl., pp. 182-188; Charles A. Barker, *The Background of the Revolution in Maryland,* New Haven, 1940—useful for its chapters on reading and educational interests in the state; William Reitzel, "The Purchasing of English Books in Philadelphia, 1790-1800," *Mod. Philol.,* XXXV (1937), 159-171; Chester T. Hallenbeck, "Book-Trade Publicity Before 1800," *Papers Bibl. Soc. Amer.,* XXXII (1939), 47-56—chiefly on Mathew Carey; and Helen M. Knubel, "Alexander Anderson and Early American Book Illustration," *Princeton Univ. Lib. Chron.,* I (1940), No. 3, 9-18; and Sinclair Hamilton, "Early American Book Illustration," *ibid.,* VI (1945), 101-126—useful groundwork for further studies in American publishing.

## Library Development

The Library of Congress, established by Act of Congress in 1800, was destroyed by fire in 1814. With the subsequent purchase of Jefferson's library of some 6,400 volumes it ceased to be merely a reference collection for the use of members. See Lucy Salamanca, *Fortress of Freedom: The Story of the Library of Congress,* Philadelphia, 1942. Other useful studies of library development and the growth of reading interests include George Watson Cole, *Early Library Development in New York State (1800-1900),* New York, 1927; Horace E. Scudder, "Public Libraries a Hundred Years Ago," in *Public Libraries in the United States of America: Their History, Condition and Management,* Washington, 1876, pp. 1-37 (Special Report, Dept. of the Interior, Bureau of Education); George G. Raddin, Jr., *An Early New York Library of Fiction, with a Checklist of the Fiction in H. Caritat's Circulating Library, No. 1 City Hotel, Broadway, New York, 1804,* New York, 1940—a document in the history of reader taste; John F. McDermott, *Private Libraries in Creole Saint Louis,* Baltimore, 1938—a catalog of books in private libraries of 56 Louisiana Creoles between 1764 and 1842, with bibl., pp. 181-186; Roger P. McCutcheon, "Libraries in New Orleans, 1771-1833," *La. Hist. Quar.,* XX (1937), 1-9; Robert F. Seybolt, "Student Libraries at Harvard, 1763-1764," *Pub. Col. Soc. Mass.,* XXVIII (1935), 449-461; Albert Goodhue, Jr., "The Reading of Harvard Students, 1770-1781, as Shown by the Records of the Speaking Club," *Essex Inst. Hist. Col.*, LXXIII (1937), 107–129; and Chester T. Hallenbeck, "A Colonial Reading List from the Union Library of Hatboro, Pennsylvania," *Pa. Mag. Hist. and Biog.*, LVI (1932), 289–340— with bibl., pp. 323–340. See also E. L. Pennington, "The Beginnings of the Library in Charles Town, South Carolina," *Proc. Amer. Antiq. Soc.*, n.s. XLIV (1934), 159–187; Richard B. Davis, "Literary Tastes in Virginia Before Poe," *Wm. and Mary Coll. Quar.*, XIX (1939), 55–68; and I. A. Leonard, "A Frontier Library, 1799," *Hispanic Amer. Hist. Rev.*, XXIII (1943), 21–51.

Material on early book collecting is available in Carl L. Cannon, *American Book Collectors and Collecting from Colonial Times to the Present*, New York, 1941—some 100 collectors in America from Thomas Prince to H. H. Bancroft; George L. McKay, "Early American Book Auctions," *Colophon*, n.s., No. 2 (1939), 71–78; and Adolf Growoll, *American Book Clubs: Their Beginnings and History, and a Bibliography of Their Publications*, New York, 1897.


## THE MID-NINETEENTH CENTURY

### LITERARY AND CULTURAL HISTORY:
*Literary Studies Specific to the Period*

Standard histories for the period include Vernon L. Parrington, *Main Currents in American Thought*, New York, 1927–1930, 3 vols.—Vol. II, *The Romantic Revolution in America*; and Fred L. Pattee, *The First Century of American Literature, 1770–1870*, New York, 1935. For the novel, see Arthur H. Quinn, *American Fiction: An Historical and Critical Survey*, New York, 1936; Carl Van Doren, *The American Novel, 1789–1939*, rev. ed., New York, 1940; Frank L. Mott, *A History of American Magazines*, Cambridge, 1938, 3 vols. (to 1885); and Harry Hartwick, *The Foreground of American Fiction*, New York, 1934. Other studies are Yvor Winters, *Maule's Curse: Seven Studies in the History of American Obscurantism—Hawthorne, Cooper, Melville, Poe, Emerson, Jones Very, Emily Dickinson, Henry James*, Norfolk, Conn., 1938; Herbert R. Brown, *The Sentimental Novel in America, 1789–1860*, Durham, N.C., 1940—a study of domestic, moral, and religious fiction; and John P. Pritchard, *Return to the Fountains: Some Classical Sources of American Criticism*, Durham, N.C., 1942—with chapters on major nineteenth century authors and with bibl. and notes, pp. 209–261.

Illuminating discussions of Spanish influence on American writers are William Charvat and Michael Kraus, *William Hickling Prescott: Representa-*

*tive Selections,* New York, 1943; and Harry Bernstein, *Origins of Inter-American Interest, 1700–1812,* Philadelphia, 1945.

Special studies include Hyder E. Rollins, *Keats' Reputation in America to 1848,* Cambridge, 1946; Julia Power, *Shelley in America* . . . , Lincoln, Nebr., 1940; William Ellery Leonard, *Byron and Byronism in America,* Boston, 1905; Annabel Newton, *Wordsworth in Early American Criticism,* Chicago, 1928; H. E. Mantz, *French Criticism of American Literature Before 1850,* New York, 1917; Augusta G. Violette, "Economic Feminism in American Literature Prior to 1848," *Univ. of Maine Studies,* 2nd ser., no. 2, (1925), 1–114; Theodore Hunt, *Le Roman Américain, 1830–1850,* Paris, 1937; George Boas, ed., *Romanticism in America,* Baltimore, 1940—a symposium on the history of taste with essays by Eric F. Goldman, Roger Gilman, George Boas, and others; Selden L. Whitcomb, "Nature in Early American Literature," *Sewanee Rev.,* II (1894), 159–179; Mary E. Woolley, "The Development of the Love of Romantic Scenery in America," *Amer. Hist. Rev.,* III (1898), 56–66; G. Harrison Orians, "The Romance Ferment After *Waverley,*" *Amer. Lit.,* III (1932), 408–431; Alexander Cowie, "The Vogue of the Domestic Novel, 1850–1870," *So. Atl. Quar.,* XLI (1942), 416–424; Samuel Kliger, "George Perkins Marsh and the Gothic Tradition in America," *New Eng. Quar.,* XIX (1946), 524–531; and Robert E. Spiller, "Critical Standards in the American Romantic Movement," *College English,* VIII (1947), 344–352. See also W. E. Sedgwick, "The Material for American Literature: A Critical Problem of the Early Nineteenth Century," *Harvard Stud. and Notes in Philol. and Lit.,* XVII (1935), 145–162.

Useful source material is in Evert A. and George L. Duyckinck, *Cyclopaedia of American Literature,* New York, 1855, 2 vols. (rev. ed., 1866). Ida G. Everson's *George Henry Calvert, American Literary Pioneer,* New York, 1944, is the biography of a writer of travel books, biography, plays, and poetry who was a friend of many of the major literary figures in his day.

## Fiction

For data on the fiction of R. M. Bird, De Forest, James Hall, Hawthorne, C. F. Hoffman, Holmes, J. P. Kennedy, Melville, Motley, Parkman, Paulding, Simms, Stowe, Bayard Taylor, and N. P. Willis, see the individual bibliographies herein. See also the bibliographies on (a) Best Sellers, (b) Regionalism and Local Color, (c) Juvenile Literature, (d) American Writers and Books Abroad, (e) Slavery and Conflict, and (f) Transcendentalism.

The early romantic fiction of Catharine Maria Sedgwick, depicting social life in New York City, include *Clarence; or, A Tale of Our Own Times* (1830), and *Linwoods; or, "Sixty Years Since" in America* (2 vols., 1835).

The fiction of Lydia Maria Child (1802–1880) is represented by *Hobomok* (1824), and *Philothea* (1836). John Greenleaf Whittier edited *Letters of Lydia Maria Child, with a Biographical Introduction,* Boston, 1883.

An early novel by Timothy Flint (1780–1840) is *Francis Berrian; or, The Mexican Patriot* (1826). See John E. Kirkpatrick, *Timothy Flint: Pioneer, Missionary, Author, Editor, 1780–1840,* Cleveland, 1911. Early examples of the intersectional novels are those by William Alexander Caruthers (1802–1846): *The Kentuckian in New-York; or, The Adventures of Three Southerns* (1834); *The Cavaliers of Virginia; or, The Recluse of Jamestown: An Historical Romance* (1834–1835); and *The Knights of the Horse-Shoe* . . . (1845; repr., New York, 1928).

The well known series of romances by "Frank Forester" (Henry William Herbert, 1807–1858) began with *The Brothers: A Tale of the Fronde* (1835). David W. Judd edited *The Life and Writings of Frank Forester,* New York, 1882, 2 vols. A recent biography is William S. Hunt, *Frank Forester (Henry William Herbert): A Tragedy in Exile,* Newark, N.J., 1933.

Washington Allston (1779–1843) is remembered by his Gothic romance, *Monaldi* (1841). Anna Cora Mowatt (1819–1870) used New York society in her setting for *The Fortune Hunter* . . . (1842). George Lippard (1822–1854) is known for his sensational exposés of vice in such novels as *The Monks of Monk Hall* (1844)—repr. as *The Quaker City* . . . (1845); and *New York: Its Upper Ten and Lower Million* (1853). New York City is the setting for *Cecil Dreeme* (1861) by Theodore Winthrop (1828–1861).

The popularity of Edward Everett Hale (1822–1909) began when his story "The Man Without a Country" first appeared in the *Atlantic Monthly* in 1863. It was first published separately in 1865, and collected with other fiction in *If, Yes, and Perhaps* . . . (1868). His Utopian satire of American society was issued as *Sybaris and Other Homes* (1869). Among his earlier fiction is *Margaret Percival in America: A Tale* (1850). Edward Everett Hale, Jr., published *The Life and Letters of Edward Everett Hale,* Boston, 1917, 2 vols. Hale's own autobiography appeared as *A New England Boyhood and Other Bits of Autobiography,* Boston, 1900; and *Memories of a Hundred Years,* New York, 1902, 2 vols.

Other novelists, popular in their day, include Laughton Osborn (*ca.* 1809–1878), whose *Sixty Years of the Life of Jeremy Levis* (2 vols., 1831) was written in the manner of *Tristram Shandy*; Joseph Holt Ingraham (1809–1860), a prolific author of historical thrillers, represented by *Lafitte; or, The Pirate of the Gulf* (1836); Charles Frederick Briggs (1804–1877), an associate of Poe's, whose autobiographical novels were published as *The Adventures of Harry Franco* . . . (1839), *Working a Passage* . . . (1844), and *The Trippings of Tom Pepper* . . . (2 vols., 1847–1850).

Elizabeth Oakes Smith (1806–1893)—"Ernest Helfenstein"—made use of the frontier for *The Western Captive* (1842), and wrote a sentimental novel of slum life published as *The Newsboy* (1854). Selections from her *Autobiography* appeared posthumously in 1924. Emily C. Judson (1817–1854)— "Fanny Forester"—wrote moralistic sketches as well as a novel, *Allen Lucas, the Self-Made Man* (1842). An extravagant tale of considerable popularity was *The Planter's Northern Bride* (2 vols., 1854), by Caroline Lee Hentz (1800–1856). The naval officer Henry Augustus Wise (1819–1869) published several melodramatic novels under the pseudonym "Harry Gringo," of which *Tales for the Marines* (1855) is one of the best. They deserve to be better known. The historical romances of Eliza Ann Dupuy (1814–1881) include *The Conspirator* (1850), and *The Huguenot Exiles* (1856).

A Newfoundland setting was chosen by Robert Traill Spence Lowell (1816–1891) for *The New Priest in Conception Bay* (1858). His experiences as headmaster of St. Mark's School are recorded in *Antony Brade: A Story of a School* (1874). Two lesser novelists were Miriam Coles Harris (1834–1925), whose *Frank Warrington* (1863) is representative of her popular tales; and Anna Elizabeth Dickinson (1842–1932), feminist and orator, who wrote *What Answer?* (1868).

*Poetry*

For data on major and other significant mid-nineteenth century poets not mentioned in the following essay, see the individual bibliographies herein.

The writers in New York City who are known as the Knickerbocker Group were associated through their similarity in tastes and their interest in polite letters. They were often represented in the *Knickerbocker Magazine* (1833–1865), which during most of its career was edited by Lewis G. and Willis G. Clark. In 1855 an anthology of selections from its issues was published as *The Knickerbocker Gallery*. Those among the group for whom individual bibliographies will be found herein include Bryant, Halleck, Hoffman, Irving, Paulding, and Willis. Also identified with it are Drake, Sands, and Sargent.

Joseph Rodman Drake (1795–1820) was an early member of the Knickerbocker Group; his only writings published during his lifetime were *Poems, By Croaker, Croaker and Co., And Croaker, Jun.* (1819), written with Fitz-Greene Halleck. They were reissued as *The Croakers* (1860). A selection from his manuscript of "Trifles in Rhyme" was published as *The Culprit Fay and Other Poems* (1835). James Grant Wilson edited *The Poetical Writings of Fitz-Greene Halleck: With Extracts from Those of Joseph Rodman Drake*, New York, 1869. Frank L. Pleadwell has recently published *The*

*Life and Works of Joseph Rodman Drake* (1795–1820): *A Memoir and Complete Text of His Poems and Prose, Including Much Never Before Printed,* Boston, 1935, with a list of manuscripts as well as a bibl., pp. 377–383. For further material, see also Nelson F. Adkins, *Fitz-Greene Halleck: An Early Knickerbocker Wit and Poet,* New Haven, 1930.

Robert Charles Sands (1799–1832) was a close friend of Bryant. Sands' essays and poems, printed during his lifetime in magazines, brought him a considerable if local contemporary reputation. His works, edited by G. C. Verplanck, were posthumously collected as *The Writings of Robert C. Sands, in Prose and Verse,* New York, 1834, 2 vols. Epes Sargent (1813–1880) established his literary reputation in Boston before settling in New York (1839–1847) to help edit the New York *Mirror* and other publications. His *Songs of the Sea with Other Poems* appeared in 1847. A minor Knickerbocker and one-time editor of the New York *Mirror* (1824) was George Pope Morris (1802–1864). His sentimental poems include "Woodman, Spare That Tree," reprinted in his *The Deserted Bride and Other Poems* (1838).

Poets whose names are associated with Poe include Sarah Helen Whitman (1803–1878), to whom Poe was at one time engaged. Her *Hours of Life, and Other Poems* (1853) was a small collection. A complete edition appeared in the year following her death. Poe's *Last Letters* to her were published in 1909. The Philadelphia poet Henry Beck Hirst (1817–1874) published *Endymion* (1848), imitative of Keats, and *The Penance of Roland* (1849). He forfeited his friendship with Poe by publishing a parody of "The Haunted Palace." John Reuben Thompson (1823–1873) of Virginia owned and edited the *Southern Literary Messenger* (1847–1860). His *Collected Poems* were not issued until 1920, and his lecture on his friend Poe appeared as *The Genius and Character of Edgar Allan Poe* (1929). The *Poems* (1845) of William Wilberforce Lord (1819–1907) were hostilely reviewed by Poe. *The Complete Poetical Works of W. W. Lord* (1938) have been edited by T. O. Mabbott.

Among New England poets, the most popular of his day, before Bryant, was James Gates Percival (1795–1856). His published work includes *Poems* (1821), *Clio* (3 vols., 1822–1827), and *The Dream of a Day, and Other Poems* (1843). In his later years Percival made contributions of some significance as a geologist. Maria Gowen Brooks (*ca.* 1794–1845) was praised by Southey and Lamb for her first volume, *Judith, Esther, and Other Poems, by a Lover of the Fine Arts* (1820). Southey's appellative "Maria of the West" she used in translation as a pseudonym for later works: "Maria del Occidente." Her epic, *Zóphiël* (1833), she wrote in Cuba. Griswold (in *The Poets and Poetry of America,* 1842) called her the foremost American poetess. The best of the verses of the Connecticut poet, James Abraham Hillhouse (1789–1841), appear in his romantic tragedy *Demetria* (2 vols., 1839). His poems were collected in *Dramas, Discourses, and Other Pieces* (1839). The Unitarian clergyman Charles Timothy Brooks (1813–1883) was best known for his translations of German poetry. His original verses include *Songs of Field and Flood* (1853). The piety and sentiment of *Occasional Pieces of Poetry* (1825), by John Gardiner Calkins Brainard (1796–1828) of Connecticut, won for them a contemporary respect. His *Fugitive Tales* were posthumously gathered in 1830, and Whittier edited his literary remains in 1832. A few poems by J. R. Lowell's wife, Maria White Lowell (1821–1853), were posthumously issued in 1855. An augmented edition appeared in 1907, and again, 1936. The *Poems* (1860) of Frederick Goddard Tuckerman (1821–1873) of Massachusetts have attracted recent attention. The best of them, together with three unpublished sonnet sequences, were published as *The Sonnets of Frederick Goddard Tuckerman* (1931) edited with an enthusiastic introduction by Witter Bynner. The fertile fancy of Elizabeth Chase Akers (Allen) (1832–1911) made her a favorite household poet. Under the pseudonym "Florence Percy" she published her earliest collection, *Forest Buds from the Woods of Maine* (1856). A late collection, *The Sunset Song, and Other Verses* (1902), includes her well known poem, "Rock Me to Sleep, Mother."

The original poems of the Boston dentist Thomas William Parsons (1819–1892) include *The Magnolia* (1866) and *The Willey House, and Sonnets* (1875). A collected edition was published in 1893, with an introduction by (Louise) Imogen Guiney and E. C. Stedman.

The poems of Sumner Lincoln Fairfield (1803–1844) deserve to be better known. *The Last Night of Pompeii* (1832) is said to have influenced Bulwer-Lytton in the choice of theme for his romance on the same subject. Fairfield's collected works appeared as *The Poems and Prose Writings of Sumner Lincoln Fairfield* (1841).

A poet who is at his best in nature descriptions of the country he knew in western New York is William Howe Cuyler Hosmer (1814–1877). A collection was published as *The Poetical Works of William H. C. Hosmer* (2 vols., 1854).

New York poets who achieved some contemporary reputation include Alice Cary (1820–1871), her sister Phoebe Cary (1824–1871), and Henry Theodore Tuckerman (1813–1871). Alice Cary enjoyed the patronage of Rufus Griswold and Horace Greeley. Phoebe Cary collaborated in writing several hymns and poems. Her own work includes *Poems and Parodies* (1854), and *Poems of Faith, Hope, and Love* (1868). Katharine Lee Bates edited *The Poems of Alice and Phoebe Cary* (1903). A biography is Mary C. Ames, *A Memorial of Alice and Phoebe Cary*, New York, 1873. The *Poems* of Tuckerman were collected and published in 1851.

In the South Stephen Collins Foster (1826–1864) had composed most of his 175 "Ethiopian songs" before 1850. They enjoyed a contemporary vogue by way of minstrel shows, and much of the popular knowledge of the South was derived by audiences who listened to them. A biography is John T. Howard, *Stephen Foster, America's Troubadour*, New York, 1934—useful as source material on native music and on the relationship of Foster to spirituals. Another biography is that by Raymond Walters, *Stephen Foster . . .*, Princeton, 1936. See also Fletcher Hodges, Jr., "Foster and the South," *So. Lit. Mes.*, II (1940), 89–96.

The versified translations of the Virginian, Philip Pendleton Cooke (1816–1850), were issued in his only published volume of poetry, *Froissart's Ballads, and Other Poems* (1847). A brief interpretive study is John D. Allen, *Philip Pendleton Cooke*, Chapel Hill, N.C., 1942—including unpublished material, a calendar of letters, and bibl., pp. 106–120. See also David K. Jackson, "Philip Pendleton Cooke . . . ," in *American Studies in Honor of William Kenneth Boyd*, Durham, N.C., 1940, pp. 282–326—with excerpts from Cooke's unpublished correspondence. Two important collections of Cooke's manuscripts are at the Peabody Institute, Baltimore, and in the Duke University Library.

The most important Charleston literary figure at the time when Charleston was the leading cultural center in the South was Hugh Swinton Legaré (1797–1843). His miscellaneous writings were collected and published in 2 vols., 1845–1846. James Mathewes Legaré (1823–1859) is represented by *Orta-Undis, and Other Poems* (1848). See Curtis Carroll Davis, ed., "Poet, Painter, and Inventor: Some Letters by James Mathewes Legaré, 1823–1859," *N.C. Hist. Rev.*, XXI (1944), 215–231. Popular in his time was the Maryland poet Edward Coote Pinkney (1802–1828). His *Poems* were issued in 1825. Thomas O. Mabbott and Frank L. Pleadwell edited *The Life and Works of Edward Coote Pinkney: A Memoir and Complete Text of His Poems and Literary Prose, Including Much Never Before Published*, New York, 1926. See also J. P. Simmons, "Edward Coote Pinkney, American Cavalier Poet," *So. Atl. Quar.*, XXVIII (1929), 406–418. The Georgia poet and Congressman Richard Henry Wilde (1789–1847) is represented by *Hesperia: A Poem* (1867).

Though John Neal (1793–1876) is principally remembered for his novels, his early effort to bring American literature to British readers and his interest in poetic criticism make his contributions to *Blackwood's Magazine* historically interesting, however false their perspective may be. See John Neal, *American Writers: A Series of Papers Contributed to Blackwood's Magazine (1824–1825)*, ed. by Fred L. Pattee, Durham, N.C., 1937—with notes and a bibliography. Other studies include W. P. Daggett, *A Down-East Yankee from the District of Maine,* Portland, Me., 1920; Joseph J. Rubin, "John Neal's Poetics as an Influence on Whitman and Poe," *New Eng. Quar.,* XIV (1941), 359–362; and John A. Pollard, "John Neal, Doctor of American Literature," *Bul. Friends' Hist. Assn.,* XXXII (1943), 5–12.

The Pennsylvania poet and painter Thomas Buchanan Read (1822–1872) published some ten volumes of verse, including *A Summer Story, Sheridan's Ride, and Other Poems* (1865). His *Poetical Works* were gathered, Philadelphia, 1866, 3 vols.

The transcendentalist poet Christopher Pearse Cranch (1813–1892) is represented by *Poems* (1844); *The Bird and the Bell, with Other Poems* (1875); and *Ariel and Caliban, with Other Poems* (1887). Leonora Cranch Scott published *The Life and Letters of Christopher Pearse Cranch,* Boston, 1917.

The familiar and comic verse of the Vermont poet John Godfrey Saxe (1816–1887) enjoyed a contemporary vogue and was issued in such volumes as *Progress: A Satirical Poem* (1846), and *Humorous and Satirical Poems* (1850).

Though Emma Lazarus (1849–1887) is best known for her *Songs of a Semite* (1882), earlier collections were *Poems and Translations* (1867) and *Admetus and Other Poems* (1871). Her published verse was collected as *The Poems of Emma Lazarus* (1889). Ralph L. Rusk edited *Letters to Emma Lazarus* (1939), important for the stature of her correspondents.

## Drama

Between 1825 and 1860 the theatrical center moved from Philadelphia to New York. The variety of plays increased, with tragedy perhaps having the most literary value. For data on three well known playwrights of the period, Robert Montgomery Bird, George Henry Boker, and Nathaniel Parker Willis, see the individual bibliographies herein.

Among dramatic writers in the early mid-century John A. Stone (1800–1834) is best known for his romantic tragedy, *Metamora; or, The Last of the Wampanoags* (1829), written for the leading American actor of the day, Edwin Forrest. Richard Penn Smith (1799–1854) is historically interesting for having introduced romantic tragedy and having used foreign sources. Representative among his original plays are *William Penn; or, The Elm Tree* (1829); and *The Triumph at Plattsburg* (1830). See Bruce W. McCullough, *The Life and Writings of Richard Penn Smith,* Menasha, Wis., 1917. The representative plays of the Philadelphia journalist and dramatist Robert Taylor Conrad (1810–1858) are *Conrad, King of Naples* (1832); and *Jack Cade* (1835). The romantic tragedies of Epes Sargent (1813–

1880) include *The Bride of Genoa* (1837); and *Velasco* (1839). Charlotte Barnes Connor (1818–1863) employed the Kentucky Tragedy as a setting for her blank-verse drama, *Octavia Brigaldi* (1837)—published in 1848. Her romantic melodramas include *The Forest Princess* (1848), first played at Liverpool, 1844.

Anna Cora Mowatt (1819–1870) established a contemporary reputation for her farcical social comedy, *Fashion* (1845). It was most recently reprinted, with an introduction, in Allan Halline, ed., *American Plays*, New York, 1935, pp. 231–272, with bibl., p. 756. Useful source material appears in her *Autobiography of an Actress; or, Eight Years on the Stage* (1854). A critical study is Arthur H. Quinn, *A History of the American Drama from the Beginning to the Civil War*, rev. ed., New York, 1943, pp. 310–319.

Among other writers of romantic blank-verse tragedy was George Henry Miles (1824–1871), represented by *Mohammed, The Arabian Prophet* (1851).

Perhaps the most successful of mid-nineteenth century dramatists was Dion Boucicault (1820–1890), the Irish-born American who contributed some 132 plays, most of them adaptations. His *Colleen Bawn* (1860) was the first of a long series of Irish comedy dramas for which he was best known. He collaborated with Joseph Jefferson, one of the most popular actors of his day, on Jefferson's great success, *Rip Van Winkle* (1865), an adaptation from Irving's story. Allardyce Nicoll and F. Theodore Clark edited Boucicault's *Forbidden Fruit and Other Plays* in Vol. I of *America's Lost Plays*, Princeton, 1940, which includes, in addition to the title piece, *Louis XI, Dot, Flying Scud, Mercy Dodd,* and *Robert Emmet.* For a critical discussion, see "The Influence of Dion Boucicault," in Arthur H. Quinn, *A History of the American Drama from the Beginning to the Civil War*, rev. ed., New York, 1943, pp. 368–392.

In addition to *Rip Van Winkle,* already mentioned, the most widely known play based on a dramatization of fiction is G. L. Aiken's version of *Uncle Tom's Cabin* (1852).

Useful as a source material on barnstorming in the mid-nineteenth century is Maud and Otis Skinner, *One Man in His Time: The Adventures of H. Watkins, Strolling Player, 1845–1863, from His Journal*, Philadelphia, 1938. Important for material on the New York, Philadelphia, and Pittsburgh stages is Francis C. Wemyss, *Twenty-six Years of the Life of an Actor and Manager*, New York, 1847, 2 vols. A rare and scarcely known item, important as source material on a colorful theatrical figure, is George Handel Hill, *Scenes from the Life of an Actor, Compiled from the Journals, Letters, and Memoranda of the Late Yankee Hill*, New York, 1853. Further valuable items are William B. Wood, *Personal Recollections of the Stage, Embracing*

*Notices of Actors, Authors, and Auditors, During a Period of Forty Years,*
Philadelphia, 1855; Sol Smith, *Theatrical Management in the West and
South for Thirty Years, Interspersed with Anecdotal Sketches: Autobio-
graphically Given,* New York, 1868; Henry D. Stone, *Personal Recollections
of the Drama; or, Theatrical Reminiscences, Embracing Sketches of Prominent Actors and Actresses, Their Chief Characteristics, Original Anecdotes
of Them, and Incidents Connected Therewith,* Albany, 1873; and Noah M.
Ludlow, *Dramatic Life as I Found It,* St. Louis, 1880—useful on the theater
in the West and South, especially St. Louis.

For secondary material dealing with the period, see Guide to Resources:
Drama.

## *The Historians*

For data on the most distinguished mid-century historians, Bancroft,
Motley, Parkman, and Prescott, see the individual bibliographies herein.

Still useful as a history of the Revolution and early national years of 1797
is Timothy Pitkin (1766–1847), *A Political and Civil History of the United
States* (2 vols., 1828). The monumental *History of the United States* (10 vols.,
1834–1876) of George Bancroft (1800–1891) exemplifies the aggressive nationalism of the era of expansion. Its final revision (6 vols., 1883–1885) includes
Bancroft's *History of the Formation of the Constitution.* A useful life is
Russel B. Nye, *George Bancroft: Brahmin Rebel,* New York, 1944. Richard
Hildreth (1807–1865) wrote *The History of the United States of America*
(6 vols., 1849–1852). It discusses events to the year 1821 with a Federalist bias.
The Virginian George Tucker (1775–1861) champions states' rights in his
historical study, *The History of the United States* (4 vols., 1856–1857). *The
History of New England* (5 vols., 1858–1890) by John Gorham Palfrey (1796–
1881) is sectional in interest, but is an early example of detailed scholarship.

Among noteworthy compilations undertaken during the century, one of
the earliest is *The Annals of America* (2 vols., 1805) by Abiel Holmes (1763–
1837). It is a chronological compilation of facts from 1492, and the second
edition (1829) records data to 1826. An annual compilation of historical and
statistical information, invaluable as source material, is the *National Calendar
and Annals of the United States* (1820–1824, 1828–1836) by Peter Force (1790–
1868). Force's *Tracts and Other Papers, Relating Principally to . . . North
America* (4 vols., 1836–1846) are reprints of scarce colonial pamphlets; and
his *American Archives* (9 vols., 1837–1853) is a collection of rare manuscript
material covering the years 1774–1776. Jedidiah Morse (1761–1826) compiled
*Annals of the American Revolution* (1824).

Jared Sparks (1789–1866) was one of the first students of American history to gather his material from manuscript sources. Though his scholarship was unscientific and marred by some bowdlerizations, his edition of *The Library of American Biography* (25 vols., 1834–1838; 1844–1847) is a skillful compilation. Among other editorial tasks he collected the writings of George Washington (12 vols., 1834–1837) and, in what is generally considered his finest editorial undertaking, collected Franklin's *Works* (10 vols., 1836–1840). Its notes are still useful, and it has been unjustly abused with little reason for its "corrections" of Franklin's text. An earlier undertaking was the compilation of *The Diplomatic Correspondence of the American Revolution* (12 vols., 1829–1830).

George Ticknor (1791–1871) is best remembered for his monumental *History of Spanish Literature* (3 vols., 1849), which was published in final revision in the year following his death. Anna Ticknor and George S. Hillard edited *Life, Letters, and Journals of George Ticknor* (2 vols., 1876), containing much documentary material on the development of historical scholarship. A study of Ticknor is Orie W. Long, "George Ticknor," in his *Literary Pioneers* . . . , Cambridge, 1935, pp. 3–62. See also Van Wyck Brooks, *The Flowering of New England,* New York, 1936, pp. 73–88; Edwin P. Whipple, "George Ticknor," in his *Recollections of Eminent Men* . . . , Boston, 1887, pp. 244–279; and Jorge Guillén, "George Ticknor, Lover of Culture," *More Books,* XVII (1942), 359–375. See also Stuart Cuthbertson, "George Ticknor's Interest in Spanish-American Literature," *Hispania,* XVI (1933), 117–126; Henry G. Doyle, "George Ticknor," *Mod. Lang. Jour.,* XXII (1937), 3–37.

## The Essay and Social Criticism

The items which follow should be supplemented by the sections dealing with the intellectual background in the preceding period (1760–1820), and in that which follows, The Late Nineteenth Century.

### General Studies

An analysis of American democracy is Ralph H. Gabriel, *The Course of American Democratic Thought: An Intellectual History Since 1815,* New York, 1940, with interesting discussions of William Graham Sumner, Henry Adams, Josiah Royce, and William James. A study of the American theory of progress is Arthur A. Ekirch, Jr., *The Idea of Progress in America, 1815–1860,* New York, 1944, with bibl., pp. 268–299. Other useful contributions to social history are E. Douglas Branch, *The Sentimental Years, 1836–1860,* New York, 1934; Henry C. Hubbart, *The Older Middle-West, 1840–1880,* New

York, 1936—emphasizing the survival of strains of Jacksonian democracy in the Copperhead movement during the Civil War and the agrarian protest after the war; Carl R. Fish, *The Rise of the Common Man, 1830–1850*, New York, 1937—with critical bibl., pp. 339–366; Albert Post, *Popular Freethought in America, 1825–1850*, New York, 1943—with emphasis on the survival of deistic thought; and Arthur M. Schlesinger, Jr., *The Age of Jackson*, Boston, 1945—a history of Jacksonian democracy. See also Henry S. Commager, "The Nineteenth-Century American," *Atl. Mo.*, CLXXVIII (1946), 71–77; and Howard M. Jones, "The Influence of European Ideas in Nineteenth-Century America," *Amer. Lit.*, VII (1935), 241–273.

For the South, the best studies are Thomas J. Wertenbaker, *The Old South: The Founding of American Civilization*, New York, 1942—an authoritative interpretation of non-English contributions; Francis P. Gaines, *The Southern Plantation: A Study in the Development and the Accuracy of a Tradition*, New York, 1925—a definitive study of the facts and the fictions; and John Donald Wade, *Augustus Baldwin Longstreet: A Study of the Development of Culture in the South*, New York, 1924.

## Science

Of the older generation of scientists, Amos Eaton (1776–1842) compiled *A Botanical Dictionary . . .* (1817), and *A Geological Nomenclature for North America* (1828). The investigations into physiology made by William Beaumont (1785–1853) were set forth in *Experiments and Observations on the Gastric Juice and the Physiology of Digestion* (1833), still considered the leading single contribution to the subject. The chief work of the naturalist (Jean) Louis (Rodolphe) Agassiz (1807–1873) is his *Contributions to the Natural History of the United States of America* (4 vols., 1857–1863). Joseph Green Cogswell (1786–1871) contributed to the literature of mineralogy and botany. As director of the Astor Library in New York (1848–1861), his bibliographical work was significant in library development. The ethnologist and founder of American anthropology, Lewis Henry Morgan (1818–1881), summarized a lifetime of careful research in his study of *Ancient Society; or, Researches in the Lines of Human Progress* (1877). An early study of semantics is Alexander Bryan Johnson's *A Treatise on Language* (1828, rev. ed. 1836), edited with an introduction by David Rynin, Berkeley, Calif., 1947.

The Smithsonian Institution was established by an Act of Congress at Washington, D.C., to sponsor government-supported scientific research in a broad field. Its first director (1846–1878) was Joseph Henry (1797–1878), whose experiments in physics were the foundation for the development of the telegraph and later electromagnetic inventions. The Institution published his scientific writings (2 vols., 1886). For a history, see George B. Goode, *The Smithsonian Institution, 1846–1896: The History of the First Half-Century* (1897)—an unsatisfactory study, but still the best published account.

An intellectual history of an unexplored field is Thomas C. Johnson, *Scientific Interests in the Old South,* New York, 1936. See also Richard B. Davis, "Forgotten Scientists in Georgia and South Carolina," *Ga. Hist. Quar.,* XXVII (1943), 271–284.

Belles-Lettres

Richard Henry Dana, Sr. (1787–1879), who had been a founder of the *North American Review,* modeled his own New York journal, *The Idle Man* (1821–1822), on Irving's *Salmagundi.* His *Poems and Prose Writings* were collected in 2 vols., 1833, and again in a revised and enlarged edition, 1850. Richard Henry Dana, Jr. (1815–1882), achieved an international reputation with the account of his journey to California and back, *Two Years Before the Mast* (1840). He described one of several later voyages in *To Cuba and Back* (1859). A collection of his addresses appeared as *Speeches in Stirring Times* (1910). Charles Francis Adams, Jr., published *Richard Henry Dana: A Biography,* Boston, 1890, 2 vols. (rev. ed., 1891). Further studies of Dana are Bliss Perry, *The Praise of Folly and Other Papers,* Boston, 1923, pp. 53–62; Van Wyck Brooks, *The Flowering of New England,* New York, 1936, pp. 303–322; James D. Hart, "The Education of Richard Henry Dana, Jr.," *New Eng. Quar.,* IX (1936), 3–25; and *idem,* "Melville and Dana," *Amer. Lit.,* IX (1937), 49–55. Hart also published a brief study of "The Other Writings of Richard Henry Dana, Jr.," *Colophon,* V (1934), Pt. XIX.

The nature essays of Susan Fenimore Cooper (1813–1894) were collected as *Rural Hours* (1850). On the life and work of Cooper's talented daughter, see Anna K. Cunningham, "Susan Fenimore Cooper: Child of Genius," *New York Hist.,* XXV (1944), 339–350.

The popular essayist Donald G. Mitchell ("Ik Marvel") (1822–1908) is best remembered for his *Reveries of a Bachelor . . .* (1850). A biography is Waldo H. Dunn, *The Life of Donald G. Mitchell: Ik Marvel,* New York, 1922. The essays and sketches of Henry Theodore Tuckerman (1813–1871) are gathered in *Leaves from the Diary of a Dreamer* (1853), and other collections.

Oliver Bell Bunce (1828–1890) edited *Appleton's Journal* (1872–1881), and his social essays thereto contributed were reprinted as *Bachelor Bluff: His Opinions, Sentiments, and Disputations* (1881).

## Philosophy

Distinguished in his day as an American philosopher was James McCosh (1811–1894), whose study of *The Scottish Philosophy* . . . (1875) supplies the background of the so-called "Princeton School." William M. Sloane edited *The Life of James McCosh: A Record Chiefly Autobiographical,* New York, 1896. Important also in their day were Andrews Norton (1786–1853), whose biblical scholarship is summarized in *The Evidences of the Genuineness of the Gospels* (3 vols., 1837–1844); and Horace Bushnell (1802–1876), whose doc-trine of the natural goodness of man is set forth in *Christian Nurture* (1847; rev. ed., 1861). For a catalog and review of the principal academic philoso-phies of the period, see Robert Blakey, "Metaphysical Writers of the United States of America," in *History of the Philosophy of Mind,* London, 1850, Vol. IV, Chap. V. See also Austin Warren, "The Concord School of Philos-ophy," *New Eng. Quar.,* II (1929), 199–233; C. P. Hotson, "Swedenborg's Influence in America," *New-Church Rev.,* XXXVII (1930), 188–207; and E. W. Todd, "Philosophical Ideas in Harvard College, 1817–1837," *New Eng. Quar.,* XVI (1943), 63–90. Further data herein will be found in the section Oratory and the Lyceum, p. 233.

## Politics and Society

Invaluable as source material on political activities during the period are the *American State Papers: Documents, Legislative and Executive, of the Congress of the United States of the Twenty-second Congress, Inclusive* . . . (17 vols., 1832–1861), ed. by Walter Lowrie and Matthew S. Clarke; and the great compilation of Thomas Hart Benton (1782–1858), *An Abridgement of the Debates of Congress from 1789 to 1856* (15 vols., 1857–1861).

In the field of political economy the work of Henry Charles Carey (1793–1879) was especially influential. His economic theory, directed against the views of Ricardo and Malthus, he set forth in such treatises as *Essay on the Rates of Wages* (1835), and *Principles of Political Economy* (3 vols., 1837–1840). His doctrines are summarized in *The Principles of Social Science* (3 vols., 1858–1859). The most popular textbook was *The Elements of Politi-cal Economy* (1837) by Francis Wayland (1796–1865), who advocated free trade in a methodical restatement of the thesis of Smith, Say, and Ricardo. His work represented the classic tradition which was followed by such well known teachers as Francis Bowen, Arthur Latham Perry, and J. Laurence Laughlin. The new school of economic thought, represented by such men as Richard T. Ely, Simon Nelson Patten, and Thomas Nixon Carver, tried to integrate economics and biology.

Contemporary observations of the American scene during the twenties, as set forth by native observers, include those of Alexander Hill Everett (1790–1847), Anne Newport Royall (1769–1854), and Theodore Dwight (1796–1866). Everett served as diplomat in Russia, Holland, and Spain from 1809 to 1828, and his experiences furnished the material for *Europe; or, A General Survey of the Principal Powers* . . . (1822), and *America; or, A General Survey of the Political Situation* . . . (1827). Later gleanings are his *Critical and Miscellaneous Essays* (2 vols., 1845–1846), a collection of contributions to the *North American Review,* of which he was an editor. Anne Royall's shrewd observations were published in *Sketches of History, Life, and Manners in the United States* (1826), and later volumes. The antidemocratic convictions of Dwight appear in his *Sketches of Scenery and Manners in the United States* (1829).

See the section below, Memoirs and Reminiscences, p. 123.

## Education

The impulses from study in German universities were transmitted by such educators as Bancroft, Cogswell, Motley, Ticknor, and Longfellow, as well as by members of the Transcendental movement. Bibliographies for Bancroft, Motley, and Longfellow, and for Transcendentalism (*post,* p. 346), will be found herein. See also the preceding section The Historians (*ante,* p. 115) and the later subsection Feminism and Reform (p. 122).

An early student of educational reform was James Gordon Carter (1795–1849), who published his views in *Essays upon Popular Education* . . . (1826). George Bancroft and Joseph Green Cogswell (1786–1871) founded the celebrated Round Hill School at Northampton, Mass. (1823–1834), modeled on the thorough training of the German *gymnasium.* A leader in the improvement of common-school education throughout the United States was Horace Mann (1796–1859). His views were published in *Lectures on Education* (1845). The advanced educational thinking of Frederick Augustus Porter Barnard (1809–1889), President of Columbia College (1864–1889), may be found in his *Letters on College Government* . . . (1855). Much documentary material on higher education appears in Anna Ticknor and George S. Hillard, eds., *Life, Letters, and Journals of George Ticknor* (2 vols., 1876). A distinguished product of the scientific education of the sixties and seventies was William James. A historical study of higher education prior to 1860 is Donald G. Tewksbury, *The Founding of American Colleges and Universities Before the Civil War, with Particular Reference to the Religious Influences Bearing upon the College Movement,* New York, 1932, with bibl., pp. 223–254. See also G. R. Lyle, "College Literary Societies in the Fifties," *Lib. Quar.,*

IX (1934), 487–494; and G. P. Schmidt, "Intellectual Cross Currents in American Colleges, 1825–1855," *Amer. Hist. Rev.,* XLII (1936), 46–67.

A standard American text widely influential in elementary schools was *A Practical System of Modern Geography* . . . (1828), compiled by Jesse Olney (1798–1872). Even more famous were the *Eclectic Readers* prepared by William Holmes McGuffey (1800–1873) in six series, 1836–1857. They supplied literary extracts and moral teachings, and were in constant use during the mid-century. Their sales numbered some 122,000,000, and their effect in shaping American culture was profound. For a biography, see Harvey C. Minnich, *William Holmes McGuffey* . . ., New York, 1936.* The popular summaries of the best known classical, European, and Oriental myths, compiled by Thomas Bulfinch (1796–1867), and published as *The Age of Fable* (1855), are still used for reference. Special studies of elementary education include Sidney L. Jackson, *America's Struggle for Free Schools: Social Tension and Education in New England and New York, 1827–1842,* Washington, 1941; and Carter G. Woodson, *The Education of the Negro Prior to 1861* . . ., New York, 1915 (rev. ed., 1928).

One of the first great city libraries to be established was the Boston Public Library, founded in 1852. See Horace G. Wadlin, *The Public Library of the City of Boston: A History,* Boston, 1911. Source material on the place of libraries in general education is in the Special Report of the Bureau of Education, *Public Libraries in the United States of America: Their History, Condition, and Management,* Washington, 1876. For an account of the intellectual interests of Southern planters, see William D. Houlette, "Plantation Libraries in the Old South," *Univ. Iowa Abstracts in History,* 1927–1934.

## The Arts

Lowell Mason (1792–1872) founded the Boston Academy of Music (1832), and was influential in establishing the teaching of music in the public schools. The first American photographer of distinction was Mathew B. Brady *(ca.* 1823–1896). He published his *Gallery of Illustrious Americans* (1850), and *Brady's National Photographic Collection of War Views* . . . (1869)— a notable assembly depicting Civil War battles and war scenes. The Boston sculptor Horatio Greenough (1805–1852) left a vivid and farseeing account of his impressions of the present and future state of American interest in art, issued as *Aesthetics in Washington* (1851). On Samuel F. B. Morse (1791–1872) see Carleton Mabee, *The American Leonardo: A Life of Samuel F. B. Morse,* New York, 1943. For references to the history of the arts in

---

* See also Richard D. Mosier, *Making the American Mind: Social and Moral Ideas in the McGuffey Readers,* New York, 1947.

America, see the appropriate sections under the various period headings herein, as well as Guide to Resources: Sources for Cultural History.

## Feminism and Reform

As a reform movement for woman's social, educational, and political equality, feminism had its beginning in the late eighteenth century. Mary Wollstonecraft's *Vindication of the Rights of Woman* (1792) is generally regarded as the first significant document. In America, both Abigail Adams and Mercy Otis Warren were in the center of politics, and as leaders and acute observers left interesting records of their ideas. Data on them appear in the section dealing with the preceding period. An early plea for women's rights is that of Hannah Mather Crocker (1752–1829), *Observations on the Real Rights of Women . . .* (1818). A pioneer in women's education was Emma (Hart) Willard (1787–1870), whose *An Address . . . Proposing a Plan for Improving Female Education* (1819) led in 1821 to the founding of a seminary in Troy, N.Y., for the higher education of women. Oberlin College led the way in granting college degrees to women (1837). For a study of the development of higher education for women, see Thomas Woody, *A History of Women's Education in the United States,* New York, 1929, 2 vols., and most recently Eleanor W. Thompson, *Education for Ladies, 1830–1860,* New York, 1947—a study of ladies' magazines as educational instruments.

The Grimké sisters were early advocates of Abolition and woman suffrage. Angelina Emily Grimké (1805–1879—Mrs. Weld) published her *Appeal to the Christian Women of the South* in 1836, and two years later appeared *Letters on the Equality of the Sexes and the Condition of Woman,* by Sarah Moore Grimké (1792–1873). A pioneer in prison reforms was Dorothea Lynde Dix (1802–1887), who presented her studies of institutional conditions as a *Memorial to the Legislature of Massachusetts* (1843). In the same decade Harriet Farley (1817–1907) edited the *Lowell Offering* (1842–1845), a periodical with material supplied by the women mill hands in Lowell, Mass. Many were collected as *Mind Amongst the Spindles* (1844). Margaret Fuller (1810–1850) surveyed the contemporary scene in *Woman in the Nineteenth Century* (1845). The first convention for woman suffrage was held at Seneca Falls, N.Y., in 1848, through the instrumentality of Lucretia Mott (1793–1880). The militant feminist magazine *Revolution* (1868–1870) was edited by Elizabeth Cady Stanton (1815–1902), who later described her career as leader in the suffrage cause in an autobiography, *Eighty Years and More . . .* (1898). Women were prominent in the cause of Abolition, and helped bring about the passage of the Fifteenth Amendment (1870).

Among the earliest of the women's clubs were the Sorosis, established in New York, 1868, and the New England Women's Club, established in the same year in Boston. The General Federation of Women's Clubs was organized in 1889.

The official organ of the National American Woman Suffrage Association was the *Woman's Journal,* founded in 1870 by Lucy Stone (1818–1893), who continued to guide its policies till the time of her death. *The History of Woman Suffrage,* published in three volumes, 1881–1886, was in part the work of Susan Brownell Anthony (1820–1906), one of the most widely known of suffragists. The labors of such people during the nineteenth century resulted in 1920 in the passage of the Nineteenth Amendment, granting nation-wide suffrage. A source collection dealing with woman's position in the nineteenth century is Clifton J. Furness, ed., *The Genteel Female,* New York, 1931. See also Eleanor Wolf Thompson, *Education for Ladies, 1830–1860: Ideas on Education in Magazines for Women,* New York, 1947.

For data on the important work as a reformer of W. L. Garrison, see Wendell P. and Francis J. Garrison, *William Lloyd Garrison, 1805–1879,* New York, 1885–1889, 4 vols. Henry Clay Dean published his *Crimes of the Civil War, and Curse of the Funding System* (1868) as a passionate attack on the Republican program, especially the management of the war debt, the national banking system, and the tariff. Important among those who instituted prison reforms was Enoch Cobb Wines (1806–1879), who published a *Report on the Prisons and Reformatories of the United States and Canada . . .* (1867). See also his *Preliminary Report of the Commissioner Appointed by the President . . .* (1871), issued in *International Congress on the Prevention and Repression of Crime . . . ,* Washington, 1872.

A recent study is Charles A. Madison, *Critics and Crusaders: A Century of American Protest,* New York, 1947, with bibl., pp. 539–554.

For further data on reform, see the three sections American Issues (p. 141), The Machine Age and the Literature of Exposure (p. 330), and Christian Socialism (p. 337).

## Memoirs and Reminiscences

Reminiscences and memoirs centering in Boston and Cambridge which are especially significant as source material include Elizabeth P. Peabody, *Record of a School, Exemplifying the General Principles of Spiritual Culture,* Boston, 1835—dealing especially with her association in education with Alcott; *idem, Reminiscences of Rev. William Ellery Channing,* Boston, 1880—source material on Boston and Cambridge intellectual history during the second quarter of the century; Joseph T. Buckingham, *Specimens of Newspaper*

*Literature: With Personal Memoirs, Anecdotes, and Reminiscences,* Boston, 1850, 2 vols.; *idem, Personal Memoirs and Recollections of Editorial Life,* Boston, 1852, 2 vols.; Samuel G. Goodrich ("Peter Parley"), *Sketches from a Student's Window,* Boston, 1851; *idem, Recollections of a Lifetime; or, Men and Things I Have Seen,* New York, 1856, 2 vols.—one of the best sources for informal literary gossip of the period; James T. Fields, *Yesterdays with Authors,* Boston, 1871; *idem, Biographical Notes and Personal Sketches,* Boston, 1882; Edwin P. Whipple, *Recollections of Eminent Men, with Other Papers,* Boston, 1887—containing chapters on Emerson, Motley, and Ticknor; Annie A. Fields, *Authors and Friends,* Boston, 1893; Edward Everett Hale, ed., *James Freeman Clarke: Autobiography, Diary and Correspondence,* Boston, 1901; Frank P. Stearns, *Cambridge Sketches,* Philadelphia, 1905.

The Saturday Club (founded in 1855) continues to be a Boston literary dinner club, whose members have included the notable figures of the times. A history of the Club to 1870 is Edward W. Emerson, *The Early Years of the Saturday Club, 1855-1870,* Boston, 1918—with biographical studies of major literary figures, contributed by specialists.

M[ark] A. De Wolfe Howe edited *Memories of a Hostess: A Chronicle of Eminent Friendships Drawn Chiefly from the Diaries of Mrs. James T. Fields,* Boston, 1922—an account of literary visitors to her Cambridge salon. See also Caroline Ticknor, *Glimpses of Authors,* Boston, 1922; Henry M. Rogers, *Memories of Ninety Years,* Boston, 1928; and Henrietta D. Skinner, *An Echo from Parnassus: Being Girlhood Memories of Longfellow and His Friends,* New York, 1928. Two volumes by Thomas W. Higginson are largely autobiographical: *Cheerful Yesterdays,* Boston, 1898; and *Old Cambridge,* New York, 1899. Mary T. Higginson edited *Letters and Journals of Thomas Wentworth Higginson, 1846-1906,* Boston, 1921.

Biographies of Concord personalities, including Alcott, Emerson, and Thoreau, are in Frank B. Sanborn's *Recollections of Seventy Years* (2 vols., 1909). Further source material is in Sanborn's *Hawthorne and His Friends* (1908).

Source material for frontier life along the Ohio during the second quarter of the century is in W. P. Strickland, ed., *Autobiography of Peter Cartwright, the Backwoods Preacher,* New York, 1856; and in Cartwright's *Fifty Years as a Presiding Elder,* New York, 1871. One of the most useful contemporary accounts of cultural life in New York City is John W. Francis, *Old New York; or, Reminiscences of the Past Sixty Years,* New York, 1858. A colorful document, even though not entirely trustworthy, is John Neal, *Wandering Recollections of a Somewhat Busy Life: An Autobiography,* Boston, 1869. Horace Greeley's *Recollections of a Busy Life . . . ,* Boston, 1868, appeared in a revised edition, New York, 1896. Oddities and anecdotes about a great variety of figures are set down in Maunsell B. Field, *Memories of Many Men and of Some Women* ..., New York, 1874. The cultural background during the second half of the century in Charleston, Boston, and New York is described in Alvan F. Sanborn, ed., *Reminiscences of Richard Lathers: Sixty Years of a Busy Life in South Carolina, Massachusetts and New York,* New York, 1907. Personal recollections of a lecturer in phrenology are in Nelson Sizer's *Forty Years in Phrenology; Embracing Recollections of History, Anecdote, and Experience,* New York, 1882. Reminiscences of many prominent literary figures are in J[ames] C. Derby, *Fifty Years Among Authors, Books, and Publishers,* New York, 1884. The best edition of *The Diary of Philip Hone, 1821-1851,* is that by Allan Nevins, New York, 1936. The diary gives a comprehensive description of New York life as recorded by a prominent citizen. A social history, principally of Charleston, by a president of South Carolina College (1845-1851) is Minnie C. Yarborough, ed., *The Reminiscences of William C. Preston,* Chapel Hill, N.C., 1933. Bayard Taylor's *Critical Essays and Literary Notes,* New York, 1880, are discursive estimates of many contemporary writers. Literary gossip and information on intellectual life, especially in Charleston, is Thomas S. Perry, ed., *The Life and Letters of Francis Lieber,* Boston, 1882. An autobiography with strong literary emphasis is Richard H. Stoddard, *Recollections Personal and Literary,* New York, 1903. George H. Putnam published *Memories of My Youth, 1844-1865,* New York, 1914. Articles which first appeared in the *Arena* during the nineties are gathered by Manley W. Kilgore and George F. Woodbury, eds., in *Personal Recollections of English and American Poets by Edward Everett Hale and Others,* Boston, 1935. Other sketches are set forth in James Grant Wilson, *Bryant and His Friends: Some Reminiscences of the Knickerbocker Writers,* New York, 1885; Jeannette L. and Joseph G. Gilder, eds., *Authors at Home,* New York, 1889; and M[ark] A. De Wolfe Howe, *American Bookmen: Sketches, Chiefly Biographical, of Certain Writers of the Nineteenth Century,* New York, 1898.

One of the distinguished autobiographies of political life is Thomas Hart Benton's *Thirty Years' View* ... *1820 to 1850* (2 vols., 1854-1856). M. M. Quaife edited *The Diary of James K. Polk* (4 vols., 1910), abridged by Allan Nevins (1929); it is valuable as the only presidential diary besides those of John Adams and John Quincy Adams. The popularity of Ulysses S. Grant's *Personal Memoirs* ... (2 vols., 1885-1886) gave it rank as a best seller in its day. It is a classic document which does not deserve its present neglect.

See also the section Slavery and Conflict: Reminiscences, p. 344.

## Foreign Observers

The classic account by a foreign observer of our manners and civilization still remains that of Count Alexis de Tocqueville. His *De la Démocratie en*

*Amérique* was first published in Paris, 1835, 2 vols., with 2 supplemental vols., 1840. Though primarily concerned with political institutions, its acute generalizations concerning the expanding nation are of great significance. The latest edition of *Democracy in America,* New York, 1945, 2 vols., is edited by Phillips Bradley from the Henry Reeve text, and includes introduction, bibliography, and notes. See George W. Pierson, *Tocqueville and Beaumont in America,* New York, 1938; and Jacob Peter Mayer, *Alexis de Tocqueville: A Biographical Essay in Political Science,* New York, 1940, transl. by M. M. Bozman and C. Hahn.

Some forty years later the English historian and diplomat James Bryce published his own notable analysis of American political institutions, *The American Commonwealth* (2 vols., 1888), after several visits to the United States and wide study of American culture and institutions. The work went through several revisions, and was last published in 1933.

Among English observers, the first woman to write her impressions of America was Frances Wright (Mme. d'Arusmont), who published her enthusiastic *Views of Society and Manners in America* (1821). Later observations during the twenties are those of Captain Basil Hall, *Travels in North America, in the Years 1827 and 1828* (3 vols., 1829); and Frances Trollope, *Domestic Manners of the Americans* (1832)—a keen but unjust record of her residence in the United States during 1827–1830. A satirical reply to Mrs. Trollope and others is *Travels in America by George Fibbleton* (1833), by Asa Greene (1789–*ca.* 1837). A vigorous attempt by a German resident to neutralize her misrepresentations is Francis J. Grund, *The Americans in Their Moral, Social, and Political Relations* (1837). George Palmer Putnam published *American Facts, Notes and Statistics, Relative to the Government, Resources, Manufactures, Commerce, Religion, Education, Literature, Fine Arts, Manners and Customs of the United States of America* (1845) to supply data on the cultural life in America correcting false British notions. For a contemporary American review of Mrs. Trollope's book, see William Gilmore Simms' *Views and Reviews in American Literature,* 2nd ser., New York, 1845, pp. 1–56.

Other English accounts during the decade of the thirties are by Thomas Hamilton, *Men and Manners in America* (1833); Carl David Arfwedson, *The United States and Canada, in 1832, 1833, and 1834* (2 vols., 1834); Frederick Marryat, *A Diary in America, with Remarks on Its Institutions* (3 vols., 1839); and James S. Buckingham, *America: Historical, Statistic, and Descriptive* (3 vols., 1841)—favorable and very detailed, written after four years' travel. Harriet Martineau is deservedly well known for the critical studies and sketches of her travels, especially *Society in America* (1837), and *Retrospect of Western Travel* (1838). George Harvey's *Scenes in the Primeval Forests of America* . . . (1841) was reprinted, Tarrytown, N.Y., 1925.

Charles Dickens made his famous first visit to America in 1842, and the trip furnished material for the unfavorable report published as *American Notes for General Circulation* (2 vols., 1842), and gave him background for *Martin Chuzzlewit* (1844).

The distinguished geologist Sir Charles Lyell set forth his antidemocratic impressions in *Travels in North America . . .* (2 vols., 1845), and continued his observations in *A Second Visit to the United States of North America* (2 vols., 1849). William Makepeace Thackeray lectured in the country on English literature and history during the winters of 1852–1853 and 1855–1856. His *Henry Esmond* (1852) was published prior to his first visit, but its sequel *The Virginians* (2 vols., 1858–1859) was based on research undertaken during the second visit. See James Grant Wilson, *Thackeray in the United States . . .* , New York, 1904, 2 vols.

Although Thomas Carlyle never visited America, he corresponded with Emerson and others, and his essays *On Heroes, Hero-Worship, and the Heroic in History* (1841) had a tremendous vogue and an impact on the theory of a "superior" race. See William S. Vance, "Carlyle in America Before *Sartor Resartus*," *Amer. Lit.*, VII (1936), 363–375, for data on Carlyle's observations.

Thomas Colley Grattan (1792–1864) was British consul at Boston, 1839–1846, and his *Civilized America* (2 vols., 1859) is important source material by a shrewd observer who, though sharply critical, admired the American character. Thomas L. Nichols traveled widely in the country between 1821 and 1861, and comments astutely in *Forty Years of American Life* (2 vols., 1864). See also Henry T. Tuckerman, *America and Her Commentators, with a Critical Sketch of Travel in the United States* (1864)—a scholarly work by the Boston-born essayist and critic. *A View of the Art of Colonization . . .* (1849), by the English colonial statesman Edward Gibbon Wakefield, is a study of great importance.

Matthew Arnold visited the United States in 1883 and again in 1886. His *Discourses in America* (1885) is a collection of lectures delivered on his tours. The impressions he gathered formed the basis for his *Civilization in the United States: First and Last Impressions of America* (1888). See Howard M. Jones, "Arnold, Aristocracy, and America," *Amer. Hist. Rev.*, XLIX (1944), 393–409.

The most useful anthology of observations by Englishmen is that of Allan Nevins, ed., *American Social History As Recorded by British Travellers*, New York, 1923. For factual histories, see Jane L. Mesick, *The English Traveller in America, 1785–1835*, New York, 1922, and its continuation, Max Berger, *The British Traveller in America, 1836–1860*, New York, 1943. Useful collateral studies are Paul M. Wheeler, *America Through British Eyes: A Study of the Attitude of 'The Edinburgh Review' Toward the United States of*

*America from 1802 Until 1861,* Rock Hill, S.C., 1935; and Clarence Gohdes, *American Literature in Nineteenth-Century England,* New York, 1944.

Important French commentaries during the 1830's and 1840's are Michel Chevalier, *Society, Manners, and Politics in the United States: Being a Series of Letters on North America* (1834; Eng. transl., 1839)—penetrating and impartial observations after two years of travel; and Guillaume Tell Poussin, *De la Puissance Américaine* (2 vols., 1843); and Philarète Chasles, *Études sur la Littérature et les Mœurs des Anglo-Américains au XIX<sup>e</sup> Siècle* (1851)— essays written between 1838 and 1850, and mainly published in the *Revue des Deux Mondes.* See Robert G. Mahieu, *Les Enquêteurs Français aux Etats-Unis de 1830 à 1837,* Paris, 1934. Later accounts are those of Jean-Jacques Antoine Ampère, *Promenade en Amérique* . . . (2 vols., 1855; rev. ed., 1860); Louis Xavier Eyma, *Excentricités Américaines* (1860); and Claudio Jannet, *Les Etats-Unis Contemporains; ou, Les Mœurs, les Institutions, et les Idées depuis la Guerre de la Sécession* (2nd ed., 1876). A bibliography for the general field is Frank Monaghan, *French Travellers in the United States, 1765-1932: A Bibliography,* New York, 1933.

Observers from other countries include the German traveler Friedrich Ludwig von Raumer, *America and Her People* (1846), transl. by William W. Turner; and the Swedish novelist Fredrika Bremer, whose extensive travels in the United States during 1849-1861 are recorded in *The Homes of the New World* (1853). Her letters from America during those years have been recently issued as *America of the Fifties* (1924), edited by Adolph B. Benson. For suggestive data on Italian travels, see Andrew J. Torrielli, *Italian Opinion on America as Revealed by Italian Travellers, 1850-1900,* Cambridge, 1941.

For an estimate of America as a concept among Europeans, restating the theory that America had no past, see Georg Wilhelm Friedrich Hegel, *The Philosophy of History* (written during the twenties) rev. transl., New York, 1900.

Further bibliographies and general studies of foreign travel will be found in the section, The Expanding Frontier: Travelers and Observers, p. 260.

INSTRUMENTS OF CULTURE AND LITERARY PRODUCTION
*Author-Publisher Relationships*

The most influential anthologist of his day was Rufus Wilmot Griswold (1815-1857), editor of *Graham's Magazine,* 1842-1843, *International Monthly Magazine,* 1850-1852, and compiler of such widely known anthologies as *The Poets and Poetry of America* (1842), *The Prose Writers of America* (1847), and *The Female Poets of America* (1849). Very valuable source material on circumstances of authorship and publication appear in William

M. Griswold, ed., *Passages from the Correspondence and Other Papers of Rufus W. Griswold* (1898). A recent biography is Joy Bayless, *Rufus Wilmot Griswold: Poe's Literary Executor,* Nashville, Tenn., 1942. A catalog of the large Griswold collection of manuscripts in the Boston Public Library is Honor McCusker, "The Correspondence of R. W. Griswold," *More Books,* XVI (1941), 105–116, 152–156, 190–196, 286–289; XVIII (1943), 67–68, 322–333.

Important source material, in the nature of correspondence often conducted between publishers and authors, is frequently available for study. In addition to the Griswold Papers, already mentioned, are the Duyckinck Papers in the New York Public Library, the Longfellow Papers in the Craigie House in Cambridge, the James T. Fields Papers in the Huntington Library, the W. H. Prescott Papers in the Massachusetts Historical Society; the Dix and Edwards Papers in the Harvard College Library—letters from authors and correspondence with G. W. Curtis, the literary adviser to the firm; and, also at Harvard, the manuscript letter books of W. D. Ticknor & Company for the years 1847–1859. Many records at present not available for study are in the possession of publishing firms.

## Copyright

Useful studies of the American and international copyright movement include Stephen P. Ladas, *The International Protection of Literary and Artistic Property,* New York, 1938, 2 vols.; Philip Wittenberg, *The Protection and Marketing of Literary Property,* New York, 1937—a discussion of legal aspects; Walter L. Pforzheimer, "Copyright and Scholarship," *English Institute Annual, 1940,* New York, 1941, pp. 164–199—the best brief treatment of the history of British and American copyright law and its relationship to bookselling and authorship. Brief studies include Andrew J. Eaton, "The American Movement for International Copyright: 1837–1860," *Lib. Quar.,* XV (1945), 95–122; Frank Freidel, "Lieber's Contribution to the International Copyright Movement," *Hunt. Lib. Quar.,* VIII (1945), 200–206; and Lawrence H. Houtchens, "Charles Dickens and International Copyright," *Amer. Lit.,* XIII (1941), 18–28.

## Book Production and Distribution

One of the large publishing organizations was the American Bible Society (founded in New York, 1816) and its kindred group, the American Tract Society (founded 1825). Together they distributed an enormous body of religious literature to Christians of all denominations.

The printer Daniel Appleton (1785–1849) founded D. Appleton & Company in New York in 1825. See G. M. Overton, *Portrait of a Publisher* (1925).

The best survey of the whole general subject is Lawrence C. Wroth, "Book Production and Distribution from the Beginning to the War Between the States," Pt. I, pp. 1–111, in Hellmut Lehmann-Haupt and others, *The Book in America* . . . , New York, 1939. A minor writer's experiences are often valuable in revealing the conditions and hardships of authorship, and such are described in Luke M. White, Jr., *Henry William Herbert and the American Publishing Scene, 1831–1858,* Newark, N.J., 1943. Further discussion of production and distribution is made in William Charvat, "James T. Fields and the Beginnings of Book Promotion, 1840–1855," *Hunt. Lib. Quar.,* VIII (1944), 75–94; Robert E. Spiller, "War with the Book Pirates," *Pub. Weekly,* CXXXII (1937), 1736–1738; Edward A. Henry, "Cincinnati as a Literary and Publishing Center, 1793–1880," *Pub. Weekly,* CXXXII (1937), 22–24, 110–112; and Lawrance Thompson, "The Printing and Publishing Activities of the American Tract Society from 1825 to 1850," *Papers Bibl. Soc. Amer.,* XXXV (1941), 81–114. A brief account of Leypoldt as founder of the *Publishers' Weekly* and producer of *The American Catalogue* (1880) is George Sheerer, "Frederick Leypoldt and the Dragon," *Amer.-Ger. Rev.,* X (Dec., 1943), 6–9. See also the Seventy-fifth Anniversary number of *Publishers' Weekly,* Jan. 18, 1947.

## Magazines and Gift Books

*Godey's Lady's Book* (1830–1898) was a Philadelphia monthly miscellany distinguished for its articles and illustrations of fashion. Under the editorship of Sarah J. Hale (1837–1877) it was widely influential as a criterion of taste. Its contributors of stories and other material were a roster of the best known writers of the day, including Emerson, Hawthorne, Holmes, Longfellow, Poe, Mrs. Stowe, and Simms. See Ruth E. Finley, *The Lady of Godey's: Sarah Josepha Hale,* Philadelphia, 1931. The *Ladies' Companion* (1834–1844) was a New York monthly similar to *Godey's,* eclectic in nature, with literary contributions from many well known authors. The *Gentleman's Magazine* (1837–1840) is remembered chiefly because Poe was the editor in its final year. The Boston *Quarterly Review* (1838–1842), founded and edited by Orestes Brownson, reflected its editor's rapidly changing views on religion and philosophy, and numbered among contributors such writers as Albert Brisbane, George Ripley, Bronson Alcott, Margaret Fuller, and Elizabeth Peabody. *Littell's Living Age* (1844–1870) was an eclectic periodical of fiction, essays, and poetry, edited until his death by Eliakim Littell (1797–1870). It continued thereafter as the *Living Age.* Poe in the short-lived

*Broadway Journal* (1845-1846), which he largely owned and to which he was the leading contributor, attacked Longfellow and many other New England writers. A popular New York monthly, which numbered important writers among its contributors, was the *Union Magazine* (1847-1852). *Harper's Monthly Magazine* (1850-current) began as an eclectic literary journal which drew frequently upon British authors. G. W. Curtis was associated with it 1853-1892, and William Dean Howells 1901-1921. For a span of 50 years (1869-1919) it was under the editorship of Henry M. Alden, and among its notable contributors were Melville, De Forest, Howells, Garland, and Henry James. *Harper's Weekly* (1857-1916) was an illustrated political and literary magazine which was notable after 1862 for the illustrations by Thomas Nast. It serialized the works of leading English and American authors. Its editors included G. W. Curtis 1863-1892 and Carl Schurz 1892-1898. The *Atlantic Monthly* (1857-current) was founded in Boston as a magazine of literature, art, and politics. Its nineteenth century editors included James Russell Lowell, J. T. Fields, W. D. Howells, and T. B. Aldrich. Notable among the contributors were Emerson, Longfellow, Whittier, and H. B. Stowe. Strongly influenced by Brownson's views, Isaac Thomas Hecker (1819-1888) founded the *Catholic World* in 1865, and remained its editor till his death. *Scribner's Monthly* was a literary journal founded in 1870 by Charles Scribner (1821-1871), with Josiah G. Holland ("Timothy Titcomb," 1819-1881) as its editor. Its contributors included E. E. Hale, Frank Stockton, Harte, Eggleston, Cable, Muir, Lanier, and Joaquin Miller. The *Century Illustrated Monthly Magazine* (1881-1930) was a continuation of *Scribner's Monthly*. Under the editorship of R. W. Gilder 1881-1909 and R. U. Johnson 1909-1913 it serialized the novels of Howells, Hay, James, and London, and published short stories by J. C. Harris and Frank Stockton. *Scribner's Magazine* (1887-1939) was a monthly founded by the younger Charles Scribner (1854-1930). Its first forty years were the most distinguished, with contributions by Harte, Stephen Crane, Edith Wharton, Henry and William James among Americans, and Stevenson and Kipling among British authors. In its later years it published stories by Hemingway and Wolfe.

For other noted magazines published during the early and middle nineteenth century, see the section herein on Bibliography of American Literature and Culture (p. 35), and Regionalism and Local Color (p. 304).

The annual miscellanies, or gift books, were designed for use as Christmas or New Year gifts. They were widely distributed during the period 1825-1865, lavishly printed, and often contained some of the best illustration and writing at a period when the monthly magazine had not achieved popularity. Notable among them were *The Atlantic Souvenir* (1826-1832); *The Token*

(1827–1842)—a Boston publication issued by S. G. Goodrich wherein first appeared Hawthorne's *Twice-Told Tales*; and *The Talisman* (1828–1830), a New York annual which published the works of Bryant, Verplanck, and R. C. Sands. Typical of the sentimental feminine verse in such volumes is that of the poetaster extravagantly praised by Poe in "The Literati": Frances Sargent Osgood (1811–1850), to be found in her volume, *The Casket of Fate* (1840). A standard study is Ralph Thompson, *American Literary Annuals and Gift Books: 1825–1865*, New York, 1936.

For an account of the history of literary production during the mid-century see Frank L. Mott, "The Business of Magazine Publishing," in *A History of American Magazines, 1850–1865*, Cambridge, 1938, II, 4–26. Special studies include Bertha-Monica Stearns, "Southern Magazines for Ladies, 1819–1860," *So. Atl. Quar.*, XXXI (1932), 70–87; and *idem*, "Philadelphia Magazines for Ladies: 1830–1860," *Pa. Mag. Hist. and Biog.*, LXIX (1945), 207–219—exclusive of *Godey's Lady's Book*.

### Newspapers and Journals

The *New York Tribune* was founded in 1841 by Horace Greeley (1811–1872), who edited it until his death. It was noted for its literary excellence, and it was the first daily to establish (1856) a regular book review department. This continued for thirty years under the editorship of George Ripley. Lurton D. Ingersoll's *The Life of Horace Greeley*, Chicago, 1873, contains primary material. Two later biographies are Don C. Seitz, *Horace Greeley: Founder of the New York Tribune*, Indianapolis, 1926; and Henry L. Stoddard, *Horace Greeley: Printer, Editor, Crusader*, New York, 1946. See especially Jeter Allen Isely, *Horace Greeley and the Republican Party, 1853–61: A Study of the New York Tribune*, Princeton, 1947.

Though short-lived, the *Spirit of the Age* (1849–1850) deserves notice as a New York weekly devoted to reforms. It was edited by W. H. Channing, and its contributors included Parke Godwin, Henry James, Sr., Albert Brisbane, and George Ripley.

The *New York Times* was founded in 1851 by Henry J. Raymond. It has continued a conservative tradition and come to be known for its accuracy and impartiality, and literary significance.

The most widely read weekly, combining features of the newspaper and the magazine, was the New York *Ledger* (1851–1903). It was owned until 1887 by Robert Bonner (1824–1899), who raised the rate of pay to authors and popularized the illustration of serialized fiction. Among the most noted contributors were Bryant, Mrs. Stowe, Longfellow, Halleck, and Edward Everett, though perhaps they were no more popular in their time than such contributors as Fanny Fern, E. D. E. N. Southworth, Lydia Sigourney, and Sylvanus Cobb, Jr.

Representative of the illustrated newspapers is *Frank Leslie's Illustrated Weekly Newspaper* (1855–1922), edited until his death by Frank Leslie himself (1821–1880). Another of the many journals and periodicals which were popular during the last part of the century is *Frank Leslie's Popular Monthly* (1876–1906), a well known miscellany.

Valuable contemporary data are given in Simon N. D. North, *History and Present Condition of the Newspaper and Periodical Press of the United States, With a Catalogue of the Publications of the Census Year,* Washington, 1884. An authoritative history of nineteenth century newspapers is Frank L. Mott, *American Journalism* . . . , New York, 1941.


## THE LATE NINETEENTH CENTURY

LITERARY AND CULTURAL HISTORY:
*Studies Specific to the Period*

For literary studies of the period, see under appropriate headings in the preceding section: The Mid-Nineteenth Century; and in the section which follows: The Twentieth Century.

The leading secondary authority on the social history of the period is Allan Nevins, *The Emergence of Modern America, 1865–1878,* New York, 1927. Significant also are Arthur M. Schlesinger, *The Rise of the City, 1878–1898,* New York, 1933—with an unusually full bibliography; Thomas C. Cochran and William Miller, *The Age of Enterprise: A Social History of Industrial America,* New York, 1942—an excellent account for the general reader; Paul Buck, *The Road to Reunion, 1865–1900,* Boston, 1937—a discussion of the variety of influences which encouraged the reintegration of the South with the nation during the period after the Civil War; and Merle Curti, *The Growth of American Thought,* New York, 1943—especially important for the study of American thought during 1875–1900 (the extensive bibliographies, pp. 755–816, are particularly valuable). Still essential is Charles E. Merriam, *American Political Ideas: Studies in the Development of American Political Thought, 1865–1917,* New York, 1920. Edward R. Lewis, *A History of American Political Thought from the Civil War to the World War,* New York, 1937, is a full and often suggestive account of a confused body of materials. One of the best accounts of national economic integration is Ida M. Tarbell, *The Nationalizing of Business, 1878–1898,* New York, 1936, with bibl., pp. 278–293. See also Edward N. Saveth, "Race and Nationalism in American

Historiography: The Late Nineteenth Century," *Pol. Sci. Quar.*, LIV (1939), 421–441.

Other useful studies are Thomas Beer, *The Mauve Decade: American Life at the End of the Nineteenth Century*, New York, 1926—an impressionistic account; and Lewis Mumford, *The Brown Decades: A Study of the Arts in America, 1865–1895*, New York, 1931—omitting discussion of sculpture, music, and drama. A study of the life of any artist and of the life of the American artist is Henry James, *William Wetmore Story and His Friends*, Boston, 1903, 2 vols. See also Matthew Josephson, *The Robber Barons: The Great American Capitalists, 1861–1901*, New York, 1934; and Harvey O'Connor, *The Astors*, New York, 1941.

The fullest listing yet made of the literary results, fictional and non-fictional, of political and economic discussion during the late nineteenth century is Lisle A. Rose, "A Bibliographical Survey of Economic and Political Writings, 1865–1900," *Amer. Lit.*, XV (1944), 381–410.

The standard monograph on western agrarian agitation is John D. Hicks, *The Populist Revolt: A History of the Farmers' Alliance and the People's Party*, Minneapolis, 1931. The most thorough effort so far to write an intellectual history of Western agrarian protest in the late nineteenth century is Chester M. Destler, *American Radicalism, 1865–1901: Essays and Documents*, New London, Conn., 1946. A valuable study of the Grange and Farmers' Alliance movements in the Middle West is in Vol. II of Logan Esarey, *A History of Indiana*, Indianapolis, 1918, 2 vols. Interesting facts about the state of literary culture in rural Illinois in the 1870's are in Ernest L. Bogart and Charles M. Thompson, *The Industrial State, 1870–1893*, Springfield, Ill., 1920 (Vol. IV of *The Centennial History of Illinois*).

A study of the attempt of freethinkers, during the period covered, to undermine the influence of the church and theology is Sidney Warren, *American Freethought, 1860–1914*, New York, 1943.

*Fiction*

Among writers of fiction who achieved distinction during the period covered, the following are treated in the individual bibliographies herein: Henry Adams, T. B. Aldrich, J. L. Allen, Bierce, Cable, C. W. Chesnutt, Clemens, Crane, Eggleston, Mary E. W. Freeman, J. C. Harris, Harte, John Hay, Howells, Henry James, S. O. Jewett, London, Norris, and T. N. Page.

The major treatment of other writers whose chief contribution was made at this time is indicated in the index. See also the sections on Best Sellers and Juvenile Literature, *post*, pp. 218 and 225.

The earliest among the collected romantic tales of Harriet Prescott Spofford (1835–1921) was *The Amber Gods, and Other Stories* (1863). A recent biography is Elizabeth K. Halbeisen, *Harriet Prescott Spofford: A Romantic Survival,* Philadelphia, 1935, with full bibl., pp. 223–263. A critical estimate is Arthur H. Quinn, *American Fiction,* New York, 1936, pp. 208–214.

Lew(is) Wallace (1827–1905) based the plot of his first published romance, *The Fair God* (1873), on the Spanish conquest of Mexico, where he had resided briefly after his service as major general in the Union Army. Its success led him to write a romance of the early Roman Empire, *Ben-Hur: A Tale of the Christ* (1880), which sold some two million copies and was widely translated. See *Lew Wallace: An Autobiography,* New York, 1906, 2 vols. A brief account of his early days is Irving McKee, "The Early Life of Lew Wallace," *Indiana Mag. of Hist.,* XXXVII (1941), 205–216.

The best known of the short stories of Frank R. Stockton (1834–1902) were published in *The Lady, or the Tiger?* (1884). *The Novels and Stories of Frank R. Stockton* were issued, New York, 1899–1904, in 23 vols. A recent biography is Martin I. Griffin, Jr., *Frank R. Stockton: A Critical Biography,* Philadelphia, 1939. For a brief critical estimate, see Arthur H. Quinn, *American Fiction,* New York, 1936, pp. 220–231. Other estimates include William Dean Howells, "Stockton's Novels and Stories," *Atl. Mo.,* LXXXVII (1901), 136–138; E. W. Bowen, "The Fiction of Frank R. Stockton," *Sewanee Rev.,* XXVIII (1920), 452–462; and "Mr. Stockton," in Arthur T. Quiller-Couch, *Adventures in Criticism,* New York, 1925, pp. 211–215.

Usually thought of as the best among the novels of (Silas) Weir Mitchell (1829–1914) is his historical novel of the Revolution, *Hugh Wynne, Free Quaker* (1897). The Author's Definitive Edition of his works was published, New York, 1913–1914, in 16 vols. Anna R. Burr published *Weir Mitchell: His Life and Letters,* New York, 1929, with bibl. A brief critical estimate is Arthur H. Quinn, "Weir Mitchell, Pioneer and Patrician," in *American Fiction,* New York, 1936, pp. 305–322. Special studies include Max Farrand, "Hugh Wynne: A Historical Novel," *Washington Quar.,* I (1907), 101–108; Felix E. Schelling, "S. Weir Mitchell, Poet and Novelist," *General Mag. and Hist. Chron.,* XXXII (1930), 323–337; and Lyon N. Richardson, "S. Weir Mitchell at Work," *Amer. Lit.,* XI (1939), 58–65.

The adroitly composed stories of Henry Cuyler Bunner (1855–1896), commonly with a New York City setting, are represented by *Short Sixes . . .* (1890). *The Poems of H. C. Bunner,* New York, 1912, were issued with an introduction by Brander Matthews. A somewhat popular biographical account is Gerard E. Jensen, *The Life and Letters of Henry Cuyler Bunner,* Durham, N.C., 1939. Further letters, edited by Jensen, are "Bunner's Letters to Gilder," *Amer. Lit.,* XVII (1945), 161–169. A brief critical summary is Arthur H. Quinn, *American Fiction,* New York, 1936, pp. 410–413. See also

Gabriel Leeb, "The United States Twist: Some Plot Revisions by Henry Cuyler Bunner," *Amer. Lit.*, IX (1938), 431–441.

A prolific author of satirical novels and plays dealing with New York Society was Edgar Fawcett (1847–1904), whose work may be represented by *Purple and Fine Linen* (1873). E. E. Hale's sister Lucretia P. Hale (1820–1900) is still remembered for her satire on Boston culture and desire for self-improvement, *The Peterkin Papers* (1880). The first of several popular novels by Arthur Sherburne Hardy (1847–1930), frequently with a European setting, was entitled *But Yet a Woman* (1883). Hardy's autobiography was published as *Things Remembered* (1923). For a brief estimate, see Arthur H. Quinn, *American Fiction,* New York, 1936, pp. 413–418.

Other late nineteenth century novelists whose writings achieved some notice are Arlo Bates (1850–1918), represented by *Mr. Jacobs* (1883) and *The Philistines* (1889); and Moncure D. Conway (1832–1907), whose *Pine and Palm* (1887) is a sectional novel of the period before the Civil War. Constance Cary Harrison (1843–1920) was widely read for her satire on social climbers, *The Anglomaniacs* (1890). Her later work includes *Belhaven Tales* (1892), and an autobiography, *Recollections Grave and Gay* (1911). Edward Eggleston's brother, George Cary Eggleston (1839–1911), wrote two romances of the ante-bellum South, *Dorothy South* (1902) and *The Master of Warlock* (1903). A representative novel by Pearl Craigie ("John Oliver Hobbes," 1867–1906) is *A Bundle of Life* (1894).

A bibliographical listing of two popular series of novels published in Boston, 1875–1900, which supplements Halkett and Laing, is Aubrey Starke, " 'No Names' and 'Round Robins,' " *Amer. Lit.*, VI (1935), 400–412.

For a discussion of the political novel, see the section The Machine Age and the Literature of Exposure, *post,* p. 330.

*Poetry*

For data on the major poets of the late nineteenth century, Emily Dickinson, Sidney Lanier, and Walt Whitman, see the individual bibliographies herein.

The poems of Edward Rowland Sill (1841–1887) were issued as *The Hermitage and Other Poems* (1868), *The Venus of Milo and Other Poems* (1883), and *Hermione and Other Poems* (1899). *The Prose of Edward Rowland Sill* (1900) was followed by *The Poems of Edward Rowland Sill* (1902). A narrative and critical biography is William B. Parker, *Edward Rowland Sill: His Life and Work,* Boston, 1915. Stanley T. Williams and Barbara D. Simison edited *Around the Horn: A Journal, December 10, 1861, to March 25, 1862,* New Haven, 1944, from the manuscript in the Yale University

Library. Reminiscences of Sill appear in Henry Holt's *Garrulities of an Octogenarian Editor,* Boston, 1923, pp. 37–40. See also Newton Arvin, "The Failure of E. R. Sill," *Bookman,* LXXII (1931), 581–589.

The earliest of the published poems of Louise Imogen Guiney (1861–1920) was *Songs at the Start* (1884). Later volumes include *The Martyrs' Idyl and Shorter Poems* (1899), and *The Princess of the Tower* (1906). Her letters were published, New York, 1926, 2 vols. Two biographical studies are Alice Brown, *Louise Imogen Guiney,* Boston, 1921; and E. M. Tenison, *Louise Imogen Guiney,* London, 1923, with a bibliography.

Lizette Woodworth Reese (1856–1935) published her first poems as *A Branch of May: Poems* (1887). Later collections are *A Handful of Lavender* (1891), *A Quiet Road* (1896), and *A Wayside Lute* (1909). Two late volumes were *White April and Other Poems* (1930), and *Pastures and Other Poems* (1933). *The Selected Poems of Lizette Woodworth Reese* were published, New York, 1926. An autobiography was published as *A Victorian Village: Reminiscences of Other Days* (1929). For a bio-bibliography, see Fred B. Millett, *Contemporary American Authors,* New York, 1940, pp. 536–537.

Though he wrote little, Philip Henry Savage (1868–1899) deserves notice for the quality of two slight collections: *First Poems and Fragments* (1895), and *Poems* (1898). Both were reprinted as *Poems of Philip Henry Savage,* edited by D. G. Mason (1901).

(William) Bliss Carman (1861–1929) issued *Low Tide on Grand Pré: A Book of Lyrics* (1893). *Songs from Vagabondia,* written with Richard Hovey, were published in three series: 1894, 1896, and 1901. Later lyrics include *Behind the Arras* (1895), *By the Aurelian Wall and Other Elegies* (1898), and *Ballads and Lyrics* (1924). A biography is Odell Shepard, *Bliss Carman,* Toronto, 1924. Brief estimates include R. H. Hathaway, "The Poetry of Bliss Carman," *Sewanee Rev.,* XXXIII (1925), 467–483; and C. G. D. Roberts, "Bliss Carman," *Dalhousie Rev.,* IX (1930), 409–417, X (1930), 1–9.

Richard Hovey (1864–1900), best known for *Songs from Vagabondia* (with Bliss Carman, 1899), also published *Launcelot and Guenevere* (1891–1907); *Seaward: An Elegy* (1893); and *Along the Trail* (1898). Brief critical estimates are Jessie B. Rittenhouse, *The Younger American Poets,* Boston, 1904, pp. 1–26; and Bruce Weirick, *From Whitman to Sandburg in American Poetry,* New York, 1924, pp. 113–124. Richard Watson Gilder (1844–1909) may be represented by *In Palestine and Other Poems* (1898), and *Poems and Inscriptions* (1901). *Letters of Richard Watson Gilder* was published, Boston, 1916. For brief estimates, see Brander Matthews, "Richard Watson Gilder," *No. Amer. Rev.,* CXCI (1910), 38–48, and Henry Holt's *Garrulities of an Octogenarian Editor,* Boston, 1923, pp. 214–215.

Edwin (Charles) Markham (1852–1940) achieved wide popular notice with the publication of *The Man with the Hoe and Other Poems* (1899). Later volumes include *Lincoln and Other Poems* (1901), and *New Poems: Eighty Songs at Eighty* (1932). A biography is William L. Stidger, *Edwin Markham*, New York, 1933. A recent critical estimate is Jesse S. Goldstein, "Two Literary Radicals: Garland and Markham in Chicago, 1893," *Amer. Lit.*, XVII (1945), 152–160. A manuscript collection is in the possession of the Edwin Markham Memorial Association, Staten Island, New York. Further manuscript material is in the Library of Congress.

Moods of the sea are expressed in such volumes of Celia Thaxter (1835–1894) as *Poems* (1872), and *Drift-Weed* (1879). An extensive gathering of manuscripts is in the Celia Thaxter Collection of the Boston Public Library. The early lyrics of Anna Hempstead Branch (1875–1937) were issued as *The Heart of the Road, and Other Poems* (1901). Ridgely Torrence edited *Last Poems of Anna Hempstead Branch*, New York, 1944—a slight gleaning. John B[anister] Tabb (1845–1909) first achieved notice with the publication of his *Poems* (1894). Further volumes of lyrics were published between 1897 and 1910. A collection of the poetry of Father Tabb appeared in 1928. The most extended biography is Francis A. Litz, *Father Tabb: A Study of His Life and Works*, Baltimore, 1923. A representative collection of the poetry of Frank Dempster Sherman (1860–1916) is *Lyrics for a Lute* (1890). Clinton Scollard edited *The Poems of Frank Dempster Sherman*, Boston, 1917, with a critical estimate. The Kentucky poet, Madison (Julius) Cawein (1865–1914), published some 36 volumes of lyrics, among which *Lyrics and Idyls* (1890) and *Kentucky Poems* (1902) are representative. An extended biography is Otto A. Rothert, *The Story of a Poet: Madison Cawein*, Louisville, Ky., 1921. The graceful sonnets of Louise Chandler Moulton (1835–1908) appeared in volumes such as *In the Garden of Dreams: Lyrics and Sonnets* (1890), and *Poems and Sonnets* (1909). See Lilian Whiting, *Louise Chandler Moulton: Poet and Friend*, Boston, 1910. There is a "Checklist of the Writings of Louise Chandler Moulton" in *Proc. Amer. Antiq. Soc.*, n.s. XLIII (1933), 234–236. See also Aubrey Starke, "Father John B. Tabb: A Checklist," *Amer. Book Collector*, VI (1935), 101–104.

## Drama (dates in parentheses are of production)

Among the score of plays by Bronson Howard (1842–1908), his most popular and successful work was *Shenandoah* (1888). It is reprinted in Montrose J. Moses' *Representative Plays . . .*, New York, 1921, with introd.; and in Arthur H. Quinn, *Representative American Plays*, rev. ed., New York, 1930, with introduction. Allan G. Halline edited *The Banker's Daughter and Other Plays*, Princeton, 1941, as Vol. X of *America's Lost Plays*. In addition to

*The Banker's Daughter* (1878), the volume includes *Hurricanes* (1878), *Old Love Letters* (1878), *Baron Rudolph* (1881), *Knave and Queen* (written *ca.* 1887), and *One of Our Girls* (1885). For a brief critical study of Howard, see Arthur H. Quinn, *A History of the American Drama from the Civil War to the Present Day,* rev. ed., New York, 1936, I, 39–65. See also Halline's introduction to *The Banker's Daughter.* A bibliography is in Halline's *American Plays,* New York, 1935, pp. 759–760.

(John) Augustin Daly (1838–1899) adapted some ninety plays for the American stage, mostly from the German and French. The best of his own compositions include *Horizon* (1871), 1885, and *Divorce* (1871), 1884. Catherine Sturtevant edited *Man and Wife and Other Plays by Augustin Daly,* Princeton, 1942, as Volume XX of *America's Lost Plays.* In addition to *Man and Wife,* the volume includes *Divorce, The Big Bonanza* (1875), 1884, *Pique* (1875), 1884, and *Needles and Pins* (1880), 1884. *Horizon* is reprinted in Allan G. Halline, *American Plays,* New York, 1935, pp. 333–376. A biography is Joseph F. Daly, *The Life of Augustin Daly,* New York, 1917. A brief critical estimate is "Augustin Daly, Constructive Artist of the Theatre," in Arthur H. Quinn, *A History of the American Drama from the Civil War to the Present Day,* rev. ed., New York, 1936, I, 1–38. A list of Daly's plays appears, *ibid.,* II, 334–340. See also "List of Daly's Plays" in *Man and Wife, and Other Plays* (ed. Sturtevant), pp. xi–xxi.

The realism of James A. Herne (1839–1901) is apparent in the early play, *Hearts of Oak* (1879), written with David Belasco. His plays were first published in a collected edition in 1928: *Shore Acres and Other Plays,* including *Margaret Fleming* (1890), *Shore Acres* (1892), *The Reverend Griffith Davenport* (1899), and *Sag Harbor* (1899—a reworking of *Hearts of Oak*). Arthur H. Quinn edited *The Early Plays of James A. Herne,* Princeton, 1940, Vol. VII of *America's Lost Plays.* It includes *Within an Inch of His Life, "The Minute Men" of 1774–1775, Drifting Apart,* and *The Reverend Griffith Davenport.* For a brief critical estimate, see "James A. Herne and the Realism of Character," in Arthur H. Quinn, *A History of the American Drama from the Civil War to the Present Day,* rev. ed., New York, 1936, I, 125–162. A further study is Dorothy S. Bucks and Arthur H. Nethercot, "Ibsen and Herne's *Margaret Fleming:* A Study of the Early Ibsen Movement in America," *Amer. Lit.,* XVII (1946), 311–333.

Usually thought the best among the popular melodramas and domestic dramas of Bartley Campbell (1843–1888) is *My Partner* (1879), depicting the California frontier. Napier Wilt has edited *The White Slave and Other Plays by Bartley Campbell,* Princeton, 1941, Vol. XIX of *America's Lost Plays.* In addition to *The White Slave* (1882), the volume contains *The Virginian, My Partner, The Galley Slave,* and *Fairfax,* all first publication. A note on the popularity of *My Partner* abroad is Horst Frenz, "Bartley Campbell's *My*

*Partner* in Berlin," *German Quar.,* XVII (1944), 32–35. Most of the plays of David Belasco (1859–1931) were written in collaboration with James A. Herne, Henry C. De Mille, Cecil B. De Mille, and others. Among the best known of his own plays are *The Heart of Maryland* (1895), and *The Girl of the Golden West* (1905). Glenn Hughes and George Savage edited *The Heart of Maryland and Other Plays by David Belasco,* Princeton, 1941, Vol. XVIII of *America's Lost Plays,* with introd. and notes. In addition to *The Heart of Maryland,* the volume includes *La Belle Russe* (1881), *The Stranglers of Paris* (1881), *The Girl I Left Behind Me* (1893), and *Naughty Anthony* (1899). Montrose J. Moses edited *Six Plays* by Belasco, with an introd. by the author, and notes by Moses, Boston, 1928. A critical estimate is "David Belasco and His Associates," in Arthur H. Quinn, *A History of the American Drama from the Civil War to the Present Day,* rev. ed., New York, 1936, I, 163–199. A full-length biography is William Winter's *The Life of David Belasco,* New York, 1918, 2 vols. Belasco's autobiography, "My Life's Story," appeared serially in *Hearst's Magazine* during 1914–1915, Vols. XXV–XXVIII.

The thirty or more popular plays of (William) Clyde Fitch (1865–1909) include *Beau Brummell* (1890), *Barbara Frietchie* (1899), and *Captain Jinks of the Horse Marines* (1901). His plays were collected and edited by Montrose J. Moses and Virginia Gerson, Boston, 1915, 4 vols. The best biography is that of Moses and Gerson, *Clyde Fitch and His Letters,* Boston, 1924. For a critical estimate, see "Clyde Fitch and the Development of Social Comedy," in Arthur H. Quinn, *A History of the American Drama from the Civil War to the Present Day,* rev. ed., New York, 1936, I, 265–296.

The poetic drama of Josephine Preston Peabody (1874–1922) includes *Marlowe* (1901), *The Piper* (1910—her best play), and *The Wolf of Gubbio* (1913). C. H. Baker edited *Diary and Letters of Josephine Preston Peabody* (1925). Her poems and plays were collected in 1927.

Among other playwrights who achieved success during this era are William Gillette (1855–1937), whose Civil War plays include *Held by the Enemy* (1886) and *Secret Service* (1895); Augustus Thomas (1857–1934), remembered for *Alabama* (1891) and *The Witching Hour* (1907).

For data on Howells as dramatist, see the individual bibliography herein.

Dramatic criticism and valuable autobiographical reminiscences appear in four books by William Winter: *Other Days* . . . (1908), *Old Friends* . . . (1909), *The Wallet of Time* . . . (1913), and *Vagrant Memories* (1915). Further significant reminiscences are in two books by Daniel Frohman: *Memories of a Manager* . . . (1911), and *Encore* (1937). The autobiography of Augustus Thomas, *The Print of My Remembrance,* New York, 1922, also gives useful primary material.

A standard history covering the drama of the period is Arthur H. Quinn, *A History of the American Drama from the Civil War to the Present Day,* rev. ed., New York, 1936.

## American Issues

The best book on intellectual, political, and economic currents from 1865 to 1900 is Adams's *The Education of Henry Adams* (1918). The observations of Edwin L. Godkin, *Reflections and Comments, 1865–1895* (1895), are a collection of Godkin's articles contributed to the *North American Review* and other periodicals. They constitute discussions of public affairs by the most distinguished editor of the day. An "official" biography, but the only printed source for Godkin's highly interesting correspondence, is Rollo Ogden, ed., *Life and Letters of Edwin Lawrence Godkin,* New York, 1907, 2 vols. Henry Holt devotes a chapter to Godkin in his autobiography, *Garrulities of an Octogenarian Editor,* Boston, 1923, pp. 282–295. See also Harold W. Stoke, "Edwin Lawrence Godkin, Defender of Democracy," *So. Atl. Quar.,* XXX (1931), 339–349.

Henry W. Grady (1850–1889) was an important influence in rebuilding the South. A posthumous collection of letters which he wrote to the New York *Ledger* was gathered as *The New South* (1890). They describe conditions in the postwar South, emphasizing economic problems and the Negro question. The standard biography is Raymond B. Nixon, *Henry W. Grady: Spokesman of the New South,* New York, 1943. See also Marvin G. Bauer, in William N. Brigance, ed., *A History and Criticism of American Public Address,* New York, 1943, I, 387–406; and John D. Wade, "Henry W. Grady," *Southern Rev.,* III (1938), 479–509.

A collaborative effort to describe the United States at the end of the century—from natural resources to government, literature, and finance—is Nathaniel S. Shaler (1841–1906), ed., *The United States of America: A Study of the American Commonwealth . . .* (3 vols., 1894). Outstanding among contributions are those of Charles Francis Adams on corporations, and W. T. Harrison on education. With the exception of Shaler's one worry about the "new immigration," there is almost no attention to Europe. See *The Autobiography of Nathaniel Southgate Shaler, with a Supplementary Memoir by His Wife,* Boston, 1909.

## Reform

The lecture of George William Curtis (1824–1892) on *The Duty of the American Scholar to Politics and the Times* (1856) was an early expression of Curtis's interest in civic and governmental reforms. Led by Curtis, Carl Schurz, and others, the Civil Service Reform was inaugurated during the Hayes administration, with the President's assistance, to counter the in-trenched spoils system of federal and local patronage. Curtis served as presi-dent of the National Civil Service Reform League from its founding in 1881 until his death. As Secretary of the Interior (1877–1881) under Hayes, Carl Schurz (1829–1906) installed a merit promotion system and fostered other important reforms. As a liberal and fearless journalist he crusaded for honest government. His *Speeches, Correspondence, and Political Papers* (6 vols., 1913) include the most important of his published writings.

To secure protective legislation for farmers, the National Grange of Patrons of Husbandry was founded in 1867. The Grange movement achieved considerable influence in the later decades of the century, and in 1889 was instrumental in establishing the Department of Agriculture.

Two liberals in the cause of penal reform were John Peter Altgeld (1847–1902), and Frederick Howard Wines (1838–1912). Altgeld published *Our Penal Machinery and Its Victims* (1884). Wines's study of crime and correc-tion was issued as *The Prevention and Repression of Crime* (1894).

In 1897 William Dwight Porter Bliss published his *Encyclopedia of Social Reform*.

Two leaders in humanitarian work at the close of the century were Booker T. Washington (1856–1915), and Jane Addams (1860–1935). Washington set forth his program for handling the Negro problem in *The Future of the American Negro* (1899). His autobiography, *Up from Slavery,* was issued two years later. It is source material for the leading Negro coeducational college, Tuskegee Normal and Industrial Institute, which he founded in 1881. Jane Addams expounded her social theories in *Democracy and Social Ethics* (1902). Primary sources for data on the Chicago social settlement, Hull-House, which she founded in 1889, appear in *Twenty Years at Hull-House* (1910), and the companion volume, *The Second Twenty Years at Hull-House* (1930).

For further data on Reform, see the sections The Machine Age and Christian Socialism, *post,* pp. 330 and 337.

Science and Scholarship

Distinguished as an ethnologist and archaeologist, Frank Hamilton Cush-ing (1857–1900) published *The Myths of Creation* (1882), and *Zuñi Folk Tales* (1901)—dealing especially with New Mexico. Theodore Low De Vinne (1828–1914) made important advances in the art of printing, both in the quality of the work from his own press, and in his writings, which include *Historic Printing Types* (1886), and *The Practice of Typography* (1900–1904).

The National Geographic Society was founded in 1888 to encourage and support geographical research. Its organ, the *National Geographic Magazine,* is amply illustrated and is popular in appeal. A classic text in astronomy is *The New Astronomy* (1888), by Samuel Pierpont Langley (1834–1906), distinguished as an astrophysicist and a scientific organizer.

Three other scientific leaders made significant contributions at the turn of the century. Alfred Thayer Mahan (1840–1914) set forth the little understood place of navies in political history in *The Influence of Sea Power upon History, 1660–1783* (1890). G[ranville] Stanley Hall (1844–1924), who founded and edited the *American Journal of Psychology* (1887–1921), influenced the United States movement toward child study, and published his important findings in *Adolescence* (1904), and other works. Josiah Willard Gibbs (1839–1903) contributed to the science of thermodynamics as professor of mathematical physics at Yale (1871–1903). An attempt to estimate his significance is Muriel Rukeyser, *Willard Gibbs,* Garden City, N.Y., 1942.

In the field of scholarship outside pure and applied science, a foundation was laid for a study of art and civilization with the incorporation, in 1870, of the Metropolitan Museum of Art, which rapidly became the largest and most important institution of its kind in the country. The Shakespearean scholar Horace Howard Furness (1833–1912) began publication of the *New Variorum* edition of Shakespeare's plays and poems in 1871. The monumental work was carried on by his son, and is still continuing under the auspices of learned societies. The philologist William Dwight Whitney (1827–1894), who ranks among the distinguished scholars of the century, contributed significantly to the development of American scholarship. His *Sanscrit Grammar* (1879) is a landmark in the study of linguistics. As a lexicographer he served as editor-in-chief of *The Century Dictionary* (1889–1891), a work which has not yet been superseded in matters of definition. As a student of English literature, Thomas Raynesford Lounsbury (1838–1915) contributed broadly to Chaucerian and Elizabethan scholarship, and published *A History of the English Language* (1879). The most notable single contributions in the field of English studies were those of Francis James Child (1825–1896). His "Observations on the Language of Chaucer" in *Memoirs of the American Academy of Arts and Sciences* (1863) was the first accurate analysis of Chaucer's metrics. He further prepared an edition of Spenser (5 vols., 1855). His chief fame rests on his edition of *The English and Scottish Popular Ballads* (5 vols., 1882–1898), the fundamental reference work for a study of the English traditional ballad.

Among editors, the work of Horace Elisha Scudder (1838–1902) deserves notice. As general editorial assistant to Houghton, Mifflin and Company from 1880 till his death, he fostered the publication of many studies in English and American literature. Under his general editorship the publishers issued the

Riverside Literature Series of British and American poets—a score of volumes, many of which still remain standard texts.

The contributions of Basil L. Gildersleeve (1831–1924) to the classical field remain important. He founded the *American Journal of Philology* (1880), and his collected contributions were published as *Essays and Studies, Educational and Literary* (1890). The first academic political periodical in the United States, the *Political Science Quarterly,* was founded by John W. Burgess (1844–1931), whose pioneer studies in the field of international law are notably represented by *Political Science and Comparative Constitutional Law* (2 vols., 1890–1891). Among the best known historical studies of Henry Osborn Taylor (1856–1941) are his *Ancient Ideals* (2 vols., 1896), and *The Mediaeval Mind* (2 vols., 1911).

John Lancaster Spalding (1840–1916), Bishop of Peoria, is remembered for his advocacy of educational traditionalism  Among his most widely read volumes were *Means and Ends of Education* (1895), and *Thoughts and Theories of Life and Education* (1897).

A leader in the scientific school of historians was Herbert Baxter Adams (1850–1901), who organized teaching at Johns Hopkins on the model of the German seminars. He was a founder of the American Historical Association (1884), and author of *The Study of History in American Colleges and Universities* (1887). His letters, published as *Historical Scholarship in the United States* (1938), include his correspondence with Woodrow Wilson and F. J. Turner. On the important historical work of Henry Adams, see the individual bibliography herein.

The first great historical scholar of the West Coast was Hubert Howe Bancroft (1832–1918), whose *History of the Pacific States* (28 vols., 1871–1890) is but one of several monumental compilations based on a great collection of source material (later donated to the University of California), and carried out by a staff who worked under his editorial supervision.

Important as a political history of the period to 1909 is the work of James Ford Rhodes (1848–1927), *History of the United States from the Compromise of 1850 [to 1909]* (1893–1928). Woodrow Wilson's *The State* appeared in 1889. Theodore Roosevelt's *The Winning of the West* (4 vols., 1889–1896) is skimpy in research. John Bach McMaster (1852–1932) placed emphasis upon social and economic history in his *A History of the People of the United States, from the Revolution to the Civil War* (8 vols., 1883–1913).

Schools of Philosophy:

1. Neo-Hegelianism

The founder of the St. Louis school of Hegelian idealism and (with Alcott) the Concord School of Philosophy was William Torrey Harris (1835–

1909), the foremost exponent of Hegel in the United States. He founded the *Journal of Speculative Philosophy* in St. Louis in 1867 and wrote prolifically on subjects dealing with secondary and higher education. His study on *Hegel's Doctrine of Reflection,* New York, 1881, was followed by such works as *Introduction to the Study of Philosophy* (1889), and *Psychologic Foundations of Education* (1898). A recent study of Harris is Edwin L. Schaub, ed., *William Torrey Harris, 1835-1935,* La Salle, Ill., 1936. For studies of the neo-Hegelians George Sylvester Morris and George Holmes Howison, see Robert M. Wenley, *Life and Work of George Sylvester Morris,* New York, 1917; and J. W. Buckham and G. M. Stratton, *George Holmes Howison: Philosopher and Teacher,* Berkeley, Calif., 1934. A collection of source materials is in Charles M. Perry, ed., *The St. Louis Movement in Philosophy,* Norman, Okla., 1930. A recent study of the movement is Frances A. B. Harmon, *The Social Philosophy of the St. Louis Hegelians,* New York, 1943. George Santayana, in *Character and Opinion in the United States,* New York, 1920, throws light on the neo-Hegelian movement as a whole and on Josiah Royce in particular. Still valuable for its discussion of the period following the Civil War is William Schuyler, "German Philosophy in St. Louis," *Educ. Rev.,* XXXIX (1905), 450-467. Denton J. Snider, *The St. Louis Movement,* St. Louis, 1920, is useful but diffuse. See also Cleon Forbes, "The St. Louis School of Thought," *Missouri Hist. Rev.,* XXV (1930-1931), 83-101, 289-305, 461-473, 609-622; XXVI (1931), 68-77.

## 2. Pragmatism and Idealism

The pragmatists used the Spencerian (Darwinian) basic concepts of organism, environment, and adaptation, and employed the language of naturalism; but in social thought they stressed the effectiveness of ideas and the possibility of novelties. For data on the chief pragmatists, William James and John Dewey, see the individual bibliographies herein.

Of increasing stature, as his works have come to be studied, is Charles Sanders Peirce (1839-1914), a founder of the school of pragmatism. The first of his works to be published was the posthumous volume *Chance, Love, and Logic,* New York, 1923, ed. by Morris R. Cohen. Charles Hartshorne and Paul Weiss have edited *Collected Papers of Charles Sanders Peirce,* Cambridge, 1931-1935, 6 vols. The fullest study is that of Justus Buchler, *Charles Peirce's Empiricism,* New York, 1939. Other estimates are Justus Buchler, "Charles Sanders Peirce, Giant in American Philosophy," *Amer. Scholar,* VIII (1939), 400-411; Charles Hartshorne, "Charles Sanders Peirce's Metaphysics of Evolution," *New Eng. Quar.,* XIV (1941), 49-63; Frederic I. Carpenter, "Charles Sanders Peirce: Pragmatic Transcendentalist," *New Eng. Quar.,* XIV (1941), 34-48; and T. A. Goudge, "Charles Peirce: Pioneer in

American Thought," *Univ. Toronto Quar.,* XII (1943), 403–414. See especially James Feibleman, *An Introduction to Peirce's Philosophy* . . ., New York, 1946.

The most significant essays of the mathematical physicist, Chauncey Wright (1830–1875), were posthumously collected by Charles Eliot Norton and published as *Chauncey Wright: Philosophical Discussions, with a Biographical Sketch,* New York, 1877. James B. Thayer edited *Letters of Chauncey Wright, with Account of His Life,* Cambridge, 1878. Recent studies are Gail Kennedy, "The Pragmatic Naturalism of Chauncey Wright," *Colo. Univ. Stud. in the Hist. of Ideas,* III (1935), 477–503. See also William James, "Chauncey Wright," in *Collected Essays and Reviews,* New York, 1920, pp. 20–25; Morris R. Cohen, in *Camb. Hist. Amer. Lit.,* III, 236; and P. P. Wiener, "Chauncey Wright's Defense of Darwin and the Neutrality of Science," *Jour. Hist. Ideas,* VI (1945), 19–45.

Though brief, the best account of pragmatism is the chapter "Development of American Pragmatism" in John Dewey, *Philosophy and Civilization,* New York, 1931.

The most distinguished philosophical idealist is Josiah Royce (1855–1916). His chief works include *The Religious Aspect of Philosophy* (1885), *The Spirit of Modern Philosophy* (1892), *The Conception of God* (1897), *The World and the Individual* (2 vols., 1900–1901), *The Philosophy of Loyalty* (1908), and *The Problem of Christianity* (2 vols., 1913). The fullest discussion of Royce appears in George Santayana's *Character and Opinion in the United States,* New York, 1920. See also "Liberty and Authority: The Idealism of Josiah Royce" in Ralph H. Gabriel, *The Course of American Democratic Thought,* New York, 1940, pp. 280–289. Contributions toward a study of Royce's philosophical position, written by leading philosophers, are gathered in *Papers in Honor of Josiah Royce* . . ., New York, 1916.

## 3. Other Philosophies

The founder of Christian Science, Mary Baker Eddy (1821–1910), published *Science and Health* (1875) as an exposition of her metaphysical system and as the official statement of the organization which soon became the Church of Christ, Scientist. The sales of the book were very large.

Benjamin Paul Blood (1832–1919) expounded a mystical concept of pluralism, induced by the use of anesthetics, in *The Anaesthetic Revelation and the Gist of Philosophy* (1874). Its publication led to an extensive correspondence with William James. Helena Petrovna Hahn Blavatsky (1831–1891) was a theosophist leader, and co-founder of the Theosophical Society. In *The Secret Doctrine* (2 vols., 1888) she presents an involved exposition of her occult theories.

*Letters, Memoirs, and Biography*

Classic documents in frontier and cultural history are the four volumes of Hamlin Garland's autobiography. *A Son of the Middle Border,* New York, 1927 (first published 1917), is the story of a "back-trailer" which is a primary source for data on the disillusionments of midwestern farmers, for a picture of Boston in the 1880's with comments on sectional attitudes of East and West, for the literary and other influences dealing with the rise of realism in fiction, and for the emergence of Chicago as a cultural center. Garland's autobiographical chronicle begins, in point of time, with *Trail-Makers of the Middle Border,* New York, 1926, and is completed in the two volumes, *A Daughter of the Middle Border,* New York, 1921, and *Back-Trailers from the Middle Border,* New York, 1928. The best of his old-age reminiscences is the first: *Roadside Meetings,* New York, 1930, covering the years 1880–1900.

Significant primary material is in *Mark Twain's Letters,* New York, 1917, 2 vols., ed. by Albert B. Paine. Brander Matthews's memoirs dealing with the cultural life of New York during 1870–1910 were issued as *These Many Years: Recollections of a New Yorker,* New York, 1917.

William Dean Howells recorded his reminiscences of the Cambridge Brahmin group and of literary Boston and New York in *Literary Friends and Acquaintance: A Personal Retrospect of American Authorship,* New York, 1900; his further reminiscences, principally of his Ohio days, appeared as *Years of My Youth,* New York, 1916.

Vivid sketches of Edward Burlingame, W. C. Brownell, Walter Berry, Henry James, and others are in Edith Wharton's autobiography, *A Backward Glance,* New York, 1934.

Other important primary material appears in Adams's *The Education of Henry Adams* (1918); Raphael Pumpelly, *My Reminiscences* (2 vols., 1918)—especially useful on the opening of the West after 1865; William James, *Memories and Studies* (1911); Anna R. Burr, ed., *Alice James: Her Brothers, Her Journal* (1934)—especially for the passing scene during the later years of Miss James (d. 1892); John S. Clark, *The Life and Letters of John Fiske* (2 vols., 1917); William R. Thayer, *The Life and Letters of John Hay* (2 vols., 1915)—an "official" view, but based on letters, and thus often revealing of the state of ideas in the Hay-Adams circle; and Charles Francis Adams, *Charles Francis Adams: An Autobiography* (1916)—with data on the industrial development. The *Letters of Charles Eliot Norton* (2 vols., 1913) reveal his friendships with artists and writers on both sides of the Atlantic. On Norton (1827–1908), see Edward W. Emerson, *Charles Eliot Norton,* Boston, 1912. Maud Howe Elliott's *This Was My Newport* (1944) includes interesting reminiscences and family letters, especially during the seventies and later.

Other reminiscences and memoirs that throw light on the literary activities of the last quarter of the century include Francis W. Halsey, *Our Literary Deluge and Some of Its Deeper Waters* (1902)—useful for author-publisher relationships; William M. Payne, *Editorial Echoes* (1902); John T. Trowbridge, *My Own Story: With Recollections of Noted Persons* (1903); William Winter, *Old Friends: Being Literary Recollections of Other Days* (1909); Lilian Whiting, *Louise Chandler Moulton: Poet and Friend* (1910)—source material on New England writers; Robert Underwood Johnson, *Remembered Yesterdays* . . . (1923); and Mark A. De Wolfe Howe, ed., *Later Years of the Saturday Club* (1927)—the Boston literary scene to 1920.

## INSTRUMENTS OF CULTURE AND LITERARY PRODUCTION
### Publishing and the Book Trade

Distinguished among publishers' memoirs is Henry Holt's *Garrulities of an Octogenarian Editor, with Other Essays Somewhat Biographical and Autobiographical,* New York, 1923. Holt, who entered Yale in 1861, seems to have known almost everyone of consequence during the last third of the century, and his observations are acute. He was especially close to John Fiske and E. L. Youmans and shared the cult of Spencer. He also knew Godkin, Francis Walker, William James, Henry Draper, O. C. Marsh, Alexander Agassiz, Whitelaw Reid, John Hay, Raphael Pumpelly, Clarence King, and Henry Adams—in a word, the leaders of American official intellectual life.

Literary reminiscences of a pioneer in international publishing are George H. Putnam, *George Palmer Putnam: A Memoir, Together with a Record of the Earlier Years of the Publishing House Founded by Him,* New York, 1912. Further material is presented in *idem, Memories of a Publisher, 1865–1915,* New York, 1915.

Discursive essays on publishing are in Walter H. Page, *A Publisher's Confession,* New York, 1905. William W. Ellsworth, an editor of the Century Company, published *A Golden Age of Authors: A Publisher's Recollections,* Boston, 1919. Light on the period 1870–1914, by the editor of *Century Magazine,* is in L[ewis] Frank Tooker, *The Joys and Tribulations of an Editor,* New York, 1924. The relationship of periodicals to general literature is set forth in Henry M. Alden, *Magazine Writing and the New Literature,* New York, 1908. Sketches of Stoddard, Stedman, Howells, and other prominent figures are in James L. Ford, *Forty-Odd Years in the Literary Shop,* New York, 1921. J[oseph] Henry Harper, in *I Remember,* New York, 1934, gives glimpses of Mark Twain, Howells, H. M. Alden, and others.

Elbert Hubbard (1856–1915) undertook some 170 *Little Journeys* to the homes of the great and the near-great. The series reflects the popular taste and was issued as chapbooks from Hubbard's own press in East Aurora, New York.

Useful history of the book trade is supplied in Raymond H. Shove, *Cheap Book Production in the United States, 1870 to 1891,* Urbana, Ill., 1937.

## THE TWENTIETH CENTURY
### LITERARY AND CULTURAL HISTORY

For historical studies dealing with philosophy, religion, education, and science—with special emphasis on the contribution and development of the twentieth century—see the section following, Background: Civilization in the United States.

*Fiction*
Primary Sources

Among major twentieth century novelists whose works are more fully discussed in the individual bibliographies, three had achieved some measure of success before the turn of the century. Hamlin Garland's earliest published prose, *Main-Travelled Roads,* appeared in 1891. Ellen Glasgow's *The Descendant* (1897) was her first published novel; and Edith Wharton's *The Greater Inclination* (1899), her first book, is a volume of short stories.

During the first decade of the century appeared Dreiser's *Sister Carrie* (1900); Upton Sinclair's *Springtime and Harvest: A Romance* (1901); Gertrude Atherton's *The Conqueror . . .* (1902); O. Henry's first book of short stories, *Cabbages and Kings* (1904); James Branch Cabell's *The Eagle's Shadow* (1904); Willa Cather's *The Troll Garden* (1905); and Zona Gale's *Romance Island* (1906).

Though Sinclair Lewis's reputation was not established until the publication of *Main Street* (1920), his first novel, *Our Mr. Wrenn,* was issued in 1914. Other writers who established their reputations during the second decade include Joseph Hergesheimer, who published his first novel, *The Lay Anthony: A Romance* (1914); Sherwood Anderson, whose earliest novel appeared in 1916 as *Windy McPherson's Son;* and Ring Lardner, whose first volume of short stories, *Gullible's Travels,* was published in 1917.

During the twenties F. Scott Fitzgerald sprang into prominence with his first volume of fiction, *This Side of Paradise* (1920); John Dos Passos, with *One Man's Initiation . . . 1917* (1920); E. E. Cummings, with his autobiographical narrative on his war experiences, *The Enormous Room* (1922); Ernest Hemingway, with his volume of short stories, *In Our Time* (1925);

William Faulkner, with *Soldiers' Pay* (1926); and Thomas Wolfe, with *Look Homeward, Angel: A Story of the Buried Life* (1929).

The era of the thirties witnessed the publication of the first published fiction by Erskine Caldwell, *The Bastard* (1930); Langston Hughes, *Not Without Laughter* (1930); James T. Farrell, *Young Lonigan: A Boyhood in Chicago Streets* (1932); William Saroyan, *The Daring Young Man on the Flying Trapeze and Other Stories* (1934); John Steinbeck, *Tortilla Flat* (1935); and Richard Wright, *Uncle Tom's Children: Four Novellas* (1938).

Less known but significant novelists during the earlier years of the century are Robert Herrick (1868–1938), who may be represented by *The Man Who Wins* (1897), *The Memoirs of an American Citizen* (1905), and *Clark's Field* (1914); and Ernest Poole (b. 1880), remembered for his first novel *The Voice of the Street* (1906), *The Harbor* (1915), *Blind: A Story of These Times* (1920), and *With Eastern Eyes* (1926). Poole has been best known abroad, where his novels have been serialized and translated into many tongues. His autobiography, *The Bridge,* appeared in 1940. Novels of early realism are those of Brand Whitlock (1869–1934), *The Thirteenth District* (1902), and *The Turn of the Balance* (1907). His autobiography appeared as *Forty Years of It* (1910). Anne Douglas Sedgwick (Mrs. Basil de Sélincourt, 1873–1935) lived mostly abroad. Her novels include *Tante* (1911), and *The Little French Girl* (1924).

Representative writers during the twenties achieved varying degrees of popular success. Two collections of the short stories of Katharine Fullerton Gerould (1879–1944) are *Vain Oblations* (1914) and *Valiant Dust* (1922). *Moon-Calf* (1920), by Floyd Dell (b. 1887) deals with a disillusioned postwar world. The first of several novels by Evelyn Scott (b. 1893), *The Narrow House,* appeared in 1921. Her autobiographical narratives were published as *Escapade* (1923), and *Background in Tennessee* (1937). *The Blind Bow-Boy* (1923), by Carl Van Vechten (b. 1880), deals with a sophisticated artistic set in New York, and his *Nigger Heaven* (1926) is a realistic picture of Harlem. Amusing stories, written from a realistic knowledge of small towns, are in *Picture Frames* (1923), by Thyra Samter Winslow (b. 1893). The romances of Brian Oswald Donn-Byrne (1889–1928) include *Blind Raftery* (1924), and *Hangman's House* (1926). The first of many novels by Louis Bromfield (b. 1896) is *The Green Bay Tree: A Novel* (1924). Well known among the novels of Edna Ferber (b. 1887) are *So Big* (1924), and *Show Boat: A Novel* (1926). Her autobiography was published as *A Peculiar Treasure* (1939). A representative collection of the short stories of Wilbur Daniel Steele (b. 1886) is *Urkey Island* (1926). Julian Green (b. 1900) wrote his psychological studies in French. Among translations are *Avarice House* (1927), and *The Dark Journey* (1929). His journal, *Personal Record* (1939), covers the decade of the thirties. His sister Anne Green (b. 1899) uses France as background in novels such as *The Selbys* (1930), concerned with expatriates. Anne Parrish (b. 1888) has written satires of manners in such novels as *The Perennial Bachelor* (1925), and *All Kneeling* (1928). *Daughter of Earth* (1929), by Agnes Smedley (b. 1890), did not become widely known. It was issued in a revised edition, 1935, with a foreword by Malcolm Cowley. Thornton (Niven) Wilder (b. 1897) published *The Cabala* in 1926, and *The Bridge of San Luis Rey* in the following year. Ben Hecht (b. 1894) selected 21 of his own stories, which he published as *The Collected Stories of Ben Hecht . . .* (1945).

Recent writers of fiction, together with a representative volume by each author, include Claude McKay (b. 1890), *Gingertown* (1932); Kay Boyle (b. 1903), *Plagued by the Nightingale* (1931); Katherine Anne Porter (b. 1894), *Flowering Judas* (1930); Dorothy Parker (b. 1893), *Here Lies: The Collected Stories of Dorothy Parker* (1939); Pearl Buck (b. 1892), *The Good Earth* (1931); Albert Halper (b. 1904), *Union Square* (1933); Nathanael West (1906–1940), *Miss Lonelyhearts* (1933—reissued by New Directions, 1946); John (Henry) O'Hara (b. 1905), *Butterfield 8* (1935); John P. Marquand (b. 1893), *The Late George Apley* (1937); and John Hersey (b. 1914), *A Bell for Adano* (1944).

Two novelists known especially for their historical romances are Kenneth (Lewis) Roberts (b. 1885), and James Boyd (b. 1888). Roberts's *Arundel* (1930), *Rabble in Arms* (1933), and later novels of colonial days, are noted for their accurate reconstruction of background. The Revolution and the Civil War furnish background for Boyd in such novels as *Drums* (1925), and *Marching On* (1927).

Further discussion of twentieth century fiction appears in the sections: Best Sellers (p. 218), Folk Tales and Humor (p. 202), Juvenile Literature (p. 225), Mingling of Tongues (p. 284), and Regionalism (p. 304).

Critical Analysis: Theory

The main body of Henry James's critical dicta, contained in prefaces to his separate volumes, has been collected and edited with an introduction by R. P. Blackmur as *The Art of the Novel: Critical Prefaces.* New York, 1934. Ellen Glasgow's discussions of the art of fiction, written originally as prefaces to her own novels, appear in *A Certain Measure: An Interpretation of Prose Fiction,* New York, 1943.

Critical Analysis: Contemporary

Two studies by Joseph Warren Beach are *The Twentieth Century Novel: Studies in Technique,* New York, 1932—dealing with contemporary writers;

and *American Fiction, 1920–1940,* New York, 1941—a study of the revolt against "bourgeois romanticism" in eight contemporaries. Maxwell Geismar's *Writers in Crisis: The American Novel Between Two Wars,* Boston, 1942, is an analysis of Lardner, Hemingway, Dos Passos, Faulkner, Wolfe, and Steinbeck, with emphasis on their cultural significance. An historical estimate, especially of the novel since Howells as an interpretation of American life, is Alfred Kazin, *On Native Grounds: An Interpretation of Modern American Prose Literature,* New York, 1942. Useful critical essays, dealing with modern aspects of the American scene, are gathered in T[homas] K. Whipple, *Study Out the Land,* Berkeley, Calif., 1943. Percy H. Boynton describes significant writers, without attempting historical assessment, in *America in Contemporary Fiction,* Chicago, 1940. Estimates by twelve critics of fifteen literary figures from Dreiser to Wolfe form the content of Malcolm Cowley, ed., *After the Genteel Tradition: American Writers Since 1910,* New York, 1937. Harlan Hatcher, *Creating the Modern American Novel,* New York, 1935, deals principally with the period 1900–1930. An earlier collection "By Twelve American Novelists"—essays in evaluation—is *The Novel of Tomorrow and the Scope of Fiction,* Indianapolis, 1922. See also Helen T. and Wilson Follett, *Some Modern Novelists: Appreciations and Estimates* (1918). Bernard A. De Voto's *The Literary Fallacy,* Boston, 1944, is a volume of unsympathetic essays on Van Wyck Brooks, Sinclair Lewis, Ernest Hemingway, and John Dos Passos.

Critical Analysis: Historical

The most detailed history of American fictional writing is Arthur H. Quinn, *American Fiction: An Historical and Critical Survey,* New York, 1936; it is a discussion, with plot summaries, of both major and minor writers of the novel and short story, with bibl., pp. 726–777. A summary history with emphasis on major writers, but with little attention to sub-literary trends, is Carl Van Doren, *The American Novel, 1789–1939,* New York, 1940. A further historical study is Harry Hartwick, *The Foreground of American Fiction* New York, 1934.

An historical survey of the short story from Irving to O. Henry is Fred L. Pattee, *The Development of the American Short Story: An Historical Survey,* New York, 1923. Other studies are Blanche C. Williams, *Our Short Story Writers,* New York, 1920, and Edward J. O'Brien, *The Advance of the American Short Story,* rev. ed., New York, 1931.

Foreign studies include Régis Michaud, *The American Novel To-day: A Social and Psychological Study,* Boston, 1928; Hermann Mohrmann, *Kultur- und Gesellschaftsprobleme des amerikanischen Romans der Nachkriegszeit,*

*1920–1927*, Giessen, 1934—a critical estimate by a German scholar of 25 "postwar" novels; and Sten Bodvar Liljegren, *The Revolt Against Romanticism in American Literature*, Upsala, 1945.

## Special Studies

Benjamin Brawley's *The Negro in Literature and Art in the United States*, New York, 1918, is a brief factual survey, with bibl., pp. 160–174. Vernon Loggins, *The Negro Author: His Development in America*, New York, 1931, a well proportioned survey, concludes with bibl., pp. 408–457. See also John H. Nelson, *The Negro Character in American Literature*, Lawrence, Kans., 1926; Nick A. Ford, *The Contemporary Negro Novel: A Study in Race Relations*, Boston, 1936; and Charles I. Glicksberg, "Negro Fiction in America," *So. Atl. Quar.*, XLV (1946), 477–488.

Other special studies include Ernest E. Leisy, "The American Historical Novel," in *Elizabethan Studies . . . in Honor of George F. Reynolds*, Boulder, Colo., 1945, pp. 307–313; Joseph Mersand, *Traditions in American Literature: A Study of Jewish Characters and Authors*, Brooklyn, N.Y., 1939; Richard A. Foster, *The School in American Literature*, Baltimore, 1930; Ima H. Herron, *The Small Town in American Literature*, Durham, N.C., 1939; Frank P. Donovan, *The Railroad in Literature: A Brief Survey . . .*, Boston, 1940; Howard W. Hintz, *The Quaker Influence in American Literature*, New York, 1940; and Morris E. Speare, *The Political Novel: Its Development in England and in America*, New York, 1924.

Brief studies include Charles I. Glicksberg, "Proletarian Fiction in the United States," *Dalhousie Rev.*, XVII (1937), 22–32; and Harold Strauss, "Realism in the Proletarian Novel," *Yale Rev.*, XXVIII (1938), 360–374. The impact of foreign literatures or writers is discussed in Carl J. Weber, "Thomas Hardy and His New England Editors," *New Eng. Quar.*, XV (1942), 681–699; Albert Schinz, "Le Livre français aux Etats-Unis," *Revue de Paris*, Feb. 15, 1936, pp. 893–906; H. H. Salls, "Joan of Arc in English and American Literature," *So. Atl. Quar.*, XXXV (1936), 167–184; R. M. Peterson, "Echoes of the Italian Risorgimento in Contemporaneous American Writers," *PMLA*, XLVII (1932), 220–240; C. F. Potter, "The Hindu Invasion of America," *Mod. Thinker*, I (1932), 16–23; Ernest R. Moore, "The Influence of the Modern Mexican Novel on the American Novel," *Revue de Littérature Comparée*, XIX (1939), 123–127; Sturgis E. Leavitt, "Latin American Literature in the United States," *ibid.*, XI (1931), 126–148; and Roy T. House, "Strong Meat in Hispanic-American Fiction," *Southwest Rev.*, XXIX (1944), 245–251. See also Francis Magyar, "American Literature in Hungary," *Books Abroad*, VI (1932), 151–152.

Anthologies

*The Best American Short Stories* . . ., a compilation begun by Edward J. O'Brien in 1915, is currently edited by Martha Foley. Blanche C. Williams began editing the annual *O. Henry Memorial Award Prize Stories* . . . in 1921; the compilation was taken over in 1944 by Herschel Brickell.

An annotated anthology, from Irving to Edna Ferber, is Fred L. Pattee, ed., *Century Readings in the American Short Story,* New York, 1927. Two earlier collections are William D. Howells, ed., *The Great Modern American Stories: An Anthology,* New York, 1920; and Alexander Jessup, ed., *Representative American Short Stories,* Boston, 1923.

Bibliography

The fullest bibliography dealing with the history of the novel is in Arthur H. Quinn, *American Fiction,* New York, 1936, pp. 726–777. A bio-bibliography of present-day writers is Fred B. Millett, *Contemporary American Authors,* New York, 1940. Two special bibliographies compiled by Janet M. Agnew are *A Southern Bibliography: Fiction, 1929–1938,* University, La., 1939, and *A Southern Bibliography: Historical Fiction, 1929–1938,* University, La., 1940.

See also the Guide to Resources: Fiction, *ante,* p. 18.

*Poetry since 1910*
Primary Sources

Of American poets who have achieved first rank in the twentieth century only Edwin Arlington Robinson had published any of his writings before 1910. His earliest volume, *The Torrent and the Night Before,* appeared in 1896. At the turn of the century the best known of the new poets were Paul Laurence Dunbar, whose *Lyrics of Lowly Life* were issued in 1896; Edwin (Charles) Markham, recognized for his two volumes, *The Man with the Hoe and Other Poems* (1899), and *Lincoln and Other Poems* (1901); William Vaughn Moody, whose first poetic play, *The Masque of Judgment,* was issued in 1900; and the California poet George Sterling, who published *The Testimony of the Suns* in 1903. Representative of the period was (Joseph) Trumbull Stickney (1874–1904), whose *Poems* (1905) were posthumously issued by W. V. Moody and others.

The so-called New Poetry movement flourished after 1910, and Chicago was one of its important centers. It was in Chicago that Harriet Monroe founded *Poetry: A Magazine of Verse* (1912), and it was through *Poetry* that recognition came to the best of the Chicago poets: Vachel Lindsay, who published *The Congo and Other Poems* in 1914; and Carl Sandburg, whose

*Chicago Poems* appeared in 1916. Sandburg's *Cornhuskers* (1918) received a special Pulitzer award in 1919. Edgar Lee Masters's Midwestern portraits were published as *Spoon River Anthology* (1915). For data on Dunbar, Lindsay, Masters, Robinson, Sandburg, and Sterling, see the individual bibliographies herein. A life of Markham (1852–1940) is William L. Stidger, *Edwin Markham,* New York, 1933.

The Imagist movement, which had started in England, was popularized in the United States through the pages of *Poetry.* The most active Imagist was Amy Lowell, whose first volume of verse, *A Dome of Many-Coloured Glass,* appeared in 1912. Hilda Doolittle ("H. D."), one of the best of the Imagists, published her first volume of verse, *Sea Garden,* in 1916. Other important members of the movement were William Carlos Williams, whose volume *The Tempers* appeared in 1913, and John Gould Fletcher, whose *Irradiations* (1915) and *Goblins and Pagodas* (1916) are representative examples of the movement. James Oppenheim (1882–1932), who edited the *Seven Arts* (1916–1917), had already published *Songs for the New Age* (1914). His collected verse appeared as *The Sea* (1924). The great influence of Ezra Pound on experimentation began to be felt during this decade. Historically important are Gertrude Stein's *Tender Buttons* (1914); *Profiles from China* (1917), by Eunice Tietjens (b. 1884); and Edna St. Vincent Millay's *Renascence and Other Poems* (1917). The fastidious poems of Adelaide Crapsey (1878–1914), written in her last year, were influenced by the Japanese *hokku,* and posthumously published as *Verse* (1915). The experimental poetry of Alfred Kreymborg (b. 1883) is represented by *Mushrooms: 16 Rhythms* (1915). It was reissued as *Mushrooms: A Book of Free Forms* (1916), and in a revised edition, 1928. Witter Bynner (b. 1881) published *Grenstone Poems* in 1917, and recognition was accorded Sara Teasdale by a special Pulitzer award in 1918 for her volume, *Love Songs* (1917). For data on Doolittle, Fletcher, Amy Lowell, Millay, Pound, Stein, Stevens, Teasdale, and Williams, see the individual bibliographies herein.

The decade of the twenties is notable for the excellence and variety of poetic achievement. T. S. Eliot published his influential volume of critical essays, *The Sacred Wood,* in 1920 and brought out what still remains one of the most distinguished volumes of poetry written in this century, *The Waste Land,* in 1922. The Pulitzer poetry prize was thrice awarded to E. A. Robinson during the decade: for his *Collected Poems* in 1922, *The Man Who Died Twice* in 1925, and *Tristram* in 1928. Robert Frost, to whom the prize was twice awarded during the thirties, first received it in 1924 for his collection *New Hampshire.* Notable work during the decade was produced by Elinor Wylie, whose sonnet sequences may be represented by her first published volume, *Nets to Catch the Wind* (1921). Other achievements during the decade are represented by Marianne Moore, *Poems* (1921); Wallace Stevens,

*Harmonium* (1923); E. E. Cummings, *Tulips and Chimneys* (1923); Robinson Jeffers, *Tamar and Other Poems* (1924); (Frederic) Ridgely Torrence, *Hesperides* (1925); Langston Hughes, *The Weary Blues* (1926); Stephen Vincent Benét, *John Brown's Body* (1928—Pulitzer Prize award, 1929); and Conrad Aiken, *Selected Poems* (1929—Pulitzer Prize award, 1930). For data on Aiken, Benét, Cummings, Eliot, Frost, Hughes, Jeffers, Moore, and Wylie, see the individual bibliographies herein.

Other representative work of the period is Countee Cullen, *Color* (1925); James Weldon Johnson, *God's Trombones: Seven Negro Sermons in Verse* (1927); Léonie Adams, *High Falcon, and Other Poems* (1929); Malcolm Cowley, *Blue Juniata* (1929); and Merrill Moore, *The Noise That Time Makes* (1929). The sonnet sequence of William Ellery Leonard, *Two Lives* (1923), is autobiographical in nature.

Perhaps the most distinguished of the younger poets during the decade of the thirties was Hart Crane, a Symbolist of originality, whose volume *The Bridge* appeared in 1930. *The Collected Poems of Hart Crane* were issued in 1933, the year following his death. Other achievement during the decade is represented by Archibald MacLeish, *Conquistador* (1932—Pulitzer Prize award, 1933); James Whaler, *Green River: A Poem for Rafinesque* (1931)—a minor classic; James Agee, *Permit Me Voyage* (1934); Clinton Scollard, *The Singing Heart* (1934); Muriel Rukeyser, *A Turning Wind: Poems* (1939); John Crowe Ransom, *Selected Poems* (1945); Howard Phelps Putnam, *The Five Seasons* (1931); Horace Gregory, *Poems, 1930–1940* (1941); Louise Bogan, *Poems and New Poems* (1941); R. P. Blackmur, *From Jordan's Delight* (1937); Allen Tate, *Selected Poems* (1937); Genevieve Taggard, *Collected Poems, 1918–1938* (1938); Laura Riding, *Collected Poems* (1938); Mark Van Doren, *Collected Poems, 1922–1938* (1939); Yvor Winters, *Poems* (1940); Kenneth Fearing, *Collected Poems of Kenneth Fearing* (1940); and John Peale Bishop, *Selected Poems* (1941). For data on Hart Crane and MacLeish, see the individual bibliographies herein. Willard Thorp compiled "Allen Tate: A Checklist," *Princeton Univ. Lib. Chron.*, III (1942), 85–98; and J. M. Patrick and R. W. Stallman, "John Peale Bishop: A Checklist," *ibid.*, VII (1946), 62–79.

The decade was also one in which southern regionalism was represented by Donald Davidson, *Lee in the Mountains, and Other Poems,* Boston, 1930; Robert Penn Warren, *Eleven Poems on the Same Theme* (1942); and Jesse Stuart, *Man with a Bull-Tongue Plow* (1934). Paul Engle's *Corn* (1939) is a volume of poems mainly inspired by the Middle West.

Of the youngest poets who have already made a contribution, John Brooks Wheelwright (1897–1940) may be represented by *Selected Poems* (1941); Karl Jay Shapiro by his first book, *Person, Place and Thing* (1942); and Delmore Schwartz by *Genesis* (1943). Other young poets whose work has shown distinction are Richard Eberhart, *Reading the Spirit* (1936); Kimball Flaccus, *The White Stranger: Poems* (1940); Howard Nutt, *Special Laughter: Poems* (1940); Howard Baker, *A Letter from the Country* (1941); Norman Macleod, *We Thank You All the Time: Poems* (1941); Randall Jarrell, *Blood for a Stranger* (1942); Kenneth Patchen, *Cloth of the Tempest* (1943), Frederic Prokosch, *Chosen Poems* (1944); and Marya Zaturenska, *The Golden Mirror* (1944).

## Anthologies

In 1912 Mitchell Kennerley published one of the earliest and most important anthologies of new poetry in *The Lyric Year: One Hundred Poems,* edited by Ferdinand Earle. It represented, according to the preface, "one year's work of a hundred American poets." William S. B. Braithwaite's *Anthology of Magazine Verse and Year Book of American Poetry* was an annual collection first issued, Boston, 1913, and continued for some fifteen years. Three Imagist anthologies were edited by Amy Lowell, all entitled *Some Imagist Poets* (1915, 1916, 1917). Alfred Kreymborg, under the title *Others,* edited three anthologies of experimental verse in 1916, 1917, and 1920. Historically interesting is Louis Zukofsky's *An "Objectivists" Anthology,* Boston, 1932. New Directions, a publishing group established in Norfolk, Connecticut, undertook to publish an annual anthology of poetry in 1940 called *Five Young American Poets,* and writers under thirty who had not published a book of verse were invited to compete for a place in it. Three volumes were issued, in 1940, 1941, and 1944. Thus a new and significant means was offered for literary experiment. Oscar Williams has edited *New Poems: An Anthology of British and American Verse,* New York, 1940–1944, 4 vols. A significant regional anthology was edited by Yvor Winters, *Twelve Poets of the Pacific,* Norfolk, Conn., 1937. Other collections are Louis Untermeyer, ed., *Modern American Poetry: A Critical Anthology,* 6th rev. ed., New York, 1942—one of the best general collections, including some nineteenth century writings; Conrad Aiken, ed., *Modern American Poets* (1922), revised and published in the Modern Library, New York, 1927; Harriet Monroe and A. C. Henderson, eds., *The New Poetry: An Anthology,* rev. and enl., New York, 1932; and Marguerite Wilkinson, ed., *Contemporary Poetry,* New York, 1923.

## Poetry Criticism

Few satisfactory histories of American poetry have been published. The most recent is Horace Gregory and Marya Zaturenska, *A History of American Poetry, 1900–1940,* New York, 1946. An early history of the Symbolist and

Imagist movements is Amy Lowell's *Tendencies in Modern American Poetry*, Boston, 1917. The reviews of the work of the new poets in the files of *Poetry* during the first decade of its publication are important. Historical studies include Edmund Wilson, *Axel's Castle: A Study in the Imaginative Literature of 1870–1930*, New York, 1931; Glenn Hughes, *Imagism and the Imagists: A Study in Modern Poetry*, Stanford Univ., Calif., 1931—a factual history with bibl., pp. 253–270; and Henry W. Wells, *The American Way of Poetry*, New York, 1943—from Freneau to the present. For a French estimate see René Taupin, *L'Influence du Symbolisme Français sur la Poésie Américaine (de 1910 à 1920)*, Paris, 1929.

The best poetry criticism published during the thirties includes Kenneth Burke, *Counter-Statement*, New York, 1931—emphasizing the psychological basis of literary forms; Allen Tate, ed., *The American Review*, Vol. III (May, 1934), 172–265—a poetry supplement with critical essays by John Crowe Ransom, Cleanth Brooks, and Robert Penn Warren; Allen Tate, *Reactionary Essays on Poetry and Ideas*, New York, 1936; Babette Deutsch, *This Modern Poetry*, New York, 1935—with bibl., pp. 295–302; R[ichard] P. Blackmur, *The Double Agent: Essays in Craft and Elucidation*, New York, 1935; Yvor Winters, *Primitivism and Decadence: A Study of American Experimental Poetry*, New York, 1937—an attack on "modernist" poetry; John Crowe Ransom, *The World's Body*, New York, 1938; and Cleanth Brooks, *Modern Poetry and the Tradition*, Chapel Hill, N.C., 1939. For a German study see Friedrich Bruns, *Die Amerikanische Dichtung der Gegenwart*, Leipzig, 1930. See also Charles I. Glicksberg, "Negro Poets and the American Tradition," *Antioch Rev.*, VI (1946), 243–253, and Herbert Read and others, "The Present State of Poetry," *Kenyon Rev.*, I (1939), 359–398.

Earlier volumes of criticism include Conrad Aiken, *Scepticisms: Notes on Contemporary Poetry*, New York, 1919; Louis Untermeyer, *American Poetry Since 1900*, New York, 1923; Llewellyn Jones, *First Impressions . . .* , New York, 1925; G[eorge] R. Elliott, *The Cycle of Modern Poetry . . .* , Princeton, 1929; Bruce Weirick, *From Whitman to Sandburg in American Poetry: A Critical Survey*, New York, 1924; and Alfred Kreymborg, *Our Singing Strength . . .* , New York, 1929, republished as *A History of American Poetry . . .* (1934))—with much attention to poetry since 1900. See also Richard F. Jones, "Nationalism and Imagism in Modern American Poetry," *Washington Univ. Stud.*, XI (1923), 97–130; and William L. Schwartz, "L'Appel de l'Extrême-Orient dans la poésie des Etats-Unis," *Revue de Littérature Comparée*, VIII (1928), 113–126.

A recent volume is Horace Gregory, *The Shield of Achilles: Essays on Beliefs in Poetry*, New York, 1944.

## Memoirs and Autobiographies

Among memoirs and autobiographies, three are useful for their personal recollection of Chicago writers, especially the poets: Harry Hansen, *Midwest Portraits: A Book of Memories and Friendships,* New York, 1923; Edgar Lee Masters, *Across Spoon River: An Autobiography,* New York, 1936; and Harriet Monroe, *A Poet's Life: Seventy Years in a Changing World,* New York, 1938—with its account of the founding of *Poetry.*

Recollections of early twentieth century poets are in Jessie B. Rittenhouse, *My House of Life: an Autobiography,* Boston, 1934. Further reminiscences are those of Malcolm Cowley, *Exile's Return . . . ,* New York, 1934; John G. Fletcher, *Life Is My Song: The Autobiography of John Gould Fletcher,* New York, 1937; Carolyn Wells, *The Rest of My Life,* Philadelphia, 1937; Eunice Tietjens, *The World at My Shoulder,* New York, 1938—with informative chapters on *Poetry* and the *Little Review*; and Louis Untermeyer, *From Another World: The Autobiography of Louis Untermeyer,* New York, 1939—with some discussion of experimental magazines.

## Bibliography

Useful bibliographies on the subject of twentieth century American poetry are Kirker Quinn and others, "American Poetry, 1930–1940: A Record of Poetry Publication in the United States During the Last Decade," *Accent,* I (1941), 213–228—a checklist; Allen Tate, *Recent American Poetry and Poetic Criticism: A Selected List of References,* Washington, 1943, 13 pp.; and *idem, Sixty American Poets, 1896–1944 . . . ,* Washington, 1945, with a bibliography of their writing compiled by Frances Cheney, 188 pp.

Bio-bibliographies for most of the writers discussed in this essay are in Fred B. Millett, *Contemporary American Authors,* New York, 1940.

## Drama:
### The Early Years (dates for plays are of production)

The poetic drama of William Vaughn Moody won him some measure of recognition at the turn of the century. For data on Moody, see the individual bibliography herein.

The *Poems and Plays* (2 vols., 1916) of Percy (Wallace) MacKaye (b. 1875) is a collection of his most representative work. On MacKaye, see "Percy MacKaye and the Drama as Spectacle," in Arthur H. Quinn, *A History of the American Drama from the Civil War to the Present Day,* rev. ed., New York, 1936, II, 27–49. A further study is "The Playwright as

Pioneer: Percy MacKaye," in Thomas H. Dickinson, *Playwrights of the New American Theater,* New York, 1925, pp. 1–55. The earliest of the dramas of Stark Young (b. 1881) is *Guenevere* (1906). The dramatic writing of Susan Glaspell (b. 1882) includes *Trifles* (1916), and *Inheritors* (1921). On MacKaye, Young, and Glaspell, see the bio-bibliographies in Fred B. Millett, *Contemporary American Authors,* New York, 1940. Langdon Mitchell (1862–1935) is best remembered for *The New York Idea* (1906). Jesse Lynch Williams (1871–1921) achieved notice with *The Stolen Story* (1906); *Why Marry?* (1917); and *Lovely Lady* (1925).

## The Twenties

On the most significant dramatists during the decade following the First World War—Eugene O'Neill, Philip Barry, and Maxwell Anderson—see the individual bibliographies herein. The first and best play of Gilbert Emery (b. 1875) is *The Hero* (1921). John Howard Lawson (b. 1895) is represented by his expressionistic plays, *Roger Bloomer* (1923), and *Processional* (1925). Sidney (Coe) Howard (1891–1939) is remembered for such plays as *They Knew What They Wanted* (1924), and *The Silver Cord* (1926). George (Edward) Kelly (b. 1887) achieved some success with *The Show-Off* (1924), *Craig's Wife* (1925), and other plays. For bio-bibliographies of Lawson, Howard, and Kelly (to 1940), see Millett.

The plays of Paul (Eliot) Green (b. 1894) include *In Abraham's Bosom* (1926), *The Field God* (1927), *The House of Connelly* (1931), and *Roll, Sweet Chariot* (1934). Barrett H. Clark's biographical sketch was published as *Paul Green,* New York, 1928. See also A. E. Malone, "An American Folk-Dramatist: Paul Green," *Dublin Mag.,* n.s. IV (1929), 31–42. A bibliography (to 1935) appears in Allan G. Halline, *American Plays,* New York, 1935, pp. 766–767.

Rachel Crothers (b. 1878) is represented by *He and She* (1920), *Nice People* (1920), *Mary the Third* (1923), *Let Us Be Gay* (1929), and *When Ladies Meet* (1932). A critical study is "Rachel Crothers and the Feminine Criticism of Life," in Arthur H. Quinn, *A History of the American Drama from the Civil War to the Present Day,* rev. ed., New York, 1936, II, 50–62. A bio-bibliography of Crothers (to 1940) is in Millett.

## Recent Playwrights

For a bibliographical account of the most significant among recent playwrights, S. N. Behrman, Clifford Odets, Elmer Rice, and William Saroyan, see the individual bibliographies herein.

The achievement of Marc(us Cook) Connelly (b. 1890) appeared most notably in his play *The Green Pastures* (1930), based on Roark Bradford's stories of the Negro's concept of Old Testament history. Lynn Riggs (b. 1899) wrote *Green Grow the Lilacs* (1931), and, more recently, *Russet Mantle* (1936). The earliest play of Martin Flavin (b. 1883), *The Blind Man* (1926), was followed, among others, by *The Criminal Code* (1930), and *Tapestry in Gray* (1936). Sidney Kingsley (b. 1906) achieved success with *Dead End* (1935), and *The World We Make* (1939). The best play of Thornton (Niven) Wilder (b. 1897) is *Our Town* (1938). For bio-bibliographies of Connelly, Riggs, Kingsley, and Wilder (to 1940), see Millett. See also Henry Adler, "Thornton Wilder's Theatre," *Horizon,* XII (1945), 89–98.

Two of the best known of the earlier plays of Robert (Emmet) Sherwood (b. 1896) are *This Is New York* (1931), and *Reunion in Vienna* (1932); more recent are *The Petrified Forest* (1935), *Idiot's Delight* (1936), and *Abe Lincoln in Illinois* (1939). Two later studies of Sherwood are Robert C. Healey, "Anderson, Saroyan, Sherwood: New Directions," *Cath. World,* CLII (1940), 174–180; and Oscar J. Campbell, "Robert Sherwood and His Times," *College English,* IV (1943), 275–280. A bio-bibliography (to 1940) is in Millett.

George S. Kaufman (b. 1889) has produced most of his plays in collaboration. For farcical satire, he may be represented by *You Can't Take It with You* (1936), written with Moss Hart; for satire of political life, by *Of Thee I Sing* (1932), with Morrie Ryskind—lyrics by Ira Gershwin; for character satire, by *The Royal Family* (1928) and *Dinner at Eight* (1932), with Edna Ferber. On Kaufman, see Thomas H. Dickinson, *Playwrights of the New American Theater,* New York, 1925, pp. 237–250; Burns Mantle, *American Playwrights of Today,* New York, 1929, pp. 86–92; Carl Carmer, "George Kaufman: Playmaker to Broadway," *Theatre Arts Monthly,* XVI (1932), 807–815; Joseph Wood Krutch, "The Random Satire of George S. Kaufman," *Nation,* CXXXVII (1933), 156–158; and Montrose J. Moses, "George S. Kaufman," *No. Amer. Rev.,* CCXXXVII (1934), 76–83. A bio-bibliography (to 1940) is in Millett.

The dramatic productions of Lillian Hellman (b. 1905) may be represented by *The Children's Hour* (1934), *The Little Foxes* (1939), and *Watch on the Rhine* (1941). The proletarian plays of Albert Maltz (b. 1908) include *Merry-Go-Round* (1932), and *Black Pit* (1935).

The Works Progress Administration operated a Federal Theatre Project during 1936–1939. It established, under the direction of Hallie Flanagan, several production units throughout the country. Among the many dramatic compositions on social and political problems, employing an experimental technique, were *Injunction Granted* (1936), and *Power* (1937). Two series of

*Federal Theatre Plays* were issued in 1938. A history of the Project is Hallie Flanagan (Davis), *Arena: The Story of the Federal Theatre* (1940).

Anthologies

Of the many collections of plays which have been issued, the best include Arthur H. Quinn, *Contemporary American Plays,* New York, 1923; *idem, Representative American Plays from 1880 to the Present Day,* New York, 1928; Thomas H. Dickinson, *Contemporary Drama: English and American,* Boston, 1925; and Richard A. Cordell, *Representative Modern Plays, British and American, from Robertson to O'Neill,* New York, 1929.

More recent anthologies are E. Bradlee Watson and Benfield Pressey, *Contemporary Drama: American Plays,* New York, Vol. I, 1931; Vol. II, 1938; John Gassner, *Twenty Best Plays of the Modern American Theatre,* New York, 1939 (Second Series, 1947); Frank W. Chandler and Richard A. Cordell, *Twentieth Century Plays, American,* New York, 1939; Harlan Hatcher, *Modern American Dramas,* New York, 1941; and Bennett Cerf and Van H. Cartmell, *Sixteen Famous American Plays,* New York, 1941.

For collections of one-act plays, there are Frank Shay, *Twenty Contemporary One-Act Plays,* New York, 1921 (rev. ed., 1922); Barrett H. Clark and Kenyon Nicholson, *The American Scene* [*A Collection of 34 Modern One-Act Plays*], New York, 1930; and William Kozlenko, *Contemporary One-Act Plays: Radio Plays, Folk Plays, Social Plays,* New York, 1938. Since 1937 Margaret G. Mayorga has published an annual volume of *The Best One-Act Plays* . . . The volumes include bibliographies and cover stage, screen, and radio.

Special collections are Frank Shay, *The Provincetown Plays,* New York, 1916, 3 vols.; George P. Baker, [*Harvard Plays*]: *Plays of the 47 Workshop,* New York, 1918–1925, 4 vols.; Alain Locke and Montgomery Gregory, *Plays of Negro Life: A Source-Book of Native American Drama,* New York, 1927 —20 plays with an introd. and bibl.; Kathryn Coe and William H. Cordell, *A New Edition of the Pulitzer Prize Plays,* New York, 1935—20 plays, from O'Neill's *Beyond the Horizon* to Sherwood's *Abe Lincoln in Illinois;* and William Kozlenko, *The Best Short Plays of the Social Theatre,* New York, 1939.

A useful collection, and one of the first to include early plays, is Arthur H. Quinn, *Representative American Plays: From 1767 to the Present Day,* 6th ed., New York, 1938; it includes introd. and bibl., and has been completely revised since it was first issued in 1917. Allan G. Halline, in *American Plays,* New York, 1935, supplies critical introds. and bibl. for the 17 selections from Royall Tyler to Paul Green. Montrose J. Moses compiled *Representative Plays by American Dramatists from 1765 to the Present Day,* New York 3 vols.: Vol. I (1918) includes the years 1765–1819; Vol. II (1925) makes selections through 1858; and Vol. III (1921) concludes with the year 1911.

## Criticism and Bibliography

Though there has been much critical writing about the American theater, comparatively little attention has been devoted to American drama. The standard history is Arthur H. Quinn, *A History of the American Drama from the Beginning to the Civil War,* rev. ed., New York, 1943 (first published in 1923), with extensive bibliographical essays and a play list, pp. 395–462. Quinn continued his study in *A History of the American Drama from the Civil War to the Present Day,* 2 vols., rev. ed., 1936 (first published in 1927), with bibliography and play list, Vol. II, pp. 305–402.

Montrose J. Moses and John M. Brown edited *The American Theatre as Seen by Its Critics, 1752–1934,* New York, 1934—chiefly valuable for the period after 1900. Moses's *The American Dramatist,* rev. ed., Boston, 1918, is useful for the period after 1870.

Other special studies include John G. Hartman, *The Development of American Social Comedy from 1787 to 1936,* Philadelphia, 1939; Margaret G. Mayorga, *A Short History of the American Drama: Commentaries on Plays Prior to 1920,* New York, 1932—with extensive bibliographies, pp. 357–472; and Douglas Gilbert, *American Vaudeville: Its Life and Times,* New York, 1940.

Two pioneer studies of twentieth century drama are Richard Burton, *The New American Drama,* New York, 1913; and Thomas H. Dickinson, *The Case of American Drama,* Boston, 1915. Later surveys include Archibald Henderson, *The Changing Drama: Contributions and Tendencies,* Cincinnati, 1919; Thomas H. Dickinson, *Playwrights of the New American Theater,* New York, 1925; idem, *An Outline of Contemporary Drama,* New York, 1927; Burns Mantle, *American Playwrights of Today,* New York, 1929, continued in idem, *Contemporary American Playwrights,* New York, 1938.

One of the best studies for the period covered is Joseph Wood Krutch, *The American Drama Since 1918: An Informal History,* New York, 1939. Other studies of recent drama include Eleanor Flexner, *American Playwrights, 1918–1938: The Theatre Retreats from Reality,* New York, 1938; Ethel T. Rockwell, *American Life as Represented in Native One-Act Plays,* Madison, Wis., 1931; Frank H. O'Hara, *Today in American Drama,* Chicago, 1939; and Clarence J. Wittler, *Some Social Trends in WPA Drama,* Washington, D.C., 1939.

Norman S. Weiser edited *The Writer's Radio Theater, 1940–1941: Outstanding Plays of the Year,* New York, 1941—ten plays written for a new medium. See also Norman Corwin, *More by Corwin: 16 Radio Dramas,* New York, 1944; and the individual bibliography on Archibald MacLeish.

Impressionistic studies include John Anderson, *Box Office,* New York, 1929; George Jean Nathan, *Testament of a Critic,* New York, 1931; and *idem, The Theatre of the Moment: A Journalistic Commentary,* New York, 1936.

The best bibliographies are those in the histories written by Quinn and by Mayorga, already mentioned. An indispensable annual is that issued by Burns Mantle since 1920: *The Best Plays . . . and the Year Book of the Drama in America.* For further bibliographical guidance, see the section Guide to Resources: Drama, *ante,* p. 19.

## The Essay and Social Criticism
Literary Journalism and the Essay

The informal or personal essay, which occupied a distinguished position in nineteenth century magazines, has been less popular since 1914. Its place has been taken by more analytical articles, often devoted to political and social problems raised by contemporary events. Nevertheless, a large number of well known writers continue to be associated with the personal essay, often presented in columns or as syndicated features of newspapers, or as sketches in such magazines as the *New Yorker, Harper's,* or the *Atlantic.* Since these essays have frequently been distinguished on the lighter side, see the section herein on Folk Tales and Humor, *post,* p. 202.

One of the earliest columnists was E(dgar) W(atson) Howe (1853–1937), editor and proprietor (1877–1911) of the Atchison, Kansas, *Daily Globe.* His column regularly appeared as "Globe Sights." Eugene Field (1850–1895) established his reputation for wit and whimsy in his column "Sharps and Flats," a feature of the Chicago *Daily News* (1883–1895). Another Chicago journalist, Bert L. Taylor (B.L.T.), conducted his column "A Line o' Type or Two" in the Chicago *Tribune* (1900–1920). He had an enthusiastic following. Finley Peter Dunne (1867–1936), also a Chicago journalist, is remembered for his shrewd dialect sketches beginning with *Mr. Dooley in Peace and in War* (1898), and concluding with *Mr. Dooley on Making a Will* (1919). Dunne served as editor of *Collier's* in 1918–1919.

Well known among later literary journalists is Don(ald Robert Perry) Marquis (1878–1937). His column "The Sun Dial" appeared in the New York *Evening Sun* from 1912 to 1920; he then transferred to the New York

*Tribune,* where his sketches appeared in "The Lantern" column for two years following. The best of his essays and verse are published as *The Old Soak* (1921), and *archy and mehitabel* (1927). The essays of Heywood (Campbell) Broun (1888–1939) were issued in such collections as *Seeing Things at Night* (1921)—a gathering of his theater criticism—and *Sitting on the World* (1924). His column in the New York *World,* "It Seems to Me," appeared during the twenties. Alexander (Humphreys) Woollcott (1887–1943) served as drama critic for the New York *Times* 1914–1922, and succeeded Heywood Broun as drama critic on the New York *World* in 1927. Representative essays by Woollcott are published in *Shouts and Murmurs* (1922) and *While Rome Burns* (1934). Ben Hecht (b. 1894) began as a reporter for the Chicago *Daily News* in 1914. Essays dealing with his observations are gathered in *A Thousand and One Afternoons in Chicago* (1922), and *Tales of Chicago Streets* (1924). Robert (Charles) Benchley (1889–1945) was associated with the New York *World* 1920–1921. He is best remembered as drama critic for *Life* (1920–1929), and for the *New Yorker.* Representative of his essays are *Of All Things* (1921), and *The Treasurer's Report* (1930). Clarence (Shepard) Day (1874–1935) contributed to *Harper's,* and later to the *New Republic* in its early years. Representative collections by Day are *This Simian World* (1920) and *Life with Father* (1935).

Franklin P(ierce) Adams (F. P. A., b. 1881) is remembered for "The Conning Tower," conducted in the New York *World* (1922–1931). The best of the essays were gathered as *The Conning Tower Book* (1926), and *The Second Conning Tower Book* (1927). More recently published is *The Melancholy Lute: Selected Songs of Thirty Years* (1936). Dorothy Parker (b. 1893), as book reviewer for the *New Yorker* (1927), conducted her column "The Constant Reader." Her stories and sketches include *Laments for the Living* (1930), and *Here Lies: The Collected Stories of Dorothy Parker* (1939).

Among the older essayists who wrote in the personal and informal tradition, two of the best known are Agnes Repplier (b. 1858), represented by the collection *Eight Decades: Essays and Episodes* (1937); and Samuel McChord Crothers (1857–1927), whose volumes include *The Gentle Reader* (1903), and *The Cheerful Giver* (1923). Important though less well known is Frank Moore Colby (1865–1925), whose early essays, *Imaginary Obligations* (1904), were gathered with later ones and edited by Clarence Day as *Colby Essays* (1926)—a minor classic. The tradition was continued by Christopher (Darlington) Morley (b. 1890): *Shandygaff . . .* (1918) is the first of his many collections of essays. Widely read among current writers in the same tradition are James Thurber (b. 1894), associated with the *New Yorker* since 1926; and E(lwyn) B(rooks) White (b. 1899), associated with

the *New Yorker* since its founding in 1925 and with *Harper's Magazine.*
Thurber's publications include *The Owl in the Attic and Other Perplexities*
(1931), and *My Life and Hard Times* (1933). White's *One Man's Meat*
(1942) is a representative collection. Elliot Paul (b. 1891) has contributed
sketches in *The Life and Death of a Spanish Town* (1937), and *Concert
Pitch* (1938)—dealing with American expatriates. Ludwig Bemelmans
(b. 1898) is represented by his collection of hotel stories, *Hotel Bemelmans'*
(1946).

Some journalists have been chiefly concerned with social and political
comment. The picturesque and vivid reporting of Richard Harding Davis
(1864–1916) appears in such a collection as *Notes of a War Correspondent*
(1910). The European news reporting of John Reed (1887–1920) was gathered as *The War in Eastern Europe* (1916), and *Ten Days That Shook the
World* (1919)—a distinguished report of the Russian Revolution. A biography
of Reed is Granville Hicks, *John Reed: The Making of a Revolutionary*
(1936). Stuart Chase (b. 1888) has dealt mainly with social and economic
problems, in such volumes as *The Tragedy of Waste* (1925), *Men and
Machines* (1929), and *Rich Land, Poor Land* (1936). Walter Lippmann
(b. 1889) was associated with the *New Republic* at its inception in 1914.
During the twenties he was the leading editorial commentator for the New
York *World,* and since 1931 has been a regular contributor to the New York
*Herald Tribune.* The first of his many political and social studies, *A Preface
to Politics* (1913), has been followed by such volumes as *A Preface to Morals*
(1929), and *The Good Society* (1937). Among this group should be named
Max Eastman, who helped found the *Masses* in 1911, and served as editor
for several years. His essays include *Journalism Versus Art* (1916), and *Art
and the Life of Action, with Other Essays* (1934). Bernard De Voto (b. 1897)
assumed charge of the column "The Easy Chair" in *Harper's* in 1935.
Representative of his journalistic essays is *Forays and Rebuttals* (1936).
Herbert Agar (b. 1897) surveyed American culture in *Land of the Free*
(1935).

Vivid first-hand reporting of observations made among the maladjusted
and incompetent is in Eleanor Rowland Wembridge's *Life Among the
Lowbrows* (1931). Two collections of sketches and stories by the journalist
and sports columnist (Alfred) Damon Runyon (1884–1946) are *Guys and
Dolls* (1932), and *Take It Easy* (1938). The best known reporting of the
journalist (James) Vincent Sheean (b. 1899) is his *Personal History* (1935)—
round-the-world impressions.

Significant war journalism is John Hersey's "Hiroshima"—a summary
account of the first atomic-bomb explosion in Japan, which occupied the
entire issue of the *New Yorker,* Aug. 31, 1946.

## Nature Essays

As a genre, the nature essay has been surprisingly undeveloped. For data on the most widely read of early twentieth century nature writers, John Burroughs and John Muir, see the individual bibliographies herein. Henry van Dyke (1852–1933) contributed such volumes as *Little Rivers* (1895); and William Beebe (b. 1877) achieved a popular notice with *Jungle Peace* (1918), and *Edge of the Jungle* (1921). Donald Culross Peattie (b. 1898) recorded his nature observations in *An Almanac for Moderns* (1935), and *A Book of Hours* (1937). Theodore Roosevelt's account of an exploration trip was published as *Through the Brazilian Wilderness* (1914).

The most useful study of nature observers during the nineteenth century is Norman Foerster, *Nature in American Literature: Studies in the Modern View of Nature,* New York, 1923—essays on the major nineteenth century observers from Bryant to Burroughs. See also P. M. Hicks, *Development of the Natural History Essay in American Literature,* Philadelphia, 1924.

## Memoirs and Autobiographies

Among the autobiographies and reminiscences dealing primarily with the literary background of which the writers were a part, several are of especial interest. Ludwig Lewisohn's *Up Stream: An American Chronicle* (1922), and *Mid-Channel: An American Chronicle* (1929) are memoirs of a novelist and critic, born in Berlin, who was brought as a child to the United States. The autobiographical works of Theodore Dreiser which describe his middle western background and his Chicago years were published as *A Traveler at Forty* (1913); *A Hoosier Holiday* (1916); *Dawn: A History of Myself* (1931)—first published as *A Book About Myself* in 1922; and *Newspaper Days: A History of Myself* (1931). Significant also are Edith Wharton, *A Backward Glance* (1934); Thomas Wolfe, *The Story of a Novel* (1936); H. L. Mencken, *Happy Days, 1880–1892* (1940), *Newspaper Days, 1899–1906* (1941), *Heathen Days, 1890–1936* (1943); George Santayana, *Persons and Places* (2 vols., 1944–1945); and Gertrude Atherton, *My San Francisco: A Wayward Biography,* Indianapolis, 1946. For data on Hamlin Garland's autobiographical chronicles, see the individual bibliography herein.

*The Autobiography of Lincoln Steffens* (3 vols., 1931) describes the part he played in the muckraking movement and his effort to expose business and government corruption. Louis Adamic, who immigrated to the United States from Yugoslavia, records his observations in *Laughing in the Jungle: The Autobiography of an Immigrant in America* (1932), and *The Native's Return . . .* (1934).

Other valuable memoirs are those of Gertrude Atherton, *Adventures of a Novelist,* New York, 1932; Mary Austin, *Earth Horizon: Autobiography* (1932); Upton Sinclair, *American Outpost: A Book of Reminiscences* (1932); Mary Ellen Chase, *A Goodly Heritage* (1932) continued in *A Goodly Fellowship* (1939); Gertrude Stein, *The Autobiography of Alice B. Toklas* (1933); and Paul Elmer More, *Pages from an Oxford Diary* (1937).

Logan Pearsall Smith's *Unforgotten Years* (1938) gives details of his Quaker boyhood in Philadelphia and his acquaintance with Whitman.

The recollections of Sherwood Anderson are valuable source material, particularly about the Chicago writers. They were published as *A Story-Teller's Story* (1924) and *Sherwood Anderson's Memoirs* (1942). Similar is Edgar Lee Masters, *Across Spoon River: An Autobiography* (1936).

Other participants in the literary scene during the twentieth century who have published memoirs and recollections include Gamaliel Bradford, *A Naturalist of Souls* (1917) and *Life and I* (1928); Waldo Frank, *Salvos: An Informal Book About Books and Plays,* New York, 1924; Floyd Dell, *Homecoming: An Autobiography* (1933); Henry S. Canby, *The Age of Confidence: Life in the Nineties* (1934); and *Alma Mater: The Gothic Age of the American College* (1936)\*; Malcolm Cowley, *Exile's Return: A Narrative of Ideas* (1934); Bliss Perry, *And Gladly Teach* (1935); Harold E. Stearns, *The Street I Know,* New York, 1935; Carl Van Doren, *Three Worlds* (1936); Albert Jay Nock, *Memoirs of a Superfluous Man* (1943); Channing Pollock, *Harvest of My Years: An Autobiography* (1943); and Mary Colum, *Life and the Dream* (1947). The wide acquaintance of William Lyon Phelps with writers of his time gives his *Autobiography with Letters* (1939) some value as source material for the period. See also M[ark] A. De Wolfe Howe, *John Jay Chapman and His Letters* (1937), and *idem, A Venture in Remembrance* (1941)—an autobiography.

Observers of the literary scene whose memoirs discuss and interpret literary personalities include Mabel Dodge Luhan (b. 1879). Her four volumes of *Intimate Memories* were issued as *Intimate Memories: Background* (1933)**,** *European Experiences* (1935), *Movers and Shakers* (1936), and *Edge of Taos Desert: An Escape to Reality* (1937); the volumes include letters from John Reed, Walter Lippmann, Gertrude Stein, and E. A. Robinson.

Letters and Journals

There are few published letters or journals of twentieth century American writers. The best are *Life and Letters of Stuart P. Sherman,* ed. by Jacob Zeitlin and Homer Woodbridge (2 vols., 1929); *The Journal of Gamaliel*

---

\* The story is carried into the 1940's in *American Memoir* (1947).

*Bradford, 1883–1932* (1933), and *The Letters of Gamaliel Bradford, 1918–1931* (1934), both edited by Van Wyck Brooks; and *Anne Douglas Sedgwick: A Portrait in Letters* (1936), edited by her husband, Basil De Selincourt.

Mark A. De Wolfe Howe edited *Holmes-Pollock Letters: The Correspondence of Mr. Justice Holmes and Sir Frederick Pollock, 1874–1932,* Cambridge, 1941, 2 vols.—well indexed, with scattered comments on books and authors—as well as *Touched with Fire: Civil War Letters and Diary of Oliver Wendell Holmes, Jr., 1861–1864,* Cambridge, 1946. The writings of Oliver Wendell Holmes (1841–1935) have been in part edited by Harry C. Shriver as *The Judicial Opinions of Oliver Wendell Holmes . . . ,* Buffalo, N.Y., 1940; and by Alfred Lief in *The Dissenting Opinions of Mr. Justice Holmes,* New York, 1929. Holmes's classic study, *The Common Law,* appeared in 1881. A biography is Silas Bent, *Justice Oliver Wendell Holmes,* New York, 1932. See also Elizabeth S. Sergeant, "Oliver Wendell Holmes," in *Fire Under the Andes,* New York, 1927, pp. 307–331; and Daniel J. Boorstin, "The Elusiveness of Mr. Justice Holmes," *New Eng. Quar.,* XIV (1941), 478–487.

## Studies of Non-Fictional Prose

An examination of prose technique through an analysis of major American writers is Gorham B. Munson, *Style and Form in American Prose,* New York, 1929. Adaline M. Conway, *The Essay in American Literature,* New York, 1914, though inadequate as a study, has a useful bibliography, pp. 85–127. See also Joseph W. Beach, *The Outlook for American Prose,* New York, 1926.

An anthology of 32 prose selections from Franklin to the date of publication is Brander Matthews, *The Oxford Book of American Essays,* New York, 1914.

A critical survey of literary journalism, biography, and autobiography is in Fred B. Millett, *Contemporary American Authors,* New York, 1940, pp. 153–180. Many of the writers discussed above are supplied with bio-bibliographies by Millett.

A useful checklist is Harry B. Weiss, "American Letter-Writers, 1698–1943," *Bul. N.Y. Pub. Lib.,* XLVIII (1944), 959–982; XLIX (1945), 36–61.

## INSTRUMENTS OF CULTURE AND LITERARY PRODUCTION
### Professional Authorship

The Authors' League of America was founded in 1912 to give protection to copyright material. The membership, numbering between four and five thousand persons, is divided among various Guilds of dramatists, artists, authors, and screen writers.

For the manner in which serious authors of the generation after 1910 earned their livings, see various biographies and autobiographies. Especially useful are Alfred Kreymborg, *Troubadour* (1925); Dorothy Dudley, *Forgotten Frontiers: Dreiser and the Land of the Free* (1932); Edgar Lee Masters, *Vachel Lindsay* (1935); *idem, Across Spoon River* (1936); Philip Horton, *Hart Crane* . . . (1937); John Gould Fletcher, *Life Is My Song* (1937); Hermann Hagedorn, *Edwin Arlington Robinson: A Biography* (1938); John S. Terry, ed., *Thomas Wolfe's Letters to His Mother* . . . (1943); Harry Hansen, *Midwest Portraits* (1943); and F. Scott Fitzgerald, *The Crack-Up* (1945), edited by Edmund Wilson. The money-making career of a big-money writer is described in Joan London, *Jack London and His Times* . . . (1939).

Publishers' confessions frequently document the position of professional writers. Among the frankest are Walter Hines Page, *A Publisher's Confession,* rev. ed., New York, 1923; and George H. Doran, *The Chronicles of Barabbas, 1884-1934,* New York, 1935. One of the best descriptions of author-publisher relationships is Roger Burlingame, *Of Making Many Books: A Hundred Years of Reading, Writing, and Publishing,* New York, 1946—including hitherto unpublished letters from Thomas Wolfe, F. Scott Fitzgerald, Edith Wharton, and others. See also the sections on author-publisher relationships and on books and the book trade in the period bibliographies preceding.

There has been no comprehensive study of authorship during the depression years of the thirties. Some of the authors' complaints are set forward in the report of the Second American Writers' Congress: *The Writer in a Changing World,* edited by Henry Hart, New York, 1937. Magazine material on the subject is plentiful, especially in the files of the *Modern Monthly,* the *New Masses,* and the *Partisan Review.* See also Burton Rascoe and Groff Conklin, eds., *The Smart Set Anthology,* New York, 1934 (and 1937).

As part of the program of the Works Progress Administration, the Federal Writers' Project was organized under the direction of Henry G. Alsberg, and functioned during the years 1935-1939. At one time some 6,600 workers were employed in state and local branches. The most enduring result was the publication of the American Guide Series, compilations which supply valuable data for all the states and many cities. There has been no book on the Federal Writers' Project. A comprehensive catalog of its American Guide Series was printed by Brentano's, New York, in 1941.

Documentary evidence of the poverty of writers and the cheapening of popular taste is in R. P. Blackmur, "The Economy of the American Writer," *Sewanee Rev.,* LV (1945), 175-185. A discussion of the sociology of the American writer is William Barrett, "The Resistance," *Partisan Rev.,* XIII (1946), 479–488.

## Books and the Book Trade

The first full-length study of all aspects of book production and distribution is Hellmut Lehmann-Haupt (with Ruth S. Granniss and Lawrence C. Wroth), *The Book in America: A History of the Making, the Selling, and the Collecting of Books in the United States,* New York, 1939, with bibl., pp. 385–422—translated from the German ed., Leipzig, 1937. See Clarence S. Brigham, "History of Book Auctions in America," *Bul. N.Y. Pub. Lib.,* XXXIX (1935), 55–89.

For mass publishing, see *Some Observations on the Future of Books,* a pamphlet by James T. Farrell (New Directions, 1946); also "Book Publishing," an article in the Aug. 15, 1945, issue of *Tide;* and "Books by the Millions," by Malcolm Cowley, *New Republic,* CIX (1943), 482–485.

For a listing of publishers, magazines, book clubs, and literary agencies, see *The Literary Marketplace,* published annually since 1941 by the R. R. Bowker Company, New York.

The fullest account of the book industry for the period covered is Orion H. Cheney, *Economic Survey of the Book Industry, 1930–1931,* New York, 1931. Documentary articles on the bureaucratic and collectivist methods of the magazines are John Bainbridge, "The Little Magazine," *New Yorker,* XXI (1945), the five issues from Nov. 17 through Dec. 15.

A brief account of a recent phenomenon is John K. Hutchens, "Publishing's Lively Child: The Twenty-five Cent Reprint," *New York Times Book Review,* May 5, 1946, pp. 3, 45. For further data on mass publishing, see the section herein on Best Sellers, *post,* p. 218.

For book clubs, see "For Better or Worse: The Book Clubs," by John K. Hutchens—the leading article in the *New York Times Book Review,* Mar. 31, 1946; "The Book-of-the-Month Club," by Richard H. Rovere, *American Mercury,* LVIII (1944), 434–441; and "Author's Jack Pot," by William Thornton Martin (Pete Martin), *Sat. Eve. Post,* July 6, 1946 (Vol. CCXIX), pp. 12–13.

The fiftieth anniversary number of the *New York Times Book Review* (Oct. 6, 1946) contains a number of well informed articles on the history of the book trade.

## Censorship

The best among general studies of censorship are Charles R. Gillett, *Burned Books . . . ,* New York, 1932; and Morris L. Ernst and William

Seagle, *To the Pure: A Study of Obscenity and the Censor,* New York, 1928, Two literary figures central in the fight against censorship were Theodore Dreiser and H. L. Mencken. See Dorothy Dudley, *Forgotten Frontiers: Dreiser and the Land of the Free,* New York, 1932; and H. L. Mencken, "Puritanism as a Literary Force"—the final chapter in his *A Book of Prefaces,* New York, 1917. See also Mencken's three volumes of autobiography, *passim.* Judge John M. Woolsey's decision lifting the ban on James Joyce's *Ulysses* is reprinted in full in the first American edition of *Ulysses* (New York, 1934). For a discussion of censorship of the movies, see Channing Pollock, "Swinging the Censor," in the *Bulletin* of the Authors' League of America, for Mar., 1917.

*Publishers' Reminiscences*

Shrewd observations on personalities and the literary scene appear in Henry Holt, *Garrulities of an Octogenarian Editor* . . . , New York, 1923— one of the most distinguished among publishers' memoirs. Some comment on the rapid growth of magazine publication during the early twentieth century is in Edward W. Bok, *The Americanization of Edward Bok,* New York, 1920. Other memoirs are Grant Overton, *Portrait of a Publisher: and The First Hundred Years of the House of Appleton, 1825–1925,* New York, 1925; George H. Doran, *Chronicles of Barabbas, 1884–1934,* New York, 1935; Frederick A. Stokes, *A Publisher's Random Notes, 1880–1935,* New York, 1935; Charles E. Goodspeed, *Yankee Bookseller: Being the Reminiscences of Charles E. Goodspeed,* Boston, 1937—largely anecdotal but well indexed; George P. Putnam, *Wide Margins: A Publisher's Autobiography,* New York, 1942; and Ferris Greenslet, *Under the Bridge: An Autobiography,* Boston, 1943—publishers' memoirs (Houghton Mifflin Company), well indexed, and source material for the years 1900–1940.

Lively sketches of literary society, especially of novelists in New York, Boston, and Chicago, is Irene and Allen Cleaton, *Books and Battles: American Literature, 1920–1930,* New York, 1937. Anecdotal literary reminiscences are in Elizabeth Jordan, *Three Rousing Cheers,* New York, 1938. For some material not elsewhere easily available on the New York literary scene during the decade 1907–1917, see Laurence J. Gomme, "The Little Book-Shop Around the Corner," *Colophon,* n.s. II (1937), 573–601. A brief history is Dorothea Lawrance Mann, *A Century of Bookselling: The Story of the Old Corner Bookstore* . . . , Boston, 1928.

# BACKGROUND

## CIVILIZATION IN THE UNITED STATES

IDEAS AND INSTITUTIONS:
*General Studies*

One of the significant studies of American history and civilization is Charles A. and Mary R. Beard, *The Rise of American Civilization,* New York, 1927, 2 vols. (rev. and enl., 1933, with Vol. III added in 1939 and Vol. IV in 1942). It deals chiefly with political aspects, stressing the economic forces which have molded society. Stimulating and informative also is Ralph H. Gabriel, *The Course of American Democratic Thought: An Intellectual History Since 1815,* New York, 1940. A critical survey of ideologies in American culture is Oscar Cargill, *Intellectual America: Ideas on the March,* New York, 1941. It essays to trace the impact of certain European ideas or modes of thought and feeling on American literature, with interest primarily centered in the period since 1900. A balanced and informed interpretation is Merle Curti, *The Growth of American Thought,* New York, 1943. Curti's *The Roots of American Loyalty,* New York, 1946, deals with the patriotic ideal. An earlier survey, written with a socialist bias, is Gustavus Myers, *The History of American Idealism,* New York, 1925. Still one of the most stimulating interpretations of American literature is Vernon L. Parrington's *Main Currents in American Thought,* New York, 1927–1930, 3 vols.

George Santayana's *Character and Opinion in the United States* (1920) discusses the conflict of materialism and idealism in American life. Interpretive essays in American literary history and scholarship are Howard M. Jones, *Ideas in America,* Cambridge, 1944. The contemporary scene is surveyed in Ralph B. Perry, *Puritanism and Democracy,* New York, 1944. See also Rushton Coulborn, Clyde Kluckhohn, and John Peale Bishop, "The American Culture: Studies in Definition and Prophecy (I—The Polity, II—The Way of Life, III—The Arts)," *Kenyon Rev.,* III (1941), 143–190. A brief but well informed estimate by an Englishman is D. W. Brogan, *The American Character,* New York, 1944.

Arthur M. Schlesinger and Dixon Ryan Fox edited *A History of American Life,* New York, 1927–1944, 12 vols., a standard survey of social growth, each volume contributed by an authority. A useful two-volume survey is Samuel E. Morison and Henry S. Commager, *The Growth of the American*

*Republic,* 3rd ed., New York, 1942, 2 vols. A social survey of America facing east is Francis P. Miller and Helen D. Hill, *The Giant of the Western World: America and Europe in a North-Atlantic Civilization,* New York, 1930. A collection of social and cultural remains, which furnishes valuable illustrations for much of American literature, is Ralph H. Gabriel, ed., *The Pageant of America: A Pictorial History of the United States,* New Haven, 1925-1929, 15 vols. An anthology of source material, preponderantly economic, is Louis M. Hacker and Helene S. Zahler, eds., *The Shaping of the American Tradition,* New York, 1947, 2 vols., with text supplied by Hacker.

Useful material dealing with the historical approach is Harry Elmer Barnes, *A History of Historical Writing,* Norman, Okla., 1937. Material on the growth of historical writing in America is furnished in Michael Kraus, *The History of American History,* New York, 1937. Invaluable is *Dictionary of American History,* ed. by James T. Adams and others, New York, 1940, 6 vols., a compilation arranged by subject headings.

A monument of cartography is Justin Winsor, ed., *Narrative and Critical History of America,* Boston, 1884-1889, 8 vols.—still useful for its notes and critical bibliography.

## Political and Economic Studies

Standard studies are Arthur M. Schlesinger, *Political and Social Growth of the American People, 1860-1940,* rev. ed., New York, 1941; Joseph Dorfman, *The Economic Mind in American Civilization, 1606-1865,* New York, 1946, 2 vols.; Peter H. Odegard and E. Allen Helms, *American Politics: A Study in Political Dynamics,* New York, 1938; Charles E. Merriam, *A History of American Political Theories,* New York, 1903—a survey from colonial times to the close of the nineteenth century; *idem, American Political Ideas,* New York, 1923—an authoritative study meagerly utilized by literary investigators; Lewis H. Haney, *History of Economic Thought . . . ,* rev. ed., New York, 1936; Fred A. Shannon, *Economic History of the People of the United States,* New York, 1934; Harold U. Faulkner, *American Political and Social History,* 4th ed., New York, 1945, with bibl., pp. 745-792; *idem, American Economic History,* 5th ed., New York, 1943—with a 52-page bibl. entirely reset; Ernest L. Bogart and Donald L. Kemmerer, *Economic History of the American People,* rev. ed., New York, 1942; Benjamin F. Wright, *American Interpretations of Natural Law: A Study in the History of Political Thought,* Cambridge, 1931—with useful discussions of the natural rights philosophy; Raymond G. Gettell, *History of American Political Thought,* New York, 1928; and Thomas A. Bailey, *A Diplomatic History of the American People,* New York, 1940. Francis W. Coker's *Recent Political Thought,* New York,

1934, is a review of dominant political ideas, both the theory and the practice, from mid-nineteenth century to date of publication. Two useful surveys are William S. Carpenter, *The Development of American Political Thought*, Princeton, 1930; and Samuel F. Bemis, *A Diplomatic History of the United States*, rev. ed., New York, 1942. A standard physiographic study is Ellen C. Semple, *American History and Its Geographic Conditions*, Boston, 1903. Nationalism is the subject of Albert K. Weinberg's *Manifest Destiny: A Study of Nationalist Expansionism in American History*, Baltimore, 1935.

Special studies dealing with the social and financial development of the United States include Morris Hillquit, *History of Socialism in the United States*, New York, 1903; Richard A. Lester, *Economics of Labor*, New York, 1941; Gustavus Myers, *History of the Great American Fortunes*, Chicago, 1910, 3 vols.—revised in one volume for the Modern Library, 1936; John R. Commons and others, *History of Labor in the United States*, New York, Vols. I and II (1918), Vols. III and IV, for the years 1896–1932 (1935); Anthony Bimba, *The History of the American Working Class*, New York, 1927—a survey from colonial times; Philip S. Foner, *History of the Labor Movement in the United States*, New York, 1947; Victor S. Clark, *History of Manufactures in the United States*, New York, 1929, 3 vols.; Adolf A. Berle, Jr., and Gardiner C. Means, *The Modern Corporation and Private Property*, New York, 1932 (rev. ed., 1937); Louis Adamic, *Dynamite: The Story of Class Violence in America*, New York, 1931—from the unorganized, spasmodic riots in the 1830's to the racketeering of the 1930's; Joseph Schafer, *The Social History of American Agriculture*, New York, 1936; Roger Burlingame, *March of the Iron Men: A Social History of Union Through Invention*, New York, 1938—a popular technological history of the influence of inventions in shaping American society down to 1865, continued in his *Engines of Democracy: Inventions and Society in Mature America*, New York, 1940; and Davis R. Dewey, *Financial History of the United States*, 12th ed., New York, 1934. Two biographical studies which treat figures important in financial and industrial development are Allan Nevins, *John D. Rockefeller: The Heroic Age of American Business*, New York, 1940, 2 vols.; and W. J. Lane, *Commodore Vanderbilt: An Epic of the Steam Age*, New York, 1942.

*Society and the Group*

Though poorly organized, a basic study is Arthur W. Calhoun, *A Social History of the American Family from Colonial Times to the Present*, Cleveland, 1917–1919, 3 vols.—reprinted in one volume, New York, 1945. Robert C. Angell, *The Integration of American Society: A Study of Groups and*

*Institutions,* New York, 1941, is an analysis of American society in terms of functional groups and their relationship. Dixon Wecter's *The Saga of American Society: A Record of Social Aspirations, 1607–1937,* New York, 1937, is national in scope and supplies useful data for the literature of manners, with bibliographical essays, pp. 485–493. Wecter discusses the rise and decline of American reputations in *The Hero in America: A Chronicle of Hero-Worship,* New York, 1941. Lillian Symes and Travers Clement, in *Rebel America: The Story of Social Revolt in the United States,* New York, 1934, trace the story from Robert Owen and David Dale to date of publication. A general appraisal of nativism is John M. Mecklin, *The Ku Klux Klan: A Study of the American Mind,* New York, 1924. See also T. V. Smith, *The American Philosophy of Equality,* Chicago, 1927. A classic study of the Negro is Gunnar Myrdal, *An American Dilemma: The Negro·Problem and Modern Democracy,* New York, 1944.

Two studies in *A History of American Life* edited by Schlesinger and Fox (*ante,* p. 173) which supply useful reference material are Harold U. Faulkner, *The Quest for Social Justice, 1898–1914,* New York, 1931, and Preston W. Slosson, *The Great Crusade and After, 1914–1928,* New York, 1930. Valuable as source material is Mark Sullivan's six-volume study of *Our Times: The United States, 1900–1925,* New York, 1926–1935. Largely devoted to the period 1900–1915 is Louis Filler, *Crusaders for American Liberalism,* New York, 1939—which supplies a link between American literature and American social history. Frederick Lewis Allen's *Only Yesterday: An Informal History of the Nineteen-Twenties,* New York, 1933, is continued in his *Since Yesterday: The Nineteen-Thirties in America,* New York, 1940. Robert S. Lynd and Helen M. Lynd analyzed a typical Midwestern community in terms of its function in *Middletown: A Study in Contemporary American Culture,* New York, 1929. Using the same "interview" technique, they restudied "Middletown" eight years later in *Middletown in Transition: A Study in Cultural Conflicts,* New York, 1937. Primary material is available in *These Are Our Lives: As Told by the People and Written by Members of the Federal Writers' Project . . . ,* Chapel Hill, N.C., 1939—confined largely to North Carolina, Tennessee, and Georgia.

Special studies include Gustavus Myers, *History of Bigotry in the United States,* New York, 1943—largely since the Civil War, with emphasis on anti-Semitism; Foster Rhea Dulles, *America Learns to Play: A History of Popular Recreation, 1607–1940,* New York, 1940, emphasizing sports, with notes on theaters and movies, and a bibl., pp. 375–390; and Arthur M. Schlesinger, *Learning How to Behave,* New York, 1946, a study of etiquette books from Cotton Mather to Emily Post. See also John A. Krout, *Annals of American Sport,* New Haven, 1929, with illustrations and bibl., pp. 338–347.

*Philosophy*

For contributions by and about William James, George Santayana, and John Dewey, see the individual bibliographies herein.

Two other leading twentieth century philosophers are William Ernest Hocking (b. 1873) and Alfred North Whitehead (1861–1947). Hocking's representative works include *The Meaning of God in Human Experience* (1912), *The Lasting Elements of Individualism* (1937), *Thoughts on Death and Life* (1937), and *Science and the Idea of God* (1944). Whitehead came to the United States in 1924. His later works include *Science and the Modern World* (1925), *Process and Reality* (1929—a major contribution), *Adventures of Ideas* (1933), and *Nature and Life* (1934).

Realists in philosophy may be represented by Walter B. Pitkin, William Pepperell Montague, and Ralph Barton Perry, who collaborated in *The New Realism: Coöperative Studies in Philosophy* (1912). Arthur O. Lovejoy and others collaborated on *Essays in Critical Realism: A Co-operative Study of the Problem of Knowledge* (1920). Lovejoy's *The Revolt Against Dualism ...* appeared in 1930. A study of values written by a layman is Walter Lippmann's *A Preface to Morals* (1929).

Representative collections include George P. Adams and William Pepperell Montague, eds., *Contemporary American Philosophy: Personal Statements,* New York, 1930, 2 vols.—professions of faith by 34 "older" philosophers; Clifford Barrett, ed., *Contemporary Idealism in America,* New York, 1932—defenses of idealism; Horace M. Kallen and Sidney Hook, eds., *American Philosophy Today and Tomorrow,* New York, 1935—professions of faith by 25 "younger" philosophers; and Paul R. Anderson and Max H. Fisch, eds., *Philosophy in America from the Puritans to James,* New York, 1939—representative selections with brief introductory essays and bibl., pp. 543–562.

A source book is Herbert Schneider, *A History of American Philosophy,* New York, 1946, a survey from early times to the present. A standard general history of schools of American philosophy is I[saac] Woodbridge Riley, *American Thought from Puritanism to Pragmatism,* rev. ed., New York, 1925. Other authoritative studies are Ralph B. Perry, *Philosophy of the Recent Past: An Outline of European and American Philosophy Since 1860,* New York, 1926; A. K. Rogers, *English and American Philosophy Since 1800,* New York, 1922; and Jay W. Fay, *American Psychology Before William James,* New Brunswick, N.J., 1939. T. V. Smith's *The Philosophic Way of Life in America,* rev. ed., New York, 1942, deals principally with the past fifty years.

Stow S. Person's *Free Religion: An American Faith,* New Haven, 1947, is a study of the evolution and influence of free religious attitudes.

*Religion*

A leading contemporary philosopher of religion is Reinhold Niebuhr (b. 1892), whose representative works include *Beyond Tragedy* (1937), *Christianity and Power Politics* (1940), *The Nature and Destiny of Man* (2 vols., 1941–1943), and *The Children of Light and the Children of Darkness* . . . (1944). Other religious leaders, together with a representative volume of their writings, include Rufus M. Jones (b. 1863), *New Studies in Mystical Religion* (1927), Harry Emerson Fosdick (b. 1878), *Christianity and Progress* (1922), and Edgar Sheffield Brightman (b. 1884), *A Philosophy of Religion* (1940).

General Studies

Authoritative surveys for the intelligent layman are Willard L. Sperry, *Religion in America,* New York, 1946, and William W. Sweet, *The Story of Religion in America,* rev. ed., New York, 1939, with bibl., pp. 599–624. An interpretive, non-sectarian history is Thomas C. Hall, *The Religious Background of American Culture,* Boston, 1930. Useful for the non-English-speaking groups' contribution to the growth of religious freedom and for a study of the separation of church and state is Evarts B. Greene, *Religion and the State: The Making and Testing of an American Tradition,* New York, 1941. Henry N. Wieman and Bernard E. Meland discuss contemporary religious thought in *American Philosophies of Religion,* Chicago, 1936. Other authoritative accounts are Frank H. Foster, *The Modern Movement in American Theology: Sketches in the History of American Protestant Thought from the Civil War to the World War,* New York, 1939; Winfred E. Garrison, *The March of Faith: The Story of Religion in America Since 1865,* New York, 1933; Henry K. Rowe, *The History of Religion in the United States,* New York, 1924; Stewart G. Cole, *The History of Fundamentalism,* New York, 1931; and Arthur S. Hoyt, *The Pulpit and American Life,* New York, 1921. An early objective account of the activities of all sects is Leonard W. Bacon, *A History of American Christianity,* New York, 1897.

New England

The standard account dealing with New England still remains Frank H. Foster, *A Genetic History of the New England Theology,* Chicago, 1907. See also *The Religious History of New England,* Cambridge, 1917—the King's Chapel Lectures on seven denominations by John W. Platner, William W. Fenn, Rufus M. Jones, and others; Joseph Haroutunian, *Piety Versus Moralism: The Passing of the New England Theology,* New York, 1932; and

Daniel D. Williams, *The Andover Liberals: A Study in American Theology,* New York, 1941.

## Denominations

Still authoritative for Congregationalism is Henry M. Dexter, *The Congregationalism of the Last Three Hundred Years, as Seen in Its Literature,* New York, 1880—with a very extensive bibliography. The standard short history is Williston Walker, *A History of the Congregational Churches in the United States,* New York, 1894, supplemented by Gaius G. Atkins and Frederick L. Fagley, *History of American Congregationalism,* Boston, 1942.

The standard source book for the Episcopal Church is William S. Perry, *The History of the American Episcopal Church: 1587–1883,* Boston, 1885, 2 vols.

Unitarianism has most recently been studied in Earl M. Wilbur, *A History of Unitarianism: Socinianism and Its Antecedents,* Cambridge, 1945. The account supplements the earlier history by George W. Cooke, *Unitarianism in America: A History of Its Origin and Development,* Boston, 1902.

For a history of the Quakers there is Rufus M. Jones, *The Faith and Practice of the Quakers,* New York, 1927.

The extensive history of Catholicism to 1866 is John G. Shea, *History of the Catholic Church in the United States,* New York, 1886–1892, 4 vols. Two brief popular surveys are George N. Shuster, *The Catholic Spirit in America,* New York, 1927, and Theodore Maynard, *The Story of American Catholicism,* New York, 1943. See also G. J. Garraghan, *The Jesuits of the Middle United States,* New York, 1938, 3 vols.

Other standard denominational histories are H. E. Jones, *A History of the Evangelical Lutheran Church in the United States,* New York, 1893; J. H. Dubbs, *History of the Reformed Church,* New York, 1895; and C. Henry Smith, *The Story of the Mennonites,* Berne, Ind., 1941. An objective and detailed life of the founder of Christian Science is that by Ernest S. Bates and J. V. Dittemore, *Mary Baker Eddy,* New York, 1932. A study of the Mormons is Nels Anderson, *Desert Saints: The Mormon Frontier in Utah,* Chicago, 1942.

Two analyses of denominations in the class structure are H[elmut] Richard Niebuhr, *The Social Sources of Denominationalism,* New York, 1929; and Elmer T. Clark, *The Small Sects in America,* Nashville, Tenn., 1938, with bibl., pp. 289–306.

A recent analysis of revivalism is William W. Sweet, *Revivalism in America: Its Origin, Growth and Decline,* New York, 1944, with bibl., pp. 183–188. An earlier account is Frank G. Beardsley, *A History of American Revivals,* New York, 1912.

## Education

The writings of Woodrow Wilson on education are significant. On Wilson, see the individual bibliography herein.

Educators who have expressed their thoughts concerning a liberal training in the modern world include Robert Maynard Hutchins (b. 1899), *The Higher Learning in America* (1936); Alexander Meiklejohn (b. 1872), *Education Between Two Worlds* (1942); and Mark Van Doren (b. 1894), *Liberal Education* (1943).

An authoritative work which deals with the history of educational thought as well as with institutions is Charles F. Thwing, *A History of Higher Education in America,* New York, 1906; supplemented by his *A History of Education in the United States Since the Civil War,* Boston, 1910. A detailed objective review is Ellwood P. Cubberley, *Public Education in the United States: A Study and Interpretation of American Educational History,* rev. and enl., Boston, 1934, with bibl. accompanying each chapter. Other standard accounts are Edgar W. Knight, *Education in the United States,* rev. ed., Boston, 1941; Paul Monroe, *Founding of the American Public School System . . . ,* New York, 1940; Elmer E. Brown, *The Making of Our Middle Schools: An Account of the Development of Secondary Education in the United States,* New York, 1903, with bibl., pp. 481–518; and Thomas Woody, *A History of Women's Education in the United States,* New York, 1929, 2 vols.—based on exhaustive research.

For over-all figures of school and college attendance during the century, see the *Statistical Abstract of the United States,* issued annually by the U.S. Department of Commerce.

Valuable surveys on teachers and teaching in the United States are Edwin E. Slosson, *The American Spirit in Education: A Chronicle of Great Teachers,* New Haven, 1921; Merle Curti, *The Social Ideas of American Educators,* New York, 1935; and Howard K. Beale, *A History of Freedom of Teaching in American Schools,* New York, 1941, with bibl., pp. 291–298.

Standard short histories of colleges are Samuel E. Morison, *Three Centuries of Harvard, 1636–1936,* Cambridge, 1936; Edward P. Cheyney, *History of the University of Pennsylvania, 1740–1940,* Philadelphia, 1940; Arthur C. Cole, *A Hundred Years of Mount Holyoke College: The Evolution of an Educational Ideal,* New Haven, 1940—with material on the crusade to make higher education available to women; and Thomas J. Wertenbaker, *Princeton, 1746–1896,* Princeton, 1946. Horace Coon, *Columbia, Colossus on the*

*Hudson,* New York, 1947, is the first in a projected American College and University Series.

Especially useful for the light it throws on the development of higher education in the United States is George H. Palmer, *The Autobiography of a Philosopher,* Boston, 1930.

Studies dealing principally with subject matter include Charles H. Handschin, *The Teaching of Modern Languages in the United States,* Washington, 1913; Benjamin Rand, "Philosophical Instruction in Harvard University from 1636 to 1906," *Harvard Graduates' Mag.,* XXXVII (1928), 29–47, 188–200, 296–311; G. Stanley Hall, "On the History of American College Text-Books and Teaching in Logic, Ethics, Psychology, and Allied Subjects," *Proc. Amer. Antiq. Soc.,* n.s. IX (1894), 137–174; and Bessie L. Pierce, *Civic Attitudes in American School Textbooks,* Chicago, 1930. Still useful is Florian Cajori, *The Teaching and History of Mathematics in the United States,* Washington, 1890. Other special studies are Robert Freeman Butts, *The College Charts Its Course: Historical Conceptions and Current Proposals,* New York, 1939—treating of the conflict between classical and utilitarian educational concepts, with bibl., pp. 427–442; and Horace M. Bond, *The Education of the Negro in the American Social Order,* New York, 1934, with bibl., pp. 465–481.

## Science

A general survey of scientific development during the nineteenth century, with chapters by specialists, is Edward S. Dana, ed., *A Century of Science in America . . . 1818–1918,* New Haven, 1918. The standard descriptive geography is Isaiah Bowman, *Forest Physiography: Physiography of the United States and Principles of Soil in Relation to Forestry,* New York, 1911. Other standard surveys are Edgar F. Smith, *Chemistry in America: Chapters from the History of the Science in the United States,* New York, 1914; George P. Merrill, *The First One Hundred Years of American Geology,* New Haven, 1924; Francis R. Packard, *History of Medicine in the United States,* New York, 1931, 2 vols.; Henry B. Shafer, *The American Medical Profession, 1733 to 1850,* New York, 1936; Richard H. Shryock, *The Development of Modern Medicine: An Interpretation of the Social and Scientific Factors Involved,* Philadelphia, 1936; David E. Smith and Jekuthiel Ginsburg, *A History of Mathematics in America Before 1900,* Chicago, 1934; and William M. and Mabel S. C. Smallwood, *Natural History and the American Mind,* New York, 1941—dealing principally with the period before 1850. See also Ralph S. Bates, *Scientific Societies in the United States,* New York, 1945.

*Historical, Scientific, and Literary Scholarship*

In addition to the many substantial studies in the history of ideas noted elsewhere throughout this essay, significant contributions to American scholarship have also been made during the twentieth century by Edward Channing (1856–1931), *History of the United States* (6 vols., 1905–1925); Charles McLean Andrews (1863–1943), *The Colonial Period of American History* (4 vols., 1934–1938); and F. S. C. Northrop (b. 1893), *The Meeting of East and West: An Inquiry Concerning World Understanding* (1946).

Influential during the twenties were James Harvey Robinson (1863–1936), *The Mind in the Making* . . . (1921); and John Herman Randall (b. 1899), *The Making of the Modern Mind* . . . (1926).

Significant archaeological contributions are James Henry Breasted (1865–1935), *A History of Egypt* (1905); Philip Ainsworth Means (b. 1892), *Ancient Civilizations of the Andes* (1931); George C. Vaillant (b. 1901), *Aztecs of Mexico: Origin, Rise and Fall of the Aztec Nation* (1941); and Sylvanus Griswold Morley (b. 1878), *The Ancient Maya* (1946). Frederick Webb Hodge (b. 1864) made important contributions to the anthropology of the Southwest, edited the *American Anthropologist* (1899–1910, 1912–1914), and headed the Bureau of Ethnology (1910–1918).

Literary scholarship in fields only incidentally allied to America is notably represented in such works as the exhaustive analysis of Samuel Taylor Coleridge's creative imagination by John Livingston Lowes (1867–1945), *The Road to Xanadu* (1927); and Arthur O. Lovejoy (b. 1873), *The Great Chain of Being: A Study of the History of an Idea* (1936).

Three of the distinguished biographies written during the twentieth century are Albert J. Beveridge (1862–1927), *The Life of John Marshall* (4 vols., 1916–1919); Carl Sandburg (b. 1878), *Abraham Lincoln* . . . (6 vols., 1926–1939); and Ralph Barton Perry (b. 1876), *The Thought and Character of William James* (1935).

THE ARTS:
*General Studies*

There are few competent studies of the development of the arts in the United States. A survey of American art from colonial times through the first quarter of the twentieth century is Eugen Neuhaus, *The History and Ideals of American Art,* Stanford University, Calif., 1931. It is supplemented by Frederick P. Keppel and Robert L. Duffus, *The Arts in American Life,* New York, 1933. Useful as a pictorial history of painting, sculpture, graphic arts, and music is Frank J. Mather, Charles R. Morey, and W. J. Henderson,

*The American Spirit in Art,* New Haven, 1927. Among the studies of Lewis Mumford which are primarily concerned with various arts allied to literature are *Sticks and Stones* . . . (1924)—an interpretation of all American civilization in terms of its architecture; *American Taste* (1929); and *The Brown Decades* . . . (1931)—a study of America's development in architecture, painting, engineering, and landscape design from the close of the Civil War to the end of the nineteenth century. Standard general studies include Theodore M. Greene, *The Arts and the Art of Criticism,* Princeton, N.J., 1940—on the interrelationship of the arts; and Katherine E. Gilbert and Helmut Kuhn, *A History of Aesthetics,* New York, 1939—a study of the general field.

## Music

A standard general survey, which supersedes earlier historical studies, is John T. Howard, *Our American Music: Three Hundred Years of It,* New York, 2nd ed., rev. and enl., 1939—well indexed, with bibl., pp. 674–700. Howard and Mendel's *Our Contemporary Composers: American Music in the Twentieth Century,* New York, 1941, continues the history and covers the decade 1930–1940. A study of American opera singers is Oscar Thompson, *The American Singer: A Hundred Years of Success in Opera,* New York, 1937. Nicolas Slonimsky's *Music Since 1900,* New York, 1938, is indexed and is useful for reference. Music of old-time fiddlers is featured in Ira W. Ford, *Traditional Music of America,* New York, 1940. William T. Upton's *Art-Song in America,* Boston, 1930, is continued by *A Supplement to Art-Song in America, 1930–1938,* Philadelphia, 1938. For studies of American hymns and hymn writing, see the section on them, *post,* p. 230.

Personal reminiscences of tin-pan alley, illustrated and indexed, with useful material on the era and subject, are Edward B. Marks, *They All Sang: From Tony Pastor to Rudy Vallée,* New York, 1935. Of special interest is Christine M. Ayars, *Contributions to the Art of Music in America by the Music Industries of Boston, 1640–1936,* New York, 1936. See also Maude Cuney-Hare, *Negro Musicians and Their Music,* Washington, 1936—a historical study, with bibl., pp. 419–423.

Henry C. Lahee's *Annals of Music in America: A Chronological Record of Significant Musical Events, from 1640 to the Present Day* . . . , Boston, 1922, includes a bibliography and is useful for reference.

## Painting and Sculpture

The best study of painting is Alan Burroughs, *Limners and Likenesses: Three Centuries of American Painting,* Cambridge, 1936. It is well illustrated and includes a bibliography, pp. 223–226. A general survey is Charles H. Caffin, *The Story of American Painting: The Evolution of Painting in America,* Garden City, N.Y., 1937. Also illustrated is Samuel Isham, *The History of American Painting,* new ed., New York, 1927. William Dunlap, who helped found the National Academy of Design (1826), wrote *A History of the Rise and Progress of the Arts of Design in the United States,* New York, 1834, 2 vols. (repr. Boston, 1918, 3 vols.)—an indispensable authority for the early period. An excellent catalog of a loan exhibition of paintings, tracing the history of the United States by way of the pictures produced by American artists, is the Metropolitan Museum's *Life in America,* New York, 1939. James T. Flexner's *America's Old Masters: First Artists of the New World,* New York, 1939, deals principally with Benjamin West, John Singleton Copley, Charles W. Peale, and Gilbert Stuart, and includes a bibliography. Of service especially to biographers seeking illustrations is *American Portraits: 1620–1825, Found in Massachusetts,* Boston, 1939, 2 vols., compiled by the Historical Records Survey of the WPA; it describes and locates the items mentioned.

Further general studies include Suzanne La Follette, *Art in America from Colonial Times to the Present Day,* New York, 1929; and Oskar F. L. Hagen, *The Birth of the American Tradition in Art,* New York, 1940.

Among special studies are Lloyd Goodrich, *Thomas Eakins: His Life and Work,* New York, 1933; *idem, Winslow Homer,* New York, 1945; Albert W. Christ-Janer, *George Caleb Bingham of Missouri: The Story of an Artist,* New York, 1940; and Jean Lipman, *American Primitive Painting,* New York, 1942.

Useful data appear in such illustrated catalogs for exhibitions of the Museum of Modern Art as *New Horizons in American Art* (1936), *Indian Art of the United States* (1941), *Americans, 1942* (1942), *Romantic Painting in America* (1943). The American Artists Series monographs issued by the Whitney Museum of American Art are important.

Though critically uneven, Lorado Taft's *The History of American Sculpture,* new ed., New York, 1930, is one of the few general histories of the subject, written by a well known sculptor. Essays by eighteen younger American artists, discussing their approach to art, form *Painters and Sculptors of Modern America,* New York, 1942, with an introduction by Monroe Wheeler. Useful for its many color plates is Peyton Boswell, Jr., *Modern American Painting,* New York, 1939. Holger Cahill and Alfred H. Barr edited *Art in America,* New York, 1935—a well illustrated but not very detailed survey of the arts of design. See also Wilhelm Reinhold Valentiner, *Origins of Modern Sculpture,* New York, 1946.

*Architecture*

A brief critical survey is Fiske Kimball, *American Architecture,* New York, 1928. A descriptive history is Thomas E. Tallmadge, *The Story of Architecture in America,* rev. ed., New York, 1936. For the modern period, see Frank Lloyd Wright, *Modern Architecture . . . ,* Princeton, 1931; and Henry R. Hitchcock, *In the Nature of Materials: 1887–1941, The Buildings of Frank Lloyd Wright,* New York, 1942—an analysis of the buildings of one of America's architects who has had great influence abroad. Talbot F. Hamlin's *The American Spirit in Architecture,* New Haven, 1926, is a pictorial history. More recently Hamlin has published *Greek Revival Architecture in America,* New York, 1944. The studies of Lewis Mumford, *Sticks and Stones* (1924) and *The South in Architecture* (1941), are suggestive.

Louis Henri Sullivan (1856–1924) was a pioneer in functional architecture. His *The Autobiography of an Idea* (1924), though rhapsodic, is indicative of trends in American architecture. See Hugh Morrison, *Louis Sullivan: Prophet of Modern Architecture,* New York, 1935.

On the work of Henry Hobson Richardson (1838–1886), one of the great nineteenth century American architects, see Henry Russell Hitchcock, Jr., *The Architecture of H. H. Richardson and His Times,* New York, 1936.

For the colonial period, see Fiske Kimball, *Domestic Architecture of the American Colonies and of the Early Republic,* New York, 1922; Joseph Jackson, *American Colonial Architecture: Its Origin and Development,* Philadelphia, 1924; and Harold D. Eberlein, *The Architecture of Colonial America,* Boston, 1915.

*Motion Pictures and the Radio*

Movies were introduced in the United States by Thomas A. Edison in 1896. The first story-film was Edwin S. Porter's *The Great Train Robbery* (1903). The first film of large scope and artistic excellence was D. W. Griffith's *The Birth of a Nation* (1915). The industry was revolutionized during the years 1927–1929 by the introduction of a synchronized sound track for spoken dialogue.

The effect of movies on the American public and of the public on the movies is studied in Margaret F. Thorp, *America at the Movies,* New Haven, 1939. A history of the subject is Lewis Jacobs, *The Rise of the American Film: A Critical History,* New York, 1939, with bibl., pp. 541–564. For an earlier analysis, see Paul Rotha, *The Film till Now: A Survey of the Cinema,* London, 1930.

The Writers' Program, New York City, began issuing *The Film Index: A Bibliography*. Volume I (1940) is devoted to "The Film as Art."

There is no competent history of the development of the radio as an art form.

## Printing

Among printers, the work of Frederic W. Goudy (1865–1947) is especially important. At his Village Press he developed notable type faces and designs for texts. His writings include *The Alphabet* (1918), and *Elements of Lettering* (1921).

The first of four projected volumes on the history of printing, intended to supersede Isaiah Thomas's *History of Printing in America* (2 vols., 1810), is Douglas C. McMurtrie, *A History of Printing in the United States: The Story of the Introduction of the Press and of Its History and Influence During the Pioneer Period in Each State of the Union,* New York, 1936. Only one volume was published. A useful compilation of selected facts is John C. Oswald, *Printing in the Americas,* New York, 1937.

See also the section, Guide to Resources in American Literary and Cultural Studies: Registries of Book Publication.

## Graphic Arts and Crafts

Frank Weitenkampf, *American Graphic Art,* new ed., New York, 1924, includes a bibl., pp. 291–298.

Scott G. Williamson, in *The American Craftsman,* New York, 1940, gives attention to glass, pottery, silver, ironwork, and welding. The volume includes useful illustrations and a bibl., pp. 219–232. For the colonial period, there is George F. Dow, *The Arts and Crafts in New England, 1704–1775,* Topsfield, Mass., 1927.

# THE AMERICAN LANGUAGE

## HISTORICAL SCHOLARSHIP

The Philological Society (*fl.* 1788-1789), a New York organization of which Noah Webster and William Dunlap were members, devoted itself informally to the promotion of an American language. The first formal study of American speech was undertaken by the linguistic scientist John Pickering in *A Vocabulary or Collection of Words and Phrases Which Have Been Supposed to Be Peculiar to the United States of America, to Which Is Prefixed an Essay on the Present State of the English Language in the United States,* Boston, 1816. In the mid-nineteenth century John R. Bartlett brought out his *Dictionary of Americanisms: A Glossary of Words and Phrases Usually Regarded as Peculiar to the United States,* New York, 1848, an important defense of American speech, prefaced by an acute discussion of the sources of Americanisms. An early and still valuable defense entitled "The English Language in America," by the American scholar Charles A. Bristed, is included in *Cambridge Essays: 1855,* London, 1855. During the winter of 1858-1859 George Perkins Marsh advocated a national independence of speech in lectures at Columbia College, published as *Lectures on the English Language,* New York, 1860 (4th ed., 1872). The study first to classify material was Maximilien Schele de Vere's *Americanisms: The English of the New World,* New York, 1872. Interest in the subject of a national language led Elias Molee to write a *Plea for an American Language; or, Germanic-English,* Chicago, 1888; and the consciousness of native forms is set forth in the compilation of John Stephen Farmer, *Americanisms—Old and New,* London, 1889.

An interesting account of British attacks upon neologisms coined by American statesmen and publicists during the early national period is given by William B. Cairns in *British Criticisms of American Writings, 1783-1815,* Madison, Wis., 1918. Such coinages were defended by Edward Everett (see Allen W. Read, "Edward Everett's Attitude Towards American English," *New Eng. Quar.* XII [1939], 112-129). The existence of a national language has been denied or deprecated until very recently. Richard Grant White attacked Bartlett's *American Glossary* (4th ed., 1877) in a series of eight extended essays in the *Atlantic Monthly,* XLI (1878), 495–502, 656–664; XLII (1878), 97–106, 342–348, 619–631; and XLIII (1879), 88–98, 379–392, 656–666. Similar views are expressed in *Americanisms and Briticisms,* New York, 1892, by Brander Matthews; and in *Academy Papers: Addresses on Language Problems . . . ,* New York, 1925, delivered before the American Academy of Arts and Letters by William C. Brownell, Brander Matthews, Henry van Dyke, and others. An account of forerunners of the Academy is Allen W. Read, "American Projects for an Academy to Regulate Speech," *PMLA,* LI (1936), 1141–1179.

More recent historical studies are Gilbert M. Tucker, *American English,* New York, 1921—marred by some careless errors; George P. Krapp, *The English Language in America,* New York, 1925, 2 vols.—eminently sound, though with emphasis on pronunciation rather than vocabulary; Fred Newton Scott, *The Standard of American Speech,* Boston, 1926; George H. McKnight, *Modern English in the Making,* New York, 1928—an excellent survey; and M(itford) M. Mathews, *The Beginnings of American English: Essays and Comments,* Chicago, 1931—a useful collection of essays by Americans written during the first fifty years of the national period, with one chapter (chap. xi) devoted to Cooper.

The most recent studies are George E. Shankle, *American Nicknames: Their Origin and Significance,* New York, 1937; Sir William A. Craigie, *The Growth of American English . . . ,* Oxford, 1940; and H(enry) L. Mencken, *The American Language: An Inquiry into the Development of English in the United States,* New York, 4th ed., 1936, corrected, enlarged, and rewritten from the 1st ed. of 1919, with its *Supplement One* (1945)— authoritative and illuminating.

SOURCE MATERIAL

A distinguished organization, founded to gather and publish material dealing with a national language, is the American Dialect Society, established by Francis James Child in 1889. The Society projected an American Dialect Dictionary in 1896. For the published results of the project, see Richard H. Thornton, *post,* p. 189. The first volume of their *Dialect Notes,* which have been issued from time to time, appeared in 1904, and the four volumes so far published are invaluable sources of material gathered by trained scholars. The first of their *Publications* was issued in 1944.

*American Speech,* a journal founded by Kemp Malone, Arthur G. Kennedy, and Louise Pound in 1925, is now issued bimonthly with a current bibliography in each issue. *Language: Journal of the Linguistic Society of America* (1925–current) is devoted to reportage of research in all aspects of scientific linguistics.

Other important articles and notes on American linguistics will be found in *S.P.E. Tracts,* published by the Society for Pure English: Nos. 1–61, Oxford, 1919–1943, 10 vols., with an Index (1934) covering Nos. 1–19. The student should also consult the issues of *Journal of American Folk-Lore,* 1888–current.

## GLOSSARIES AND DICTIONARIES

Noah Webster published *An American Dictionary of the English Language . . . ,* New York, 1828, and though he devoted relatively little attention to Americanisms as such, he assembled much material on pronunciation. The definitive biography is Harry R. Warfel, *Noah Webster: Schoolmaster to America,* New York, 1936.

Strongly opposed to Webster's innovations was Joseph Emerson Worcester (1784–1865), whose *Comprehensive Pronouncing and Explanatory Dictionary of the English Language* (1830) uncompromisingly held to orthodox British examples of spelling and pronunciation. Webster's charges of plagiarism led to the long "War of Dictionaries." Worcester's conservatism prevailed at Harvard College until mid-century, but no important revision of his dictionary appeared after 1860.

John R. Bartlett's *Dictionary of Americanisms . . . ,* New York, 1848, went through four editions by 1877, and was reprinted as late as 1896. Other early glossaries are Alfred L. Elwyn, *Glossary of Supposed Americanisms,* New York, 1859; Charles L. Norton, *Political Americanisms: A Glossary of Terms and Phrases Current at Different Periods in American Politics,* New York, 1890; and Sylva Clapin, *A New Dictionary of Americanisms: Being a Glossary of Words Supposed to Be Peculiar to the United States and the Dominion of Canada,* New York, 1902.

The first of many philological works on Americanisms to have scientific value is the compilation of Richard H. Thornton, *An American Glossary: Being an Attempt to Illustrate Certain Americanisms upon Historical Principles.* Vols. I and II were published, London, 1912; Vol. III, ed. by Percy W. Long, was published in *Dialect Notes,* VI (1931–1939), pts. iii–xviii.

*A Dictionary of American English on Historical Principles,* compiled and ed. by Sir William Craigie and James R. Hurlbert, Chicago, 1938–1944, with a large staff of collaborating specialists, is the standard work.

Other recent compilations of use in special fields are H(erbert) W. Horwill, *An Anglo-American Interpreter: A Vocabulary and Phrase Book,* Oxford, 1939; Lester V. Berrey and Melvin Van den Bark, *The American Thesaurus of Slang: A Complete Reference Book of Colloquial Speech,* New York, 1942 *; John S. Kenyon and Thomas A. Knott, *A Pronouncing Dic-*

* Revised edition, 1947.

*tionary of American English,* Springfield, Mass., 1944; and Harold Wentworth, *American Dialect Dictionary,* New York, 1944.

An excellent linguistic study of Spanish loan-words is Harold W. Bentley, *A Dictionary of Spanish Terms in English, with Special Reference to the American Southwest,* New York, 1932, with bibl., pp. 241–243.

Histories of the subject are by Stewart A. Steger, *American Dictionaries . . . ,* Baltimore, 1913, with bibliog., pp. 121–125; and M(itford) M. Mathews, *A Survey of English Dictionaries,* New York, 1933, in which the chapter on the nineteenth century is primarily concerned with American dictionaries.

## USAGE

The first American textbook of English for use in colleges was William C. Fowler, *The English Language in Its Elements and Forms,* New York, 1850; but no scientific analysis, drawing inductively upon Americanisms, was made until George O. Curme published his *Syntax,* Boston, 1931, and his *Parts of Speech and Accidence,* Boston, 1935. W(illiam) Cabell Greet, *Usage and Abusage: A Guide to Good English,* New York, 1942, is an excellent study. H(erbert) W. Horwill's *A Dictionary of Modern American Usage,* Oxford, 1935, is not authoritative.

A careful study of the contents of grammar texts appears in Robert C. Pooley, *Grammar and Usage in Textbooks on English,* Madison, Wis., 1933; and Rollo L. Lyman issued *English Grammar in American Schools Before 1850,* Washington, 1922 (*Bul. Bureau of Education,* No. 12, Dept. Interior).

The standard style book is that issued by the University of Chicago Press, *A Manual of Style,* 10th rev. ed., 1937 (first published in 1906).

## PRONUNCIATION

One of the first scientific studies is Robert J. Menner, "The Pronunciation of English in America," *Atlantic Mo.,* CXV (1915), 360–366. Later and more extended studies are George P. Krapp, *The Pronunciation of Standard English in America,* New York, 1919; Joshua H. Neumann, *American Pronunciation According to Noah Webster (1783) . . . ,* New York, 1924; John S. Kenyon, *American Pronunciation: A Textbook of Phonetics for Students of English,* Ann Arbor, Mich., 8th rev. ed., 1940; and W(illiam) Cabell Greet, *World Words: Recommended Pronunciation,* New York, 1944. Some of the national radio systems prepare manuals of pronunciation which are standard for broadcasting. See Jane D. Zimmerman, *Radio Pronunciations: A Study of Two Hundred Educated Non-professional Radio Speakers,* New York, 1946.

## REGIONAL SPEECH AND LOCALISMS

B. W. Green compiled a *Word-Book of Virginia Folk-Speech,* Richmond, Va., 1899. There is a good index to scattered passages relating to American speech as noted by early travelers in Jane L. Mesick, *The English Traveller in America, 1785-1835,* New York, 1922, pp. 240-245. Other useful compilations are Anders Orbeck, *Early New England Pronunciation as Reflected in Some Seventeenth Century Town Records of Eastern Massachusetts,* Ann Arbor, Mich., 1927; Charles C. Fries, *American English Grammar: The Grammatical Structure of Present-Day American English, with Especial Reference to Social Differences or Class Dialects,* New York, 1940; Harold Wentworth, *American Dialect Dictionary,* New York, 1944. A brief checklist is C. Alphonso Smith, "Dialect in America," *Camb. Hist. Amer. Lit.,* II (1918), 615—useful to date of publication. See also Kenneth L. Pike, *The Intonation of American English,* Ann Arbor, Mich., 1945. Lewis H. and Marguerite Herman have prepared a *Manual of American Dialects,* New York, 1947.

## LINGUISTIC GEOGRAPHY

Hans Kurath and others have issued a *Linguistic Atlas of New England,* Providence, 1939 (with bibliographies, pp. 55-61, 105-121), together with a *Handbook of the Linguistic Geography of New England,* Providence, 1939.

## BIBLIOGRAPHY

The "Bibliography" of American English in each issue of *American Speech* is an invaluable guide to the articles, pamphlets, and books in the field of speech and linguistics. The listing begins with Volume XIII (1938), and concurrently *PMLA* ceased listing language items in its annual "American Bibliography" (March Supplement). Previous to 1922, the standard listing is that of Arthur G. Kennedy, *A Bibliography of Writings on the English Language . . . ,* Cambridge, 1927, which covers the American field on pp. 336-416. Other bibliographical listings will be found in the issues of *Dialect Notes.* There is a checklist (to 1921) by Harry M. Ayres, "The English Language in America," *Camb. Hist. Amer. Lit.,* IV (1921), 810-813; and an annotated checklist (repr. from *Bul. N.Y. Public Library,* 1936-1938) in William J. Burke, *The Literature of Slang,* New York, 1939.

# FOLK LITERATURE

## SONGS AND BALLADS

Folklore collections in the United States properly began with the first issue of the *Journal of American Folk-Lore* (1888). Publications by dozens of regional and state folklore societies are augmented by hundreds of folk-song volumes, multitudes of newspaper and magazine articles, and most recently by the thousands of recordings deposited in the Archive of American Folk Song of the Library of Congress. The material has multiplied vastly during the past twenty years alone, and the listings which follow are highly selective.

### GENERAL STUDIES AND COLLECTIONS

With the publication of John A. Lomax, *Cowboy Songs and Other Frontier Ballads,* New York, 1910, the serious and widespread study of folk literature in America had its beginning. The volume, issued with a foreword by Theodore Roosevelt and an introduction by Barrett Wendell, made the claim that the origins and folklore traits of ballads in this country were comparable to those of traditional English ballads. The claim was not substantiated by the work of Louise Pound, who believed the cowboy material to be largely adaptations. Her *American Ballads and Songs,* New York, 1922, is a collection representative of the various song-types, and of their regions, with authoritative critical comment. Carl Sandburg's collection, *The American Songbag,* New York, 1927, presents appealing selections, with sensitive critical commentaries. The product of long field experience is John A. and Alan Lomax, *American Ballads and Folk Songs,* New York, 1934. It has been supplemented by the same authors' *Our Singing Country: A Second Volume of American Ballads and Folk Songs,* New York, 1941, with bibl., pp. 405–410. Other recent general collections are George P. Jackson, *Spiritual Folk-Songs of Early America: Two Hundred and Fifty Tunes and Texts with an Introduction and Notes,* New York, 1937; Carl L. Carmer, *America Sings: Stories and Songs of Our Country's Growing,* New York, 1942; Philip D. Jordan and Lillian Kessler, *Songs of Yesterday: A Song Anthology of American*

*Life,* Garden City, N.Y., 1941—lively and informative; and Benjamin A. Botkin, *A Treasury of American Folklore: Stories, Ballads, and Traditions of the People,* New York, 1944—the most representative collection of American folklore to be found in one volume.

*Folk-Say: A Regional Miscellany,* Norman, Okla., 1929–1932, 4 vols., was edited by B. A. Botkin. The four volumes, published annually, contain significant folklore, many examples of the creative use of folk material, and essays by distinguished folklorists and writers.

The greatest single medium for the publication of American folklore is the *Journal of American Folk-Lore,* mentioned above. Of the many regional and state folklore societies that have been organized and are still active, a few have published extensively. Among them should be mentioned the Texas Folk-Lore Society, whose *Publications* have been issued since 1916. Three important additions to the periodical literature of American folklore are the *Southern Folklore Quarterly* (1937–current), *California Folklore Quarterly* (1942–current), and *New York Folklore Quarterly* (1945–current).

Useful appreciations of the folklore heritage in America are in Bernard De Voto's *Mark Twain's America,* Boston, 1932, and Van Wyck Brooks, *The World of Washington Irving,* New York, 1944. Knowledge and appreciation of folk elements in American drama appear in Arthur H. Quinn's *A History of the American Drama from the Beginning to the Civil War,* rev. ed., New York, 1943; and in his *A History of the American Drama from the Civil War to the Present Day,* rev. ed., New York, 1936. Similarly understanding are Fred L. Pattee's *The New American Literature, 1890–1930,* New York, 1930, and Vernon L. Parrington's *Main Currents in American Thought,* New York, 1927–1930—though Parrington is skeptical about the folklore authenticity of the Davy Crockett legend.

One of the most concise and authoritative studies of folk literature in America is Martha W. Beckwith, *Folklore in America: Its Scope and Method,* Poughkeepsie, N.Y., 1931. Other important contributions are William W. Newell, "On the Field and Work of a Journal of American Folk-Lore," *Jour. Amer. Folk-Lore,* I (1888), 3-7; Charles M. Skinner, *American Myths and Legends,* Philadelphia, 1903, 2 vols.—"processed" folklore, but valuable; Phillips Barry, "Native Balladry in America," *Jour. Amer. Folk-Lore,* XXII (1909), 365-373; *idem,* "The Transmission of Folk-Song," *ibid.,* XXVII (1914), 67-76; Louise Pound, "New World Analogues of the English and Scottish Popular Ballads," *Mid-West Quar.,* III (1916), 171-187—a denial of the theory of communal composition of cowboy songs; Reed Smith, "The Traditional Ballad in America, 1936," *Southern Folklore Quar.,* I (1937), 13-17; and Mary Austin, "American Folk," *Folk-Say,* 1930, pp. 287-290.

The fundamental reference work for study of the English traditional ballad is the monumental collection edited by Francis James Child, *The English and Scottish Popular Ballads,* Boston, 1882–1898, 5 vols., with a few American texts. An inexpensive one-volume abridgment of Child's great collection is Helen Child Sargent and George Lyman Kittredge, eds., *English and Scottish Popular Ballads,* Boston, 1932. For general background see A. H. Krappe, *The Science of Folk-Lore,* London, 1930, and Gordon H. Gerould, *The Ballad of Tradition,* Oxford, 1932.

Further studies of folklore, particularly as they touch upon the folk tale, will be found in the section Folk Tales and Humor, *post,* p. 202.

SPECIFIC STUDIES AND COLLECTIONS:
*The North Atlantic Seaboard to Maryland*

The French folksongs of the Northeast are collected in Marius Barbeau and Edward Sapir, *Folk Songs of French Canada,* New Haven, 1925. A variety of good songs, with a lively discussion of their relation to the singers, is Fannie H. Eckstorm and Mary W. Smyth, *Minstrelsy of Maine: Folk-Songs and Ballads of the Woods and the Coast,* Boston, 1927. An excellent collection, devoted entirely to ballads of the Child type, is Phillips Barry, Fannie H. Eckstorm, and Mary W. Smyth, *British Ballads from Maine: The Development of Popular Songs, with Texts and Airs,* New Haven, 1929. Phillips Barry's *The Maine Woods Songster,* Cambridge, 1939, supplies the airs for all songs included. *Down-East Spirituals and Others,* New York, 1943, collected and edited by George P. Jackson, is a compilation from old New England and New York singing books with a discussion of their dissemination through the country. The long tradition of singing in Vermont is recorded in Helen H. Flanders and others, *The Green Mountain Songster: Traditional Folk Songs of Vermont,* New Haven, 1939. Eloise H. Linscott compiled *Folksongs of Old New England,* New York, 1939, with the airs harmonized. Further material will be found in Worthington C. Ford, *Broadsides, Ballads, etc. Printed in Massachusetts, 1639–1800,* Boston, 1922. The importance of folklore in the lives of New Englanders is suggested in Gladys H. Carroll, *Dunnybrook,* New York, 1943. See also Alice M. Earle, "Old-Time Marriage Customs in New England," *Jour. Amer. Folk-Lore,* VI (1893), 97–102.

A collection of New York folklore is that of Emelyn E. Gardner, *Folklore from the Schoharie Hills, New York,* Ann Arbor, Mich., 1937. A thorough treatment of Pennsylvania folksongs and tales is George Korson, ed., *Minstrels of the Mine Patch: Songs and Stories of the Anthracite Industry,* Philadelphia, 1938; and his companion volume, *Coal Dust on the Fiddle: Songs and Stories of the Bituminous Industry,* Philadelphia, 1943. Henry W.

Shoemaker, *Mountain Minstrelsy of Pennsylvania,* Philadelphia, 1931, is a revised and enlarged edition of his *North Pennsylvania Minstrelsy.* A comprehensive representation is that of John B. Stoudt, *The Folklore of the Pennsylvania Germans,* Philadelphia, 1916—a discussion of nursery songs, counting-out rhymes, riddles, and ballads. See also his "Pennsylvania German Riddles and Nursery Rhymes," *Jour. Amer. Folk-Lore,* XIX (1906), 113–121.

A full treatment of beliefs, customs, and superstitions in Maryland is Annie W. Whitney and Caroline C. Bullock, *Folk-Lore from Maryland,* New York, 1925.

*The South*

A classic study and collection, first published in 1917, is Cecil J. Sharp, *English Folk Songs from the Southern Appalachians,* Oxford, 1932, including 273 songs and ballads, with 968 tunes gathered by Olive Dame Campbell. Another, varied and full, is also one of the earliest scholarly editions: John H. Cox, *Folk-Songs of the South,* Cambridge, 1925. Especially useful for its critical introduction to the ballad and to ballad problems is Reed Smith, *South Carolina Ballads, with a Study of the Traditional Ballad To-day,* Cambridge, 1928. One of the notable collections restricted to ballads of the Child type is Arthur K. Davis, Jr., *Traditional Ballads of Virginia,* Cambridge, 1929. George P. Jackson's *White Spirituals in the Southern Uplands: The Story of the Fasola Folk, Their Songs, Singings, and "Buckwheat Notes,"* Chapel Hill, N.C., 1933, is a study of "spiritual folksongs." Authentic folk material is gathered in Vance Randolph, *From an Ozark Holler: Stories of Ozark Mountain Folk,* New York, 1933. The Deep South is represented in the excellent collection of Arthur P. Hudson, *Folksongs of Mississippi and Their Background,* Chapel Hill, N.C., 1936—157 items, including native as well as imported ballads and songs, with bibliography and indexes. It is supplemented by his *Folk Tunes from Mississippi,* New York, 1937 and 1938, with music ed. by George Herzog. Two other all-round collections are Dorothy Scarborough, *A Song Catcher in Southern Mountains: American Folk Songs of British Ancestry,* New York, 1937; and Mellinger E. Henry, *Folk-Songs from the Southern Highlands,* New York, 1938—193 songs, with variants, and 40 tunes.

Josiah H. Combs edited *Folk-Songs du Midi des Etats-Unis,* Paris, 1927—Kentucky, Virginia, West Virginia, Tennessee, Arkansas, Oklahoma, and Texas folksongs, with a useful account of their background (texts in English, study portions in French). Ralph S. Boggs edited "North Carolina Folktales Current in the 1820's" and "North Carolina White Folktales and Riddles,"

*Jour. Amer. Folk-Lore,* LXVII (1934), 269–328—valuable material with a bibliography. Other compilations are Harvey H. Fuson, *Ballads of the Kentucky Highlands,* London, 1931; Mellinger E. Henry, *Beech Mountain,* [N.C.] *Folk Songs and Ballads,* New York, 1936; John H. Cox, *Folk-Songs Mainly from West Virginia* . . . , New York, 1939; Louis W. Chappell, *Folk-Songs of Roanoke and the Albemarle,* Morgantown, W.Va., 1939; and Irène T. Whitfield, *Louisiana French Folk Songs,* University, La., 1939. An important early collection is that of Alcée Fortier, *Louisiana Folk-Tales in French Dialect and English Translation,* Boston, 1895 (Vol. II, *Memoirs of the American Folk-Lore Society*).

Useful special studies are Arthur P. Hudson, "The Singing South: Folk-Song in Recent Fiction Describing Southern Life," *Sewanee Rev.,* XLIV (1936), 268–295; Marie Campbell, "Survivals of Old Folk Drama in the Kentucky Mountains," *Jour. Amer. Folk-Lore,* LI (1938), 10–24; and Maurice Zolotow, "Hillbilly Boom," *Sat. Eve. Post,* Feb. 12, 1944, pp. 22–23, 36, 38. An autobiography with a folklore background is Wayman Hogue, *Back Yonder: An Ozark Chronicle,* New York, 1932. Of historic importance is H. E. Taliaferro, *Fisher's River* [N.C.], *Scenes and Characters, By "Skitt," "Who Was Raised Thar,"* New York, 1859.

## The Northwest Territory and the Central West

Collections having their origin in what geographically was first known as the Northwest Territory have only recently been published. They include Mary O. Eddy, *Ballads and Songs from Ohio,* New York, 1939; Emelyn E. Gardner and Geraldine J. Chickering, *Ballads and Songs of Southern Michigan,* Ann Arbor, Mich., 1939; Paul G. Brewster, *Ballads and Songs of Indiana,* Bloomington, Ind., 1940; Charles Neely, *Tales and Songs of Southern Illinois,* Menasha, Wis., 1938; and Theodore C. Blegen and Martin B. Ruud, *Norwegian Emigrant Songs and Ballads,* Minneapolis, 1936—translated by the editors and harmonized by Gunnar J. Malmin. An interesting example of adaptation is studied in Archer Taylor, "An Old-World Tale from Minnesota," *Jour. Amer. Folk-Lore,* XXXI (1918), 555–556.

One of the distinguished collections, gathered from material in the Central West, is Henry M. Belden, ed., *Ballads and Songs Collected by the Missouri Folk-Lore Society,* Columbia, Mo., 1940. A comprehensive collection is Joseph M. Carrière, *Tales from the French Folk-Lore of Missouri,* Evanston, Ill., 1937. Earl J. Stout's *Folklore from Iowa,* New York, 1936, contains 112 ballads and songs of varied types and 1,351 examples of "Current Beliefs." An early study is that of G. W. Weippiert, "Legends of Iowa," *Jour. Amer. Folk-Lore,* II (1889), 287–290, which suggests how quickly a new country can develop its own legends. A useful early checklist of original material is Louise Pound, *Folk-Song of Nebraska and the Central West: A Syllabus*, Lincoln, Nebr., 1915.

## The Plains, the Southwest, and the Far West

John A. and Alan Lomax's *Cowboy Songs and Other Frontier Ballads*, New York, 1938, is a revised and enlarged edition of John A. Lomax's *Cowboy Songs* (1910). Music is added, and the notes are useful. The work is supplemented by John A. Lomax, *Songs of the Cattle Trail and Cow Camp*, New York, 1919. Many of the songs in N. Howard Thorp, *Songs of the Cowboys*, Boston, 1921, are by known authors. Two other compilations are Charles J. Finger, *Frontier Ballads*, Garden City, N.Y., 1927; and Fred W. Allsopp, *Folklore of Romantic Arkansas*, New York, 1931, 2 vols.

Spanish material is recorded in Aurora Lucero-White, *The Folklore of New Mexico*, Santa Fe, 1941—in Spanish. Other collections and studies of Spanish material are Juan B. Rael, "Cuentos Españoles de Colorado y de Nuevo Méjico," *Jour. Amer. Folk-Lore*, LII (1939), 227–323; Gustavo Durán and others, *Fourteen Traditional Spanish Songs from Texas*, Washington, 1942; Aurelio M. Espinosa, "New Mexican Spanish Folk-Lore," *Jour. Amer. Folk-Lore*, XXVI (1913), 97–122, XXVIII (1915), 319–352; *idem*, "Romancero Nuevomejicano," *Revue Hispanique*, XXXIII (1915), 446–560, XL (1917), 215–227; *idem*, "Traditional Spanish Ballads in New Mexico," *Hispania*, XV (Mar., 1932), 89–102; and J. Frank Dobie, "El Canción del Rancho de Los Olmos," *Jour. Amer. Folk-Lore*, XXXVI (1923), 192–195.

A good selection from old western songsters is contained in Eleanora Black and Sidney Robertson, *The Gold Rush Song Book, Comprising a Group of Twenty-five Authentic Ballads as They Were Sung by the Men Who Dug for Gold in California During the Period of the Great Gold Rush of 1849, with Music*, San Francisco, 1940. See also Duncan Emrich, *Casey Jones and Other Ballads of the Mining West*, Denver, 1942; and Wayland D. Hand, "Folklore from Utah's Silver Mining Camps," *Jour. Amer. Folk-Lore*, LIV (1941), 132–161.

### NEGRO FOLKLORE

Still important both in the representation and in the critical study of the Negro spiritual is Henry E. Krehbiel, *Afro-American Folksongs: A Study in Racial and National Music*, New York, 1914. One of the most thorough studies of historical and critical problems presented in a collection of authentic texts is Newman I. White, *American Negro Folk-Songs*, Cambridge, 1928.

James W. Johnson, in *The Book of American Negro Spirituals,* New York, 1925, makes more absolute claims of folk origin than Krehbiel, but they are not substantiated by the studies of Newman I. White and Guy B. Johnson. A large, representative collection, with good handling of the music, is John W. Work, *American Negro Songs and Spirituals: A Comprehensive Collection of 230 Folk Songs, Religious and Secular,* New York, 1940. One of the best collections of folk tales among the Gullahs and other Negroes is Elsie C. Parsons, *Folk-Lore of the Sea Islands, South Carolina,* New York, 1923. Negro folk tales from Mississippi, some of them independent traditional versions of the Uncle Remus stories, are retold by John B. Sale, *The Tree Named John,* Chapel Hill, N.C., 1929. The dialect and narrative are well rendered. New evidence of African elements in Negro folksongs is offered in Lydia E. Parrish, *Slave Songs of the Georgia Sea Islands,* New York, 1942. Howard W. Odum's *Rainbow Round My Shoulder: The Blue Trail of Black Ulysses,* Indianapolis, 1928, is the result of a folklorist-sociologist's attempt to treat his material imaginatively. Authoritative treatments of Negro secular songs and their implications are to be found in two compilations by Howard W. Odum and Guy B. Johnson: *The Negro and His Songs,* Chapel Hill, N.C., 1925, and *Negro Workaday Songs,* Chapel Hill, N.C., 1926. An important contribution not only to folklore but to American cultural history is George P. Jackson, *White and Negro Spirituals, Their Life Span and Kinship, Tracing 200 Years of Untrammeled Song Making and Singing Among Our Country Folk, with 116 Songs as Sung by Both Races,* New York, 1943. Two further studies of the Gullah Negroes are Guy B. Johnson, *Folk Culture on St. Helena Island,* Chapel Hill, N.C., 1930; and Mason Crum, *Gullah: Negro Life in the Carolina Sea Islands,* Durham, N.C., 1940. Further material on Negro folklore may be found in the issues of the *Journal of Negro History* (1916–current). Authentic, if "treated," folklore is Edward C. L. Adams, *Congaree Sketches: Scenes from Negro Life in the Swamps of the Congaree and Tales by Tad and Scip of Heaven and Hell with Other Miscellany* (Introduction by Paul Green), Chapel Hill, N.C., 1927. See also the novels of Julia Peterkin.

For special studies see Dorothy Scarborough and Ola L. Gulledge, *On the Trail of Negro Folk Songs,* Cambridge, 1925—a fresh and intimate presentation; Guy B. Johnson, "Negro Folk Songs," in *Culture in the South,* ed. by W. T. Couch, Chapel Hill, N.C., 1934; Muriel D. Longini, "Folk Songs of Chicago Negroes," in *Jour. Amer. Folk-Lore,* LII (1939), 96; and John J. Niles, *Singing Soldiers,* New York, 1927—largely Negro songs of World War I.

Early collections are William Francis Allen and others, *Slave Songs of the United States* (1867)—one of the earliest books to contain both words and music set down from slaves; G. D. Pike, *The Jubilee Singers* (1873); and William E. Barton, *Old Plantation Hymns: A Collection of Hitherto Unpublished Melodies of the Slave and the Freedman*, Boston, 1899. One of the earliest critical studies is that of Thomas W. Higginson, "Negro Spirituals," *Atl. Mo.*, XIX (1867), 685–694. Joel Chandler Harris's *Uncle Remus and His Friends: Old Plantation Stories, Songs and Ballads, with Sketches of Negro Character*, was published in Boston, 1892. An annotated checklist is Myrtle Funkhouser, "Folk-Lore of the American Negro: A Bibliography," *Bul. Bibl.*, XVI (1937–1939), 28–29, 49–51, 72–73, 108–110, 136–137, 159–160.

## RIVER SONGS AND SEA CHANTIES

A standard collection is Joanna C. Colcord, *Songs of American Sailormen*, New York, 1938, with an introduction by Lincoln Colcord. It is a revised and enlarged edition of *Roll and Go: Songs of American Sailormen* (1924). Attractively illustrated but without music is Frank Shay, *Iron Men and Wooden Ships: Deep Sea Chanties*, New York, 1924. Robert W. Neeser has compiled *American Naval Songs and Ballads*, New Haven, 1938, with a bibliog. of early songbooks, pp. 359–361.

Two recent collections of river songs and tales are Charles E. Brown, *Old Man River, Upper Mississippi River Steamboating Days Stories: Tales of the Old Time Steamboats and Steamboatmen*, Madison, Wis., 1940; and Mary Wheeler, *Steamboatin' Days: Folk Songs of the River Packet Era*, Baton Rouge, La., 1944. Excellent treatment of folk material along the Mississippi is Walter J. Blair and Franklin J. Meine, *Mike Fink, King of Mississippi Keelboatmen*, New York, 1933. See also Carl L. Carmer, *Songs of the Rivers of America*, New York, 1942, with musical accompaniment. The New York publishers Farrar & Rinehart began publication late in the 1930's of the Rivers of America Series. Some thirty-one volumes had been published by February, 1947, and all treat, with varying degrees of fullness and reliability, the folklore of the rivers and regions described. See also Alvin F. Harlow, *Old Towpaths: The Story of the American Canal Era*, New York 1926.

## FOLKLORE OF THE LUMBERJACK

Three standard collections of lumberjack ballads are Franz Rickaby, *Ballads and Songs of the Shanty-Boy*, Cambridge, 1926; Roland P. Gray, *Songs and Ballads of the Maine Lumberjacks with Other Songs from Maine*, Cambridge, 1925; and Earl C. Beck, *Songs of the Michigan Lumberjacks . . .*, Ann Arbor, 1941. Charles E. Brown compiled *Whiskey Jack*

*Yarns: Short Tales of the Old Time Lumber Raftsmen of the Wisconsin River and Their Mythical Hero* . . . , Madison, Wis., 1940.

The well known legendary Paul Bunyan has been the subject of several studies. James Stevens's *Paul Bunyan,* New York, 1925, has been criticized for its sophistication of material, but it is an early and important handling of the legend. See also Stevens' *The Saginaw Paul Bunyan,* New York, 1932. Other studies are Esther Shephard, *Paul Bunyan,* New York, 1925; Ida V. Turney, *Paul Bunyan Comes West,* New York, 1928; K. Bernice Stewart and Homer A. Watt, "Legends of Paul Bunyan, Lumberjack," *Trans. Wis. Acad. Sciences, Arts, and Letters,* XVIII (1915), 639–651; and Louis Le Fevre, "Paul Bunyan and Rip Van Winkle," *Yale Rev.,* XXXVI (1946), 66–76. A recent gathering is Stanley D. Newton, *Paul Bunyan of the Great Lakes,* Chicago, 1946.

## FOLK PLAYS

A classic study and collection of play-party songs and games is William W. Newell, *Games and Songs of American Children,* rev. ed., New York, 1911. The most thorough treatment since Newell's work is Benjamin A. Botkin, *The American Play-Party Song, with a Collection of Oklahoma Texts and Tunes,* Lincoln, Nebr., 1937, with a useful bibliography, pp. 383–389.

The Carolina Playmakers of the University of North Carolina, since 1918, have been giving dramatic treatment of folk material and have taken the folk drama to the people. Frederick H. Koch has published the results of this work in *The Carolina Play-Book* (1927–current), in *American Folk Plays,* New York, 1939, and in *Carolina Folk Plays* (3 series), New York, 1941. Other collections are Bernice K. Harris, *Folk Plays of Eastern Carolina* . . . , Chapel Hill, N.C., 1940, with bibl., pp. 271–287; Kate P. Lewis, *Alabama Folk Plays,* Chapel Hill, N.C., 1943; and Altona Trent-Johns, *Play Songs of the Deep South,* Washington, 1944.

Special studies of interest are John G. Bourke, "The Miracle Play of the Rio Grande," *Jour. Amer. Folk-Lore,* VI (1893), 89–95; Antoinette Taylor, "An English Christmas Play," *Jour. Amer. Folk-Lore,* XXII (1909), 389–394; and M. R. Cole, ed. and transl., *Los Pastores: A Mexican Play of the Nativity,* Boston, 1907, with illustrations and music.

## LITERARY BALLADS

Of the various conscious attempts at composing ballads on American themes the most successful are to be found in Vachel Lindsay's *Collected*

*Poems,* rev. ed., New York, 1927; and in the works of Stephen Vincent Benét, especially his *John Brown's Body,* New York, 1928, and his *Ballads and Poems, 1915–1930,* Garden City, N.Y., 1931. Roark Bradford's *John Henry,* New York, 1931, an account of the legendary Negro hero, was dramatized by the author in 1940. His *Ol' Man Adam an' His Chillun* (1928) was adapted by Marc Connelly in the most noted American play dealing with folk material, *The Green Pastures* (1930).

George S. Jackson's compilation, *Early Songs of Uncle Sam,* Boston, 1933, reprints songs contained in popular collections printed in the United States, 1825–1850. The collection includes no dialect songs and is without music. The introduction is written by Kenneth B. Murdock.

BIBLIOGRAPHY

The fundamental tool for the scientific study of folklore is Stith Thompson, *Motif-Index of Folk-Literature: A Classification of Narrative Elements in Folk-Tales, Ballads* . . . , Bloomington, Ind., 1932–1936, 6 vols. Other useful bibliographies and checklists are Alan Lomax and Sidney R. Cowell, *American Folk Song and Folk Lore: A Regional Bibliography,* New York, 1942; Mellinger E. Henry, *A Bibliography for the Study of American Folk-Songs* . . . , London, 1937; Ralph S. Boggs, *Bibliography of Latin American Folklore,* New York, 1940; and Helen H. Flanders, "Index of Ballads and Folk-Songs in the Archives of Vermont Folk-Songs at Smiley Manse, Springfield, Vermont," *Proc. Vt. Hist. Soc.,* VII (1939), 73–98—with a "First Supplement," *Proc. Vt. Hist. Soc.,* VII (1939), 279–285. Good bibliographies are supplied in almost all the leading collections which have been listed above.

A "Folk Lore Bibliography . . ." has been compiled by Ralph S. Boggs annually in the March issue of the *Southern Folklore Quar.,* 1938–current. Prior to 1938 it was a part of the "American Bibliography" of *PMLA.*

The key to a great treasury is the *Check-list of Recorded Songs in the English Language in the Archive of American Folk Song to July, 1940,* Washington, 1942, 3 vols. The very extensive musical recordings were made largely by John A. and Alan Lomax, and the checklist was published by the Music Division of the Library of Congress with geographical index.

For information about projects having folkloristic connections see the *Catalogue* of the WPA Writers' Program Publications: the American Guide Series; and the American Life Series, September, 1941. The *Index* of the Research Projects is in three volumes.

## FOLK TALES AND HUMOR

### GENERAL STUDIES

A pioneering study of the native subliterary source of the American cultural heritage is Constance M. Rourke, *American Humor: A Study of National Character,* New York, 1931. Her posthumously published volume, *The Roots of American Culture and Other Essays,* New York, 1942, consists of brief studies toward an unwritten history of the folk origins of American culture. Jennette Tandy's *Crackerbox Philosophers in American Humor and Satire,* New York, 1925, traces the evolution of pioneer yarns and the anecdotes of the hero as "philosopher." Useful general studies are Napier Wilt, *Some American Humorists,* New York, 1929; Walter Blair, introd. to *Native American Humor, 1800–1900,* New York, 1937; and *idem, Horse Sense in American Humor from Benjamin Franklin to Ogden Nash,* Chicago, 1942. Thomas L. Masson, *Our American Humorists,* rev. ed., New York, 1931, covers principally the years since 1900. For studies of graphic humor there are the two volumes of William Murrell, *A History of American Graphic Humor . . . ,* New York, 1933–1938—covering the years 1747–1938. See also Carl Holliday, *The Wit and Humor of Colonial Days . . . ,* Philadelphia, 1912.

Further studies are J. De Lancey Ferguson, "The Roots of American Humor," *Amer. Scholar,* IV (1935), 41–49; Walter Blair, "The Popularity of Nineteenth-Century American Humorists," *Amer. Lit.,* III (1931), 175–194; Will D. Howe, "Early Humorists," *Camb. Hist. Amer. Lit.,* II (1918), 148–159; "American Humor," in Stephen Leacock, *Essays and Literary Studies,* New York, 1916, pp. 97–136; and James R. Masterson, "Travellers' Tales of Colonial Natural History," *Jour. Amer. Folk-Lore,* LIX (1946), 51–67, 174–188—evidence of tall tales prior to the Revolution. Two early studies are J. L. Ford, "A Century of American Humor," *Munsey's Mag.,* XXV (1901), 482–490; and Henry C. Lukens, "American Literary Comedians," *Harper's Mag.,* LXXX (1890), 783–797.

The fullest bibliographies of material dealing with American humor are in Walter Blair, *Native American Humor, 1800–1900,* New York, 1937; and in Harold W. Thompson, *Body, Boots, and Britches,* Philadelphia, 1940.

### REGIONAL TALES AND THE FOLK HERO

*A Narrative of the Life of David Crockett . . . Written by Himself* (1834) passes as the autobiography of David Crockett (1786–1836), and is a fine example of exaggeration and farce in the tall tale which has come to be especially associated with the Old Southwest. It evidently was stimulated by such books as *Sketches and Eccentricities of Col. David Crockett* (1833), which were the work of Whig journalists who attributed the authorship to Crockett, in an attempt to make Crockett the politician into a frontier hero. The *Narrative* is one of the earliest books to use the American language with assurance and racy distinction. An important biographical study is Constance Rourke, *Davy Crockett,* New York, 1934. An excellent collection of tales built around Crockett is Richard M. Dorson, *Davy Crockett: American Comic Legend,* New York, 1939. Hamlin Garland edited *The Autobiography of David Crockett* for the Modern Student's Library, New York, 1923. See also Walter Blair, "Six Davy Crocketts," *Southwest Rev.,* XXV (1940), 443–462.

Mike Fink *(ca.* 1770 to *ca.* 1823), the keelboatman on the Ohio and Mississippi rivers, became as fabulous for the tall tales of his exploits as Crockett and Paul Bunyan. The orally transmitted accounts of his adventures found their way into print as early as 1829. Literary use has been made of Fink in Emerson Bennett, *Mike Fink* (1848); John G. Neihardt, *The River and I* (1910), and many other sketches. A valuable treatment of frontier annals is Walter Blair and Franklin J. Meine, *Mike Fink, King of Mississippi Keelboatmen,* New York, 1933—with a bibliography, pp. 273-283.

For tales about Paul Bunyan, the giant hero of the many lumberjack tales of the Great Lakes region and the Pacific Northwest, see the section above, Folklore of the Lumberjack, p. 199. Robert Frost's "Paul's Wife" is a treatment of the subject. The southern counterpart of Bunyan is Tony Beaver, whose mythical exploits are located "way up in the Smokies," or "up Eel River" in the Cumberland Mountains. Margaret Montague has recorded his adventures in *Up Eel River* (1928).

John Henry *(ca.* 1870) continues to be the hero of a cycle of Negro ballads and tall tales. Two studies are Roark Bradford, *John Henry* (1931); and Guy B. Johnson, *John Henry: Tracking Down a Negro Legend* (1931).

For general treatment of the American folk hero, see Frank Shay, *Here's Audacity! American Legendary Heroes,* New York, 1930.


THE OLD SOUTHWEST: FROM THE
SAVANNAH RIVER TO THE MISSISSIPPI

American comic legends and tall tales developed early in the Old Southwest. One of the earliest collections of picaresque sketches is Henry Junius Nott (1797–1837), *Novelettes of a Traveller; or, Odds and Ends from the Knapsack of Thomas Singularity, Journeyman Printer* (2 vols., 1834). The first work in a definite literary tradition dealing with the rough-and-tumble frontier is Augustus Baldwin Longstreet (1790–1870), *Georgia Scenes, Characters, Incidents* . . . (1835). A valuable study is John D. Wade, *Augustus Baldwin Longstreet: A Study of the Development of Culture in the South,* New York, 1924, with bibliography, pp. 373–383. See also Vernon L. Parrington, *Main Currents in American Thought,* New York, 1927–1930, II, 166–172.

Another early collection of tall tales of the Old Southwest is Johnson Jones Hooper *(ca.* 1815–1863), *Some Adventures of Captain Simon Suggs, Late of the Tallapoosa Volunteers* (1845); and *idem, The Widow Rugby's Husband* . . . (1851). Especially noted for their literary merit are the writings of T[homas] B[angs] Thorpe (1815–1878), which include *The Mysteries of the Backwoods* (1846) and *The Hive of 'The Bee-Hunter'* (1854). His stories, "The Big Bear of Arkansas" (1841) and "Tom Owen, the Bee-Hunter" have often been reprinted. William T[rotter] Porter (1809–1858) edited *The Big Bear of Arkansas and Other Sketches* (1845)—an early anthology of humor. He established *The Spirit of the Times* (1831–1858), a magazine devoted to the collection of humorous material dealing with the Old Southwest and the frontier. It included the writings of Captain Martin Scott, Albert Pike, M. C. Field, Colonel C. F. M. Noland, and others. Joseph M. Field (1810–1856) published tales of frontier humor, including "Mike Fink, the Last of the Boatmen," in *The Drama in Pokerville* . . . (1847). Two other collections of the same period are John S. Robb, *Streaks of Squatter Life, and Far-West Scenes* . . . (1847); and T. A. Burke, *Polly Peaseblossom's Wedding* (1851).

The most famous of the lawless-frontier collections, and a landmark in the development of humor of the Old Southwest, is Joseph G. Baldwin (1815–1864), *The Flush Times of Alabama and Mississippi: A Series of Sketches,* New York, 1853. In the following year appeared the tall tales of Sol(omon Franklin) Smith (1801–1869): *Sol Smith's Theatrical Apprenticeship* (1854), and *The Theatrical Journey-Work* . . . *of Sol Smith* (1854). Noted for its prank-playing, rough-neck humor is the volume of George Washington Harris (1814–1869), *Sut Lovingood: Yarns Spun by a "Nat'ral Born Durn'd Fool"* (1867). Harris's book was well known to Mark Twain, whose own most famous contributions to humor of the Old Southwest appeared in the same year: *The Celebrated Jumping Frog of Calaveras County and Other Sketches.* A careful study of Mark Twain's place in folk literature is Victor Royce West, *Folklore in the Works of Mark Twain,* Lincoln, Nebr., 1930.

## COLLECTIONS

Five important collections of early tales and narrative humor are Franklin J. Meine, *Tall Tales of the Southwest: An Anthology of Southern and*

*Southwestern Humor, 1830–1860,* New York, 1930; Walter Blair, *Native American Humor, 1800–1900,* New York, 1937—with an extensive selected bibliography, pp. 163-196; Harold W. Thompson, *Body, Boots, and Britches,* Philadelphia, 1940—a rich, mixed collection from New York state presented vivaciously; James R. Masterson, *Tall Tales of Arkansaw,* Boston, 1942—a study of folk tales of the Old Southwest, with extensive notes and bibliography, pp. 306-425; and Richard M. Dorson, *Jonathan Draws the Long Bow: New England Popular Tales and Legends,* Cambridge, 1946—a collection of neglected New England folklore.

Other authoritative anthologies dealing with particular regions are Earl A. Collins, *Folk Tales of Missouri,* Boston, 1935; Mody C. Boatright, *Tall Tales from Texas,* Dallas, 1934; and Victor L. O. Chittick, *Ring-Tailed Roarers: Tall Tales of the American Frontier, 1830–60,* Caldwell, Idaho, 1941. See also Joseph L. French, *The Best of American Humor from Mark Twain to Benchley: A Prose Anthology,* Garden City, N.Y., 1938.

A fine collection of legends of the Southwest is J. Frank Dobie, *Coronado's Children: Tales of Lost Mines and Buried Treasures of the Southwest,* Dallas, Texas, 1931. See also Dobie's "Texas-Mexican Border Broadsides," *Jour. Amer. Folk-Lore,* XXXVI (1928), 185-191.

Studies of folk humor on the frontier are Thomas D. Clark, *The Rampaging Frontier: Manners and Humors of Pioneer Days in the South and the Middle West,* Indianapolis, 1939—a popular survey with bibliography, pp. 343-350; Mary Austin, "The Folk Story in America," *So. Atl. Quar.,* XXXIII (1934), 10-19; Mody C. Boatright, "The Tall Tale in Texas," *So. Atl. Quar.,* XXX (1931), 271-279; C. Grant Loomis, "The American Tall Tale and the Miraculous," *Calif. Folklore Quar.,* IV (1945), 109-128; and Richard Chase, "The Jack Tales," *Southern Folklore Quar.,* I–V (1937–1941), *passim*—one of the largest and most piquant cycles current in American tradition. A vivacious account of the major American folk heroes and of American history in relation to them is Walter Blair, *Tall Tale America: A Legendary History of Our Humorous Heroes,* New York, 1944.

## CRACKER-BOX PHILOSOPHERS

Humor in the more urbane tradition, often employing conscious literary devices with the intent of gently satirizing institutions or passing events, was an early part of American literary output. Comic writers usually published their sketches first in the columns of newspapers, and many of them were columnists who came to have national reputations as wits and humorists. One of the earliest humorists of this type was the Philadelphia journalist, Joseph Clay Neal (1807-1847), whose first book was published as *Charcoal Sketches; or, Scenes in a Metropolis* (1838). Benjamin Penhallow Shillaber

(1814–1890) created the character of Mrs. Partington in 1847 for a Boston newspaper. Her malapropisms were more widely disseminated in the popular volume *Life and Sayings of Mrs. Partington* . . . , 1854. Shillaber founded in Boston the humorous weekly, the *Carpet-Bag* (1851–1853)—an important journal in developing the "cracker-box" type of American humor. It was through the pages of the *Carpet-Bag* that Mark Twain was first introduced to the public. Other early collections of humorous sketches are W(illiam) E(vans) Burton (1802–1860), *A Yankee Among the Mermaids* . . . (1854); Mortimer Neal Thom[p]son (1831–1875), *Doesticks: What He Says* (1855); Frederick Swartwout Cozzens (1818–1869), *The Sparrowgrass Papers; or, Living in the Country* (1856); and Frances Miriam Whitcher (1814–1852), *The Widow Bedott Papers* (1856)—the first American treatment at length of a female comic figure.

Next to Mark Twain the most famous mid-nineteenth century humorist was Charles Farrar Browne ("Artemus Ward," 1834–1867), whose first book, *Artemus Ward: His Book* (1862) portrays "Down East" characters. For Browne, see the individual bibliography herein. Almost as well known was Henry Wheeler Shaw ("Josh Billings," 1818–1885). *Josh Billings: Hiz Sayings* (1866) was his first published collection. His *Farmer's Allminax* was issued annually, 1869–1880; and *Josh Billings: His Works, Complete* was issued, New York, 1888, with a biographical introduction. A revised edition of *The Complete Works of Josh Billings* was published, Chicago, 1919. A life of Billings is Cyril Clemens, *Josh Billings: Yankee Humorist*, Webster Groves, Mo., 1932. See also Joseph Jones, "Josh Billings: Some Yankee Notions on Humor," *Studies in English, Univ. of Texas, 1943*, pp. 148–161.

Comic interpretations of the Civil War were made popular by the New York journalist Robert Henry Newell ("Orpheus C. Kerr," 1836–1901). The sketches were collected and published as *The Orpheus C. Kerr Papers*, New York, 1862–1871, 5 vols. Well known as a northern War satirist was David Ross Locke ("Petroleum V. Nasby," 1833–1888). The first of several collections was published as *The Nasby Papers* (1864). *The Nasby Letters* were posthumously issued in 1893. James Russell Lowell's second series of *The Biglow Papers* (1867) was the most distinguished collection of satirical humor dealing with the Civil War. The North was best satirized in the humor of Charles Henry Smith ("Bill Arp," 1826–1903). His first collection was published as *Bill Arp, So-Called* (1866). It was followed by such other collections as *Bill Arp's Peace Papers* (1873). Humorous descriptions of Civil War events are in *Miles O'Reilly His Book* (1864), by Charles Graham Halpine (1820–1868).

The best of far western humor during the mid-nineteenth century is that of George Horatio Derby ("John Phoenix," 1823–1861), whose contributions were made first to California newspapers (1849–1856). *Phoenixiana; or, Sketches and Burlesques* (1856) was followed by *The Squibob Papers* (1865). *Phoenixiana* has been reprinted from time to time, most recently edited by Francis P. Farquhar, San Francisco, 1937. An authoritative biographical study of Derby is George R. Stewart, *John Phoenix, Esq., The Veritable Squibob: A Life of Captain George H. Derby, U.S.A.,* New York, 1937, with a bibliography of Derby's writings, pp. 209–217.

Very popular as a lecturer was Edgar Watson Nye ("Bill Nye," 1850–1896). His writings include *Bill Nye and Boomerang* . . . (1881). Frank W. Nye edited *Bill Nye: His Own Life Story,* New York, 1926. See also "Letters of Riley and Bill Nye," *Harper's Mag.,* CXXXVIII (1919), 473–484. Other humorous collections of the period include Melville de Lancey Landon ("Eli Perkins," 1839–1910), *Thirty Years of Wit* . . . (1891); James Mont-gomery Bailey (1841–1894), *Life in Danbury* . . . (1873)—a collection from early Danbury, Conn., newspaper columns; and Robert Jones Burdette (1844–1914), *Hawk-Eyes* (1879). Burdette's well known lecture on "The Rise and Fall of the Mustache" was first printed in *The Rise and Fall of the Mustache and Other Hawkeyetems* (1877).

Especially well known were the writings of Marietta Holley (1836–1926), whose character Samantha Allen, or "Josiah Allen's Wife," dominated the series of books that began with *My Opinions and Betsy Bobbet's* (1873) and concluded with *Josiah Allen on the Woman Question* (1914).

Humorous collections that deal with practical jokes are represented by George Wilbur Peck (1840–1916), *Peck's Bad Boy and His Pa* (1883). The newspaper whimsy of Eugene Field (1850–1895), who was associated with the Chicago *Morning News* and *Record* during 1883–1895, was gathered and published in *Tribune Primer* (1882), *Culture's Garland* (1887), and other volumes. *The Writings in Prose and Verse of Eugene Field* was issued, New York, 1898–1901, 12 vols. For biography and criticism of Field see Charles H. Dennis, *Eugene Field's Creative Years,* New York, 1924; and Slason Thompson, *The Life of Eugene Field, the Poet of Childhood,* New York, 1927.

The extravagant farcical tales of John Kendrick Bangs (1862–1922) began with the publication of *Tiddledywink Tales* (1891). Best known is *A House-Boat on the Styx* . . . (1896). For biography see Francis H. Bangs, *John Kendrick Bangs: Humorist of the Nineties,* New York, 1941. The most in-cisive humorous satirist at the turn of the century was Finley Peter Dunne (1867–1936). The first and best of his many "Mr. Dooley" volumes, written in an Irish brogue, was *Mr. Dooley in Peace and in War* (1898). The last was entitled *Mr. Dooley on Making a Will, and Other Necessary Evils* (1919). Selections have been edited by Elmer Ellis, *Finley Peter Dunne: Mr. Dooley at His Best,* New York, 1938, with a foreword by F. P. Adams. A biography, containing the only printing of Dunne's unfinished memoirs, is Elmer Ellis, *Mr. Dooley's America: A Life of Finley Peter Dunne,* New York, 1941. See also "Imported Horse Sense: Mr. Dooley," in Walter Blair, *Horse Sense in American Humor* . . . , Chicago, 1942, pp. 240–255.

The best literary examples of the language of slang are in the various published writings of George Ade, whose first *Fables in Slang* appeared in 1900. For further details, see the individual bibliography on Ade herein. The Canadian humorist Stephen (Butler) Leacock (1869–1944) was widely known in the United States. His first volume, *Literary Lapses,* was published in 1910; *Last Leaves* appeared in 1945. Other twentieth century humorists who have been especially popular include Irvin S(hrewsbury) Cobb (1876–1944), whose autobiography *Exit Laughing* was published in 1941; Robert (Charles) Benchley (1889–1945)—at his best in such sketches of the average man as *Of All Things* (1921); and Will(iam) Rogers (1879–1935), who wrote in the tradition of Artemus Ward and Mr. Dooley. See P. J. O'Brien's *Will Rogers* (1935). Frank McKinney Hubbard ("Abe Martin," 1868–1930) was known as a midwestern humorist, and published *Abe Martin, Hoss Sense and Nonsense* (1926). See "Abe Martin and Will Rogers," in Walter Blair, *Horse Sense in American Humor,* Chicago, 1942, pp. 256–273.

Among recent humorists, Clarence Day (1874–1935) published *This Simian World* in 1920, but is best remembered for his later autobiographical essays, the first of which were published in *God and My Father* (1932). Don(ald) Marquis (1878–1937) published several volumes of humorous verse; his *archy and mehitabel* (1927) and its sequels—free-verse essays in which the principals, a cockroach and an alley cat, furnish Marquis with a medium for expressing his ideas on contemporary events and manners—continue to have a loyal following. Collections of the humor of Franklin P(ierce) Adams (b. 1881) are *The Melancholy Lute: Selected Songs of Thirty Years* (1936). James (Grover) Thurber (b. 1894) issued *The Owl in the Attic and Other Perplexities* (1931), and more recently *Cream of Thurber* (1939). One of the first of the humorous volumes of E(lwyn) B(rooks) White (b. 1899) was *The Fox of Peapack and Other Poems* (1938); and a representative collection of the writings of Ogden Nash (b. 1902) is *I'm a Stranger Here Myself* (1938).

REGIONAL HUMORISTS

The tradition of the Down East Yankee is best remembered in the creations of Seba Smith ("Major Jack Downing," 1792–1868), one of the earliest of the "funny" men in the tradition of the illiterate and naïvely humorous characters. *The Life and Writings of Major Jack Downing of Downing-*

*ville* . . . was first published in 1833. See also Charles A. Davis, *Letters of J. Downing, Major* . . . (1934). Two other early writers in the Down East tradition are Ann Sophia Stephens (1813–1886), who published *High Life in New York* (1843), and Thomas Chandler Haliburton (1796–1865), the Canadian humorist who influenced writers in the United States through the use of Down East humor and speech. His *Sam Slick's Wise Saws and Modern Instances* . . . (1853) has been edited by Ray P. Baker, New York, 1923, with a bibliography.

Dialect humor of the Pennsylvania Germans is best represented by Charles Godfrey Leland (1824–1903). His *Meister Karl's Sketch-Book* (1855) was followed by the well known *Hans Breitmann's Party with Other Ballads* (1868). For critical studies of Leland, see Sculley Bradley, " 'Hans Breitmann' in England and America," *Colophon,* n.s. II, No. 1 (1936), 65–81; Marianne Thalmann, "Hans Breitmann," *PMLA,* LIV (1939), 579–588; and Charles I. Glicksberg, "Charles Godfrey Leland and *Vanity Fair,*" *Pa. Mag. Hist. and Biog.,* LXII (1938), 309–323. The Leland manuscripts are deposited in the Boston Public Library and in the Library Company of Philadelphia. See Joseph Jackson, *A Bibliography of the Work of Charles Godfrey Leland,* Philadelphia, 1927. Another representative of the "scrapple English" of the Pennsylvania Germans is Charles Follen Adams (1842–1918). His earliest sketches were published as *Leedle Yawcob Strauss, and Other Poems* (1878). A collection, *Yawcob Strauss and Other Poems* was issued in 1910.

Collections of humorous tales found in the South are William C. Hendricks, ed., *Bundle of Troubles, and Other Tarheel Tales,* Durham, N.C., 1943—gathered in North Carolina; *South Carolina Folk Tales: Stories of Animals and Supernatural Beings,* in the *Bul. Univ. S.C.* for Oct., 1941; and Vance Randolph, *Ozark Mountain Folks,* New York, 1932—yarns from the Ozarks. One of the earliest writers to picture the Georgia "cracker" was William Tappan Thompson (1812–1882). His *Major Jones's Courtship* was first published in 1843, and the character appears in later collections. Joel Chandler Harris's Uncle Remus stories, originally published in the Atlanta *Constitution,* were the first significant notice of Negro folk tales. For studies of Harris, see the individual bibliography herein. Early humor dealing with Louisiana is represented by "Madison Tensas, M.D." (pseud. of Henry Clay Lewis), *Odd Leaves from the Life of a Louisiana "Swamp Doctor"* (1843); D. Corcoran, *Pickings from the . . . "Picayune"* (1846); and George M. Wharton, *The New Orleans Sketch Book* (1853). The best collection of humorous tales from the Deep South is that of Arthur P. Hudson, *Humor of the Old Deep South,* New York, 1936. A valuable regional collection for the Northwest is William J. Snelling, *Tales of the Northwest,* edited with an introduction by John T. Flanagan, Minneapolis, 1936. It was first published anonymously in 1830 as *Tales of the Northwest; or, Sketches of Indian Life and Character, by a Resident beyond the Frontier.*

The dialect tales of the mining and cattle-raising frontier, by Alfred Henry Lewis ("Dan Quin," 1858–1914), are represented by *Wolfville* (1897), and later volumes of the "Wolfville" series. The journalist Prentice Mulford (1834–1891) described humorously his life in California in *Prentice Mulford's Story* (1889).

## MAGAZINES

Four humorous weeklies have maintained notable standards in their writing and illustrations. *Puck* (1877–1918) was a comic weekly distinguished during the first two decades of its existence for its incisive wit; among its editors were H. C. Bunner, 1878–1896; Harry Leon Wilson, 1896–1902, and J. K. Bangs, 1904–1905. *Judge* (1881–1939) carried on in the comic tradition of *Puck,* and was especially successful during the period 1910–1930. *Life* (1883–1936), a humorous and satirical weekly noted for its drawings, enjoyed its greatest circulation and popularity before the First World War. The *New Yorker* (1925–current) is well known for the sophisticated wit of its drawings and for the fiction and verse of Ring Lardner, Robert Benchley, Dorothy Parker, James Thurber, Ogden Nash, and others.

## MINSTREL HUMOR AND JOKE BOOKS

Minstrel shows originated in the United States, and were popular here and in Europe during the nineteenth century. The blackface song "Jim Crow" (1830) was introduced by an early performer, Thomas Dartmouth Rice (1808–1860). Dan(iel Decatur) Emmett (1815–1904) was an early minstrel and song writer who is said to have composed "Dixie." Among his other songs are "Old Dan Tucker" and "Walk Along." Edwin P. Christy (1815–1862) organized a well known troupe, Christy's Minstrels, which toured widely here and abroad during the forties and fifties. Stephen Foster wrote several of his minstrel songs under Christy's name.

A lively and informal treatment of minstrel humor is Dailey Paskman and Sigmund Spaeth, *"Gentlemen, Be Seated!" A Parade of the Old-Time Minstrels,* Garden City, N.Y., 1928. Anecdotes illustrative of folklore backgrounds of famous actors are in Brander Matthews and Laurence Hutton, eds., *Actors and Actresses of Great Britain and the United States from the Days of David Garrick to the Present Time,* New York, 1886, 5 vols. See also Laurence Hutton, *Curiosities of the American Stage,* New York, 1891. Two important histories of vaudeville and the minstrel stage are Douglas Gilbert,

*American Vaudeville: Its Life and Times,* New York, 1940; and Carl F. Wittke, *Tambo and Bones: A History of the American Minstrel Stage,* Chapel Hill, N.C., 1930. Two examples of the old minstrel joke books are *Bones: His Gags and Stump Speeches; Nigger and Dutch Stories and Dialogues . . . "Broken China" Dialect Pieces, and Other Conundrums,* New York, 1879; and *Uncle Si's Black Jokes,* New York, n.d. An example of what "Ethiopian Opera" was like is *The Darkey Drama: A Collection of Approved Ethiopian Acts, Scenes, and Interludes: As played with complete success by the Christy's, Bryant's, Wood's, Charley White's, Buckley's, Morris and Bell's, Duprez and Green's, Hooley's, Sharpley's "Iron Clads," Birch's, Leon and Kelly's, and other first-class Negro Minstrel Troupes,* 10 parts in 3 vols., London and New York (Samuel French, n.d.).

Few traces of American humor appear in the early published jest books until 1831, with the publication of *The American Comic Almanac for 1831,* Boston. For studies of early jest books, see Howard M. Chapin, "Colonial Humor," *Amer. Collector,* V (1928), No. 6; James H. Thompson, "The First American Humorist," *Reading and Collecting,* II (1938), No. 3; and Walter Blair, *Native American Humor, 1800–1900,* New York, 1937. See also the bibliography on American almanacs, *post,* p. 240. The best general study is Harry B. Weiss, *A Brief History of American Jest Books,* New York, 1943.

## PROVERB LITERATURE

There is need for further investigation of the use of American proverbs by American writers other than Mark Twain. The best known examples of the early proverb literature are the Poor Richard almanacs issued by Franklin, 1733–1758. A facsimile reproduction of many has been issued with a foreword by Phillips Russell, New York, 1928. Lively examples of the role of almanacs in disseminating folklore are in George Lyman Kittredge, *The Old Farmer and His Almanack . . . ,* Cambridge, 1924. A good midwestern collection is Emma Snapp, "Proverbial Lore in Nebraska," *Univ. Nebr. Studies in Lang., Lit., and Crit.,* No. 13 (1933). See also Margaret Hardie, "Proverbs and Proverbial Expressions Current in the United States East of Missouri and North of the Ohio River," *Amer. Speech,* IV (1929), 461–472; and Richard Jente, "A Review of Proverb Literature Since 1920," in *Corona: Studies in Celebration of the 80th Birthday of Samuel Singer . . . ,* ed. by Arno Schirokauer and Wolfgang Paulsen, Durham, N.C., 1941. An entire chapter on proverbs current in New York state is in Harold W. Thompson, *Body, Boots, and Britches,* Philadelphia, 1940.

# INDIAN LORE AND ANTIQUITIES

Though early Indian missionaries, beginning with John Eliot, were deeply concerned with reform and conversion among the aborigines, they contributed little to a study of Indian culture. A recognition of its importance and beauty developed late, and texts of Indian songs and tales are therefore often very fragmentary, passed orally from one generation to another by a dwindling race.

The first American learned society to emphasize ethnology was the American Antiquarian Society (founded 1812). Vol. I (1820) of its *Transactions* is largely devoted (pp. 105–299) to a study by Caleb Atwater, "Description of the Antiquities Discovered in the State of Ohio and Other Western States." It remained, however, for Henry Rowe Schoolcraft (1793–1864) to initiate the broader study of Indian culture, following his appointment in 1822 as government superintendent of Indian Affairs in the northwestern frontiers. His first study, dealing with the geographic area of the Allegheny and Atlantic, he called *Algic Researches, Comprising Inquiries Respecting the Mental Characteristics of the North American Indians,* New York, 1839, 2 vols., later edited (Philadelphia, 1856) with some additions and omissions, and published with the title *The Myth of Hiawatha.* His *Onéota; or, The Red Race of America,* issued in 8 numbers in 1844–1845, was revised and published as *The American Indians: Their History, Condition, and Prospects, from Original Notes and Manuscripts* . . . , Rochester, N.Y., 1851 (and later eds., with varying titles). His greatest work remains the *Historical and Statistical Information Respecting the History, Condition, and Prospects of the Indian Tribes of the United States* . . . , Philadelphia, 1851–1857, 6 parts (with varying titles in later printings), a monumental study which, in spite of some erroneous conclusions and even inventions, provided the foundation for later researches. The relationship of Longfellow to Schoolcraft's collection, as well as to the present-day folklore of the Ojibwa Indians, is set forth in Stith Thompson, "The Indian Legend of Hiawatha," *PMLA,* XXXVII (1922), 128–140. An interesting, though verbose, account of Schoolcraft's activities is provided by Chase S. and Stellanova Osborn, *Schoolcraft—Longfellow—Hiawatha,* Lancaster, Pa., 1943.

Important also among early collectors and interpreters of Indian lore was Albert Gallatin (1761–1849), who may be said to have created the science of American linguistics in "A Synopsis of the Indian Tribes of North America," *Trans. Amer. Antiq. Soc.*, II (1836), 9–422. A sumptuous compilation of Indian portraits, with biographical sketches, was issued by Thomas L. McKenney (1785–1859) and James Hall (1793–1868), *History of the Indian Tribes of North America* . . . (3 vols., 1836–1844). Other pioneer work was done by Alexander W. Bradford (1815–1867) in *American Antiquities* . . . (1841). The American Ethnological Society, sponsored by Gallatin, was founded in 1842 and issued the first of its *Transactions* in 1845. The Smithsonian Institution was established by an Act of Congress in 1846, with a primary interest in furthering ethnological studies. The report by Ephraim George Squier and E. H. Davis, *Ancient Monuments of the Mississippi Valley* (1848), was issued as the first of the *Smithsonian Contributions to Knowledge*. Lewis H. Morgan (1818–1881), who may be said to have established in this country the study of American anthropology, began his researches with investigations about Indian matters. His *League of the Ho-dé-no-sau-nee, or Iroquois* (1851), is important as the earliest scientific account of an Indian tribe. Among his many articles on matters related to ethnology may be mentioned "The 'Seven Cities of Cibola,' " *No. Amer. Rev.*, CVIII (1869), 457–498. The first basic synthesis of a half-century of work on Indians was the compilation *The Native Races of the Pacific States of North America* (5 vols., 1875–1876), the leading contributor to which was Hubert Howe Bancroft (1832–1918). The interest thus created in western antiquities led to the establishment in 1879 of the Archaeological Institute of America, an organization which placed a study of the archaeology of the Southwest on a modern footing. Popular interest in American antiquities is shown by publication in *Century Magazine* during 1882–1883 of a series of articles by Frank Hamilton Cushing on "My Adventures in Zuñi." Two other ethnologists whose monographs on the Indians are significant are John G. Bourke (1843–1896) and Adolph F. A. Bandelier (1840–1914). Many of Bandelier's studies were published in the *Reports* of the Peabody Museum of Archaeology and Ethnology.

The work of Daniel G. Brinton (1837–1899) on *The Myths of the New World: A Treatise on the Symbolism and Mythology of the Red Race of America,* New York, 1868 (3rd ed., rev., 1896), is a good example of the symbolic interpretation of American Indian myths fashionable two generations ago. Brinton edited the *Library of Aboriginal American Literature,* Philadelphia, 1882–1890, 8 vols., a collection containing almost all that is available from early Spanish records, including the standard edition of the *Walam Olum*. His *Aboriginal American Authors and Their Productions,* Philadelphia, 1883, is an early survey. Some texts may be found in Reuben

G. Thwaites, ed., *The Jesuit Relations* . . . , Cleveland, 1896–1901, 73 vols.

By the end of the nineteenth century the study begun by anthropologists and ethnologists was continued by musicians and students of literature in great numbers. One of the earliest among such students was Alice C. Fletcher, who published first *A Study of Omaha Indian Music,* Cambridge, 1893, with the songs and music, pp. 79–151; it was followed by her *Indian Story and Song, from North America,* Boston, 1900, and *Indian Games and Dances, with Native Songs,* Boston, 1915. Later collections are those of Natalie (Curtis) Burlin, *The Indians' Book* . . . , New York, 1907—material gathered from the recitation of descendants of earlier tribes which, though somewhat shaped by contact with the civilization of the white man, essentially preserves the aboriginal spirit—and George W. Cronyn, ed., *The Path on the Rainbow: An Anthology of Songs and Chants from the Indians of North America,* New York, 1918.

A standard study of the general field is the authoritative compilation of Stith Thompson, *Tales of the North American Indians,* Cambridge, 1929—a selection of nearly 100 widely distributed tales, with introduction, extensive comparative notes (pp. 271–360), and bibliography (pp. 371–386). It is complemented by Clark Wissler, *The Indians of the United States: Four Centuries of Their History and Culture,* New York, 1940. Other collections are John R. Swanton, *Myths and Tales of the Southeastern Indians,* Washington, 1929; and Grenville Goodwin, *Myths and Tales of the White Mountain Apache,* New York, 1939.

Other collections have recently been made of important Indian tales. Such a work as Ruth Benedict, *Zuñi Mythology,* New York, 1935, 2 vols., may fairly represent the type of collections made by Leonard Bloomfield, George A. Dorsey, A. L. Kroeber, Robert H. Lowie, Edward Sapir, and Clark Wissler.

A number of monographs on particular Indian tales have been published, in the nature of such articles as Dorothy Demetracopoulou, "The Loon Woman Myth: A Study in Synthesis," *Jour. Amer. Folk-Lore,* XLVI (1933), 101–128, and A. H. Gayton, "The Orpheus Myth in North America," *ibid.,* XLVIII (1935), 263–293.

Mary Austin's *The American Rhythm: Studies and Reëxpressions of Amerindian Songs,* Boston, 1930 (enlarged from 1st ed. of 1923), argues that the uniformity of native Indian feeling creates a rhythm characteristic of aboriginal literature as well as of the literature of white men in the same locality, and hence becomes fundamentally a part of all American literature. The study is based on many years of contact with Indians in the deserts of the Southwest, but its thesis is not generally accepted by American Indian scholars.

The most thorough student of songs and music of particular tribes has been Frances Densmore. Her *Chippewa Music,* Washington, 1910–1913, is the first of a considerable series of bulletins on Indian music and tribal customs, published by the Bureau of American Ethnology, that include examination of the Teton Sioux, Northern Ute, Papago, Yuman, Menominee, Nootka, Quileute, Mandan, and Pawnee. An epitome of her work is published as *The American Indians and Their Music,* New York, 1926, an authoritative survey.

The monumental work, in which a study of all the incidents in the myths of the North Pacific Coast pointed the way for all future studies, is that of the distinguished anthropologist Franz Boas, *Tsimshian Mythology,* pp. 29–1037 of *Report of the Bureau of American Ethnology,* No. 31, Washington, 1916. He followed it with similar studies of the tales of other tribes, such as the Kwakiutl, Salishan, Sahaptin, Kutenai, and Keresan.

Special studies of interest are T. T. Waterman, "The Explanatory Element in the Folk-Tales of the North-American Indians," *Jour. Amer. Folk-Lore,* XXVII (1914), 1–54, a basic treatment showing that the explanatory element in many American Indian tales is incidental rather than primary; Ruth M. Underhill, *Singing for Power,* Berkeley, Calif., 1938, an excellent presentation of Indian poetry and oratory; Father Berard Haile, *Origin Legend of the Navaho Flintway,* Chicago, 1943, a study of particular ceremonials based on the most recent researches; and Archer Taylor, "American Indian Riddles," *Jour. Amer. Folk-Lore,* LVII (1944), 1–15, an assembly of the rather scant evidences of American Indian riddles.

A collection is Margot Astrov, ed., *The Winged Serpent: An Anthology of American Indian Prose and Poetry,* New York, 1947.

## COLLATERAL STUDIES

No single satisfactory study of Indian contributions to American ideas has been published. The problem is touched on in Gilbert Chinard, *L'Amérique et le Rêve Exotique dans la Littérature Française au XVIIᵉ et au XVIIIᵉ Siècle,* Paris, 1913—the cult of the Indian in romantic literature; Mary M. Atkeson, "A Study of the Local Literature of the Upper Ohio Valley, with Especial Reference to the Early Pioneer and Indian Tales, 1820–1840," *Ohio State Univ. Bul.,* XXVI (Sept., 1921), 1–62; Benjamin Bissell, *The American Indian in English Literature of the Eighteenth Century,* New Haven, 1925; William E. Stafford, "Our Heritage from the American Indians," *Annual Report Smithsonian Inst.,* Washington, 1927, pp. 405–410; Hoxie N. Fairchild, *The Noble Savage,* New York, 1928—an extensive study of the Indian in English literature; Albert Keiser, *The Indian in American Literature,* New York, 1933—the Indian as interpreted by American writers, with a bibl., pp. 300–305; Julian P. Boyd, ed., *Indian Treaties Printed by Benjamin Franklin, 1736–1762,* Philadelphia, 1938, with an introduction by Carl Van Doren—a documented and authoritative study of Indian political relationships in the colonial period; Mabel Morris, "Jefferson and the Language of the American Indian," *Mod. Lang. Quar.,* VI (1945), 31–34; and G. E. E. Lindquist and others, *The Indian in American Life,* New York, 1944.

RESOURCES

The leading publications in which authoritative studies and monographs appear are the Bulletins and especially the Reports of the Bureau of Ethnology, and the *Journal of American Folk-Lore,* founded by Franz Boas in 1888. A large and increasing collection of recorded music of American Indian songs and dances is available for study in the Library of Congress. Other important publications are the Columbia University Contributions to Anthropology, the Publications of the Jessup North Pacific Expedition, and the University of California Publications in American Archaeology and Ethnology.

Especially important collections of Indian source material are in the National Archives Building, Washington, including confidential archives and government imprints, census records for the years 1790 to 1870, and the field records of the Federal Theater Project. The Ayer Collection in the Newberry Library, Chicago, is outstanding for material relating to Indian history. Other important holdings are in the libraries of the American Philosophical Society, the Historical Society of Pennsylvania, and the Brinton and Berendt Collections in the University of Pennsylvania.

AUTHENTIC FICTIONAL STUDIES

*The Delight Makers,* New York, 1890, by Adolph F. A. Bandelier, is a remarkable re-creation by an anthropologist of Pueblo life in the Southwest before the coming of the white man. Hamlin Garland's short stories, *The Book of the American Indian,* New York, 1923, deals especially with the Cheyennes and the Sioux. Oliver La Farge wrote *Laughing Boy,* 1929, and *All the Young Men,* 1935, from his acquaintance with the Navajos, Apaches, and other Indians. Dama M. Smith's *Hopi Girl,* Stanford Univ., Calif., 1931, is a reliable study. A realistic picture of the modern Navajo is Edwin Corle, *People on the Earth,* 1937. A valuable presentation of the Great Lakes Indians is Iola Fuller, *The Loon Feather,* New York, 1940. One of the most recent fictional studies is Charles L. McNichols, *Crazy Weather,* New York, 1944.

BIBLIOGRAPHY

A useful checklist to 1921 of "Non-English Writings: Aboriginal," is compiled by Mary Austin in *Cambridge Hist. Amer. Lit.,* IV (1921), 610–634. The student should further consult the bibliography in Stith Thompson, *Tales of the North American Indians,* Cambridge, 1929, pp. 371–386. Morris Swadesh and others compile a "Bibliography of American Indian Linguistics," published, from time to time since 1936, in *Language.* There is also Elizabeth G. Dennis, *The Indians of America: A Reference List for Schools and Libraries* . . . , Boston, 1928.

# POPULAR LITERATURE

## BEST SELLERS

### HISTORICAL SURVEY

Books which enjoy unusual popularity are generally referred to as best sellers. The popularity may be brief, or extend over a period of years. Although usually ephemeral and often subliterary, the best seller may at times be a volume of substantial merit. For example, the best-selling book in the United States continues to be the Bible. Among religious sects founded in America, two have sponsored volumes representing cornerstones of their faiths, and each continues to sell widely: *The Book of Mormon* (1830), which is said to have been revealed in 1827 to Joseph Smith (1805–1844), founder of the Church of Jesus Christ of Latter-Day Saints; and *Science and Health with Key to the Scriptures* (1875), the authorized textbook of Christian Science, compiled and published by Mary Baker Eddy (1821–1910).

The earliest best sellers of the colonial period were the almanacs (see Almanacs and Chapbooks, *post,* p. 239.) Michael Wigglesworth's *The Day of Doom* (1662) was immensely popular in England as well as in the colonies. Among Indian captivities, a form of literature generally popular, John Williams's *The Redeemed Captive Returned to Zion* (1707) was widely sold (see the section Indian Captivities, *post,* p. 273).

Among school texts, the *New England Primer,* issued prior to 1690, is said to have sold some 5,000,000 copies. Noah Webster's *The American Spelling Book* (1787) long continued in wide use, and is estimated to have sold some 60,000,000 copies by 1890. Other best-selling texts include Jedidiah Morse, *Geography Made Easy* (1784), Caleb Bingham (1757–1817), *The American Preceptor* (1794) and *The Columbian Orator* (1797), and William Holmes McGuffey (1800–1873), *Eclectic Readers* (1836–1857). For data on the dictionaries of Webster and of Joseph Worcester, see the section The American Language, *ante,* p. 187. See also the section Juvenile Literature, *post,* p. 225.

### POETRY

The most widely known poems of the nineteenth century include such varied selections as "Ben Bolt" (1843), by Thomas Dunn English (1819–

1902); Longfellow's *The Song of Hiawatha* (1855); "Nothing to Wear" (1857), the satirical verses of William Allen Butler (1825–1902); Bret Harte's "Plain Language from Truthful James" (1870); and *Poems of Passion* (1883), by Ella Wheeler Wilcox (1850–1919), whose later poems and sketches continued to market readily. Best sellers among twentieth century verse writers include James Whitcomb Riley, who is discussed herein in an individual bibliography, and Edgar A. Guest (b. 1881), whose widely syndicated verses have been gathered in collections such as *Just Folks* (1917).

Important as a study of popular poetic taste is Hazel Felleman, comp., *The Best Loved Poems of the American People,* New York, 1936.

## FICTION

Susanna Rowson's *Charlotte (Temple): A Tale of Truth,* first published in London (1791), has gone through some 160 editions in the United States alone. The sales of Irving's *The Sketch Book* (1819–1820) have been continuous to the present.

An extraordinary case of plagiarism followed the publication of *The Asylum; or, Alonzo and Melissa* (1811), by Isaac Mitchell (*ca.* 1759–1812), a work which achieved great popularity in the almost verbatim rendering by one Daniel Jackson in the same year. The second edition of Mitchell's romance (1824) recaptured for it the reputation it had in fact won. The first edition exists in a unique copy in the Henry E. Huntington Library.

Timothy Shay Arthur (1809–1885) was the author of nearly one hundred moral tracts. His *Temperance Tales* (1844) were followed by other fictional pieces devoted to the temperance cause. His novel *Ten Nights in a Bar-Room and What I Saw There* (1854) was successfully dramatized four years later by William W. Pratt. The *Autobiography* (1845-rev. eds., 1859, 1869) of John B. Gough (1817–1886), English-born lecturer and reformed drunkard, takes its place among the most widely sold volumes of the century.

Sentimental feminine fiction achieved great popularity. The sixty domestic romances of E(mma) D(orothy) E(liza) N(evitte) Southworth (1819–1899) made her a household name. Representative are *The Curse of Clifton* . . . (1852), and *The Hidden Hand* (1859). A recent biography is Regis L. Boyle, *Mrs. E. D. E. N. Southworth: Novelist,* Washington, 1939 Sara Jane Lippincott ("Grace Greenwood," 1823–1904), was popular as poet, essayist, and journalist, and her sketches were collected in *Greenwood Leaves* . . . (1850) and other volumes. Sara Payson Willis ("Fanny Fern, 1811–1872) was the sister of N. P. Willis and the wife of the biographer James Parton. Very popular in its day was her first volume of witty sketches, *Fern Leaves from Fanny's Portfolio* (1853). Mary Jane Holmes (1825–1907) produced nearly forty sentimental stereotyped novels of which some 2,000,000 copies are said to have been sold. Best known among them is *Lena Rivers* (1856). The enormously popular *St. Elmo* (1866) was written by Augusta Jane Evans (1835–1909), the Alabama novelist; her sentimental, moralistic tales include also *Inez: A Tale of the Alamo* (1855).

The New England novelist Sylvanus Cobb, Jr. (1823–1887), who produced some thirteen hundred short stories and novelettes, is said to have been the first writer in the country to undertake the wholesale production of popular fiction. His novels include *The Bravo's Secret . . .* (1851) and *The Patriot Cruiser* (1859).

No American novel of the century matched the popularity or sales of Harriet Beecher Stowe's *Uncle Tom's Cabin* (1852). It was the first novel by an American to sell over a million copies, and its translation into many tongues gave Mrs. Stowe a world-wide fame.

Less well remembered today are the novels of Maria Susanna Cummins (1827–1866), whose moralistic romances include *The Lamplighter* (1854); Elizabeth Stuart Phelps Ward (1844–1911), who achieved great popularity with her fervid religious novels, best known of which is *The Gates Ajar* (1868); Edward Payson Roe (1838–1888), whose novels of sentimental piety were widely read, notably *Barriers Burned Away* (1872); and Archibald Clavering Gunter (1847–1907), who wrote some forty novels of which *Mr. Barnes of New York* (1887) sold more than a million copies. About thirty of his books were translated into Swedish. The theme of *Ben-Hur: A Tale of the Christ* (1880), a historical romance by Lew(is) Wallace (1827–1905), gave it immense popularity. It has been translated into many languages, and its sales are numbered in the millions.

Stories now considered classics, which continue to sell widely, include *The Man Without a Country* (1865—first printed in the *Atlantic Monthly,* 1863), by Edward Everett Hale (1822–1909); Mark Twain's *The Adventures of Tom Sawyer* (1876); and the Utopian socialistic romance *Looking Backward, 2000–1887* (1888), by Edward Bellamy, a work which, widely translated, made the author internationally famous, and led to the founding of a Nationalist party that advocated the principles which the novel set forth.

In 1896 the Congregational pastor Charles Monroe Sheldon (1857–1946) published his story of a modern minister who follows the example of Christ in his daily living: *In His Steps*. The book is said to be the most popular of all modern novels. In the fifty years since publication it has sold some 20,000,000 copies, and has been translated into more than twenty languages.

Other novelists and story-writers at the turn of the century whose stories were best sellers, together with a representative story by each, include Amelia Edith Barr (1831–1919), *Jan Vedder's Wife* (1885); Henry van Dyke (1852–

1933), *The Story of the Other Wise Man* (1896); Richard Harding Davis (1864–1916), *Soldiers of Fortune* (1897); Silas Weir Mitchell (1829–1914), *Hugh Wynne, Free Quaker* (1897); Charles Major (1856–1913), *When Knighthood Was in Flower* (1898); Edward Noyes Westcott (1846–1898), *David Harum: A Story of American Life* (1898); Paul Leicester Ford (1865–1902), *Janice Meredith* (1899); Elbert Hubbard (1856–1915), *A Message to Garcia* (1899); Mary Johnston (1870–1936), *To Have and to Hold* (1900); Irving Bacheller (b. 1859), *Eben Holden: A Tale of the North Country* (1900); George Barr McCutcheon (1866–1928), *Graustark* (1901); Owen Wister (1860–1938), *The Virginian* (1902); John Fox, Jr. (1863–1919), *The Little Shepherd of Kingdom Come* (1902); Jack London, *The Call of the Wild* (1903); Harold MacGrath (1871–1932), *The Man on the Box* (1904); Winston Churchill (1871–1947), *The Crossing* (1904); Gene Stratton-Porter (1868–1924), *Freckles* (1904); Joseph C. Lincoln (1870–1944), *Partners of the Tide* (1905); Thomas Dixon (1864–1946), *The Clansman* (1905)—on which was based *The Birth of a Nation* (1915), the first large screen spectacle; Robert W. Chambers (1865–1933), *The Fighting Chance* (1906); Rex (Ellingwood) Beach (b. 1877), *The Spoilers* (1906); Grace Livingston Hill (1865–1947), *The Enchanted Barn* (1918); and Harold Bell Wright (1872–1944), *The Winning of Barbara Worth* (1911)—a romance which, like his others, *The Shepherd of the Hills* (1907) and *The Calling of Dan Matthews* (1909), continues occasionally to be found in lists of best sellers.

Before 1920 Kathleen (Thompson) Norris (b. 1880) had established her popularity with *Mother* (1911); and Harry Leon Wilson (1867–1939) with *Bunker Bean* (1912) and *Ruggles of Red Gap* (1915). Some sixty western adventure stories by Zane Grey (1875–1939) have sold nearly 15,000,000 copies. Representative of his romances is *Riders of the Purple Sage* (1912). *Dere Mable: Love Letters of a Rookie* (1918), by Edward Streeter (b. 1891), sold widely if briefly at the conclusion of the First World War.

More recent successes include *The Covered Wagon* (1922), by Emerson Hough (1857–1923); *Gentlemen Prefer Blondes* (1926), by Anita Loos (b. 1893); and the long picaresque novel *Anthony Adverse* (1933), by (William) Hervey Allen (b. 1889).

The fastest selling story in history has been Margaret Mitchell's only novel, *Gone with the Wind* (1936), a long romance of the Civil War. Its vogue has been immense and continuing both here and abroad. Some million and a half copies were sold during the first year. To date more than 3,000,000 copies have been sold in this country alone, and the story has been translated into a score of foreign languages. Lloyd C. Douglas (b. 1877) continues to turn out popular successes, a recent representative of which is *The Robe* (1942).

*Bibliography*

A study of best sellers, especially during the twentieth century, is Alice P. Hackett, *Fifty Years of Best Sellers, 1895-1945,* New York, 1945, with chapters on "The Structure of the Best Seller," "Best Seller Subjects," and "Best Sellers Before 1880." Useful also is Asa D. Dickinson, *The Best Books of the Decade, 1926-1935: A Later Clue to the Literary Labyrinth,* New York, 1937. Brief studies are Edward A. Weeks, "The Best Sellers Since 1875," *Pub. Weekly,* CXXV (1934), 1503-1506, and Margaret C. Banning, "The Problem of Popularity," *Sat. Rev. Lit.,* XIV (May 2, 1936), 3-4, 16-17. See also Robert S. and Helen M. Lynd, *Middletown* (1929), and *Middletown in Transition* (1937), on popular reading habits; and Louis R. Wilson, *The Geography of Reading . . . ,* Chicago, 1938—a survey of American libraries.

### DRAMA

Nineteenth century plays which won special popularity include William Henry Smith (1806-1872), *The Drunkard; or, The Fallen Saved* (1844)—written as a sentimental plea for temperance; Joseph Jefferson and Dion Boucicault's dramatization of Irving's *Rip Van Winkle* (1865)—famous especially for Jefferson's acting in the title role; and Augustin Daly's *Under the Gaslight* (1867). *The Old Homestead* (1886), by Denman Thompson (1833-1911), remained a popular success for more than twenty years. *A Trip to Chinatown,* by Charles Hale Hoyt (1860-1900), produced in 1891, was a popular farce. *Sherlock Holmes* (1899) was an arrangement of the Conan Doyle stories by the actor William Gillette (1855-1937), who continued to act the title role for some thirty-five years.

The romantic Indian play, *The Squaw Man* (1905), by Edwin Milton Royle (1862-1942), was popular in its day. It was adapted as the libretto of a musical play, *White Eagle* (1927). *Lightnin'* (1918), by Winchell Smith and Frank Bacon, enjoyed one of the longest continuous runs in American dramatic history, though its record was broken when Anne Nichols's *Abie's Irish Rose* (1924) had a continuous New York run of 2,532 performances.

Two recent plays that have broken previous records are Erskine Caldwell's *Tobacco Road* (dramatized in 1933), and Clarence Day's *Life with Father,* first produced in 1939, and continuously produced into 1947.

### DIME NOVELS

Inexpensive thrillers, dealing with romantic historical themes, border warfare, or violent action in general, achieved great popularity in the later decades of the nineteenth century until they were superseded, around 1900, by pulp magazines, juvenile series such as those concerning the Rover Boys, and by the comic strip. The Boston publisher and author Maturin Murray Ballou (1820–1895) was noted for his mass production of popular literature, and his formula for a set type of plot construction made him a forerunner of dime-novel publishers. Orville James Victor (1827–1910) became well known as a publisher of dime novels. His wife, Metta Victoria Victor (1831–1886), was author of such volumes as *Lives of the Female Mormons* (1856). The most famous publisher of dime novels was Erastus Beadle (1821–1894), who made a highly profitable career of publishing cheap books which he sold by the millions. The first from his press, Ann S. Stephens's *Malaeska: The Indian Wife of the White Hunter* (1860), is said to have sold 300,000 copies in the first year.

Popular writers of dime novels include Edward S. Ellis (1840–1916), who in six months sold nearly half a million copies of *Seth Jones; or, The Captives of the Frontier* (1860); and William Henry Thomas (1824–1895), who established a highly successful Boston publishing firm and wrote such melodramatic works as *A Slaver's Adventures* (1872).

Most of the boys' thrillers that preceded the modern comic books were published by Street & Smith. Upton Sinclair wrote some of them; Theodore Dreiser for a year was one of the editors. The names signed to them are practically all pseudonyms which, together with some of the real names as well, became the property of the publishers. All the Street & Smith books were written on a salary of $75 to $100 a week for 20,000 words. Among the most widely read were those written about the imaginative detective Nick Carter, a character created by John Russell Coryell in the 1880's. Most of the 1,076 Nick Carter stories were written by Frederick Van Rensselaer Dey. The stories appeared in seventeen languages, and had a real influence on serious French writers among the Dadaists and Surrealists.

Prentiss Ingraham (1843–1904) turned out some 600 dime novels, a third of which featured his friend Buffalo Bill. It was Edward Zane Carroll Judson (1823–1886)—"Ned Buntline"—who, meeting W. F. Cody in 1869, endowed him with the name "Buffalo Bill," and made him the hero of a series of novels. Edward L. Wheeler was author of the Deadwood Dick series, dealing with the exploits of the Indian fighter Richard W. Clarke (1845–1930), to whom they were later attributed.

The Tarzan stories, dealing with the adventures of a white boy adopted by apes of the African jungle, are the creation of Edgar Rice Burroughs (b. 1875). They have probably been the most lucrative continuation of the dime-novel tradition in the twentieth century. Translated into fifty-six languages, their foreign vogue has been immense.

## Bibliography

A popular survey of subliterary novels is Edmund Pearson, *Dime Novels; or, Following an Old Trail in Popular Literature,* Boston, 1929. A brief study of their social significance is Merle Curti, "Dime Novels and the American Tradition," *Yale Rev.,* XXVI (1937), 761–778. The fullest bibliography is Charles Bragin, *Dime Novels: Bibliography, 1860–1928,* Brooklyn, 1938. For a listing of Beadle's publications, continued in fact through 1875, see Ralph Admari, "The House That Beadle Built: 1859 to 1869," *Amer. Book Collector,* IV (1933), 221–226, 288–291; V (1934), 22–25, 60–63, 92–94, 147–149, 215–217.

### DETECTIVE STORIES

Detective stories are often avidly read by connoisseurs of mystery, murder, and the art of detection, but the sales of such books have seldom been extensive enough to put them in the best-seller class.

Edgar Allan Poe is said to have written the first modern detective stories, including such tales as "The Murders in the Rue Morgue" (1841), "The Mystery of Marie Rogêt" (1842–1843), and "The Purloined Letter" (1845). In France, Poe's method was admired, followed and further developed by such writers as Emile Gaboriau; and in England by Wilkie Collins, and later by Arthur Conan Doyle.

The first American writer to establish the formula and popularity of the detective story was Anna Katharine Green (1846–1935). Deservedly well known among her stories is the first she wrote, *The Leavenworth Case* (1878). Allan Pinkerton (1819–1884) founded his own private detective agency. Records written up from his own personal investigations are published in his *Criminal Reminiscences and Detective Sketches* (1879), and *Thirty Years a Detective . . .* (1884). John Russell Coryell (*ca.* 1852–1924) treated the character of the detective Nick Carter in the 1880's. The name was later appropriated by other writers, and some thousand titles of the Carter novelettes have been issued. Further data on them will be found above on p. 223.

The most successful twentieth century writers of detective stories include Willard Huntington Wright ("S. S. Van Dine," 1888–1939), whose novel *The Benson Murder Case* (1926) was followed by several other Philo Vance stories; Earl Derr Biggers (1884–1933), whose proverb-quoting Chinese detective, Charlie Chan, is featured in *The Chinese Parrot* (1926) and similar stories; Frances Noyes Hart (b. 1890), remembered for *The Bellamy Trial* (1927); and Dashiell Hammett (b. 1894), who introduced realism and hard-boiled dialogue in such stories as *The Maltese Falcon* (1930) and *The*

*Thin Man* (1932). Under the pseudonym of Ellery Queen, Frederic Dannay and Manfred Lee have written *The French Powder Mystery* (1930) and other stories. John P. Marquand (b. 1893) created Mr. Moto, a subtle Japanese sleuth, for a series of tales.

The so-called "pulpwood," or thriller, magazines have increased in number during the century, and their sales are very wide. A recent study of them is Harold B. Hersey, *Pulpwood Editor: The Fabulous World of the Thriller Magazines Revealed by a Veteran Editor and Publisher,* New York, 1937.

A history of detective-story writing, from Poe to the present, is Howard Haycraft, *Murder for Pleasure: The Life and Times of the Detective Story,* New York, 1941, with bibl., pp. 279–297.

For further data, see the sections American Writers and Books Abroad, *post,* p. 356, and Juvenile Literature following.

## JUVENILE LITERATURE

### INDIVIDUAL WRITERS

Children's literature in America began as an aid to piety, addressed to an audience of youthful adults. Such, for example, was John Cotton's *Milk for Babes* (1646). The *New England Primer* (*ca.* 1683) included the well known children's prayer beginning, "Now I lay me down to sleep." Most of the early children's songs and poems were imported or reprinted, the best known being *Songs for the Nursery; or, Mother Goose's Melodies,* London, 1760, derived from English and French sources. Much of the juvenile literature was handed down orally in the form of ballads which developed with new versions and additions. They were usually in the tradition of Old World fairy tales, folklore, and tales of chivalry.

It is true, of course, that many books written for adults have been enthusiastically read by children. Outstanding among such works are the writings of Irving, Cooper, Dana, and Mark Twain.

One of the earliest consciously produced children's poems, still widely known, is Clement Clarke Moore's "A Visit from St. Nicholas" (1823). Sarah Josepha Hale (1788–1879) published *Poems for Our Children* (1830), which included "Mary Had a Little Lamb."

The beginning of the modern period of juvenile literature may be seen in the writing of "Peter Parley," Samuel Griswold Goodrich (1793–1860), and of Jacob Abbott (1803–1879). Goodrich, though he wrote some hundred moralistic books, broke away from religious didacticism and may be represented by his earliest juvenile, *The Tales of Peter Parley About America*

(1827). Hawthorne's *Twice-Told Tales* (1837), and his later juvenile fiction, were written under the encouragement of Goodrich. They are an attempt to avoid the moral and didactic, and to understand the child's mind. Abbott, who wrote to entertain and instruct, was the author of the well known "Rollo Series," 28 vols., the first of which appeared in 1834. An early example of non-religious juvenile fiction is *The Young Emigrants* (1830), by Susan (Ridley) Sedgwick (1789–1867).

No American writer is better known for the retelling of old stories than Hawthorne. His adaptation from Greek myth, *A Wonder-Book for Girls and Boys* (1852), was followed by a similar collection, *Tanglewood Tales* (1853). Sidney Lanier published *The Boy's Froissart* (1879), *The Boy's King Arthur* (1880), *The Boy's Mabinogion* (1881), *The Boy's Percy* (1882), for which he wrote the prefaces.

Christopher Pearse Cranch's *The Last of the Huggermuggers* (1856) and *Kobboltozo: A Sequel . . .* (1857) are important juveniles.

Two mid-nineteenth century writers who early appealed to love of adventure were Daniel Pierce Thompson (1795–1868) and (Thomas) Mayne Reid (1818–1883), the Irish-born romancer. Thompson's *The Green Mountain Boys* (1839) continues to be reprinted. See J. E. Flitcroft, *Daniel Pierce Thompson: The Novelist of Vermont . . .* , Cambridge, 1929. Representative of Reid's adventure stories are *The Scalp Hunters* (1851), and *The Boy Hunters* (1852). "Elizabeth Wetherell," Susan Bogert Warner (1819–1885), wrote juveniles stressing sentimental piety, such as *Queechy* (1852). Patriotism and adventure were the themes of the well known "Oliver Optic," William Taylor Adams (1822–1897). His Boat Club Series (1854) was followed by the Army and Navy Series and many later series of like kind. John Townsend Trowbridge (1827–1916) published *Cudjo's Cave* in 1864, and Mary Mapes Dodge (1831–1905) is still remembered for *Hans Brinker; or, The Silver Skates: A Story of Life in Holland* (1865). No writer of juveniles has been more widely read than Horatio Alger, Jr. (1834–1899). In the year of his death he claimed to have written about seventy books, mostly juveniles, but more than a hundred titles are issued over his signature. It is supposed that no fewer than 20,000,000 copies were published in the Ragged Dick Series (1867 ff.), the Luck and Pluck Series (1869 ff.), the Tattered Tom Series (1871 ff.), etc. For a recent biography, see Herbert R. Mayes, *Alger: A Biography Without a Hero,* New York, 1928. Louisa May Alcott's *Little Women* (1868–1869) was followed by *Little Men* (1871). For further data on Alcott, see the individual bibliography herein.

Martha F. Finley ("Martha Farquharson," 1828–1909), wrote some hundred novels for children. The best known of her characters, Elsie Dinsmore, appeared in twenty-eight Elsie Dinsmore books (1867–1905). See Janet

E. Brown, *The Saga of Elsie Dinsmore: A Study in Nineteenth Century Sensibility* (Monographs in English, No. 4, 1945, Univ. of Buffalo).

Frank R. Stockton (1834–1902) may be represented by *Ting-a-Ling* (1870). T. B. Aldrich's *The Story of a Bad Boy* (1870) still claims youthful readers. Less well remembered is Isabella Alden (1841–1930), who published some seventy-five juveniles under the pseudonym "Pansy."

An early western adventure writer was Noah Brooks (1830–1903), who published *The Boy Emigrants* in 1876. Joel Chandler Harris's Uncle Remus stories first appeared in 1880. For Harris, see the individual bibliography herein. Charles Carleton Coffin (1823–1896) was well known in the last quarter of the nineteenth century for his patriotic adventure tales, *The Boys of '61: Or, Four Years of Fighting* (1881) and *The Boys of '76: A History of the Battles of the Revolution* (1876). Harriet Mulford Stone Lothrop (1844–1924) brought out *Five Little Peppers and How They Grew* in 1881, the first of a series that achieved wide popularity. Howard Pyle (1853–1911) is best remembered for the illustrations with which he furnished his texts. His first volume was published as *The Merry Adventures of Robin Hood* (1883). Edward Eggleston's *The Hoosier Schoolboy* appeared in 1883. The best known juvenile story of Frances Hodgson Burnett (1849–1924), and one which set an unhappy fashion at the time in the style of boys' clothing, was *Little Lord Fauntleroy* (1886). Other writers of juveniles during the eighties were Charles E. Carryl (1842–1920), *Davy and the Goblin . . .* (1885); Sarah Orne Jewett, *The Story of the Normans* (1887); Kirk Munroe (1850–1930), *The Flamingo Feather* (1887); Palmer Cox (1840–1924), *The Brownies: Their Book* (1887); and Frances C. Baylor (1848–1920), *Juan and Juanita* (1888).

William O. Stoddard (1835–1925) published some seventy books for boys of the nature of *Little Smoke: A Tale of the Sioux* (1891). Eugene Field's poems of childhood were issued as *With Trumpet and Drum* (1892). Authentic pictures of pioneer life on the Maine coast are the Elm Island Stories of Elijah Kellogg (1813–1901), initiated with *Lion Ben of Elm Island* (1896). Before the turn of the century, there had appeared *Master Skylark. A Story of Shakespeare's Time* (1897) by John Bennett (b. 1865); *Fables for the Frivolous* (1898) by Guy Wetmore Carryl (1873–1904), who wrote many later tales; *Court-Martialed* (1898), the earliest of several boys' books by Upton Sinclair; and the first of the juveniles of Peter Newell (1862–1924), *Peter Newell's Pictures and Rhymes* (1899).

Syndication of juvenile literature was first undertaken by Edward Stratemeyer (1863–1930), who founded the Stratemeyer Literary Syndicate, and produced such books as the well known Rover Boys Series, Motor Boys Series, and Tom Swift Series.

(George William) Gilbert Patten ("Burt L. Standish," 1866–1945), began his widely known Frank Merriwell Series, dealing with wholesome college youth at work and at play, in 1896. The series, perhaps the most extended in all juvenile literature, includes more than two hundred novels, and is said to have sold more than 25,000,000 copies. See John L. Cutler, *Gilbert Patten and His Frank Merriwell Saga: A Study in Sub-Literary Fiction, 1896–1913,* Orono, Me., 1934.

The "Oz Books" were written by Lyman Frank Baum (1856–1919), and were initiated with *The Wonderful Wizard of Oz* (1900). Gelett Burgess (b. 1866) published *Goops and How to Be Them* (1900). Other popular writers for children during the first decade of the twentieth century, together with a representative work of each, are Alice Hegan Rice (1870–1942), *Mrs. Wiggs of the Cabbage Patch* (1901); Stewart Edward White (b. 1873), *The Magic Forest* (1903); Kate Douglas Wiggin (1856–1923), *Rebecca of Sunnybrook Farm* (1903); Thornton W. Burgess (b. 1874), *Old Mother West Wind* (1910); and Owen M. Johnson (b. 1878), *The Varmint* (1910).

*The Dutch Twins* (1911) and *The French Twins* (1918) are representative stories by Lucy F. Perkins (1865–1937), written with the purpose of creating in children an understanding of foreign cultures. Jean Webster (1876–1916) published *Daddy-Long-Legs* in 1912. The first of Booth Tarkington's Penrod books, *Penrod,* was issued in 1914. Mary Ellen Chase (b. 1887) published *The Girl from the Big Horn Country* in 1916.

Recent writers of juvenile.fiction, with a representative work of each, are Carl Sandburg (b. 1878), *Rootabaga Stories* (1922); Rachel Lyman Field (1894–1942), *Eliza and the Elves* (1926); Thames (Ross) Williamson (b. 1894), *Opening Davy Jones's Locker . . .* (1930); Laura Adams Armer (b. 1874), *Waterless Mountain* (1931); Dorothy Kunhardt, *Junket Is Nice* (1933); Phil Stong (b. 1899), *Farm Boy . . .* (1934); and Evelyn (D.) Scott (b. 1893), *Billy, the Maverick* (1934).

CHILDREN'S MAGAZINES

The *Juvenile Magazine . . .* , Philadelphia, 1802–1803, is alleged to be the first magazine for children published in the United States. Lydia Maria Child edited the well known child's magazine, the *Juvenile Miscellany,* 1826–1834.

No other magazines for children achieved the distinction or the longevity of the *Youth's Companion* (1827–1929). It had reached a circulation of a half-million copies at its peak in 1890, and included among its writers such distinguished contributors as Whittier, Garland, Howells, London, and later Theodore Roosevelt and Woodrow Wilson.

*Parley's Magazine* (1833–1844), edited by S. G. Goodrich, was merged into *Merry's Museum* . . . (1841–1872), edited by Louisa May Alcott in 1867. It, in turn, was merged into the *Youth's Companion*.

Other nineteenth century juvenile magazines of distinction include the *Little Pilgrim* (1854–1868?), edited by "Grace Greenwood" (Sara J. Lippincott); *Oliver Optic's Magazine: Our Boys and Girls* (1867–1875) and *Harper's Young People* (1879–1895). The most distinguished juvenile, next to *Youth's Companion*, was *St. Nicholas* (1873–1940), edited by Mary Mapes Dodge during the first thirty-two years of its publication. It established a contributors' department of fiction, essays, and verse for youthful readers, and some of the earliest writing of E. B. White, Faulkner, Fitzgerald, Lardner, Wylie, and Edmund Wilson appeared in its columns.

The tenth United States Census Report (1880) indicates that some 217 children's periodicals were published in the United States in the last quarter of the nineteenth century. The number rapidly declined.

The *American Boy* (1899–1941) absorbed the *Youth's Companion* in 1929. At present *Boys' Life: The Boy Scouts' Magazine* (1911–current) is one of the few juvenile magazines of particular distinction.

## SPECIAL STUDIES

Histories and special studies of juvenile literature are Rosalie V. Halsey, *Forgotten Books of the American Nursery* . . . , Boston, 1911; Montrose J. Moses, *Children's Books and Reading*, New York, 1907; Abraham S. W. Rosenbach, *Early American Children's Books, with Bibliographical Descriptions of the Books in His Private Collection*, Portland, Me., 1933; Harry B. Weiss, "Samuel Wood (1760–1844) and Sons, Early New York Publishers of Children's Books," *Bul. N.Y. Pub. Lib.*, XLVI (1942), 755–771; and Harriet L. Matthews, "Children's Magazines," *Bul. Bibl.*, I (1899), 133–136.

## BIBLIOGRAPHY

Checklists are Algernon Tassin, "Books for Children," *Camb. Hist. Amer. Lit.*, II (1918), 631–638; Charles F. Heartman, *American Primers* . . . , Highland Park, N.J., 1935; and *idem, The New-England Primer Issued Prior to 1830* . . . , New York, 1934.

A standard catalog is Helen G. Cushing, *Children's Song Index: An Index to More Than 22,000 Songs in 189 Collections Comprising 222 Volumes*, New York, 1936. Useful also is Elva S. Smith, *The History of Children's Literature: A Syllabus with Selected Bibliographies*, Chicago, 1937—covering English and American writing to 1900; Siri Andrews and others, comps.,

*Children's Catalog* . . . , 6th edition rev., New York, 1941—annually supplemented and frequently revised.

## HYMNS AND HYMN WRITING

### EARLY WRITERS AND COMPILERS

The seventeenth century Puritans restricted their church music to the singing of traditional psalms. The first American collection, as well as the earliest book issued in the colonies, was *The Whole Booke of Psalmes Faithfully Translated into English Metre,* Cambridge, 1640. Generally known as the *Bay Psalm Book,* it was the compilation of Thomas Weld, John Eliot, and Richard Mather, and it remained for a century the most widely used published collection. Later translations of the Psalms, undertaken for the most part to refine the meter, include those of Cotton Mather, *Psalterium Americanum* (1718), and Thomas Prince (1687–1758), *The Psalms, Hymns, and Spiritual Songs of the Old and New Testaments* (1758).

The pamphlet by John Tufts (1689–1750), *An Introduction to the Singing of Psalm Tunes in a Plain and Easy Method* (1712), advocates "a new way" —a revival of "regular singing," that is, by note. Further impetus was given to regular singing by Cotton Mather's nephew, Thomas Walter (1696–1725), with the publication of his *The Grounds and Rules of Musick Explained; or, An Introduction to the Art of Singing by Note* (1721).

The first hymnbook (as distinguished from psalmbooks) printed in America was *Collection of Psalms and Hymns,* Charleston, 1737, prepared by John Wesley during his missionary residence in the South. The tunes and verses are of English origin. Indeed, American hymnody from the earliest times to the present has been directly stimulated by English usage, and, apart from psalmody, dates from the compilations of Isaac Watts, whose influence extended to America during the second decade of the eighteenth century. Amended versions of Watts's popular collection of *Psalms and Hymns* were published by Joel Barlow (1785) and Timothy Dwight (1801). By mid-century the Congregationalists had admitted hymns, which might be, as they were with Mather Byles, original religious songs. A new epoch in church music, which lasted for a century and coincided with the passing of the *Bay Psalm Book,* was inaugurated by *Urania; or, A Choice Collection of Psalm-Tunes, Anthems, and Hymns* (1762), compiled by James Lyon (1735–1794) shortly after his graduation from Princeton in 1759. The Boston tanner William Billings (1746–1800) attempted to reform the bare hymnody with publication of *The New England Psalm-Singer* (1770), original and sometimes quaint settings of religious poetry. His patriotic hymns and anthems written during the Revolution include the belligerent "Chester," and paraphrases of the Psalms invoking God's mercy exclusively for the patriot cause. An even more influential compilation by Billings was *The Singing-Master's Assistant* (1778). The first Presbyterian hymn writer was Samson Occom (1723-1792), the Mohegan Indian educated by Eleazar Wheelock. Occom visited England (1766-1767) as a preacher in the interests of Dartmouth College. Several hymns in his *A Choice Collection of Hymns and Spiritual Songs* (1774) are said to be original compositions.

The considerable body of Lutheran hymnody, traditional among the Pennsylvania Germans (and in some degree among the Swedish settlers), dates from the late seventeenth century, and includes the first original tunes and hymns produced in the American colonies, many of which still remain in manuscript. The collection made by Johannes Kelpius (1673-1708) was first printed, reproduced in facsimile, in Volume I of *Church Music and Musical Life in Pennsylvania in the Eighteenth Century* (1926). The highest level of musical activity in the colonies was attained by the Moravians in and near Bethlehem, Pa., where varied instruments as well as original compositions have been traditional from the early years of the eighteenth century to the present. Little or no trace of the influence of Lutheran hymnody upon the development of American hymnody in general has been found.

### THE LATER HYMNODISTS

Among patriotic hymns, the most famous is "The Star-Spangled Banner" (1814), by Francis Scott Key (1779-1843), adopted as the national anthem by an Act of Congress in 1931, though officially so used by the Army and Navy since the Spanish-American War. It was composed following the bombardment of Fort McHenry, near Baltimore, during the night of Sept. 13-14, 1814. Immediately published as a broadside, entitled "The Bombardment of Fort McHenry," it was first collected in a volume of songs and devotional pieces posthumously published as the author's *Poems* . . . (1857). The Boston Baptist clergyman Samuel Francis Smith (1808-1895), while still a student at Andover Theological Seminary, composed "America" (1831). It was first sung at a Fourth of July celebration in 1832, and published in *The Choir* (1832), a collection edited by Lowell Mason. It is gathered in Smith's *Poems of Home and Country* (1895). The "Battle-Hymn of the Republic" was written by Julia Ward Howe (1819-1910) during a visit to McClellan's headquarters in December, 1861, and was published in the *Atlantic Monthly* in the following February. Katharine Lee Bates (1859-1929) wrote "America the Beautiful" in 1893. It was published in the *Congregationalist*, July 4

1895. Later revised, it was collected in her *America the Beautiful and Other Poems* (1911). Some sixty tunes have been composed for it.

The best known composer of hymns and compiler of hymnals was Lowell Mason (1792–1872), the founder of the Boston Academy of Music (1832), and an influential figure in establishing the teaching of music in public schools. He compiled some fifty books of music, and among his most popular compositions are "The Missionary Hymn" ("From Greenland's Icy Mountains"), and "Bethany" ("Nearer, My God, to Thee"). Similarly important was the work of the New York composer and choir conductor Thomas Hastings (1784–1872). Much of his original work is collected in *Devotional Hymns and Religious Poems* (1850). With Lowell Mason he edited his first collection, *Spiritual Songs for Social Worship* (1831–1832). The foremost Universalist preacher of his day was Hosea Ballou (1771–1852), who edited collections of hymns and himself composed nearly two hundred.

An extensive contribution to American hymnody has been made by Unitarians. Considered as a leading poet in his day, John Pierpont (1785–1866) published *Airs of Palestine* (1816) in praise of sacred music, and later brought out religious hymns and odes. John Quincy Adams (1767–1848) issued *Poems of Religion and Society* in the year of his death. It represents a selection of his verses which Adams himself valued highly. Much the most important Unitarian hymn writers were Samuel Longfellow (1819–1892)—the younger brother of H. W. Longfellow—and Samuel Johnson (1822–1882). Together they brought out *A Book of Hymns* (1846), and *Hymns of the Spirit* (1864). Among the many published books by Frederic Henry Hedge (1805–1890) are his *Hymns for the Church of Christ* (1853). It was he who translated in 1853 Luther's "Ein' feste Burg" in the notable stanzas beginning "A mighty fortress is our God." The collection made by James Freeman Clarke (1810–1888), *The Disciples' Hymn Book* (1844), includes original songs of his own. Other hymn writers whose verses achieved popularity in their day include Eliza Lee Cabot Follen (1787–1860); George Washington Doane (1799–1859), Bishop of New Jersey, 1832–1859; and Adoniram Judson (1788–1850), the distinguished Baptist missionary to Burma.

Almost every poet and poetaster of the nineteenth century wrote hymns or religious lyrics which could be set to music. The pious verses of Lydia Huntley Sigourney (1791–1865) were widely known. A representative volume of the nearly sixty books which she issued, chiefly devoted to moral or religious themes, is *Moral Pieces in Prose and Verse* (1815). Harriet Beecher Stowe's *Religious Poems* appeared in 1867. The original verses of the Congregational minister Ray Palmer (1808–1887) were published in *Hymns and Sacred Pieces* (1865) and other collections. Alice and Phoebe Cary collaborated on hymns and poems, and issued a compilation of *Hymns for All*

*Christians* (1869). Lucy Larcom (1824–1893) published popular verses, some of which were set to music. A collected edition of her poems appeared in 1885. More enduring are the occasional verses of Bryant and H. W. Longfellow, which, though not intended for hymnals, were later included in them and are still sung. Many of the poems of Whittier were set to music as hymns, and remain among the best contributions to American hymnody. The contributions of Phillips Brooks (1835–1893) were considerable, and include the well loved "O Little Town of Bethlehem" (1868). Of collections during the mid-nineteenth century none achieved wider circulation than the compilation of Henry Ward Beecher, issued as the *Plymouth Collection* (1855). At the turn of the century, the compilations of Frederick Lucian Hosmer (1840–1929) were widely adopted and have permanent merit.

Folk hymnody, which has survived in revival meetings, is well represented in its early collections by Jeremiah Ingalls, comp., *The Christian Harmony; or, Songster's Companion* (1805), including much of American origin. Though generally out of use, the gospel songs of Fanny Jane Crosby (1820–1915) were greatly in demand by publishers during the late nineteenth century, and she is said to have written some 8,000 pieces. The evangelist Dwight Lyman Moody (1837–1899) collaborated with his organist and singer Ira D. Sankey (1840–1908) to compile selections of hymns that remained very popular during the century. See Sankey's *My Life and the Story of the Gospel Hymns* (1906). For data on the enduring Negro spirituals, see the section on Folk Literature: Songs and Ballads, *ante*, p. 192.

A useful collection is W. Garrett Horder, *The Treasury of American Sacred Song*, New York, 1896. See also Frank J. Metcalf, *American Writers and Compilers of Sacred Music*, New York, 1925. The most careful history of the subject is Henry W. Foote, *Three Centuries of American Hymnody*, Cambridge, 1940, with estimates of the aesthetics of hymnody. An earlier account is Edward S. Ninde, *The Story of the American Hymn*, New York, 1921. See also Hamilton C. Macdougall, *Early New England Psalmody: An Historical Appreciation, 1620–1820*, Brattleboro, Vt., 1940.


## ORATORY AND THE LYCEUM

### ORATORY AND DEBATING: TO 1820
#### Oratory

The techniques of oratory and debate have been cultivated in America from the earliest periods. The New England pulpit furnished the best oratory down to the middle of the eighteenth century. Notable exemplars of the art include John Cotton, Jonathan Edwards, Thomas Hooker, Increase Mather, and Thomas Shepard. Data on all of them will be found in individual bibliographies herein. Mather Byles, grandson of Increase Mather, continued the family tradition of pulpit oratory. On Byles, see the section herein, The Colonial Period to 1760: Poetry, *ante,* p. 80. The most dynamic preaching of the eighteenth century seems to have been that of George Whitefield (1714–1770), the English evangelist instrumental in promoting the Great Awakening (1739). He attracted large audiences during his several visits to the colonies in the fifties and sixties. A selection of his works was published in several volumes in the two years following his death. Among others during the late eighteenth century who established reputations as orators are John Witherspoon (1723–1794), president of the College of New Jersey (Princeton) from 1768 until the Revolution; and Ezra Stiles (1727–1795), president of Yale College, 1778–1795. Witherspoon's writings were collected in 9 vols., 1804. See V. L. Collins, *President Witherspoon* (2 vols., 1925). Stiles published little during his lifetime. A biography is that by his son-in-law, Abiel Holmes, *The Life of Ezra Stiles* (1798). *Discourses on Various Subjects* (2 vols., 1779), by the Anglican clergyman Jacob Duché (1737–1798), contains some of his famous sermons.

Distinguished orators among statesmen of the Revolution include John Adams, Alexander Hamilton, William Livingston, and James Otis. Each of them is supplied with an individual bibliography herein. For data on others, notably Patrick Henry, see the section herein: The Forming of the Republic: Historical and Political Writing, *ante,* p. 87.

The leading orator and pamphleteer of New England Federalism was Fisher Ames (1758–1808). His writings, first issued in the year following his death, were later published in an enlarged edition (2 vols., 1854). The Virginia statesman Richard Henry Lee (1732–1794) was a commanding figure in parliamentary debate. See J. C. Ballagh, ed., *The Letters of Richard Henry Lee* (2 vols., 1911–1914). Forceful also were John Jay (1745–1829) and Gouverneur Morris (1752–1816). H. P. Johnston edited *Correspondence and Public Papers of John Jay* (4 vols., 1890–1893). Jared Sparks wrote a life of Morris (3 vols., 1832). On John Quincy Adams, see the section on Debating, below.

An early anthology is E. B. Williston, *Eloquence of the United States* (5 vols., 1827). A brief study is George V. Bohman, "Political Oratory in Pre-Revolutionary America," *Quar. Jour. Speech,* XXIII (1937), 243–250.

## Debating

One of the earliest debating clubs, organized under the stimulus of the visit of Bishop Berkeley, was the Literary and Philosophical Society of Newport (1730–1747). The influence of the Linonia (Literary and Debating) Society, allegedly founded at Yale in September, 1753, is said to have been great. The Calliopean Society (1788–1831), a New York debating society and library, included among its members Washington Irving and C. F. Hoffman. The college debating societies flourished in the early years of the nineteenth century and later, and were important factors in shaping the intellectual culture of undergraduates. Cooper Union (Cooper Institute), founded in New York in 1859 by Peter Cooper, was famous for its courses in debating and oratory.

John Quincy Adams (1767–1848) was known in his day as a peerless parliamentary debater. He published in his *Lectures on Rhetoric and Oratory* (2 vols., 1810) the substance of the lectures he delivered as first Boylston Professor of Rhetoric and Oratory at Harvard. His son Charles Francis Adams published the *Memoirs of John Quincy Adams* (12 vols., 1874–1877)— important as studies of politics and of American letters. Allan Nevins has edited *The Diary of John Quincy Adams, 1794–1845*, New York, 1929. See also Donald M. Goodfellow, "The First Boylston Professor of Rhetoric and Oratory," *New Eng. Quar.*, XIX (1946), 372–389; and Horace G. Rahskopf, "John Quincy Adams: Speaker and Rhetorician," *Quar. Jour. Speech*, XXXII (1946), 435–441.

Useful material is in David Potter, *Debating in the Colonial Chartered Colleges: An Historical Survey, 1642 to 1900*, New York, 1944; and in J. N. Beam, *The American Whig Society*, Princeton, 1933.

## MID-NINETEENTH CENTURY AND AFTER
### The Rostrum

Among statesmen, the most distinguished orators and debaters of the century included Henry Clay, John C. Calhoun, Daniel Webster, and Lincoln. Each of them is discussed in an individual bibliography herein.

Also highly respected in his day was the educator and statesman Edward Everett (1794–1865). His *Orations and Speeches on Various Occasions* (4 vols., 1836, 1850–1868) include most of his public utterances. A recent biography is Paul R. Frothingham, *Edward Everett: Orator and Statesman*, Boston, 1925. Other studies include Foster Stearns, in Samuel F. Bemis, ed., *The American Secretaries of State and Their Diplomacy*, New York, 1928, VI, 117–141; Orie W. Long, *Literary Pioneers . . .*, Cambridge, 1935, pp. 63–76; and Allen W. Read, "Edward Everett's Attitude Towards American English," *New Eng. Quar.*, XII (1939), 112–129.

The *Orations and Speeches* of Charles Sumner (1811–1874) were published, Boston, 1850, 2 vols. His *Works* were collected twenty years later (15 vols., 1870–1883). Edward L. Pierce published *Memoir and Letters of*

*Charles Sumner* (4 vols., 1877–1893). Two lives are Moorfield Storey, *Charles Sumner,* Boston, 1900, and George H. Haynes, *Charles Sumner,* Philadelphia, 1909. On Sumner as an orator, see R. Elaine Pagel and Carl Dallinger, in William N. Brigance, ed., *A History and Criticism of American Public Address,* New York, 1943, II, 751–776, with selected bibliography.

The oratory of Stephen A. Douglas (1813–1861) is represented in *The Lincoln-Douglas Debates of 1858* (1910), ed. by Edwin E. Sparks. Douglas's *Autobiography* (1838) was reprinted by the Illinois State Hist. Soc. (1913).

As journalist and orator, Henry Woodfin Grady (1850–1889) was an important influence in rebuilding the South. His published writings include *The New South and Other Addresses* (1904), and *The Complete Orations and Speeches of Henry W. Grady* (1910).

Though William Jennings Bryan (1860–1925) is more closely associated with twentieth century politics and statecraft, his power as orator is in the tradition of the preceding century. The *Speeches of William Jennings Bryan* were issued in 1913, 2 vols., and he published his memoirs in the year of his death. A biography is Paxton Hibben, *Bryan: The Peerless Leader* (1929). On Bryan as orator, see Myron G. Phillips, in William N. Brigance, ed., *op. cit.,* II, 891–918.

The oratory of recent years has found a new medium of expression in the radio. The wartime addresses of Franklin Delano Roosevelt (1882–1945), many of them memorable, were often conversational in manner, and included an entire nation as audience.

### The Pulpit

Two of the notable pulpit orators of the century were Theodore Parker and Henry Ward Beecher. For data on them, see the individual bibliographies herein.

Others include Phillips Brooks (1835–1893), who won an international reputation as a leader in the Episcopal faith. His *Essays and Addresses* were published in the year before his death. Alexander V. G. Allen issued *The Life and Letters of Phillips Brooks* (3 vols., 1900). A recent brief study is William Lawrence, *Life of Phillips Brooks,* New York, 1930. For a discussion of Brooks as orator, see Marie Hochmuth and Norman W. Mattis, in William N. Brigance, ed., *op. cit.,* I, 294–328, with selective bibliography.

### The Bar

Distinguished among orators before the bar were Rufus Choate (1799–1859) and William M. Evarts (1818–1901).

Samuel G. Brown published *The Life and Writings of Rufus Choate,* Boston, 1862. A recent biography is Claude M. Fuess, *Rufus Choate: The Wizard of the Law,* New York, 1928. On Choate as orator, see John W. Black, in William N. Brigance, ed., *op. cit.,* I, 434–458, with selective bibliography.

*The Arguments and Speeches of William M. Evarts* were published, New York, 1919, 3 vols. A recent biography is Chester L. Barrows, *William M. Evarts: Lawyer, Diplomat, Statesman,* Chapel Hill, N.C., 1941. On Evarts as orator, see Lester Thonssen, in William N. Brigance, ed., *op. cit.,* I, 483–499, with selective bibliography.

### The Platform

Two leading orators who made a cause of social reform were Wendell Phillips (1811–1884) and Robert G. Ingersoll (1833–1899).

Phillips's *Speeches, Lectures, and Letters* (2 vols., 1863–1891) are source material for liberal causes in the mid-century. Two biographies are those of George L. Austin, *The Life and Times of Wendell Phillips,* Boston, 1884, and Lorenzo Sears, *Wendell Phillips: Orator and Agitator,* New York, 1909. On Phillips as an orator, see W(illard) Hayes Yeager, in William N. Brigance, ed., *op. cit.,* I, 329–362, with selective bibliography.

*The Works of Robert G. Ingersoll* were published, New York, 1900, 12 vols. The most recent biography is that of Cameron Rogers, *Colonel Bob Ingersoll: A Biographical Narrative of the Great American Orator and Agnostic,* New York, 1927. Sidelights on Ingersoll appear in Hamlin Garland's *Roadside Meetings* (1930), pp. 42–54. On Ingersoll as orator, see Wayland M. Parrish and Alfred D. Huston, in William N. Brigance, ed., *op. cit.,* I, 363–386, with selective bibliography.

### THE LYCEUM

Josiah Holbrook (1788–1854) founded the first American lyceum at Millbury, Mass., in 1826, and remained a leader in the lyceum movement until his death. He published *The American Lyceum; or, Society for the Improvement of Schools and Diffusion of Useful Knowledge,* Boston, 1829—a description of his project—and beginning in 1830 he issued a series of tracts, *Scientific Tracts Designed for Instruction and Entertainment* . . . For a time he edited the *Family Lyceum* (1832) as a weekly newspaper. Holbrook established some 100 branches before 1829, and within the next seven years he set up nearly 3,000 more branches. The notable lecturers of the time included all the best known figures in statecraft, education, and literature. Data on

Beecher, Clemens, Emerson, Holmes, Lowell, Parker, Bayard Taylor, Thoreau, and Daniel Webster will be found in the individual bibliographies herein.

In his own day Edwin Percy Whipple (1819–1886) ranked with Poe and Lowell as an authoritative American critic and was regarded as a leading lyceum lecturer. Representative of his published works are *Lectures on Subjects Connected with Literature and Life* (1850). A recent study is Denham Sutcliffe, " 'Our Young American Macaulay': Edwin Percy Whipple, 1819–1886," *New Eng. Quar.*, XIX (1946), 3–18.

By 1868 the lyceum had become a commercial lecture bureau, and in that year the journalist and leading lecture promoter James Redpath (1833–1891) founded the Boston (later Redpath) Lyceum Bureau. A study of the lyceum during the period after the Civil War is Charles F. Horner, *The Life of James Redpath and the Development of the Modern Lyceum,* New York, 1926.

In 1874 Lewis Miller and John H. Vincent established the Chautauqua Assembly on the shore of Lake Chautauqua, New York, as a program and assembly for religious and educational instruction, later extended to include musical and dramatic entertainments. The Chautauqua Institution undertook to extend its facilities by way of an annual summer school, correspondence courses, and book publication; and from 1880 to 1914 issued its own organ, *The Chautauquan.* After 1890 Chautauqua societies replaced the lyceums and continued to flourish in small communities throughout the country well into the twentieth century, though with increased attention to entertainment.

The main outlines are sketched in John S. Noffsinger, *Correspondence Schools, Lyceums, Chautauquas,* New York, 1926; and Cecil B. Hayes, *The American Lyceum: Its History and Contribution to Education,* Washington, 1932. For an authentic early account, see John H. Vincent, *The Chautauqua Movement* (1886). Useful also is Jesse Lyman Hurlbut, *The Story of Chautauqua,* New York, 1921. A. Augustus Wright edited *Who's Who in the Lyceum,* Philadelphia, 1906, with a foreword (pp. 5–57) containing an enthusiastic brief history of the movement.

### History and Criticism

The fullest critical survey of American oratory is William N. Brigance, ed., *A History and Criticism of American Public Address,* New York, 1943, 2 vols. Chapters, written by collaborating specialists, are devoted to individual orators. Included in the historical survey (I, 3–210), is a section by Doris G. Yoakam on "Women's Introduction to the American Platform" (pp. 153–

192). See also Francis Pendleton Gaines, *Southern Oratory: A Study in Idealism,* University, Ala., 1946.

Other useful studies are Warren C. Shaw, *History of American Oratory,* Indianapolis, 1928, and Herbert A. Wichelns, "The Literary Criticism of Oratory," in *Studies in Honor of James A. Winans . . . ,* New York, 1925, pp. 181–216. For a study of the lyceum and popular spokesmen of the mid-nineteenth century, see Constance M. Rourke, *Trumpets of Jubilee,* New York, 1927. Samuel B. Harding edited *Select Orations Illustrating American History,* New York, 1924. In the nature of source material are Edward G. Parker, *The Golden Age of American Oratory* (1857), and Thomas Wentworth Higginson, *American Orators and Oratory* (1901).

Special studies of some value are H. H. Hoeltje, "Notes on the History of Lecturing in Iowa, 1855–1885," *Iowa Jour. Hist. and Politics,* XXV (1927), 62–131; William D. Hoyt, Jr., "Richard Henry Dana [Sr.] and the Lecture System, 1841," *New Eng. Quar.,* XVIII (1945), 93–96; and Elmer E. Stoll, "The Downfall of Oratory: Our Undemocratic Arts," *Jour. Hist. Ideas,* VII (1946), 3–34.

Useful background material is in Gerald W. Johnson, *America's Silver Age,* New York, 1939.

A bibliographical listing is Albert C. Baird, "A Selected Bibliography of American Oratory," *Quar. Jour. Speech Educ.,* XII (1926), 352–356.

## ALMANACS AND CHAPBOOKS

### ALMANACS

With the exception of a broadside, the first work printed in the British colonies was *An Almanack for New England for the Year 1639.* It was issued from the Cambridge press of Stephen Day. As in England, almanacs began as calendars with astronomical data added. They were the most widely distributed items issued from the colonial press and today are notable for their rarity. In the early years Boston was the center of almanac making. John Tulley of Saybrook, Conn., added humorous matter in his almanac of 1687. For an annotated bibliography of Tulley's almanacs, see Alfred B. Page, "John Tulley's Almanacks, 1687–1702," *Pub. Col. Soc. Mass.,* XIII (1910), 207–223. Later almanacs featured popular science and included proverbs, jests, and practical information. The almanacs of New England were often edited by young Harvard graduates, who used the pages to feature their own verse or give up-to-date popular scientific instruction. The first recorded exposition of the Copernican system in New England seems to be that of Zechariah

Brigden, "A breif Explication and proof of the Philolaick Systeme," in the *Almanack* issued at Cambridge, 1659, reprinted in *New Eng. Quar.,* VII (1934), 9–12.

Almanac making in Philadelphia dates from 1687. Almanacs were there issued by Daniel Leeds (1652–1720), and by his son Titan Leeds (1699–1738).

Among the notable almanacs in the early years of the eighteenth century were those issued at Dedham, Mass., by Nathaniel Ames (1708–1764), and continued by his son, as *Astronomical Diary and Almanack* (1725–1775). Their importance as source material on the rural intellectual interests in the colonies is the subject of Samuel Briggs, *The Essays, Humor, and Poems of Nathaniel Ames, Father and Son, of Dedham, Massachusetts, from Their Almanacks, 1726–1775* . . ., Cleveland, 1891. James Franklin published *The Rhode Island Almanack* (1728–1758). Benjamin Franklin's Poor Richard almanacs (1733–1758) are probably the best known of all. Robert Bailey Thomas (1766–1846) began publication of the *Farmer's Almanack* in 1793. Under the title *The Old Farmer's Almanac,* it is still published. Its importance as a source of information on New England life and manners is set forth in George L. Kittredge, *The Old Farmer and His Almanack* (1904).

The Crockett almanacs were issued by various publishers and purported to be the work of Davy Crockett or his "heirs." Some fifty appeared between 1835 and 1856, featuring tall tales concerning Crockett, Mike Fink, Daniel Boone, and others. Notable collections of early almanacs are in the library of the American Antiquarian Society at Worcester, and in the Library of Congress. At present *The World Almanac and Book of Facts* is issued annually as a standard compendium by the New York *World-Telegram.*

Studies of American almanacs are Clarence S. Brigham, "An Account of American Almanacs and Their Value for Historical Study," *Proc. Amer. Antiq. Soc.,* n.s. XXXV (1925), 1–25, 194–209; Chester N. Greenough, "New England Almanacs, 1766–1775, and the American Revolution," *Proc. Amer. Antiq. Soc.,* n.s. XLV (1935), 288–316; and N. W. Lovely, "Notes on New England Almanacs," *New Eng. Quar.,* VIII (1935), 264–277. Checklists and bibliographies are Hugh A. Morrison, *Preliminary Check List of American Almanacs, 1639–1800,* Washington, 1907; Charles L. Nichols, "Checklist of Maine, New Hampshire and Vermont Almanacs," *Proc. Amer. Antiq. Soc.,* n.s. XXXVIII (1928), 63–163; Albert C. Bates, "Checklist of Connecticut Almanacs, 1709–1850, with Introduction and Notes," *Proc. Amer. Antiq. Soc.,* n.s. XXIV (1914), 93–215; Victor H. Paltsits, "The Almanacs of Roger Sherman, 1750–1761," *Proc. Amer. Antiq. Soc.,* n.s. XVIII (1907), 213–258; Howard M. Chapin, "Check List of Rhode Island Almanacs, 1643–1850, with Introduction and Notes," *Proc. Amer. Antiq. Soc.,* n.s. XXV (1915), 19–54; Alexander J. Wall, "A List of New York Almanacs, 1694–1850," *Bul. N.Y.*

*Pub. Lib.*, XXIV (1920), 287–296, 335–355, 389–413, 443–460, 508–519, 543–559, 620–641; Charles F. Heartman, *Preliminary Checklist of Almanacs Printed in New Jersey Prior to 1850*, Metuchen, N.J., 1929; and Douglas C. McMurtrie, "A Check-List of Kentucky Almanacs, 1789–1830," *Register Ky. State Hist. Soc.*, July, 1932, pp. 237–259.

CHAPBOOKS

Chapbooks were pamphlet editions of popular literature such as jokes, ballads, fables, moral tales, and orations. They were widely distributed, often by peddlers on foot or on horseback, in the early years of the nineteenth century, and together with the newspaper and the almanac were an important instrument in the dissemination of popular literature. The best known publisher of chapbooks was the Worcester printer and historian, Isaiah Thomas. For some thirty years Mason Locke Weems (1759–1825) acted as book agent and peddler of chapbooks for Mathew Carey. For a study of American chapbooks, see Harry B. Weiss, *American Chapbooks, 1722–1842*, New York, 1945.

# BIBLIOGRAPHIES: MOVEMENTS AND INFLUENCES

# CHRONICLES OF THE FRONTIER: LITERATURE
# OF TRAVEL AND WESTWARD MIGRATION

The written records dealing with the discovery and settlement of America are by far the most voluminous and ramifying body of material that touches upon American civilization. For four centuries America remained a frontier, during which time its conquest, settlement, and expansion were a vital concern to great numbers who were directly affected at home and abroad, as well as to others who saw the New World as another chance to create a civilization which might avoid the admitted failures of the past.

Of the large number of published books and tracts dealing with America, a small part has now been studied. Much yet remains to be said of the contributions made by Italian, Spanish, Portuguese, Dutch, and Scandinavian commentators and travelers. Studies of English, French, and German influences are somewhat more advanced. The extensive bibliography in Joseph Sabin's *A Dictionary of Books Relating to America* (29 vols., 1868–1936), though making no attempt to list periodical articles, is so vast in its coverage that students have not yet had opportunity to make full use of it.

The output in the sixteenth, seventeenth, and eighteenth centuries was aimed to meet particular demands. Writers sought first to satisfy curiosity, to promote settlements by furnishing guides to the natural history of the wilderness and the manners of the inhabitants, and to inform travelers of conditions they could expect when impelled to undertakings in the New World. Thus the utilitarian character of much early writing. Later appeared the comments upon society and manners, both critical and enthusiastic. Along with them appeared a sprinkling of "escape" literature, sometimes trivial, often entertaining. Finally, in the late eighteenth century, appeared the works which deal with America as idea, as a Utopia. Three centuries of colonization had resulted in a national experiment. How should American society be analyzed? Could it survive? Should the democratic experiment, bound to be "contagious," be transplanted to Europe, and if so, would it be beneficial? The discovery of America had had an explosive effect. Unlike the continents of Asia and Africa, it was a *new world* in fact, for men to conquer, exploit, shape. It offered a new chance. A recent and useful general presentation of America studied in the field of ideas is Eugène Déprez, "Les Grands Voyages et les Grandes Découvertes jusqu'à la Fin du XVIIIᵉ Siècle: Origines, Déve-loppement, Conséquences," *Bul. du Comité International des Sciences His-toriques,* No. 9 (June, 1930), pp. 555–614.

In addition to the vast amount of material dealing with the European impact, there are the records of the generations of settlers themselves who, in the process of westward migration across the continent, were no longer European, whatever their racial origin. These are the accounts written by men and women who had now become Americans. Whatever the literary merit of such writing, it deserves the study and analysis it is increasingly receiving. Such material can be found in the thousands of travel narratives and the journals and letters of explorers, settlers, missionaries, fur traders, emigrants, and observers whose writings have been separately issued or pub-lished in the collections of state and local historical societies. Much still remains in manuscript.

The titles which follow are highly selective. They represent works which (a) are historical documents of primary significance; (b) as domestic or for-eign comment on society remain the source of much that is known or believed about American culture; and (c) typify the variety and complexity of America as frontier. The selection is necessarily arbitrary and suggestive only. The items here listed must be supplemented by reference to material elsewhere herein recorded. See especially the sections on American Writers and Books Abroad, *post,* p. 356; Mingling of Tongues, *post,* p. 284; The Colonial Period to 1760: Cultural History, *ante,* p. 72; Regionalism and Local Color, *post,* p. 304; and Utopian Ventures, *post,* p. 348. Data on bibliographical centers and registries of book publication appear in the Guide to Resources, pp. 3–13, 21–25.

## EASTERN UNITED STATES TO THE MISSISSIPPI

### THE EARLIEST EXPLORATIONS

A thirteenth century manuscript, narrating the story of Leif Ericsson (*fl.* 999–1003) and of his father Eric the Red, is the earliest extant record of explorations to North America. The story of their attempted colonization of Vineland, usually identified with Maine, Massachusetts, and other parts of New England, has been rendered into English by Arthur M. Reeves in *The Finding of Wineland the Good: The History of the Icelandic Discovery of America,* London, 1890. The translation includes *The Saga of Eric the Red* and *The Wineland History of the Flatey Book*. These accounts are most accessible in the *Original Narratives of Early American History*, New York, 1906, and later, a series published under the general editorship of John Franklin Jameson.

The first written record dating from the New World is Columbus's description of his voyage from Aug. 3, 1492, to Mar. 15, 1493, published in Spanish at Barcelona in Apr., 1493. The famous letter may conveniently be found in the Original Narratives Series, edited by Edward G. Bourne.

North American travel literature may be said to start with Alvar Núñez Cabeza de Vaca's account of his overland trek from Florida to the Southwest during the years 1528-1536, first printed as *La Relación y Comentarios . . .* , Zamora, 1542. The first part of *La Relación* was rendered into English by Buckingham Smith as *The Narrative of Alvar Nuñez Cabeça de Vaca*, Washington, 1851. There are several other reasonably accurate translations and reprints, the most conveniently accessible of which is Frederick W. Hodge and Theodore H. Lewis, eds., *The Spanish Explorers in the Southern United States, 1528-1543*, New York, 1907 (Orig. Narr. Ser.). Cabeza de Vaca's account of the legendary "Seven Cities of Cibola" excited the curiosity of Francisco Vásquez Coronado, who then began his famous march from Mexico into the "Southwest" in 1540—across Texas, Oklahoma, and Kansas. The story of the expedition was published in Francisco López de Gómara, *La Historia General de las Indias* (1552 and later). It also was reported by Pedro de Casteñeda in *Relación de le Jornada de Cibola*. The latter text remained in manuscript until 1896, when the Spanish text was printed, with an English translation, by George P. Winship. The famous story of Hernando de Soto's discovery of the Mississippi was told by de Soto's companion, the anonymous "Gentleman of Elvas," in *Relaçam Verdadeira . . .* (1557). It is best rendered from the Portuguese in Richard Hakluyt's *Virginia Richly Valued . . .* , (1609). The tragic history of the Huguenot colony in Florida, conceived by Admiral Coligny and planted by Jean Ribaut, which ended in a massacre by the Spaniards, is told in René Goulaine de Laudonnière's *L'Histoire Notable de la Floride . . .* , Paris, 1586, edited and in part written by Martin Basanier. It was translated into English in 1587, and is most accessible in B. F. French, ed., *Historical Collections of Louisiana and Florida*, n.s. New York, 1869, pp. 165-362.

Notable also is the account by Antonio de Espejo of his California (i.e., New Mexico) expeditions made in 1582-1583. The original Spanish and French editions are very rare, and the unique English edition, London, 1587, is in the Henry E. Huntington Library. It is entitled *New Mexico: Otherwise, the voiage of Anthony of Espeio . . . Translated out of the Spanish copie printed first at Madreel, 1586, and afterward at Paris, in the same yeare.*

Hakluyt included it among his collections of travels, and it has recently been made accessible, edited by Frederick W. Hodge, Lancaster, Pa., 1928.

The accounts of Jacques Cartier's journeys up the St. Lawrence, in his effort to discover a northwest passage to Cathay, begin with *Brief Recit, et Succincte Narration, de la Navigation Faicte es Yles de Canada . . .*, Paris, 1545, a record of his second voyage. Accounts of the first voyage (1534) were published in Italian (1556), in English (1580), and in French (1598) as *Discours du Voyage fait par le capitaine Jacques Cartier aux Terres-Neufves de Canadas . . .*, at Rouen. John Florio was the translator of the earliest English version, which was later included in Hakluyt's *The Principal Navigations . . .*, London, 1600, as *The First Relation of Jaques Carthier of S. Malo . . . 1534.* This account is included in *Early English and French Voyages, Chiefly from Hakluyt, 1534-1608,* ed. by Henry S. Burrage, New York, 1906 (Orig. Narr. Ser.), pp. 4-31. A critical edition of the *Brief Recit* (1545), from manuscript, has been published by the University of Toronto. The best English version is that of James Phinney Baxter, Portland, Me., 1906. Useful studies of Cartier, by Henry P. Biggar, are in *Publ. of the Public Archives of Canada,* No. 5 (1911), and No. 14 (1930).

No collections of early voyages are more important or more deservedly famous than those of Richard Hakluyt (1552-1616), the English scholar, geographer, and editor. The first of his published works was *Divers Voyages Touching the Discovery of America . . .*, London, 1582. Continuing his interest in assembling source material dealing with English discoveries and colonization, Hakluyt published *The Principall Navigations, Voiages, and Discoveries of the English Nation . . .*, London, 1589. During 1598-1600 appeared the final, reconstructed, and greatly enlarged edition of this latter work, entitled *The Principal Navigations, Voyages, Traffiques and Discoveries of the English Nation,* in 3 vols. The *Divers Voyages,* edited with introduction and notes by John Winter Jones, was reprinted, London, 1850. Recent reprints of *The Principal Navigations,* among the many that have appeared since 1600, are the Glasgow 1903-1905 ed. in 12 vols.; the London 1907 ed. in 8 vols.; and the London 1926-1931 ed. in 8 vols., issued in Everyman's Library. Hakluyt bequeathed his unused material to Samuel Purchas, who utilized it in compiling *Hakluytus Posthumus; or, Purchas His Pilgrimes . . .*, London, 1625, 4 vols. This continuation is based in part on Hakluyt's manuscripts, not always carefully or judiciously used. None of Purchas's works was reprinted until the Glasgow 1905-1907 reissue in 20 volumes of the 1625 edition of the *Pilgrimes.*

No early book of travels and exploration is more important as literature than Thomas Hariot, *A Briefe and True Report of the New Found Land of Virginia . . .*, London, 1588. This history of the North Carolina coast by a professional mathematician and geographer is the first English book on the first English colony in what is now the United States. Hariot's fellow colonist John White (*fl.* 1585–1593) contributed imaginative drawings, made from eyewitness knowledge, to the De Bry (1590) edition. The account is included in Hakluyt's collection, and appeared in many later editions. A facsimile reproduction of the 1588 edition, with an introduction by Randolph G. Adams, was issued Ann Arbor, Mich., 1931. See especially the volume recently edited and annotated by Stefan Lorant, *The New World: The First Pictures of America, Made by John White and Jacques Le Moyne, with Contemporary Narratives of the Huguenot Settlement in Florida, 1562–1565, and the Virginia Colony, 1585–1590*, New York, 1946.

Many of the early explorations already described, together with other published reprints, are accessible in whole or in part in volumes of the Original Narratives Series: *The Spanish Explorers in the Southern United States, 1528–1543*, New York, 1907, ed. by Frederick W. Hodge and Theodore H. Lewis; *Early English and French Voyages, Chiefly from Hakluyt, 1534–1608*, New York, 1906, ed. by Henry S. Burrage; and *Spanish Exploration in the Southwest, 1542–1706*, New York, 1916, ed. by Herbert E. Bolton.

### THE NORTH AND NORTHWEST

The various accounts by Samuel de Champlain (1567–1635) of his voyages and travels furnish the most complete and vivid contemporary record of the early history of French Canada (1603–1635). The explorations were very extensive, and Champlain's descriptions are detailed and authentic. His first voyage, described in the historically valuable record entitled *Des Sauvages; ou, Voyage de Samuel Champlain de Brouage Fait en la France Nouvelle,* was soon translated into English and included in the 1625 edition of *Purchas His Pilgrimes.* The 1613 edition of his *Voyages* reports his mapping of New England. Important among the later accounts is *Voyages et Descouvertures . . .*, Paris, 1619, the second edition of which (1627) reports his trips through upper New York State in 1615. The final summing up, and his last and longest book, is *Les Voyages de la Nouvelle France . . .*, Paris, 1632. Many editions of the writings have been published, but no accurate English translation was made until that of Annie N. Bourne, in *The Voyages and Explorations of Samuel de Champlain, 1604–1616, Narrated by Himself,* New York, 1922, 2 vols., ed. with introd. and bibl. footnotes by Edward G. Bourne. The most nearly definitive edition of the *Works* was published by the Champlain Society, Toronto, 1922–1927, 6 vols., ed. by Henry P. Biggar. Most easily accessible is William L. Grant, ed., *The Voyages of Samuel de Champlain, 1604–1618*, New York. 1907 (Orig. Narr. Ser.).

Foremost among the Franciscan Recollects was Gabriel Sagard-Théodat, historian of the Hurons. His *Histoire du Canada* . . . , Paris, 1636 (reprinted, Paris, 1866, 4 vols.), sums up his previous work and describes the arrival of Etienne Brulé at Mackinac and the Sault in 1619. The work is translated as *The Long Journey to the Country of the Hurons, by Father Gabriel Sagard,* Toronto, 1939, ed. by George M. Wrong.

One of the monumental collections of documentary reports relating to North America is that known as *The Jesuit Relations and Allied Documents: Travels and Explorations of the Jesuit Missionaries in New France, 1610–1791* . . . , translated into English, ed. by Reuben G. Thwaites, Cleveland, 1896–1901, in 73 vols. They are the reports on the Great Lakes area in the seventeenth and eighteenth centuries, written to the Superiors of the Jesuit Order by the missionaries in New France; and the regions and peoples described include those in the present states of New York, Michigan, Illinois. Wisconsin, and Minnesota. Some of them were originally published annually in Paris during the period 1632 through 1673; in the latter year publication was discontinued after forty volumes had been issued. The Canadian government republished those already in print, in 1858, in 3 vols. The *Relations* furnished the source for Parkman's *The Jesuits in North America in the Seventeenth Century* (1867), but the first complete text in English is that assembled by Thwaites. Inevitably the quality of writing and the acuteness with which regions and events are depicted vary, but important among the many chroniclers are such names as Paul Le Jeune, Barthélemy Vimont, Jérôme Lalament, Paul Ragueneau, Claude Jean Allouez, Claude Dablon, Jean de Brébeuf, and Jacques Marquette. A full discussion of these *Relations,* together with useful bibl. data, is Lawrence C. Wroth, "The Jesuit Relations from New France," *Papers Bibl. Soc. Amer.,* XXX (1936), 110–149.

A readable and reliable account of work in the Upper Mississippi Valley, especially in Minnesota, is that of the most widely read of Recollects, Father Louis Hennepin, *Description de la Louisiane* . . . , Paris, 1683. It was translated into English, New York, 1880; but the authoritative rendering is that of Marion E. Cross, Minneapolis, 1938. An important compilation, which published the original account of La Salle's voyages (especially his first) down the Mississippi, is that of the Recollect, Chrétien Le Clercq, *Premier Etablissement de la Foy dans la Nouvelle France* . . . , Paris, 1691, 2 vols. It is translated into English by John G. Shea, New York, 1881, 2 vols. La Salle's discoveries are controversial. They have recently been reexamined by Jean Delanglez, *Some La Salle Journeys,* Chicago, 1938.

A notable analysis of the American Indian as observed in the seventeenth century is that of Louis-Armand de Lorn d'Arce, Baron de Lahontan, *Nouveaux Voyages de M. le Baron de Lahontan,* La Haye, 1703, 2 vols. It was immediately translated into English and has been reissued in some fifty editions. A reprint of the English edition of 1703 was brought out by Reuben G. Thwaites, Chicago, 1905, 2 vols.

Some of the better known material has been made accessible in *Early Narratives of the Northwest, 1634–1699,* New York, 1917 (Orig. Narr. Ser.), ed. by Louise P. Kellogg. The collection includes Father Allouez's Wisconsin journey, 1669–1670; the Mississippi voyage of Jolliet and Marquette, 1673; and La Salle's discoveries, 1678–1693. The best general account of many of the earliest voyages is still that of Justin Winsor, *Narrative and Critical History of America,* Boston, 1884–1889, 8 vols.

## NEW ENGLAND

The two earliest descriptions of New England are those of John Brereton and James Rosier. Brereton's *A Briefe and True Relation of the Discoverie of the North Part of Virginia* . . . , London, 1602, is reprinted in *Coll. Mass. Hist. Soc.,* 3rd ser., VIII (1843), 83–123; and Rosier's *A True Relation* . . . , London, 1605, describing the coast of Maine, is reprinted, *ibid.,* pp. 125–157.

Much of the writing set down in the first years of the New England settlements is "promotion" literature, accounts written to draw settlers to the new colonies. Such are the well designed and still neglected descriptions of John Smith. Especially interesting are *A Description of New-England* . . . , London, 1616; *New Englands Trials,* London, 1620; *The Generall Historie of Virginia, New-England, and the Summer Isles* . . . , London, 1624; and *Advertisements for the Unexperienced Planters of New-England, or Anywhere,* London, 1631—containing the earliest account of the Anglican Church in America. An excellent edition of Smith's writings is that of Edward Arber, *Travels and Works of Captain John Smith,* Birmingham, Eng., 1884, reprinted with some corrections and an introduction by Arthur G. Bradley, Edinburgh, 1910, 2 vols. For details of the many reprints of Smith's writings and of data about Smith, see the individual bibliography herein.

John White (1575–1648) was one of the English merchants who helped establish the Massachusetts Bay Colony. His report, published as *The Planters Plea* . . . , London, 1630, defends the economic and social values of settling the colony, and recounts its early history. It is reprinted in *Proc. Mass. Hist. Soc.,* LXII (1930), 367–425, and is edited by M. H. Saville in facsimile, Rockport, Mass., 1930. A detailed life is Frances Rose-Troup, *John White: The Patriarch of Dorchester and the Founder of Massachusetts, 1620–1630,* New York, 1931.

Part of a journal of the first Salem minister, Francis Higginson (1586–

1630), details the hardships of the first winter in the Bay Colony, and gives the initial reaction of Englishmen to the new scene. This part was published as *New-Englands Plantation* . . . , London, 1630, and has most recently been reprinted in *Proc. Mass. Hist. Soc.,* LXII (1930), 301–321. The complete journal is printed in the *Life* (1891) by Thomas W. Higginson. Another deservedly well known early description is William Wood's *New Englands Prospect* . . . , London, 1634. It has been reprinted, Boston, 1865, ed. by Charles Deane; and Boston, 1898, ed. by Henry W. Boynton.

Writing of primary value by participants in the colonizing of New England is that of William Bradford, John Winthrop, and Edward Johnson. Individual bibliographies of Bradford and Winthrop are herein included. Edward Johnson (1598–1672) published *A History of New-England: From the English Planting in the Yeere 1628 untill the Yeere 1652* . . . , London, 1654. It is better known by its running title *The Wonder-Working Providence of Sions Saviour in New England*. Written by a layman and militia captain, it especially represents the viewpoint of the rank and file. Of various reprints, the latest is that edited by J. F. Jameson, in the Orig. Narr. Ser., New York, 1910. The earliest published account of the Plymouth Colony is Robert Cushman's *A Sermon Preached at Plimmoth* . . . , London, 1622.

The unpublished writing of William Bradford and Edward Winslow was used by Nathaniel Morton in his *New-England's Memoriall* . . . , Cambridge, 1669. It has been reprinted in Scholars' Facsimiles and Reprints, New York, 1937, ed. by Howard J. Hall.

Several important accounts have been left by observers who themselves never became settlers. Thomas Morton's *New English Canaan or New Canaan,* Amsterdam, 1637, is a riotous attack on Puritans by a gentleman of questionable antecedents who clashed with authorities of both Plymouth and Massachusetts Bay, and was expelled for conduct considered both immoral and dangerous. The best edited reprint is that of Charles Francis Adams, published with introduction and notes in the *Pub. Prince Soc. of Boston,* XIV (1883).

The first professional lawyer in Massachusetts Bay was Thomas Lechford (*fl.* 1629–1642), debarred from practice in 1641 for trying to influence a jury. No Puritan, he had little sympathy with the conduct of colonial affairs, and returned to England in 1642. He left an invaluable record of daily life in "Note-Book Kept by Thomas Lechford, Esq., Lawyer, in Boston, Massachusetts Bay, from June 27, 1638, to July 29, 1641," ed. by E. E. Hale in *Trans. and Coll. Amer. Antiq. Soc.,* VII (1885). His entertaining *Plain Dealing; or, Newes from New-England,* London, 1642, though an attack on the Puritan, is judicious. It has been edited by J. H. Trumbull in *Library of New England History,* No. 4, Boston, 1867, and appears also in *Coll. Mass.*

*Hist. Soc.,* 3rd ser., III (1833), 55–128. A similarly non-Puritan viewpoint, critical and refreshingly candid, is that of John Josselyn, the naturalist and traveler. He left two interesting accounts of New England in *New Englands Rarities Discovered: in Birds, Beasts, Fishes, Serpents, and Plants of That Country,* London, 1672; and *An Account of Two Voyages to New-England,* London, 1674. The first-named volume was reprinted, ed. by E. Tuckerman, in *Trans. and Coll. Amer. Antiq. Soc.,* IV (1860), 133–238; and the second in *Coll. Mass. Hist. Soc.,* 3rd ser., III (1833), 211–354. A valuable record left by a Catholic priest is that of Father Gabriel Dreuillettes, "Narrative of a Journey to New England, 1650," in *The Jesuit Relations . . . ,* ed. by Reuben G. Thwaites, XXXVI, 83–111.

Among the early historians who were observers of the men and events they describe, one of the most considerable is William Hubbard (1621–1704). His earliest record is *A Narrative of the Troubles with the Indians in New-England . . . ,* Boston, 1677. More important is his *A General History of New-England from the Discovery to MDCLXXX . . . ,* first printed in *Coll. Mass. Hist. Soc.,* 2nd ser., V–VI (1815). The best edition is that of 1848, supplemented by the sheets issued in 1878. Hubbard's account was written in 1680 at the request of and by subsidy from the General Court. Though the account is based chiefly on the earlier works of Morton, Bradford, and Winthrop, it inserts matter not found elsewhere. It was used by Cotton Mather and Thomas Prince in compiling their histories. Two critical estimates of Hubbard are Randolph G. Adams, "William Hubbard's 'Narrative,' 1677: A Bibliographical Study," *Papers Bibl. Soc. Amer.,* XXXIII (1939), 25–39; and Kenneth B. Murdock, "William Hubbard and the Providential Interpretation of History," *Proc. Amer. Antiq. Soc.,* LII (1943), 15–37.

A monumental work of scholarship, accurate and perceptive, is Cotton Mather's *Magnalia Christi Americana . . . ,* London, 1702. This folio volume of nearly a thousand pages might equally well be classified as biography, narrative history, or intellectual history. It is discussed by Kenneth B. Murdock, in Thomas J. Holmes, *Cotton Mather: A Bibliography,* Cambridge, 1940, II, 589–591.

The scholarship of Thomas Prince (1687–1758) is displayed in *A Chronological History of New-England . . . ,* Boston, 1736–1755, 2 vols., carefully based on good sources and set down in the form of annals with exactness and brevity. Some supplementary material is reprinted in *Coll. Mass. Hist. Soc.,* 2nd ser., VII (1818), 189–295.

Samuel Penhallow's *The History of the Wars of New-England, with the Eastern Indians,* Boston, 1726, is vivid and realistic. A monument of early historical scholarship is the three-volume work of Isaac Backus, *History of*

*New England, with Particular Reference to the Denomination of Christians Called Baptists* (1777–1796), 3 vols., though it is biased and awkward in style.

What may properly be termed the final compilations of material dealing with the New England frontier, assembled by one who both knew and participated in the history of the colonial period, are the productions of Thomas Hutchinson, the last royal governor of the Massachusetts Bay (1771–1774). He gathered *A Collection of Original Papers Relative to the History of the Colony of Massachusets-Bay,* Boston, 1769 (reprinted, Albany, 1865, 2 vols.), an invaluable collection, containing documents of fundamental importance, the originals of which were lost during the Revolution. Also based on extensive study of manuscript sources is *The History of . . . Massachusetts-Bay,* 3 vols.: I–II, Boston, 1764–1767; III, London, 1828. An excellent modern edition, made from the author's own copies of the first two volumes and from his manuscript of vol. III, is that of Lawrence S. Mayo, Cambridge, 1936, 3 vols., with memoirs and additional notes supplied by the editor. For bibliographical and critical details, see Charles Deane, *Hutchinson Bibliography* (1857), and Lawrence S. Mayo's account in *Proc. Amer. Antiq. Soc.,* n.s. XLI (1931), 321–339.

Collections of source material are Alexander Young, ed., *Chronicles of the Pilgrim Fathers . . . from 1602 to 1625,* Boston, 1841, and *idem, Chronicles of the First Planters of the Colony of Massachusetts Bay, from 1623 to 1636,* Boston, 1846—both critical reprintings; Samuel G. Drake, ed., *The Old Indian Chronicle: Being a Collection of Exceeding Rare Tracts Written and Published in the Time of King Philip's War, by Persons Residing in the Country . . . ,* Boston, 1836 (and also 1867), with introd. and notes; William H. Whitmore, ed., *The Andros Tracts: Being a Collection of Pamphlets and Official Papers,* Boston, 1868–1874, 3 vols.—important as source material and original narrative concerning the Andros regime, 1686–1689, and the Revolution of 1689. A recent collection is Charles H. Lincoln, ed., *Narratives of the Indian Wars, 1675–1699,* New York, 1913 (Orig. Narr. Ser.), including accounts by Cotton Mather and Mary Rowlandson.

NEW NETHERLAND

Emanuel van Meteren, in his *Historie der Nederlandschen en Haar Nabueren Oorlogen,* Amsterdam, 1652, affords the earliest published account of Henry Hudson's voyage up the Hudson River in 1609, told as part of the Netherland history. The first work devoted solely to a discussion of Dutch colonies, of which New Amsterdam was but one, is *Nieuwe Wereldt, ofte Beschrijvinghe van West-Indien,* Leyden, 1625, the work of Johann de Laet, a director of the West India Company and an associate of the publishing house of the Elzevirs. Robert Juet's account of New Netherland is in the third volume of *Purchas His Pilgrimes* (1625), published as *Henry Hudson's Third Voyage*. The first complete, printed description of the Dutch province is that of Adriaen van der Donck, the fiery lawyer and remonstrant, in *Beschryvinge van Nieuw-Nederlant . . .* , Amsterdam, 1655. His "Remonstrance," written as a protest against the despotism of the Stuyvesant regime, was entitled *Vertoogh van Nieu-Neder-Land . . . . . .,* 's Gravenhage, 1650. It is vigorously and ably written, and deserves to be better known.

An interesting personality, as it is revealed in his writing, is that of the navigator, colonizer, and geographer, David Pietersz. De Vries. His *Korte Historiael . . .* , Hoorn, 1655 ("Short Historical Notes from the Logbook of Voyages in the Four Quarters of the Globe"), presents the first sensitive impressions of the beauty of the Hudson River. The picture of New Netherland manners and people is vivid, and the style is salty. The account is significant among early descriptions.

The earliest separate publication in English describing the province is Daniel Denton's *A Brief Description of New York: Formerly Called New Netherlands . . .* , London, 1670. It has been often reprinted, and is best edited by Victor H. Paltsits, for the Scholars' Facsimile Text Soc., New York, 1937.

A very entertaining account of colonial manners in New England and New York is that written by two Dutch observers, Jasper Danckaerts and Peter Sluyter. The *Journal* of their travel in 1679–1680 along the seaboard from Boston to Delaware was first printed from manuscript by the Long Island Historical Soc. (1867), and is most easily accessible in the volume edited by Bartlett B. James and John Franklin Jameson for the Orig. Narr. Ser., New York, 1913. A later traveler's account of some interest was written by Charles Wolley, *A Two Years Journal in New-York,* London, 1701, reprinted in facsimile, ed. by Edward G. Bourne, Cleveland, 1902. Convenient reprints of several early narratives and descriptions, including selections from the writing of Juet, Laet, De Vries, and van der Donck, are in *Narratives of New Netherland, 1609–1664,* New York, 1909 (Orig. Narr. Ser.), ed. by John Franklin Jameson. William Smith (the younger), *The History of the Province of New-York . . .* , London, 1757, chronicles events to 1732, with emphasis on the eighteenth century. The edition of 1829 includes a continuation by Smith. The manuscript of the *History* is in the New York Public Library.

The most authentic and detailed study of New Netherland manners and literature is that of Ellis L. Raesly, *Portrait of New Netherland,* New York, 1945. Isaac N. Phelps Stokes, *The Iconography of Manhattan Island . . .* ,

New York, 1915–1928, 6 vols., is immensely useful for its data regarding the early history of New Netherland. See also Georg M. Asher, *A Bibliographical and Historical Essay on the Dutch Books and Pamphlets Relating to New-Netherland* . . . , Amsterdam, 1854–1867 (2 parts).

MIDDLE ATLANTIC COLONIES

Like much of the early writing dealing with New England, a great deal of that relating to the settlement of Pennsylvania, New Jersey, Delaware, and Maryland is promotional in character. Such is the intent of much of the writing of William Penn, the English Quaker who secured the grant of Pennsylvania in 1681, and personally organized the colony. For data on Penn, see the individual bibliography herein.

The Quaker Thomas Budd emigrated to New Jersey in 1678. His *Good Order Established in Pennsylvania and New Jersey* . . . , Philadelphia, 1685, 39 pp., giving an account of conditions in the region, is excellent promotion literature. It was reprinted, Cleveland, 1902, with introduction and notes by Frederick J. Shepard. A further useful record is Gabriel Thomas's *An Historical and Geographical Account of . . . Pensilvania,* London, 1698, reprinted in part, Harrisburg, Pa., 1935.

The first "dissertation" about Pennsylvania by a native Pennsylvanian is Tobias Erick Biörck, *Dissertatio Gradualis de Plantatione Ecclesiae Svecanae in America* . . . , Upsala, 1731, 34 pp.

One of the most important and influential of early colonizers was Francis Daniel Pastorius. This German-born lawyer, teacher, scholar, and linguist emigrated in 1683 as agent for some Frankfort Quakers (Mennonites) to establish a settlement in and near Germantown. His *Umständige Geographische Beschreibung Pensylvaniae,* Frankfort, 1700, is an important description of the colonization. On Pastorius, see the individual bibliography herein.

Authoritative studies are assembled in Ralph Wood, ed., *The Pennsylvania Germans,* Princeton, 1942, with essays on their cultural achievements contributed by eight specialists. A discussion of early promotion tracts is Hope Frances Kane, "Notes on Early Pennsylvania Promotion Literature," *Pa. Mag. Hist. and Biog.,* LXIII (1939), 144–168.

An account of Swedish settlements on the Delaware, in the years 1653–1654, is Peter Mårtensson Lindeström, *Geographia Americae,* Philadelphia, 1925, translated from the original manuscript. The most noted reporter of settlements and events along the "South" or "Delaware" River is David Pietersz. De Vries, already mentioned for his accounts of New Netherland. Though his reliability has been questioned, his narratives are vivid; the *Korte*

*Historiael* (1655) is as indispensable source material for the early history of the middle Atlantic colonies as John Smith's chronicles are for Virginia and New England. The first detailed report of Swedish settlements on the Delaware, collected from journals and accounts of members of the colony, is that of Tomas Campanius Holm, *Kort Beskrifning om Provincien Nya Swerige . . .*, Stockholm, 1702. Holm himself had never been in the colony. The work was translated, Philadelphia, 1844.

The best of the Swedish chroniclers was Israel Acrelius (1714-1800), pastor at Christiana (Wilmington, Del.). His *Beskrifning om . . . Nya Swerige . . .*, Stockholm, 1759, was translated by W. M. Reynolds, Philadelphia, 1874.

*Narratives of Early Pennsylvania, Delaware, and West Jersey, 1630-1708*, ed. by Albert C. Myers, New York, 1912 (Orig. Narr. Ser.), includes accounts by De Vries, Acrelius, Penn, Thomas, and Pastorius.

A listing of fundamental Swedish material is *New Sweden, 1638-1938: Being a Catalogue of Rare Books and Manuscripts Relating to the Swedish Colonization on the Delaware River*, Philadelphia, 1938, issued by the Historical Society of Pennsylvania.

Three narratives of early settlements in Maryland are significant. The Jesuit Father Andrew White set down *A Relation of . . . Lord Baltimore's Plantation in Maryland*, London, 1634: good Catholic promotion literature, with much said about Christianity and little about Catholicism. John Hammond's *Leah and Rachel; or, The Two Fruitfull Sisters, Virginia and Mary-Land . . .*, London, 1656, is a racy and vigorous tract contrasting living conditions in England and the colonies. It is reprinted in the Force *Tracts*, III (1844), No. 14, 30 pp. George Alsop's *A Character of the Province of Mary-Land . . .*, London, 1666, is a jocular and vivacious mixture of prose and verse describing the country and the Indians. Alsop was an indentured servant and wished to set forth the arrangements by which other poor people might conveniently emigrate to America. The work was edited by John G. Shea, New York, 1869, and most recently by Clayton C. Hall, New York, 1910. The White, Hammond, and Alsop accounts are included among *Narratives of Early Maryland, 1633-1684*, New York, 1910 (Orig. Narr. Ser.), ed., by Clayton C. Hall.

One of the very best pictures of life in any colony is given by Ebenezer Cooke (*fl.* 1708-1732) in his satirical poem *The Sot-Weed Factor . . .*, London, 1708. A facsimile ed. of *The Maryland Muse* (1731) has been edited by Lawrence C. Wroth, *Proc. Amer. Antiq. Soc.*, XLIV (1934), 267-335.

A discussion of early promotion literature is Lawrence C. Wroth, "The Maryland Colonization Tracts," in *Essays Offered to Herbert Putnam . . . .* New Haven, 1929, pp. 539-555.

SOUTH ATLANTIC COLONIES

John Smith was only twenty-six years old when the Virginia Company received its patent, but he energetically took part in promoting and organizing the enterprise and long remained the actual, if not the titular, head of the colony. His vivid and substantially true report is the earliest first-hand account of the settlement, published as *A True Relation of Such Occurrences and Accidents of Note as Hath Hapned in Virginia since the First Planting of That Colony,* London, 1608. He continued the story of his governorship in *A Map of Virginia, with a Description of the Country,* London, 1612, and reworked his earlier writings in *The Generall Historie of Virginia, New-England, and the Summer Isles* . . . , London, 1624, wherein is given an extended account of the Pocahontas story. For data regarding the many reprints and special studies of Smith, see the individual bibliography herein.

The first secretary of the Virginia colony and its earliest historian was William Strachey, whose well written account, entitled *The Historie of Travail into Virginia Britannia* . . . , was inscribed to Francis Bacon (1618). It remained in manuscript until 1849, when it was published by the Hakluyt Society.

Edward Maria Wingfield, a patentee of Virginia in 1606, accompanied the first colonists to Jamestown in the following year. His amplified diary, *A Discourse of Virginia* . . . , transcribed from the manuscript in the Lambeth Palace Library, was first published in the American Antiquarian Society's *Archaeologia Americana,* IV (1860), 67–103, ed. with introd. and notes by Charles Deane. Ralph Hamor's *A True Discourse of the Present State of Virginia* . . . , London, 1615 (reprinted, Albany, 1860), is an authentic early account; so also is *Good Newes from Virginia,* London, 1613, by Alexander Whitaker, the clergyman who converted Pocahontas. The latter volume was reprinted in facsimile, New York, 1936.

Of especial significance are the Burwell Papers, a manuscript account of (Nathaniel) Bacon's Rebellion (1676), the Virginia revolt against the dictatorial policy of Sir William Berkeley. Though the original appears to have been lost, a copy was found among the papers of Captain Nathaniel Burwell and sent by Josiah Quincy in 1812 to the Massachusetts Historical Society, where it was first printed in the Society's *Collections* in 1814, and again, more accurately, in 1866, under the title, *The History of Bacon's and Ingram's Rebellion.* The manuscript was then given to the Virginia Historical Society. The *History,* together with the poems included in it, is now attributed to John Cotton of "Queen's Creek," or to his wife Ann. See Jay B. Hubbell, "John and Ann Cotton, of 'Queen's Creek,' Virginia," *Amer. Lit.,* X (1938), 179–201.

A neglected work of some importance is Robert Beverley, *The History and Present State of Virginia* . . . , London, 1705 (enl., 1722). It is a lively account, with shrewd observations on the southern planters and the earlier historians and critics. Of the various reprints, the best is that edited with introduction by Charles Campbell, Richmond, Va., 1855. Beverley is discussed in Moses C. Tyler, *A History of American Literature During the Colonial Time,* rev. ed., New York, 1897, II, 264–267, and most recently in Louis B. Wright, "Beverley's History . . . of Virginia (1705): A Neglected Classic," *William and Mary Quar.,* ser. 3, I (1944), 49–64—a bibliographical and critical account.

The best reporting of contemporary social history is in the sprightly monograph written by the historian and mathematics professor Hugh Jones, *The Present State of Virginia,* London, 1724. William Stith's *The History of the First Discovery and Settlement of Virginia* . . . , Williamsburg, 1747, is the earliest "secondary" history written in the colony. It is systematic and scholarly, and based on the accounts of John Smith, Robert Beverley, and the records of the Virginia Company.

Convenient collections of early reports are in *Narratives of Early Virginia, 1606–1625,* New York, 1907 (Orig. Narr. Ser.), ed. by Lyon G. Tyler.

Four seventeenth century accounts of discovery and settlement along the southern seaboard deserve notice. William Hilton, *A Relation of a Discovery Lately Made on the Coast of Florida,* London, 1664, deals especially with the region of South Carolina. So do the brief tracts by Samuel Wilson, *An Account of the Province of Carolina,* London, 1682, 22 pp., and Thomas Ash, *Carolina* . . . , London, 1682, 40 pp.—a carefully written monograph reprinted, Tarrytown, N.Y., 1917. An excellent discussion of the geology and natural history of the Appalachian Divide is John Lederer, *The Discoveries of John Lederer in Three Several Marches from Virginia to the West of Carolina* . . . , London, 1672, originally written in Latin.

A brief but carefully written report of the region as it appeared in the early years of the eighteenth century is John Archdale, *A New Description of . . . Carolina,* London, 1707, 32 pp. (reprinted, Charleston, S.C., 1822).

Deservedly the best known Carolina reporter is John Lawson (d. 1712), the English explorer, surveyor, and colonist, who penetrated the unexplored territory in the Carolinas and Georgia. He published the record of his observations as *A New Voyage to Carolina* . . . , London, 1709, reissued in 1714, and later, as *The History of North Carolina,* though it had first appeared in John Stevens, *A New Collection of Voyages and Travels,* London, 1708, Vol. I. As a description of frontier life, it contributes especially to the ethnology of the region. The best recent reprint is that edited by Frances L. Harriss, Richmond, Va., 1937.

Convenient reprints of early chronicles, including those of Ash, Hilton,

Wilson, and Archdale, are in *Narratives of Early Carolina, 1650–1708,* New York, 1911 (Orig. Narr. Ser.), ed. by Alexander S. Salley, Jr.

Well written promotional tracts dealing with settlements in Georgia were published by Benjamin Martyn. Among them might be mentioned *Reasons for Establishing the Colony of Georgia . . .,* London, 1733, and *An Impartial Enquiry into the State and Utility of the Province of Georgia,* London, 1741.

The most carefully documented early account is that of Patrick Tailfer, *A True and Historical Narrative of the Colony of Georgia . . . ,* Charleston, 1741, written with the assistance of Hugh Anderson and David Douglass, and intended primarily as a satire upon the Oglethorpe administration.

Valuable studies of colonization and promotion tracts are Verner W. Crane, *The Southern Frontier, 1670–1732,* Durham, N.C., 1928, with bibl., pp. 335–356; and *idem,* "The Promotion Literature of Georgia," in *Bibliographical Essays: A Tribute to Wilberforce Eames,* Cambridge, 1924, pp. 281–298.

The fullest studies of Smith, Strachey, and John Pory (*ca.* 1570–1635) are in Howard M. Jones, "The Literature of Virginia in the Seventeenth Century," in *Memoirs Amer. Acad. Arts and Sciences,* Boston, 1946, pp. 16–28.

### COLLECTIONS

In addition to the regional collections described herein under the appropriate headings, other general collections are Peter Force, *Tracts and Other Papers, Relating Principally to the Origin, Settlement, and Progress of Colonies in North America,* Washington, 1836–1846, 4 vols.—reprints of scarce, early pamphlets; Albert B. Hart, ed., *American History Told by Contemporaries . . .*, New York, 1897–1931, 5 vols.; and John B. McMaster, ed., *Trail Makers: Library of History and Exploration,* New York, 1903–1906, 17 vols.

### THE EXPANDING FRONTIER: TRAVELERS AND OBSERVERS

The journal of Pierre François Xavier de Charlevoix, first published in Paris, 1744, as part of his *Histoire de la Nouvelle France,* was anonymously translated and published in London, 1761, 2 vols., as *Journal of a Voyage to North-America . . .* It is one of the best French accounts of North America in the eighteenth century, and is available in reprint, Louise P. Kellogg, ed., in 2 vols., Chicago, 1923. Other significant eighteenth century accounts are John Bartram, *Observations on the Inhabitants, Climate, Soil . . . Made by John Bartram in His Travels from Pensilvania to . . . Lake Ontario,* London, 1751; and James Adair, *The History of the American Indians, Particularly*

*Those Nations Adjoining to the Mississippi, East and West Florida, South and North Carolina, and Virginia* . . . , London, 1775 (reprinted by Samuel C. Williams as *Adair's History of the American Indians,* Johnson City, Tenn., 1930)—an excellent description of the Southern Mississippi Valley before the Revolution.

Jonathan Carver's *Travels Through the Interior Parts of North America, in the Years 1766, 1767, and 1768,* London, 1778, later published as *Three Years Travels* . . . , is important as the product of the first English-speaking traveler to explore west of the Mississippi. For data on Carver and the authenticity of the record, see Edward G. Bourne, "The Travels of Jonathan Carver," *Amer. Hist. Rev.,* XI (1906), 287–302, and especially Louise P. Kellogg, "The Mission of Jonathan Carver," *Wis. Mag. Hist.,* XII (1928), 127–145. Jacques Pierre Brissot de Warville published an account of his *Nouveau Voyage dans les Etats-Unis de l'Amérique,* Paris, 1791, 3 vols. It was a sympathetic and authentic picture of manners in the early years of the national period. The first two volumes were translated in the following year by Joel Barlow as *New Travels in the United States of America*—reprinted most recently in Bowling Green, Ohio, 1919. François René Chateaubriand visited the United States during July–December, 1791, and recorded his impressions in his romantic tales, *Atala* (1801), *René* (1802), and *Les Natchez* (1826). See Gilbert Chinard, "Chateaubriand en Amérique," *Mod. Philol.,* IX (1911), 129–149.

Also important is John Filson, *The Discovery, Settlement, and Present State of Kentucke* . . . , Wilmington, Del., 1784, reprinted by Willard R. Jillson as *Filson's Kentucke: A Facsimile Reproduction of the Original Wilmington Edition of 1784, with Paged Critique, Sketch of Filson's Life, and Bibliography,* Louisville, Ky., 1929. The sketch is unsystematic, but the facts have been industriously gathered.

William Bartram deals extensively with the South in *Travels Through North and South Carolina, Georgia, East and West Florida* . . . , Philadelphia, 1791; and Gilbert Imlay with the Ohio valley in *Topographical Description of the Western Territory of North America: Containing a Succinct Account of Its Soil, Climate, Natural History, Population, Agriculture, Manners, and Customs* . . . , London, 1792—the third edition of which (London, 1797) reprints additional miscellaneous material. The most thorough account of Imlay's checkered career in Kentucky, London, and Paris, gathered from scattered and incomplete sources, is Ralph L. Rusk, *The Adventures of Gilbert Imlay,* Bloomington, Ind., 1923 (Ind. Univ. Stud., X, No. 57). See also O. F. Emerson, "Notes on Gilbert Imlay, Early American Writer," *PMLA.,* XXXIX (1924), 406–439.

The scientist and physician Daniel Drake (1785–1852), who founded the

Ohio Medical College (1819), made an important contribution to natural and social history in his *Natural and Statistical View; or, Picture of Cincinnati . . .* (1815). His son Charles D. Drake edited *Pioneer Life in Kentucky: A Series of Reminiscential Letters . . .* , Cincinnati, 1870.

In the early national period English travelers, interested in settlements, left extensive records. Henry Wansey's *The Journal of an Excursion to the United States of North America in the Summer of 1794,* Salisbury, Eng., 1796, devotes pp. 284–290 to "Literature." Thomas Ashe published his *Travels in America, Performed in 1806, for the Purpose of Exploring the Rivers Alleghany, Monongahela, Ohio, and Mississippi . . .* , London (and Newburyport, Mass.), 1808.

Charles W. Janson's *The Stranger in America, 1793–1806,* London, 1807, is an authentic picture of the American citizen; the volume was edited with introduction and notes by Carl S. Driver, New York, 1935. The English actor-manager John Bernard kept a journal of his American tour, edited from MS. by Mrs. Bayle Bernard and published with introduction, notes, and index by Laurence Hutton and Brander Matthews, New York, 1887, under the title *Retrospections of America, 1797–1811.* John Melish, *Travels in the United States, 1806–7,* London, 1818, is a description of conditions before 1812 by an impartial British traveler. A volume which early turned attention to the prairie was Morris Birkbeck, *Notes on a Journey in America, from the Coast of Virginia to the Territory of Illinois,* London, 1818. It became widely known through the criticism of Cobbett, who was in the pay of eastern land speculators. Birkbeck's *Letters from Illinois,* Philadelphia, 1818, was designed to attract other British settlers. E. B. Washburne edited George Flower's *History of the English Settlement in Edwards County, Illinois, Founded in 1817 and 1818, by Morris Birkbeck (Coll. Chicago Hist. Soc.),* Chicago, 1882, vol. I. Though Flower later quarreled with his associate, the *History* is a valuable account of the settlement of the prairie region and, later, of the controversy over slavery in Illinois.

Four other accounts are William Tell Harris, *Remarks Made During a Tour Through the United States of America in the Years 1817, 1818, and 1819,* London, 1821; John M. Duncan, *Travels Through Part of the United States and Canada in 1818 and 1819,* New York, 1823, 2 vols.—a minute study of social conditions in northeastern America by an unprejudiced Scotsman; William N. Blane, *An Excursion Through the United States and Canada During the Years 1822–23,* London, 1824; and Thomas Hamilton, *Men and Manners in America,* Philadelphia, 1833. Basil Hall's *Travels in North America in the Years 1827 and 1828* (1829) was one of the most widely read accounts written about the young republic.

Several notable travel accounts have been set down by Americans. One of the earliest is Timothy Dwight, *Travels in New-England and New-York*, New Haven, 1821–1822, 4 vols.—shrewd in its perceptions. One of the best known accounts of life along the Ohio and Mississippi is Timothy Flint (1780–1840), *Recollections of the Last Ten Years, Passed in Occasional Residences and Journeyings in the Valley of the Mississippi, from Pittsburg [sic] and the Missouri to the Gulf of Mexico, and from Florida to the Spanish Frontier . . .* , Boston, 1826; reprint ed. by C. Hartley Grattan, New York, 1932 (for factual material, see John E. Kirkpatrick, *Timothy Flint, Pioneer. Missionary, Author, Editor, 1780–1840 . . .* , Cleveland, 1911). Also dealing with the Ohio Valley is Henry M. Brackenridge, *Recollections of Persons and Places in the West, 1800–1821*, Philadelphia, 1868 (the second and best ed.; first ed. publ. in 1834). Charles Fenno Hoffman's *A Winter in the West*, New York, 1835, describes a horseback trip through the sparsely settled areas of Michigan and Illinois. See John F. McDermott, "Henry Marie Brackenridge and His Writings," *Western Pa. Hist. Mag.*, XX (1937), 181-196.

The most ambitious collection of reprints of early narratives of travel and description, with introduction and notes, is Reuben G. Thwaites, ed., *Early Western Travels, 1748–1846: A Series of Annotated Reprints of Some of the Best and Rarest Contemporary Volumes of Travel . . .* , Cleveland, 1904–1907, 32 vols. The two final volumes supply an analytic index which gives access to an impressive body of first-hand information about frontier conditions.

A recently published collection is W. F. Horn, *The Horn Papers: Early Westward Movement on the Monongahela and Upper Ohio, 1765–1795*, Waynesburg, Pa., 1946, 3 vols.*

A classic of humor of the old Southwest is Augustus B. Longstreet (1790–1870), *Georgia Scenes, Characters, Incidents, etc., in the First Half Century of the Republic*, Augusta, Ga., 1835 (and many later eds.). Intimate knowledge of frontier life may be gathered from the extracts of John J. Audubon's *Journal*, ed. by Francis H. Herrick and entitled *Delineations of American Scenery and Character*, New York, 1926; the *Journal of John James Audubon*, Boston, 1929, 2 vols., is ed. by Howard Corning. The tales of Caroline M. Kirkland (1801–1864), *A New Home—Who'll Follow? Or, Glimpses of Western Life*, New York, 1839; *Forest Life . . .* , New York, 1842, 2 vols.; and *Western Clearings . . .* , New York, 1845, are authentic sketches of pioneer life in Michigan. A fine account of prairie life in Illinois and Missouri before 1845 is Sarah J. Cummins's *Autobiography and Reminiscences*, La Grande, Ore., 1914. For a picture of pioneer society in Kentucky, Tennessee, Indiana, and Ohio, there are Peter Cartwright's *Autobiography*

---

* These are demonstrated to be forgeries. See *William and Mary Quarterly*, 3rd ser., IV (Oct., 1947).

of *Peter Cartwright, the Backwoods Preacher,* New York, 1856, ed. by W. P. Strickland, and his *Fifty Years as a Presiding Elder,* New York, 1871, ed. by W. S. Hooper. George C. Eggleston's reminiscences of Edward Eggleston in *The First of the Hoosiers,* Philadelphia, 1903, are worth consulting.

## THE TRANS-MISSISSIPPI WEST

### EARLY EXPLORATION AND TRADING EXPEDITIONS

The definitive work of scholarship on the Lewis and Clark expedition is Reuben G. Thwaites, ed., *Original Journals of the Lewis and Clark Expedition, 1804–1806* . . . , New York, 1904–1905, 8 vols. It includes every item known to the editor, and prints the journals of Charles Floyd and Joseph Whitehouse for the first time. Thwaites's introduction and notes cover every aspect of the expedition with great care. The first edition of the work was *The History of the Expedition Under the Command of Captains Lewis and Clark,* published in 1814, edited by Paul Allen. Most of the work of compilation was done by Nicholas Biddle, who worked from the manuscript journals turned over to him by Clark after the death of Lewis. Elliott Coues published an edition in New York, 1893, 4 vols. Notable among the very early accounts of expeditions into the interior parts of New Spain, written in English, is Zebulon M. Pike's *An Account of Expeditions to the Sources of the Mississippi, and Through the Western Parts of Louisiana, to the Sources of the Arkansaw, Kans, La Platte, and Pierre Jaun Rivers; Performed by Order of the Government of the United States During the Years 1805, 1806, and 1807* . . . , Philadelphia, 1810. It is reprinted, ed. by Elliott Coues, as *The Expedition of Zebulon Montgomery Pike,* New York, 1895, 3 vols., with copious, if somewhat arbitrary, notes and an introduction.

The gathering of furs by the roving trader and solitary trapper long remained the only business of importance in the entire western region. Pierre Gaultier de Varennes, Sieur de La Vérendrye (1685–1749), was one of the earliest and most important French Canadian explorers of western Canada who entered the region on the promise of a fur-trade monopoly in the regions he might discover. He built a fort on the site of what is now Winnipeg and went overland to the upper Missouri River, perhaps as far as the present state of Wyoming. His *Journals and Letters,* Toronto, 1927, were edited with introduction and notes by Lawrence J. Burpee. The expeditions sent out by John Jacob Astor, and the founding of Astoria, are events therefore of deep national significance. The standard authorities on the first part of the over-land Astorian expedition and the contemporary events along the Missouri

River are John Bradbury, *Travels in the Interior of America, 1797–1811,* Liverpool, 1817 (2nd ed., London, 1819), reprinted as Vol. V of Thwaites's *Early Western Travels . . .* , Cleveland, 1904; and Henry M. Brackenridge, *Views of Louisiana, Together with a Journal of a Voyage Up the Missouri River in 1811,* Pittsburgh, 1814. Brackenridge's *Journal* is reprinted in Vol. VI of Thwaites's *Early Western Travels,* pp. 19–166, from a version revised, enlarged, and separately issued in 1816 under the title, *Journal of a Voyage Up the River Missouri . . .* It is a first-hand account of the French cultural legacy in the Mississippi Valley. See R. H. True, "A Sketch of the Life of John Bradbury, Including His Unpublished Correspondence with Thomas Jefferson," *Proc. Amer. Phil. Soc.,* LXVIII (1929), 133–150.

The authoritative account of the North-West Company of Canada, with headquarters at Astoria, is [*Gabriel*] *Franchère's Narrative of a Voyage to the Northwest Coast, 1811–1814,* Montreal, 1820, reprinted in New York, 1854, and included in Thwaites, *Early Western Travels . . .* , Cleveland, 1904, VI, 167–410. James's redaction of Long's expedition is Edwin James, *Account of an Expedition from Pittsburgh to the Rocky Mountains, Performed in the Years 1819, 1820, by Order of the Hon. J. C. Calhoun, Secretary of War, Under the Command of Maj. S[tephen] H. Long, of the U.S. Top Engineers,* Philadelphia, 1822–1823, 2 vols. (London, 1823, 3 vols.), and reprinted from the London ed. in Thwaites, *Early Western Travels,* Cleveland 1905, Vols. XIV–XVII. James compiled the narrative on the basis of journals kept by Long and other members of the party, in addition to his own notes. Two later accounts by foreign observers, which are especially detailed and accurate, are Ross Cox, *Adventures on the Columbia River, Including the Narrative of a Residence of Six Years on the Western Side of the Rocky Mountains . . .* , London, 1831, 2 vols.; and George Catlin, *Letters and Notes on the Manners, Customs, and Conditions of the North American Indians . . .* , London, 1841, 2 vols. (Edinburgh, 1926). Also important is Thomas L. McKenney's *History of the Indian Tribes of North America,* Philadelphia, 1836–1844, 3 vols., written in collaboration with James Hall.

### THE OVERLAND TRAIL

It is significant that before 1840 both Irving and Cooper had turned their interest to the West. Though Cooper's *The Prairie: A Tale* (1827) is certainly romanticized (see John T. Flanagan, "The Authenticity of Cooper's *The Prairie,*" *Mod. Lang. Quar.,* II [1941], 99–104), his depiction of the Ishmael Bush family is a valuable commentary on frontier character; and the book was important in influencing the eastern mind about the West. Even though Irving's *A Tour on the Prairies* (1835) is somewhat sentimentalized, it is first-hand and factual. Supplemented by his manuscript journals of the same trip, now published as *The Western Journals of Washington Irving,* ed. by John F. McDermott, Norman, Okla., 1944, it is one of the important contributions to frontier literature.

Probably the most comprehensive and accurate summary accounts written on the subject of the fur trade and the opening up of the West are those of Washington Irving, and of Josiah Gregg (1806-1850)—the outstanding authority on the Santa Fe Trail. The literary quality of their productions gives them unique value in the field they cover. Irving's *Astoria; or, Anecdotes of an Enterprise Beyond the Rocky Mountains,* Philadelphia, 1836, 2 vols., and his digest from the journal of Captain B. L. E. Bonneville, *The Rocky Mountains . . .* (1837), are descriptions of the northwestern states and of the fur trade. Gregg published *Commerce of the Prairies; or, The Journal of a Santa Fé Trader, During Eight Expeditions Across the Great Western Prairies, and a Residence of Nearly Nine Years in Northern Mexico,* New York, 1844, 2 vols. It is reprinted in Thwaites, *Early Western Travels . . . ,* Cleveland, 1905, Vols. XIX–XX. Another edition was reprinted by the Southwest Press, Dallas, Tex., 1933. Maurice G. Fulton has edited the *Diary and Letters of Josiah Gregg,* Norman, Okla., 1941-1944, 2 vols., with an introduction by Paul Horgan which supplies valuable biographical information about a man who has remained somewhat mysterious despite the enormous reputation of his *Commerce of the Prairies.*

The source from which the American public got its first impressions of the Overland Trail and the Pacific Coast was John C. Frémont's *Report of the Exploring Expedition to the Rocky Mountains in the Year 1842, and to Oregon and North California in the Years 1843-44 . . . ,* Washington, 1845 (U.S. 28th Congress, 2nd Session, House Exec. Doc. No. 166). Though it remains authentic, it should be supplemented by Joseph N. Nicollet's *Report Intended to Illustrate a Map of the Hydrographical Basin of the Upper Mississippi River . . . ,* Washington, 1843 (U.S. 26th Congress, 2nd Session, Senate Doc. No. 237); and the journals of James Clyman: Charles L. Camp, ed., *James Clyman, American Frontiersman, 1792-1881: The Adventures of a Trapper and Covered Wagon Emigrant as Told in His Own Reminiscences and Diaries,* San Francisco, 1928. Other accounts, both interesting and significant, are Robert Stuart, *The Discovery of the Oregon Trail: Robert Stuart's Narratives of His Overland Trip Eastward from Astoria in 1812-13 . . . ,* New York, 1935, ed. by Philip Ashton Rollins from the Stuart manuscript journal in the Astoria files of the New York Public Library; Harrison C. Dale, ed., *The Ashley-Smith Explorations and the Discovery of a Central Route to the Pacific, 1822-1829, with the Original Journals,* rev. ed., Glendale, Calif., 1941 —the narratives and journals of William Henry Ashley, Jedediah Strong

Smith, and Harrison G. Rogers, as important as Clyman's *Adventures,* and often more entertaining. The Oregon historian Frances Fuller Victor has recorded an excellent narrative, especially of the mountain traders during the 1830's, in *The River of the West: Life and Adventure in the Rocky Mountains and Oregon* . . . , San Francisco (and Hartford, Conn.), 1870. W. F. Wagner has edited *Leonard's Narrative: Adventures of Zenas Leonard, Fur Trader and Trapper, 1831–1836,* Cleveland, 1904, from the rare original edition of 1839; it has most recently been edited by Milo M. Quaife, *Narrative of the Adventures of Zenas Leonard, Written by Himself,* Chicago, 1934.

Though not entirely authentic, two accounts are especially interesting, and have a real foundation in fact: James Ohio Pattie, *The Personal Narrative of James O. Pattie, of Kentucky, During an Expedition from St. Louis, through the Vast Regions Between That Place and the Pacific Ocean* . . . , ed. by Timothy Flint, Cincinnati, 1831; and David H. Coyner, *The Lost Trappers: A Collection of Interesting Scenes and Events in the Rocky Mountains, Together with a Short Description of California* . . . , Cincinnati, 1847. Pattie's *Narrative* is included in Thwaites, *Early Western Travels* . . . , Cleveland, 1905, Vol. XVIII, and has been edited by Milo M. Quaife, Chicago, 1930.

Important as accounts written by a participant are Alexander Ross, *Adventures of the First Settlers on the Oregon or Columbia River: Being a Narrative of the Expedition Fitted Out by John Jacob Astor, to Establish the "Pacific Fur Company"* . . . , London, 1849 (ed. by Milo M. Quaife, Chicago, 1923); and *The Fur Hunters of the Far West: A Narrative of Adventures in the Oregon and Rocky Mountains,* London, 1855, 2 vols.—one of very few first-hand published journals (Vol. I has been edited by Milo M. Quaife, Chicago, 1924). Of similar import is James P. Beckwourth, *The Life and Adventures of James P. Beckwourth, Mountaineer, Scout, Pioneer, and Chief of the Crow Nation of Indians, Written from His Own Dictation by T. D. Bonner,* New York, 1856, and reprinted, New York, 1931, in facsimile of the 1856 edition.

For reliable and well conceived descriptions of the Rio Grande Valley and of Mexico, including the capital, in the 1840's, there is George W. Kendall, *Narrative of the Texan Santa Fé Expedition, Comprising a Description of a Tour Through Texas and Across the Great Southwestern Prairies* . . . , New York, 1844, 2 vols. A facsimile reprint is in the *Original Narratives of Texas History and Adventure,* Austin, Tex., 1935, 2 vols. Fayette Copeland, *Kendall of the Picayune* . . . , Norman, Okla., 1943, is good biography, with comments on the development of journalism in New Orleans. Another significant early narrative is John Lloyd Stephens, *Incidents of Travel in Central America, Chiapas, and Yucatan,* New York, 1841.

During the thirties and forties many emigrant guide books were issued. Among the best are John Mason Peck, *Guide for Emigrants* (1831), and Lansford W. Hastings, *The Emigrants' Guide to Oregon and California . . . ,* Cincinnati, 1845—reproduced in facsimile by Charles H. Carey, Princeton, 1932, with historical notes and a bibliography. Very well known is Overton Johnson and William H. Winter, *Route Across the Rocky Mountains . . . of the Emigration of 1843,* reprinted with preface and notes by Carl L. Cannon, Princeton, 1932, from the first (1846) edition. Excellent factual reporting about California is Richard H. Dana's *Two Years Before the Mast . . . ,* 1840.

A good contemporary account of the Doniphan expedition, by a participant, is John T. Hughes, *Doniphan's Expedition, Containing an Account of the Conquest of New Mexico . . . ,* Cincinnati, 1847, reprinted in William E. Connelley, *Doniphan's Expedition and the Conquest of New Mexico and California,* Topeka, Kans., 1907, pp. 113–524. Significant is Edwin Bryant, *What I Saw in California: Being the Journal of a Tour, by the Emigrant Route and South Pass of the Rocky Mountains, Across the Continent of North America, the Great Desert Basin, and Through California in the Years 1846, 1847,* New York, 1848. Bryant left Louisville, Ky., Apr. 18, 1846, joined Frémont's California Battalion, and was alcalde of San Francisco under the military occupation. He returned overland with Gen. S. H. Kearny to Leavenworth, Kans., Aug. 22, 1847. Francis Parkman's *The California and Oregon Trail,* New York, 1849, reveals how the Far West looked to a somewhat unsympathetic young Boston Brahmin.

An outstanding contemporary account of life in the southern Rockies in the 1840's, with unusually fine reporting on the Mountain Men, was written by Lewis H. Garrard, *Wah-To-Yah, and the Taos Trail . . . ,* Cincinnati, 1850. It was reprinted by Ralph P. Bieber as Vol. VI of the Southwest Historical Series, Glendale, Calif., 1938. Bieber's introduction dealing with Garrard's life, and his textual notes, are models of editorial thoroughness. Rufus B. Sage recorded the impression of his travels in *Scenes in the Rocky Mountains . . . ,* Philadelphia, 1846. The young English explorer, George Frederick Ruxton, traveling northward from Mexico City, spent the winter of 1846–1847 at or near Pueblo, a fur-trading post on the Arkansas River, where he met Garrard and learned much about the Mountain Men. His *Adventures in Mexico and the Rocky Mountains,* London, 1847 (and later reprints), is excellent reporting. Ruxton's *Life in the Far West,* New York, 1849 (reprinted ed. by Horace Kephart, New York, 1915), though fictionalized, has more of the atmosphere of the West than his *Adventures.* Another Englishman, Frederick Marryat, left records of his impressions of the West in *A Diary in America, with Remarks on Its Institutions,* London, 1839, 3 vols. (Philadelphia, 1839, 2 vols.). For a recent account of James Bridger

(1804–1881), see Stanley Vestal, *Jim Bridger: Mountain Man,* New York, 1946.

## THE CONTINENT AS OBSERVED FROM ABROAD

Among travel narratives written by continental observers of the American frontier during the second quarter of the nineteenth century, those of Beltrami, Sealsfield, and Prince Maximilian should be named. Giacomo Costantino Beltrami (1779–1835), the Italian traveler and political refugee, like Schoolcraft undertook in 1823 further search for the true source of the Mississippi, and left an important record of his adventures in *La Découverte des Sources du Mississippi et de la Rivière Sanglante,* New Orleans, 1824. Charles Sealsfield (Karl Anton Postl), whose life is still not clearly understood, came from Moravia and traveled in the South and Southwest in 1823–1824. He published *Die Vereinigten Staaten von Nordamerika, nach ihren politischen, religiösen, und gesellschaftlichen Verhältnisse betrachtet,* Stuttgart, 1827, translated in London, 1827–1828, in two parts: *The United States of North America as They Are,* and *The Americans as They Are.* (For further details, see the individual bibliography on Sealsfield herein.) Alexander Philipp Maximilian, Prince of Wied-Neuwied, wrote a most reliable account of the early history of the American Fur Company on the upper Missouri, in *Reise in das innere Nord-America in den Jahren 1832 bis 1834,* Coblenz, 1839–1841, 2 vols. It was translated by H. Evans Lloyd, London, 1843, and the Lloyd text is reprinted in Thwaites, *Early Western Travels . . . ,* Cleveland, 1906, Vols. XXII–XXV.

Typical of the German travel comments, before the great emigration of 1848, are Friedrich Schmidt, *Versuch über den politischen Zustand der Vereinigten Staaten von Nord Amerika* (1822); Jonas Heinrich Gudehus, *Meine Auswanderung nach Amerika im Jahre 1822, und meine Rückkehr in die Heimath im Jahre 1825* (2 vols., 1829); and Hermann Achenbach, *Tagebuch meiner Reise nach den Nord-amerikanischen Freistaaten; oder, Das neue Kanaan* (1835).

## THE LATER ACCOUNTS

Outstanding as a detailed description of the overland emigration during the second quarter of the century, highly authentic and very readable, is William L. Manly, *Death Valley in '49: An Important Chapter of California Pioneer History . . . ,* San Jose, Calif., 1894 (ed. by Milo M. Quaife, Chicago, 1927). Detailed and authentic also is Jessy Q. Thornton, *Oregon and California in 1848 . . . ,* New York, 1849, 2 vols.

Henry R. Schoolcraft (1793–1864) is important aside from the literary use that Longfellow made of him. His *Scenes and Adventures in the Semi-Alpine Region of the Ozark Mountains of Missouri and Arkansas, Which Were First Traversed by De Soto, in 1541*, Philadelphia, 1853, reprints (pp. 153–197), with some corrections, his *A View of the Lead-Mines of Missouri*, first published in 1819.

Two representative narratives of the late overland crossings, 1849–1853, are John R. Bartlett, *Personal Narrative of Explorations and Incidents in Texas, New Mexico, California . . . During the Years 1850, '51, '52, '53 . . .*, New York, 1854, 2 vols.; and Alonzo Delano, *Across the Plains and Among the Diggings*, ed. by Rufus R. Wilson, with photographs by Louis Palenske, New York, 1936 (first published in 1854, as *Life on the Plains and Among the Diggings*).

Of the numerous published accounts of the gold-mining days and of pioneer and frontier life in California, a few items merit special notice. Georgia W. Read and Ruth Gaines have edited *Gold Rush: The Journals, Drawings, and Other Papers of J. Goldsborough Bruff, Captain, Washington City and California Mining Association, April 2, 1849, to July 20, 1851*, New York, 1944, 2 vols. An excellent account of gold discovery is John Steele, *In Camp and Cabin: Mining Life and Adventure, in California During 1850 and Later*, Lodi, Wis., 1901. It is a sequel to *Across the Plains in 1850*, ed. by Steele (Chicago, 1930), from an account attributed to Lieut. Andrew Jackson Lindsay, originally published serially in the *Lodi Valley News* in 1899. A classic account of the California mines is *California in 1851 [and 1852]: The Letters of Dame Shirley*, ed. by Carl I. Wheat, San Francisco, 1933, 2 vols. The letters, written by Mrs. Louise Smith Clappe to her sister Mary Jane, in Massachusetts, during 1851–1852, are signed "Dame Shirley." They were originally published serially in the *Pioneer*, 1854–1855, and were first issued in book form by T. C. Russell, as *The Shirley Letters from California Mines in 1851-52* (1922). Indispensable as a contemporary picture of a frontier city in the 1850's is Frank Soulé and others, *The Annals of San Francisco . . .*, New York, 1855, 824 pp. Equally important for Los Angeles during the same period is Horace Bell, *Reminiscences of a Ranger; or, Early Times in Southern California*, Santa Barbara, 1927, with a foreword by Arthur M. Ellis. Jessie Benton Frémont's *A Year of American Travel*, New York, 1878, and her *Far West Sketches . . .*, Boston, 1890, were written from first-hand observation.

## LITERARY EXPLOITATION

Bayard Taylor left New York in June, 1849, as special correspondent for the *Tribune*, and returned nine months later. His *Eldorado; or, Adventures in the Path of Empire, Comprising a Voyage to California, via Panama; Life in San Francisco and Monterey; Pictures of the Gold Region, and Experiences of Mexican Travel,* New York, 1850 (and many later editions), is based in part on his dispatches. His *At Home and Abroad . . . ,* New York, 1860, is a slightly later picture of California. On Taylor, see the individual bibliography herein.

Novels and romances, based on both first- and second-hand knowledge or observation of the prairies and Far West, by mid-century were appearing in large numbers. One of the most prolific, as well as authentic, of the romancers is Emerson Bennett (1822–1905). Between his *The Bandits of the Osage: A Western Romance,* Cincinnati, 1847, and *Forest and Prairie; or, Life on the Frontier,* Philadelphia, 1860, he published some dozen tales with similar theme and background. See R. V. Mills, "Emerson Bennett's Two Oregon Novels," *Oregon Hist. Quar.,* XLI (1940), 367–381.

Theodore Winthrop (1828–1861) wrote an authentic early novel of western life, *John Brent* (1862), describing a cross-country trip. His *The Canoe and the Saddle* (1863) is a vivid sketch of a journey in the Northwest.

Horace Greeley, like Taylor, made a trip west for the *Tribune,* but did so overland, most of the way by stage, from eastern Kansas to Denver, thence to California by way of Laramie, Salt Lake City, and Truckee Pass. From the material of his dispatches he published *An Overland Journey, from New York, to San Francisco, in the Summer of 1859,* New York, 1860. Henry Villard's *The Past and Present of the Pike's Peak Gold Regions* (St. Louis, 1860), was edited with introduction and notes by Le Roy R. Hafen, Princeton, 1932. Of some interest is Albert D. Richardson, *Beyond the Mississippi: From the Great River to the Great Ocean: Life and Adventure on the Prairies, Mountains, and Pacific Coast . . . 1857–1867,* New York, 1867.

Samuel Bowles, reporting for the Springfield, Mass., *Republican,* went northwestward to Portland, Oregon, and on his return published *Across the Continent: A Summer's Journey to the Rocky Mountains, the Mormons, and the Pacific States, with Speaker Colfax,* Springfield, Mass., 1865. He added material on the basis of a second trip in 1868, again with Schuyler Colfax, and published *Our New West: Records of Travel Between the Mississippi River and the Pacific Ocean . . . ,* Hartford, Conn., 1869. By this time the frontier was being reported by newspapermen who could travel across most of the continent by rail, and did so for summer adventure and diversion.

The railroad surveys of the late 1850's are voluminous and, along with many trivia, include a great amount of information essential to a complete understanding of the opening of the frontier. Representative of the best of such registers is *Appleton's Railway and Steam Navigation Guide, . . . A Commercial Register,* New York (*ca.* 1850), ed. by G. F. Thomas. The best one-volume survey of railroading in the West is Glenn C. Quiett, *They Built the West: An Epic of Rails and Cities,* New York, 1934, with bibl. essays, pp. 543–550.

The publication of Mark Twain's *Roughing It* (1872)—a classic assessment of frontier values—and Clarence King's *Mountaineering in the Sierra Nevada* (1871) represents the high-water mark of frontier literature that belongs properly to belles-lettres.

The account by King (1842–1901) is a record of scientific explorations in the sixties of the little known California mountains. Two recent studies by David H. Dickason are "Clarence King's First Western Journey," *Hunt. Lib. Quar.,* VII (1943), 71–88, and "Henry Adams and Clarence King: The Record of a Friendship," *New Eng. Quar.,* XVII (1944), 229–254. An absorbing scientific account of western exploration, as well as a fine example of excellent government reporting, is the record set forth in *Report of the Geological Exploration of the Fortieth Parallel,* Washington, 1870–1880, 7 vols., ed. by Clarence King, with contributions also by John Wesley Powell, George M. Wheeler, and Ferdinand Hayden. It describes their exploration of the Cordilleran range from eastern Colorado to California.

John Wesley Powell (1834–1902), under the direction of the Smithsonian Institution, explored the Colorado River, 1869–1872, and his account was published by the Institution in 1875. It was edited in part by Horace Kephart as *First Through the Grand Canyon . . . : Being the Record of the Pioneer Exploration of the Colorado River in 1869–70,* New York, 1915. The first step in the formation of the Reclamation Service is described by Powell in his *Report on the Lands of the Arid Region of the United States, with a More Detailed Account of the Lands of Utah,* Washington, 1878. Bernard De Voto discusses Powell as an intellectual force in the West in *The Literary Fallacy,* Boston, 1944, pp. 124–135.

Increasingly important as they are viewed in the light of more recent studies are the works of William Gilpin (1813–1894): *The Central Gold Region . . .* (1860), later reprinted as *Mission of the North American People . . .* (1873–1874) and expanded in *The Cosmopolitan Railway Compacting and Fusing Together All the World's Continents,* San Francisco, 1890.

There are perhaps no more vigorous descriptions than those of Clarence E. Dutton (1841–1912). His *Report on the Geology of the High Plateaus of Utah* was published as part of the *Geographical and Geological Survey of the Rocky Mountain Region* by the Department of the Interior, Washington, 1880. His account of *The Physical Geology of the Grand Canyon District* is part of the 1882 *Annual Report* (II, 47–166) of the director of the United States Geological Survey. Two other monographs are *The Tertiary History* of the Grand Canyon District, U.S. Geological Survey Monograph, II (1882); and Mount Taylor and the Zuñi Plateau, U.S. Geological Survey Annual Report, VI, 105–198 (1886). A brief biography, with an estimate of Dutton as a man of letters, is Wallace Stegner, Clarence Edward Dutton: An Appraisal, Salt Lake City, 1936, 23 pp. Both Muir and Burroughs leaned heavily on Dutton for their data.

The writings of King, Powell, Gilpin, and Dutton may fittingly be called the endpieces to the literature of discovery in continental United States.

An encyclopedic record of all available information which has been useful to emigrants, explorers, adventurers, and settlers was published, in 1312 pages, by Linus P. Brockett: Our Western Empire; or, The New West Beyond the Mississippi . . . , Philadelphia, 1881. Basic as social history is William Wright (Dan De Quille), The Big Bonanza: An Authentic Account of the Discovery, History, and Working of the Comstock Lode of Nevada (1876). It has been reprinted, New York, 1947, with an introduction by Oscar Lewis.

Indispensable as a subject bibliography for the period it covers is Henry R. Wagner, Henry R. Wagner's The Plains and the Rockies: A Bibliography of Original Narratives of Travel and Adventure, 1800–1865, rev. and enl. by Charles L. Camp, San Francisco, 1937, which is a model of thoroughness. The arrangement is chronological, and the entries contain descriptive notes. Wagner also compiled The Spanish Southwest, 1542–1794: An Annotated Bibliography, Albuquerque, 1937, 2 vols. The compilation of Charles W. Smith, Pacific Northwest Americana: A Checklist of Books and Pamphlets Relating to the History of the Pacific Northwest, New York, 1921, should also be consulted.

## INDIAN CAPTIVITIES

Indian captivities form a separate and extensive body of literature, peculiar to the American frontier. Whether true or fictionalized, they were a steadily profitable publishing venture as long as the border Indian existed. They enjoyed great popularity among readers eager for narrative accounts in the picaresque tradition, dealing adventurously with material of frontier life. Religious groups not only approved of them, but themselves published accounts as examples of Christian fortitude or martyrdom. Promoters saw in them a means to advertise Indian territory to settlers. A few are still remembered as best sellers in their day and later, such as Mary Rowlandson's The Sovereignty and Goodness of God . . . Being a Narrative of the Captivity and Restauration of Mrs. Mary Rowlandson, Cambridge, 1682, and John

Williams's *The Redeemed Captive Returning to Zion* . . . , Boston, 1707, written at the urgent request of Cotton Mather. The epistolary novel of Ann Eliza Bleecker (1752–1783), *The History of Maria Kittle* (1797), deals with the capture of an American woman.

The most famous of the captivities deal with the frontiers of New England, the Alleghenies (Pennsylvania, Virginia, and Carolina), Ohio, Texas (overland to California, Oregon, and Santa Fe), and with the Spirit Lake uprising in Iowa and the Sioux massacres in Minnesota. The extent to which they were published is indicated by the two catalogs of the Ayer Collection, wherein are listed some 500 narratives and editions: Clara A. Smith, comp., *Narratives of Captivity Among the Indians of North America: A List of Books . . . in the Edward E. Ayer Collection of the Newberry Library*, Chicago, 1912; and the *Supplement*, issued in 1928. Further items are included in the bookseller's catalog of Edward Eberstadt & Sons, *Indian Captivities and Massacres: . . . Books, Pamphlets, and Broadsides Offered for Sale*, New York, 1943. Many others, more briefly recounted, found their way into newspapers and magazines, and a few have been published in the journals and collections of historical societies.

A few samples indicate by their titles the variety of narratives: William Biggs, *Narrative of the Captivity of William Biggs Among the Kickapoo Indians in Illinois in 1788, Written by Himself*, New York, 1922; *Narrative of the Singular Adventures and Captivity of Mr. Thomas Barry, Among the Monsipi Indians, in the Unexplored Regions of North America* (1800)— largely fictitious; James E. Seaver, *A Narrative of the Life of Mrs. Mary Jemison* . . . , Canandaigua, N.Y., 1824—often reprinted, most recently in 1929; Milo M. Quaife, ed., *The Indian Captivity of O. M. Spencer*, Chicago, 1922 (Lakeside Classics)—an account originally written for the Cincinnati *Western Christian Advocate* in 1834, and first issued in book form in 1835; and Edwin Eastman, *Seven and Nine Years Among the Camanches and Apaches: An Autobiography*, Jersey City, 1873.

One of the earliest collections among the large number subsequently compiled is Cotton Mather's *Good Fetch'd Out of Evil: A Collection of Memorables Relating to Our Captives*, Boston, 1706. Other examples are Samuel L. Metcalfe, *A Collection of Some of the Most Interesting Narratives of Indian Warfare in the West* . . . , Lexington, Ky., 1821 (reprinted, New York, 1913); Alexander S. Withers, *Chronicles of Border Warfare; or, A History of the Settlement by the Whites, of North-Western Virginia* . . . , Clarksburg, Va., 1831; and Samuel G. Drake, *Indian Captivities; or, Life in the Wigwam: Being True Narratives of Captives Who Have Been Carried Away by the Indians from the Frontier Settlements* . . . , Auburn, 1850 (and many later editions), first published in 1841 as *Tragedies of the Wilder-*

*ness* . . . Other memorable accounts are in *The Jesuit Relations* (ed. Thwaites, 1896–1901), especially the relations of Fathers Jogues and Jean de Brébeuf. A convenient collection is *Narratives of the Indian Wars, 1675–1699*, New York, 1913 (Orig. Narr. Ser.), ed. by Charles H. Lincoln, including Mary Rowlandson's account.

A useful collection of hitherto unpublished journals, surveys, and letters, selected by John Franklin Jameson, is Isabel M. Calder, ed., *Colonial Captivities, Marches, and Journeys*, New York, 1935.

Among special studies should be named Emma L. Coleman, *New England Captives Carried to Canada Between 1677 and 1760, During the French and Indian Wars*, Portland, Me., 1925, 2 vols.; J. Almus Russell, "The Narratives of Indian Captivities," *Education*, LI (1930), 84–88; Dorothy A. Dondore, "White Captives Among the Indians," *N.Y. Hist.*, XIII (1932), 292–300; Carl Rister, *Border Captives: The Traffic in Prisoners by Southern Plains Indians, 1835–1875*, Norman, Okla., 1940, with a bibl., pp. 199–206; Phillips D. Carleton, "The Indian Captivity," *Amer. Lit.*, XV (1943), 169–180—a brief survey; and Roy H. Pearce, "The Significance of the Captivity Narrative," *Amer. Lit.*, XIX (1947), 1–20.

No bibliography of the general subject has been published.

## INDIAN TREATIES

Indian treaties are a body of material unique in the literature of the world. Composed by no single author, the treaties occupy a place in prose comparable in many ways to the popular ballads in the history of poetry. Their provenance, structure, the metaphors and even the rites of their composition and style deserve extensive analysis. Scholarship in the subject at present is singularly meager.

A great many treaties were made between the Indians and the colonial governors, with the object of retaining Indian friendship, since the tribes were known to act as buffers between the British and French colonies, and in time of war the Indians were invaluable allies. A large number of the treaties were printed, but the issues of each text were very limited. An outstanding pioneer study of them is the carefully compiled *Indian Treaties Printed by Benjamin Franklin, 1736–1762*, Philadelphia, 1938, ed. with an introduction by Carl Van Doren and extensive historical and bibliographical notes by Julian P. Boyd. Henry F. De Puy compiled *A Bibliography of the English Colonial Treaties with the American Indians, Including a Synopsis of Each Treaty*, New York, 1917. It includes a total of fifty-four titles of the exceedingly rare documents, printed between 1677 and 1769, listing councils held at such key points as Falmouth, Mass., Albany, N.Y., Philadelphia, and Easton, Pa.

Further material will be found in the journals of the governors and councils of the various colonies and the proceedings of the legislative bodies. "Indian Deeds to the Agreements with William Penn" are scattered through the *Pennsylvania Archives*, 1st ser., I (1852). No single person is more important in the history of Indian diplomatic relations than Conrad Weiser of Philadelphia. A recent full-length biography is Paul A. W. Wallace. *Conrad Weiser, 1696-1760: Friend of Colonist and Mohawk*, Philadelphia. 1945. An earlier study, with emphasis on factual detail, is Joseph S. Walton. *Conrad Weiser and the Indian Policy of Colonial Pennsylvania*, Philadelphia, 1900. Further summaries of treaties, based upon the *Pennsylvania Archives and Colonial Documents*, are given in Chester H. Sipe, *The Indian Wars of Pennsylvania*, Harrisburg, Pa., 1929. George A. Cribbs, *The Frontier Policy of Pennsylvania*, Pittsburgh, 1919, is a concise account of Indian affairs to 1800, with bibl. notes, and a bibliography, pp. 96-102. See also Peter S. Du Ponceau, "A Memoir on the History of the Celebrated Treaty Made by William Penn with the Indians . . . 1682," *Penn. Hist. Soc. Memoirs*, III, pt. 2 (1836), 145-212.

The pioneer study of the treaties as literature is Lawrence C. Wroth, "The Indian Treaty as Literature," *Yale Rev.*, XVII (1928), 749-766.


## REGIONALISM IN FRONTIER LITERATURE

Much interesting fictional use was made of the Indian and frontier material. James A. Jones, *Traditions of the North American Indians*, London, 1830, is the revised edition of his *Tales of an Indian Camp* (1829). John T. Flanagan edited William J. Snelling (1804-1848), *Tales of the Northwest; or, Sketches of Indian Life and Character*, Minneapolis, 1936, with an introduction reprinted from the original edition published in Boston, 1830. Three well known volumes of stories that derive their material from the frontier during the second quarter of the nineteenth century are James K. Paulding, *Westward Ho! A Tale*, New York, 1832; Augustus B. Longstreet, *Georgia Scenes, Characters, Incidents, etc. . . . .*, Augusta, 1835, and Robert Montgomery Bird, *Nick of the Woods; or, the Jibbenainosay*, Philadelphia, 1837. The last named volume has been recently edited by Cecil B. Williams, New York, 1939 (Amer. Fiction Ser.), with an introduction and bibliography. Benjamin Drake (1795-1841), *Tales and Sketches from the Queen City*, Cincinnati, 1838, deserves to be noted, as does William Leggett (1802-1839), *Tales and Sketches*, New York, 1829. Among the more interesting of Tim othy Flint's novels are *Francis Berrian; or, the Mexican Patriot,* Boston, 1826; *George Mason, the Young Backwoodsman* . . . , Boston, 1829; *The Shoshonee Valley: A Romance,* Cincinnati, 1830. The border romances of Cooper and Simms are well known.

Authors of books and contributors to periodicals and newspapers in the colonies and along the expanding western frontier at first made conscious effort to conform to established patterns of language and literature. William D. Gallagher's brief preface to *Selections from the Poetical Literature of the West,* Cincinnati, 1841, is an apology for presenting the 109 poems by thirty-eight Ohio Valley poets. In Columbus, Ohio, William T. Coggeshall followed his plea for regionalism, *The Protective Policy in Literature* (1859), with an anthology entitled, *The Poets and Poetry of the West: With Biographical and Critical Notices,* Columbus, 1860; it was intended to correct the neglect of western writers by Rufus W. Griswold in his widely known collection of *The Poets and Poetry of America,* Philadelphia, 1842, and by Evert A. and George L. Duyckinck in their even more inclusive *Cyclopaedia of American Literature,* New York, 1855. Meanwhile James Hall published *Legends of the West,* Cincinnati, 1854, a collection of stories and sketches representing Hall's effort to make literary use of the materials of frontier life in the Ohio Valley. Percy H. Boynton discusses the place occupied by the frontier in literary criticism and fiction in *The Rediscovery of the Frontier,* Chicago, 1931; and Lucy L. Hazard applies the theory of F. J. Turner to literary history in *The Frontier in American Literature,* New York, 1927. See also Jay B. Hubbell, "The Frontier," in Norman Foerster, ed., *The Reinterpretation of American Literature,* New York, 1928, pp. 39–61.

The standard factual account of the early culture of the Ohio and Upper Mississippi valleys is Ralph L. Rusk, *The Literature of the Middle Western Frontier,* New York, 1925, 2 vols.; it is a guide to travel and description as well as to the literary productions of the regions, with a very extensive bibliography, II, 39–364. William H. Venable's *Beginnings of Literary Culture in the Ohio Valley: Historical and Biographical Sketches,* Cincinnati, 1891, though unsystematic, is a pioneer work, with sketches of Timothy Flint, James Hall, Daniel Drake, and other figures of the early Northwest, and with notes on early western magazines. Further studies of the region have been made by Mary M. Atkeson, "A Study of the Local Literature of the Upper Ohio Valley, with Especial Reference to the Early Pioneer and Indian Tales, 1820–1840," *Ohio State Univ. Bul.,* XXVI (Sept., 1921), 1–62; Willard R. Jillson, *Early Kentucky Literature, 1750–1840,* Frankfort, Ky., 1931—a descriptive history with bibliographies; Aubrey Starke, "Books in the Wilderness," *Jour. Ill. State Hist. Soc.,* XXIX (1936), 258–270—reading records of the upper Mississippi Valley before 1833; Leon Howard, "Literature and the Frontier: The Case of Sally Hastings," *Jour. of Eng. Lit. Hist.,* VII (1940), 68–82—her trip into the West in 1808; and John T. Flanagan, *James Hall, Literary Pioneer of the Ohio Valley,* Minneapolis, 1941—excellent as an introduction to the pioneering literary and journalistic efforts in that region. Also useful as a study of regional literature is Carle B. Spotts, "The Development of Fiction on the Missouri Frontier, 1830–1860," *Mo. Hist. Rev.,* XXVIII (1934), 195–205, 275–286; XXIX (1934), 17–26; XXIX (1935), 100–108, 186–194, 279–294. An unpublished dissertation is that of Harold A. Blaine, "The Frontiersman in American Prose Fiction, 1800–1860," Western Reserve, 1936. J(ames) Frank Dobie, *Guide to Life and Literature of the Southwest . . . ,* Austin, Tex., 1943, includes bibliographies and is authoritative. A collection of writing from the trans-Mississippi West, from the earliest times to the present, is Rufus A. Coleman, *Western Prose and Poetry,* New York, 1932. See also Henry S. Commager, "The Literature of the Pioneer West," *Minnesota Hist.,* VIII (1927), 319–328.

Bibliographies of state histories are numerous. Among the most useful are Earl G. Swem, *A Bibliography of Virginia . . . ,* Richmond, 1916–1919, 3 vols.—a notable compilation, as is his monumental *Virginia Historical Index,* Roanoke, Va., 1934, 2 vols., especially useful for the colonial period. The extent to which published first-hand material of the westward effort is available may be seen in such compilations as Solon J. Buck, *Travel and Description, 1765–1865, Together with a List of County Histories, Atlases, and Biographical Collections,* Springfield, Ill., 1914—dealing with Illinois. Frank L. Mott's *Literature of Pioneer Life in Iowa . . . with a Partially Annotated Bibliography,* Iowa City, 1923, includes a finding list. Two others are C. W. Raines, *A Bibliography of Texas . . . ,* Austin, Tex., 1896; and Robert E. and R. G. Cowan, *A Bibliography of the History of California, 1510–1930,* San Francisco, 1933. The monumental work still standard for reference is that compiled under the direction of the historian and anthropologist Hubert H. Bancroft (1832–1918). His *Works* (San Francisco, 1882–1890, 39 vols.) incorporate material dealing with Central America, Mexico, and the far western part of the United States and Canada. See John W. Caughey, *Hubert Howe Bancroft: Historian of the West,* Berkeley, Calif., 1946. A useful checklist is Edith J. R. Hawley, "Bibliography of Literary Geography," *Bul. Bibl.,* X (1918), 34–38, 58–60, 76, 93–94, 104–105.

Under the guidance of the Historical Records Survey during the 1930's an inventory was made, state by state, of books that have been issued bearing American imprints. The results of this great accumulation have been published, and the checklist will be found in Douglas C. McMurtrie, "The Bibliography of American Imprints," *Publishers' Weekly,* CXLIV (1943), 1939–1944; it lists all items issued from 1937 to 1942. Other good bibliographies of frontier literature will be found in Mabel Major and others, *Southwest Heritage: A Literary History with Bibliography,* Albuquerque, N.M., 1938— a selective list of some 1,000 titles; Levette J. Davidson, *Rocky Mountain Life in Literature: A Descriptive Bibliography,* Denver, 1936; and Oscar O. Winther, *The Trans-Mississippi West: A Guide to Its Periodical Literature, 1811–1938,* Bloomington, Ind., 1943.

Also useful are Hannah Logasa, *Regional United States: A Subject List,* Boston, 1942, and the section on "Pioneering," pp. 1–21, in Otis W. Coan and Richard G. Lillard, *America in Fiction: An Annotated List of Novels That Interpret Aspects of Life in the United States,* Stanford Univ., Calif., 1945. Reference material for study of western frontier literary history is George D. Lyman, *The Saga of the Comstock Lode: Boom Days in Virginia City,* New York, 1934. Studies in the influence of disillusionment on agricultural frontiers in the development of "realism" in American fiction, particularly such men as E. W. Howe, Joseph Kirkland, and Hamlin Garland, have been made in an unpublished dissertation by Carlton F. Culmsee, "The Rise of the Concept of Hostile Nature in Novelists of the American Frontier," University of Iowa, 1940. A linguistic compilation is that of Ramon F. Adams, *Western Words: A Dictionary of the Range, Cow Camp, and Trail,* Norman, Okla., 1944.

See also the section Regionalism and Local Color, *post,* p. 304.

## SECONDARY SOURCES

When Frederick J. Turner (1861–1932) read his paper on "The Significance of the Frontier in American History" before the American Historical Society in Chicago in 1893, he inaugurated a new study and interpretation of the West. His volume *The Frontier in American History,* New York, 1920, traces its movement from Massachusetts Bay through the Ohio and Mississippi valleys to the Far West, and his final work, *The Significance of Sections in American History,* New York, 1932, was a posthumous recipient of the Pulitzer Prize. James G. Leyburn, *Frontier Folkways,* New Haven, 1935, challenges the Turner thesis. Still standard is Frederic L. Paxson, *History of the American Frontier, 1763–1893,* Boston, 1924, an elaboration of Turner's ideas.

For the earliest period, Herbert E. Bolton's *The Colonization of North America, 1492–1783,* New York, 1936, is authoritative; the fullest treatment is the four-volume documented study of Charles M. Andrews, *The Colonial Period of American History,* New Haven, 1934–1938: the first three volumes devoted to "The Settlements," and the last to "England's Commercial and

Colonial Policy." Andrews's *Our Earliest Colonial Settlements: Their Diversities of Origin and Later Characteristics,* New York, 1933, gives many data in brief compass. See also Archer B. Hulbert, *Frontiers: The Genius of American Nationality . . . ,* Boston, 1929; Fulmer Mood, "The English Geographers and the Anglo-American Frontier in the Seventeenth Century," *Univ. Calif. Pub. Geography,* VI (1944), No. 9, pp. 363–395; Clifford K. Shipton, "The New England Frontier," *New Eng. Quar.,* X (1937), 25–36; and Carl Bridenbaugh, *Cities in the Wilderness: The First Century of Urban Life in America, 1625–1742,* New York, 1939—a documented study of intellectual life in colonial towns. Clarence Haring, *The Spanish Empire in America,* New York, 1947, incorporates work from his earlier studies.

Standard sectional histories of the expanding frontier are Lois K. Mathews (Mrs. M. B. Rosenberry), *Expansion of New England: The Spread of New England Settlement and Institutions to the Mississippi River, 1620–1865,* Boston, 1909; Herbert I. Priestley, *The Coming of the White Man, 1492–1848,* New York, 1930, with bibl. essay, pp. 351–386; Thomas J. Wertenbaker, *The First Americans, 1607–1690,* New York, 1927, with bibl. essay, pp. 317–338; Dixon R. Fox, ed., *Sources of Culture in the Middle West: Backgrounds Versus Frontier,* with essays by Benjamin F. Wright, Avery Craven, John Hicks, and Marcus L. Hansen; James M. Miller, *The Genesis of Western Culture: The Upper Ohio Valley, 1800–1825,* Columbus, Ohio, 1938, with bibl., pp. 165–176. The region north of the Ohio is treated in Walter Havighurst, *Land of Promise: The Story of the Northwest Territory,* New York, 1946. See also Burke A. Hinsdale, *The Old Northwest . . . ,* New York, 1899 (rev. ed.).

For the Deep South, Charles Etienne Arthur Gayarré, *A History of Louisiana* (1851–1866, 4 vols.), though somewhat fictionalized, is a monumental study, vivid and authentic in its descriptions, and is still standard for the colonial and early periods. A recent study is Verner W. Crane, *The Southern Frontier, 1670–1732,* Philadelphia, 1929. A brief treatment of the region south of the Ohio is Archibald Henderson, *The Conquest of the Old Southwest: The Romantic Story of the Early Pioneers into Virginia, the Carolinas, Tennessee, and Kentucky, 1740–1790,* New York, 1920. The story is carried farther west in Justin Winsor, *The Westward Movement: The Colonies and the Republic West of the Alleghanies, 1763–1798,* Boston, 1897, and in Arthur P. Whitaker, *The Spanish-American Frontier, 1783–1795: The Westward Movement and the Spanish Retreat in the Mississippi Valley,* Boston, 1927. Useful selections with bibliographies on the changing frontier are in Ina F. Woestemeyer and J. Montgomery Gambrill, eds., *The Westward Movement: A Book of Readings on Our Changing Frontiers,* New York, 1930.

The definitive treatment of Jefferson's concerted effort to secure information about Louisiana, and the organization of expeditions such as those of Pike and of Lewis and Clark, is Isaac J. Cox, *The Early Exploration of Louisiana,* in Cincinnati Univ. Stud., II (1906), No. 1. It is supplemented by Cardinal Goodwin, *The Trans-Mississippi West, 1803-1853: A History of Its Acquisition and Settlement,* New York, 1922. See also Jeannette Mirsky, *The Westward Crossings: Balboa, Mackenzie, Lewis and Clark,* New York, 1946. The regions now comprising Kansas, Oklahoma, Texas, and New Mexico are treated in Carl C. Rister, *The Southwestern Frontier, 1865-1881,* Cleveland, 1928.

Indispensable on the opening up of the Far West is Hiram M. Chittenden, *The American Fur Trade of the Far West: A History of Pioneer Trading Posts and Early Fur Companies of the Missouri Valley and Rocky Mountains and of the Overland Commerce with Santa Fé,* rev. ed., New York, 1935, 2 vols. Other standard studies are Archer B. Hulbert, *Forty-Niners: The Chronicle of the California Trail,* Boston, 1931; Ralph P. Bieber, ed., *Southern Trails to California in 1849,* Glendale, Calif., 1937; Frederic L. Paxson, *The Last American Frontier,* New York, 1910—from the Mississippi to the Pacific Ocean; Theodore Roosevelt, *The Winning of the West,* New York, 1889-1896, 4 vols.—from 1763 through the explorations of Lewis and Clark and of Pike; Joseph Schafer, *The History of the Pacific Northwest,* New York, 1905; and Otis W. Freeman and Howard H. Martin, *The Pacific Northwest,* New York, 1942—a detailed geographical study. Hubert H. Bancroft's monumental *History of the Pacific States of North America,* San Francisco, 1882-1890, 34 vols., is still standard for reference; as is Nathaniel P. Langford, *Vigilante Days and Ways; The Pioneers of the Rockies; The Makers and Making of Montana and Idaho,* Boston, 1890, 2 vols. (reprinted Chicago, 1912).

Further items include George B. Utley, "Theodore Roosevelt's *Winning of the West:* Some Unpublished Letters," *Miss. Valley Hist. Rev.,* XXX (1944), 495-507; J. Frank Dobie, *Guide to the Life and Literature of the Southwest . . . ,* Austin, Tex., 1943; Glenn C. Quiett, *Pay Dirt: A Panorama of American Gold-Rushes,* New York, 1936; and Everett N. Dick, *The Sod House Frontier, 1854-1890 . . . ,* New York, 1937.

The rivers and lakes of America from the first have been an essential means of transportation. Farrar & Rinehart began publication late in the 1930's of the Rivers of America Series, each volume written by an author chosen for his special knowledge of his subject. By February, 1947, thirty-one volumes had been published. The American Lakes Series published by Bobbs-Merrill, Indianapolis, is under way. The volume *Lake Ontario* (1945) has been edited by Arthur Pound with bibliographical notes. Further systematic research into this most important subject is necessary. Representative of special studies at present are Hiram M. Chittenden, *History of Early Steamboat Navigation on the Missouri River* . . . , Cleveland, 1903, 2 vols.; Fred E. Dayton, *Steamboat Days,* New York, 1925; Herbert and Edward Quick, *Mississippi Steamboatin': A History of Steamboating on the Mississippi and its Tributaries,* New York, 1926; and Leland D. Baldwin, *The Keelboat Age on Western Waters,* Pittsburgh, 1941, with bibl., pp. 237-252.

Other secondary sources of importance in a study of American frontier culture are Edward Eggleston, *The Transit of Civilization from England to America in the Seventeenth Century,* New York, 1901, a work which broke new ground by showing the need for studying the cultural development of the American people; Philip Ashton Rollins, *The Cowboy: An Unconventional History of Civilization on the Old-Time Cattle Range,* New York, 1936 (rev. and enl.); Walter P. Webb, *The Great Plains,* Boston, 1931—the outstanding study of the growth of society in the plains area, with a chapter devoted to its literature (pp. 453-484); Constance Rourke, *Davy Crockett,* New York, 1937; and Bernard De Voto, *The Year of Decision, 1846,* Boston, 1943, presenting the thesis that in that year America was transformed from an agrarian nation into an empire.

Further material will be found in De Voto's *Mark Twain's America,* Boston, 1932; and Everett N. Dick, *Vanguards of the Frontier* . . . , New York, 1941. See also Peter G. Mode, *The Frontier Spirit in American Christianity,* New York, 1923.


## BIBLIOGRAPHY

For travel accounts set down by foreign observers of American manners, together with supplemental general studies of them, see the appropriate sections under the Bibliographies by Period and Type.

The best general survey of the history of travel and travelers in America is still Seymour Dunbar, *A History of Travel in America* . . . , Indianapolis, 1915, 4 vols., with bibl., IV, 1445-1481. The field of such studies at present is limited. For a recent study, see Howard M. Jones, "The Colonial Impulse: An Analysis of the 'Promotion' Literature of Colonization," *Proc. Amer. Philos. Soc.,* XC (1946), 131-161.

A bibliography relating to Turner's historical hypothesis is Everett E. Edwards, *References on the Significance of the Frontier in American History,* Washington, 1939. An excellent general guide to the literature of discovery is Edward G. Cox, *A Reference Guide to the Literature of Travel* . . . (Seattle, 1938, 2 vols.), Vol. II: *The New World.* Useful checklists are supplied in *Camb. Hist. Amer. Lit.*, as follows: George P. Winship and Maude E. C. Covell, "Travellers and Explorers, 1583–1763," I, 365–380; Lane Cooper, "Travellers and Observers, 1763–1846," I, 468–490; and Frederick S. Dellenbaugh, "Travellers and Explorers, 1846–1900," IV, 681–728.

Ralph L. Rusk, *The Literature of the Middle Western Frontier*, New York, 1925, 2 vols., provides bibliographies of "Narratives of Adventurers and Travellers from the Eastern States and from Europe," and "Travel and Observation by Western Writers," II, 101–136. Special studies are Dorothy A. Dondore, *The Prairies and the Making of Middle America: Four Centuries of Description*, Cedar Rapids, Iowa, 1926—encyclopedic and valuable as a bibliographical aid; and Willard R. Jillson, "A Bibliography of Early Western Travel in Kentucky: 1674–1824," *Ky. State Hist. Soc. Reg.*, XLII (1945), 99–119.

Solon J. Buck, *Travel and Description, 1765–1865 . . .* , Springfield, Ill., 1914, is a useful key to the literature of travel in the Mississippi Valley before the Civil War, with a chronological list of travel narratives, a library census, and an index.

For the Southwest, in addition to the compilations of Wagner and of Smith (see *ante*, p. 273), there is Jesse L. Rader, comp., *South of Forty, from the Mississippi to the Rio Grande: A Bibliography*, Norman, Okla., 1947—useful but not exhaustive. See also the section Regionalism in Frontier Literature, *ante*, p. 276.

Supplemental material is Charles O. Paullin, *Atlas of the Historical Geography of the United States*, Washington, 1932. It is a compilation of 688 maps edited by John K. Wright, published jointly by the Carnegie Institution and the American Geographical Society of New York. John G. Bartholomew, *A Literary and Historical Atlas of America*, London, 1930, is published in Everyman's Library, and is useful for both hemispheres.

# MINGLING OF TONGUES:
# WRITING OTHER THAN ENGLISH

## GENERAL STUDIES

The literary productivity of foreign groups in the United States includes the writing of immigrants who were immediately assimilated and who wrote without primary reference to the foreign culture of which they had been a part. Such writers as Jacob Riis (Danish-American) and Edward Bok (Dutch-American) are properly not a part of "foreign" culture. There were also, especially in the earlier periods, bilinguists, such as Francis Daniel Pastorius, who made no conscious effort to preserve the heritage of a foreign culture but nevertheless were influential in their expression of an alien rather than an indigenous point of view.

Of primary importance among foreign influences has been that of the "cultural island," that is, the relatively isolated foreign community, present as a factor in American literary history from the earliest colonial times. Of these groups the best known are the German (including the Pennsylvania German), the French of New Orleans, the Scandinavian in the Midwest, the Spanish in California and the Southwest, and the Hebrew and Yiddish cultures centered in New York City. There are in addition other European and Asiatic cultures of considerable importance, which have yet to be explored. Any study, therefore, which attempts to estimate the extent and importance of such foreign influences must at the present time be tentative.

The material on particular immigrant groups is voluminous but frequently of indifferent quality. No full study, for example, of English immigration to the United States exists.

An important general study touching upon foreign cultural influences is David F. Bowers, ed., *Foreign Influences in American Life: Essays and Critical Bibliographies,* Princeton, 1944—eight essays illustrating the cultural impact upon American institutions since colonial times, with extensive bibliography, pp. 175–254. Other studies touching particularly upon literary influences are "The Influence of European Ideas in Nineteenth-Century America," in Howard M. Jones, *Ideas in America,* Cambridge, 1944, pp. 125–139; Ralph P. Boas and Katherine Burton, *Social Backgrounds of American Literature,* Boston, 1939; Carl Wittke, "Melting-Pot Literature," *College*

*English,* VII (1946), 189–197; "The Immigrant Pioneer in Fiction," in Percy H. Boynton, *The Rediscovery of the Frontier,* Chicago, 1931, Chapter IV; Michael Kraus, "Literary Relations Between Europe and America in the Eighteenth Century," *William and Mary Quar.,* I (1944), 210–234; and George S. Gordon, *Anglo-American Literary Relations,* New York, 1942— six essays dealing with the contemporary scene. Useful also as a study of the interconnections of American and British literature is H. V. Routh, *Towards the Twentieth Century: Essays in the Spiritual History of the Nineteenth,* New York, 1937.

One of the best general interpretations of the non-English contribution to the American cultural heritage is Thomas J. Wertenbaker, *The Founding of American Civilization: The Middle Colonies,* New York, 1938. Further material is in the same author's *The Old South,* New York, 1942, Chapter V. Samuel Bercovici, *L'Amérique Inconnue,* Paris, 1933, is a study of alien colonies in the United States. See also Carl Wittke, *We Who Built America: The Saga of the Immigrant,* New York, 1939. Maurice R. Davie, *World Immigration,* New York, 1936, contains a bibliography, pp. 563–571, which lists immigrant biographies, as well as fiction dealing with the immigrant. Useful also is Francis J. Brown and Joseph S. Roucek, eds., *One America: The History, Contributions, and Present Problems of Our Racial and National Minorities,* rev. ed., New York, 1945, with a 42-page bibliography. Standard treatments of alien groups are John R. Commons, *Races and Immigrants in America,* rev. ed., New York, 1920—a general survey through the nineteenth century; and William C. Smith, *Americans in the Making: The Natural History of the Assimilation of Immigrants,* New York, 1939, with a checklist of immigrant biographies, pp. 432–439. Isaac B. Berkson in *Theories of Americanization,* New York, 1920, argues the "ethnic federation" theory of racial assimilation.

A well documented study of the "old" immigration to 1860 is Marcus L. Hansen, *The Atlantic Migration, 1607–1860,* Cambridge, 1940. A good treatment of the "new" immigration is Peter Roberts, *The New Immigration,* New York, 1912, emphasizing the social problems of assimilation after the 1880's. Other useful studies are Marcus L. Hansen, *The Immigrant in American History,* Cambridge, 1940; George M. Stephenson, *A History of American Immigration: 1820–1924,* Boston, 1926; and Oscar Handlin, *Boston's Immigrants, 1790–1865: A Study in Acculturation,* Cambridge, 1941.

Two studies attempting to account for the failure of the "melting pot" are Henry P. Fairchild, *The Melting Pot Mistake,* Boston, 1926; and Edward A. Ross, *The Old World in the New,* New York, 1914. The best account of Irish immigration is William F. Adams, *Ireland and Irish Emigration to the New World from 1815 to the Famine,* New Haven, 1932. Two other studies dealing with immigration from the United Kingdom are S. C. Johnson, *A History of Emigration from the United Kingdom to North America, 1763-1912*, London, 1913; and Henry J. Ford, *The Scotch Irish in America*, Princeton, 1915.

No full bibliography of non-English writings has been published. Still useful is the brief checklist by Albert B. Faust and others, "Non-English Writings: German, French, Yiddish, Aboriginal," *Camb. Hist. Amer. Lit.*, IV (1921), 813-827. For the subject of immigration itself, see W. Ralph Janeway, *Bibliography of Immigration in the United States, 1900-1930*, Columbus, Ohio, 1934.

*Index Translationum* . . . : *International Bibliography of Translations*, is a quarterly list published in Paris from July, 1932, to January, 1940. It furnishes some clues to intercultural relations.

A valuable recent study of foreign contributions to American life and culture is Louis Adamic, *A Nation of Nations*, New York, 1945, with bibl., pp. 353-362.

## GERMAN AND PENNSYLVANIA GERMAN

GERMAN: PRIMARY SOURCES
*Prose*

At the present time the most fully explored "foreign" culture is that of the Germans. Their settlements date from the seventeenth century, and German travelers and historians have frequently recorded their impressions of the American scene since the early colonial period. Important among such historians is the colonist, lawyer, linguist, and poet, Francis Daniel Pastorius (1651 to *ca.* 1720), the founder of Quietist Germantown in 1683, whose contribution to colonial literature deserves to be better known. His works are described in an individual bibliographical essay herein. An early history of German settlements is John Kelpius (1673-1708), *The Diarium of Magister Johannes Kelpius*, first published, Lancaster, Pa., 1917, ed. by Julius F. Sachse. The Georgia settlements of the Saltzburgers are described in Samuel Urlsperger (1685-1772), *Ausführliche Nachricht von den Saltzburgischen Emigranten, die sich in America niedergelassen haben*, Halle, 1735-1752, 3 vols. Other travels of importance are those of Gottlieb Mittelberger, *Reise nach Pennsylvanien im Jahr 1750* . . . , Frankfort, 1756—translated by Carl T. Eben, Philadelphia, 1898; Gottfried Achenwall, *Einige Anmerkungen über Nordamerika* . . . , Frankfort, 1769—translated by J. G. Rosengarten, Philadelphia, 1903; and Johann David Schöpf, *Reise durch einige der mittlern und südlichen vereinigten nordamerikanischen Staaten,* Erlangen, 1788, 2 vols.—translated by A. J. Morrison, Philadelphia, 1911. The voluminous reports of seventeen Lutheran pastors in Pennsylvania known as the *Hallesche Nachrichten,* Halle, 1787, are significant. These have been translated, Philadelphia, 1880–1881, 2 vols. History and travel in the nineteenth century include Moritz von Fürstenwärther, *Der Deutsche in Nord-Amerika,* Stuttgart, 1818; Ludwig Gall, *Meine Auswanderung nach den Vereinigten-Staaten* . . . (1819), Trier, 1822; Bernhard zu Sachsen-Weimar-Eisenach, *Reise* . . . *durch Nord Amerika,* Philadelphia, 1828; Gottfried Duden, *Bericht über eine Reise nach den westlichen Staaten Nordamerikas,* Elberfeld, 1829; F. L. G. von Raumer, *Die Vereinigten Staaten von Nordamerika,* Leipzig, 1845, 2 vols.—translated by W. W. Turner, New York, 1846; Johann G. Büttner, *Briefe aus und über Nordamerika* . . . , Dresden, 1845; Franz von Löher, *Geschichte und Zustände der Deutschen in Amerika,* Cincinnati and Leipzig, 1847; Moritz Busch, *Wanderungen zwischen Hudson und Mississippi, 1851 und 1852,* Stuttgart, 1854; and Julius Fröbel, *Aus Amerika* . . . , Leipzig, 1857–1858, 2 vols. Popular pictorial books were those of Karl Knortz, *Amerikanische Lebensbilder,* Zurich, 1884; and Rudolf Cronau, *Von Wunderland zu Wunderland* . . . , Leipzig, 1885.

Travel volumes, reminiscences, and romances, especially written to depict American life during the nineteenth century, were published in some number. One of the earliest was Ernst Willkomm, *Die Europamüden,* Leipzig, 1838. One of the most important writers was Charles Sealsfield, whose works are described in an individual bibliography herein. Rivaling Sealsfield in popularity was Friedrich Gerstäcker (1816–1872), whose 150 travel and adventure books include *Streif- und Jagdzüge durch die Vereinigten Staaten Nordamerikas* (1844); *Die Regulatoren von Arkansas* (1845); *Die Flusspiraten des Mississippi* (1847–1848); *Gold, ein Californisches Lebensbild* (1854); and *Nach Amerika! Ein Volksbuch* (1855). Early translations of Gerstäcker's narratives and romances include *The Wanderings and Fortunes of Some German Emigrants* (1848); *The Daughter of the Riccarees* (1851); *Narrative of a Journey Round the World* (1853); *The Regulators of Arkansas* (1857); and *The Young Gold-Digger* (1860). Other representative works of the same period are Ferdinand Kürnberger, *Der Amerikamüde,* Frankfort, 1855; Karl Büchile, *Land und Volk der Vereinigten Staaten* (1855); Otto Ruppius, the best of whose fifteen volumes of collected works are *Der Pedlar* (1857), *Das Vermächtnis des Pedlars* (1859), *Der Prärie Teufel* (1861), *Ein Deutscher* (1862); Karl Peter Heinzen, *Die Deutschen und die Amerikaner,* Boston, 1860—primary reminiscences; and Reinhold Solger, *Anton in Amerika,* Bromberg, 1862.

The works of Friedrich Armand Strubberg (1806–1889), who wrote under the pseudonym "Armand," have not been translated. More than a score of his novels deal with America, especially with German colonization in the Southwest, slavery, the Mexican War, and the frontier in general. Among the best of them are *Sklaverei in Amerika; oder, Schwarzes Blut* (1862); *Carl Scharnhorst: Abenteuer eines deutschen Knaben in Amerika* (1872); *Der Sprung vom Niagarafall* (1864); *Friedrichsburg: Die Colonie des deutschen Fürstenvereins in Texas* (1867); *Die Fürstentochter* (1872); and *Die geraubten Kinder: Eine Erzählung aus Texas, für die Kinder* (1875). For a study of Strubberg see Preston A. Barba, "Friedrich Armand Strubberg," *Ger.-Amer. Annals,* n.s. X (1912), 175-225; XI (1913), 3-63, 115-142.

The "German Cooper," Heinrich Balduin Möllhausen (1825-1905), described frontier life in some fifty romances. Best known are his trilogy of frontier life: *Der Halb Indianer,* 1861; *Der Flüchtling,* 1861; *Der Majordomo,* 1863. The best of his romances include *Das Mormonenmädchen,* 1864; *Die Kinder des Sträflings,* 1876; *Der Piratenlieutenant,* 1877; *Der Leuchtthurm am Michigan . . . ,* 1883; *Wildes Blut,* 1886; and *Die Familie Neville: Roman aus der Zeit des nordamerikanischen Bürgerkrieges,* 1889. The sole translation of a Möllhausen work is his *Diary of a Journey from the Mississippi to . . . the Pacific,* 1858.

Reminiscences of frontier life in the latter part of the nineteenth century are Gert Göbel, *Länger als ein Menschenleben in Missouri,* St. Louis, 1877. An early socialistic novel is Max Arlberg, *Joseph Freifeld, Ein Social-Roman aus dem deutschamerikanischen Leben,* Milwaukee, 1887.

Robert Reitzel (1849-1898) has been considered among the most brilliant of German-American writers. His writings have been collected in three volumes as *Des Armen Teufel gesammelte Schriften,* Detroit, 1913. His autobiography, *Abenteuer eines Grünen,* was published, Chicago, 1902. See Adolf E. Zucker, "Robert Reitzel as Poet," *Ger.-Amer. Annals,* n.s. XIII (1915), 49-66.

Other items of interest are Hugo Bertsch, *Die Geschwister,* Stuttgart, 1903; Rudolph Puchner, *Anna Ruland,* 1903; and Henry F. Urban, *Aus dem Dollarlande,* 1906, and *Lederstrumpfs Erben,* Berlin, 1908. *The Reminiscences of Carl Schurz* were published, New York, 1907-1908, 3 vols., and a year later Gustav Philipp Körner published his *Memoirs,* Cedar Rapids, Ia., 1909, 2 vols. Among the most recent reminiscences are those of Johannes Gillhoff (1861-1930), *Jürnjacob Swehn, der Amerikafahrer,* Berlin, 1918.

Some observers have been especially interested in American industrial and scientific development. See for example Friedrich Ratzel, *Kulturgeographie der Vereinigten Staaten von Nord-America,* Munich, 1878-1880, 2 vols.; Ludwig Max Goldberger, *Das Land der unbergenzten Mög-*

*lichkeiten,* Berlin, 1903; Wilhelm von Polenz, *Das Land der Zukunft,* 4th ed., Berlin, 1904; and Georg von Skal, *Das amerikanische Volk,* Berlin, 1908.

## Poetry

Chicago was long the poetic capital, and fully half of the output has been published there. Chiefly lyrical in character, most of it has been written in High German and still remains scattered largely in German-American periodicals and newspapers, and in small booklets. Some has been collected in anthologies such as Konrad Nies and Herman Rosenthal's *Deutsch-amerikanische Dichtung,* 1888–1890, 2 vols.; Gustav A. Zimmermann's *Deutsch in Amerika,* Chicago, 1894; G. A. Neeff's *Vom Lande des Sternenbanners,* Heidelberg, 1905; Heinrich A. Rattermann, *Deutsch-amerikanisches Biographikon und Dichteralbum,* Cincinnati, 1911, 3 vols. Among local studies or collections, that by Selma Marie Metzenthin Raunick, *Deutsche Schriften in Texas,* 1935–1936, 2 vols., is typical.

Of the older generation of poets, the most gifted and versatile were Konrad Nies and Udo Brachvogel. More modern are Martin Drescher (*Gedichte,* Chicago, 1909), Fernande Richter (pseud. Edna Fern), and George Sylvester Viereck, who has himself rendered his verse and plays into English.

Epic poetry, usually less excellent than the lyric, is typified by Julius Bruck, *Ahasver,* 1875; Ernst Henrici, *Aztekenblume;* Rudolf Puchner, *Aglaja,* 1887; Rudolf Thomann, *Leben und Thaten von Hannes Schaute,* 1873; Ferdinand Schreiber, *Armanda,* 1882; Gustav Brühl, *Charlotte,* 1883; and Theodor Kirchoff, *Hermann,* 1898.

## Drama

The German theater, established in New York in 1840, has had a long and continuous existence. Though most of the plays have been German classics, some have been German-American. Geza Berger's *Barbara Ubryk* was a sensational success. Other playwrights include Kaspar Butz, *Florian Geyer;* Ernst Anton Zündt, who chose historical themes such as *Jugurtha, Rienzi, Galilie;* Emil Schneider, *Ulfila;* Friedrich Schnake, *Montezuma;* Viktor Precht, *Jacob Leisler;* and Friedrich Ernst, *Peter Mühlenberg; oder, Bibel und Schwert.*

Of plays with a setting near home, there is Adolf Philipp's comedy, *Der Corner Grocer aus der Avenue A,* and his *Also das ist New York;* and Lotta L. Leser, *Der Glücksuchende in Amerika.*

Studies of the German-American theater are Edwin H. Zeydel, "The

German Theater in New York City . . ." (from 1840 to 1914), in *Jahrbuch der Deutsch-Amerikanischen Historischen Gesellschaft von Illinois,* XV (1915), 255–309; Albert B. Faust, *The German Element in the United States,* Boston, 1909, II (Chapter VII); *Das Buch der Deutschen in Amerika . . . ,* Philadelphia, 1909, pp. 421–470; Alfred H. Nolle, "The German Drama on the St. Louis Stage," *Ger.-Amer. Annals,* n.s. XV (1917), 29–65, 73–112; and John C. Andressohn, "Die literarische Geschichte des Milwaukeer deutschen Bühnenwesens, 1850–1911," *Ger.-Amer. Annals,* n.s. X (1912), 65–88, 150–170.

PENNSYLVANIA GERMAN: PRIMARY SOURCES

The Pennsylvania Germans early developed a literary and cultural tradition. Their writings for the most part have been published in periodicals and newspapers. The best known and best loved among dialect poets was Henry Harbaugh, many of whose writings were collected in *Harbaugh's Harfe,* 1870. Other well known writers, whose works have been separately issued, are Henry Lee Fisher, whose works include *Die alte Zeite,* 1879; and *Kurzweil und Zeitvertreib,* 1882 and 1896; Thomas Hess Harter, *Boonastiel . . . [A Volume of Legend, Story and Song],* 1893 (rev. ed. 1942). Harvey M. Miller's *Pennsylvania-German Poems,* 1906, was followed by *Pennsylvania-German Stories,* 1907 (and later), and *G'shbos und Arnsht,* 1939.

Collections have not yet been made of the writings of Ezra Grumbine, Matthias Sheeleigh, Thomas J. Rhoads, and John Birmelin—chief of the new writers.

Anthologies of Pennsylvania German writing include Daniel Miller, *Pennsylvania German,* Reading, Pa., 1904, 2 vols. (reprinted 1911); Heinz Kloss and A. M. Aurand, *Lewendiche Schtimme aus Pennsilveni,* Stuttgart and New York, 1929; *idem, Ich schwetz in der Muttersproch,* 1936; Harry Hess Reichard, *Pennsylvania German Verse,* 1940; and several collections by A. M. Aurand.

Studies of the Pennsylvania German language have most recently been made in J. William Frey, *Pennsylvania-Dutch Grammar,* 1942; Albert F. Buffington, "A Grammatical and Linguistic Study of Pennsylvania German . . . ," unpublished dissertation, Harvard University, 1939; and Marcus B. Lambert, *A Dictionary of Non-English Words of the Pennsylvania-German Dialect,* 1924. Earlier studies are Abraham Horne, *The Pennsylvania German Manual for Pronouncing, Speaking and Writing English,* Allentown, Pa., 1875 (reissued 1910); Marion D. Learned, *The Pennsylvania German Dialect,* Baltimore, 1889; James C. Lins, *A Common-Sense Penn-*

*sylvania German Dictionary,* 1887; Edward H. Rauch, *A Pennsylvania Dutch Hand-Book: A Book of Instruction,* 1879; and S. S. Haldemann, *Pennsylvania Dutch, a Dialect of South Germany with an Infusion of English,* 1872.

The best literary history is that of Earl F. Robacker, *Pennsylvania German Literature: Changing Trends from 1683 to 1942,* Philadelphia, 1943—a survey of the evolution of High German, English, and dialect writing, with a 14-page bibliography. A good brief literary study is that of Harry H. Reichard, "Pennsylvania German Literature," in Ralph Wood, ed., *The Pennsylvania Germans,* Princeton, 1942, pp. 165–224. See also Reichard's "Pennsylvania German Dialect Writings and Writers," *Proc. and Addresses Pennsylvania German Soc.,* XXVI (1918); Heinz Kloss, *Die Pennsylvania-deutsche Literatur,* 1931; and Friedrich Schön, *Deutschsprachige Mundartdichtung in Amerika,* 1931.

The dialect stories of Elsie Singmaster (Mrs. Elsie S. Lewars) are well known. Her first published story was *Katy Gaumer* (1914). By 1940 she had published some 250 stories. Helen Reimensnyder Martin wrote *Tillie, a Mennonite Maid* (1904). The best among the published stories of Katharine Riegel Loose ("Georg Schock") are *Hearts Contending* (1910) and *The House of Yost* (1923). Among other recent dialect fiction writers are Mildred Jordan and Joseph Yoder.

Aside from the poetry of the Pennsylvania Germans, there is a considerable body of other German dialect poetry, most of it humorous. Among the better examples are Carl Münter, *Nu sünd wi in Amerika: en plattdütsch Reimels,* 1878; Ferdinand W. Lafrentz, *Nordische Klänge: Plattdeutsche Reimels,* 1881 and 1882; Karl Adler, *Mundartlich Heiteres* (1886); Charles G. Leland, *Hans Breitmann Ballads,* written between 1856 and 1895, and gathered and published as a single volume in 1914; and the humorous poems of Kurt M. Stein, *Die Schönste Lengewitch* (1925), *Gemixte Pickles* (1927), and *Limburger Lyrics* (1932). Adler's, Leland's, and Stein's verses are a kind of *Kauderwelsch,* or mixture of broken English and German dialect.

SECONDARY SOURCES: HIGH GERMAN AND DIALECT
*Literary Exploitation*

Novels which have made use of German and Czech settlements and immigrants, especially in the Middle West, include Willa Cather's *O Pioneers!* (1913); and *My Ántonia* (1918); Sidney H. Small, *Fourscore* (1924); Ruth Suckow, *Country People* (1924); Hope W. Sykes, *The Joppa Door* (1937); and Hester Pine, *The Waltz Is Over* (1943).

*German-American Scholarship*

The most notable of foundations currently fostering German-American scholarship is the Carl Schurz Memorial Foundation, 420 Chestnut Street, Philadelphia. For the Pennsylvania German groups there are the Pennsylvania German Society and the Pennsylvania German Folklore Society, and several Pennsylvania German county historical associations. Throughout the country are numerous county and local historical associations devoted to the preservation and study of German culture in America. University studies and linguistic researches are carried on in many states, especially in those where the German population has become numerous. Further data, often of an antiquarian nature, will be found in the columns of the German newspapers. A notable collection of German-American printing is in the Library of Congress. Particularly rich depositories of German-Americana are the Library of Congress, the New York Public Library, and, somewhat less extensive, the libraries of the University of Illinois and University of Wisconsin.

*Newspapers*

The leading German newspapers in the United States during the nineteenth century were *Staats-Zeitung* (New York, 1834); the St. Louis *Anzeiger des Westens* (1835); and the Cincinnati *Volksblatt* (1836). See Daniel Miller, *Early German American Newspapers,* Lancaster, Pa., 1911; J. F. L. Raschen, "American-German Journalism a Century Ago," *Amer.-Ger. Rev.,* XII (June, 1946), 13–15; and *Bibliography of Foreign Language Newspapers and Periodicals Published in Chicago,* Chicago, 1942, published by the Chicago Public Library.

*General Studies*

Among significant and readily accessible studies of German-American literature are Harold S. Jantz, "German Thought and Literature in New England, 1620–1820; A Preliminary Survey," *Jour. of Eng. and Ger. Philol.,* XLI (1942), 1–46; Bayard Q. Morgan, "Sources of German Influences on American Letters," *Amer.-Ger. Rev.,* X (Feb., 1944), 4–7, 35—a consideration of books in German, in translation, and critical and popular exposition; *idem,* "Traces of German Influence in American Letters," *ibid.,* X (Apr., 1944), 15–18. Other literary studies include Scott H. Goodnight, *German Literature in American Magazines Prior to 1846,* Madison, Wis., 1907; Martin H. Haertel, *German Literature in American Magazines, 1846–1880,*

Madison, Wis., 1908; Frederick H. Wilkens, "Early Influence of German Literature in America," *Americana Germanica*, III (1899), 103–205; John S. Flory, *Literary Activity of the German Baptist Brethren in the Eighteenth Century*, Elgin, Ill., 1908; and Albert B. Faust, "Non-English Writings: German," *Camb. Hist. Amer. Lit.*, IV (1921), 572–590.

General cultural studies of Germans in America appear in *Der deutsche Pionier*, Cincinnati, 1869–1887, 18 vols.—valuable source material, especially on the "New Germans"; Albert B. Faust, *The German Element in the United States* . . . , New York, 1927, 2 vols. (first published 1909)—standard but dated: it is supplemented for the earlier German migration by W. A. Knittle's *Early Eighteenth Century Palatine Emigration*, Philadelphia, 1937, and by many articles in *Pub. and Proc. Pa. Ger. Soc.* (1891–1940); Ludwig Fulda, "Die Deutschen in Amerika: Ein Kulturproblem," *Germanistic Soc. Quar.*, I (1914), 10–35; John A. Walz, *German Influence in American Education and Culture*, Philadelphia, 1936—a brief study; John A. Hawgood, *The Tragedy of German America: The Germans in the United States of America During the Nineteenth Century and After*, New York, 1940; and Rachel Davis-DuBois and Emma Schweppe, *The Germans in American Life*, New York, 1936—a brief factual account.

Other general works on Germans in the United States, often with sections on German writers in America, include Rudolf Cronau, *Drei Jahrhunderte deutschen Lebens in Amerika: Eine Geschichte der Deutschen in den Vereinigten Staaten*, Berlin, 1909; Georg von Bosse, *Das deutsche Element in den Vereinigten Staaten*, New York, 1908; Gustav Körner, *Das deutsche Element in den Vereinigten Staaten von Nordamerika, 1818–1848*, Cincinnati, 1880; Frederick F. Schrader, *The Germans in the Making of America*, Boston, 1924; Rudolf Cronau, *German Achievements in America*, New York, 1916; and Max Heinrici, ed., *Das Buch der Deutschen in Amerika*, Philadelphia, 1909.

Indispensable as source material for a study of the Pennsylvania Germans are the *Proceedings* of the Pennsylvania German Society (1891–1940), 48 vols. Other valuable source books are W. A. Helffrich, *Lebensbild aus dem pennsylvanisch-deutschen Predigerstand*, Allentown, Pa., 1906—one of the "High German" books on the Pennsylvania Germans; and the issues of *The Pennsylvania German*, published as *Penn-Germania* for the years 1900–1915.

Other studies devoted primarily to the Pennsylvania Germans are H. E. Jacobs, *A History of the Evangelical Lutheran Church in the United States*, 2nd ed., New York, 1919—standard on the subject; and Thomas J. Wertenbaker, *The Founding of American Civilization: The Middle Colonies*, New York, 1938. See also James O. Knauss, *Social Conditions Among the Penn-*

*sylvania Germans in the Eighteenth Century, as Revealed in German News-
papers Published in America*, Lancaster, Pa., 1922; and E. M. Fogel, *Beliefs
and Superstitions of the Pennsylvania Germans*, Philadelphia, 1915.

Special studies include A. D. Graeff, *Old World Backgrounds of American Civilization*, Philadelphia, 1941; John P. Hoskins, "German Influence
on Religious Life and Thought During the Colonial Period," *Princeton
Theol. Rev.*, V (1907), 49-79, 210-241; and William A. Haussmann, *German-
American Hymnology, 1683-1800*, in *Americana Germanica*, II (1899), 1-16.

## BIBLIOGRAPHY

"Anglo-German Bibliography . . ." has been issued annually in the
*American-German Rev.* (1941–current). An annual bibliography for the
years 1933–1940 will be found in *Jour. Eng. and Ger. Philol.*, Vols. XXXIV-
XL. An authoritative study is Bayard Q. Morgan, *A Critical Bibliography
of German Literature in English Translation, 1481-1927, with Supplement
Embracing the Years 1928-1935*, Stanford Univ., Calif., 1938. Other valuable
bibliographies and checklists are Oswald Seidensticker, *The First Century
of German Printing in America, 1728-1830—Preceded by a Notice of the
Literary Work of F. D. Pastorius*, Philadelphia, 1893; Paul H. Baginsky,
*German Works Relating to America, 1493-1800: A List Compiled from the
Collections of the New York Public Library*, New York, 1942; and Emil
Meynen, *Bibliography on German Settlements in Colonial North America*,
Leipzig, 1937—indispensable for research in the German and Pennsylvania-
German field.

## FRENCH

### PRIMARY SOURCES

No other French cultural island was ever established in the United States
comparable to the one in New Orleans, where the writings were confined
to the Creoles of Louisiana. One of the most distinguished of the early writers
was Charles Etienne Arthur Gayarré, who is treated in an individual bibliography herein. His *History of Louisiana* (1866), though somewhat fictional, is
still standard for the colonial and early national periods. Alcée Fortier's *A History of Louisiana* (4 vols., 1904) equals Gayarré's in importance. Other histories include Alexandre Barde (*ca.* 1811–1863), *Histoire des Comités de Vigilance aux Attakapas St. Jean Baptiste* (1861); and Henry Rémy (1812–1867),
who published part of his voluminous *Histoire de la Louisiane* in his journal
*Saint-Michel* (1854–1856). His notes on Mexican life were published in

*Tierra Caliente* (1859). Early drama may be represented by Auguste Lussan (d. 1842), *Martyrs de la Louisiane* (1839); Louis-Placide Canonge (1822–1893), *France et Espagne; ou, La Louisiane en 1768 et 1769* (1850). A mid-nineteenth century novel is Louis-Armand Garreau (1817–1865), *Louisiana: Episode emprunté à la Domination Française en Amérique* (1862).

The earliest literary productions from the Louisiana press were two volumes of poems published at New Orleans in 1777, written by Julien Poydras (1746–1824): *Le Dieu et les Nayades du Fleuve St. Louis . . .* , and *Epitre à Don Bernard de Galvez.* For a study of Poydras, see Edward L. Tinker, *Louisiana's Earliest Poet: Julien Poydras and the Paeans to Gálvez,* New York, 1933.

Among poets and romancers Charles Oscar Dugué (1821–1872) published *Essais Poétiques* (1847). The most prolific was Charles Testut (*ca.* 1819 to *ca.* 1892), whose *Veillées Louisianaises: Série de Romans Historiques sur la Louisiane* was published 1849 in 2 vols. His poems were issued as *Les Echos* (1849), and *Fleurs d'Eté* (1851). In addition to several novels he left brief sketches of 52 contemporary Louisiana writers, published as *Portraits Littéraires* (1850). The best lyrics are those of François-Dominique Rouquette (1810–1890), *Meschacébéenes* (1836), *Fleurs d'Amérique* (1856); and Adrien-Emmanuel Rouquette (1813–1887), *Les Savanes* (1841), *Wild Flowers* (1848), and *La Nouvelle Atala* (1879).

An extensive collection of French-speaking tales from Missouri has been compiled by Joseph M. Carrière, *Tales from the French Folk-Lore of Missouri,* Evanston and Chicago, 1937.

An important linguistic analysis, written by an unknown author, has been edited by Jay K. Ditchy, *Les Acadiens Louisianais et leur Parler,* Washington, 1932. Another study is that of Alfred Mercier, *Etude sur la Langue Créole* (1877).

Studies of the French drama, for the most part plays imported or adapted from France, are Lewis P. Waldo, *The French Drama in America in the Eighteenth Century and Its Influence on the American Drama of That Period, 1701–1800,* Baltimore, 1942; Harold W. Schoenberger, *American Adaptations of French Plays on the New York and Philadelphia Stages from 1790 to 1833,* Philadelphia, 1924; and Ralph H. Ware, *American Adaptations of French Plays on the New York and Philadelphia Stages from 1834 to the Civil War,* Philadelphia, 1930. A useful reference volume is Hamilton Mason, *French Theatre in New York: A List of Plays, 1899–1939,* New York, 1940.

GENERAL STUDIES

The most extensive study of American and French cultural relations is Howard M. Jones, *America and French Culture, 1750–1848,* Chapel Hill,

1927, with a bibliography pp. 573–602. Beginnings toward a study of Creole literature are Alcée Fortier, *Louisiana Studies . . .* , New Orleans, 1894; and Ruby van A. Caulfield, *The French Literature of Louisiana,* New York, 1929. See also Edward J. Fortier, "Non-English Writings: French," *Camb. Hist. Amer. Lit.,* IV (1921), 590–598; and Grace B. Sherrer, "French Culture as Presented to Middle-Class America by *Godey's Lady's Book,* 1830–1840," *Amer. Lit.,* III (1931), 277–286. Of interest as source material toward a study of the French cultural legacy in the Mississippi Valley is Rufus Babcock, ed., *Memoir of John Mason Peck, D.D.,* Philadelphia, 1864.

A useful study of libraries and reading is John F. McDermott, *Private Libraries in Creole St. Louis,* Baltimore, 1938.

The influence of important French writers in America has been made the subject of special study in Robert G. Mahieu, *Sainte-Beuve aux Etats-Unis,* Princeton, 1945; Paul M. Spurlin, *Montesquieu in America, 1760–1801,* University, La., 1940; Richmond L. Hawkins, *Madame de Staël and the United States,* Cambridge, 1930; *idem, Auguste Comte and the United States, 1816–1853,* Cambridge, 1936; Mary-Margaret H. Barr, *Voltaire in America, 1744–1800,* Baltimore, 1941; Jacob Canter, "The Literary Reputation of Baudelaire in England and America, 1857–1934," unpublished dissertation, Harvard Univ., 1940; and Benjamin Griffith, *Balzac aux Etats-Unis,* Paris, 1931.

The best pictures of the Creoles of New Orleans as presented in fictional studies are in the works of George Washington Cable, Kate Chopin, Lafcadio Hearn, and Grace King. See in addition to Grace King's fictional studies her picture of Charles Gayarré in *Creole Families of New Orleans,* New York, 1921; and the study of "Ante-Bellum New Orleans," in her *New Orleans: The Place and the People,* New York, 1911.

BIBLIOGRAPHY

A list of some 350 French writers is in Edward L. Tinker, *Les Écrits de la Langue Française en Louisiane au XIXᵉ Siècle: Essais Biographiques et Bibliographiques,* Paris, 1932. Albert L. Rabinovitz has compiled an *Index to Early American Periodical Literature, 1728–1870: French Fiction,* New York, 1943. The most thorough guide to French periodicals and newspapers is that compiled by Edward L. Tinker, "Bibliography of the French Newspapers and Periodicals of Louisiana," *Proc. Amer. Antiq. Soc.,* n.s. XLII (1932), 247–370. See also Augustus H. Shearer and others, "French Newspapers in the United States Before 1800," *Papers Bibl. Soc. Amer.,* XIV (1920), 45–147.

## SPANISH AND ITALIAN

### SPANISH

No survey has yet been made of the Spanish contribution in America. Spanish oral literature and religious drama have had a continuous history since 1598. Some progress has been made toward a study of the literature and culture in Aurora Lucero-White, *Folk-Dances of the Spanish-Colonials of New Mexico,* rev. ed., Santa Fe, 1940; Mabel Major and others, *Southwest Heritage: A Literary History with Bibliography,* Albuquerque, 1938; and (Miss) James Ellen Stiff, "The Spanish Element in Southwestern Fiction," unpublished dissertation, Southern Methodist Univ., 1928. Some information may be gleaned in the Federal Writers Project state guides for Texas, California, and other southwestern states.

### Literary Exploitation

The treatment of Spanish folk varies from highly romantic pictures of the early discoveries and exploitations of California to realistic presentation of modern peons. Authors who have dealt especially with the Spanish include Gertrude Atherton, Willa Cather, Kyle Crichton, Richard A. Summers, John Steinbeck, and Harvey Fergusson.

Useful bibliographical material is in Remigio U. Pane, *English Translations from the Spanish, 1484–1943: A Bibliography,* New Brunswick, N.J., 1944; Henry R. Wagner, *The Spanish Southwest, 1542–1794: An Annotated Bibliography,* Albuquerque, 1937, 2 vols.; Robert E. Cowan, *A Bibliography of the Spanish Press of California, 1833–1845,* San Francisco, 1919; Paul T. Manchester, *A Bibliography and Critique of the Spanish Translations from the Poetry of the United States,* Nashville, Tenn., 1927; and Raymond L. Grismer, *A Reference Index to 12,000 Spanish-American Authors,* New York, 1939.

### ITALIAN

No competent study has yet been made of the Italian literary and cultural contribution to America, and what little work has been done is confined mostly to New York City. The Federal Writers Project published *The Italians of New York,* a survey touching upon the intellectual and cultural life.

The most distinguished Italian writer in America was Lorenzo da Ponte

(1749–1838), who had been Mozart's librettist before he came to New York and initiated the study of Italian at King's College (Columbia University). He published *Storia della Lingua e Letteratura Italiana in New-York* . . . , New York, 1827. The *Memorie di Lorenzo da Ponte* . . . , New York, 1823–1827, 4 vols., was translated by Elizabeth Abbott, and edited and annotated by Arthur Livingston, Philadelphia, 1929. A biography is Joseph L. Russo, *Lorenzo da Ponte: Poet and Adventurer,* New York, 1922, with bibl., pp. 147–157.

An authoritative study of Italian immigration is Robert F. Foerster, *The Italian Emigration of Our Time,* Cambridge, 1919. See also Giovanni Schiavo, *The Italians in America Before the Civil War,* New York, 1934. Fictional treatment of the Italian in America will be found in the works of Guido d'Agostino, Pietro di Donato, Louis Forgione, John Fante, Sidney Meller, Pascal D'Angelo, and Jo Pagano.

Some information on literary activities of Italians in the United States may be gleaned from Giovanni Schiavo, *op. cit.;* Bruno Roselli, *Italian Yesterday and Today,* Boston, 1935; Howard R. Marraro, "The Teaching of Italian in America in the Eighteenth Century," *Mod. Lang. Jour.,* XXV (1941), 120–125; and *idem,* "Pioneer Italian Teachers of Italian in the United States," *ibid.,* XXVIII (1944), 555–582.

## SCANDINAVIAN

### GENERAL STUDIES

George L. White, Jr., has published *Scandinavian Themes in American Fiction,* Philadelphia, 1937, with bibl., pp. 225–231. The best general survey is that of Kendric C. Babcock, *The Scandinavian Element in the United States,* Urbana, Ill., 1914.

### NORWEGIAN

The Norwegian literature is excellent, though it is for the most part a recent one. The earliest Norwegian newspaper, *Nordlyset,* was published in Muskego, Wis., 1847. Of the 500 newspapers since then, two major ones survive—one of which was founded in Brooklyn in 1891.

Material dealing with the distinguished Norwegian-American authors O. E. Rölvaag and H. H. Boyesen will be found listed in the individual bibliographies herein.

After the Civil War some 100 Norwegian-American novels were published during the nineteenth century. Very few of them have been translated nor is their literary importance commensurate with their value as historical or social documents. Norwegian-American fiction properly begins with Tellef Grundysen during the seventies. See "Tellef Grundysen and the Beginnings of Norwegian-American Fiction," in Laurence M. Larson, *The Changing West and Other Essays,* Northfield, Minn., 1937, pp. 49-66.

Those who have left records of their travels include Simon Johnson, *From Fjord to Prairie; or, In the New Kingdom* (1916), and Dorthea Dahl, *Returning Home* (1920). The historical works of Ole A. Buslett (1855-1924) have not been translated, nor have those of Peer O. Strømme (1856-1921).

Among novelists, Johannes B. Wist (1864-1923) wrote under the pseudonym "Arnljot." His trilogy of Norwegian immigrant culture is *Nykommenbilleder* (1920); *Hjemmet paa Praerien* (1921); and *Jonasville* (1922). Two novels of Waldemar Ager (1869-1941) have been translated: *Christ Before Pilate: An American Story* (1910, tr. 1924); and *I Sit Alone,* New York, 1931. Jon Norstog (1878-1942) has published poetry.

The Norwegian-American Historical Association at Northfield, Minn., has issued ten volumes of publications under the title, *Norwegian-American Studies and Records* (1926-1943). For studies of Norwegian-American literature see Richard Beck, "Norwegian-American Literature," in Giovanni Bach and others, *The History of the Scandinavian Literatures,* New York, 1938, pp. 74-84; Aagot D. Hoidahl, "Norwegian-American Fiction, 1880-1928," *Nor.-Amer. Stud. and Records,* V (1930), 61-83; Albert O. Barton, "Alexander Corstvet and Anthony M. Rud, Norwegian-American Novelists," *Nor.-Amer. Stud. and Records,* VI (1931); Theodore C. Blegen and Martin B. Ruud, *Norwegian Emigrant Songs and Ballads,* Minneapolis, 1936; and Harry Sundby-Hansen, *Norwegian Immigrant Contributions to America's Making,* New York, 1921. In addition see Annette Anderson, "Ibsen in America," *Scand. Stud. and Notes,* XIV (1937), 65-109, 115-155, and Jacob Hodnefield, "Some Recent Publications Relating to Norwegian-American History," *Nor.-Amer. Stud. and Records,* V-XI (1930-1938)—a current bibliography. Fictional exploitation of Norwegian pioneers is Katherine Forbes, *Mamma's Bank Account* (1943).

The authoritative studies of Norwegian immigration are those of Theodore C. Blegen, *Norwegian Migration to America, 1825-1860,* Northfield, Minn., 1931; and *Norwegian Migration to America: The American Transition,* Northfield, Minn., 1940. See also Carlton C. Qualey, *Norwegian Settlement in the United States,* Northfield, Minn., 1938.

## SWEDISH

An account of the Swedish settlements in Delaware in 1653-1654 is Peter Mårtensson Lindeström's *Geographica Americae,* Philadelphia, 1925, translated from the original manuscript. Other early accounts are those of Tomas Campanius Holm (1702) and Israel Acrelius (1759).

Among Swedish-American writers during the nineteenth century are Hans Mattson (1832–1893), whose *Reminiscences: The Story of an Emigrant* (1891) are available in a good translation. The poetry of Johan G. R. Banér (b. 1861) is not translated, nor is Vilhelm Berger's history of the Swedes in the United States. Other writers include Oliver A. Linder (b. 1862), Carl Wilhelm Andeer (b. 1870), Axel August Swärd, and Gustav Wicklund. More recent is the work of Johan Person and (Oscar) Leonard Strömberg, one of whose novels, *The Ice Is Breaking* (1925), has been translated.

Johan Alfred Enander's stories have been published in *Hemlandet,* a leading Swedish immigrant journal. Anders Schön has edited *Prärieblommen,* a literary annual. Skulda V. Banér's tales of Swedes are centered in mining communities in upper Michigan.

A study of Swedish-American fiction is Holger Lundbergh, "New Swedish Note in American Fiction," *Amer. Swed. Mo.* (Nov., 1944), 12–13, 24–25. An unpublished thesis is Walter W. Gustafson, "The Swedish Language in the United States," New York University, 1929. See also Adolph B. Benson and Naboth Hedin, eds., *The Swedes in America, 1836–1938,* New Haven, 1938; and George M. Stephenson, *The Religious Aspects of Swedish Immigration: A Study of Immigrant Churches,* Minneapolis, 1932. A bibliography of items published for the most part during the first quarter of the eighteenth century is Arthur G. Renstrom, "The Earliest Swedish Imprints in the United States," *Papers Bibl. Soc. Amer.,* XXXIX (1945), 181–191.

## DANISH AND ICELANDIC

The most distinguished literary contribution by a Danish-American is Jacob A. Riis, *The Making of an American* (1901). Other Danish-American authors are Adam Dan, Carl Hansen, Enok Mortensen, John Volk, and Anton Kvist.

Among Icelandic-American authors should be mentioned Stephan G. Stephansson (1853–1927), and Johann Magnús Bjarnason.

## JEWISH: YIDDISH AND HEBREW

Virtually all Yiddish literature appeared originally in the Yiddish press which reached its peak between 1910 and 1940. Since 1870, over six hundred Yiddish periodicals have been published. The Yiddish daily, the extant *Jewish Daily Forward,* founded in 1897 and edited by Abraham Cahan (1860–1951) for nearly half a century, has served as a champion of Yiddish literature. Although Cahan edited the most important Yiddish newspaper, he wrote his fiction almost exclusively in English. His novel, *The Rise of David Levinsky,* New York, 1917, remains the Jewish immigrant classic. Other works include *Yekl: A Tale of the New York Ghetto* (1899) and *The Imported Bridegroom and Other Stories of the New York Ghetto* (1898). Cahan's major work in Yiddish is his five-volume autobiography, *Bleter fun mayn lebn* (1926–1931).

For data on the Yiddish novelist, Sholem Asch, see the individual bibliography herein. In addition to Asch, the major novelists are the brothers I. J. Singer (*The Brothers Ashkenazi,* trans. 1936) and Isaac Bashevis Singer (*The Family Moskat,* trans. 1950).

Among the writers of short fiction were the early realists "Solomon Libin" (Israel Hurwitz), *Gewehlte werk* (1915–1916), 4 vols., and Leon Kobrin, *Gezamelte shriftn* (1910), 4 vols. Of the "young" school of "esthetic" writers, David Ignatov and Joseph Opatoshu are the best known. "Sholem Aleichem" (Solomon Rabinowitz) has achieved world renown as a writer of short fiction: *Alle werk fun sholem aleichem* (1909–1917).

Leading Yiddish poets are Morris Rosenfeld, *Songs from the Ghetto,* (Boston, 1898), David Edelstadt, Morris Winchevsky, and A. Liesin. "Yehoash" (Solomon Blumgarten), translator of *Hiawatha* into Yiddish in 1906, achieved distinction with his Yiddish translation of the Bible.

The more important of the Yiddish playwrights have been Jacob Gordin, David Pinski, Halper Leivick (*Der golem*), "S. Ansky" (Solomon Rappaport) (*Der dybbuk*), and Peretz Hirschbein. For a time, Maurice Schwartz's Yiddish Art Theater produced only serious Yiddish plays.

Hebrew poets include Menachem Mendel Dolitsky, Simon Halkin, Naphtali Herz Imber (best known for *Hatikvah,* the Zionist anthem), Isaac Rabinowitz, and Gerson Rosenzweig. *Ha-tsofeh ba-arets ha-chadasha* (1871–1876) was the first Hebrew periodical. *Hatoren* (1913–1925), *Miklat* (1917–1920), the weekly *Hadoar* (1921–    ), and *Bitzaron* (1939–) are among the best literary journals.

The most useful histories of Jews in America are Peter Wiernik, *History of the Jews in America from the Period of the Discovery of the New World to the Present Time,* New York, 1931; Lee M. Friedman, *Early American Jews,* Cambridge, 1934—with bibliography, pp. 211–219; Lee J. Levinger, *A History of the Jews in the United States,* Cincinnati, 1930; and Oscar I. Janowsky, ed., *The American Jews: A Composite Picture,* New York, 1942.

Bibliographical studies are Rebecca Schneider, *Bibliography of Jewish Life in the Fiction of America and England,* Albany, N.Y., 1916; Nathaniel Buchwald, "Non-English Writings: Yiddish," *Camb. Hist. Amer. Lit.,* IV (1921), 598–609; and A. S. W. Rosenbach, *An American Jewish Bibliography . . . (to 1850),* Baltimore, 1926.

## OTHER EUROPEAN AND NEAR EAST CULTURES

The following listing is necessarily incomplete because the extent of the literary culture of other European and Near East races has not yet been determined. The most thoroughly studied of minor racial cultures is the Finnish-American. Phil Stong's novel, *The Iron Mountain* (1942), is a colorful picture of the life of Finns in Minnesota. See Evert A. Louhi, *The Delaware Finns* . . . , New York, 1925; and John Ilmari Kolehmainen, "The Finnish Pioneers in Minnesota," *Minnesota Hist.*, XXV (1944), 317–318; and *idem,* "The Finns of Wisconsin," *Wis. Mag. Hist.*, XXVII (1944), 391–399.

The contributions of Polish writers have been mostly in journalism. The travel writings of Venceslaus Gasiorowski (1869–1940) and the poetry of Victoria Janda have been separately published. See Avrahm Yarmolinsky, *Early Polish Americana: A Bibliographical Study,* New York, 1937. A useful study of Polish immigration is that of William I. Thomas and Florian Znaniecki, *The Polish Peasant in Europe and America,* New York, 1918–1920, 2 vols. The best single index of the nature and quality of Polish-American verse is the *Antologia Poezzi Polsko-Amerykanskiej* (1936).

A beginning has been made toward a study of the Russian contribution by Avrahm Yarmolinsky, *Russian Americana, Sixteenth to Eighteenth Centuries: A Bibliographical and Historical Study,* New York, 1943. A picture of America as seen by transplanted Russians is George Papashvily and Helen Waite, *Anything Can Happen* (1944). See also Royal A. Gettman, *Turgenev in England and America,* Urbana, Ill., 1941; and Jerome Davis, *The Russian Immigrant,* New York, 1922.

Pioneer study of Portuguese cultures is Donald R. Taft, *Two Portuguese Communities in New England,* New York, 1923. For other cultures see Thomas Capek, *The Czechs (Bohemians) in America* . . . , Boston, 1920, Louis Adamic, *My America* (1938), and Michael Pupin, *From Immigrant to Inventor* (1923)—impressions recorded by Central Europeans; Philip K. Hitti, *The Syrians in America,* New York, 1924; Malcolm M. Vartan, *The Armenians in America,* Boston, 1919. William Saroyan's *My Name Is Aram* (1940) is an authentic presentation of Armenian-American life. Saroyan has edited *Hairenik, 1934–1939: An Anthology of Short Stories and Poems by Young Armenian Writers in the United States, and Translations of Selected Short Stories from the Original Armenian,* Boston, 1939, collected from issues of the *Hairenik Weekly* (1934–1938).

Other studies include Henry Pratt Fairchild, *Greek Immigration to the United States,* New Haven, 1911; and John Paul von Grueningen, ed., *The Swiss in the United States.* Madison, Wis., 1940.

## MEXICAN AND LATIN AMERICAN

The cultural relations between nations of the Western Hemisphere are expanding, and the Latin and South American interest in the literary culture of the United States is growing. See Manuel Gamio, *Mexican Immigration to the United States: A Study of Human Migration and Adjustment,* Chicago, 1930; Emory S. Bogardus, *The Mexican in the United States,* Los Angeles, 1934; and James A. Granier, *Latin American Belles-Lettres in English Translation: A Selective and Annotated Guide,* Washington, 1942.

## ORIENTAL

### CHINESE

An exploratory study of the Chinese as pictured in American literature, and the attitude expressed toward the Chinese immigrant in imaginative writing by Americans, is William P. Fenn, *Ah Sin and His Brethren in American Literature,* Peiping, China, 1933. See also William R. North, *Chinese Themes in American Verse,* Philadelphia, 1937, with bibl., pp. 123–175; Mary R. Coolidge, *Chinese Immigration,* New York, 1909—an older study but valuable; and George H. Danton, *Culture Contacts of the United States and China,* New York, 1931.

### JAPANESE

The influence of Japanese literature and art on the United States has been transmitted principally through the studies and appreciations of American scholars who have lived or traveled extensively in Japan. For the invaluable contributions of Lafcadio Hearn, see the individual bibliography on Hearn. Ernest F. Fenollosa (1853–1908) taught for twelve years in Japan and was a pioneer in the study of Oriental literature and art. Two racial studies are Yamato Ichihashi, *Japanese in the United States: A Critical Study of the Problems of the Japanese Immigrants and Their Children,* Stanford Univ., Calif., 1932, and Edward K. Strong, *The Japanese in California,* Stanford Univ., Calif., 1933.

A most valuable social history of Asian influence is that of Arthur E. Christy, ed., *The Asian Legacy and American Life: Essays,* New York, 1945, with bibliographical notes.

# REGIONALISM AND LOCAL COLOR

## GENERAL STUDIES

In general, local color emphasizes the setting as characteristic of a district, region, or era, and reproduces the customs, dialect, costumes, landscapes, and other peculiarities which have not been standardized. Genre writing, often associated with local color and regionalism, may be said to refer to a specific style, dealing realistically with scenes from everyday life. It is true that from the earliest times writing reflected the locale, but as representatives of a movement the local colorists did not attract attention until after the Civil War, when they were associated with humor, with frontier tall tales, and with local traditions. Bret Harte's *The Luck of Roaring Camp* (1868) has often been designated as the first local color story. For folk element in regionalism and local color, see that part of the Folk Literature section of the bibliography (*ante,* pp. 197–201) dealing with regional-racial fiction. See also the general bibliographical essay on Mingling of Tongues, *ante,* pp. 284–303.

The term "regionalism" as it has applied recently in the South refers to an intellectual movement which approached local color with the theory that particular sections have cultural, geographical, and economic entity. The southern regionalists have attempted a study of the relation of folklore to literature and have been preoccupied with a critical interpretation of historical backgrounds rather than with photographic realism. Donald Davidson's *The Attack on Leviathan: Regionalism and Nationalism in the United States,* Chapel Hill, N.C., 1938, is a volume of discursive essays by a southern agrarian on the relationship of regionalism to American literary and social culture. Howard W. Odum and Harry E. Moore attempt an integration of historical, ethnic, cultural, and physiographic factors in *American Regionalism: A Cultural-Historical Approach to National Integration,* New York, 1938, with bibl., pp. 643–675. See also Cary McWilliams, *The New Regionalism in American Literature,* Seattle, 1930. A French estimate is Pierre Brodin, *Le Roman régionaliste américain: Esquisse d'une géographie morale et pittoresque des Etats-Unis,* Paris, 1937. Attention is given to development of local color fiction in Fred L. Pattee, *The Development of the American Short Story,* New York, 1923. See also Horace S. Fiske, *Provincial Types in Ameri-*

*can Fiction,* New York, 1903, and Elizabeth A. Green, *The Negro in Contemporary American Literature,* Chapel Hill, N.C., 1928.

Other regional studies are Theodore Hornberger, "Three Self-Conscious Wests," *Southwest Rev.,* XXVI (1941), 428–448; Henry W. Boynton, "Literature by Piecemeal," *Eng. Jour.,* XXIII (1934), 179–188; Cary McWilliams, "Localism in American Criticism," *Southwest Rev.,* XIX (1934), 410–428; Benjamin A. Botkin, "Regionalism: Cult or Culture?" *Eng. Jour.,* XXV (1936), 181–185; John N. Oldham, "Anatomy of Provincialism," *Sewanee Rev.,* XLIV (1936), 68–75, 145–152, 296–302; Ima H. Herron, "The Blight of Romanticism," *Southwest Rev.,* XXVI (1941), 449–453; and Charles C. Walcutt, "The Regional Novel and Its Future," *Arizona Quar.,* I (1945), No. 2, 17–27. See also Norman McLeod and others, "Regionalism: A Symposium," *Sewanee Rev.,* XXXIX (1931), 456–483.

A regional anthology of selections from the works of thirty-eight writers, from James Hall to Zona Gale, is Harry R. Warfel and G. Harrison Orians, eds., *American Local-Color Stories,* New York, 1941. Useful information on regional literature will be found in the various state guides prepared under the supervision of the Works Progress (Work Projects) Administration during the 1930's. See also Oscar O. Winther, *The Trans-Mississippi West: A Guide to Its Periodical Literature, 1811–1938,* Bloomington, Ind., 1943.

*Midland,* a regional journal, was founded at Iowa City in 1915, and published much good native material. In 1920, *Frontier: A Regional Literary Quarterly* was established at Missoula, Mont. The two magazines were merged in 1933 under the title *Frontier and Midland,* and continued publication until 1939. *Utah Humanities Review: A Regional Quarterly* was established in 1947.

## NEW ENGLAND

Regional writing with local setting in New England, though it dates from the early part of the nineteenth century, became most prominent during the years 1870–1890. Authentic detail appears in the writing of Mary E. Wilkins Freeman, Hawthorne, Holmes, Howells, Henry James, Sarah Orne Jewett, James Russell Lowell, Harriet Beecher Stowe, and Edith Wharton—all of whom are supplied with individual bibliographies herein.

Realistic pictures of social customs in the early nineteenth century are in the writings of Catharine Maria Sedgwick (1789–1867). Her best known works include *A New-England Tale: or, Sketches of New-England Characters and Manners* (1822); *Redwood: A Tale* (1824); *Tales and Sketches* (1835). An early study is Mary E. Dewey, *Life and Letters of Catharine M.*

*Sedgwick,* New York, 1871. See also Bertha-Monica Stearns, "Miss Sedgwick Observes Harriet Martineau," *New Eng. Quar.,* VII (1934), 533–541. A bibliography is that of Sister Mary M. Welch, *Catharine Maria Sedgwick . . .* (1937).

Sylvester Judd (1813–1853) supplied realistic background in *Margaret: A Tale of the Real and Ideal . . .* (1845) and in *Richard Edney and the Governor's Family . . .* (1850), a tale of the Maine timber country. Other authentic localized settings are in Elizabeth Stuart Phelps (1815–1852), *The Sunny Side; or, the Country Minister's Wife* (1851); Julia C. R. Dorr (1825–1913), *Farmingdale* (1854), and *Lanmere* (1856)—savage novels of Down East; Seba Smith (1792–1868), *'Way Down East; or, Portraitures of Yankee Life* (1854)—local color tales by "Major Jack Downing"; George Lunt (1803–1885), *Eastford; or, Household Sketches* (1855); John Turvill Adams (1805–1882), *The Lost Hunter* (1856)—nineteenth century Connecticut; and Elizabeth Drew Barstow Stoddard (1823–1902, the wife of Richard Henry Stoddard), whose first novel, *The Morgesons* (1862), deals realistically with New England, as do her later stories.

Celia (Laighton) Thaxter (1835–1894) portrayed her life off the New Hampshire coast in such works as *Among the Isles of Shoals* (1873) and *An Island Garden* (1894). A Connecticut writer important in the development of locale in the short story is Rose Terry Cooke (1827–1892), whose works include *Root-Bound* (1885), *Happy Dodd . . .* (1887), and, most important, *Huckleberries Gathered from New England Hills* (1891). Annie Trumbull Slosson (1838–1926) is remembered for *Dumb Foxglove, and Other Stories* (1898) and *A Local Colorist* (1912).

The Vermont Quaker, Rowland Evans Robinson (1833–1900), was well known in his day for *Uncle Lisha's Shop: Life in a Corner of Yankeeland* (1887) and *A Danvis Pioneer* (1900). Both volumes were reprinted, Rutland, Vt., 1933, with introductions by Fred L. Pattee and Dorothy Canfield Fisher. *Danvis Folks* (1894) and *A Hero of Ticonderoga* (1898) were reprinted, Rutland, Vt., 1934, with introductions by Walter P. Eaton and John Farrar.

The stories of Dorothy Canfield Fisher (b. 1879) with Vermont settings are represented by *Hillsboro People* (1915) and *The Brimming Cup* (1916). Alice Brown (b. 1857) made use of her native New England in *Meadow-Grass: Tales of New England Life* (1895) and *Tiverton Tales* (1899).

More recent stories with a Maine setting are *Mary Peters* (1934) and *Silas Crockett* (1936), by Mary Ellen Chase (b. 1887); *As the Earth Turns* (1933), by Gladys H. Carroll (b. 1904); *Time Out of Mind* (1935), by Rachel (Lyman) Field (b. 1894); and *Red Sky in the Morning* (1935), by Robert P. Tristram Coffin (b. 1892). Eugene O'Neill, George Santayana, and John P. Marquand have turned to the decadent aspects of New England for their portrayals. Others who have used authentic Vermont and New Hampshire background include Zephine Humphrey (Fahnestock) (b. 1874), *Mountain Verities* (1923), Ernest Poole (b. 1880), *One of Us* (1923), and Le Grand Cannon (b. 1899), *Look to the Mountain* (1942).

Two early anthologies indicating regional interest are Charles J. Fox, ed., *The New Hampshire Book: Being Specimens of the Literature of the Granite State,* Nashua, N.H., 1842, and Charles W. Everest, ed., *The Poets of Connecticut; with Biographical Sketches,* New York, 1864.

For a study of the place of New England in American literature, there is Helene Widenmann, *Neuengland in der erzählenden Literatur Amerikas,* Halle, 1935. See also Babette M. Levy, "Mutations in New England Local Color," *New Eng. Quar.,* XIX (1946), 338–358.

Useful local bibliographies are Walter J. Coates, *A Bibliography of Vermont Poetry, and Gazetteer of Vermont Poets,* Montpelier, Vt., 1942—a partial listing; and Joseph Williamson, *A Bibliography of the State of Maine from the Earliest Period to 1891,* Portland, Me., 1896, 2 vols.

## NEW YORK TO DELAWARE

There has been relatively less exploitation of the east-central seaboard states by local colorists than of New England and the South. Irving and Paulding confined themselves largely in their settings to Manhattan Island and its environs. Cooper chose the country which he knew around Cooperstown to describe the old manorial society and the anti-rent war. Solon Robinson (1803–1880) wrote of upstate New York in *Hot Corn-Life Scenes in New York* (1854), as did Bayard Taylor in *Hannah Thurston* (1863). The Adirondacks furnish the setting for *Adventures in the Wilderness; or, Camp-Life in the Adirondacks* (1869), by William H. H. Murray (1840–1904); and for the realistic sketches by Philander Deming (1829–1915), in *Adirondack Stories* (1880), and in *Tompkins and Other Folks* (1885). Harold Frederic's *Seth's Brother's Wife* (1887) is an authentic and vivid portrayal of upstate politics and farm life, as is Irving Bacheller's *Eben Holden . . .* (1900).

More recently Walter D. Edmonds (b. 1903) has given a picture of the old Erie Canal in *Rome Haul* (1929), and has used other local settings in *Mostly Canallers: Collected Stories* (1934), and *Drums Along the Mohawk* (1936). Carl (Lamson) Carmer (b. 1893) drew on New York State folklore for *Listen for a Lonesome Drum* (1936), and *Genesee Fever* (1941). Other authentic settings are in the stories of Henry James and Edith Wharton; also in Hilda Morris, *The Main Stream* (1939); Burke Boyce (b. 1901), *The Perilous Night* (1942); and George F. Hummel (b. 1882), *Subsoil* (1924), and *Heritage* (1935)—both with Long Island backgrounds.

The best known writers who have chosen New York City and northern New Jersey for their sketches include H. C. Bunner, Richard Harding Davis, O. Henry,* Brander Matthews, F. Hopkinson Smith, and Frank R. Stockton. See Arthur B. Maurice, *The New York of the Novelists,* New York, 1916. A study of regional characteristics is Dixon Ryan Fox, *Yankees and Yorkers,* New York, 1940, with data on literary differences and conflicts.

Pennsylvania and Delaware furnish background for Bayard Taylor's *Joseph and His Friend* (1870), and *Beauty and the Beast and Tales of Home* (1872). Helen Hunt Jackson's later short stories, *Between Whiles* (1887), draw on the Saranac region in New York, and Lancaster County, Pennsylvania. George Alfred Townsend (1841–1914) is best remembered for his local color stories, *Tales of the Chesapeake* (1880). S. Weir Mitchell (1829–1914) is best remembered for *Hugh Wynne, Free Quaker* (1897), one of several romances with a Philadelphia setting.

Margaret Deland (1857–1945) chose the country near Pittsburgh for two of her best known collections of local color sketches, *Old Chester Tales* (1898) and *Dr. Lavendar's People* (1903); as did Joseph Hergesheimer in *Mountain Blood* (1915). Elsie Singmaster's authentic Pennsylvania German dialect stories may be represented by *Katy Gaumer* (1914).

Two early regional studies are M. Katherine Jackson, *Outlines of the Literary History of Colonial Pennsylvania,* Lancaster, Pa., 1906; and Ellis P. Oberholtzer, *The Literary History of Philadelphia,* Philadelphia, 1906— largely antiquarian in interest. One of the earliest regional histories is Joshua Francis Fisher, "Some Account of the Early Poets and Poetry of Pennsylvania," pp. 53–103, in *Memoirs of the Historical Society of Pennsylvania,* II, pt. 2 (1830). Scattered references to Middle States regionalism are frequent in Arthur H. Quinn, *American Fiction* (1936), and in Fred L. Pattee, *A History of American Literature Since 1870* (1915).

A useful anthology of selections from early New York writers is Kendall B. Taft, ed., *Minor Knickerbockers: Representative Selections, with Introduction, Bibliography, and Notes,* New York, 1947 (Amer. Writers Ser.).

## THE SOUTH AND DEEP SOUTH

GENERAL STUDIES:
*Literary Regionalism*

No section of the country has been more conscious of its regionalism than the South. Though not entirely reliable, the best general study still remains Montrose J. Moses, *The Literature of the South,* New York, 1910. An appre-

* Some of his best regional stories have their setting in the Southwest.

ciative account is Carl Holliday, *A History of Southern Literature,* New York, 1906. Special studies include Charles Alphonso Smith, *Southern Literary Studies . . . ,* Chapel Hill, N.C., 1927; Jay B. Hubbell, "Literary Nationalism in the Old South," in *American Studies in Honor of William Kenneth Boyd,* Durham, N.C., 1940—a documented study showing the early plea for a distinctive southern literature; *I'll Take My Stand: The South and the Agrarian Tradition,* New York, 1930—a symposium by John Crowe Ransom, Donald Davidson, Allen Tate, John Donald Wade, and others; Edd W. Parks, *Segments of Southern Thought,* Athens, Ga., 1938—informal studies of southern life and literature from the point of view of a "distributist-agrarian"; Shields McIlwaine, *The Southern Poor-White from Lubberland to Tobacco Road,* Norman, Okla., 1939—social portraiture in literature, from Byrd to Caldwell. A first-hand account, chiefly of contemporary southern writers, is Emily Clark, *Innocence Abroad,* New York, 1931. Earlier studies include Sidney E. Bradshaw, *On Southern Poetry Prior to 1860,* Richmond, Va., 1900, with bibl., pp. 148–157; William M. Baskervill, *Southern Writers: Biographical and Critical Studies,* Nashville, Tenn., 1897–1903, 2 vols.; and Esther P. Ellinger, *The Southern War Poetry of the Civil War,* Philadelphia, 1918, with bibl., pp. 49–192.

The most distinguished of southern periodicals, all still current, are the *Sewanee Review* (founded 1892), the *South Atlantic Quarterly* (1902), and the *Virginia Quarterly Review* (1925). The *Southern Review* (1935–1942) was important, though short-lived.

*Anthologies*

Still indispensable because of its inclusiveness, though uncritical and sometimes unreliable, is Edwin A. Alderman and others, *Library of Southern Literature: Compiled Under the Direct Supervision of Southern Men of Letters,* Atlanta, 1907–1923, 17 vols. Volumes XV–XVI include "Biographical Dictionary of Authors" and an "Author Bibliography." Useful sectional anthologies are Edd W. Parks, ed., *Southern Poets: Representative Selections, with Introduction, Bibliography, and Notes,* New York, 1936 (Amer. Writers Ser.); (Clarence) Addison Hibbard, ed., *The Lyric South: An Anthology of Recent Poetry from the South,* New York, 1928—devoted principally to the previous decade; *idem,* ed., *Stories of the South, Old and New,* Chapel Hill, N.C., 1931; Robert Penn Warren, ed., *A Southern Harvest: Short Stories by Southern Writers,* Boston, 1937; Richmond C. Beatty and William P. Fidler, eds., *Contemporary Southern Prose,* Boston, 1940; and Gregory Paine, ed., *Southern Prose Writers: Representative Selections, with Introduction, Bibliography, and Notes,* New York, 1947 (Amer. Writers Ser.).

Regional checklists are Carvel E. Collins, "Nineteenth Century Fiction of the Southern Appalachians," *Bul. Bibl.,* XVII (1942–1943), 186–190, 215–218; James G. Johnson, *Southern Fiction Prior to 1860: An Attempt at a First-Hand Bibliography,* Charlottesville, Va., 1909; and Janet M. Agnew, *A Southern Bibliography: Poetry, 1929–1938,* University, La., 1940.

### Cultural Studies

Two recent analyses are Charles S. Johnson and others, *Into the Main Stream,* Chapel Hill, N.C., 1947; and Howard W. Odum, *The Way of the South: Toward the Regional Balance of America,* New York, 1947.

Edgar W. Knight's *Public Education in the South,* Boston, 1922, furnishes a bibliography for each chapter. Edwin Mims, in *The Advancing South: Stories of Progress and Reaction,* Garden City, N.Y., 1926, contrasts old and new forces in southern life. Ellis M. Coulter, *College Life in the Old South,* New York, 1928, includes a bibl., pp. 361–369. Broadus Mitchell and George S. Mitchell, *The Industrial Revolution in the South,* Baltimore, 1930, studies the social effects of the growth of the cotton textile industry in the South. A symposium by thirty-one scholars in a wide range of aspects is William T. Couch, comp., *Culture in the South,* Chapel Hill, N.C., 1934. Two other interpretive regional studies are Benjamin B. Kendrick and Alex M. Arnett, *The South Looks at Its Past,* Chapel Hill, N.C., 1935; and John Dollard, *Caste and Class in a Southern Town,* New Haven, 1937. An attempt to account historically for the southern mentality of the present day, which develops the thesis that Reconstruction in the South established a "savage ideal" of intolerance and rigid traditionalism, is Wilbur J. Cash, *The Mind of the South,* New York, 1941. See also William Hesseltine, *The South in American History,* rev. ed., New York, 1943.

### VIRGINIA

Sketches of southern customs and manners appear in the writings of William Wirt (1772–1834), typified by *The Rainbow* (1804). John P. Kennedy compiled *Memoirs of the Life of William Wirt,* Philadelphia, 1849, 2 vols. Three important series of essays by Wirt, written for Richmond newspapers, have been identified in Jay B. Hubbell, "William Wirt and the Familiar Essay in Virginia," *William and Mary Coll. Quar.,* XXIII (1943), 136–152. See also "The Influence of William Wirt," in Richard B. Davis, *Francis Walker Gilmer . . . ,* Richmond, Va., 1939; and *idem,* "Poe and William Wirt," *Amer. Lit.,* XVI (1944), 212–220.

The regional fiction of Nathaniel Beverley Tucker (1784–1851) is represented by *George Balcombe* (1836) and *The Partisan Leader: A Tale of the*

*Future* (1836). A sketch of Tucker is Maude H. Woodfin, "Nathaniel Beverley Tucker," *Richmond College Historical Papers*, II (1917), 9–42. See also John F. McDermott, "Nathaniel Beverley Tucker in Missouri," *William and Mary Coll. Quar.*, XX (1940), 504–507. Collections of Tucker's manuscripts are in the Duke University Library and in the library of the College of William and Mary.

John Esten Cooke (1830–1886) is regarded as the best of the Virginia novelists before the Civil War. His works include *The Virginia Comedians* (1854), *The Last of the Foresters* . . . (1856), *Surry of Eagle's Nest* (1866), and *Stories of the Old Dominion* . . . (1879). A documented life is John O. Beaty, *John Esten Cooke, Virginian*, New York, 1922. See Jay B. Hubbell, "The War Diary of John Esten Cooke," *Jour. So. Hist.*, VII (1941), 536–540; and Carvel Collins, "John Esten Cooke and Local-Color," *So. Lit. Mess.*, VI (1944), 82–84. Oscar Wegelin has compiled *A Bibliography of the Separate Writings of John Esten Cooke of Virginia, 1830–1886*, rev. ed., Hattiesburg, Miss., 1941.

The pre-Civil War sketches by George William Bagby (1828–1883), who edited the *Southern Literary Messenger* 1860–1864, were edited by Thomas Nelson Page (1910). A biography by Joseph L. King, Jr., *Dr. George William Bagby: A Study in Virginia Literature, 1850–1880*, New York, 1927, includes a bibliography, pp. 189–193.

The local color interest of Francis Hopkinson Smith (1838–1915) is typified in *Colonel Carter of Cartersville* (1891). Two analyses of Smith as artist-novelist are Theodore Hornberger, "The Effect of Painting on the Fiction of F. Hopkinson Smith (1838–1915)," *Studies in English, Univ. of Texas, 1943* (1944), 162–192; and *idem*, "Painters and Painting in the Writings of F. Hopkinson Smith," *Amer. Lit.*, XVI (1944), 1–10.

Mary Johnston (1870–1936) wrote a score of popular romances, several of which use a Civil War setting; well known are *The Long Roll* (1911) and *Cease Firing* (1912).

Individual bibliographies for three well known Virginia writers—Thomas Nelson Page, Ellen Glasgow, and James Branch Cabell—will be found herein.

Richmond established a place for itself as a literary center when Thomas H. White there founded the *Southern Literary Messenger* (1834–1864), the magazine which Poe edited 1835–1837. It maintained its regional interest under the editorships of Benjamin B. Minor (1843–1847), J. R. Thompson (1847–1860), and G. W. Bagby (1860–1864). The Richmond *Reviewer* (1921–1925), well known as an experimental magazine, was founded by Emily Clark and discovered such writers as Julia Peterkin, DuBose Heyward, and Paul Green. See Jay B. Hubbell, *Virginia Life in Fiction*, Dallas, Tex., 1922, with bibl., pp. 55–78. A regional anthology is Armistead C. Gordon, Jr., *Virginian Writers of Fugitive Verse,* New York, 1923.

## KENTUCKY

On James Lane Allen, see the individual bibliography herein. One of the most prolific of Kentucky regionalists was Madison (Julius) Cawein (1865–1914). His *Blooms of the Berry* (1887) was brought to public attention when it was reviewed by William Dean Howells in *Harper's Magazine* in May, 1888. Other poetic collections include *Lyrics and Idyls* (1890), *Intimations of the Beautiful* (1894), and *The Vale of Tempe* (1905). See William Dean Howells, "The Poetry of Mr. Madison Cawein," *No. Amer. Rev.,* CLXXXVII (1908), 124–128. Irving S. Cobb's *Old Judge Priest* (1915) figures in later collections. John (William) Fox, Jr. (1863–1919), became one of the most widely read among best-seller novelists at the turn of the twentieth century with such stories of Kentucky mountain folk as *A Cumberland Vendetta and Other Stories* (1895), *The Little Shepherd of Kingdom Come* (1903), and *The Trail of the Lonesome Pine* (1908).

Elizabeth Madox Roberts (1886–1941) was a regionalist who reproduced the speech and folk customs of the Kentucky mountaineers in *The Time of Man* (1926), *Not by Strange Gods* (1941), and other fiction. See Alexander M. Buchan, "Elizabeth Madox Roberts," *Southwest Rev.,* XXV (1940), 463–481, and Allen Tate, "The Elizabeth Madox Roberts Papers," *Lib. Cong. Quar. Jour. of Current Acquisitions,* I (1943), 29–31.

Other regionalists include Henry Watterson (1840–1921), who published his autobiography, *Marse Henry* (1919); Olive Tilford Dargan, whose short stories include *Highland Annals* (1925); and most recently, Jesse Stuart (b. 1907), represented by *Man with a Bull-Tongue Plow* (1934) and *Head o' W-Hollow* (1936).

Willard R. Jillson's *Early Kentucky Literature, 1750–1840,* Frankfort, Ky., 1931, is a descriptive history with bibliographies.

## TENNESSEE AND ALABAMA

For Mary N. Murfree ("Charles Egbert Craddock"), see the individual bibliography. Other Tennessee regional novels are represented by Sarah Barnwell Elliott (1848–1928) in *Jerry* (1891) and *The Durket Sperret* (1898); John Trotwood Moore (1858–1929) in *Songs and Stories from Tennessee* (1897); and T(homas) S(igismund) Stribling (b. 1881) in his bitterly realistic *Teeftallow* (1926) and *Bright Metal* (1928). Especially noteworthy is his trilogy dealing with life in Alabama: *The Forge* (1931), *The Store* (1932), and *Un-*

*finished Cathedral* (1934). A French study of Stribling is Maurice Le Breton, "L'Evolution sociale dans les Etats du Sud, d'après les romans de T. S. Stribling," *Etudes Anglaises,* I (1937), 36–52.

The novels and stories about the South by Caroline Gordon (b. 1895) have authentic Tennessee settings, and may be represented by *Penhally* (1931), and *None Shall Look Back* (1937).

An unpublished dissertation is Frank J. Ray, "Tennessee Writers: A Bibliographical Index," Univ. Tenn., 1929.

## GEORGIA

One of the earliest of Georgia regionalists was Augustus Baldwin Longstreet (1790–1870), who is best known for his *Georgia Scenes, Characters, Incidents . . .* (1835). A later humorous local colorist was Richard Malcolm Johnston (1822–1898), the best of whose sketches, frankly imitative of Longstreet, were published as *Georgia Sketches* (1864), revised as *Dukesborough Tales* (1871). His *Autobiography* was published in 1900. The Georgia tales of Harry Stillwell Edwards (1854–1938) are typified by *Two Runaways, and Other Stories* (1889). For material on Erskine Caldwell, see the individual bibliography herein.

The Atlanta Junior Members Round Table of the American Library Association prepared a *Georgia Author Bibliography, 1900–1940,* Atlanta, 1942. See also Rabun L. Brantley, *Georgia Journalism of the Civil War Period,* Nashville, Tenn., 1929.

## SOUTH CAROLINA

Charleston was one of the earliest and most flourishing among regional centers of literary culture. It was in Charleston that Hugh Swinton Legaré (1797–1843) founded the *Southern Review* (1828–1832), published as a quarterly literary magazine with contributions chiefly from southern writers. See Linda Rhea, *Hugh Swinton Legaré: A Charleston Intellectual,* Chapel Hill, N.C., 1934. Other early Charleston publications were the *Charleston Mercury* (1820–1868); and the *Southern Literary Journal and Monthly Magazine* (1835–1838)—strongly sectional in character. Simms edited the *Southern and Western Monthly Magazine and Review* (1845) until it was absorbed by the *Southern Literary Messenger.* Here also James D. B. De Bow founded *De Bow's Review* (1846–1880). The most notable of all Charleston periodicals was *Russell's Magazine* (1857–1860), edited by Paul Hamilton Hayne. It took its name from its publisher, John Russell, who maintained a bookshop in Charleston during the fifties where met the "Russell's Bookstore Group"—

an informal literary association which included Timrod, Hayne, Simms, and W. J. Grayson.

Recent writers who have made use of regional material include DuBose Heyward (1885–1940), whose portrayal of Negro life is best known in *Porgy* (1925) and *Mamba's Daughters* (1929); and Julia (Mood) Peterkin (b. 1880), who has made use of the Gullah Negro folklore of the Carolina Islands in *Scarlet Sister Mary* (1928). See R. A. Law, "Mrs. Peterkin's Negroes," *Southwest Rev.,* XIV (1929), 455–461.

William S. Hoole compiled *A Check-List and Finding-List of Charleston Periodicals, 1732–1864,* Durham, N.C., 1936.

NORTH CAROLINA

Early literary exploitation of North Carolina will be found in the sketches of Harden E. Taliaferro (1818–1875), *Fisher's River Scenes and Characters* (1859). Frances Christine Fisher Tiernan (1846–1920) described her life in many novels and sketches such as *The Land of the Sky* . . . (1876), and *A Summer Idyl* (1878). Albion W. Tourgée (1838–1905) chose the turbulent Reconstruction era for his autobiographic novel *A Fool's Errand* (1879) and later stories. See Roy F. Dibble, *Albion W. Tourgée,* New York, 1921. Among the many regional novels of Constance Fenimore Woolson (1840–1894), *For the Major* (1883) was written with a North Carolina background. A recent study is John D. Kern, *Constance Fenimore Woolson: Literary Pioneer,* Philadelphia, 1934, with bibl., pp. 180–194.

Paul (Eliot) Green (b. 1894) uses regional setting for his plays *In Abraham's Bosom* (1927), and *The House of Connelly* (1931). The most distinguished North Carolina writer, Thomas Wolfe, drew on his native background in *Look Homeward, Angel* (1929), and in *Of Time and the River* (1935) and later novels. For Wolfe, see the individual bibliography herein.

LOUISIANA

One of the chief centers of the local color movement in the United States during the nineteenth century was New Orleans, whose romantic past figures in the works of several significant writers. Mary Ashley Townsend (1832–1901) found material there for her novel *The Brother Clerks* (1857) and her poems *The Captain's Story* (1874). George Washington Cable's *Old Creole Days* (1879) inspired Grace (Elizabeth) King (1852–1932) to attempt a more faithful delineation of Creole life and character in *Monsieur Motte* (1888), *Balcony Stories* (1893), and other sketches. Grace King's autobiography, *Memories of a Southern Woman of Letters,* was published, New York, 1932. Even as Grace King drew principally upon the Creoles—the American-born descendants of French and Spanish settlers of Latin America—so Kate (O'Flaherty) Chopin (1851–1904) drew for local color upon the Cajuns, heirs of the Acadian exiles. She is best remembered for such books as *Bayou Folk* (1894), and *A Night in Acadie* (1897). Daniel S. Rankin, *Kate Chopin and Her Creole Stories*, Philadelphia, 1932, contains a full bibl., pp. 296–307.

A popular writer of post-bellum Negro dialect stories was Ruth McEnery Stuart (1849–1917), whose work is represented by *A Golden Wedding and Other Tales* (1893), and *In Simpkinsville: Character Tales* (1897).

Many of the stories of Lafcadio Hearn center in New Orleans. For a picture of literary New Orleans during the era 1890–1930, see Grace King's *Memories* . . ., New York, 1932.

Studies of New Orleans as a cultural center are Roger P. McCutcheon, "Books and Booksellers in New Orleans, 1730–1830," *Louisiana Hist. Quar.*, XX (1937), 3–15; and Nelle Smither, "A History of the English Theatre at New Orleans, 1806–1842," *Louisiana Hist. Quar.*, XXVIII (1945), 85–276, 361–572. See Max L. Griffin, "A Bibliography of New Orleans Magazines," *Louisiana Hist. Quar.*, XVIII (1935), 493–556. A useful general study is Arlin Turner, "Fiction of the Bayou Country," *Sat. Rev. Lit.*, XVIII (Apr. 30, 1938), 3–4, 16.

A factual narrative dealing with Louisiana is Edward King, *The Great South: A Record of Journeys in Louisiana, Texas* . . . , Hartford, 1875—first serialized in *Scribner's Mag.* in 1874.

A recently published regional anthology is Lizzie C. McVoy, ed., *Louisiana in the Short Story*, University, La., 1940. See also Lizzie C. McVoy and Ruth B. Campbell, *A Bibliography of Fiction by Louisianians and on Louisiana Subjects*, University, La., 1935, and Thomas P. Thompson, *Louisiana Writers Native and Resident, Including Others Whose Books Belong to a Bibliography of That State* . . ., New Orleans, 1904.

## MISSISSIPPI

Two collections of Southern tales by Sherwood Bonner (Katherine Sherwood Bonner MacDowell, 1849–1883) are *Dialect Tales* (1883) and *Suwanee River Tales* (1884). Her novel with a Mississippi setting was published as *Like Unto Like* (1879).

The Mississippi poet Irwin Russell (1853–1879) is remembered for his accurate rendering of the Negro dialect. Joel Chandler Harris edited *Poems by Irwin Russell* (1888), a volume reissued and enlarged in 1917 as *Christmas-Night in the Quarters, and Other Poems*. On Russell, see William M. Baskervill, *Southern Writers* . . ., Nashville, 1897, I, 1–40; J. S. Kendall, "Irwin Russell in New Orleans," *Louisiana Hist. Quar.*, XIV (1931), 321–345; A. A.

Kern, "Biographical Notes on Irwin Russell," *Texas Rev.*, II (1916), 140–149; and L. D. S. Harrell, "A Bibliography of Irwin Russell," *Jour. Miss. Hist.*, VIII (1946), 3–23.

Roark Bradford (b. 1896) chose Mississippi for the setting of *Ol' Man Adam an' His Chillun* (1928), and *Let the Band Play Dixie, and Other Stories* (1934). For data concerning the most significant Mississippi novelist, William Faulkner, see the individual bibliography herein. The novel *River House* (1929) by Stark Young (b. 1881) makes authentic use of his own early background.

FLORIDA

Constance Fenimore Woolson (1840–1894), Cooper's grandniece, used Florida as a background for some of her sketches in *Rodman the Keeper: Southern Sketches* (1880), and for her novel *East Angels* (1886). John D. Kern's *Constance Fenimore Woolson: Literary Pioneer,* Philadelphia, 1934, is a life, with bibl., pp. 180–194. See also Fred L. Pattee, "Constance Fenimore Woolson and the South," *So. Atl. Quar.*, XXXVIII (1939), 130–141; Lyon N. Richardson, "Constance Fenimore Woolson: 'Novelist Laureate' of America," *So. Atl. Quar.*, XXXIX (1940), 18–36; and Jay B. Hubbell, ed., "Some New Letters of Constance Fenimore Woolson," *New Eng. Quar.*, XIV (1941), 715–735—fifteen letters to Paul Hamilton Hayne.

Maurice Thompson's southern romances include *A Tallahassee Girl* (1881), and *At Love's Extremes* (1885).

Most recently the Florida of Marjorie Kinnan Rawlings (b. 1896) has been popularized in *South Moon Under* (1933), *The Yearling* (1938), and other stories.

Though Paul Laurence Dunbar and Charles Waddell Chesnutt did not write with a particular region in mind, Dunbar's *Lyrics of Lowly Life* (1896) and Chesnutt's *The Conjure Woman* (1899) make use of authentic Negro dialect.


*THE MIDDLE WEST*

GENERAL STUDIES

The central area of the United States, stretching westward from the Ohio River to the Rocky Mountains, includes the Prairie and Plains regions, and has furnished some of the most significant of regional and local color literature. Two recent anthologies dealing with regional literature of the Middle West give evidence of the growing interest in the field: John T. Frederick, ed.,

*Out of the Midwest: A Collection of Present-Day Writing,* New York, 1944; and John T. Flanagan, *America Is West: An Anthology of Midwestern Life and Literature,* Minneapolis, 1945. The standard factual history of the middle western frontier literature is Ralph L. Rusk, *The Literature of the Middle Western Frontier,* New York, 1925, 2 vols., with extensive bibliographies. Two recent brief studies by John T. Flanagan are "The Middle Western Farm Novel," *Minnesota Hist.,* XXIII (1942), 113-125, and "The Middle Western Historical Novel," *Jour. Ill. State Hist. Soc.,* XXXVII (1944), 7-47. A useful bibliography is Flanagan's "A Bibliography of Middle Western Farm Novels," *Minnesota Hist.,* XXIII (1942), 156-158.

Emerson Hough (1857-1923) is remembered for his popular historical romances of the West, which include *The Mississippi Bubble* (1902) and *The Covered Wagon* (1922). His personal recollections are incorporated in *The Passing of the Frontier* (1918). See Lee A. Stone, *Emerson Hough: His Place in American Letters,* Chicago, 1925.

A regional collection of plays is E. P. Conkle, *Crick Bottom Plays: Five Mid-Western Sketches,* New York, 1930.

## OHIO

Cincinnati was a center of literary regionalism as early as 1830. For a pioneer study, see William H. Venable, *Beginnings of Literary Culture in the Ohio Valley . . .,* Cincinnati, 1891, with its sketches of Timothy Flint, James Hall, Daniel Drake, and other figures of the early Northwest, and its notes on early western magazines. Recent fictional exploitation is in the writings of Sherwood Anderson, especially in his stories of small-town life, *Winesburg, Ohio* (1919); and in Louis Bromfield's *The Farm* (1933).

Further discussion of important regional writers will be found in the bibliography on Chronicles of the Frontier, *ante,* p. 245. A survey of authors, with a bibliography of an early regional school at Cincinnati, is Lucille B. Emch, "Ohio in Short Stories, 1824-1839," *Ohio Arch. and Hist. Quar.,* LII (1944), 209-250. See also W. Ralph Janeway, *A Selected List of Ohio Authors, and Their Books,* Columbus, 1933—a preliminary checklist.

## INDIANA

A discussion of the whole Hoosier School is in Meredith Nicholson, *The Hoosiers* (1900). Theodore Dreiser's recollections are set forth in *A Hoosier Holiday* (1916). For other important Hoosier writers, Edward Eggleston, James Whitcomb Riley, George Ade, and Dreiser, see the individual bibliographies herein.

John James Piatt (1835-1917), the Indiana poet and journalist, issued

*Poems of Two Friends* (1860) with W. D. Howells, and later published *Western Windows and Other Poems* (1869) and *Idyls and Lyrics of the Ohio Valley* (1881). (James) Maurice Thompson (1844–1901), in *Hoosier Mosaics* (1875), gives authentic dialect sketches of Indiana. His *Alice of Old Vincennes* (1900) has its setting in the Northwest Territory. Meredith Nicholson's *A Hoosier Chronicle* (1912) is a semi-autobiographical novel.

Widely known among writers whose stories frequently have been given a Hoosier setting is Booth Tarkington (1869–1946). His portrayal of life in a midwestern city is recorded in the trilogy, *The Turmoil* (1915), *The Magnificent Ambersons* (1918), and *The Midlander* (1923)—all published under the title *Growth* (1927). On Tarkington, see Percy H. Boynton, *Some Contemporary Americans,* Chicago, 1924, pp. 108–125; and Arthur H. Quinn, *American Fiction,* New York, 1936, pp. 596–606. Two early lives are Asa D. Dickinson, *Booth Tarkington . . .*, New York, 1926, and Robert C. Holliday, *Booth Tarkington,* New York, 1918. Barton Currie has compiled *Booth Tarkington: A Bibliography,* New York, 1932.

An early regional anthology is Benjamin S. Parker, *Poets and Poetry of Indiana,* New York, 1900. For a recent study, see Richard A. Cordell, "Limestone, Corn, and Literature: The Indiana Scene and Its Interpreters," *Sat. Rev. Lit.,* XIX (Dec. 17, 1938), 3–4, 14–15.

## ILLINOIS

Writers who have belonged to the "Chicago School" include Dreiser, Herrick, Masters, Sandburg, Lindsay, Sinclair Lewis, Sherwood Anderson, Hemingway, and Farrell. It was in Chicago that Harriet Monroe founded *Poetry* in 1912, and here also that Louis Sullivan established the Chicago School in architecture which influenced urban construction by way of the skyscraper. Frank Lloyd Wright's "prairie style" of domestic architecture was designed as appropriate to midwestern landscape. One of the most important of publishing houses was Stone and Kimball. Valuable material for the historian of literary culture is in Sidney Kramer, *A History of Stone and Kimball and Herbert S. Stone & Co.: With a Bibliography of Their Publications, 1893–1905,* Chicago, 1940. Much of the writing of Eugene Field (1850–1895) was inspired by his life in and near Chicago and is recorded in his volume *A Little Book of Western Verse* (1889). See John T. Flanagan, "Eugene Field After Sixty Years," *Univ. Kan. City Rev.,* XIII (1945), 167–173.

One of the earliest novels to treat Chicago realistically was *The Cliff-Dwellers* (1893), by Henry B. Fuller (1857–1929). Fuller's other novels with a Chicago setting may be represented by *Under the Skylights* (1901), and *On the Stairs* (1918). For a discussion of his fiction, see Arthur H. Quinn, *American Fiction,* New York, 1936, pp. 424–432.

Chicago has been the scene of "exposure literature," notably in Frank Norris's *The Pit* (1903)—dealing with the grain market; Upton Sinclair's *The Jungle* (1906)—the meat packing industry; and Robert Herrick's *Chimes* (1926)—the University of Chicago. A colorful drama with a newspaper background is Ben Hecht and Charles MacArthur, *The Front Page* (1928). Authentic pictures of the South Side and the underworld furnish the background for James T. Farrell's *Studs Lonigan: A Trilogy* (1938), which was begun with *Young Lonigan: A Boyhood in Chicago Streets* (1932).

Other panoramas of Chicago life are in Janet A. Fairbank, *The Smiths* (1925); William Riley Burnett, *Little Caesar* (1929); and Margaret Ayer Barnes, *Years of Grace* (1930) and *Within This Present* (1933).

For studies of the Chicago School, see Harry Hansen, *Midwest Portraits* (1923), and Lloyd Lewis and H. J. Smith, *Chicago: The History of Its Reputation* (1929). Primary material dealing with Chicago will also be found in the works of Hamlin Garland. See further Fred L. Pattee, *The New American Literature, 1890–1930,* New York, 1930, pp. 18–35.

Realistic novels portraying the Middle West, with settings principally in Illinois, were written by Joseph Kirkland (1830–1894), chief of which are *Zury: The Meanest Man in Spring County* (1887) and its sequel, *The McVeys* (1888). No adequate study of Kirkland has yet been published. Two useful brief estimates are by John T. Flanagan: "Joseph Kirkland, Pioneer Realist," *Amer. Lit.,* XI (1939), 273–284; and "A Note on Joseph Kirkland," *ibid.,* XII (1940), 107–108.

The Illinois frontier is the subject of John Hay's *Pike County Ballads, and Other Pieces* (1871), which depicts the traditional Pike character who came to be indigenous in Illinois, Missouri, Arkansas, Texas, and California.

Mary Hartwell Catherwood (1847–1902) achieved success with regional stories, among which *The Spirit of an Illinois Town* (1897) is representative. See Robert Price, "Mrs. Catherwood's Early Experiments with Critical Realism," *Amer. Lit.,* XVII (1945), 140–151, and *idem,* "Mary Hartwell Catherwood: A Bibliography," *Jour. Ill. State Hist. Soc.,* XXXIII (1940), 68–77.

The Federal Works Agency compiled a *Bibliography of Illinois Poets Since 1900,* Chicago, 1942.

## MICHIGAN

The sentimental verses of Will Carleton (1845–1912) were widely read, and depict one aspect of regional life as Carleton saw it. They include *Farm Ballads* (1873), *Farm Legends* (1875), and *City Ballads* (1885). For a life of Carleton, see A. E. Corning, *Will Carleton,* New York, 1917.

Realistic romances of Michigan lumber camps and of the Northwest are in Stewart Edward White's *The Blazed Trail* (1902), and other stories. James

Stevens (b. 1892) has made a study of the tall tales of lumbermen, in *Paul Bunyan* (1925) and *The Saginaw Paul Bunyan* (1932). The North Woods stories of James Oliver Curwood (1878–1927), typified by *The Grizzly King* (1916), were immensely popular.

More recent fiction depicting Michigan farm life is in Arthur Pound (b. 1884), *Once a Wilderness* (1934), and Della T. Lutes, *Millbrook* (1938).

For a study of Michigan regionalism, see Arnold Mulder, "Authors and Wolverines," *Sat. Rev. Lit.*, XIX (Mar. 4, 1939), 3–4, 16.

### IOWA

Alice French (1850–1934), under the pseudonym "Octave Thanet," was widely read at the turn of the twentieth century. Her novel *Knitters in the Sun* (1887) was followed by collections of stories dealing with Iowa and Arkansas, *Stories of a Western Town* (1893), and *A Captured Dream, and Other Stories* (1897). Well known as an Iowa regionalist is Herbert Quick (1861–1925): his *Vandemark's Folly* (1922) was followed by a sequel, *The Hawkeye* (1923). Quick's autobiography, *One Man's Life* (1925), is source material for the frontier West.

Ruth Suckow (b. 1892) is another Iowa regionalist, and her short stories and novels include *Iowa Interiors* (1926) and *The Folks* (1934). See J. T. Frederick, "Ruth Suckow and the Middle Western Literary Movement," *English Jour.*, XX (1931), 1–8, and Joseph E. Baker, "Regionalism in the Middle West," *American Review*, IV (1935), 603–614.

Paul Corey (b. 1903) began his realistic trilogy of Iowa farm life with *Three Miles Square* (1939), and continued it in *The Road Returns* (1940) and *County Seat* (1941).

A brief study of Iowa regionalism is Wallace Stegner, "The Trail of the Hawkeye: Literature Where the Tall Corn Grows," *Sat. Rev. Lit.*, XVIII (July 30, 1938), 3–4, 16–17. Alice Marple has compiled *Iowa Authors and Their Works: A Contribution Toward a Bibliography,* Des Moines, 1918. An unpublished dissertation is Rowena Longmire, "Dictionary Catalogue of the Short Stories of Arkansas, Missouri, and Iowa from 1869 to 1900," Univ. of Chicago, 1932.

### WISCONSIN, MINNESOTA, AND NEBRASKA

Hamlin Garland, who knew and exploited middle western regionalism, chose Wisconsin and neighboring states for such books as *Main-Travelled Roads* (1891), *Prairie Folks* (1893), and *Rose of Dutcher's Coolly* (1895). *Birth* (1918), by Zona Gale (1874–1938), is a realistic study of a Wisconsin village. Glenway Wescott (b. 1901) is represented by *The Grandmothers* . . .

(1927) and *Good-bye, Wisconsin* (1928); and August Derleth (b. 1909), by *Restless Is the River* (1939) and *Village Year: A Sac Prairie Journal* (1941).

Oscar Wegelin has compiled "Wisconsin Verse: A Compilation of the Titles of Volumes of Verse Written by Authors Born or Residing in the State of Wisconsin," *Papers Bibl. Soc. Amer.*, VII (1913), 90–114.

A picture of political graft dealing with the Indian lands of Minnesota is Honoré Willsie Morrow (1880–1940), *Lydia of the Pines* (1917). The most noted Minnesota regionalist is Sinclair Lewis, whose *Main Street* (1920) satirically depicts town and village life, as his *Babbitt* (1922) portrays that of the larger city. The fiction of Martha Ostenso (b. 1900) based on Norwegian immigrant life is represented by *Wild Geese* (1925).

Swiss immigrant life in Nebraska is the subject of Mari Sandoz (b. 1900), *Old Jules* (1935) and *Slogum House* (1937).

The North Woods—the lumber country of Michigan, Wisconsin, and northern Minnesota—has been authentically used as setting for the fiction of Stewart Edward White (b. 1873) in *The Claim Jumpers* (1901) and *The Blazed Trail* (1902); by Kenneth Roberts in his historical romance, *Northwest Passage* (1937); and much earlier by Constance Fenimore Woolson in *Castle Nowhere: Lake-Country Sketches* (1875)—dealing with the French inhabitants along the Great Lakes. Mary Hartwell Catherwood published the first of a series of romances dealing with French Canada and the Middle West in *The Romance of Dollard* (1889). One of her best collections of short stories is *The Chase of Saint Castin, and Other Stories of the French in the New World* (1894).

## THE PLAINS REGION

Olivier Gloux ("Gustave Aimard," 1818–1883) sailed as a boy from France, and for ten years lived in Arkansas and elsewhere as hunter, trapper, and miner. Among his twenty-five novels and tales, many are based on his adventures in the United States. Representative are *Loyal Heart; or, The Trappers of Arkansas* (1858), and *The Pirates of the Prairies* (1858).

Among recent fictional representations, *Cimarron* (1930), by Edna Ferber (b. 1887), is a romance reconstructing pioneer life in Oklahoma. John Steinbeck's *The Grapes of Wrath* (1939) depicts the Dust Bowl era and the migration of the "Okies" to California.

E(dgar) W(atson) Howe (1853–1937) wrote an early realistic novel of Kansas: *The Story of a Country Town* (1883). Kansas is also the setting of *In Our Town* (1906) and *A Certain Rich Man* (1909), by William Allen White (1868–1944).

Notable studies of Nebraska pioneer life are Willa Cather's *O Pioneers!* (1913) and *My Ántonia* (1918).

Classic portrayals of cowboy life are the novels and sketches of Andy Adams (1859-1935), represented by *The Log of a Cowboy* (1903). *The Wind Blew West* (1935), by Edwin M. Lanham (b. 1904), has its setting in Texas, as does his *Thunder in the Earth* (1941).

Two regional compilations are Mary H. Marable and Elaine Boylan, *A Handbook of Oklahoma Writers*, Norman, Okla., 1939; and Sophia J. Lammers, *A Provisional List of Nebraska Authors*, Lincoln, Nebr., 1918.

## THE SOUTHWEST

One of the most popular romances of its day was *Ramona: A Story* (1884), by Helen Hunt Jackson (1831-1885), dealing with the Mission Indians of southern California. For biographical and critical studies, see Ruth Odell, *Helen Hunt Jackson*, New York, 1939; Louise Pound, "Biographical Accuracy and 'H.H.,'" *Amer. Lit.*, II (1931), 418-421; and Allan Nevins, "Helen Hunt Jackson: Sentimentalist vs. Realist," *Amer. Scholar*, X (1941), 269-285. Authentic fiction of the southwestern frontier are the stories of Alfred Henry Lewis ("Dan Quin," 1857-1914), the first of whose six volumes of Wolfville stories is *Wolfville* (1897). Eugene Manlove Rhodes (1869-1934) was a novelist of the cattlemen, and may be represented by *Good Men and True* (1910) and *Once in the Saddle* (1927). The earliest of Mary Austin's many studies of the Southwest is *The Land of Little Rain* (1903). Katherine Anne Porter (b. 1894), in *Flowering Judas* (1930), makes use of the Southwest and Mexico for setting. See Lodowick Hartley, "Katherine Anne Porter," *Sewanee Rev.*, XLVIII (1940), 201-216, and Robert P. Warren, "Katherine Anne Porter: Irony with a Center," *Kenyon Rev.*, IV (1942), 29-42.

Oliver La Farge (b. 1901), *Laughing Boy* (1929), depicts the Navajo Indians. The Southwest furnishes the setting for some of the writings of Stephen Crane, Willa Cather, Paul Horgan, and Maxwell Anderson. Mary Austin's wide acquaintance with the Far West appears in her *Earth Horizon: Autobiography*, Boston, 1932. Thomas M. Pearce and Telfair Hendon have edited *America in the Southwest: A Regional Anthology*, Albuquerque, N.M., 1933. A further useful collection is Alice C. Henderson, *The Turquoise Trail: An Anthology of New Mexico Poetry*, Boston, 1928. J(ames) Frank Dobie, *Guide to Life and Literature of the Southwest . . .*, Austin, Tex., 1943, is authoritative, as is Mabel Major and others, *Southwest Heritage: A Literary History with Bibliography*, Albuquerque, N.M., 1938—with a selective bibliography of some 600 titles. An appreciative study is Laura A. Armer, *Southwest*, New York, 1935. See also Lyle Saunders, "A Guide to the Literature of the Southwest," *New Mex. Quar. Rev.*, XV (1945), 397-404, XVI (1946), 240-246, 399-408, 523-527; and John T. Flanagan and Raymond L.

Grismer, "Mexico in American Fiction Prior to 1850," *Hispania,* XXIII (:940), 307–318. A recent anthology is Thomas M. Pearce and A. P. Thomason, comps., *Southwesterners Write,* Albuquerque, N.M., 1947.

## THE PACIFIC NORTHWEST

The Idaho regionalist, Vardis Fisher (b. 1895), has dealt realistically with the hardships of western pioneer life in his tetralogy *In Tragic Life* (1932), *Passions Spin the Plot* (1934), *We Are Betrayed* (1935), *No Villain Need Be* (1936).

The far western explorer, Jedediah Strong Smith (1798–1831), who was a member of the Ashley expedition up the Missouri in 1823, is the central figure in John G. Neihardt's novel, *The Splendid Wayfaring* (1920). Sketches and legends of the Montana Crow Indians are gathered in Frank B. Linderman, *Old Man Coyote* (1931).

The opening up of Oregon and the establishment of John Jacob Astor's fur-trading empire is the subject of Washington Irving's *Astoria* (1836). Joaquin Miller describes his association with the Indians of southwest Oregon and northwest California in *Life Amongst the Modocs* (1873). A romance with authentic background dealing with the Oregon question, is by Emerson Hough (1857–1923): *54-40 or Fight!* (1909). The Oregon pioneer, Marcus Whitman (1802–1847), is the subject of Honoré Willsie Morrow's novel *We Must March* (1925); and a realistic picture of the Oregon homesteaders, 1906–1908, is Harold L. Davis, *Honey in the Horn* (1935).

Archie Binns (b. 1899) has chosen the logging business for background in *The Timber Beast* (1944) and other Washington novels. Robert Cantwell (b. 1908), in *Laugh and Lie Down* (1931), depicts life in a Washington mill city.

The North Woods stories of Jack London have been widely read. Less well known is Elizabeth Robins (b. 1862), *The Magnetic North* (1904).

A recent regional anthology is Stewart H. Holbrook, *Promised Land: A Collection of Northwest Writing,* New York, 1945. Lancaster Pollard has compiled "A Check List of Washington Authors," *Pacific Northwest Quar.,* XXXI (1940), 3–96, XXXV (1944), 233–266.

## CALIFORNIA AND THE FAR WEST

One of the earliest and most important of the centers of regional culture was San Francisco. Here was published the *Golden Era* (1852–1893), a newspaper and literary journal in which appeared the early writings of Bret Harte.

Mark Twain, C. W. Stoddard, Alonzo Delano, Joaquin Miller, and others. It was distinguished principally during the first decade of its existence. The *Overland Monthly* (1868–1875, 1883–1933), was similarly important in its early years. Bret Harte edited it 1868–1870, and among its contributors were C. W. Stoddard, Ina Coolbrith, E. R. Sill, Edwin Markham, George Sterling, Jack London, and John Muir. At one time or another some of the most distinguished writers have been associated with San Francisco, including Frank Norris, Bierce, Bret Harte, and, most important of all, Mark Twain. A useful regional history is Franklin Walker, *San Francisco's Literary Frontier,* New York, 1939—with new material on various figures, including Ina Coolbrith, Charles Warren Stoddard, and Henry George.

The early days of western mining are authentically depicted in Mary Hallock Foote (1847–1938), *The Led-Horse Claim: A Romance of a Mining Camp* (1883). The only novel of the philosopher Josiah Royce (1855–1916) is a regional California tale, *The Feud of Oakfield Creek* (1887), which deserves to be better known.

A classic romance of the Wyoming cowboy is *The Virginian* (1902), by Owen Wister (1860–1938). Wister elsewhere makes use of his knowledge of the Far West in his stories and sketches. *The Writings of Owen Wister,* New York, 1928, 11 vols., include material first published in book form.

G. R. MacMinn's "The Gentleman from Pike in Early California," *Amer. Lit.,* VIII (1936), 160–169, deals chiefly with George H. Derby's characterization of the Pike, with some data on early ballad and newspaper treatments of the character.

The fiction of Chester Bailey Fernald (1869–1938), with settings in San Francisco's Chinatown, is represented by *The Cat and the Cherub* . . . (1896) and *Chinatown Stories* (1899). Stewart Edward White (1873–1946) first published his historical trilogy, *The Story of California* (1927), as *Gold: A Tale of the Forty-niners* (1913), *The Gray Dawn* (1915), and *The Rose Dawn* (1920).

John Steinbeck's *Tortilla Flat* (1935) depicts the life of the Monterey *paisanos.*

Short stories by Gertrude Atherton (b. 1857) dealing with California regionalism are collected in *The Splendid Idle Forties: Stories of Old California* (1902); and George R. Stewart, Jr. (b. 1895), has recently reconstructed the early California frontier in *Ordeal by Hunger: The Story of the Donner Party* (1936) and *East of the Giants* (1938).

Levette J. Davidson and Prudence Bostwick have compiled *The Literature of the Rocky Mountain West, 1803–1903,* Caldwell, Idaho, 1939—an anthology with critical essay and a bibliography.* A collection of writings from the trans-Mississippi West, from the early times to the present, is Rufus A. Coleman, *Western Prose and Poetry*, New York, 1932. Edgar J. Hinkel and William E. McCann have prepared *Biographies of California Authors and Indexes of California Literature*, Oakland, Calif., 1942, 2 vols. Further useful bibliographical material is Levette J. Davidson, *Rocky Mountain Life in Literature: A Descriptive Bibliography*, Denver, 1936. Six bibliographical compilations by Edgar J. Hinkel are *Bibliography of California . . . Drama . . .* , Oakland, Calif., 1938; *Bibliography of California Fiction . . .*, Oakland, Calif., 1938; *Bibliography of California . . . Poetry . . .* , Oakland, Calif., 1938; *Criticism of California Literature . . . Drama: A Digest and Bibliography*, Oakland, Calif., 1940; *Criticism of California Literature: Fiction . . . A Digest and Bibliography*, Oakland, Calif., 1940; *Criticism of California Literature: Poetry . . . A Digest and Bibliography*, Oakland, Calif., 1940. See also Eva F. Wheeler, "A Bibliography of Wyoming Writers," *Univ. Wyo. Pub.*, VI (1939), No. 2, 11–37.

* It is supplemented by further regional material in Levette J. Davidson and Forrester Blake, comps., *Rocky Mountain Tales*, Norman, Okla., 1947.

# SCIENCE AND SOCIAL CRITICISM

## SOCIAL DARWINISM AND THE BACKGROUND OF NATURALISM IN LITERATURE

### SOCIAL DARWINISM

The two English scientists of the nineteenth century who did most to undermine existing scientific concepts as they had been handed down to modern times were Sir Charles Lyell and Charles Darwin. Lyell's *The Principles of Geology* (3 vols., 1830–1833) revolutionized ideas about the age of the earth by demonstrating the gradual process of natural laws. The publication in 1859 of Darwin's ideas *On the Origin of Species by Means of Natural Selection* . . . carried Lyell's concepts over from geology into biology, and led to the beginning of scientific positivism: the belief that science alone gives the truth; that science should describe, not explain; and that metaphysical speculation is vain. The positivistic concepts were carried forward in France by Auguste Comte; in England, by John Stuart Mill and Karl Pearson; and in America, by the mathematical physicist Chauncey Wright. As a result, interest in America turned more and more to scientific problems, led to Charles Sanders Peirce's doctrine of "fallibilism," to Henry Adams's mechanical formula for history, to the religious agnosticism of Robert G. Ingersoll, and to naturalism in literature. For discussions of the influence of French positivism, see R. L. Hawkins, *Auguste Comte and the United States, 1816–1853,* Cambridge, 1936; and *idem, Positivism in the United States,* Cambridge, 1938.

The most noted popularizer of Darwinism was Herbert Spencer. His vogue was enormous, and his influence on the founders of American sociology was very great. Articles by or about him were sprinkled through the popular magazines, especially during the years 1840–1890. He coined the phrase "survival of the fittest," stood staunchly against state interference, argued that human perfection is inevitable, that a technological community is best, and that the poor should not be aided but eliminated. Among industrialists Andrew Carnegie was his most prominent disciple. It was largely through Spencer's influence that literary language itself developed scientific metaphor, and his influence on the naturalistic writers was direct. Lined up against his philosophy of scientific progress were publicists of all sorts, including social Utopians and Marxists.

Materialistic determinism by way of Lyell, Darwin, and Spencer was popularized in America by John Fiske, Henry Ward Beecher, Carl Schurz, William Graham Sumner, Edward Livingston Youmans, and Asa Gray, who was the acknowledged interpreter of American opinion after 1870. Louis Agassiz, alone among noted American naturalists, never accepted Darwinism or evolution in any form; but James Dwight Dana in his *Manual of Geology* (1864; 4th ed., 1895) introduced natural selection, and came to be accepted as dean of American geologists. By the early 1870's the transmutation of species and natural selection dominated the outlook of American naturalists, and became part of the thinking of most enlightened writers.

John Fiske became the leading American expounder and popularizer of Darwinism. His *Outlines of Cosmic Philosophy* (1874) was widely read. For Fiske, see the individual bibliography herein. Charles W. Eliot (1834-1926), a young chemist trained in the Darwinian tradition, assumed the presidency of Harvard College in 1869, and Fiske was now able to lecture under university aegis. William Graham Sumner, at Yale, employed Spencer's *Study of Sociology* as a text even though President Noah Porter forbade it as antitheistic; but by 1877 President Porter was convinced of its soundness. The English Darwinian, Thomas Huxley, made a lecture tour during the seventies which received a wide press notice. By this time popular magazines took up the controversy of Darwinism. *Appleton's Journal,* founded in 1867, was an outlet for Fiske and Youmans, and the publishing house of Appleton led in the support of evolution. In 1872 Youmans founded the *Popular Science Monthly.* E. L. Godkin's *Nation* lent support. The founding of Johns Hopkins University in 1876, under the presidency of Daniel C. Gilman, gave compelling force to the Darwinian hypothesis.

## THE MECHANISTIC APPROACH

An important founder of modern sociology was Lester Frank Ward (1841-1913). His *Dynamic Sociology* (2 vols., 1883) was a forerunner of social planning and the first comprehensive sociological treatise written in America. His influential writings include *Outlines of Sociology* (1898), and *Glimpses of the Cosmos* (6 vols., 1913-1918).

William Graham Sumner (1840-1910) was an economic conservative who battled for competitive individualism. His *What Social Classes Owe to Each Other* (1883) was an early expression of his views. Albert G. Keller and Maurice R. Davie edited *Essays of William Graham Sumner,* New Haven, 1934, 2 vols. A brief study of Sumner's influence is "William Graham Sumner, Critic of Romantic Democracy," in Ralph H. Gabriel, *The Course of American Democratic Thought,* New York, 1940, pp. 237-250. Two other important pioneers were Albion W. Small (1854-1926) and Franklin H. Giddings

(1855–1931). Small founded the *American Journal of Sociology* in 1895, and edited it until his death. He published *The Meaning of Social Science* in 1910. Giddings's views are expressed in *The Principles of Sociology* (1896).

Chauncey Wright (1830–1875) defended the Darwinian hypothesis in *Philosophical Discussions* (1877) and was deeply influential among philosophers. See Philip P. Wiener, "Chauncey Wright's Defense of Darwin and the Neutrality of Science," *Jour. Hist. Ideas,* VI (1945), 19–45; and Joseph L. Blau, "Chauncey Wright: Radical Empiricist," *New Eng. Quar.,* XIX (1946), 495–517. David G. Croly (1829–1889), a follower of Comte, coined the word "miscegenation" and introduced it when he published *Miscegenation: The Theory of the Blending of the Races . . .* (1864).

Among mathematicians and physicists, the positivist position was championed by (Josiah) Willard Gibbs (1839–1903). His *Elementary Principles in Statistical Mechanics* was published in 1902. For a study of Gibbs's important contribution, see Muriel Rukeyser, *Willard Gibbs,* Garden City, 1942.

The search for a mechanistic theory of history was attempted by Brooks Adams in *Law of Civilization and Decay* (1895). His edition of Henry Adams's *The Degradation of the Democratic Dogma* (1919) includes Adams's "A Letter to American Teachers of History" and "The Rule of Phase in History." Charles Sanders Peirce (1839–1914) developed the theory of "fallibilism": the doctrine of an evolutionary universe in which the reality of chance and the principle of continuity are absolute, as is the dependence of logic on ethics. His first separately published volume was posthumously issued in 1923 as *Chance, Love, and Logic.* Justus Buchler published *Charles Peirce's Empiricism,* New York, 1939, and edited *The Philosophy of Peirce: Selected Writings,* New York, 1940. James Feibleman has published *An Introduction to Peirce's Philosophy, Interpreted as a System,* New York, 1946. For a recent study, see Philip P. Wiener, "Peirce's Metaphysical Club and the Genesis of Pragmatism," *Jour. Hist. Ideas,* VII (1946), 218–233.

### RECONCILIATION AND CONFLICT WITH RELIGION

The attempt to reconcile science and religion was made by the theologian and Princeton president, James McCosh (1811–1894), in *Christianity and Positivism* (1871), and by the foremost Darwinian scientist, Asa Gray (1810–1888), in *Natural Science and Religion* (1880). Henry Ward Beecher published *Evolution and Religion* (2 vols., 1885); and Lyman Abbott, *The Theology of an Evolutionist* (1897). The casuistic length to which writers were driven to effect a compromise between religion and science appears in the symposium by Simon Newcomb, Noah Porter, James Freeman Clarke, and James McCosh, "Law and Design in Nature," *No. Amer. Rev.,* CXXVIII (1879),

537–562. The revolution in scientific thinking was reflected in a new biblical scholarship popularized by works such as Washington Gladden's *Who Wrote the Bible?* (1891).

The attempt to base religion on science was publicized in Francis Elling-wood Abbot's *Scientific Theism* (1885), and John Fiske's *Through Nature to God* (1899)—works which upheld the Spencerian thesis that science and religion are two different approaches to the same problem.

Andrew Dickson White (1832–1918), the first president of Cornell University, summarized the principal issues in *A History of the Warfare of Science with Theology in Christendom* (2 vols., 1896); and Richard Theodore Ely (1854–1943) published *Social Aspects of Christianity and Other Essays* (1889).

The virulent hostility to the Darwinian hypothesis was manifest especially in the sixties and seventies. A popular exposition of anti-Darwinism was Charles Hodge's *What is Darwinism?* (1874). The evangelism of the fundamentalist, Dwight L. Moody (1837–1899), exerted a tremendous influence.

The other extreme, an impulse toward agnosticism and atheism, was epitomized in the writings and lectures of Robert G. Ingersoll (1833–1899), whose *Works* were collected in 12 vols. (1900).

## NATURALISM IN LITERATURE

Toward the end of the century literature was filled with Darwinian terms. Significant as a pioneering work in naturalistic fiction is *The Story of a Country Town* (1883) by E(dgar) W(atson) Howe (1854–1937), whose frankness was not equaled until the publication of Sinclair Lewis's *Main Street* (1920). For data on the writers influenced most by the movement: Harold Frederic, Hamlin Garland, Stephen Crane, Frank Norris, Jack London, Theodore Dreiser, William Faulkner, and James T. Farrell, see the individual bibliographies herein. For a study of the direct influence of European literary naturalism, especially the French, upon American writers, see Matthew Josephson, *Zola and His Time* . . ., New York, 1928.

## SECONDARY STUDIES

The best brief introduction to a study of Social Darwinism is the account given in Merle Curti, *The Growth of American Thought,* New York, 1943. A highly suggestive monograph on the vogue of racial inequality and the beginning of the dogma of the superior race is Richard Hofstadter, *Social Darwinism in American Thought, 1860–1915,* Philadelphia, 1944, with bibl., pp. 177–186—concerning the reception of Darwinism in the United States.

The influences of scientific determinism on modern fiction are discussed in Harry Hartwick, *The Foreground of American Fiction*, New York, 1934, with bibl., pp. 410–430. See also Oscar Cargill, *Intellectual America: Ideas on the March*, New York, 1941, pp. 48–175; and Alfred Kazin, *On Native Grounds*, New York, 1942, especially for his discussion of Norris, Crane, Dreiser, and London. Valuable background material is in Merle Curti, *The Social Ideas of American Educators*, New York, 1935.

Brief studies include John L. Gillen, "The Development of Sociology in the United States," *Publ. Amer. Sociol. Soc.*, XXI (1926), 1–25; Herbert Edwards, "Zola and the American Critics," *Amer. Lit.*, IV (1932), 114–129; Sidney Ratner, "Evolution and the Rise of the Scientific Spirit in America," *Philosophy of Science*, III (1936), 104–122; Bert J. Loewenberg, "Darwinism Comes to America, 1859–1900," *Miss. Valley Hist. Rev.* (1941), 339–368; Herbert W. Schneider, "Evolution and Theology in America," *Jour. Hist. Ideas*, VI (1945), 3–18; and Morton G. White, "The Revolt Against Formalism in American Social Thought of the Twentieth Century," *ibid.*, VIII (1947), 131–152.

A general survey is David F. Bowers, "Hegel, Darwin, and the American Tradition," in *Foreign Influences in American Life* (ed. by Bowers), Princeton, 1944, pp. 146–171, with a critical bibl., pp. 235–254.

## THE MACHINE AGE AND THE LITERATURE OF EXPOSURE

### FICTIONAL EXPLOITATION

One of the earliest novelists to make fictional use of the industrial era was Rebecca Harding Davis (1831–1910). Her story of wage slavery in mills, "Life in the Iron Mills," was published in the *Atlantic Monthly*, VII (1861), 430–451. The same magazine published serially "A Story of Today" (Vols. VIII and IX, 1861–1862), written with similar intent to expose the evils of social inequality. Her novel *John Andross* (1874) was written to expose the whiskey trust.

The most important journal to devote itself to the cause of civil service and tariff reform was the New York weekly *Nation*, founded by Edwin Lawrence Godkin (1831–1902) in 1865. Godkin continued as editor until 1881.

Several important novels directed against various forms of corruption were published during the seventies. Elizabeth Stuart Phelps Ward's *The Silent Partner* (1871) was written to expose wage slavery in factories. The fraudulent speculation in western land was the subject of *The Gilded Age* (1873) by Mark Twain and Charles Dudley Warner; of Edward Eggleston's

*The Mystery of Metropolisville* (1873); and of David Ross Locke's *A Paper City* (1878). Mining fraud is the background for John F. Swift's *Robert Greathouse* (1876). Josiah G. Holland's *Sevenoaks: A Story of Today* (1875) deals with dishonest oil speculation. Henry Adams in *Democracy* (1879) centered his interest on political corruption. Edward Bellamy's brother Charles wrote *The Breton Mills* (1879)—a very early novel on industrial class struggle.

*The Stillwater Tragedy* (1880), by Thomas Bailey Aldrich, was written to demonstrate the calamity and futility of strikes, and John Hay's *The Bread-Winners* (1884) was an attack on organized labor. Henry Francis Keenan intended his *The Money-Makers: A Social Parable* (1885) as a reply to Hay's *The Bread-Winners,* demonstrating the corrupting influence of big business. Keenan's novel and Howells's *The Rise of Silas Lapham* (1885) are two of the earliest novels which center their plots on big business. In the same year John T. Trowbridge used oil swindles as the basis for *Farnell's Folly.*

Injustices and corruption in the management of factories, mills, railroads, department stores, and indeed government, were the themes of such novels as Amanda Douglas, *Hope Mills; or, Between Friend and Sweetheart* (1880); Thomas S. Denison, *An Iron Crown: A Tale of the Great Republic* (1885)— one of the darkest pictures of monopoly; George T. Dowling, *The Wreckers: A Social Study* (1886); Martin A. Foran, *The Other Side: A Social Study Based on Fact* (1886); Hamlin Garland, *A Member of the Third House* (1892)—one of the best novels on political corruption; and Ignatius Donnelly, *The Golden Bottle* (1892)—dealing with trusts.

H. H. Boyesen concerned himself with human values in the social struggle in such novels as *The Mammon of Unrighteousness* (1891) and *The Social Strugglers* (1893). F. Hopkinson Smith attacked organized labor in *Tom Grogan* (1896). False values and the struggle of force against force are treated in such novels as Will Payne, *The Money Captain* (1898); Harold Frederic, *The Market Place* (1899); and Margaret Sherwood, *Henry Worthington, Idealist* (1899). Charles Dudley Warner emphasized the folly of acquiring wealth without values in his trilogy, *A Little Journey in the World* (1889), *The Golden House* (1895), and *That Fortune* (1899).

## The Political Novel

Mark Twain and Charles Dudley Warner (1829–1900) furnished a name for an era of political corruption in the title of their book *The Gilded Age* (1873), which depicts the unscrupulous acquisitiveness in Washington and elsewhere during the boom times after the Civil War. Washington during Grant's administration is the setting of John W. De Forest's *Playing the Mis-*

*chief* (1875) and *Honest John Vane* (1875). Abuse of political power is the theme of *Democracy* (1879), by Henry Adams, a scathing indictment of corruption in contemporary Washington. *Through One Administration* (1883), by Frances Hodgson Burnett (1849–1924), is similar in theme and setting.

Sectional political activities furnished material for several novelists. Albion W. Tourgée (1838–1905) deals with the political status of the South during the period of Reconstruction in *A Fool's Errand* (1879), *Bricks Without Straw* (1880), and *The Invisible Empire* (1883)—the Ku Klux Klan. Francis Marion Crawford (1854–1909) chose Boston for his setting in *An American Politician* (1884), and Hamlin Garland's *A Spoil of Office* (1892) centers on corruption in the Middle West and the organization of the Grange and the Farmers' Alliance. One of the best political novels is *The Honorable Peter Stirling* (1894), by Paul Leicester Ford (1865–1902), dealing with ward politics in New York City. See "Paul Leicester Ford and the Industry of Politics," in Morris E. Speare, *The Political Novel* . . . (1924), pp. 322–333; and Arthur H. Quinn, *American Fiction* (1936), pp. 494–496. Ellen Glasgow's *The Voice of the People* (1900) is the first of many novels depicting the political background in Virginia from 1850 to 1940. The most popular writer of political romances, Winston Churchill (1871–1947), created his striking figure Jethro Bass as the central character in *Coniston* (1906)—concerned with mid-nineteenth century New Hampshire politics. Midwestern politics is featured in *The Crisis* (1901) and *A Far Country* (1915). *Mr. Crewe's Career* (1908) centers on railroad monopoly. See "Winston Churchill and Civic Righteousness," in John C. Underwood, *Literature and Insurgency* (1914), pp. 299–345, and "Mr. Winston Churchill and the Novel of Political Reform," in Morris E. Speare, *The Political Novel* . . . (1924), pp. 306–321.

*The Thirteenth District* (1902), by Brand Whitlock (1869–1934), is concerned with the professional politician; and Jack London's *The Iron Heel* (1908), dealing with the theme of dictatorship, foreshadows Sinclair Lewis's *It Can't Happen Here* (1935). One of the most recent exposés of political chicanery is the novel *Revelry* (1926), by Samuel Hopkins Adams (b. 1871), centering on Washington during the Harding administration. For data on the fiction of Upton Sinclair, much of which is intended to expose political corruption, see the individual bibliography on Sinclair herein.

No satisfactory study of the American political novel as such has been published. Morris E. Speare, *The Political Novel in England and America,* New York, 1924, touches briefly on the subject. Useful material is in Fred H. Harrington, "Literary Aspects of American Anti-Imperialism, 1898–1902," *New Eng. Quar.,* X (1937), 650–667, especially on the writings of Howells, Clemens, Aldrich, and Garland. See Secondary Studies. *post,* p. 334.

## NON-FICTIONAL WRITING

Henry Adams and Charles Francis Adams, Jr., exposed growing corruption in *Chapters of Erie, and Other Essays* (1871). The most important work of protest against the domination of big business was Henry George, *Progress and Poverty: An Inquiry into the Cause of Industrial Depressions, and of Increase of Want with Increase of Wealth* (1879). George's critical arguments were his greatest contribution, but his constructive proposal of a single tax on land, amounting to the whole or almost the whole of economic rent, has given rise to an organized movement that is still in existence. Henry Demarest Lloyd (1847–1903) first won notice with "The Story of a Great Monopoly," *Atl. Mo.,* XLVII (1881), 317–334. It was not until some dozen years later that Lloyd published a classic in the "literature of exposure," *Wealth Against Commonwealth* (1894)—a fully documented attack on monopolies, particularly the Standard Oil Company. His earlier volume, *A Strike of Millionaires Against Miners* (1890), was an appeal for industrial justice. Other notable inquiries into social inequalities are Jacob A. Riis, *How the Other Half Lives* (1890)—dealing with his experiences in the New York slums—and Charles B. Spahr, *An Essay on the Present Distribution of Wealth in the United States* (1896), and *America's Working People* (1900).

The most original American economist on an issue of outstanding importance was Thorstein Veblen (1857–1929). His trenchant attack on commercialism was published as *The Theory of the Leisure Class* (1899), followed by *The Theory of Business Enterprise* (1904). *The Engineers and the Price System* (1921) is a discussion of the American industrial system at the end of the First World War. Joseph Dorfman's biography, *Thorstein Veblen and His America,* New York, 1934, contains a survey of economic thought in the United States during Veblen's formative years (the 1880's and 1890's), and is the best available substitute for a full-length history of American economic thought in these decades.

The social reformer Benjamin O. Flower (1858–1918) founded the *Arena,* a journal of economic and social discussion, in 1889, and edited it until 1898. His views are expressed in *Righting the People's Wrongs* . . . (1917).

Two notable world's fairs were organized during the last quarter of the century to celebrate America's industrial majority. The first was held in Philadelphia in 1876. For reports of the Director-General and other officers, see *United States Centennial Commission: International Exhibition, 1876,* Washington, 1880, 9 vols. A somewhat confusing but lavishly illustrated description of the various exhibits is *The Masterpieces of the Centennial International Exhibition,* Philadelphia, 1875–1876, 3 vols. The World's Columbian Exposition was held in Chicago in 1893. For a full narrative account, see *Report of the President to the Board of Directors of the World's Columbian Exposition, Chicago, 1892–1893*, Chicago, 1898. Highly commendatory contemporary accounts are Henry Van Brunt, "The Columbian Exposition and American Civilization," *Atl. Mo.*, LXXI (1893), 577–588, and Alice Freeman Palmer, "Some Lasting Results of the World's Fair," *Forum*, XVI (1893), 517–523—the latter essay representing genteel Easterners' approval of the West's supposed refinement and new interest in things of the spirit.

The industrialist Andrew Carnegie (1835–1919) epitomizes the era of big business. His essay *The Gospel of Wealth* (1889) sets forth his idea that the rich are trustees for the public good. A collection of his magazine articles and addresses was published as *The Empire of Business* (1902). Written with a good deal of literary ability, they afford one of the best statements of the point of view of a relatively enlightened and humane business leader. The volume includes the famous addresses on "The Road to Business Success" and "The Common Interest of Labour and Capital."

### SECONDARY STUDIES

Walter F. Taylor, *The Economic Novel in America*, Chapel Hill, N.C., 1942, is a discussion of the novel as a product of the machine age and emphasizes the importance of a native democratic tradition as compared with European radicalism in the leading critics of Big Business. It contains a bibliography, pp. 341–365, which is supplemented by Lisle A. Rose, "A Bibliographical Survey of Economic and Political Writings, 1865–1900," *Amer. Lit.*, XV (1944), 381–410. Useful treatment of the subject is in A(lfred) Whitney Griswold, *The American Cult of Success*, Baltimore, 1934. See also John Chamberlain, *Farewell to Reform*, New York, 1932; and Edward E. Cassady, "Muckraking in the Gilded Age," *Amer. Lit.*, XIII (1941), 134–141.

Published dissertations which are devoted to the novel in the Machine Age include George A. Dunlap, *The City in the American Novel, 1789–1900: A Study of American Novels Portraying Contemporary Conditions in New York, Philadelphia, and Boston*, Philadelphia, 1934; Claude R. Flory, *Economic Criticism in American Fiction, 1792 to 1900*, Philadelphia, 1936; and James H. Barnett, *Divorce and the American Divorce Novel, 1858–1937: A Study in Literary Reflections of Social Influences*, Philadelphia, 1939. Unpublished material is Edward E. Cassady, "The Business Man in the American Novel, 1865–1900," Univ. Calif., 1939; John Hollenbach, "Economic Individualism in the American Novel, 1865–1888," Univ. Wis., 1941; and George Mayberry, "Industrialism and the Industrial Worker in the American Novel, 1814–1890," Harvard Univ., 1942.

See also Edward J. O'Brien, *The Dance of the Machines: The American*

*Short Story and the Industrial Age,* New York, 1929—an indictment of taste for "formula" stories.

## LITERATURE OF THE MUCKRAKING MOVEMENT

The muckraking movement was so named by Theodore Roosevelt in 1906 in his attack on corruption in politics and business. It began as a movement in 1902, reached its climax some ten years later, and ended in 1916. The leading vehicle for the muckrakers was *McClure's Magazine* (1901–1912), with its staff of brilliant writers and investigators headed by Lincoln Steffens (its managing editor, 1902–1906), Ida M. Tarbell, and Ray Stannard Baker. Other journals associated with the movement were the *Arena, Independent, Collier's, Cosmopolitan, American Magazine,* and *Everybody's*—on the last two of which Steffens was for a time an associate editor. A few influential newspapers sponsored the movement, notably the New York *World* and the Kansas City *Star*.

Steffens himself turned his attention especially to corruption in municipal politics. His best known works include *The Shame of the Cities* (1904), *The Struggle for Self-Government* (1906), and *The Upbuilders* (1909). A posthumous collection of his later writings is in *Lincoln Steffens Speaking* (1936). Ida M. Tarbell's *The History of the Standard Oil Company,* New York, 1904, 2 vols., was a carefully documented study of a great monopoly and one of the most important of the early contributions to the influence of the movement. Samuel Hopkins Adams (b. 1871), who was associated with *McClure's* and with *Collier's,* published *The Great American Fraud* (1906)—an exposure of patent nostrums. For the support given to the movement by Theodore Roosevelt, see Henry F. Pringle, *Theodore Roosevelt: A Biography,* New York, 1931.

The ablest novelist associated with the muckrakers was David Graham Phillips (1867–1911). Among the most important of his novels dealing with exposure, *The Cost* (1904) and *The Deluge* (1905) are about Wall Street manipulations; *The Plum Tree* (1905), about the operations of a political boss; and *Light-Fingered Gentry* (1907), about insurance scandals. Frank Norris's *The Octopus* (1901) dealt with railroad monopolies, and *The Pit* (1903) pictured manipulations in the Chicago grain market. Robert Herrick (1868–1938), in *The Memoirs of an American Citizen* (1905), was concerned with ethics in the Chicago meat-packing business. Other Herrick novels dealing with conflicts in American society between success and integrity include *The Common Lot* (1904) and *A Life for a Life* (1910). Most widely read was his *The Master of the Inn* (1908). For studies of Herrick see William Dean Howells, "The Novels of Robert Herrick," *No. Amer. Rev.,*

CLXXXIX (1909), 812–820; "Two Studies of Robert Herrick," in Edwin A. Björkman, *Voices of Tomorrow. . . .*, New York, 1913, pp. 260–289; Harry Hansen, *Midwest Portraits . . .*, New York, 1923, pp. 225–251, and Newton Arvin, "Homage to Robert Herrick," *New Repub.,* LXXXII (Mar. 6, 1935), 93–95.

Upton Sinclair associated himself with the movement and published *The Jungle* (1906), on the Chicago meat-packing industry, and *The Money Changers* (1908), dealing with Wall Street. John Spargo's exposure of tenement conditions was *The Bitter Cry of the Children* (1906). The most notable literary contributions were Theodore Dreiser's Chicago studies, *The Financier* (1912) and its sequel, *The Titan* (1914). One of the most popular of muckraking novels was Winston Churchill's *The Inside of the Cup* (1912), dealing with the church.

The chief reform writing of William Allen White (1868–1944) appeared in the columns of his Emporia *Gazette* as well as in articles for numerous magazines. His fiction with reformist purposes includes *Stratagems and Spoils* (1901), *A Certain Rich Man* (1909), and *In the Heart of a Fool* (1918). See especially Everett Rich, *William Allen White,* New York, 1941, which contains extensive bibliographies. Most of the exposure writing of Thomas Edward Watson (1856–1922) appeared in the columns of *Tom Watson's Magazine* (New York, 1905–1906), in his *Weekly Jeffersonian,* and in *Watson's Jeffersonian Magazine* (Atlanta, 1907–1917). Much of the reformist writing of Moorfield Storey (1845–1929) appeared in innumerable pamphlets, articles, and public letters attacking political corruption. His book *The Conquest of the Philippines by the United States, 1898–1925,* written with M. P. Lichauco, was published in 1926.

Material on the muckraking movement will be found in Mark Sullivan's autobiography, *The Education of an American* (1938), dealing with muckraking journalism; and various writings of Burton J. Hendrick, whose *The Age of Big Business,* New Haven, 1919, contains much scathing commentary on early business operations. His contributions to *McClure's* between 1905 and 1913 often dealt with the amassing of great American fortunes. Norman Hapgood (1868–1937) edited *Collier's* 1903–1912, during its muckraking period. His autobiography, *The Changing Years* (1930), is source material on the movement. For an account of conditions during 1900–1910, see especially C(ornelius) C. Regier, *The Era of the Muckrakers,* Chapel Hill, N.C., 1932, with bibliography, pp. 217–241. An incisive critique of the period is that of John Chamberlain, *Farewell to Reform . . .*, New York, 1932. Lincoln Steffens's *Autobiography* (1931) is one of the best histories of the development of the muckraking movement. Other useful studies are Upton Sinclair, *The Brass Check* (1919), and Louis Filler, *Crusaders for American Liberalism,* New York, 1939.

## CHRISTIAN SOCIALISM

The social gospel movement was an attempt to apply the teachings of Jesus to social problems. It called attention to danger spots in American civilization and spoke forthrightly for social betterment, particularly as regarded slums, immigration, social and financial inequalities. A pioneer treatise on Christian Socialism is *Our Country* (1885) by the Congregational minister Josiah Strong (1847-1916). This outline of his "social gospel" was followed by *Religious Movements for Social Betterment* (1900). See Edward T. Root, "Josiah Strong: A Modern Prophet of the Kingdom of God," *New-Church Rev.*, XXIX (1922), 47-54. Another early exponent of Christian Socialism was George Davis Herron (1862-1925), whose essays on Christian sociology are set forth in *The Christian Society* (1894), *The Christian State* (1895), and *The Social Meanings of Religious Experience* . . . (1896). On Herron's later years, see Mitchell P. Briggs, *George D. Herron and the European Settlement,* Stanford Univ., 1932. The Baptist minister Walter Rauschenbusch (1861-1918) was a leader of the Christian Socialist movement. His works include *Christianity and the Social Crisis* (1907), *Christianizing the Social Order* (1912), and *Theology of the Social Gospel* (1917). See Vernon P. Bodein, *The Social Gospel of Walter Rauschenbusch and Its Relation to Religious Education,* New Haven, 1944, with bibl., pp. 158-163.

Lyman Abbott (1835-1922) championed rationality and scientific views which reconciled Darwinian theory and Christianity. As editor of the *Outlook* he gained a wide audience, and his views are expressed in such books as *The Evolution of Christianity* (1892), and *Christianity and Social Problems* (1896).

Another pioneer in the Christian Socialist movement was Octavius B. Frothingham (1822-1895). His *The Religion of Humanity* (1872) is an early and important document. See also his *Recollections and Impressions, 1822-1890,* New York, 1891. The Congregational minister Washington Gladden (1836-1918) championed the same causes in works such as *Applied Christianity: Moral Aspects of Social Questions* (1886). Important also in the movement was Francis G. Peabody (1847-1936), whose published works include *Jesus Christ and the Social Question* (1900) and *The Approach to the Social Question* . . . (1909). An important study of the movement is Daniel D. Williams, *The Andover Liberals: A Study in American Theology,* New York, 1941, with bibl., pp. 193-199.

An approach to the same problem made by sociologists and political economists may be observed in the works of Henry George and Edward Bellamy. For data on George and Bellamy, see the individual bibliographies herein. Other important writings in the field are the works of Richard T. Ely

(1854–1943), *Social Aspects of Christianity* (1889) and *Socialism and Social Reform* (1894); and William D. P. Bliss (1856–1926), *What Is Christian Communism?* (1890). Bliss edited *The Encyclopaedia of Social Reform* (1897; rev. ed., 1907).

The impulse toward Christian Socialism appears in such novels as Albion W. Tourgée's *Murvale Eastman, Christian Socialist* (1890); and in the novel of Charles M. Sheldon (1857–1946), *In His Steps* (1896)—which is alleged to be the most popular modern novel, having sold some twenty million copies and been translated into a score of languages.

An important study of the social gospel movement is Charles H. Hopkins, *The Rise of the Social Gospel in American Protestantism, 1865–1915,* New Haven, 1940—an account of the development of a sense of responsibility for social justice in the leading Protestant churches in America. James Dombrowski's *The Early Days of Christian Socialism in America,* New York, 1936, with bibl., pp. 195–202, includes chapters on Ely, George, and Bellamy. See further John W. Buckham, *Progressive Religious Thought in America,* New York, 1919; Arthur C. McGiffert, *The Rise of Modern Religious Ideas,* New York, 1922; and John Chamberlain, *Farewell to Reform . . . ,* New York, 1932.

# SLAVERY AND CONFLICT

## EARLY ANTISLAVERY LITERATURE

Protests against the institution of slavery had been voiced in the early days of colonial settlement. Samuel Sewall's *The Selling of Joseph* (1700) remonstrated against the slave traffic. The humanitarian philosophy of Anthony Benezet (1713–1784) was expressed in *Observations on the Inslaving, Importing and Purchasing of Negroes* (1759); and in the early days of the republic Crèvecœur devoted the ninth of his *Letters from an American Farmer* (1782) to the antislavery cause. Franklin, as president of the Abolition Society, signed the memorial presented to the House of Representatives of the United States on February 12, 1789, urging it as his last public act to discourage the traffic in slaves. His opinions are recorded in his essay "On the Slave-Trade" (1790). The prominent Virginia lawyer St. George Tucker (1752–1827) pleaded for the gradual emancipation of slaves in his *Dissertation on Slavery* (1796). For a study of early attempts at slavery reform, see Michael Kraus, "Slavery Reform in the Eighteenth Century: An Aspect of Transatlantic Intellectual Cooperation," *Pa. Mag. Hist. and Biog.*, LX (1936), 53–66.

## ABOLITIONIST MAGAZINES AND PROPAGANDA

During the 1830's the slavery issue became vital. William Lloyd Garrison (1805–1879) and others organized the New England Anti-Slavery Society in 1832; and in 1833 the American Anti-Slavery Society was established at Philadelphia and included such members as Wendell Phillips, Whittier, Edmund Quincy, and James G. Birney. Garrison expressed himself forcibly in *Thoughts on African Colonization* (1832). Important primary material on Garrison is published in Wendell P. and Francis J. Garrison, *William Lloyd Garrison, 1805–1879, The Story of His Life As Told by His Children,* New York, 1885–1889, 4 vols. Later studies are those of Lindsay Swift, *William Lloyd Garrison,* Philadelphia, 1911; and John J. Chapman, *William Lloyd Garrison,* New York, 1913. Lydia Maria Child (1802–1880) made *An Appeal in Favor of That Class of Americans Called Africans* (1833), which received wide contemporary notice. Whittier contributed a biographical introduction

339

to *Letters of Lydia Maria Child,* Boston, 1882. In the South James G. Birney (1792–1857) was an early antislavery leader whose *Letter on the Political Obligations of Abolitionists* (1839) won him recognition. Two volumes of his letters were published in 1938. Theodore Dwight Weld (1803–1895), the Massachusetts reformer, was an early and influential Abolitionist. Together with his wife Angelina Grimké he wrote and lectured effectively to consolidate antislavery feeling and convert others who became influential. His tract *The Bible Against Slavery* (1837) was followed by *American Slavery As It Is* (1839), which is alleged to have inspired Mrs. Stowe's *Uncle Tom's Cabin* (1852). James K. Paulding's *Slavery in the United States* (1836) is a vehement defense of "the institution" by a northerner.

William Lloyd Garrison as a militant pacifist was the spearhead of New England Abolitionism. He edited the *Genius of Universal Emancipation* (1829–1830), and established the *Liberator* at Boston in 1831, a periodical which continued under his editorship for the next thirty-four years to be an instrument of great significance in the cause of Abolition. Important among antislavery periodicals and newspapers was the *Liberty Bell* (1839–1858), a gift book devoted to antislavery literature, sponsored by Maria Weston Chapman. It secured as contributors Emerson, Longfellow, Lowell, Theodore Parker, Wendell Phillips, Bayard Taylor, and Harriet Beecher Stowe. The *National Enquirer and Constitutional Advocate of Universal Liberty* was founded in 1836 by the Quaker Abolitionist Benjamin Lundy, whose book, *The War in Texas* (1836), had been an exposé of the war as a slaveholders' scheme. In 1838 the *National Enquirer* became the *Pennsylvania Freeman,* for two years thereafter under the editorship of Whittier. Elijah Parish Lovejoy first edited the antislavery *Observer* (1833) at St. Louis. He moved his press in 1836 to Alton, Illinois, where it was mobbed four times, and he was killed defending it. The *National Era* (1847–1860) was edited from Washington by Gamaliel Bailey as an antislavery journal. Among its literary contributors were Hawthorne and Whittier, and it is best remembered for its serialization of *Uncle Tom's Cabin.* Frederick Douglass (1817–1895), born into slavery, escaped to Massachusetts in 1838. His lectures before antislavery societies made him well known, and his *Narrative of the Life of Frederick Douglass: An American Slave* (1845) was widely read. This early ex-slave biography was revised and published in 1855 as *My Bondage and My Freedom.* Booker T. Washington wrote a biography, *Frederick Douglass,* Philadelphia, 1906–1907. The most recent life is Shirley Graham, *There Was Once a Slave,* New York, 1947. Douglass founded the *North Star* (1847–1864), a newspaper noted for its good journalism, differing from the *Liberator* by favoring peaceful political methods. The organ of the New York Anti-Slavery Society was the *National Anti-Slavery Standard* (1840–1872). Lowell, during the two years in which he was its editor (1848–1849), contributed to it some of his *Biglow Papers*. It was for a time edited by Parker Pillsbury, whose *Acts of the Anti-Slavery Apostles* (1883) is a source book in the history of the Abolition movement. Of some significance was the Boston *Commonwealth*, an antislavery journal founded by Samuel Gridley Howe and his wife Julia Ward Howe.

The vehement and effective oratory of Charles Sumner (1811–1874) made him a leader of the New England liberal opposition to the South. His *Works* were published, Boston, 1870–1883, 15 vols. Other leading antislavery orators include Wendell Phillips, whose *Speeches, Lectures and Letters* were collected and published in 1863; the elder William Ellery Channing, whose philosophical attacks on slavery were issued as pamphlets and gathered in *The Works of William E. Channing*, Boston, 1841–1843, 6 vols.; Theodore Parker, whose passionate speeches and sermons opposing slavery and war are best remembered by his representative essay, *A Letter to the People of the United States Touching the Matter of Slavery*, Boston, 1848, and were gathered in *The Collected Works of Theodore Parker*, London, 1873–1874, 14 vols.; Henry Ward Beecher, whose ardent antislavery lectures in England were effective pro-Union propaganda and have most recently been edited by Newell D. Hillis as *Lectures and Orations by Henry Ward Beecher*, New York, 1913; and William Cullen Bryant, who as editor of the New York *Evening Post* and as orator was a spokesman for the antislavery cause. His *Orations and Addresses* were published New York, 1873.

One of the most circumstantial accounts of the institution of slavery to be found is that of the English traveler Ebenezer Davies, *American Scenes and Christian Slavery: A Tour of Four Thousand Miles in the United States*, London, 1849. Robert Dale Owen published *The Wrong of Slavery . . . ,* Philadelphia, 1864. His *The Policy of Emancipation* (1863) allegedly influenced Lincoln's views. See also Joshua Reed Giddings, *The History of the Rebellion*, New York, 1864—an Abolitionist's account.

FICTION OF THE NORTH

Although Harriet Beecher Stowe's *Uncle Tom's Cabin* (1852) is the best known of all novels based on slavery, it is in fact but one of many creditable productions. One of the earliest antislavery novels was Sarah Josepha (Buell) Hale's *Northwood; or, Life North and South* (1827). Asa Greene (1789 to *ca.* 1837) published his fictional autobiography, *A Yankee Among the Nullifiers* (1833)—an authentic depiction of his travel observations in South Carolina. Richard Hildreth's very popular *The Slave; or, Memoirs of Archy Moore* (1836) was frequently republished. Mary Hayden Pike (1824–1908) wrote two antislavery novels, *Ida May* (1854) and *Caste* (1856). John Townsend Trowbridge included among his forty novels for boys two that were antislavery propaganda: *Neighbor Jackwood* (1857) and *Cudjo's Cave* (1864). Whitman's friend William Douglas O'Connor (1832–1889) is remembered for his Abolitionist novel, *Harrington* (1860).

Studies dealing with antislavery novels and propaganda are Lorenzo D. Turner, *Anti-Slavery Sentiment in American Literature Prior to 1865*, Washington, 1929—with a bibliography pp. 153–182; Janet Wilson, "The Early Anti-Slavery Propaganda," *More Books*, XIX (1944), 393–405; and Oscar Sherwin, "The Armory of God," *New Eng. Quar.*, XVIII (1945), 70–82. A useful checklist is Rebecca W. Smith, "Catalogue of the Chief Novels and Short Stories by American Authors Dealing with the Civil War and Its Effects, 1861–1899," *Bul. Bibl.*, XVI (1939), 193–194; XVII (1940–1941), 10–12, 33–35, 53–55, 72–75. The compilation by Benjamin A. Botkin, *Lay My Burden Down: A Folk History of Slavery*, Chicago, 1945, is made up from the Slave Narrative Collection of the Federal Writers' Project.

## POETRY OF THE NORTH

Poetry as well as prose was made the vehicle of ardent sentiments about the issues of union, secession, and slavery. Whittier's *Poems Written During the Progress of the Abolition Question* (1838) was followed by his *Voices of Freedom* (1846), which includes his well known "Massachusetts to Virginia." Longfellow's *Poems on Slavery* (1842) includes "The Arsenal at Springfield." Holmes's "Brother Jonathan's Lament for Sister Caroline" (1861) is a patriotic poem on the secession of South Carolina. Julia Ward Howe's "Battle-Hymn of the Republic" was published in 1862. Poe's intimate friend William Ross Wallace (1819–1881) published *The Liberty Bell* (1862) —militant poems supporting the Union. Henry Howard Brownell (1820–1872), a Connecticut lawyer who served as secretary to Farragut during the war, issued two volumes of poems inspired by the battles he had witnessed: *Lyrics of a Day; or, Newspaper-Poetry* (1864); and *War-Lyrics and Other Poems* (1866). Of the many early patriotic anthologies of war poetry the best are those compiled by Frank Moore (1828–1904): *Lyrics of Loyalty* (1864), *Rebel Rhymes and Rhapsodies* (1864), and others. The finest verse to receive its inspiration from the issues and conflict was that of Whitman. His *Drum-Taps* (1865) was followed by *Sequel to Drum-Taps* (1865–1866). His *Memoranda During the War* (1875) is reprinted in *Specimen Days and Collect* (1882). For a checklist of northern war poetry see Will D. Howe, "Poets of the Civil War, I: The North," *Camb. Hist. Amer. Lit.*, II (1918), 582–585.

LITERATURE OF THE SOUTHERN CAUSE

The most powerful spokesman for the South, especially in his orations and addresses, was John C. Calhoun, whose advocacy of slavery and States' Rights is recorded in *Speeches of John C. Calhoun,* New York, 1843, and in Richard K. Crallé, ed., *The Works of John C. Calhoun,* New York, 1851–1856, 6 vols. William Gilmore Simms defended slavery in his orations and essays, particularly as editor of the *Southern Quarterly Review* (1856–1857). *Works of William Gilmore Simms* was published, New York, 1853–1866, 20 vols. James D. B. De Bow was influential as editor of the *Southern Quarterly Review* (1844–1845), and as founder and editor of *De Bow's Review* (1846–1880). His *Industrial Resources of the Southern and Western States* (1853), 3 vols., reprints important articles from his *Review.* The "fire-eater" of the Confederacy was William Lowndes Yancey (1814–1863), who lectured in favor of a nonpartisan union of the South against northern antislavery agitation. The Virginia lawyer George Fitzhugh (1806–1881) published two proslavery tracts: *Sociology for the South; or, The Failure of Free Society* (1854) and *Cannibals All! or, Slaves Without Masters* (1857). Violently anti-Negro were the tracts of Hinton Rowan Helper (1829–1909) of North Carolina: *The Impending Crisis of the South: How to Meet It* (1857); and *Nojoque: A Question for a Continent* (1867).

Much of the best writing in the literature of conflict will be found in the novels and poems of southern partisans. Nathaniel Beverley Tucker's *George Balcombe* (1836) gives a realistic picture of contemporary Virginia and Missouri; and his novel *The Partisan Leader* (1836) was reissued as propaganda during the Civil War. Hugh Swinton Legaré (1797–1843), the literary leader of Charleston during the 1830's, was widely read, and his writings were collected, 1845–1846, 2 vols. William John Grayson (1788–1863) wrote *Letters of Curtius* (1851) in defense of slavery. He is best known for his didactic poem *The Hireling and the Slave* (1854). A volume of his *Selected Poems* (1907) was published by his daughter Mrs. William H. Armstrong. Jeremiah Clemens (1814–1865) of Alabama deserves to be better known for his novel of the Civil War, *Tobias Wilson: A Tale of the Great Rebellion* (1865). The war novels of John Esten Cooke (1830–1886) include *Surry of Eagle's Nest* (1866), *Hilt to Hilt* (1869), and *Mohun* (1869). His *The Heir of Gaymount* (1870) is a plea for agrarianism. Mary Virginia Terhune (1830–1922), who wrote under the pseudonym Marion Harland, produced some twenty-five popular romantic novels dealing for the most part with the South before and during the war. The best among them are *Alone* (1854), *Sunnybank* (1866), and *A Gallant Fight* (1888).

The best loved among the poets of the Confederacy was Henry Timrod

(1828–1867). In his lifetime only a slim volume of *Poems* (1860) was published. His friend Paul Hamilton Hayne issued *The Poems of Henry Timrod*, New York, 1873. Hayne's own martial lyrics were issued as *Legends and Lyrics* (1872). Other poets of the Confederacy were Margaret Junkin Preston (1820–1897), who wrote *Beechenbrook: A Rhyme of the War* (1865), *Old Song and New* (1870), and *Cartoons* (1875); and Abram Joseph Ryan (1838–1886), the Maryland poet and priest whose mystical lyrics were issued as *Father Ryan's Poems* (1879). Song writers include James Ryder Randall (1839–1908), author of "Maryland, My Maryland" (1861), and Dan(iel Decatur) Emmett (1815–1904) who is said to have written "Dixie."

*Virginians of the Valley, and Other Poems* (1879), by Francis Orray Ticknor (1822–1874) is a collection posthumously edited by P. H. Hayne; it deserves to be better known. *The Poems of Francis Orray Ticknor* (1911) is edited by M. T. Ticknor.

Of the twenty or more anthologies of southern war poetry, the best is that compiled by William Gilmore Simms, *War Poetry of the South,* New York, 1867. See Jennette R. Tandy, "Pro-Slavery Propaganda in American Fiction of the Fifties," *So. Atl. Quar.,* XXI (1922), 41–50, 170–178. For a checklist see Edwin Mims, "Poets of the Civil War, II: The South," *Camb. Hist. Amer. Lit.,* II (1918), 585–588.

REMINISCENCES

Honest representation by a northern visitor will be found in the writings of Frederick Law Olmsted (1822–1903): *A Journey in the Seaboard Slave States* (1856), *A Journey Through Texas* (1857), and *A Journey in the Back Country* (1860). These works were condensed and issued as *The Cotton Kingdom* (2 vols. 1861). Two other fascinating accounts are those of John Sergeant Wise (1846–1913), *The End of the Era* (1899), and Edward Porter Alexander (1835–1910), *Military Memoirs of a Confederate* (1907)—comprehensive and authoritative.

Henry Morford (1823–1881), the New York journalist, narrates his experiences during the war in *Red-Tape and Pigeon-Hole Generals as Seen from the Ranks* (1864). Three of his novels describe the incompetence and venality in the northern army: *Shoulder Straps* (1863), *The Coward* (1863), and *The Days of Shoddy* (1864). John Pendleton Kennedy supported the Union in *Mr. Ambrose's Letters on the Rebellion* (1865). Augustine J. H. Duganne (1823–1884) gives a vivid account of war experiences in *Camps and Prisons* (1865). Lew(is) Wallace (1827–1905) rose to the rank of major general in the Union Army. *Lew Wallace: An Autobiography* (1906), completed by his wife, is a valuable memoir. Similarly authentic are Gen. John Beatty's *Memoirs of a Volunteer, 1861–1863* (1879), recently edited by Harvey S.

Ford, with an introduction by Lloyd Lewis, New York, 1946. George Cary Eggleston (1839–1911) served with the Confederates, and later published his autobiography, *A Rebel's Recollections* (1874). Herman Melville's poems, *Battle-Pieces and Aspects of the War* (1866), deal with events and impressions of the war. The Presbyterian minister William Mumford Baker (1825–1883) wrote a novel, *Inside: A Chronicle of Secession* (1866), under the pseudonym of George F. Harrington. The book is in fact the autobiography of a northerner in the South during the war. The frontier novelist John Beauchamp Jones (1810–1866) founded the *Southern Monitor* at Philadelphia (1858) in the interests of the South. His *A Rebel War Clerk's Diary at the Confederate Capital* (1866) deals authentically with the scenes described. The Connecticut-born novelist John William De Forest drew on his war experiences to write the finest of the realistic fiction of the Civil War and the years following. Best known is *Miss Ravenel's Conversion from Secession to Loyalty* (1867). His other novels and tales include *Kate Beaumont* (1872), *Honest John Vane* (1875), *Playing the Mischief* (1875), and *The Bloody Chasm* (1881). Sidney Lanier recorded his experiences in the war in his novel *Tiger-Lilies* (1867). Rebecca Harding Davis's *Waiting for the Verdict* (1868) is pro-Negro propaganda. The Connecticut Abolitionist Samuel Joseph May (1797–1871) published *Some Recollections of Our Antislavery Conflict* (1869). Thomas Wentworth Higginson led the first regiment of Negro soldiers through the war and set forth his views of Negro rights in *Army Life in a Black Regiment* (1870). The Union officer Albion Winegar Tourgée (1838–1905) wrote his pro-Negro novels from his experience as an ardently Republican carpetbagger in North Carolina. They include *'Toinette* (1874—reprinted as *A Royal Gentleman*, 1881), *Figs and Thistles* (1879), *A Fool's Errand* (1879), *Bricks Without Straw* (1880), *John Eax and Memelon* (1882), *Hot Plowshares* (1883), and *Pactolus Prime* (1890). The most widely performed drama inspired by the war is the well known play *Allatoona* (ca. 1875), by Judson Kilpatrick and J. O. Moore, later revived as *The Blue and the Gray; or, War Is Hell*.

## SOCIAL STUDIES

The classic sociological study of the Negro is William E. B. Du Bois, *The Souls of Black Folk: Essays and Sketches* (1903—17th ed., 1931). Other useful studies are Benjamin G. Brawley, *A Short History of the American Negro,* New York, rev. ed., 1939, with a bibliography pp. 265–272; and Ulrich B. Phillips, *American Negro Slavery* . . . , New York, 1918. A standard history of the period is that of Arthur C. Cole, *The Irrepressible Conflict: 1850–1865,* New York, 1934, with an annotated bibliography (pp. 408–450) to all aspects of the social history of the period.

# TRANSCENDENTALISM
# AND UTOPIAN VENTURES

The transcendental movement in New England was the earliest and most indigenous expression of romanticism as an individualistic, unsystematic attitude toward the world of nature and man, and it was set forth by way of the language of Oriental mysticism and German romanticism. It was especially associated with Concord, Massachusetts, during the years 1836 to 1860, though it had been foreshadowed from the time of Jonathan Edwards's first published sermon (1731) and was continued in the Unitarianism developed by William Ellery Channing and others. Emerson, in *Nature* (1836) and *The American Scholar* (1837), wrote two of the earliest transcendental documents. Thoreau's *Walden* (1854) is of similar, primary significance in the movement. Full bibliographical details concerning the major transcendental writers—Emerson, Thoreau, Alcott, Fuller, Very, Parker, and Brownson— will be found elsewhere herein. Though Hawthorne was never centrally tied into the movement, he at one time briefly associated himself with it. Indeed, it may be said that no major writer of the period escaped its influence, including Bryant, Longfellow, Lowell, Melville, Whitman, and Whittier. Other transcendentalists include Elizabeth Palmer Peabody (1804-1894), William Ellery Channing the younger (1818-1901), William Henry Channing (1810-1884), George Ripley (1802-1880), Christopher Pearse Cranch (1813-1892), Frederic Henry Hedge (1805-1890), and James Freeman Clarke (1810-1888). Octavius B. Frothingham contributed two studies: *George Ripley*, Boston, 1882, and *Memoir of William H. Channing*, Boston, 1886. The only biography of Cranch is Leonora Cranch Scott, *The Life and Letters of Christopher Pearse Cranch*, Boston, 1917. A large collection of Cranch manuscripts is in the Boston Public Library. A useful study of Hedge, who organized the Transcendental Club and introduced German transcendentalism to American thinkers, is Orie W. Long, *Frederic Henry Hedge: A Cosmopolitan Scholar*, Portland, Me., 1939. A recent documented study is Ronald V. Wells, *Three Christian Transcendentalists: James Marsh, Caleb Sprague Henry, Frederic Henry Hedge*, New York, 1943, containing a printing of a few Hedge letters, pp. 202-216, and a bibl., pp. 217-224. The earliest transcendental periodical was the *Western Messenger* (1835-1841), edited from Cincinnati and Louisville by W. H. Channing, assisted (1836-1839) by James Freeman Clarke. It offered transcendental and Unitarian discussion, with interpretations of German and Oriental literature contributed by Emerson and other notable writers. The chief organ of the New England transcendental movement was the *Dial* (1840-1844), edited by Margaret Fuller, and later (1842) by Emerson. For further discussion of the *Dial,* see the section Definition, History, and Criticism: "The American Scholar" to *Leaves of Grass, ante,* p. 45. A literary journal continuing the same name and purposes was published in Cincinnati in 1860, edited by Moncure Conway. It received contributions from a few of the same writers, though it did not achieve the distinction of its earlier namesake. A full discussion of periodicals of the movement is Clarence F. Gohdes, *The Periodicals of American Transcendentalism,* Durham, N.C., 1931.

There is need for a further study of American transcendentalism. At present the best accounts will be found in "Transcendentalism," in Theodore Parker, *Lessons from the World of Matter and the World of Man,* Boston, 1865—a contemporary interpretation by a leading participant; Octavius B. Frothingham, *Transcendentalism in New England: A History,* New York, 1876—with attention to origins in Germany, France, and England; Harold C. Goddard, *Studies in New England Transcendentalism,* New York, 1908, with bibl., pp. 207-212. The subject receives attention in Henry D. Gray, *Emerson: A Statement of New England Transcendentalism as Expressed in the Philosophy of Its Chief Exponent,* Stanford, Calif., 1917; Isaac Woodbridge Riley, *American Thought from Puritanism to Pragmatism,* 2nd ed., New York, 1923, Chaps. II, VI; "The Genteel Tradition in American Philosophy," in George Santayana, *Winds of Doctrine,* New York, 1913; and "The Golden Age of Transcendentalism," in Lucy L. Hazard, *The Frontier in American Literature,* New York, 1927, pp. 147-180. Many of the chapters of Van Wyck Brooks, *The Flowering of New England, 1815-1865,* New York, rev. ed. 1941, deal directly with the subject.

Judith K. Johnson has edited *The Journals of Charles King Newcomb,* Providence, 1946, with a biographical and critical introduction.

A study of the sources of Orientalism is Arthur E. Christy, *The Orient in American Transcendentalism: A Study of Emerson, Thoreau, and Alcott,* New York, 1932. Other studies of indebtedness to foreign influences include Walter L. Leighton, *French Philosophers and New-England Transcendentalism,* Charlottesville, Va., 1908; William Girard, "De l'influence exercée par Coleridge et Carlyle sur la formation du transcendentalisme," *Univ. Calif. Publ. Mod. Philol.,* IV (1916), 404-411; Frank T. Thompson, "Emerson's Indebtedness to Coleridge," *Stud. Philol.,* XXIII (1926), 55-76; *idem,* "Emerson and Carlyle," *ibid.*, XXIV (1927), 438–453. Two recent studies of the German influence are by René Wellek: "The Minor Transcendentalists and German Philosophy," *New Eng. Quar.*, XV (1942), 652–680; and "Emerson and German Philosophy," *ibid.*, XVI (1943), 41–62. See also Merle Curti, "The Great Mr. Locke: America's Philosopher, 1783–1861," *Hunt. Lib. Bul.*, XI (1937), 107–155. Background studies are Clarence H. Faust, "The Background of the Unitarian Opposition to Transcendentalism," *Modern Philology*, XXXV (1938), 297–324; and Edgeley W. Todd, "Philosophical Ideas at Harvard College, 1817–1837," *New Eng. Quar.*, XVI (1943), 63–90. A collection of transcendentalist verse was edited by George W. Cooke, *The Poets of Transcendentalism: An Anthology*, Boston, 1903, including forty-four representatives with brief biographical notes.

## UTOPIAN VENTURES

An outgrowth of a German pietist sect which had been persecuted abroad was the Harmony Society established by George Rapp in Pennsylvania during the first decade of the nineteenth century. In 1815 the society moved to Indiana and settled as the New Harmony community on the Wabash River under the leadership of Robert Dale Owen (1801–1877). The group published the *New-Harmony Gazette* (1825–1835), a weekly periodical which outlasted the community, itself disbanded in 1828 through dissension. The magazine continued with broadened scope under the guidance of Owen and Frances Wright (Mme. d'Arusmont, 1795–1852) and after 1829 became *Free Enquirer*, a socialist periodical. Two recent studies of Owen and the New Harmony movement are Richard W. Leopold, *Robert Dale Owen: A Biography*, Cambridge, 1940—a documented life; and Marguerite Young, *Angel in the Forest: A Fairy Tale of Two Utopias*, New York, 1945. An earlier study is George B. Lockwood, *The New Harmony Movement*, New York, 1905.

In the same decade Nashoba Community (1825–1828) was founded in Tennessee by Frances Wright to emancipate the Negroes gradually by educating them for the responsibility of freedom. She returned to England to lecture on her work, and published her talks as *Course of Popular Lectures*, London, 1829, with a supplemental volume five years later. See A. J. G. Perkins and Theresa Wolfson, *Frances Wright, Free Enquirer*, New York, 1939; and William R. Waterman, *Frances Wright*, New York, 1924.

Among early published suggestions for carrying out Utopian ventures is John A. Etzler, *The Paradise Within the Reach of All Men, Without Labor, by Powers of Nature and Machinery*, Pittsburgh, 1833. The book was reviewed at some length by Thoreau, "Paradise (to Be) Regained," *Democratic Rev.*, XIII (1843), 451–463.

John Humphrey Noyes (1811–1886) established a group of "Bible Communists"—a socioreligious community of perfectionists at Putney, Vermont (1836–1846), and shortly thereafter the Oneida Community (1848–1879) in central New York State. The latter group issued the *Oneida Circular* (1864–1876), and published *Handbook of the Oneida Community . . .* , Wallingford, Conn., 1867. Noyes published an account of Utopian ventures as *History of American Socialisms,* Philadelphia, 1870. See George W. Noyes, *John Humphrey Noyes: The Putney Community,* Oneida, N.Y., 1931.

The most notable venture in community living was the establishment of Brook Farm (1841–1847), a cooperative community near West Roxbury, Massachusetts. Under the leadership of George Ripley it was intended as a transcendental club and was known as "Brook Farm Institute of Agriculture and Education." Here at one time or another during its brief existence were associated most of the chief figures of the transcendental movement. Hawthorne chose the venture as the setting for his *Blithedale Romance* (1852). Elizabeth P. Peabody's *Last Evening with Allston, and Other Papers,* Boston, 1886, includes essays on Brook Farm and allied subjects. A recent study is Katherine Burton, *Paradise Planters: The Story of Brook Farm,* New York, 1939. A brief early account is Lindsay Swift, *Brook Farm: Its Members, Scholars, and Visitors,* New York, 1900. John T. Codman's *Brook Farm: Historic and Personal Memoirs,* Boston, 1894, is an account by a young participant. The Brook Farm Papers are deposited in the Boston Public Library. Published letters dealing with Brook Farm are Marianne Dwight Orvis, *Letters from Brook Farm, 1844–1847,* ed. by Amy L. Reed, Poughkeepsie, N.Y., 1928; Zoltán Haraszti, *The Idyll of Brook Farm: As Revealed by Unpublished Letters in the Boston Public Library,* Boston, 1937, 46 pp.; and Clarence H. Gohdes, "Three Letters by James Kay Dealing with Brook Farm," *Philological Quar.,* XVII (1938), 377–388.

The leading Fourierist was Parke Godwin (1816–1904), who succeeded Bryant as editor of the New York *Evening Post* in 1878. His two early discussions of the movement were published at New York in 1844: *A Popular View of the Doctrine of Charles Fourier,* and *Democracy, Constructive and Pacific.* Emerson discussed Fourierism at some length in "Historic Notes of Life and Letters in New England," in *Works,* Concord ed., X, 348–370. See also his essay "The Transcendentalist," *ibid.,* I, 327–359.

Under the leadership of Albert Brisbane (1809–1890), Brook Farm became the Brook Farm Phalanx and the center of Fourierist propaganda. Here were published the Fourierist organs, the *Phalanx* (1843–1845) and the *Harbinger* (1845–1849). Brisbane's *Social Destiny of Man; or, Association and Reorganization of Industry . . .* , Philadelphia, 1840, was one of the earliest American studies of Fourierism. Brisbane's book, together with his popularization of the movement through his column in the New York *Tribune,* was instrumental in the formation of other socialized communities. The most scientifically planned of Fourierist ventures was the North American Phalanx founded at Red Bank, New Jersey, by Brisbane with the advice of Parke Godwin, W. H. Channing, Greeley, and Ripley. It is described in Charles Sears, *The North American Phalanx: An Historical and Descriptive Sketch . . . with an introduction by Edward Howland,* Prescott, Wis., 1886. Its records are deposited with the Monmouth County Historical Society, Freehold, New Jersey. An unpublished thesis is Arthur E. Bestor, Jr., "American Phalanxes: A Study of Fourierist Socialism in the United States," Yale Univ., 1938. See also George K. Smart, "Fourierism in Northampton: Two Documents," *New Eng. Quar.,* XII (1939), 370–374. Contemporary data on Fourierism will be found in the writings of the elder Henry James (1811–1882)—for example, his *Christianity the Logic of Creation* (1857). A fictional account of A. B. Alcott's part in establishing Fruitlands (1842) at Harvard, Massachusetts, is the sketch by his daughter Louisa in her *Silver Pitchers* (1876), entitled "Transcendental Wild Oats." For accounts of other communist ventures, see the two volumes by Frederick W. Evans: *Autobiography of a Shaker,* Mt. Lebanon, N.Y., 1869, and *Shaker Communism,* London, 1871. A recent study is Marguerite F. Melcher, *The Shaker Adventure,* Princeton, 1941. For bibliography see John P. McLean, *A Bibliography of Shaker Literature . . . ,* Columbus, O., 1905.

Further contemporary studies of Utopian communities and ventures are Charles Nordhoff, *The Communistic Societies of the United States . . . ,* New York, 1875; William A. Hinds, *American Communities: Brief Sketches,* New York, 1878; Alcander Longley, *Communism: The Right Way, and the Best Way, for All to Live,* St. Louis, 1880; Charles W. Hubner, *Modern Communism,* Atlanta, 1880; and Albert Shaw, *Icaria: A Chapter in the History of Communism,* New York, 1884. The influence of such ventures on Utopian romances is discussed in Laurence Gronlund, *The Co-operative Commonwealth: An Exposition of Modern Socialism,* Boston, 1884.

The Mormon adventure in socialized living has been made the subject of an enormous literature, almost all of it controversial. Although E. D. Howe's *Mormonism Unveiled* (1834) is anti-Mormon, it is one of the earliest accounts, and is remarkably trustworthy as source material. Among histories, still useful is W. A. Linn, *The Story of the Mormons* (1902). Two recent studies are Nels Anderson, *Desert Saints: The Mormon Frontier in Utah,* Chicago, 1942; and Fawn M. Brodie, *No Man Knows My History: The Life of Joseph Smith, the Mormon Prophet,* New York, 1945. Valuable reference to literature based on Mormonism is "List of Works in the New York Public Library Relating to the Mormons," *Bul. N.Y. Pub. Lib.,* XIII (1909), 183–239.

See also *Catalogue of Books, Early Newspapers and Pamphlets on Mormonism* (1898), 48 pp., collected by William Berrian.

A general survey of Utopian literature is Frances Theresa Russell, *Touring Utopia: The Realm of Constructive Humanism,* New York, 1932, with a bibliography. A popular study with new material is Victor F. Calverton, *Where Angels Dared to Tread,* New York, 1941. Chapters on Utopian communities appear in Morris Hillquit, *History of Socialism in the United States,* New York, 1903. Lewis Mumford, *The Story of Utopias,* New York, 1922, touches slightly on the American scene. Other studies include Robert J. Hendricks, *Bethel and Aurora: An Experiment in Communism as Practical Christianity,* New York, 1933; and Frederick A. Bushee, "Communistic Societies in the United States," *Pol. Sci. Quar.,* XX (1905), 625–664. Utopian ventures are touched on in two standard studies: Claude R. Flory, *Economic Criticism in American Fiction, 1792–1900,* Philadelphia, 1936; and Walter F. Taylor, *The Economic Novel in America,* Chapel Hill, N.C., 1942.

## UTOPIAN FICTION

The French communist Etienne Cabet published *Voyage et Aventures de Lord William Carisdall en Icarie,* Paris, 1840, a widely read Utopian romance which was responsible for Icarian communities which flourished from 1854 to 1895 in Chiltenham, Missouri; Cloverdale, California; Corning, Iowa, and elsewhere. The best of the Utopian romances during the last half of the nineteenth century include Edward Everett Hale, *Sybaris and Other Homes* (1869); John Macnie, *The Diothas* (1880); Alfred D. Cridge, *Utopia; or, The History of an Extinct Planet* (1884); Ignatius Donnelly, *Caesar's Column: A Story of the Twentieth Century* (1891); Chauncey Thomas, *Crystal Button . . .* (1891); Amos K. Fiske, *Beyond the Bourne . . .* (1891); John Bell Bouton, *The Enchanted . . .* (1891); Henry Olerich, *A Cityless and Countryless World,* Holstein, Ia., 1893; Edward Bellamy, *Equality* (1897); and Albert A. Merrill, *The Great Awakening: The Story of the Twenty-second Century* (1899). Two of Howells's novels deal with the subject of social Utopia: *A Traveler from Altruria* (1894) and *Through the Eye of the Needle* (1907).

Laurence Gronlund's *The Coöperative Commonwealth* (1884), though not a novel, furnished the background for the most famous of all futurity stories, Edward Bellamy's *Looking Backward, 2000–1887* (1888).

Sylvester Judd (1813–1853) wrote a transcendental novel *Margaret: A Tale of the Real and Ideal . . .* (1845); and a didactic metaphysical epic, *Richard Edney and the Governor's Family: A Rus-Urban Tale* (1850). See Philip J. Brockway, "Sylvester Judd (1813–1853): Novelist of Transcendentalism," Orono, Me., 1941.

Few studies of the Utopian novel have been published. Two are Robert L. Shurter, "The Utopian Novel in America, 1888–1900," *So. Atl. Quar.*, XXXIV (1935), 137–144; and Allyn B. Forbes, "The Literary Quest for Utopia, 1880–1900," *Social Forces*, VI (1927), 179–189. Three useful unpublished dissertations are Robert L. Shurter, "The Utopian Novel in America, 1865–1900," Western Reserve, 1936; Margaret Thal-Larsen, "Political and Economic Ideas in American Utopian Fiction," Univ. Calif., 1941; and Vernon L. Parrington, Jr., "The Utopian Novel in America," Brown Univ., 1943.

# BOHEMIA: ESCAPISM AND AESTHETICISM

PRIMARY SOURCES

The most notable of early gathering places for literary Bohemians was Pfaff's Cellar in New York City on Broadway above Bleecker Street. Here during the 1850's assembled such figures as Whitman, Bayard Taylor, Fitz-James-O'Brien, William Winter, George Arnold, Henry Clapp, Adah Menken, and the "Queen of Clapp's Bohemia"—the famous beauty Jane McElheney (pseud. Ada Claire). See Henry Clapp's *The Pioneer; or, Leaves from an Editor's Portfolio,* New York, 1846. The writings of George Arnold (1834–1865) were largely burlesque in prose and verse. Arnold's poems were gathered by William Winter and published as *Drift: A Sea-Shore Idyl and Other Poems* (1866), and *Poems, Grave and Gay* (1867). The Civil War brought an end to the gatherings, which are officially reported in Bayard Taylor's *The Echo Club and Other Literary Diversions* (1876). A recent biography of O'Brien is Francis Wolle, *Fitz-James O'Brien: A Literary Bohemian of the Eighteen-Fifties,* Boulder, Colo., 1944, with bibl., pp. 252–293. O'Brien's stories have been collected in *The Diamond Lens and Other Stories* . . ., ed. with introd. by Gilbert Seldes, New York, 1932. William Dean Howells's *Literary Friends and Acquaintance* (1900) includes a chapter on Whitman and the old New York Bohemia. Similarly important has been the Bohemian Club in San Francisco, established in 1872, and still a vigorous literary and musical organization. Charles Warren Stoddard is one of the early California authors associated with aestheticism. See the individual bibliography herein. His *Summer Cruising in the South Seas* (1874), as well as his autobiographical novel, *For the Pleasure of His Company* (1903), typifies his conscious attention to a delicately wrought style. During the 1880's Ambrose Bierce was associated with the San Francisco *Examiner* as a free-lance journalist. It was at this time that he established his reputation as a wit and as the literary dictator of the West Coast, strongly influencing many younger writers. A useful study of periodicals and personalities in California literature during the second half of the nineteenth century is Franklin Walker, *San Francisco's Literary Frontier,* New York, 1939; it includes material on Bierce and Stoddard and on the western variety of Bohemianism.

During the early decades of the twentieth century the section of New York City known as Greenwich Village became a literary and artistic colony, identified with Bohemianism. It fostered a succession of "little magazines," including the *Little Review* and *Seven Arts*. For a fuller discussion of the place of "little magazines" in American literary history, see the bibliography on Experimental Magazines, *ante,* p. 64.

Chief among writers who developed a polished style and a concern for artistry, often of an exotic and unconventional nature, were Lafcadio Hearn and Edgar Saltus. On Hearn and Saltus, see the individual bibliographies herein. The credo of the famed artist and controversialist James A. McNeill Whistler (1834–1903) is set forth in his collected writings, *The Gentle Art of Making Enemies* (1890), which includes the "Ten o'Clock" lecture. Stuart Fitzrandolph Merrill (1863–1915) translated the prose poems of various French symbolists in *Pastels in Prose* (1890). The volume was published with an introduction by Howells. The exotic furnished escapist material for John Boyle O'Reilly (1844–1890), an Irish political exile who had become a Boston journalist and whose poems were gathered in *Songs from Southern Seas* (1873). Best known of writers who took to the "open road" was Richard Hovey (1864–1900). With Bliss Carman he published *Songs from Vagabondia* (1894) and later volumes. Carman (1861–1929) edited *The Chap-Book* (1894–1898), one of the first of the "little magazines." His verse was early collected, Boston, 1905, 2 vols. A recent selection has been published as *Bliss Carman's Poems,* New York, 1932.

The leading expatriate aesthete was Henry Harland (1861–1905). After publishing realistic fiction dealing with Jewish life in New York City he broke with his literary past, went to England, and became the editor of the most noted of "little magazines," the *Yellow Book* (1894). His later fiction includes *Grey Roses* (1895), *Comedies and Errors* (1898), *The Cardinal's Snuff-Box* (1900), and *My Friend Prospero* (1904).

The best known among literary critics associated with aestheticism was James Gibbons Huneker, who served as a critic of taste in art, literature, drama, and music on the New York *Sun* from 1900 to 1917. On Huneker, see the individual bibliography herein. Others include Walter Blackburn Harte, whose *Meditations in Motley* (1894) are bookish essays by a forgotten critic who edited the Boston *Flyleaf*. Outstanding among critics was Harry Thurston Peck (1856–1914), who served as professor of Latin at Columbia for many years and edited the *Bookman* from 1895 to 1902. His literary essays, mainly on contemporaries, were published as *The Personal Equation* (1898). (Charles) Vance Thompson founded and, with Huneker, edited the little magazine *M'lle New York*. A reprint of essays contributed to the magazine was published as *French Portraits: Being Appreciations of the Writers of*

*Young France* (1900), with illustrations from Remy de Gourmont's *Livre des masques*. Gelett Burgess's *Are You a Bromide? or the Sulphitic Theory* (1906) was a widely popular attack on philistinism which originally appeared in the *Smart Set*. Henry E. Krehbiel (1854–1923), who served as music critic on the New York *Tribune* from 1880 to 1923, was a leading interpreter who did much to raise the standards of musical criticism in America. (Joseph) Percival Pollard (1869–1911) was one of the earliest interpreters of European literature at the beginning of the twentieth century. His *Masks and Minstrels of New Germany* (1911) was a pioneer study of contemporary German literature which influenced the works of Bierce and Mencken. Little of his magazine writing has been collected, and his plays remain unpublished. One of the most elaborate critical apologies for escapism in literature is James Branch Cabell, *Beyond Life: Dizain des Demiurges,* New York, 1919.

SECONDARY SOURCES

An informative illustrated account of Bohemianism is Albert Parry, *Garrets and Pretenders: A History of Bohemianism in America,* New York, 1933. A brilliant study is Thomas Beer, *The Mauve Decade: American Life at the End of the Nineteenth Century,* New York, 1926, though its approach to the subject is entirely impressionistic. Lloyd Lewis and Henry Justin Smith, *Oscar Wilde Discovers America, 1882,* New York, 1936, mainly based on contemporary newspapers, cuts across the subject of American aestheticism in an illuminating way. A social and economic study is Caroline F. Ware, *Greenwich Village, 1920–1930: A Comment on American Civilization in the Post-War Years,* Boston, 1935. Other useful treatments are in Alfred Kazin, *On Native Grounds . . . ,* New York, 1942, pp. 51–72; Bernard Smith, *Forces in American Criticism,* New York, 1939, pp. 261–285; and Oscar Cargill, *Intellectual America: Ideas on the March,* New York, 1941, pp. 176–229, 418–456, 473–516.

Informed essays on Bierce and Hearn appear in Percy H. Boynton, *More Contemporary Americans,* Chicago, 1927. The same authors also are discussed in Matthew Josephson, *Portrait of the Artist as American,* New York, 1930. Allusions to Huneker and Mencken appear in Edmund Wilson, "Thoughts on Being Bibliographed," *Princeton Univ. Lib. Chron.* V (1944), 51–61.

For further data, see the section American Writers and Books Abroad—Expatriates, *post,* p. 366.

# AMERICAN WRITERS AND BOOKS ABROAD

Any discussion of the literature written to interpret foreign countries must at present be very incomplete, for few investigations of the subject have been undertaken. The following tentative lists place emphasis upon writers whose works have literary merit or whose observations upon the foreign scene deserve more attention than they have previously been accorded.

## COMMENTATORS ON EUROPE

Several of the most distinguished or best known nineteenth century men of letters published their impressions of European culture and manners. Irving's *Tales of a Traveller* (1824) are built mainly about his tour of Germany (1822–1823). The four volumes of Cooper's *Gleanings in Europe* (1837–1838) furnish brilliant social criticism. N. P. Willis traveled widely in Europe and the Near East, and his *Loiterings of Travel* (3 vols., 1840), and *Pencillings by the Way* (3 vols., 1844), are collections of letters describing his acquaintances. Bayard Taylor was one of the most widely traveled writers of his day, and the letters which he wrote for the New York *Tribune* were the basis for such collections as *Views A-foot* (1846) and many later volumes. Margaret Fuller's *At Home and Abroad* (1856) followed James Russell Lowell's "Leaves from My Journal" (1854); and during the same decade appeared John W. De Forest's *European Acquaintance . . .* (1858). The first of Henry James's travel essays, *Transatlantic Sketches* (1875), was followed by *Portraits of Places* (1883). Mark Twain's travels in Germany, Italy, and Switzerland were recorded in *A Tramp Abroad* (1880). Henry Adams has much to say of his life in Germany and England during the mid-nineteenth century in *The Education of Henry Adams* (1907). T. B. Aldrich's nostalgic account of his travels was published as *From Ponkapog to Pesth* (1883). Data about all the foregoing will be found in individual bibliographies herein.

The leading journalists of the century include Willis, Taylor, Clemens, and Adams, already mentioned. In addition, Horace Greeley in his *Glances at Europe* . . . (1851) devotes much attention to the Great Exhibition. The New York journalist and political leader Thurlow Weed (1797–1882) published *Letters from Europe and the West Indies, 1843–1862* (1866). The first of ten travel books by Charles Dudley Warner (1829–1900) appeared under the title *Saunterings* (1872). Other interesting accounts of travel in Central Europe are J. Ross Browne (1821–1875), *An American Family in Germany* (1866)—shrewd and humorous—and Poultney Bigelow (b. 1855), *Paddles and Politics down the Danube* (1892).

Generally acknowledged as the leading journalistic reporter of his time was Richard Harding Davis (1864–1916). Such volumes as *The Rulers of the Mediterranean* (1893), *About Paris* (1895), and *With the Allies* (1914) reached a wide reading public. *The Novels and Stories of Richard Harding Davis* were issued, New York, 1916, in 12 vols. Some of his letters appear in Charles B. Davis, *Adventures and Letters of Richard Harding Davis,* New York, 1917. A recent biography is Fairfax Downey, *Richard Harding Davis: His Day,* New York, 1933.

During the century congregations might send their pastors to Europe for "culture," and it was popular for clergymen to record rapid impressions of their trips abroad, sometimes dedicated to their parishioners. Such writing usually constitutes light, pleasant reading. Among the best such impressions are those of the Unitarian pastor William Ware (1797–1852), *Sketches of European Capitals* (1851); "Letters from Europe," in Henry Ward Beecher's *Star Papers; or, Experiences of Art and Nature* (1855), pp. 9–89; John E. Edwards (1814–1891), *Random Sketches and Notes of European Travel in 1856* (1857), with an entertaining preface; Henry W. Bellows (1814–1882), *The Old World in Its New Face: Impressions of Europe in 1867–1868* (2 vols., 1868–1869); and Phillips Brooks (1835–1893), *Letters of Travel* (1893)—describing his journeys in the sixties and eighties.

Accounts of scientific travel are important, for they reflect the growing interest in study abroad of art and science. The most influential scientist in America during the first half of the nineteenth century was Benjamin Silliman (1779–1864) of Yale. His observations on university life and achievements in scholarship he recorded in *A Journal of Travels in England, Holland, and Scotland* (1810), and later in *A Visit to Europe in 1851* (2 vols., 1853). Walter Channing (1786–1876), the brother of William Ellery Channing, is representative of the students of medicine who gained their training in Edinburgh, London, and elsewhere abroad. Channing's record of an extended European tour he published as *A Physician's Vacation* (1856).

Other interesting and well written accounts are those of Mordecai Manuel Noah (1785–1851), *Travels in England, France, Spain, and the Barbary States* (1819)—a record of the period he served as consul to Tunis (1813–1815);

the Philadelphia lawyer Horace Binney Wallace (1817–1852), *Art, Scenery and Philosophy in Europe* (1855); David Ross Locke ("Petroleum V. Nasby," 1833–1888), *Nasby in Exile* . . . (1882)—shrewd comments on manners and morals; and Francis Hopkinson Smith (1838–1915), *Well-Worn Roads of Spain, Holland, and Italy* (1887).

The sentimental and nostalgic appeal of Europe is presented in the works of such representative writers as Sara Jane Lippincott ("Grace Greenwood"), *Haps and Mishaps of a Tour in Europe* (1854); Erastus C. Benedict (1800–1880), *A Run Through Europe* (1860); Edward Everett Hale, *Ninety Days' Worth of Europe* (1861); and Helen Hunt Jackson, *Glimpses of Three Coasts* (1886).

Some published accounts were of an advisory nature, often factual letters which stressed special information. Among such publications might be named James Freeman Clarke's *Eleven Weeks in Europe, and What May Be Seen in That Time* (1852), C(yrus) A(ugustus) Bartol (1813–1900), *Pictures of Europe, Framed in Ideas* (1855)—largely on the theory of travel; J. H. B. Latrobe (1803–1891), *Hints for Six Months in Europe* . . . (1869); C. C. Fulton, *Europe Viewed Through American Spectacles* (1874); Joel Cook (1842–1910), *A Holiday Tour in Europe* (1879); and W. W. Nevin (1836–1899), *Vignettes of Travel* . . . (1891).

For a study of foreign travel of American Indians, see Carolyn T. Foreman, *Indians Abroad, 1493–1938,* Norman, Okla., 1943, with a bibliography.


## EDUCATIONAL INFLUENCES

One of the earliest educational leaders who studied abroad and helped initiate the German influence on American literature and education was George Ticknor, who with Edward Everett studied and traveled abroad during the years 1815–1819. Ticknor's notable *History of Spanish Literature* was published in 1849 in three volumes. See especially "George Ticknor's Wanderjahre," in Van Wyck Brooks's *The Flowering of New England,* New York, 1936, pp. 73–88. Longfellow studied in Germany and elsewhere abroad in the years 1826–1829. See Lawrance Thompson, *Young Longfellow, 1807–1843,* New York, 1938. Calvin Ellis Stowe (1802–1886), after a tour of European school systems, published his *Report on Elementary Instruction in Europe* (1837), a work which had a very real effect on American school systems. For a study of European influences, particularly the German, on American education and literature, see Orie W. Long, *Literary Pioneers: Early American Explorers of European Culture,* Cambridge, 1935, with chapters on Ticknor, Everett, Cogswell, Bancroft, Longfellow, and Motley.

## STUDIES OF INDIVIDUAL COUNTRIES

### ENGLAND

One of the earliest American travel books to attempt a description of England as a foreign country was the *Journal of Travels to England . . .* (1810) of Benjamin Silliman (1779–1864). See also the English and French sections of *Audubon and His Journals,* by Maria R. Audubon, New York, 1900, 2 vols. *Letters from London,* Boston, 1804, by William Austin (1778–1841), are sketches by a New Englander of the English. Irving's *The Sketch Book* (1819–1820) and *Bracebridge Hall* (1822) are well known. Two works which deserve mention are *Sketches of Society in Great Britain and Ireland* (2 vols., 1834), by the Rev. Charles S. Stewart (1795–1870), and *Walks and Talks of an American Farmer in England* (1852), by the landscape architect Frederick Law Olmsted (1822–1903). Harriet Beecher Stowe's *Sunny Memories of Foreign Lands* (1854) was widely read and deals principally with her reception in England. Emerson's famous *English Traits* (1856), a collection of essays delivered first as lectures in 1848, contains notable studies in cultural anthropology. Hawthorne, in *Our Old Home* (1863) and *Passages from the English Notebooks* (1870), recorded his own shrewd observations on the English. Elihu Burritt (1810–1879), "the learned blacksmith," set forth observations in an attempt to improve rural conditions at home in *A Walk from London to Land's End and Back* (1865). See Merle Curti, *The Learned Blacksmith: The Letters and Journals of Elihu Burritt,* New York, 1937. The Yale professor James M. Hoppin discussed art and manners in *Old England: Its Scenery, Art and People* (1867). The alleged advantages of the English over the Americans formed the subject of Richard Grant White's *England Without and Within* (1881).

A standard study of the period covered is Robert E. Spiller, *The American in England During the First Half Century of Independence,* New York, 1926, with bibliographies. A readable account is Robert Balmain Mowat, *Americans in England,* Boston, 1935. A recent study is Robert C. Le Clair, *Three American Travellers in England . . .,* Philadelphia, 1945, with bibl., pp. 215–219—dealing with Lowell, Henry Adams, and Henry James.

### FRANCE AND GERMANY

The best of the earlier accounts of travels in France are largely devoted to discussions and descriptions of Paris. Among them are such works as Augustus K. Gardner (1821–1876), *Old Wine in New Bottles . . .* (1848)—describing student life; James Jackson Jarves (1818–1888), *Parisian Sights*

(1852); Phebe H. Gibbons (b. 1821), *French and Belgians* (1879); and Richard Harding Davis, *About Paris* (1895). Henry James widens the horizon in *A Little Tour of France* (1885). An unpublished dissertation is Robert C. L. Scott, "American Travellers in France, 1830–1860," Yale Univ., 1940.

For references to travel in Germany, see especially the sections herein on Educational Influences (*ante,* p. 358), Europe in Fiction (*post,* p. 361), and Commentators on Europe (*ante,* p. 356).

### ITALY

Some of the most significant literature of travel during the nineteenth century concerned itself with Italy. *Notes on Italy* (1831), by the painter Rembrandt Peale (1778–1860), is based on his residence abroad in 1828–1830. Italian political changes during the mid-century increased American interest in Italy, and are discussed in *Letters from Italy* (1845) by Joel Tyler Headley (1813–1897). He published a new and revised edition in 1853. The Boston sculptor Horatio Greenough (1805–1852) lived in Italy for some time and set down his impressions in *The Travels, Observations, and Experience of a Yankee Stonecutter* (1852). One of the most widely quoted of all travel books was George S. Hillard (1808–1879), *Six Months in Italy* (1853).

Of considerable significance are the travel books and critical studies of Italian art by James Jackson Jarves, which may be represented by *Italian Sights* (1856). Significant also are the books on Italy by the American sculptor who resided there, William Wetmore Story (1819–1895), among which should be named *Roba di Roma* (1862) and *Vallombrosa* (1881). William Dean Howells, who resided four years as consul at Venice, recorded his valuable impressions in *Venetian Life* (1866), *Italian Journeys* (1867), and *Modern Italian Poets* (1887). Hawthorne's *Passages from the French and Italian Notebooks* (1868) are well known.

Further interesting material appears in Eugene Benson (1839–1908), *Art and Nature in Italy* (1882); Charles Dudley Warner, *Our Italy* (1891); and F. Hopkinson Smith, *Gondola Days* (1897). The *Notes of Travel and Study in Italy* (1860) by Charles Eliot Norton (1827–1908) are somewhat prejudiced and narrow.

For a discussion of American travelers and expatriates in Italy during the 1850's, see "The Romantic Exiles," in Van Wyck Brooks, *The Flowering of New England,* New York, 1936, pp. 460–477.

### SPAIN

Irving's *A Chronicle of the Conquest of Granada* (1829) and *The Alhambra* (1832) continued to be the best known travel accounts of Spain written during the nineteenth century. John Hay's *Castilian Days* (1871) are vivid observations. Other outstanding accounts include those of Henry Willis Baxley (1803–1876), *Spain . . .* (2 vols., 1875); James Albert Harrison (1848–1911), *Spain in Profile: A Summer Among the Olives and Aloes* (1879); George Parsons Lathrop (1851–1898), *Spanish Vistas* (1883); Edward Everett Hale, *Seven Spanish Cities, and the Way to Them* (1883); and Henry M. Field (1822–1907), *Old Spain and New Spain* (1888). James Russell Lowell's posthumously published *Impressions of Spain* (1899) were written after he had served as minister to Spain (1877–1880).

A survey of travel in Spain is Carrie Farnham, *American Travellers in Spain,* New York, 1921.

## EUROPE IN FICTION

Three early representatives of fictional material with European settings are Cooper's *The Bravo* (1831), *The Heidenmauer* (1832), and *The Headsman* (1833). William Starbuck Mayo (1812–1895) recorded his careful first-hand observations of Moorish life in his novel, *The Berber* (1850). Theodore Sedgwick Fay (1807–1898) deserves further study; among his novels dealing with Europe is *The Countess Ida: A Tale of Berlin* (1840).

Hawthorne's *The Marble Faun* (1860) uses his Italian acquaintance for plot and setting.

Harriet Beecher Stowe's *Agnes of Sorrento* (1862) is a historical novel with an Italian setting. Distinguished among the novels and tales with English and European settings are those of Henry James, beginning with *The American* (1877) and *An International Episode* (1879). Later writers whose fictional material was based largely upon European backgrounds are Henry Blake Fuller (1857–1929) and Francis Marion Crawford. Fuller's *The Chevalier of Pensieri-vani* (1890) and *The Châtelaine of La Trinité* (1892) depict European court life. Hitherto unpublished Fuller material appears in Constance M. Griffin, *Henry Blake Fuller: A Critical Biography,* Philadelphia, 1939. Carl Van Vechten published *Henry B. Fuller,* Chicago, 1929.

No American novelist knew Italy better or portrayed it with more skill than Francis Marion Crawford (1854–1909). Among his forty novels with Italian background should be noticed *A Roman Singer* (1884), and *Saracinesca* (1887). His *Greifenstein* (1889), a story of German university life, is representative of his other European novels. A recent biography is Maud H. Elliott, *My Cousin, F. Marion Crawford,* New York, 1934. Other studies of Crawford as novelist include Arthur H. Quinn, *American Fiction,* New York, 1936, pp. 385–403; William P. Trent, "Mr. Crawford's Novels," *Sewanee Rev,* II (1894), 239–256; Hugh Walpole, "The Stories of Francis Marion Crawford," *Yale Rev.*, XII (1923), 674–691; and Adolph B. Benson, "Marion Crawford's *Dr. Claudius,*" *Scand. Studies and Notes*, XII (1933), 77–85.

Constance Fenimore Woolson (1840–1894) lived in Italy after 1879. Her collection *Dorothy and Other Italian Stories* (1896) deals with Americans in Italy.

See Howard R. Marraro, "American Travellers in Rome, 1811–1850," *Cath. Hist. Rev.*, XXIX (1944), 470–509; and the collection edited by Philip Rahv, *Discovery of Europe: The Story of American Experience in the Old World*, Boston, 1947.

THE NEAR EAST

Observations on travel in the Near East frequently had the romantic fascination of the exotic. David Porter (1780–1843) was minister to Turkey under Jackson, and his letters to James K. Paulding were later published as *Constantinople and Its Environs* (2 vols., 1835). John Lloyd Stephens (1805–1852) wrote *Incidents of Travel in Egypt, Arabia, Petraea, and the Holy Land* (1837), and *Incidents of Travel in Greece, Turkey, Russia, and Poland* (1838).

Some of the best descriptive comments of travel in the Near East were made by George William Curtis (1824–1892), written first when he was correspondent for the New York *Tribune*. His amusing impressions were published as *Nile Notes of a Howadji* (1851) and *The Howadji in Syria* (1852). Charles Eliot Norton edited *The Orations and Addresses of George William Curtis*, New York, 1894, 3 vols.; George W. Cooke edited *Early Letters of George William Curtis to John S. Dwight*, New York, 1898, and Caroline Ticknor, "Some Early Letters of George W. Curtis," *Atl. Mo.*, CXIV (1914), 363–376. See also Elizabeth L. Adams, "George William Curtis and His Friends," *More Books*, XIV (1939), 291–303, 353–366, for a new estimate based on a large number of letters to him. The only biography is Edward Cary, *George William Curtis*, Boston, 1894.

John W. De Forest's travels in Syria are recorded in *Oriental Acquaintance . . .* (1856), and accounts of Bayard Taylor's tours of the Near East were published as *The Lands of the Saracen* (1855) and *Travels in Greece and Russia* (1859). Mark Twain's masterpiece of shrewd comments, *The Innocents Abroad; or, The New Pilgrim's Progress* (1869), was immediately popular and has maintained its rank among the best of American observations of travel abroad.

Other items of merit are William Goodell (1792–1867), *Forty Years in the Turkish Empire; or, Memoirs of Rev. William Goodell*, New York, 1876; Charles Dudley Warner, *My Winter on the Nile* (1876); Thomas Gold Appleton (1812–1884), *A Nile Journal* (1876); and Charles A. Dana (1819–1897), *Eastern Journeys* . . . (1898).

Melville's *Clarel* (1876) was inspired by his trip to the Holy Land; his diary of the trip was only recently published as *Journal Up the Straits* (1935).

## THE ORIENT

The missionary, Samuel Wells Williams (1812–1884), published *The Middle Kingdom: A Survey of the . . . Chinese Empire and Its Inhabitants* (2 vols., 1848), a work which long remained the standard history of China written in English. Bayard Taylor's travels into the Far East were published as *A Visit to India, China, and Japan, in the Year 1853* (1855).

Commodore Matthew Calbraith Perry (1794–1858) published *Narrative of the Expedition of an American Squadron to the China Seas and Japan* (3 vols., 1856), a readable summary of his career, dealing with scientific as well as political matters. See Samuel Wells Williams, *A Journal of the Perry Expedition to Japan (1853–1854)*, Yokohama, 1910. A recent biography is Edward M. Barrows, *The Great Commodore: The Exploits of Matthew Calbraith Perry*, Indianapolis, 1935.

The best known and most sympathetic interpreter of Japan was Lafcadio Hearn. For data on Hearn, see the individual bibliography herein. John La Farge (1835–1910) published *An Artist's Letters from Japan* (1897)—acute observations; and the Salem zoologist, Edward Sylvester Morse (1838–1925), recorded his thoughtful impressions in *Japan Day by Day, 1877 . . . 1883* (1917), and *Glimpses of China and Chinese Homes* (1902). William Sturgis Bigelow (1850–1926) journeyed to Japan in 1882, where for seven years he studied and collected the material which he brought back to Boston. His *Buddhism and Immortality* (1908), though it is but a brief 78-page monograph, is important as interpretation. Ernest Francisco Fenollosa (1853–1908) journeyed in 1878 to Japan, where he taught and, like Bigelow, became a student of Japanese art. His poems were published as *East and West: The Discovery of America and Other Poems* (1893). His important studies of Oriental art were posthumously issued as *Epochs of Chinese and Japanese Art* (2nd ed., 2 vols., 1912). Ezra Pound became Fenollosa's literary executor and edited *Cathay* (1915)—mainly translations by Fenollosa of Japanese poetry.

Percival Lowell (1855–1916) pictured the Far East in four travel volumes, beginning with *Chosön* (1885) and concluding with *Occult Japan* (1895).

The linguist and student of comparative literatures, Thomas Sergeant Perry (1845–1928), taught English in Japan 1898–1901. Edwin Arlington Robinson edited *Selections from the Letters of Thomas Sergeant Perry,* New York, 1929.

## OCEANIA

Studies of the travels of such significant figures as Henry Adams, Clemens, London, Melville, and C. W. Stoddard will be found herein in the individual bibliographies of those authors.

One of the earliest and most important journals of travel in the Pacific written by Americans is John Ledyard (1751–1789), *A Journal of Captain Cook's Last Voyage to the Pacific Ocean* (1783). They are acute observations by the young adventurer and explorer who left off his studies at Dartmouth College to travel, and subsequently accompanied Captain James Cook to the Sandwich Islands. Jared Sparks wrote a *Life of John Ledyard* (1828). Other important accounts by early voyagers are those of Captain David Porter (1780–1843), whose *Journal of a Cruise Made to the Pacific Ocean . . . in the Years 1812, 1813, and 1814 . . .* (2 vols., 1815) suggested one of the sketches in Melville's "The Encantadas"; Amasa Delano (1763–1823), whose *A Narrative of Voyages and Travels in the Northern and Southern Hemispheres . . .* (1817) was the source for Melville's "Benito Cereno"; and Samuel Patterson (b. 1785), who published the *Narrative . . .* (1817) of his adventures. Benjamin Morrell (1795–1839), in *A Narrative of Four Voyages to the South Sea . . .* (1832), covers trips into many oceans. James Jackson Jarves, whose accounts of travel in Europe have already been noted, left an interesting record of an eight-year residence in Hawaii in his *History of the Hawaiian or Sandwich Islands* (1843) and other volumes. Other early travel accounts of some importance are George Washington Bates, *Sandwich Island Notes* (1854); Henry Willis Baxley, *What I Saw on the West Coast of South and North America and at the Hawaiian Islands* (1865)—viewed from the standpoint of a physician; and Edward T. Perkins, *Na Motu; or, Reef-Rovings in the South Seas . . .* (1854).

Many of the diaries and journals of missionaries have been published. Many more, still unpublished, remain to be studied. Among the best published items should be mentioned two accounts by the Rev. Charles S. Stewart: *Private Journal of a Voyage to the Pacific Ocean, and Residence at the Sandwich Islands . . .* (1828), and *A Visit to the South Seas . . .* (2 vols., 1831). Hiram Bingham (1789–1869) published *A Residence of Twenty-one Years in the Sandwich Islands* (1847), and Henry T. Cheever (1814–1897) wrote *Life in the Sandwich Islands; or, The Heart of the Pacific as It Was and Is* (1851). A recent study of missionary enterprise in the Pacific is Louis B. Wright and Mary I. Fry, *Puritans in the South Seas,* New York, 1936.

Later interesting sketches were contributed by John La Farge in *Reminiscences of the South Seas* (1912). Among the volumes of poetry by John Boyle O'Reilly (1844–1890) are his *Songs from Southern Seas* (1873).

Recent accounts are Frederick O'Brien (1869–1932), *White Shadows in the South Seas* (1919) and *Atolls of the Sun* (1922); and Willard Price (b. 1887), *The South Sea Adventure* (1936).

## OTHER TRAVELS

Further interesting accounts, chiefly in Central and South America, include the travel narrative of the naval officer Hiram Paulding (1797–1878), *Bolivar in His Camp* (1834)—the record of a 1,500-mile horseback trip in the Andes in 1824; Richard Henry Dana, Jr., *Two Years Before the Mast* (1840)—the trip made in 1834–1836 from Boston by way of Cape Horn to California and back; John Lloyd Stephens (1805–1852), *Incidents of Travel in Central America, Chiapas and Yucatan* (1841)—an account of the most extensive travels executed at that time, and still important as a study.

Bayard Taylor's *A Journey to Central Africa* was issued in 1854. The Reverend Charles S. Stewart made an excursion to South America recorded in *Brazil and La Plata: The Personal Record of a Cruise*, New York, 1856. Dana's *To Cuba and Back* (1859) lacks the interest of his earlier account.

*The Mexican Guide* (1886), by Thomas Allibone Janvier (1849–1913) was a standard sketch which went into a fifth edition in 1893. Further published records of his travels in Europe and elsewhere are also authentic. F. Hopkinson Smith's *A White Umbrella in Mexico* (1889) is an amusing account. One of the most vivid and sprightly volumes is Charles M. Flandrau (1871–1938), *Viva Mexico!* (1908).

More recent accounts of travel in South America are those of Theodore Roosevelt, *Through the Brazilian Wilderness* (1914); and Blair Niles, *Casual Wanderings in Ecuador* (1923), and *Colombia, Land of Miracles* (1924).

## SCIENTIFIC EXPLORERS

An early and still interesting account of exploration is that of Henry M. Brackenridge (1786–1871), *Voyage to South America, performed by order of the American Government, in the years 1817 and 1818 . . .* , Baltimore, 1819. The notable expedition of Captain Charles Wilkes (1798–1877) was published as *Narrative of the United States Exploring Expedition, During the Years 1838, 1839, 1840, 1841, 1842*, Philadelphia (6 vols., 1845; 5 vols., 1850). The archaeologist Ephraim George Squier (1821–1888) made record of his journeys in *Nicaragua* (1852), *The States of Central America* (1858), and *Peru* (1877).

The geologist Raphael Pumpelly (1837–1923) published *Across America and Asia: Notes of a Five Years' Journey Around the World* . . . , 5th rev. ed., New York, 1870; and *Explorations in Turkestan* . . . , Washington, 1905–1908, 3 vols. His autobiography, *My Reminiscences,* New York, 1918, 2 vols., deserves to be better known. On Pumpelly, see Henry Holt's *Garrulities of an Octogenarian Editor,* Boston, 1923, pp. 226–230.

A standard and excellently written scientific account is Clarence E. Dutton (1841–1912), *Hawaiian Volcanoes,* published in the *Annual Report* of the United States Geological Survey, IV (1884), 75–219. Alexander Agassiz (1835–1910) gives a fascinating picture of his scientific explorations in *A Contribution to American Thalassography: Three Cruises of the* . . . *"Blake"* . . . (1888). George R. Agassiz has edited *Letters and Recollections of Alexander Agassiz,* Boston, 1913.

The discovery of the North Pole by Robert E. Peary (1856–1920) is recorded in his book *The North Pole* (1910). The best picture of Eskimo life is that of Vilhjalmur Stefansson, *My Life with the Eskimo* (1913). No better account of travels in Alaska has been published than that of John Muir, *Travels in Alaska* (1915).

### EXPATRIATES

Among American men of letters of the nineteenth century who at one period of their life or another chose Europe for extended residence are Irving, Cooper, Willis, Bret Harte, and Mark Twain. Edith Wharton was educated abroad, and in 1907 moved to France. The painters John Singleton Copley, Benjamin West, and Washington Allston, and the sculptor William Wetmore Story, took up residence abroad as young men; and some of them stayed. Three leading American writers of the twentieth century—Henry James, George Santayana, and T. S. Eliot—turned permanently toward England and Europe. Logan Pearsall Smith (1865–1946), though born and reared in a Philadelphia Quaker atmosphere, became identified with England where he resided after 1888.

A useful account of expatriates in Italy is in Henry James's *William Wetmore Story and His Friends,* Boston, 1903, 2 vols. Howard O. Sturgis (1855–1920), though Boston-bred, lived mostly in England. His novels, usually written with an English setting, may be represented by *Belchamber* (1904).

The two best known expatriates of the twentieth century are Ezra Pound and Gertrude Stein. For data on them, see the individual bibliographies herein. See also the section Bohemia: Escapism and Aestheticism (*ante*, p. 353) for further material

Two accounts of expatriates, especially in Paris, during the generation of the twenties are Harold E. Stearns, *The Street I Know*, New York, 1935, and Malcolm Cowley, *Exile's Return: A Narrative of Ideas*, New York, 1934.

Selections from fifty-two representative expatriates and American residents abroad are in Peter Neagoe, ed., *Americans Abroad: An ·Anthology*, The Hague, Holland, 1932.

The best brief historical summary is R. P. Blackmur, "The American Literary Expatriate," in David F. Bowers, ed., *Foreign Influences in American Life* . . . , Princeton, 1944, pp. 126–145, with critical bibl., pp. 233–234.

## AMERICAN BOOKS ABROAD

Interest abroad in American literature during the nineteenth century was expressed for the most part in analysis and criticism of individual authors. The interest was extensive, and the student is referred to the individual bibliographies herein, especially to those dealing with Bryant, Clemens, Cooper, Eggleston, Emerson, Margaret Fuller, Harte, Hawthorne, Irving, Henry James, Longfellow, Melville, Norris, Poe, H. B. Stowe, Thoreau, and Whitman. Further pertinent data will be found in the sections: Chronicles of the Frontier—The Continent as Observed from Abroad (*ante*, p. 269); The Forming of the Republic—Foreign Influences (*ante*, p. 94); The Mid-Nineteenth Century—Foreign Observers (*ante*, p. 125); and Best Sellers (*ante*, p. 218).

Three surveys of American writing by Englishmen are D(avid) H. Lawrence, *Studies in Classic American Literature*, New York, 1923—challenging attacks on major authors; J(ohn) C. Squire, ed., *Contemporary American Authors*, New York, 1928; and A(lfred) C. Ward, *American Literature, 1880–1930*, New York, 1932—a brief survey. Three factual studies are Chalmers Roberts, "American Books in England," *World's Work*, VIII (1904), 5430–5431; Gertrude Atherton, "The American Novel in England," *Pub. Weekly*, LXXVII (Feb. 12, 1910), 933; and Lovat Dickson, "The American Novel in England," *ibid.*, CXXXIV (Oct. 29, 1938), 1586–1590. See also William B. Cairns, *British Criticism of American Writings, 1815–1833*, Madison, Wis., 1922; *idem*, "British Republication of American Writings, 1783–1833," *PMLA*, XLIII (1928), 303–310; Amy Cruse, *The Victorians and Their Reading*, New York, 1935; Marjorie Plant, *The English Book Trade*, London, 1939; George S. Gordon, *Anglo-American Literary Relations*, London, 1942; and James Lansdale Hodson, *And Yet I Like America*, London,

1943. See also Walter Fischer, "Angloamerikanische Kultur- und Litera-turbeziehungen in neuer Zeit," *Archiv für das Studium der neueren Sprachen und Literaturen,* CLXXXIV (1943), 11–31. An unpublished dissertation is Louise H. Johnson, "America in the Thought of Leading British Men of Letters, 1830–1890," Univ. Wis., 1943.

A useful study of German histories of American literature is John H. Nelson, "Some German Surveys of American Literature," *Amer. Lit.,* I (1929), 149–160. See also Lida von Krockow, "American Characters in Ger-man Novels," *Atl. Mo.,* LXVII (1891), 824–838; E. A. C. Keppler, "America in the Popular and Student Poetry of Germany," *PMLA,* XVIII (1903), appendix, xxvii–xxviii; Grace I. Colbron, "The American Novel in Germany," *Bookman,* XXXIX (1914), 45–49; Clement Vollmer, "The American Novel in Germany, 1871–1913," *German American Annals,* n.s. XV (1917), 113–144, 165–219, with bibl., pp. 177–219; Lawrence M. Price, *The Reception of Eng-lish Literature in Germany,* Berkeley, Calif., 1932; H. Lüdeke, "American Literature in Germany: A Report of Recent Research and Criticism, 1931–1933," *Amer. Lit.,* VI (1934), 168–175; and Lydia E. Wagner, "The Reserved Attitude of the Early German Romanticists Toward America," *Germanic Quar.,* XVI (1943), 8–12.

Among contemporary interpretations by French observers are Charles Cestre, "American Literature Through French Eyes," *Yale Rev.,* n.s. X (1920), 85–98, and André Siegfried, *America Comes of Age: A French Analysis,* transl. by H. H. and Doris Hemming, New York, 1927. Régis Michaud's *Panorama de la Littérature Américaine Contemporaine,* Paris, 1928, covers the decade to date of publication. For a summary of French studies through 1934, see Jean Simon, "French Studies in American Literature and Civiliza-tion," *Amer. Lit.,* VI (1934), 176–190. Three recent studies are André Gide, *Imaginary Interviews,* New York, 1944, Chap. 16, "The New American Novelists"; Charles Cestre, *La Littérature Américaine,* Paris, 1945—a short survey, with a brief bibliography of French studies in American literature; and Jean-Paul Sartre, "American Novelists in French Eyes," *Atl. Mo.,* CLXXVIII (1946), 114–118. A French anthology of new American literature appeared as a special issue of *Fontaine,* published during the war in Algiers; another appeared as a 400-page issue of *L'Arbalète,* ed. by Marcel Duhamel. The latter is reviewed in the March, 1945, issue of *Confluences.* For further studies, see Lander MacClintock, "Sainte-Beuve and America," *PMLA,* LX (1945), 427–436; and Carlos Lynes, Jr., "The *Nouvelle Revue Française* and American Literature, 1909–1940," *French Rev.,* XIX (1946), 159–167.

The beginning of interest abroad in American literature as a whole, as distinguished from analyses of individual writers, is seen in the work of the Swedish critic Ruben G. Berg, *Moderna Amerikaner* (1925). The acceptance speech by Sinclair Lewis at the time of the Nobel award (1930), together with the address of welcome by Erik Axel Karlfeldt of the Swedish Academy —both valuable documents—was reprinted as a pamphlet by Harcourt, Brace and Company, New York, 1931.

Other European studies include the Danish survey by Frederik Schyberg, *Moderne Amerikansk Litteratur, 1900–1930* (1930); and a survey by the Czech scholar Otakar Vočadlo, *Současná Literatura Spojených Státu* (1934). A Norwegian estimate dealing especially with twentieth century writers is Arne Kildal, *Amerikas Stemme: Fra Amerikansk Litteratur og Kulturliv* (1935). See also Henning Larsen and Einar Haugen, "Björnson and America: A Critical Review," *Scand. Studies and Notes*, XIII (Feb., 1934), 1–12. Reception of American literature in Russia is discussed in A. Yarmolinsky, "The Russian View on American Literature," *Bookman*, XLIV (1916), 44; Sergei Dinamov, "American Literature in Russia," *Modern Quar.*, V (1929), 367–368; Andrew J. Steiger, "American Authors Popular in Soviet Russia," in the third (Mar., 1936) issue of the English edition of *International Literature* (Moscow); Alexander Anikst, "Soviet Finds Modernity in American Authors," *Lib. Jour.*, LXX (1945), 10–12; and Robert Magidoff, "American Literature in Russia," *Sat. Rev. Lit.*, XXIX (Nov. 2, 1946), 9–11, 45–46. Further interest as exhibited by translations is set forth in A. Vaicinlaitis, "American Writers in Lithuania," *Books Abroad*, XVII (1943), 334–337.

General studies include Camillo von Klenze, "The United States in European Literature," *PMLA*, XXIV (1909), appendix, xiii–xiv; and H. Houston Peckham, "Is American Literature Read and Respected in Europe?" *So. Atl. Quar.*, XIII (1914), 382–388.

Other useful studies appear in Angelina La Piana, *La Cultura Americana e l'Italia*, Torino, 1938; John T. Reid, "As the Other Americans See Our Literature," *So. Atl. Quar.*, XL (1941), 211–219; David F. Bowers, ed., *Foreign Influences in American Life*, Princeton, 1944; and John Graham Brooks, *As Others See Us: A Study of Progress in the United States*, New York, 1908, with a condensed but useful bibliography, pp. 347–353. See also "American Culture Abroad," *Comparative Literature News-Letter*, IV (1946), 41–45— for the years 1931–1945.

The most complete listing of American books in translation appears in *Index Translationum . . . : International Bibliography of Translations,* a quarterly publication issued at Paris, 1932–1940.

An early study, dealing particularly with major nineteenth century authors, is (John) De Lancey Ferguson, *American Literature in Spain*, New York, 1916.

Interpretations by observers in Mexico and Latin America include Edmundo O'Gorman, *Fundamentos de la Historia de America*, Mexico City,

1942; and William Rex Crawford, *A Century of Latin-American Thought,*
Cambridge, 1944.

A bibliography is William T. Spoerri, *The Old World and the New:
A Synthesis of Current European Views on American Civilization,* Zurich,
1938.

# BIBLIOGRAPHIES:
# INDIVIDUAL AUTHORS

# HENRY (BROOKS) ADAMS
*1838–1918*

SEPARATE WORKS

*Chapters of Erie, and Other Essays* (with Charles Francis Adams, Jr.), 1871; *Essays in Anglo-Saxon Law*, 1876; *Documents Relating to New England Federalism, 1800–1815*, 1877; *Democracy: An American Novel*, 1879; *The Life of Albert Gallatin*, 1879; *The Writings of Albert Gallatin*, 1879; *John Randolph*, 1882; *Esther: A Novel*, 1884; *History of the United States of America During the Administration of Thomas Jefferson*, 1884–1885; *History of the United States of America During the Administration of James Madison*, 1888–1889; *Historical Essays*, 1891; *Memoirs of Marau Taaroa . . .* (1893); *Mont-Saint-Michel and Chartres*, 1904; *The Education of Henry Adams: An Autobiography*, 1907; *The Life of George Cabot Lodge*, 1911; *The Degradation of the Democratic Dogma*, 1919.

Essays and reviews, many of which have never been reprinted, appear in the following newspapers and periodicals (the dates are inclusive): *Harvard Magazine*, 1855–1858; *Boston Courier*, 1860–1861; *Boston Daily Advertiser*, 1860–1861; *New York Times*, 1861; *North American Review*, 1867–1876; *Nation*, 1868–1877; *Edinburgh Review*, 1869; *Westminster Review*, 1870; *American Historical Review*, 1895; *Proceedings Massachusetts Historical Society*, 1910. Adams also contributed an essay on King in *Clarence King Memoirs . . .*, New York, 1904.

The most important published collections of Adams letters are Worthington C. Ford, ed., *A Cycle of Adams Letters, 1861–1865*, Boston, 1920, 2 vols.; *idem*, ed., *Letters of Henry Adams, 1858–1891*, Boston, 1930; *idem*, ed., *Letters of Henry Adams, 1892–1918*, Boston, 1938; and Harold Dean Cater, ed., *Henry Adams and His Friends: A Collection of His Unpublished Letters*, Boston, 1947. Gleanings will be found in *Letters of John Hay and Extracts from Diary*, Washington, 1908, 3 vols.—selected but not edited by Henry Adams; Mabel La Farge, ed., *Letters to a Niece and Prayer to the Virgin of Chartres*, Boston, 1920; Frederick B. Luquiens, ed., "Seventeen Letters of Henry Adams," *Yale Rev.*, X (1920), 111–130; Albert S. Cook, ed., "Six Letters of Henry Adams," *ibid.*, 131–140; "Three Letters from Henry Adams to Albert S. Cook," *Pacific Rev.*, II (1921), 273–275; Stephen Gwynn, ed.,

*The Letters and Friendships of Sir Cecil Spring-Rice,* Boston, 1929, 2 vols.;
Paul H. Bixler, "A Note on Henry Adams," *Colophon,* Pt. 17, No. 2 (1934);
"Letters of Henry Adams," *Yale Rev.,* XXIV (1934), 112–117—to Moreton
Frewen, with a note by Shane Leslie; John E. Alden, "Henry Adams as
Editor: A Group of Unpublished Letters Written to David A. Wells," *New
Eng. Quar.,* XI (1938), 146–152; W. Stull Holt, "Henry Adams and the Johns
Hopkins University," *ibid.,* 632–638—letters to President Gilman, 1875–1878;
and Max I. Baym, "Henry Adams and Henry Vignaud," *New Eng. Quar.,*
XVII (1944), 442–449.

### EDITED TEXTS AND REPRINTS

There is no collected edition of Adams's works, and the need is pressing
for an inexpensive, complete, annotated reissue of his writings. At present reprints may be found as follows:

*Documents Relating to New England Federalism, 1800–1815* (1877), ed.
by Adams, was reprinted Boston, 1905. *Democracy* (1879), first published
anonymously, has been reprinted many times; it was brought out in 1908
with a foreword by Henry Holt, and was last reprinted with the foreword
in 1925. *John Randolph* (1882), in the American Statesmen Series, edited by
J. T. Morse, Jr., has been frequently reprinted. *Esther* (1884), published under
the pseudonym Frances Snow Compton, was reprinted in facsimile, with an
introduction by Robert E. Spiller, New York, 1938. The 4-volume *History . . .
During the Administration of Thomas Jefferson* (privately printed, Cambridge, 1884–1885; published, New York, 1889–1890) together with the 5-vol-
ume *History . . . During the Administration of James Madison* (privately
printed, Cambridge, 1888–1889; published, New York, 1890–1891) was reprinted in 4 vols. with an introduction by Henry S. Commager, New York,
1930. A condensation has been edited by Herbert Agar as *The Formative
Years . . . ,* Boston, 1947, 2 vols. *Memoirs of Arii . . . ,* never published,
was privately printed in Paris in 1901, as a revision of *Memoirs of Marau
Taaroa, Last Queen of Tahiti,* n.p., privately printed, 1893. A facsimile reproduction of the Paris 1901 edition, with variant readings from the 1893 edition,
is that of Robert E. Spiller, ed., *Tahiti: Memoirs of Arii Taimai,* New York,
1947. *Mont-Saint-Michel and Chartres,* first privately printed, Washington,
1904, revised and privately printed, Washington, 1912, was published, Boston,
1913, with an introduction by Ralph Adams Cram; it was reprinted, Boston,
1919, and has since been reprinted many times. The *Education,* privately
printed, Washington, 1907, was published, Boston, 1918, with a preface by
Adams himself, signed by Henry Cabot Lodge; it has been reprinted many
times, and was issued in the Modern Library, 1931, with a preface by James
T. Adams. *The Life of George Cabot Lodge,* Boston, 1911, was reprinted

in full in Edmund Wilson, ed., *The Shock of Recognition* . . . , New York, 1943. Adams's Presidential Address to the American Historical Association, "The Tendency of History" (*Report*, 1894), was expanded into *A Letter to American Teachers of History*, privately printed, Baltimore, 1910. This in turn was included, with an additional essay by Adams and an introduction by Brooks Adams, in *The Degradation of the Democratic Dogma*, New York, 1919, and was reprinted, New York, 1928, as *The Tendency of History* (without the introduction).

Arthur W. Silver edited "Henry Adams's 'Diary of a Visit to Manchester,' " *Amer. Hist. Rev.*, LI (1945), 74–89—first published in the Boston *Courier*, Dec. 16, 1861.

BIOGRAPHY AND CRITICISM

At present there is no life of Adams which attempts to explore the sources of his ideas or evaluate his aesthetic philosophy. James T. Adams's narrative biography *Henry Adams*, New York, 1933, is brief and is based mainly on the *Education*.

Work on the sources of Adams's ideas, particularly in his reading, is yet to be done. His thoughts need closer correlation with intellectual history both in this country and abroad, particularly with reference to his aesthetic philosophy. Until primary material has been released for study, critical estimates must be tentative. In general Adams criticism has suffered most by the acceptance of his own judgment of himself as a "failure." The issue on this point has not been openly joined, but because Adams's major work is autobiographical, critics have not distinguished clearly between the man (whom they admittedly have not understood) and his works (which they increasingly appreciate).

Analyses of Adams's thought are Robert E. Spiller, introduction to *Esther*, New York, 1938; R. P. Blackmur, "Henry and Brooks Adams: Parallels to Two Generations," *Southern Rev.*, V (1939), 308–334; and *idem*, "Henry Adams: Three Late Moments," *Kenyon Rev.*, II (1940), 7–29.

As a historian and interpreter of the scientific phenomena of his age he has been studied by James Truslow Adams, "Henry Adams and the New Physics: Its Effect on His Theory of History," *Yale Rev.*, XIX (1929), 283–302; Henry S. Commager, "Henry Adams" in William T. Hutchinson, ed., *The Marcus W. Jernegan Essays in American Historiography*, Chicago, 1937, pp. 191–206—outstanding as a study of Adams as historian; Roy F. Nichols, "The Dynamic Interpretation of History," *New Eng. Quar.*, VIII (1935), 163–178; "Frederick Jackson Turner vs. Henry Adams," in Ralph H. Gabriel, *The Course of American Democratic Thought* . . . , New York, 1940, pp. 251–268; "Tendencies in History," in Muriel Rukeyser, *Willard Gibbs*, New

York, 1942, pp. 403–428; and Charles A. Beard, "Historians at Work: Brooks and Henry Adams," *Atl. Mo.*, CLXXI (1943), 87–98. Other studies of the subject are George H. Sabine, "Henry Adams and the Writing of History," *Univ. Calif. Chron.*, XXVI (1924), 31–46; Maurice F. Neufield, "The Crisis in Prospect," *Amer. Scholar*, IV (1935), 397–408; Max I. Baym, "William James and Henry Adams," *New Eng. Quar.*, X (1937), 717–742; James Stone, "Henry Adams's Philosophy of History," *New Eng. Quar.*, XIV (1941), 538–548; Herbert Edwards, "The Prophetic Mind of Henry Adams," *College English*, III (1942), 708–721; and Nathalia Wright, "Henry Adams's Theory of History: A Puritan Defense," *New Eng. Quar.*, XVII (1945), 204–210.

Penetrating contemporary reviews of the *Education* are Robert M. Lovett, "The Betrayal of Henry Adams," *Dial*, LXV (1918), 468–472; Carl Becker, "The Education of Henry Adams," *Amer. Hist. Rev.*, XXIV (1919), 422–434; and Stuart P. Sherman, "Evolution in the Adams Family," *Nation*, CX (1920), 473–477. Studies of Adams as a man of letters are "The Pioneer American Political Novel of Henry Adams," in Morris E. Speare, *The Political Novel . . .* , New York, 1924, pp. 287–305; Louis Zukofsky, "Henry Adams: A Criticism in Autobiography," *Hound and Horn*, III (1930), 333–357, 518–530, IV (1930), 46–72; Max I. Baym, "The 1858 Catalogue of Henry Adams's Library," *Colophon*, n.s. III (1938), No. 4, 483–489; and Robert A. Hume, "The Style and Literary Background of Henry Adams, with Attention to *The Education of Henry Adams,*" *Amer. Lit.*, XVI (1945), 296–315.

Other special studies are Stewart Mitchell, "Henry Adams and Some of His Students," *Proc. Mass. Hist. Soc.*, LXVI (1942), 294–310—a good portrait of Adams at Harvard drawn from the letters and memories of his students; Dixon Wecter, "Harvard Exiles," *Virginia Quar. Rev.*, X (1934), 244–257—Adams as an "academic Tory"; Charles I. Glicksberg, "Henry Adams Reports on a Trades-Union Meeting," *New Eng. Quar.*, XV (1942), 724–728—Adams as a correspondent in the sixties; "Henry Adams and the Hand of the Fathers," in Ferner Nuhn, *The Wind Blew from the East*, New York, 1942, pp. 164–194—the European influence on Adams; and Max I. Baym, "Henry Adams and the Critics," *Amer. Scholar*, XV (1945), 79–89.

Estimates of Adams interesting to the extent that the authors are spokesmen of their times are "Henry Adams," in Paul Elmer More, *Shelburne Essays: Eleventh Series*, Boston, 1921, pp. 117–140; "Henry Adams," in Thomas K. Whipple, *Spokesmen . . .* , New York, 1928, pp. 23–43 (with bibl., pp. 43–44); Vernon L. Parrington, *Main Currents in American Thought . . .* , New York, III (1930), 214–227; "The Miseducation of Henry Adams," in Van Wyck Brooks, *Sketches in Criticism*, New York, 1932, pp. 197–210; *idem, New England: Indian Summer, 1865–1915*, New York, 1940, pp. 250–275, 354–372, 474–490—three "episodes" in the life of Adams, with a re-creation of the people and the thoughts that influenced him.

PRIMARY SOURCES

Most of the Adams family papers are impounded in the library of the Massachusetts Historical Society. There are a few letters in the Houghton Library of Harvard University, and many, not all available, in the possession of the family and associates. Until family restrictions are lifted, scholars will work chiefly from printed sources.

The outstanding manuscript collection is that of the Massachusetts Historical Society, which, in addition to the papers noted above, includes Adams's own books, many of them with marginalia. Here too are most of the privately printed first editions of his works—editions limited, in some instances, to fewer than ten copies. A much less important collection is the one which Adams presented, a few items at a time, to Adelbert College of Western Reserve University. The great collection of Adams Papers in the Boston Public Library includes John Adams's personal library, with annotations in Henry Adams's hand.

Among published sources of primary material, most significant are Ward Thoron, ed., *The Letters of Mrs. Henry Adams, 1865–1883*, Boston, 1936; Charles F. Adams, *Charles Francis Adams, 1835–1915: An Autobiography*, Boston, 1916; and James T. Adams, *The Adams Family*, Boston, 1931.

Important as source material are the memoirs of friends and associates, among which are those of C. F. Adams, Margaret Chanler, E. L. Godkin, John Hay, Henry Holt, Henry James, Clarence King, John La Farge, J. Laurence Laughlin, Henry Cabot Lodge, Whitelaw Reid, H. H. Richardson, Augustus Saint-Gaudens, Carl Schurz, Cecil Spring-Rice, Lindsay Swift, Henry Osborn Taylor, and Charles F. Thwing.

BIBLIOGRAPHY

The "Bibliography of the Writings of Henry Adams," in James T. Adams, *Henry Adams*, New York, 1933, pp. 213–229, is the most serviceable listing at present.

# JOHN ADAMS
## 1735–1826

SEPARATE WORKS

*Essay on Canon and Feudal Law*, 1768; *History of the Dispute with America*, 1774; *Thoughts on Government*, 1776; *A Collection of State Papers*,

1782; *A Defence of the Constitutions of Government of the United States of America,* 1787–1788, 1794; *A Selection of Patriotic Addresses,* 1798; *Discourses on Davila,* 1805; *The Inadmissible Principles,* 1809; *Novanglus and Massachusettensis; or, Political Essays,* 1819.

COLLECTED WORKS

The standard collection still remains the edition prepared by Adams's grandson Charles Francis Adams, *The Works of John Adams,* Boston, 1850–1856, 10 vols.; it includes material from several diaries and from his autobiography. Adams's writings constitute the best introduction to the study of republics as interpreted by an American statesman.

Letters of Adams published during his lifetime are *Twenty-six Letters, upon Interesting Subjects,* New York, 1789; *Four Letters,* Boston, 1802; *Correspondence . . . Concerning the British Doctrine of Impressment,* Baltimore, 1809; *Correspondence Between the Hon. John Adams . . . and the Late Wm. Cunningham . . . ,* Boston, 1823—letters not included in the C. F. Adams edition of John Adams's *Works.*

Correspondence published after Adams's death includes the deservedly well known *Letters of John Adams Addressed to His Wife,* Boston, 1841, 2 vols.; and *Familiar Letters of John Adams and His Wife,* New York, 1876—both edited by Charles Francis Adams. These overlap considerably. The latter stops with 1783, but is fuller for the decade preceding 1783 than the former, which continues to the year 1801. The *Warren-Adams Letters* fill two volumes of *Coll. Mass. Hist. Soc.,* LXXII–LXXIII (1917–1923). More recent collections are Paul Wilstach, ed., *Correspondence of John Adams and Thomas Jefferson,* Indianapolis, 1925; and Worthington C. Ford, ed., *Statesman and Friend: Correspondence of John Adams with Benjamin Waterhouse, 1784–1822,* Boston, 1927. Gleanings are in "Letters of John Adams and John Quincy Adams, 1776–1838," *Bul. N.Y. Pub. Lib.,* IX (1906), 227–250.

A useful volume of selections is *The Selected Writings of John and John Quincy Adams.* New York, 1946, edited, with introduction, by Adrienne Koch and William Peden.

BIOGRAPHY AND CRITICISM

The *Life* of John Adams in Vol. I of Charles Francis Adams's edition of *The Works of John Adams* (1850–1856) is important as an exposition of his public services. It was reprinted, Philadelphia, 1871, 2 vols., and again issued in 1874, in a revised and corrected edition. Of the 640-odd pages of this edition the first 87 are the work of John Quincy Adams. The greater part was written by the editor, Charles Francis Adams. Mellen Chamberlain's *John*

*Adams: The Statesman of the American Revolution* . . . , Boston, 1899, is an essay evaluating Adams's political character. A full-length intellectual study, very usefully documented, is Correa M. Walsh, *The Political Science of John Adams* . . . , New York, 1915. Gilbert Chinard's *Honest John Adams*, Boston, 1933, is the only recent life. James T. Adams surveys the dynasties in *The Adams Family*, Boston, 1930. The best brief sketch is that of Worthington C. Ford in *Dict. Amer. Biog.* (1928).

Brief studies of aspects of Adams's political thought are Francis N. Thorpe, "The Political Ideas of John Adams," *Pa. Mag. Hist. and Biog.*, XLIV (1920), 1–46; "John Adams as a Britannic Statesman," in Randolph G. Adams, *Political Ideas of the American Revolution* . . . , Durham, N.C., 1922, pp. 86–108; and Joseph Dorfman, "The Regal Republic of John Adams," *Pol. Sci. Quar.*, LIX (1944), 227–247.

Adams is treated as a man of letters in Dorothy M. Robathan, "John Adams and the Classics," *New Eng. Quar.*, XIX (1946), 91–98; and in Moses C. Tyler, *The Literary History of the American Revolution*, New York, 1897, I, 93–98. A catalogue of Adams's library was printed by the Boston Public Library in 1917.

PRIMARY SOURCES

*The History of the Administration of John Adams* . . . , New York, 1802, is a contemporary estimate by John Wood. George Gibbs's *Memoirs of the Administrations of Washington and John Adams* . . . , New York, 1846, 6 vols., is violently anti-Federalist.

The published writings of Washington, Jefferson, Hamilton, Franklin, Madison, and Monroe are important sources in interpretation of Adams.

The leading collection of Adams papers, especially the personal papers, is in the Boston Public Library. A very large collection is deposited in the Library of Congress, much of it unpublished. There is much manuscript material among the Adams Papers in the Massachusetts Historical Society. Some letters are in the Bancroft Collection of the New York Public Library. The most important of Adams's published state papers are reprinted in James D. Richardson, *A Compilation of the Messages and Papers of the Presidents, 1789–1902*, New York, 1903.

BIBLIOGRAPHY

No full bibliography of Adams's works or related material has been published. Printed sources are listed in C. F. Adams's edition of the *Works* (1850–1856) and need to be brought to date. The bibliographical guide in *Dict. Amer. Biog.* is necessarily brief.

# GEORGE ADE
*1866–1944*

SEPARATE WORKS

*Artie*, 1896; *Pink Marsh*, 1897; *Doc' Horne*, 1899; *Fables in Slang*, 1900; *More Fables*, 1900; *Forty Modern Fables*, 1901; *The Girl Proposition*, 1902; *People You Know*, 1903; *Circus Day*, 1903; *Handsome Cyril*, 1903; *Clarence Allen*, 1903; *In Babel*, 1903; *Rollo Johnson*, 1904; *Breaking into Society*, 1904; *True Bills*, 1904; *In Pastures New*, 1906; *The Slim Princess*, 1907; *I Knew Him When—*, 1910; *Hoosier Hand Book*, 1911; *Verses and Jingles*, 1911; *Knocking the Neighbors*, 1912; *Ade's Fables*, 1914; *Hand-Made Fables*, 1920; *Single Blessedness and Other Observations*, 1922; *Stay with Me Flagons*, 1922; *Bang! Bang!* 1928; *The Old-Time Saloon*, 1931; *Revived Remarks on Mark Twain*, 1936; *One Afternoon ·with Mark Twain*, 1939.

Among the published plays by George Ade are: *The Sultan of Sulu*, 1903; *Marse Covington*, 1918; *Nettie*, 1923; *Speaking to Father*, 1923; *The Mayor and the Manicure*, 1923; *Just Out of College*, 1924; *Father and the Boys*, 1924; *The College Widow*, 1924; *The County Chairman*, 1924.

Reprints appear in Franklin J. Meine, ed., *Stories of the Streets and of the Town from the Chicago Record, 1893–1900*, Chicago, 1941; and Fred C. Kelly, ed., *The Permanent Ade . . .*, New York, 1947.

A biography is Fred C. Kelly, *George Ade: Warmhearted Satirist*, Indianapolis, 1947. Critical estimates are "Old Wisdom in a New Tongue: George Ade," in Carl Van Doren, *Many Minds*, New York, 1924, pp. 18–33; and "George Ade," in H. L. Mencken, *Prejudices: First Series*, New York, 1919, pp. 113–122.

A definitive listing of printed material by and about Ade is Dorothy R. Russo, *A Bibliography of George Ade, 1866–1944*, Indianapolis, 1947, published by the Indiana Historical Society.

# CONRAD (POTTER) AIKEN
*b. 1889*

SEPARATE WORKS

*Earth Triumphant and Other Tales in Verse*, 1914; *Turns and Movies and Other Tales in Verse*, 1916; *The Jig of Forslin: A Symphony*, 1916; *Nocturne of Remembered Spring and Other Poems*, 1917; *The Charnel Rose, Senlin (A Biography), and Other Poems*, 1918; *Scepticisms*, 1919; *The*

*House of Dust: A Symphony*, 1920; *Punch: The Immortal Liar*, 1921; *Priapus and the Pool*, 1922; *The Pilgrimage of Festus*, 1923; *Bring! Bring!* 1925; *Blue Voyage*, 1927; *Costumes by Eros*, 1928; *Prelude*, 1929; *Selected Poems*, 1929; *John Deth, A Metaphysical Legend, and Other Poems*, 1930; *Gehenna*, 1930; *The Coming Forth by Day of Osiris Jones*, 1931; *Preludes for Memnon*, 1931; *Great Circle*, 1933; *Among the Lost People*, 1934; *Landscape West of Eden*, 1935; *King Coffin*, 1935; *Time in the Rock*, 1936; *A Heart for the Gods of Mexico*, 1939; *And in the Human Heart*, 1940; *Conversation, or, Pilgrims' Progress*, 1940; *Brownstone Eclogues and Other Poems*, 1942; *The Soldier: A Poem*, 1944; *The Kid*, 1947.

BIOGRAPHY AND CRITICISM

The only full-length biography of Aiken is Houston Peterson, *Melody of Chaos*, New York, 1931.

Critical estimates are "Conrad Aiken," in Louis Untermeyer, *American Poetry Since 1900*, New York, 1923, pp. 170–182; Alfred Kreymborg, *Our Singing Strength . . .*, New York, 1929, pp. 429–437; Stanley J. Kunitz, "The Poetry of Conrad Aiken," *Nation*, CXXXIII (1931), 393–395; Marianne Moore, "If a Man Die," *Hound and Horn*, V (1932), 313–320; and Harlan Hatcher, *Creating the Modern American Novel*, New York, 1935, pp. 183–187. A checklist of Aiken's writings and of writings relating to him appears in Fred B. Millett's *Contemporary American Authors*, New York, 1940, pp. 213–216. The most recent checklist of his writings is compiled by Frances Cheney, in Allen Tate, *Sixty American Poets, 1896–1944*, Washington, 1945, pp. 3–6.

# AMOS BRONSON ALCOTT
## *1799–1888*

SEPARATE WORKS

*Observations on the Principles and Methods of Infant Instruction*, 1830; *The Doctrine and Discipline of Human Culture*, 1836; *Conversations with Children on the Gospels*, 1836–1837; *Tablets*, 1868; *Concord Days*, 1872; *Table-Talk*, 1877; *New Connecticut: An Autobiographical Poem*, 1881; *Ralph Waldo Emerson*, 1882; *Sonnets and Canzonets*, 1882.

COLLECTED WORKS

Odell Shepard has edited *The Journals of Bronson Alcott*, Boston, 1938. *Orphic Sayings . . .*, were reprinted from the *Dial*, with an introduction by William P. Randel, Mt. Vernon, N.Y., 1939; and David P. Edgell edited

"Bronson Alcott's 'Autobiographical Index,'" *New Eng. Quar.*, XIV (1941), 704–715—notes concerning the Fruitlands experiment.

## BIOGRAPHY AND CRITICISM

The most inclusive biography is Odell Shepard, *Pedlar's Progress: The Life of Bronson Alcott*, Boston, 1937. A narrative account is Hubert H. Hoeltje, *Sheltering Tree: A Story of the Friendship of Ralph Waldo Emerson and Amos Bronson Alcott*, Durham, N.C., 1943—based on their letters and diaries. Other lives are Frank B. Sanborn and William T. Harris, *A. Bronson Alcott: His Life and Philosophy*, Boston, 1893, 2 vols.—with copious excerpts from Alcott's letters and diary; Honoré W. Morrow, *The Father of Little Women*, Boston, 1927—an account of his educational career; and Dorothy McCuskey, *Bronson Alcott, Teacher*, New York, 1940. The sketch of Alcott in the *New Amer. Cyclopaedia* (1858) was written by Emerson.

Studies of Alcott and Utopian projects are Clara E. Sears, comp., *Bronson Alcott's Fruitlands*, Boston, 1915—with a reprint of Louisa May Alcott's *Transcendental Wild Oats;* Harold C. Goddard, in *Camb. Hist. Amer. Lit.*, I (1917), 336–339—brief but discriminating; Arthur E. Christy, *The Orient in American Transcendentalism . . .* , New York, 1933; "Alcott, Margaret Fuller, Brook Farm," in Van Wyck Brooks, *The Flowering of New England*, New York, 1936, pp. 228–251; Frederic I. Carpenter, "Bronson Alcott: Genteel Transcendentalist—An Essay in Definition," *New Eng. Quar.*, XIII (1940), 34–48; David P. Edgell, "Bronson Alcott's 'Gentility,'" *New Eng. Quar.*, XIII (1940), 699–705—a further definition.

Bronson Alcott as a teacher is the theme of George E. Haefner, *A Critical Estimate of the Educational Theories and Practices of A. Bronson Alcott*, New York, 1937. Further studies are Austin Warren, "The Orphic Sage: Bronson Alcott," *Amer. Lit.*, III (1931), 3–13; Hubert H. Hoeltje, "Amos Bronson Alcott in Iowa," *Iowa Jour. Hist. and Pol.*, XXIX (1931), 375–401; Clarence Gohdes, "Alcott's 'Conversation' on the Transcendental Club and *The Dial*," *Amer. Lit.*, III (1931), 14–27.

## PRIMARY SOURCES

Elizabeth P. Peabody's *Record of a School . . .* , Boston, 1835, is based on Alcott's theory and practice. The journals of Emerson and Thoreau record much about Alcott. Further material is in F. L. H. Willis, *Alcott Memoirs . . .* , Boston, 1915; Thomas W. Higginson, *Contemporaries*, Boston, 1899, pp. 23–33; and *idem, Carlyle's Laugh . . .* , Boston, 1909, pp. 75–91.

# LOUISA MAY ALCOTT
*1832–1888*

### SEPARATE WORKS

*Flower Fables,* 1855; *Hospital Sketches,* 1863; *On Picket Duty and Other Tales,* 1864; *The Rose Family,* 1864; *Moods,* 1865; *The Mysterious Key and What It Opened,* 1867; *Morning-Glories, and Other Stories,* 1868; *Kitty's Class Day,* 1868; *Aunt Kipp,* 1868; *Nelly's Hospital,* 1868 (?); *Psyche's Art,* 1868; *Little Women; or, Meg, Jo, Beth, and Amy,* 1868; *Little Women; or, Meg, Jo, Beth, and Amy: Part Second,* 1869; *An Old-Fashioned Girl,* 1870; *Little Men: Life at Plumfield with Jo's Boys,* 1871; *Aunt Jo's Scrap-Bag* 1872–1882, 6 vols.; *Work,* 1873; *Eight Cousins; or, The Aunt-Hill,* 1875; *Silver Pitchers: And Independence, A Centennial Love Story,* 1876; *Rose in Bloom: A Sequel to "Eight Cousins,"* 1876; *A Modern Mephistopheles,* 1877; *Under the Lilacs,* 1878; *Meadow Blossoms,* 1879; *Sparkles for Bright Eyes,* 1879; *Water Cresses,* 1879; *Jack and Jill: A Village Story,* 1880; *Proverb Stories,* 1882; *Spinning-Wheel Stories,* 1884; *Jo's Boys and How They Turned Out: A Sequel to "Little Men,"* 1886; *A Garland for Girls,* 1888; *A Modern Mephistopheles and A Whisper in the Dark,* 1889.

### COLLECTED WORKS

*Louisa May Alcott: Her Life, Letters and Journals,* was edited by Ednah D. Cheney, Boston, 1889 (also 1900 and 1928). No further collections have been made. Many of her stories, popular ever since they were first published, continue to be frequently reprinted as books for children.

### BIOGRAPHY AND CRITICISM

Louisa May Alcott has been a popular subject for biographies, the quality of which in general has been uncritical and enthusiastic. A recent narrative life, more discriminating than most, is Katharine Anthony, *Louisa May Alcott,* New York, 1938. Brief estimates appear in Gamaliel Bradford, *Portraits of American Women,* Boston, 1919, pp. 167–194; "Miss Alcott's New England," in Katharine Fullerton Gerould, *Modes and Morals,* New York, 1920, pp. 182–198; Odell Shepard, "The Mother of *Little Women,*" *No. Amer. Rev.,* CCXLV (1938), 391–398; and Marion Talbot, "Glimpses of the Real Louisa May Alcott," *New Eng. Quar.,* XI (1938), 731–738.

Five studies by Madeleine B. Stern are documented: "Louisa Alcott, Trouper: Experiences in Theatricals, 1848–1880," *New Eng. Quar.,* XVI (1943), 175–197; "Louisa May Alcott: Civil War Nurse," *Americana* XXXVII (1943), 296–325; "Louisa M. Alcott's Contributions to Periodicals,

1868–1888," *More Books,* XVIII (1943), 411–420—with an enumerative bibl., pp. 415–420; "The Witch's Cauldron to the Family Hearth: Louisa M. Alcott's Literary Development, 1848–68," *More Books,* XVIII (1943), 363–380 —with a selective bibl. for the twenty years preceding publication of *Little Women* (1868); and "Louisa M. Alcott's Self-Criticism," *More Books,* XX (1945), 339–345. Other recent studies are Elizabeth L. Adams, "Louisa Alcott's Doomed Manuscript," *More Books,* XVII (1942), 221–222; and Leona Rostenberg, "Some Anonymous and Pseudonymous Thrillers of Louisa M. Alcott," *Papers Bibl. Soc. Amer.,* XXXVII (1943), 131–140—an identification of several titles. For reference, May L. Becker has compiled *Louisa Alcott's People,* New York, 1936.

PRIMARY SOURCES

Among published memoirs dealing with the Alcott family are Maria S. Porter, *Recollections of Louisa May Alcott . . . ,* Boston, 1893; Clara Gowing, *The Alcotts as I Knew Them,* Boston, 1909; Frank B. Sanborn, *Recollections of Seventy Years,* Boston, 1909; *idem,* "Reminiscences of Louisa M. Alcott," *Independent,* LXXII (1912), 496–502; and Caroline Ticknor, *May Alcott: A Memoir,* Boston, 1928—a life of her sister. Further material may be found in works dealing with her father, Amos Bronson Alcott.

Many of her letters are in the Houghton Library of Harvard University.

BIBLIOGRAPHY

Lucile Gulliver compiled *Louisa May Alcott: A Bibliography,* Boston, 1932. See also above the studies of Stern and of Rostenberg.

## THOMAS BAILEY ALDRICH
### *1836–1907*

SEPARATE WORKS

*The Bells: A Collection of Chimes,* 1855; *Daisy's Necklace: And What Came of It,* 1857; *The Course of True Love Never Did Run Smooth,* 1858; *The Ballad of Babie Bell and Other Poems,* 1859; *Pampinea and Other Poems,* 1861; *Out of His Head: A Romance,* 1862; *Poems,* 1863; *The Poems of Thomas Bailey Aldrich,* 1865; *Pansy's Wish: A Christmas Fantasy,* 1870; *The Story of a Bad Boy,* 1870; *Marjorie Daw, and Other People,* 1873; *Prudence Palfrey: A Novel,* 1874; *Flower and Thorn: Later Poems,* 1877; *The Queen of Sheba,* 1877; *A Midnight Fantasy and the Little Violinist,* 1877; *The Stillwater Tragedy,* 1880; *The Poems of Thomas Bailey Aldrich,* 1882; *From Ponkapog to Pesth,* 1883; *Mercedes and Later Lyrics,* 1884; *Poems: House-*

*hold Edition*, 1885; *The Second Son: A Novel*, 1888; *Wyndham Towers*, 1890; *The Sisters' Tragedy, with Other Poems, Lyrical and Dramatic*, 1891; *An Old Town by the Sea*, 1893; *Two Bites at a Cherry, with Other Tales*, 1894; *Mercedes: A Drama in Two Acts*, 1894; *Unguarded Gates and Other Poems*, 1895; *Judith and Holofernes*, 1896; *A Sea Turn and Other Matters*, 1902; *Ponkapog Papers*, 1903; *Judith of Bethulia: A Tragedy*, 1904.

*Cloth of Gold, and Other Poems*, Boston, 1874, is a reprint of "all the poems which the author cares to retain of the edition published . . . in 1865," important because the Aldrich canon was here fixed. Other volumes of selected reprints are *Friar Jerome's Beautiful Book, and Other Poems*, Boston, 1881; *Later Lyrics*, Boston, 1896; and *A Book of Songs and Sonnets*, Boston, 1906. *The Story of a Bad Boy* (1870) was reprinted, New York, 1930, in the Modern Readers' Ser., with an introduction by V. L. O. Chittick; and most lately, New York, 1936; *Marjorie Daw* (1873) has been reprinted many times, as lately as 1923.

*The Writings of Thomas Bailey Aldrich* were collected, Cambridge, 1897, in 8 vols., and again, Boston, 1907, reissued with a 9th vol. added.

Published letters from Aldrich to William Winter are in Winter's *Old Friends: Being Literary Recollections of Other Days*, New York, 1909, pp. 132–152, 351–376.

Ferris Greenslet wrote *The Life of Thomas Bailey Aldrich*, Boston, 1908. There are very few critical studies of Aldrich; the two most recent are "Aldrich and His Circle," in Van Wyck Brooks, *New England: Indian Summer*, New York, 1940, pp. 296–315; and Alexander Cowie, "Indian Summer Novelist," *New Eng. Quar.*, XV (1942), 608–621. Earlier studies and appreciations are Bliss Perry, *Park Street Papers*, Boston, 1908, pp. 143–170; Paul E. More, *Shelburne Essays, Seventh Series*, New York, 1910, pp. 138–152; and C. Hartley Grattan, "Thomas Bailey Aldrich," *Amer. Mercury*, V (1925), 41–45. The narrative sketch in *Dict. Amer. Biog.* (1928) is by William B. Parker.

Aldrich's *An Old Town by the Sea*, Boston, 1893, is autobiographical. His wife, Lilian W. Aldrich, recorded further reminiscences in *Crowding Memories*, Boston, 1920. Most of the Aldrich manuscripts are deposited in the T. B. Aldrich Birthplace, Portsmouth, N.H. Other collections are in the Henry E. Huntington Library, Harvard College Library, and Princeton University Library.

A seven-page *Annotated List of the Works of Thomas Bailey Aldrich*, New York, 1907, is compiled by Annette P. Ward. A bibliography of original editions is in the Greenslet *Life* (1908), pp. 261–292. Other bibliographical data are in *A Catalogue of the Works of Thomas Bailey Aldrich, Collected by Francis Bartlett*, Merrymount Press, 1898; and Ernest D. North, "A

Bibliography of the Original Editions of the Works of Thomas Bailey Aldrich," *Book Buyer*, n.s., XXII (1901), 296–303.


## JAMES LANE ALLEN
### *1849–1925*

SEPARATE WORKS

*Flute and Violin*, 1891; *Sister Dolorosa and Posthumous Fame*, 1892; *The Blue-Grass Region of Kentucky*, 1892; *John Gray: A Kentucky Tale of the Olden Time*, 1893; *A Kentucky Cardinal*, 1895; *Aftermath*, 1896; *Summer in Arcady*, 1896; *The Choir Invisible*, 1897; *Two Gentlemen of Kentucky*, 1899; *Chimney Corner Graduates*, 1900; *The Reign of Law: A Tale of the Kentucky Hemp Fields*, 1900; *The Mettle of the Pasture*, 1903; *The Bride of the Mistletoe*, 1909; *The Doctor's Christmas Eve*, 1910; *The Heroine in Bronze*, 1912; *The Last Christmas Tree*, 1914; *The Sword of Youth*, 1915; *A Cathedral Singer*, 1916; *The Kentucky Warbler*, 1918; *The Emblems of Fidelity: A Comedy in Letters*, 1919; *The Alabaster Box*, 1923; *The Landmark*, 1925.

BIOGRAPHY AND CRITICISM

The best study of Allen is in Grant C. Knight, *James Lane Allen and the Genteel Tradition*, Chapel Hill, N.C., 1935. See also Chap. XXI of Arthur H. Quinn, *American Fiction*, New York, 1936. An earlier narrative account is John W. Townsend, *James Lane Allen*, Louisville, Ky., 1927. Brief studies and appreciations are L. W. Payne, Jr., "The Stories of James Lane Allen," *Sewanee Rev.*, VIII (1900), 45–55; "James Lane Allen: A Study," in John B. Henneman, *Shakespearean and Other Papers*, Sewanee, Tenn., 1911, pp. 115–166; "James Lane Allen," in Harry A. Toulmin, *Social Historians*, Boston, 1911, pp. 101–130; and Grant C. Knight, "Allen's Christmas Trilogy and Its Meaning," *Bookman*, LXVIII (1928), 411–415.

A chronological list of Allen's writings, together with secondary sources, is in Knight's *James Lane Allen* (1935), pp. 288–304.


## MAXWELL ANDERSON
### *b. 1888*

SEPARATE WORKS *

PLAYS: *White Desert* (1923); *What Price Glory* (with Laurence Stallings) (1924), 1926; *First Flight* (with Laurence Stallings) (1925), 1926;

---

\* Dates in parentheses are of production when it differs from publication or when publication has not occurred.

*The Buccaneer* (with Laurence Stallings) (1925), 1926; *Chicot the King* (1926); *Saturday's Children*, 1927; *Gods of the Lightning* (with Harold Hickerson), 1928; *Outside Looking In* (1925), 1928; *Gypsy* (1929); *The Marriage Recipe* (1929); *Elizabeth the Queen*, 1930; *Night over Taos*, 1932; *The Princess Renegade* (1932); *Both Your Houses*, 1933; *Mary of Scotland* (1933), 1934; *Valley Forge*, 1934; *Winterset*, 1935; *The Masque of Kings*, 1936; *The Wingless Victory*, 1936; *High Tor* (1936), 1937; *The Star-Wagon*, 1937; *The Feast of Ortolans*, 1938; *Knickerbocker Holiday*, 1938; *Key Largo*, 1939; *Journey to Jerusalem*, 1940; *Second Overture*, 1940; *Candle in the Wind*, 1941; *The Eve of St. Mark*, 1942; *Storm Operation*, 1944; *Joan of Lorraine* (1946), 1947.

ESSAYS: *The Bases of Artistic Creation*, 1942; *The Essence of Tragedy and Other Footnotes and Papers*, 1939; *Off Broadway*, 1947.

POEMS: *You Who Have Dreams*, 1925.

COLLECTED WORKS

The three plays written in collaboration with Laurence Stallings are published as *Three American Plays*, New York, 1926. *Eleven Verse Plays*, New York, 1940, includes the most important written between 1929 and 1939.

BIOGRAPHY AND CRITICISM

Critical estimates are in Arthur H. Quinn, *A History of the American Drama from the Civil War to the Present Day*, New York, 1936, II, 233-236, 266-271; "Maxwell Anderson," in Eleanor Flexner, *American Playwrights* . . ., New York, 1938, pp. 78-129; and "The Poetic Drama: Maxwell Anderson," in Joseph Wood Krutch, *The American Drama Since 1918* . . ., New York, 1939, pp. 286-318.

Two earlier appreciations are Barrett H. Clark, *Maxwell Anderson: The Man and His Plays*, New York, 1933; and Carl Carmer, "Maxwell Anderson: Poet and Champion," *Theatre Arts Mo.*, XVII (1933), 437-446.

More recent special studies are Edith J. R. Isaacs, "Maxwell Anderson," *English Jour.*, XXV (1936), 795-804; Herbert E. Childs, "Playgoer's Playwright, Maxwell Anderson," *English Jour.*, XXVII (1938), 475-485; Robert C. Healey, "Anderson, Saroyan, Sherwood: New Directions," *Catholic World*, CLII (1940), 174-180; Harold Rosenberg, "Poetry and the Theatre," *Poetry*, LVII (1941), 258-263; Vincent Wall, "Maxwell Anderson: The Last Anarchist," *Sewanee Rev.*, XLIX (1941), 339-369; E. Foster, "Core of Belief: Interpretation of the Plays of Maxwell Anderson," *Sewanee Rev.*, L (1942), 87-100; Allan G. Halline, "Maxwell Anderson's Dramatic Theory," *Amer. Lit.*, XVI (1944), 63-81; Ainslie Harris, "Maxwell Anderson," *Madison Quar.*, IV (1944), 30-44—an analysis of his tragedies; Arthur M. Sampley,

"Theory and Practice in Maxwell Anderson's Poetic Tragedies," *College English*, V (1944), 412–418; H. E. Woodbridge, "Maxwell Anderson," *So. Atl. Quar.*, XLIV (1945), 55–68; and Samuel Kliger, "Hebraic Lore in Maxwell Anderson's *Winterset*," *Amer. Lit.*, XVIII (1946), 219–232.

Montrose J. Moses, ed., *Dramas of Modernism and Their Forerunners*, Boston, 1941, includes a bibliography, pp. 931–933, of contemporary reviews and studies. It is supplemented by the listing in Fred B. Millett, *Contemporary American Authors*, New York, 1940, pp. 219–221.

## SHERWOOD ANDERSON
### *1876–1941*

SEPARATE WORKS

*Windy McPherson's Son*, 1916; *Marching Men*, 1917; *Mid-American Chants*, 1918; *Winesburg, Ohio*, 1919; *Poor White*, 1920; *The Triumph of the Egg*, 1921; *Many Marriages*, 1923; *Horses and Men*, 1923; *A Story Teller's Story*, 1924; *Dark Laughter*, 1925; *The Modern Writer*, 1925; *Sherwood Anderson's Notebook*, 1926; *Tar: A Midwest Childhood*, 1926; *A New Testament*, 1927; *Alice and the Lost Novel*, 1929: *Hello Towns!* 1929; *Nearer the Grass Roots*, 1929; *The American County Fair*, 1930; *Perhaps Women*, 1931; *Beyond Desire*, 1932; *Death in the Woods*, 1933; *No Swank*, 1934; *Puzzled America*, 1935; *Kit Brandon: A Portrait*, 1936; *Plays, Winesburg and Others*, 1937; *Home Town*, 1940; *Sherwood Anderson's Memoirs*, 1942.

REPRINTS

*Winesburg, Ohio* (1919) was reissued in the Modern Library in the year it was first published. *Poor White* (1920) was reprinted in the Modern Library in 1926.

BIOGRAPHY AND CRITICISM

There is no adequate study of Sherwood Anderson. Nathan Bryllion Fagin published *The Phenomenon of Sherwood Anderson: A Study in American Life and Letters*, Baltimore, 1927. Other early appreciations and critical estimates are Harry Hansen, *Midwest Portraits*, New York, 1923, pp. 109–179—a good appraisal of the early writing; Alyse Gregory, "Sherwood Anderson," *Dial*, LXXV (1923), 243–246; Victor F. Calverton, "Sherwood Anderson," *Modern Quar.*, II (1924), 82–118; "Sherwood Anderson," in Paul Rosenfeld, *Port of New York*, New York, 1924, pp. 175–197; "Sherwood Anderson: A Study in Sociological Criticism," in Victor F. Calverton, *The Newer Spirit . . .*, New York, 1925, pp. 52–118—a useful treatment of one important aspect of Anderson's writing; Carl Van Doren, "Sinclair Lewis and Sherwood Anderson: A Study of Two Moralists," *Century Mag.,* CX (1925), 362-369; "Sherwood Anderson's Tales of the New Life," in Stuart P. Sherman, *Critical Woodcuts,* New York, 1926, pp. 5-17; Cleveland B. Chase, *Sherwood Anderson,* New York, 1927; "Sherwood Anderson," in David Karsner, *Sixteen Authors to One,* New York, 1928, pp. 45-66; "Sherwood Anderson, Poet," in Rebecca West, *The Strange Necessity,* London, 1928, pp. 281-290; "Sherwood Anderson," in Thomas K. Whipple, *Spokesmen . . . ,* New York, 1928, pp. 115-138.

More recent studies are Harry Hartwick, *The Foreground of American Fiction,* New York, 1934, pp. 111-150; "Sherwood Anderson," in Harlan Hatcher, *Creating the Modern American Novel,* New York, 1935, pp. 155-171; Robert M. Lovett, "Sherwood Anderson," in Malcolm Cowley, ed., *After the Genteel Tradition,* New York, 1936, pp. 88-99; C. John McCole, *Lucifer at Large,* London, 1937, pp. 125-150; "Sherwood Anderson" in Percy H. Boynton, *America in Contemporary Fiction,* Chicago, 1940, pp. 113-130; Lionel Trilling, "Sherwood Anderson," *Kenyon Rev.,* III (1941), 293-302; "The New Realism: Sherwood Anderson and Sinclair Lewis," in Alfred Kazin, *On Native Grounds . . . ,* New York, 1942, pp. 205-226; Nathan Bryllion Fagin, "Sherwood Anderson," *So. Atl. Quar.,* XLIII (1944), 256-262; and "Anderson: Psychoanalyst by Default," in Frederick J. Hoffman, *Freudianism and the Literary Mind,* Baton Rouge, La., 1945, pp. 230-255.

The three autobiographical volumes of Anderson are *A Story Teller's Story,* New York, 1924; *Tar: A Midwest Childhood,* New York, 1926; and *Sherwood Anderson's Memoirs,* New York, 1942—posthumously published.

Some Anderson manuscripts are deposited in the library of Stanford University.

A bibliographical listing is in Fred B. Millett, *Contemporary American Authors,* New York, 1940, pp. 221-225.

## SHOLEM ASCH
### b. 1880

SEPARATE WORKS IN ENGLISH

*Mottke, the Vagabond,* 1917; *America,* 1918; *The God of Vengeance,* 1918; *Uncle Moses: A Novel,* 1920; *Kiddush Ha-Shem: An Epic of 1648,* 1926; *Sabbatai Zevi,* 1930; *The Mother,* 1930; *Three Cities,* 1933; *Salvation,* 1934; *In the Beginning,* 1935; *The Calf of Paper* (American ed., *The War Goes On*), 1936; *Three Novels: Uncle Moses; Chaim Lederer's Return; Judge*

*Not—*, 1938; *Song of the Valley*, 1939; *The Nazarene*, 1939; *What I Believe*, 1941; *Children of Abraham*, 1942; *The Apostle*, 1943; *East River*, 1946.

*Winter the Sinner*, in *Six Plays of the Yiddish Theatre* . . ., was translated and edited by Isaac Goldberg, Boston, 1916.

COLLECTED WORKS

Much that Asch has written is not available in English translation. His *Works (Gezammelte Shriften)* were collected in Yiddish, Warsaw, 1937, 28 vols.

BIOGRAPHY AND CRITICISM

A useful narrative sketch is the one by Louis Rittenberg in *Universal Jewish Encyclopedia* (1939). Three recent studies are John Cournos, "Three Novelists: Asch, Singer, and Schneour," *Menorah Jour.*, XXV (1937), 81–91; Charles A. Madison, "Sholem Asch," *Poet Lore*, XLVI (1940), 303–337—an extended sketch with critical comments, comparisons, and epitomes of the translated books; and Harry Slochower, "Franz Werfel and Sholom Asch: The Yearning for Status," *Accent*, V (1945), 73–82. An earlier estimate is Herbert S. Gorman's "Yiddish Literature, and the Case of Shalom Asch," *Bookman*, LVII (1923), 394–400.

# JOHN JAMES AUDUBON
## *1780–1851*

SEPARATE WORKS

*The Birds of America from Original Drawings*, 1827–1838; *Ornithological Biography; or, An Account of the Habits of the Birds of the United States of America*, 1831–1839; *A Synopsis of the Birds of America*, 1839; *The Birds of America from Drawings Made in the United States and Their Territories*, 1840–1844; *The Viviparous Quadrupeds of North America*, 1845–1848; *The Quadrupeds of North America*, 1849–1854.

COLLECTED WORKS

Robert Buchanan, ed., *Life and Adventures of Audubon the Naturalist*, London, 1868, in spite of the fact that it is bowdlerized, is an important early collection made from the notes kept by Mrs. Audubon. Mrs. Audubon issued a nearly identical publication: Lucy G. Audubon, ed., *The Life of John James Audubon, the Naturalist*, New York, 1869, with an introduction by James Grant Wilson—often reprinted. The text from two portions of Audubon's journals was edited by Howard Corning: *Journal of John James Audubon*

*Made During His Trip to New Orleans in 1820–1821,* Boston, 1929, with fore-word by Ruthven Deane; and *Journal of John James Audubon Made While Obtaining Subscriptions to His "Birds of America," 1840–1843,* Boston, 1929. John W. Audubon edited *Audubon's Western Journal, 1849–1850 . . . ,* Cleveland, 1906. Howard Corning edited *Letterᶜ of John James Audubon, 1826–1840,* Boston, 1930, 2 vols.

EDITED TEXTS AND REPRINTS

Audubon's narrative skill is well shown in a volume of extracts reprinted from his *Ornithological Biography* (1831–1839) as *Delineations of American Scenery and Character,* New York, 1926, with introduction and brief bibliog-raphy by Francis H. Herrick. The most recent volume of selections is Donald C. Peattie, ed., *Audubon's America: The Narratives and Experiences of John James Audubon,* Boston, 1940.

BIOGRAPHY AND CRITICISM

Audubon has been fortunate in his biographers. The authoritative life is still Francis H. Herrick, *Audubon the Naturalist: A History of His Life and Time,* New York, 1917, 2 vols., a work which later biographers acknowledge for its careful use of source material. The critical study by Constance Rourke, *Audubon,* New York, 1936, is important as a study of the frontier; and Donald C. Peattie, *Singing in the Wilderness: A Salute to John James Audubon,* New York, 1935, is an evaluation of Audubon as a scientific observer.

The first published life is Mrs. Horace St. John, *Audubon: The Naturalist of the New World . . . ,* London, 1856. The study by John Burroughs, *John James Audubon,* Boston, 1902, is appreciative. Other recent lives are Edward A. Muschamp, *Audacious Audubon: The Story of a Great Pioneer, Artist, Naturalist and Man,* New York, 1929; and Stanley C. Arthur, *Audubon: An Intimate Life of the American Woodsman,* New Orleans, 1937.

Other studies and appreciations are Irving T. Richards, "Audubon, Joseph R. Mason, and John Neal," *Amer. Lit.,* VI (1934), 122–140; Mangum Weeks, "On John James Audubon," *So. Atl. Quar.,* XLI (1942), 76–87; Henry L. Savage, "John James Audubon: A Backwoodsman in the Salon," *Princeton Univ. Lib. Chron.,* V (1944), 129–136; "Aububon," in Van Wyck Brooks, *The World of Washington Irving,* New York, 1944, pp. 176–194; Donald A. Shelley, "Audubon to Date," *N.Y. Hist. Soc. Quar.,* XXX (1946), 168–173; and George A. Zabriskie, "The Story of a Priceless Art Treasure: The Origi-nal Water Colors of John James Audubon," *ibid.,* pp. 69–76. Alice J. Taylor, *I Who Should Command All,* New Haven, 1937, reexamines the moot ques-tion of his ancestry and birth.

PRIMARY SOURCES

There is useful source material in Maria R. Audubon, *Audubon and His Journals,* New York, 1897, 2 vols., with zoological notes by Elliott Coues. The first appearance of an autobiographical piece entitled "Myself" was in Maria R. Audubon, "Audubon's Story of His Youth," *Scribner's Mag.,* XIII (1893), 267–287.

The originals of all but two of Audubon's long series of journals were destroyed by members of his family. The chief manuscript depository is the Museum of Comparative Zoology, Harvard University.

BIBLIOGRAPHY

The most complete Audubon bibliography is in Francis H. Herrick's *Audubon* (1917), II, 401–456 (2nd ed., 1938, pp. 401–461). In the same volume is a list of "Familiar Letters," pp. 415–417.

# IRVING BABBITT
## *1865–1933*

WORKS

*Literature and the American College: Essays in Defense of the Humanities,* 1908; *The New Laokoön: An Essay on the Confusion of the Arts,* 1910; *The Masters of Modern French Criticism,* 1912; *Rousseau and Romanticism,* 1919; *Democracy and Leadership,* 1924; *On Being Creative, and Other Essays,* 1932; *Spanish Character, and Other Essays,* 1940.

Though many of Babbitt's scattered articles and studies are gathered into the volumes of essays named above, much of his writing remains uncollected.

BIOGRAPHY AND CRITICISM

Frederick Manchester and Odell Shepard brought together a collection of independent memoirs by thirty-nine contributors to present a portrait of Babbitt in *Irving Babbitt: Man and Teacher,* New York, 1941.

The most significant critical studies of Babbitt, written at the height of the neo-humanist controversy, are T. S. Eliot, "The Humanism of Irving Babbitt," *Forum,* LXXX (1928), 37–44; Bernard Bandler, 2nd, "The Individualism of Irving Babbitt," *Hound and Horn,* III (1929), 57–70; Mary M. Colum, "Literature, Ethics, and the Knights of Good Sense," *Scribner's Mag.,* LXXXVII (1930), 599–608; Edmund Wilson, "Notes on Babbitt and More," *New Republic,* LXII (1930), 115–120; *idem,* "Sophocles, Babbitt, and Freud," *New Republic,* LXV (1930), 68–70; Francis E. McMahon, *The Humanism of Irving Babbitt,* Washington, 1931; James L. Adams, "Humanism and Creation," *Hound and Horn*, VI (1932), 173–196; Alexander P. Cappon, "Irving Babbitt and His Fundamental Thinking," *New Humanist*, VI (1933), 9–13; Frances T. Russell, "The Romanticism of Irving Babbitt," *So. Atl. Quar.*, XXXII (1933), 399–411.

Interest abroad in Babbitt's critical position is demonstrated in Louis J. A. Mercier, *Le Mouvement Humaniste aux Etats-Unis: W. C. Brownell, Irving Babbitt, Paul Elmer More*, Paris, 1928; Christian Richard, *Le Mouvement Humaniste en Amérique et les Courants de Pensée Similaire en France*, Paris, 1934; Folke Leander, *Humanism and Naturalism: A Comparative Study of Ernest Seillière, Irving Babbitt, and Paul Elmer More*, Göteborg, 1937; Viktor Lange and Hermann Boeschenstein, *Kulturkritik und Literaturbetrachtung in Amerika*, Breslau, 1938—containing an analysis of Babbitt's principles. Two early notices by Europeans are Hans Hecht, in *Englische Studien*, LV (1921), 447–457—a review of *Rousseau and Romanticism;* and Lynn H. Hough, "Dr. Babbitt and Vital Control," *Lond. Quar. Rev.*, CXLVII (1927), 1–15.

Recent evaluations are R. P. Blackmur, "Humanism and Symbolic Imagination: Notes on Rereading Irving Babbitt," *Southern Rev.*, VII (1941), 309–325; Wylie Sypher, "Irving Babbitt: A Reappraisal," *New Eng. Quar.*, XIV (1941), 64–76; and "Irving Babbitt," in John P. Pritchard, *Return to the Fountains* . . . , Durham, N.C., 1942, pp. 170–179—the influence of the classics on his thinking evaluated.

Studies chiefly biographical and appreciative are Frank J. Mather, Jr., "Irving Babbitt," *Harv. Grad. Mag.*, XLII (1933), 65–84; Hoffman Nickerson, "Irving Babbitt," *Amer. Rev.*, II (1934), 385–404; Paul E. More, "Irving Babbitt," *Amer. Rev.*, III (1934), 23–40; William F. Giese, "Irving Babbitt, Undergraduate," *Amer. Rev.*, VI (1935), 65–94; Donald MacCampbell, "Irving Babbitt: Some Entirely Personal Impressions," *Sewanee Rev.*, XLIII (1935), 164–174; and three essays in *Amer. Rev.* by G. R. Elliott: "Irving Babbitt as I Knew Him," VIII (1936), 36–60; "T. S. Eliot and Irving Babbitt," VII (1936), 442–454; and "The Religious Dissension of Babbitt and More," IX (1937), 252–265.

BIBLIOGRAPHY

The most complete listing of Babbitt's published writings is by Frederick Manchester and others in his *Spanish Character* . . . , Boston, 1940, pp. 249–259. The same work contains an "Index to the Collected Works of Irving Babbitt," pp. 263–361. Further material is in Fred B. Millett, *Contemporary American Authors*, New York, 1940, pp. 231–234.

# GEORGE BANCROFT
*1800–1891*

### SEPARATE WORKS

*Poems*, 1823; *A History of the United States, from the Discovery of the American Continent*, 1834–1875; *History of the Colonization of the United States*, 1838–1857; *Literary and Historical Miscellanies*, 1855; *The American Revolution*, 1860–1875; *Joseph Reed: A Historical Essay*, 1867; *History of the Formation of the Constitution of the United States of America*, 1882; *A Plea for the Constitution of the United States*, 1886; *Martin Van Buren to the End of His Public Career*, 1889; *History of the Battle of Lake Erie and Miscellaneous Papers*, 1891.

### COLLECTED WORKS

*A History of the United States*, Boston, was completed in 10 vols. in 1875. It was revised to 6 vols. in the next year, and received its last author-revision, New York, 1883–1885, 6 vols.

The first collection of letters was made in Mark A. De Wolfe Howe, *The Life and Letters of George Bancroft*, New York, 1908, 2 vols. Further gatherings appear in an exchange of correspondence between Van Buren and Bancroft (no title) printed in *Proc. Mass. Hist. Soc.*, XLII (1909), 381–442; and in John S. Bassett, "Correspondence of George Bancroft and Jared Sparks, 1823–32," *Smith Coll. Stud. in Hist.*, II (1917), No. 2, pp. 67–143.

### BIOGRAPHY AND CRITICISM

The best critical biography is Russel B. Nye, *George Bancroft: Brahmin Rebel*, New York, 1944. An earlier account is *The Life and Letters* mentioned above.

For Bancroft's part in establishing the Naval Academy at Annapolis, the fullest account is James R. Soley, *Historical Sketch of the United States Naval Academy*, Washington, 1876. Other studies of Bancroft as public servant are given in Thomas H. Hittell, "George Bancroft and His Services to California," in *Papers Calif. Hist. Soc.*, I (1893), pt. 4, 20 pp.; John S. Bassett, *The Middle Group of American Historians*, New York, 1917—useful on Bancroft as politician; and Otto zu Stolberg-Wernigerode, *Germany and the United States During the Era of Bismarck*, Reading, Pa., 1937—on Bancroft as diplomat.

The best study of Bancroft and German culture is "George Bancroft," in Orie W. Long, *Literary Pioneers*, Cambridge, 1936, pp. 108–158. Further material is given in Harold S. Jantz, "German Thought and Literature in New England," *Jour. Eng. and Ger. Philol.*, XLI (1942), 1–46.

Other special studies are Norman H. Dawes and Franklin T. Nichols, "Revaluing Bancroft," *New Eng. Quar.,* VI (1933), 278-293; Michael Kraus, "George Bancroft, 1834-1934," *New Eng. Quar.,* VII (1934), 662-682; Van Wyck Brooks, *The Flowering of New England,* New York, 1936, pp. 111-134.

PRIMARY SOURCES

For Bancroft's relations with Boston and Cambridge society there is material in the correspondence, journals, and biographies of Emerson, Longfellow, and others of the Concord and Cambridge groups. Allan Nevins, ed., *Polk: The Diary of a President, 1845-1849,* New York, 1929, supplies data on Bancroft as a cabinet member. Bancroft's unpublished essay "Of the Liberal Education of Boys" is in the New York Public Library.

The leading collections of Bancroft manuscripts are in the New York Public Library, the library of the Massachusetts Historical Society, and the National Archives. Further material, principally letters, is in the Library of Congress, the Boston Public Library, the Henry E. Huntington Library, and the American Antiquarian Society Library.

BIBLIOGRAPHY

The fullest listing of Bancroft's writings and of works relating to him is in Russel B. Nye, *George Bancroft* (1944), pp. 327-330, 337-340.

## JAMES NELSON BARKER
### *1784-1858*

PLAYS *

*The Spanish Rover,* written 1804—unfinished; *America,* written 1805; *Tears and Smiles* (1807), 1808; *The Embargo; or, What News?* (1808); *The Indian Princess; or, La Belle Sauvage,* 1808; *Marmion; or, The Battle of Flodden Field* (1812), 1816; *The Armourer's Escape; or, Three Years at Nootka Sound* (1817); *How to Try a Lover,* 1817 (acted as *A Court of Love,* 1836); *Superstition; or, The Fanatic Father* (1824), 1826.

*Tears and Smiles* is reprinted in Musser's life of Barker; *The Indian Princess,* in Montrose J. Moses, *Representative Plays by American Dramatists,* New York, 1918, I, 567-628, with an introduction; and *Superstition,* in Arthur H. Quinn, *Representative American Plays,* rev. ed., New York, 1930, pp. 109-140, and in Allan G. Halline, *American Plays,* New York, 1935, pp. 117-152—both with introductions.

* Dates in parentheses are of production when it differs from publication or when publication has not occurred.

BIOGRAPHY AND CRITICISM

A factual biography is Paul H. Musser, *James Nelson Barker, 1784-1858,* Philadelphia, 1929, with special attention to sources. See also "James Nelson Barker and the Native Plays, 1805-1825," in Arthur H. Quinn, *A History of American Drama from the Beginning to the Civil War,* rev. ed., New York, 1943, pp. 136-162.

Barker's manuscripts are in the Library of the Pennsylvania Historical Society, the University of Pennsylvania Library, and the Library Company of Philadelphia. William Dunlap's *A History of the American Theatre,* New York, 1832, II, 308-316, includes a letter from Barker giving an account of his own work.

The fullest bibliography of primary and secondary material is in Musser's life, pp. 211-223.


# JOEL BARLOW
## 1754-1812

WORKS

*The Vision of Columbus,* 1787; *Advice to the Privileged Orders in the Several States of Europe,* 1792-1793; *The Hasty Pudding,* 1796; *The Political Writings of Joel Barlow,* 1796; *Prospectus for a National Institution . . . ,* 1806. *The Columbiad,* 1807, was a final revision of *The Vision of Columbus.*

Theodore A. Zunder edited "Six Letters of Joel Barlow to Oliver Wolcott," *New Eng. Quar.,* II (1929), 475-489. Other gleanings are Ezra K. Maxfield, "A Newly Discovered Letter from Joel Barlow to His Wife, from Algiers," *Amer. Lit.,* IX (1938), 442-449—supplemented by M. Ray Adams, in *Amer. Lit.,* X (1938), 224-227; and Theodore A. Zunder, "A New Barlow Poem," *Amer. Lit.,* XI (1939), 206-209.

BIOGRAPHY AND CRITICISM

Barlow's early career is well treated in Theodore A. Zunder, *The Early Days of Joel Barlow, a Connecticut Wit: His Life and Works from 1754 to 1787,* New Haven, 1934. New material is added in Leon Howard, *The Connecticut Wits,* Chicago, 1943, pp. 133-165; 271-341, especially for Barlow's later years. An extensive review of Barlow's services is "Citizen Barlow of the Republic of the World," in John Dos Passos, *The Ground We Stand On,* New York, 1941, pp. 256-380.

Three early studies are "The Literary Strivings of Mr. Joel Barlow," in Moses C. Tyler, *Three Men of Letters,* New York, 1895, pp. 129-180; Charles

B. Todd, *Life and Letters of Joel Barlow: Poet, Statesman, Philosopher* . . . , New York, 1886—still useful for material quoted from primary sources; and A. C. Baldwin, "Joel Barlow," *New Englander*, XXXII (1873), 413–437.

Significant contemporary estimates of Barlow are "Joel Barlow" in *Public Characters of 1806*, London, 1806, pp. 152–180; P. S. Du Pont de Nemours, "Notice sur la vie de M. Barlow," *Mercure de France*, Apr. 10, 1813; and Konrad E. Oelsner, *Notice sur la Vie et les Ecrits de M. Joel Barlow*, Paris, 1813.

Special studies of Barlow's career are Vernon P. Squires, "Joel Barlow: Patriot, Democrat, and Man of Letters," *Quar. Jour. Univ. No. Dakota*, IX (1919), 299–308; Adolph B. Benson, "An American Poet-Enemy of Gustavus III of Sweden," *Scand. Stud. and Notes*, X (1928), 104–110; Theodore A. Zunder, "Joel Barlow and George Washington," *Mod. Lang. Notes*, XLIV (1929), 254–256; Victor C. Miller, *Joel Barlow: Revolutionist, London, 1791–92*, Hamburg, 1932; Maria dell' Isola, "Joel Barlow: Précurseur de la Société des Nations," *Rev. de Litt. Comp.*, Avril-Juin, 1934, pp. 283–296; Theodore A. Zunder, "Notes on the Friendship of Joel Barlow and Tom Paine," *Amer. Book Coll.*, VI (1935), 96–99; M. Ray Adams, "Joel Barlow, Political Romanticist," *Amer. Lit.*, IX (1937), 113–152; Leon Howard, "Joel Barlow and Napoleon," *Hunt. Lib. Quar.*, II (1938), 37–52; Ezra K. Maxfield, "The Tom Barlow Manuscript of the *Columbiad*," *New Eng. Quar.*, XI (1938), 834–842; Percy H. Boynton, "Joel Barlow Advises the Privileged Orders," *New Eng. Quar.*, XII (1939), 477–499; Dixon Wecter, "Joel Barlow and the Sugar Beets," *Colorado Mag.*, XVIII (1941), 179–181; Harry R. Warfel, "Charles Brockden Brown's First Poem," *Amer. Notes & Queries*, II (1941), 19–20; and Joseph Dorfman, "Joel Barlow: Trafficker in Trade and Letters," *Pol. Sci. Quar.*, LIX (1944), 83–100.

PRIMARY SOURCES

The most extensive as well as most important collection of Barlow manuscripts is that in the Harvard College Library, including his manuscript diary, and letters to and from eminent citizens. Other collections are in the Pequot Library of Southport, Conn.; the Library of Congress; and the library of the Connecticut Historical Society.

BIBLIOGRAPHY

A full checklist of the writings of Barlow, together with a description of extant manuscripts, is in Leon Howard, *The Connecticut Wits*, Chicago, 1943, pp. 421–424. Useful for secondary items is the checklist in Theodore A. Zunder, *The Early Days of Joel Barlow*, New Haven, 1934, pp. 308–311. Reference to printed archives in Howard's work is useful especially for the years of Barlow's residence abroad.

## PHILIP BARRY
### b. 1896

PLAYS *

You and I, 1923; The Youngest (1924), 1925; In a Garden (1925), 1926; White Wings (1926), 1927; John (1927), 1929; Paris Bound (1927), 1929; Cock Robin (with Elmer Rice) (1928), 1929; Holiday (1928), 1929; Hotel Universe, 1930; Tomorrow and Tomorrow, 1931; The Animal Kingdom, 1932; The Joyous Season, 1934; Bright Star (1935); Spring Dance, 1936; Here Come the Clowns (1938), 1939; The Philadelphia Story (1939); Liberty Jones (1941); Without Love (1943).

Here Come the Clowns was novelized as War in Heaven, 1938.

Plays reprinted in anthologies include Paris Bound, in Arthur H. Quinn, ed., Representative American Plays, New York, rev. ed., 1930; and You and I, in Allan G. Halline, ed., American Plays, New York, 1935. Both include critical estimates.

The fullest bio-bibliographical account is Fred B. Millett, Contemporary American Authors, New York, 1940, pp. 235–236.

## JOHN AND WILLIAM BARTRAM
### 1699–1777          1739–1823

SEPARATE WORKS

(John Bartram) Observations on the Inhabitants, Climate, Soil, Rivers . . . Made by Mr. John Bartram in His Travels from Pensilvania to . . . Lake Ontario, 1751; (William Bartram) Travels Through North and South Carolina, Georgia, East and West Florida, 1791.

COLLECTED WORKS

John Bartram's Observations, London, 1751, was reprinted, Geneva, N.Y., 1895. Further material is in William Stork, A Description of East Florida, with a Journal Kept by John Bartram . . . , 3rd ed., London, 1769; and in Francis Harper, ed., "John Bartram: Diary of a Journey Through the Carolinas, Georgia, and Florida . . . ," Trans. Amer. Philos. Soc., XXXIII (1944),

* Dates in parentheses are of production when it differs from publication or when publication has not occurred.

1–120—the authoritative text, with extensive annotations. Extracts from the *Journal* publ. by Stork are printed in the *Annual Report* of the Smithsonian Inst., 1875, pp. 393 ff.

William Bartram's "Observations on the Creek and Cherokee Indians, 1789," was publ. in *Trans. Amer. Ethnol. Soc.*, III (1853), 1–81. Mark Van Doren edited the *Travels* (1791), New York, 1928, in an edition reprinted in 1940 with an introduction by John L. Lowes. The authoritative text of the *Travels*, ed. from the MSS, is that of Francis Harper, in *Trans. Amer. Philos. Soc.*, XXXIII (1944), 121–242.

### BIOGRAPHY AND CRITICISM

A brief narrative account of the Bartrams is Ernest Earnest, *John and William Bartram: Botanists and Explorers* . . . , Philadelphia, 1940. Though not wholly accurate, William Darlington's *Memorials of John Bartram and Humphry Marshall* . . . , Philadelphia, 1849, is important for its printing of correspondence between John Bartram and Peter Collinson. The best brief account of John Bartram is that of Donald C. Peattie in *Dict. Amer. Biog.* (1929).

A study of William Bartram's work and literary influence is Nathan Bryllion Fagin, *William Bartram: Interpreter of the American Landscape*, Baltimore, 1933. An early recognition of William Bartram's literary art and influence is Ernest H. Coleridge, "Coleridge, Wordsworth, and the American Botanist, William Bartram," *Trans. Royal Soc. of Lit.*, XXVII (1906), 69–92. A good brief account is that of Lane Cooper in *Dict. Amer. Biog.* (1929). See also John L. Lowes, *The Road to Xanadu*, Boston, 1927.

### PRIMARY SOURCES

The great bulk of the source material relating to the Bartrams is unpublished, and deserves to be assembled. The chief manuscript depository is the Historical Society of Pennsylvania. Other collections in Philadelphia are in the Bartram Memorial Library at the University of Pennsylvania, the library of the Academy of Natural Sciences, and the archives of the American Philosophical Society. Further papers are in the possession of the Royal Society of London.

### BIBLIOGRAPHY

A complete checklist of the published writings of William Bartram is in the *Bartonia* (Philadelphia Botanical Club), for Dec. 31, 1931. A checklist especially useful for secondary material is in N. B. Fagin, *William Bartram* (1933), pp. 205–215.

# HENRY WARD BEECHER
*1813–1887*

SEPARATE AND COLLECTED WORKS

*Seven Lectures to Young Men,* 1844; *Star Papers; or, Experiences of Art and Nature,* 1855 (contributions to the *Independent*); *New Star Papers; or, Views and Experiences of Religious Subjects,* 1859 (further contributions to the *Independent*); *Plain and Pleasant Talk About Fruits, Flowers, and Farming,* 1859; *Eyes and Ears,* 1862 (contributions to the New York *Ledger*); *Freedom and War,* 1863 (discourses on the topics of the times); *Norwood; or, Village Life in New England,* 1867; *Sermons,* 1869, 2 vols.; *The Life of Jesus, the Christ,* 1870—part I only published; *Lecture Room Talks,* New York, 1872—compiled by Truman J. Ellinwood; *Yale Lectures on Preaching,* 1872; *ibid., Second Series,* 1873; *ibid., Third Series,* 1874; *Evolution and Religion,* 1885, 2 vols.; *Patriotic Addresses in America and England,* 1887. Newell D. Hillis edited *Lectures and Orations by Henry Ward Beecher,* New York, 1913.

BIOGRAPHY AND CRITICISM

Many biographies of Beecher have been published, but none is thoroughly satisfactory. The latest is Paxton Hibben, *Henry Ward Beecher: An American Portrait,* New York, 1927, based on good sources with new material, but sharply critical of Beecher. Lyman Abbott's *Henry Ward Beecher* (1903) is sympathetic but discriminating. The sketch in *Dict. Amer. Biog.* (1929) is written by Harris B. Starr. See also Lyman B. Stowe, *Saints, Sinners, and Beechers,* Indianapolis, 1934.

Of the many earlier laudatory biographies, the best include Lyman Abbott and S. B. Halliday, *Henry Ward Beecher: A Sketch of His Career . . . ,* Hartford, Conn., 1887; and William C. Beecher and Samuel Scoville, *A Biography of Rev. Henry Ward Beecher,* New York, 1888.

A good monograph on Beecher as a man of letters is Lionel G. Crocker, *Henry Ward Beecher's Art of Preaching,* Chicago, 1934. Crocker also contributed the chapter on Beecher in William N. Brigance, ed., *A History and Criticism of American Public Address,* New York, 1943, I, 265–293. "Henry Ward Beecher," in Lewis O. Brastow, *Representative Modern Preachers,* New York, 1904, pp. 98–142, is an analysis of Beecher's qualities as a preacher.

Reports on the Tilton-Beecher case will be found in *Theodore Tilton vs. Henry Ward Beecher . . . Verbatim Report by the Official Stenographer,* New York, 1875, 3 vols.; and Austin Abbott, *Official Report of the Trial of Henry Ward Beecher,* New York, 1875, 2 vols.

Much autobiographical material will be found in the sermons and addresses. Truman J. Ellinwood edited *Autobiographical Reminiscences of Henry Ward Beecher,* New York, 1898.

A list of Beecher's writings, compiled by W. E. Davenport, is in Lyman Abbott's *Henry Ward Beecher* (1903), pp. xvii–xxxviii. Further items are listed in Crocker, pp. 132–138.


# S(AMUEL) N(ATHANIEL) BEHRMAN
## *b. 1893*

PLAYS *

*Bedside Manners* (with Kenyon Nicholson), 1924; *A Night's Work* (with Kenyon Nicholson), 1926; *The Second Man,* 1927; *Meteor* (1929), 1930; *Brief Moment,* 1931; *Biography* (1932), 1933; *Three Plays . . . : Serena Blandish; Meteor; The Second Man,* 1934; *Rain from Heaven* (1934), 1935; *End of Summer,* 1936; *Wine of Choice, 1938; No Time for Comedy,* 1939; *The Talley Method,* 1941; *The Pirate,* 1943.

Behrman also has made adaptations of other plays and written motion picture scripts.

BIOGRAPHY AND CRITICISM

Significant criticism of Behrman is Joseph W. Krutch, *The American Drama Since 1918: An Informal History,* New York, 1939, pp. 180–205. See also Eleanor Flexner, *American Playwrights: 1918–1938,* New York, 1938, pp. 59–77; Burns Mantle, *Contemporary American Playwrights,* New York, 1938, pp. 108–115; and Arthur H. Quinn, *A History of the American Drama from the Civil War to the Present Day,* rev. ed., New York, 1936, II, 291–294.

A bio-bibliography is in Fred B. Millett, *Contemporary American Authors,* New York, 1940, pp. 244–245.


# EDWARD BELLAMY
## *1850–1898*

SEPARATE WORKS

*Six to One: A Nantucket Idyl,* 1878; *Dr. Heidenhoff's Process,* 1880; *Miss Ludington's Sister: A Romance of Immortality,* 1884; *Looking Backward:*

---

* Dates in parentheses are of production when it differs from publication or when publication has not occurred.

*2000–1887*, 1888; *Equality*, 1897; *The Blindman's World and Other Stories*, 1898; *The Duke of Stockbridge: A Romance of Shays' Rebellion*, 1900; *The Religion of Solidarity*, 1940.

EDITED TEXTS AND REPRINTS

*Looking Backward* was published in the Modern Library, New York, 1942, with an introduction by Heywood Broun; and in University Classics, Chicago, 1943, ed. by Frederic R. White. It was published in London, 1945. Earlier issues are a "Memorial Edition," Boston (1898), 1917, and an edition in the Riverside Lib., Boston, 1931, both with an introduction by Sylvester Baxter. *Equality*, the sequel to *Looking Backward*, was reprinted, New York, 1933. *The Religion of Solidarity* was first published, Yellow Springs, Ohio, 1940, edited by Arthur E. Morgan.

Reprints of articles have been gathered in *Edward Bellamy Speaks Again: Articles, Public Addresses, Letters*, Kansas City, Mo., 1937, with an introd. by R. Lester McBride. *Talks on Nationalism*, Chicago, 1938, is made up of articles first published in the *New Nation*, 1891–1893.

BIOGRAPHY AND CRITICISM

The first biography of Bellamy is Arthur E. Morgan, *Edward Bellamy*, New York, 1944, a documented study. Excerpts from Bellamy's writing, analyzed to emphasize his social philosophy, comprise Arthur E. Morgan, *The Philosophy of Edward Bellamy*, New York, 1945. See also William D. Howells, "Edward Bellamy," *Atl. Mo.*, LXXXII (1898), 253–256.

Special studies are Robert L. Shurter, "The Literary Work of Edward Bellamy," *Amer. Lit.*, V (1933), 229–234; "Edward Bellamy: Religion in Utopia," in James Dombrowski, *The Early Days of Christian Socialism in America*, New York, 1936, pp. 84–95; John H. Franklin, "Edward Bellamy and the Nationalist Movement," *New Eng. Quar.*, XI (1938), 739–772; Robert L. Shurter, "The Writing of *Looking Backward*," *So. Atl. Quar.*, XXXVIII (1939), 255–261; "Edward Bellamy," in Walter F. Taylor, *The Economic Novel in America*, Chapel Hill, N.C., 1942, pp. 184–213; Charles A. Madison, "Edward Bellamy, Social Dreamer," *New Eng. Quar.*, XV (1942), 444–466; Elizabeth Sadler, "One Book's Influence: Edward Bellamy's *Looking Backward*," *New Eng. Quar.*, XVII (1944), 530–555; and Albert W. Levi, "Edward Bellamy: Utopian," *Ethics*, LV (1945), 131–144.

Useful as background studies are Allyn B. Forbes, "The Literary Quest for Utopia, 1880–1900," *Social Forces*, VI (1927), 179–189; Vernon L. Parrington, *Main Currents in American Thought*, New York, III (1930), 302–315; and "Minority Report of the Novelists," in John Chamberlain, *Farewell to Reform* . . ., New York, 1932.

The principal manuscript depository is the Harvard College Library. A bibliographical listing is in Arthur E. Morgan, *Edward Bellamy* (1944), pp. 421–439.

# STEPHEN VINCENT BENÉT
## 1898–1943

SEPARATE WORKS

*Five Men and Pompey*, 1915; *The Drug-Shop; or, Endymion in Edmonstoun*, 1917; *Young Adventure*, 1918; *Heavens and Earth*, 1920; *The Beginning of Wisdom*, 1921; *Young People's Pride*, 1922; *Ballad of William Sycamore, 1790–1880*, 1923; *Jean Huguenot*, 1923; *King David*, 1923; *Tiger Joy*, 1925; *Spanish Bayonet*, 1926; *John Brown's Body*, 1928; *The Barefoot Saint*, 1929; *The Litter of the Rose Leaves*, 1930; *A Book of Americans* (with Rosemary Benét), 1933; *James Shore's Daughter*, 1934; *Burning City*, 1936; *Thirteen O'Clock*, 1937; *The Devil and Daniel Webster*, 1937; *The Headless Horseman: An Operetta in One Act*, 1937; *Johnny Pye and the Fool Killer*, 1938; *Tales Before Midnight*, 1939; *The Ballad of the Duke's Mercy*, 1939; *Nightmare at Noon*, 1940; *Listen to the People*, 1941; *A Summons to the Free*, 1941; *They Burned the Books*, 1942; *America*, 1944; *Prayer: A Child Is Born*, 1944; *Western Star*, 1945; *The Last Circle*, 1946.

*Western Star*, complete in itself at the time of the author's death, is the first section of a projected narrative poem covering America's history.

COLLECTED WORKS AND REPRINTS

*Ballads and Poems, 1915–1930*, Garden City, N.Y., 1931, is a volume of selections taken mainly from earlier published works. *We Stand United, and Other Radio Scripts*, New York, 1945, is a posthumous collection. Two other gatherings are *Selected Works of Stephen Vincent Benét*, New York, 1942, 2 vols.; and *Twenty-five Short Stories*, Garden City, N.Y., 1943. Mabel A. Bessey edited and annotated *John Brown's Body*, New York, 1941.

BIOGRAPHY AND CRITICISM

Critical estimates of Benét are Louis Untermeyer, *American Poetry Since 1900*, New York, 1923, pp. 242–246; Robert M. Lovett, "The American Conflict," *New Repub.*, LVI (1928), 51–52; Harriet Monroe, "A Cinema Epic," *Poetry*, XXXIII (1928), 91–96; Alfred Kreymborg, *Our Singing Strength*, New York, 1929, pp. 607–611; Sidney R. Daniels, "A Saga of the American Civil War," *Contemp. Rev.*, CXLVI (1934), 466–471; Morton D. Zabel, "The American Grain," *Poetry*, XLVIII (1936), 276–282; Christopher La Farge,

"The Narrative Poetry of Stephen Vincent Benét," *Sat. Rev. Lit.*, XXVII (Aug. 5, 1944), 106–108; and Paul L. Wiley, "The Phaeton Symbol in *John Brown's Body*," *Amer. Lit.*, XVII (1945), 231–242.

A symposium by ten contemporaries who knew Benét is "As We Remember Him," *Sat. Rev. Lit.*, XXVI (Mar. 27, 1943), 7–11.

The most recent bibliography is that compiled by Frances Cheney, in Allen Tate, *Sixty American Poets, 1896–1944*, Washington, 1945, pp. 11–16, with location of copies. See also William R. Benét and John Farrar, *Stephen Vincent Benét . . .*, New York, 1943, pp. 37–39; and Jacob Blanck, *Merle Johnson's American First Editions*, rev. ed., New York, 1942. Material by and about Benét is listed in Fred B. Millett, *Contemporary American Authors*, New York, 1940, pp. 246–249. Manuscripts are in the Yale University Library.


## AMBROSE (GWINNETT) BIERCE
### *1842–1914?*

### SEPARATE WORKS

*The Fiend's Delight*, 1872; *Nuggets and Dust*, 1872; *Cobwebs from an Empty Skull*, 1873; *The Dance of Death*, 1877; *Tales of Soldiers and Civilians*, 1891; *The Monk and the Hangman's Daughter* (with G. A. Danziger), 1892; *Black Beetles in Amber*, 1892; *Can Such Things Be?* 1893; *Fantastic Fables*, 1899; *Shapes of Clay*, 1903; *The Cynic's Word Book*, 1906; *The Shadow on the Dial*, 1909; *Write It Right*, 1909; *Battle Sketches*, 1930.

### COLLECTED WORKS

*Collected Works of Ambrose Bierce*, Washington and New York, 1909–1912, 12 vols., was published by Walter Neale. The *Prospectus* contains relevant biographical material.

The letters have been published as follows: Bertha C. Pope, ed., *The Letters of Ambrose Bierce*, San Francisco, 1921; S. Loveman, ed., *Twenty-one Letters of Ambrose Bierce*, Cleveland, 1922; "A Collection of Bierce Letters," *Univ. Calif. Chron.*, XXXIV (1932), 30–48; and Stanley T. Williams, ed., "Ambrose Bierce and Bret Harte," *Amer. Lit.*, XVII (1945), 179–180—a letter to Harte.

### EDITED TEXTS AND REPRINTS

*Tales of Soldiers and Civilians* (San Francisco, 1891) was printed in New York under the title *In the Midst of Life* (1898), and reprinted, with omissions and additions, in a new edition (1918). It was published under the latter title, with an introduction by George Sterling, in the Modern Library (1927).

*The Monk and the Hangman's Daughter* (1892) was reprinted with *Fantastic Fables* (1899) in 1926, in Boni's American Library. For details of the controversy over authorship of the story, see Frank Monaghan, "Ambrose Bierce and the Authorship of *The Monk and the Hangman's Daughter*," *Amer. Lit.*, II (1931), 337-349. *Can Such Things Be?* (1893) was reprinted in Boni's Amer. Lib., New York, 1906. *The Cynic's Word Book* (1906) was reprinted as *The Devil's Dictionary* (1911). *The Shadow on the Dial* (1909), a collection of newspaper articles, mainly political, was edited with an introduction by S. O. Howes and reprinted as the eleventh volume of the collected works. Specimens of Bierce's work as a newspaper paragrapher appear in Carroll D. Hall, ed., *Selections from "Prattle,"* Book Club of California: California Literary Pamphlets, No. 3 (1936). *Ten Tales*, London, 1925, has an interesting introduction by A. J. A. Symons. Clifton Fadiman edited *The Collected Writings of Ambrose Bierce*, New York, 1946 (810 pp.).

BIOGRAPHY AND CRITICISM

The best rounded biographical account is Carey McWilliams, *Ambrose Bierce: A Biography*, New York, 1929. A critical monograph is C. Hartley Grattan, *Bitter Bierce: A Mystery of American Letters*, New York, 1929. The pioneer appreciation is Vincent Starrett, *Ambrose Bierce*, Chicago, 1920. Walter Neale, the editor of Bierce's *Collected Works*, published *The Life of Ambrose Bierce*, New York, 1929. The most recent account is Joseph Noel, *Footloose in Arcadia; A Personal Record of Jack London, George Sterling, Ambrose Bierce*, New York, 1940. Personal reminiscences of Bierce are George Sterling, "The Shadow Maker," *Amer. Mercury*, VI (1925), 10-19; Franklin Walker, *Ambrose Bierce, the Wickedest Man in San Francisco*, 1941—anecdotes, with a replica of Bierce's paper, *The Wasp;* and *idem, San Francisco's Literary Frontier*, New York, 1939.

Two critical estimates of Bierce are "The Letters of Ambrose Bierce," in Van Wyck Brooks, *Emerson and Others*, New York, 1927, pp. 147-157; and "Ambrose Bierce," in Percy H. Boynton, *More Contemporary Americans*, Chicago, 1927, pp. 75-94.

Other studies are Adolphe de Castro, *Portrait of Ambrose Bierce*, New York, 1929; Leroy J. Nations, "Ambrose Bierce: The Gray Wolf of American Letters," *So. Atl. Quar.*, XXV (1926), 253-268; Napier Wilt, "Ambrose Bierce and the Civil War," *Amer. Lit.*, I (1929), 260-285; Arthur M. Miller, "The Influence of Edgar Allan Poe on Ambrose Bierce," *Amer. Lit.*, IV (1932), 130-150; Carroll D. Hall, *Bierce and the Poe Hoax*, San Francisco, 1934; George Snell, "Poe Redivivus," *Arizona Quar.*, I (1945), No. 2, 49-57; and Clifton Fadiman, "Portrait of a Misanthrope," *Sat. Rev. Lit.*, XXIX (Oct. 12, 1946), 11-13, 61-62.

PRIMARY SOURCES

The chief depository of Bierce manuscripts is the Henry E. Huntington Library—22 vols. of material, including some 360 letters. Other collections are in the libraries of Stanford University and the University of Southern California.

BIBLIOGRAPHY

Vincent Starrett published *A Bibliography of the Writings of Ambrose Bierce*, Philadelphia, 1929. Another, much fuller listing, including a full record of Bierce's published articles, is Joseph Gaer, ed., *Ambrose Bierce*, in Monograph No. 4 of *Calif. Lit. Research Project* (1935).

# ROBERT MONTGOMERY BIRD
## *1806–1854*

SEPARATE WORKS *

*Calavar; or, The Knight of the Conquest*, 1834; *The Infidel; or, The Fall of Mexico*, 1835; *The Hawks of Hawk-Hollow*, 1835; *Sheppard Lee*, 1836; *Nick of the Woods*, 1837; *Peter Pilgrim; or, A Rambler's Recollections*, 1838; *The Adventures of Robin Day*, 1839; *A Broker of Bogota* (1834), 1917; *Pelopidas*, 1919; *The Gladiator* (1831), 1919; *Oralloossa* (1832), 1919; *The City Looking Glass: A Philadelphia Comedy* (written 1828), 1933; *The Cowled Lover* (written 1827), 1941; *Caridorf; or, The Avenger* (written 1827), 1941; *News of the Night; or, A Trip to Niagara* (written *ca.* 1827), 1941; *'Twas All for the Best; or, 'Tis All a Notion* (written 1827), 1941.

EDITED TEXTS AND REPRINTS

*A Broker of Bogota* was first published in Arthur H. Quinn, *Representative American Plays*, New York, 1917, and was reprinted in Clement E. Foust's *Life* (1919). *Pelopidas, The Gladiator*, and *Oralloossa* were first published in Foust's *Life*. Arthur H. Quinn first published *The City Looking Glass*, New York, 1933, ed. with an introduction. The four most recently published plays, here printed for the first time, were ed. by Edward H. O'Neill in *The Cowled Lover, and Other Plays*, Princeton, 1941, Vol. XII of *America's Lost Plays. The Gladiator* was reprinted in Allan G. Halline, *American Plays*, New York, 1935.

The best modern text of *Nick of the Woods; or, The Jibbenainosay: A Tale of Kentucky*, is that edited by Cecil B. Williams, New York, 1939 (Amer.

* For plays, dates in parentheses are of production unless otherwise stated.

Fiction Ser.), with introd., chronol., and bibl. There is also an edition, New York, 1928.

## BIOGRAPHY AND CRITICISM

Clement E. Foust, *The Life and Dramatic Works of Robert Montgomery Bird,* New York, 1919, is documented and authoritative. The best brief sketch is that of Arthur H. Quinn, in *Dict. Amer. Biog.* (1929). A standard estimate of Bird as dramatist is "Robert Montgomery Bird and the Rise of the Romantic Play, 1825–1850," in Arthur H. Quinn, *A History of the American Drama from the Beginning to the Civil War,* rev. ed., New York, 1943, pp. 220–268.

The introduction in Williams's ed. of *Nick of the Woods* (1939) furnishes the best criticism of Bird as a novelist.

## PRIMARY SOURCES

C. Seymour Thompson edited the "Life of Robert Montgomery Bird: Written by His Wife, Mary Mayer Bird, Edited from Her Manuscript . . . ," *Univ. Pa. Lib. Chron.,* XII (1944) and XIII (1945), in five installments, with selections from Bird's correspondence.

Among contemporary memoirs and biographies significant as source material are James Rees, *The Dramatic Authors of America,* Philadelphia, 1845; Francis C. Wemyss, *Twenty-six Years of the Life of an Actor and Manager,* New York, 1847, 2 vols.; and William R. Alger, *The Life of Edwin Forrest,* Philadelphia, 1877, 2 vols. For others, see the listing in Foust's *Life* (1919), pp. 161–167.

The chief manuscript depository is in the Library of the University of Pennsylvania. It consists of manuscripts of plays, poems, and biographical material, including the manuscript life of Bird recently edited by Thompson.

## BIBLIOGRAPHY

The bibliographical listing in Foust's *Life* (1919), pp. 161–167, includes Bird's contributions to magazines, and is especially useful for references to published items, both primary and secondary. The listing in *Camb. Hist. Amer. Lit.* is in Vol. I (1917), 493–494. The most recent bibliography is in Allan G. Halline, *American Plays* (1935), pp. 754–755, and lists unpublished as well as published plays.

# GEORGE HENRY BOKER
*1823–1890*

SEPARATE WORKS *

*The Lesson of Life and Other Poems*, 1848; *Calaynos: A Tragedy* (1849), 1848; *Anne Boleyn: A Tragedy*, 1850; *The Podesta's Daughter and Other Poems*, 1852; *The Betrothal* (written 1850), 1856; *The World a Mask* (1851), 1856; *Leonor de Guzman* (1853), 1856; *The Widow's Marriage* (1852), 1856; *Francesca da Rimini* (1855), 1856; *The Bankrupt* (1855); *Poems of the War*, 1864; *Königsmark: The Legend of the Hounds and Other Poems*, 1869; *The Book of the Dead: Poems* (written *ca.* 1858–1860), 1882; *Nydia* (written 1885), 1929; *Glaucus* (written *ca.* 1885), 1940.

COLLECTIONS, EDITED TEXTS AND REPRINTS

An edition of *Plays and Poems*, Boston, 1856, 2 vols., in addition to the poems, includes the following plays: *Calaynos, Anne Boleyn, Leonor de Guzman, Francesca da Rimini, The Betrothal, The Widow's Marriage*, the last four here published for the first time.

Leigh Hunt and S. Adams Lee edited *The Book of the Sonnet*, London, 1867, 2 vols., which included a few of Boker's sonnets in Vol. II, and an essay, "The American Sonnet," I, 95–131, which Boker helped Lee to write. The greatest number of Boker's sonnets, recently recovered in manuscript, were first published by Edward Sculley Bradley, ed., *Sonnets: A Sequence on Profane Love*, Philadelphia, 1929. Modern reprints of *Francesca da Rimini* are included in Tremaine McDowell, ed., *The Romantic Triumph, 1830–1860*, New York, 1933, pp. 636–699; and in Allan G. Halline, ed., *American Plays*, New York, 1935, pp. 273–332. Sculley Bradley edited *Glaucus and Other Plays*, Princeton, 1940, with introduction and notes. The volume includes, in addition to the title play, here first published, *The World a Mask* and *The Bankrupt*.

There is no collection of Boker's letters. A few gleanings are in Jay B. Hubbell, ed., "George Henry Boker, Paul Hamilton Hayne, and Charles Warren Stoddard: Some Unpublished Letters," *Amer. Lit.*, V (1933), 146–165; and *idem*, "Five Letters from George Henry Boker to William Gilmore Simms," *Pa. Mag. Hist. and Biog.*, LXIII (1939), 66–71.

BIOGRAPHY AND CRITICISM

The only full-length biography is Edward Sculley Bradley, *George Henry Boker: Poet and Patriot*, Philadelphia, 1927, authoritative and fully docu-

---

* Dates in parentheses are of production when it differs from publication or when publication has not occurred.

mented. The best brief account is that by Arthur H. Quinn in *Dict. Amer. Biog.* (1929). An early critical estimate of Boker as playwright is Quinn's "The Dramas of George Henry Boker," *PMLA*, XXXII (1917), 233–266. Quinn also treats of Boker at some length in *A History of the American Drama from the Beginning to the Civil War*, rev. ed., New York, 1943, pp. 337–367. Another earlier estimate is Joseph Wood Krutch, "George Henry Boker, a Little Known American Dramatist," *Sewanee Rev.*, XXV (1917), 457–468.

Special studies are Edward Sculley Bradley, "A Newly Discovered American Sonnet Sequence," *PMLA*, XL (1925), 910–920; Richmond C. Beatty, "Bayard Taylor and George H. Boker," *Amer. Lit.*, VI (1934), 316–327; Sculley Bradley, "George Henry Boker and Angie Hicks," *Amer. Lit.*, VIII (1936), 258–265. Studies of individual plays are Bradley's introduction to *Glaucus and Other Plays* (1940); Gertrude Urban, "Paolo and Francesca in History and Literature," *Critic*, XL (1902), 425–438; and J. C. Metcalf, "An Old Romantic Triangle: Francesca da Rimini in Three Dramas," *Sewanee Rev.*, XXIX (1921), 45–58.

PRIMARY SOURCES

Source material on Boker as a man of letters is found in the memoirs and biographies of Bayard Taylor, Edmund C. Stedman, Charles G. Leland, and Robert Montgomery Bird. A large share of his manuscripts is in the Princeton University Library. The Boker-Taylor correspondence is in the Cornell University Library. Other material is in the Henry E. Huntington Library and the Duke University Library.

BIBLIOGRAPHY

A chronological list of Boker's writings and of biographical and critical material is in Edward Sculley Bradley, *George Henry Boker: Poet and Patriot*, Philadelphia, 1927, pp. 343–355.

## RANDOLPH (SILLIMAN) BOURNE
### *1886–1918*

SEPARATE WORKS

*Youth and Life*, 1913; *The Gary Schools*, 1916; *Towards an Enduring Peace* (with others), 1916; *Education and Living*, 1917.

*Untimely Papers*, New York, 1919, were edited by James Oppenheim; and *History of a Literary Radical, and Other Essays*, New York, 1920, was edited with an introduction by Van Wyck Brooks.

COLLECTED WORKS

Three collections of letters have been published in *Twice a Year:* "Randolph Bourne: Some Pre-War Letters, 1912–1914," No. 2 (1939), 79–102; "Randolph Bourne: Letters, 1913–1914," Nos. 5–6 (1940–1941), 79–80, followed by "Diary for 1901," pp. 89–98; and "Randolph Bourne: Letters, 1913–1914," No. 7 (1941), 76–90.

BIOGRAPHY AND CRITICISM

A documented critical study is Louis Filler, *Randolph Bourne*, Washington, 1943. The sketch in *Dict. Amer. Biog.* (1929) is by Ernest S. Bates. A useful study of Bourne's intellectual development is Max Lerner, "Randolph Bourne and Two Generations," *Twice a Year*, Nos. 5 and 6 (1940–1941), 54–78. Two other appreciations are "Randolph Bourne," in Van Wyck Brooks. *Emerson and Others*, New York, 1927, pp. 121–145; and Paul Rosenfeld. "Randolph Bourne," *Dial*, LXXV (1923), 545–560.

The fullest bibliography is in Filler's *Randolph Bourne* (1943), pp 152–155.

# HJALMAR HJORTH BOYESEN
## *1848–1895*

SEPARATE WORKS IN ENGLISH

*Gunnar*, 1874; *A Norseman's Pilgrimage*, 1875; *Tales from Two Hemispheres*, 1876; *Falconberg*, 1879; *Goethe and Schiller*, 1879; *Queen Titania*, 1881; *Ilka on a Hilltop*, 1881 (play 1884); *Idyls of Norway*, 1882; *A Daughter of the Philistines*, 1883; *The Story of Norway*, 1886; *The Modern Vikings*, 1887; *The Light of Her Countenance*, 1889; *Vagabond Tales*, 1889; *Against Heavy Odds*, 1890; *A Fearless Trio*, 1890; *The Mammon of Unrighteousness*, 1891; *A Golden Calf*, 1892; *Essay on German Literature*, 1892; *Boyhood in Norway*, 1892; *The Social Strugglers*, 1893; *Norseland Tales*, 1894; *A Commentary on the Writings of Henrik Ibsen*, 1894; *Literary and Social Silhouettes*, 1894; *Essays on Scandinavian Literature*, 1895.

BIOGRAPHY AND CRITICISM

The sketch of Boyesen in *Dict. Amer. Biog.* (1929) was contributed by Ernest H. Wright. Recent studies are "Struggle and Flight," in Granville Hicks, *The Great Tradition*, rev. ed., New York, 1935, pp. 131–163; "Hjalmar Hjorth Boyesen," in Laurence M. Larson, *The Changing West and Other Essays*, Northfield, Minn., 1937, pp. 82–115; and George L. White, "H. H. Boyesen : A Note on Immigration," *Amer. Lit.*, XIII (1942), 363–371.

Early studies and appreciations are B. W. Wells, "Hjalmar Hjorth Boyesen," *Sewanee Rev.*, IV (1896), 299–311; Theodore Stanton, "Professor Boyesen at Cornell University," *Open Court*, X (1896), 4812–4814; G. M. Hyde, "In Gratitude to Professor Boyesen," *Dial*, XIX (1895), 323–324. There are early references to Boyesen in the letters and memoirs of William D. Howells.

No full-length bibliography of Boyesen has been published. Some further secondary items are included at the end of the sketch of Boyesen in *Dict. Amer. Biog.* (1929).

## HUGH HENRY BRACKENRIDGE
### *1748–1816*

SEPARATE WORKS

*A Poem on the Rising Glory of America*, 1772; *A Poem on Divine Revelation*, 1774; *The Battle of Bunkers-Hill*, 1776; *The Death of General Montgomery*, 1777; *Six Political Discourses*, 1778; *An Eulogium of the Brave Men Who Have Fallen in the Contest with Great Britain*, 1779; *Narrative of a Late Expedition Against the Indians*, 1783; *Modern Chivalry*, 1792–1815; *Political Miscellany*, 1793; *Incidents of the Insurrection in the Western Parts of Pennsylvania in the Year 1794*, 1795; *The Standard of Liberty*, 1802(?); *An Epistle to Walter Scott*, 1811; *Law Miscellanies*, 1814.

Parts 1 and 2 of *Modern Chivalry* were published in 1792; Parts 3 and 4, in 1793 and 1797; the work was revised in 1805, and completed in 1815, with final additions and revisions. It is conveniently obtainable, edited with introduction, chronology, and bibliography, by Claude M. Newlin, New York, 1937 (American Fiction Ser.).

BIOGRAPHY AND CRITICISM

The authoritative biography of Brackenridge is that of Claude M. Newlin, *The Life and Writings of Hugh Henry Brackenridge*, Princeton, 1932. Newlin contributed the brief sketch to the *Dict. Amer. Biog.* (1929). The standard treatment of Brackenridge as dramatist is Arthur H. Quinn, *A History of the American Drama from the Beginning to the Civil War*, rev. ed., New York, 1943, pp. 50–53. Other useful general studies are Moses C. Tyler, *The Literary History of the American Revolution*, New York, 1897, II, 210–224, 297–302; and Vernon L. Parrington, *Main Currents in American Thought*, New York, 1927, I, 390–395.

The best study of *Modern Chivalry* is in the Newlin edition of the volume (1937), pp. ix–xi. Other useful special studies are Lyon N. Richardson, *A*

*History of Early American Magazines, 1740–1789,* New York, 1931, pp. 197–210—the best account of Brackenridge's association with the *United States Magazine;* Myrl I. Eakin, "Hugh Henry Brackenridge, Lawyer," *Western Pa. Hist. Mag.,* X (1927), 163–175; Martha Connor, "Hugh Henry Brackenridge at Princeton University," *ibid.,* X (1927), 146–162; Mildred Williams, "Hugh Henry Brackenridge as a Judge of the Supreme Court of Pennsylvania, 1799–1816," *ibid.,* 210–223; and Thomas P. Haviland, "The Miltonic Quality of Brackenridge's *Poem on Divine Revelation," PMLA,* LVI (1941), 588–592.

### PRIMARY SOURCES

There is autobiographical material in *Incidents of the Insurrection* (1795), and in the pages of the *Gazette Publications* (1806). His son, Henry Marie Brackenridge, contributed "Biographical Notice of H. H. Brackenridge . . .," *So. Lit. Mess.,* VIII (1842), 1–19. Other writings of H. M. Brackenridge are important sources, especially his *Recollections of Persons and Places in the West* (1834). Further primary material is in David P. Brown, *The Forum . . .,* Philadelphia, 1856, 2 vols.

The two large manuscript collections are those in the Library of Congress and the library of the University of Pittsburgh.

### BIBLIOGRAPHY

The authoritative bibliographical study is Charles F. Heartman, *A Bibliography of the Writings of Hugh Henry Brackenridge Prior to 1825,* New York, 1917. The best sources for secondary items are Newlin's *Life* (1932), pp. 309–315, and his edition of *Modern Chivalry* (1937), pp. xlii–xliv.

## WILLIAM BRADFORD
### 1589/90–1657

### SEPARATE WORKS

*Mourt's Relation* (with Edward Winslow), 1622; *Of Plimoth Plantation,* 1856; "A Dialogue," 1841; "A Third Dialogue," 1871; "A Descriptive and Historical Account . . .," 1794; "A Word to New Plymouth," 1794; "Of Boston in New England," 1838; "A Word to New England," 1838.

### EDITED TEXTS AND REPRINTS

*Mourt's Relation,* so called from the name of its compiler, George Morton, was first published as *A Relation or Journall of the Beginning and Proceedings of the English Plantation Setled at Plimoth,* London, 1622. It was abbreviated in *Purchas his Pilgrims,* London, 1625, Bk. X, chap. iv. It was reprinted in *Coll. Mass. Hist. Soc.,* 1st ser., VIII (1802), 203–239; and was edited by Henry M. Dexter, Boston, 1865. A minute diary of events from November, 1620, to December, 1621, it is now generally thought to be the joint work of Bradford and Edward Winslow, who continues the account in his *Good Newes from New England.* It has been often reprinted.

*Of Plimoth Plantation,* begun in 1630 and continuing the record to 1646, remained in manuscript for two centuries, though used by Nathaniel Morton (1669) and later by Thomas Prince and Cotton Mather for their histories. Rediscovered, it was first printed complete in *Coll. Mass. Hist. Soc.,* 4th ser., III (1856), with notes by Charles Deane. It was reproduced in facsimile from the original manuscript with an introduction by John A. Doyle, London, 1896; and again reproduced from manuscript, when it was returned from England and presented to the State of Massachusetts, as *Bradford's History "Of Plimoth Plantation,"* Boston, 1898. The best edition is that of Worthington C. Ford, Boston, 1912, in 2 vols. It also has been edited somewhat abridged for the Original Narratives Series (New York, 1908) by William T. Davis.

Bradford wrote "A Dialogue, or the Sum of a Conference Between Some Young Men Born in New England and Sundry Ancient Men That Came Out of Holland and Old England" (*ca.* 1648), first printed in Alexander Young, *Chronicles of the Pilgrim Fathers,* Boston, 1841, pp. 409–458; it was most recently reprinted in *Pub. Col. Soc. Mass.,* XXII (1923), 115–141. A "Second Dialogue" was lost and has never been published. "A Dialogue or Third Conference," written *ca.* 1652, was edited by Charles Deane, in *Proc. Mass. Hist. Soc.,* 1st ser., XI (1871), 396–464.

Other published items written by Bradford are "A Descriptive and Historical Account of New England in Verse," issued first in *Coll. Mass. Hist. Soc.,* 1st ser., III (1794), 77–84, and later in *Proc. Mass. Hist. Soc.,* 1st ser., XI (1871), 465–482; "A Word to New Plymouth," *Coll. Mass. Hist. Soc.,* 1st ser., III (1794), 478–482; "Of Boston in New England," *ibid.,* 3rd ser., VII (1838), 27–28; and "A Word to New England," *idem.*

A fragmentary "Letter-Book, 1624–1630," is in *Coll. Mass. Hist. Soc.,* 1st ser., III (1794), 27–84. "Letters of William Bradford" to John Winthrop were issued *ibid.,* 4th ser., VI (1863), 156–161. An important item also is "A Letter of William Bradford and Isaac Allerton, 1623," *Amer. Hist. Rev.,* VIII (1903), 294–301.

## BIOGRAPHY AND CRITICISM

No good biography of Bradford has been written. Two narrative studies are James Shepard, *Governor William Bradford, and His Son Major William Bradford,* New Britain, Conn., 1900; and Albert H. Plumb, *William Bradford of Plymouth,* Boston, 1920. The best brief estimate is that of Samuel E. Morison in *Dict. Amer. Biog.* (1929). Other authoritative estimates are Moses C. Tyler, *A History of American Literature During the Colonial Period,* New York, rev. ed., 1897, I, 116-125; and Williston Walker, *Ten New England Leaders,* New York, 1901, pp. 3-45. Important among early accounts is Cotton Mather, "The Life of William Bradford," in *Magnalia,* London, 1702, Bk. II, chap. i.

The study of Bradford as a literary artist begun by E. F. Bradford, "Conscious Art in Bradford's *History of Plymouth Plantation*," *New Eng. Quar.,* I (1928), 133-157, could profitably be extended.

PRIMARY SOURCES

Bradford's *History* still remains the principal source of his life. The manuscript of the *History* is in the Massachusetts State Library. Further manuscripts are in the possession of the Massachusetts Historical Society.

Important published source material may be gleaned from *Records of the Colony of New Plymouth in New England,* Boston, 1855-1861, 12 vols., ed. by Nathaniel B. Shurtleff (vols. 1-8) and David Pulsifer (vols. 9-12). His will, inventory, and marriage record are given in *Mayflower Descendant,* II (1900), 228-234, and *ibid.,* IX (1907), 115-117.

BIBLIOGRAPHY

No satisfactory bibliography for Bradford has been published. The introductions to the various editions of the *History* are helpful.


# ANNE BRADSTREET
## *1612?-1672*

COLLECTED WORKS

The writings of Anne Bradstreet have been published in five editions. The first, issued in London, 1650, without her supervision, was the only edition published in her lifetime: *The Tenth Muse Lately Sprung Up in America.* . . . The second, a revised and enlarged edition of the first, including the "Contemplations," is entitled *Several Poems Compiled with Great Variety of Wit and Learning,* Boston, 1678. The Boston 1758 edition is a reprint of the second. The fourth edition was edited by John H. Ellis as *The Works of Anne Bradstreet in Prose and Verse,* Charlestown, Mass., 1867 (reprinted, New York, 1932); it contains new material and is copiously supplied with biographical and critical notes. The fifth edition, edited with an introduction by Charles Eliot Norton as *The Poems of Mrs. Anne Bradstreet,*

*Together with Her Prose Remains,* New York, 1897, supplies the most accurate text, though it does not supersede the Ellis edition.

### EDITED TEXTS AND REPRINTS

*A Dialogue Between Old England and New, and Other Poems* was issued in *Old South Leaflets,* VII (1905), No. 159. Selections from her writings are included in nearly all anthologies of American literature, somewhat extensively in Perry Miller and Thomas H. Johnson, *The Puritans,* New York, 1938, pp. 561–579.

### BIOGRAPHY AND CRITICISM

A narrative biography is Helen S. Campbell, *Anne Bradstreet and Her Time,* Boston, 1891. The best brief narrative and critical sketches are Moses C. Tyler, *A History of American Literature During the Colonial Period,* rev. ed., New York, 1897, I, 277–292; Lyon N. Richardson, in *Dict. Amer. Biog.* (1929); and "Mistress Anne Bradstreet," in Samuel E. Morison, *Builders of the Bay Colony,* Boston, 1930, pp. 320–336. Further data appear in Metta Bradstreet, "Anne Bradstreet: Her Life and Works," *Hist. Coll. Topsfield* (Mass.) *Hist. Soc.,* I (1895), 3–9; and George F. Whicher, ed., *Alas, All's Vanity; or, A Leaf from the First American Edition of Several Poems . . .,* New York, 1942, with a brief introductory essay.

### BIBLIOGRAPHY

Oscar Wegelin has compiled "A List of Editions of the Poems of Anne Bradstreet, with Several Additional Books Relating to Her," *Amer. Book Collector,* IV (1933), 15–16. A further item is J. Kester Svendsen, "Anne Bradstreet in England: A Bibliographical Note," *Amer. Lit.,* XIII (1941), 63–65. A brief critical bibliography accompanies the sketch in *Dict. Amer. Biog.* (1929).

There is an important manuscript collection of Anne Bradstreet material in Harvard College Library.

## VAN WYCK BROOKS
### b. 1886

### SEPARATE WORKS

*Verses by Two Undergraduates* (with John Hall Wheelock), 1905; *The Wine of the Puritans: A Study of Present-Day America,* 1908; *The Soul: An Essay Towards a Point of View,* 1910; *The Malady of the Ideal: Obermann, Maurice de Guérin and Amiel,* 1913; *John Addington Symonds: A Biographical Study,* 1914; *America's Coming-of-Age,* 1915; *The World of H. G.*

*Wells,* 1915; *Letters and Leadership,* 1918; *The Ordeal of Mark Twain,* 1920; *The Pilgrimage of Henry James,* 1925; *Emerson and Others,* 1927; *Sketches in Criticism,* 1932; *The Life of Emerson,* 1932; *Three Essays on America,* 1934; *The Flowering of New England, 1815–1865,* 1936; *New England: Indian Summer, 1865–1915,* 1940; *Opinions of Oliver Allston,* 1941; *On Literature Today,* 1941; *The World of Washington Irving,* 1944; *The Times of Melville and Whitman,* 1947.

REPRINTS

*The Flowering of New England* was published in a revised edition, New York, 1940, and was issued in the Modern Library, New York, 1941. *The Flowering of New England* and *New England: Indian Summer* were reprinted in one volume, Garden City, 1944. A revision of *The Ordeal of Mark Twain* was published in 1933.

BIOGRAPHY AND CRITICISM

Earlier estimates of Brooks as critic are Mary M. Colum, "An American Critic: Van Wyck Brooks," *Dial,* LXXVI (1924), 33–41; "Van Wyck Brooks," in Paul Rosenfeld, *Port of New York,* New York, 1924, pp. 19–63; Edmund Wilson, "Imaginary Conversations: Mr. Van Wyck Brooks and Mr. Scott Fitzgerald," *New Repub.,* XXXVIII (1924), 249–254; Edna Kenton, "Henry James and Mr. Van Wyck Brooks," *Bookman,* LXII (1925), 153–157; Gorham B. Munson, "Van Wyck Brooks: His Sphere and His Encroachments," *Dial,* LXXVIII (1925), 28–42; "Scientific Jargon: Mr. Van Wyck Brooks," in Joseph W. Beach, *The Outlook for American Prose,* Chicago, 1926, pp. 28–32; Norman Foerster, *Toward Standards,* New York, 1928, pp. 110–119; Seward Collins, "Criticism in America: The Origins of a Myth," *Bookman,* LXXI (1930), 241–256, 353–364; and Norman Foerster, "The Literary Prophets," *ibid.,* LXXII (1930), 35–44.

Estimates of the later critical thinking of Brooks are found in Howard M. Jones, "The Pilgrimage of Van Wyck Brooks," *Va. Quar. Rev.,* VIII (1932), 439–442; Charles I. Glicksberg, "Van Wyck Brooks," *Sewanee Rev.,* XLIII (1935), 175–186; Theodore Maynard, "Van Wyck Brooks," *Catholic World,* CXL (1935), 412–421; Bernard Smith, "Van Wyck Brooks," in Malcolm Cowley, ed., *After the Genteel Tradition,* New York, 1936, pp. 64–78; John D. Wade, "The Flowering of New England," *So. Rev.,* II (1937), 807–814; Dayton Kohler, "Van Wyck Brooks: Traditionally American," *College English,* II (1941), 629–639; Bernard Smith, "Van Wyck Brooks," *College English,* IV (1942), 93–99; René Wellek, "Van Wyck Brooks and a National Literature," *Amer. Prefaces,* VII (1942), 292–306; and Oscar Cargill, "The Ordeal of Van Wyck Brooks," *College English,* VIII (1946), 55–61.

BIBLIOGRAPHY

A checklist of Brooks's writings, including the books he has edited as well as those he has translated, is in Fred B. Millett, *Contemporary American Authors*, New York, 1940, pp. 262–264, together with references to secondary material.

## CHARLES BROCKDEN BROWN
### *1771–1810*

SEPARATE WORKS

*Alcuin*, 1798; *Wieland*, 1798; *Ormond*, 1799; *Arthur Mervyn*, 1799; *Edgar Huntly*, 1799; *Clara Howard*, 1801; *Jane Talbot*, 1801; *Memoirs of Carwin, The Biloquist*, 1815.

COLLECTED WORKS

*The Novels of Charles Brockden Brown* . . . were published, Boston, 1827, 7 vols., and reprinted, Philadelphia, 1887, 6 vols.

Brown's correspondence for the most part is still unpublished. An exchange of letters concerning a book, presumably *Wieland*, is William Peden, "Thomas Jefferson and Charles Brockden Brown," *Maryland Quar.*, II (1944), 65–68.

EDITED TEXTS AND REPRINTS

Three of Brown's novels, together with *Alcuin* (a treatise on women's rights) and some of his uncollected writings, have been recently published in edited texts. *Alcuin: A Dialogue*, New Haven, 1935, is a facsimile reprint of the first edition, edited with an introduction by LeRoy E. Kimball. Fred L. Pattee edited *Wieland; or, The Transformation, Together with Memoirs of Carwin the Biloquist: A Fragment*, New York, 1926 (American Authors Ser.). Ernest Marchand edited *Ormond*, New York, 1937 (American Fiction Ser.), with introduction, chronology, and bibliography. David L. Clark edited *Edgar Huntly; or, Memoirs of a Sleep-Walker*, New York, 1928 (Modern Readers' Ser.). Harry R. Warfel edited *The Rhapsodist and Other Uncollected Writings*, New York, 1943, for Scholars' Facsimiles and Reprints.

BIOGRAPHY AND CRITICISM

No satisfactory biography of Brown has yet been published. On Brown's important work as an editor, see Frank L. Mott, *A History of American Magazines, 1741–1850*, New York, 1930, *passim*. One of the first studies of him that attempt historical criticism is Martin S. Vilas, *Charles Brockden Brown:*

*A Study of Early American Fiction,* Burlington, Vt., 1904. William Dunlap's *The Life of Charles Brockden Brown* . . . , Philadelphia, 1815, 2 vols., is an original source of information. The work, begun by Paul Allen, was completed by Brown's friend Dunlap, though the title page does not acknowledge Allen's share. The work is in fact extremely inaccurate, but it has usually been followed by later writers. It was issued in an abridgment as *Memoirs of Charles Brockden Brown* . . . , London, 1822.

For brief studies, in addition to the introductions to the edited reprints described above, there is the sketch by Carl Van Doren in *Dict. Amer. Biog.* (1929).

Two early estimates of Brown, still useful, are "Memoir of Charles Brockden Brown, the American Novelist," in William H. Prescott, *Biographical and Critical Miscellanies,* New York, 1845, pp. 1–56; and "The Novels of Charles Brockden Brown," in Richard H. Dana, Sr., *Poems and Prose Writings,* New York, 1850, II, 325–343.

More recent general studies are "Charles Brockden Brown," in Annie R. Marble, *Heralds of American Literature,* Chicago, 1907, pp. 279–318—best of the earlier studies; Lillie D. Loshe, *The Early American Novel,* New York, 1907, pp. 29–58; Warren B. Blake, "Brockden Brown and the Novel," *Sewanee Rev.,* XVIII (1910), 431–443; "Charles Brockden Brown," in John Erskine, *Leading American Novelists,* New York, 1910, pp. 3–49; "Charles Brockden Brown," in George E. Woodberry, *Literary Memoirs of the Nineteenth Century,* New York, 1921, pp. 275–282; Arthur H. Quinn, *American Fiction,* New York, 1936, pp. 25–39; and Fred L. Pattee, *The First Century of American Literature,* New York, 1935, pp. 96–106, 190–193. There is also Max Fricke, *Charles Brockden Browns Leben und Werke,* Hamburg, 1911, 95 pp.

Special studies are Carl Van Doren, "Minor Tales of Brockden Brown, 1798–1800," *Nation,* C (1915), 46–47; David L. Clark, "Brockden Brown and the Rights of Women," *Univ. Texas Bul.,* 2212 (1922); *idem,* "Brockden Brown's First Attempt at Journalism," *Univ. Tex. Studies in English,* VII (1927), 155–174; M. T. Solve, "Shelley and the Novels of Brown," in *The Fred Newton Scott Anniversary Papers,* Chicago, 1929, pp. 141–156; F. C. Prescott, *"Wieland* and *Frankenstein," Amer. Lit.,* II (1930), 172–173; Eleanor Sickels, "Shelley and Charles Brockden Brown," *PMLA,* XLV (1930), 1116–1128; Ernest Marchand, "The Literary Opinions of Charles Brockden Brown," *Studies in Philol.,* XXXI (1934), 541–566—a documented account, based on uncollected reviews and essays; B. M. Stearns, "A Speculation Concerning Charles Brockden Brown," *Pa. Mag. Hist. and Biog.,* LIX (1935), 99–105; Harry R. Warfel, "Charles Brockden Brown's German Sources," *Mod. Lang. Quar.,* I (1940), 357–365; Thomas P. Haviland, "Préciosité Crosses the Atlantic," *PMLA,* LIX (1944), 131–141; and Mabel Morris, "Charles Brockden Brown and the American Indian," *Amer. Lit.,* XVIII (1946), 244–247.

PRIMARY SOURCES

The bulk of Brown's manuscripts is collected in the Library of Congress. A description of those deposited in the Historical Society of Pennsylvania will be found in "Supplement to the Guide to the Manuscript Collections in the Historical Society of Pennsylvania," *Pa. Mag. Hist. and Biog.,* LXVIII (1944), 98–111.

BIBLIOGRAPHY

Two recent selective bibliographies of secondary items are in the Marchand ed. of *Ormond,* New York, 1937, pp. xlvii–li; and in the Warfel ed. of *The Rhapsodist,* New York, 1943. Still useful is the listing in *Camb. Hist. Amer. Lit.,* I (1917), 527–529.

# CHARLES FARRAR BROWNE
## ("ARTEMUS WARD")
### *1834–1867*

WORKS

Two books only were published by Ward during his lifetime: *Artemus Ward: His Book,* New York, 1862; *Artemus Ward: His Travels,* New York, 1865. Posthumous items are *Artemus Ward in London, and Other Papers,* London, 1867; *Sandwiches,* New York, 1869; and *Artemus Ward's Lecture,* New York, 1869, ed. by T. W. Robertson and E. P. Hingston. *The Complete Works of Artemus Ward,* New York, 1903, is one of the latest of the many editions of Ward's "complete" works. *Artemus Ward's Best Stories,* New York, 1912, was edited by Clifton Johnson with an introduction by William Dean Howells. The best selected reprint is *Selected Works of Artemus Ward,* New York, 1924, edited with an introduction by Albert J. Nock. *Letters of Artemus Ward to Charles E. Wilson, 1858–1861,* was issued at Cleveland, 1900, 86 pp.

BIOGRAPHY AND CRITICISM

A full-length life is Don C. Seitz, *Artemus Ward (Charles Farrar Browne): A Biography and Bibliography,* New York, 1919. The sketch in *Dict. Amer. Biog.* (1929) is by Stephen Leacock.

Two good recent studies are by Albert J. Nock: "Artemus Ward," *Sat. Rev. Lit.,* I (Oct. 4, 1924), 157–158; and "Artemus Ward's America," *Atl. Mo.,*

CLIV (1934), 273–281. Other useful estimates are Jennette Tandy, *Cracker-box Philosophers*, New York, 1925, pp. 132–157, and P. H. Belknap, "Our Unique Humorist: Artemus Ward," *Dial*, LXVII (1919), 433–434.

Early estimates are given in Frederic Hudson, *Journalism in the United States . . .*, New York, 1873, pp. 688–696; H. R. Haweis, *American Humorists*, London, 1883, pp. 137–162; and Mark A. De Wolfe Howe, *American Bookmen*, New York, 1898, pp. 163–171.

Edward P. Hingston, *The Genial Showman . . .*, New York, 1870, was written from intimate knowledge of Artemus Ward. See also memoirs and reminiscences of Mark Twain and William Winter.

The bibliography in Don C. Seitz, *Artemus Ward* (1919), pp. 319–338, includes a calendar of Artemus Ward's many contributions to newspapers and periodicals from 1852 to his death.

# WILLIAM C(RARY) BROWNELL
## *1851–1928*

### SEPARATE WORKS

*French Traits: An Essay in Comparative Criticism*, 1889; *French Art: Classic and Contemporary Painting and Sculpture*, 1892; *Victorian Prose Masters*, 1901; *American Prose Masters*, 1909; *Criticism*, 1914; *Standards*, 1917; *The Genius of Style*, 1924; *Democratic Distinction in America*, 1927.

### REPRINTS

*American Prose Masters* was edited with an introduction by Stuart P. Sherman, for the Modern Students' Lib., New York, 1923. G. H. Brownell edited *William Crary Brownell: An Anthology of His Writings, Together with Biographical Notes and Impressions of the Later Years*, New York, 1933.

### BIOGRAPHY AND CRITICISM

Estimates of Brownell as critic are appreciative for the most part. Among them are Russell Sturgis, "William Crary Brownell as Critic on Fine Art," *Internat. Mo.*, V (1902), 448–467; "An American Critic: W. C. Brownell," in George M. Harper, *John Morley and Other Essays*, Princeton, 1920, pp. 93–110; "W. C. Brownell," in Stuart P. Sherman, *Points of View*, New York, 1924, pp. 89–126; "Mr. Brownell on the Quest for Perfection," in *idem, Critical Woodcuts*, New York, 1926, pp. 111–121; Louis J. A. Mercier, *Le Mouvement Humaniste aux Etats-Unis: W. C. Brownell, Irving Babbitt, Paul Elmer More*, Paris, 1928; Edith Wharton, "William C. Brownell," *Scribner's Mag.*, LXXXIV (1928), 596–602; Bernard Bandler II, "The Humanism of W. C.

Brownell," *Hound and Horn*, II (1929), 205-222; *W. C. Brownell: Tributes and Appreciations*, New York, 1929—essays by Edith Wharton, Agnes Repplier, Bliss Perry, and others; and Louis J. A. Mercier, "W. C. Brownell and Our Neo-Barbarism," *Forum*, LXXXI (1929), 376-381. John P. Pritchard, *Return to the Fountains*, Durham, N.C., 1942, pp. 159-169, is a study of the influence of the classics upon Brownell's criticism.

No life of Brownell has been published. The sketch in *Dict. Amer. Biog.* is by Ernest S. Bates. Many of his manuscripts are in the library of the University of Virginia.

## ORESTES (AUGUSTUS) BROWNSON
### *1803-1876*

WORKS

*New Views of Christianity, Society, and the Church*, 1836; *Charles Elwood; or, the Infidel Converted*, 1840; *The Mediatorial Life of Jesus*, 1842; *Essays and Reviews*, 1852; *The Spirit-Rapper: An Autobiography*, 1854; *The Convert; or Leaves from My Experience*, 1857; *The American Republic: Its Constitution, Tendencies, and Destiny*, 1865.

*The Works of Orestes A. Brownson* were collected and arranged by his son Henry F. Brownson, Detroit, 1882-1907, 20 vols. Uncollected material can be found in the magazines he edited, particularly the *Boston Quarterly Review* (1838-1842); and *Brownson's Quarterly Review* (1844-1864, 1873-1875).

BIOGRAPHY AND CRITICISM

Two recent biographies are especially useful: Arthur M. Schlesinger, Jr., *Orestes A. Brownson: A Pilgrim's Progress*, Boston, 1939—a record particularly of the externals bearing on Brownson's life and thought; and Theodore Maynard, *Orestes Brownson: Yankee, Radical, Catholic*, New York, 1943—with emphasis on the years after Brownson's conversion to Catholicism.

Important as source material is the early biography of Brownson by his son Henry F. Brownson, *Orestes A. Brownson's Early Life, Middle Life, Latter Life*, Detroit, 1898-1900, 3 vols. See also Virgil G. Michel, *The Critical Principles of Orestes A. Brownson*, Washington, 1918.

Special studies of interest include "Orestes A. Brownson and *The Boston Quarterly Review*," in Clarence F. Gohdes, *The Periodicals of American Transcendentalism*, Durham, N.C., 1931; Paul R. Conroy, "The Role of the American Constitution in the Political Philosophy of Orestes A. Brownson," *Catholic Hist. Rev.*, XXV (1939), 271-286; Helen S. Mims, "Early American Democratic Theory and Orestes Brownson," *Science and Society*, III (1939),

166–188; Arthur M. Schlesinger, Jr., "Orestes Brownson: An American Marxist Before Marx," *Sewanee Rev.,* XLVII (1939), 317–323; Wilfred Parsons, "Brownson, Hecker, and Hewit," *Catholic World,* CLIII (1941), 396–408; Thomas I. Cook and Arnaud B. Leavelle, "Orestes A. Brownson's *The American Republic,*" *Review of Politics,* IV (1942), 77–90; Dagmar R. Le Breton, "Orestes Brownson's Visit to New Orleans in 1855," *Amer. Lit.,* XVI (1944), 110–114; A. Robert Caponigri, "Brownson and Emerson: Nature and History," *New Eng. Quar.,* XVIII (1945), 368–390; and Thomas Ryan, "Brownson and the Papacy," *Amer. Eccles. Rev.,* CXIV (1946), 114–122.

An important manuscript collection is in the library of the University of Notre Dame. Very adequate bibliographies of both primary and secondary material are in the lives of Brownson by Schlesinger (1939), pp. 299–305; and by Maynard (1943), pp. 433–443.

## WILLIAM CULLEN BRYANT
### 1794–1878

SEPARATE WORKS

*The Embargo; or, Sketches of the Times: A Satire,* 1808; *The Embargo . . . and Other Poems,* 1809; *An Oration Delivered at Stockbridge,* 1820; *Poems,* 1821; *Poems,* 1832; *Poems,* 1834; *Poems,* 1836; *Poems,* 1839; *Popular Considerations on Homoeopathia,* 1841; *The Fountain and Other Poems,* 1842; *An Address to the People of the United States in Behalf of the American Copyright Club,* 1843; *The White-Footed Deer and Other Poems,* 1844; *Letters of a Traveller; or, Notes of Things Seen in Europe and America,* 1850; *Reminiscences of The Evening Post,* 1851; *A Discourse on the Life and Genius of James Fenimore Cooper,* 1852; *Poems,* 1854; *Letters of a Traveller: Second Series,* 1859; *A Discourse on the Life, Character, and Genius of Washington Irving,* 1860; *Thirty Poems,* 1864; *Hymns,* 1864; *Hymns,* 1869; *Some Notices of the Life and Writings of Fitz-Greene Halleck,* 1869; *Letters from the East,* 1869; *A Discourse on the Life, Character, and Writings of Gulian Crommelin Verplanck,* 1870; *The Iliad of Homer, Translated into English Blank Verse,* 1870; *Poems,* 1871; *The Odyssey of Homer,* 1871–1872; *Poems,* 1875; *The Flood of Years,* 1878.

The first draft of "Thanatopsis" was written in 1811. The poem was first published in the *North American Review,* 1817, in an expanded version; it is included, with additions, in *Poems* (1821).

The 1832 ed. of *Poems* is a reissue of the 1821 ed., enlarged and rearranged. The editions of 1834 and 1836 both contain a few additional poems; and that of 1839, one addition, "The Battlefield." Reprints during the next fifteen years show no changes. A few additions appear in the 1854 ed., and revisions and additions are made in the 1871 ed. The last collection is *Poems,* 1875, 3 vols. The third volume contains poems written after 1854, and incorporates *Thirty Poems* of 1864 and some further additions.

The 1869 ed. of *Hymns* is a reissue of the 1864 ed., with a few additions.

COLLECTIONS EDITED BY BRYANT

Among literary collections which Bryant edited are *Selections from the American Poets,* New York, 1840; *A Library of Poetry and Song,* New York, 1871—reissued frequently, and as recently as 1925; *Picturesque America; or, The Land We Live In,* New York, 1872–1874, 2 vols.—the compilation chiefly done by Oliver B. Bunce, but with introduction written and proof sheets read by Bryant; *A New Library of Poetry and Song,* New York, 1876, 2 vols., reissued as recently as 1903; and *A Popular History of the United States . . . ,* New York, 1876–1881, 4 vols., for which Bryant wrote the introduction and read proof.

COLLECTED WORKS

Many of Bryant's poems and a few of his prose tales are still either unpublished or uncollected. Most of his prose, principally reviews and editorials, is not available, since it has not been republished from the literary collections which he edited or to which he contributed, or from the columns of the New York *Evening Post,* which he served as assistant editor 1826–1829, and as editor 1829–1878. A volume of his *Orations and Addresses* was published, New York, 1873. *The Poetical Works of William Cullen Bryant,* New York, 1876, was the last collected edition, hence the final text, which Bryant himself provided. His son-in-law Parke Godwin edited *The Poetical Works of William Cullen Bryant,* New York, 1883, 2 vols., to which some new material was added, together with some textual changes and useful notes. Godwin also edited *Prose Writings of William Cullen Bryant,* New York, 1884, 2 vols. The most inclusive one-volume edition is that of H. C. Sturges and R. H. Stoddard, *The Poetical Works of William Cullen Bryant,* New York, 1903, known as the Roslyn Edition. A few uncollected items were issued in *Unpublished Poems by Bryant and Thoreau,* Boston, 1907. Further gleanings of unpublished items are Tremaine McDowell, "The Juvenile Verse of William Cullen Bryant," *Studies in Philol.,* XXVI (1929), 96–116; *idem, William Cullen Bryant: Representative Selections . . . ,* New York, 1935; and " 'Dictionary of the New York Dialect of the English Tongue,' " *Amer. Speech,* XVI (1941), 157–158—a comic dictionary probably compiled by Bryant *ca.* 1818, during his earliest visit to New York.

No extensive collection of Bryant's letters has been made since the publication of Parke Godwin, ed., *A Biography of William Cullen Bryant, with Extracts from His Private Correspondence,* New York, 1883, 2 vols., containing many hitherto unpublished poems and letters. Other collections are Tremaine McDowell, "William Cullen Bryant and Yale," *New Eng. Quar.,* III (1930), 706–716—early letters, previously unpublished; Frank Smith, "Schoolcraft, Bryant, and Poetic Fame," *Amer. Lit.,* V (1933), 170–172—a letter to Schoolcraft from Bryant written in 1852; Helen L. Drew, "Unpublished Letters of William Cullen Bryant," *New Eng. Quar.,* X (1937), 346–355; Charles I. Glicksberg, "Letters by William Cullen Bryant, 1826–1827," *Americana,* XXXIII (1939), 23–41; William D. Hoyt, Jr., "Some Unpublished Bryant Correspondence," *New York Hist.,* XXI (1940), 63–70, 193–204—largely personal, some dealing with public affairs, especially the Civil War; and Jay B. Hubbell, "A New Letter by William Cullen Bryant," *Ga. Hist. Quar.,* XXVI (1942), 288–290.

EDITED TEXTS AND REPRINTS

After the publication of *Poems* (1832), republication of the same collected items was frequent during his lifetime. Occasionally a well known poem was separately issued; for example, *A Forest Hymn* (1860), *Voices of Nature* (1865), *The Song of the Sower* (1871), *The Story of the Fountain* (1872), *The Little People of the Snow* (1873), and *Among the Trees* (1874).

The best selected text is Tremaine McDowell, *William Cullen Bryant: Representative Selections, with Introduction, Bibliography, and Notes,* New York, 1935 (Amer. Writers Ser.)—containing all the well known poems, as well as hitherto unpublished or unavailable selections from Bryant's poetry, reviews, editorials, and correspondence. Other recent reprints are *Poems of William Cullen Bryant,* New York, 1914 (the Oxford Edition), and J. P. Simmons, ed., *Thanatopsis and Other Poems,* Boston, 1930 (Riverside Lit. Ser.).

BIOGRAPHY AND CRITICISM

No biography of Bryant has been published in forty years, and critical estimates are not numerous. The standard life still remains Parke Godwin, *A Biography of William Cullen Bryant, with Extracts from His Private Correspondence,* New York, 1883, 2 vols. It is uncritical and adulatory, but useful as a portrait by a younger associate who supplies many contemporary data. John Bigelow's *William Cullen Bryant,* Boston, 1890 (Amer. Men of Letters Ser.), was written from personal acquaintance. William A. Bradley's *William Cullen Bryant,* New York, 1905 (Eng. Men of Letters Ser.), supplies no new biographical material but is useful for its criticism of individual poems.

The best brief narrative biography is that of Allan Nevins in the *Dict Amer. Biog.* (1929); a good critical summary is Tremaine McDowell's introduction to *William Cullen Bryant: Representative Selections* (1935), pp. xiii-lxviii.

Significant contemporary criticism and reviews of Bryant's writing are listed in McDowell, pp. 363–388, and a summary of early criticism of Bryant in English periodicals is in William B. Cairns, *British Criticism of American Writings, 1815–1833*, Madison, Wis., 1922, pp. 158–164. Later estimates of Bryant by men of letters are "William Cullen Bryant," in Edmund C. Stedman, *Poets of America*, Boston, 1885, pp. 62–94; "Mr. Bryant's *Thirty Poems*" and "Mr. Bryant's *Homer*," in *idem, Genius and Other Essays*, New York, 1911, pp. 111–140; William E. Leonard, "Bryant," in *Camb. Hist. Amer. Lit.*, New York, 1917, I, 260–278; Rémy de Gourmont, *Deux Poètes de la Nature: Bryant et Emerson*, Paris, 1925, pp. 25–50; and "New York: Bryant," in Van Wyck Brooks, *The World of Washington Irving*, 1944, pp. 234–261.

Special studies, chiefly biographical, are Tremaine McDowell, "The Ancestry of William Cullen Bryant," *Americana*, XXII (1928), 408–420; *idem*, "Cullen Bryant Prepares for College," *So. Atl. Quar.*, XXX (1931), 125–133; *idem*, "Cullen Bryant at Williams College," *New Eng. Quar.*, I (1928), 443–466; and George V. Bohman, "A Poet's Mother: Sarah Snell Bryant in Illinois," *Jour. Ill. State Hist. Soc.*, XXXIII (1940), 166–189.

The fullest treatment of Bryant as editor is Allan Nevins, *The Evening Post: A Century of Journalism*, New York, 1922; it supplies new material and corrects earlier accounts. Two further studies, by Charles I. Glicksberg, are "Bryant and the *United States Review*," *New Eng. Quar.*, VII (1934), 687–701—on Bryant as co-editor and contributor to the literary monthly—and "William Cullen Bryant and the American Press," *Journalism Quar.*, XVI (1940), 356–365.

Studies of "Thanatopsis" are Carl Van Doren, "The Growth of Thanatopsis," *Nation*, CI (1915), 432–433; W. F. Johnson, "Thanatopsis, Old and New," *No. Amer. Rev.*, CCXXIV (1927), 556–572—dealing with revisions in it; Charles W. Nichols, "A Passage in 'Thanatopsis,'" *Amer. Lit.*, XI (1939), 217–218; and Arthur I. Ladu, "A Note on *Childe Harold* and 'Thanatopsis,'" *Amer. Lit.*, XI (1939), 80–81.

Other useful studies are A. H. Herrick, "William Cullen Bryants Beziehungen zur Deutschen Dichtung," *Modern Language Notes*, XXXII (1917), 344–351—a tabulation of German material in his writings; "The Centenary of Bryant's Poetry," in Fred L. Pattee, *Side-Lights on American Literature*, New York, 1922, pp. 293–326; "Bryant," in Norman Foerster, *Nature in American Literature*, New York, 1923, pp. 1–19; "William Cullen Bryant: Puritan Liberal," in Vernon L. Parrington, *Main Currents in American Thought*, New York, II (1927), 238–246; Tremaine McDowell, "Bryant and *The North American Review*," *Amer. Lit.*, I (1929), 14–26—on the details of publishing his poetry and prose; Joseph S. Schick, "William Cullen Bryant and Théophile Gautier," *Modern Language Jour.*, XVII (1933), 260–267; Charles I. Glicksberg, "William Cullen Bryant: A Reinterpretation," *Rev. Anglo-Amér.*, XI (1934), 495–503; "William Cullen Bryant," in Gay W. Allen, *American Prosody*, New York, 1935, pp. 27–55; Marvin T. Herrick, "Rhetoric and Poetry in Bryant," *Amer. Lit.*, VII (1935), 188–194; Tremaine McDowell, "Bryant's Practice in Composition and Revision," *PMLA*, LII (1937), 474–502; J(oseph) Chesley Mathews, "Bryant's Knowledge of Dante," *Italica*, XVI (1939), 115–119; William P. Hudson, "Archibald Alison and William Cullen Bryant," *Amer. Lit.*, XII (1940), 59–68; and "William Cullen Bryant," in John P. Pritchard, *Return to the Fountains*, Durham, N.C., 1942, pp. 13–25— the influence of the classics on his writings. Two further studies by Charles I. Glicksberg are "William Cullen Bryant and Fanny Wright," *Amer. Lit.*, VI (1935), 427–432, and "Bryant on Emerson the Lecturer," *New Eng. Quar.*, XII (1939), 530–534.

PRIMARY SOURCES

In addition to the record of Bryant's views expressed in his many editorials and reviews and in his correspondence, there are the two series of his *Letters of a Traveller* (1850, 1859), and his *Reminiscences of The Evening Post* (1851). The memoirs and biographies of other leading American writers of the nineteenth century almost invariably record estimates or appreciations of Bryant. R. C. Waterston's *Tribute to William Cullen Bryant*, Boston, 1878, is the address of a friend before the Massachusetts Historical Society. George W. Curtis, *The Life, Character, and Writings of William Cullen Bryant*, New York, 1879, is likewise a memorial address. James Grant Wilson's *Bryant and His Friends* . . . , New York, 1885, is useful as source material. Further data are published in Amanda Mathews, "The Diary of a Poet's Mother," *Mag. of Hist.*, II (1905), 206–209; George Cary Eggleston, *Recollections of a Varied Life*, 1910; and Keith Huntress and Fred W. Lorch, "Bryant and Illinois: Further Letters of the Poet's Family," *New Eng. Quar.*, XVI (1943), 634–647.

A large collection of Bryant manuscripts is in the New York Public Library. Further material is in the Henry E. Huntington Library, the Massachusetts Historical Society Library, and the Harvard College Library. Some letters are in the Longfellow House, Cambridge.

BIBLIOGRAPHY

H. C. Sturges's list of writings by Bryant in the Roslyn Edition of the *Poetical Works* (1903) is useful in spite of the fact that it is incomplete and inaccurate. Errors are noted in A. H. Herrick, "Chronology of a Group of

Poems by W. C. Bryant," *Modern Language Notes*, XXXII (1917), 180–182. The bibliography in *Camb. Hist. Amer. Lit.*, I (1917), 517–521, does not carry beyond the year 1911. The listing in Tremaine McDowell, *Representative Selections* (1935), pp. lxxiii–lxxxii, includes contemporary reviews and criticisms and is selective and annotated. See also the list by Harry Hartwick in Walter F. Taylor, *A History of American Letters*, New York, 1936, pp. 499–501; and Harry H. Clark, ed., *Major American Poets*, New York, 1936, pp. 788–792—useful for annotations.

## JOHN BURROUGHS
### *1837–1921*

SEPARATE WORKS

*Notes on Walt Whitman as Poet and Person*, 1867; *Wake-Robin*, 1871; *Winter Sunshine*, 1876; *Birds and Poets*, 1877; *Locusts and Wild Honey*, 1879; *Pepacton*, 1881; *Fresh Fields*, 1885; *Signs and Seasons*, 1886; *Indoor Studies*, 1889; *Riverby*, 1894; *Whitman: A Study*, 1896; *The Light of Day*, 1900; *Literary Values*, 1902; *John James Audubon*, 1902; *Far and Near*, 1904; *Ways of Nature*, 1905; *Bird and Bough*, 1906; *Camping with President Roosevelt*, 1906; *Leaf and Tendril*, 1908; *Time and Change*, 1912; *The Summit of the Years*, 1913; *The Breath of Life*, 1915; *Under the Apple-Trees*, 1916; *Field and Study*, 1919; *Accepting the Universe*, 1920; *Under the Maples*, 1921; *The Last Harvest*, 1922; *My Boyhood*, 1922; *My Dog Friends*, 1928; *The Heart of Burroughs's Journals*, 1928; *The Slabsides Book of John Burroughs*, 1931.

COLLECTED WORKS AND BIOGRAPHY

*The Writings of John Burroughs* were published, Boston, 1904–1922, 23 vols. Published correspondence appears in *John Burroughs and Ludella Peck*, New York, 1925, covering the years 1892–1912; and Clara Barrus, *The Life and Letters of John Burroughs*, Boston, 1925, 2 vols. *The Heart of Burroughs's Journals*, Boston, 1928, was edited by Clara Barrus. A further selection is needed. The official biography of Burroughs is that of his literary executor Clara Barrus, *The Life and Letters of John Burroughs*, Boston, 1925, 2 vols. She has also written *John Burroughs: Boy and Man*, New York, 1920; and *Whitman and Burroughs, Comrades*, Boston, 1931. Other biographical studies include extracts from Burroughs's writings, published as *John Burroughs at Troutbeck*, Amenia, N.Y., 1926; Dallas Lore Sharp, *The Seer of Slabsides*, Boston, 1921; and Clifford H. Osborne, *The Religion of John Burroughs*, Boston, 1930.

The most important study of Burroughs as a man of letters is "Burroughs," in Norman Foerster, *Nature in American Literature,* New York, 1923, pp. 264–305. A good brief estimate is "John Burroughs," in Bliss Perry, *The Praise of Folly and Other Papers,* Boston, 1923, pp. 63–72. The sketch of Burroughs in *Dict. Amer. Biog.* (1929) was contributed by Norman Foerster.

For estimates of Burroughs as a naturalist see Henry F. Osborn, *Impressions of Great Naturalists,* New York, 1924, pp. 183–198; Philip M. Hicks, *The Development of the Natural History Essay in American Literature,* Philadelphia, 1924, pp. 124–158; and Henry C. Tracy, *American Naturalists,* New York, 1930, pp. 86–99.

PRIMARY SOURCES

Clara Barrus's *Our Friend, John Burroughs,* Boston, 1914, incorporates autobiographical sketches by Burroughs. Julian Burroughs edited his father's biography, *My Boyhood,* Garden City, N.Y., 1922, to which he contributed a chapter, "My Father." Reminiscences of Burroughs are in Robert J. H. De Loach, *Rambles with John Burroughs,* Boston, 1912; Clifton Johnson, *John Burroughs Talks: His Reminiscences and Comments,* Boston, 1922—readable and generally accurate; and William Sloane Kennedy, *The Real John Burroughs: Personal Recollection and Friendly Estimate,* New York, 1924. Almost all of Burroughs's writings are autobiographical in nature. See especially Horace L. Traubel, *With Walt Whitman in Camden,* Boston, 1906–1914, 3 vols.

No bibliography of Burroughs has been published.


## (HAROLD) WITTER BYNNER
### b. 1881

SEPARATE WORKS

*An Ode to Harvard and Other Poems,* 1907; *Tiger,* 1913; *The Little King,* 1914; *The New World,* 1915; *Spectra* (with A. D. Ficke), 1916; *Grenstone Poems: A Sequence,* 1917; *A Canticle of Praise,* 1918; *The Beloved Stranger,* 1919; *Snickerty Nick,* 1919; *A Canticle of Pan,* 1920; *Pins for Wings,* 1920; *A Book of Plays,* 1922; *Caravan,* 1925; *Cake: An Indulgence,* 1926; *Roots,* 1929; *Indian Earth,* 1929; *The Persistence of Poetry,* 1929; *Eden Tree,* 1931; *Against the Cold,* 1933; *Guest Book,* 1935; *Against the Cold and Other Poems,* 1940; *Take Away the Darkness,* 1947. Translations include Euripides, *Iphigenia in Taurus* (1915); and *The Jade Mountain: A Chinese Anthology* (1929)—300 poems from the T'ang dynasty, A.D. 618–906.

*Selected Poems by Witter Bynner* was edited by Robert Hunt, New York, 1936 (2nd ed., rev., 1943), with critical preface by Paul Horgan.

Critical estimates are Babette Deutsch, "Two Solitudes," *Dial*, LXXI (1919), 301–302; James Oppenheim, "The Poetry of Witter Bynner," in *The Borzoi, 1925*, New York, 1925, pp. 150–152; Harriet Monroe, "Mr. Bynner in the South-West," *Poetry*, XXXVI (1930), 276–278; Richard P. Blackmur, "Versions of Solitude," *Poetry*, XXXIX (1932), 217–221; and Hildegarde Flanner, "Witter Bynner's Poetry," *University Rev.*, VI (1940), 269–274.

Bynner manuscripts are in the Stanford University Library, Harvard College Library, and the Lockwood Memorial Library, University of Buffalo.

A bibliographical listing is in Fred B. Millett, *Contemporary American Authors*, New York, 1940, pp. 274–276.

## WILLIAM BYRD II
### *1674-1744*

WORKS

*The History of the Dividing Line* was printed first in *The Westover Manuscripts: Containing the History of the Dividing Line Betwixt Virginia and North Carolina; A Journey to the Land of Eden, A.D. 1733; and A Progress to the Mines*, Petersburg, Va., 1841, ed. by Edmund Ruffin. A second edition was brought out by T. H. Wynne, ed., *History of the Dividing Line and Other Tracts*, Richmond, Va., 1866, 2 vols. John S. Bassett provided a standard text of *The Writings of "Colonel William Byrd, of Westover in Virginia, Esqʳ,"* New York, 1901. The definitive edition is that of William K. Boyd, *William Byrd's Histories of the Dividing Line Betwixt Virginia and North Carolina*, Raleigh, N.C., 1929, with introduction and notes, including a transcript of *The Secret History of the Line*, hitherto unpublished. An excerpt from the *History* is Earl G. Swem, ed., *Description of the Dismal Swamp and a Proposal to Drain the Swamp*, Metuchen, N.J., 1922. Mark Van Doren edited *A Journey to the Land of Eden and Other Papers*, New York, 1928, as a popular reprint.

Richmond C. Beatty and William J. Mulloy translated *Neu-Gefundenes Eden* (Bern, 1737) as *William Byrd's Natural History of Virginia; or, The Newly Discovered Eden*, Richmond, Va., 1940, edited with an introduction.

Byrd's shorthand manuscript diary dealing with his private and official life was decoded and edited by Louis B. Wright and Marion Tinling as *The Secret Diary of William Byrd of Westover, 1709–1712*, Richmond, Va., 1941. In the following year Maude H. Woodfin edited *Another Secret Diary of William Byrd of Westover, 1739–1741, with Letters and Literary Exercises, 1696–1726*, Richmond, Va., 1942, decoded and collated by Marion Tinling. Further gleanings from manuscript sources are Louis B. Wright, ed., "William Byrd's Defense of Sir Edmund Andros," *William and Mary Quar.*, II

(1945), 47–62; and *idem,* in the appendix to *An Essay Upon the Government of the English Plantations . . . (1701),* San Marino, Calif., 1945.

Byrd's letters have been published as follows: "Letters of Colonel William Byrd," *Amer. Hist. Rev.,* I (1895), 88–90; "Letters of William Byrd, 2d, of Westover, Va.," *Va. Mag. Hist. and Biog.,* IX (1901–1902), 113–130, 225–251; and "Letters of the Byrd Family," *ibid.,* XXXV (1927), 221–245, 371–389, XXXVI (1928), 36–44, 113–123, 209–222, 353–362, XXXVII (1929), 28–33, 101–118, 242–252, 301–315, XXXVIII (1930), 51–63, 145–156, 347–360, XXXIX (1931), 139–145, 221–229.

Rebecca Johnston edited "William Byrd Title Book," *ibid.,* XLVIII (1940), 31–56, 107–129, 222–237, 328–340, XLIX (1941), 37–50, 174–180, 269–278, 354–363, L (1942), 169–179, 238–263.

BIOGRAPHY AND CRITICISM

A full-length biography is Richmond C. Beatty, *William Byrd of Westover,* Boston, 1932. A good brief account is that of John S. Bassett in his edition of Byrd's *Writings* (1901). Other brief general studies are Philip A. Bruce, *The Virginia Plutarch,* Chapel Hill, N.C., 1929, I, 135–154; Louis B. Wright, *The First Gentlemen of Virginia,* San Marino, Calif., 1940, pp. 312–347; and Moses C. Tyler, *A History of American Literature During the Colonial Period,* rev. ed., New York, 1897, II, 270–278. The sketch in *Dict. Amer. Biog.* (1929) is by Thomas J. Wertenbaker.

Special studies include Maude H. Woodfin, "William Byrd and the Royal Society," *Va. Mag. Hist. and Biog.,* XL (1932), 23–34, 111–123; Kenneth B. Murdock, "William Byrd and the Virginian Author of *The Wanderer,*" *Harvard Studies and Notes in Philol. and Lit.,* XVII (1935), 129–136; James R. Masterson, "William Byrd in Lubberland," *Amer. Lit.,* IX (1937), 153–170; Carl L. Cannon, "William Byrd II of Westover," *Colophon,* n.s. III (1938), No. 2, 291–302—on Byrd's library; Louis B. Wright and Marion Tinling, "William Byrd of Westover, an American Pepys," *So. Atl. Quar.,* XXXIX (1940), 259–274; Maude H. Woodfin, "The Missing Pages of William Byrd's 'Secret History of the Line,'" *William and Mary Quar.,* II (1945), 63–70; and Louis B. Wright, "William Byrd's Opposition to Governor Francis Nicholson," *Jour. So. Hist.,* XI (1945), 68–79.

PRIMARY SOURCES

Important manuscript holdings, including much of the "Diary," are in the Henry E. Huntington Library. Further manuscript material is in the Library of Congress, and the libraries of the University of North Carolina, and the Virginia Historical Society. The last named institution possesses a third portion of the diary, covering the years 1717–1721.

Essential source material is in the files of Correspondence of the Board of Trade, in the Public Records Office, in London. See also R. A. Brock, ed., *The Official Letters of Alexander Spotswood*, Richmond, Va., 1885.

An extensive listing of secondary material is in the bibliography of Beatty's *William Byrd* (1932), pp. 225-229.

# (JAMES) BRANCH CABELL
*b. 1879*

### SEPARATE WORKS

*The Eagle's Shadow*, 1904; *The Line of Love*, 1905; *Gallantry*, 1907; *The Cords of Vanity*, 1909; *Chivalry*, 1909; *The Soul of Melicent*, 1913 (revised as *Domnei*, 1920); *The Rivet in Grandfather's Neck*, 1915; *From the Hidden Way*, 1916; *The Certain Hour*, 1916; *The Cream of the Jest*, 1917; *Beyond Life*, 1919; *Jurgen*, 1919; *The Jewel Merchants*, 1921; *Figures of Earth*, 1921; *The Lineage of Lichfield*, 1922; *The High Place*, 1923; *Straws and Prayer-Books*, 1924; *The Silver Stallion*, 1926; *The Music from Behind the Moon*, 1926; *Something About Eve*, 1927; *The White Robe*, 1928; *The Way of Ecben*, 1929; *Sonnets from Antan*, 1929; *Some of Us: An Essay in Epitaphs*, 1930; *These Restless Heads*, 1932; *Special Delivery: A Packet of Replies*, 1933; *Smirt: An Urban Nightmare*, 1934; *Ladies and Gentlemen*, 1934; *Smith: A Sylvan Interlude*, 1935; *Preface to the Past*, 1936; *Smire: An Acceptance in the Third Person*, 1937; *The King Was in His Counting House*, 1938; *Hamlet Had an Uncle*, 1940; *The First Gentleman of America: A Comedy of Conquest*, 1942; *The St. Johns: A Parade of Diversities*, 1943 (Rivers of Amer. Ser.); *There Were Two Pirates*, 1946; *Let Me Lie*, 1947.

### COLLECTED WORKS AND REPRINTS

The Storisende ed. of *The Works of James Branch Cabell* was published, New York, 1927-1930, 18 vols. *The Cream of the Jest* (1917) was reprinted in the Modern Library, New York, 1927; *Beyond Life* (1919), 1923; *Jurgen* (1919), 1934; *The High Place* (1923) in Bonibooks, New York, 1931. *Chivalry* (1909) was rev. and enl., and published with an introduction by Burton Rascoe, New York, 1921. John Macy edited *Between Dawn and Sunrise: Selections from the Writings of James Branch Cabell*, New York, 1930.

### BIOGRAPHY AND CRITICISM

No life of Cabell has been published. Before *Jurgen* (1919) critical notice of Cabell's writing was negligible. Two estimates by Wilson Follett appeared in the *Dial:* "A Gossip on James Branch Cabell," LXIV (1918), 393–396; and "Ten Times One Makes One," LXVI (1919), 225–228.

During the twenties the following evaluations of his writings appeared: "James Branch Cabell," in Blanche C. Williams, *Our Short Story Writers,* New York, 1920, pp. 22–40; Hugh Walpole, *The Art of James Branch Cabell,* New York, 1920, 32 pp.; Robert M. Lovett, "Mr. James Branch Cabell," *New Repub.,* XXVI (1921), 187–189; Aleister Crowley, "Another Note on Cabell," *Reviewer,* III (1923), 907–914; Don M. Bregenzer and Samuel Loveman, eds., *A Round Table in Poictesme: A Symposium,* Cleveland, 1924; Joseph W. Beach, "Pedantic Study of Two Critics," *Amer. Speech,* I (1926), 299–306; *idem,* "Mr. Cabell," in his *The Outlook for American Prose,* Chicago, 1926, pp. 63–80; H. L. Mencken, *James Branch Cabell,* New York, 1927 (pamphlet); Joseph Hergesheimer, "James Branch Cabell," *Amer. Mercury,* XIII (1928), 38–47; Régis Michaud, "James Branch Cabell and the Escape to Poictesme," and "James Branch Cabell on the High Place," in his *The American Novel To-day,* Boston, 1928, pp. 200–237; Warren A. McNeill, *Cabellian Harmonics,* New York, 1928—with an introduction by Cabell; "James Branch Cabell," in David Karsner, *Sixteen Authors to One,* New York, 1928, pp. 27–44; and Edward N. Hooker, "Something About Cabell," *Sewanee Rev.,* XXXVII (1929), 193–203. The legal proceedings that followed the publication of *Jurgen* are published in Guy Holt, *Jurgen and the Law: A Statement with Exhibits, Including the Court's Opinion, and the Brief for the Defendants on Motion to Direct an Acquittal,* New York, 1923.

Later critical estimates are "James Branch Cabell," in Henry S. Canby, *American Estimates,* New York, 1929, pp. 70–79; Vernon L. Parrington, *Main Currents in American Thought,* New York, III (1930), 335–345; Clara F. McIntyre, "Mr. Cabell's Cosmos," *Sewanee Rev.,* XXXVIII (1930), 278–285; Gay W. Allen, "Jurgen and Faust," *Sewanee Rev.,* XXXIX (1931), 485–492; "James Branch Cabell," in Emily Clark, *Innocence Abroad,* New York, 1931, pp. 35–52; Carl Van Doren, *James Branch Cabell,* New York, 1925 (rev. ed., 1932); William R. Parker, "A Key to Cabell," *English Jour.,* XXI (1932), 431–440; Clifton Fadiman, "(James) Branch Cabell," *Nation,* CXXXVI (1933), 409–410; Maurice Le Breton, "James Branch Cabell, romancier: I. Les Premières Œuvres," *Rev. Anglo-Amér.,* XI (1933–1934), 112–128, and "II. Les Romans de Poictesme," *ibid.,* 223–237—an important study by a European; Leon Howard, "Figures of Allegory: A Study of James Branch Cabell," *Sewanee Rev.,* XLII (1934), 54–66; "The Journeys of Jurgen," in Harry Hartwick, *The Foreground of American Fiction,* New York, 1934, pp. 177–186; "James Branch Cabell," in Harlan Hatcher, *Creating the Modern American Novel,* New York, 1935, pp. 191–201; Peter Monro Jack, "The James Branch Cabell Period," *New Repub.,* LXXXIX (1937), 323–326; and Camille John McCole, *Lucifer at Large,* London, 1937, pp. 57–81.

Among recent studies are Ernst T. Sehrt, "Die Weltanschauung James Branch Cabells, im Anschluss an seinen *Figures of Earth," Englische Studien,* LXXII (1938), 355–399—one of the most searching studies to date; "James Branch Cabell," in Percy H. Boynton, *America in Contemporary Fiction,* Chicago, 1940, pp. 73–90; Carl Van Doren, *The American Novel,* rev. and enl., New York, 1940, pp. 315–322; and Alfred Kazin, *On Native Grounds,* New York, 1942, pp. 231–238.

BIBLIOGRAPHY

The fullest listing to date of Cabell's writings is Jacob Blanck, *Merle Johnson's American First Editions,* 4th ed., New York, 1942. There is also Isidore R. Brussel, *A Bibliography of the Writings of James Branch Cabell: A Revised Bibliography,* Philadelphia, 1932. The fullest listing of secondary items is Fred B. Millett, *Contemporary American Authors,* New York, 1940, pp. 276–280.

## GEORGE W(ASHINGTON) CABLE
### *1844–1925*

SEPARATE WORKS

*Old Creole Days,* 1879; *The Grandissimes,* 1880; *Madame Delphine,* 1881; *The Creoles of Louisiana,* 1884; *Dr. Sevier,* 1885; *The Silent South,* 1885; *Bonaventure,* 1888; *Strange True Stories of Louisiana,* 1889; *The Negro Question,* 1890; *The Busy Man's Bible,* 1891; *John March: Southerner,* 1894; *Strong Hearts,* 1899; *The Cavalier,* 1901; *Bylow Hill,* 1902; *Kincaid's Battery,* 1908; *"Posson Jone'" and Père Raphaël,* 1909; *Gideon's Band,* 1914; *The Amateur Garden,* 1914; *The Flower of the Chapdelaines,* 1918; *Lovers of Louisiana,* 1918.

*Old Creole Days* was published with an introduction by Lucy L. C. Biklé, New York, 1937 (reprinted 1943).

BIOGRAPHY AND CRITICISM

The official biography is that written by his daughter Lucy L. C. Biklé, *George W. Cable: His Life and Letters,* New York, 1928. The best brief sketch is that of Fred L. Pattee in *Dict. Amer. Biog.* (1929).

Other general studies are "George Washington Cable," in Harry A. Toulmin, *Social Historians,* Boston, 1911, pp. 35–36; Fred L. Pattee, *A History of American Literature Since 1870,* New York, 1915, pp. 246–253; and Arthur H. Quinn, *American Fiction,* New York, 1936, pp. 345–351. An early estimate is "George W. Cable," in William M. Baskervill, *Southern Writers,* Nashville, 1897, I, 299–356.

Special studies are Lafcadio Hearn, "The Scenes of Cable's Romances,' *Century Mag.*, XXVII (1883), 40–47; George S. Wykoff, "The Cable Family in Indiana," *Amer. Lit.* I (1929), 183–195—genealogical data; Edward L. Tinker, "Cable and the Creoles," *Amer. Lit.*, V (1934), 313–326; Harry R. Warfel, "George W. Cable Amends a Mark Twain Plot," *Amer. Lit.*, VI (1934), 328–331; and Arlin Turner, "George Washington Cable's Literary Apprenticeship," *Louisiana Hist. Quar.*, XXIV (1941), 168–186—an analysis of Cable's "Drop Shot" column in the New Orleans *Daily Picayune*, 1870–1871.

The case against Cable, as a writer who was somewhat unjust in his treatment of Creole characters, is well set forth in Grace King, *Memories of a Southern Woman of Letters*, New York, 1932.

A checklist of Cable's books, magazine articles, and separately printed stories is in Mrs. Biklé's *Life* (1928), pp. 303–306.

# ERSKINE (PRESTON) CALDWELL
### b. 1903

SEPARATE WORKS

*The Bastard*, 1929; *Poor Fool*, 1930; *American Earth*, 1931; *Tobacco Road*, 1932; *God's Little Acre*, 1933; *We Are the Living*, 1933; *Journeyman*, 1935; *Kneel to the Rising Sun*, 1935; *Some American People*, 1935; *You Have Seen Their Faces*, 1937; *Southways*, 1938; *North of the Danube*, 1939; *Trouble in July*, 1940; *Jackpot*, 1940; *Say, Is This the U.S.A.*, 1941; *All Night Long: A Novel of Guerrilla Warfare in Russia*, 1942; *All-Out on the Road to Smolensk*, 1942; *Georgia Boy*, 1943; *Tragic Ground*, 1944; *A House in the Uplands*, 1946; *The Sure Hand of God*, 1947.

*God's Little Acre* (1933) was reprinted in the following year in the Modern Library. *Journeyman* (1935) was issued in a revised edition, New York, 1938. Henry S. Canby edited *Stories by Erskine Caldwell*, New York, 1944, with an introduction.

BIOGRAPHY AND CRITICISM

Recent studies of Caldwell's fiction include Kenneth Burke, "Caldwell: Maker of Grotesques," *New Repub.*, LXXXII (1935), 232–235; Maurice E. Coindreau, "Erskine Caldwell," *Nouvelle Rev. Française*, XLVII (1936), 908–912; John D. Wade, "Sweet Are the Uses of Degeneracy," *Southern Rev.*, I (1936), 449–466; Vernon Loggins, *I Hear America*, New York, 1937, pp. 221–224; William T. Couch, "Landlord and Tenant," *Virginia Quar. Rev.*, XIV (1938), 309–312; Donald Davidson, "Erskine Caldwell's Picture Book," *South-*

*ern Rev.,* IV (1938), 15–25; Joseph Wood Krutch, "The Case of Erskine Caldwell," *Nation,* CXLVI (1938), 190; Peter A. Carmichael, "Jeeter Lester," *Sewanee Rev.,* XLVIII (1940), 21–29; Malcolm Cowley, "The Two Erskine Caldwells," *New Repub.,* CXI (1944), 599–600; John M. Maclachlan, "Folk and Culture in the Novels of Erskine Caldwell," *Southern Folklore Quar.,* IX (1945), 93–101; and W. M. Frohock, "Erskine Caldwell: Sentimental Gentleman from Georgia," *Southwest Rev.,* XXX (1946), 351–359.

A bio-bibliography is in Fred B. Millett, *Contemporary American Authors,* New York, 1940, pp. 281–282.

## JOHN CALDWELL CALHOUN
### *1782–1850*

WORKS

*A Disquisition on Government,* 1851; *Discourse on the Constitution and Government of the United States,* 1851. The only separate volume printed in Calhoun's lifetime known to be by him was *Speeches of John C. Calhoun,* New York, 1843, published to promote his Presidential candidacy. Richard K. Crallé edited *The Works of John C. Calhoun,* New York, 1851–1856, 6 vols. J. F. Jameson edited "Correspondence of John C. Calhoun," *Amer. Hist. Assn. Annual Report for 1899,* II (1900), 71–218, including a calendar of published correspondence. Further gleanings are "Letters from John C. Calhoun to Charles Tait," *Gulf States Hist. Mag.,* I (1902), 92–104, and Thomas R. Hay, ed., "John C. Calhoun and the Presidential Campaign of 1824: Some Unpublished Calhoun Letters," *Amer. Hist. Rev.,* XL (1934–1935), 82–96, 287–300.

*Life of John C. Calhoun,* New York, 1843, published at the time of Calhoun's campaign for the Presidency, is in fact autobiographical.

BIOGRAPHY AND CRITICISM

An authoritative life is Charles M. Wiltse, *John C. Calhoun, Nationalist, 1782–1828,* Indianapolis, 1944. Earlier lives are Arthur Styron, *The Cast-Iron Man: John C. Calhoun and American Democracy,* New York, 1935; William M. Meigs, *The Life of John Caldwell Calhoun,* New York, 1917, 2 vols.— the most elaborate study; and Gaillard Hunt, *John C. Calhoun,* Philadelphia, 1908, still one of the best. The sketch in *Dict. Amer. Biog.* (1929) is by Ulrich B. Phillips.

Special studies are St. George L. Sioussat, "John Caldwell Calhoun," in Samuel F. Bemis, ed., *The American Secretaries of State and Their Diplomacy,* New York, 1928, V, 127–233; Richard N. Current, "John C. Calhoun,

Philosopher of Reaction," *Antioch Rev.,* III (1943), 223–234; "John Caldwell Calhoun," in William P. Trent, *Southern Statesmen of the Old Régime,* New York, 1897, pp. 153–193; "John Caldwell Calhoun," in Gamaliel Bradford, *As God Made Them,* Boston, 1929, pp. 87–128; "A Footnote on John C. Calhoun," in Ralph H. Gabriel, *The Course of American Democratic Thought,* New York, 1940, pp. 103–110; and Gerald W. Johnson, *America's Silver Age: The Statecraft of Clay, Webster, Calhoun,* New York, 1939.

Calhoun as a man of letters is discussed in Vernon L. Parrington, *Main Currents in American Thought,* New York, 1927, II, 69–82. Useful background material is in David F. Houston, *A Critical Study of Nullification in South Carolina,* New York, 1896; Claude G. Bowers, *The Party Battles of the Jackson Period,* Boston, 1922; and Hermann E. von Holst, *John C. Calhoun,* Boston, 1882 (Amer. Statesmen Ser.). Thomas Hart Benton's *A Thirty Years' View . . . ,* New York, 1854–1856, 2 vols., is especially valuable as source material.

The bulk of the Calhoun manuscripts is in the Library of Congress, the National Archives, Yale University Library, and the library of Clemson College, South Carolina.

A bibliography is in Charles M. Wiltse, *John C. Calhoun* (1944), pp. 443–453.

# WILLA (SIBERT) CATHER
## *1875–1947*

### SEPARATE WORKS

*April Twilights,* 1903; *The Troll Garden,* 1905; *Alexander's Bridge,* 1912; *O Pioneers!* 1913; *My Autobiography,* by S. S. McClure, 1914; *The Song of the Lark,* 1915; *My Ántonia,* 1918; *Youth and the Bright Medusa,* 1920; *One of Ours,* 1922; *A Lost Lady,* 1923; *The Professor's House,* 1925; *My Mortal Enemy,* 1926; *Death Comes for the Archbishop,* 1927; *Shadows on the Rock,* 1931; *Obscure Destinies,* 1932; *Lucy Gayheart* 1935; *Not Under Forty,* 1936; *Sapphira and the Slave Girl,* 1940.

### COLLECTED WORKS AND EDITED REPRINTS

*The Novels and Stories of Willa Cather* were published, Boston, 1937–1941, 13 vols., as a "Library Edition." *April Twilights and Other Poems,* New York, 1933, is a new edition of the 1903 volume, with added material. Reprints have been issued of *Alexander's Bridge* (1912), Boston, 1922, with a preface by the author; *O Pioneers!* (1913), Boston, 1929, in the Riverside Lib.; *The Song of the Lark* (1915), New York, 1932, in the Travellers' Lib., with a preface by the author; *One of Ours* (1922), New York, 1926, with introduction by Stanley T. Williams; and *Death Comes for the Archbishop* (1927), New York, 1931 (Modern Library), and also New York, 1945. Various of her novels and stories have been translated into French and German.

BIOGRAPHY AND CRITICISM

There is no published life of Willa Cather. Criticism of her writings was negligible for the twenty years following the publication of her first book in 1903. She received the Pulitzer Prize for *One of Ours* in 1922. One of the earliest critical notices is Lloyd Morris, "Willa Cather," *No. Amer. Rev.*, CCXIX (1924), 641–652. In the next three years three estimates appeared: Thomas Beer, "Miss Cather," in *The Borzoi, 1925*, New York, 1925, pp. 23–30; "Willa Cather and the Changing World," in Stuart P. Sherman, *Critical Woodcuts*, New York, 1926, pp. 32–48; and "Willa Cather," in Elizabeth S. Sergeant, *Fire Under the Andes*, New York, 1927, pp. 261–282.

Estimates published in the decade following *Death Comes for the Archbishop* (1927) are Alexander Porterfield, "Willa Cather," in J. C. Squire, ed., *Contemporary American Authors*, New York, 1928, pp. 45–67; "Willa Cather," in Thomas K. Whipple, *Spokesmen*, New York, 1928, pp. 139–160; Edward Wagenknecht, "Willa Cather," *Sewanee Rev.*, XXXVII (1929), 221–239; René Rapin, *Willa Cather*, New York, 1930; Pierre Chamaillard, "Le Cas de Marian Forrester," *Revue Anglo-Amér.*, VIII (1931), 419–427; Louis Kronenberger, "Willa Cather," *Bookman*, LXXIV (1931), 134–140; Clifton Fadiman, "Willa Cather: The Past Recaptured," *Nation*, CXXXV (1932), 563–565; Archer Winsten, "A Defense of Willa Cather," *Bookman*, LXXIV (1932), 634–640; Granville Hicks, "The Case Against Willa Cather," *English Jour.*, XXII (1933), 703–710; "Simplicity with Glory," in Harry Hartwick, *The Foreground of American Fiction*, New York, 1934, pp. 389–404; Edward K. Brown, "Willa Cather and the West," *Univ. Toronto Quar.*, V (1936), 544–566; and Lionel Trilling, "Willa Cather," in Malcolm Cowley, ed., *After the Genteel Tradition*, New York, 1937, pp. 52–63.

Most recent are Howard M. Jones, "The Novels of Willa Cather," *Sat. Rev. Lit.*, XVIII (Aug. 6, 1938), 3–4; Robert H. Footman, "The Genius of Willa Cather," *Amer. Lit.*, X (1938), 123–141; "Willa Cather," in Carl Van Doren, *The American Novel*, rev. and enl., New York, 1940, pp. 281–293; "Willa Cather," in Percy H. Boynton, *America in Contemporary Fiction*, Chicago, 1940, pp. 150–163; "Trends of the Future in Willa Cather," in Nellie Elizabeth Monroe, *The Novel and Society*, Chapel Hill, N.C., 1941, pp. 225–245; "Elegy and Satire: Willa Cather and Ellen Glasgow," in Alfred Kazin, *On Native Grounds*, New York, 1942, pp. 247–257; and E. K. Brown, "Homage to Willa Cather," *Yale Rev.*, XXXVI (1946), 77–92.

PRIMARY SOURCES

Some autobiographical data are in "My First Novels—There Were Two," *Colophon*, Pt. 6, No. 4 (1931), 4 pp. Her will specifies that her correspondence may never be published.

BIBLIOGRAPHY

A compilation covering first editions is in Jacob Blanck, *Merle Johnson's American First Editions*, 4th ed., New York, 1942. The fullest listing of secondary items is Fred B. Millett, *Contemporary American Authors*, New York, 1940, pp. 289–292. Frederick B. Adams, Jr., "Willa Cather, Middle Years: The Right Road Taken," *Colophon*, new graphic ser., I (1939), No. 4, 103–108, supplies data on editions.

# WILLIAM ELLERY CHANNING
## 1780–1842

SEPARATE WORKS

Significant among the separate works of Channing are *A Sermon on War*, 1816; *The Moral Argument Against Calvinism*, 1820; *A Discourse on the Evidences of Revealed Religion*, 1821; *Sermons and Tracts, including the Analysis of the Character of Napoleon, and Remarks on the Life and Writings of John Milton*, 1828; "The Importance and Means of a National Literature," 1830; *Discourses, Reviews, and Miscellanies*, 1830; *Discourses*, 1832; *Slavery*, 1835; *A Letter to the Abolitionists*, 1837; *A Letter to the Hon. Henry Clay, on the Annexation of Texas to the United States*, 1837; *Character of Napoleon, and Other Essays, Literary and Philosophical*, 1837, 2 vols.; *Self-Culture*, 1838; *Remarks on the Slavery Question*, 1839; *Lecture on War*, 1839; *Emancipation*, 1840; *Lectures on the Elevation of the Labouring Portion of the Community*, 1840; *The Duty of Free States; or, Remarks Suggested by the Case of the Creole*, 1842; *Conversations in Rome: Between an Artist, a Catholic, and a Critic*, 1847.

The writings of Channing were steadily issued during his lifetime both in this country and abroad. Several went through many reprints during the course of the nineteenth century.

COLLECTED WORKS

*The Works of William E. Channing*, Boston, 1841–1843, 6 vols., went through seventeen editions by 1867. They were issued in a new revised edition, Boston, 1875. A new and "complete" edition was issued in one volume, 1,060 pages, Boston, 1886.

*Correspondence of William Ellery Channing and Lucy Aikin, from 1826 to 1842,* London and Boston, 1874, was edited by Anna L. Le Breton. Extracts from his correspondence and manuscripts are in William H. Channing, *Memoir of William Ellery Channing . . . ,* Boston, 1848, 3 vols. *Dr. Channing's Note-Book: Passages from the Unpublished Manuscripts of William Ellery Channing,* was published, Boston, 1887. A collection of Channing's *Discourses on War* was issued, Boston, 1903.

BIOGRAPHY AND CRITICISM

In his own day Channing was regarded, especially in England, as one of the leading American literary figures. Since that time he has generally been evaluated as a publicist and spokesman of Unitarianism. Channing as a literary figure needs new evaluation. Two early biographies are William H. Channing, *The Life of William Ellery Channing,* Boston, 1880; and John W. Chadwick, *William Ellery Channing, Minister of Religion,* Boston, 1903. See also "William Ellery Channing," in Daniel D. Addison, *The Clergy in American Life and Letters,* New York, 1900, pp. 191–228; Charles W. Eliot, *Four American Leaders,* Boston, 1906, pp. 57–72; and Vernon L. Parrington, *Main Currents in American Thought,* New York, 1927–1930, II, 328–338. The sketch of Channing in *Dict. Amer. Biog.* (1930) is by Samuel M. Crothers. Among special studies, that of Robert E. Spiller, "A Case for W. E. Channing," *New Eng. Quar.,* III (1930), 55–81, recognizes Channing as a man of letters. Other special studies are Granville Hicks, "Dr. Channing and the Creole Case," *Amer. Hist. Rev.,* XXXVII (1932), 516–525; Herbert W. Schneider, "The Intellectual Background of William Ellery Channing," *Church Hist.,* VII (1938), 3–23; William P. Randel, "Hawthorne, Channing, and Margaret Fuller," *Amer. Lit.,* X (1939), 472–476; Arthur I. Ladu, "Channing and Transcendentalism," *Amer. Lit.,* XI (1939), 129–137; Neal F. Doubleday, "Channing on the Nature of Man," *Journal of Religion,* XXIII (1943), 245–257; and Marie Hochmuth, "William Ellery Channing, New England Conversationalist," *Quar. Jour. of Speech,* XXX (1944), 429–439.

Useful contemporary evaluations and reminiscences are Elizabeth P. Peabody, *Reminiscences of Rev. William Ellery Channing,* Boston, 1880; Theodore Parker, *The American Scholar,* Boston, 1907, pp. 126–171—ed. by George W. Cooke; and Russell N. Bellows, ed., *The Channing Centenary . . . ,* Boston, 1881.

No bibliography of Channing has been published.

# CHARLES W(ADDELL) CHESNUTT
*1858–1932*

### SEPARATE WORKS

*The Conjure Woman*, 1899; *The Wife of His Youth*, 1899; *Frederick Douglass*, 1899; *The House Behind the Cedars*, 1900; *The Marrow of Tradition*, 1901; *The Colonel's Dream*, 1905.

### BIOGRAPHY AND CRITICISM

The most extensive critical study of Chesnutt's writings is "Maturing of Negro Literature," in Benjamin G. Brawley, *The Negro Genius . . .*, New York, 1937, pp. 143–170. An estimate of Chesnutt as artist and social force is Jay Saunders Redding, *To Make a Poet Black*, Chapel Hill, N.C., 1939, pp. 68–76. His work is briefly discussed by Vernon Loggins, *The Negro Author*, New York, 1931, pp. 310–313, and John Chamberlain, "The Negro as Writer," *Bookman*, LXX (1930), 603–611. An early recognition was that of William Dean Howells, "Mr. Charles W. Chesnutt's Stories," *Atl. Mo.*, LXXXV (1900), 699–701. See also Carolyn Shipman, "The Author of *The Conjure Woman*," *Critic*, XXXV (1899), 632–634.

An autobiographical account of Chesnutt's standard in writing is "Post-Bellum—Pre-Harlem," *Colophon*, New York, 1931, Pt. 5, 8 pp.

A bibliographical listing is in Jacob Blanck, *Merle Johnson's American First Editions*, 4th ed., New York, 1942.

# THOMAS HOLLEY CHIVERS
*1809–1858*

### SEPARATE WORKS

*The Path of Sorrow*, 1832; *Conrad and Eudora*, 1834; *Nacoochee*, 1837; *The Lost Pleiad and Other Poems*, 1845; *Search After Truth*, 1848; *Eonchs of Ruby: A Gift of Love*, 1851; *Memoralia*, 1853; *Virginalia*, 1853; *A Gift of the Beautiful*, 1853; *Atlanta*, 1853; *Birth-Day Song of Liberty*, 1856; *The Sons of Usna: A Tragi-Apotheosis in Five Acts*, 1858.

Lewis Chase edited *Thomas Holley Chivers: A Selection*, Oglethorpe, Ga., 1929. Selections from Chivers's poetry are given in Damon's life of Chivers (1930).

### BIOGRAPHY AND CRITICISM

The most extensive critical treatment of Chivers as a lyric poet is S(amuel) Foster Damon, *Thomas Holley Chivers, Friend of Poe: With Selections from*

*His Poems* . . ., New York, 1930. A brief estimate is R. L. Pitfield, "Thomas Holley Chivers: 'The Wild Mazeppa of Letters,'" *Gen. Mag. and Hist Chron.*, XXXVII (1934), 73–92. The sketch of Chivers in *Dict. Amer. Biog.* (1930) is contributed by S. Foster Damon.

The Poe-Chivers controversy has been explored by Landon C. Bell, *Poe and Chivers*, Columbus, 1931; George E. Woodberry, ed., "The Poe-Chivers Papers," *Century Mag.*, LXV (1903), 435–447; Alphonso G. Newcomer, "The Poe-Chivers Tradition Reëxamined," *Sewanee Rev.*, XII (1904), 20–35.

PRIMARY SOURCES

Manuscripts of Chivers are in the Boston Public Library and the library of Duke University. Source material regarding Chivers will be found in the biographies of Poe. See also Thomas O. Mabbott's edition of Poe's *Politian*, Richmond, 1923; and *Passages from the Correspondence and Other Papers of Rufus W. Griswold* (1898), edited by William M. Griswold.

The best bibliography of Chivers is that in Damon's life (1930), pp. 283–288.


# HENRY CLAY
## *1777–1852*

COLLECTED WORKS

*The Works of Henry Clay*, New York, 1857, 6 vols., were edited by Calvin Colton, and republished with additional material, New York, 1896, 7 vols. The later edition includes over two volumes of correspondence, four volumes of speeches, and an introduction by the editor. Early separate collections were Colton's edition of *The Private Correspondence of Henry Clay*, New York, 1855; Daniel Mallory, ed., *The Life and Speeches of Henry Clay*, New York, 1843, 2 vols.—including Clay's most important speeches to 1842; and Richard Chambers, ed., *Speeches of the Hon. Henry Clay, of the Congress of the United States*, Cincinnati, 1842.

BIOGRAPHY AND CRITICISM

Still indispensable as a study of Clay's whole career is the two-volume life by Carl Schurz, *Henry Clay*, Boston, 1887, prepared for the American Statesmen Series. Three recent studies are Bernard Mayo, *Henry Clay: Spokesman of the New West*, Boston, 1937—with emphasis on the years prior to the War of 1812; George R. Poage, *Henry Clay and the Whig Party*, Chapel Hill, N.C., 1936—dealing mainly with Clay's later political career; and Glyndon G. Van Deusen, *The Life of Henry Clay*, Boston, 1937. The biography by Clay's grandson Thomas H. Clay, *Henry Clay*, Philadelphia, 1910, was completed by Ellis P. Oberholtzer. The sketch of Clay in *Dict. Amer. Biog.* (1930) was contributed by E. Merton Coulter.

Clay as a man of letters is best treated by Ernest J. Wrage, "Henry Clay," in William N. Brigance, ed., *A History and Criticism of American Public Address*, New York, 1943, II, 603-638. See also Vernon L. Parrington, *Main Currents in American Thought*, New York, 1927, II, 142-144.

Special studies include Willard R. Jillson, *Henry Clay's Defense of Aaron Burr in 1806: An Episode of Early Western Adventure*, Frankfort, Ky., 1943, 11 pp.; Mary P. Follett, "Henry Clay as Speaker of the House of Representatives," in the *Annual Report* of the Amer. Hist. Assn. for 1891 (1892), pp. 257-265; and Hubert B. Fuller, *The Speakers of the House*, Boston, 1909. Clay as statesman is treated in Gerald W. Johnson, *America's Silver Age: The Statecraft of Clay, Webster, Calhoun*, New York, 1939.

The great bulk of Clay's manuscripts is deposited in the Library of Congress. Further manuscript material is in the library of the University of Chicago.

Published material of a primary nature is in Epes Sargent, *The Life and Public Services of Henry Clay*, New York, 1842—republished with additional material in 1848; Calvin Colton, *The Life and Times of Henry Clay*, New York, 1846, 2 vols.—for which Clay read proof; Edward G. Parker, *The Golden Age of American Oratory*, Boston, 1857; William Mathews, *Oratory and Orators*, Chicago, 1879; and Oliver Dyer, *Great Senators in the United States Forty Years Ago*, New York, 1889. George D. Prentice, *Biography of Henry Clay*, Hartford, 1831, was published as a campaign biography. Further material of primary nature will be found in the reminiscences and biographies of Horace Greeley and Robert C. Winthrop.

The fullest bibliographical listing of primary and secondary material is in Bernard Mayo's biography (1937), pp. 527-548. See also the study by Poage (1936), pp. 279-283. A selective bibliography concludes the study of Clay as orator by Ernest J. Wrage in Brigance's *A History and Criticism of American Public Address* (1943), II, 635-638.


# SAMUEL L(ANGHORNE) CLEMENS
## ("MARK TWAIN")
### *1835-1910*

SEPARATE WORKS

*The Celebrated Jumping Frog of Calaveras County and Other Sketches,* 1867; *The Innocents Abroad*, 1869; *Mark Twain's (Burlesque) Autobiography*, 1871; *Roughing It*, 1872; *The Gilded Age* (with Charles Dudley

Warner), 1873; *Mark Twain's Sketches: New and Old*, 1875; *The Adventures of Tom Sawyer*, 1876; *A True Story*, 1877; *Punch, Brothers, Punch!* 1878; *A Tramp Abroad*, 1880; *The Prince and the Pauper*, 1882; *The Stolen White Elephant, etc.*, 1882; *Life on the Mississippi*, 1883; *The Adventures of Huckleberry Finn*, 1885; *A Connecticut Yankee in King Arthur's Court*, 1889; *The American Claimant*, 1892; *Merry Tales*, 1892; *The £1,000,000 Bank-Note*, 1893; *Tom Sawyer Abroad*, 1894; *The Tragedy of Pudd'nhead Wilson*, 1894; *Personal Recollections of Joan of Arc*, 1896; *Tom Sawyer Abroad, Tom Sawyer, Detective, and Other Stories*, 1896; *Following the Equator*, 1897; *How to Tell a Story and Other Essays*, 1897; *The Man That Corrupted Hadleyburg and Other Stories and Essays*, 1900; *A Double Barrelled Detective Story*, 1902; *My Début as a Literary Person*, 1903; *A Dog's Tale*, 1904; *Extracts from Adam's Diary*, 1904; *King Leopold's Soliloquy*, 1905; *What Is Man?* 1906; *The $30,000 Bequest*, 1906; *Eve's Diary*, 1906; *Christian Science*, 1907; *A Horse's Tale*, 1907; *Is Shakespeare Dead?* 1909; *Extract from Captain Stormfield's Visit to Heaven*, 1909; *The Mysterious Stranger*, 1916; *What Is Man? and Other Essays*, 1917; *The Curious Republic of Gondour*, 1919; *The Mysterious Stranger and Other Stories*, 1922; *Europe and Elsewhere*, 1923.

COLLECTED WORKS

The definitive edition of the collected works is that edited by Albert B. Paine, *The Writings of Mark Twain*, New York, 1922-1925, 37 vols. Other collections are the "Author's National Edition" of *The Writings of Mark Twain*, New York, 1907-1918, 25 vols.; the "Autograph Edition" of *The Writings of Mark Twain*, Hartford, Conn., 1899-1900, 22 vols.; the "Underwood Edition" of *The Writings of Mark Twain*, New York, 1901-1907, 25 vols.; and *Mark Twain's Works*, New York, 1933, 23 vols.

*Mark Twain's Autobiography*, New York, 1924, 2 vols., was edited by Albert B. Paine, with an introduction; it was dictated to Paine, and in 1924 family permission was given for publication of most of the dictated material; it should be used cautiously—see Delancey Ferguson, "The Uncollected Portions of Mark Twain's *Autobiography*," *Amer. Lit.*, VIII (1936), 37-46. Bernard De Voto edited from source material what constitutes in effect a third volume of the autobiography: *Mark Twain in Eruption: Hitherto Unpublished Pages About Men and Events*, New York, 1940, including significant new material.

*Mark Twain's Speeches*, New York, 1910, includes an introduction by Albert B. Paine and an appreciation by William D. Howells. Paine edited *Mark Twain's Notebook*, New York, 1935.

The surreptitiously printed item, *1601; or, Conversation as It Was by the*

*Social Fireside in the Time of the Tudors* . . . , was edited with a bibliography by Franklin J. Meine, Chicago, 1939.

Collections of Mark Twain's contributions to newspapers have been made by G. Ezra Dane, ed., *Letters from the Sandwich Islands, Written for the Sacramento Union,* San Francisco, 1937 (and Stanford Univ., Calif., 1938); Franklin Walker, ed., *The Washoe Giant in San Francisco, Being Heretofore Uncollected Sketches* . . . , San Francisco, 1938; Ivan Benson, *Mark Twain's Western Years, Together with Hitherto Unreprinted Clemens Western Items,* Stanford Univ., Calif., 1938; Thomas Nickerson, ed., *Letters from Honolulu, Written for the Sacramento Union,* Honolulu, 1939—written in 1866, and here first published with an introduction by John W. Vandercook; Franklin Walker and G. Ezra Dane, eds., *Mark Twain's Travels with Mr. Brown, Being Heretofore Uncollected Sketches Written by Mark Twain for the San Francisco Alta California in 1866 and 1867* . . . , New York, 1940; Cyril Clemens, ed., *Republican Letters,* Webster Groves, Mo., 1941—contributions to the *Chicago Republican* in 1868; Edgar M. Branch, ed., *Mark Twain's Letters in the Muscatine Journal,* Chicago, 1942—five letters, 1853–1855. Other gleanings are Minnie M. Brashear, "Mark Twain Juvenilia," *Amer. Lit.,* II (1930), 25–53—early writings from Hannibal, Mo., newspapers; Walter Blair, "Mark Twain, New York Correspondent," *Amer. Lit.,* XI (1939), 247–259—travel letters from the San Francisco *Alta California* of 1867; Cyril Clemens, "Mark Twain's Washington in 1868," *Mark Twain Quar.,* V (1942), 1–16—correspondence from Washington; and Ernest E. Leisy, "Mark Twain and Isaiah Sellers," *Amer. Lit.,* XIII (1942), 398–405—on two letters in the New Orleans *True Delta,* 1859.

The bulk of Mark Twain's personal correspondence now in print appears in Albert B. Paine, ed., *Mark Twain's Letters, Arranged with Comment,* New York, 1917, 2 vols., supplemented by Bernard De Voto, ed., *Mark Twain in Eruption* . . . , New York, 1940, and by Albert B. Paine, *Mark Twain, A Biography* . . . , New York, 1912, 3 vols. Fred W. Lorch, "Mark Twain's Early Nevada Letters," *Amer. Lit.,* X (1939), 486–488, offers bibliographical data to clear up certain of Paine's editorial inaccuracies. Further unpublished letters appear in Clara Clemens, *My Father, Mark Twain,* New York, 1931; Cyril Clemens, *Mark Twain, the Letter Writer,* Boston, 1932; Theodore Hornberger, ed., *Mark Twain's Letters to Will Bowen: "My First and Oldest and Dearest Friend,"* Austin, Tex., 1941. Further gleanings are Minnie M. Brashear, "An Early Mark Twain Letter," *Modern Language Notes,* XLIV (1929), 256–259; Fred W. Lorch, "A Mark Twain Letter," *Iowa Jour. Hist. and Politics,* XXVIII (1930), 268–276; William B. Gates, "Mark Twain to His English Publishers," *Amer. Lit.,* XI (1939), 78–81; (anon.), *A Letter from Mark Twain to His Publishers, Chatto and Windus* . . . , San Francisco,

1929; John R. Schultz, "New Letters of Mark Twain," *Amer. Lit.,* VIII, (1936), 47–51—to Bayard Taylor; James C. Olson, "Mark Twain and the Department of Agriculture," *Amer. Lit.,* XIII (1942), 408–410; Lawrence C. Powell, "An Unpublished Mark Twain Letter," *Amer. Lit.,* XIII (1942), 405–407; Bernard De Voto, ed., "Letter from the Recording Angel," *Harper's Mag.,* CXCII (1946), 106–109; and Ernest E. Leisy, ed., *The Letters of Quintus Curtius Snodgrass,* Dallas, Tex., 1946—ten humorous letters first published in 1861 in the New Orleans *Daily Crescent.*

De Voto has also edited "Fenimore Cooper's Further Literary Offenses," *New Eng. Quar.,* XIX (1946), 291–301—a hitherto unpublished continuation of "Fenimore Cooper's Literary Offenses," first published in *No. Amer. Rev.,* July, 1895. See also G. H. Brownell, "Two Hitherto Unknown Twain Tales . . .," *Twainian,* V (Nov.-Dec., 1946), 1–2.

EDITED TEXTS AND REPRINTS

A volume of selections, edited by Albert B. Paine, is *Moments with Mark Twain,* New York, 1920. Three other collected one-volume editions are *The Family Mark Twain,* New York, 1935 (1,462 pp.), with biographical summary by Albert B. Paine and a foreword by Owen Wister; *The Mark Twain Omnibus: Drawn from the Works of Mark Twain,* New York, 1935, edited by Max J. Herzberg, 441 pp.; and *The Portable Mark Twain,* New York, 1946, edited by Bernard De Voto—including a few hitherto unpublished letters. A serviceable volume is Fred L. Pattee, ed., *Mark Twain: Representative Selections, with Introduction and Bibliography,* New York, 1935 (Amer. Writers Ser.), though it contains no later work.

Separate published works are available: *A Connecticut Yankee in King Arthur's Court,* New York, 1930 (Modern Classics), ed. by W. N. Otto, and New York, 1942, with a foreword by John T. Winterich. *The Innocents Abroad,* New York, 1927 (Modern Readers' Ser.), with introduction by Albert B. Paine. *Jim Smiley and His Jumping Frog,* Chicago, 1940—republished from the original newsprint in 1865. *Life on the Mississippi,* New York, 1923 (Modern Classics), with an introduction by J. W. Rankin, and an abridged ed. prepared by Edwin V. Knickerbocker, New York, 1935; and as one of the "Bantam Books," New York, 1946. *The Prince and the Pauper,* New York, 1920 (Modern Classics), with introduction by Arthur H. Quinn, and New York, 1931 (Modern Classics), with new introduction by Emily F. Barry and Herbert B. Bruner. *Tom Sawyer* and *Huckleberry Finn* have been issued and reissued many times. They are available together in one-volume editions, New York, 1932 (Modern Classics), and similarly issued, New York, 1940 (Modern Library). A text edition of *Tom Sawyer,* Cambridge, 1939, is issued with introduction by Bernard De Voto, including as prologue the "Boy's

Manuscript," here first printed, with illustrations by Thomas Hart Benton. It is also in the Modern Lit. Ser., Boston, 1931. *Huckleberry Finn* is issued, New York, 1931 (Modern Classics), and New York, 1942, with an introduction by Bernard De Voto.

BIOGRAPHY AND CRITICISM

The authorized biography is Albert B. Paine, *Mark Twain, A Biography: The Personal and Literary Life of Samuel Langhorne Clemens,* New York, 1912, 3 vols., without letters. Paine was Clemens's secretary, and the study is ardently appreciative. Two recent studies by Bernard De Voto, based on careful use of fresh source material, are *Mark Twain's America,* Boston, 1932, with bibl., pp. 323-334 (dealing with his environment before coming East), and *Mark Twain at Work,* Cambridge, 1942 (three essays on Mark Twain as literary artisan). Other general studies are Edward C. Wagenknecht, *Mark Twain: The Man and His Work,* New Haven, 1935; William D. Howells, *My Mark Twain: Reminiscences and Criticisms,* New York, 1910—useful still as criticism and source material; Van Wyck Brooks, *The Ordeal of Mark Twain,* New York, 1920 (rev. ed., 1933)—presenting Mark Twain as a thwarted genius; Minnie M. Brashear, *Mark Twain: Son of Missouri,* Chapel Hill, N.C., 1934, with bibl., pp. 264-284—an exhaustive study of his reading; and J(ohn) De Lancey Ferguson, *Mark Twain: Man and Legend,* Indianapolis, 1943—the most recent study. Other biographical portraits are supplied by Archibald Henderson, *Mark Twain,* London, 1911; Clara Clemens (Gabrilowitsch), *My Father: Mark Twain,* New York, 1931—important as source material; Stephen Leacock, *Mark Twain,* New York, 1933; Edgar Lee Masters, *Mark Twain: A Portrait,* New York, 1938; and Samuel C. Webster, *Mark Twain: Business Man,* Boston, 1946.

Brief critical estimates, interesting to the extent to which the authors are spokesmen of their times, are "Democracy and Mark Twain," in John C. Underwood, *Literature and Insurgency* . . . , New York, 1914, pp. 1-40; "The Democracy of Mark Twain," in Stuart P. Sherman, *On Contemporary Literature,* New York, 1917, pp. 18-49; "Mark Twain," *idem,* in *Camb. Hist. Amer. Lit.,* III (1921), 1-20; "Mark Twain's Last Phase," in *idem, The Main Stream,* New York, 1927, pp. 80-88; Carl Van Doren, in *Dict. Amer. Biog.* (1930); Theodore Dreiser, "Mark the Double Twain," *English Jour.,* XXIV (1935), 615-627—on his complex personality; and Owen Wister, "In Homage to Mark Twain," *Harper's Mag.,* CLXXI (1935), 547-556.

Studies devoted to Mark Twain's use of language are Katherine Buxbaum, "Mark Twain and American Dialect," *Amer. Speech,* II (1927), 233-236; Frances G. Emberson, "Mark Twain's Vocabulary: A General Survey," *Univ. Mo. Studies,* X (1935), No. 3, pp. 1-53, with bibl., pp. 35-53; Ada M. Klett,

"Meisterschaft, or The True State of Mark Twain's German," *Amer.-German Rev.*, VII (1941), No. 2, pp. 10–11; and Dixon Wecter, "Mark Twain as Translator from the German," *Amer. Lit.*, XIII (1941), 257–263. An extensive compilation is Robert L. Ramsay and Frances G. Emberson, *A Mark Twain Lexicon*, Columbia, Mo., 1938 (*Univ. Mo. Studies*, XIII, No. 1, 278 pp.).

Four studies of the influence of Mark Twain are Edgar H. Hemminghaus, *Mark Twain in Germany*, New York, 1939—covering the years 1874 to the present, with extensive bibliography; Archibald Henderson, "The International Fame of Mark Twain," *No. Amer. Rev.*, CXCII (1910), 805–815; Stephen Leacock, "Mark Twain and Canada," *Queen's Quar.*, XLII (1935), 68–81; and Adolph B. Benson, "Mark Twain's Contacts with Scandinavia," *Scand. Studies and Notes*, XIV (1937), 159–167.

A significant early French estimate of Mark Twain is Marie Thérèse Blanc (pseud., Th. Bentzon), "Les Humoristes Américains: I. Mark Twain," *Revue des Deux Mondes*, C (1872), 313–335.

Other studies of special aspects of Mark Twain's career are G. W. James, "Mark Twain and the Pacific Coast," *Pacific Mo.*, XXIV (1910), 115–132; H. Houston Peckham, "The Literary Status of Mark Twain, 1877–1890," *So. Atl. Quar.*, XIX (1920), 332–340; "Mark Twain and the Theater," in Brander Matthews, *Playwrights on Playmaking*, New York, 1923, pp. 159–184; Harold Meyer, "Mark Twain on the Comstock," *Southwest Rev.*, XII (1927), 197–207; Fred W. Lorch, "Mark Twain in Iowa," *Iowa Jour. of Hist. and Politics*, XXVII (1929), 408–456, 507–547—on Mark Twain as lecturer; Herbert L. Stewart, "Mark Twain on the Jewish Question," *Dalhousie Rev.*, XIV (1934), 455–458; Hyatt H. Waggoner, "Science in the Thought of Mark Twain," *Amer. Lit.*, VIII (1937), 357–370; J[ohn] De Lancey Ferguson, "The Case for Mark Twain's Wife," *Univ. of Toronto Quar.*, IX (1939), 9–21; Dudley R. Hutcherson, "Mark Twain as a Pilot," *Amer. Lit.*, XII (1940), 353–355; Fred W. Lorch, "Mark Twain and the 'Campaign That Failed,'" *Amer. Lit.*, XII (1941), 454–470—on Mark Twain's brief experience as a Rebel soldier in Missouri; "Mark Twain," in Walter F. Taylor, *The Economic Novel in America*, Chapel Hill, N.C., 1942, pp. 116–147; Max Lederer, "Mark Twain in Vienna," *Mark Twain Quar.*, VII (1945), 1–12; Edgar H. Hemminghaus, "Mark Twain's German Provenience," *Modern Language Quar.*, VI (1945), 459–478; and George I. Bidewell, "Mark Twain's Florida Years," *Missouri Hist. Rev.*, XL (1946), 159–173. See also Effie Mona Mack, *Mark Twain in Nevada*, New York, 1947—the three years 1861–1863.

Themes, sources, and other topics relating directly to the works of Mark Twain are Olin H. Moore, "Mark Twain and Don Quixote," *PMLA*, XXXVII (1922), 324–346; Victor R. West, "Folklore in the Works of Mark

Twain," *Univ. of Nebr. Studies in Lang., Lit., and Crit.,* Lincoln, Nebr., 1930, No. 10—an 87-page study, with index; Dixon Wecter, "Mark Twain and the West," *Hunt. Lib. Quar.,* VIII (1945), 359–377—the influence of the Nevada and California years on his literary career; Gladys C. Bellamy, "Mark Twain's Indebtedness to John Phoenix," *Amer. Lit.,* XIII (1941), 29–43; G. Harrison Orians, "Walter Scott, Mark Twain, and the Civil War," *So. Atl. Quar.,* XL (1941), 342–359.

Studies relating to separate stories are Alma B. Martin, *A Vocabulary Study of "The Gilded Age,"* Webster Groves, Mo., 1930, with an introduction by Robert L. Ramsay, a foreword by Hamlin Garland, and a brief bibliography; Franklin Walker, "An Influence from San Francisco on Mark Twain's *The Gilded Age,*" *Amer. Lit.,* VIII (1936), 63–66; Ernest E. Leisy, "Mark Twain's Part in *The Gilded Age,*" *Amer. Lit.,* VIII (1937), 445–447; Jacob Blanck, *"The Gilded Age:* A Collation," *Pub. Weekly,* CXXXVIII (1940), 186–188; Walter F. Taylor, "Mark Twain and the Machine Age," *So. Atl. Quar.,* XXXVII (1938), 384–396; and Frank C. Willson, "That *Gilded Age* Again: An Attempt to Unmuddle the Mystery of the Fifty-seven Variants," *Papers Bibl. Soc. Amer.,* XXXVII (1943), 141–156. Five items dealing with *Huckleberry Finn* are W. Beck, "Huckleberry Finn *versus* the Cash Boy," *Education,* XLIX (1928), 1–13; De Lancey Ferguson, "Huck Finn Aborning," *Colophon,* n.s. III (1938), no. 2, 171–180; Arthur L. Vogelback, "The Publication and Reception of *Huckleberry Finn* in America," *Amer. Lit.,* XI (1939), 260–272; Fred W. Lorch, "A Note on Tom Blankenship (Huckleberry Finn)," *Amer. Lit.,* XII (1940), 351–353; and "Mark Twain, Hank, and Huck," in Walter Blair, *Horse Sense in American Humor . . . ,* Chicago, 1942, pp. 195–217. Studies of *Tom Sawyer* are J. Christian Bay, "Tom Sawyer, Detective: The Origin of the Plot," in *Essays Offered to Herbert Putnam . . .* (ed. by William W. Bishop and Andrew Keogh), New Haven, 1929, pp. 80–88; Howard S. Mott, Jr., "The Origin of Aunt Polly," *Pub. Weekly,* CXXXIV (1938), 1821–1823; Walter Blair, "On the Structure of *Tom Sawyer,*" *Modern Philol.,* XXXVII (1939), 75–88; Theodore Hornberger, ed., *Mark Twain's Letters to Will Bowen . . . ,* Austin, Tex., 1941—which supplies data on *Tom Sawyer;* and John B. Hoben, "Mark Twain's *A Connecticut Yankee:* A Genetic Study," *Amer. Lit.,* XVIII (1946), 197–218.

Other studies are Frederick A. G. Cowper, "The Hermit Story, as Used by Voltaire and Mark Twain," in *Papers . . . in Honor of . . . Charles Frederick Johnson . . .* (ed. by Odell Shepard and Arthur Adams), Hartford, Conn., 1928, pp. 313–337; Fred W. Lorch, "A Source for Mark Twain's 'The Dandy Frightening the Squatter,'" *Amer. Lit.,* III (1931), 309–313; Arthur L. Vogelback, *"The Prince and the Pauper:* A Study in Critical Standards," *ibid.,* XIV (1942), 48–54; George Feinstein, "Mark Twain's Idea of Story Structure," *ibid.*, XVIII (1946), 160–163; C. Grant Loomis, "Dan De Quille's Mark Twain," *Pacific Hist. Rev.*, XV (1946), 336–347—on the influence of his friendship with Dan De Quille (William Wright); Mary A. Wyman, "A Note on Mark Twain," *College Eng.*, VII (1946), 438–442; and Sven B. Liljegren, "The Revolt Against Romanticism in American Literature as Evidenced in the Works of S. L. Clemens," in *Essays and Studies on Amer. Lang. and Lit.* (Publ. Amer. Inst. Univ. Upsala, No. 1, 1947), 60 pp.

PRIMARY SOURCES

In addition to Mark Twain's published autobiography, letters, and notebooks, source material is most readily found in William D. Howells, *My Mark Twain: Reminiscences and Criticisms,* New York, 1910; Clara Clemens (Gabrilowitsch), *My Father, Mark Twain,* New York, 1931; and in an early biography, Will M. Clemens, *Mark Twain, His Life and Work: A Biographical Sketch,* San Francisco, 1892 (New York, 1894). Other scattered sources are Elizabeth Wallace, *Mark Twain and the Happy Island,* Chicago, 1913; Henry W. H. Fischer, *Abroad with Mark Twain and Eugene Field: Tales They Told to a Fellow Correspondent,* New York, 1922; Mary Lawton, *A Lifetime with Mark Twain: The Memoirs of Katy Leary, for Thirty Years His Faithful and Devoted Servant,* New York, 1925; William R. Gillis, *Gold Rush Days with Mark Twain,* New York, 1930; Opie P. Read, *Mark Twain and I,* Chicago, 1940; and Cyril Clemens, *Young Sam Clemens,* Portland, Me., 1943—chiefly anecdotal.

Brief published reminiscences are Joseph H. Twichell, "Mark Twain," *Harper's Mag.*, XCII (1896), 817–827; "Mark Twain Number," *Bookman,* XXXI (June, 1910); "Memories of Mark Twain," in Brander Matthews, *The Tocsin of Revolt and Other Essays,* New York, 1922, pp. 251–294; "Mark Twain Number," *Mentor,* XII (1924), 3–58—profusely illustrated; William R. Gillis, *Memories of Mark Twain and Steve Gillis,* Sonora, Calif., 1924—a record of mining experiences; Absalom Grimes, "Campaigning with Mark Twain," *Missouri Hist. Rev.*, XXI (1927), 188–201—edited by Milo M. Quaife; and George Ade, *One Afternoon with Mark Twain,* Chicago, 1939.

The bulk of the manuscripts of Mark Twain is owned by the Mark Twain Estate: see Bernard De Voto, "The Mark Twain Papers," *Sat. Rev. Lit.*, XIX (Dec. 10, 1938), 3–4, 14–15. On the Hannibal Papers presented to the State Historical Society of Missouri, at Columbia, see C. J. Armstrong, "Mark Twain's Early Writings Discovered," *Missouri Hist. Rev.*, XXIV (1930), 485–501. An account of the Frear Collection of Mark Twain material at Yale is given by Gilbert M. Troxell, "Samuel Langhorne Clemens, 1835–1910," *Yale Univ. Lib. Gazette,* XVIII (1943), 1–5. Important holdings are in the

Library of Congress. Lesser collections are in the Henry E. Huntington Library, the Boston Public Library, and the Princeton University Library.

BIBLIOGRAPHY

The most thorough bibliography of the printing of works of Mark Twain is Merle Johnson, *A Bibliography of the Works of Mark Twain, Samuel Langhorne Clemens: A List of First Editions in Book Form and of First Printings in Periodicals and Occasional Publications of His Varied Literary Activities,* New York, 1935—rev., with new material added, from orig. ed. of 1910. A bibliography of books and articles dealing with Mark Twain between 1869 and 1910 appears in Archibald Henderson, *Mark Twain,* London, 1911, pp. 215–230. Further listings are included in Bernard De Voto, *Mark Twain's America,* Boston, 1932, pp. 323–334; Minnie M. Brashear, *Mark Twain, Son of Missouri,* Chapel Hill, N.C., 1934, pp. 264–284; Edward C. Wagenknecht, *Mark Twain: The Man and His Work,* New Haven, 1935, pp. 281–290; Fred L. Pattee, ed., *Mark Twain: Representative Selections . . . ,* New York, 1935, pp. liii–lxi; Ivan Benson, *Mark Twain's Western Years . . . ,* Stanford Univ., Calif., 1938—including "Periodical Bibliography: Bibliography of the Writings of Mark Twain in the Newspapers and Magazines of Nevada and California, 1861–1866," pp. 165–174; and Edgar M. Branch, "A Chronological Bibliography of the Writings of Samuel Clemens to June 8, 1867," *Amer. Lit.,* XVIII (1946), 109–159. See also Harry Hartwick, in Walter F. Taylor, *A History of American Letters,* New York, 1936, pp. 545–549.

Two Mark Twain societies have issued publications. The Mark Twain Society, Webster Groves, Mo., has issued the *Mark Twain Quarterly* since 1936. The *Twainian,* a mimeographed publication of the Mark Twain Society of Chicago, appeared during 1939–1940.

# JAMES FENIMORE COOPER
## *1789–1851*

SEPARATE WORKS

*Precaution: A Novel,* 1820; *The Spy: A Tale of the Neutral Ground,* 1821; *The Pioneers; or, The Sources of the Susquehanna: A Descriptive Tale,* 1823; *Tales for Fifteen,* 1823; *The Pilot: A Tale of the Sea,* 1823; *Lionel Lincoln; or, The Leaguer of Boston,* 1825; *The Last of the Mohicans: A Narrative of 1757,* 1826; *The Prairie: A Tale,* 1827; *The Red Rover: A Tale,* 1828; *Notions of the Americans, Picked Up by a Travelling Bachelor,* 1828; *The Wept of Wish-ton-Wish: A Tale,* 1829; *The Water-Witch; or, The Skimmer of the Seas,* 1831; *The Bravo: A Tale,* 1831; *The Heidenmauer; or, The Benedictines: A Legend of the Rhine,* 1832; *The Headsman; or, The Abbaye des*

*Vignerons: A Tale*, 1833; *A Letter to His Countrymen*, 1834; *The Monikins*, 1835; *Sketches of Switzerland*, 1836; *Sketches of Switzerland: Part Second*, 1836; *Gleanings in Europe* (France), 1837; *Gleanings in Europe: England*, 1837; *Gleanings in Europe: Italy*, 1838; *The American Democrat*, 1838; *Homeward Bound; or, The Chase: A Tale of the Sea*, 1838; *Home as Found*, 1838; *The History of the Navy of the United States of America*, 1839; *The Pathfinder; or, The Inland Sea*, 1840; *Mercedes of Castile; or, The Voyage to Cathay*, 1840; *The Deerslayer; or, The First War-Path*, 1841; *The Two Admirals: A Tale*, 1842; *The Wing-and-Wing; or, Le Feu-Follet: A Tale*, 1842; *Le Mouchoir: An Autobiographical Romance*, 1843; *Wyandotté; or, The Hutted Knoll: A Tale*, 1843; *Ned Myers; or, A Life Before the Mast*, 1843; *Afloat and Ashore; or, The Adventures of Miles Wallingford* (two series), 1844; *Satanstoe; or, The Littlepage Manuscripts: A Tale of the Colony*, 1845; *The Chainbearer; or, The Littlepage Manuscripts*, 1845; *Lives of Distinguished American Naval Officers*, 1846; *The Redskins; or, Indian and Injin: Being the Conclusion of the Littlepage Manuscripts*, 1846; *The Crater; or, Vulcan's Peak: A Tale of the Pacific*, 1847; *Jack Tier; or, The Florida Reef*, 1848; *The Oak Openings; or, The Bee-Hunter*, 1848; *The Sea Lions; or, The Lost Sealers*, 1849; *The Ways of the Hour: A Tale*, 1850.

## COLLECTED WORKS

*The Works of J. Fenimore Cooper*, New York, 1849–1851, 12 vols., is the Author's Revised Edition. The first definitive edition of Cooper's *Works*, containing all novels except *Ned Myers* but no non-fiction prose or short tales, was published in 32 vols., with illustrations by F. O. C. Darley, important for identification, New York, 1859–1861. The Household Edition of the *Works*, New York, 1876–1884, 32 vols., was published with introductions to many of the volumes by the author's daughter Susan Fenimore Cooper. The most easily procurable text is *The Works of James Fenimore Cooper*, New York, 1895–1900, 33 vols.

The author's grandson, James F. Cooper, edited the *Correspondence of James Fenimore Cooper*, New Haven, 1922, 2 vols., compiled for the most part from letters to Cooper. The scattered gleanings of Cooper's published letters are calendared by Robert E. Spiller, *James Fenimore Cooper: Representative Selections* . . . , New York, 1936, pp. lxxxix–cii. A recent collection is Susan E. Lyman, "'I Could Write You a Better Book Than That Myself': Twenty-five Unpublished Letters of James Fenimore Cooper," *Bul. N.Y. Hist. Soc.*, XXIX (1945), 213–241.

## EDITED TEXTS AND REPRINTS

Modern reprints of the following have been published: *The Spy* (1821), ed. by Tremaine McDowell, New York, 1931 (Modern Student's Lib.); *The*

*Pioneers* (1823), London, 1907 (Everyman); *The Last of the Mohicans* (1826), London, 1906 (Everyman), and ed. with an introduction by Fred L. Pattee, New York, 1927 (Modern Readers' Ser.); *The Prairie* (1827), London, 1907 (Everyman); *Gleanings in Europe* (France and England, 1837), ed. with an introduction by Robert E. Spiller, New York, 1928–1930, 2 vols.; *The American Democrat* (1838), ed. with an introduction by H. L. Mencken, New York, 1931; *The Pathfinder* (1840), London, 1906 (Everyman); *The Deerslayer* (1841), London, 1906 (Everyman), and ed. with an introduction by Gregory Paine, New York, 1927 (Amer. Authors Ser.); *Satanstoe* (1845), ed. with chronology and bibl. by Robert E. Spiller and J. D. Coppock, New York, 1937 (Amer. Fiction Ser.).

The most serviceable one-volume text of the non-fiction prose is Robert E. Spiller, *James Fenimore Cooper: Representative Selections, with Introduction, Bibliography, and Notes,* New York, 1936.

BIOGRAPHY AND CRITICISM

Thomas R. Lounsbury's *James Fenimore Cooper,* Boston, 1882, is not yet superseded. The biography of Robert E. Spiller, *Fenimore Cooper: Critic of His Times,* New York, 1931, gives data on Cooper's relationship with publishers and on his European travels, places emphasis on his social thought, and concludes with a bibliographical note (pp. 319–325); it is supplemented by his introduction to *James Fenimore Cooper: Representative Selections . . . ,* New York, 1936. The best short biography is William B. Shubrick Clymer's *James Fenimore Cooper,* Boston, 1900. Among recent estimates, new material is included in the narrative (not critical) life by Henry W. Boynton, *James Fenimore Cooper,* New York, 1931.

Estimates of Cooper by other men of letters, significant to the extent that the authors are spokesmen of their times, are those of Poe in J. B. Moore, ed., *Selections from Poe's Literary Criticism,* New York, 1926, pp. 126–142; "The Writings of James Fenimore Cooper," in William Gilmore Simms, *Views and Reviews in American Literature,* New York, 1845, first ser., pp. 210–238; Francis Parkman, "James Fenimore Cooper," *No. Amer. Rev.,* CLIV (1852), 147–161; William Cullen Bryant, *Orations and Addresses,* New York, 1873, pp. 45–91; Mark Twain, "Fenimore Cooper's Literary Offenses," *No. Amer. Rev.,* CLXI (1895), 1–12—a classic attack; William D. Howells, *Heroines of Fiction,* New York, 1901, I, 102–112; Mark A. De Wolfe Howe, *American Bookmen,* New York, 1902, pp. 29–51; Edmund C. Stedman, "Poe, Cooper, and the Hall of Fame," *No. Amer. Rev.,* CLXXXV (1907), 801–812; "Cooper," in William C. Brownell, *American Prose Masters,* New York, 1909, pp. 3–60; "James Fenimore Cooper," in John Erskine, *Leading American Novelists,* New York, 1910, pp. 51–129; Brander Matthews, *Gateways to Literature,* New York, 1912, pp. 243–276; Joseph Conrad, *Notes on Life and*

*Letters,* New York, 1921, pp. 53–57; "James Fenimore Cooper," in Carl Van Doren, *The American Novel,* New York, 1921 (rev. ed., 1940), pp. 21–42; Vernon L. Parrington, *Main Currents in American Thought,* New York, 1927–1930, II, 222–237; Henry S. Canby, *Classic Americans,* New York, 1931, pp. 97–142; Van Wyck Brooks, *The World of Washington Irving,* New York, 1944—(three chapters: "Cooper: The First Phase," "Irving and Cooper Abroad," and "New York: Cooper," pp. 214–233, 315–336, 399–425). Further estimates will be found in Marcel Clavel, *Fenimore Cooper and His Critics* . . . , and in his detailed biographical study: *Fenimore Cooper, sa vie et son œuvre: La Jeunesse (1789–1826)*, both issued at Aix-en-Provence, 1938.

Four studies of Cooper as social critic by Robert E. Spiller are "Fenimore Cooper, Critic of His Times: New Letters from Rome and Paris, 1830–31," *Amer. Lit.,* I (1929), 131–148; "Fenimore Cooper's Defense of Slave-Owning America," *Amer. Hist. Rev.,* XXXV (1930), 575–582; "Fenimore Cooper and Lafayette: 'The Finance Controversy of 1831–1832," *Amer. Lit.,* III (1931), 28–44; and "Fenimore Cooper and Lafayette: Friends of Polish Freedom, 1830–1832," *Amer. Lit.,* VII (1935), 56–75. Further material revealing Cooper in his own times is in Dorothy Waples, *The Whig Myth of James Fenimore Cooper,* New Haven, 1938. John F. Ross has published *The Social Criticism of Fenimore Cooper,* Berkeley, Calif., 1933.

Cooper's influence abroad is the subject of Preston A. Barba, *Cooper in Germany,* Bloomington, Ind., 1914; E. P. Dargan, "Balzac and Cooper: *Les Chouans,*" *Modern Philol.,* XIII (1915), 193–213; J. De Lancey Ferguson, *American Literature in Spain,* New York, 1916, pp. 32–54; Robert E. Spiller, *The American in England,* New York, 1926, pp. 300–345; Margaret M. Gibb, *Le Roman de Bas-de-Cuir: Etude sur Fenimore Cooper et Son Influence en France,* Paris, 1927; Georgette Bosset, *Fenimore Cooper et le Roman d'Aventure en France vers 1830* . . . , Paris, 1928; Emilio Goggio, "Cooper's *Bravo* in Italy," *Romanic Rev.,* XX (1929), 222–230.

Themes and sources in Cooper's novels are discussed in Ernest E. Leisy, *The American Historical Novel . . . The Early Novels of James Fenimore Cooper, 1821–1831,* Urbana, Ill., 1926; Albert Keiser, *The Indian in American Literature,* New York, 1933, pp. 101–143; and Jason A. Russell, "Cooper: Interpreter of the Real and the Historical Indian," *Jour. Amer. Hist.,* XXIII (1930), 41–71. Studies of individual novels have been made, as follows:

Of *The Spy* (1821): Tremaine McDowell, "The Identity of Harvey Birch," *Amer. Lit.,* II (1930), 111–120; *idem,* introduction to Modern Student's Lib. ed. of *The Spy,* New York, 1931.

Of *The Pioneers* (1823): Andrew Nelson, "James Cooper and George Croghan," *Philological Quar.,* XX (1941), 69–73.

Of *The Prairie* (1827): John T. Flanagan, "The Authenticity of Cooper's *The Prairie,*" *Modern Lang. Quar.,* II (1941), 99–104.

Of *The Red Rover* (1828): John D. Gordan, *"The Red Rover* Takes the Boards," *Amer. Lit.,* X (1938), 66-75.

Of *The Headsman* (1833): Thomas R. Palfrey, "Cooper and Balzac: *The Headsman," Modern Philol.,* XXIX (1932), 335-341.

Of *Mercedes of Castile* (1840): Donald M. Goodfellow, "The Sources of *Mercedes of Castile," Amer. Lit.,* XII (1940), 318-328.

Of *Satanstoe* (1845); Dorothy Dondore, "The Debt of Two Dyed-in-the-Wool Americans to Mrs. Grant's *Memoirs:* Cooper's *Satanstoe* and Paulding's *The Dutchman's Fireside," Amer. Lit.,* XII (1940), 52-58.

Three studies of the Leatherstocking Tales are: James Routh, "The Model of the Leatherstocking Tales," *Modern Language Notes,* XXVIII (1913), 77-79; Gregory L. Paine, "The Indians of the Leatherstocking Tales," *Studies in Philol.,* XXIII (1926), 16-39; and Louise Pound, "The Dialect of Cooper's Leatherstocking," *Amer. Speech,* II (1927), 479-488.

Other discussions that throw light on Cooper's life and work are Harold H. Scudder, "What Mr. Cooper Read to His Wife," *Sewanee Rev.,* XXXVI (1928), 177-194 (see G. E. Hastings' reply below); E. R. Outland, *The Effingham Libels on Cooper,* Univ. Wis. Studies in Language and Lit., No. 28 (1929)—including an appendix with documents on the war with the press; Robert E. Spiller, "Cooper's Notes on Language," *Amer. Speech,* IV (1929), 294-300; Tremaine McDowell, "James Fenimore Cooper as Self-Critic," *Studies in Philol.,* XXVII (1930), 508-516; Gregory Paine, "Cooper and *The North American Review," Studies in Philol.,* XXVIII (1931), 799-809; John A. Kouwenhoven, "Cooper's 'Upside Down' Turns Up," *Colophon,* n.s. III (1938), No. 4, 524-530—on his first and only play; "Fenimore Cooper, or The Ruins of Time," in Yvor Winters, *Maule's Curse . . . ,* Norfolk, Conn., 1938, pp. 25-50; Louis H. Bolander, "The Naval Career of James Fenimore Cooper," *Proc. U.S. Naval Inst.,* LXVI (1940), 541-550; George E. Hastings, "How Cooper Became a Novelist," *Amer. Lit.,* XII (1940), 20-51; Emilio Goggio, "The Italy of James Fenimore Cooper," *Modern Language Jour.,* XXIX (1945), 66-71; George Snell, "The Shaper of American Romance," *Yale Rev.,* XXXIV (1945), 482-494; Granville Hicks, "Landlord Cooper and the Anti-Renters," *Antioch Rev.,* V (1945), 95-109; William H. Bonner, "Cooper and Captain Kidd," *Modern Language Notes,* LXI (1946), 21-27; Russell Kirk, "Cooper and the European Puzzle," *College Eng.,* VII (1946), 198-207; and H. Lüdeke, "James Fenimore Cooper and the Democracy of Switzerland," *Eng. Studies,* XXVII (1946), 33-34.

PRIMARY SOURCES

*The Cooper Gallery; or, Pages and Pictures from the Writings of James Fenimore Cooper,* New York, 1865, with notes by Susan Fenimore Cooper, is important. Susan Fenimore Cooper's published reminiscences, "A Glance Backward" and "A Second Glance Backward," *Atl. Mo.*, LIX (1887), 199–206, and LX (1887), 474–486, add further details. W. R. Littell edited *A History of Cooperstown*, Cooperstown, N.Y., 1929; and James F. Cooper's *The Legends and Traditions of a Northern County* supplies notes and documents relating to Cooperstown.

The bulk of Cooper's manuscripts, until recently in the hands of the family, has now been deposited in the Yale University Library. In the library of the Historical Society of Pennsylvania, and in the Historical Society at Burlington, N.J., there are deposited copies of a manuscript dictionary of characters in Cooper's novels, compiled by Thomas Chalkley Matlock, together with plot summaries and excerpts from contemporary criticism.

BIBLIOGRAPHY

*A Descriptive Bibliography of the Writings of James Fenimore Cooper*, New York, 1934, by Robert E. Spiller and Philip C. Blackburn, provides in its introduction data on copyright conditions and on correspondence of Cooper with his publishers. A selective and annotated bibliography, useful for secondary sources and for scattered letters and correspondence, is provided in Robert E. Spiller, *James Fenimore Cooper: Representative Selections . . .*, New York, 1936, pp. lxxxix–cii. In the Cooper Collection at Yale, in manuscript, is "A Bibliography of James Fenimore Cooper," prepared by Cooper's grandson James F. Cooper, with some entries not found elsewhere. Preston A. Barba compiled a list of "German Translations of Cooper's Works," in *Cooper in Germany*, Bloomington, Ind., 1914, pp. 93–104.

# JOHN COTTON
## 1584–1652

SEPARATE WORKS

*Gods Promise to His Plantation*, 1630; *An Abstract of the Lawes of New England*, 1641; *The Way of Life*, 1641; *A Briefe Exposition of the Whole Book of Canticles*, 1642; *The Powrring Out of the Seven Vials*, 1642; *A Letter . . . to Mr. Williams*, 1643; *The Keyes of the Kingdom of Heaven*, 1644; *The Covenant of Gods Free Grace*, 1645; *The Way of the Churches of Christ in New-England*, 1645; *The Controversie Concerning Liberty of Conscience in Matters of Religion*, 1646; *Milk for Babes*, 1646; *The Bloudy Tenent, Washed, and Made White in the Bloud of the Lambe*, 1647; *The Way of Congregational Churches Cleared*, 1648; *Christ the Fountaine of Life*, 1651; *A Briefe Exposition . . . of Ecclesiastes*, 1654; *The New Covenant*, 1654; *An*

*Exposition upon the Thirteenth Chapter of the Revelation,* 1655; *The Cove-nant of Grace,* 1655; *A Brief Exposition . . . of Canticles,* 1655; *A Practical Commentary . . . upon the First Epistle Generall of John,* 1656.

### EDITED TEXTS AND REPRINTS

No collection of Cotton's works has been made. Individual works were often reprinted during the seventeenth century. Modern reprints may be found as follows: Edwin D. Mead, "John Cotton's Farewell Sermon to Winthrop's Company at Southampton," *Proc. Mass. Hist. Soc.,* 3rd ser., I (1908), 101–115—a reprint of *Gods Promise,* with introduction; *An Abstract of the Lawes,* commonly known as "Moses His Judicials," in Thomas Hutch-inson, *A Collection of Original Papers . . . ,* 1769, in *Coll. Mass. Hist. Soc.,* 1st ser., V (1798), 173–192, and in Force, *Tracts,* III (1844), No. 9. The pamphlets Cotton wrote in the Cotton-Williams controversy are reprinted in Vols. I–IV of *The Writings of Roger Williams,* Providence, 1866–1870. The "Copy of a Letter from Mr. Cotton to Lord Say and Seal in the Year 1636," is in Thomas Hutchinson, *The History of the Colony and Province of Massachusetts-Bay* (1764), ed. Mayo, I (1936), 414–417. Three letters are printed in Alexander Young, *Chronicles of the First Planters . . . ,* Boston, 1846, pp. 419–444, together with a contemporary biographical sketch attributed to Samuel Whiting.

### BIOGRAPHY AND CRITICISM

All the authoritative biographies of Cotton are brief; the best life is that of Williston Walker in *Ten New England Leaders,* New York, 1901, pp. 49–94. The sketch in *Dict. Amer. Biog.* (1930) is written by James T. Adams.

The Cotton-Williams controversy is the subject of two useful studies: Henry B. Parkes, "John Cotton and Roger Williams Debate Toleration, 1644–1652," *New Eng. Quar.,* IV (1931), 735–756; and Elizabeth Hirsch, "John Cotton and Roger Williams: Their Controversy Concerning Re-ligious Liberty," *Church Hist.,* X (1941), 38–51. The fullest treatment of the historical background is that of Charles M. Andrews, "Religious and Political Difficulties in the Bay Colony," Chap. XXI in *The Colonial Period of American History,* New Haven, I (1934), 462–495.

The best account of Cotton and the Antinomian affair is Charles F. Adams, *Three Episodes of Massachusetts History,* Boston, 1892, 2 vols.

Other studies are Moses C. Tyler, in *A History of American Literature During the Colonial Period,* rev. ed., New York, 1897, I, 210–216; Isabel M. Calder, "John Cotton and the New Haven Colony," *New Eng. Quar.,* III (1930), 82–94; and Theodore Hornberger, "Puritanism and Science: The Relationship Revealed in the Writings of John Cotton," *New Eng. Quar.*, X (1937), 503–515.

Studies of *An Abstract of the Lawes of New England* (1641) are Worthington C. Ford, "Cotton's 'Moses His Judicials,'" *Proc. Mass. Hist. Soc.*, 2nd ser., XVI (1903), 274–284; and Isabel M. Calder, "John Cotton's 'Moses His Judicials,'" *Pub. Col. Soc. Mass.*, XXVIII (1935), 86–94. Isabel M. Calder's "The Authorship of a Discourse About Civil Government . . . ," *Amer. Hist. Rev.*, XXXVII (1932), 267–269, gives evidence that the work is by Davenport.

## PRIMARY SOURCES

A contemporary biographical sketch will be found in what is said to be the first American biography, John Norton's life of Cotton: *Abel Being Dead Yet Speaketh*, Cambridge, 1657, reprinted with notes by Enoch Pond, Boston, 1834, and discussed in Dana K. Merrill, "The First American Biography," *New Eng. Quar.*, XI (1938), 152–154. Cotton Mather's life of his grandfather, included in the *Magnalia*, was first published as *Johannes in Eremo: Memoirs Relating to . . . John Cotton*, Boston, 1695.

There is an important manuscript collection of Cotton Papers in the Boston Public Library. Other Cotton manuscripts are in the library of Bowdoin College.

## BIBLIOGRAPHY

An authoritative bibliography is Julius H. Tuttle, "Writings of Rev. John Cotton," in *Bibliographical Essays: A Tribute to Wilberforce Eames*, Cambridge, 1924, pp. 363–380.

## (HAROLD) HART CRANE
### *1899–1932*

## SEPARATE WORKS

*White Buildings: Poems*, 1926; *The Bridge: A Poem*, 1930.

## COLLECTED WORKS

Waldo Frank edited *The Collected Poems of Hart Crane*, New York, 1933, with an introduction. The volume includes uncollected early and later poems.

## BIOGRAPHY AND CRITICISM

Philip Horton's *Hart Crane: The Life of an American Poet*, New York, 1937, is a balanced critical biography based on information from Crane's literary associates and on his correspondence. The best brief sketch is that of F. O. Matthiessen in *Dict. Amer. Biog., Supplement One* (1944).

Allen Tate contributed the introduction to *White Buildings* (1926). The fullest critical estimates are "Hart Crane," in Allen Tate, *Reactionary Essays on Poetry and Ideas,* New York, 1936, pp. 26-42; "New Thresholds, New Anatomies: Notes on a Text by Hart Crane," in R(ichard) P. Blackmur, *The Double Agent,* New York, 1935, pp. 121-140. Other sympathetic studies are Gorham B. Munson, *Destinations,* New York, 1928, pp. 160-177; Morton D. Zabel, "The Book of Hart Crane," *Poetry,* XLII (1933), 33-39; Babette Deutsch, *This Modern Poetry,* New York, 1935, pp. 150-157; Howard Moss, "Disorder as Myth: Hart Crane's *The Bridge,*" *Poetry,* LXII (1943), 32-45; Hyatt H. Waggoner, "Hart Crane's Bridge to Cathay," *Amer. Lit.,* XVI (1944), 115-130; and *idem,* "Hart Crane and the Broken Parabola," *Univ. Kansas City Rev.,* VIII (1945), 173-177.

Less sympathetic estimates are Max Eastman, *The Literary Mind,* New York, 1931, *passim;* Howard Blake, "Thoughts on Modern Poetry," *Sewanee Rev.,* LIII (1935), 187-196; and Yvor Winters, "The Progress of Hart Crane," *Poetry,* XXXVI (1930), 153-165.

A collection of the Crane-Munson correspondence is in the Library of Ohio State University. A bibliographical listing is in Fred B. Millett, *Contemporary American Authors,* New York, 1940, pp. 305-306. See also the recent compilation by Frances Cheney, in Allen Tate, *Sixty American Poets, 1896-1944,* Washington, 1945, p. 24.

## STEPHEN CRANE
### *1871-1900*

SEPARATE WORKS

*Maggie: A Girl of the Streets,* 1892; *The Black Riders and Other Lines* [Poems], 1895; *The Red Badge of Courage,* 1895; *A Souvenir and a Medley,* 1896; *The Little Regiment,* 1896; *George's Mother,* 1896; *The Third Violet,* 1897; *The Open Boat and Other Tales of Adventure,* 1898; *Active Service,* 1899; *War Is Kind* [Poems], 1899; *The Monster and Other Stories,* 1899; *Wounds in the Rain,* 1900; *Whilomville Stories,* 1900; *Great Battles of the World,* 1901; *Last Words,* 1902; *The O'Ruddy* (with Robert Barr), 1903; *A Battle in Greece,* 1936.

COLLECTED WORKS

*The Work of Stephen Crane,* New York, 1925-1926, 12 vols., ed. by Wilson Follett, has introductions by various hands, some personal reminiscence, some critical. Follett also edited *The Collected Poems of Stephen Crane,* New York, 1930. No collection of Crane's letters has been made. Those now published will be found in "Some Letters of Stephen Crane," *Academy,* LIX (Aug. 11, 1900), 116; *Two Letters from Stephen Crane to Joseph Conrad,* London, 1926; and "A Stephen Crane Letter . . . ," *Colophon,* No. 6, 1930. See also Lyndon U. Pratt, "An Addition to the Canon of Stephen Crane," *Research Studies State Coll. Wash.,* VII (1939), 55–58.

EDITED TEXTS AND REPRINTS

*Men, Women, and Boats,* New York, 1921, and *Maggie: A Girl of the Streets, and Other Stories,* New York, 1933, are volumes of selections in the Modern Library, with introductions by Vincent Starrett. *The Red Badge of Courage* was issued in the Modern Library, New York, 1942, and in Pocket Books, New York, 1942; and it was included in the Modern Literature Series, New York, 1926, with an introduction by Max J. Herzberg. Carl Van Doren's selection of *Twenty Stories . . . ,* New York, 1940, contains most of Crane's memorable work with the exception of *The Red Badge of Courage.* Another volume of selections is *Maggie, Together with George's Mother and The Blue Hotel,* New York, 1931, with an introduction by Henry Hazlitt.

BIOGRAPHY AND CRITICISM

Thomas Beer's *Stephen Crane: A Study in American Letters,* New York, 1923, remains the best portrait to date, and supersedes the pioneer biographical study of Thomas L. Raymond, *Stephen Crane,* Newark, N.J., 1923. Critical estimates will be found in the introductions to the several volumes of *The Works of Stephen Crane* (New York, 1925-1926) contributed as follows: Carl Van Doren, Vol. IV; Amy Lowell, Vol. VI; Willa Cather, Vol. IX; and H. L. Mencken, Vol. X.

Other studies of Crane's technique are "Prose for Fiction: Stephen Crane," in Gorham B. Munson, *Style and Form in American Prose,* New York, 1929, pp. 159-170; "The Voyage of Stephen Crane," in Matthew Josephson, *Portrait of the Artist as American,* New York, 1930, pp. 232-264; Harry Hartwick, *The Foreground of American Fiction,* New York, 1934, pp. 21-44—with emphasis on science and determinism; Henry Lüdeke, "Stephen Cranes Gedichte," *Anglia,* LXII (1938), 410-422; Russel B. Nye, "Stephen Crane as Social Critic," *Modern Quar.,* XI (1940), 48-54; David H. Dickason, "Stephen Crane and the *Philistine,*" *Amer. Lit.,* XV (1943), 279-287.

Source and theme are investigated in Lyndon U. Pratt, "A Possible Source for *The Red Badge of Courage,*" *Amer. Lit.,* XI (1939), 1-10; and H. T. Webster, "Wilbur F. Hinman's *Corporal Si Klegg* and Stephen Crane's *The Red Badge of Courage,*" *Amer. Lit.,* XI (1939), 285-293.

Estimates and appreciations by other men of letters are H. G. Wells, "Stephen Crane from an English Standpoint," *No. Amer. Rev.*, CLXXI (1900), 233–242; Hamlin Garland, "Stephen Crane as I Knew Him," *Yale Rev.*, n.s. III (1914), 494–506; Joseph Conrad, "Stephen Crane: A Note Without Dates," *Bookman*, L (1920), 529–531; Edward Garnett, *Friday Nights*, New York, 1922, pp. 201–217; Carl Van Doren, "Stephen Crane," *Amer. Mercury*, I (1924), 11–14; and "Stephen Crane," in Ford Madox Ford, *Portraits from Life*, Boston, 1937, pp. 21–37.

Three studies of Crane as an undergraduate are Harvey Wickham, "Stephen Crane at College," *Amer. Mercury*, VII (1926), 291–297; Claude Jones, "Stephen Crane at Syracuse," *Amer. Lit.*, VII (1935), 82–84; and Lyndon U. Pratt, "The Formal Education of Stephen Crane," *Amer. Lit.*, X (1939), 460–471.

Other brief studies of Crane are Harriet Monroe, "Stephen Crane," *Poetry*, XIV (1919), 148–152; Vincent Starrett, *Buried Caesars*, Chicago, 1923, pp. 73–86; Floyd Dell, "Stephen Crane and the Genius Myth," *Nation*, CXIX (1924), 637–638; Wilson Follett, "The Second Twenty-eight Years," *Bookman*, LXVIII (1929), 532–537; Don C. Seitz, "Stephen Crane: War Correspondent," *Bookman*, LXXVI (1933), 137–140; and William L. Werner, "Stephen Crane and *The Red Badge of Courage*," *New York Times Book Rev.*, Sept. 30, 1945, p. 4.

### PRIMARY SOURCES

The introductions in two of the volumes of the *Work* (1925–1926) are especially important as reminiscences: that in Vol. II, by Robert Hobart Davis, and that in Vol. XII, by Charles Michelson. Ralph D. Paine has left a record of intimate acquaintance with Crane in *Roads of Adventure*, Boston, 1922. Other sources are Edwin W. Chubb, *Stories of Authors*, New York, 1910, pp. 361–363; containing excerpts from two letters of Crane that have biographical interest; Jessie Conrad, "Recollections of Stephen Crane," *Bookman*, LXIII (1926), 134–137; Carl Bohnenberger and N. M. Hill, eds., "The Letters of Joseph Conrad to Stephen and Cora Crane," *Bookman*, LXIX (1929), 225–235, 367–374; Thomas Beer, "Mrs. Stephen Crane," *Amer. Mercury*, XXXI (1934), 289–295; Helen R. Crane, "My Uncle, Stephen Crane," *Amer. Mercury*, XXXI (1934), 24–29.

The Stephen Crane Association, in Newark, N.J., has memorabilia and other material of interest.

### BIBLIOGRAPHY

Vincent Starrett, *Stephen Crane: A Bibliography*, Philadelphia, 1923, is standard, as is Benjamin J. R. Stolper, *Stephen Crane: A List of His Writ-*

*ings and Articles About Him,* Newark, N.J., 1930. The latest checklist is Claude E. Jones, "Stephen Crane: A Bibliography of His Short Stories and Essays," *Bul. Bibl.,* XV (1935), 149–150; XV (1936), 170.

# (MICHEL-GUILLAUME JEAN) ST. JEAN DE CRÈVECŒUR
## *1735–1813*

### SEPARATE WORKS

*Letters from an American Farmer,* 1782; *Voyage dans la Haute Pensyl-vanie et dans l'Etat de New-York,* 1801; *Sketches of Eighteenth Century America,* 1925.

*Lettres d'un Cultivateur Américain,* Paris, 1783, is a translation and expansion of the London, 1782, edition. The *Sketches* . . . , New Haven, 1925, edited with an introduction by Henri L. Bourdin, Ralph H. Gabriel, and Stanley T. Williams, are more and better "Letters" found by Bourdin in Paris in 1922, that were suppressed in 1782 either by Crèvecœur or by his publisher, and are an important supplement. The story of their recovery is told by Bourdin and Williams, "The Unpublished Manuscripts of Crève-cœur," *Studies in Philol.,* XXII (1925), 425–432. Bourdin and Williams edited four other printings of Crèvecœur material: "Crèvecœur on the Susque-hanna," *Yale Rev.,* XIV (1925), 552–584; "Crèvecœur, the Loyalist; The Grotto: An Unpublished Letter from The American Farmer," *Nation,* CXXI (1925), 328–330; "Hospitals (During the Revolution)," *Philological Quar.,* V (1926), 157–165; and "Sketch of a Contrast Between the Spanish and English Colonies," *Univ. Calif. Chron.,* XXVIII (1926), 152–163.

### REPRINTS

The *Letters from an American Farmer,* edited with a preface by William P. Trent and an introduction by Ludwig Lewisohn, New York, 1925 (first publication, 1904), is a reprint of the English edition of 1793. They were published, London, 1912, in Everyman's Lib.

### BIOGRAPHY AND CRITICISM

The most complete biographical studies are Julia P. Mitchell, *St. Jean de Crèvecœur,* New York, 1916; and Howard C. Rice, *Le Cultivateur Améri-cain: Etude sur l'Œuvre de Saint John de Crèvecœur,* Paris, 1933. There is also Robert de Crèvecœur, *Saint John de Crèvecœur: Sa Vie et ses Ou-vrages* . . . , Paris, 1883.

The best brief sketch is that of Stanley T. Williams in *Dict. Amer. Biog.* (1930). Standard studies of Crèvecœur as a man of letters are Moses C. Tyler,

*The Literary History of the American Revolution,* New York, 1897, II, 347–358; and Vernon L. Parrington, *Main Currents in American Thought,* New York, 1927, I, 140–147.

Special studies are Henri L. Bourdin and Stanley T. Williams, "The American Farmer Returns," *No. Amer. Rev.,* CCXXII (1925), 135–140; and James R. Masterson, "The Tale of the Living Fang," *Amer. Lit.,* XI (1939), 66–73.

A full bibliography is in Howard C. Rice, *Le Cultivateur Américain* (1933), pp. 231–254.

## E(DWARD) E(STLIN) CUMMINGS
### *b. 1894*

SEPARATE WORK

*Eight Harvard Poets,* 1917; *The Enormous Room,* 1922; *Tulips and Chimneys,* 1923; *&,* 1925; *XLI Poems,* 1925; *Is 5,* 1926; *Him,* 1927; *Christmas Tree,* 1928; (no title), 1930; *CIOPW,* 1931; *VV (Viva: Seventy New Poems),* 1931; *Eimi,* 1933; *Tom: A Ballet,* 1935; *No Thanks,* 1935; *1/20 (One Over Twenty): Poems,* 1936; *50 Poems,* 1940 *1 x 1,* 1944; *Anthropos: The Future of Art,* 1945; *Santa Claus: A Morality,* 1946.

*The Enormous Room* was reissued, New York, 1934, with a new introduction, in the Modern Library.

*Collected Poems . . . ,* was published, New York, 1938.

CRITICISM

The "Cummings Number" of the *Harvard Wake,* No. 5 (Spring, 1946), 90 pp., includes the first appearance of three Cummings items and critical estimates by fifteen poets and critics.

Early evaluations of Cummings's poetry are John Dos Passos, "Off the Shoals," *Dial,* LXXIII (1922), 97–102; Paul Rosenfeld, *Men Seen . . . ,* New York, 1925, pp. 191–200; and Maurice Lesemann, "The Poetry of E. E. Cummings," *Poetry,* XXIX (1926), 164–169.

Later estimates are Allen Tate, "Personal Conversation," *Poetry,* XXXIX (1932), 332–337; "Notes on E. E. Cummings' Language," in R. P. Blackmur, *The Double Agent,* New York, 1935, pp. 1–29; Babette Deutsch, *This Modern Poetry,* New York, 1935, pp. 226–229; John P. Bishop, "The Poems and Prose of E. E. Cummings," *So. Rev.,* IV (1938), 173–186; Samuel I. Hayakawa, "Is Indeed 5," *Poetry,* LII (1938), 284–292; and John Finch, "New England Prodigal," *New Eng. Quar.,* XII (1939), 643–653. The most recent critical studies are Paul Rosenfeld, "The Enormous Cummings," *Twice a Year,* Nos. 3–4 (1939–1940), 271–280; John Arthos, "The Poetry of E. E. Cummings,

*Amer. Lit.*, XIV (1943), 372–383; and Joseph Axelrod, "Cummings and Phonetics," *Poetry*, LXV (1944), 88–94.

Some manuscripts are in the Harvard College Library.

A bio-bibliography is in Fred B. Millett, *Contemporary American Authors*, New York, 1940, pp. 310–311. The most recent checklist is that compiled by Frances Cheney, in Allen Tate, *Sixty American Poets, 1896–1944*, Washington, 1945, pp. 25–27.

## JOHN W(ILLIAM) DE FOREST
*1826–1906*

### SEPARATE WORKS

*History of the Indians of Connecticut*, 1851; *Oriental Acquaintance*, 1856; *European Acquaintance*, 1858; *Seacliff*, 1859; *Miss Ravenel's Conversion from Secession to Loyalty*, 1867; *Overland*, 1871; *Kate Beaumont*, 1872; *The Wetherel Affair*, 1873; *Honest John Vane*, 1875; *Playing the Mischief*, 1875; *Irene the Missionary*, 1879; *The Bloody Chasm*, 1881; *A Lover's Revolt*, 1898; *The De Forests of Avesnes*, 1900; *The Downing Legends*, 1901; *Poem: Medley and Palestina*, 1902. De Forest's novel, *Witching Times*, was serialized in *Putnam's Monthly Mag.*, VIII (1856), 570–594, IX (1857), 11–28, 188–207, 297–317, 394–413, 515–524, 621–630, X (1857), 62–74, 218–231, 393–404. *Miss Ravenel's Conversion* was reprinted, New York, 1939, with an introduction by Gordon S. Haight. *A Volunteer's Adventures: A Union Captain's Record of the Civil War*, New Haven, 1946, consists of letters to his wife, and selections from his journals and magazine articles

### BIOGRAPHY AND CRITICISM

The earliest recognition of De Forest as a significant American novelist was by William Dean Howells. His review of *Miss Ravenel's Conversion* is in *Atl. Mo.*, XX (1867), 120–122; of *Kate Beaumont, ibid.*, XXIX (1872), 364–365; and of *The Wetherel Affair, ibid.*, XXXIV (1874), 229. Two later general estimates by Howells appear in *My Literary Passions*, New York, 1895, pp. 223–224, and *Heroines of Fiction*, New York, 1901, II, 152–163. Another early estimate is Clarence Gordon, "Mr. De Forest's Novels," *Atl. Mo.*, XXXII (1873), 611–621.

Recent evaluations are Gordon S. Haight's introduction to *Miss Ravenel's Conversion*, New York, 1939, pp. ix–xvi; Arthur H. Quinn, *American Fiction*, New York, 1936, pp. 166–174—with useful references to magazine publication of De Forest's stories; Van Wyck Brooks, *New England: Indian Summer . . .* , New York, 1940, pp. 239–243.

An unpublished dissertation is James H. Croushore, "John William De

Forest: A Biographical and Critical Study to the Year 1868," Yale Univ., 1944. The sketch of De Forest in *Dict. Amer. Biog.* (1930) is by H. E. Starr.

Some biographical data of a primary nature are supplied by De Forest in his genealogical study, *The De Forests of Avesnes* . . . , New Haven, 1900. No bibliography or checklist dealing with De Forest has been published.

## JOSEPH DENNIE
### 1768–1812

SEPARATE WORKS AND REPRINTS

*The Lay Preacher; or, Short Sermons for Idle Readers,* 1796, 1817; *Desultory Reflections on the New Political Aspects of Public Affairs,* 1800; *The Spirit of the Farmer's Museum, and Lay Preacher's Gazette,* 1801.

A reprint of both the 1796 and 1817 edition of *The Lay Preacher* was edited by Milton Ellis for the Scholars' Facsimiles and Reprints, New York, 1943, with an introduction and a bibliographical note. *The Spirit of the Farmer's Museum,* Walpole, N.H., 1801, was a selection of material from the periodical, mainly the work of Dennie. *The Letters of Joseph Dennie, 1768–1812,* were edited by Laura G. Pedder, in *Univ. of Maine Studies,* 2nd ser., No. 36, XXXVIII (1936), xxii, 212 pp.

BIOGRAPHY AND CRITICISM

The only full-length biography of Dennie is (Harold) Milton Ellis, *Joseph Dennie and His Circle: A Study of American Literature from 1792 to 1812,* Austin, Texas, 1915. Also useful is "Joseph Dennie: 'The Lay Preacher,' " in Annie R. Marble, *Heralds of American Literature,* Chicago, 1907, pp. 193–231. The sketch of Dennie in *Dict. Amer. Biog.* (1930) is by George F. Whicher. An early account is William W. Clapp, Jr., *Joseph Dennie* . . . , Cambridge, 1880, 41 pp. Contemporary estimates and appreciations were published in John Elihu Hall, *The Philadelphia Souvenir* . . . , Philadelphia, 1826; and in the *Port Folio* issue of Feb., 1812.

Dennie edited the *Port Folio* from 1801 till his death. In addition to the study by Ellis, there is Randolph C. Randall, "Authors of the *Port Folio* Revealed by the Hall Files," *Amer. Lit.,* XI (1940), 379–416, which identifies hitherto uncollected pieces by Dennie and others. Earlier studies of the magazine are Albert H. Smyth, *The Philadelphia Magazines and Their Contributors,* Philadelphia, 1872; and "The Port Folio," in Ellis P. Oberholtzer, *The Literary History of Philadelphia,* Philadelphia, 1906, pp. 168–188. A useful study of Dennie as editor of the *Port Folio* is in Frank L. Mott, *A History of*

*American Magazines,* Cambridge, 1938, Vol. I. Lewis Leary, "Leigh Hunt in Philadelphia: An American Literary Incident of 1803," *Pa. Mag. Hist. and Biog.,* LXX (1946), 270–280, deals with the reprinting of some Hunt poems in the *Port Folio.*

Other brief studies include Andrew P. Peabody, "The Farmer's Weekly Museum," *Proc. Amer. Antiq. Soc.,* n.s. VI (1890), 106–129; and Lewis Leary, "Wordsworth in America: Addenda," *Modern Language Quar.,* LVIII (1943), 391–393.

## JOHN DEWEY
### *b. 1859*

#### SEPARATE WORKS

*Psychology,* 1887; *Outlines of a Critical Theory of Ethics,* 1891; *The School and Society,* 1899; *The Educational Situation,* 1902; *Studies in Logical Theory* (with others), 1903; *Ethics* (with J. H. Tufts), 1908; *The Influence of Darwin on Philosophy, and Other Essays,* 1910; *How We Think,* 1910; *Educational Essays,* 1910; *Interest and Effort in Education,* 1913; *German Philosophy and Politics,* 1915; *Schools of To-morrow* (with Evelyn Dewey), 1915; *Democracy and Education: An Introduction to the Philosophy of Education,* 1916; *Essays in Experimental Logic,* 1916; *Reconstruction in Philosophy,* 1920; *Letters from China and Japan,* 1920; *Human Nature and Conduct,* 1922; *Experience and Nature,* 1925; *The Public and Its Problems,* 1927; *The Quest for Certainty,* 1929; *Impressions of Soviet Russia and the Revolutionary World: Mexico, China, Turkey,* 1929; *Characters and Events: Popular Essays in Social and Political Philosophy,* 1929; *Individualism, Old and New,* 1930; *Philosophy and Civilization,* 1931; *A Common Faith,* 1934; *Art as Experience,* 1934; *Logic, the Theory of Inquiry,* 1938; *Experience and Education,* 1938; *Freedom and Culture,* 1939; *Education Today,* 1940; *Problems of Men,* 1946.

#### EDITED TEXTS AND REPRINTS

*The School and Society* (1899) was issued in a revised edition, Chicago, 1915; *Ethics* (1908), New York, 1932. *Human Nature and Conduct* (1922) was issued in the Modern Library, New York, 1930.

J. J. Findlay edited selections from the educational essays of Dewey in *The School and the Child,* London, 1907. Two other selected reprints are Joseph Ratner, ed., *The Philosophy of John Dewey,* New York, 1928; and *idem,* ed., *Intelligence in the Modern World: John Dewey's Philosophy,* New York, 1939 (Modern Library).

BIOGRAPHY AND CRITICISM

A collection of critical essays, with a detailed reply by Dewey, is Paul A. Schilpp, ed., *The Philosophy of John Dewey*, Chicago, 1939. Other recent significant estimates of Dewey are Sidney Hook, *John Dewey: An Intellectual Portrait*, New York, 1939; William T. Feldman, *The Philosophy of John Dewey: A Critical Analysis*, Baltimore, 1934; and *John Dewey: The Man and His Philosophy*, Cambridge, 1930—a symposium of eleven addresses by contemporary philosophers. See also Morton G. White, *The Origin of Dewey's Instrumentalism*, New York, 1943; George Santayana, *Obiter Scripta*, New York, 1936; and Scudder Klyce, *Dewey's Suppressed Psychology . . .*, Winchester, Mass., 1928.

Studies devoted to the philosophical, psychological, and religious aspects of Dewey's thinking include Morris R. Cohen, "On American Philosophy: John Dewey and the Chicago School," *New Repub.*, XXII (1920), 82–86; Thomas V. Smith, "Dewey's Theory of Value," *Monist*, XXXII (1922), 339–354; Paul Crissman, "Dewey's Theory of the Moral Good," *Monist*, XXXVIII (1928), 592–619; Julius Seelye Bixler, "Professor Dewey Discusses Religion," *Harvard Theol. Rev.*, XXIII (1930), 213–233; Henry N. Wieman, "Religion in John Dewey's Philosophy," *Jour. of Religion*, XI (1931), 1–19; George H. Mead, "The Philosophy of John Dewey," *International Jour. Ethics*, XLVI (1935), 64–81; Edna A. Shearer, "Dewey's Esthetic Theory," *Jour. Philos.*, XXXII (1935), 617–627, 650–664; Horace S. Fries, "The Method of Proving Ethical Realism," *Philosophical Rev.*, XLVI (1937), 485–502; Eduard Baumgarten, *Der Pragmatismus: R. W. Emerson, W. James, J. Dewey*, Frankfort on the Main, 1938; William E. Hocking, "Dewey's Concepts of Experience and Nature," *Philosophical Rev.*, XLIX (1940), 228–244; Stephen S. White, *A Comparison of the Philosophies of F. C. S. Schiller and John Dewey*, Chicago, 1940; E. T. Mitchell, "Dewey's Theory of Valuation," *Ethics*, LV (1945), 287–297; and James K. Feibleman, "Influence of Peirce on Dewey's Logic," *Education*, LXVI (1945), 18–24. See also Delton T. Howard, *John Dewey's Logical Theory*, New York, 1918.

Useful background studies are Warner Fite, *Moral Philosophy: The Critical View of Life*, New York, 1925; William Y. Elliott, *The Pragmatic Revolt in Politics: Syndicalism, Fascism, and the Constitutional State*, New York, 1928; and Mortimer J. Adler, *Art and Prudence: A Study in Practical Philosophy*, New York, 1937.

Two studies devoted to Dewey's educational theory are Jesse H. Newlon, "John Dewey's Influence in the Schools," *School and Soc.*, XXX (1929), 691–700; and Ernest C. Moore, "John Dewey's Contribution to Educational Theory," *School and Soc.*, XXXI (1930), 37–47.

Estimates of Dewey as a man of letters are Joseph Warren Beach, *The*

*Outlook for American Prose,* Chicago, 1926, pp. 41–52; Folke Leander, "John Dewey and the Classical Tradition," *Amer. Rev.,* IX (1937), 504–527; and V. C. Aldrich, "John Dewey's Use of Language," *Jour. Philos.,* XLI (1944), 261–271.

A brief estimate of Dewey's international influence is Isaac L. Kandel, "Influence of Dewey Abroad," *School and Soc.,* XXX (1929), 700–704.

Other brief studies include Forrest O. Wiggins, "William James and John Dewey," *Personalist,* XXIII (1942), 182–198; Max Eastman, "John Dewey," *Atl. Mo.,* CLXVIII (1941), 671–685; Frank H. Knight, "Pragmatism and Social Action," *International Jour. Ethics,* XLVI (1936), 229–236; "The Winnowing Fan," in Harvey Wickham, *The Unrealists,* New York, 1930, pp. 196–218; Wilmon H. Sheldon, "Professor Dewey: The Protagonist of Democracy," *Jour. Philos.,* XVIII (1921), 309–320; and "John Dewey," in Edwin E. Slosson, *Six Major Prophets,* Boston, 1917, pp. 252–289.

An early bibliography dealing with primary and secondary material is Milton H. Thomas and Herbert W. Schneider, *A Bibliography of John Dewey,* New York, 1929. A somewhat later extended listing is in Paul A. Schilpp, ed., *The Philosophy of John Dewey,* Chicago, 1939, pp. 609–676. See also the listing in Fred B. Millett, *Contemporary American Authors,* New York, 1940, pp. 318–327.


# EMILY DICKINSON
### 1830–1886

COLLECTED WORKS

Only five poems of Emily Dickinson were published during her lifetime, and they appeared anonymously in periodicals. *Poems by Emily Dickinson, Edited by Two of Her Friends, Mabel Loomis Todd and T. W. Higginson,* Boston, 1890, contains a preface by Higginson. A 16th edition was published in 1898; a 17th, in 1904; and the volume was reissued as lately as 1920. *Poems by Emily Dickinson, Second Series, Edited by Two of Her Friends, T. W. Higginson and Mabel Loomis Todd,* Boston, 1891, contains a preface by Mrs. Todd; it was issued in a 5th ed. in 1893, and was currently reissued down to 1920. The "Poems, 1890," and "Poems, Second Series" were combined into one volume, Boston, 1893. *Poems by Emily Dickinson, Third Series, Edited by Mabel Loomis Todd* was issued, Boston, 1896.

The three volumes contained 449 poems, and 102 additional poems or parts of poems were included in *Letters of Emily Dickinson,* Boston, 1894, 2 vols., edited by Mabel L. Todd. All these poems, constituting the Dickinson canon until 1914, were issued between 1890 and 1896. The three volumes before the

*Letters* are generally referred to as "Poems, 1890," "Poems, Second Series," and "Poems, Third Series."

Further poems were published in *The Single Hound: Poems of a Lifetime,* Boston, 1914, ed. by Martha D. Bianchi. *The Complete Poems of Emily Dickinson,* Boston, 1924, ed. by Martha D. Bianchi, contains the three series, together with those in *The Single Hound,* and five additional poems. A volume of newly edited poems appeared with the publication of *Further Poems of Emily Dickinson Withheld from Publication by Her Sister Lavinia,* Boston, 1929, ed. by Martha D. Bianchi and Alfred L. Hampson. The same editors issued *The Poems of Emily Dickinson,* Boston, 1930, compiled from the three series, together with those in *The Single Hound* and the *Further Poems* collections, with one omission and with one additional poem. Still another collection was made of *Unpublished Poems of Emily Dickinson,* Boston, 1936, ed. by Martha D. Bianchi and Alfred L. Hampson. The same editors issued *The Poems of Emily Dickinson,* Boston, 1937, combining the texts of all preceding collections with that of *Unpublished Poems,* here called "Additional Poems."

From a new source, 668 hitherto unpublished poems and fragments were gathered in *Bolts of Melody: New Poems of Emily Dickinson,* New York, 1945, ed. by Mabel Loomis Todd and Millicent Todd Bingham. See also Mrs. Bingham's "Poems of Emily Dickinson: Hitherto Published Only in Part," *New Eng. Quar.,* XX (1947), 3–50.

The text of Emily Dickinson's poems has yet to be established. Only that in *Bolts of Melody* (1945) approaches accuracy. The text of the Todd-Higginson series and of the Bianchi-Hampson groups has been inaccurately transcribed and often bowdlerized.

### LETTERS

*Letters of Emily Dickinson, Edited by Mabel Loomis Todd,* Boston, 1894, 2 vols., includes 102 poems or parts of poems. It was reissued, New York, 1931, in a new and enlarged edition. Martha D. Bianchi's *The Life and Letters of Emily Dickinson,* Boston, 1924, includes (Part I) letters not elsewhere available and (Part II) a bowdlerization of an unauthorized reprinting of Mrs. Todd's collection. Important corrections are made in the 5th printing (1929). The serious inaccuracies in the text are set forth in Morris U. Schappes, "Errors in Mrs. Bianchi's Edition of Emily Dickinson's *Letters,*" *Amer. Lit.,* IV (1933), 369–384. Important additional mate.ial, especially in letters to the brothers Clark, is in Mrs. Todd's 1931 new and enlarged edition of *Letters of Emily Dickinson.* Further publication was undertaken by Martha D. Bianchi, ed., *Emily Dickinson Face to Face: Unpublished Letters with Notes and Reminiscences,* Boston, 1932; some of these letters are not included elsewhere.

Gleanings are in Helen H. Arnold, " 'From the Garden We Have Not Seen': New Letters of Emily Dickinson," *New Eng. Quar.*, XVI (1943), 363–375; and Frank Davidson, "Some Emily Dickinson Letters," *Indiana Quar. for Bookmen*, I (1945), 113–118—three unpublished letters.

SELECTED REPRINTS

Conrad Aiken compiled *Selected Poems of Emily Dickinson*, London, 1924, with an introduction; the poems are chosen from the Todd-Higginson series. Two other reprints are *Emily Dickinson*, ed. by Louis Untermeyer, New York, 1927 (Pamphlet Poets Ser.), and *Poems for Youth*, ed. by Alfred L. Hampson, Boston, 1934.

BIOGRAPHY AND CRITICISM

The most useful life is George F. Whicher, *This Was a Poet: A Critical Biography of Emily Dickinson*, New York, 1938. Other narrative and critical studies are Martha D. Bianchi, *The Life and Letters of Emily Dickinson*, Boston, 1924—revised with additions and corrections, 1924, 1925, 1929; Mac-Gregor Jenkins, *Emily Dickinson, Friend and Neighbor*, Boston, 1930 (new ed., 1939)—largely reminiscences; Genevieve Taggard, *The Life and Mind of Emily Dickinson*, New York, 1930; Josephine Pollitt, *Emily Dickinson: The Human Background of Her Poetry*, New York, 1930—with some new data and an untrustworthy account of Emily Dickinson's supposed love affair; and Emilio Cecchi, *Emily Dickinson*, Morcelliana (Brescia), 1939.

Special studies mainly critical are Anna M. Wells, "Early Criticism of Emily Dickinson," *Amer. Lit.*, I (1929), 243–259; "Emily Dickinson," in Gay W. Allen, *American Prosody*, New York, 1935, pp. 307–321; Grace B. Sherrer, "A Study of Unusual Verb Constructions in the Poems of Emily Dickinson," *Amer. Lit.*, VII (1935), 37–46; "Emily Dickinson," in Allen Tate, *Reactionary Essays on Poetry and Ideas*, New York, 1936, pp. 3–26; Yvor Winters, *Maule's Curse . . .*, Norfolk, Conn., 1938, pp. 149–165; "Emily Dickinson: Notes on Prejudice and Fact," in R. P. Blackmur, *The Expense of Greatness*, New York, 1940, pp. 106–138; Milton Hindus, "Emily's Prose: A Note," *Kenyon Rev.*, II (1940), 88–91; Mary E. Barbot, "Emily Dickinson Parallels," *New Eng. Quar.*, XIV (1941), 689–696; Donald F. Connors, "The Significance of Emily Dickinson," *College Eng.*, III (1942), 624–633; Eunice Glenn, "Emily Dickinson's Poetry: A Revaluation," *Sewanee Rev.*, LI (1943), 574–588. Early estimates are "Emily Dickinson," in Gamaliel Bradford, *Portraits of American Women*, Boston, 1919, pp. 229–257; Jean Catel, "Emily Dickinson: Essai d'Analyse Psychologique," *Revue Anglo-Amér.*, II (1925), 394–405; and *idem*, "Emily Dickinson: L'Œuvre," *ibid.*, 105–120.

Special studies, chiefly biographical, are Sydney R. McLean, "Emily Dickinson at Mount Holyoke," *New Eng. Quar.*, VII (1934), 25–42; "Emily Dickinson," in Van Wyck Brooks, *New England: Indian Summer*, New York, 1940, pp. 316–329; and S. Baldi, "Appunti per uno studio sulle poesia della Dickinson," *Letteratura*, VI (1942), 76–88. See also Carl J. Weber, "Two Notes from Emily Dickinson," *Colby College Quar.*, XV (1946), 239–240.

The controversy in the matter of editing Emily Dickinson's poems is treated at length in Millicent T. Bingham, *Ancestors' Brocades: The Literary Début of Emily Dickinson*, New York, 1945. Briefer studies are Frederick J. Pohl, "The Emily Dickinson Controversy," *Sewanee Rev.*, XLI (1933), 467–482; John Erskine, "The Dickinson Saga," *Yale Rev.*, XXXV (1945), 74–83; F. O. Matthiessen, "The Problem of the Private Poet," *Kenyon Rev.*, VII (1945), 584–597; and George F. Whicher, "In Emily Dickinson's Garden," *Atl. Mo.*, CLXXVII (1946), 64–70.

PRIMARY SOURCES

Among published writings of interest as source material are Thomas W. Higginson, *Carlyle's Laugh and Other Surprises*, Boston, 1909, pp. 247–283; and Mary T. Higginson, *Thomas Wentworth Higginson . . .*, Boston, 1914.

The large part of Emily Dickinson's manuscripts is in private hands. The greater part of such material in public depositories is in the Galatea Collection of the Boston Public Library, as are the T. W. Higginson letters. Some material is in Harvard College Library.

BIBLIOGRAPHY

George F. Whicher has added a "Bibliographical Postscript," pp. 311–329, to his biography *This Was a Poet* (1938). There is also *Emily Dickinson: . . . A Bibliography*, Amherst, Mass., 1930, comp. by the Jones Library, with a foreword by George F. Whicher. A useful annotated bibliography is Harry H. Clark, ed., *Major American Poets*, New York, 1936, pp. 894–897. See also Harry Hartwick, in Walter F. Taylor, *A History of American Letters*, New York, 1936, pp. 553–555.

# JOHN DICKINSON
## 1732–1808

SEPARATE WORKS

*A Protest Against the Appointment of Benjamin Franklin*, 1764; *A Reply to the Speech of Joseph Galloway*, 1764; *A Petition to the King from the Inhabitants of Pennsylvania*, 1764; *The Resolutions and Declaration of Rights*

*Adopted by the Stamp Act Congress,* 1765; *A Petition to the King from the Stamp Act Congress,* 1765; *The Late Regulations Respecting the British Colonies . . . Considered,* 1765; *An Address to the Committee of Correspondence in Barbados,* 1766; *Letters from a Farmer in Pennsylvania to the Inhabitants of the British Colonies,* 1768; "A Song for American Freedom (Liberty Song)," 1768; *An Address Read at a Meeting of Merchants to Consider Non-Importation,* 1768; *Two Letters on the Tea-Tax,* 1773; *Address of Congress to the Inhabitants of the Province of Quebec,* 1774; *An Essay on the Constitutional Power of Great-Britain over the Colonies in America,* 1774; *A Declaration by the Representatives of the United Colonies,* 1775; *An Essay for a Frame of Government in Pennsylvania,* 1776; *Address of Congress to the Several States on the Present Situation of Affairs,* 1779; *The Letters of Fabius . . .* (2 series), 1788, 1797; *An Address on the Past, Present, and Eventual Relations of the United States to France,* 1803.

COLLECTED WORKS AND REPRINTS

*The Political Writings of John Dickinson, Esq. . . . ,* Wilmington, Del., 1801, 2 vols., was reprinted, 1814. Paul L. Ford edited *The Writings of John Dickinson: Vol. I, Political Writings, 1764–1774,* Philadelphia, 1895; no more volumes were published. Ford also edited "The Letters of Fabius," in *Pamphlets on the Constitution of the United States,* Brooklyn, 1888, pp. 163–216. R. T. H. Halsey edited *Letters from a Farmer in Pennsylvania,* New York, 1903.

BIOGRAPHY AND CRITICISM

The standard biography is Charles J. Stillé, *The Life and Times of John Dickinson, 1732–1808,* Philadelphia, 1891. Two useful studies of Dickinson as a man of letters are Vernon L. Parrington, *Main Currents in American Thought,* New York, I (1927), 219–232, and Moses C. Tyler, *The Literary History of the American Revolution,* New York, 1897, I, 234–241, II, 21–34. The sketch in *Dict. Amer. Biog.* (1930) was contributed by James T. Adams.

Other studies of Dickinson are Isaac Sharpless, *Political Leaders of Provincial Pennsylvania,* New York, 1919, pp. 224–243; Robert H. Richards, "The Life and Character of John Dickinson," *Papers Hist. Soc. Del.,* III (1901), No. 30, 26 pp.; Wharton Dickinson, "John Dickinson, LL.D., the Great Colonial Essayist," *Mag. Amer. Hist.,* X (1883), 223–234; Richard J. Hooker, "John Dickinson on Church and State," *Amer. Lit.,* XVI (1944), 82–98; and John H. Powell, "John Dickinson, President of the Delaware State, 1781–1782," *Delaware Hist.,* Jan. and July, 1946, pp. 1–54, 111–134. An unpublished dissertation is John H. Powell, "John Dickinson, Penman of the American

Revolution," State Univ. of Iowa, 1938. For a brief bibliography of primary and secondary items see Harry Hartwick in Walter F. Taylor, *A History of American Letters,* New York, 1936, pp. 486–487.


# HILDA DOOLITTLE (ALDINGTON)
## ("H. D.")
### *b. 1886*

WORKS

*Sea Garden,* 1916; *Hymen,* 1921; *Heliodora and Other Poems,* 1924; *Palimpsest,* 1926; *Hippolytus Temporizes,* 1927; *Hedylus,* 1928; *Red Roses for Bronze,* 1929; *The Hedgehog,* 1936; *Ion of Euripides* (translation), 1937; *The Walls Do Not Fall,* 1944; *Tribute to the Angels,* 1945; *The Flowering of the Rod,* 1946.

*Choruses from the Iphigeneia in Aulis and the Hippolytus of Euripides* were translated by H. D., London, 1919. *Collected Poems of H. D.,* New York, 1925, were reprinted, 1940.

BIOGRAPHY AND CRITICISM

Useful critical estimates are H. P. Collins, *Modern Poetry,* New York, 1925, pp. 154–202; Douglas Bush, *Mythology and the Romantic Tradition in English Poetry,* Cambridge, 1937, pp. 497–506; May Sinclair, "The Poems of 'H. D.,' " *Fortnightly Rev.,* n.s. CXXI (1927), 329–345; "H. D.," in René Taupin, *L'Influence du Symbolisme Français sur la Poésie Américaine,* Paris, 1929, pp. 158–165; Frank A. Doggett, "H. D.: A Study in Sensitivity," *Sewanee Rev.,* XXXVII (1929), 1–9; "H. D.: The Perfect Imagist," in Glenn Hughes, *Imagism and the Imagists,* Stanford Univ., Calif., 1931, pp. 109–124; R. P. Blackmur, "The Lesser Satisfactions," *Poetry,* XLI (1932), 94–100. Standard estimates are Louis Untermeyer, *American Poetry Since 1900,* New York, 1923, pp. 309–316; and Alfred Kreymborg, *Our Singing Strength,* New York, 1929, pp. 347–353.

Evaluations by other contemporary poets include Amy Lowell, *Tendencies in Modern American Poetry,* New York, 1917, pp. 235–243; "H. D.," in Harriet Monroe, *Poets and Their Art,* New York, 1926, pp. 92–99; John Gould Fletcher, "From 75 B.C. to 1925 A.D.," *Sat. Rev. Lit.,* III (1927), 482; and Babette Deutsch, *This Modern Poetry,* New York, 1935, pp. 66–72.

Manuscripts of H. D. are in the Harvard College Library and the libraries of the University of Chicago and the University of Buffalo. Personal reminiscences are included in John Gould Fletcher, *Life Is My Song,* New York, 1937, and Richard Aldington, *Life for Life's Sake,* New York, 1941.

The fullest bibliographical listing of primary and secondary items is in Fred B. Millett, *Contemporary American Authors*, New York, 1940, pp. 328–329. A recent list, including a description of special editions, is by Frances Cheney, in Allen Tate, *Sixty American Poets, 1896–1944*, Washington, 1945, pp. 7–9.

## JOHN (RODERIGO) DOS PASSOS
### *b. 1896*

SEPARATE WORKS

*One Man's Initiation . . . 1917*, 1920; *Three Soldiers*, 1921; *Rosinante to the Road Again*, 1922; *A Pushcart at the Curb*, 1922; *Streets of Night*, 1923; *Manhattan Transfer*, 1925; *The Garbage Man*, 1926; *Orient Express*, 1927; *Airways, Inc.*, 1928; *The 42nd Parallel*, 1930; *1919*, 1932; *In All Countries* 1934; *Three Plays*, 1934; *The Big Money*, 1936; *Journeys Between Wars*, 1938; *Adventures of a Young Man*, 1939; *The Ground We Stand On*, 1941; *Number One: A Novel*, 1943; *State of the Nation*, 1944; *Tour of Duty*, 1946.

REPRINTS

*Three Soldiers* (1921) was reprinted, New York, 1932, in the Modern Lib.; *The 42nd Parallel* (1930), New York, 1937, in the Modern Lib., with an introduction by the author. *U S A*, New York, 1937, is a reprint of *The 42nd Parallel*, *1919*, and *The Big Money*. *Journey Between Two Wars*, New York, 1938, is a selection from three previous travel books, with additions about Spain in 1937. *One Man's Initiation . . .* (1920) was reprinted as *First Encounter*, New York, 1945. *U S A* was reprinted, Boston, 1947, 3 vols.

BIOGRAPHY AND CRITICISM

Few substantial estimates of Dos Passos as a man of letters were made in the twenties. Among the earliest is Sinclair Lewis, "Manhattan at Last!" *Sat. Rev. Lit.*, II (Dec. 5, 1925), 361. An early study is Werner Neuse, *Die literarische Entwicklung von John Dos Passos*, Giessen, 1931.

Later evaluations are Granville Hicks, "John Dos Passos," *Bookman*, LXXV (1932), 32–42; Alan Calmer, "John Dos Passos," *Sewanee Rev.*, XL (1932), 341–349; Michael Gold, "The Education of John Dos Passos," *English Jour.*, XXII (1933), 87–97; Bernard De Voto, "John Dos Passos: Anatomist of Our Time," *Sat. Rev. Lit.*, XIV (Aug. 8, 1936), 3–4, 12–13; Harlan Hatcher, *Creating the Modern American Novel*, New York, 1935, pp. 132–139; "Dos Passos: Poet Against the World," in Malcolm Cowley, *After the Genteel Tradition*, New York, 1937, pp. 168–185; C. John McCole, *Lucifer at Large*,

London, 1937, pp. 175–200; John T. Reid, "Spain as Seen by Some Contemporary Writers," *Hispania*, XX (1937), 139–150; Mason Wade, "Novelist of America: John Dos Passos," *No. Amer. Rev.*, CCXLIV (1937), 349–367; Delmore Schwartz, "John Dos Passos and the Whole Truth," *Southern Rev.*, IV (1938), 351–367; John Chamberlain, *John Dos Passos: A Biographical and Critical Essay*, New York, 1939, 19 pp.; and James T. Farrell, "Dos Passos and the Critics," *Amer. Mercury*, XLVIII (1939), 489–494.

The most recent estimates are Carl Van Doren, *The American Novel*, rev. ed., New York, 1940, pp. 334–338; "John Dos Passos," in Percy H. Boynton, *America in Contemporary Fiction*, Chicago, 1940, pp. 185–203; Milton Rugoff, "Dos Passos, Novelist of Our Time," *Sewanee Rev.*, XLIX (1941), 453–468; "John Dos Passos: Conversion of a Hero," in Maxwell Geismar, *Writers in Crisis*, Boston, 1942, pp. 87–140—the most comprehensive estimate to date; "Dos Passos and the U.S.A.," in Thomas K. Whipple, *Study Out the Land*, Berkeley, Calif., 1943, pp. 85–92.

The fullest bibliographical listing is Fred B. Millett, *Contemporary American Authors*, New York, 1940, pp. 329–332—especially useful for secondary sources.

## THEODORE (HERMAN ALBERT) DREISER
### *1871–1945*

SEPARATE WORKS

*Sister Carrie*, 1900; *Jennie Gerhardt*, 1911; *The Financier*, 1912; *A Traveller at Forty*, 1913; *The Titan*, 1914; *The "Genius,"* 1915; *Plays of the Natural and the Supernatural*, 1916; *A Hoosier Holiday*, 1916; *Free and Other Stories*, 1918; *The Hand of the Potter*, 1918; *Twelve Men*, 1919; *Hey Rub-a-Dub-Dub*, 1920; *A Book About Myself*, 1922; *The Color of a Great City*, 1923; *An American Tragedy*, 1925; *Moods, Cadenced and Declaimed*, 1926; *Chains*, 1927; *Dreiser Looks at Russia*, 1928; *A Gallery of Women*, 1929; *The Aspirant*, 1929; *My City*, 1929; *Epitaph*, 1929; *Fine Furniture*, 1930; *Dawn*, 1931; *Tragic America*, 1931; *America Is Worth Saving*, 1941; *The Bulwark*, 1946; *The Stoic*, 1947.

REPRINTS

There is no collected edition of Dreiser's work. Reprints have appeared as follows:

*Sister Carrie* (1900): New York, 1917 (Modern Lib.—reprinted, 1931, with a new preface by the author).

*Jennie Gerhardt* (1911): Garden City, N.Y., 1934 (Star Books).

*The Financier* (1912): New York, 1927, rev. ed.; Cleveland, Ohio, 1946.

*The Titan* (1914): Garden City, N.Y., 1935 (Star Books); Cleveland, Ohio, 1946.

*The "Genius"* (1915): Garden City, N.Y., 1935 (Star Books).

*Free and Other Stories* (1918): New York, 1925 (Modern Lib., with an introduction by Sherwood Anderson).

*The Hand of the Potter* (1918): New York, 1927, rev. ed.

*Twelve Men* (1919): New York, 1928 (Modern Lib.).

*An American Tragedy* (1925): Garden City, N.Y., 1934 (Star Books).

*Moods, Cadenced and Declaimed* (1926): revised and enlarged as *Moods, Philosophic and Emotional, Cadenced and Declaimed,* New York, 1935.

Howard Fast edited *The Best Short Stories of Theodore Dreiser,* Cleveland, Ohio, 1947.

BIOGRAPHY AND CRITICISM

Critical notices of Dreiser's work were slow to appear. Among the earliest are John Cowper Powys, "Theodore Dreiser," *Little Rev.,* II (1915), 7–13; H. L. Mencken, "The Dreiser Bugaboo," *Seven Arts,* II (1917), 507–517; "Theodore Dreiser," in *idem, A Book of Prefaces,* New York, 1917, pp. 67–148—the first extended critical recognition; "The Barbaric Naturalism of Theodore Dreiser," in Stuart P. Sherman, *On Contemporary Literature,* New York, 1917, pp. 85–101—an unsympathetic appraisal which first appeared in the *Nation,* Dec. 2, 1915; Frank Harris, *Contemporary Portraits,* 2nd ser., New York, 1919, pp. 81–106; Randolph Bourne, *History of a Literary Radical and Other Essays,* New York, 1920, pp. 195–204; and Edward H. Smith, "Dreiser, After Twenty Years," *Bookman,* LIII (1921), 27–39.

Stuart P. Sherman's revised judgment appears in *The Main Stream,* New York, 1927 (pp. 134–144—"Mr. Dreiser in Tragic Realism"). Other estimates during the late twenties are Burton Rascoe, *Theodore Dreiser,* New York, 1925; "Theodore Dreiser," in Thomas K. Whipple, *Spokesmen . . . ,* New York, 1928, pp. 70–93; "Theodore Dreiser," in David Karsner, *Sixteen Authors to One,* New York, 1928, pp. 3–26; and Milton Waldman, "Theodore Dreiser," in J. C. Squire, ed., *Contemporary American Authors,* New York, 1928, pp. 97–120.

Later appraisals are Robert Shafer, "An American Tragedy," in Norman Foerster, ed., *Humanism and America,* New York, 1930, pp. 149–169; Dorothy Dudley, *Forgotten Frontiers: Dreiser and the Land of the Free,* New York, 1932—a study of postwar literature, centering on Dreiser; Charles Le Verrier, "Un Grand Romancier Américain: Theodore Dreiser," *Revue Hebdomadaire,* Jan. 21, 1933, pp. 280–294; Harry Hartwick, *The Foreground of American Fiction,* New York, 1934, pp. 85–110; "Theodore Dreiser," in

Harlan Hatcher, *Creating the Modern American Novel,* New York, 1935, pp. 34–57; John Chamberlain, "Theodore Dreiser," in Malcolm Cowley, ed., *After the Genteel Tradition* . . . , New York, 1936, pp. 27–36; "Dreiser," in Ford Madox Ford, *Portraits from Life,* Boston, 1937, pp. 164–182; C. John McCole, *Lucifer at Large,* London, 1937, pp. 17–54; John F. Huth, Jr., "Theodore Dreiser: 'The Prophet,' " *Amer. Lit.,* IX (1937), 207–217; *idem,* "Theodore Dreiser, Success Monger," *Colophon,* n.s. III (1938), No. 1, pp. 120–133; Myrta L. Avary, "Success, and Dreiser," *ibid.,* No. 4, pp. 598–604; John F. Huth, Jr., "Dreiser and Success: An Additional Note," *ibid.,* No. 3, 406–410; and Eliseo Vivas, "Dreiser, an Inconsistent Mechanist," *International Jour. Ethics,* XLVIII (1938), 498–508.

The most recent studies are "Theodore Dreiser," in Percy H. Boynton, *America in Contemporary Fiction,* Chicago, 1940, pp. 131–149; "Theodore Dreiser," in Carl Van Doren, *The American Novel,* rev. ed., New York, 1940, pp. 245–259; Charles C. Walcutt, "The Three Stages of Theodore Dreiser's Naturalism," *PMLA,* LV (1940), 266–289; "Two Educations: Edith Wharton and Theodore Dreiser," in Alfred Kazin, *On Native Grounds,* New York, 1942, pp. 73–90; Cyrille Arnavon, "Theodore Dreiser and Painting," *Amer. Lit.,* XVII (1945), 113–126; Granville Hicks, "Theodore Dreiser," *Amer. Mercury,* LXII (1946), 751–756; Woodburn O. Ross, "Concerning Dreiser's Mind," *Amer. Lit.,* XVIII (1946), 233–243; and Lionel Trilling, "Dreiser and the Liberal Mind," *Nation,* CLXII (1946), 466, 468–472.

Five recent evaluations by James T. Farrell are "A Literary Behemoth Against the Backdrop of His Era," *New York Times Book Review,* July 4, 1943, p. 3—a revaluation of *Sister Carrie; "An American Tragedy," ibid.,* May 6, 1945, pp. 6, 16; "Some Aspects of Dreiser's Fiction," *ibid.,* Apr. 29, 1945, pp. 7, 28—an estimate of Dreiser's social determinism; "Theodore Dreiser: In Memoriam," *Sat. Rev. Lit.,* XXIX (Jan. 12, 1946), 16–17, 27–28. See also John T. Flanagan, "Theodore Dreiser in Retrospect," *Southwest Rev.,* XXXI (1946), 408–411.

PRIMARY SOURCES

A large manuscript collection is in the University of Pennsylvania Library.

The most important published source material is in the four volumes of autobiography, here arranged in order of biographical sequence: *Dawn,* New York, 1931; *A Book About Myself,* New York, 1922—reissued as *Newspaper Days,* New York, 1931; *A Traveller at Forty,* New York, 1913; and *A Hoosier Holiday,* New York, 1916. Background studies of the Chicago Dreiser wrote about will be found in the autobiography of a former mayor, Carter H. Harrison, *Stormy Years,* Indianapolis, 1930; and in Lloyd Wendt and Herman Kogan, *Lords of the Levee,* Indianapolis, 1943—a biography of Michael

Kenna and John J. Coughlin. Dreiser himself contributed "The Early Adventures of *Sister Carrie,*" to the *Colophon,* Pt. 5 (1931), pp. 1–4.

BIBLIOGRAPHY

An early listing of Dreiser's works is Edward D. McDonald, *A Bibliography of the Writings of Theodore Dreiser,* Philadelphia, 1928. Errata and addenda are given in Vrest Orton, *Dreiserana: A Book About His Books,* New York, 1929. Further material is in Fred B. Millett, *Contemporary American Authors,* New York, 1940, pp. 332–337.

## PAUL LAURENCE DUNBAR
### *1872–1906*

SEPARATE WORKS

*Oak and Ivy,* 1893; *Majors and Minors,* 1895; *Lyrics of Lowly Life,* 1896; *Folks from Dixie,* 1898; *The Uncalled,* 1898; *Poems of Cabin and Field,*\* 1899; *Lyrics of the Hearthside,* 1899; *The Strength of Gideon and Other Stories,* 1900; *The Love of Landry,* 1900; *Candle-Lightin' Time,*\* 1901; *The Fanatics,* 1901; *The Sport of the Gods,* 1902; *Lyrics of Love and Laughter,* 1903; *In Old Plantation Days,* 1903; *Li'l' Gal,*\* 1904; *The Heart of Happy Hollow,* 1904; *Lyrics of Sunshine and Shadow,* 1905; *Howdy, Honey, Howdy,*\* 1905; *Joggin' Erlong,*\* 1906; *Chris'mus Is A-Comin',*\* 1907.

COLLECTED WORKS AND REPRINTS

*The Complete Poems of Paul Laurence Dunbar,* published New York, 1913, and several times reprinted, includes Howells's introduction to *Lyrics of Lowly Life* (1896). Selected reprints are Benjamin G. Brawley, ed., *The Best Stories of Paul Laurence Dunbar,* New York, 1938.

BIOGRAPHY AND CRITICISM

A full-length biography is Benjamin G. Brawley, *Paul Laurence Dunbar: Poet of His People,* Chapel Hill, N.C., 1936. Other recent studies are Jay Saunders Redding, *To Make a Poet Black,* Chapel Hill, N.C., 1939, pp. 56–67; "Paul Laurence Dunbar," in Benjamin G. Brawley, *Negro Builders and Heroes,* Chapel Hill, N.C., 1937, pp. 158–166; and Vernon Loggins, *The Negro Author . . . ,* N.Y., 1931, pp. 313–324 and 344–352.

Special studies are Louis T. Achille, "Paul Laurence Dunbar, Poète Nègre," *Revue Anglo-Amér.,* XI (1934), 504–519; John Chamberlain, "The

\* Starred items are illustrated gift-book editions of verse, largely reprints of previously published material.

Negro as Writer," *Bookman*, LXX (1930), 603–611; Charles Eaton Burch, "The Plantation Negro in Dunbar's Poetry," *Southern Workman*, L (1921), 227–229; and *idem*, "Dunbar's Poetry in Literary English," *ibid.*, pp. 469–473.

The early review by William Dean Howells of *Majors and Minors* (1895), which was important in bringing Dunbar to the notice of the public, appeared in *Harper's Weekly*, XL (1896), 630.

The Schomburg Collection in the 135th Street Branch of the New York Public Library contains manuscript letters and first editions of Dunbar. Published material of a primary nature is Edward F. Arnold, "Some Personal Reminiscences of Paul Laurence Dunbar," *Jour. Negro Hist.*, XVII (1932), 400–408.

Andrew M. Burris has compiled a "Bibliography of Works by Paul Laurence Dunbar . . . ," *Amer. Collector*, V (1927), 69–73. Later bibliographical listings of primary and secondary material are in Brawley's biography (1936) and in Jacob Blanck, *Merle Johnson's American First Editions*, 4th ed., New York, 1942.

## WILLIAM DUNLAP
### 1766–1839

SEPARATE WORKS

The published plays of Dunlap, not including translations, follow. Dates in parentheses are of production when it differs from publication.

*The Father; or, American Shandyism*, 1789; *Darby's Return*, 1789; *The Fatal Deception; or, The Progress of Guilt* (1794), published as *Leicester*, 1806; *Fontainville Abbey* (1795), 1806; *The Archers; or, Mountaineers of Switzerland*, 1796; *The Mysterious Monk* (1796), published as *Ribbemont; or, The Feudal Baron*, 1803; *The Knight's Adventure* (1797), 1807; *André*, 1798; *The Italian Father* (1799), 1810; *The Glory of Columbia Her Yeomanry!* (1803), 1817; *Yankee Chronology; or, Huzza for the Constitution!* 1812; *A Trip to Niagara; or, Travellers in America* (1828), 1830.

Among the many translations of popular German and French dramas, Dunlap's version of Kotzebue's *The Stranger* (1798) had a tremendous vogue. For a list of Dunlap's dramatic translations, see Oral S. Coad, *William Dunlap* (1917), 289–293. Two translations, *False Shame* and *Thirty Years*, were edited by Coad in Vol. II of *America's Lost Plays*, Princeton, 1940.

*André* was reprinted in Allan G. Halline, *American Plays*, New York, 1935, pp. 41–74. Dunlap's published writings other than plays are *Memoirs of George Fred. Cooke*, London, 1813, 2 vols.—rev. ed., London, 1815, 2 vols.;

*A Narrative of the Event Which Followed Bonaparte's Campaign in Russia,*
Hartford, Conn., 1814; *The Life of Charles Brockden Brown,* Philadelphia,
1815, 2 vols. (abridged as *Memoirs of Charles Brockden Brown,* London,
1822); *A History of the American Theatre,* London, 1833, 2 vols. (first pub.,
1832)—source material of great value, especially for the New York stage;
*A History of the Rise and Progress of the Arts of Design in the United States,*
New York, 1834, 2 vols. (reprinted, Boston, 1918, 3 vols.)—an indispensable
authority; *Thirty Years Ago; or, The Memoirs of a Water Drinker,* 1836;
*A History of New York, for Schools,* 1837, 2 vols.—events to 1789; *History
of the New Netherlands,* 1839–1840, 2 vols. Dorothy C. Barck edited the *Diary
of William Dunlap (1766–1839)* . . . , New York, 1930, 3 vols., from eleven
of Dunlap's thirty or more extant manuscript diaries.

BIOGRAPHY AND CRITICISM

A detailed narrative biography of Dunlap is Oral S. Coad, *William Dun-
lap: A Study of His Life and Works and of His Place in Contemporary
Culture,* New York, 1917. A standard estimate of Dunlap as dramatist is
"William Dunlap, Playwright and Producer," in Arthur H. Quinn, *The
History of the American Drama from the Beginning to the Civil War,*
rev. ed., New York, 1943, pp. 74–112.

Other general estimates are "William Dunlap and His Circle," in Van
Wyck Brooks, *The World of Washington Irving,* New York, 1944, pp. 152–
175; and Theodore S. Woolsey, "The American Vasari," *Yale Rev.,* III (1914),
778–789.

Special studies are Oral S. Coad, "The Gothic Element in American Lit-
erature Before 1835," *Jour. English and Germanic Philol.,* XXIV (1925), 72–
93; Mary R. Bowman, "Dunlap and the 'Theatrical Register' of the *New-York
Magazine,*" *Studies in Philol.,* XXIV (1927), 413–425; Adolph B. Benson,
"Scandinavian Influences in the Works of William Dunlap and Richard
Alsop," *Scandinavian Studies and Notes,* IX (1927), 239–257; and *idem,* "The
Sources of William Dunlap's *Ella, A Norwegian Tale,*" *ibid.,* XIX (1946),
136–143. Important background material is in George C. D. Odell, *Annals
of the New York Stage,* New York, Vols. I and II (1927).

PRIMARY SOURCES

The two chief depositories of Dunlap manuscripts are the New York Historical Society Library and the Yale University Library. Parts of Dunlap's
manuscript diary for the years 1786–1834 are in each library. For description,
see "Diary of William Dunlap," *Coll. N.Y. Hist. Soc.,* LXII–LXIV, and
Oral S. Coad, "The Dunlap Diaries at Yale," *Studies in Philol.,* XXIV (1927),
403–412—digest of the unpublished material. Autobiographical informa-

tion appears in Dunlap's *A History of the American Theatre,* and *A History of . . . the Arts of Design.*

BIBLIOGRAPHY

A checklist of all Dunlap's dramatic writings is given in the introduction to Coad's edition of *False Shame* (1940). See also Halline, *American Plays* (1935), pp. 752–753; Oscar Wegelin, *A Bibliographical Checklist of the Plays and Miscellaneous Writings of William Dunlap,* is in Vol. I of *Bibliographica Americana,* New York, 1916.

TIMOTHY DWIGHT

*1752–1817*

SEPARATE WORKS

*A Dissertation on the History, Eloquence, and Poetry of the Bible,* 1772; *The Conquest of Canäan; A Poem in Eleven Books,* 1785; *The Triumph of Infidelity: A Poem,* 1788; *Greenfield Hill: A Poem in Seven Parts,* 1794; *The Nature, and Danger, of Infidel Philosophy,* 1798; *Remarks on the Review of Inchiquin's Letters,* 1815; *Theology Explained and Defended,* 1818–1819; *Travels in New-England and New-York,* 1821–1822. Dwight is perhaps the author of *America; or, A Poem on the Settlement of the British Colonies,* 1770.

BIOGRAPHY AND CRITICISM

The first full-length biography, well documented, is Charles E. Cuningham, *Timothy Dwight, 1752–1817: A Biography,* New York, 1942. Two further recent studies are "Timothy Dwight" and "President Timothy Dwight," in Leon Howard, *The Connecticut Wits,* Chicago, 1943, pp. 79–111, 342–401. The biographical sketch in *Dict. Amer. Biog.* (1930) is written by Harris E. Starr.

Significant contemporary estimates of Dwight are Denison Olmsted, "Biographical Memoir of the Rev. Timothy Dwight," *Port Folio,* IV (1817), 355–369; Benjamin Silliman, *A Sketch of the Life and Character of President Timothy Dwight,* New Haven, 1817; William T. and Sereno Dwight, "Memoir of the Life of President Dwight," incorporated as a preface to Timothy Dwight's *Theology,* I (1818), 3–61; and William B. Sprague, *Annals of the American Pulpit,* New York, 1857, II, 152–165—incorporating memorials written by Dwight's contemporaries.

Later critical estimates of Dwight are "A Great College President and What He Wrote," in Moses C. Tyler, *Three Men of Letters,* New York,

1895, pp. 71-127; "Timothy Dwight," in Daniel D. Addison, *The Clergy in American Life and Letters,* New York, 1900, pp. 157-190; Vernon L. Parrington, *Main Currents in American Thought,* I (1927), pp. 360-363; and "Timothy Dwight, the Elder, of Yale," in Mark A. De Wolfe Howe, *Classic Shades,* Boston, 1928, pp. 1-40.

Biographical information is supplied by Franklin B. Dexter, *Biographical Sketches of the Graduates of Yale College,* New York, III (1903); and by William B. Sprague, "Life of Timothy Dwight," in Jared Sparks, ed., *American Biography,* 2nd ser., IV (1845), 225-364.

Useful special studies are Benson J. Lossing, "Timothy Dwight and the Greenfield Academy," *Amer. Hist. Reg.,* II (1873), 385-387; Theodore A. Zunder, "Noah Webster and *The Conquest of Canäan,*" *Amer. Lit.,* I (1929), 200-202; A. Whitney Griswold, "Three Puritans on Prosperity," *New Eng. Quar.,* VII (1934), 475-493; Percy H. Boynton, "Timothy Dwight and His Connecticut," *Modern Philology,* XXXVIII (1940), 193-203—on his *Travels;* and Lewis E. Buchanan, "The Ethical Ideas of Timothy Dwight," *Research Studies State Coll. of Wash.,* XIII (1945), 185-199.

PRIMARY SOURCES

There is no really important manuscript collection of Dwight material. The most extensive is that in the Yale University Library. Other material is in the New York Public Library. A calendar of the Dwight manuscripts, in public and private hands, is in Cuningham's biography.

Printed source material will be found in Franklin B. Dexter, ed., *The Literary Diary of Ezra Stiles,* New Haven, 1901; and in Benjamin Silliman, *A Sketch of the Life and Character of President Timothy Dwight,* New Haven, 1817.

BIBLIOGRAPHY

The most convenient checklist of Dwight's writings is that in Leon Howard, *The Connecticut Wits,* Chicago, 1943, pp. 416-418. Further secondary items are given in Dexter's *Biographical Sketches,* Vol. III (1903).

## JONATHAN EDWARDS
### *1703-1758*

SEPARATE WORKS

*God Glorified in the Work of Redemption,* 1731; *A Divine and Supernatural Light,* 1734; *A Faithful Narrative,* 1737; *Discourses on Various Important Subjects,* 1738; *The Distinguishing Marks of a Work of the Spirit of*

*God,* 1741; *Sinners in the Hands of an Angry God,* 1741; *Some Thoughts Concerning the Present Revival of Religion in New England,* 1742; *A Treatise Concerning Religious Affections,* 1746; *An Humble Attempt to Promote Explicit Agreement,* 1747; *An Account of the Life of the Late Reverend Mr. David Brainerd,* 1749; *An Humble Inquiry into the Rules of the Word of God Concerning . . . Communion,* 1749; *A Farewell Sermon Preached at the First Precinct in Northampton,* 1751; *True Grace,* 1753; *A Careful and Strict Enquiry Into . . . Freedom of Will . . . ,* 1754; *The Great Christian Doctrine of Original Sin Defended,* 1758; *Two Dissertations:* I. *Concerning the End for Which God Created the World;* II. *The Nature of True Virtue,* 1765; *Charity and Its Fruits,* 1852; *Selections from the Unpublished Writings* (ed. Grosart), 1865; *Observations Concerning the Scripture Oeconomy* (ed. Smyth), 1880; *An Unpublished Essay of Edwards on the Trinity* (ed. Fisher), 1903.

COLLECTED WORKS AND LETTERS

The first collected edition of Edwards's works is still the best, but it is the most difficult to procure: *The Works of President Edwards,* edited by Edward Williams and Edward Parsons, Leeds, 1806–1811, 8 vols.—reprinted in 1817, and again in 1847, with two "Supplementary Volumes." It supplies the fullest and least altered text. The first American edition is that of Samuel Austin, *The Works of President Edwards,* Worcester, Mass., 1808–1809, 8 vols. —reprinted, New York, 1843, 4 vols. The text is trustworthy. The most accessible edition is Sereno E. Dwight's *The Works of President Edwards: With a Memoir of His Life,* New York, 1829–1830, 10 vols. The text is bowdlerized. Volume I is *The Life of President Edwards,* by Dwight. Edward Hickman edited *The Works of Jonathan Edwards, With an Essay [by Henry Rogers] on His Genius and Writings,* London, 1834, 2 vols.—reprinted many times. Sets of any edition are somewhat scarce. From time to time new material has appeared, and a complete text of Edwards's published writings therefore will be found in very few depositories. The most complete holdings are in the libraries of the Presbyterian Historical Society, Philadelphia; Princeton University (together with Princeton Theological Seminary); and Yale University.

Edwards's letters are uncollected. Many, needing reediting, are in Dwight's *Life.* A few have been edited by Clarence H. Faust and Thomas H. Johnson, *Jonathan Edwards: Representative Selections . . . ,* New York, 1935, pp. 382–415; and by Stanley T. Williams, "Six Letters of Jonathan Edwards to Joseph Bellamy," *New England Quar.,* I (1928), 226–242. Others are listed in Thomas H. Johnson, *The Printed Writings of Jonathan Edwards . . . ,* Princeton, 1940, pp. 15–17.

EDITED TEXTS AND REPRINTS

Texts not previously published are Tryon Edwards, ed., *Charity and Its Fruits,* New York, 1852; Alexander B. Grosart, ed., *Selections from the Unpublished Writings of Jonathan Edwards, of America,* Edinburgh, 1865; Egbert C. Smyth, ed., *Observations Concerning the Scripture Oeconomy of the Trinity and Covenant of Redemption,* New York, 1880; and George P. Fisher, ed., *An Unpublished Essay of Edwards on the Trinity, with Remarks on Edwards and His Theology,* New York, 1903.

Egbert C. Smyth reproduced from manuscript, with facsimiles, "Some Early Writings of Jonathan Edwards, A.D. 1714–1726," *Proc. Amer. Antiq. Soc., n.s.* X (1896), 212–247. H. Norman Gardiner, in editing *Selected Sermons of Jonathan Edwards,* New York, 1904, included a sermon preached in 1737, here first published from manuscript. Carl Van Doren edited *Benjamin Franklin and Jonathan Edwards: Selections from Their Writings,* New York, 1920 (Modern Student's Lib.).

The most easily available selections appear in Clarence H. Faust and Thomas H. Johnson, *Jonathan Edwards: Representative Selections, with Introduction, Bibliography, and Notes,* New York, 1935 (Amer. Writers Ser.).

BIOGRAPHY AND CRITICISM

The narrative biography of Ola E. Winslow, *Jonathan Edwards, 1703–1758: A Biography,* New York, 1940, is fully documented and authoritative. Arthur C. McGiffert's *Jonathan Edwards,* New York, 1932, discusses his theology, though it does not supersede Alexander V. G. Allen, *Jonathan Edwards,* Boston, 1889, which is still the fullest treatment of Edwards as theologian. A briefer general study is the introduction to Clarence H. Faust and Thomas H. Johnson, *Jonathan Edwards: Representative Selections . . . ,* New York, 1935, pp. xi–cxv.

Special studies of Edwards's theological and philosophical position are: William H. Channing, "Jonathan Edwards and the Revivalists," *Christian Examiner,* XLIII (1857), 4th ser., 374–394; Egbert C. Smyth, "Jonathan Edwards' Idealism," *Amer. Jour. Theology,* I (1897), 950–964; H. Norman Gardiner, "The Early Idealism of Jonathan Edwards," *Philos. Rev.,* IX (1900), 573–596; Williston Walker, *Ten New England Leaders,* New York, 1901, pp. 217–263; John H. MacCracken, "The Sources of Jonathan Edwards' Idealism," *Philos. Rev.,* XI (1902), 26–42; Frank H. Foster, *A Genetic History of the New England Theology,* Chicago, 1907; I. Woodbridge Riley, *American Philosophy . . . ,* New York, 1907, pp. 126–190; Herbert W. Schneider, *The Puritan Mind,* New York, 1930, 102–155; Frederick I. Carpenter, "The Radicalism of Jonathan Edwards," *New Eng. Quar.,* IV (1931), 629–644; Joseph G. Haroutunian, "Jonathan Edwards: A Study in Godliness," *Jour. Religion,*

XI (1931), 400–419; Rufus Suter, "The Concept of Morality in the Philosophy of Jonathan Edwards," *Jour. Religion,* XIV (1934), 265–272; Perry Miller, "Jonathan Edwards to Emerson," *New Eng. Quar.,* XIII (1940), 589–617; Conrad Wright, "Edwards and the Arminians on the Freedom of the Will," *Harvard Theological Rev.,* XXXV (1942), 241–261; and Joseph G. Haroutunian, "Jonathan Edwards: Theologian of the Great Commandment," *Theology Today,* I (1944), 361–377.

Edwards's interest in science is discussed by Henry C. McCook, "Jonathan Edwards as a Naturalist," *Presbyterian and Reformed Rev.,* I (1890), 393–402; Clarence H. Faust, "Jonathan Edwards as a Scientist," *Amer. Lit.,* I (1930), 393–404; Theodore Hornberger, "The Effect of the New Science upon the Thought of Jonathan Edwards," *Amer. Lit.,* IX (1937), 196–207; and Harvey G. Townsend, "Jonathan Edwards' Later Observations of Nature," *New Eng. Quar.,* XIII (1940), 510–518.

As a man of letters, Edwards is treated in Thomas H. Johnson, "Jonathan Edwards' Background of Reading," *Pub. Colonial Soc. Mass.,* XXVIII (1931), 193–222.

Useful background studies are Joseph Tracy, *The Great Awakening: A History of the Revival of Religion in the Time of Edwards and Whitefield,* Boston, 1841—with important source material from diaries, letters, and elsewhere; Ezra Byington, *The Puritan in England and New England,* Boston, 1896—a summary statement of the Calvinism of the founders of New England; Thomas H. Billings, "The Great Awakening," *Essex Institute Hist. Coll.,* LXV (1929), 89–104; W. M. Gewehr, *The Great Awakening in Virginia 1740–1790,* Durham, N.C., 1930; Clarence Gohdes, "Aspects of Idealism in Early New England," *Philosophical Rev.,* XXXIX (1930), 537–555; and William E. Rowley, "The Puritans' Tragic Vision," *New Eng. Quar.,* XVII (1944), 394–417.

PRIMARY SOURCES

Edwards's disciple Samuel Hopkins wrote *The Life and Character of the Late . . . Mr. Jonathan Edwards . . . ,* Boston, 1765, an admiring tribute. Sereno E. Dwight's *The Life of President Edwards,* New York, 1829, though outdated as biography, contains material not elsewhere available. "Jonathan Edwards' Last Will, and the Inventory of His Estate," appears in *Bibliotheca Sacra,* XXXIII (1876), 438–443.

The bulk of Edwards manuscripts, principally sermons, is in the Yale University Library and the Andover-Harvard Theological Seminary Library, Cambridge. They are described in detail, together with items scattered in other collections, in Ola E. Winslow, *Jonathan Edwards . . . ,* New York, 1940, pp. 373–378. Franklin B. Dexter, "On the Manuscripts of Jonathan Edwards," *Proc. Mass. Hist. Soc.,* XV (1902), 2 ser., 2–16, is an early survey.

Of use still is William P. Upham, "On the Shorthand Notes of Jonathan Edwards," *ibid.*, pp. 514–521.

BIBLIOGRAPHY

The bibliography in *Camb. Hist. Amer. Lit.*, New York (1917), I, 428–432, is supplemented by the "Selected Bibliography" in Ola E. Winslow, *Jonathan Edwards . . .* , New York, 1940, pp. 373–393. The bibliography in Clarence H. Faust and Thomas H. Johnson, *Jonathan Edwards: Representative Selections . . .* , New York, 1935, pp. cxix–cxlii, is annotated. A collation of his works is undertaken in Thomas H. Johnson, *The Printed Writings of Jonathan Edwards, 1703–1758: A Bibliography*, Princeton, 1940.

# EDWARD EGGLESTON
## *1837–1902*

SEPARATE WORKS

*Mr. Blake's Walking-Stick: A Christmas Story for Boys and Girls*, 1870; *Book of Queer Stories and Stories Told on a Cellar Door*, 1871; *The Hoosier School-Master: A Novel*, 1871; *The End of the World: A Love Story*, 1872; *The Mystery of Metropolisville*, 1873; *The Circuit Rider: A Tale of the Heroic Age*, 1874; *The Schoolmaster's Stories, for Boys and Girls*, 1874; *Roxy*, 1878; *The Hoosier School-Boy*, 1883; *Queer Stories for Boys and Girls*, 1884; *The Graysons: A Story of Illinois*, 1888; *The Faith Doctor: A Story of New York*, 1891; *Duffels*, 1893.

Eggleston's *A History of the United States and Its People*, 1888, appeared in later reissues with various titles. His *The Beginners of a Nation* was published in 1896; and *The Transit of Civilization from England to America in the Seventeenth Century*, 1901, was reprinted, 1933. Eggleston compiled other histories for elementary schools, and collaborated in compilations of religious books and other works. *The Hoosier School-Boy* was reprinted, New York, 1936; and *The Hoosier School-Master* was issued in the Modern Readers' Series, 1928. *The Schoolmaster's Stories, for Boys and Girls* (1874) is a reprint for the most part of *The Book of Queer Stories* (1871), with some additional material.

BIOGRAPHY AND CRITICISM

A full-length narrative and critical biography is William Peirce Randel, *Edward Eggleston: Author of 'The Hoosier School-Master,'* New York, 1946. The best brief sketch is that of Ralph L. Rusk in *Dict. Amer. Biog.* (1931). Two studies by John T. Flanagan are "The Novels of Edward Eggleston," *College Eng.*, V (1944), 250–258; and "The Hoosier Schoolmaster in

Minnesota," *Minnesota Hist.*, XVIII (1937), 347–370. Other special studies include Edward Stone, "Edward Eggleston's Religious Transit," *Univ. Texas Studies in Eng.*, No. 3926 (1939), pp. 210–218; Charles Hirschfeld, "Edward Eggleston: Pioneer in Social History," in Eric F. Goldman, ed., *Historiography and Urbanization: Essays in American History in Honor of W. Stull Holt*, Baltimore, 1941, pp. 189–210; Benjamin T. Spencer, "The New Realism and a National Literature," *PMLA*, LVI (1941), 1116–1132; James A. Rawley, "Edward Eggleston: Historian," *Indiana Mag. Hist.*, XL (1944), 341–352; William Peirce Randel, "Zoroaster Higgins: Edward Eggleston as a Political Satirist in Verse," *Amer. Lit.*, XVII (1945), 255–260; and *idem*, "Edward Eggleston's Library at Traverse des Sioux," *Minnesota Hist.*, XXVI (1945), 242–247. Two linguistic studies are Margaret Bloom, "Eggleston's Notes on Hoosier Dialect," *Amer. Speech*, IX (1934), 319–320, and John M. Haller, "Edward Eggleston, Linguist," *Philological Quar.*, XXIV (1945), 175–186.

*The Hoosier School-Master* was translated in whole or in part into Danish (1878), French (1879)—reprinted from *Revue des Deux Mondes*, CII (1872), 125–176—German, and Swedish.

PRIMARY SOURCES

The bulk of the Eggleston manuscripts is in the Collection of Regional History, at Cornell University. Published source material may be found in George C. Eggleston's *The First of the Hoosiers* . . ., Philadelphia, 1903—reminiscences about Eggleston by his brother; and in the same writer's *A Rebel's Recollections*, New York, 1875. See also Meredith Nicholson, *The Hoosiers*, New York, 1900; the letters of E. C. Stedman and of W. D. Howells; and the autobiographies of Hamlin Garland. James A. Rawley's "Some New Light on Edward Eggleston," *Amer. Lit.*, XI (1940), 453–458, is a letter written in the 1880's by George C. Eggleston to a friend.

BIBLIOGRAPHY

The fullest bibliography is that in Randel's biography (pp. 263–313). It locates manuscripts, lists the books, pamphlets, and periodical contributions by Eggleston, and supplies secondary items through 1941.

JOHN ELIOT

*1604–1690*

SEPARATE WORKS

*The Glorious Progress of the Gospel Amongst the Indians*, 1649; *A Late and Further Manifestation*, 1655; *The Christian Commonwealth*, 1659; *A Further Accompt of the Progresse of the Gospel Amongst the Indians*, 1659;

*The New Testament . . . Translated into the Indian Language,* 1661; *The Holy Bible . . . Translated into the Indian Language,* 1663; *Communion of Churches,* 1665; *The Indian Grammar Begun,* 1666; *The Indian Primer,* 1669; *A Brief Narrative of the Progress of the Gospel,* 1671; *Indian Dialogues,* 1671; *The Logic Primer,* 1672; *The Harmony of the Gospels,* 1678; *A Brief Answer to a Small Book Written by John Narcot,* 1679.

EDITED TEXTS AND REPRINTS

There is no collected edition of Eliot's works. Reprints have been issued as follows: *The Glorious Progress* (1649), in *Coll. Mass. Hist. Soc.,* 3rd ser., IV (1834), 68–98; *A Late and Further Manifestation* (1655), *ibid.,* 261–287; *The Christian Commonwealth* (1659), *ibid.,* IX (1846), 127–164, and in Photostat Americana, No. 34, 1937; *A Further Accompt* (1659), New York, 1865; *The Indian Grammar Begun* (1666), *Coll. Mass. Hist. Soc.,* 2nd ser., IX (1832), 243–366; *A Brief Narrative* (1671), edited with an introduction by W. T. R. Marvin, Boston, 1868; *The Logic Primer* (1672), edited with an introduction by Wilberforce Eames, Cleveland, 1904.

*Tears of Repentance,* written with Thomas Mayhew, is printed in *Coll. Mass. Hist. Soc.,* 3rd ser., IV (1834), 197–260.

Eliot's published letters for the most part were written to report his progress as missionary. They may be found as follows: "Letters to Robert Boyle," *Coll. Mass. Hist. Soc.,* 1st ser., III (1794), 177–188—nine letters written during the years 1670–1688; "An Account of Indian Churches in New-England . . .," *Coll. Mass. Hist. Soc.,* 1st ser., X (1809), 124–129—from a letter written in 1673; Henry Whitfield, *A Farther Discovery . . .,* New York, 1865, including five letters from Eliot; Charles A. Briggs, ed., "John Eliot's Description of New England in 1650," *Proc. Mass. Hist. Soc.,* 2nd ser., II (1885), 44–50—from a letter transcribed from manuscript; "A Letter of John Eliot, 1644," *Pub. Rhode Island Hist. Soc.,* n.s. VI (1898), 110–117; Wilberforce Eames, ed., *John Eliot and the Indians, 1652–1657: Being Letters Addressed to Rev. Jonathan Hanmer of Barnstable, England,* New York, 1915—reproduced from MS; "Three Letters of John Eliot . . .," *Bul. John Rylands Lib.,* V (1920), 102–110; George P. Winship, ed., "Letters of John Eliot, the Apostle," *Proc. Mass. Hist. Soc.,* LIII (1920), 189–192—with bibliographical data; and Frederick J. Powicke, ed., "Some Unpublished Correspondence of the Rev. Richard Baxter and the Rev. John Eliot, 'the Apostle to the American Indians,' 1656–1682," *Bul. John Rylands Lib.,* XV (1931), 138–176, 442–466.

BIOGRAPHY AND CRITICISM

The best account of Eliot is the brief one by Ezra H. Byington, "John Eliot, the Puritan Missionary to the Indians," *Papers Amer. Soc. Church Hist.,* VIII (1897), 109–145; supplemented by "John Eliot, the Apostle to the

Indians," in *idem, The Puritan as a Colonist and Reformer,* Boston, 1899, pp. 205–270. Other authoritative sketches are "John Eliot," in Williston Walker, *Ten New England Leaders,* New York, 1901; "John Eliot, Apostle to the Indians," in Mary G. Humphreys, ed., *Missionary Explorers Among the American Indians,* New York, 1913, pp. 3–28; "John Eliot," in Samuel E. Morison, *Builders of the Bay Colony,* Boston, 1930, pp. 289–319; and the accounts by H. R. Tedder in the *Dict. Nat. Biog.* and James T. Adams in *Dict. Amer. Biog.* (1931).

Early lives are to be found in "The Historical Account of John Eliot . . . ," *Coll. Mass. Hist. Soc.,* 1st ser., VIII (1802), 5–35; Convers Francis, *Life of John Eliot, the Apostle to the Indians,* New York, 1849; and Robert B. Caverly, *History of the Indian Wars of New England, with Eliot the Apostle Fifty Years in the Midst of Them,* Boston, 1882.

PRIMARY SOURCES

Cotton Mather wrote an early life, *The Triumphs of the Reformed Religion in America: The Life and Death of the Renown'd Mr. John Eliot,* London, 1691, reprinted in the *Magnalia.* George P. Winship edited *The New England Company of 1649 and John Eliot,* Boston, 1920, with an introduction —a reproduction from MS of a ledger (1650–1660) and record books of the Corporation for the Propagation of the Gospel in New England.

BIBLIOGRAPHY

An excellent bibliography of Eliot's Indian works, together with many facsimile photographs of title pages and other published and manuscript items, has been compiled by Wilberforce Eames in James C. Pilling, *Bibliography of the Algonquian Languages,* U.S. Bureau of Ethnology, Bul. No. 13 (1891), pp. 127–184. A careful study of the vexed authorship problems of many Eliot tracts is George P. Winship, "The Eliot Indian Tracts," in *Bibliographical Essays: A Tribute to Wilberforce Eames,* Cambridge, 1924, pp. 179–192. Further data are supplied in Wilberforce Eames, "Discovery of a Lost Cambridge Imprint: John Eliot's *Genesis,* 1655," *Pub. Colonial Soc. Mass.,* XXXIV (1943), 11–12, and in the Eliot bibliography in *Camb. Hist. Amer. Lit.,* I (1917), 390–393.


# T(HOMAS) S(TEARNS) ELIOT
### *b. 1888*

SEPARATE WORKS

*Prufrock and Other Observations,* 1917; *Ezra Pound: His Metric and Poetry,* 1917; *Poems,* 1919; *Poems,* 1920; *The Sacred Wood: Essays on Poetry and Criticism,* 1920; *The Waste Land,* 1922; *Homage to John Dryden,* 1924; *The Journey of the Magi,* 1927; *Shakespeare and the Stoicism of Seneca,* 1927; *A Song for Simeon,* 1928; *For Lancelot Andrewes: Essays on Style and Order,* 1928; *Animula,* 1929; *Dante,* 1929; *Ash-Wednesday,* 1930; *Marina,* 1930; *Charles Whibley: A Memoir,* 1931; *Triumphal March,* 1931; *Thoughts After Lambeth,* 1931; *John Dryden the Poet, the Dramatist, the Critic,* 1932; *Sweeney Agonistes,* 1932; *The Use of Poetry and the Use of Criticism,* 1933; *After Strange Gods,* 1934; *The Rock: A Pageant Play,* 1934; *Elizabethan Essays,* 1934; *Murder in the Cathedral,* 1935; *Essays, Ancient and Modern,* 1936; *The Idea of a Christian Society,* 1939; *The Family Reunion: A Play,* 1939; *Old Possum's Book of Practical Cats,* 1939; *East Coker,* 1940; *The Dry Salvages,* 1941; *Little Gidding,* 1942; *The Music of Poetry,* 1942; *The Classics and the Man of Letters,* 1942.

COLLECTIONS AND REPRINTS

*Ara Vos Prec,* London, 1919, is a collection of the two previous volumes of poetry (*Prufrock,* 1917, and *Poems,* 1919), reproduced with one exception in *Poems,* 1920. *Poems, 1909–1925,* London, 1925, includes all the previous poetical works, with the addition of "The Hollow Men." *Selected Essays, 1917–1932,* New York, 1932, was published in a second edition, revised and enlarged, London, 1934, which included the bulk of the four earlier volumes of essays, together with several additional pieces. *Essays, Ancient and Modern,* London, 1936, was an enlarged collection of material published in part as *For Lancelot Andrewes* (1928). Four later poetical collections are *Collected Poems, 1909–1935,* London and New York, 1936; *The Waste Land and Other Poems,* London, 1940; *Later Poems, 1925–1935,* London, 1941; and *Four Quartets,* London, 1943—the group *Burnt Norton, East Coker, The Dry Salvages,* and *Little Gidding.*

*Points of View* (1941) is a selection of Eliot's critical writings, edited by John Hayward.

Eliot has contributed introductions to selected writings of Dryden (1928), Baudelaire (1930), Johnson (1930), Tennyson (1936), Joyce (1942), Kipling (1942), and others.

BIOGRAPHY AND CRITICISM

A revealing critique of Eliot's poetry, and the most extensive treatment to date, is F(rancis) O. Matthiessen's *The Achievement of T. S. Eliot: An Essay on the Nature of Poetry,* Boston, 1935. Among early estimates are D. MacCarthy, "T. S. Eliot," *New Statesman,* XVI (1921), 418–420; Edmund Wilson, "The Poetry of Drouth," *Dial,* LXXIII (1922), 611–616; I. A. Richards, "The Poetry of T. S. Eliot," *Living Age,* CCCXXIX (1926), 112–115; "T. S. Eliot," in Bonamy Dobrée, *The Lamp and the Lute,* Oxford,

1929, pp. 107–133; "Deuxième Phase de l'Imagisme: T. S. Eliot," in René Taupin, *L'Influence du Symbolisme Français sur la Poésie Américaine* . . . , Paris, 1929, pp. 211–240; and "T. S. Eliot and The Waste Land," in Alfred Kreymborg, *Our Singing Strength,* New York, 1929, pp. 523–538.

Later studies are Morton D. Zabel, "T. S. Eliot in Mid-Career," *Poetry,* XXXVI (1930), 330–337; *idem,* "The Still Point," *ibid.,* XLI (1932), 152–158; Allen Tate, "Irony and Humility," *Hound and Horn,* IV (1931), 290–297; "T. S. Eliot," in Edmund Wilson, *Axel's Castle,* New York, 1931, pp. 93–131 —an evaluation of Eliot's accomplishment to date; W. E. Collin, "T. S. Eliot," *Sewanee Rev.,* XXXIX (1931), 13–24; *idem,* "T. S. Eliot the Critic," *Sewanee Rev.,* 419–424; Thomas McGreevy, *Thomas Stearns Eliot: A Study,* London, 1931; Louis Grudin, *Mr. Eliot Among the Nightingales,* Paris, 1932; Hugh Ross Williamson, *The Poetry of T. S. Eliot,* London, 1932; F. R. Leavis, *New Bearings in English Poetry* . . . , London, 1932, pp. 75–132; René Taupin, "The Classicism of T. S. Eliot," *Symposium,* III (1932), 64–82; Theodore Spencer, "The Poetry of T. S. Eliot," *Atl. Mo.,* CLI (1933), 60–68; J. R. Daniells, "T. S. Eliot and His Relation to T. E. Hulme," *Univ. Toronto Quar.,* II (1933), 380–396; Richard P. Blackmur, "T. S. Eliot in Prose," *Poetry,* XLII (1933), 44–49; "T. S. Eliot," in Edith Sitwell, *Aspects of Modern Poetry,* London, 1934, pp. 99–140; Malcolm Cowley, "The Religion of Art," *New Repub.,* LXXVII (1934), 216–218; G. M. Turnell, "Tradition and T. S. Eliot," *Colosseum,* I (1934), 44–54; "T. S. Eliot, Pseudoist," in Wyndham Lewis, *Men Without Art,* London, 1934, pp. 65–100; Allardyce Nicoll, "Mr. T. S. Eliot and the Revival of Classicism," *English Jour.,* XXIII (1934), 269–278; Conrad Aiken, "After *Ash-Wednesday,*" *Poetry,* XLV (1934), 161–165; "T. S. Eliot: From *Ash-Wednesday* to *Murder in the Cathedral,*" in Richard P. Blackmur, *The Double Agent,* New York, 1935, pp. 184–218; Hans W. Häusermann, "T. S. Eliots Religiöse Entwicklung," *Englische Studien,* LXIX (1935), 373–391; Babette Deutsch, *This Modern Poetry,* New York, 1935, pp. 123–139; Calvin S. Brown, Jr., "T. S. Eliot and *Die Droste,*" *Sewanee Rev.,* XLVI (1938), 492–500; Theodore Morrison, "*Ash Wednesday:* A Religious History," *New Eng. Quar.,* XI (1938), 266–286; Edward K. Brown, "Mr. Eliot and Some Enemies," *Univ. Toronto Quar.,* VIII (1938), 69–84; and W. Harvey-Jellie, "T. S. Eliot Among the Prophets," *Dalhousie Rev.,* XVIII (1938), 83–90.

The most recent estimates are Babette Deutsch, "T. S. Eliot and the Laodiceans," *Amer. Scholar,* IX (1940), 19–30; C. L. Barber, "T. S. Eliot After Strange Gods," *Southern Rev.,* VI (1940), 387–416; "T. S. Eliot: The Historical Critic," in John Crowe Ransom, *The New Criticism,* 1941, pp. 135–208; "Orpheus in Hell: T. S. Eliot," in Ferner Nuhn, *The Wind Blew from the East,* New York, 1942, pp. 195–255; Philip Wheelwright, "The Burnt

Norton Trilogy," *Chimera*, I (1942), 7–18; Leonard Unger, "T. S. Eliot's Rose Garden: A Persistent Theme," *Southern Rev.*, VII (1942), 667–689; F. O. Matthiessen, "Eliot's Quartets," *Kenyon Rev.*, V (1943), 161–178—an analysis of the latest poems; "T. S. Eliot: or, The Illusion of Reaction," in Yvor Winters, *The Anatomy of Nonsense*, Norfolk, Conn., 1943, pp. 120–167; Hyatt H. Waggoner, "T. S. Eliot and *The Hollow Men*," *Amer. Lit.*, XV (1943), 101–126; Leo Kirschbaum, "Eliot's *Sweeney Among the Nightingales*," *Explicator*, II (1943), No. 3; Harry M. Campbell, "An Examination of Modern Critics: T. S. Eliot," *Rocky Mt. Rev.*, VIII (1944), 128–138; R(ichard) P. Blackmur and others, "Mr. Eliot and Notions of Culture: A Discussion," *Partisan Rev.*, XI (1944), 302–312—a symposium on Eliot's "Notes on Culture"; Eliseo Vivas, "The Objective Correlative of T. S. Eliot," *Amer. Bookman*, I (1944), 7–18; Peter Monro Jack, "A Review of Reviews: T. S. Eliot's *Four Quartets*," *ibid.*, 91–99; Genevieve W. Foster, "The Archetypal Imagery of T. S. Eliot," *PMLA*, LX (1945), 567–585; William A. Nitze, "The Waste Land: A Celtic Arthurian Theme," *Modern Philology*, XLIII (1945), 58–62; Delmore Schwartz, "T. S. Eliot as the International Hero," *Partisan Rev.*, XII (1945), 199–206; Wallace Fowlie, "Eliot and Tchelitchew," *Accent*, V (1945), 166–170; Sidney Hook, "The Dilemma of T. S. Eliot," *Nation*, CLX (1945), 69–71; John C. Pope, "Prufrock and Raskolnikov," *Amer. Lit.*, XVII (1945), 213–230—the influence of Dostoevski's *Crime and Punishment*; Hermann Peschmann, "The Later Poetry of T. S. Eliot," *English*, V (1945), 180–188; Roy P. Basler, "Psychological Patterns in 'The Love Song of J. Alfred Prufrock,'" in William S. Knickerbocker, ed., *Twentieth Century English*, New York, 1946, pp. 384–400; William Blissett, "The Argument of T. S. Eliot's *Four Quartets*," *University of Toronto Quar.*, XV (1946), 115–126; A. K. Coomaraswamy, "Primordial Images," *PMLA*, LXI (1946), 601–602; Michael F. Moloney, "Mr. Eliot and Critical Tradition," *Thought*, XXI (1946), 455–474; F. J. Smith, "A Reading of *East Coker*," *ibid.*, 272–286; Grover Smith, "Observations on Eliot's 'Death by Water,'" *Accent*, VI (1946), 257–263; and T. Weiss, "T. S. Eliot and the Courtyard Revolution," *Sewanee Rev.*, LIV (1946), 289–307. See also Raymond Preston, *'Four Quartets' Rehearsed: A Commentary on T. S. Eliot's Cycle of Poems*, New York, 1946, 64 pp. An evaluation of *The Waste Land* is in Cleanth Brooks, *Modern Poetry and the Tradition*, Chapel Hill, N.C., 1939.

A few Eliot manuscripts are in the Harvard College Library.

A useful Eliot bibliography is Donald C. Gallup, *A Catalogue of English and American First Editions of Writings by T. S. Eliot, Exhibited in the Yale University Library* . . ., New Haven, 1937, 42 pp. Varian Fry, "A Bibliography of the Writings of Thomas Stearns Eliot," *Hound and Horn*, I (1928), 214–218, 320–324, is more detailed in its descriptions than Gallup, but less comprehensive for the period covered. A recent checklist is compiled by Frances Cheney, in Allen Tate, *Sixty American Poets, 1896–1944*, Washington, 1945. pp. 31–42.


# RALPH WALDO EMERSON
### *1803–1882*

SEPARATE WORKS

*Letter . . . to the Second Church and Society*, 1832; *A Historical Discourse Delivered Before the Citizens of Concord, 12th September, 1835*, 1835; *Nature*, 1836; *The American Scholar*, 1837; *An Address Delivered Before the Senior Class in Divinity College, Cambridge . . .*, 1838; *An Oration Delivered Before the Literary Societies of Dartmouth College*, 1838; *The Method of Nature*, 1841; *Essays*, 1841; *Man the Reformer*, 1842; *The Young American*, 1844; *Nature: An Essay, and Lectures of the Times*, 1844; *An Address Delivered in . . . Concord . . .*, 1844; *Orations, Lectures and Addresses*, 1844; *Essays: Second Series*, 1844; *Poems*, 1847; *Representative Men: Seven Lectures*, 1850; *English Traits*, 1856; *The Conduct of Life*, 1860; *May-Day and Other Pieces*, 1867; *Society and Solitude*, 1870; *Letters and Social Aims*, 1876; *Selected Poems*, 1876; *Fortune of the Republic*, 1878; *The Preacher*, 1880; *Lectures and Biographical Sketches*, 1884; *The Senses and the Soul*, 1884; *Natural History of the Intellect and Other Papers*, 1893; *Two Unpublished Essays*, 1896; *Tantalus*, 1903.

COLLECTED WORKS

Two collected editions appeared in Emerson's lifetime: *The Complete Works of Emerson*, London, 1866, 2 vols., and *The Prose Works of Emerson*, Boston, 1869, 2 vols., to which a third volume was added in 1878. Following his death there was issued *The Writings of Emerson*, Cambridge, 1883–1887, 16 vols. The standard edition is still the authoritative Centenary Edition, prepared, with notes, by his son Edward Waldo Emerson, and issued as *The Complete Works of Ralph Waldo Emerson*, Boston, 1903–1904, 12 vols. *The Uncollected Writings: Essays, Addresses, Poems, Reviews and Letters by Ralph Waldo Emerson*, New York, 1912, edited by Charles C. Bigelow, contains supplementary material. More recently further material has been published: Clarence F. Gohdes, ed., *Uncollected Lectures by Ralph Waldo Emerson*, New York, 1933; Arthur C. McGiffert, ed., *Young Emerson Speaks: Unpublished Discourses on Many Subjects*, Boston, 1938—twenty-five sermons, chronologically arranged, with useful notes and a bibliography; and Jeanne Kronman, "Three Unpublished Lectures of Ralph Waldo Emerson," *New Eng. Quar.*, XIX (1946), 98–110.

*The Journals of Ralph Waldo Emerson* were edited by E. W. Emerson and W. E. Forbes, Boston, 1909–1914, 10 vols., in a format uniform with the Centenary Edition of the *Works*.

Emerson's very extensive correspondence has been published as follows: *The Correspondence of Thomas Carlyle and Ralph Waldo Emerson, 1834–1872*, Boston, 1883, 2 vols., edited by Charles E. Norton, with supplementary letters published in 1886, and a revised edition issued in 1888; Frank B. Sanborn, ed., "The Emerson-Thoreau Correspondence," *Atl. Mo.,* LXIX (1892), 577–596, 736–753; *A Correspondence Between John Sterling and Ralph Waldo Emerson,* Boston, 1897, ed. by E. W. Emerson; *Letters from Ralph Waldo Emerson to a Friend* (Samuel Gray Ward), Boston, 1899, ed. by Charles E. Norton; and "Correspondence Between Ralph Waldo Emerson and Herman Grimm," *Atl. Mo.,* XCI (1903), 467–479, edited by Frederick W. Holls. The inclusive edition is that of Ralph L. Rusk, ed., *The Letters of Ralph Waldo Emerson,* New York, 1939, 6 vols.—as complete a calendar of Emerson letters as possible, including some 2,000 hitherto unpublished letters, with corrected versions of several hundred others; this annotated and indexed collection is prefaced by an excellent introduction and supplied with a checklist of all correspondence hitherto published, and full texts of letters not elsewhere available. Gleanings may be found in A. Warren Stearns, "Four Emerson Letters to Dr. Daniel Parker," *Tuftonian,* I (1940), 6–9; Barbara D. Simison, "The Letters of Ralph Waldo Emerson: Addenda," *Modern Language Notes,* LV (1940), 425–427; Ralph L. Rusk, ed., *Letters to Emma Lazarus in the Columbia University Library,* New York, 1939; Zoltán Haraszti, ed., *Letters by T. W. Parsons,* Boston, 1940; William P. Randel, ed., "A Late Emerson Letter," *Amer. Lit.,* XII (1941), 496–497; and Carlos Baker, "The Road to Concord: Another Milestone in the Whitman-Emerson Friendship," *Princeton Univ. Lib. Chron.,* VII (1946), 100–117—a newly discovered letter by Emerson concerning his estimate of Whitman.

"Three Unpublished Lectures of Ralph Waldo Emerson" are edited by Jeanne Kronman, *New Eng. Quar.,* XIX (1946), 98–110.

### EDITED TEXTS AND REPRINTS

Emerson's *Nature* (1836) was edited by Kenneth W. Cameron in the Scholars' Facsimiles and Reprints, New York, 1940, with an introduction, index-concordance, and bibliography. Selections were made by Bliss Perry, *The Heart of Emerson's Journals,* Boston, 1926; Arthur H. Quinn, *Emerson's Essays and Poems,* New York, 1926; Bliss Perry, *The Heart of Emerson's Essays: Selections from His Complete Works,* Boston, 1933, with introduction and notes. *The Complete Writings of Ralph Waldo Emerson* were made available in a single-volume edition by William H. Wise & Co., New York, 1929, in 1,435 pp. Brooks Atkinson edited *The Complete Essays and Other*

*Writings of Ralph Waldo Emerson,* with a biographical introduction, for the Modern Library, New York, 1940.

A good general text is supplied by Frederic I. Carpenter, ed., *Ralph Waldo Emerson: Representative Selections, with Introduction, Bibliography, and Notes,* New York, 1934 (Amer. Writers Ser.). Mark Van Doren edited *The Portable Emerson,* New York, 1946; and Eduard C. Lindeman edited *Emerson: The Basic Writings of America's Sage,* New York, 1947.

BIOGRAPHY AND CRITICISM

No definitive biography of Emerson has been written, even though the material for such a life has long been available. The best brief biography is still that of George E. Woodberry, *Ralph Waldo Emerson,* English Men of Letters Ser., New York, 1907, containing excellent criticism. George W. Cooke's early biography, published in the last year of Emerson's life, *Ralph Waldo Emerson: His Life, Writings, and Philosophy,* Boston, 1881, is especially interesting as a contemporary interpretation, with stress on the writings. Emerson's literary executor, James E. Cabot, published *A Memoir of Ralph Waldo Emerson,* Boston, 1887, 2 vols., which, though it omits criticism and interpretation, is the best portrait of the man. A European who has interpreted Emerson well is Marie Dugard, *Ralph Waldo Emerson: Sa Vie et Son Œuvre,* Paris, 1907. Among more recent studies, Oscar W. Firkins's *Ralph Waldo Emerson,* Boston, 1915, is vivid if critically uneven; Bliss Perry's *Emerson Today,* Princeton, 1931, is a sympathetic interpretation and the best introduction to the subject. Van Wyck Brooks, *The Life of Emerson,* New York, 1932, draws heavily upon the *Journals.*

The leading studies of Emerson as philosopher and critic are those of Henry D. Gray, *Emerson: A Statement of New England Transcendentalism as Expressed in the Philosophy of Its Chief Exponent,* Stanford Univ., Calif., 1917; Régis Michaud, *L'Esthétique d'Emerson,* Paris, 1927; Paul Sakmann, *Emersons Geisteswelt,* Stuttgart, 1927; "Emerson," chap. iii in Norman Foerster, *Nature in American Literature,* Boston, 1923, pp. 37–68, and "Emerson," chap. ii in *idem, American Criticism,* Boston, 1928, pp. 52–110— both excellent brief studies; Frederic I. Carpenter, *Emerson and Asia,* Cambridge, 1930—a study of Emerson's Orientalism and his Neo-Platonism; "Introduction" in *idem,* ed., *Ralph Waldo Emerson: Representative Selections . . . ,* New York, 1934, pp. xi–xlviii; and "From Emerson to Thoreau," in F(rancis) O. Matthiessen, *American Renaissance . . . ,* New York, 1941, pp. 3–175, which, though unsympathetic, is one of the best critical studies.

Three recent unpublished theses are especially useful: John C. Gerber, "Emerson's Economics" (Univ. of Chicago, 1941), analyzes Emerson's conservative laissez-faire economics on the level of the senses as they relate to his transcendental liberalism on the level of the ideal; Vivian C. Hopkins, "The Aesthetic Theory of Ralph Waldo Emerson" (Univ. of Mich., 1943), canvasses the subject thoroughly; and Stephen E. Whicher, "The Lapse of Uriel: A Study in the Evolution of Emerson's Thought, with Special Reference to the Years 1833–1847" (Harvard Univ., 1943), provides an analysis of Emerson's formative period.

Brief studies of significant aspects of Emerson's philosophic position will be found in Frederic I. Carpenter, "Points of Comparison Between Emerson and William James," *New Eng. Quar.,* II (1929), 458–474; Clarence Hotson, "Emerson and the Swedenborgians," *Studies in Philol.,* XXVII (1930), 517–545; Chester E. Jorgenson, "Emerson's Paradise Under the Shadow of Swords," *Philological Quar.,* XI (1932), 274–292—Emerson's views of evil; Frederick B. Tolles, "Emerson and Quakerism," *Amer. Lit.,* X (1938), 142–165—its importance in his formative years; Frederic I. Carpenter, "William James and Emerson," *Amer. Lit.,* XI (1939), 39–57; George H. Hartwig, "Emerson on Historical Christianity," *Hibbert Jour.,* XXXVII (1939), 405–412; Alexander C. Kern, "Emerson and Economics," *New Eng. Quar.,* XIII (1940), 678–696; Perry Miller, "Edwards to Emerson," *New Eng. Quar.,* XIII (1940), 589–617—on the continuity of New England thought; Mildred Silver, "Emerson and the Idea of Progress," *Amer. Lit.,* XII (1940), 1–19—a summary of the development of his philosophy; Robert P. Falk, "Emerson and Shakespeare," *PMLA,* LVI (1941), 532–543—an analysis of the adverse judgment of the final estimate in *Representative Men*; William A. Huggard, "Emerson's Philosophy of War and Peace," *Philological Quar.,* XXII (1943), 370–375; Merrell R. Davis, "Emerson's 'Reason' and the Scottish Philosophers," *New Eng. Quar.,* XVII (1944), 209–228; Henry A. Pochmann, "Emerson and the St. Louis Hegelians," *Amer.-Ger. Rev.,* X (Feb., 1944), 14–17—on Emerson's meeting with the group in 1867; Stuart G. Brown, "Emerson's Platonism," *New Eng. Quar.,* XVIII (1945), 325–345; A. Robert Caponigri, "Brownson and Emerson: Nature and History," *New Eng. Quar.,* XVIII (1945), 368–390; and Hermann Hummel, "Emerson and Nietzsche," *New Eng. Quar.,* XIX (1946), 63–84.

Brief critical estimates of Emerson, significant to the extent to which the authors are spokesmen of their times, are: "Emerson," in Matthew Arnold, *Discourses in America,* London, 1885, pp. 138–207; Edmund C. Stedman, *Poets of America,* Boston, 1885, pp. 133–179; "Emerson," in John M. Robertson, *Modern Humanists . . .,* London, 1895, pp. 112–136; *The Centenary of the Birth of Ralph Waldo Emerson,* Concord, 1903—fifteen addresses by Le Baron R. Briggs, Charles Eliot Norton, Thomas W. Higginson, William James, Hugo Münsterberg, and others; "Emerson," in William C. Brownell, *American Prose Masters,* New York, 1909, pp. 131–204; Paul E.

More, "Emerson," in *Cambridge Hist. of Amer. Lit.*, New York, I (1917), 349–362; "The Emersonian Liberation," in Stuart P. Sherman, *Americans*, New York, 1922, pp. 63–121; "Emerson," in Vernon L. Parrington, *Main Currents in American Thought*, New York, 1927, II, 386–399; Percy H. Boynton, "Emerson in His Period," *International Jour. of Ethics*, XXXIX (1929), 177–189; "Emerson," in Henry S. Canby, *Classic Americans*, New York, 1931, pp. 143–183; and "Emerson," in H. W. Garrod, *Poetry and the Criticism of Life*, Cambridge, 1931, pp. 85–107.

Brief essays by four philosophers are especially noteworthy: "Emerson," in George Santayana, *Interpretations of Poetry and Religion*, New York, 1900, pp. 217–233; William James and Hugo Münsterberg, in *The Centenary of the Birth of . . . Emerson* (see paragraph above); Hugo Münsterberg, "Emerson as Philosopher," *Harvard Psychological Stud.*, II (1906), 16–31; and John Dewey, "Emerson," in *Characters and Events . . .* , New York, 1929, 2 vols., I, 69–77.

Emerson as a man of letters is the subject of Emerson G. Sutcliffe's "Emerson's Theories of Literary Expression," *Univ. of Illinois Studies in Lang. and Lit.*, VIII (1923), 9–143. Allied aspects of the subject are treated in Norman Foerster, "Emerson on the Organic Principle in Art," *PMLA*, XLI (1926), 193–208; Robert M. Gay, *Emerson: A Study of the Poet as Seer*, New York, 1928; "Ralph Waldo Emerson," in Gay W. Allen, *American Prosody*, New York, 1935, pp. 91–126; Charles Cestre, "Emerson Poète," *Etudes Anglaises*, IV (1940), 1–14; and Herbert A. Wichelns, "Ralph Waldo Emerson," in William N. Brigance, ed., *A History and Criticism of American Public Address*, New York, 1943, I, 501–525—a classification and analysis of several types of Emerson's speeches. Further brief treatments are found in Jean Gorely, "Emerson's Theory of Poetry," *Poetry Rev.*, XXII (1931), 263–273; Ralph Thompson, "Emerson and *The Offering for 1829*," *Amer. Lit.*, VI (1934), 151–157; John T. Flanagan, "Emerson as a Critic of Fiction," *Philological Quar.*, XV (1936), 30–45; Emerson: Wood-Notes," in Van Wyck Brooks, *The Flowering of New England*, New York, 1936, pp. 252–267; Kenneth Burke, "Acceptance and Rejection," *Southern Rev.*, II (1937), 600–632; J. D. Yohannan, "Emerson's Translations of Persian Poetry from German Sources," *Amer. Lit.*, XIV (1943), 407–420—with a checklist; and Walter Blair and Clarence Faust, "Emerson's Literary Method," *Modern Philol.*, XLII (1944), 79–95—emphasizing Emerson's dependence for method and dialectic on Plato's "chain of being."

An exhaustive study of the sources of Emerson's thought is Kenneth W. Cameron, *Emerson the Essayist*, Raleigh, N.C., 1945, 2 vols., with reprintings from rare books which interested him, particularly those on New England idealism and Swedenborgianism; this work supersedes the author's *Ralph Waldo Emerson's Reading . . .* , Raleigh, N.C., 1941. Other studies of Emerson's background of reading are contained in John S. Harrison, *The Teachers of Emerson*, New York, 1910—Plato and the Neo-Platonists; Régis Michaud, *Autour d'Emerson*, Paris, 1924—on his relationship to Nietzsche, Achille Murat, and Swedenborg; and Arthur E. Christy, *The Orient in American Transcendentalism*, New York, 1932, pp. 61–185—a documented study. Briefer studies of influences are John B. Moore, "Emerson on Wordsworth," *PMLA*, XLI (1926), 179–192; Frederic I. Carpenter, "Immortality from India," *Amer. Lit.*, I (1929), 234–242; Harriet R. Zink, "Emerson's Use of the Bible," *Univ. of Nebr. Studies in Lang., Lit., and Crit.*, No. 14 (1935), with reference-index, pp. 61–74, and bibliography; Norman A. Brittin, "Emerson and the Metaphysical Poets," *Amer. Lit.*, VIII (1936), 1–21; Fred B. Wahr, "Emerson and the Germans," *Monatshefte für deutschen Unterricht*, XXXIII (1941), 49–63; "Ralph Waldo Emerson," in John P. Pritchard, *Return to the Fountains . . .*, Durham, N.C., 1942, pp. 44–60—the influence of the classics; René Wellek, "Emerson and German Philosophy," *New Eng. Quar.*, XVI (1943), 41–62; and J. D. Yohannan, "The Influence of Persian Poetry upon Emerson's Work," *Amer. Lit.*, XV (1943), 25–41. Emerson's debt to individual writers is presented in Fred B. Wahr, *Emerson and Goethe*, Ann Arbor, Mich., 1915—a documented study; Frank T. Thompson, "Emerson's Indebtedness to Coleridge," *Studies in Philol.*, XXIII (1926), 55–76; *idem*, "Emerson and Carlyle," *ibid.*, XXIV (1927), 438–453; *idem*, "Emerson's Theory and Practice of Poetry," *PMLA*, XLIII (1928), 1170–1184—his debt to Coleridge and Wordsworth; Richard C. Pettigrew, "Emerson and Milton," *Amer. Lit.*, III (1931), 45–59; Joe D. Pollitt, "Ralph Waldo Emerson's Debt to John Milton," *Marshall Rev.*, III (1939), 13–21; Charles L. Young, *Emerson's Montaigne*, New York, 1941; J. Chesley Mathews, "Emerson's Knowledge of Dante," *Univ. of Texas Studies in Eng.*, No. 4226 (1942), pp. 171–198; Carl F. Strauch, "Gérando: A Source for Emerson," *Modern Language Notes*, LVIII (1943), 64–67; and Mary C. Turpie, "A Quaker Source for Emerson's Sermon on the Lord's Supper," *New Eng. Quar.*, XVII (1944), 95–101.

Studies of *The American Scholar* (1837) have been made by Bliss Perry ("Emerson's Most Famous Speech," in his *The Praise of Folly and Other Papers*, Boston, 1923, pp. 81–113) and by Henry Nash Smith ("Emerson's Problem of Vocation: A Note on *The American Scholar*," *New Eng. Quar.*, XII (1939), 52–67). The "Divinity School Address" (1838) is the subject of two studies: Clarence F. Gohdes, "Some Remarks on Emerson's 'Divinity School Address,'" *Amer. Lit.*, I (1929), 27–31; and Henry S. Commager, "Tempest in a Boston Tea Cup," *New Eng. Quar.*, VI (1933), 651–675. "The Background for Emerson's 'Boston Hymn,'" is presented by Carl F. Strauch, in *Amer. Lit.*, XIV (1942), 36–47.

Emerson's friendships are the subject of three substantial volumes: Horace

Howard Furness, ed., *Records of a Lifelong Friendship, 1807–1882: Ralph Waldo Emerson and William Henry Furness,* Boston, 1910—in which Emerson's juvenile poem "Fortus" is printed; André Bruel, *Emerson et Thoreau,* Paris, 1929; and Hubert H. Hoeltje, *Sheltering Tree: A Story of the Friendship of Ralph Waldo Emerson and Amos Bronson Alcott,* Durham, N.C., 1943—based on letters and diaries. Briefer studies are Clarence F. Gohdes, "Whitman and Emerson," *Sewanee Rev.,* XXXVII (1929), 79–93; "Emerson and Margaret Fuller," in George E. De Mille, *Literary Criticism in America . . . ,* New York, 1931, pp. 118–132; Carlos Baker, "Emerson and Jones Very," *New Eng. Quar.,* VII (1934), 90–99; Harry R. Warfel, "Margaret Fuller and Ralph Waldo Emerson," *PMLA,* L (1935), 576–594; and George H. Hartwig, "An Immortal Friendship: Carlyle and Emerson," *Hibbert Jour.,* XXXVIII (1939), 102–114. Emerson's life in Concord is set forth by Van Wyck Brooks—"Emerson and Six Episodes," in his *Emerson and Others,* New York, 1927, pp. 1–105. See also John B. McNulty, "Emerson's Friends and the Essay on Friendship," *New Eng. Quar.* XIX (1946), 390–394.

Records of Emerson's personality on the lecture platform have been given by James Russell Lowell—"Emerson the Lecturer," in his *My Study Windows,* Boston, 1871, pp. 375–384; Annie Fields, "Mr. Emerson in the Lecture Room," *Atl. Mo.,* LI (1883), 818–832—full notes on his "History of the Intellect" lectures; and Charles I. Glicksberg, "Bryant on Emerson the Lecturer," *New Eng. Quar.,* XII (1939), 530–534. Material on Emerson as lecturer in the West has been gathered by Willard Thorp, "Emerson on Tour," *Quar. Jour. of Speech,* XVI (1930), 19–34; Ernest Marchand, "Emerson and the Frontier," *Amer. Lit.,* III (1931), 149–174; Louise Hastings, "Emerson in Cincinnati," *New Eng. Quar.,* XI (1938), 443–469; Russel B. Nye, "Emerson in Michigan and the Northwest," *Michigan Hist. Mag.,* XXVI (1942), 159–172; Eleanor B. Scott, "Emerson Wins the Nine Hundred Dollars," *Amer. Lit.,* XVII (1945), 78–85—Emerson in Iowa; and C. J. Wasung, "Emerson Comes to Detroit," *Michigan Hist. Mag.,* XXIX (1945), 59–72. The story of Emerson's reception in England, particularly by the Carlyles, is told by Townsend Scudder III, in *The Lonely Wayfaring Man: Emerson and Some Englishmen,* New York, 1936. Scudder has published further factual detail on Emerson in the British Isles with articles on "Emerson in Dundee," *Amer. Scholar,* IV (1935), 331–344; "Emerson's British Lecture Tour, 1847–1848," *Amer. Lit.,* VII (1935), 15–36, 166–180; "A Chronological List of Emerson's Lectures on His British Lecture Tour of 1847–1848," *PMLA,* LI (1936), 243–248; and "Emerson in London and the London Lectures," *Amer. Lit.,* VIII (1936), 22–36.

Some measure of Emerson's influence abroad may be observed by such studies as C. Andler, *Nietzsche: Sa Vie et Sa Pensée,* Paris, 1920, 2 vols., I,

340-371; Maurice Chazin, "Quinet: An Early Discoverer of Emerson," *PMLA,* XLVIII (1933), 147-163; Besse D. Howard, "The First French Estimate of Emerson," *New Eng. Quar.,* X (1937), 447-463; Margaret Gilman, "Baudelaire and Emerson," *Romanic Rev.,* XXXIV (1943), 211-222; and S. L. Jackson, "A Soviet View of Emerson," *New Eng. Quar.,* XIX (1946), 236-243.

Other studies of Emerson's career having special interest are Raymer McQuiston, *The Relation of Ralph Waldo Emerson to Public Affairs,* Lawrence, Kans., 1923; Harry H. Clark, "Emerson and Science," *Philological Quar.,* X (1931), 225-260; Joseph Warren Beach, "Emerson and Revolution," *Univ. Toronto Quar.,* III (1934), 474-497; Donald MacRea, "Emerson and the Arts," *Art Bul.,* XX (1938), 78-95; Emilio Goggio, "Emerson's Interest in Italy," *Italica,* XVII (1940), 97-103; Marjory M. Moody, "The Evolution of Emerson as an Abolitionist," *Amer. Lit.,* XVII (1945), 1-21; Mentor L. Williams, " 'Why Nature Loves the Number Five': Emerson Toys with the Occult," *Papers Michigan Acad. Sci., Arts, and Letters,* XXX (1944), 639-649; G. R. Foster, "The Natural History of the Will," *Amer. Scholar,* XV (1946), 277-287—a comparison of Emerson's and Nietzsche's ideas of the will; Eduard C. Lindeman, "Emerson's Pragmatic Mood," *ibid.,* XVI (1946), 57-64; and Egbert S. Oliver, "Emerson's 'Days,' " *New Eng. Quar.,* XIX (1946), 518-524.

Studies useful as background material are William Braswell, "Melville as a Critic of Emerson," *Amer. Lit.,* IX (1937), 317-334; Clarence H. Faust, "The Background of the Unitarian Opposition to Transcendentalism," *Modern Philol.,* XXXV (1938), 297-324; and Clarence Hotson, "The Christian Critics and Mr. Emerson," *New Eng. Quar.,* XI (1938), 29-47.

PRIMARY SOURCES

The following early studies of Emerson, most of which are in the nature of reminiscences, are useful as source material: Fredrika Bremer, *The Homes of the New World: Impressions of America,* New York, 1853—a record of conversations with Emerson, written in 1849; George Searle Phillips (*pseud.* January Searle), *Emerson: His Life and Writings,* London, 1855—the earliest biography; Amos Bronson Alcott, *Ralph Waldo Emerson: Philosopher and Seer,* Boston, 1882; Moncure D. Conway, *Emerson at Home and Abroad* Boston, 1882; Alexander Ireland, *Ralph Waldo Emerson: His Life, Genius and Writings,* London, 1882; Oliver Wendell Holmes, *Ralph Waldo Emerson,* Boston, 1884; James B. Thayer, *A Western Journey with Emerson* Boston, 1884; Frank B. Sanborn, ed., *The Genius and Character of Emerson* Boston, 1885—sixteen essays by various writers, including A. B. Alcott, W. T Harris, Julian Hawthorne, Elizabeth P. Peabody, and Julia Ward Howe,

"Some Recollections of Ralph Waldo Emerson," in Edwin P. Whipple, *Recollections of Eminent Men . . .* , Boston, 1887, pp. 119–154; Edward W. Emerson, *Emerson in Concord: A Memoir,* Boston, 1889; C. J. Woodbury, *Talks with Emerson,* London, 1890; "Emerson Sixty Years After," in John J. Chapman, *Emerson and Other Essays,* New York, 1898, pp. 3–108; "Ralph Waldo Emerson," in Thomas W. Higginson, *Contemporaries,* Boston, 1899, pp. 1–22; John Albee, *Remembrances of Emerson,* New York, 1901; Edward Everett Hale, *Memoirs of a Hundred Years,* New York, 1902, 2 vols., II, 230–240; Frank B. Sanborn, *The Personality of Emerson,* Boston, 1903; "Emerson as I Saw Him" and "In Emerson's and Thoreau's Town," in Joel Benton, *Persons and Places,* New York, 1905, pp. 1–7, 67–77.

The manuscripts which Emerson himself preserved, including his journals, sermons, and lectures, have been deposited in the Houghton Library of Harvard University; his literary executor, James E. Cabot, and his son, Edward W. Emerson, provided the present arrangement of them. A typescript of the journals, with indications of published and unpublished passages, is deposited with the manuscripts. Ralph L. Rusk's edition of the *Letters* provides a calendar of all letters known to be extant.

The manuscripts of the early lectures and sermons are nearly intact, but Emerson's increasing habit of mining his own writings for later work has left the later manuscripts in a cut and somewhat confused state. The commonplace books and journals are in bound notebooks and are therefore in better condition, but Emerson's practice of keeping several books simultaneously injures their continuity. The edition of the *Journals* prepared by his son and grandson makes them into a more nearly continuous work by constructing a mosaic of scattered passages. The best and most revealing passages from the *Journals* are included in this edition with only slight editorial changes; but passages previously printed either in substance or in full are omitted.

Until recently Emerson's library, many volumes of which contain marginal notations, was cataloged and kept by the Ralph Waldo Emerson Memorial Association in the replica of his study in the Concord Antiquarian Society. A part of this library has now been moved to the Houghton Library, Harvard University. Other manuscripts are in the Henry E. Huntington Library, the Longfellow House at Cambridge, Mass., and the T. B. Aldrich Birthplace at Portsmouth, N.H.

### BIBLIOGRAPHY

A full bibliography for Emerson is needed. At present the following compilations are serviceable: George W. Cooke, *A Bibliography of Ralph Waldo Emerson,* Boston, 1908; *The Cambridge History of American Literature,*

New York, I (1917), 551–566; *The Stephen H. Wakeman Collection of Books of Nineteenth Century American Writers*, New York, 1924—American Art Association catalog, containing a list of Emerson ephemera, etc.; Frederic I. Carpenter, ed., *Ralph·Waldo Emerson: Representative Selections . . .* , New York, 1934, pp. xlix–lvi—selective and annotated; Harry H. Clark, ed., *Major American Poets*, New York, 1936, pp. 817–823—selective and annotated; and *Index to Early American Periodical Literature, 1728–1870: Part 4, Ralph Waldo Emerson, 1803–1882*, New York, 1942. See also Harry Hartwick, in Walter F. Taylor, *A History of American Letters*, New York, 1936, pp. 509–513.

Henry A. Pochmann, in "The Emerson Canon," *Univ. of Toronto Quar.*, XII (1943), 476–484, raises the question of restudy of Emerson in the light of the quantity of new source material available.

A concordance of the prose works of Emerson is needed, similar to the one compiled by G. S. Hubbell, *A Concordance to the Poems of Ralph Waldo Emerson*, New York, 1932.

## JAMES T(HOMAS) FARRELL
### b. 1904

SEPARATE WORKS

*Young Lonigan: A Boyhood in Chicago Streets*, 1932; *Gas-House McGinty*, 1933; *The Young Manhood of Studs Lonigan*, 1934; *Calico Shoes and Other Stories*, 1934; *Judgment Day*, 1935; *Guillotine Party and Other Stories*, 1935; *A Note on Literary Criticism*, 1936; *A World I Never Made*, 1936; *Can All This Grandeur Perish?* 1937; *No Star Is Lost*, 1938; *Tommy Gallagher's Crusade*, 1939; *Father and Son*, 1940; *Ellen Rogers*, 1941; *$1,000 a Week, and Other Stories*, 1942; *My Days of Anger*, 1943; *To Whom It May Concern*, 1944; *The League of Frightened Philistines, and Other Papers*, 1945; *Bernard Clare*, 1946; *When Boyhood Dreams Come True*, 1946; *Literature and Morality*, 1947; *The Life Adventurous*, 1947.

*Studs Lonigan: A Trilogy . . . with a New Introduction by the Author*, was published in the Modern Library, New York, 1938. Two further volumes of reprinted selections are *The Short Stories of James T. Farrell*, New York, 1937; and *Fifteen Selected Stories*, New York, 1943.

CRITICISM

One of the fullest critical estimates is Oscar Cargill, *Intellectual America: Ideas on the March*, New York, 1941, pp. 159–171. Other evaluations are Robert M. Lovett, "James T. Farrell," *English Jour.*, XXVI (1937), 347–354;

C. John McCole, *Lucifer at Large*, London, 1937, pp. 277–290; Earle Birney, "The Fiction of James T. Farrell," *Canadian Forum*, XIX (1939), 21–24; Carl Van Doren, *The American Novel . . .* , rev. ed., New York, 1940, pp. 355–356; Ruth Hatfield, "The Intellectual Honesty of James T. Farrell," *College Eng.*, III (1942), 337–346; and Calder Willington, "Note on James T. Farrell," *Quar. Rev. Lit.*, II (1946), 120–124.

Farrell contributed a brief essay on his literary method, "A Novelist Begins," *Atl. Mo.*, CLXII (1938), 330–334.

A bio-bibliography is in Fred B. Millett, *Contemporary American Authors*, New York, 1940, pp. 345–346.

## WILLIAM FAULKNER
### b. 1897

### WORKS

*The Marble Faun*, 1924; *Soldiers' Pay*, 1926; *Mosquitoes*, 1927; *The Sound and the Fury*, 1929; *Sartoris*, 1929; *As I Lay Dying*, 1930; *Sanctuary*, 1931; *These 13*, 1931; *Idyll in the Desert*, 1931; *Salmagundi*, 1932; *This Earth*, 1932; *Miss Zilphia Gant*, 1932; *Light in August*, 1932; *A Green Bough*, 1933; *Doctor Martino and Other Stories*, 1934; *Pylon*, 1935; *Absalom, Absalom!* 1936; *The Unvanquished*, 1938; *The Wild Palms*, 1939; *The Hamlet*, 1940; *Go Down, Moses, and Other Stories*, 1942.

*Sanctuary* was reprinted, New York, 1932, in the Modern Library. A collected edition, *The Portable Faulkner*, New York, 1946, is edited with a critical introduction by Malcolm Cowley.

### BIOGRAPHY AND CRITICISM

Significant estimates of Faulkner's writing did not appear until the late twenties. Among the earliest are Evelyn Scott, *On William Faulkner's "The Sound and the Fury,"* New York, 1929, 10 pp.; Granville Hicks, "The Past and the Future of William Faulkner," *Bookman*, LXXIV (1931), 17–24; Marshall L. Smith, "Faulkner of Mississippi," *ibid.*, 411–417; Henry S. Canby, "The School of Cruelty," *Sat. Rev. Lit.*, VII (1931), 673–674; Alan R. Thompson, "The Cult of Cruelty," *Bookman*, LXXIV (1932), 477–487; and A. Wigfall Green, "William Faulkner at Home," *Sewanee Rev.*, XL (1932), 294–306.

Later studies are Pelham Edgar, *The Art of the Novel*, New York, 1933, pp. 338–351; Morris U. Schappes, "Faulkner as Poet," *Poetry*, XLIII (1933), 48–52; "William Faulkner, the Moralist with a Corn Cob," in Wyndham Lewis, *Men Without Art*, London, 1934, pp. 42–64; Harry Hartwick, *The Foreground of American Fiction*, New York, 1934, pp. 160–166; Lawrence

S. Kubie, "William Faulkner's *Sanctuary:* An Analysis," *Sat. Rev. Lit.,* XI (Oct. 20, 1934), 218, 224–226—an extended study; "Counterpoint: *Light in August,*" in James W. Linn and Houghton W. Taylor, *A Foreword to Fiction,* New York, 1935, pp. 144–157; Harlan Hatcher, *Creating the Modern American Novel,* New York, 1935, pp. 234–243; Maurice Le Breton, "Technique et Psychologie chez William Faulkner," *Etudes Anglaises,* I (1937), 418–438; C. John McCole, *Lucifer at Large,* London, 1937, pp. 203–228; and George M. O'Donnell, "Faulkner's Mythology," *Kenyon Rev.,* I (1939), 285–299.

Among more recent criticisms are Percy H. Boynton, *America in Contemporary Fiction,* Chicago, 1940, pp. 103–112; Burton Rascoe, "Faulkner's New York Critics," *Amer. Mercury,* L (1940), 243–247; Warren Beck, "Faulkner and the South," *Antioch Rev.,* I (1941), 82–94; *idem,* "Faulkner's Point of View," *College Eng.,* II (1941), 736–749; *idem,* "A Note on Faulkner's Style," *Rocky Mt. Rev.,* VI (1942), 5–14; Delmore Schwartz, "The Fiction of William Faulkner," *Southern Rev.,* VII (1941), 145–160; "William Faulkner: The Negro and the Female," in Maxwell Geismar, *Writers in Crisis,* Boston, 1942, pp. 141–184—the most comprehensive study to date; and John M. Maclachlan, "William Faulkner and the Southern Folk," *Southern Folklore Quar.,* IX (1945), 153–167. Two useful re-appraisals by Malcolm Cowley are "William Faulkner's Human Comedy," *N.Y. Times Book Rev.,* Oct. 29, 1944, p. 4; "William Faulkner Revisited," *Sat. Rev. Lit.,* Apr. 14, 1945, pp. 13–16; and George Snell, "The Fury of William Faulkner," *Western Rev.,* XI (autumn, 1946), 29–40.

BIBLIOGRAPHY

The fullest bibliographical listing to date is Robert W. Daniel, *A Catalogue of the Writings of William Faulkner,* New Haven, 1942, 32 pp. Earlier listings are Aubrey Starke, "An American Comedy: An Introduction to a Bibliography of William Faulkner," *Colophon,* Pt. 19 (1934), 12 pp.; and Fred B. Millett, *Contemporary American Authors,* New York, 1940, pp. 346–348—useful for books and articles about Faulkner.

# JOHN FISKE
### *1842–1901*

SEPARATE WORKS

*Tobacco and Alcohol,* 1869; *Myths and Myth-Makers,* 1872; *Outlines of Cosmic Philosophy,* 1874; *The Unseen World, and Other Essays,* 1876; *Darwinism and Other Essays,* 1879; *Excursions of an Evolutionist,* 1884; *The*

*Destiny of Man Viewed in the Light of His Origin,* 1884; *American Political Ideas Viewed from the Standpoint of Universal History,* 1885; *The Idea of God as Affected by Modern Knowledge,* 1886; *The Critical Period of American History, 1783–1789,* 1888; *The Beginnings of New England,* 1889; *The War of Independence,* 1890; *Civil Government in the United States,* 1890; *The American Revolution,* 1891; *The Discovery of America,* 1892; *Edward Livingston Youmans, Interpreter of Science for the People,* 1894; *A History of the United States for Schools,* 1894; *Old Virginia and Her Neighbors,* 1897; *The Dutch and Quaker Colonies in America,* 1899; *The Origin of Evil,* 1899; *A Century of Science and Other Essays,* 1899; *Through Nature to God,* 1899; *The Mississippi Valley in the Civil War,* 1900; *Life Everlasting,* 1901; *Essays, Historical and Literary,* 1902; *New France and New England,* 1902; *Colonization of the New World,* 1902; *Independence of the New World,* 1902; *Modern Development of the New World,* 1902; *How the United States Became a Nation,* 1904.

COLLECTED WORKS

*The Writings of John Fiske,* 24 vols., were issued in Cambridge, 1902, the year following his death. *Unpublished Orations* were issued Boston, 1909.

Three collections of his letters have been made. John S. Clark, *The Life and Letters of John Fiske,* Boston, 1917, 2 vols., contains a full index. *The Letters of John Fiske,* New York, 1940, edited by his daughter Ethel F. Fisk, stress the daily affairs, but the book lacks introduction, index, and notes. *The Personal Letters of John Fiske,* Cedar Rapids, Iowa, 1939, has no index.

BIOGRAPHY AND CRITICISM

An early life is that of Thomas S. Perry, *John Fiske, Boston,* 1906. An early estimate of Fiske by a historian is Albert B. Hart, "The Historical Service of John Fiske," *Connecticut Mag.,* VII (1902–1903), 611–617. A recent evaluation is Henry S. Commager, "John Fiske: An Interpretation," *Proc. Mass. Hist. Soc.,* LXVI (1942), 332–345. The sketch of Fiske in *Dict. Amer. Biog.* (1931) is by James T. Adams. See also J. B. Sanders, "John Fiske," *Mississippi Valley Hist. Rev.,* XVII (1930), 264–277; and Josiah Royce, "John Fiske," *Unpopular Rev.,* X (1918), 160–189.

Special studies include Lawrence C. Powell, "John Fiske, Bookman," *Papers Bibl. Soc. Amer.,* XXXV (1941), 221–254; Russel B. Nye, "John Fiske and His Cosmic Philosophy," *Papers Michigan Acad. Science, Arts, and Letters,* XXVIII (1943), 685–698; and Josiah Royce, "John Fiske as Thinker," *Harvard Graduates' Mag.,* X (1901), 23–33.

Many of Fiske's manuscripts are in the Harvard College Library. A few are in Princeton University Library. Reminiscences and appreciations are

Samuel S. Green, "Reminiscences of John Fiske," *Proc. Amer. Antiq. Soc.* n.s. XVI (1902), 421–428—with bibl. footnotes; William R. Thayer, "Memoir of John Fiske," *Proc. Mass. Hist. Soc.*, XLVI (1913), 167–174; and Henry Holt, *Garrulities of an Octogenarian Editor* . . . , New York, 1923, pp. 321–351— shrewd observations by one who knew Fiske well.

There is a brief bibliography in Thomas S. Perry, *John Fiske* (1906), pp. 103–105.

## F(RANCIS) SCOTT (KEY) FITZGERALD
### *1896–1940*

SEPARATE WORKS

*This Side of Paradise*, 1920; *Flappers and Philosophers*, 1920; *Tales of the Jazz Age*, 1922; *The Beautiful and Damned*, 1922; *The Vegetable; or, From President to Postman*, 1923; *The Great Gatsby*, 1925; *All the Sad Young Men*, 1926; *Tender Is the Night*, 1934; *Taps at Reveille*, 1935.

COLLECTED WORKS AND REPRINTS

*The Last Tycoon: An Unfinished Novel*, New York, 1941, was published in an edition including *The Great Gatsby* and *Selected Stories*. Edmund Wilson edited *The Crack-Up*, Norfolk, Conn., 1945, a volume of uncollected pieces, notebooks, and unpublished Fitzgerald letters, together with letters to Fitzgerald from Gertrude Stein and others. *The Great Gatsby* was reprinted in the Modern Lib., New York, 1934; and again, New York, 1945, with an introduction by Lionel Trilling. The most recent collection is the *Portable F. Scott Fitzgerald*, New York, 1945, selected by Dorothy Parker, with an introduction by John O'Hara.

BIOGRAPHY AND CRITICISM

No life of Fitzgerald has yet been published. Early criticism includes Edmund Wilson, "Imaginary Conversations: Mr. Van Wyck Brooks and Mr. Scott Fitzgerald," *New Repub.*, XXXVIII (1924), 249–254; "F. Scott Fitzgerald," in Ernest Boyd, *Portraits: Real and Imaginary*, New York, 1924, pp. 217–226; John Farrar, *The Literary Spotlight*, New York, 1924, pp. 125– 134; William R. Benét, "An Admirable Novel," *Sat. Rev. Lit.*, I (May 9, 1925), 739–740—a review of *The Great Gatsby*; and "F. Scott Fitzgerald," in Paul Rosenfeld, *Men Seen* . . . , New York, 1925, pp. 215–224.

Later estimates are A. C. Ward, *American Literature, 1880–1930*, London, 1932, pp. 136–138; Harlan Hatcher, *Creating the Modern American Novel*, New York, 1935, pp. 79–82; John P. Bishop, "The Missing All," *Virginia*

*Quar. Rev.,* XIII (1937), 106–121; and Irene and Allen Cleaton, *Books and Battles,* Boston, 1937, pp. 9–14, 232–235, and *passim.*

Recent critical studies are Margaret Marshall, "Notes by the Way," *Nation,* CLII (1941), 159–160; Charles Weir, Jr., "An Invite with Gilded Edges," *Virginia Quar. Rev.,* XX (1944), 100–113—an estimate of Fitzgerald as a novelist; William Troy, "Scott Fitzgerald: The Authority of Failure," *Accent,* VI (1945), 56–60; John Berryman, "F. Scott Fitzgerald," *Kenyon Rev.,* VIII (1946), 103–112; and Arthur Mizener, "Scott Fitzgerald and the Imaginative Possession of American Life," *Sewanee Rev.,* LIV (1946), 66–86. Mizener also contributed "F. Scott Fitzgerald: The Poet of Borrowed Time," to Willard Thorp, ed., *The Lives of Eighteen from Princeton,* Princeton, 1946, pp. 333–353.

A symposium "In Memory of Scott Fitzgerald," *New Repub.,* CIV (1941), 213–217, 311–313, contains the personal reminiscences of Glenway Wescott, John Dos Passos, John O'Hara, and Budd Schulberg.

There are Fitzgerald manuscripts in the Princeton University Library.

A bibliographical listing is in Fred B. Millett, *Contemporary American Authors,* New York, 1940, pp. 354–356.

# JOHN GOULD FLETCHER
## *b. 1886*

### SEPARATE WORKS

*Fire and Wine,* 1913; *Fool's Gold,* 1913; *The Book of Nature,* 1913; *The Dominant City,* 1913; *Visions of the Evening,* 1913; *Irradiations: Sand and Spray,* 1915; *Goblins and Pagodas,* 1916; *The Tree of Life,* 1918; *Japanese Prints,* 1918; *Breakers and Granite,* 1921; *Paul Gauguin: His Life and Art,* 1921; *Parables,* 1925; *Branches of Adam,* 1926; *The Black Rock,* 1928; *John Smith—Also Pocahontas,* 1928; *The Two Frontiers: A Study in Historical Psychology,* 1930; *XXIV Elegies,* 1935; *Life Is My Song,* 1937; *South Star,* 1941; *The Burning Mountain,* 1946; *Arkansas,* 1947.

### REPRINTS

*Preludes and Symphonies,* Boston, 1922 (and New York, 1930), is a reissue of both *Irradiations* (1915) and *Goblins and Pagodas* (1916). *Selected Poems by John Gould Fletcher* was issued, New York, 1938.

### BIOGRAPHY AND CRITICISM

Critical estimates are Dorothy Dudley, "Poet and Theorist," *Poetry,* IX (1916), 43–47; Amy Lowell, *Tendencies in Modern American Poetry,* Boston,

1917, pp. 235–343; "Possessor and Possessed: John Gould Fletcher," in Conrad Aiken, *Scepticisms*, New York, 1919, pp. 105–114; Louis Grudin, "A Naïve Mystic," *Poetry*, XXI (1923), 270–275; "John Gould Fletcher," in Harriet Monroe, *Poets and Their Art*, New York, 1926, pp. 86–91; Alfred Kreymborg, *Our Singing Strength*, New York, 1929, pp. 361–367; "John Gould Fletcher," in René Taupin, *L'Influence du Symbolisme Français sur la Poésie Améri-caine*, Paris, 1929, pp. 193–210; "John Gould Fletcher: Pictorialist and Mystic," in Glenn Hughes, *Imagism and the Imagists*, Stanford University, Calif., 1931, pp. 125–152; Robert P. Warren, "A Note on Three Southern Poets," *Poetry*, XL (1932), 103–113; Richard P. Blackmur, "Versions of Fletcher," *Poetry* XLVII (1936), 344–347; Babette Deutsch, "A Lost Address," *Poetry*, LII (1938), 347–351; and Baucum Fulkerson, "John Gould Fletcher," *Sewanee Rev.* XLVI (1938), 275–287.

A bibliographical listing is in Fred B. Millett, *Contemporary American Authors*, New York, 1940, pp. 356–358. See also the recent list by Frances Cheney, in Allen Tate, *Sixty American Poets*, 1896–1944, Washington, 1945, pp. 49–51.

# BENJAMIN FRANKLIN
## *1706-1790*

### SEPARATE WORKS

A listing of all the separate pieces written by Franklin is impossible within the scope of this bibliography. Some here included were never printed separately, strictly speaking; but they are important items and are included for convenience of identification.

It should be noted that the commonly entitled *Poor Richard's Almanack* is a composite designation. It was *Poor Richard* from 1732 through 1747, and *Poor Richard Improved* from 1747 through later issues. *The Way to Wealth* (1757) is the title later given to the preface to *Poor Richard Improved* for 1758.

*Essay on Human Vanity* (1735) is not surely by Franklin, who said that it was written by an unknown author. *An Historical Review* (1759), often attributed to Franklin, is now believed certainly not to be his work, and is here omitted.

*The Dogood Papers*, 1722; editorial preface to the *New England Courant*, 1723; *A Dissertation on Liberty and Necessity*, 1725; *Journal of a Voyage from London to Philadelphia*, 1726; *Articles of Belief and Acts of Religion*, 1728; *Rules for a Club*, 1728; *Busybody Papers*, 1728–1729; *A Modest Enquiry into . . . Paper Currency*, 1729; preface to *Pennsylvania Gazette*, 1729; *A Dialogue Between Philocles and Horatio*, 1730; *A Second Dialogue . . .* ,

1730; *A Witch Trial at Mount Holly*, 1730; *An Apology for Printers*, 1731; introduction to Logan's *Cato's Moral Distiches*, 1735; *Essay on Human Vanity*, 1735; *A Proposal for Promoting Useful Knowledge*, 1743; *An Account of the New Invented Pennsylvania Fire-Places*, 1744; preface to Logan's translation of Cicero's *Cato Major*, 1744; *Advice to a Young Man on Choosing a Mistress*, 1745; *Reflections on Courtship and Marriage*, 1746; *Plain Truth*, 1747; *Proposals Relating to the Education of Youth in Pensilvania*, 1749; *Experiments and Observations on Electricity*, 1751–1753; *Poor Richard's Almanack*, 1732–1764, *Idea of the English School*, 1751; *Some Account of the Pennsylvania Hospital*, 1754; *An Act for the Better Ordering and Regulating . . . for Military Purposes*, 1755; *A Dialogue Between X, Y, and Z*, 1755; *Observations Concerning the Increase of Mankind*, 1755; *Plan for Settling the Western Colonies*, 1756?; *The Way to Wealth*, 1757; *Some Account of . . . Small-Pox*, 1759; *The Interest of Great Britain Considered*, 1760; *Advice to a Young Tradesman*, 1762; *A Parable Against Persecution*, 1764; *Cool Thoughts*, 1764; *A Narrative of the Late Massacres*, 1764; preface to the *Speech of Joseph Galloway, Esq.*, 1764; *The Examination of Dr. Benjamin Franklin*, 1766; *Physical and Meteorological Observations*, 1766; *Remarks and Facts Concerning American Paper Money*, 1767; *Causes of the American Discontent Before 1768*, 1768; preface to Dickinson's *Letters from a Farmer*, 1768; *Art of Swimming*, 1768; *A Scheme for a New Alphabet*, 1768; *An Edict of the King of Prussia*, 1773; preface to *An Abridgement of the Book of Common Prayer*, 1773; *Rules by Which a Great Empire May Be Reduced to a Small One*, 1773; notes to Whatley's *Principles of Trade*, 1774; *Account of Negotiations in London*, 1775; *Articles of Confederation*, 1775; *The Ephemera*, 1778; *The Morals of Chess*, 1779; *The Whistle*, 1779; *Dialogue Between Franklin and the Gout*, 1780; *The Handsome and the Deformed Leg*, 1780; *Journal of the Negotiations for Peace*, 1782; *Information to Those Who Would Remove to America*, 1784; *Remarks Concerning the Savages of North America*, 1784; *Maritime Observations*, 1785; *Observations on the Causes and Cure of Smoky Chimneys*, 1785; *Art of Procuring Pleasant Dreams*, 1786; *Observations Relative to . . . the Academy in Philadelphia*, 1789; *Autobiography*, 1791–1868.

COLLECTED WORKS

Important collected editions of Franklin's writings published in his lifetime, and prepared with his knowledge and consent, include *Political, Miscellaneous, and Philosophical Pieces . . .*, London, 1779, edited by Benjamin Vaughan. Its notes are useful source material. The editions published in 1769 and 1774 of *Experiments and Observations on Electricity* (1751–1753) contain numerous philosophical writings outside scientific subjects; so do the

*Œuvres* in French, Paris, 1775, all of which Franklin attended to in detail. *Philosophical and Miscellaneous Papers* . . . , London, 1787, edited by Edward Bancroft, also were brought together with Franklin's consent.

*Mémoires de la Vie Privée de Benjamin Franklin* . . . , Paris, 1791, were continued in *Memoirs of the Life and Writings of Benjamin Franklin,* London, 1817-1819, 6 vols.; 1818, 3 vols., in a garbled edition by William Temple Franklin. The same material was published in Philadelphia, 1818, 6 vols., edited by William Duane, with some added material. The bibliography of these editions is still confused, but the best work in setting them straight is that of Paul L. Ford, *Franklin Bibliography* (1889).

Jared Sparks's edition of Franklin's *Works,* Boston, 1836-1840, 10 vols., has been abused with little reason for his "corrections" of Franklin's text; its notes are still useful, and it includes some pieces possibly written by Franklin which are omitted in the Smyth edition.

John Bigelow edited a *Life,* Philadelphia, 1874, 3 vols., including the *Autobiography,* with later extracts from autobiographical writings arranged as a continuation. Bigelow's edition of *The Complete Works,* New York, 1887-1889, 10 vols., corrects errors in the Sparks edition and adds much new material, all here first arranged chronologically.

The standard edition still remains *The Writings of Benjamin Franklin,* New York, 1905-1907, 10 vols., edited by Albert H. Smyth; it is marred by some omissions, but the introduction and the *Life* in Vol. X. are useful.

A new edition of Franklin's collected works is needed, or at least a supplement to the Smyth edition which will incorporate the many letters, pamphlets, contributions to newspapers and periodicals which have been identified in the Ford *Bibliography* (1889) or since discovered in print or manuscript.

Franklin's correspondence has been separately collected in the following editions: William Temple Franklin, ed., *The Private Correspondence of Benjamin Franklin,* London, 1817, 2 vols. (for the years 1753-1790); William Duane, *Letters to Benjamin Franklin, from His Family and Friends, 1751-1790,* New York, 1859; Theodore Diller, ed., *Franklin's Contribution to Medicine* . . . , Brooklyn, N.Y., 1912—letters of Franklin bearing on medicine; Gilbert Chinard, ed., *Les Amitiés Américaines de Madame d'Houdetot d'après sa Correspondance Inédite avec Benjamin Franklin et Thomas Jefferson,* Paris, 1924; Luther S. Livingston, ed., *Benjamin Franklin's Letters to Madame Helvétius and Madame La Freté,* Cambridge, 1924; W. S. Mason, ed., "Franklin and Galloway: Some Unpublished Letters," *Proc. Amer. Antiq. Soc.,* n.s. XXXIV (1924), 227-258—many letters on Pennsylvania colonial history, not in Smyth; James M. Stifler, ed., *"My Dear*

*Girl": The Correspondence of Benjamin Franklin with Polly Stevenson, Georgiana and Catherine Shipley,* New York, 1927—some hitherto unpublished letters; George S. Eddy, ed., "Correspondence between Dr. Benjamin Franklin and John Walker, Regarding the Logographic Process of Printing," *Proc. Amer. Antiq. Soc.,* n.s. XXXVIII (1929), 349-363; Nathan G. Goodman, ed., *The Ingenious Dr. Franklin: Selected Scientific Letters of Benjamin Franklin,* Philadephia, 1931—a few hitherto uncollected pieces. See also *Letters and Papers of Benjamin Franklin and Richard Jackson, 1753-1785,* Philadelphia, 1947, edited and annotated, with an introduction, by Carl Van Doren.

Jared Sparks's *A Collection of the Familiar Letters and Miscellaneous Papers of Benjamin Franklin,* Boston, 1833, contains a few fragments not elsewhere available.

### EDITED TEXTS AND REPRINTS

*A Dissertation on Liberty and Necessity* (1725) was issued in facsimile, edited by Lawrence C. Wroth, New York, 1930. There have been a great many selected reprints of *Poor Richard's Almanack* (1732-1764); among the best are the collection of *The Sayings of Poor Richard* . . . , Brooklyn, N.Y., 1890, edited by Paul L. Ford, with an essay on colonial almanacs; and Nathan G. Goodman, ed., *Profile of Genius: Poor Richard Pamphlets,* Philadelphia, 1938. The six numbers of Franklin's *The General Magazine and Historical Chronicle for All the British Plantations in America,* issued in 1741, were reproduced for the Facsimile Text Society, New York, 1938, edited by Lyon N. Richardson, with a bibliographical note. Harold D. Carew edited *Advice to a Young Man on Choosing a Mistress* (1745), Sierra Madre, Calif., 1930, with a foreword. *Plain Truth* (1747) was reproduced in *Photostat Americana,* 2nd ser., No. 31, Boston, 1937. *Proposals Relating to the Education of Youth* (1749) were reprinted, Ann Arbor, Mich., 1927, and Philadelphia, 1931, edited by William Pepper. The important *Experiments and Observations on Electricity* (1751-1753) were edited with bibliographical footnotes and a bibliography by I. Bernard Cohen, Cambridge, 1941. *The Way to Wealth* (1757), one of the most popular and most frequently reprinted essays of Franklin, was reproduced under its title *Father Abraham's Speech,* in *Photostat Americana,* 2nd ser., No. 104, Boston, 1940. Luther S. Livingston edited *A Parable Against Persecution* (1764), Cambridge, 1916, with a bibliography; it was also reprinted, Boston, 1927, and New York, 1943. *Advice to a Young Tradesman* (1762) was reproduced in *Photostat Americana,* 2nd ser., No. 117, Boston, 1940. *An Address to the Good People of Ireland . . . 1778* was edited by Paul L. Ford, Brooklyn, N.Y., 1891. Luther S. Livingston edited *The Whistle* (1779), Cambridge, 1922, with a bibliography to 1820. A convenient collection of Franklin's lighter pieces, including some of the surreptitious ones, is Paul McPharlin, ed., *Satires and Bagatelles,* Detroit, 1937.

One of the most frequently edited pieces, in whole or in part, among all items in American literature is Franklin's *Autobiography.* Its first complete publication began when John Bigelow acquired the manuscript and edited it, with additions from Franklin's correspondence and other writings, in 1868. Another edition, Philadelphia, 1888, 3 vols., was published under the title *The Life of Benjamin Franklin, Written by Himself.* Three recent printings are Oral S. Coad, ed., *The Autobiography of Benjamin Franklin,* New York, 1927 (Modern Readers' Ser.); *Autobiography of Benjamin Franklin and Selections from His Other Writings,* New York, 1932 (Modern Lib.); and Henry S. Commager, ed., *The Autobiography of Benjamin Franklin and Selections from His Writings,* New York, 1944. The extraordinary story of the circumstances of composition and publication of the *Autobiography* has been told by Max Farrand, "Benjamin Franklin's Memoirs," *Huntington Lib. Bul.,* No. 10 (1936), 49–78, and *idem,* "Self-Portraiture: the Autobiography," *Jour. Franklin Inst.,* CCXXXIII (1942), 1–16.

George S. Eddy has edited the *Account Books Kept by Benjamin Franklin,* New York, 1928–1929, 2 vols.

Three volumes have been prepared by Carl Van Doren: *Benjamin Franklin and Jonathan Edwards: Selections from Their Writings,* New York, 1920; *Benjamin Franklin: The Autobiography, with Sayings of Poor Richard, Hoaxes, Bagatelles, Essays, and Letters,* New York, 1940 (Pocket Books); and *Benjamin Franklin's Autobiographical Writings,* New York, 1945, 810 pp.—including 100 hitherto unpublished or uncollected pieces.

A serviceable volume of selections is Frank L. Mott and Chester E. Jorgenson, *Benjamin Franklin: Representative Selections, with Introduction, Bibliography, and Notes,* New York, 1936 (Amer. Writers Ser.); as is Nathan G. Goodman, ed., *A Benjamin Franklin Reader,* New York, 1945.

BIOGRAPHY AND CRITICISM

The best one-volume study of Franklin is Carl Van Doren, *Benjamin Franklin,* New York, 1938—fully documented. Though superseded at many points by later investigations, James Parton's *Life and Times of Benjamin Franklin,* New York, 1864, 2 vols., is still the most comprehensive biography, narrative rather than critical. Among brief studies, and indeed a model of its kind, is the sketch in *Dict. Amer. Biog.* (1931) by Carl L. Becker. Other important lives are Paul L. Ford, *The Many-Sided Franklin,* New York, 1899—a survey of Franklin's career under the heads of his varied activities; Verner W. Crane, *Benjamin Franklin: Englishman and American,* Balti-

more, 1936—Franklin's development as a student of public affairs; Edward
E. Hale and E. E. Hale, Jr., *Franklin in France,* Boston, 1887–1888, 2 vols.—
the fullest account of the French period, with a collection of letters to Franklin; John T. Morse, Jr., *Benjamin Franklin,* Boston, 1889—stressing his political and diplomatic career; and John B. McMaster, *Benjamin Franklin as a
Man of Letters,* Boston, 1887. Further recent studies are William C. Bruce,
*Benjamin Franklin, Self-Revealed . . . ,* New York, 1917; J. Henry Smythe,
Jr., *The Amazing Benjamin Franklin,* New York, 1929; the two biographies
by Bernard Faÿ, *Franklin: The Apostle of Modern Times,* Boston, 1929,
and *The Two Franklins: Fathers of American Democracy,* Boston, 1933;
and Evarts S. Scudder, *Benjamin Franklin: A Biography,* London, 1939.

Estimates of Franklin, significant to the extent that the authors are spokes-
men of their times, are Moses C. Tyler, *The Literary History of the American
Revolution,* New York, 1897, II, 359–381; Paul E. More, *Benjamin Franklin,* New York, 1900; "Franklin and the Age of Enlightenment," in
Stuart P. Sherman, *Americans,* New York, 1922, pp. 28–62; Vernon L.
Parrington, *Main Currents in American Thought,* New York, I (1927), 164–
178; and Henry S. Canby, *Classic Americans,* New York, 1931, pp. 34–45.
The collection of papers, *Meet Dr. Franklin,* Philadelphia, 1943, is a series of
talks printed for the Franklin Institute, with contributions covering many
aspects of Franklin's career by Carl Van Doren, R. A. Millikan, Max Farrand,
Conyers Read, Verner W. Crane, Robert E. Spiller, George W. Pepper,
Bernhard Knollenberg, Gilbert Chinard, Lawrence C. Wroth, C. R. Woodward, and Julian P. Boyd.

Recent studies of Franklin as statesman and public servant are Ruth L.
Butler, *Doctor Franklin: Postmaster General,* Garden City, N.Y., 1928; Mal-
colm R. Eiselen, *Franklin's Political Theories,* Garden City, N.Y., 1928; Jean
J. Jusserand, "Franklin in France," in *Essays Offered to Herbert Putnam . . . ,*
New Haven, 1929, pp. 226–247; Eduard Baumgarten, *Benjamin Franklin:
Der Lehrmeister der amerikanischen Revolution,* Frankfurt am Main, 1936;
James B. Nolan, *General Benjamin Franklin: The Military Career of a
Philosopher,* Philadelphia, 1936; *idem, Benjamin Franklin in Scotland and
Ireland, 1759 and 1771,* Philadelphia, 1938; *Indian Treaties Printed by Benja-
min Franklin, 1736–1762,* with an introduction by Carl Van Doren, and with
historical and bibliographical notes by Julian P. Boyd, Philadelphia, 1938—
an important study of a little known subject; A. Stuart Pitt, "Franklin and
the Quaker Movement Against Slavery," *Bul. Friends' Hist. Assoc.,* XXXII
(1943), 13–31—a documented account of Franklin's antislavery activities.

Franklin's interest in science and learning is dealt with by Francis N.
Thorpe, ed., *Benjamin Franklin and the University of Pennsylvania,* Washington, 1893; A. W. Wetzel, "Benjamin Franklin as an Economist," *Johns*

*Hopkins Univ. Studies in Hist. and Pol. Science,* XIII (1895), 425–440—still important; I. Woodbridge Riley, *American Philosophy: The Early Schools,* New York, 1907, pp. 229–265; William Pepper, *The Medical Side of Benjamin Franklin,* Philadelphia, 1911; Lewis J. Carey, *Franklin's Economic Views,* Garden City, N.Y., 1928; Thomas Woody, ed., *Educational Views of Benjamin Franklin,* New York, 1931; Austin K. Gray, *Benjamin Franklin's Library: ... A Short Account of the Library Company of Philadelphia, 1731–1931,* New York, 1936; Edward P. Cheyney, *History of the University of Pennsylvania, 1740–1940,* Philadelphia, 1940—the standard account; Dixon Wecter, "Burke, Franklin, and Samuel Petrie," *Huntington Lib. Quar.,* III (1940), 315–338; *idem,* "Benjamin Franklin and an Irish 'Enthusiast,' " *Huntington Lib. Quar.,* IV (1941), 205–234; Carl Van Doren, "The Beginnings of the American Philosophical Society," *Proc. Amer. Philos. Soc.,* LXXXVII (1943), 277–289—Franklin's part in shaping it; and I. Bernard Cohen, "How Practical Was Benjamin Franklin's Science?" *Pa. Mag. Hist. and Biog.,* LXIX (1945), 284–293. The files of the *Journal* of the Franklin Institute contain much that is important to a study of Franklin's intellectual activities.

Two items concern themselves primarily with Franklin as printer: Luther S. Livingston, *Franklin and His Press at Passy,* New York, 1914; and John C. Oswald, *Benjamin Franklin, Printer,* Garden City, N.Y., 1917.

Studies of sources and themes of individual items are Worthington C. Ford, "Franklin's *New England Courant,*" *Proc. Mass. Hist. Soc.,* LVII (1924), 336–353; George F. Horner, "Franklin's *Dogood Papers* Re-examined," *Studies in Philol.,* XXXVII (1940), 501–523; Chester E. Jorgenson, "The Source of Benjamin Franklin's Dialogues Between Philocles and Horatio (1730)," *Amer. Lit.,* VI (1934), 337–339; Paul McPharlin, "Franklin's 'Cato Major,' 1744," *Publishers' Weekly,* CXLIV (1943), 2111–2118; John F. Ross, "The Character of Poor Richard: Its Source and Alteration," *PMLA,* LV (1940), 785–794; George S. Wykoff, "Problems Concerning Franklin's 'A Dialogue Between Britain, France, Spain, Holland, Saxony, and America,' " *Amer. Lit.,* X (1940), 439–448; A. Stuart Pitt, "The Sources, Significance, and Date of Franklin's 'An Arabian Tale,' " *PMLA,* LVII (1942), 155–168; and Verner W. Crane, "Three Fables by Benjamin Franklin," *New Eng. Quar.,* IX (1936), 499–504.

Other recent studies are Verner W. Crane, "Benjamin Franklin on Slavery and American Liberties," *Pennsylvania Mag. Hist. and Biog.,* LXII (1938), 1–11; Richard I. Shelling, "Benjamin Franklin and the Dr. Bray Associates," *ibid.,* LXIII (1939), 282–293; Conyers Read, "The English Elements in Benjamin Franklin," *ibid.,* LXIV (1940), 314–330; Louis B. Wright, "Franklin's Legacy to the Gilded Age," *Virginia Quar. Rev.,* XX

(1946), 268–279; and T. A. Distler, "Franklin's Two Colleges," *General Mag. and Hist. Chron.,* XLVIII (1946), 117–124.

PRIMARY SOURCES

The principal manuscript collection, containing some 13,000 items in nine languages, is in the possession of the American Philosophical Society, in 76 vols. For a description, see I. Minis Hays, *Calendar of the Papers of Benjamin Franklin in the Library of the American Philosophical Society,* Philadelphia, 1908. Many valuable manuscripts have been acquired since publication of Hays's *Calendar.* The collection of papers in the Library of Congress, second in importance, is in the Stevens Collection: 14 vols., totaling some 3,000 documents (for a description, see Worthington C. Ford, *List of the Benjamin Franklin Papers in the Library of Congress,* Washington, 1905). It has been augmented by addition of the Lavoisier manuscripts— see Donald H. Mugridge, "Scientific Manuscripts of Benjamin Franklin," *Lib. of Congress Jour. of Current Acquisitions,* IV (1947), 12–21. The holdings of the Library of the University of Pennsylvania are considerable, and are calendared by Hays in an appendix to his *Calendar of the Papers of Benjamin Franklin . . . ,* pp. 399–546. The other large collection in Philadelphia is in the Library of the Historical Society of Pennsylvania. The Mason-Franklin collection, formed by William Smith Mason, is in the Yale University Library and includes manuscript books and pamphlets and the correspondence with Joseph Galloway and the Shipley family. See George S. Eddy, "Ramble Through the Mason-Franklin Collection," *Yale Univ. Lib. Gaz.,* X (1936), 65–90; and Dorothy W. Bridgewater, "Notable Additions to the Franklin Collection," *ibid.,* XX (1945), 21–28. The William L. Clements Library at the University of Michigan has further Galloway correspondence and other letters to and from Franklin among the Lansdowne (Shelburne) Papers. The holograph of the *Autobiography,* together with other material, is in the Huntington Library. Letters to Catherine Ray Greene (privately owned) are deposited in the John Carter Brown Library, Providence, R.I. The Morgan Library owns letters to Peter Collinson and correspondence between William Temple Franklin and Louis Le Veillard. There are further manuscripts and letters in public and private collections in the United States. In England the leading Franklin collections are in the British Museum, the Public Records Office, and the libraries of the Royal Society and of King's College, Cambridge. In France there is much material in the Archives du Ministère des Affaires Etrangères, the Bibliothèque du Ministère de la Marine, the Bibliothèque Nationale, and in private collections. For details of Franklin letters in European public collections, see the introduction to Stevens, *Facsimiles . . . ,* below.

BIBLIOGRAPHY

The definitive work to the date of publication is Paul L. Ford's *Franklin Bibliography: A List of Books Written by or Relating to Benjamin Franklin,* Brooklyn, N.Y., 1889. For European material, B. F. Stevens's *Facsimiles of Manuscripts in European Archives Relating to America, 1773–1783,* Washington, 1889–1898, 25 vols., is essential.

Verner W. Crane in "Certain Writings of Benjamin Franklin on the British Empire and the American Colonies," *Papers Bibl. Soc. Amer.,* XXVIII (1934), 1–27, identifies a body of Franklin papers that more than doubles the known existing canon at that time. H. F. De Puy, *A Bibliography of the English Colonial Treaties with the American Indians, Including a Synopsis of Each Treaty,* New York, 1917, includes several Franklin imprints. Comments on the state of Franklin scholarship, with directions for possible research, were presented by George S. Eddy in the *Colophon,* n.s. II (1937), No. 4, 602–616.

Further bibliographical data can be gathered from "List of Works in the New York Public Library by or Relating to Benjamin Franklin," *Bul. N.Y. Pub. Lib.,* X (1906), 29–83; Eleanor Conway, "Dr. Abeloff's Franklin Collection," *Quar. Bul. N.Y. Hist. Soc.,* XXVI (1942), 65–66; and George S. Eddy, "A Work Book of the Printing House of Benjamin Franklin and David Hall, 1759–1766," *Bul. N.Y. Pub. Lib.,* XXXIV (1930), 575–589.

A list of portraits and association objects will be found in John C. Oswald, *Benjamin Franklin in Oil and Bronze,* New York, 1926; and in *Benjamin Franklin and His Circle: A Catalogue of an Exhibition at the Metropolitan Museum of Art, New York,* New York, 1936. W. J. Campbell prepared *A Short-Title Check List of All the Books, Pamphlets, Broadsides, etc. Known to Have Been Printed by Benjamin Franklin,* Philadelphia, 1918, and compiled *The Collection of Franklin Imprints in the Museum of the Curtis Publishing Company,* Philadelphia, 1918. I. Minis Hays compiled *The Chronology of Benjamin Franklin . . . ,* Philadelphia, 1913.

# HAROLD FREDERIC
## *1856–1898*

SEPARATE WORKS

*Seth's Brother's Wife,* 1887; *The Lawton Girl,* 1890; *In the Valley,* 1890; *The Young Emperor: William II of Germany,* 1891; *The Return of the O'Mahony,* 1892; *The New Exodus: A Study of Israel in Russia,* 1892; *The Copperhead,* 1893; *Marsena, and Other Stories of the Wartime,* 1894; *Mrs. Albert Grundy: Observations in Philistia,* 1896; *The Damnation of Theron*

*Ware*, 1896; *March Hares*, 1896; *The Deserter and Other Stories*, 1898; *Gloria Mundi*, 1898; *The Market-Place*, 1899.

*The Damnation of Theron Ware* (1896) was reprinted, New York, 1924, with an introduction by Robert M. Lovett. *In the Sixties* (1897) is a reprint of *The Copperhead* (1893) and *Marsena* (1894), but it includes an introduction herein first printed.

## BIOGRAPHY AND CRITICISM

Very few studies of Frederic's writings have been published. Though brief, the estimate in Arthur H. Quinn, *American Fiction*, New York, 1936, pp. 449-452, is one of the most extensive general estimates. A useful evaluation of *The Damnation of Theron Ware* is the introduction by Robert M. Lovett in the 1924 reprint. The biographical sketch in *Dict. Amer. Biog.* (1932) is by Ernest S. Bates.

Two early evaluations are those of Frank Harris, "Harold Frederic," *Sat. Rev.*, LXXXVI (1898), 526-528, and Louise Imogen Guiney, "Harold Frederic: A Half-Length Sketch from the Life," *Book Buyer*, XVII n.s. (1898-1899), 600-604.

More recent studies are Carey McWilliams, "Harold Frederic: 'A Country Boy of Genius,'" *Univ. Calif. Chron.*, XXXV (1933), 21-34—a somewhat unfavorable estimate, not entirely accurate in detail—and Charles C. Walcutt, "Harold Frederic and American Naturalism," *Amer. Lit.*, X (1939), 11-22. Anecdotal reminiscences appear in "Harold Frederic," in Charles L. Hind, *More Authors and I*, New York, 1922, pp. 113-117.

The fullest bibliographical checklist is that in Jacob Blanck, *Merle Johnson's American First Editions*, 4th ed., New York, 1942.

## MARY E(LEANOR) WILKINS FREEMAN
### *1852-1930*

## SEPARATE WORKS

*Decorative Plaques*, 1883; *The Adventures of Ann*, 1886; *A Humble Romance*, 1887; *A New England Nun and Other Stories*, 1891; *The Pot of Gold and Other Stories*, 1892; *Young Lucretia and Other Stories*, 1892; *Giles Corey, Yeoman*, 1893; *Jane Field*, 1893; *Pembroke*, 1894; *Comfort Pease and Her Gold Ring*, 1895; *Madelon*, 1896; *Jerome: A Poor Man*, 1897; *Once Upon a Time, and Other Child-Verses*, 1897; *Silence and Other Stories*, 1898; *The People of Our Neighborhood*, 1898; *In Colonial Times*, 1899; *The Jamesons*, 1899; *The Heart's Highway*, 1900; *The Love of Parson Lord and Other Stories*, 1900; *Understudies*, 1901; *The Portion of Labor*, 1901; *Six Trees*, 1903; *The Wind in the Rose-Bush*, 1903; *The Givers*, 1904; *The*

*Debtor*, 1905; *"Doc" Gordon*, 1906; *By the Light of the Soul*, 1906; *The Fair Lavinia*, 1907; *The Shoulders of Atlas*, 1908; *The Winning Lady*, 1909; *The Green Door*, 1910; *The Butterfly House*, 1912; *The Yates Pride*, 1912; *The Copy-Cat and Other Stories*, 1914; *An Alabaster Box* (with Florence M. Kingsley), 1917; *Edgewater People*, 1918.

A compilation of *The Best Stories of Mary E. Wilkins*, New York, 1927, was edited with an introduction by Henry W. Lanier.

### BIOGRAPHY AND CRITICISM

No life of Mrs. Freeman has been published. The biographical sketch in *Dict. Amer. Biog.* (1931) was contributed by Elizabeth D. Hanscom.

Standard estimates are Arthur H. Quinn, *American Fiction*, New York, 1936, pp. 433–441; and Fred L. Pattee, *A History of American Literature Since 1870*, New York, 1915, pp. 235–240.

Two valuable early studies are Marie Thérèse Blanc (pseud., Th. Bentzon), "Un Romancier de la Nouvelle-Angleterre: Mary E. Wilkins," *Revue des Deux Mondes*, CXXXVI (1896), 544–569; and Charles M. Thompson, "Miss Wilkins: An Idealist in Masquerade," *Atl. Mo.*, LXXXIII (1899), 665–675. See also Blanche C. Williams, *Our Short Story Writers*, New York, 1920, pp. 160–181. An unpublished dissertation is Edward R. Foster, "Mary Wilkins Freeman: A Critical and Biographical Study," Harvard Univ., 1935.

A bibliographical listing is in Jacob Blanck, *Merle Johnson's American First Editions*, 4th ed., New York, 1942.

## PHILIP (MORIN) FRENEAU
### *1752–1832*

### SEPARATE WORKS

*A Poem on the Rising Glory of America*, 1772; *The American Village*, 1772; *American Liberty*, 1775; *A Voyage to Boston*, 1775; *General Gage's Confession*, 1775; *The British Prison-Ship: A Poem*, 1781; *The Poems of Philip Freneau*, 1786; *A Journey from Philadelphia to New York*, 1787; *The Miscellaneous Works of Mr. Philip Freneau*, 1788; *The Village Merchant*, 1794; *Poems Written Between the Years 1768 & 1794*, 1795; *Letters on Various Interesting and Important Subjects*, 1799; *Poems . . . Third Edition*, 1809; *A Collection of Poems*, 1815; *Some Account of the Capture of the Ship "Aurora,"* 1899.

### COLLECTED WORKS AND EDITED REPRINTS

Fred L. Pattee has provided a good edition of *Poems of Philip Freneau, Poet of the American Revolution*, Princeton, 1902–1907, 3 vols. It is supplemented by *The Last Poems of Philip Freneau,* ed. by Lewis Leary, New Brunswick, N.J., 1946—uncollected version, 1815-1827. *The American Village* was edited in facsimile from the 1772 ed., with introduction by Harry L. Koopman and bibliographical data by Victor H. Paltsits, Providence, 1906. *Letters on Various Interesting and Important Subjects* was reproduced from the 1799 ed., with bibliography, by Harry H. Clark for the Scholars' Facsimiles and Reprints, New York, 1943. Charles F. Heartman edited *Unpublished Freneauana,* New York, 1918. *Poems of Freneau,* ed. by Harry H. Clark, New York, 1929, is a selection of Freneau's best verse, with an introduction, pp. xiii-lviii. Philip Marsh edited a letter: "Philip Freneau to Peter Freneau," *Jour. Rutgers Univ. Lib.,* X (1946), 28-30.

Two early reprints, still useful, are *Poems on Various Subjects,* London, 1861, a reprint of the 1786 *Poems,* with an English preface; and Evert A. Duyckinck, ed., *Poems Relating to the American Revolution by Philip Freneau,* New York, 1865, with a good introduction and invaluable notes.

### BIOGRAPHY AND CRITICISM

A full-length critical study, based on new material, is Lewis Leary, *That Rascal Freneau: A Study in Literary Failure,* New Brunswick, N.J., 1941. It includes an appendix on "Freneau's Reading," pp. 411-417. The first one hundred and twelve pages of Pattee's *Poems of Philip Freneau . . .* contain a biography. The best brief sketch is that by Pattee in *Dict. Amer. Biog.* (1931). A documented study of Freneau's activities in politics is Samuel E. Forman, "The Political Activities of Philip Freneau," *Johns Hopkins Univ. Studies in Hist. and Pol. Sci.,* XX (1902), Nos. 9 and 10. An earlier life is Mary S. Austin, *Philip Freneau . . . ,* New York, 1901.

Useful general estimates are Moses C. Tyler, *The Literary History of the American Revolution,* I (1897), 171-183, 413-426; "Philip Freneau: America's First Poet," in Annie R. Marble, *Heralds of American Literature,* Chicago, 1907, pp. 61-104; "Philip Freneau," in Paul E. More, *Shelburne Essays,* 5th ser., New York, 1908, pp. 86-105; "The Modernness of Philip Freneau," in Fred L. Pattee, *Side-Lights on American Literature,* New York, 1922, pp. 250-292; Vernon L. Parrington, *Main Currents in American Thought,* New York, I (1927), 368-381; Victor F. Calverton, "Philip Freneau: Apostle of Freedom," *Modern Mo.,* VII (1933), 533-546.

Special studies dealing with Freneau as a man of letters are S. B. Hustvedt, "Philippic Freneau," *Amer. Speech,* IV (1928), 1-18; Harry H. Clark, "The Literary Influences of Philip Freneau," *Studies in Philol.,* XXII (1925), 1-33; *idem,* "What Made Freneau the Father of American Poetry?" *ibid.,* XXVI (1929), 1-22; *idem,* "What Made Freneau the Father of American Prose?" *Transactions Wisconsin Acad. Sci., Arts, and Letters,* XXV (1930), 39-50;

Adolph B. Benson, "The Misconception of Philip Freneau's 'Scandinavian War Song,' " *Journal Eng. and Ger. Philol.*, XXVIII (1929), 111-116; Joseph M. Beatty, Jr., "[Charles] Churchill and Freneau," *Amer. Lit.*, II (1930), 121-130; Frank Smith, "Philip Freneau and *The Time-Piece and Literary Companion*," *Amer. Lit.*, IV (1932), 270-287; E. G. Ainsworth, "An American Translator of Ariosto: Philip Freneau," *Amer. Lit.*, IV (1933), 393-395; "Philip Freneau," in Gay W. Allen, *American Prosody*, New York, 1935, pp. 1-26; Philip M. Marsh, "Was Freneau a Fighter?" *Proc. New Jersey Hist. Soc.*, LVI (1938), 211-218; and Dorothy Dondore, "Freneau's *The British Prison-Ship* and Historical Accuracy," *English Jour.*, XXVIII (1939), 228-230. Four studies by Philip M. Marsh are "Freneau and Jefferson: The Poet-Editor Speaks for Himself About the *National Gazette* Episode," *Amer. Lit.*, VIII (1936), 180-189; "Philip Freneau and His Circle, *Pennsylvania Mag. Hist. and Biog.*, LXIII (1939), 37-59; "Philip Freneau's Personal File of The Freeman's Journal," *Proc. New Jersey Hist. Soc.*, LVII (1939), 163-170; and "A Broadside of Freneau's *The British Prison-Ship*," *Amer. Lit.*, X (1939), 476-480—with Milton Ellis.

Among the latest special studies, several are by Lewis Leary: "Philip Freneau in Charleston," *South Carolina Hist. and Geneal. Mag.*, XLII (1941), 89-98—a checklist, with an introduction, of Freneau's contributions to Charleston's newspapers, 1785-1806; "*The Time-Piece*: Philip Freneau's Last Venture in Newspaper Editing," *Princeton Univ. Lib. Chron.*, II (1941), 65-74; "The Log of the Brig *Rebecca*, October 15-November 7, 1779," *Jour. Rutgers Univ. Lib.*, V (1942), 65-70—Freneau's account of his voyage to the Canary Islands; "Philip Freneau on the Cession of Florida," *Florida Hist. Quar.*, XXI (1942), 40-43—an uncollected poem of his later years; "The Manuscript of Philip Freneau's *The British Prison-Ship*," *Jour. Rutgers Univ. Lib.*, VI (1942), 1-28; "Philip Freneau's Captain Hanson," *Amer. Notes and Queries*, II (1942), 51-53; and "Father Bombo's Pilgrimage," *Pennsylvania Mag. Hist. and Biog.*, LXVI (1942), 459-478. Other recent special studies are Rudolf Kirk, "Freneau's 'View' of Princeton," *Jour. Rutgers Univ. Lib.*, III (1939), 20-25; Thomas P. Haviland, "A Measure for the Early Freneau's Debt to Milton," *PMLA*, LV (1940), 1033-40; V. E. Gibbens, "A Note on Three Lyrics of Philip Freneau," *Modern Language Notes*, LIX (1944), 313-315. Several recent studies by Philip M. Marsh are "Freneau and the Bones of Columbus," *Modern Language Notes*, LX (1945), 121-124; "Freneau's 'Hezekiah Salem,' " *New Eng. Quar.*, XVIII (1945), 256-259; "The Griswold Story of Freneau and Jefferson," *Amer. Hist. Rev.*, LI (1945), 68-73; "Philip Freneau and Francis Hopkinson," *Proc. New Jersey Hist. Soc.*, LXIII (1945), 141-149; "Philip Freneau's Manuscript of 'The Spy,' " *Jour. Rutgers Univ. Lib.*, IX (1945), 23-27; "From 'Ezekiah Salem' to 'Robert Slender' . . . ,"

*Modern Language Notes,* LXI (1946), 447–451; "Madison's Defense of Freneau," *William and Mary Quar.,* 3d ser., III (1946), 269–280; and "Philip Freneau, Our Sailor Poet," *Amer. Neptune,* VI (1946), 115–120.

Very few Freneau manuscripts are extant. The best collections are in the Rutgers University Library and the Historical Society of Pennsylvania. A full description of manuscript depositories is in Leary's biography, pp. 409–411.

### BIBLIOGRAPHY

The fullest listing of the writings of Freneau is in Leary's biography, pp. 418–480. An early compilation is that of Victor H. Paltsits, *A Bibliography of the Separate and Collected Works of Philip Freneau,* New York, 1903. An annotated bibliography is Harry H. Clark, ed., *Major American Poets,* New York, 1936, pp. 781–782. See also Harry Hartwick, in Walter F. Taylor, *A History of American Letters,* New York, 1936, pp. 490–491.


## ROBERT (LEE) FROST
### *b. 1874*

### SEPARATE WORKS

*A Boy's Will,* 1913; *North of Boston,* 1914; *Mountain Interval,* 1916; *New Hampshire: A Poem with Notes and Grace Notes,* 1923; *West-Running Brook,* 1928; *A Way Out,* 1929; *The Cow's in the Corn,* 1929; *Two Letters Written on His Undergraduate Days at Dartmouth College in 1892,* 1931; *Three Poems,* 1935; *A Further Range,* 1936; *A Witness Tree,* 1942; *A Masque of Reason,* 1945; *Steeple Bush,* 1947; *A Masque of Mercy,* 1947.


### COLLECTED WORKS

*Collected Poems of Robert Frost* was published, New York, 1930; it was issued in 1939 with additions.


### REPRINTS

*Selected Poems by Robert Frost,* New York, 1923, was issued in a 3rd ed., 1934. *Selected Poems by Robert Frost,* London, 1936, includes introductory essays by W. H. Auden, Paul Engle, and others. Louis Untermeyer edited *Come In, and Other Poems,* New York, 1943, with biographical introduction.


### BIOGRAPHY AND CRITICISM

An analysis of Frost as poet is Lawrance Thompson, *Fire and Ice: The Art and Thought of Robert Frost,* New York, 1942. Earlier studies are Gorham B. Munson, *Robert Frost: A Study in Sensibility and Good Sense,* New

York, 1927, and Caroline Ford, *The Less Traveled Road: A Study of Robert Frost*, Cambridge, 1935, 58 pp. Excerpts from two decades of critical reviews have been compiled by Richard Thornton, *Recognition of Robert Frost: Twenty-fifth Anniversary*, New York, 1937. An estimate is "The Northeast Corner," in Louis Untermeyer, *From Another World*, New York, 1939, pp. 206–228.

Among early estimates are "Robert Frost," in Amy Lowell, *Tendencies in Modern American Poetry*, Boston, 1917, pp. 79–136; Edward Garnett, *Friday Nights*, New York, 1922, pp. 221–242; "Robert Frost," in Louis Untermeyer, *American Poetry Since 1900*, New York, 1923, pp. 15–41; Dorothy Dudley, "The Acid Test," *Poetry*, XXIII (1924), 328–335; "Robert Frost," in Percy H. Boynton, *Some Contemporary Americans*, Chicago, 1924, pp. 33–49; "The Soil of the Puritans," in Carl Van Doren, *Many Minds*, New York, 1924, pp. 50–66; Llewellyn Jones, *First Impressions*, New York, 1925, pp. 37–52; Charles Cestre, "Amy Lowell, Robert Frost, and Edwin Arlington Robinson," *Johns Hopkins Alumni Mag.*, XIV (1926), 363–388; "Robert Frost," in Harriet Monroe, *Poets and Their Art*, New York, 1926, pp. 56–62; "Robert Frost," in Elizabeth S. Sergeant, *Fire Under the Andes*, New York, 1927, pp. 285–303; John Freeman, "Robert Frost," in J. C. Squire, ed., *Contemporary American Authors*, New York, 1928, pp. 15–44; "Robert Frost," in Thomas K. Whipple, *Spokesmen*, New York, 1928, pp. 94–114; Sidney Cox, *Robert Frost: Original "Ordinary Man*,*"* New York, 1929; George R. Elliott, *The Cycle of Modern Poetry*, Princeton, 1929, pp. 112–134; "The Fire and Ice of Robert Frost," in Alfred Kreymborg, *Our Singing Strength*, New York, 1929, pp. 316–332.

Later general studies are Gorham B. Munson, "Robert Frost and the Humanistic Temper," *Bookman*, LXXI (1930), 419–422; James S. Wilson, "Robert Frost: American Poet," *Virginia Quar. Rev.*, VII (1931), 316–320; James McBride Dabbs, "Robert Frost and the Dark Woods," *Yale Rev.*, XXIII (1934), 514–520; Babette Deutsch, *This Modern Poetry*, New York, 1935, pp. 40–46; Mark Van Doren, "The Permanence of Robert Frost," *Amer. Scholar*, V (1936), 190–198; Merrill Moore, "Poetic Agrarianism, Old Style," *Sewanee Rev.*, XLV (1937), 507–509; and John Gould Fletcher, "Robert Frost the Outlander," *Mark Twain Quar.*, III (1940), 5–8.

European studies of Frost are Albert Feuillerat, "Poètes américains d'aujourd'hui: M. Robert Frost," *Revue des Deux Mondes*, XVII (1923), 185–210; and Alfredo Ortiz-Vargas, "Perfiles Anglo-Americanos," *Revista Iberoamericana*, IV (1941), 163–176. See also the "Frost Number" of the *New Hampshire Troubadour*, XVI (November, 1946).

Special studies are George O. Aykroyd, "The Classical in Robert Frost," *Poet-Lore*, XL (1929), 610–614; Robert S. Newdick, "The Early Verse of

Robert Frost and Some of His Revisions," *Amer. Lit.*, VII (1935), 181–187; *idem,* "Robert Frost and the Dramatic," *New Eng. Quar.*, X (1937), 262–269; *idem,* "Robert Frost and the Sound of Sense," *Amer. Lit.*, IX (1937), 289–300; Robert P. T. Coffin, *New Poetry of New England: Frost and Robinson,* Baltimore, 1938; Bernard De Voto, "The Critics and Robert Frost," *Sat. Rev. Lit.*, XVII (Jan. 1, 1938), 3–4, 14–15; Robert S. Newdick, "Robert Frost Looks at War," *So. Atl. Quar.*, XXXVIII (1939), 52–59; *idem,* "Robert Frost and the Classics," *Classical Jour.*, XXXV (1940), 403–416; *idem,* "Robert Frost's Other Harmony," *Sewanee Rev.*, XLVIII (1940), 409–418; Hyatt H. Waggoner, "The Humanistic Idealism of Robert Frost," *Amer. Lit.*, XIII (1941), 207–223; Robert G. Berkelman, "Robert Frost and the Middle Way," *College Eng.*, III (1942), 347–353; Reginald L. Cook, "Robert Frost: A Time to Listen," *College Eng.*, VII (1945), 66–71; and Charles H. Foster, "Robert Frost and the New England Tradition," in *Elizabethan Studies . . . in Honor of George F. Reynolds,* Boulder, Colo., 1945, pp. 370–381.

PRIMARY SOURCES

There are manuscripts of Frost in the Harvard College Library; in the Jones Library, Amherst, Mass.; and in the Lockwood Memorial Library, Univ. of Buffalo.

BIBLIOGRAPHY

The most recent bibliography is Louis and Esther Mertins, *The Intervals of Robert Frost: A Critical Bibliography,* Berkeley, Calif., 1947. See also W. B. Shubrick Clymer and Charles R. Green, *Robert Frost: A Bibliography,* Amherst, Mass., 1937. Lawrance Thompson compiled *Robert Frost: A Chronological Survey,* Middletown, Conn., 1936. Further data appear in Frederic G. Melcher, "Robert Frost and His Books," *Colophon,* No. 2, 1930, pp. 1–7; and in Robert S. Newdick, "Three Poems by Robert Frost," *Amer. Lit.*, VII (1935), 329. Useful for secondary sources is Fred B. Millett, *Contemporary American Authors,* New York, 1940, pp. 362–366. See also the checklist by Frances Cheney, in Allen Tate, *Sixty American Poets, 1896–1944,* Washington, 1945, pp. 53–58.

# (SARAH) MARGARET FULLER (OSSOLI)
### *1810–1850*

SEPARATE WORKS

The original works consist of *Summer on the Lakes, in 1843,* 1844; *Woman in the Nineteenth Century,* 1845; *Papers on Literature and Art,* 1846.

She translated *Eckermann's Conversations with Goethe,* 1839, and (in part) *Correspondence of Fräulein Günderode and Bettina von Arnim,* 1842. She edited *At Home and Abroad,* 1856; and *Life Without and Life Within,* 1859.

## COLLECTED WORKS

All of Margaret Fuller's writings were out of print until Mason Wade edited *The Writings of Margaret Fuller,* New York, 1941, a one-volume collection of essays, letters, and miscellaneous items, with reprint of *Woman in the Nineteenth Century* and an abbreviated version of *Summer on the Lakes.* *Love-Letters of Margaret Fuller, 1845–1846,* New York, 1903, was edited with an introduction by Julia Ward Howe, and includes reminiscences by Emerson, Horace Greeley, and Charles T. Congdon.

Gleanings of unpublished letters are Granville Hicks, "Margaret Fuller to Sarah Helen Whitman: An Unpublished Letter," *Amer. Lit.,* I (1930), 419–421; Willard E. Martin, Jr., "A Last Letter of Margaret Fuller Ossoli," *ibid.,* V (1933), 66–69; and J. W. Thomas, "A Hitherto Unpublished Poem by Margaret Fuller," *ibid.,* XV (1944), 411–415.

## BIOGRAPHY AND CRITICISM

A standard life is Mason Wade, *Margaret Fuller: Whetstone of Genius,* New York, 1940. Madeleine B. Stern, *The Life of Margaret Fuller,* New York, 1942, though a fictional biography, is full and accurate in detail. Earlier lives are Margaret Bell, *Margaret Fuller: A Biography,* New York, 1930; and Katharine Anthony, *Margaret Fuller: A Psychological Biography,* New York, 1920. Katharine Anthony contributed a sketch of Margaret Fuller to *Dict. Amer. Biog.* (1931).

Brief general studies are "Alcott, Margaret Fuller, Brook Farm," in Van Wyck Brooks, *The Flowering of New England,* rev. ed., New York, 1940, pp. 228–251; Vernon L. Parrington, *Main Currents in American Thought,* New York, II (1927), 426–434; "Margaret Fuller Ossoli," in Gamaliel Bradford, *Portraits of American Women,* Boston, 1919, pp. 133–163; and "Margaret Fuller," in Andrew Macphail, *Essays in Puritanism,* London, 1905, pp. 116–167—dealing especially with her life in Italy.

Among the earlier special studies are Karl Knortz, *Brook Farm und Margaret Fuller,* New York, 1886; "Margaret Fuller Ossoli," in George M. Gould, *Biographic Clinics,* Philadelphia, 1904, II, 271–281—a study of her maladies; Frederick A. Braun, *Margaret Fuller and Goethe . . . ,* New York, 1910; and Richard V. Carpenter, "Margaret Fuller in Northern Illinois," *Jour. Illinois State Hist. Soc.,* II (1910), 7–22.

Later estimates are Helen N. McMaster, "Margaret Fuller as a Literary Critic," *Univ. Buffalo Studies,* VII (1928), No. 3; "Emerson and Margaret Fuller," in George E. DeMille, *Literary Criticism in America,* New York,

1931, pp. 118–132; Harry Slochower, "Margaret Fuller and Goethe," *Germanic Rev.,* VII (1932), 130–144; Harry R. Warfel, "Margaret Fuller and Ralph Waldo Emerson," *PMLA,* L (1935), 576–584; Frances M. Barbour, "Margaret Fuller and the British Reviewers," *New Eng. Quar.,* IX (1936), 618–625; and William P. Randel, "Hawthorne, Channing, and Margaret Fuller," *Amer. Lit.,* X (1939), 472–476.

Among recent studies four are by Madeleine B. Stern: "Margaret Fuller's Stay in Providence, 1837–1838," *Americana,* XXXIV (1940), 353–369; "Margaret Fuller's Schooldays in Cambridge," *New Eng. Quar.,* XIII (1940), 207–222; "Margaret Fuller and *The Dial,*" *So. Atl. Quar.,* XL (1941), 11–21; and "Margaret Fuller's Summer in the West, 1843," *Michigan Hist. Mag.,* XXV (1941), 300–330. Other recent studies are Leona Rostenberg, "Margaret Fuller's Roman Diary," *Jour. Modern Hist.,* XII (1940), 209–220; Charles A. Madison, "Margaret Fuller: Transcendental Rebel," *Antioch Rev.,* II (1942), 422–438; Arthur R. Schultz, "Margaret Fuller: Transcendentalist Interpreter of American Literature," *Monatshefte für deutschen Unterricht,* XXXIV (1942), 169–182; and Roland C. Burton, "Margaret Fuller's Criticism of the Fine Arts," *College Eng.,* VI (1944), 18–23.

### PRIMARY SOURCES

The two large collections of Margaret Fuller's manuscripts are in the Boston Public Library and the Harvard College Library. Many of the original texts of letters and journals were scattered and have been lost. Those which have been preserved have often been mutilated by her earlier biographers: Emerson, William Henry Channing, and James Freeman Clarke. The *Memoirs of Margaret Fuller Ossoli,* Boston, 1852, 2 vols., edited by Emerson, Channing, and Clarke, were compiled from her manuscripts, but the text is bowdlerized.

Early biographies, of use principally as primary material, are Julia Ward Howe, *Margaret Fuller, Marchesa Ossoli,* Boston, 1883, and Thomas W. Higginson, *Margaret Fuller Ossoli,* Boston, 1884 (Amer. Men of Letters).

Data of a primary nature will be found in the various studies of Brook Farm and the Transcendental movement; and especially in the memoirs, journals, and biographies of Amos Bronson Alcott, Horace Greeley, James Freeman Clarke, Julia Ward Howe, William W. Story, Poe, Hawthorne, and Emerson.

Six letters to Margaret Fuller were edited by Leona Rostenberg, "Mazzini to Margaret Fuller, 1847–1849," *Amer. Hist. Rev.,* XLVII (1941), 73–80. A discussion of further material is Evelyn W. Orr, "Two Margaret Fuller Manuscripts," *New Eng. Quar.,* XI (1938), 794–802.

BIBLIOGRAPHY

A calendar of Margaret Fuller's contributions to periodicals is in the Wade edition of the *Writings* (1941), 595–600. For useful secondary material see Mason Wade, *Margaret Fuller* (1940), 294–297. An extensive listing of primary and secondary material is in Madeleine B. Stern, *Margaret Fuller* (1942), 493–523.

## ZONA GALE
### *1874–1938*

SEPARATE WORKS

*Romance Island*, 1906; *The Loves of Pelleas and Etarre*, 1907; *Friendship Village*, 1908; *Friendship Village Love Stories*, 1909; *Mothers to Men*, 1911; *Christmas: A Story*, 1912; *When I Was a Little Girl*, 1913; *Neighborhood Stories*, 1914; *Heart's Kindred*, 1915; *A Daughter of the Morning*, 1917; *Birth*, 1918; *Peace in Friendship Village*, 1919; *Miss Lulu Bett*, 1920; *The Secret Way*, 1921; *Uncle Jimmy*, 1922; *Faint Perfume*, 1923; *Mister Pitt*, 1925; *The Neighbors*, 1926; *Preface to a Life*, 1926; *Yellow Gentians and Blue*, 1927; *Portage, Wisconsin, and Other Essays*, 1928; *Borgia*, 1929; *Bridal Pond*, 1930; *Evening Clothes*, 1932; *Papa La Fleur*, 1933; *Old-Fashioned Tales*, 1933; *Faint Perfume: A Play with a Prologue*, 1934; *Light Woman*, 1937; *Frank Miller of Mission Inn*, 1938; *Magna*, 1939.

REPRINTS

There is no collection of the writings of Zona Gale. *Miss Lulu Bett* (1920) was issued in the Modern Lib., New York, 1928.

BIOGRAPHY AND CRITICISM

August Derleth's *Still Small Voice: The Biography of Zona Gale*, New York, 1940, is appreciative and well written. Its criticisms of Zona Gale's writing are virtually all that have been published. Wilson Follett issued a pamphlet, *Zona Gale: An Artist in Fiction*, New York, 1923. Brief discussion appears in Régis Michaud, *The American Novel To-day*, Boston, 1928, pp. 248–254.

PRIMARY SOURCES

Zona Gale's own reminiscences are *When I Was a Little Girl* (1913) and *Portage, Wisconsin, and Other Essays* (1928). "The Unfinished Autobiography" is published in Derleth's biography, pp. 272–305. There are a few manuscripts in the Princeton University Library.

A bibliography is in Fred B. Millett, *Contemporary American Authors,* New York, 1940, pp. 366–368.

## (HANNIBAL) HAMLIN GARLAND
### *1860–1940*

SEPARATE WORKS

*Under the Wheel: A Modern Play in Six Scenes,* 1890; *Main-Travelled Roads,* 1891; *A Member of the Third House,* 1892; *Jason Edwards: An Average Man,* 1892; *A Little Norsk: or, Ol' Pap's Flaxen,* 1892; *A Spoil of Office,* 1892; *Prairie Folks,* 1893; *Prairie Songs,* 1893; *Crumbling Idols,* 1894; *Rose of Dutcher's Coolly,* 1895; *Wayside Courtships,* 1897; *Ulysses S. Grant: His Life and Character,* 1898; *The Spirit of Sweetwater,* 1898; *The Trail of the Goldseekers,* 1899; *Boy Life on the Prairie,* 1899; *The Eagle's Heart,* 1900; *Her Mountain Lover,* 1901; *The Captain of the Gray Horse Troop,* 1902; *Hesper,* 1903; *The Light of the Star,* 1904; *The Tyranny of the Dark,* 1905; *The Long Trail,* 1907; *Money Magic,* 1907; *The Shadow World,* 1908; *The Moccasin Ranch,* 1909; *Cavanagh, Forest Ranger,* 1910; *Other Main-Travelled Roads,* 1910; *Victor Ollnee's Discipline,* 1911; *The Forester's Daughter,* 1914; *They of the High Trails,* 1916; *A Son of the Middle Border,* 1917; *A Daughter of the Middle Border,* 1921; *A Pioneer Mother,* 1922; *The Book of the American Indian,* 1923; *Trail-Makers of the Middle Border,* 1926; *Memories of the Middle Border,* 1926; *The Westward March of American Settlement,* 1927; *Back-Trailers from the Middle Border,* 1928; *Roadside Meetings,* 1930; *Companions on the Trail,* 1931; *My Friendly Contemporaries,* 1932; *Afternoon Neighbors,* 1934; *Iowa, O Iowa!* 1935; *Forty Years of Psychic Research,* 1936; *The Mystery of the Buried Crosses,* 1939.

REPRINTS

There is no collected edition of Garland's works. *Main-Travelled Roads,* Boston, 1891, the collection of Wisconsin and Iowa tales which made Garland's reputation, was reissued with additional material, New York, 1907. Its sequel in what is called the "Veritist" series is *Other Main-Travelled Roads,* New York, 1910, a volume including *Prairie Folks* (1893) and *Wayside Courtships* (1897). *Jason Edwards* (1892) is a novelized form of *Under the Wheel* (1890). *Witch's Gold,* New York, 1906, is a new and enlarged version of *The Spirit of Sweetwater* (1898). The realistic novel *Rose of Dutcher's Coolly,* New York, 1895, was published in a revised edition, New York, 1899; and *Boy Life on the Prairie,* New York, 1899, Garland's first book in point of writing, was revised in 1908; it uses the material which was later culled in *A Son of the Middle Border* (1917). *The Long Trail* (1907) was edited by Barbara G. Spayd, New York, 1935. *A Son of the Middle Border* (1917) was edited by E. H. K. McComb, New York, 1927, in the Modern Readers' Series.

## BIOGRAPHY AND CRITICISM

No adequate study of Garland has yet been published. A thorough analysis of his thought, reading, and friendships is the unpublished thesis of Benjamin F. Gronewold, "The Social Criticism of Hamlin Garland," New York Univ., 1943. Another unpublished thesis dealing with his early years is Eldon C. Hill, "A Biographical Study of Hamlin Garland from 1860–1895," Ohio State Univ., 1940.

Brief general criticism is in Edwin W. Bowen, "Hamlin Garland, the Middle-West Short-Story Writer," *Sewanee Rev.,* XXVII (1919), 411–422; "Hamlin Garland," Blanche C. Williams, in *Our Short Story Writers,* New York, 1920, pp. 182–199; Carl Van Doren, *Contemporary American Novelists,* New York, 1922, pp. 38–47; Fred L. Pattee, *The Development of the American Short Story,* New York, 1923, pp. 313–317; Ruth M. Raw, "Hamlin Garland, the Romanticist," *Sewanee Rev.,* XXXVI (1928), 202–210; Vernon L. Parrington, *Main Currents in American Thought,* New York, 1930, III, 288–300; Claude Simpson, "Hamlin Garland's Decline," *Southwest Rev.,* XXVI (1941), 223–234; "Hamlin Garland," in Walter F. Taylor, *The Economic Novel in America,* Chapel Hill, N.C., 1942, pp. 148–183; and Jesse S. Goldstein, "Two Literary Radicals: Garland and Markham in Chicago, 1893," *Amer. Lit.,* XVII (1945), 152–160. One of the earliest studies of Garland is Marie Thérèse Blanc, "Un Radical de la Prairie: Hamlin Garland," *Rev. des Deux Mondes,* CLVII (1900), 139–180. See also William D. Howells, "Mr. Garland's Books," *No. Amer. Rev.,* CXCVI (1912), 523–528.

Studies of Garland and the frontier are Allan Nevins, "Garland and the Prairies," *Literary Rev.,* II (1922), 881–882; Lucy L. Hazard, *The Frontier in American Literature,* New York, 1927, pp. 261–267; Frank L. Mott, "Exponents of the Pioneers," *Palimpsest,* XI (Feb., 1930), 61–66; and Albert Keiser, *The Indian in American Literature,* New York, 1933, pp. 279–292.

## PRIMARY SOURCES

Garland's autobiographical chronicle begins in point of time with *Trail-Makers of the Middle Border,* New York, 1926, the story of his father's migration from Maine to Wisconsin; it is continued in the most distinguished of his works, *A Son of the Middle Border,* New York, 1917; and is completed in the two volumes, *A Daughter of the Middle Border,* New York, 1921; and *Back-Trailers from the Middle Border,* New York, 1928.

His old-age reminiscences were written in chronological sequence: *Roadside Meetings,* New York, 1930—the best of the four, covering the years 1880–1900; *Companions on the Trail: A Literary Chronicle,* New York, 1931—for the years 1900–1913; *My Friendly Contemporaries: A Literary Log,* New York, 1932—for the decade 1913–1923; and *Afternoon Neighbors: Further Excerpts from a Literary Log,* New York, 1934, the concluding volume of the series, beginning with November, 1922.

Further uncollected items by Garland of an autobiographical nature are "Sanity in Fiction," *No. Amer. Rev.,* CLXXVI (1903), 336–348—an appreciation of Howells; "My Aim in *Cavanagh,*" *World's Work,* XX (1910). 13569; "Books of My Childhood," *Sat. Rev. Lit.,* VII (1930), 347; and "Some of My Youthful Enthusiasms," *English Jour.,* XX (1931), 355–364—reminiscences of Howells and of Boston as a cultural hub. Statements by Garland on his literary position are "The West in Literature," *Arena,* VI (1892), 669–676 —an application of Taine's theory to American literary history; "The Future of Fiction," *Arena,* VII (1893), 513–524—the place of fiction in literary history and the influence of Taine and evolution; "Productive Conditions of American Literature," *Forum,* VII (1894), 690–698—a clear statement of his position as a "verist"; and "Limitations of Authorship in America," *Bookman,* LIX (1924), 257–262—a statement of his position as veritist and "aristocrat in literature." An early influence upon his critical theories, and probable source of the term "veritism," is Eugène Véron, *L'Esthétique* (2nd ed., 1883).

Sketches and reminiscences of Garland are in *Mark Twain Quar.,* IV (Summer, 1940), by Irving Bacheller and others. More material is in John T. Flanagan, "Hamlin Garland, Occasional Minnesotan," *Minnesota Hist.,* XXII (1941), 157–168.

The chief collection of unpublished manuscripts is that of the Doheny Library of the University of Southern California, Los Angeles. It includes diaries, notebooks, letters to and copies of letters from Garland, together with some marginalia. The Garland-Gilder correspondence is in the New York Public Library.

BIBLIOGRAPHY

The best listing of Garland first editions is in Jacob Blanck, *Merle Johnson's American First Editions,* 4th ed., New York, 1942. The fullest listing of secondary material is in Fred B. Millett, *Contemporary American Authors,* New York, 1940, pp. 368–372.

# CHARLES ÉTIENNE ARTHUR GAYARRÉ
*1805–1895*

WORKS

*Essai historique sur la Louisiane,* 1830–1831, 2 vols., is largely a translation of F. X. Martin's *History of Louisiana.* It was revised and enlarged as *Histoire de la Louisiane,* 1846–1847, 2 vols., and was afterwards rewritten in English. *Romance of the History of Louisiana,* 1848, later became "first series" in Vol. I of *History of Louisiana,* 1851–1866. The four volumes of the *History of Louisiana,* 1851–1866, were first issued separately as (1) *Louisiana; Its Colonial History and Romance* (1851), (2) *Louisiana; Its History as a French Colony* (1852), (3) *History of Louisiana: The Spanish Domination* (1854), (4) *History of Louisiana: The American Domination* (1866). The fourth edition (1903) contains a biography by Grace King and a bibliography by William Beer. *Philip II of Spain* (1866) is a psychological study.

Gayarré's fiction includes *The School for Politics: A Dramatic Novel* (1854); *Fernando de Lemos—Truth and Fiction: A Novel* (1872)—in part autobiographical; *Aubert Dubayet; or, The Two Sister Republics* (1882)—a sequel to *Fernando de Lemos.* His one published play is *Dr. Bluff in Russia; or, The Emperor Nicholas and the American Doctor* (1865).

Among Gayarré's pamphlets, the most significant and most frequently cited are *Address of Charles Gayarré, to the People of the State, on the Late Frauds Perpetrated at the Election Held on the 7th Nov., 1853, in the City of New Orleans* (1853), 16 pp.; *Influence of Mechanic Arts on the Human Race: Two Lectures . . .* (1854), 86 pp.; *A Sketch of General Jackson, by Himself,* New Orleans, 1857, 21 pp.; *The Creoles of History and the Creoles of Romance: A Lecture . . .* (1885), 15 pp.—the controversy against G. W. Cable.

"Four Letters from Charles Gayarré" were published in *Louisiana Hist. Quar.,* XII (1929), 28–32. A useful study is Charles R. Anderson, "Charles Gayarré and Paul Hayne: The Last Literary Cavaliers," in *American Studies in Honor of William Kenneth Boyd*; ed. by David Kelly Jackson, Durham, N.C., 1940, pp. 221–281—with bibliographical footnotes and quotations from many letters. Also useful is Edward L. Tinker, "Charles Gayarré, 1805–95," *Papers Bibliographical Soc. Amer.,* XXVII (1933), 24–64, with bibliography (pp. 54–64).

BIOGRAPHY AND CRITICISM

Useful earlier estimates are John H. Nelson, "Charles Gayarré, Historian and Romancer," *Sewanee Rev.,* XXXIII (1925), 427–438; John S. Kendall,

"The Last Days of Charles Gayarré," *Louisiana Hist. Quar.*, XV (1932), 359–375; and "Charles Gayarré," in Grace E. King, *Creole Families of New Orleans*, New York, 1921, pp. 269–290. Eulogistic essays appear in *Pub. Louisiana Hist. Soc.*, III, Pt. 4, 1906, 7–45. The sketch in *Dict. Amer. Biog.* (1931) was contributed by Ernest S. Bates. For data on Gayarré's activities in collecting documents, see Carl L. Cannon in *American Book Collectors and Collecting*, New York, 1941, pp. 243–244.

Other early studies include Paul Hamilton Hayne, "Charles Gayarré: The Statesman," *Southern Bivouac*, n.s. II (June, 1886), 28–37; *idem*, "Charles Gayarré: The Author," *ibid.*, n.s. II (July, Aug., 1886), 108–112, 172–176; Charles Aldrich, "Louisiana's Veteran Author," *Critic*, n.s. XIII (1890), 29–30; and Alcée Fortier, *Louisiana Studies* . . . , New Orleans, 1894, pp. 24–25, 92–93, 102, 113–114.

Manuscript letters written by Gayarré and Paul Hamilton Hayne are in the Duke University Library, as is also the manuscript of Gayarré's autobiographical sketch. For a discussion of the authenticity of the sketch, see the item by Charles R. Anderson mentioned above. Gayarré's business, legal, literary, and personal papers are deposited in the Department of Archives, Louisiana State University. Useful published primary material is Frank D. Richardson, "A Last Evening with Judge Gayarré," in *Louisiana Hist. Quar.*, XIV (1931), 81–85; and Grace E. King, *Memories of a Southern Woman of Letters*, New York, 1932, pp. 30–45.

Bibliographies are included in the 4th ed. (1903) of *History of Louisiana*, compiled by William Beer, and in the biographical sketches by Anderson and by Tinker mentioned above.

# HENRY GEORGE
*1839–1897*

### SEPARATE WORKS

*Our Land and Land Policy*, 1871; *Progress and Poverty*, 1879; *The Irish Land Question*, 1881; *Social Problems*, 1883; *Protection or Free Trade*, 1886; *The Condition of Labor*, 1891; *A Perplexed Philosopher*, 1892; *The Science of Political Economy*, 1897.

Many of the ideas which George proposed were first developed in numerous periodical articles, especially in his own weekly, the *Standard* (1886–1892) which gave him national hearing as well as the support of labor in his two unsuccessful New York mayoralty campaigns.

### COLLECTIONS AND REPRINTS

*The Writings of Henry George*, New York, 1898–1901, 10 vols., were edited by his son. The same material was again published in the "Library Edition" of *The Complete Works of Henry George,* Garden City, N.Y., 1906-1911, 10 vols.

*Progress and Poverty* was translated into many languages soon after its publication in 1880. It has been frequently reprinted and has been available in the Modern Library since 1938. Several other works have been made available by recent reprints. A convenient volume of selections from *Progress and Poverty* is that edited by Harry G. Brown, *Significant Paragraphs from Henry George's Progress and Poverty,* New York, 1928.

BIOGRAPHY AND CRITICISM

*The Life of Henry George,* edited by Henry George, Jr., was published, New York, 1911, 2 vols. Useful background material for social ideals of the period following the Civil War is in George R. Geiger, *The Philosophy of Henry George,* New York, 1933. Albert J. Nock published *Henry George: An Essay,* New York, 1939. An important study is A. N. Young, *The Single Tax Movement in the United States,* Princeton, 1916. The sketch of George in *Dict. Amer. Biog.* (1931) was contributed by Broadus Mitchell.

Early studies of George are George Gunton, "The Economic Heresies of Henry George," *Forum,* III (1887), 15-28; Herbert Spencer, "Unpublished Letters . . . , the Henry George Controversy," *Independent,* LVI (1904), 1169-1174, 1471-1478; Edgar H. Johnson, "The Economics of Henry George's *Progress and Poverty,*" *Jour. Pol. Econ.,* XVIII (1910), 714-735; and Alexander Mackendrick, "Henry George's Teaching," *Westminster Rev.,* CLXXII (1912), 133-142.

More recent studies include John Dewey's introduction to *Significant Paragraphs from Henry George's Progress and Poverty,* New York, 1928; McAlister Coleman, *Pioneers of Freedom,* New York, 1929, pp. 109-122; Ida M. Tarbell, "New Dealers of the Seventies," *Forum,* XCII (1934), 133-139; "Henry George: A Prophet of Social Justice," in James Dombrowski, *The Early Days of Christian Socialism in America,* New York, 1936, pp. 35-49; George R. Geiger, "The Forgotten Man: Henry George," *Antioch Rev.,* I (1941), 291-307; and Charles A. Madison, "Henry George, Prophet of Human Rights," *So. Atl. Quar.,* XLIII (1944), 349-360. In the large body of the literature of controversy regarding George's social theories some is still intrinsically important. See for example George B. Dixwell, *"Progress and Poverty": A Review of the Doctrines of Henry George;* Arnold Toynbee, *"Progress and Poverty": A Criticism of Mr. Henry George,* London, 1883; Thomas H. Huxley, "Capital—the Mother of Labour," *Nineteenth Century,* XXVII (1890), 513-532; and John Bagot, "Progress and Poverty," *Westminster Rev.,* CLXXII (1909), 371-375.

There are many autobiographical references in Henry George, Jr., *The*

*Life of Henry George* (1900), and in George's own works, especially *Pro-tection or Free Trade* (1886) and *The Science of Political Economy* (1897). See also Louis F. Post, *The Prophet of San Francisco* . . . : *Personal Memories and Interpretations of Henry George,* New York, 1930 (first issued, Chicago, 1904).

A full bibliography of primary and secondary sources, including a large number of items in the literature of ideas during the last two decades of the nineteenth century, is Rollin A. Sawyer, *Henry George and the Single Tax: A Catalogue of the Collection in the New York Public Library,* New York, 1926, 90 pp. For a checklist of press opinions of *Progress and Poverty* see Louis F. Post, *The Prophet of San Francisco* (1904), pp. 49–61.

# ELLEN (ANDERSON GHOLSON) GLASGOW
## *1874-1945*

SEPARATE WORKS

*The Descendant,* 1897; *Phases of an Inferior Planet,* 1898; *The Voice of the People,* 1900; *The Freeman and Other Poems,* 1902; *The Battle-Ground,* 1902; *The Deliverance,* 1904; *The Wheel of Life,* 1906; *The Ancient Law,* 1908; *The Romance of a Plain Man,* 1909; *The Miller of Old Church,* 1911; *Virginia,* 1913; *Life and Gabriella,* 1916; *The Builders,* 1919; *One Man in His Time,* 1922; *The Shadowy Third and Other Stories,* 1923; *Barren Ground,* 1925; *The Romantic Comedians,* 1926; *They Stooped to Folly,* 1929; *The Sheltered Life,* 1932; *Vein of Iron,* 1935; *In This Our Life,* 1941; *A Certain Measure: An Interpretation of Prose Fiction,* 1943.

COLLECTED WORKS AND REPRINTS

Two collected editions have been made: *The Works of Ellen Glasgow,* Garden City, N.Y., 1929–1933, 8 vols.—the "Old Dominion Ed.," each volume of which has been revised, with a new preface; and *The Works of Ellen Glasgow,* New York, 1938, 12 vols.—the "Virginia Ed."

*Barren Ground* (1925) was published in the Modern Lib., New York, 1936.

BIOGRAPHY AND CRITICISM

There is no published life of Ellen Glasgow. Very few informed critical estimates of her writing were made during the twenty-five years following publication of her first book in 1897. Among the earliest are "Ellen Glasgow: The Fighting Edge of Romance," in Stuart P. Sherman, *Critical Woodcuts,* New York, 1926, pp. 73–82; and Edwin Mims, "The Social Philosophy of

Ellen Glasgow," *Social Forces,* IV (1926), 495–503. Two appreciations published at about the same time are Louise M. Field, *Ellen Glasgow, Novelist of the Old and the New South: An Appreciation,* Garden City, 1923—a pamphlet; and Dorothea L. Mann, "Ellen Glasgow, Citizen of the World," *Bookman,* LXIV (1926), 265–271.

Later estimates are Sara Haardt, "Ellen Glasgow and the South," *Bookman,* LXIX (1929), 133–139; "Two Sides of the Shielded: A Note as to Ellen Glasgow," in James Branch Cabell, *Some of Us,* New York, 1930, pp. 47–58; "Ellen Glasgow," in Emily Clark, *Innocence Abroad,* New York, 1931, pp. 55–69; William R. Parker, "Ellen Glasgow: A Gentle Rebel," *English Jour.,* XX (1931), 187–194; Léonie Villard, "L'Œuvre d'Ellen Glasgow, romancière américaine," *Revue Anglo-Amér.,* XI (1933), 97–111; Harlan Hatcher, *Creating the Modern American Novel,* New York, 1935, pp. 94–98; Arthur H. Quinn, *American Fiction,* New York, 1936, pp. 670–682.

Most recent evaluations are Marjorie K. Rawlings, "Regional Literature of the South," *College Eng.,* I (1940), 381–389—which gives her first place among southern regionalists; "Contemplation of Manners in Ellen Glasgow," in Nellie Elizabeth Monroe, *The Novel and Society,* Chapel Hill, N.C., 1941, pp. 139–187; and "Elegy and Satire: Willa Cather and Ellen Glasgow," in Alfred Kazin, *On Native Grounds,* New York, 1942, pp. 247–264.

BIBLIOGRAPHY

The fullest listing of Ellen Glasgow's writings is William H. Egly, "Bibliography of Ellen Anderson Gholson Glasgow," *Bul. Bibl.,* XVII (1940), 47–50. The listing in *A Certain Measure* (1943), pp. 265–272, includes her contributions to books and periodicals up to the date of publication. For secondary items, see Fred B. Millett, *Contemporary American Authors,* New York, 1940, pp. 374–376.

## THOMAS GODFREY
### 1736–1763

SEPARATE WORKS

*The Court of Fancy: A Poem,* 1762; *Juvenile Poems on Various Subjects, with The Prince of Parthia: A Tragedy,* 1765 (*The Prince of Parthia* was produced in 1767).

EDITED REPRINTS

*The Prince of Parthia* was reprinted first in Arthur H. Quinn, *Representative American Plays,* New York, 1917. It was also edited by Archibald

Henderson, with a critical introduction, Boston, 1917; and has been reprinted by Montrose J. Moses, *Representative Plays by American Dramatists,* New York, 1918.

BIOGRAPHY AND CRITICISM

The best study of Godfrey as playwright is in Arthur H. Quinn, *A History of the American Drama from the Beginning to the Civil War,* rev. ed., New York, 1943, pp. 16–27. A further estimate is that of Moses C. Tyler, *A History of American Literature During the Colonial Period,* rev. ed., New York, 1897, II, 244–251. The sketch of Godfrey in *Dict. Amer. Biog.* (1931) is by Arthur H. Quinn. An earlier estimate is George O. Seilhamer, *A History of the American Theatre, 1749–1797,* Philadelphia, 1888–1891, I, 185–195.

Two special studies by C. Lennart Carlson are: "Thomas Godfrey in England," *Amer. Lit.,* VII (1935), 302–309, and "A Further Note on Thomas Godfrey in England," *ibid.,* IX (1937), 73–77. Other special studies are Thomas C. Pollock, "Rowe's *Tamerlane* and *The Prince of Parthia,*" *ibid.,* VI (1934), 158–162; Henry B. Woolf, "Thomas Godfrey: Eighteenth-Century Chaucerian," *ibid.,* XII (1941), 486–490; and Albert F. Gegenheimer, "Thomas Godfrey: Protégé of William Smith," *Pennsylvania Hist.,* IX (1942), 233–251, X (1943), 26–43.

Contemporary sketches of Godfrey are by William Smith in the *American Magazine,* I (1758), 602–604, and by Nathaniel Evans, introduction to Godfrey's *Juvenile Poems* (1765).

The best bibliography is in Quinn's *A History of the American Drama . . . to the Civil War* (1943), p. 404.

# JAMES HALL
### *1793–1868*

SEPARATE WORKS

*Trial and Defense of First Lieutenant James Hall,* 1820; *Letters from the West,* 1828; *Winter Evenings,* 1829; *Legends of the West,* 1832; *The Soldier's Bride and Other Tales,* 1833; *The Harpe's Head: A Legend of Kentucky,* 1833; *Sketches of History, Life, and Manners in the West,* 1834; *Tales of the Border,* 1835; *A Memoir of the Public Services of William Henry Harrison of Ohio,* 1836; *Statistics of the West,* 1836; *History of the Indian Tribes of North America* (with Thomas L. McKenney), 1836–1844; *The Wilderness and the War Path,* 1846; *The West: Its Commerce and Navigation,* 1848.

Hall edited the *Illinois Gazette,* 1820–1822, the *Illinois Intelligencer,* 1829–

1832, and founded the first literary periodical west of the Ohio, the *Illinois Monthly Magazine* (1830), which became the *Western Monthly Magazine* when he moved it to Cincinnati in 1832; he continued as its editor until 1836. He edited *The Western Souvenir,* Cincinnati, 1829, the earliest annual published in the West; all its contributors were western authors.

### REPRINTS

Hall issued a revised edition of *Legends of the West* (1832), New York, 1853. *The Harpe's Head* (Philadelphia, 1833) was published as *Kentucky: A Tale,* London, 1834. The *History of the Indian Tribes of North America* (Philadelphia, 1836–1844, 3 vols.) was reprinted, Edinburgh, 1933–1934, with an introduction by Frederick W. Hodge.

### BIOGRAPHY AND CRITICISM

John T. Flanagan, *James Hall, Literary Pioneer of the Ohio Valley,* Minneapolis, 1941, is the first adequate study of Hall's career as writer. Other studies are Esther Shultz, "James Hall in Shawneetown," *Jour. Ill. State Hist. Soc.,* XXII (1929), 388–400—Hall's early life in Illinois; *idem,* "James Hall in Vandalia," *ibid.,* XXIII (1930), 92–112; R. P. Eckert, Jr., "The Path of the Pioneer," *Colophon,* n.s. No. 3 (1936), 404–421; John T. Flanagan, "An Early Collection of American Tales," *Huntington Lib. Quar.,* III (1939), 103–105—dealing with *Winter Evenings*; and *idem,* "James Hall and the Antiquarian and Historical Society of Illinois," *Jour. Ill. State Hist. Soc.,* XXXIV (1941), 439–452. See also Ralph L. Rusk, *The Literature of the Middle Western Frontier,* New York, 1925, 2 vols.

A collection of unpublished letters is in the library of the Historical and Philosophical Society of Ohio, at the University of Cincinnati.

A complete and accurate bibliography of Hall's writings is in Peter G. Thompson, *A Bibliography of the State of Ohio,* Cincinnati, 1880, pp. 140–145. Useful especially for secondary sources is the bibliographical listing in Flanagan, *James Hall* (1941), pp. 207–211.

# FITZ-GREENE HALLECK
*1790–1867*

### SEPARATE WORKS

*Poems, by Croaker, Croaker & Co., and Croaker, Jun.,* 1819; *Fanny,* 1819; *Marco Bozzaris,* 1825; *Alnwick Castle, with Other Poems,* 1827; *The Recorder, with Other Poems,* 1833; *Young America: A Poem,* 1865; *Lines to the Recorder,* 1866; *A Letter . . . to Joel Lewis Griffing,* 1921.

*Poems, by Croaker . . .*, written in collaboration with Joseph Rodman Drake, was reissued as *The Croakers,* New York, 1860.

COLLECTED WORKS

*The Poetical Works of Fitz-Greene Halleck,* New York, 1847, were reissued in 1852, 1858, and 1859. Each of the new editions included some new material. James G. Wilson edited *The Poetical Writings of Fitz-Greene Halleck: With Extracts from Those of Joseph Rodman Drake,* New York, 1869. In the same year Wilson published *The Life and Letters of Fitz-Greene Halleck.* Uncollected letters and poems were first published in Adkins's life (1930).

BIOGRAPHY AND CRITICISM

A full-length biography is Nelson F. Adkins, *Fitz-Greene Halleck: An Early Knickerbocker Wit and Poet,* New Haven, 1930. The sketch of Halleck in *Dict. Amer. Biog.* (1932) was contributed by Walter C. Bronson. See also Kendall B. Taft, "The First Printing of Halleck's 'The Winds of March Are Humming,'" *N.Y. Hist. Soc. Quar. Bul.,* XXVII (1943), 35-36.

PRIMARY SOURCES

Contemporary estimates of Halleck by his New York associates are Evert A. Duyckinck; *Fitz-Greene Halleck,* New York, 1868; Frederic S. Cozzens, *Fitz-Greene Halleck: A Memorial,* New York, 1868; William Cullen Bryant, *Some Notices of the Life and Writings of Fitz-Greene Halleck,* New York, 1869; Bayard Taylor, *Critical Essays and Literary Notes,* New York, 1880, pp. 233-257; and James G. Wilson, *Bryant and His Friends,* New York, 1886, pp. 245-279. See also George P. Lathrop, "Fitz-Greene Halleck," *Atl. Mo.,* XXXIX (1877), 718-729.

The fullest bibliography is that in Adkins's life (1930), pp. 376-387. It includes a checklist of portraits and engravings.

# ALEXANDER HAMILTON
## *1757-1804*

SEPARATE WORKS

*A Full Vindication of the Measures of the Congress,* 1774; *The Farmer Refuted,* 1775; *Letters from "Phocion,"* 1784; *The Federalist* (with Madison and Jay), 1787-1788; *Report on Public Credit,* 1790; *Report on Manufactures,* 1791; *Letters by "An American,"* 1792; *"Pacificus" Letters,* 1793; *"Americanus" Letters,* 1794; *"Camillus" Letters,* 1795-1796; *A Defence of the Treaty of Amity, Commerce, and Navigation* (with Rufus King and John Jay), 1795;

*Letter . . . Concerning the Public Conduct and Character of John Adams,*
1800; *An Address to the Electors of the State of New-York,* 1801; *The Examination of the President's Message . . . 1801,* 1802.

COLLECTED WORKS

The Federalist Edition of *The Works of Alexander Hamilton,* ed. by
Henry Cabot Lodge, New York, 1904, 12 vols., is at present the most authoritative. It was first issued, New York, 1885–1886, 9 vols. Some material not
included in the Lodge edition is published in John C. Hamilton, ed., *The
Works of Alexander Hamilton . . . ,* New York, 1850–1851, 7 vols. The
earliest collection is *The Works of Alexander Hamilton: Comprising His
Most Important Official Reports . . . ,* New York, 1810, 3 vols.

A new edition of Hamilton's works would add much material, especially
letters still uncollected. Those published are Gertrude Atherton, ed., *A Few
of Hamilton's Letters, Including His Description of the Great West Indian
Hurricane of 1772,* New York, 1903; *The Fate of Major André: A Letter
from Alexander Hamilton to John Laurens,* New York, 1916; and Arthur H.
Cole, ed., *Industrial and Commercial Correspondence of Alexander Hamilton, Anticipating His Report on Manufactures,* Chicago, 1928—exhibiting
Hamilton's careful investigation and his use of material.

EDITED TEXTS AND REPRINTS

Selections from Hamilton's official reports have been edited by Felix
Flügel, *Documents Relating to American Economic History . . . ,* Berkeley,
Calif., 1929. Samuel McKee, Jr., edited *Papers on Public Credit, Commerce,
and Finance,* New York, 1934. Selected writings are gathered in James T.
Adams, ed., *Jeffersonian Principles and Hamiltonian Principles: Extracts
from the Writings of Thomas Jefferson and Alexander Hamilton,* Boston,
1932, with introduction; and in Frederick C. Prescott, ed., *Alexander Hamilton and Thomas Jefferson: Representative Selections, with Introduction,
Bibliography, and Notes,* New York, 1934 (Amer. Writers Ser.).

Editions and reprints of the *Federalist* are numerous. The best edited text
remains that of Paul L. Ford, New York, 1898, well indexed. The text prepared by Henry Cabot Lodge, New York, 1888 and many later printings,
includes a bibliography. It was published in Everyman's Lib., 1911, and in the
Modern Lib., New York, 1941. John S. Bassett edited *Selections from the
Federalist,* with introduction, New York, 1921, for the Modern Student's Lib.

BIOGRAPHY AND CRITICISM

A recent nonpartisan life is Nathan Schachner, *Alexander Hamilton,* New
York, 1946. John T. Morse, Jr., *The Life of Alexander Hamilton,* Boston,
1876, 2 vols., still remains among the best narrative biographies, partisan but

balanced. Henry Cabot Lodge, *Alexander Hamilton,* Boston, 1882 (and later), though well informed, is strongly biased in favor of Hamiltonian principles. The early years, to 1776, are presented in George Shea, *The Life and Epoch of Alexander Hamilton: A Historical Study,* Boston, 1881 (3rd ed.), and in Henry D. Baker, *West Indian Birth and Boyhood of Alexander Hamilton* . . ., New York, 1929. Gertrude Atherton's well known novel *The Conqueror: A Dramatized Biography of Alexander Hamilton,* New York, 1902, is based on a study of sources. Some fresh interpretations, together with several inaccuracies, appear in Henry J. Ford, *Alexander Hamilton,* New York, 1920. John C. Hamilton's *History of the Republic . . . as Traced in the Writings of Alexander Hamilton and of His Contemporaries,* New York, 1857–1864, 7 vols., is not well digested, but the documentation is formidable. Both William Graham Sumner, *Alexander Hamilton,* New York, 1890, and James Schouler, *Alexander Hamilton,* Boston, 1901, are more impartial than Lodge and Morse. The best brief account is the sketch by Allan Nevins in *Dict. Amer. Biog.* (1932). Another recent life is David G. Loth, *Alexander Hamilton: Portrait of a Prodigy* . . ., New York, 1939. There is need for a biography that will make full use of the Hamilton Papers in the Library of Congress.

An analysis of Hamilton as political economist is Lynton K. Caldwell, *The Administrative Theories of Hamilton and Jefferson: Their Contribution to Thought on Public Administration,* Chicago, 1944. An important study of the impact abroad of Hamilton's fiscal policies is Pieter Jan van Winter, *Het Aandeel van den Amsterdamschen Handel aan den Opbouw van het Amerikaansche Gemeenebest* . . ., The Hague, 1927–1933, 2 vols. Charles A. Beard's *Economic Origins of Jeffersonian Democracy,* New York, 1915, is indispensable. Other studies of Hamilton as political economist are C. F. Dunbar, "Financial Precedents Followed by Hamilton," *Quar. Jour. Econ.,* III (1888), 32–59; Anson D. Morse, "Alexander Hamilton," *Pol. Sci. Quar.,* V (1890), 1–23; Edward G. Bourne, "Alexander Hamilton and Adam Smith," *Quar. Jour. Econ.,* VIII (1894), 328–344; Edward C. Lunt, "Hamilton as a Political Economist," *Jour. Pol. Econ.,* III (1895), 289–310.

Further studies of Hamilton as public servant are William S. Culbertson, *Alexander Hamilton: An Essay,* New Haven, 1911—an important interpretation; Alex Bein, *Die Staatsidee Alexander Hamiltons in ihrer Entstehung und Entwicklung* . . ., Munich, 1927; "Alexander Hamilton and the Federalist Party," in John Fiske, *Essays, Historical and Literary,* New York, 1902, I, 99–142; and Worthington C. Ford, ed., "Alexander Hamilton's Notes in the Federal Convention of 1787," *Amer. Hist. Rev.,* X (1904), 97–109.

The best general criticism of Hamilton's financial policy is Ugo Rabbeno, *The American Commercial Policy: Three Historical Essays,* London, 1895, Pt. III, chap. I—translated from the Italian. James O. Wettereau has dealt authoritatively with aspects of the subject in three essays: "Letters from Two Businessmen to Alexander Hamilton on Federal Fiscal Policy, November, 1789," *Jour. Economic and Business Hist.*, III (1931), 667–686; "New Light on the First Bank of the United States," *Pennsylvania Mag. Hist. and Biog.*, LXI (1937), 263–285—a pioneer study; and "Branches of the First Bank of the United States," *Jour. Economic Hist.*, II (1942), Dec. Supplement.

Hamilton's relation to the press is covered in Allan Nevins, *The Evening Post: A Century of Journalism*, New York, 1922.

Other studies important for students of Hamilton are Samuel F. Bemis, *Jay's Treaty: A Study in Commerce and Diplomacy*, New York, 1923; *idem*, *Pinckney's Treaty: A Study of America's Advantage from Europe's Distress, 1783–1800*, Baltimore, 1926; Robert A. East, *Business Enterprise in the American Revolutionary Era*, New York, 1938; and Leland D. Baldwin, *Whiskey Rebels: The Story of a Frontier Uprising*, Pittsburgh, 1939.

As a man of letters, Hamilton is treated in Vernon L. Parrington, *Main Currents in American Thought*, New York, I (1927), 292–307; Bower Aly, *The Rhetoric of Alexander Hamilton*, New York, 1941—an analysis of the Poughkeepsie speeches, with a bibl., pp. 199–213; and Ora Davisson, "The Early Pamphlets of Alexander Hamilton," *Quar. Jour. Speech*, XXX (1944), 168–173.

The public lives of Hamilton and Jefferson were so closely tied until Hamilton's death in 1804 that general studies touching upon one necessarily concern the other at many points. In addition to the studies here named, the student should consult the bibliographical essay on Jefferson, where he will find much material bearing upon the career and statecraft of Hamilton.

PRIMARY SOURCES

*The Life of Alexander Hamilton*, New York, 1834–1840, 2 vols., written by Hamilton's son, John C. Hamilton, supplies source material to 1787, at which point it stops. The *Life* is expanded and continued in John C. Hamilton's *History of the Republic* . . ., noticed earlier. Other published sources are William Coleman, *A Collection of the Facts and Documents, Relative to the Death of Major-General Alexander Hamilton* . . ., New York, 1804— reprinted, Boston, 1904; Edgar S. Maclay, ed., *Journal of William Maclay* . . ., New York, 1890—with many interesting sidelights on Hamilton; and Allan M. Hamilton, *The Intimate Life of Alexander Hamilton, Based Chiefly upon Original Family Letters and Other Documents* . . ., New York, 1910—containing some new material gathered by his grandson. The published writings of Washington, Adams, Jefferson, Madison, and Monroe, all are important sources in an interpretation of Hamilton.

Hamilton's manuscripts are for the greatest part in the Library of Congress, which purchased them in 1849. Some manuscripts are in the Stevens

Institute of Technology, Hoboken, N.J. Others are scattered throughout the country, notably in the Historical Society of Pennsylvania and the Connecticut Historical Society.

BIBLIOGRAPHY

No extensive listing has appeared since Paul L. Ford's *Bibliotheca Hamiltoniana: A List of Books Written by, or Relating to Alexander Hamilton*, New York, 1886. The listing should be brought to date. That in Prescott's *Representative Selections* (1934), pp. lxxiii–lxxix, is selective and annotated.

## JOEL CHANDLER HARRIS
### *1848–1908*

SEPARATE WORKS

*Uncle Remus: His Songs and His Sayings*, 1881; *Nights with Uncle Remus*, 1883; *Mingo and Other Sketches in Black and White*, 1884; *Free Joe*, 1887; *Daddy Jake the Runaway*, 1889; *Balaam and His Friends*, 1892; *On the Plantation*, 1892; *Uncle Remus and His Friends*, 1892; *Little Mr. Thimblefinger and His Queer Country*, 1894; *Mr. Rabbit at Home*, 1895; *Sister Jane*, 1896; *Stories of Georgia*, 1896; *The Story of Aaron*, 1896; *Aaron in the Wildwoods*, 1897; *Tales of the Home Folks in Peace and War*, 1898; *Plantation Pageants*, 1899; *The Chronicles of Aunt Minervy Ann*, 1899; *On the Wing of Occasions*, 1900; *Gabriel Tolliver*, 1902; *The Making of a Statesman*, 1902; *Wally Wanderoon and His Story-Telling Machine*, 1903; *A Little Union Scout*, 1904; *The Tar-Baby and Other Rhymes of Uncle Remus*, 1904; *Told by Uncle Remus: New Stories of the Old Plantation*, 1905; *Uncle Remus and Brer Rabbit*, 1907; *The Bishop and the Boogerman*, 1909; *The Shadow Between His Shoulder-Blades*, 1909; *Uncle Remus and the Little Boy*, 1910; *Uncle Remus Returns*, 1918; *The Witch Wolf*, 1921.

EDITED TEXTS AND REPRINTS

A convenient collection is that edited by Julia C. Harris, *Joel Chandler Harris: Editor and Essayist: Miscellaneous Literary, Political, and Social Writings*, Chapel Hill, N.C., 1931. Robert L. Wiggins, *The Life of Joel Chandler Harris . . .*, Nashville, Tenn., 1918, is a collection of Harris's early significant writings.

The "Uncle Remus" stories have been frequently reprinted. *Uncle Remus: His Songs and His Sayings* was issued, New York, 1931, for the Modern Lit. Ser. Recent reprints are *Tales from Uncle Remus*, Boston, 1935, and *Brer Rabbit: Stories from Uncle Remus*, New York, 1941.

BIOGRAPHY AND CRITICISM

Robert L. Wiggins, *The Life of Joel Chandler Harris from Obscurity in Boyhood to Fame in Early Manhood* (1918), is a study of Harris's literary development before the publication of *Uncle Remus* (1881). The standard biography is that by his daughter-in-law, Julia C. Harris, *The Life and Letters of Joel Chandler Harris,* Boston, 1918. A recent life is Alvin F. Harlow, *Joel Chandler Harris (Uncle Remus): Plantation Storyteller,* New York, 1941. The sketch in *Dict. Amer. Biog.* (1932) is by George H. Genzmer. Among recent critical estimates are "Joel Chandler Harris and the Fiction of Folklore," in Arthur H. Quinn, *American Fiction,* New York, 1936, pp. 374–384; John D. Wade, "Profits and Losses in the Life of Joel Chandler Harris," *Amer. Rev.,* I (1933), 17–35; "Joel Chandler Harris," in Charles Alphonso Smith, *Southern Literary Studies,* Chapel Hill, N.C., 1927, pp. 128–157; and "Uncle Remus Arrives," in John H. Nelson, *The Negro Character in American Literature,* Lawrence, Kans., 1926, pp. 107–119.

Earlier general studies are "Joel Chandler Harris," in William M. Baskervill, *Southern Writers: Biographical and Critical Studies,* Nashville, 1902, pp. ¡1–88; Ray Stannard Baker, "Joel Chandler Harris," *Outlook,* LXXVIII (1904), 595–603; "Joel Chandler Harris," in Harry A. Toulmin, *Social Historians,* Boston, 1911, pp. 133–164; H. E. Harman, "Joel Chandler Harris: The Prose Poet of the South," *So. Atl. Quar.,* XVII (1918), 243–248; and T. E. Ferguson, "Joel Chandler Harris," *Texas Rev.,* VI (1921), 214–221.

Special studies are F. M. Warren, " 'Uncle Remus' and 'The Roman de Renard,' " *Modern Language Notes,* V (1890), 258–270; Elsie C. Parsons, "Joel Chandler Harris and Negro Folklore," *Dial,* LXVI (1919), 491–493; John Stafford, "Patterns of Meaning in *Nights with Uncle Remus,*" *Amer. Lit.,* XVIII (1946), 89–108; and T. H. English, "Joel Chandler Harris's Earliest Literary Project," *Emory Univ. Quar.,* II (1946), 176–185.

Useful background material is Francis P. Gaines, *The Southern Plantation: A Study in the Development and the Accuracy of a Tradition,* New York, 1924; and Howard W. Odum, *An American Epoch,* New York, 1930.

PRIMARY SOURCES

The major manuscript collection is in the Emory University Library, at Atlanta. Some material is in the Duke University Library.

Reminiscences of Harris are in James C. Derby, *Fifty Years Among Authors,* New York, 1884, pp. 433–440; Lucian L. Knight, *Reminiscences of Famous Georgians,* Atlanta, I (1907), 482–492; Ivy L. Lee, comp., *"Uncle Remus": Joel Chandler Harris as Seen and Remembered by a Few of His Friends . . . ,* n.p., 1908; and Caroline Ticknor, *Glimpses of Authors,* Boston, 1922, pp. 152–168.

BIBLIOGRAPHY

The bibliography in Julia C. Harris's *Life* (1918), pp. 603–610, was compiled by Katherine H. Wootten (1907) and revised by Julia C. Harris. There is a listing of primary and secondary items in Robert L. Wiggins's *Life* (1918), pp. 429–444. An account of certain rare printings is in Julia C. Harris, "Uncle Remus at Home and Abroad," *Southern Lit. Mess.*, II (1940), 84–86.

# (FRANCIS) BRET(T) HARTE
### *1836–1902*

SEPARATE WORKS

*The Lost Galleon and Other Tales*, 1867; *Condensed Novels*, 1867; *The Luck of Roaring Camp*, 1870; *Plain Language from Truthful James (The Heathen Chinee)*, 1870; *Poems*, 1871; *East and West Poems*, 1871; *Stories of the Sierras*, 1872; *The Little Drummer*, 1872; *Mrs. Skaggs's Husbands*, 1873; *Tales of the Argonauts*, 1875; *Echoes of the Foot-Hills*, 1875; *Wan Lee: The Pagan*, 1876; *Two Men of Sandy Bar*, 1876; *Gabriel Conroy*, 1875–1876; *Thankful Blossom*, 1877; *The Story of a Mine*, 1878; *Drift from Two Shores*, 1878; *The Twins of Table Mountain*, 1879; *Poetical Works*, 1880; *Flip and Found at Blazing Star*, 1882; *In the Carquinez Woods*, 1883; *On the Frontier*, 1884; *By Shore and Sedge*, 1885; *Maruja*, 1885; *The Queen of the Pirate Isle*, 1886; *Snow-Bound at Eagle's*, 1886; *The Crusade of the Excelsior*, 1887; *A Millionaire of Rough-and-Ready*, 1887; *A Phyllis of the Sierras*, 1888; *The Argonauts of North Liberty*, 1888; *Cressy*, 1889; *The Heritage of Dedlow Marsh*, 1889; *A Ward of the Golden Gate*, 1890; *A Waif of the Plains*, 1890; *A Sappho of Green Springs*, 1891; *A First Family of Tasajara*, 1891; *Colonel Starbottle's Client*, 1892; *Susy: A Story of the Plains*, 1893; *Sally Dows*, 1893; *A Protégée of Jack Hamlin's*, 1894; *The Bell-Ringer of Angel's*, 1894; *Clarence*, 1895; *In a Hollow of the Hills*, 1895; *Poetical Works of Bret Harte*, 1896; *Barker's Luck and Other Stories*, 1896; *Three Partners*, 1897; *Some Later Verses*, 1898; *Tales of Trail and Town*, 1898; *Stories in Light and Shadow*, 1898; *Mr. Jack Hamlin's Meditation*, 1899; *From Sand Hill to Pine*, 1900; *Under the Redwoods*, 1901; *Condensed Novels: Second Series*, 1902; *Sue: A Play in Three Acts*, 1902; *Openings in the Old Trail*, 1902; *Trent's Trust*, 1903; *The Story of Enriquez*, 1924.

COLLECTED WORKS

Harte himself began the collection and revision of *The Complete Works of Bret Harte*, London, 1880–1912, 10 vols. The Standard Library Edition, *The Writings of Bret Harte*, Boston, 1896–1914, 19 vols., includes in the final volume a biographical sketch, glossary of Far West terms, and indexes of characters. The Argonaut Edition, *The Works of Bret Harte,* New York, 1914, 25 vols., includes *By Shore and Sedge* and *On the Frontier,* omitted from the Standard Edition.

Charles M. Kozlay edited *Stories and Poems and Other Uncollected Writings by Bret Harte,* Boston, 1914, with an introductory account of Harte's early contributions to the California press.

The last collected edition of Harte's poetry is *The Complete Poetical Works of Bret Harte,* Boston, 1899. Other gatherings are Charles M. Kozlay, ed., *The Lectures of Bret Harte,* Brooklyn, 1909; *idem,* ed., *Sketches of the Sixties,* San Francisco, 1926—Bret Harte (and Mark Twain) material from the *Californian,* 1864–1867 (a new ed., 1927, contains added titles); and Geoffrey Bret Harte, ed., *The Letters of Bret Harte,* Boston, 1926. Gleanings are Bradford A. Booth, ed., "Unpublished Letters of Bret Harte," *Amer. Lit.,* XVI (1944), 131–142.

EDITED TEXTS AND REPRINTS

Selections have been issued in *The Luck of Roaring Camp . . . and Selected Stories and Poems,* New York, 1928, with introduction by George R. Stewart, Jr.; *The Luck of Roaring Camp, Californian Tales and Poems . . . ,* London, 1929 (Everyman's Lib.); *Concerning "Condensed Novels,"* Stanford Univ., Calif., 1929, with introduction and bibliographical notes by Nathan Van Patten; *The Heathen Chinee; Plain Language from Truthful James,* San Francisco, 1934, with introduction by Ina Coolbrith and bibliography by Robert E. Cowan; *Bret Harte's Stories of the Old West,* selected by W. Harper and A. M. Peters, Boston, 1940; *Tales of the Gold Rush,* New York, 1944, with introduction by Oscar Lewis.

A serviceable collection is Joseph B. Harrison, ed., *Bret Harte: Representative Selections, with Introduction, Bibliography, and Notes,* New York, 1941 (Amer. Writers Ser.).

BIOGRAPHY AND CRITICISM

The authoritative life is George R. Stewart, Jr., *Bret Harte: Argonaut and Exile,* Boston, 1931. Earlier accounts are Henry W. Boynton, *Bret Harte,* New York, 1903—vigorous and discriminating if not sympathetic; Henry C. Merwin, *The Life of Bret Harte, with Some Account of the California Pioneers,* Boston, 1911—a narrative biography. A standard estimate is Arthur H. Quinn, *American Fiction,* New York, 1936, pp. 232–242.

Special studies are "Bret Harte," in John Erskine, *Leading American Novelists,* New York, 1910, pp. 325–369; Heinrich Kessler, "Die Verwendung der Mundart bei Bret Harte," in *Beiträge zur Erforschung der Sprache . . . ,*

Breslau, V (1928), 181–262; Archer B. Hulbert, *Forty-niners: The Chronicle of the California Trail,* Boston, 1931, pp. 323–333—a list of publications and manuscripts dealing with the Overland Trail and the California of the Argonauts; Joseph B. Harrison, *Bret Harte: Representative Selections . . . ,* New York, 1941, pp. xi–cxii—a critical essay. Franklin Walker, *San Francisco's Literary Frontier,* New York, 1939, contains a dependable account of Harte's career, especially in San Francisco.

PRIMARY SOURCES

The two accounts of Thomas Edgar Pemberton, *Bret Harte: A Treatise and a Tribute,* London, 1900, and *The Life of Bret Harte,* New York, 1903, are written by a friend who knew Harte especially in his later years. William D. Howells and others, "Reminiscences of Bret Harte," *Overland Mo.,* XL (1902), 220–239; and Thomas D. Beasley, *A Tramp Through the Bret Harte Country,* San Francisco, 1914, supply further data.

The chief depositories of Bret Harte's manuscripts are the William Andrews Clark Memorial Library of the University of California at Los Angeles, and the Morgan Library. Other material is in the Henry E. Huntington Library.

BIBLIOGRAPHY

George R. Stewart, Jr., provides a bibliography in his life, *Bret Harte* (1931), pp. 337–365; and has also prepared "A Bibliography of the Writings of Bret Harte in the Magazines and Newspapers of California, 1857–1871," *Univ. Calif. Pub. in English,* III (1933), 119–170. Further data are in Joseph Gaer, ed., *Bret Harte* (Calif. Lit. Research Monograph, No. 10, 1935). Clarence Gohdes has compiled "A Check-List of Bret Harte's Works in Book Form Published in the British Isles," *Bul. Bibl.,* XVIII (1943), 19, 36–39. The listing in Joseph B. Harrison, *Bret Harte: Representative Selections,* New York, 1941, pp. cxiii–cxxv, is selective and annotated.

# NATHANIEL HAWTHORNE
## *1804–1864*

SEPARATE WORKS

*Fanshawe: A Tale,* 1828; *Peter Parley's Universal History,* 1837; *Twice-Told Tales,* 1837; *Grandfather's Chair,* 1841; *Famous Old People, Being the Second Epoch of Grandfather's Chair,* 1841; *Liberty Tree, with the Last Words of Grandfather's Chair,* 1841; *Biographical Stories for Children,* 1842; *The Celestial Rail-Road,* 1843; *Mosses from an Old Manse,* 1846; *The Scarlet*

*Letter*, 1850; *True Stories from History and Biography*, 1851; *The House of the Seven Gables*, 1851; *A Wonder-Book for Girls and Boys*, 1852; *The Snow-Image and Other Twice-Told Tales*, 1852; *The Blithedale Romance*, 1852; *Life of Franklin Pierce*, 1852; *Tanglewood Tales for Girls and Boys*, 1853; *The Marble Faun*, 1860; *Our Old Home*, 1863; *Pansie: A Fragment*, 1864; *Septimius Felton; or, The Elixir of Life*, 1872; *The Dolliver Romance and Other Pieces*, 1876; *Fanshawe and Other Pieces*, 1876; *Dr. Grimshawe's Secret*, 1883; *The Ghost of Doctor Harris*, 1900.

"The Ancestral Footstep" was first published as part of the volume of "Sketches and Studies" in *The Complete Works* (1883).

COLLECTED WORKS

There is pressing need for a new edition of Hawthorne's works, one which will incorporate edited texts of his journals, notebooks, and correspondence. Such an edition must wait upon publication of the remaining unedited notebooks (French and Italian) now under way. At present *The Complete Works of Nathaniel Hawthorne, with Introductory Notes*, Boston, 1883, 12 vols., ed. by George P. Lathrop is regarded as the standard (Riverside) edition. The Autograph Edition of the *Complete Writings* was published in Boston, 1900, 22 vols.

The editing of the notebooks was first undertaken by Mrs. Hawthorne as follows: *Passages from the American Note-Books*, Boston, 1868; *Passages from the Note-Books of the Late Nathaniel Hawthorne*, London, 1869; *Passages from the English Note-Books*, Boston, 1870, 2 vols.; *Passages from the French and Italian Note-Books*, Boston, 1872, 2 vols. Mrs. Hawthorne bowdlerized the manuscript text, and omitted many personal allusions. Excellent editions of *The American Notebooks of Nathaniel Hawthorne*, New Haven, 1932, and of *The English Notebooks*, New York, 1941, have been edited from manuscript sources by Randall Stewart.

Further uncollected items are Samuel T. Pickard, ed., *Hawthorne's First Diary, with an Account of Its Discovery*, Boston, 1897, the authenticity of which is still in question; Newton Arvin, ed., *The Heart of Hawthorne's Journals*, Boston, 1929—the text needs reediting in the light of more recent studies; Elizabeth L. Chandler, "Hawthorne's 'Spectator,'" *New Eng. Quar.*, IV (1931), 288–330—a reprint of a manuscript weekly of verse and prose in 1820; Norman H. Pearson, "A Sketch by Hawthorne," *New Eng. Quar.*, VI (1933), 136–144; Donald C. Gallup, "On Hawthorne's Authorship of 'The Battle-Omen,'" *New Eng. Quar.*, IX (1936), 690–699—a reprint of a sketch probably by Hawthorne; and Arlin Turner, *Hawthorne as Editor: Selections from His Writings in The American Magazine for Useful and Entertaining Knowledge*, University, La., 1941. Randall Stewart edited "Hawthorne's Contributions to *The Salem Advertiser," Amer. Lit.*, V (1934), 327–341, and "Two Uncollected Reviews by Hawthorne," *New Eng. Quar.*, IX (1936), 504–509. See also Nelson F. Adkins, "The Early Projected Works of Nathaniel Hawthorne," *Papers Bibl. Soc. Amer.*, XXXIX (1945), 119–155.

## LETTERS

Hawthorne is notably distinguished as·a letter writer, though his letters at present are uncollected. Those already published may be found scattered as follows: Julian Hawthorne, *Nathaniel Hawthorne and His Wife*, Boston, 1885, 2 vols.; Samuel Longfellow, *Life of Henry Wadsworth Longfellow*, Boston, 1887; Horatio Bridge, *Personal Recollections of Nathaniel Hawthorne*, New York, 1893; *Love Letters of Nathaniel Hawthorne, 1839–41 and 1841–63* (to Sophia Peabody), Chicago, 1907, with preface by Roswell Field; *Letters of Hawthorne to William D. Ticknor, 1851–1864*, Newark, N.J., 1910, 2 vols.; Caroline Ticknor, *Hawthorne and His Publisher*, Boston, 1913; Randall Stewart, "Hawthorne and Politics: Unpublished Letters to William B. Pike," *New Eng. Quar.*, V (1932), 237–263; Edward B. Hungerford, "Hawthorne Gossips About Salem," *New Eng. Quar.*, VI (1933), 445–469— letters to his cousin John S. Dike, 1830–1831; Manning Hawthorne, "Nathaniel Hawthorne Prepares for College," *New Eng. Quar.*, XI (1938), 66–88; *idem*, "Hawthorne's Early Years," *Essex Institute Hist. Coll.*, LXXIV (1938), 1–21; *idem*, "Hawthorne and Utopian Socialism," *New Eng. Quar.*, XII (1939), 726–730; *idem*, "Nathaniel and Elizabeth Hawthorne, Editors," *Colophon*, New Graphic Ser., No. 3 (1939), 12 pp.; Harold Blodgett, "Hawthorne as Poetry Critic: Six Unpublished Letters to Lewis Mansfield," *Amer. Lit.*, XII (1940), 173–184; Randall Stewart, "The Hawthornes at the Wayside, 1860–1864," *More Books*, XIX (1944), 263–279; *idem*, "Hawthorne's Last Illness and Death," *ibid.*, XIX (1944), 303–313. A brief description of the 164 letters and fragments of letters written to Sophia Peabody Hawthorne from 1839 to 1863, now part of the Huntington Library collection, is given by Randall Stewart, "Letters to Sophia," *Huntington Lib. Quar.*, VII (1944), 387–395.

## EDITED TEXTS AND REPRINTS

Newton Arvin, ed., *The Heart of Hawthorne's Journals* (1929), and Arlin Turner, ed., *Hawthorne as Editor: Selections from His Writings . . .* (1941), have been described above among the collected works, as have *The American Notebooks* (1932) and *The English Notebooks* (1941), excellently edited by Randall Stewart. Arvin's edition of *Hawthorne's Short Stories*, New York, 1946, is especially useful for its text of twenty-nine stories, and for the introduction. A brief text of selections, edited chiefly from the sketches and tales, is Austin Warren, *Nathaniel Hawthorne: Representative Selections, with Introduction, Bibliography, and Notes,* Amer. Writers Ser., New York, 1934.

Satisfactory edited texts of separate works are yet to be made. The text of *Dr. Grimshawe's Secret* was published by Julian Hawthorne, Boston, 1883, with a preface and notes. The following reprints have been published:

*The Blithedale Romance,* London, 1912 (Everyman's Lib.). *The House of the Seven Gables,* London, 1907 (Everyman's Lib.); London, 1924 (World's Classics); New York, 1930 (New Pocket Classics). *The Marble Faun,* London, 1910 (Everyman's Lib.). *Mosses from an Old Manse,* New York, 1908 (Pocket Classics). *The Scarlet Letter,* London, 1907 (Everyman's Lib.); ed. by Stuart P. Sherman, New York, 1919 (Modern Student's Lib.); New York, 1920 (Pocket Classics); New York, 1927 (Modern Lib.); New York, 1927 (Modern Readers' Ser.); ed. E. E. Leisy, New York, 1929 (Nelson's English Ser.). *Tanglewood Tales,* New York, 1907 (Pocket Classics). *Twice-Told Tales,* London, 1911 (Everyman's Lib.). *Selections from Twice-Told Tales,* New York, 1930 (New Pocket Classics). *Wonder-Book,* New York, 1905 (Pocket Classics). *A Wonder Book and Tanglewood Tales,* London, 1907 (Everyman's Lib.).

Collections of tales and romances are *Tales by Nathaniel Hawthorne,* ed. by Carl Van Doren, London, 1928 (World's Classics); *The Great Stone Face and Other Tales of the White Mountains,* Boston, 1935; *Legends of the Province House,* New York, 1936; *The Complete Novels and Selected Tales of Nathaniel Hawthorne,* ed. by Norman H. Pearson, New York, 1939 (Modern Lib.); and *The Best Known Works of Nathaniel Hawthorne, Including The Scarlet Letter, The House of the Seven Gables, The Best of the Twice-Told Tales,* Garden City, N.Y., 1941 (Blue Ribbon Books).

### BIOGRAPHY AND CRITICISM

Few good biographical estimates of Hawthorne have been published, and a definitive life cannot be written until editions of the letters and journals are available.

The best general estimate of Hawthorne is still that of George E. Woodberry, *Nathaniel Hawthorne,* Boston, 1902. Other general studies are Henry James, *Hawthorne,* New York, 1879; Moncure D. Conway, *Life of Nathaniel Hawthorne,* London, 1890; Newton Arvin, *Hawthorne,* Boston, 1929; Edward A. Mather Jackson, *Nathaniel Hawthorne: A Modest Man,* New York, 1940.

Contributions to special biographical studies are Manning Hawthorne, "Nathaniel Hawthorne at Bowdoin," *New Eng. Quar.,* XIII (1940), 246–279; G. E. Jepson, "Hawthorne in the Boston Custom House," *Bookman,* XIX

(1904), 573–580; W. S. Nevins, "Nathaniel Hawthorne's Removal from the Salem Custom House," *Essex Institute Hist. Coll.*, LIII (1917), 97–132; John B. Osborne, "Nathaniel Hawthorne as American Consul," *Bookman*, XVI (1902), 461–464; Arlin Turner, "Hawthorne at Martha's Vineyard," *New Eng. Quar.*, XI (1938), 394–400. See also the section "Letters," *ante*, p. 546.

Appraisals of Hawthorne by critics and men of letters, significant to the extent that the estimates are made by spokesmen for their times, are Edgar Allan Poe's reviews of *Twice-Told Tales* in *Graham's Magazine*, XX (1842), 254, 298–300, hailing Hawthorne's "originality," and Poe's later unfavorable reaction, "Tale Writing: Nathaniel Hawthorne," *Godey's Lady's Book*, XXXV (1847), 252–256; "Hawthorne," in Edwin P. Whipple, *Character and Characteristic Men*, Boston, 1866, pp. 218–242—an early and an acute analysis of Hawthorne's mind and art; "Nathaniel Hawthorne," in Leslie Stephen, *Hours in a Library*, New York, 1875, I, 204–237; Anthony Trollope, "The Genius of Nathaniel Hawthorne," *No. Amer. Rev.*, CXXIX (1879), 203–222; "Hawthorne," in Lewis E. Gates, *Studies and Appreciations*, New York, 1900, pp. 92–109; "The Solitude of Hawthorne" and "The Origins of Hawthorne and Poe," in Paul E. More, *Shelburne Essays*, first series, New York, 1904, pp. 22–50, 51–70; "Hawthorne," in William C. Brownell, *American Prose Masters*, New York, 1909, pp. 63–130; John Erskine, "Hawthorne," in *Camb. Hist. Amer. Lit.*, II (1918), 16–31; "Hawthorne," in George E. Woodberry, *Literary Memoirs . . .* , New York, 1921, pp. 201–214; and "Hawthorne: A Puritan Critic of Puritanism," in Stuart P. Sherman, *Americans*, New York, 1922, pp. 122–152. More recent estimates will be found in Herbert W. Schneider, *The Puritan Mind*, New York, 1930, pp. 256–264; "Hawthorne in Salem," in Van Wyck Brooks, *The Flowering of New England . . .* , New York, 1936, pp. 210–227; and "Nathaniel Hawthorne," in Carl Van Doren, *The American Novel . . .* , New York, 1940, pp. 58–83.

Analysis of Hawthorne's art is ably set forth by F(rancis) O. Matthiessen, "Hawthorne," in *American Renaissance . . .* , New York, 1941, pp. 179–368. Other important studies are Edward Davidson, "The Last Phase of Hawthorne's Art" (unpublished thesis, Yale Univ., 1940)—a critical examination of the manuscripts of the posthumous novels, with a discussion of their importance in the decline of Hawthorne's artistic powers; Leland Schubert, *Hawthorne the Artist: Fine-Art Devices in Fiction*, Chapel Hill, N.C., 1944 —analysis of his writings as an expression of his understanding of the technique of art; and Lawrence S. Hall, *Hawthorne: Critic of Society*, New Haven, 1944—on Hawthorne as an observer of his own times. Brief special studies are "Hawthorne's Supernaturalism," in Prosser H. Frye, *Literary Reviews and Criticisms*, New York, 1908, pp. 114–129; Arlin Turner, "Hawthorne's Literary Borrowings," *PMLA*, LI (1936), 543–562; *idem*, "Hawthorne as Self-Critic," *So. Atl. Quar.*, XXXVII (1938), 132–138; *idem*, "Hawthorne's Methods of Using His Source Materials," in *Studies for William A. Read*, University, La., 1940, pp. 301–312; Manning Hawthorne, "Hawthorne and 'The Man of God,'" *Colophon*, II (1937), n.s., no. 2, pp. 262–282; "Maule's Curse, or Hawthorne and the Problem of Allegory," in Yvor Winters, *Maule's Curse . . .*, Norfolk, Conn., 1938, pp. 3–22; Vladimir Astrov, "Hawthorne and Dostoevski as Explorers of the Human Conscience," *New Eng. Quar.*, XV (1942), 296–319; Walter Blair, "Color, Light and Shadow in Hawthorne's Fiction," *New Eng. Quar.*, XV (1942), 74–94; Neal F. Doubleday, "Hawthorne's Satirical Allegory," *College Eng.*, III (1942), 325–337; and Charles H. Foster, "Hawthorne's Literary Theory," *PMLA*, LVII (1942), 241–254.

Sources and themes have been explored by Elizabeth L. Chandler, *A Study of the Sources of the Tales and Romances Written by Nathaniel Hawthorne Before 1853*, Northampton, Mass., 1926 (Vol. VII, no. 4, *Smith Coll. Studies in Modern Languages*)—limited to notebooks and letters; Randall Stewart, ed., *The American Notebooks*, New Haven, 1932, and *The English Notebooks*, New York, 1941—with prefaces important for their study of sources and themes in the novels. Other brief general source studies are Randall Stewart, "Hawthorne and *The Faerie Queene*," *Philological Quar.*, XII (1933), 196–206; Neal F. Doubleday, "Hawthorne's Criticism of New England Life," *College Eng.*, II (1941), 639–653; and Philip Rahv, "The Dark Lady of Salem," *Partisan Rev.*, VIII (1941), 362–381. Studies bearing upon individual tales and novels are Arlin Turner, "Autobiographical Elements in Hawthorne's *The Blithedale Romance*," *Univ. Texas Studies in Eng.*, XV (1935), 39–63; "Hawthorne at North Adams," in Bliss Perry, *The Amateur Spirit*, Boston, 1904, pp. 119–139—background for "Ethan Brand"; Randall Stewart, "Ethan Brand," *Sat. Rev. Lit.*, V (Apr. 27, 1929), 967—a study of sources; John A. Kouwenhoven, "Hawthorne's Notebooks and *Doctor Grimshawe's Secret*," *Amer. Lit.*, V (1934), 349–358; Louise Hastings, "An Origin for 'Dr. Heidegger's Experiment,'" *Amer. Lit.*, IX (1938), 403–410; Neal F. Doubleday, "The Theme of Hawthorne's 'Fancy's Show Box,'" *Amer. Lit.*, X (1938), 341–343; Philip E. Burnham, "Hawthorne's *Fanshawe* and Bowdoin College," *Essex Institute Hist. Coll.*, LXXX (1944), 131–138; G. Harrison Orians, "Scott and Hawthorne's *Fanshawe*," *New Eng. Quar.*, XI (1938), 388–394; J. S. Goldstein, "The Literary Source of Hawthorne's *Fanshawe*," *Modern Language Notes*, LX (1945), 1–8; Alfred A. Kern, "The Sources of Hawthorne's *Feathertop*," *PMLA*, XLVI (1931), 1253–1259; G. Harrison Orians, "The Sources and Themes of Hawthorne's 'The Gentle Boy,'" *New Eng. Quar.*, XIV (1941), 664–678; Karl G. Pfeiffer, "The Prototype of the Poet in 'The Great Stone Face,'" *Research Studies State Coll. of Wash.* IX

(1941), 100–108; G. Harrison Orians, "The Angel of Hadley in Fiction: A Study of the Sources of Hawthorne's 'The Grey Champion,'" *Amer. Lit.,* IV (1932), 257–269; Harold P. Miller, "Hawthorne Surveys His Contemporaries," *Amer. Lit.,* XII (1940), 228–235—on revising "The Hall of Fantasy"; Thomas M. Griffiths, "'Montpelier' and 'Seven Gables': Knox's Estate and Hawthorne's Novel," *New Eng. Quar.,* XVI (1943), 432–443; Thomas M. Griffiths, *Maine Sources in "The House of the Seven Gables,"* Waterville, Me., 1945–49 pp., documented; Fannye N. Cherry, "A Note on the Source of Hawthorne's 'Lady Eleanore's Mantle,'" *Amer. Lit.,* VI (1935), 437–439; Dorothy Waples, "Suggestions for Interpreting *The Marble Faun,*" *Amer. Lit.,* XIII (1941), 224–239; Nathalia Wright, "Hawthorne and the Praslin Murder," *New Eng. Quar.,* XV (1942), 5–14—on *The Marble Faun*; G. Harrison Orians, "Hawthorne and 'The Maypole of Merry Mount,'" *Modern Language Notes,* LIII (1938), 159–167; Alice L. Cooke, "The Shadow of Martinus Scriblerus in Hawthorne's 'The Prophetic Pictures,'" *New Eng. Quar.,* XVII (1944), 597–604; Amy L. Reed, "Self-Portraiture in the Works of Nathaniel Hawthorne," *Studies in Philol.,* XXIII (1926), 40–54—sources for "The Prophetic Pictures"; G. Harrison Orians, "The Source of Hawthorne's 'Roger Malvin's Burial,'" *Amer. Lit.,* X (1938), 313–318; Frederic I. Carpenter, "Scarlet A Minus," *College Eng.,* V (1944), 173–180—on *The Scarlet Letter*; John C. Gerber, "Form and Content in *The Scarlet Letter,*" *New Eng. Quar.,* XVII (1944), 25–55; Herbert Read, "Hawthorne," *Hound and Horn,* III (1930), 213–229—possible source for *The Scarlet Letter*; Julian Hawthorne, "The Making of *The Scarlet Letter,*" *Bookman,* LXXIV (1931), 401–411; William L. Werner, "The First Edition of Hawthorne's *The Scarlet Letter,*" *Amer. Lit.,* V (1934), 359; Neal F. Doubleday, "Hawthorne's Hester and Feminism," *PMLA,* LIV (1939), 825–827; Françoise Dony, "Romantisme et Puritanisme chez Hawthorne, à propos de la 'Lettre Pourpre,'" *Etudes Anglaises,* IV (1940), 15–30; M. A. De Wolfe Howe, "The Tale of Tanglewood," *Yale Rev.,* XXXII (1942), 323–336; Horace E. Thorner, "Hawthorne, Poe, and a Literary Ghost," *New Eng. Quar.,* VII (1934), 146–154—on Poe's charge of plagiarism in *Twice-Told Tales*; G. Harrison Orians, "New England Witchcraft in Fiction," *Amer. Lit.,* II (1930), 54–71—on sources for "Young Goodman Brown"; Fannye N. Cherry, "The Sources of Hawthorne's 'Young Goodman Brown,'" *Amer. Lit.,* V (1934), 342–348; and Richard H. Fogle, "Ambiguity and Clarity in Hawthorne's 'Young Goodman Brown,'" *New Eng. Quar.,* XVIII (1945), 448–465.

Hawthorne's reading background, and possible influences upon him, are studied in "Books Read by Hawthorne, 1828–50: From the 'Charge Books' of the Salem Athenaeum," *Essex Institute Hist. Coll.,* LXVIII (1932), 65–87; Austin Warren, "Hawthorne's Reading," *New Eng. Quar.,* VIII (1935), 480–497; Alice L. Cooke, "Some Evidences of Hawthorne's Indebtedness to

Swift," *Univ. Texas Studies in Eng.*, No. 3826 (1938), 140–162; William P. Randel, "Hawthorne, Channing, and Margaret Fuller," *Amer. Lit.*, X (1939), 472–476; M. J. Griswold, "American Quaker History in the Works of Whittier, Hawthorne, and Longfellow," *Americana*, XXXIV (1940), 220–263; J. Chesley Mathews, "Hawthorne's Knowledge of Dante," *Univ. Texas Studies in Eng.*, No. 4026 (1940), 157–165; "Nathaniel Hawthorne," in John P. Pritchard, *Return to the Fountains* . . ., Durham, N.C., 1942, pp. 68–78— on the influence of the classics; and Frank Davidson, "Hawthorne's Hive of Honey," *Modern Language Notes*, LXI (1946), 14–21.

Other studies include Randall Stewart, "Hawthorne in England: The Patriotic Motive in the Note-Books," *New Eng. Quar.*, VIII (1935), 3–13; *idem*, "Hawthorne's Speeches at Civic Banquets," *Amer. Lit.*, VII (1936), 415–423; *idem*, "Hawthorne and the Civil War," *Studies in Philol.*, XXXIV (1937), 91–106; Bertha Faust, *Hawthorne's Contemporaneous Reputation: A Study of Literary Opinion in America and England, 1828–1864*, Washington, 1940; Leroy H. Buckingham, "Hawthorne and the British Income Tax," *Amer. Lit.*, XI (1940), 451–453; Manning Hawthorne, "The Friendship Between Hawthorne and Longfellow," *English Leaflet*, XXXIX (1940), 25–30; Robert F. Metzdorf, "Hawthorne's Suit Against Ripley and Dana," *Amer. Lit.*, XII (1940), 235–241; Neal F. Doubleday, "Hawthorne and Literary Nationalism," *Amer. Lit.*, XII (1941), 447–453; Arlin Turner, "Hawthorne and Reform," *New Eng. Quar.*, XV (1942), 700–714; L. J. Merrill, "The Puritan Policeman," *Amer. Sociological Rev.*, X (1945), 766–776; Neal F. Doubleday, "Hawthorne's Use of Three Gothic Patterns," *College Eng.*, VII (1946), 250–262; Gilbert P. Voight, "Hawthorne and the Roman Catholic Church," *New Eng. Quar.*, XIX (1946), 394–398; Jane Lundblad, *Nathaniel Hawthorne and the Tradition of Gothic Romance (Essays and Studies on Amer. Lang. and Lit.*, IV), Amer. Institute Univ. Upsala, 1946; Harrison Hayford, "Hawthorne, Melville, and the Sea," *New Eng. Quar.*, XIX (1946), 435–452; Allan Pryce-Jones, "Hawthorne in England," *Life and Letters*, L (1946), 71–80; and Manning Hawthorne, "A Glimpse of Hawthorne's Boyhood," *Essex Institute Hist. Coll.*, LXXXIII (1947), 178–184.

PRIMARY SOURCES

Among printed studies, reminiscent and critical, the following are useful as source material: Mary R. Mitford, *Recollections of a Literary Life*, New York, 1852; Samuel G. Goodrich, *Recollections of a Lifetime*, New York, 1857, 2 vols.; Edward Dicey, "Nathaniel Hawthorne," *Macmillan's Mag.*, X (1864), 241–246; "Hawthorne," in Amos Bronson Alcott, *Concord Days*, Boston, 1872, pp. 193–197; Alexander Japp (*pseud.*, H. A. Page), *Memoir of Nathaniel Hawthorne* . . ., London, 1872; George P. Lathrop, *A Study of Hawthorne*, Boston, 1876; James T. Fields, *Yesterdays with Authors*, Boston,

1881, pp. 41–124; Julian Hawthorne, *Nathaniel Hawthorne and His Wife,* Boston, 1885, 2 vols.; Horatio Bridge, *Personal Recollections of Nathaniel Hawthorne,* New York, 1893; Rose Hawthorne Lathrop, *Memories of Hawthorne,* Boston, 1897; Julian Hawthorne, *Hawthorne and His Circle,* New York, 1903; Richard H. Stoddard, "My Acquaintance with Hawthorne," in *Recollections . . . ,* New York, 1903, pp. 116–133; Frank B. Sanborn, *Hawthorne and His Friends,* Cedar Rapids, Iowa, 1908; Helen A. Clarke, *Hawthorne's Country,* New York, 1910—topographical descriptions, well illustrated; Caroline Ticknor, *Hawthorne and His Publisher,* Boston, 1913; John B. Moore, ed., *Selections from Poe's Literary Criticism,* New York, 1926; Samuel E. Morison, ed., "Melville's 'Agatha' Letter to Hawthorne," *New Eng. Quar.,* II (1929), 296–307; Manning Hawthorne, "Maria Louisa Hawthorne," *Essex Institute Hist. Coll.,* LXXV (1939), 103–134—on Hawthorne's sister; and *idem,* "Parental and Family Influences on Hawthorne," *ibid.,* LXXVI (1940), 1–13. Further studies by Randall Stewart include: "Recollections of Hawthorne by His Sister Elizabeth," *Amer. Lit.,* XVI (1945), 316–331; "Editing Hawthorne's Notebooks: Selections from Mrs. Hawthorne's Letters to Mr. and Mrs. Fields, 1864–1868," *More Books,* XX (1945), 299–315; "Mrs. Hawthorne's Financial Difficulties: Selections from Her Letters to James T. Fields, 1865–1868," *ibid.,* XXI (1946), 43–53; and "Mrs. Hawthorne's Quarrel with James T. Fields," *ibid.,* pp. 254–263—further letters.

The chief collections of Hawthorne manuscripts are deposited in the Boston Public Library, the Morgan Library, and the Henry E. Huntington Library— see Randall Stewart, "Letters to Sophia," *Huntington Lib. Quar.,* VII (1944), 387–395. The Manning Collection is in the Essex Institute, Salem, Mass., and a substantial collection is in the New York Public Library. Two volumes of official letters, concerning Hawthorne during his years as American consul, are on file in the National Archives, Washington.

BIBLIOGRAPHY

A full bibliography of Hawthorne is greatly needed. Until it appears the following lists are serviceable: Nina E. Browne, *A Bibliography of Nathaniel Hawthorne,* Boston, 1905; Wallace H. Cathcart, *Bibliography of the Works of Nathaniel Hawthorne,* Cleveland, 1905; J. C. Chamberlain, *First Editions of the Works of Nathaniel Hawthorne,* New York, 1905. Further items are included in the Hawthorne bibliography in the *Camb. Hist. Amer. Lit.,* II (1918), 415–424. The bibliography in Austin Warren, *Nathaniel Hawthorne: Representative Selections . . . ,* New York, 1934, pp. lxxv–lxxxix, is annotated and selective. See also Harry Hartwick, in Walter F. Taylor, *A History of American Letters,* New York, 1936, pp. 515–519.

A collation of the first and second editions of *The Scarlet Letter* has been made by David A. Randall and John T. Winterich, *Publishers' Weekly,* CXXXVII (1940), 1181–1182.

*An Analytical Index to the Works of Nathaniel Hawthorne . . .*, Boston, 1882, was compiled by Evangeline M. O'Connor, by proper names and by topics.

## JOHN (MILTON) HAY
### *1838–1905*

### SEPARATE WORKS

*Jim Bludso of the Prairie Belle, and Little Breeches,* 1871; *Castilian Days,* 1871; *Pike County Ballads,* 1871; *The Bread-Winners,* 1884; *Abraham Lincoln: A History* (with John G. Nicolay), 1890; *Poems,* 1890; *In Praise of Omar,* 1898.

### COLLECTED WORKS

Clarence L. Hay edited his father's poetry, with an introduction, in *The Complete Poetical Works of John Hay, Including Many Poems Now First Collected,* Boston, 1916. Except for a slim volume of *Addresses of John Hay* (1907), his many political speeches remain uncollected.

Hay destroyed a very large number of his personal letters. His wife edited *Letters of John Hay and Extracts from Diary . . .*, Washington, 1908, 3 vols., selected by Henry Adams, and covering the period 1860–1905; but they were inadequately proofread and must be used cautiously. Later editions of letters are Caroline Ticknor, ed., *A Poet in Exile: Early Letters of John Hay,* Boston, 1910; William Roscoe Thayer, *The Life and Letters of John Hay,* Boston, 1915, 2 vols.; *A College Friendship: A Series of Letters from John Hay to Hannah Angell,* Boston, 1938; and Tyler Dennett, ed., *Lincoln and the Civil War in the Diaries and Letters of John Hay,* New York, 1939.

### BIOGRAPHY AND CRITICISM

The most authoritative life of Hay is Tyler Dennett, *John Hay: From Poetry to Politics,* New York, 1933. Earlier biographies are William Roscoe Thayer, *The Life and Letters of John Hay,* Boston, 1915, 2 vols.; and Lorenzo Sears, *John Hay: Author and Statesman,* New York, 1914. The best brief sketch is that by Alfred L. P. Dennis in the *Dict. Amer. Biog.* (1932).

Studies of Hay as a man of letters are William D. Howells, "John Hay in Literature," *No. Amer. Rev.,* CLXXXI (1905), 343–351; Henry B. Van Hoesen, "John Hay and the Historian's Use of Newspapers," in Deoch Fulton, ed., *Bookmen's Holiday . . .*, New York, 1943, pp. 395–398; and Sister St. Ignatius Ward, *The Poetry of John Hay,* Washington, 1930.

Special studies of aspects of Hay's public career are Alfred L. P. Dennis, "John Hay," in Samuel F. Bemis, ed., *The American Secretaries of State and Their Diplomacy*, New York, IX (1929), 115–189; Tyler Dennett, *Americans in Eastern Asia*, New York, 1922; and idem, *Roosevelt and the Russo-Japanese War*, Garden City, N.Y., 1925.

Other studies are Brooks Adams, "John Hay," *McClure's Mag.*, XIX (1902), 173–182; A. S. Chapman, "The Boyhood of John Hay," *Century Mag.*, LXXVIII (1909), 444–454—useful illustrations; Theodore Stanton, "John Hay and the Bread-Winners," *Nation*, CIII (1916), 130–131; and Granville Hicks, "The Conversion of John Hay," *New Repub.*, LXVII (1931), 100–101.

PRIMARY SOURCES

The best source materials are Hay's letters and diaries. There is further important material in the memoirs, letters, and biographies of Henry Adams, Theodore Roosevelt, Whitelaw Reid, Sir Cecil Spring-Rice, William McKinley, Baron von Eckardstein, and other public figures of the day. Joseph B. Bishop published "A Friendship with John Hay," *Century Mag.*, LXXI (1906), 773–780.

The most important collections of Hay manuscripts in public depositories are those in the Library of Congress and the National Archives. Further material is to be found among the Charles Sumner Papers in Harvard College Library.

BIBLIOGRAPHY

The fullest listing of works relating to Hay is in Dennett's *John Hay* (1933), pp. 445–449. "A Short List of His Writings," comp. by William E. Louttit, Jr., *ibid.*, pp. 451–456, is the most complete to date.

# PAUL HAMILTON HAYNE
## 1830–1886

SEPARATE WORKS

*Poems*, 1855; *Sonnets and Other Poems*, 1857; *Avolio: A Legend of the Island of Cos*, 1860; *Legends and Lyrics*, 1872; *The Mountain of the Lovers*, 1875; *Lives of Robert Young Hayne and Hugh Swinton Legaré*, 1878; *The Broken Battalions*, 1885.

COLLECTED WORKS

No properly edited collection of Hayne's poetry has been published, though a volume of *Collected Poems* was issued four years before his death, with a biographical introductory sketch by Margaret J. Preston. His contributions to *Russell's Magazine* (1857–1860), which he helped found and also edited, remain uncollected, as do his contributions to other periodicals. He wrote a sympathetic introduction to *The Poems of Henry Timrod*, rev. ed., New York, 1873.

Some 250 letters mostly from Hayne have been edited by Daniel M. McKeithan, *A Collection of Hayne Letters*, Austin, Texas, 1944. Charles Duffy edited *The Correspondence of Bayard Taylor and Paul Hamilton Hayne*, Baton Rouge, La., 1945—46 letters, most of them previously unpublished—with introductory notes and index. Gleanings are Aubrey H. Starke, "Sidney Lanier and Paul Hamilton Hayne: Three Unpublished Letters," *Amer. Lit.*, I (1929), 32–39; Jay B. Hubbell, "George Henry Boker, Paul Hamilton Hayne, and Charles Warren Stoddard: Some Unpublished Letters," *Amer. Lit.*, V (1933), 146–165; J. Delancey Ferguson, "A New Letter of Paul Hamilton Hayne," *Amer. Lit.*, V (1934), 368–371; and Rufus A. Coleman, "Hayne Writes to [John T.] Trowbridge," *Amer. Lit.*, X (1939), 483–486.

### BIOGRAPHY AND CRITICISM

There is no adequate biography of Hayne. The most recent biographical sketch is that in *Dict. Amer. Biog.* (1932). Special studies are W. H. Hayne, "Paul H. Hayne's Methods of Composition," *Lippincott's Mag.*, L (1892), 793–796; Daniel M. McKeithan, "Paul Hamilton Hayne's Reputation in Augusta at the Time of His Death," *Univ. Texas Studies in Eng.*, No. 3826 (1939), 163–173; *idem*, "A Note on Hayne's Ancestry," *Georgia Hist. Quar.*, XXIV (1940), 166–167; *idem*, "A Correspondence Journal of Paul Hamilton Hayne," *ibid.*, XXVII (1942), 249–272; Charles R. Anderson, "Charles Gayarré and Paul Hayne: The Last Literary Cavaliers," in *American Studies in Honor of William Kenneth Boyd*, Durham, N.C., 1940, pp. 221–281; and Max L. Griffin, "Whittier and Hayne: A Record of Friendship," *Amer. Lit.*, XIX (1947), 41–58.

Early studies and appreciations are Sidney Lanier, *Music and Poetry*, New York, 1898, pp. 197–211; "Paul Hamilton Hayne: Poet Laureate of the South," in Samuel A. Link, *Pioneers of Southern Literature*, Nashville, Tenn., I (1899), 43–87; J. T. Brown, Jr., "Paul Hamilton Hayne," *Sewanee Rev.*, XIV (1906), 236–247; and Charles W. Hubner, *Representative Southern Poets*, New York, 1906, pp. 55–82.

### PRIMARY SOURCES

Two extensive collections of Hayne manuscripts are at Cornell University and Duke University. Scattered material is at the University of North

Carolina, Emory University, University of Texas, Yale University, and elsewhere. Fifteen letters to Hayne were edited by Jay B. Hubbell, "Some New Letters of Constance Fenimore Woolson," *New Eng. Quar.*, XIV (1941), 715–735. See also Daniel M. McKeithan, *Selected Letters: John Garland James to Paul Hamilton Hayne and Mary Middleton Michel Hayne*, Austin, Texas, 1947.

There is no published Hayne bibliography.

## LAFCADIO HEARN
*1850–1904*

SEPARATE WORKS

During Hearn's lifetime the following were published: *Stray Leaves from Strange Literature*, 1884; *Some Chinese Ghosts*, 1887; *Chita*, 1889; *Two Years in the French West Indies*, 1890; *Youma*, 1890; *Glimpses of Unfamiliar Japan*, 1894; *"Out of the East,"* 1895; *Kokoro*, 1896; *Gleanings in Buddha-Fields*, 1897; *Exotics and Retrospectives*, 1898; *Japanese Fairy Tales*, 1898–1903; *In Ghostly Japan*, 1899; *Shadowings*, 1900; *A Japanese Miscellany*, 1901; *Kottō*, 1902; *Kwaidan*, 1904; *Japan: An Attempt at Interpretation*, 1904.

COLLECTED WORKS

The posthumous writings of Hearn are compilations of his early newspaper contributions, lectures as recorded by his students, letters, extracts from diaries, and other miscellaneous items. New material is constantly being published. It is impossible at present to be sure the listings are complete, since much of the recently published material has been compiled in Tokyo.

*The Writings of Lafcadio Hearn*, Boston, 1922, 16 vols., is a collection known as the Koizumi edition which gathers the writings already in print and includes the Bisland *Life and Letters* (Boston, 1906, 2 vols.).

Some seventeen volumes of Hearn's lectures have been published, a large part of them recorded from verbatim reports set down by his students at the University of Tokyo. Five volumes, covering lectures for the years 1896–1902, are edited by John Erskine: *Interpretations of Literature*, New York, 1915, 2 vols.; *Appreciations of Poetry*, New York, 1916; *Life and Literature*, New York, 1917; and *Pre-Raphaelite and Other Poets*, New York, 1922. Ryuji Tanabé and others edited seven more volumes: *Some Strange English Literary Figures* . . ., Tokyo, 1926; *A History of English Literature* . . ., Tokyo, 1927, 2 vols. (5th rev. ed., 1941); *Romance and Reason*, Tokyo, 1928; *Complete Lectures on Art, Literature, and Philosophy*, Tokyo, 1932; *On Poetry*, Tokyo, 1934; and *On Poets*, Tokyo, 1934. Other collections of lectures are in *Lectures on Prosody*, Tokyo, 1929; *Victorian Philosophy*, Tokyo, 1930;

T. Ochiai, ed., *On Literature*, Tokyo, 1922; Iwao Inagaki, ed., *Lectures on Shakespeare*, Tokyo, 1931; and Shigetsugu Kishi, ed., *Lafcadio Hearn's Lectures on Tennyson*, Tokyo, 1941.

Several volumes have been compiled from the sketches, essays, and editorials which Hearn contributed to Cincinnati and New Orleans newspapers, principally during the years 1878–1887. Charles W. Hutson edited *Fantastics, and Other Fancies*, Boston, 1914; *Creole Sketches*, Boston, 1924; and *Editorials*, Boston, 1926. Albert Mordell edited *Essays in European and Oriental Literature*, New York, 1923; and *Occidental Gleanings*, New York, 1925. Six volumes from the same sources have been compiled by Ichiro Nishizaki, *Literary Essays*, Tokyo, 1939; *Lafcadio Hearn's American Articles*, Tokyo, 1939—the fullest collection of Hearn's scattered journalism; *Barbarous Barbers, and Other Stories*, Tokyo, 1939; *Buying Christmas Toys, and Other Essays*, Tokyo, 1939; *The New Radiance*, Tokyo, 1939; and *Oriental Articles*, Tokyo, 1939. Other gatherings are *Karma*, New York, 1918; Ryuji Tanabé, ed., *Facts and Fancies*, Tokyo, 1929; Sanki Ichikawa, ed., *Essays on American Literature*, Tokyo, 1929; and *Letters from Shimane and Kyushu*, Kyoto, 1934 —reprinted from the Japan *Weekly Mail*.

Hearn's published diaries and letters are in part as follows: Milton Bronner, ed., *Letters from the Raven: Being the Correspondence of Lafcadio Hearn with Henry Watkin*, New York, 1907; Elizabeth Bisland, ed., *The Japanese Letters of Lafcadio Hearn*, Boston, 1910; Nina H. Kennard, *Lafcadio Hearn*, London, 1911—with letters to Hearn's half-sister, Mrs. Atkinson; Ferris Greenslet, ed., *Leaves from the Diary of an Impressionist: Early Writings by Lafcadio Hearn*, Boston, 1911; M. Ōtani, ed., *Letters from Tokyo*, Tokyo, 1920; Ryuji Tanabé, *Diaries and Letters*, Tokyo, 1921; Sanki Ichikawa, ed., *Some New Letters and Writings of Lafcadio Hearn*, Tokyo, 1925. Other collections are *Letters to a Pagan*, Detroit, 1933; O. Edwards, "Some Unpublished Letters of Lafcadio Hearn," *Transactions and Proc. Japan Soc.*, XVI (1917–1918), 16–35; E. C. Beck, "Letters of Lafcadio Hearn to His Brother," *English Jour.*, XX (1931), 287–292, and *Amer. Lit.*, IV (1932), 167–173.

Miscellaneous items posthumously published are *The Romance of the Milky Way, and Other Studies and Stories*, Boston, 1905; Albert Mordell, ed., *An American Miscellany: . . . Articles and Stories Now First Collected*, New York, 1924, 2 vols.; and *idem*, ed., *Sketches and Tales from the French*, Tokyo, 1935—translations by Hearn.

### REPRINTS

*Some Chinese Ghosts* (1887) was issued in the Modern Lib., with an introduction by Manuel Komroff, New York, 1927. Edward L. Tinker wrote a prologue for *Japanese Fairy Tales* (1898–1903), Mt. Vernon, N.Y., 1936. Further reprints are *A Japanese Miscellany* (1901), Boston, 1919; *Kwaidan* (1904), Boston, 1930; John Erskine, ed., *Talks to Writers,* New York, 1920—material which first appeared in *Interpretations of Literature* (1915) and *Life and Literature* (1917); *idem,* ed., *Books and Habits,* New York, 1921—reprints from earlier collections. *Karma and Other Stories and Essays* was issued, London, 1924.

BIOGRAPHY AND CRITICISM

Vera McWilliams, *Lafcadio Hearn,* Boston, 1946, is a well balanced biography. Elizabeth Bisland's *The Life and Letters of Lafcadio Hearn,* Boston, 1906, 2 vols., was authorized and utilizes indispensable material, though it is apologetic and glosses over important facts. A detailed factual study is Nina H. Kennard, *Lafcadio Hearn,* London, 1911. A lively and solid account of the earlier years is Edward L. Tinker, *Lafcadio Hearn's American Days,* New York, 1924—well illustrated; rev. ed., 1925. The most satisfactory brief biographical sketch is that by Tinker in *Dict. Amer. Biog.* (1932).

One of the earliest critical essays on Hearn, chiefly as a stylist, is Paul E. More, *Shelburne Essays, Second Series,* New York, 1905, pp. 46–72. A study of Lafcadio Hearn's maladies and the effect of eye strain is "Lafcadio Hearn," in George M. Gould, *Biographic Clinics,* Philadelphia, 1906, IV, 209–237. Gould's *Concerning Lafcadio Hearn,* Philadelphia, 1908, is a biased attack, with some new facts.

Appreciative estimates are Yone Noguchi, *Lafcadio Hearn in Japan,* Yokohama, 1910—including Mrs. Hearn's "Reminiscences"; Jean Temple, *Blue Ghost: A Study of Lafcadio Hearn,* New York, 1931—sensitive impressions; and Kenneth P. Kirkwood, *Unfamiliar Lafcadio Hearn,* Tokyo, 1936.

Among early interpretive essays are Joseph de Smet, *Lafcadio Hearn: L'Homme et l'Œuvre,* Paris, 1911; Edward Thomas, *Lafcadio Hearn,* Boston, 1912; D. H. Langton, "Lafcadio Hearn," *Manchester Quar.,* XXXI (1912), 1–23; M. Monahan, "Lafcadio Hearn: A French Estimate," *Forum,* XLIX (1913), 356–366.

Later critical estimates are "Lafcadio Hearn," in Percy H. Boynton, *More Contemporary Americans,* Chicago, 1927, pp. 51–74; Oscar Lewis, *Hearn and His Biographers: The Record of a Literary Controversy,* San Francisco, 1930; Katherine Anne Porter, "A Disinherited Cosmopolitan," *N.Y. Herald Tribune Books,* Feb. 16, 1930, p. 22; "An Enemy of the West: Lafcadio Hearn," in Matthew Josephson, *Portrait of the Artist as American,* New York, 1930, pp. 199–231; H. Masamuné, "New Light on Lafcadio Hearn," *Contemporary Japan,* II (1933), 270–280; Albert Parry, *Garrets and Pretenders,* New York, 1933, pp. 163–166.

The most recent studies are Fritz van Briessen, "Lafcadio Hearn: Decadent? Aesthet? Exotist?" *Englische Studien*, LXXI (1937), 372–382; *idem*, *Stil und Form bei Lafcadio Hearn*, Giessen, 1937.

PRIMARY SOURCES

The most important source material is contained in Hearn's letters and diaries, many of which are still unpublished. Reminiscences have been published by his son Kazuo Koizumi, *Father and I: Memories of Lafcadio Hearn*, Boston, 1935, and his wife Setsuko Koizumi, *Reminiscences of Lafcadio Hearn*, Boston, 1918. The account by Hearn's son is charming, but both volumes are trivial.

Other published items useful as source material are Kazuo Koizumi, ed., *Letters from Basil Hall Chamberlain to Lafcadio Hearn*, Tokyo, 1936; *idem*, *More Letters from Basil Hall Chamberlain to Lafcadio Hearn . . .*, Tokyo, 1937; Léona Q. Barel, *The Idyl: My Personal Reminiscences of Lafcadio Hearn*, Tokyo, 1933, 65 pp.; E. Foxwell, "Reminiscences of Lafcadio Hearn," *Transactions and Proc. Japan Soc.*, VIII (1907–1909), 68–94; and Caroline Ticknor, *Glimpses of Authors*, Boston, 1922.

A large number of Hearn's manuscripts are in Japan, many of them presumably at the University of Tokyo. The largest collection outside Japan is in the Houghton Library of Harvard University. Much material also is in the New York Public Library. Further items are in the Henry E. Huntington Library and the Library of Congress.

BIBLIOGRAPHY

P. D. and Ione Perkins, *Lafcadio Hearn: A Bibliography of His Writings*, Boston, 1934, is a reliable compilation; but the subject is complicated and almost endless, since new material is still being brought out in Japan. Martha H. Sisson has compiled "A Bibliography of Lafcadio Hearn," *Bul. Bibl.*, XV (1933–1934), 6–7, 32–34, 55–56, 73–75—also trustworthy. A ready reference to first editions, compilations, translations, and books with contributions by Hearn (though not complete) is Jacob Blanck, *Merle Johnson's American First Editions*, 4th ed., New York, 1942.

## ERNEST (MILLER) HEMINGWAY
### b. 1898

SEPARATE WORKS

*Three Stories & Ten Poems*, 1923; *In Our Time: Stories*, 1924 (enlarged ed., 1925); *The Torrents of Spring*, 1926; *Today Is Friday*, 1926; *The Sun*

*Also Rises,* 1926; *Men Without Women,* 1927; *A Farewell to Arms,* 1929; *Death in the Afternoon,* 1932; *God Rest You Merry Gentlemen,* 1933; *Winner Take Nothing,* 1933; *Green Hills of Africa,* 1935; *To Have and Have Not,* 1937; *The Spanish Earth,* 1938; *The Fifth Column and the First Forty-nine Stories,* 1938; *For Whom the Bell Tolls,* 1940.

Hemingway edited *Men at War: The Best War Stories of All Time,* New York, 1942.

REPRINTS

*The Sun Also Rises* (1926) was published, New York, 1930, in the Modern Lib., with an introduction by Henry S. Canby. *A Farewell to Arms* (1929) also was reprinted in the Modern Lib., New York, 1932, with an introd. by Ford Madox Ford. *For Whom the Bell Tolls* (1940), was reprinted, Princeton, 1942, with an introduction by Sinclair Lewis. Selected items were included in the Modern Lib. under the title *The Short Stories of Ernest Hemingway,* New York, 1942; and Malcolm Cowley edited another selection for the Viking Portable Lib. in *The Portable Hemingway,* New York, 1944, with introduction and notes.

BIOGRAPHY AND CRITICISM

There is no biography of Hemingway, and no important critical recognition was accorded to him until after publication of *The Sun Also Rises,* in 1926. Early estimates are Robert Littell, "Notes on Hemingway," *New Repub.,* LI (1927), 303–306; Paul Rosenfeld, *By Way of Art,* New York, 1928, pp. 151–163; L. W. Dodd, "Simple Annals of the Callous," *Sat. Rev. Lit.,* IV (Nov. 19, 1927), 322–323; and Robert Herrick, "What Is Dirt?" *Bookman,* LXX (1929), 258–262.

Critical studies during the early thirties are Henry S. Canby, "Chronicle and Comment," *Bookman,* LXX (1930), 641–647; Arthur Dewing, "The Mistake About Hemingway," *No. Amer. Rev.,* CCXXXII (1931), 364–371; Lawrence Leighton, "An Autopsy and a Prescription," *Hound and Horn,* V (1932), 519–539; Robert M. Lovett, "Ernest Hemingway," *English Jour.,* XXI (1932), 609–617; Gertrude Stein, *The Autobiography of Alice B. Toklas,* New York, 1933, pp. 261–271; Lincoln Kirstein, "The Canon of Death," *Hound and Horn,* VI (1933), 336–341; "Bull in the Afternoon," in Max Eastman, *Art and the Life of Action,* New York, 1934, pp. 87–101; Harry Hartwick, *The Foreground of American Fiction,* New York, 1934, pp. 153–159; Storm Jameson, "The Craft of the Novelist," *English Rev.,* LVIII (1934), 28–43; and "Ernest Hemingway, the 'Dumb Ox,'" in Wyndham Lewis, *Men Without Art,* London, 1934, pp. 17–41.

Later estimates are C. John McCole, *Lucifer at Large,* London, 1937, pp.

153-172; John T. Reid, "Spain as Seen by Some Contemporary Writers," *Hispania*, XX (1937), 139-150; John P. Bishop, "The Missing All," *Virginia Quar. Rev.*, XIII (1937), 107-121; Elliot Paul, "Hemingway and the Critics," *Sat. Rev. Lit.*, XVII (Nov. 6, 1937), 3-4; Delmore Schwartz, "Ernest Hemingway's Literary Situation," *Southern Rev.*, III (1938), 769-782; J. Donald Adams, "Ernest Hemingway," *English Jour.*, XXVIII (1939), 87-94; Edmund Wilson, "Ernest Hemingway: Bourdon Gauge of Morale," *Atl. Mo.*, CLXIV (1939), 36-46; Carl Van Doren, *The American Novel, 1789-1939*, New York, 1940, pp. 334-348; Edgar Johnson, "Farewell the Separate Peace," *Sewanee Rev.*, XLVIII (1940), 289-300—with stress on his intellectual growth; and Maxwell Geismar, "No Man Alone Now," *Virginia Quar. Rev.*, XVII (1941), 517-534.

The most recent studies are Alfred Kazin, *On Native Grounds*, New York, 1942, pp. 327-341; "Ernest Hemingway: You Could Always Come Back," in Maxwell Geismar, *Writers in Crisis*, Boston, 1942, pp. 37-86; James T. Farrell, "Ernest Hemingway, Apostle of a 'Lost Generation,'" *N.Y. Times Book Rev.*, Aug. 1, 1943, pp. 6, 14—a revaluation of *The Sun Also Rises*; Edward Fenimore, "English and Spanish in *For Whom the Bell Tolls*," *Jour. English Lit. Hist.*, X (1943), 73-86; Ray B. West, Jr., "Ernest Hemingway: Death in the Evening," *Antioch Rev.*, IV (1944), 569-580; E. Cecchi, "Ernest Hemingway," *Mercurio*, II (1945), 111-123; Robert Penn Warren, "Hemingway," *Kenyon Rev.*, IX (1947), 1-28; and W. M. Frohock, "Ernest Hemingway: Violence and Discipline," *Southwest Rev.*, XXXII (1947), 89-97, 184-193.

**BIBLIOGRAPHY**

An exhaustive listing of Hemingway's writings, to 1931, is Louis H. Cohn, *A Bibliography of the Works of Ernest Hemingway*, New York, 1931. An earlier brief listing is Vrest Orton, "Some Notes Bibliographical and Otherwise on the Books of Ernest Hemingway," *Publishers' Weekly*, CXVII (1930), 884-886. A more recent listing is Fred B. Millett, *Contemporary American Authors*, New York, 1940, pp. 385-388.

# JOSEPH HERGESHEIMER
b. *1880*

**SEPARATE WORKS**

*The Lay Anthony*, 1914; *Mountain Blood*, 1915; *The Three Black Pennys*, 1917; *Gold and Iron*, 1918; *The Happy End*, 1919; *Linda Condon*, 1919; *Java Head*, 1919; *San Cristóbal de la Habana*, 1920; *Cytherea.* 1922; *The*

*Bright Shawl*, 1922; *The Presbyterian Child*, 1923; *Balisand*, 1924; *From an Old House*, 1925; *Tampico*, 1926; *Quiet Cities*, 1928; *Swords and Roses*, 1929; *Triall by Armes*, 1929; *The Party Dress*, 1930; *The Limestone Tree*, 1931; *Sheridan: A Military Narrative*, 1931; *Berlin*, 1932; *Love in the United States and the Big Shot*, 1932; *Tropical Winter*, 1933; *The Foolscap Rose*, 1934.

EDITED TEXTS AND REPRINTS

The Sun Dial Lib., Garden City, N.Y., reprinted three novels: *The Lay Anthony* (1914), 1928; *Mountain Blood* (1915), 1928; and *The Bright Shawl* (1922), 1928. *Swords and Roses* (1929) was issued by Blue Ribbon Books, New York, 1931.

BIOGRAPHY AND CRITICISM

Early estimates of Hergesheimer are James Branch Cabell, "In Respect to Joseph Hergesheimer," *Bookman*, L (1919), 267–273; Wilson Follett, "Factualist Versus Impressionist," *Dial*, LXVI (1919), 449–451; "Joseph Hergesheimer," in Blanche C. Williams, *Our Short Story Writers*, New York, 1920, pp. 223–236; Llewellyn Jones, *Joseph Hergesheimer: The Man and His Books*, New York, 1920, 33 pp.; J. B. Cabell, *Joseph Hergesheimer: An Essay in Interpretation*, Chicago, 1921, 27 pp.; "Mr. Hergesheimer's *Cytherea*," in Henry S. Canby, *Definitions*, first ser., New York, 1922, pp. 217–223; "Joseph Hergesheimer," in Carl Van Doren, *Contemporary American Novelists*, New York, 1922, pp. 122–131; "Joseph Hergesheimer," in S. P. B. Mais, *Some Modern Authors*, New York, 1923, pp. 70–74; "Diversions of the Anchorite," in James Branch Cabell, *Straws and Prayer-Books*, New York, 1924, pp. 193–221.

Later evaluations are "Hergesheimer," in H. L. Mencken, *Prejudices: Fifth Series*, New York, 1926, pp. 42–49; Berthe Gagnot, "Un Romancier Américain: Joseph Hergesheimer," *Revue Anglo-Amér.*, III (1926), 505–510; "The Ivory Tower," in Upton Sinclair, *Money Writes!* New York, 1927, pp. 92–99; "Joseph Hergesheimer," in Percy H. Boynton, *More Contemporary Americans*, Chicago, 1927, pp. 137–156; Jerome B. Gray, "An Author and His Town: West Chester and Joseph Hergesheimer Get Used to Each Other," *Bookman*, LXVII (1928), 159–164; J. B. Priestley, "Joseph Hergesheimer," in John C. Squire, ed., *Contemporary American Authors*, New York, 1928, pp. 179–203; Sara Haardt, "Joseph Hergesheimer's Methods," *Bookman*, LXIX (1929), 398–403; "Un Roman d'Aventures: *Tampico* de Joseph Hergesheimer," in André Levinson, *Figures Américaines*, Paris, 1929, pp. 139–149; "About One and Another: A Note as to Joseph Hergesheimer," in James Branch Cabell, *Some of Us*, New York, 1930, pp. 91–104; "Joseph

Hergesheimer," in Stephen Graham, *The Death of Yesterday,* London, 1930, pp. 71–78; Fred L. Pattee, *The New American Literature,* New York, 1930, pp. 345–350; "Joseph Hergesheimer," in Emily Clark, *Innocence Abroad,* New York, 1931, pp. 87–106; "Point of View: Hergesheimer," in Joseph W. Beach, *The Twentieth Century Novel,* New York, 1932, pp. 280–286; Geoffrey West, "Joseph Hergesheimer," *Virginia Quar. Rev.,* VIII (1932), 95–108; Ludwig Lewisohn, *Expression in America,* New York, 1932, pp. 531–538; Leon Kelley, "America and Mr. Hergesheimer," *Sewanee Rev.,* XL (1932), 171–193.

The most recent studies are "Costumes by Hergesheimer," in Harry Hartwick, *The Foreground of American Fiction,* New York, 1934, pp. 187–199; "Facing Two Worlds: Joseph Hergesheimer," in Harlan Hatcher, *Creating the Modern American Novel,* New York, 1935, pp. 202–210; and "Joseph Hergesheimer," in Percy H. Boynton, *America in Contemporary Fiction,* Chicago, 1940, pp. 53–72.

PRIMARY SOURCES

*The Presbyterian Child* (1923) is an autobiography, and there is further source material in *From an Old House* (1925). A few of Hergesheimer's manuscripts are in the Princeton University Library.

BIBLIOGRAPHY

The fullest bibliographical listing is in Fred B. Millett, *Contemporary American Authors,* New York, 1940, pp. 390–392.

## CHARLES FENNO HOFFMAN
### *1806–1884*

SEPARATE WORKS

*A Winter in the West,* 1835; *Wild Scenes in the Forest and Prairie,* 1839; *Greyslaer: A Romance of the Mohawk,* 1840; *The Vigil of Faith, and Other Poems,* 1842; *The Echo; or, Borrowed Notes for Home Circulation,* 1844; *Lays of the Hudson,* 1846; *Love's Calendar, Lays of the Hudson, and Other Poems,* 1847; *The Pioneers of New York,* 1848.

Hoffman established the *Knickerbocker Magazine,* 1833. He edited the *American Monthly Magazine,* 1835–1837; the *New York Mirror,* 1837; and the *Literary World* for several months, 1847–1848. Magazines to which he contributed include *The Wintergreen* (1843), *The Opal* (1844), and *The Gift* (1844). He edited an early regional anthology, *The New York Book of Poetry* (1837).

*The Poems of Charles Fenno Hoffman*, Philadelphia, 1873, were edited by his nephew Edward F. Hoffman.

BIOGRAPHY AND CRITICISM

A recent biographical study is Homer F. Barnes, *Charles Fenno Hoffman*, New York, 1930. The sketch in *Dict. Amer. Biog.* (1932) was contributed by Lucius H. Holt.

Source material is in Hoffman's autobiography, *A Winter in the West*, New York, 1835. He is discussed in Poe's *The Literati*, New York, 1850. For further source material see James Grant Wilson, *Bryant and His Friends*, New York, 1886, pp. 409–413.

An extensive bibliographical listing is in Barnes's biography. See also Jacob Blanck, *Merle Johnson's American First Editions*, 4th ed., New York, 1942.


# OLIVER WENDELL HOLMES
## *1809–1894*

SEPARATE WORKS

*The Harbinger: A May-Gift*, 1833; *Poems*, 1836; *Boylston Prize Dissertations for . . . 1836 and 1837*, 1838; *Homoeopathy, and Its Kindred Delusions*, 1842; *The Contagiousness of Puerperal Fever*, 1843; *The Position and Prospects of the Medical Student*, 1844; *Urania: A Rhymed Lesson*, 1846; *Poems*, 1846; *Introductory Lecture, Delivered . . . Harvard University, Nov. 3, 1847*, 1847; *Poems*, 1849; *Astraea: The Balance of Illusions*, 1850; *A Poem . . . Delivered at . . . the Pittsfield Cemetery, Sept. 9, 1850*, 1850; *The Benefactors of the Medical School of Harvard University*, 1850; *The Poetical Works of Oliver Wendell Holmes*, 1852; *Songs of the Class of MDCCCXXIX*, 1854; *Oration Delivered Before the New England Society*, 1856; *Valedictory Address, etc., March 10th, 1858*, 1858; *The Autocrat of the Breakfast-Table*, 1858; *Songs and Poems of the Class of 1829: Second Edition*, 1859; *The Professor at the Breakfast-Table*, 1860; *Currents and Counter-Currents in Medical Science*, 1860; *Elsie Venner: A Romance of Destiny*, 1861; *Songs in Many Keys*, 1862; *The Poems of Oliver Wendell Holmes*, 1862; *Border Lines of Knowledge in . . . Medical Science*, 1862; *Oration . . . on the Fourth of July, 1863*, 1863; *Soundings from the Atlantic*, 1864; *Humorous Poems*, 1865; *The Gurdian Angel*, 1867; *Teaching from the Chair and at the Bedside*, 1867; *Songs and Poems of the Class of Eighteen Hundred and Twenty-nine: Third Edition*, 1868; *The Medical Profession in Massachusetts*, 1869; *Mechanism in Thought and Morals*, 1871; *Valedictory Address . . . March 2, 1871*, 1871;

*The Claims of Dentistry*, 1872; *The Poet at the Breakfast-Table*, 1872; *Songs of Many Seasons, 1862–1874*, 1875; *Poetical Works*, 1877; *An Address Delivered at . . . the Boston Microscopical Society*, 1877; *John Lothrop Motley: A Memoir*, 1879; *The School-Boy*, 1879; *The Iron Gate and Other Poems*, 1880; *Address Delivered at . . . the Boston Medical Library Association, December 3, 1878*, 1881; *Medical Highways and By-Ways*, 1882; *Farewell Address . . . to the Medical School of Harvard University, November 28, 1882*, 1882; *Medical Essays 1842–1882*, 1883; *Pages from an Old Volume of Life*, 1883; *A Mortal Antipathy*, 1885; *Ralph Waldo Emerson*, 1885; *Illustrated Poems*, 1885; *Our Hundred Days in Europe*, 1887; *Before the Curfew and Other Poems*, 1888; *Over the Teacups*, 1891; *Memoir of Henry Jacob Bigelow*, 1891; *A Dissertation on Acute Pericarditis*, 1937.

COLLECTED WORKS

The "Handy Volume Edition" of *The Poetical Works of Oliver Wendell Holmes*, Boston, 1881 (and later), 2 vols., brought together the greatest part of the material written to that date. The Riverside Edition of *The Writings of Oliver Wendell Holmes*, Boston, 1891, 13 vols., furnished the plates for the Standard Library Edition: *The Works of Oliver Wendell Holmes*, Boston, 1892, 13 vols., increased to 15 vols. in 1896 by the addition of John T. Morse's *Life and Letters of Oliver Wendell Holmes*. The standard one-volume edition of the poems is that edited by Horace E. Scudder, *The Complete Poetical Works of Oliver Wendell Holmes*, Boston, 1895, containing a chronological list of poems, pp. 341–344.

Morse's *Life and Letters*, mentioned above, includes the bulk of Holmes's published correspondence. Other gleanings may be found in George W. Curtis, ed., *The Correspondence of John Lothrop Motley*, New York, 1889, 2 vols.; Joseph E. Adams Smith, *The Poet Among the Hills: Oliver Wendell Holmes in Berkshire . . .* , Pittsfield, Mass., 1895—especially useful for uncollected speeches and short poems; anon., "A Letter from Dr. Holmes [to Arthur Gilman, Oct. 29, 1874]," *Atlantic Mo.*, C (1907), 715; Esther B. Carpenter, *South-County Studies . . .* , Boston, 1924, including twenty-six letters, 1869–1886; and anon., "Four Letters of Dr. Holmes [addressed to Charles Coleman Sellers of Philadelphia]," *Yale Rev.*, n.s., XIV (1925), 410–413.

EDITED TEXTS AND REPRINTS

The work by which Holmes is most widely known, *The Autocrat of the Breakfast-Table* (1858), has been frequently reprinted. The most recent separate reprint is that edited by Franklin T. Baker, New York, 1928 (Modern Readers' Ser.). It was also published in Pocket Classics, New York, 1914;

and Everyman's Lib., London, 1906. A London reprint of 1904 has an introduction by G. K. Chesterton and notes by E. H. Blakeney. *The Professor at the Breakfast-Table* (1860) was issued in both Everyman's Lib. and World's Classics, London, 1906, and was edited by Clement K. Shorter, London, 1928. *The Poet at the Breakfast-Table* (1872) was issued in both Everyman's Lib. and World's Classics, London, 1906. Josiah H. Castleman edited *Selections from the Poems of Oliver Wendell Holmes,* New York, 1907.

*Oliver Wendell Holmes: Representative Selections, with Introduction, Bibliography, and Notes,* ed. by Samuel I. Hayakawa and Howard M. Jones, New York, 1939 (Amer. Writers Ser.), is easily available, and is the most trustworthy text of selections.

BIOGRAPHY AND CRITICISM

An authoritative assessment, stressing Holmes's psychological insight, is Mark A. De Wolfe Howe, *Holmes of the Breakfast-Table,* New York, 1939. Still important is William L. Schroeder, *Oliver Wendell Holmes: An Appreciation,* London, 1909. Among brief general studies are Mark A. De Wolfe Howe, in *Dict. Amer. Biog.* (1932); Samuel I. Hayakawa and Howard M. Jones, introduction to their edition of *Oliver Wendell Holmes: Representative Selections,* New York, 1939; Harry H. Clark, "Dr. Holmes: A Reinterpretation," *New Eng. Quar.,* XII (1939), 19–34; and H. D. Fuller, "Holmes," in John Macy, ed., *American Writers on American Literature,* New York, 1931, pp. 153–163.

Studies of Holmes as a man of letters, significant to the extent that the writers are spokesmen of their time, include Edmund C. Stedman, *Poets of America,* Boston, 1885, pp. 273–303; George W. Curtis, *Literary and Social Essays,* New York, 1895, pp. 205–236; Leslie Stephen, *Studies of a Biographer,* London, 1907, II, 149–182; "Holmes," in John Macy, *The Spirit of American Literature,* New York, 1913, pp. 155–171; Brander Matthews, "Holmes," in *Camb. Hist. Amer. Lit.,* II (1918), 224–240; Vernon L. Parrington, *Main Currents in American Thought,* II (1927), 451–460; and "Dr. Holmes" and "The Autocrat," in Van Wyck Brooks, *The Flowering of New England,* New York, 1940 (rev. ed.), pp. 343–358, 478–498.

Estimates of Holmes as physician, scientist, and teacher are an important part of the special studies. *The Psychiatric Novels of Oliver Wendell Holmes,* New York, 1943, is an abridgment of *Elsie Venner, The Guardian Angel,* and *A Mortal Antipathy,* with critical introductions and annotations by Clarence P. Oberndorf, a clinical professor of psychiatry. Tributes to Holmes are Sir William Osler, "Oliver Wendell Holmes," *Johns Hopkins Hosp. Bul.,* V (1894), 85–88; D. W. Cheever, "Oliver Wendell Holmes the Anatomist," *Harvard Grad. Mag.,* III (1894), 154–159; Charles W. Eliot, "Oliver Wendell

Holmes," *ibid.,* XXXI (1923), 457–465; and E. M. Bick, "A Note on the Medical Works of Oliver Wendell Holmes," *Annals Medical Hist.,* IV (1932), 487–490. See also Henry R. Viets, "Oliver Wendell Holmes, Physician," *Amer. Scholar,* III (1934), 5–11; and Nelson F. Adkins, " 'The Chambered Nautilus': Its Scientific and Poetic Backgrounds," *Amer. Lit.,* IX (1938), 458–465.

Holmes's religious position is the subject of Emory S. Turner, "The Autocrat's Theology: Unpublished Letters of Oliver Wendell Holmes," *Putnam's Mag.,* VI (1909), 662–667; and A. H. Strong, *American Poets and Their Theology,* Philadelphia, 1916, pp. 319–367.

Other special studies include W. G. Ballantine, "Oliver Wendell Holmes as a Poet and as a Man," *No. Amer. Rev.,* CXC (1909), 178–193; W. S. Knickerbocker, "His Own Boswell: A Note on the Poetry of Oliver Wendell Holmes," *Sewanee Rev.,* XLI (1933), 454–466; "Oliver Wendell Holmes," in Gay W. Allen, *American Prosody,* New York, 1935, pp. 193–216; Samuel I. Hayakawa, "Holmes's Lowell Institute Lectures," *Amer. Lit.,* VIII (1936), 281–290—his opinion of the English romantic poets; Hjalmar O. Lokensgard, "Oliver Wendell Holmes's 'Phrenological Character,' " *New Eng. Quar.,* XIII (1940), 711–718; *idem,* "Holmes Quizzes the Professors," *Amer. Lit.,* XIII (1941), 157–162; John P. Pritchard, *Return to the Fountains,* Durham, N.C., 1942, pp. 90–98; Thomas Franklin Currier, "The Autocrat of the Breakfast-Table: A Bibliographical Study," *Papers Bibl. Soc. Amer.,* XXXVIII (1944), 284–311; *idem,* "Oliver Wendell Holmes, Poet Laureate of Harvard," *Proc. Mass. Hist. Soc.,* LXVII (1945), 436–451; Edouard Roditi, "Oliver Wendell Holmes as Novelist," *Ariz. Quar.,* I (1945), No. 4, 23–33; and George Arms, " 'To Fix the Image All Unveiled and Warm,' " *New Eng. Quar.,* XIX (1946), 534–537. See also Edward W. Emerson, *The Early Years of the Saturday Club, 1855–1870,* Boston, 1918, *passim.*

PRIMARY SOURCES

Published estimates of Holmes as he was known to the writers include William Sloane Kennedy, *Oliver Wendell Holmes: Poet, Littérateur, Scientist,* Boston, 1883; E. E. Brown, *Life of Oliver Wendell Holmes,* Boston, 1884; the Holmes Number of the *Critic,* n.s. II (Aug. 30, 1884); "Oliver Wendell Holmes: Personal Recollections and Unpublished Letters," in Annie A. Fields, *Authors and Friends,* Boston, 1893, pp. 107–157; John T. Morse, *Life and Letters of Oliver Wendell Holmes,* Boston, 1896, 2 vols.—a source book; John T. Trowbridge, "Recollections of Oliver Wendell Holmes," *Atl. Mo.,* XCI (1903), 600–605; and "Dr. Holmes," in Frank P. Stearns, *Cambridge Sketches,* Philadelphia, 1905, pp. 142–161. The reminiscences of Thomas W. Higginson include references to Holmes, some of them extensive: *Old Cambridge,* New York, 1899; *Contemporaries,* Boston, 1899; and *Cheerful Yesterdays,* Boston, 1901. William D. Howells devotes a chapter to Holmes in *Literary Friends and Acquaintance,* New York, 1900, pp. 146–177. Much pertinent material appears in Caroline Ticknor, ed., *Dr. Holmes's Boston,* Boston, 1915.

The chief depositories of the Holmes manuscripts are the Library of Congress and the Morgan Library. Items are also in the Henry E. Huntington Library, the Massachusetts Historical Society Library, the Boston Public Library, and the Harvard College Library.

BIBLIOGRAPHY

The compilation of George B. Ives, *A Bibliography of Oliver Wendell Holmes,* Boston, 1907, is exhaustive to that date, and lists many uncollected items. The listing in Hayakawa and Jones's *Oliver Wendell Holmes: Representative Selections* (1939), pp. cxvii–cxxix, is selective and annotated, as is that in Harry H. Clark, ed., *Major American Poets,* New York, 1936, pp. 882–886. See also Harry Hartwick, in Walter F. Taylor, *A History of American Letters,* New York, 1936, pp. 530–533; and Jacob Blanck, ed., *Merle Johnson's American First Editions,* 4th ed., New York, 1942, pp. 257–261.

# THOMAS HOOKER
## 1586–1647

SEPARATE WORKS

*The Poore Douting Christian,* 1629; *The Soules Preparation for Christ,* 1632; *The Equall Wayes of God,* 1632; *The Soules Humiliation,* 1637; *The Soules Implantation,* 1637; *The Soules Ingrafting into Christ,* 1637; *The Soules Effectuall Calling to Christ,* 1637; *The Soules Exaltation,* 1638; *Heaven's Treasury Opened, in a Faithful Exposition of the Lord's Prayer,* 1638; *The Unbeleevers Preparing for Christ,* 1638; *Foure Godly and Learned Treatises,* 1638; *The Christians Two Chiefe Lessons,* 1640; *The Danger of Desertion,* 1641; *The Saints Guide,* 1645; *A Survey of the Summe of Church-Discipline,* 1648; *The Covenant of Grace Opened,* 1649; *The Saints Dignitie, and Duty,* 1651; *The Application of Redemption,* 1656.

EDITED TEXTS AND REPRINTS

There is no collection of Hooker's works, nor are there reprints of his treatises, some of them of great consequence in the history of thought. Hooker's sermon *The Poore Douting Christian* (1629) is reprinted in part in Edwin D. Mead, "Thomas Hooker's Farewell Sermon in England," *Proc.*

*Mass. Hist. Soc.,* XLVI (1913), 253–274. His letters have not been printed with the exception of "Rev. Thomas Hooker's Letter, in Reply to Governor Winthrop," *Proc. Connecticut Hist. Soc.,* I (1860), 2–18. A few selections from his treatises are given in Perry Miller and Thomas H. Johnson, *The Puritans,* New York, 1938, pp. 290–313.

BIOGRAPHY AND CRITICISM

There is great need for adequate study of one of the leading thinkers and writers of the seventeenth century. No study has yet superseded the narrative life written by George L. Walker, *Thomas Hooker, Preacher, Founder, Democrat,* New York, 1891. A nineteen-page brochure is Warren S. Archibald, "Thomas Hooker," New Haven, 1933, in the *Pubs. Tercentenary Commission State of Conn.* The sketch in *Dict. Amer. Biog.* was written by James T. Adams. Cotton Mather's account, entitled *Piscator Evangelicus; or, The Life of Mr. Thomas Hooker,* Boston, 1695, is also to be found in the *Magnalia.* The best study of Hooker as a political force is "The Beginnings of Connecticut," in Charles M. Andrews, *The Colonial Period of American History,* New Haven, II (1936), 67–99. Significant also is Perry Miller, "Thomas Hooker and the Democracy of Early Connecticut," *New Eng. Quar.,* IV (1931), 663–712. Hooker as a man of letters is treated by Moses C. Tyler, *A History of American Literature During the Colonial Time,* rev. ed., New York, 1897, I, 193–203.

BIBLIOGRAPHY

No satisfactory bibliography of Hooker's works has been published. The listings in Joseph Sabin, *A Dictionary of Books Relating to America . . . ,* are supplemented by the lists compiled by J. Hammond Trumbull, "Thomas Hooker's Published Works," in George L. Walker's biography, pp. 184–195. Further useful secondary material will be found in *Camb. Hist. Amer. Lit.,* I (1917), 395–397.

## FRANCIS HOPKINSON
### *1737–1791*

SEPARATE WORKS

*An Exercise,* 1761; *Science: A Poem,* 1762; *A Collection of Psalm Tunes,* 1762; *Errata; or, The Art of Printing Incorrectly,* 1763; *A Psalm of Thanksgiving,* 1766; *The Psalms of David . . . in Metre,* 1767; *A Pretty Story: Written . . . by Peter Grievous, Esq.,* 1774; *The Battle of the Kegs,* 1779; *Account of the Grand Federal Procession,* 1788; *An Ode,* 1788; *A Set of*

*Eight Songs,* 1788; *An Oration,* 1789; *Judgments in the Admiralty of Pennsylvania,* 1789; *Ode from Ossian's Poems,* 1794.

COLLECTED WORKS AND REPRINTS

*The Miscellaneous Essays and Occasional Writings of Francis Hopkinson,* Philadelphia, 1792, 3 vols., was collected by Hopkinson, and includes only a small part of his verse and prose. *The Battle of the Kegs* (1779), first published in the *Pennsylvania Packet,* Mar. 4, 1778, was reprinted, Philadelphia, 1866. *A Pretty Story* (1774) was reprinted as *The Old Farm and the New Farm: A Political Allegory,* New York, 1857, edited with introduction and notes by Benson J. Lossing.

Many of Hopkinson's contributions to the *Pennsylvania Packet,* the *Pennsylvania Magazine,* and other periodicals have not yet been collected. See Hastings, *Life* (1926), pp. 475–480, for identifications of probable writings by Hopkinson.

Harold V. Milligan edited some of the music and songs of Hopkinson in *The First American Composer,* Boston, 1919.

Two further items are Albert F. Gegenheimer, "An Unpublished Letter of Francis Hopkinson to George Washington," *Amer. Lit.,* XIV (1942), 308–310, and George E. Hastings, "Two Uncollected Essays by Francis Hopkinson," *General Mag. and Hist. Chron.,* XLI (1939), 416–422.

BIOGRAPHY AND CRITICISM

One of the few extensive biographies of literary figures of the Middle Colonies is George E. Hastings, *The Life and Works of Francis Hopkinson,* Chicago, 1926. The authoritative study of Hopkinson as musician is Oscar G. T. Sonneck, *Francis Hopkinson: The First American Poet-Composer ...,* Washington, 1905. The sketch of Hopkinson in *Dict. Amer. Biog.* (1932) is a brief epitome by George E. Hastings of his own biography. Important brief studies are Charles R. Hildeburn, "Francis Hopkinson," *Pennsylvania Mag. Hist. and Biog.,* II (1878), 314–324; and Moses C. Tyler, *The Literary History of the American Revolution,* New York, 1897, I, 162–171, II, 130–157.

Two special studies by George E. Hastings are "Francis Hopkinson and the Anti-Federalists," *Amer. Lit.,* I (1930), 405–418, and "Francis Hopkinson and the Flag," *Americana,* XXXIII (1939), 1–23. Other special studies are Dixon Wecter, "Francis Hopkinson and Benjamin Franklin," *Amer. Lit.,* XII (1940), 200–217—letters to Franklin and a poem; Lewis Leary, "Francis Hopkinson, Jonathan Odell, and 'The Temple of Cloacina': 1782," *Amer. Lit.,* XV (1943), 183–191; and Albert F. Gegenheimer, "The Pirating of Francis Hopkinson's *Science,*" *Amer. Lit.,* XVII (1945), 170–173.

The two chief depositories of Hopkinson manuscripts are the Henry E.

Huntington Library and the library of the American Philosophical Society. Other manuscripts are owned by the Historical Society of Pennsylvania, the Massachusetts Historical Society, the Library Company of Philadelphia, and the Library of Congress.

The best bibliography of Hopkinson is in Hastings's *Life* (1926), pp. 481–496, which includes a calendar of the manuscripts.

# WILLIAM DEAN HOWELLS
## *1837–1920*

SEPARATE WORKS

Fiction: *Their Wedding Journey*, 1872; *A Chance Acquaintance*, 1873; *A Foregone Conclusion*, 1875; *The Lady of the Aroostook*, 1879; *The Undiscovered Country*, 1880; *Doctor Breen's Practice*, 1881; *A Fearful Responsibility, and Other Stories*, 1881; *A Modern Instance*, 1882; *A Woman's Reason*, 1883; *The Rise of Silas Lapham*, 1885; *Indian Summer*, 1886; *The Minister's Charge*, 1887; *April Hopes*, 1888; *Annie Kilburn*, 1888; *A Hazard of New Fortunes*, 1890; *The Shadow of a Dream*, 1890; *An Imperative Duty*, 1892; *The Quality of Mercy*, 1892; *Christmas Every Day and Other Stories Told for Children*, 1893; *The World of Chance*, 1893; *The Coast of Bohemia*, 1893; *A Traveler from Altruria*, 1894; *The Day of Their Wedding*, 1896; *A Parting and a Meeting*, 1896; *The Landlord at Lion's Head*, 1897; *An Open-Eyed Conspiracy: An Idyl of Saratoga*, 1897; *The Story of a Play*, 1898; *Ragged Lady*, 1899; *Their Silver Wedding Journey*, 1899; *A Pair of Patient Lovers*, 1901; *The Kentons*, 1902; *The Flight of Pony Baker*, 1902; *Questionable Shapes*, 1903; *Letters Home*, 1903; *The Son of Royal Langbrith*, 1904; *Miss Bellard's Inspiration*, 1905; *Through the Eye of the Needle*, 1907; *Between the Dark and the Daylight*, 1907; *Fennel and Rue*, 1908; *New Leaf Mills*, 1913; *The Daughter of the Storage*, 1916; *The Leatherwood God*, 1916; *The Vacation of the Kelwyns*, 1920; *Mrs. Farrell*, 1921.

Poetry: *Poems of Two Friends* (with John J. Piatt), 1860; *No Love Lost: A Romance of Travel*, 1869; *Poems*, 1873; *Stops of Various Quills*, 1894; *The Mother and the Father: Dramatic Passages*, 1909.

Travel, Criticism, Biography, etc.: *Lives and Speeches of Abraham Lincoln and Hannibal Hamlin*, 1860; *Venetian Life*, 1866; *Italian Journeys*, 1867; *Suburban Sketches*, 1871; *Sketch of the Life and Character of Rutherford B. Hayes (etc.)*, 1876; *A Day's Pleasure and Other Sketches*, 1876; *Three Villages*, 1884; *A Little Girl Among the Old Masters*, 1884; *Niagara Revisited*, 1884; *Tuscan Cities*, 1886; *Modern Italian Poets*, 1887; *A Boy's Town*, 1890; *Criticism and Fiction*, 1891; *A Little Swiss Sojourn*, 1892; *My Year in a Log Cabin,* 1893; *My Literary Passions,* 1895; *Impressions and Experiences,* 1896; *Stories of Ohio,* 1897; *Literary Friends and Acquaintance,* 1900; *Heroines of Fiction,* 1901; *Literature and Life,* 1902; *London Films,* 1905; *Certain Delightful English Towns,* 1906; *Roman Holidays and Others,* 1908; *Seven English Cities,* 1909; *Imaginary Interviews,* 1910; *My Mark Twain,* 1910; *Familiar Spanish Travels,* 1913; *The Seen and the Unseen at Stratford-on-Avon,* 1914; *Years of My Youth,* 1916; *Eighty Years and After,* 1921; *Life in Letters of William Dean Howells,* 1928.

Plays: *The Parlor Car,* 1876; *Out of the Question,* 1877; *A Counterfeit Presentment,* 1877; *The Sleeping Car,* 1883; *The Register,* 1884; *The Elevator,* 1885; *The Garroters,* 1886; *A Sea-Change; or, Love's Stowaway,* 1888; *The Mouse-Trap and Other Farces,* 1889; *The Albany Depot,* 1892; *A Letter of Introduction,* 1892; *The Unexpected Guests,* 1893; *Evening Dress,* 1893; *A Likely Story,* 1894; *A Previous Engagement,* 1897; *Room Forty-five,* 1900; *Bride Roses,* 1900; *The Smoking Car,* 1900; *An Indian Giver,* 1900; *Parting Friends,* 1911.

Among the collections Howells edited are *Library of Universal Adventure by Sea and Land* . . . , New York, 1888, and *The Great Modern American Stories: An Anthology,* New York, 1920, to which he contributed an introduction.

REPRINTS

No collection of Howells's writings has been published. Reprints from previously published stories, plays, and sketches have been issued under the following titles: *Five O'Clock Tea,* New York, 1894; *Doorstep Acquaintance, and Other Sketches,* Boston, 1900; *Buying a Horse,* Boston, 1916; *Hither and Thither in Germany,* New York, 1920. Reprints of separate items are *A Modern Instance* (1882), Boston, 1909, in Riverside Literature Ser.; *The Parlor Car* (1876) *and The Sleeping Car* (1883), Boston, 1918, in Riverside Lit. Ser.; *The Rise of Silas Lapham* (1885), ed. by James M. Spinning, Boston, 1928, in Riverside Lit. Ser., and also, Boston, 1937, with an introduction by Booth Tarkington; *Annie Kilburn* (1888), New York, 1919, in Modern Classics, with an introduction by William B. Cairns; and *A Hazard of New Fortunes* (1890), New York, 1917, in the Modern Lib. The campaign biography written for and corrected by Lincoln, published as *Lives and Speeches of Abraham Lincoln and Hannibal Hamlin,* Columbus, Ohio, 1860, was reissued in facsimile in part as *Life of Abraham Lincoln,* Springfield, Ill., 1938.

LETTERS AND OTHER COLLECTED ITEMS

There still remain in manuscript many Howells letters. The largest collection yet published is that edited by his daughter Mildred Howells, *Life in*

*Letters of William Dean Howells,* New York, 1928, 2 vols., with a bibl., II, 403–409. Further important letters are included in Albert B. Paine, *Mark Twain: A Biography,* New York, 1912, 3 vols., and in Percy Lubbock, ed., *The Letters of Henry James,* New York, 1920, 2 vols. Howells contributed an introductory letter to Charles Warren Stoddard's *South Sea Idyls,* Boston, 1892. A printing of manuscript letters relative to *A Woman's Reason* (1883) is George W. Arms, "A Novel and Two Letters," *Jour. Rutgers Univ. Lib.,* VIII (1944), 9–13 and *idem,* " 'Ever Devotedly Yours': The Whitlock-Howells Correspondence," *ibid.,* X (1946), 1–19. See also F. C. Marston, Jr., "An Early Howells Letter," *Amer. Lit.,* XVIII (1946), 163–165.

Five unpublished prefaces, written for a projected thirty-volume collected "Library Edition" (1911) of Howells's writings—of which only six volumes were published—were edited by George W. Arms, "Howells' Unpublished Prefaces," *New Eng. Quar.,* XVII (1944), 580–591.

## BIOGRAPHY AND CRITICISM

The large collections of Howells manuscripts that have become available since his death in 1920, together with the many special studies published since that time, make the need for further narrative and critical biographical estimates especially pressing. The most satisfactory study is Delmar G. Cooke, *William Dean Howells: A Critical Study,* New York, 1922. The last general study was that of Oscar W. Firkins, *William Dean Howells: A Study,* Cambridge, 1924. Three years before Howells's death appeared Alexander Harvey's *William Dean Howells: A Study of the Achievement of a Literary Artist,* New York, 1917, factually inaccurate. The best brief narrative sketch is that of Firkins in *Dict. Amer. Biog.* (1932).

Estimates of Howells as a man of letters, important to the extent that the authors are spokesmen of their times, are Horace E. Scudder, "The East and the West in Recent Fiction," *Atl. Mo.,* LII (1883), 704–706; *idem,* "James, Crawford, and Howells," *ibid.,* LVII (1886), 850–857; "Mr. Howells' Novels," in John M. Robertson, *Essays Towards a Critical Method,* London, 1889, pp. 149–199; Horace E. Scudder, "Mr. Howells's Literary Creed," *Atl. Mo.,* LXVIII (1891), 566–569; "Mr. Howells and Romanticism," in William P. Trent, *The Authority of Criticism and Other Essays,* New York, 1899, pp. 257–268; Brander Matthews, "Mr. Howells as a Critic," *Forum,* XXXII (1902), 629–638; Hamlin Garland, "Sanity in Fiction," *No. Amer. Rev.,* CLXXVI (1903), 336–348; Mark Twain, "William Dean Howells," *Harper's Mag.,* CXIII (1906), 221–225; Henry M. Alden, "William Dean Howells," *Bookman,* XLIX (1919), 549–554; H. L. Mencken, *Prejudices: First Series,* New York, 1919, pp. 52–58; Edmund Gosse, "The Passing of William Dean Howells," *Living Age,* CCCVI (1920), 98–100; Carl Van Doren, in *Camb. Hist. Amer. Lit.,* III (1921), 77–85; Vernon L. Parrington, *Main Currents in*

*American Thought,* New York, III (1930), 241-253; Hamlin Garland, "Howells," in John Macy, ed., *American Writers on American Literature,* New York, 1931, pp. 285-297; Van Wyck Brooks, three chapters in *New England: Indian Summer,* New York, 1940: "Howells in Cambridge," pp. 204-223; "Howells and James," pp. 224-249; and "Howells in New York," pp. 373-394—a trilogy of estimates which together form the most substantial of recent studies.

Howells as a social critic is most fully treated in Walter F. Taylor, *The Economic Novel in America,* Chapel Hill, N.C., 1942, pp. 214-281; and in the unpublished thesis of George W. Arms, "The Social Criticism of William Dean Howells," New York University, 1939—which stresses the influence of Tolstoy, Morris, George, Bellamy, and others. One of the earliest discussions of the subject is Altha L. Bass, "The Social Consciousness of William Dean Howells," *New Repub.,* XXVI (1921), 192-194. Later studies of the subject are J. W. Getzels, "William Dean Howells and Socialism," *Science and Society,* II (1938), 376-386; Conrad Wright, "The Sources of Mr. Howells's Socialism," *ibid.,* pp. 514-517—the influence of Laurence Gronlund; George W. Arms, "Further Inquiry into Howells's Socialism," *ibid.,* III (1939), 245-248; and *idem,* "The Literary Background of Howells's Social Criticism," *Amer. Lit.,* XIV (1942), 260-276.

The best discussion of Howells as dramatist is "William Dean Howells and the Approach to Realism," in Arthur H. Quinn, *A History of the American Drama from the Civil War to the Present Day,* New York, 1936, I, 66-81.

Among earlier studies of Howells, still useful are "William Dean Howells," in Harry T. Peck, *The Personal Equation,* New York, 1898, pp. 3-49; A. Schade Van Westrum, "Mr. Howells and American Aristocracies," *Bookman,* XXV (1907), 67-73; "William Dean Howells as Man of Letters," in William C. Wilkinson, *Some New Literary Valuations,* New York, 1909, pp. 11-73.

In Howells's late lifetime appeared W. B. Trites, "William Dean Howells," *Forum,* XLIX (1913), 217-240; "Howells," in John Macy, *The Spirit of American Literature,* Garden City, N.Y., 1913, pp. 278-295; "William Dean Howells and Altruria," in John C. Underwood, *Literature and Insurgency,* New York, 1914, pp. 87-129; and Helen T. and Wilson Follett, *Some Modern Novelists,* New York, 1918, pp. 99-123.

Later studies are John Erskine, "William Dean Howells," *Bookman,* LI (1920), 385-389; May Tomlinson, "Fiction and Mr. Howells," *So. Atl. Quar.,* XX (1921), 360-367; James F. Muirhead, "Howells and Trollope," *Living Age,* CCCVIII (1921), 304-309; Régis Michaud, *The American Novel Today,* Boston, 1928, pp. 61-70; C. Hartley Grattan, "Howells: Ten Years

After," *Amer. Mercury*, XX (1930), 42–50; Herbert Edwards, "Howells and the Controversy over Realism in American Fiction," *Amer. Lit.*, III (1931), 237–248; Aubrey H. Starke, "William Dean Howells and Sidney Lanier," *Amer. Lit.*, III (1931), 79–82; "Howells" in George E. De Mille, *Literary Criticism in America*, New York, 1931, pp. 182–205; Harry Hartwick, *The Foreground of American Fiction*, New York, 1934, pp. 315–340; Bernard Smith, "Howells: The Genteel Radical," *Sat. Rev. Lit.*, XI (Aug. 11, 1934), 41–42; Arthur H. Quinn, *American Fiction*, New York, 1936, pp. 257–278; Walter F. Taylor, "William Dean Howells: Artist and American," *Sewanee Rev.*, XLVI (1938), 288–303; and Bernard Smith, *Forces in American Criticism*, New York, 1939, pp. 158–175.

The most recent studies are "Howells and Realism," in Carl Van Doren, *The American Novel*, rev. ed., New York, 1940, pp. 115–136; Alfred Kazin, "Howells: A Late Portrait," *Antioch Rev.*, I (1941), 216–233; "William Dean Howells," in John P. Pritchard, *Return to the Fountains*, Durham, N.C., 1942, pp. 135–147—the influence of the classics; Edwin H. Cady, "William Dean Howells and the *Ashtabula Sentinel*," *Ohio State Arch. and Hist. Quar.*, LIII (1944), 39–51—some shaping forces in Howells's early years; *idem*, "A Note on Howells and 'The Smiling Aspects of Life,'" *Amer. Lit.*, XVII (1945), 175–178; Edwin H. Cady, "The Neuroticism of William Dean Howells," *PMLA*, LXI (1946), 229–238; George Snell, "Howells' Grasshopper," *College Eng.*, VII (1946), 444–452; and William M. Gibson, "Materials and Form in Howells's First Novels," *Amer. Lit.*, XIX (1947), 158–166.

PRIMARY SOURCES

The most important source material is in Howells's letters, his travel books, and his autobiographical novels and studies: *A Boy's Town*, New York, 1890; *My Year in a Log Cabin*, New York, 1893; *Impressions and Experiences*, New York, 1896; *Literary Friends and Acquaintance*, New York, 1900; and *Years of My Youth*, New York, 1916—reminiscences, chiefly of the Ohio days. Other biographical material is in *A Day's Pleasure* (1876) and *New Leaf Mills* (1913). William Cooper Howells's *Recollections of Life in Ohio from 1813 to 1840*, Cincinnati, 1895, are reminiscences of his father, with an introduction by William Dean Howells. Hamlin Garland's *Roadside Meetings* (1930) and *My Friendly Contemporaries* (1932) contain much source material about Howells. An early article of Van Wyck Brooks is "Mr. Howells at Work at Seventy-two . . . ," *World's Work*, XVIII (1909), 11547–11549. A recent collection is George W. Arms and William M. Gibson, eds., "Five Interviews with William Dean Howells," *Americana*, XXXVII, No. 2 (Apr., 1943)—impressions gathered by Stephen Crane, Theodore Dreiser, and others.

The letters, memoirs, and biographies of Mark Twain, James Russell

Lowell, Henry James, Henry Holt, and other nineteenth and twentieth century American writers and editors often contain significant references to Howells.

Two major manuscript collections are in the Harvard College Library and the National Archives at Washington. Other collections are in the Longfellow House, Cambridge; the W. D. Howells House, Kittery, Me.; the T. B. Aldrich Birthplace, Portsmouth, N.H.; the Henry E. Huntington Library; and the Boston Public Library. Further material is in the Princeton University Library and the Rutgers University Library.

BIBLIOGRAPHY

A listing and collation, with a few exceptions, of all Howells's books and periodical publications is William M. Gibson and George Arms, comps., "A Bibliography of William Dean Howells," which began in the *Bul. N.Y. Pub. Lib.,* L, 675–698 (Sept., 1946). This checklist is continued in successive issues of the *Bulletin,* ending in Aug., 1947. Earlier listings are Oscar W. Firkins, *William Dean Howells: A Study* (1924), pp. 339–346; Delmar G. Cooke, *William Dean Howells* (1922), pp. 257–272; and *Camb. Hist. Amer. Lit.,* IV (1921), 663–666. A bibliography of secondary Howells items is needed.

## (JAMES) LANGSTON HUGHES
### b. 1902

WRITINGS

Poems: *The Weary Blues,* 1926; *Fine Clothes to the Jew,* 1927; *Dear Lovely Death,* 1931; *The Negro Mother,* 1931; *Scottsboro Limited,* 1932; *The Dream Keeper,* 1932; *A New Song,* 1938; *Shakespeare in Harlem,* 1942; *Freedom's Plow,* 1943; *Fields of Wonder,* 1947.

Fiction: *Not Without Laughter,* 1930; *The Ways of White Folks,* 1934. *The Big Sea,* 1940, is an autobiography to the year 1930.

BIOGRAPHY AND CRITICISM

Early estimates are Frank L. Schoell, "Un Poète Nègre," *Revue Politique et Littéraire,* LXVII (1929), 436–438; James W. Johnson, *Black Manhattan,* New York, 1930, pp. 271–273; and John Chamberlain, "The Negro as Writer," *Bookman,* LXX (1930), 603–611. More recent criticism is Jay Saunders Redding, *To Make a Poet Black,* Chapel Hill, N.C., 1939, pp. 113–117; and "Shakespeare in Harlem," in Edwin R. Embree, *Thirteen Against the Odds,* New York, 1944, pp. 117–138.

Manuscript poems of Hughes are in the Lockwood Memorial Library, University of Buffalo.

A bio-bibliography is Fred B. Millett, *Contemporary American Authors,* New York, 1940, pp. 403–404.

## DAVID HUMPHREYS
### *1752–1818*

*Poems by Col. David Humphreys,* 1789; *The Miscellaneous Works of Colonel Humphreys,* 1790 (and 1804); *The Yankey in England: A Drama in Five Acts,* 1816?; *Letters from the Hon. David Humphreys, F.R.S.,* 1817.

The most recent study of Humphreys is "David Humphreys" and "The Honorable David Humphreys," in Leon Howard, *The Connecticut Wits,* Chicago, 1943, pp. 112–132, 241–270. The sketch in *Dict. Amer. Biog.* (1932) is by Stanley T. Williams.

Valuable as a source of original material is Frank L. Humphreys, *The Life and Times of David Humphreys,* New York, 1917, 2 vols. The most valuable collection of Humphreys manuscripts is in the National Archives. Other material is in the Library of Congress, the Massachusetts Historical Society, the Historical Society of Pennsylvania, and the Yale University Library.

A checklist of Humphreys's writings, together with a description of the manuscript writings, is in Leon Howard, *The Connecticut Wits* (1943), pp. 419–420. Further secondary items follow the sketch of Humphreys in the *Dict. Amer. Biog.* (1932).

## JAMES GIBBONS HUNEKER
### *1860–1921*

SEPARATE WORKS

*Mezzotints in Modern Music,* 1899; *Chopin: The Man and His Music,* 1900; *Melomaniacs,* 1902; *Overtones,* 1904; *Iconoclasts,* 1905; *Visionaries,* 1905; *Egoists,* 1909; *Promenades of an Impressionist,* 1910; *Franz Liszt,* 1911; *The Pathos of Distance,* 1913; *Old Fogy,* 1913; *Ivory, Apes, and Peacocks,* 1915; *New Cosmopolis,* 1915; *The Development of Piano Music,* 1915–1916; *Unicorns,* 1917; *The Philharmonic Society of New York,* 1917; *The Steinway Collection of Paintings,* 1919; *Bedouins,* 1920; *Steeplejack,* 1920; *Painted Veils,* 1920; *Variations,* 1921.

COLLECTED WORKS

Only Huneker's letters have been collected and edited by his wife, Josephine Huneker, in two volumes: *Letters of James Gibbons Huneker,* New York, 1022, and *Intimate Letters of James Gibbons Huneker,* New York,

1924 (reprinted, 1936). An additional letter is in *Letters to Conrad,* London 1926.

REPRINTS

Huneker's only novel, *Painted Veils* (1920) was reprinted by the Modern Lib., New York, 1932. A good selection of material is H. L. Mencken, ed., *Essays by James Huneker,* New York, 1929.

BIOGRAPHY AND CRITICISM

Benjamin De Casseres has written a brief monograph: *James Gibbons Huneker,* New York, 1925. The best narrative sketch is that of William J. Henderson in *Dict. Amer. Biog.* (1932). Two early critical appreciations by H. L. Mencken are: "James Huneker," *A Book of Prefaces,* New York, 1917, pp. 151–194; and "James Huneker," *Prejudices,* 3rd ser., New York, 1922, pp. 65–83.

Later estimates are "Huneker," in George E. De Mille, *Literary Criticism in America,* New York, 1931, pp. 206–244; Van Wyck Brooks, *Sketches in Criticism,* New York, 1932, pp. 230–235; Bernard Smith, "Huneker, Man of the Tribe," *Sat. Rev. Lit.,* X (Aug. 19, 1933), 49–50; Albert Parry, *Garrets and Pretenders,* New York, 1933, pp. 114–119.

Most recent evaluations are Eliot C. Fay, "Huneker's Criticisms of French Literature," *French Rev.,* XIV (1940), 130–137, and Alfred Kazin, *On Native Grounds,* New York, 1942, pp. 62–66.

PRIMARY SOURCES

Huneker's autobiography, *Steeplejack,* New York, 1920, 2 vols., is casual and discursive, but supplements his letters as source material.

The fullest bibliographical listing is in Jacob Blanck, *Merle Johnson's American First Editions,* 4th ed., New York, 1942.

# WASHINGTON IRVING
## *1783–1859*

SEPARATE WORKS

*Letters of Jonathan Oldstyle, Gent.,* 1802–1803; *Salmagundi; or, The Whim-Whams and Opinions of Launcelot Langstaff, Esq., and Others* (with J K. Paulding and William Irving), 1807–1808; *A History of New York from the Beginning of the World to the End of the Dutch Dynasty,* 1809; biographical sketch of Thomas Campbell in *The Poetical Works of Thomas Campbell,* 1810; contributions to the *Analectic Magazine,* 1813–1815; *The Sketch Book of Geoffrey Crayon, Gent.,* 1819–1820; *Bracebridge Hall; or, The*

*Humorists,* 1822; *Tales of a Traveller,* 1824; *A History of the Life and Voyages of Christopher Columbus,* 1828; *A Chronicle of the Conquest of Granada,* 1829; *Voyages and Discoveries of the Companions of Columbus,* 1831; *The Alhambra,* 1832; *The Crayon Miscellany (A Tour on the Prairies, Abbotsford and Newstead Abbey, Legends of the Conquest of Spain),* 1835; *Astoria,* 1836; *The Rocky Mountains,* 1837; *The Life of Oliver Goldsmith with Selections from His Writings,* 1840; *Biography and Poetical Remains of the Late Margaret Miller Davidson,* 1841; *Mahomet and His Successors,* 1850; *The Life of George Washington,* 1855–1859; *Wolfert's Roost and Other Papers,* 1855; *Spanish Papers and Other Miscellanies,* 1866; *Abu Hassan,* 1924; *The Wild Huntsman,* 1924.

COLLECTED WORKS

The author's uniform revised (standard) edition is *The Works of Washington Irving,* New York, 1860–1861, 21 vols. The same text is to be found in *The Works of Washington Irving,* New York, 1881, 12 vols., a more easily procurable set. Other editions are *Works of Washington Irving,* Philadelphia, 1870–1871, 27 vols. (Knickerbocker Edition); *Irving's Works,* New York, 1882–1884, 27 vols. (Hudson Edition); and *Works of Washington Irving,* New York, 1910, 40 vols.

Pierre M. Irving edited some unpublished material and reprints in *Spanish Papers and Other Miscellanies Hitherto Unpublished or Uncollected,* New York, 1866, 2 vols.

The first publication of *Abu Hassan* and of *The Wild Huntsman* was undertaken by George S. Hellman, Boston, 1924. He edited each with an introduction.

William R. Langfeld edited *The Poems of Washington Irving Brought Together from Various Sources and for the First Time,* New York, 1931—also in *Bul. N.Y. Pub. Lib.,* XXXIV (1930), 763–779.

PRINTED LETTERS

The earliest collections of printed letters were made by Evert A. Duyckinck, ed., *Irvingiana: A Memorial to Washington Irving . . . ,* New York, 1860, and by Charles R. Leslie, *Autobiographical Recollections,* Boston, 1860. A large collection is that of Pierre M. Irving, ed., *The Life and Letters of Washington Irving,* New York, 1862–1864, 4 vols. Other collections have appeared as follows: William W. Waldron, ed., *Washington Irving and Cotemporaries . . . ,* New York, 1867; Thatcher T. Payne Luquer, ed., "Correspondence of Washington Irving and John Howard Payne," *Scribner's Mag.,* XLVIII (1910), 461–482, 597–616; *Letters from Washington Irving to Mrs. William Renwick, and to Her Son James Renwick . . . ,* New York, 1910; George S. Hellman, ed., *The Letters of Washington Irving to Henry*

*Brevoort,* New York, 1915, 2 vols. (1918, 1 vol.); Killis Campbell, ed., "The Kennedy Papers: A Sheaf of Unpublished Letters from Washington Irving," *Sewanee Rev.,* XXV (1917), 1–19; George S. Hellman, *Washington Irving, Esquire: Ambassador at Large from the New World to the Old,* New York, 1925; Stanley T. Williams, ed., *Letters from Sunnyside and Spain by Washington Irving,* New Haven, 1928—written during middle life, 1840–1845; *idem,* ed., *Washington Irving and the Storrows: Letters from England and the Continent,* Cambridge, 1933; Coleman O. Parsons, ed., "Washington Irving Writes from Granada," *Amer. Lit.,* VI (1935), 439–443; Stanley T. Williams and Leonard B. Beach, "Washington Irving's Letters to Mary Kennedy," *Amer. Lit.,* VI (1934), 44–65; *idem,* "Washington Irving and Andrew Jackson," *Yale Univ. Lib. Gaz.,* XIX (1945), 67–69; and Clara and Rudolf Kirk, eds., "Seven Letters of Washington Irving," *Jour. Rutgers Univ. Lib.,* IX (1945), 1–22—written in 1804–1805; continued, *ibid.,* pp. 36–58, and X (1946), 20–27.

JOURNALS AND DIARIES

Irving has been fortunate in the editorial coverage of his notes and journals. The following have been published: William P. Trent and George S. Hellman, eds., *The Journals of Washington Irving, from July, 1815, to July, 1842,* Boston, 1919, 3 vols.; William P. Trent, ed., *Notes and Journal of Travel in Europe, 1804–1805,* New York, 1921, 3 vols.; Clara L. Penny, ed., *Washington Irving Diary: Spain, 1828–29,* New York, 1926. Five volumes of journals and notes have been edited with critical introductions by Stanley T. Williams: *Tour in Scotland, 1817, and Other Manuscript Notes by Washington Irving,* New Haven, 1927—including the *Excursion to Runcorn* and *Fragments; Notes While Preparing Sketch Book, etc. . . . . 1817, by Washington Irving,* New Haven, 1927; *Journal of Washington Irving, 1823–1824,* Cambridge, 1931—including a recently discovered manuscript by Irving on William the Conqueror, pp. 245–257; *Journal, 1803, by Washington Irving,* New York, 1934; and *Journal of Washington Irving, 1828, and Miscellaneous Notes on Moorish Legend and History,* New York, 1937. John F. McDermott edited *The Western Journals of Washington Irving,* Norman, Okla., 1944—an annotated transcript of the five unpublished journals which Irving kept on his trip in 1832 to the country west of Arkansas (the first was published by Trent and Hellman in a different version in their three-volume edition of the *Journals*).

EDITED TEXTS AND REPRINTS

A verbatim reprint of the 1809 edition of *A History of New York,* with critical introduction, was edited by Stanley T. Williams and Tremaine

McDowell, New York, 1927 (Amer. Authors Ser.); selections from it are given in Edwin Greenlaw, ed., *Knickerbocker's History,* New York, 1923 (Pocket Classics).

*The Sketch Book* (1819–1820) has been reprinted very frequently. Among recent issues are those edited by H. Y. Moffett, New York, 1929 (New Pocket Classics), and T. Williamson, New York, 1929 (Modern Readers' Ser.).

*Letters of Jonathan Oldstyle* (1802–1803), edited from the original text by Stanley T. Williams, was reproduced by the Facsimile Text Society, No. 52, New York, 1941.

*The Conquest of Granada* (1829) and *Mahomet and His Successors* (1850) were published in Everyman's Lib., London, 1910 and 1911. *Tales by Washington Irving,* a selection by Carl Van Doren, was issued in World's Classics, London, 1928.

A serviceable one-volume selected text is Henry A. Pochmann, ed., *Washington Irving: Representative Selections, with Introduction, Bibliography, and Notes,* New York, 1934 (Amer. Writers Ser.). Saxe Commins edited *Selected Writings of Washington Irving,* New York, 1945, for the Modern Library.

BIOGRAPHY AND CRITICISM

The definitive biography is Stanley T. Williams, *The Life of Washington Irving,* New York, 1935, 2 vols., a detailed study of the man and of literary life in his times. The standard history until 1935 was Pierre M. Irving's *The Life and Letters of Washington Irving, By His Nephew* . . ., New York, 1862–1864, 4 vols., issued in a People's Edition in 1869. Other biographies are those of Charles Adams, New York, 1870; David J. Hill, New York, 1879; Richard H. Stoddard, New York, 1886; Francis H. Underwood, Philadelphia, 1890; Charles Dudley Warner, Boston, 1890; and Henry W. Boynton, Boston, 1901. There is also the study of George S. Hellman, *Washington Irving, Esquire: Ambassador at Large from the New World to the Old,* New York, 1925.

Special studies, useful for the light they shed on European sources and on Irving's contacts and influence abroad, are Henry A. Pochmann's introduction to *Washington Irving: Representative Selections* . . ., New York, 1934, pp. xi–xcii; George D. Morris, *Washington Irving's Fiction in the Light of French Criticism,* Bloomington, Ind., 1916; Adolph B. Benson, "Scandinavians in the Works of Washington Irving," *Scandinavian Studies and Notes,* IX (1927), 207–223; Emilio Goggio, "Washington Irving and Italy," *Romanic Rev.,* XXI (1930), 26–33; Stanley T. Williams, "The First Version of the Writings of Washington Irving in Spanish," *Modern Philol.,* XXVIII (1930),

185–201; *idem,* "Washington Irving and Fernán Caballero," *Jour. English and Germanic Philol.,* XXIX (1930), 352–366—a companion article to the last named; *idem,* "Washington Irving's First Stay in Paris," *Amer. Lit.,* II (1930), 15–20; Henry A. Pochmann, "Irving's German Tour and Its Influence on His Tales," *PMLA,* XLV (1930), 1150–1187; Edwin H. Zeydel," Washington Irving and Ludwig Tieck," *ibid.,* XLVI (1931), 946–947—a supplemental article to the last named; Ernest Boll, "Charles Dickens and Washington Irving," *Modern Language Quar.,* V (1944), 453–467; William C. Desmond Pacey, "Washington Irving and Charles Dickens," *Amer. Lit.,* XVI (1945), 332–339; Louise M. Hoffman, "Irving's Use of Spanish Sources in *The Conquest of Granada,*" *Hispania,* XXVIII (1945), 483–498; and Christof Wegelin, "Dickens and Irving," *Modern Language Quar.,* VII (1946), 83–91.

There are four studies dealing with the Knickerbocker History: Edwin Greenlaw, "Washington Irving's Comedy of Politics," *Texas Rev.,* I (1916), 291–306; Tremaine McDowell, "General James Wilkinson in the *Knickerbocker History of New York,*" *Modern Language Notes,* XLI (1926), 353–359; Clarence M. Webster, "Irving's Expurgation of the 1809 *History of New York,*" *Amer. Lit.,* IV (1932), 293–295; and Charlton G. Laird, "Tragedy and Irony in *Knickerbocker's History,*" *Amer. Lit.,* XII (1940), 157–172. For *The Sketch Book* there is Henry A. Pochmann, "Irving's German Sources in *The Sketch Book,*" *Studies in Philol.,* XXVII (1930), 477–507.

Other special studies are G. E. Hastings, "John Bull and His American Descendants," *Amer. Lit.,* I (1929), 40–68; Jason A. Russell, "Irving: Recorder of Indian Life," *Jour. Amer. Hist.,* XXV (1931), 185–195; Albert Keiser, *The Indian in American Literature,* New York, 1933, pp. 52–64; Stanley T. Williams, "Washington Irving, Matilda Hoffman, and Emily Foster," *Modern Language Notes,* XLVIII (1933), 182–186; Stanley T. Williams and Ernest E. Leisy, eds., "Polly Holman's Wedding: Notes by Washington Irving," *Southwest Rev.,* XIX (1934), 449–454; Irving T. Richards, "John Neal's Gleanings in Irvingiana," *Amer. Lit.,* VIII (1936), 170–179; Francis P. Smith, "Washington Irving, the Fosters, and Some Poetry," *Amer. Lit.,* IX (1937), 228–232; J. Chesley Mathews, "Washington Irving's Knowledge of Dante," *Amer. Lit.,* X (1939), 480–483; George Snell, "Washington Irving: A Revaluation," *Modern Language Quar.,* VII (1946), 303–309; Thomas A. Kirby, "Carlyle and Irving," *Jour. of English Lit. Hist.,* XIII (1946), 59–63; James L. Wilson, "Washington Irving's 'Celebrated English Poet,'" *Amer. Lit.,* XVIII (1946), 247–249—a note on Southey; Jacob Blanck, *"Salmagundi* and Its Publisher," *Papers Bibl. Soc. Amer.,* XLI (1947), 1–32; and Thomas A. Kirby, "Irving and Moore: A Note on Anglo-American Literary Relations," *Mod. Lang. Notes,* LXII (1947), 251–255.

Contemporary estimates and recollections of interest are "Irving's Conquest of Granada," in William H. Prescott, *Biographical and Critical Miscellanies,* Philadelphia, 1845, pp. 82–113; Evert A. Duyckinck, ed., *Irvingiana . . . ,* New York, 1860; Charles R. Leslie, *Autobiographical Recollections,* Boston, 1860, pp. 204–302; and Henry W. Longfellow, and others, "Tributes to Irving," *Proc. Mass. Hist. Soc.,* 1st ser., IV (1860), 393–424. George S. Hellman edited *Letters of Henry Brevoort to Washington Irving, Together with Other Unpublished Brevoort Papers,* New York, 1916, 2 vols. (1-vol. ed., 1918). Further reminiscences are in M. C. Yarborough, "Rambles with Washington Irving: Quotations from an Unpublished Autobiography of William C. Preston," *So. Atl. Quar.,* XXIX (1930), 423–439.

Other published source material is in Stanley T. Williams and Leonard B. Beach, eds., *The Journal of Emily Foster,* New York, 1938; Leonard B. Beach and others, eds., "Peter Irving's Journals," *Bul. N.Y. Pub. Lib.,* XLIV (1940), 591–608, 649–670, 745–772, 814–842, 888–914—the extant record of the travels of Irving's oldest brother in 1807. Henry L. Ellsworth's *Washington Irving on the Prairie; or, A Narrative of a Tour of the Southwest in the Year 1832,* ed. by Stanley T. Williams and Barbara D. Simison, New York, 1937, is a more accurate account than Irving's *A Tour on the Prairies* (1835).

The three chief manuscript collections, in order of their importance, are: the Seligman and George S. Hellman Collections in the New York Public Library (see *The Seligman Collection of Irvingiana,* New York, 1926, and *Catalogue of the Hellman Collection of Irvingiana,* New York, 1929); the Irving Collection in the Sterling Memorial Library of Yale University; and the collection in the Henry E. Huntington Library. The Irving-Storrow letters are in the Harvard College Library; Irving's diplomatic correspondence is in the Library of Congress and in the files of the National Archives.

Stanley T. Williams and Mary E. Edge have compiled *A Bibliography of the Writings of Washington Irving: A Check List,* New York, 1936, very complete, with listings of secondary material as well to date of publication. A collector's bibliography, with many data on issues and conditions, is William R. Langfeld and Philip C. Blackburn, "Washington Irving: A Bibliography," *Bul. N.Y. Pub. Lib.,* XXXVI (1932), 415–422, 487–494, 561–571, 627–636, 683–689, 755–778, 828–841. The listing in Henry A. Pochmann, *Washington Irving: Representative Selections . . . ,* New York, 1934, pp. xciii–cx, is selective and annotated.

# HENRY JAMES
## 1843–1916

SEPARATE WORKS

*A Passionate Pilgrim and Other Tales*, 1875; *Transatlantic Sketches*, 1875; *Roderick Hudson*, 1876; *The American*, 1877; *Watch and Ward*, 1878 (James's first novel, serialized in 1871); *French Poets and Novelists*, 1878; *The Europeans*, 1878; *Daisy Miller*, 1879; *An International Episode*, 1879; *The Madonna of the Future and Other Tales*, 1879; *Hawthorne*, 1879; *The Diary of a Man of Fifty, and A Bundle of Letters*, 1880; *Confidence*, 1880; *Washington Square*, 1881; *The Portrait of a Lady*, 1881; *The Siege of London, The Pension Beaurepas, and The Point of View*, 1883; *Portraits of Places*, 1883; *Tales of Three Cities*, 1884; *A Little Tour in France*, 1885; *Stories Revived*, 1885; *The Bostonians*, 1886; *The Princess Casamassima* 1886; *Partial Portraits*, 1888; *The Aspern Papers, Louisa Pallant, and The Modern Warning*, 1888; *The Reverberator*, 1888; *A London Life, The Patagonia, The Liar, and Mrs. Temperley*, 1889; *The Tragic Muse*, 1890; *The Lesson of the Master, The Marriages, etc.*, 1892; *The Private Life, etc.*, 1893; *The Wheel of Time, etc.*, 1893; *The Real Thing and Other Tales*, 1893; *Picture and Text*, 1893; *Essays in London and Elsewhere*, 1893; *Theatricals: Two Comedies—Tenants, and Disengaged*, 1894; *Theatricals, Second Series*, 1895; *Terminations, The Death of the Lion, etc.*, 1895; *Embarrassments*, 1896; *The Other House*, 1896; *The Spoils of Poynton*, 1897; *What Maisie Knew*, 1897; *The Two Magics, The Turn of the Screw, and Covering End*, 1898; *In the Cage*, 1898; *The Awkward Age*, 1899; *The Soft Side*, 1900; *The Sacred Fount*, 1901; *The Wings of the Dove*, 1902; *William Wetmore Story and His Friends*, 1903; *The Better Sort*, 1903; *The Ambassadors*, 1903; *The Golden Bowl*, 1904; *The Question of Our Speech, and The Lesson of Balzac*, 1905; *English Hours*, 1905; *The American Scene*, 1907; *Views and Reviews*, 1908; *Julia Bride*, 1909; *Italian Hours*, 1909; *The Finer Grain*, 1910; *The Outcry*, 1911; *A Small Boy and Others*, 1913; *Notes on Novelists*, 1914; *Notes of a Son and Brother*, 1914; *The Ivory Tower*, 1917; *The Middle Years*, 1917; *The Sense of the Past*, 1917; *Within the Rim and Other Essays, 1914–1915*, 1918; *Gabrielle de Bergerac*, 1918; *Travelling Companions*, 1919.

COLLECTED WORKS

*The Novels and Tales of Henry James*, New York, 1907–1917, 26 vols., is a uniformly bound issue of James's works, and the only collected American edition. It contains the first printing of *Julia Bride, The Jolly Corner*, and *Fordham Castle*. It was issued, with many added titles, London, 1921–1923, 35 vols.

*The Letters of Henry James,* New York, 1920, 2 vols., were edited by Percy Lubbock. Reviews of these *Letters,* which should be consulted, are Edith Wharton, "Henry James in His Letters," *Quar. Rev.,* CCXXXIV (1920), 188–202, and Pelham Edgar, "The Letters of Henry James," *Queen's Quar.,* XXVIII (1921), 283–287. Other published collections of the letters are *The Letters of Henry James to Walter Berry,* Paris, 1928; E(dward) F. Benson, ed., *Henry James: Letters to A. C. Benson and Auguste Monod, Now First Published,* London, 1930; and Elizabeth Robins, ed., *Theatre and Friendship: Some Henry James Letters, with a Commentary,* New York, 1932. Gleanings are J. C. Squire, ed., "Three Unpublished Letters and a Monologue by Henry James," *London Mercury,* VI (1922), 492–501; James McLane, ed., "A Henry James Letter," *Yale Rev.,* n.s., XIV (1924), 205–208; "Two Unpublished Letters," *Hound and Horn,* VII (1934), 414–416; and Louise Boit, "Henry James as Landlord," *Atl. Mo.,* CLXXVIII (1946), 118–121.

*The Notebooks of Henry James* were edited, with an introduction, by F. O. Matthiessen and Kenneth B. Murdock, New York, 1947—a record of James's progress from 1878 until his later years.

### EDITED TEXTS AND REPRINTS

A collection of early reviews, appearing 1864–1866, is gathered by Pierre de Chaignon la Rose, ed., *Notes and Reviews by Henry James,* Cambridge, 1921. The main body of James's critical dicta, contained in prefaces to separate volumes, has been collected, with an introduction, in R(ichard) P. Blackmur, *The Art of the Novel: Critical Prefaces,* New York, 1934. F(rancis) O. Matthiessen has edited *Stories of Writers and Artists,* New York, 1944, with an introduction originally published in *Partisan Rev.,* XI (1944), 71–87. Other recent collections, indicating an increased and widening interest in James, are Philip Rahv, ed., *The Great Short Novels of Henry James,* New York, 1944; and Clifton Fadiman, ed., *The Short Stories of Henry James,* New York, 1945 —a selection of seventeen short stories, written during 1877–1909.

A convenient one-volume text is Lyon N. Richardson, ed., *Henry James: Representative Selections, with Introduction, Bibliography, and Notes,* New York, 1941 (Amer. Writers Ser.).

Edna Kenton's "'The Ambassadors': Project of Novel," *Hound and Horn,* VII (1934), 541–562, is a partial printing of an unpublished manuscript which James sent to his publishers in 1900.

Reprints of individual novels and stories are *The Ambassadors,* New York 1930 (Modern Classics); *The American,* Boston, 1907 (Riverside College Classics); *Daisy Miller,* New York, 1918 (Modern Library)—with introduction by William Dean Howells; *Daisy Miller, and An International Episode,* New York, 1927 (Modern Readers' Series); *The Portrait of a Lady,* New York, 1936 (Modern Library); *The Spoils of Poynton,* Norfolk, Conn., 1943

(New Classic Series); *The Turn of the Screw, and The Lesson of the Master*, New York, 1930 (Modern Library); *The Turn of the Screw, and The Aspern Papers*, London, 1935 (Everyman's Library); *The Bostonians*, New York, 1945, edited by Philip Rahv; *The American Scene*, New York, 1946, with an introduction by W. H. Auden; and *The American Novels and Stories of Henry James*, edited with an introduction by F. O. Matthiessen, New York, 1947.

BIOGRAPHY AND CRITICISM

The standard descriptive and critical biography is Pelham Edgar, *Henry James: Man and Author*, London, 1927. Two earlier studies are Ford Madox Ford, *Henry James: A Critical Study*, London, 1913; and Rebecca West, *Henry James*, New York, 1916. Van Wyck Brooks, *The Pilgrimage of Henry James*, New York, 1925, lays emphasis on the stress, shown in his characters, set up by the pull between Europe and the United States. Significant European evaluations of James are Léon Edel, *Henry James: Les Années Dramatiques*, Paris, 1931; and Sten Bodvar Liljegren, *American and European in the Works of Henry James*, Lund, 1920.

Special studies of aspects of individual novels and stories are Stephen Spender, "The School of Experience in the Early Novels," *Hound and Horn*, VII (1934), 417–433; Royal A. Gettman, "Henry James's Revision of *The American*," *Amer. Lit.*, XVI (1945), 279–295; Francis Fergusson, "The Drama in *The Golden Bowl*," *Hound and Horn*, VII (1934), 407–413; F. O. Matthiessen, "The Painter's Sponge and Varnish Bottle: Henry James's Revision of *The Portrait of a Lady*," *Amer. Bookman*, I (1944), No. 1, 49–68; Hélène Harvitt, "How Henry James Revised *Roderick Hudson*: A Study in Style," *PMLA*, XXXIX (1924), 203–227; supplemented by Raymond D. Havens, "The Revision of *Roderick Hudson*," *PMLA*, XL (1925), 433–434; Edmund Wilson, "The Ambiguity of Henry James," *Hound and Horn*, VII (1934), 385–406—a discussion of *The Turn of the Screw;* Robert L. Wolff, "The Genesis of *The Turn of the Screw*," *Amer. Lit.*, XIII (1941), 1–8; and R. P. Blackmur, "The Sacred Fount," *Kenyon Rev.*, IV (1942), 328–352—a critical appraisal of aspects not elsewhere treated.

James in his relation to France is the subject of Marie R. Garnier, *Henry James et la France*, Paris, 1927—a documented study; Léon Edel, "A Note on the Translations of H. James in France," *Revue Anglo-Amér.*, VII (1930), 539–540; Charles Cestre, "La France dans l'Œuvre de Henry James," *Revue Anglo-Amér.*, X (1932), 1–13, 112–122; and W. C. D. Pacey, "Henry James and His French Contemporaries," *Amer. Lit.*, XIII (1941), 240–256.

An extensive study of James as a man of letters is F(rancis) O. Matthiessen, *Henry James: The Major Phase*, New York, 1944, based not only upon the novels but upon an examination of James's working notebooks. R(ichard) P. Blackmur's analysis of "The Critical Prefaces," *Hound and Horn,* VII (1934), 444-477, is found also as the introduction to his edition of the prefaces published as *The Art of the Novel . . .,* New York, 1934. Three other expositions of James's methods in fiction are Léon Edel, *The Prefaces of Henry James,* Paris, 1931; Morris Roberts, *Henry James's Criticism,* Cambridge, 1929; and "The Enchanted Kingdom of Henry James," in Ferner Nuhn, *The Wind Blew from the East,* New York, 1942, pp. 87-163.

Studies of James's technique and development are Joseph W. Beach, *The Method of Henry James,* New Haven, 1918; "The Education of Henry James," "A 'Passionate Pilgrim,'" and "The Return of Henry James"—chaps. iii, iv, viii, in Matthew Josephson, *Portrait of the Artist as American,* New York, 1930; Cornelia P. Kelley, *The Early Development of Henry James,* Urbana, Ill., 1930; C(linton) Hartley Grattan, *The Three Jameses . . .,* New York, 1932, pp. 208-357; Edwin M. Snell, *The Modern Fables of Henry James,* Cambridge, 1935; Arthur J. A. Waldock, *James, Joyce, and Others,* London, 1937; "Maule's Well; or, Henry James and the Relation of Morals to Manners," in Yvor Winters, *Maule's Curse . . .,* Norfolk, Conn., 1938, pp. 169-216; Lyon N. Richardson, introduction to *Henry James: Representative Selections . . .,* New York, 1941, pp. ix-xc; and Robert P. Warren, ed., the Henry James Number, *Kenyon Rev.,* V (1943), 481-617—a symposium of nine critical essays.

Other discussions treating special aspects of James's art and technique are Dorothy Bethurum, "Morality and Henry James," *Sewanee Rev.,* XXXI (1923), 324-330; Joseph W. Beach, *The Twentieth Century Novel: Studies in Technique,* New York, 1932, pp. 177-228; "The Special Case of Henry James," in Stuart P. Sherman, *The Emotional Discovery of America . . .,* New York, 1932, pp. 35-47; Harry Hartwick, *The Foreground of American Fiction,* New York, 1934, pp. 341-368; Edna Kenton, "Henry James in the World," *Hound and Horn,* VII (1934), 506-513; Lawrence Leighton, "Armor Against Time," *ibid.,* pp. 373-384; L. C. Knights, "Henry James and the Trapped Spectator," *Southern Rev.,* IV (1939), 600-615; Carl Van Doren, *The American Novel . . .,* New York, 1940, pp. 163-189; Randall Stewart, "The Moral Aspects of Henry James's 'International Situation,'" *University Rev.,* IX (1943), 109-113; F. O. Matthiessen, "Henry James' Portrait of the Artist," *Partisan Rev.,* XI (1944), 71-87; and Saul Rosenzweig, "The Ghost of Henry James," *Partisan Rev.,* XI (1944), 436-455—a psychoanalytical study.

Brief estimates of James, significant to the extent the authors are spokesmen of their times, are William Dean Howells, "Henry James, Jr.," *Century Mag.,* n.s. III (1882), 25-29; *idem,* "Mr. Henry James's Later Work," *No. Amer. Rev.,* CLXXVI (1903), 125-137; Joseph Conrad, "Henry James: An

Appreciation," *No. Amer. Rev.,* CLXXX (1905), 102–108; "Henry James," in William C. Brownell, *American Prose Masters,* New York, 1909, pp. 339–400; A(rthur) C. Benson, "Henry James," *Cornhill Mag.,* n.s. XL (1916), 511–519; "The Aesthetic Idealism of Henry James," in Stuart P. Sherman, *On Contemporary Literature,* New York, 1917, pp. 226–255; Henry James Number of the *Little Review,* V (Aug., 1918)—with contributions by Ezra Pound, T. S. Eliot, and others; Edmund Gosse, "Henry James," *Scribner's Mag.,* LXVII (1920), 422–430, 548–557; Van Wyck Brooks, "Henry James: The American Scene," *Dial,* LXXV (1923), 29–42; "Henry James: The Arch-Enemy of 'Low-Company,' " in Wyndham Lewis, *Men Without Art,* London, 1934, pp. 138–157; "Henry James, the Master," in Ford Madox Ford, *Portraits from Life,* Boston, 1937, pp. 1–20; Van Wyck Brooks, *New England: Indian Summer,* New York, 1940, pp. 224–249, 276–295, 395–408; "Henry James," in Dorothy M. Hoare, *Some Studies in the Modern Novel,* Litchfield, Conn., 1940, pp. 3–35; Stephen Spender, "A World Where the Victor Belonged to the Spoils," *N.Y. Times Book Rev.,* Mar. 12, 1944, p. 3; and Malcolm Cowley, "The Two Henry Jameses," *New Repub.,* CXII (1945), 177–180. F. W. Dupee edited *The Question of Henry James: A Collection of Critical Essays,* New York, 1945—estimates by Howells, Conrad, Lubbock, Eliot, Wilson, and others.

Accounts of James's interest in the theater will be found in "Henry James and the Theater," in Brander Matthews, *Playwrights and Playmaking . . . ,* New York, 1923, pp. 185–204, and Allen Wade, "Henry James as Dramatic Critic," *Theatre Arts Mo.,* XXVII (1943), 735–740, as well as in his own scattered notes on the theater, and the letters collected by Elizabeth Robins, *Theatre and Friendship . . . ,* New York, 1932.

Other studies of interest are "Henry James, Expatriate," in John C. Underwood, *Literature and Insurgency,* New York, 1914, pp. 41–86; Ralph B. Perry, "Henry James in Italy," *Harvard Grad. Mag.,* XLI (1933), 189–200; Léon Edel, "The Exile of Henry James," *Univ. Toronto Quar.,* II (1933), 520–532; Newton Arvin, "Henry James and the Almighty Dollar," *Hound and Horn,* VII (1934), 434–443; Marianne Moore, "Henry James as a Characteristic American," *ibid.,* 363–372; Léon Edel, "Henry James: The War Chapter, 1914–1916," *Univ. Toronto Quar.,* X (1941), 125–138; Daniel Lerner, "The Influence of Turgenev on Henry James," *Slavonic Year-Book,* XX (1941), 28–54; Richard N. Foley, *Criticism in American Periodicals of the Works of Henry James from 1866 to 1916,* Washington, 1944—a survey and summary of reviews; V. A. Young, "The Question of James," *Arizona Quar.,* I (winter, 1945), 57–62; Mervyn Jones-Evans, "Henry James's Year in France," *Horizon,* XIV (1946), 52–60; E. K. Brown, "James and Conrad," *Yale Rev.,* XXXV (1946), 265–285; Katherine Hoskins, "Henry James and the Future of the

Novel," *Sewanee Rev.*, LIV (1946), 87-101; R. W. Short, "The Sentence Structure of Henry James," *Amer. Lit.*, XVIII (1946), 71-88; Adeline R. Tintner, "The Spoils of Henry James," *PMLA*, LXI (1946), 239-251; Quentin Anderson, "Henry James and the New Jerusalem," *Kenyon Rev.*, VIII (1946), 515-566—on James as a moralist; Elizabeth F. Hoxie, "Mrs. Grundy Adopts Daisy Miller," *New Eng. Quar.*, XIX (1946), 474-484; and Morris Roberts, "Henry James and the Art of Foreshortening," *Rev. English Studies*, XXII (1946), 207-214.

PRIMARY SOURCES

Most of the Henry James manuscripts in public depositories are in the Harvard College Library and Library of Congress collections.

James gives an account of his boyhood days in Europe in *A Small Boy and Others*, New York, 1913. His early life through the Cambridge period is set down in *Notes of a Son and Brother*, New York, 1914; and *The Middle Years*, New York, 1917, carries the story approximately to the twentieth century. His published letters are mentioned above under Collected Works. James's secretary for many years, Theodora Bosanquet, has published *Henry James at Work*, London, 1924.

There are many important references to Henry James in published material relating to other members of the James family: Henry James (William James's son), ed., *The Letters of William James*, Boston, 1920; C(linton) Hartley Grattan, *The Three Jameses: A Family of Minds . . .*, New York, 1932; Anna R. Burr, ed., *Alice James: Her Brothers, Her Journal*, New York, 1934; Austin Warren, *The Elder Henry James*, New York, 1934; and Ralph B. Perry, *The Thought and Character of William James . . .*, Boston, 1935, 2 vols.

Reminiscences appear in Edith Wyatt, "Henry James: An Impression," *No. Amer. Rev.*, CCIII (1916), 592-599; E. S. Nadal, "Personal Recollections of Henry James," *Scribner's Mag.*, LXVIII (1920), 89-97; Robert Herrick, "A Visit to Henry James," in *The Manly Anniversary Studies in Language and Literature*, Chicago, 1923, pp. 229-242—with reference to James's change in style when he began dictation; "Henry James," in A(rthur) C. Benson. *Memories and Friends*, London, 1924, pp. 192-204; Mildred Howells, ed., *Life in Letters of William Dean Howells*, New York, 1928, *passim;* Edith Wharton, *A Backward Glance*, New York, 1934, pp. 169-196; and Compton Mackenzie, "Henry James," *Life and Letters Today*, XXXIX (1943), 147-155.

BIBLIOGRAPHY

LeRoy Phillips, *A Bibliography of the Writings of Henry James*, rev. ed., New York, 1930, is complete to that date. Gleanings appear in Edna Kenton,

"Some Bibliographical Notes on Henry James," *Hound and Horn*, VII (1934), 535–540. The bibliography in Lyon N. Richardson, *Henry James: Representative Selections* . . . , New York, 1941, is selective and annotated. I. R. Brussel, *Anglo-American First Editions: West to East*, New York, 1936, establishes American and English priorities of many items.

# WILLIAM JAMES
## 1842–1910

WORKS

*The Principles of Psychology*, 1890; *Psychology: Briefer Course*, 1892; *The Will to Believe, and Other Essays in Popular Philosophy*, 1897; *Human Immortality: Two Supposed Objections to the Doctrine*, 1898; *Talks to Teachers on Psychology*, 1899; *The Varieties of Religious Experience: A Study in Human Nature*, 1902; *The Sentiment of Rationality*, 1905; *Pragmatism: A New Name for Some Old Ways of Thinking*, 1907; *A Pluralistic Universe*, 1909; *The Meaning of Truth*, 1909.

*Some Problems of Philosophy: A Beginning of an Introduction to Philosophy*, New York, 1911, was prepared for the press by H. M. Kallen from the unfinished manuscript, and edited with prefatory note by his son, Henry James. The latter also edited *Memories and Studies*, New York, 1911, with a prefatory note.

*The Letters of William James*, Boston, 1920, 2 vols., was edited with a biographical introduction and notes by his son. Further letters have been published in Mary E. Raymond, "Memories of William James," *New Eng. Quar.*, X (1937), 419–429, and J. Seelye Bixler, "Letters from William James to Théodule A. Ribot," *Colby Lib. Quar.*, I (1945), 153–161.

Several volumes of James's writings have been collected and edited by Ralph Barton Perry: the most important is the critical biography, *The Thought and Character of William James, as Revealed in Unpublished Correspondence and Notes, Together with His Published Writings*, Boston, 1935, 2 vols.; earlier articles are reprinted with a preface in *Essays in Radical Empiricism*, New York, 1912, and with a preface and notes in *Collected Essays and Reviews*, New York, 1921. Perry's most recent selections from previously published material by James are *Essays on Faith and Morals*, New York, 1943, and *Pragmatism . . . Together with Four Related Essays . . .*, New York, 1943.

Volumes which are made up of reprinted material are *On Some of Life's Ideals*, New York, 1912, and *Habit*, Boston, 1915. *The Principles of Psychology* was issued in the Amer. Science Ser., New York, 1931, 2 vols. *Talks to Teachers on Psychology* was reprinted, New York, 1938, with an introduction by John Dewey and William H. Kilpatrick. Elizabeth P. Aldrich edited *As William James Said: Extracts from the Published Writings of William James,* New York, 1942. Two volumes have been issued in the Modern Library: *The Philosophy of William James: Drawn from His Own Works,* New York, 1925, with an introduction by Horace M. Kallen, and *The Varieties of Religious Experience,* New York, 1936. *Selected Papers on Philosophy,* New York, 1917, was edited by C. M. Bakewell for Everyman's Library.

## BIOGRAPHY AND CRITICISM

The authoritative full-length biography of James is Ralph Barton Perry, *The Thought and Character of William James . . . ,* Boston, 1935, 2 vols. A further critical study by Perry is *In the Spirit of William James,* New Haven, 1938. Perry also contributed the sketch of James to *Dict. Amer. Biog.* (1932). Two important gatherings of critical essays have recently been published. *In Commemoration of William James, 1842–1942,* New York, 1942, is a symposium of sixteen addresses by J. Seelye Bixler, John Dewey, Horace M. Kallen, Ralph B. Perry, Herbert W. Schneider, and others. *William James: The Man and the Thinker,* Madison, Wis., 1942, is a volume of centenary addresses by J. Seelye Bixler, John Dewey, Max C. Otto, and others. Among the critical estimates of James as a philosopher published during his lifetime are Dickinson S. Miller, "'The Will to Believe' and the Duty to Doubt," *International Jour. Ethics,* IX (1899), 169–195; Ettie Stettheimer, *The Will to Believe as a Basis for the Defense of Religious Faith,* New York, 1907; and "The Pragmatism of William James," in Paul Elmer More, *Shelburne Essays,* 7th Ser., New York, 1910, pp. 195–212.

Among studies of James published since 1910 are Etiènne Emile Boutroux, *William James,* Paris, 1911—translated, New York, 1912, by Archibald and Barbara Henderson; Arthur O. Lovejoy, "William James as Philosopher," *International Jour. Ethics,* XXI (1911), 125–153; Théodore Flournoy, *The Philosophy of William James,* New York, 1917—first published in French, 1911; Josiah Royce, *William James and Other Essays on the Philosophy of Life,* New York, 1912; Henri Reverdin, *La Notion d'Expérience d'après William James,* Geneva, 1913; Howard V. Knox, *The Philosophy of William James,* London, 1914; and Horace M. Kallen, *William James and Henri Bergson: A Study in Contrasting Theories of Life,* Chicago, 1914.

Later studies of various aspects of James as a philosopher are Ethel E. Sabin, *William James and Pragmatism,* Lancaster, Pa., 1918; J. E. Turner, *An Examination of William James's Philosophy: A Critical Essay for the General Reader,* Oxford, 1919; "William James," in George Santayana, *Character and Opinion in the United States,* New York, 1920, pp. 64–96; Jean A. Wahl, *Les Philosophies Pluralistes d'Angleterre et d'Amérique,* Paris, 1920; Emmanuel Leroux, *Le Pragmatisme Américain et Anglais:*

*Etudes Historique et Critique,* Paris, 1922; Floris Delattre, "William James: Bergsonien," *Revue Anglo-Amér.,* I (1923), 135-144; Julius Seelye Bixler, *Religion in the Philosophy of William James,* Boston, 1926—with bibliographical footnotes; Charles K. Trueblood, "The Education of William James," *Dial,* LXXXIII (1927), 301-314; Maurice Le Breton, *La Personnalité de William James,* Paris, 1929; Frederic I. Carpenter, "Points of Comparison Between Emerson and William James," *New Eng. Quar.,* II (1929), 458-474; "William James," in John Dewey, *Characters and Events,* New York, 1929, I, 107-122; Maurice Baum, "The Attitude of William James Toward Science," *Monist,* XLII (1932), 585-604; Julius Seelye Bixler, "William James and Our Changing World," *Amer. Scholar,* I (1932), 392-400; Maurice Baum, "The Development of James's Pragmatism Prior to 1879," *Jour. Philos.,* XXX (1933), 43-51; Henry B. Parkes, "William James," *Hound and Horn,* VII (1933), 6-28; and "Sur le Pragmatisme de William James," in Henri Bergson, *La Pensée et le Mouvant: Essais et Conférences,* Paris, 1934.

The most recent studies are Max I. Baym, "William James and Henry Adams," *New Eng. Quar.,* X (1937), 717-742—Adams's marginal comments on his copy of James's *Principles of Psychology*; Eduard Baumgarten, *Der Pragmatismus: R. W. Emerson, W. James, J. Dewey,* Frankfort, 1938; John M. Moore, *Theories of Religious Experience with Special Reference to James, Otto, and Bergson,* New York, 1938; "The Creative Individual: The Pragmatism of William James," in Ralph H. Gabriel, *The Course of American Democratic Thought,* New York, 1940, pp. 280-289; Justus Buchler, "The Philosopher, the Common Man and William James," *Amer. Scholar,* XI (1942), 416-426; Irwin Edman, "For a New World," *New Repub.;* CVIII (1943), 224-228; and M. C. Otto, "On a Certain Blindness in William James," *Ethics,* LIII (1943), 184-191. Interest in James in South America is demonstrated by A. L. Delle Piane, *William James,* Montevideo, 1943.

James as a man of letters is the subject of "William James, Man of Letters," in John Macy, *The Critical Game,* New York, 1922, pp. 175-189; Van Wyck Brooks, *Sketches in Criticism,* New York, 1932, pp. 37-45; William S. Ament, "William James as a Man of Letters," *Personalist,* XXIII (1942), 199-206; and Jacques Barzun, "William James as Artist," *New Repub.,* CVIII (1943), 218-220.

Other studies are Elizabeth G. Evans, "William James and His Wife," *Atl. Mo.,* CXLIV (1929), 374-387; and "Things Jimsian," in Harvey Wickham, *The Unrealists,* New York, 1930, pp. 29-67.

PRIMARY SOURCES

The bulk of all James manuscripts is deposited in the Harvard College Library. Published items of interest as source material are the autobiographical writings of William James's brother Henry, and the biographical studies of members of the James family that have recently been issued. For details see the listing under "Primary Sources" in the bibliographical essay on Henry James. John Jay Chapman devoted a chapter to William James in *Memories and Milestones,* New York, 1915, pp. 19–28.

## BIBLIOGRAPHY

Ralph Barton Perry prepared an *Annotated Bibliography of the Writings of William James,* New York, 1920, 69 pp., including a calendar of all reviews and special articles written by James. There is no extensive listing of writings about James.

## (JOHN) ROBINSON JEFFERS
### *b. 1887*

SEPARATE WORKS

*Flagons and Apples,* 1912; *Californians,* 1916; *Tamar and Other Poems,* 1924; *Roan Stallion, Tamar, and Other Poems,* 1925; *The Women at Point Sur,* 1927; *Poems,* 1928; *An Artist,* 1928; *Cawdor,* 1928; *Dear Judas and Other Poems,* 1929; *Stars,* 1930; *Apology for Bad Dreams,* 1930; *Descent to the Dead,* 1931; *Thurso's Landing,* 1932; *Give Your Heart to the Hawks,* 1933; *Return: An Unpublished Poem,* 1934; *Solstice and Other Poems,* 1935; *The Beaks of Eagles,* 1936; *Such Counsels You Gave to Me,* 1937; *Hope Is Not for the Wise: An Unpublished Poem,* 1937; *Two Consolations,* 1940; *Be Angry at the Sun,* 1941; *Medea,* 1946.

REPRINTS

*Roan Stallion, Tamar, and Other Poems* was issued in the Modern Lib., New York, 1935. A volume of *The Selected Poetry of Robinson Jeffers* was published, New York, 1938.

BIOGRAPHY AND CRITICISM

Lawrence C. Powell's *Robinson Jeffers: The Man and His Work,* Los Angeles, 1934, was published in a revised and improved version, Pasadena, Calif., 1940. It supersedes the author's *An Introduction to Robinson Jeffers,* Dijon, 1932. Other general studies are Rudolph Gilbert, *Shine, Perishing Republic: Robinson Jeffers and the Tragic Sense in Modern Poetry,* Boston, 1936; Melba B. Bennett, *Robinson Jeffers and the Sea,* San Francisco, 1936—including some of Jeffers's sea poetry; George Sterling, *Robinson Jeffers: The Man and the Artist,* New York, 1926, 40 pp.—the first study of Jeffers; and Louis Adamic, *Robinson Jeffers: A Portrait,* Seattle, 1929, 35 pp.

Among the earliest special studies of Jeffers's poetry are James Daly,

"Roots Under the Rocks," *Poetry*, XXVI (1925), 278–285; Charles Cestre, "Robinson Jeffers," *Revue Anglo-Amér.*, IV (1927), 489–502—an important French estimate; Benjamin DeCasseres, "Robinson Jeffers: Tragic Terror," *Bookman*, LXVI (1927), 262–266; Harold L. Davis, "Jeffers Denies Us Twice," *Poetry*, XXXI (1928), 274–279; Lloyd S. Morris, "Robinson Jeffers: The Tragedy of a Modern Mystic," *New Repub.*, LIV (1928), 386–390; Benjamin H. Lehman, "The Most Significant Tendency in Modern Poetry," *Scripps College Papers*, No. 2 (1929), 1–12; and Morton D. Zabel, "The Problem of Tragedy," *Poetry*, XXXIII (1929), 336–340.

Later estimates are Yvor Winters, "Robinson Jeffers," *Poetry*, XXXV (1930), 279–286; Benjamin H. Lehman, "Robinson Jeffers," *Sat. Rev. Lit.*, VIII (Sept. 5, 1931), 97–99; Rolfe Humphries, "Two Books by Jeffers," *Poetry*, XL (1932), 154–158; Harlan Hatcher, "The Torches of Violence," *English Jour.*, XXIII (1934), 91–99; John G. Fletcher, "The Dilemma of Robinson Jeffers," *Poetry*, XLIII (1934), 338–342; Babette Deutsch, *This Modern Poetry*, New York, 1935, pp. 206–213; Rolfe Humphries, "Robinson Jeffers," *Modern Mo.*, VIII (1935), 680–689, 748–753; Hildegarde Flanner, "Two Poets: Jeffers and Millay," *New Repub.*, LXXXIX (1937), 379–382; Louis Wann, "Robinson Jeffers: Counterpart of Walt Whitman," *Personalist*, XIX (1938), 297–308; William Van Wyck, *Robinson Jeffers*, Los Angeles, 1938, 17 pp.; Hyatt H. Waggoner, "Science and the Poetry of Robinson Jeffers," *Amer. Lit.*, X (1938), 275–288; Walter Gierasch, "Robinson Jeffers," *English Jour.*, XXVIII (1939), 284–295; Delmore Schwartz and Frajam Taylor, "The Enigma of Robinson Jeffers," *Poetry*, LV (1939), 30–38; and Jeanne Wronecki, "Un Poète Américain d'Aujourd'hui: Robinson Jeffers," *Revue de France*, II (1939), 283–286

The most recent studies are Frederic I. Carpenter, "The Values of Robinson Jeffers," *Amer. Lit.*, X (1940), 353–366; *idem*, "Death Comes for Robinson Jeffers," *University Rev.*, VII (1941), 97–105; Harold Watts, "Robinson Jeffers and Eating the Serpent," *Sewanee Rev.*, XLIX (1941), 39–55; R. W. Short, "The Tower Beyond Tragedy," *Southern Rev.*, VII (1941), 132–144; William S. Johnson, "The 'Savior' in the Poetry of Robinson Jeffers," *Amer. Lit.*, XV (1943), 159–168; Rudolph Gilbert, *Four Living Poets*, Santa Barbara, 1944—including an essay on Jeffers.

PRIMARY SOURCES

The *Carmelite* issued a "Robinson Jeffers Supplement," Dec. 12, 1928, edited by Ella Winter, with tributes by Lincoln Steffens, Carl Sandburg, Edgar Lee Masters, and others. Jeffers's own comments on his earliest published writing appeared in *Colophon*, Pt. 10, Art. 1 (1932), pp. 1–8. Further reminiscences are "Jeffers the Neighbor," in Lincoln Steffens, *Lincoln*

*Steffens Speaking,* New York, 1936, pp. 76–83; and Edith Greenan, *Of Una Jeffers,* Los Angeles, 1939.

A collection of Jeffers manuscripts and first editions is in Occidental College Library; some manuscripts are in the University of Buffalo.

BIBLIOGRAPHY

An exhaustive bibliographical listing to 1933 is Sydney S. Alberts, *A Bibliography of the Works of Robinson Jeffers,* New York, 1933, with a foreword by Jeffers. Later listings are in *Robinson Jeffers, 1905–1935: An Exhibition Commemorating the Thirtieth Anniversary of His Graduation from Occidental College* . . . (1935); and William White, on some unnoticed Jeffers poems, in *Papers Bibl. Soc. Amer.,* XXXIV (1940), 362–363. For secondary items see Fred B. Millett, *Contemporary American Authors,* 1940, pp. 406–409. The most recent listing is by Frances Cheney, in Allen Tate, *Sixty American Poets, 1896–1944,* Washington, 1945, pp. 64–68.

## THOMAS JEFFERSON
### *1743–1826*

SEPARATE WORKS

*A Summary View of the Rights of British America,* 1774; *The Declaration of Independence,* 1776; *Notes on the Establishment of a Money Unit,* 1784; *Notes on the State of Virginia,* 1784–1785; *An Appendix to the Notes on Virginia Relative to the Murder of Logan's Family,* 1800; *A Manual of Parliamentary Practice,* 1801; *The Address of Thomas Jefferson to the Senate* . . . *on the 4th* . . . *of March, 1801* . . . , 1801; *Life of Captain* [*Meriwether*] *Lewis,* 1817.

COLLECTED WORKS

Public announcement has been made of a complete edition of the writings of Jefferson, sponsored by Princeton University, to be published by the Princeton University Press, under the editorship of Julian P. Boyd. It is a body of writing that upon completion is expected to run to some fifty volumes. Until it has been published the best text is that of Paul L. Ford, ed., *The Writings of Thomas Jefferson,* New York, 1892–1899, 10 vols. The fullest collection is that of Andrew A. Lipscomb and Albert E. Bergh, eds., *The Writings of Thomas Jefferson,* Washington, 1903, 20 vols., with many facsimiles; but the misprints, unindicated omissions, and bowdlerizations limit its usefulness. Other early collections are Thomas Jefferson Randolph, ed., *Memoir, Correspondence, and Miscellanies, from the Papers of Thomas Jeffer-*

*son,* Charlottesville, Va., 1829, 4 vols.—the earliest collection; Henry A. Washington, ed., *The Writings of Thomas Jefferson* . . . , Washington, 1853–1854, 9 vols., reprinted verbatim in the Lipscomb and Bergh edition.

The best edition of Jefferson's autobiography is that of Paul L. Ford, *Autobiography of Thomas Jefferson* . . . , New York, 1914, with introduction and notes. Prepared in 1821, the autobiography was first published in Randolph's *Memoir* . . . (1829).

Two items have been edited by Gilbert Chinard: *The Commonplace Book of Thomas Jefferson: A Repertory of His Ideas on Government,* Baltimore, 1926; and *The Literary Bible of Thomas Jefferson: His Commonplace Book of Philosophers and Poets,* Baltimore, 1928—the missing complement of Jefferson's Bible.

Extracts from a journal dealing with utilitarian farming supplemented by further data were compiled by Edwin M. Betts, *Thomas Jefferson's Garden Book, 1766–1824, with Relevant Extracts from His Other Writings,* Philadelphia, 1944.

CORRESPONDENCE

A register of letters to and from Jefferson, with manuscript locations and other supplementary data, is the *Calendar of the Correspondence of Thomas Jefferson,* Washington, 1894–1903, 3 vols.

Published correspondence, some of which at present is uncollected, may be found in several separately issued items. A very early collection is that of Nathaniel Francis Cabell, *Early History of the University of Virginia, as Contained in the Letters of Thomas Jefferson and Joseph C. Cabell,* Richmond, 1856. Charles F. Jenkins edited *Jefferson's Germantown Letters, Together with Other Papers Relating to His Stay in Germantown During the Month of November, 1793,* Philadelphia, 1906. There are also Max J. Kohler, "Unpublished Correspondence Between Thomas Jefferson and Some American Jews," *Pub. Amer. Jewish Hist. Soc.,* XX (1911), 11–30; *The Confidential Letters from Thomas Jefferson to William Wirt* . . . , Philadelphia, 1912; Worthington C. Ford, ed., *Thomas Jefferson Correspondence, Printed from the Originals in the Collections of William K. Bixby,* Boston, 1916—including letters not in collected works; and Vol. II of *Official Letters of the Governors of the State of Virginia* . . . (1928)—for Jefferson's period as governor.

Six gatherings of letters, most of which appear in the collected works, have been edited by Gilbert Chinard: *Les Amitiés Américaines de Madame d'Houdetot, d'Après Sa Correspondance Inédite avec Benjamin Franklin et Thomas Jefferson,* Paris, 1924; *Jefferson et les Idéologues d'Après Sa Correspondance Inédite avec Destutt de Tracy, Cabanis, J.-B. Say et Auguste Comte,* Baltimore, 1925; *Trois Amitiés Françaises de Jefferson, d'Après Sa*

*Correspondance Inédite avec Madame de Bréhan, Madame de Tessé, et Madame de Corny,* Paris, 1927; *Volney et l'Amérique, d'Après des Documents Inédites et Sa Correspondance avec Jefferson,* Baltimore, 1923; *The Letters of Lafayette and Jefferson,* Baltimore, 1929; and *The Correspondence of Jefferson and Du Pont de Nemours, with an Introduction on Jefferson and the Physiocrats,* Baltimore, 1931.

Further published letters are Paul Wilstach, ed., *Correspondence of John Adams and Thomas Jefferson,* Indianapolis, 1925; Dumas Malone, ed., *Correspondence Between Thomas Jefferson and Pierre Samuel du Pont de Nemours, 1798-1817,* Boston, 1930—with translations by Linwood Lehman; Bernard Mayo, ed., *Thomas Jefferson and His Unknown Brother Randolph . . . ,* Charlottesville, Va., 1942—an exchange of twenty-eight letters, 1807-1815, here first printed; Howard R. Marraro, ed., "Jefferson Letters Concerning the Settlement of Mazzei's Virginia Estate," *Mississippi Valley Hist. Rev.,* XXX (1943), 235-242—see also Marraro, "The Four Versions of Jefferson's Letter to Mazzei," *William and Mary Coll. Quar.,* 2nd ser., XXII (1942), 18-29; and Marie Kimball, "Jefferson's Farewell to Romance," *Virginia Quar. Rev.,* IV (1928), 402-419—his "sentimental interlude" with Maria Cosway. Helen D. Bullock's *My Head and My Heart: A Little History of Thomas Jefferson and Maria Cosway,* New York, 1945, includes twenty-five hitherto unpublished letters exchanged by Jefferson and Mrs. Cosway during the years 1786-1789. The text must be checked. A recent collection is Richard B. Davis, ed., *Correspondence of Thomas Jefferson and Francis Walker Gilmer, 1814-1826,* Columbia, S.C., 1946.

Gleanings are Frank H. Severance, ed., "A Bundle of Thomas Jefferson's Letters, Now First Published," *Pub. Buffalo Hist. Soc.,* VII (1904), 1-32—to François Adriaan van der Kemp, 1790-1825; Marie Dickoré, ed., *Two Letters from Thomas Jefferson to His Relatives the Turpins . . . ,* Oxford, Ohio, 1941; and Sigmund Diamond, "Some Jefferson Letters," *Mississippi Valley Hist. Rev.,* XXVIII (1941), 224-242.

Further letters are scattered through the collected works and the various memoirs and lives.

EDITED TEXTS AND REPRINTS

Jefferson's *A Summary View* is reproduced from the first edition, Williamsburg, Va., 1774, in Scholars' Facsimiles and Reprints, New York, 1943.

Two extensive compilations are Adrienne Koch and William Peden, *The Life and Selected Writings of Thomas Jefferson,* New York, 1944 (Modern Lib.)—containing hundreds of letters, some from manuscript sources, and a useful introduction; and Saul K. Padover, ed., *The Complete Jefferson: Containing His Major Writings, Published and Unpublished, Except His Let-*

*ters* . . . , New York, 1943. A further general selected text is Frederick C. Prescott, *Alexander Hamilton and Thomas Jefferson: Representative Selections, with Introduction, Bibliography, and Notes,* New York, 1934 (Amer. Writers Ser.).

Selections of particular material are Joseph G. de Roulhac Hamilton, ed., *The Best Letters of Thomas Jefferson,* Boston, 1926; Charles F. Arrowood, ed., *Thomas Jefferson and Education in a Republic,* New York, 1930—reprint of Jefferson's statements on education; James T. Adams, ed., *Jeffersonian Principles* . . . , Boston, 1932—with introduction; Saul K. Padover, ed., *Democracy, by Thomas Jefferson* . . . , New York 1939—selected statements of Jefferson on the rights of man; John Dewey, ed., *The Living Thoughts of Thomas Jefferson,* New York, 1940—with an interesting introductory essay; Edward Boykin, *The Wisdom of Thomas Jefferson* . . . , New York, 1941—including the Jefferson Bible; and Bernard Mayo, ed., *Jefferson Himself: The Personal Narrative* . . . , Boston, 1942—important for its chronological account of Jefferson's stated views, with "notes and sources," pp. 347–365.

John P. Foley has prepared *The Jefferson Cyclopedia: A Comprehensive Collection of the Views of Thomas Jefferson, Classified and Arranged in Alphabetical Order Under Nine Thousand Titles* . . . , New York, 1900.

### BIOGRAPHY AND CRITICISM

The most satisfactory one-volume interpretation of Jefferson's whole intellectual career is Adrienne Koch, *The Philosophy of Thomas Jefferson,* New York, 1943, a study which arrives at conclusions somewhat different from those in Gilbert Chinard's *Thomas Jefferson: The Apostle of Americanism,* Boston, 1929, the best one-volume study to that date. The three volumes of Claude G. Bowers furnish the longest and most detailed study of Jefferson and are frankly partisan in their sympathies: *The Young Jefferson, 1743–1789,* New York, 1945; *Jefferson and Hamilton: The Struggle for Democracy in America,* Boston, 1925; and *Jefferson in Power: The Death Struggle of the Federalists,* Boston, 1936, but they must be checked for factual errors. They were published as a trilogy in chronological order, Boston, 1945.

Among earlier biographies, still very useful are Theodore Dwight, *The Character of Thomas Jefferson as Exhibited in His Own Writings,* Boston, 1839—a hostile Federalist view; Henry S. Randall, *The Life of Thomas Jefferson,* New York, 1858, 3 vols.—the most comprehensive source book; James Parton, *Life of Thomas Jefferson* . . . , Boston, 1874; and William E. Curtis, *The True Thomas Jefferson,* Philadelphia, 1901.

Other recent lives are Francis W. Hirst, *Life and Letters of Thomas Jefferson,* New York, 1926; Albert Jay Nock, *Jefferson,* New York, 1926;

and James T. Adams, *The Living Jefferson,* New York, 1936; Marie Kimball, *Jefferson: The Road to Glory, 1743 to 1776,* New York, 1943, and *Jefferson: War and Peace,* New York, 1947, are the first two of a projected series of three volumes.

The sketch of Jefferson by Dumas Malone in the *Dict. Amer. Biog.* (1933) is the best brief account.

The authoritative study of Jefferson's presidential years, as well as the finest piece of writing in the whole Jefferson canon, is Henry Adams, *History of the United States . . . During the First and Second Administrations of Thomas Jefferson,* New York, 1889–1890, 4 vols.—remarkably objective, considering Adams's Federalist bias, in presenting Jefferson's principles. An excellent special study is Carl Becker, *The Declaration of Independence: A Study in the History of Political Ideas,* New York, 1922. It is complemented by Julian P. Boyd, *The Declaration of Independence: The Evolution of the Text as Shown in Facsimiles of Various Drafts by Its Author . . . ,* Princeton, 1945, with bibliographical footnotes.

Other standard studies of Jefferson's political career are "Thomas Jefferson, the Conservative Reformer," in John Fiske, *Essays, Historical and Literary,* New York, I, 1902, pp. 143–182; Edward Channing, *The Jeffersonian System, 1801–1811,* New York, 1906; Charles A. Beard, *Economic Origins of Jeffersonian Democracy,* New York, 1915—indispensable; Samuel F. Bemis, "Thomas Jefferson," in *The American Secretaries of State . . . ,* New York, 1927, II, 3–93; Louis M. Sears, *Jefferson and the Embargo,* Durham, N.C., 1927; William K. Woolery, *The Relation of Thomas Jefferson to American Foreign Policy, 1783–1793,* Baltimore, 1927; Charles M. Wiltse, *The Jeffersonian Tradition in American Democracy,* Chapel Hill, N.C., 1935; and Lynton K. Caldwell, *The Administrative Theories of Hamilton and Jefferson . . . ,* Chicago, 1944.

Standard and authoritative studies in the general field are Carl R. Fish, *The Civil Service and the Patronage,* Cambridge, 1904; Charles R. Lingley, "The Transition in Virginia from Colony to Commonwealth," *Columbia Univ. Studies in Hist., Econ., and Pub. Law,* XXXVI (1910), 325–535; Hamilton J. Eckenrode, *The Revolution in Virginia,* Boston, 1916; Albert J. Beveridge, *The Life of John Marshall,* Boston, 1916–1919, 4 vols.; Isaac J. Cox, *The West Florida Controversy . . . ,* Baltimore, 1918; Everett S. Brown, ed., *William Plumer's Memorandum . . . ,* New York, 1923; Louise B. Dunbar, *A Study of "Monarchical" Tendencies in the United States from 1776 to 1801,* Urbana, Ill., 1923; Charles E. Merriam, ed., *A History of Political Theories . . . ,* New York, 1924; and Bernard Faÿ, *The Revolutionary Spirit in France and America . . . ,* New York, 1927.

Notes on Jefferson as a man of letters are Gilbert Chinard, ed., *The Com-*

*monplace Book* . . . , Baltimore, 1926—with an introduction on Jefferson's early reading; Stuart P. Sherman, *The Main Stream,* New York, 1927, pp. 17–36; Vernon L. Parrington, *Main Currents in American Thought,* New York, I (1927), 342–356; "Thomas Jefferson, Librarian," in Randolph G. Adams, *Three Americanists* . . . , Philadelphia, 1939, pp. 69–96; and Albert C. Baugh, "Thomas Jefferson, Linguistic Liberal," in *Studies for William A. Read* . . . , University, La., 1940, pp. 88–108.

Authoritative studies of Jefferson's concern with education are Herbert B. Adams, *Thomas Jefferson and the University of Virginia* . . . , Washington, 1888; John C. Henderson, *Thomas Jefferson's Views on Public Education,* New York, 1890; and Roy J. Honeywell, *The Educational Work of Thomas Jefferson,* Cambridge, 1931.

Jefferson as a scientist is presented in William E. Curtis, *The True Thomas Jefferson,* Philadelphia, 1901; Alexander Chamberlain, "Thomas Jefferson's Ethnological Opinions and Activities," *Amer. Anthropologist,* n.s. IX (1907), 499–509; George T. Surface, "Thomas Jefferson: A Pioneer Student of American Geography," *Bul. Amer. Geographical Soc.,* XLI (1909), 743–750; William I. Wyman, "Thomas Jefferson and the Patent System," *Jour. Patent Office Soc.,* I (Sept., 1918); Frederic A. Lucas, "Thomas Jefferson: Palaeontologist," *Natural Hist.,* XXVI (1926), 328–330; Henry F. Osborn, "Thomas Jefferson, the Pioneer of American Paleontology," *Science,* LXIX (1929), 410–413; H. C. Montgomery, "Thomas Jefferson as a Philologist," *Amer. Jour. Philol.,* LXV (1944), 367–371; and Mabel Morris, "Jefferson and the Language of the American Indian," *Modern Language Quar.,* VI (1945), 31–34.

Useful investigations into Jefferson's interest in and knowledge of architecture have been made by Fiske Kimball, *Thomas Jefferson: Architect,* Boston, 1916—Jefferson presented by a professional architect; William A. Lambeth and Warren H. Manning, *Thomas Jefferson as an Architect and a Designer of Landscapes,* Boston, 1913—with plates; Paul Wilstach, *Jefferson and Monticello,* Garden City, N.Y., rev. ed., 1931; and, most recently, Ihna T. Frary, *Thomas Jefferson, Architect and Builder,* Richmond, Va., 1931—well illustrated. See also Fiske Kimball, "Form and Function in the Architecture of Jefferson," *Mag. of Art,* XL (1947), 150–153.

Other studies of Jefferson's career are Dumas Malone, "Polly Jefferson and Her Father," *Virginia Quar. Rev.,* VII (1931), 81–95; W. D. Gould, "The Religious Opinions of Thomas Jefferson," *Mississippi Valley Hist. Rev.,* XX (1933), 191–209—based on unpublished material; Charles M. Wiltse, "Thomas Jefferson on the Law of Nations," *Amer. Jour. International Law,* XXIX (1935), 66–81; Maude H. Woodfin, "Contemporary Opinion in Virginia of Thomas Jefferson," in Avery Craven, ed., *Essays in Honor of William E.*

*Dodd,* Chicago, 1935, pp. 30–85; Frank L. Mott, *Jefferson and the Press,* Baton Rouge, La., 1943; Philip Marsh, "Jefferson and Journalism," *Huntington Lib. Quar.,* IX (1946), 209–212; A. Whitney Griswold, "The Agrarian Democracy of Thomas Jefferson," *Amer. Pol. Sci. Rev.,* XL (1946), 657–681; Philip Marsh, " 'The Vindication of Mr. Jefferson,' " *So. Atl. Quar.,* XLV (1946), 61–67; and E. T. Martin, "Thomas Jefferson's Interest in Science and Useful Arts," *Emory Univ. Quar.,* II (1946), 65–73.

Jefferson on tour is the subject of Edward Dumbauld, *Thomas Jefferson: American Tourist,* Norman, Okla., 1946; Marie G. Kimball, "Thomas Jefferson's Rhine Journey," *Amer.-Ger. Rev.,* XIII, (Oct., 1946) 4–7, (Dec., 1946) 11–14; and Edith R. Bevan, ed., "Thomas Jefferson in Annapolis . . . ," *Maryland Hist. Mag.,* XLI (1946), 115–124.

A significant reprint with introduction is Charles A. Sainte-Beuve's *Thomas Jefferson et Tocqueville,* Princeton, 1943, edited by Gilbert Chinard from the original, first printed in *Le Temps,* April 7, 1835.

Symposia, commemorating the Jefferson bicentennial, are the "Jefferson Issue" of *Ethics,* LIII (1943), 237–310, with contributions by Claude G. Bowers, Herbert W. Schneider, Gilbert Chinard, H. M. Kallen, and others; the "Jefferson Number" of the *Mississippi Valley Hist. Rev.,* XXX (1943), 159–214, with articles by Charles A. Beard, George H. Knoles, Gilbert Chinard, and Lynn W. Turner; and the gathering of papers in the *Proc. Amer. Philos. Soc.,* LXXXVII (1943), 199–289, by Carl Becker, Louis B. Wright, Harlow Shapley, Fiske Kimball, Gilbert Chinard, Carl Van Doren, and others, with an introduction by Edwin G. Conklin, and bibliographical footnotes.

Recently two studies of the Jefferson library interests have been made by William H. Peden, "Some Notes Concerning Thomas Jefferson's Libraries," *William and Mary Quar.,* 3rd ser., I (1944), 265–272; and an editing of *The 1828 Catalogue of the Library of the University of Virginia,* Ann Arbor, 1945.

PRIMARY SOURCES

In addition to the published memoirs and contemporary lives already described, further material will be found in B. L. Rayner, *Sketches of . . . Thomas Jefferson . . . ,* New York, 1832; George Tucker, *The Life of Thomas Jefferson . . . ,* Philadelphia, 1837, 2 vols.—the first important biography, written by a friend from local sources; and Sarah N. Randolph, *The Domestic Life of Thomas Jefferson,* New York, 1871—composed by Jefferson's great-granddaughter from family letters and reminiscences, including material not elsewhere in print. Of first importance are the published writings of Washington, Adams, Hamilton, Madison, and Monroe.

A union list of Jefferson manuscripts, under way during the past ten years, is located at the University of Virginia. The two greatest collections of manuscripts are in the Library of Congress and the library of the Massachusetts Historical Society. The first of these consists of 236 large folio volumes of some 27,000 pieces, and much of Jefferson's own library is deposited in the same place. The second comprises some 10,000 items, rich in letters and papers relating to Jefferson's private and personal affairs, given to the Society in 1898, representing letters equally divided between those written and received by Jefferson for the years 1770–1826. (See "The Jefferson Papers," *Coll. Mass. Hist. Soc.,* 7th ser., I (1900)—the entire volume.) Further important manuscript holdings are at the University of Virginia, the American Philosophical Society, the Historical Society of Pennsylvania, and the Missouri Historical Society. Scattered material may be found in the Henry E. Huntington Library and in the library of the College of William and Mary. Some still remains in private hands.

A summary of present knowledge about the Jefferson manuscripts and bibliography is Randolph G. Adams's account in *Colophon,* n.s. III (1938), 134–136; and an account of the history of the manuscripts is Helen D. Bullock, "The Papers of Thomas Jefferson," *Amer. Archivist,* IV (1941), 238–249.

BIBLIOGRAPHY

An early listing of published items is Hamilton B. Tompkins, *Bibliotheca Jeffersoniana: A List of Books Written by or Relating to Thomas Jefferson,* New York, 1887. Vol. I of Paul L. Ford's *The Writings of Thomas Jefferson,* New York, 1892–1899, 10 vols., includes a list of the printed works, as well as the best bibliography of Jefferson's *Notes on the State of Virginia* (1784–1785). A 73-page bibliography is included in Vol. XX of the Lipscomb and Bergh ed. of the *Writings* (1903). The listing in Prescott's *Alexander Hamilton and Thomas Jefferson: Representative Selections* (1934) is selective and annotated. The most recent guide is William H. Peden, *Some Aspects of Jefferson Bibliography* . . . , Lexington, Va., 1941, 22 pp.


# SARAH ORNE JEWETT
## *1849–1909*

SEPARATE WORKS

*Deephaven,* 1877; *Old Friends and New,* 1879; *Country By-Ways,* 1881; *The Mate of the Daylight and Friends Ashore,* 1883; *A Country Doctor,* 1884; *A Marsh Island,* 1885; *A White Heron, and Other Stories,* 1886; *The King of Folly Island, and Other People,* 1888; *Strangers and Wayfarers,* 1890;

*A Native of Winby, and Other Tales,* 1893; *The Life of Nancy,* 1895; *The Country of the Pointed Firs,* 1896; *The Queen's Twin, and Other Stories,* 1899; *The Tory Lover,* 1901.

Miss Jewett's numerous books for children include *The Story of the Normans,* 1887. *Verses by Sarah Orne Jewett* was privately printed by friends in 1916.

## COLLECTED WORKS AND REPRINTS

*Stories and Tales,* Boston, 1910, was issued in 7 vols. The best approach to Miss Jewett's writings is through *The Best Stories of Sarah Orne Jewett,* Boston, 1925, 2 vols., edited with an appreciative foreword by Willa Cather. *The Country of the Pointed Firs* was reprinted in the Riverside Library, Boston, 1929; and London, 1939, with a preface by Willa Cather. *The Night Before Thanksgiving, A White Heron, and Selected Stories by Sarah Orne Jewett,* Boston, 1911, was issued in the Riverside Literature Ser., with introductory notes by K. H. Shute. *Tales of New England* (1890) was a selection from the earlier writings. Many of the less important stories, published from time to time in magazines, still remain uncollected. Annie Fields edited *Letters of Sarah Orne Jewett,* Boston, 1911.

## BIOGRAPHY AND CRITICISM

The most substantial study is F(rancis) O. Matthiessen, *Sarah Orne Jewett,* Boston, 1929. Matthiessen also contributed the biographical sketch in *Dict. Amer. Biog.* (1933). A brief standard estimate is Arthur H. Quinn, *American Fiction . . . ,* New York, 1936, pp. 324–330.

Special studies are Charles M. Thompson, "The Art of Miss Jewett," *Atl. Mo.,* XCIV (1904), 485–497; Edward M. Chapman, "The New England of Sarah Orne Jewett," *Yale Rev.,* n.s. III (1913), 157–172; Martha H. Shackford, "Sarah Orne Jewett," *Sewanee Rev.,* XXX (1922), 20–26; Carl J. Weber, "Whittier and Sarah Orne Jewett," *New Eng. Quar.,* XVIII (1945), 401–407; and *idem,* "Sarah Orne Jewett's First Story," *ibid.,* XIX (1946), 85–90.

Further material, chiefly reminiscent, is in Edward Garnett, *Friday Nights,* New York, 1922, pp. 189–198; Mark A. De Wolfe Howe, *Memories of a Hostess,* Boston, 1922—based on the journals of Mrs. James T. Fields; and Willa Cather, "Miss Jewett," in *Not Under Forty,* New York, 1936, pp. 76–95. Also useful is the sketch by Esther Forbes in the *Boston Transcript,* May 16, 1925.

Jewett manuscripts may be found in the Thomas Bailey Aldrich Birthplace, Portsmouth, N.H.; in the Harvard College Library; and in the Library of Colby College, Waterville, Maine.

The most accurate checklist of Miss Jewett's writings is in the preface to Matthiessen's biography (1929).

# JOHN PENDLETON KENNEDY
## 1795–1870

### SEPARATE WORKS

*The Red Book*, 1818–1819; *Swallow Barn*, 1832; *Horse-Shoe Robinson*, 1835; *Rob of the Bowl*, 1838; *Quodlibet*, 1840; *Defense of the Whigs*, 1843; *Memoirs of the Life of William Wirt*, 1849; *The Border States*, 1861; *Mr. Ambrose's Letters on the Rebellion*, 1865.

### COLLECTED WORKS AND REPRINTS

An edition of *The Works of John Pendleton Kennedy* was issued, New York, 1854, in 3 vols. *The Collected Works of John Pendleton Kennedy*, New York, 1871, 10 vols., includes the *Life* by Henry T. Tuckerman. Further collected material appeared in *At Home and Abroad: A Series of Essays, with a Journal in Europe in 1867-68*, New York, 1872; *Political and Official Papers*, New York, 1872; and *Occasional Addresses*, New York, 1872.

*Swallow Barn* was edited for the Amer. Authors Ser., with introduction, by Jay B. Hubbell, New York, 1929. Ernest E. Leisy edited *Horse-Shoe Robinson*, with introduction, chronology, and bibl., for the Amer. Fiction Ser., New York, 1937.

### BIOGRAPHY AND CRITICISM

Henry T. Tuckerman, *The Life of John Pendleton Kennedy*, New York, 1871, is an authorized portrait, and though inadequate, remains the only full-length study. The biographical sketch by Hubbell in his edition of *Swallow Barn* (1929) is useful, as is the introduction by Ernest E. Leisy in his edition of *Horse-Shoe Robinson* (1937).

Other general estimates are those of Vernon L. Parrington, *Main Currents in American Thought*, New York, 1927, II, 46–56; and Mary W. Williams in *Dict. Amer. Biog.* (1933). Edward M. Gwathmey's *John Pendleton Kennedy*, New York, 1931, is brief and adds little not in Tuckerman.

Special studies other than those in the Hubbell and the Leisy editions, already mentioned, are John E. Uhler, "Kennedy's Novels and His Posthumous Works," *Amer. Lit.*, III (1932), 471–479; John R. Moore, "Kennedy's *Horse-Shoe Robinson*: Fact or Fiction?" *Amer. Lit.*, IV (1932), 160–166; and Henry C. Forman, "The Rose Croft in Old St. Mary's," *Maryland Hist. Mag.*, XXXV (1940), 26–31.

An extensive manuscript collection of Kennedy material is in the Peabody Institute, Baltimore. It includes letters from and to Kennedy, seventeen volumes of diaries covering the years 1829–1839, 1847–1869, and an uncompleted autobiography. Killis Campbell, "The Kennedy Papers," *Sewanee Rev.,* XXV (1917), 1–19, 193–208, 348–360, reprints letters to Kennedy from Irving and several other American and English authors. John Wynne, a Baltimore friend, contributed "John P. Kennedy" to *Harper's Mag.,* XXV (1862), 335–340. See also Robert C. Winthrop, "Tributes to the Memory of John Pendleton Kennedy," *Proc. Massachusetts Hist. Soc.,* XI (1870), 354–369; and *Annual Report of the Secretary of the Navy* for 1852.

A checklist of Kennedy's writings is in Jacob Blanck, *Merle Johnson's American First Editions,* 4th ed., New York, 1942. The most useful selective bibliography is that in Ernest E. Leisy, ed., *Horse-Shoe Robinson,* New York, 1937, pp. xxix–xxxii.

# SIDNEY LANIER
## *1842–1881*

SEPARATE WORKS

During Lanier's lifetime the following items were published: *Tiger-Lilies: A Novel,* 1867; *Florida: Its Scenery, Climate, and History,* 1875; *The Centennial Meditation of Columbia, 1776–1876 . . . A Cantata . . . ,* 1876; *Poems,* 1877; *The Science of English Verse,* 1880.

Lanier wrote prefaces only for *The Boy's Froissart,* 1879; *The Boy's King Arthur,* 1880; *The Boy's Mabinogion,* 1881; *The Boy's Percy,* 1882.

*The English Novel and the Principle of Its Development,* 1883, was edited by W. H. Browne; Mary D. Lanier brought out a revised edition, 1897.

*Poems of Sidney Lanier* (1884) were edited by his wife, with a memorial by William H. Ward. The edition of 1891 added seven poems; the edition of 1916, two further poems.

Henry W. Lanier edited *Music and Poetry: Essays upon Some Aspects and Inter-Relations of the Two Arts,* 1898; *Bob: The Story of Our Mocking-Bird,* 1899; *Retrospects and Prospects: Descriptive and Historical Essays,* 1899; *Shakespeare and His Forerunners: Studies in Elizabethan Poetry and Its Development from Early English,* 1902, 2 vols.

COLLECTED AND SELECTED WORKS

*The Centennial Edition of Sidney Lanier,* Baltimore, 1945, 10 vols., under the general editorship of Charles R. Anderson, is the first uniform set of

Lanier's works. It includes a large number of previously unpublished or uncollected essays and poems, and some thousand letters, most of which are here first published. The editorial staff includes Paull F. Baum, Kemp Malone, Clarence Gohdes, Garland Greever, Cecil Abernethy, Philip Graham, and Aubrey H. Starke. Lanier thus becomes the first American author whose collected works and letters have been made available by scholars, with authoritative texts, full introductions, and notes. In addition, there is *A Concordance to the Poems of Sidney Lanier: Including the 'Poem Outlines' and Certain Uncollected Items,* Austin, Texas, 1939, compiled by Philip Graham and Joseph Jones.

The most recent volume of selections is that edited by Henry W. Lanier, *Selections from Sidney Lanier: Prose and Verse,* New York, 1916. Henry W. Lanier also edited *Poem Outlines,* New York, 1908. Earlier selections are: Mary E. Burt, *The Lanier Book* . . . , New York, 1904; Morgan Callaway, Jr., ed., *Select Poems of Sidney Lanier,* New York, 1895, with introductions, notes, and bibliography. *Hymns of the Marshes* was published, New York, 1907. Jay B. Hubbell edited "A Commencement Address by Sidney Lanier," *Amer. Lit.,* II (1931), 385–404.

### LETTERS

Letters in print before the publication of *The Centennial Edition* are Henry W. Lanier, ed., *Letters of Sidney Lanier* . . . , New York, 1899—selections from his correspondence during the years 1866–1881; George H. Clarke, ed., *Some Reminiscences and Early Letters of Sidney Lanier,* Macon, Ga., 1907; Aubrey H. Starke, "Sidney Lanier and Paul Hamilton Hayne: Three Unpublished Letters," *Amer. Lit.,* I (1929), 32–39; J. De Witt Hankins, "Unpublished Letters of Sidney Lanier," *Southern Literary Messenger,* II (1940), 5–11; and Margaret L. Wiley, ed., *Letters: Sidney Lanier to Col. John G. James,* Austin, Texas, 1942.

### BIOGRAPHY AND CRITICISM

The best of the early biographies is that of Edwin Mims, *Sidney Lanier,* Boston, 1905—a sympathetic study. A documented and detailed biography is Aubrey H. Starke, *Sidney Lanier: A Biographical and Critical Study,* Chapel Hill, N.C., 1933—including some unpublished poems, and a bibliography, pp. 455–473. Richard Webb and Edwin R. Coulson, *Sidney Lanier, Poet and Prosodist,* Athens, Ga., 1941, is a belated publication of Webb's 1903 essay on Lanier's poetics supplemented by Coulson's essay on Lanier in the light of modern criticism. Mary C. Jones has compiled *Sidney Lanier: A Chronological Record of Authenticated Facts,* Macon, Ga., 1940.

Historical estimates of Lanier appear in Fred L. Pattee, *A History of*

*American Literature Since 1870,* New York, 1915, pp. 274-288; Percy H. Boynton, *History of American Literature,* Boston, 1919, pp. 349-358; Gamaliel Bradford, *American Portraits, 1875-1900,* Boston, 1922, pp. 59-83; Norman Foerster, *Nature in American Literature,* New York, 1923, pp. 221-237; Stanley T. Williams, "Sidney Lanier," in John Macy, ed., *American Writers on American Literature,* New York, 1931, pp. 327-341; Robert Penn Warren, "The Blind Poet: Sidney Lanier," *Amer. Rev.,* II (1933), 27-45; and John Crowe Ransom, "Hearts and Heads," *Amer. Rev.,* II (1934), 554-571.

Early studies of Lanier were Charles W. Kent, "A Study of Lanier's Poems," *PMLA,* VII (1892), 33-63; "Sidney Lanier," in William M. Baskervill, *Southern Writers,* Nashville, 1897, pp. 137-298; Thomas W. Higginson, *Contemporaries,* New York, 1899, pp. 85-101; John Spencer Bassett, "The Struggles of Sidney Lanier," *Methodist Rev.,* XLIX (1900), 3-17; and William P. Trent, ed., *Southern Writers,* New York, 1905, pp. 404-407.

A French estimate is Thérèse Bentzon (Mme. Blanc), "Un Musicien Poète: Sidney Lanier," in *Revue des Deux Mondes,* CXLV (1898), 307-341—translated in *Littell's Living Age,* CCXVII (1898), 411-423, 517-524.

Two studies of Lanier as prosodist are George Saintsbury, *History of English Prosody,* London, 1910, III, 493-497; and "Sidney Lanier," in Gay W. Allen, *American Prosody,* New York, 1935, pp. 277-306. Special studies by Philip Graham are "Lanier's Reading," *Univ. Texas Studies in English,* XI (1931), 63-89; "Lanier and Science," *Amer. Lit.,* IV (1932), 288-292; and "A Note on Lanier's Music," *Univ. Texas Studies in English,* XVII (1937), 107-111. Two studies by Aubrey H. Starke are "Sidney Lanier: Man of Science in the Field of Letters," and "Lanier's Appreciation of Whitman," *Amer. Scholar,* II (1933), 389-408. Other special studies include James S. Snoddy, "Color and Motion in Lanier," *Poet-Lore,* XII (1900), 558-570; H. E. Harman, "A Study of Sidney Lanier's 'The Symphony,'" *So. Atl. Quar.,* XVII (1918), 32-39; Ernest P. Kuhl, "Sidney Lanier and Edward Spencer," *Studies in Philol.,* XXVII (1930), 462-476; John C. French, "First Drafts of Lanier's Verse," *Modern Language Notes,* XLVIII (1933), 27-31; John S. Mayfield, "Sidney Lanier's Immortal Bird," *Amer. Book Collector,* VI (1935), 200-203; Gay W. Allen, "Sidney Lanier as a Literary Critic," *Philological Quar.,* XVII (1938), 121-138; Lewis Leary, "The Forlorn Hope of Sidney Lanier," *So. Atl. Quar.,* XLVI (1947), 263-271; and Nathalia Wright, "The East Tennessee Background of Sidney Lanier's *Tiger-Lilies,*" *Amer. Lit.,* XIX (1947), 127-138.

Aspects of Lanier's career are studied in John W. Wayland, *Sidney Lanier at Rockingham Springs,* Dayton, Va., 1912; J. Saulsbury Short, "Sidney Lanier at Johns Hopkins," *Johns Hopkins Alumni Mag.,* V (1916), 7-24;

John S. Mayfield, "Lanier's Trail in Texas," *Texas Mo.*, III (1929), 329–337; *idem, Some New Facts Concerning Sidney Lanier in Florida*, Baltimore, 1935; Lena E. Jackson and Aubrey H. Starke, "New Light on the Ancestry of Sidney Lanier," *Virginia Mag. Hist. and Biog.*, XLIII (1935), 160–168; *idem*, "Sidney Lanier in Florida," *Florida Hist. Soc. Quar.*, XV (1936), 118–124; and Leola S. Beeson, *Sidney Lanier at Oglethorpe University*, Macon, Ga., 1936.

PRIMARY SOURCES

Most of the Lanier manuscripts are in the Lanier Room of the Johns Hopkins University Library. Scattered manuscripts are in the Duke University Library and Harvard College Library.

Published reminiscences of a primary nature include Clifford A. Lanier, "Reminiscences of Sidney Lanier," *Chautauquan*, XXI (1895), 403–409; Daniel Coit Gilman, "Sidney Lanier: Reminiscences and Letters," *So. Atl. Quar.*, IV (1905), 115–122; Milton H. Northrup, "Sidney Lanier: Recollections and Letters," *Lippincott's Mag.*, LXXV (1905), 302–315; George H. Clarke, "Some Early Letters and Reminiscences of Sidney Lanier," *Independent*, LXI (1906), 1092–1098; and Hamlin Garland, *Roadside Meetings*, New York, 1930, pp. 144–153.

BIBLIOGRAPHY

Philip Graham and Frieda C. Thies have compiled the most complete bibliography for *The Centennial Edition*, VI (1945), 379–412, including collected prose, poetry, and letters; the first printing of poems and short prose; a listing of unpublished manuscripts; a full citation of biography and criticism; and selected reviews of Lanier's published volumes. See also Harry H. Clark, ed., *Major American Poets*, New York, 1936, pp. 903–907—an annotated listing; and Harry Hartwick, in Walter F. Taylor, *A History of American Letters*, New York, 1936, pp. 550–553.

# RING (RINGGOLD WILMER) LARDNER
## *1885–1933*

SEPARATE WORKS

*Bib Ballads*, 1915; *You Know Me Al*, 1916; *Gullible's Travels*, 1917; *My Four Weeks in France*, 1918; *Treat 'Em Rough*, 1918; *Own Your Own Home*, 1919; *Regular Fellows I Have Met*, 1919; *The Real Dope*, 1919; *The Young Immigrunts*, 1920; *Symptoms of Being 35*, 1921; *The Big Town*, 1921; *Say It with Oil*, 1923; *How to Write Short Stories (with Samples)*, 1924; *What of It?* 1925; *The Love Nest and Other Stories*, 1926; *The Story of a Wonder*

*Man,* 1927; *Round Up,* 1929; *June Moon* (with George S. Kaufman), 1930; *Lose with a Smile,* 1933; *First and Last,* 1934.

## REPRINTS AND COLLECTIONS

*Ring Lardner's Best Stories* . . ., Garden City, 1938, with a foreword by William McFee, is a collection made from the stories in *The Big Town* (1921) and *Round Up* (1929). Gilbert Seldes edited selections as *First and Last,* New York, 1934; and *The Portable Ring Lardner,* New York, 1946. The Modern Lib. issue of *The Collected Short Stories of Ring Lardner,* New York, 1941, is a reprint of *Round Up.*

## BIOGRAPHY AND CRITICISM

The best biographical sketch of Lardner is that of Nelson F. Adkins in *Dict. Amer. Biog., Suppl. One* (1944). Very few critical estimates of Lardner were published during his lifetime. Four of some significance are "Beyond Grammar: Ring Lardner," in Carl Van Doren, *Many Minds,* New York, 1924, pp. 167–180; "Mr. Dooley, Meet Mr. Lardner," in Gilbert Seldes, *The Seven Lively Arts,* New York, 1924, pp. 111–126; "Ring Lardner: Hard-Boiled Americans," in Stuart P. Sherman, *The Main Stream,* New York, 1927, pp. 168–175; and Clifton Fadiman, "Ring Lardner and the Triangle of Hate," *Nation,* CXXXVI (1933), 315–317.

The most recent recognition is "Ring Lardner: Like Something Was Going to Happen," in Maxwell Geismar, *Writers in Crisis,* Boston, 1942, pp. 1–36—the fullest treatment to date; and James T. Farrell, "Ring Lardner's Success-Mad World," *N.Y. Times Book Rev.,* June 18, 1944, pp. 3, 18.

## PRIMARY SOURCES

Lardner's *The Story of a Wonder Man* (1927) is a burlesque autobiography.

## BIBLIOGRAPHY

The fullest bibliographical listing of items by and about Lardner is in Fred B. Millett, *Contemporary American Authors,* New York, 1940, pp. 429–431.

## (HARRY) SINCLAIR LEWIS
### *b. 1885*

## SEPARATE WORKS

*Hike and the Aeroplane,* 1912; *Our Mr. Wrenn,* 1914; *The Trail of the Hawk,* 1915; *The Job,* 1917; *The Innocents,* 1917; *Free Air,* 1919; *Main Street,*

1920; *Babbitt*, 1922; *Arrowsmith*, 1925; *Mantrap*, 1926; *Elmer Gantry*, 1927; *The Man Who Knew Coolidge*, 1928; *Dodsworth: A Novel*, 1929; *Ann Vickers*, 1933; *Work of Art*, 1934; *Jayhawker: A Play in Three Acts* (with Lloyd Lewis), 1935; *Selected Short Stories*, 1935; *It Can't Happen Here*, 1935; *The Prodigal Parents*, 1938; *Bethel Merriday*, 1940; *Gideon Planish*, 1943; *Cass Timberlane*, 1945; *Kingsblood Royal*, 1947.

REPRINTS

Four novels were issued as the Nobel Prize Edition of the Novels of Sinclair Lewis: *Main Street, Babbitt, Elmer Gantry, Dodsworth*, New York, 1931. *Babbitt* (1922) was published in the Modern Lib., New York, 1942; *Arrowsmith* (1925) was edited by Barbara G. Spayd, New York, 1933, with bibliographical notes; and published in the Modern Lib., New York, 1933. Other reprints are *Selected Short Stories of Sinclair Lewis*, Garden City, N.Y., 1935; and *Seven Selected Short Stories*, New York, 1943.

BIOGRAPHY AND CRITICISM

Critical estimates of Lewis's work made before the Nobel Prize award (1930) are "Sinclair Lewis," in Carl Van Doren, *The American Novel . . .*, New York, 1921 (rev. ed., 1940), pp. 303–314; Archibald Marshall, "Gopher Prairie," *No. Amer. Rev.*, CCXV (1922), 394–402; Stuart P. Sherman, *The Significance of Sinclair Lewis*, New York, 1922, 28 pp.; Oliver Harrison (Harrison Smith), *Sinclair Lewis*, New York, 1925, 28 pp.; Percy H. Boynton, *More Contemporary Americans*, Chicago, 1927, pp. 179–198; "Sinclair Lewis," in Walter Lippmann, *Men of Destiny*, New York, 1927, pp. 71–92; Vernon L. Parrington, *Sinclair Lewis: Our Own Diogenes*, Seattle, 1927, 27 pp.; Régis Michaud, *The American Novel To-day*, Boston, 1928, pp. 128–153; Milton Waldman, in J. C. Squire and others, *Contemporary American Authors*, New York, 1928, pp. 71–94; "Sinclair Lewis," in Thomas K. Whipple, *Spokesmen . . .*, New York, 1928, pp. 208–229; Frances T. Russell, "The Young Mr. Lewis," *Univ. Calif. Chron.*, XXX (1928), 417–427; *idem*, "The Growing Up of Sinclair Lewis," *ibid.*, XXXII (1930), 319–324; "Sinclair Lewis," in David Karsner, *Sixteen Authors to One*, New York, 1928, pp. 67–82; Emory S. Bogardus, "Social Distances in Fiction: Analysis of Main Street," *Sociology and Social Research*, IX (1929), 174–180; "Goblins in Winnemac: A Note as to Sinclair Lewis," in James Branch Cabell, *Some of Us*, New York, 1930, pp. 61–73; and Vernon L. Parrington, *Main Currents in American Thought*, New York, III (1930), 360–369.

Later estimates are Henry S. Canby, "Sinclair Lewis," *Amer.-Scandinavian Rev.*, XIX (1931), 73–76; Christian S. Gauss, "Sinclair Lewis *vs*. His Education," *Sat. Eve. Post*, CCIV (Dec. 26, 1931), pp. 20–21, 54–56; Howard M.

Jones, "Mr. Lewis's America," *Virginia Quar. Rev.,* VII (1931), 427-432; Lewis Mumford, "The America of Sinclair Lewis," *Current Hist.,* XXXIII (1931), 529-533; Bernard De Voto, "Sinclair Lewis," *Sat. Rev. Lit.,* IX (Jan. 28, 1933), 397-398; Carl Van Doren, *Sinclair Lewis: A Biographical Sketch,* Garden City, N.Y., 1933; William Rose Benét, "The Earlier Lewis," *Sat. Rev. Lit.,* X (Jan. 20, 1934), 421-422; Victor F. Calverton, "Sinclair Lewis: The Last of the Literary Liberals," *Modern Mo.,* VIII (1934), 77-86; Henry S. Canby, "Sinclair Lewis's Art of Work," *Sat. Rev. Lit.,* X (Feb. 10, 1934), 465, 473; Harry Hartwick, *The Foreground of American Fiction,* New York, 1934, pp. 250-281; Lionel Crocker, "Sinclair Lewis on Public Speaking," *Quar. Jour. Speech,* XXI (1935), 232-237; "Sinclair Lewis," in Harlan Hatcher, *Creating the Modern American Novel,* New York, 1935, pp. 109-126; Robert Cantwell, "Sinclair Lewis," in Malcolm Cowley, ed., *After the Genteel Tradition . . . ,* New York, 1936, pp. 112-126; Granville Hicks, "Sinclair Lewis and the Good Life," *English Jour.,* XXV (1936), 265-273; Lloyd R. Morris, "Sinclair Lewis: His Critics and the Public," *No. Amer. Rev.,* CCXLV (1938), 381-390; Joseph E. Baker, "Sinclair Lewis, Plato, and the Regional Escape," *English Jour.,* XXVIII (1939), 460-468; "Sinclair Lewis," in Percy H. Boynton, *America in Contemporary Fiction,* Chicago, 1940, pp. 164-184; Thomas D. Horton, "Sinclair Lewis: The Symbol of an Era," *No. Amer. Rev.,* CCXLVIII (1940), 374-393; Benjamin Stolberg, "Sinclair Lewis," *Amer. Mercury,* LIII (1941), 450-460; "The New Realism: Sherwood Anderson and Sinclair Lewis," in Alfred Kazin, *On Native Grounds . . . ,* New York, 1942, 205-226; Leo and Miriam Gurko, "The Two Main Streets of Sinclair Lewis," *College English,* IV (1943), 288-292.

Critical estimates of Lewis as observed abroad are "Sinclair Lewis Introduces Elmer Gantry," in Rebecca West, *The Strange Necessity,* London, 1928, pp. 269-280; Luc Durtain, "Un Témoin des Etats-Unis: Le Romancier Sinclair Lewis," *Revue Hebdomadaire,* XXXVIII (1929), 554-564; Harry L. Binsse and John J. Trounstine, "Europe Looks at Sinclair Lewis," *Bookman,* LXXII (1931), 453-457; Leo von Hibler, "Sinclair Lewis und die Amerikanische Wirtschaft, zum 50. Geburtstag des Autors," *Anglia,* LIX (1935), 448-460; R. De Villeneuve, "Le Nationalisme de Sinclair Lewis," *Mercure de France,* CCLXXX (1937), 286-307; and Jean Loiseau, "La Croisade de Sinclair Lewis," *Etudes Anglaises,* II (1938), 120-133.

Some manuscripts of Sinclair Lewis are at Los Angeles in the library of the University of Southern California.

An early bibliographical listing of Lewis material is in Carl Van Doren, *Sinclair Lewis,* Garden City, 1933, pp. 77-187, compiled by Harvey Taylor. Useful especially for secondary material is the listing in Fred B. Millett, *Contemporary American Authors,* New York, 1940, pp. 436-441.

# LUDWIG LEWISOHN
b. *1882*

SEPARATE WORKS

*The Broken Snare*, 1908; *A Night in Alexandria*, 1909; *The Modern Drama: An Essay in Interpretation*, 1915; *The Spirit of Modern German Literature*, 1916; *The Poets of Modern France*, 1918; *The Drama and the Stage*, 1922; *Up Stream: An American Chronicle*, 1922; *Don Juan*, 1923; *The Creative Life*, 1924; *Israel*, 1925; *The Case of Mr. Crump*, 1926; *Cities and Men*, 1927; *The Defeated*, 1927; *Roman Summer*, 1927; *Adam: A Dramatic History*, 1929; *Mid-Channel: An American Chronicle*, 1929; *Stephen Escott*, 1930; *The Golden Vase*, 1931; *The Last Days of Shylock*, 1931; *Expression in America*, 1932; *This People*, 1933; *An Altar in the Fields: A Novel*, 1934; *The Permanent Horizon: A New Search for Old Truths*, 1934; *Trumpet of Jubilee: A Novel*, 1937; *The Answer: The Jew and the World, Past, Present, and Future*, 1939; *For Ever Wilt Thou Love*, 1939; *Haven*, 1940; *Renegade*, 1942; *Breathe Upon These*, 1944.

REPRINTS

Lewisohn edited *A Modern Book of Criticism*, selections, with an introduction, for Modern Lib., New York, 1919. The first volume of his autobiographical trilogy, *Up Stream* (1922), was reprinted in Modern Lib., New York, 1926. *The Defeated* (London, 1927) was issued in America as *The Island Within*, New York, 1928, and in the Modern Lib., New York, 1940. James W. Wise edited *A Jew Speaks: An Anthology from Ludwig Lewisohn*, New York, 1931. *Expression in America* (1932) was revised under the title *The Story of American Literature*, New York, 1937, and included under that title in the Modern Lib., New York, 1939; it is a companion history, in Freudian terms, to his *Creative America: An Anthology*, New York, 1933. The first American trade edition of *The Case of Mr. Crump* was published, New York, 1947.

BIOGRAPHY AND CRITICISM

Up to the present, studies of Lewisohn as novelist and critic are negligible. One of the earliest is Amy Lowell, "The Case of Modern Poetry Versus Professor Lewisohn," *Bookman*, XLVIII (1919), 558–566. Two more recent studies are Dorothea Brande, "Mr. Lewisohn Interprets America," *Amer. Rev.*, II (1933), 189–198; and Ernest S. Bates, "Lewisohn into Crump," *Amer. Mercury*, XXXI (1934), 441–450. The fullest accounts of his life are his autobiographical studies: *Up Stream* (1922), *Mid-Channel* (1929), and *Haven* (1940).

Bibliographical listings are in Fred B. Millett, *Contemporary American Authors,* New York, 1940, pp. 441–444—useful especially for Lewisohn's work as translator and editor.

## ABRAHAM LINCOLN
### 1809–1865

#### COLLECTED WORKS

The numerous sets of Lincoln's writings which are called "Complete Works" are in fact far from complete, and their accuracy cannot be trusted. An edition of Lincoln's complete writings has been publicly announced, co-sponsored by the Rutgers University Press and the Abraham Lincoln Association of Springfield, Illinois.

At present the most important collection is *Abraham Lincoln: Complete Works* . . ., New York, 1905, 12 vols., actually edited by Francis D. Tandy, though bearing the names of John G. Nicolay and John Hay, since it is a new and enlarged redaction, with a general introduction by Richard W. Gilder, of the two-volume edition first published in 1894 by Nicolay and Hay. No other collections are comparable in scope or accuracy.

#### LETTERS AND ADDRESSES

The correspondence in the *Complete Works* (1905) mentioned above is supplemented by Gilbert A. Tracy, ed., *Uncollected Letters of Abraham Lincoln* . . ., Boston, 1917, with an introduction by Ida M. Tarbell; Paul M. Angle, ed., *New Letters and Papers of Lincoln,* Boston, 1930; and Vol. II of Emanuel Hertz's *Abraham Lincoln: A New Portrait,* New York, 1931—derivative and frequently inaccurate.

Lincoln forgeries have been numerous. Among them are the letters purporting to be correspondence between Lincoln and Ann Rutledge, published in *Atl. Mo.,* Dec., 1928, to Feb., 1929.

#### SELECTIONS AND REPRINTS

A very useful volume of selections, including a sound introduction, is Roy P. Basler, ed., *Abraham Lincoln: His Speeches and Writings,* Cleveland, 1946. Philip Van Doren Stern's edition of *The Life and Writings of Abraham Lincoln,* New York, 1942, for the Modern Lib., has an introduction by Allan Nevins. Three other recent volumes of selected reprints are *The Literary Works of Abraham Lincoln,* New York, 1942, edited with a foreword by Carl Van Doren; *Selected Writings and Speeches* . . ., Chicago, 1943, ed. by T. Harry Williams; and Philip S. Foner, ed., *Abraham Lincoln: Selections from His Writings,* New York, 1944. Earlier selections were published in the

Riverside Literature Ser., Boston, 1926; the Modern Student's Lib., New York, 1927; and the New Pocket Classics, New York, 1930. *Speeches and Letters,* New York, 1929, are in Everyman's Lib.

The *Lincoln-Douglas Debates of 1858,* Springfield, Ill., 1910, were edited with an introduction by Edwin E. Sparks. *An Autobiography of Abraham Lincoln . . . ,* Indianapolis, 1926, was compiled from autobiographical portions of his writings by Nathaniel W. Stephenson.

The most recent editions of selections help meet the need, expressed by Roy P. Basler, "Abraham Lincoln: Artist," *No. Amer. Rev.,* CCXLV (1938), 144–153, for a good edition of Lincoln's writings prepared for students of literature as well as of history. Addenda appear in Rufus Rockwell Wilson, ed., *Uncollected Works of Abraham Lincoln,* Elmira, N.Y., 1947.

BIOGRAPHY AND CRITICISM

The best of the early biographies is the voluminous history written by the men who had been Lincoln's presidential secretaries, John G. Nicolay and John Hay, *Abraham Lincoln: A History,* New York, 1890, 10 vols. It is an authorized account, set down from first-hand knowledge by great admirers. The most vivid and poetic life—and a classic among American biographies— is Carl Sandburg, *Abraham Lincoln: The Prairie Years,* New York, 1926, 2 vols., completed by *Abraham Lincoln: The War Years,* New York, 1939, 4 vols. A sound and thorough historical investigation is Albert J. Beveridge, *Abraham Lincoln, 1809–1858,* Boston, 1928, 2 vols. An authentic analysis of the early presidential years, based on documentary evidence much of which is here first used, is James G. Randall, *Lincoln the President: Springfield to Gettysburg,* New York, 1945, 2 vols., continued in Randall's *Lincoln the Liberal Statesman,* New York, 1947. Also written from material drawn from primary sources is William E. Baringer, *A House Dividing: Lincoln as President Elect,* Springfield, Ill., 1945. The best brief biographical and critical sketch is that of James G. Randall in *Dict. Amer. Biog.* (1933).

The several biographical studies by William E. Barton, published between 1920 and 1930, are based on thorough research. Lord Charnwood's one-volume life, *Abraham Lincoln,* New York, 1916, is well proportioned. A popular life is Ida M. Tarbell, *The Life of Abraham Lincoln,* New York, 1917, 2 vols.

For listings of the voluminous special political studies, the reader is referred to the bibliographies below. The *Abraham Lincoln Quarterly* (1940– current) continues the *Bulletin* published by the Abraham Lincoln Association of Springfield, Illinois (1923–1939). Both periodicals are devoted to a variety of special studies.

Lincoln as a man of letters is best treated in Roy P. Basler, ed., *Abraham Lincoln: His Speeches and Writings,* New York, 1946; an earlier study is

Daniel K. Dodge, *Abraham Lincoln: Master of Words,* New York, 1924. Standard estimates are Nathaniel W. Stephenson, "Lincoln," *Camb. Hist. Amer. Lit.,* III (1921), 367–384; and Vernon L. Parrington, *Main Currents in American Thought,* New York, II (1927), 152–160. Other special studies are Roy P. Basler, "Abraham Lincoln's Rhetoric," *Amer. Lit.,* XI (1939), 167–182; Paul M. Angle, "Lincoln's Power with Words," *Abraham Lincoln Assn. Papers for 1934,* pp. 59–87; and Benjamin P. Thomas, "Lincoln's Humor: An Analysis," *ibid.,* 1935, pp. 61–90.

Lincoln as orator is the subject of two studies: Mildred F. Berry, "Abraham Lincoln: His Development in the Skills of the Platform," in William N. Brigance, ed., *A History and Criticism of American Public Address,* New York, 1943, II, 828–858; and Earl W. Wiley, "Abraham Lincoln: His Emergence as the Voice of the People," *ibid.,* II, 859–877.

Paul M. Angle edited *The Lincoln Reader,* New Brunswick, N.J., 1947— one hundred seventy-nine authoritative biographical articles about Lincoln, especially in the pre-presidential years.

## PRIMARY SOURCES

A classic picture of the prairie years is W. H. Herndon and J. W. Weik, *Herndon's Lincoln: The True Story of a Great Life,* Chicago, 1889, 3 vols.— to be used in Paul M. Angle's edition (1930). Other early lives, still meritorious, are those of J. G. Holland (1866), Ward H. Lamon (1872—actually written by Chauncey F. Black), Isaac N. Arnold (1885), Carl Schurz (1891), and J. T. Morse (1893). Useful reminiscences are those of U. F. Linder, A. K. McClure, A. T. Rice, Joshua F. Speed, James Speed, W. O. Stoddard, and H. C. Whitney. There are also the diaries of John Hay, Gideon Welles, Salmon P. Chase, Edward Bates, and Orville Hickman Browning.

The largest and most useful collections of Lincolniana are those of the Illinois State Historical Library, Springfield, Ill.; Henry E. Huntington Library, San Marino, Calif.; Lincoln National Life Foundation, Fort Wayne, Ind.; Brown University Library, Providence, R.I.; and Lincoln Memorial University, Harrowgate, Tenn. The most important collection of unused manuscripts is the voluminous file of Lincoln papers in the Library of Congress, deposited several years ago, and only recently available.

## BIBLIOGRAPHY

The first adequate listing of the tremendous quantity of Lincoln literature is Jay Monaghan, *Lincoln Bibliography, 1839–1939,* Springfield, Ill., 1945, 2 vols. Paul M. Angle, *A Shelf of Lincoln Books,* New Brunswick, N.J., 1946, is a critical appraisal of eighty-one biographies, monographs, and collections of Lincoln's writings. Valuable bibliographies are those prepared by Randall, following his sketch of Lincoln in *Dict. Amer. Biog.* (1933), and in Vol. II of his *Lincoln the President,* New York, 1945. See also Ernest J. Wessen, "Debates of Lincoln and Douglas: A Bibliographical Discussion," *Papers Bibl. Soc. Amer.,* XL (1946), 91–106.

# (NICHOLAS) VACHEL LINDSAY
## *1879–1931*

### SEPARATE WORKS

*The Tramp's Excuse and Other Poems,* 1909; *Rhymes to Be Traded for Bread,* 1912; *General William Booth Enters into Heaven and Other Poems,* 1913; *Adventures While Preaching the Gospel of Beauty,* 1914; *The Congo and Other Poems,* 1914; *The Art of the Moving Picture,* 1915; *A Handy Guide for Beggars,* 1916; *The Chinese Nightingale and Other Poems,* 1917; *The Golden Whales of California, and Other Rhymes in the American Language,* 1920; *The Golden Book of Springfield,* 1920; *Going-to-the-Sun,* 1923; *Going-to-the-Stars,* 1926; *The Candle in the Cabin: A Weaving Together of Script and Singing,* 1926; *The Litany of Washington Street,* 1929; *Every Soul Is a Circus,* 1929.

### COLLECTIONS AND SELECTED WORKS

*The Daniel Jazz and Other Poems,* London, 1920, is a selection of previously published poems. *Collected Poems,* New York, 1923, was revised and issued as an illustrated edition, New York, 1925.

*Letters of Nicholas Vachel Lindsay to A. Joseph Armstrong,* Waco, Tex., 1940, was edited by Armstrong.

*Selected Poems of Vachel Lindsay,* New York, 1931 (Modern Readers' Ser.), was edited with an introduction by Hazelton Spencer.

A revised edition of *The Art of the Moving Picture* (1915) was issued in 1922 with added material.

A partial list of the numerous pamphlets and broadsides which Lindsay printed for distribution during his minstrel days is in Jacob Blanck, *Merle Johnson's American First Editions,* 4th ed., New York, 1942, pp. 316–317.

### BIOGRAPHY AND CRITICISM

Edgar Lee Masters's *Vachel Lindsay: A Poet in America,* New York, 1935, is a narrative and critical biography written by a friend who had also been a participant in the poetry movement centering in Chicago.

One of the earliest estimates of Lindsay as poet is the introduction written by Harriet Monroe for *The Congo and Other Poems,* New York, 1914. Others written during Lindsay's lifetime are "The Higher Vaudeville: Vachel Lindsay," in Conrad Aiken, *Scepticisms,* N.Y., 1919, pp. 155-159; Marianne Moore, "An Eagle in the Ring," *Dial,* LXXV (1923), 498-505; Louis Untermeyer, *American Poetry Since 1900,* New York, 1923, pp. 88-112; Herbert S. Gorman, "Vachel Lindsay, Evangelist of Poetry," *No. Amer. Rev.,* CCXIX (1924), 123-128; Carl Van Doren, *Many Minds,* New York, 1924, pp. 151-166; Llewellyn Jones, *First Impressions,* New York, 1925, pp. 85-96; Clement Wood, *Poets of America,* New York, 1925, pp. 229-245; "Vachel Lindsay," in Harriet Monroe, *Poets and Their Art,* New York, 1926, pp. 21-28; Charles Davies and Llewellyn Lucas, "Two Aspects of Vachel Lindsay," *Poetry and the Play,* XI (1927), 294-303; Edward Davison, "Nicholas Vachel Lindsay," in J. C. Squire, ed., *Contemporary American Authors,* New York, 1928, pp. 207-236; Albert E. Trombly, "Vachel Lindsay's Prose," *Southwest Rev.,* XIII (1928), 459-468; "Vachel Lindsay," in Thomas K. Whipple, *Spokesmen,* New York, 1928, pp. 184-207; Alfred Kreymborg, *Our Singing Strength,* New York, 1929, pp. 368-378; and "Vachel Lindsay," in Stephen Graham, *The Death of Yesterday,* London, 1930, pp. 92-98.

Later estimates are Henry S. Canby, "Vachel Lindsay," *Sat. Rev. Lit.,* VIII (Jan. 9, 1932), 437; Henry M. Robinson, "The Ordeal of Vachel Lindsay: A Critical Reconstruction," *Bookman,* LXXV (1932), 6-9; Hazelton Spencer, "The Life and Death of a Bard," *Amer. Mercury,* XXV (1932), 455-462; Jessie B. Rittenhouse, "Vachel Lindsay," *So. Atl. Quar.,* XXXII (1933), 266-282; John Drinkwater, "Two American Lives," *Quar. Rev.,* CCLXVI (1936), 122-135; William R. Moses, "Vachel Lindsay: Ferment of the Poet's Mind," *Southern Rev.,* I (1936), 828-836; C. P. Lee, "Adulation and the Artist," *Sat. Rev. Lit.,* Aug. 10, 1940, pp. 7, 18-19; and Austin Warren, "The Case of Vachel Lindsay," *Accent,* VI (1946), 230-239.

PRIMARY SOURCES

Lindsay's autobiography, *Adventures While Preaching the Gospel of Beauty,* New York, 1914, and his *A Handy Guide for Beggars,* New York, 1916, give accounts of his early struggle to gain recognition as a modern minstrel. Other source material is in Stephen Graham, *Tramping with a Poet in the Rockies,* New York, 1922; Albert E. Trombly, *Vachel Lindsay, Adventurer,* Columbia, Mo., 1929; Aubrey Starke and others, "They Knew Vachel Lindsay: A Symposium of Personal Reminiscences," *Latin Quarter-ly,* I (1934), 128-140; and A. Joseph Armstrong, "Vachel Lindsay as I Knew Him," *Mark Twain Quar.,* V (1943), No. 3, pp. 6-11. See also the autobiographies of Edgar Lee Masters, Harriet Monroe, and other Chicago writers.

Lindsay manuscripts are deposited in Harvard College Library, Dartmouth College Library, and the library of the University of Buffalo.

BIBLIOGRAPHY

Bibliographical listings are in Fred B. Millett, *Contemporary American Authors,* New York, 1940, pp. 445–449. See also the listing by Frances Cheney in Allen Tate, *Sixty American Poets, 1896–1944,* Washington, 1945. For an annotated bibliography, see Harry H. Clark, ed., *Major American Poets,* New York, 1936, pp. 929–931.

# WILLIAM LIVINGSTON
## *1723–1790*

SEPARATE WORKS

*Philosophic Solitude; or, The Choice of a Rural Life: A Poem,* 1747; *A Review of the Military Operations in North-America,* 1757; *A Soliloquy,* 1770; *Observations on Government,* 1787.

*A Review of the Military Operations . . .* was reprinted in *Coll. Mass. Hist. Soc.,* VII (1801), 67–163. *A Brief Consideration of New York with Respect to Its Natural Advantages,* Metuchen, N.J., 1925—a reprint of articles from the *Independent Reflector* (1753) attributed to Livingston—was probably written by William Smith, Jr. (see Lyon N. Richardson, *A History of Early American Magazines,* New York, 1931, p. 80).

BIOGRAPHY AND CRITICISM

Theodore Sedgwick, Jr., published *A Memoir of the Life of William Livingston . . .* (1833), making use of family papers, but the errors are numerous. Livingston as a man of letters is discussed by Moses C. Tyler in *The Literary History of the American Revolution,* New York, 1897, II, 17–20; and, most recently and fully, by Lyon N. Richardson, *A History of Early American Magazines, 1741–1789,* New York, 1931, pp. 75–91. The sketch in *Dict. Amer. Biog.* (1933) is by John A. Krout. Further material is in Franklin B. Dexter, *Biographical Sketches of the Graduates of Yale College,* New Haven, I (1885). Two useful historical studies of Livingston are in Carl L. Becker, *The History of Political Parties in the Province of New York, 1760–1776,* Madison, Wis., 1909, and Charles H. Levermore, "The Whigs of Colonial New York," *Amer. Hist. Rev.,* I (1896), 238–250.

Most of Livingston's manuscripts are in the possession of the Massachusetts Historical Society. Further primary material has been published in Edwin B. Livingston, *The Livingstons of Livingston Manor,* New York, 1910.

No satisfactory bibliography of Livingston has been published.

# JACK (JOHN GRIFFITH) LONDON
## 1876–1916

SEPARATE WORKS

*The Son of the Wolf, Tales of the Far North*, 1900; *The God of His Fathers and Other Stories*, 1901; *A Daughter of the Snows*, 1902; *Children of the Frost*, 1902; *The Cruise of the Dazzler*, 1902; *The Call of the Wild*, 1903; *The Kempton-Wace Letters* (with Anna Strunsky), 1903; *The People of the Abyss*, 1903; *The Faith of Men and Other Stories*, 1904; *The Sea-Wolf*, 1904; *War of the Classes*, 1905; *The Game*, 1905; *Tales of the Fish Patrol*, 1905; *Moon-Face and Other Stories*, 1906; *White Fang*, 1906; *Scorn of Women*, 1906; *Before Adam*, 1906; *Love of Life and Other Stories*, 1906; *The Road*, 1907; *The Iron Heel*, 1907; *Martin Eden*, 1909; *Revolution*, 1909; *Revolution and Other Essays*, 1910; *Lost Face*, 1910; *Burning Daylight*, 1910; *Theft*, 1910; *When God Laughs and Other Stories*, 1911; *Adventure*, 1911; *The Cruise of the Snark*, 1911; *South Sea Tales*, 1911; *A Son of the Sun*, 1912; *The House of Pride and Other Tales of Hawaii*, 1912; *Smoke Bellew*, 1912; *The Night-Born*, 1913; *The Abysmal Brute*, 1913; *John Barleycorn*, 1913; *The Valley of the Moon*, 1913; *The Strength of the Strong (and Other Pieces)*, 1914; *The Mutiny of the Elsinore*, 1914; *The Scarlet Plague*, 1915; *The Star Rover*, 1915; *The Little Lady of the Big House*, 1916; *The Turtles of Tasman*, 1916; *The Acorn-Planter*, 1916; *The Human Drift*, 1917; *Jerry of the Islands*, 1917; *Michael, Brother of Jerry*, 1917; *The Red One*, 1918; *On the Makaloa Mat*, 1919; *Hearts of Three*, 1920; *Dutch Courage and Other Stories*, 1922.

No collection has been made of London's works. Reprints of separate items have appeared from time to time, uniformly bound in the so-called "Sonoma Edition." Most of these reprints are no longer in print. Many of the more popular stories have been translated, some of them into several languages. "Tramping with Kelly Through Iowa: A Jack London Diary," appeared, with a comment by John E. Briggs, in the *Palimpsest*, VII (May, 1926), 129–164. London's first published book, *The Son of the Wolf: Tales of the Far North*, was issued in the Riverside Library, Boston, 1930. *The Call of the Wild* has been reprinted in many editions, separately and in collections. It is most easily available in Frank L. Mott, ed., *The Call of the Wild and Other Stories*, Modern Readers' Ser., New York, 1935. Other selections are Franklin K. Mathiews, ed., *Brown Wolf and Other Jack London Stories*, New York, 1920; Leonard D. Abbott, ed., *London's Essays of Revolt*, New York, 1926; and *Best Short Stories of Jack London*, Sun Dial Press, Garden City, N.Y., 1945.

Charmian (Kittredge) London's *The Book of Jack London,* New York, 1921, 2 vols., is a well documented biography, necessarily prejudiced, and strongest for the period of her marriage to Jack London. The account by his daughter, Joan London, *Jack London and His Times: An Unconventional Biography,* New York, 1939, is also prejudiced, and supplements and offsets the Charmian London story. It is the fullest statement of the middle period, especially the two years of his marriage to Bess Maddern, and is especially useful on the influence of his reading and of contemporary movements. The only unprejudiced life is that of Irving Stone, *Sailor on Horseback: The Biography of Jack London,* Boston, 1938, popular, but based on original sources.

Further biographical essays, written during his lifetime, are H. M. Bland, "Jack London: Traveler, Novelist and Social Reformer," *Craftsman,* IX (1906), 607–619; Martin E. Johnson, *Through the South Seas with Jack London,* New York, 1913; and Bailey Millard, "Jack London, Farmer," *Bookman,* XLIV (1916), 151–156.

In the year following London's death, several other studies appeared, most of them in the nature of reminiscences: Grace I. Colbron, "Jack London: What He Was, and What He Accomplished," *Bookman,* XLIV (1917), 441–451; E. Preston Dargan, "Jack London in Chancery," *New Republic,* X, Apr. 21, 1917, Pt. 2, pp. 7–8; L. S. Friedland, "Jack London as Titan," *Dial,* LXII, 49–51 (Jan. 25, 1917); George W. James, "A Study of Jack London in His Prime," *Overland Mo.,* LXIX (1917), 361–399; R. W. Lane, "Life and Jack London," a serial in *Sunset,* reaching from Oct., 1917 (pp. 17–20), to May, 1918 (pp. 28–32); Wilfrid Lay, "'John Barleycorn' Under Psychoanalysis," *Bookman,* XLV (1917), 47–54; Leon R. Livingston, *From Coast to Coast with Jack London* . . ., Erie, Pa., 1917; Frank Pease, "Impressions of Jack London," *Seven Arts,* I (1917), 522–530; and Anna S. Walling, "Memories of Jack London," *Masses,* X (1917), No. 9, Issue 73.

Among more recent studies, the two most extensive are Georgia L. Bamford, *The Mystery of Jack London: Some of His Friends, Also a Few Letters —A Reminiscence,* Oakland, Calif., 1931; and Joseph Noel, *Footloose in Arcadia: A Personal Record of Jack London, George Sterling, Ambrose Bierce,* New York, 1940.

Other biographical studies and reminiscences are "Jack London," in Stephen Graham, *The Death of Yesterday,* London, 1930, pp. 53–61; Upton Sinclair, "Is This Jack London?" *Occult Rev.,* LII (1930), 394–400, LIII (1931), 10–14; George S. Viereck, "The Ghost of Jack London," *Liberty,* VIII (Oct. 10, 1931, pp. 15–18); "Jack London Number," *Overland Mo.,* XC (May, 1932); David H. Dickason, "A Note on Jack London and David Starr

Jordan," *Indiana Mag. Hist.*, XXXVIII (1942), 407–410; and Hobart Bosworth, "My Jack London," *Mark Twain Quar.*, V (1943), No. 2, pp. 2–5, 24.

Analyses of London as a writer are H[enry] L. Mencken, *Prejudices,* 1st ser., New York, 1919, pp. 236–239; E. W. Bowen, "Jack London's Place in American Literature," *Reformed Church Rev.*, 4th ser., XXIV (1920), 306–315; "Jack London," in Blanche C. Williams, *Our Short Story Writers,* New York, 1920, pp. 256–277; Lewis Mumford, "Jack London," *New Republic,* XXX (Mar. 29, 1922), 145–147; "The Prophet of the Last Frontier," in Fred L. Pattee, *Side-Lights on American Literature,* New York, 1922, pp. 98–160; Stephen Graham, "Jack London," *English Rev.*, XXXVIII (1924), 732–737; Clara Margolin, *Jack London's Short Stories: Ihre Form und ihr Gehalt . . .*, Heidelberg, 1926; K. Groos, "Die Verwendung der Eidetik als Kunstmittel in J. Londons Roman *Martin Eden," Zeitschrift für angewandte Psychologie,* XXXIII (1929), 417–438; C. Hartley Grattan, "Jack London," *Bookman,* LXVIII (1929), 667–671; Harry Hartwick, *The Foreground of American Fiction,* New York, 1934, pp. 67–84; Charles C. Walcutt, "Naturalism and the Superman in the Novels of Jack London," *Papers Michigan Acad. Science, Arts and Letters,* XXIV (1938), Pt. IV, pp. 89–107; and "Jack London, Wonder Boy," in Thomas K. Whipple, *Study Out the Land,* Berkeley, Calif., 1943, pp. 93–104.

An unpublished thesis which thoroughly reviews and analyzes London's work is Margaret I. Pope, "Jack London: A Study in Twentieth-Century Values" (Univ. of Wisconsin, 1935).

PRIMARY SOURCES

Many London manuscripts are in the Cresmer Collection at the University of Southern California. Further manuscript material is in the Henry Huntington Library; the University of California, Berkeley; and the Charlotte Ashley Felton Memorial Library, Stanford University.

In addition to source material—reminiscences of London—already listed above, London's autobiography, *John Barleycorn,* New York, 1913, should be consulted; and also Charmian (Kittredge) London's *The Log of the Snark,* New York, 1915, *Our Hawaii,* New York, 1917 (revised in 1922 to eliminate the bulk of the personal memoirs, incorporated in *The Book of Jack London,* New York, 1921), and *The New Hawaii,* London, 1923—a continuation of Jack London's tale, "My Hawaiian Aloha." Further material appears in Robert Herrick, *The Memoirs of an American Citizen,* New York, 1905.

BIBLIOGRAPHY

No adequate bibliography for Jack London is available. Joseph Gaer has compiled biographical and bibliographical data in *Jack London* (n.p.), 1934:

Monograph No. 1, of *California Literary Research Project,* mimeographed. Though inaccurate, it is a convenient collection of essential facts. A "Jack London Bibliography" is included in Charmian (Kittredge) London, *The Book of Jack London,* New York, 1921, II, 397–414.

# HENRY WADSWORTH LONGFELLOW
## *1807–1882*

### SEPARATE WORKS

*Elements of French Grammar,* 1830; *French Exercises,* 1830; *Novelas Españolas,* 1830; *Manuel de Proverbes Dramatiques,* 1830; *Syllabus de la Grammaire Italienne,* 1832; *Saggi de' Novellieri Italiani,* 1832; *Coplas de Don Jorge Manrique,* 1833; *Outre-Mer: A Pilgrimage Beyond the Sea,* 1833–1834; *Hyperion: A Romance,* 1839; *Voices of the Night,* 1839; *Ballads and Other Poems,* 1842; *Poems on Slavery,* 1842; *The Spanish Student: A Play in Three Acts,* 1843; *Poems,* 1845; *The Belfry of Bruges,* 1846; *Evangeline: A Tale of Acadie,* 1847; *Kavanagh: A Tale,* 1849; *The Seaside and the Fireside,* 1850; *The Golden Legend,* 1851; *The Song of Hiawatha,* 1855; *The Courtship of Miles Standish and Other Poems,* 1858; *The New England Tragedy,* 1860; *Tales of a Wayside Inn,* 1863; *Noël,* 1864; *The Divine Comedy of Dante Alighieri,* 1865–1867; *Household Poems,* 1865; *Flower-de-Luce,* 1867; *The New England Tragedies,* 1868; *The Alarm-Bell of Atri,* 1871; *The Divine Tragedy,* 1871; *Three Books of Song,* 1872; *Christus: A Mystery,* 1872; *Aftermath,* 1873; *The Hanging of the Crane,* 1874; *The Masque of Pandora and Other Poems,* 1875; *Kéramos,* 1877; *Kéramos and Other Poems,* 1878; *Bayard Taylor,* 1879; *From My Arm-Chair,* 1879; *Ultima Thule,* 1880; *In the Harbor: Ultima Thule—Part II,* 1882; *Michael Angelo,* 1882–1883; *There Was a Little Girl,* 1883.

### COLLECTED WORKS

Two collected editions were issued during the poet's life: his *Prose Works,* Boston, 1857, 2 vols., and *The Early Poems of Henry Wadsworth Longfellow,* London, 1878, ed. by R. H. Shepherd. The Riverside Edition of the *Complete Poetical and Prose Works* was published in 11 vols., Boston, 1886. The standard Library Edition, edited by Samuel Longfellow, including the *Life* by the editor, is *The Works of Henry Wadsworth Longfellow,* Boston, 1886–1891, 14 vols. Horace E. Scudder edited *The Complete Poetical Works of Henry W. Longfellow,* Boston, 1893, in one volume. The Craigie Edition of the *Complete Works* (Boston, 1904) is uniform with the Riverside Edition, but illustrated.

Other collections, all including material therein first collected, are R. W. Pettengill, ed., *Longfellow's Boyhood Poems,* Saratoga Springs, N.Y., 1925; James T. Hatfield, "An Unknown Prose Tale by Longfellow," *Amer. Lit.,* III (1931), 136–148 (reprint of "The Wondrous Tale of a Little Man in Gosling Green," from the *New Yorker,* Nov., 1834); Ralph Thompson, "Additions to Longfellow Bibliography, Including a New Prose Tale," *Amer. Lit.,* III (1931), 303–308; Bertram H. Flanders, "An Uncollected Longfellow Translation," *Amer. Lit.,* VII (1935), 205–207; Lawrance Thompson, "An Inquiry into the Importance of 'Boston Prize-Poems,'" *Colophon,* New Graphic ser., I (1940), No. 4, pp. 55–62—identifying a hitherto unknown poem.

Extracts from Longfellow's *Journal,* together with many letters, were published in the *Life* by Samuel Longfellow (Boston, 1886–1891). See also Julius Clausen, "Longfellow and Scandinavia: . . . With Some Unpublished Letters," *Amer.-Scandinavian Rev.,* XVI (1928), 732–740; James T. Hatfield, ed., "The Longfellow-Freiligrath Correspondence," *PMLA,* XLVIII (1933), 1223–1293; Merle E. Curti, "Henry Wadsworth Longfellow and Elihu Burritt," *Amer. Lit.,* VII (1935), 315–328; Irving T. Richards, "Longfellow in England: Unpublished Extracts from His Journal," *PMLA,* LI (1936), 1123–1140; Maud Howe Elliott, *Uncle Sam Ward and His Circle,* New York, 1938 (a first printing of fifty letters from Longfellow to Ward); W. Fischer, "An Unpublished Letter by Longfellow to a German Correspondent," in *Studies for William A. Read,* University, La., 1940; and Philip A. Shelley, "An Exchange of Letters with Longfellow," *PMLA,* LX (1945), 611–616—correspondence with Niclas Müller, the German publicist and translator, in 1864.

EDITED TEXTS AND REPRINTS

Though innumerable selections from Longfellow have been issued in the past fifty years, very few have usefulness today. The most serviceable edited volume is Odell Shepard, ed., *Henry Wadsworth Longfellow: Representative Selections, with Introduction, Bibliography, and Notes,* New York, 1934 (Amer. Writers Ser.). *The Sonnets of Henry Wadsworth Longfellow* were edited by Ferris Greenslet, Boston, 1907, with an introduction. *The Poems of Longfellow* was included in the Modern Lib., New York, 1945.

BIOGRAPHY AND CRITICISM

*The Life of Henry W. Longfellow* by the poet's brother Samuel Longfellow, Boston, 1886, 2 vols., though inaccurate, is primary and still indispensable. It is supplemented by the same author's *Final Memorials of Henry Wadsworth Longfellow,* Boston, 1887, later (1891) published as Vol. III of the *Life.* Other early biographies still useful are Eric S. Robertson, *The Life of Henry Wadsworth Longfellow,* London, 1887; G. R. Carpenter, *Henry*

*Wadsworth Longfellow*, Boston, 1901; William P. Trent, *Longfellow and Other Essays*, New York, 1908; Oliphant Smeaton, *Longfellow and His Poetry*, London, 1919. For the years covered, Lawrance Thompson, *Young Longfellow, 1807-1843*, New York, 1938, is excellent analysis, based on original sources.

The fullest treatment of Longfellow and his European relationships are those of James T. Hatfield, *New Light on Longfellow, with Special Reference to His Relations to Germany*, Boston, 1933—based in part on fresh material; Orie W. Long, *Literary Pioneers*, Cambridge, 1935—especially on Longfellow's early education in Germany; "Longfellow," in Clarence Gohdes, *American Literature in Nineteenth-Century England*, New York, 1944, pp. 99-126; Edmond Estève, *Longfellow et la France (Bowdoin Coll. Bul.*, No. 146), 1925; and Iris L. Whitman, *Longfellow and Spain*, New York, 1927. Briefer studies are those of Willis A. Chamberlin, "Longfellow's Attitude Toward Goethe," *Modern Philol.*, XVI (1918), 57-76; Julius Clausen, "Longfellow and Scandinavia: . . . With Some Unpublished Letters," *Amer.-Scandinavian Rev.*, XVI (1928), 732-740; Margaret Di Giovanni, "The Italian Friends of Longfellow," *Italia*, XVII (1940), 144-147; John E. Englekirk, "Notes on Longfellow in Spanish America," *Hispania*, XXV (1942), 295-308; Emilio Goggio, "Italian Influences on Longfellow's Works," *Romanic Rev.*, XVI (1925), 208-222; and George L. White, Jr., "Longfellow's Interest in Scandinavia During the Years 1835-1847," *Scandinavian Studies*, XVII (1942), 70-82.

Studies of themes and sources are M. G. Hill, "Some of Longfellow's Sources for the Second Part of *Evangeline*," *PMLA*, XXXI (1916), 161-180; Stith Thompson, "The Indian Legend of Hiawatha," *PMLA*, XXXVII (1922), 128-140—the relation of Longfellow to Schoolcraft's collection, as well as to the present-day folklore of the Ojibwa Indians; Wilbur L. Schramm, "*Hiawatha* and Its Predecessors," *Philological Quar.*, XI (1932), 321-343; Chase S. and Stellanova Osborn, *Schoolcraft—Longfellow—Hiawatha*, Lancaster, Pa., 1943; A. H. Appelmann, "Longfellow's *Poems on Slavery* in Their Relationship to Freiligrath," *Modern Language Notes*, XXX (1915), 101-102; John Van Schaick, Jr., *The Characters in Tales of a Wayside Inn*, Boston, 1939; and J. T. Krumpelman, "Longfellow's 'Golden Legend' and the 'Arme Heinrich' Theme in Modern German Literature," *Jour. English and Germanic Philol.*, XXV (1926), 137-192. A brief study of "A Psalm of Life" and "Excelsior" is in William Charvat's "Let Us Then Be Up and Doing," *English Jour.*, XXVIII (1939), 374-383. See also George Arms, "The Revision of 'My Lost Youth,'" *Modern Language Notes*, LXI (1946), 389-392.

Critical estimates of Longfellow valuable to the extent that the authors are spokesmen of their times are J. B. Moore, ed., *Selections from Poe's*

*Literary Criticism,* New York, 1926, pp. 64–81—mainly from *The Literati* (1850); "Longfellow," in William M. Rossetti, *Lives of Famous Poets,* London, 1878, pp. 338–391; James Russell Lowell, *The Function of the Poet and Other Essays,* Boston, 1920, pp. 115–126; Bayard Taylor, *Critical Essays and Literary Notes,* New York, 1880, pp. 296–298; Anthony Trollope, "Henry Wadsworth Longfellow," *No. Amer. Rev.,* CXXXII (1881), 383–406; "Henry Wadsworth Longfellow," in Edmund C. Stedman, *Poets of America,* Boston, 1885, pp. 180–224; "Longfellow," in Thomas W. Higginson, *Old Cambridge,* New York, 1899, pp. 109–144; "The White Mr. Longfellow," in William Dean Howells, *Literary Friends and Acquaintance,* New York, 1900, pp. 178–211; *idem,* "The Art of Longfellow," *No. Amer. Rev.,* CLXXXIV (1907), 472–485; Bliss Perry, *Park-Street Papers,* Boston, 1908, pp. 107–140; "Longfellow" in William P. Trent, *Longfellow and Other Essays,* New York, 1910, pp. 1–36; "Longfellow," in George E. Woodberry, *Literary Memoirs . . . ,* New York, 1921, pp. 215–226; "Henry Wadsworth Longfellow," in Gamaliel Bradford, *Biography and the Human Heart,* Boston, 1932, pp. 37–62; George Saintsbury, *Prefaces and Essays,* London, 1933, pp. 324–344; and Van Wyck Brooks, "Longfellow in Cambridge" and "Cambridge: Longfellow, Dana the Younger, Lowell" (chaps. viii and xvi), in *The Flowering of New England,* New York, 1936.

Other special studies of interest are Carl L. Johnson, *Professor Longfellow of Harvard,* Eugene, Ore., 1944—a documented study of his years as teacher, 1836–1854; *idem,* "Three Notes on Longfellow," *Harvard Studies and Notes in Philol. and Lit.,* XIV (1932), 249–271; John P. Pritchard, "The Horatian Influence upon Longfellow," *Amer. Lit.,* IV (1932), 22–38; "Henry Wadsworth Longfellow," in Gay W. Allen, *American Prosody,* New York, 1935, pp. 154–192; M. J. Griswold, "American Quaker History in the Works of Whittier, Hawthorne, and Longfellow," *Americana,* XXXIV (1940), 220–263; Manning Hawthorne, "The Friendship Between Hawthorne and Longfellow," *English Leaflet,* XXXIX (1940), 25–30; Clarence Gohdes, "Longfellow and His Authorized British Publishers," *PMLA,* LV (1940), 1165–1179; William Charvat, "Longfellow's Income from His Writings, 1840–1852," *Papers Bibl. Soc. Amer.,* XXXVIII (1944), 9–21; Samuel Longfellow, "The Old Portland Academy: Longfellow's Fitting School," *New Eng. Quar.,* XVIII (1945), 247–251; David Hecht, "Longfellow in Russia," *ibid.,* XIX (1946), 531–534; and *idem,* "Lavrov and Longfellow," *Russian Rev.,* V (1946), 90–96.

PRIMARY SOURCES

The bulk of Longfellow material, including letters to and from him, is in the Longfellow (Craigie) House, Cambridge. It is available for restricted use.

A further important collection is in the Bowdoin College Library. The Longfellow manuscript material in the Harvard College Library includes deposits from his library. Further collections are in the Boston Public Library and the Henry E. Huntington Library. Some material will be found in the Thomas B. Aldrich Birthplace, Portsmouth, N.H.

Among printed sources, primary material will be found in D. Gilbert Dexter, *Life and Works of Henry W. Longfellow,* Cambridge, 1882; W. Sloane Kennedy, *Henry W. Longfellow,* Boston, 1882; Francis H. Underwood, *Henry Wadsworth Longfellow: A Biographical Sketch,* Boston, 1882; Thomas W. Higginson, *Henry Wadsworth Longfellow,* Boston, 1902; Richard H. Stoddard, *Recollections Personal and Literary,* New York, 1903; Frank P. Stearns, *Cambridge Sketches,* Philadelphia, 1905; Charles E. Norton, *Henry Wadsworth Longfellow: A Sketch of His Life,* Boston, 1907; William Winter, *Old Friends . . . ,* New York, 1909; Ernest W. Longfellow (the poet's son), *Random Memories,* Boston, 1922; Mrs. H. D. Skinner, *An Echo from Parnassus,* New York, 1928.

BIBLIOGRAPHY

There is no definitive bibliography for Longfellow. The following compilations may be consulted: L. S. Livingston, *A Bibliography of the First Editions in Book Form of the Writings of Henry Wadsworth Longfellow,* New York, 1908; *The Cambridge History of American Literature,* New York, 1917, II, 425–436; *The Stephen H. Wakeman Collection of Books of Nineteenth Century American Writers . . . ,* New York, 1924; Ralph Thompson, "Additions to Longfellow Bibliography . . . ," *Amer. Lit.,* III (1931), 303–308; Clarence Gohdes, "A Check-List of Volumes by Longfellow Published in the British Isles During the Nineteenth Century," *Bul. Bibl.,* XVII (1940–1941), 46, 67–69, 93–96.

Annotated checklists are in Odell Shepard, ed., *Henry Wadsworth Longfellow: Representative Selections . . . ,* New York, 1934, pp. lvii–lxii; and Harry H. Clark, ed., *Major American Poets,* New York, 1936, pp. 847–850. See also Harry Hartwick, in Walter F. Taylor, *A History of American Letters,* New York, 1936, pp. 523–526.

## AMY LOWELL
### *1874–1925*

SEPARATE WORKS

*Dream Drops; or, Stories from Fairy Land,* 1887; *A Dome of Many-Coloured Glass,* 1912; *Sword Blades and Poppy Seed,* 1914; *Six French Poets,*

1915; *Men, Women and Ghosts,* 1916; *Tendencies in Modern American Poetry,* 1917; *Can Grande's Castle,* 1918; *Pictures of the Floating World,* 1919; *Legends,* 1921; *A Critical Fable,* 1922; *What's O'Clock,* 1925; *John Keats,* 1925; *East Wind,* 1926; *Ballads for Sale,* 1927; *The Madonna of Carthagena,* 1927; *Fool o' the Moon,* 1927; *Poetry and Poets: Essays,* 1930.

*Selected Poems of Amy Lowell* were edited by John Livingston Lowes, Boston, 1928.

Harley F. MacNair edited *Florence Ayscough and Amy Lowell: Correspondence of a Friendship,* Chicago, 1945—letters for the most part written during 1917-1925.

BIOGRAPHY AND CRITICISM

The most comprehensive narrative and critical study is S. Foster Damon, *Amy Lowell: A Chronicle, with Extracts from Her Correspondence,* Boston, 1935. The best brief account is that of John Livingston Lowes in *Dict. Amer. Biog.* (1933).

Appreciations by other poets are John Gould Fletcher, "Miss Lowell's Discovery: Polyphonic Prose," *Poetry,* VI (1915), 32-36; "The Technique of Polyphonic Prose: Amy Lowell" and "Amy Lowell as Critic," in Conrad Aiken, *Scepticisms . . . ,* New York, 1919, pp. 115-125, 251-257; Archibald MacLeish, "Amy Lowell and the Art of Poetry," *No. Amer. Rev.,* CCXXI (1925), 508-521; and "Amy Lowell," in Harriet Monroe, *Poets and Their Art,* New York, 1926, pp. 78-85.

Other estimates of her work before her death in 1925 are Winifred Bryher, *Amy Lowell: A Critical Appreciation,* London, 1918, 47 pp.; Helen B. Kizer, "Amy Lowell: A Personality," *No. Amer. Rev.,* CCVII (1918), 736-747; William M. Patterson, "New Verse and New Prose," *ibid.,* 257-267; Josephine Hammond, "Amy Lowell and the Pretorian Cohorts," *Personalist,* I (1920), 14-36; James W. Tupper, "The Poetry of Amy Lowell," *Sewanee Rev.,* XXVIII (1920), 37-53; Richard Hunt and Royall H. Snow, *Amy Lowell: Sketches Biographical and Critical,* New York, 1921, 28 pp.; "Amy Lowell," in Louis Untermeyer, *American Poetry Since 1900,* New York, 1923, pp. 135-156; "Amy Lowell," in Percy H. Boynton, *Some Contemporary Americans,* Chicago, 1924, pp. 72-88; and John Farrar, *The Literary Spotlight,* New York, 1924, pp. 51-64.

Later studies are John Livingston Lowes, "The Poetry of Amy Lowell," *Sat. Rev. Lit.,* II (Oct. 3, 1925), 169-170, 174-175; Charles Cestre, "L'Œuvre Poétique d'Amy Lowell," *Revue Anglo-Amér.,* II (1925), 481-500; Clement Wood, *Amy Lowell,* New York, 1926, 185 pp.; Florence Ayscough, "Amy Lowell and the Far East," *Bookman,* LXIII (1926), 11-18; Charles Cestre, "Amy Lowell, Robert Frost, and Edwin Arlington Robinson," *Johns Hopkins*

*Alumni Mag.,* XIV (1926), 363–388; "Amy Lowell," in Elizabeth S. Sergeant, *Fire Under the Andes,* New York, 1927, pp. 11–32; William L. Schwartz, "A Study of Amy Lowell's Far Eastern Verse," *Modern Language Notes,* XLIII (1928), 145–152; Pierre Isoré, "L'Originalité d'Amy Lowell," *Revue Anglo-Amér.,* VI (1929), 317–326; Alfred Kreymborg, *Our Singing Strength,* New York, 1929, pp. 353–360; "Amy Lowell," in René Taupin, *L'Influence du Symbolisme Français sur la Poésie Américaine,* Paris, 1929, pp. 166–192; Herman C. Hoskier, *"The Bronze Horses": A Comment on the Prose-Poem of Amy Lowell,* Portland, Me., 1930, 17 pp.; "Amy Lowell: The Success," in Glenn Hughes, *Imagism and the Imagists,* Stanford, Calif., 1931, pp. 197–223; Winfield T. Scott, "Amy Lowell After Ten Years," *New Eng. Quar.,* VIII (1935), 320–330; and "Storm Center in Brookline," in Louis Untermeyer, *From Another World,* New York, 1939, pp. 99–125. See also Ferris Greenslet, *The Lowells and Their Seven Worlds,* Boston, 1946.

PRIMARY SOURCES

The bulk of Amy Lowell's manuscripts, together with her complete library, is in the Harvard College Library. Other material is in the Princeton University Library and in the libraries of the University of Virginia and the University of Buffalo.

BIBLIOGRAPHY

An extensive checklist is Frances Kemp, "Bibliography of Amy Lowell," *Bul. Bibl.,* XV (1933–1934), 8–9, 25–26, 50–53. There are further listings in Fred B. Millett, *Contemporary American Authors,* New York, 1940, pp. 452–457. "A List of Publications" is in Damon's *Amy Lowell* (1935), pp. 729–742. Most recent is the listing by Frances Cheney, in Allen Tate, *Sixty American Poets, 1896–1944,* Washington, 1945.

## JAMES RUSSELL LOWELL
### *1819–1891*

SEPARATE WORKS

*Class Poem,* 1838 (pamphlet); *A Year's Life, and Other Poems,* 1841; *Poems,* 1844; *Conversations on Some of the Old Poets,* 1845; *Poems: Second Series,* 1848; *A Fable for Critics,* 1848; *The Biglow Papers,* first series, 1848; *The Vision of Sir Launfal,* 1848; *Fireside Travels,* 1864; *Ode Recited at the Commemoration of the Living and Dead Soldiers of Harvard University,* 1865; *The Biglow Papers,* second series, 1867; *Under the Willows, and Other Poems,* 1869; *The Cathedral,* 1870; *Among My Books,* 1870; *My Study*

*Windows,* 1871; *Among My Books: Second Series,* 1876; *Three Memorial Poems,* 1877; *Democracy and Other Addresses,* 1887; *The English Poets; Lessing, Rousseau,* 1888; *Political Essays,* 1888; *Heartsease and Rue,* 1888; *Books and Libraries, and Other Papers,* 1889.

Lowell served as co-editor, with Robert Carter, of the *Pioneer: A Literary and Critical Magazine* (1843), which was discontinued after three months. His antislavery editorials appeared in the *Pennsylvania Freeman* and the *National Anti-Slavery Standard* during the forties and early fifties. He was the first editor of the *Atlantic Monthly* (1857–1861), and joint editor with Charles Eliot Norton of the *North American Review* from 1864 to 1868. His association with the latter magazine continued until 1872.

COLLECTED WORKS

The most comprehensive collection is the Elmwood Edition of *The Complete Writings of James Russell Lowell,* Boston, 1904, 16 vols., edited by Charles Eliot Norton. It includes the *Letters* (3 vols.), first published in 2 vols. by Norton in 1894, and Scudder's *Life* (2 vols.). The Riverside Edition of *The Writings of James Russell Lowell,* Boston, 1890, 10 vols., is the first important edition of Lowell's collected works. The material was revised by the author. Volumes XI and XII were added in 1891 and 1892—*Latest Literary Essays and Addresses of James Russell Lowell* and *The Old English Dramatists,* edited by Norton. The latter is a gathering of six Lowell Institute lectures first published in *Harper's Magazine,* 1892.

A useful collection of the poems is the Cambridge Edition, edited by Horace E. Scudder: *The Complete Poetical Works of James Russell Lowell,* Boston, 1897, 1917—valuable for headnotes and chronology (pp. 481–484). Other early collections are *The Early Poems of James Russell Lowell,* New York, 1892—with a biographical sketch by Nathan Haskell Dole; and *Early Prose Writings of James Russell Lowell,* London, 1902, edited by E. E. Hale, with an introduction by Walter Littlefield.

Three posthumously published titles edited by Charles Eliot Norton, in addition to the two mentioned above, are *Letters of James Russell Lowell,* New York, 1894, 2 vols., enlarged, Boston, 1904, 3 vols.—the latter collection supersedes the earlier; *Last Poems of James Russell Lowell,* Boston, 1895—two here published for the first time; and *The Power of Sound: A Rhymed Lecture,* New York, 1896.

Other items are *American Ideas for English Readers,* Boston, 1892—eleven addresses delivered in England, 1880–1888; *Lectures on English Poets,* Cleveland, 1897—Lowell Institute lectures delivered in 1855, reprinted from the Boston *Daily Advertiser; Impressions of Spain,* Boston, 1899—compiled from the Diplomatic Correspondence by Joseph B. Gilder, with an introduction by A. A. Adee; *The Anti-Slavery Papers of James Russell Lowell*, Boston, 1902, 2 vols.—some fifty articles contributed to newspapers during 1844-1850, not included in the collected works; *The Round Table*, Boston, 1913—nine uncollected reviews; *The Function of the Poet, and Other Essays*, Boston, 1920—early essays and reviews edited by Albert Mordell; and *New Letters of James Russell Lowell*, New York, 1932—important additions to the Lowell canon, edited by Mark A. DeWolfe Howe. Carl J. Weber, "Lowell: Poet and Friendly Critic," *Colby Lib. Quar.*, I (1943), 19–23, is a publication from manuscript of letters to a niece.

Much of Lowell's prose and verse is still uncollected. The pieces may be located in periodicals and newspapers through the bibliography by Cooke. See also Killis Campbell, "Lowell's Uncollected Poems," *PMLA*, XXXVIII (1923), 933–937; and *idem*, "Three Notes on Lowell," *Modern Language Notes*, XXXVIII (1923), 121–122.

## REPRINTS

Selections from the prose and poetry of Lowell have appeared in many anthologies, or have been published in separate editions for limited or popular distribution, or for use as school texts at all levels. Harry H. Clark and Norman Foerster have recently edited a serviceable collection: *James Russell Lowell: Representative Selections, with Introduction, Bibliography, and Notes*, New York, 1947. Other reprints include *Conversations on Some of the Old Poets*, New York, 1901, with an introduction by Fred L. Pattee; *The Vision of Sir Launfal and Other Poems*, New York, 1929, edited by Herbert Bates and revised by Harold Y. Moffett (New Pocket Classics); *Fireside Travels*, New York, 1906, with an introduction by William P. Trent, and London, 1915, with an introduction by E. V. Lucas; *Among My Books*, New York, 1912 (Everyman's Lib.); *Democracy and Other Addresses*, Boston, 1931; *Selected Literary Essays from James Russell Lowell*, Boston, 1914 (Riverside Literature Ser.), with an introduction by Will D. Howe and Norman Foerster. There are also Ernest G. Hoffsten, ed., *The Earlier Essays of James Russell Lowell*, New York, 1916 (Pocket Classics); and Tucker Brooke, ed., *Two Essays of James Russell Lowell: On a Certain Condescension in Foreigners, and Democracy*, New York, 1927.

## BIOGRAPHY AND CRITICISM

Still the most authentic and complete biography is that of Horace E. Scudder, *James Russell Lowell: A Biography*, Cambridge, 1901, 2 vols. Ferris Greenslet, *James Russell Lowell: His Life and Work*, Boston, 1905 (American Men of Letters), is brief but reliable, as is the estimate by Mark A. De Wolfe Howe in *Dict. Amer. Biog.* (1933). The most recent appraisal is Richmond C. Beatty, *James Russell Lowell*, Nashville, Tenn., 1942.

Estimates of Lowell as a man of letters, significant to the extent that the authors are spokesmen of their times, are Poe's comments, reprinted in John B. Moore, ed., *Selections from Poe's Literary Criticism*, New York, 1926, pp. 82–92; "Lowell," in Bayard Taylor, *Critical Essays and Literary Notes*, New York, 1880, pp. 298–301; H. D. Traill, "Mr. J. R. Lowell," *Fortnightly Rev.*, n.s. XXXVIII (1885), 79–89; "James Russell Lowell," in Edmund C. Stedman, *Poets of America*, Boston, 1885, pp. 304–348; Bret Harte, "A Few Words About Mr. Lowell," *New Rev.*, V (1891), 193–201; "James Russell Lowell," in Henry James, *Essays in London and Elsewhere*, New York, 1893, pp. 44–80; C. E. Norton, "James Russell Lowell," *Harper's Mag.*, LXXXVI (1893), 846–857; "Studies of Lowell," in William D. Howells, *Literary Friends and Acquaintance*, New York, 1900, pp. 212–250; "James Russell Lowell," in George E. Woodberry, *Makers of Literature*, New York, 1900, pp. 324–349; B. O. Flower, "James Russell Lowell as a Poet of Freedom and Human Rights," *Arena*, XLI (1909), 309–317; "Lowell," in William C. Brownell, *American Prose Masters*, New York, 1909, pp. 271–335—an excellent critique; "Lowell," in John Macy, *The Spirit of American Literature*, New York, 1913, pp. 189–209; Ashley H. Thorndike, "Lowell," in *Camb. Hist. Amer. Lit.*, II (1918), 245–257; "James Russell Lowell," in Bliss Perry, *The Praise of Folly and Other Papers*, Boston, 1923, pp. 130–150; "Lowell," in Norman Foerster, *Nature in American Literature*, New York, 1923, pp. 143–175; "Lowell, Cambridge Brahmin," in Vernon L. Parrington, *Main Currents in American Thought*, II (1927), pp. 460–472; Robert M. Lovett, "Lowell," in John Macy, ed., *American Writers on American Literature*, New York, 1931, pp. 177–189; and "Lowell's Essays," in Van Wyck Brooks, *The Flowering of New England*, New York, 1936, pp. 505–525. Useful excerpts from contemporary criticism appear in C. W. Moulton, ed., *Library of Literary Criticism*, Buffalo, 1905, VIII, 17–42.

Special studies of Lowell as poet and critic are W. C. Wilkinson, *A Free Lance in the Field of Life and Letters*, New York, 1874, pp. 50–183; Ray Palmer, "James Russell Lowell and Modern Literary Criticism," *International Rev.*, IV (1877), 264–281—a contemporary review of both series of Lowell's *Among My Books*; "Lowell as a Critic," in William Watson, *Excursions in Criticism*, London, 1893, pp. 89–96; Ferris Lockwood, "Mr. Lowell on Art-Principles," *Scribner's Mag.*, XV (1894), 186–189; Alexis F. Lange, "James Russell Lowell as a Critic," *Univ. Calif. Chron.*, VIII (1906), 352–364; William H. Hudson, *Lowell and His Poetry*, London, 1914; Joseph J. Reilly, *James Russell Lowell as a Critic*, New York, 1915; John M. Robertson, "Lowell as Critic," *No. Amer. Rev.*, CCIX (1919), 246–262; Harry H. Clark, "Lowell's Criticism of Romantic Literature," *PMLA*, XLI (1926), 209–228; "Lowell," in Norman Foerster, *American Criticism*, Boston, 1928, pp. 111–156—one of the major estimates; Austin Warren, "Lowell on Thoreau," *Studies in Philol.*,

XXVII (1930), 442–461; "Lowell," in George E. De Mille, *Literary Criticism in America,* New York, 1931, pp. 49–85; Dorothy L. Werner, *The Idea of Union in American Verse, 1776–1876,* Philadelphia, 1932—dealing with Lowell's political verse (*passim,* see index); and Richard C. Pettigrew, "Lowell's Criticism of Milton," *Amer. Lit.,* III (1932), 457–464. "Lowell's Mental Growth," by Harry H. Clark, and "Lowell as Critic," by Norman Foerster, supply the introduction (pp. xi–cxxxix) for Clark and Foerster's *James Russell Lowell: Representative Selections . . . ,* New York, 1947.

Among studies of individual works, several deal with *The Biglow Papers:* Charles H. Grandgent, "From Franklin to Lowell: A Century of New England Pronunciation," *PMLA,* XIV (1899), 207–239; Edward M. Chapman, *"The Biglow Papers* Fifty Years After," *Yale Rev.,* n.s. VI (1916), 120–134; F. D. Smith, "Mr. Wilbur's Posthumous Macaronics," *Quar. Jour. Univ. No. Dakota,* X (1920), 436–443; "Permanent Values in *The Biglow Papers,"* in L. H. Chrisman, *John Ruskin, Preacher, and Other Essays,* New York, 1921, pp. 163–176; "The Biglow Papers," in Jennette R. Tandy, *Crackerbox Philosophers in American Humor and Satire,* New York, 1925, pp. 43–64; Marie Killheffer, "A Comparison of the Dialect of *The Biglow Papers* with the Dialect of Four Yankee Plays," *Amer. Speech,* III (1928), 222–236; Russel B. Nye, "Lowell and American Speech," *Philological Quar.,* XVIII (1939), 249–256; and "A Brahmin Dons Homespun," in Walter Blair, *Horse Sense in American Humor,* Chicago, 1942, pp. 77–101. An extended European study is J. A. Heil, *Die Volkssprache im Nordosten der Vereinigten Staaten von Amerika, dargestellt auf Grund der Biglow Papers von James Russell Lowell,* in *Giessener Beiträge zur Erforschung der Sprache und Kultur Englands und Nordamerikas,* Breslau, 1927, III, No. 2, 205–311—see also the review by A. G. Kennedy, *Amer. Speech,* III (1928), 426–427.

Other studies of individual works include Claude M. Fuess, "Some Forgotten Political Essays by Lowell," *Proc. Mass. Hist. Soc.,* LXII (1930), 3–12; E. J. Nichols, "Identification of Characters in Lowell's *A Fable for Critics,"* *Amer. Lit.,* IV (1932), 191–194; William White, "Two Versions of Lowell's 'Function of the Poet,'" *Philological Quar.,* XX (1941), 587–596; Louise Pound, "Lowell's 'Breton Legend,'" *Amer. Lit.,* XII (1940), 348–350; H. V. Bail, "James Russell Lowell's [Commemoration] Ode," *Papers Bibl. Soc. Amer.,* XXXVII (1943), 169–202; Arthur W. M. Voss, "The Evolution of Lowell's 'The Courtin,'" *Amer. Lit.,* XV (1943), 42–50; *idem,* "Lowell's 'A Legend of Brittany,'" *Modern Language Notes,* LXI (1946), 343–345; and Richard B. Davis, "A Variant of Lowell's 'I Go to the Ridge in the Forest,'" *ibid.,* pp. 392–395.

Lowell's religious thought is well analyzed in L. M. Shea, *Lowell's Religious Outlook,* Washington, 1926. It is further studied in A. H. Strong,

*American Poets and Their Theology,* Philadelphia, 1916, pp. 265–317; E. J. Bailey, *Religious Thought in the Greater American Poets,* Boston, 1922, pp. 158–182; and Gilbert P. Voigt, *The Religious and Ethical Element in the Major American Poets (Bul. Univ. So. Carolina),* 1925, pp. 100–123.

Records of Lowell as a teacher are presented by H. E. Scudder, "Mr. Lowell as a Teacher," *Scribner's Mag.,* X (1891), 645–649; "Mr. Lowell as a Teacher," in Barrett Wendell, *Stelligeri and Other Essays Concerning America,* New York, 1893, pp. 205–217; Charles W. Eliot, "James Russell Lowell as a Professor," *Harvard Grad. Mag.,* XXVII (1919), 492–497; and William R. Thayer, "James Russell Lowell as a Teacher: Recollections of His Last Pupil," *Scribner's Mag.,* LXVIII (1920), 473–480.

Other special studies are E. D. Mead, "Lowell's *Pioneer,*" *New Eng. Mag.,* n.s. V (1891), 235–258; Edward Grubb, "The Socialism of James Russell Lowell," *ibid.,* VI (1892), 676–678; Edwin Mims, "Lowell as a Citizen," *So. Atl. Quar.,* I (1902), 27–40; Edward S. Parsons, "Lowell's Conception of Poetry," *Colorado Coll. Pub., Language Ser.,* II, No. 20 (1908), 67–84; Gustav Pollak, *The International Perspective in Criticism . . . ,* New York, 1914, pp. 58–83; R. E. Roberts, "James Russell Lowell: A British Estimate," *Living Age,* CCCI (1919), 231–235; "Lowell's Addresses," in George E. Woodberry, *Literary Memoirs of the Nineteenth Century,* New York, 1921, 303–320; H. T. Henry, "Music in Lowell's Prose and Verse," *Musical Quar.,* XXIV (1924), 546–572; Harry C. Clark, "Lowell: Humanitarian, Nationalist, or Humanist?" *Studies in Philol.,* XXVII (1930), 411–441; Warren G. Jenkins, "Lowell's Criteria of Political Values," *New Eng. Quar.,* VII (1934), 115–141; Gay W. Allen, *American Prosody,* New York, 1935, pp. 244–276; George Wurfl, *Lowell's Debt to Goethe: A Study of Literary Influence,* State College, Pa., 1936; Edward G. Bernard, "New Light on Lowell as Editor," *New Eng. Quar.,* X (1937), 337–341; Lincoln R. Gibbs, "A Brahmin's Version of Democracy," *Antioch Rev.,* I (1941), 50–62; John P. Pritchard, *Return to the Fountains,* Durham, N.C., 1942, pp. 99–118—the influence of the classics; Richard D. Altick, "Was Lowell an Historical Critic?" *Amer. Lit.,* XIV (1942), 250–259; Richmond C. Beatty, "Lowell's Commonplace Books," *New Eng. Quar.,* XVIII (1945), 391–401; and William A. Jackson, "James Russell Lowell and John Locke," *ibid.,* XIX (1946), 113–114.

See also Beckles Willson, *America's Ambassadors to England, 1785–1929,* New York, 1929; and Ferris Greenslet, *The Lowells and Their Seven Worlds,* Boston, 1946—a study of several generations of the Lowell family.

PRIMARY SOURCES

A large collection of Lowell manuscripts, little used, is in the Harvard College Library. Some sixty letters are deposited in the Henry E. Huntington

Library. Lowell's diplomatic correspondence, also little used, is in the National Archives in Washington. Two other important collections are in the Morgan Library, and at Elmwood House, Cambridge.

Published source material includes Ethel Golann, "A Lowell Autobiography," *New Eng. Quar.*, VII (1934), 356–364—written for the Harvard Class Book in 1838; J. Franklin Jameson and others, "James Russell Lowell: A Composite Character Sketch," *Review of Reviews*, IV (1891), 287–310; Edward Everett Hale, *James Russell Lowell and His Friends*, Boston, 1899; Thomas W. Higginson, *Old Cambridge*, New York, 1899, pp. 145–196; Rollo Ogden, ed., *Life and Letters of Edwin Lawrence Godkin*, New York, 1907, 2 vols.; William R. Thayer, ed., *Letters of John Holmes to James Russell Lowell and Others*, Boston, 1917. A special Lowell number of the *Critic* was issued, February 23, 1889. Some data regarding his diplomatic career will be found in *Papers Relating to the Foreign Relations of the United States, 1877–1885*, published by the Department of State.

BIBLIOGRAPHY

Invaluable to the date of its publication is George W. Cooke, *A Bibliography of James Russell Lowell*, Boston, 1906, for both primary and secondary material. It can be supplemented by Luther S. Livingston, *A Bibliography of the First Editions in Book Form of the Writings of James Russell Lowell . . .*, New York, 1914; the checklist in H. E. Scudder's biography (II, 421–427); and H. E. Joyce, "A Bibliographical Note on James Russell Lowell," *Modern Language Notes*, XXXV (1920), 249–250. There are further additions in Killis Campbell, "Bibliographical Notes on Lowell," *Univ. Texas Studies in English*, IV (1924), 115–119. Selective and annotated is the listing in Harry H. Clark and Norman Foerster, eds., *James Russell Lowell: Representative Selections . . .*, New York, 1947, pp. cxliii–clxvi. See also Harry Hartwick, in Walter F. Taylor, *A History of American Letters*, New York, 1936, pp. 526–530.


ARCHIBALD MacLEISH
*b. 1892*

SEPARATE WORKS

*Songs for a Summer's Day*, 1915; *Tower of Ivory*, 1917; *The Happy Marriage and Other Poems*, 1924; *The Pot of Earth*, 1925; *Nobodaddy*, 1926; *Streets in the Moon*, 1926; *The Hamlet of A. MacLeish*, 1928; *Einstein*, 1929; *New Found Land*, 1930; *Conquistador*, 1932; *Frescoes for Mr. Rockefeller's City*, 1933; *Poems*, 1933; *Panic*, 1935; *Public Speech*, 1936; *The Fall of the*

*City*, 1937; *Air Raid*, 1938; *Land of the Free*, 1938; *America Was Promises*, 1939; *The Irresponsibles: A Declaration*, 1940; *The American Cause*, 1941.

COLLECTED WORKS

Four collected items are *Poems, 1924-1933*, Boston, 1933; *A Time to Speak: The Selected Prose of Archibald MacLeish*, Boston, 1941; *A Time to Act: Selected Addresses*, Boston, 1943; and *The American Story: Ten Broadcasts*, New York, 1944.

BIOGRAPHY AND CRITICISM

There is little significant criticism of MacLeish's writing until 1930. Three estimates by Morton D. Zabel are "The Compromise of A. MacLeish," *Poetry*, XXXVI (1930), 270-275; "Cinema of Hamlet," *ibid.*, XLIV (1934), 150-159; and "The Poet on Capitol Hill," *Partisan Rev.*, VIII (1941), 2-19, 128-145. Other early studies are Harriet Monroe, "Archibald MacLeish," *Poetry*, XXXVIII (1931), 150-155; George Dangerfield, "Archibald Mac-Leish: An Appreciation," *Bookman*, LXXII (1931), 493-496; Dudley Fitts, "'To Karthage Then I Came,'" *Hound and Horn*, IV (1931), 637-641; Lincoln Kirstein, "Arms and Men," *ibid.*, V (1932), 484-492; Morris U. Schappes, "The Direction of A. MacLeish," *Symposium*, III (1932), 476-494; Frances Gillmor, "The Curve of a Continent," *New Mexico Quar.*, IV (1934), 114-122; Rolfe Humphries, "Archibald MacLeish," *Modern Mo.*, VIII (1934), 264-270, 274; Howard Blake, "Thoughts on Modern Poetry," *Sewanee Rev.*, XLIII (1935), 187-196; Llewellyn Jones, "Archibald MacLeish: A Modern Metaphysical," *English Jour.*, XXIV (1935), 441-451; Babette Deutsch, *This Modern Poetry*, New York, 1935, pp. 229-237; Horace Gregory, "Poets in the Theatre," *Poetry*, XLVIII (1936), 221-228; Wellington E. Aiken, "Poetic Form in *Conquistador*," *Modern Language Notes*, LI (1936), 107-109; Mason Wade, "The Anabasis of A. MacLeish," *No. Amer. Rev.*, CCXLIII (1937), 330-343; and Merrill Denison, "Radio and the Writer," *Theatre Arts Mo.*, XXII (1938), 365-370.

Among more recent estimates are Arthur Mizener, "The Poetry of Archibald MacLeish," *Sewanee Rev.*, XLIV (1938), 501-519—an analysis of MacLeish's whole poetic career; Dorothy Van Ghent, "The Poetry of Archibald MacLeish," *Science and Society*, II (1938), 500-511; Harold Rosenberg, "The God in the Car," *Poetry*, LII (1938), 334-342; Dayton Kohler, "MacLeish and the Modern Temper," *So. Atl. Quar.*, XXXVIII (1939), 416-426; Elizabeth Donnald, "An Ideal Confidence Reflected by Some Contemporary American Poets," *Furman Bul.*, XXII (1940), No. 7, 3-17; and Edwin Honig, "History, Document, and Archibald MacLeish," *Sewanee Rev.*, XLVIII (1940), 385-396.

The most recent studies are Eleanor M. Sickels, "Archibald MacLeish and American Democracy," *Amer. Lit.,* XV (1943), 223–227; and Hyatt H. Waggoner, "Archibald MacLeish and the Aspect of Eternity," *College Eng.,* IV (1943), 402–412—a statement of his philosophic position.

PRIMARY SOURCES

There are collections of MacLeish manuscripts in the Princeton University Library, the Library of Congress, and the Harvard College Library.

BIBLIOGRAPHY

Full bibliographical details of first editions to 1938, including data about books and periodicals with contributions by MacLeish, are in Arthur Mizener, *Catalogue of the First Editions of Archibald MacLeish* . . . , New Haven, 1938, 30 pp. An annotated list for the general reader through 1939 is Gerrish Thurber, "MacLeish Published Books," *Library Jour.,* LXIV (1939), 864, 866. Most recent is the extensive checklist by Frances Cheney, in Allen Tate, *Sixty American Poets, 1896–1944,* Washington, 1945, pp. 89–97.

## JAMES MADISON
### 1751–1836

COLLECTED WORKS

The standard collection of Madison papers is Gaillard Hunt, ed., *The Writings of James Madison, Comprising His Public Papers and His Private Correspondence* . . . , New York, 1900–1910, 9 vols. For the most part it supersedes earlier editions and includes a great part of his private correspondence. Volumes III and IV include the "Journal of the Constitutional Convention." The collection also gathers his speeches in the Virginia Convention, 1788; his speeches in Congress; and many papers written while he was Secretary of State and President. *Letters and Other Writings of James Madison,* Philadelphia, 1865, 4 vols., known as the "Congress Edition," includes some letters not in Hunt. Letters not found elsewhere are gathered in Edmund C. Burnett, ed., *Letters of Members of the Continental Congress,* Washington, 1921–1936, 8 vols.—from Aug., 1774, to July, 1789; Henry D. Gilpin, ed., *The Papers of James Madison, Purchased by Order of Congress* . . . , Washington, 1840, 3 vols.; and Henry Adams, ed., *The Writings of Albert Gallatin,* Philadelphia, 1879, 3 vols. *Calendar of the Correspondence of James Madison,* Washington, 1894, supplies further details.

More recent collected material is Gaillard Hunt, ed., *The Journal of the Debates in the Convention Which Framed the Constitution of the United*

*States, May–September, 1787, as Recorded by James Madison,* New York, 1908, 2 vols.; James B. Scott, ed., *James Madison's Notes of Debate in the Federal Convention of 1787* . . . , New York, 1918—with bibl. notes, pp. xvii–xviii; Arthur T. Prescott, comp., *Drafting the Federal Constitution: A Rearrangement of Madison's Notes* . . . , University, La., 1941. For data on *The Federalist,* see the Hamilton bibliography, *ante,* p. 537. The first printing of "James Madison's Autobiography," ed. by Douglass Adair, is in *William and Mary Quar.,* II (1945), 191–209.

BIOGRAPHY AND CRITICISM

The most recent studies of Madison are Irving Brant, *James Madison, the Virginia Revolutionist,* Indianapolis, 1941; Edward M. Burns, *James Madison: Philosopher of the Constitution,* New Brunswick, N.J., 1938; and Abbot E. Smith, *James Madison: Builder* . . . , New York, 1937.

Still standard are Gaillard Hunt, *The Life of James Madison,* New York, 1902—with little attempt at interpretation; and William C. Rives, *History of the Life and Times of James Madison,* Boston, 1859–1868, 3 vols. Rives's *Life,* never completed, ends in 1797, but it is reliably written from personal acquaintance. Studies of Madison as a man of letters are Wilbur E. Moore, "James Madison, the Speaker," *Quar. Jour. Speech,* XXXI (1945), 155–162—describing his platform technique; and Louis C. Schaedler, "James Madison, Literary Craftsman," *William and Mary Quar.,* III (1946), 515–533. The sketch in *Dict. Amer. Biog.* (1933) was written by Julius W. Pratt. A recent estimate is Douglass Adair, "James Madison," in Willard Thorp, ed., *The Lives of Eighteen from Princeton,* Princeton, 1946, pp. 137–157—a summary estimate.

Henry Adams, *History of the United States of America During the Administration of James Madison,* New York, 1890–1891, 9 vols., is indispensable for the years of Madison's service as Secretary of State and President; it was reprinted with an introduction by Henry S. Commager, New York, 1930. Other estimates of Madison as statesman are Charles E. Hill, "James Madison," in Samuel F. Bemis, ed., *The American Secretaries of State and Their Diplomacy,* Vol. III, New York, 1927; Julius W. Pratt, *Expansionists of 1812,* New York, 1925. Further studies are "James Madison," in Henry C. Lodge, *Historical and Political Essays,* Boston, 1892; Clarence W. Bowen, ed., *The History of the Centennial Celebration of the Inauguration of George Washington* . . . , New York, 1892; and John L. McLeish, *James Madison at Princeton,* New York, 1895. Other general studies of importance which cover the early years of the republic, during which Madison's statesmanship is significant, are itemized in the bibliographies herein of Washington, Adams, Jefferson, and Hamilton.

PRIMARY SOURCES

The most extensive collection of manuscripts is that owned by the Library of Congress. It includes the bulk of Madison's correspondence, largely covered by printed and manuscript calendars; the famous notes; miscellaneous manuscripts; and some printed matter. There are files of official papers in the National Archives. Some manuscripts are in the New York Public Library, the Historical Society of Pennsylvania and the Princeton University Library. A few are scattered elsewhere. Manuscript data on Madison as an undergraduate have been compiled by V. Lansing Collins, "Princeton University Alumni Records," in the office of the Secretary of Princeton University.

Letters to Madison are in Joseph Jones, *Letters of Joseph Jones, of Virginia, 1777–1787*, Washington, 1889. *Memoirs and Letters of Dolly Madison* were compiled by her grandniece, Lucia B. Cutts, Boston, 1887.

BIBLIOGRAPHY

The fullest bibliographical listing is in Irving Brant, *James Madison* (1941), pp. 401–450. Also useful for primary and secondary sources is the listing in Edward M. Burns, *James Madison* (1938), pp. 201–206.

# EDGAR LEE MASTERS
### b. 1869

SEPARATE WORKS

*A Book of Verses*, 1898; *Maximilian: A Play*, 1902; *The New Star Chamber and Other Essays*, 1904; *The Blood of the Prophets*, 1905; *Althea: A Play*, 1907; *The Trifler: A Play*, 1908; *The Leaves of the Tree: A Play*, 1909; *Songs and Sonnets*, 1910; *Eileen: A Play*, 1910; *The Locket: A Play*, 1910; *The Bread of Idleness: A Play*, 1911; *Spoon River Anthology*, 1915; *Songs and Satires*, 1916; *The Great Valley*, 1916; *Toward the Gulf*, 1918; *Starved Rock*, 1919; *Mitch Miller*, 1920; *Domesday Book*, 1920; *The Open Sea*, 1921; *Children of the Market Place*, 1922; *Skeeters Kirby*, 1923; *The Nuptial Flight*, 1923; *Mirage*, 1924; *The New Spoon River*, 1924; *Selected Poems*, 1925; *Lee: A Dramatic Poem*, 1926; *Kit O'Brien*, 1927; *Levy Mayer and the New Industrial Era*, 1927; *Jack Kelso: A Dramatic Poem*, 1928; *The Fate of the Jury: An Epilogue to Domesday Book*, 1929; *Lichee Nuts*, 1930; *Gettysburg, Manila, Acoma*, 1930; *Lincoln, the Man*, 1931; *Godbey: A Dramatic Poem*, 1931; *The Serpent in the Wilderness*, 1933; *The Tale of Chicago*, 1933; *Dramatic Duologues: Four Short Plays . . .* , 1934; *Richmond: A Dramatic Poem*, 1934; *Invisible Landscapes*, 1935; *Vachel Lindsay:*

*A Poet in America,* 1935; *Poems of People,* 1936; *Across Spoon River,* 1936; *The Golden Fleece of California,* 1936; *Whitman,* 1937; *The Tide of Time,* 1937; *The New World,* 1937; *Mark Twain, A Portrait,* 1938; *More People,* 1939; *Illinois Poems,* 1941; *Along the Illinois,* 1942; *The Sangamon,* 1942.

COLLECTED WORKS

Thirty-two new poems were added to the second edition of *Spoon River Anthology* (1916). No collected edition has been issued since the publication of *Selected Poems,* New York, 1925.

BIOGRAPHY AND CRITICISM

Recognition of Masters as a poet was slow until the publication of *Spoon River Anthology* (1915). During the decade that followed, reviews and criticisms included Lawrence Gilman, "Moving Picture Poetry," *No. Amer. Rev.,* CCII (1915), 271–276; Willard H. Wright, "Mr. Masters' Spoon River Anthology: A Criticism," *Forum,* LV (1916), 109–113; "Edgar Lee Masters and Carl Sandburg," in Amy Lowell, *Tendencies in Modern American Poetry,* Boston, 1917, pp. 139–232—the earliest extended analysis by a competent poet and critic; Julius W. Pratt, "Whitman and Masters: A Contrast," *So. Atl. Quar.,* XVI (1917), 155–158; "The Two Magics: Edgar Lee Masters," in Conrad Aiken, *Scepticisms,* New York, 1919, pp. 65–75; J. C. Chandler, "The Spoon River Country," *Jour. Illinois State Hist. Soc.,* XIV (1921–1922), 252–329; "Edgar Lee Masters," in Louis Untermeyer, *American Poetry Since 1900,* New York, 1923, pp. 113–132; Harry Hansen, *Midwest Portraits,* New York, 1923, pp. 225–251; Percy H. Boynton, *Some Contemporary Americans,* Chicago, 1924, pp. 50–62; John Farrar, ed., *The Literary Spotlight,* New York, 1924, pp. 222–231; Llewellyn Jones, *First Impressions,* New York, 1925, pp. 69–84; and Clement Wood, *Poets of America,* New York, 1925, pp. 163–180.

Later estimates are "Edgar Lee Masters," in Harriet Monroe, *Poets and Their Art,* New York, 1926, pp. 46–55; "Edgar Lee Masters," in David Karsner, *Sixteen Authors to One,* New York, 1928, pp. 125–144; Alfred Kreymborg, *Our Singing Strength,* New York, 1929, pp. 379–385; John C. Powys, "Edgar Lee Masters," *Bookman,* LXIX (1929), 650–656; R. Altrocchi, "Edgar Lee Masters and Joinville," *Modern Language Notes,* XLV (1930), 360–362; Herbert E. Childs, "Agrarianism and Sex: Edgar Lee Masters and the Modern Spirit," *Sewanee Rev.,* XLI (1933), 331–343; and John G. Fletcher, "Masters and Men," *Poetry,* XLIX (1937), 343–347.

PRIMARY SOURCES

Masters's autobiography, *Across Spoon River: An Autobiography,* New

York, 1936, is important as source material dealing with the Chicago writers. Masters has also published "Introduction to Chicago," *Amer. Mercury*, XXXI (1934), 49–59; and "The Genesis of Spoon River," *ibid.*, XXVIII (1933), 38–55.

Manuscripts are deposited in the library of the University of Southern California, at Los Angeles, and in the libraries of Harvard University and the University of Buffalo.

### BIBLIOGRAPHY

A checklist of Masters's writing, together with secondary material, is in Fred B. Millett, *Contemporary American Authors*, New York, 1940, pp. 476–480. See also the recent list by Frances Cheney, in Allen Tate, *Sixty American Poets, 1896–1944*, Washington, 1945, pp. 99–103.

## COTTON MATHER
### *1663–1728*

### SEPARATE WORKS

Of the 444 printed items that are known to be productions of Mather, the following works are generally accounted the most significant: *A Poem Dedicated to the Memory of . . . Urian Oakes*, 1682; *The Declaration of the Gentlemen*, 1689; *Memorable Providences, Relating to Witchcrafts and Possessions*, 1689; *The Present State of New England*, 1690; *The Way to Prosperity*, 1690; *The Wonderful Works of God Commemorated*, 1690; *Little Flocks Guarded Against Grievous Wolves*, 1691; *Some Considerations on the Bills of Credit*, 1691; *The Triumphs of the Reformed Religion in America*, 1691 (in later eds., *The Life and Death of the Renown'd Mr. John Eliot*, 1691); *Fair Weather*, 1692; *A Midnight Cry*, 1692; *Ornaments for the Daughters of Zion*, 1692; *The Return of Several Ministers*, 1692; *Winter-Meditations*, 1693; *The Wonders of the Invisible World*, 1693; *The Short History of New England*, 1694; *Durable Riches*, 1695; *Johannes in Eremo*, 1695; *Humiliations Follow'd with Deliverances*, 1697; *Pietas in Patriam: The Life of His Excellency, Sir William Phips*, 1697; *Eleutheria; or, An Idea of the Reformation in England*, 1698; *Decennium Luctuosum*, 1699; *A Family Well-Ordered*, 1699; *The Everlasting Gospel*, 1700; *Reasonable Religion*, 1700; *Christianus Per Ignem*, 1702; *Magnalia Christi Americana; or, The Ecclesiastical History of New-England*, 1702; *A Faithful Man Described and Rewarded*, 1705; *The Negro Christianized*, 1706; *A Memorial of the Present Deplorable State of New England*, 1707; *Corderius Americanus: An Essay upon the Good Education of Children*, 1708; *The Deplorable State of New-England*, 1708; *Winthropi Justa*, 1708; *Theopolis Americana*, 1710; *Boni-*

*facius*, 1710 (Essays to Do Good); *Curiosa Americana*, 1712-1724; *Duodecennium Luctuosum*, 1714; *Fair Dealing*, 1716; *Psalterium Americanum*, 1718; *Concio ad Populum*, 1719; *Mirabilia Dei*, 1719; *The Accomplished Singer*, 1721; *The Christian Philosopher*, 1721; *India Christiana*, 1721; *Some Account of . . . Inoculating . . . the Small Pox* (with Zabdiel Boylston), 1721; *Parentator*, 1724; *Une Grande Voix du Ciel à la France*, 1725; *Manuductio ad Ministerium*, 1726; *Ratio Disciplinae Fratrum Novanglorum*, 1726; *Boanerges*, 1727; "Political Fables," 1825, 1926.

### EDITED TEXTS AND REPRINTS

No collected edition of the works of Cotton Mather exists. The *Diary of Cotton Mather*, ed. by Worthington C. Ford, was first published in 1911–1912 in *Coll. Mass. Hist. Soc.*, 7th ser., vols. VII-VIII. A carefully chosen and prepared text is that of Kenneth B. Murdock, ed., *Selections from Cotton Mather*, New York, 1926.

Recent reprints of separate works are as follows: *Memorable Providences* (1689), ed. by George L. Burr, in part, in *Narratives of the Witchcraft Cases*, New York, 1914, pp. 91-143; *The Wonders of the Invisible World* (1693), *ibid.*, pp. 209-251—and many other earlier reprints; *The Life of Sir William Phips* (1697), ed. by Mark Van Doren, New York, 1929, and included in Murdock, *Selections*, pp. 149-283; *Magnalia* (1702), Hartford, 1853-1855, 2 vols., ed. by Thomas Robbins—the Introduction and Book II are included in Murdock, *Selections*, pp. 1-283; *The Deplorable State of New-England* (1708), *Coll. Mass. Hist. Soc.*, 5th ser., VI (1879), 97-131; *Bonifacius*, later generally known as *Essays To Do Good* (1710), in many reprints, the latest New York, 1838; *The Christian Philosopher* (1721), excerpts in Murdock, *Selections*, pp. 285-362; *Parentator* (1724), extracts in *Andros Tracts*, VII (1874), 121-187; *Manuductio*, issued by Facsimile Text Society, with bibliographical notes by T. J. Holmes and K. B. Murdock, New York, 1938; "Political Fables" (MS *ca.* 1692), first published in *Coll. Mass. Hist. Soc.*, 3rd ser., I (1825), 126-133, also in Murdock, *Selections*, pp. 363-371.

### BIOGRAPHY AND CRITICISM

Still the best biography of Mather is Barrett Wendell, *Cotton Mather: The Puritan Priest*, New York, 1891 (also 1926); other full-length studies are Abijah P. Marvin, *The Life and Times of Cotton Mather*, Boston, 1892, and Ralph P. and Louise Boas, *Cotton Mather*, New York, 1928. Among brief biographical studies of significance, that of Kenneth B. Murdock in *Dict. Amer. Biog.* (1933) is the most recent. John L. Sibley's account in *Biographical Sketches of Graduates of Harvard University*, vol. III, Cambridge, 1885, pp. 6-158, is also authoritative. Earlier monographs are Chandler

Robbins, *A History of the Second Church, or Old North, in Boston,* Boston, 1852, pp. 67–115; and W. B. O. Peabody, "Cotton Mather," in Jared Sparks, ed., *American Biography,* VI (1836), 161–350. Contemporary estimates are Benjamin Colman, *The Holy Walk . . . ,* Boston, 1728, and Samuel Mather, *The Life of . . . Cotton Mather,* Boston, 1729.

Studies of Mather as a man of letters are the introduction in Kenneth B. Murdock, ed., *Selections from Cotton Mather,* New York, 1926, pp. ix–lviii; *idem,* "Cotton Mather, Parson, Scholar and Man of Letters," in Albert B. Hart, ed., *Commonwealth History of Massachusetts,* II (1928), 323–354; Moses C. Tyler, *A History of American Literature During the Colonial Period,* II (1878), 73–89; "The Mather Dynasty," in Vernon L. Parrington, *Main Currents in American Thought,* New York, I (1927), 98–117; Julius H. Tuttle, "The Libraries of the Mathers," *Proc. Amer. Antiq. Soc.,* n.s., XX (1910), 269–356; and Thomas J. Holmes, *The Mather Literature,* Cleveland, 1927.

Individual works have been studied in Charles Deane, "The Light Shed upon Cotton Mather's *Magnalia* by His Diary," *Proc. Mass. Hist. Soc.,* 1st ser., VI (1863), 404–414; Chester N. Greenough, "A Letter Relating to the Publication of Cotton Mather's *Magnalia," Pub. Colonial Soc. Mass.,* XXVI (1927), 296–312; David Davies, "Coleridge's Marginalia in Mather's *Magnalia," Huntington Lib. Quar.,* II (1939), 233–240; Reginald E. Watters, "Biographical Technique in Cotton Mather's *Magnalia," William and Mary Quar.,* 3rd ser., II (1945), 154–163; Matt B. Jones, "Some Bibliographical Notes on Cotton Mather's *The Accomplished Singer," Pub. Colonial Soc. Mass.,* XXVIII (1935), 186–193; Theodore Hornberger, "Cotton Mather's Annotations on the First Chapter of Genesis," *Univ. Texas Pub. No. 3826, Studies in Eng.,* (1938), 112–122; Thomas J. Holmes, "The Surreptitious Printing of One of Cotton Mather's Manuscripts," *Bibliographical Essays: A Tribute to Wilberforce Eames,* Cambridge, 1924, pp. 149–160 *(A Brand Plucked from the Burning)*; and Howard C. Rice, "Cotton Mather Speaks to France: American Propaganda in the Age of Louis XIV," *New Eng. Quar.,* XVI (1943), 198–233 *(Une Grande Voix du Ciel).*

Aspects of Mather's lifelong interest in science are treated in Julius H. Tuttle, "William Whiston and Cotton Mather," *Pub. Colonial Soc. Mass.,* XIII (1912), 197–204; George L. Kittredge, "Some Lost Works of Cotton Mather," *Proc. Mass. Hist. Soc.,* XLV (1912), 418–479; *idem,* "Further Notes on Cotton Mather and the Royal Society," *Pub. Colonial Soc. Mass.,* XIV (1913), 281–292; *idem,* "Cotton Mather's Election into the Royal Society," *ibid.,* 81–114; *idem,* "Cotton Mather's Scientific Communications to the Royal Society," *Proc. Amer. Antiq. Soc.,* n.s. XXVI (1916), 18–57—identified and annotated; and Theodore Hornberger, "The Date, the Source, and the Significance of Cotton Mather's Interest in Science," *Amer. Lit.*, VI (1935), 413–420.

Mather's part in the witchcraft delusion is the subject of two early studies: William F. Poole, "Cotton Mather and Salem Witchcraft," *No. Amer. Rev.*, CVIII (1869), 337–397; and Samuel F. Haven, *The Mathers and the Witchcraft Delusion*, Worcester, 1874. More recent treatments are George L. Kittredge, "Notes on Witchcraft," *Proc. Amer. Antiq. Soc.*, XVIII (1907), 148–212; Thomas J. Holmes, "Cotton Mather and His Writings on Witchcraft," *Papers Bibl. Soc. Amer.*, XVIII (1925), 30–59; and Zoltán Haraszti, "Cotton Mather and the Witchcraft Trials," *More Books*, XV (1940), 179–184.

Kuno Francke has contributed three articles on Mather and his German correspondent: "Cotton Mather and August Hermann Francke," *Harvard Studies and Notes in Philol. and Lit.*, V (1896), 57–67; "Further Documents . . . ," *Americana Germanica*, I (1897), 31–66; and "The Beginning of Cotton Mather's Correspondence with August Hermann Francke," *Philological Quar.*, V (1926), 193–195.

Other studies are Henry W. Haynes, "Cotton Mather and His Slaves," *Proc. Amer. Antiq. Soc.*, n.s. VI (1889–1890), 191–195; Williston Walker, "The Services of the Mathers," *Papers Amer. Soc. Church Hist.*, V (1893), 61–85; Lee M. Friedman, "Cotton Mather and the Jews," *Pub. Amer. Jewish Hist. Soc.*, No. 26 (1918), 201–210; Philip G. Nordell, "Cotton Mather in Love," *Harper's Mag.*, CLIII (1926), 556–572; Kenneth B. Murdock, "Cotton Mather and the Rectorship of Yale College," *Pub. Colonial Soc. Mass.*, XXVI (1927), 388–401; and A. Whitney Griswold, "Three Puritans on Prosperity," *New Eng. Quar.*, VII (1934), 475–493.

PRIMARY SOURCES

The chief depositories of Mather's manuscripts are the American Antiquarian Society—with very large holdings; the Massachusetts Historical Society—also with large holdings, much of them unpublished; and the Boston Public Library. Other important holdings are in Harvard College Library; the Congregational Library, in Boston; and the Royal Society, in London. There are scattered holographs elsewhere. A calendar of Mather's manuscripts has been published by William S. Piper, Appendix B, in Thomas J. Holmes, *Cotton Mather: A Bibliography of His Works*, Cambridge, 1940 (3 vols.), III, 1301–1311.

BIBLIOGRAPHY

The Holmes bibliography, mentioned above, is definitive and monumental. Besides the listings and analyses, it is supplied with notes and appendices by Theodore Hornberger, Kenneth B. Murdock, Lloyd A. Brown, Perry Miller, and others, who have prepared critical as well as bibliographical notes on the major works, and supplied calendars of Mather's prefaces, newspaper contributions, and letters.

## INCREASE MATHER
### 1639–1723

SEPARATE WORKS

Of the 102 whole works known to be Mather's the following are generally accounted the most significant: *The Life and Death of . . . Richard Mather*, 1670; *Some Important Truths About Conversion*, 1674; *The Times of Men Are in the Hand of God*, 1675; *A Brief History of the Warr with the Indians in New-England*, 1676; *A Relation of the Troubles Which Have Hapned in New-England*, 1677; *A Call from Heaven to the Present and Succeeding Generations*, 1679; *Heaven's Alarm to the World*, 1681; *Kometographia; or, A Discourse Concerning Comets*, 1683; *An Arrow Against Profane and Promiscuous Dancing*, 1684; *The Doctrine of Divine Providence, Opened and Applyed*, 1684; *An Essay for the Recording of Illustrious Providences*, 1684; *A Brief Discourse Concerning the Unlawfulness of the Common-Prayer-Worship*, 1686; *A Testimony Against Several Prophane and Superstitious Customs*, 1687; *De Successu Evangelii apud Indos in Nova-Anglia*, 1688; *A Narrative of the Miseries of New England*, 1688; *A Brief Relation of the State of New England*, 1689; *A Brief Account Concerning Several of the Agents of New-England*, 1691; *Cases of Conscience Concerning Evil Spirits Personating Men*, 1693; *The Great Blessing of Primitive Counsellours*, 1693; *Angelographia*, 1696; *The Surest Way to the Greatest Honour*, 1699; *The Order of the Gospel*, 1700; *The Excellency of a Publick Spirit*, 1702; *Ichabod*, 1702; *A Discourse Concerning Earthquakes*, 1706; *A Disquisition Concerning Ecclesiastical Councils*, 1716; *Several Reasons Proving That Inoculating . . . the Small Pox Is a Lawful Practice*, 1721.

EDITED TEXTS AND REPRINTS

No collection of Mather's works has been made. *The Mather Papers*, to the extent they have been published, are gathered in *Collections of the Mass. Hist. Soc.*, 4th ser., VIII (1868). Extracts of *Diary by Increase Mather . . .*, ed. by Samuel A. Green, Cambridge, 1900, compass the years 1674–1687. Certain of the individual works have been reprinted during the past century: *The Life and Death of . . . Richard Mather* (1670), in *Coll. Dorchester Antiq. and Hist. Soc.*, No. 3, Boston, 1850; *A Brief History of the Warr with the Indians* (1676), ed. by Samuel G. Drake, reprinted as *History of King Philip's War,* Boston and Albany, 1862; *A Relation of the Troubles* (1677), ed. by Drake as *Early History of New England,* Albany, 1864; *An Essay for the Recording of Illustrious Providences* (1684) is reprinted with an introduction by George Offor under the title *Remarkable Providences,* London, 1856 and 1890; *A Narrative of the Miseries of New England* (1688) appears in *Andros Tracts,* II, 1–11 (Boston, 1869), and in *Old South Leaflets,* II, No. 3 (1884); *A Brief Relation of the State of New England* (1689) is published in *Coll. Mass. Hist. Soc.,* 3rd ser., I (1825), 93–101—in an earlier draft than that published in 1689; also in Peter Force, *Tracts,* IV, No. 11 (1846), and in the *Andros Tracts,* II, 149–170 (Boston, 1869); *A Brief Account Concerning Several of the Agents* (1691) has been most recently reprinted, with introduction and notes by Charles M. Andrews, in *Narratives of the Insurrection, 1675–1690,* New York, 1915; *Several Reasons Proving That Inoculating . . . the Small Pox Is a Lawful Practice* (1721) was edited with introduction by George L. Kittredge, Cleveland, 1921.

## BIOGRAPHY AND CRITICISM

The definitive biography of Mather is Kenneth B. Murdock, *Increase Mather: The Foremost American Puritan,* Cambridge, 1925, detailed, with a full list of sources. Brief authoritative sketches are those by Murdock in *Dict. Amer. Biog.* (1933), and by John L. Sibley, *Biographical Sketches of Graduates of Harvard University,* Cambridge, I (1873), 410–470. Critical estimates, significant to the extent that the authors are spokesmen of their times, are Moses C. Tyler, *A History of American Literature During the Colonial Period,* New York, 1878, II, pp. 67–72; "Increase Mather," in Williston Walker, *Ten New England Leaders,* New York, 1901, pp. 175–213; and "The Mather Dynasty," in Vernon L. Parrington, *Main Currents in American Thought . . .,* New York, I (1927), 98–117. Two contemporary sketches are those by Cotton Mather, *Parentator,* Boston, 1724, and by Samuel Mather (of Witney), *Memoirs of . . . Increase Mather,* London, 1725.

On Mather's books and reading there are Julius H. Tuttle, "The Libraries of the Mathers," *Proc. Amer. Antiq. Soc.,* n.s. XX (1910), 269–356; and Henry J. Cadbury, "Harvard College Library and the Libraries of the Mathers," *ibid.,* L (1940), 20–48—with a checklist of titles probably owned by Increase Mather.

Other special studies are John A. Walz, "Increase Mather and Dr. Faust, an American 'Faustsplitter,'" *Germanic Rev.,* XV (1940), 20–31; and C. Grant Loomis, "An Unnoted German Reference to Increase Mather," *New Eng. Quar.,* XIV (1941), 374–376. See also Harold S. Jantz, "Henning Witte and Increase Mather," *New Eng. Quar.,* XVIII (1945), 408.

In addition there is Kenneth B. Murdock, *The Portraits of Increase Mather* . . ., Cleveland, 1924.

PRIMARY SOURCES

The bulk of Mather's manuscripts is deposited in the library of the American Antiquarian Society, which holds Mather's manuscript autobiography and most of his diaries. Further important collections of manuscripts are in the library of the Massachusetts Historical Society, including the lesser part of the diaries. There is also material in the Huntington Library. Much of Mather's diaries has yet to be published.

BIBLIOGRAPHY

Thomas J. Holmes, *Increase Mather: A Bibliography of His Works*, Cleveland, 1931, 2 vols., is complete and authoritative. It is supplied with an introduction by George P. Winship, and supplementary material by Kenneth B. Murdock and George F. Dow. Here also are calendared Mather's prefaces, newspaper contributions, and published letters.

## CORNELIUS MATHEWS
### *1817–1889*

SEPARATE WORKS

*The Motley Book: A Series of Tales and Sketches*, 1838; *Behemoth: A Legend of the Mound-Builders* (a romance laid in the Mississippi Valley), 1839; *The True Aims of Life*, 1839; *The Politicians: A Comedy*, 1840; *Wakondah, The Master of Life: A Poem*, 1841; *The Career of Puffer Hopkins* (a novel dealing with New York City), 1842; *Poems on Man, in His Various Aspects under the American Republic*, 1843; *Big Abel and the Little Manhattan* (a novel dealing with New York City), 1845; *Moneypenny; or, The Heart of the World: A Romance of the Present Day*, 1850; *Chanticleer: A Thanksgiving Story of the Peabody Family*, 1850; *Witchcraft: A Tragedy*, 1852; *A Pen-and-Ink Panorama of New York City*, 1853; *False Pretences; or, Both Sides of Good Society: A Comedy*, 1856 (produced in 1855).

*Witchcraft: A Tragedy* was performed at Philadelphia in 1846 as "Witchcraft; or, the Martyrs of Salem." The other tragedy, *Jacob Leisler* (1848), has not been published. A collection was made of *The Various Writings of Cornelius Mathews*, New York, 1843.

Mathews compiled various volumes of Indian legends and tales from material supplied by Henry R. Schoolcraft. The most important collection is *The Enchanted Moccasins and Other Legends of the American Indians*, New

York, 1877, originally published in 1856 as *The Indian Fairy Book*. After 1836 Mathews contributed to the *American Monthly Magazine*, the *New York Review*, and the *Knickerbocker Magazine*. With Evert A. Duyckinck he founded and edited *Arcturus* (1840). He was a contributing editor of the New York *Dramatic Mirror* from 1882 until his death.

## BIOGRAPHY AND CRITICISM

No full-length study of Mathews has been published. The best brief biographical sketch is that contributed by Theodore F. Jones to the *Dict. Amer. Biog.* (1933). Some discussion of Mathews as dramatist is in Arthur H. Quinn, *A History of the American Drama from the Beginning to the Civil War*, rev. ed., New York, 1943, pp. 276–277, 285, 322.

# HERMAN MELVILLE
## *1819–1891*

## SEPARATE WORKS

*Typee*, 1846; *Omoo*, 1847; *Mardi*, 1849; *Redburn*, 1849; *White-Jacket*, 1850; *Moby-Dick*, 1851; *Pierre*, 1852; *Israel Potter*, 1855; *The Piazza Tales*, 1856; *The Confidence-Man*, 1857; *Battle-Pieces*, 1866; *Clarel*, 1876; *John Marr and Other Sailors*, 1888; *Timoleon*, 1891; *Billy Budd and Other Prose Pieces*, 1924; *Poems*, 1924; *Journal Up the Straits*, 1935.

## COLLECTED WORKS

The first volume of a projected fourteen-volume edition of Melville's writings, each volume prepared by a specialist, is Howard P. Vincent, ed., *Collected Poems of Herman Melville*, Chicago, 1947. It includes hitherto unpublished and uncollected poems, as well as the poetry of the novels. At present the only collected edition is *The Works of Herman Melville*, London, 1922–1924, 16 vols. Vol. XIII, ed. by Raymond M. Weaver, contains hitherto unpublished prose, including *Billy Budd*.

Published letters, as yet uncollected, are scattered through many books and periodicals. The chief gatherings are in Meade Minnigerode, ed., *Some Personal Letters of Herman Melville . . .*, New York, 1922—an inaccurately transcribed text; Victor H. Paltsits, ed., *Family Correspondence of Herman Melville, 1830–1904*, New York, 1929—especially useful for genealogy; and Willard Thorp, ed., *Herman Melville: Representative Selections . . .*, New York, 1938, pp. 368–404. Samuel E. Morison, ed., "Melville's 'Agatha' Letter to Hawthorne," *New Eng. Quar.*, II (1929), 296–307, is important for a study of Melville's technique. The most recent to appear is Harrison Hayford, ed.,

"Two New Letters of Herman Melville," *Jour. of Eng. Literary Hist.*, XI (1944), 76–83. The bibliography in Thorp, ed., *Herman Melville . . .*, records other gleanings.

The only transcription of *Journal Up the Straits, October 11, 1856–May 5, 1857* is that of Raymond M. Weaver, New York, 1935, inaccurately edited. The journal of his trip to California in 1860 is printed as "Journal of Melville's Voyage in a Clipper Ship," *New Eng. Quar.*, II (1929), 120–125.

The need for a new collected edition of Melville's works is especially pressing.

### EDITED TEXTS AND REPRINTS

Two of the novels have been carefully edited: *Pierre; or, The Ambiguities* (ed. by Robert S. Forsythe, New York, 1930, 1941), and *Moby Dick; or, The White Whale* (ed. by Willard Thorp, New York, 1947). An easily available selective text is Willard Thorp, ed., *Herman Melville: Representative Selections, with Introduction, Bibliography, and Notes,* New York, 1938 (Amer. Writers Ser.); it includes poems and hitherto unpublished letters. The notes are especially useful since they deal with a major author as yet insufficiently explicated.

Other reprints have been published as follows: *Typee* (1846), Boston, 1902, with an introduction by William P. Trent; London, 1907 (Everyman's Lib.), 1924 (World's Classics). *Mardi* (1849), New York; 1925, ed. by R. M. Weaver. *Redburn* (1849), New York, 1924, ed. by R. M. Weaver. *White-Jacket* (1850), London, 1929, ed. by Carl Van Doren (World's Classics). *Moby-Dick* (1851), London, 1907 (Everyman's Lib.), 1920 (ed. by Viola Meynell—World's Classics); New York, 1926 (Modern Lib.), 1929 (ed. by Ralph Dow, 2 vols.—Modern Readers' Ser.), 1943. *Pierre* (1852), New York, 1929, with an introduction by John B. Moore. *Israel Potter* (1855), New York, 1924. *The Piazza Tales* (1856), New York, 1929. *John Marr and Other Poems,* Princeton, 1922, with an introduction by Henry Chapin—a selection from all Melville's poetical works. *The Apple-Tree Table and Other Sketches,* Princeton, 1922, with an introduction by Henry Chapin—ten prose pieces originally published in periodicals, 1850–1856. *The Encantadas; or, Enchanted Isles* (reprinted from *The Piazza Tales,* 1856), with an introduction, critical epilogue, and bibl. notes, ed. by Victor W. von Hagen, Burlingame, Calif., 1940. Raymond M. Weaver edited the *Shorter Novels of Herman Melville,* New York, 1928, including *Billy Budd,* and William Plomer edited *Selected Poems . . .,* London, 1943 (New Hogarth Lib.).

### BIOGRAPHY AND CRITICISM

A full-length study from the sources is Jean Simon, *Herman Melville, Marin, Métaphysicien et Poète*, Paris, 1939. The author worked in the United

States, and the bibliography is especially useful for its listing of translations and foreign criticisms. The most balanced and informed narrative biography of Melville is William E. Sedgwick, *Herman Melville: The Tragedy of Mind,* Cambridge, 1944. The first full-length life was Raymond M. Weaver, *Herman Melville: Mariner and Mystic,* New York, 1921. Later researches have increased the material and altered many judgments. Much of the source for John Freeman's *Herman Melville* (London, 1926) was Weaver, but the critical estimates are sound for its time. Lewis Mumford's *Herman Melville,* New York, 1929, is best at integration, but is undocumented. When Evert A. and George L. Duyckinck edited their *Cyclopaedia of American Literature* (1855), they wrote what might be termed a brief "official" biography of their close friend (II, 672–676). J. E. A. Smith's *Herman Melville. Written for the Evening Journal,* Pittsfield, Mass., 1891, is a 30-page biographical sketch by an old friend. The sketch of Melville in *Dict. Amer. Biog.* (1933) was written by Van Wyck Brooks.

In addition to the study by Sedgwick, mentioned above, the chief interpretations of Melville's thought and art are William Braswell, *Melville's Religious Thought: An Essay in Interpretation,* Durham, N.C., 1943; "Melville," in F(rancis) O. Matthiessen, *American Renaissance . . . ,* New York, 1941, pp. 371–514; and the introduction (pp. xi–cxxix) in Willard Thorp, *Herman Melville: Representative Selections . . . ,* New York, 1938. Significant studies also are Vega Curl, "Pasteboard Masks: Fact as Spiritual Symbol in the Novels of Hawthorne and Melville," Radcliffe Honors thesis, 1931; Viola C. White, "Symbolism in the Writings of Herman Melville," Univ. of North Carolina dissertation, 1934; Karl H. Sundermann, *Herman Melvilles Gedankengut . . . ,* Berlin, 1937; Luther S. Mansfield, *Herman Melville: Author and New Yorker, 1844–1851,* Chicago, 1938; Stanley Geist, "Herman Melville: The Tragic Vision and the Heroic Ideal," Harvard Honors thesis, 1939; and Wilbur S. Scott, "Melville's Originality: A Study of Some of the Sources of *Moby Dick,*" Princeton Univ. dissertation, 1943. Further important studies are G. C. Homans, "The Dark Angel: The Tragedy of Herman Melville," *New Eng. Quar.,* V (1932), 699–730; Luther S. Mansfield, "Glimpses of Herman Melville's Life in Pittsfield, 1850–1851: Some Unpublished Letters of Evert A. Duyckinck," *Amer. Lit.,* IX (1937), 26–48; Willard Thorp, "Herman Melville's Silent Years," *University Rev.,* III (1937), 254–262; "Herman Melville and the Problems of Moral Navigation," in Yvor Winters, *Maule's Curse . . . ,* Norfolk, Conn., 1938, pp. 53–89; "The Craft of Herman Melville: A Putative Statement," in R(ichard) P. Blackmur, *The Expense of Greatness . . . ,* New York, 1940, pp. 139–166; "Melville, Critic of Mid-Nineteenth Century Beliefs," in Ralph H. Gabriel, *The Course of American Democratic Thought,* New York, 1940, pp. 67–77; and Reginald E. Watters, "Melville's Metaphysics of Evil," *University of Toronto Quar.,* IX (1940), 170–182.

Studies of Melville, significant to the extent to which the authors are spokesmen of their times, are H. S. Salt, "Herman Melville," *Scottish Art Rev.,* II (1889), 186–190—an early recognition; Richard H. Stoddard, "Herman Melville," New York *Mail and Express,* Oct. 8, 1891, p. 5—a significant contemporary judgment; W. C. Russell, "A Claim for American Literature," *No. Amer. Rev.,* CLIV (1892), 138–149—another of the few contemporary recognitions. The first comprehensive survey of Melville's whole work is F. J. Mather, Jr., "Herman Melville," *Review,* I (1919), 276–278, 298–301—a turning point in Melville criticism. More recent studies are "Herman Melville," in Carl Van Doren, *The American Novel* . . . , New York, rev. ed., 1940, pp. 84–102; "Conrad and Melville," in Henry S. Canby, *Definitions,* 1st ser., New York, 1922, pp. 257–268; Carl Van Vechten, "The Later Work of Herman Melville," *Double Dealer,* III (1922), 9–20; "Herman Melville," in J. W. N. Sullivan, *Aspects of Science,* 2nd ser., New York, 1926, pp. 190–205; "Herman Melville," in Percy H. Boynton, *More Contemporary Americans,* Chicago, 1927, pp. 29–50; "Herman Melville," in Vernon L. Parrington, *Main Currents in American Thought* . . . , New York, II (1927), 258–267; "Hawthorne and Melville," in Henry S. Canby, *Classic Americans,* New York, 1931, pp. 226–262.

Surveys of Melville's reputation and contemporary vogue are O. W. Riegel, "The Anatomy of Melville's Fame," *Amer. Lit.,* III (1931), 195–203, with corrections in William Braswell, "A Note on 'The Anatomy of Melville's Fame,'" *Amer. Lit.,* V (1934), 360–364. Other surveys are H. W. Hetherington, "The Reputation of Herman Melville in America," Univ. of Michigan dissertation, 1933; Charles R. Anderson, "Contemporary American Opinions of *Typee* and *Omoo,*" *Amer. Lit.,* IX (1937), 1–25; and Willard Thorp, "'Grace Greenwood' Parodies *Typee,*" *Amer. Lit.,* IX (1938), 455–457.

Melville as lecturer is the subject of John H. Birss, "'Travelling': A New Lecture by Herman Melville," *New Eng. Quar.,* VII (1934), 725–728; George Kummer, "Herman Melville and the Ohio Press," *Ohio State Archaeol. and Hist. Quar.,* XLV (1936), 34–36; Merrell R. Davis, "Melville's Midwestern Lecture Tour, 1859," *Philological Quar.,* XX (1941), 46–57; Francis V. Lloyd, Jr., "Melville's First Lectures," *Amer. Lit.,* XIII (1942), 391–395; Charles Duffy, "Toward the Whole Evidence on Melville as a Lecturer," *Amer. Notes and Queries,* II (1942), 58; (anon.), "Melville and His Public," *ibid.,* pp. 67–71; (anon.), "Toward the Whole Evidence on Melville as a Lecturer," *ibid.,* pp. 111–112; John Birss, "Toward the Whole Evidence on Melville as a Lecturer," *ibid.,* III (1943), 11–12; and Tyrus Hillway, "A Note on Melville's Lecture in New Haven," *Modern Language Notes,* LX (1945), 55–57.

Studies of Melville's journeyings in the Pacific are Charles R. Anderson, *Melville in the South Seas,* New York, 1939—the 1841–1844 journeyings and their bearing on the South Seas novels; Jean Simon, *La Polynésie dans l'Art et la Littérature de l'Occident,* Paris, 1939; Daniel Aaron, "Melville and the Missionaries," *New Eng. Quar.,* VIII (1935), 404–408; Robert S. Forsythe, "Herman Melville in Honolulu," *ibid.,* 99–105; *idem,* "Herman Melville in the Marquesas," *Philological Quar.,* XV (1936), 1–15; and Clarence Gohdes, "Gossip About Melville in the South Seas," *New Eng. Quar.,* X (1937), 526–531.

The sources and themes of individual works, together with further data, are supplied as follows:

*Typee:* Bernard De Voto, "Editions of *Typee,*" *Sat. Rev. Lit.,* V (Nov. 24, 1928), 406; Nelson F. Adkins, "A Note on Herman Melville's *Typee,*" *New Eng. Quar.,* V (1932), 348–351; Russell Thomas, "Yarn for Melville's *Typee,*" *Philological Quar.,* XV (1936), 16–29; Victor H. Paltsits, "Herman Melville's Background and New Light on the Publication of *Typee,*" in *Bookmen's Holiday . . . ,* New York, 1943, pp. 248–268.

*Omoo:* Robert S. Forsythe, "Herman Melville in Tahiti," *Philological Quar.,* XVI (1937), 344–357; *idem,* "Herman Melville's Father Murphy," *Notes and Queries,* CLXXII (1937), 254–258, 272–276; *idem,* "More upon Herman Melville in Tahiti," *Philological Quar.,* XVII (1938), 1–17.

*Mardi:* John H. Birss, "A Note on Melville's *Mardi,*" *Notes and Queries,* CLXII (1932), 404; Stephen A. Larrabee, "Melville Against the World," *So. Atl. Quar.,* XXXIV (1935), 410–418; David Jaffé, "Some Sources of Melville's *Mardi,*" *Amer. Lit.,* IX (1937), 56–69; Leon Howard, "Melville's Struggle with the Angel," *Modern Language Quar.,* I (1940), 195–206; Merrell R. Davis, "The Flower Symbolism in *Mardi,*" *Modern Language Quar.,* II (1942), 625–638; Gordon Mills, "The Significance of 'Arcturus' in *Mardi,*" *Amer. Lit.,* XIV (1942), 158–161; Tyrus Hillway, "Taji's Abdication in Herman Melville's *Mardi,*" *Amer. Lit.,* XVI (1944), 204–207; *idem,* "Taji's Quest for Certainty," *Amer. Lit.,* XVIII (1946), 27–34.

*Redburn:* Willard Thorp, "Redburn's Prosy Old Guide Book," *PMLA,* LIII (1938), 1146–1156; Keith Huntress, "A Note on Melville's *Redburn,*" *New Eng. Quar.,* XVIII (1945), 259–260.

*White-Jacket:* Albert Mordell, "Melville and *White-Jacket,*" *Sat. Rev. Lit.,* VII (July 4, 1931), 946; Charles R. Anderson, "A Reply to Melville's *White-Jacket* by Rear-Admiral Thomas O. Selfridge, Sr.," *Amer. Lit.,* VII (1935), 123–144; Keith Huntress, "Melville's Use of a Source for *White-Jacket,*" *Amer. Lit.,* XVII (1945), 66–74.

*Moby-Dick:* "Notes on Herman Melville," in Van Wyck Brooks, *Emerson and Others,* New York, 1927, pp. 171–205; S. Foster Damon, "Why Ishmael Went to Sea," *Amer. Lit.,* II (1930), 281–283; William S. Ament, "Some Americanisms in *Moby Dick,*" *Amer. Speech,* VII (1932), 365–367; *idem,*

"Bowdler and the Whale: Some Notes on the First English and American Editions of *Moby-Dick*," *Amer. Lit.*, IV (1932), 39-46; Leon Howard, "A Predecessor of Moby-Dick," *Modern Language Notes*, XLIX (1934), 310-311; Frederick B. Adams, Jr. (on "The Mast-head" chapter), in *Colophon*, n.s. II (1936), 148-154; Lorena M. Gary, "Rich Colors and Ominous Shadows," *So. Atl. Quar.*, XXXVII (1938), 41-45; Charles Olson, "Lear and Moby Dick," *Twice a Year*, No. 1 (1938), 165-189; David Potter, "Reviews of *Moby-Dick*," *Jour. Rutgers Univ. Lib.*, III (1940), 62-65; Sumner W. D. Scott, "Some Implications of the Typhoon Scenes in *Moby Dick*," *Amer. Lit.*, XII (1940), 91-98; Charles Duffy, "A Source for the Conclusion of Melville's *Moby Dick*," *Notes and Queries*, CLXXXI (1941), 278-279; Thomas O. Mabbott, "A Source for the Conclusion of Melville's *Moby Dick*," *ibid.*, 47-48; Henry A. Myers, "Captain Ahab's Discovery: The Tragic Meaning of *Moby Dick*," *New Eng. Quar.*, XV (1942), 15-34; F. Pirano, "*Moby Dick* di Herman Melville," *Convivium*, XV (1943), 209-243; Charles C. Walcutt, "The Fire Symbolism in *Moby Dick*," *Modern Language Notes*, LIX (1944), 304-310; J. C. McCloskey, "*Moby-Dick* and the Reviewers," *Philological Quar.*, XXV (1946), 20-31; Sophie Hollis, "*Moby Dick*: A Religious Interpretation," *Catholic World*, CLXIII (1946), 158-162; Montgomery Belgion, "Heterodoxy on Moby Dick?" *Sewanee Rev.*, LV (1947), 108-125; Charles Olson, *Call Me Ishmael*, New York, 1947—the influence of Shakespeare.

*Pierre*: S. Foster Damon, "Pierre the Ambiguous," *Hound and Horn*, II (1929), 107-118; E. L. G. Watson, "Melville's *Pierre*," *New Eng. Quar.*, III (1930), 195-234; Merton M. Sealts, "Herman Melville's 'I and My Chimney,'" *Amer. Lit.*, XIII (1941), 142-154.

*Israel Potter*: Roger P. McCutcheon, "The Technique of Melville's *Israel Potter*," *So. Atl. Quar.*, XXVII (1928), 161-174; W. S. Holden, "Some Sources of Herman Melville's *Israel Potter*," Columbia Univ. master's thesis, 1932.

*Piazza Tales*: Harold H. Scudder, "Melville's *Benito Cereno* and Captain Delano's Voyages," *PMLA*, XLIII (1928), 502-532; Leon Howard, "Melville and Spenser: A Note on Criticism," *Modern Language Notes*, XLVI (1931), 291-292; Russell Thomas, "Melville's Use of Some Sources in *The Encantadas*," *Amer. Lit.*, III (1932), 432-456; Merton M. Sealts, "The Publication of Melville's *Piazza Tales*," *Modern Language Notes*, LIX (1944), 56-59; Egbert S. Oliver, "A Second Look at 'Bartleby,'" *College Eng.*, VI (1945), 431-439.

*The Confidence-Man*: Egbert S. Oliver, "Melville's Picture of Emerson and Thoreau in *The Confidence-Man*," *College Eng.*, VIII (1946), 61-72.

*Clarel*: Henry W. Wells, "Herman Melville's *Clarel*," *College Eng.*, IV (1943), 478-483.

*Billy Budd*: E. L. G. Watson, "Melville's Testament of Acceptance," *New*

*Eng. Quar.*, VI (1933), 319–327; Charles R. Anderson, "The Genesis of *Billy Budd.*, *Amer. Lit.*, XII (1940), 329–346; E. Barron Freeman, "The Enigma of Melville's 'Daniel Orme,'" *Amer. Lit.*, XVI (1944), 208–211; Charles Weir, Jr., "Malice Reconciled: A Note on *Billy Budd*," *University of Toronto Quar.*, XIII (1944), 276–285. Other individual works are studied in E. H. Eby, "Herman Melville's 'Tartarus of Maids,'" *Modern Language Quar.*, I (1940), 95–100; and Douglas Sackman, "The Original of Melville's Apple-Tree Table," *Amer. Lit.*, XI (1940), 448–451.

Further special studies of value are Daniel Aaron, "An English Enemy of Melville," *New Eng. Quar.*, VIII (1935), 561–567; Jean Simon, "Recherches Australiennes sur Herman Melville," *Revue Anglo-Amér.*, XIII (1935), 114–129; Oscar Wegelin, "Herman Melville as I Recall Him," *Colophon*, n.s. I, No. 1 (1935), 21–24—on the sale of Melville's library; Frederic I. Carpenter, "Puritans Preferred Blondes: The Heroines of Melville and Hawthorne," *New Eng. Quar.*, IX (1936), 253–272; William Braswell, "Melville as a Critic of Emerson," *Amer. Lit.*, IX (1937), 317–334; James D. Hart, "Melville and Dana," *Amer. Lit.*, IX (1937), 49–55; Luther S. Mansfield, "Melville's Comic Articles on Zachary Taylor," *Amer. Lit.*, IX (1938), 411–418; Charles R. Anderson, "Melville's English Debut," *Amer. Lit.*, XI (1939), 23–38; William Braswell, "Melville's Use of Seneca," *Amer. Lit.*, XII (1940), 98–104; Nathalia Wright, "Biblical Allusion in Melville's Prose," *Amer. Lit.*, XII (1940), 185–199; Jean Giona, "Pour Salver Melville," *Nouvelle Revue Française*, XXVIII (1940), 433–458; James M. Purcell, "Melville's Contribution to English," *PMLA*, LVI (1941), 797–808—lists of some 180 words; Willard Thorp, "Did Melville Review *The Scarlet Letter?*" *Amer. Lit.*, XIV (1942), 302–305; William Charvat, "Melville's Income," *Amer. Lit.*, XV (1943), 251–261; Clarence Gohdes, "Melville's Friend 'Toby,'" *Modern Language Notes*, LIX (1944), 52–55; Henry F. Pommer, "Melville as Critic of Christianity," *Friends' Intelligencer*, CII (1945), 121–123; Reginald E. Watters, "Melville's Sociality," *Amer. Lit.*, XVII (1945), 33–49; *idem*, "Melville's 'Isolatoes,'" *PMLA*, LX (1945), 1138–1148; Elizabeth S. Foster, "Melville and Geology," *Amer. Lit.*, XVII (1945), 50–65; Egbert S. Oliver, "Melville's Goneril and Fanny Kemble," *New Eng. Quar.*, XVIII (1945), 489–500; Robert Penn Warren, "Melville the Poet," *Kenyon Rev.*, VIII (1946), 208–223; and Harrison Hayford, "Hawthorne, Melville, and the Sea," *New Eng. Quar.*, XIX (1946), 435–452.

A bibliography of reviews and criticisms of Melville's writings published during his lifetime is given in Willard Thorp, *Herman Melville: Representative Selections*, pp. cxli–cliii.

PRIMARY SOURCES

In the Houghton Library of Harvard University is the collection of Melville material formerly owned by Melville's granddaughter, Eleanor Melville Metcalf. Among these papers are many Melville letters relating to the publication of his books, letters to Melville, holograph manuscripts of his later poems and prose pieces and of the 1849 and 1856 journals. The Harvard College Library also possesses books from Melville's library, many of them annotated by him.

Three Melville collections are in the New York Public Library: the Gansevoort-Lansing Collection, in which are the important letters of Melville and his wife to members of the Gansevoort family (his mother's); the extensive Duyckinck Collection of letters and holograph manuscripts of reviews which Melville contributed to the Duyckincks' *Literary World,* together with other important material; and the Berg Collection, which contains Melville letters, and books that were owned by Melville and his family.

Other important Melville material is in the Lemuel Shaw Collection of the Massachusetts Historical Society and in the Princeton University Library.

BIBLIOGRAPHY

There is no full Melville bibliography at present. The selective listings in Willard Thorp, *Herman Melville: Representative Selections,* pp. cxxxiii–clxi, are annotated. Checklists are given in William S. Ament, "Bowdler and the Whale . . .," *Amer. Lit.,* IV (1932), 39–46; Meade Minnigerode, *Some Personal Letters of Herman Melville* . . ., New York, 1922, pp. 101–195; Michael Sadleir, *Excursions in Victorian Bibliography,* London, 1922, pp. 217–234; Raymond M. Weaver, *Herman Melville* . . ., New York, 1921; and Jean Simon, *Herman Melville* . . ., Paris, 1939, pp. 587–602.

## H(ENRY) L(OUIS) MENCKEN
### *b. 1880*

SEPARATE WORKS

*Ventures into Verse,* 1903; *George Bernard Shaw: His Plays,* 1905; *The Philosophy of Friedrich Nietzsche,* 1908; *What You Ought To Know About Your Baby* (with L. K. Hirshberg), 1910; *Men Versus the Man* (with R. R. La Monte), 1910; *The Artist,* 1912; *Europe After 8:15* (with G. J. Nathan and W. H. Wright), 1914; *A Little Book in C Major,* 1916; *A Book of Burlesques,* 1916; *A Book of Prefaces,* 1917; *Damn! A Book of Calumny,* 1918; *In Defense of Women,* 1918; *The American Language,* 1919; *Prejudices: First Series,* 1919; *Prejudices: Second Series,* 1920; *The American Credo* (with G. J. Nathan), 1920; *Heliogabalus* (with G. J. Nathan), 1920; *Prejudices: Third Series,* 1922; *Prejudices: Fourth Series,* 1924; *Notes on Democracy,*

1926; *Prejudices: Fifth Series,* 1926; *Prejudices: Sixth Series,* 1927; *Treatise on the Gods,* 1930; *Making a President,* 1932; *Treatise on Right and Wrong,* 1934; *Happy Days, 1880–1892,* 1940; *Newspaper Days, 1899–1906,* 1941; *A New Dictionary of Quotations on Historical Principles,* 1942; *Heathen Days, 1890–1936,* 1943; *Christmas Story,* 1946.

REPRINTS AND COLLECTIONS

*A Book of Burlesques* (1916) is reprinted in Borzoi Pocket Books, New York, 1924; *In Defense of Women* (1918), in Star Books, Garden City, N.Y., 1931. *The American Language* . . . (1919) has greatly increased in bulk and in authority; the 4th ed., New York, 1936, is standard at present, with much material added in *Supplement One,* New York, 1945. The six series of *Prejudices* (1919–1927) have been culled for *Selected Prejudices,* New York, 1930 (Modern Lib.).

*Criticism in America: Its Function and Status,* New York, 1924, is an important collection of critical essays by nine contributors including Mencken.

A revised edition of *Treatise on the Gods* was issued, New York, 1946, with added material.

BIOGRAPHY AND CRITICISM

Isaac Goldberg has written *The Man Mencken: A Biographical and Critical Survey,* New York, 1925. There is at present very little judicious criticism of Mencken. Studies through 1928 are especially inclined to a bias. Among those which are useful as expressions of their times are Burton Rascoe and others, *H. L. Mencken: Fanfare* . . ., New York, 1920; Edmund Wilson, "H. L. Mencken," *New Repub.,* XXVII (June 1, 1921), 10–13; "A Critic in C Major," in Fred L. Pattee, *Side-Lights on American Literature,* New York, 1922, pp. 56–97; "Mr. Mencken, the Jeune Fille, and the New Spirit in Letters," in Stuart P. Sherman, *Americans,* New York, 1922, pp. 1–12; "H. L. Mencken: Critic," in Frank Harris, *Contemporary Portraits,* 4th ser., New York, 1923, pp. 143–154; "Smartness and Light: H. L. Mencken," in Carl Van Doren, *Many Minds,* New York, 1924, pp. 120–135; "The Vaudeville Critic: H. L. Mencken," in Victor F. Calverton, *The Newer Spirit,* New York, 1925, pp. 165–179; Joseph Hergesheimer, "Mr. H. L. Mencken," in *The Borzoi, 1925,* New York, 1925, pp. 102–106; "Mr. Mencken," in Joseph W. Beach, *The Outlook for American Prose,* Chicago, 1926, pp. 81–92; William Salisbury, "Mencken, the Foe of Beauty," *Amer. Parade,* I (July, 1926), 34–49; "H. L. Mencken as Liberator," in Stuart P. Sherman, *Critical Woodcuts,* New York, 1926, pp. 235–243; Ernest A. Boyd, *H. L. Mencken,* New York, 1927; Walter Lippmann, *Men of Destiny,* New York, 1927, pp. 61–70; "H. L. Mencken" in Elizabeth S. Sergeant, *Fire Under the Andes,* New York, 1927.

pp. 239–257; and Irving Babbitt, "The Critic and American Life," *Forum*, LXXIX (1928), 161–176.

Later criticism is somewhat more detached. Estimates have been made by Henry S. Canby, *American Estimates*, New York, 1929, pp. 58–61; James B. Cabell, "Dreams on Cosmogony: A Note as to H. L. Mencken," in his *Some of Us*, New York, 1930, pp. 107–118; Benjamin De Casseres, *Mencken and Shaw* . . ., New York, 1930, pp. 3–103; I. J. Semper, "H. L. Mencken and Catholicism," *Catholic World*, CXXXI (1930), 641–650; Emily Clark, "H. L. Mencken," in her *Innocence Abroad*, New York, 1931, pp. 109–126; Van Wyck Brooks, "Mr. Mencken and the Prophets," in his *Sketches in Criticism*, New York, 1932, pp. 26–33; Louis Kronenberger, "H. L. Mencken," in Malcolm Cowley, ed., *After the Genteel Tradition*, New York, 1936, pp. 100–111; and Bernard Smith, "The Urban Tory: Mencken," in his *Forces in American Criticism*, New York, 1939, pp. 304–312.

PRIMARY SOURCES

Mencken's three volumes of autobiography are *Happy Days* (1940), *Newspaper Days* (1941), and *Heathen Days* (1943). He has also compiled *Menckeniana: A Schimpflexikon*, New York, 1928—denunciatory press comments. Further source material is in George J. Nathan, *The Intimate Notebooks of George Jean Nathan*, New York, 1932, pp. 94–121.

The chief collection of Mencken manuscripts is in the Library of Congress. Further material is in the Princeton University Library.

BIBLIOGRAPHY

No bibliography of Mencken attempting coverage of the large number of pamphlets and contributed introductions and prefaces has yet been published. Some minor and fugitive pieces are included in Jacob Blanck, *Merle Johnson's American First Editions*, 4th ed., New York, 1942, pp. 358–361. Further material, especially of a secondary nature, is in Fred B. Millett, *Contemporary American Authors*, New York, 1940, pp. 480–486. An early listing is Carroll Frey, *A Bibliography of the Writings of H. L. Mencken*, Philadelphia, 1924.

# EDNA ST. VINCENT MILLAY
### *b. 1892*

SEPARATE WORKS

*Renascence*, 1917; *A Few Figs from Thistles*, 1920; *The Lamp and the Bell*, 1921; *Aria da Capo*, 1921; *Second April*, 1921; *Two Slatterns and a King*, 1921; *The Ballad of the Harp-Weaver*, 1922; *The Harp-Weaver and Other*

*Poems*, 1923; *Distressing Dialogues*, 1924; *The King's Henchman*, 1927; *The Buck in the Snow and Other Poems*, 1928; *Fatal Interview*, 1931; *The Princess Marries the Page*, 1932; *Wine from These Grapes*, 1934; *Conversation at Midnight*, 1937; *Huntsman, What Quarry?* 1939; *Make Bright the Arrows*, 1940; *The Murder of Lidice*, 1942.

The play *Aria da Capo*, first published as a separate item in New York, 1921, originally appeared in *The Chapbook* (London) No. 14, Aug., 1920, filling the entire issue. *Distressing Dialogues* (1924) was published under the pseudonym "Nancy Boyd."

COLLECTED WORKS

*Collected Sonnets of Edna St. Vincent Millay*, New York, 1941, and *Collected Lyrics of Edna St. Vincent Millay*, New York, 1943, assemble much previously published material. *Three Plays*, New York, 1926, assembles the three earliest plays, all published in 1921: *The Lamp and the Bell, Aria da Capo, Two Slatterns and a King*.

BIOGRAPHY AND CRITICISM

Early studies of Miss Millay's verse include "Edna St. Vincent Millay," in Louis Untermeyer, *American Poetry Since 1900*, New York, 1923, pp. 214–220; Harriet Monroe, "Edna St. Vincent Millay," in *Poetry*, XXIV (1924), 260–266; Witter Bynner, "Edna St. Vincent Millay," in *New Repub.*, XLI (Dec. 10, 1924), Winter Literary Section, pp. 14–15; John Farrar, ed., *The Literary Spotlight*, New York, 1924, pp. 77–90; "Edna St. Vincent Millay" in Harriet Monroe, *Poets and Their Art*, New York, 1926, pp. 63–71; "Minority Report," in Lee Simonson, *Minor Prophecies*, New York, 1927, pp. 119–135—on *The King's Henchman*; John H. Preston, "Edna St. Vincent Millay," *Virginia Quar. Rev.*, III (1927), 342–355; Edward Davison, "Edna St. Vincent Millay," *English Jour.*, XVI (1927), 671–682; and Alfred Kreymborg, *Our Singing Strength*, New York, 1929, pp. 438–446.

Later estimates are Edd W. Parks, "Edna St. Vincent Millay," *Sewanee Rev.*, XXXVIII (1930), 42–49; Rica Brenner, *Ten Modern Poets*, New York, 1930, pp. 63–81; Harriet Monroe, "Advance or Retreat?" *Poetry*, XXXVIII (1931), 216–221; Allen Tate, "Miss Millay's *Sonnets*," *New Repub.*, LXVI (1931), 335–336; Arthur E. Du Bois, "Edna St. Vincent Millay," *Sewanee Rev.*, XLIII (1935), 80–104; Hildegarde Flanner, "Two Poets: Jeffers and Millay," *New Repub.*, LXXXIX (1937), 379–382; Elizabeth Atkins, *Edna St. Vincent Millay and Her Times*, Chicago, 1936—a general estimate; John C. Ransom, "The Poet as Woman," *Southern Rev.*, II (1937), 783–806; James M. Dabbs, "Edna St. Vincent Millay: Not Resigned," *So. Atl. Quar.*, XXXVII (1938), 54–66; Thomas C. Chubb, "Shelley Grown Old," *No. Amer. Rev.*, CCXLV (1938), 170–180.

BIBLIOGRAPHY

Karl Yost, *A Bibliography of the Works of Edna St. Vincent Millay*, New York, 1937, is carefully compiled and includes some Millay material here first published. It is supplemented by John S. Van E. Kohn, "Some Undergraduate Printings of Edna St. Vincent Millay," *Publishers' Weekly*, CXXXVIII (Nov. 30, 1940), 2026–2029. The best listing of secondary material is Fred B. Millett, *Contemporary American Authors*, New York, 1940, pp. 487–491. For a listing of many poems published in various anthologies, see Jacob Blanck, *Merle Johnson's American First Editions*, 4th ed., New York, 1942. The most recent checklist is compiled by Frances Cheney, in Allen Tate, *Sixty American Poets, 1896–1944*, Washington, 1945, pp. 104–109.

## JOAQUIN (CINCINNATUS HEINE [HINER]) MILLER
### *1841(?)–1913*

SEPARATE WORKS

*Specimens*, 1868; *Joaquin, et al.*, 1869; *Pacific Poems*, 1871; *Songs of the Sierras*, 1871; *Songs of the Sun-Lands*, 1873; *Life Amongst the Modocs: Unwritten History*, 1873; *Arizonian*, 1874; *First Fam'lies in the Sierras*, 1875; *The Ship in the Desert*, 1875; *The One Fair Woman*, 1876; *The Baroness of New York*, 1877; *Songs of Italy*, 1878; *Songs of Far-Away Lands*, 1878; *Shadows of Shasta*, 1881; *William Brown of Oregon*, 1883; *The Silent Man: A Comedy Drama*, 1883; *Memorie and Rime*, 1884; *'49: The Gold-Seeker of the Sierras*, 1884; *The Destruction of Gotham*, 1886; *Songs of the Mexican Seas*, 1887; *In Classic Shades and Other Poems*, 1890; *Songs of Summer Lands*, 1892; *The Building of the City Beautiful*, 1893; *An Illustrated History of the State of Montana*, 1894; *Songs of the Soul*, 1896; *Chants for the Boer*, 1900; *True Bear Stories*, 1900; *As It Was in the Beginning*, 1903; *Light: A Narrative Poem*, 1907; *Trelawney with Shelley and Byron*, 1922.

Life Amongst the Modocs (1873) was reissued with new titles as follows: *Unwritten History: Life Among the Modocs* (1874); *Paquita: The Indian Heroine* (1881); *My Own Story* (1890); and *Joaquin Miller's Romantic Life Amongst the Indians* (1898).

Plays: *First Fam'lies in the Sierras* (1875) was revised as the most popular of Miller's plays, *The Danites in the Sierras* (1882). Other published plays are *Forty-nine* (1882); *Tally Ho!* (1910); and *An Oregon Idyll* (1910).

COLLECTED WORKS AND REPRINTS

*The Complete Poetical Works of Joaquin Miller*, San Francisco, 1897 (rev.

ed., 1902), includes a brief account of his literary life. The so-called "Bear Edition" of *Joaquin Miller's Poems* was published in San Francisco, 1909–1910, 6 vols.

Miller's autobiography has recently been edited by Sidney G. Firman, *Overland in a Covered Wagon: An Autobiography*, New York, 1930—useful but untrustworthy. Other recent material will be found in Alfred Powers, ed., *A Royal Highway of the World*, Portland, Ore., 1932; and John S. Richards, ed., *Joaquin Miller: His California Diary* . . . , Seattle, 1936—for the years 1855–1857.

No full collection of Miller's letters has been published. Gleanings will be found in Beatrice B. Beebe, ed., "Letters of Joaquin Miller," *Frontier*, XII (1932), 121–124, 223–228, 344–347; and Clarence Gohdes, "Some Letters of Joaquin Miller to Lord Houghton," *Modern Language Quar.*, III (1942), 297–306.

Stuart P. Sherman edited *The Poetical Works of Joaquin Miller*, New York, 1923, a volume of selections, with a useful critical introduction on Miller as poet. *The Danites in the Sierras* was reprinted in Allan G. Halline, *American Plays* (1935), pp. 377–406, with introduction.

## BIOGRAPHY AND CRITICISM

The most recent life is Martin S. Peterson, *Joaquin Miller, Literary Frontiersman*, Stanford Univ., Calif., 1937. Miller's friend Harr Wagner published an admiring biography, *Joaquin Miller and His Other Self*, San Francisco, 1929. A useful unpublished dissertation is Roger R. Walterhouse, "Bret Harte, Joaquin Miller, and the Western Local Color Story," Univ. of Chicago, 1939. A standard estimate of Miller as dramatist is Arthur H. Quinn, *A History of the American Drama from the Civil War to the Present Day*, rev. ed., New York, 1936, I, 116–118. The sketch of Miller in *Dict. Amer. Biog.* (1933) was written by Ernest S. Bates. An important critical estimate is "Joaquin Miller: Poetical Conquistador of the West," in Stuart P. Sherman, *Americans*, New York, 1923, pp. 186–238—used by Sherman as an introduction to his edition of *The Poetical Works* (1923).

Other general studies are Bruce Weirick, *From Whitman to Sandburg in American Poetry*, New York, 1924, pp. 83–94; George Sterling, "Joaquin Miller," *Amer. Mercury*, VII (1926), 220–229; and Van Wyck Brooks, *Sketches in Criticism*, New York, 1932, pp. 236–240.

Special studies include Fred W. Lorch, "A Note on Joaquin Miller," *Amer. Lit.*, III (1931), 75–78; Albert Keiser, *The Indian in American Literature*, New York, 1933, pp. 233–248; G. E. Veach, "The Indiana Boyhood of the Poet of the Sierras," *Indiana Mag. Hist.*, XXX (1934), 153–160; J. S. Richards, "Joaquin Miller's California Diary," *Frontier and Midland*, XVI (Autumn, 1935),

35–40; and Arlin Turner, "Joaquin Miller in New Orleans," *Louisiana Hist. Quar.*, XXII (1939), 216–225.

PRIMARY SOURCES

Many Miller papers, including his diary, are at Claremont College, Claremont, Calif. Among his writings, source material will be found in *Life Amongst the Modocs* (1873); *Memorie and Rime* (1884); and in his autobiography, *Overland in a Covered Wagon* (1930). Miller contributed "How I Came to Be a Writer of Books," *Lippincott's*, XXXVIII (1886), 106–110. *Overland Monthly*, Vol. LXXV, had a "Joaquin Miller Number," Feb., 1920. Yone Noguchi gives a first-hand account of Miller in *The Story of Yone Noguchi Told by Himself*, London, 1914, pp. 55–83. Hamlin Garland describes Miller as he knew him in *Roadside Meetings* (1930), pp. 207–223, 379–387. There are also the volume by Juanita Miller, *My Father C. H. Joaquin Miller, Poet*, Oakland, Calif., 1941, and H. C. Thompson's "Reminiscences of Joaquin Miller and Canyon City," *Oregon Hist. Quar.*, XLV (1944), 326–336.

BIBLIOGRAPHY

The fullest bibliographical listing is that in Martin S. Peterson, *Joaquin Miller* (1937), pp. 179–191. A drama bibliography is in Allan G. Halline, *American Plays* (1935), p. 758.

## WILLIAM VAUGHN MOODY
### 1869–1910

SEPARATE WORKS

*The Masque of Judgment*, 1900; *Poems*, 1901; *The Fire-Bringer*, 1904; *The Great Divide: A Play*, 1909; *The Faith Healer: A Play*, 1909.

With Robert Morss Lovett, Moody wrote *A History of English Literature*, 1902. Moody edited the poetry of Milton. He also edited selections from the poetry of Scott and the prose of De Quincey, as well as an edition of Homer. *The Great Divide* was first produced (1906) as *A Sabine Woman*.

COLLECTED WORKS AND REPRINTS

*The Poems and Plays of William Vaughn Moody* were edited with an introduction by John M. Manly, Boston, 1912, 2 vols. Daniel G. Mason edited *Some Letters of William Vaughn Moody*, Boston, 1913, with an introduction. Thomas H. Dickinson edited *Four Hitherto Unpublished Letters of William Vaughn Moody*, Madison, Wis., 1915. The important collection of letters to his wife, Harriet Converse Moody, was edited by Percy MacKaye, *Letters to Harriet,* Boston, 1935, with a 68-page introduction. Some twenty unpublished letters, together with previously unpublished early poems, are included in David D. Henry's life of Moody (1934), pp. 223–261.

Reprints include *Selected Poems of William Vaughn Moody,* Boston, 1931, edited by Robert M. Lovett; *The Great Divide* in Thomas H. Dickinson, ed., *Chief Contemporary Dramatists,* 1st ser., Boston, 1915, pp. 283–315; and *The Faith Healer* in Arthur H. Quinn, *Representative American Plays,* New York, 1917, pp. 805–839.

### BIOGRAPHY AND CRITICISM

General studies of Moody as poet and dramatist are David D. Henry, *William Vaughn Moody: A Study,* Boston, 1934; Robert M. Lovett, introduction to *Selected Poems* (1931), ix–xcii; Paul Shorey, "The Poetry of William Vaughn Moody," *University [of Chicago] Record,* XIII (1927), 172–200; Charlton M. Lewis, "William Vaughn Moody," *Yale Rev.,* n.s. II (1913), 688–703; Bruce Weirick, *From Whitman to Sandburg in American Poetry,* New York, 1924, pp. 128–142; and Alfred Kreymborg, *Our Singing Strength,* New York, 1929, pp. 286–293. The sketch of Moody in *Dict. Amer. Biog.* (1934) was contributed by Walter P. Eaton.

Early special studies include George Soule, "A Great Pilgrim-Pagan," *Little Rev.,* I (1914), 2–9; C. R. Walker, "The Poetry of William Vaughn Moody," *Texas Rev.,* I (1915), 144–153; M. H. Shackford, "Moody's *The Fire Bringer* for To-day," *Sewanee Rev.,* XXVI (1918), 407–416; J. W. Buckham, "The Doubt and Faith of William Vaughn Moody," *Homiletic Rev.,* LXXV (1918), 349–353; Gorham B. Munson, "The Limbo of American Literature," *Broom,* II (1922), 259–260; and Nelson F. Adkins, "The Poetic Philosophy of William V. Moody," *Texas Rev.,* IX (1924), 97–112.

Two recent studies of Moody's "Ode" are D. M. McKeithan, "A Note on William Vaughn Moody's 'An Ode in Time of Hesitation,'" *Amer. Lit.,* IX (1937), 349–351; and Francis J. and Adaline Glasheen, "Moody's 'An Ode in Time of Hesitation,'" *College Eng.,* V (1943), 121–129.

Estimates of Moody as dramatist are Arthur H. Quinn, *A History of the American Drama from the Civil War to the Present Day,* rev. ed., 1936, II, 1–26; Thomas H. Dickinson, *Playwrights of the New American Theater,* New York, 1925, pp. 134–144; and Nash O. Barr and Charles H. Caffin, "William Vaughn Moody: A Study," *Drama,* No. 2 (1911), 177–211.

### PRIMARY SOURCES

Some Moody manuscripts are in the Princeton University Library. Reminiscences and appreciations are Bliss Perry, "William Vaughn Moody," in

*Commemorative Tributes to Thomas Wentworth Higginson . . .*, New York, 1922, pp. 14–17; Robert M. Lovett, "Memories of William Vaughn Moody," *Atl. Mo.*, CXLVII (1931), 385–393; and Hamlin Garland, *Companions of the Trail*, New York, 1931, pp. 87–94.

BIBLIOGRAPHY

The bibliographical listing in David D. Henry's life (1934), pp. 263–272, includes newspaper and periodical reviews of Moody's writings. See also Percy MacKaye, *Letters to Harriet* (1935), pp. 439–443; and Jacob Blanck, *Merle Johnson's American First Editions*, 4th ed., New York, 1942.

## MARIANNE (CRAIG) MOORE
### b. *1887*

SEPARATE WORKS

*Poems*, 1921; *Observations*, 1924; *Selected Poems*, 1935; *The Pangolin and Other Verse*, 1936; *What Are Years*, 1941; *Nevertheless*, 1944.

The *Poems* (1921) were arranged by Hilda Doolittle ("H. D.") and others. *Observations* (1924) is a reprint, with additions, of *Poems*. *Selected Poems* (1935) has an introduction by T. S. Eliot.

BIOGRAPHY AND CRITICISM

Two of the earliest reactions to the poetry of Marianne Moore are Harriet Monroe, "Symposium on Marianne Moore," *Poetry*, XIX (1922), 208–216, and Louis Untermeyer, *American Poetry Since 1900*, New York, 1923, pp. 362–368. Other early estimates are William Carlos Williams, "Marianne Moore," *Dial*, LXXVIII (1925), 393–401; "Marianne Moore," in Paul Rosenfeld, *Men Seen*, New York, 1925, pp. 165–173; Gorham B. Munson, *Destinations*, New York, 1928, pp. 90–100; "Marianne Moore," in René Taupin, *L'Influence du Symbolisme Français sur la Poésie Américaine*, Paris, 1929, pp. 273–275; and Alfred Kreymborg, *Our Singing Strength*, New York, 1929, pp. 490–494.

More recent studies are "The Method of Marianne Moore," in R(ichard) P. Blackmur, *The Double Agent*, New York, 1935, pp. 141–171; Morton D. Zabel, "A Literalist of the Imagination," in Morton D. Zabel, ed., *Literary Opinion in America*, New York, 1937, pp. 426–436; and Kenneth Burke, "Motives and Motifs in the Poetry of Marianne Moore," *Accent*, II (1942), 157–169. See also T. S. Eliot's introduction to *Selected Poems* (1935).

Manuscript poems of Marianne Moore are deposited in the Lockwood Memorial Library at the University of Buffalo.

A checklist, especially useful for secondary material, is in Fred B. Millett, *Contemporary American Authors*, New York, 1940, pp. 491–492. The most recent compilation of primary items is that of Frances Cheney, in Allen Tate, *Sixty American Poets, 1896–1944,* Washington, 1945, pp. 110–111.

## PAUL ELMER MORE
### *1864–1937*

SEPARATE WORKS

*Helena and Occasional Poems,* 1890; *The Great Refusal,* 1894; *Benjamin Franklin,* 1900; *The Jessica Letters* (with Cora M. Harris), 1904; *Shelburne Essays,* 1904, 1905, 1906, 1908, 1909, 1910, 1913, 1915, 1919, 1921; *Nietzsche,* 1912; *The Drift of Romanticism,* 1913 (*Shelburne Essays,* 8th ser.); *Aristocracy and Justice,* 1915 (*Shelburne Essays,* 9th ser.); *Platonism,* 1917; *With the Wits,* 1919 (*Shelburne Essays,* 10th ser.); *The Religion of Plato,* 1921 (The Greek Tradition, I); *A New England Group and Others,* 1921 (*Shelburne Essays,* 11th ser.); *Hellenistic Philosophies,* 1923 (The Greek Tradition, II); *The Christ of the New Testament,* 1924 (The Greek Tradition, III); *Christ the Word,* 1927 (The Greek Tradition, IV); *The Demon of the Absolute,* 1928 (New Shelburne Essays, I); *The Catholic Faith,* 1931 (The Greek Tradition, V); *The Sceptical Approach to Religion,* 1934 (New Shelburne Essays, II); *On Being Human,* 1936 (New Shelburne Essays, III); *Pages from an Oxford Diary,* 1937.

REPRINTS

Almost all of the essays included in the two "Shelburne Essays" series are reprints in part of material first issued in periodicals. The 3rd ed. of *Platonism* (1917) was issued in 1931 as a "Complementary Volume" to "The Greek Tradition" series. *The Catholic Faith* (1931) was reprinted, London, 1932, as *Christian Mysticism: A Critique. Selected Shelburne Essays,* New York, 1935, in World's Classics, included essays from 11 vols. of the first series (1904–1921).

BIOGRAPHY AND CRITICISM

An extended study of More as critic is Robert Shafer, *Paul Elmer More and American Criticism,* New Haven, 1935. More's place in the neo-humanist movement is also the subject of Louis J. A. Mercier, *Le Mouvement Humaniste aux Etats-Unis: W. C. Brownell, Irving Babbitt, Paul Elmer More,* Paris, 1928; and Folke Leander, *Humanism and Naturalism: A Comparative Study of Ernest Seillière, Irving Babbitt, and Paul Elmer More,* Göteborg, 1937.

Among earlier studies are Clarissa Rinaker, "The Dualism of Mr. P. E. More," *Philosophical Rev.,* XXVI (1917), 409–420; Harvey W. Peck, "Some Aspects of the Criticism of Paul Elmer More," *Sewanee Rev.,* XXVI

(1918), 63–84; and "An Imaginary Conversation with Mr. P. E. More," in Stuart P. Sherman, *Americans*, New York, 1922, pp. 316–336.

More recent are Jacob Zeitlin, ed., "Stuart P. Sherman and Paul Elmer More: Correspondence," *Bookman*, LXX (1929), 43–53; Philip S. Richards, "An American Platonist," *Nineteenth Cent.*, CV (1929), 479–489; Allen Tate, "The Fallacy of Humanism," *Hound and Horn*, III (1930), 234–258; G. S. Brett, "Paul Elmer More: A Study," *Univ. Toronto Quar.*, IV (1935), 279–295; W. Norman Pittenger, "Paul Elmer More as Theologian," *Amer. Church Mo.*, XLI (1937), 353–361; Rudolf Stamm, "Paul Elmer Mores Suche nach einer Lebendigen Tradition," *Englische Studien*, LXXII (1937), 58–72; "Paul E. More and the Gentle Reader," in George R. Elliott, *Humanism and Imagination*, Chapel Hill, N.C., 1938, pp. 46–65; Folke Leander, "More: Puritan *à rebours*," *Amer. Scholar*, VII (1938), 438–453; Stuart G. Brown, "Toward an American Tradition," *Sewanee Rev.*, XLVII (1939), 476–497; "Paul Elmer More," in John P. Pritchard, *Return to the Fountains*, Durham, N.C., 1942, pp. 180–190; Horace Gregory, "On Paul Elmer More and His Shelburne Essays," *Accent*, IV (1944), 140–149; J. Oates Whitney, in Willard Thorp, ed., *The Lives of Eighteen from Princeton*, Princeton, 1946, pp. 302–317; and M. D. C. Tait, "The Humanism of Paul Elmer More," *Univ. Toronto Quar.*, XVI (1947), 109–122.

Reminiscences are Louis T. More, "Shelburne Revisited: An Intimate Glimpse of Paul Elmer More," *Sewanee Rev.*, XLVIII (1940), 457–460; and J. Duncan Spaeth, "Conversations with Paul Elmer More," *Sewanee Rev.*, LI (1943), 532–545.

BIBLIOGRAPHY

An inclusive bibliography is Malcolm Young, *Paul Elmer More: A Bibliography*, Princeton, 1941.

## JOHN LOTHROP MOTLEY
### *1814–1877*

SEPARATE WORKS

*Morton's Hope; or, The Memoirs of a Provincial*, 1839; *Merry-Mount: A Romance of the Massachusetts Colony*, 1849; *The Rise of the Dutch Republic*, 1856; *History of the United Netherlands, from the Death of William the Silent, to the Twelve Years' Truce—1609*, 1860–1867; *The Life and Death of John of Barneveld*, 1874.

COLLECTED WORKS

The Netherlands Edition of *The Writings of John Lothrop Motley*,

London and New York, 1900, 17 vols., was edited by George W. Curtis. It omits several titles.

The correspondence of Motley, to the extent it has been published, is in Oliver Wendell Holmes, *John Lothrop Motley: A Memoir,* Boston, 1879; George W. Curtis, ed., *The Correspondence of John Lothrop Motley,* New York, 1889, 2 vols.—an invaluable supplement to Holmes's *Memoir;* Susan and Herbert A. St. J. Mildmay, eds., *John Lothrop Motley and His Family: Further Letters and Records,* London, 1910—prepared by his daughter and son-in-law; and James P. Grund, "Bismarck and Motley: With Correspondence Till Now Unpublished," *No. Amer. Rev.,* CLXVII (1898), 360–376, 481–496, 569–572.

EDITED TEXTS AND REPRINTS

*The Rise of the Dutch Republic,* London, 1856, 3 vols., has been reprinted many times; it is in the Everyman's Lib., London, 1906. *History of the United Netherlands,* London, 1860–1867, 4 vols., was published almost simultaneously in New York, 1861–1868. It has often been reprinted—most recently, New York, 1909.

A convenient reprint of selections is Chester P. Higby and Bradford T. Schantz, *John Lothrop Motley: Representative Selections, with Introduction, Bibliography, and Notes,* New York, 1939 (Amer. Writers Ser.).

BIOGRAPHY AND CRITICISM

No definitive life of Motley has been published. The most complete biography is that of Oliver Wendell Holmes, *John Lothrop Motley: A Memoir,* Boston, 1879, prepared at the request of the Massachusetts Historical Society, and first published in *The Writings of Oliver Wendell Holmes,* Boston, 1878, XI, 329–526. It is the work of a friend, written from close personal acquaintance.

The best brief biographical sketch is that of Edward P. Cheyney in *Dict. Amer. Biog.* (1934). Two analyses of Motley as man of letters are "John Lothrop Motley," in Orie W. Long, *Literary Pioneers,* Cambridge, 1935, pp. 199–224—with emphasis upon his life and studies abroad; and "The Boston Historians: Motley," in Van Wyck Brooks, *The Flowering of New England,* New York, 1936, pp. 323–342. A further critical analysis is that of Higby and Schantz in their *John Lothrop Motley: Representative Selections* (1939), pp. xi–cxxxi.

Two earlier studies are "John Lothrop Motley," in John S. Bassett, *The Middle Group of American Historians,* New York, 1917, pp. 223–232; and Ruth Putnam, "Motley," in *Camb. Hist. Amer. Lit.,* II (1918), 131–147.

Special studies are "Motley's Correspondence," in George E. Woodberry, *Literary Memoirs,* New York, 1921, pp. 227–238; and Bradford T. Schantz,

"Motley's 'The Chevalier de Sataniski,'" *Amer. Lit.*, XIII (1941), 155–157—
dealing with a story published serially in *Graham's Magazine* (1844).

PRIMARY SOURCES

The most important published source material is Motley's own correspondence. Essential also are the Holmes's *Memoir* (1879), and the Mildmay
records assembled in *John Lothrop Motley and His Family* (1910). Reminiscences of Motley are in the biographies and published journals of other
New England men of letters during the mid-nineteenth century. Three useful studies are "Motley, the Historian," in Edwin P. Whipple, *Recollections
of Eminent Men,* Boston, 1887, pp. 155–203; William D. Howells, *Literary
Friends and Acquaintance,* New York, 1900, pp. 93–97; and Henry C. Lodge,
"Some Early Memoirs," *Scribner's Mag.,* LIII (1913), 714–729—including
two letters not found elsewhere.

The two chief collections of manuscripts are in the library of the Massachusetts Historical Society, and in the National Archives.

BIBLIOGRAPHY

The bibliography in Higby and Schantz, *John Lothrop Motley: Representative Selections* (1939), pp. cxxxv–clxi, is annotated and selective, and the
fullest listing to date. An earlier bibliography is that in the *Camb. Hist. Amer.
Lit.,* II (1918), 501–503.

## JOHN MUIR
### *1838–1914*

SEPARATE WORKS

*The Mountains of California,* 1894; *Our National Parks,* 1901; *Stickeen,*
1909; *Edward Henry Harriman,* 1911; *My First Summer in the Sierra,* 1911;
*The Yosemite,* 1912; *The Story of My Boyhood and Youth,* 1913.

Muir's writings published posthumously include *Letters to a Friend:
Written to Mrs. Ezra S. Carr, 1866–1879,* Boston, 1915; *Travels in Alaska,*
1915; *A Thousand-Mile Walk to the Gulf,* 1916—a journal of his trip made
in 1868. William F. Badé edited *The Cruise of the Corwin,* Boston, 1918,
and *Steep Trails,* Boston, 1918. Muir also edited *Picturesque California and
the Region West of the Rocky Mountains, from Alaska to Mexico,* San
Francisco, 1888—a lavishly illustrated western guidebook.

COLLECTED WORKS

William F. Badé edited *The Writings of John Muir,* Boston, 1916–1924,

10 vols. He further edited *The Life and Letters of John Muir*, Boston, 1923–1924, 2 vols. Hitherto unpublished journals were recently edited by Linnie M. Wolfe, *John of the Mountains: The Unpublished Journals of John Muir*, Boston, 1938.

BIOGRAPHY AND CRITICISM

*Son of the Wilderness: The Life of John Muir*, New York, 1945, by Linnie M. Wolfe, is an admiring biography. The sketch in *Dict. Amer. Biog.* (1934) was contributed by William F. Badé. A very useful study is "Muir," in Norman Foerster, *Nature in American Literature*, New York, 1923, pp. 238–263.

Material of a primary nature is in S[amuel] Hall Young, *Alaska Days with John Muir*, New York, 1915. See also John Muir's *The Story of My Boyhood and Youth*, Boston, 1913. A checklist of first editions is in Jacob Blanck, *Merle Johnson's American First Editions*, 4th ed., New York, 1942. A checklist of secondary sources especially useful for published memoirs and reminiscences is in Linnie M. Wolfe's *Life* (1945), pp. 349–350.

# MARY NOAILLES MURFREE
## ("CHARLES EGBERT CRADDOCK")
### *1850–1922*

SEPARATE WORKS

*In the Tennessee Mountains*, 1884; *Where the Battle Was Fought*, 1884; *Down the Ravine*, 1885; *The Prophet of the Great Smoky Mountains*, 1885; *In the Clouds*, 1886; *The Story of Keedon Bluffs*, 1887; *The Despot of Broomsedge Cove*, 1888; *In the "Stranger People's" Country*, 1891; *His Vanished Star*, 1894; *The Mystery of Witch-Face Mountain*, 1895; *The Phantoms of the Foot-Bridge*, 1895; *The Young Mountaineers*, 1897; *The Juggler*, 1897; *The Bushwhackers*, 1899; *The Story of Old Fort Loudon*, 1899; *The Champion*, 1902; *A Spectre of Power*, 1903; *The Frontiersmen*, 1904; *The Storm Centre*, 1905; *The Amulet*, 1906; *The Windfall*, 1907; *The Fair Mississippian*, 1908; *The Raid of the Guerilla*, 1912; *The Ordeal*, 1912; *The Story of Duciehurst*, 1914.

Several stories still remain uncollected.

BIOGRAPHY AND CRITICISM

A recent critical biography is Edd W. Parks, *Charles Egbert Craddock (Mary Noailles Murfree)*, Chapel Hill, N.C., 1941. The sketch in *Dict. Amer. Biog.* (1934) was contributed by Charles L. Lewis.

Brief estimates are Arthur H. Quinn, *American Fiction* . . . , New York, 1936, pp. 368–371 and Fred L. Pattee, *A History of American Literature Since 1870,* New York, 1915, pp. 308–316. See also Montrose J. Moses, *The Literature of the South,* New York, 1910, pp. 464–468.

Special studies are Milton T. Adkins, "The Mountains and Mountaineers of Craddock's Fiction," *Mag. Amer. Hist.,* XXIV (1890), 305–309; "Charles Egbert Craddock," in William M. Baskervill, *Southern Writers* . . . , Nashville, I (1897), 357–404; and "Charles Egbert Craddock," in Harry A. Toulmin, *Social Historians,* Boston, 1911, pp. 59–97.

A European study is Alfred Reichert, *Charles Egbert Craddock und die Amerikanische Short-Story,* Leipzig, 1912.

The leading manuscript collection is in Emory University Library at Atlanta.

The best bibliographical listing of primary and secondary material is in Edd W. Parks's life, pp. 237–249.


## (BENJAMIN) FRANK(LIN) NORRIS
### *1870–1902*

SEPARATE WORKS

*Yvernelle,* 1891; *Moran of the Lady Letty,* 1898; *McTeague,* 1899; *Blix,* 1899; *A Man's Woman,* 1900; *The Octopus,* 1901; *The Pit,* 1903; *The Responsibilities of the Novelist,* 1903; *A Deal in Wheat,* 1903; *The Joyous Miracle,* 1906; *The Third Circle,* 1909; *Vandover and the Brute,* 1914; *The Surrender of Santiago,* 1917; *Frank Norris of "The Wave": Stories and Sketches from the San Francisco Weekly, 1893–1897,* 1931 (ed. by Oscar Lewis).


COLLECTED WORKS AND REPRINTS

*The Complete Works of Frank Norris,* Garden City, N.Y., 1928, was issued in 10 vols., of which Vol. X is "Collected Writings Hitherto Unpublished in Book Form." Willard E. Martin, Jr., edited "Two Uncollected Essays by Frank Norris," *Amer. Lit.,* VIII (1936), 190–198. Two novels by Norris have been published in the Modern Lib.: *McTeague* (1918); and *The Pit* (1934). *The Octopus* was reprinted in 1947.


BIOGRAPHY AND CRITICISM

A narrative and critical life is Franklin Walker, *Frank Norris: A Biography,* New York, 1932. The latest biography is Ernest Marchand, *Frank Norris: A Study,* Stanford Univ., Calif., 1942. Two studies of French influence on Norris are Marius Biencourt, *Une Influence du Naturalisme Français en Amérique: Frank Norris,* Paris, 1933; and L. Ahnebrink, *The Influence of Emile Zola on Frank Norris,* Cambridge, 1947.

Other critical studies are C. Hartley Grattan, "Frank Norris," *Bookman,* LXIX (1929), 506–510; Vernon L. Parrington, *Main Currents in American Thought,* New York, III (1930), 329–334; Herbert Edwards, "Zola and the American Critics," *Amer. Lit.,* IV (1932), 114–129; Paul H. Bixler, "Frank Norris's Literary Reputation," *Amer. Lit.,* VI (1934), 109–121; Harry Hartwick, *The Foreground of American Fiction,* New York, 1934, pp. 45–66; Willard E. Martin, Jr., "Frank Norris's Reading at Harvard College," *Amer. Lit.,* VII (1935), 203–204; Edward E. Cassady, "Muckraking in the Gilded Age," *Amer. Lit.,* XIII (1941), 134–141; Charles C. Walcutt, "Frank Norris on Realism and Naturalism," *Amer. Lit.,* XIII (1941), 61–63; and "Frank Norris," in Walter F. Taylor, *The Economic Novel in America,* Chapel Hill, N.C., 1942, pp. 282–306.

Special studies of *The Octopus* are Willard E. Martin, Jr., "The Establishment of the Order of Printings . . . ," *Amer. Lit.,* V (1933), 17–28; H. Willard Reninger, "Norris Explains *The Octopus:* A Correlation of His Theory and Practice," *Amer. Lit.,* XII (1940), 218–227; and George W. Meyer, "A New Interpretation of *The Octopus," College Eng.,* IV (1943), 351–359.

Few early critical studies are significant. Two studies which recognize Norris as an artist are William D. Howells, "Frank Norris," *No. Amer. Rev.,* CLXXV (1902), 769–778; and Denison H. Clift, "The Artist in Frank Norris," *Pacific Mo.,* XVII (1907), 313–322. A longer study is "Frank Norris," in John C. Underwood, *Literature and Insurgency,* New York, 1914, pp. 130–178. See also C. C. Dobie, "Frank Norris, Or Up from Culture," *Amer. Mercury,* XIII (1928), 412–424.

## BIBLIOGRAPHY

Many of Norris's letters were destroyed, and no collection of them has been published. The fullest bibliographical listings are in Ernest Marchand, *Frank Norris: A Study* (1942), pp. 241–249; and Marius Biencourt, *Une Influence . . .* (1933), 233–244—especially useful for the listing of French studies. Other listings are Joseph Gaer, ed., *Frank Norris: Bibliography and Biographical Data,* Calif. Lit. Research Proj., Monograph No. 3, 1934; and Harvey Taylor, *Frank Norris: Two Poems and 'Kim' Reviewed, with a Bibliography,* San Francisco, 1930.

# CLIFFORD ODETS
*b. 1906*

PLAYS *

*Awake and Sing,* 1935; *Three Plays* . . . : *Awake and Sing; Waiting for Lefty; Till the Day I Die,* 1935; *Paradise Lost* (1935), 1936; *Golden Boy,* 1937; *Rocket to the Moon* (1938), 1939; *Night Music,* 1940; *Clash by Night* (1941), 1942.

*Six Plays of Clifford Odets* is a reprint in the Modern Library, New York, 1939.

BIOGRAPHY AND CRITICISM

Significant criticism of Odets as playwright is Joseph W. Krutch, *The American Drama Since 1918: An Informal History,* New York, 1939, pp. 263–277. See also Burns Mantle, *Contemporary American Playwrights,* New York, 1938, pp. 115–121; John McCarten, "Revolution's Number One Boy," *New Yorker,* Jan. 22, 1938, pp. 21–27; Edith J. R. Isaacs, "Clifford Odets: First Chapters," *Theatre Arts Mo.,* XXIII (1939), 257–264; and R. S. Warshow, "Poet of the Jewish Middle Class," *Commentary,* I (1946), 17–22.

A bio-bibliography is in Fred B. Millett, *Contemporary American Authors,* New York, 1940, pp. 512–514.

# EUGENE (GLADSTONE) O'NEILL
*b. 1888*

SEPARATE WORKS

*Thirst and Other One Act Plays,* 1914; *Bound East for Cardiff,* 1916; *Before Breakfast,* 1916; *The Moon of the Caribbees, and Six Other Plays of the Sea,* 1919; *Beyond the Horizon,* 1920; *Gold,* 1920; *The Emperor Jones, Diff'rent,* and *The Straw,* 1921; *The Hairy Ape, Anna Christie,* and *The First Man,* 1922; *The Dreamy Kid,* 1922; *All God's Chillun Got Wings,* 1924; *Welded,* 1924; *Desire Under the Elms,* 1925; *The Great God Brown, The Fountain,* and *The Moon of the Caribbees, and Other Plays,* 1926; *Marco Millions,* 1927; *Lazarus Laughed,* 1927; *Strange Interlude,* 1928; *Dynamo,* 1929; *Mourning Becomes Electra,* 1931; *Ah! Wilderness,* 1933; *Days Without End,* 1934; *The Iceman Cometh,* 1946.

* Dates in parentheses are of production when it differs from publication or when publication has not occurred.

Dates of production for O'Neill's plays through 1934 may be identified in the volume by Arthur H. Quinn mentioned below, pp. 384-386.

## COLLECTED WORKS

Editions of O'Neill's collected works have been issued as follows: *The Complete Works of Eugene O'Neill*, New York, 1924, 2 vols.; *Complete Works*, New York, 1925, 4 vols.; *Plays*, New York, 1925-26, 5 vols.; *Plays*, New York, 1941, 3 vols. The most complete collection is *The Plays of Eugene O'Neill*, New York, 1934-1935, 12 vols.

## REPRINTS

Separate plays have been reprinted, sometimes with introductions, in almost every American drama collection issued since 1914. The Modern Library includes four separate O'Neill collections, as follows: *The Moon of the Caribbees and Six Other Plays of the Sea*, with an introduction by George J. Nathan, New York, 1923; *The Emperor Jones and The Straw*, with an introduction by Dudley Nichols, New York, 1928; *The Long Voyage Home: Seven Plays of the Sea*, New York, 1940; and *Nine Plays . . . Selected by the Author*, with an introduction by Joseph Wood Krutch, New York, 1941.

Some published letters of O'Neill appear in Isaac Goldberg, *The Theatre of George Jean Nathan . . .* , New York, 1926.

## BIOGRAPHY AND CRITICISM

Two important studies of O'Neill as dramatist are "Eugene O'Neill, Poet and Mystic," in Arthur H. Quinn, *A History of the American Drama from the Civil War to the Present Day*, rev. ed., New York, 1936, II, 165-206; and "Tragedy: Eugene O'Neill," in Joseph Wood Krutch, *The American Drama Since 1918 . . .* , New York, 1939, pp. 73-133. Other general studies are Sophus Keith Winther, *Eugene O'Neill: A Critical Study*, New York, 1934; Richard D. Skinner, *Eugene O'Neill: A Poet's Quest . . .* , New York, 1935; Barrett H. Clark, *Eugene O'Neill: The Man and His Plays*, rev. ed., New York, 1947; "Eugene O'Neill," in Eleanor Flexner, *American Playwrights . . .* , New York, 1938, pp. 130-197; Otto Koischwitz, *O'Neill*, Berlin, 1938.

Three studies of O'Neill abroad have been made by Horst Frenz, "Eugene O'Neill in Russia," *Poet-Lore*, XLIX (1943), 241-247; "A List of Foreign Editions and Translations of Eugene O'Neill's Dramas," *Bul. Bibl.*, XVIII (1943), 33-34; "Eugene O'Neill in France," *Books Abroad* (Spring, 1944), 140-141.

Other studies are "The Playwright Unbound: Eugene O'Neill," in Thomas H. Dickinson, *Playwrights of the New American Theater*, New

York, 1925, pp. 56–123; "Eugene O'Neill," in Thomas K. Whipple, *Spokesmen*, New York, 1928, pp. 230–253; Elizabeth S. Sergeant, *Fire Under the Andes*, New York, 1927, pp. 81–104; I. N. Hayward, "Strindberg's Influence on Eugene O'Neill," *Poet-Lore*, XXXIX (1928), 596–604; Charles Cestre, "Eugène O'Neill et les Surgissements du Tréfond," *Revue Anglo-Amér.*, VI (1928), 131–144; Walter P. Eaton, *The Drama in English*, New York, 1930, pp. 331–343; Francis Ferguson, "Eugene O'Neill," *Hound and Horn*, III (1930), 145–160; Barrett H. Clark, "Aeschylus and O'Neill," *English Jour.*, XXI (1932), 699–710; Lionel Trilling, "Eugene O'Neill," in Malcolm Cowley, ed., *After the Genteel Tradition*, New York, 1937, pp. 127–141; Walter P. Eaton, "O'Neill: 'New Risen Attic Stream,'" *Amer. Scholar*, VI (1937), 304–312; Homer E. Woodbridge, "Eugene O'Neill," *So. Atl. Quar.*, XXXVII (1938), 22–35; Clara Blackburn, "Continental Influences on Eugene O'Neill's Expressionistic Drama," *Amer. Lit.*, XIII (1941), 109–133; Frederic I. Carpenter, "The Romantic Tragedy of Eugene O'Neill," *College Eng.*, VI (1945), 250–258; Eric Bentley, "The Return of Eugene O'Neill," *Atl. Mo.*, CLXXVIII (1946), 64–66; and George J. Nathan, "O'Neill: A Critical Summation," *Amer. Mercury*, LXIII (1946), 713–719.

PRIMARY SOURCES

There is a large collection of O'Neill manuscripts in the Princeton University Library, including the holographs of many plays, in the O'Neill collection; see Marguerite L. McAneny, "Eleven Manuscripts of Eugene O'Neill," *Princeton Univ. Lib. Chron.*, IV (1943), 86–89. Further important material is in the Yale University Library; see Walter P. Eaton, "The Eugene O'Neill Collection," *Yale Univ. Lib. Gaz.*, XVIII (1943), 5–8.

BIBLIOGRAPHY

Ralph Sanborn and Barrett H. Clark prepared *A Bibliography of the Works of Eugene O'Neill*, New York, 1931, including 51 pages of hitherto unpublished poetry. The listing of primary and secondary material in Allan G. Halline, *American Plays*, New York, 1935, pp. 763–766, is useful.


# JAMES OTIS
## *1725-1783*

WORKS

*The Rudiments of Latin Prosody* . . . *and the Principles of Harmony in Poetic and Prosaic Composition*, 1760; *A Vindication of the Conduct of the House of Representatives*, 1762; *The Rights of the British Colonies Asserted and Proved*, 1764; *Considerations on Behalf of the Colonists, in a Letter to a Noble Lord, 1765; Brief Remarks on the Defence of the Halifax Libel on the British-American Colonies*, 1765; *A Vindication of the British Colonies . . .*, 1765.

All the political pamphlets have been edited, with an introduction, by Charles F. Mullett, *Some Political Writings of James Otis,* Columbia, Mo., 1929, 2 vols. Otis contributed many articles, signed and unsigned, to the *Boston Gazette* during the years 1761–1769.

### BIOGRAPHY AND CRITICISM

The best brief sketch of Otis is that in *Dict. Amer. Biog.* (1934), contributed by Samuel E. Morison. No biography has yet superseded William Tudor's *The Life of James Otis . . .*, Boston, 1823. Francis Bowen wrote the sketch in Jared Sparks, *The Library of American Biography,* 2nd ser., Vol. II (1847).

A study of Otis as a man of letters is Moses C. Tyler, *The Literary History of the American Revolution, 1763–1783,* New York, 1897, I, 30–51, 75–79, 86–90. Two studies of Otis as political statesman are J. H. Ellis, "James Otis," *Amer. Law Rev.,* III (1869), 641–665; and Benjamin F. Wright, Jr., *American Interpretations of Natural Law . . .*, Cambridge, 1931, pp. 64–70.

### PRIMARY SOURCES

The Otis family manuscripts and papers are in the Massachusetts Historical Society, though very few were written by James Otis, since he corresponded very little and destroyed all his papers before his death. For an unsympathetic contemporary estimate, see the account in Thomas Hutchinson, *The History of the Colony and Province of Massachusetts-Bay* (ed. Lawrence Shaw Mayo), Cambridge, 1936, III, 63–82.

The fullest bibliographical listing, especially of secondary sources, is that of Samuel E. Morison in *Dict. Amer. Biog.* (1934).

## THOMAS NELSON PAGE
### 1853–1922

### SEPARATE WORKS

*In Ole Virginia*, 1887; *Befo' de War* (dialect verses, with A. C. Gordon), 1888; *Two Little Confederates*, 1888; *On Newfound River*, 1891; *Among the Camps*, 1891; *Elsket and Other Stories*, 1891; *The Old South*, 1892; *The Burial of the Guns*, 1894; *Pastime Stories*, 1894; *The Old Gentleman of the Black Stock*, 1897; *Social Life in Old Virginia*, 1897; *Two Prisoners*, 1898;

*Red Rock,* 1898; *Santa Claus's Partner,* 1899; *Gordon Keith,* 1903; *Bred in the Bone,* 1904; *The Negro: The Southerner's Problem,* 1904; *The Coast of Bohemia,* 1906; *Under the Crust,* 1907; *The Old Dominion: Her Making and Her Manners,* 1908; *Robert E. Lee: The Southerner,* 1908; *Tommy Trot's Visit to Santa Claus,* 1908; *John Marvel: Assistant,* 1909; *Robert E. Lee: Man and Soldier,* 1911; *The Land of the Spirit,* 1913; *Italy and the World War,* 1920; *Dante and His Influence,* 1922; *Washington and Its Romance,* 1923; *The Red Riders,* 1924.

*The Novels, Stories, Sketches and Poems of Thomas Nelson Page* were published, New York, 1906–1918, 18 vols.

#### BIOGRAPHY AND CRITICISM

Page's brother Rosewell Page wrote *Thomas Nelson Page: A Memoir of a Virginia Gentleman,* New York, 1923. A good brief sketch is that of John H. Nelson in *Dict. Amer. Biog.* (1934). Standard critical estimates are Fred L. Pattee, *A History of American Literature Since 1870,* New York, 1915, pp. 265–269; and Arthur H. Quinn, *American Fiction,* New York, 1936, pp. 357–362. See also Charles W. Kent, "Thomas Nelson Page," *So. Atl. Quar.,* VI (1907), 263–271; Edwin Mims, "Thomas Nelson Page," *Atl. Mo.,* C (1907), 109–115; Harry A. Toulmin, *Social Historians,* Boston, 1911, pp. 1–32; and Montrose J. Moses, *The Literature of the South,* New York, 1910, pp. 446–448.

The chief manuscript depository is the library of Duke University. It has more than 9,000 items. Autobiographical material appears especially in *Two Little Confederates* (1888) and *The Burial of the Guns* (1894).

Bibliographical data are in Jacob Blanck, *Merle Johnson's American First Editions,* 4th ed., New York, 1942.

## THOMAS PAINE
### *1737–1809*

#### SEPARATE WORKS

*The Case of the Officers of Excise,* 1772, 1793; *Epistle to the People Called Quakers,* 1776; *Common Sense,* 1776; *The Crisis,* 1776–1783; *Public Good,* 1780; *Letter Addressed to the Abbé Raynal,* 1782; *Dissertation on Government, the Affairs of the Bank, and Paper-Money,* 1786; *Prospects on the Rubicon,* 1787; *The Rights of Man,* 1791–1792; *A Letter Addressed to the Addressers,* 1792; *Reasons for Wishing to Preserve the Life of Louis Capet,* 1793; *The Age of Reason,* 1794–1796; *Dissertation on First-Principles of Government,* 1795; *The Decline and Fall of the English System of Finance,* 1796; *Letter to George Washington,* 1796; *Agrarian Justice,* 1797; *Letter to the*

*People of France and the French Armies,* 1797; *Compact Maritime,* 1801; *Letters to the Citizens of the United States of America,* 1802–1803; *Letter to the People of England,* 1804; *Examination of the Passages in the New Testament,* 1807; *On the Origin of Freemasonry,* 1810; *Miscellaneous Poems,* 1819,

COLLECTED WORKS

The first critical and complete gathering of Paine's works is still the standard text: Moncure D. Conway, ed., *The Writings of Thomas Paine,* New York, 1894–1896, 4 vols. Others are Daniel E. Wheeler, ed., *Life and Writings of Thomas Paine,* New York, 1908, 10 vols., with a biographical introduction by Thomas C. Rickman, and appreciations by Leslie Stephen and others; and William M. Van der Weyde, ed., *The Life and Works of Thomas Paine,* New Rochelle, N.Y., 1925, 10 vols. Some material in the later collections, not always carefully identified, is omitted in the Conway edition. Early collections are *The Writings of Thomas Paine,* Albany, N.Y., 1792; *The Political Writings of Thomas Paine,* Charlestown, Mass., 1824, 2 vols., and *The Theological Works of Thomas Paine,* Boston, 1834.

Gatherings of Paine's letters are in the Silas Deane Papers, *Coll. Connecticut Hist. Soc.,* II (1870), 127–368, XXIII (1930), *passim;* and in Deane Papers, *Coll. New-York Hist. Soc.,* XIX–XXIII (1887–1890), *passim.* Other published correspondence is in *Coll. New-York Hist. Soc.,* XI (1878), 470–488— to Robert Morris; Moncure D. Conway, ed., "Unpublished Letters of Thomas Paine," *Nation,* LXII (1896), 471–472; Louise P. Kellogg, ed., "Letter of Thomas Paine, 1793," *Amer. Hist. Rev.,* XXIX (1924), 501–505; Dixon Wecter, "Thomas Paine and the Franklins," *Amer. Lit.,* XII (1940), 306–317 —letters showing their agreement in the cause of independence; and Harold W. Landin, "Some Letters of Thomas Paine and William Short on the Nootka Sound Crisis," *Jour. Modern Hist.,* XIII (1941), 357–374.

REPRINTS

Three recent reprints have made the writings of Paine easily available: Harry H. Clark, ed., *Thomas Paine: Representative Selections, with Introduction, Bibliography, and Notes,* New York, 1944 (Amer. Writers Ser.)— with full documentation; Howard Fast, ed., *The Selected Work of Tom Paine, Set in the Framework of His Life,* New York, 1945—"Common Sense," "Rights of Man," "The Age of Reason," "Letter to Washington," and some of the "Crisis Papers," with running commentary; and Philip S. Foner, ed., *The Complete Writings of Thomas Paine,* New York, 1945, 2 vols., arranged by subject, and containing material not in previous collections. Harry H. Clark edited *Six New Letters of Thomas Paine: Being Pieces on the Five Per Cent Duty Addressed to the Citizens of Rhode Island,*

Madison, Wis., 1939—here first reprinted from the Providence *Gazette and Country Journal* of 1782 and 1783. Other reprints are Carl Van Doren, ed., *Selections from the Writings of Thomas Paine,* New York, 1922 (Modern Lib.); Arthur W. Peach, ed., *Selections from the Works of Thomas Paine,* New York, 1928 (Amer. Authors Ser.); *Complete and Unabridged Selections from the Writings of Thomas Paine,* Washington, 1935; John Dos Passos, ed., *The Living Thoughts of Tom Paine,* London, 1940; and *Basic Writings of Thomas Paine: Common Sense, Rights of Man, Age of Reason,* New York, 1942.

### BIOGRAPHY AND CRITICISM

*The Life of Thomas Paine* . . . , by Moncure D. Conway, New York, 1892, 2 vols., is a work of extensive research and, though not discriminating, remains the standard biography. It is supplemented by additional material in a translation: *Thomas Paine (1737–1809) et la Révolution dans les Deux Mondes,* Paris, 1900. Other lives recently published are Hesketh Pearson, *Tom Paine, Friend of Mankind,* New York, 1937; Marie A. Pardee, *Thomas Paine, 1737–1809, d'Après ses Écrits et les Archives* . . . , Paris, 1938; Frank Smith, *Thomas Paine, Liberator,* New York, 1938; and William E. Woodward, *Tom Paine: America's Godfather, 1737–1809,* New York, 1945. Earlier lives are Ellery Sedgwick, *Thomas Paine,* Boston, 1899, and Mary A. Best, *Thomas Paine, Prophet and Martyr of Democracy* . . . , New York, 1927.

Estimates of Paine have usually been made with strong bias. During his lifetime two very hostile biographies were published: George Chalmers, *The Life of Thomas Paine* . . . , London, 1791, and James Cheetham, *The Life of Thomas Paine* . . . , New York, 1809. The best of the early lives is Thomas C. Rickman, *The Life of Thomas Paine,* London, 1814, written in part to counterbalance Cheetham. It is less adulatory than Calvin Blanchard, *Life of Thomas Paine* . . . , New York, 1860 (and 1877). Three documented articles by Frederick Sheldon add some material not given elsewhere: "Thomas Paine's Second Appearance in the United States," *Atl. Mo.,* IV (1859), 1–17; "Tom Paine's First Appearance in America," *ibid.,* 565–575—especially for the years 1774–1787; and "Thomas Paine in England and France," *ibid.,* 690–709—a good account of the years 1787–1802.

The two most authoritative brief accounts are by Leslie Stephen, in *Dict. Nat. Biog.,* and Crane Brinton, in *Dict. Amer. Biog.* (1934). The introduction in Harry H. Clark, ed., *Thomas Paine: Representative Selections,* New York, 1944, pp. xi–cxviii, is a documented summary of Paine's political, religious, and ethical ideas and of his literary theory and practice.

Studies of Paine as a man of letters are Harry H. Clark, "Thomas Paine's Theories of Rhetoric," *Trans. Wisconsin Acad. Sci., Arts, and Letters,*

XXVIII (1933), 307-339; and Moses C. Tyler, *The Literary History of the American Revolution,* I (1897), 452-474.

Paine as a political economist is presented in C. E. Merriam, Jr., "Thomas Paine's Political Theories," *Pol. Sci. Quar.,* XIV (1899), 389-403; C. E. Persinger, "The Political Philosophy of Thomas Paine," *Univ. Nebraska Grad. Bul.,* 6th ser., No. 3 (1901), 54-74; Albert Matthews, "Thomas Paine and the Declaration of Independence," *Proc. Mass. Hist. Soc.,* XLIII (1910), 241-253; Norman Sykes in F. J. C. Hearnshaw, ed., *The Social and Political Ideas . . . of the Revolutionary Era,* London, 1931, pp. 100-140; Joseph Dorfman, "The Economic Philosophy of Thomas Paine," *Pol. Sci. Quar.,* LIII (1938), 372-386; Howard Penniman, "Thomas Paine, Democrat," *Amer. Pol. Sci. Rev.,* XXXVII (1943), 244-262.

Studies of Paine's religious thinking are Harry H. Clark, "An Historical Interpretation of Thomas Paine's Religion," *Univ. Calif. Chron.,* XXXV (1933), 56-87; and two articles by Robert B. Falk: "Thomas Paine: Deist or Quaker," *Pennsylvania Mag. Hist. and Biog.,* LXII (1938), 52-63; and "Thomas Paine and the Attitude of the Quakers to the American Revolution," *ibid.,* LXIII (1939), 302-310.

Examinations of Paine's reputation both during his life and since are Harry H. Clark, "Toward a Reinterpretation of Thomas Paine," *Amer. Lit.,* V (1933), 133-145; and Dixon Wecter, "Hero in Reverse," *Virginia Quar. Rev.,* XVIII (1942), 243-259.

Other studies of aspects of Paine's life and writing are Caroline Hogue, "The Authorship and Date of 'The American Patriot's Prayer,'" *Amer. Lit.,* II (1930), 168-172—on a poem wrongly ascribed to Paine; Frank Smith, "New Light on Thomas Paine's First Year in America, 1775," *Amer. Lit.,* I (1930), 347-371; *idem,* "The Authorship of 'An Occasional Letter Upon the Female Sex,'" *Amer. Lit.,* II (1930), 277-280; Marjorie Nicholson, "Thomas Paine, Edward Nares, and Mrs. Piozzi's Marginalia," *Huntington Lib. Bul.,* No. 10 (1936), 103-135; Harry H. Clark, "Thomas Paine's Relation to Voltaire and Rousseau," *Revue Anglo-Amér.,* IX (1932), 305-318, 393-405; R. R. Palmer, "Tom Paine, Victim of the Rights of Man," *Pennsylvania Mag. Hist. and Biog.,* LXVI (1942), 161-175; Darrel Abel, "The Significance of the Letter to the Abbé Raynal in the Progress of Thomas Paine's Thought," *ibid.,* 176-190; V. E. Gibbens, "Tom Paine and the Idea of Progress," *ibid.,* 191-204; and J. J. Meng, "Thomas Paine: French Propagandist in the United States," *Records Amer. Catholic Hist. Soc.,* Philadelphia, LVII (1946), 1-21.

PRIMARY SOURCES

A shrewd contemporary rebuttal of *The Rights of Man* is "Letters of

Publicola," in the *Writings of John Quincy Adams* (ed. W. C. Ford), I (1913), 65–110. References to Paine and material about him are scattered through the collected works of statesmen of the Revolution.

A large part of Paine's unpublished letters and papers was destroyed by fire while in the possession of General Bonneville. Some manuscripts are in the Rutgers University Library.

BIBLIOGRAPHY

No full bibliography of Paine has been published. The listing in Harry H. Clark, ed., *Thomas Paine: Representative Selections,* New York, 1944, pp. cxxv–cli, is selective and annotated, and useful especially for secondary sources.

# THEODORE PARKER
## *1810–1860*

SEPARATE WORKS

*A Discourse of Matters Pertaining to Religion,* 1842; *A Letter to the People of the United States Touching the Matter of Slavery,* 1848; *Speeches, Addresses, and Occasional Sermons,* 1852; *Ten Sermons of Religion,* 1853; *Sermons of Theism, Atheism, and the Popular Theology,* 1853; *Additional Speeches, Addresses, and Occasional Sermons,* 1855; *The Trial of Theodore Parker, for the "Misdemeanor" of a Speech in Faneuil Hall Against Kidnapping,* 1855.

Parker edited the *Massachusetts Quarterly Review,* 1848–1850.

COLLECTED WORKS

The early posthumous collections of Parker's writings include *Prayers,* Boston, 1862; *Lessons from the World of Matter and the World of Man,* Boston, 1865, edited with a preface by Rufus Leighton; *Historic Americans,* Boston, 1870; *Views of Religion,* 1885. *The Collected Works of Theodore Parker,* London, 1863–1874, 14 vols., is poorly edited and incomplete. The Centenary Edition of *The Works of Theodore Parker,* Boston, 1907–1913, 15 vols., is not complete, but it is well edited; each volume is supplied with preface and notes, individually prepared by George W. Cooke, Samuel A. Eliot, Thomas W. Higginson, James K. Hosmer, Frank B. Sanborn, Samuel B. Stewart, and Charles W. Wendte.

Many of Parker's letters are in John Weiss's *Life* (2 vols., 1864), but no recent collection has been made; a few more are included in Joseph Fort Newton, *Lincoln and Herndon,* Cedar Rapids, Iowa, 1910.

BIOGRAPHY AND CRITICISM

Parker was widely known and appreciated abroad, and biographies of him were published in several languages. The most authoritative of recent studies is Henry S. Commager, *Theodore Parker,* Boston, 1936. The best of the early lives is Octavius Brooks Frothingham, *Theodore Parker: A Biography,* Boston, 1874. The earliest is John Weiss, *Life and Correspondence of Theodore Parker,* New York, 1864, 2 vols., invaluable as source material. John W. Chadwick published *Theodore Parker, Preacher and Reformer,* Boston, 1900.

The study of Parker in Vernon L. Parrington, *Main Currents in American Thought,* New York, II (1927), 414-425, is brief but significant. The sketch of Parker in *Dict. Amer. Biog.* (1934), is by Francis A. Christie.

Special studies include that of Roy C. McCall in William N. Brigance, ed., *A History and Criticism of American Public Address,* New York, 1943, I, 238-264; Francis A. Christie, "Theodore Parker and Modern Theology," *Meadville Jour.,* XXV (1930), no. 1, 3-17; Henry S. Commager, "The Dilemma of Theodore Parker," *New Eng. Quar.,* VI (1933), 257-277; *idem,* "Tempest in a Boston Tea Cup," *ibid.,* 651-675; *idem,* "Theodore Parker, Intellectual Gourmand," *Amer. Scholar,* III (1934), 257-265; and Arthur I. Ladu, "The Political Ideas of Theodore Parker," *Studies in Philol.,* XXXIII (1941), 106-123. Useful for background are "Theodore Parker," in S. B. Stewart, *Unitarianism: Its Origin and History,* Boston, 1890, pp. 220-244; and "Theodore Parker," in Daniel D. Addison, *The Clergy in American Life and Letters,* New York, 1900, pp. 229-267.

PRIMARY SOURCES

The two chief manuscript depositories are the Massachusetts Historical Society, with some twenty volumes of material, and the Boston Public Library, with nearly as much manuscript and Parker's own library of some 15,000 volumes.

Parker's "Letter to the Twenty-eighth Congregational Society: 'Theodore Parker's Experience as a Minister,'" not only is the best brief account of his public career, but is immensely important as a study of the intellectual life of Boston during the forties and fifties.

The memoirs and biographies of Parker's contemporaries are valuable as source material, especially those of Emerson, W. E. Channing, George Ripley, A. B. Alcott, George Bancroft, and Margaret Fuller.

BIBLIOGRAPHY

The extensive bibliographical listing by Charles W. Wendte in Vol. XV (1913) of the Centenary Edition of Parker's *Works* includes a calendar of his reviews, pamphlets, and memorial articles. The fullest listing of secondary material is in Henry S. Commager, *Theodore Parker* (1936), pp. 311–331. Still useful is the bibliography in John W. Chadwick, *Theodore Parker* (1900).

# FRANCIS PARKMAN
*1823–1893*

### SEPARATE WORKS

*The California and Oregon Trail,* 1849; *History of the Conspiracy of Pontiac and the War of the North American Tribes,* 1851; *Vassall Morton: A Novel,* 1856; *The Book of Roses,* 1866; *Pioneers of France in the New World,* 1865; *The Jesuits in North America in the Seventeenth Century,* 1867; *The Discovery of the Great West,* 1869; *The Old Regime in Canada,* 1874; *Count Frontenac and New France Under Louis XIV,* 1877; *Montcalm and Wolfe,* 1884; *A Half Century of Conflict,* 1892.

After 1879, *The Discovery of the Great West* (1869) was published as *La Salle and the Discovery of the Great West.*

### COLLECTED WORKS

Any authorized edition published after 1893 supplies a good text. The Champlain Edition of *The Works of Francis Parkman,* Boston, 1897–1901, 21 vols., contains an introduction by John Fiske. The Frontenac Edition of *The Works of Francis Parkman,* Boston, 1902, 20 vols., includes Farnham's *Life.* The most recent collection is the Centenary Edition of *The Works of Francis Parkman,* Boston, 1922, 12 vols.

Mason Wade edited *The Journals of Francis Parkman,* New York, 1947, 2 vols.—recently discovered, intrinsically important as part of the Parkman canon and for study of Parkman as historian and man of letters.

The letters of Parkman are published only in part. Many are reproduced in the biographies by Farnham and by Sedgwick, together with excerpts from Parkman's diary for the years 1841–1846. Two other gatherings are Don C. Seitz, ed., *Letters from Francis Parkman to E. G. Squier . . . ,* Cedar Rapids, Iowa, 1911, with biography and bibliographical footnotes; and John S. Bassett, ed., "Letters of Francis Parkman to Pierre Margry," in *Smith College Studies in Hist.,* VIII (1923), Nos. 3 and 4—some eighty-five letters, with introductory notes.[*]

Excerpts from Parkman's autobiography are printed in *Proc. Mass. Hist. Soc.,* 2nd ser., VIII (1893), 350–360.

---

[*] A great number have recently been discovered in the attic study of his Chestnut Street home.

### EDITED TEXTS AND REPRINTS

*The Oregon Trail* (1849) was edited from Parkman's notebooks by Mason Wade, New York, 1943. Other earlier reprints are New York, 1930, in Modern Readers' Ser., with an introduction by Hamlin Garland; New York, 1910, with an introduction by William E. Leonard; and New York, 1910, with notes and introduction by Ottis B. Sperlin.

*The Conspiracy of Pontiac* (1851) was reprinted, London and New York, 1927, 2 vols., in Everyman's Lib.; and also New York, 1929, with an introduction by Joseph Schafer, in the Modern Readers' Ser.

The most convenient selected text is that of Wilbur L. Schramm, *Francis Parkman: Representative Selections, with Introduction, Bibliography, and Notes,* New York, 1938.

### BIOGRAPHY AND CRITICISM

Mason Wade, *Francis Parkman, Heroic Historian,* New York, 1942, is an interpretive biography based on careful study of sources. Charles H. Farnnam, *A Life of Francis Parkman,* Boston, 1900, is the best of the earlier critical accounts. Henry D. Sedgwick, *Francis Parkman,* Boston, 1904 (Amer. Men of Letters), is a source book rather than a critical interpretation, with long excerpts from Parkman's diary.

The best brief narrative sketch is that of James T. Adams in *Dict. Amer. Biog.* (1934). The critical introduction in Wilbur L. Schramm, *Francis Parkman: Representative Selections* (1938), pp. xiii–cxvi, is important as a supplement to other interpretations.

Estimates of Parkman by Canadian historians are Henri R. Casgrain, "Francis Parkman," in *Biographies Canadiennes,* Quebec, 1875; George M. Wrong, "Francis Parkman," *Canadian Hist. Rev.,* IV (1923), 289–303; and Aegidius Fauteux, "Francis Parkman," *Bul. des Recherches Historiques,* XXXI (1925), 177–183.

Other estimates of Parkman as historian are John Fiske, "Francis Parkman," in *A Century of Science, and Other Essays,* Boston, 1899, pp. 194–264—to be found also in the Champlain Edition of Parkman's *Works,* Vol. I (1897); John S. Bassett, "Francis Parkman, the Man," *Sewanee Rev.,* X (1902), 285–301—an interpretive résumé; James Sullivan, "Sectionalism in Writing History," *Jour. N.Y. State Hist. Assn.,* II (1921), 73–88; and Clarence W. Alvord, "Francis Parkman," *Nation,* CXVII (1923), 394–396—a centennial estimate.

Studies of Parkman as a man of letters are William D. Howells, "Mr. Parkman's Histories," *Atl. Mo.,* XXXIV (1874), 602–610; Bliss Perry, "Some Personal Qualities of Francis Parkman," *Yale Rev.,* n.s. XIII (1924), 443–448—an analysis of the effect of Parkman's early reading; and "Francis

Parkman," in Van Wyck Brooks, *New England: Indian Summer,* New York, 1940, pp. 169–183.

Other special studies are "Francis Parkman," George M. Gould, in *Biographic Clinics,* Philadelphia, 1904, II, 131–202—on Parkman's maladies; Doane Robinson, "Parkman Not in Dakota," *So. Dakota Hist. Coll.,* XII (1924), 103–107; Joseph Schafer, "Francis Parkman, 1823–1923," *Mississippi Valley Hist. Rev.,* X (1924), 351–364; J. A. Russell, "Francis Parkman and the Real Indians," *Jour. Amer. Hist.,* XXII (1928), 121–129—Parkman's accuracy; Wilbur L. Schramm, "Parkman's Novel," *Amer. Lit.,* IX (1937), 218–227; *idem,* "A New Englander on the Road to Oregon," *New Eng. Quar.,* XIII (1940), 49–64; and Howard H. Peckham, "The Sources and Revisions of Parkman's *Pontiac,*" *Papers Bibl. Soc. Amer.,* XXXVII (1943), 293–307—a critical account of Parkman's use and evaluation of his sources.

PRIMARY SOURCES

Tributes and reminiscences published at the time of Parkman's death include O. B. Frothingham, "Memoir of Francis Parkman, LL.D.," *Proc. Mass. Hist. Soc.,* 2nd ser., VIII (1894), 520–562; J. M. Le Moine, "Reminiscences of Francis Parkman at Quebec," *Canadian Mag.,* III (1894), 493–497; Daniel D. Slade, "In the White Mountains with Francis Parkman in 1841," *New Eng. Mag.,* n.s. XI (1894), 94–99; Barrett Wendell, "Francis Parkman," *Proc. Amer. Acad. Arts and Sci.,* XXIX (1893–1894), 435–447; and Edward Wheelwright, "Memoir of Francis Parkman," *Pub. Col. Soc. Mass.,* I (1894), 304–350—documented biographical data. More recent reminiscences are Henry C. Lodge, "Francis Parkman," *Proc. Mass. Hist. Soc.,* 2nd ser. LVI (1923), 319–335.

The largest and most complete manuscript collection is deposited with the Massachusetts Historical Society. See their *Transactions,* 2nd ser., I, 360–362; III, 152–153; VI, 105, 391–392; VII, 348–349; VIII, 171. For the many other small, scattered collections, see Mason Wade, *Francis Parkman* (1942), p. ix.

BIBLIOGRAPHY

The biographies by Wade, pp. 453–456, and by Farnham, pp. xii–xiii, 359–364, both include checklists of Parkman's contributions to periodicals. That in Schramm's *Representative Selections* (1938), pp. cxxi–cxliv, is annotated and selective, and lists Parkman's reviews, prefaces, and sketches.

# FRANCIS DANIEL PASTORIUS
## *1651 to ca. 1720*

PRINTED WORKS

*Disputatio Inauguralis de Rasura Documentorum . . . pro Licentia Summos in utroque jure Honores ac Privilegia Doctoralia more Mayorum vite capessendi d. 23, Nov. 1676* (Altdorf—Juridical thesis); *Copia, eines von einem Sohn an seine Eltern aus America, abgelossenen Brieffes . . .* , dated Philadelphia, March 7, 1684—a published letter of the same date as *Sichere Nachricht auss America, wegen der Landschafft Pennsylvania. . . .* A full translation of this "Report," printed as *Pastorius' First Account of Pennsylvania,* is given in A. C. Myer, ed., *Narratives of Early Pennsylvania . . . ,* New York, 1912, pp. 392–411. A photo-facsimile of the original is in M. D. Learned, *The Life of Francis Daniel Pastorius . . . ,* Philadelphia, 1908, p. 128. *Vier kleine doch ungemeine und sehr nützliche Tractätlein . . . ,* Germantown, 1690; *Ein Send-Brieff offenhertziger Liebsbezeugung an die sogenannte Pietisten in Hoch-Teutschland,* Amsterdam, 1697; *Henry Bernhard Koster, William Davis, Thomas Rutter and Thomas Bowyer: Four Boasting Disputers of this World briefly rebuked . . . ,* New York, 1697; *A New Primmer or Methodical Directions to Attain the True Spelling, Reading, and Writing of English,* New York, *ca.* 1698; *Umständige geographische Beschreibung der zu allerletzt erfundenen Provintz Pensylvaniae,* Frankfurt and Leipzig, 1700 (translated fully by Gertrude S. Kimball in A. C. Myer, ed., *Narratives of Early Pennsylvania . . . ,* New York, 1912, pp. 353–448 as "Circumstantial Geographical Description of Pennsylvania," with an introduction by J. F. Jameson).

WRITINGS IN MANUSCRIPT

Much that is significant in the writing of Pastorius remains in the five volumes of manuscripts which are deposited in the Historical Society of Pennsylvania. The so-called "Beehive," a compendium of miscellaneous learning and quotation collected for his children, was begun in 1696. It is important for original verse which has yet to be critically evaluated. A discussion and partial reproduction of the contents is in Learned's *Life,* pp. 236–274.

BIOGRAPHY AND CRITICISM

A full-length biography, containing many reproductions of title pages and texts with extensive bibliographical information, is Marion Dexter Learned, *The Life of Francis Daniel Pastorius, the Founder of Germantown . . . with* an *Appreciation of Pastorius by Samuel Whitaker Pennypacker*, Philadelphia, 1908. The sketch of Pastorius in *Dict. Amer. Biog.* (1934) was contributed by George H. Genzmer. Some account of Pastorius's background, immigration, and his place as a literary figure is in Levi O. Kuhns, *The German and Swiss Settlements of Colonial Pennsylvania*, new ed., New York, 1914.

Chapter iii of Samuel Whitaker Pennypacker, *The Settlement of Germantown*, Philadelphia, 1899, gives an extended biographical account of Pastorius with lists of his writings, printed and in manuscript, and facsimiles of title pages. Chapter iv contains a translation of the *Sichere Nachricht* (1684). See also Oswald Seidensticker, *Die erste deutsche Einwanderung in Amerika und die Gründung von Germantown im Jahre 1683* . . . , Philadelphia, 1883, and *Bilder aus der Deutsch-pennsylvänischen Geschichte*, New York, 1885.

One of the earliest protests against slavery (see Myer, ed., *Narratives of Early Pennsylvania*, p. 356) is thought to have been composed by Pastorius. The protest is the subject of Whittier's poem, *The Pennsylvania Pilgrim*, the preface to which contains a translation of Pastorius's Latin prologue to the Germantown book of records.

"The Writings of Franz Daniel Pastorius," exclusive of the 1684 letters, are listed in Oswald Seidensticker, *The First Century of German Printing in America, 1728–1830, Preceded by a Notice of the Literary Work of F. D. Pastorius*, Philadelphia, 1893, pp. 1–5.

## JAMES KIRKE PAULDING
### 1778–1860

SEPARATE WORKS

*Salmagundi; or, The Whim-Whams and Opinions of Launcelot Langstaff, Esq., and Others* (with Washington and William Irving), 1807–1808; *The Diverting History of John Bull and Brother Jonathan*, 1812; *The Lay of the Scottish Fiddle: A Tale of Havre de Grace, Supposed to Be Written by Walter Scott, Esq.*, 1813; *Letters from the South*, 1817; *The Backwoodsman: A Poem*, 1818; *Salmagundi: Second Series*, 1819–1820; *A Sketch of Old England*, 1822; *Koningsmarke: The Long Finne, A Story of the New World*, 1823; *John Bull in America; or, The New Munchausen*, 1825; *The Merry Tales of the Three Wise Men of Gotham*, 1826; *The New Mirror for Travellers, and a Guide to the Springs*, 1828; *Tales of the Good Woman*, 1829; *Chronicles of the City of Gotham from the Papers of a Retired Common Councilman*, 1830; *The Dutchman's Fireside: A Tale*, 1831; *Westward Ho!* 1832; *A Life of Washington*, 1835; *Slavery in the United States*, 1836; *The Book of Saint Nicholas*, 1836; *A Gift from Fairy-Land*, 1838; *The Old Con-*

*tinental: or, The Price of Liberty,* 1846; *American Comedies* (with W. I Paulding), 1847; *The Puritan and His Daughter,* 1849.

COLLECTED WORKS

No recent collection of Paulding's work has been published. Two early collections, long out of print, are very rare: New York, 1835–1837, 14 vols.; and New York, 1867–1868, 4 vols., selected and edited by his son William Irving Paulding.

*The Bucktails,* first published in *American Comedies* (1847), has recently been reprinted in Allan Halline's *American Plays,* New York, 1935, pp. 75–116, with an introduction.

BIOGRAPHY AND CRITICISM

William Irving Paulding published a biography of his father, *The Literary Life of James K. Paulding,* New York, 1867, still valuable as a source book. A more recent critical estimate is Amos L. Herold, *James Kirke Paulding: Versatile American,* New York, 1926, brief but documented. Herold also contributed the sketch of Paulding to *Dict. Amer. Biog.* (1934). A useful independent study is Vernon L. Parrington, *Main Currents in American Thought,* New York, II (1927), 212–221.

Studies of Paulding as dramatist, in addition to Halline's mentioned above, are Arthur H. Quinn, *A History of the American Drama from the Beginning to the Civil War,* rev. ed., New York, 1943, pp. 293–294; and Nelson F. Adkins, "James K. Paulding's *Lion of the West,*" *Amer. Lit.,* III (1931), 249–258—his lost play. Among other studies of Paulding as author are Frank Davidson, "Paulding's Treatment of the Angel of Hadley," *Amer. Lit.,* VII (1935), 330–332; and W. T. Conklin, "Paulding's Prose Treatment of Types and Frontier Life Before Cooper," *Univ. Texas Studies in Eng.,* No. 3926 (1940), pp. 163–171.

PRIMARY SOURCES

An authorized contemporary sketch is that in Evert A. and George L. Duyckinck, *Cyclopaedia of American Literature,* II (1855), 1–10. See also "James K. Paulding," in James G. Wilson, *Bryant and His Friends,* New York, 1886, pp. 129–156. Other source material will be found in the memoirs and letters of Washington Irving and Henry Brevoort.

BIBLIOGRAPHY

The checklist of Paulding's writings in Amos L. Herold, *James Kirke Paulding* (1926), pp. 148–160, includes Paulding's contributions to magazines. Oscar Wegelin compiled "A Bibliography of the Separate Publications of

James Kirke Paulding, Poet, Novelist, Humorist, Statesman, 1779–1860,"
*Papers Bibl. Soc. Amer.,* XII (1918), 34–40, which is useful but should be
checked. See also the drama bibliography in Allan Halline's *American Plays*
(1935), p. 753; and Nelson F. Adkins, "A Study of James K. Paulding's
'Westward Ho!'" *Amer. Collector,* III (1927), 221–229.

# JOHN HOWARD PAYNE
## *1791–1852*

### SEPARATE WORKS

*Julia; or, The Wanderer,* 1806; *Brutus; or, The Fall of Tarquin,* 1818;
*Clari; or, The Maid of Milan,* 1823; "Home, Sweet Home," 1823; *Charles the
Second; or, The Merry Monarch* (with Irving), 1824; *Richelieu: A Domestic
Tragedy* (with Irving), 1826.

Eleven plays, all first published from manuscript, were edited by Codman
Hislop and W. R. Richardson in Vols. V and VI of *America's Lost Plays,*
Princeton, 1940. They are: (Vol. V) *Trial Without Jury, Mount Savage, The
Boarding Schools, The Two Sons-in-Law, Mazeppa, The Spanish Husband;*
(Vol. VI) *The Last Duel in Spain, Woman's Revenge, The Italian Bride,
Romulus the Shepherd King,* and *The Black Man; or, The Spleen.*

Payne published the *Thespian Mirror* (1805–1806), one of the earliest of
theatrical reviews, and *The Pastime* (1807–1808).

### EDITED TEXTS AND REPRINTS

*Charles the Second* was reprinted in Arthur H. Quinn, *Representative
American Plays,* New York, 1917. Copies of several of Payne's plays are still
available in the Samuel French reprints.

"Correspondence of Washington Irving and John Howard Payne" was
published in *Scribner's Mag.,* XLVIII (1910), 461–482, 597–616. T. T. P.
Luquer edited "When Payne Wrote 'Home! Sweet Home!': Letters from
Paris, 1822–1823," *Scribner's Mag.,* LVIII (1915), 742–754. See also A. Bass,
"From the Note-Books of John Howard Payne," *Frontier and Midland,* XIV
(1934), 139–146.

One of the earliest biographies of a dramatist is Gabriel Harrison, *John
Howard Payne, Dramatist, Poet, Actor, and Author of "Home Sweet Home":
His Life and Writings,* Philadelphia, 1884 (rev. ed., 1885). The best brief
estimate of Payne as dramatist is "John Howard Payne and the Foreign
Plays, 1805–1825," in Arthur H. Quinn, *A History of the American Drama
from the Beginning to the Civil War,* rev. ed., New York, 1943, pp. 163–198.
Valuable for the early years is W. T. Hanson, *The Early Life of John Howard*

*Payne,* Boston, 1913. See also Rosa P. Chiles, *John Howard Payne,* Washington, 1930.

Special studies include *The Romance of Mary Wollstonecraft Shelley, John Howard Payne, and Washington Irving,* Boston, 1907; M. Morris, "Mary Shelley and John Howard Payne," *London Mercury,* XXII (1930), 443–450; Bertha-Monica Stearns, "John Howard Payne as an Editor," *Amer. Lit.,* V (1933), 215–228; and Allan R. MacDougall, "John Howard Payne (1791–1852)," *Americana,* XXXIII (1939), 463–475.

Fourteen volumes of Payne's manuscripts are in the Edward E. Ayer Collection of the Newberry Library, Chicago. For a contemporary portrait see *Memoirs of John Howard Payne, the American Roscius,* London, 1815. Further primary material is in Stanley T. Williams, *The Life of Washington Irving,* New York, 1935, 2 vols.

The best checklist is Charles F. Heartman and Harry B. Weiss, "Notes Toward a Bibliography of John Howard Payne," *Amer. Book Collector,* III (1933), 181–184, 224–228, 305–307, IV (1933), 27–29, 79–82, 138–141.

# WILLIAM PENN
## *1644–1718*

### SEPARATE WORKS

Among the separately published writings of Penn, the most important are *No Cross, No Crown,* 1669; *The Great Cause of Liberty of Conscience,* 1670; *Quakerism: A New Nick-Name for Old Christianity,* 1672; *A Brief Account of the Province of Pennsylvania,* 1682; *Information and Direction to Such Persons as Are Inclined to America,* 1684; *The Excellent Priviledge of Liberty and Property,* 1687; *Some Fruits of Solitude,* 1693; *Fruits of a Father's Love,* 1693; *An Essay Towards the Present and Future Peace of Europe,* 1693–1694; *An Account of W. Penn's Travails in Holland and Germany,* 1694; *A Brief Account of the Rise and Progress of the People Called Quakers,* 1695; *The Harmony of Divine and Heavenly Doctrines,* 1696; *The Christian Quaker and His Divine Testimony,* 1699.

### COLLECTED WORKS AND EDITED TEXTS

The most nearly complete edition of Penn's writings is *A Collection of the Works of William Penn,* London, 1726, 2 vols., with a biographical introduction by Joseph Besse. *The Select Works of William Penn,* London, 1782, is in 5 vols. Facsimile reproductions (Boston, 1924) have been made of *A Brief Account of the Province of Pennsylvania* and *Information and Direction to Such Persons as Are Inclined to America. The Excellent Priviledge of Liberty and Property* was reprinted, Philadelphia, 1897. *Some Fruits of Solitude* was published in some later reprints as *Reflections and Maxims. An Essay Towards the Present and Future Peace of Europe* (1693–1694) has been reprinted, Washington, 1912; New York, 1943; and Philadelphia, 1944. Albert C. Myers edited *William Penn: His Own Account of the Lenni Lenape or Delaware Indians, 1683,* Moylan, Pa., 1937. Elizabeth J. Gray prepared an edition of *Fruits of a Father's Love,* Philadelphia, 1944, which includes also the *Letter to His Wife and Children,* written in 1682, and published first in 1761.

Henry J. Cadbury edited "William Penn's Journal: Kent and Sussex, 1672," *Pennsylvania Mag. Hist. and Biog.,* LXVIII (1944), 419–429, as well as "Intercepted Correspondence of William Penn," *ibid.,* LXX (1946), 349–372. Deborah Logan and Edward Armstrong edited *Correspondence Between William Penn and James Logan . . . ,* Philadelphia, 1870–1872, 2 vols.—Vols. IX–X in *Publ. Hist. Soc. Pennsylvania.* Further letters appear in *Memoirs Pennsylvania Hist. Soc.,* I (1826), 411–422, II (1827), 239–247. J. Francis Fisher edited "Inedited Letters of William Penn," *ibid.,* III (1834), 281–292, IV (1840), 167–212.

BIOGRAPHY AND CRITICISM

The best life of Penn is William Hull, *William Penn: A Topical Biography,* New York, 1937. The most authoritative account of the founding of the province is "The Proprietary Province of Pennsylvania," in Charles M. Andrews, *The Colonial Period of American History,* New Haven, III (1937), pp. 268–328. A well written brief life is William W. Comfort, *William Penn, 1644–1718: A Tercentenary Estimate,* Philadelphia, 1944. Especially useful as a study of Penn's life before 1770 is Mabel R. Brailsford, *The Making of William Penn,* New York, 1930. The sketch in *Dict. Amer. Biog.* (1934) is by Rayner W. Kelsey. Earlier biographies are by Thomas Clarkson (1813; 2nd ed., 1814, 2 vols.) and Samuel N. Janney (1852)—with extensive quotation from Penn's letters. Others, useful as compilations, are by S. G. Fisher (1900), J. W. Graham (1917), Bonamy Dobrée (1930), and Arthur Pound (1932)—especially for Penn's family background.

A study of Penn's social ideas is Edward C. O. Beatty, *William Penn as a Social Philosopher,* New York, 1939, with a foreword by Marcus W. Jernegan. Other special studies are Luella M. Wright, "William Penn and the Royal Society," *Bul. Friends' Hist. Assn.,* XXX (1941), 8–10, and John H. Powell, "William Penn's Writings: An Anniversary Essay," *Pennsylvania Hist.,* XI (1944), 233–259.

The "Penn Number" of the *Pennsylvania Mag. Hist. and Biog.,* LXVIII (Oct., 1944) includes studies contributed by William W. Comfort, Henry J.

Cadbury, Thomas E. Drake, Thomas R. White, and William E. Lingelbach.

The two chief depositories of Penn's manuscripts are the Friends' Library, Euston Road, London, and the Historical Society of Pennsylvania.

Mary K. Spence published *William Penn: A Bibliography,* Harrisburg, Pa., 1932. Further material appears in the *Bulletin* of the Department of Public Instruction of Pennsylvania, No. 1 (1932), and in William Hull's *Eight First Biographies* (1936).

## EDGAR ALLAN POE
### *1809–1849*

### SEPARATE WORKS

*Tamerlane and Other Poems,* 1827; *Al Aaraaf, Tamerlane and Minor Poems,* 1829; *Poems,* 1831; *The Narrative of Arthur Gordon Pym,* 1838; *The Conchologist's First Book,* 1839; *Tales of the Grotesque and Arabesque,* 1840; *The Murders in the Rue Morgue, and The Man That Was Used Up,* 1843; *The Raven and Other Poems,* 1845; *Tales,* 1845; *Eureka: A Prose Poem,* 1848; *The Literati,* 1850; *Politian: An Unfinished Tragedy,* 1923.

### COLLECTED WORKS

No American writer has been more competently studied and edited than Poe, and there is need for a new collected edition of his works to incorporate the letters, never collected, and assemble other new material now available. By far the most complete edition is that of James A. Harrison, *The Complete Works of Edgar Allan Poe,* Virginia Edition, New York, 1902, 17 vols., reprinted as the Monticello Edition in the same year—both out of print. Some new material first appeared in *The Works of the Late Edgar Allan Poe: With a Memoir by Rufus Wilmot Griswold and Notices of His Life and Genius by N. P. Willis and J. R. Lowell,* New York, 1850–1856, 4 vols. Three other collected editions were published during the nineteenth century: John H. Ingram, *The Works of Edgar Allan Poe,* Edinburgh, 1874–1875, 4 vols.; Richard H. Stoddard, *The Works of Edgar Allan Poe,* New York, 1884, 6 vols.; and George E. Woodberry and Edmund C. Stedman, *The Works of Edgar A. Poe,* Chicago, 1894–1895, 10 vols. Further Poe material was first collected in the last named *Works.* Charles F. Richardson edited *The Complete Works of Edgar Allan Poe,* New York, 1902, 10 vols.; and Nathan Haskell Dole supervised a ten-volume edition in 1908. The best edition of Poe's poems is that of Killis Campbell, *The Poems of Edgar Allan Poe,* Boston, 1917. James H. Whitty edited *The Complete Poems . . . ,* Boston, 1911, rev. 1917.

Poe's correspondence, not collected, is published in part. In addition to letters gathered in some of the collected works named above, there are published items as follows: George E. Woodberry, "Selections from the Correspondence of Edgar Allan Poe," *Century Mag.*, XLVIII (1894), 572–583, 725–737, 854–866; Eugene Field, ed., *Some Letters of Edgar Allan Poe to E. H. N. Patterson* . . . , Chicago, 1898; James A. Harrison, ed., *Last Letters of Edgar Allan Poe to Sarah Helen Whitman,* New York, 1909; *Some Edgar Allan Poe Letters,* St. Louis, Mo., 1915—printed for private distribution, from originals in the collection of W. K. Bixby; James S. Wilson, ed., "The Letters of Edgar A. Poe to George W. Eveleth," *Alumni Bul. Univ. Va.,* XVII (Jan., 1924), 34–39; Mary N. Stanard, ed., *Edgar Allan Poe Letters Till Now Unpublished, in the Valentine Museum, Richmond, Virginia,* Philadelphia, 1925; Lewis Chase, "A New Poe Letter," *Amer. Lit.,* VI (1934), 66–69; John W. Ostrom, "A Poe Correspondence Re-edited," *Americana,* XXXIV (1940), 409–446— letters to Joseph E. Snodgrass; Arthur H. Quinn and Richard H. Hart, eds., *Edgar Allan Poe Letters and Documents in the Enoch Pratt Free Library,* New York, 1941 (Scholars' Facsimiles and Reprints).

Checklists of letters appear in John W. Ostrom, *Check List of Letters to and from Poe,* Charlottesville, Va., 1941—a calendar of some 750 items.

EDITED TEXTS AND REPRINTS

*Politian: An Unfinished Tragedy,* ed. by Thomas O. Mabbott, was first published complete, Richmond, Va., 1923. For corrections see Mabbott, "The Text of Poe's Play *Politian,*" *Notes and Queries,* CLXXXIX (July 14, 1945), 14. An edition of *The Gold Bug,* foreword by Hervey Allen and notes by Thomas O. Mabbott, was issued in New York, 1928. The Facsimile Text Society of New York has reproduced four first editions: *Al Aaraaf, Tamerlane and Minor Poems* (1829 ed.), with bibl. and notes by Thomas O. Mabbott, New York, 1933; *Poems* (1831 ed.), with bibliographical notes by Killis Campbell, New York, 1936; *Tamerlane and Other Poems* (1827 ed.), with bibl. and notes by Thomas O. Mabbott, New York, 1941; and *The Raven and Other Poems* (1845 ed.), with introduction by Thomas O. Mabbott, New York, 1942.

Other edited texts are those of Frederick C. Prescott, *Selections from the Critical Writings of Edgar Allan Poe,* New York, 1909; Killis Campbell, *Poe's Short Stories,* New York, 1927 (Amer. Authors Ser.); James S. Wilson, *Tales of Edgar Allan Poe,* New York, 1927; Jacob E. Spannuth, *Doings of Gotham* . . . , Pottsville, Pa., 1929, with introduction by Thomas O. Mabbott —Poe's contributions to the *Columbia Spy*; and John G. Varner, Jr., *Edgar Allan Poe and the Philadelphia Saturday Courier,* Charlottesville, Va., 1933— a facsimile reproduction of the first texts of Poe's earliest tales. A serviceable selected text is that of Margaret Alterton and Hardin Craig, eds., *Edgar Allan Poe: Representative Selections, with Introduction, Bibliography, and Notes,* New York, 1935 (Amer. Writers Ser.).

The Modern Library includes *The Complete Tales and Poems of Edgar Allan Poe* (1938); and Philip Van Doren Stern has edited *Edgar Allan Poe* in the Viking Portable Library, New York, 1945. Arthur H. Quinn and Edward H. O'Neill have edited *The Complete Poems and Stories of Edgar Allan Poe, with Selections from His Critical Writings,* New York, 1946, 2 vols.

The revived *Southern Literary Messenger* (1939–current) frequently re-produces articles which Poe first published in that journal.

BIOGRAPHY AND CRITICISM

Still the best written general study is George E. Woodberry, *The Life of Edgar Allan Poe, Personal and Literary, with His Chief Correspondence with Men of Letters,* 1885 (rev. ed., Boston, 1909, 2 vols.), even though some of its facts have been superseded. John H. Ingram, *Edgar Allan Poe: His Life, Letters, and Opinions,* London, 1880, 2 vols., is an early life. The pioneer work in French criticism of Poe was the three essays of Charles Baudelaire: "Edgar Allan Poe: Sa Vie et Ses Œuvrages," in *Revue de Paris* (March–April, 1852); "Edgar Poe: Sa Vie et Ses Œuvres," in *Histoires Extraordinaires par Edgar Poe,* Paris, 1856 (transl. by H. C. Curwin, London, 1872); and "Notes Nouvelles sur Edgar Poe," in *Nouvelles Histoires Extraordinaires par Edgar Poe,* Paris, 1857. Despite gaps in Baudelaire's knowledge of Poe's life, these essays supply criticism of the finest quality. Emile Lauvrière's *Edgar Poe: Sa Vie et Son Œuvre . . .,* Paris, 1904, 2 vols., has been partly superseded by Camille Mauclair, *La Génie d'Edgar Poe . . .,* Paris, 1925.

The most recent Poe biography is Arthur H. Quinn, *Edgar Allan Poe: A Critical Biography,* New York, 1941, based on primary sources, and informative of the actual conditions under which Poe worked. Killis Campbell, *The Mind of Poe, and Other Studies,* Cambridge, 1933, was written from knowledge of Poe material. Other studies are Hervey Allen, *Israfel: The Life and Times of Edgar Allan Poe,* New York, 1926, 2 vols.; Joseph Wood Krutch, *Edgar Allan Poe: A Study in Genius,* New York, 1926—psychoanalytical in approach; and Mary E. Phillips, *Edgar Allan Poe: The Man,* Philadelphia, 1926, 2 vols., profusely illustrated.

In addition to the estimates of Poe by earlier critics (see Collected Works, *ante,* p. 689), interesting to the extent to which the authors are spokesmen of their times, there are other brief general estimates that represent viewpoints worthy of record. Among them are "Edgar Allan Poe," in Edmund C. Stedman, *Poets of America,* Boston, 1885, pp. 225–272; "Poe," in John M. Robertson, *New Essays Towards a Critical Method,* London, 1889, pp. 55–130;

"Edgar Allan Poe," in Lewis E. Gates, *Studies and Appreciations,* New York, 1900, pp. 110–128; "The Origins of Hawthorne and Poe," in Paul E. More, *Shelburne Essays,* 1st ser., New York, 1904, pp. 51–70; "Poe," in William C. Brownell, *American Prose Masters,* New York, 1909, pp. 207–267; "The Centenary of Poe," in William P. Trent, *Longfellow and Other Essays,* New York, 1910, pp. 211–244; André Fontainas, *La Vie d'Edgar A. Poe,* Paris, 1919; George Saintsbury, "Edgar Allan Poe," *Dial,* LXXXIII (1927), 453–463; "Poe," in Henry S. Canby, *Classic Americans,* New York, 1931, pp. 263–307; "Poe," in George E. De Mille, *Literary Criticism in America . . . ,* New York, 1931, pp. 86–117; and two chapters in Van Wyck Brooks, *The World of Washington Irving,* New York, 1944: "Poe in the South," pp. 337–361, and "Poe in the North," pp. 443–456. Pertinent here is "Biographies of Poe," in John Macy, *The Critical Game,* New York, 1922, pp. 193–200.

Special studies of aspects of Poe as a man of letters are Margaret Alterton, *Origins of Poe's Critical Theory,* Iowa City, 1925; Norman Foerster, "Quantity and Quality in Poe's Aesthetic," *Studies in Philol.,* XX (1923), 310–335; *idem,* "Poe," in his *American Criticism . . . ,* Boston, 1928, pp. 1–51; Henry M. Belden, "Observation and Imagination in Coleridge and Poe: A Contrast," in *Papers . . . in Honor of . . . Charles Frederick Johnson,* Hartford, Conn., 1928, pp. 131–175; Floyd Stovall, "Poe's Debt to Coleridge," *Univ. Texas Studies in Eng.,* X (1930), 70–127; David K. Jackson, *Poe and the Southern Literary Messenger,* Richmond, Va., 1934; "Edgar Allan Poe," in Gay W. Allen, *American Prosody,* New York, 1935, pp. 56–90; "Edgar Allan Poe: A Crisis in the History of American Obscurantism," in Yvor Winters, *Maule's Curse . . . ,* Norfolk, Conn., 1938, pp. 93–122; May G. Evans, *Music and Edgar Allan Poe . . . ,* Baltimore, 1939; "Edgar Allan Poe," in John P. Pritchard, *Return to the Fountains . . . ,* Durham, N.C., 1942, pp. 26–43—Poe's debt to the classics; and John E. Cooke, *Poe as a Literary Critic,* Baltimore, 1946, edited by N. Bryllion Fagin.

Poe as a humorist is presented in Napier Wilt, "Poe's Attitude Toward His Tales: A New Document," *Modern Philol.,* XXV (1927), 101–105, which, taken with James S. Wilson, "The Devil Was in It," *Amer. Mercury,* XXIV (1931), 215–220, conclusively demonstrates the burlesque intent of Poe's early work. There is also Walter F. Taylor, "Israfel in Motley: A Study of Poe's Humor," *Sewanee Rev.,* XLII (1934), 330–340.

Textual studies are Dudley Hutcherson, "The Philadelphia *Saturday Museum* Text of Poe's Poems," *Amer. Lit.,* V (1933), 36–48; Kenneth Rede, "Poe Notes: From an Investigator's Notebook," *Amer. Lit.,* V (1933), 49–54; Cullen B. Colton, "George Hooker Colton and the Publication of 'The Raven,'" *Amer. Lit.,* X (1938), 319–330; John C. Wyllie, "A List of the Texts of Poe's Tales," in *Humanistic Studies in Honor of John Calvin Metcalf,*

Charlottesville, Va., 1941, pp. 322-338—including translations; Edward H. O'Neill, "The Poe-Griswold-Harrison Texts of the 'Marginalia,'" *Amer. Lit.*, XV (1943), 238-250; and Jay B. Hubbell, "'O, Tempora! O, Mores!' A Juvenile Poem by Edgar Allan Poe," *Univ. Colo. Studies*, ser. B., II (1945), 314-321.

Discussions of source and theme in the individual tales and poems are Floyd Stovall, "An Interpretation of Poe's 'Al Aaraaf,'" *Univ. Texas Studies in Eng.*, IX (1929), 106-133—answered by Richard C. and Marie M. Pettigrew, *Amer. Lit.*, VIII (1937), 439-445; Bradford A. Booth, "The Identity of Annabel Lee," *College Eng.*, VII (1945), 17-19; Fred A. Dudley, "Tintinnabulation: And a Source of Poe's 'The Bells,'" *Amer. Lit.*, IV (1932), 296-300; Arthur E. Du Bois, "The Jazz Bells of Poe," *College Eng.*, II (1940), 230-244; Joseph S. Schick, "The Origin of 'The Cask of Amontillado,'" *Amer. Lit.*, VI (1934), 18-21; Louise Pound, "On Poe's 'The City in the Sea,'" *Amer. Lit.*, VI (1934), 22-27, and again on the same, *ibid.*, VIII (1936), 70-71; Oral S. Coad, "The Meaning of Poe's 'Eldorado,'" *Modern Language Notes*, LIX (1944), 59-61; Thomas O. Mabbott, "The Sources of Poe's 'Eldorado,'" *Modern Language Notes*, LX (1945), 312-314; *idem*, "Poe's 'Israfel,'" *Explicator*, II (1944), Item 57; Arlin Turner, "Another Source of Poe's 'Julius Rodman,'" *Amer. Lit.*, VIII (1936), 69-70; Roy P. Basler, "The Interpretation of 'Ligeia,'" *College Eng.*, V (1944), 363-372; Walter Blair, "Poe's Conception of Incident and Tone in the Tale," *Modern Philol.*, XLI (1944), 228-240—a study of the structure of "The Masque of the Red Death"; John R. Moore, "Poe, Scott, and 'The Murders in the Rue Morgue,'" *Amer. Lit.*, VIII (1936), 52-58; Keith Huntress, "Another Source for Poe's 'Narrative of Arthur Gordon Pym,'" *Amer. Lit.*, XVI (1944), 19-25; David L. Clark, "The Sources of Poe's 'The Pit and the Pendulum,'" *Modern Language Notes*, XLIV (1929), 349-356; Robert S. Forsythe, "Poe's 'Nevermore': A Note," *Amer. Lit.*, VII (1936), 439-452; Oscar Cargill, "A New Source for 'The Raven,'" *Amer. Lit.*, VIII (1936), 291-294; Edna B. Triplett, "A Note on Poe's 'The Raven,'" *Amer. Lit.*, X (1938), 339-341; Fannye N. Cherry, "The Source of Poe's 'Three Sundays in a Week,'" *Amer. Lit.*, II (1930), 232-235; Joe E. Jones, "Poe's 'Nicéan Barks,'" *Amer. Lit.*, II (1931), 433-438; Frank M. Durham, "A Possible Relationship Between Poe's 'To Helen' and Milton's *Paradise Lost*, Book IV," *Amer. Lit.*, XVI (1945), 340-343; Roy P. Basler, "Poe's 'Ulalume,'" *Explicator*, II (1944), Item 49. Miscellaneous items are Earl L. Griggs, "Five Sources of Edgar Allan Poe's 'Pinakidia,'" *Amer. Lit.*, I (1929), 196-199; David K. Jackson, "Poe Notes: 'Pinakidia' and 'Some Ancient Greek Authors,'" *Amer. Lit.*, V (1933), 258-267; Kenneth L. Daughrity, "Poe's 'Quiz on Willis,'" *Amer. Lit.*, V (1933), 55-62; Henry M. Belden, "Poe's 'The City in the Sea' and Dante's City of Dis," *Amer. Lit.*, VII

(1935), 332–334; Roy P. Basler, "Byronism in Poe's 'To One in Paradise,'"
*Amer. Lit.*, IX (1937), 232–236; Walter G. Neale, Jr., "The Source of Poe's
'Morella,'" *Amer. Lit.*, IX (1937), 237–239; Frank Davidson, "A Note on
Poe's 'Berenice,'" *Amer. Lit.*, XI (1939), 212–213; and James O. Bailey, "Poe's
'Palaestine,'" *Amer. Lit.*, XIII (1941), 44–58.

Poe's reception abroad needs further study. The groundwork has been
laid by Célestin P. Cambiaire, *The Influence of Edgar Allan Poe in France*,
New York, 1927; Léon Lemonnier, *Edgar Poe et la Critique Française de 1845
à 1875*, Paris, 1928; *idem*, *Les Traducteurs d'Edgar Poe en France . . .*, Paris,
1928; *idem*, *Edgar Poe et les Poètes Français*, Paris, 1932; John E. Englekirk,
*Edgar Allan Poe in Hispanic Literature*, New York, 1934; and "Situation de
Baudelaire," in Paul Valéry, *Variété II* (1930), pp. 141–174—a distillation of
the French estimate of Poe. See also Louis Seylaz, *Edgar Poe et les Premiers
Symbolistes Français*, Lausanne, 1923; Mozelle Scaff Allen, "Poe's Debt to
Voltaire," *Univ. Texas Studies in Eng.*, XV (July, 1935), 63–75; Percy G.
Adams, "Poe, Critic of Voltaire," *Modern Language Notes*, LVII (1942),
273–275; F. Hippe, *Edgar Allan Poes Lyrik in Deutschland*, Münster, 1913;
and Gustav Gruener, "Notes on the Influence of E. T. A. Hoffmann upon
Edgar Allan Poe," *PMLA*, XIX (1904), 1–25.

Poe's interest in the mysterious and in cryptography is the theme of
Edward Hungerford, "Poe and Phrenology," *Amer. Lit.*, II (1930), 209–231;
William F. Friedman, "Edgar Allan Poe, Cryptographer," *Amer. Lit.*, VIII
(1936), 266–280; William K. Wimsatt, Jr., "Poe and the Chess Automaton,"
*Amer. Lit.*, XI (1939), 138–151; *idem*, "What Poe Knew About Cryptog-
raphy," *PMLA*, LVIII (1943), 754–779; and Clarence S. Brigham, "Edgar
Allan Poe's Contributions to *Alexander's Weekly Messenger*," *Proc. Amer.
Antiq. Soc.*, LII (1943), 45–123—an extensive study.

On the Poe-Chivers controversy, see the bibliography of Chivers herein,
*ante*, p. 441. Other personal relationships are discussed by Aubrey Starke,
"Poe's Friend Reynolds," *Amer. Lit.*, XI (1939), 152–159; Richard B. Davis,
"Poe and William Wirt," *Amer. Lit.*, XVI (1944), 212–220; William H.
Gravely, Jr., "An Incipient Libel Suit Involving Poe," *Modern Language
Notes*, LX (1945), 308–311; and "Thomas Dunn English's *Walter Woofe*: A
Reply to 'A Minor Poe Mystery,'" *Princeton Univ. Lib. Chron.*, V (1944),
108–114.

Other studies are Paul E. More, "A Note on Poe's Method," *Studies in
Philol.*, XX (1923), 302–309; Edith Philips, "The French of Edgar Allan Poe,"
*Amer. Speech*, II (1927), 270–274; James S. Wilson, "Poe's Philosophy of
Composition," *No. Amer. Rev.*, CCXXIII (1927), 675–684; Léon Lemonnier,
"Edgar Poe et le Théâtre de Mystère et de Terreur," *Grande Revue*, CXXX
(1929), 379–396; Killis Campbell, "Poe's Knowledge of the Bible," *Studies in*

*Philol.*, XXVII (1930), 546–552; W. O. Clough, "The Use of Color Words by Edgar Allan Poe," *PMLA*, XLV (1930), 598–613; William L. Werner, "Poe's Theories and Practice in Poetic Technique," *Amer. Lit.*, II (1930), 157–165; Percy H. Boynton, "Poe and Journalism," *English Jour.*, XXI (1932), 345–352; DeLancey Ferguson, "Charles Hine and His Portrait of Poe," *Amer. Lit.*, III (1932), 465–470; Richard C. Pettigrew, "Poe's Rime," *Amer. Lit.*, IV (1932), 151–159; Killis Campbell, "Three Notes on Poe," *Amer. Lit.*, IV (1933), 385–388; Joy Bayless, "Another Rufus W. Griswold as a Critic of Poe," *Amer. Lit.*, VI (1934), 69–72—Rufus White Griswold; Ernest Marchand, "Poe as Social Critic," *Amer. Lit.*, VI (1934), 28–43; Emma K. Norman, "Poe's Knowledge of Latin," *Amer. Lit.*, VI (1934), 72–77; Leonard B. Hurley, "A New Note in the War of the Literati," *Amer. Lit.*, VII (1936), 376–394; Ruth L. Hudson, "Poe and Disraeli," *Amer. Lit.*, VIII (1937), 402–416; David K. Jackson, "Poe's Knowledge of Law During the *Messenger* Period . . .," *Amer. Lit.*, X (1938), 331–339; Charles C. Walcutt, "The Logic of Poe," *College Eng.*, II (1941), 438–444; P. M. Jones, "Poe, Baudelaire, and Mallarmé: A Problem of Literary Judgment," *Modern Language Rev.*, XXXIX (1944), 236–246; Marcel Françon, "Poe et Baudelaire," *PMLA*, LX (1945), 841–859; William H. Gravely, Jr., "An Incipient Libel Suit Involving Poe," *Modern Language Notes*, LX (1945), 308–311; Malcolm Cowley, "Aidgarpo," *New Repub.*, CXIII (1945), 607–610; Joseph S. Schick, "Poe and Jefferson," *Virginia Mag. Hist. and Biog.*, LIV (1946), 316–320; and George Snell, "First of the New Critics," *Quar. Rev. Lit.*, II (1946), 333–340.

PRIMARY SOURCES

Locations of the chief depositories of Poe manuscripts are fully described in Heartman and Rede, *A Census . . .* (see Bibliography, below), and discussed in Arthur H. Quinn, *Edgar Allan Poe . . .*, New York, 1941, *passim*.

Especially useful as source material are Sarah H. Whitman, *Edgar Poe and His Critics*, New York, 1860 (also Providence, 1885); Thomas O. Mabbott, ed., "The Letters from George W. Eveleth to Edgar Allan Poe," *Bul. New York Pub. Lib.*, XXVI (1922), 171–195; Hervey Allen and Thomas O. Mabbott, eds., *Poe's Brother: The Poems of William Henry Leonard Poe*, New York, 1926; Amanda P. Schulte, *Facts About Poe: Portraits and Daguerreotypes . . .*, Charlottesville, Va., 1926; and Thomas O. Mabbott, ed., "Letters from Mary E. Hewitt to Poe," *Christmas Books*, Hunter College, New York, 1937, pp. 116–121.

Bibliographies of source material are in George E. Woodberry, "The Poe-Chivers Papers," *Century Mag.*, LXV (1903), 435–447, 545–558; Killis Campbell, "Poe Documents in the Library of Congress," *Modern Language Notes*, XXV (1910), 127–128—the Ellis-Allen letters; *idem*, "Some Unpublished Documents Relating to Poe's Early Years," *Sewanee Rev.*, XX (1912), 201–202; *idem,* "The Poe Canon," in his *The Mind of Poe . . .* , Cambridge, 1933, pp. 187–238; and Honor McCusker, "The Correspondence of R. W. Griswold," *More Books,* XVI (1941), 105–116, 152–156, 190–196, 286–289—the beginning of a list of autograph letters in the Griswold Collection of the Boston Public Library.

See also the recently published lecture on Poe by John Reuben Thompson (1823–1873), *The Genius and Character of Edgar Allan Poe* (1929).

BIBLIOGRAPHY

Bibliographical studies relating to Poe are Charles F. Heartman and Kenneth Rede, *A Census of First Editions and Source Materials by Edgar Allan Poe in American Collections,* Metuchen, N.J., 1932—with a calendar of Poe's contributions to annuals and periodicals; John W. Robertson, *Bibliography of the Writings of Edgar A. Poe,* San Francisco, 1934, 2 vols.—a chronological list, 1827–1850, including many rare items, supplemented with additions and corrections by David Randall in *Publishers' Weekly,* CXXV (1934), 1540–1543; May G. Evans, *Music and Edgar Allan Poe: A Bibliographical Study,* Baltimore, 1939; Charles F. Heartman and James R. Canny, *A Bibliography of First Printings of the Writings of Edgar Allan Poe . . .* , Hattiesburg, Miss., 1943; *Index to Early American Periodical Literature, 1728–1870: Part 2, Edgar Allan Poe,* New York, 1941. Three other sources are Killis Campbell, "Gleanings in the Bibliography of Poe," *Modern Language Notes,* XXXII (1917), 267–272; *idem,* "Recent Books About Poe," *Studies in Philol.,* XXIV (1927), 474–479; and Claire-Eliane Engel, "L'Etat des travaux sur Poe en France," *Modern Philol.,* XXIX (1932), 482–488. The brief bibliography in the Alterton-Craig *Edgar Allan Poe: Representative Selections* (1935) is selective and annotated, as is that in Harry H. Clark, ed., *Major American Poets,* New York, 1936, pp. 834–839. See also Harry Hartwick, in Walter F. Taylor, *A History of American Letters,* New York, 1936, pp. 501–506.

Bradford A. Booth and Claude E. Jones have compiled *A Concordance of the Poetical Works of Edgar Allan Poe,* Baltimore, 1941.

# WILLIAM SYDNEY (SIDNEY) PORTER
## ("O. HENRY")
### *1862–1910*

SEPARATE WORKS

*Cabbages and Kings,* 1904; *The Four Million,* 1906; *The Trimmed Lamp,* 1907; *Heart of the West,* 1907; *The Voice of the City,* 1908; *The Gentle*

*Grafter,* 1908; *Roads of Destiny,* 1909; *Options,* 1909; *Strictly Business,* 1910; *Whirligigs,* 1910; *Let Me Feel Your Pulse,* 1910; *Sixes and Sevens,* 1911; *Rolling Stones,* 1912; *Waifs and Strays,* 1917.

## COLLECTED WORKS AND REPRINTS

The great popularity of O. Henry's stories is reflected in the number of collected editions and reprints of his writings. *The Complete Writings of O. Henry,* Garden City, N.Y., 1917, 14 vols., was the first uniform collected edition. Later editions are O. Henry Biographical Edition, Garden City, 1929, 18 vols.; *The Complete Works of O. Henry,* Garden City, 1927, with critical and biographical comment, pp. 1319-1385; *The Complete Works of O. Henry,* Garden City, 1937, 1,653 pp., with foreword by W. L. Phelps.

Further collections are *O. Henryana: Seven Odds and Ends, Poetry and Short Stories,* Garden City, 1920—many here first collected; *Letters to Lithopolis, from O. Henry to Mabel Wagnalls,* Garden City, 1922; *Postscripts,* New York, 1923, edited with introduction by Florence Stratton from material first published in the *Houston Post,* 1895-1896. Mary S. Harrell edited *O. Henry Encore: Stories and Illustrations Usually Under the Name, The Post Man,* Dallas, Texas, 1936, and New York, 1939—chiefly anonymous material reprinted from the *Houston Post,* 1895-1896, and attributed by the editor to O. Henry.

There is no full collection of O. Henry letters. Clarence Gohdes edited "Some Letters by O. Henry," *So. Atl. Quar.,* XXXVIII (1939), 31-39.

Further selections are C. Alphonso Smith, ed., *Selected Stories from O. Henry,* Garden City, 1922; Hyder E. Rollins, ed., *Heart of the West,* Garden City, 1925, 2 vols., with notes; *The Voice of the City and Other Stories by O. Henry,* New York, 1935, with an introduction by Clifton Fadiman; and *Best Short Stories of O. Henry,* New York, 1945, selected, with introduction, by Bennett Cerf and Van H. Cartmell, for the Modern Library.

## BIOGRAPHY AND CRITICISM

The authorized life is C. Alphonso Smith, *O. Henry Biography,* New York, 1916. There is also Robert H. Davis and Arthur B. Maurice, *The Caliph of Bagdad . . . ,* New York, 1931.

Useful among early studies and appreciations are Hyder E. Rollins, "O. Henry," *Sewanee Rev.,* XXII (1914), 213-232; "The Amazing Genius of O. Henry," in Stephen Leacock, *Essays and Literary Studies,* New York, 1916, pp. 233-266; "William Sydney Porter," in Blanche C. Williams, *Our Short Story Writers,* New York, 1920, pp. 200-222; and "The Age of O. Henry," in Fred L. Pattee, *Side-Lights on American Literature,* New York, 1922, pp. 3-55.

Recent general estimates are "O. Henry," in Fred L. Pattee, *The New American Literature*, New York, 1930, pp. 160–179; Arthur H. Quinn, *American Fiction*, New York, 1936, pp. 545–549; and Heinz Noack, *O. Henry als Mystiker*, Berlin, 1937. The sketch in *Dict. Amer. Biog.* (1935) is by Carl Van Doren.

Special studies include L. W. Payne, Jr., "The Humor of O. Henry," *Texas Rev.*, IV (1918), 18–37; Hyder E. Rollins, "O. Henry's Texas," *ibid.*, 295–307; Alexander Woollcott, "O. Henry, Playwright," *Bookman*, LVI (1922), 152–157; Paul S. Clarkson, "A Decomposition of *Cabbages and Kings*," *Amer Lit.*, VII (1935), 195–202—on its composition; John A. Lomax, "Harry Steger and O. Henry," *Southwest Rev.*, XXIV (1939), 299–316; Duncan Robinson and others, "O. Henry's Austin," *ibid.*, 388–410; Margetta Jung, "O. Henry in Manhattan," *ibid.*, 411–415; Trueman O'Quinn, "O. Henry in Austin," *Southwestern Hist. Quar.*, XLIII (1939), 143–157; Luther W. Courtney, "O. Henry's Case Reconsidered," *Amer. Lit.*, XIV (1943), 361–371; and William B. Gates, "O. Henry and Shakspere," *Shakespeare Assn. Bul.*, XIX (1944), 20–25.

The records of O. Henry's trial have been reproduced from the originals of the United States Circuit Court of Appeals at New Orleans in *W. S. Porter, Plaintiff in Error, vs. United States, Defendant in Error . . .* , Austin Texas, 1940.

PRIMARY SOURCES

A few O. Henry manuscripts are in the Princeton University Library. Published material of a primary nature is in Seth Moyle, *My Friend O. Henry*, New York, 1914; Archibald Henderson, *O. Henry: A Memorial Essay*, Raleigh, N.C., 1914; Al (Alphonso J.) Jennings, *Through the Shadows with O. Henry*, New York, 1921—useful for the Honduras and penitentiary years; *O. Henry Papers: Containing Some Sketches of His Life Together with an Alphabetical Index to His Complete Works*, rev. ed., Garden City, N.Y., 1925; and William W. Williams, "The Quiet Lodger of Irving Place," *Amer. Book Coll.*, V (1934), 72–76, 118–122, 136–139.

BIBLIOGRAPHY

The most complete bibliographical listing is Paul S. Clarkson, *A Bibliography of William Sydney Porter (O. Henry)*, Caldwell, Idaho, 1938. See also Hyder E. Rollins's review, *Amer. Lit.*, XI (1940), 107–109, for corrections and additions. Other listings are in *Waifs and Strays* (1917), which contains a representative selection of criticism and biographical comment and an index of short stories. Further data may be found in *O. Henry Papers* (1925), pp. 42–44.

# EZRA POUND
*b. 1885*

SEPARATE WORKS

Poetry: *A Lume Spento*, 1908; *Personae*, 1909; *Exultations*, 1909; *Provença*, 1910; *Canzoni*, 1911; *Ripostes*, 1912; *Lustra*, 1916; *Quia Pauper Amavi*, 1919; *Umbra*, 1920; *Hugh Selwyn Mauberley*, 1920; *Poems, 1918-21*, 1921; *A Draft of XVI. Cantos*, 1925; *A Draft of Cantos 17-27*, 1928; *A Draft of XXX Cantos*, 1930; *Eleven New Cantos: XXXI-XLI*, 1934; *Homage to Sextus Propertius*, 1934; *The Fifth Decad of Cantos*, 1937; *Cantos LII-LXXI*, 1940.

Prose: *The Spirit of Romance*, 1910; *Pavannes and Divisions*, 1918; *Instigations*, 1920; *Indiscretions*, 1923; *Antheil and the Treatise on Harmony*, 1924; *Imaginary Letters*, 1930; *How to Read*, 1931; *A B C of Economics*, 1933; *A B C of Reading*, 1934; *Make It New*, 1934; *Jefferson and/or Mussolini*, 1935; *Polite Essays*, 1937; *Culture*, 1938.

*Gaudier-Brzeska* (1916) is a biography. Translations from the Chinese, based on the notes of Fenollosa, are *Cathay*, 1915; *Noh—or, Accomplishment*, 1916; and *Certain Noble Plays of Japan*, 1916. Among other translations are *The Sonnets and Ballate of Guido Cavalcanti*, 1912.

*Personae: The Collected Poems*, 1926, is a reprint of *Personae* (1909), *Exultations* (1909), *Ripostes* (1912), *Lustra* (1916), *Homage to Sextus Propertius* (1934), and *Hugh Selwyn Mauberley* (1920).

Among works edited by Pound are *Des Imagistes*, 1914, *Profile: An Anthology*, 1932; and *Active Anthology*, 1933—book of modern verse. T. S. Eliot has edited *Selected Poems of Ezra Pound*, 1928.

BIOGRAPHY AND CRITICISM

One of the best brief studies of the writing of Pound is Alice S. Amdur, *The Poetry of Ezra Pound*, Cambridge, 1936. Among the earliest estimates recognizing Pound as poet and critic are Carl Sandburg, "The Work of Ezra Pound," *Poetry*, VII (1916), 249-257; T. S. Eliot, *Ezra Pound: His Metric and Poetry*, New York, 1917, 31 pp.; "A Pointless Pointillist: Ezra Pound," in Conrad Aiken, *Scepticisms*, New York, 1919, pp. 136-142; and May Sinclair, "The Reputation of Ezra Pound," *No. Amer. Rev.*, CCXI (1920), 658-668.

Later estimates are "Ezra Pound," in Louis Untermeyer, *American Poetry Since 1900*, New York, 1923, pp. 157-169; Herbert S. Gorman, "Bolingbroke of Bards," *No. Amer. Rev.*, CCXIX (1924), 855-865; "Ezra Pound," in Harriet Monroe, *Poets and Their Art*, New York, 1926, pp. 12-20; "Ezra

Pound," in René Taupin, *L'Influence du Symbolisme français sur la Poésie américaine,* Paris, 1929, pp. 133–158; Allen Tate, "Ezra Pound's Golden Ass," *Nation,* CXXXII (1931), 632–634; Louis Zukovsky, "The Cantos of Ezra Pound," *Criterion,* X (1931), 424–440; René Taupin, "La Poésie d'Ezra Pound," *Revue Anglo-Amér.,* VIII (1931), 221–236; Marianne Moore, "The Cantos," *Poetry,* XXXIX (1931), 37–50; Dudley Fitts, "Music Fit for the Odes," *Hound and Horn,* IV (1931), 278–289; Iris Barry, "The Ezra Pound Period," *Bookman,* LXXIV (1931), 159–171; "Ezra Pound: Poet, Pedagogue, Propagandist, etc.," in Glenn Hughes, *Imagism and the Imagists,* Stanford Univ., Calif., 1931, pp. 224–249; and John L. Brown, "A Troubadour at Hamilton," *Hamilton Lit. Mag.,* LXII (1932), 53–63.

Among the most recent studies are F. R. Leavis, *New Bearings in English Poetry,* London, 1932, pp. 133–157; "Ezra Pound," in Edith Sitwell, *Aspects of Modern Poetry,* London, 1934, pp. 178–214; Horace Gregory, "The A. B. C. of Ezra Pound," *Poetry,* XLVI (1935), 279–285; "Masks of Ezra Pound," in Richard P. Blackmur, *The Double Agent,* New York, 1935, pp. 30–67; Babette Deutsch, *This Modern Poetry,* New York, 1935, pp. 61–66, 75–86, 119–124; "Ezra Pound," in Allen Tate, *Reactionary Essays on Poetry and Ideas,* New York, 1936, pp. 43–51; Martin Gilkes, "Discovery of Ezra Pound," *English,* II (1938), pp. 74–83; L. Berti, "Poesia e minetismo con Ezra Pound," *Letteratura,* IV (1940), 140–145, V (1941), 123–134; and T. S. Eliot, "Ezra Pound," *Poetry,* LXVIII (1946), 326–339.

PRIMARY SOURCES AND BIBLIOGRAPHY

An important collection of letters is in the Lockwood Memorial Library at the University of Buffalo.

Checklists of works by and about Pound are in Alice S. Amdur, *The Poetry of Ezra Pound* (1936), pp. 103–106; Fred B. Millett, *Contemporary American Authors,* New York, 1940, pp. 529–533; and Frances Cheney, in Allen Tate, *Sixty American Poets, 1896–1944,* Washington, 1945, pp. 115–122.

# WILLIAM HICKLING PRESCOTT
## *1796–1859*

SEPARATE WORKS

*History of the Reign of Ferdinand and Isabella, the Catholic,* 1837; *History of the Conquest of Mexico,* 1843; *Biographical and Critical Miscellanies,* 1845; *History of the Conquest of Peru,* 1847; *History of the Reign of Philip the Second,* 1855–1858—incomplete at Prescott's death.

COLLECTED WORKS

The Montezuma Edition of *The Works of William H. Prescott,* Philadelphia, 1904, 22 vols., ed. by Wilfred H. Munro, is the last complete ed. of Prescott's writings. The edition of Prescott's *Works,* Philadelphia, 1874, 16 vols., by John Foster Kirk, includes Kirk's emendations and Prescott's important revisions of the *Conquest of Mexico.*

*The Correspondence of William Hickling Prescott, 1833–1847,* Boston, 1925, is a well edited selection from the original drafts in the Mass. Hist. Soc., prepared by Prescott's great-grandson Roger Wolcott. It is supplemented, especially for the remaining years of Prescott's life, by Clara L. Penney, ed., *Prescott: Unpublished Letters to Gayangos in the Library of the Hispanic Society of America,* New York, 1927, with material on Prescott's methods as a scholar. A long and important letter from Prescott, previously unpublished, is Fulmer Mood and Granville Hicks, eds., "Letters to Dr. Channing on Slavery and the Annexation of Texas, 1837," *New Eng. Quar.,* V (1932), 587–601.

A checklist of Prescott's lesser works, together with titles of his reviews and sketches, is in the Charvat and Kraus *William Hickling Prescott: Representative Selections* (1943), pp. cxxxi–cxxxv.

EDITED TEXTS AND REPRINTS

The *Conquest of Mexico* and the *Conquest of Peru* were issued in one volume, New York, 1936, in the Modern Lib. Earlier reprints of the *Conquest of Mexico* were issued, New York, 1934, with an introduction by Carl Van Doren; and in Everyman's Lib., New York, 1933, 2 vols. An edition of the *Conquest of Peru* was issued in Everyman's Lib. in the same year.

The most serviceable selected text of Prescott is William Charvat and Michael Kraus, *William Hickling Prescott: Representative Selections, with Introduction, Bibliography, and Notes,* New York, 1943 (Amer. Writers Ser.).

BIOGRAPHY AND CRITICISM

Still standard is George Ticknor, *Life of William Hickling Prescott,* Boston, 1864, though it makes little use of manuscript material. It includes letters and documents, and a useful appendix of translations of Prescott's writings. Rollo Ogden prepared *William Hickling Prescott,* Boston, 1904, for the Amer. Men of Letters Ser. It is a short life based in part on manuscript material. The biography by Harry T. Peck, *William Hickling Prescott,* New York, 1905 (Eng. Men of Letters Ser.), attempts a critical analysis of Prescott as a man of letters.

The best brief narrative sketch of Prescott is that of Roger B. Merriman, in *Dict. Amer. Biog.* (1935). The introduction in the Charvat and Kraus

*William Hickling Prescott: Representative Selections* (1943), pp. xi–cxxviii, is the fullest and most recent critical appraisal.

One of the best early estimates of Prescott as historian is that of Theodore Parker, in *The Collected Works of Theodore Parker,* ed. by F. P. Cobbe, London, X (1865), 81–153. P. A. Means, "A Re-examination of Prescott's Account of Early Peru," *New Eng. Quar.,* IV (1931), 645–662, is a favorable revaluation by a specialist in the literature of Peru.

Prescott as a man of letters is the subject of "Prescott's *Ferdinand and Isabella,*" in Van Wyck Brooks, *The Flowering of New England,* New York, 1936, pp. 135–146. Harry H. Clark's "Literary Criticism in the *North American Review, 1815–1835,*" *Trans. Wisconsin Acad. Sci., Arts, and Letters,* XXXII (1940), 299–350, summarizes Prescott's contributions.

PRIMARY SOURCES

Tributes and memoirs are published in the *Proc. Mass. Hist. Soc.,* IV (1860). A description of Prescott's eye trouble by one of his physicians is James Jackson, *Another Letter to a Young Physician,* Boston, 1861, pp. 130–156. An anecdotal account is Samuel Eliot, "William Hickling Prescott," *New Eng. Mag.,* IX (1893), 515–529. Further reminiscences are Edward W. Emerson, *Early Years of the Saturday Club,* Boston, 1918, pp. 180–187.

The chief depository of Prescott manuscripts, including notes, correspondence, and diaries throughout his life, is the Massachusetts Historical Society. Other important manuscript items are in the Henry E. Huntington Library, and in the Hispanic Society of America.

BIBLIOGRAPHY

The bibliography of Prescott in Charvat and Kraus, *William Hickling Prescott: Representative Selections* (1943), pp. cxxxi–cxlii, is selective and annotated. Data about his Spanish and other translations will be found in the biography by Ticknor, and in J. DeLancey Ferguson, *American Literature in Spain,* New York, 1916, pp. 148–157.

# ELMER (L.) RICE
### b. 1892

PLAYS *

*On Trial,* 1914; *The Home of the Free,* 1917; *The Adding Machine,* 1923; *Wake Up, Jonathan* (with Hatcher Hughes) (1921), 1928; *Close Harmony; or, The Lady Next Door* (with Dorothy Parker) (1924), 1929; *Cock Robin*

---

* Dates in parentheses are of production when it differs from publication or when publication has not occurred.

(with Philip Barry) (1928), 1929; *Street Scene,* 1929; *The Subway,* 1929; *See Naples and Die* (1929), 1930; *Counsellor-at-Law,* 1931; *The Left Bank,* 1931; *The House in Blind Alley,* 1932; *We, the People,* 1933; *Judgment Day,* 1934; *The Passing of Chow-Chow,* 1934; *Three Plays Without Words,* 1934; *Between Two Worlds* (1934), 1935; *Not for Children,* 1935; *Black Sheep* (1932), 1938; *American Landscape* (1938), 1939; *Two on an Island,* 1940; *Flight to the West,* 1941; *A New Life,* 1944; *Dream Girl* (1945), 1946.

Other writings of Rice include *A Voyage to Purilia,* 1930, and *Imperial City: A Novel,* 1937.

BIOGRAPHY AND CRITICISM

Significant criticism of Rice as dramatist is that of Joseph W. Krutch, *The American Drama Since 1918: An Informal History,* New York, 1939, pp. 229–239, 248–250. See also Burns Mantle, *Contemporary American Playwrights,* New York, 1938, pp. 54–61, and Arthur H. Quinn, *A History of the American Drama from the Civil War to the Present Day,* rev. ed., New York, 1936, pp. 262–264.

A bio-bibliography is in Fred B. Millett, *Contemporary American Authors,* New York, 1940, pp. 539–541.

## JAMES WHITCOMB RILEY
### *1849–1916*

SEPARATE WORKS

*"The Old Swimmin'-Hole," and 'Leven More Poems,* 1883; *Character Sketches, The Boss Girl, A Christmas Story, and Other Sketches,* 1886; *Afterwhiles,* 1887; *Nye and Riley's Railway Guide,* 1888; *Old-Fashioned Roses,* 1888; *Pipes o' Pan at Zekesbury,* 1888; *Rhymes of Childhood,* 1890; *Neghborly Poems,* 1891; *The Flying Islands of the Night,* 1891; *Green Fields and Running Brooks,* 1892; *Poems Here at Home,* 1893; *Armazindy,* 1894; *The Days Gone By and Other Poems,* 1895; *A Tinkle of Bells and Other Poems,* 1895; *A Child-World,* 1897; *Rubaiyat of Doc Sifers,* 1897; *Riley Love-Lyrics,* 1899; *Home-Folks,* 1900; *The Book of Joyous Children,* 1902; *His Pa's Romance,* 1903; *A Defective Santa Claus,* 1904; *Riley Songs o' Cheer,* 1905; *While the Heart Beats Young,* 1906; *Morning,* 1907; *The Boys of the Old Glee Club,* 1907; *Old School Day Romances,* 1909; *A Hoosier Romance, 1868,* 1910; *Fugitive Pieces,* 1914; *Early Poems,* 1914.

COLLECTED WORKS

The Homestead Edition of *The Poems and Prose Sketches of James Whitcomb Riley* was published, New York, 1897–1914, 16 vols., and the

Greenfield Edition, Indianapolis, 1900–1916, 14 vols. Edmund H. Eitel edited the Biographical Edition of *The Complete Works of James Whitcomb Riley,* Indianapolis, 1913, 6 vols. The most recent collection of the whole works is *The Complete Poetical Works of James Whitcomb Riley,* Indianapolis, 1937, a one-volume reprint of a reissue of the Biographical Edition.

*Letters of James Whitcomb Riley* were edited by William L. Phelps, Indianapolis, 1930. Other gatherings are Edmund H. Eitel, ed., "Letters of Riley and Bill Nye," *Harper's Mag.,* CXXXVIII (1919), 473–484; and *Love Letters of the Bachelor Poet, James Whitcomb Riley, to Miss Elizabeth Kahle . . . ,* Boston, 1922.

BIOGRAPHY AND CRITICISM

The most useful narrative sketches of Riley are the companion volumes of Marcus Dickey, *The Youth of James Whitcomb Riley,* Indianapolis, 1919; and *The Maturity of James Whitcomb Riley,* Indianapolis, 1922. Two others are Edmund H. Eitel's account in the Biographical Edition of *The Complete Works* (1913); and Meredith Nicholson, "James Whitcomb Riley," *Atl. Mo.,* CXVIII (1916), 503–514.

Estimates and special studies are Louise P. Richards, "James Whitcomb Riley on a Country Newspaper," *Bookman,* XX (1904), 18–24; Harriet Monroe, "James Whitcomb Riley," *Poetry,* VIII (1916), 305–307; Bliss Carman, *James Whitcomb Riley: An Essay,* New York, 1918; Brander Matthews, *Introduction to American Literature,* New York, 1918, pp. 233–237; "The Singer of the Old Swimmin' Hole," in Henry A. Beers, *The Connecticut Wits and Other Essays,* New Haven, 1920, pp. 31–43; Edgar Lee Masters, "James Whitcomb Riley: A Sketch of His Life and an Appraisal of His Works," *Century Mag.,* CXIV (1927), 704–715; Alfred Kreymborg, *Our Singing Strength,* New York, 1929, pp. 242–243; and Robert Price, "James Whitcomb Riley in 1876," *Indiana Mag. Hist.,* XXV (1939), 129–140. A discussion of the whole Hoosier School is in Meredith Nicholson, *The Hoosiers* (1900).

PRIMARY SOURCES

Published memoirs and reminiscences incorporating useful material about Riley are Hamlin Garland, *Roadside Meetings,* New York, 1930, pp. 224–239; Clara E. Laughlin, *Reminiscences of James Whitcomb Riley,* New York, 1916; George S. Cottman, "Some Reminiscences of James Whitcomb Riley," *Indiana Mag. Hist.,* XIV (1918), 99–107; Daniel L. Marsh, *The Faith of the People's Poet; James Whitcomb Riley,* Indianapolis, 1920; Jeannette C. Nolan, *James Whitcomb Riley, Hoosier Poet,* New York, 1941; and Minnie B. Mitchell, *Hoosier Boy: James Whitcomb Riley,* Indianapolis, 1942.

The chief collection of Riley manuscripts is in the Indiana State Library. Other collections are those in the Indianapolis Public Library; the Library of Congress; and the library of Emory University.

### BIBLIOGRAPHY

A definitive bibliography for Riley has been compiled by Anthony J. and Dorothy R. Russo, *A Bibliography of James Whitcomb Riley*, Indianapolis, 1944.

## EDWIN ARLINGTON ROBINSON
*1869–1935*

### SEPARATE WORKS

*The Torrent and the Night Before*, 1896; *The Children of the Night*, 1897; *Captain Craig*, 1902 (rev. with additional poems, 1915); *The Town Down the River*, 1910; *Van Zorn*, 1914; *The Porcupine*, 1915; *The Man Against the Sky*, 1916; *Merlin*, 1917; *The Three Taverns*, 1920; *Lancelot* 1920; *Avon's Harvest*, 1921; *Roman Bartholow*, 1923; *The Man Who Died Twice*, 1924; *Dionysus in Doubt*, 1925; *Tristram*, 1927; *Sonnets 1889–1927*, 1928; *Three Poems*, 1928; *Fortunatus*, 1928; *Modred: A Fragment*, 1929; *The Prodigal Son*, 1929; *Cavender's House*, 1929; *The Glory of the Nightingales*, 1930; *Matthias at the Door*, 1931; *Nicodemus*, 1932; *Talifer*, 1933; *Amaranth*, 1934; *King Jasper*, 1935; *Hannibal Brown: Posthumous Poem*, 1936.

### COLLECTED WORKS

The earliest edition of *Collected Poems*, New York, 1921, was issued in one volume. It was followed by *Collected Poems of Edwin Arlington Robinson*, 5 vols., Cambridge, 1927. A one-volume *Collected Poems of Edwin Arlington Robinson*, New York, 1929, includes *Cavender's House*, separately issued in the same year. Bliss Perry edited *Edwin Arlington Robinson: Poems*, New York, 1931—selections, with a preface and Robinson's notes on his own poetry, here first printed. The latest and most inclusive edition is *Collected Poems of Edwin Arlington Robinson*, New York, 1937—a "complete edition with additional poems."

### LETTERS

Ridgely Torrence edited *Selected Letters of Edwin Arlington Robinson*, New York, 1940, with an introduction. Further letters have been published by Carl J. Weber, ed., *Letters of Edwin Arlington Robinson to Howard George Schmitt*, Waterville, Me., 1943. William T. Walsh, "Some Recollections of E. A. Robinson," *Catholic World*, CLV (1942), 522–531, includes some Robinson letters.

## BIOGRAPHY AND CRITICISM

The most recent estimate is Yvor Winters, *Edwin Arlington Robinson*, New York, 1947. Mark Van Doren's study, *Edwin Arlington Robinson*, was published in New York, 1927. Hermann Hagedorn's *Edwin Arlington Robinson: A Biography*, New York, 1938, was written from close acquaintance. An early biography is Ben R. Redman, *Edwin Arlington Robinson*, New York, 1926.

The most recent extended analysis of Robinson's philosophic development is Estelle Kaplan, *Philosophy in the Poetry of Edwin Arlington Robinson*, New York, 1940, with bibliography, pp. 145–153. Earlier estimates are Lloyd R. Morris, *The Poetry of Edwin Arlington Robinson: An Essay in Appreciation*, New York, 1923, with a bibliography compiled by W. V. R. Whitall, pp. 81–112; Lucius M. Beebe, *Aspects of the Poetry of Edwin Arlington Robinson*, Cambridge, 1928, with bibliography by Bradley Fisk, pp. 71–107; and Charles Cestre, *An Introduction to Edwin Arlington Robinson*, New York, 1930. Briefer critical estimates are "Edwin Arlington Robinson," in Percy H. Boynton, *Some Contemporary Americans . . .* , Chicago, 1924, pp. 16–32; "Edwin Arlington Robinson," in John Farrar, *The Literary Spotlight*, New York, 1924, pp. 116–124, 348; "Edwin Arlington Robinson," in J(ohn) C. Squire, *Contemporary American Authors*, New York, 1928, pp. 121–148; and "Edwin Arlington Robinson," in Thomas K. Whipple, *Spokesmen . . .* , New York, 1928, pp. 45–69. Estimates and appreciations by other poets are "Edwin Arlington Robinson," in Amy Lowell, *Tendencies in Modern American Poetry*, Boston, 1917, pp. 3–75—one of the earliest and still significant; "A Bird's-Eye View of Edwin Arlington Robinson," in *idem, Poetry and Poets*, Boston, 1930, pp. 210–232—a later companion-piece; Harriet Monroe's two essays, "Edwin Arlington Robinson," in her *Poets and Their Art*, New York, 1926, pp. 1–11; and "Robinson as Man and Poet," *Poetry*, XLVI (1935), 150–157; "Edwin Arlington Robinson," in John Drinkwater, *The Muse in Council*, New York, 1925, pp. 248–262; and Robert P. T. Coffin, *New Poetry of New England: Frost and Robinson*, Baltimore, 1938.

Recent brief critical studies are David Brown, "E. A. Robinson's Later Poems," *New Eng. Quar.*, X (1937), 487–502; Frederic I. Carpenter, "Tristram the Transcendent," *New Eng. Quar.*, XI (1938), 501–523; Floyd Stovall, "The Optimism Behind Robinson's Tragedies," *Amer. Lit.*, X (1938), 1–23; Hyatt H. Waggoner, "E. A. Robinson and the Cosmic Chill," *New Eng. Quar.*, XIII (1940), 65–84; Louise Dauner, "Vox Clamantis: Edwin Arlington Robinson as a Critic of American Democracy," *ibid.*, XV (1942), 401–426, and

"The Pernicious Rib: E. A. Robinson's Concept of Feminine Character," *Amer. Lit.*, XV (1943), 139–158; and Horace Gregory and Marya Zaturenska, "The Vein of Comedy in E. A. Robinson's Poetry," *Amer. Bookman*, I (1944), No. 2, 43–64—a brief evaluation of his poetic career.

Sources and themes have been made the study of Lucius M. Beebe, *Edwin Arlington Robinson and the Arthurian Legend*, Cambridge, 1927; E. Edith Pipkin, "The Arthur of Edwin Arlington Robinson," *English Jour.*, XIX (1930), 183–195; David Brown, "A Note on *Avon's Harvest*," *Amer. Lit.*, IX (1937), 343–349; C. Elta Van Norman, "Captain Craig," *College Eng.*, II (1941), 462–475; Louise Dauner, "Avon and Cavender: Two Children of the Night," *Amer. Lit.*, XIV (1942), 55–65; and W. Denham Sutcliffe, "The Original of Robinson's 'Captain Craig,'" *New Eng. Quar.*, XVI (1943), 407–431. Five studies by Charles Cestre are "Le *Tristan* d'Edwin Arlington Robinson," *Revue Anglo-Amér.*, V (1927–1928), 97–110, 219–228; "Le Dernier Poème d'Edwin Arlington Robinson: *Cavender's House*," *ibid.*, VI (1929), 489–507; "L'Œuvre Poétique d'Edwin Arlington Robinson," *ibid.*, I (1924), 279–294; "Amy Lowell, Robert Frost, and Edwin Arlington Robinson," *Johns Hopkins Alumni Mag.*, XIV (1926), 363–388; and "Récit, Drame, et Symbole chez Edwin Arlington Robinson," *Revue Anglo-Amér.*, IX (1932), 406–412.

Other evaluations are "Edwin Arlington Robinson," in Louis Untermeyer, *American Poetry Since 1900*, New York, 1923, pp. 42–66; "The Wise Music of Robinson," in Alfred Kreymborg, *Our Singing Strength*, New York, 1929, pp. 297–315; David Brown, "Some Rejected Poems of Edwin Arlington Robinson," *Amer. Lit.*, VII (1936), 395–414; Carl J. Weber, "Three Newly Discovered Articles by Edwin Arlington Robinson," *Colby Mercury*, VII (1941), 69–72; Winifred Burns, "Edwin Arlington Robinson in the Hands of the Reviewers," *Poet Lore*, XLVIII (1942), 164–175—with a bibliography (pp. 171–175) of reviews of each of his volumes; Carl J. Weber, "Poet and President," *New Eng. Quar.*, XVI (1943), 615–626; Esther W. Bates, *Edwin Arlington Robinson and His Manuscripts*, Waterville, Me., 1944—on his method of preparing them; Hoyt H. Hudson, "Robinson and Praed," *Poetry*, LXI (1943), 612–620—W. M. Praed's influence on Robinson's poetry; Richard Crowder, "'Here Are the Men . . . ;' E. A. Robinson's Male Character Types," *New Eng. Quar.*, XVIII (1945), 346–367; Yvor Winters, "Religious and Social Ideas in the Didactic Work of E. A. Robinson," *Arizona Quar.*, I (1945), No. 1, 70–85; and Richard Crowder, "E. A. Robinson's Craftsmanship: Opinions of Contemporary Poets," *Modern Language Notes*, LXI (1946), 1–14, and "The Emergence of E. A. Robinson," *So. Atl. Quar.*, XLV (1946), 89–98. See also the *Colby Lib. Quar.*, Ser. II (Feb. 1947), pp. 1–13.

PRIMARY SOURCES

Among printed sources, useful especially as reminiscences, are Laura E. Richards, *E. A. R.*, Cambridge, 1936; Rollo W. Brown, *Next Door to a Poet: A Friendly Glimpse of Edwin Arlington Robinson*, New York, 1937; Olivia H. D. Torrence, "The Poet at the Dinner Table," *Colophon*, n.s. III (1938), no. 1, pp. 92–99; and Fredericka Beatty, "Edwin Arlington Robinson as I Knew Him," *So. Atl. Quar.*, XLIII (1944), 375–381.

The most important collection of Robinson manuscripts is in the Library of Congress. Further manuscript material is in the Harvard College Library, the Princeton University Library, Williams College Library, and the Alderman Library, University of Virginia.

BIBLIOGRAPHY

Lillian Lippincott, *A Bibliography of the Writings and Criticisms of Edwin Arlington Robinson*, Boston, 1937, which is very complete, is supplemented by Charles B. Hogan, "Edwin Arlington Robinson: New Bibliographical Notes," *Papers Bibliog. Soc. Amer.*, XXXV (1941), 115–144. Volumes of biography and criticism which contain useful bibliographical items are noted above, under that heading. See also Leonidas W. Payne, Jr., "The First Edition of E. A. Robinson's *The Peterborough Idea*," *Univ. of Texas Studies in Eng.*, No. 3926 (1939), pp. 219–231.

Two useful bibliographies have been compiled by Harry H. Clark, ed., *Major American Poets*, New York, 1936, pp. 938–940 (annotated), and Harry Hartwick, in Walter F. Taylor, *A History of American Letters*, New York, 1936, pp. 569–570.

# O. E. (OLE EDVART) RÖLVAAG
## 1876–1931

SEPARATE WORKS IN ENGLISH

*Giants in the Earth*, 1927; *Peder Victorious*, 1929; *Pure Gold*, 1930; *Their Father's God*, 1931; *The Boat of Longing*, 1933.

REPRINTS

A text edition of *Giants in the Earth* was prepared with introduction by Vernon L. Parrington, New York, 1929, for Harper's Modern Classics. No collection of Rölvaag's writings has been published.

BIOGRAPHY AND CRITICISM

Theodore Jorgenson and Nora O. Solum published a full-length biography, *Ole Edvart Rölvaag: A Biography,* New York, 1939. It quotes many letters from Rölvaag, and is indexed, but contains no bibliography. The sketch of Rölvaag in *Dict. Amer. Biog.* (1935) was contributed by Einar I. Haugen.

Among earlier estimates of Rölvaag are Julius E. Olson, "Rölvaag's Novels of Norwegian Pioneer Life in the Dakotas," *Scandinavian Studies and Notes,* IX (1926), 45-55; Vernon L. Parrington, *Main Currents in American Thought,* III (1930), 387-396; and Einar I. Haugen, "Rölvaag: Norwegian-American," *Norwegian-Amer. Stud. and Records,* VII (1933), 53-73.

Recent studies are George L. White, Jr., "O. E. Rölvaag: Prophet of a People," in *Scandinavian Themes in American Fiction,* Philadelphia, 1937, pp. 97-108; Theodore Jorgenson, "The Main Factors in Rölvaag's Authorship," *Norwegian-Amer. Studies and Records,* X (1938), 135-151; Kenneth Bjørk, "The Unknown Rölvaag: Secretary in the Norwegian-American Historical Association," *ibid.,* XI (1940), 114-149; "Ole Edvart Rölvaag," in Percy H. Boynton, *America in Contemporary Fiction,* New York, 1940, pp. 225-240; and Joseph E. Baker, "Western Man Against Nature: *Giants in the Earth,*" *College Eng.,* IV (1942), 19-26.

PRIMARY SOURCES

The files of the Norwegian-American Historical Association, Northfield, Minn., hold the bulk of Rölvaag's manuscripts. They are described in Nora O. Solum, "The Sources of the Rølvaag Biography," *Norwegian-Amer. Studies and Records,* XI (1940), 150-159. An interview by Lincoln Colcord, who knew Rölvaag well, is "Rölvaag the Fisherman Shook His Fist at Fate," *Amer. Mag.,* CV (1928), 37, 188-192.

BIBLIOGRAPHY

The fullest bibliographical listing is in Fred B. Millett, *Contemporary American Authors,* New York, 1940, pp. 554-556. It includes a list of Rölvaag's writings in Norwegian which have not been translated. There is a partial bibliographical listing in Parrington's edition of *Giants* (1929), pp. 467-468.

# EDGAR (EVERTSON) SALTUS
## *1855-1921*

SEPARATE WORKS

*Balzac,* 1884; *The Philosophy of Disenchantment,* 1885; *The Anatomy of Negation,* 1886; *Mr. Incoul's Misadventure,* 1887; *The Truth About Tristrem Varick,* 1888; *Eden,* 1888; *A Transaction in Hearts,* 1889; *A Transient Guest and Other Episodes,* 1889; *The Pace that Kills,* 1889; *Love and Lore,* 1890;

*Mary Magdalen*, 1891; *Imperial Purple*, 1892; *Facts in the Curious Case of H. Hyrtle, Esq.*, 1892; *Madame Sapphira*, 1893; *Enthralled*, 1894; *When Dreams Come True*, 1894; *Purple and Fine Women*, 1903; *The Pomps of Satan*, 1904; *The Perfume of Eros*, 1905; *Vanity Square*, 1906; *Historia Amoris*, 1906; *The Lords of the Ghostland*, 1907; *Daughters of the Rich*, 1909; *The Monster*, 1912; *Oscar Wilde: An Idler's Impression*, 1917; *The Paliser Case*, 1919; *The Imperial Orgy*, 1920; *The Gardens of Aphrodite*, 1920; *The Ghost Girl*, 1922; *Parnassians Personally Encountered*, 1923; *The Uplands of Dream*, 1925; *Victor Hugo and Golgotha*, 1925; *Poppies and Mandragora*, 1926.

REPRINTS

The writings of Saltus published posthumously were edited by his wife, Marie Saltus. Reprints of his books are *The Anatomy of Negation* (1886), New York, 1925; *Mr. Incoul's Misadventure* (1887), New York, 1925; *Purple and Fine Women* (1903), Chicago, 1925, with an introduction by W. L. George; *The Imperial Orgy* (1920), in the Modern Lib., New York, 1927. Selected reprints are *Wit and Wisdom from Edgar Saltus*, London, 1905. Some of the novels have been translated into French.

BIOGRAPHY AND CRITICISM

The best brief narrative sketch of Saltus is that of Granville Hicks in *Dict. Amer. Biog.* (1935). The biography by his third wife, Marie Saltus, *Edgar Saltus, the Man*, Chicago, 1925, is lushly appreciative and deals with his later years. One of the earliest critical estimates is Ramsay Colles, "A Publicist: Edgar Saltus," *Westminster Rev.*, CLXII (1904), 463–474. An appreciation by Carl Van Vechten is "Edgar Saltus," in *Excavations*, New York, 1926, pp. 89–128. Others are Gorham B. Munson, "The Limbo of American Literature," *Broom*, II (1922), 250–260; "Edgar Saltus," in Arthur Symons, *Dramatis Personae*, London, 1925, pp. 263–268; and Charles Honce, introduction to *The Uplands of Dream* (1925).

PRIMARY SOURCES

Factual data are in *Who's Who in America*, 1920–1921, and Ethel S. Ludington, *Ludington-Saltus Records*, New York, 1925, ed. by Louis E. De Forest. James G. Huneker's autobiography *Steeplejack* (1919) is useful; and Saltus figures as a minor character in Huneker's only novel, *Painted Veils* (1920). The typescript of *The Imperial Orgy* is in the Henry E. Huntington Library.

BIBLIOGRAPHY

The most satisfactory bibliographical listing is in Jacob Blanck, *Merle Johnson's American First Editions*, 4th ed., New York, 1942.

# CARL (CHARLES AUGUST) SANDBURG
*b. 1878*

**SEPARATE WORKS**

*In Reckless Ecstasy*, 1904; *Chicago Poems*, 1916; *Cornhuskers*, 1918; *Smoke and Steel*, 1920; *Slabs of the Sunburnt West*, 1922; *Rootabaga Stories*, 1922; *Rootabaga Pigeons*, 1923; *Abraham Lincoln: The Prairie Years*, 1926; *Good Morning, America*, 1928; *Steichen, the Photographer*, 1929; *Potato Face*, 1930; *Early Moon*, 1930; *Mary Lincoln, Wife and Widow* (with Paul M. Angle), 1932; *The People, Yes*, 1936; *A Lincoln and Whitman Miscellany*, 1938; *Abraham Lincoln: The War Years*, 1939. Sandburg edited a ballad collection, *The American Songbag*, 1927.

**COLLECTIONS**

*Selected Poems of Carl Sandburg*, London, 1926, was edited by Rebecca West with a critical introduction. A second collection, *Early Moon*, New York, 1930, was published especially for children. *Home Front Memo*, New York, 1943, is a gathering of pamphlets, speeches, broadcasts, and other miscellaneous writings.

**BIOGRAPHY AND CRITICISM**

Karl W. Detzer, *Carl Sandburg: A Study in Personality and Background*, New York, 1941, is a narrative biography. The earliest extended critical recognition is "Edgar Lee Masters and Carl Sandburg," in Amy Lowell, *Tendencies in Modern American Poetry*, Boston, 1917, pp. 139–232, written immediately upon the publication of *Chicago Poems* (1916). Other estimates of Sandburg's writings, before the publication of the first part of the Lincoln biography in 1926, are "Poetic Realism: Carl Sandburg," in Conrad Aiken, *Scepticisms*, New York, 1919, pp. 143–148; Stuart P. Sherman, *Americans*, New York, 1922, pp. 239–245; Harry Hansen, *Midwest Portraits*, New York, 1923, pp. 15–91—an extended account; "Carl Sandburg," in Louis Untermeyer, *American Poetry Since 1900*, New York, 1923, pp. 67–87; Carl Van Doren, *Many Minds*, New York, 1924, pp. 136–150; Percy H. Boynton, *Some Contemporary Americans*, Chicago, 1924, pp. 62–69; Gorham B. Munson, "The Single Portent of Carl Sandburg," *Double Dealer*, VII (1924), 17–26; "Carl Sandburg," in Paul Rosenfeld, *Port of New York*, New York, 1924, pp. 65–81; Llewellyn Jones, *First Impressions*, New York, 1925, pp. 53–68; and Bruce Weirick, *From Whitman to Sandburg in American Poetry: A Critical Survey*, New York, 1924, pp. 210–221.

Later estimates are "Carl Sandburg," in Harriet Monroe, *Poets and Their Art*, New York, 1926, pp. 29–38; Rebecca West, "The Voice of Chicago," *Sat.*

*Rev. Lit.,* III (Sept. 4, 1926), 81–83—reprinted as the introduction to *Selected Poems* (1926); Constance L. Skinner, "Songs That Give Reason for Singing," *No. Amer. Rev.,* CCXXIII (1926), 695–700; Howard M. Jones, "Backgrounds of Sorrow," *Virginia Quar. Rev.,* III (1927), 111–123; "Carl Sandburg," in Thomas K. Whipple, *Spokesmen,* New York, 1928, pp. 161–183; "Carl Sandburg," in David Karsner, *Sixteen Authors to One,* New York, 1928, pp. 145–158; Alfred Kreymborg, *Our Singing Strength,* New York, 1929, pp. 382–394; Charles H. Compton, "Who Reads Carl Sandburg?" *So. Atl. Quar.,* XXVIII (1929), 190–200; Morton D. Zabel, "Sandburg's Testament," *Poetry,* XLIX (1936), 33–45; Newton Arvin, "Carl Sandburg," in Malcolm Cowley, ed., *After the Genteel Tradition,* New York, 1936, pp. 79–87; and Babette Deutsch, "Poetry for the People," *English Jour.,* XXVI (1937), 265–274.

There are Sandburg manuscripts in the Harvard College Library.

William P. Schenk compiled "Carl Sandburg: A Bibliography," *Bul. Bibl.,* XVI (1936), 4–7. Further bibliographical material is in Fred B. Millett, *Contemporary American Authors,* New York, 1940, pp. 557–561. See also the checklist by Frances Cheney, in Allen Tate, *Sixty American Poets, 1896–1944,* Washington, 1945, pp. 143–147.

## GEORGE SANTAYANA
### b. 1863

SEPARATE WORKS

*Sonnets and Other Verses,* 1894; *The Sense of Beauty,* 1896; *Lucifer: A Theological Tragedy,* 1899; *Interpretations of Poetry and Religion,* 1900; *A Hermit of Carmel and Other Poems,* 1901; *The Life of Reason,* 1905–1906; *Three Philosophical Poets: Lucretius, Dante, and Goethe,* 1910; *Winds of Doctrine,* 1913; *Egotism in German Philosophy,* 1916; *Character and Opinion in the United States,* 1920; *Soliloquies in England and Later Soliloquies,* 1922; *Poems,* 1922; *Scepticism and Animal Faith,* 1923; *Dialogues in Limbo,* 1925; *Platonism and the Spiritual Life,* 1927; *The Realm of Essence,* 1927; *The Realm of Matter,* 1930; *The Genteel Tradition at Bay,* 1931; *Five Essays,* 1933; *The Last Puritan,* 1935; *Obiter Scripta,* 1936; *The Realm of Truth,* 1937; *The Realm of Spirit,* 1940; *The Idea of Christ in the Gospels,* 1946.

The first two volumes of Santayana's autobiography, *Persons and Places,* have been published as *The Background of My Life,* New York, 1944; and *The Middle Span,* New York, 1945.

COLLECTED WORKS AND REPRINTS

*The Works of George Santayana* were issued, New York, 1936–1937,

14 vols. *The Realm of Being,* New York, 1942, 4 vols., includes the four "Realms": *Essence* (1927), *Matter* (1930), *Truth* (1937), *Spirit* (1940). Logan P. Smith edited *Little Essays Drawn from the Writings of George Santayana,* London, 1920. Irwin Edman edited *The Philosophy of Santayana: Selections,* New York, 1936, which was included in the Modern Lib., New York, 1942.

Several letters of Santayana to William James are in Ralph Barton Perry, *The Thought and Character of William James,* Boston, 1935.

BIOGRAPHY AND CRITICISM

Paul A. Schilpp in *The Philosophy of George Santayana,* Chicago, 1940, edited a series of critical essays on Santayana's thought, with the philosopher's own extended reply. Other recent studies of Santayana as philosopher are George W. Howgate, *George Santayana,* Philadelphia, 1938; and Van Meter Ames, *Proust and Santayana: The Aesthetic Way of Life,* Chicago, 1937.

Among early estimates of Santayana are Morris R. Cohen, "On American Philosophy: George Santayana," *New Repub.,* XXIII (1920), 221-223; Horace M. Kallen, "America and the Life of Reason," *Jour. Philos.,* XVIII (1921), 533-551, 568-575; Joseph Ratner, "George Santayana's Theory of Religion," *Jour. Religion,* III (1923), 458-475; Marten Ten Hoor, "George Santayana's Theory of Knowledge," *Jour. Philos.,* XX (1923), 197-211; and Joseph Ratner, "George Santayana: A Philosophy of Piety," *Monist,* XXXIV (1924), 236-259.

Later studies include Katherine Gilbert, "Santayana's Doctrine of Aesthetic Expression," *Philosophical Rev.,* XXV (1926), 221-235; Daniel Cory, "A Study of Santayana . . . ," *Jour. Philosophical Studies,* II (1927), 349-364; Sterling P. Lamprecht, "Santayana, Then and Now," *Jour. Philos.,* XXV (1928), 533-550; Edward I. Watkins, "The Philosophy of George Santayana," *Dublin Rev.,* CLXXXII (1928), 32-45; Hugo T. Saglio, "Implications of *The Life of Reason,"* *Jour. Philos.,* XXVIII (1931), 533-544; John H. Randall, Jr., "The Latent Idealism of a Materialist," *ibid.,* 645-660; Sterling P. Lamprecht, "Naturalism and Agnosticism in Santayana," *ibid.,* XXX (1933), 561-574.

Santayana as poet and man of letters is the subject of John C. Ransom, "Art and Mr. Santayana," *Virginia Quar. Rev.,* XIII (1937), 420-436; Philip B. Rice, "George Santayana: The Philosopher as Poet," *Kenyon Rev.,* II (1940), 460-475. Earlier studies are "George Santayana," in William Archer, *Poets of the Younger Generation,* New York, 1902, pp 373-384; Jessie B. Rittenhouse, *The Younger American Poets,* Boston, 1904, pp. 94-109; George O'Neill, "Poetry, Religion, and Professor Santayana," *Studies,* X (1921), 451-463. Other studies are Dickinson S. Miller, "Mr. Santayana and William James," *Harvard Grad. Mag.,* Mar., 1921, pp. 348-364; Herbert W. Smith. "George

Santayana," *Amer. Rev.*, I (1923), 190–204; "The Tower of Irony: George Santayana," in Carl Van Doren, *Many Minds*, New York, 1924, pp. 83–101; Margaret Münsterberg, "Santayana at Cambridge," *Amer. Mercury*, I (1924), 69–74; John B. Priestley, *Figures in Modern Literature*, London, 1924, pp. 165–187; Harold A. Larrabee, "George Santayana . . . ," *Sewanee Rev.*, XXXIX (1931), 209–221, 325–339; *idem*, "Robert Bridges and George Santayana," *Amer. Scholar*, I (1932), 167–182; Irwin Edman, "Santayana at Seventy," *Sat. Rev. Lit.*, X (Dec. 16, 1933), 349–350; George W. Howgate, "Santayana and Humanism," *Sewanee Rev.*, XLIII (1935), 49–57; Donald MacCampbell, "Santayana's Debt to New England," *New Eng. Quar.*, VIII (1935), 203–214; Archibald A. Bowman, *A Sacramental Universe . . .*, Princeton, 1939—with a special chapter on the philosophical system of Santayana; William S. Knickerbocker, "Figaro Among the Philosophers: George Santayana," *Sewanee Rev.*, L (1941), 250–265; George W. Howgate, "The Essential Santayana," *Mark Twain Quar.*, V (1942), 7–18; Paul Hoffman, "Santayanas *The Last Puritan* und seine Kulturkritik des Amerikanismus," *Germanisch-Romanische Monatschrift*, XXX (1942), 21–39; J. Glenn Gray, "Plato the Greek and Santayana the Cosmopolitan," *Amer. Scholar*, XII (1943), 186–204; Daniel Cory, "Santayana in Europe," *Atl. Mo.*, CLXXIV (1944), 53–62—his life in Rome; and Stanley Dell, "Truth of History . . . ," *Chimera*, V (1944), 41–51.

The best source material will be found in Santayana's autobiography, *Persons and Places* (1944–1945), and in the few published letters mentioned above under Collected Works.

A bibliography of his writings to October, 1940, is compiled by Shohig Terzian, in Paul A. Schilpp, *The Philosophy of George Santayana*, Chicago, 1940, pp. 607–668. For secondary items, see Fred B. Millett, *Contemporary American Authors*, New York, 1940, pp. 561–565. There is a checklist in George W. Howgate, *George Santayana* (1938), pp. 349–352.

# WILLIAM SAROYAN
## b. 1908

### SHORT STORIES AND NOVELS

*The Daring Young Man on the Flying Trapeze, and Other Stories*, 1934; *Inhale and Exhale*, 1936; *Three Times Three*, 1936; *Little Children*, 1937; *Love, Here Is My Hat*, 1938; *A Native American*, 1938; *The Trouble with Tigers*, 1938; *Peace, It's Wonderful*, 1939; *My Name Is Aram*, 1940; *Saroyan's Fables*, 1941; *The Human Comedy*, 1943; *Dear Baby*, 1944; *The Adventures of Wesley Jackson*, 1946.

PLAYS *

*The Hungerers,* 1939; *My Heart's in the Highlands* (1939), 1940; *The Time of Your Life* (1939), 1940; *The Ping-Pong Game,* 1940; *Subway Circus,* 1940; *Love's Old Sweet Song* (1939), 1940; *Three Plays by William Saroyan: The Beautiful People, Sweeney in the Trees, and Across the Board on To-morrow Morning,* 1941; *Razzle Dazzle,* 1942; *Get Away, Old Man* (1943), 1944; *Jim Dandy,* 1947.

REPRINTS

*The Daring Young Man on the Flying Trapeze* was reprinted in the Modern Library, New York, 1941. *Forty-eight Saroyan Stories,* New York, 1942, is a reprint of *Love, Here Is My Hat* and *Peace, It's Wonderful. Best Stories of William Saroyan* was published in London, 1942.

BIOGRAPHY AND CRITICISM

Studies of Saroyan as novelist and playwright include Harlan Hatcher, "William Saroyan," *English Jour.,* XXVIII (1939), 169–177; Edmund Wilson, "The Boys in the Back Room: William Saroyan," *New Repub.,* CIII (1940), 697–698; George J. Nathan, "Saroyan: Whirling Dervish of Fresno," *Amer. Mercury,* LI (1940), 303–308; Joseph Mersand, "William Saroyan and the American Imagination," *Players Mag.,* XVII (Jan., 1941), 9; Edwin B. Burgum, "The Lonesome Young Man on the Flying Trapeze," *Virginia Quar. Rev.,* XX (1944), 392–403; and Philip Rahv, "William Saroyan: A Minority Report," *Amer. Mercury,* LVII (1943), 371–377.

A bio-bibliography is in Fred B. Millett, *Contemporary American Authors,* New York, 1940, pp. 567–569.


# CHARLES SEALSFIELD
## (Karl Anton Postl)
### *1793–1864*

WORKS

Translations of Sealsfield's German works are scattered and incomplete. English versions of his accepted masterpiece, *Das Cajütenbuch,* are *The Cabin Book* . . ., tr. by C. F. Mersch, New York, 1844, and tr. by Sarah Powell, London, 1852.

Sealsfield's own redaction of *Die Vereinigten Staaten* . . ., 1827 (Vol. I), was published as *The United States of North America as They Are* . . ., 1827. An abbreviated version of Vol. II of this work was published as *The*

* Dates in parentheses are of production when it differs from publication.

*Americans As They Are . . .*, 1828. Other translations include *Austria As It Is . . .*, 1828; *Tokeah; or, The White Rose . . .*, 1829, recast as *Der Legitime und die Republikaner*, 1833. Sealsfield's novel of Mexico, *Der Virey und die Aristokraten . . .*, 1835, is not reproduced in a complete English translation.

The following novels on "American" themes were published under various serial titles: *Transatlantische Reiseskizzen; Lebensbilder aus beiden Hemisphären*, etc. As separate items they are known as *George Howard's Esq. Brautfahrt*, 1834; *Christophorus Bärenhäuter*, 1834; *Morton, oder die grosse Tour*, 1835; *Ralph Doughby's Esq. Brautfahrt*, 1835; *Pflanzerleben*, 1836; *Die Farbigen*, 1836; and *Nathan, der Squatter-Regulator*, 1837.

His later works include *Die deutsch-amerikanischen Wahlverwandtschaften*, 1839–1840; *Das Cajütenbuch, oder nationale Charakteristiken*, 1841; *Süden und Norden*, 1842–1843—a historical novel of Mexico during the years of the early republic; and *Die Grabesschuld, nachgelassene Erzählung*, 1873.

Sealsfield's collected works, *Gesammelte Werke von Charles Sealsfield*, Stuttgart, 1845–1847, 15 vols., are not complete. No definitive edition has yet been published. Albert B. Faust has made available the largest collection of Sealsfield letters in "Unpublished Letters of Charles Sealsfield," *PMLA*, IX (1894), 343–402, and *Charles Sealsfield, der Dichter beider Hemisphären*, Weimar, 1897.

### BIOGRAPHY AND CRITICISM

The most comprehensive biography of Sealsfield to date is that of Albert B. Faust, *Charles Sealsfield, der Dichter beider Hemisphären*, Weimar, 1897. Still important as appreciation is F. Hardman, "The Writings of Charles Sealsfield," *Foreign Quar. Rev.*, XXXVII (1846), 416–448. Further primary material is in K. M. Kertbery, *Erinnerung an Charles Sealsfield*, Brussels and Leipzig, 1864. One of the earliest scholarly studies is Albert B. Faust, *Charles Sealsfield (Carl Postl) Materials for a Biography; A Study of His Style; His Influence upon American Literature . . .*, Baltimore, 1892.

A valuable contemporary estimate is Saint-René Taillandier, "Charles Sealsfield: Le Romancier de la Démocratie Américaine," *Revue des Deux Mondes*, XXIII (1848), 461–499.

Early brief studies are Otto Heller, "Some Sources of Sealsfield," *Modern Philol.*, VII (1910), 587–592; Preston A. Barba, "Sealsfield Sources," *German Amer. Annals*, n.s. IX (1911), 31–39; and Bernhard A. Uhlendorf, *Charles Sealsfield: Ethnic Elements and Natural Problems in His Works*, Chicago, 1922.

Recent studies include William P. Dallman, *The Spirit of America as Interpreted in the Works of Charles Sealsfield*, St. Louis, 1935; Otto Heller, "Charles Sealsfield, a Forgotten Discoverer of the Mississippi," *Missouri Hist. Rev.*, XXXI (1937), 382–401; *idem, The Language of Charles Sealsfield: A*

*Study of Atypical Usage,* St. Louis, 1941; Karl J. Arndt and Henry Groen, "Sealsfield, the 'Greatest American Author,'" *Amer.-German Rev.,* VII (June, 1941), 12–15; Karl J. Arndt, "The Cooper-Sealsfield Exchange of Criticism," *Amer. Lit.,* XV (1943), 16–24; and *idem,* "Sealsfield's Early Reception in England and America," *Germanic Rev.,* XVIII (1943), 176–195.

An unpublished dissertation is Nanette M. Ashby, "The Sealsfield Controversy: A Study of Publication Conditions Affecting the Reception in America of the Works of Charles Sealsfield," Stanford Univ., 1939.

A standard bibliographical and reference guide is Otto Heller and Theodore H. Leon, *Charles Sealsfield: Bibliography of His Writings, Together with a Classified and Annotated Catalogue of Literature Relating to His Works and Life,* St. Louis, 1939, 88 pp.

# SAMUEL SEWALL
## *1652–1730*

### SEPARATE WORKS

*The Revolution in New England Justified* (with Edward Rawson), 1691; *Phaenomena quaedam Apocalyptica,* 1697; *The Selling of Joseph,* 1700; *Proposals Touching the Accomplishment of Prophecies,* 1713; *Diary of Samuel Sewall,* 1878–1882.

### COLLECTED WORKS

"A Memorial Relating to the Kennebec Indians," dated Boston, 1721, is published in *Coll. Maine Hist. Soc.,* 1st ser., III (1853), 351–353. *Diary of Samuel Sewall, 1674–1729,* 3 vols., *Coll. Mass. Hist. Soc.,* 5th ser., V–VII (1878–1882), needs reediting. The *Letter-Book of Samuel Sewall,* 2 vols., is in *Coll. Mass. Hist. Soc.,* 6th ser., I–II (1886–1888). George L. Kittredge edited "Letters of Samuel Lee and Samuel Sewall Relating to New England and the Indians," *Pub. Colonial Soc. Mass.,* XIV (1913), 142–155.

An abridgment of *Samuel Sewall's Diary* was edited by Mark Van Doren, New York, 1927.

### BIOGRAPHY AND CRITICISM

Nathan H. Chamberlain, *Samuel Sewall and the World He Lived In,* Boston, 1897, is a narrative biography. John L. Sibley's account in *Biographical Sketches of Graduates of Harvard University,* Cambridge, II (1881), 345–364, is still authoritative. The sketch in *Dict. Amer. Biog.* (1935) is by James T. Adams.

Sewall as a man of letters is the subject of "A Puritan Pepys," in Henry C. Lodge, *Studies in History,* Boston, 1884, pp. 21–84; Moses C. Tyler, *A*

*History of American Literature During the Colonial Period,* rev. ed., New York, 1897, II, 99–103; Vernon L. Parrington, *Main Currents in American Thought* . . . , New York, I (1927), 88–97; Henry W. Lawrence, "Samuel Sewall: Revealer of Puritan New England," *So. Atl. Quar.,* XXXIII (1934), 20–37; and Karl W. Dykema, "Samuel Sewall Reads John Dryden," *Amer. Lit.,* XIV (1942), 157–161. Further data are in Cecil H. C. Howard, "Chief Justice Samuel Sewall," *Essex Institute Hist. Coll.,* XXXVII (1901), 161–176; and George P. Winship, "Samuel Sewall and the New England Company," *Proc. Mass. Hist. Soc.,* LXVII (1945), 55–110.

The bulk of Sewall's manuscript material, his diary and other papers, is in the library of the Massachusetts Historical Society. His commonplace book is in the Boston Public Library.

## THOMAS SHEPARD
### *1605–1649*

SEPARATE WORKS

*The Sincere Convert,* 1640; *New Englands Lamentation for Old Englands Present Errours,* 1645; *The Day-Breaking,* 1647; *Certain Select Cases Resolved,* 1648; *The Clear Sun-shine of the Gospel,* 1648; *The First Principles of the Oracles of God,* 1648; *The Sound Beleever,* 1649; *Theses Sabbaticae,* 1649; *Four Necessary Cases of Conscience,* 1651; *A Defence of the Answer* (with John Allin), 1652; *Subjection to Christ,* 1652; *A Short Catechism,* 1654; *The Parable of the Ten Virgins,* 1660; *The Church-Membership of Children,* 1663; *Wine for Gospel Wantons,* 1668.

COLLECTED WORKS

One of the very few collected editions of works of seventeenth century New England divines is John A. Albro, ed., *The Works of Thomas Shepard* . . . , Boston, 1853, 3 vols.; it contains a life of Shepard by the editor. Thomas Prince collected some of Shepard's treatises in *Three Valuable Pieces* . . . , Boston, 1747. *The Autobiography of Thomas Shepard* . . . was first edited from manuscript by Nehemiah Adams, Boston, 1832. A sermon outline, from a manuscript now lost, is "Thomas Shepard's Election Sermon, in 1638," *New Eng. Hist. Geneal. Reg.,* XXIV (1870), 361–366. A letter from "Thomas Shepard to Hugh Peter, 1645," was published in *Amer. Hist. Rev.,* IV (1898), 105–107.

EDITED TEXTS AND REPRINTS

Reprints of the following separate works have been made: *The Day-Breaking* (1647), *Coll. Mass. Hist. Soc.,* 3rd ser., IV (1834), 1–23; *The Clear*

*Sun-shine* (1648), *ibid.,* pp. 25–67; also New York, 1865. *A Short Catechism* (1654) was reproduced in Photostat Americana, No. 251 (1930). "The Autobiography of Thomas Shepard," prefaced by a complete bibliography, was reprinted in *Pub. Colonial Soc. Mass.,* XXVII (1932), 345–400.

BIOGRAPHY AND CRITICISM

John A. Albro wrote *The Life of Thomas Shepard,* Boston, 1847. It also appears in Vol. I of Albro's collection of Shepard's *Works* (1853). The best brief sketch is Samuel E. Morison, "Master Thomas Shepard," in *Builders of the Bay Colony,* Boston, 1930, pp. 105–134. Cotton Mather's narrative account was published in Bk. III of the *Magnalia* (1702). Other studies are Moses C. Tyler, *A History of American Literature During the Colonial Period,* rev. ed., New York, 1897, I, 204–209; Andrew M. Davis, "A Few Words About the Writings of Thomas Shepard," *Pub. Cambridge Hist. Soc.,* III (1908), 79–89; and *idem,* "Hints of Contemporary Life in the Writings of Thomas Shepard," *Pub. Colonial Soc. Mass.,* XII (1911), 136–162.

PRIMARY SOURCES

Shepard's manuscript "Autobiography" is in the possession of the First Church, Cambridge. Unpublished manuscripts are in the possession of the New York Public Library (including a diary), the American Antiquarian Society, the New England Historic Genealogical Society, and the Massachusetts Historical Society.

BIBLIOGRAPHY

The most authoritative bibliographical listing of both primary and secondary material is in the preface to the edition of the "Autobiography," *Pub. Colonial Soc. Mass.,* XXVII (1932), 347–350.

# STUART P(RATT) SHERMAN
## *1881–1926*

SEPARATE WORKS

*Matthew Arnold: How To Know Him,* 1917; *On Contemporary Literature,* 1917; *Americans,* 1922; *The Genius of America: Studies in Behalf of the Younger Generation,* 1923; *Men of Letters of the British Isles* (with Theodore Spicer-Simson), 1924; *Points of View,* 1924; *My Dear Cornelia,* 1924; *Letters to a Lady in the Country* . . . (with Garreta Busey), 1925; *Critical Woodcuts,* 1926; *The Main Stream,* 1927; *Shaping Men and Women: Essays on Literature and Life,* 1928; *The Emotional Discovery of America and Other Essays,* 1932.

BIOGRAPHY AND CRITICISM

Within three years of Sherman's death a biography, important for its collection of letters, was published by two friends and associates, Jacob Zeitlin and Homer Woodbridge, *Life and Letters of Stuart P. Sherman*, New York, 1929, 2 vols., with a bibliography, II, 801–860, exhaustive for Sherman's own writings.

Few critical essays dealt significantly with Sherman during his life. One of the earliest was Charles Heaton, "A Philosophical Litterateur," *Monist*, XXVIII (1918), 608–612. Others were "The Great and Good Tradition. Stuart P. Sherman," in Carl Van Doren, *Many Minds*, New York, 1924, pp. 67–82; "Mr. Sherman," in Joseph W. Beach, *The Outlook for American Prose*, Chicago, 1926, pp. 92–108; Gerald Carson, "Mr. Stuart Sherman Discovers Aphrodite Pandemos," *Bookman*, LXIII (1926), 389–396; and Mary M. Colum, "Stuart P. Sherman," *Sat. Rev. Lit.*, II (June 26, 1926), 881–882.

Later studies were George E. De Mille, "Stuart P. Sherman: The Illinois Arnold," *Sewanee Rev.*, XXXV (1927), 78–93; Henry S. Canby, "Stuart P. Sherman: 'The American Scholar,'" *Sat. Rev. Lit.*, VI (Oct. 5, 1929), 201–202, 205–206; Jacob Zeitlin, ed., "Stuart P. Sherman and Paul Elmer More: Correspondence," *Bookman*, LXX (1929), 43–53—a publication of further letters; Newton Arvin, "Stuart Sherman," *Hound and Horn*, III (1930), 304–313; Edwin B. Burgum, "Stuart Sherman," *English Jour.*, XIX (1930), 137–150; Norman Foerster, "The Literary Historians," *Bookman*, LXXI (1930), 365–374; Austin Warren, "Humanist into Journalist: Stuart Sherman," *Sewanee Rev.*, XXXVIII (1930), 357–365; "Sherman," in George E. De Mille, *Literary Criticism in America*, New York, 1931, pp. 245–276; "Stuart Sherman and the War Age," in George R. Elliott, *Humanism and Imagination*, Chapel Hill, N.C., 1938, pp. 66–85; "Stuart Pratt Sherman," in John P. Pritchard, *Return to the Fountains*, Durham, N.C., 1942, pp. 191–199.

The fullest bibliographical listing to date of publication is in Zeitlin and Woodbridge, *Life and Letters* . . . (1929), II, 801–860. More recent items are in Fred B. Millett, *Contemporary American Authors*, New York, 1940, pp. 575–578.

# WILLIAM GILMORE SIMMS
## *1806–1870*

SEPARATE WORKS

Fiction: *The Book of My Lady*, 1833; *Martin Faber: The Story of a Criminal*, 1833; *Guy Rivers: A Tale of Georgia*, 1834; *The Yemassee: A Romance of Carolina*, 1835; *The Partisan: A Tale of the Revolution*, 1835; *Mellichampe: A Legend of the Santee*, 1836; *Richard Hurdis: or. The Avenger of Blood*, 1838; *Pelayo: A Story of the Goth*, 1838; *Carl Werner:*

*An Imaginative Story*, 1838; *The Damsel of Darien*, 1839; *Border Beagles: A Tale of Mississippi*, 1840; *The Kinsmen; or, The Black Riders of Congaree*, 1841; *Confession; or, The Blind Heart*, 1841; *Beauchampe; or, The Kentucky Tragedy*, 1842; *Castle Dismal; or, The Bachelor's Christmas*, 1844; *The Prima Donna: A Passage from City Life*, 1844; *Helen Halsey; or The Swamp State of Conelachita*, 1845; *Count Julian; or, The Last Days of the Goth*, 1845; *The Wigwam and the Cabin: First Series*, 1845; *Second Series*, 1845; *The Lily and The Totem; or, The Huguenots in Florida*, 1850; *Flirtation at the Moultrie House*, 1850; *Katharine Walton; or, The Rebel of Dorchester*, 1851; *The Golden Christmas: A Chronicle of St. John's, Berkeley*, 1852; *The Sword and the Distaff; or, "Fair, Fat, and Forty,"* 1852; *As Good as a Comedy; or, The Tennesseean's Story*, 1852; *Marie De Berniere*, 1853; *Vasconselos: A Romance of the New World*, 1853; *Southward Ho! A Spell of Sunshine*, 1854; *The Forayers; or, The Raid of the Dog-Days*, 1855; *Charlemont; or The Pride of the Village*, 1856; *Eutaw*, 1856; *The Cassique of Kiawah*, 1859.

Poetry: *Monody on the Death of Gen. Charles Cotesworth Pinckney*, 1825; *Lyrical and Other Poems*, 1827; *Early Lays*, 1827; *The Vision of Cortes, Cain, and Other Poems*, 1829; *The Tri-Color; or, The Three Days of Blood in Paris*, 1830; *Atalantis*, 1832; *Southern Passages and Pictures*, 1839; *Donna Florida*, 1843; *Grouped Thoughts and Scattered Fancies*, 1845; *Areytos; or, Songs of the South*, 1846; *Lays of the Palmetto*, 1848; *The Cassique of Accabee*, 1848; *Charleston, and Her Satirists: A Scribblement*, 1848; *Sabbath Lyrics; or, Songs from Scripture*, 1849; *The City of the Silent*, 1850; *Poems: Descriptive, Dramatic, Legendary and Contemplative*, 1853.

History, Biography, and Miscellaneous: *The Remains of Maynard Davis Richardson*, 1833; *Slavery in America*, 1838; *The History of South Carolina*, 1840; *The Geography of South Carolina*, 1843; *The Life of Francis Marion*, 1844; *The Views and Reviews in American Literature, History and Fiction*, 1845; *The Life of Captain John Smith*, 1846; *The Life of the Chevalier Bayard*, 1847; *The Life of Nathanael Greene*, 1849; *Father Abbott; or, The Home Tourist*, 1849; *Norman Maurice; or, The Man of the People*, 1851; *Michael Bonham; or, The Fall of Bexar*, 1852; *South Carolina in the Revolutionary War*, 1853; *Egeria; or, Voices of Thought and Counsel for the Woods and the Wayside*, 1853; *Sack and Destruction of the City of Columbia, S.C.*, 1865.

*Carl Werner* (1838), a collection of eight tales, was published in two volumes. *The Wigwam and the Cabin: First Series* (1845) is a collection of seven stories; the *Second Series* (1845) comprises six stories.

The Revolutionary romances are seven in number: *The Partisan* (1835), *Mellichampe* (1836), *Katharine Walton* (1851)—a trilogy; and *The Kinsmen* (1841) later called *The Scout* (1854), *The Sword and the Distaff* (1852) revised and renamed *Woodcraft; or, Hawks About the Dovecote* (1854), *The Forayers* (1855), and its sequel *Eutaw* (1856).

The best of the romances of colonial and Indian life are *The Yemassee* (1835), *The Cassique of Kiawah* (1859), and many of the tales in *Carl Werner* and *The Wigwam and the Cabin*.

The border romances—novels of colonial and nineteenth century life in the South—are *Guy Rivers* (1834), *Richard Hurdis* (1838) and its sequel *Border Beagles* (1840), *Beauchampe* (1842), and *Helen Halsey* (1845). A portion of *Beauchampe,* considerably rewritten, was renamed *Charlemont* (1856) and published as a separate novel.

Romances of Spanish history are *Pelayo* (1838), *The Damsel of Darien* (1839), *Count Julian* (1845), and *Vasconselos* (1853).

"Joscelyn: A Tale of the Revolution" (1867), "Voltmeier; or, The Mountain Men" (1869), and "The Cub of the Panther: A Mountain Legend" were printed in periodicals but never in book form.

### COLLECTED WORKS AND REPRINTS

*Works of William Gilmore Simms,* New York, 1853–1866, 20 vols., includes all the full-length stories up to 1866, except *Martin Faber, The Damsel of Darien, Pelayo,* and *Count Julian.* It also includes *Southward Ho!* (short stories), *The Wigwam and the Cabin* (collected tales), and a volume of verse. Many of the stories were collected or revised and supplied with new prefaces. No inclusive edition of Simms's complete works has ever been issued, nor is there a complete edition of the romances.

His letters are uncollected. Nine letters written to Evert A. Duyckinck in 1865–1867 are edited by Alfred T. Odell, "William Gilmore Simms in the Post-War Years," *Bul. Furman Univ.,* XXIX (1946), No. 3, pp. 5–20.

Alexander Cowie edited *The Yemassee,* New York, 1937, with valuable introduction, chronology, and bibl., for the Amer. Fiction Series. The romance was edited earlier by M. Lyle Spencer, Richmond, 1911.

### BIOGRAPHY AND CRITICISM

No adequate biography of Simms has been published. The standard life is William P. Trent, *William Gilmore Simms,* Boston, 1892 (Amer. Men of Letters). The sketch in *Dict. Amer. Biog.* (1935) was contributed by Carl Van Doren, who also wrote the study of Simms in *Camb. Hist. Amer. Lit.,* I (1917), 312–318. A useful independent study is that of Vernon L. Parrington in *Main Currents in American Thought,* New York, II (1927), 125–136. Two further general studies of interest are "Charleston and the Southwest: Simms," in Van Wyck Brooks, *The World of Washington Irving,* New York, 1944, pp. 291–314; and "William Gilmore Simms," in John Erskine, *Leading American Novelists,* New York, 1910, pp. 131–177.

Special studies include Hampton M. Jarrell, "Falstaff and Simms's Porgy," *Amer. Lit.*, III (1931), 204–212; *idem*, "Simms's Visits to the Southwest," *Amer. Lit.*, V (1933), 29–35; Albert Keiser, *The Indian in American Literature*, New York, 1933, pp. 154–174; William S. Hoole, "A Note on Simms's Visits to the Southwest," *Amer. Lit.*, VI (1934), 334–336; *idem*, "William Gilmore Simms's Career as Editor," *Georgia Hist. Quar.*, XIX (1935), 47–54; Raven I. McDavid, Jr., "*Ivanhoe* and Simms' *Vasconselos*," *Modern Language Notes*, LVI (1941), 294–297; William S. Hoole, "Simms' *Michael Bonham*: A 'Forgotten' Drama of the Texas Revolution," *Southwestern His. Quar.*, XLVI (1942), 255–261; John W. Higham, "The Changing Loyalties of William Gilmore Simms," *Jour. Southern Hist.*, IX (1943), 210–223; Floyd H. Deen, "The Genesis of *Martin Faber* in *Caleb Williams*," *Modern Language Notes*, LIX (1944), 315–317—the debt to Godwin; *idem*, "A Comparison of Simms's *Richard Hurdis* with Its Sources," *ibid.*, LX (1945), 406–408.

For a study of *The Yemassee*, see the introduction to Cowie's edition, New York, 1937. An authoritative study of "The Yamassee War, 1715–1716" is in Verner W. Crane, *The Southern Frontier, 1670–1732*, Durham, N.C., 1928, pp. 162–186.

Depositories of Simms's manuscripts are the University of North Carolina, Duke University, and the Library of Congress.

### BIBLIOGRAPHY

A valuable compilation is Oscar Wegelin, *A Bibliography of the Separate Writings of William Gilmore Simms of South Carolina, 1806–1870*, 3rd ed. rev., Hattiesburg, Miss., 1941, which includes finding lists. A. S. Salley compiled a *Catalogue of the Salley Collection of the Works of Wm. Gilmore Simms*, Columbia, S.C., 1943, 121 pp.—a bibliographical description of the large and important collection. The fullest listing of secondary material is in Alexander Cowie's edition of *The Yemassee*, New York, 1937. Other bibliographical information will be found in Oscar Wegelin, "Simms's First Publication," *New York Hist. Soc. Quar. Rev.*, XXV (1941), 26–27; and in J. Allen Morris, "The Stories of William Gilmore Simms," *Amer. Lit.*, XIV (1942), 20–35—a canon of fifty-eight stories, listed chronologically.

# UPTON SINCLAIR
### b. 1878

### SEPARATE WORKS

Novels: *Springtime and Harvest: A Romance* (also published as *King Midas: A Romance*), 1901; *The Journal of Arthur Stirling*, 1903; *Prince Hagen: A Phantasy*, 1903; *Manassas: A Novel of the War*, 1904; *A Captain of Industry*, 1906; *The Jungle*, 1906; *The Overman* (short stories), 1907; *The Metropolis*, 1908; *The Moneychangers*, 1908; *Samuel the Seeker*, 1910; *Love's Pilgrimage*, 1911; *Sylvia*, 1913; *Sylvia's Marriage*, 1914; *King Coal*, 1917; *Jimmie Higgins: A Story*, 1919; *100%: The Story of a Patriot*, 1920 (English edition, *The Spy*, 1921); *They Call Me Carpenter: A Tale of the Second Coming*, 1922; *Oil!* 1927; *Boston*, 1928; *Mountain City*, 1930; *Roman Holiday*, 1931; *The Wet Parade*, 1931; *Co-op: A Novel of Living Together*, 1936; *Little Steel*, 1938; *Our Lady*, 1938.

The Lanny Budd series includes *World's End*, 1940; *Between Two Worlds*, 1941; *Dragon's Teeth*, 1942; *Wide Is the Gate*, 1943; *The Presidential Agent*, 1944; *Dragon Harvest*, 1945; *A World to Win*, 1946; *Presidential Mission*, 1947. An *Index to the Lanny Budd Story* (1943) covers the first four volumes of the series.

*The Jungle* was issued with a new introduction by the author, New York, 1946.

Plays: *Plays of Protest*, 1912; *Hell: A Verse Drama and Photoplay*, 1923; *Singing Jailbirds*, 1924; *Bill Porter: A Drama of O. Henry in Prison*, 1925; *Depression Island*, 1935; *Marie Antoinette*, 1939.

Political and Social Studies: *The Industrial Republic*, 1907; *The Profits of Religion*, 1918; *The Brass Check: A Study of American Journalism*, 1919; *The Book of Life, Mind and Body*, 1921; *Love and Society* (Vol. II of *The Book of Life*), 1922; *The Goose-Step: A Study of American Education*, 1923; *The Goslings: A Study of the American Schools*, 1924; *Mammonart*, 1925; *Money Writes!* 1927; *I, Governor of California: . . . A True Story of the Future*, 1933; *The Way Out*, 1933; *The EPIC Plan for California*, 1934; *The Book of Love*, 1934.

Sinclair's autobiography, *American Outpost: A Book of Reminiscences*, 1932, was published in England in the same year under the title *Candid Reminiscences: My First Thirty Years*. In addition to the items named, he has published children's books and a great many pamphlets dealing with social problems. In 1915 he edited *The Cry for Justice: An Anthology of the Literature of Social Protest*. I. O. Evans compiled *An Upton Sinclair Anthology* (1934), with a preface by Sinclair. See also *Upton Sinclair Anthology*, New York, 1947, with introduction by Irving Stone and Lewis Browne.

BIOGRAPHY AND CRITICISM

An early study of Sinclair is Floyd Dell, *Upton Sinclair: A Study in Social Protest*, New York, 1927. Other early estimates of Sinclair are Frank Harris, *Contemporary Portraits*, 3rd ser., New York, 1920, pp. 15–30; Curtice N. Hitchcock, "*The Brass Check* . . .," *Jour. Polit. Econ.*, XXIX (1921), 336–348; "The Novels of Upton Sinclair," in Van Wyck Brooks, *Emerson and*

*Others,* New York, 1927, pp. 207-217; Robert M. Lovett, "Upton Sinclair," *English Jour.,* XVII (1928), 706-714; Walter Lippmann, "Upton Sinclair," *Sat. Rev. Lit.,* IV (Mar. 3, 1928), 641-643; and "Upton Sinclair," in David Karsner, *Sixteen Authors to One,* New York, 1928, pp. 265-280.

Later evaluations are J. H. Whyte, "Upton Sinclair: Puritan and Socialist," *Modern Scot,* III (1932), 149-155; Harry Hartwick, *The Foreground of American Fiction,* New York, 1934, pp. 231-249; Harlan Hatcher, *Creating the Modern American Novel,* New York, 1935, pp. 127-132; Arthur H. Quinn, *American Fiction,* New York, 1936, pp. 652-656; Robert Cantwell, "Upton Sinclair," in Malcolm Cowley, ed., *After the Genteel Tradition,* New York, 1936, pp. 37-51; and Carl Van Doren, *The American Novel,* rev. ed., New York, 1940, pp. 240-242.

Manuscript letters from Sinclair are deposited in the Charlotte Ashley Felton Memorial Library of Stanford University.

Sinclair himself published *Books of Upton Sinclair in Translations and Foreign Editions: A Bibliography of 772 Titles in 47 Languages, 39 Countries,* 2nd ed., Monrovia, Calif., 1938. The fullest bibliographical listing of primary and secondary sources to 1940 is in Fred B. Millett, *Contemporary American Authors,* New York, 1940, pp. 579-586. See also Joseph Gaer, *Upton Sinclair,* Monograph No. 6 of Calif. Lit. Research Project (1935); and Elizabeth Bantz, "Upton Sinclair: Book Reviews and Criticisms Published in German and French Periodicals and Newspapers," *Bul. Bibl.,* XVIII (1946), 204-206.

# JOHN SMITH
## *1579/80-1631*

SEPARATE WORKS

*A True Relation of . . . Virginia,* 1608; *A Map of Virginia, with a Description of the Countrey,* 1612; *A Description of New England,* 1616; *New Englands Trials,* 1620; *The Generall Historie of Virginia, New-England, and the Summer Isles,* 1624; *An Accidence; or, The Pathway to Experience Necessary for All Young Seamen,* 1626; *The True Travels, Adventures, and Observations of Captaine John Smith,* 1630; *Advertisements for the Unexperienced Planters of New-England, or Any Where,* 1631.

COLLECTED WORKS

The best collection of Smith's writings is *Travels and Works of Captain John Smith . . . ,* Birmingham, Eng., 1884, ed. by Edward Arber, reprinted with some corrections and an introduction by Arthur G. Bradley, Edinburgh, 1910, 2 vols. Charles Deane edited "The 'Last Will and Testament' of Captain

John Smith," with his epitaph, in *Proc. Mass. Hist. Soc.*, 1st ser., IX (1867), 451–456.

### EDITED TEXTS AND REPRINTS

A convenient reprint, including many selections from Smith, is Henry S. Burrage, ed., *Early English and French Voyages,* Original Narratives Ser., New York, 1906. *A True Relation* and *A Map of Virginia* are included in Lyon G. Tyler, ed., *Narratives of Early Virginia,* Orig. Narr. Ser., New York, 1907, pp. 30–71, 76–118; *A Description of New England,* in *Coll. Mass. Hist. Soc.,* 3rd ser., VI (1837), 95–140; *New Englands Trials,* ed. by Charles Deane, *Proc. Mass. Hist. Soc.,* XII (1873), 449 ff.; *The Generall Historie,* often reprinted, most recently was issued in Glasgow, 1907, 2 vols.; *The True Travels* was edited with an introduction by John Gould Fletcher and bibl. notes by Lawrence C. Wroth, New York, 1930; and *Advertisements for the Unexperienced Planters* is in *Coll. Mass. Hist. Soc.,* 3rd ser., III (1833), 1–53.

### BIOGRAPHY AND CRITICISM

Biographies of Smith are uncritical and say little of his work for New England. The two most recent are Edward Keble Chatterton, *Captain John Smith,* New York, 1927, and John Gould Fletcher, *John Smith—Also Pocahontas,* New York, 1928—the best account. Earlier accounts are those of William Gilmore Simms, *The Life of Captain John Smith . . . ,* New York, 1846; George S. Hillard, "The Life and Adventures of Captain John Smith," in Jared Sparks, ed., *American Biography,* 1st ser., II (1854), 171–407; Charles Dudley Warner, *Captain John Smith . . . ,* New York, 1881; Katherine P. Woods, *The True Story of Captain John Smith,* New York, 1901; and Arthur G. Bradley, *Captain John Smith . . . ,* London, 1905.

Smith is best treated in brief accounts, especially those of J. A. Doyle in *Dict. Nat. Biog.,* James T. Adams in *Dict. Amer. Biog.* (1935), and Samuel E. Morison in *Builders of the Bay Colony,* Boston, 1930, pp. 3–20. Also important are the comments of Charles M. Andrews in *The Colonial Period of American History,* New Haven, I (1934), *passim.*

The controversy over his veracity properly begins with Henry Adams, "Captain John Smith," *No. Amer. Rev.,* CIV (1867), 1–30—Adams's first historical essay and a noted examination of the Pocahontas episode—and continued by Lewis L. Kropf's devastating examination of Smith's earlier travels in *Amer. Hist. Rev.,* III (1898), 737–738. The issues are best summarized in Jarvis M. Morse, "John Smith and His Critics: A Chapter in Colonial Historiography," *Jour. Southern Hist.,* I (1935), 123–137. See also Keith Glenn, "Captain John Smith and the Indians," *Virginia Mag. Hist. and Biog.,* LII (1944), 228–248.

Smith is best treated as a man of letters in Howard M. Jones, "The Literature of Virginia in the Seventeenth Century," in *Memoirs Amer. Acad. Arts and Sciences*, Boston, 1946, pp. 16–23. See also Moses C. Tyler, *A History of American Literature During the Colonial Period*, rev. ed., New York, 1897, I, 18–38.

BIBLIOGRAPHY

A model of bibliographical scholarship in dealing with an extraordinarily complex subject is Wilberforce Eames's collation and description of Smith's works, published in 1927 as Part CXVII of Joseph Sabin's *Dictionary of Books Relating to America*, XX, 218–265. A brief critical bibliography follows the sketch of Smith in *Dict. Amer. Biog.* (1935).

# EDMUND CLARENCE STEDMAN
## *1833–1908*

SEPARATE WORKS

*Poems, Lyrical and Idyllic*, 1860; *The Battle of Bull Run*, 1861; *Alice of Monmouth: An Idyl of the Great War, with Other Poems*, 1864; *The Blameless Prince and Other Poems*, 1869; *Victorian Poets*, 1875; *Octavius Brooks Frothingham and the New Faith*, 1876; *Hawthorne and Other Poems*, 1877; *Lyrics and Idylls, with Other Poems*, 1879; *Songs and Ballads*, 1884; *Poets of America*, 1885; *The Nature and Elements of Poetry*, 1892; *Poems Now First Collected*, 1897; *Mater Coronata*, 1901; *Genius and Other Essays*, 1911.

WORKS EDITED BY STEDMAN

Chief among the works edited by Stedman are *A Library of American Literature from the Earliest Settlement to the Present Time* (with Ellen M. Hutchinson), New York, 1889–1890, 11 vols.—an inclusive selection that is still useful for reference; *The Works of Edgar A. Poe* (with George E. Woodberry), Chicago, 1894–1895, 10 vols.; *A Victorian Anthology, 1837–1895*, Boston, 1895; and *An American Anthology, 1787–1900*, Boston, 1900—the editor's critical review of American poetry. The publication of these works was important in increasing an interest in and appreciation of American and English literature. Stedman further edited the works of Lanier (with T. B. Aldrich), and of Robert Browning, E. B. Browning, and Austin Dobson. His guidebooks to Europe and the Paris Exposition sold widely. He also edited *The New York Stock Exchange: Its History*, New York, 1905.

COLLECTED WORKS

The first collection of Stedman's poems was published when he was forty:

*The Poetical Works of Edmund Clarence Stedman,* Boston, 1873. Another edition, including later poems, was issued in 1885; and a final collection, *The Poems of Edmund Clarence Stedman,* Boston, 1908. A gathering of his letters was edited by Laura Stedman and George M. Gould, *Life and Letters of Edmund Clarence Stedman,* New York, 1910, 2 vols., with a full bibliography compiled by Alice Marsland, II, 613–654. Further "Selections from the Literary Correspondence of Edmund Clarence Stedman," were published in *Magazine of History,* XXV (1917), 140–151.

BIOGRAPHY AND CRITICISM

The fullest life of Stedman is that by Laura Stedman and George M. Gould, mentioned above. The best brief account is that of Ernest S. Bates in *Dict. Amer. Biog.* (1935). Special studies are J. J. Piatt, "Mr. Stedman's Poetry," *Atl. Mo.,* XLI (1878), 313–319—a review of *Hawthorne and Other Poems* (1877); H. C. Vedder, *American Writers of To-day,* New York, 1899, pp. 3–26; George E. De Mille, "Stedman, Arbiter of the Eighties," *PMLA,* XLI (1926), 756–766, reprinted in his *Literary Criticism in America,* New York, 1931, pp. 133–157; and "Edmund Clarence Stedman," in John P. Pritchard, *Return to the Fountains,* Durham, N.C., 1942, pp. 119–134.

PRIMARY SOURCES

Reminiscences and appreciations of Stedman are Theodore Dreiser, "Edmund Clarence Stedman at Home," *Munsey's Mag.,* XX (1899), 931–938; John Hay, "Edmund Clarence Stedman," in *Addresses of John Hay,* New York, 1907, pp. 227–234; "Edmund Clarence Stedman," in Thomas W. Higginson, *Carlyle's Laugh,* Boston, 1909, pp. 137–156; "Edmund Clarence Stedman as Man of Letters," in William C. Wilkinson, *Some New Literary Valuations,* New York, 1909, pp. 253–290; and Caroline Ticknor, *Glimpses of Authors,* Boston, 1922, pp. 200–212. Anna Bowman Dodd and J. L. and J. B. Gilder describe the New York town house and Stedman as a personality in *Authors at Home,* New York, 1889, pp. 275–290. See also Henry Holt, *Garrulities of an Octogenarian Editor,* Boston, 1923, pp. 113–116.

The chief collection of Stedman manuscripts is in the Columbia University Library. Other manuscript material is in the Henry E. Huntington Library and the Princeton University Library.

The fullest bibliography of Stedman's writings is that compiled by Alice Marsland in the *Life and Letters,* mentioned above.

# GERTRUDE STEIN
*1874–1946*

## SEPARATE WORKS

*Three Lives: Stories of the Good Anna, Melanctha, and the Gentle Lena,*
1909; *Tender Buttons: Objects, Food, Rooms,* 1914; *Geography and Plays,*
1922; *The Making of Americans: Being a History of a Family's Progress,*
1925; *A Book Concluding with As a Wife Has a Cow,* 1926; *Composition as
Explanation,* 1926; *A Village: Are You Ready Yet Not Yet: A Play in Four
Acts,* 1928; *Useful Knowledge . . . ,* 1928; *An Acquaintance with Description,* 1929; *Lucy Church Amiably,* 1930; *Dix Portraits,* 1930; *How to Write,*
1931; *Operas and Plays,* 1932; *Matisse, Picasso, and Gertrude Stein, with Two
Shorter Stories,* 1933; *The Autobiography of Alice B. Toklas,* 1933; *Four
Saints in Three Acts,* 1934; *Portraits and Prayers,* 1934; *Narration: Four Lectures,* 1935; *Lectures in America,* 1935; *The Geographical History of America,*
1936; *Everybody's Autobiography,* 1937; *A Wedding Bouquet: Ballet,* 1938;
*Anciens et Modernes: Picasso,* 1938; *The World Is Round,* 1939; *Paris France,*
1940; *What Are Masterpieces,* 1940; *Ida: A Novel,* 1941; *Wars I Have Seen,*
1945; *Brewsie and Willie,* 1946; *Four in America,* 1947.

*Three Lives* (1909) was reprinted in the Modern Library, New York, 1933,
with an introduction by Carl Van Vechten. *The Making of Americans* (1925)
was reissued, New York, 1934, in an abridged edition with a preface by
Bernard Faÿ. Carl Van Vechten edited *Selected Writings of Gertrude Stein,*
New York, 1946, with an introduction.

## BIOGRAPHY AND CRITICISM

A full-length appreciative biography is Bravig Imbs, *Confessions of
Another Young Man,* New York, 1936.

Among early critical estimates are "A Note on Gertrude Stein," in Stuart
P. Sherman, *Points of View,* New York, 1924, pp. 261–268; Paul Rosenfeld,
*By Way of Art,* New York, 1928, pp. 111–131; "Gertrude Stein," in Edmund
Wilson, *Axel's Castle: A Study in the Imaginative Literature of 1870–1930,*
New York, 1931, pp. 237–256; and Edith Sitwell, *Aspects of Modern Poetry,*
London, 1934, pp. 215–226. Three studies by Laura Riding are *A Survey of
Modernist Poetry,* London, 1927, pp. 274–287; *Contemporaries and Snobs,*
New York, 1928, pp. 123–199; and *Experts Are Puzzled,* London, 1930, pp.
95–110.

Among recent studies are Harvey Eagleson, "Gertrude Stein: Method in
Madness," *Sewanee Rev.,* XLIV (1936), 164–177; Vernon Loggins, *I Hear
America . . . ,* New York, 1937, pp. 323–328; Carl Van Doren, *The American*

*Novel,* rev. ed., New York, 1940, pp. 338–341; Oscar Cargill, *Intellectual America* . . . , New York, 1941, pp. 293–299, 312–322; Henry Rago, "Gertrude Stein," *Poetry,* LXIX (1946), 93–97; and Malcolm Cowley, "Gertrude Stein: Writer or Word Scientist," *N.Y. Herald Tribune Weekly Book Rev.,* Nov. 24, 1946, p. 1.

For the manuscript collection in the Yale University Library see Norman H. Pearson, "The Gertrude Stein Collection," *Yale Univ. Lib. Gaz.,* XVI (1942), 45–47. Further material was added after her death in 1946. Gertrude Stein's autobiography was written purportedly by her secretary and published as *The Autobiography of Alice B. Toklas,* New York, 1933. Source material has been published in Mabel Dodge Luhan's *European Experiences,* New York, 1935, and *Movers and Shakers,* New York, 1936, which includes ten letters from Gertrude Stein.

Very comprehensive bibliographies are Robert B. Haas and Donald C. Gallup, *A Catalogue of the Published and Unpublished Writings of Gertrude Stein: Exhibited in the Yale University Library 22 February to 29 March 1941,* New Haven, 1941; and Julian Sawyer, "Gertrude Stein (1874–    ): A Check-List Comprising Critical and Miscellaneous Writings About Her Work, Life and Personality from 1913 to 1943," *Bul. Bibl.,* XVII (1943), 211–212, XVIII (1943), 11–13. A recent checklist by Frances Cheney is in Allen Tate, *Sixty American Poets, 1896–1944,* Washington, 1945, pp. 150–15

# JOHN (ERNST) STEINBECK
## b. 1902

### SEPARATE WORKS

*Cup of Gold: A Life of Henry Morgan, Buccaneer, with Occasional Reference to History,* 1929; *The Pastures of Heaven,* 1932; *To a God Unknown,* 1933; *Tortilla Flat,* 1935; *In Dubious Battle,* 1936; *Saint Katy the Virgin,* 1936; *Of Mice and Men,* 1937; *The Red Pony,* 1937; *"Their Blood Is Strong,"* 1938; *The Long Valley,* 1938; *The Grapes of Wrath,* 1939; *The Forgotten Village,* 1941; *Sea of Cortez,* 1941; *The Moon Is Down,* 1942; *Bombs Away,* 1942; *Cannery Row,* 1945; *The Wayward Bus,* 1947; *The Pearl,* 1947.

### REPRINTS

Four Steinbeck novels have been reprinted in the Modern Library: *Tortilla Flat,* 1937; *Of Mice and Men,* 1938; *In Dubious Battle,* 1939; *The Grapes of Wrath,* 1941. *The Pastures of Heaven* was issued in Penguin Books, New York, 1942. *Thirteen Great Short Stories from The Long Valley* was published, New York, 1943. Pascal Covici compiled a volume of selections, *The Portable Steinbeck,* New York, 1943.

BIOGRAPHY AND CRITICISM

A useful general study is "John Steinbeck: Of Wrath or Joy," in Maxwell Geismar, *Writers in Crisis,* Boston, 1942, pp. 237-270. An earlier estimate is Harry T. Moore, *The Novels of John Steinbeck: A First Critical Study,* Chicago, 1939, 102 pp. Other general estimates of value are "John Steinbeck," in Percy H. Boynton, *America in Contemporary Fiction,* Chicago, 1940, pp. 241-257; Lincoln R. Gibbs, "John Steinbeck, Moralist," *Antioch Rev.,* II (1942), 172-184; Stanley E. Hyman, "Some Notes on John Steinbeck," *ibid.,* 185-200; "Steinbeck: Through a Glass, Though Brightly," in Thomas K. Whipple, *Study Out the Land,* Berkeley, Calif., 1943, pp. 105-111; and Carlos Baker, *"In Dubious Battle* Revalued," *N.Y. Times Book Rev.,* July 25, 1943, pp. 4, 16. Among early estimates of Steinbeck are Lewis Gannett's preface to a reissue of Steinbeck's first published work, *Cup of Gold,* 1936; Edmund C. Richards, "The Challenge of John Steinbeck," *No. Amer. Rev.,* CCXLIII (1937), 406-413; and Burton Rascoe, "John Steinbeck," *English Jour.,* XXVII (1938), 205-216.

More recent brief estimates are Claude E. Jones, "Proletarian Writing and John Steinbeck," *Sewanee Rev.,* XLVIII (1940), 445-456; Frederic I. Carpenter, "The Philosophical Joads," *College Eng.,* II (1941), 315-325; *idem,* "John Steinbeck: American Dreamer," *Southwest Rev.,* XXVI (1941), 454-467; Martin S. Shockley, "The Reception of *The Grapes of Wrath* in Oklahoma," *Amer. Lit.,* XV (1944), 351-361; Lewis Gannett, "John Steinbeck: Novelist at Work," *Atl. Mo.,* CLXXVI (1945), 55-61; W. M. Frolock, "John Steinbeck's Men of Wrath," *Southwest Rev.,* XXXI (1946), 144-152; Woodburn Ross, "John Steinbeck: Earth and Stars," *Univ. Missouri Studies in Honor of A. H. R. Fairchild* (1946), pp. 177-191; and Edwin B. Burgum, "The Sensibility of John Steinbeck," *Sci. and Soc.,* X (1946), 132-147.

Bibliographies and checklists are in Lawrence C. Powell, "Toward a Bibliography of John Steinbeck," *Colophon,* n.s. III (1938), 558-568; Jacob Blanck, *Merle Johnson's American First Editions,* 4th ed., New York, 1942; and Fred B. Millett, *Contemporary American Authors,* New York, 1940, pp. 596-597—especially useful for secondary items.

# GEORGE STERLING
## *1869-1926*

SEPARATE WORKS

*The Testimony of the Suns and Other Poems,* 1903; *The Triumph of Bohemia: A Forest Play,* 1907; *A Wine of Wizardry and Other Poems,* 1909; *The House of Orchids and Other Poems,* 1911; *Beyond the Breakers and Other Poems,* 1914; *Ode on the Opening of the Panama-Pacific International*

*Exposition*, 1915; *The Evanescent City*, 1915; *Yosemite: An Ode*, 1916; *The Caged Eagle and Other Poems*, 1916; *Songs*, 1916; *The Play of Everyman*, 1917; *The Binding of the Beast and Other War Verse*, 1917; *Thirty-five Sonnets*, 1917; *Lilith: A Dramatic Poem*, 1919; *Rosamund*, 1920; *To a Girl Dancing*, 1921; *Sails and Mirage and Other Poems*, 1921; *Truth*, 1923; *Robinson Jeffers: The Man and the Artist*, 1926; *Strange Waters*, 1926; *Five Poems*, 1927; *Sonnets to Craig*, 1928; *Poems to Vera*, 1938; *After Sunset*, 1939.

A volume of *Selected Poems* was issued, New York, 1923.

### BIOGRAPHY AND CRITICISM

There is no biography of Sterling. The best brief narrative sketch is by Carey McWilliams in *Dict. Amer. Biog.* (1935). Studies and appreciations are Louis Untermeyer, *American Poetry Since 1900*, New York, 1923, pp. 290–292; Mary Austin, "George Sterling at Carmel," *Amer. Mercury*, XI (1927), 65–72; Upton Sinclair, introduction to *Sonnets to Craig*, New York, 1928; Albert Parry, *Garrets and Pretenders*, New York, 1933, pp. 233–239; and "Laureate of Bohemia: George Sterling," in Miriam A. De Ford, *They Were San Franciscans*, Caldwell, Idaho, 1941, pp. 295–321.

*The Letters of Ambrose Bierce*, San Francisco, 1921, ed. by Bertha C. Pope, include a memoir of Bierce by Sterling. Reminiscences about Sterling are in Joseph Noel, *Footloose in Arcadia: A Personal Record of Jack London, George Sterling, Ambrose Bierce*, New York, 1940; Irving Stone, *Sailor on Horseback: The Biography of Jack London*, Boston, 1938; and Upton Sinclair, "My Friend George Sterling," *Bookman*, LXVI (1927), 30–32.

A large collection of Sterling manuscripts is in the Library of Congress. Other manuscripts are at Stanford University. Many letters are still in private hands.

Cecil Johnson has published *A Bibliography of the Writings of George Sterling*, San Francisco, 1931.


# WALLACE STEVENS
*b. 1879*

### SEPARATE WORKS

*Harmonium*, 1923; *Ideas of Order*, 1935; *Owl's Clover*, 1936; *The Man with the Blue Guitar and Other Poems*, 1937; *Parts of a World*, 1942; *Notes Toward a Supreme Fiction*, 1942; *Esthétique du Mal*, 1945; *Transport to Summer*, 1947.

*Harmonium* was issued in a second edition (1931) with a dozen added poems. No collected edition of Stevens's work has been published.

BIOGRAPHY AND CRITICISM

All criticism of Stevens's poetry down to 1935 is based on the poems in *Harmonium*. It includes Llewelyn Powys, "The Thirteenth Way," *Dial*, LXXVII (1924), 45–50; "Wallace Stevens," in Paul Rosenfeld, *Men Seen . . .*, New York, 1925, pp. 151–162; Gorham Munson, "The Dandyism of Wallace Stevens," *Dial*, LXXIX (1925), 413–417; "Wallace Stevens," in Harriet Monroe, *Poets and Their Art*, New York, 1926, pp. 39–45; "Wallace Stevens," in René Taupin, *L'Influence du Symbolism Français sur la Poésie Américaine . . .*, Paris, 1929, pp. 275–278; Morton D. Zabel, "The Harmonium of Wallace Stevens," *Poetry*, XXXIX (1931), 148–154; R. P. Blackmur, "Examples of Wallace Stevens," *Hound and Horn*, V (1932), 223–255; and Hoffman R. Hays, "Laforgue and Wallace Stevens," *Romanic Rev.*, XXV (1934), 242–248.

An appreciation of Stevens is Alfred Kreymborg, *Our Singing Strength*, New York, 1929, pp. 500–504. An unfavorable estimate is that of Louis Untermeyer in *American Poetry Since 1900*, New York, 1923, pp. 323–328.

The Wallace Stevens Number of the *Harvard Advocate*, CXXVII, no. 3 (Dec., 1940), included poems by Stevens and articles and statements by Delmore Schwartz, Morton D. Zabel, Theodore Spencer, Cleanth Brooks, Harry Levin, F. O. Matthiessen, Marianne Moore, Allen Tate, Robert Penn Warren, William Carlos Williams, Hi Simons, and others. The most extensive recent estimate is "Wallace Stevens; or, The Hedonist's Progress," in Yvor Winters, *The Anatomy of Nonsense*, Norfolk, Conn., 1943, pp. 88–119. A study of *Ideas of Order* (1935) is Howard Baker, "Wallace Stevens and Other Poets," *Southern Rev.*, I (1935), 373–389. Other recent studies are Marianne Moore, "Unanimity and Fortitude," *Poetry*, XLIX (1937), 268–272; Julian Symons, "A Short View of Wallace Stevens," *Life and Letters Today*, XXVI (1940), 215–224; Harvey Breit, "Sanity That Is Magic," *Poetry*, LXII (1943), 48–50; Wylie Sypher, "Connoisseur in Chaos: Wallace Stevens," *Partisan Rev.*, XIII (1946), 83–94; and L. L. Martz, "Wallace Stevens: The Romance of the Precise," *Yale Poetry Rev.*, II (Aug. 1946), 13–20.

Four critical estimates by Hi Simons are " 'The Comedian as the Letter C': Its Sense and Its Significance," *Southern Rev.*, V (1940), 453–468; "The Humanism of Wallace Stevens," *Poetry*, LXI (1942), 448–452; "The Genre of Wallace Stevens," *Sewanee Rev.*, LIII (1945), 566–579; and "Wallace Stevens and Mallarmé," *Modern Philol.*, XLIII (1946), 235–259.

The Lockwood Memorial Library at the University of Buffalo contains an important manuscript collection.

A bio-bibliography is in Fred B. Millett, *Contemporary American Authors*, New York, 1940, pp. 597–598. A further checklist compiled by Frances

Cheney is in Allen Tate, *Sixty American Poets, 1896–1944,* Washington, 1945, pp. 156–157.

## CHARLES WARREN STODDARD
### *1843–1909*

SEPARATE WORKS

*Poems,* 1867; *South Sea Idyls,* 1873; *Mashallah! A Flight into Egypt,* 1881; *The Lepers of Molokai,* 1885; *A Troubled Heart,* 1885; *Hawaiian Life,* 1894; *The Wonder-Worker of Padua,* 1896; *A Cruise Under the Crescent: From Suez to San Marco,* 1898; *In the Footprints of the Padres,* 1902; *For the Pleasure of His Company,* 1903; *Exits and Entrances,* 1903; *The Island of Tranquil Delights,* 1904.

The volume of *Poems* (1867) was edited by Bret Harte. *South Sea Idyls* (1873) was published in England as *Summer Cruising in the South Seas,* London, 1874.

COLLECTED WORKS

Ina Coolbrith edited *The Poems of Charles Warren Stoddard,* New York, 1917. Some of Stoddard's sketches were published as *Apostrophe to the Skylark* . . ., Los Angeles, 1909, in the Calif. Classics Ser., with an appreciation by George W. James. *Charles Warren Stoddard's Diary of a Visit to Molokai in 1884* . . ., San Francisco, 1933, was published with an introduction by Oscar Lewis.

BIOGRAPHY AND CRITICISM

No life of Stoddard has been published. The best narrative sketch is that by Carl G. Stroven in *Dict. Amer. Biog.* (1936). Material on Stoddard's relations with other California writers, together with some biographical data and critical estimates, is scattered through Franklin Walker, *San Francisco's Literary Frontier,* New York, 1939 (see the index). Two special studies are Jay B. Hubbell, "George Henry Boker, Paul Hamilton Hayne, and Charles Warren Stoddard: Some Unpublished Letters," *Amer. Lit.,* V (1933), 146–165; and the appreciation by Harry M. Bland, "Charles Warren Stoddard and His Place in American Literature," *Univ. Calif. Chron.,* Oct., 1909. Carl G. Stroven's unpublished thesis, a life of Stoddard, is at Duke University (1932).

PRIMARY SOURCES

In addition to Stoddard's travel books and the published parts of his diary, there is the story of his conversion to Catholicism as he tells it in *A Troubled*

*Heart* (1885). *For the Pleasure of His Company* (1903) is an autobiographical novel. Factual data are supplied in *Who's Who in America,* 1908–1909.

Stoddard manuscripts are in the Bishop Museum, Honolulu, at Stanford University, in the Henry E. Huntington Library, and at Notre Dame University.

No bibliography of works by or relating to Stoddard has been published.

## RICHARD HENRY STODDARD
### *1825–1903*

SEPARATE WORKS

*Foot-Prints,* 1849; *Poems,* 1852; *Songs of Summer,* 1857; *The Life, Travels and Books of Alexander von Humboldt,* 1859; *The Lovers and Heroines of the Poets,* 1861; *The King's Bell,* 1863; *Abraham Lincoln: An Horatian Ode,* 1865; *The Book of the East and Other Poems,* 1871; *Poets' Homes* (with others), 1877; *The Poems of Richard Henry Stoddard,* 1880; *The Life of Washington Irving,* 1886; *The Lion's Cub, with Other Verse,* 1890; *Under the Evening Lamp,* 1892; *Recollections, Personal and Literary,* 1903.

EDITORIAL AND CRITICAL WORKS

Stoddard reviewed for the New York *World,* 1860–1870, and served as literary editor for the New York *Mail and Express,* 1880–1903. He edited the Golden Leaves Series, the Sans-Souci Series, the Treasure-Trove Series, and the Bric-a-Brac Series, in which were published reminiscences of Lamb, Hazlitt, Young, Moore, Constable, Gillies, and others; anecdote biographies of Shelley, Thackeray, and Dickens; and selections from Swinburne. He edited the writings of Bryant and of Poe, Greville's memoirs, and brought up to date Rufus W. Griswold's *The Poets and Poetry of America* (1873), *The Female Poets of America* (1874), and *The Poets and Poetry of England* (1875). One of his last editorial compilations was an edition of *English Verse,* New York, 1883, 5 vols., in collaboration with W. J. Linton.

BIOGRAPHY AND CRITICISM

There are few biographical or critical estimates of Stoddard, and all of them are brief. A. R. Macdonough, "Richard Henry Stoddard," *Scribner's Mo.,* XX (1880), 686–694, still remains useful. There are also "Stoddard's Poems" and "Stoddard's Last Poem," in Edmund C. Stedman, *Genius and Other Essays,* New York, 1911, pp. 141–153, 166–173; and William P. Fenn, "Richard Henry Stoddard's Chinese Poems," *Amer. Lit.,* X (1940), 417–438. Stoddard's own *Recollections* (1903) are source material for the New York literary world of the seventies and eighties. Two large collections of his manuscripts are in the Cornell University Library and the Library of the American Antiquarian Society.

A full bibliographical listing to 1870 is in Allibone's *Dictionary* (1870—with suppl., 1891). A later listing may be found in *Who's Who in America* for 1901–1902.

## HARRIET (ELIZABETH) BEECHER STOWE
### *1811–1896*

SEPARATE WORKS

*Prize Tale: A New England Sketch,* 1834; *An Elementary Geography,* 1835; *The Mayflower; or, Sketches of Scenes and Characters Among the Descendants of the Pilgrims,* 1843; *Uncle Tom's Cabin,* 1852; *A Key to Uncle Tom's Cabin,* 1853; *Uncle Sam's Emancipation, etc.,* 1853; *Sunny Memories of Foreign Lands,* 1854; *Geography for My Children,* 1855; *Dred: A Tale of the Great Dismal Swamp,* 1856; *Our Charley and What to Do with Him,* 1858; *The Minister's Wooing,* 1859; *The Pearl of Orr's Island,* 1862; *Agnes of Sorrento,* 1862; *A Reply . . . in Behalf of the Women of America, etc.,* 1863; *The Ravages of a Carpet,* 1865; *House and Home Papers,* 1865; *Little Foxes,* 1866; *Stories About Our Dogs,* 1865; *Religious Poems,* 1867; *Queer Little People,* 1867; *Daisy's First Winter and Other Stories,* 1867; *The Chimney-Corner,* 1868; *Men of Our Times,* 1868; *Oldtown Folks,* 1869; *The American Woman's Home,* 1869; *Lady Byron Vindicated,* 1870; *Little Pussy Willow,* 1870; *My Wife and I,* 1871; *Pink and White Tyranny,* 1871; *Sam Lawson's Oldtown Fireside Stories,* 1872; *Palmetto-Leaves,* 1873; *Woman in Sacred History,* 1873; *We and Our Neighbors,* 1875; *Betty's Bright Idea, etc.,* 1876; *Footsteps of the Master,* 1876; *Poganuc People,* 1878; *A Dog's Mission,* 1881; *Our Famous Women,* 1884.

COLLECTED WORKS AND REPRINTS

*The Writings of Harriet Beecher Stowe* were collected and published, Boston, 1896, 16 vols. Convenient reprints of *Uncle Tom's Cabin* are obtainable in Everyman's Lib., London, 1909; Modern Readers' Ser., New York, 1926, ed. by Francis P. Gaines; and most recently, New York, 1938, ed. by Raymond Weaver.

For her letters, see the following paragraph.

BIOGRAPHY AND CRITICISM

A complete and documented life is Forrest Wilson, *Crusader in Crinoline:*

*The Life of Harriet Beecher Stowe,* Philadelphia, 1941. Another recent biography is Catherine Gilbertson, *Harriet Beecher Stowe,* New York, 1937. The brief sketch in *Dict. Amer. Biog.* (1936) is by Katharine Anthony. Among "official" biographies are Charles E. Stowe, *Life of Harriet Beecher Stowe: Compiled from Her Journals and Letters,* Boston, 1889; Annie A. Fields, *Life and Letters of Harriet Beecher Stowe,* Boston, 1897; and Charles E. and Lyman Beecher Stowe, *Harriet Beecher Stowe: The Story of Her Life,* Boston, 1911.

Brief general estimates are "Harriet Beecher Stowe," in John Erskine, *Leading American Novelists,* New York, 1910, pp. 275-323; "Harriet Beecher Stowe," in William P. Trent, *Great American Writers,* New York, 1912, pp. 197-211; "Harriet Beecher Stowe," in Gamaliel Bradford, *Portraits of American Women,* Boston, 1919, pp. 101-130; "Harriet Beecher Stowe," in Constance M. Rourke, *Trumpets of Jubilee,* New York, 1927, pp. 87-148—especially interesting among the briefer essays; and Vernon L. Parrington, *Main Currents in American Thought,* New York, II (1927), 371-378.

Special studies include James F. Rhodes, *History of the United States from the Compromise of 1850,* I (1893), *passim*—discussions of the reception of *Uncle Tom's Cabin* at home and abroad; Grace E. Maclean, *"Uncle Tom's Cabin" in Germany,* New York, 1910 (Vol. X of *Americana Germanica*); E. K. Maxfield, " 'Goody Goody' Literature and Mrs. Stowe," *Amer. Speech,* IV (1929), 189-202; Tremaine McDowell, "The Use of Negro Dialect by Harriet Beecher Stowe," *ibid.,* VI (1931), 322-326; Frank J. Klingberg, "Harriet Beecher Stowe and Social Reform in England," *Amer. Hist. Rev.,* XLIII (1938), 542-552; and Wayne Burns and Emerson G. Sutcliffe, *"Uncle Tom* and Charles Reade," *Amer. Lit.,* XVII (1946), 334-347. An unpublished dissertation is John R. Adams, "A Critical Study of the Works of Harriet B. Stowe," Univ. So. Calif., 1939.

PRIMARY SOURCES

Mrs. Stowe's own account of her trip abroad was published as *Sunny Memories of Foreign Lands,* Boston, 1854, 2 vols. Charles Beecher edited *Autobiography . . . of Lyman Beecher,* London, 1863-1865, 2 vols. (New York, 1864, 2 vols.)—the account left by her father. Further source material is in Annie A. Fields, *Authors and Friends,* Boston, 1896; and Lyman B. Stowe, *Saints, Sinners, and Beechers,* Indianapolis, 1934.

The chief manuscript depository is the Henry E. Huntington Library. Other manuscript collections are in Harvard College Library, Yale University Library, the Library of Congress, and the Boston Public Library. For a calendar of her manuscripts, see Forrest Wilson, *Crusader in Crinoline* (1941), pp. 643-657.

BIBLIOGRAPHY

The most complete and authoritative bibliography of Mrs. Stowe's writings before 1860, including translations of and contemporary works on *Uncle Tom's Cabin*, is that in Joseph Sabin, *A Dictionary of Books Relating to America*, XXIV (1933), 33–73—comp. by Wilberforce Eames. A collation of editions of *Uncle Tom's Cabin* is in David A. Randall and John T. Winterich, "One Hundred Good Novels: Stowe, Harriet Beecher: *Uncle Tom's Cabin*," *Pub. Weekly*, CXXXVII (1940), 1931–1932. Further material is in William Talbot, "*Uncle Tom's Cabin*: First English Editions," *Amer. Book Coll.*, III (1933), 292–297.

# BAYARD TAYLOR
## 1825–1878

SEPARATE WORKS

*Ximena; or, The Battle of the Sierra Morena and Other Poems*, 1844; *Views Afoot; or, Europe Seen with Knapsack and Staff*, 1846; *Rhymes of Travel, Ballads and Poems*, 1849; *Eldorado; or, Adventures in the Path of Empire*, 1850; *A Book of Romances, Lyrics and Songs*, 1852; *A Journey to Central Africa*, 1854; *The Lands of the Saracen*, 1855; *Poems of the Orient*, 1855; *A Visit to India, China, and Japan in the Year 1853*, 1855; *Poems of Home and Travel*, 1855; *Cyclopaedia of Modern Travel*, 1856; *Northern Travel*, 1858; *Travels in Greece and Russia*, 1859; *At Home and Abroad*, 1860; *The Poet's Journal*, 1862; *Hannah Thurston: A Story of American Life*, 1863; *The Poems of Bayard Taylor*, 1864; *John Godfrey's Fortunes, Related by Himself: A Story of American Life*, 1864; *The Story of Kennett*, 1866; *The Picture of St. John*, 1866; *Colorado: A Summer Trip*, 1867; *The Golden Wedding: A Masque*, 1868; *By-Ways of Europe*, 1869; *Joseph and His Friend*, 1870; *Faust* (translation), 1870–1871; *Beauty and the Beast and Tales of Home*, 1872; *The Masque of the Gods*, 1872; *Lars: A Pastoral of Norway*, 1873; *The Prophet: A Tragedy*, 1874; *A School History of Germany*, 1874; *Egypt and Iceland in the Year 1874*, 1874; *Home Pastorals, Ballads, and Lyrics*, 1875; *The Echo Club and Other Literary Diversions*, 1876; *Prince Deukalion: A Lyrical Drama*, 1878; *Studies in German Literature*, 1879; *Critical Essays, and Literary Notes*, 1880.

Taylor's translation of *Faust* is included in the World's Classics series.

COLLECTED WORKS

Two collections of Taylor's works are *The Dramatic Works of Bayard Taylor*, Boston, 1880, and *The Poetical Works of Bayard Taylor*, Boston, 1880.

A carefully edited collection of letters is John R. Schultz, ed., *The Unpublished Letters of Bayard Taylor in the Huntington Library,* San Marino, Calif., 1937. Letters are included in the Hansen-Taylor and Scudder biography (1884). Gleanings are H. W. Lanier, ed., "Letters Between Two Poets: The Correspondence of Bayard Taylor and Sidney Lanier," *Atl. Mo.,* LXXXIII (1899), 791–807, LXXIV (1899), 127–141. Robert Warnock offers data on letters and lectures in "Bayard Taylor's Unpublished Letters to His Sister Annie," *Amer. Lit.,* VII (1935), 47–55—a description of some 120 letters in private hands—and "Unpublished Lectures of Bayard Taylor," *Amer. Lit.,* V (1933), 123–132. A further item is A. J. Prahl, ed., "An Unpublished Letter of Bayard Taylor," *Modern Language Notes,* LXI (1946), 55–57. A recent collection is Charles Duffy, *The Correspondence of Bayard Taylor and Paul Hamilton Hayne,* Baton Rouge, La., 1945—46 letters, mostly unpublished, with introduction and notes.

BIOGRAPHY AND CRITICISM

The most recent life of Taylor is Richmond C. Beatty, *Bayard Taylor: Laureate of the Gilded Age,* Norman, Okla., 1936. A conscientious factual account is Marie Hansen-Taylor and Horace E. Scudder, *Life and Letters of Bayard Taylor,* Boston, 1884, 2 vols.—with much valuable primary material. Other accounts are Albert H. Smyth, *Bayard Taylor,* Boston, 1896 (Amer. Men of Letters), and Russell H. Conwell, *The Life, Travels, and Literary Career of Bayard Taylor,* Boston, 1879—largely hack work. The best brief account is that of Carl Van Doren in *Dict. Amer. Biog.* (1936).

Special studies are Juliana C. S. Haskell, *Bayard Taylor's Translation of Goethe's Faust,* New York, 1908, a careful study of the work on which his reputation chiefly rests; Hamilton Wright Mabie, "Bayard Taylor: Adventurer," *Bookman,* XLIII (1916), 51–59; F. W. C. Lieder, "Bayard Taylor's Adaptation of Schiller's *Don Carlos,*" *Jour. English and Germanic Philol.,* XVI (1917), 27–52; John T. Flanagan, "Bayard Taylor's Minnesota Visits," *Minnesota Hist.,* XIX (1938), 399–418; Horst Frenz, "Bayard Taylor and the Reception of Goethe in America," *Jour. English and Germanic Philol.,* XLI (1942), 121–139; John T. Krumpelmann, "The Genesis of Bayard Taylor's Translation of Goethe's *Faust,*" *ibid.,* XLII (1943), 551–562; A. J. Prahl, "Bayard Taylor and Goethe," *Modern Language Quar.,* VII (1946), 205–217; and *idem,* "Bayard Taylor's Letters from Russia," *Huntington Lib. Quar.,* IX (1946), 411–418.

PRIMARY SOURCES

Taylor's own travel books and his letters are chiefly important among published source materials. He is mentioned in the memoirs and biographies of almost all the writers of his day. Further material is in Marie Hansen-Taylor and Lilian Bayard Taylor Kiliani, *On Two Continents: Memories of Half a Century,* New York, 1905. Especially worthy of mention are "Bayard Taylor," in William Winter, *Old Friends, Being Literary Recollections of Other Days,* New York, 1909, pp. 153–180; "Bayard Taylor," in George E. Woodberry, *Literary Memoirs,* New York, 1921, pp. 239–248; "Bayard Taylor," in Edmund C. Stedman, *Poets of America,* Boston, 1885, pp. 396–434; and James G. Wilson, *Bryant and His Friends,* New York, 1886, pp. 347–375.

The chief collections of Taylor manuscripts are in the Boker-Taylor correspondence at Cornell University, in the Henry E. Huntington Library, and in the Chester, Pennsylvania, libraries and societies. Other material is in the Boston Public Library and the Harvard College Library.

### BIBLIOGRAPHY

A thorough bibliography of Taylor's writings is in Albert H. Smyth's life (1896), pp. 299–307. Beatty's biography (1936) is the best source on secondary material to date of publication, pp. 363–374.

# EDWARD TAYLOR
## 1645?–1729

### EDITED TEXTS

The poetry of Taylor remained in manuscript until 1937. Though much of it is still unpublished, all that has been issued is edited by Thomas H. Johnson, as follows: *The Poetical Works of Edward Taylor,* New York, 1939—including the extended verse sequence "God's Determinations," and several of the "Sacramental Meditations"; "Some Edward Taylor Gleanings," *New Eng. Quar.,* XVI (1943), 280–296; and "The Topical Verses of Edward Taylor," *Pub. Colonial Soc. Mass.,* XXXIV (1943), 513–554. Extracts from Taylor's diary, now apparently lost, are printed as the "Diary of Edward Taylor," *Proc. Mass. Hist. Soc.,* XVIII (1881), 4–18. A letter from "Edward Taylor to Increase Mather" is in the *Coll. Mass. Hist. Soc.,* 4th ser., VIII (1868), 629–631.

### BIOGRAPHY AND CRITICISM

A biographical and critical sketch is Thomas H. Johnson, "Edward Taylor: A Puritan 'Sacred Poet,'" *New Eng. Quar.,* X (1937), 290–322, including some data not elsewhere assembled, together with the first selections of Taylor's poetry to be published. Still useful is the brief account in

John L. Sibley, *Biographical Sketches of Graduates of Harvard University*, Cambridge, II (1881), 397–412, 534–536. John T. Terry published *Rev. Edward Taylor,* New York (n.d.).

Further narrative and critical data are supplied in Thomas H. Johnson, "The Discovery of Edward Taylor's Poetry," *Colophon,* New Graphic Ser., I (1939), No. 2, pp. 101–106; *idem,* "A Seventeenth-Century Printing of Some Verses of Edward Taylor," *New Eng. Quar.,* XIV (1941), 139–141—two stanzas surreptitiously issued; Austin Warren, "Edward Taylor's Poetry: Colonial Baroque," *Kenyon Rev.,* III (1941), 355–371; Wallace C. Brown, "Edward Taylor: An American 'Metaphysical,' " *Amer. Lit.,* XVI (1944), 186–197; Nathalia Wright, "The Morality Tradition in the Poetry of Edward Taylor," *Amer. Lit.,* XVIII (1946), 1–17; and Willie T. Weathers, "Edward Taylor: Hellenistic Puritan," *ibid.,* pp. 18–26.

PRIMARY SOURCES

Most of Taylor's manuscripts, including the holograph of the "Poetical Works," are in the Yale University Library. Some scattered notes and sermons are in the Boston Public Library and the library of the Massachusetts Historical Society. The Yale collection is calendared in *The Poetical Works,* pp. 221–228, 229. The inventory of Taylor's library is in the same volume, pp. 201–220.

BIBLIOGRAPHY

Bibliographical listings are in John L. Sibley, *Biographical Sketches,* II (1881), 410–412; in *The Poetical Works* (1939), pp. 229–231; and at the conclusion to the sketch of Taylor in *Dict. Amer. Biog.,* Supplement One (1944).

# SARA TEASDALE
## *1884–1933*

SEPARATE WORKS

*Sonnets to Duse and Other Poems,* 1907; *Helen of Troy and Other Poems,* 1911; *Rivers to the Sea,* 1915; *Love Songs,* 1917; *Flame and Shadow,* 1920; *Dark of the Moon,* 1926; *Stars To-night,* 1930; *A Country House,* 1932; *Strange Victory,* 1933.

*Helen of Troy* (1911) was reissued with revisions, New York, 1922. *Flame and Shadow* (1920) was reissued in a revised edition, London, 1924. Sara Teasdale edited several poetry anthologies.

*The Collected Poems of Sara Teasdale* was published, New York, 1937.

No full-length biography has been published. The sketch in *Dict. Amer. Biog.* (1936) was contributed by Harriet Monroe. An early critical estimate is "Sara Teasdale," in Louis Untermeyer, *American Poetry Since 1900*, New York, 1923, pp. 206–213. Harriet Monroe discusses the poetry of Sara Teasdale in her *Poets and Their Art*, New York, 1926, pp. 72–77, and in *Poetry*, XXV (1925), 262–268, XLII (1933), 30–33. See also Conrad Aiken, "'It Is in Truth a Pretty Toy,'" *Dial*, LXXVIII (1925), 107–114; and Babette Deutsch, "The Solitary Ironist," *Poetry*, LI (1937), 148–153.

Manuscript collections are in the Lockwood Memorial Library of the University of Buffalo (with many letters), in the Harvard College Library, and in the Yale University Library.

A bio-bibliography is in Fred B. Millett, *Contemporary American Authors*, New York, 1940, pp. 610–613. See also the checklist by Frances Cheney, in Allen Tate, *Sixty American Poets, 1896–1944*, Washington, 1945, pp. 165–167.


# HENRY DAVID THOREAU
## *1817–1862*

### SEPARATE WORKS

*A Week on the Concord and Merrimack Rivers*, 1849; *Walden; or, Life in the Woods*, 1854; *Excursions*, 1863; *The Maine Woods*, 1864; *Cape Cod*, 1865; *Letters to Various Persons*, 1865; *A Yankee in Canada, with Anti-Slavery and Reform Papers*, 1866; *Early Spring in Massachusetts*, 1881; *Summer*, 1884; *Winter*, 1888; *Autumn*, 1892; *Miscellanies*, 1894; *Familiar Letters of Henry David Thoreau*, 1894; *Poems of Nature*, 1895; *The Service*, 1902; *Sir Walter Raleigh*, 1905; *Journal*, 1906; *The Moon*, 1927; *The Transmigration of the Seven Brahmans: A Translation*, 1932.


### COLLECTED WORKS

No collection of Thoreau's writings was published until many years after his death. *The Writings of Henry David Thoreau, with Bibliographical Introductions and Full Indexes* was published as the Riverside Edition, Cambridge, 1894, 10 vols., with Vols. V–VIII ed. by Harrison G. O. Blake. In the same year Frank B. Sanborn edited *Familiar Letters . . .* , which was added as Vol. XI, and the set now issued (1894) as the Cambridge Edition, reissued, Boston, 1932. Frank B. Sanborn edited *The First and Last Journeys of Thoreau, Lately Discovered Among His Unpublished Journals and Manuscripts*, Boston, 1905, 2 vols. In 1906 the Manuscript Edition was published (with a sheet of manuscript bound in before the frontispiece of Vol. I), and from the plates were printed *The Writings of Henry David Thoreau*, Boston, 1906, 20 vols.—the standard Walden Edition: Vol. VI is the *Familiar Letters* volume, ed. by Sanborn, and Vols. VII–XX contain the *Journals* (1837–1861), ed. by Bradford Torrey. Harrison G. O. Blake edited *Thoreau's Complete Works*, Boston, 1929, 5 vols. (Concord Edition).

A much needed text, including "every available piece of genuine verse," is Carl Bode, ed., *Collected Poems of Henry Thoreau*, Chicago, 1943, published in a trade edition and a critical one.

Collections of letters are Ralph Waldo Emerson, ed., *Letters to Various Persons*, Boston, 1865 (also 1881); Frank B. Sanborn, ed., *Familiar Letters* . . . , Boston, 1894, with notes; and Elias Harlow Russell, "A Bit of Unpublished Correspondence Between Henry D. Thoreau and Isaac T. Hecker," *Proc. Amer. Antiq. Soc.*, n.s. XV (1904), 58–69. Recently published letters edited by Carl Bode are "Thoreau Finds a House," *Sat. Rev. Lit.*, XXIX (July 20, 1946), p. 15; and "Thoreau's Last Letter" (dated April 2, 1862), *New Eng. Quar.*, XIX (1946), 244.

EDITED TEXTS AND REPRINTS

Edited texts of separate items are Odell Shepard, ed., *A Week on the Concord and Merrimack Rivers*, New York, 1921 (Modern Students' Lib.); Frank B. Sanborn, ed., *The Service*, Boston, 1902; Henry Aiken Metcalf, ed., *Sir Walter Raleigh*, Boston, 1905; *On the Duty of Civil Disobedience*, New Haven, 1928; Arthur E. Christy, ed., *The Transmigration of the Seven Brahmans: A Translation from the Harivansa of Langlois*, New York, 1932, from manuscript with introduction and notes. Reprints of *Walden* are very numerous: the most recent and available are Walter Raymond, ed., London, 1908 (Everyman's Lib.); Joseph L. King, ed., New York, 1929 (Mod. Readers' Ser.); Henry S. Canby, ed., Boston, 1936; Brooks Atkinson, ed., New York, 1937 (Modern Lib.); and Gordon S. Haight, ed., New York, 1942 (Classics Club).

Selected works appear in James MacKaye, ed., *Thoreau, Philosopher of Freedom: Writings on Liberty*, New York, 1930; Theodore Dreiser, ed., *The Living Thoughts of Thoreau*, New York, 1939; Bertha Stevens, ed., *Thoreau, Reporter of the Universe: A Selection of His Writings* . . . New York, 1939; and *The Works of Henry D. Thoreau, with a Biographical Sketch by Ralph Waldo Emerson*, New York, 1940 (incl. *Walden, Cape Cod, A Week on the Concord and Merrimack Rivers*, and *The Maine Woods*).

Standard texts are Odell Shepard, ed., *The Heart of Thoreau's Journals*, Boston, 1927; Henry S. Canby, ed., *The Works of Thoreau, Selected and Edited*, Boston, 1937; Bartholow V. Crawford, *Henry David Thoreau: Representative Selections, with Introduction, Bibliography, and Notes*, New York,

1934 (Amer. Writers Ser.); Henry Seidel Canby, ed., *The Works of Thoreau,* Boston, 1947—the Cambridge Edition; and Carl Bode, ed., *The Portable Thoreau,* New York, 1947.

BIOGRAPHY AND CRITICISM

The most recent full-length biography is Henry S. Canby, *Thoreau,* Boston, 1939, especially useful on Thoreau as a writer. (Justin) Brooks Atkinson's *Henry Thoreau, The Cosmic Yankee,* New York, 1927, is a narrative biography. Interest in Thoreau abroad was met by "Henry David Thoreau: His Character and Opinions," in Robert Louis Stevenson's *Familiar Studies of Men and Books,* London, 1882, pp. 129–171; and Henry S. Salt, *The Life of Henry David Thoreau,* London, 1890. F(rancis) O. Matthiessen gave the fullest treatment of Thoreau's aesthetic in "From Emerson to Thoreau," Book I of his *American Renaissance* . . . , New York, 1941, pp. 3–175. Other studies of Thoreau as literary artist and moralist are "Thoreau's *Journal,*" in Paul E. More, *Shelburne Essays,* 5th ser., New York, 1908, pp. 106–131; Norman Foerster, "Thoreau as Artist," *Sewanee Rev.,* XXIX (1921), 2–13, an analysis of his prose; Raymond Adams, "Thoreau's Literary Apprenticeship," *Studies in Philol.,* XXIX (1932), 617–629; William D. Templeton, "Thoreau, Moralist of the Picturesque," *PMLA,* XLVII (1932), 864–889; Bartholow V. Crawford, introduction to *Henry David Thoreau: Representative Selections* . . . , New York, 1934, pp. xi–lvii; "Thoreau," in Van Wyck Brooks, *The Flowering of New England* . . . , New York, 1940 (rev. ed.), pp. 286–302; Charles C. Walcutt, "Thoreau in the Twentieth Century," *So. Atl. Quar.,* XXXIX (1940), 168–184; Charles A. Madison, "Henry David Thoreau: Transcendental Individualist," *Ethics,* LIV (1944), 110–123; Henry W. Wells, "An Evaluation of Thoreau's Poetry," *Amer. Lit.,* XVI (1944), 99–109; and George F. Whicher, *Walden Revisited* . . . , Chicago, 1945.

Thoreau as a reporter and interpreter of nature is fully discussed in "Thoreau," in Norman Foerster, *Nature in American Literature* . . . , New York, 1923, pp. 69–142; and Léon Bazalgette, *Henry Thoreau: Bachelor of Nature,* New York, 1924, translated by Van Wyck Brooks from *Henry Thoreau, Sauvage* . . . , Paris, 1924. Other studies of these aspects of Thoreau are Jason A. Russell, "Thoreau: The Interpreter of the Real Indian," *Queen's Quar.,* XXXV (1927), 37–48, with excerpts from unpublished notebooks; Edward B. Hinckley, "Thoreau and Beston: Two Observers of Cape Cod," *New Eng. Quar.,* IV (1931), 216–229; "Thoreau at Walden," in Van Wyck Brooks, *The Flowering of New England* . . . , New York, 1940 (rev. ed.), pp. 359–373; Reginald L. Cook, *The Concord Saunterer: Including a Discussion of the Nature Mysticism of Thoreau* . . . , Middlebury, Vt., 1940; and

Edward S. Deevey, Jr., "A Re-examination of Thoreau's *Walden,*" *Quar. Rev. Biology,* XVII (1942), 1–11—an evaluation of Thoreau as a leading limnologist.

Thoreau's intellectual development is the subject of Norman Foerster, "The Intellectual Heritage of Thoreau," *Texas Rev.,* II (1917), 192–212; Clarence Gohdes, "Henry Thoreau, Bachelor of Arts," *Classical Jour.,* XXIII (1928), 323–336—as a classical scholar; Charles Cestre, "Thoreau et Emerson," *Revue Anglo-Amér.,* VII (1930), 215–230; John B. Moore, "Thoreau Rejects Emerson," *Amer. Lit.,* IV (1932), 241–256; Grant Loomis, "Thoreau and Zimmermann," *New Eng. Quar.,* X (1937), 789–792; Francis L. Utley, "Thoreau and Columella: A Study in Reading Habits," *New Eng. Quar.,* XI (1938), 171–180; Raymond Adams, "Thoreau at Harvard: Some Unpublished Records," *New Eng. Quar.,* XIII (1940), 24–33; "Emerson and Thoreau," in Ralph H. Gabriel, *The Course of American Democratic Thought* . . . , New York, 1940, pp. 39–51; "Henry David Thoreau," in John P. Pritchard, *Return to the Fountains* . . . , Durham, N.C., 1942, pp. 61–67; and Joseph J. Kwiat, "Thoreau's Philosophical Apprenticeship," *New Eng. Quar.,* XVIII (1945), 51–69. Other influences are treated in Arthur E. Christy, *The Orient in American Transcendentalism* . . . , New York, 1933; Adolph B. Benson, "Scandinavian Influences in the Writings of Thoreau," *Scand. Studies,* XVI (1941), 201–211, 241–256. Ernest E. Leisy has identified some borrowings in "Thoreau and Ossian," *New Eng. Quar.,* XVIII (1945), 96–98, and in "Francis Quarles and Henry D. Thoreau," *Modern Language Notes,* LX (1945), 335–336. Further sources are identified in Raymond Adams, "Thoreau's Sources for 'Resistance to Civil Government,'" *Studies in Philol.,* XLII (1945), 640–653.

Other studies are Thomas M. Raysor, "The Love Story of Thoreau," *Studies in Philol.,* XXIII (1926), 457–463; Albert Keiser, "New Thoreau Material," *Modern Language Notes,* XLIV (1929), 253–254; Henry S. Salt, "Gandhi and Thoreau," *Nation and Athenaeum,* XLVI (Mar. 1, 1930), 728; Raymond Adams, "A Bibliographical Note on *Walden,*" *Amer. Lit.,* II (1930), 166–168; Austin Warren, "Lowell on Thoreau," *Studies in Philol.,* XXVII (1930), 442–461; James P. Wood, "English and American Criticism of Thoreau," *New Eng. Quar.,* VI (1933), 733–746; Viola C. White, "Thoreau's Opinion of Whitman," *New Eng. Quar.,* VIII (1935), 262–264; Frank Buckley, "Thoreau and the Irish," *ibid.,* XIII (1940), 389–400; Robert L. Straker, "Thoreau's Journey to Minnesota," *New Eng. Quar.,* XIV (1941), 549–555; Clarence A. Manning, "Thoreau and Tolstoi," *New Eng. Quar.,* XVI (1943), 234–243; Randall Stewart, "The Growth of Thoreau's Reputation," *College Eng.,* VII (1946), 208–214; James P. Brawner, "Thoreau as Wit and Humorist," *So. Atl. Quar.,* XLIV (1945), 170–194; Ernest E. Leisy,

"Sources of Thoreau's Borrowings in *A Week,*" *Amer. Lit.,* XVIII (1946), 37–44; Nick Aaron Ford, "Henry David Thoreau, Abolitionist," *New Eng. Quar.,* XIX (1946), 359–371; Madeleine B. Stern, "Approaches to Biography," *So. Atl. Quar.,* XLV (1946), 362–371; Hubert H. Hoeltje, "Thoreau as Lecturer," *New Eng. Quar.,* XIX (1946), 485–494; and S. T. Hyman, "Henry Thoreau in Our Time," *Atl. Mo.,* CLXXVIII (1946), 137–146.

Some eighty photographs of Walden Pond and vicinity are published in Henry Bugbee Kane, *Thoreau's Walden: A Photographic Register,* New York, 1946. The quest and discovery of the actual site of Thoreau's hut are set forth in Roland Wells Robbins, *Discovery at Walden,* Stoneham, Mass., 1947.

PRIMARY SOURCES

A significant early appreciation is Ralph Waldo Emerson, "Thoreau," *Atl. Mo.,* X (1862), 239–249. Invaluable source material presented by an intimate friend and companion is William E. Channing, *Thoreau, the Poet-Naturalist: With Memorial Verses,* Boston, 1873, rev. and enlarged by Frank B. Sanborn, Boston, 1902. Emerson's son Edward Waldo Emerson published *Henry Thoreau as Remembered by a Young Friend,* Boston, 1917; and, for the American Men of Letters Series, Frank B. Sanborn wrote *The Life of Henry David Thoreau, Including Many Essays Hitherto Unpublished, and Some Account of His Family and Friends,* Boston, 1917.

The leading depositories of Thoreau manuscripts are the Harvard College Library, the Henry E. Huntington Library, and the Morgan Library. Further items are in the Abernethy Library of Middlebury College.

BIBLIOGRAPHY

The best bibliography to 1908, superseding earlier works, is Francis H. Allen, *A Bibliography of Henry David Thoreau,* Boston, 1908. It is supplemented by Joseph S. Wade, "A Contribution to a Bibliography from 1909 to 1936 of Henry David Thoreau," *Jour. N.Y. Entomological Soc.,* XLVII (1939), 163–203. Further material appears in William White, "A Henry David Thoreau Bibliography, 1908–1937," *Bul. Bibl.,* XVI (1938–1939), 90–92, 111–113, 131–132, 163, 181–182, 199–202; and in Walter Harding, "A Bibliography of Thoreau in Poetry, Fiction, and Drama," *Bul. Bibl.,* XVIII (1943), 15–18. The bibliography in Bartholow V. Crawford, *Henry David Thoreau: Representative Selections* . . . , New York, 1934, pp. lix–lxix, is selective and annotated. See also Evadene B. Swanson, "The Manuscript Journal of Thoreau's Last Journey," *Minnesota Hist.,* XX (1939), 169–173. To be continued is Philip E. Burnham and Carvel Collins, "Contribution to a Bibliography of Thoreau, 1938–1945," *Bul. Bibl.,* XIX (1946), 16–18.

# HENRY TIMROD
*1828-1867*

SEPARATE AND COLLECTED WORKS

Timrod's only publication during his life was the volume of *Poems*, Boston, 1860. His friend Paul Hamilton Hayne edited *The Poems of Henry Timrod*, New York, 1873, with a sketch of his life. The poem *Katie*, New York, 1884, was addressed to his wife, Kate (Goodwin) Timrod (d. 1913). The Memorial Edition of *Poems of Henry Timrod* was issued, Boston, 1899 (and Richmond, 1901).

Jay B. Hubbell edited *The Last Years of Henry Timrod, 1864-1867: Including Letters of Timrod to Paul Hamilton Hayne and Letters About Timrod by William Gilmore Simms, John R. Thompson, John Greenleaf Whittier, and Others*, Durham, N.C., 1941—including heretofore uncollected items. Guy A. Cardwell, Jr., edited *The Uncollected Poems of Henry Timrod*, Athens, Ga., 1942, with an introduction and a bibl. of earlier collections, pp. 111-114. Edd W. Parks edited *The Essays of Henry Timrod*, Athens, Ga., 1942, with introduction and notes which reveal how Timrod analyzed and tried to refute Poe's aesthetic. Eleven letters are in William Fidler's "Unpublished Letters of Henry Timrod," *Southern Literary Messenger*, II (1940), 532-534.

BIOGRAPHY AND CRITICISM

There is no full-length biography of Timrod. Some of the best critical estimates appear in the volumes of collected writings named above. The best brief sketch is that by Armistead C. Gordon, Jr., in *Dict. Amer. Biog.* (1936). Other studies are George A. Wauchope, *Henry Timrod, Man and Poet: A Critical Study*, Columbia, S.C., 1915, 30 pp.; and Henry E. Shepherd, "Henry Timrod: Literary Estimate and Bibliography," *Pub. Southern Hist. Assn.*, III (1899), 267-280—the bibl. compiled by A. S. Salley, Jr.

Admiring tributes are published in Virginia P. Clare, *Harp of the South*, Oglethorpe Univ., Ga., 1936; and Henry T. Thompson, *Henry Timrod: Laureate of the Confederacy*, Columbia, S.C., 1928—with selections from his verse and prose.

Special studies are Gilbert P. Voigt, "Timrod's Essays in Literary Criticism," *Amer. Lit.*, VI (1934), 163-167; *idem*, "Timrod in the Light of Newly Revealed Letters," *So. Atl. Quar.*, XXXVII (1938), 263-269; Edd W. Parks, "Timrod's College Days," *Amer. Lit.*, VIII (1936), 294-296; and William Fidler, "Henry Timrod: Poet of the Confederacy," *Southern Literary Messenger*, II (1940), 527-532. Earlier estimates are Henry Austin, "Henry Timrod," *International Rev.,* IX (1880), 310–319; Charles H. Ross, "The New Edition of Timrod," *Sewanee Rev.,* VII (1899), 414–420; and James E. Routh, Jr., "The Poetry of Henry Timrod," *So. Atl. Quar.,* IX (1910), 267–274. Good background is furnished in Jay B. Hubbell, "Literary Nationalism in the Old South," in *American Studies in Honor of William Kenneth Boyd,* Durham, N.C., 1940, pp. 175–220. Further material is in William P. Trent, *William Gilmore Simms,* Boston, 1892.

The largest collection of Timrod manuscripts is in the Paul Hamilton Hayne Collection at the Duke University Library. Further items are in the Charleston (S.C.) Library Society, the University of South Carolina, and the University of Alabama. Items of interest about the Timrod family are Rupert Taylor, "Henry Timrod's Ancestress, Hannah Caesar," *Amer. Lit.,* IX (1938), 419–430; and Guy A. Cardwell, Jr., "William Henry Timrod, the Charleston Volunteers, and the Defense of St. Augustine," *N.C. Hist. Rev.,* XVIII (1941), 23–37.

The most serviceable bibliography is that compiled by A. S. Salley, Jr., for the article by Henry E. Shepherd, named above.

## JOHN TRUMBULL
### *1750–1831*

### SEPARATE WORKS

*An Essay on the Use and Advantages of the Fine Arts,* 1770; *An Elegy on the Death of Mr. Buckingham St. John,* 1771; *The Progress of Dulness* (*Part First,* 1772, *Part Second,* 1773, *Part Third,* 1773); *M'Fingal: A Modern Epic Poem, Canto First,* 1775; *M'Fingal . . . in Four Cantos,* 1782.

### COLLECTED WORKS

*The Poetical Works of John Trumbull,* Hartford, 1820, 2 vols., was published under Trumbull's supervision, prefaced by a memoir which is probably autobiographical.

### EDITED TEXTS AND REPRINTS

*M'Fingal* was edited by Benson J. Lossing, New York, 1864, with detailed notes. The 1820 ed. of *The Poetical Works* was the basis for a reprint of Trumbull's writings, ed. by Arthur H. Nason, in Vol. XIV of *The Colonnade,* New York, 1922, published for the Andiron Club.

### BIOGRAPHY AND CRITICISM

An authoritative life is Alexander Cowie, *John Trumbull: Connecticut*

*Wit,* Chapel Hill, N.C., 1936. Trumbull receives extensive notice in "John Trumbull," in Leon Howard, *The Connecticut Wits,* Chicago, 1943, pp. 37–78. The best brief account is that by Cowie in *Dict. Amer. Biog.* (1936). Moses C. Tyler, *The Literary History of the American Revolution,* New York, 1897, I, 187–221, 426–450, is excellent on Trumbull as a man of letters; "John Trumbull: Satirist and Scholar," in Annie R. Marble, *Heralds of American Literature,* Chicago, 1907, pp. 107–145, is good general criticism; and Vernon L. Parrington, *Main Currents in American Thought,* New York, I (1927), 248–252, is a brief statement of Trumbull's political views.

Special studies are James H. Trumbull, *The Origin of M'Fingal,* Morrisania, N.Y., 1868; Alexander Cowie, "John Trumbull as Revolutionist," *Amer. Lit.,* III (1931), 287–295; and Lennox Grey, "John Adams and John Trumbull in the 'Boston Cycle,'" *New Eng. Quar.,* IV (1931), 509–514. Two more recent studies by Alexander Cowie are "John Trumbull as a Critic of Poetry," *New Eng. Quar.,* XI (1938), 773–793, and "John Trumbull Glances at Fiction," *Amer. Lit.,* XII (1940), 69–73.

PRIMARY SOURCES

In addition to the "Memoir" which prefaces the 1820 ed. of *The Poetical Works,* there is the *Biographical Sketch of the Character of Governor Trumbull,* Hartford, 1809, known to be Trumbull's work.

The two important manuscript collections are the "Tyler Papers" in Cornell University Library, and the "Woodbridge Papers" in the Burton Historical Collection of the Detroit Public Library. There are scattered materials in possession of the Connecticut Historical Society and the Yale University Library. A calendar of letters written by Trumbull is in Cowie's life, pp. 222–223. A recently published letter is Katharine A. Conley, "A Letter of John Trumbull," *New Eng. Quar.,* XI (1938), 372–374.

BIBLIOGRAPHY

The fullest bibliographical listing is in Cowie's life, pp. 215–223; some later additions are made in Leon Howard, *The Connecticut Wits,* Chicago, 1943, pp. 413–415.

# ROYALL TYLER
*1757–1826*

WORKS

*The Contrast* (produced, 1787), 1790; *The Algerine Captive,* 1797; *The Yankey in London,* 1809.

*The Contrast* is reprinted in Arthur H. Quinn, *Representative American Plays* (1917); Montrose Moses, *Representative Plays* (1918); and Allan G. Halline, *American Plays* (1935). It was separately edited by James B. Wilbur, Boston, 1920, with introduction and bibl. by Helen Tyler Brown. Arthur W. Peach and George F. Newbrough edited *Four Plays by Royall Tyler,* Princeton, 1941, as Volume XV of *America's Lost Plays.* It includes *The Island of Barrataria, The Origin of the Feast of Purim, Joseph and His Brethren,* and *The Judgment of Solomon.*

BIOGRAPHY AND CRITICISM

No full-length life of Tyler has yet been published. The sketch in *Dict. Amer. Biog.* (1936) is by Arthur H. Quinn. Further general criticism is in Arthur H. Quinn, *A History of the American Drama from the Beginning to the Civil War,* rev. ed., New York, 1943, pp. 64-73; and Arthur H. Nethercot, "The Dramatic Background of Royall Tyler's *The Contrast,*" *Amer. Lit.,* XII (1941), 435-446.

A further study is Frederick Tupper, "Royall Tyler: Man of Law and Man of Letters," *Vermont Hist. Soc. Proc.* (1926-1928), pp. 65-101. Helen Tyler Brown and Frederick Tupper edited *Grandmother Tyler's Book: The Recollections of Mary Palmer Tyler . . . ,* New York, 1925—Royall Tyler's wife.

The Royall Tyler Papers are deposited in the Vermont Historical Society Library, Montpelier, but are not now available.

For a list of Tyler's unpublished plays see Allan G. Halline, *American Plays,* New York, 1935, pp. 751-752.

# JONES VERY
## *1813-1880*

WORKS

*Essays and Poems,* Boston, 1839, prepared under Emerson's guidance, was the only volume published in Very's lifetime. It was issued "completely" by James Freeman Clarke in 1886, with a biographical sketch by Clarke and a preface by C. A. Bartol, in an edition of some 600 poems. *Poems by Jones Very,* Boston, 1883, has an introductory memoir by William P. Andrews.

BIOGRAPHY AND CRITICISM

An authoritative biographical and critical study is William I. Bartlett, *Jones Very: Emerson's "Brave Saint,"* Durham, N.C., 1942, including a large number of poems here first printed. Special studies are Clarence Gohdes,

"Alcott's 'Conversation' on the Transcendental Club and *The Dial,*" *Amer. Lit.,* III (1931), 14–28; "Jones Very," in Gamaliel Bradford, *Biography and the Human Heart,* Boston, 1932, pp. 187–212; Carlos Baker, "Emerson and Jones Very," *New Eng. Quar.,* VII (1934), 90–99; "Jones Very and R. W. Emerson: Aspects of New England Mysticism," in Yvor Winters, *Maule's Curse,* Norfolk, Conn., 1938, pp. 125–165. In the last-named work is "A Brief Selection of the Poems of Jones Very," pp. 219–232. A calendar of Very's poetical contributions to the Salem *Observer* (1833–1840) and the *Western Messenger* (1839–1840) is in Bartlett's *Jones Very* (1942), pp. 210–217. The sketch in *Dict. Amer. Biog.* (1936) is by Carlos Baker.

Most of Very's letters were burned after his death. Most of his extant manuscripts are in the Andover Theological Library, Cambridge, Mass., and the Brown University Library. Other important material is in the files of the Essex Institute, Salem, Mass., and in Emerson's published and unpublished letters and journals.

A full bibliographical listing of primary and secondary sources is in Bartlett's *Jones Very* (1942), pp. 209–227.

## NATHANIEL WARD
### *1578?–1652*

#### SEPARATE WORKS

*The Simple Cobler of Aggawam in America,* 1647; *A Religious Retreat Sounded to a Religious Army,* 1647; *A Word to Mr. Peters,* 1647.

#### EDITED TEXTS AND REPRINTS

Reprints of *The Simple Cobler* have been frequent. The best is the most recent, edited by Lawrence C. Wroth for the Scholars' Facsimiles and Reprints, New York, 1937, with full bibliographical data. "A Coppie of the Liberties of the Massachusets Colonie in New England" was first published in *Coll. Mass. Hist. Soc.,* 3rd ser., VIII (1843), 216–237; it is also No. 25 of *American History Leaflets,* ed. by A. B. Hart and E. Channing (1896), and was edited by W. H. Whitmore, Boston, 1889. The "Letters of Nathaniel Ward . . . to John Winthrop" are in *Coll. Mass. Hist. Soc.,* 4th ser., VII (1865), 23–29.

#### BIOGRAPHY AND CRITICISM

A narrative biography is John Ward Dean, *A Memoir of the Rev. Nathaniel Ward . . . ,* Albany, 1868, with a bibl., pp. 168–177. The best brief sketch is "Nathaniel Ward, Lawmaker and Wit," in Samuel E. Morison,

*Builders of the Bay Colony,* Boston, 1930, pp. 217–243. Ward as a man of letters is treated by Moses C. Tyler, *A History of American Literature During the Colonial Period,* rev. ed., New York, I (1897), 227–240. An unpublished dissertation is Shirley Wilcox Harvey, "Nathaniel Ward: His Life and Works, Together with an Edited Edition of His *Simple Cobler,"* Boston Univ., 1935.

# GEORGE WASHINGTON
## *1732–1799*

COLLECTED WORKS

Publication of the definitive collection of Washington's writings, ed. by John C. Fitzpatrick, has been completed: *The Writings of George Washington from the Original Manuscript Sources, 1745–1799: Prepared Under the Direction of the United States George Washington Bicentennial Commission,* Washington, 1931–1944, 39 vols., with a general index in the two final volumes. It is complete and inclusive, and supersedes all earlier collections. Until its publication, the most useful collection was *The Writings of George Washington,* New York, 1889–1893, 14 vols., ed. by Worthington C. Ford. The earliest important collection was that of Jared Sparks, *The Writings of George Washington,* Boston, 1834–1837, 12 vols., which included some hundreds of letters not in the Ford ed., but was marred by textual alterations and unnoted omissions. Fitzpatrick began the groundwork for preparing his edition by publishing a *Calendar of the Correspondence of George Washington . . . with the Continental Congress,* Washington, 1906; and *Calendar of the Correspondence of George Washington . . . with the Officers,* Washington, 1915, 4 vols.

Other useful collections are John C. Fitzpatrick, ed., *The Diaries of George Washington, 1748–1799,* Boston, 1925, 4 vols.; *idem, George Washington, Colonial Traveller, 1732–1775,* Indianapolis, 1927—a compilation of extracts from Washington's papers of his travels through the United States, arranged chronologically with editorial notes; William S. Baker, *Itinerary of General Washington,* Philadelphia, 1892—extracts covering the years 1775–1783; and Archer B. Hulbert, ed., *Washington and the West: Being George Washington's Diary of September, 1784 . . . ,* New York, 1905, and Cleveland, 1911. A calendar of Washington's travels, compiled from his writings, is William S. Baker, *Washington After the Revolution, 1784–99,* Philadelphia, 1898. Two other useful collections are John C. Fitzpatrick, ed., *George Washington's Accounts of Expenses While Commander-in-Chief . . . ,* Boston, 1917—a facsimile rendering of account books for the years 1775–1783, with annotations; and Stephen Decatur, Jr., *Private Affairs of George Washington, from the Records and Accounts of Tobias Lear, Esquire, His Secretary,* Boston, 1933—the cash accounts of the President's expenses for the years 1789–1792.

*The Journal of Major George Washington,* ed. by Randolph G. Adams, New York, 1940, was published in Scholars' Facsimiles and Reprints from the Williamsburg ed., 1754, and covers the period Oct., 1753, to Jan., 1754. *Washington's Farewell Address, in Facsimile, with Transliterations of All the Drafts of Washington, Madison, and Hamilton* . . . , New York, 1935, ed. by Victor H. Paltsits, gives valuable emphasis to the evolution of Washington as writer and thinker.

BIOGRAPHY AND CRITICISM

Somewhat less than half of all that Washington wrote was in print before publication (1931–1944) of the Fitzpatrick collected edition. The most recent studies of Washington have therefore an important advantage in easily accessible material of the greatest significance. The most detailed of such biographies is Nathaniel W. Stephenson and Waldo H. Dunn, *George Washington,* New York, 1940, 2 vols.—balanced and authoritative. Bernhard Knollenberg, *Washington and the Revolution: A Reappraisal* . . . , New York, 1940, freshly evaluates the war years, and is based on new material from manuscript. John C. Fitzpatrick's *George Washington Himself,* Indianapolis, 1933, appraises Washington's character in the light of new manuscript evidence.

Among earlier lives, still standard are William R. Thayer, *George Washington,* Boston, 1922; Woodrow Wilson, *George Washington,* New York, 1903; Henry C. Lodge, *George Washington,* Boston, 1889, 2 vols.—more detailed than the lives by Thayer and Wilson but based, as are they, on a partial publication of the *Writings.* Much interesting material is in Paul L. Ford, *The True George Washington,* Philadelphia, 1896 (reprinted as *George Washington,* 1924), but it is undocumented. The well known "debunking" biography by Rupert Hughes, *George Washington,* New York, 1926–1930, 3 vols., is to be used cautiously, though its bibliographical aids have value.

*The Life of George Washington,* in Vol. I (1837) of Jared Sparks's ed. of Washington's *Writings,* was published separately in 1839. It is historically interesting. Deservedly well known is Washington Irving's *Life of George Washington,* New York, 1855–1859, 5 vols., though it places excessive reliance on Sparks. Ranking with Irving is John Marshall's *The Life of George Washington,* Philadelphia, 1804–1807, 5 vols., which is the earliest of important lives and is significant also as source material, though the Presidential years are treated with Federalist sympathies. The famous life by Mason L

Weems, *A History of the Life and Death, Virtues and Exploits, of General George Washington,* Philadelphia, 1800 (reprinted, New York, 1927), is largely fabrication and thus is thoroughly unreliable.

The sketch of Washington in *Dict. Amer. Biog* (1936) is by John C. Fitzpatrick.

Recent special studies, all reliable, are Eugene E. Prussing, *The Estate of George Washington, Deceased,* Boston, 1927—an evaluation of his fortune; Thomas G. Frothingham, *Washington, Commander-in-Chief,* Boston, 1930; Charles H. Ambler, *George Washington and the West,* Chapel Hill, N.C., 1936; and Gilbert Chinard, *George Washington as the French Knew Him,* Princeton, 1940—an edited collection of useful texts.

Earlier studies are Paul Wilstach, *Mount Vernon: Washington's Home and the Nation's Shrine,* Garden City, 1916—useful on his home life; Paul L. Haworth, *George Washington, Farmer,* Indianapolis, 1915 (reprinted as *George Washington, Country Gentleman . . .* , 1925); and Henry B. Carrington, *Battles of the American Revolution, 1775-1781,* New York, 1876—collateral material for the military side.

To the present very little attention has been devoted to Washington as a man of letters. Studies of the subject are "George Washington as Diarist," in Stuart P. Sherman, *Critical Woodcuts,* New York, 1926, pp. 296-310; James H. Penniman, *George Washington as Man of Letters,* n.p., 1918, 52 pp.; and Paul L. Ford, *Washington, and the Theatre,* New York, 1899. See also G. R. Frey, "George Washington in German Fiction," *Amer.-Ger. Rev.,* XII (June, 1946), 25-26, 37.

PRIMARY SOURCES

A description of the great collection of Washington manuscripts in the Library of Congress, consisting of over 400 volumes, is in the Fitzpatrick ed. of the *Writings,* introduction, Vol. I. Further details, especially of manuscripts elsewhere, are in the bibliography following the sketch of Washington in *Dict. Amer. Biog.* Much of Washington's library was deposited in the Boston Athenaeum: see Appleton P. C. Griffin, *A Catalogue of the Washington Collection in the Boston Athenaeum,* Cambridge, 1897. The Washington portraits are best described in Gustav Eisen, *Portraits of Washington,* New York, 1932, 3 vols.; and the sculptures in Frances D. Whittemore, *George Washington in Sculpture,* Boston, 1933.

Other source material is Louis Gottschalk, ed., *The Letters of Lafayette to Washington, 1777-1799,* New York, 1944; S. M. Hamilton, *Letters to Washington, 1752-1775,* New York, 1898-1902, 4 vols.; Jared Sparks, *Correspondence of the American Revolution: Being Letters of Eminent Men to George Washington,* Boston, 1853, 4 vols.; and George W. P. Custis,

*Recollections and Private Memoirs of Washington,* New York, 1860—a source of much unprovable tradition about Washington.

BIBLIOGRAPHY

There is need for a Washington bibliography to date. Useful are William S. Baker, *Bibliotheca Washingtoniana: A Descriptive List of the Biographies and Bibliographical Sketches of George Washington,* Philadelphia, 1889; and Margaret B. Stillwell, "Checklist of Eulogies and Funeral Orations on the Death of George Washington . . .," *Bul. N.Y. Pub. Lib.,* XX (1916), 403–450.

# DANIEL WEBSTER
## *1782–1852*

COLLECTED WORKS

J. W. McIntyre edited *The Writings and Speeches of Daniel Webster,* Boston, 1903, 18 vols., known as the National Edition—an effort at complete publication of Webster's works. An early collection published during Webster's lifetime is Edward Everett, ed., *The Works of Daniel Webster,* Boston, 1851, 6 vols.

The fullest collection of published correspondence is C. H. Van Tyne, *The Letters of Daniel Webster . . . ,* New York, 1902. Fletcher Webster's edition of *The Private Correspondence of Daniel Webster,* Boston, 1857, 2 vols., includes Webster's brief autobiography, as written in 1829. A. R. M. Lower edited "An Unpublished Letter of Daniel Webster," *New Eng. Quar.,* XII (1939), 360–364.

BIOGRAPHY AND CRITICISM

The fullest biography is Claude M. Fuess, *Daniel Webster,* Boston, 1930, 2 vols. Samuel Hopkins Adams's *The Godlike Daniel,* was published in New York in the same year. Of the many earlier biographies of Webster, those deserving mention are S. G. Fisher, *The True Daniel Webster,* Philadelphia, 1911; John B. McMaster, *Daniel Webster,* New York, 1902; and Henry C. Lodge, *Daniel Webster,* Boston, 1883, the first brief formal study. The sketch of Webster in *Dict. Amer. Biog.* (1936) is by Arthur C. Cole. Useful general estimates are "Daniel Webster," in Gamaliel Bradford, *As God Made Them,* Boston, 1929, pp. 1–42; Vernon L. Parrington, *Main Currents in American Thought,* New York, II (1927), 304–316; and Henry C. Lodge, "Webster," *Camb. Hist. Amer. Lit.,* II (1918), 92–103.

Special studies are E. P. Wheeler, *Daniel Webster: The Expounder of the Constitution,* New York, 1905; Robert L. Carey, *Daniel Webster as an*

*Economist*, New York, 1929; Clyde A. Duniway, "Daniel Webster," in Samuel F. Bemis, ed., *The American Secretaries of State and Their Diplomacy*, New York, 1928, V, 3–64, VI, 77–113; and Gerald W. Johnson, *America's Silver Age: The Statecraft of Clay, Webster, Calhoun*, New York, 1939.

Webster as orator and man of letters is discussed in William N. Brigance, ed., *A History and Criticism of American Public Address*, New York, 1943, II, 665–733 (by Wilbur S. Howell and Hoyt H. Hudson); "Daniel Webster as a Master of English Style," in Edwin P. Whipple, *American Literature and Other Papers*, Boston, 1887, pp. 139–233; "Daniel Webster as an Orator" and "A Glance at Daniel Webster," in Mellen Chamberlain, *John Adams ... with Other Essays*, Boston, 1899, pp. 329–342, 357–368; and Glen E. Mills, "Misconceptions Concerning Daniel Webster," *Quar. Jour. of Speech*, XXIX (1943), 423–428—a correction of popular misconceptions about Webster as orator.

Other special studies are "Daniel Webster and the Sentiment of Union," in John Fiske, *Essays, Historical and Literary*, New York, 1902, I, 363–409; H. D. Foster, "Webster's Seventh of March Speech and the Secession Movement, 1850," *Amer. Hist. Rev.*, XXVII (1922), 245–270; and Clyde A. Duniway, "Webster and the West," *Minnesota Hist.*, IX (Mar., 1928), 3–15.

PRIMARY SOURCES

The largest collection of Webster manuscripts is in the New Hampshire Historical Society at Concord. Other collections are in the library of Dartmouth College, and Phillips Exeter Academy. Further material is filed in the National Archives. The manuscripts dealing with Webster in the Library of Congress consist mostly of letters written to him.

Contemporary published reminiscences and memoirs of interest are Samuel L. Knapp, *A Memoir of the Life of Daniel Webster*, Boston, 1831; Charles Lanman, *The Private Life of Daniel Webster* (1852)—a biography by Webster's private secretary which the family tried to suppress; Charles W. March, *Reminiscences of Congress* (1850)—reprinted as *Daniel Webster and His Contemporaries* (1852). Other personal reminiscences are those of Peter Harvey (1877) and George T. Curtis (1870).

BIBLIOGRAPHY

Bibliographies of primary and secondary material are in Fuess, *Daniel Webster*, pp. 419–430, and *Camb. Hist. Amer. Lit.*, II (1918), pp. 480–488. Other important bibliographical listings are Clifford B. Clapp, "The Speeches of Daniel Webster: A Bibliographical Review," *Papers Bibl. Soc. Amer.*, XIII (1919), 3–63; Fletcher Webster, "A Chronological List of the Writings and Speeches of Daniel Webster," in the *Writings*, XVIII (1903), 579–619; and

Charles H. Hart, *Bibliographia Websteriana: A List of the Publications Occasioned by the Death of Daniel Webster*, Philadelphia, 1883, 4 pp.

## EDITH (NEWBOLD JONES) WHARTON
### *1862–1937*

SEPARATE WORKS

*The Decoration of Houses* (with Ogden Codman, Jr.), 1897; *The Greater Inclination*, 1899; *The Touchstone*, 1900; *Crucial Instances*, 1901; *The Valley of Decision*, 1902; *Sanctuary*, 1903; *Italian Villas and Their Gardens*, 1904; *The Descent of Man and Other Stories*, 1904; *Italian Backgrounds*, 1905; *The House of Mirth*, 1905; *Madame de Treymes*, 1907; *The Fruit of the Tree*, 1907; *A Motor-Flight Through France*, 1908; *The Hermit and the Wild Woman, and Other Stories*, 1908; *Artemis to Actaeon and Other Verse*, 1909; *Tales of Men and Ghosts*, 1910; *Ethan Frome*, 1911; *The Reef*, 1912; *The Custom of the Country*, 1913; *Fighting France: From Dunkerque to Belfort*, 1915; *Xingu and Other Stories*, 1916; *Summer*, 1917; *The Marne*, 1918; *French Ways and Their Meaning*, 1919; *The Age of Innocence*, 1920; *In Morocco*, 1920; *The Glimpses of the Moon*, 1922; *A Son at the Front*, 1923; *Old New York*, 1924; *The Mother's Recompense*, 1925; *The Writing of Fiction*, 1925; *Here and Beyond*, 1926; *Twelve Poems*, 1926; *Twilight Sleep*, 1927; *The Children*, 1928; *Hudson River Bracketed*, 1929; *Certain People*, 1930; *The Gods Arrive*, 1932; *Human Nature*, 1933; *A Backward Glance*, 1934; *The World Over*, 1936; *Ghosts*, 1937; *The Buccaneers*, 1938.

EDITED TEXTS AND REPRINTS

There is no collected edition of Edith Wharton's writings. Of her novels *The House of Mirth* (1905) was reprinted in World's Classics, London, 1936. *Ethan Frome* (1911) has been most frequently reprinted; it is in the Modern Student's Lib., New York, 1922, with an important introduction contributed by the author. More recently it was edited by Bernard De Voto, New York, 1938, and by Clifton Fadiman, New York, 1939. *The Age of Innocence* (1920) was edited by Orton Lowe for the Mod. Lit. Ser., New York, 1932, and was issued in the Modern Lib., New York, 1943. Many of her novels have been made available in good French translations. Outstanding is *The House of Mirth (Chez les Heureux du Monde*, Paris, 1908), with an important critical introduction by Paul Bourget.

BIOGRAPHY AND CRITICISM

The most extensive study is Edward K. Brown, *Edith Wharton: Etude*

*Critique,* Paris, 1935. Among critical estimates before publication of *The Age of Innocence* (1920), generally considered Mrs. Wharton's best work, are Charles Waldstein, "Social Ideals," *No. Amer. Rev.,* CLXXXII (1906), 840–852, CLXXXIII (1906), 125–126—an important early study of *The House of Mirth;* "Mrs. Wharton," in Henry D. Sedgwick, *The New American Type and Other Essays,* Boston, 1908, pp. 53–96; "The Greater Edith Wharton," in Edwin A. Björkman, *Voices of Tomorrow,* New York, 1913, pp. 290–304; Henry James, *Notes on Novelists,* New York, 1914, pp. 280–283; "Culture and Edith Wharton," in John C. Underwood, *Literature and Insurgency,* New York, 1914, pp. 346–390; Percy Lubbock, "The Novels of Edith Wharton," *Quar. Rev.,* CCXXIII (1915), 182–201; "Edith Wharton," in Helen T. and Wilson Follett, *Some Modern Novelists,* New York, 1919, pp. 291–311; "Edith Wharton," in Blanche C. Williams, *Our Short Story Writers,* New York, 1920, pp. 337–357; and Charles K. Trueblood, "Edith Wharton," *Dial,* LXVIII (1920), 80–91.

Later estimates are "Edith Wharton," in Percy H. Boynton, *Some Contemporary Americans,* Chicago, 1924, pp. 89–107; Robert M. Lovett, *Edith Wharton,* New York, 1925—a critical appreciation; Wilbur L. Cross, "Edith Wharton," *Bookman,* LXIII (1926), 641–646; Régis Michaud, *The American Novel To-day,* Boston, 1928, pp. 54–60; "Edith Wharton: Costuming the Passions," in Stuart P. Sherman, *The Main Stream,* New York, 1927, pp. 204–212; Osbert Burdett, "Edith Wharton," in J. C. Squire, ed., *Contemporary American Authors,* New York, 1928, pp. 151–178; Robert Sencourt, "The Poetry of Edith Wharton," *Bookman,* LXXIII (1931), 478–486; Frances T. Russell, "Melodramatic Mrs. Wharton," *Sewanee Rev.,* XL (1932), 425–437; *idem,* "Edith Wharton's Use of Imagery," *English Jour.,* XXI (1932), 452–461; "Edith Wharton," in Pelham Edgar, *The Art of the Novel,* New York, 1933, pp. 196–205; and Harry Hartwick, *The Foreground of American Fiction,* New York, 1934, pp. 369–388.

Since her death, summaries of her place in the world of letters are Henry S. Canby, "Edith Wharton," *Sat. Rev. Lit.,* XVI (Aug. 21, 1937), 6–7; Edmund Wilson, "Justice to Edith Wharton," *New Repub.,* XCV (1938), 209–213—an important analysis; Edward K. Brown, "Edith Wharton," *Etudes Anglaises,* II (1938), 12–26; "Moral Situation in Edith Wharton," in Nellie Elizabeth Monroe, *The Novel and Society,* Chapel Hill, N.C., 1941, pp. 111–138; and "Two Educations: Edith Wharton and Theodore Dreiser," in Alfred Kazin, *On Native Grounds,* New York, 1942, pp. 73–90—an estimate with the advantage of perspective.

PRIMARY SOURCES

The most important source material is in Edith Wharton's autobiography,

*A Backward Glance* (1934); in her statement of artistic credo, *The Writing of Fiction* (1925); and in her travel books. She contributed "The Writing of *Ethan Frome*," to Colophon, Pt. II (1931), 1–4. There is further significant material in the memoirs and biographies of William D. Howells, Henry James, and Charles E. Norton.

Percy Lubbock's *Portrait of Edith Wharton,* New York, 1947, is portraiture by one who knew her well.

The majority of Edith Wharton manuscripts are deposited in the Yale University Library, but will not be available for inspection until 1968.

BIBLIOGRAPHY

The fullest listing of books and articles by and relating to Edith Wharton is in Fred B. Millett, *Contemporary American Authors,* New York, 1940, pp. 633–639. Useful data are supplied by Lavinia R. Davis, *A Bibliography of the Writings of Edith Wharton,* Portland, Me., 1933, 63 pp., and Lawson M. Melish, *A Bibliography of the Collected Writings of Edith Wharton,* New York, 1927—limited in use by its date of compilation. See also the bibliography in Edward K. Brown, *Edith Wharton: Etude Critique,* Paris, 1935, pp. 331–340.

# WALT(ER) WHITMAN
*1819–1892*

SEPARATE WORKS

*Franklin Evans,* 1842; *Leaves of Grass,* 1855, 1856, 1860–1861, 1867, 1871, 1872, 1876, 1881–1882, 1882, 1888, 1889, 1891–1892; *Drum-Taps,* 1865; *Democratic Vistas,* 1871; *Passage to India,* 1871; *After All, Not to Create Only,* 1871; *As a Strong Bird on Pinions Free,* 1872; *Memoranda During the War,* 1875–1876; *Two Rivulets,* 1876; *Specimen Days and Collect,* 1882–1883; *November Boughs,* 1888; *Good-bye My Fancy,* 1891; *Autobiographia,* 1892; *Notes and Fragments,* 1899; *An American Primer,* 1904; *Lafayette in Brooklyn,* 1905; *Criticism: An Essay,* 1913; *Pictures,* 1927; *A Child's Reminiscence,* 1930.

COLLECTIONS

*Calamus: Letters . . . ,* 1897; *The Wound Dresser,* 1898; *Walt Whitman's Diary in Canada,* 1904; *Uncollected Poetry and Prose . . . ,* 1921; *The Half-Breed, and Other Stories,* 1927; *Rivulets of Prose,* 1928; *Walt Whitman's Workshop,* 1928; *I Sit and Look Out,* 1932; *New York Dissected,* 1936.

Whitman rewrote and expanded *Leaves of Grass* so that each printing is in fact a new edition. The method and manner of the publication is complicated to such an extent that a descriptive bibliography may never be able to place issues and priorities definitively. Later editions cannot be described accurately as 8th, 9th, 10th, etc. The important printings made during Whitman's lifetime are as follows: *First edition,* Brooklyn, 1855, no publisher, 95 pages, containing the noted preface on the poet as seer, later omitted or largely absorbed into his poems, and including among its twelve poems those later entitled "Song of Myself," "I Sing the Body Electric," and "There Was a Child Went Forth." *Second edition,* Brooklyn, Fowler and Wells, 1856, 384 pages, containing twenty additional poems, including "By Blue Ontario's Shore" (which, in verse form, incorporates some of the preface to the first edition), "Crossing Brooklyn Ferry," and "Song of the Broad-Axe," as well as the fulsome reply to Emerson's laudatory letter of July, 1855, in part here printed, concluding "I greet you at the beginning of a great career. R. W. Emerson"—the phrase also quoted on the backstrip. *Third edition,* Boston, Thayer and Eldridge, 1860–1861, 456 pages, containing 122 new poems, together with two new sections: "Calamus" and "Children of Adam." *Fourth edition,* New York, 1867, no publisher, 338 pages, reprinting in the latest copies from the press the poems published as *Drum-Taps* (1865) and *Sequel to Drum-Taps* (1865), including the elegiacs on Lincoln. *Fifth edition,* Washington, no publisher, 1871, 384 pages, reissued in 1872, with the addition of "Passage to India" and "After All, Not to Create Only," both separately published in 1871. The Author's or Centennial Edition was published, Camden, 1876, in 2 vols.—the first a reprint of the 1871 edition without added material, and the second entitled *Two Rivulets.* The so-called "Suppressed Edition" was undertaken by James R. Osgood and Co., Boston, 1881, 382 pages, including new poems, but it was withdrawn from circulation when the publisher was threatened with prosecution. Whitman, from the same plates, issued an "Author's Edition," Camden, 1882, while waiting for the publication of the same material to be undertaken by Rees Welsh and Co., Philadelphia, in the same year. In 1889 the Philadelphia publisher David McKay issued a special pocket edition, 404 pages, incorporating *November Boughs* (1888) in a section called "Annex to Preceding Pages," and here entitled "Sands at Seventy"; the prose preface to *November Boughs*—"A Backward Glance o'er Travel'd Roads"—was transferred as epilogue to the present volume, and the whole put out as a birthday souvenir.

The final edition of *Leaves of Grass* to be issued under the author's supervision, the so-called "Deathbed Edition," was published by David McKay, Philadelphia, 1891–1892, incorporating as a second "annex" *Good-bye My Fancy,* separately published in 1891.

### COLLECTED WORKS

Whitman himself oversaw the publishing of the *Complete Poems and*

*Prose of Walt Whitman, 1855–1888,* Philadelphia, 1888–1889—which includes the so-called "Tenth Edition" of *Leaves of Grass*—and arranged for the publication of his *Complete Prose Works,* Philadelphia, 1892. His literary executors, Horace L. Traubel, Richard M. Bucke, and Thomas B. Harned, collected further material which they issued as *In Re Walt Whitman,* Philadelphia, 1893, including in it three early reviews of *Leaves of Grass* written by Whitman himself and published anonymously. They edited the first extensive collection, *The Complete Writings of Walt Whitman,* New York, 1902, 10 vols., with bibl. and critical material supplied by Oscar L. Triggs.

There is no collected edition of Whitman letters. Those published are Thomas B. Harned, ed., *Letters Written by Walt Whitman to His Mother from 1866 to 1872,* New York, 1902; *idem,* ed., *The Letters of Anne Gilchrist and Walt Whitman,* Garden City, N.Y., 1918; Emory Holloway, ed., "Some New Whitman Letters," *Amer. Mercury,* XVI (1929), 183–188; Rollo G. Silver, ed., "Seven Letters of Walt Whitman," *Amer. Lit.,* VII (1935), 76–81; *idem,* ed., "Thirty-one Letters of Walt Whitman," *ibid.,* VIII (1937), 417–438—important additions; and Oral S. Coad, ed., "Seven Whitman Letters," *Jour. Rutgers Univ. Lib.,* VIII (1944), 18–26—complete printing of the letters to William Sloane Kennedy, 1885–1891. For further items see the section following.

EDITED TEXTS AND REPRINTS

Whitman's literary executor Richard M. Bucke edited three volumes with introduction before the turn of the century: *Calamus* . . . , Boston, 1897—a collection of letters to Doyle, not the poetry; *The Wound Dresser,* Boston, 1898—a series of letters written during the hospital days in Washington; and *Notes and Fragments,* 1899—printed for private circulation. Horace Traubel edited *An American Primer,* Boston, 1904, with a facsimile of the original manuscript. William Sloane Kennedy edited *Walt Whitman's Diary in Canada,* Boston, 1904, with extracts from other of his diaries and literary notebooks. Editorials, essays, and reviews written for the Brooklyn *Daily Eagle* in 1846–1847 were collected by Cleveland Rodgers and John Black as *The Gathering of the Forces,* New York, 1920. Further gleanings have appeared in Emory Holloway, ed., *The Uncollected Poetry and Prose of Walt Whitman,* New York, 1921, 2 vols.

Recent texts, all competently edited, are *Pictures: An Unpublished Poem of Walt Whitman,* New York, 1927, ed. by Emory Holloway from a manuscript of about 1850, with introduction and notes; *The Half-Breed, and Other Stories,* New York, 1927, ed. by Thomas O. Mabbott—four short stories, first published in the New York *Aristidean* (1845); *Walt Whitman's Workshop,* ed. with introduction and notes by Clifton J. Furness, Cambridge, 1928—a collection of unpublished manuscripts, including *The Eighteenth Presidency:*

*Voice of Walt Whitman to Each Young Man in the Nation, North, South, East, and West*—a pamphlet written for the presidential campaign of 1856, which was in fact first discovered by Jean Catel, translated into French by Adrienne Monnier, in the March, 1926, issue of *Navire d'Argent,* and separately printed, Paris, 1928; *Rivulets of Prose: Critical Essays,* New York, 1928, ed. by Carolyn Wells and Alfred F. Goldsmith; *Franklin Evans; or, The Inebriate: A Tale of the Times,* New York, 1929, ed. by Emory Holloway, with an introduction; *A Child's Reminiscence,* Seattle, 1930, collected and ed. by Thomas O. Mabbott and Rollo G. Silver, with introduction and notes, including some items published anonymously in the New York *Saturday Press* during 1859–1860; *I Sit and Look Out,* New York, 1932, ed. by Emory Holloway and Vernolian Schwarz—editorials from the Brooklyn *Daily Times; Walt Whitman and the Civil War: A Collection of Original Articles and Manuscripts,* Philadelphia, 1933, ed. by Charles I. Glicksberg; *New York Dissected,* New York, 1936, ed. by Emory Holloway and Ralph Adimari—a collection of articles published in *Life Illustrated,* 1855–1856; Jean Catel, ed., "Un Inédit de Walt Whitman," *Etudes Anglaises,* III (1939), 359–360; and Katherine Molinoff, ed., *An Unpublished Whitman Manuscript: The Record Book of the Smithtown Debating Society, 1837–1838,* New York, 1941, with introduction by Oscar Cargill.

*Walt Whitman's Backward Glances,* Philadelphia, 1947, is a critical edition prepared by Sculley Bradley and John A. Stevenson, showing the evolution of "A Backward Glance o'er Travel'd Roads" from the four constituent articles: "A Backward Glance on My Own Road," "How 'Leaves of Grass' Was Made," "How I Made a Book," and "My Book and I."

The best volume of selected reprints to 1938 is Emory Holloway, ed., *Complete Poetry and Selected Prose and Letters,* London, 1938. Mark Van Doren edited *The Viking Portable Library Walt Whitman,* New York, 1945, 698 pages, including ninety-five poems, with Whitman's prefaces and the best of *Specimen Days. Leaves of Grass* has been issued in many editions, most recently edited by Carl Sandburg for the Illustrated Modern Lib., New York, 1944. Other reprints are Stuart P. Sherman, ed., New York, 1922 (Modern Student's Lib.), John Valente, ed., New York, 1928 (Modern Readers' Ser.), and Sherwood Anderson, ed., New York, 1933. The first (1855) edition was edited with introduction by Clifton J. Furness for the Facsimile Text Soc., New York, 1939. *Leaves of Grass: The Collected Poems* was edited by Emory Holloway for Blue Ribbon Books, Garden City, N.Y., 1942.

Other selections are Louise Pound, ed., *Specimen Days, Democratic Vistas, and Other Prose,* Garden City, N.Y., 1935; and Christopher Morley, ed., *Walt Whitman in Camden: A Selection of Prose from Specimen Days,* Camden, N.J., 1938.

A serviceable volume is Floyd Stovall, ed., *Walt Whitman: Representative Selections, with Introduction, Bibliography, and Notes*, New York, rev. ed., 1939 (Amer. Writers Ser.).

BIOGRAPHY AND CRITICISM

The most recent critical estimate of Whitman is Henry S. Canby, *Walt Whitman, An American: A Study in Biography*, Boston, 1943. Less comprehensive, though similarly important as critical studies, are: Bliss Perry, *Walt Whitman: His Life and Works*, Boston, 1906, and Emory Holloway, *Whitman: An Interpretation in Narrative*, New York, 1926. Three general studies which express the point of view of foreign critics are Léon Bazalgette, *Walt Whitman: L'Homme et Son Œuvre*, Paris, 1908—with an English translation by Ellen Fitzgerald, New York, 1920; Jean Catel, *Walt Whitman: La Naissance du Poète*, Paris, 1929; and Frederik Schyberg, *Walt Whitman*, Copenhagen, 1933. Other valuable general studies are Henry B. Binns, *A Life of Walt Whitman*, New York, 1905, and Newton Arvin, *Whitman*, New York, 1938. There is need for a full-length biographical study of Whitman which will make use of the large number of important specialized studies.

Among early appreciations which deserve notice are John Addington Symonds, *Walt Whitman: A Study*, London, 1893; John Burroughs, *Whitman: A Study*, Boston, 1896; and Basil De Selincourt, *Walt Whitman: A Critical Study*, London, 1914.

Among critical studies of Whitman, primarily as a man of letters, the extended analysis "Whitman," in F(rancis) O. Matthiessen, *American Renaissance . . .*, New York, 1941, pp. 517–656, is important. Norman Foerster's two essays "Whitman," in *Nature in American Literature . . .*, New York, 1923, pp. 176–220, and "Whitman," in *American Criticism . . .*, Boston, 1928, pp. 157–222, are excellent studies. Other revealing discussions are "Whitman and Taine," in Francis B. Gummere, *Democracy and Poetry,* Boston, 1911, pp. 96–148, and Léon Bazalgette, *Le Poème-Evangile de Walt Whitman*, Paris, 1921. A summary estimate appears in "Biographies of Whitman," in John Macy, *The Critical Game*, New York, 1922, pp. 203–211.

Significant to the extent the authors are spokesmen for their times are "The Poetry of Democracy: Walt Whitman," in Edward Dowden, *Studies in Literature, 1789–1877*, London, 1878, pp. 468–523; Robert Louis Stevenson, "The Gospel According to Walt Whitman," *New Quar.*, X (1879), 461–481; Richard M. Bucke, *Walt Whitman*, Philadelphia, 1883; "Walt Whitman," in Edmund C. Stedman, *Poets of America*, Boston, 1883, pp. 349–395; "Walt Whitman," in Havelock Ellis, *The New Spirit*, London, 1890; "Walt Whitman," in Thomas W. Higginson, *Contemporaries*, Boston, 1899, pp. 72–84; "Walter Whitman," in Andrew Macphail, *Essays in Puritanism*, London,

1905, pp. 168–206; Henry James, *Views and Reviews,* Boston, 1908, pp. 101–110; "Walt Whitman," in Arthur C. Benson, *Escape and Other Essays,* New York, 1915, pp. 63–90; "Walt Whitman," in Stuart P. Sherman, *Americans,* New York, 1922, pp. 153–185; "Walt Whitman," in Harriet Monroe, *Poets and Their Art,* New York, 1926, pp. 179–184; Amy Lowell, "Walt Whitman and the New Poetry," *Yale Rev.,* XVI (1927), 502–519; "Walt Whitman," in Henry S. Canby, *Classic Americans,* New York, 1931, pp. 308–351; and "Walt Whitman," in Gamaliel Bradford, *Biography and the Human Heart,* Boston, 1932, pp. 65–93.

One of the first studies of Whitman's technique was undertaken by the earliest of French vers-librists, Edouard Dujardin, "Les Premiers Poètes du Vers Libre," *Mercure de France,* CXLVI (1921), 577–621. Later studies are John Erskine, "Whitman's Prosody," *Studies in Philol.,* XX (1923), 336–344; Autrey N. Wiley, "Reiterative Devices in *Leaves of Grass,*" *Amer. Lit.,* I (1929), 161–170; Jean Catel, *Rythme et Langage dans la Première Edition des "Leaves of Grass" (1855),* Paris, 1930; "Walt Whitman," in Gay W. Allen, *American Prosody,* New York, 1935, pp. 217–243; Sculley Bradley, "The Fundamental Metrical Principle in Whitman's Poetry," *Amer. Lit.,* X (1938), 437–459; and Detlev W. Schumann, "Enumerative Style and Its Significance in Whitman, Rilke, Werfel," *Modern Language Quar.,* III (1942), 171–204.

Whitman's recognition abroad, especially in France, dates from the third quarter of the nineteenth century. One of the earliest important European critical estimates is Marie Thérèse Blanc (pseud., Th. Bentzon), "Un Poète Américain: Walt Whitman," *Revue des Deux Mondes,* XCIX (1872), 565–582. Jules Laforgue translated the opening passages of *Leaves of Grass* and other material in *La Vogue,* I (1886), 325–328, II (1886), 73–76. Three further translations into French were made by Francis Vielé-Griffin, in *Revue Indépendante,* IX (1888), 279–286. Five useful French estimates have appeared in *Revue Anglo-Américaine.* The first two, by Jean Catel, are entitled "Le Roman d'Amour de Walt Whitman," I (1924), 197–212; and "Walt Whitman Pendant la Guerre de Sécession: d'Après des Documents Inédits," III (1926), 410–419. Three, by Charles Cestre, are "Walt Whitman, l'Inadapté," VII (1930), 385–408; "Walt Whitman: Le Mystique, le Lyrique," VII (1930), 481–504; and "Walt Whitman, le Poète," VIII (1930), 19–41.

Other studies of Whitman in relation to France include P. M. Jones, "Whitman in France," *Modern Language Rev.,* X (1915), 1–27; *idem,* "The Influence of Walt Whitman on the Origin of the 'Vers Libre,'" *ibid.,* XI (1916), 186–194; F. Baldensperger, "Walt Whitman and France," *Columbia Univ. Quar.,* XXI (1919), 298–309; Gay W. Allen, "Walt Whitman and Jules Michelet," *Etudes Anglaises,* I (1937), 230–237; S. A. Rhodes, "The Influence of Walt Whitman on André Gide," *Romanic Rev.*, XXXI (1940), 156-171; and W. T. Starr, "Jean Giono and Walt Whitman," *French Rev.*, XIV (1940), 118-129. An unpublished dissertation is Oreste Francesco Pucciani, "The Literary Reputation of Walt Whitman in France," Harvard Univ., 1943.

The influence of Whitman in Germany is presented in R. H. Riethmueller, *Walt Whitman and the Germans*, Philadelphia, 1906; O. E. Lessing, "Walt Whitman and His German Critics," *Jour. English and Germanic Philol.*, IX (1910), 85-98; *idem*, "Walt Whitman and His German Critics Prior to 1910," *Amer. Collector*, III (1926), 7-15; E. Thorstenberg, "The Walt Whitman Cult in Germany," *Sewanee Rev.*, XIX (1911), 71-86; G. D. Clark, "Walt Whitman in Germany," *Texas Rev.*, VI (1921), 123-137; A. Jacobsen, "Walt Whitman in Germany Since 1914," *Germanic Rev.*, I (1926), 132-141; Harry Law-Robertson, "Walt Whitman in Deutschland," *Giessener Beiträge zur Deutschen Philologie*, XLII (1935); and Otto Springer, "Walt Whitman and Ferdinand Freiligrath," *Amer.-German Rev.*, XI (Dec., 1944), 22-26, 38—Whitman in German translation.

Studies dealing with Whitman's reputation in England include Harold Blodgett, *Walt Whitman in England*, Ithaca, N.Y., 1934—incorporating material from earlier studies by the same author; Clarence Gohdes and P. E. Baum, eds., *Letters of W. M. Rossetti Concerning Whitman, Blake, and Shelley*, Durham, N.C., 1934; and P. M. Jones, "Whitman and Verhaeren," *Aberystwyth Studies* (Aberystwyth, Wales), II (1914), 71-106. Three studies of Swinburne and Whitman are Georges Lafourcade, "Swinburne and Walt Whitman," *Modern Language Rev.*, XXII (1927), 84-86; William B. Cairns, "Swinburne's Opinion of Whitman," *Amer. Lit.*, III (1931), 125-135; and W. S. Monroe, "Swinburne's Recantation of Walt Whitman," *Revue Anglo-Amér.*, VIII (1931), 347-351.

A South American study is Luis Franco, *Walt Whitman*, Buenos Aires, 1945.

Further studies of Whitman's foreign reputation are Frederick Schyberg, *Walt Whitman*, Copenhagen, 1933; A. Parry, "Walt Whitman in Russia," *Amer. Mercury*, XXXIII (1934), 100-107; Joseph Remenyi, "Walt Whitman in Hungarian Literature," *Amer. Lit.*, XVI (1944), 181-185; Horst Frenz, "American Literature and World Literature," *Comparative Literature News-Letter*, II (Feb. 1944), 4-6—the vogue of Whitman in Europe; Fernando Alegría, "Walt Whitman en Hispanoamérica," *Revista Iberoamér.*, VIII (1944), 343-356; and Gay W. Allen, "Walt Whitman's Reception in Scandinavia," *Papers Bibl. Soc. Amer.*, XL (1946), 259-275.

Studies of influences upon Whitman are O. Zarek, "Walt Whitman and German Poetry," *Living Age*, CCCXVI (1923), 334-337; Louise Pound, "Walt Whitman and the Classics," *Southwest Rev.*, X (1925), 75-83; *idem*, "Walt

Whitman and Italian Music," *Amer. Mercury,* VI (1925), 58–62; John B. Moore, "The Master of Whitman," *Studies in Philol.,* XXIII (1926), 77–89—Emerson; Mody C. Boatright, "Whitman and Hegel," *Univ. Texas Studies in Eng.,* IX (1929), 134–150; Adolph B. Benson, "Walt Whitman's Interest in Swedish Writers," *Jour. English and Germanic Philol.,* XXXI (1932), 332–345; Joseph C. Mathews, "Walt Whitman's Reading of Dante," *Univ. Texas Studies in Eng.,* No. 3926 (1939), 177–179; Fred M. Smith, "Whitman's Poet-Prophet and Carlyle's Hero," *PMLA,* LV (1940), 1146–1164; R. P. Falk, "Walt Whitman and German Thought," *Jour. English and Germanic Philol.,* XL (1941), 315–330; and Olive W. Parsons, "Whitman the Non-Hegelian," *PMLA,* LVIII (1943), 1073–1093. See also Gay W. Allen, "Biblical Echoes in Whitman's Works," *Amer. Lit.,* VI (1934), 302–315—with an index; Esther Shephard, *Walt Whitman's Pose,* New York, 1938—especially useful for sources; David Goodale, "Some of Whitman's Borrowings," *Amer. Lit.,* X (1938), 202–213; Joseph J. Rubin, "Whitman and Carlyle," *Modern Language Notes,* LIII (1938), 370–371; Gregory Paine, "The Literary Relations of Whitman and Carlyle, with Especial Reference to Their Contrasting Views on Democracy," *Studies in Philol.,* XXXVI (1939), 550–563; W. B. Fulghum, Jr., "Whitman's Debt to Joseph Gostwick," *Amer. Lit.,* XII (1941), 491–496; Clarence Gohdes, "A Note on Whitman's Use of the Bible as a Model," *Modern Language Quar.,* II (1941), 105–108; and Fred M. Smith, "Whitman's Debt to Carlyle's *Sartor Resartus,*" *Modern Language Quar.,* III (1942), 51–65.

The friendships of Whitman are the subject of Clarence Gohdes, "Whitman and Emerson," *Sewanee Rev.,* XXXVII (1929), 79–93; Clara Barrus, *Whitman and Burroughs, Comrades,* New York, 1931; and E. G. Berry, "Whitman's Canadian Friend," *Dalhousie Rev.,* XXIV (1944), 77–82—Richard M. Bucke.

Some approach has been made to the study of Whitman as journalist in Portia Baker, "Walt Whitman and *The Atlantic Monthly,*" *Amer. Lit.,* VI (1934), 283–301; *idem,* "Walt Whitman's Relations with Some New York Magazines," *Amer. Lit.,* VII (1935), 274–301; and Joseph J. Rubin, "Whitman's *New York Aurora,*" *Amer. Lit.,* X (1939), 214–217.

Other studies are William Sloane Kennedy, *The Fight of a Book for the World,* West Yarmouth, Mass., 1926—some account of the reception given to *Leaves of Grass;* Edward Hungerford, "Walt Whitman and His Chart of Bumps," *Amer. Lit.,* II (1931), 350–384; Clifton J. Furness, "Walt Whitman's Estimate of Shakespeare," *Harvard Studies and Notes in Philol. and Lit.,* XIV (1932), 1–33; Sculley Bradley, "Walt Whitman on Timber Creek," *Amer. Lit.,* V (1933), 235–246; Charles I. Glicksberg, "Walt Whitman in 1862," *Amer. Lit.,* VI (1934), 264–282; Edward G. Bernard, "Some New

Whitman Manuscript Notes," *Amer. Lit.,* VIII (1936), 59–63; William L. Werner, "Whitman's 'The Mystic Trumpeter' as Autobiography," *Amer. Lit.,* VII (1936), 455–458; Joseph J. Rubin, "Whitman in 1840: A Discovery," *Amer. Lit.,* IX (1937), 239–242; George L. Sixbey, " 'Chanting the Square Deific': A Study in Whitman's Religion," *Amer. Lit.,* IX (1937), 171–195; Joseph J. Rubin, "Whitman and the Boy-Forger," *Amer. Lit.,* X (1938), 214–215; Maurice O. Johnson, "Walt Whitman as a Critic of Literature," *Studies in Language Lit., and Criticism,* Univ. of Nebr., No. 16 (1938), 73 pp.; "Whitman and the Civil War," in Ralph H. Gabriel, *The Course of American Democratic Thought . . .,* New York, 1940, pp. 123–131; Frederic I. Carpenter, "Walt Whitman's 'Eidolon,'" *College Eng.,* III (1942), 534–545; Katherine Molinoff, *Whitman's Teaching at Smithtown, 1837-1838,* New York, 1942; Julia Spiegelman, "Walt Whitman and Music," *So. Atl. Quar.,* XLI (1942), 167–176; Edna D. Romig, "More Roots for *Leaves of Grass,*" in *Elizabethan Studies . . . in Honor of George F. Reynolds,* Boulder, Colo., 1945, pp. 322–327; Courtland Y. White, "A Whitman Ornithology," *Cassinia,* XXXV (1945), 12–22; Alice L. Cooke, "Notes on Whitman's Musical Background," *New Eng. Quar.,* XIX (1946), 224–235; Carlos Baker, "The Road to Concord: Another Milestone in the Whitman-Emerson Friendship," *Princeton Univ. Lib. Chron.,* VII (1946), 100–117; Malcolm Cowley, "Walt Whitman: The Miracle," *New Repub.,* CXIV (1946), 385–388; *idem,* "Walt Whitman: The Secret," *ibid.,* 481–484; Charles I. Glicksberg, "Walt Whitman and 'January Searle,'" *Amer. Notes and Queries,* VI (1946), 51–53; Sister Mary Eleanor, "Hedge's *Prose Writers of Germany* as a Source of Whitman's Knowledge of German Philosophy," *Modern Language Notes,* LXI (1946), 381–388; and Richmond C. Beatty, "Whitman's Political Thought," *So. Atl. Quar.,* XLVI (1947), 72–83.

PRIMARY SOURCES

The most important published source material is to be found in Whitman's letters and notebooks, in the reminiscent material in *Specimen Days and Collect* (1882–1883), and in the occasional notes of the *Complete Poems and Prose* (1888–1889). The *Autobiographia* (1892) was published in the year of Whitman's death. Other primary published material is in J. T. Trowbridge, "Reminiscences of Walt Whitman," *Atl. Mo.,* LXXXIX (1902), 163–175; and in the three-volume study by Horace L. Traubel, *With Walt Whitman in Camden,* Vol. I, Boston, 1906; Vols. II and III, New York, 1908–1914. There are also the early reminiscences of John Burroughs, *Notes on Walt Whitman as Poet and Person,* New York, 1867 (rev. ed., 1871); Sadakichi Hartmann, *Conversations with Walt Whitman,* New York, 1895; William Sloane Kennedy, *Reminiscences of Walt Whitman,* Boston, 1896; Edward

Carpenter, *Days with Walt Whitman,* London, 1906; W. E. Walling, *Whitman and Traubel,* New York, 1916; Elizabeth L. Keller, *Walt Whitman in Mickle Street,* New York, 1921; Harrison S. Morris, *Walt Whitman: A Brief Biography with Reminiscences,* Cambridge, 1929; Katherine Molinoff, *Some Notes on Whitman's Family* . . ., New York, 1941; and Jennie A. Morgan, "Early Reminiscences of Walt Whitman," *Amer. Lit.,* XIII (1941), 9–17.

The chief depositories of Whitman manuscripts are the Library of Congress; the National Archives; the Walt Whitman Foundation Museum, Camden, N.J.; the Boston Public Library; the Sterling Memorial Library, Yale University (see Stanley T. Williams, "The Adrian Van Sinderen Collection of Walt Whitman," *Yale Univ. Lib. Gaz.,* XV [1941], 49–53); the Duke University Library (see Ellen F. Frey, *Catalogue of the Whitman Collection in the Duke University Library* . . ., Durham, N.C., 1945); and the library of the University of Pennsylvania. Scattered material is in the Henry E. Huntington Library; the Historical Society of Pennsylvania; the Longfellow House, Cambridge, Mass.; and the libraries of Harvard University, Johns Hopkins University, Columbia University, and Rutgers University.

BIBLIOGRAPHY

The bibliography prepared by Oscar L. Triggs in Traubel's ed. of *The Complete Writings* . . ., New York, 1902, is still useful for the notes. More recent are: Emory Holloway and H. S. Saunders, in *Camb. Hist. Amer. Lit.,* II (1918), 551–581—basic, including prose and poetry published in periodicals; Frank Shay, *The Bibliography of Walt Whitman,* New York, 1920—omitting works about Whitman; Carolyn Wells and Alfred F. Goldsmith, *A Concise Bibliography of the Works of Walt Whitman, with a Supplement of 50 Books About Whitman,* Boston, 1922 (a limited edition); *Index to Early American Periodical Literature, 1728–1870: Part 3, Walt Whitman,* New York, 1941 (New York Univ. Libraries); Rea McCain, "Walt Whitman in Italy: A Bibliography," *Bul. Bibl.,* XVII (1941), 66–67, 92–93—annotated. The listing in Floyd Stovall, ed., *Walt Whitman: Representative Selections* . . . , New York, 1934, is selective and annotated, as is that in Harry H. Clark, ed., *Major American Poets,* New York, 1936, pp. 914–919. See also Harry Hartwick, in Walter F. Taylor, *A History of American Letters,* New York, 1936, pp. 536–541.

The indispensable compilation of works dealing with recent Whitman scholarship is Gay W. Allen, *Twenty-five Years of Walt Whitman Bibliography, 1918–1942,* Boston, 1943. Allen's *Walt Whitman Handbook,* Chicago, 1946, is a descriptive bibliography and topical discussion.

# JOHN GREENLEAF WHITTIER
## 1807–1892

### SEPARATE WORKS

Legends of New-England, 1831; Moll Pitcher, 1832; Justice and Expediency, 1833; Mogg Megone, 1836; Poems Written . . . Between . . . 1830 and 1838 . . ., 1837; Narrative of James Williams, 1838; Poems, 1838; Moll Pitcher, and the Minstrel Girl, 1840; Lays of My Home, 1843; The Song of the Vermonters, 1843?; Ballads and Other Poems, 1844; The Stranger in Lowell, 1845; Voices of Freedom, 1846; The Supernaturalism of New England, 1847; Poems, 1849; Leaves from Margaret Smith's Journal, 1849; Old Portraits and Modern Sketches, 1850; Songs of Labor and Other Poems, 1850; The Chapel of the Hermits, 1853; Literary Recreations and Miscellanies, 1854; The Panorama, 1856; The Sycamores, 1857; Home Ballads, 1860; In War Time, 1864; National Lyrics, 1865; Snow-Bound, 1866; The Tent on the Beach, 1867; Among the Hills, 1869; Miriam, 1871; The Pennsylvania Pilgrim, 1872; Hazel-Blossoms, 1875; Mabel Martin, 1876; The Vision of Echard, 1878; The King's Missive, 1881; The Bay of Seven Islands, 1883; Saint Gregory's Guest, 1886; At Sundown, 1890; A Legend of the Lake, 1893; The Demon Lady, 1894.

### COLLECTED WORKS

The earliest collection attempting completeness is The Poetical Works of John Greenleaf Whittier, Boston, 1857, 2 vols. It was followed by Prose Works of John Greenleaf Whittier, Boston, 1866, 2 vols. With Whittier's cooperation, Horace E. Scudder edited The Writings of John Greenleaf Whittier, Boston, 1888–1889, 7 vols.; it includes many early poems, selected by Whittier, here first collected; the later (1894) issue is the standard library edition, and a full account of its editing is given by Eleanor M. Tilton, "Making Whittier Definitive," New Eng. Quar., XII (1939), 281–314. This edition was the basis for Scudder's one-volume Cambridge Edition: The Complete Poetical Works of John Greenleaf Whittier, Boston, 1894. A more recent collection is W. Garrett Horder, ed., The Poetical Works of John Greenleaf Whittier, with Notes . . ., London, 1919.

Letters of Whittier were first published by Samuel T. Pickard, Life and Letters of John Greenleaf Whittier, Boston, 1894, 2 vols. (rev. ed., 1907). Pickard also edited Whittier as a Politician: Illustrated by His Letters to Professor Elizur Wright, Jr., Boston, 1900. Further collections are John Albree, ed., Whittier Correspondence from the Oak Knoll Collections, 1830–1892, Salem, Mass., 1911; Marie V. Denervaud, ed., Whittier's Unknown Romance:

*Letters to Elizabeth Lloyd,* Boston, 1922; Thomas F. Currier, ed., *Elizabeth Lloyd and the Whittiers: A Budget of Letters,* Cambridge, 1939, which expands the collection made in *Whittier's Unknown Romance.* Further gleanings appear in Earl L. Griggs, "John Greenleaf Whittier and Thomas Clarkson," *Amer. Lit.,* VII (1936), 458–460; Edward D. Snyder, "Whittier's Letters to Ann Elizabeth Wendell," *Bul. Friends' Hist. Assn.,* XXIX (1940), 69–92; Jay B. Hubbell, *The Last Years of Henry Timrod* . . . , Durham, N.C., 1941; and Raymond M. Bennett, "An Unpublished Whittier Letter," *Jour. Rutgers Univ. Lib.,* IX (1945), 30–32. Four poems not in Whittier's collected works have been edited by Henry J. Cadbury, "Whittier's Early Quaker Poems," *New Eng. Quar.,* XVIII (1945), 251–256.

For the many separate broadsides, leaflets, and contributions to books, largely uncollected, see the Currier *Bibliography* and *Merle Johnson's American First Editions* (ed. Jacob Blanck), 4th ed., New York, 1942.

### EDITED TEXTS AND REPRINTS

The most easily available edited text is Harry H. Clark, *John Greenleaf Whittier: Representative Selections, with Introduction, Bibliography, and Notes,* New York, 1935 (Amer. Writers Ser.).

Selections of Whittier's prose and poetry, often edited, have been published frequently in school-text editions and in anthologies and collections. The most recent publication is *The Poems of John Greenleaf Whittier,* ed. with a commentary by Louis Untermeyer, New York, 1945.

### BIOGRAPHY AND CRITICISM

Still the best biography is Samuel T. Pickard, *Life and Letters of John Greenleaf Whittier,* Boston, 1894, 2 vols. (rev. ed., 1907). The most authoritative of recent studies is Albert Mordell, *Quaker Militant: John Greenleaf Whittier,* Boston, 1933—with a bibl., pp. 333–343. Whitman Bennett's *Whittier, Bard of Freedom,* Chapel Hill, N.C., 1941, stresses the early years and includes valuable bibliographical data. Among early lives, that of Francis H. Underwood, *John Greenleaf Whittier: A Biography,* Boston, 1884, was in part authorized. William Sloane Kennedy's narrative biography, *John Greenleaf Whittier: His Life, Genius, and Writings,* Boston, 1882, was revised and enlarged in 1892. A first printing of many early poems is included in Samuel T. Pickard, *Whittier-Land* . . . , Boston, 1904.

Estimates of Whittier, important to the extent that the authors are spokesmen of their times, are "John Greenleaf Whittier," in Edmund C. Stedman, *Poets of America,* Boston, 1885, pp. 95–132; "John Greenleaf Whittier," in Barrett Wendell, *Stelligeri, and Other Essays Concerning America,* New York, 1893, pp. 147–202; "John Greenleaf Whittier," in Thomas W. Higginson, *Contemporaries,* Boston, 1899, pp. 60–71; "John Greenleaf Whittier," in George E. Woodberry, *Makers of Literature,* New York, 1901, pp. 302–323; George Rice Carpenter, *John Greenleaf Whittier* (Amer. Men of Letters), Boston, 1903; Bliss Perry, *John Greenleaf Whittier: A Sketch of His Life ...,* Boston, 1907; and William M. Payne, "Whittier," in *Camb. Hist. Amer. Lit.,* II (1918), 42–54.

Studies of Whittier's religious and philosophical thinking are Chauncey J. Hawkins, *The Mind of Whittier: A Study of Whittier's Fundamental Religious Ideas,* New York, 1904; Iola K. Eastburn, *Whittier's Relation to German Life and Thought ...,* Philadelphia, 1915; "Whittier," in Norman Foerster, *Nature in American Literature ...,* New York, 1923, pp. 20–36; James S. Stevens, *Whittier's Use of the Bible,* Orono, Me., 1930; Arthur E. Christy, "Orientalism in New England: Whittier," *Amer. Lit.,* I (1930), 372–392; *idem,* "The Orientalism of Whittier," *ibid.,* V (1933), 247–257; M. Jane Griswold, "American Quaker History in the Works of Whittier, Hawthorne, and Longfellow," *Americana,* XXXIV (1940), 220–263; Rufus M. Jones, "Whittier's Fundamental Religious Faith," in Howard H. Brinton, ed., *Byways in Quaker History ...,* Wallingford, Pa., 1944, pp. 19–40; Henry J. Cadbury, "Whittier as Historian of Quakerism," *ibid.,* pp. 41–66; and C. Marshall Taylor, "Whittier the Quaker Politician," *ibid.,* pp. 67–76.

Whittier's technique as poet is presented in Frances M. Pray, *A Study of Whittier's Apprenticeship as a Poet ... Between 1825 and 1835 ...,* Bristol, N.H., 1930—a collection of some 100 youthful poems, from local newspapers and publications; Winfield T. Scott, "Poetry in American: A New Consideration of Whittier's Verse," *New Eng. Quar.,* VII (1934), 258–275; "John Greenleaf Whittier," in Gay W. Allen, *American Prosody,* New York, 1935, pp. 127–153; Desmond Powell, "Whittier," *Amer. Lit.,* IX (1937), 335–342; and Kathryn A. McEuen, "Whittier's Rhymes," *Amer. Speech,* XX (1945), 51–57.

Other useful studies are "Whittier," in George M. Gould, *Biographic Clinics ...,* Philadelphia, 1904, II, 253–267—with reference to eyestrain and illness; Nelson F. Adkins, "Two Uncollected Prose Sketches of Whittier," *New Eng. Quar.,* VI (1933), 364–371; Thomas F. Currier, "Whittier and the *New England Weekly Review,*" *ibid.,* 589–597; Albert Mordell, "Whittier and Lucy Hooper," *ibid.,* VII (1934), 316–324; Nathaniel L. Sayles, "A Note on Whittier's *Snow-Bound,*" *Amer. Lit.,* VI (1934), 336–337; Thomas F. Currier, "Whittier and the Amesbury-Salisbury Strike," *New Eng. Quar.,* VIII (1935), 105–112; *idem,* "Whittier's 'The Demon Lady,'" *ibid.,* X (1937), 776–780—with the text; *idem,* "Whittier's Philadelphia Friends in 1838," *Bul. Friends' Hist. Assn.,* XXVII (1938), 58–72; Edward D. Snyder, "Whittier Returns to Philadelphia After a Hundred Years," *Pennsylvania Mag. Hist. and Biog.,* LXII (1938), 140–161—on the Nicholson collection at Haverford

College, with a table of contents of Vol. I of the Nicholson-Whittier Note-books; Charles A. Hawley, "John Greenleaf Whittier and His Middle Western Correspondents," *Bul. Friends' Hist. Assn.,* XXVIII (1939), No. 1, 19–29; Bertha-Monica Stearns, "John Greenleaf Whittier, Editor," *New Eng. Quar.,* XIII (1940), 280–304; Carl J. Weber, "Whittier and Sarah Orne Jewett," *ibid,* XVIII (1945), 401–407; Cora Dolbee, "Kansas and 'The Prairied West' of John G. Whittier," *Essex Institute Hist. Coll.,* LXXXI (1945), 307–347, LXXXII (1946), 49–68, 153–173; C. Marshall Taylor, "Whittier vs. Garrison," *ibid.,* LXXXII (1946), 249–278; and Kenneth Scott, "The Source of Whittier's 'The Dead Ship of Harpswell,'" *Amer. Neptune,* VI (1946), 223–227.

PRIMARY SOURCES

Published memoirs and reminiscences of some significance are Mary B. Claflin, *Personal Recollections of John G. Whittier,* New York, 1893; Annie A. Fields, *Whittier: Notes of His Life and of His Friendships,* New York, 1893; Charlotte F. Grimké, "Personal Recollections of Whittier," *New Eng. Mag.,* n.s. VIII (1893), 468–476; Annie A. Fields, *Authors and Friends,* Boston, 1897; Robert S. Rantoul, "Some Personal Reminiscences of the Poet Whittier," *Essex Institute Hist. Coll.,* XXXVII (1901), 129–144; Thomas W. Higginson, *John Greenleaf Whittier* (Eng. Men of Letters), New York, 1902; Abby J. Woodman, "Reminiscences of John Greenleaf Whittier's Life at Oak Knoll, Danvers, Mass.," *Essex Inst. Hist. Coll.,* XLIV (1908), 97–122; Elizabeth F. Hume, "Summers with a Poet: Recollections of John Greenleaf Whittier," *Essex Inst. Hist. Coll.,* LXXV (1939), 313–325; and *idem,* "Neighbor to a Poet: Recollections of John Greenleaf Whittier," *ibid.,* LXXVI (1940), 345–354.

The principal depositories of Whittier manuscripts are the Essex Institute, Salem, Mass. (the Oak Knoll Collection, extensive and only recently used); the Haverhill, Mass., Public Library; the Morgan Library; and Haverford College (the Nicholson-Whittier Collection). Other manuscript material is in Harvard College Library; the Boston Public Library; the Longfellow House, Cambridge, Mass.; and the T. B. Aldrich Birthplace, Portsmouth, N.H.

BIBLIOGRAPHY

The definitive Whittier bibliography, and one of the finest single-author American bibliographies, is Thomas F. Currier, *A Bibliography of John Greenleaf Whittier,* Cambridge, 1937. An annotated selective listing is Harry H. Clark, ed., *Major American Poets,* New York, 1936, pp. 798–802. See also Harry Hartwick, in Walter F. Taylor, *A History of American Letters,* New York, 1936, pp. 519–521.

# MICHAEL WIGGLESWORTH
## *1631–1705*

### SEPARATE WORKS

*The Day of Doom*, 1662?, 1666; *Meat Out of the Eater*, 1670; *Riddles Un-riddled; or, Christian Paradoxes* (first published in the 1689 edition of *Meat Out of the Eater*).

### COLLECTED WORKS

No collection as such of Wigglesworth's writing has been made. Letters from "Michael Wigglesworth to Increase Mather" are published in *The Mather Papers, Coll. Mass. Hist. Soc.*, 4th ser., VIII (1868), 645–647. A poem, "God's Controversy with New-England," written in 1662, was first published in *Proc. Mass. Hist. Soc.*, 1st ser., XII (1873), 83–93. "The prayse of Eloquence," a college declamation transcribed from manuscript, was first reproduced in Samuel E. Morison, *Harvard College in the Seventeenth Century*, Cambridge, 1936, I, 180–183.

### EDITED TEXTS AND REPRINTS

No copy of the first edition of *The Day of Doom*, believed to have been published in Cambridge in 1662, has been positively identified. The work went through many editions into the first quarter of the eighteenth century. It was edited by J. W. Dean and W. H. Burr, New York, 1867, and published with a critical introduction by Kenneth B. Murdock, New York, 1929. Nearly all anthologies of American literature include selections of Wigglesworth's poetry; he is amply represented in Perry Miller and Thomas H. Johnson, *The Puritans*, New York, 1938, pp. 585–629.

### BIOGRAPHY AND CRITICISM

The most inclusive biography, especially useful for the supplementary material, is John W. Dean, *Sketch of the Life of Rev. Michael Wigglesworth, A.M., with a Fragment of His Autobiography, Some of His Letters, and a Catalogue of His Library*, Albany, 1863 (2nd ed., 1871, with a slightly varying title). The best brief sketch is that of Kenneth B. Murdock in *Dict. Amer. Biog.* (1936). Still useful is that of John L. Sibley in *Biographical Sketches of Graduates of Harvard University*, Cambridge, I (1873), 259–286. Cotton Mather's funeral sermon on Wigglesworth is published as *A Faithful Man Described and Rewarded* . . ., Boston, 1705. In addition to the introduction to the Murdock edition of *The Day of Doom*, mentioned above, a good critical study of Wigglesworth as a man of letters is F. O. Matthiessen, "Michael

Wigglesworth: A Puritan Artist," *New Eng. Quar.*, I (1928), 491–504. The earlier account in Moses C. Tyler, *A History of American Literature During the Colonial Period,* rev. ed., New York, 1897, II, 23–37, is still useful.

PRIMARY SOURCES

There are two important collections of Wigglesworth manuscripts, containing much unpublished material. That in the library of the New England Historic Genealogical Society includes two volumes of manuscript notes, together with notebooks Wigglesworth kept in college (from which "The prayse of Eloquence" was printed). In the library of the Massachusetts Historical Society are autobiographical notes and records of his spiritual growth.

BIBLIOGRAPHY

In addition to the brief critical bibliography accompanying the sketch in *Dict. Amer. Biog.,* there is a useful listing in Sibley. Further studies are Samuel A. Green's essay on *The Day of Doom,* in *Publ. Mass. Hist. Soc.,* 2nd ser., IX (1895), 269–275; and two contributions by Matt B. Jones, "Notes for a Bibliography of Michael Wigglesworth's *Day of Doom* and *Meat Out of the Eater*," *Proc. Amer. Antiq. Soc.,* n.s. XXXIX (1930), 77–84; and "Michael Wigglesworth's *Meat Out of the Eater*," *Yale Univ. Lib. Gaz.,* V (1931), 45–47.

# ROGER WILLIAMS
## *ca. 1603–1683*

SEPARATE WORKS

*A Key into the Language of America,* 1643; *Mr. Cottons Letter Lately Printed, Examined and Answered,* 1644; *The Bloudy Tenent of Persecution, for Cause of Conscience, Discussed,* 1644; *Queries of Highest Consideration,* 1644; "Christenings Make Not Christians," written *ca.* 1645; *The Bloody Tenent Yet More Bloody,* 1652; *The Fourth Paper Presented by Major Butler,* 1652; *The Hireling Ministry None of Christs,* 1652; *Experiments of Spiritual Life and Health,* 1652; *George Fox Digged Out of His Burrowes,* 1676; *An Answer to a Letter Sent from Mr. Coddington . . . ,* 1678.

COLLECTED WORKS

Williams is one of the very few colonial authors whose works have been collected. *The Writings of Roger Williams,* Providence, 1866–1874, 6 vols., published by the Narragansett Club, reprints most of the letters and separate works. Vol. VI, ed. by John R. Bartlett, prints the *Letters of Roger Williams,*

*1632–1682.* Scattered collections are "Letter to Major Mason, 1670," *Coll. Mass. Hist. Soc.,* I (1792), 275–283; "Letters from 1632 to 1675" (to John Winthrop), *ibid.,* 4th ser. VI (1863), 184–311; *Letters and Papers of Roger Williams, 1629–1682,* Boston, 1924; and "Important Roger Williams Letter," *Coll. Rhode Island Hist. Soc.,* XXVII (1934), 85–92.

EDITED TEXTS AND REPRINTS

*A Key into the Language of America* (London, 1643) is reprinted in part in *Coll. Mass. Hist. Soc.,* III (1794), 203–238, and V (1798), 80–106, and in full in *Coll. R.I. Hist. Soc.,* I (1827), 17–163. See especially the reprint edited by Howard M. Chapin, Providence, R.I., 1936. Henry M. Dexter edited *Roger Williams' "Christenings Make Not Christians," R.I. Hist. Tracts,* 1st ser., No. 14 (1881); and Clarence S. Brigham edited *The Fourth Paper . . . ,* (London, 1652), Providence, 1903.

BIOGRAPHY AND CRITICISM

Though Williams has frequently been the subject of narrative and critical biographies, his character and career have not yet been fully depicted. The best life at present is Samuel H. Brockunier, *The Irrepressible Democrat: Roger Williams,* New York, 1940. Other twentieth century studies are Edmund J. Carpenter, *Roger Williams: A Study of the Life, Times and Character of a Political Pioneer,* New York, 1909; May E. Hall, *Roger Williams,* Boston, 1917; Emily Easton, *Roger Williams: Prophet and Pioneer,* New York, 1930—with stress on the early, little known years; James E. Ernst, *Roger Williams: New England Firebrand,* New York, 1932—detailed, but to be checked for accuracy; and Charles S. Longacre, *Roger Williams: His Life, Work, and Ideals,* Washington, 1940—also to be checked for accuracy. Among the early biographies, that of James D. Knowles, *Memoir of Roger Williams . . . ,* Boston, 1834, is still useful. Other studies are William Gammell, *Life of Roger Williams . . . ,* Boston, 1846; Romeo Elton, *Life of Roger Williams,* London, 1852; and Oscar S. Straus, *Roger Williams: The Pioneer of Religious Liberty,* New York, 1894. Among brief sketches that in *Dict. Amer. Biog.* is contributed by Samuel H. Brockunier (1936); two other estimates are those of Moses C. Tyler, *A History of American Literature During the Colonial Period,* rev. ed., New York, 1897, I, 241–263; and Vernon L. Parrington, *Main Currents in American Thought,* New York, I (1927), 62–75. See also "Roger Williams and the Planting of the Commonwealth in America," in John Dos Passos, *The Ground We Stand On,* New York, 1941, pp. 21–183.

Studies of Williams's political and religious thought are "Roger Williams and the Founding of Rhode Island," in Charles M. Andrews, *The Colonial Period of American History,* New Haven, II (1936), 1–36—one of the most informed and balanced in spite of its brevity; and James E. Ernst, *The*

*Political Thought of Roger Williams,* Seattle, 1929. Other studies of special aspects of his career are Charles Deane, "Roger Williams and the Massachusetts Charter," *Proc. Mass. Hist. Soc.,* XII (1873), 341–358; Henry M. Dexter, *As to Roger Williams, and His 'Banishment' from the Massachusetts Plantation,* Boston, 1876—valuable on Williams's liberalism; Michael Freund, *Die Idee der Toleranz im England der Grossen Revolution,* Halle, 1927—dealing largely with Milton and Williams; Henry S. Burrage, "Why Was Roger Williams Banished?" *Amer. Jour. Theol.,* V (1901), 1–17; Howard M. Chapin, *Roger Williams and the King's Colors: The Documentary Evidence,* Providence, 1928; James E. Ernst, "New Light on Roger Williams' Life in England," *Coll. R.I. Hist. Soc.,* XXII (1929), 97–103; *idem,* "Roger Williams and the English Revolution," *ibid.,* XXIV (1931), 1–58, 118–128; Henry B. Parkes, "John Cotton and Roger Williams Debate Toleration, 1644–1652," *New Eng. Quar.,* IV (1931), 735–756; Michael Freund, "Roger Williams, Apostle of Complete Religious Liberty," *Coll. R.I. Hist. Soc.,* XXVI (1933), 101–133; George A. Stead, "Roger Williams and the Massachusetts-Bay," *New Eng. Quar.,* VII (1934), 235–257; Frederick B. Wiener, "Roger Williams' Contribution to Modern Thought," *Coll. R.I. Hist. Soc.,* XXVIII (1935), 1–20; Reuben E. E. Harkness, "Roger Williams: Prophet of Tomorrow," *Jour. Religion,* XV (1935), 400–425; Elizabeth Hirsch, "John Cotton and Roger Williams: Their Controversy Concerning Religious Liberty," *Church Hist.,* X (1941), 38–51; and B. F. Swan, "Roger Williams and the Insane," *Rhode Island Hist.,* V (1946), 65–70.

PRIMARY SOURCES

Some manuscript material may be found in the library of the Massachusetts Historical Society.

BIBLIOGRAPHY

A working bibliography to 1917 will be found in *Camb. Hist. Amer. Lit.,* I (1917), 393–395. Howard M. Chapin has published a *List of Roger Williams' Writings,* Providence, 1918. Further material may be found in *The Writings . . . ,* Providence, 1866–1874, 6 vols.

# WILLIAM CARLOS WILLIAMS
### b. 1883

SEPARATE WORKS

*Poems,* 1909; *The Tempers,* 1913; *A Book of Poems, Al Que Quiere!* 1917; *Kora in Hell: Improvisations,* 1920; *Sour Grapes: A Book of Poems,* 1921; *Spring and All,* 1923; *Go Go,* 1923; *The Great American Novel,* 1923; *In the*

*American Grain*, 1925; *A Voyage to Pagany*, 1928; *The Knife of the Times and Other Stories*, 1932; *A Novelette, and Other Prose, 1921–1931*, 1932; *The Cod Head*, 1932; *An Early Martyr, and Other Poems*, 1935; *Adam & Eve & The City*, 1936; *White Mule*, 1937; *Life Along the Passaic River*, 1938; *In the Money: White Mule, Part II*, 1940; *The Broken Span*, 1941; *The Wedge*, 1944; *Paterson*, 1946.

## COLLECTED WORKS

*Collected Poems, 1921–1931*, New York, 1934, was issued with preface by Wallace Stevens. *The Complete Collected Poems of William Carlos Williams: 1906–1938*, Norfolk, Conn., 1938, is an inclusive edition.

## BIOGRAPHY AND CRITICISM

Early critical estimates are Louis Untermeyer, *American Poetry Since 1900*, New York, 1923, pp. 343–345; "William Carlos Williams," in Paul Rosenfeld, *Port of New York*, New York, 1924, pp. 103–115; Kenneth Burke, "William Carlos Williams, The Methods of," *Dial*, LXXXII (1927), 94–98; and Carl Rakosi, "William Carlos Williams," *Symposium*, IV (1933), 439–447.

Among more recent studies are Babette Deutsch, *This Modern Poetry*, New York, 1935, pp. 72–75; "Dr. Williams' Position," in Ezra Pound, *Polite Essays*, London, 1937, pp. 67–81; Yvor Winters, *Primitivism and Decadence*, New York, 1937 (see index); Paul Rosenfeld, "Williams the Stylist," *Sat. Rev. Lit.*, XIX (Feb. 11, 1939), 16; and Ruth Lechlitner, "The Poetry of William Carlos Williams," *Poetry*, LIV (1939), 326–335.

An important collection of letters and manuscripts is in the Lockwood Memorial Library at the University of Buffalo.

## BIBLIOGRAPHY

A bibliographical listing is in Fred B. Millett, *Contemporary American Authors*, New York, 1940, pp. 646–647, including reviews in *Poetry* of Williams's various separately published titles. The most recent checklist is compiled by Frances Cheney, in Allen Tate, *Sixty American Poets, 1896–1944*, Washington, 1945, pp. 177–179.

# NATHANIEL PARKER WILLIS
## 1806–1867

## SEPARATE WORKS

*Sketches*, 1827; *Fugitive Poetry*, 1829; *Poem Delivered Before the Society of United Brothers*, 1831; *Melanie, and Other Poems*, 1835; *Pencillings by the Way*, 1835; *Inklings of Adventure*, 1836; *Bianca Visconti; or, The Heart*

*Overtasked: A Tragedy* (produced, 1837), 1839; *Tortesa; or, The Usurer Matched*, 1839; *A l'Abri; or, The Tent Pitch'd*, 1839; *Loiterings of Travel*, 1840; *The Sacred Poems*, 1843; *Poems of Passion*, 1843; *The Lady Jane, and Other Poems*, 1843; *Lecture on Fashion*, 1844; *Poems, Sacred, Passionate, and Humorous*, 1845; *Dashes at Life with a Free Pencil*, 1845; *Poems of Early and After Years*, 1848; *Rural Letters and Other Records of Thought at Leisure*, 1849; *Hurry-graphs*, 1851; *Health Trip to the Tropics*, 1853; *Famous Persons and Famous Places*, 1854; *Out-Doors at Idlewild*, 1855; *The Rag-Bag: A Collection of Ephemera*, 1855; *Paul Fane: A Novel*, 1857; *The Convalescent*, 1859.

COLLECTED WORKS AND REPRINTS

No really complete edition of Willis's writings has ever been published, incorporating material from the files of the *Corsair*, the New York *Mirror*, and the *Home Journal*, which he served as a regular member of their editorial staffs. The first edition that claimed to assemble all material was *The Complete Works of N. P. Willis*, New York, 1846. The best edition is that published in uniform style, New York, 1849–1859, 13 vols.

Most of Willis's published writing was reprinted frequently during the nineteenth century. *Letters from Under a Bridge, and Poems* (1840) is a reprint of *A l'Abri* (1839). *Summer Cruise in the Mediterranean* (1853) is a reprint in part of *Pencillings by the Way* (1835). Reprints of earlier short stories were gathered in *People I Have Met* (1850), *Life Here and There* (1850), and *Fun-Jottings* (1853). One of the latest and best editions of his poems is *The Poetical Works of N. P. Willis*, London, 1888. A selection of the *Prose Writings of Nathaniel Parker Willis*, New York, 1885, was ed. by Henry A. Beers. *Pencillings by the Way* was reprinted, London, 1942.

BIOGRAPHY AND CRITICISM

Henry A. Beers published a life, *Nathaniel Parker Willis*, Boston, 1885 (Amer. Men of Letters). An unpublished dissertation is Kenneth L. Daughrity, "The Life and Works of Nathaniel Parker Willis," Univ. of Va., 1934. Daughrity contributed the sketch of Willis to the *Dict. Amer. Biog.* (1936).

Other general estimates are Fred L. Pattee, *The Development of the American Short Story*, New York, 1923, pp. 78–88; Granville Hicks, "A Literary Swell," *Amer. Mercury*, XVI (1929), 361–369; Allan G. Halline, *American Plays*, New York, 1935, pp. 201–205, 755–756; and "N. P. Willis," in Van Wyck Brooks, *The World of Washington Irving*, New York, 1944, pp. 426–442.

Special studies of Willis are Kenneth L. Daughrity, "Poe's 'Quiz on Willis,'" *Amer. Lit.*, V (1933), 55–62; William P. Fenn, "The Source of One of Willis's Sketches," *Amer. Lit.*, VI (1935), 421–426; and Harold H. Scudder, "Thackeray and N. P. Willis," *PMLA*, LVII (1942), 589–592. Discussion of Willis abroad is also in Robert E. Spiller, *The American in England*, New York, 1926, *passim*.

Among early estimates are Edward F. Hayward, "Nathaniel Parker Willis," *Atl. Mo.*, LIV (1884), 212–222; James G. Wilson, *Bryant and His Friends*, New York, 1886, pp. 312–333; and G. Paston, "The Penciller by the Way: Nathaniel Parker Willis," *Cornhill Mag.*, n.s. XI (1901), 326–345.

PRIMARY SOURCES

Material on Willis appears in the biographies and memoirs of many of the chief literary figures of the nineteenth century, both in England and America.

The bulk of all his papers is in the Morristown, N.J., Public Library. Further manuscript material is in the Yale University Library.

BIBLIOGRAPHY

A list of first editions of Willis's writings is in Beers's life (1885). The bibliography of his plays is in Allan G. Halline, *American Plays* (1935), 755–756. Further references follow the sketch of Willis in *Dict. Amer. Biog.* (1936).

# (THOMAS) WOODROW WILSON
## *1856–1924*

SEPARATE WORKS

*Congressional Government*, 1885; *The State: Elements of Historical and Practical Politics*, 1889; *Division and Reunion, 1829–1889*, 1893; *An Old Master and Other Political Essays*, 1893; *Mere Literature and Other Essays*, 1896; *George Washington*, 1896; *A History of the American People*, 1902; *Constitutional Government in the United States*, 1908.

COLLECTED WORKS AND REPRINTS

The most important edition of Wilson's published writings is *The Public Papers of Woodrow Wilson*, Garden City, N.Y., 1925–1927, 6 vols., ed. by Ray Stannard Baker and William E. Dodd. They include *College and State* (2 vols.), *The New Democracy* (2 vols.), and *War and Peace* (2 vols.). The campaign speeches of 1912 are included in *The New Freedom* (1913). A convenient gathering of Wilson's writings is *Selected Literary and Political Papers and Addresses of Woodrow Wilson*, New York, 1925–1927, 3 vols.

The most extensive collection of published letters, taken from original sources, is that ed. by Ray Stannard Baker, *Woodrow Wilson: Life and Letters,* Garden City, N.Y., 1927–1939, 8 vols.

BIOGRAPHY AND CRITICISM

A beginning toward an extended critical biography of Wilson is Arthur S. Link, *Wilson: The Road to the White House,* Princeton, 1947. The fullest account of Wilson's life is that in Baker's *Woodrow Wilson: Life and Letters* (1927–1939). The best brief sketch is that of Charles Seymour in *Dict. Amer. Biog.* (1936). Following the sketch is an important bibliography of secondary items especially useful for memoirs and biographies dealing with Wilson as university teacher and administrator, and as politician, statesman, and peacemaker. It includes also contemporary foreign and domestic estimates. Among early studies that of Ray Stannard Baker, *Woodrow Wilson and World Settlement . . . ,* Garden City, N.Y., 1922, 3 vols., is a survey of Wilson at the Peace Conference, primarily useful for the documents it presents. Other studies and brief biographies are William W. Hollingsworth, *Woodrow Wilson's Political Ideals as Interpreted from His Works,* Princeton, 1918; George Creel, *The War, the World, and Wilson,* New York, 1920; Josephus Daniels, *The Life of Woodrow Wilson, 1856–1924,* Philadelphia, 1924; David Lawrence, *The True Story of Woodrow Wilson,* New York, 1924; William Allen White, *Woodrow Wilson: The Man, His Times, and His Task,* Boston, 1924; John R. Bolling, *Chronology of Woodrow Wilson . . . ,* New York, 1927; and William E. Dodd, *Woodrow Wilson and His Work,* rev. ed., New York, 1932.

Among recent studies is Herbert C. F. Bell, *Woodrow Wilson and the People,* Garden City, N.Y., 1945, a biography written from the point of view of Wilson's contact with the public. A useful study of the politics behind the movement in the United States in favor of the League, and the politics of its defeat, is Ruhl J. Bartlett, *The League to Enforce Peace,* Chapel Hill, N.C., 1944. Other studies of the political scene are James Kerney, *The Political Education of Woodrow Wilson,* New York, 1926, and Josephus Daniels, *The Wilson Era,* Chapel Hill, N.C., 1944. Two studies, somewhat unfavorable to Wilson, are Thomas A. Bailey, *Woodrow Wilson and the Lost Peace,* New York, 1944, and *Woodrow Wilson and the Great Betrayal,* New York, 1945.

In view of the acknowledged rank of Wilson as a man of letters among statesmen, very few estimates have been made of Wilson as a historical student. The most useful are "Woodrow Wilson as a Man of Letters," in Bliss Perry, *The Praise of Folly and Other Papers,* Boston, 1923, pp. 151–170; Marjorie L. Daniel, "Woodrow Wilson: Historian," *Mississippi Valley Hist. Rev.,* XXI (1934), 361–374; and Stockton Axson, *Woodrow Wilson as Man of Letters . . . ,* Houston, Texas, 1935. See also Michael Kraus, *The History of American History,* New York, 1937, pp. 454–461; and Dayton D. McKean,

"Woodrow Wilson," in William N. Brigance, ed., *A History and Criticism of American Public Address,* New York, 1943, II, 968–992.

PRIMARY SOURCES

There are three important collections of Woodrow Wilson papers. The collection in the Manuscript Division of the Library of Congress was for the most part gathered and used by Ray Stannard Baker in writing his biography. For an account of this collection see *Library of Congress Quar. Jour. of Current Acquisitions,* II (Feb., 1945). The most complete accumulation of material by and about Wilson is the Woodrow Wilson Collection in the library of Princeton University. It is open to scholars, subject only to restrictions imposed by the donors. Permission to use the papers in the Princeton University Archives may be obtained from the Secretary of the University.

The library of the Woodrow Wilson Foundation, in New York City, has specialized in books and documents that relate in particular to the League of Nations and in general to international affairs.

The unpublished Wilson-House correspondence in the Yale University Library is open to restricted use. There are also collections of state papers in the National Archives.

Much material of a primary nature appears in the published memoirs and biographies of public figures associated with Wilson during his years in the White House. Among them may be named J. P. Tumulty (1921), D. F. Houston (1926), Edward M. House (1926–1928), Bainbridge Colby (1930), Edith Reid (1934), I. H. Hoover (1934), and Ray Stannard Baker (1945). See also Oswald Garrison Villard, *Fighting Years,* New York, 1939, and Josephus Daniels, *The Wilson Era: Years of War and After,* Chapel Hill, N.C., 1946.

Some account of Wilson as a man of letters and a teacher is Charles G. Osgood, "Woodrow Wilson," in Willard Thorp, ed., *The Lives of Eighteen from Princeton,* Princeton, 1946, pp. 282–301; William S. Myers, ed., *Woodrow Wilson: Some Princeton Memories,* Princeton, 1946—a symposium, concerning Wilson chiefly during the years 1905–1910; Bliss Perry, *And Gladly Teach,* Boston, 1935; and "Woodrow Wilson, Princeton Schoolmaster," in Alfred P. Dennis, *Gods and Little Fishes,* Indianapolis, 1931, pp. 84–117. A volume by Wilson's sister-in-law is Margaret R. Elliott, *My Aunt Louisa and Woodrow Wilson,* Chapel Hill, N.C., 1934.

BIBLIOGRAPHY

Harry Clemens, *An Essay Towards a Bibliography of the Published Writings and Addresses of Woodrow Wilson, 1875–1910* (1913), was continued, to cover the later writings, by G. D. Brown (1917) and H. S. Leach (1922). The fullest listing to date of secondary material is that by Charles Seymour in *Dict. Amer. Biog.* (1936).

# JOHN WINTHROP
## 1588–1649

SEPARATE WORK.

"A Modell of Christian Charity," written *ca.* 1630; *A Short Story of the . . . Antinomians,* 1644; *A Declaration of Former Passages,* 1645; *Conclusions,* 1769; *The History of New England,* 1790.

EDITED TEXTS AND REPRINTS

"A Modell of Christian Charity," written on board the *Arbella* during 1630, was first published in full in *Coll. Mass. Hist. Soc.,* 3rd ser., VII (1838), 31–48; it is most accurately transcribed in the *Winthrop Papers,* Boston, II (1931), 282–295. *A Short Story of the . . . Antinomians,* London, 1644, is reprinted in Charles F. Adams, ed., *Antinomianism in the Colony of Massachusetts Bay,* Boston, 1894, pp. 67–233. *A Declaration of Former Passages and Proceedings Betwixt the English and the Narrowgansets,* Boston, 1645, is reproduced in Photostat Americana, Mass. Hist. Soc., Boston, 1936. *Winthrop's Conclusions for the Plantation in New England* (1769) is reprinted with critical notes by Robert C. Winthrop in *Old South Leaflets,* II (1896), No. 50.

The first two volumes of Winthrop's manuscript journal, a chronicle of the years 1630–1649, were first printed at Hartford, 1790, as *A Journal of the Transactions and Occurrences in the Settlement of Massachusetts. . . .* The third manuscript volume was discovered and the whole published as *The History of New England from 1630 to 1649,* Boston, 1825–1826, 2 vols., ed. by James Savage. Savage made some revisions and issued the work again in 2 vols., Boston, 1853, the edition which long remained the only complete and authoritative text. It was not superseded by the edition of James K. Hosmer, in the Original Narratives of Early American History, New York, 1908, 2 vols. The journal is now being published definitively under the general editorship of Allyn B. Forbes for the Mass. Hist. Soc., in the *Winthrop Papers:* Vol. I (1929) covers the years 1498–1628; II (1931), 1623–1630; III (1943), 1631–1637; IV (1944), 1637–1644. These *Papers,* concerning the most important single family in colonial New England, are unequaled in scope and quantity by any similar collection, and their publication is an enterprise of consequence. "The First Year, 1630–1631, of the Journal of John Winthrop," will also be found in *Proc. Mass. Hist. Soc.,* LXII (1929), 329–361.

BIOGRAPHY AND CRITICISM

The standard though uncritical narrative biography is Robert C. Winthrop, *Life and Letters of John Winthrop,* Boston, 1864–1867 (2nd ed., 1869), 2 vols. It includes many original papers. Joseph H. Twichell edited *Some Old Puritan Love-Letters: John and Margaret Winthrop, 1618–1638,* New York, 1893; and wrote *John Winthrop, First Governor of the Massachusetts Colony,* New York, 1891. The most authoritative brief accounts are Albert B. Hart, "John Winthrop, Commonwealth Builder," in Albert B. Hart, ed., *Commonwealth History of Massachusetts,* New York, I (1927), 159–190; "John Winthrop, Esquire," in Samuel E. Morison, *Builders of the Bay Colony,* Boston, 1930, pp. 51–104; and the sketch by James T. Adams in *Dict. Amer. Biog.* (1936). Other useful accounts are Moses C. Tyler, *A History of American Literature During the Colonial Period,* New York, rev. ed., I (1897), 128–136; "John Winthrop," in Andrew Macphail, *Essays in Puritanism,* London, 1905, pp. 52–115; and Vernon L. Parrington, *Main Currents in American Thought,* New York, I (1927), 38–50. Cotton Mather includes "The Life of John Winthrop," in his *Magnalia,* London, 1702, Bk. II, ch. iv.

Special studies are Stanley Gray, "The Political Thought of John Winthrop," *New Eng. Quar.,* III (1930), 681–705; Edgar A. J. Johnson, "Economic Ideas of John Winthrop," *ibid.,* 235–250; and Frank W. Grinnell, "John Winthrop and the Constitutional Thinking of John Adams," *Proc. Mass. Hist. Soc.,* LXIII (1931), 91–119. Collateral studies are William B. Weeden, *Economic and Social History of New England, 1620–1782,* Boston, 1890, 2 vols.; Charles M. Andrews, *The Colonial Period of American History,* New Haven, I (1934); and Alice M. Earle, *Margaret Winthrop,* New York, 1895.

PRIMARY SOURCES

Almost all Winthrop's letters and other personal papers are deposited in the library of the Massachusetts Historical Society. For an account of their provenance and scope, see the introduction to *Winthrop Papers,* Vol. I, Boston, 1929.

BIBLIOGRAPHY

The brief bibliographical essay for Winthrop in *Dict. Amer. Biog.* is as extensive and useful as any yet prepared.

## JOHN WISE
### *1652–1725*

SEPARATE WORKS

*The Churches Quarrel Espoused,* 1710; *A Vindication of the Government of New England Churches,* 1717; *A Word of Comfort to a Melancholy Country,* 1721.

### EDITED TEXTS AND REPRINTS

*The Churches Quarrel* and *A Vindication* were reissued together in one volume in 1772 and again in 1862, and had wide influence as defenses of the democratic principle. *The Churches Quarrel* was also published separately, with introduction by J. S. Clark, Boston, 1860. Wise's "Instructions for Emigrants from Essex County, Mass., to South Carolina, 1697," is printed in *New Eng. Hist. Geneal. Reg.,* XXX (1876), 64–67. Two narratives of the expedition of Sir William Phips against Canada in 1690, in *Proc. Mass. Hist. Soc.,* 2nd ser., XV (1902), include "The Narrative of Mr. John Wise," pp. 281–296.

### BIOGRAPHY AND CRITICISM

No life of John Wise has been published. Narrative summaries are John L. Sibley, *Biographical Sketches of Graduates of Harvard University,* Cambridge, II (1881), 428–441; Thomas F. Waters, "John Wise of Chebacco," *Pub. Ipswich Hist. Soc.,* No. 26 (1927), 1–23; and Irving C. Story, "John Wise: Congregational Democrat," *Pacific Univ. Bul.,* XXXVI (1939), No. 3, 11 pp. The sketch in *Dict. Amer. Biog.* (1936) is by James T. Adams. A contemporary appreciation is John White, *The Gospel Treasure in Earthen Vessels . . . ,* Boston, 1725, preached as a funeral sermon.

As a man of letters Wise is presented in Moses C. Tyler, *A History of American Literature During the Colonial Period,* New York, rev. ed., 1897, II, 104–116; and in Vernon L. Parrington, *Main Currents in American Thought,* New York, I (1927), 118–125. See also Paul S. McElroy, "John Wise: The Father of American Independence," *Essex Institute Hist. Coll.,* LXXXI (1945), 201–226—Wise's contribution to the cause of civil liberty.

### BIBLIOGRAPHY

There is no bibliography of Wise later than that in *Camb. Hist. Amer. Lit.,* I (1917), 425. That in Sibley, *Biographical Sketches,* II (1881), 440–441, remains the best for secondary sources.

## THOMAS (CLAYTON) WOLFE
### *1900–1938*

### WORKS

*Look Homeward, Angel: A Story of the Buried Life,* 1929; *Of Time and the River: A Legend of Man's Hunger in His Youth,* 1935; *From Death to*

*Morning*, 1935; *The Story of a Novel*, 1936; *The Web and the Rock*, 1939; *A Note on Experts: Dexter Vespasian Joyner*, 1939; *You Can't Go Home Again*, 1940; *The Hills Beyond*, 1941—with a note on Thomas Wolfe by Edward C. Aswell; *Gentlemen of the Press: A Play*, 1942.

*Thomas Wolfe's Letters to His Mother, Julia Elizabeth Wolfe*, New York, 1943, was edited by John S. Terry. "Writing Is My Life: Letters of Thomas Wolfe," *Atl. Mo.*, CLXXVIII (1946), 60–66, is the first of a series of three installments of letters addressed to Mrs. J. M. Roberts, his teacher during school days.

Reprints include *Look Homeward, Angel*, New York, 1934 (Modern Lib.); *The Face of a Nation: Poetical Passages from the Writings of Thomas Wolfe*, New York, 1939; *Stories by Thomas Wolfe*, New York, 1944; *The Hills Beyond*, New York, 1944; *A Stone, a Leaf, a Door: Poems by Thomas Wolfe*, 1945, ed. by John S. Barnes; and *The Portable Thomas Wolfe*, ed. by Maxwell Geismar, New York, 1946.

BIOGRAPHY AND CRITICISM

Earlier critical estimates include Robert Penn Warren, "A Note on the Hamlet of Thomas Wolfe," *Amer. Rev.*, V (1935), 191–208; Hamilton Basso, "Thomas Wolfe," in Malcolm Cowley, ed., *After the Genteel Tradition*, New York, 1936, pp. 202–212; C. John McCole, *Lucifer at Large*, London, 1937, pp. 231–254; Ernest S. Bates, "Thomas Wolfe," *English Jour.*, XXVI (1937), 519–527; Thurston Macauley, "Thomas Wolfe: A Writer's Problems," *Publishers' Weekly*, CXXXIV (1938), 2150–2152; William Braswell, "Thomas Wolfe Lectures and Takes a Holiday," *College Eng.*, I (1939), 11–22; John P. Bishop, "The Sorrows of Thomas Wolfe," *Kenyon Rev.*, I (1939), 7–17; Dayton Kohler, "Thomas Wolfe: Prodigal and Lost," *College Eng.*, I (1939), 1–10; and S. L. Solon, "The Ordeal of Thomas Wolfe," *Modern Quar.*, XI (1939), No. 5, 45–53.

More recent estimates are "Thomas Wolfe," in Percy H. Boynton, *America in Contemporary Fiction*, Chicago, 1940, pp. 204–224; "Thomas Wolfe," in Carl Van Doren, *The American Novel*, rev. ed., New York, 1940, pp. 343–348; Carlos Baker, "Thomas Wolfe's Apprenticeship," *Delphian Quar.*, XXIII (1940), 20–25; Claude M. Simpson, Jr., "A Note on Wolfe," *Fantasy*, VI (1940), No. 2, 17–21; *idem*, "Thomas Wolfe: A Chapter in His Biography," *Southwest Rev.*, XXV (1940), 308–321; E. K. Brown, "Thomas Wolfe: Realist and Symbolist," *Univ. Toronto Quar.*, X (1941), 153–166; Thomas L. Collins, "Thomas Wolfe," *Sewanee Rev.*, L (1942), 487–504; Robert Falk, "Thomas Wolfe and the Critics," *College Eng.*, V (1944), 186–192; Monroe M. Stearns, "The Metaphysics of Thomas Wolfe," *ibid.*, VI (1945), 193–199; Desmond Powell, "Of Thomas Wolfe," *Arizona Quar.*, I

(1945), No. 1, 28–36; John M. Maclachlan, "Folk Concepts in the Novels of Thomas Wolfe," *Southern Folklore Quar.*, IX (1945), 175–186; Edwin B. Burgum, "Thomas Wolfe's Discovery of America," *Virginia Quar. Rev.*, XXII (1946), 421–437; Maxwell Geismar, "Thomas Wolfe: The Hillman and the Furies," *Yale Rev.*, XXXV (1946), 649–665; Anne W. Armstrong, "As I Saw Thomas Wolfe," *Arizona Quar.*, II (Spring, 1946), 5–14; and F. I. Carpenter, "Thomas Wolfe: The Autobiography of an Idea," *Univ. Kansas City Rev.*, XII (1946), 179–188. See also Hayden Norwood, *The Marble Man's Wife: Thomas Wolfe's Mother*, New York, 1947—recollections by Mrs. Wolfe.

An extended evaluation is "Thomas Wolfe: The Unfound Door," in Maxwell Geismar, *Writers in Crisis*, Boston, 1942, pp. 185–236. The "Profile" of Maxwell Perkins by Malcolm Cowley in the *New Yorker*, Apr. 8, 1944, pp. 30–43, deals extensively with Perkins's part in the development of Wolfe as a novelist. See also L. Ruth Middlebrook, "Reminiscences of Tom Wolfe," *Amer. Mercury*, LXIII (1946), 544–549; LXIV (1947), 413–420.

There are extensive manuscript collections of unpublished material in the Harvard College Library.

George R. Preston, Jr., *Thomas Wolfe: A Bibliography*, New York, 1943, is a collation of Wolfe's writings, with magazine location of the short stories, critical articles, and reviews. Also useful is Bernice Kauffman, "Bibliography of Periodical Articles on Thomas Wolfe," *Bul. Bibl.*, XVII (1942), 162–165.

# GEORGE EDWARD WOODBERRY
## *1855–1930*

### WORKS

*A History of Wood-Engraving*, 1883; *Edgar Allan Poe*, 1885; *The North Shore Watch and Other Poems*, 1890; *Studies in Letters and Life*, 1890; *Wild Eden*, 1899; *Heart of Man*, 1899; *Makers of Literature*, 1900; *Nathaniel Hawthorne*, 1902; *Poems*, 1903; *America in Literature*, 1903; *The Torch*, 1905; *Swinburne*, 1905; *Ralph Waldo Emerson*, 1907; *The Appreciation of Literature*, 1907; *Great Writers*, 1907; *Life of Edgar Allan Poe*, 1909; *The Inspiration of Poetry*, 1910; *Two Phases of Criticism, Historical and Aesthetic*, 1914; *The Flight and Other Poems*, 1914; *North Africa and the Desert*, 1914; *Ideal Passion: Sonnets*, 1917; *The Roamer and Other Poems*, 1920; *Literary Essays*, 1920; *Literary Memoirs of the Nineteenth Century*, 1921.

Woodberry's *Life of Edgar Allan Poe* (1909) is a new work, not a reprint of his *Edgar Allan Poe* (1885). Woodberry edited the works of Shelley (1892) and, with E. C. Stedman, the works of Poe (1894–1895, 10 vols.).

*Selected Poems of George Edward Woodberry* were published, Boston, 1933. *Selected Letters of George Edward Woodberry,* Boston, 1933, were edited with an introduction by Walter de La Mare. *A Scholar's Testament: Two Letters from George Edward Woodberry to J. E. Spingarn,* Amenia, N.Y., 1931, was published with an introductory note by Lewis Mumford. They deserve to be more widely known.

BIOGRAPHY AND CRITICISM

There is no adequate life of Woodberry. Louis V. Ledoux, *George Edward Woodberry: A Study of His Poetry,* Cambridge, 1917, is useful. The sketch in *Dict. Amer. Biog.* (1936) is by Joel E. Spingarn.

Studies and appreciations include "George E. Woodberry," in John Macy, *The Critical Game,* New York, 1922, pp. 215–224; John Erskine, "George Edward Woodberry, 1855–1930: An Appreciation . . . ," *Bul. N.Y. Pub. Lib.,* XXXIV (1930), 275–279; Charles F. Thwing, "George Edward Woodberry," *Harvard Graduates' Mag.,* XXXVIII (1930), 433–443; Harold Kellock, "Woodberry, a Great Teacher," *Nation,* CXXX (1930), 120–122; and "George Edward Woodberry," in John P. Pritchard, *Return to the Fountains,* Durham, N.C., 1942, pp. 148–158—a study of Woodberry as a student of the classics.

There are deposited in the Harvard College Library some 1,500 letters to and about Woodberry and some 30 written by him. A checklist of Woodberry's writings is in Louis V. Ledoux, *George Edward Woodberry* (1917), 57–72. P. R. Hawkins, "A List of Writings by and About George Edward Woodberry," *Bul. N.Y. Pub. Lib.,* XXXIV (1930), 279–296, is the fullest listing to date.

# JOHN WOOLMAN
## 1720–1772

SEPARATE WORKS

*Some Considerations on the Keeping of Negroes,* 1754 (second part, 1762); *Considerations on Pure Wisdom and Human Policy,* 1768; *Considerations on the True Harmony of Mankind,* 1770; *An Epistle to the Quarterly and Monthly Meetings of Friends,* 1772; *A Plea for the Poor,* 1793.

COLLECTED WORKS AND REPRINTS

*The Works of John Woolman* were published, Philadelphia, 1774 (and 1818). The best and most complete edition of *The Journal and Essays of John Woolman* is that of Amelia M. Gummere, New York, 1922, edited from the original manuscripts. The *Journal* itself was first published in the Philadelphia edition of the *Works* (1774). It was rewritten twice, and all three manuscripts are preserved. More than twoscore editions have been issued, among which is that published in Boston, 1871, with an introduction by John Greenleaf Whittier; and *The Journal with Other Writings of John Woolman* was edited by Vida D. Scudder for Everyman's Library, London, 1910.

The first publication of a manuscript on war was that edited by Robert E. Spiller, "John Woolman on War," *Jour. Rutgers Univ. Lib.*, V (1941), 60–91.

BIOGRAPHY AND CRITICISM

The fullest and most accurate account of Woolman's life is by Amelia M. Gummere in the introduction to her edition of *The Journal* (1922). The most recent study is Janet Whitney, *John Woolman: American Quaker*, Boston, 1942. Two other studies are Frank V. Morley, *The Tailor of Mount Holly: John Woolman*, London, 1926; and W. Teignmouth Shore, *John Woolman: His Life and Our Times* . . . , London, 1913. The brief sketch in *Dict. Amer. Biog.* (1936) is by John E. Pomfret.

Special studies of Woolman are "The Christianity of Woolman," in Addison P. Russell, *Characteristics: Sketches and Essays,* Boston, 1884, pp. 160–194; Moses C. Tyler, *The Literary History of the American Revolution,* New York, 1897, II, 339–347; E. C. Wilson, "John Woolman: A Social Reformer of the Eighteenth Century," *Economic Rev.,* XI (1901), 170–189; "John Woolman, the Quaker," in George M. Trevelyan, *Clio, a Muse, and Other Essays,* London, 1913, pp. 133–142; Ann Sharpless, *John Woolman: A Pioneer in Labor Reform,* Philadelphia, 1920, 22 pp.; "John Woolman," in Llewelyn Powys, *Thirteen Worthies,* New York, 1923, pp. 169–179; Muriel Kent, "John Woolman, Mystic and Reformer," *Hibbert Jour.,* XXVI (1928), 302–313; "The Journal of John Woolman," in Willard L. Sperry, *Strangers and Pilgrims* . . . , Boston, 1939, pp. 137–165; and Frederick B. Tolles, "John Woolman's List of 'Books Lent,'" *Bul. Friends' Hist. Assn.,* XXXI (1942), 72–81.

The bulk of Woolman's manuscripts is in the Friends' Historical Library, Swarthmore College. Important material is in the library of the Pennsylvania Historical Society and in the library of Rutgers University.

The most complete bibliography of Woolman's works is in the Gummere edition of the *Journal* (1922), pp. 610–630. Further bibliographical listing is in Janet Whitney, *John Woolman* (1942), pp. 435–440.

# RICHARD WRIGHT
*b. 1908*

## WRITINGS

*Uncle Tom's Children: Four Novellas*, 1938, was enlarged and reissued as *Uncle Tom's Children: Five Long Stories*, 1940. *Native Son*, 1940, was reissued in the Modern Lib., 1942. Later works are *Twelve Million Black Voices*, 1941; and *Black Boy*, 1945, an autobiography.

## BIOGRAPHY AND CRITICISM

Two earlier estimates are David L. Cohn, "The Negro Novel: Richard Wright," *Atl. Mo.*, CLXV (1940), 659–661; and Edwin B. Burgum, "The Promise of Democracy and The Fiction of Richard Wright," *Science and Society*, VII (1943), 338–352. More recent studies are Ralph Ellison, "Richard Wright's Blues," *Antioch Rev.*, V (1945), 198–211—valuable criticism—and Horace Cayton, "Frightened Children of Frightened Parents," *Twice a Year*, XII–XIII (1945), 262–269.

Primary material is in Richard Wright and Antonio R. Frasconi, "Exchange of Letters," *Twice a Year*, XII–XIII (1945), 255–261. A biographical sketch is "Native Son," in Edwin R. Embree, *Thirteen Against the Odds*, New York, 1944, pp. 25–46.


# ELINOR (HOYT) WYLIE
*1885–1928*

## SEPARATE WORKS

*Incidental Numbers*, 1912; *Nets to Catch the Wind*, 1921; *Black Armour: A Book of Poems*, 1923; *Jennifer Lorn: A Sedate Extravaganza*, 1923; *The Venetian Glass Nephew*, 1925; *The Orphan Angel*, 1926; *Mr. Hodge & Mr. Hazard*, 1928; *Trivial Breath*, 1928; *Angels and Earthly Creatures: A Sequence of Sonnets*, 1928.

*Mortal Image* is the title of the English edition (1927) of *The Orphan Angel*.

## COLLECTED WORKS

William R. Benét edited *Collected Poems of Elinor Wylie*, New York, 1932. *Collected Prose of Elinor Wylie*, New York, 1933, includes her best known pieces, with biographical and critical prefaces by S. V. Benét, W. R. Benét, Isabel Patterson, Carl Van Doren, and Carl Van Vechten. *Last Poems of Elinor Wylie,* New York, 1943, includes unpublished verses transcribed by Jane D. Wise, and some hitherto uncollected pieces, with a foreword by William R. Benét.

A partial list of items issued as pamphlets, and others in anthologies, miscellanies, and collections, is in Jacob Blanck, *Merle Johnson's American First Editions,* 4th ed., New York, 1942.

## BIOGRAPHY AND CRITICISM

Elinor Wylie's sister, Nancy Hoyt, included previously unpublished material in *Elinor Wylie: The Portrait of an Unknown Lady,* Indianapolis, 1935. The sketch in *Dict. Amer. Biog.* (1936) was contributed by Carl Van Doren. Useful critical evaluations are Herbert S. Gorman, "Daughter of Donne," *No. Amer. Rev.,* CCXIX (1924), 679–686; "Elinor Wylie" in Elizabeth S. Sergeant, *Fire Under the Andes,* New York, 1927, pp. 107–121; Harriet Monroe, "Elinor Wylie," *Poetry,* XXXIII (1929), 266–272; James Branch Cabell, "Sanctuary in Porcelain: A Note as to Elinor Wylie," *Virginia Quar. Rev.,* VI (1930), 335–341; "Elinor Wylie," in Emily Clark, *Innocence Abroad,* New York, 1931, pp. 167–184; Morton D. Zabel, "The Pattern of the Atmosphere," *Poetry,* XL (1932), 273–282; William R. Benét, *The Prose and Poetry of Elinor Wylie,* Norton, Mass., 1934, 24 pp.; Carl Van Doren, "Elinor Wylie: A Portrait from Memory," *Harper's Mag.,* CLXXIII (1936), 358–367; Dayton Kohler, "Elinor Wylie: Heroic Mask," *So. Atl. Quar.,* XXXVI (1937), 218–228; H. Lüdeke, "Venetian Glass: The Poetry and Prose of Elinor Wylie," *English Studies,* XX (1938), 241–250; and Julia Cluck, "Elinor Wylie's Shelley Obsession," *PMLA,* LVI (1941), 841–860.

## PRIMARY SOURCES

A very large part of all Elinor Wylie manuscripts, except those privately owned, is in the Library of Congress. Other manuscripts are in the Lockwood Memorial Library, Univ. of Buffalo. The memoirs and biographies of contemporary poets should be consulted.

## BIBLIOGRAPHY

No full bibliography of Wylie has yet been published. A listing of her own writings is in Jacob Blanck, *Merle Johnson's American First Editions,* 4th ed., New York, 1942. A listing of primary and secondary material is Fred B. Millett, *Contemporary American Authors,* New York, 1940, pp. 661–663. See also Frances Cheney, in Allen Tate, *Sixty American Poets, 1896–1944,* Washington, 1945, pp. 182–184.

LITERARY HISTORY
OF THE
UNITED STATES:

*BIBLIOGRAPHY SUPPLEMENT*

# PREFACE

This volume began as a supplement of approximately one hundred pages, designed as an addendum to a future reprinting of Volume III of *Literary History of the United States*. The editors wished to accomplish two aims: to bring the 1948 bibliography volume up to date—that is, to cover the decade 1948–1958—and to expand the index. After a few months of work, it soon became apparent that scholarship in the areas of American literature and history had so burgeoned in the post-war years that even with the most ruthless pruning we could not hope to offer a useful compilation in so small a space. Our publishers, therefore offered to issue a separate volume, permitting us to extend the coverage in depth as well as to add sixteen new individual biographies. This volume, however, is still a *selective* bibliography. The coverage, within the limits of selectivity, attempts to be complete through 1957. As many 1958 items as possible were added to the manuscript during the typescript and proof stages.

The scholar preparing comprehensive listings is encouraged to use these volumes in conjunction with this bibliography: Jacob Blanck's multivolumed *Bibliography of American Literature;* Lewis Leary's *Articles on American Literature, 1900–1950;* James Woodress' *Dissertations in American Literature, 1891–1955;* the bibliographical survey edited by Floyd Stovall, *Eight American Authors: A Review of Research and Criticism;* the *Harvard Guide to American History,* edited by Oscar Handlin and others; and the continuing bibliographies in such journals as *American Literature, American Quarterly, Newsletter of the European Association for American Studies* (first issued, 1955), *Bulletin of the British Association for American Studies* (first issued, 1956), and *Jahrbuch für Amerikastudien* (first issued, 1956).

Some readers may be confused by the boldface numbers preceding each rubric, for example, on the opening page: **3.** BIBLIOGRAPHICAL CENTERS; **13.** PUBLISHED CATALOGS AND DIRECTORIES; **14.** UNION LISTS AND SPECIAL COLLECTIONS, and so on. These numbers refer the reader to that page in the original bibliography for the initial discussion of this topic, to which we have now added the most recent titles.

For specific entries, we wish to acknowledge assistance from Carlos Baker, James F. Beard, Jr., Whitfield J. Bell, Jr., R. P. Blackmur, Rufus A. Blanchard, Julian P. Boyd, L. H. Butterfield, Frederick S. Crews, David Donald, Donald Gallup, Caroline Gordon, Leland Jamison, Howard Mumford Jones, Rudolf Kirk, Arthur S. Link, A. Walton Litz, Robert B. Martin, James B. Meriwether, Arthur Mizener, Merrill D. Peterson, Henry A. Pochmann, Paul Ramsey, Moses Rischin, M. L. Rosenthal, Robert W. Stallman, Mark Schorer, Allen Tate, Lawrance R. Thompson, and James L. Woodress. The staff of the Princeton University Library was, as always, generous with its time and information, particularly Frederick L. Arnold, Dorothy R. Crawford, Elizabeth Burch Jones, Alexander D. Wainwright, and Eleanor V. Weld. For preparation of the typescript, Mary Bertagni deserves special acknowledgment.

Princeton University                               Richard M. Ludwig
December, 1958

# GUIDE TO RESOURCES

## 3. BIBLIOGRAPHICAL CENTERS

CENTRAL:
### The Washington Area

The first annual *National Union Catalog, A Cumulative Author List* was issued in Washington in 1957. It lists all the books card-catalogued during 1956 by the Library of Congress as well as by 200 cooperating libraries in North America. An important research tool, this compilation carries on the first of the published cumulative indexes, *A Catalog of Books Represented by Library of Congress Printed Cards, Issued to July 31, 1942* (167 vols., published 1942–1946), which was followed by *Supplement . . . Cards Issued August 1, 1942–December 31, 1947; The Library of Congress Author Catalog, 1948–1952;* and *The Library of Congress Catalog—Books: Authors,* issued annually 1953, 1954, 1955. Quinquennial cumulations of the *National Union Catalog* will continue to be published, as well as annual issues (the cumulation for 1957 appearing only in the 1953–1957 gathering).

Care must be taken in using these volumes, however. A book published in the last year covered by any series does not automatically appear in the appropriate volume; it frequently is listed in the succeeding series.

## 13. PUBLISHED CATALOGS AND DIRECTORIES

In addition to the *National Union Catalog,* the student should consult the *Cumulative Book Index,* New York, 1898–current, and *Books in Print,* New York, 1948–current, an author-title-series index to the *Publishers' Trade List Annual.*

The British Museum *General Catalogue of Printed Books,* a new edition begun in 1931, has reached 51 volumes (1954); alphabetically it proceeds only to "Dezw." The Bibliothèque Nationale *Catalogue Général des Livres Imprimés,* Paris, 1900–current, covers 183 volumes (1955) through "Tendil."

## 14. UNION LISTS AND SPECIAL COLLECTIONS

A second supplement to *Union List of Serials in Libraries in the United States and Canada* was published in 1953; it lists chiefly new titles from 1944 through 1949.

*New Serial Titles: A Union List of Serials Commencing Publication After December 31, 1949* appeared in 1956, planned as a successor to *Union List of Serials* under the sponsorship of the Joint Committee on the Union List of Serials. Over 200 libraries contributed to these volumes. *New Serial Titles* will appear in twelve monthly issues and in annual cumulations which are self-cumulative over five-year periods.

## 16. *GUIDES TO PROFESSIONAL STUDIES AND BIBLIOGRAPHIES*

### GUIDES TO REFERENCE BOOKS AND THESES

The tenth edition of Tom P. Cross, *Bibliographical Guide to English Studies* was published in Chicago, 1951. A more recent study of bibliographical research problems is Jacques Barzun and Henry F. Graff, *The Modern Researcher,* New York, 1957.

There are several excellent research guides for scholars. *Guide to Reference Books,* 7th ed., edited by Constance M. Winchell, Chicago, 1951 (followed by *Supplement, 1950–1952* and *Second Supplement, 1953–1955*), is a publication of the American Library Association; it is the standard guide to reference books. Robert W. Murphey, *How and Where to Look It Up: A Guide to Standard Sources for Information,* New York, 1958, is designed for laymen as well as professional scholars. A clear explanation of the proper use of reference books, with brief general lists, is Mary Neill Barton, comp., *Reference Books: A Brief Guide for Students,* 3d ed., Enoch Pratt Free Library, Baltimore, 1954.

Theodore Besterman, *A World Bibliography of Bibliographies,* 3d ed., 4 vols., Geneva, 1955–1956, lists over 80,000 separately published bibliographies. The *Bibliographic Index,* New York, 1937–current, is a cumulative bibliography of bibliographies, appearing in semi-annual and annual volumes. The *Bulletin of Bibliography,* Boston, 1897–current, is a medium for the publication of articles, bibliographies, and reading lists. L. N. Malclès, Curator of the Library of the Sorbonne, prepared *Bibliographical Services Throughout the World,* Paris, 1955, the first and second annual reports of the International Advisory Committee on Bibliography organized by UNESCO in 1953.

### 17. SOURCES SPECIFIC TO AMERICAN LITERATURE AND HISTORY:
*General Studies*

James Woodress edited *Dissertations in American Literature, 1891–1955,* Durham, N.C., 1957. "Research in Progress" continues to appear as a regular feature in the journal *American Literature,* published quarterly.

Lewis Leary's *Articles on American Literature Appearing in Current Periodicals, 1920–1945,* Durham, N.C., 1947, has been superseded by his more recent compilation, *Articles on American Literature, 1900–1950,* Durham, N.C., 1954. Each issue of *American Literature* continues to list "Articles on American Literature Appearing in Current Periodicals," compiled by the Committee on Bibliography of the American Literature Group of the Modern Language Association. The "Annual Bibliography" in the April issues of *PMLA* continues to devote one section to articles on American literature. In addition, "Articles in American Studies" began to appear annually with the Summer, 1955, issue of *American Quarterly.* This annotated survey of over 200 periodicals is prepared by the Committee on Bibliography of the American Studies Association of Metropolitan New York. Thomas F. Marshall compiled *An Analytical Index to American Literature, Volumes I–XX, March, 1929–January, 1949,* Durham, N.C., 1954. See also *Report of the Committee on Trends in Research in American Literature, 1940–1950,* published by the American Literature Group of the Modern Language Association, 1951.

A subject-guide and helpful general reference is Howard Mumford Jones, *Guide to American Literature and Its Backgrounds Since 1890,* Cam· bridge, Mass., 1953. Floyd Stovall edited *Eight American Authors: A Review of Research and Criticism,* New York, 1956, prepared by eight American scholars. Chapters of annotated listings are devoted to Poe, Emerson, Hawthorne, Thoreau, Melville, Whitman, Twain, and James.

### 18. *Fiction*

Lyle H. Wright, *American Fiction, 1774–1850: A Contribution Toward a Bibliography,* San Marino, Calif., 1939, was revised in 1948; it now includes 2,772 titles. He has followed it with *American Fiction, 1851–1875: A Contribution Toward a Bibliography,* San Marino, Calif., 1957, covering 2,832 titles. A fourth edition of Otis W. Coan and Richard G. Lillard, *America in Fiction* . . . appeared in Stanford, 1956. Elizabeth M. Kerr prepared *Bibliography of the Sequence Novel,* Minneapolis, 1950. Maxwell Whiteman edited *A Century of Fiction by American Negroes, 1853–1952: A Descriptive Bibliography,* Philadelphia, 1955.

Firkins' *Index to Short Stories* has been superseded by Dorothy E. Cook and Isabel S. Monro, eds., *Short Story Index,* New York, 1953, with a supplement in 1956 edited by Dorothy E. Cook and Estelle A. Fidell.

Dorothy E. Cook and others, *Fiction Catalog,* New York, 1942–current, continues to list works by author, title, and subject; the analytic index is especially helpful.

**19.** *Poetry*

Raymond J. Dixon, ed., *Granger's Index to Poetry*, 4th ed., New York, 1953 (a 474-page supplement appeared in 1957), is the standard index to poetry printed in anthologies. Karl Shapiro prepared *A Bibliography of Modern Prosody*, Baltimore, 1948. Kenton Kilmer prepared the revised edition (1954) of Allen Tate, *Sixty American Poets, 1896–1944*, Washington, 1945, a helpful check list. The student of modern poetry will find much use for George Arms and Joseph M. Kuntz, *Poetry Explication: A Checklist of Interpretation Since 1925 of British and American Poems Past and Present*, New York, 1950.

**19.** *Drama*

George C. D. Odell, *Annals of the New York Stage*, 15 vols., New York, 1927–1949, is an indispensable account of the history of the theatre in New York City from 1699–1894. Continuations of Odell's listings, without his analytical detail, are in *The Best Plays of 1894–1899*, eds. John Chapman and Garrison P. Sherwood, New York, 1955; *The Best Plays of 1899–1909*, eds. Burns Mantle and Garrison P. Sherwood, New York, 1944; and *The Best Plays of 1909–1919*, eds. Burns Mantle and Garrison P. Sherwood, New York, 1933.

*Play Index: 1949–1952*, eds. Dorothy H. West and Dorothy M. Peake, New York, 1953, is a partial continuation of Firkins' *Index of Plays* (fifteen years remain uncovered). Joseph T. Shipley, *Guide to Great Plays*, Washington, 1956, gives a brief history of 660 plays by world dramatists. *Dramatic Index*, Boston, 1910–current, continues to appear separately and as Part II of *Annual Magazine Subject Index*.

**21.** *REGISTRIES OF PUBLICATION*

BOOKS

The first volume of Jacob Blanck's *Bibliography of American Literature* was published in New Haven, 1955, the second in 1957. It will extend to more than eight volumes, and it furnishes a descriptive bibliography of all American authors who "enjoyed something resembling recognition" between 1780–1950. Supervised by the Bibliographical Society of America, the work will cover 35,000 items by 300 authors; emphasis is on belles-lettres. Listings are generously annotated, especially first editions.

**25. PERIODICALS AND NEWSPAPERS**

The *Union List of Serials,* its two supplements, and its successor, *New Series Titles* (see p. 4), continue to be of first importance as periodical guides. *Ulrich's Periodicals Directory,* 8th ed., New York, 1956, is a classified guide to a selected list of current periodicals, foreign and domestic. Consult Winchell or Murphey (described p. 4 above) for more specialized listings.

*Editor and Publisher: International Yearbook Number,* New York, 1920–current, is a comprehensive annual guide to the newspapers of the United States and Canada. Along with *Editor and Publisher Market Guide,* New York, 1924–current, it lists over 1500 daily newspapers. *N. W. Ayer and Son's Directory of Newspapers and Periodicals* remains, however, the most complete guide to the American press.

## 27. DICTIONARIES AND DIGESTS

BIOGRAPHICAL

"Supplement Two" of the *Dictionary of American Biography* was issued in New York, 1958, Robert Livingston Schuyler, editor. It contains 585 sketches of American men and women who died between 1935–1940. A concise *DAB* is in preparation.

The *National Cyclopedia of American Biography,* New York, 1892–1955, now extends to 39 volumes. Marion Dargan compiled *Guide to American Biography,* Albuquerque, 1949, 1952. Part One covers 1607–1815; Part Two covers 1815–1933. *Biography Index* (1946–current) is a quarterly index to biographical material in books and magazines. The first permanent cumulation, edited by Bea Joseph and Charlotte Warren Squires, covers Jan., 1946–July, 1949.

## 29. REFERENCE

James D. Hart, *The Oxford Companion to American Literature,* New York, 1956, is a third and largely revised edition. Phyllis Hartnoll compiled *The Oxford Companion to the Theatre,* New York, 1951; a second edition appeared in 1957. The first supplement to Stanley Kunitz, ed., *Twentieth Century Authors* appeared in New York, 1955, bringing the original biographies and bibliographies up to date as well as adding 700 new biographies, mostly of authors who have come into prominence since 1942.

Additional useful reference volumes are William Rose Benét, ed., *The Reader's Encyclopedia*, New York, 1948; Joseph T. Shipley, ed., *Dictionary of World Literature: Criticism, Forms, Technique*, rev. ed., New York, 1953; and S. H. Steinberg, ed., *Cassell's Encyclopaedia of Literature*, 2 vols., New York, 1953.

## 31. SOURCES FOR CULTURAL HISTORY

The *Harvard Guide to American History*, ed. Oscar Handlin and others, Cambridge, Mass., 1954, is the long-awaited successor to Channing, Hart, and Turner, *Guide to the Study and Reading of American History* (1912). It is a selective listing of books and articles published up to December 31, 1950. American history is here construed in its widest sense.

In recent years, five other reference volumes have appeared which are helpful for work in American studies: William Carl Spielman, *Introduction to Sources of American History*, New York, 1951; Michael Martin and Leonard Gelber, *The New Dictionary of American History*, New York, 1952; Irving S. Kull and Nell M. Kull, *A Short Chronology of American History, 1492–1950*, New Brunswick, N.J., 1952; Richard B. Morris, *Encyclopedia of American History*, New York, 1953; and Gorton Carruth and others, *The Encyclopedia of American Facts and Dates*, New York, 1956. Under the auspices of the American Studies Association Committee on Microfilm Bibliography, David R. Weimer compiled *Bibliography of American Culture, 1493–1875*, Ann Arbor, University Microfilms, 1957.

*Writings on American History*, Washington, 1906–current, continues as an annual bibliography, except for the years 1941–1947 which have not yet been covered. These invaluable compilations appear as a supplement to the *Annual Report* of the American Historical Association. An *Index to the Writings on American History, 1902–1940* appeared in Washington, 1956, under the auspices of the American Historical Association. H. Hale Bellot, *American History and American Historians: A Review of Recent Contributions to the Interpretation of the History of the United States*, Norman, Okla., 1952, covers the years 1890–1940. Extensive bibliographies are included.

Tremaine McDowell, *American Studies*, Minneapolis, 1948, is a survey and analysis of academic programs for the study of American civilization. Robert H. Walker, ed., *American Studies in the United States: A Survey of College Programs*, Baton Rouge, 1958, is both a detailed directory of nearly one hundred institutions offering programs in American civilization and a discussion of the history and the current problems of American studies. Sigmund Skard surveys the European counterpart of our American civiliza-

tion programs in *American Studies in Europe,* 2 vols., Philadelphia, 1958;
he ranges from England to Russia, from the time of the American Revolution to 1957, from secondary school to graduate studies. See also the chapters
on American literature in Lewis Leary, ed., *Contemporary Literary Scholarship: A Critical Review,* New York, 1958.

# BIBLIOGRAPHIES: LITERATURE
AND CULTURE

Howard Mumford Jones, *The Theory of American Literature*, Ithaca, 1948, is a historical study of American literary histories. John Paul Pritchard, *Criticism in America*, Norman, Okla., 1956, is a survey of American literary theory "from the early period of the republic to the middle years of the twentieth century." Floyd Stovall edited a collaborative book for the American Literature Group of the Modern Language Association, *The Development of American Literary Criticism*, Chapel Hill, 1955—five studies of American criticism from 1800 to 1952. A history of American literary criticism which also treats the changing pattern of American culture is Benjamin T. Spencer, *The Quest for Nationality: An American Literary Campaign*, Syracuse, 1957. A treatment of the impact of culture on literature, touching upon all the major critical movements since World War I, is Solomon Fishman, *The Disinherited of Art: Writer and Background*, Berkeley, 1953. Stanley Edgar Hyman's study of twelve modern critics, *The Armed Vision: A Study in the Methods of Modern Literary Criticism*, New York, 1948, is described by the author as "biased and selective." See also, *passim*, William K. Wimsatt, Jr., and Cleanth Brooks, *Literary Criticism: A Short History*, New York, 1957.

## 55. *Collections*

Volumes devoted to a cross section of American critical essays (as well as essays on literary theory) are numerous: Allen Tate, ed., *A Southern Vanguard*, New York, 1947; Robert W. Stallman, ed., *Critiques and Essays in Criticism: 1920–1948*, New York, 1949; *idem, The Critic's Notebook*, Minneapolis, 1950; John Crowe Ransom, ed., *The Kenyon Critics*, New York, 1951; Charles I. Glicksberg, ed., *American Literary Criticism, 1900–1950*, New York, 1951; Morton D. Zabel, ed., *Literary Opinion in America*, rev. ed., New York, 1951, still the most broadly representative of twentieth-century collections; R. S. Crane, ed., *Critics and Criticism, Ancient and Modern*, Chicago, 1952; Ray B. West, Jr., ed., *Essays in Modern Literary Criticism*, New York, 1952; John W. Aldridge, ed., *Critiques and Essays on Modern Fiction, 1920–1951*, New York, 1952; Clarence A. Brown, ed., *The Achievement of American Criticism*, New York, 1954; and Albert D. Van Nostrand, ed., *Literary Criticism in America*, New York, 1957, the last two covering the entire history from Colonial times to the present.

### 57. *Critical Analysis: Literature and American Life*

Malcolm Cowley in *The Literary Situation*, New York, 1954, discusses current literary conditions and trends as well as the plight of the writer in our society. Allan Angoff edited *American Writing Today: Its Independence and Vigor*, New York, 1957, the contents of which appeared as a special number of the London *Times Literary Supplement*.

Recent criticism, to some extent based on social and psychological premises, includes James T. Farrell, *Literature and Morality*, New York, 1947; Howard Fast, *Literature and Reality*, New York, 1950; F. O. Matthiessen, *The Responsibilities of the Critic*, New York, 1952, a posthumous collection of essays; Allen Tate, *The Man of Letters in the Modern World*, New York, 1955; Frederick J. Hoffman, *Freudianism and the Literary Mind*, rev. ed., Baton Rouge, 1957; and two volumes of collected essays by Edmund Wilson: *The Shores of Light: A Literary Chronicle of the Twenties and Thirties*, New York, 1952, and *Classics and Commercials: A Literary Chronicle of the Forties*, New York, 1950.

### 59. *Critical Analysis: Literature and the American Past*

A comprehensive survey of our literary heritage is Arthur Hobson Quinn, Kenneth B. Murdock, Clarence Gohdes, and George F. Whicher, *The Literature of the American People: A Historical and Critical Survey*, New York, 1951. The Library of Congress card lists it under Quinn.

Van Wyck Brooks completed his five-volume study, *Makers and Finders: A History of the Writer in America, 1800–1915*, with *The Times of Melville and Whitman*, New York, 1947, and *The Confident Years: 1885–1915*, New York, 1952. Grant C. Knight studies transition years in *The Critical Period in American Literature* [1890–1900], Chapel Hill, 1951, and *The Strenuous Age in American Literature* [1900–1910], Chapel Hill, 1954. Essays by seven scholars in symposium, prepared (with one exception) for the American Literature Group of the Modern Languages Association, are *Transitions in American Literary History*, ed. Harry Hayden Clark, Durham, N.C., 1953. Jay B. Hubbell makes an encyclopedic study in *The South in American Literature, 1607–1900*, Durham, N.C., 1954; the bibliographies are impressive. Robert E. Spiller's short history, *The Cycle of American Literature: An Essay in Historical Criticism*, New York, 1955, develops a theory of a single organic movement in American letters. Walter F. Taylor's *A History of American Letters* (1936) was expanded and revised to *The Story of American Letters*, Chicago, 1956.

Two general historical studies by foreign scholars are of high quality and keen perception: Heinrich Straumann, *American Literature in the Twentieth*

*Century,* London, 1951, and Marcus Cunliffe, *The Literature of the United States,* London, 1954.

Specialized treatments of American literary history are R. W. B. Lewis, *The American Adam: Innocence, Tragedy, and Tradition in the Nineteenth Century,* Chicago, 1955; Frederic I. Carpenter, *American Literature and the Dream,* New York, 1955; Leslie A. Fiedler, *An End to Innocence,* Boston, 1955; and Randall Stewart, *American Literature and Christian Doctrine,* Baton Rouge, 1958.

## 61. The Analytical and Aesthetic Movement

Three recent studies of symbolism are Charles Feidelson, Jr., *Symbolism and American Literature,* Chicago, 1953; Philip Wheelwright, *The Burning Fountain: A Study in the Language of Symbolism,* Bloomington, Ind., 1954; and William York Tindall, *The Literary Symbol,* New York, 1955.

Critical analyses on a variety of subjects are Austin Warren, *Rage for Order: Essays in Criticism,* Chicago, 1948; Philip Rahv, *Image and Idea: Fourteen Essays on Literary Themes,* Norfolk, Conn., 1949; and Eliseo Vivas, *Creation and Discovery: Essays in Criticism and Aesthetics,* New York, 1955.

A specialized compilation is William Elton, *A Glossary of the New Criticism,* Chicago, 1949.

## 62. Magazines of Criticism

*American Literature* (1929–current) and *American Quarterly* (1949–current) are essential journals for the American literary scholar. In addition to publishing critical articles, they act as clearing-houses for continuing bibliographies and important miscellaneous information. Critical articles on American literary-historical subjects appear in these journals, not previously listed in *LHUS,* III, 62–64: *Publications of the Modern Language Association* (1884–current), *American Historical Review* (1895–current), *South Atlantic Quarterly* (1902–current), *Southwest Review* (1915–current; formerly *Texas Review*), *New England Quarterly* (1928–current), *American Scholar* (1932–current), *University of Kansas City Review* (1934–current; formerly *University Review*), *Western Review* (1937–current; formerly *Rocky Mountain Review*), *College English* (1939–current), *Chicago Review* (1946–current), *Pacific Spectator* (1947–1956), *Western Humanities Review* (1947–current), *Hudson Review* (1948–current), *Modern Fiction Studies* (1955–current), and *Texas Quarterly* (1958–current).

## 64. Experimental Magazines

Carolyn F. Ulrich and Eugenia Patterson compiled *Little Magazines, a List,* New York, 1947, covering the years 1890–1946 from the materials in the large collection of the New York Public Library. *Index to Little Magazines, 1948,* compiled by Avalon Smith, Harriet[t] Colegrove, and Alan Swallow, Denver, 1949, indexes 31 magazines not included in *Readers' Guide* or *International Index.* Succeeding annual issues for 1949, 1950, 1951, 1952 increased the number of magazines listed; the compilers altered with each issue. The sixth issue is a three-year cumulation; the seventh covers two years.

Margaret Anderson edited 150 selections from the files in *The Little Review Anthology,* New York, 1953. Paul R. Stewart, *The Prairie Schooner Story: A Little Magazine's First 25 Years,* Lincoln, Neb., 1955; and John M. Bradbury, *The Fugitives: A Critical Account,* Chapel Hill, 1958, *passim,* are valuable historical studies.

## 68. *Anthologies:*
### General Surveys

Among the many recent survey-anthologies of American literature are Joe Lee Davis, John T. Frederick, and Frank Luther Mott, eds., *American Literature: An Anthology and Critical Survey,* 2 vols., New York, 1948–1949; Edwin Harrison Cady, Frederick J. Hoffman, and Roy Harvey Pearce, eds., *The Growth of American Literature,* 2 vols., New York, 1956; and Sculley Bradley, Richmond Croom Beatty, and E. Hudson Long, eds., *The American Tradition in Literature,* 2 vols., New York, 1956.

## 69. Special Surveys and Collections

Richmond Croom Beatty, Floyd C. Watkins, and Thomas Daniel Young edited *The Literature of the South,* Chicago, 1952. Willard Thorp compiled *A Southern Reader,* New York, 1955, a cross section documentary survey of life in the South.

The most satisfactory collection of American poetry is F. O. Matthiessen, ed., *The Oxford Book of American Verse,* New York, 1950. Oscar Williams edited *A Little Treasury of American Poetry,* New York, 1948; George Mayberry edited *A Little Treasury of American Prose,* New York, 1949.

*The American Treasury, 1455–1955,* New York, 1955, an unconventional anthology which doubles as a reference book and a collection of quotations, was prepared by Clifton Fadiman with the assistance of Charles Van Doren.

## 69. INSTRUMENTS OF LITERARY PRODUCTION
### Magazines

The fourth volume of Frank Luther Mott's *A History of American Magazines,* Cambridge, Mass., 1957, carries the study from 1885–1905. James Playsted Wood, *Magazines in the United States,* 2nd ed., New York, 1956, is a brief one-volume history, but it covers the twentieth century. Theodore Peterson, *Magazines in the Twentieth Century,* Urbana, Ill., 1956, a study limited to commercial magazines, is edited for the lay public.

Two biographies of magazine editors are John Tebbel, *George Horace Lorimer and the Saturday Evening Post,* Garden City, N.Y., 1948, and Dale Kramer, *Ross and the New Yorker,* New York, 1951.

## 70. *The Press*

Frank Luther Mott's *American Journalism,* revised in 1950, includes a new section covering the 1940's. His more recent volume, *The News in America,* Cambridge, Mass., 1952, is "exposition, not a controversial tract," as he explains in the preface. A one-volume history, which attempts to cover the years 1690–1945, is Robert W. Jones, *Journalism in the United States,* New York, 1947. As a supplement to established histories, Edwin H. Ford and Edwin Emery, *Highlights in the History of the American Press: A Book of Readings,* Minneapolis, 1954, reprints 27 significant articles from 17 periodicals published during the past one hundred years.

Specialized studies of newspaper men and their papers are Gerald W. Johnson, *An Honorable Titan: A Biographical Study of Adolph S. Ochs,* New York, 1946; Jeter Allen Isely, *Horace Greeley and the Republican Party, 1853–1861: A Study of the New York Tribune,* Princeton, 1947; and Francis Brown, *Raymond of the Times,* New York, 1951. Meyer Berger prepared, for the centennial year, *The Story of the New York Times, 1851–1951,* New York, 1951. Philip Kinsley continued his *The Chicago Tribune: Its First Hundred Years,* Vol. III (1880–1900), Chicago, 1946. A history of the *Christian Science Monitor* is Erwin D. Canham, *Commitment to Freedom,* Boston, 1958.

Four allied studies are Commission on Freedom of the Press, *A Free and Responsible Press: A General Report on Mass Communication . . . ,* Chicago 1947; William E. Hocking, *Freedom of the Press,* Chicago, 1947; Herbert Brucker, *Freedom of Information,* New York, 1949; and William L Chenery, *Freedom of the Press,* New York, 1955.

## BIBLIOGRAPHIES BY PERIOD AND TYPE

### 72. *THE COLONIAL PERIOD TO 1760*

CULTURAL HISTORY:
*General Studies*

Robert E. Spiller's anthology of Colonial writing, *The Roots of National Culture: American Literature to 1830,* was revised by Spiller and Harold Blodgett, New York, 1949. Richard M. Dorson edited two collections: *America Begins: Early American Writing,* New York, 1950, and *America Rebels: Narratives of the Patriots,* New York, 1953. Jarvis M. Morse, *American Beginnings: Highlights and Sidelights of the Birth of the New World,* Washington, 1952, is a guided tour of original writings, mostly pre-1700.

Three general studies of the colonial period are R. V. Coleman, *The First Frontier,* New York, 1948 (beginnings to the 1660's); *idem, Liberty and Property,* New York, 1951 (from the British conquest of New Netherland in 1664 through the Stamp Act Congress of 1765); and Daniel J. Boorstin, *The Americans: The Colonial Experience,* New York, 1958. Carl Bridenbaugh followed his *Cities in the Wilderness* (1938) with *Cities in Revolt: Urban Life in America, 1743–1776,* New York, 1955. Louis B. Wright's contributions to the history of this period include *The Atlantic Frontier: Colonial American Civilization, 1607–1763,* New York, 1947, and *The Cultural Life of the American Colonies, 1607–1763,* New York, 1957. Perry Miller calls the ten chapters in his *Errand into the Wilderness,* Cambridge, Mass., 1956, "a rank of spotlights on the massive narrative of the movement of European culture into the vacant wilderness of America." Ola Elizabeth Winslow, *Meetinghouse Hill, 1630–1783,* New York, 1952, is a social history with focus on the community meetinghouse. More specialized studies are Penfield Roberts, *The Quest for Security, 1715–1740,* New York, 1947; Leonard Woods Labaree, *Conservatism in Early American History,* New York, 1948; Frederick B. Tolles, *Meeting House and Counting House: The Quaker Merchants of Colonial Philadelphia, 1682–1763,* Chapel Hill, N.C., 1948; and Clinton Rossiter, *Seedtime of the Republic: The Origin of the American Tradition of Political Liberty,* New York, 1953.

### 73. *New England*

Perry Miller has followed *The New England Mind: The Seventeenth Century* (1939) with *The New England Mind: From Colony to Province,* Cambridge, Mass., 1953. The second edition of Samuel Eliot Morison's *The Puritan Pronaos* (1936) was published in New York, 1956, under the title

*The Intellectual Life of Colonial New England.* Four other interpretations of the period are Thomas J. Wertenbaker, *The Puritan Oligarchy,* New York, 1947, a study of the Massachusetts Bible state; George M. Stephenson, *The Puritan Heritage,* New York, 1952; Alan Simpson, *Puritanism in Old and New England,* Chicago, 1955, and Edwin Scott Ganstad, *The Great Awakening in New England,* New York, 1957. See also Robert E. Brown, *Middle-Class Democracy and the Revolution in Massachusetts, 1691–1780,* Ithaca, 1955.

George F. Willison followed his *Saints and Strangers, Being the Lives of the Pilgrim Fathers and Their Families . . . ,* New York, 1945, with *The Pilgrim Reader,* New York, 1953, eyewitness accounts from the Scrooby beginnings to the death of Bradford.

## 74. The South

Wesley Frank Craven, *The Southern Colonies in the Seventeenth Century, 1607–1689,* Baton Rouge, 1949, is the first volume of *A History of the South,* Wendell Holmes Stephenson and E. Merton Coulter, general editors. Clarence Ver Steeg's *The Southern Colonies in the Eighteenth Century, 1689–1763* is in preparation. Two studies by Carl Bridenbaugh are *Seat of Empire: The Political Role of Eighteenth Century Williamsburg,* Williamsburg, 1950, and *Myths and Realities: Societies of the Colonial South,* Baton Rouge, 1952.

## 76. EDUCATION AND SCIENCE

A recent study is Brooke Hindle, *The Pursuit of Science in Revolutionary America, 1735–1789,* Durham, N.C., 1956.

## 79. LITERARY CULTURE:
### General Studies

Kenneth B. Murdock, *Literature and Theology in Colonial New England,* Cambridge, Mass., 1949, deals with "the colonial Puritans' successes and failures as artists." A survey of primeval America in literature is John Bakeless, *The Eyes of Discovery: The Pageant of North America As Seen by the First Explorers,* Philadelphia, 1950.

The *Bay Psalm Book* was reproduced in facsimile from the 1640 edition, Chicago, 1956, accompanied by a companion volume by Zoltán Haraszti, *The Enigma of the Bay Psalm Book,* Chicago, 1956, which provides an analysis of the background and a critical examination of the text.

## 86. *THE FORMING OF THE REPUBLIC: 1760–1820*

CULTURAL HISTORY:
*General Studies*

Surveys of the period include Merrill Jensen, *The New Nation: A History of the United States During the Confederation, 1781–1789,* New York, 1950; Julius W. Pratt, *America's Colonial Experiment,* New York, 1950; Nathan Schachner, *The Founding Fathers,* New York, 1954; Edmund S. Morgan, *The Birth of the Republic, 1763–1789,* Chicago, 1956; and Wesley Frank Craven, *The Legend of the Founding Fathers,* New York, 1956. A standard textbook is David M. Potter and Thomas G. Manning, eds., *Nationalism and Sectionalism in America, 1775–1877: Select Problems in Historical Interpretation,* New York, 1949.

Two specialized studies by Leonard D. White are *The Federalists: A Study in Administrative History,* New York, 1948, and *The Jeffersonians: A Study in Administrative History, 1801–1829,* New York, 1951. See also Manning J. Dauer, *The Adams Federalists,* Baltimore, 1953.

### 87. *Historical and Political Writing*

John Adams, Franklin, Hamilton, Jefferson, Madison, and Washington are treated in individual bibliographies. Histories of the Revolution are numerous and varied: John C. Miller, *Triumph of Freedom, 1775–1783,* Boston, 1948; Oliver M. Dickerson, *The Navigation Acts and the American Revolution,* Philadelphia, 1951; Christopher Ward, *The War of the Revolution,* ed. John Richard Alden, 2 vols., New York, 1952; John Richard Alden, *The American Revolution, 1775–1783,* New York, 1954; Lawrence Henry Gipson, *The Coming of the Revolution, 1763–1775,* New York, 1954; Elisha P. Douglass, *Rebels and Democrats: The Struggle for Equal Political Rights and Majority Rule During the American Revolution,* Chapel Hill, N.C., 1955; Eric Robson, *The American Revolution in Its Political and Military Aspects, 1763–1783,* New York, 1955; John Richard Alden, *The South in the Revolution, 1763–1789,* Baton Rouge, 1957; and Howard H. Peckham, *The War for Independence: A Military History,* Chicago, 1958.

Henry Steele Commager and Richard B. Morris edited *The Spirit of 'Seventy-Six: The Story of the American Revolution as told by Participants,* 2 vols., Indianapolis, 1958.

### 90. *The Religious Impact*

A good general study is William Warren Sweet, *Religion in the Development of American Culture, 1765–1840*, New York, 1952. The selected bibliography is especially helpful.

### 107. *THE MID-NINETEENTH CENTURY*
*Fiction*

Mid-nineteenth century fiction, and its relation to social forces, is studied in Helen McMahon, *Criticism of Fiction: A Study of Trends in the Atlantic Monthly, 1857–1898*, New York, 1952, and Robert A. Lively, *Fiction Fights the Civil War: An Unfinished Chapter in the Literary History of the American People*, Chapel Hill, N.C., 1957. David Brion Davis calls his *Homicide in American Fiction, 1798–1860*, Ithaca, 1957, a study in social values.

### 116. *The Essay and Social Criticism:*
General Studies

A social history of the period is Robert E. Riegel, *Young America, 1830–1840*, Norman, Okla., 1949. George Dangerfield, *The Era of Good Feelings*, New York, 1952, is a study of political transition from Jeffersonian republicanism to Jacksonian democracy. Three studies of John Quincy Adams are Samuel Flagg Bemis, *John Quincy Adams and the Foundations of American Foreign Policy*, New York, 1949; *idem, John Quincy Adams and the Union*, New York, 1956; and George A. Lipsky, *John Quincy Adams: His Theory and Ideas*, New York, 1950. Political-social histories of the Jacksonian era are numerous: Leonard D. White, *The Jacksonians: A Study in Administrative History, 1829–1861*, New York, 1954; Harold C. Syrett, *Andrew Jackson: His Contribution to the American Tradition*, Indianapolis, 1953; John William Ward, *Andrew Jackson: Symbol for an Age*, New York, 1955, a study of the popular image; and Marvin Meyers, *The Jacksonian Persuasion: Politics and Belief*, Stanford, 1957. More specialized are Harry R. Stevens, *The Early Jackson Party in Ohio*, Durham, N.C., 1957, and Joseph L. Blau, ed., *Social Theories of Jacksonian Democracy: Representative Writings of the Period 1825–1850*, New York, 1947.

Clement Eaton has written two comprehensive surveys of the South: *A History of the Old South*, New York, 1949 (with an impressive bibliography), and *A History of the Southern Confederacy*, New York, 1954. Francis Butler Simkins, *A History of the South*, New York, 1953, was originally published as *The South, Old and New: A History, 1820–1947*,

New York, 1947. Pertinent volumes in the projected ten-volume *A History of the South* (Wendell Holmes Stephenson and E. Merton Coulter, general editors) are Charles S. Sydnor, *The Development of Southern Sectionalism, 1819-1848*, Baton Rouge, 1948; Avery O. Craven, *The Growth of Southern Nationalism, 1848-1861*, Baton Rouge, 1953; and E. Merton Coulter, *The Confederate States of America, 1861-1865*, Baton Rouge, 1950. Militarism in the South is treated in John Hope Franklin, *The Militant South, 1800-1861*, Cambridge, Mass., 1956.

Western America during this period is studied in Ray Allen Billington, *The Far Western Frontier, 1830-1860*, New York, 1956.

### 123. *Memoirs and Reminiscences*

Allan Nevins and Milton Halsey Thomas edited *The Diary of George Templeton Strong*, New York, 1952. The four volumes of this illuminating document are titled *Young Man in New York, 1835-1849; The Turbulent Fifties, 1850-1859; The Civil War, 1860-1865;* and *Post-War Years, 1865-1875.*

### 133. *THE LATE NINETEENTH CENTURY*

LITERARY AND CULTURAL HISTORY:
*Studies Specific to the Period*

Arthur M. Schlesinger's *Political and Social Growth of the American People, 1865-1940* (first published with this title, 1941) has been revised, in its fourth edition, to *The Rise of Modern America, 1865-1951*, New York, 1951. Two studies by C. Vann Woodward are *Origins of the New South, 1877-1913*, Baton Rouge, 1951, and *Reunion and Reaction: The Compromise of 1877 and the End of Reconstruction*, Boston, 1951. A popular social history is Stewart H. Holbrook, *The Age of the Moguls*, New York, 1953. More specialized aspects of American society are treated in James J. Martin, *Men Against the State: The Expositors of Individualist Anarchism in America, 1827-1908*, De Kalb, Ill., 1953; Edward Chase Kirkland, *Men, Cities, and Transportation: A Study in New England History, 1820-1900*, 2 vols., Cambridge, Mass., 1948; and *idem, Dream and Thought in the Business Community, 1860-1900*, Ithaca, 1956.

### 134. *Fiction*

Two standard volumes on the changes in literary mode in the latter part of the century are Lars Åhnebrink, *The Beginnings of Naturalism in Ameri-*

*can Fiction*, Uppsala, Sweden, 1950, and Charles Child Walcutt, *American Literary Naturalism, A Divided Stream*, Minneapolis, 1956.

## 136. *Poetry*

An analytical survey is Carlin T. Kindilien, *American Poetry in the Eighteen Nineties*, Providence, 1956.

## 138. *Drama*

Eleanor Ruggles has written a popular biography of one of the principal actors of the nineteenth century, *Prince of Players: Edwin Booth*, New York, 1953. Richard Moody's *The Astor Place Riot*, Bloomington, Ind., 1958, concerns the rivalry between William Macready and Edwin Forrest. A much-needed study of the century's greatest producer is Marvin Felheim, *The Theater of Augustin Daly*, Cambridge, Mass., 1956.

Relevant chapters in these histories illuminate the period in a more general sense: A. Nicholas Vardac, *Stage to Screen: Theatrical Method from Garrick to Griffith*, Cambridge, Mass., 1949; Glenn Hughes, *A History of the American Theatre, 1700–1950*, New York, 1951; Lloyd R. Morris, *Curtain Time: The Story of the American Theater*, New York, 1953; and Richard Moody, *America Takes the Stage: Romanticism in American Drama and Theatre, 1750–1900*, Bloomington, Ind., 1955.

## 151. *THE TWENTIETH CENTURY*

LITERARY AND CULTURAL HISTORY
*Fiction:*
Critical Analysis: Contemporary

Maxwell Geismar continues his study of the novel in the twentieth century with *The Last of the Provincials, 1915–1925*, Boston, 1947; *Rebels and Ancestors, 1890–1915*, Boston, 1953; and *American Moderns: From Rebellion to Conformity*, New York, 1958. Percy Lubbock's *The Craft of Fiction* (1921) was reprinted in New York, 1945, 1957.

It is difficult to select representative critical studies published since 1948; it is even more difficult to classify them. Four volumes of strongly personal opinions are Bernard DeVoto, *The World of Fiction*, Boston, 1950; John W. Aldridge, *After the Lost Generation: A Critical Study of the Writers of Two Wars*, New York, 1951; *idem, In Search of Heresy: American Literature in an Age of Conformity*, New York, 1956; and Edmund Fuller, *Man in Modern Fiction: Some Minority Opinions on Contemporary*

*American Writing,* New York, 1958. Three excellent specialized studies are Robert Humphrey, *Stream of Consciousness in the Modern Novel,* Berkeley, 1954; Leon Edel, *The Psychological Novel, 1900–1950,* New York, 1955; and Melvin Friedman, *Stream of Consciousness: A Study in Literary Method,* New Haven, 1955. Studies of the modern novel which are partly devoted to the American writer are Seán O'Faoláin, *The Vanishing Hero: Studies in Novelists of the Twenties,* London, 1956; Frank O'Connor, *The Mirror in the Roadway: A Study of the Modern Novel,* New York, 1956; John McCormick, *Catastrophe and Imagination: An Interpretation of the Recent English and American Novel,* London, 1957; and Morton D. Zabel, *Craft and Character: Texts, Method, and Vocation in Modern Fiction,* New York, 1957. French critics who have surveyed our novels in the twentieth century include Charly Guyot, *Les Romanciers Américains d'Aujourd'hui,* Paris, 1948; Claude-Edmonde Magny, *L'Age du Roman Américain,* Paris, 1948; and Jean Simon, *Le Roman Américain au XX$^e$ Siècle,* Paris, 1950. Four provocative collections of critiques are William Van O'Connor, ed., *Forms of Modern Fiction,* Minneapolis, 1948; Harold C. Gardiner, S.J., ed., *Fifty Years of the American Novel: A Christian Appraisal,* New York, 1951; Granville Hicks, ed., *The Living Novel,* New York, 1957; and Charles Shapiro, ed., *Twelve Original Essays on Great American Novels,* Detroit, 1958.

## 152. Critical Analysis: Historical

Alexander Cowie, *The Rise of the American Novel,* New York, 1948, and Edward Wagenknecht, *Cavalcade of the American Novel,* New York, 1952, are standard surveys. Richard Chase, *The American Novel and Its Tradition,* Garden City, N.Y., 1957, is a recent, brief study, more an essay in definition than a historical treatment. Ernest E. Leisy's *The American Historical Novel,* Norman, Okla., 1950, is especially valuable for its appendix listings. Frederick J. Hoffman, *The Modern Novel in America,* Chicago, 1951, covers the years 1900–1950. Highly personal criticism which must be taken with caution is George Snell, *The Shapers of American Fiction, 1798–1947,* New York, 1947.

The short story is studied in Seán O'Faoláin, *The Short Story,* London, 1948; H. E. Bates, *The Modern Short Story: A Critical Survey,* New York, 1950; and Ray B. West, Jr., *The Short Story in America, 1900–1950,* Chicago, 1952.

## 153. Special Studies

Particular aspects of the novel in America are treated in Edwin Berry Burgum, *The Novel and the World's Dilemma,* New York, 1946; Blanche Housman Gelfant, *The American City Novel,* Norman, Okla., 1954; Kenneth Lynn, *The Dream of Success,* Boston, 1955, a study of Dreiser, London, Phillips, Norris, and Herrick; Joseph L. Blotner, *The Political Novel,* New York, 1955; Walter B. Rideout, *The Radical Novel in the United States, 1900–1954,* Cambridge, Mass., 1956; Irving Howe, *Politics and the Novel,* New York, 1957; W. M. Frohock, *The Novel of Violence in America,* rev. ed., Dallas, 1957; George Bluestone, *Novels into Film,* Baltimore, 1957; and Robert A. Bone, *The Negro Novel in America,* New Haven, 1958.

## 157. *Poetry Since 1910:*
Anthologies

The most satisfactory collection of modern American poetry, complete with notes and an analysis of the modern idiom, is Kimon Friar and John Malcolm Brinnin, eds., *Modern Poetry: American and British,* New York, 1951. Other excellent collections are John Ciardi, ed., *Mid-Century American Poets,* New York, 1950; W. H. Auden, *The Criterion Book of Modern American Verse,* New York, 1956; Louis Untermeyer, Karl Shapiro, and Richard Wilbur, eds., *New Modern American and Modern British Poetry,* rev. ed., New York, 1957; James K. Robinson and Walter B. Rideout, eds., *A College Book of Modern Verse,* Evanston, Ill., 1958; and David Cecil and Allen Tate, eds., *Modern Verse in English, 1900–1950,* New York, 1958.

## 157. Poetry Criticism

A brief survey of the period is Louise Bogan, *Achievement in American Poetry, 1900–1950,* Chicago, 1951. Two specialized historical studies are Stanley K. Coffman, *Imagism: A Chapter for the History of Modern Poetry,* Norman, Okla., 1951, and John M. Bradbury, *The Fugitives: A Critical Account,* Chapel Hill, N.C., 1958.

Critical essays which, for the most part, treat individual poets are R. P. Blackmur, *Language as Gesture: Essays in Poetry,* New York, 1952; Randall Jarrell, *Poetry and the Age,* New York, 1953; Murray Krieger, *The New Apologists for Poetry,* Minneapolis, 1956; Leonard Unger, *The Man in the Name: Essays on the Experience of Poetry,* Minneapolis, 1956; and Stuart Holroyd, *Emergence from Chaos,* Boston, 1957. More general analyses—historical, critical, and semantic—include William Van O'Connor, *Sense and Sensibility in Modern Poetry,* Chicago, 1948; Muriel Rukeyser, *The Life of Poetry,* New York, 1949; William Joseph Rooney, *The Problem of "Poetry and Belief" in Contemporary Criticism,* Washington, 1949; Hyatt Howe Waggoner, *The Heel of Elohim: Science and Values in Modern American Poetry,* Norman, Okla., 1950; Babette Deutsch, *Poetry in Our Time,* New York, 1952; and W. K. Wimsatt, Jr., *The Verbal Icon: Studies in the Meaning of Poetry,* Lexington, Ky., 1954. See also Stephen Spender,

*The Making of a Poem*, London, 1955, pp. 166–192. A provocative collection is *Poets at Work*, New York, 1948, with essays by Rudolf Arnheim, W. H. Auden, Karl Shapiro, and Donald A. Stauffer. A comprehensive guide to the craft of poetry is Babette Deutsch, *Poetry Handbook*, New York, 1957, a dictionary of terms.

## 159. Bibliography

Allen Tate, *Sixty American Poets, 1896–1944*, Washington, 1945, was revised in 1954. George Arms and Joseph M. Kuntz compiled *Poetry Explication: A Checklist of Interpretation Since 1925 of British and American Poems Past and Present*, New York, 1950.

## 162. *Drama:*
Anthologies

John Gassner has edited a series of anthologies of American plays: *25 Best Plays of the Modern American Theatre—Early Series, 1916–1929*, New York, 1949; *20 Best Plays of the Modern American Theatre, 1930–1939*, New York, 1955; *Best Plays of the Modern American Theatre—Second Series, 1939–1946*, New York, 1947; *Best American Plays—Third Series, 1945–1951*, New York, 1952; and *Best American Plays—Fourth Series, 1951–1957*, New York, 1958. In 1947, Joseph Wood Krutch revised Montrose J. Moses' *Representative American Dramas National and Local* (1933). Frederic G. Cassidy, ed., *Modern American Plays*, New York, 1949; Barrett H. Clark and William H. Davenport, eds., *Nine Modern American Plays*, New York, 1951; Robert Warnock, ed., *Representative Modern Plays, American*, New York, 1952; Harlan Hatcher, ed., *A Modern Repertory*, New York, 1953; and Jack Gaver, ed., *Critics' Choice: New York Drama Critics' Circle Prize Plays, 1935–55*, New York, 1955, are additional collections.

## 163. Criticism and Bibliography

Joseph Wood Krutch's study, *The American Drama Since 1918* (first published, 1939), was revised in New York, 1957. A brief historical study of the period is Alan S. Downer, *Fifty Years of American Drama, 1900–1950*, Chicago, 1951. See also the relevant chapters in Glenn Hughes, *A History of the American Theatre, 1700–1950*, New York, 1951, and Barrett H. Clark and George Freedley, *A History of Modern Drama*, New York, 1947. Ward Morehouse, *Matinee Tomorrow: Fifty Years of Our Theatre* [1898–1948], New York, 1949, is a popular account of the romance of the theatre. Edmond M. Gagey, *Revolution in American Drama*, New York, 1947, is a kaleidoscopic survey of the Broadway theatre between 1917–1947.

An ambitious specialized treatment of the era is W. David Sievers, *Freud on Broadway: A History of Psychoanalysis and the American Drama*, New York, 1955. Other studies of various aspects of the American theatre are Felix Sper, *From Native Roots: A Panorama of Our Regional Drama*, Caldwell, Idaho, 1948; Cecil Smith, *Musical Comedy in America*, New York, 1950; Abel Green and Joe Laurie, Jr., *Show Biz: From Vaude to Video*, New York, 1951; and Robert Gard, *Grassroots Theater: A Search for Regional Arts in America*, Madison, Wis., 1955.

Volumes of drama criticism—essays on the modern theatre, on dramatic form and technique, on changing modes—include Maxwell Anderson, *Off Broadway: Essays About the Theater*, New York, 1947; Joseph Wood Krutch, *"Modernism" in Modern Drama: A Definition and an Estimate*, Ithaca, 1953; Eric Bentley, *The Dramatic Event: An American Chronicle*, New York, 1954; Walter Kerr, *How Not to Write a Play*, New York, 1955; and Mary McCarthy, *Sights and Spectacles 1937–1956*, New York, 1956. John Gassner has published two recent studies: *The Theatre in Our Times: A Survey of the Men, Materials, and Movements in the Modern Theatre*, New York, 1954, and *Form and Idea in Modern Theatre*, New York, 1956.

Critical biographies of prominent theatrical figures are Craig Timberlake, *The Bishop of Broadway: The Life & Work of David Belasco*, New York, 1954; Archie Binns in collaboration with Olive Kooken, *Mrs. Fiske and the American Theatre*, New York, 1955; and Wisner Payne Kinne, *George Pierce Baker and the American Theatre*, Cambridge, Mass., 1954. *The Theatre of Robert Edmond Jones*, Middletown, Conn., 1958, is a series of essays on Jones' work, edited by Ralph Pendleton. *Ten Talents in the American Theatre*, ed. David H. Stevens, Norman, Okla., 1957, is a collection of essays by directors, producers, and playwrights. Margo Jones describes her own theatre in *Theatre-in-the-Round*, New York, 1951; Edith J. R. Isaacs, *The Negro in the American Theatre*, New York, 1947, covers the last hundred years.

Burns Mantle died in 1948. His annual series, *The Best Plays . . . and the Year Book*, was continued by John Chapman through 1952 and by Louis Kronenberger after that date. An index to Mantle's *Best Plays*, covering the years 1899–1950, was published in New York, 1950.

George Jean Nathan, *The Theatre Book of the Year, 1942–1943*, New York, 1943, is the first of an annual record which continued until 1951. In 1953, Nathan published *The Theatre in the Fifties*.

John Chapman began an annual series, *Theatre '53*, New York, 1953, which, in 1957, changed its title to *Broadway's Best: 1957: The Complete Record of the Theatrical Year*.

Daniel Blum has compiled several pictorial records of the American theatre: *Theatre World* has been an annual since 1945; *A Pictorial History of the American Theatre, 1900–1950*, New York, 1950, has been revised in

1951, 1953, and 1956; *Great Stars of the American Stage* was published in New York, 1952.

**169.** *The Essay and Social Criticism*
Studies of Non-Fictional Prose

A general survey is James Gray, May Brodbeck, and Walter Metzger, *American Non-Fiction, 1900–1950,* Chicago, 1952. Dana Kinsman Merrill, *American Biography: Its Theory and Practice,* Portland, Me., 1957, uses representative works from Colonial times to the present.

**171.** INSTRUMENTS OF CULTURE AND LITERARY PRODUCTION
*Books and the Book Trade*

Hellmut Lehmann-Haupt's classic study, *The Book in America,* has appeared in a second edition, New York, 1951, with the collaboration of Lawrence C. Wroth and Rollo G. Silver. The bibliography is especially helpful. William Miller, *The Book Industry,* New York, 1949, is a concise analysis of trade-book publishing in the United States. A similar and more recent study is Chandler B. Grannis, ed., *What Happens in Book Publishing,* New York, 1957. Harold K. Guinzberg, Robert W. Frase, and Theodore Waller, *Books and the Mass Market,* Urbana, Ill., 1953, is a volume of lectures on the economic aspects of publishing. A historical study is Madeleine B. Stern, *Imprints on History: Book Publishers and American Frontiers,* Bloomington, Ind., 1956. The phenomenon of paperbound books is surveyed in Freeman Lewis, *Paperbound Books in America,* New York, 1952, and Frank L. Schick, *The Paperbound Book in America and Its European Antecedents,* New York, 1958.

**171.** Censorship

In recent years, studies in censorship have been understandably numerous. This listing is no more than an introduction to the bibliography: Zechariah Chafee, Jr., *Free Speech in the United States,* Cambridge, Mass., 1941; Clair Wilcox, ed., *Civil Liberties Under Attack,* Philadelphia, 1951; Merle Miller, *The Judges and the Judged,* New York, 1952; Harold L. Cross, *The People's Right to Know: Legal Access to Public Records and Proceedings,* New York, 1953; Walter M. Daniels, ed., *The Censorship of Books,* New York, 1954; Elmer Davis, *But We Were Born Free,* Indianapolis, 1954; Anne Lyon Haight, *Banned Books,* rev. ed., New York, 1955; and Paul Blanshard, *The Right to Read: The Battle Against Censorship,* Boston, 1955.

# BACKGROUND

## 173. *CIVILIZATION IN THE UNITED STATES*

IDEAS AND INSTITUTIONS:
*General Studies*

The projected sixteen volumes of the Library of Congress Series in American Civilization will constitute a comprehensive survey of the American scene in the first half of the twentieth century. Ralph Henry Gabriel is the general editor. Eight volumes have been published in Cambridge, Mass.: John I. H. Baur, *Revolution and Tradition in Modern American Art*, 1951; Herbert Wallace Schneider, *Religion in 20th Century America*, 1952; Frank Luther Mott, *The News in America*, 1952; Merle Curti, ed., *American Scholarship in the Twentieth Century*, 1953; John Sirjamaki, *The American Family in the Twentieth Century*, 1953; Oscar Handlin, *The American People in the Twentieth Century*, 1954; Lowry Nelson, *American Farm Life*, 1954; and Thomas C. Cochran, *The American Business System: A Historical Perspective, 1900–1955*, 1957. A thirteenth volume has been added to the series called *A History of American Life*, Arthur M. Schlesinger and Dixon Ryan Fox, general editors: Dixon Wecter, *The Age of the Great Depression, 1929–1941*, New York, 1948.

One of the most ambitious studies in recent years is Max Lerner's huge one-volume survey, *America as a Civilization: Life and Thought in the United States Today*, New York, 1957. Equally important to the student of American civilization are Dwight L. Dumond, *America in Our Time, 1896–1946*, New York, 1947; Arthur M. Schlesinger, *Paths to the Present*, New York, 1949; Henry Steele Commager, *The American Mind: An Interpretation of American Thought and Character Since the 1880's*, New Haven, 1950; Harvey Wish, *Society and Thought in America*, 2 vols., New York, 1950–1952; Richard D. Mosier, *The American Temper: Patterns in Our Intellectual Heritage*, Berkeley, 1952; Morris R. Cohen, *American Thought: A Critical Sketch*, ed., Felix S. Cohen, Glencoe, Ill., 1954; Merle Curti, *Probing Our Past*, New York, 1955; and Stow Persons, *American Minds: A History of Ideas*, New York, 1958. A recent comprehensive history is William Miller, *A New History of the United States*, New York, 1958. Marshall B. Davidson, *Life in America*, 2 vols., Boston, 1951, is a popular, well-illustrated survey. Two foreign observers are Harold J. Laski, *The American Democracy*, New York, 1948, and D. W. Brogan, *American Themes*, London, 1948.

Symposia on the American tradition include John W. Chase, ed., *Years of the Modern: An American Appraisal*, New York, 1949; Dixon Wecter,

F. O. Matthiessen, and others, *Changing Patterns in American Civilization,* Philadelphia, 1949; Daniel Aaron, ed., *America in Crisis: Fourteen Crucial Episodes in American History,* New York, 1952; Newton Arvin, Jacques Barzun, Max Lerner, and others, *America and the Intellectuals,* New York, 1953; Edward Saveth, ed., *Understanding the American Past,* Boston, 1954; and Frank Thistlethwaite, *The Great Experiment,* Cambridge, Eng., 1955. Guy A. Cardwell edited *Readings from the Americas: An Introduction to Democratic Thought,* New York, 1947. Isabel Leighton assembled a valuable collection of contemporaneous essays in *The Aspirin Age, 1919–1941,* New York, 1949.

More specialized histories are Frederick J. Hoffman, *The Twenties: American Writing in the Postwar Decade,* New York, 1955; Leo Gurko, *The Angry Decade* [the 30's], New York, 1947; and Eric F. Goldman, *The Crucial Decade: America 1945–1955,* New York, 1956. Studies of reform and reformers include Daniel Aaron, *Men of Good Hope: A Story of American Progressives,* New York, 1951; Eric F. Goldman, *Rendezvous with Destiny: A History of Modern American Reform,* New York, 1952; and Richard Hofstadter, *The Age of Reform: From Bryan to F.D.R.,* New York, 1955.

Michael Kraus' *A History of American History* (1937) was expanded and revised to *The Writing of American History,* Norman, Okla., 1953. See also Social Science Research Council Bulletin No. 54, *Theory and Practice in Historical Study: A Report of the Committee on Historiography,* New York, 1946; H. Hale Bellot, *American History and American Historians: A Review of Recent Contributions to the Interpretation of the History of the United States,* Norman, Okla., 1952; and Social Science Research Council Bulletin No. 64, *The Social Sciences in Historical Study: A Report of the Committee on Historiography,* New York, 1954. Louis Gottschalk, *Understanding History: A Primer of Historical Method,* Chicago, 1950, and Jacques Barzun and Henry F. Graff, *The Modern Researcher,* New York, 1957, are basic guides.

## 174. Political and Economic Studies

The *Economic History of the United States* is a projected nine-volume survey edited by a board of five American scholars. To date, five volumes have appeared: George Rogers Taylor, *The Transportation Revolution, 1815–1860,* New York, 1951; Fred A. Shannon, *The Farmer's Last Frontier: Agriculture, 1860–1897,* New York, 1945; Harold U. Faulkner, *The Decline of Laissez-Faire: 1897–1917,* New York, 1951; George Henry Soule, *Prosperity Decade: From War to Depression, 1917–1929,* New York, 1947; and Broadus Mitchell, *Depression Decade: From New Era Through New Deal, 1929–1941,* New York, 1947. The third volume of Joseph Dorfman's *The Economic Mind in American Civilization* was published in New York,

1949. It covers the years 1865–1918. Other general economic histories include John Kenneth Galbraith, *American Capitalism: The Concept of Countervailing Power*, Boston, rev. ed., 1956; Merle Fainsod and Lincoln Gordon, *Government and the American Economy*, rev. ed., New York, 1948; Adolf A. Berle, Jr., *The 20th Century Capitalist Revolution*, New York, 1954; and Charles H. Hession, S. M. Miller, and Curwen Stoddard, *The Dynamics of the American Economy*, New York, 1956.

Histories of American political thought are numerous. Surveys varying in scope are Richard Hofstadter, *The American Political Tradition and the Men Who Made It*, New York, 1948; Herbert Agar, *The Price of Union*, Boston, 1950; Daniel J. Boorstin, *The Genius of American Politics*, Chicago, 1953; Louis Hartz, *The Liberal Tradition in America: An Interpretation of American Political Thought Since the Revolution*, New York, 1955; and Ralph Henry Gabriel, *The Course of American Democratic Thought*, rev. ed., 1956. A foreign observer's report is D. W. Brogan, *Politics in America*, New York, 1954 (published in London as *An Introduction to American Politics*, 1954). Samuel Lubell, *The Future of American Politics*, New York, 1952, and Chester Bowles, *American Politics in a Revolutionary World*, Cambridge, Mass., 1956, discuss political theory. Robert S. Allen has edited two collections of essays on political conditions: *Our Fair City*, New York, 1947, and *Our Sovereign State*, New York, 1949. Political liberty is the subject of Alan Barth, *The Loyalty of Free Men*, New York, 1951; *idem, Government by Investigation*, New York, 1955; A. Powell Davies, *The Urge to Persecute*, Boston, 1953; Ferdinand Lundberg, *The Treason of the People*, New York, 1954; and Henry Steele Commager, *Freedom, Loyalty, and Dissent*, New York, 1954. More specialized studies are V. O. Key, Jr., with the assistance of Alexander Heard, *Southern Politics in State and Nation*, New York, 1949; Lionel Gelber, *The American Anarchy: Democracy in an Era of Bigness*, New York, 1953; Willmoore Kendall and Austin Ranney, *Democracy and the American Party System*, New York, 1956; and V. O. Key, Jr., *Politics, Parties, and Pressure Groups*, 4th ed., New York, 1958. Two useful collections of documents are Thomas I. Emerson and David Haber, eds., *Political and Civil Rights in the United States: A Collection of Legal and Related Materials*, Buffalo, 1952, and Henry A. Turner, ed., *Politics in the United States: Readings in Political Parties and Pressure Groups*, New York, 1955.

The most ambitious and comprehensive survey of socialism, from the seventeenth century to the present, was edited by Donald Drew Egbert and Stow Persons, *Socialism and American Life*, 2 vols., Princeton, 1952. The first volume contains fourteen chapters by fourteen authorities on American civilization; the second volume is an invaluable descriptive and critical bibliography prepared by T. D. Seymour Bassett. Three briefer histories are Ira Kipnis, *The American Socialist Movement, 1897–1912*, New York,

1952; Howard H. Quint, *The Forging of American Socialism: Origins of the Modern Movement,* Columbia, S.C., 1953; and David A. Shannon, *The Socialist Party of America: A History,* New York, 1955. Communism in America is studied in Gabriel A. Almond, *The Appeals of Communism,* Princeton, 1954; Max M. Kampelman, *The Communist Party vs. The C.I.O.: A Study in Power Politics,* New York, 1957; and Irving Howe and Lewis Coser, assisted by Julius Jacobson, *The American Communist Party: A Critical History, 1919–1957,* Boston, 1958. See also Samuel A. Stouffer, *Communism, Conformity, and Civil Liberties,* New York, 1955. Related general historical studies are Arthur A. Ekirch, *The Decline of American Liberalism,* New York, 1955, and Harvey Goldberg, ed., *American Radicals: Some Problems and Personalities,* New York, 1957.

Sumner Welles and Donald C. McKay were the general editors of the American Foreign Policy Library, published by the Harvard University Press, a multivolumed series begun after World War II, frequently revised and reprinted. Dexter Perkins has made a historical survey in *The Evolution of American Foreign Policy,* New York, 1948. Two studies by George F. Kennan are *American Diplomacy, 1900–1950,* Chicago, 1951, and *Realities of American Foreign Policy,* Princeton, 1954. More general studies are Thomas A. Bailey, *The Man in the Street: The Impact of American Public Opinion on Foreign Policy,* New York, 1948; Gabriel A. Almond, *The American People and Foreign Policy,* New York, 1950; and Max Beloff, *Foreign Policy and the Democratic Process,* Baltimore, 1955. Ruhl J. Bartlett edited *The Record of American Diplomacy: Documents and Readings in the History of American Foreign Relations,* rev. ed., New York, 1954.

## 175. Society and the Group

C. Wright Mills has produced three valuable sociological studies in the last decade: *The New Men of Power, America's Labor Leaders,* written with Helen Schneider, New York, 1948; *White Collar: The American Middle Classes,* New York, 1951; and *The Power Elite,* New York, 1956. David Riesman's *The Lonely Crowd,* written with Reuel Denney and Nathan Glazer, New Haven, 1950, was followed by *Faces in the Crowd: Individual Studies in Character and Politics,* with Nathan Glazer, New Haven, 1952, and *Individualism Reconsidered and Other Essays,* Glencoe, Ill., 1954. Joseph Wood Krutch edited a symposium, *Is the Common Man Too Common?,* Norman, Okla., 1954. Other general studies of American society include Geoffrey Gorer, *The American People: A Study in National Character,* New York, 1948; Frederick Martin Stern, *Capitalism in America: A Classless Society,* New York, 1951; Robin M. Williams, Jr., *American Society: A Sociological Interpretation,* New York, 1951; and David M. Potter, *People of Plenty: Economic Abundance and the American Character,*

Chicago, 1954. Excellent collections are Kingsley Davis, Harry C. Brede-meier, and Marion J. Levy, Jr., eds., *Modern American Society,* New York, 1949, and Reinhard Bendix and Seymour M. Lipset, eds., *Class, Status and Power: A Reader in Social Stratification,* Glencoe, Ill., 1953.

In recent years, American scholars, editors, and free-lance writers have analyzed our society in a number of informative and entertaining volumes written for the layman but nevertheless helpful for the student: Andrew Tully, *Era of Elegance,* New York, 1947; Cleveland Amory, *The Proper Bostonians,* New York, 1947; Lloyd R. Morris, *Postscript to Yesterday: America: the Last Fifty Years,* New York, 1947; *idem, Not So Long Ago,* New York, 1949; Cleveland Amory, *The Last Resorts,* New York, 1952; Frederick Lewis Allen, *The Big Change: America Transforms Itself, 1900–1950,* New York, 1952; Sidney Ditzion, *Marriage, Morals, and Sex in America: A History of Ideas,* New York, 1953; Leo Gurko, *Heroes, High-brows and the Popular Mind,* Indianapolis, 1953; Russell Lynes, *The Taste-makers,* New York, 1954; *idem, A Surfeit of Honey,* New York, 1957; and A. C. Spectorsky, *The Exurbanites,* Philadelphia, 1955. More specialized studies are Irvin G. Wyllie, *The Self-Made Man in America: The Myth of Rags to Riches,* New Brunswick, N.J., 1954, and Robert H. Bremner, *From the Depths: The Discovery of Poverty in the United States,* New York, 1956.

Studies of discrimination in the United States have been numerous since the end of World War II: Arnold and Caroline Rose, *America Divided: Minority Group Relations in the United States,* New York, 1948; S. Andhil Fineberg, *Punishment Without Crime,* Garden City, N.Y., 1949; Arnold Forster, *A Measure of Freedom,* Garden City, N.Y., 1950; Carey McWilliams, *Brothers Under the Skin,* rev. ed., Boston, 1951; Charles F. Marden, *Minori-ties in American Society,* New York, 1952; and Stewart G. and Mildred Wiese Cole, *Minorities and the American Promise,* New York, 1954. Two symposia on the subject are R. M. MacIver, ed., *Discrimination and National Welfare,* New York, 1949, and Joseph B. Gittler, ed., *Understanding Minority Groups,* New York, 1956. Studies devoted to the subject of anti-Semitism in America include Carey McWilliams, *A Mask for Privilege,* Boston, 1948; Oscar and Mary F. Handlin, *Danger in Discord: Origins of Anti-Semitism in the United States,* New York, 1948; and Ruth G. Wein-traub, *How Secure These Rights? Anti-Semitism in the United States in 1948,* New York, 1949. Discrimination against the Negro is the subject of Earl Conrad, *Jim Crow America,* New York, 1947; Harry S. Ashmore, *The Negro and the Schools,* Chapel Hill, N.C., 1954; Lee Nichols, *Break-through on the Color Front,* New York, 1954; Charles Abrams, *Forbidden Neighbors,* New York, 1955; and C. Vann Woodward, *The Strange Career of Jim Crow,* New York, rev. ed., 1957. See also Robert C. Weaver, *The Negro Ghetto,* New York, 1948, and Rayford W. Logan, *The Negro in American Life and Thought: The Nadir, 1877–1901,* New York, 1954. James

McBride Dabbs, *The Southern Heritage,* New York, 1958, is an important statement of the Southern view of race relations in historical perspective.

Two of the most comprehensive studies of the Negro in the American heritage are John Hope Franklin, *From Slavery to Freedom: A History of American Negroes,* New York, 1947, and E. Franklin Frazier, *The Negro in the United States,* rev. ed., New York, 1957. Briefer histories are Frank Tannenbaum, *Slave and Citizen: The Negro in the Americas,* New York, 1946; Roi Ottley, *Black Odyssey: The Story of the Negro in America,* New York, 1948; Arnold Rose, *The Negro in America,* New York, 1948; Maurice R. Davie, *Negroes in American Society,* New York, 1949; and two volumes by J. Saunders Redding: *They Came in Chains: Americans from Africa,* Philadelphia, 1950, and *The Lonesome Road: The Story of the Negro's Part in America,* New York, 1958. Herbert Aptheker edited *A Documentary History of the Negro People in the United States,* New York, 1951.

### 177. *Philosophy*

John Dewey, Williams James, and George Santayana are treated in individual bibliographies. Two recent studies of Alfred North Whitehead are A. H. Johnson, *Whitehead's Theory of Reality,* Boston, 1952, and Nathaniel Lawrence, *Whitehead's Philosophical Development: A Critical History of the Background of* Process and Reality, Berkeley, 1956. F. S. C. Northrop and Mason W. Gross selected *Alfred North Whitehead: An Anthology,* New York, 1953. Lucien Price recorded *Dialogues of Alfred North Whitehead,* Boston, 1954.

Histories of American philosophy include W. H. Werkmeister, *A History of Philosophical Ideas in America,* New York, 1949; Joseph L. Blau, *Men and Movements in American Philosophy,* New York, 1952; and Stow Persons, *American Minds: A History of Ideas,* New York, 1958. Richard D. Mosier analyzes the American mind from Puritanism to pragmatism in *The American Temper: Patterns of Our Intellectual Heritage,* Berkeley, 1952. A posthumous volume of Morris R. Cohen, *American Thought: A Critical Sketch,* Glencoe, Ill., 1954, was edited by his son, Felix S. Cohen. Morton G. White, *Social Thought in America: The Revolt Against Formalism,* New York, 1949, traces the development of the leading ideas of Charles A. Beard, John Dewey, Oliver Wendell Holmes, Jr., James Harvey Robinson, and Thorstein Veblen. Two studies of pragmatism are Philip P. Wiener, *Evolution and the Founders of Pragmatism,* Cambridge, Mass., 1949, and Harry K. Wells, *Pragmatism, Philosophy of Imperialism,* New York, 1954. Phases in the history of idealism are studied in Henry A. Pochmann, *New England Transcendentalism and St. Louis Hegelianism,* Philadelphia, 1948.

Three useful collections are Marvin Farber, ed., *Philosophic Thought in France and the United States,* Buffalo, 1950; Max H. Fisch, ed., *Classic*

*American Philosophers: Selections from Their Writings with Introductory Essays,* New York, 1951; and Ralph B. Winn, ed., *American Philosophy,* New York, 1955. There are suggested readings following each essay in the latter volume.

## 178. *Religion:*
General Studies

William W. Sweet, *The Story of Religion in America,* New York, 1950, is a second revised edition of a valuable general historical study. Anson Phelps Stokes, *Church and State in the United States,* 3 vols., New York, 1950, is a monumental and indispensable work. James Hastings Nichols, *Democracy and the Churches,* Philadelphia, 1951, and Leo Pfeffer, *Church, State, and Freedom,* Boston, 1953, are also of primary importance. See also William W. Sweet, *American Culture and Religion: Six Essays,* Dallas, 1951.

## 178. New England

The standard works are Perry Miller, *The New England Mind: From Colony to Province,* Cambridge, Mass., 1953, and *The New England Mind: The Seventeenth Century,* New York, 1939, reprinted Cambridge, Mass., 1954. John T. McNeill, *The History and Character of Calvinism,* New York, 1954, is a thorough study.

## 179. Denominations

A basic reference which covers all major groups is Philip Schaff and others, eds., *The American Church History Series,* 13 vols., 1893–1897. The best brief general survey is F. E. Mayer, *The Religious Bodies of America,* St. Louis, 1954; the bibliography is excellent. A provocative discussion is Will Herberg, *Protestant, Catholic, Jew: An Essay in American Religious Sociology,* Garden City, N.Y., 1955.

James Thayer Addison, *The Episcopal Church in the United States, 1789–1931,* New York, 1951; Gaius Jackson Slosser, ed., *They Seek a Country: The American Presbyterians, Some Aspects,* New York, 1955; and Conrad Wright, *The Beginnings of Unitarianism in America* [to 1805], Boston, 1955, are important denominational studies.

A thorough evaluation of the total Catholic contribution to American life is Theodore Maynard, *The Catholic Church and the American Idea,* New York, 1953. Carefully documented studies, with impressive bibliographies, are John T. Ellis, *American Catholicism,* Chicago, 1956, and Robert D. Cross, *The Emergence of Liberal Catholicism in America,* Cambridge, Mass., 1958. By all odds the most controversial study is Paul Blanshard,

*American Freedom and Catholic Power,* Boston, 1949, rev. ed., 1958. The most balanced reply is James M. O'Neill, *Catholicism and American Freedom,* New York, 1952.

Other denominational histories are Thomas O'Dea, *The Mormons,* Chicago, 1957, and Ray B. West, *Kingdom of the Saints: The Story of Brigham Young and the Mormons,* New York, 1957; Charles S. Braden, *Christian Science Today,* Dallas, 1958; on revivalism, Bernard A. Weisberger, *They Gathered at the River,* Boston, 1958; on small sects, Charles S. Braden, *These Also Believe,* New York, 1949. An economic history of the Latter-Day Saints is Leonard J. Arrington, *Great Basin Kingdom,* Cambridge, Mass., 1958.

Two useful bibliographies are Henry J. Browne, "American Catholic History: A Progress Report on Research and Study," *Church History,* XXVI (1957), 372–380, and Robert T. Handy, "Survey of Recent Literature: American [Protestant] Church History," *Church History,* XXVII (1958), 161–165.


180. *Education*

The history of educational institutions in America is treated in Newton Edwards and Herman G. Richey, *The School in the American Social Order,* Boston, 1947; Edgar W. Knight, *Fifty Years of American Education,* New York, 1952; and George P. Schmidt, *The Liberal Arts College: A Chapter in American Cultural History,* New Brunswick, N.J., 1957. See also R. Freeman Butts, *A Cultural History of Western Education,* New York, 1955, *passim.* Various aspects of American colleges and graduate schools are discussed in Richard Hofstadter and C. DeWitt Hardy, *The Development and Scope of Higher Education in the United States,* New York, 1952; Ernest Earnest, *Academic Procession: An Informal History of the American College, 1636 to 1953,* Indianapolis, 1953; and Richard J. Storr, *The Beginnings of Graduate Education in America,* Chicago, 1953. Two informative collections of essays are John Guy Fowlkes, ed., *Higher Education in American Society: Papers Delivered at the National Education Conference . . . , 1948,* Madison, Wis., 1949, and Sidney J. French, ed., *Accent on Teaching: Experiments in General Education,* New York, 1954. Richard G. Axt, *The Federal Government and Financing Higher Education,* New York, 1952, treats a subject of increasing importance. Surveys of the relation between religion and education in America include V. T. Thayer, *Religion in Public Education,* New York, 1947; R. Freeman Butts, *The American Tradition in Religion and Education,* Boston, 1950; and F. Ernest Johnson, ed., *American Education and Religion: The Problem of Religion in the Schools,* New York, 1952, a symposium representing a number of different opinions.

Studies which can be classified under the broad heading of the philosophy of education include Howard Mumford Jones, *Education and World*

*Tragedy,* Cambridge, Mass., 1946; James Bryant Conant, *Education in a Divided World,* Cambridge, Mass., 1948; Horace M. Kallen, *The Education of Free Men,* New York, 1949; Theodore Brameld, *Ends and Means in Education,* New York, 1950; Robert M. Hutchins, *The Conflict in Education in a Democratic Society,* New York, 1953; David H. Stevens, *The Changing Humanities,* New York, 1953; Theodore Meyer Greene, *Liberal Education Reconsidered,* Cambridge, Mass., 1953; Theodore Brameld, *Philosophies of Education in Cultural Perspective,* New York, 1955; David Riesman, *Constraint and Variety in American Education,* Lincoln, Neb., 1956; Merle Curti, *American Paradox: The Conflict of Thought and Action,* New Brunswick, N.J., 1956; and Howard Mumford Jones, *American Humanism: Its Meaning for World Survival,* New York, 1957.

The "crisis in education," an increasing problem in the 1950's, is approached in Benjamin Fine, *Our Children Are Cheated,* New York, 1947, and Paul Woodring, *Let's Talk Sense About Our Schools,* New York, 1953. Arthur E. Bestor studies the crisis and its cure in *Educational Wastelands,* Urbana, Ill., 1952, and *The Restoration of Learning,* New York, 1955.

Academic freedom and related issues are treated in George R. Stewart and others, *The Year of the Oath, The Fight for Academic Freedom at the University of California,* Garden City, N.Y., 1950; Richard Hofstadter and Walter P. Metzger, *The Development of Academic Freedom in the United States,* New York, 1955; Robert M. MacIver, *Academic Freedom in Our Time,* New York, 1955; and Russell Kirk, *Academic Freedom: An Essay in Definition,* Chicago, 1955.

## 181. Science

Historical studies include Dirk J. Struik, *Yankee Science in the Making,* Boston, 1948; I. Bernard Cohen, *Some Early Tools of American Science,* Cambridge, Mass., 1950; and Whitfield J. Bell, Jr., *Early American Science: Needs and Opportunities for Study,* Williamsburg, 1955. A more specialized discussion is Edward A. White, *Science and Religion in American Thought: The Impact of Naturalism,* Stanford, 1952. Individual studies of prominent men in American science include Donald Fleming, *John William Draper and the Religion of Science,* Philadelphia, 1950; Thomas Coulson, *Joseph Henry: His Life and Work,* Princeton, 1950; Lynde P. Wheeler, *Josiah Willard Gibbs: The History of a Great Mind,* rev. ed., New Haven, 1952; Donald Fleming, *William H. Welch and the Rise of Modern Medicine,* Boston, 1954; and Otho T. Beall, Jr., and Richard H. Shryock, *Cotton Mather: First Significant Figure in American Medicine,* Baltimore, 1954. John E. Burchard edited *Mid-Century: The Social Implications of Scientific Progress,* Cambridge, Mass., 1950, a verbatim account of the discussions held at Massachusetts Institute of Technology on its mid-century convocation.

Mitchell Wilson compiled a fascinating pictorial history, *American Science and Invention,* New York, 1954. J. O. Bailey, *Pilgrims Through Space and Time: Trends and Patterns in Scientific and Utopian Fiction,* New York, 1947, discusses the contributions of Hawthorne, Bierce, Howells, and other American writers to the genre as well as the sources and the influence of Poe's "scientific" tales.

## 182. THE ARTS:
### General Studies

John A. Kouwenhoven, *Made in America: The Arts in Modern Civilization,* New York, 1948, analyzes the relation of art in general to life in the machine age. John I. H. Baur describes his *Revolution and Tradition in Modern American Art,* Cambridge, Mass., 1951, as "an attempt to define and trace the development of the chief movements in our painting and sculpture during the last fifty years, with occasional excursions into architecture and the graphic arts." Lewis Mumford, Peter Viereck, William Schuman, and others contributed to *The Arts in Renewal,* Philadelphia, 1951, a symposium.

The arts as mass media are studied by Gilbert Seldes in *The Great Audience,* New York, 1950, and *The Public Arts,* New York, 1956, and by Erik Barnouw in *Mass Communication: Television, Radio, Film, Press,* New York, 1956. Bernard Rosenberg and David Manning White edited a wide selection of essays, *Mass Culture: The Popular Arts in America,* Glencoe, Ill., 1957. Changes in American taste are surveyed in Frederick Lewis Allen, *The Big Change: America Transforms Itself 1900–1950,* New York, 1952, and Russell Lynes, *The Tastemakers,* New York, 1954. Marshall B. Davidson, *Life in America,* 2 vols., Boston, 1951, illustrates profusely reflections of American society in art forms.

Two studies of the American comic strip are Coulton Waugh, *The Comics,* New York, 1947, and, in part, Lancelot Hogben, *From Cave Painting to Comic Strip: A Kaleidoscope of Human Communication,* New York, 1949. Frederic Wertham, *Seduction of the Innocent,* New York, 1954, is an analysis of comic books. Scholars of American civilization will also want to inspect Philip Graham, *Showboats: The History of an American Institution,* Austin, Tex., 1951, and Walter Terry, *The Dance in America,* New York, 1956.

A heterogeneous anthology of readings in contemporary aesthetics, mainly from the philosophers' viewpoint, is *The Problem of Aesthetics,* eds. Eliseo Vivas and Murray Krieger, New York, 1953.

## 183. Music

John Tasker Howard, *Our American Music: Three Hundred Years of It,* 3d. ed., rev. and enl., New York, 1946, is still the standard general survey of music in the United States. Two more recent histories are Gilbert Chase, *America's Music from the Pilgrims to the Present,* New York, 1955, and John Tasker Howard and George Kent Bellows, *A Short History of Music in America,* New York, 1957. Musical organizations are studied in Mary E. Peltz, *Behind the Gold Curtain: The Story of the Metropolitan Opera, 1883-1950,* New York, 1950, and John H. Mueller, *The American Symphony Orchestra: A Social History of Musical Taste,* Bloomington, Ind., 1951. Oscar G. T. Sonneck's *Early Concert-Life in America* (1731-1800), first published in Leipzig, 1907, was reprinted in New York, 1949. Philip D. Jordan, *Singin' Yankees,* Minneapolis, 1946; Richard B. Harwell, *Confederate Music,* Chapel Hill, N.C., 1950; and *idem, Songs of the Confederacy,* New York, 1951, are volumes on music in nineteenth-century America. Howard Thurman, *The Negro Spiritual Speaks of Life and Death,* New York, 1947, is a series of lectures. See also, *passim,* Calvin S. Brown, *Music and Literature: A Comparison of the Arts,* Atlanta, 1948; Cecil Smith, *Worlds of Music,* New York, 1953; Jacques Barzun, *Music in American Life,* New York, 1956; and Irving Kolodin, *The Musical Life,* New York, 1958.

In the last decade, surveys of jazz have been numerous. Barry Ulanov followed his well-informed *A History of Jazz in America,* New York, 1952, with *A Handbook of Jazz,* New York, 1957. Marshall W. Stearns begins his study, *The Story of Jazz,* New York, 1956, with the African and West Indian origins. David Noakes translated André Hodier's *Hommes et Problèmes du Jazz* under the title *Jazz: Its Evolution and Essence,* New York, 1956. A second, revised edition of Rudi Blesh, *Shining Trumpets: A History of Jazz,* appeared in 1958. Blesh has also written, with Harriet Janis, *They All Played Ragtime,* New York, 1950, a pre-jazz study. Nat Shapiro and Nat Hentoff edited *Hear Me Talkin' to Ya: The Story of Jazz by the Men Who Made It,* New York, 1955. *Eddie Condon's Treasury of Jazz,* eds. Eddie Condon and Richard Gehman, New York, 1956, is a collection of essays and reminiscences. A useful reference volume is Leonard Feather, *The Encyclopedia of Jazz,* New York, 1955.

Roland Gelatt, *The Fabulous Phonograph,* Philadelphia, 1955, is a social history of recordings.

Of bibliographical interest is William H. Seltsam, ed., *Metropolitan Opera Annals,* New York, 1949, which covers the years 1883 (first performance) to 1947. The *First Supplement* (*1947-1957*) appeared in New York, 1957.

### 183. *Painting and Sculpture*

Among recent comprehensive surveys of American art are Oliver W. Larkin, *Art and Life in America,* New York, 1949; Virgil Barker, *American Painting: History and Interpretation,* New York, 1950; E[dgar] P[reston] Richardson, *Painting in America: The Story of 450 Years,* New York, 1956; and Alexander Eliot, *Three Hundred Years of American Painting,* New York, 1957. James T. Flexner followed his *America's Old Masters* (1939) with *First Flowers of Our Wilderness,* Boston, 1947; *A Short History of American Painting,* Boston, 1950; and *The Light of Distant Skies, 1760–1835,* New York, 1954. Two studies of art in the last century are David Howard Dickason, *The Daring Young Men: The Story of the American Pre-Raphaelites,* Bloomington, Ind., 1953, and John I. H. Baur, *American Painting in the Nineteenth Century,* New York, 1953. Wolfgang Born made specialized studies in *Still-Life Painting in America,* New York, 1947, and *American Landscape Painting: An Interpretation,* New Haven, 1948. An impressive bibliography and catalogue is *M. and M. Karolik Collection of American Paintings, 1815 to 1865,* Cambridge, Mass., 1949, printed for the Museum of Fine Arts, Boston.

The development of American painting in the twentieth century is recorded in Frederick S. Wight, *Milestones of American Painting in Our Century,* New York, 1949; Milton W. Brown, *American Painting from the Armory Show to the Depression,* Princeton, 1955; and Rudi Blesh, *Modern Art USA: Men, Rebellion, Conquest, 1900–1956,* New York, 1956. Abstractionist art is specifically treated in T. B. Hess, *Abstract Painting: Background and American Phase,* New York, 1951, and Andrew C. Ritchie, *Abstract Painting and Sculpture in America,* New York, 1951. Useful for its plates especially is *American Painting Today,* ed. Nathaniel Pousette-Dart, New York, 1956.

Among individual studies of American artists are James T. Flexner, *John Singleton Copley,* Boston, 1948, and *Gilbert Stuart,* New York, 1955; Theodore Sizer, *The Works of Colonel John Trumbull,* New Haven, 1950; Edgar Preston Richardson, *Washington Allston: A Study of the Romantic Artist in America,* Chicago, 1948; Harold McCracken, *Frederic Remington, Artist of the Old West,* Philadelphia, 1947; Alfred Frankenstein, *After the Hunt: William Harnett and Other American Still Life Painters, 1870–1900,* Berkeley, 1953; Lloyd Goodrich, *John Sloan,* New York, 1952; Van Wyck Brooks, *John Sloan,* New York, 1955; and McKinley Helm, *John Marin,* Boston, 1948.

C. Ludwig Brummé, *Contemporary American Sculpture,* New York, 1948, and Jacques P. Schnier, *Sculpture in Modern America,* Berkeley, 1948, are comprehensive studies. See also Albert Ten Eyck Gardner, *Yankee Stonecutters: The First American School of Sculpture, 1800–1850*, New York, 1945, and Margaret Cresson, *Journey into Fame: The Life of Daniel Chester French*, Cambridge, Mass., 1947.

## 185. Architecture

Three general studies of American architecture, both domestic and commercial, are James Marston Fitch, *American Building: The Forces That Shape It*, Boston, 1948; Ernest Pickering, *The Homes of America As They Have Expressed the Lives of Our People for Three Centuries*, New York, 1951; and Wayne Andrews, *Architecture, Ambition, and Americans*, New York, 1955. Thomas H. Creighton edited *Building for Modern Man*, Princeton, 1949, a symposium on planning man's physical environment. See also, *passim*, Talbot F. Hamlin, ed., *Forms and Functions of Twentieth-Century Architecture*, 4 vols., New York, 1952.

Specialized studies include Carl Bridenbaugh, *Peter Harrison: First American Architect*, Chapel Hill, N.C., 1949; Hugh Morrison, *Early American Architecture*, New York, 1952; Thomas Tileston Waterman, *The Dwellings of Colonial America*, Chapel Hill, N.C., 1950; John F. Kelly, *Early Connecticut Meeting Houses*, New York, 1948; Fiske Kimball, *Mr. Samuel McIntire, Carver: The Architect of Salem*, Portland, Me., 1940; Agnes Addison Gilchrist, *William Strickland: Architect and Engineer, 1788–1854*, Philadelphia, 1950; Henry C. Forman, *The Architecture of the Old South: The Medieval Style, 1585–1850*, Cambridge, Mass., 1948; Antoinette F. Downing and Vincent J. Scully, Jr., *The Architectural Heritage of Newport, Rhode Island, 1640–1915*, Cambridge, Mass., 1952; Richard Hubbard Howland and Eleanor P. Spencer, *The Architecture of Baltimore: A Pictorial History*, ed., Wilbur Harvey Hunter, Jr., Baltimore, 1953; and Walter H. Kilham, *Boston After Bulfinch: An Account of Its Architecture, 1800–1900*, Cambridge, Mass., 1946. Carl Wilbur Condit discusses the twentieth-century phenomenon, *The Rise of the Skyscraper*, Chicago, 1952. Two critical analyses of prefabricated suburbia in this century are Bernard Rudofsky, *Behind the Picture Window*, New York, 1955, and John Keats, *The Crack in the Picture Window*, Boston, 1956. Lewis Mumford edited *Roots of Contemporary American Architecture*, New York, 1952, 37 essays (1850–1950) by various hands. See also Lewis Mumford, *Art and Technics*, New York, 1952, and *From the Ground Up: Observations on Contemporary Architecture, Housing, Highway Building, and Civic Design*, New York, 1956.

Louis H. Sullivan's *Kindergarten Chats and Other Writings* (1901) was reprinted in 1947, his *Autobiography of an Idea* (1924) in 1949. The most recent study of Sullivan is John Szarkowski, *The Idea of Louis Sulli-*

*van*, Minneapolis, 1956. The writings of Frank Lloyd Wright include *The Future of Architecture*, New York, 1953; *An American Architecture*, New York, 1955; and *A Testament*, New York, 1957. Bernard Karpel has prepared a Wright bibliography, *What Men Have Written About Frank Lloyd Wright . . . 1900 to 1955*, New York, 1955.

### 185. *Motion Pictures, Radio, and Television*

Histories of the films are Martin Quigley, *Magic Shadows*, Washington, 1948, which traces the invention and development of the movie camera; Arthur Knight, *The Liveliest Art: A Panoramic History of the Movies*, New York, 1957; Bosley Crowther, *The Lion's Share*, New York, 1957, the story of MGM; and Richard Griffith and Arthur Mayer, *The Movies*, New York, 1957, an attempt to survey the movies from pre-nickelodeon days to the present, chiefly through 1500 photographs. Social-psychological studies are Parker Tyler, *Magic and Myth of the Movies*, New York, 1947; Hortense Powdermaker, *Hollywood, the Dream Factory*, Boston, 1950; and Martha Wolfenstein and Nathan Leites, *Movies: A Psychological Study*, Glencoe, Ill., 1950. Sergei M. Eisenstein, *The Film Sense*, New York, 1942, and *Film Form*, New York, 1949, both ed. and trans. by Jay Leyda, are classic studies of technical and aesthetic problems. Raymond Spottiswoode, *Film and Its Technique*, Berkeley, 1951, is a comprehensive and illuminating account. Two special studies are A. Nicholas Vardac, *Stage to Screen: Theatrical Method from Garrick to Griffith*, Cambridge, Mass., 1949, and George Bluestone, *Novels into Film*, Baltimore, 1957. See also these volumes from London: Ernest Lindgren, *The Art of the Film*, 1948; Basil Wright, *The Use of the Film*, 1948; Roger Manvell, *A Seat at the Cinema*, 1951; and John Montgomery, *Comedy Films*, 1954.

General studies of radio are Judith Cary Waller, *Radio, The Fifth Estate*, Boston, 1946; Charles A. Siepmann, *Radio's Second Chance*, Boston, 1946; and Llewellyn White, *The American Radio: A Report on the Broadcasting Industry in the United States from the Commission on Freedom of the Press*, Chicago, 1947. Radio in conjunction with its new competitor is discussed in Charles A. Siepmann, *Radio, Television, and Society*, New York, 1950; Herbert L. Marx, ed., *Television and Radio in American Life*, New York, 1953; and Giraud Chester and Garnet R. Garrison, *Television and Radio: An Introduction*, New York, 1956.

Leo Bogart, *The Age of Television*, New York, 1956, is a general introduction to the new medium. Max Wylie calls his *Clear Channels: Television and the American People*, New York, 1955, a report to set owners Other studies of the effects of the newest medium of communication on society are Robert Shayon, *Television and Our Children*, New York, 1951;

William Y. Elliott, ed., *Television's Impact on American Culture,* East Lansing, Mich., 1956, a collection of twelve essays; and Charles A. Siepmann, *TV and Our School Crisis,* New York, 1958.

For discussion of all three media, see Gilbert Seldes above, p. 832.

## 186. Graphic Arts and Crafts

Erwin O. Christensen, *The Index of American Design,* New York, 1950, is a handsomely illustrated examination of the crafts and of popular and folk arts; it has a selected bibliography. Other surveys are Alice Ford, *Pictorial Folk Art, New England to California,* New York, 1949, and Jean Lipman, *American Folk Decoration,* New York, 1951. Her *American Folk Art in Wood, Metal and Stone,* New York, 1948, is more specialized, as are Carl Bridenbaugh, *The Colonial Craftsmen,* New York, 1950, and Erwin O. Christensen, *Early American Wood Carving,* New York, 1952.

## 187. THE AMERICAN LANGUAGE
### HISTORICAL SCHOLARSHIP

*Supplement Two* to Mencken's *American Language* appeared in New York, 1948.

General historical studies in varying degrees of coverage are Thomas Pyles, *Words and Ways of American English,* New York, 1952; Donald J. Lloyd and Harry R. Warfel, *American English in Its Cultural Setting,* New York, 1956; and Albert H. Marckwardt, *American English,* New York, 1958. Charles Kenneth Thomas, *An Introduction to the Phonetics of American English,* New York, 1947, is a study of the pronunciation of English in the United States. John B. Carroll, *The Study of Language: A Survey of Linguistics and Related Disciplines in America,* Cambridge, Mass., 1953, reviews American scholarship.

### 189. GLOSSARIES AND DICTIONARIES

Noah Webster's *Dissertations on the English Language* (1789) was reprinted in facsimile, Gainesville, Fla., 1951, with an introduction by Harry R. Warfel. The most recent study of Webster is K. E. Lindblad, *Noah Webster's Pronunciation and Modern New England Speech: A Comparison,* Cambridge, Mass., 1954.

Joseph A. Weingarten has written *Supplementary Notes . . . ,* New York, 1948, to Craigie and Hurlbert's *Dictionary of American English on Historical Principles* (1938–1944).

The 50,000 entries in M. M. Mathews' *A Dictionary of Americanisms on*

*Historical Principles,* 2 vols., Chicago, 1951, stress the distinctive additions the Americans have made to the English language. Recent compilations in special fields are Joseph A. Weingarten, *An American Dictionary of Slang and Colloquial Speech,* New York, 1954; David Kin, *Dictionary of American Maxims,* and *Dictionary of American Proverbs,* both New York, 1955; and Homer Hogan, *Dictionary of American Synonyms,* New York, 1956.

### 190. USAGE

Margaret Nicholson's *A Dictionary of American-English Usage,* New York, 1957, is based on H. W. Fowler's *Modern English Usage* (1926). Bergen Evans and Cornelia Evans, *A Dictionary of Contemporary American Usage,* New York, 1957, is equally authoritative.

### 191. REGIONAL SPEECH AND LOCALISMS

Southern dialects, folk speech, and place names are studied in M. M. Mathews, *Some Sources of Southernisms,* University, Ala., 1948; Lorenzo Dow Turner, *Africanisms in the Gullah Dialect,* Chicago, 1949; Vance Randolph and George P. Wilson, *Down in the Holler: A Gallery of Ozark Folk Speech,* Norman, Okla., 1953; E. Wallace McMullen, *English Topographic Terms in Florida, 1563–1874,* Gainesville, Fla., 1953; and Norman E. Eliason, *Tarheel Talk: An Historical Study of the English Language in North Carolina to 1860,* Chapel Hill, N.C., 1956. Ramon F. Adams compiled *Western Words: A Dictionary of the Range, Cow Camp and Trail,* Norman, Okla., 1944. A. F. Hubbell analyzed *The Pronunciation of English in New York City,* New York, 1950. Other special studies are Nils G. Holmer, *John Campanius' Lutheran Catechism in the Delaware Language,* Upsala, Sweden, 1946, chiefly a linguistic analysis of the 1696 publication of Campanius' translation of Luther's Small Catechism into the American-Virginia language, and Einar Haugen, *The Norwegian Language in America: A Study in Bilingual Behavior,* 2 vols., Philadelphia, 1953. Lewis Helmar Herman and Marguerite Shalett Herman compiled *Manual of American Dialects for Radio, Stage, Screen and Television,* New York, 1947.

### 191. LINGUISTIC GEOGRAPHY

Hans Kurath followed his *Linguistic Atlas of New England,* 3 vols., 1939–1943, with *A Word Geography of the Eastern United States,* Ann Arbor, Mich., 1949. See also E. Bagby Atwood, *A Survey of Verb Forms in the Eastern United States,* Ann Arbor, Mich., 1953.

## 192. FOLK LITERATURE

### *SONGS AND BALLADS*
GENERAL STUDIES AND COLLECTIONS

John A. and Alan Lomax followed their *Our Singing Country* (1941) with *Folksongs U.S.A.: The III Best American Ballads,* New York, 1947. Other general collections are Margaret Bradford Boni, *The Fireside Book of Folk Songs,* New York, 1947; Tristram P. Coffin, *The British Traditional Ballad in North America,* Philadelphia, 1950; George Pullen Jackson, *Another Sheaf of White Spirituals,* Gainesville, Fla., 1952; Burl Ives, *The Burl Ives Song Book: American Song in Historical Perspective,* New York, 1953; and John Greenway, *American Folksongs of Protest,* Philadelphia, 1953. See also, *passim,* MacEdward Leach, *The Ballad Book,* New York, 1955.

John A. Lomax, *Adventures of a Ballad Hunter,* New York, 1947, is an informal account by an eminent collector. G. Malcolm Laws, Jr., *Native American Balladry,* Philadelphia, 1950, is both a descriptive study and a bibliographical syllabus. He has also compiled, in similar fashion, *American Balladry from British Broadsides,* Philadelphia, 1957.

### 194. SPECIFIC STUDIES AND COLLECTIONS:
*The North Atlantic Seaboard to Maryland*

Helen Hartness Flanders and Marguerite Olney, *Ballads Migrant in New England,* New York, 1953, has an introduction by Robert Frost. George Korson collected *Pennsylvania Songs and Legends,* Philadelphia, 1949.

### 195. *The South*

Gladys Vee Jameson, *Wake and Sing,* New York, 1955, is a slim anthology of the music of Appalachian America. Other regional collections are Lucien L. McDowell, *Memory Melodies: A Collection of Folk Songs from Middle Tennessee,* Smithville, Tenn., 1947; Byron Arnold, *Folksongs of Alabama,* University, Ala., 1950; Alton C. Morris, *Folksongs of Florida,* Gainesville, Fla., 1950; and Jean Ritchie, *A Garland of Mountain Song,* New York, 1953.

### 197. *The Plains, the Southwest, and the Far West*

John A. Lomax's *Songs of the Cattle Trail and Cowcamp,* New York, 1919, 1950, is not to be confused with his better-known *Cowboy Songs* (1910, 1938).

Vance Randolph compiled four volumes of *Ozark Folksongs,* Columbia, Mo., 1946–1950. William A. Owens, *Texas Folk Songs,* Austin, 1950, is limited to 118 songs of Anglo-American origin.

### 197. NEGRO FOLKLORE

Howard Thurman, *The Negro Spiritual Speaks of Life and Death,* New York, 1947, is a series of lectures. Miles Mark Fisher edited *Negro Slave Songs in the United States,* Ithaca, 1953; Allen M. Garret edited, from William A. Logan's collection, *Road to Heaven: Twenty-Eight Negro Spirituals,* University, Ala., 1955.

### 199. RIVER SONGS AND SEA CHANTIES

A new edition of Frank Shay's *Iron Men and Wooden Ships* (1924) appeared in New York, 1948, under the title *American Sea Songs and Chanteys from the Days of Iron Men and Wooden Ships.*

### 199. FOLKLORE OF THE LUMBERJACK

Earl C. Beck, ed., *Lore of the Lumber Camps,* Ann Arbor, Mich., 1948, is chiefly ballads and songs.

Daniel G. Hoffman, *Paul Bunyan, Last of the Frontier Demigods,* Philadelphia, 1952, throws much new light on the history of the legend. Harold W. Felton edited *Legends of Paul Bunyan,* New York, 1947, a generous collection; Earl C. Beck compiled *They Knew Paul Bunyan,* Ann Arbor, Mich., 1956, songs and anecdotes of Roaring Jim, Billy the Bum, Blowhard Ike, and others.

### 201. BIBLIOGRAPHY

Charles Haywood has prepared a monumental index of almost 1200 pages, *A Bibliography of North American Folklore and Folksong,* New York, 1951. It is carefully subdivided and copiously indexed.

Levette J. Davidson, *A Guide to American Folklore,* Denver, Colo., 1951, is a brief descriptive introduction with basic reading lists. A more specialized listing is Arthur K. Davis, *Folk-Songs of Virginia: A Descriptive*

*Index and Classification,* Durham, N.C., 1949. See also G. Malcolm Laws above, p. 45.

Recordings are catalogued in *A List of American Folksongs Currently Available on Records,* compiled by The Archive of American Folksong of the Library of Congress, Washington, 1953, and *Folksongs on Records,* eds. Ben Gray Lumpkin and others, Boulder, Colo., 1950.


## 202. FOLK TALES AND HUMOR
### REGIONAL TALES AND THE FOLK HERO

Two recent studies of David Crockett are Marion Michael Null, *The Forgotten Pioneer, The Life of Davy Crockett,* New York, 1954, and James Atkins Shackford, *David Crockett: The Man and the Legend,* ed. John B. Shackford, Chapel Hill, N.C., 1956.

Walter Blair and Franklin J. Meine edited *Half Horse, Half Alligator: The Growth of the Mike Fink Legend,* Chicago, 1956, the original narratives on which the editors based their 1933 study.

The adventures and opinions of Nebraska's legendary hero have been compiled by Paul R. Beath, *Febold Feboldson: Tall Tales from the Great Plains,* Lincoln, Neb., 1948. A study of the legendary Texan is Joseph Leach, *The Typical Texan: Biography of an American Myth,* Dallas, 1952. See also Chris Emmett, *Shanghai Pierce: A Fair Likeness,* Norman, Okla., 1953.

A reliable account of still another folk hero is Robert Price, *Johnny Appleseed: Man and Myth,* Bloomington, Ind., 1954.

A valuable general study is Stith Thompson, *The Folk Tale,* New York, 1946.


### 203. THE OLD SOUTHWEST

Recent studies of Hooper and Porter are W. Stanley Hoole, *Alias Simon Suggs: The Life and Times of Johnson Jones Hooper,* University, Ala., 1952, and Norris W. Yates, *William T. Porter and* The Spirit of the Times: *A Study of the Big Bear School of Humor,* Baton Rouge, 1957.


### 204. COLLECTIONS

B. A. Botkin followed his *Treasury of American Folklore* (1944) with five other generous collections, all published in New York: *A Treasury of New England Folklore,* 1947; *A Treasury of Southern Folklore,* 1949; *A Treasury of Western Folklore,* 1951; *A Treasury of Railroad Folklore* (with Alvin F. Harlow), 1953; and *A Treasury of Mississippi River Folklore*

1955. In 1954, he edited *Sidewalks of America: Folklore, Legends, . . . of City Folk*, Indianapolis. Ben C. Clough, ed., *The American Imagination at Work: Tall Tales and Folk Tales*, New York, 1947; Martha Foley and Abraham Rothberg, eds., *U. S. Stories: Regional Stories from the Forty-Eight States*, New York, 1949; Mody C. Boatright and others, eds., *Folk Travelers: Ballads, Tales, and Talk*, Austin and Dallas, 1953; and John T. Flanagan and Arthur Palmer Hudson, eds., *Folklore in American Literature*, Evanston, Ill., 1958, are additional general anthologies.

Horace P. Beck has made a survey of *The Folklore of Maine*, Philadelphia, 1957. The folk literature of Michigan is treated by Richard M. Dorson in *Bloodstoppers & Bearwalkers, Folk Traditions of the Upper Peninsula*, Cambridge, Mass., 1952, and *Negro Folktales in Michigan*, Cambridge, Mass., 1956. Tales collected in Perry and Leslie counties, Kentucky, are in Leonard W. Roberts, *South from Hell-Fer-Sartin: Kentucky Mountain Folk Tales*, Lexington, Ky., 1955. Vance Randolph has compiled four collections of Ozark stories: *We Always Lie to Strangers: Tall Tales from the Ozarks*, New York, 1951; *Who Blowed Up the Church House? . . .*, New York, 1952; *The Devil's Pretty Daughter . . .*, New York, 1955; and *The Talking Turtle . . .*, New York, 1957. See also his *Ozark Superstitions*, New York, 1947.

Newman Ivey White, Paull F. Baum, and others edited *The Frank C. Brown Collection of North Carolina Folklore*, 4 vols., Durham, N.C., 1952–1957, containing ballads, songs, the music of the ballads, and a miscellaneous volume of tales, legends, proverbs, riddles, games, and rhymes. Three more volumes are in preparation.

Lyle Saxon, Edward Dreyer, and Robert Tallant compiled *Gumbo Ya-Ya: A Collection of Louisiana Folk Tales*, Boston, 1945. Texas tales are collected in J. Mason Brewer, *The Word on the Brazos: Negro Preacher Tales from the Brazos Bottoms of Texas*, Austin, 1953; Mody C. Boatright, Wilson M. Hudson, and Allen Maxwell, *Texas Folk and Folklore*, Dallas, 1954; and J. Frank Dobie, *Tales of Old-Time Texas*, Boston, 1955.

## 205. CRACKER-BOX PHILOSOPHERS

Cyril Clemens, *Shillaber*, Webster Groves, Mo., 1946, discusses the creation of Mrs. Partington and the founding of *The Carpet Bag*. Duncan Emrich edited *Comstock Bonanza*, New York, 1950, a collection of the humorous writings of Mark Twain and seven of his friends of the Virginia City boom days. Donald Day edited *The Autobiography of Will Rogers*, Boston, 1949, and selections from Rogers' newspaper column, *Sanity Is Where You Find It*, Boston, 1955.

**208.** REGIONAL HUMORISTS

Generous samplings of American humor can be found in James R. Aswell, ed., *Native American Humor,* New York, 1947; Mody C. Boatright, ed., *Folk Laughter on the American Frontier,* New York, 1949, both an anthology and an analysis; James N. Tidwell, ed., *A Treasury of American Folk Humor,* New York, 1956; and Kenneth S. Lynn, ed., *The Comic Tradition in America,* Garden City, N.Y., 1958.


## 212. INDIAN LORE AND ANTIQUITIES

STUDIES AND COLLECTIONS

General historical surveys are John Collier, *The Indians of the Americas,* New York, 1947; D'Arcy McNickle, *They Came Here First: The Epic of the American Indian,* Philadelphia, 1949; Ruth Murray Underhill, *Red Man's America: A History of Indians in the United States,* Chicago, 1953; and Roy Harvey Pearce, *The Savages of America: A Study of the Indian and the Idea of Civilization,* Baltimore, 1953. Clark Wissler's *The American Indian: An Introduction to the Anthropology of the New World* (1917) is in its third edition, New York, 1950. Studies which treat the antiquity of Indian life are Kenneth MacGowan, *Early Man in the New World,* New York, 1950, and Frank C. Hibben, *Treasure in the Dust,* Philadelphia, 1951.

Howard H. Peckham, *Pontiac and the Indian Uprising,* Princeton, 1947, utilizes documents which have been uncovered since the publication of Francis Parkman's *History of the Conspiracy of Pontiac* (1851). Stanley Vestal's *Sitting Bull, Champion of the Sioux,* Norman, Okla., 1957, is an expanded edition of his classic biography (1932).

Specialized studies of individual tribes or areas are these volumes from the Civilization of American Indian Series, all published in Norman, Okla.: Edward Everett Dale, *The Indians of the Southwest,* 1949; Stanley A. Stubbs, *Bird's-Eye View of the Pueblos,* 1950; Ernest Wallace and E. Adamson Hoebel, *The Comanches,* 1952; Walter Collins O'Kane, *The Hopis,* 1953; R. S. Cotterill, *The Southern Indians,* 1954; Francis Haines, *The Nez Percés: Tribesmen of the Columbia Plateau,* 1955; Ruth Murray Underhill, *The Navajos,* 1956; George Bird Grinnell, *The Fighting Cheyennes,* 1956; George E. Hyde, *A Sioux Chronicle,* 1956; Edwin C. McReynolds, *The Seminoles,* 1957; William T. Hagan, *The Sac and Fox Indians,* 1958; and John C. Ewers, *The Blackfeet,* 1958.

Ella E. Clark collected *Indian Legends of the Pacific Northwest,* Berkeley, 1953.

## 222. POPULAR LITERATURE

*BEST SELLERS*
*Bibliography*

Frank Luther Mott, *Golden Multitudes: The Story of Best Sellers in the United States,* New York, 1947, and James D. Hart, *The Popular Book: A History of America's Literary Taste,* New York, 1950, are standard treatments of the subject. The latter covers 1620–1950 and emphasizes social history. See also Alice Payne Hackett, *60 Years of Best Sellers, 1895–1955,* New York, 1956. Mary Noel, *Villains Galore: The Heyday of the Popular Story Weekly,* New York, 1954, though undocumented is a detailed study of the revolution in literary taste in America in the 1830's and after. A specialized study is Helen Waite Papashvily, *All the Happy Endings: A Study of the Domestic Novel in America . . . ,* New York, 1956. See also Malcolm Cowley, *The Literary Situation,* New York, 1954, and Bernard Rosenberg and David M. White, eds., *Mass Culture: The Popular Arts in America,* Glencoe, Ill., 1957.

### 224. DIME NOVELS
*Bibliography*

Two histories of American publishing houses are Albert Johannsen, *The House of Beadle and Adams and Its Dime and Nickel Novels: The Story of a Vanished Literature,* 2 vols., Norman, Okla., 1950, and Quentin Reynolds, *The Fiction Factory, or From Pulp Row to Quality Street,* New York, 1955, a history of Street & Smith.

## 235. ORATORY AND THE LYCEUM

### MID-NINETEENTH CENTURY AND AFTER
*The Rostrum*

Francis Pendleton Gaines, *Southern Oratory: A Study in Idealism,* University, Ala., 1946, is a brief volume, four lectures which consider oratory as a "consequence of the artistic impulse."

### 237. *The Platform*

Two new studies of Robert G. Ingersoll have appeared: Clarence H. Cramer's sympathetic interpretation, *Royal Bob,* Indianapolis, 1952, and Eva Ingersoll Wakefield's edition of *The Letters of Robert G. Ingersoll,* New

York, 1951. See also Ralph H. Gabriel, *The Course of American Democratic Thought*, New York, 2nd edition, 1956, for sidelights on Ingersoll.

### 237. THE LYCEUM

Historical studies are David Mead, *Yankee Eloquence in the Middle West: The Ohio Lyceum, 1850–1870*, East Lansing, Mich., 1951, and the only recent full treatment of the subject, Carl Bode, *The American Lyceum: Town Meeting of the Mind*, New York, 1956. Victoria and Robert Ormond Case, *We Called It Culture: The Story of Chautauqua*, New York, 1948, and Harry P. Harrison as told to Karl Detzer, *Culture Under Canvas: The Story of Tent Chautauqua*, New York, 1958, are informal treatments of this American phenomenon.

### 238. *History and Criticism*

The third volume of *A History and Criticism of American Public Address* (1943) appeared in New York, 1955, edited by Marie Hochmuth, William N. Brigance, and Donald C. Bryant.

Wayland Maxfield Parrish and Marie Hochmuth edited *American Speeches*, New York, 1954, selections ranging from Jonathan Edwards to Franklin Delano Roosevelt. *American Public Addresses, 1740–1952*, ed. A. Craig Baird, New York, 1957, covers almost the same period.

# BIBLIOGRAPHIES: MOVEMENTS
AND INFLUENCES

## 260. CHRONICLES OF THE FRONTIER: LITERATURE OF TRAVEL AND WESTWARD MIGRATION

### *EASTERN UNITED STATES TO THE MISSISSIPPI*
#### THE EXPANDING FRONTIER: TRAVELERS AND OBSERVERS

Daniel Drake's *Discourse on the History, Character, and Prospects of the West* (1834) was reprinted in facsimile, with an introduction by Perry Miller, Gainesville, Fla., 1955.

George Bradshaw edited *A Collection of Travel in America, by Various Hands,* New York, 1948, which includes essays by Thoreau, Melville, Henry James and others. A collection larger in scope is Oscar Handlin, ed., *This Was America: True Accounts . . . by European Travelers to the Western Shore in the Eighteenth, Nineteenth and Twentieth Centuries,* Cambridge, Mass., 1949. Warren S. Tryon compiled *A Mirror for Americans: Life and Manners in the United States, 1790-1870, as Recorded by American Travelers,* 3 vols., Chicago, 1952.

Useful bibliographies of this literature are E. Merton Coulter, *Travels in the Confederate States: A Bibliography,* Norman, Okla., 1948, a listing of more than 500 accounts, and Thomas D. Clark and others, eds., *Travels in the Old South: A Bibliography,* 2 vols., Norman, Okla., 1956, covering the years 1527–1825.

### 264. *THE TRANS-MISSISSIPPI WEST*
#### EARLY EXPLORATION AND TRADING EXPEDITIONS

Bernard DeVoto edited *The Journals of Lewis and Clark,* Boston, 1953, a one-volume condensation of the 1904–1905 Thwaites edition.

Loyd Haberly, *Pursuit of the Horizon,* New York, 1948, is a study of George Catlin, American traveler and painter of Indian life.

### 265. THE OVERLAND TRAIL

John Francis McDermott prepared a new edition of Washington Irving's *A Tour on the Prairies,* Norman, Okla., 1956. Max L. Moorhead edited Josiah Gregg's *Commerce of the Prairies* (1844), Norman, Okla., 1954.

The reminiscences of the Stevens Party of 1844, first published in 1888, were recently edited by George R. Stewart, *The Opening of the California Trail . . .* , Berkeley, 1953. See also Robert Eccleston's diary, *Overland to California on the Southwestern Trail,* 1849, eds. George P. Hammond and Edward H. Howes, Berkeley, 1950, and *The Road to Sante Fe: The Journal and Diaries of George Champlin Sibley and Others . . . , 1825–1827,* ed. Kate L. Gregg, Albuquerque, 1952.

Aubrey L. Haines re-edited Osborne Russell's account of the Rocky Mountain fur trade, 1834–1843, *Journal of a Trapper,* Portland, Ore., 1955. William H. Ellison and Francis Price edited *The Life and Adventures in California of Don Agustín Janssens, 1834–1856,* San Marino, Calif., 1953; the translation of this manuscript, known as "Vida y Aventuras" by Agustín Janssens, is by Francis Price.

**269.** THE LATER ACCOUNTS

Josiah Royce's *California, from the Conquest in 1846 to the Second Vigilance Committee in San Francisco: A Study of American Character* (1886) was reprinted with an introduction by Robert Glass Cleland, New York, 1948.

John E. Pomfret edited, from manuscripts in the Huntington Library, *California Gold Rush Voyages, 1848–1849: Three Original Narratives,* San Marino, Calif., 1954. Also from a manuscript in the Huntington Library is *California Gold Rush Merchant: The Journal of Stephen Chapin Davis,* ed. Benjamin B. Richards, San Marino, Calif., 1956.

## 273. *INDIAN CAPTIVITIES*

Howard H. Peckham edited *Captured by Indians: True Tales of Pioneer Survivors,* New Brunswick, N. J., 1954, fourteen narratives dating from 1676 to 1864, retold in shorter form.

## 279. *SECONDARY SOURCES*

Bernard DeVoto's *The Course of Empire,* Boston, 1952, the first volume of a trilogy, is a history and description of the continental experience from 1492 to 1805. *Across the Wide Missouri,* Boston, 1947, treating the years 1832–1838, and *The Year of Decision, 1846,* Boston, 1943, continue his study of continentalism. R. V. Coleman, *The First Frontier,* New York, 1948, is a history of the early settlements along the Atlantic seaboard. Stewart H. Holbrook, *The Yankee Exodus: An Account of Migration from New*

*England*, New York, 1950, emphasizes the movement west of the Mississippi.

The opening of the south and southwest is studied in Everett Dick, *The Dixie Frontier: A Social History of the Southern Frontier from the First Transmontane Beginnings to the Civil War*, New York, 1948; Ohland Morton, *Terán and Texas: A Chapter in Texas-Mexican Relations*, Austin, 1948; Barnes F. Lathrop, *Migration into East Texas, 1835-1860*, Austin, 1949; William C. Binkley, *The Texas Revolution*, Baton Rouge, 1952; Wayne Gard, *The Chisholm Trail*, Norman, Okla., 1954; Paul I. Wellman, *Glory, God, and Gold: A Narrative History*, Garden City, N.Y., 1954; and Noel M. Loomis, *The Texan–Sante Fé Pioneers*, Norman, Okla., 1958. See also Paul Horgan, *Great River: The Rio Grande in North American History*, 2 vols., New York, 1954.

Ray Allen Billington has published two volumes on the movement to the far west: *Westward Expansion: A History of the American Frontier*, New York, 1949, and *The Far Western Frontier, 1830-1860*, New York, 1956; the latter has a good descriptive bibliography. Two volumes by Oscar O. Winther are *The Great Northwest: A History*, New York, 1947, and *The Old Oregon Country: A History of Frontier Trade, Transportation, and Travel*, Stanford, 1950. Further studies include R. Carlyle Buley, *The Old Northwest: Pioneer Period, 1815-1840*, 2 vols., Bloomington, Ind., 1950; J. Roderic Korns, ed., *West from Fort Bridger: The Pioneering of the Immigrant Trails Across Utah, 1846-1850*, Salt Lake City, 1951; Louis B. Wright, *Culture on the Moving Frontier*, Bloomington, Ind., 1955; Norman A. Graebner, *Empire on the Pacific: A Study in American Continental Expansion*, New York, 1955; Walter Havighurst, *Wilderness for Sale: The Story of the First Western Land Rush*, New York, 1956; Irving Stone, *Men to Match My Mountains: The Opening of the Far West, 1840-1900*, New York, 1956; and Dorothy O. Johansen and Charles M. Gates, *Empire of the Columbia: A History of the Pacific Northwest*, New York, 1957.

The California gold rush is treated in Rodman W. Paul, *California Gold: The Beginning of Mining in the Far West*, Cambridge, Mass., 1947; John W. Caughey, *Gold Is the Cornerstone*, Berkeley, 1948; and *passim*, Charles Howard Shinn, *Mining Camps: A Study in American Frontier Government*, New York, 1948. Papers describing the first discovery are in *California Gold Discovery: Centennial Papers of the Time, the Site and Artifacts*, San Francisco, 1947. See also collected papers in John W. Caughey, ed., *Rushing for Gold*, Berkeley, 1949. Of allied interest is Oscar Lewis, *Sea Routes to the Goldfields: The Migration by Water to California in 1849-1852*, New York, 1949. A pictorial record of the era is Joseph Henry Jackson, ed., *Gold Rush Album*, New York, 1949.

Specialized studies are Oscar Lewis, *Silver Kings: The Lives and Times of Mackay, Fair, Flood, and O'Brien, Lords of the Nevada Comstock Lode*,

New York, 1947; W. W. Robinson, *Land in California: The Story of Mission Lands, Ranchos, Squatters . . .* , Berkeley, 1948; Edward Hungerford, *Wells Fargo: Advancing the American Frontier*, New York, 1949; Morris E. Garnsey, *America's New Frontier*, New York, 1950, *passim*, an economic history of "the mountain West"; Raymond W. Settle and Mary Lund Settle, *Saddles and Spurs: The Pony Express Saga*, Harrisburg, Pa., 1955; and James P. Shannon, *Catholic Colonization on the Western Frontier*, New Haven, 1957.

Earl Pomeroy, *In Search of the Golden West: The Tourist in Western America*, New York, 1957, is an anecdotal history of tourism in the west from the opening of the transcontinental railroads; the illustrations are excellent. Robert Taft, *Artists and Illustrators of the Old West, 1850–1900*, New York, 1953, treats generally neglected but valuable material. The cowboy is studied in Joe B. Frantz and Julian Ernest Choate, Jr., *The American Cowboy: The Myth and the Reality*, Norman, Okla., 1955, and *The Best of the American Cowboy*, ed. Ramon F. Adams, Norman, Okla., 1957. Robert West Howard edited an informal group of essays, *This Is the West*, New York, 1957.

Henry Nash Smith's *Virgin Land: The American West as Symbol and Myth*, Cambridge, Mass., 1950, is a pioneering study in symbolism as the expression of a culture.

## 282. BIBLIOGRAPHY

R. W. G. Vail, *The Voice of the Old Frontier*, Philadelphia, 1949, is a brief descriptive study prefaced to "A Bibliography of North American Frontier Literature, 1542–1800," a listing of almost 400 pages.

## 284. MINGLING OF TONGUES:
## WRITING OTHER THAN ENGLISH

### GENERAL STUDIES

Survey histories of the peopling of our land include Oscar Handlin, *The Uprooted: The Epic Story of the Great Migrations That Made the American People*, Boston, 1951; John Higham, *Strangers in the Land: Patterns of American Nativism, 1860–1925*, New Brunswick, N.J., 1955; and Barbara Miller Solomon, *Ancestors and Immigrants: A Changing New England Tradition*, Cambridge, Mass., 1956. More specialized studies are Edward N. Saveth, *American Historians and European Immigrants, 1875–1925*, New York, 1948; Edward George Hartmann, *The Movement to Americanize the Immigrant,* New York, 1948; Robert Ernst, *Immigrant Life in New York City, 1825–1863,* New York, 1949; and Charlotte Erickson, *American Industry and the European Immigrant, 1860–1885,* Cambridge, Mass., 1957. The legal problems are treated in William S. Bernard, ed., *American Immigration Policy,* New York, 1950; Milton R. Konvitz, *Civil Rights in Immigration,* Ithaca, 1953; and Robert A. Divine, *American Immigration Policy, 1924–1952,* New Haven, 1957.

Accounts of immigration from the United Kingdom include Rowland Tappan Berthoff, *British Immigrants in Industrial America, 1790–1950,* Cambridge, Mass., 1953; Carl Wittke, *The Irish in America,* Baton Rouge, 1956; Ian C. C. Graham, *Colonists from Scotland: Emigration to North America, 1707–1783,* Ithaca, 1956; Wilbur S. Shepperson, *British Emigration to North America: Projects and Opinions in the Early Victorian Period,* Minneapolis, 1957; Leonard Patrick O'Connor Wibberley, *The Coming of the Green,* New York, 1958; and Arnold Schrier, *Ireland and the American Emigration, 1850–1900,* Minneapolis, 1958.

The arrival of the Dutch in America is studied in Arnold Mulder, *Americans from Holland,* Philadelphia, 1947, and Henry S. Lucas, *Netherlanders in America: Dutch Immigration to the United States and Canada, 1789–1950,* Ann Arbor, Mich., 1955.

More recent problems of immigration are described in C. Wright Mills (in collaboration with Clarence Senior and Rose Kohn Goldsen), *The Puerto Rican Journey: New York's Newest Migrants,* New York, 1950; Maurice R. Davie and others, *Refugees in America,* New York, 1947; Donald Peterson Kent, *The Refugee Intellectual: The Americanization of the Immigrants of 1933–1941,* New York, 1953; and Christopher Rand, *The Puerto Ricans,* New York, 1958.

## 292. *GERMAN AND PENNSYLVANIA GERMAN*
### General Studies

Henry A. Pochmann and others, *German Culture in America: Philosophical and Literary Influences, 1600–1900,* Madison, Wis., 1957, is a comprehensive exploration of Germanic influences on thought and art in America's cultural development.

Two specialized studies by Carl Wittke are *Refugees of Revolution: The German Forty-Eighters in America,* Philadelphia, 1952, and *The German–Language Press in America,* Lexington, Ky., 1957. See also Dieter Cunz, *The Maryland Germans,* Princeton, 1948, and John Wesley Thomas, *James Freeman Clarke: Apostle of German Culture to America,* Boston. 1949.

*Anglo-German and American-German Crosscurrents,* ed. Philip Allison

Shelley, Arthur O. Lewis, Jr., and William W. Betts, Jr., Chapel Hill, N.C., 1957, seven essays by the editors and others, is the first volume of the Penn State Project on Anglo-German and American-German Literary and Cultural Relations.

Frederic Klees, *The Pennsylvania Dutch,* New York, 1950, is a good introduction for the general reader.

## 294. BIBLIOGRAPHY

Henry A. Pochmann, comp., and Arthur R. Schultz, ed., *Bibliography of German Culture in America to 1940,* Madison, Wis., 1953, is a compilation of over 12,000 entries.

## 296. *FRENCH*

### BIBLIOGRAPHY

Adrian H. Jaffe compiled *Bibliography of French Literature in American Magazines in the 18th Century,* East Lansing, Mich., 1951. Henry Putney Beers, *The French in North America: A Bibliographical Guide to French Archives, Reproductions, and Research Missions,* Baton Rouge, 1957, is also a history of the principal depositories in France of material relating to the United States.

## 297. *SPANISH AND ITALIAN*

Stanley T. Williams, *The Spanish Background of American Literature,* 2 vols., New Haven, 1955, is a much-needed study of the influence of Spain in the Americas from 1607–1950. See also Irving A. Leonard, *Books of the Brave: Being an Account of Books and of Men in the Spanish Conquest and Settlement of the Sixteenth-Century New World,* Cambridge, Mass., 1949.

More strictly historical treatments are C. H. Haring, *The Spanish Empire in America,* New York, 1947; Carey McWilliams, *North from Mexico: The Spanish-Speaking People of the United States,* New York, 1949; and Lewis Hanke, *The Spanish Struggle for Justice in the Conquest of America,* Philadelphia, 1949.

Olga Peragallo, *Italian-American Authors and Their Contribution to American Literature,* ed. Anita Peragallo, New York, 1949, contains sixty bio-bibliographical sketches. Lawrence Frank Pisani, *The Italian in America: A Social Study and History,* New York, 1957, is a general survey with descriptive bibliography.

## 298. *SCANDINAVIAN*

NORWEGIAN

Studies of Norwegian immigration are Theodore C. Blegen, *Grass Roots History*, Minneapolis, 1947, *passim*, and Leola Nelson Bergmann, *Americans from Norway*, Philadelphia, 1950. Theodore C. Blegen edited *Land of Their Choice: The Immigrants Write Home*, Minneapolis, 1955, a collection of Norwegian immigrant letters from 1820–1870. See also Einar Haugen, *The Norwegian Language in America: A Study in Bilingual Behavior*, 2 vols., Philadelphia, 1953.

### 299. SWEDISH

Swedish immigration is studied in Adolph B. Benson and Naboth Hadin, *Americans from Sweden*, Philadelphia, 1950, and Eric W. Fleisher and Jörgen Weibull, *Viking Times to Modern: The Story of Swedish Exploring and Settlement in America . . .* , Minneapolis, 1953.

A treatment of Swedish drama in America is Henriette C. K. Naeseth, *The Swedish Theatre of Chicago, 1868–1950*, Rock Island, Ill., 1951.

A useful bibliography is O. Fritiof Ander, ed., *The Cultural Heritage of the Swedish Immigrant: Selected References*, Rock Island, Ill., 1956.

## 300. *JEWISH: YIDDISH AND HEBREW*

The first volumes of the Library of Jewish Classics are Jacob S. Minkin, *The World of Moses Maimonides*, New York, 1957, and *In This World and the Next: Selected Writings by I. L. Peretz*, trans. Mosche Spiegel, New York, 1958.

General histories include Lee M. Friedman, *Pilgrims in a New Land*, Philadelphia, 1948; Anita Libman Lebeson, *Pilgrim People*, New York, 1950; Oscar Handlin, *Adventure in Freedom: Three Hundred Years of Jewish Life in America*, New York, 1954; and Rufus Learsi (Israel Goldberg), *The Jews in America: A History*, Cleveland, 1954. More specialized studies are Albert I. Gordon, *Jews in Transition*, Minneapolis, 1949; Morris U. Schappes, ed., *A Documentary History of the Jews in the United States, 1654–1875*, New York, 1950, 159 documents, some published here for the first time, accompanied by notes with a Marxist bias; Jacob Rader Marcus, *Early American Jewry* [1649–1794], 2 vols., Philadelphia, 1951–1952; *idem, Memoirs of American Jews, 1775–1865*, 3 vols., Philadelphia, 1955–1956; Eric E. Hirshler, *Jews from Germany in the United States*, New York, 1955; and Theodore Friedman and Robert Gordis, eds., *Jewish Life in America*, New York, 1955, 18 essays by various hands.

Moses Rischin prepared *An Inventory of American Jewish History,* Cambridge, Mass., 1954. For further bibliography see these periodicals: *Publications of the American Jewish Historical Society* (1893–current), *The American Jewish Yearbook* (1899–current), *The Menorah Journal* (1915–current), *Jewish Social Studies* (1939–current), *Commentary* (1945–current), and *The American Jewish Archives* (1948–current).

## 303. MEXICAN AND LATIN AMERICAN

Three historical-political studies by Arthur P. Whitaker are *The United States and South America,* Cambridge, Mass., 1948; *The Western Hemisphere Idea: Its Rise and Decline,* Ithaca, 1954; and *The United States and Argentina,* Cambridge, Mass., 1954.

## 303. ORIENTAL

### CHINESE

Francis L. K. Hau, *Americans and Chinese: Two Ways of Life,* New York, 1953, is a comparative study from an anthopological approach which considers literary causes and effects.

### 303. JAPANESE

A much-needed literary history is Earl Miner, *The Japanese Tradition in British and American Literature,* Princeton, 1958. Two social studies are Bradford Smith, *Americans from Japan,* Philadelphia, 1948, and Morton Grodzins, *Americans Betrayed: Politics and the Japanese Evacuation,* Chicago, 1949.

## 304. REGIONALISM AND LOCAL COLOR

## GENERAL STUDIES

Merrill Jensen edited *Regionalism in America,* Madison, Wis., 1951, a symposium. From French Canada comes one of the first full-scale analyses of our regional fiction: Harry Bernard, *Le Roman Régionaliste aux Etats-Unis, 1913–1940,* Montreal, 1949.

Within the scope of this supplement, individual regions and states cannot be given full treatment bibliographically. The listing which follows is *highly selective;* descriptions are omitted.

## 305. *NEW ENGLAND*

Henry Beston, ed., *White Pine and Blue Water: A State of Maine Reader,* New York, 1950; Robert N. Linscott, ed., *State of Mind: A Boston Reader,* New York, 1948.

## 307. *NEW YORK TO DELAWARE*

John A. Kouwenhoven, ed., *The Columbia Historical Portrait of New York* [City], New York, 1953.

## 308. *THE SOUTH AND DEEP SOUTH*

Jay B. Hubbell, *The South in American Literature, 1607–1900,* Durham, N.C., 1954; Louis D. Rubin, Jr., and Robert D. Jacobs, eds., *Southern Renascence: The Literature of the Modern South,* Baltimore, 1953; Donald Davidson, *Southern Writers in the Modern World,* Athens, Ga., 1958; Louis D. Rubin, Jr., and James Jackson Kilpatrick, eds., *The Lasting South: Fourteen Southerners Look at Their Home,* Chicago, 1957; Willard Thorp, ed., *A Southern Reader,* New York, 1955; Richard Walser, ed., *North Carolina in the Short Story,* Chapel Hill, N.C., 1948; *idem, North Carolina Poetry,* rev. ed., Chapel Hill, 1951; *idem, North Carolina Drama,* Richmond, 1956; Etolia S. Basso, ed., *The World of Jackson Square: A New Orleans Reader,* New York, 1948.

## 316. *THE MIDDLE WEST*

R. E. Banta, *Indiana Authors and Their Books, 1816–1916,* Crawfordsville, Ind., 1949; A. J. Liebling, *Chicago: The Second City,* New York, 1952; Elijah L. Jacobs and Forrest E. Wolverton, *Missouri Writers: A Literary History of Missouri, 1780–1955,* St. Louis, 1955.

## 322. *THE SOUTHWEST*

T. M. Pearce and A. P. Thomason, eds., *Southwesterners Write: The American Southwest in Stories and Articles by Thirty-Two Contributors,* Albuquerque, 1946; J. Frank Dobie, *Guide to Life and Literature of the Southwest,* rev. ed., Dallas, 1952; Walter S. Campbell (Stanley Vestal),

*The Book Lover's Southwest: A Guide to Good Reading,* Norman, Okla., 1955.

### 323. THE PACIFIC NORTHWEST

V. L. O. Chittick, *Northwest Harvest: A Regional Stock-Taking,* New York, 1948; Sidney Warren, *Farthest Frontier: The Pacific Northwest,* New York, 1949.

### 323. CALIFORNIA AND THE FAR WEST

Levette J. Davidson, ed., *Poems of the Old West: A Rocky Mountain Anthology,* Denver, Colo., 1951; Franklin Walker, *A Literary History of Southern California,* Berkeley, 1950; Ramon F. Adams, comp., *Six-Guns and Saddle Leather: A Bibliography of Books and Pamphlets on Western Outlaws and Gunmen,* Norman, Okla., 1954.

## SCIENCE AND SOCIAL CRITICISM

### 329. SOCIAL DARWINISM AND THE BACKGROUND OF NATURALISM IN LITERATURE
SECONDARY STUDIES

See Frederick W. Conner, *Cosmic Optimism: A Study of the Interpretation of Evolution by American Poets from Emerson to Robinson,* Gainesville, Fla., 1949, and Stow Persons, ed., *Evolutionary Thought in America,* New Haven, 1950, a collection of essays by various hands.

Basic studies of naturalism in the novel are Lars Åhnebrink, *The Beginnings of Naturalism in American Fiction,* Upsala, Sweden, 1950, and Charles Child Walcutt, *American Literary Naturalism, A Divided Stream,* Minneapolis, 1956.

### 334. THE MACHINE AGE AND THE LITERATURE OF EXPOSURE
SECONDARY STUDIES

See pp. 24–25 above for studies of the political and economic novel.

**335.** LITERATURE OF THE MUCKRAKING MOVEMENT

David Graham Phillips, *The Treason of the Senate,* New York, 1953, is a reprinting of the series of articles which were originally published in *Cosmopolitan Magazine* between March and November, 1906.

Louis Filler, *Crusades for American Liberalism,* New York, 1950, is a reissue, with a new introduction, of a valuable study of the muckraking period.

## 344. SLAVERY AND CONFLICT

REMINISCENCES

Arthur M. Schlesinger edited Frederick Law Olmsted's 1861 volume, *The Cotton Kingdom: A Traveller's Observations on Cotton and Slavery in the American Slave States,* New York, 1953.

**345.** SOCIAL STUDIES

A general history is Kenneth M. Stampp, *The Peculiar Institution: Slavery in the Ante-Bellum South,* New York, 1956. More specialized studies are Russel B. Nye, *Fettered Freedom: Civil Liberties and the Slavery Controversy, 1830–1860,* East Lansing, Mich., 1949; James Benson Sellers, *Slavery in Alabama,* University, Ala., 1950; T. E. Drake, *Quakers and Slavery in America,* New Haven, 1950; Vincent C. Hopkins, *Dred Scott's Case,* New York, 1951; and W. D. Postell, *The Health of Slaves on Southern Plantations,* Baton Rouge, 1951.

## 346. TRANSCENDENTALISM AND UTOPIAN VENTURES

A valuable anthology of source material until now not easily available is Perry Miller, *The Transcendentalists,* Cambridge, Mass., 1950. Three studies are Henry A. Pochmann, *New England Transcendentalism and St. Louis Hegelianism,* Philadelphia, 1948; F. DeWolfe Miller, *Christopher Pearce Cranch and His Caricatures of New England Transcendentalism,* Cambridge, Mass., 1951; and Stanley M. Vogel, *German Literary Influences on the American Transcendentalists,* New Haven, 1955.

Two surveys of Utopian ventures are Vernon L. Parrington, Jr., *American Dreams: A Study of American Utopias,* Providence, 1947, and Mark Holloway, *Heavens on Earth: Utopian Communities in America, 1680–1880,* New York, 1951. A more specific study is Arthur Eugene Bestor, Jr.,

*Backwoods Utopias: The Sectarian and Owenite Phases of Communitarian Socialism in America, 1663-1829,* Philadelphia, 1950.

## 356. AMERICAN WRITERS AND BOOKS ABROAD

European-American intellectual relations are discussed in Philip Rahv, ed., *Discovery of Europe: The Story of American Experience in the Old World,* Boston, 1947; Michael Kraus, *The Atlantic Civilization: Eighteenth-Century Origins,* Ithaca, 1949; and Margaret Denny and William H. Gilman, eds., *The American Writer and the European Tradition,* Minneapolis, 1950. More specialized studies are Esther E. Brown, *The French Revolution and the American Man of Letters,* Columbia, Mo., 1951, and William L. Sachse, *The Colonial American in Britain,* Madison, Wis., 1956.

The impact of American writers, travelers, and culture on Europe has been discussed, in recent years, in a wide variety of ways. This listing is only an introduction to the bibliography:

*General:* Henry Steele Commager, ed., *America in Perspective: The United States Through Foreign Eyes,* New York, 1947, essays by 37 authors from Crèvecoeur to Madariaga; Halvdan Koht, *The American Spirit in Europe: A Survey of Transatlantic Influences,* Philadelphia, 1949; Bertrand Russell, John Lehmann, and others, *The Impact of America on European Culture,* Boston, 1951; *America and the Mind of Europe,* New York, 1952, essays by various hands, all from the *Saturday Review of Literature,* with an introduction by Lewis Galantière; André Siegfried, *America at Mid-Century,* trans. Margaret Ledésert, New York, 1955; and Sigmund Skard, *American Studies in Europe,* 2 vols., Philadelphia, 1958.

*British:* Allan Nevins, ed., *America Through British Eyes,* New York, 1948, and Allan Angoff, ed., *American Writing Today,* New York, 1957, a symposium which first appeared in the London *Times Literary Supplement.*

*French:* Cyrille Arnavon, *Les Lettres Américaines devant la Critique Française, 1887-1917,* Paris, 1951, and Durand Echeverria, *Mirage in the West: A History of the French Image of American Society to 1815,* Princeton, 1957.

*German:* Richard Mönnig, *Amerika und England im Deutschen, Österreichischen und Schweizerischen Schrifttum der Jahre 1945-1949: Eine Bibliographie,* Stuttgart, 1951, a listing of 4406 titles; Paul Hartig, ed., *Amerikakunde,* 2d ed., Frankfurt am Main, 1952, twelve German scholars writing a guide to American cultural history; and Kaspar T. Locher, *German Histories of American Literature,* Chicago, 1955, a chronological description covering the years 1800-1950, in microcard edition.

*Swiss:* Emil Graf, *Die Aufnahme der Englischen und Amerikanischen Literatur in der Deutschen Schweiz von 1800–1830,* Zürich, 1951.

*Swedish:* Carl L. Anderson, *The Swedish Acceptance of American Literature,* Philadelphia, 1957.

*Japanese:* Takashi Sugiki, *A Backward Glance at the Study of American Literature in Japan,* Tokyo, 1952, a bibliographical survey of the last hundred years.

# BIBLIOGRAPHIES:
# INDIVIDUAL AUTHORS

# HENRY (BROOKS) ADAMS

**374.** EDITED TEXTS AND REPRINTS

There is still no collected edition of Adams' work. The Cornell University Press reprinted the first six chapters of Adams' *History of the United States of America During the Administration of Thomas Jefferson* under the title *The United States in 1800*, Ithaca, 1955. From the same press is *Chapters of Erie*, Ithaca, 1956, containing "A Chapter of Erie" (Charles Francis Adams, Jr.), "The New York Gold Conspiracy" (Henry Adams), and "An Erie Raid" (Charles Francis Adams, Jr.).

Elizabeth Stevenson edited, with an introduction, *A Henry Adams Reader*, New York, 1958.

Newton Arvin edited *The Selected Letters of Henry Adams*, New York, 1951. See also Samuel Eliot Morison, ed., "A Letter and a Few Reminiscences of Henry Adams," *NEQ*, XXVII (1954), 95-97.

**375.** BIOGRAPHY AND CRITICISM

Two biographies have appeared in recent years. Ernest Samuels' *The Young Henry Adams*, Cambridge, Mass., 1948 (taking him through the apprentice years, from the Harvard of 1854 to the Washington of 1877), is followed by *Henry Adams: The Middle Years, 1877-1891*, Cambridge, Mass., 1958. Elizabeth Stevenson, *Henry Adams, A Biography*, New York, 1955, is a full-length portrait.

Two studies combining biography with extensive critical analysis are Robert A. Hume, *Runaway Star: An Appreciation of Henry Adams*, Ithaca, 1951, and J. C. Levenson, *The Mind and Art of Henry Adams*, Boston, 1957. Specialized studies are Max I. Baym, *The French Education of Henry Adams*, New York, 1951; William H. Jordy, *Henry Adams: Scientific Historian*, New Haven, 1952; and Henry Wasser, *The Scientific Thought of Henry Adams*, Thessaloniki, 1956. See also Thornton Anderson, *Brooks Adams: Constructive Conservative*, Ithaca, 1951; and Robert C. LeClair, *Three American Travellers in England: James Russell Lowell, Henry Adams, Henry James*, Philadelphia, 1954.

Briefer studies are R. F. Miller, "Henry Adams and the Influence of Woman," *AL*, XVIII (1947), 291-298; Charles I. Glicksberg, "Henry Adams and the Modern Spirit," *DR*, XXVII (1947), 299-309; Charles I. Glicksberg, "Henry Adams the Journalist," *NEQ*, XXI (1948), 232-236; Evelyn Page, "The Diary and the Public Man," *NEQ*, XXII (1949), 147-172; John

Lydenberg, "Henry Adams and Lincoln Steffens," *SAQ*, XLVIII (1949), 42–64; Herbert Edwards, "Henry Adams: Politician and Statesman," *NEQ*, XXII (1949), 49–60; W. R. Taylor, "Historical Bifocals on the Year 1800," *NEQ*, XXIII (1950), 172–186; Richard Greenleaf, "History, Marxism and Henry Adams," *SciS*, XV (1951), 193–208; M. W. Hess, "The Atomic Age and Henry Adams," *CathW*, CLXXII (1951), 256–263; William Jordy, "Henry Adams and Francis Parkman," *AQ*, III (1951), 52–68.

More recent studies are R. P. Blackmur, "The Virgin and the Dynamo," *Mag. of Art*, XLV (Apr., 1952), 147–153; *idem*, "Harmony of True Liberalism: Henry Adams' *Mont-Saint-Michel and Chartres*," *SR*, LX (1952), 1–27; Florence M. Burns, "Henry Adams's Appreciation of Nature," *NEQ*, XXVI (1953), 237–243; Vern Wagner, "The Lotus of Henry Adams," *NEQ*, XXVII (1954), 75–94; R. P. Blackmur, "Adams Goes to School: I. The Problem Laid Out," *KR*, XVII (1955), 597–623; Benjamin M. Price, "That Baffling Diary," *SAQ*, LIV (1955), 56–64; Warner B. Berthoff and David Bonnell Green, "Henry Adams and Wayne MacVeagh," *PMHB*, LXXX (1956), 493–512; Edward N. Saveth, "The Heroines of Henry Adams," *AQ*, VIII (1956), 231–242; and Henry S. Kariel, "The Limits of Social Science: Henry Adams' Quest for Order," *Am Pol Sci Rev*, L (1956), 1074–1092.

**377. BIBLIOGRAPHY**

There are valuable check lists and secondary bibliography in the volumes by Baym, Jordy, Samuels, and Stevenson above. See also Jacob Blanck's *Bibliography of American Literature*, New Haven, 1955, I, 1–11.

# JOHN ADAMS

**378. COLLECTED WORKS**

In October, 1954, the Adams Manuscript Trust announced the opening to the public of "the papers of President John Adams, President John Quincy Adams, and Charles Francis Adams, together with the papers of their wives and children," an estimated 300,000 pages of material dated 1630–1920. A plan for publication, under the editorship of Lyman H. Butterfield, was arranged by the Adams Manuscript Trust (at that time the owner), the Massachusetts Historical Society (the sponsor of the edition and, since 1956, the owner of the papers), the Harvard University Press (the publisher), and Time, Inc. (the donor of funds). The first stage, a microfilm edition of the entire contents of the family archive, was begun in 1954 and is still in course of publication; it is copyrighted by the Adams Manuscript Trust but is unrestrictedly free for research purposes. Later stages will be a multiple series of volumes to be published by the Harvard University Press and a serial publication in *Life* of excerpts which have general public interest. See Walter Muir Whitehill, "The Adams Papers: The Record of Two Centuries of a Harvard Family," *Harvard Alumni Bul.*, LVII (Oct. 23, 1954), 117–119, 123–124; the illustrated article in *Life*, XXXVII (Oct. 25, 1954), 39–41; Lyman H. Butterfield, "The Adams Papers," *Daedalus*, LXXXVI (May, 1955), 62–71; and, for a more extensive account, *idem*, "The Papers of the Adams Family: Some Account of Their History," *PMHS*, LXXI (1953–57), 329–356.

Gleanings of John and Abigail Adams correspondence are in William Van Lennep, ed., "John Adams to a Young Playwright: An Unpublished Letter to Samuel Judah," *HLB*, I (1947), 117–118; Stewart Mitchell, ed., *New Letters of Abigail Adams, 1788–1801*, Boston, 1947; Lyman H. Butterfield, "The Jefferson-Adams Correspondence in the Adams Manuscript Trust," *LCQJ*, V (Feb., 1948), 3–6; Charles Warren, "The Doctored Letters of John Adams," *PMHS*, LXVIII (1952), 160–170; and Howard C. Rice, Jr., ed., *The Adams Family in Auteuil, 1784–1785; As Told in the Letters of Abigail Adams*, Boston, 1956.

BIOGRAPHY AND CRITICISM

Two biographies are Catherine Drinker Bowen, *John Adams and the American Revolution*, Boston, 1950, and Alfred Iacuzzi, *John Adams, Scholar*, New York, 1952. Specialized studies are Zoltán Haraszti, *John Adams and the Prophets of Progress*, Cambridge, Mass., 1952; Manning Julian Dauer, *The Adams Federalists*, Baltimore, 1953; and Stephen G. Kurtz, *The Presidency of John Adams*, New York, 1957.

See also Janet Whitney, *Abigail Adams*, Boston, 1947, *passim*; John C. Miller, *Crisis in Freedom: The Alien and Sedition Acts*, Boston, 1951; James Morton Smith, *Freedom's Fetters: The Alien and Sedition Laws and American Civil Liberties*, Ithaca, 1956; and John Dos Passos, *The Men Who Made the Nation*, New York, 1957. Briefer studies are B. Knollenberg, "John Adams, Knox, and Washington," *PAAS*, LVI (1946), 207–238; R. Von Abele, "The World of John Adams," *Am Merc*, LXVII (July, 1948), 66–73; Lyman H. Butterfield, "The Dream of Benjamin Rush: The Reconciliation of John Adams and Thomas Jefferson," *YR*, XL (1950), 297–319; George Peek, Jr., "John Adams on the Nature of Man and Government," *MAQR*, LVIII (Dec., 1951), 70–76; Adrienne Koch, "Hamilton, Adams, and the Pursuit of Power," *RPol*, XVI (Jan., 1954), 37–66; J. Charles, "Adams and Jefferson: The Origins of the American Party System," *WMQ*, XII (1955), 410–430; D. H. Stewart and G. P. Clark, "Misanthrope or Humanitarian? John Adams in Retirement," *NEQ*, XXVIII (1955), 216–236; and C. Rossiter, "The Legacy of John Adams," *YR*, XLVI (1957), 528–550.

# GEORGE ADE

**380. CRITICISM**

Recent critical studies are J. A. Clark, "Ade's Fables in Slang: An Appreciation," *SAQ*, XLVI (1947), 537–544; Bergen Evans, "George Ade, Rustic Humorist," *Am Merc*, LXX (1950), 321–329; and Fred C. Kelly, "George Ade, Master of Warm-hearted Satire," *MAQR*, LXI (1955), 156–160.

# CONRAD (POTTER) AIKEN

**380. SEPARATE WORKS**

*The Divine Pilgrim*, 1949; *Skylight One: Fifteen Poems*, 1949; *The Short Stories of Conrad Aiken*, 1950; *Ushant: An Essay*, 1952; *Collected Poems*, 1953; *A Letter from Li Po and Other Poems*, 1955; *Mr. Arcularis: A Play*, 1957; *Sheepfold Hill: Fifteen Poems*, 1958; *Collected Criticism . . . from 1916 to the Present: A Reviewer's ABC* (ed. Rufus A. Blanshard), 1958.

Aiken edited the following: *Modern American Poets*, London, 1922 (New York, 1927; enlarged as *Twentieth-Century American Poetry*, New York, 1944); *Emily Dickinson: Selected Poems*, London, 1924 (New York, 1948); *American Poetry, 1671–1928*, New York, 1929 (enlarged as *A Comprehensive Anthology of American Poetry*, New York, 1944); and *An Anthology of Famous English and American Poetry* (with William Rose Benét), New York, 1945.

**381. BIOGRAPHY AND CRITICISM**

*Wake 11* (New York, 1952) is a Conrad Aiken number. In addition to nine poems, a fragment from *Ushant*, and a review (reprinted) of Eliot's *The Waste Land*, all by Aiken, it includes ten articles, chiefly critical, by various hands and a check list (see below).

Critical estimates are Dan G. Hoffman, "Poetic Symbols from the Public Domain," *SFQ*, XII (1948), 293–297; C. S. Brown, "Music and Conrad Aiken," *GaR*, II (1948), 40–51; Eric W. Carlson, "The Range of Symbolism in Poetry," *SAQ*, XLVIII (1949), 442–451; S. M. Fitzgerald, "Aiken's Search for Self-Awareness," *Commonweal*, LVII (Nov. 14, 1952), 143–146; R. P. Blackmur, "Conrad Aiken: The Poet," *Atl*, CXCII (Dec., 1953), 77–82; Edward Dahlberg, "A Long Lotus Sleep," *Poetry*, LXXXI (1953), 313–321; Joseph Warren Beach, "Conrad Aiken and T. S. Eliot: Echoes and Overtones," *PMLA*, LXIX (1954), 753–762; Calvin S. Brown, "The Poetry of Conrad Aiken," *GaR*, VIII (1954), 315–322; Frederick L. Gwynn, "The Functional Allusions in Conrad Aiken's *Mr. Arcularis*," *TCL*, II (Apr.,

1956), 21–25; Seymour L. Gross, "The Reflection of Poe in Conrad Aiken's 'Strange Moonlight,'" *MLN*, LXXII (1957), 185–189; and Rufus A. Blanchard, "Metamorphosis of a Dream," *SR*, LXV (1957).

For a listing of explications of individual poems see George Arms and Joseph M. Kuntz, *Poetry Explication*, New York, 1950, p. 25.

The most recent check lists are R. W. Stallman, "Annotated Checklist on Conrad Aiken: A Critical Study," *Wake 11*, New York, 1952, pp. 114–121, and Allen Tate, *Sixty American Poets, 1896–1944*, rev. ed., Washington, 1954, pp. 2–5.


## AMOS BRONSON ALCOTT

### 382. BIOGRAPHY AND CRITICISM

Recent studies are David Mead, "Some Ohio Conversations of Amos Bronson Alcott," *NEQ*, XXII (1949), 358–372; Kurt F. Leidecker, "Amos Bronson Alcott and the Concord School of Philosophy," *Personalist*, XXXIII (1952), 242–256; Sherman Paul, "Alcott's Search for the Child," *BPLQ*, IV (1952), 88–96; John B. Wilson, "Bronson Alcott, Platonist or Pestalozzian?" *SchS*, LXXXI (Feb. 19, 1955), 49–53; John C. Broderick, "Bronson Alcott's 'Concord Book,'" *NEQ*, XXIX (1956), 365–380; *idem*, "Thoreau, Alcott, and the Poll Tax," *SP*, LIII (1956), 612–626.

Of bibliographical interest are Shirley W. Dinwiddie and Richard L. Herrnstadt, "Amos Bronson Alcott: A Bibliography," *BB*, XXI (1954), 64–67, 92–96; and Jacob Blanck, *Bibliography of American Literature*, New Haven, 1955, I, 20–26.


## LOUISA MAY ALCOTT

### 383. BIOGRAPHY AND CRITICISM

A documented, full-length study is Madeleine B. Stern, *Louisa May Alcott*, Norman, Okla., 1950. A more recent biography is Marjorie Worthington, *Miss Alcott of Concord*, New York, 1958. Briefer studies are W. P. Sears, Jr., "Educational Theories of Louisa May Alcott," *DR*, XXVII (1947), 327–334; Madeleine B. Stern, "Louisa's *Wonder Book*: A Newly Discovered Alcott Juvenile," *AL*, XXVI (1954), 384–390; and Eleanor Perényi, "Dear Louisa," *Harper's*, CCXI (Oct., 1955), 69–72.

### 384. BIBLIOGRAPHY

The most recent listing is Jacob Blanck, *Bibliography of American Literature*, New Haven, 1955, I, 27–45.

## THOMAS BAILEY ALDRICH

**384.** BIOGRAPHY AND CRITICISM

Samuel Sloan Duryee, Jr., *Thomas Bailey Aldrich (1836–1907): Inspired Poet of the Piscataqua,* New York, 1951, is an address printed for The Newcomen Society of England in North America.

Two critical-bibliographical studies are G. J. L. Gomme, "T. B. Aldrich and 'Household Words,'" *PBSA,* XLII (1948), 70–72, and Richard Cary, "Thomas Bailey Aldrich Writes to an English Eccentric," *CLQ,* Series III (1954), 244–253.

A full listing is Jacob Blanck, *Bibliography of American Literature,* New Haven, 1955, I, 46–77.

## MAXWELL ANDERSON

**386.** SEPARATE WORKS *

PLAYS: *Anne of the Thousand Days,* 1948; *Lost in the Stars* (1949), 1950; *Barefoot in Athens,* 1951; *The Bad Seed* (1954), 1955; *The Day the Money Stopped* (with Brendan Gill) (1958); *The Golden Six* (1958).

**387.** BIOGRAPHY AND CRITICISM

The first full-length study is Mabel Driscoll Bailey, *Maxwell Anderson: The Playwright as Prophet,* New York, 1957.

Briefer studies are Pauline Steiner and Horst Frenz, "Anderson and Stallings' *What Price Glory?* and Carl Zuckmayer's *Rivalen,*" *Ger. Quar,* XX (1947), 239–251; Moody E. Prior, *The Language of Tragedy,* New York, 1947, *passim;* Patrick J. Rice, "Maxwell Anderson and the Eternal Dream," *CathW,* CLXXVII (1953), 364–370; Jacob H. Adler, "Shakespeare in *Winterset,*" *ETJ,* VI (1954), 241–248; Robert E. Sherwood, "'White Desert' to 'Bad Seed,'" *TArts,* XXXIX (March, 1955), 28–29, 93; Dale Riepe, "The Philosophy of Maxwell Anderson," *NDQ,* XXIV (Spring, 1956), 45–50; and Robert C. Roby, "Two Worlds: Maxwell Anderson's *Winterset,*" *CE,* XVIII (1957), 195–202.

The *North Dakota Quarterly,* XXV (Spring, 1957), is a special Maxwell Anderson issue.

---

* Dates in parentheses are of production when it differs from publication or when publication has not occurred.

# SHERWOOD ANDERSON

**388.** CORRESPONDENCE

Howard Mumford Jones and Walter B. Rideout edited *Letters of Sherwood Anderson,* Boston, 1953, from the collection in the Newberry Library, Chicago.

REPRINTS

The *Sherwood Anderson Reader* was edited, with an introduction. by Paul Rosenfeld, Boston, 1947.

BIOGRAPHY AND CRITICISM

Two recent studies are James E. Schevill, *Sherwood Anderson, His Life and Work,* Denver, 1951, and Irving Howe, *Sherwood Anderson,* New York, 1951. *Newberry Library Bulletin,* Second Ser., No. 2 (Dec., 1948), is a Sherwood Anderson memorial number, including a description of the Anderson papers now deposited in the library.

Briefer estimates are Paul Rosenfeld, "Sherwood Anderson's Work," *Anglica,* I (Apr.–June, 1946), 66–88; W. A. Sutton, "Sherwood Anderson: The Clyde Years," *NOQ,* XIX (July, 1947), 99–114; *idem,* "Sherwood Anderson: The Spanish-American War Years," *ibid.,* XX (Jan., 1948), 20–36; *idem,* "Sherwood Anderson: The Cleveland Year, 1906-1907," *ibid.,* XXII (Winter, 1949–50), 39–44; *idem,* "Sherwood Anderson: The Advertising Years, 1900-1906," *ibid.,* XXII (Summer, 1950), 120–157; John T. Flanagan, "The Permanence of Sherwood Anderson," *SWR,* XXXV (1950), 170–177; George Schloss, "Sherwood Anderson," *HudR,* IV (1951), 477–480; Brom Weber, "Anderson and 'The Essence of Things,'" *SR,* LIX (1951), 678–692; William L. Phillips, "How Sherwood Anderson Wrote *Winesburg, Ohio,*" *AL,* XXIII (1951), 7–30; Charles C. Walcutt, "Sherwood Anderson: Impressionism and the Buried Life," *SR,* LX (1952), 28–47; William Faulkner, "Sherwood Anderson: An Appreciation," *Atl,* CXCI (June, 1953), 27–29; A. Chapman, "Sherwood Anderson and Eduardo Mallea," *PMLA,* LXIX (1954), 34–45; James T. Farrell, "A Memoir on Sherwood Anderson," *Perspective,* VII (Summer, 1954), 83–88; Simon O. Lesser, "The Image of the Father: A Reading of 'My Kinsman, Major Molineux' and 'I Want to Know Why,'" *PR,* XXII (1955), 370–390; John T. Flanagan, "Hemingway's Debt to Sherwood Anderson," *JEGP,* LIV (1955), 507–520; Bernard Raymund, "The Grammar of Not-Reason: Sherwood Anderson," *ArQ,* XII (1956), 48–60, 137–148; Jarvis Thurston, "Anderson and *Winesburg:* Mysticism and Craft," *Accent,* XVI (1956), 107–128; John J. Mahoney, "An Analysis of *Winesburg, Ohio,*" *JAAC,* XV (1956).

245–252; and Earl Hilton, "Sherwood Anderson and 'Heroic Vitalism,'" *NOQ,* XXIX (1957), 97–107.

A selective bibliography is R. D. Gozzi, "A Bibliography of Sherwood Anderson's Contributions to Periodicals," *Newberry Lib. Bul.,* Second Ser., No. 2 (Dec., 1948), 71–82.

# SHOLEM ASCH
### d. 1957

**389.** SEPARATE WORKS IN ENGLISH

*Tales of My People,* 1948; *Mary,* 1949; *Moses,* 1951; *A Passage in the Night,* 1953; *The Prophet,* 1955.

*Salvation,* translated by Willa and Edwin Muir (1934), was completely revised and enlarged, New York, 1951.

**390.** BIOGRAPHY AND CRITICISM

Recent studies are Oscar Cargill, "Sholem Asch: Still Immigrant and Alien," *CE,* XII (1950), 67–74; and R. W. George, "Sholem Asch—Man of Letters and Prophet," *Religion in Life,* XX (1950), 106–113.

Of bibliographical interest is *Catalogue of Hebrew and Yiddish Manuscripts and Books from the Library of Sholem Asch Presented to Yale University by Louis M. Rabinowitz,* comp. Leon Nemoy, with an introductory essay by Sholem Asch, New Haven, 1945.

# JOHN JAMES AUDUBON

**390.** COLLECTED WORKS

Alice Ford compiled and edited *Audubon's Butterflies, Moths, and Other Studies,* New York, 1952, the first publication of a heretofore unknown Audubon sketchbook of fifteen pages of insect and reptile drawings.

See also H. M. Hunter, "Unpublished Audubon," *Nat. Hist.,* LIX (1950), 285.

**391.** EDITED TEXTS AND REPRINTS

*Audubon's Animals: The Quadrupeds of North America,* ed. Alice Ford, New York, 1951, is a reprinting of the plates of *The Vivaparous Quadrupeds of North America* (1845–1848) and excerpts from the text. Alice Ford also edited *The Bird Biographies of John James Audubon,* New York, 1957, a new edition of *Ornithological Biography* (1831–1839) which deletes some of the original text and adds several passages from the seven-volume octavo edition (1840–1844) of Audubon's great folio, *The Birds of America.*

BIOGRAPHY AND CRITICISM

George Clyde Fisher, *The Life of Audubon*, New York, 1949, is illustrated with paintings and drawings by Audubon from the permanent collection of the American Museum of Natural History.

John Francis McDermott edited *Up the Missouri with Audubon: The [1843] Journal of Edward Harris*, Norman, Okla., 1951, making this journal available in its entirety for the first time.

Briefer studies are J. E. Graustein, "Audubon and Nuttall," *Sci Mo*, LXXIV (1952), 84–90; and Malcolm Bell, Jr., "Eye Witnesses to a Vanished America," *GaR*, X (1956), 13–23.

The articles on Audubon and his work in *Audubon Magazine* (formerly *Bird Lore*, 1899–current) are too numerous to list separately here.

**392. BIBLIOGRAPHY**

Of bibliographical interest are these catalogues for centennial exhibits: *An Audubon Anthology . . . : An Exhibition, Princeton University Library . . .*, Princeton, 1950; *John J. Audubon Centennial Exhibition*, Lyman Allyn Museum, New London, Conn., 1951; and three *Audubon Centennial Exhibitions*, National Audubon Society, New York City, 1951.

## IRVING BABBITT

**392. BIOGRAPHY AND CRITICISM**

Three recent studies are Russell Kirk, "The Conservative Humanism of Irving Babbitt," *PrS*, XXVI (1952), 245–255; L. J. A. Mercier, "Was Irving Babbitt a Naturalist?" *NSch*, XXVII (Jan., 1953), 39–71; and Folke Leander, "Irving Babbitt and Benedetto Croce: The Philosophical Basis of the New Humanism in American Criticism," *Göteborgs Studier I: Litteraturhistoria* (1954), pp. 147–168.

## GEORGE BANCROFT

**394. BIOGRAPHY AND CRITICISM**

Three recent estimates are C. Carroll Hollis, "Brownson on George Bancroft," *SAQ*, XLIX (1950), 42–52; John W. Rathburn, "George Bancroft on Man and History," *TWASAL*, XLIII (1954), 51–73; and Ralph M. Alderman, "The Case of James Cook: A Study of Political Influence in 1840," *EIHC*, XCII (1956), 59–67.

A full bibliographical listing is in Jacob Blanck, *Bibliography of American Literature*, New Haven, 1955, I, 118–138.

# JOEL BARLOW

**396.** BIOGRAPHY AND CRITICISM

The first full-length biography is James Woodress, *A Yankee's Odyssey: The Life of Joel Barlow*, Philadelphia, 1958.

Critical studies are Joseph L. Blau, "Joel Barlow, Enlightened Religionist," *JHI*, X (1949), 430–444; and Merton A. Christensen, "Deism in Joel Barlow's Early Work: Heterodox Passages in *The Vision of Columbus*," *AL*, XXVII (1956), 509–520.

More specialized studies are Lewis Leary, "Joel Barlow and William Hayley: A Correspondence," *AL*, XXI (Nov., 1949), 325–334; Robert F. Durden, "Joel Barlow in the French Revolution," *WMQ*, VIII (1951), 327–354; and David V. Erdman, "William Blake's Debt to Joel Barlow," *AL*, XXVI (1954), 94–98.

**397.** BIBLIOGRAPHY

For a check list, see Jacob Blanck, *Bibliography of American Literature*, New Haven, 1955, I, 169–184.

# PHILIP BARRY
### d. 1949

**398.** SEPARATE WORKS

*Second Threshold* (with revisions by Robert E. Sherwood), 1951.

BIOGRAPHY AND CRITICISM

Gerald Hamm, *The Drama of Philip Barry* was published in Philadelphia, 1948. A recent brief critical study is Monroe Lippman, "Philip Barry and His Socio-Political Attitudes," *QJS*, XLII (1956), 151–156.

# JOHN AND WILLIAM BARTRAM

**399.** BIOGRAPHY AND CRITICISM

A biographical essay by a novelist is Josephine Herbst, *New Green World*, New York, 1954.

Briefer studies are Francis Harper, "William Bartram and the American Revolution," *PAPS*, XCVII (1953), 571–577; Richard M. Gummere, "William Bartram, a Classical Scientist," *CJ*, L (1955), 167–170; Francis D. West, "John Bartram and Slavery," *SCHM*, LVI (1955), 115–119; Malcolm Bell, Jr., "Eye Witnesses to a Vanished America," *GaR*, X (1956), 13–23;

Francis D. West, "John Bartram and the American Philosophical Society," *PH*, XXIII (1956), 463–466; Winifred Notman Prince, "John Bartram in the Cedar Swamps," *PMHB*, LXXXI (1957), 86–88; and Francis D. West, "Sweden Honors John Bartram," *ibid.*, LXXXI (1957), 88–90.

## HENRY WARD BEECHER

#### 400. BIOGRAPHY AND CRITICISM

A special study of five years of Beecher's life is Robert Shaplen, *Free Love and Heavenly Sinners: The Story of the Great Henry Ward Beecher Scandal*, New York, 1954.

Briefer studies are David Mead, "The Humiliation of Henry Ward Beecher in the West," *OSAHQ*, LVIII (1949), 94–100; and Marvin Felheim, "Beecher's Two Views of the Stage; or, The Theory and Practice of Henry Ward Beecher," *NEQ*, XXV (1952), 314–326.

## S(AMUEL) N(ATHANIEL) BEHRMAN

#### 401. SEPARATE WORKS *

*Dunnigan's Daughter* (1945), 1946; *Jane* (based on a Somerset Maugham story), 1952; *Fanny* (with Joshua Logan; based on the trilogy of Marcel Pagnol) (1954), 1955; *The Cold Wind and the Warm* (1958).

*Duveen*, 1952, is a biographical sketch of Lord Duveen; *The Worcester Account*, 1954, is autobiography.

#### BIOGRAPHY AND CRITICISM

A brief critical study is Charles Kaplan, "S. N. Behrman: The Quandary of the Comic Spirit," *CE*, XI (1950), 317–323.

## EDWARD BELLAMY

#### 402. EDITED TEXTS AND REPRINTS

Joseph Schiffman edited *Edward Bellamy: Selected Writings on Religion and Society*, New York, 1955.

#### BIOGRAPHY AND CRITICISM

Sylvia E. Bowman, *The Year 2000*, New York, 1958, is a critical biography of Bellamy.

Brief studies are Louis Filler, "Edward Bellamy and the Spiritual Un-

---

* Dates in parentheses are of production when it differs from publication or when publication has not occurred.

rest," *AJES*, VIII (1949), 239–249; Joseph Schiffman, "Edward Bellamy's Religious Thought," *PMLA*, LXVIII (1953), 716–732; George J. Becker, "Edward Bellamy: Utopia, American Plan," *AR*, XIV (1954), 181–194; Joseph Schiffman, "Edward Bellamy's Altruistic Man," *AQ*, VI (1954), 195–209; and Joseph L. Blau, "Bellamy's Religious Motivation for Social Reform," *Rev. Religion*, XXI (1957), 156–166.

The most recent bibliographical listing is Jacob Blanck, *Bibliography of American Literature*, New Haven, 1955, I, 192–196.

## STEPHEN VINCENT BENÉT

### 403. BIOGRAPHY AND CRITICISM

The first biography is Charles Fenton, *Stephen Vincent Benét: The Life and Times of an American Man of Letters, 1898–1943*, New York, 1958. Of biographical interest is "Epic on an American Theme: Stephen Vincent Benét and the Guggenheim Foundation," *New Col*, II, Part 5 (Jan., 1949), 1–12, letters by Benét, dated 1925–1927 from Paris.

Critical estimates are Leon Spitz, "Stephen Vincent Benét," *AHeb*, CLVII (Feb. 13, 1948), 8, 13; Eugene O'Neill, Jr., "S. V. Benét: 'John Brown's Body,'" *SRL*, XXXII (Aug. 6, 1949), 34–35; Eleanor M. Sickels, "Stephen Vincent Benét," *CE*, XIV (1953), 440–446; and Frederick H. Jackson, "Stephen Vincent Benét and American History," *Historian*, XVII (1954), 67–75.

Two bibliographical listings are Gladys Louise Maddocks, "Stephen Vincent Benét: A Bibliography," *BB*, XX (1951), 142–146, (1952), 158–160; and Allen Tate, *Sixty American Poets, 1896–1944*, rev. ed., Washington, 1954, pp. 7–13.

## AMBROSE (GWINNETT) BIERCE

### 404. COLLECTED WORKS

For more Bierce letters see M. E. Grenander, ed., "Seven Ambrose Bierce Letters," *YULG*, XXII (1957), 12–18.

### 405. BIOGRAPHY AND CRITICISM

Paul Fatout has published two studies of Bierce: *Ambrose Bierce, the Devil's Lexicographer*, Norman, Okla., 1951, a biography; and *Ambrose Bierce and the Black Hills*, Norman, Okla., 1956, based on the unpublished "Black Hills Correspondence."

Briefer studies are Marcus Klein, "San Francisco and Her Hateful

Ambrose Bierce," *HR*, VII (1954), 392–407; and Paul Fatout, "Ambrose Bierce, Civil War Topographer," *AL*, XXVI (1954), 391–400.

The most recent bibliographical listing is Jacob Blanck, *Bibliography of American Literature*, New Haven, 1955, I, 216–227.

## ROBERT MONTGOMERY BIRD

**407.** BIOGRAPHY AND CRITICISM

Two critical studies are Cecil B. Williams, "R. M. Bird's Plans for Novels of the Frontier," *AL*, XXI (1949), 321–324; and Robert L. Bloom, "Robert Montgomery Bird, Editor," *PMHB*, LXXVI (1952), 123–141.

BIBLIOGRAPHY

The most recent listing is Jacob Blanck, *Bibliography of American Literature*, New Haven, 1955, I, 228–234.

## RANDOLPH (SILLIMAN) BOURNE

**409.** SEPARATE WORKS

*History of a Literary Radical, and Other Essays,* first published in 1920 (edited by Van Wyck Brooks), was reprinted in New York, 1956, as *History of a Literary Radical, and Other Papers* with a few minor changes in Brooks' introduction.

**410.** BIOGRAPHY AND CRITICISM

Brief studies are C. A. Madison, "The Man in the Black Cape: Randolph Bourne, a Literary Radical," *ASch*, XV (1946), 338–347; and Samuel Sillen, "The Challenge of Randolph Bourne," *MM*, VI (Dec., 1953), 24–32.

## HJALMAR HJORTH BOYESEN

**410.** BIOGRAPHY AND CRITICISM

Of special interest is Arlin Turner, ed., "A Novelist Discovers a Novelist: The Correspondence of H. H. Boyesen and George W. Cable," *WHR*, V (1951), 343–372.

A full listing of Boyesen's writings is in Jacob Blanck, *Bibliography of American Literature*, New Haven, 1955, I, 251–260.

# HUGH HENRY BRACKENRIDGE

**411.** BIOGRAPHY AND CRITICISM

Philip M. Marsh has published three studies of Brackenridge: "Hugh Henry Brackenridge: More Essays in the *National Gazette*," *WPHM*, XXIX (1946), 147–152; "Hugh Henry Brackenridge: The 'Direct Primary' of 1792," *ibid.*, XXXII (1949), 115–116; and "Brackenridge's 'Resignation,'" *ibid.*, XXXIX (1956), 279–282.

**412.** BIBLIOGRAPHY

A recent listing is Jacob Blanck, *Bibliography of American Literature*, New Haven, 1955, I, 261–268.

# WILLIAM BRADFORD

**412.** EDITED TEXTS AND REPRINTS

*Of Plymouth Plantation* has been re-edited from the complete text, with notes and an introduction, by Samuel Eliot Morison, New York, 1952.

**413.** BIOGRAPHY AND CRITICISM

A recent biography is Bradford Smith, *Bradford of Plymouth*, Philadelphia, 1952.

# ANNE BRADSTREET

**415.** BIOGRAPHY AND CRITICISM

Brief studies are Elizabeth Wade White, "The Tenth Muse—A Tercentenary Appraisal of Anne Bradstreet," *WMQ*, VIII (1951), 355–377; and Richard Crowder, "Anne Bradstreet and Keats," *N&Q*, III (1956), 386–388.

BIBLIOGRAPHY

Of bibliographical interest is Buchanan Charles, "Colonial Manuscript Back Home," *LJ*, LXXXI (Jan. 15, 1956), 148–149.

# VAN WYCK BROOKS

**415.** SEPARATE WORKS

*The Confident Years: 1885–1915*, 1952; *The Writer in America*, 1953; *Scenes and Portraits: Memories of Childhood and Youth*, 1954; *John Sloan:*

*A Painter's Life*, 1955; *Helen Keller: Sketch for a Portrait*, 1956; *Days of the Phoenix: The Nineteen-Twenties I Remember*, 1957; *From a Writer's Note-book*, 1958; *The Dream of Arcadia: American Writers and Artists in Italy, 1760–1915*, 1958.

### 416. REPRINTS

*The Malady of the Ideal: Obermann, Maurice de Guérin, and Amiel* (1913) was reprinted in Philadelphia, 1947. *A Chilmark Miscellany*, New York, 1948, is a selection of previously published writings with the exception of a few of the "Notes from a Journal." *Our Literary Heritage: A Pictorial History of the Writer in America* (with Otto L. Bettmann), New York, 1956, is an abridgment of Brooks' five-volume study, *Makers and Finders: A History of the Writer in America, 1800–1915*.

BIOGRAPHY AND CRITICISM

See Stanley Edgar Hyman, "Van Wyck Brooks and Biographical Criti cism," *Accent*, VII (1947), 131–149.

## CHARLES BROCKDEN BROWN

### 417. COLLECTED WORKS AND CORRESPONDENCE

For more letters see David Lee Clark, ed., "Unpublished Letters of Charles Brockden Brown and W. W. Wilkins," *UTSE*, XVII (June, 1948), 75–107, and Clark's biography of Brown, below.

BIOGRAPHY AND CRITICISM

Two biographies are Harry R. Warfel, *Charles Brockden Brown, Ameri-can Gothic Novelist*, Gainesville, Fla., 1949, and David Lee Clark, *Charles Brockden Brown, Pioneer Voice of America*, Durham, N.C., 1952.

Briefer estimates are Charles C. Cole, Jr., "Brockden Brown and the Jef-ferson Administration," *PMHB*, LXXII (1948), 253–263; John G. Frank, "The Wieland Family in Charles Brockden Brown's 'Wieland,'" *Monats-hefte*, XLII (1950), 347–353; Eleanor M. Tilton, "'The Sorrows' of Charles Brockden Brown," *PMLA*, LXIX (1954), 1304–1308; and W. B. Berthoff, "Adventures of a Young Man: An Approach to Charles Brockden Brown," *AQ*, IX (1957), 421–434.

### 419. BIBLIOGRAPHY

A full listing is in Jacob Blanck, *Bibliography of American Literature*, New Haven, 1955, I, 302–309.

# CHARLES FARRAR BROWNE
## ("ARTEMUS WARD")

**419.** BIOGRAPHY AND CRITICISM

Brief studies are Irving McKee, "Artemus Ward in California and Nevada, 1863–1864," *PHR*, XX (Feb., 1951), 11–23; Stanley T. Williams, "Artemus the Delicious," *VQR*, XXVIII (1952), 214–227; Fred W. Lorch, "Mark Twain's 'Artemus Ward' Lecture on the Tour of 1871–1872," *NEQ*, XXV (1952), 327–343; John Q. Reed, "Civil War Humor: Artemus Ward," *Civil War Hist.*, II (Sept., 1956), 87–101; and Bryson L. Jaynes, "Artemus Ward Among the Mormons," *RSSCW*, XXV (1957), 75–84.

A bibliographical listing is Jacob Blanck, *Bibliography of American Literature*, New Haven, 1955, I, 312–324.

# ORESTES (AUGUSTUS) BROWNSON

**421.** WORKS

Alvan S. Ryan edited, with an introduction, *The Brownson Reader*, New York, 1955.

BIOGRAPHY AND CRITICISM

Brief studies are Thomas R. Ryan, "Brownson on Salvation and the Church," *AER*, CXVII (1947), 117–124; *idem*, "Brownson's Love of Truth," *CathW*, CLXVI (1948), 537–544; *idem*, "Brownson's Technique in Apologetics," *AER*, CXVIII (1948), 12–22; Edward J. Power, "Orestes A. Brownson," *RACHSP*, LXII (1951), 72–95; *idem*, "Brownson's Theory of Education," *ibid.*, LXII (1951), 142–171; *idem*, "Brownson's Views on Responsibility for Education," *ibid.*, LXII (1951), 221–253; *idem*, "Brownson's Attitude Toward Catholic Education," *ibid.*, LXIII (1952), 110–128; M. A. Fitzsimons, "Brownson's Search for the Kingdom of God: The Social Thought of an American Radical," *RPol*, XVI (1954), 22–36; Stanley J. Parry, "The Premises of Brownson's Political Theory," *RPol*, XVI (1954), 194–211; Chester A. Soleta, "The Literary Criticism of Orestes A. Brownson," *RPol*, XVI (1954), 334–351; Carl F. Krummel, "Catholicism, Americanism, Democracy, and Orestes Brownson," *AQ*, VI (1954), 19–31; Thomas R. Ryan, "Orestes A. Brownson and the Irish," *M-A*, XXVIII (July, 1956), 156–172.

# WILLIAM CULLEN BRYANT

**423.** COLLECTED WORKS AND CORRESPONDENCE

Gleanings of letters are Herman E. Spivey, ed., "William Cullen Bryant Changes His Mind: An Unpublished Letter About Thomas Jefferson,"

*NEQ,* XXII (1949), 528–529; John C. Guilds, ed., "Bryant and Simms: A New Letter to Simms," *GHQ,* XXXVII (1953), 142–146; Benjamin Lease, ed., "William Cullen Bryant: An Unpublished Letter," *N&Q,* CXCVIII (1953), 396–397.

**424. EDITED TEXTS AND REPRINTS**

The 1808 and 1809 editions of *The Embargo* were reproduced in facsimile, with an introduction and notes by Thomas O. Mabbott, Gainesville, Fla., 1955.

BIOGRAPHY AND CRITICISM

A recent biography is Harry Houston Peckham, *Gotham Yankee: A Biography of William Cullen Bryant,* New York, 1950.

Critical and historical estimates are William Cullen Bryant, II, "The Genesis of 'Thanatopsis,'" *NEQ,* XXI (1948), 163–184; Max L. Griffin, "Bryant and the South," *TSE,* I (1949), 53–80; George Arms, "William Cullen Bryant: A Respectable Station on Parnassus," *UKCR,* XV (1949), 215–223; Charles I. Glicksberg, "William Cullen Bryant: Champion of Simple English," *JQ,* XXVI (1949), 299–303; Donald A. Ringe, "Kindred Spirits: Bryant and Cole," *AQ,* VI (1954), 233–244; *idem,* "William Cullen Bryant and the Science of Geology," *AL,* XXVI (1955), 507–514; Donald A. Ringe, "Bryant's Use of the American Past," *PMASAL,* LXI (1956), 323–331; *idem,* "Bryant and Whitman: A Study in Artistic Affinities," *BUSE,* II (1956), 85–94; Charles L. Sanford, "The Concept of the Sublime in the Works of Thomas Cole and William Cullen Bryant," *AL,* XXVIII (1957), 434–448; and William Cullen Bryant, II, "The Waterfowl in Retrospect," *NEQ,* XXX (1957), 181–189.

**426. BIBLIOGRAPHY**

A recent listing is Jacob Blanck, *Bibliography of American Literature,* New Haven, 1955, I, 331–384.

# JOHN BURROUGHS

**427. COLLECTED WORKS AND BIOGRAPHY**

Farida A. Wiley edited, with an introduction, *John Burroughs' America: Selections from the Writings of the Hudson River Naturalist,* New York, 1951.

Two biographical studies are Leonora Sill Ashton, "John Burroughs— Neighbor," *Audubon Mag.,* LIII (Mar.–Apr., 1951), 96–101, 136; and Rufus A. Coleman, "Trowbridge and Burroughs," *MLQ,* XIV (1953), 154–162.

**428.** BIBLIOGRAPHY

A full listing is in Jacob Blanck, *Bibliography of American Literature,* New Haven, 1955, I, 433-448.

# (HAROLD) WITTER BYNNER

**428.** SEPARATE WORKS

*Journey with Genius: Recollections and Reflections Concerning the D. H. Lawrences,* 1951.

Bynner's translation of Euripides, *Iphigenia in Taurus* (1915) was reprinted in Chicago, 1956.

# WILLIAM BYRD II

**429.** SEPARATE WORKS

The third part of Byrd's diaries, covering the middle years, has been edited by Louis B. Wright and Marion Tinling, *The London Diary (1717-1721) and Other Writings,* New York, 1958.

**430.** BIOGRAPHY AND CRITICISM

Special studies are Willie T. Weathers, "William Byrd: Satirist," *WMQ,* IV (1947), 27-41; Lewis Leary, "A William Byrd Poem," *WMQ,* IV (1947), 356; St. George Sioussat, "The *Philosophical Transactions* of the Royal Society in the Libraries of William Byrd of Westover, Benjamin Franklin, and the American Philosophical Society," *PAPS,* XCIII (1949), 99-113; and Floyd C. Watkins, "James Kirke Paulding and the Manuscripts of William Byrd," *MLN,* LXVII (1952), 56-57.

# (JAMES) BRANCH CABELL
## *d. 1958*

**431.** SEPARATE WORKS

*The Devil's Own Dear Son,* 1949; *Quiet, Please,* 1952; *As I Remember It: Some Epilogues in Recollection,* 1955.

COLLECTED WORKS AND REPRINTS

*The Witch-Woman: A Trilogy About Her,* New York, 1948, reprints *The Music from Behind the Moon* (1926), *The White Robe* (1928), and *The Way of Ecben* (1929).

Brief estimates are Raymond Himelick, "Cabell, Shelley, and the 'Incorrigible Flesh,'" *SAQ,* XLVII (1948), 88–95; Edward Wagenknecht, "Cabell: A Reconsideration," *CE,* IX (1948), 238–246; Edd Winfield Parks, "James Branch Cabell," *Southern Renascence,* ed. Louis D. Rubin, Jr., and Robert D. Jacobs, Baltimore, 1953, pp. 251–261; Edmund Wilson, "The James Branch Cabell Case Reopened," *NY,* XXXII (Apr. 21, 1956), 140–168; and Raymond Himelick, "Figures of Cabell," *MFS,* II (1956–1957), 214–220.

### 433. BIBLIOGRAPHY

Two full listings are Frances Joan Brewer, *James Branch Cabell: A Bibliography of His Writings, Biography and Criticism,* Charlottesville, 1957, and the companion volume, Matthew J. Bruccoli, *Notes on the Cabell Collection at the University of Virginia,* Charlottesville, 1957.

## GEORGE W(ASHINGTON) CABLE

### 433. CORRESPONDENCE

Cable letters can be found in Kjell Ekström, ed., "The Cable-Howells Correspondence," *Studia Neophilologica,* XXII (1950), 48–61; and Guy A. Cardwell, *Twins of Genius: Letters of Mark Twain, George W. Cable, and Others,* East Lansing, Mich., 1953. See also Mattie Russell, ed., "George Washington Cable Letters in Duke University Library," *DULN,* No. 25 (Jan., 1951), 1–13.

### REPRINTS

*A Southerner Looks at Negro Discrimination: Selected Writings of George W. Cable* is a pamphlet edited, with a biographical sketch, by Isabel Cable Manes, New York, 1946. Arlin Turner edited *The Negro Question, A Selection of Writings on Civil Rights in the South* by George W. Cable, New York, 1958; six of the selections are published for the first time, from manuscripts in the Cable Collection at the Tulane University Library.

### BIOGRAPHY AND CRITICISM

Arlin Turner, *George W. Cable, a Biography,* Durham, N.C., 1956, is the most recent full-length study. Kjell Ekström, *George Washington Cable,* Upsala, Sweden, and Cambridge, Mass., 1950, is a study of Cable's early life and work.

Briefer estimates are Philip Butcher, "George W. Cable and Booker T. Washington," *JNE,* XVII (1948), 462–468; *idem,* "George W. Cable and Negro Education," *JNH,* XXXIV (1949), 119–134; Fred W. Lorch, "Cable and His Reading Tour with Mark Twain in 1884–1885," *AL*, XXIII (1952), 471–486; Joseph G. Tregle, Jr., "Early New Orleans Society: A Reappraisal," *JSH*, XVIII (1952), 20–36; Richard Chase, "Cable and His *Grandissimes*," *KR*, XVIII (1956), 373–383; and Edmund Wilson, "The Ordeal of George Washington Cable," *NY*, XXXIII (Nov. 9, 1957), 172–216.

A bibliographical listing is in Jacob Blanck, *Bibliography of American Literature*, New Haven, 1957, II, 1–14.


# ERSKINE (PRESTON) CALDWELL

**434.** SEPARATE WORKS

*This Very Earth*, 1948; *Place Called Estherville*, 1949; *Episode in Palmetto*, 1950; *Call It Experience: The Years of Learning How to Write*, 1951; *A Lamp for Nightfall*, 1952; *The Courting of Susie Brown*, 1952; *Love and Money*, 1954; *Gretta*, 1955; *Gulf Coast Stories*, 1956; *Certain Women*, 1957; *Molly Cottontail*, 1958.

*The Humorous Side of Erskine Caldwell*, New York, 1951, is an anthology compiled by Robert Cantwell. *The Complete Stories of Erskine Caldwell* appeared in 1953. Reprints of individual novels are numerous.

BIOGRAPHY AND CRITICISM

Brief estimates are Louis-Marcel Raymond, "Erskine Caldwell," *Nouvelle Relève*, V (1947), 497–505; anon., "America's Most Censored Author—An Interview with Erskine Caldwell," *Pub. Weekly*, CLV (Mar. 19–May 14, 1949), 1312, 1438, 1512–1515, 1519, 1805–1806, 1876, 1960–1961; Robert Hazel, "Notes on Erskine Caldwell," *Southern Renascence*, ed. Louis D. Rubin, Jr., and Robert D. Jacobs, Baltimore, 1953, pp. 316–324; and Carl Bode, "Erskine Caldwell: A Note for the Negative," *CE*, XVII (1956), 357–359.


# JOHN CALDWELL CALHOUN

**435.** SEPARATE WORKS AND CORRESPONDENCE

A projected fifteen-volume edition of the papers of John C. Calhoun is in progress at the University of South Carolina.

*A Disquisition on Government* was reprinted, with an introduction by Naphtaly Levy, New York, 1947. John M. Anderson edited *Calhoun: Basic Documents*, State College, Pa., 1952, which contains the *Disquisition on Government* and eleven speeches. *A Disquisition on Government and Selections from the Discourse*, New York, 1953, was edited by C. Gordon Post.

For Calhoun correspondence see Alice Noble Waring, ed., "Letters of

John C. Calhoun to Patrick Noble, 1812–1837," *JSH*, XVI (1950), 64–73; and Jay B. Hubbell, ed., "James Kirke Paulding's Last Letter to John C. Calhoun," *NCHR*, XXXII (1955), 410–414.

BIOGRAPHY AND CRITICISM

Charles M. Wiltse's *John C. Calhoun, Nationalist, 1782–1828* (1944) has been followed by his *John C. Calhoun, Nullifier, 1829–1839*, Indianapolis, 1949, and *John C. Calhoun, Sectionalist, 1840–1850*, Indianapolis, 1951. A briefer biography is Margaret L. Coit, *John C. Calhoun, American Portrait*, Boston, 1950.

A special study is August O. Spain, *The Political Theory of John C. Calhoun*, New York, 1951. See also Matthew A. Fitzsimons, "Calhoun's Bid for the Presidency, 1841–1844," *MVHR*, XXXVIII (1951), 39–60; Harold Schultz, "A Century of Calhoun Biographies," *SAQ*, L (1951), 248–254; Margaret L. Coit, "Calhoun and the Downfall of States' Rights," *VQR*, XXVIII (1952), 191–208; and Magdalen Eichert, "John C. Calhoun's Land Policy of Cession," *SCHM*, LV (1954), 198–209.

# WILLA (SIBERT) CATHER

**436.** SEPARATE WORKS

*The Old Beauty and Others*, 1948; *On Writing: Critical Studies on Writing as an Art*, 1949.

COLLECTED WORKS AND EDITED REPRINTS

James R. Shively edited *Writings from Willa Cather's Campus Years*, Lincoln, Neb., 1950. George N. Kates provided an introduction and notes to *Willa Cather in Europe: Her Own Story of the First Journey*, New York, 1956. *Early Stories of Willa Cather* were edited by Mildred R. Bennett, New York, 1957.

**437.** BIOGRAPHY AND CRITICISM

Biographical studies have been numerous since Willa Cather's death. Leon Edel completed E. K. Brown's *Willa Cather: A Critical Biography*, New York, 1953. Edith Lewis provided *Willa Cather Living: A Personal Record*, New York, 1953, and Elizabeth Shepley Sergeant, *Willa Cather: A Memoir*, Philadelphia, 1953. Mildred R. Bennett's *The World of Willa Cather*, New York, 1951, must be used with care; it needs more careful editing and substantiation.

The first full-length critical study is David Daiches, *Willa Cather: A Critical Introduction*, Ithaca, 1951. See also Josephine Lurie Jessup, *The Faith of Our Feminists: A Study in the Novels of Edith Wharton, Ellen*

*Glasgow, Willa Cather,* New York, 1950, and Maxwell Geismar, "Willa Cather: Lady in the Wilderness," *The Last of the Provincials: The American Novel, 1915–1925,* Boston, 1947, pp. 153–220. Briefer studies are Dayton Kohler, "Willa Cather: 1876–1947," *CE,* IX (1947), 8–18; George Seibel, "Miss Willa Cather from Nebraska," *New Col,* II (Sept., 1949), 195–208; Flora Bullock, "Willa Cather, Essayist and Dramatic Critic: 1891–1895," *PrS,* XXIII (1949), 393–400; Bernard Baum, "Willa Cather's Waste Land," *SAQ,* XLVIII (1949), 589–601; E. A. and L. D. Bloom, "Willa Cather's Novels of the Frontier: A Study in Thematic Symbolism," *AL,* XXI (1949), 71–93; *idem,* "Willa Cather's Novels of the Frontier: The Symbolic Function of 'Machine-Made Materialism,'" *UTQ,* XX (1950), 45–60; John P. Hinz, "A Lost Lady and *The Professor's House,*" *VQR,* XXIX (1953), 70–85; and Witter Bynner, "A Willa Cather Triptych," *NMQ,* XXIII (1953), 330–338.

More recent studies are Leon Edel, "Willa Cather's *The Professor's House:* An Inquiry into the Use of Psychology in Literary Criticism," *LP,* IV (Nov., 1954), 66–79; E. A. and L. D. Bloom, "The Genesis of *Death Comes for the Archbishop,*" *AL,* XXVI (1955), 479–506; Frederick J. Hoffman, "Willa Cather's Two Worlds," *The Twenties,* New York, 1955, pp. 153–162; Curtis Dahl, "An American *Georgic:* Willa Cather's *My Ántonia,*" *CL,* VII (1955), 43–51; Curtis Bradford, "Willa Cather's Uncollected Short Stories," *AL,* XXVI (1955), 537–551; E. A. and L. D. Bloom, "*Shadows on the Rock:* Notes on the Composition of a Novel," *TCL,* II (1956), 70–85; and Eleanor M. Smith, "The Literary Relationship of Sarah Orne Jewett and Willa Sibert Cather," *NEQ,* XXIX (1956), 472–492.

### 438. BIBLIOGRAPHY

Of bibliographical interest are E. K. Brown, "Willa Cather: The Benjamin D. Hitz Collection," *Newberry Lib. Bul.,* No. 5 (Dec., 1950), 158–160; and Phyllis Martin Hutchinson, "The Writings of Willa Cather: A List of Works By and About Her," *BNYPL,* LX (June–Aug., 1956), 267–288, 338–356, 378–400.

## WILLIAM ELLERY CHANNING

### 439. BIOGRAPHY AND CRITICISM

A recent biographical study is Arthur W. Brown, *Always Young for Liberty: A Biography of William Ellery Channing,* Syracuse, 1956. David P. Edgell's *William Ellery Channing: An Intellectual Portrait,* Boston, 1955, sees Channing as a "synthesizer of intellectual and ethical theories." A study of Channing as an atypical Unitarian is Robert Leet Patterson, *The Philosophy of William Ellery Channing,* New York, 1952.

Briefer studies are Lenthiel H. Downs, "Emerson and Dr. Channing:

Two Men from Boston," *NEQ*, XX (1947), 516–534; Reino Virtanen, "Tocqueville and William Ellery Channing," *AL*, XXII (1950), 21–28; and John E. Reinhardt, "The Evolution of William Ellery Channing's Sociopolitical Ideas," *AL*, XXVI (1954), 154–165.

The first full bibliographical listing of Channing's work is in Jacob Blanck, *Bibliography of American Literature*, New Haven, 1957, II, 129–133.

## CHARLES W(ADDELL) CHESNUTT

### 440. BIOGRAPHY AND CRITICISM

An extensive study is Helen M. Chesnutt, *Charles Waddell Chesnutt, Pioneer of the Color Line*, Chapel Hill, 1952. Briefer estimates are Samuel Sillen, "Charles W. Chesnutt: A Pioneer Negro Novelist," *MM*, VI (Feb. 1953), 8–14; and Russell Ames, "Social Realism in Charles W. Chesnutt, *Phylon*, XIV (1953), 199–206.

## THOMAS HOLLEY CHIVERS

### 440. SEPARATE WORKS

*Virginalia* was reprinted in facsimile, Brooklyn, 1942. Richard Beale Davis edited *Chivers' Life of Poe* from the Huntington Library manuscripts, New York, 1952.

### BIOGRAPHY AND CRITICISM

A recent critical study is Charles Henry Watts, *Thomas Holley Chivers, His Literary Career and His Poetry*, Athens, Ga., 1956.

Jacob Blanck, *Bibliography of American Literature*, New Haven, 1957, II, 157–159 is a valuable listing.

## HENRY CLAY

### 441. COLLECTED WORKS AND CORRESPONDENCE

The Henry Clay papers are being prepared for publication in a projected ten-volume edition by James F. Hopkins at the University of Kentucky.

For Clay correspondence, see Bernard Mayo, ed., "Henry Clay, Patron and Idol of White Sulphur Springs: His Letters to James Caldwell," *VMHB*, LV (1947), 301–317; and Sarah Agnes Wallace, ed., "Last Letters of Henry Clay," *KSHSR*, L (1952), 307–318.

BIOGRAPHY AND CRITICISM

A recent study is Clement Eaton, *Henry Clay and the Art of American Politics,* Boston, 1957.

Briefer estimates are Rebecca Kinsman Monroe, "Bills for Reception of Henry Clay at Salem, 1833," *EIHC,* LXXXVIII (1952), 366; Glyndon G. Van Deusen, "Henry Clay, 1852–1952," *FCHQ,* XXVI (1952), 338–346; Harry R. Stevens, "Henry Clay, the Bank, and the West in 1824," *AHR,* LX (1955), 843–848; and Richard Laverne Troutman, "Henry Clay and His 'Ashland' Estate," *FCHQ,* XXX (1956), 159–174.

# SAMUEL L(ANGHORNE) CLEMENS
## ("MARK TWAIN")

**443.** COLLECTED WORKS, REPRINTS, AND CORRESPONDENCE

Three collections of basic materials were edited by the late Dixon Wecter: *Mark Twain in Three Moods,* San Marino, Calif., 1948; *The Love Letters of Mark Twain,* New York, 1949; and *Mark Twain to Mrs. Fairbanks,* San Marino, Calif., 1949. *Report from Paradise,* also edited by Dixon Wecter, New York, 1952, contains two opening chapters of *Captain Stormfield's Visit to Heaven* and "Letter from the Recording Angel."

Walter Francis Frear's *Mark Twain and Hawaii,* Chicago, 1947, is a collection of, as well as commentary on, Twain's writing on Hawaii. Henry Nash Smith and Frederick Anderson, eds., *Mark Twain of the Enterprise,* Berkeley, 1957, is a collection of newspaper articles and other documents by Twain, 1862–1864.

Guy A. Cardwell, *Twins of Genius,* East Lansing, Mich., 1953, prints eighteen letters from Twain to George W. Cable and twenty letters from Cable to Twain, 1881–1906. The introduction by Oscar Lewis to his edition of Dan De Quille [William Wright], *The Big Bonanza,* New York, 1947, contains some hitherto unpublished letters by Twain. See also the first, second, and third of "American Travel Letters, Series Two," reprinted from the *Alta California,* in *The Twainian* (1947, 1949); "Mark Twain's Letters in the San Francisco *Call,*" *The Twainian* (1949, 1952); and "An Unpublished Twain Letter," *MTQ,* VII (Spring–Summer, 1947), 19; VIII (Summer–Fall, 1948), 13.

The first collection of Twain's shorter fiction is *The Complete Short Stories,* ed. Charles Neider, New York, 1957.

**446.** BIOGRAPHY AND CRITICISM

Dixon Wecter followed Albert Bigelow Paine and Bernard De Voto as editor for the Mark Twain Estate. Before his untimely death, he had planned a multi-volume biography. Only *Sam Clemens of Hannibal,* Boston, 1952, has appeared, published posthumously.

Gladys C. Bellamy, *Mark Twain as Literary Artist,* Norman, Okla., 1950, is the most ambitious of recent books on Twain as artist. Specialized studies are E. M. Branch, *The Literary Apprenticeship of Mark Twain,* Urbana, Ill., 1950, and Kenneth Andrews, *Nook Farm: Mark Twain's Hartford Circle,* Cambridge, Mass., 1950. Two comparative critiques are Henry Seidel Canby, *Turn West, Turn East: Mark Twain and Henry James,* Boston, 1951, and Guy A. Cardwell, *Twins of Genius,* East Lansing, Mich., 1953. Two studies from France are Simon Hornstein, *Mark Twain: La Faillite d'un Idéal,* Paris, 1950, and Roger Asselineau, *The Literary Reputation of Mark Twain from 1910 to 1950: A Critical Essay and a Bibliography,* Paris, 1954. See also Arthur L. Scott, ed., *Mark Twain, Selected Criticism,* Dallas, 1955, and E. Hudson Long, *Mark Twain Handbook,* New York, 1957.

Briefer studies are William M. Gibson, "Mark Twain and Howells: Anti-Imperialists," *NEQ,* XX (1947), 435-470; L. T. Dickinson, "Marketing a Best Seller: Mark Twain's *Innocents Abroad,*" *PBSA,* XLI (1947), 107-122; *idem,* "Mark Twain's Revisions in Writing *The Innocents Abroad,*" *AL,* XIX (1947), 139-157; Charles J. Lovell, "The Background of Mark Twain's Vocabulary," *ASp,* XXII (1947), 88-98; C. O. Parsons, "The Devil and Samuel Clemens," *VQR,* XXIII (1947), 582-606; A. L. Vogelback, "Mark Twain: Newspaper Contributor," *AL,* XX (1948), 111-128; S. C. Webster, "Ghost Life on the Mississippi," *PS,* II (1948), 485-490; R. B. West, Jr., "Mark Twain's Idyl of Frontier America," *UKCR,* XV (1948), 92-104; Mentor L. Williams, "Mark Twain's Joan of Arc," *MAQR,* LIV (1948), 243-250; R. H. Wilson, "Malory in the *Connecticut Yankee,*" *UTSE,* XXVII (1948), 185-206; Alexander Cowie, "Mark Twain," *The Rise of the American Novel,* New York, 1948, pp. 599-652; D. M. McKeithan, "Mark Twain's *Tom Sawyer Abroad* and Jules Verne's *Five Weeks in a Balloon,*" *UTSE,* XXVIII (1949), 257-270; Asher Brynes, "Boy-Men and Man-Boys," *YR,* XXXVIII (1949), 223-233; Joseph Jones, "Utopia as Dirge," *AQ,* II (1950), 214-226; Edgar M. Branch, "The Two Providences: Thematic Form in 'Huckleberry Finn,'" *CE,* XI (1950), 188-195; Fred W. Lorch, "Mark Twain's Lecture from *Roughing It,*" *AL,* XXII (1950), 290-307; Tom Burnam, "Mark Twain and the Paige Typesetter: A Background for Despair," *WHR,* VI (1951-52), 29-36; Fred W. Lorch, "Cable and His Reading Tom with Mark Twain in 1884-1885," *AL,* XXIII (1952), 471-486; John Hinz, "Huck and Pluck: 'Bad' Boys in American Fiction," *SAQ,* LI (1952), 120-129; Edwin S. Fussell, "The Structural Problem of *The Mysterious Stranger,*" *SP,* XLIX (1952), 95-104; Fred W. Lorch, "Mark Twain's 'Artemus Ward' Lecture on the Tour of 1871-1872," *NEQ,* XXV (1952), 327-343; Arthur L. Scott, "Mark Twain Looks at Europe," *SAQ,* LII (1953), 399-413; John C. McCloskey, "Mark Twain as Critic in *The Innocents Abroad,*"

*AL,* XXV (1953), 139–151; D. M. McKeithan, "Mark Twain's Letters of Thomas Jefferson Snodgrass," *PQ,* XXXII (1953), 353–365; Leo Marx, "Mr. Eliot, Mr. Trilling, and *Huckleberry Finn,*" *ASch,* XXII (1953), 423–440; and Paul Schmidt, "Mark Twain's Satire on Republicanism," *AQ,* V (1953), 344–356.

More recent studies are Edgar H. Goold, Jr., "Mark Twain on the Writing of Fiction," *AL,* XXVI (1954), 141–153; Lewis Leary, "Tom and Huck: Innocence on Trial," *VQR,* XXX (1954), 417–430; James M. Cox, "Remarks on the Sad Initiation of Huckleberry Finn," *SR,* LXII (1954), 389–405; Alexander E. Jones, "Mark Twain and Freemasonry," *AL,* XXVI (1954), 363–373; Edwin S. Fussell, "Hemingway and Mark Twain," *Accent,* XIV (1954), 199–206; Tom Burnam, "Mark Twain and the Austrian Edison," *AQ,* VI (1954), 364–372; John Gerber, "Mark Twain's 'Private Campaign,'" *Civil War Hist.,* I (Mar., 1955), 37–60; Arthur L. Scott, "Mark Twain: Critic of Conquest," *DR,* XXXV (1955), 45–53; Frances V. Brownell, "The Role of Jim in *Huckleberry Finn,*" *BUSE,* I (1955), 74–83; Henry Nash Smith, "'That Hideous Mistake of Poor Clemens's,'" *HLB,* IX (1955), 145–180; Frank Baldanza, "The Structure of *Huckleberry Finn,*" *AL,* XXVII (1955), 347–355; Arthur L. Scott, "The *Century Magazine* Edits *Huckleberry Finn,* 1884–1885," *AL,* XXVII (1955), 356–362; Leslie Fiedler, "'As Free as Any Cretur . . . ,'" *New Rep,* CXXXIII (Aug. 15, 1955), 17–18; (Aug. 22, 1955), 16–18; F. R. Leavis, "Mark Twain's Neglected Classic [*Pudd'nhead Wilson*]," *Commentary,* XXI (Feb., 1956), 128–136; Howard G. Baetzhold, "Mark Twain: England's Advocate," *AL,* XXVIII (1956), 328–346; Alexander E. Jones, "Mark Twain and Sexuality," *PMLA,* LXXI (1956), 595–616; Charles Kaplan, "Holden and Huck: The Odysseys of Youth," *CE,* XVIII (1956), 76–80; Leo Marx, "The Pilot and the Passenger: Landscape Conventions and the Style of *Huckleberry Finn,*" *AL,* XXVIII (1956), 129–146; Alexander E. Jones, "Mark Twain and the Determinism of *What is Man?*" *AL,* XXIX (1957), 1–17; Thomas Arthur Gullason, "The 'Fatal' Ending of Huckleberry Finn," *AL,* XXIX (1957), 86–91; Richard Chase, "Mark Twain and the Novel," *The American Novel and Its Tradition,* New York, 1957, pp. 139–156; Edgar Branch, "Mark Twain and J. D. Salinger: A Study in Literary Continuity," *AQ,* IX (1957), 144–158; and Henry Nash Smith, "Mark Twain's Images of Hannibal: From St. Petersburg to Eseldorf," *UTSE,* XXXVII (1958), 3–23.

### 449. PRIMARY SOURCES

Henry Nash Smith of the University of California at Berkeley is the successor to Dixon Wecter as literary editor of the unpublished papers of the Mark Twain Estate. The Moffett Collection of the University of California is described in the New York *Times,* Sept. 19, 1954. Important manuscripts are in the Berg Collection of the New York Public Library. Twain's letters to Howells are in the William Dean Howells Papers at Harvard University.

**450.** BIBLIOGRAPHY

Harry Hayden Clark has compiled a critical selected bibliography for *Eight American Authors: A Review of Research and Criticism,* ed. Floyd Stovall, New York, 1956. Roger Asselineau, *The Literary Reputation of Mark Twain from 1910 to 1950,* Paris, 1954, includes a bibliography of 1,333 items. See also the Twain listings in Jacob Blanck, *Bibliography of American Literature,* New Haven, 1957, II, 173–254.

Of special interest is *Mark Twain: An Exhibition Selected Mainly from the Papers Belonging to the Samuel L. Clemens Estate on Deposit in the Huntington Library,* San Marino, Calif., 1947. See also the *Mark Twain Quarterly,* published since 1936, and *The Twainian,* published intermittently since 1939, for further listings.

# JAMES FENIMORE COOPER

**451.** COLLECTED WORKS AND CORRESPONDENCE

James F. Beard, Jr., is preparing a multi-volumed edition of the Cooper letters and journals, to be published by the Harvard University Press. See also W. T. Bandy, ed., "Two Uncollected Letters of James Fenimore Cooper," *AL,* XX (1949), 441–442.

EDITED TEXTS AND REPRINTS

*Autobiography of a Pocket Handkerchief* (*Le Mouchoir: An Autobiographical Romance,* 1843), not included in the collected editions, was edited by George F. Horner and Raymond Adams in a limited edition, Chapel Hill, N.C., 1949.

*Early Critical Essays, 1820–1822* was reproduced in facsimile from *The Literary and Scientific Repository, and Critical Review* with an introduction and headnotes by James F. Beard, Jr., Gainesville, Fla., 1955.

*The American Democrat* (1838), first reprinted in 1931 with an introduction by H. L. Mencken, reappeared in New York, 1955, with an additional introductory note by Robert E. Spiller.

Reprints of the novels are numerous.

**452.** BIOGRAPHY AND CRITICISM

Marcel Clavel, *Fenimore Cooper: Sa vie et son oeuvre: La jeunesse* (*1789–1826*), Aix-en-Provence, 1938, is a doctoral thesis which has been described as "the most detailed biographical work on Cooper yet produced, with respect to both his life and his writings, up to the time he sailed for Europe." The most recent biography is James Grossman, *James Fenimore Cooper*, New York, 1949.

In 1951 at Cooperstown, the New York State Historical Association devoted its annual meeting to the centennial of Cooper's death. *New York History*, XXV (Oct., 1954), is a specially-bound issue (*James Fenimore Cooper: A Re-appraisal*, with an introduction by Howard Mumford Jones) of papers read at the three-day meeting.

Georg Fridén, *James Fenimore Cooper and Ossian*, Upsala, Sweden, and Cambridge, Mass., 1949, is a brief specialized study. Other critical and historical estimates are Roy Harvey Pearce, "The Leatherstocking Tales Re-examined," *SAQ*, XLVI (1947), 524-536; Harold H. Scudder, "Cooper and the Barbary Coast," *PMLA*, LXII (1947), 784-792; idem, "Cooper's *The Crater*," *AL*, XIX (1947), 109-126; Richard H. Ballinger, "Origins of James Fenimore Cooper's *The Two Admirals*," *AL*, XX (1948), 20-30; E. S. Muszynska-Wallace, "The Sources of *The Prairie*," *AL*, XXI (1949), 191-200; Walter Sutton, "Cooper as Found—1949," *UKCR*, XVI (1949), 3-10; W. B. Gates, "Cooper's 'The Sea Lions' and Wilkes' 'Narrative,'" *PMLA*, LXV (1950), 1069-1075; Max L. Griffin, "Cooper's Attitude Toward the South," *SP*, XLVIII (1951), 67-76; James Grossman, "James Fenimore Cooper: An Uneasy American," *YR*, XL (1951), 696-709; C. Hugh Holman, "The Influence of Scott and Cooper on Simms," *AL*, XXIII (1951), 203-218; W. B. Gates, "Cooper's Indebtedness to Shakespeare," *PMLA*, LXVII (1952), 716-731; Howard Mumford Jones, "Prose and Pictures: James Fenimore Cooper," *TSE*, III (1952), 133-154; idem, "James Fenimore Cooper and the Hudson River School," *Mag. of Art*, XLV (1952), 243-251; Marius Bewley, "Revaluations: James Fenimore Cooper," *Scrutiny*, XIX (1952-1953), 98-125; and James F. Beard, Jr., "The First History of Greater New York: Unknown Portions of Fenimore Cooper's Last Work," *NYHSQB*, XXXVII (1953), 109-145.

More recent studies are Marius Bewley, "Fenimore Cooper and the Economic Age," *AL*, XXVI (1954), 166-195; George J. Becker, "James Fenimore Cooper and American Democracy," *CE*, XVII (1956), 325-334; Marvin Meyers, "The Great Descent: A Version of Fenimore Cooper," *PS*, X (1956), 367-381; and John T. Frederick, "Cooper's Eloquent Indians," *PMLA*, LXXI (1956), 1004-1017.

### 455.  BIBLIOGRAPHY

The most recent listing is Jacob Blanck, *Bibliography of American Literature*, New Haven, 1957, II, 276-310.

# (HAROLD) HART CRANE

**457.** COLLECTED WORKS AND CORRESPONDENCE

The Waldo Frank edition of *Collected Poems* (1933) was reprinted in New York, 1946.

Brom Weber edited *The Letters of Hart Crane, 1916–1932*, New York, 1952.

BIOGRAPHY AND CRITICISM

Brom Weber, *Hart Crane: A Biographical and Critical Study*, New York, 1948, contains an appendix of Crane's uncollected poetry and prose, the work sheets of "Atlantis," and a selected bibliography.

For briefer estimates see Yvor Winters, "The Significance of *The Bridge*, by Hart Crane; or, What Are We to Think of Professor X?" *In Defense of Reason*, New York, 1947, pp. 577–603; Karl Shapiro, "The Meaning of the Discarded Poem," *Poets at Work* (by Rudolph Arnheim and others), New York, 1948, pp. 83–121 (a study of "Cape Hatteras"); Ray B. West, "Portrait of the Artist as American," *WR*, XII (1948), 247–251; Martin S. Shockley, "Hart Crane's 'Lachrymae Christi,'" *UKCR*, XVI (1949), 31–36; Brewster Ghiselin, "Bridge into the Sea," *PR*, XVI (1949), 679–686; Alan Swallow, "Hart Crane," *UKCR*, XVI (1949), 103–118; Joseph Frank, "Hart Crane: American Poet," *SR*, LVII (1949), 156–159; Hyatt Howe Waggoner, "Hart Crane: Beyond All Sesames of Science," *The Heel of Elohim: Science and Values in Modern Poetry*, Norman, Okla., 1950, pp. 155–192; Barbara Herman, "The Language of Hart Crane," *SR*, LVIII (1950), 52–67; Stanley K. Coffman, Jr., "Symbolism in *The Bridge*," *PMLA*, LXVI (1951), 65–77; Herbert Martey, "Hart Crane's 'The Broken Tower': A Study in Technique," *UKCR*, XVIII (1952), 199–205.

More recent studies are H. C. Morris, "Crane's 'Voyages' as a Single Poem," *Accent*, XIV (1954), 291–299; Frederick J. Hoffman, "Hart Crane's *The Bridge*: The Crisis in Experiment," *The Twenties*, New York, 1955, pp. 223–239; John R. Willingham, "'Three Songs' of Hart Crane's *The Bridge*: A Reconsideration," *AL*, XXVII (1955), 62–68; Lawrence Dembo, "The Unfractioned Idiom of Hart Crane's *The Bridge*," *AL*, XXVII (1955), 203–224; Joseph Warren Beach, "Hart Crane and Moby Dick," *WR*, XX (1956), 183–196; and A. Alvarez, "The Lyric of Hart Crane," *TC*, CLX (1956), 506–517.

For a listing of explications of individual poems see George Arms and Joseph M. Kuntz, *Poetry Explication*, New York, 1950, pp. 48–50.

BIBLIOGRAPHY

H. D. Rowe compiled *Hart Crane, a Bibliography,* Denver, 1955. An additional listing is Allen Tate, *Sixty American Authors, 1896–1944,* rev. ed., Washington, 1954, pp. 18–19.

See also Jethro Robinson, "The Hart Crane Collection," *CLC,* IV (Feb., 1955), 3–7.

## STEPHEN CRANE

### 458. COLLECTED WORKS AND CORRESPONDENCE

Robert W. Stallman's *Stephen Crane: An Omnibus,* New York, 1952, contains, in addition to novels, short stories, poems, and newspaper articles, 120 letters, 57 of which were never before published.

Edwin H. Cady and Lester G. Wells edited *Love Letters to Nellie Crouse, with Six Other Letters . . . ,* Syracuse, 1954. See also Herbert Faulkner West, *A Stephen Crane Collection,* Hanover, N.H., 1948, pp. 20–22; and Robert W. Stallman, ed., "Stephen Crane's Letters to Ripley Hitchcock," *BNYPL,* LX (1956), 318–322.

Daniel G. Hoffman's *The Poetry of Stephen Crane,* New York, 1957, a critical analysis drawing upon the manuscripts in the Columbia University Libraries, publishes seventeen poems for the first time.

For a full account of unpublished Crane prose in the Berg Collection of the New York Public Library, in the Crane Collection of the Columbia University Libraries, and in the private collection of Clifton Waller Barrett (now in the University of Virginia Library), see Robert W. Stallman, "Stephen Crane: Some New Stories," *BNYPL,* LX (1956), 455–462, 477–486; LXI (1957), 36–46. Daniel G. Hoffman describes "Stephen Crane's New Jersey Ghosts: Two Newly-Recovered Sketches," *PNJHS,* LXXI (1953), 239–253; and John D. Gordan speculates about Crane's collaboration on "*The Ghost* at Brede Place," *BNYPL,* LVI (1952), 591–595.

### 459. EDITED TEXTS AND REPRINTS

A new collected edition of Crane is needed. The Wilson Follett twelve-volume edition (1925–1926) omits some work of interest and is now out of print. Reprints of the individual novels and stories, however, are numerous.

Melvin Schoberlin edited *The Sullivan County Sketches,* Syracuse, 1949.

### BIOGRAPHY AND CRITICISM

A recent critical biography is John Berryman, *Stephen Crane,* New York, 1950. For a full-length analysis of the poems, see Daniel G. Hoffman, above.

For critical notes and introductions to all of Crane's work, see Robert W. Stallman's omnibus volume, above.

Edwin H. Cady edited, with an introduction, Corwin K. Linson's memoir, *My Stephen Crane,* Syracuse, 1958.

There are chapters on Crane's work in Lars Åhnebrink, *The Beginnings of Naturalism in American Fiction,* Upsala, 1950; Maxwell Geismar, *Rebels and Ancestors: The American Novel, 1890–1915,* Boston, 1953; and Charles Child Walcutt, *American Literary Naturalism, A Divided Stream,* Minneapolis, 1956.

Briefer studies are Ames W. Williams, "Stephen Crane, War Correspondent," *New Col,* I (1948), 113–124; V. A. Elconin, "Stephen Crane at Asbury Park," *AL,* XX (1948), 275–289; Willa Cather, "When I Knew Stephen Crane," *PrS,* XXIII (1949), 231–237; Caroline Gordon, "Stephen Crane," *Accent,* IX (1949), 153–157; John W. Schroeder, "Stephen Crane Embattled," *UKCR,* XVII (1950), 119–129; Morgan Blum, "Berryman as Biographer, Stephen Crane as Poet," *Poetry,* LXXVIII (1951), 298–307; John W. Stevenson, "The Literary Reputation of Stephen Crane," *SAQ,* LI (1952), 286–300; Walter Sutton, "Pity and Fear in 'The Blue Hotel,'" *AQ,* IV (1952), 73–78; Joseph J. Kwiat, "Stephen Crane and Painting," *AQ,* IV (1952), 331–338; Daniel G. Hoffman, "An Unwritten Life of Stephen Crane," *CLC,* II (1953), 12–16; John E. Hart, "*The Red Badge of Courage* as Myth and Symbol," *UKCR,* XIX (1953), 249–256; E. A. Gillis, "A Glance at Stephen Crane's Poetry," *PrS,* XXVIII (1954), 73–79; Edith R. Jones, "Stephen Crane at Brede," *Atl,* CXCIV (1954), 57–61; Richard P. Adams, "Naturalistic Fiction: 'The Open Boat,'" *TSE,* IV (1954), 137–146.

More recent studies are Robert W. Stallman, "Stephen Crane's Revision of *Maggie: A Girl of the Streets,*" *AL,* XXVI (1955), 528–536; *idem,* "'The Red Badge of Courage': A Collation of Two Pages of Manuscript Expunged from Chapter XII," *PBSA,* XLIX (1955), 273–277; James B. Colvert, "The Origins of Stephen Crane's Literary Credo," *UTSE,* XXXIV (1955), 179–188; M. Solomon, "Stephen Crane: A Critical Study," *MM,* IX (Jan., 1956), 25–42; (Mar., 1956), 31–47; Joseph N. Satterwhite, "Stephen Crane's 'The Blue Hotel': The Failure of Understanding," *MFS,* II (1956–1957), 238–241; James M. Cox, "*The Pilgrim's Progress* as a Source for Stephen Crane's *The Black Riders,*" *AL,* XXVIII (1957), 478–487; James Trammell Cox, "Stephen Crane as Symbolic Naturalist: An Analysis of 'The Blue Hotel,'" *MFS,* III (1957), 147–158; Lillian Gilkes and Joan H. Baum, "Stephen Crane's Last Novel: *The O'Ruddy,*" *CLC,* VI (1957), 41–48; and Edward Stone, "The Many Suns of *The Red Badge of Courage,*" *AL,* XXIX (1957), 322–326.

**460.** BIBLIOGRAPHY

The most complete bibliography is Ames W. Williams and Vincent Starrett, *Stephen Crane: A Bibliography,* Glendale, Calif., 1948. See also the Crane listings in Jacob Blanck, *Bibliography of American Literature,* New Haven, 1957, II, 329–338.

A check list is in Stallman's omnibus volume, above; a bibliographical note is in Berryman, above.

The George Matthew Adams collection of Crane, at Dartmouth College, is described in West, above. The George Arents collection at Syracuse University is described in Cady and Wells, above. See also *Stephen Crane (1871–1900): An Exhibition of His Writings Held in the Columbia University Libraries September 17–November 30, 1956,* arranged and described by Joan H. Baum, New York, 1956. This exhibition drew on the Berg and the Barrett collections as well as the Columbia University Crane material.


# (MICHEL-GUILLAUME JEAN) ST. JEAN DE CRÈVECŒUR

**461.** BIOGRAPHY AND CRITICISM

Special studies are Percy G. Adams, "Crèvecœur and Franklin," *PH,* XIV (1947), 273–279; *idem,* "Notes on Crèvecœur," *AL,* XX (1948), 327–333; Léon Rey, "Crèvecœur and the First Franco-American Packet Line," *NYHSQB,* XXXV (1951), 171–194 (trans. and ed. Kent Forster); and Percy G. Adams, "The Historical Value of Crèvecœur's *Voyage dans la haute Pensylvanie et dans [l'état de] New York,*" *AL,* XXV (1953), 152–168.


# E(DWARD) E(STLIN) CUMMINGS

**462.** SEPARATE WORKS

*Xaîpe,* 1950; *i: six nonlectures,* 1953; *Poems, 1923–1954,* 1954; *95 Poems,* 1958.

George James Firmage edited, with an introduction, *e. e. cummings: A Miscellany,* New York, 1958, which contains critical prose by Cummings on a variety of subjects.

BIOGRAPHY AND CRITICISM

The first biographical study is Charles Norman, *The Magic-Maker: E. E. Cummings,* New York, 1958.

Critical estimates are R. M. Adams, "grasshopper's waltz: the poetry of e. e. cummings," *Cronos,* I (1947), 1–7; M. N. S. Whiteley, "Savagely a

Maker," *Poetry*, LXX (1947), 211–217; Karl Shapiro, "Prosody as the Meaning," *Poetry*, LXXIII (1949), 336–351; George Haines, "::2:1: The World and E. E. Cummings," *SR*, LIX (1951), 206–227; Theodore Spencer, "Technique as Joy," *Perspectives USA*, No. 2 (Winter, 1953), 23–29; S. V. Baum, "E. E. Cummings: The Technique of Immediacy," *SAQ*, LIII (1954), 70–88; Eleanor M. Sickels, "The Unworld of E. E. Cummings," *AL*, XXVI (1954), 223–238; Robert E. Maurer, "Latter-Day Notes on E. E. Cummings' Language," *BuR*, V (May, 1955), 1–23; Carl Bode, "E. E. Cummings: The World of 'Un,'" *Poetry*, LXXXVI (1955), 358–363; Rudolph Von Abele, "'Only to Grow': Change in the Poetry of E. E. Cummings," *PMLA*, LXX (1955), 913–933; Robert E. Maurer, "E. E. Cummings' *Him*," *BuR*, VI (May, 1956), 1–27; Barbara Watson, "The Dangers of Security: E. E. Cummings' Revolt against the Future," *KR*, XVIII (1956), 519–537; and Norman Friedman, "Diction, Voice, and Tone: The Poetic Language of E. E. Cummings," *PMLA*, LXXII (1957), 1036–1059.

For a listing of explications of individual poems see George Arms and Joseph M. Kuntz, *Poetry Explication*, New York, 1950, pp. 51–52.

Paul Lauter compiled a mimeographed bibliography, *E. E. Cummings: Index to First Lines and Bibliography of Works by and about the Poet*, Denver, 1955. See also Allen Tate, *Sixty American Poets, 1896–1944*, rev. ed., Washington, 1954, pp. 19–21.

# JOHN W(ILLIAM) DE FOREST

### 463. SEPARATE WORKS AND CORRESPONDENCE

James H. Croushore and David Morris Potter edited, with an introduction and notes, *A Union Officer in the Reconstruction*, New Haven, 1948. These papers on the South during the Reconstruction first appeared as a series of magazine articles, May, 1868–Feb., 1869. They were later revised by De Forest and gathered with other materials into a single manuscript, now in the Yale University Library under the title, *The Bureau Major*.

For De Forest correspondence see E. R. Hagemann, ed., "John William De Forest and *The Galaxy*, Some Letters, 1867–1872," *BNYPL*, LIX (1955), 175–194.

### BIOGRAPHY AND CRITICISM

A brief estimate is Thomas O'Donnell, "De Forest, Van Petten, and Stephen Crane," *AL*, XXVII (1956), 578–580.

For bibliographical listings see E. R. Hagemann, "A Checklist of the Writings of John William De Forest (1826–1906)," *SB*, VIII (1956), 185–194; and Jacob Blanck, *Bibliography of American Literature*, New Haven, 1957, II, 432–437.

## JOSEPH DENNIE

**464.** BIOGRAPHY AND CRITICISM

Two brief studies are Lewis Leary, "Joseph Dennie on Benjamin Franklin: A Note on Early American Literary Criticism," *PMHB*, LXXII (1948), 240–246; and Thomas P. Govan, "The Death of Joseph Dennie: A Memoir by Nicholas Biddle," *ibid.*, LXXV (1951), 36–46.

A listing of Dennie's works is in Jacob Blanck, *Bibliography of American Literature*, New Haven, 1957, II, 438–442.

## JOHN DEWEY
### *d. 1952*

**465.** SEPARATE WORKS

*Knowing and the Known* (with Arthur F. Bentley), 1949.

EDITED TEXTS AND REPRINTS

*The Public and Its Problems* (1927) was reprinted, Chicago, 1946. *The Influence of Darwin on Philosophy, and Other Essays* (1910) was reprinted, New York, 1951.

Irwin Edman edited selections from the works of Dewey in *John Dewey: His Contribution to the American Tradition*, Indianapolis, 1955.

**466.** BIOGRAPHY AND CRITICISM

Specialized studies are numerous: Benjamin Wolstein, *Experience and Valuation: A Study in John Dewey's Naturalism*, New York, 1949; Jerome Nathanson, *John Dewey: The Reconstruction of the Democratic Life*, New York, 1951; H. S. Thayer, *The Logic of Pragmatism: An Examination of John Dewey's Logic*, New York, 1952; Norbert J. Fleckenstein, *A Critique of John Dewey's Theory of the Nature and the Knowledge of Reality in the Light of the Principles of Thomism*, Washington, 1954; Melvin C. Baker, *Foundations of John Dewey's Educational Theory*, New York, 1955; Manford George Gutzke, *John Dewey's Thought and Its Implications for Christian Education*, New York, 1956; and Paul K. Crosser, *The Nihilism of John Dewey*, New York, 1955. See also James Oliver Buswell, *The Philosophies of F. R. Tennant and John Dewey*, New York, 1950; and Folke Leander, *Estetik och Kunskapsteori: Croce, Cassirer, Dewey*, Göteborg, 1950.

Three volumes of critical essays contain significant estimates. *Value: A Cooperative Inquiry*, ed. Ray Lepley, New York, 1949, is a collection of fourteen essays (mostly on Dewey's theory of value) by various hands, including Dewey, occasioned by Lepley's article, "Some Questions about

Value," *JP*, XLI (1944), 449–455. Sidney Hook edited a volume of twenty essays, *John Dewey: Philosopher of Science and Freedom; A Symposium*, New York, 1950. Kenneth D. Benne and William O. Stanley edited six studies in *Essays for John Dewey's Ninetieth Birthday*, Urbana, Ill., 1950.

Briefer estimates are George Dykhuizen, "An Early Chapter in the Life of John Dewey," *JHI*, XIII (1952), 563–572; George Santayana, "Three American Philosophers," *ASch*, XXII (1953), 281–284; Robert E. Fitch, "John Dewey—the 'Last Protestant,'" *PS*, VII (1953), 224–230; Van Meter Ames, "John Dewey as Aesthetician," *JAAC*, XII (1953), 145–168; George Boas, "Communication in Dewey's Aesthetics," *ibid.*, XII (1953), 177–183; S. C. Pepper, "The Concept of Fusion in Dewey's Aesthetic Theory," *ibid.*, XII (1953), 169–176; and Gail Kennedy, "Science and the Transformation of Common Sense: The Basic Problem of Dewey's Philosophy," *JP*, LI (1954), 313–325.

## EMILY DICKINSON

### 467. COLLECTED WORKS

Thomas H. Johnson edited *The Poems of Emily Dickinson, Including Variant Readings Critically Compared with All Known Manuscripts*, 3 vols., Cambridge, Mass., 1955. This work establishes finally the texts of Emily Dickinson's poems.

Earlier printings, of textual interest, are Millicent Todd Bingham, "Poems of Emily Dickinson: Hitherto Published Only in Part," *NEQ*, XX (1947), 3–50; William White, "Two Unlisted Emily Dickinson Poems," *CLQ*, Series III (1948), 69–70; George F. Whicher, "Some Uncollected Poems of Emily Dickinson," *AL*, XX (1949), 436–440; and Millicent Todd Bingham, "Prose Fragments of Emily Dickinson," *NEQ*, XXVIII (1955), 291–318.

### 468. LETTERS

*The Letters of Emily Dickinson*, 3 vols., Cambridge, Mass., 1958, were edited by Thomas H. Johnson; Theodora Ward, associate editor. This edition publishes 1,150 letters and prose fragments, approximately 100 for the first time. It supersedes all previous texts.

Three earlier volumes are Theodora Van Wagenen Ward, ed., *Emily Dickinson's Letters to Dr. and Mrs. Josiah Gilbert Holland*, Cambridge, Mass., 1951; Millicent Todd Bingham, *Emily Dickinson: A Revelation*, New York, 1954; and *idem, Emily Dickinson's Home: Letters of Edward Dickinson and His Family*, New York, 1955.

*Letters of Emily Dickinson*, ed. Mabel Loomis Todd (1894), was reissued, with an introduction by Mark Van Doren, Cleveland, 1951.

### 469. BIOGRAPHY AND CRITICISM

Two recent critical studies are Richard Chase, *Emily Dickinson,* New York, 1951; and Thomas H. Johnson, *Emily Dickinson: An Interpretive Biography,* Cambridge, Mass., 1955.

Other studies are Henry W. Wells, *Introduction to Emily Dickinson,* Chicago, 1947; Ruth Flanders McNaughton, *The Imagery of Emily Dickinson,* Lincoln, 1949 (University of Nebraska Studies, n. s. No. 4); Donald E. Thackrey, *Emily Dickinson's Approach to Poetry,* Lincoln, 1954 (University of Nebraska Studies, n. s. No. 13); and the two volumes by Millicent Todd Bingham, above.

Rebecca Patterson's *The Riddle of Emily Dickinson,* Boston, 1951, is untrustworthy.

Briefer estimates are Edwin Moseley, "The Gambit of Emily Dickinson," *UKCR,* XVI (1949), 11–19; Herbert Ellsworth Childs, "Emily Dickinson, Spinster," *WHR,* III (1949), 303–309; Sister Mary Humiliata, "Emily Dickinson—Mystic Poet?" *CE,* XII (1950), 144–149; Herbert Ellsworth Childs, "Emily Dickinson and Sir Thomas Browne," *AL,* XXII (1951), 455–465; Myron Ochshorn, "In Search of Emily Dickinson," *NMQ,* XXIII (1953), 94–106; Thomas H. Johnson, "Emily Dickinson: Creating the Poems," *HLB,* VII (1953), 257–270; Frederic I. Carpenter, "Emily Dickinson and the Rhymes of Dream," *UKCR,* XX (1953), 113–120; Theodora Van Wagenen Ward, "Emily Dickinson and T. W. Higginson," *BPLQ,* V (1953), 3–18; André Maurois, "Emily Dickinson, poétesse et recluse," *Rev. de Paris,* LX (Nov., 1954), 1–13; Theodora Ward, "Ourself Behind Ourself: An Interpretation of the Crisis in the Life of Emily Dickinson," *HLB,* X (1956), 5–39; Lewis Leary, "The Poems of Emily Dickinson," *Thought,* XXXI (1956), 282–286; and William Howard, "Emily Dickinson's Poetic Vocabulary," *PMLA,* LXXII (1957), 225–248.

Essay-reviews of the 1955 edition of *Poems* are R. P. Blackmur, "Emily Dickinson's Notation," *KR,* XVIII (1956), 224–237; John Crowe Ransom, "Emily Dickinson," *Perspectives USA,* No. 15 (1956), 5–20; and Austin Warren, "Emily Dickinson," *SR,* LXV (1957), 565–586.

For a listing of explications of individual poems see George Arms and Joseph M. Kuntz, *Poetry Explication,* New York, 1950, pp. 53–56.

### 470. PRIMARY SOURCES

The Alfred L. Hampson Collection of Dickinson manuscripts (bequeathed to him by Martha Dickinson Bianchi) was presented in 1950 by Gilbert H. Montague to the Houghton Library of Harvard University. The Mabel Loomis Todd Collection of Dickinson manuscripts was presented in 1956 by Millicent Todd Bingham to Amherst College Library. These two assemblages comprise the bulk of all Dickinson manuscripts.

BIBLIOGRAPHY

See William White and Charles R. Green, "Homage to Emily Dickinson," *BB,* XX (1951), 112–115; Thomas H. Johnson, "Establishing a Text: The Emily Dickinson Papers," *SB,* V (1952–53), 21–32; and Jacob Blanck, *Bibliography of American Literature,* New Haven, 1957, II, 446–454.

## JOHN DICKINSON

**471.** BIOGRAPHY AND CRITICISM

Brief studies are Frederick B. Tolles, "Light on John Dickinson," *Friends Intelligencer,* CIV (Feb., 1947), 56; William G. Soler, "John Dickinson's 'Ode, On the French Revolution,'" *AL,* XXV (1953), 287–292; and Richard M. Gummere, "John Dickinson, the Classical Penman of the Revolution," *CJ,* LII (1956), 81–88.

## HILDA DOOLITTLE (ALDINGTON)
## ("H. D.")

**472.** SEPARATE WORKS

*By Avon River,* 1949; *Tribute to Freud: With Unpublished Letters by Freud to the Author,* 1956.

BIOGRAPHY AND CRITICISM

See Harold H. Watts, "H. D. and the Age of Myth," *SR,* LVI (1948), 287–303; William Carlos Williams, "Something for a Biography," *GMHC,* L (1948), 211–213; and Stanley K. Coffman, Jr., *Imagism,* Norman, Okla., 1951, *passim.*

For a listing of explications of individual poems see George Arms and Joseph M. Kuntz, *Poetry Explication,* New York, 1950, pp. 62–63.

## JOHN (RODERIGO) DOS PASSOS

**473.** SEPARATE WORKS

*The Grand Design,* 1949; *The Prospect Before Us,* 1950; *Chosen Country,* 1951; *Most Likely to Succeed,* 1954; *The Head and Heart of Thomas Jefferson,* 1954; *The Theme Is Freedom,* 1956; *The Men Who Made the Nation,* 1957; *The Great Days,* 1958.

*District of Columbia,* Boston, 1952, is a reprint of the trilogy: *Adventures of a Young Man* (1939), *Number One* (1943), and *The Grand Design* (1949).

BIOGRAPHY AND CRITICISM

The first full-length study is Georges-Albert Astre, *Thèmes et structures dans l'œuvre de John Dos Passos,* Paris, 1956.

Briefer critical estimates are Joseph Warren Beach, "Dos Passos: 1947," *SR,* LV (1947), 406–418; Jean-Paul Sartre, "À propos de John Dos Passos," *Situation,* I (1947), 14–25; W. M. Frohock, "John Dos Passos: Of Time and Frustration," *SWR,* XXXIII (1948), 71–80, 170–179; Granville Hicks, "Dos Passos and His Critics," *Am Merc,* LXVIII (1949), 623–630; *idem,* "The Politics of John Dos Passos," *AR,* X (1950), 85–98; *idem,* "John Dos Passos: Liberty and the Father-Image," *AR,* X (1950), 99–106; and Herbert Marshall McLuhan, "John Dos Passos: Technique vs. Sensibility," *Fifty Years of the American Novel: A Christian Appraisal,* ed. Harold C. Gardiner, S.J., New York, 1951, pp. 151–164.

More recent studies are Deming Brown, "Dos Passos in Soviet Criticism," *CL,* V (1953), 332–350; Blanche Housman Gelfant, "John Dos Passos: The Synoptic Novel," *The American City Novel,* Norman, Okla., 1954, pp. 133–174; Eugene Arder, "*Manhattan Transfer:* An Experiment in Technique," *UKCR,* XXII (1955), 153–158; Martin Kallich, "John Dos Passos, Fellow-Traveller: A Dossier with Commentary," *TCL,* I (1956), 173–190; and Charles Child Walcutt, *American Literary Naturalism, A Divided Stream,* Minneapolis, 1956, pp. 280–289.

Jack Potter compiled *A Bibliography of John Dos Passos,* Chicago, 1950. See also Martin Kallich, "Bibliography of John Dos Passos," *BB,* XIX (1949), 231–235; and William White, "More Dos Passos: Bibliographical Addenda," *PBSA,* XLV (1951), 156–158.


# THEODORE (HERMAN ALBERT) DREISER

**475.** BIOGRAPHY AND CRITICISM

Two critical biographies are Robert H. Elias, *Theodore Dreiser: Apostle of Nature,* New York, 1949; and F. O. Matthiessen, *Theodore Dreiser,* New York, 1951. Of biographical interest is Helen Dreiser, *My Life with Dreiser,* Cleveland, 1951.

Robert H. Elias is preparing a three-volume edition of the Dreiser letters, to be published by the University of Pennsylvania Press.

Alfred Kazin and Charles Shapiro edited a collection of essays on Dreiser,

*The Stature of Theodore Dreiser: A Critical Survey of the Man and His Work,* Bloomington, Ind., 1955.

Studies of Dreiser are in Lionel Trilling, *The Liberal Imagination,* New York, 1950; Lars Åhnebrink, *The Beginnings of Naturalism in American Fiction,* Upsala, Sweden, 1950; Maxwell Geismar, *Rebels and Ancestors: The American Novel, 1890-1915,* Boston, 1953; Blanche Housman Gelfant, *The American City Novel,* Norman, Okla., 1954; Kenneth S. Lynn, *The Dream of Success,* Boston, 1955, pp. 13-74; and Charles Child Walcutt, *American Literary Naturalism, A Divided Stream,* Minneapolis, 1956.

Briefer studies are H. L. Mencken, "The Life of an Artist," *New Yorker,* XXIV (Apr. 17, 1948), 43-57; Van Wyck Brooks, "Theodore Dreiser," *UKCR,* XVI (1950), 187-197; Albert Mordell, *My Relations with Theodore Dreiser . . . ,* Girard, Kansas, 1951; Joseph J. Kwiat, "Dreiser and the Graphic Artist," *AQ,* III (1951), 127-141; George Steinbrecher, Jr., "Inaccurate Accounts of *Sister Carrie," AL,* XXIII (1952), 490-493; Alexander Kern, "Dreiser's Difficult Beauty," *WR,* XVI (1952), 129-136; Joseph J. Kwiat, "Dreiser's *The 'Genius'* and Everett Shinn, the 'Ash-Can' Painter," *PMLA,* LXVII (1952), 15-31; *idem,* "The Newspaper Experience: Crane, Norris, and Dreiser," *NCF,* VIII (1953), 99-117; Lars Åhnebrink, "Dreiser's *Sister Carrie* and Balzac," *Symposium,* VII (1953), 306-322.

More recent studies are Walter Blackstock, "Dreiser's Dramatizations of American Success," *Florida State Univ. Stud.,* No. 14 (1954), 107-130; John Lydenberg, "Theodore Dreiser: Ishmael in the Jungle," *Monthly Rev.,* VII (1955), 124-136; George J. Becker, "Theodore Dreiser: The Realist as Social Critic," *TCL,* I (1955), 117-127; Bernard Rosenberg, "Mr. Trilling, Theodore Dreiser (and Life in the U. S.)," *Dissent,* II (1955), 171-178; Gerhard Friedrich, "Theodore Dreiser's Debt to Woolman's *Journal," AQ,* VII (1955), 385-392; Gerhard Friedrich, "A Major Influence on Theodore Dreiser's *The Bulwark," AL,* XXIX (1957), 180-193; *idem,* "The Dreiser-[Rufus M.] Jones Correspondence," *BFHA,* XLVI (1957), 23-34; J. D. Thomas, "The Natural Supernaturalism of Dreiser's Novels," *RIP,* XLIV (1957), 112-125; and Gerald Willen, "Dreiser's Moral Seriousness," *UKCR,* XXIII (1957), 181-187.

### 476. PRIMARY SOURCES

See Robert H. Elias, "The Library's Dreiser Collection," *UPLC,* XVII (1950), 78-80.

### 477. BIBLIOGRAPHY

"A Selected Bibliography of Dreiser Biography and Criticism" is in Alfred Kazin and Charles Shapiro, eds., *The Stature of Theodore Dreiser,* Bloomington, Ind., 1955, pp. 271-303.

## PAUL LAURENCE DUNBAR

**477.** BIOGRAPHY AND CRITICISM

Virginia Cunningham, *Paul Laurence Dunbar and His Song*, New York, 1948, is the most recent biography.

A bibliographical listing is in Jacob Blanck, *Bibliography of American Literature*, New Haven, 1957, II, 498–505.

## TIMOTHY DWIGHT

**480.** BIOGRAPHY AND CRITICISM

Brief studies are Lewis Leary, "The Author of *The Triumph of Infidelity*," *NEQ*, XX (1947), 377–385; Alfred O. Aldridge, "Timothy Dwight's Posthumous Gift to British Theology," *AL*, XXI (1950), 479–481; Vincent Freimarck, "Timothy Dwight's *Dissertation* on the Bible," *AL*, XXIV (1952), 73–76; and Abe C. Ravitz, "Timothy Dwight: Professor of Rhetoric," *NEQ*, XXIX (1956), 63–72.

**481.** BIBLIOGRAPHY

The most recent listing is Jacob Blanck, *Bibliography of American Literature*, New Haven, 1957, II, 519–530.

## JONATHAN EDWARDS

**482.** COLLECTED WORKS AND LETTERS

The Yale University Press edition of *The Works of Jonathan Edwards* is under the general editorship of Perry Miller. *Freedom of the Will*, ed. Paul Ramsey, New Haven, 1957, is the first volume to be published.

Edwards' letters are still uncollected. A recent publication is George R. Clark, ed., "An Unpublished Letter by Jonathan Edwards," *NEQ*, XXIX (1956), 228–233.

**483.** EDITED TEXTS AND REPRINTS

*Images or Shadows of Divine Things*, ed. Perry Miller, New Haven, 1948, is the first publication of a Yale manuscript to which Edwards gave various titles. *The Life and Diary of David Brainerd*, edited with a biographical sketch by Philip E. Howard, Jr., Chicago, 1949, is a reprinting of Edwards' *An Account of the Life of the Late Reverend M. David Brainerd* (1749).

Vergilius Ferm edited *Puritan Sage: Collected Writings of Jonathan Edwards*, New York, 1953.

BIOGRAPHY AND CRITICISM

The most recent critical biography is Perry Miller, *Jonathan Edwards*, New York, 1949. See also Harvey G. Townsend, ed., *The Philosophy of Jonathan Edwards from His Private Notebooks*, Eugene, Ore., 1955.

Briefer studies are A. O. Aldridge, "Jonathan Edwards and William Godwin on Virtue," *AL*, XVIII (1947), 308–318; Harvey G. Townsend, "The Will and the Understanding in the Philosophy of Jonathan Edwards," *CH*, XVI (1947), 210–220; Frank Davidson, "Three Patterns of Living," *AAUP*, XXXIV (1948), 364–374; Edward H. Cady, "The Artistry of Jonathan Edwards," *NEQ*, XXII (1949), 61–72; A. O. Aldridge, "Edwards and Hutcheson," *HTR*, XLIV (1951), 35–53; Thomas A. Schafer, "Jonathan Edwards and Justification by Faith," *CH*, XX (1951), 55–67; Donald H. Rhoades, "Jonathan Edwards: America's First Philosopher," *Personalist*, XXXIII (1952), 135–147; Vincent Thomas, "The Modernity of Jonathan Edwards," *NEQ*, XXV (1952), 60–84; Howard C. Rice, Jr., "Jonathan Edwards at Princeton: With a Survey of Edwards Material in the Princeton University Library," *PULC*, XV (1954), 69–89; and Thomas A. Schafer, "Jonathan Edwards' Conception of the Church," *CH*, XXIV (1955), 51–66.

**485.** BIBLIOGRAPHY

See the survey by Howard C. Rice, Jr., above.

## EDWARD EGGLESTON

**485.** BIOGRAPHY AND CRITICISM

Brief estimates are Robert W. Johannsen, "Literature and History: The Early Novels of Edward Eggleston," *IMH*, XLVIII (1952), 37–54; W. P. Randel, "Edward Eggleston's Minnesota Fiction," *MH*, XXXIII (1953), 189–193; *idem*, "The Kit Carson of the Northwest," *MH*, XXXIII (1953), 269–281; and *idem*, "Edward Eggleston on Dialect," *ASp*, XXX (1955), 111–114.

## T(HOMAS) S(TEARNS) ELIOT

**488.** SEPARATE WORKS

*Reunion by Destruction: Reflections on a Scheme for Church Union in South India*, 1943; *What Is a Classic?* 1945; *On Poetry*, 1947; *A Practical Possum*, 1947; *Milton*, 1947; *Notes Toward the Definition of Culture*, 1948; *From Poe to Valéry*, 1948; *A Sermon Preached in Magdalene College Chapel*,

1948; *The Aims of Poetic Drama*, 1949; *The Cocktail Party*, 1950; *Talk on Dante*, 1950; *Poetry and Drama*, 1951; *The Value and Use of Cathedrals in England Today*, 1951; "*Those Who Need Privacy and Those Whose Need Is Company*," 1951; *The Film of Murder in the Cathedral* (with George Hoellering), 1952; *The Three Voices of Poetry*, 1953; *American Literature and the American Language*, 1953; *The Confidential Clerk*, 1954; *The Cultivation of Christmas Trees*, 1954; *Religious Drama: Mediaeval and Modern*, 1954; *The Literature of Politics*, 1955; *The Frontiers of Criticism*, 1956; *On Poetry and Poets*, 1957; *The Elder Statesman*, 1958.

### 489. COLLECTIONS AND REPRINTS

*Poems Written in Early Youth* was compiled by John Hayward and printed privately in Stockholm, 1950. *The Complete Poems and Plays* appeared in New York in 1952. It reprints *Collected Poems, 1909–1935; Four Quartets; Old Possum's Book of Practical Cats;* and three plays: *Murder in the Cathedral, The Family Reunion,* and *The Cocktail Party. On Poetry and Poets*, New York, 1957, is a collection of sixteen essays, all previously published separately except for the Ballard Matthews Lectures (delivered at University College, North Wales, in 1944) on "Samuel Johnson as Poet and Critic" and the 1955 Hamburg University lecture on "Goethe as the Sage" (published in Germany but not in England or America).

*Selected Essays, 1917–1932* has undergone several revisions. A second edition was published in London in 1934, a third in 1951. *Selected Essays*, New York, 1950, is the second American edition. It omits the dates in the original title and adds four essays from *Essays, Ancient and Modern:* "In Memoriam," "Religion and Literature," "The *Pensées* of Pascal," and "Modern Education and the Classics."

Other reprintings and translations of Eliot's work are too numerous to list here.

### BIOGRAPHY AND CRITICISM

F. O. Matthiessen's *The Achievement of T. S. Eliot*, 2d ed., rev. and enl., Boston, 1947, is still one of the major studies of Eliot's poetry; a third edition, in 1958, has a chapter on Eliot's later work by C. L. Barber. There have been many others in recent years. From America: Elizabeth Drew, *T. S. Eliot: The Design of His Poetry*, New York, 1949; George Williamson, *A Reader's Guide to T. S. Eliot: A Poem-by-Poem Analysis*, New York, 1953; and Grover Smith, Jr., *T. S. Eliot's Poetry and Plays: A Study in Sources and Meaning*, Chicago, 1956. From England: Francis A. C. Wilson, *Six Essays on the Development of T. S. Eliot*, London, 1948; Helen Louise Gardner, *The Art of T. S. Eliot*, London, 1949; and D. E. S. Maxwell, *The Poetry of T. S. Eliot*, London, 1952. From France: Georges Cattaui, *Trois poètes: Hopkins, Yeats, Eliot*, Paris, 1947; Claire Éliane Engel, *Esquisses anglaises: Charles Morgan, Graham Greene, T. S. Eliot,* Paris, 1949; and Edward J. H. Greene, *T. S. Eliot et la France,* Paris, 1951. From Germany and Austria: Egon Fritz, *Die Selbstbehauptung des Abenlandes im Werk von T. S. Eliot,* Hamburg, 1948; Grete und Hans Heinrich Schaeder, *Ein Weg zu T. S. Eliot,* Hameln, 1948; Heinz Günther Klatt, *Sanatorium einer Ehe: Versuch einer Deutung von T. S. Eliots "Cocktail-Party,"* Hannover, 1952; and Ernst Beer, *Thomas Stearns Eliot und der Antiliberalismus des XX. Jahrhunderts,* Wien, 1953. From Italy: Silvio Policardi, *La poesia di T. S. Eliot,* Milano, 1949; Giovanni Freddi, *Idea di religione in T. S. Eliot,* Brecia, 1953; and Spartaco Gamberini, *La poesia di T. S. Eliot,* Genova, 1954. From Norway: Kristian Smidt, *Poetry and Belief in the Work of T. S. Eliot,* Oslo, 1949.

Collections of essays on Eliot's work are Balachandra Rajan, ed., *T. S. Eliot: A Study of His Writings by Several Hands,* London, 1947; Richard March and Tambimuttu, eds., *T. S. Eliot: A Symposium,* London, 1948; and Leonard Unger, ed., *T. S. Eliot: A Selected Critique,* New York, 1948. Specialized studies are Victor H. Brombert, *The Criticism of T. S. Eliot: Problems of an "Impersonal Theory" of Poetry,* New Haven, 1949; David Buchan Morris, *The Poetry of Gerard Manley Hopkins and T. S. Eliot in the Light of the Donne Tradition,* Bern, 1953; Richard Aldington, *Ezra Pound and T. S. Eliot: A Lecture,* Hurst, Berkshire, England, 1954; and Percival William Martin, *Experiment in Depth: A Study of the Work of Jung, Eliot, and Toynbee,* New York, 1955. The severest judgments passed on Eliot in recent years are in Rossell Hope Robbins, *The T. S. Eliot Myth,* New York, 1951, and Albert Mordell, *T. S. Eliot's Deficiencies as a Social Critic* . . . , Girard, Kansas, 1951.

Chapters devoted to Eliot can be found in Horace Gregory and Marya Zaturenska, *A History of American Poetry: 1900–1940,* New York, 1946; Stanley Edgar Hyman, *The Armed Vision,* New York, 1948; George Hamilton Rostrevor, *The Telltale Article: A Critical Approach to Modern Poetry,* London, 1949; Hyatt Howe Waggoner, *The Heel of Elohim,* Norman, Okla., 1950; R. P. Blackmur, *Language as Gesture,* New York, 1952; Frederick J. Hoffman, *The Twenties,* New York, 1955; and Leonard Unger, *The Man in the Name,* Minneapolis, 1956.

For a listing of explications of individual poems, see George Arms and Joseph M. Kuntz, *Poetry Explication,* New York, 1950, pp. 64–73.

Briefer studies are David Daiches, "Some Aspects of T. S. Eliot," *CE,* IX (1947), 115–122; Francis Fergusson, "Action as Passion: *Tristan* and *Murder in the Cathedral,*" *KR,* IX (1947), 201–221; L. L. Martz, "The Wheel and the Point: Aspects of Imagery and Theme in Eliot's Later Poetry," *SR,* LV (1947), 126–147; W. Y. Tindall, "The Recantation of T. S. Eliot," *ASch,* XVI (1947), 431–437; R. W. Flint, "The *Four Quartets* Reconsidered," *SR,* LVI (1948), 69–81; D. B. Brotman, "T. S. Eliot: 'The Music of Ideas,'" *UTQ*, XVIII (1948), 20–29; Hugh Kenner, "Eliot's Moral Dialectic," *HudR*, II (1949), 421–448; David Daiches, "T. S. Eliot," *YR*, XXXVIII (1949), 460–470; John Peter, "'The Family Reunion,'" *Scrutiny*, XVI (1949), 219–230; Arthur Wormhoudt, "A Psychoanalytical Interpretation of 'The Love Song of J. Alfred Prufrock,'" *Perspective*, II (1949), 109–117; Anne Ward, "Speculations on Eliot's Time-World: An Analysis of *The Family Reunion* in Relation to Hulme and Bergson," *AL*, XXI (1949), 18–34; Jane Worthington, "The Epigraphs to the Poetry of T. S. Eliot," *AL*, XXI (1949), 1–17; Curtis Bradford, "Journeys to Byzantium," *VQR*, XXV (1949), 205–225; L. A. Cormican, "Mr. Eliot and Social Biology," *Scrutiny*, XVII (1950), 2–13; William Arrowsmith, "English Verse Drama (II): *The Cocktail Party*," *HudR*, III (1950), 411–430; Patricia M. Adair, "Mr. Eliot's 'Murder in the Cathedral,'" *Cambridge Jour.*, IV (1950), 83–95; Ruth C. Child, "The Early Critical Work of T. S. Eliot: An Assessment," *CE*, XII (1951), 269–275; Giorgio Melchiori, "Echoes in 'The Waste Land,'" *ES*, XXXII (1951), 1–11; R. P. Blackmur, "In the Hope of Straightening Things Out," *KR*, XIII (1951), 303–314; John M. Bradbury, "Four Quartets: The Structural Symbolism," *SR*, LIX (1951), 254–270; George A. Knox, "Quest for the Word in Eliot's *Four Quartets*," *ELH*, XVIII (1951), 310–321; and Donald F. Theall, "Traditional Satire in Eliot's 'Coriolan,'" *Accent*, XI (1951), 194–206.

Other studies are Sarah Watson Emery, "Saints and Mr. Eliot," *EUQ*, VII (1951), 129–142; Morris Weitz, "T. S. Eliot: Time as a Mode of Salvation," *SR*, LX (1952), 48–64; Harold E. McCarthy, "T. S. Eliot and Buddhism," *Phil. East & West*, II (1952), 31–55; R. Ames, "Decadence in the Art of T. S. Eliot," *SciS*, XVI (1952), 193–221; Grover Smith, "Mr. Eliot's New 'Murder,'" *NMQ*, XXII (1952), 331–339; Frank Wood, "Rilke and Eliot: Tradition and Poetry," *GR*, XXVII (1952), 246–259; Charles Moorman, "Order and Mr. Eliot," *SAQ*, LII (1953), 73–87; Robert B. Heilman, "*Alcestis* and *The Cocktail Party*," *CL*, V (1953), 105–116; E. Schwartz, "Eliot's *Cocktail Party* and the New Humanism," *PQ*, XXXII (1953), 58–68; William Blissett, "Pater and Eliot," *UTQ*, XXII (1953), 261–268; Ray B. West, Jr., "Personal History and the 'Four Quartets,'" *NMQ*, XXIII (1953), 269–282; R. L. Beare, "T. S. Eliot and Goethe," *GR*, XXVIII (1953), 243–253; B. A. Morrissette, "T. S. Eliot and Guillaume Apollinaire," *CL*, V (1953), 262–268; John Peter, "Murder in the Cathedral," *SR*, LXI (1953), 362–383; Stephen Spender, "Rilke and the Angels, Eliot and the Shrines," *SR*, LXI (1953), 557–581; Morton Seif, "The Impact of T. S. Eliot on Auden and Spender," *SAQ*, LIII (1954), 61–69; Robert Martin Adams, "Donne and Eliot: Metaphysicals," *KR*, XVI (1954), 278–291; David W. Evans, "T. S. Eliot, Charles Williams, and the Sense of the Occult," *Accent*, XIV (1954), 148–155; R. D. Wagner, "The Meaning of Eliot's Rose-Garden," *PMLA*, LXIX (1954), 22–33; Joseph Warren Beach, "Conrad

Aiken and T. S. Eliot: Echoes and Overtones," *PMLA*, LXIX (1954), 753-762; David L. Stevenson, "An Objective Correlative for T. S. Eliot's Hamlet," *JAAC*, XIII (1954), 69-79; and Delmore Schwartz, "T. S. Eliot's Voice and His Voices," *Poetry*, LXXXV (1954, 1955), 170-176, 232-242.

More recent studies are Armour H. Nelson, "The Critics and *The Waste Land*, 1922-1949," *ES*, XXXVI (1955), 1-15; William Arrowsmith, "Transfiguration in Eliot and Euripides," *SR*, LXIII (1955), 421-442; Charles J. Glicksberg, "The Journey That Must Be Taken: Spiritual Quest in T. S. Eliot's Plays," *SWR*, XL (1955), 203-210; Sears Jayne, "Mr. Eliot's Agon," *PQ*, XXXIV (1955), 395-414; David Holbrook, "Mr. Eliot's Chinese Wall," *EIC*, V (1955), 418-426; René Wellek, "The Criticism of T. S. Eliot," *SR*, LXIV (1956), 398-443; A. F. Beringause, "Journey Through *The Waste Land*," *SAQ*, LVI (1957), 79-90; Arthur Mizener, "To Meet Mr. Eliot," *SR*, LXV (1957), 34-49; J. E. Hardy, "An Antic Disposition," *SR*, LXV (1957), 50-60; Frank Kermode, "Dissociation of Sensibility," *KR*, XIX (1957), 169-194; Robert A. Colby, "Orpheus in the Counting House: *The Confidential Clerk*," *PMLA*, LXXII (1957), 791-802; and Robert L. Beare, "Notes on the Text of T. S. Eliot: Variants from Russell Square," *SB*, IX (1957), 21-49.

#### 491. BIBLIOGRAPHY

The most complete bibliography to date is Donald C. Gallup, *T. S. Eliot: A Bibliography, Including Contributions to Periodicals and Foreign Translations*, New York, 1953, which supersedes his 1947 check list. A useful listing is Allen Tate, *Sixty American Poets, 1896-1944*, rev. ed., Washington, 1954, pp. 24-39.

There are important Eliot collections in the libraries of Brown, Harvard, Princeton, Yale, and the University of Virginia.

## RALPH WALDO EMERSON

#### 492. COLLECTED WORKS AND CORRESPONDENCE

In 1954, Kenneth Walter Cameron edited Emerson's college poem "Indian Superstition" with a "dissertation on Emerson's orientalism at Harvard," Hanover, N.H.

Further publications of Emerson's correspondence are Kenneth Walter Cameron, ed., "A Sheaf of Emerson Letters," *AL*, XXIV (1953), 476-480; and Howard M. Fish, Jr., ed., "Five Emerson Letters," *AL*, XXVII (1955), 25-30.

**493.** EDITED TEXTS

Frank Davidson has edited with notes and an introduction *Napoleon; or, The Man of the World,* Bloomington, Ind. (Indiana University Publications Humanities Series, No. 16), 1947. Herbert Faulkner West has edited *Emerson at Dartmouth; A Reprint of His Oration: Literary Ethics,* Hanover, N.H., 1956.

**494.** BIOGRAPHY AND CRITICISM

The major biography is Ralph L. Rusk, *The Life of Ralph Waldo Emerson,* New York, 1949; it makes use of unpublished as well as published manuscript materials.

Frederic I. Carpenter has prepared a useful *Emerson Handbook,* New York, 1953. It is a guide to both biography and criticism.

Two important studies of Emerson's philosophy are Sherman Paul, *Emerson's Angle of Vision: Man and Nature in American Experience,* Cambridge, Mass., 1952, and Stephen E. Whicher, *Freedom and Fate: An Inner Life of Ralph Waldo Emerson,* Philadelphia, 1953. For recent scholarship on Emerson's aesthetics see Vivian C. Hopkins, *Spires of Form: A Study of Emerson's Aesthetic Theory,* Cambridge, Mass., 1951; Charles R. Metzger, *Emerson and Greenough: Transcendental Pioneers of an American Esthetic,* Berkeley, 1954; and Joseph R. Reaver, *Emerson as Mythmaker,* Gainesville, Fla., 1954. Every student of Emerson's religious theories will want to use Perry Miller's *The Transcendentalists: An Anthology,* Cambridge, Mass., 1950.

Of special interest are chapters on Emerson in Frederick William Conner, *Cosmic Optimism,* Gainesville, Fla., 1949; Daniel Aaron, *Men of Good Hope,* New York, 1951; Joseph L. Blau, *Men and Movements in American Philosophy,* New York, 1952; Charles Feidelson, Jr., *Symbolism and American Literature,* Chicago, 1953; and R. W. B. Lewis, *The American Adam,* Chicago, 1955, *passim.* A brief but provocative analysis of Emerson is Howard Mumford Jones, *The Iron String,* Cambridge, Mass., 1950.

Two attacks on Emersonian philosophy are in Henry Bamford Parkes, *The American Experience,* New York, 1947, and Yvor Winters, *In Defense of Reason,* Denver, 1947.

Briefer studies are Carlos Baker, "The Road to Concord: Another Milestone in the Whitman–Emerson Friendship," *PULC,* VII (1946), 100–117; E. Lindeman, "Emerson's Pragmatic Mood," *ASch,* XVI (1946–47), 57–64; L. H. Downs, "Emerson and Dr. Channing: Two Men from Boston," *NEQ,* XX (1947), 516–534; Sculley Bradley, "Lowell, Emerson and the *Pioneer,*" *AL,* XIX (1947), 231–244; S. G. Brown, "Emerson," *UKCR,* XV (1948), 27–37; N. F. Adkins, "Emerson and the Bardic Tradition," *PMLA,* LXIII

(1948), 662–677; Kathryn Anderson McEuen, "Emerson's Rhymes," *AL*, XX (1948), 31–42; T. A. Perry, "Emerson, The Historical Frame, and Shakespeare," *MLQ*, IX (1948), 440–447; J. R. Roberts, "Emerson's Debt to the Seventeenth Century," *AL*, XXI (1949), 298–310; J. C. Gerber, "Emerson and the Political Economists," *NEQ*, XXII (1949), 336–357; Patrick F. Quinn, "Emerson and Mysticism," *AL*, XXI (1950), 397–414; Kenneth Walter Cameron, "An Early Prose Work of Emerson," *AL*, XXII (1950), 332–338; G. Ferris Cronkhite, "The Transcendental Railroad," *NEQ*, XXIV (1951), 306–328; Kenneth Walter Cameron, "Coleridge and the Genesis of Emerson's 'Uriel,' " *PQ*, XXX (1951), 212–217; Robert T. Harris, "Nature: Emerson and Mill," *WHR*, VI (1951–52), 1–13; Carl F. Strauch, "The Daemonic and Experimental in Emerson," *Personalist*, XXXIII (1952), 40–55; Kenneth Walter Cameron, "Emerson, Thoreau, and the Society of Natural History," *AL*, XXIV (1952), 21–30; Vern Wagner, "No Tumult of Response: Emerson's Reception as a Lyceum Lecturer," *WHR*, VI (1952), 129–135; and Franklin B. Newman, "Emerson and Buonarroti," *NEQ*, XXV (1952), 524–535.

More recent studies are William T. Stafford, "Emerson and the James Family," *AL*, XXIV (1953), 433–461; Douglas C. Stenerson, "Emerson and the Agrarian Tradition," *JHI*, XIV (1953), 95–115; Perry Miller, "Emersonian Genius and the American Democracy," *NEQ*, XXVI (1953), 27–44; Ralph L. Rusk, "Emerson and the Stream of Experience," *CE*, XIV (1953), 373–379; John O. McCormick, "Emerson's Theory of Human Greatness," *NEQ*, XXVI (1953), 291–314; S. G. Brown, "Emerson: 1803–1953," *Ethics*, LXIV (1954), 217–225; R. P. Adams, "Emerson and the Organic Metaphor," *PMLA*, LXIX (1954), 117–130; J. O. Eidson, "Charles Stearns Wheeler: Emerson's 'Good Grecian,' " *NEQ*, XXVII (1954), 472–483; R. H. Super, "Emerson and Arnold's Poetry," *PQ*, XXXIII (1954), 396–403; Morton Cronin, "Some Notes on Emerson's Prose Diction," *ASp*, XXIX (1954), 105–113; Seymour L. Gross, "Emerson and Poetry," *SAQ*, LIV (1955), 82–94; John Q. Anderson, "Emerson and 'Manifest Destiny,' " *BPLQ*, VII (1955), 23–33; Andrew Schiller, "Gnomic Structure in Emerson's Poetry," *PMASAL*, XL (1955), 313–320; T. M. Brown, "Greenough, Paine, Emerson and the Organic Aesthetic," *JAAC*, XIV (1956), 304–317; D. M. Murray, "Emerson's 'Language as Fossil Poetry': An Analogy from Chinese," *NEQ*, XXIX (1956), 204–215; Carl F. Strauch, "Emerson's 'New England Capitalist,' " *HLB*, X (1956), 245–253; Conrad Wright, "Emerson, Barzillai Frost, and the Divinity School Address," *HTR*, XLIX (1956), 19–43; William Hedges, "A Short Way Around Emerson's Nature," *TWASAL*, XLIV (1956), 21–27; Kenneth Walter Cameron, "History and Biography in Emerson's Unpublished Sermons," *PAAS*, LXVI (1957), 103–118; V. L. O. Chittick, "Emerson's 'Frolic Health,' " *NEQ*, XXX (1957), 209–234; B

Bernard Cohen, "Emerson and Hawthorne on England," *BPLQ*, IX (1957), 73–85; and Robert C. Pollock, "A Reappraisal of Emerson," *Thought*, XXXII (1957), 86–132.

### 500. BIBLIOGRAPHY

A full bibliography for Emerson is still not completed. Floyd Stovall has prepared a useful annotated bibliography for *Eight American Authors: A Review of Research and Criticism*, ed. Floyd Stovall, New York, 1956. See also the classified lists of Frederic I. Carpenter's *Emerson Handbook*, New York, 1953; and John D. Gordan, "Ralph Waldo Emerson, 1803–1882: Catalogue of an Exhibition from the Berg Collection," *BNYPL*, LVII (1953), 392–408, 433–460.

The first issue of the *Emerson Society Quarterly* appeared in 1955. It is edited by Kenneth Walter Cameron of Trinity College, Hartford. See separate issues for a variety of bibliographical entries.


## JAMES T(HOMAS) FARRELL

### 501. SEPARATE WORKS

*The Road Between*, 1949; *An American Dream Girl* [*and Other Stories*], 1950; *This Man and This Woman*, 1951; *Yet Other Waters*, 1952; *The Face of Time*, 1953; *Reflections at Fifty, and Other Essays*, 1954; *French Girls Are Vicious, and Other Stories*, 1955; *My Baseball Diary*, 1957; *A Dangerous Woman, and Other Stories*, 1957; *It Has Come to Pass*, 1958.

*The Short Stories of James T. Farrell* (1937) was reprinted, New York, 1945 and 1951. *An Omnibus of Short Stories*, New York, 1956, is a one-volume edition of *$1,000 a Week* (1942), *To Whom It May Concern* (1944), and *The Life Adventurous* (1947).

### BIOGRAPHY AND CRITICISM

*The Coming of Age of a Great Book*, New York, 1953, is a collection of criticism of *Studs Lonigan* by various hands. Other brief estimates are Charles Child Walcutt, "Naturalism in 1946: Dreiser and Farrell," *Accent*, VI (1946), 263–268; Irving Howe, "James T. Farrell: The Critic Calcified," *PR*, XIV (1947), 545–546 ff.; W. M. Frohock, "James Farrell: The Precise Content," *SWR*, XXXV (1950), 39–48; Charles I. Glicksberg, "The Criticism of James T. Farrell," XXXV (1950), 189–196; Irwin Stock, "Farrell and His Critics," *ArQ*, VI (1950), 328–338; Charles Child Walcutt, "James T. Farrell and the Reversible Topcoat," *ArQ*, VII (1951), 293–310; Frank O'Malley, "James T. Farrell: Two Twilight Images," *Fifty Years of the American Novel: A Christian Appraisal*, ed. Harold C. Gardiner, S.J., New York, 1951, pp. 237–256; Blanche Housman Gelfant, "James T. Farrell: The Ecological Novel," *The American City Novel*, Norman, Okla., 1954, pp. 175–227; and C. Hartley Grattan, "James T. Farrell: Moralist," *Harper's*, CCIX (Oct. 1954), 93–98.

The James T. Farrell Collection of Manuscripts is in the University of Pennsylvania Library.

# WILLIAM FAULKNER

**502. SEPARATE WORKS**

*Intruder in the Dust*, 1948; *Knight's Gambit*, 1949; *Collected Stories*, 1950; *Requiem for a Nun*, 1951; *A Fable*, 1954; *Big Woods*, 1955; *The Town*, 1957.

*Notes on a Horsethief*, published in a limited edition, Greenville, Miss., 1951, is an episode which appeared, somewhat revised, in *A Fable*. *The Faulkner Reader*, 1954, contains *The Sound and the Fury*, the Nobel Prize address, short stories, and excerpts from novels.

The sketches Faulkner contributed to the New Orleans *Times-Picayune* in 1925 are edited by Carvel Collins, *William Faulkner: New Orleans Sketches*, New Brunswick, N.J., 1958, superseding incomplete collections published in Minneapolis, 1953 and 1955, and Tokyo, 1955.

*Faulkner at Nagano*, ed. Robert A. Jelliffe, Tokyo, 1956, contains interviews, the text of seminars, and other material related to the 1955 Nagano Seminars in which Faulkner took part.

**BIOGRAPHY AND CRITICISM**

There is as yet no biography. Three book-length critical studies are Harry Modean Campbell and Ruel E. Foster, *William Faulkner: A Critical Appraisal*, Norman, Okla., 1951; Irving Howe, *William Faulkner: A Critical Study*, New York, 1952; and William Van O'Connor, *The Tangled Fire of William Faulkner*, Minneapolis, 1954. A special study is Ward L. Miner, *The World of William Faulkner*, Durham, N.C., 1952. Collected critical essays are Frederick J. Hoffman and Olga W. Vickery, eds., *William Faulkner: Two Decades of Criticism*, East Lansing, Mich., 1951, and Alan Downer, ed., *English Institute Essays: 1952*, New York, 1954.

Four journals published special Faulkner issues: *Perspective*, II (Summer, 1949) and III (Autumn, 1950); *Harvard Advocate*, CXXXV (Nov., 1951); *Modern Fiction Studies*, II (Autumn, 1956); and *Princeton University Library Chronicle*, XVIII (Spring, 1957). *Faulkner Studies* began publication in Denver, Colo., Vol. I, No. 1 (Spring, 1952); it ceased publication in Minneapolis, Minn., Vol. III, No. 4 (Winter, 1954), after eleven issues.

General critical studies are Caroline Gordon, "Notes on Faulkner and Flaubert," *HudR*, I (1948), 222–231; Dayton Kohler, "William Faulkner and the Social Conscience," *CE*, XI (1949), 119–127; Robert Bunker, "Faulkner: A Case for Regionalism," *NMQR*, XIX (1949), 108–115; Charles I. Glicksberg, "The World of William Faulkner," *ArQ*, V (1949), 46–58; W. M. Frohock, *The Novel of Violence in America, 1920–1950*, Dallas, 1950, pp. 101–124; R. W. B. Lewis, "The Hero in the New World: William Faulkner's *The Bear*," *KR*, XIII (1951), 641–660; Walter Sullivan, "The Tragic Design of *Absalom, Absalom!*" *SAQ*, L (1951), 552–566; Cleanth Brooks, "*Absalom, Absalom!:* The Definition of Innocence," *SR*, LIX (1951), 543–558; Walton Litz, "William Faulkner's Moral Vision," *SWR*, XXXVII (1952), 200–209; John Lydenberg, "Nature Myth in Faulkner's 'The Bear,'" *AL*, XXIV (1952), 62–72; Wright Morris, "The Violent Land: Some Observations on the Faulkner Country," *Mag. of Art*, XLV (1952), 99–103; Robert Humphrey, "Form and Function of Stream of Consciousness in William Faulkner's 'The Sound and the Fury,'" *UKCR*, XIX (1952), 34–40; Frederick L. Gwynn, "Faulkner's Prufrock—and Other Observations," *JEGP*, LII (1953), 63–70; Robert M. Adams, "Poetry in the Novel; or, Faulkner Esemplastic," *VQR*, XXIX (1953), 419–434; Arthur L. Scott, "The Faulknerian Sentence," *PrS*, XXVII (1953), 91–98; Robert D. Jacobs, "Faulkner's Tragedy of Isolation," *Southern Renascence*, eds. Louis D. Rubin, Jr., and Robert D. Jacobs, Baltimore, 1953, pp. 170–191; Maurice-Edgar Coindreau, "William Faulkner in France," *Yale French Stud.*, No. 10 (1953), 85–91; A. C. Hoffman, "Point of View in *Absalom, Absalom!*" *UKCR*, XIX (1953), 233–239; Peter Swiggart, "Moral and Temporal Order in *The Sound and the Fury*," *SR*, LXI (1953), 221–237.

More recent studies are Melvin Backman, "Sickness and Primitivism: A Dominant Pattern in William Faulkner's Work," *Accent*, XIV (1954), 61–73; R. W. Flint, "Faulkner as Elegist," *HudR*, VII (1954), 246–257; Karl E. Zink, "William Faulkner: Form as Experience," *SAQ*, LIII (1954), 384–403; Carvel Collins, "Faulkner and Certain Earlier Southern Fiction," *CE*, XVI (1954), 92–97; Norman Holmes Pearson, "Faulkner's Three 'Evening Suns,'" *YULG*, XXIX (1954), 61–70; Carl Benson, "Thematic Design in *Light in August*," *SAQ*, LIII (1954), 540–555; Olga W. Vickery, "*The Sound and the Fury*: A Study in Perspective," *PMLA*, LXIX (1954), 1017–1037; Jack Gordon Goellner, "A Closer Look at 'As I Lay Dying,'" *Perspective*, VII (1954), 42–54; Viola Hopkins, "William Faulkner's 'The Hamlet': A Study in Meaning and Form," *Accent*, XV (1955), 125–144; Andrew Lytle, "The Son of Man: He Will Prevail," *SR*, LXII (1955), 114–137; William Webb Pusey, "William Faulkner's Works in Germany to 1940: Translations and Criticism," *GR*, XXX (1955), 211–226; Carl Galharn, "Faulkner's Faith: Roots from *The Wild Palms*," *TCL*, I (1955), 139–160; Ilse D. Lind, "The Design and Meaning of *Absalom, Absalom!*" *PMLA*, LXX (1955), 887–912; Linton Massey, "Notes on the Unrevised Galleys of Faulkner's *Sanctuary*," *SB*, VIII (1956), 195–208; Randall Stewart, "Hawthorne and Faulkner," *CE*, XVII (1956), 258–262; Karl E. Zink, "Flux and the Frozen Moment: The Imagery of Stasis in Faulkner's Prose," *PMLA*, LXXI (1956), 285–301; James Hafley, "Faulkner's *Fable:* Dream and Transfiguration," *Accent*, XVI (1956), 3–14; Jean Stein, "William Faulkner: The Art of Fiction [Interview]," *Paris Rev.*, No. 12 (1956), 28–52; Beekman W. Cottrell, "Christian Symbols in 'Light in August,'" *MFS*, II (1956–1957), 207–213; Olga W. Vickery, "Faulkner's First Novel," *WHR*, XI (1957), 251–256; T. Y. Greet, "The Theme and Structure of Faulkner's *The Hamlet*," *PMLA*, LXXII (1957), 775–790; John L. Langley, Jr., "Joe Christmas: The Hero in the Modern World," *VQR*, XXXIII (1957), 233–249; and Andrew Lytle, "*The Town:* Helen's Last Stand," *SR*, LXV (1957), 475–484.

**503.** BIBLIOGRAPHY

The most complete listing of Faulkner's work is James B. Meriwether, *William Faulkner: A Check List*, Princeton University Library, 1957. Two listings of critical studies are the bibliography compiled by Olga W. Vickery for *William Faulkner: Two Decades of Criticism*, East Lansing, Mich., 1951, pp. 269–280, and Maurice Beebe, "Criticism of William Faulkner: A Selected Checklist with an Index to Studies of Separate Works," *MFS*, II (1956), 150–164.

## F(RANCIS) SCOTT (KEY) FITZGERALD

**505.** COLLECTED WORKS AND REPRINTS

*Afternoon of an Author*, Princeton, 1957, is a volume of fourteen uncollected stories and six essays from the Princeton University Library Fitzgerald Collection, with an introduction and notes by Arthur Mizener.

Malcolm Cowley selected *The Stories of F. Scott Fitzgerald*, New York, 1951. A major reprinting is *Three Novels: The Great Gatsby* (with an introduction by Malcolm Cowley), *Tender Is the Night* (with the author's final revisions; edited by Malcolm Cowley), *The Last Tycoon: An Unfinished Novel* (edited by Edmund Wilson), New York, 1953.

The *Princeton University Library Chronicle*, XII (Summer, 1951), is an F. Scott Fitzgerald issue.

BIOGRAPHY AND CRITICISM

A full-length biography is Arthur Mizener, *The Far Side of Paradise, A Biography of F. Scott Fitzgerald*, Boston, 1951. James E. Miller, *The Fictional Technique of Scott Fitzgerald*, The Hague, 1957, is a critical analysis of the first three novels.

Alfred Kazin edited *F. Scott Fitzgerald: The Man and His Work*, Cleveland, 1951, a collection of critical essays by various hands.

Briefer studies are Maxwell Geismar, *The Last of the Provincials: The American Novel, 1915-1925*, Boston, 1947, pp. 287-352; Maurice Hindus, "F. Scott Fitzgerald and Literary Anti-Semitism," *Commentary*, III (1947), 508-516, IV (1947), 188-189; Martin Kallich, "F. Scott Fitzgerald: Money or Morals," *UKCR*, XV (1949), 271-280; Katherine Brégy, "F. Scott Fitzgerald —Tragic Comedian," *CathW*, CLXXIII (1951), 86-91; Henry Dan Piper, "Fitzgerald's Cult of Disillusion," *AQ*, III (1951), 69-80; D. W. Harding, "Scott Fitzgerald," *Scrutiny*, XVIII (1951-1952), 166-174; Tom Burnam, "The Eyes of Dr. Eckleburg: A Re-examination of 'The Great Gatsby,'" *CE*, XIV (1952), 7-12; Edwin S. Fussell, "Fitzgerald's Brave New World," *ELH*, XIX (1952), 291-306; Henry Wechsler, *The Theme of Failure in F. Scott Fitzgerald*, Washington, Pa., 1952; Charles S. Holmes, "Fitzgerald: The American Theme," *PS*, VI (1952), 243-252; Malcolm Cowley, "F. Scott Fitzgerald: The Romance of Money," *WR*, XVII (1953), 245-255; Douglas Taylor, "*The Great Gatsby:* Style and Myth," *UKCR*, XX (1953), 30-40.

More recent studies are F. C. Watkins, "Fitzgerald's Jay Gatz and Young Ben Franklin," *NEQ*, XXVII (1954), 249-252; Marius Bewley, "Scott Fitzgerald's Criticism of America," *SR*, LXII (1954), 223-246; Norman Friedman, "Versions of Form in Fiction: *Great Expectations* and *The Great Gatsby*," *Accent*, XIV (1954), 246-264; Frederick J. Hoffman, *The Twenties*, New York, 1955, pp. 111-119; Albert J. Lubell, "The Fitzgerald Revival," *SAQ*, LIV (1955), 95-106; W. M. Frohock, "Morals, Manners, and Scott Fitzgerald," *SWR*, XL (1955), 220-228; Robert W. Stallman, "Conrad and *The Great Gatsby*," *TCL*, I (1955), 5-12; Robert W. Stallman, "Gatsby and the Hole in Time," *MFS*, I (1955), 2-16; Andrew W. Turnbull, "Scott Fitzgerald at La Paix," *NY*, XXXII (Apr. 7, 1956), 98-109; *idem*, "Further Notes on Fitzgerald at La Paix," *NY*, XXXII (Nov. 17, 1956), 153-165; Henry Dan Piper, "Frank Norris and Scott Fitzgerald," *HLQ*, XIX (1956), 393-400; Robert Ornstein, "Scott Fitzgerald's Fable of East and West," *CE*, XVIII (1956), 139-143; Thomas A. Hanzo, "The Theme and the Narrator of 'The Great Gatsby,'" *MFS*, II (1956-1957), 183-190; Barbara Giles, "The Dream of F. Scott Fitzgerald," *Mainstream*, X (1957), 1-12; and John Henry Raleigh, "Fitzgerald's *The Great Gatsby:* Legendary Bases and Allegorical Significances," *UKCR*, XXIII (1957), 283-291.

## 506. BIBLIOGRAPHY

A valuable bibliography is Henry Dan Piper, "F. Scott Fitzgerald: A Check List," *PULC*, XII (1951), 196-208. See also Arthur Mizener, "The F. Scott Fitzgerald Papers," *ibid.*, XII (1951), 190-195.

# JOHN GOULD FLETCHER
*d. 1950*

**506.** BIOGRAPHY AND CRITICISM

Charlie May Simon, *Johnswood*, New York, 1953, is a personal memoir by Fletcher's wife. See also Donald Davidson, "In Memory of John Gould Fletcher," *Poetry*, LXXVII (1950), 154–161; Richard Crowder, "John Gould Fletcher as Cassandra," *SAQ*, LII (1953), 88–92; Norreys J. O'Conor, "Impressions of John Gould Fletcher," *SWR*, XXXVIII (1953), 238–243; and Ralph Behrens, "John Gould Fletcher and Rimbaud's 'Alchime du Verbe,'" *CL*, VIII (1956), 46–62.

A bibliographical listing is in Allen Tate, *Sixty American Poets, 1896–1944*, rev. ed., Washington, 1954, pp. 43–45.


# BENJAMIN FRANKLIN

**508.** COLLECTED WORKS AND CORRESPONDENCE

*The Papers of Benjamin Franklin*, a new edition of his writings, is now in preparation for publication under the auspices of the American Philosophical Society and Yale University. The general editors are Leonard W. Labaree and Whitfield J. Bell, Jr. The edition, to include all of Franklin's writing as well as all significant communications addressed to him, will run to more than twenty-five volumes. *Mr. Franklin: A Selection from His Personal Letters*, New Haven, 1956, is a preliminary sampling, published on the occasion of the two hundred and fiftieth anniversary of Franklin's birth. For details see Leonard W. Labaree, "The Papers of Benjamin Franklin," *Manuscripts*, VII (1954), 34–39; *idem*, "The Papers of Benjamin Franklin," *Daedalus*, LXXXVI (1955), 57–62; Whitfield J. Bell, Jr., "Franklin's Papers and *The Papers of Benjamin Franklin*," *PH*, XXII (1955), 1–17; William E. Lingelbach, "Benjamin Franklin's Papers and the American Philosophical Society," *PAPS*, XCIX (1955), 359–380; and Leonard W. Labaree and Whitfield J. Bell, Jr., "The Papers of Benjamin Franklin: A Progress Report," *ibid.*, CI (1957), 532–534.

Several collections of letters have appeared in recent years: Verner W. Crane, ed., *Benjamin Franklin's Letters to the Press, 1758–1775*, Chapel Hill, 1948; William Greene Roelker, ed., *Benjamin Franklin and Catherine Ray Greene, Their Correspondence, 1775–1790*, Philadelphia, 1949; and Carl Van Doren, ed., *Letters of Benjamin Franklin and Jane Mecom*, Princeton, 1950. See also Frederic R. Kirkland, ed., "Three Franklin Letters," *PMHB*, LXXII (1948), 70–76; *idem*, "Three Mecom-Franklin Letters," *ibid.*, LXXII (1948), 264–272; Antonio Pace, ed., "The Franklin-Volta Correspondence:

Legend or Fact?" *PAPS*, XCIX (1955), 436–439; Robert L. Kahn, ed., "Some Unpublished Raspe-Franklin Letters," *ibid.*, XCIX (1955), 127–132; *idem,* "Three Franklin-Raspe Letters," *ibid.*, XCIX (1955), 397–400; *idem,* "Addendum Concerning a Lost Franklin-Raspe Letter," *ibid.*, C (1956), 279; and Whitfield J. Bell, Jr., ed., " 'All Clear Sunshine': New Letters of Franklin and Mary Stevenson Hewson," *ibid.*, C (1956), 521–536.

### 510. EDITED TEXTS AND REPRINTS

Max Farrand, ed., *The Autobiography of Benjamin Franklin: A Restoration of a "Fair Copy,"* Berkeley, 1949, is based upon four source texts: the William Temple Franklin edition (1818), the Bigelow edition (1868), the French translation by Louis Guillaume le Veillard, and the French translation of the first part published by Buisson (1791). Max Farrand, ed., *Benjamin Franklin's Memoirs: Parallel Text Edition,* Berkeley, 1949, comprises the text of Franklin's original manuscript, the French translation by Louis Guillaume le Veillard, the French translation published by Buisson, and the version edited by William Temple Franklin.

Carl Van Doren edited *The Will of Benjamin Franklin, 1757,* Philadelphia, 1949. Perry Miller provided an introduction to *The New England Courant: A Selection of Certain Issues Containing Writings of Benjamin Franklin or Published by Him During His Brother's Imprisonment,* Boston, 1956. Richard E. Amacher edited *Franklin's Wit and Folly: The Bagatelles,* New Brunswick, N.J., 1953. Reprintings of the *Autobiography* are too numerous to list separately.

### 511. BIOGRAPHY AND CRITICISM

Carl L. Becker, *Benjamin Franklin,* Ithaca, 1946, is a biographical sketch, reprinted from the *Dictionary of American Biography.* Fuller studies of Franklin's life are I. Bernard Cohen, *Benjamin Franklin: His Contribution to the American Tradition,* Indianapolis, 1953; Verner W. Crane, *Benjamin Franklin and a Rising People,* Boston, 1954; and Nelson Beecher Keyes, *Benjamin Franklin, an Affectionate Portrait,* New York, 1956.

Recent specialized studies are Gilbert Chinard, *L'Apothéose de Benjamin Franklin,* Paris, 1955; William Bell Clark, *Benjamin Franklin's Privateers, A Naval Epic of the American Revolution,* Baton Rouge, 1956; I. Bernard Cohen, *Franklin and Newton: An Inquiry into Speculative Newtonian Experimental Science and Franklin's Work in Electricity as an Example Thereof,* Philadelphia, 1956; and Alfred Owen Aldridge, *Franklin and His French Contemporaries,* New York, 1957.

Four special Franklin issues, in commemoration of the two hundred and fiftieth anniversary of his birth, are *Proceedings of the American Philosophical Society,* XCIX (Dec., 1955), and C (Aug., 1956); the *Journal of the Franklin Institute,* CCLXI (Jan., 1956); and the *Pennsylvania Magazine of History and Biography,* LXXX (Jan., 1956).

Briefer studies are Percy G. Adams, "Crèvecœur and Franklin," *PH,* XIV (1947), 273–279; Frederic R. Kirkland, "Jefferson and Franklin," *PMHB,* LXXI (1947), 218–222; Antonio Pace, "Franklin and Machiavelli," *Symposium,* I (1947), 36–42; A. D. McKillop, "Some Newtonian Verses in *Poor Richard,*" *NEQ,* XXI (1948), 383–385; Maurice J. Quinlan, "Dr. Franklin Meets Dr. Johnson," *PMHB,* LXXIII (1949), 34–44; Alfred Owen Aldridge, "The Debut of American Letters in France," *FAR,* III (1950), 1–23; *idem,* "Franklin and the Ghostly Drummer of Tedworth," *WMQ,* VII (1950), 559–567; Thomas Coulson, "Benjamin Franklin and the Post Office," *JFI,* CCL (1950), 191–212; Lyman H. Butterfield, "B. Franklin's Epitaph," *New Col,* III (1950), 9–39; Alfred Owen Aldridge, "Benjamin Franklin and Philosophical Necessity," *MLQ,* XII (1951), 292–309; Charles W. Meister, "Franklin as a Proverb Stylist," *AL,* XXIV (1952), 157–166; Thomas Coulson, "Franklin's Wit and Wisdom," *JFI,* CCLIV (1952), 13–16; Clinton Rossiter, "The Political Theory of Benjamin Franklin," *PMHB,* LXXVI (1952), 259–293; Merton A. Christensen, "Franklin on the Hemphill Trial: Deism versus Presbyterian Othodoxy," *WMQ,* X (1953), 422–440; Gerald Stourzh, "Reason and Power in Benjamin Franklin's Political Thought," *Am Pol Sci Rev,* XLVII (1953), 1092–1115; Frederick B. Tolles, "Franklin and the Pulteney Mission: An Episode in the Secret History of the American Revolution," *HLQ,* XVII (1953), 37–58; and Charles L. Sanford, "An American's *Pilgrim's Progress,*" *AQ,* VI (1954), 297–310.

More recent studies are Leonard W. Labaree, "Benjamin Franklin and His Scientific Friends," *BuR,* V (1955), 1–18; Gilbert Chinard, "Franklin en France," *FR,* XXIX (1956), 281–289; Harold A. Larrabee, "Poor Richard in an Age of Plenty," *Harper's,* CCXII (Jan., 1956), 64–68; J. Bennett Nolan, "Monsieur Franklin," *PH,* XXIII (1956), 347–375; Dorothy F. Grimm, "Franklin's Scientific Institution," *PH,* XXIII (1956), 437–462; Jack C. Barnes, "A Moral Epistle: A Probable Addition to the Franklin Canon," *NEQ,* XXX (1957), 73–84; Richard D. Miles, "The American Image of Benjamin Franklin," *AQ,* IX (1957), 117–143; and Morris Bishop, "Franklin in France," *Daedalus,* LXXXVI (1957), 214–230.

## 515. BIBLIOGRAPHY

See F. S. Philbrick, "Notes on Early Editions and Editors of Franklin," *PAPS,* XCVII (1953), 525–564; *The Benjamin Franklin Collection of Autograph Letters, Documents, Books, and Almanacs . . . Together with Other Material by His Contemporaries, Collection Formed by the Late Arthur Bloch . . . ,* New York, 1954 (a catalogue of the Parke-Bernet auction, Oct. 20, 1954); *Benjamin Franklin, The Two Hundred and Fiftieth Anniversary of His Birth, 1706–1956,* Philadelphia, 1956 (an exhibition in the Library of Congress); and *Bibliothèque Nationale, Benjamin Franklin et la France,* Paris, 1956 (catalogue of the exhibition at the Bibliothèque Nationale).

## MARY E(LEANOR) WILKINS FREEMAN

### 517. BIOGRAPHY AND CRITICISM

The first biography of Mrs. Freeman is Edward Foster, *Mary E. Wilkins Freeman,* New York, 1956.

See also Babette M. Levy, "Mutations in New England Local Color," *NEQ,* XIX (1946), 338–358.

## PHILIP (MORIN) FRENEAU

### 517. SEPARATE WORKS

See Philip M. Marsh, "A Freneau Fragment," *JRUL,* X (1947), 60–62, and *idem,* "A Lost Fragment of Freneau's 'The Spy,'" *ibid.,* XIII (1950), 61–63.

### COLLECTED WORKS AND EDITED REPRINTS

*The Prose of Philip Freneau* was selected and edited by Philip M. Marsh, New Brunswick, N.J., 1955. Mr. Marsh also edited [*James*] *Monroe's Defense of Jefferson and Freneau Against Hamilton,* Oxford, Ohio, 1948.

### 518. BIOGRAPHY AND CRITICISM

A special study is Nelson F. Adkins, *Philip Freneau and the Cosmic Enigma: The Religious and Philosophical Speculations of an American Poet,* New York, 1949.

Five studies by Philip M. Marsh are "Jefferson and Freneau," *ASch,* XVI (1947), 201–210; "Philip Freneau and James Madison, 1791–1793," *PNJHS,* LXV (1947), 189–194; "Philip Freneau and the Theatre," *ibid.,* LXVI (1948), 96–105; "Indian Folklore in Freneau," *ibid.,* LXXI (1953), 125–135; and "The Freneau-Hopkinson Quarrel," *ibid.,* LXXIV (1956), 304–314.

Two studies by Lewis Leary are "The First Biography of Philip Freneau," *PNJHS,* LXV (1947), 117–125, and "Philip Freneau and Monmouth County," *Monmouth County Hist. Assn. Bul.,* I (1948), 59–82. See also Ruth W. Brown, "Classical Echoes in the Poetry of Philip Freneau," *CJ,* XLV (1949), 29–35.

For a listing of explications of individual poems see George Arms and Joseph M. Kuntz, *Poetry Explication,* New York, 1950, p. 75.

The most recent bibliographical study is Owen P. Thomas, "Philip Freneau: A Bibliography," *PNJHS*, LXXV (1957), 197–205.

## ROBERT (LEE) FROST

### 520. COLLECTED WORKS

*Complete Poems of Robert Frost* was published in New York, 1949.

### REPRINTS

*The Road Not Taken: An Introduction to Robert Frost*, New York, 1951, is a selection of Frost's poems, with a biographical preface and running commentary by Louis Untermeyer. *Aforesaid*, New York, 1954, is a limited edition of selected poems, printed for Frost's eightieth birthday.

### BIOGRAPHY AND CRITICISM

A recent biographical study is Sidney Cox, *Swinger of Birches: A Portrait of Robert Frost*, New York, 1957. A full-length critical study is Reginald L. Cook, *The Dimensions of Robert Frost*, New York, 1958.

Briefer estimates are W. G. O'Donnell, "Robert Frost and New England: A Revaluation," *YR*, XXXVII (1948), 698–712; Lawrance Thompson, "An Early Frost Broadside," *New Col*, I (1948), 5–12; Yvor Winters, "Robert Frost; or, The Spiritual Drifter as Poet," *SR*, LVI (1948), 564–596; William O'Donnell, "Parable in Poetry," *VQR*, XXV (1949), 269–282; Hyatt Howe Waggoner, *The Heel of Elohim: Science and Values in Modern American Poetry*, Norman, Okla., 1950, pp. 41–60; C. M. Bowra, "Robert Frost," *Adelphi*, XXVII (1950), 46–64; Ray Nash, "The Poet and the Pirate," *New Col*, II (1950), 311–321; Louis Landré, "Premières critiques de Robert Frost," *EA*, V (May, 1952), 143–151; and Howard Sergeant, "The Poetry of Robert Frost," *English* (London), IX (Spring, 1952), 13–16.

More recent studies are Randall Jarrell, *Poetry and the Age*, New York, 1953, pp. 28–69; Robert Francis, "Robert Frost from His Green Mountain," *DR*, XXXIII (1953), 117–127; Joseph Warren Beach, "Robert Frost," *YR*, XLIII (1954), 204–217; Eleanor Farjeon, "Edward Thomas and Robert Frost," *London Mag.*, I (May, 1954), 50–61; Harold H. Watts, "Robert Frost and the Interrupted Dialogue," *AL*, XXVII (1955), 69–87; William Mulder, "Freedom and Form: Robert Frost's Double Discipline," *SAQ*, LIV (1955), 386–393; Harold H. Watts, "Three Entities and Robert Frost," *BuR*, V (Dec., 1955), 19–38; Seymour Chatman, "Robert Frost's 'Mowing': An Inquiry into Prosodic Structure," *KR*, XVIII (1956), 421–438; and Carlos Baker, "Frost on the Pumpkin," *GaR*, XI (1957), 117–131.

For a listing of explications of individual poems see George Arms and Joseph M. Kuntz, *Poetry Explication,* New York, 1950, pp. 76–78.

**522.** BIBLIOGRAPHY

Of bibliographical interest is *The Earle J. Bernheimer Collection of First Editions of American Authors, Featuring a Remarkable Collection of the Writings of Robert Frost, Printed and in Manuscript, Including the Unique Copy of Twilight,* New York, 1950 (a catalogue of the Parke-Bernet auction, Dec., 1950).

# (SARAH) MARGARET FULLER (OSSOLI)

**522.** SEPARATE WORKS

Three studies by J. Wesley Thomas contribute new information on Margaret Fuller's writing: "A Hitherto Unpublished Textual Criticism by James Freeman Clarke of Margaret Fuller's Translation of *Tasso,*" *Monatshefte,* XLI (Feb., 1949), 89–92; "New Light on Margaret Fuller's Projected 'Life of Goethe,'" *GR,* XXIV (1949), 216–223; and "James Freeman Clarke, Margaret Fuller, and Emma Keats, Some Previously Unpublished Manuscripts," *FCHQ,* XXVIII (1954), 21–27.

**523.** COLLECTED WORKS AND CORRESPONDENCE

Leopold Wellisz, *The Friendship of Margaret Fuller D'Ossoli and Adam Mickiewicz,* New York, 1947, prints, for the first time, ten letters from Mickiewicz to Miss Fuller. This brochure supplements the letters edited by Emma Detti, *Margaret Fuller Ossoli e suoi Corrispondenti,* Firenze, 1942.

BIOGRAPHY AND CRITICISM

The most recent biography is Faith Chipperfield, *In Quest of Love: The Life and Death of Margaret Fuller,* New York, 1957.

For critical estimates see M. Whitcomb Hess, "Margaret Fuller and Browning's 'Childe Roland,'" *Personalist,* XXVIII (1947), 376–383; Edward Nicholas, "It Is I: Margaret Fuller," *Harper's,* CXCIX (July, 1949), 66–76; Margaret Munsterberg, "Margaret Fuller Centenary," *BPLQ,* II (1950), 245–268; Thomas H. McNeal, "Poe's *Zenobia:* An Early Satire on Margaret Fuller," *MLQ,* XI (1950), 205–216; Edward G. Berry, "Margaret Fuller Ossoli, 1810–1850," *DR,* XXX (1951)), 369–376; Wilma R. Ebbitt, "Margaret Fuller's Ideas on Criticism," *BPLQ,* III (1951), 171–187; Eileen S. Barr, "Margaret Fuller D'Ossoli," *WHR,* VI (1951–1952), 37–52; E. A. Hoyt and

L. S. Brigham, "Glimpses of Margaret Fuller: The Green Street School and Florence," *NEQ,* XXIX (1956), 87–98; and Perry Miller, "'I Find No Intellect Comparable to My Own,'" *AH,* VIII (Feb., 1957), 22–25, 96–99.

# (HANNIBAL) HAMLIN GARLAND

**526.** REPRINTS AND CORRESPONDENCE

*Crumbling Idols* (1894) was reprinted in facsimile, with an introduction by Robert E. Spiller, Gainesville, Fla., 1952. *Main-Travelled Roads* (1891) reappeared, with a new preface by B. R. McElderry and the 1893 introduction by William Dean Howells, New York, 1956.

For Garland letters, see John T. Flanagan, ed., "Hamlin Garland Writes to His Chicago Publisher," *AL,* XXIII (1952), 447–457; and Lars Åhnebrink, ed., "Paris in Times of Turmoil: Three Letters of Hamlin Garland to His Parents in 1899," *EA,* IX (1956), 246–251.

**527.** BIOGRAPHY AND CRITICISM

Two studies which treat Garland as naturalist are Lars Åhnebrink, *The Beginnings of Naturalism in American Fiction,* Upsala, 1950, pp. 63–89 and *passim;* and Charles Child Walcutt, *American Literary Naturalism, A Divided Stream,* Minneapolis, 1956, 53–65 and *passim.*

Other estimates are Clyde E. Henson, "Joseph Kirkland's Influence on Hamlin Garland," *AL,* XXIII (1952), 458–463; B. R. McElderry, "Hamlin Garland and Henry James," *AL,* XXIII (1952), 433–446; Bernard L. Duffey, "Hamlin Garland's 'Decline' from Realism," *AL,* XXV (1953), 69–74; C. E. Schorer, "Hamlin Garland's First Published Story," *AL,* XXV (1953), 89–92; John R. Dove, "The Significance of Hamlin Garland's First Visit to England," *UTSE,* XXXII (1953), 96–109; Donald Pizer, "Hamlin Garland in the *Standard,*" *AL,* XXVI (1954), 401–415; C. E. Schorer, "Hamlin Garland of Wisconsin," *WMH,* XXXVII (1954), 147–150, 182–185; Donald Pizer, "Crane Reports Garland on Howells," *MLN,* LXX (1955), 37–39; B. R. McElderry, "Hamlin Garland's View of Whitman," *Personalist,* XXXVI (1955), 369–378; Lars Åhnebrink, "Garland and Dreiser: An Abortive Friendship," *MJ,* VII (1955–1956), 285–292; and Herbert Edwards, "Herne, Garland, and Henry George," *AL,* XXVIII (1956), 359–367.

A recent bibliographical study is Donald Pizer, "Hamlin Garland: A Bibliography of Newspaper and Periodical Publications (1885–1895)," *BB,* XXII (1957), 41–44.

# CHARLES ÉTIENNE ARTHUR GAYARRÉ

**529.** BIOGRAPHY AND CRITICISM

The *Louisiana Historical Quarterly,* XXXIII (Apr., 1950), is a Charles Gayarré number. It prints "Some Letters of Charles Étienne Gayarré on Literature and Politics, 1854–1855" (twenty letters from the New York Public Library collections); "Tribunals of Criminal Jurisdiction in Ancient Rome" (from the original unedited Gayarré manuscript in the Bibliotheca Parsoniana, New Orleans); and four articles on Gayarré.

# HENRY GEORGE

**530.** COLLECTIONS AND REPRINTS

*Progress and Poverty* (1879) was reprinted, New York, 1955.

**531.** BIOGRAPHY AND CRITICISM

Anna George De Mille's *Henry George, Citizen of the World,* Chapel Hill, 1950, was edited for publication, after the author's death, by Don C. Shoemaker. A more ambitious study than this personal memoir is Charles Albro Barker's historical biography, *Henry George,* New York, 1955, which draws heavily on the Henry George Collection, given by Anna George De Mille to the New York Public Library.

Briefer estimates are Ransom E. Noble, Jr., "Henry George and the Progressive Movement," *AJES,* VIII (1949), 259–269; Elwood P. Lawrence, "Henry George's British Mission," *AQ,* III (1951), 232–243; and Herbert Edwards, "Herne, Garland, and Henry George," *AL,* XXVIII (1956), 359–367.

# ELLEN (ANDERSON GHOLSON) GLASGOW

**532.** SEPARATE WORKS

*The Woman Within,* 1954.

COLLECTED WORKS AND CORRESPONDENCE

*Letters of Ellen Glasgow,* New York, 1958, was compiled and edited with an introduction and notes by Blair Rouse.

BIOGRAPHY AND CRITICISM

For critical estimates see Josephine Lurie Jessup, *The Faith of Our Feminists: A Study in the Novels of Edith Wharton, Ellen Glasgow, Willa*

*Cather,* New York, 1950, and these briefer studies: H. Blair Rouse, "Ellen Glasgow in Retrospect," *EUQ,* VI (1950), 30–40; Frederick P. W. Mac-Dowell, "Ellen Glasgow and the Art of the Novel," *PQ,* XXX (1951), 328–347; Maxwell Geismar, *Rebels and Ancestors: The American Novel, 1890–1915,* Boston, 1953, pp. 219–283; John Edward Hardy, "Ellen Glasgow," *Southern Renascence,* ed. Louis D. Rubin, Jr., and Robert D. Jacobs, Baltimore, 1953, pp. 236–250; and Barbara Giles, "Character and Fate: The Novels of Ellen Glasgow," *Midstream,* IX (Sept., 1956), 20–31.

## JAMES HALL

**535.** BIOGRAPHY AND CRITICISM

Brief studies are David Donald, "The Autobiography of James Hall, Western Literary Pioneer," *OSAHQ,* LVI (1947), 295–304; John T. Flanagan, "Folklore in the Stories of James Hall," *MF,* V (1955), 159–168; and Edgeley W. Todd, "James Hall and the Hugh Class Legend," *AQ,* VII (1955), 362–370.

## ALEXANDER HAMILTON

**537.** COLLECTED WORKS

Harold C. Syrett is executive editor of the papers of Alexander Hamilton now being prepared for publication at Columbia University.

EDITED TEXTS AND REPRINTS

*Alexander Hamilton and the Founding of the Nation,* New York, 1957, is a selection of his writings based on the Hamilton manuscripts in the Library of Congress and on his many newspaper articles, edited with an introduction and headnotes by Richard B. Morris. Saul K. Padover edited *The Mind of Hamilton,* New York, 1958, which contains all of his public papers, a selection from his private papers, and a biographical introduction by the editor.

BIOGRAPHY AND CRITICISM

The first volume of a two-volume biography is Broadus Mitchell, *Alexander Hamilton: Youth to Maturity, 1755–1788,* New York, 1957. Louis M. Hacker, *Alexander Hamilton in the American Tradition,* New York, 1957, is a biographical essay on the man and his age. Broadus Mitchell, *Heritage from Hamilton,* New York, 1957, is three lectures on Hamilton and a selection of letters, some published for the first time. See also, *passim,* Nathan Schachner, *The Founding Fathers,* New York, 1954, and Philip M.

Marsh, ed., *[James] Monroe's Defense of Jefferson and Freneau Against Hamilton,* Oxford, Ohio, 1948.

The *William and Mary Quarterly,* XIII (1955), is a Hamilton Bicentennial number containing seven articles.

Briefer studies are Nathan Schachner, "Alexander Hamilton Viewed by His Friends: The Narratives of Robert Troup and Hercules Mulligan," *WMQ,* IV (1947), 203–225; Philip M. Marsh, "Hamilton and Monroe," *MVHR,* XXXIV (1947), 459–468; *idem,* "Hamilton's Neglected Essays, 1791–1793," *NYHSQB,* XXXII (1948), 280–300; Gilbert L. Lycan, "Alexander Hamilton and the North Carolina Federalists," *NCHR,* XXV (1948), 442–465; Harold Larson, "Alexander Hamilton: The Fact and Fiction of His Early Years," *WMQ,* IX (1952), 139–151; Milton Halsey Thomas, "Alexander Hamilton's Unfought Duel of 1795," *PMHB,* LXXVIII (1954), 342–352; James Morton Smith, "Alexander Hamilton, the Alien Law, and Seditious Libels," *RPol,* XVI (1954), 305–333; and Albert H. Bowman, "Jefferson, Hamilton, and American Foreign Policy," *PSQ,* LXXI (1956), 18–41.

## JOEL CHANDLER HARRIS

### 540. EDITED TEXTS AND CORRESPONDENCE

Thomas H. English edited Harris' unfinished novel (begun *c.* 1900) from a manuscript in the Emory University Library: "Qua: A Romance of the Revolution," *Emory Univ. Pub.: Sources and Reprints,* Series III, Atlanta, 1946. "Seven Tales of Uncle Remus," ed. Thomas H. English, *ibid.,* Series V, Atlanta, 1948, is a group of previously uncollected tales printed for the centennial of Harris' birth. Another centenary volume is *The Favorite Uncle Remus,* eds. George Van Santvoord and Archibald C. Coolidge, Boston, 1948. See also "An Uncollected Uncle Remus Sketch," *EUQ,* X (1954), 266–270.

Benjamin Lease edited "A Newly-Discovered Joel Chandler Harris Letter," *GHQ,* XXXVII (1953), 345–346. See also Thomas H. English, ed., "Mark Twain to Uncle Remus, 1881–1885," *Emory Univ. Pub.: Sources and Reprints,* Series VII, Atlanta, 1953.

### 541. BIOGRAPHY AND CRITICISM

Stella Brewer Brookes, *Joel Chandler Harris, Folklorist,* Athens, Ga., 1950, is a critical biography. Briefer estimates are Julia Collier Harris, "Joel Chandler Harris: The Poetic Mind," *EUQ,* III (1947), 21–29; Louise Dauner, "Myth and Humor in the Uncle Remus Fables," *AL,* XX (1948), 129–143; Thomas H. English, "The Twice-Told Tale and Uncle Remus," *GaR,* II (1948), 447–460; Wenzell Brown, "Anansi and Brer Rabbit," *Am Merc,*

LXIX (1949), 438–443; Bernard Wolfe, "Uncle Remus and the Malevolent Rabbit," *Commentary*, VIII (July, 1949), 31–41; and Sumner Ives, "Dialect Differentiation in the Stories of Joel Chandler Harris," *AL*, XXVII (1955), 88–96.

# (FRANCIS) BRET(T) HARTE

**542.** COLLECTED WORKS AND CORRESPONDENCE

More gleanings of Harte letters are Bradford A. Booth, ed., "Bret Harte Goes East: Some Unpublished Letters," *AL*, XIX (1948), 318–335.

**543.** BIOGRAPHY AND CRITICISM

Special studies are Ernst R. May, "Bret Harte and the *Overland Monthly*," *AL*, XXII (1950), 260–271; J. H. Young, "Anna Dickinson, Mark Twain, and Bret Harte," *PMHB*, LXXVI (1952), 39–46; Margaret Duckett, "Bret Harte's Portrayal of Half-Breeds," *AL*, XXV (1953), 193–212; Bradford A. Booth, "Mark Twain's Comments on Bret Harte's Stories," *AL*, XXV (1954), 492–495; Louis Martin Sears, "Bret Harte as Consul," *MTJ*, IX (Summer, 1954), 17–24; Margaret Duckett, "Bret Harte and the Indians of Northern California," *HLQ*, XVIII (1954), 59–83; C. Grant Loomis, "Bret Harte's Folklore," *WF*, XV (1956), 19–22; and Margaret Duckett, "Plain Language from Bret Harte," *NCF*, XI (1957), 241–260.

# NATHANIEL HAWTHORNE

**545.** COLLECTED WORKS

The French and Italian notebooks are still unedited. A complete collection of Hawthorne's letters is being prepared by Norman Holmes Pearson and Randall Stewart.

There are Hawthorne letters in James C. Austin, *Fields of the Atlantic Monthly*, San Marino, Calif., 1953. See also Ralph M. Aderman, ed., "Newly Located Hawthorne Letters," *EIHC*, LXXXVIII (1952), 163–165.

**546.** EDITED TEXTS

Edward H. Davidson has edited *Doctor Grimshawe's Secret*, Cambridge, Mass., 1954, in which he prints different versions of this unfinished romance.

Malcolm Cowley edited *The Portable Hawthorne*, New York, 1948, and Mark Van Doren selected *The Best of Hawthorne*, New York, 1951.

There are numerous reprintings of individual novels.

**547. BIOGRAPHY AND CRITICISM**

There are two recent biographies: Randall Stewart, *Nathaniel Hawthorne: A Biography,* New Haven, 1948, is the culmination of years of study of the Hawthorne papers. Robert Cantwell, *Nathaniel Hawthorne: The American Years,* New York, 1948, is the first volume of a projected two-volume biography. See also Louise Hall Tharp, *The Peabody Sisters of Salem,* Boston, 1950, and Vernon Loggins, *The Hawthornes: The Story of Seven Generations of an American Family,* New York, 1951.

Mark Van Doren, *Nathaniel Hawthorne,* New York, 1949, combines a biographical with a critical reading. Richard H. Fogle's *Hawthorne's Fiction: The Light and the Dark,* Norman, Okla., 1952; Hyatt H. Waggoner's *Hawthorne, A Critical Study,* Cambridge, Mass., 1955; and Roy R. Male, Jr., *Hawthorne's Tragic Vision,* Austin, Tex., 1957, are recent critical analyses. Specialized studies are Jane Lundblad, *Nathaniel Hawthorne and European Literary Tradition,* Upsala, Sweden and Cambridge, Mass., 1947; Edward H. Davidson, *Hawthorne's Last Phase,* New Haven, 1949; William Bysshe Stein, *Hawthorne's Faust, a Study of the Devil Archetype,* Gainesville, Fla., 1953; Alfred S. Reid, *The Yellow Ruff & The Scarlet Letter: A Source of Hawthorne's Novel,* Gainesville, Fla., 1955; and Rudolph Von Abele, *The Death of the Artist: A Study of Hawthorne's Disintegration,* The Hague, 1955. See also Marion Louise Kesselring, *Hawthorne's Reading, 1828-1850,* New York, 1949.

Portions of the following books contribute to any survey of recent criticism on Hawthorne: Austin Warren, *Rage for Order,* Chicago, 1948; Marius Bewley, *The Complex Fate,* London, 1952; Charles Feidelson, Jr., *Symbolism and American Literature,* Chicago, 1953; R. W. B. Lewis, *The American Adam,* Chicago, 1955; and Richard Chase, *The American Novel and Its Tradition,* New York, 1957.

Shorter studies are Frank Davidson, "Thoreau's Contributions to Hawthorne's *Mosses*," *NEQ,* XX (1947), 535-542; Christof Wegelin, "Europe in Hawthorne's Fiction," *ELH,* XIV (1947), 219-245; Malcolm Cowley, "Hawthorne in the Looking Glass," *SR,* LVI (1948), 545-563; Barriss Mills, "Hawthorne and Puritanism," *NEQ,* XXI (1948), 78-102; Roy Harvey Pearce, "Hawthorne and the Twilight of Romance," *YR,* XXXVII (1948), 487-506; Robert B. Heilman, "Hawthorne's 'The Birthmark': Science as Religion," *SAQ,* XLVIII (1949), 575-583; John T. Flanagan, "The Durable Hawthorne," *JEGP,* XLIX (1950), 88-96; Donald A. Ringe, "Hawthorne's Psychology of the Head and the Heart," *PMLA,* LXV (1950), 120-132; John W. Shroeder, "'That Inward Sphere': Notes on Hawthorne's Heart Imagery and Symbolism," *PMLA,* LXV (1950), 106-119; Carl Bode, "Hawthorne's *Fanshawe:* The Promising of Greatness," *NEQ,* XXIII (1950), 235-242; John E. Hart, "*The Scarlet Letter:* One Hundred Years After,"

*NEQ,* XXIII (1950), 381–395; Darrel Abel, "The Theme of Isolation in Hawthorne. Parts I & II," *Personalist,* XXXII (1951), 42–59, 182–190; Q. D. Leavis, "Hawthorne as Poet," *SR,* LIX (1951), 179–205, 426–458; Chester E. Eisinger, "Pearl and the Puritan Heritage," *CE,* XII (1951), 323–329; Rudolph Von Abele, " 'The Scarlet Letter': A Reading," *Accent,* XI (1951), 211–227; Harold Orel, "The Double Symbol," *AL,* XXIII (1951), 1–6.

Other studies are D. M. McKeithan, "Hawthorne's 'Young Goodman Brown': An Interpretation," *MLN,* LXVII (1952), 93–96; G. Harrison Orians, "Hawthorne and Puritan Punishments," *CE,* XIII (1952), 424–432; Randall Stewart, "Melville and Hawthorne," *SAQ,* LI (1952), 436–446; Frank Davidson, "Toward a Re-evaluation of *The Blithedale Romance,*" *NEQ,* XXV (1952), 374–383; D. K. Anderson, Jr., "Hawthorne's Crowds," *NCF,* VII (1952), 39–50; Leon Howard, "Hawthorne's Fiction," *ibid.,* VII (1953), 237–250; Charles Child Walcutt, " 'The Scarlet Letter' and Its Modern Critics," *ibid.,* VII (1953), 251–264; Darrel Abel, "Hawthorne's Scepticism about Social Reform: With Special Reference to *The Blithedale Romance,*" *UKCR,* XIX (1953), 181–193; *idem,* "Hawthorne's House of Tradition," *SAQ,* LII (1953), 561–578; Henry S. Kariel, "Man Limited: Nathaniel Hawthorne's Classicism," *ibid.,* LII (1953), 528–542; Clark Griffith, "Substance and Shadow: Language and Meaning in *The House of the Seven Gables,*" *MP,* LI (1953), 187–195; John W. Bicknell, "*The Marble Faun* Reconsidered," *UKCR,* XX (1954), 193–199; Morton Cronin, "Hawthorne on Romantic Love and the Status of Women," *PMLA,* LXIX (1954), 89–98; S. R. Price, "The Head, the Heart, and 'Rappaccini's Daughter,' " *NEQ,* XXVII (1954), 399–403; Roy Harvey Pearce, "Hawthorne and the Sense of the Past, or the Immortality of Major Molineux," *ELH,* XXI (1954), 327–349.

The most recent studies are Hugh N. MacLean, "Hawthorne's *Scarlet Letter:* 'The Dark Problem of This Life,' " *AL,* XXVII (1955), 12–24; Jesse Bier, "Hawthorne on the Romance: His Prefaces Related and Examined," *MP,* LIII (1955), 17–24; Marvin Laser, " 'Head,' 'Heart,' and 'Will' in Hawthorne's Psychology," *NCF,* X (1955), 130–140; James E. Miller, Jr., "Hawthorne and Melville: The Unpardonable Sin," *PMLA,* LXX (1955), 91–114; Michael Lloyd, "Hawthorne, Ruskin, and the Hostile Tradition," *EM,* VI (1955), 109–133; Alfred H. Marks, "Who Killed Judge Pyncheon? The Role of the Imagination in *The House of the Seven Gables,*" *PMLA,* LXXI (1956), 355–369; Leo Marx, "The Machine in the Garden," *NEQ,* XXIX (1956), 27–42; Bernard J. Paris, "Optimism and Pessimism in *The Marble Faun,*" *BUSE,* II (1956), 95–112; Robert Stanton, "Hawthorne, Bunyan, and the American Romances," *PMLA,* LXXI (1956), 155–165; Maurice Beebe, "The Fall of the House of Pyncheon," *NCF,* XI (1956), 1–17; Henry G. Fairbanks, "Sin, Free Will, and 'Pessimism' in Hawthorne," *PMLA,* LXXI (1956), 975–989; Frederick C. Crews, "A New Reading of *The Blithe-*

*dale Romance," AL,* XXIX (1957), 147–170; Edward Stone, "The Antique Gentility of Hester Prynne," *PQ,* XXXVI (1957), 90–96; B. Bernard Cohen, "Emerson and Hawthorne on England," *BPLQ,* IX (1957), 73–85; and Richard P. Adams, "Hawthorne's *Provincial Tales," NEQ,* XXX (1957), 39–57.

**552.** BIBLIOGRAPHY

A full annotated bibliography is being prepared by Nouvart Tashjian and Dwight Eckerman. For a bibliographical essay see Walter Blair's com, pilation for *Eight American Authors: A Review of Research and Criticism* ed. Floyd Stovall, New York, 1956.

## PAUL HAMILTON HAYNE

**554.** COLLECTED WORKS AND CORRESPONDENCE

Previously unpublished texts are in Richard Beale Davis, "An Unpublished Poem by Paul Hamilton Hayne," *AL,* XVIII (1947), 327–329; *idem,* "An Uncollected Elegy by Paul Hamilton Hayne," *SCHM,* LII (1951), 52–54; and H. Blair Rouse and Floyd C. Watkins, "Some Manuscript Poems by Paul Hamilton Hayne," *EUQ,* VIII (1952), 83–91.

For more letters see Richard Beale Davis, ed., "Paul Hamilton Hayne to Dr. Francis Peyre Porcher," *SP,* XLIV (1947), 529–548; D. M. McKeithan, ed., "Paul Hamilton Hayne Writes to the Grand-daughter of Patrick Henry," *GHQ,* XXXII (1948), 22–28; Richard Beale Davis, ed., "The Southern Dilemma: Two Unpublished Letters of Paul Hamilton Hayne," *JSH,* XVII (1951), 64–70; Charles Duffy, ed., "A Southern Genteelist: Letters by Paul Hamilton Hayne to Julia C. R. Dorr," *SCHM,* LII (1951), 65–73, 154–165, 207–217; LIII (1952), 19–30; and Francis B. Dedmond, ed., "Editor Hayne to Editor Kingsbury: Three Significant Unpublished Letters," *NCHR,* XXXII (1955), 92–101.

**555.** BIOGRAPHY AND CRITICISM

The first adequate biography is Kate Harbes Becker, *Paul Hamilton Hayne: Life and Letters,* Belmont, N.C., 1951.

Briefer estimates are Charles R. Anderson, "Poet of the Pine Barrens," *GaR,* I (1947), 280–293; Max L. Griffin, "Whittier and Hayne: A Record of Friendship," *AL,* XIX (1947), 41–58; Richard B. Harwell, "A Confederate View of the Southern Poets," *AL,* XXIV (1952), 51–61; Francis B. Dedmond, "The Poems of Paul Hamilton Hayne to Frances Christine Fisher," *NCHR,* XXVIII (1951), 408–413; and Edd Winfield Parks, "When Paul Hamilton Hayne Fought a Duel," *GaR,* XI (1957), 80–84.

# LAFCADIO HEARN

**556.** COLLECTED WORKS

Another volume of newspaper sketches, originally printed in the Cincinnati *Enquirer* and Cincinnati *Commercial*, 1874–1877, is *Children of the Levee*, ed. O. W. Frost, Lexington, Ky., 1957.

Some Hearn scholars have rejected *Letters to a Pagan*, Detroit, 1933, as spurious.

**557.** REPRINTS

*Japan: An Attempt at Interpretation* (1904) was reprinted in Rutland, Vt., 1955.

Henry Goodman edited *The Selected Writings of Lafcadio Hearn*, with an introduction by Malcolm Cowley, New York, 1949.

**558.** BIOGRAPHY AND CRITICISM

General estimates are Daniel Stempel, "Lafcadio Hearn: Interpreter of Japan," *AL*, XX (1948), 1–19; John J. Espey, "The Two Japans of Lafcadio Hearn," *PS*, IV (1950), 342–351; O. W. Frost, "The Birth of Lafcadio Hearn," *AL*, XXIV (1952), 372–377; Albert J. Salvan, "Lafcadio Hearn's Views on the Realism of Zola," *PMLA*, LXVII (1952), 1163–1167; Ulick O'Connor, "Lafcadio Hearn," *DM*, XXIX (1953), 31–37; Sidonia C. Rosenbaum, "The Utopia of Lafcadio Hearn—Spanish America," *AQ*, VI (1954), 76–78; Allen E. Tuttle, "Lafcadio Hearn and the Soul of the Far East," *Contemp. Japan*, XXIII (1955), 529–552; and *idem*, "The Achievement of Lafcadio Hearn," *DM*, XXXII (1956), 6–13.

# ERNEST (MILLER) HEMINGWAY

**559.** SEPARATE WORKS

*Across the River and Into the Trees*, 1950; *The Old Man and the Sea*, 1952.

**560.** COLLECTIONS

In 1953, Charles Scribner's Sons began issuing a uniform edition of the collected works. Charles Poore edited *The Hemingway Reader*, New York, 1953.

BIOGRAPHY AND CRITICISM

Charles A. Fenton, *The Apprenticeship of Ernest Hemingway: The Early Years*, New York, 1954, is chiefly biography.

A full-length critical study is Carlos Baker, *Hemingway: The Writer as Artist*, Princeton, 1952 (second edition, 1956, with an additional chapter on *The Old Man and the Sea*). Philip Young, *Ernest Hemingway*, New York, 1952, is a short critical study. John K. M. McCaffery, ed., *Ernest Hemingway: The Man and His Work*, Cleveland, 1950, is a collection of twenty-five essays by various hands. John Alfred Atkins, *The Art of Ernest Hemingway: His Work and Personality*, appeared in London in 1952.

Recent critical articles are George Snell, *Shapers of American Fiction*, New York, 1947, pp. 156–172; Robert Penn Warren, "Novelists-Philosophers —X," *Horizon*, XV (1947), 156–180; Robert Daniel, "Hemingway and His Heroes," *QQ*, LIV (1947–48), 471–485; D. S. Savage, "Ernest Hemingway," *HudR*, I (1948), 380–401; Mario Praz, "Hemingway in Italy," *PR*, XV (1948), 1086–1100; George Hemphill, "Hemingway and James," *KR*, XI (1949), 50–60; Caroline Gordon, "Notes on Hemingway and Kafka," *SR*, LVII (1949), 215–226; W. M. Frohock, *The Novel of Violence in America, 1920–1950*, Dallas, 1950, pp. 167–199; Frederick J. Hoffman, *The Modern Novel in America, 1900–1950*, Chicago, 1951, pp. 89–103; Isaac Rosenfeld, "A Farewell to Hemingway," *KR*, XIII (1951), 147–155; Harry Levin, "Observations on the Style of Hemingway," *KR*, XIII (1951), 581–609; Leo Gurko, "The Achievement of Ernest Hemingway," *CE*, XIII (1952), 368–375; William White, "Father and Son: Comments on Hemingway's Psychology," *DR*, XXXI (1952), 276–284; Edmund Wilson, *The Shores of Light*, New York, 1953, pp. 115–124, 339–344, 616–629; John McCormick, "Hemingway and History," *WR*, XVII (1953), 87–98; Deming Brown, "Hemingway in Russia," *AQ*, V (1953), 143–156; Frederick Carpenter, "Hemingway Achieves the Fifth Dimension," *PMLA*, LXIX (1954), 711–718; Edwin Fussell, "Hemingway and Mark Twain," *Accent*, XIV (1954), 199–206.

More recent studies are John T. Flanagan, "Hemingway's Debt to Sherwood Anderson," *JEGP*, LIV (1955), 507–520; Leon Edel, "The Art of Evasion," *Folio*, XX (1955), 18–20; Philip Young, "Hemingway: A Defense," *ibid.*, XX (1955), 20–22; James B. Colvert, "Ernest Hemingway's Morality in Action," *AL*, XXVII (1955), 372–385; Delmore Schwartz, "The Fiction of Ernest Hemingway," *Perspectives USA*, No. 13 (1955), 70–88; Warren Beck, "The Short Happy Life of Mrs. Macomber," *MFS*, I (Nov., 1955), 28–37; André Maurois, "Ernest Hemingway," *Rev. de Paris*, LXII (Mar., 1955), 3–16; Leo Gurko, "The Old Man and the Sea," *CE*, XVII (1955), 11–15; E. M. Halliday, "Hemingway's Ambiguity: Symbolism and Irony," *AL*, XXVIII (1956), 1–22; William B. Bache, "Craftsmanship in 'A Clean Well-Lighted Place,' " *Personalist*, XXXVII (1956), 60–64; Eugene Goodheart, "The Legacy of Ernest Hemingway," *PrS*, XXX (1956), 212–218; Leo J. Hertzel, "Hemingway and the Problem of Belief," *CathW*, CLXXXIV (Oct., 1956), 29–33; Ivan Kashkeen, "Alive in the Midst of Death," *Soviet Lit.*, No. 7 (1956), 160–172; Charles C. Walcutt, *American*

*Literary Naturalism,* Minneapolis, 1956, pp. 258–289; C. Hugh Holman, "Hemingway and Vanity Fair," *CaQ,* VIII (Summer, 1956), 31–37; Arthur L. Scott, "In Defense of Robert Cohn," *CE,* XVIII (1957), 309–314; Robert C. Hart, "Hemingway on Writing," *ibid.,* XVIII (1957), 314–320; Otto Friedrich, "Ernest Hemingway: Joy Through Strength," *ASch,* XXVI (1957), 470 ff.; Morton D. Zabel, *Craft and Character in Fiction,* New York, 1957, pp. 317–326.

*Modern Fiction Studies,* I (Aug., 1955), is a special issue devoted to Hemingway.

**561.** BIBLIOGRAPHY

A recent bibliographical guide is Lee Samuels, *A Hemingway Check List,* New York, 1951, with a preface by Hemingway. See also Maurice Beebe, "Criticism of Ernest Hemingway: A Selected Checklist with an Index to Studies of Separate Works," *MFS,* I (Aug., 1955), 36–45.


## OLIVER WENDELL HOLMES

**565.** COLLECTED WORKS AND CORRESPONDENCE

Alexander E. Jones edited "An Uncollected Poem by Oliver Wendell Holmes," *BPLQ,* VII (1955), 107–110.

More letters can be found in R. G. Kent, ed., "An Unpublished Letter of Oliver Wendell Holmes," *AL,* XX (1948), 333–336; and Mark De Wolfe Howe, ed., "The Holmes-Laski Letters," *Atl,* CXC (Sept.–Oct., 1952), 29–34, 70–74. See also Charles R. Anderson, ed., "Two Letters from Lanier to Holmes," *AL,* XVIII (1947), 321–326.

**566.** BIOGRAPHY AND CRITICISM

The most recent biographical study is Eleanor M. Tilton, *Amiable Autocrat: A Biography of Dr. Oliver Wendell Holmes,* New York, 1947.

George E. Hamilton, *Oliver Wendell Holmes, His Pioneer Stereoscope and the Later Industry,* New York, 1949, is an address printed for the Newcomen Society of England in North America. Other special studies are Reginald Fitz, "President Eliot and Dr. Holmes Leap Forward," *HLB,* I (1947), 212–220; Alexander C. Kern, "Dr. Oliver Wendell Holmes Today," *UKCR,* XIV (1948), 191–199; Harold H. Scudder, "The 'Contentment' of Dr. Holmes," *AL,* XX (1949), 443–446; Neille Shoemaker, "The Contemporaneous Medical Reputation of Oliver Wendell Holmes," *NEQ,* XXVI (1953), 477–493; and Charles Boewe, "Reflex Action in the Novels of Oliver Wendell Holmes," *AL,* XXVI (1954), 303–319.

**568.** BIBLIOGRAPHY

Eleanor M. Tilton completed and edited Thomas Franklin Currier's *Bibliography of Oliver Wendell Holmes,* New York, 1953.

## THOMAS HOOKER

**569.** BIOGRAPHY AND CRITICISM

Recent studies are Clinton Rossiter, "Thomas Hooker," *NEQ,* XXV (1952), 459–488; and Everett H. Emerson, "Notes on the Thomas Hooker Canon," *AL,* XXVII (1956), 554–555.

## FRANCIS HOPKINSON

**570.** BIOGRAPHY AND CRITICISM

See Thomas P. Haviland, "Francis Hopkinson and the Grammarians," *PMHB,* LXXVI (1952), 63–70; and Philip Marsh, "The Freneau-Hopkinson Quarrel," *PNJHS,* LXXIV (1956), 304–314.

## WILLIAM DEAN HOWELLS

**572.** REPRINTS

Clara Marburg Kirk and Rudolf Kirk edited, with an introduction, notes, and bibliography, *William Dean Howells: Representative Selections,* New York, 1950. Henry Steele Commager edited *Selected Writings of William Dean Howells,* New York, 1950. Reprints of individual novels are numerous.

LETTERS AND OTHER COLLECTED ITEMS

Further gleanings of Howells correspondence are in Kjell Ekstrom, ed., "The Cable-Howells Correspondence," *SN,* XXII (1950), 48–61; Arthur A. Adrian, ed., "Augustus Hoppin to William Dean Howells," *NEQ,* XXIV (1951), 84–89; John W. Ward, ed., "Another Howells Anarchist Letter," *AL,* XXII (1951), 489–490; James Woodress, ed., "The Lowell-Howells Friendship: Some Unpublished Letters," *NEQ,* XXVI (1953), 523–528; Robert W. Ayers, ed., "W. D. Howells and Stephen Crane: Some Unpublished Letters," *AL,* XXVIII (1957), 469–477; and Clara and Rudolf Kirk, eds., "Two Howells Letters," *JRUL,* XXI (1957), 1–7.

*Prefaces to Contemporaries (1882–1920),* ed. George Arms, William M. Gibson, and Frederic C. Marston, Jr., Gainesville, Fla., 1957, contains facsimile reproductions of thirty-four of Howells' prefaces to books by contemporary authors.

**573. BIOGRAPHY AND CRITICISM**

A critical-biographical study of one phase of Howells' development is James Woodress, *Howells and Italy,* Durham, 1952. Howells' early life is treated in Edwin H. Cady, *The Road to Realism: The Early Years, 1837–1885, of William Dean Howells,* Syracuse, 1956. A more general study of Howells as novelist is Everett Carter, *Howells and the Age of Realism,* Philadelphia, 1954.

Briefer estimates are William M. Gibson, "Mark Twain and Howells: Anti-imperialists," *NEQ,* XX (1947), 435–470; *idem,* "Materials and Form in Howells's First Novels," *AL,* XIX (1947), 158–166; George Arms, "Howells' New York Novel: Comedy and Belief," *NEQ,* XXI (1948), 313–325; Edwin H. Cady, "Howells in 1948," *UKCR,* XV (1948), 83–91; Alexander Cowie, *The Rise of the American Novel,* New York, 1948, pp. 653–701; Lloyd Morris, "Conscience in the Parlor: William Dean Howells," *AS,* XVIII (1949), 407–416; D. M. Rein, "Howells and the *Cosmopolitan,*" *AL,* XXI (1949), 49–55; John K. Reeves, "The Way of a Realist: A Study of Howells' Use of the Saratoga Scene," *PMLA,* LXV (1950), 1035–1052; Louis J. Budd, "William Dean Howells' Debt to Tolstoy," *ASEER,* IX (1950), 292–301; Herbert Edwards, "Howells and Herne," *AL,* XXII (1951), 432–441; Lionel Trilling, "W. D. Howells and the Roots of Modern Taste," *PR,* XVIII (1951), 516–536; Edd Winfield Parks, "Howells and the Gentle Reader," *SAQ,* L (1951), 239–247; Louis J. Budd, "Howells, the *Atlantic Monthly,* and Republicanism," *AL,* XXIV (1952), 139–156; William F. Ekstrom, "The Equalitarian Principle in the Fiction of William Dean Howells," *AL,* XXIV (1952), 40–50; Leonard Lutwack, "William Dean Howells and the 'Editor's Study,'" *AL,* XXIV (1952), 195–207; and Arnold B. Fox, "Howells as a Religious Critic," *NEQ,* XXV (1952), 199–216.

More recent studies are Edd Winfield Parks, "A Realist Avoids Reality: W. D. Howells and the Civil War Years," *SAQ,* LII (1953), 93–97; Harry H. Clark, "The Role of Science in the Thought of W. D. Howells," *TWASAL,* XLII (1953), 263–303; W. J. Meserve, "Truth, Morality, and Swedenborg in Howells' Theory of Realism," *NEQ,* XXVII (1954), 252–257; Earl B. Braly, "William Dean Howells, Author and Journalist," *Jour. Quar.,* XXXII (1955), 456–462; Ernest Sirluck, "Howells' *A Modern Instance,*" *MAR,* X (1956), 66–72; Anne W. Amacher, "The Genteel Primitivist and the Semi-Tragic Octoroon," *NEQ,* XXIX (1956), 216–227; Leo P. Coyle, "Mark Twain and William Dean Howells," *Ga. Rev.,* X (1956), 302–311; Claudio Gorlier, "William Dean Howells e le definizioni del realismo," *Studi Americani,* II (1956), 83–125; John Roland Dove, "Howells' Irrational Heroines," *UTSE,* XXXV (1956), 64–80; Harrison T. Meserole, "The Dean in Person: Howells' Lecture Tour," *WHR,* X (1956), 337–347; Thomas A. Gullason, "New Light on the Crane-Howells Relationship," *NEQ,* XXX

(1957), 389–392; and Kenneth E. Eble, "Howells' Kisses," *AQ*, IX (1957), 441–447.

### 576. BIBLIOGRAPHY

The most complete listing is William M. Gibson and George Arms, *A Bibliography of William Dean Howells*, New York, 1948. See also Edwin H. Cady, "William Dean Howells in Italy: Some Bibliographical Notes," *Symposium*, VII (1953), 147–153; and "The Literary Manuscripts of William Dean Howells: A Descriptive Finding List," comp. John K. Reeves, *BNYPL*, LXII (June–July, 1958), 267–278 ff.

On March 8, 1951, Clara M. and Rudolf Kirk began issuing intermittently *The Howells Sentinel*, New Brunswick, N.J., a mimeographed bulletin for The Howells Group of MLA in which addenda to the Gibson-Arms bibliography have appeared as well as notes on projected editions and collections of Howells.

# (JAMES) LANGSTON HUGHES

### 576. SEPARATE WORKS

Poems: *One-Way Ticket*, 1949; *Montage of a Dream Deferred*, 1951.

Fiction: *Simple Speaks His Mind*, 1950; *Laughing to Keep from Crying*, 1952; *Simple Takes a Wife*, 1953; *Simple Stakes a Claim*, 1957; *Tambourines to Glory*, 1958.

Miscellaneous: *The Poetry of the Negro, 1746–1949: An Anthology* (with Arna Bontemps), 1949; *The Sweet Flypaper of Life* (with Roy de Carava), 1955; *A Pictorial History of the Negro in America* (with Milton Meltzer), 1956; *I Wonder as I Wander: An Autobiographical Journey*, 1956.

*The Langston Hughes Reader*, New York, 1958, contains the libretto of Hughes' musical comedy, *Simply Heavenly;* a one-act play, *Soul Gone Home;* the text of a pageant, *The Glory of Negro History;* and excerpts from previously published work.

### BIOGRAPHY AND CRITICISM

Critical estimates are John W. Parker, " 'Tomorrow' in the Writings of Langston Hughes," *CE*, X (1949), 438–441; Arthur P. Davis, "The Harlem of Langston Hughes' Poetry," *Phylon*, XIII (1952), 276–283; *idem*, "Jesse B. Semple: Negro American," *ibid.*, XV (1954), 21–28; *idem*, "The Tragic Mulatto Theme in Six Works of Langston Hughes," *ibid.*, XVI (1955), 195–204.

The most recent bibliographical listing is Allen Tate, *Sixty American Poets, 1896–1944*, rev. ed., Washington, 1954, pp. 52–54.

## JAMES GIBBONS HUNEKER

**578. BIOGRAPHY AND CRITICISM**

Brief studies are John Paul Pritchard and John M. Raines, "James Gibbons Huneker, Critic of the Seven Arts," *AQ*, II (1950), 53–61; Arnold T. Schwab, "Irish Author and American Critic: George Moore and James Huneker," *NCF*, VIII (1954), 256–271; IX (1954), 22–37; *idem*, "Joseph Conrad's American Friend: Correspondence with James Huneker," *MP*, LII (1955), 222–232; and *idem*, "James Huneker's Criticism of American Literature," *AL*, XXIX (1957), 64–78.

## WASHINGTON IRVING

**579. PRINTED LETTERS**

Printings of single items are M. B. Seigler, ed., "Washington Irving to William C. Preston: An Unpublished Letter," *AL*, XIX (1947), 256–259; anon., "Letter from Washington Irving to George A. Ward, 1842," *EIHC*, LXXXIII (1947), 85; and Thomas R. Adams, ed., "Washington Irving— Another Letter from Spain," *AL*, XXV (1953), 354–358.

**580. EDITED TEXTS AND REPRINTS**

Barbara Damon Simison edited "Washington Irving's Notebook of 1810," *YULG*, XXIV (1949), 1–16, 74–94. Howard C. Horsford edited "Illustration to the Legend of Prince Ahmed: An Unpublished Sketch by Washington Irving," *PULC*, XIV (1952), 30–36. Andrew Breen Myers edited "Washington Irving's Madrid Journal 1827–1828 and Related Letters," *BNYPL*, LXII (May–Aug., 1958), 217–227 ff.

*Tales of the Alhambra*, with an introduction and notes by Ricardo Villa-Real, Granada, 1955, is a reprinting of *The Alhambra* (1832).

**581. BIOGRAPHY AND CRITICISM**

A recent study is Walter A. Reichart, *Washington Irving and Germany*, Ann Arbor, Mich., 1957.

Brief analyses are George R. Price, "Washington Irving's Librettos," *Music & Letters*, XXIX (1948), 348–355; Leonard B. Beach, "Washington Irving," *UKCR*, XIV (1948), 259–266; R. B. Van Wart, "Washington Irving and Scotland," *Blackwood's Mag.*, CCLXVI (1949), 257–263; K. A. Spaulding, "A Note on *Astoria*: Irving's Use of the Robert Stuart Manuscript," *AL*, XXII (1950), 150–157; Richard Beale Davis, "Washington Irving and Joseph C. Cabell," *Univ. Va. Stud.*, IV (1951), 7–22; Harry Miller Lydenberg, "Irving's Knickerbocker and Some of Its Sources,"

*BNYPL*, LVI (1952), 544–553, 596–619; Daniel G. Hoffman, "Irving's Use of American Folklore in 'The Legend of Sleepy Hollow,'" *PMLA*, LXVIII (1953), 425–435; Charles W. Jones, "Knickerbocker Santa Claus," *NYHSQB*, XXXVIII (1954), 357–383; Stanley T. Williams, *The Spanish Background of American Literature*, New Haven, 1955, II, 3–45 and *passim;* John C. Fiske, "The Soviet Controversy over Pushkin and Washington Irving," *CL*, VII (1955), 25–31; William L. Hedges, "Irving's *Columbus:* The Problem of Romantic Biography," *AmF*, XIII (1956), 127–140; Walter A. Reichart, "The Early Reception of Washington Irving's Works in Germany," *Anglia*, LXXIV (1956), 345–363; John F. McDermott, "Washington Irving and the Journal of Captain Bonneville," *MVHR*, XLIII (1956), 459–467; and S. P. Rhodes, "Washington Irving's Use of Traditional Folklore," *SFQ*, XX (1956), 143–153.

### 583. BIBLIOGRAPHY

Of bibliographical interest are Jacob Blanck, "*Salmagundi* and Its Publishers," *PBSA*, XLI (1947), 1–32; and Vincent L. Eaton, "The Leonard Kebler Gift of Washington Irving First Editions," *LCQJ*, V (1948), 9–13.


# HENRY JAMES

### 584. COLLECTED WORKS AND CORRESPONDENCE

*The Complete Plays of Henry James,* ed. Leon Edel, Philadelphia, 1949, is, a definitive edition.

*The Selected Letters of Henry James,* New York, 1955, was edited by Leon Edel. Janet Adam Smith edited *Henry James and Robert Louis Stevenson: A Record of Friendship and Criticism,* New York, 1949. Leon Edel and Gordon Ray edited *Henry James and H. G. Wells: A Record of Their Friendship, Their Debate on the Art of Fiction, and Their Quarrel,* Urbana, 1958, a volume of articles, excerpts from books, and all extant James-Wells letters, many never before published. See also Mark De Wolfe Howe, ed., "The Letters of Henry James to Mr. Justice Holmes," *YR*, XXXVIII (1949), 410–433; John La Farge, "Henry James's Letters to the La Farges," *NEQ*, XXII (1949), 173–192; Richard C. Harrier, ed., "Letters of Henry James, Transcribed from the Original Manuscripts in the Colby College Library," *CLQ*, Series III (1953), 153–164; and Leon Edel and Lyall H. Powers, eds., "Henry James and the *Bazar* Letters," *Howells and James: A Double Billing,* New York, 1958, pp. 27–55. Two recent articles on Henry James and Vernon Lee (Violet Paget) print important unpublished letters: Carl J. Weber, "Henry James and His Tiger-Cat," *PMLA*, LXVIII (1953), 672–687; and Burdett Gardner, "An Apology for Henry James's 'Tiger-Cat,'" *PMLA*, LXVIII (1953), 688–695.

A guide to letters not in Percy Lubbock's 1920 two-volume collection is B. R. McElderry, Jr., "The Published Letters of Henry James: A Survey," *BB*, XX (1952), 165-171, 187.

### 585. EDITED TEXTS AND REPRINTS

*Eight Uncollected Tales of Henry James,* ed. Edna Kenton, New Brunswick, N.J., 1950, reprints for the first time five of James' early tales.

Selections of critical essays by James are Morris Roberts, ed., *The Art of Fiction and Other Essays,* New York, 1948; John L. Sweeney, ed., *The Painter's Eye: Notes and Essays on the Pictorial Arts,* Cambridge, Mass., 1956; Leon Edel, ed., *Henry James: The Future of the Novel: Essays on the Art of Fiction,* New York, 1956; and Albert Mordell, ed., *Literary Reviews and Essays: American, English, and French Literature,* New York, 1957. A selection of dramatic criticism is *The Scenic Art, Notes on Acting and the Drama,* ed. Allan Wade, New Brunswick, N.J., 1948.

*A Little Tour in France* was reprinted, illustrated, in London, 1949, with an introduction by Michael Swan. *Portraits of Places,* New York, 1948, was reprinted with an "Essay on James as a Traveller" by George Alvin Finch. Leon Edel and Ilse Dusoir Lind edited *Parisian Sketches: Letters to the New York Tribune, 1875-1876,* New York, 1957. Morton Dauwen Zabel edited *The Art of Travel: Scenes and Journeys in America, England, France, and Italy from the Travel Writings of Henry James,* New York, 1958.

Anthologies of James' fiction are numerous. In 1946, David Garnett selected *Fourteen Stories by Henry James* (London); in 1948, Michael Swan compiled *Ten Short Stories of Henry James* (London); *Henry James: Selected Stories,* London, 1957, was chosen, with an introduction, by Gerard Hopkins. Leon Edel edited *The Ghostly Tales of Henry James,* New Brunswick, N.J., 1948, and *Selected Fiction,* New York, 1953. Morton Dauwen Zabel assembled *The Portable Henry James,* New York, 1951. Reprints of single novels are too numerous to list separately.

Ruth and Augustus Goetz adapted *Washington Square* for the stage: *The Heiress,* New York, 1948. *The Innocents,* New York, 1950, is an adaptation of *The Turn of the Screw* by William Archibald. Guy Bolton's *Child of Fortune,* New York, 1956, is an adaptation of *The Wings of the Dove.*

### 586. BIOGRAPHY AND CRITICISM

Three specialized volumes of biographical material are F. O. Matthiessen, *The James Family,* New York, 1947 (containing selections from the writings of Henry, Sr., William, Alice, and Henry James, Jr.); Simon Harcourt Nowell-Smith, *The Legend of the Master,* London, 1947 (chiefly reminiscenses and letters of persons who knew James); and Frederick W. Dupee, ed., *Henry James: Autobiography,* New York, 1956 (which reprints *A Small Boy and Others, Notes of a Son and Brother,* and *The Middle Years*).

The first volume of a projected three-volume biography is Leon Edel, *Henry James: The Untried Years, 1843–1870*, Philadelphia, 1953. One-volume biographies are Frederick W. Dupee, *Henry James*, New York, 1951; Michael Swan, *Henry James*, London, 1952; and Robert C. LeClair, *Young Henry James, 1843–1870*, New York, 1955. Henry Seidel Canby makes a comparative study of James and Twain in *Turn West, Turn East*, Boston, 1951.

Full-length critical analyses are Osborn Andreas, *Henry James and the Expanding Horizon: A Study of the Meaning and Basic Themes of James' Fiction*, Seattle, 1948; Elizabeth Stevenson, *The Crooked Corridor: A Study of Henry James*, New York, 1949; Edwin T. Bowden, *The Themes of Henry James: A System of Observation through the Visual Arts*, New Haven, 1956; Charles G. Hoffman, *The Short Novels of Henry James*, New York, 1957; Frederick C. Crews, *The Tragedy of Manners: Moral Drama in the Later Novels of Henry James*, New Haven, 1957; and Quentin Anderson, *The American Henry James*, New Brunswick, 1957. See also F. R. Leavis, *The Great Tradition*, London, 1948, pp. 126–172; Austin Warren, *Rage for Order*, Chicago, 1948, pp. 142–161; Alexander Cowie, *The Rise of the American Novel*, New York, 1948, pp. 702–742; Marius Bewley, *The Complex Fate*, London, 1952, pp. 1–149; and Richard Chase, *The American Novel and Its Tradition*, New York, 1957, pp. 117–137. An enlarged edition, 1954, of Joseph Warren Beach, *The Method of Henry James*, New Haven, 1918, contains corrections and new bibliographies.

Two special Henry James issues are *Modern Fiction Studies*, III (Spring, 1957), and *Nineteenth Century Fiction*, XII (June, 1957).

Briefer studies are W. H. Auden, "Henry James's 'The American Scene,'" *Horizon*, XV (1947), 77–90; Joseph Warren Beach, "The Sacred and Solitary Refuge," *Furioso*, III (1947), 23–37; S. G. Putt, "A Henry James Jubilee, II," *CM*, CLXII (1947), 284–297; Morris Roberts, "Henry James's Final Period," *YR*, XXXVII (1947), 60–67; Robert B. Heilman, "'The Turn of the Screw' as Poem," *UKCR*, XIV (1948), 277–289; Heidi Specker, "The Change of Emphasis in the Criticism of Henry James," *ES*, XXIX (1948), 33–47; Edward Wagenknecht, "Our Contemporary Henry James," *CE*, X (1948), 123–132; Lawrence Barrett, "Young Henry James, Critic," *AL*, XX (1949), 385–400; Edwin Clark, "Henry James and the Actress," *PS*, III (1949), 84–99; George Hemphill, "Hemingway and James," *KR*, XI (1949), 50–60; B. R. McElderry, Jr., "The Uncollected Stories of Henry James," *AL*, XXI (1949), 279–291; Claire J. Raeth, "Henry James's Rejection of 'The Sacred Fount,'" *ELH*, XVI (1949), 308–324; Oliver Evans, "James's Air of Evil: 'The Turn of the Screw,'" *PR*, XVI (1949), 175–187; Graham Greene, "Henry James," *TR*, XXIX (1950), 9–22; B. R. McElderry, Jr., "Henry James and 'The Whole Family,'" *PS*, IV (1950), 352–360; Viola R. Dunbar, "The Revision of *Daisy Miller*," *MLN*, LXV (1950), 311–317; H.

Blair Rouse, "Charles Dickens and Henry James: Two Approaches to the Art of Fiction," *NCF*, V (1950), 151–157; Robert E. Young, "An Error in *The Ambassadors*," *AL*, XXII (1950), 245–253; R. W. Short, "Some Critical Terms of Henry James," *PMLA*, LXV (1950), 667–680; David Kerner, "A Note on *The Beast in the Jungle*," *UKCR*, XVII (1950), 109–118; John Henry Raleigh, "Henry James: The Poetics of Empiricism," *PMLA*, LXVI (1951), 107–123; Henry Popkin, "The Two Theatres of Henry James," *NEQ*, XXIV (1951), 69–83; Leon Edel, "The Architecture of James's 'New York Edition,'" *NEQ*, XXIV (1951), 169–178; Joseph J. Firebaugh, "The Pragmatism of Henry James," *VQR*, XXVII (1951), 419–435; R. P. Blackmur, "The Loose and Baggy Monsters of Henry James," *Accent*, XI (1951), 129–146; Ilse Dusoir Lind, "The Inadequate Vulgarity of Henry James," *PMLA*, LXVI (1951), 886–910.

Other studies are Arthur L. Scott, "A Protest against the James Vogue," *CE*, XIII (1952), 194–201; Herbert Edwards, "Henry James and Ibsen," *AL*, XXIV (1952), 208–223; Donald M. Murray, "Henry James and the English Reviewers, 1882–1890," *AL*, XXIV (1952), 1–20; Ward S. Worden, "Henry James's *What Maisie Knew*: A Comparison with the Plans in *The Notebooks*," *PMLA*, LXVIII (1953), 371–383; Bradford A. Booth, "Henry James and the Economic Motif," *NCF*, VIII (1953), 141–150; Charles G. Hoffmann, "Innocence and Evil in James' *The Turn of the Screw*," *UKCR*, XX (1953), 97–105; R. W. Short, "Henry James's World of Images," *PMLA*, LXVIII (1953), 943–960; Dorothea Krook, "The Method of the Later Works of Henry James," *London Mag.*, I (1954), 54–70; *idem, "The Wings of the Dove,"* *Camb. Jour.*, VII (Aug., 1954), 671–689; Maurice Beebe, "The Turned Back of Henry James," *SAQ*, LIII (1954), 521–539; Priscilla Gibson, "The Uses of James's Imagery: Drama Through Metaphor," *PMLA*, LXIX (1954), 1076–1084; Max F. Schulz, "The Bellegarde's Feud with Christopher Newman," *AL*, XXVII (1955), 42–55; Patrick F. Quinn, "Morals and Motives in *The Spoils of Poynton*," *SR*, LXII (1954), 563–577; Michael Swan, "Henry James and the Heroic Young Master," *London Mag.*, II (1955), 78–86; Francis Fergusson, "*The Golden Bowl* Revisited," *SR*, LXIII (1955), 13–28; Caroline Gordon, "Mr. Verver, Our National Hero," *SR*, LXIII (1955), 29–47; Charles R. Anderson, "James's Portrait of the Southerner," *AL*, XXVII (1955), 309–331; Christof Wegelin, "Henry James: The Expatriate as American," *Symposium*, IX (1955), 46–55.

More recent studies are Alfred R. Ferguson, "The Triple Quest of Henry James: Fame, Art, and Fortune," *AL*, XXVII (1956), 475–498; Oscar Cargill, "*The Princess Casamassima*: A Critical Reappraisal," *PMLA*, LXXI (1956), 97–117; Harold T. McCarthy, "Henry James and 'The Personal Equation,'" *CE*, XVII (1956), 272–278; Harris W. Wilson, "What *Did* Maisie Know?" *CE*, XVII (1956), 279–282; Leon Edel, "'A Tragedy of Error': James's First Story," *NEQ*, XXIX (1956), 291–317; Jean Kimball, "The

Abyss and the Wings of the Dove: The Image as Revelation," *NCF,* X (1956), 281–300; Leo B. Levy, "Henry James's *Confidence* and the Development of the Idea of the Unconscious," *AL,* XXVIII (1956), 347–358; Robert Rogers, "The Beast in Henry James," *AI,* XIII (1956), 427–454; Robert W. Stallman, "Time and the Unnamed Article in *The Ambassadors,*" *MLN,* LXXII (1957), 27–32; Jean Kimball, "Henry James's Last Portrait of a Lady: Charlotte Stant in *The Golden Bowl,*" *AL,* XXVIII (1957), 449–468; Robert L. Gale, "Art Imagery in Henry James's Fiction," *AL,* XXIX (1957), 47–63; John Silver, "A Note on the Freudian Reading of 'The Turn of the Screw,'" *AL,* XXIX (1957), 207–211; and B. R. McElderry, Jr., "Henry James's 'The Art of Fiction,'" *RSSCW,* XXV (1957), 91–100.

### 589. BIBLIOGRAPHY

A full bibliography, with collations of first editions, is Leon Edel and Dan H. Laurence, *A Bibliography of Henry James,* New York, 1958, which replaces the LeRoy Phillips listings (1906, 1930).

A selected critical bibliography was prepared by Robert E. Spiller for *Eight American Authors: A Review of Research and Criticism,* ed. Floyd Stovall, New York, 1956. Maurice Beebe and William T. Stafford compiled "Criticism of Henry James: A Selected Checklist with an Index to Studies of Separate Works" for *Modern Fiction Studies,* III (1957), paying special attention to post-1950 scholarship. Selective listings are in *The Notebooks of Henry James,* ed., F. O. Matthiessen and Kenneth B. Murdock, New York, 1947; Michael Swan, *Henry James,* London, 1950; and Leon Edel, ed., *Selected Fiction,* New York, 1953.

For supplementary listings see Eunice C. Hamilton, "Biographical and Critical Studies of Henry James, 1941–1948," *AL,* XX (1949), 424–435; and Viola R. Dunbar, "Addenda to 'Biographical and Critical Studies of Henry James, 1941–1948,'" *AL,* XXII (1950), 56–61. Of specialized interest are Alfred R. Ferguson, "Some Bibliographical Notes on the Short Stories of Henry James," *AL,* XXI (1949), 292–297; and John R. Russell, "The Henry James Collection," *Univ. Rochester Lib. Bul.,* XI (1956), 50–52.

## WILLIAM JAMES

### 590. WORKS

Ralph Barton Perry's edition of *Pragmatism . . . Together with Four Related Essays . . .* (1943) was reprinted, New York, 1949. *The Principles of Psychology* (1890) was reprinted, Chicago, 1952. *Essays in Pragmatism by William James,* ed. Alburey Castell, New York, 1948, is a reprinting of seven papers in one volume to provide an introduction to James' philosophy.

F. O. Matthiessen, *The James Family,* New York, 1947, includes selections from the writings of Henry James, Sr., William, Henry, and Alice James.

**591.** BIOGRAPHY AND CRITICISM

The most recent full-length study is Lloyd R. Morris, *William James, the Message of a Modern Mind*, New York, 1950.

Briefer studies are Ronald B. Levinson, "Swigart's *Logik* and William James," *JHI*, VIII (1947), 475–483; Jane Mayhall, "William James and the Modern Mood," *AR*, VIII (1948), 291–305; Leo Stein, "Exercises in Criticism . . . William James," *AS*, XVII (1948), 161–165; John K. McCreary, "William James and Modern Value Problems," *Personalist*, XXXI (1950), 126–134; J. B. Shouse, "David Hume and William James: A Comparison," *JHI*, XIII (1952), 514–527; and Milic Capek, "The Reappearance of the Self in the Last Philosophy of William James," *Phil. Rev.*, LXII (1953), 526–544.

## (JOHN) ROBINSON JEFFERS

**593.** SEPARATE WORKS

*The Double Axe and Other Poems*, 1948; *Hungerfield and Other Poems*, 1954.

BIOGRAPHY AND CRITICISM

A recent critical study is Radcliffe Squires, *The Loyalties of Robinson Jeffers*, Ann Arbor, Mich., 1956.

Briefer estimates are Charles I. Glicksberg, "The Poetry of Doom and Despair," *Humanist*, VII (1947), 69–76; Hyatt Howe Waggoner, *The Heel of Elohim: Science and Values in Modern Poetry*, Norman, Okla., 1950, pp. 105–132; Barbara Nauer Folk, "Robinson Jeffers Taken to Task," *CathW*, CLXXIX (1954), 270–273; and Lawrence Clark Powell, "The Double Marriage of Robinson Jeffers," *SWR*, XLI (1956), 278–282.

For a listing of explications of individual poems see George Arms and Joseph M. Kuntz, *Poetry Explication*, New York, 1950, p. 93.

**595.** BIBLIOGRAPHY

The most recent listing is Allen Tate, *Sixty American Poets, 1896–1944*, rev. ed., Washington, 1954, pp. 55–59.

## THOMAS JEFFERSON

**595.** COLLECTED WORKS

Fifteen volumes of the projected fifty-two of *The Papers of Thomas Jefferson* have appeared under the editorship of Julian P. Boyd, Princeton, 1950–1958. An index to Volumes I–VI has been compiled by Elizabeth J.

Sherwood and Ida T. Hopper, Princeton, 1954, and to Volumes VII–XII by Elizabeth J. Sherwood, Princeton, 1958. See also Lyman H. Butterfield, "The Papers of Thomas Jefferson," *Amer. Archivist,* XII (1949), 131–145.

### 596. CORRESPONDENCE

Elizabeth Cometti edited *Jefferson's Ideas on a University Library: Letters from the Founder of the University of Virginia to a Boston Bookseller,* Charlottesville, 1950. See also Lyman H. Butterfield, "The Jefferson-Adams Correspondence in the Adams Manuscript Trust," *LCQJ,* V (1948), 3–6; Lyman H. Butterfield and Howard C. Rice, Jr., eds., "Jefferson's Earliest Note to Maria Cosway . . . ," *WMQ,* V (1948), 26–33; Jessie R. Lucke, ed., "Some Correspondence with Thomas Jefferson Concerning the Public Printers," *SB,* I (1948–1949), 25–38; Thomas A. Kirby, ed., "Jefferson's Letters to Pickering," *Philologica: The Malone Anniversary Studies,* Baltimore, 1949, pp. 256–268; and Rush Welter, "The Adams-Jefferson Correspondence, 1812–1826," *AQ,* II (1950), 234–250.

### 597. EDITED TEXTS AND REPRINTS

A new edition of Jefferson's *Life and Morals of Jesus of Nazareth* (the so-called Jefferson Bible, first published in 1903) was edited by Henry Wilder Foote, Boston, 1951. John Cook Wyllie edited *Thomas Jefferson's Prayer Book,* Charlottesville, 1952. *Thomas Jefferson's Farm Book, with Commentary and Relevant Extracts from Other Writings* was compiled by Edwin M. Betts, Princeton, 1953. William Peden edited Jefferson's *Notes on the State of Virginia,* Chapel Hill, 1955, the first separate reprinting in more than sixty years of Jefferson's only full-length book. *The Political Writings of Thomas Jefferson: Representative Selections,* New York, 1955, was compiled by Edward Dumbauld.

### 598. BIOGRAPHY AND CRITICISM

Biographies of Jefferson in recent years have been numerous. Before her death in 1956, Marie Kimball published the third volume of her uncompleted series, *Jefferson: The Scene of Europe, 1784 to 1789,* New York, 1950. Dumas Malone has begun a projected five-volume study, to be called *Jefferson and His Time;* the first two to be published are *Jefferson the Virginian,* Boston, 1948, and *Jefferson and the Rights of Man,* Boston, 1951. Nathan Schachner published a two-volume life, *Thomas Jefferson: A Biography,* New York, 1951. Other recent lives are John Dos Passos, *The Head and the Heart of Thomas Jefferson,* Garden City, N.Y., 1954, and Phillips Russell, *Jefferson, Champion of the Free Mind,* New York, 1956.

Specialized studies are Eleanor Davidson Berman, *Thomas Jefferson Among the Arts: An Essay in Early American Esthetics,* New York, 1947; Karl Lehmann-Hartleben, *Thomas Jefferson, American Humanist,* New

York, 1947; Howard C. Rice, [Jr.], *L'Hotel de Langeac: Jefferson's Paris Residence* (a bilingual edition), Paris and Monticello, 1947; Daniel Joseph Boorstin, *The Lost World of Thomas Jefferson*, New York, 1948; Max Beloff, *Thomas Jefferson and American Democracy*, London, 1948; Adrienne Koch, *Jefferson and Madison, the Great Collaboration*, New York, 1950; Edwin T. Martin, *Thomas Jefferson: Scientist*, New York, 1952; and Caleb Perry Patterson, *The Constitutional Principles of Thomas Jefferson*, Austin, Tex., 1953.

Further studies of the Jefferson library interests are *Catalogue of the Library of Thomas Jefferson*, 4 vols., compiled with annotations by E. Millicent Sowerby, Washington, 1952-1955, and E. Millicent Sowerby, "Thomas Jefferson and His Library," *Papers Bibl. Soc. Amer.*, L (1956), 213-228. *Jefferson's Fine Arts Library for the University of Virginia, with Additional Notes on Architectural Volumes Known to Have Been Owned by Jefferson*, Charlottesville, 1956, was edited by William B. O'Neal.

Briefer studies are E. D. Berman and E. C. McClintock, "Thomas Jefferson and Rhetoric," *QJS*, XXXIII (1947), 1-8; Frederic R. Kirkland, "Jefferson and Franklin," *PMHB*, LXXI (1947), 218-222; Adrienne Koch, "Philosopher-Statesman of the Republic," *SR*, LV (1947), 384-405; Philip M. Marsh, "Jefferson and Freneau," *AS*, XVI (1947), 201-210; Anthony Marc Lewis, "Jefferson and Virginia's Pioneers, 1774-1781," *MVHR*, XXXIV (1948), 551-588; Mina R. Bryan, "Thomas Jefferson Through the Eyes of His Contemporaries," *PULC*, IX (1948), 219-224; Anthony Marc Lewis, "Jefferson's Summary View as a Chart of Political Union," *WMQ*, V (1948), 34-51; Julian P. Boyd, "Thomas Jefferson's Empire of Liberty," *VQR*, XXIV (1948), 538-554; *idem*, "Thomas Jefferson and the Police State," *NCHR*, XXV (1948), 233-253; Ralph H. Gabriel, "Thomas Jefferson and Twentieth-Century Rationalism," *VQR*, XXVI (1950), 321-335; Lyman H. Butterfield, "The Dream of Benjamin Rush: The Reconciliation of John Adams and Thomas Jefferson," *YR*, XL (1951), 297-319; Howard C. Rice, Jr., "Jefferson in Europe a Century and a Half Later," *PULC*, XII (1951), 19-35; *idem*, "Jefferson's Gift of Fossils to the Museum of Natural History in Paris," *PAPS*, XCV (1951), 597-627; Merrill D. Peterson, "The Jefferson Image, 1829," *AQ*, III (1951), 204-220; Julian P. Boyd, "Thomas Jefferson Survives," *ASch*, XX (1951), 163-173; and *idem*, "The Relevance of Thomas Jefferson for the Twentieth Century," *ibid.*, XXII (1952-1953), 61-76.

More recent studies are Edd Winfield Parks, "Jefferson as a Man of Letters," *GaR*, VI (1952), 450-459; *idem*, "Jefferson's Attitude toward History," *GHQ*, XXXVI (1952), 336-341; Gordon E. Baker, "Thomas Jefferson on Academic Freedom," *AAUP* XXXIX (1953), 377-387; H. H. Bellot, "Thomas Jefferson in American Historiography," *Trans. Royal Hist. Soc.*, IV (1954), 135-155; George E. Sensabaugh, "Jefferson's Use of Milton in the Ecclesiastical Controversies of 1776," *AL*, XXVI (1955), 552-559; J. G.

deRoulhac Hamilton, "The Pacificism of Thomas Jefferson," *VQR*, XXI (1955), 607–620; Bernhard Fabian, "Jefferson's *Notes on Virginia:* The Genesis of Query XVII, *The Different Religions Received into that State?*" *WMQ*, XII (1955), 124–138; Arthur Bestor, *Three Presidents and Their Books*, Urbana, Ill., 1955, pp. 1–44; R. R. Palmer, ed., "A Neglected Work: Otto Vossler on Jefferson and the Revolutionary Era," *WMQ*, XII (1955), 462–471; *idem*, "The Dubious Democrat: Thomas Jefferson in Bourbon France," *PSQ*, LXXII (1957), 388–404; H. Trevor Colbourn, "Thomas Jefferson's Use of the Past," *WMQ*, XV (1958), 56–70; and Julian P. Boyd, "Two Diplomats Between Revolutions: John Jay and Thomas Jefferson," *VMHB*, LXVI (1958), 131–146.

#### 601. PRIMARY SOURCES

*The Jefferson Papers of the University of Virginia*, Charlottesville, 1948, is a calendar compiled by Constance E. Thurlow and Francis L. Berkeley, Jr., with an appended essay by Helen D. Bullock on the papers of Thomas Jefferson. Frank J. and Frank W. Klingberg, eds., *The Correspondence between Henry Stephens Randall and Hugh Blair Grigsby, 1856–1861*, Berkeley, 1952, contains much information on Jefferson's papers and the progress of Randall's biography. See also Rayford W. Logan, ed., *Memoirs of a Monticello Slave as Dictated to Charles Campbell in the 1840's by Isaac, One of Thomas Jefferson's Slaves*, Charlottesville, 1951.

#### 602. BIBLIOGRAPHY

Recent listings are Coolie Verner, *A Further Checklist on the Separate Editions of Jefferson's Notes on the State of Virginia*, Charlottesville, 1950, and *idem*, "Mr. Jefferson Distributes His *Notes:* A Preliminary Checklist of the First Edition," *BNYPL*, LVI (1952), 159–186.

## SARAH ORNE JEWETT

#### 603. COLLECTED WORKS AND CORRESPONDENCE

*Lady Ferry*, Waterville, Me., 1950, is a reprinting, with an introduction by Annie E. Mower, of a short story first published in *Old Friends and New* (1879).

Many of the Jewett letters in the Colby College Library are now in print. Carl J. Weber edited *Letters of Sarah Orne Jewett*, Waterville, Me., 1947, a collection of thirty-three, most of them printed for the first time. Richard Cary edited a volume of ninety-four letters, more than half appearing for the first time: *Sarah Orne Jewett Letters*, Waterville, Me., 1956. See also Carl J. Weber, ed., "More Letters from Sarah Orne Jewett," *CLQ*, Series II (1949), 201–206; *idem*, "Three More Jewett Letters," *ibid.*, Series II (1950), 216–218;

*idem,* "Three More Letters of Sarah Orne Jewett," *ibid.,* Series III (1952), 106–114; and John Alden, ed., "Sarah Orne Jewett to Mellen Chamberlain," *BPLQ,* IX (1957), 86–96.

BIOGRAPHY AND CRITICISM

A recent monograph is A. M. Buchan, *"Our Dear Sarah": An Essay on Sarah Orne Jewett,* Washington University Studies, No. 24, St. Louis, 1953. Briefer studies are John Austin Parker, "Sarah Orne Jewett's 'Boat Song,'" *AL,* XXIII (1951), 133–136; Ferman Bishop, "Henry James Criticizes *The Tory Lover,*" *AL,* XXVII (1955), 262–264; Richard Cary, "Jewett, Tarkington, and the Maine Line," *CLQ,* Series IV (1956), 89–95; Eleanor M. Smith, "The Literary Relationship of Sarah Orne Jewett and Willa Sibert Cather," *NEQ,* XXIX (1956), 472–492; and Ferman Bishop, "Sarah Orne Jewett's Idea of Race," *NEQ,* XXX (1957), 243–249.

A full listing is *A Bibliography of the Published Writings of Sarah Orne Jewett,* Waterville, Me., 1949, compiled by Clara Carter Weber and Carl J. Weber.


# JOHN PENDLETON KENNEDY

**604.** BIOGRAPHY AND CRITICISM

Brief studies are F. X. Gallagher, "The Gentleman from Maryland," *Evergreen Quar.,* V (1948), 48–55; and Charles H. Bohner, *"The Red Book, 1819–1821,* a Satire on Baltimore Society," *MHM,* LI (1956), 175–187.

**605.** PRIMARY SOURCES

Of bibliographical interest is Lloyd W. Griffin, "The John Pendleton Kennedy Manuscripts," *MHM,* XLVIII (1953), 327–336.


# SIDNEY LANIER

**605.** COLLECTED WORKS

Stark Young provided a preface for *Selected Poems,* New York, 1947.

**606.** LETTERS

Three recent publications are Charles R. Anderson, ed., "Two Letters from Lanier to Holmes," *AL,* XVIII (1947), 321–326; Walter Harding, ed., "Sidney Lanier and Virginia Hawkins, Two Letters," *GHQ,* XXXVIII (1954), 290–294; and David Bonnell Green, ed., "Two Letters of Sidney Lanier," *MHM,* LI (1956), 54–56.

BIOGRAPHY AND CRITICISM

Brief studies are Charles R. Anderson, "Poet of the Pine Barrens," *GaR*, I (1947), 280–293; Nathalia Wright, "The East Tennessee Background of Sidney Lanier's *Tiger-Lilies*," *AL*, XIX (1947), 127–138; Lewis Leary, "The Forlorn Hope of Sidney Lanier," *SAQ*, XLVI (1947), 263–271; R. N. Daniel, "Sidney Lanier," *Furman Stud.*, XXXI (1948), 35–45; Boyd Guest, "Sidney Lanier's Feminine Ideal," *GHQ*, XXXII (1948), 175–178; John G. Fletcher, "Sidney Lanier," *UKCR*, XVI (1949), 97–102; Charles R. Anderson, "Lanier and Science: Addenda," *MLN*, LXVI (1951), 395–398; Joseph Beaver, "Lanier's Use of Science for Poetic Imagery," *AL*, XXIV (1953), 520–533; North Callahan, "The Life of Sidney Lanier as Related to His Work," *So. Observer*, II (1954), 169–179; and Ronald F. Howell, "Poet Bleckley, Friend of Sidney Lanier," *GaR*, X (1956), 321–332.

For a listing of explications of individual poems, see George Arms and Joseph M. Kuntz, *Poetry Explication*, New York, 1950, p. 101.

## RING (RINGGOLD WILMER) LARDNER

**609.** BIOGRAPHY AND CRITICISM

The first biography is Donald Elder, *Ring Lardner*, Garden City, N.Y., 1956.

Briefer studies are M. C. Kasten, "The Satire of Ring Lardner," *EJ*, XXXVI (1947), 192–195; Mark Harris, "Ring Lardner Confidential," *Provincial*, I (Oct., 1956), 2–6; John Berryman, "The Case of Ring Lardner: Art and Entertainment," *Commentary*, XXII (1956), 416–423; and Delmore Schwartz, "Ring Lardner: Highbrow in Hiding," *Reporter*, XV (Aug. 9, 1956), 52–54.

BIBLIOGRAPHY

Robert H. Goldsmith has compiled "Ring W. Lardner: A Checklist of His Published Work," *BB*, XXI (1954), 104–106.

## (HARRY) SINCLAIR LEWIS
*d. 1951*

**609.** SEPARATE WORKS

*The God-Seeker*, 1949; *World So Wide*, 1951.

**610.** REPRINTS

Harry E. Maule and Melville H. Cane edited a Sinclair Lewis reader, *The Man from Main Street: Selected Essays and Other Writings, 1904–1950*, New York, 1953. Reprints of individual novels are numerous.

BIOGRAPHY AND CRITICISM

There is no full-length biography or critical study of Lewis. Mark Schorer is preparing a comprehensive critical biography. Grace Hegger Lewis published a memoir of her husband, *With Love from Gracie; Sinclair Lewis: 1912–1925*, New York, 1955. Harrison Smith edited, with an introduction, *From Main Street to Stockholm: Letters of Sinclair Lewis, 1919–1930*, New York, 1952.

Brief critical studies are Maxwell Geismar, *The Last of the Provincials: The American Novel, 1915–1925*, Boston, 1947, pp. 69–150; John T. Flanagan, "A Long Way to Gopher Prairie: Sinclair Lewis's Apprenticeship," *SWR*, XXXII (1947), 403–413; Warren Beck, "How Good is Sinclair Lewis?" *CE*, IX (1948), 173–180; Russell Ames, "Sinclair Lewis Again," *CE*, X (1948), 77–80; Perry Miller, "The Incorruptible Sinclair Lewis," *Atl*, CLXXXVII (Apr., 1951), 30–34; Dorothy Thompson, "Sinclair Lewis: A Postscript," *Atl*, CLXXXVII (June, 1951), 73–74; George J. Becker, "Sinclair Lewis: Apostle to the Philistines," *Accent*, XXI (1952), 423–432; Deming Brown, "Sinclair Lewis: The Russian View," *AL*, XXV (1953), 1–12; Lyon N. Richardson, "Revision in Sinclair Lewis's *The Man Who Knew Coolidge*," *AL*, XXV (1953), 326–333; Franklin Walker, "Jack London's Use of Sinclair Lewis Plots, Together with a Printing of Three of the Plots," *HLQ*, XVII (1953), 59–74; Dale Warren, "Notes on a Genius: Sinclair Lewis at His Best," *Harper's*, CCVIII (Jan., 1954), 61–69; Frederick F. Manfred, "Sinclair Lewis: A Portrait," *ASch*, XXIII (1954), 162–184; Sheldon Grebstein, "Sinclair Lewis' Minnesota Boyhood," *MH*, XXXIV (1954), 85–89; Donald Gallup, "Two Early Manuscripts of Sinclair Lewis," *YULG*, XXIX (1954), 37–40.

More recent studies are Frederic I. Carpenter, "Sinclair Lewis and the Fortress of Reality," *CE*, XVI (1955), 416–423; Lyon N. Richardson, "*Arrowsmith*: Genesis, Development, Versions," *AL*, XXVII (1955), 225–244; Sheldon Grebstein, "The Education of a Rebel: Sinclair Lewis at Yale," *NEQ*, XXVIII (1955), 372–382; and Mark Schorer, "Sinclair Lewis and the Method of Half-Truths," *Society and Self in the Novel; English Institute Essays: 1955*, ed. Mark Schorer, New York, 1956, pp. 117–144.

# LUDWIG LEWISOHN
*d. 1955*

**612. SEPARATE WORKS**

*Goethe: The Story of a Man,* 1949; *The American Jew: Character and Destiny,* 1950.

BIOGRAPHY AND CRITICISM

See Theodore Friedman, "Ludwig Lewisohn: In Memoriam," *Judaism,* V (1956), 173.

# ABRAHAM LINCOLN

**613. COLLECTED WORKS**

Co-sponsored by the Rutgers University Press and the Abraham Lincoln Association of Springfield, Illinois, *The Collected Works of Abraham Lincoln,* 8 vols., New Brunswick, N.J., 1953, was edited by Roy P. Basler and his assistant editors, Marion Dolores Pratt and Lloyd A. Dunlap. An index volume appeared in 1955. This edition was made possible only by the opening in 1947 of the Robert Todd Lincoln Collection in the Library of Congress, with its hundreds of Lincoln holographs. It supersedes all previous collections of Lincoln's writings. For a critical review by David Donald, see *AHR,* LIX (1953), 142–149; for review-articles, see T. Harry Williams, "Abraham Lincoln—Principle and Pragmatism in Politics," *MVHR,* XL (1953), 89–106; and Edmund Wilson, "Abraham Lincoln: The Union as Religious Mysticism," *NY,* XXIX (Mar. 14, 1953), 116–136.

A one-volume redaction of the *Collected Works* is *The Living Lincoln: The Man, His Mind, His Times, and the War He Fought, Reconstructed from His Own Writings,* ed. Paul M. Angle and Earl Schenck Miers, New Brunswick, N.J., 1955. Addenda appear in Rufus Rockwell Wilson, ed., *Uncollected Works of Abraham Lincoln,* 2 vols., Elmira, N.Y., 1947–1948.

LETTERS AND ADDRESSES

*Created Equal? The Complete Lincoln-Douglas Debates of 1858* was edited with an introduction by Paul M. Angle, Chicago, 1958. *The Illinois Political Campaign of 1858,* Washington, 1958, is a facsimile of the printer's copy as edited and prepared for the press by Abraham Lincoln, first published in 1860 under the title *Political Debates between Hon. Abraham Lincoln and Hon. Stephen A. Douglas, in the Celebrated Campaign of 1858, in Illinois.* Paul M. Angle also edited *Lincoln's Speeches and Letters,* New York, 1958.

Paul M. Angle edited *Abraham Lincoln: His Autobiographical Writings Now Brought Together for the First Time,* Kingsport, Tenn., 1947. *The Lincoln Encyclopedia: The Spoken and Written Words of A. Lincoln Arranged for Ready Reference,* New York, 1950, was compiled by Archer H. Shaw.

*Herndon's Life of Lincoln* (1889) reappeared with an introduction and notes by Paul M. Angle, Cleveland, 1949.

## 614. BIOGRAPHY AND CRITICISM

James G. Randall's biography, *Lincoln the President: Springfield to Gettysburg,* 2 vols., New York, 1945, is completed in two more volumes, *Lincoln the President: Midstream,* New York, 1952, and, with the assistance of Richard N. Current, *Lincoln the President: Last Full Measure,* New York, 1955. Two excellent one-volume studies are Benjamin P. Thomas, *Abraham Lincoln, a Biography,* New York, 1952, and Carl Sandburg, *Abraham Lincoln: The Prairie Years and the War Years* (1926 and 1939), reduced to a single volume, New York, 1954. James G. Randall, *Mr. Lincoln,* ed. Richard N. Current, New York, 1957, is composed of "those parts of the larger work which deal primarily with Lincoln the man and with his personal relationships." Richard Current has also written a profile of Lincoln in *The Lincoln Nobody Knows,* New York, 1958. Herbert Mitgang, ed., *Lincoln As They Saw Him,* New York, 1956, is a collection of contemporaneous reports and editorials in newspapers and periodicals.

Five specialized biographical studies are Donald W. Riddle, *Lincoln Runs for Congress,* New Brunswick, N.J., 1948, and *Congressman Abraham Lincoln,* Urbana, Ill., 1957; T. Harry Williams, *Lincoln and His Generals,* New York, 1952; and Ruth Painter Randall, *Mary Lincoln: Biography of a Marriage,* Boston, 1953, and *Lincoln's Sons,* Boston, 1955.

Benjamin P. Thomas, *Portrait for Posterity: Lincoln and His Biographers,* New Brunswick, N.J., 1947, is "the story behind the Lincoln books, based on the correspondence of Lincoln's biographers."

Historical, political, and military studies are numerous: James G. Randall, *Lincoln and the South,* Baton Rouge, 1946; W. B. Hesseltine, *Lincoln and the War Governors,* New York, 1948; Kenneth P. Williams, *Lincoln Finds a General,* 4 vols., New York, 1949–1956; Helen Nicolay, *Lincoln's Secretary,* New York, 1949; Allan Nevins, *The Emergence of Lincoln,* 2 vols., New York, 1950; Bruce Catton's triology: *Mr. Lincoln's Army,* New York, 1951, *Glory Road,* New York, 1952, and *A Stillness at Appomattox,* New York, 1953; Robert S. Harper, *Lincoln and the Press,* New York, 1951; Harlan Hoyt Horner, *Lincoln and Greeley,* Urbana, Ill., 1953; Allan Nevins, *The Statesmanship of the Civil War,* New York, 1953;

William F. Zornow, *Lincoln and the Party Divided,* Norman, Okla., 1954; Robert V. Bruce, *Lincoln and the Tools of War,* Indianapolis, 1956; David Donald, *Lincoln's Herndon,* New York, 1948, and *Lincoln Reconsidered: Essays on the Civil War Era,* New York, 1956; and David M. Silver, *Lincoln's Supreme Court,* Urbana, Ill., 1956.

Briefer studies are V. M. Scanlan, "A Southerner's View of Abraham Lincoln," *IMH,* XLIII (1947), 141–158; Robert Fortenbaugh, "Lincoln as Gettysburg Saw Him," *PH,* XIV (1947), 1–12; Richard Hofstadter, "Abraham Lincoln and the Self-Made Myth," *The American Political Tradition and the Men Who Made It,* New York, 1948; Reinhard H. Luthin, "Lincoln and the American Tradition," *MJ,* III (1950–1951), 1–10; Robert Berkelman, "Lincoln's Interest in Shakespeare," *Shak. Quar.,* II (1951), 303–312; Stewart Mitchell, "Lincoln and 'The Devil's Advocate,'" *PMHS,* LXVIII (1952), 350–376; Clarence A. Brown, "Walt Whitman and Lincoln," *JISHS,* XLVII (1954), 176–184; and David C. Mearns, *Three Presidents and Their Books,* Urbana, Ill., 1955.

### 615. PRIMARY SOURCES

David C. Mearns, *The Lincoln Papers: The Story of the Collection with Selections to July 4, 1861,* 2 vols., New York, 1948, is an account of the disposition of the President's papers, and a selection of more than five hundred documents representing "a cross-section of American society in Lincoln's time."

Other collections are described in Carl Sandburg, *Lincoln Collector: The Story of Oliver R. Barrett's Great Private Collection,* New York, 1949; *The Immortal Autograph Letters, Documents, Manuscripts . . . Collected by Oliver R. Barrett,* New York, 1952 (the catalogue of the Parke-Bernet sale, Feb. 19–20, 1952); Clyde C. Walton, Jr., *The Bollinger Lincoln Lectures,* Iowa City, 1953 (addresses given at the dedication of the Lincoln Library collected by James W. Bollinger and bequeathed to the State University of Iowa); and Frederick R. Goff, "Lincolniana Added to the Stern Collection," *LCQJ,* XII (1955), 53–58.

### BIBLIOGRAPHY

For guidance through the bibliographical wilderness of Lincoln studies (now more than 4,000 items), consult the *Journal of the Illinois State Historical Society* (1908–current); the *Lincoln Herald* (1938–current), published by the Lincoln Memorial University Press, Harrogate, Tenn.; the *Abraham Lincoln Quarterly* (1940–1952), published by the Abraham Lincoln Association, Springfield, Ill.; and *Lincoln Lore,* the weekly bulletin of the Lincoln National Life Foundation, Fort Wayne, Ind.

# (NICHOLAS) VACHEL LINDSAY

**616.** BIOGRAPHY AND CRITICISM

An "interpretive biography of Vachel Lindsay and Springfield, Illinois" is Mark Harris, *City of Discontent*, Indianapolis, 1952. Briefer studies are Davis Edwards, "The Real Source of Vachel Lindsay's Poetic Technique," *QJS*, XXXIII (1947), 182–195; Emmett L. Avery, "Vachel Lindsay in Spokane," *PS*, III (1949), 338–353; N. E. Enkvist, "The Folk Element in Vachel Lindsay's Poetry," *ES*, XXXII (1951), 241–249; Carl Carmer, "Three Aprils and a Poet," *Atl*, CXCVII (1956), 69–71; and Emmett L. Avery, "Vachel Lindsay: Spokane Journalist," *RSSCW*, XXV (1957), 101–110.

For a listing of explications of individual poems see George Arms and Joseph M. Kuntz, *Poetry Explication*, New York, 1950, pp. 101–102.

**618.** BIBLIOGRAPHY

The most recent bibliographical listing is Allen Tate, *Sixty American Poets, 1896–1944*, rev. ed., Washington, 1954, pp. 67–70. A mimeographed *Inventory of the Lindsayana Collection in Springfield, Illinois* was published by Mrs. N. V. Lindsay in Hartford, Conn., 1949, preparatory to sale.

# WILLIAM LIVINGSTON

**618.** BIOGRAPHY AND CRITICISM

See Dorothy Rita Dillon, *The New York Triumvirate: A Study of the Legal and Political Careers of William Livingston, John Morin Scott, William Smith, Jr.*, New York, 1949.

# JACK (JOHN GRIFFITH) LONDON

**620.** BIOGRAPHY AND CRITICISM

Philip S. Foner edited *Jack London, American Rebel: A Collection of His Social Writings Together with an Extensive Study of the Man and His Times*, New York, 1947. Three full estimates of London as novelist are Maxwell Geismar, *Rebels and Ancestors: The American Novel, 1890–1915*, Boston, 1953, pp. 139–216; Kenneth S. Lynn, *The Dream of Success*, Boston, 1955, pp. 75–118; and Charles Child Walcutt, *American Literary Naturalism, A Divided Stream*, Minneapolis, 1956, pp. 87–113 and *passim*.

Briefer critical studies are Robert H. Woodward, "Jack London's Code of Primitivism," *Folio*, XVIII (May, 1953), 39–44; Franklin Walker, "Jack London's Use of Sinclair Lewis Plots, Together with a Printing of Three of the Plots," *HLQ*, XVII (1953), 59–74; Sam S. Baskett, "A Source of *The Iron Heel*," *AL*, XXVII (1955), 268–270; *idem*, "Jack London on the Oakland Waterfront," *AL*, XXVII (1955), 363–371; and Gordon Mills, "Jack London's Quest for Salvation," *AQ*, VII (1955), 3–14.

## HENRY WADSWORTH LONGFELLOW

**623.** BIOGRAPHY AND CRITICISM

A recent biography is Edward Wagenknecht, *Longfellow: A Full-Length Portrait*, New York, 1955. Of biographical interest are Edward Wagenknecht, ed., *Mrs. Longfellow: Selected Letters and Journals of Fanny Appleton Longfellow (1817–1861)*, New York, 1956, and Andrew Hilen, ed., *The Diary of Clara Crowninshield: A European Tour with Longfellow, 1835–1836*, Seattle, 1956.

A specialized critical study is Andrew Hilen, *Longfellow and Scandinavia: A Study of the Poet's Relationship with the Northern Languages and Literature*, New Haven, 1947. See also Carl Hammer, Jr., *Longfellow's 'Golden Legend' and Goethe's 'Faust,'* Baton Rouge, 1952.

Briefer studies are Manning Hawthorne and Henry Wadsworth Longfellow Dana, "The Origin of Longfellow's *Evangeline*," *PBSA*, XLI (1947), 165–203; C. L. Johnson, "Longfellow's Beginnings in Foreign Languages," *NEQ*, XX (1947), 317–328; H. W. L. Dana and Manning Hawthorne, "'The Maiden Aunt of the Whole Human Race,': Fredrika Bremer's Friendship with Longfellow and Hawthorne," *ASR*, XXXVII (1949), 217–229; J. Chesley Mathews, "Echoes of Dante in Longfellow's Poetry," *Italica*, XXVI (1949), 242–259; Waino Nyland, "*Kalevala* as a Reputed Source of Longfellow's *Song of Hiawatha*," *AL*, XXII (1950), 1–20; Norman Holmes Pearson, "Both Longfellows," *UKCR*, XVI (1950), 245–253.

More recent studies are James C. Austin, "J. T. Fields and the Revision of Longfellow's Poems: Unpublished Correspondence," *NEQ*, XXIV (1951), 239–250; Rose M. Davis, "'The Tents of Grace' in Longfellow's *Evangeline*: Their History and Fate," *PH*, XVIII (1951), 269–292; Rudolph Von Abele, "A Note on Longfellow's Poetic," *AL*, XXIV (1952), 77–83; Andrew Hilen, "Longfellow's 'A Lay of Courage,'" *PMLA*, LXVII (1952), 949–959; Edward N. Waters, "Liszt and Longfellow," *Musical Quar.*, XLI (1955), 1–25; Joseph E. O'Neill, "Longfellow: Preacher and Poet," *Thought*, XXXI (1956–1957), 567–600; John M. Fein, "Longfellow, Sarmiento, and Two Unpublished Letters," *AmF*, XII (1956), 299–302.

For a listing of explications of individual poems, see George Arms and Joseph M. Kuntz, *Poetry Explication*, New York, 1950, p. 102.

# AMY LOWELL

**626.** COLLECTED WORKS

Louis Untermeyer edited, with an introduction, *The Complete Poetical Works of Amy Lowell*, Boston, 1955.

**627.** BIOGRAPHY AND CRITICISM

A recent biography is Horace Gregory, *Amy Lowell: Portrait of the Poet in Her Time*, New York, 1958.

Briefer studies are John A. Lomax, "Amy Lowell at Baylor," *SWR*, XXXII (1947), 133–134; Eric W. Carlson, "The Range of Symbolism in Poetry," *SAQ*, XLVIII (1949), 442–451; and Norreys Jephson O'Conor, "Amy Lowell: A Reminiscence," *ArQ*, VIII (1952), 145–157.

A listing of explications of individual poems is in George Arms and Joseph M. Kuntz, *Poetry Explication*, New York, 1950, p. 103.

**628.** BIBLIOGRAPHY

The most recent listing is Allen Tate, *Sixty American Poets, 1896–1944*, rev. ed., Washington, 1954, pp. 71–73.

# JAMES RUSSELL LOWELL

**629.** COLLECTED WORKS

Thelma M. Smith edited *Uncollected Poems of James Russell Lowell*, Philadelphia, 1950.

M. A. De Wolfe Howe and G. W. Cottrell, Jr., edited *The Scholar-Friends: Letters of Francis James Child and James Russell Lowell*, Cambridge, Mass., 1952. Other collections of letters are W. H. G. Armytage, ed., "Some New Letters of James Russell Lowell," *N&Q*, CXCV (May 13, 1950), 207–208; James L. Woodress, ed., "Comfort Me, O My Publisher: Some Unpublished Letters from James Russell Lowell to James T. Fields," *HLQ*, XV (1951), 73–86; Arthur Voss, ed., "An Uncollected Letter of Lowell's Parson Wilbur," *NEQ*, XXVI (1953), 396–399; James L. Woodress, ed., "The Lowell-Howells Friendship: Some Unpublished Letters," *NEQ*, XXVI (1953), 523–528; and Louis J. Budd, ed., "More New Letters of James Russell Lowell," *DULN*, No. 28 (1953), 1–13.

**630.** REPRINTS

William Smith Clark II selected and edited *Essays, Poems, and Letters*, New York, 1948.

BIOGRAPHY AND CRITICISM

A full-length critical analysis is Leon Howard, *Victorian Knight-Errant: A Study of the Early Literary Career of James Russell Lowell*, Berkeley, 1952.

Briefer studies are Sculley Bradley, "Lowell, Emerson, and the *Pioneer*," *AL*, XIX (1947), 231–244; K. A. McEuen, "Lowell's Puns," *ASp*, XXII (1947), 24–33; Arthur Voss, "James Russell Lowell," *UKCR*, XV (1949), 224–233; John Paul Pritchard, "A Glance at Lowell's Classical Reading," *AL*, XXI (1950), 442–455; Arthur Voss, "Backgrounds of Lowell's Satire in 'The Biglow Papers,'" *NEQ*, XXIII (1950), 47–64; Max L. Griffin, "Lowell and the South," *TSE*, II, (1950), 75–102; Nils Erik Enkvist, "The Biglow Papers in Ninteenth-Century England," *NEQ*, XXVI (1953), 219–236; and Jayne Crane Harder, "James Russell Lowell: Linguistic Patriot," *ASp*, XXIX (1954), 181–186.

634. BIBLIOGRAPHY

Brief notes are F. De Wolfe Miller, "Twenty-eight Additions to the Canon of Lowell's Criticism," *SB*, IV (1951), 205–210; and James L. Woodress, "A Note on Lowell Bibliography: The Review of Howells' *Venetian Life*," *SB*, IV (1951), 210–211.

## ARCHIBALD MacLEISH

634. SEPARATE WORKS

*Actfive, and Other Poems*, 1948; *Poetry and Opinion: The Pisan Cantos of Ezra Pound: A Dialogue on the Role of Poetry*, 1950; *Freedom Is the Right to Choose: An Inquiry into the Battle for the American Future*, 1951; *The Trojan Horse*, 1952; *This Music Crept by Me upon the Waters*, 1953; *Songs for Eve*, 1954; *J. B.*, 1958.

635. COLLECTED WORKS

*Collected Poems, 1917–1952* appeared in Boston, 1952.

BIOGRAPHY AND CRITICISM

Brief estimates are Kenneth Lash, "Myth and the Conquest of Mexico," *NMQ*, XVII (1947), 38–44; Hyatt Howe Waggoner, *The Heel of Elohim: Science and Values in Modern American Poetry*, Norman, Okla., 1950, pp. 133–154; John Ciardi, "The Poetry of Archibald MacLeish," *Atl*, CXCI (May, 1953), 67–68; and Reed Whittemore, "MacLeish and Democratic Pastoral," *SR*, LXI (1953), 700–709.

For a listing of explications of individual poems see George Arms and Joseph M. Kuntz, *Poetry Explication*, New York, 1950, p. 104.

**636.** BIBLIOGRAPHY

The most recent listing is Allen Tate, *Sixty American Poets, 1896–1944*, rev. ed., Washington, 1954, pp. 73–80.


# JAMES MADISON

**636.** COLLECTED WORKS AND REPRINTS

The papers of James Madison are being edited at the University of Chicago; about twenty-five volumes are projected.

Saul K. Padover edited, with an introduction, *The Complete Madison: His Basic Writings*, New York, 1953.

BIOGRAPHY AND CRITICISM

Irving Brant's *James Madison, the Virginia Revolutionist* (1941) is followed by four more volumes, all published in Indianapolis: *James Madison, the Nationalist, 1780–1787*, 1948; *James Madison, Father of the Constitution, 1787–1800*, 1950; *James Madison, the Secretary of State, 1800–1809*, 1953; and *James Madison, the President, 1809–1812*, 1956. A specialized study is Adrienne Koch, *Jefferson and Madison, the Great Collaboration*, New York, 1950.

Briefer studies are Philip M. Marsh, "Philip Freneau and James Madison, 1791–1793," *PNJHS*, LXV (1947), 189–194; Lyon G. Tyler, "Madison and the War of 1812: Circumstances that Prolonged the War," *Tyler's Quar. Hist. & Gen. Mag.*, XXIX (1948), 159–165; Theodore Bolton, "The Life Portraits of James Madison," *WMQ*, VIII (1951), 25–47; Alpheus T. Mason, "The Federalist—A Split Personality," *AHR*, LVII (1952), 625–643; Neal Riemer, "The Republicanism of James Madison," *PSQ*, LXIX (1954), 45–64; *idem*, "James Madison's Theory of the Self-Destructive Features of Republican Government," *Ethics*, LXV (1954), 34–43; and Adrienne Koch, "James Madison and the Workshop of Liberty," *RPol*, XVI (1954), 175–193.


# EDGAR LEE MASTERS
*d. 1950*

**639.** BIOGRAPHY AND CRITICISM

A recent study is Kimball Flaccus, *The Vermont Background of Edgar Lee Masters*, New York, 1955. See also Gertrude Claytor, "Edgar Lee Masters in the Chelsea Years," *PULC*, XIV (1952), 1–29; and John T. Flanagan, "The Spoon River Poet," *SWR*, XXXVIII (1953), 226–237.

For a listing of explications of individual poems see George Arms and Joseph M. Kuntz, *Poetry Explication*, New York, 1950, p. 108.

## COTTON MATHER

**641.** BIOGRAPHY AND CRITICISM

Mather's interest in science is elaborated in Otho T. Beall, Jr., and Richard H. Shryock, *Cotton Mather, First Significant Figure in American Medicine,* Baltimore, 1954.

Briefer studies are Conway Zirkle, "The Theory of Concentric Spheres: Edmund Halley, Cotton Mather, and John Cleves Symmes," *Isis,* XXXVII (1947), 155-159; Victor Hugo Paltsits, "New Light on *Publick Occurrences:* America's First Newspaper," *PMHS,* LIX (1949), 75-88; Richard M. Dorson, "Five Directions in American Folklore," *MF,* I (1951), 158-160; Ernest Benz, "Pietist and Puritan Sources of Early Protestant World Missions," *CH,* XX (1951), 28-55; Dagobert DeLevie, "Cotton Mather, Theologian and Scientist," *AQ,* III (1951), 362-365; John B. Blake, "The Inoculation Controversy in Boston: 1721-1722," *NEQ,* XXV (1952), 489-506; Richard Dean Hathaway, " 'Ye Scheme to Bagge Penne': A Forged Letter Smears Cotton Mather," *WMQ,* X (1953), 403-421; Elizabeth Bancroft Schlesinger, "Cotton Mather and His Children," *WMQ,* X (1953), 181-189; Katherine Anne Porter, "A Bright Particular Faith, A.D. 1700: A Portrait of Cotton Mather," *Perspectives USA,* No. 7 (Spring, 1954), 83-92; and Laurence Farmer, "When Cotton Mather Fought the Smallpox," *AH,* VIII (Aug., 1957), 40-43, 109.

## INCREASE MATHER

**644.** EDITED TEXTS AND REPRINTS

*A Testimony Against Several Prophane and Superstitious Customs* (1687) was reprinted with an introduction and notes by William Peden, and a bibliographical note by Lawrence Starkey, in Charlottesville, 1953.

## HERMAN MELVILLE

**647.** COLLECTED WORKS

Four more volumes in the projected *Complete Works* (Hendricks House) have appeared: Egbert S. Oliver, ed., *Piazza Tales,* New York, 1948; Henry A. Murray, ed., *Pierre; or, The Ambiguities,* New York, 1949; Luther S. Mansfield and Howard P. Vincent, eds., *Moby-Dick,* New York, 1952; and Elizabeth S. Foster, *The Confidence-Man: His Masquerade,* New York, 1954.

Letters by, to, and about Melville are in Eleanor Melville Metcalf, ed., *Herman Melville: Cycle and Epicycle,* Cambridge, Mass., 1953.

The only transcription of *Journal of a Visit to London and the Continent, 1849–1850* is that of Eleanor Melville Metcalfe, Cambridge, Mass., 1948. A new edition (re-titled) of *Journal Up the Straits* is Howard C. Horsford, ed., *Journal of a Visit to Europe and the Levant,* Princeton, 1955, which corrects Weaver's text and is fully annotated.

## 648. EDITED TEXTS

F. Barron Freeman, ed., *Melville's Billy Budd,* Cambridge, Mass., 1948, is an attempt at a transcription, with all variant readings, of the novel and of the unpublished short story, "Baby Budd, Sailor." The text is unfortunately still inexact.

Jay Leyda edited *The Complete Stories of Herman Melville,* New York, 1949, and *The Portable Melville,* New York, 1952. Reprints of individual novels are too numerous to list separately.

Two dramatizations of *Billy Budd* are Louis O. Coxe and Robert H. Chapman, *Uniform of Flesh,* Princeton, 1947 (mimeographed), and the rewritten version, *Billy Budd,* Princeton, 1951. *Billy Budd, An Opera in Four Acts,* London, 1952, has a libretto by E. M. Forster and Eric Crozier, music by Benjamin Britten.

### BIOGRAPHY AND CRITICISM

Two interdependent biographies are Leon Howard's formal narrative, *Herman Melville,* Berkeley, 1951, and Jay Leyda's *The Melville Log: A Documentary Life of Herman Melville, 1819–1891,* 2 vols., New York, 1951. They are separate yet related studies. Three European scholars writing of Melville's life are Geoffrey Stone, *Melville,* New York, 1949; Pierre Frédérix, *Herman Melville,* Paris, 1950; and Ronald Mason, *The Spirit Above the Dust: A Study of Herman Melville,* London, 1951. A specialized study is Merton M. Sealts, *Melville as Lecturer,* Cambridge, Mass., 1957.

Studies which are as much criticism as biography are Richard Chase, *Herman Melville,* New York, 1949; Newton Arvin, *Herman Melville,* New York, 1950; and William H. Gilman, *Melville's Early Life and Redburn,* New York, 1951. Three highly individualistic critiques are Charles Olson, *Call Me Ishmael,* New York, 1947; Lawrance Thompson, *Melville's Quarrel with God,* Princeton, 1952; and Milton R. Stern, *The Fine Hammered Steel of Herman Melville,* Urbana, Ill., 1957. To these should be added the work on Melville in Charles Feidelson, Jr., *Symbolism and American Literature,* Chicago, 1953, and R. W. B. Lewis, *The American Adam,* Chicago, 1955.

Studies dealing chiefly with sources and related matters are Howard Vincent, *The Trying-Out of Moby-Dick,* Boston, 1949; Nathalia Wright, *Melville's Use of the Bible,* Durham, N.C., 1949; Tyrus Hillway, *Melville and the Whale*, Stonington, Conn., 1950; Merrell R. Davis, *Melville's Mardi: A Chartless Voyage*, New Haven, 1952. Of more general interest are M. O. Percival, *A Reading of Moby-Dick*, Chicago, 1950; Gabriele Baldini, *Melville o le ambiguità*, Milan, 1952; C. L. R. James, *Mariners, Renegades, and Castaways: The Story of Herman Melville and the World We Live In*, New York, 1953; Edward H. Rosenberry, *Melville and the Comic Spirit*, Cambridge, Mass., 1955; and James Baird, *Ishmael*, Baltimore, 1956.

*Moby-Dick, Centennial Essays*, eds. Tyrus Hillway and Luther S. Mansfield, Dallas, 1953, is a collection of nine essays printed for the Melville Society. The *Princeton University Library Chronicle*, XIII (Winter, 1952), is a special Melville issue. *American Literature*, XXV (Jan., 1954), is devoted solely to Melville.

Briefer studies are Alexander Eliot, "Melville and Bartleby," *Furioso*, III (1947), 11–21; Willard Thorp, ed., *Moby-Dick*, New York, 1947, pp. ix–xvii; Newton Arvin, "A Note on the Background of *Billy Budd*," *AL*, XX (1948), 51–55; Henry F. Pommer, "Herman Melville and the Wake of the *Essex*," *AL*, XX (1948), 290–304; Tyrus Hillway, "Melville and the Spirit of Science," *SAQ*, XLVIII (1949), 77–88; Sherman Paul, "Melville's 'The Town Ho's Story,'" *AL*, XXI (1949), 212–221; R. W. Short, "Melville as Symbolist," *UKCR*, XV (1948), 38–46; Howard P. Vincent, "'White Jacket': An Essay in Interpretation," *NEQ*, XXII (1949), 304–315; Newton Arvin, "Melville's Shorter Poems," *PR*, XVI (1949), 1034–1046; Walter Weber, "Some Characteristic Symbols in Herman Melville's Works," *ES*, XXX (1949), 217–224; Merton M. Sealts, "Melville and the Shakers," *SB*, II (1949–50), 105–114; Alfred Kazin, "On Melville as Scripture," *PR*, XVII (1950), 67–75; Dan G. Hoffman, "Melville's 'Story of China Aster,'" *AL*, XXII (1950), 137–149; R. W. B. Lewis, "Melville on Homer," *AL*, XXII (1950), 166–176; Joseph Schiffman, "Melville's Final Stage, Irony: A Re-examination in *Billy Budd* Criticism," *AL*, XXII (1950), 128–136; Joseph Schiffman, "Critical Problems in Melville's 'Benito Cereno,'" *MLQ*, XI (1950), 317–324; Dan G. Hoffman, "Melville in the American Grain," *SFQ*, XIV (1950), 185–191; Harry Slochower, "*Moby Dick*: The Myth of Democratic Expectancy," *AQ*, II (1950), 259–269; Donald Weeks, "Two Uses of *Moby Dick*," *AQ*, II (1950), 155–164; Philip Rahv, "Melville and His Critics," *PR*, XVII (1950), 732–735; Edward G. Lueders, "The Melville-Hawthorne Relationship in *Pierre* and *The Blithedale Romance*," *WHR*, IV (1950), 323–334; Harry Slochower, "Freudian Motifs in *Moby-Dick*," *Complex*, III (1950), 16–25; W. H. Auden, *The Enchaféd Flood*, New York, 1950, *passim*.

Other studies are Harrison Hayford, "The Sailor Poet of *White-Jacket*," *BPLQ*, III (1951), 221–228; Norman Holmes Pearson, "Billy Budd: 'The King's Yarn,'" *AQ*, III (1951), 99–114; J. W. Shroeder, "Sources and Symbols for Melville's *Confidence-Man*," *PMLA*, LXVI (1951), 363–380;

Nathalia Wright, "The Head and the Heart in Melville's *Mardi*," *PMLA*, LXVI (1951), 351-362; Millicent Bell, "Pierre Bayle and *Moby-Dick*," *PMLA*, LXVI (1951), 626-648; Charles A. Fenton, "'The Bell-Tower': Melville and Technology," *AL*, XXIII (1951), 219-232; John J. Gross, "The Rehearsal of Ishmael: Melville's 'Redburn,'" *VQR*, XXVII (1951), 581-600; Henry A. Murray, "In Nomine Diaboli," *NEQ*, XXIV (1951), 435-452; John W. Nichol, "Melville and the Midwest," *PMLA*, LXVI (1951), 613-625; F. X. Canfield, "Moby Dick and the Book of Job," *CathW*, CLXXIV (1952), 254-260; Edward Fiess, "Melville as a Reader and Student of Byron," *AL*, XXIV (1952), 186-194; Richard H. Fogle, "The Monk and the Bachelor: Melville's *Benito Cereno*," *TSE*, III (1952), 155-178; Howard C. Horsford, "Evidence of Melville's Plans for a Sequel to *The Confidence-Man*," *AL*, XXIV (1952), 85-89; Randall Stewart, "Melville and Hawthorne," *SAQ*, LI (1952), 436-446; C. Merton Babcock, "The Vocabulary of *Moby Dick*," *ASp*, XXVII (1952), 91-101; Tyrus Hillway, "Billy Budd: Melville's Human Sacrifice," *PS*, VI (1952), 342-347; R. B. West, Jr., "The Unity of *Billy Budd*," *HudR*, V (1952), 120-127; Charles Moorman, "Melville's *Pierre* and the Fortunate Fall," *AL*, XXV (1953), 13-30; Charles G. Hoffman, "The Shorter Fiction of Herman Melville," *SAQ*, LII (1953), 414-430; Frederic I. Carpenter, "Melville: The World in a Man-of-War," *UKCR*, XIX (1953), 257-264; Perry Miller, "Melville and Transcendentalism," *VQR*, XXIX (1953), 556-575; Leo Marx, "Melville's Parable of the Walls," *SR*, LXI (1953), 602-627; Marius Bewley, "A Truce of God for Melville," *SR*, LXI (1953), 682-700; Stanley Edgar Hyman, "Melville the Scrivener," *NMQ*, XXIII (1953), 381-415.

More recent studies are Don Geiger, "Melville's Black God: Contrary Evidence in 'The Town-Ho's Story,'" *AL*, XXV (1954), 464-471; George R. Stewart, "The Two Moby-Dicks," *AL*, XXV (1954), 417-448; James Dean Young, "The Nine Gams of the *Pequod*," *AL*, XXV (1954), 449-463; Walter E. Bezanson, "Melville's 'Clarel': The Complex Passion," *ELH*, XXI (1954), 146-159; Joseph J. Firebaugh, "Humorist as Rebel: The Melville of *Typee*," *NCF*, IX (1954), 108-120; Walter E. Bezanson, "Melville's Reading of Arnold's Poetry," *PMLA*, LXIX (1954), 365-391; B. R. McElderry, Jr., "Three Earlier Treatments of the *Billy Budd* Theme," *AL*, XXVII (1955), 251-257; Laurence Barrett, "The Differences in Melville's Poetry," *PMLA*, LXX (1955), 606-623; Dorothee Grdseloff, "A Note on the Origin of Fedallah in *Moby-Dick*," XXVII (1955), 396-403; James E. Miller, Jr., "Hawthorne and Melville: The Unpardonable Sin," *PMLA*, LXX (1955), 91-114; John Parke, "Seven *Moby-Dicks*," *NEQ*, XXVIII (1955), 319-338; William Van O'Connor, "Melville on the Nature of Hope," *UKCR*, XXII (1955), 123-130; Joseph Warren Beach, "Hart Crane and *Moby-Dick*," *WR*, XX (1956), 183-196; Lillian Beatty, "Typee and Blithedale: Rejected Ideal Communities," *Personalist*, XXXVII (1956), 367-378; Alfred Kazin,

"Ishmael and Ahab," *Atl*, CXCVIII (Nov., 1956), 81–85; Perry Miller, *The Raven and the Whale*, New York, 1956, *passim;* Gene B. Montague, "Melville's *Battle-Pieces*," *UTSE*, XXXV (1956), 106–115; John B. Noone, Jr., "*Billy-Budd:* Two Concepts of Nature," *AL*, XXIX (1957), 249–262; David Jaffé, "Some Origins of *Moby-Dick:* New Finds in an Old Source," *AL*, XXIX (1957), 263–277; John G. Cawelti, "Some Notes on the Structure of *The Confidence-Man*," *AL*, XXIX (1957), 278–288; Sidney Kaplan, "Herman Melville and the American National Sin: The Meaning of *Benito Cereno*," *JNH*, XLII (1957), 11–37; Maurice B. Cramer, "*Billy Budd* and *Billy Budd*," *JGE*, X (1957), 78–91; and William Braswell, "Melville's *Billy Budd* as 'An Inside Narrative,'" *AL*, XXIX (1957), 133–146.

#### 654. BIBLIOGRAPHY

There is no complete bibliography of Melville's work. Stanley T. Williams prepared a bibliographical essay for *Eight American Authors: A Review of Research and Criticism*, ed. Floyd Stovall, New York, 1956. Recent additions to existing check lists are in Merton M. Sealts, *Melville's Reading: A Check-List of Books Owned and Borrowed*, Cambridge, Mass., 1950; Herbert Cahoon, "Herman Melville: A Check List of Books and Manuscripts in the Collections of the New York Public Library," *BNYPL*, LV (1951), 263–275, 325–338; Gordon H. Mills, "American First Editions at TxU: VII. Herman Melville (1819–1891)," *UTLC*, IV (1951), 89–92; the *Annual Melville Bibliography, 1951* (1952), *1952–53* (1954), sponsored by the Melville Society and compiled by S. C. Sherman, J. H. Birss, and Gordon Roper; and Milton R. Stern, *The Fine Hammered Steel of Herman Melville*, Urbana, Ill., 1957, pp. 252–291 (covering the scholarship up to 1954).

The *Melville Society Newsletter* was first published, mimeographed, in March, 1945; beginning with Vol. IV (Mar., 1949), it became a printed leaflet.

## H(ENRY) L(OUIS) MENCKEN
### d. 1956

#### 654. SEPARATE WORKS

*A Mencken Chrestomathy*, 1949; *Minority Report: H. L. Mencken's Notebooks*, 1956.

#### 655. REPRINTS AND COLLECTIONS

*The Days of H. L. Mencken*, New York, 1947, is a one-volume edition of *Happy Days* (1940), *Newspaper Days* (1941), and *Heathen Days* (1943). Malcolm Moos edited *A Carnival of Buncombe*, Baltimore, 1956, which reprints sixty-nine of Mencken's political pieces from the Baltimore *Evening*

*Sun.* James T. Farrell edited *Prejudices: A Selection,* New York, 1958. Robert McHugh collected *The Bathtub Hoax and Other Blasts and Bravos from the Chicago Tribune,* New York, 1958.

BIOGRAPHY AND CRITICISM

Two biographies are Edgar Kemler, *The Irreverent Mr. Mencken,* Boston, 1950, and William Manchester, *Disturber of the Peace: The Life of H. L. Mencken,* New York, 1951. Charles Angoff's *H. L. Mencken: A Portrait from Memory,* New York, 1956, is a personal memoir.

Briefer studies are Maxwell Geismar, *The Last of the Provincials: The American Novel, 1915–1925,* Boston, 1947, pp. 3–66; Raymond L. Francis, "Mark Twain and H. L. Mencken," *PrS,* XXIV (1950), 31–39; Van Wyck Brooks, "Mencken in Baltimore," *ASch,* XX (1951), 409–421; Oscar Cargill, "Mencken and the South," *GaR,* VI (1952), 369–376; Edward Stone, "Baltimore's Friendly Dragon," *GaR,* VIII (1954), 347–353; Alistair Cooke, "The Last Happy Days of H. L. Mencken," *Atl,* CXCVII (1956), 33–38; and Joseph Wood Krutch, "This Was Mencken: An Appreciation," *Nation,* CLXXXII (Feb. 11, 1956), 109–110.

## EDNA ST. VINCENT MILLAY
### d. 1950

**656.** SEPARATE WORKS

*Mine the Harvest,* 1954.

**657.** COLLECTED WORKS AND CORRESPONDENCE

Norma Millay edited *Collected Poems,* New York, 1956. *Letters of Edna St. Vincent Millay,* New York, 1952, was edited by Allan Ross Macdougall.

REPRINTS

*A Few Figs from Thistles* (1920) was reprinted in New York, 1950, with several poems not included in other editions.

BIOGRAPHY AND CRITICISM

The first biographical study is Vincent Sheean, *The Indigo Bunting: A Memoir of Edna St. Vincent Millay,* New York, 1951. Edmund Wilson supplements this work with "a kind of counter-memoir": "Epilogue, 1952: Edna St. Vincent Millay," *The Shores of Light,* New York, 1952, pp. 744–793.

Briefer estimates are John Ciardi, "Edna St. Vincent Millay: A Figure of Passionate Living," *SRL,* XXXIII (Nov. 11, 1950), 8–9, 77; and Mary M.

Colum, "Edna Millay and Her Time," *New Rep*, CXXIV (Mar. 12, 1951), 17–18.

A listing of explications of individual poems is in George Arms and Joseph M. Kuntz, *Poetry Explication*, New York, 1950, pp. 109–110.

**658.** BIBLIOGRAPHY

The most recent listing is Allen Tate, *Sixty American Poets, 1896–1944*, rev. ed., Washington, 1954, pp. 85–89.

## JOAQUIN (CINCINNATUS HEINE [HINER]) MILLER

**658.** COLLECTED WORKS AND CORRESPONDENCE

Additional letters were edited by John Raine Dunbar, "Some Letters of Joaquin Miller to Frederick Locker," *MLQ*, XI (1950), 438–444.

**659.** BIOGRAPHY AND CRITICISM

The latest biographical study is M. Marion Marberry, *Splendid Poseur: Joaquin Miller—American Poet*, New York, 1953.

Special studies are John Raine Dunbar, "Joaquin Miller: Sedition and Civil War," *PHR*, XIX (1950), 31–36; William W. Winn, "Joaquin Miller's 'Real Name,'" *Calif. Hist. Soc. Quar.*, XXXIII (1954), 143–146; and Margaret Duckett, "Carlyle, 'Columbus,' and Joaquin Miller," *PQ*, XXXV (1956), 443–447.

## WILLIAM VAUGHN MOODY

**660.** COLLECTED WORKS AND CORRESPONDENCE

Of general interest is Edwin S. Fussell, "Robinson to Moody: Ten Unpublished Letters," *AL*, XXIII (1951), 173–187.

**661.** BIOGRAPHY AND CRITICISM

See Thomas Riggs, Jr., "Prometheus 1900," *AL*, XXII (1951), 399–423.

## MARIANNE (CRAIG) MOORE

**662.** SEPARATE WORKS

*Collected Poems*, 1951; *Predilections*, 1955; *Like a Bulwark*, 1956.

Two translations are *Rock Crystal: A Christmas Tale*, 1945 (with Elizabeth Mayer, from the German of Adalbert Stifter), and *The Fables of La Fontaine*, 1954.

BIOGRAPHY AND CRITICISM

Brief estimates are Wallace Fowlie, "Marianne Moore," *SR*, LX (1952), 537–547; Randall Jarrell, "Thoughts about Marianne Moore," *PR*, XIX (1952), 687–700; Louise Bogan, "Reading Contemporary Poetry," *CE*, XIV (1953), 255–260; Frederick J. Hoffman, "Marianne Moore: Imaginary Gardens and Real Toads," *Poetry*, LXXXIII (1953), 152–157; W. D. Snodgrass, "Elegance in Marianne Moore," *WR*, XIX (1954), 57–64; Thomas B. Brumbaugh, "Concerning Marianne Moore's Museum," *TCL*, I (1956), 191–195; Bette Richart, "Marianne Moore: In the Grand Tradition," *Commonweal*, LXV (Dec. 28, 1956), 338–339; Elder Olson, "The Poetry of Marianne Moore," *ChiR*, XI (Spring, 1957), 100–104; Ralph Rees, "The Armor of Marianne Moore," *BuR*, VII (May, 1957), 27–40; Winthrop Sergeant, "Humility, Concentration, and Gusto," *NY*, XXXII (Feb. 16, 1957), 38 ff.; and Clarence Brown, ed., "Department of Amplification," *NY*, XXXIII (Apr. 13, 1957), 140–146. The *Quarterly Review of Literature*, IV (n.d.), is a Marianne Moore issue.

A listing of explications of individual poems is in George Arms and Joseph M. Kuntz, *Poetry Explication*, New York, 1950, pp. 112–114.

A bibliographical listing is in Allen Tate, *Sixty American Poets, 1896–1944*, rev. ed., Washington, 1954, pp. 89–91. For a full bibliographical essay see "The Achievement of Marianne Moore: A Bibliography," comp. Eugene P. Sheehy and Kenneth A. Lohf, *BNYPL*, LXII (Mar.–May, 1958), 131–149 ff.

# PAUL ELMER MORE

**663.** COLLECTED WORKS AND REPRINTS

Arthur Hazard Dakin edited selections from More's anonymous works, *A Paul Elmer More Miscellany*, Portland, Me., 1950.

*The Sceptical Approach to Religion* (1934) was reprinted in Princeton, 1958; *Pages from an Oxford Diary* (1937) reappeared in Princeton, 1951.

BIOGRAPHY AND CRITICISM

Two studies are Robert Schafer, "Paul Elmer More: A Note on His Verse and Prose Written in Youth, with Two Unpublished Poems," *AL*, XX (1948), 43–51; and Joan N. Harding, "An American Thinker," *ConR*, No. 1057 (Jan., 1954), 34–39.

## JOHN MUIR

**666.** COLLECTED WORKS

*Studies in the Sierra,* San Francisco, 1950, with an introduction by William E. Colby, is a collection of seven articles by Muir which appeared in 1874-1875 in the *Overland Monthly.*

Edwin Way Teale compiled, with an introduction and interpretive comments, *The Wilderness World of John Muir,* Boston, 1954.

## (BENJAMIN) FRANK(LIN) NORRIS

**668.** COLLECTED WORKS AND REPRINTS

A collection of seventy-four letters has been edited by Franklin Walker in a limited edition, *The Letters of Frank Norris,* San Francisco, 1956.

*Six Essays on the Responsibilities of the Novelist,* Yonkers, N.Y., 1949, is a reprint from the 1903 volume.

BIOGRAPHY AND CRITICISM

Five critics have given Norris special attention in their studies of American fiction: Lars Åhnebrink, *The Beginnings of Naturalism in American Fiction,* Upsala, 1950, pp. 104-124, 277-308, 381-407, and *passim;* Maxwell Geismar, *Rebels and Ancestors: The American Novel, 1890-1915,* Boston, 1953, pp. 3-66; Kenneth S. Lynn, *The Dream of Success,* Boston, 1955, pp. 158-207; Charles Child Walcutt, *American Literary Naturalism, A Divided Stream,* Minneapolis, 1956, pp. 114-156; and Richard Chase, *The American Novel and Its Tradition,* New York, 1957, pp. 185-204.

Other critical studies are Irving McKee, "Notable Memorials to Mussel Slough," *PHR,* XVII (Jan., 1948), 19-27; Charles Kaplan, "Norris's Use of Sources in *The Pit,*" *AL,* XXV (1953), 75-84; J. J. Kwiat, "The Newspaper Experience: Crane, Norris, and Dreiser," *NCF,* VIII (1953), 99-117; Charles Kaplan, "Fact into Fiction in *McTeague,*" *HLB,* VIII (1954), 381-385; J. J. Kwiat, "Frank Norris: The Novelist as Social Critic and Literary Theorist," *NS,* Heft 9 (1954), 385-392; Charles G. Hoffman, "Norris and the Responsibility of the Novelist," *SAQ,* LIV (1955), 508-515; Donald Pizer, "Another Look at *The Octopus,*" *NCF,* X (1955), 217-224; and Henry Dan Piper, "Frank Norris and Scott Fitzgerald," *HLQ,* XIX (1956), 393-400.

## CLIFFORD ODETS

**670.** PLAYS *

*The Big Knife,* 1949; *The Country Girl* (1950), 1951; *The Flowering Peach* (1954).

*The Country Girl* was published in London, 1955, as *Winter Journey.*

BIOGRAPHY AND CRITICISM

See John Gassner, "The Long Journey of a Talent," *TArts,* XXXIII (July, 1949), 25-30.

## EUGENE (GLADSTONE) O'NEILL
### *d. 1953*

**670.** SEPARATE WORKS *

*A Moon for the Misbegotten* (1947), 1952; *Long Day's Journey into Night,* 1956; *A Touch of the Poet,* 1957.

Lawrence Gellert collected one three-act and four one-act plays, dated 1913-1915, in *Lost Plays,* New York, 1950, reprinted as *Lost Plays of Eugene O'Neill,* New York, 1958.

**671.** BIOGRAPHY AND CRITICISM

Agnes Boulton, *Part of a Long Story,* New York, 1958, is the memoirs of O'Neill's first wife.

A full-length critical analysis is Edwin A. Engel, *The Haunted Heroes of Eugene O'Neill,* Cambridge, Mass., 1953. A more recent study is Doris V. Falk, *Eugene O'Neill and the Tragic Tension,* New Brunswick, N.J., 1958.

Briefer studies are Horst Frenz, "Eugene O'Neill on the London Stage," *QQ,* LIV (1947), 223-230; Woodrow Geier, "O'Neill's Miracle Play," *Religion in Life,* XVI (1947), 515-526; Joseph Wood Krutch, "O'Neill's Tragic Sense," *ASch,* XVI (1947), 283-290; Rudolf Stamm, "The Dramatic Experiments of Eugene O'Neill," *ES,* XXVIII (1947), 1-15; Sverre Arestad, "*The Iceman Cometh* and *The Wild Duck,*" *SS,* XX (1948), 1-11; Hamilton Basso, "The Tragic Sense," *NY,* XXIII (Feb. 28, Mar. 6, Mar. 13, 1948), 34-38 ff., 34-38 ff., 37-40; Bonamy Dobrée, "Mr. O'Neill's Latest Play," *SR,* LVI (1948), 118-126; John Lovell, Jr., "Eugene O'Neill's Darker Brother," *TArts,* XXXII (Feb., 1948), 45-48; Rudolf Stamm, "A New Play by Eugene O'Neill," *ES,* XXIX (1948), 138-145; William Peery, "Does the

* Dates in parentheses are of production when it differs from publication or when publication has not occurred.

Buskin Fit O'Neill?" *UKCR*, XV (1949), 281–287; Rudolf Stamm, "The Orestes Theme in Three Plays by Eugene O'Neill, T. S. Eliot, and Jean-Paul Sartre," *ES*, XXX (1949), 244–255; Vivian C. Hopkins, "'The Iceman' Seen Through 'The Lower Depths,'" *CE*, XI (1949), 81–87; Alan S. Downer, "Eugene O'Neill as Poet of the Theatre," *TArts*, XXXV (Feb., 1951), 22–23; Eric Bentley, "Trying to Like O'Neill," *KR*, XIV (1952), 476–492; Joseph Wood Krutch, "Eugene O'Neill, The Lonely Revolutionary," *TArts*, XXXVI (Apr., 1952), 29–30, 78; Gustav Kirchner, "Das Lustspiel O'Neills: Ah Wilderness!" *NS*, Heft 1 (1952), 1–10; Doris M. Alexander, "*Strange Interlude* and Schopenhauer," *AL*, XXV (1953), 213–228; Bernard Baum, "*The Tempest* and *The Hairy Ape:* The Literary Incarnation of Mythos," *MLQ*, XIV (1953), 258–273; Horst Frenz, "Eugene O'Neill on the German Stage," *Theatre Annual 1953*, XI, 24–34; Hans Galinsky, "Eugene O'Neill, die Wendung des modernen amerikanischen Theaters zur Tragödie," *NS*, Heft 6 (1953), 233–246; Doris M. Alexander, "Hugo of *The Iceman Cometh:* Realism and O'Neill," *AQ*, V (1953), 357–366; *idem*, "Psychological Fate in *Mourning Becomes Electra*," *PMLA*, LXVIII (1953), 923–934.

More recent studies are Joseph Wood Krutch, "O'Neill the Inevitable," *TArts*, XXXVIII (Feb., 1954), 66–69; Roy Walker, "The Right Kind of Pity," *TC*, CLV (1954), 79–86; Lester Cole and John Howard Lawson, "Two Views on O'Neill," *MM*, VII (June, 1954), 56–63; N. Bryllion Fagin, "Eugene O'Neill," *AR*, XIV (1954), 14–26; Doris M. Alexander, "Eugene O'Neill as Social Critic," *AQ*, VI (1954), 349–363; Ivan H. Walton, "Eugene O'Neill and Folkways of the Sea," *WF*, XIV (1955), 153–169; Reg Skene, "*The Bacchae* of Euripides and *The Great God Brown*," *Manitoba Arts Rev.*, X (1956), 55–65; Horst Frenz, "Eugene O'Neill in Deutschland," *Euphorion*, L (1956), 307–327; Joseph Wood Krutch, "Domestic Drama with Some Difference," *TArts*, XL (Apr., 1956), 25, 89–91; Frederic Fleisher, "Strindberg and O'Neill," *Symposium*, X (1956), 84–94; Doris M. Alexander, "*Lazarus Laughed* and Buddha," *MLQ*, XVII (1956), 357–365; Annette Rubinstein, "The Dark Journey of Eugene O'Neill," *Mainstream*, X (Apr., 1957), 29–33; and Edwin A. Engel, "Eugene O'Neill's Long Day's Journey into Light," *MAQR*, LXIII (1957), 348–354.

## THOMAS NELSON PAGE

**674. BIOGRAPHY AND CRITICISM**

Unpublished letters are in William M. E. Rachal, ed., "Some Letters of Thomas Nelson Page," *VMHB*, LXI (1953), 179–185; and John R. Roberson, ed., "Two Virginia Novelists on Woman's Suffrage: An Exchange of Letters between Mary Johnston and Thomas Nelson Page," *ibid.,* LXIV (1956), 286–290.

See also Marshall W. Fishwick, "Virginia Honors Thomas Nelson Page in Centennial," *Commonwealth,* XX (Apr., 1953), 39, 52; and John R. Roberson, "The Manuscript of Page's 'Marse Chan,'" *SB,* IX (1957), 259–262.

# THOMAS PAINE

### 675. REPRINTS

*The Rights of Man* (1791–1792) was reprinted with an introduction by George Jacob Holyoake, New York, 1951.

### 676. BIOGRAPHY AND CRITICISM

Two special studies are Joseph Lewis, *Thomas Paine, Author of the Declaration of Independence,* New York, 1947, and Brother Dominic Elder, *The Common Man Philosophy of Thomas Paine: A Study of the Political Ideas of Paine,* Notre Dame, Ind., 1951.

Briefer studies are James Woodress, "The 'Cold War' of 1790–1791: Documented by a Collection of Eighteenth-Century Pamphlets in the Duke University Library," *DULN,* No. 20 (July, 1948), 7–18; Alfred Owen Aldridge, "Why Did Thomas Paine Write on the Bank?" *PAPS,* XCIII (1949), 309–315; W. H. G. Armytage, "Thomas Paine and the Walkers: An Early Episode in Anglo-American Co-operation," *PH,* XVIII (1951), 16–30; Cecilia M. Kenyon, "Where Paine Went Wrong," *Am Pol Sci Rev,* XLV (1951), 1086–1099; Alfred Owen Aldridge, "Thomas Paine and the New York *Public Advertiser,*" *NYHSQB,* XXXVII (1953), 361–382; Adrian Brunel, "Thomas Paine," *ConR,* CLXXXVIII (1955), 52–56; Alfred Owen Aldridge, "The Poetry of Thomas Paine," *PMHB,* LXXIX (1955), 81–99; Harrison T. Meserole, "W. T. Sherwin: A Little-Known Paine Biographer," *PBSA,* XLIX (1955), 268–272; T. M. Brown, "Greenough, Paine, Emerson and the Organic Aesthetic," *JAAC,* XIV (1956), 304–317; Richard M. Gimbel, "New Political Writings by Thomas Paine," *YULG,* XXX (1956), 94–107; and Alfred Owen Aldridge, "Thomas Paine's Plan for a Descent on England," *WMQ,* XIV (1957), 74–84.

### 678. BIBLIOGRAPHY

Richard Gimbel compiled *Thomas Paine: A Bibliographical Check List of Common Sense, with an Account of Its Publication,* New Haven, 1956.

# THEODORE PARKER

**679.** BIOGRAPHY AND CRITICISM

Two special studies are Jean Schorer, *Deux grands américains: W. Channing [et] T. Parker*, Geneva, 1947, and John Edward Dirks, *The Critical Theology of Theodore Parker*, New York, 1948.

See also G. F. Newbrough, "Reason and Understanding in the Works of Theodore Parker," *SAQ*, XLVII (1948), 64–75; Theodore Mead, "Theodore Parker in Ohio," *NOQ*, XXI (1949–1949), 18–23; and H. Shelton Smith, "Was Theodore Parker a Transcendentalist?" *NEQ*, XXIII (1950), 351–364.

# FRANCIS PARKMAN

**680.** COLLECTED WORKS AND CORRESPONDENCE

Additional letters are in Howard Doughty, ed., "Parkman's Dark Years: Letters to Mary Dwight Parkman," *HLB*, IV (1950), 53–85.

**681.** EDITED TEXTS AND REPRINTS

*The Battle for North America*, ed. John Tebbel, Garden City, N.Y., 1948, is an abridgment of Parkman's *France and England in North America* (thirteen volumes of the Frontenac Edition). Samuel Eliot Morison edited *The Parkman Reader*, Boston, 1955.

BIOGRAPHY AND CRITICISM

A recent critical estimate is Otis A. Pease, *Parkman's History: The Historian as Literary Artist*, New Haven, 1953.

Briefer studies are Bernard DeVoto, "The Easy Chair," *Harper's*, CXCVIII (Apr., 1949), 52–55; William Jordy, "Henry Adams and Francis Parkman," *AQ*, III (1951), 52–68; Dean Moor, "The Paxton Boys: Parkman's Use of the Frontier Hypothesis," *M-A*, XXXVI (1956), 211–219; James D. Hart, "Patrician Among Savages: Francis Parkman's *The Oregon Trail*," *GaR*, X (1956), 69–73.

**682.** BIBLIOGRAPHY

See James E. Walsh, "*The California and Oregon Trail:* A Bibliographical Study," *New Col*, III (1950), 279–285.

# JAMES KIRKE PAULDING

**684.** SEPARATE WORKS

James N. Tidwell edited a newly discovered Paulding play, *The Lion of the West; Retitled, The Kentuckian; or, A Trip to New York, a Farce in Two Acts,* revised by John Augustus Stone and William Bayle Bernard, Stanford, 1954. See also Francis Hodge, "Biography of a Lost Play: *Lion of the West,*" *TA,* XII (1954), 48–61.

**685.** COLLECTED WORKS AND CORRESPONDENCE

Jay B. Hubbell edited "James Kirke Paulding's Last Letter to John C. Calhoun," *NCHR,* XXXII (1955), 410–414.

BIOGRAPHY AND CRITICISM

Brief studies are Arlin Turner, "James K. Paulding and Timothy Flint," *MVHR,* XXXIV (1947), 105–111; M. L. Williams, "Paulding Satirizes Owenism," *IMH,* XLIV (1948), 355–365; *idem,* "Paulding's Contributions to the *Columbia Magazine,*" *AL,* XXI (1949), 222–227; *idem,* "A Tour of Illinois in 1842," *JISHS,* XLII (1949), 292–312; Floyd C. Watkins, "The Political Career of James Kirke Paulding," *EUQ,* VI (1950), 225–235; *idem,* "James Kirke Paulding's Creole Tale," *LHQ,* XXXIII (1950), 364–379; *idem,* "James Kirke Paulding and the South," *AQ,* V (1953), 219–230; Ralph M. Aderman, "James Kirke Paulding on Literature and the West," *AL,* XXVII (1955), 97–101; and *idem,* "The Case of James Cook: A Study of Political Influence in 1840," *EIHC,* XCII (1956), 59–67.

BIBLIOGRAPHY

J. Albert Robbins compiled "Some Unrecorded Poems of James Kirke Paulding: An Annotated Check-List," *SB,* III (1950), 229–240.

# JOHN HOWARD PAYNE

**686.** BIOGRAPHY AND CRITICISM

The most recent studies are Lewis Leary and Arlin Turner, "John Howard Payne in New Orleans," *LHQ,* XXXI (1948), 110–122; Lewis Leary, "John Howard Payne's Southern Adventure: 1835," *DULN,* No. 19 (1948), 2–11; S. H. Blakely, "John Howard Payne's *Thespian Mirror,* New York's First Theatrical Magazine," *SP,* XLVI (1949), 577–602; and Veddei Morris Gilbert, "The Stage Career of John Howard Payne," *NOQ,* XXIII (1950–1951), 59–74.

# WILLIAM PENN

**687.** COLLECTED WORKS AND EDITED TEXTS

Of special interest is Herman Blum, *William Penn, 1644–1718: New Light Thrown on the Quaker Founder of Pennsylvania, Through Heretofore Unpublished Documents in the Blumhaven Library,* Philadelphia, 1950, the catalogue of an exhibition of holograph letters and autograph documents.

Frederick B. Tolles and Gordon Alderfer compiled a volume of selected excerpts, *The Witness of William Penn,* New York, 1957.

**688.** BIOGRAPHY AND CRITICISM

Two special studies are William W. Comfort, *William Penn and Our Liberties,* Philadelphia, 1947, and Rachel McMasters Hunt, *William Penn, Horticulturist,* Pittsburgh, 1953.

See also H. J. Cadbury, "Penn, Collison, and the Royal Society," *BFHA,* XXXVI (1947), 19–24; Beach Langston, "William Penn and Chaucer," *N&Q,* I (1954), 49–50; and Mary Maples, "William Penn, Classical Republican," *PMHB,* LXXXI (1957), 138–156.

# EDGAR ALLAN POE

**689.** COLLECTED WORKS

John W. Ostrom has edited, in two volumes, *The Letters of Edgar Allen Poe,* Cambridge, Mass., 1948. He published a "Supplement to *The Letters of Poe,*" *AL,* XXIV (1952), 358–366, and "Second Supplement to *The Letters of Poe,*" *AL,* XXIX (1957), 79–86. See also E. R. Hagemann, ed., "Two 'Lost' Letters by Poe, with Notes and Commentary," *AL,* XVIII (1957), 507–510.

**691.** BIOGRAPHY AND CRITICISM

Sarah Helen Whitman's *Edgar Poe and His Critics* (1860) has been reissued, New Brunswick, N.J., 1949, with an introduction and notes by Oral Sumner Coad. Princess Marie Bonaparte's *Edgar Poe: étude psychoanalytique,* Paris, 1933, has been translated into English by John Rodker and published in 1949 as *The Life and Works of Edgar Poe.* Richard Beale Davis edited *Chivers' Life of Poe,* San Marino, Calif., 1952, from manuscripts in the Huntington Library, first published in part by George E. Woodberry. Baudelaire's three essays on Poe (1852, 1856, 1857) are now translated and edited by Lois and Francis E. Hyslop, Jr., *Baudelaire on Poe,* State College, Pa., 1952.

The most recent biographical study is N. Bryllion Fagin, *The Histrionic*

*Mr. Poe*, Baltimore, 1949. See also Jay B. Hubbell, *The South in American Literature, 1607–1900*, Durham, 1954, pp. 528–550 and *passim*, and Perry Miller, *The Raven and the Whale*, New York, 1956, *passim*.

The most comprehensive critique is Edward H. Davidson, *Poe: A Critical Study*, Cambridge, Mass., 1957. For a discussion of Poe's reputation outside of America, see Haldeen Braddy's *Glorious Incense: The Fulfillment of Edgar Allan Poe*, Washington, 1953. Poe's influence in England is studied in H. H. Kühnelt's *Die Bedeutung von Edgar Allan Poe für die Englische Literatur*, Innsbruck, 1949. Poe and France are treated in Léon Lemmonier, *Edgar Poe et les conteurs français*, Paris, 1947, and Patrick Francis Quinn, *The French Face of Edgar Poe*, Carbondale, Ill., 1957.

Allen Tate published two essays on Poe in *The Forlorn Demon*, New York, 1953; T. S. Eliot writes somewhat harshly of Poe in *From Poe to Valéry*, New York, 1948. Of specialized interest is Joseph Chiari, *Symbolisme from Poe to Mallarmé: The Growth of a Myth*, London, 1956.

Briefer critical studies are S. E. Lind, "Poe and Mesmerism," *PMLA*, LXII (1947), 1077–1094; S. C. Worthen, "Poe and the Beautiful Cigar Girl," *AL*, XX (1948), 305–312; J. O. Bailey, "The Geography of Poe's 'Dream-Land' and 'Ulalume,'" *SP*, XLV (1948), 512–523; Marvin Laser, "The Growth and Structure of Poe's Concept of Beauty," *ELH*, XV (1948), 69–84; H. B. Parkes, "Poe, Hawthorne, Melville: An Essay in Sociological Criticism," *PR*, XVI (1949), 157–165; Darrel Abel, "Edgar Poe: A Centennial Estimate," *UKCR*, XVI (1949), 77–96; *idem*, "A Key to the House of Usher," *UTQ*, XVIII (1949), 176–185; Gerald G. Grubb, "The Personal and Literary Relationships of Dickens and Poe," *NCF*, V (1950), 1–22, 101–120, 209–221; Marie Bonaparte, "The Black Cat," *PR*, XVII (1950), 834–860; Philip Young, "The Earlier Psychologists and Poe," *AL*, XXII (1951), 442–454; Montgomery Belgion, "The Mystery of Poe's Poetry," *EIC*, I (1951), 51–66; Ada B. Nisbet, "New Light on the Dickens-Poe Relationship," *NCF*, V (1951), 295–302; Patrick F. Quinn, "Poe's Imaginary Voyage," *HR*, IV (1952), 562–585; N. Bryllion Fagin, "Edgar Allan Poe," *SAQ*, LI (1952), 276–285.

More recent studies are Albert J. Lubell, "Poe and A. W. Schlegel," *JEGP*, LII (1953), 1–12; Leo Spitzer, "A Reinterpretation of 'The Fall of the House of Usher,'" *CL*, IV (1952), 351–363; Boyd Carter, "Poe's Debt to Charles Brockden Brown," *PrS*, XXVII (1953), 190–196; Anthony Caputi, "The Refrain in Poe's Poetry," *AL*, XXV (1953), 169–178; Francis B. Dedmond, "The War of the Literati: Documents of the Legal Phase," *N&Q*, CXCVIII (1953), 303–308; J. Woodrow Hassell, Jr., "The Problem of Realism in 'The Gold Bug,'" *AL*, XXV (1953), 179–192; Robert A. Colby, "Poe's Philosophy of Composition," *UKCR*, XX (1954), 211–214; Francis B. Dedmond, "'The Cask of Amontillado' and the War of the Literati," *MLQ*, XV (1954), 137–146; Clark Griffith, "Poe's 'Ligeia' and the

English Romantics," *UTQ,* XXIV (1954), 8–25; Thomas P. Haviland, "How Well Did Poe Know Milton?" *PMLA,* LXIX (1954), 841–860; James Miller, Jr., " 'Ulalume' Resurrected," *PQ,* XXXIV (1955), 197–205; Howard Mumford Jones, "Poe, 'The Raven,' and the Anonymous Young Man," *WHR,* IX (1955), 127–138; George Kelly, "Poe's Theory of Beauty," *AL,* XXVII (1956), 521–536; Sidney P. Moss, "Poe and His Nemesis—Lewis Gaylord Clark," *AL,* XXVIII (1956), 30–49; Maurice Beebe, "The Fall of the House of Pyncheon," *NCF,* XI (1956), 1–17; and William Whipple, "Poe's Political Satire," *UTSE,* XXXV (1956), 81–95.

**696.** BIBLIOGRAPHY

A bibliographical essay by Jay B. Hubbell is in *Eight American Authors: A Review of Research and Criticism,* ed. Floyd Stovall, New York, 1956. See also John D. Gordan, "Edgar Allan Poe: An Exhibition on the Centenary of His Death, October 7, 1849. A Catalogue of the First Editions, Manuscripts, Autograph Letters from the Berg Collection," *BNYPL,* LIII (1949), 471–491.

# WILLIAM SYDNEY (SIDNEY) PORTER
## ("O. HENRY")

**697.** COLLECTED WORKS AND REPRINTS

*The Complete Works of O. Henry,* 2 vols., with a foreword by Harry Hansen, was reprinted in Garden City, N.Y., 1953.

BIOGRAPHY AND CRITICISM

Three biographies have appeared in recent years: Eugene Hudson Long, *O. Henry, the Man and His Work,* Philadelphia, 1949; Dale Kramer, *The Heart of O. Henry,* New York, 1954; and Gerald Langford, *Alias O. Henry: A Biography of William Sidney Porter,* New York, 1957.

Brief studies are Edward C. Echols, "O. Henry's 'Shaker of the Attic Salt,'" *CJ,* XLIII (1948), 488–489; *idem,* "O. Henry and the Classics—II," *ibid.,* XLIV (1948), 209–211; Walter Carroll, "An Afternoon with O. Henry's Widow," *PrS,* XXVI (1952), 138–143; Dan McAllister, " 'Negligently, Perhaps; Criminally, Never,'" *SAQ,* LI (1952), 562–573; Deming Brown, "O. Henry in Russia," *RusR,* XII (1953), 253–258; and J. S. Gallegly, "Background and Pattern of O. Henry's Texas Badman Stories," *RIP,* XLII (1955), 1–31.

# EZRA (LOOMIS) POUND

**699.** SEPARATE WORKS

Poetry: *The Pisan Cantos* [74–84], 1948; *The Cantos of Ezra Pound* [1–84], 1948; *Section: Rock-Drill, 85–95 de los Cantares,* 1956. Cantos 96 and 97 have appeared in *The Hudson Review,* IX (1956), 1–19, 387–398; Canto 98 in *L'Illustrazione Italiana,* Anno 85, N. 9 (Sept. 1958), 35–39; Canto 99 in *The Virginia Quarterly Review,* XXXIV (1958), 339–354. *Personae: The Collected Poems,* New York, 1950, is a re-issue of the 1926 Liveright edition with the addition of two appendices.

Prose: *Money Pamphlets by Pound,* London, 1950–1952, is a series of six pamphlets, all previously published as follows: *Social Credit: An Impact,* London, 1935; *What Is Money For?,* London, 1939; *Carta de Visita,* Rome, 1942; *L'America, Roosevelt e le Cause della Guerra Presente,* Venice, 1944; *Introduzione alla Natura Economica degli S. U. A.,* Venice, 1944; *Oro e Lavoro,* Rapallo, 1944. Other prose volumes are *"If This Be Treason . . . ,"* Siena, 1948; *Patria Mia,* Chicago, 1950 (written prior to 1913; now published for the first time); *Secondo Biglietto da Visita,* Rome, 1953; and *The Literary Essays of Ezra Pound,* Norfolk, Conn., 1954 (a selection edited with an introduction by T. S. Eliot). *Pavannes and Divagations* appeared in New York, 1958.

Translations: *Confucius: The Unwobbling Pivot and the Great Digest,* 1947; *The Translations of Ezra Pound,* 1953; *The Classic Anthology Defined by Confucius,* 1954; and *Sophocles: Women of Trachis,* 1957.

BIOGRAPHY AND CRITICISM

Three book-length studies are Hugh Kenner, *The Poetry of Ezra Pound,* Norfolk, Conn., 1951; H. H. Watts, *Ezra Pound and the Cantos,* Chicago, 1952; and John J. Espey, *Ezra Pound's Mauberley: A Study in Composition,* Berkeley, 1955. Single essays published separately are Archibald Mac-Leish, *Poetry and Opinion: The Cantos of Ezra Pound, a Dialogue on the Role of Poetry,* Urbana, Ill., 1950, and Richard Aldington, *Ezra Pound and T. S. Eliot: A Lecture,* Hurst, Berkshire, England, 1954. Volumes of collected essays are Peter Russell, ed., *An Examination of Ezra Pound: A Collection of Essays,* Norfolk, Conn., 1950, and Lewis Leary, ed., *Motive and Method in the Cantos of Ezra Pound: English Institute Essays,* New York, 1954. Of biographical interest is Charles Norman, *The Case of Ezra Pound,* New York, 1948. John Hamilton Edwards and William Vasse, Jr., compiled an *Annotated Index to the Cantos of Ezra Pound,* Berkeley, 1957.

*Quarterly Review of Literature,* V (1949), is a special Pound issue. *Analyst* (Northwestern Univ.) has published guides to the Cantos by various critics. See Nos. I–VIII (1953–1955), No. XI (1956), No. XIII (1957)

*The Pound Newsletter* (Univ. of Calif., Berkeley), Nos. 1–9 (Jan., 1954–Jan., 1956), was a clearing-house for criticism, notes, collations, check lists, and bibliography on Pound. A special issue of *Nuova Corrente:* 5–6 (Genoa, June, 1956), contains sixteen critical articles, notes, and poems on Pound by American, Italian, and British critics.

Shorter critical studies are Lawrence Richardson, "Ezra Pound's Homage to Propertius," *Yale Poetry Rev.*, VI (1947), 21–29; Charles I. Glicksberg, "Ezra Pound and the Fascist Complex," *SAQ*, XLVI (1947), 349–358; H. W. Häusermann, "W. B. Yeats's Criticism of Ezra Pound," *Eng. Stud.*, XXIX (Aug., 1948), 97–109; Allen Tate, *On the Limits of Poetry*, New York, 1948, pp. 350–357; Jacques Valette, "Ezra Pound," *Mercure de France*, CCCV (Jan., 1949), 160–163; D. P. Williams, "The Background of *The Pisan Cantos*," *Poetry*, LXXIII (1949), 216–221; John Berryman, "The Poetry of Ezra Pound," *PR*, XVI (1949), 377–394; Margaret Schlauch, "The Anti-Humanism of Ezra Pound," *SciS*, XIII (1949), 258–269.

Of special interest on Pound and the Bollingen Prize controversy are Samuel Sillen, "A Prize for Ezra Pound," *MM*, II (Apr., 1949), 3–6; William Barrett, "A Prize for Ezra Pound," *PR*, XVI (1949), 344–347; Robert Hillyer, "Treason's Strange Fruit: The Case of Ezra Pound and the Bollingen Award," *SRL*, XXXII (June 11, 1949), 9–11, 28; *idem*, "Poetry's New Priesthood," *SRL*, XXXII (June 18, 1949), 7–9, 38; Hayden Carruth, "The Bollingen Award: What Is It?" *Poetry*, LXXIV (1949), 154–156; *idem*, "The Anti-Poet All Told," *Poetry*, LXXIV (1949), 274–285; anon., "Bollingen Prize in Poetry," *Annual Report, Librarian of Congress*, June 30, 1949, pp. 88–94; *The Case Against the Saturday Review of Literature* (a pamphlet published by *Poetry*, Oct., 1949); Malcolm Cowley, "The Battle over Ezra Pound," *New Rep*, CXXI (Oct. 3, 1949), 17–20.

Later studies are Warren Ramsey, "Pound, Laforgue, and Dramatic Structure," *CL*, III (1951), 47–56; Frederick Morgan, "A Note on Ezra Pound," *HudR*, IV (1951), 156–160; R. W. Flint, "Pound and the Lyric," *HudR*, IV (1951), 293–304; Sister M. Bernetta Quinn, "Ezra Pound and the Metamorphic Tradition," *WR*, XV (1951), 169–181; Peter Viereck, "Pure Poetry, Impure Politics, and Ezra Pound," *Commentary*, XI (1951), 340–346; Stanley K. Coffman, Jr., "Ezra Pound and Imagist Theory," *Imagism*, Norman, Okla., 1951, pp. 120–162; Ronald Bottrall, "Ezra Pound," *Adelphi*, XXVIII (1952), 618–623; Hugh Kenner, "Pound on Joyce," *Shenandoah*, III (Autumn, 1952), 3–8; Leonard Casper, "Apprenticed in Provence," *Poetry*, LXXXI (1952), 203–211; R. P. Blackmur, *Language as Gesture*, New York, 1952, pp. 124–162; Babette Deutsch, *Poetry in Our Time*, New York, 1952, pp. 119–151; Richard G. Stern, "Pound as Translator," *Accent*, XIII (1953), 265–268; A. Bronson Feldman, "The Critical Canons of Ezra Pound," *PL*, LVII (1953), 226–246; Herbert Read, *The True Voice of Feeling*, London, 1953, pp. 116–138; Allen Tate, *The Forlorn Demon*, Chicago,

1953, pp. 156–160; Dan Pinck, "A Visit with Ezra Pound," *Reporter*, X (Feb. 2, 1954), 40–43; Thomas Parkinson, "Yeats and Pound: The Illusion of Influence," *CL*, VI (1954), 256–264; William Carlos Williams, *Selected Essays*, New York, 1954, pp. 162–169; Frederick J. Hoffman, "Eza Pound's *Hugh Selwyn Mauberley*," *The Twenties*, New York, 1955, pp. 36–46; Herbert Bergman, "Ezra Pound and Walt Whitman," *AL*, XXVII (1955), 56–61; Victor L. Ferkiss, "Ezra Pound and American Fascism," *JPol*, XVII (1955), 173–197; Edwin Honig, "That Mutation of Pound's," *KR*, XVII (1955), 349–356; Donald Davie, "Yeats and Pound," *DM*, XXX (Oct., 1955), 17–21; Sam Hynes, "The Case of Ezra Pound," *Commonweal*, LXIII (1955), 251–254; Gordon Ringer, "Notes on the Present State of Pound Studies," *Shenandoah*, VI (Summer, 1955), 64–66; Louise Bogan, *Selected Criticism*, New York, 1955, pp. 138–141, 178–183; Marianne Moore, *Predilections*, New York, 1955, pp. 62–83.

More recent studies are Thomas E. Connolly, "Ezra Pound's 'Near Perigord': The Background of a Poem," *CL*, VIII (1956), 110–121; William P. Tucker, "Ezra Pound, Fascism, and Populism," *RPol*, XVIII (1956), 105–107; A. Alvarez, "Ezra Pound: The Qualities and Limitations of Translation-Poetry," *EIC*, VI (1956), 171–189; Hayden Carruth, "The Poetry of Ezra Pound," *Perspectives USA*, No. 16 (1956), 129–159; Thomas E. Connolly, "Further Notes on *Mauberley*," *Accent*, XVI (1956), 59–67; Robert Fitzgerald, "Gloom and Gold in Ezra Pound," *Encounter*, VII (July, 1956), 16–22; *idem*, "A Note on Ezra Pound," *KR*, XVIII (1956), 505–518; Robert Pack, "The Georgians, Imagism, and Ezra Pound: A Study in Revolution," *ArQ*, XII (1956), 250–265; Donald Davie, "Adrian Stokes and Pound's *Cantos*," *TC*, CLX (1956), 419–436; Richard H. Rovere, "The Question of Ezra Pound," *Esquire*, XLVIII (Sept., 1957), 66 ff.; and Forrest Read, "The Pattern of the *Pisan Cantos*," *SR*, LXV (1957), 400–419.

For explications of individual poems see the listing in George Arms and Joseph M. Kuntz, *Poetry Explication*, New York, 1950, pp. 120–121.

700. BIBLIOGRAPHY

The most complete listing is John H. Edwards, *A Preliminary Checklist of the Writings of Ezra Pound*, New Haven, 1953. See also *The Pound Newsletter* (Univ. of Calif., Berkeley), Nos. 1–9 (Jan., 1954–Jan., 1956), especially Nos. 5–7; Allen Tate, *Sixty American Poets, 1896–1944*, rev. ed., Washington, 1954, pp. 93–101; and Myles Slatin, "More by Ezra Pound," *YULG*, XXX (1955), 74–80.

Important Pound collections are in the Brown University Library, the Chapin Library at Williams College, and the Grosvenor Library in Buffalo, New York.

# WILLIAM HICKLING PRESCOTT

**701. BIOGRAPHY AND CRITICISM**

See D. A. Ringe, "The Artistry of Prescott's 'The Conquest of Mexico,'" *NEQ*, XXVI (1953), 454–476.

# ELMER (L.) RICE

**702. SEPARATE WORKS ***

*The Show Must Go On: A Novel*, 1949; *The Grand Tour: A Play in Two Acts* (1951), 1952; *The Winner: A Play in Four Scenes*, 1954.

The first collection of Rice's plays is *Seven Plays*, New York, 1950. *Not for Children*, first published in 1935, was rewritten and revised, New York, 1951.

**703. BIOGRAPHY AND CRITICISM**

See Ralph L. Collins, "The Playwright and the Press: Elmer Rice and His Critics," *TA*, VII (1948–1949), 35–58.

# JAMES WHITCOMB RILEY

**704. BIOGRAPHY AND CRITICISM**

Jeannette Covert Nolan, Horace Gregory, and James T. Farrell contributed to *Poet of the People: An Evaluation of James Whitcomb Riley*, Bloomington, Ind., 1951. A more recent study is Richard Crowder, *Those Innocent Years: The Legacy and Inheritance of a Hero of the Victorian Era, James Whitcomb Riley*, Indianapolis, 1957.

See also Katherine Reeves, "The Publick Reader," *VQR*, XXVII (1951), 403–409.

# EDWIN ARLINGTON ROBINSON

**705. COLLECTED WORKS**

*Tilbury Town, Selected Poems of Edwin Arlington Robinson*, New York, 1953, was edited with an introduction and notes by Lawrance Thompson.

* Dates in parentheses are of production when it differs from publication.

LETTERS

Denham Sutcliffe edited *Untriangulated Stars: Letters of Edwin Arlington Robinson to Harry deForest Smith, 1890–1905,* Cambridge, Mass., 1947. See also Edwin S. Fussell, ed., "Robinson to Moody: Ten Unpublished Letters," *AL,* XXIII (1951), 173–187; and R. L. Lowe, "Two Letters of Edwin Arlington Robinson: A Note on His Early Critical Reception," *NEQ,* XXVII (1954), 257–261.

### 706. BIOGRAPHY AND CRITICISM

Three critical studies are Emery Neff, *Edwin Arlington Robinson,* New York, 1948; Ellsworth Barnard, *Edwin Arlington Robinson: A Critical Study,* New York, 1952; and Edwin S. Fussell, *Edwin Arlington Robinson: The Literary Background of a Traditional Poet,* Berkeley, 1954.

Briefer studies are Richard Crowder, "E. A. Robinson's Camelot," *CE,* IX (1947), 72–79; W. T. Scott, "'Great and Austere Poet,'" *Poetry,* LXX (1947), 94–98; Malcolm Cowley, "Edwin Arlington Robinson: Defeat and Triumph," *New Rep,* CXIX (Dec. 6, 1948), 26–30; Lewis M. Isaacs, "E. A. Robinson Speaks of Music," *NEQ,* XXII (1949), 499–510; Richard Crowder, "E. A. Robinson's Symphony: 'The Man Who Died Twice,'" *CE,* XI (1949), 141–144; anon., "Two Friends of Robinson," *CLQ,* Series II (Feb., 1949), 147–152; Willis D. Jacobs, "E. A. Robinson's 'Mr. Flood's Party,'" *CE,* XII (1950), 77–82; Richard Crowder, "'Man Against the Sky,'" *CE,* XIV (1953), 269–276; Louis O. Coxe, "E. A. Robinson: The Lost Tradition," *SR,* LXII (1954), 247–266; Conrad Aiken, "On Edwin Arlington Robinson," *CLQ,* Series IV (Feb., 1956), 95–97; Robert W. Hill, "Moonlight on a Shadowy Figure: A. H. Louis, the Original of E. A. Robinson's 'Captain Craig,'" *BNYPL,* LX (1956), 373–377; and Winfield Townley Scott, "To See Robinson," *NMQ,* XXVI (1956), 161–178.

For a listing of explications of individual poems see George Arms and Joseph M. Kuntz, *Poetry Explication,* New York, 1950, pp. 124–126.

### 708. PRIMARY SOURCES

See *Edwin Arlington Robinson: A Descriptive List of the Lewis M. Isaacs Collection of Robinsoniana,* New York, 1948, with an introduction by Edith J. R. Isaacs; and Léonie Adams, "The Ledoux Collection of Edwin Arlington Robinson Manuscripts," *LCQJ,* VII (Nov., 1949), 9–13. James Humphry, III, compiled *The Library of Edwin Arlington Robinson: A Descriptive Catalogue,* Waterville, Me., 1950.

BIBLIOGRAPHY

A bibliographical listing is Allen Tate, *Sixty American Poets, 1896–1944,* rev. ed., Washington, 1954, pp. 107–113.

# EDGAR (EVERTSON) SALTUS

**710.** BIOGRAPHY AND CRITICISM

See Eric McKitrick, "Edgar Saltus of the Obsolete," *AQ*, III (1951), 22–35.

# CARL (CHARLES AUGUST) SANDBURG

**711.** SEPARATE WORKS

*The Photographs of Abraham Lincoln* (with Frederick Hill Meserve), 1944; *Remembrance Rock*, 1948; *Lincoln Collector: The Story of Oliver R. Barrett's Great Private Collection* (edited by Sandburg), 1949; *Complete Poems*, 1950; *Carl Sandburg's New American Songbag*, 1950; *Always the Young Strangers*, 1953.

COLLECTIONS AND REPRINTS

*Storm over the Land*, New York, 1942, is a "profile of the Civil War" taken mainly from the four volumes of *Abraham Lincoln: The War Years* (1939); some sections are rewritten and half of the photographs are here published for the first time.

*Poems of the Midwest*, New York, 1946, is a reprinting of *Chicago Poems* (1916) and *Cornhuskers* (1918).

*Abraham Lincoln: The Prairie Years and the War Years*, New York, 1954, is a one-volume distillation of the six-volume biography.

*The Sandburg Range*, New York, 1957, is a representative selection from his entire work: excerpts from his novel, his autobiography, the biography of Lincoln, the children's stories, the seven volumes of poems, in addition to ten new poems, two new children's stories, and "A Lincoln Preface."

BIOGRAPHY AND CRITICISM

Recent estimates are Horace Gregory and Marya Zaturenska, *A History of American Poetry, 1900–1940*, New York, 1946, pp. 242–251 and *passim;* Henry W. Wells, *The American Way of Poetry*, New York, 1943, pp. 135–147 and *passim;* Charles Allen, "Cadenced Free Verse," *CE*, IX (1948), 195–199; Dan G. Hoffman, "Sandburg and 'The People': His Literary Populism Reappraised," *AR*, X (1950), 265–278; Alan Jenkins, "Portrait of a Poet at College," *SAQ*, XLIX (1950), 478–482; William Carlos Williams, "Carl Sandburg's Complete Poems," *Poetry*, LXXVIII (1951), 345–351; and P. Stroud, "Sandburg the Young Stranger," *PrS*, XXVII (1953), 320–328.

The *Journal of the Illinois State Historical Society*, LXV (Winter, 1952), is a Carl Sandburg issue, a tribute on his 75th birthday.

For a listing of explications of individual poems see George Arms and Joseph M. Kuntz, *Poetry Explication*, New York, 1950, p. 127.

Thomas S. Shaw compiled *Carl Sandburg: A Bibliography*, Washington, 1948. More recent listings are Ralph G. Newman, "A Selective Checklist of Sandburg's Writings," *JISHS*, LXV (1952), 402–406, and Allen Tate, *Sixty American Poets, 1896–1944*, rev. ed., Washington, 1954, pp. 114–119.

# GEORGE SANTAYANA
## d. 1952

**712. SEPARATE WORKS**

*Dominations and Powers: Reflections on Liberty, Society and Government*, 1951.

The third and final volume of Santayana's autobiography, *Persons and Places*, is *My Host the World*, New York, 1953.

*The Poet's Testament*, New York, 1953, collects all of Santayana's poetry not hitherto published, in addition to two plays, *The Marriage of Venus* and *Philosophers at Court*.

**COLLECTED WORKS, REPRINTS, AND CORRESPONDENCE**

*The Life of Reason* (1905–1906) has been reprinted in a one-volume edition, revised by the author in collaboration with Daniel Cory, New York, 1954.

Irwin Edman's *The Philosophy of Santayana: Selections* (1936) was reprinted, New York, 1953, in a greatly enlarged edition with a new preface and introductory essay. Irving Singer edited *Essays in Literary Criticism*, New York, 1956, being selections from Santayana's works. *The Idler and His Works, and Other Essays*, ed. Daniel Cory, New York, 1957, prints twelve essays never before published in book form.

Daniel Cory also edited, with an introduction and commentary, *The Letters of George Santayana*, New York, 1955.

**713. BIOGRAPHY AND CRITICISM**

Four full-length studies are Jacques Duron, *La pensée de George Santayana: Santayana en Amérique*, Paris, 1950; Willard E. Arnett, *Santayana and the Sense of Beauty*, Bloomington, Ind., 1955; Richard Butler, *The Mind of Santayana*, London, 1956; and Irving Singer, *Santayana's Aesthetics: A Critical Introduction*, Cambridge, Mass., 1957.

The *Journal of Philosophy*, LI (Jan. 21, 1954), is a special Santayana issue. Other brief studies are B. F. Hazen, "The Last Puritan," *Cronos*, I (1947), 1–5; Concha Zardoya, "Poesía y Estilo de George Santayana," *Cuadernos Americanos* (Mexico), XLIX (1950), 130–156; Jacques Valette,

"Santayana," *MdF*, CCCXI (1951), 726–729; Emile Bréhier, "La philosophie de George Santayana," *Revue Philosophique*, CXLII (1952), 245–248; Marcel Brion, "George Santayana," *Revue des Deux Mondes*, No. 24 (1952), 710–716; Luis Farré, "El pensamiento de Santayana," *Cuadernos Hispanoamericanos* (Madrid), No. 36 (1952), 224–236; Clemente J. López, "Santayana, poeta," *ibid.*, No. 36 (1952), 237–245; Russell Kirk, "The Politics of George Santayana," *PS*, VII (1953), 62–69; George Biddle, "Last Talks with Santayana," *Reporter*, VIII (Apr. 28, 1953), 35–40; Daniel Cory, "Santayana's Last Year," *Atl*, CXCI (Apr., 1953), 66–70; T. G. Henderson, "Santayana Awaiting Death," *JP*, L (1953), 201–206; Wilbert Snow, "A Last Visit with Santayana," *Am Merc*, LXXVI (Mar.–Apr., 1953), 28–33; Henry David Aiken, "George Santayana: Natural Historian of Symbolic Forms," *KR*, XV (1953), 337–356; Charles T. Harrison, "Santayana's 'Literary Psychology,'" *SR*, LXI (1953), 206–220; Padraic Colum, "George Santayana," *DM*, XXIX (Oct.–Dec., 1953), 14–20; Mario Tassoni, "Profilo spirituale di G. Santayana," *Pensiero Critico*, No. 7–8 (Dec., 1953), 11–14; Roberto Giammanco, "La Concezione dell'arte in George Santayana," *SA*, I (1955), 309–316; Gerald Weales, "A Little Faith, A Little Envy: A Note on Santayana and Auden," *ASch*, XXIV (1955), 340–347; and C. T. Harrison, "Aspects of Santayana," *SR*, LXV (1957), 141–146.

Of bibliographical interest is Daniel Cory, "The 'George Santayana Collection,'" *CLC*, V (Feb., 1956), 23–25.

# WILLIAM SAROYAN

### 714. SHORT STORIES AND NOVELS

*The Assyrian, and Other Stories*, 1950; *Rock Wagram*, 1951; *Tracy's Tiger*, 1951; *The Laughing Matter*, 1953; *Mama, I Love You*, 1956; *The Whole Voyald, and Other Stories*, 1956; *Papa, You're Crazy*, 1957.

### 715. PLAYS *

*Don't Go Away Mad, and Two Other Plays: Sam Ego's House* [*and*] *A Decent Birth, a Happy Funeral*, 1949; *The Cave Dwellers* (1957), 1958.

#### MEMOIRS

*The Twin Adventures: The Adventures of William Saroyan, a Diary; The Adventures of Wesley Jackson, a Novel*, 1950; *The Bicycle Rider in Beverly Hills*, 1952.

#### REPRINTS

*The Saroyan Special*, New York, 1948, is a collection of ninety-two stories selected by the author. *The William Saroyan Reader*, New York,

* Dates in parentheses are of production when it differs from publication.

1958, reprints *Tracy's Tiger, The Time of Your Life,* and excerpts from other works.

BIOGRAPHY AND CRITICISM

Two studies are Frederic I. Carpenter, "The Time of William Saroyan's Life," *PS,* I (1947), 88–96, and William J. Fisher, "What Ever Happened to Saroyan?" *CE,* XVI (1955), 336–340, 385.

## CHARLES SEALSFIELD
## ("KARL ANTON POSTL")

**716.** CORRESPONDENCE

See Harold Jantz, "Charles Sealsfield's Letter to Joel R. Poinsett," *GR,* XXVII (1952), 155–164.

BIOGRAPHY AND CRITICISM

The most recent biography is Eduard Castle, *Der Grosse Unbekannte: Das Leben von Charles Sealsfield (Karl Postl),* Vienna, 1952.

Brief studies are A. E. Schroeder, "New Sources of Charles Sealsfield," *JEGP,* XLVI (1947), 70–74, and these by Karl J. Arndt: "Sealsfield's Command of the English Language," *MLN,* LXVII (1952), 310–313; "Charles Sealsfield and the *Courrier des Etats-Unis,*" *PMLA,* LXVIII (1953), 170–188; "Recent Sealsfield Discoveries," *JEGP,* LIII (1954), 160–171; and "Plagiarism: Sealsfield or Simms?" *MLN,* LXIX (1954), 577–581.

## SAMUEL SEWALL

**717.** BIOGRAPHY AND CRITICISM

See W. Lawrence Thompson, "Classical Echoes in Sewall's Diaries: 1674–1729," *NEQ,* XXIV (1951), 374–377, and Freeman Tilden, "Four Widows and One Judge," *AH,* V (Spring, 1954), 10–11, 50–51.

## WILLIAM GILMORE SIMMS

**722.** COLLECTED WORKS AND REPRINTS

*The Letters of William Gilmore Simms,* 5 vols., Columbia, S.C., 1952–1956, were collected and edited by Mary C. Simms Oliphant, Alfred Taylor Odell, and T. C. Duncan Eaves, with an introduction by Donald Davidson and a biographical sketch by Alexander S. Salley. See also John C. Guilds, "Bryant in the South: A New Letter to Simms," *GHQ,* XXXVII (1953),

142–146, and Arlin Turner, "William Gilmore Simms in His Letters," *SAQ*, LIII (1954), 404–415.

BIOGRAPHY AND CRITICISM

Recent studies are J. Allen Morris, "Gullah in the Stories and Novels of William Gilmore Simms," *ASp*, XXII (1947), 46–53; Edward Stone, " 'Caleb Williams' and 'Martin Faber': A Contrast," *MLN*, LXII (1947), 480–483; C. Hugh Holman, "William Gilmore Simms' Picture of the Revolution as a Civil Conflict," *JSH*, XV (1949), 441–462; Max L. Griffin, "Bryant and the South," *TSE*, I (1949), 53–80; C. Hugh Holman, "Simms and the British Dramatists," *PMLA*, LXV (1950), 346–359; *idem,* "The Influence of Scott and Cooper on Simms," *AL*, XXIII (1951), 203–218; Edd Winfield Parks, "Simms's Edition of the Shakespeare Apocrypha," *Stud. Shak.* (1953), 30–39; Stanley T. Williams, "Spanish Influences on the Fiction of William Gilmore Simms," *HR*, XXI (1953), 221–228; Karl J. Arndt, "Plagiarism: Sealsfield or Simms?" *MLN*, LXIX (1954), 577–581; Jay B. Hubbell, *The South in American Literature, 1607–1900,* Durham, 1954, pp. 572–602; Edward P. Vandiver, Jr., "Simms's Porgy and Cooper," *MLN*, LXX (1955), 272–274; John C. Guilds, "Simms's First Magazine: *The Album,*" *SB*, VIII (1956), 169–183; John C. Guilds, "William Gilmore Simms and the *Cosmopolitan,*" *GHQ*, XLI (1957), 31–41; and S. P. C. Duvall, "W. G. Simms's Review of Mrs. Stowe," *AL*, XXX (1958), 107–117.

## UPTON SINCLAIR

**723.** SEPARATE WORKS

Novels: *Another Pamela; or, Virtue Still Rewarded,* 1950; *It Happened to Didymus,* 1958.

The Lanny Budd series continues with *One Clear Call,* 1948; *O Shepherd, Speak!* 1949; *The Return of Lanny Budd,* 1953.

Plays: *The Enemy Had It Too,* 1950.

Political and social studies: *The Cup of Fury,* 1956.

**724.** BIOGRAPHY AND CRITICISM

Special studies are Albert Mordell, "Haldeman-Julius and Upton Sinclair," *Critic & Guide,* IV (Feb., 1950), 94–119; Leon Spitz, "Upton Sinclair on Zionism," *AHeb,* CLVIII (Dec. 31, 1951), 6, 15; J. D. Koerner, "The Last of the Muckrake Men," *SAQ*, LV (1956), 221–232; and Howard H. Quint, "Upton Sinclair's Quest for Artistic Independence—1909," *AL*, XXIX (1957), 194–202.

# JOHN SMITH

**726.** EDITED TEXTS AND REPRINTS

A recent reprinting is Ben Clyde McCary, *John Smith's Map of Virginia, with a Brief Account of Its History,* Williamsburg, 1957.

BIOGRAPHY AND CRITICISM

The fullest biographical study in recent years is Bradford Smith, *Captain John Smith, His Life and Legend,* Philadelphia, 1953. A briefer treatment is Marshall W. Fishwick, *Virginians on Olympus: A Cultural Analysis of Four Great Men,* Richmond, 1951. See also J. P. C. Southall, "Captain John Smith (1580-1631) and Pocahontas (1595?-1617)," *Tyler's Quar. Hist. & Gen. Mag.,* XXVIII (1947), 209-225.

# EDMUND CLARENCE STEDMAN

**728.** BIOGRAPHY AND CRITICISM

See Edward M. Williams, "Edmund Clarence Stedman at Home," *NEQ,* XXV (1952), 242-247.

# GERTRUDE STEIN

**729.** SEPARATE WORKS

*Kisses Can,* 1947; *Literally True,* 1947; *The Mother of Us All* (with Virgil Thomson), 1947; *Two (Hitherto Unpublished) Poems,* 1948; *Blood on the Dining Room Floor,* 1948; *Last Operas and Plays,* 1949; *Things as They Are, A Novel in Three Parts,* 1950; *Absolutely Bob Brown; or, Bobbed Brown,* 1955; *To Bobchen Haas,* 1957.

The Yale Edition of the Unpublished Writings of Gertrude Stein is under the general editorship of Carl Van Vechten. Eight volumes have been published in New Haven, all from the Gertrude Stein Collection in the Yale University Library: *Two: Gertrude Stein and Her Brother, and Other Early Portraits (1908-1912),* with a foreword by Janet Flanner, 1951; *Mrs. Reynolds, and Five Earlier Novelettes,* with a foreword by Floyd Frankenberg, 1952; *Bee Time Vine, and Other Pieces (1913-1927),* with a preface and notes by Virgil Thomson, 1953; *As Fine as Melanchtha (1914-1930),* with a foreword by Natalie Clifford Barney, 1954; *Painted Lace, and Other Pieces (1914-1937),* with an introduction by Daniel-Henry Kahnweiler, 1955; *Stanzas in Meditation and Other Poems (1929-1933),* with a preface by Donald Sutherland, 1956; *Alphabets and Birthdays,* with an introduction by Donald Gallup, 1957; and *A Novel of Thank You*, with an introduction by Carl Van Vechten, 1958.

BIOGRAPHY AND CRITICISM

William Garland Rogers has written a personal memoir, utilizing many Stein letters to the author, *When This You See, Remember Me: Gertrude Stein in Person*, New York, 1948. The major biographical study is Elizabeth Sprigge, *Gertrude Stein, Her Life and Work*, New York, 1957.

Donald Gallup edited, with notes and introductions, *The Flowers of Friendship: Letters Written to Gertrude Stein*, New York, 1953.

The first full-length critical study of Stein is Donald Sutherland, *Gertrude Stein, a Biography of Her Work*, New Haven, 1951. Rosalind S. Miller's *Gertrude Stein: Form and Intelligibility*, New York, 1949, contains the Radcliffe themes edited from the manuscripts in the Yale University Library.

Briefer critical studies are Oliver Evans, "Gertrude Stein as Humorist," *PrS*, XXI (1947), 97–101; Katherine Anne Porter, "Gertrude Stein: A Self-Portrait," *Harper's*, CXCV (1947), 519–528; Josephine Herbst, "Miss Porter and Miss Stein," *PR*, XV (1948), 568–572; Oliver Evans, "The Americanism of Gertrude Stein," *PrS*, XXII (1948), 70–74; Donald Gallup, "A Book Is a Book Is a Book," *New Col*, I (1948), 67–80; *idem*, "Always Gtrde Stein," *SWR*, XXXIV (1949), 254–258; George Haines, IV, "Gertrude Stein and Composition," *SR*, LVII (1949), 411–424; Donald Gallup, "The Making of *The Making of Americans*," *New Col*, III (1950), 54–74; Ben Reid, "Gertrude Stein's Critics," *UKCR*, XIX (1952), 121–130; Donald Gallup, "Gertrude Stein and the *Atlantic*," *YULG*, XXVIII (1954), 109–128; Harry R. Garvin, "Sound and Sense in *Four Saints in Three Acts*," *BuR*, V (1954), 1–11; and Allegra Stewart, "The Quality of Gertrude Stein's Creativity," *AL*, XXVIII (1957), 488–506.

BIBLIOGRAPHY

The most complete listing is George James Firmage, *A Check-List of the Published Writings of Gertrude Stein*, Amherst, 1954. See also Julian Sawyer, "Gertrude Stein: A Bibliography, 1941–1948," *BB*, XIX (1948), 152–156, 183–187; and Donald Gallup, "The Gertrude Stein Collection," *YULG*, XXII (1947), 22–32.

# JOHN (ERNST) STEINBECK

**730.** SEPARATE WORKS

*A Russian Journal* (with Robert Capa), 1948; *Burning Bright*, 1950; *East of Eden*, 1952; *Sweet Thursday*, 1954; *The Short Reign of Pippin IV*, 1957; *Once There Was a War*, 1958.

*Pipe Dream* (1955) is a Rodgers and Hammerstein musical comedy based on *Sweet Thursday*.

REPRINTS

*The Log from the Sea of Cortez*, New York, 1951, is the narrative portion of *Sea of Cortez* (1941) here reissued with a profile "About Ed Ricketts." *The Short Novels of John Steinbeck*, New York, 1953, are reprinted with an introduction by Joseph Henry Jackson. Reprints of individual novels are too numerous to list separately.

**731.** BIOGRAPHY AND CRITICISM

The first full-length critical study is Peter Lisca, *The Wide World of John Steinbeck*, New Brunswick, N.J., 1958. E. W. Tedlock, Jr., and C. V. Wicker edited *Steinbeck and His Critics, a Record of Twenty-Five Years*, Albuquerque, 1957.

Briefer studies are Freeman Champney, "John Steinbeck, Californian," *AR*, VII (1947), 345–362; Marie Forestier, "Steinbeck et son œuvre," *Revue Nouvelle*, V (1947), 253–261; Frederick Bracher, "Steinbeck and the Biological View of Man," *PS*, II (1948), 14–29; Woodburn O. Ross, "John Steinbeck: Naturalism's Priest," *CE*, X (1949), 432–437; Blake Nevius, "Steinbeck: One Aspect," *PS*, III (1949), 302–310; Claude-Edmonde Magny, "*East of Eden*," *Perspectives USA*, No. 5 (1953), 146–152; Bernard Bowron, " 'The Grapes of Wrath': A 'Wagons West' Romance," *ColQ*, III (1954), 84–91; Ward Moore, "Cannery Row Revisited: Steinbeck and the Sardine," *Nation*, CLXXIX (1954), 325–327; Warren G. French, "Another Look at *The Grapes of Wrath*," *ColQ*, III (1955), 337–343; and Martin Shockley, "Christian Symbolism in *The Grapes of Wrath*," *CE*, XVIII (1956), 87–90.

Of bibliographical interest is Georges Remords, "John Steinbeck—note bibliographique," *Bulletin de la Faculté des Lettres de Strasbourg*, XXVIII (Apr., 1950), 301–305.

## WALLACE STEVENS
### d. 1955

**732.** SEPARATE WORKS

*Three Academic Pieces: The Realm of Resemblance, Someone Puts a Pineapple Together, Of Ideal Time and Choice*, 1947; *A Primitive Like an Orb, A Poem*, 1948; *The Auroras of Autumn*, 1950; *The Relations Between Poetry and Painting*, 1951; *The Necessary Angel: Essays on Reality and the Imagination*, 1951; *Selected Poems* (London), 1953; *Raoul Dufy, A Note*, 1953; *Collected Poems*, 1954; *Opus Posthumous*, 1957.

*Collected Poems* (1954) was published to honor Stevens on his seventy-fifth birthday. It contains *Harmonium* (as revised in 1931 and reissued in 1947), *Ideas of Order* (as reissued in 1952), *The Man with the Blue Guitar* (as reissued in 1952, except for "Owl's Clover"), *Parts of a World* (as first published except for two short poems), *Transport to Summer* and *The Auroras of Autumn* (as first published), and "The Rock" (a section of twenty-five poems never before included in a book).

Of the poems and essays in *Opus Posthumous* (1957), edited with an introduction by Samuel French Morse, about one-third are here published for the first time.

### 733. BIOGRAPHY AND CRITICISM

Two critical analyses are William Van O'Connor, *The Shaping Spirit: A Study of Wallace Stevens,* Chicago, 1950, and Robert Pack, *Wallace Stevens: An Approach to His Poetry and Thought,* New Brunswick, N.J., 1958.

The *Trinity Review* (Hartford, Conn.) published "A Celebration for Wallace Stevens," VIII (May, 1954), containing poems by Stevens and articles, poems, and letters by various hands. *Perspective*, VII (Autumn, 1954), is a special Wallace Stevens issue.

Brief critical estimates are Fred Laros, "Wallace Stevens Today," *BaR*, II (1947), 8–15; Robert Lowell, "Imagination and Reality," *Nation*, CLXVI (1947), 400–407; Bernard Heringman, "Two Worlds and Epiphany," *BaR*, II (1948), 156–159; Marius Bewley, "The Poetry of Wallace Stevens," *PR*, XVI (1949), 895–915; J. V. Cunningham, "The Poetry of Wallace Stevens," *Poetry*, LXXV (1949), 149–165; Bernard Heringman, "Wallace Stevens: The Use of Poetry," *ELH*, XVI (1949), 325–336; Randall Jarrell, "Reflections on Wallace Stevens," *PR*, XVIII (1951), 335–344; Roy Harvey Pearce, "Wallace Stevens: The Life of the Imagination," *PMLA*, LXVI (1951), 561–582; Harold H. Watts, "Wallace Stevens and The Rock of Summer," *KR*, XIV (1952), 122–140; R. P. Blackmur, "Wallace Stevens— An Abstraction Blooded," "On Herbert Read and Wallace Stevens," *Language as Gesture*, New York, 1952, pp. 250–254, 255–259; C. Roland Wagner, "The Idea of Nothingness in Wallace Stevens," *Accent*, XII (1952), 111–121; Warren Carrier, "Wallace Stevens' Pagan Vantage," *Accent*, XIII (1953), 165–168; Donald Davie, "'Essential Gaudiness': The Poems of Wallace Stevens," *TC*, CLIII (1953), 455–462.

More recent studies are Steve Feldman, "Reality and the Imagination: The Poetic of Wallace Stevens' 'Necessary Angel,'" *UKCR*, XXI (1954), 35–43; R. P. Blackmur, "The Substance That Prevails," *KR*, XVII (1955), 94–110; Elder Olson, "The Poetry of Wallace Stevens," *CE*, XVI (1955), 395–402; Randall Jarrell, "The Collected Poems of Wallace Stevens," *YR*, XLIV (1955), 340–353; Marius Bewley, "The Poetry of Wallace Stevens," *Commonweal*, LXII (1955), 617–622; Glanco Cambon, "Le 'Notes Toward a Supreme Fiction' di Wallace Stevens," *SA*, I (1955), 205–233; Robert

Pack, "The Abstracting Imagination of Wallace Stevens: Nothingness and the Hero," *ArQ*, XI (1955), 197–209; William J. Smith, "Modern Poetry: Texture and Text," *Shenandoah*, VI (1955), 6–16; William Carlos Williams, "Wallace Stevens," *Poetry*, LXXXVII (1956), 234–239; Samuel French Morse, "Wallace Stevens: Some Ideas About the Thing Itself," *BUSE*, II (1956), 55–64; Howard Nemerov, "The Poetry of Wallace Stevens," *SR*, LXV (1957), 1–14; Richard Ellmann, "Wallace Stevens' Ice-Cream," *KR*, XIX (1957), 89–105; and Northrop Frye, "The Realistic Oriole: The Poetry of Wallace Stevens," *HudR*, X (1957), 353–370.

For a listing of explications of individual poems, see George Arms and Joseph M. Kuntz, *Poetry Explication*, New York, 1950, pp. 141–146.

BIBLIOGRAPHY

The major bibliographical listing is Samuel French Morse, *Wallace Stevens: A Preliminary Checklist of His Published Writings, 1898–1954*, New Haven, 1954. See also William Van O'Connor, *The Shaping Spirit: A Study of Wallace Stevens*, Chicago, 1950, pp. 141–146, and Allen Tate, *Sixty American Poets, 1896–1944*, rev. ed., Washington, 1954, pp. 127–129.

There are Stevens manuscripts in the Library of Congress and the Lockwood Memorial Library of the University of Buffalo.

## HARRIET (ELIZABETH) BEECHER STOWE

### 736. BIOGRAPHY AND CRITICISM

Two special studies are Harry Birdoff, *The World's Greatest Hit: Uncle Tom's Cabin*, New York, 1947, and Charles H. Foster, *The Rungless Ladder: Harriet Beecher Stowe and New England Puritanism*, Durham, 1954. See also Joseph C. Furnas, *Goodbye to Uncle Tom*, New York, 1956, *passim*.

Briefer estimates are C. H. Foster, "The Genesis of Harriet Beecher Stowe's 'The Minister's Wooing,'" *NEQ*, XXI (1948), 493–517; Alexander Cowie, *The Rise of the American Novel*, New York, 1948, pp. 447–463; Grace Seiler, "Harriet Beecher Stowe," *CE*, XI (1949), 127–137; Barnard Hewitt, "Uncle Tom and Uncle Sam: New Light from an Old Play," *QJS*, XXXVII (1951), 63–70; Margaret Wyman, "Harriet Beecher Stowe's Topical Novel on Woman Suffrage," *NEQ*, XXV (1952), 383–391; Frank Rahill, "America's Number One Hit," *TArts*, XXXVI (1952), 18–24; A. M. Drummond and Richard Moody, "The Hit of the Century: Uncle Tom's Cabin: 1852–1952," *ETJ*, IV (1952), 315–322; Ruth Suckow, "An Almost Lost American Classic," *CE*, XIV (1953), 315–325; Frederick H. Jackson, "*Uncle Tom's Cabin* in Italy," *Symposium*, VII (1953), 323–332; J. P. Roppolo, "Uncle Tom in New Orleans: Three Lost Plays," *NEQ*, XXVII

(1954), 213–226; Herbert G. Nicholas, "Uncle Tom's Cabin, 1852–1952," *GaR*, VIII (1954), 140–149; Margaret C. Banning, *"Uncle Tom's Cabin* by Harriet Beecher Stowe," *GaR*, IX (1955), 461–465; William Reardon and John Foxen, "Civil War Theater: The Propaganda Play," *Civil War Hist.*, I (1955), 281–293; and S. P. C. Duvall, "W. G. Simms's Review of Mrs. Stowe," *AL*, XXX (1958), 107–117.

## BAYARD TAYLOR

**738.** COLLECTED WORKS AND REPRINTS

*Eldorado; or, Adventures in the Path of Empire* (1850) was reprinted, with an introduction by Robert Glass Cleland, New York, 1949.

**739.** BIOGRAPHY AND CRITICISM

The most recent biographical study is Richard Cary, *The Genteel Circle: Bayard Taylor and His New York Friends,* Ithaca, 1952.

Special studies are Raymond Himelick, "Bayard Taylor and Browning's 'Holy Vitus,'" *SAQ*, L (1951), 542–551; F. De Wolfe Miller, "Lowell the Author of Bayard Taylor's Review of *Laus Veneris,*" *AL*, XXVII (1955), 106–109; John T. Krumpelmann, "Bayard Taylor and Schiller," *Contributions to the Humanities, 1954* (La. State Univ. Stud., Humanistic Ser.), No. 5 (1955), 11–24; *idem,* "Bayard Taylor as a Literary Mediator between Germany and the South Atlantic States," *NS,* Heft 9 (1955), 415–418; and Horst Frenz and Philip Allison Shelley, "Bayard Taylor's German Lecture on American Literature," *JA,* II (1957), 89–133.

## EDWARD TAYLOR

**740.** EDITED TEXTS

Printings of Yale manuscript poems not included in Thomas H. Johnson's *The Poetical Works of Edward Taylor,* New York, 1939, are Morris A. Neufield, "A Meditation upon the Glory of God," *YULG*, XXV (1951), 110–111; Barbara Damon Simison, "Poems by Edward Taylor," *YULG,* XXVIII (1954), 93–102, 161–170; XXIX (1954), 25–34, 71–80; Donald E. Stanford, "Sacramental Meditations by Edward Taylor," *YULG,* XXXI (1956), 61–75; and *idem,* "Nineteen Unpublished Poems by Edward Taylor," *AL,* XXIX (1957), 18–46.

BIOGRAPHY AND CRITICISM

Recent critical studies are Sidney E. Lind, "Edward Taylor: A Revaluation," *NEQ,* XXI (1948), 518–530; Roy Harvey Pearce, "Edward Taylor·

The Poet as Puritan," *NEQ*, XXIII (1950), 31–46; Herbert Blau, "Heaven's Sugar Cake: Theology and Imagery in the Poetry of Edward Taylor," *NEQ*, XXVI (1953), 337–360; Willie T. Weathers, "Edward Taylor and the Cambridge Platonists," *AL*, XXVI (1954), 1–31; William B. Goodman, "Edward Taylor Writes His Love," *NEQ*, XXVII (1954), 510–515; Donald E. Stanford, "Edward Taylor and the Lord's Supper," *AL*, XXVII (1955), 172–178; Mindele Black, "Edward Taylor: Heavens Sugar Cake," *NEQ*, XXIX (1956), 159–181; and Biancamaria Tedeschini Lalli, "Edward Taylor," *SA*, II (1956), 9–43.

A listing of explications of individual poems is in George Arms and Joseph M. Kuntz, *Poetry Explication*, New York, 1950, pp. 149–151.

## HENRY DAVID THOREAU

### 742. COLLECTED WORKS

A new edition of the fourteen volumes of journals, edited by Bradford Torrey and first published as part of the standard Walden Edition, 1906, is Francis H. Allen, ed., *The Journals of Henry David Thoreau*, Boston, 1949.

Perry Miller edited, with a commentary, *Consciousness in Concord: The Text of Thoreau's Hitherto Lost Journal (1840–1841)*, Boston, 1958.

### 743. EDITED TEXTS AND CORRESPONDENCE

James Lyndon Shanley's *The Making of Walden, with the Text of the First Version*, Chicago, 1957, is based on a transcription of Huntington Manuscript 924, the version that Thoreau wrote in 1846–47. Joseph Jones compiled *Index to Walden*, Austin, Tex., 1955. Oscar Cargill has edited *Selected Writings on Nature and Liberty*, New York, 1952.

Walter Harding and Carl Bode edited *The Correspondence of Henry David Thoreau*, New York, 1958.

### 744. BIOGRAPHY AND CRITICISM

Three biographical studies are Joseph Wood Krutch, *Henry David Thoreau*, New York, 1948; William M. Condry, *Thoreau*, New York, 1954; and Henry Beetle Hough, *Thoreau of Walden*, New York, 1956. Of biographical interest are Robert F. Stowell, *A Thoreau Gazetteer*, Calais, Vt., 1948, and Leonard Kleinfeld, *Henry David Thoreau Chronology*, New York, 1950 (limited private edition).

Sherman Paul's *The Shores of America: Thoreau's Inward Exploration*, Urbana, Ill., 1958, called "a spiritual biography or a biography of a vocation," is at the same time a comprehensive critical study.

Of general critical importance are Ethel Seybold, *Thoreau: The Quest and the Classics*, New Haven, 1951; Reginald L. Cook, *The Concord*

*Saunterer*, 1940, revised and expanded as *Passage to Walden*, Boston, 1949; and Leo Stoller, *After Walden: Thoreau's Changing Views on Economic Man*, Stanford, 1958. Walter Harding has collected a cross section of critical studies in *Thoreau: A Century of Criticism*, Dallas, 1954.

Briefer studies are Reginald L. Cook, "Thoreau in Perspective," *UKCR*, XIV (1947), 117–125; James M. Dabbs, "Thoreau: The Adventurer as Economist," *YR*, XXXVI (1947), 667–672; Frank Davidson, "Thoreau's Contribution to Hawthorne's *Mosses*," *NEQ*, XX (1947), 535–542; Robert Francis, "Thoreau's Mask of Serenity," *Forum*, CVII (1947), 72–77; Hubert H. Hoeltje, "Thoreau and the Concord Academy," *NEQ*, XXI (1948), 103–109; W. P. Glick, "Thoreau and the *Herald of Freedom*," *NEQ*, XXII (1949), 193–204; C. C. Hollis, "Thoreau and the State," *Commonweal*, L (1949), 530–533; John H. Holmes, "Thoreau's 'Civil Disobedience,'" *Chri Century*, LXVI (1949), 787–789; Heinz Elau, "Wayside Challenger—Some Remarks on the Politics of Henry David Thoreau," *AR*, IX (1949), 509–522; Sherman Paul, "The Wise Silence: Sound as the Agency of Correspondence in Thoreau," *NEQ*, XXII (1949), 511–527; Kathryn Whitford, "Thoreau and the Woodlots of Concord," *NEQ*, XXIII (1950), 291–306; J. Chesley Mathews, "Thoreau's Reading in Dante," *Italica*, XXVII (1950), 77–81; G. Ferris Cronkhite, "The Transcendental Railroad," *NEQ*, XXIV (1951), 306–328; Walter Harding, "Thoreau on the Lecture Platform," *NEQ*, XXIV (1951), 365–374; Philip and Kathryn Whitford, "Thoreau: Pioneer Ecologist and Conservationist," *Sci Mo*, LXXIII (1951), 291–296; Kenneth Walter Cameron, "Emerson, Thoreau, and the Society of Natural History," *AL*, XXIV (1952), 21–30; Joseph L. Blau, *Men and Movements in American Philosophy*, New York, 1952, pp. 131–141; Kenneth Walter Cameron, "Thoreau Discovers Emerson: A College Reading Record," *BNYPL*, LVII (1953), 319–334; G. M. Ostrander, "Emerson, Thoreau, and John Brown," *MVHR*, XXXIX (1953), 713–726; Sherman Paul, "Resolution at Walden," *Accent*, XIII (1953), 101–113; Carl Bode, "Thoreau the Actor," *AQ*, V (1953), 247–252; Francis B. Dedmond, "Economic Protest in Thoreau's *Journal*," *SN*, XXVI (1953–54), 65–76.

More recent studies are Frank Davidson, "Melville, Thoreau, and 'The Apple-Tree Table,'" *AL*, XXV (1954), 479–488; Alec Lucas, "Thoreau, Field Naturalist," *UTQ*, XXIII (1954), 227–232; E. B. White, "Walden—1954," *YR*, XLIV (1954), 13–22; John O. Eidson, "Charles Stearns Wheeler: Emerson's 'Good Grecian,'" *NEQ*, XXVII (1954), 472–483; Christopher McKee, "Thoreau: A Week on Mt. Washington and in Tuckerman Ravine," *Appalachia*, XXX (1954), 169–183; Samuel Sillen, "Thoreau in Today's America," *MM*, VII (1954), 1–9; Raymond Adams, "Thoreau's Mock-Heroics and the American Natural History Writers," *SP*, LII (1955), 86–97; A. Schiller, "Thoreau and Whitman: The Record of a Pilgrimage," *NEQ*, XXVIII (1955), 186–197; John C. Broderick, "Thoreau's Proposals for Legislation," *AQ*, VII (1955), 285–290; Sherman Paul, "Thoreau's 'The Landlord': 'Sublimely Trivial for the Good of Men,'" *JEGP*, LIV (1955), 587–590; Lawrence Willson, "Thoreau and Roman Catholicism," *CathHR*, XLII (1956), 157–172; John C. Broderick, "Thoreau, Alcott, and the Poll Tax," *SP*, LIII (1956), 612–626; George Hendrick, "The Influence of Thoreau's 'Civil Disobedience' on Gandhi's *Satyagraha*," *NEQ*, XXIX (1956), 462–471; Sreebrishna Sarma, "A Short Study of Oriental Influences upon H. D. Thoreau with Special Reference to His 'Walden,'" *JA*, I (1956), 76–92; Walter L. Fertig, "John Sullivan Dwight's Pre-publication Notice of *Walden*," *NEQ*, XXX (1957), 84–90; C. Grant Loomis, "Henry David Thoreau as Folklorist," *WF*, XVI (1957), 90–106; and Carl F. Hovde, "Nature into Art: Thoreau's Use of His Journals in *A Week*," *AL*, XXX (1958), 165–184.

## 746. BIBLIOGRAPHY

See the critical selected bibliography compiled by Lewis Leary for *Eight American Authors: A Review of Research and Criticism*, ed. Floyd Stovall, New York, 1956.

Since 1941, Walter Harding has been contributing "Additions to the Thoreau Bibliography" to each issue of the *Thoreau Society Bulletin*. See also his "The Thoreau Collection of the Pierpont Morgan Library of New York City," *Thoreau Soc. Bul.*, No. 19 (1947), 2; "A Check List of Thoreau's Lectures," *BNYPL*, LII (1948), 78–87; "A Preliminary Checklist of the Editions of *Walden*," *Thoreau Soc. Bul.*, No. 39 (1952), 2–3; *A Centennial Check-List of the Editions of Henry David Thoreau's Walden*, Charlottesville, 1954, and *Thoreau's Library*, Charlottesville, 1957.

Additional bibliographical information is in Philip E. Burnham and Carvel Collins, "Contributions to a Bibliography of Thoreau," *BB*, XIX (1947), 37–39; Raymond Adams, "The Bibliographical History of Thoreau's *A Week on the Concord and Merrimack Rivers*," *PBSA*, XLII (1949), 39–47; Francis B. Dedmond, "A Check List of Manuscripts Relating to Thoreau in the Huntington Library, the Houghton Library of Harvard University, and the Berg Collection of the New York Public Library," *Thoreau Soc. Bul.*, No. 43 (1953), 3–4; Walter Scott Houston, "An Index to the First Ten Years of Thoreau Society Publications," *Thoreau Soc. Booklet*, No. 8 (1953), 1–2; Mrs. H. W. Kent, "A Catalog of the Thoreau Collection in the Concord Antiquarian Society," *Thoreau Soc. Bul.*, No. 47 (1954), 1–4; and Walter Harding and Carl Bode, "Henry David Thoreau: A Check List of His Correspondence," *BNYPL*, LIX (1955), 253–258.

# HENRY TIMROD

**747.** COLLECTED WORKS AND CORRESPONDENCE

Additional letters are William Fidler, ed., "[Seven Unpublished Letters of Henry Timrod]," *AlaR*, II (1949), 139–149.

BIOGRAPHY AND CRITICISM

Three brief studies are M. B. Seigler, "Henry Timrod and Sophie Sosnowski," *GHQ*, XXXI (1947), 171–180; Edd Winfield Parks, "Timrod's Concept of Dreams," *SAQ*, XLVIII (1949), 584–588; and Jay B. Hubbell, *The South in American Literature, 1607–1900*, Durham, 1954, pp. 466–474.

# JOHN TRUMBULL

**748.** BIOGRAPHY AND CRITICISM

Special studies are H. W. Starr, "A Note on Gray and Trumbull," *N&Q*, CXCII (1947), 254–255; *idem*, "Trumbull and Gray's *Bard*," *MLN*, LXII (1947), 116–119; and Bruce I. Granger, "John Trumbull and Religion," *AL*, XXIII (1951), 57–79.

# JONES VERY

**750.** BIOGRAPHY AND CRITICISM

Two special studies are W. B. Berthoff, "Jones Very: New England Mystic," *BPLQ*, II (1950), 63–76; and Kenneth W. Cameron, "A College Poem by Jones Very," *Emerson Soc. Quar.*, No. 5 (1956), 12–13. For a listing of explications of individual poems see George Arms and Joseph M. Kuntz, *Poetry Explication*, New York, 1950, pp. 155–156.

# GEORGE WASHINGTON

**752.** COLLECTED WORKS, REPRINTS, AND CORRESPONDENCE

Don Marshall Larrabee edited *A Reprint of the Journals of George Washington and His Guide, Christopher Gist . . . November–December, 1753,* Williamsport, Pa., 1950. *Washington's Inaugural Address of 1789,* Washington, 1952, is a National Archives Facsimile edition. Additional studies of Washington manuscripts are Roland Baughman, "Washington's Manuscript Diaries of 1795 and 1798," *PBSA*, XLV (1951), 117–124; and Nathan E.

Stein, "The Discarded Inaugural Address of G. Washington," *Manuscripts,* X (Spring, 1958), 2–17.

Saxe Commins edited *The Basic Writings of George Washington,* New York, 1948. Saul K. Padover edited *The Washington Papers: Selections from the Public and Private Writings of George Washington,* New York, 1955.

For Washington correspondence see Gertrude Richards, ed., "New Letters of George Washington to Benjamin Lincoln," *HLB,* X (1956), 39–72.

**753. BIOGRAPHY AND CRITICISM**

Before his death in 1953, Douglas Southall Freeman completed six volumes of *George Washington, a Biography,* New York, 1948–1954. The seventh and final volume, *George Washington: First in Peace,* New York, 1957, was completed by his assistants, John Alexander Carroll and Mary Wells Ashworth. A condensation of this work into one volume is being planned by the publishers.

A recent critical biography by a British scholar is Marcus Cunliffe, *George Washington, Man and Monument,* Boston, 1958. More popular treatments are Howard Swiggett, *The Great Man: George Washington As a Human Being,* Garden City, N.Y., 1953, and John Tebbel, *George Washington's America,* New York, 1954. A specialized study is Hugh Cleland, *George Washington in the Ohio Valley,* Pittsburgh, 1955.

Two historical-political estimates are James Hart, *The American Presidency in Action, 1789: A Study in Constitutional History,* New York, 1948, and Curtis P. Nettels, *George Washington and American Independence,* Boston, 1951.

Of literary interest are Samuel Blaine Shirk, *The Characterization of George Washington in American Plays Since 1875,* Philadelphia, 1949, and William Alfred Bryan, *George Washington in American Literature, 1775–1865,* New York, 1952.

Briefer studies are John R. Frey, "George Washington in American Fiction," *VMHB,* LV (1947), 342–349; John P. Dix, "George Washington, Father of His Country," *Soc. Stud.,* XXXIX (1948), 68–76; James Douglas Anderson, "Washington and Lincoln: Two Ill-Mated Spirits of the 'Freedom' Train," *Tyler's Quar. Hist. & Gen. Mag.,* XXX (1948), 5–20; William A. Bryan, "George Washington: Symbolic Guardian of the Republic, 1850–1861," *WMQ,* VII (1950), 53–63; Marshall Smelser, "George Washington and the Alien and Sedition Acts," *AHR,* LIX (1954), 322–334; *idem,* "George Washington Declines the Part of El Libertador," *WMQ,* XI (1954), 42–51; William D. Houlette, "Books of the Virginia Dynasty," *LQ,* XXIV (1954), 226–239; Reginald C. McGrane, "George Washington: An Anglo-American Hero," *VMHB,* LXIII (1955), 3–14; Saul K. Padover, "George Washington—Portrait of a True Conservative," *Soc. Research,* XXII (1955),

199–222; Arthur N. Holcombe, "The Role of Washington in the Framing of the Constitution," *HLQ*, XIX (1956), 317–334; and Alexander DeConde, "Washington's Farewell, the French Alliance, and the Election of 1796," *MVHR*, XLIII (1957), 641–658.

## DANIEL WEBSTER

### 755. BIOGRAPHY AND CRITICISM

Two special studies are Richard N. Current, *Daniel Webster and the Rise of National Conservatism*, Boston, 1955, and Howard A. Bradley and James A. Winans, *Daniel Webster and the Salem Murder*, Columbia, Mo., 1956.

John Sloan Dickey, *Eleazar Wheelock, 1711–1779, Daniel Webster, 1782–1852, and Their Pioneer Dartmouth College*, New York, 1954, is an address printed for The Newcomen Society of England in North America.

See also Robert Gray Gunderson, "Webster in Linsey-Woolsey," *QJS*, XXXVII (1951), 23–30.

## EDITH (NEWBOLD JONES) WHARTON

### 757. EDITED TEXTS AND REPRINTS

Arthur Hobson Quinn edited, with an introduction, *An Edith Wharton Treasury*, New York, 1950, including *The Age of Innocence, The Old Maid*, and ten short stories. Wayne Andrews edited *The Best Short Stories of Edith Wharton*, New York, 1958.

### BIOGRAPHY AND CRITICISM

A full-length critical analysis is Blake Nevius, *Edith Wharton: A Study of Her Fiction*, Berkeley, 1953. See also Josephine Lurie Jessup, *The Faith of Our Feminists: A Study of the Novels of Edith Wharton, Ellen Glasgow, Willa Cather*, New York, 1950.

Briefer studies are Louis Auchincloss, "Edith Wharton and Her New Yorks," *PR*, XVIII (1951), 411–419; Hilda Fife, "Letters from Edith Wharton to Vernon Lee," *CLQ*, Series III (1953), 139–144; Nancy R. Leach, "Edith Wharton's Unpublished Novel," *AL*, XXV (1953), 334–353; R. B. Dooley, "A Footnote to Edith Wharton," *AL*, XXVI (1954), 78–85; John Harvey, "Contrasting Worlds: A Study in the Novels of Edith Wharton," *EA*, VII (1954), 190–198; Winifred Lynskey, "The 'Heroes' of Edith Wharton," *UTQ*, XXIII (1954), 354–361; Louis O. Coxe, "What Edith Wharton Saw in Innocence," *New Rep*, CXXXII (June 27, 1955), 16–18; J. D. Thomas, "Marginalia on *Ethan Frome*," *AL*, XXVII (1955), 405–409;

Norman Friedman, "Point of View in Fiction: The Development of a Critical Concept," *PMLA*, LXX (1955), 1160-1184; William Van O'Connor, "The Novel of Experience," *Critique*, I (1956), 37-44; Larry Rubin, "Aspects of Naturalism in Four Novels by Edith Wharton," *TCL*, II (1957), 182-192; Nancy R. Leach, "New England in the Stories of Edith Wharton," *NEQ*, XXX (1957), 90-98; Millicent Bell, "A James 'Gift' to Edith Wharton," *MLN*, LXXII (1957), 182-185; and Walter B. Rideout, "Edith Wharton's *The House of Mirth*," *Twelve Original Essays on Great American Novels*, ed. Charles Shapiro, Detroit, 1958, pp. 148-176.

**759.** BIBLIOGRAPHY

See Blake Nevius, " 'Pussie' Jones's Verses: A Bibliographical Note on Edith Wharton," *AL*, XXIII (1952), 494-497, and *idem, Edith Wharton: A Study of Her Fiction*, Berkeley, 1953, pp. 260-265.


## WALT(ER) WHITMAN

**760.** COLLECTED WORKS AND CORRESPONDENCE

There is still no variorum edition of *Leaves of Grass*. Three volumes help to untangle the publishing problems: Gay Wilson Allen, *Walt Whitman Handbook*, New York, 1946; Frederick Schyberg, *Walt Whitman*, New York, 1951; and Roger Asselineau, *L'Evolution de Walt Whitman*, Paris, 1954.

A recent reprinting of letters is *The Wound Dresser: Letters Written to His Mother from the Hospitals in Washington During the Civil War*, ed. Richard M. Bucke, New York, 1949. *Faint Clews and Indirections*, ed. Clarence Gohdes and Rollo G. Silver, Durham, N.C., 1949, prints fragmentary notes for poems, versions of prose passages, and letters by members of the Whitman family, all from the Trent Collection of the Library of Duke University. Other letters are in Horst Frenz, ed., *Whitman and [Thomas William Hazen] Rolleston, A Correspondence*, Bloomington, Ind., 1951, and *With Walt Whitman in Camden, January 21 to April 7, 1889*, by Horace Traubel, ed. Sculley Bradley, Philadelphia, 1953 (the fourth volume of Traubel's work, published posthumously). See also Horst Frenz, "Walt Whitman's Letters to Karl Knortz," *AL*, XX (1948), 155-163; Carl Roos, "Walt Whitman's Letters to a Danish Friend," *Orbis Litterarum*, VII (1949), 31-60; Roger Asselineau, "Walt Whitman, Child of Adam? Three Unpublished Letters to Whitman," *MLQ*, X (1949), 91-95; and Walter Harding, "A Sheaf of Whitman Letters," *SB*, V (1952-53), 203-210.

Edwin H. and Rosalind S. Miller compiled *Walt Whitman's Correspondence: A Checklist*, New York, 1957, in which they list over 3,500 items, arranged chronologically. Professor Miller is planning to edit the entire correspondence for the prospective New York University edition of Whitman's writings.

### 761. EDITED TEXTS

A re-issue of the "Deathbed Edition" is *The Complete Prose and Poetry of Walt Whitman*, with an introduction by Malcolm Cowley, 2 vols., New York, 1948. Louis Untermeyer edited *The Poetry and Prose of Walt Whitman*, New York, 1949.

Fredson Bowers edited, with notes and an introduction, a parallel text edition, *Whitman's Manuscripts: "Leaves of Grass"* (*1860*), Chicago, 1955. The standard "Inclusive Edition" of *Leaves of Grass*, edited in 1924 by Emory Holloway from the 1902 *Complete Writings*, has been reprinted, New York, 1954. There are numerous other reprintings of *Leaves of Grass*, hardcover and paperback.

*Walt Whitman of the New York Aurora: Editor at Twenty-Two*, eds. Joseph Jay Rubin and Charles H. Brown, State College, Pa., 1950, is a collection of recently discovered writings. *Walt Whitman Looks at the Schools*, ed. Florence Bernstein Freedman, New York, 1950, is a group of articles on schools and the education of youth which appeared in the Brooklyn *Evening Star* and the Brooklyn *Daily Eagle*. *The Eighteenth Presidency!* has been re-edited by Edward F. Grier, Lawrence, Kansas, 1956.

Two useful collections are *The Best of Whitman*, ed. Harold W. Blodgett, New York, 1953, and *The Whitman Reader*, ed. Maxwell Geismar, New York, 1955. *Walt Whitman's Poems*, eds. Gay Wilson Allen and Charles T. Davis, New York, 1955, is the first volume of selections which also provides the student with detailed critical notes to each poem and general guidance in a full introduction to Whitman's poetry.

### 763. BIOGRAPHY AND CRITICISM

The most inclusive biography is Gay Wilson Allen, *The Solitary Singer, A Critical Biography*, New York, 1955. An enormously detailed work which is equally biography and criticism is Roger Asselineau, *L'Evolution de Walt Whitman après la première édition des Feuilles d'Herbes*, Paris, 1954. The Danish scholar Frederick Schyberg published *Walt Whitman* in Copenhagen, 1933; in 1951 it was translated into English by Evie Allison Allen, with an introduction by Gay Wilson Allen. Taken together, these three volumes are an invaluable addition to Whitman studies.

Recent full-length critical analyses are not as numerous as one might expect. The second part of Roger Asselineau's *L'Evolution de Walt Whitman* ("La Création d'une Œuvre") is especially useful. Richard Chase's *Walt Whitman Reconsidered*, New York, 1955, places the poet among his nineteenth-century contemporaries. James E. Miller, Jr., *A Critical Guide to Leaves of Grass,* Chicago, 1957, is a series of essays on the major poems. Two collections of critical essays also appeared in the centennial year: Leaves of Grass *One Hundred Years After,* Stanford, 1955 (containing essays by various critics), and *Walt Whitman: Man, Poet, and Philosopher,* Washington, 1955 (three lectures delivered at the Library of Congress by Gay Wilson Allen, Mark Van Doren, and David Daiches). Gay Wilson Allen also edited *Walt Whitman Abroad: Critical Essays from Germany, France . . . ,* Syracuse, 1955.

Specialized studies are Nathan Resnick, *Walt Whitman and the Authorship of the Good Gray Poet,* New York, 1948; Charles B. Willard, *Whitman's American Fame: The Growth of His Reputation in America After 1892,* Providence, 1950; Joseph Beaver, *Walt Whitman, Poet of Science,* New York, 1951; R. D. Faner, *Walt Whitman and Opera,* Philadelphia, 1951; and Fernando Alegría, *Walt Whitman en Hispanoamérica,* Mexico City, 1954. Edwin Harold Eby's *Concordance of Walt Whitman's Leaves of Grass and Selected Prose Writings,* Seattle, 1949–1954, published in five fascicles, is now complete.

Briefer critical studies are Joseph Beaver, "Walt Whitman, Star-Gazer," *JEGP,* XLVIII (1949), 307–319; Leo Spitzer, "'Explication de Texte' Applied to Walt Whitman's 'Out of the Cradle Endlessly Rocking,'" *ELH,* XVI (1949), 229–249; William L. Finkel, "Walt Whitman's Manuscript Notes on Oratory," *AL,* XXII (1950), 29–53; Alice L. Cooke, "A Note on Whitman's Symbolism in 'Song of Myself,'" *MLN,* LXV (1950), 228–232; R. W. B. Lewis, "The Danger of Innocence: Adam as Hero in American Literature," *YR,* XXXIX (1950), 473–490; Charles H. Brown, "Young Editor Whitman: An Individualist in Journalism," *JQ,* XXVII (1950), 141–148; Edward F. Grier, "Walt Whitman, The *Galaxy,* and *Democratic Vistas,*" *AL,* XXIII (1951), 332–350; Ferner Nuhn, *"Leaves of Grass* Viewed as an Epic," *ArQ,* VII (1951), 324–338; Alfred Marks, "Whitman's Triadic Imagery," *AL,* XXIII (1951), 99–126; Floyd Stovall, "Whitman's Knowledge of Shakespeare," *SP,* XLIX (1952), 643–669; *idem,* "Whitman, Shakespeare, and Democracy," *JEGP,* LI (1952), 457–472; W. Gordon Milne, "William Douglas O'Connor and the Authorship of *The Good Gray Poet,*" *AL,* XXV (1953), 31–42; Esther Shephard, "An Inquiry into Whitman's Method of Turning Prose into Poetry," *MLQ,* XIV (1953), 43–59; *idem,* "Possible Sources of Some of Whitman's Ideas and Symbols in *Hermes Mercurius Trismegistus* and Other Works," *MLQ,* XIV (1953), 60–81; Randall Jarrell, "Some Lines from Whitman," *Poetry and the Age,* New York, 1953, pp. 112–132; Fredson Bowers, "Whitman's Manuscripts for the Original 'Calamus' Poems," *SB,* VI (1953–54), 257–265.

Other studies are W. D. Templeman, "Hopkins and Whitman: Evidence of Influence and Echoes," *PQ,* XXXIII (1954), 48–65; Stanley K. Coffman, Jr., "'Crossing Brooklyn Ferry': A Note on the Catalogue Technique in

Whitman's Poetry," *MP*, LI (1954), 225–232; G. Ferris Cronkhite, "Walt Whitman and the Locomotive," *AQ*, VI (1954), 164–172; Georgiana Pollak, "The Relationship of Music to 'Leaves of Grass,'" *CE*, XV (1954), 384–394; Herbert Bergman, "Whitman and Tennyson," *SP*, LI (1954), 492–504; Fredson Bowers, "The Manuscript of Walt Whitman's 'A Carol of Harvest, for 1867,'" *MP*, LII (1954), 29–51; Floyd Stovall, "Notes on Whitman's Reading," *AL*, XXVI (1954), 337–362; Herbert Bergman, "Ezra Pound and Walt Whitman," *AL*, XXVII (1955), 56–61; Emory Holloway, "Walt Whitman Pursued," *AL*, XXVII (1955), 1–11; Richard P. Adams, "Whitman: A Brief Revaluation," *TSE*, V (1955), 111–149; R. W. Flint, "The Living Whitman," *PR*, XXII (1955), 391–399; A. Schiller, "Thoreau and Whitman: The Record of a Pilgrimage," *NEQ*, XXVIII (1955), 186–197; Stanley K. Coffman, Jr., "Form and Meaning in Whitman's 'Passage to India,'" *PMLA*, LXX (1955), 337–349; James E. Miller, Jr., "'Song of Myself' as Inverted Mystical Experience," *PMLA*, LXX (1955), 636–661; Phyl and Pierre Hentgès, "Walt Whitman, poète d'un nouveau monde," *Nouvelle Critique*, No. 68 (Sept.–Oct., 1955), 84–104; B. R. McElderry, Jr., "Hamlin Garland's View of Whitman," *Personalist*, XXXVI (1955), 369–378; Maurice Mendelson, "Leaves of Grass," *Soviet Literature* (Moscow), No. 7 (1955), 161–167; Perry Miller, "The Shaping of the American Character," *NEQ*, XXVIII (1955), 435–454; Egbert S. Oliver, "'The Seas Are All Cross'd': Whitman on America and World Freedom," *WHR*, IX (1955), 303–312; and Charles A. Allen, "The Whitman Centenary: A Publisher's View," *NMQ*, XXV (1955–56), 387–392.

More recent studies are C. E. Pulos, "Whitman and Epictetus: The Stoical Element in *Leaves of Grass*," *JEGP*, LV (1956), 75–84; Joseph J. Kwiat, "Robert Henri and the Emerson-Whitman Tradition," *PMLA*, LXXI (1956), 617–636; George A. Peek, Jr., "Walt Whitman and Politics," *MAQR*, LXII (1956), 254–261; Lorenzo D. Turner, "Walt Whitman and the Negro," *CJF*, XV (1956), 5–11; Sholom J. Kahn, "Whitman's 'Black Lucifer': Some Possible Sources," *PMLA*, LXXI (1956), 932–944; B. R. McElderry, Jr., "The Inception of 'Passage to India,'" *PMLA*, LXXI (1956), 837–839; Samuel Sillen, "Walt Whitman, poète de la démocratie américaine," *La Pensée*, No. 69 (Sept., 1956), 77–91; No. 70 (Dec., 1956), 69–82; Harry R. Warfel, "Whitman's Structural Principles in 'Spontaneous Me,'" *CE*, XVIII (1957), 190–195; Sydney J. Krause, "Whitman, Music, and *Proud Music of the Storm*," *PMLA*, LXXII (1957), 705–721; and Fredson Bowers, "The Earliest Manuscript of Whitman's 'Passage to India' and Its Notebook," *BNYPL*, LXI (1957), 319–352.

## 768. BIBLIOGRAPHY

In addition to Gay Wilson Allen's *Walt Whitman Handbook* (1946), the most useful critical bibliography is by Willard Thorp in *Eight*

*American Authors: A Review of Research and Criticism,* ed. Floyd Stovall, New York, 1956. Roger Asselineau's *L'Evolution de Walt Whitman,* Paris, 1954, contains a seventeen-page bibliography. Evie A. Allen and Gay Wilson Allen prepared a "Walt Whitman Bibliography, 1944–1954" for the *Walt Whitman Foundation Bulletin* (Apr., 1955); it is especially useful for a study of Whitman's reputation since World War II. See also Harold W. Blodgett, "Bibliographical Description as a Key to Whitman," *Walt Whitman Newsletter,* II (Mar.–June, 1956), 8–9; and William White, "Bibliography," *Walt Whitman Newsletter,* II (Sept., 1956), 29; III (Mar., 1957), 13–14.

Catalogues of Whitman exhibitions and collections are vital to the Whitman bibliography. More than 1,000 items owned by the Library of Congress are listed in *Walt Whitman, a Catalog Based upon the Collections of the Library of Congress* (with notes on Whitman Collections and Collectors), Washington, 1955. Charles E. Feinberg, one of the great Whitman collectors, compiled for the Detroit Library Exhibition *Walt Whitman: A Selection of the Manuscripts, Books, and Association Items Gathered by Charles E. Feinberg,* Detroit, 1955. For the London Whitman Exhibit, Mr. Feinberg drew on eleven American collections; the United States Information Service issued the catalogue: *Walt Whitman: Catalogue of an Exhibition held at the American Library, London, March–April, 1954.* Lewis M. Stark and John D. Gordan compiled *Walt Whitman's Leaves of Grass: A Centenary Exhibition from the Lion Whitman Collection and the Berg Collection of the New York Public Library,* New York, 1955. Ernest Francis Amy has written *An Evaluation of Ohio Wesleyan University's Recently Acquired Walt Whitman Collection* (published separately as an off-print from the *Ohio Wesleyan Magazine,* June, 1955).

See also anon., "The Whitman Collection: Some New Manuscripts," *LCUP,* XIV (Apr., 1957), 29–31; Dorothy Bowen and Philip Durham, "Walt Whitman Materials in the Huntington Library," *HLQ,* XIX (Nov., 1955), 81–96; and Charles B. Willard, "The Saunders Collection of Whitmania in the Brown University Library," *Books at Brown,* XVIII (May, 1956), 14–22.


## JOHN GREENLEAF WHITTIER

**769.** COLLECTED WORKS AND CORRESPONDENCE

Walter McIntosh Merrill edited "Uncollected Early Poems by John Greenleaf Whittier," *EIHC,* XCI (1955), 128–146.

Martha Hale Shackford compiled *Whittier and the Cartlands, Letters and Comments,* Wakefield, Mass., 1950. Additional letters are Max L. Griffin, ed., "Whittier and Hayne: A Record of Friendship," *AL*, XIX (1947), 41–58; and R. Craig Fabian, ed., "Some Uncollected Letters of John Greenleaf Whittier to Gerritt Smith," *AL*, XXII (1950), 158–163.

770. BIOGRAPHY AND CRITICISM

The most recent full-length study is John A. Pollard, *John Greenleaf Whittier, Friend of Man*, Boston, 1949.

Briefer studies are Arlin Turner, "Whittier Calls on George W. Cable," *NEQ*, XXII (1949), 92–96; Osborn T. Smallwood, "The Historical Significance of Whittier's Anti-Slavery Poems as Reflected by Their Political and Social Background," *JNH*, XXXV (1950), 150–173; Arlin Thaler, "Whittier and the English Poets," *NEQ*, XXIV (1951), 53–68; C. Marshall Taylor, "Whittier Set to Music," *EIHC*, LXXXVIII (1952), 24–27; Cecil B. Williams, "Whittier's Relation to Garrison and the 'Liberator,'" *NEQ*, XXV (1952), 248–254; Joseph M. Ernest, Jr., "Whittier and Whitman: Uncongenial Personalities," *BFHA*, XLII (1953), 85–89; Edward D. Snyder, "Seventy Years of Whittier Biographies," *ibid.*, XLIII (1954), 1–14; and J. Zanger, "A Note on Skipper Ireson's Ride," *NEQ*, XXIX (1956), 236–238.

772. BIBLIOGRAPHY

Of biographical interest is C. Marshall Taylor, "Some Whittier First Editions Published in the British Isles," *Jour. Friends' Hist. Soc.*, XLII (1950), 41–45.

## MICHAEL WIGGLESWORTH

773. EDITED TEXTS AND REPRINTS

Edmund S. Morgan edited "The Diary of Michael Wigglesworth," *Pub. Colonial Soc. Mass. (Transactions 1942–1946)*, XXXV (1951), 311–444.

## ROGER WILLIAMS

775. BIOGRAPHY AND CRITICISM

A recent biographical study is Ola Elizabeth Winslow, *Master Roger Williams: A Biography*, New York, 1957. Perry Miller's *Roger Williams, His Contribution to the American Tradition*, Indianapolis, 1953, deals more directly with Williams' influence.

Briefer studies are Clinton Rossiter, "Roger Williams on the Anvil of Experience," *AQ*, III (1951), 14–21; Maxwell H. Morris, "Roger Williams and the Jews," *Amer. Jewish Archives*, III (1951), 24–27; Randall Stewart, "Rhode Island Literature," *RIH*, XII (1953), 97–105; Mauro Calamandrei,

"Neglected Aspects of Roger Williams' Thought," *CH*, XXI (1952), 239–258; and Alan Simpson, "How Democratic Was Roger Williams?" *WMQ*, XIII (1956), 53–67.

## WILLIAM CARLOS WILLIAMS

776. SEPARATE WORKS

*Paterson, Book II*, 1948; *A Dream of Love*, 1948; *The Clouds*, 1948; *Paterson, Book III*, 1949; *The Pink Church*, 1949; *Paterson, Book IV*, 1951; *The Autobiography of William Carlos Williams*, 1951; *The Build-Up*, 1952; *The Desert Music, and Other Poems*, 1954; *Journey to Love*, 1955; *John Marin* (with Duncan Phillips and others), 1956; *Paterson, Book V*, 1958. *Many Loves*, a play, was produced in 1958.

777. COLLECTED WORKS AND CORRESPONDENCE

*The Collected Later Poems of William Carlos Williams* appeared in New York, 1950, *The Collected Earlier Poems of William Carlos Williams* in New York, 1951. *Make Light of It*, New York, 1950, is a collection of short stories. *Selected Essays* appeared in New York, 1954.

Randall Jarrell provided an introduction to *Selected Poems*, New York, 1949.

John C. Thirlwall edited *The Selected Letters of William Carlos Williams*, New York, 1957.

BIOGRAPHY AND CRITICISM

The first full-length study is Vivienne Koch, *William Carlos Williams*, Norfolk, Conn., 1950.

*Briarcliff Quarterly*, III (Oct., 1946), is a Williams issue containing five contributions (prose and poetry) by Williams and twelve articles, letters, comments on Williams by various hands. *Western Review*, XVII (Summer, 1953), contains "American Letters: A Symposium," which is an article by Russell Roth, "In the American Grain," followed by comments on this article by Elizabeth Hardwick, Robert B. Heilman, and William Van O'Connor. *Perspective*, VI (Autumn–Winter, 1953), is a Williams issue containing seven critical studies.

Other estimates are Frederick Morgan, "William Carlos Williams: Imagery, Rhythm, Form," *SR*, LV (1947), 675–690; Robert Lowell, "Paterson II," *Nation*, CLXVI (June 19, 1948), 692–694; Randall Jarrell, "A View of Three Poets," *PR*, XVIII (1951), 691–700; Joseph Bennett, "The Lyre and the Sledgehammer," *HudR*, V (1952), 295–307; Richard Ellmann, "William Carlos Williams: The Doctor in Search of Himself," *KR*, XIV (1952), 510–512; Vivienne Koch, "William Carlos Williams: The Man and the

Poet," *KR*, XIV (1952), 502–510; *idem*, "Williams: The Social Mask," *Poetry*, LXXX (1952), 89–95; R. L. Beum, "The Neglect of Williams," *Poetry*, LXXX (1952), 291–293; Frederick J. Hoffman, "Williams and His Muse," *Poetry*, LXXXIV (1954), 23–27; Frank Thompson, "The Symbolic Structure of *Paterson*," *WR*, XIX (1955), 285–293; Paola Bompard, "Profilo di William Carlos Williams," *SA*, I (1955), 235–255; and Sister M. Bernetta Quinn, "William Carlos Williams: A Testament of Perpetual Change," *PMLA*, LXX (1955), 292–322.

For a listing of explications of indiviual poems see George Arms and Joseph M. Kuntz, *Poetry Explication*, New York, 1950, pp. 161–162.

BIBLIOGRAPHY

A recent listing is Allen Tate, *Sixty American Poets, 1896–1944*, rev. ed., Washington, 1954, pp. 143–146. Edith Heal, ed., *I Wanted to Write a Poem: The Autobiography of the Works of a Poet*, Boston, 1958, is a catalogue-bibliography of Williams' books and pamphlets with the poet's own reminiscences of their publication and an account of his writing methods.

# (THOMAS) WOODROW WILSON

### 779. COLLECTED WORKS AND REPRINTS

Arthur S. Link is editor in chief of the comprehensive edition of the Wilson letters and papers being prepared for publication by the Woodrow Wilson Foundation. John Wells Davidson is associate editor. The project is expected to total thirty volumes.

*Cabinet Government in the United States* (first published in the *International Review*, Aug., 1879) was reprinted, with an introduction by Thomas K. Finletter, Stamford, Conn., 1947. *Leaders of Men*, now first published from an 1890 manuscript in the Woodrow Wilson Collection in the Library of Congress, was edited with an introduction and notes by T. H. Vail Motter, Princeton, 1952. *The Study of Public Administration* (first published in the *Political Science Quarterly*, June, 1887) was reprinted with an introduction by Ralph Purcell, Washington, 1955. *Congressional Government: A Study in American Politics* (1885) was reprinted, with an introduction by Walter Lippmann, New York, 1956.

John Wells Davidson edited *A Crossroads of Freedom: The 1912 Campaign Speeches of Woodrow Wilson*, New Haven, 1956. Additional speeches are in *The Politics of Woodrow Wilson: Selections from His Speeches and Writings*, ed. August Heckscher, New York, 1956.

Two compilations of Wilson's writings are *Woodrow Wilson's Own Story*, selected and edited by Donald Day, Boston, 1952, and *The Wilson Reader*, edited by Frances Farmer, New York, 1956, containing a biographical sketch by the editor and excerpts from Wilson's writings as well as from contemporaneous writing about Wilson.

### 780. BIOGRAPHY AND CRITICISM

Arthur S. Link continues his extended biography in *Wilson: The New Freedom*, Princeton, 1956. A more recent lengthy study is Arthur Walworth, *Woodrow Wilson*, 2 vols., New York, 1958. Herbert Hoover writes from personal experience in *The Ordeal of Woodrow Wilson*, New York, 1958.

Briefer lives are E. M. Hugh-Jones, *Woodrow Wilson and American Liberalism*, New York, 1948; McMillan Lewis, *Woodrow Wilson of Princeton*, Narberth, Pa., 1952; John Arthur Garraty, *Woodrow Wilson: A Great Life in Brief*, New York, 1956; Alexander L. and Juliette L. George, *Woodrow Wilson and Colonel House: A Personality Study*, New York, 1956; John Morton Blum, *Woodrow Wilson and the Politics of Morality*, Boston, 1956; and Silas Bent McKinley, *Woodrow Wilson: A Biography*, New York, 1957.

Studies of the political scene include Tien-yi Li, *Woodrow Wilson's China Policy, 1913–1917*, New York, 1952; Edward H. Buehrig, *Woodrow Wilson and the Balance of Power*, Bloomington, Ind., 1955; Paul Mantoux, *Les délibérations du conseil des quatres*, 2 vols., Paris, 1955; Victor S. Mamatey, *The United States and East Central Europe, 1914–1918: A Study in Wilsonian Diplomacy and Propaganda*, Princeton, 1957; and two volumes by Arthur S. Link: *Woodrow Wilson and the Progressive Era, 1910–1917*, New York, 1954, and *Wilson the Diplomatist: A Look at His Major Foreign Policies*, Baltimore, 1957.

See also, *passim*, John Morton Blum, *Joe Tumulty and the Wilson Era*, Boston, 1951; Jonathan Daniels, *The End of Innocence*, Philadelphia, 1954; and George F. Kennan, *Soviet-American Relations, 1917–1920*, 2 vols., Princeton, 1956–1958 (a third volume to follow).

Special issues of journals and collections of essays and speeches commemorated the Wilson centennial. See Em Bowles Alsop, ed., *The Greatness of Woodrow Wilson, 1856–1956*, New York, 1956; *Centenaire Woodrow Wilson, 1856–1956*, Geneva, 1956; *Florida State University Studies*, No. 23, *Woodrow Wilson Centennial Issue*, ed. Victor S. Mamatey, Tallahassee, 1956; *Lectures and Seminar at the University of Chicago . . . in Celebration of the Centennial of Woodrow Wilson, 1856–1956*, Chicago, 1956; Arthur P. Dudden, ed., *Woodrow Wilson and the World Today*, Philadelphia, 1957; Edward H. Buehrig, ed., *Wilson's Foreign Policy in Perspective*, Bloomington, Ind., 1957; and these journals: *Johns Hopkins Magazine*. VII (Mar., 1956); *Princeton University Library Chronicle*, XVII (Spring, 1956); *Virginia Quarterly Review*, XXXII (Autumn, 1956); and *Confluence*, V (Autumn, 1956, and Winter, 1957).

Briefer studies are Dexter Perkins, "Woodrow Wilson: An Interpretation," *Trans. Royal Hist. Soc.*, XXIX (1947), 115-134; John L. Snell, "Wilson's Peace Program and German Socialism, Jan.-Mar., 1918," *MVHR*, XXXVIII (1951), 187-214; Wesley M. Bagby, "Woodrow Wilson, a Third Term, and the Solemn Referendum," *AHR*, LX (1955), 567-575; Charles Seymour, "Woodrow Wilson in Perspective," *For. Affairs*, XXXIV (1956), 175-186; Louis Brownlow, "Woodrow Wilson and Public Administration," *Pub. Admin. Rev.*, XVI (1956), 77-81; George C. Osborn, "Woodrow Wilson and Frederick Jackson Turner," *PNJHS*, LXXIV (1956), 208-229; Robert H. Ferrell, "Woodrow Wilson: Man and Statesman," *RPol*, XVIII (1956), 131-145; Henry A. Turner, "Woodrow Wilson as Administrator," *Pub. Admin. Rev.*, XVI (1956), 249-257; Raymond B. Fosdick, "Woodrow Wilson Among His Friends," *Harper's*, CCXIII (1956), 57-63; Dwight L. Dumond, "Woodrow Wilson: A Century View," *MAQR*, LXIII (1956), 64-74; Edward Younger, "Woodrow Wilson—The Making of a Leader," *VMHB*, LXIV (1956), 387-401; and Earl Pomeroy, "Woodrow Wilson: The End of His First Century," *Oregon Hist. Quar.*, LVII (1956), 315-332.

By far the best survey of recent Wilson studies is Richard L. Watson, "Woodrow Wilson and His Interpreters, 1947-1957," *MVHR*, XLIV (1957), 207-236.

**781.** PRIMARY SOURCES

See Alexander P. Clark, "The Woodrow Wilson Collection: A Survey of Additions Since 1945," *PULC*, XVII (1956), 173-184.

BIBLIOGRAPHY

Laura Shearer Turnbull, *Woodrow Wilson: A Selected Bibliography of His Published Writings, Addresses, and Public Papers*, Princeton, 1948, lists 1,061 items and in addition includes "Newspaper Reports of Woodrow Wilson's Speeches, Statements, and Papers, 1910-1912" (compiled by Arthur S. Link) and "Books in the Woodrow Wilson Field" (compiled by Katherine E. Brand).

More recent bibliographical articles are Katherine E. Brand, "Woodrow Wilson, in His Own Time," *LCQJ*, XIII (1956), 61-72, and anon., "Catalog of the Woodrow Wilson Centennial Exhibit," *ibid.*, 73-105. Arthur S. Link's *Woodrow Wilson and the Progressive Era*, New York, 1954, contains a bibliographical essay.

# JOHN WINTHROP

**782.** EDITED TEXTS AND REPRINTS

The publication of the *Winthrop Papers*, Vol. V (1947), covering the years 1645-1649, completes the edition of Winthrop's manuscript journal begun in 1929 under the general editorship of Allyn B. Forbes for the Massachusetts Historical Society.

BIOGRAPHY AND CRITICISM

A recent study is Edmund S. Morgan, *The Puritan Dilemma: The Story of John Winthrop,* Boston, 1958. See also Milton Rubincam, "A Winthrop-Bernadotte Pedigree," *NEGHR,* CIII (1949), 246–253; and B. Katherine Brown, "A Note on the Puritan Concept of Aristocracy," *MVHR,* XLI (1954), 105–112.

## JOHN WISE

**784.** BIOGRAPHY AND CRITICISM

A biographical study is George Allan Cook, *John Wise, Early American Democrat,* New York, 1952. See also Clinton L. Rossiter, "John Wise: Colonial Democrat," *NEQ,* XXII (1949), 3–32; and R. M. Gummere, "John Wise: A Classical Controversialist," *EIHC,* XCII (1956), 265–278.

## THOMAS (CLAYTON) WOLFE

**784.** SEPARATE WORKS

*Mannerhouse: A Play in a Prologue and Three Acts,* 1948; ". . . The Years of Wandering in Many Lands and Cities,"* 1949; *A Western Journal: A Daily Log of the Great Parks Trip, June 20–July 2, 1938,* 1951.

COLLECTED WORKS, CORRESPONDENCE, AND REPRINTS

*The Letters of Thomas Wolfe* were collected and edited by Elizabeth Nowell, New York, 1956. A briefer volume is *The Correspondence of Thomas Wolfe and Homer Andrew Watt,* eds. Oscar Cargill and Thomas Clark Pollock, New York, 1954. See also "The Last Letter of Thomas Wolfe and the Reply to It," *HLB,* I (1947), 278–279; and Robert D. Meade, ed., " 'You Can't Escape Autobiography': New Letters of Thomas Wolfe," *Atl,* CLXXXVI (Nov., 1950), 80–83.

Maxwell Geismar edited *The Portable Thomas Wolfe,* New York, 1950. Reprints of individual novels are too numerous to list separately.

**785.** BIOGRAPHY AND CRITICISM

Full-length studies are Herbert J. Muller, *Thomas Wolfe,* Norfolk, Conn., 1947; Pamela Hansford Johnson, *Hungry Gulliver: An English Critical Appraisal of Thomas Wolfe,* New York, 1948 (published in England under the title *Thomas Wolfe: A Critical Study);* Daniel L. Delakas,

*Thomas Wolfe, la France et les romanciers français,* Paris, 1950; Karin Pfister, *Zeit und Wirklichkeit bei Thomas Wolfe,* Heidelberg, 1954; Louis D. Rubin, *Thomas Wolfe, the Weather of His Youth,* Baton Rouge, 1955; George M. Reeves, Jr., *Thomas Wolfe et l'Europe,* Paris, 1955; and Floyd C. Watkins, *Thomas Wolfe's Characters,* Norman, Okla., 1957.

Collections of essays on Wolfe are Richard Walser, ed., *The Enigma of Thomas Wolfe: Biographical and Critical Selections,* Cambridge, Mass., 1953, and Thomas Clark Pollock and Oscar Cargill, eds., *Thomas Wolfe at Washington Square,* New York, 1954.

Briefer studies are Maxwell E. Perkins, "Thomas Wolfe," *Harvard Lib. Bul.,* I (1947), 269–277; Edward C. Aswell and J. S. Terry, "En Route to a Legend: Two Interpretations of Thomas Wolfe," *SRL,* XXXI (Nov. 27, 1948), 1–3, 34–36; W. M. Frohock, "Thomas Wolfe: Of Time and Neurosis," *SR,* XXXIII (1948), 349–360; B. R. McElderry, Jr., "The Autobiographical Problem in Thomas Wolfe's Earlier Novels," *ArQ,* IV (1948), 315–324; W. W. Pusey, III, "The German Vogue of Thomas Wolfe," *GR,* XXIII (1948), 131–148; Richard Walser, "Some Notes on Wolfe's Reputation Abroad," *CaQ,* I (1949), 37–48; W. P. Albrecht, "Time as Unity in Thomas Wolfe," *NMQR,* XIX (1949), 320–329; Oscar Cargill, "Gargantua Fills His Skin," *UKCR,* XVI (1949), 20–30; Margaret Church, "Thomas Wolfe: Dark Time," *PMLA,* LXIV (1949), 629–638; W. P. Albrecht, "The Title of *Look Homeward, Angel: A Story of the Buried Life,*" *MLQ,* XI (1950), 50–57; Richard S. Kennedy, "Thomas Wolfe at Harvard, 1920–1923," *HLB,* IV (1950), 172–190, 304–319; Struthers Burt, "Catalyst for Genius: Maxwell Perkins, 1884–1947," *SRL,* XXXIV (June 9, 1951), 6–8, 36–39; Edward C. Aswell, "Thomas Wolfe Did Not Kill Maxwell Perkins," *SRL,* XXXIV (Oct. 11, 1951), 16–17, 44–46; Paul Jaffard, "L'Œuvre de Thomas Wolfe," *Critique,* VII (1951), 686–693; Marcel Brion "Thomas Wolfe," *Revue des Deux Mondes,* No. 16 (1952), 731–740; Louis D. Rubin, Jr., "Thomas Wolfe in Time and Place," *Southern Renascence,* ed. Louis D. Rubin, Jr., and Robert D. Jacobs, Baltimore, 1953, pp. 290–305; Walter Fuller Taylor, "Thomas Wolfe and the Middle-Class Tradition," *SAQ,* LII (1953), 543–554; George W. McCoy, "Asheville and Thomas Wolfe," *NCHR,* XXX (1953), 200–217; Floyd C. Watkins, "Thomas Wolfe and the Nashville Agrarians," *GaR,* VII (1953), 410–423; Edward Stone, "The Paving Stones of Paris: Psychometry from Poe to Proust," *AQ,* V (1953), 121–131; Horst Frenz, "Bemerkungen über Thomas Wolfe," *NS,* Heft 9 (1953), 371–377; H. M. Ledig-Rowohlt, "Thomas Wolfe in Berlin," *ASch,* XXII (1953), 185–201.

More recent studies are B. R. McElderry, Jr., "The Durable Humor of *Look Homeward, Angel,*" *ArQ,* XI (1955), 123–128; Eugene Tedd, "'Hours of Hell and Anguish,'" *PrS,* XXIX (1955), 95–108; Cecil B. Williams, "Thomas Wolfe Fifteen Years After," *SAQ,* LIV (1955), 523–537; Martin

Maloney, "A Study of Semantic States: Thomas Wolfe and the Faustian Sickness," *Gen. Semantics Bul.*, Nos. 16 & 17 (1955), 15–25; F. David Martin, "The Artist, Autobiography, and Thomas Wolfe," *BuR*, V (1955), 15–28; Horst Frenz, "A German Home for 'Mannerhouse,'" *TArts*, XL (Aug., 1956), 62–63, 95; Malcolm Cowley, "The Life and Death of Thomas Wolfe," *New Rep*, CXXXV (Nov. 19, 1956), 17–21; Floyd C. Watkins, "Thomas Wolfe's High Sinfulness of Poetry," *MFS*, II (1956–1957), 197–206; Maurice Natanson, "The Privileged Moment: A Study in the Rhetoric of Thomas Wolfe," *QJS*, XLIII (1957), 143–150; and Daniel L. Delakas, "Thomas Wolfe and Anatole France: A Study of Some Unpublished Experiments," *CL*, IX (1957), 33–50.

Of bibliographical interest is Thomas Little, "The Thomas Wolfe Collection of William B. Wisdom [at Harvard College Library]," *HLB*, I (1947), 280–287.

# GEORGE EDWARD WOODBERRY

### 787. BIOGRAPHY AND CRITICISM

Three studies are Richard B. Hovey, "George Edward Woodberry: Genteel Exile," *NEQ*, XXIII (1950), 504–526; Martha Hale Shackford, "George Edward Woodberry as Critic," *NEQ*, XXIV (1951), 510–527; and James Thurber, "Photograph Album: Man with a Pipe," *NY*, XXVII (Aug. 25, 1951), 33–41.

*Addresses at the University Convocation in Honor of George Edward Woodberry, 12 May 1948* was published by the Columbia University Press, New York, 1948.

### BIBLIOGRAPHY

The most recent check list is Joseph Doyle, "George Edward Woodberry: A Bibliography," *BB*, XXI (1955), 136–139, 163–168, 176–181, 209–214. See also Joseph Doyle, "A Finding List of Manuscript Materials Relating to George Edward Woodberry," *PBSA*, XLVI (1952), 165–168.

# JOHN WOOLMAN

### 787. SEPARATE WORKS

The most recent edition of *The Journal of John Woolman* is that of Janet Whitney, Chicago, 1950.

788. BIOGRAPHY AND CRITICISM

A study which combines criticism with text is Reginald Reynolds, *The Wisdom of John Woolman, with a Selection from His Writings as a Guide to the Seekers of Today,* London, 1948. Catherine Owens Peare, *John Woolman: Child of Light,* New York, 1954, is a biographical study.

Briefer estimates are P. Douglas, "Two Eighteenth-Century Philadelphians: Benjamin Franklin and John Woolman," *GMHC.* LIV (1952), 131–138; and Gerhard Friedrich, "Theodore Dreiser's Debt to Woolman's *Journal,*" *AQ,* VII (1955), 385–392.


# RICHARD WRIGHT

789. WRITINGS

*The Outsider,* 1953; *Black Power: A Record of Reactions in a Land of Pathos,* 1954; *The Color Curtain, a Report on the Bandung Conference,* 1956; *Pagan Spain,* 1957; *White Man, Listen!,* 1957; *The Long Dream,* 1958.

See also Richard Crossman, ed., *The God That Failed,* New York, 1949, pp. 115–162.

BIOGRAPHY AND CRITICISM

Recent estimates are Alain Locke, "From *Native Son* to *Invisible Man:* A Review of the Literature of the Negro for 1952," *Phylon,* XIV (1953), 34–44; Nick Aaron Ford, "The Ordeal of Richard Wright," *CE,* XV (1953), 87–94; *idem,* "Four Popular Negro Novelists," *Phylon,* XV (1954), 29–39; Alfred Maund, "The Negro Novelist and the Contemporary Scene," *CJF,* XIII (1954), 28–34; Arthur P. Davis, " 'The Outsider' as a Novel of Race," *MJ,* VII (1955–1956), 320–326; and Nathan A. Scott, "Search for Beliefs: Fiction of Richard Wright," *UKCR,* XXIII (1956), 19–24, 131–138.

M. D. Sprague prepared "Richard Wright: A Bibliography," *BB,* XXI (1953), 39.

# BIBLIOGRAPHIES: ADDITIONAL INDIVIDUAL AUTHORS

John Peale Bishop
R. P. Blackmur
Kenneth Burke
James Gould Cozzens
Caroline Gordon
J. P. Marquand
John O'Hara
John Crowe Ransom
Robert E. Sherwood
Booth Tarkington
Allen Tate
Albion W. Tourgée
Carl Van Vechten
Robert Penn Warren
Thornton Wilder
Edmund Wilson

# JOHN PEALE BISHOP
*1891–1944*

SEPARATE WORKS

Poetry: *Green Fruit,* 1917; *Now with His Love,* 1933; *Minute Particulars,* 1935; *Selected Poems,* 1941.

Fiction: *Many Thousands Gone,* 1931; *Act of Darkness,* 1935.

Miscellaneous: *The Undertaker's Garland* (with Edmund Wilson), 1922; *American Harvest, Twenty Years of Creative Writing in the United States* (edited with Allen Tate), 1942.


COLLECTIONS

*The Collected Poems of John Peale Bishop* was edited with a preface and a personal memoir by Allen Tate, New York, 1948. *The Collected Essays of John Peale Bishop* was edited with an introduction by Edmund Wilson, New York, 1948. *A Southern Vanguard: The John Peale Bishop Memorial Volume,* ed. Allen Tate, New York, 1947, is an anthology of stories, poems, and critical essays offered for the John Peale Bishop Memorial Prize.


BIOGRAPHY AND CRITICISM

Critical estimates are Robert Penn Warren, "Working Toward Freedom," *Poetry,* XLIII (1934), 342–346; Allen Tate, *Reactionary Essays on Poetry and Ideas,* New York, 1936, pp. 52–63; anon., "John Peale Bishop '17," *PULC,* VII (1946), 55–56; Robert W. Stallman, "The Poetry of John Peale Bishop," *WR,* XI (1946), 4–19; Joseph Frank, "Force and Form: A Study of John Peale Bishop," *SR,* LV (1947), 71–107; Allen Tate, "John Peale Bishop: A Personal Memoir," *WR,* XII (1948), 67–71; Stanley Edgar Hyman, "Notes on the Organic Unity of John Peale Bishop," *Accent,* IX (1949), 102–113; William Arrowsmith, "An Artist's Estate," *HudR,* II (1949), 118–127; Robert W. Stallman, "The Poetry of John Peale Bishop," *Southern Renascence,* ed. Louis D. Rubin, Jr., and Robert D. Jacobs, Baltimore, 1953, pp. 368–391; Jesse Bier, "John Peale Bishop: The Memory Lingers On," *WHR,* IX (1955), 243–248.

For a listing of explications of specific poems, see George Arms and Joseph M. Kuntz, *Poetry Explication,* New York, 1950, pp. 30–32.

A bibliographical listing is in Fred B. Millett, *Contemporary American Authors,* New York, 1940, pp. 252–253. See also J. Max Patrick and Robert W. Stallman, "John Peale Bishop: A Checklist," *PULC,* VII (1946), 62–79; and Allen Tate, *Sixty American Poets, 1869–1944,* rev. ed., Washington, D.C., 1954, pp. 13–14.

# R(ICHARD) P(ALMER) BLACKMUR
*b. 1904*

SEPARATE WORKS

Essays: *The Double Agent*, 1935; *The Expense of Greatness*, 1940; *Language as Gesture*, 1952; *The Lion and the Honeycomb*, 1955; *Anni Mirabiles, 1921–1925*, 1956.

Poetry: *From Jordan's Delight*, 1937; *The Second World*, 1942; *The Good European and Other Poems*, 1947.

Pamphlets: *For Any Book*, 1924; *T. S. Eliot*, 1928; *Dirty Hands; or, The True-Born Censor*, 1930; *Psyche in the South*, 1934.

Editions: *The Art of the Novel, Critical Prefaces by Henry James* (with a critical introduction), 1934; *John Wheelwright: Selected Poems* (with a prefatory note), 1941.

BIOGRAPHY AND CRITICISM

Early critical estimates are C. H. Grattan, ed., *Critique of Humanism*, New York, 1930, pp. 237–254; Horace Gregory, "Two Critics in Search of an Absolute," *Nation*, CXXXVIII (1934), 189–191; P. B. Rice, "Death as an Island," *Nation*, CXLIV (1937), 512–514; Allen Tate, "R. P. Blackmur and Others," *SoR*, III (1937), 183–198; Delmore Schwartz, "The Critical Method of R. P. Blackmur," *Poetry*, LIII (1938), 28–39; Alfred Kazin, *On Native Grounds*, New York, 1942, pp. 431, 438–440; R. B. West, Jr., "An Examination of Modern Critics: R. P. Blackmur," *RMR*, VIII (1945), 139–145; Stanley Edgar Hyman, *The Armed Vision*, New York, 1948, pp. 239–271.

More recent studies are C. I. Glicksberg, *American Literary Criticism, 1900–1950*, New York, 1951, pp. 378–380; R. W. B. Lewis, "Casella as Critic: A Note on R. P. Blackmur," *KR*, XIII (1951), 458–474; Randall Jarrell, *Poetry and the Age*, New York, 1953, pp. 166–170; Louise Bogan, *Selected Criticism*, New York, 1955, pp. 191–194; Floyd Stovall, ed., *Development of Literary Criticism*, Chapel Hill, N.C., 1955, pp. 236–239; J. P. Pritchard, *Criticism in America*, Norman, Okla., 1956, pp. 256–261; Allan Angoff, ed., *American Writing Today*, New York, 1957, pp. 35-37.

For listing of explication of specific poems, see George Arms and Joseph M. Kuntz, *Poetry Explication*, New York, 1950, p. 32.

Bibliographical listings are Carlos Baker, "R. P. Blackmur: A Checklist," *PULC*, III (1942), 99–106; and Allen Tate, *Sixty American Poets, 1896–1944*, rev. ed., Washington, 1954, pp. 15-16.

# KENNETH (DUVA) BURKE
*b. 1897*

SEPARATE WORKS

Fiction: *The White Oxen and Other Stories*, 1924; *Towards a Better Life, Being a Series of Epistles or Declamations*, 1932.

Non-fiction: *Counter-Statement*, 1931; *Permanence and Change, An Anatomy of Purpose*, 1935; *Attitudes Toward History*, 1937; *The Philosophy of Literary Form*, 1941; *A Grammar of Motives*, 1945; *A Rhetoric of Motives*, 1950.

Poetry: *Book of Moments, Poems 1915–1954*, 1955.

Translations: *Death in Venice*, trans. from the German of Thomas Mann, 1925; *Genius and Character*, trans. from the German of Emil Ludwig, 1927; *Saint Paul*, trans. from the French of Emile Baumann, 1929.

BIOGRAPHY AND CRITICISM

Critical estimates are William Carlos Williams, "Kenneth Burke," *Dial*, LXXVI (1929), 6–8; Austin Warren, "Kenneth Burke: His Mind and Art," *SR*, XLI (1933), 344–364; A. E. DuBoise, "Accepting and Rejecting Kenneth Burke," *SR*, XLV (1937), 343–356; C. I. Glicksberg, "Kenneth Burke: The Critic's Critic," *SAQ*, XXXVI (1937), 74–84; H. B. Parkes, "Attitudes Toward History," *So. Rev.*, III (1938), 693–706; John Crowe Ransom, "An Address to Kenneth Burke," *KR*, IV (1942), 219–237; Howard Nemerov, "The Agon of Will as Idea: A Note on the Terms of Kenneth Burke," *Furioso*, II (Spring, 1947), 29–42; Marius Bewley, "Kenneth Burke as Literary Critic," *Scrutiny*, XV (1948), 254–277; B. I. Duffey, "Reality as Language: Kenneth Burke's Theory of Poetry," *WR*, XII (1948), 132–145; Stanley Edgar Hyman, *The Armed Vision*, New York, 1948, pp. 347–394; Allen Tate, "A Note on Autotelism," *KR*, XI (1949), 13–16; Marie Hochmuth, "Kenneth Burke and the 'New Rhetoric,'" *QJS*, XXXVIII (1952), 133–144; H. D. Duncan, *Language and Literature in Society*, Chicago, 1953, pp. 84–100; Herbert Blau, "Kenneth Burke: Tradition and the Individual Critic," *AQ*, VI (1954), 323–336; and L. Virginia Holland, "Kenneth Burke's Dramatistic Approach in Speech Criticism," *QJS*, XLI (1955), 352–358.

A bibliographical listing is in Fred B. Millett, *Contemporary American Authors*, New York, 1940, pp. 268–269.

# JAMES GOULD COZZENS
*b. 1903*

SEPARATE WORKS

*Confusion*, 1924; *Michael Scarlett*, 1925; *Cock Pit*, 1928; *The Son of Perdition*, 1929; *S. S. San Pedro*, 1931; *The Last Adam*, 1933; *Castaway*, 1934; *Men and Brethren*, 1936; *Ask Me Tomorrow*, 1940; *The Just and the Unjust*, 1942; *Guard of Honor*, 1948; *By Love Possessed*, 1957.

BIOGRAPHY AND CRITICISM

Critical estimates are Robert Van Gelder, "James Gould Cozzens at Work," *NYTBR*, June 23, 1940, p. 14; Stanley Edgar Hyman, "My Favorite Forgotten Book [*Castaway*]," *Tomorrow*, VII (May, 1947), 58–59; *idem*, "James Gould Cozzens and the Art of the Possible," *NMQ*, XIX (1949), 476–498; Bernard De Voto, "The Easy Chair," *Harper's*, CXCVIII (Feb., 1949), 72–73; Granville Hicks, "The Reputation of James Gould Cozzens," *CE*, XI (1950), 177–183; Frederick Bracher, "Of Youth and Age: James Gould Cozzens," *PS*, V (1951), 48–62; Orville Prescott, *In My Opinion: An Inquiry into the Contemporary Novel*, Indianapolis, 1952, pp. 180–191; Francis Fergusson, "Three Novels," *Perspectives USA*, No. 6 (1954), 30–44; Louis O. Coxe, "The Complex World of James Gould Cozzens," *AL*, XXVII (1955), 157–171; Chester E. Eisinger, "The American War Novel: An Affirming Flame," *PS*, IX (1955), 272–287; John Fischer, "Nomination for a Nobel Prize," *Harper's*, CCXV (Sept., 1957), 14–15, 18, 20; John W. Ward, "James Gould Cozzens and the Condition of Modern Man," *ASch*, XXVII (1957), 92–99; Richard M. Ludwig, "A Reading of the James Gould Cozzens Manuscripts," *PULC*, XIX (1957), 1–14; John Lydenberg, "Cozzens and the Critics," *CE*, XIX (1957), 99–104; Dwight Macdonald, "By Cozzens Possessed," *Commentary*, XXV (1958), 36–47; and Irving Howe, "James Gould Cozzens: Novelist of the Republic," *New Rep*, CXXXVIII (Jan. 20, 1958), 15–19.

*Critique: Studies in Modern Fiction* (Univ. of Minnesota), I (Winter, 1958), is a James Gould Cozzens issue. For this issue, James B. Meriwether prepared "A James Gould Cozzens Check List," the most complete bibliography to date.

# CAROLINE GORDON
*b. 1895*

SEPARATE WORKS

Novels: *Penhally*, 1931; *Aleck Maury, Sportsman*, 1934; *The Garden of Adonis*, 1937; *None Shall Look Back*, 1937; *Green Centuries*, 1941; *The*

*Women on the Porch*, 1944; *The Strange Children*, 1951; *The Malefactors*, 1956.

Short stories: *The Forest of the South*, 1945.

Criticism: *How to Read a Novel*, 1957.

Texts: *The House of Fiction, An Anthology of the Short Story* (edited with Allen Tate), 1950.

BIOGRAPHY AND CRITICISM

Two early studies are Andrew Lytle, "Caroline Gordon and the Historic Image," *SR*, LVII (1949), 560–586; and Vivienne Koch, "The Conservatism of Caroline Gordon," *Southern Renascence*, ed. Louis D. Rubin, Jr., and Robert D. Jacobs, Baltimore, 1953, pp. 325–337.

The first issue of *Critique: Studies in Modern Fiction*, published in 1956 at the University of Minnesota, is devoted exclusively to Caroline Gordon. Later studies are Lawrence T. King, "The Novels of Caroline Gordon," *CathW*, CLXXXI (1955), 274–279; and Willard Thorp, "The Way Back and the Way Up: The Novels of Caroline Gordon," *BuR*, VI (1956), 1–15.

A bibliographical listing is Joan Griscom, "A Bibliography of Caroline Gordon," *Critique* (Minneapolis), I (Winter, 1956), 74–78.

# J(OHN) P(HILLIPS) MARQUAND
## b. 1893

SEPARATE WORKS

Fiction: *The Unspeakable Gentleman*, 1922; *Four of a Kind*, 1923; *The Black Cargo*, 1925; *Do Tell Me, Doctor Johnson*, 1928; *Warning Hill*, 1930; *Haven's End*, 1933; *Ming Yellow*, 1935; *No Hero*, 1935; *Thank You, Mr. Moto*, 1936; *The Late George Apley*, 1937; *Think Fast, Mr. Moto*, 1937; *Mr. Moto Is So Sorry*, 1938; *Wickford Point*, 1939; *Don't Ask Questions*, 1941; *H. M. Pulham, Esquire*, 1941; *Last Laugh, Mr. Moto*, 1942; *So Little Time*, 1943; *It's Loaded, Mr. Bauer*, 1943; *Repent in Haste*, 1945; *B. F.'s Daughter*, 1946; *Point of No Return*, 1949; *Melville Goodwin, USA*, 1951; *Thirty Years*, 1954; *Sincerely, Willis Wayde*, 1955; *Stopover: Tokyo*, 1957; *Life at Happy Knoll*, 1957; *Women and Thomas Harrow*, 1958.

Plays: *The Late George Apley* (with George S. Kaufman), 1946 (first performed, 1944). Paul Osborn, *Point of No Return*, 1952, is based on the Marquand novel.

Miscellaneous: *Prince and Boatswain: Sea Tales from the Recollection of Rear-Admiral Charles E. Clark* (with James Morris Morgan), 1915; *Lord Timothy Dexter of Newburyport, Mass.*, 1925; *Federalist Newburyport; or, Can Historical Fiction Remove a Fly from Amber*, 1952.

COLLECTIONS

*North of Grand Central*, 1956, is a re-issue of *The Late George Apley, Wickford Point*, and *H. M. Pulham, Esquire* in one volume. *Mr. Moto's Three Aces*, 1956, is a one-volume edition of *Thank You, Mr. Moto, Think Fast, Mr. Moto*, and *Mr. Moto Is So Sorry*.

BIOGRAPHY AND CRITICISM

Philip Hamburger, *J. P. Marquand, Esquire: A Portrait in the Form of a Novel*, Boston, 1952, is a biographical profile.

Early critical estimates are C. M. Fiske, "John P. Marquand: Something of an Apley Himself," *SRL*, XIX (Dec. 10, 1938), 10–11; Harlan Hatcher, "John Phillips Marquand," *CE*, I (1939), 107–118; Percy H. Boynton, "The Novel of Puritan Decay: From Mrs. Stowe to John Marquand," *NEQ*, XIII (1940), 626–637; Herschel Brickell, "Miss Glasgow and Mr. Marquand," *VQR*, XVII (1941), 405–417; T. D. Bisbee, "John P. Marquand's Tales of Two Cities," *SRL*, XXIV (July 5, 1941), 11, 14; Joseph Warren Beach, *American Fiction, 1920–1940*, New York, 1942, pp. 253–270; G. T. Hellman, "How to Take the World in Your Stride (After Being Tipped Off by John P. Marquand)," *NY*, XIX (Oct. 23, 1943), 20–21; Roger Butterfield, "John P. Marquand: America's Famous Novelist of Manners," *Life*, XVII (1944), 64–73; Robert Van Gelder, "Marquand Unburdens Himself," *Writers and Writing*, New York, 1946, pp. 38–41; William White, "Mr. Marquand's 'Mr. Moto,'" *ASp*, XXIII (1948), 157–158.

More recent studies are Granville Hicks, "Marquand of Newburyport," *Harper's*, CC (Apr., 1950), 101–108; William White, "On Collecting John P. Marquand," *Amateur Book Coll.*, I (1951), 5; Leo Gurko, "The High-Level Formula of J. P. Marquand," *Am. School*, XXI (1952), 443–453; Robert F. Haugh, "The Dilemma of John P. Marquand," *MAQR*, LIX (1952), 19–24; E. C. Wagenknecht, *Cavalcade of the American Novel*, New York, 1952, pp. 438–448; Harvey Breit, *Writer Observed*, Cleveland, 1956, pp. 47–51. Of special interest is John P. Marquand, "Apley, Wickford Point, and Pulham: My Early Struggles," *Atl*, CXCVIII (1956), 71–74.

Of bibliographical interest are William White, "John P. Marquand: A Preliminary Checklist," *BB*, XIX (1949), 268–271; *idem*, "Marquandiana," *BB*, XX (1950), 8–12; and *idem*, "John P. Marquand since 1950," *BB*, XXI (1956), 230–234.

# JOHN (HENRY) O'HARA
*b. 1905*

SEPARATE WORKS

Novels: *Appointment in Samarra*, 1934; *Butterfield 8*, 1935; *Hope of Heaven*, 1938; *Pal Joey*, 1940; *A Rage to Live*, 1949; *The Farmer's Hotel*, 1951; *Ten North Frederick*, 1955; *A Family Party*, 1956; *From the Terrace*, 1958.

Short Stories: *The Doctor's Son and Other Stories*, 1935; *Files on Parade*, 1939; *Pipe Night*, 1945; *Hellbox*, 1947.

Plays: *Pal Joey* (with Lorenz Hart and Richard Rodgers), 1940; published 1952.

Essays: *Sweet and Sour*, 1954.

COLLECTIONS

*Here's O'Hara*, Cleveland, 1946, is a collection in one volume of twenty short stories and three novels: *Butterfield 8, Hope of Heaven*, and *Pal Joey*.

BIOGRAPHY AND CRITICISM

Critical estimates are Wolcott Gibbs, "Watch Out for Mr. O'Hara," *SRL*, XVII (Feb. 19, 1938), 10–12; Robert Van Gelder, *Writers and Writing*, New York, 1946, pp. 59–61; Edmund Wilson, *Classics and Commercials*, New York, 1950, pp. 22–26; Orville Prescott, *In My Opinion*, Indianapolis, 1952, pp. 50–74; John Mason Brown, *As They Appear*, New York, 1952, pp. 233–237; Clifton Fadiman, *Party of One*, Cleveland, 1955, pp. 446–454; and Harvey Breit, *Writer Observed*, Cleveland, 1956, pp. 81–83.

A bibliographical listing is Fred B. Millett, *Contemporary American Authors*, New York, 1940, p. 514.

# JOHN CROWE RANSOM
*b. 1888*

SEPARATE WORKS

Poetry: *Poems About God*, 1919; *Chills and Fever*, 1924; *Grace After Meat* (London), 1924; *Two Gentlemen in Bonds*, 1927; *Selected Poems*, 1945; *Poems and Essays*, 1955.

Essays: *God Without Thunder: An Unorthodox Defense of Orthodoxy*, 1930; *I'll Take My Stand: The South and the Agrarian Tradition, by Twelve Southerners*, 1930; *The World's Body*, 1938; *The New Criticism*, 1941.

Miscellaneous: *American Rhodes Scholars, Oxford, 1910–1913* (with Christopher Morley and Elmer Davis), 1913; *Shall We Complete the Trade?*

*A Proposal for the Settlement of Foreign Debts to the United States,* 1933; *Topics for Freshman Writing* (edited by Ransom), 1935; *A College Primer for Writing* (edited by Ransom), 1943; *The Kenyon Critics: Studies in Modern Literature from the Kenyon Review* (edited by Ransom), 1951.

BIOGRAPHY AND CRITICISM

Early critical estimates are Alice C. Henderson, "An American Georgian," *Poetry,* XVI (1920), 51–52; Allen Tate, "Poetry and the Absolute," *SR,* XXXV (1927), 41–52; Marie Luhrs, "A Conjurer," *Poetry,* XXX (1927), 162–165; William S. Knickerbocker, "Theological Homebrew," *SR,* XXXIX (1931), 103–111; *idem,* "Mr. Ransom and the Old South," *SR,* XXXIX (1931), 222–239; Robert Penn Warren, "A Note on Three Southern Poets," *Poetry,* XL (1932), 103–113; and *idem,* "John Crowe Ransom: A Study in Irony," *VQR,* XI (1935), 93–112.

Later estimates are H. M. Campbell, "John Crowe Ransom," *SWR,* XXIV (1939), 476–489; J. E. Baker, "The Philosopher and the 'New Critic,'" *SR,* L (1942), 167–171; Donald A. Stauffer, "Critical Principles and a Sonnet," *ASch,* XII (1943), 52–62; Robert Penn Warren, "Pure and Impure Poetry," *KR,* V (1943), 228–254; Yvor Winters, "John Crowe Ransom and Thunder Without God," *The Anatomy of Nonsense,* Norfolk, Conn., 1943, pp. 168–228; R. C. Beatty, "John Crowe Ransom as Poet," *SR,* LII (1944), 344–366; Winifred Lynskey, "A Critic in Action: Mr. Ransom," *CE,* V (1944), 239–249; E. B. Burgum, "An Examination of Modern Critics: John Crowe Ransom," *RMR,* VIII (1944), 87–93; Catherine Cater, "Four Voices Out of the South," *MAQR,* L (1944), 166–173; H. Trowbridge, "Aristotle and the 'New Criticism,'" *SR,* LII (1944), 537–555 (with a rejoinder by Ransom, "The Bases of Criticism," 556–571); Robert W. Stallman, "The New Criticism and the Southern Critics," *A Southern Vanguard,* ed. Allen Tate, New York, 1947, pp. 28–51; D. S. Carne-Ross, "Ransom's 'Judith of Bethulia,'" *Nine,* II (1950), 91–95; N. F. Ford, "Empson's and Ransom's Mutilations of Texts," *PQ,* XXIX (1950), 81–84; and Morgan Blum, "The Fugitive Particular: John Crowe Ransom, Critic," *WR,* XIV (1950), 85–102.

The most recent estimates are John M. Bradbury, "Ransom as Poet," *Accent,* XI (1951), 45–57; Babette Deutsch, *Poetry in Our Time,* New York, 1952, pp. 204–209; Vivienne Koch, "The Poetry of John Crowe Ransom," *Modern American Poetry,* ed. B. Rajan, New York, 1952, pp. 33–65; Isabel Gamble, "Ceremonies of Bravery: John Crowe Ransom," *Hopkins Rev.,* VI (Spring–Summer, 1953), 105–115; J. P. Pritchard, *Criticism in America,* Norman, Okla., 1956, pp. 238–246; G. R. Warrerman, "The Irony of John Crowe Ransom," *UKCR,* XXIII (1956), 151–160; Martin C. Battestin, "John Crowe Ransom and *Lycidas:* A Reappraisal," *CE,* XVIII (1956), 223–228.

"Homage to John Crowe Ransom: Essays on His Work as Poet and

Critic, Prepared and Here Collected in Honor of His Sixtieth Birthday" appeared in *Sewanee Review*, LVI (1948), 365–476.

A guide to explication of individual poems can be found in George Arms and Joseph M. Kuntz, *Poetry Explication*, New York, 1950, pp. 122–124.

Bibliographical listings are Fred B. Millett, *Contemporary American Authors*, New York, 1940, pp. 535–536; Allen Tate, *Sixty American Poets, 1896–1944*, rev. ed., Washington, 1954, pp. 103–104; and Robert W. Stallman, "John Crowe Ransom: A Checklist," *SR*, LVI (1948), 442–476.

# ROBERT E(MMET) SHERWOOD
## *1896–1955*

SEPARATE WORKS

\* Plays: *The Road to Rome*, 1927; *The Queen's Husband*, 1928; *Waterloo Bridge*, 1930; *This Is New York*, 1931; *Reunion in Vienna*, 1932; *The Petri-fied Forest*, 1935; *Idiot's Delight*, 1936; *Abe Lincoln in Illinois*, 1939; *There Shall Be No Night*, 1940; *Small War on Murray Hill* (1957).

Fiction: *The Virtuous Knight*, 1931; *Unending Crusade*, 1932.

Non-fiction: *Roosevelt and Hopkins: An Intimate History*, 1948.

Miscellaneous: *The Best Moving Pictures of 1922–23: Who's Who in the Movies and The Year Book of the American Screen*, 1923; *E. V. Lucas: Appreciations* (with J. Farrar, C. Overton and L. Jones), 1925; *Tovarich* by Jacques Deval (adapted and translated by Sherwood), 1937; *Second Threshold* by Philip Barry (with revisions and a preface by Sherwood), 1951.

BIOGRAPHY AND CRITICISM

Critical estimates are Max Lerner, *Ideas Are Weapons*, New York, 1939, pp. 48–53; F. H. O'Hara, *Today in American Drama*, Chicago, 1939, pp. 102–108; Edith J. R. Isaacs, "Robert Sherwood," *TArts*, XXIII (1939), 31–40; R. C. Healey, "Anderson, Saroyan, Sherwood: New Directions," *CathW*, CLII (1940), 174–180; John Gassner, "Robert Emmet Sherwood," *Atl.*, CLXIX (1942), 26–33; O. J. Campbell, "Robert Sherwood and His Times," *CE*, IV (1943), 275–280; Harvey Breit, "An Interview with Robert E. Sherwood," *NYTBR*, Feb. 13, 1949, p. 23; John Mason Brown, *Still Seeing Things*, New York, 1951, pp. 13–23; John Gassner, *The Theatre in Our Times*, New York, 1954, pp. 311–321; Maxwell Anderson, "Robert Sherwood," *TArts*, XL (1956), 26–27, 87.

A bibliographical listing is in Fred B. Millett, *Contemporary American Authors*, New York, 1940, pp. 578–579.

\* Dates in parentheses are of production when publication has not occurred.

# BOOTH TARKINGTON
### 1869–1946

SEPARATE WORKS

Fiction: *The Gentleman from Indiana*, 1899; *Monsieur Beaucaire*, 1900; *The Two Vanrevels*, 1902; *Cherry*, 1903; *In the Arena: Stories of Political Life*, 1905; *The Beautiful Lady*, 1905; *The Conquest of Canaan*, 1905; *His Own People*, 1907; *The Guest of Quesnay*, 1908; *Beasley's Christmas Party*, 1909; *The Flirt*, 1913; *Penrod*, 1914; *The Turmoil*, 1915; *Penrod and Sam*, 1916; *Seventeen*, 1916; *The Magnificent Ambersons*, 1918; *Ramsey Milholland*, 1919; *Alice Adams*, 1921; *Harlequin and Columbine*, 1921; *Gentle Julia*, 1922; *The Fascinating Stranger and Other Stories*, 1923; *The Midlander*, 1924; *Women*, 1925; *The Plutocrat*, 1927; *Claire Ambler*, 1928; *Young Mrs. Greeley*, 1929; *Penrod Jashber*, 1929; *Mirthful Haven*, 1930; *Mary's Neck*, 1932; *Wanton Mally*, 1932; *Presenting Lily Mars*, 1933; *Little Orvie*, 1934; *Mr. White, The Red Barn, Hell, and Bridewater*, 1935; *The Lorenzo Bunch*, 1936; *Rumbin Galleries*, 1937; *The Heritage of Hatcher Ide*, 1941; *The Fighting Littles*, 1941; *Kate Fennigate*, 1943; *Image of Josephine*, 1945; *The Show Piece* (unfinished novel, published posthumously), 1947; *Three Selected Short Novels* (previously uncollected: *Walterson, Uncertain Molly Collicut, Rennie Peddigoe*), 1947.

* Plays: *The Man from Home* (with Harry Leon Wilson; printed, but not published, in 1907 as *The Guardian*), 1908; *Cameo Kirby* (with Harry Leon Wilson) (1908); *Foreign Exchange* (1909); *If I Had Money (Getting a Polish)* (1909); *Springtime* (1909); *Your Humble Servant* (with Harry Leon Wilson) (1909); *Beauty and the Jacobin*, 1912; *The Man on Horseback*, (1912); *The Gibson Upright* (with Harry Leon Wilson), 1919; *Up from Nowhere* (with Harry Leon Wilson) (1919); ** *Poldekin*, 1920; *Clarence*, 1921; *The Intimate Strangers*, 1921; *The Country Cousin* (with Julian Street; printed, but not published, in 1916 as *The Ohio Lady*), 1921; *The Wren*, 1922; *The Ghost Story*, 1922; *Rose Briar* (1922); *The Trysting Place*, 1923; *Magnolia* (1923); *Tweedles* (with Harry Leon Wilson), 1924; *Bimbo, the Pirate*, 1926; *The Travelers*, 1927; *Station YYYY*, 1927; *How's Your Health?* (with Harry Leon Wilson), 1930; *Colonel Satan* (1932); *The Help Each Other Club*, 1933; *Mister Antonio* (first produced in 1916), 1935; *Lady Hamilton and Her Nelson*, 1945.

Non-fiction: *The Collector's Whatnot* (with Hugh Kahler and Kenneth Roberts), 1923; *Looking Forward and Others*, 1926; *The World Does Move*, 1928; *Some Old Portraits*, 1939; *Your Amiable Uncle: Letters to His Nephews*, 1949.

* Dates in parentheses are of production when publication has not occurred.
** Published serially only, *McClure's*, March–July, 1920.

COLLECTED WORKS

*The Works of Booth Tarkington,* Autograph Edition, New York, 1918–1932, 27 vols., was limited to 565 numbered copies. All but two volumes were reissues of earlier published books. *The Works of Booth Tarkington,* Seawood Edition, New York, 1922–1932, 27 vols., was limited to 1075 copies. Both editions were initiated by Doubleday, Page and completed by Doubleday, Doran and Company. Less comprehensive collections are Scribner's 6-vol. set published in 1915; Review of Review Company's 4-vol. set published in 1915; the Doubleday, Page Leather-bound Edition, 8 vols., 1920; the Doubleday, Page Royalty Edition, 10 vols., 1922; the Collier Hoosier Edition, 8 vols., 1927; and the popular, inexpensive Doubleday One-by-One Edition, 7 vols., 1933.

In 1927, Doubleday, Page published *Growth* which combined three novels: *The Magnificent Ambersons, The Turmoil,* and *National Avenue* (called *The Midlander* when it first appeared in 1924). In 1931, Doubleday, Doran published *Penrod: His Complete Story,* including a "Dedicatory Word by the Author," followed by the text of *Penrod, Penrod and Sam,* and *Penrod Jashber* with some new insertions and some omissions. John Beecroft, ed., *The Gentleman from Indianapolis,* New York, 1957, is a collection of seven short stories, three complete novels, and excerpts from three novels.

BIOGRAPHY AND CRITICISM

The first full-length critical biography is James Woodress, *Booth Tarkington: Gentleman from Indiana,* Philadelphia, 1955. It is based largely on the collection of papers given by Tarkington's widow to Princeton University. For a description of this material see anon., "The Booth Tarkington Papers," *PULC,* XII (Winter, 1951), 91–92, and James Woodress, "The Tarkington Papers," *PULC,* XVI (Winter, 1955), 45–53. There are clipping files of Tarkington material in Indianapolis in the state and public libraries. Tarkington began his own memoirs in "As I Seem to Me," *Sat. Eve. Post,* CCXIV (July 5–Aug. 23, 1941), but he completed only the first part: youth and literary apprenticeship.

Further studies, chiefly reminiscences, are C. H. Garrett, "Booth Tarkington," *Outlook,* LXXII (Dec. 6, 1902), 817–819; "John-a-Dreams" [R. T. Sloss], "The Real Booth Tarkington and Some of His Poems and Drawings," *Pearson's Magazine,* IX (Mar., 1903), 211–220; anon., "The Personal Tarkington," *Bookman,* XLII (Jan., 1916), 505–510; Robert Cortes Holliday, *Booth Tarkington,* New York, 1918; Asa Don Dickinson, *Booth Tarkington,* New York, 1926; A. P. Dennis, "Getting Booth Tarkington Educated," *World's Work,* LIX (Jan., 1930), 57–60; Kenneth Roberts, "A Gentleman from Maine and Indiana," *Sat. Eve. Post,* CCIV (Aug. 8, 1931), 14–15, 50, 54, 57.

Studies of Tarkington as a dramatist are Clayton M. Hamilton, *Seen on the Stage*, New York, 1920, pp. 192–203; B. H. Clark, "Booth Tarkington, Dramatist," *Outlook*, CXXXII (1922), 202–204; Margaret G. Mayorga, *A Short History of the American Drama*, New York, 1932, pp. 260–264; and Albert D. Van Nostrand, "The Plays of Booth Tarkington," *PULC*, XVII (1955), 13–39.

Other studies are A. H. Quinn, *American Fiction*, New York, 1936, pp. 596–622; Carl Van Doren, *The American Novel, 1789–1939*, New York, 1940, pp. 260–280; Edward Wagenknecht, *Cavalcade of the American Novel*, New York, 1952, pp. 244–251; James L. Woodress, "Booth Tarkington's Political Career," *AL*, XXVI (1954), 209–222; *idem*, "Booth Tarkington's Attack on American Materialism," *GaR*, VIII (1954), 440–446; *idem*, "Tarkington's New York Literary Debut: Letters Written to His Family in 1899," *PULC*, XVI (1955), 54–79; Barton Currie, "An Editor in Pursuit of Booth Tarkington," *PULC*, XVI (1955), 80–88; Richard Cary, "Jewett, Tarkington, and the Maine Line," *CLQ*, Series IV, No. 5 (Feb., 1956), 89–95; and Winfield Townley Scott, "Tarkington and the 1920's," *ASch*, XXVI (1957), 181–194.

BIBLIOGRAPHY

The first check list of Tarkington's writing is Barton Currie, *Booth Tarkington: A Bibliography*, New York, 1932. The Committee on Bibliography of the Indiana Historical Society commissioned a complete bibliography: Dorothy Ritter Russo and Thelma L. Sullivan, *A Bibliography of Booth Tarkington: 1869–1946*, Indianapolis, 1949. This volume gives abundant information about all of Tarkington's work. Additional data are in Fred B. Millett, *Contemporary American Authors*, New York, 1944, pp. 604–609, and anon., "Additions to the Tarkington Bibliography," *PULC*, XVI (1955), 89–94.

# (JOHN ORLEY) ALLEN TATE
*b. 1899*

SEPARATE WORKS

Poetry: *Mr. Pope and Other Poems*, 1928; *Three Poems*, 1930; *Poems: 1928–1931*, 1932; *The Mediterranean and Other Poems*, 1936; *Selected Poems*, 1937; *Sonnets at Christmas*, 1941; *Pervigilium Veneris, The Vigil of Venus* (translated by Tate), 1943; *The Winter Sea*, 1944; *Poems: 1920–1945* (London), 1947; *Poems: 1922–1947*, 1948; *Two Conceits for the Eye to Sing, If Possible*, 1950.

Biography: *Stonewall Jackson, The Good Soldier*, 1928; *Jefferson Davis: His Rise and Fall*, 1929.

Fiction: *The Fathers*, 1938.

Essays: *I'll Take My Stand: The South and the Agrarian Tradition*, by *Twelve Southerners*, 1930; *Reactionary Essays on Poetry and Ideas*, 1936; *Reason in Madness, Critical Essays*, 1941; *On the Limits of Poetry, Selected Essays: 1928-1948*, 1948; *The Hovering Fly and Other Essays*, 1949; *The Forlorn Demon, Didactic and Critical Essays*, 1953; *The Man of Letters in the Modern World, Selected Essays: 1928-1955*, 1955.

Miscellaneous: *Who Owns America? A New Declaration of Independence* (edited with Herbert Agar), 1936; *America Through the Essay* (edited with A. Theodore Johnson), 1938; *Invitation to Learning* (with Huntington Cairns and Mark Van Doren), 1941; *American Harvest: Twenty Years of Creative Writing* (edited with John Peale Bishop), 1942; *The Language of Poetry: Essays by Philip Wheelwright and Others* (edited by Tate), 1942; *Princeton Verse Between Two Wars* (edited by Tate), 1942; *Recent American Poetry and Poetic Criticism* (compiled by Tate), 1943; *Sixty American Poets, 1896-1944* (selected with a preface and critical notes by Tate), 1945; *A Southern Vanguard: The John Peale Bishop Memorial Volume* (edited by Tate), 1947; *The Collected Poems of John Peale Bishop* (edited with a preface and memoir by Tate), 1948; *The House of Fiction: An Anthology of the Short Story* (with Caroline Gordon), 1950.

BIOGRAPHY AND CRITICISM

Early critical estimates are Morton D. Zabel, "A Critic's Poetry," *Poetry*, XXXIII (1929), 281-284; William S. Knickerbocker, "The Return of the Native," *SR*, XXXVIII (1930), 479-483; Robert Shafer, "Humanism and Impudence," *Bookman*, LXX (1930), 489-498; Morton D. Zabel, "The Creed of Memory," *Poetry*, XL (1932), 34-39; Frank C. Flint, "*Poems: 1928-1931*," *Symposium*, III (1932), 407-414; idem, "Five Poets," *SoR*, I (1936), 650-674; C. I. Glicksberg, "Allen Tate and Mother Earth," *SR*, XLV (1937), 284-295; Kenneth Burke, "Tentative Proposal," *Poetry*, L (1937), 96-100; Cleanth Brooks and Mark Van Doren, "Modern Poetry [A Symposium]," *Amer. Rev.*, VIII (1937), 427-456; Samuel French Morse, "Second Reading," *Poetry*, LI (1938), 262-266.

Later studies are Delmore Schwartz, "The Poetry of Allen Tate," *SoR*, V (1940), 419-438; Joe Horrell, "Some Notes on Conversion in Poetry," *SoR*, VII (1941), 117-131; F. Roelinger, "Two Theories of Poetry as Knowledge," *SoR*, VII (1942), 690-705; Catherine Cater, "Four Voices Out of the South," *MAQR*, L (1944), 166-173; Horace Gregory and Marya Zaturenska, *A History of American Poetry, 1900-1940*, New York, 1946, pp. 372-379; Robert W. Stallman, "The New Criticism and the Southern Critics," *A Southern Vanguard*, ed. Allen Tate, New York, 1947, pp. 28-51; Arthur Mizener, "'The Fathers' and Realistic Fiction," *Accent*, VII (1947), 101-109; R. C. Beatty, "Allen Tate as Man of Letters," *SAQ*, XLVII (1948), 226-241;

Frederick Morgan, "Recent Poetry," *HudR,* I (1948), 258–266; Howard Nemerov, "The Current of the Frozen Stream: An Essay on the Poetry of Allen Tate," *Furioso,* III (Fall, 1948), 50–61; Clifford Amyx, "The Aesthetics of Allen Tate," *WR,* XIII (1949), 135–145; Vivienne Koch, "The Poetry of Allen Tate," *KR,* XI (1949), 355–378; Monroe K. Spears, "The Criticism of Allen Tate," *SR,* LXVII (1949), 317–334.

The most recent criticism is Peter Russell, "A Note on the Poetry of Allen Tate," *Nine,* II (1950), 89–91; Alwyn Berland, "Violence in the Poetry of Allen Tate," *Accent,* XI (1951), 161–171; Rudd Fleming, "Dramatic Involution: Tate, Husserl, and Joyce," *SR,* LX (1952), 445–464; Babette Deutsch, *Poetry in Our Time,* New York, 1952, pp. 195–202; Wade Donahoe, "Allen Tate and the Idea of Culture," *Hopkins Rev.,* VI (1953), 116–131; Louis D. Rubin, Jr., "The Serpent in the Mulberry Bush," *Hopkins Rev.,* VI (1953), 132–147; Katherine Bregy, "Allen Tate—Paradoxical Pilgrim," *CathW,* CLXXX (1954), 121–125; Willard Burdett Arnold, *The Social Ideas of Allen Tate,* Boston, 1955; Eliseo Vivas, *Creation and Discovery,* New York, 1955, pp. 267–281; J. P. Pritchard, *Criticism in America,* Norman, Okla., 1956, pp. 246–250; and Richard Foster, "Narcissus as Pilgrim: Allen Tate," *Accent,* XVII (1957), 158–171.

Listings of explication of individual poems can be found in George Arms and Joseph M. Kuntz, *Poetry Explication,* New York, 1950, pp. 147–149.

Bibliographical listings are in Fred B. Millett, *Contemporary American Authors,* New York, 1940, pp. 609–610; Willard Thorp, "Allen Tate: A Checklist," *PULC,* III (1942), 85–98; and Allen Tate, *Sixty American Poets, 1896–1944,* rev. ed., Washington, 1954, pp. 131–134.

# ALBION W(INEGAR) TOURGÉE
## *1838–1905*

SEPARATE WORKS

Fiction: *Toinette,* 1875 (under pseudonym, Henry Churton; republished as *A Royal Gentleman,* 1881); *Figs and Thistles,* 1879; *A Fool's Errand,* 1880; *Bricks Without Straw,* 1880; *'Zouri's Christmas,* 1881; *John Eax and Marmelon,* 1882; *Hot Plowshares,* 1883; *An Appeal to Caesar,* 1884; *Button's Inn,* 1887; *Letters to a King,* 1888; *Pactolus Prime,* 1890.

Non-fiction: *The Veteran and His Pipe,* 1886; *The War of the Standards: Coin and Credit Versus Coin Without Credit,* 1896; *The Story of a Thousand: A History of the 105th Volunteer Infantry: 1862–1865,* 1896.

BIOGRAPHY AND CRITICISM

The only book-length study is Roy Floyd Dibble, *Albion W. Tourgée*, New York, 1921. More recent criticism is R. B. Nye, "Judge Tourgée and Reconstruction," *OSAHQ*, L (1941), 101–114; George J. Becker, "Albion W. Tourgée: Pioneer in Social Criticism," *AL*, XIX (1947), 59–72; Alexander Cowie, *Rise of the American Novel*, New York, 1948, pp. 521–535; and Robert A. Lively, *Fiction Fights the Civil War*, Chapel Hill, 1957, *passim*.

# CARL VAN VECHTEN
*b. 1880*

SEPARATE WORKS

Fiction: *Peter Whiffle, His Life and Works*, 1922; *The Blind Bow-Boy*, 1923; *The Tattooed Countess*, 1924; *Firecrackers*, 1925; *Nigger Heaven*, 1926; *Spider Boy*, 1928; *Parties*, 1930.

Essays: *Sacred and Profane Memories*, 1932.

Books on music: *Five Old English Ditties, with Music*, 1904; *Music After the Great War and Other Studies*, 1915; *Music and Bad Manners*, 1916; *Interpreters and Interpretations*, 1917; *The Merry-Go-Round*, 1918; *The Music of Spain*, 1918; *In the Garret*, 1920; *My Musical Life* by Nikolay Andreyevich Rimsky-Korsakoff (edited with an introduction by Van Vechten), 1923; *Red: Papers on Musical Subjects*, 1925; *Excavations*, 1926; *Last Operas and Plays* by Gertrude Stein (edited with an introduction by Van Vechten), 1949.

Books on cats: *The Tiger in the House*, 1920; *Lords of the Housetops*, 1921; *Feathers*, 1930.

BIOGRAPHY AND CRITICISM

The first full-length study is Edward Lueders, *Carl Van Vechten and the Twenties*, Albuquerque, 1955.

Early studies are Charles G. Baldwin, "Carl Van Vechten," *The Men Who Make Our Novels*, rev. ed., New York, 1924, pp. 523–529; Gertrude Stein, "One: Carl Van Vechten," *Geography and Plays*, Boston, 1922, pp. 199–200; *idem*, "Van or Twenty Years After," *Reviewer*, IV (1924), 176–177; Joseph Warren Beach, "The Peacock's Tail," *ASp*, I (1925), 65–73; Emily Clark, "Carl Van Vechten," *Innocence Abroad*, New York, 1931, pp. 129–145; Harlan Hatcher, *Creating the Modern American Novel*, New York, 1935, pp. 72–86; Peter Monro Jack, "The James Branch Cabell Period," *New Rep*, LXXXIX (1937), 323–326.

More recent criticism is Oscar Cargill, "The Intelligentsia: Carl Van Vechten," *Intellectual America*, New York, 1941, pp. 507–511; Alfred Kazin,

"The Exquisites: Coda," *On Native Grounds,* New York, 1942, pp. 244–246; anon., "Carl Van Vechten," *PULC,* V (1944), 79–80; H. M. Gloster, "The Van Vechten Vogue," *Phylon,* VI (1945), 310–314; *idem, Negro Voices in American Fiction,* Chapel Hill, 1948, pp. 157–173; G. S. Schuyler, "Carl Van Vechten," *Phylon,* XI (1950), 362–368; Edmund Wilson, *Shores of Light,* New York, 1952, pp. 68–72; and Frederick J. Hoffman, *The Twenties,* New York, 1955, *passim.*

Of special interest is John D. Gordan, "Carl Van Vechten: Notes for an Exhibition in Honor of His Seventy-fifth Birthday," *BNYPL,* LIX (1955), 331–366.

Bibliographical listings are Scott Cunningham, *A Bibliography of the Writings of Carl Van Vechten,* Philadelphia, 1924; Fred B. Millett, *Contemporary American Authors,* New York, 1940, pp. 626–628; and Klaus W. Jonas, *Carl Van Vechten: A Bibliography,* New York, 1955.


# ROBERT PENN WARREN
### b. 1905

## SEPARATE WORKS

Fiction: *Night Rider,* 1939; *At Heaven's Gate,* 1943; *All the King's Men,* 1946; *The Circus in the Attic and Other Stories,* 1947; *World Enough and Time,* 1950; *Band of Angels,* 1955.

Poetry: *Thirty-Six Poems,* 1935; *Eleven Poems on the Same Theme,* 1942; *Selected Poems, 1923–1943,* 1944; *Brother to Dragons, A Tale in Verse and Voices,* 1953; *Promises: Poems, 1954–1956,* 1957.

Biography: *John Brown, the Making of a Martyr,* 1929.

Essays: *William Faulkner and His South,* 1951; *Segregation, the Inner Conflict in the South,* 1956; *Selected Essays,* 1958.

Miscellaneous: *An Approach to Literature* (with Cleanth Brooks and J. T. Purser), 1936; *A Southern Harvest, Short Stories by Southern Writers* (edited by Warren), 1937; *Understanding Poetry* (with Cleanth Brooks), 1938; *Understanding Fiction* (with Cleanth Brooks), 1943; *Modern Rhetoric, with Readings* (with Cleanth Brooks), 1949, 2d ed., 1957; *Fundamentals of Good Writing, a Handbook of Modern Rhetoric* (with Cleanth Brooks), 1950; *A New Southern Harvest* (edited by Warren), 1957.

## BIOGRAPHY AND CRITICISM

Early critical estimates are Morton D. Zabel, "Problems of Knowledge," *Poetry,* XLVIII (1936), 37–41; Cleanth Brooks and Mark Van Doren, "Modern Poetry [Symposium]," *Amer. Rev.,* VIII (1937), 427–456; Catherine Cater, "Four Voices Out of the South," *MAQR,* L (1944), 166–173; Irene Hendry, "The Regional Novel: The Example of Robert Penn

Warren," *SR*, LIII (1945), 84–102; W. P. Southard, "The Religious Poetry of Robert Penn Warren," *KR*, VII (1945), 653–676; Joseph E. Baker, "Irony in Fiction: 'All the King's Men,'" *CE*, IX (1947), 122–130; N. R. Girault, "The Narrator's Mind as Symbol: An Analysis of 'All the King's Men,'" *Accent*, VII (1947), 220–234; Oscar Cargill, "Anatomist of Monsters," *CE*, IX (1947), 1–8; R. B. Heilman, "Melpomene as Wallflower; or, The Reading of Tragedy," *SR*, LV (1947), 154–166; William Van O'Connor, "Robert Penn Warren: 'Provincial Poet,'" *A Southern Vanguard*, ed. Allen Tate, New York, 1947, pp. 92–99; Eric Bentley, "The Meaning of Robert Penn Warren's Novels," *KR*, X (1948), 407–424; Howard Nemerov, "The Phoenix in the World," *Furioso*, III (Spring, 1948), 36–46; J. L. Stuart, "The Achievement of Robert Penn Warren," *SAQ*, XLVII (1948), 560–579; William Van O'Connor, "Robert Penn Warren's Short Fiction," *WR*, XII (1948), 251–253.

More recent studies are W. M. Frohock, "Mr. Warren's Albatross," *SWR*, XXXVI (1951), 48–59; R. B. Heilman, "Tangled Web," *SR*, LIX (1951), 107–119; Sam Hynes, "Robert Penn Warren: The Symbolic Journey," *UKCR*, XVII (1951), 279–285; Joseph Frank, "Romanticism and Reality in Robert Penn Warren," *HudR*, IV (1951), 248–258; Charles R. Anderson, "Violence and Order in the Novels of Robert Penn Warren," *Hopkins Rev.*, VI (Winter, 1953), 88–105; H. M. Campbell, "Warren as Philosopher in *World Enough and Time*," *Hopkins Rev.*, VI (1953), 106–116; John M. Bradbury, "Robert Penn Warren's Novels: The Symbolic and Textual Patterns," *Accent*, XIII (1953), 77–89; Michel Mohrt, "Robert Penn Warren and the Myth of the Outlaw," *Yale French Stud.*, No. 10 (1953), 70–84; Wallace W. Douglas, "Drug Store Gothic: The Style of Robert Penn Warren," *CE*, XV (1954), 265–272; Francis Fergusson, "Three Novels," *Perspectives USA*, No. 6 (1954), 30–44; Newell F. Ford, "Kenneth Burke and Robert Penn Warren: Criticism by Obsessive Metaphor," *JEGP*, LIII (1954), 172–177; Louis D. Rubin, Jr., "All the King's Meanings," *GaR*, VIII (1954), 422–434; Robert White, "Robert Penn Warren and the Myth of the Garden," *Faulkner Stud.*, III (1954), 59–67; Frederick P. W. McDowell, "Psychology and Theme in Brother to Dragons," *PMLA*, LXX (1955), 565–586; *idem*, "Robert Penn Warren's Criticism," *Accent*, XV (1955), 173–196; F. Cudworth Flint, "Mr. Warren and the Reviewers," *SR*, LXIV (1956), 632–645; James Magner, S.J., "Robert Penn Warren's Quest for an Angel," *CathW*, CLXXXIII (1956), 178–183; Norman Kelvin, "The Failure of Robert Penn Warren," *CE*, XVIII (1957), 355–364; and William Wasserstrom, "Robert Penn Warren: From Paleface to Redskin," *PrS*, XXXI (1957), 323–333.

For a listing of explications of individual poems see George Arms and Joseph M. Kuntz, *Poetry Explication*, New York, 1950, pp. 156–157.

The most recent bibliographical listing is Robert W. Stallman, "Robert

Penn Warren: A Checklist of His Critical Writings," *UKCR*, XIV (1947), 78–83. See also Fred B. Millett, *Contemporary American Authors*, New York, 1940, pp. 628–629; and Allen Tate, *Sixty American Poets, 1896–1944*, rev. ed., 1954, pp. 140–142.

# THORNTON (NIVEN) WILDER
## *b. 1897*

### SEPARATE WORKS

Novels: *The Cabala*, 1926; *The Bridge of San Luis Rey*, 1927; *The Woman of Andros*, 1930; *Heaven's My Destination*, 1935; *The Ides of March*, 1948.

\* Plays: *The Angel That Troubled the Waters and Other Plays*, 1928; *The Long Christmas Dinner and Other Plays in One Act* (including *Queens of France; Pullman Car Hiawatha; Love, and How to Cure It; Such Things Only Happen in Books; The Happy Journey to Trenton and Camden*), 1931; *Our Town*, 1938; *The Merchant of Yonkers* (1938), 1939; *The Skin of Our Teeth*, 1942; *The Matchmaker* (a re-written version of *The Merchant of Yonkers*) (1954), 1957; *A Life in the Sun* (*The Alcestiad*) (1955); *Bernice* (1957); *The Wreck on the 5:25* (1957); *The Drunken Sisters* (1957).

### COLLECTIONS

*Three Plays*, New York, 1957, combines *Our Town, The Skin of Our Teeth*, and *The Matchmaker* in one volume.

### BIOGRAPHY AND CRITICISM

Early estimates are John Farrar, "The Editor Recommends—," *Bookman*, LXIII (1926), 478; L. W. Dodd, "The Ways of Man to Man," *SRL*, IV (Dec. 3, 1927), 371; Edmund Wilson, "Thornton Wilder," *New Rep*, LV (1928), 303–305; St. John Adcock, "Thornton Wilder," *Bookman* (London), LXXV (1929), 316–319; Pierre Loving, "The Bridge of Casuistry," *This Quarter*, II (1929), 150–161; anon., "The Economic Interpretation of Wilder," *New Rep*, LXV (1930), 31–32; Henry Hazlitt, "Communist Criticism," *Nation*, CXXXI (1930), 583–584; Michael Gold, "Wilder: Prophet of the Genteel Christ," *New Rep*, LXIV (1930), 266–267; E. G. Twitchett, "Mr. Thornton Wilder," *London Merc.*, XXII (1930), 32–39; R. P. Blackmur, "Thornton Wilder," *Hound & Horn*, III (1930), 586–589.

Later criticism is Walter Tritsch, "Thornton Wilder in Berlin," *Living Age*, CCCXLI (1931), 44–47; Robert McNamara, "Phases of American Religion in Thornton Wilder and Willa Cather," *CathW*, CXXXV (1932),

---

\* Dates in parentheses are of production when it differs from publication or when publication has not occurred.

641-649; Granville Hicks, *The Great Tradition*, New York, 1933, pp. 257-292; Harlan Hatcher, *Creating the Modern American Novel*, New York, 1935, pp. 247-261; E. K. Brown, "A Christian Humanist: Thornton Wilder," *UTQ*, IV (1935), 356-370; Walther Fischer, "Thornton Wilders *The Bridge of San Luis Rey* und Prosper Mérimées *Le Car[r]osse du Saint-Sacrement,*" *Anglia*, LX (1936), 234-240; Ross Parmenter, "Novelist into Playwright," *SRL*, XVIII (June 11, 1938), 10-11; John Mason Brown, *Two on the Aisle*, New York, 1938, pp. 187-193; Dayton Kohler, "Thornton Wilder," *EJ*, XXVIII (1939), 1-11; Martin Gardner, "Thornton Wilder and the Problem of Providence," *Univ. Rev.*, VII (1940), 83-91; Joseph Campbell and H. M. Robinson, "The Skin of Whose Teeth? The Strange Case of Mr. Wilder's New Play and 'Finnegan's Wake,'" *SRL*, XXV (Dec. 19, 1942), 3-4, XXVI (Feb. 13, 1943), 16, 18-19; Edith J. R. Isaacs, "Thornton Wilder in Person," *TArts*, XXVII (1943), 21-30; Henry Alder, "Thornton Wilder's Theatre," *Horizon*, XII (1945), 89-99; Henry Seidel Canby, *American Memoir*, Boston, 1947, pp. 330-338; and E. M. Gagey, *Revolution in American Drama*, New York, 1947, pp. 71-119.

More recent estimates are John Mason Brown, "Wilder: 'Our Town,'" *SRL*, XXXII (Aug. 6, 1949), 33-34; J. J. Firebaugh, "The Humanism of Thornton Wilder," *PS*, IV (1950), 426-438; Edmund Wilson, *Classics and Commercials*, New York, 1950, pp. 81-86; *idem*, *Shores of Light*, New York, 1952, pp. 442-450, 587-592; Winfield Townley Scott, "'Our Town' and the Golden Veil," *VQR*, XXIX (1953), 103-117; Elio Vittorini, "Teatro americano in Italia," *Galleria*, IV (1954), 303-306; Erwin Stürzl, "Weltbild und Lebensphilosophie Thornton Wilders," *NS*, Heft 8 (1955), 341-351; Tyrone Guthrie, "The World of Thornton Wilder," *N.Y. Times Mag.*, Nov. 27, 1955, pp. 26-27, 64-68; Edgar Neis, "Thornton Wilders Novelle, *The Bridge of San Luis Rey*: Versuch einer Interpretation," *NS*, Heft 1 (1956), 18-26; Malcolm Cowley, "The Man Who Abolished Time," *Sat. Rev.*, XXXIX (Oct. 6, 1956), 13-14, 50-52; Francis Fergusson, "Three Allegorists: Brecht, Wilder, and Eliot," *SR*, LXIV (1956), 544-573; Arthur H. Ballet, "'In Our Living and in Our Dying,'" *EJ*, XLV (1956), 243-249; Mary McCarthy, *Sights & Spectacles*, New York, 1956, pp. 21-29, 53-56; Richard H. Goldstone, "Thornton Wilder: The Art of Fiction [Interview]," *Paris Rev.*, No. 15 (1957), 36-57.

A bibliographical listing is in Fred B. Millett, *Contemporary American Authors*, New York, 1940, pp. 643-645.

# EDMUND WILSON
*b. 1895*

### SEPARATE WORKS

Criticism: *Axel's Castle: A Study in the Imaginative Literature of 1870–1930*, 1931; *The Triple Thinkers: Ten Essays on Literature*, 1938; *The Wound and the Bow: Seven Studies in Literature*, 1941; *The Boys in the Back Room: Notes on California Novelists*, 1941; *Notebooks of Night*, 1942; *Classics and Commercials: A Literary Chronicle of the Forties*, 1950; *The Shores of Light: A Literary Chronicle of the Twenties and Thirties*, 1952.

Essays: History and travel: *The American Jitters: A Year of the Slump*, 1932; *Travels in Two Democracies*, 1936; *To the Finland Station*, 1940; *Europe Without Baedeker*, 1947; *The Scrolls from the Dead Sea*, 1955; *Red, Black, Blond, and Olive: Studies in Four Civilizations*, 1956; *A Piece of My Mind: Reflections at Sixty*, 1956; *The American Earthquake: A Documentary of the Jazz Age, The Great Depression, and the New Deal*, 1958.

Fiction: *I Thought of Daisy*, 1929; *Memoirs of Hecate County*, 1946.

Plays and dialogues: *Discordant Encounters*, 1929; *This Room and This Gin and These Sandwiches*, 1937; *The Little Blue Light*, 1950; *Five Plays* (only *Cyprian's Prayer* never before published), 1954.

Poems: *Poets, Farewell*, 1929.

Miscellaneous: *The Undertaker's Garland* (with John Peale Bishop), 1922; *The Shock of Recognition: The Development of Literature in the United States Recorded by the Men Who Made It* (edited by Wilson), 1943; *The Crack-Up, with Other Uncollected Pieces, Notebooks, and Unpublished Letters of F. Scott Fitzgerald* (edited by Wilson), 1945; *The Collected Essays of John Peale Bishop* (edited by Wilson), 1948; *The Last Tycoon, An Unfinished Novel by F. Scott Fitzgerald* (edited by Wilson), 1953.

### BIOGRAPHY AND CRITICISM

Early critical studies are Morton D. Zabel, "Marginalia of a Critic," *Poetry*, XXXV (1930), 222–226; Bernard De Voto, "My Dear Edmund Wilson," *SRL*, XV (Feb. 13, 1937), 8, 20; F. C. Flint, "A Critique of Experimental Poetry," *VQR*, XIII (1937), 453–457; C. I. Glicksberg, "Edmund Wilson: Radicalism at the Crossroads," *SAQ*, XXXVI (1937), 466–477; T. C. Wilson, "The Muse and Edmund Wilson," *Poetry*, LII (1938), 144–152; Norma McCarty, "Edmund Wilson," *Nor. Am. Rev.*, CCXLVI (1938), 192–197; F. W. Dupee, "Edmund Wilson's Criticism," *PR*, IV (1938), 48–51; Ernest Boyd, "Edmund Wilson's Essays," *SRL*, XVII (Mar. 26, 1938), 10; J. A. Clark, "The Sad Case of Edmund Wilson," *Commonweal*, XXVIII (1938), 292–295; Joseph Freeman, "Edmund Wilson's Globe of Glass,"

*New Masses*, XXVII (1938), 73–79; V. J. Jerome, "Edmund Wilson: To the Munich Station," *New Masses*, XXXI (Apr. 4, 1939), 23–26; Edward Fiess, "Edmund Wilson: Art and Ideas," *AR*, I (1941), 356–367.

Later estimates are Delmore Schwartz, "The Writing of Edmund Wilson," *Accent*, II (1942), 177–186; George Snell, "An Examination of Modern Critics, II: Edmund Wilson, 'The Historical Critic,'" *RMR*, VIII (1944), 36–44; Christian Gauss, "Edmund Wilson, the Campus, and the Nassau 'Lit,'" *PULC*, V (1944), 41–50; Granville Hicks, "The Intransigence of Edmund Wilson," *Am. Rev.*, VI (1946), 550–562.

The following reports concern the *Memoirs of Hecate County* court trial: *Pub. Weekly*, CL (1946), 2608, 2726, 3104, 3106; CLI (1947), 2499; CLIII (1948), 1457–1458; CLIV (1948), 1974–1975.

The most recent criticism is R. Adams, "Masks and Delays: Edmund Wilson as Critic," *SR*, LVI (1948), 272–286; Stanley Edgar Hyman, *The Armed Vision*, New York, 1948, pp. 19–48; C. I. Glicksberg, *American Literary Criticism, 1900–1950*, New York, 1951, pp. 482–485; Theodore B. Dolmatch, "Edmund Wilson as Literary Critic," *UKCR*, XVII (1951), 213–219; Seymour Krim, "A Trademark of Equality," *HudR*, IV (1951), 150–155; William Phillips, "The Wholeness of Literature: Edmund Wilson's Essays," *Am Merc*, LXXV (1952), 103–107; F. O. Matthiessen, *The Responsibilities of the Critic*, New York, 1952, pp. 159–161; Gilbert Highet, *People, Places and Books*, New York, 1953, pp. 29–36; Edwin Honig, "Edmund Wilson's Chronicles," *NMQ*, XXIV (1954), 99–105; Murray Kempton, *Part of Our Time*, New York, 1955, pp. 110–149; Alfred Kazin, *The Inmost Leaf*, New York, 1955, pp. 93–97; Harvey Breit, *Writer Observed*, Cleveland, 1956, pp. 267–269; J. P. Pritchard, *Criticism in America*, Norman, Okla., 1956, pp. 269–276. Of special interest is Edmund Wilson, "The Author at Sixty," *A Piece of My Mind*, New York, 1956, pp. 209–239.

Bibliographical listings are in Fred B. Millett, *Contemporary American Authors*, New York, 1940, pp. 649–651; and Arthur Mizener, "Edmund Wilson: A Checklist," *PULC*, V (1944), 62–78.

# LITERARY HISTORY
OF THE
# UNITED STATES:

## *BIBLIOGRAPHY SUPPLEMENT II*

# PREFACE

In 1948, *Literary History of the United States* was published in three volumes by The Macmillan Company of New York. The first two volumes were composed of 81 chapters written by 56 scholars. The third volume, also a joint undertaking, was devoted entirely to bibliographies. The Editorial Board, which was first organized in 1940, assumed responsibility for all parts of the work, but each member made his individual contribution throughout: Robert E. Spiller, the Chairman, was in charge of policy and planning; Willard Thorp edited the text of the two-volume history; Thomas H. Johnson compiled and edited the bibliographies; Henry S. Canby served as senior adviser. Three editorial associates reviewed all the work in these three volumes: Howard Mumford Jones, Dixon Wecter, and Stanley T. Williams.

In 1953, a second edition was published in two volumes. The text of the history, originally in two volumes, was combined into one and an additional chapter was added in order to treat the years 1945–1953. The bibliography volume remained unchanged. By 1956, it was evident that updating of this bibliography was called for, and I joined the Editorial Board to prepare a supplement which appeared as a separate volume in 1959, covering the decade 1948–1958. When it came time to issue a third edition, in 1963, we combined this supplement with the original bibliography to form Volume Two, but we did not change the pagination of either book. Volume One, the history, remained unchanged except for the last chapter. In order to cover the years 1945–1962, the final chapter of the second edition was completely revised and broken into two. The first of these, by Willard Thorp and Robert E. Spiller, dealt with those authors whose careers were mainly in the period between the two world wars and who could therefore be discussed with historical perspective. The second, by Ihab Hassan, attempted a preliminary estimate of those authors whose careers began after 1945.

This second bibliographical supplement is designed, therefore, to be used in conjunction with the third edition. It aims at covering the years 1958–1970, but it also picks up pre-1958 items which were missed in the first supplement and includes some 1971 entries which were added to the manuscript during the typescript and proof stages. In planning the first supplement, we decided to increase by sixteen the number of individual author bibliographies. In this supplement, we have again added sixteen new bibliographies of authors not previously treated at length. Some readers may be confused by the boldface numbers preceding each rubric, for example, on the opening page: **3.** BIBLIO-

GRAPHICAL CENTERS; 13. PUBLISHED CATALOGS AND DIRECTORIES; 14. UNION LISTS AND SPECIAL COLLECTIONS, and so on. In both supplements, these numbers refer the reader to that page in the original bibliography volume for the initial discussion of this topic, to which we have now added the most recent titles. In choosing these addenda, I have obviously had to be selective. If I have missed major works, I shall expect to hear from the reader who discovers the omission, just as I expect to be advised of any errors.

If the scholar is attempting to prepare comprehensive listings on any subject, he will want to inspect other guides in addition to this volume: Jacob Blanck's multivolumed *Bibliography of American Literature*; Charles H. Nilon's *Bibliography of Bibliographies in American Literature*; Donald H. Mugridge and Blanche P. McCrum's *Guide to the Study of the United States of America*; Lewis Leary's two compilations, *Articles on American Literature, 1900–1950* and *Articles on American Literature, 1950–1967*; James Woodress's annual reviews of scholarship, beginning with *American Literary Scholarship: An Annual/1963*, and his standard reference work, *Dissertations in American Literature, 1891–1966*; the bibliographical survey edited by Floyd Stovall, *Eight American Authors*, and the complementary volume edited by Jackson R. Bryer, *Fifteen Modern American Authors*; and the continuing bibliographies in such journals as *American Literature, American Quarterly, PMLA, American Historical Review, American Studies, Bulletin of the British Association for American Studies, Newsletter of the European Association for American Studies, Jahrbuch für Amerikastudien*, and *Studi Americani*.

Throughout the preparation of this work, I have had much assistance not only from my associate editors but from colleagues and students. For advice on specific entries, I wish to thank Carlos Baker, Michael D. Bell, Sculley Bradley, Michael J. Capek, Donald Gallup, William Howarth, Howard Mumford Jones, Arthur S. Link, A. Walton Litz, James M. McPherson, Charles A. Miller, Monroe K. Spears, Lawrance Thompson, and Emily Mitchell Wallace. The staff of Princeton University Library was, as always, generous with advice and quick to respond, especially Frederick L. Arnold, Frances Chen, Mary Ann Jensen, Jay Lucker, and Eleanor V. Weld. In the early stages of preparing this manuscript, I had invaluable help from research assistants: Susan Gossett, Mary Elizabeth Gray, Peter Hatch, Peter Kopf, Lee Van Valkenburgh, Gary Williams, C. Webster Wheelock, and especially Robert W. Coxe. For preparation of the typescript, Mary Bertagni deserves special acknowledgment. The Macmillan Company could not have provided me with a better editor than Ray A. Roberts.

Princeton University                                         Richard M. Ludwig
August, 1971

# GUIDE TO RESOURCES

## 3. BIBLIOGRAPHICAL CENTERS

### The Washington Area

The *National Union Catalog; A Cumulative Author List* continues to be published in monthly, quarterly, and annual cumulations. Quinquennial cumulations have appeared for 1953–1957, 28 vols., Ann Arbor, Mich., 1958; 1958–1962, 54 vols., New York, 1963; and 1963–1967, 67 vols., Ann Arbor, Mich., 1969.

The first volume of the *National Union Catalog: Pre-1956 Imprints* was issued in Chicago, 1968. Since it is "a repertory of the cataloged holdings of selected portions of the cataloged collections of the major research libraries of the United States and Canada, plus the more rarely held items in the collections of selected smaller and specialized libraries," it will comprise, when completed in 1978, about 13,000,000 entries in a series of about 610 volumes. All entries post-1956 will be found in the quinquennial cumulations described above, with certain overlapping for the years 1953–1956.

The *National Union Catalog of Manuscript Collections, 1959–1961*, Ann Arbor, Mich., 1962, prints "reproductions of cards for nearly 7,300 manuscript collections issued by the Library of Congress during the years 1959–1961." It is the first of a series of what are now annual and cumulative issuances. Three important guides for material beyond the Washington area are Philip M. Hamer's annotated checklist, *A Guide to Archives and Manuscripts in the United States,* New Haven, Conn., 1961; a compilation by the Committee on Manuscript Holdings of the American Literature Group in the Modern Language Association of America, *American Literary Manuscripts: A Checklist of Holdings in Academic, Historical, and Public Libraries in the United States,* Austin, Tex., 1960; and Bernard R. Crick and Miriam Alman, eds., *A Guide to Manuscripts Relating to America in Great Britain and Ireland,* London, 1961. See also Philip C. Brooks, *Research in Archives: The Use of Unpublished Primary Sources,* Chicago, 1969.

### 5. NORTHEAST:

### The New York Area

*A Guide to the Principal Sources for American Civilization, 1800–1900, in the City of New York,* 2 vols., New York, 1960–1962, was compiled by Harry J. Carman and Arthur W. Thompson as a sequel to the Evarts B. Greene–Richard B. Morris survey covering the years 1600–1800 (2nd ed., 1953).

## 13. *PUBLISHED CATALOGS AND DIRECTORIES*

The British Museum *General Catalogue of Printed Books*, begun in 1931, was completed in 263 volumes (1966), and has been followed by a *Ten-Year Supplement, 1956–1965*, 50 vols., London, 1968. The Bibliothèque Nationale *Catalogue Général des Livres Imprimés*, Paris, 1900–current, covers 208 volumes (1970); alphabetically it proceeds to "Vifvinfros."

## 14. *UNION LISTS AND SPECIAL COLLECTIONS*

The third and final edition of *Union List of Serials in Libraries of the United States and Canada*, 5 vols., New York, 1965, was edited by Edna Brown Titus. It covers periodicals through December 31, 1949. Its successor is *New Serial Titles: A Union List of Serials Commencing Publication after December 31, 1949*, a monthly, quarterly, and annual publication issued by the Library of Congress. A two-volume gathering covering the years 1950–1960 was published in Washington, D.C., 1961, followed by *New Serial Titles, 1961–1965*, 2 vols., New York, 1966; and *New Serial Titles, 1966–1968*, 2 vols., Washington, D.C., 1969.

## 16. *GUIDES TO PROFESSIONAL STUDIES AND BIBLIOGRAPHIES*

GUIDES TO REFERENCE BOOKS AND THESES

The standard work on the subject, Constance M. Winchell's *Guide to Reference Books*, has been reissued in an eighth edition, Chicago, 1967, followed by *Supplement* (*1965–1966*), ed. Eugene P. Sheehy, Chicago, 1968. Future supplements are to be expected every two years. The British equivalent of this volume is *Guide to Reference Material*, ed. A. J. Walford and L. M. Payne, 3 vols., London, 1966. Two briefer compilations, interpretive guides designed for college students, are Saul Galin and Peter Spielberg, *Reference Books: How to Select and Use Them*, New York, 1969; and Jean Key Gates, *Guide to the Use of Books and Libraries*, New York, 1962. See also Robert B. Downs and Frances B. Jenkins, eds., *Bibliogra-*

*phy: Current State and Future Trends,* Urbana, Ill., 1967; Richard D. Altick, *The Art of Literary Research,* New York, 1963; and Jacques Barzun and Henry F. Graff, *The Modern Researcher,* rev. ed., New York, 1970.

The fourth edition of Theodore Besterman's *World Bibliography of Bibliographies,* 5 vols., Lausanne, 1965–1966, lists 117,000 items. Two European guides are Louise N. Malclès, *Les sources du travail bibliographique,* 4 vols., Geneva, 1950–1958; and Wilhelm Totok and Rolf Weitzel, *Handbuch der bibliographischen Nachschlagewerke,* 3rd ed., Frankfurt am Main, 1966. In addition to the *Bibliographic Index* (1937–current) and the *Bulletin of Bibliography* (1897–current), scholars will also want to consult the annual publication of the Bibliographical Society of the University of Virginia, *Studies in Bibliography,* Charlottesville, Va., (1948–current), especially for the selective checklist of bibliographical scholarship published during the preceding year.

**17. SOURCES SPECIFIC TO AMERICAN LITERATURE AND HISTORY:**
*General Studies*

The most ambitious general listing is *A Guide to the Study of the United States of America: Representative Books Reflecting the Development of American Life and Thought,* Washington, D.C., 1960, almost 1,200 pages of annotated bibliography prepared by Donald H. Mugridge and Blanche P. McCrum under the supervision of Roy P. Basler. A supplement is in preparation. Charles H. Nilon's *Bibliography of Bibliographies in American Literature,* New York, 1970, lists 6,500 entries in four sections: Bibliography, Authors, Genres, and Auxiliary, the latter rubric having 30 subheads.

Of the briefer listings, Clarence Gohdes's *Bibliographical Guide to the Study of the Literature of the U.S.A.,* 3rd ed., Durham, N.C., 1970, is invaluable. For the students of English and American literature, the following are helpful: Arthur G. Kennedy and Donald B. Sands, *A Concise Bibliography for Students of English,* 4th ed., Stanford, Calif., 1960; Richard D. Altick and Andrew Wright, *Selective Bibliography for the Study of English and American Literature,* 4th ed., New York, 1971; and David McPherson and Robert L. Montgomery, Jr., *A Student's Guide to British and American Literature,* Austin, Tex., 1967. More specialized listings can be found in Richard Beale Davis, *American Literature through Bryant, 1585–1830,* New York, 1969; Harry Hayden Clark, *American Literature: Poe through Hamlin Garland,* New York, 1970; Howard Mumford Jones and Richard M. Ludwig, *Guide to American Literature and Its Backgrounds since 1890*, 3rd ed., Cambridge, Mass., 1964; Louis D. Rubin, Jr., ed., *A Bibliographical Guide to the Study of Southern Literature*, Baton Rouge, La., 1969; and Darwin T. Turner, *Afro-American Writers*, New York, 1970.

Each issue of *American Literature* (quarterly, Duke University Press) continues to list "Articles on American Literature Appearing in Current Periodicals," compiled by the Committee on Bibliography of the American Literature Section of the Modern Language Association. Lewis Leary's first compilation of these listings, *Articles on American Literature, 1900–1950* (Durham, N.C., 1954) has been followed by *Articles on American Literature, 1950–1967* (Durham, N.C., 1970). The summer supplements of *American Quarterly* (American Studies Association and the University of Pennsylvania) publish "annual annotated interdisciplinary bibliographies of current articles in American Studies" as well as an annual review of books. The "Annual Bibliography" in the May issues of *PMLA* continues to devote one section to articles on American literature. In 1964, the title was changed to "MLA International Bibliography." In 1970, this bibliography began to appear in a new multivolume format, separate from, but published by, its parent journal *PMLA*. The bibliography for American literature is included in Volume I of the four-volume set. *American Literary Realism, 1870–1910* (three times annually, 1967–current) publishes "comprehensive annotated bibliographies of secondary comment on those literary figures of the designated period who have not received adequate coverage elsewhere." *America: History and Life: A Guide to Periodical Literature* (1964–current) prints abstracts of articles concerning all phases of American civilization. *American Literature Abstracts* (1967–current) is "a review of current scholarship in the field of American literature." Scholars will also want to consult annual, quarterly, or monthly listings in such periodicals as *Abstracts of English Studies* (1958–current); *The Year's Work in English Studies* (1954–current); *The Annual Bibliography of English Language and Literature* (1920–current); *Twentieth Century Literature* (1955–current); *Modern Fiction Studies* (1955–current); *Modern Drama* (1958–current); and *Abstracts of Folklore Studies* (1963–current). Thomas F. Marshall compiled *An Analytical Index to American Literature*, Durham, N.C., 1963. It covers Volumes I–XXX (1929–1959) of the journal *American Literature*.

James Woodress originated an annual review of scholarship as a supplement to the listings in *PMLA*. The first volume, *American Literary Scholarship: An Annual/1963*, Durham, N.C., 1965, includes essays by various scholars on the year's work on Emerson, Thoreau, Hawthorne, Melville, Whitman, Twain, Henry James, Faulkner, Hemingway, and Fitzgerald, along with nine general topics such as "Nineteenth-Century Poetry" and

"Fiction: 1930 to the Present." With the appearance of the survey of the year 1968 (Durham, N.C., 1970), J. Albert Robbins assumed the editorship. The volumes are vital for their descriptive reviews.

*Eight American Authors: A Review of Research and Criticism,* ed. Floyd Stovall, New York, 1956, was reprinted in 1963 with a bibliographical supplement, covering 1955–1962, a selective checklist compiled by J. Chesley Matthews. Jackson R. Bryer edited a companion volume to the Stovall survey, *Fifteen Modern American Authors: A Survey of Research and Criticism,* Durham, N.C., 1969. The authors included are Sherwood Anderson, Cather, Hart Crane, Dreiser, Eliot, Faulkner, Fitzgerald, Frost, Hemingway, O'Neill, Pound, Robinson, Steinbeck, Stevens, and Wolfe.

European surveys of studies in American literature include *Eine Bibliographie der Aufnahme Amerikanischer Literatur in Deutschen Zeitschriften 1945–1960,* comp. Gerhard H. W. Zuther, Munich, 1965; *Russian Studies of American Literature: A Bibliography,* comp. Valentina A. Libman, trans. Robert V. Allen, ed. Clarence Gohdes, Chapel Hill, N.C., 1969; and *Repertorio bibliografico della letteratura Americana in Italia,* Rome, 1966, comp. Robert Perrault and Alessandra Pinto Surdi for Centro di Studi Americani.

James Woodress, with the assistance of Marian Koritz, revised and enlarged his standard reference work, *Dissertations in American Literature 1891–1966,* Durham, N.C., 1968. Since the first edition appeared in 1957, the number of dissertations in the field has almost doubled. A valuable addendum is the list compiled by Lawrence F. McNamee, *Dissertations in English and American Literature: Theses Accepted by American, British and German Universities, 1865–1964,* New York, 1968. "Research in Progress" continues to appear as a regular feature in the journal *American Literature.*

Donna Gerstenberger and George Hendrick supplanted their *Directory of Periodicals Publishing Articles in English and American Literature and Language,* Denver, Colo., 1959, with *Second Directory . . . ,* Denver, Colo., 1965 (listing 417 periodicals with commentary on each) and *Third Directory . . . ,* Chicago, 1970 (listing 547 periodicals). Richard A. Gray compiled *A Guide to Book Review Citations: A Bibliography of Sources,* Columbus, Ohio, 1969.

18. *Fiction*

Lyle H. Wright, *American Fiction, 1774–1850: A Contribution toward a Bibliography,* San Marino, Calif., 1939, rev. ed., 1948, was revised again in 1969. He has followed it with *American Fiction, 1851–1875,* San Marino, Calif., 1957, rev. ed., 1969; and *American Fiction, 1876–1900*, San Marino, Calif., 1966. A fifth edition of Otis W. Coan and Richard G. Lillard, *America in Fiction: An Annotated List of Novels That Interpret Aspects of Life in the U.S., Canada, and Mexico* appeared in Palo Alto, California, 1967. *Short Story Index*, ed. Dorothy E. Cook and Isabel S. Monro, New York, 1953, has had supplements in 1956 and 1960. The *Supplement, 1959–1963*, New York, 1965, was prepared by Estelle A. Fidell.

Students seeking checklists of books and articles on general studies of fiction as well as studies of individual novelists will want to consult C. Hugh Holman, *The American Novel through Henry James*, New York, 1966; Blake Nevins, *The American Novel: Sinclair Lewis to the Present*, New York, 1970; and Donna Gerstenberger and George Hendrick, *The American Novel 1789–1959: A Checklist of Twentieth-Century Criticism*, Denver, Colo., 1961 (a second volume, covering 1960–1968, is published under the title *The American Novel: A Checklist of Criticism on Novels Written since 1789*, Chicago, 1970). Warren S. Walker edited *Twentieth-Century Short Story Explication: Interpretations, 1900–1960 Inclusive, of Short Fiction since 1800*, Hamden, Conn., 1961, with supplements in 1963 and 1965. A second edition (1967) extended the listing through 1966. The first supplement to this edition includes explications published 1967–1969. See also Jarvis Thurston *et al.*, *Short Fiction Criticism: A Checklist of Interpretation since 1925 of Stories and Novelettes (American, British, Continental), 1800–1958*, Denver, Colo., 1960.

## 19. Poetry

*Granger's Index to Poetry*, ed. Raymond J. Dixon, 5th ed., New York, 1962, indexes 574 anthologies of verse by title, first line, author, and subject. Alex Preminger, Frank J. Warnke, and O. B. Hardison, Jr., eds., *Encyclopedia of Poetry and Poetics*, Princeton, N.J., 1965, divides more than 1,000 entries by various scholars under four headings: history of poetry, techniques of poetry, poetics and criticism, and poetry and its relationship to other fields of interest. The *Concise Encyclopedia of English and American Poets and Poetry*, ed. Stephen Spender and Donald Hall, New York, 1963, prints contributions by a variety of authorities on individual poets as well as general topics. *Contemporary Poets of the English Language*, ed. Rosalie Murphy, Chicago and London, 1970, provides biographical and bibliographical information for 1,100 poets. *Literary Recordings: A Checklist of the Archive of Recorded Poetry and Literature in the Library of Congress*, Washington, D.C., 1966, brings the inventory up through June, 1965.

For listings of articles on poetry, the major source is Joseph M. Kuntz,

*Poetry Explication: A Checklist of Interpretations since 1925 of British and American Poems Past and Present,* rev. ed., Denver, Colo., 1962. See also the June issues of *Explicator* (1942–current).

### 19. *Drama*

Listings of books on the theatre are numerous. The major comprehensive annotated bibliography dealing with all aspects of world theatre is Blanch M. Baker's *Theatre and Allied Arts: A Guide to Books Dealing with the History, Criticism, and Technic of the Drama and Theatre, and Related Arts and Crafts,* New York, 1952. More specialized are Pat M. Ryan, *American Drama Bibliography: A Checklist of Publications in English,* Fort Wayne, Ind., 1969; E. Hudson Long, *American Drama from Its Beginnings to the Present,* New York, 1970; Carl J. Stratman, *Bibliography of the American Theatre: Excluding New York City,* Chicago, 1965; Clarence Gohdes, *Literature and Theater of the States and Regions of the U.S.A.: An Historical Bibliography,* Durham, N.C., 1967; and Carl J. Stratman, *American Theatrical Periodicals, 1798–1967: A Bibliographical Guide,* Durham, N.C., 1970.

Checklists of plays include Joseph A. Weingarten, *Modern American Playwrights, 1918–1948,* 2 vols., New York, 1946–1947; G. William Bergquist, ed., *Three Centuries of English and American Plays: A Checklist; England: 1500–1800; United States: 1714–1830,* New York, 1963; and the second supplement to Firkins's *Index of Plays,* Estelle A. Fidell and Dorothy M. Peake, eds., *Play Index, 1953–1960,* New York, 1963.

Guides to dramatic criticism are Irving Adelman and Rita Dworkin, *Modern Drama: A Checklist of Critical Literature on 20th Century Plays,* Metuchen, N.J., 1967; James M. Salem, *A Guide to Critical Reviews,* New York, 1966 (twentieth century only); and Arthur Coleman and Gary R. Tyler, *Drama Criticism,* I, Denver, Colo., 1966 (English and American, since 1940). A multivolume edition of *New York Times Theatre Reviews, 1920–1970,* has been announced for publication in 1971.

### 21. *REGISTRIES OF PUBLICATION*

BOOKS

Descriptive bibliographies of 300 authors who died before 1931 are being compiled by Jacob Blanck. The fifth volume (Washington Irving to Henry Wadsworth Longfellow) of *Bibliography of American Literature* was published in New Haven, 1969; the first appeared in 1955.

The 12 volumes of Charles Evans's *American Bibliography: A Chrono-*

*logical Dictionary of All Books, Pamphlets, and Periodical Publications Printed in the United States* (Chicago, 1903–1934) cover the years 1639–1799. They were reprinted in Gloucester, Massachusetts, in 1941. To complete Evans's original task, Clifford K. Shipton edited a thirteenth volume, 1799–1800, Worcester, Mass., 1955. Roger Pattrell Bristol prepared a fourteenth volume, an index, Worcester, Mass., 1959, as well as two separate publications, *Index to Printers, Publishers, and Booksellers Indicated by Charles Evans in His American Bibliography*, Charlottesville, Va., 1961, and *Supplement to Charles Evans' American Bibliography*, Charlottesville, Va., 1962. The latter adds 11,200 entries which escaped the notice of Evans and Shipton. Lewis M. Stark and Maud D. Cole have added a *Checklist of Additions to Evans' American Bibliography in the Rare Book Room of the New York Public Library*, New York, 1960. *National Index of American Imprints through 1800*, ed. Clifford K. Shipton and James E. Mooney, Worcester, Mass., 1969, is subtitled *The Short-Title Evans*.

To bridge the gap between Evans's work and Orville A. Roorbach's *Bibliotheca Americana* (covering 1820–1848, first published in 1849), Ralph R. Shaw and Richard H. Shoemaker have compiled from secondary sources *American Bibliography: A Preliminary Checklist for 1801–1819*, 22 vols., New York, 1958–1966. Shoemaker began adding to these listings with *A Checklist of American Imprints for 1820*, New York, 1964. His latest volumes are *A Checklist of American Imprints for 1827*, Metuchen, N.J., 1970; and *A Checklist of American Imprints for 1828*, Metuchen, N.J., 1971. More are in progress.

### 25. PERIODICALS AND NEWSPAPERS

In addition to the *Union List of Serials* and the *New Serial Titles* (described above), consult the *Union List of Little Magazines*, Chicago, 1956; and *Ulrich's International Periodicals Directory*, ed. Merle Rohinsky, 2 vols., 14th ed., New York, 1971, plus annual supplements. For the history of earlier magazines, Benjamin M. Lewis compiled *A Register of Editors, Printers, and Publishers of American Magazines, 1741–1810*, New York, 1957.

The best comprehensive guides to the newspapers of the United States and Canada continue to be *N. W. Ayer and Son's Directory of Newspapers and Periodicals* (1880–current), *Editor and Publisher International Yearbook* (1920–current), and *Journalism Quarterly* (1924–current). Equally invaluable is the *New York Times Index* (1913–current). Roland E. Wolseley's *The Journalist's Book Shelf: An Annotated and Selected Bibliography of U.S. Journalism* (1939) is in its seventh edition, Chicago, 1961.

## 27. *DICTIONARIES AND DIGESTS*
BIOGRAPHICAL

*The Concise Dictionary of American Biography* (New York, 1964) was prepared under the direction of Joseph G. E. Hopkins. It is a one-volume abridgement of all 14,780 articles in the original dictionary and supplements. *The National Cyclopaedia of American Biography,* New York, 1892–1967, now extends to 63 volumes and is still in progress. *A Dictionary of North American Authors Deceased before 1950,* comp. W. Stewart Wallace, Detroit, Mich., 1968, is a reprint of a reference work, first published in 1951, which is a useful supplement to the *Dictionary of American Biography* and the *National Cyclopaedia. American Authors and Books, 1640–1940,* by W. J. Burke and Will D. Howe, New York, 1943, was augmented and revised by Irving R. Weiss, New York, 1962. See also *Biography Index* (1946–current) and *Contemporary Authors* (1962–current).

## 29. REFERENCE

The standard reference-handbooks are still James D. Hart, *The Oxford Companion to American Literature,* 4th ed., New York, 1965; and Phyllis Hartnoll, *The Oxford Companion to the Theatre,* 3rd ed., New York, 1967. Additional useful references are *The Reader's Encyclopedia,* ed. William Rose Benét, 2nd ed., New York, 1965; and *The Reader's Adviser,* ed. Winifred F. Courtney, 2 vols., 11th ed., New York, 1968. *The Reader's Encyclopedia of American Literature,* prepared by Max J. Herzberg and the staff of the Thomas Y. Crowell Company, New York, 1962, is a curiously uneven and erratic reference volume, but it is nevertheless a useful supplement to the others available.

## 31. *SOURCES FOR CULTURAL HISTORY*

The five-volume *Dictionary of American History,* ed. James T. Adams, 2nd ed., New York, 1946, has been followed by Volume VI, *Supplement One,* ed. J. G. E. Hopkins and Wayne Andrews, New York, 1961, covering the years 1940–1960. *The Concise Dictionary of American History,* ed. Wayne Andrews, New York, 1962, is a one-volume redaction of the earlier six.

Richard B. Morris's *Encyclopedia of American History* (1953) has had a revised and enlarged edition, New York, 1965. Gorton Carruth *et al., The*

*Encyclopedia of American Facts and Dates* (1956) is in its fifth edition, New York, 1970. The most recent additions to these major reference volumes are Thomas H. Johnson's *Oxford Companion to American History*, New York, 1966; and Howard L. Hurwitz, *An Encyclopedic Dictionary of American History*, New York, 1968.

The best bibliography on books on American history is Michael Kraus's chapter in *The American Historical Association's Guide to Historical Literature*, ed. George F. Howe *et al.*, New York, 1961. Henry P. Beers's *Bibliographies in American History: Guide to Materials for Research* (1938) has had a revised edition, Paterson, N.J., 1959.

Additional reference volumes for the study of American culture are Bert F. Hoselitz, ed., *A Reader's Guide to the Social Sciences*, Glencoe, Ill., 1959; Hans Sperber and Travis Trittschuh, *American Political Terms: An Historical Dictionary*, Detroit, Mich., 1962; and John T. Ellis, *A Guide to American Catholic History*, Milwaukee, Wis., 1959.

Analyses of both theory and method of academic programs for the study of American civilization can be found in Edwin T. Bowden, ed., *American Studies: Problems, Promises, and Possibilities*, Austin, Tex., 1958; Joseph T. Kwait and Mary C. Turpie, eds., *Studies in American Culture: Dominant Ideas and Images*, Minneapolis, Minn., 1960; *New Voices in American Studies*, ed., Ray B. Browne *et al.*, Lafayette, Ind., 1966; *U.S.A. in Focus: Recent Reinterpretations*, ed. Sigmund Skard, Oslo, 1966; Marshall W. Fishwick, ed., *American Studies in Transition*, rev. ed., Philadelphia, 1968; A. N. J. Hollander and Sigmund Skard, eds., *American Civilisation: An Introduction*, London, 1968; *American Studies: Essays on Theory and Method*, ed. Robert Meredith, Columbus, Ohio, 1968; and *Frontiers of American Culture*, ed. Ray B. Browne *et al.*, Lafayette, Ind., 1968. Sigmund Skard's *The American Myth and the European Mind: American Studies in Europe, 1776–1960*, Philadelphia, 1961, is a 110-page distillation of his two-volume survey, *American Studies in Europe* (1958).

For continuing bibliographies on American culture, see *Writings on American History* (1902–current), *American Historical Review* (1895–current), *Journal of American History* (1914–current), *American Quarterly* (1949–current), *American Studies: An International Newsletter* (1962–current), *Bulletin of the British Association for American Studies* (1956–current), *Newsletter of the European Association for American Studies* (1955–current), *Jahrbuch für Amerikastudien* (1956–current), and *Studi Americani* (1955–current).

# BIBLIOGRAPHIES: LITERATURE
AND CULTURE

Howard Mumford Jones's *The Theory of American Literature* (1948) has been reissued, Ithaca, N.Y., 1965, with a chapter about recent developments in criticism: mythical, New Critical, psychoanalytical. Edd W. Parks covers the years 1785–1861, but omits Poe, in *Ante-Bellum Southern Literary Critics*, Athens, Ga., 1962. John Paul Pritchard's *Literary Wisemen of Gotham*, Baton Rouge, La., 1963, concentrates on "criticism in New York, 1815–1860." Richard Ruland's *The Rediscovery of American Literature*, Cambridge, Mass., 1967, discusses "the premises of critical taste, 1900–1940" with emphasis on Stuart Pratt Sherman, the New Humanists, H. L. Mencken, and F. O. Matthiessen. Walter E. Sutton's *Modern American Criticism*, Englewood Cliffs, N.J., 1963, is a valuable outline and summary of five representative groups: New Humanists, psychological and myth critics, liberal and radical critics, New Critics, and neo-Aristotelians. Keith F. McKean, *The Moral Measure of Literature,* Denver, Colo., 1961, has chapters on Irving Babbitt, Paul Elmer More, and Yvor Winters. The third and fourth volumes of René Wellek's *A History of Modern Criticism, 1750–1950*, New Haven, Conn., 1965, treat Poe, Emerson, Whitman, Lowell, Howells, and Henry James among others. A fifth volume is in preparation. Hans-Joachim Lang surveys American criticism from Barrett Wendell to Van Wyck Brooks in *Studien zur Entstehung der neueren amerikanischen Literaturkritik*, Hamburg, 1961.

From the mid-1880's to the present, interest in a variety of literary movements has risen and declined. The following volumes trace the changing modes of literary art: Donald Pizer, *Realism and Naturalism in Nineteenth-Century American Literature,* Carbondale, Ill., 1966; Harold H. Kolb, Jr., *The Illusion of Life: American Realism as a Literary Form,* Charlottesville, Va., 1969; Sydney J. Krause, ed., *Essays on Determinism in American Literature*, Kent, Ohio, 1964 (seven papers, Twain to Dos Passos); Daniel Aaron, *Writers on the Left: Episodes in American Literary Communism*, New York, 1961 (from 1912 to the early 1940's); James B. Gilbert, *Writers and Partisans: A History of Literary Radicalism in America*, New York, 1968; Robert Weimann, *"New Criticism" und die Entwicklung bürgerlicher Literaturwissenschaft*, Halle, 1962; Louis Fraiberg, *Psychoanalysis and American Literary Criticism,* Detroit, Mich., 1960 (Van Wyck Brooks, Edmund Wilson, Kenneth Burke, and Lionel Trilling among others); Claudia C. Morrison, *Freud and the Critic: The Early Use of Depth Psychology in Literary Criticism,* Chapel Hill, N.C., 1968; Norman N. Holland, *The Dynamics of Literary Response,* New York, 1968; Sidney Finkelstein, *Existentialism and Alienation in American Literature,* New York, 1965 (O'Neill to Mailer); Richard Foster, *The New Romantics: A Reappraisal of the New Criticism,* Bloomington, Ind., 1962; and Renato Poggioli, *The Theory of the Avant-Garde,* trans. Gerald Fitzgerald, Cambridge, Mass., 1968. See also the June issues of *Journal of Aesthetics and Art Criticism* (1941–current) for annual bibliographies.

### 55. *Collections*

*Literary Opinion in America,* ed. Morton D. Zabel, 2 vols., 3rd rev. ed., New York, 1962, is still the most generous collection of essays and contains the best bibliography on twentieth-century American criticism, but see also Charles Feidelson, Jr., and Paul Brodtkorb, Jr., eds., *Interpretations of American Literature,* New York, 1959; Irving Howe, ed., *Modern Literary Criticism: An Anthology,* Boston, 1958; Bernard S. Oldsey and Arthur O. Lewis, eds., *Visions and Revisions in Modern American Literary Criticism,* New York, 1962; Walter Sutton and Richard Foster, eds., *Modern Criticism: Theory and Practice,* New York, 1963; Richard Ellmann and Charles Feidelson, Jr., eds., *The Modern Tradition,* New York, 1965; and A. Walton Litz and Lawrence I. Lipking, eds., *Modern Literary Criticism, 1900–1970,* New York, 1971 (concentrating on Pound, Eliot, I. A. Richards, and Northrop Frye).

### 57. *Critical Analysis: Literature and American Life*

Literary criticism based on social and psychological premises is by necessity varied in scope and content. The following volumes are a cross-section of recent work. Wilson O. Clough, *The Necessary Earth: Nature and Solitude in American Literature,* Austin, Tex., 1964, concentrates on "the degree to which the long experience with an open frontier has entered into native American literature." Leo Marx's *The Machine in the Garden: Technology and the Pastoral Ideal in America,* New York, 1964, analyses the American image as "a contradiction between peaceful rustic paradise and complex urban and industrial juggernaut." Somewhat the same theme is discussed in Thomas Reed West's *Flesh of Steel: Literature and the Machine in American Culture,* Nashville, Tenn., 1967. W. M. Frohock argues a thesis that "recent American literature is about the central paradox in American culture: the presence of variety amid monotony" in *Strangers*

*to This Ground: Cultural Diversity in Contemporary American Writing,*
Dallas, Tex., 1961.

David Madden has assembled three useful collections of essays on social
comment in American writing, all published in Carbondale, Illinois: *Proletarian Writers of the Thirties* (1968), *Tough Guy Writers of the Thirties*
(1968), and *American Dreams, American Nightmares* (1970). Albert
Parry has revised his *Garrets and Pretenders: A History of Bohemianism in
America* (1933) with two new chapters, "Greenwich Village Revisited:
1948" by Parry and "Enter Beatniks: The Boheme of 1960" by Harry T.
Moore, New York, 1961. The Beat Generation writers are elaborately
discussed in John Clellon Holmes, *Nothing More to Declare*, New York,
1967; Elias Wilentz, ed., *The Beat Scene*, New York, 1960; Thomas F.
Parkinson, ed., *A Casebook on the Beat*, New York, 1961; and Bruce Cook,
*The Beat Generation*, New York, 1971. More recent American literature is
the subject of Isaac Rosenfeld's *An Age of Enormity: Life and Writings in
the Forties and Fifties*, ed. Theodore Solotaroff, Cleveland, Ohio, 1962; and
Theodore Solotaroff, *The Red-Hot Vacuum and Other Pieces on the Writing
of the Sixties*, New York, 1970.

Leslie Fiedler's three-part study in "literary anthropology" is *Love and
Death in the American Novel*, New York, 1960, rev. ed., 1966; *Waiting for
the End,* New York, 1964; and *The Return of the Vanishing American*,
New York, 1968. Richard Chase offered "a dialogue on life and letters in
contemporary America" in *Democratic Vista*, New York, 1958. More social commentary from literary critics is available in Irving Howe's *A World
More Attractive: A View of Modern Literature and Politics*, New York,
1963; and Elizabeth Hardwick, *A View of My Own: Essays in Literature
and Society,* New York, 1962.

## 59. *Critical Analysis: Literature and the American Past*

Leon Howard's *Literature and the American Tradition*, Garden City,
N.Y., 1960, is a comprehensive survey which sets out to answer the question "Does the literary history of America reveal the existence of an attitude of mind consistent and durable enough to be called an aspect of the
national character?" Robert E. Spiller, *The Cycle of American Literature*
(1955) has been reissued, New York, 1967, with an "Epilogue" (1950–
1965). Willis Wager's *American Literature: A World View,* New York,
1968, is an abbreviated history of our literary writers designed for popular
consumption or as a guide for foreign students. Histories by foreign scholars include Cyrille Arnavon. *Histoire littéraire des États Unis*, Paris, 1953;
Carlo Izzo, *Storia della letteratura nord-americana,* Milan, 1957; Henry

Lüdeke, *Geschichte der amerikanischen Literatur*, Bern, 1963; and Walter F. Schirmer, *Kurze Geschichte der englischen und amerikanischen Literatur*, Tübingen, 1964. Rod W. Horton and Herbert W. Edwards, *Backgrounds of American Literary Thought*, 2nd ed., New York, 1967, is an exposition of movements from Puritanism to existentialism. Other critical histories are best divided chronologically, since they are limited to certain periods of our history:

Seventeenth and Eighteenth Centuries: Howard Mumford Jones, *The Literature of Virginia in the Seventeenth Century*, 2nd ed., Charlottesville, Va., 1968; Moses Coit Tyler, *A History of American Literature, 1607–1783*, abr. and ed. Archie H. Jones, Chicago, 1967; and Russel B. Nye, *American Literary History: 1607–1830*, New York, 1970.

Early Nineteenth Century: James T. Callon, *Kindred Spirits: Knickerbocker Writers and American Artists, 1807–1855*, Chapel Hill, N.C., 1967.

Mid-Nineteenth Century: Robert Edson Lee, *From West to East: Studies in the Literature of the American West*, Urbana, Ill., 1966; Edwin Fussell, *Frontier: American Literature and the American West*, Princeton, N.J., 1965; Edmund Wilson, *Patriotic Gore: Studies in the Literature of the American Civil War*, New York, 1962; and Howard Mumford Jones, *History and the Contemporary: Essays in Nineteenth-Century Literature*, Madison, Wis., 1964.

Late Nineteenth Century: Jay Martin, *Harvests of Change: American Literature 1865–1914*, Englewood Cliffs, N.J., 1967; Larzer Ziff, *The American 1890's: Life and Times of a Lost Generation*, New York, 1966; and Warner Berthoff, *The Ferment of Realism: American Literature 1884–1919*, New York, 1965.

Twentieth Century: Willard Thorp, *American Writing in the Twentieth Century*, Cambridge, Mass., 1960; Heinrich Straumann, *American Literature in the Twentieth Century*, 3rd rev. ed., New York, 1965; Robert E. Spiller, ed., *A Time of Harvest: American Literature 1910–1960*, New York, 1962 (Voice of America broadcasts); and Anthony Hilfer, *The Revolt from the Village, 1915–1930*, Chapel Hill, N.C., 1969.

The interaction of history and literature in critical judgment is the subject, variously treated, of Roy Harvey Pearce, *Historicism Once More: Problems and Occasions for the American Scholar*, Princeton, N.J., 1969; Robert E. Spiller, *The Third Dimension*, New York, 1965; and *The Oblique Light*, New York, 1968, two collections of studies in literary history and biography; David Levin, *In Defense of Historical Literature: Essays on American History, Autobiography, Drama, and Fiction*, New York, 1967; and Robert H. Bremner, ed., *Essays on History and Litera-*

*ture,* Columbus, Ohio, 1966. Franz H. Link, *Amerikanische Literatur-geschichtsschreibung, Ein Forschungsbericht,* Stuttgart, 1963, is a critical review of the recent theory and practice of American literary historiography, focusing on *Literary History of the United States;* Robert Weimann, "Tradition und Krise Amerikanischer Literarhistorie. Zur ihrer Methodologie und Geschichte," *Weimarer Beiträge,* Berlin, 1965, is a reply from the Marxist point of view. More specialized are Howard Mumford Jones, *Belief and Disbelief in American Literature,* Chicago, 1967; Allan Guttmann, *The Conservative Tradition in America,* New York, 1967 (Irving to Eliot); Carl Bode, ed., *The Young Rebel in American Literature,* New York, 1960 (Thoreau to Faulkner); and *idem,* ed., *The Great Experiment in American Literature,* London, 1961, lectures delivered at the U.S. embassy in London. *Amerika: Vision und Wirklichkeit,* ed. Franz H. Link, Frankfurt am Main, 1968, is a collection of essays reflecting German scholarship in American literature during the past 20 years.

## 61. The Analytical and Aesthetic Movement

An important contribution to the understanding of symbolism is John Senior's *The Way Down and Out: The Occult in Symbolist Literature,* Ithaca, N.Y., 1959.

Critical analyses on a variety of subjects, ranging from James Fenimore Cooper to James Baldwin, can be found in Wright Morris, *The Territory Ahead,* New York, 1958; Joseph Frank, *The Widening Gyre,* New Brunswick, N.J., 1963; Ralph Ellison *Shadow and Act,* New York, 1964; Norman Podhoretz, *Doings and Undoings,* New York, 1964; F. W. Dupee, *The King of Cats and Other Remarks,* New York, 1965; R. W. B. Lewis, *Trials of the Word,* New Haven, Conn., 1965; Ray B. West, Jr., *The Writer in the Room,* East Lansing, Mich., 1968; and John F. Lynen, *The Design of the Present,* New Haven, Conn., 1969. Two primary contributions to analyses of style in our literature are Richard Bridgman, *The Colloquial Style in America,* New York, 1966; and Richard Poirier, *A World Elsewhere: The Place of Style in American Literature,* New York, 1966.

From England come several important analytical studies: Tony Tanner, *The Reign of Wonder: Naivety and Reality in American Literature,* Cambridge, 1965; Martin Green, *Reappraisals: Some Commonsense Readings in American Literature,* New York, 1965; and Denis Donoghue, *The Ordinary Universe: Soundings in Modern Literature,* New York, 1968. From Italy come Cesare Pavese's collected essays on American authors, translated by Edwin Fussell under the title *American Literature: Essays and Opinion,* Berkeley, Calif., 1970; and 18 articles by Agostino Lombardo,

*Realismo e simbolismo: saggi di letteratura americana contemporanea,* Rome, 1957.

## 62. Magazines of Criticism

Critical articles on American literary-historical subjects appear in these journals not previously listed here: *TDR: Tulane Drama Review* (1957–1967), *Criticism* (1959–current), *Midway* (1960–current), *Drama Survey* (1961–current), *American Notes and Queries* (1962–current), *English Language Notes* (1963–current), *Studies in Short Fiction* (1963–current), *Tri-Quarterly* (1964–current), *Novel: A Forum on Fiction* (1967–current), *American Literary Realism, 1870–1910* (1967–current), *TDR: The Drama Review,* formerly *Tulane Drama Review,* (1968–current), *New Literary History* (1969–current), *Studies in the Novel* (1969–current), *Journal of Modern Literature* (1970–current), *Resources for American Literary Study* (1971–current).

*Southern Review* (1935–1942) was revived in Baton Rouge, Louisiana, in 1965 and is still current. *Kenyon Review,* founded in 1938, ceased publication in 1968.

Two new English journals, both edited in Manchester, are *Critical Quarterly* (1959–current) and *Journal of American Studies* (1967–current).

## 64. Experimental Magazines

The *Index to Little Magazines* continues to appear biannually as a two-year cumulation, compiled by various editors. The latest volume, covering 1966–1967 (Chicago, 1970), brings the coverage to the quarter-century mark. Stephen H. Goode is now at work continuing, retrospectively, the work begun with the first issue in this series—*Index to Little Magazines, 1948* (Denver, Colo., 1949). His first volume, *Index to Little Magazines, 1943–1947* (Denver, Colo., 1965), was followed by *Index to Little Magazines, 1940–1942* (New York, 1967). In ten projected volumes he will cover the years 1900–1948.

Kenneth A. Lohf and Eugene P. Sheehy prepared *An Index to the Little Review, 1914–1929,* New York, 1961.

Frederick J. Hoffman *et al., The Little Magazine: A History and a Bibliography,* 2nd ed., Princeton, N.J., 1966, is still the standard reference; but see also J. B. May, *Twigs as Varied Bent,* Corona, N.Y., 1954; and Leonard V. Fulton, *Directory of Little Magazines,* 2nd ed., El Cerrito, Calif., 1966. Three informative critical histories are G. A. M. Janssens, *The American Literary Review,* The Hague, 1966; Leonard Greenbaum,

*The Hound and Horn: The History of a Literary Quarterly,* The Hague, 1966; and James B. Gilbert, *Writers and Partisans,* New York, 1968, on the *Partisan Review*.

## 68. *Anthologies:*
### General Surveys

Among the many recent survey-anthologies of American literature are *Masters of American Literature,* ed. Leon Edel, Thomas H. Johnson, Sherman Paul, and Claude Simpson, 2 vols., Boston, 1959; *Major Writers of America,* gen. ed., Perry Miller, New York, 1962; *Voices from America's Past,* ed. Richard B. Morris and James L. Woodress, 3 vols., New York, 1963; *American Literature,* ed. Richard Poirier and William J. Vance, 2 vols., Boston, 1970; and *The Literature of America,* ed. Irving Howe, Mark Schorer, and Larzer Ziff, 3 vols., New York, 1970.

## 69. Special Surveys and Collections

Early American literature can be studied in three convenient collections: George F. Horner and Robert A. Bains, eds., *Colonial and Federalist American Writings,* New York, 1966; Robert E. Spiller, ed., *The American Literary Revolution, 1783–1837,* New York, 1967; and Roy Harvey Pearce, *Colonial American Writing,* 3rd ed., New York, 1969.

Nineteenth-century writers are reprinted in Richard H. Fogle, ed., *The Romantic Movement in American Writing,* New York, 1966; Bruce R. McElderry, Jr., *The Realistic Movement in American Writing,* New York, 1965; Wallace Stegner, ed., *Selected American Prose, 1841–1900: The Realistic Movement,* New York, 1958; Willard Thorp, ed., *Great Short Works of the American Renaissance,* New York, 1968, and *Great Short Works of American Realism,* New York, 1968; and Van Wyck Brooks, ed., *A New England Reader,* New York, 1962.

The South is represented in *Southern Writing in the Sixties: Fiction,* ed. John W. Corrington and Miller Williams, Baton Rouge, La., 1966; *South: Modern Southern Literature in Its Cultural Setting,* ed. Louis D. Rubin, Jr., and Robert D. Jacobs, Garden City, N.Y., 1961; *The Southwest in Life and Literature,* ed. Charles L. Sonnichsen, New York, 1962.

William T. Stafford surveys contemporary authors in *Twentieth Century American Writing,* New York, 1965. More specialized collections are Harvey Swados, ed., *The American Writer and the Great Depression,* Indianapolis, Ind., 1966; and Jack Salzman, ed., *Years of Protest: A Collection of American Writing of the 1930's,* New York, 1967.

**69.** INSTRUMENTS OF LITERARY PRODUCTION:
*Magazines*

The fifth volume of Frank Luther Mott's *A History of American Magazines*, Cambridge, Mass., 1968, is titled *Sketches of 21 Magazines, 1905–1930*. It was assembled by his daughter from notes left after his death in 1964. An extensive index for the entire series appears in this final volume. See also Theodore Peterson, *Magazines in the Twentieth Century*, 2nd ed., Urbana, Ill., 1964; and Roland E. Wolseley, *Understanding Magazines*, 2nd ed., Ames, Iowa, 1969. Theodore P. Greene, *America's Heroes: The Changing Models of Success in American Magazines*, New York, 1970, is "a capsule history of American magazines" as well as a study of individualism in America.

Histories of particular American magazines have appeared in abundance: Harold S. Wilson, *McClure's Magazine and the Muckrakers*, Princeton, N.J., 1970; Carl R. Dolmetsch, *The Smart Set: A History and Anthology*, New York, 1966; John Tebbel, *The American Magazine: A Compact History*, New York, 1969; three volumes on *The Dial*: Nicholas Joost, *Years of Transition: The Dial, 1912–1920*, Barre, Mass., 1967; *idem*, *Scofield Thayer and The Dial: An Illustrated History*, Carbondale, Ill., 1964; and William Wasserstrom, *The Time of The Dial*, Syracuse, N.Y., 1963; Susan J. Turner, *A History of The Freeman: Literary Landmark of the Early Twenties*, New York, 1963; and Robert T. Elson, *Time, Inc.: The Intimate History of a Publishing Empire, 1923–1941*, New York, 1968.

Biographies of magazine editors include Peter Lyon, *Success Story: The Life of S. S. McClure*, New York, 1963; Max Putzel, *The Man in the Mirror: William Marion Reedy and His Magazine*, Cambridge, Mass., 1963; and John Kobler, *Luce: His Time, Life, and Fortune*, New York, 1968. Contemporary editors reminisce: Norman Cousins about the *Saturday Review* in *Present Tense: An American Editor's Odyssey*, New York, 1967; Edward Weeks about the *Atlantic Monthly* in *In Friendly Candor*, Boston, 1959; and Otto Friedrich about the demise of the *Saturday Evening Post* in *Decline and Fall*, New York, 1970.

Frequently better than histories are samplings of a magazine's pages. A cross-section of our publishing tastes can be seen in *The Federalist Literary Mind: Selections from The Monthly Anthology and Boston Review, 1803–1811*, ed. Lewis P. Simpson, Baton Rouge, La., n.d.; *Gentlemen, Scholars and Scoundrels: A Treasury of the Best of Harper's Magazine from 1850 to the Present*, ed. Horace Knowles, New York, 1959; *Jubilee: One Hundred Years of the Atlantic*, ed. Edward Weeks and Emily Flint, Boston, 1957; *One Hundred Years of The Nation: A Centennial Anthology*,

*1865–1965*, ed. Henry M. Christman and Abraham Feldman, New York, 1965; *The Muckrakers: The Era in Journalism That Moved America to Reform—The Most Significant Magazine Articles of 1902–1912*, ed. Arthur Myron Weinberg and Lila Weinberg, New York, 1961; *Echoes of Revolt: The Masses 1911–1917*, ed. William L. O'Neill, Chicago, 1966; *A Dial Miscellany*, ed. William Wasserstrom, Syracuse, N.Y., 1963; *The Saturday Review Gallery*, with an introduction by John T. Winterich, New York, 1959; and *The Partisan Review Anthology*, ed. William Phillips and Philip Rahv, New York, 1962. Jesse Kornbluth edited *Notes from the Underground: An Anthology*, New York, 1970, "a comprehensive guide to the new crop of Anti-Establishment periodicals."

## 70. The Press

Frank Luther Mott's *American Journalism: A History, 1690–1960*, 3rd ed., New York, 1962, is still the standard history. But see also Bernard A. Weisberger, *The American Newspaperman*, Chicago, 1961; Alvin Silverman's pamphlet *The American Newspaper*, New York, 1964; and Edwin Emery, ed., *The Story of America as Reported by Its Newspapers, 1690–1965*, New York, 1965.

Specialized histories are Arthur M. Schlesinger, Sr., *Prelude to Independence: The Newspaper War on Britain, 1764–1776*, New York, 1958; Gottfried Dietze, *The Federalist: A Classic on Federalism and Free Government*, Baltimore, Md., 1960; Hodding Carter, *Their Words Were Bullets: The Southern Press in War, Reconstruction, and Peace*, Athens, Ga., 1969; Robert F. Karolevitz, *Newspapering in the Old West: A Pictorial History of Journalism and Printing on the Frontier*, Seattle, Wash., 1965; Julian S. Rammelkamp, *Pulitzer's Post-Dispatch, 1878–1883*, Princeton, N.J., 1967; Charles H. Brown, *The Correspondents' War: Journalists in the Spanish-American War*, New York, 1967; and Robert J. Glessing, *The Underground Press in America*, Bloomington, Ind., 1970.

Newsmen and observers have discussed special aspects of the press, chiefly contemporary: James Reston, *The Artillery of the Press: Its Influence on American Foreign Policy*, New York, 1967; Bernard C. Cohen, *The Press and Foreign Policy*, Princeton, N.J., 1963; John Hohenberg, *The New Front Page*, New York, 1966; Jonathan Daniels, *They Will Be Heard: America's Crusading Newspaper Editors*, New York, 1965; and Carl E. Lindstrom, *The Fading American Newspaper*, Garden City, N.Y., 1960. Two collections are especially valuable for their diverse opinions on large subjects: *The Press in Perspective*, ed. Ralph D. Casey, Baton Rouge, La., 1963; and *The Black American and the Press*, ed. Jack Lyle, Los Angeles, 1968.

Biographies illuminate still other aspects of journalism. Calder M. Pickett describes the conservative Middle West in *Ed Howe: Country Town Philosopher*, Lawrence, Kan., 1969. Two studies of Joseph Pulitzer analyze "the new style journalism" and its source: W. A. Swanberg, *Pulitzer*, New York, 1967; and George Juergens, *Joseph Pulitzer and the New York World*, Princeton, N.J., 1966. See also Homer W. King, *Pulitzer's Prize Editor: A Biography of John A. Cockerill, 1845–1896*, Durham, N.C., 1965. Roger Burlingame offers a popular account of "the life and times of Elmer Davis" in *Don't Let Them Scare You*, Philadelphia, 1961. Three former members of the New York *Times*'s staff survey that paper: Arthur Krock, *Memoirs: Sixty Years on the Firing Line*, New York, 1968; Turner Catledge, *My Life and The Times*, New York, 1971; and Gay Talese, *The Kingdom and the Power: The Story of the Men Who Influence the Institution That Influences the World—The New York Times*, New York, 1969. J. David Stern discusses the New York *Post* among other matters in *Memoirs of a Maverick Publisher*, New York, 1962. A running account of British and American journalists engaged in reporting current events from the Crimean War to the present is John Hohenberg's *Foreign Correspondence: The Great Reporters and Their Times*, New York, 1964.

Warren C. Price compiled *The Literature of Journalism: An Annotated Bibliography*, Minneapolis, Minn., 1959, concerned chiefly with newspapers and magazines of the United States, followed by a supplement (with Calder M. Pickett), *Annotated Journalism Bibliography, 1958–1968*, Minneapolis, Minn., 1970. More specialized is Ralph E. McCoy's *Freedom of the Press: An Annotated Bibliography*, Carbondale, Ill., 1968.

## 72. *THE COLONIAL PERIOD TO 1760*

CULTURAL HISTORY:
*General Studies*

Samuel Eliot Morison has begun a three-volume study with *The European Discovery of America: The Northern Voyages, A.D. 500–1600*, New York, 1971. Howard Mumford Jones traces the influence of the European Renaissance and the classical tradition on the American experience in *O Strange New World: American Culture: The Formative Years*, New York, 1964. A commendably concise treatment of our early years, written by an English scholar, is G. R. Crone's *The Discovery of America*, London, 1969.

Two important histories of the colonies are Clarence L. Ver Steeg, *The Formative Years, 1607–1763*, New York, 1964; and Wesley Frank Craven, *The Colonies in Transition, 1660–1713*, New York, 1968. Peter Gay analyzes the major historical works of leading Puritans—William Bradford, Cotton Mather, and Jonathan Edwards—in *A Loss of Mastery: Puritan Historians in Colonial America*, Berkeley, Calif., 1966. The church and state relationship, particularly the Church of England's influence in the colonies, is the subject of Carl Bridenbaugh's *Mitre and Sceptre: Trans-Atlantic Faiths, Ideas, Personalities, and Politics, 1689–1775*, New York, 1962. On more specialized topics, note must be made of Howard H. Peckham, *The Colonial Wars, 1689–1762*, Chicago, 1964; William H. Nelson, *The American Tory*, New York, 1961; and Richard M. Gummere, *The American Colonial Mind and the Classical Tradition*, Cambridge, Mass., 1963. Collections of essays include *Law and Authority in Colonial America*, ed. George Athan Billias, Barre, Mass., 1965; *Seventeenth-Century America: Essays in Colonial History*, ed. James Morton Smith, Chapel Hill, N.C., 1959; and *Politics and Society in Colonial America*, ed. Michael G. Kammen, New York, 1967. For general reference, Mark Mayo Boatner's *Encyclopedia of the American Revolution*, New York, 1966, is invaluable.

*The Colonial Image: Origins of American Culture*, ed. John C. Miller, New York, 1962, is a volume of generous selections from John Smith and William Bradford to Franklin and Crèvecoeur. The first volume of *Pamphlets of the American Revolution, 1750–1776*, edited by Bernard Bailyn with the assistance of Jane N. Garrett, Cambridge, Mass., 1965, prints 72 pamphlets from the years 1750–1765. Three more volumes will follow.

### 73. *New England*

The transition from colonist to American is the subject of two recent studies of the New England colonies: Richard Bushman, *From Puritan to Yankee: Character and the Social Order in Connecticut, 1690–1765*, Cambridge, Mass., 1967; and Richard S. Dunn, *Puritans and Yankees: The Winthrop Dynasty of New England, 1630–1717*, Princeton, N.J., 1962. Domestic life is studied in John Demos, *A Little Commonwealth: Family Life in Plymouth Colony*, New York, 1970; and Darrett B. Rutman, *Winthrop's Boston: Portrait of a Puritan Town, 1630–1649*, Chapel Hill, N.C., 1965. Peter N. Carroll's *Puritanism and the Wilderness*, New York, 1969, focuses on "the intellectual significance of the New England frontier, 1629–1700."

### 74. *The South*

Richard L. Morton's *Colonial Virginia*, 2 vols., Chapel Hill, N.C., 1960, covers the years 1607–1763 and has been called "incomparably the best political history" of the growth of the colony. Richard Beale Davis's *Intellectual Life in Jefferson's Virginia, 1790–1830*, Chapel Hill, N.C., 1964, ranges widely over law, politics, science, religion, fine arts, and literature. Hennig Cohen, *The South Carolina Gazette, 1732-1775*, Columbia, S.C., 1953, is a study of the literary culture of the colonial South as well as a history of a newspaper.

### 86. *THE FORMING OF THE REPUBLIC: 1760–1820*

CULTURAL HISTORY:
*General Studies*

Daniel J. Boorstin continues his history of the American people, begun in *The Americans: The Colonial Experience* (1958), with a survey from the Revolution to the Civil War, *The Americans: The National Experience*, New York, 1965. A third volume is projected. Jackson Turner Main examines four different kinds of societies—frontier, subsistence farm, commercial farm, and urban—in *The Social Structure of Revolutionary America*, Princeton, N.J., 1965. Russel B. Nye's *The Cultural Life of the New Nation, 1776–1830*, New York, 1960, covers "the transition from the age of Locke and Jefferson to the age of Coleridge and Emerson." Adrienne Koch discusses the character and thought of John Adams, Franklin, Hamilton, Jefferson, and Madison in *Power, Morals, and the Founding Fathers: Essays in the Interpretation of the American Enlightenment*, Ithaca, N.Y., 1961.

## 87. *Historical and Political Writing*

John Adams, Franklin, Hamilton, Jefferson, Madison, and Washington are treated in individual bibliographies below.

Five recent histories, most of them concise accounts and all of them general interpretive surveys, cover these 60 years more than adequately: Bernhard Knollenberg, *Origin of the American Revolution, 1759–1766*, New York, 1960; Forrest McDonald, *E Pluribus Unum: The Formation of the American Republic, 1776–1790*, Boston, 1965; Gordon S. Wood, *The Creation of the American Republic, 1776–1787*, Chapel Hill, N.C., 1969; John C. Miller, *The Federalist Era, 1789–1801*, New York, 1960; and Marcus Cunliffe, *The Nation Takes Shape, 1789–1837*, Chicago, 1959.

Histories of the Revolution continue to proliferate. John R. Alden argues a need "for a modern and relatively detailed book" that deals "with things social, economic, political, military, and diplomatic" between 1763 and 1789. He has succeeded nobly in creating that book: *A History of the American Revolution*, New York, 1969. Merrill Jensen's *The Founding of a Nation: A History of the American Revolution, 1763–1776*, New York, 1962, is essentially a political history. More specialized treatments of the era are Bernard Bailyn, *The Ideological Origins of the American Revolution*, Cambridge, Mass., 1967; H. Trevor Colbourn, *The Lamp of Experience: Whig History and the Intellectual Origins of the American Revolution*, Chapel Hill, N.C., 1965; David Hawke, *In the Midst of a Revolution*, Philadelphia, 1961; and Richard B. Morris, *The American Revolution Reconsidered*, New York, 1967. Catherine Drinker Bowen, in *Miracle at Philadelphia*, Boston, 1966, confines herself to "the story of the Constitutional Convention, May to September, 1787." Much new material, unfortunately of minor writers, is uncovered in Bruce Ingham Granger's *Political Satire in the American Revolution, 1763–1783*, Ithaca, N.Y., 1960. Students of American history will also want to consult R. R. Palmer's massive synthesis, *The Age of the Democratic Revolution*, 2 vols., Princeton, N.J., 1959–1964, subtitled *A Political History of Europe and America, 1760–1800*.

More specialized histories, concerned with sectionalism, are Francis S. Philbrick, *The Rise of the West, 1754–1830*, New York, 1965; Thomas P. Abernethy, *The South in the New Nation, 1789–1819*, Baton Rouge, La., 1961; and Norman K. Risjord, *The Old Republicans: Southern Conserva-*

*tism in the Age of Jefferson,* New York, 1965. Harold and James Kirker's *Bulfinch's Boston, 1787–1817,* New York, 1964, is a history of the city as well as of the architect's total involvement in Boston life.

## 99. *Poetry*

Gordon E. Bigelow develops general theories as well as critical analyses in *Rhetoric and American Poetry of the Early National Period,* Gainesville, Fla., 1960. Two useful anthologies of the period are *Colonial American Poetry,* ed. Kenneth Silverman, New York, 1968; and *Seventeenth-Century American Poetry,* ed. Harrison T. Meserole, Garden City, N.Y., 1968. See also the relevant chapters in Hyatt H. Waggoner's *American Poets from the Puritans to the Present,* Boston, 1968.

## 102. *Drama*

Hugh F. Rankin's *The Theatre in Colonial America,* Chapel Hill, N.C., 1965, is the first full-length study based on original sources and written from the historian's viewpoint. Brooks McNamara has provided an important architectural history, *The American Playhouse in the Eighteenth Century,* Cambridge, Mass., 1969, tracing major changes from the first playhouse (in Williamsburg, about 1716) to the end of the century.

## 107. *THE MID-NINETEENTH CENTURY*

LITERARY AND CULTURAL HISTORY:
*Fiction*

Five of the major studies of this period are Marius Bewley's "cultural polemic," *The Eccentric Design,* New York, 1959, with important chapters on Cooper, Hawthorne, and Henry James among others; Harry Levin, *The Power of Blackness,* New York, 1958, concentrating on Poe, Hawthorne, and Melville; Daniel G. Hoffman, *Form and Fable in American Fiction,* New York, 1961, a thematic treatment of Irving, Hawthorne, Melville, and Twain; Joel Porte, *The Romance in America,* Middletown, Conn., 1969, studies from Cooper to James; and D. E. S. Maxwell, *American Fiction: The Intellectual Background,* New York, 1963, a survey from Cooper to Wharton. A. N. Kaul treats "actual and ideal society in 19th-century fiction" in *The American Vision,* New Haven, Conn., 1963. David W. Noble is somewhat more specialized in *The Eternal Adam and the New World Garden: The Central Myth in the American Novel since 1830,* New York,

1968. See also *Six American Novelists of the Nineteenth Century: An Introduction*, ed. Richard Foster, Minneapolis, Minn., 1968, a gathering of Minnesota pamphlets.

Regional studies include Edwin W. Gaston, *The Early Novel of the Southwest*, Albuquerque, N.M., 1961; and James G. Johnson, *Southern Fiction prior to 1860*, New York, 1968. H. Bruce Franklin assembled an anthology with historical-critical introductions in *Future Perfect: American Science Fiction of the Nineteenth Century*, New York, 1966. The legacy of Jeffersonian idealism is the focus of Howard Mumford Jones's *Jeffersonianism and the American Novel*, New York, 1966. Two religio-philosophical studies are Terence Martin, *The Instructed Vision: Scottish Common Sense Philosophy and the Origins of American Fiction*, Bloomington, Ind., 1961; and John T. Frederick, *The Darkened Sky: Nineteenth-Century Novelists and Religion*, Notre Dame, Ind., 1969. Nathalia Wright investigates some of our expatriate authors in *American Novelists in Italy: The Discoverers: Allston to James*, Philadelphia, 1965. See also the relevant pages on fiction in Edmund Wilson's *Patriotic Gore: Studies in the Literature of the American Civil War*, New York, 1962.

## 109. *Poetry*

Lee Steinmetz edited *The Poetry of the American Civil War*, East Lansing, Mich., 1960, an anthology of little-known pieces.

## 113. *Drama*

Three specialized histories contribute significant knowledge of our cultural patterns: David Grimsted, *Melodrama Unveiled: American Theater and Culture, 1800–1850*, Chicago, 1968; James H. Dormon, Jr., *Theater in the Ante-Bellum South: 1815–1861*, Chapel Hill, N.C., 1967; and Francis Hodge, *Yankee Theatre: The Image of America on the Stage, 1825–1850*, Austin, Tex., 1964. Richard Moody's *Edwin Forrest: First Star of the American Stage*, New York, 1960, is the first full-scale biography. Charles H. Shattuck's *The Hamlet of Edwin Booth*, Urbana, Ill., 1969, is detailed acting history.

## 116. *The Essay and Social Criticism:*
General Studies

Among the important intellectual histories are Irving H. Bartlett, *The American Mind in the Mid-Nineteenth Century*, New York, 1967; and

Clement Eaton, *The Mind of the Old South*, Baton Rouge, La., 1964. Clifford S. Griffin concentrates on the Calvinist tradition in *Their Brothers' Keepers: Moral Stewardship in the United States, 1800–1865*, New Brunswick, N.J., 1960. Frank Thistlethwaite's *The Anglo-American Connection in the Early Nineteenth Century*, Philadelphia, 1959, is concerned with intercultural communication. Fred Somkin describes "some of the contradictions that appeared in American life during the first half of the 19th century" in *Unquiet Eagle: Memory and Desire in the Idea of Freedom, 1815–1860*, Ithaca, N.Y., 1967. Timothy L. Smith treats one phase of our cultural history in *Revivalism and Social Reform in Mid-Nineteenth Century America*, New York, 1957. *American Life in the 1840's*, ed. Carl Bode, New York, 1967, reprints historical documents about the daily life of the average American.

Specialized histories include George Dangerfield, *The Awakening of American Nationalism, 1815–1828*, New York, 1965; Glyndon G. Van Deusen, *The Jacksonian Era, 1828–1848*, New York, 1959; Avery O. Craven, *Civil War in the Making, 1815–1860*, Baton Rouge, La., 1959; Douglas T. Miller, *Jacksonian Aristocracy: Class and Democracy in New York, 1830–1860*, New York, 1967; Roy F. Nichols, *The Stakes of Power, 1845–1877*, New York, 1961; and David Donald, *The Politics of Reconstruction, 1863–1867*, Baton Rouge, La., 1965.

Two of the most ambitious books on Southern history during this period are Clement Eaton, *The Growth of Southern Civilization, 1790–1860*, New York, 1961; and Thomas D. Clark and Albert D. Kirwan, *The South since Appomattox: A Century of Regional Change*, New York, 1967. Charles P. Roland's *The Confederacy*, Chicago, 1960, is a concise treatment of the subject. The image of the South in Northern literary art is the subject of Howard R. Floan's *The South in Northern Eyes, 1831 to 1861*, Austin, Tex., 1958. William R. Taylor pursues the history and development of stereotypes in *Cavalier and Yankee: The Old South and American National Character*, New York, 1961.

Coping with the subject of the Civil War from either a literary or a sociohistorical viewpoint is impossible here. Students are urged to consult *Civil War Books: A Critical Bibliography*, compiled by Allan Nevins, James I. Robertson, Jr., and Bell I. Wiley, 2 vols., Baton Rouge, La., 1967–1969, a listing of over 5,000 annotated titles with a cross-referenced index. For quick reference to names and dates, see Mark Mayo Boatner, *The Civil War Dictionary*, New York, 1959; and Henry E. Simmons, *A Concise Encyclopedia of the Civil War*, New York, 1965. Social history of the ante-bellum South (1825–1860) is indexed in the third volume of *Travels in the Old South: A Bibliography*, ed. Thomas D. Clark, Norman, Okla., 1956–1959.

## 133. *THE LATE NINETEENTH CENTURY*

*Studies Specific to the Period*

One of the most comprehensive cultural histories of the period is Howard Mumford Jones's *The Age of Energy: Varieties of American Experience, 1865–1915*, New York, 1971. A politico-economic history of the same period is Ray Ginger's *Age of Excess: The United States from 1877–1914*, New York, 1965. Robert H. Wiebe discusses "the reconstruction of American society" during the period in *The Search for Order, 1877–1920*, New York, 1967. Christopher Lasch's *The New Radicalism in America, 1889–1963*, New York, 1965, focuses on "the intellectual as a social type." See also Frederic Cople Jaher, *Doubters and Dissenters: Cataclysmic Thought in America, 1885–1918*, London, 1964.

Several volumes of collected essays add important appraisals and reappraisals of the history of this period: H. Wayne Morgan, ed., *The Gilded Age*, rev. ed., Syracuse, N.Y., 1970; Ari and Olive Hoogenboom, eds., *The Gilded Age*, Englewood Cliffs, N.J., 1967; Ray Ginger, ed., *The Nationalizing of American Life, 1877–1900*, New York, 1965; and John Tipple, ed., *The Capitalist Revolution: A History of American Social Thought, 1890–1919*, New York, 1970.

Two volumes concentrate on the years immediately following the Civil War: John Hope Franklin, *Reconstruction: After the Civil War*, Chicago, 1961; and Rembert W. Patrick, *The Reconstruction of the Nation*, New York, 1967. Hugh C. Bailey discusses Southern social reformers and the progressive movement, beginning in the 1890's, in *Liberalism in the New South*, Coral Gables, Fla., 1969. See also the pertinent chapters in C. Vann Woodward's *The Burden of Southern History*, Baton Rouge, La., 1960.

More specialized political histories are J. Rogers Hollingsworth, *The Whirligig of Politics: The Democracy of Cleveland and Bryan*, Chicago, 1963; Paul W. Glad, *The Trumpet Soundeth: William Jennings Bryan and His Democracy, 1896–1912*, Lincoln, Neb., 1960; and Ray Ginger, *Altgeld's America: The Lincoln Ideal versus Changing Realities*, New York, 1958, which illuminates the change from rural to urban America, particularly Altgeld's Chicago, 1892–1905. Economic history can be found in Walter T. K. Nugent's *Money and American Society, 1865–1880*, New York, 1968; international affairs in Ernest R. May, *From Imperialism to Isolationism, 1898–1919*, New York, 1964, and in Robert L. Beisner, *Twelve against Empire: The Anti-Imperialists, 1898–1900*, New York, 1968. The power of the press and contemporary journalism in moving

America to reform is the focus of David M. Chalmers's *The Social and Political Ideas of the Muckrakers,* New York, 1964; and Arthur and Lila Weinberg's collection of "the most significant magazine articles of 1902–1912," *The Muckrakers,* New York, 1961.

Two highly specialized cultural studies important for contemporaneous reflections of late nineteenth-century American society are John Henry Raleigh, *Matthew Arnold and American Culture,* Berkeley, Calif., 1957; and Helen Howe, *The Gentle Americans, 1864–1960: Biography of a Breed,* New York, 1965.

Social history of the postwar South (1865–1900) is indexed in the first volume of *Travels in the New South: A Bibliography,* ed. Thomas D. Clark, Norman, Okla., 1962.

### 134. Fiction

New developments in the novel, particularly social fiction, are the focus of Robert Falk, *The Victorian Mode in American Fiction, 1865–1885,* East Lansing, Mich., 1965; Gordon O. Taylor, *The Passages of Thought: Psychological Representation in the American Novel, 1870–1900,* New York, 1969; and Robert W. Schneider, *Five Novelists of the Progressive Era,* New York, 1965. See also the relevant chapters in Gordon Milne, *The American Political Novel,* Norman, Okla., 1966; William Wasserstrom, *Heiress of All the Ages: Sex and Sentiment in the Genteel Tradition,* Minneapolis, Minn., 1959; and Sergio Perosa, *Le vie della narrativa americana,* Milan, 1965, especially the chapters on Henry James and Stephen Crane. Jan W. Dietrichson's *The Image of Money in the American Novel of the Gilded Age,* Oslo, 1969, is limited to James and Howells. Marianne Debouzy's *La genèse de l'esprit de révolte dans le roman américain, 1875–1915,* Paris, 1968, treats the novel from Howells through Upton Sinclair.

### 136. Poetry

Two critical surveys of the period are Aaron Kramer, *The Prophetic Tradition in American Poetry, 1835–1900,* Rutherford, N.J., 1968; and Robert H. Walker, *The Poet and the Gilded Age,* Philadelphia, 1963. Useful anthologies are *The Poetry of the American Civil War,* ed. Lee Steinmetz, East Lansing, Mich., 1960; and *The American Poets, 1800–1900,* ed. Edwin Cady, Glenview, Ill., 1966.

### 138. Drama

No single volume treats only this period, but relevant chapters in these histories are important for the scholar: Walter J. Meserve, *An Outline*

*History of American Drama,* Totowa, N.J., 1965; Alfred L. Bernheim, *The Business of the Theatre: An Economic History . . . 1750–1932,* New York, 1964; Jack Poggi, *Theater in America: The Impact of Economic Forces, 1870–1967,* Ithaca, N.Y., 1968; Brooks Atkinson, *Broadway,* New York, 1970; Ima Honaker Herron, *The Small Town in American Drama,* Dallas, Tex., 1969; and Daniel C. Blum, *A Pictorial History of the American Theatre: 100 Years, 1860–1960,* Philadelphia, 1960, rev. ed., ed. John Willis, New York, 1969.

## 151. *THE TWENTIETH CENTURY*

LITERARY AND CULTURAL HISTORY:
*Fiction*
Critical Analysis: Contemporary

Several volumes, among the many treating this subject, aim at general considerations of contemporary fiction: Michael Millgate, *American Social Fiction: James to Cozzens,* New York, 1964; Nelson Manfred Blake, *Novelists' America: Fiction as History, 1910–1940,* Syracuse, N.Y., 1969; John W. Aldridge, *Time to Murder and Create: The Contemporary Novel in Crisis,* New York, 1966; Arthur Mizener, *The Sense of Life in the Modern Novel,* Boston, 1964; and Walter Allen, *The Modern Novel in Britain and the United States,* New York, 1964. Jack Ludwig's *Recent American Novelists,* Minneapolis, Minn., 1962, is a pamphlet. See also the relevant chapters in Willard Thorp's *American Writing in the Twentieth Century,* Cambridge, Mass., 1960.

Chief among the studies treating the fiction of mid-century and after are Ihab Hassan, *Radical Innocence: Studies in the Contemporary American Novel,* Princeton, N.J., 1961; Marcus Klein, *After Alienation: American Novels in Mid-Century,* Cleveland, Ohio, 1964; Jonathan Baumbach, *The Landscape of Nightmare,* New York, 1965; Robert Scholes, *The Fabulators,* New York, 1967; Helen A. Weinberg, *The New Novel in America: The Kafkan Mode in Contemporary Fiction,* Ithaca, N.Y., 1969; and Tony Tanner, *City of Words: American Fiction, 1950–1970,* New York, 1971. But see also David D. Galloway, *The Absurd Hero in American Fiction: Updike, Styron, Bellow, Salinger,* Austin, Tex., 1966; Howard M. Harper, Jr., *Desperate Faith: A Study of Bellow, Salinger, Mailer, Baldwin, and Updike,* Chapel Hill, N.C., 1967; Irving Malin, *New American Gothic,* Carbondale, Ill., 1962; and Max F. Schulz, *Radical Sophistication: Studies in Contemporary Jewish-American Novelists,* Athens, Ohio, 1969. M. Mendelson has written a Russian study of five writers (1939–1962) in *The Contemporary American Novel*, Moscow, 1964.

Among the many collections of critical essays are *The Idea of an American Novel*, ed. Louis D. Rubin, Jr., and John Rees Moore, New York, 1961, selected documents "that bear on our long-standing self-consciousness about the American novel"; *The American Novel: From James Fenimore Cooper to William Faulkner*, ed. Wallace Stegner, New York, 1965 (Voice of America broadcasts); *Seven Modern American Novelists: An Introduction*, ed. William Van O'Connor, Minneapolis, Minn., 1964; 18 essays on newer novelists, *Contemporary American Novelists*, ed. Harry T. Moore, Carbondale, Ill., 1964; *The Creative Present: Notes on Contemporary American Fiction*, ed. Nona Balakian and Charles Simmons, Garden City, N.Y., 1963; and *Seven Contemporary Authors: Essays on Cozzens, Miller, West, Golding, Heller, Albee, and Powers*, ed. Thomas B. Whitbread, Austin, Tex., 1966.

## 152. Critical Analysis: Historical

Leslie A. Fiedler, *Love and Death in the American Novel*, New York, 1960, rev. ed., 1966, is a highly individual psychological study of fiction from 1789 to 1959. James B. Gilbert writes a "history of literary radicalism" in *Writers and Partisans*, New York, 1968.

Still one of the best general surveys of the short story, Fred Lewis Pattee's *The Development of the American Short Story* (1923) has been reprinted, New York, 1966. Austin M. Wright's *The American Short Story in the Twenties*, Chicago, 1961, concentrates on Anderson, Fitzgerald, Hemingway, Faulkner, and Katherine Anne Porter. William Peden's *The American Short Story*, Boston, 1964, is a historical and bibliographical study.

## 153. Special Studies

Regional studies include four books on the South: Frederick J. Hoffman, *The Art of Southern Fiction: A Study of Some Modern Novelists*, Carbondale, Ill., 1967; C. Hugh Holman, *Three Modes of Modern Southern Fiction: Ellen Glasgow, William Faulkner, Thomas Wolfe*, Athens, Ga., 1966; Louis D. Rubin, Jr., *The Faraway Country: Writers of the Modern South* [from Cable to Styron], Seattle, Wash., 1963; Louise Y. Gossett, *Violence in Recent Southern Fiction*, Durham, N.C., 1965; and three books on the West: Roy W. Meyer, *The Middle Western Farm Novel in the Twentieth Century*, Lincoln, Neb., 1965; Nicholas J. Karolides, *The Pioneer in the*

*American Novel, 1900–1950*, Norman, Okla., 1967; and James K. Folsom, *The American Western Novel*, New Haven, Conn., 1966.

Stanley Cooperman offers a thematic treatment in *World War I and the American Novel*, Baltimore, Md., 1967; a brief European view of the same subject is Ulrich Steuerwald's *Der Americanische Weltkriegsroman, 1919–1939*, Bern, 1965. Warren French concentrates on naturalism in *The Social Novel at the End of an Era* [ca. 1940], Carbondale, Ill., 1966. Chester E. Eisinger analyses the next decade in *Fiction of the Forties*, Chicago, 1963. Louis Auchincloss studies nine women novelists (from Sarah Orne Jewett to Mary McCarthy) in *Pioneers and Caretakers*, Minneapolis, Minn., 1965. Joseph Blotner spans the years 1900–1960 in *The Modern American Political Novel*, Austin, Tex., 1966. Albert D. Van Nostrand studies "the relation between commercial pressures and artistic purposes in marketing books" in *The Denatured Novel*, Indianapolis, Ind., 1960. John O. Lyons's *The College Novel in America*, Carbondale, Ill., 1962, is a survey of more than 200 novels from the early nineteenth century to the present. Anne M. Springer's *The American Novel in Germany*, Hamburg, 1961, offers not only an important bibliography but studies of our fiction between the wars, from London to Hemingway. See also the relevant chapters in Alma Elizabeth Murch, *The Development of the Detective Novel*, New York, 1958; and Kingsley Amis, *New Maps of Hell: A Survey of Science Fiction*, New York, 1960.

Studies of the Negro writer include Edward Margolies, *Native Sons: A Critical Study of Twentieth-Century Negro American Authors*, Philadelphia, 1968; *Anger and Beyond: The Negro Writer in the United States*, ed. Herbert Hill, New York, 1966; and *Five Black Writers: Essays on Wright, Ellison, Baldwin, Hughes, and LeRoi Jones*, ed. Donald B. Gibson, New York, 1971. John H. Clarke, ed., *William Styron's Nat Turner: Ten Black Writers Respond*, Boston, 1968, is a violent reaction against Styron's novel, *The Confessions of Nat Turner* (1967). *Images of the Negro in American Literature*, ed. Seymour L. Gross and John Edward Hardy, Chicago, 1966, reprints articles with a valuable introduction and checklist of criticism and scholarship by Gross.

## 154. Bibliography

For the major bibliographies, see pages 7–8 above. Additional specialized listings are A. T. Dickinson, Jr., *American Historical Fiction*, 3rd ed., New York, 1971, almost 2,000 titles classified into periods of American history from Colonial times to 1962; and W. Tasker Witham, *The Adolescent in the American Novel: 1920–1960*, New York, 1964, over 500 works with brief critical commentary.

**157.** *Poetry Since 1910:*

Anthologies

Choosing the best from among the score of good anthologies is impossible. Two well-made hard-cover collections are *Twentieth Century Poetry: American and British (1900–1970)*, ed. John Malcolm Brinnin and Bill Read with photographs by Rollie McKenna, rev. ed., New York, 1970; and *Chief Modern Poets of England and America*, ed. Gerald De Witt Sanders, John Herbert Nelson, and M. L. Rosenthal, 5th ed., New York, 1970. Two early paper-bound gatherings of the poetry of the fifties and sixties are totally different in viewpoint: the academic poets appear in *New Poets of England and America*, ed. Donald Hall, Robert Pack, and Louis Simpson, New York, 1957, rev. ed., 1962; the Beat poets and the more experimental appear in *The New American Poetry, 1945–1960*, ed. Donald M. Allen, New York, 1960. Since that time other commendable collections have appeared: *Today's Poets*, ed. Chad Walsh, New York, 1964; *A Controversy of Poets*, ed. Paris Leary and Robert Kelly, Garden City, N.Y., 1965; *Poems of Our Moment*, ed. John Hollander, New York, 1968; *The Contemporary American Poets*, ed. Mark Strand, New York and Cleveland, Ohio, 1969; *Naked Poetry: Recent American Poetry in Open Forms*, ed. Stephen Berg and Robert Mezey, Indianapolis, Ind., 1969; and *The Young American Poets*, ed. Paul Carroll, Chicago, 1968. Generous selections of Negro poetry are available in *New Negro Poets: U.S.A.*, ed. Langston Hughes, Bloomington, Ind., 1964; *American Negro Poetry*, ed. Arna Bontemps, New York, 1963; and *Black Fire: An Anthology of Afro-American Writing*, ed. LeRoi Jones and Larry Neal, New York, 1968.

**157.** Poetry Criticism

The most ambitious historical survey is Hyatt H. Waggoner's *American Poets from the Puritans to the Present*, Boston, 1968. Roy Harvey Pearce stresses the relation of American poetry to American culture through analyses of selected poets from Edward Taylor to Wallace Stevens in *The Continuity of American Poetry*, Princeton, N.J., 1961. A perceptive "survey" of contemporary poetry is in two books by M. L. Rosenthal: *The Modern Poets: A Critical Introduction*, New York, 1960, and *The New Poets: American and British Poetry since World War II*, New York, 1967. For briefer comments see Stephen Stepanchev, *American Poetry since 1945*, New York, 1965; and Glauco Cambon's pamphlet, *Recent American Poetry*, Minneapolis, Minn., 1962.

Critical essays which treat individual poets, for the most part, are in Richard Howard's comprehensive *Alone with America*, New York, 1969;

and in Ralph J. Mills, Jr.'s considerably briefer *Contemporary American Poetry*, New York, 1965. Michael Yatron, in *America's Literary Revolt*, New York, 1959, concentrates on Masters, Lindsay, Sandburg, and Populism. J. Hillis Miller studies Eliot, Stevens, and William Carlos Williams in the company of Europeans in *Poets of Reality*, Cambridge, Mass., 1965. A. D. Van Nostrand is especially informative on Whitman and Hart Crane in *Everyman His Own Poet*, New York, 1968; Glauco Cambon focuses on Stevens, Williams, and Hart Crane in *The Inclusive Flame*, Bloomington, Ind., 1963; and Karl Shapiro attacks Pound, Eliot, and other moderns in the pages of *In Defense of Ignorance*, New York, 1960. Joseph Warren Beach's posthumous volume, *Obsessive Images*, ed. William Van O'Connor, Minneapolis, Minn., 1960, is confined to "symbolism in poetry of the 1930's and 1940's." The Beat Generation—Ginsberg, Ferlinghetti, Snyder, Corso, and others—is chronicled in *A Casebook on the Beat*, ed. Thomas Parkinson, New York, 1961; *The Beat Scene*, ed. Elias Wilentz with photographs by Fred McDarrah, New York, 1960; and Bruce Cook, *The Beat Generation*, New York, 1971.

*Dionysus and the City: Modernism in Twentieth-Century Poetry*, New York, 1970, is an elaborate exposition by Monroe K. Spears of the term "modernism." L. S. Dembo works out philosophical theory in *Conceptions of Reality in Modern American Poetry*, Berkeley, Calif., 1966. Harvey Gross "approaches the union of form, meaning, and sound through a study of prosody" in *Sound and Form in Modern Poetry*, Ann Arbor, Mich., 1964. One of the most original studies of the nature of the poetic imagination is Stanley Burnshaw's *The Seamless Web*, New York, 1970.

Among the composite volumes—collected essays by various hands on a variety of subjects and poets—these are useful: *Start with the Sun: Studies in Cosmic Poetry*, ed. James E. Miller, Jr., Karl Shapiro, and Bernice Slote, Lincoln, Neb., 1960; *Poets in Progress*, ed. Edward Hungersford, Evanston, Ill., 1962; *Aspects of American Poetry*, ed. Richard M. Ludwig, Columbus, Ohio, 1963; *The Contemporary Poet as Artist and Critic*, ed. Anthony Ostroff, Boston, 1964; *American Poetry*, ed. Irvin Ehrenpreis, New York, 1965; *Poets on Poetry*, ed. Howard Nemerov, New York, 1966 (Voice of America lectures by 19 poets); and *The Poet as Critic*, ed. F. P. W. McDowell, Evanston, Ill., 1967.

European scholars have provided a variety of critical volumes. From England: A. Alvarez, *The Shaping Spirit*, London, 1958 (published the same year in New York under the title *Stewards of Excellence*); Denis Donoghue, *Connoisseurs of Chaos*, New York, 1965; and *The Ordinary Voice*, New York, 1968. From Italy: Ruggero Bianchi, *La poetica dell' imagismo*, Milan, 1965; and Vito Amoruso, *La letteratura beat americana*, Bari, 1969. From Germany: Klaus Heinrich Kohring, *Die Formen des*

*"Long Poem"* in der Modernen Amerikanischen Literatur, Heidelberg, 1967.

An important guide to poetics and the terms of poetic analysis is Karl Shapiro and Robert Beum, *A Prosody Handbook*, New York, 1965.

### 159. Bibliography

Two reference volumes of biographical and bibliographical information are Stephen Spender and Donald Hall, eds., *The Concise Encyclopedia of English and American Poets and Poetry,* London, 1963; and Rosalie Murphy, ed., *Contemporary Poets of the English Language,* Chicago, 1970. The major reference work for history, types, movements, prosody, and critical terminology is *Encyclopedia of Poetry and Poetics,* ed. Alex Preminger, Frank J. Warnke, and O. B. Hardison, Jr., Princeton, N.J., 1965.

### 162. *Drama:*
Anthologies

*America's Lost Plays,* ed. Barrett H. Clark *et al.,* 20 vols., 1940, have been reissued in ten volumes, Bloomington, Ind. 1963–1965. A twenty-first volume was recently added to the collection: *Satiric Comedies: America's Lost Plays,* ed. William R. Reardon and Walter J. Meserve, Bloomington, Ind., 1969.

Useful collections of plays are *Dramas from the American Theatre, 1762–1909,* ed. Richard Moody, Cleveland, Ohio, 1966; *The Black Crook and Other Nineteenth-Century American Plays,* ed. Myron Matlaw, New York, 1967; and *American Dramatic Literature,* ed. Jordan Y. Miller, New York, 1961, an anthology of dramatic art since 1918. Contemporary drama can be found in Robert W. Corrigan's selection, *New American Plays,* I, New York, 1970, followed by William M. Hoffman's *New American Plays,* II and III, New York, 1970. See also *Theatre Experiment,* comp. Michael Benedikt, New York, 1967; and *Eight Plays from Off-Off Broadway,* ed. Nick Orzel and Michael Smith, Indianapolis, Ind., 1966.

### 163. Criticism

General surveys of the period are Joseph Golden, *The Death of Tinker Bell: The American Theatre in the 20th Century,* Syracuse, N.Y., 1967; Alan S. Downer, *Recent American Drama,* Minneapolis, Minn., 1961; and Brooks Atkinson, *Broadway,* New York, 1970. See also Walter J. Meserve, *An Outline History of American Drama,* Totowa, N.J., 1965. Three volumes concentrate on the 1930's: Jane DeHart Mathews, *The Federal Theatre, 1935–1939: Plays, Relief, and Politics,* Princeton, N.J., 1967; Morgan Y. Himelstein, *Drama Was a Weapon: The Left-Wing Theatre in New York, 1929–1941,* New Brunswick, N.J., 1963; and Gerald Rabkin, *Drama and Commitment: Politics in the American Theatre of the Thirties,* Bloomington, Ind., 1964. Gerald Weales treats in great detail the post–1945 theatre: *American Drama since World War II,* New York, 1962, and *The Jumping-Off Place: American Drama in the 1960's,* New York, 1969. Even more specialized are Allan Lewis, *American Plays and Playwrights of the Contemporary Theatre,* New York, 1965, covering the period 1957–1964; C. E. W. Bigsby, *Confrontation and Commitment: A Study of Contemporary American Drama, 1959–1966,* London, 1967, Columbia, Mo., 1968; and William Goldman, *The Season* [1967–1968]: *A Candid Look at Broadway,* New York, 1969.

Julia S. Price chronicles the other part of New York theatre, *The Off-Broadway Theater,* New York, 1962; and Julius Novick makes a critical study of 50 resident professional theatre companies in *Beyond Broadway: The Quest for Permanent Theatres,* New York, 1968. Two important studies of Negro contributions to the theatre are Loften Mitchell, *Black Drama: The Story of the American Negro in the Theatre,* New York, 1967; and Doris E. Abramson, *Negro Playwrights in the American Theatre, 1925–1959,* New York, 1969. Musical comedy is the focus of Lehman Engel's *The American Musical Theater: A Consideration,* New York, 1967. Peripheral studies useful to the student of American culture include Albert F. McLean, Jr., *American Vaudeville as Ritual,* Lexington, Ky., 1965; Marian Spitzer, *The Palace,* New York, 1969, a history of the vaudeville house on Broadway at Forty-seventh Street that opened in 1913; Irving Zeidman, *The American Burlesque Show,* New York, 1967; and George K. Chindahl, *A History of the Circus in America,* Caldwell, Idaho, 1959.

Thomas E. Porter studies nine plays beginning with O'Neill in *Myth and Modern Drama,* Detroit, Mich., 1969. Louis Broussard focuses on "contemporary allegory from Eugene O'Neill to Tennessee Williams" in *American Drama,* Norman, Okla., 1962; and Denis Donoghue treats "modern British and American verse drama" in *The Third Voice,* Princeton, N.J., 1959. Collections of critical essays include Horst Frenz, ed., *American Playwrights on Drama,* New York, 1965; Alan S. Downer, ed. *American Drama and Its Critics,* Chicago, 1965; John Russell Brown and Bernard Harris, eds., *American Theatre,* New York, 1967; and Alan S. Downer, ed., *The American Theatre Today,* New York, 1967 (originally Voice of America broadcasts).

Some of the best criticism of the American theatre comes, naturally, from notes and reviews. In recent years, important collections of essays and second thoughts have appeared: Walter Kerr, *Pieces at Eight,* New York, 1957; *The Theater in Spite of Itself,* New York, 1963; and *Thirty Plays Hath November,* New York, 1969; Robert Brustein, *The Theatre of Revolt,* Boston, 1964; *Seasons of Discontent,* New York, 1967; and *The Third Theatre,* New York, 1969; Harold Clurman, *The Naked Image: Observations in the Modern Theatre,* New York, 1966; Richard Gilman, *Common and Uncommon Masks: Writings on Theatre, 1961–1970,* New York, 1970; Richard Schechner, *Public Domain,* Indianapolis, Ind., 1969; Martin Gottfried, *A Theater Divided: The Postwar American Stage,* Boston, 1968; and John Lahr, *Up Against the Fourth Wall,* New York, 1970.

### 163. Bibliography

The annals of the Broadway theatre can be followed by the *Best Plays* series, annual volumes begun 1920 and edited for many years by Burns Mantle. From 1953–1961, Louis Kronenberger edited the series; from 1962–1964, Henry Hewes; from 1965, Otis L. Guernsey, Jr.

Daniel Blum died in 1965. Since that time his annual *Theatre World* has been edited by John Willis. *Pictorial History of the American Theatre, 1860–1970,* ed. John Willis, New York, 1969 [*sic*], is a third and enlarged edition of the pictorial record Daniel Blum began in 1950.

For the major checklists of plays and guides to dramatic criticism, see page 9 above. Among the useful dictionaries and encyclopedias are the invaluable *Biographical Encyclopedia and Who's Who of the American Theatre,* ed. Walter Rigdon, New York, 1966; Bernard Hewitt, *Theatre, U.S.A., 1688–1857,* New York, 1959; John Gassner and Edward Quinn, eds., *The Reader's Encyclopedia of World Drama,* New York, 1969; and Allan Lewis, *American Plays and Playwrights of the Contemporary Theatre,* New York, 1965, covering the years 1957–1964. Play digests are available in John Lovell, *Digests of* [100] *Great American Plays,* New York, 1961; and Theodore J. Shank, *A Digest of 500 Plays,* New York, 1963

### 171. INSTRUMENTS OF CULTURE AND LITERARY PRODUCTION:
*Books and the Book Trade*

Charles A. Madison's *Book Publishing in America,* New York, 1966, is concerned primarily with the cultural rather than the financial aspects of the trade. A vital guide to all aspects of the business is Herbert S. Bailey, Jr., *The Art and Science of Book Publishing,* New York, 1970. See also Datus C. Smith, Jr. *et al., A Guide to Book Publishing,* New York, 1966;

and Chandler B. Grannis, ed., *What Happens in Book Publishing,* 2nd ed., New York, 1967. *Bowker Lectures on Book Publishing,* New York, 1957, prints 17 given at the New York Public Library, 1935–1956. *Trends in American Publishing,* ed. Kathryn Luther Henderson, Urbana, Ill., 1968, is a gathering of symposium papers.

Historical studies are more limited in scope. Rollo G. Silver's *The American Printer, 1787–1825,* Charlottesville, Va., 1967, "describes the condition of the American printer . . . , his methods of work, the equipment he used, and the policies by which he conducted his business." See also his *Typefounding in America, 1787–1825,* Charlottesville, Va., 1965. The economics of authorship and the domination of the New York-Philadelphia publishing axis is the subject of William Charvat's *Literary Publishing in America, 1790–1850,* Philadelphia, 1959. His collected papers were published posthumously as *The Profession of Authorship in America, 1800–1870,* ed. Matthew J. Bruccoli, Columbus, Ohio, 1968. Walter Sutton concentrates on Cincinnati as a nineteenth-century publishing center in *The Western Book Trade,* Columbus, Ohio, 1961. A variety of short papers on publishing history are gathered in *Books in America's Past,* ed. David Kaser, Charlottesville, Va., 1966.

More specialized and contemporary matters are discussed in Jesse W. Markham *et al., An Economic Media Study of Book Publishing,* New York, 1966; Gene R. Hawes, *To Advance Knowledge: A Handbook on American University Press Publishing,* New York, 1967; Aubert J. Clark, *The Movement for International Copyright in Nineteenth-Century America,* Washington, D.C., 1960; and Charles Lee, *The Hidden Public: The Story of the Book-of-the-Month Club,* Garden City, N.Y., 1958.

Histories of individual publishing houses include David Kaser, *Messrs. Carey & Lea of Philadelphia: A Study in the History of the Book Trade,* Philadelphia, 1957; Raymond L. Kilgour, *Lee and Shepard: Publishers for the People,* Hamden, Conn., 1965; Eugene Exman, *The Brothers Harper,* New York, 1965, and *The House of Harper,* New York, 1967; Roger Burlingame, *Endless Frontiers: The Story of McGraw-Hill,* New York, 1959; and Ellen B. Ballou, *The Building of the House: Houghton Mifflin's Formative Years,* Boston, 1970.

Biographies of book publishers and sellers over the last hundred years include W. S. Tryon, *Parnassus Corner: A Life of James T. Fields, Publisher to the Victorians,* Boston, 1963; Carl J. Weber, *The Rise and Fall of James Ripley Osgood: A Biography,* Waterville, Me., 1959; Charles A. Madison, *The Owl among Colophons: Henry Holt as Publisher and Editor,* New York, 1966; Walker Gilmer, *Horace Liveright: Publisher of the Twenties,* New York, 1970; and W. G. Rogers, *Wise Men Fish Here: The Story of Frances Steloff and the Gotham Book Mart,* New York, 1964.

Reminiscences by publishers and dealers include William Jovanovich, *Now, Barabbas,* New York, 1964; Harold S. Latham, *My Life in Publishing,* New York, 1965; Victor Weybright, *The Making of a Publisher: A Life in the 20th-Century Book Revolution,* New York, 1967; David A. Randall, *Dukedom Large Enough: Reminiscences of a Rare Book Dealer, 1929–1956,* New York, 1969; and Cass Canfield, *The Publishing Experience,* Philadelphia, 1969.

## 171. Censorship

Investigations of this subject have been so numerous in recent years that subdivisions are advisable:

History: Leonard W. Levy, *Legacy of Suppression: Freedom of Speech and Press in Early American History,* Cambridge, Mass., 1960; Ronald Pearsall, *The Worm in the Bud,* Toronto, 1969 (on the double standards of Victorian middle- and upper-class sexual life); and Paul S. Boyer, *Purity in Print: The Vice-Society Movement and Book Censorship in America,* New York, 1968.

General: Terence J. Murphy, *Censorship: Government and Obscenity,* Baltimore, Md., 1963; Morris L. Ernst and Alan U. Schwartz, *Censorship: The Search for the Obscene,* New York, 1964; and Harry M. Clor, *Obscenity and Public Morality: Censorship in a Liberal Society,* Chicago, 1969.

Collections: *The First Freedom: Liberty and Justice in the World of Books and Reading,* ed. Robert B. Downs, Chicago, 1960; *Literary Censorship: Principles, Cases, Problems,* ed. Kingsley and Eleanor Widmer, San Francisco, 1961; *Versions of Censorship,* ed. with commentary John McCormick and Mairi MacInnes, Chicago, 1962; and *Censorship in the United States,* ed. Grant S. McClellan, New York, 1967.

Special Problems: Jack Nelson and Gene Roberts, Jr., *The Censors and the Schools,* Boston, 1963; Harold C. Gardiner, S.J., *Catholic Viewpoint on Censorship,* New York, 1958.

Special cases: E. R. Hutchison, *Tropic of Cancer on Trial,* New York, 1968; Charles Rembar, *The End of Obscenity,* New York, 1968; and Robert W. Haney, *Comstockery in America: Patterns of Censorship and Control,* Boston, 1960 (especially *Ulysses* and *Lady Chatterley's Lover*).

# BACKGROUND

## 173. *CIVILIZATION IN THE UNITED STATES*

IDEAS AND INSTITUTIONS:
*General Studies*

The Library of Congress Series in American Civilization continues with
I. L. Kandel, *American Education in the Twentieth Century*, Cambridge,
Mass., 1957; Willard Thorp, *American Writing in the Twentieth Century*,
Cambridge, Mass., 1960; *American Perspectives: The National Self-Image
in the Twentieth Century*, ed. Robert E. Spiller and Eric Larrabee, Cam-
bridge, Mass., 1961; and William Clyde DeVane, *Higher Education in
Twentieth-Century America*, Cambridge, Mass., 1965.

Perry Miller's *The Life of the Mind in America: From the Revolution to
the Civil War*, New York, 1965, is a posthumous volume, printing two
sections and part of a third of a multivolume work Miller had projected
before his death. His *Nature's Nation*, Cambridge, Mass., 1967, is a collection of essays tracing the movement of European culture into America from
the seventeenth to the nineteenth century. Carl N. Degler's *Out of Our Past*,
New York, 1959, is subtitled *The Forces That Shaped Modern America*. It
moves from the Puritan Colonies to the Great Depression of the 1930's,
with emphasis on the role of ideas. Russel B. Nye's *This Almost Chosen
People*, East Lansing, Mich., 1966, is also a group of "essays in the history
of American ideas." Don W. Wolfe's *The Image of Man in America*, Dallas, Tex., 1957, discusses 22 Americans from Jefferson to John Dewey,
carefully omitting religious views. Ursula Brumm concentrates on religious
symbolism derived from Puritan forms in *American Thought and Religious
Typology*, New Brunswick, N.J., 1970; and Austin Warren traces the history (1620–1920) and pathology of conscience in *The New England Conscience*, Ann Arbor, Mich., 1966. Charles L. Sanford offers a history and
analysis of the Edenic myth in America, with emphasis on Franklin, Jefferson, Bryant, and Cole, in *The Quest for Paradise: Europe and the American Moral Imagination*, Urbana Ill., 1961. Loren Baritz's *City on a Hill: A
History of Ideas and Myths in America*, New York, 1964, moves from John
Winthrop to Herman Melville with emphasis on the intellectual significance
of six Americans. In *The Distorted Image*, Cleveland, Ohio, 1968, Thomas
L. Hartshorne analyzes "the changing conceptions of the American character since Turner." John Morton Blum's "historical inquiry," *The Promise
of America*, Boston, 1965, also treats the meaning of the American experience. John William Ward's collected essays, *Red, White, and Blue*, New

York, 1969, concentrates on "the way in which history and the imagination shape each other and the meaning of individual freedom in American history." See also Daniel J. Boorstin, *The Americans: The National Experience,* New York, 1965; Frank Freidel, *America in the Twentieth Century,* 3rd ed., New York, 1971; and Thomas D. Clark, *The Emerging South,* 2nd ed., New York, 1968. On more specialized topics, though still concerned with the whole history of the American people, are Hans Huth, *Nature and the American: Three Centuries of Changing Attitudes,* Berkeley, Calif., 1957; John G. Cawelti, *Apostles of the Self-Made Man,* Chicago, 1965; Richard Hofstadter, *Anti-Intellectualism in American Life,* New York, 1963; and W. Lloyd Warner, *Living and Dead: A Study of the Symbolic Life of Americans,* New Haven, Conn., 1959. Roger Butterfield's *The American Past,* New York, 1966, is a "history of the United States from Concord to the Great Society" told through 1,100 pictures with text. One of the best general histories, for the literary scholar, is Samuel Eliot Morison's *The Oxford History of the American People,* New York, 1965. Robert Allen Skotheim treats the major interpreters of our history and their methodology in *American Intellectual Histories and Historians,* Princeton, N.J., 1966.

The last seven decades are studied in such a variety of detailed histories that this listing can only suggest some of the more prominent titles. They are arranged chronologically.

The early years of the century are the subject of Walter Lord, *The Good Years: From 1900 to the First World War,* New York, 1960; Henry F. May, *The End of American Innocence . . . 1912–1917,* New York, 1959; and Ernest Earnest, *The Single Vision: The Alienation of American Intellectuals, 1910–1930,* New York, 1970.

The years 1915–1930 are surveyed in Frederick J. Hoffman, *The Twenties,* New York, 1955; William Edward Leuchtenburg, *The Perils of Prosperity, 1914–1932,* Chicago, 1958; Anthony Channell Hilfer, *The Revolt from the Village, 1915–1930,* Chapel Hill, N.C., 1969; Andrew Sinclair, *Prohibition: The Era of Excess,* Boston, 1962; and Loren Baritz, ed., *The Culture of the Twenties,* Indianapolis, Ind., 1970.

The thirties are treated from the economic and social as well as literary viewpoint in Lester V. Chandler, *America's Greatest Depression, 1929–1941,* New York, 1970; Studs Terkel, *Hard Times: An Oral History of the Great Depression,* New York, 1970; Robert Bendiner, *Just Around the Corner: A Highly Selective History of the Thirties,* New York, 1967; Edwin P. Hoyt, *The Tempering Years* [1929–1939], New York, 1963; Edmund Wilson, *The American Earthquake: A Documentary of the Twenties and Thirties,* New York, 1964; and Malcolm Cowley, *Think Back on*

*Us: A Contemporary Chronicle of the 1930's* [essays from the *New Republic*], ed. Henry Dan Piper, Carbondale, Ill., 1967.

The forties are discussed in John Brooks, *The Great Leap: The Past Twenty-Five Years in America,* New York, 1966; and Herbert Agar, *The Unquiet Years: U.S.A. 1945–1955,* London, 1957.

The fifties and sixties are the focus of Max Lerner, *The Unfinished Country: A Book of American Symbols,* New York, 1959; Murray Kempton, *America Comes of Middle Age,* Boston, 1963; Ronald Berman, *America in the Sixties: An Intellectual History,* New York, 1968; William L. O'Neill, *Coming Apart: An Informal History of America in the 1960's,* Chicago, 1971; and Andrew Hacker, *The End of the American Era,* New York, 1970, the latter volume elaborating the idea that "the United States has ceased to serve as a moral model for the rest of the world."

Collections by various hands of brief essays on American civilization range from organized symposia to reprints of magazine articles. Hennig Cohen culled two important volumes from the pages of the *American Quarterly: The American Experience* (Boston, 1968) and *The American Culture* (Boston, 1968), both subtitled *Approaches to the Study of the United States. America Now,* ed. John G. Kirk, New York, 1968, discusses "assumptions about our culture, society, government, and economy" in 22 essays by scholars and public officials. Gordon Mills edited *Innocence and Power: Individualism in Twentieth-Century America,* Austin, Tex., 1965, five essays from the *Texas Quarterly* and two written for this volume. Other collections include *The Search for Identity: Essays on the American Character,* ed. Roger L. Shinn, New York, 1964; *The Southerner as American,* ed. Charles Grier Sellers, Jr., Chapel Hill, N.C., 1960; *Change in the Contemporary South,* ed. Allan P. Sindler, Durham, N.C., 1963; and *The American Enlightenment: The Shaping of the American Experiment and a Free Society,* ed. Adrienne Koch, New York, 1965.

Observations of our contemporary culture by social historians, journalists, and novelists include John A. Kouwenhoven, *The Beer Can by the Highway: Essays on What's "American" about America,* New York, 1961; Richard Rovere, *The American Establishment and Other Reports, Opinions, and Speculations,* New York, 1962; Wright Morris, *A Bill of Rites, a Bill of Wrongs, a Bill of Goods,* New York, 1968; Gore Vidal, *Reflections upon a Sinking Ship,* Boston, 1969; John Keats, *The New Romans: An American Experience,* Philadelphia, 1967; William K. Zinsser, *Pop Goes America,* New York, 1966; and Tom Wolfe's essays on "the scruffy margins of American culture": *The Kandy-Kolored Tangerine-Flake Streamline Baby,* New York, 1965; *The Pump House Gang,* New York, 1968; and *The Electric Kool-Aid Acid Test,* New York, 1968.

Anti-Establishment writers, under various rubrics, have reported equally thoroughly on the continuing revolution in our culture: Thomas Hayden, *Rebellion and Repression*, New York, 1969, and *Trial*, New York, 1970; Mark Gerzon, *The Whole World Is Watching: A Young Man Looks at Youth's Dissent*, New York, 1969; Noam Chomsky, *American Power and the New Mandarins*, New York, 1969; Noam Chomsky et al., *Trials of the Resistance*, New York, 1970; Charles A. Reich, *The Greening of America*, New York, 1970; Richard Kostelanetz, ed., *Beyond Left and Right: Radical Thought for Our Times*, New York, 1968; and Theodore Roszak, *The Making of a Counter Culture: Reflections on the Technocratic Society and Its Youthful Opposition*, New York, 1969.

Three volumes deal with our manners and morals: Bradford Smith, *Why We Behave Like Americans*, Philadelphia, 1957; Gerald Carson, *The Polite Americans: A Wide-Angle View of Our More or Less Good Manners over 300 Years*, New York, 1966; and *American Manners and Morals: A Picture History of How We Behaved and Misbehaved* by the editors of *American Heritage*, Marion, Ohio, 1969.

America in foreign eyes is another country, or so it seems from reading Jacques Maritain, *Reflections on America*, New York, 1958; Helmut Schoek, *U.S.A.: Motive und Strukturen*, Stuttgart, 1958; R. L. Bruckberger, *Image of America*, trans. C. G. Paulding and Virgilia Peterson, New York, 1959; D. W. Brogan, *America in the Modern World*, New Brunswick, N.J., 1960, and *American Aspects*, New York, 1964; Alistair Cooke, *Talk about America*, New York, 1968; Jean-Jacques Servan-Schreiber, *The American Challenge*, New York, 1968; Ronald Segal, *The Americans: A Conflict of Creed and Reality*, New York, 1969 (published in England under the title *America's Receding Future: The Collision of Creed and Reality*); and Jean-François Revel, *Without Marx or Jesus: The New American Revolution Has Begun*, trans. J. F. Bernard, New York, 1971.

### 174. Political and Economic Studies

*The Economic History of the United States,* published by Holt, Rinehart, and Winston, Inc., now projected in ten volumes, has added three titles since 1951: Paul W. Gates, *The Farmer's Age: Agriculture, 1815–1860*, New York, 1960; Edward C. Kirkland, *Industry Comes of Age: Business, Labor, and Public Policy, 1860–1897*, New York, 1961; and Curtis P. Nettels, *The Emergence of a National Economy, 1775–1815*, New York, 1962. The fourth and fifth volumes of Joseph Dorfman's *The Economic Mind in American Civilization*, New York, 1959, covering the years 1918–1933, complete this series. Harold U. Faulkner's *American Economic History* is in its eighth edition, New York, 1960; its bibliographies are extensive. Seymour E.

Harris has edited a composite *American Economic History*, New York, 1961: 16 chapters by 16 contributors. More specialized studies of interest to the student of American civilization are Douglas C. North, *Growth and Welfare in the American Past*, Englewood Cliffs, N.J., 1966; Eliot Janeway, *The Economics of Crisis: War, Politics, and the Dollar*, New York, 1968; Milton Friedman's and Anna Jacobson Schwartz's definitive *Monetary History of the United States, 1867–1960*, Princeton, N.J., 1963; and Herbert Stein, *The Fiscal Revolution in America*, Chicago, 1964.

Paul A. Samuelson's *Stability and Growth in the American Economy*, Stockholm, 1963, is "a concise study of the main American economic problems since World War II, addressed to a European audience." Three important books by John Kenneth Galbraith are *The Affluent Society*, Boston, 1958, rev. ed., 1969; *Economic Development in Perspective*, Cambridge, Mass., 1962; and *The New Industrial State*, Boston, 1967. Arthur M. Okun's *The Political Economy of Prosperity*, Washington, D.C., 1970, "explores the areas of agreement and disagreement among economists on the unparalleled growth in U. S. economy." See also Robert L. Heilbroner, *Between Capitalism and Socialism: Essays in Political Economics*, New York, 1970; and George J. Stigler, *Essays in the History of Economics*, Chicago, 1965.

Histories of American political thought continue to proliferate. Broadus Mitchell and Louise Pearson Mitchell have written, for the nonspecialist, *A Biography of the Constitution of the United States: Its Origin, Formation, Adoption, Interpretation*, New York, 1964. Written from the legal rather than the historical standpoint is Arthur E. Sutherland's *Constitutionalism in America: Origin and Evolution of Its Fundamental Ideas*, New York, 1965. See also Donald G. Morgan, *Congress and the Constitution: A Study of Responsibility*, Cambridge, Mass., 1966; Max Beloff, *The American Federal Government*, New York, 1959; Roy F. Nichols, *The Invention of the American Political Parties* [to 1860], New York, 1967; and Clinton Rossiter, *Parties and Politics in America*, Ithaca, N.Y., 1960.

Important political histories that concentrate on shorter periods are Bernard Bailyn, *The Origins of American Politics*, New York, 1968; David Hackett Fischer, *The Revolution of American Conservatism: The Federalist Party in the Era of Jeffersonian Democracy*, New York, 1965; William E. Leuchtenburg, ed., *The New Deal: A Documentary History*, New York, 1968; Daniel Bell, *The End of Ideology: On the Exhaustion of Political Ideas in the Fifties*, rev. ed., New York, 1962; and James L. Sundquist, *Politics and Policy: The Eisenhower, Kennedy, and Johnson Years*, Washington, D.C., 1968. For a variety of viewpoints on the subject of political theory, see Richard Hofstadter, *The Paranoid Style in American Politics and Other Essays*, New York, 1965; Harvey Wheeler, *Democracy in a*

*Revolutionary Era: The Political Order Today,* New York, 1968; Lawrence H. Chamberlain *et al., Theory and Practice in American Politics,* ed. William H. Nelson with the collaboration of Frances L. Loewenheim, Chicago, 1964; Gottfried Dietze, *America's Political Dilemma: From Limited to Unlimited Democracy,* Baltimore, Md., 1968; Hans Kohn, *American Nationalism: An Interpretive Essay,* New York, 1957; Samuel Lubell, *The Hidden Crisis in American Politics,* New York, 1970; Arnold M. Rose, *The Power Structure: Political Process in American Society,* New York, 1967; and Dexter Perkins, *The Diplomacy of a New Age: Major Issues in U. S. Policy since 1945,* Bloomington, Ind., 1967.

Specialized studies of the Supreme Court include Paul A. Freund, *The Supreme Court of the United States: Its Business, Purposes, and Performance,* Cleveland, Ohio, 1961; Robert J. Harris, *The Quest for Equality: The Constitution, Congress, and the Supreme Court,* Baton Rouge, La., 1960; Charles A. Miller, *The Supreme Court and the Uses of History,* Cambridge, Mass., 1969; an analytical history by Richard H. McCloskey, *The American Supreme Court,* Chicago, 1960; and a recent critical analysis of *The Warren Court,* edited by Richard H. Sayler, Barry B. Boyer, and Robert E. Goodring, Jr., New York, 1969.

Studies of the presidency and presidential powers are so numerous it is difficult to do more than indicate the range: Edward S. Corwin, *The President: Office and Powers, 1787-1957,* 4th ed., New York, 1957; Wilfred E. Binckley, *President and Congress,* 3rd ed., New York, 1962; James MacGregor Burns, *Presidential Government,* Boston, 1966; Theodore C. Sorensen, *Decision-Making in the White House: The Olive Branch or the Arrows,* New York, 1963; and Thomas E. Cronin and Sanford D. Greenberg, eds., *The Presidential Advisory System,* New York, 1969. No recent journalistic reports on this subject can improve on Theodore H. White's three volumes, *The Making of the President, 1960,* New York, 1961; *The Making of the President, 1964,* New York, 1965; and *The Making of the President, 1968,* New York, 1969.

Autobiographical views of recent politics are available in many volumes, notably Lewis Strauss, *Men and Decisions,* Garden City, N.Y., 1962; Dwight David Eisenhower, *The White House Years,* 2 vols., Garden City, N.Y., 1963-1965; David E. Lilienthal, *The Journals of David E. Lilienthal,* 5 vols., New York, 1964-1971; Dean Acheson, *Present at the Creation: My Years in the State Department,* New York, 1969; George F. Kennan, *Memoirs, 1925-1950,* Boston, 1967; and Charles Frankel, *High on Foggy Bottom: An Outsider's Inside View of Government,* New York, 1969.

Milton R. Konvitz is general editor of the Cornell Studies in Civil Liberty. Three additions to the series are his own *Fundamental Liberties of a*

*Free People: Religion, Speech, Press, Assembly*, Ithaca, N.Y., 1957; Richard P. Longaker, *The Presidency and Individual Liberties*, Ithaca, N.Y., 1961; and Wilson Record, *Race and Radicalism: The NAACP and the Communist Party in Conflict*, Ithaca, N.Y., 1964. See also Henry J. Abraham, *Freedom and the Court: Civil Rights and Liberties in the United States*, New York, 1967; Norman Dorsen, *Frontiers of Civil Liberties*, New York, 1969; and John H. McCord, ed., *With All Deliberate Speed: Civil Rights Theory and Reality*, Urbana, Ill., 1969.

The extremes in American politics are discussed in Clinton Rossiter, *Conservatism in America: The Thankless Persuasion*, 2nd ed., New York, 1962; Daniel Bell, ed., *The Radical Right*, Garden City, N.Y., 1963; Christopher Lasch, *The Agony of the American Left*, New York, 1969; and Clinton Rossiter, *Marxism: The View from America*, New York, 1960. More specialized histories are James Weinstein, *The Decline of Socialism in America, 1912–1925*, New York, 1967; Patrick Renshaw, *The Wobblies: The Story of Syndicalism in the United States*, Garden City, N.Y., 1967; David A. Shannon, *The Decline of American Communism: A History of the Communist Party in the United States since 1945*, New York, 1959; and Earl Latham, *The Communist Controversy in Washington: From the New Deal to McCarthy*, Cambridge, Mass., 1966. Theodore Draper's *The Roots of American Communism*, New York, 1957, is the first volume of a projected two-volume study and quite separate from his *American Communism and Soviet Russia: The Formative Period*, New York, 1960.

## 175. Society and the Group

What with integration, minority groups, urban renewal, crime in the streets, and drug addiction becoming household words, sociological studies during the last decade have increased enormously. The following list is obviously selective and is divided into 12 rubrics for convenience only. Overlapping is unavoidable.

General: Peter F. Drucker, *The Age of Discontinuity: Guidelines to Our Changing Society*, New York, 1969; W. Lloyd Warner *et al.*, *The Emergent American Society*, New Haven, Conn., 1967; Clarence Morris, ed., *Trends in Modern Society* [Benjamin Franklin Lectures], Philadelphia, 1962; Ashley Montagu, *The American Way of Life*, New York, 1967; John Greenway, *The Inevitable Americans*, New York, 1964; James Sellers, *Public Ethics: American Morals and Manners*, New York, 1970; John Kenneth Galbraith, *The Affluent Society*, Boston, 1958; Alvin Toffler, *The Culture Consumers*, New York, 1964, and *Future Shock*, New York, 1970; and three books by Marshall McLuhan: *Understanding Media: The Extensions of Man*, New York, 1964; *The Medium Is the Massage* (with Quentin

Fiore), New York, 1967; and *Culture Is Our Business*, New York, 1970.

The City: Lewis Mumford, *The Urban Prospect*, New York, 1968; Constance McLaughlin Green, *American Cities in the Growth of the Nation*, New York, 1957, and *The Rise of Urban America*, New York, 1965; Jane Jacobs, *The Death and Life of Great American Cities*, New York, 1961, and *The Economy of Cities*, New York, 1969; Blake McKelvey, *The Urbanization of America, 1860–1915*, New Brunswick, N.J., 1963, and *The Emergence of Metropolitan America, 1915–1966*, New Brunswick, N.J., 1968; Charles N. Glabb and A. Theodore Brown, *A History of Urban America*, New York, 1967; Raymond Vernon, *The Myth and the Reality of Our Urban Problems*, Cambridge, Mass., 1966; and Martin Anderson, *The Federal Bulldozer: A Critical Analysis of Urban Renewal, 1949–1962*, Cambridge, Mass., 1964. Robert Gutman has compiled a brief bibliography, *Urban Sociology*, New Brunswick, N.J., 1963.

Rural Society: Edward C. Higbee, *Farms and Farmers in an Urban Age*, New York, 1963; Wayne E. Fuller, *RFD: The Changing Face of Rural America*, Bloomington, Ind., 1964; M. Lee Taylor and Arthur R. Jones, *Rural Life and Urbanized Society*, New York, 1964; and James H. Copp, ed., *Our Changing Rural Society: Perspectives and Trends*, Ames, Iowa, 1964.

Social Classes: Joseph A. Kahl, *The American Class Structure*, New York, 1957; Seymour Martin Lipset and Reinhard Bendix, *Social Mobility in Industrial Society*, Berkeley, Calif., 1959; Leonard Reissman, *Class in American Society*, Glencoe, Ill., 1959; William M. Dobriner, *Class in Suburbia*, Englewood Cliffs, N.J., 1963; E. Digby Baltzell, *An American Business Aristocracy*, New York, 1962; Ralph E. Lapp, *The New Priesthood: The Scientific Elite and the Uses of Power*, New York, 1965; Vance Packard, *The Status Seekers*, New York, 1959; Cleveland Amory, *Who Killed Society?*, New York, 1960; and Nathaniel Burt, *First Families: The Making of an American Aristocracy*, Boston, 1970.

Ethnic Groups: Stanley Lieberson, *Ethnic Patterns in American Cities*, Glencoe, Ill., 1963; Hubert M. Blalock, *Toward a Theory of Minority-Group Relations*, New York, 1967; Nathan Glazer and Daniel Patrick Moynihan, *Beyond the Melting Pot: The Negroes, Puerto Ricans, Jews, Italians, and Irish of New York City*, 2nd ed., Cambridge, Mass., 1970; Oscar Handlin, *The Newcomers: Negroes and Puerto Ricans in a Changing Metropolis*, Cambridge, Mass., 1959; Arthur J. Rubel, *Across the Tracks: Mexican-Americans in a Texas City*, Austin, Tex., 1966; and a textbook of selected readings: Milton L. Barron, ed., *American Minorities*, New York, 1957.

Race Relations: Oscar Handlin, *Race and Nationality in American Life*,

Garden City, N.Y., 1957; Thomas F. Gossett, *Race: The History of an Idea in America*, rev. ed., Dallas, Tex., 1965; Dennis Clark, *The Ghetto Game: Racial Conflicts in the City,* New York, 1962; Earl Raab, ed., *American Race Relations Today,* Garden City, N.Y., 1962; and Bernard E. Segal, ed., *Racial and Ethnic Relations*, New York, 1966.

Segregation: Gustavus Myers, *History of Bigotry in the United States,* rev. ed., New York, 1960; Jacob K. Javits, *Discrimination—U.S.A.,* rev. ed., New York, 1962; Melvin M. Tumin, *Desegregation: Readiness and Resistance,* Princeton, N.J., 1958; Lewis M. Killian, *The Impossible Revolution,* New York, 1968; Reed Sarratt, *The Ordeal of Desegregation: The First Decade,* New York, 1966; Marvin Brooks Norfleet, *Forced School Integration in the U.S.A.,* New York, 1961; Joseph E. O'Neill, ed., *A Catholic Case against Segregation,* New York, 1961; and Albert P. Blaustein and Clarence Clyde Ferguson, Jr., *Desegregation and the Law,* 2nd ed., New Brunswick, N.J., 1962. For bibliography, see Meyer Weinberg, *Desegregation Research: An Appraisal,* Bloomington, Ind., 1970.

Poverty: Robert H. Bremner, *From the Depths: The Discovery of Poverty in the United States,* New York, 1956; Michael Harrington, *The Other America: Poverty in the United States,* New York, 1962; David R. Hunter, *The Slums: Challenge and Response,* Glencoe, Ill., 1964; Thomas Gladwin, *Poverty U.S.A.,* Boston, 1967; Chaim Isaac Waxman, comp., *Poverty: Power and Politics,* New York, 1968; John C. Donovan, *The Politics of Poverty,* New York, 1967; and Gerald D. Suttles, *The Social Order of the Slum: Ethnicity and Territory in the Inner City,* Chicago, 1968, concerning the Chicago poor.

Population: Lincoln H. Day and Alice Taylor Day, *Too Many Americans,* New York, 1965; Conrad F. Taeuber and Irene B. Taeuber, *The Changing Population of the United States,* New York, 1958, a highly technical study; and Ronald Freedman, *Population: The Vital Revolution,* Chicago, 1965.

The Sexual Revolution: Charles E. Winick, *The New People: Desexualization in American Life,* New York, 1968; P. A. Sorokin, *The American Sex Revolution,* Boston, 1957; Myron Brenton, *The American Male,* New York, 1966; Eleanor Flexner, *Century of Struggle: The Women's Rights Movement in the United States,* Cambridge, Mass., 1959; Andrew Sinclair, *The Better Half: The Emancipation of the American Woman,* New York, 1965 (paperback edition, 1966, drops the first half of the title); U.S. President's Commission on the Status of Women, *American Women,* ed. Margaret Mead and Frances Balgley Kaplan, New York, 1965; Robert E. Riegel, *American Women: A Story of Social Change,* Rutherford, N.J., 1970; Seymour M. Farber and Roger H. Wilson, eds., *The Challenge to Women,* New York, 1966; and two widely circulated studies, Betty

Friedan, *The Feminine Mystique,* New York, 1963; and Kate Millett, *Sexual Politics,* New York, 1970.

Mass Communication: Joseph T. Klapper, *The Effects of Mass Communication,* Glencoe, Ill., 1960; Lewis A. Dexter and David Manning White, eds., *People, Society, and Mass Communications,* New York, 1964; and Charles R. Wright, *Mass Communication: A Sociological Perspective,* New York, 1959.

Crime and Violence: Richard Hofstadter and Michael Wallace, *American Violence: A Documentary History,* New York, 1971; Ramsey Clark, *Crime in America: Observations on Its Nature, Causes, Prevention and Control,* New York, 1970; Edwin M. Schur, *Our Criminal Society: The Social and Legal Sources of Crime in America,* Englewood Cliffs, N.J., 1969; William A. Westley, *Violence and the Police: A Sociological Study of Law, Custom, and Morality,* Cambridge, Mass., 1970; Saul Bernstein, *Alternatives to Violence,* New York, 1967; and two studies by Richard Harris, *The Fear of Crime,* New York, 1969; and *Justice: The Crisis of Law, Order, and Freedom in America,* New York, 1970.

### 176. *The Negro*

The tremendous increase in scholarship and general interest in Negro history and culture is cause for this new subdivision. So many important books have appeared in the last decade that the student should seek out first the three comprehensive bibliographies of the subject if he wishes complete coverage: *The Negro in America,* comp. Elizabeth W. Miller, Cambridge, Mass., 1966, 2nd ed., comp. Mary L. Fisher, Cambridge, Mass., 1970, enlarged to 6,500 entries; *The Negro in the United States,* comp. Dorothy B. Porter, Washington, D.C., 1970, 1,827 entries under 40 heads; and *Blacks in America: Bibliographical Essays,* ed. James M. McPherson *et al.,* Garden City, N.Y., 1971, especially important for the annotations.

For the student interested in important representative titles, this highly selective list will serve.

General history: John Hope Franklin, *From Slavery to Freedom: A History of American Negroes,* 3rd ed., New York, 1967, the standard book in the field; August Meier and Elliott M. Rudwick, *From Plantation to Ghetto: An Interpretive History of American Negroes,* New York, 1969; and Richard Bardolph, *The Negro Vanguard,* New York, 1959, Negro "movers and shakers from Crispus Attucks to Ralph Bunche."

History to 1865: Winthrop D. Jordan, *White over Black: American Attitudes toward the Negro, 1550-1812,* Chapel Hill, N.C., 1968; *idem, The Negro versus Equality, 1762-1826,* Chicago, 1969; Henry Allen Bullock, *A History of Negro Education in the South: From 1619 to the*

*Present*, Cambridge, Mass., 1967; Leon F. Litwack, *North of Slavery: The Negro in the Free States, 1790–1860*, Chicago, 1961; Kenneth M. Stampp, *The Peculiar Institution: Slavery in the Ante-Bellum South*, New York, 1956; Stanley M. Elkins, *Slavery: A Problem in American Institutional Life*, Chicago, 1959; James M. McPherson, *The Negro's Civil War: How American Negroes Felt and Acted during the War for the Union*, New York, 1965; and *idem, The Struggle for Equality: Abolitionists and the Negro in the Civil War and Reconstruction*, Princeton, N.J., 1964.

History from 1865 to 1970: August Meier, *Negro Thought in America, 1880–1915: Racial Ideologies in the Age of Booker T. Washington*, Ann Arbor, Mich., 1963; Gilbert Osofsky, *Harlem: The Making of a Ghetto: Negro New York, 1690–1930*, New York, 1966; C. Vann Woodward, *The Strange Career of Jim Crow*, 2nd rev. ed., New York, 1966; and Arthur I. Waskow, *From Race Riot to Sit-In 1919 and the 1960's: A Study in the Connections between Conflict and Violence*, Garden City, N.Y., 1966.

Black Nationalism: Essien U. Essien-Udom, *Black Nationalism: A Search for an Identity in America*, Chicago, 1962; Benjamin Muse, *The American Negro Revolution: From Nonviolence to Black Power, 1963–1967*, Bloomington, Ind., 1968; Theodore Draper, *The Rediscovery of Black Nationalism*, New York, 1970; Anthony Lewis, *Portrait of a Decade: The Second American Revolution*, New York, 1964; and two collections of essays: *The Black Power Revolt*, ed. Floyd B. Barbour, Boston, 1968; and *Black Nationalism in America*, ed. John Bracey, Jr., August Meier, and Elliott Rudwick, Indianapolis, Ind., 1970.

Race Relations: Charles E. Silberman, *Crisis in Black and White*, New York, 1964; and Kenneth B. Clark, *Dark Ghetto: Dilemmas of Social Power*, New York, 1965.

Specialized Topics: Benjamin Muse, *Ten Years of Prelude: The Story of Integration since the Supreme Court's 1954 Decision*, New York, 1964; Donald R. Matthews and James W. Prothro, *Negroes and the New Southern Politics*, New York, 1966; and Harold Cruse, *The Crisis of the Negro Intellectual*, New York, 1967.

Spokesmen: James Baldwin, *The Fire Next Time*, New York, 1963; Ralph Ellison, *Shadow and Act*, New York, 1964; Malcolm Little, *The Autobiography of Malcolm X*, New York, 1965; Eldridge Cleaver, *Soul on Ice*, New York, 1967; *idem, Post-Prison Writings and Speeches*, ed. Robert Scheer, New York, 1969; Whitney M. Young, Jr., *Beyond Racism: Building an Open Society*, New York, 1969; and Stokely Carmichael and Charles V. Hamilton, *Black Power: The Politics of Liberation in America*, New York, 1967, described by the authors as "a political framework and ideology which represents the last reasonable opportunity for this society to work out its racial problems short of prolonged destructive guerrilla warfare."

177. *Philosophy*

John Dewey, William James, and George Santayana are treated in individual bibliographies, below. Murray G. Murphey's *The Development of Peirce's Philosophy*, Cambridge, Mass., 1961, is "an examination of Charles Sanders Peirce's biography in order to elucidate the systematic nature of his philosophy." See also Vincent G. Potter, S.J., *Charles S. Peirce on Norms and Ideals*, Amherst, Mass., 1967; and *Studies in the Philosophy of Charles Sanders Peirce, Second Series*, ed. Edward C. Moore and Richard S. Robin, Amherst, Mass., 1964. A recent study of Josiah Royce is Peter Fuss's *The Moral Philosophy of Josiah Royce*, Cambridge, Mass., 1965. Recent studies of Alfred North Whitehead include A. H. Johnson, *Whitehead's Philosophy of Civilization*, Boston, 1958; Ivor Leclerc, *Whitehead's Metaphysics*, New York, 1958; Victor Lowe, *Understanding Whitehead*, Baltimore, Md., 1962, a general introduction and interpretation; Donald W. Sherburne, *A Whiteheadian Aesthetic: Some Implications of Whitehead's Metaphysical Speculation*, New Haven, Conn., 1961, New York, 1970; Paul F. Schmidt, *Perception and Cosmology in Whitehead's Philosophy*, New Brunswick, N.J., 1967; and Edward Pols, *Whitehead's Metaphysics: A Critical Examination of Process and Reality*, Carbondale, Ill., 1967.

Still invaluable as a source book is Herbert W. Schneider, *A History of American Philosophy*, New York, 1946, 2nd ed., 1963. Other general studies include John E. Smith, *The Spirit of American Philosophy*, New York, 1963; Robert Clifton Whittemore, *Makers of the American Mind*, New York, 1964; and Edward H. Madden, *Civil Disobedience and Moral Law in Nineteenth-Century American Philosophy*, Seattle, Wash., 1968. H. B. Van Wesep's *Seven Sages: The Story of American Philosophy*, New York, 1960, is a semipopular study from Franklin to Whitehead.

Studies of pragmatism have sprouted during the last decade. Paul K. Conkin's *Puritans and Pragmatists: Eight Eminent American Thinkers*, New York, 1968, spans more than two centuries, from Jonathan Edwards to John Dewey. Alfred J. Ayer's *The Origins of Pragmatism*, San Francisco, 1968, concentrates on Peirce and William James; Edward C. Moore adds Dewey to his study of three philosophers in *American Pragmatism*, New York, 1961. Edward H. Madden treats a neglected predecessor of James in *Chauncey Wright and the Foundations of Pragmatism*, Seattle, Wash., 1963. *The Chicago Pragmatists* by Egbert Darnell Rucker, Minneapolis, Minn., 1969, discusses John Dewey, George Herbert Mead, James Hayden Tufts, and James Rowland Angell between 1895-1930. Horace S. Thayer surveys the history of the term in *Meaning and Action: A Critical History of Pragmatism*, Indianapolis, Ind., 1968.

Max Black collected essays by various hands in *Philosophy in America*, Ithaca, N.Y., 1965. Two volumes originating in England that aim at presenting "a cross-section of the philosophical thinking that has been taking place on the American scene" are *Contemporary American Philosophy*, ed. George P. Adams and William Pepperell Montague, New York, 1962; and *Contemporary American Philosophy: Second Series*, ed. John E. Smith, New York, 1970.

## 178. *Religion:*
General Studies

The most ambitious undertaking in recent years is a "comprehensive-interpretive survey [by more than twenty scholars] of the formative religious dimensions of American culture" called *Religion in American Life*, ed. James Ward Smith and A. Leland Jamison, Princeton, N.J., 1961: Volume I, *The Shaping of American Religion;* Volume II, *Religious Perspectives in American Culture;* Volume III, not yet published; Volume IV, in two parts, *A Critical Bibliography of Religion in America,* comp. Nelson R. Burr. Important one-volume surveys are Winthrop S. Hudson's *Religion in America*, New York, 1965; and Edwin S. Gaustad, *A Religious History of America,* New York, 1966. See also William A. Clebsch, *From Sacred to Profane America: The Role of Religion in American History,* New York, 1968. Collected essays can be found in *The Shaping of American Religion*, ed. James Ward Smith and A. Leland Jamison, Princeton, N.J., 1961; *Reinterpretation in American Church History,* ed. J. C. Brauer, Chicago, 1968; and *Religious Issues in American History*, ed. Edwin S. Gaustad, New York, 1968.

Church-state relations in the United States are discussed in Roy F. Nichols, *Religion and American Democracy*, Baton Rouge, La., 1959; Loren P. Beth, *The American Theory of Church and State*, Gainesville, Fla., 1958; Mark DeWolfe Howe, *The Garden and the Wilderness*, Chicago, 1965; William O. Douglas, *The Bible and the Schools,* Boston, 1966; and Milton R. Konvitz, *Religious Liberty and Conscience: A Constitutional Inquiry,* New York, 1968.

Theological problems in literature are the central concern of Amos Wilder's *Theology and Modern Literature*, Cambridge, Mass., 1958; Howard Mumford Jones, *Belief and Disbelief in American Literature,* Chicago, 1967; Arnold Smithline, *Natural Religion in American Literature,* New Haven, Conn., 1966; and two volumes by Nathan A. Scott, Jr.: *Modern Literature and the Religious Frontier,* New York, 1958; and *The Broken Center: Studies in the Theological Horizon of Modern Literature*, New Haven, 1966.

178. New England

The major work following Perry Miller's basic studies is Alan Heimert, *Religion and the American Mind: From the Great Awakening to the Revolution,* Cambridge, Mass., 1966. A study of "the pathology of conscience" designed for the general reader is Austin Warren, *The New England Conscience,* Ann Arbor, Mich., 1966. William G. McLoughlin concentrates on "the Baptists and the separation of church and state" in *New England Dissent, 1630–1833,* 3 vols., Cambridge, Mass., 1971.

179. Denominations

Three general studies are Robert M. Miller, *American Protestantism and Social Issues, 1919–1939,* Chapel Hill, N.C., 1958; Winthrop S. Hudson, *American Protestantism,* Chicago, 1961; and Kenneth K. Bailey, *Southern White Protestantism in the Twentieth Century,* New York, 1964.

John T. Ellis has revised his important study, *American Catholicism* (1956), Chicago, 1969; and he has also prepared *A Guide to American Catholic History,* Milwaukee, Wis., 1959. Studies of early Catholic history include Ellis's *Catholics in Colonial America,* Baltimore, Md., 1965; Aaron I. Abell, *American Catholicism and Social Action: A Search for Social Justice, 1865–1950,* Garden City, N.Y., 1960; and David J. O'Brien, *American Catholics and Social Reform: The New Deal Years,* New York, 1968. Changes in the church are the subject of three vastly different studies: Robert D. Cross, *The Emergence of Liberal Catholicism in America,* Cambridge, Mass., 1958; Philip Gleason, ed., *Contemporary Catholicism in the United States,* Notre Dame, Ind., 1969; and Francine du Plessix Gray, *Divine Disobedience: Profiles in Catholic Radicalism* [Ivan Illich, the Brothers Berrigan, and others], New York, 1970.

Other denominational histories are Conrad Wright, *The Beginnings of Unitarianism in America,* rev. ed., Boston, 1966; Raymond W. Albright, *A History of the Protestant Episcopal Church,* New York, 1964; Frederick B. Tolles, *Quakers and the Atlantic Culture,* New York, 1960; Gillian Lindt Gollin, *Moravians in Two Worlds: A Study of Changing Communities,* New York, 1967; E. Franklin Frazier, *The Negro Church in America,* New York, 1963; three studies of the Mormon world: Leonard J. Arrington, *Great Basin Kingdom: An Economic History of the Latter-Day Saints, 1830–1900,* Cambridge, Mass., 1958; William Mulder, *Homeward to Zion: The Mormon Migration from Scandinavia,* Minneapolis, Minn., 1957; and *Among the Mormons: Historic Accounts by Contemporary Observers,* ed. William Mulder and A. Russell Mortenson, New York, 1958; and four volumes on individual church leaders: James F. Findlay, Jr., *He*

*Gathered Them at the River: Dwight L. Moody: American Evangelist, 1837–1899*, Chicago, 1969; William G. McLoughlin, Jr., *Modern Revivalism: Charles Grandison Finney to Billy Graham*, New York, 1959; Robert T. Handy, ed., *The Social Gospel in America: Gladden, Ely, and Rauschenbusch*, New York, 1966; and Donald Meyer, *The Positive Thinkers: A Study of the American Quest for Health, Wealth and Personal Power from Mary Baker Eddy to Norman Vincent Peale*, Garden City, N.Y., 1965.

Useful guides and bibliographical accumulations are Edwin S. Gaustad, *Historical Atlas of Religion in America*, New York, 1962; Harold H. Watts, *The Modern Reader's Guide to Religions*, New York, 1964; and Frank Spencer Mead, *Handbook of Denominations in the United States*, 5th rev. ed., New York, 1970.

## 180. *Education*

The history of education in America is surveyed in *American Higher Education: A Documentary History*, 2 vols., Chicago, 1961, a collection of readings and historical sources edited by Richard Hofstadter and Wilson Smith; and Frederick Rudolph, *The American College and University: A History*, New York, 1962. Bernard Bailyn explores our early schools in *Education in the Forming of American Society: Needs and Opportunities for Study*, Chapel Hill, N.C., 1960. Lawrence A. Cremin provides the definitive study in *American Education: The Colonial Experience, 1607–1783*, New York, 1970. Histories of more recent developments are Russell Brown Thomas, *The Search for a Common Learning: General Education, 1800–1960*, New York, 1962; Lawrence A. Cremin, *The Transformation of the School: Progressivism in American Education, 1876–1957*, New York, 1961; George E. Peterson, *The New England College in the Age of the University* [roughly 1881–1894], Amherst, Mass., 1964; Theodore R. Sizer, *Secondary Schools at the Turn of the Century*, New Haven, Conn., 1964; and William Clyde DeVane, *Higher Education in Twentieth-Century America*, Cambridge, Mass., 1965. Howard Mumford Jones's *One Great Society: Humane Learning in the United States*, New York, 1959, is both a historical and theoretical study. Politics and history inform the analyses in Allan Nevins's *The State Universities and Democracy*, Urbana, Ill., 1962; Rush Welter, *Popular Education and Democratic Thought in America*, New York, 1962; and Sidney W. Tiedt, *The Role of the Federal Government in Education*, New York, 1966. Merle Curti's *The Social Ideas of American Educators* (1935) has been revised, New York, 1960, with a chapter on the last 25 years.

Ex-presidents, ex-deans, ex-chancellors have been loquacious on a subject they knew at firsthand. A. Whitney Griswold (Yale) published *Liberal*

*Education and the Democratic Ideal and Other Essays*, New Haven, Conn., 1959; Clark Kerr (University of California) discusses *The Uses of the University*, Cambridge, Mass., 1963; James A. Perkins (Cornell) prescribes the role of contemporary higher education in *The University in Transition*, Princeton, N.J., 1967; James Bryant Conant (Harvard) is concerned with specific remedies in *Shaping Educational Policy*, New York, 1964; as is Jacques Barzun (Columbia) in *The American University: How It Runs, Where It Is Going*, New York, 1968; and Harold Taylor (Sarah Lawrence) offers a blueprint for radical change in *Students without Teachers: The Crisis in the University*, New York, 1969.

Teacher preparation is the subject of James Bryant Conant's *The Education of American Teachers*, New York, 1963; James D. Koerner, *The Miseducation of American Teachers*, Boston, 1963; and Harold Taylor, *The World as Teacher*, New York, 1969. In the first of two projected volumes, Christopher Jencks and David Riesman discuss "the transforming effect on education of professionalism in graduate schools, with its emphasis on research over teaching": *The Academic Revolution*, New York, 1968. Two vital reports on the same subject are Bernard Berelson's *Graduate Education in the United States*, New York, 1960; and Don Cameron Allen's *The Ph.D. in English and American Literature*, New York, 1968.

Among the widely read attacks on our educational system, these volumes are primary. They are written, however, from vastly different experiences and viewpoints: Paul Goodman, *The Community of Scholars*, New York, 1962; Hyman George Rickover, *American Education—A National Failure*, New York, 1963; Jonathan Kozol, *Death at an Early Age*, Boston, 1967; James Ridgeway, *The Closed Corporation: American Universities in Crisis*, New York, 1968; Charles E. Silberman, *Crisis in the Classroom: The Remaking of American Education*, New York, 1970; and Herbert R. Kohl, *The Open Classroom: A Practical Guide to a New Way of Teaching*, New York, 1970.

The rise of student activism in recent years began at the University of California at Berkeley in 1964 and continued to spread during the rest of the decade. The history of campus confrontations which assumed national prominence is recorded in Hal Draper, *Berkeley: The New Student Revolt*, New York, 1965; Phillip Abbott Luce, *The New Left: A Resurgence of Radicalism among American Students*, New York, 1966; Jerry L. Avorn and Members of the Columbia *Daily Spectator*, *Up against the Ivy Wall*, New York, 1969; Roger Kahn, *The Battle for Morningside Heights*, New York, 1970; Gary R. Weaver and James H. Weaver, eds., *The University and Revolution*, Englewood Cliffs, N.J., 1969; and Lawrence E. Eichel *et al.*, *The Harvard Strike*, Boston, 1970. Faculty commentary on many of the same issues can be found in Seymour Martin Lipset, ed., *Student Politics*,

New York, 1967; Daniel Bell *et al., Confrontation: The Student Rebellion and the Universities,* New York, 1969; Joseph J. Schwab, *College Curriculum and Student Protest,* Chicago, 1969; Nathan Glazer, *Remembering the Answers: Essays on the American Student Revolt,* New York, 1970; Lewis S. Fener, *The Conflict of Generations: The Character and Significance of Student Movements,* New York, 1969; and Seymour Martin Lipset and Philip G. Altbach, eds., *Students in Revolt,* Boston, 1970. Some of the most staunchly conservative arguments against student discontent were voiced by George F. Kennan in an article, "Rebels without a Program," in the *New York Times Magazine* in January, 1968. It is reprinted with a cross-section of student and faculty replies in *Democracy and the Student Left,* Boston, 1968. John Hersey, the novelist and former master at Yale, tries to interpret these years for the older generation in *Letter to the Alumni,* New York, 1970.

The problems of urban education, ghetto schools, and minority groups have been discussed widely in the last decade. James E. Coleman's 737-page report to the U.S. Office of Education is a primary document: *Equality of Educational Opportunity,* Washington, D.C., 1966. Among other important publications are Meyer Weinberg, ed., *Integrated Education,* Beverly Hills, Calif., 1968; Abram J. Jaffe *et al., Negro Higher Education in the 1960's,* New York, 1968; James McEvoy and Abraham Miller, *Black Power and Student Rebellion,* Belmont, Calif., 1969; and William M. Birenbaum, *Overlive: Power, Poverty, and the University,* New York, 1969.

Recent discussions of academic freedom include Walter P. Metzger *et al., Dimensions of Academic Freedom,* Urbana, Ill., 1969; and Sidney Hook, *Academic Freedom and Academic Anarchy,* New York, 1970. The "shape of the future" is the subject of two lively collections of essays: *How Many Roads? The 70s,* ed. Herman A. Estrin and Esther Lloyd-Jones, Beverly Hills, Calif., 1970; and *Campus 1980,* ed. Alvin Eurich and the Staff of the Academy for Educational Development, New York, 1968.

## 181. *Science*

Historical studies span American society from its founding to the present: Richard H. Shryock, *Medicine and Society in America, 1660–1860,* New York, 1960; Brooke Hindle, *The Pursuit of Science in Revolutionary America, 1735–1789,* Chapel Hill, N.C., 1956; William R. Stanton, *The Leopard's Spots: Scientific Attitudes toward Race in America, 1815–1859,* Chicago, 1960; Nathan Reingold, ed., *Science in Nineteenth-Century America,* New York, 1964; George H. Daniels, *American Science in the Age of Jackson,* New York, 1968; William H. Goetzmann, *Explora-*

*tion and Empire: The Explorer and the Scientist in the Winning of the American West,* New York, 1966; H. J. Habakkuk, *American and British Technology in the Nineteenth Century: The Search for Labour-Saving Inventions,* Cambridge, Eng., 1962; L. Sprague DeCamp, *The Heroic Age of American Invention,* Garden City, N.Y., 1961, a popular account chiefly on the nineteenth century; A. Hunter Dupree, ed., *Science and the Emergence of Modern America, 1865–1916,* New York, 1963; and two books by James Harvey Young: *The Toadstool Millionaires: A Social History of Patent Medicines in America before Federal Regulation,* Princeton, N.J., 1961, and *The Medical Messiahs: A Social History of Health Quackery in Twentieth-Century America,* Princeton, N.J., 1967.

Sociopolitical investigations include *Science and Society in the United States,* ed. David D. Van Tassel and Michael G. Hall, Homewood, Ill., 1966; *The Politics of Science,* ed., William R. Nelson, New York, 1968; *The Politics of American Science, 1939 to the Present,* ed. James L. Penick *et al.,* New York, 1965; and A. Hunter Dupree, *Science in the Federal Government,* Cambridge, Mass., 1957. Academic relationships are studied in Boyd R. Keenan, ed., *Science and the University,* New York, 1966; and Frederick Seitz *et al.,* eds., *Science, Government, and the Universities,* Seattle, Wash., 1966, papers delivered at a 1965 meeting of the National Academy of Science. Eli Ginzberg, with Miriam Ostow, made a special study of "the changing structure of health services in the United States," *Men, Money, Medicine,* New York, 1970.

Important papers on methods of analysis are collected in *The Philosophy of Science,* ed. Peter H. Nidditch, London, 1968. Three volumes which treat the future of scientific study, particularly in America, are H. L. Nieburg, *In the Name of Science,* New York, 1966; Nigel Calder, *Technopolis: Social Control of the Uses of Science,* New York, 1970; and Zbigniew Brzezinski, *Between Two Ages: America's Role in the Technetronic Era,* New York, 1970.

Individual studies of prominent American scientists include Brooke Hindle, *David Rittenhouse,* Princeton, N.J., 1964; A. Hunter Dupree, *Asa Gray, 1810–1888,* Cambridge, Mass., 1959; Edward Lurie, *Louis Agassiz: A Life in Science,* Chicago, 1960; Saul Benison, *Tom Rivers: Reflections on a Life in Medicine and Science,* Cambridge, Mass., 1967; Nuel Pharr Davis, [Ernest Orlando] *Lawrence and* [J. Robert] *Oppenheimer,* New York, 1968; and Spencer Klaw, *The New Brahmins: Scientific Life in America,* New York, 1968.

Three scientific reference volumes which will serve the student of American culture are the *McGraw-Hill Encyclopedia of Science and Technology,* 15 vols., New York, 1960 (annual supplements are found under *McGraw-Hill Yearbook of Science and Technology*); the *Harper Encyclopedia of*

*Science,* ed. James R. Newman, rev. ed., New York, 1967; and *Van Nostrand's Scientific Encyclopedia,* 4th ed., Princeton, N.J., 1968.

## 182. THE ARTS:
*General Studies*

Short general histories of the various arts in America, from the Colonial period to the present, are Richard McLanathan's profusely illustrated *The American Tradition in the Arts,* New York, 1968; and William H. Pierson, Jr., and Martha Davidson, eds., *Arts of the United States: A Pictorial Survey,* New York, 1960, 18 essays and a 300-page illustrated catalogue. Histories of the arts in the early years of the republic include Louis B. Wright *et al., The Arts in America: The Colonial Period,* New York, 1966; Harold E. Dickson, *Arts of the Young Republic: The Age of William Dunlap,* Chapel Hill, N.C., 1968; Neil Harris, *The Artist in American Society: The Formative Years, 1790–1860,* New York, 1966; and Walter M. Whitehill, *The Arts in Early American History* [to 1862], Chapel Hill, N.C., 1966, with a 115-page bibliography by Wendell D. Garrett and Jane N. Garrett. Surveys of the nineteenth century are more varied in their approach: Lillian B. Miller, *Patrons and Patronism: The Encouragement of the Fine Arts in the United States, 1790–1860,* Chicago, 1966; Carl Bode, *The Anatomy of American Popular Culture, 1840–1861,* Berkeley, Calif., 1959; Henry Nash Smith, *Popular Culture and Industrialism, 1865–1890,* New York, 1967; Lewis Mumford, *The Brown Decades: A Study of the Arts in America, 1865–1895,* 2nd rev. ed., New York, 1955; and Russell Lynes, *The Art-Makers of Nineteenth-Century America,* New York, 1970.

Critical surveys of the popular arts are Russel Nye's comprehensive *The Unembarrassed Muse,* New York, 1970; and Barry Ulanov's *The Two Worlds of American Art,* New York, 1965. More specialized, in the sense of not being surveys, are Gifford Phillips, *The Arts in a Democratic Society,* Santa Barbara, Calif., 1966; Leonard B. Meyer, *Music, the Arts, and Ideas: Patterns and Predictions in Twentieth-Century Culture,* Chicago, 1967; and Roy McMullen, *Art, Affluence, and Alienation: The Fine Arts Today,* New York, 1968. Collected essays can be found in *Culture for the Millions: Mass Media in Modern Society,* ed. Norman Jacobs, Princeton, N.J., 1961; *Modern Culture and the Arts,* ed. James B. Hall and Barry Ulanov, New York, 1967; *The Arts and the Public,* ed. James E. Miller, Jr., and Paul D. Herring, Chicago, 1967; *The American Imagination: A Critical Survey of the Arts* [excerpts from the *Times Literary Supplement*], London, 1960; and a symposium on "The Visual Arts Today" in the Winter, 1960, issue of *Daedalus.* Changes in America's taste are recorded in Ishbel Ross, *Taste in America: An Illustrated History,* New York, 1967; Marjorie Longley, Louis Silverstein, and Samuel A. Tower, *America's Taste, 1851–1959,* New York, 1960; and Russell Lynes, *The Domesticated Americans,* New York, 1963. Popular accounts of collectors are Aline B. Saarinen, *The Proud Possessors,* New York, 1958; and Alvin Toffler, *The Culture Consumers: A Study of Art and Affluence in America,* New York, 1964. Two important economic studies are William J. Baumol and William G. Bowen, *Performing Arts: The Economic Dilemma,* New York, 1966; and Rockefeller Brothers Fund, *The Performing Arts: Problems and Prospects,* New York, 1965.

Among the individual critics of our culture, oriented toward the arts, these cover wide ground: Harold Rosenberg, *The Tradition of the New,* New York, 1959, and *The Anxious Object: Art Today and Its Audience,* New York, 1964; Clement Greenberg, *Art and Culture: Critical Essays,* Boston, 1961; Marshall McLuhan, *Understanding Media,* New York, 1964; Dwight Macdonald, *Against the American Grain,* New York, 1962; Susan Sontag, *Against Interpretation,* New York, 1966; William Snaith, *The Irresponsible Arts,* New York, 1964, an attack on "current tendencies in the arts and their 'establishments'"; and Reuel Denney, *The Astonished Muse,* Chicago, 1957.

Surveys of our humorists are Jesse Bier, *The Rise and Fall of American Humor,* New York, 1968; Richard Boyd Hauck, *A Cheerful Nihilism: Confidence and "The Absurd" in American Humorous Fiction,* Bloomington, Ind., 1971; Willard Thorp, *American Humorists,* Minneapolis, Minn., 1964; and Norris W. Yates, *The American Humorist: Conscience of the Twentieth Century,* Ames, Iowa, 1964. Stephen Becker's *Comic Art in America,* New York, 1959, is described as "a social history of the funnies, the political cartoons, magazine humor, sporting cartoons, and animated cartoons." See also Pierre Couperie *et al., A History of the Comic Strip,* New York, 1968; and David Manning White and Robert H. Abel, eds., *The Funnies: An American Idiom,* New York, 1963.

The place of photography in cultural history is the subject of Beaumont Newhall's *The History of Photography from 1839 to the Present,* rev. ed., New York, 1964; John Szarkowski, *The Photographer and the American Landscape,* New York, 1963; and Edward Steichen, *A Life in Photography,* Garden City, N.Y., 1963.

## 183. Music

John Tasker Howard's *Our American Music,* 4th ed., New York, 1965, is still the standard survey; but see also Gilbert Chase, *America's Music from the Pilgrims to the Present,* 2nd rev. ed., New York, 1966; Irving L. Sablosky, *American Music,* Chicago, 1969; Virgil Thomson, *American Music since 1910,* New York, 1971; and Paul Henry Lang, ed., *One Hundred Years of Music in America,* New York, 1961. More specialized histories are Irving Lowens, *Music and Musicians in Early America,* New York, 1964; P. A. Scholes, *The Puritans and Music in England and New England,* New York, 1962; Julian Mates, *The American Musical Stage before 1800,* New Brunswick, N.J., 1962; Stanley Green, *The World of Musical Comedy,* New York, 1960; and Ronald L. Davis, *A History of Opera in the American West,* Englewood Cliffs, N.J., 1965.

Among the many studies and collections of folksongs, these are representative: Bruno Nettl, *An Introduction to Folk Music in the United States,* 2nd ed., Detroit, Mich., 1962; Harold Courlander, *Negro Folk Music, U.S.A.,* New York, 1963; and Donald K. Wilgus, *Anglo-American Folksong Scholarship since 1898,* New Brunswick, N.J., 1959.

Gunther Schuller is preparing a comprehensive history of jazz. The first of two volumes is *Early Jazz: Its Roots and Musical Development,* New York, 1967, covering the beginnings to 1930. See also Winthrop Sargent, *Jazz: A History,* rev. ed., New York, 1964; Neil Leonard, *Jazz and the White Americans,* Chicago, 1962; Whitney Balliett, *Dinosaurs in the Morning: 41 Pieces on Jazz,* Philadelphia, 1962; and *Jazz: New Perspectives . . . ,* ed. Nat Hentoff and Albert J. McCarthy, New York, 1959. The newer rock music is treated in Charlie Gillett, *The Sound of the City: The Rise of Rock and Roll,* New York, 1970; and Jonathan Eisen, ed., *The Age of Rock,* New York, 1969, and *The Age of Rock Two: Sights and Sounds of the American Cultural Revolution,* New York, 1970.

Two musical anthologies of note are W. Thomas Marrocco and Harold Gleason, eds., *Music in America . . . 1620–1865,* New York, 1964; and Lester S. Levy, *Grace Notes in American History: Popular Sheet Music from 1820 to 1900,* Norman, Okla., 1967.

Good reference works are numerous. Willi Apel's *Harvard Dictionary of Music,* 2nd rev. and enl. ed., Cambridge, Mass., 1969, is the standard authoritative work; but John Owen Ward's *The Oxford Companion to Music,* 10th ed., New York, 1970, is also a primary reference volume. Leonard Feather edited two vital compendia: *The Encyclopedia of Jazz,* rev. ed., New York, 1960; and *The Encyclopedia of Jazz in the Sixties,* New York, 1967. David Ewen's *New Complete Book of the American Musical Theater,* New York, 1971, is a historical guide to more than 300 productions. Robert S. Gold compiled *A Jazz Lexicon,* New York, 1964. Two bibliographical volumes are Nat Shapiro, ed., *Popular Music: An Annotated Index,* New York, 1964; and Robert Reisner, *The Literature of Jazz: A Selective Bibliography,* rev. ed., New York, 1959.

## 183. *Painting*

Two of the major comprehensive surveys have had new editions: Oliver W. Larkin, *Art and Life in America,* rev. and enl. ed., New York, 1960 (with an important bibliography); and E[dgar] P[reston] Richardson, *Painting in America: From 1502 to the Present,* 2nd ed., New York, 1965. See also Lloyd Goodrich, *Three Centuries of American Art,* New York, 1966; Daniel M. Mendelowitz, *A History of American Art,* New York, 1960; Samuel M. Green, *American Art: A Historical Survey,* New York, 1966; and *American Painting,* Volume I, *From Its Beginning to the Armory Show* by Jules David Prown; Volume II, *The Twentieth Century* by Barbara Rose, New York, 1969.

More specialized histories include John C. Ewers, *Artists of the Old West,* Garden City, N.Y., 1965; Barbara Novak, *American Painting of the Nineteenth Century,* New York, 1969; Lloyd Goodrich and John I. Baur, *American Art of Our Century,* New York, 1961; Sam Hunter, *Modern American Painting and Sculpture,* New York, 1959; Henry Geldzahler, *American Painting in the Twentieth Century,* New York, 1965; Virgil Baker, *From Realism to Reality in Recent American Painting,* Lincoln, Neb., 1959; Cedric Dover, *American Negro Art,* New York, 1960; and Dorothy Dunn, *American Indian Painting of the Southwest and Plains Area,* Albuquerque, N.M., 1968.

Among individual studies of American artists, these are representative: Charles M. Mount, *Gilbert Stuart: A Biography,* New York, 1964; Jules David Prown, *John Singleton Copley,* 2 vols., Cambridge, Mass., 1966; John Francis McDermott, *George Caleb Bingham, River Portraitist,* Norman, Okla., 1959; Lloyd Goodrich, *Albert P. Ryder,* New York, 1959; Albert Ten Eyck Gardner, *Winslow Homer,* New York, 1961, Bennard B. Perlman, *The Immortal Eight: American Painting from Eakins to the Armory Show (1870–1913),* New York, 1962; William Innes Homer, *Robert Henri and His Circle,* Ithaca, N.Y., 1969; Ira Glackens, *William Glackens and the Ashcan Group,* New York, 1957; Martin Friedman *et al., Charles Sheeler,* Washington, D.C., 1969; Ernst Scheyer, *Lyonel Feininger: Caricature and Fantasy,* Detroit, Mich., 1964; and Yvon Bizardel, *American Painters in Paris,* trans. Richard Howard, New York, 1960. Thomas Hart Benton surveys his own career in *An American in Art: A Professional and Technical Autobiography,* Lawrence, Kan., 1969. Aaron Bohrod provides an illustrated autobiographical study in *A Decade of Still Life,* Madison, Wis., 1966.

Useful reference works include George C. Groce and David H. Wallace, *The New York Historical Society's Dictionary of Artists in America,*

*1564–1860*, New Haven, Conn., 1957; Paul Cummings, *A Dictionary of Contemporary American Artists,* New York, 1966; Hayward and Blanche Cirker, eds., *Dictionary of American Portraits,* New York, 1967; and Albert Ten Eyck Gardner and Stuart P. Feld, *American Painting,* Greenwich, Conn., 1965, a catalogue of the collection of the Metropolitan Museum of Art.

### 183. *Sculpture*

The major comprehensive study is Wayne Craven's *Sculpture in America,* New York, 1968. It spans four centuries and concludes with an invaluable bibliography of surveys, period studies, expositions, and 100 individual artists. Margaret F. Thorp's *The Literary Sculptors,* Durham, N.C., 1965, discusses the lives and work of American artists between 1825 and 1876, notably Horatio Greenough, William Wetmore Story, Harriet Hosmer, and Hiram Powers. Allan I. Ludwig made a scholarly study of Puritan iconography in *Graven Images: New England Stonecarving and Its Symbols, 1650–1815,* Middletown, Conn., 1966. Maurice Tuchman edited *American Sculpture of the* [Nineteen] *Sixties,* Los Angeles, 1967. See also Sam Hunter, *Modern American Painting and Scultpure,* New York, 1959.

Studies of individual artists include Nathalia Wright, *Horatio Greenough: The First American Sculptor,* Philadelphia, 1963; Robert L. Gale, *Thomas Crawford, American Sculptor,* Pittsburgh, 1964; David H. Wallace, *John Rogers, The People's Sculptor,* Middletown, Conn., 1967; and Louise Hall Tharp, *Saint-Gaudens and the Gilded Age,* Boston, 1969.

Albert Ten Eyck Gardner's *American Sculpture,* Greenwich, Conn., 1965, is a catalogue of the more than 350 pieces in the Metropolitan Museum of Art.

### 185. *Architecture*

Several important surveys have appeared in recent years. Carl W. Condit's history of structural forms and techniques, *American Building Art: The Nineteenth Century,* New York, 1960, was followed by his *American Building Art: The Twentieth Century,* New York, 1961, and by his popular history, *American Building: Materials and Techniques from the First Colonial Settlements to the Present,* Chicago, 1968. Important for background studies is John Burchard and Albert Bush-Brown, *The Architecture of America: A Social and Cultural History,* Boston, 1961. An important photographic history, as supplement to the above, is Wayne Andrews's *Architecture in America,* New York, 1960. See also William A. Coles and Henry Hope Reed, Jr., *Architecture in America: A Battle of*

*Styles,* New York, 1961; Alan Gowans, *Images of American Living: Four Centuries of Architecture and Furniture as Cultural Expression,* Philadelphia, 1964; Ian McCallum, *Architecture U.S.A.,* New York, 1959, a biographical approach; and the chapters on America in Sigfried Giedion, *Space, Time, and Architecture: The Growth of a New Tradition,* 5th enl. ed., Cambridge, Mass., 1967; and John Jacobus, *Twentieth-Century Architecture: The Middle Years, 1940–1965,* New York, 1966.

Regional studies abound. Of New England: Marian Card Donnelly, *The New England Meeting Houses of the Seventeenth Century,* Middletown, Conn., 1968; and Bainbridge Bunting, *Houses of Boston's Back Bay: An Architectural History 1840–1917,* Cambridge, Mass., 1967. Of the Eastern seaboard: John W. Reps, *Monumental Washington: The Planning and Development of the Capital Center,* Princeton, N.J., 1967; Constance McLaughlin Green, *Washington,* Volume I, *Village and Capital 1800–1878;* Volume II, *Capital City, 1879–1950,* Princeton, N.J., 1962–1963; and William B. O'Neal, *Architecture in Virginia,* New York, 1968. Of the Middle West: Wayne Andrews, *Architecture of Michigan,* Detroit, Mich., 1967, and *Architecture in Chicago and Mid-America,* New York, 1968, both photographic surveys; Carl W. Condit, *The Chicago School of Architecture,* Chicago, 1964, covering the years 1875–1925. Of the West: Harold Kirker, *California's Architectural Frontier: Style and Tradition in the Nineteenth Century,* San Marino, Calif., 1960; and Robert M. Fogelson, *The Fragmented Metropolis: Los Angeles, 1850–1930,* Cambridge, Mass., 1967.

Varieties of architectural theories are treated in James Early, *Romanticism and American Architecture,* New York, 1965; Don Gifford, ed., *The Literature of Architecture: The Evolution of Architectural Theory and Practice in Nineteenth-Century America,* New York, 1966; James Marston Fitch, *Architecture and the Esthetics of Plenty,* New York, 1961; Henry Hope Reed, Jr.'s attack on modern architecture, *The Golden City,* New York, 1958; and *Who Designs America?,* ed. Laurence B. Holland, Garden City, N.Y., 1966.

Three major city-planning studies are John W. Reps, *The Making of Urban America: A History of City Planning in the United States,* Princeton, N.J., 1965; Edmund N. Bacon, *Design of Cities,* New York, 1967; and Mel Scott, *American City Planning since 1890,* Berkeley, Calif., 1969.

Maurice English edited *The Testament of Stone: Themes of Idealism and Indignation from the Writings of Louis Sullivan,* Evanston, Ill., 1963. See also Sherman Paul, *Louis Sullivan: An Architect in American Thought,* Englewood Cliffs, N.J., 1962; and Willard Connely, *Louis Sullivan as He Lived,* New York, 1960. Edgar Kaufmann and Ben Raeburn selected the contents of *Frank Lloyd Wright: Writings and Buildings,* New York, 1960, a handbook for the study of Wright's work. Finis Farr wrote the first full-length biography, *Frank Lloyd Wright*, New York, 1961. See also Herbert Jacobs, *Frank Lloyd Wright: America's Greatest Architect*, New York, 1965; and Olgivanna Lloyd Wright, *Frank Lloyd Wright: His Life, His Work, His Words*, New York, 1966. The most recent study of New England's Bulfinch is Harold Kirker's *The Architecture of Charles Bulfinch*, Cambridge, Mass., 1969, including a catalogue and description of all known commissions.

Frank J. Roos, Jr., *Bibliography of Early American Architecture* (1943) has been revised, updated, and extensively annotated, Urbana, Ill., 1968.

### 185. Motion Pictures

Books on the film industry and art have multiplied so rapidly in the last decade that the following notations can suggest only a few of the major titles. All books on individual actors, directors, and producers, many volumes of criticism, and almost all textbooks have had to be omitted. Unfortunately, no comprehensive bibliography of film scholarship and criticism exists.

Recent histories of the films include Kevin Brownlow, *The Parade's Gone By*, New York, 1968; Edward Wagenknecht, *The Movies in the Age of Innocence*, Norman, Okla., 1962; Albert R. Fulton, *Motion Pictures: The Development of an Art from Silent Films to the Age of Television*, Norman, Okla., 1960; Richard Schickel, *Movies: The History of an Art and an Institution*, New York, 1964; George N. Fenin and William K. Everson, *The Western: From Silents to Cinerama*, New York, 1962; Penelope Houston, *The Contemporary Cinema*, Baltimore, Md., 1963; Sheldon Renan, *An Introduction to the American Underground Film*, New York, 1967; and Parker Tyler, *Underground Film: A Critical History*, New York, 1969. Two important reissues bring major works back into print: Terry Ramsaye, *A Million and One Nights: A History of the Motion Picture* (1926), New York, 1964; and Paul Rotha, *The Film Till Now: A Survey of World Cinema* (1930), New York, 1963.

The director's art and techniques is the subject of Andrew Sarris, *The American Cinema: Directors and Directions 1929–1968*, New York, 1969; John Russell Taylor, *Cinema Eye, Cinema Ear: Some Key Film-makers of the Sixties*, New York, 1964; Eric Sherman and Martin Rubin, *The Director's Event: Interviews with Five American Film-makers*, New York, 1970; Andrew Sarris, ed., *Interviews with Film Directors*, Indianapolis, Ind., 1968.

The aesthetics of film making are treated in Rudolph Arnheim, *Film as*

*Art,* Berkeley, Calif., 1958; Pierre L'Herminier, ed., *L'Art du cinéma,* Paris, 1960; Siegfried Kracauer, *Theory of Film,* New York, 1960; Lo Duca, *L'Erotisme au cinéma,* Paris, 1962; Ernest Lindgren, *The Art of the Film,* 2nd rev. ed., New York, 1963; Jean Mitry, *Esthétique et psychologie du cinéma,* Paris, 1963; John Howard Lawson, *Film: The Creative Process,* New York, 1964; Parker Tyler, *The Three Faces of the Film,* rev. ed., South Brunswick, N.J., 1967; André Bazin, *What Is Cinema?,* selected and translated by Hugh Gray, Berkeley, Calif., 1967; I. C. Jarvie, *Movies and Society,* New York, 1970; and Peter Wollen, *Signs and Meaning in the Cinema,* Bloomington, Ind., 1969. From among the practicing film critics come several informative volumes: Robert Warshow, *The Immediate Experience,* Garden City, N.Y., 1962; Pauline Kael, *I Lost It at the Movies,* Boston, 1965; Stanley Kauffmann, *A World on Film,* New York, 1966; Dwight Macdonald, *Dwight Macdonald on Movies,* Englewood Cliffs, N.J., 1969; and Andrew Sarris, *Confessions of a Cultist: On the Cinema, 1955–1969,* New York, 1970.

Robert Gessner's *The Moving Image: A Guide to Cinematic Literacy,* New York, 1968, is a detailed analysis of selected film scripts aimed at discovering "the unique patterns and structures that, through the visualization of ideas and emotions, make cinema an art." Haig P. Manoogian's *The Film-maker's Art,* New York, 1966, is an anatomy as well as a theoretical discussion. Kenneth Macgowan combines technical discussion with history in *Behind the Screen,* New York, 1965.

The complex problems of censorship are the focus of Murray Schumach's *The Face on the Cutting Room Floor,* New York, 1964; Ira H. Carmen, *Movies, Censorship, and the Law,* Ann Arbor, Mich., 1966; and Richard S. Randall, *Censorship of the Movies: The Social and Political Control of a Mass Medium,* Madison, Wis., 1968.

For reference volumes, see Leslie Halliwell, *The Filmgoer's Companion,* 3rd rev. ed., New York, 1970; P. J. Graham, *A Dictionary of the Cinema,* rev. ed., New York, 1968; and Richard B. Dimmitt, *A Title Guide to the Talkies: A Comprehensive Listing of 16,000 Feature-Length Films from October, 1927, until December, 1963,* New York, 1965. *The New York Times Film Reviews, 1913–1968,* New York, 1970, is a five-volume reprinting of more than 16,000 reviews. The sixth volume, *The New York Times Film Reviews Appendix-Index,* New York, 1971, contains addenda, awards, a portrait gallery, and a 1,000-page index.

## 185. *Radio and Television*

Erik Barnouw has written a definitive three-volume *History of Broadcasting in the United States.* The first volume, *A Tower in Babel,* New

York, 1966, takes the story to 1933; the second volume, *The Golden Web,* New York, 1969, covers the years 1933–1953; *The Image Empire,* New York, 1970, brings the story to the present. Briefer histories are Poyntz Tyler, ed., *Television and Radio,* New York, 1961; and Wilson P. Dizard, *Television: A World View,* Syracuse, N.Y., 1966.

Socioeconomic studies of the television medium include Gary A. Steiner, *The People Look at Television: A Study of Audience Attitudes,* New York, 1963; Harry J. Skornia, *Television and Society: An Inquest and Agenda for Improvement,* New York, 1965; Leon Arons and Mark A. May, eds., *Television and Human Behavior: Tomorrow's Research in Mass Communication,* New York, 1963; and David Manning White and Richard Averson, *Sight, Sound, and Society,* Boston, 1968. More specialized studies are Robert MacNeil, *The People Machine: The Influence of Television on American Politics,* New York, 1968; Kurt and Gladys E. Lang, *Politics and Television,* New York, 1968; Solomon S. Simonson, *Crisis in Television: A Study of the Private Judgment and the Public Interest,* New York, 1966; Patrick D. Hazard, ed., *TV as Art: Some Essays in Criticism,* Champaign, Ill., 1966; Norton S. Parker, *Audiovisual Script Writing,* New Brunswick, N.J., 1968; Lola Gola Yoakem, ed., *TV and Screen Writing,* Berkeley, Calif., 1958; Meyer Weinberg, *TV in America: The Morality of Hard Cash,* New York, 1962; and John W. Powell, *Channels of Learning: The Story of Educational Television,* Washington, D.C., 1962.

Fred W. Friendly, former president of CBS News, writes about television from the inside in *Due to Circumstances beyond Our Control,* New York, 1967; and Newton N. Minow, former chairman of the Federal Communications Commission, discusses "the private broadcasters and the public interest" in *Equal Time,* ed. Lawrence Laurent, New York, 1964. Informal critical writing on the medium can be found in Charles Sopkin's satires, *Seven Glorious Days, Seven Fun-Filled Nights: One Man's Struggle to Survive a Week Watching Commercial Television,* New York, 1968; and Michael J. Arlen's 36 *New Yorker* essays, *Living-Room War: Writings about Television,* New York, 1969.

## 186. *Graphic Arts and Crafts*

Peter C. Welsh's *American Folk Art: The Art and Spirit of a People,* Washington, D.C., 1965, is an illustrated discussion concentrating on the nineteenth century. See also Ellen Sabine, *American Folk Art,* Princeton, N.J., 1958; and Mary Black and Jean Lipman, *American Folk Painting,* New York, 1967. Regional studies include Edwin Tunis, *Colonial Craftsmen and the Beginning of American Industry,* Cleveland, Ohio, 1965; Priscilla Sawyer Lord and Daniel J. Foley, *The Folk Arts and Crafts of New*

*England*, Philadelphia, 1965; and Henry Kauffman, *Pennsylvania Dutch American Folk Art*, New York, 1964. Henry Glassie's *Pattern in the Material Folk Culture of the Eastern United States*, Philadelphia, 1968, is especially valuable for its 73-page bibliography.

American furniture makers are well illustrated in Alan Gowans, *Images of American Living: Four Centuries of Architecture and Furniture as Cultural Expression*, Philadelphia, 1964; Joseph Downs, *American Furniture: Queen Anne and Chippendale Periods*, New York, 1952; Charles F. Montgomery, *American Furniture: The Federal Period*, New York, 1966; and Edward Deming Andrews and Faith Andrews, *Religion in Wood: A Book of Shaker Furniture*, Bloomington, Ind., 1966.

## 187. THE AMERICAN LANGUAGE
HISTORICAL SCHOLARSHIP

H. L. Mencken's *The American Language*, 4th ed. and two supplements (1936–1948) has been abridged by Raven I. McDavid, Jr., and David W. Maurer, New York, 1963. Albert H. Marckwardt's revision of George Philip Krapp's *Modern English: Its Growth and Present Use* (1909) was published in New York, 1968.

Among the general studies are W. Nelson Francis, *The Structure of American English* (with a chapter on American English dialects by Raven I. McDavid, Jr.), New York, 1958; Louise M. Myers, *Guide to American English*, 4th ed., Englewood Cliffs, N.J., 1966, and *Roots of Modern English*, Boston, 1966; Thomas Pyles, *The Origins and Development of the English Language* (with a chapter on recent British and American English), 2nd ed., New York, 1971; Kellogg W. Hunt and Paul Stoakes, *Our Living Language*, 2nd ed., Boston, 1967; Max Black, *The Labyrinth of Language*, New York, 1968; and Charlton Laird, *Language in America*, New York, 1970. Black also edited a collection of essays by various hands on the language of politics, religion, poetry, law: *The Importance of Language*, Ithaca, N.Y., 1962. More specialized studies are Charles Kenneth Thomas, *Introduction to the Phonetics of American English*, 2nd ed., New York, 1958; Hans Kurath, *A Phonology and Prosody of Modern English*, Ann Arbor, Mich., 1964; Arthur J. Bronstein, *The Pronunciation of English: An Introduction to Phonetics*, New York, 1960; Richard R. Lodwig and Eugene F. Barrett, *The Dictionary and the Language*, New York, 1967; and Noam Chomsky and Morris Halle, *The Sound Pattern of English*, New York, 1968. *Language and Life in the U.S.A.* by Gladys G. Doty and Janet Ross is a guide to American English for foreign students, Evanston, Ill., 1960.

189. GLOSSARIES AND DICTIONARIES

From the 50,000 entries in his *Dictionary of Americanisms* (1951), M[itford] M. Mathews prepared *Americanisms: A Dictionary of Selected Americanisms on Historical Principles,* Chicago, 1966.

Dictionaries of slang are surprisingly numerous: Harold Wentworth and Stuart Berg Flexner, eds., *Dictionary of American Slang,* New York, 1960 (a supplement by Flexner was added to the 1967 edition); Eric Partridge, ed., *A Dictionary of Slang and Unconventional English,* 6th ed., New York, 1967; M. J. Leitner and J. R. Lanen, eds., *Dictionary of French and American Slang,* New York, 1965; Hyman E. Goldin and Frank O'Leary, eds., *Dictionary of American Underworld Lingo,* New York, 1950.

From London come two standard references which are concerned, of course, with British English, but are nevertheless important to American scholars: *The Oxford Dictionary of English Etymology,* ed. C. T. Onions, New York, 1966; and Eric Partridge, *Origins: A Short Etymological Dictionary of Modern English,* New York, 1962.

George R. Stewart compiled *Names on the Land,* rev. ed., Boston, 1958, followed by *American Place-Names: A Concise and Selective Dictionary for the Continental United States of America,* New York, 1970. More specialized listings are Harold C. Whitford, *A Dictionary of American Homophones and Homographs,* New York, 1966; and Eric Pugh, *A Dictionary of Acronyms and Abbreviations in Management, Technology, and Information Science,* rev. ed., Hamden, Conn., 1970.

190. USAGE

The most ambitious guides are William and Mary Morris, *Dictionary of Word and Phrase Origins,* 3 vols., New York, 1962–1971; and Wilson Follett's *Modern American Usage,* edited and completed by Jacques Barzun *et al.,* New York, 1966. See also Robert C. Whitford and James R. Foster, *Concise Dictionary of American Grammar and Usage,* New York, 1955; Margaret M. Bryant, ed., *Current American Usage,* New York, 1962; and Theodore M. Bernstein's lively and witty "guides to better writing emanating from the News Room of the New York *Times*": *Watch Your Language,* Great Neck, N.Y., 1958; *More Language That Needs Watching,* Manhasset, N.Y., 1962; and *The Careful Writer,* New York, 1965. H. W. Fowler's *Modern English Usage* (1926), compiled for British users, has had a second edition by Sir Ernest Gowers, New York, 1965.

191. REGIONAL SPEECH AND LOCALISMS

For dialectical studies see Hans Kurath and Raven I. McDavid, Jr., *The Pronunciation of English in the Atlantic States*, Ann Arbor, Mich., 1961; and Carroll E. Reed, *Dialects of American English*, Cleveland, Ohio, 1967. Joshua A. Fishman and others have compiled a group of essays on *Language Loyalty in the United States: The Maintenance and Perpetuation of Non-English Mother Tongues by American Ethnic and Religious Groups*, New York, 1967. More specialized listings of local speech are recorded in Archer Taylor and Bartlett Jere Whiting, *A Dictionary of American Proverbs and Proverbial Phrases, 1820–1880*, Cambridge, Mass., 1958.

191. BIBLIOGRAPHY

Vito J. Brenni prepared *American English: A Bibliography*, Philadelphia, 1964. For more complete listings see the continuing annual bibliographies published in *American Speech: A Quarterly of Linguistics* (1925–current).

## 192. FOLK LITERATURE

### SONGS AND BALLADS
GENERAL STUDIES AND COLLECTIONS

Alan Lomax edited *Folk Songs of North America*, New York, 1960, and (with Elizabeth Poston) *The Penguin Book of American Folk Songs*, Baltimore, Md., 1965. More specialized collections are two volumes by Irwin Silber: *Songs of the Civil War*, New York, 1960, and *Songs of the Great American West*, New York, 1967. A revised edition of John A. Lomax and Alan Lomax's *Cowboy Songs and Other Frontier Ballads* appeared in New York, 1966. Arthur Kyle Davis, Jr., edited *More Traditional Ballads of Virginia*, Chapel Hill, N.C., 1960.

Thomas K. Scherman edited Russell A. Ames's *The Story of American Folk Song*, New York, 1960. G. Malcolm Laws, Jr., *Native American Balladry*, rev. ed., Philadelphia, 1964, is both history and reference volume. Two considerations of the current popularity of folksong are Oscar Brand, *The Ballad Mongers: Rise of the Modern Folk Song*, New York, 1962; and David A. DeTurk and A. Pulin, Jr., eds., *The American Folk Scene: Dimensions of the Folksong Revival*, New York, 1967. *The Singing Sixties* by Willard A. Heaps and Porter W. Heaps, Norman, Okla., 1960, focuses on "the spirit of Civil War days drawn from the music of the times." Alan Lomax edited *Folk Song Style and Culture*, Washington, D.C., 1968, a report from the staff of the Cantometrics Project of Columbia University which argues that "song style symbolizes and reinforces certain important aspects of social structure in all cultures."

### 197. NEGRO FOLKLORE

Among the volumes devoted to various aspects of the history of Negro music are Lindsay Patterson, comp., *The Negro in Music and Art*, New York, 1967; Harold Courlander, *Negro Folk Music, U.S.A.*, New York, 1963; Thomas W. Talley, comp., *Negro Folk Rhymes, Wise and Otherwise*, Port Washington, N.Y., 1968; and Hans Nathan, *Dan Emmett and the Rise of Early Negro Minstrelsy*, Norman, Okla., 1962.

### 201. BIBLIOGRAPHY

Still basic is Charles Haywood, *A Bibliography of North American Folklore and Folksong*, 2 vols., 2nd rev. ed., New York, 1961. Ray M. Lawless's *Folksingers and Folksongs in America*, rev. ed., New York, 1965, is a "handbook of biography, bibliography, and discography." Donald K. Wilgus surveys almost every important British or American collection or article on folksong before 1959 in *Anglo-American Folksong Scholarship since 1898*, New Brunswick, N.J., 1959, an invaluable guide through the forest of publications.

### 202. FOLK TALES AND HUMOR
#### GENERAL STUDIES

The bibliography of folk-tale collections and studies of American folklore is now so extensive that the suggested titles which follow must be described merely as basic works. They are not for "the folklore fraternity," as Richard M. Dorson calls his colleagues who use, as their guides, the pages of the *Journal of American Folklore, Western Folklore*, and the *Southern Folklore Quarterly* among others.

Students of American civilization will want to consult Richard M. Dorson's *American Folklore*, Chicago, 1959, a comprehensive survey (limited to prose narrative) ranging from Colonial times to the present. The scope of international folklore scholarship is demonstrated in Alan Dundes's anthology, *The Study of Folklore*, Englewood Cliffs, N.J., 1965. Jan

Harold Brunvand has assembled basic materials for demonstrating how to organize a folklore course in *The Study of American Folklore: An Introduction*, New York, 1968. Regional studies are the focus of Richard M. Dorson's *Buying the Wind: Regional Folklore in the United States*, Chicago, 1964; and Frank R. Kramer, *Voices in the Valley: Mythmaking and Folk Belief in the Shaping of the Middle West*, Madison, Wis., 1964 (particularly good for its bibliographical notes). See also Mody C. Boatright, Robert B. Downs, and John T. Flanagan, *The Family Saga and Other Phases of American Folklore,* Urbana, Ill., 1958.

The pages of the *Journal of American Folklore* have provided the material for two important collections: *Folklore of America*, sel. and ed. Tristram P. Coffin and Hennig Cohen, New York, 1966; and *Folklore of the Great West*, sel. and ed. John Greenway, Palo Alto, Calif., 1969. "The artistic use of folklore by American authors" is the focus of a collection of "representative selections of prose and verse," *Folklore in American Literature*, ed. John T. Flanagan and Arthur Palmer Hudson, Evanston, Ill., 1958. B. A. Botkin's valuable *Treasury of New England Folklore* (1947) has had a revised edition, New York, 1965. Langston Hughes and Arna Bontemps have edited a group of tales, poems, and songs in *The Book of Negro Folklore*, New York, 1958. Richard M. Dorson's collection is *American Negro Folktales,* Greenwich, Conn., 1967. John Mason Brewer compiled *American Negro Folklore*, Chicago, 1968.

### 202. BIBLIOGRAPHY

One of the basic volumes, now in a second revised edition, is Charles Haywood's *A Bibliography of North American Folklore and Folksong,* 2 vols., New York, 1961. Stith Thompson compiled a classification of "narrative elements" in *A Motif-Index of Folk Literature*, 6 vols., rev. ed., Bloomington, Ind., 1955–1958. Marjorie Tallman edited a *Dictionary of American Folklore*, New York, 1960. See also the relevant pages in *A Guide to the Study of the United States of America*, ed. Donald H. Mugridge and Blanche P. McCrum, Washington, D.C., 1960; and for annual bibliographies the March issues of *Southern Folklore Quarterly*, the April supplements of *Journal of American Folklore*.

### 208. REGIONAL HUMORISTS

Wade Hall's *The Smiling Phoenix*, Gainsville, Fla., 1965, is a summarizing assessment of Southern humor from 1865–1914. John Q. Anderson culled newspapers and magazines between 1835 and 1860 to sample popular humor of the Old South in *With the Bark On*, Nashville, Tenn., 1967. Two studies of the "Big Bear" school of humor are Milton Rickel's biography of its creator, *Thomas Bangs Thorpe: Humorist of the Old Southwest,* Baton Rouge, La., 1962; and Norris W. Yates's *William T. Porter and the Spirit of the Times*, Baton Rouge, La., 1957, an analysis of the magazine as well as a portrait of its owner. Hennig Cohen and William B. Dillingham edited a generous sampling in *Humor of the Old Southwest*, Boston, 1964.

John S. Robb's *Streaks of Squatter Life, and Far-West Scenes*, ed. John Francis McDermott, Gainesville, Fla., 1962, is a facsimile reproduction of humorous sketches, with the original illustrations, from the St. Louis *Weekly Reveille* of 1844–1846. It was originally published in 1847. John Q. Anderson edited *Louisiana Swamp Doctor: The Writings of Henry Clay Lewis Alias "Madison Tenas, M.D.,"* Baton Rouge, La., 1962. M. Thomas Inge edited *High Times and Hard Times: Sketches and Tales by George Washington Harris*, Nashville, Tenn., 1967.

## 212. INDIAN LORE AND ANTIQUITIES

STUDIES AND COLLECTIONS

Early Indian history is the subject of Harold E. Driver, ed., *The Americas on the Eve of Discovery*, Englewood Cliffs, N.J., 1964; Jack D. Forbes, *The Indian in America's Past*, Englewood Cliffs, N.J., 1964; Alvin M. Josephy, Jr., *The Indian Heritage of America*, New York, 1968; and Robert Wauchope, *Lost Tribes and Sunken Continents: Myth and Method in the Study of American Indians*, Chicago, 1962. Ethnic and cultural studies include William T. Hagan, *American Indians*, Chicago, 1961 (emphasis on Indian-white relations); Fred Eggan, *The American Indian: Perspectives for the Study of Social Change*, Chicago, 1966; Harold E. Driver, *Indians of North America*, Chicago, 1961, 2nd rev. ed., 1969; D'Arcy McNickle, *The Indian Tribes of the United States: Ethnic and Cultural Survival*, New York, 1962; and Stuart Levine and Nancy Oestreich Lurie, eds., *The American Indian Today*, Deland, Fla., 1968. Roy Harvey Pearce's study, *The Savages of America* (1953), has been revised under the title *Savages and Civilization*, Baltimore, Md., 1965. John Tebbel concentrates on a special aspect of Indian-white relations in *The Compact History of the Indian Wars*, New York, 1966. The most recent general study is Dee Brown's *Bury My Heart at Wounded Knee: An Indian History of the American West*, New York, 1970.

Area studies range from prehistoric to modern times: William V.

Kinietz, *The Indians of the Western Great Lakes, 1615–1760*, Ann Arbor, Mich., 1965; Mary Jourdan Atkinson, *Indians of the Southwest*, 4th ed., San Antonio, Tex., 1963; William W. Newcomb, *The Indians of Texas*, Austin, Tex., 1961; Robert E. Ditzler, *The Indian People of Arizona*, New York, 1967; Alvin M. Josephy, Jr., *The Nez Percé Indians and the Opening of the Northwest*, New Haven, Conn., 1965; Tom McFeat, ed., *Indians of the North Pacific Coast*, Seattle, Wash., 1967; and Robert I. Burns, *The Jesuits and the Indian Wars of the Northwest*, New Haven, Conn., 1966.

For specialized studies of individual tribes consult first the Civilization of the American Indian Series published by the University of Oklahoma Press. Begun in 1932, the list has reached, by 1969, a total of 100 titles. See also Laura Gilpin, *The Enduring Navaho*, Austin, Tex., 1968; and John Stands in the Timber and Margot Liberty, *Cheyenne Memories*, New Haven, Conn., 1967. Other specialized books and collections include *Indian Tales of North America*, ed., Tristram P. Coffin, Philadelphia, 1961; Alice Marriot and Carol K. Rachlin, *American Indian Mythology*, New York, 1969; Dorothy Dunn, *American Indian Painting*, Albuquerque, N.M., 1968; Bill Holm [Oscar William Holm], *Northwest Coast Indian Art: An Analysis of Form*, Seattle, Wash., 1965; Julia Seton, *American Indian Arts: A Way of Life*, New York, 1962; John Francis McDermott, *Seth Eastman: Pictorial Historian of the Indian*, Norman, Okla., 1961; and Harold McCracken, *George Catlin and the Old Frontier*, New York, 1959.

For general reference volumes, see John Leeds Stoutenburgh, *Dictionary of the American Indian*, New York, 1960; Bernard Klein and Daniel Icolari, eds., *Reference Encyclopedia of the American Indian*, New York, 1967; and Roger C. Owen *et al.*, eds., *The North American Indians: A Sourcebook*, New York, 1967.

## 222. POPULAR LITERATURE

### BEST SELLERS

*Bibliography*

Carl Bode discusses best sellers, among other subjects, in his miscellany, *The Half-World of American Culture*, Carbondale, Ill., 1965. See also Alice Payne Hackett, *70 Years of Best Sellers, 1895–1965*, New York, 1967.

**224.** DIME NOVELS:
*Bibliography*

Charles Bragin compiled *Bibliography: Dime Novels, 1860–1964,* Brooklyn, N.Y., 1964.

## 235. *ORATORY AND THE LYCEUM*

MID-NINETEENTH CENTURY AND AFTER:
*The Rostrum*

Francis Lea McCurdy describes "the forms and traditions of speechmaking developed to meet the needs of frontiersmen" in *Stump, Bar and Pulpit: Speechmaking on the Missouri Frontier*, Columbia, Mo., 1969.

**237.** THE LYCEUM

The most recent treatment of the popular education system which lasted until the 1920's is Joseph E. Gould's *The Chautauqua Movement: An Episode in the Continuing American Revolution*, New York, 1961. Edward Weeks describes a Boston "counterpart" in *The Lowells and Their Institute*, Boston, 1966.

# BIBLIOGRAPHIES: MOVEMENTS
# AND INFLUENCES

## 260. CHRONICLES OF THE FRONTIER: LITERATURE OF TRAVEL AND WESTWARD MIGRATION

### EASTERN UNITED STATES TO THE MISSISSIPPI

THE EXPANDING FRONTIER: TRAVELERS AND OBSERVERS

Thomas D. Clark has concluded *Travels in the Old South: A Bibliography* (2 vols., 1956) with a third volume covering the years 1825–1860, Norman, Okla., 1959.

### 264. *THE TRANS-MISSISSIPPI WEST*

EARLY EXPLORATION AND TRADING EXPEDITIONS

Donald Jackson edited *Letters of the Lewis and Clark Expedition, with Related Documents, 1783–1854,* Urbana, Ill., 1962, and *The Journals of Zebulon Montgomery Pike, with Letters and Related Documents,* 2 vols., Norman, Okla., 1966. *The Letters of George Catlin and His Family: A Chronicle of the American West,* Berkeley, Calif., 1966, was edited by Marjorie Catlin Roehm.

### 265. THE OVERLAND TRAIL

James Hall's *Letters from the West* (1828) has been reprinted with an introduction by John T. Flanagan, Gainesville, Fla., 1967. Firsthand accounts of life in the Far West include *Man of the Plains: Recollections of Luther North, 1856–1882,* ed. Donald F. Danker, Lincoln, Neb., 1961; *The West of William H. Ashley: The International Struggle for the Fur Trade of the Missouri, the Rocky Mountains, and the Columbia, with Explorations beyond the Continental Divide, Recorded in the Diaries and Letters of William H. Ashley and His Contemporaries, 1822–1838,* ed. Dale L. Morgan, Denver, Colo., 1964; *Adventures of Zenas Leonard, Fur Trader,* ed. John C. Ewers, Norman, Okla., 1959; and *Fifty Years on the Trail: The True Story of Western Life, the Adventures of John Young Nelson as Described to Harrington O'Reilly,* Norman, Okla., 1963, "the autobiography of a mountain man who survived prairie fires, Indian massacres, Mormon avenging angels, and at least nine Sioux wives." Marvin Lewis edited *The Mining Frontier: Contemporary Accounts for the American West in the Nineteenth Century,* Norman, Okla., 1967, "a scrapbook of 56 items, mostly newspaper articles."

**269.** THE LATER ACCOUNTS

*Owen Wister Out West: His Journals and Letters*, Chicago, 1958, was edited by his daughter, Fanny Kemble Wister. It covers the period 1885–1895.

## 279. *SECONDARY SOURCES*

In the last 20 years, several American presses have begun publishing organized series of books on the American frontier. It is impossible to list them all here. The student is urged, therefore, to investigate these series as a preliminary to what follows under this rubric of secondary sources: The Western Frontier Library, The Civilization of the American Indian Series, and The American Exploration and Travel Series published by the University of Oklahoma Press; The Western Americana Series published by Yale University Press; The Pioneer Heritage Series published by the University of Nebraska Press; The Histories of the American Frontier Series published by Holt, Rinehart and Winston, Inc.; The American Trails Library published by McGraw-Hill Book Company; and The Far West and Rockies Historical Series published by Arthur H. Clark Company.

Dale Van Every's *Forth to the Wilderness: The First American Frontier, 1754–1774*, New York, 1961, is the first volume of four devoted to the history of American expansion. It was followed by *A Company of Heroes* [1775–1783], New York, 1962; *Ark of Empire* [1784–1803], New York, 1963; and *The Final Challenge* [1804–1845], New York, 1964. John R. Alden's *Pioneer America*, New York, 1966, portrays "American society as it developed up to the close of the Civil War," a complementary study to Walter LaFeber's *The New Empire: An Interpretation of American Expansion, 1860–1898*, Ithaca, N.Y., 1963. Other volumes concerned with the whole story of westward exploration are Thomas D. Clark, *Frontier America: The Story of the Westward Movement*, 2nd ed., New York, 1969; John A. Hawgood, *The American West*, London, 1967; and William H. Goetzmann, *Exploration and Empire*, New York, 1966. Collections of essays on this subject include *The Frontier in Perspective*, ed. Walker D. Wyman and Clifton B. Kroeber, Madison, Wis., 1957; *The Frontier Re-Examined*, ed. John Francis McDermott, Urbana, Ill., 1967; *The Frontier in American History and Literature*, ed. Hans Galinsky, Frankfurt am Main, 1960; *The American West: A Reorientation*, ed. Gene M. Gressley, Laramie, Wyo., 1966. C. Merton Babcock has compiled a volume of readings illustrating "the social and literary record" in *The American Frontier*, New York, 1965; as have also Robert W. Richmond and Robert W. Mardock in *A Nation Moving West*, Lincoln, Neb., 1966.

The latest appraisals of Frederick Jackson Turner and his theories are Ray Allen Billington, *The Frontier Thesis: Valid Interpretation of American History?*, New York, 1966; *idem, America's Frontier Heritage,* New York, 1966; and Richard Hofstadter and Seymour M. Lipset, eds., *Turner and the Sociology of the Frontier,* New York, 1968. See also the relevant pages in Wilbur R. Jacobs, John W. Caughey, and Joe B. Frantz, *Turner, Bolton, and Webb: Three Historians of the American Frontier,* Seattle, Wash., 1965. Wilbur R. Jacobs edited *Frederick Jackson Turner's Legacy: Unpublished Writings in American History,* San Marino, Calif., 1965.

Early frontier days are described in Alden T. Vaughan, *New England Frontier: Puritans and Indians, 1620–1675,* Boston, 1965; and Douglas Edward Leach, *The Northern Colonial Frontier, 1607–1763,* New York, 1966. The opening of the South and Southwest is the subject of Odie B. Faulk, *Land of Many Frontiers: A History of the American Southwest,* New York, 1968; and John Anthony Caruso, *The Mississippi Valley Frontier: The Age of French Exploration and Settlement,* New York, 1966. C. L. Sonnichsen has compiled selections from over 40 authors, covering four centuries, in *The Southwest in Life and Literature,* New York, 1962. Expansion into the Far West can be closely studied in John A. Hawgood, *America's Western Frontiers: The Exploration and Settlement of the Trans-Mississippi West,* New York, 1967; Robert G. Athearn, *High Country Empire,* New York, 1960, a study of the history of the region from Kansas to Montana over the last 200 years; Wallace Stegner, *The Gathering of Zion: The Story of the Mormon Trail,* New York, 1964; Francis P. Farquhar, *History of the Sierra Nevada,* Berkeley, Calif., 1966, beginning with the arrival of Spanish explorers in 1772 to the present day; George R. Stewart, *The California Trail: An Epic with Many Heroes,* New York, 1962; Earl Pomeroy, *The Pacific Slope: A History of California, Oregon, Washington, Idaho, Utah, and Nevada,* New York, 1965; Raymond A. Wohlrabe, *The Pacific Northwest,* New York, 1968; Frederick Merk, *The Oregon Question: Essays in Anglo-American Diplomacy and Politics,* Cambridge, Mass., 1967; and Morgan B. Sherwood, *Exploration of Alaska, 1865–1900,* New Haven, Conn., 1965.

Biographies of individual explorers and settlers include Paul Russell Cutright, *Lewis and Clark: Pioneering Naturalists,* Urbana, Ill., 1969; Wallace Stegner, *Wolf Willow: A History, a Story, and a Memory of the Last Plains Frontier,* New York, 1962; Randolph C. Randall, *James Hall: Spokesman of the New West,* Columbus, Ohio, 1964; Don Russell, *The Lives and Legends of Buffalo Bill* [William F. Cody], Norman, Okla., 1960; and Kent Ladd Steckmesser, *The Western Hero in History and Legend,* Norman, Okla., 1965.

Recent literary-historical studies are widely divergent in approach and cannot be easily grouped together, but these are informative for the student of American civilization: Edwin Fussell, *Frontier: American Literature and the American West*, Princeton, N.J., 1965; Walter Allen, *The Urgent West: The American Dream and Modern Man*, New York, 1969; Roderick Nash, *Wilderness and the American Mind*, New Haven, Conn., 1967; G. Edward White, *The Eastern Establishment and the Western Experience: The West of Frederick Remington, Theodore Roosevelt, and Owen Wister*, New Haven, Conn., 1968; Robert Edson Lee, *From West to East: Studies in the Literature of the American West*, Urbana, Ill., 1966; and Wallace Stegner, *The Sound of Mountain Water: The Changing American West*, Garden City, N.Y., 1969.

Specialized studies are subdivided under 23 individual rubrics in the valuable bibliography of frontier history (a listing of over 600 titles) included in Nelson Klose's *Concise Study Guide to the American Frontier*, Lincoln, Neb., 1964. The following list is only a suggestion:

Mining camps: Duane A. Smith, *Rocky Mountain Mining Camps: The Urban Frontier*, Bloomington, Ind., 1967.

Cattlemen: John T. Schlebecker, *Cattle-Raising of the Plains, 1900–1961*, Lincoln, Neb., 1963; Gene M. Gressley, *Bankers and Cattlemen*, New York, 1966; and Henry Sinclair Drago, *Great American Cattle Trails*, New York, 1965.

Fur traders: Paul Chrisler Phillips, *The Fur Trade*, 2 vols., Norman, Okla., 1961; Lewis O. Saum, *The Fur Trader and the Indian*, Seattle, Wash., 1965; John E. Sunder, *The Fur Trade on the Upper Missouri, 1840–1865*, Norman, Okla., 1965; and Walter O'Meara, *Daughters of the Country: The Women of the Fur Traders and Mountain Men*, New York, 1968.

Forts: Robert W. Frazer, *Forts of the West*, Norman, Okla., 1965; and Robert G. Athearn, *Forts of the Upper Missouri*, Englewood Cliffs, N.J., 1967.

The Army: Robert M. Utley, *Frontiersmen in Blue: The United States Army and the Indian, 1848–1865*, New York, 1967; and William H. Goetzman, *Army Exploration in the American West, 1803–1863*, New Haven, Conn., 1959.

The Cities: Richard C. Wade, *The Urban Frontier: The Rise of Western Cities, 1790–1830*, Cambridge, Mass., 1959; and A. Theodore Brown, *Frontier Community: Kansas City to 1870*, Columbia, Mo., 1963.

Domestic and Commercial Life: Edward Everett Dale, *Frontier Ways: Sketches of Life in the Old West*, Austin, Tex., 1959; T. Scott Miyakawa, *Protestants and Pioneers: Individualism and Conformity on the American Frontier*, Chicago, 1964; Henry Pickering Walker, *The Wagonmasters: High Plains Freighting from the Earliest Days of the Santa Fe Trail to*

*1880,* Norman, Okla., 1966; Ralph Moody, *Stagecoach West,* New York, 1967; Richard A. Van Orman, *A Room for the Night: Hotels of the Old West,* Bloomington, Ind., 1966; and H. G. Merriam, ed., *Way Out West: Recollections and Tales,* Norman, Okla., 1969.

## 282. BIBLIOGRAPHY

O. O. Winther compiled *A Classified List of the Periodical Literature of the Trans-Mississippi West, 1811–1957,* Bloomington, Ind., 1961, a bibliography of 9,000 articles, over half of them since 1958. Ramon F. Adams evaluates over 400 accounts "of supposedly authentic Western history" in *Burs under the Saddle: A Second Look at Books and Histories of the West,* Norman, Okla., 1964. More specialized listings are Henry Putney Beers, *The French and British in the Old Northwest: A Bibliographical Guide to Archive and Manuscript Sources,* Detroit, 1964; and Ramon F. Adams, *The Rampaging Herd: A Bibliography of Books and Pamphlets on Men and Events in the Cattle Industry,* Norman, Okla., 1959.

## 284. MINGLING OF TONGUES:

## WRITING OTHER THAN ENGLISH

### GENERAL STUDIES

Oscar Handlin has followed *The Uprooted* (1951) with *Immigration as a Factor in American History,* Englewood Cliffs, N.J., 1959, and *Children of the Uprooted,* New York, 1966. For general analyses see also Maldwyn Allen Jones, *American Immigration,* Chicago, 1960; and Michael Kraus, *Immigration, the American Mosaic: From Pilgrims to Modern Refugees,* Princeton, N.J., 1966. Arthur Mann has compiled a volume of readings on the subject: *Immigrants in American Life,* Boston, 1968. Henry Steele Commager edited *Immigration and American History: Essays in Honor of Theodore C. Blegen,* Minneapolis, Minn., 1961. More specialized studies are David S. Wyman, *Paper Walls: America and the Refugee Crisis, 1938–1941,* Amherst, Mass., 1968; Laura Fermi, *Illustrious Immigrants: The Intellectual Migration from Europe, 1930–1941,* Chicago, 1968; and Donald Fleming and Bernard Bailyn, eds., *The Intellectual Migration: Europe and America, 1930–1960,* Cambridge, Mass., 1969.

Accounts of immigration from the United Kingdom include George Pot-

ter, *To the Golden Door: The Story of the Irish in Ireland and America,*
Boston, 1960; William V. Shannon, *The American Irish,* rev. ed., New
York, 1966, concentrating on the twentieth century; Earl F. Niehaus, *The
Irish in New Orleans, 1800–1860,* Baton Rouge, La., 1965; Thomas N.
Brown, *Irish-American Nationalism, 1870–1890,* Philadelphia, 1966; Alan
Conway, ed., *The Welsh in America: Letters from the Immigrants,*
Minneapolis, Minn., 1961; and A. L. Rowse, *The Cousin Jacks: The
Cornish in America,* New York, 1969.

Arrivals from other countries, not discussed individually under the
rubrics below, are documented in E. Wilder Spaulding, *The Quiet Invaders:
The Story of the Austrian Impact upon America,* Vienna, 1968; Theodore
Saloutos, *The Greeks in the United States,* Cambridge, Mass., 1964; Gerald
Gilbert Govorchin, *Americans from Yugoslavia,* Gainesville, Fla., 1961;
two volumes by Joseph A. Wytrwal, *America's Polish Heritage: A Social
History of the Poles in America,* Detroit, Mich., 1961, and *Poles in Ameri-
can History and Tradition,* Detroit, Mich., 1969; A. William Hoglund,
*Finnish Immigrants in America, 1880–1920,* Madison, Wis., 1960; and
Ralph J. Jalkanen, ed., *The Finns in North America: A Social Symposium,*
East Lansing, Mich., 1969.

## 292. *GERMAN AND PENNSYLVANIA GERMAN*

### General Studies

Richard O'Connor's *The German-Americans,* Boston, 1968, is a commendably readable history of "the contributions of the German element in
the building of America." Theodore Huebener tries to cover the same
ground in too brief an account, *The Germans in America,* Philadelphia,
1962. More specialized studies are Henry M. Adams, *Prussian-American
Relations, 1775–1871,* Cleveland, Ohio, 1960; Philip Gleason, *The Conservative Reformers: German-American Catholics and the Social Order,*
Notre Dame, Ind., 1968; René Wellek, *Confrontations: Studies in the Intellectual and Literary Relations between Germany, England, and the United
States during the Nineteenth Century,* Princeton, N.J., 1965; Peter
Bauland, *The Hooded Eagle: Modern German Drama on the New York
Stage,* Syracuse, N.Y., 1968, covering the years 1894–1965; Jurgen
Herbst, *The German Historical School in American Scholarship: A Study
in the Transfer of Culture,* Ithaca, N.Y., 1965, primarily in history and
social sciences, 1870–1900; and Robert E. Cazden, *German Exile Litera-*

*ture in America, 1933–1950: A History of the Free German Press and Book Trade,* Chicago, 1970.

*Anglo-German and American-German Crosscurrents,* II, ed. Philip Allison Shelley and Arthur O. Lewis, Jr., Chapel Hill, N.C., 1962, contains two essays of special interest to American studies. W. La Marr Kopp's *German Literature in the United States, 1945–1960,* Chapel Hill, N.C., 1967, is a third volume in this series but is a unified work by one scholar and not a collection of studies by several hands. It includes an extensive "Title List of German Literature in English Translation published in the United States, 1945–1960." Bayard Q. Morgan also prepared *A Critical Bibliography of German Literature in English Translation,* 2 vols., New York, 1965, covering the years 1481–1955.

The Pennsylvania German Society celebrated its seventy-fifth anniversary with a volume demonstrating its contributions to American civilization: Homer Tope Rosenberger, *The Pennsylvania Germans, 1891–1965,* Allentown, Penna., 1966. See also William I. Schreiber, *Our Amish Neighbors,* Chicago, 1962; and John A. Hostetler, *Amish Society,* Baltimore, Md., 1963.

## 295. FRENCH

### GENERAL STUDIES

Crane Brinton's *The Americans and the French,* Cambridge, Mass., 1968, is a brief study "addressed to Americans who have little prior knowledge of the subject." *French Tradition in America,* ed. Yves F. Zoltvany, Columbia, S.C., 1969, contains more than 60 documents that deal with "the foundation and organization of a colonial empire." More extended examinations of smaller subjects are William C. Stinchcombe, *The American Revolution and the French Alliance,* Syracuse, N.Y., 1969; Henry Blumenthal, *A Reappraisal of Franco-American Relations, 1830–1871,* Chapel Hill, N.C., 1959; and John Francis McDermott, ed., *The French in the Mississippi Valley,* Urbana, Ill., 1965.

## 296. BIBLIOGRAPHY

Hamilton Mason compiled *French Theatre in New York: A List of Plays, 1899–1939,* New York, 1966. Frank Monaghan's *French Travellers in the United States, 1765–1932* (1933) has been reprinted with a supplement by Samuel L. Marino, New York, 1961.

## 297. *SPANISH AND ITALIAN*

Studies in early American history include Charles Gibson, *Spain in America,* New York, 1966; and Lewis Hanke, *The Spanish Struggle for Justice in the Conquest of America,* Boston, 1966. Allan Guttmann's *The Wound in the Heart: America and the Spanish Civil War,* Glencoe, Ill., 1962, discusses the literature of those years as well as the ideological issues posed by the war.

Italian participation in the opening of our frontier is recorded in Andrew F. Rolle's *The Immigrant Upraised: Italian Adventurers and Colonists in an Expanding America,* Norman, Okla., 1968. Joseph Lopreato's *Italian Americans,* New York, 1970, is "a sociologist's efforts to summarize . . . the major aspects of the Italian Americans' social experiences as they bear on their continuing assimilation."

## 299. *SCANDINAVIAN*

SWEDISH

See Finis Harbert Capps, *From Isolationism to Involvement: The Swedish Immigrant Press in America, 1914–1945,* Chicago, 1966.

## 300. *JEWISH: YIDDISH AND HEBREW*

Collections of literary texts include *The Golden Land: A Literary Portrait of American Jewry, 1654 to the Present,* ed. Azriel Eisenberg, New York, 1964; *The Rise of American Jewish Literature: An Anthology of Selections from the Major Novels,* ed. Charles Angoff and Meyer Levin, New York, 1970; and *Breakthrough: A Treasury of Contemporary American-Jewish Literature,* ed. Irving Malin and Irwin Stark, Philadelphia, 1963. Leo Rosten's *The Joys of Yiddish,* New York, 1968, is a "relaxed lexicon of Yiddish, Hebrew, and Yinglish words" combined with anecdotes and history. Irving Malin treats seven modern American Jewish writers (Saul Bellow, Bernard Malamud, Philip Roth, Delmore Schwartz, Leslie Fiedler, Karl Shapiro, and Isaac Rosenfeld) in *Jews and Americans,* Carbondale, Ill., 1965. See also Sol Liptzin, *The Jew in American Literature,* New York, 1966; and Bernard Sherman, *The Invention of the Jew: Jewish-American Education Novels (1916–1964),* New York, 1969.

The major historical study is *The Jews of the United States, 1790–1840,* ed. Joseph L. Blau and Salo W. Baron, 3 vols., New York, 1963. A briefer history is Deborah Pessin, *History of the Jews in America,* New York, 1958. More specialized studies are *A Documentary History of the Jews in the United States, 1654–1875,* ed. Morris U. Schappes, 3rd ed., New York, 1970, with important bio- and bibliographic data; Moses Rischin, *The Promised City: New York City's Jews, 1870–1914,* Cambridge, Mass., 1962; Ronald Sanders, *The Downtown Jews: Portraits of an Immigrant Generation,* New York, 1969; and Judd L. Teller, *Strangers and Natives: The Evolution of the American Jew from 1921 to the Present,* New York, 1968. Nathan Glazer's *American Judaism,* Chicago, 1957, traces historical development theologically and communally.

Among the sociological studies are Marshall Sklare, ed., *The Jews: Social Patterns of an American Group,* Glencoe, Ill., 1958; Samuel H. Dresner, *The Jew in American Life,* New York, 1963; Stuart E. Rosenberg, *America Is Different: The Search for Jewish Identity in America,* New York, 1965; and James Yaffe, *The American Jews,* New York, 1968. Stephen Birmingham has written two widely popular historical biographies with sociological overtones: *Our Crowd: The Great Jewish Families of New York,* New York, 1967, and *The Grandees: America's Sephardic Elite,* New York, 1970.

## 303. *MEXICAN AND LATIN AMERICAN*

The most ambitious survey in recent years is *A Documentary History of the Mexican Americans,* ed. Wayne Moquin and Charles Van Doren, New York, 1971. Cecil Robinson analyzes stereotypes in *With the Ears of Strangers: The Mexican in American Literature,* Tucson, Ariz., 1963. Nancie L. Gonzalez's *The Spanish-Americans of New Mexico: A Heritage of Pride,* rev. ed., Albuquerque, N.M., 1969, is "a sociological analysis of a unique ethnic group."

## 303. *ORIENTAL*

CHINESE

Sociohistorical studies are S. W. Kung, *Chinese in American Life: Some Aspects of Their History, Status, Problems, and Contributions,* Seattle, Wash., 1962; and Gunther Barth, *Bitter Strength: A History of the Chinese in the United States, 1850–1870,* Cambridge, Mass., 1964.

### 303. JAPANESE

The first biographical study of Ernest Fenollosa, American philosopher, historian, and world's leading authority on Japanese art history, is Lawrence W. Chisolm's *Fenollosa: The Far East and American Culture*, New Haven, Conn., 1963. Bill Hosokawa has written a history of Japanese-Americans in *Nisei: The Quiet Americans*, New York, 1969.

### 308. REGIONALISM AND LOCAL COLOR

#### THE SOUTH AND DEEP SOUTH

John M. Bradbury, *Renaissance in the South: A Critical History of the Literature, 1920–1960*, Chapel Hill, N.C., 1963; Louis D. Rubin, Jr., *The Faraway Country: Writers of the Modern South*, Seattle, Wash., 1963; R. C. Simonini, Jr., ed., *Southern Writers: Appraisals in Our Time*, Charlottesville, Va., 1964; Frank E. Vandiver, ed., *The Idea of the South: Pursuit of a Central Theme*, Chicago, 1964; John C. McKinney and Edgar T. Thompson, eds., *The South in Continuity and Change*, Durham, N.C., 1965; Jay B. Hubbell, *South and Southwest: Literary Essays and Reminiscences*, Durham, N.C., 1965; and Louis D. Rubin, Jr., and Robert D. Jacobs, eds., *South: Modern Southern Literature in Its Cultural Setting*, Garden City, N.Y., 1961.

The Fugitives and Agrarians are the subject of four critical studies: John Bradbury, *The Fugitives*, Chapel Hill, N.C., 1958; Louise Cowan, *The Fugitive Group: A Literary History*, Baton Rouge, La., 1959; John L. Stewart, *The Burden of Time: The Fugitives and Agrarians*, Princeton, N.J., 1965; and Alexander Karanikas, *Tillers of a Myth: Southern Agrarians as Social and Literary Critics*, Madison, Wis., 1966.

See also Louis D. Rubin, Jr.'s, invaluable *Bibliographical Guide to the Study of Southern Literature*, Baton Rouge, La., 1969, compiled by 100 scholars.

### 316. *THE MIDDLE WEST*

Roy W. Meyer, *The Middle Western Farm Novel in the Twentieth Century*, Lincoln, Neb., 1965; Dale Kramer, *Chicago Renaissance: The Literary Life in the Midwest, 1900–1930*, New York, 1966.

### 323. *CALIFORNIA AND THE FAR WEST*

Robert E. Lee, *From West to East: Studies in the Literature of the Far West*, Urbana, Ill., 1966; James K. Folsom, *The American Western Novel*, New Haven, Conn., 1966.

### 334. SCIENCE AND SOCIAL CRITICISM

*THE MACHINE AGE AND THE LITERATURE OF EXPOSURE*

SECONDARY STUDIES

See pp. 33–35 above for studies of the political and economic novel.

### 335. LITERATURE OF THE MUCKRAKING MOVEMENT

In addition to David M. Chalmers's *The Social and Political Ideas of the Muckrakers*, New York, 1964, see Arthur Weinberg and Lila Weinberg, eds., *The Muckrakers: The Era in Journalism That Moved America to Reform*, New York, 1961; Herbert Shapiro, ed., *The Muckrakers and American Society*, Boston, 1968; and Harold S. Wilson, *McClure's Magazine and the Muckrakers*, Princeton, N.J., 1970.

### 344. SLAVERY AND CONFLICT

REMINISCENCES

The "confessions" of Nat Turner (1831) are printed in two recent volumes: Herbert Aptheker, *Nat Turner's Slave Rebellion*, New York, 1966; and Frank R. Johnson, *The Nat Turner Slave Insurrection*, Murfreesboro, N.C., 1966. *To Be a Slave*, ed. Julius Lester, New York, 1968, is "a compilation, selected from various sources and arranged chronologically, of the reminiscences of slaves and ex-slaves about their experiences from the leaving of Africa through the Civil War and into the early twentieth century." Harvey Wish edited *Slavery in the South: First Hand Accounts of the Ante-Bellum American Southland from Northern and Southern Whites, Negroes, and Foreign Observers,* New York, 1964. See also Herbert Aptheker's *One Continual Cry: David Walker's Appeal to the Colored Citizens of the World, 1829–1830, Its Setting and Its Meaning . . . ,* New York, 1965.

### 345. SOCIAL STUDIES

The most general of the many recent books on slavery are David B. Davis, *The Problem of Slavery in Western Culture,* Ithaca, N.Y., 1966; Barnett Hollander, *Slavery in America,* New York, 1963; Stanley M. Elkins, *Slavery: A Problem in American Institutional and Intellectual Life,* 2nd ed., Chicago, 1968; Owen A. Sherrard, *Freedom from Fear: The Slave and His Emancipation,* New York, 1961; and Eugene D. Genovese, *The Political Economy of Slavery: Studies in the Economy and Society of the Slave South,* New York, 1965. William O. Douglas's *Mr. Lincoln and the Negroes: The Long Road to Equality,* New York, 1963, contains texts of documents from 1776 to 1963 in a 100-page appendix.

The abolition movement is seen from many angles in Louis Filler, *The Crusade against Slavery, 1830–1860,* New York, 1960; Dwight L. Dumond, *Antislavery: The Crusade for Freedom in America,* Ann Arbor, Mich., 1961; Lawrence Lader, *The Bold Brahmins: New England's War against Slavery, 1831–1863,* New York, 1961; Martin B. Duberman, ed., *The Antislavery Vanguard: New Essays on the Abolitionists,* Princeton, N.J., 1965; and Louis Ruchames, ed., *The Abolitionists: A Collection of Their Writings,* New York, 1963.

More specialized studies are Richard C. Wade, *Slavery in the Cities: The South, 1820–1860,* New York, 1964; Edgar J. McManus, *A History of Negro Slavery in New York,* Syracuse, N.Y., 1966; Hans L. Trefousse, *The Radical Republicans: Lincoln's Vanguard for Racial Justice,* New York, 1969; Eric L. McKitrick, ed., *Slavery Defended: The Views of the Old South,* Englewood Cliffs, N.J., 1963; and Merton L. Dillon, *Benjamin Lundy and the Struggle for Negro Freedom,* Urbana, Ill., 1966.

Dwight L. Dumond has compiled *A Bibliography of Antislavery in America,* Ann Arbor, Mich., 1961.

## 346. TRANSCENDENTALISM AND UTOPIAN VENTURES

The most important publication on this subject in recent years is William R. Hutchison's *The Transcendentalist Ministers: Church Reform in the New England Renaissance*, Boston, 1959. It ignores Thoreau, puts Emerson on the periphery, and concentrates on Theodore Parker, Andrews Norton, and the theological background. A recent biography of the founder of Brook Farm is Charles Crowe's *George Ripley: Transcendentalist and Utopian Socialist*, Athens, Ga., 1967. Myron Simon and Thornton H. Parsons have gathered ten essays on Emerson, Dickinson, Thoreau, and others in *Transcendentalism and Its Legacy*, Ann Arbor, Mich., 1966. A good study of the intellectual origins and related works is Elémire Zolla's *Le origini del trascendentalismo*, Rome, 1963. Kenneth W. Cameron has compiled important resources for the study of Emerson, Thoreau, and their contemporaries in *Transcendentalists and Minerva* (1958), *Transcendental Climate* (1963), and *Transcendental Epilogue* (1965), all published in Hartford, Conn. See also the pages of the *Emerson Society Quarterly* and the *American Transcendental Quarterly*.

Recent studies devoted to American Utopias include William E. Wilson, *The Angel and the Serpent: The Story of New Harmony*, Bloomington, Ind., 1964; and Paul K. Conkin, *Two Paths to Utopia: The Hutterites and the Llano Colony*, Lincoln, Neb., 1964. The following titles investigate the general subject in a variety of ways: Robert C. Elliott, *The Shape of Utopias: Studies in a Literary Genre*, Chicago, 1970; Chad Walsh, *From Utopia to Nightmare*, New York, 1962; W. H. G. Armytage, *Yesterday's Tomorrow: A Historical Survey of Future Societies*, London, 1968; Jean Servier, *Histoire de l'utopie*, Paris, 1967; Nell P. Eurich, *Science in Utopia: A Mighty Design*, Cambridge, Mass., 1967; William Nelson, ed., *Twentieth-Century Interpretations of Utopia: A Collection of Critical Essays*, Englewood Cliffs, N.J., 1968; and Frank E. Manuel, ed., *Utopias and Utopian Thought*, Boston, 1966.

## 356. AMERICAN WRITERS AND BOOKS ABROAD

European observations of our culture are the focus of *As Others See Us: The United States through Foreign Eyes*, ed. Franz M. Joseph, Princeton, N.J., 1959; Edward W. Chester, *Europe Views America: A Critical Evaluation*, Washington, D.C., 1962; and Henri Baudet, *Paradise on Earth: Some Thoughts on European Images of the Non-European Man*, trans. Elizabeth Wentholt, New Haven, Conn., 1965.

The American experience of Europe is discussed in Ernest P. Earnest, *Expatriates and Patriots: American Artists, Scholars, and Writers in Europe*, Durham, N.C., 1968; Frank MacShane, ed., *The American in Europe*, New York, 1965; Van Wyck Brooks, *The Dream of Arcadia: American Writers and Artists in Italy, 1760–1915*, New York, 1958; Paul R. Baker, *The Fortunate Pilgrims: Americans in Italy, 1800–1860*, Cambridge, Mass., 1964; and Stephen A. Larrabee, *Hellas Observed: The American Experience of Greece, 1775–1865*, New York, 1957.

The impact of American literary writers on world literature is the subject of a variety of studies. They can be managed best by listing them by country:

German: Lawrence Marsden Price, *The Reception of United States Literature in Germany*, Chapel Hill, N.C., 1966; Harvey W. Hewitt-Thayer, *American Literature as Viewed in Germany, 1818–1861*, Chapel Hill, N.C., 1958; Eugene F. Timpe, *American Literature in Germany, 1861–1872*, Chapel Hill, N.C., 1965; and Earl R. Beck, *Germany Rediscovers America*, Tallahassee, Fla., 1968. Richard Mummendey has compiled a bibliography of translations from Benjamin Franklin to 1957: *Belles Lettres of the United States of America in German Translations*, Charlottesville, Va., 1961. See also Gerhard H. W. Zuther, *Eine Bibliographie der Aufnahme amerikanischer Literatur in deutschen Zeitschriften 1945–1960*, Munich, 1965.

Italian: Donald Heiney, *America in Modern Italian Literature*, New Brunswick, N.J., 1964. *Repertorio bibliografico della letteratura americana in Italia*, Rome, 1966, is an extensive checklist in two volumes, covering the years 1945–1954, compiled by the Centro di Studi Americani under the direction of Biancamaria Tedeschini Lalli. A third volume, covering 1955–1959, appeared in Rome in 1969.

Spanish: Arnold Chapman, *The Spanish-American Reception of United States Fiction, 1920–1940*, Berkeley, Calif., 1966; Concha Zardoya, *Historia de la literatura norteamericana*, Barcelona, 1956.

Norwegian: Sigmund Skard, ed., *U.S.A. in Focus: Recent Re-interpretations*, Oslo, 1966; A. N. J. den Hollander and Sigmund Skard, eds., *American Civilisation: An Introduction*, Harlow, 1968; Sigmund Skard and Henry H. Wasser, eds., *Americana Norvegica: Norwegian Contributions to American Studies*, 2 vols., Philadelphia, 1966–1968. See also continuing issues of *Norwegian-American Studies and Records* (1926–current).

Russian: Deming B. Brown, *Soviet Attitudes toward American Writing*, Princeton, N.J., 1962; Alayne P. Reilly, *America in Soviet Literature*, New York, 1971. Valentina A. Libman compiled *Russian Studies of American Literature: A Bibliography*, trans. Robert V. Allen, ed. Clarence Gohdes, Chapel Hill, N.C., 1969.

Hungarian: Lázló Kardos and Mihály Sukösd, eds., *Az Amerikai Irdalom a XX. Szazadban* [American Literature in the Twentieth Century], 2nd ed., Budapest, 1965.

Indian: C. D. Narasimhaiah, ed., *Indian Response to American Literature*, New Delhi, 1967.

For a continuing listing of translations of American literature into foreign languages, see *Index Translationum: International Bibliography of Translations*, 21 vols., Paris, 1932–current.

BIBLIOGRAPHIES:
INDIVIDUAL AUTHORS

# HENRY (BROOKS) ADAMS

**373. SEPARATE WORKS**

For more Adams letters, see C. Waller Barrett, ed., "The Making of a History: Letters of Henry Adams to Henry Vignaud and Charles Scribner, 1879–1913," *PMHS*, LXXI (1959), 204–271; Max I. Baym, "An Historian Prods a Philologist: The Letters of Henry Adams to William Dwight Whitney," *YULG*, XLII (1967), 77–101; Charles Vandersee, "Henry Adams behind the Scene: Civil War Letters to Frederick W. Seward," *BNYPL*, LXXI (1967), 245–264; Jean et Evelyne de Chazeaux, trans., "Lettres de Henry Adams: Tahiti, 1891," *RDM*, I (Sept., 1968), 85–100; and Charles Vandersee, "Henry Adams' Education of Martha Cameron: Letters, 1888–1916," *TSLL*, X (1968), 233–293. See also André Monchoux, "Propos inédits sur la France dans les lettres de Henry Adams," *RLC*, XLI (1967), 238–274.

**374. EDITED TEXTS AND REPRINTS**

In addition to numerous reprints of individual Adams titles, two collections have appeared: *The Great Secession Winter of 1860–61 and Other Essays,* ed. George Hochfield, New York, 1958; and *The Education of Henry Adams and Other Selected Writings*, ed. Edward N. Saveth, New York, 1965.

**375. BIOGRAPHY AND CRITICISM**

Ernest Samuels has completed his three-volume biography with *Henry Adams: The Major Phase*, Cambridge, Mass., 1964.

Vern Wagner's *The Suspension of Henry Adams: A Study of Manner and Matter,* Detroit, Mich., 1969, pays particular attention to Adams's style and humor in the major works. John Conder's *A Formula of His Own: Henry Adams's Literary Experiment*, Chicago, 1970, concentrates on *The Education* and *Mont-Saint-Michel*; Melvin Lyon's *Symbol and Idea in Henry Adams*, Lincoln, Neb., 1970, concentrates on influences, particularly medieval. George Hochfield's *Henry Adams*, New York, 1962, is exactly what its subtitle calls it: an introduction and interpretation. More specialized studies are Timothy Paul Donovan, *Henry Adams and Brooks Adams: The Education of Two American Historians,* Norman, Okla., 1961; and Robert F. Sayre, *The Examined Self: Benjamin Franklin, Henry Adams, and Henry James*, Princeton, N.J., 1964.

Briefer studies are Edward N. Saveth, "Henry Adams: Waning of America's Patriciate," *Com,* XXIV (1957), 302–309; John C. Cairns, "The Successful Quest of Henry Adams," *SAQ,* LVII (1958), 168–193; Lynn White, Jr., "Dynamo and Virgin Reconsidered," *ASch,* XXVII (1958),

183–194; Howard M. Munford, "Henry Adams and the Tendency of History," *NEQ*, XXXII (1959), 79–90; Bernhard Fabian, "Henry Adams: Ein Forschungsbericht 1918–1958," *AKG*, XLI (1959), 218–259; D. R. Welland, "Henry Adams as Novelist," *RMS*, III (1959), 25–50; Tony Tanner, "The Lost America—The Despair of Henry Adams and Mark Twain," *ModA*, V (1961), 299–310; Millicent Bell, "Adams' *Esther*: The Morality of Taste," *NEQ*, XXXV (1962), 147–161; John P. McIntyre, S.J., "Henry Adams and the Unity of *Chartres*," *TCL*, VII (1962), 159–171; Lewis Mumford, "Apology to Henry Adams," *VQR*, XXXVIII (1962), 196-217; Ernst Scheyer, "The Aesthete Henry Adams," *Criticism*, IV (1962), 313–327; James K. Folsom, "Mutation as Metaphor in *The Education of Henry Adams*," *ELH*, XXX (1963), 162–174; Robert Mane, "Henry Adams et la science," *EA*, XVI (1963), 1–10; and Merrill D. Peterson, "Henry Adams on Jefferson the President," *VQR*, XXXIX (1963), 187–201.

More recent studies are Michael Colacurcio, "The Dynamo and the Angelic Doctor: The Bias of Henry Adams' Medievalism," *AQ*, XVII (1965), 696–712; Richard Ruland, "Tocqueville's *De la démocratie en Amérique* and *The Education of Henry Adams*," *CLS*, II (1965), 195–207; Richard C. Vitzthum, "Henry Adams' Paraphrase of Sources in the *History of the United States*," *AQ*, XVII (1965), 81–91; Harry M. Campbell, "Academic Criticism on Henry Adams: Confusion about Chaos," *MASJ*, VII (1966), 3–14; Abraham Blinderman, "Henry Adams and the Jews," *CJF*, XXV (1966), 3–8; Peter Shaw, "Blood Is Thicker than Irony: Henry Adams' *History*," *NEQ*, XL (1967), 163–187; Charles Vandersee, "The Pursuit of Culture in Adams' *Democracy*," *AQ*, XIX (1967), 239–248; J. C. Levenson, "Henry Adams and the Art of Politics," *SoR*, IV (1968), 50–58; Earl N. Harbert, "Henry Adams' New England View: A Regional Angle of Vision," *TSE*, XVI (1968), 107–134; Howard M. Munford, "Henry Adams: The Limitations of Science," *SoR*, IV (1968), 59–71; and Eusebio Rodrigues, "Out of Season for Nirvana: Henry Adams and Buddhism," *Indian Essays in American Literature*, ed. S. Mukherjee and D. K. V. Raghavacharyulu, Bombay, 1969, pp. 179–194.

# JOHN ADAMS

### 378. COLLECTED WORKS

Publication of *The Adams Papers*, under the editorship of Lyman H. Butterfield, began in 1961. More than 100 volumes will be forthcoming from Harvard University Press, in four series. The first to be published are:

Series I: Diaries
*Diary and Autobiography of John Adams (1755-1804)*, ed. L. H. Butterfield *et al.*, 4 vols., 1961; *The Earliest Diary of John Adams (1753-1759)*, a supplement to the *Diary and Autobiography*, ed. L. H. Butterfield *et al.*, 1966; *Diary of Charles Francis Adams (1820-1880)*: Volumes I and II, ed. Aïda DiPace Donald and David Donald, 1964; Volumes III and IV, ed. Marc Friedlander and L. H. Butterfield, 1968; 20 volumes to follow.

Series II: Family Correspondence
*Adams Family Correspondence*, Volumes I and II (1761-1778), ed. L. H. Butterfield *et al.*, 1963.

Series III: General Correspondence and Other Papers of the Adams Statesmen
*Legal Papers of John Adams*, ed. L. Kinvin Wroth and Hiller B. Zobel, 3 vols., 1965.

Series IV: Adams Family Portraits
*Portraits of John and Abigail Adams*, by Andrew Oliver, 1967.

A 608-reel microfilm edition of the entire contents of the Adams archive is available in most large libraries. The history of the papers, past and present, is told by Lyman H. Butterfield in the introduction to the first volume of *Diary and Autobiography of John Adams*, cited above. See also Bernard Bailyn, "Butterfield's Adams: Notes for a Sketch," *WMQ*, XIX (1962), 238-256.

The complete correspondence between Thomas Jefferson and Abigail and John Adams has been edited by Lester J. Cappon in a reader's edition, *The Adams-Jefferson Letters*, 2 vols., Chapel Hill, N.C., 1959.

BIOGRAPHY AND CRITICISM

The first biography to appear since the opening of the Adams papers is Page Smith's lengthy *John Adams*, 2 vols., Garden City, N.Y., 1962. *The John Adams Papers*, selected, edited, and interpreted by Frank Donovan, New York, 1965, is an attempt at a portrait via excerpts from the microfilm edition accompanied by running commentary. Gilbert Chinard's *Honest John Adams* (1933) was reprinted in Boston in 1964.

Of primary importance among recent critical volumes is John R. Howe,

*The Changing Political Thought of John Adams*, Princeton, N.J., 1966. Of more specialized interest are John Murray Allison, *Adams and Jefferson: The Story of a Friendship*, Norman, Okla., 1966; and Edward Handler, *America and Europe in the Political Thought of John Adams*, Cambridge, Mass., 1964. Adrienne Koch, ed., *Adams and Jefferson: "Posterity Must Judge,"* Chicago, 1963, is a 60-page pamphlet in the Berkeley Series in American History. Howard F. Bremer compiled a brief research tool for the student, *John Adams, 1735-1826: Chronology—Documents—Bibliographical Aids*, Dobbs Ferry, N.Y., 1967. Briefer studies are John W. Ellsworth, "John Adams: The American Revolution as a Change of Heart?" *HLQ*, XXVIII (1965), 293-300; Linda K. Kerber and Walter J. Morris, "Politics and Literature: The Adams Family and the *Port Folio*," *WMQ*, XXIII (1966), 450-476; Earl N. Harbert, "John Adams' Private Voice: The *Diary and Autobiography*," *TSE*, XV (1967), 89-105; and Susan Ford, "Thomas Jefferson and John Adams on the Classics," *Arion*, VI (1967), 116-132.

# GEORGE ADE

**380.** SEPARATE WORKS

*Fables in Slang* and *More Fables in Slang* were reprinted, jointly, with an introduction by E. F. Bleiler, New York, 1960. Franklin J. Meine edited *Chicago Stories* with an introduction, Chicago, 1963; James T. Farrell did the same for *Artie* and *Pink Marsh*, Chicago, 1963. A good introduction, for new readers, is *The America of George Ade (1866-1944): Fables, Short Stories, Essays*, ed. Jean Shepherd, New York, 1960.

The first full-length critical study is Lee Coyle, *George Ade*, New York, 1964. For briefer estimates see Richard F. Bauerle, "A Look at the Language of George Ade," *AS*, XXXIII (1958), 77-79; R. Balfour Daniels, "George Ade as Social Critic," *MissQ*, XII (1959), 194-204; Lowell Matson, "Ade—Who Needed None," *LitR*, V (1961), 99-114; and Jack Brenner, "Howells and Ade," *AL*, XXXVIII (1966), 198-207.

# CONRAD (POTTER) AIKEN
## d. 1973
**380.** SEPARATE WORKS

*The Morning Song of Lord Zero: Poems Old and New*, 1963; *A Seizure of Limericks*, 1964; *Thee: A Poem*, 1967.

*Cats and Bats and Things with Wings*, New York, 1965; and *Tom, Sue and the Clock*, London, 1966, are children's verse.

Aiken revised and enlarged his edition of *Twentieth-Century American Poetry*, New York, 1963.

### 381. COLLECTED WORKS

*Selected Poems* appeared in New York, 1961; a second edition of *Collected Poems* in New York, in 1970. Mark Schorer wrote a preface for *Collected Short Stories*, Cleveland, Ohio, 1960, R. P. Blackmur for *The Collected Novels of Conrad Aiken* [*Blue Voyage, Great Circle, King Coffin, A Heart for the Gods of Mexico, Conversation*], New York, 1964. *Three Novels: Blue Voyage, Great Circle, King Coffin* is a paperback edition with a preface by the author, New York, 1966.

### 381. BIOGRAPHY AND CRITICISM

In lieu of a recent biography, see Ashley Brown, "An Interview with Conrad Aiken, *Shen*, XV (1963), 18–40; Conrad Aiken, "Please Continue, Mr. Aiken," *Phoenix*, No. 1 (1966), pp. 18–29; Patricia R. Willis, "Unabashed Praise of a Poet," *GaR*, XXI (1967), 373–380; and Alexander A. Lawrence, "228 Habersham Street," *GaR*, XXII (1968), 317–334.

The major critical work is Jay Martin, *Conrad Aiken: A Life of His Art*, Princeton, N.J., 1962. Frederick J. Hoffman published a perceptive study, *Conrad Aiken*, New York, 1962; Reuel Denney's *Conrad Aiken*, Minneapolis, Minn., 1964, is a pamphlet.

For briefer studies see Rufus A. Blanshard, "Pilgrim's Progress: Conrad Aiken's Poetry," *TQ*, I (1958), 135–148; James Dickey, "A Gold-mine of Consciousness," *Poetry*, XCIV (1959), 41–44; E. P. Bollier, "From Scepticism to Poetry: A Note on Conrad Aiken and T. S. Eliot," *TSE*, XIII (1963), 95–104; Ann Gossman, "'Silent Snow, Secret Snow': The Child as Artist," *SSF*, I (1964), 123–128; James W. Tuttleton, "Aiken's 'Mr. Arcularis': Psychic Regression and the Death Instinct," *AI*, XX (1963), 295–314; Vance Mizelle, "Conrad Aiken's 'Music Strangely Subtle,'" *GaR*, XIX (1965), 81–92; John R. Moore, "Conrad Aiken: The Egotistical Sublime?," *SR*, LXXIV (1966), 694–709; Jennifer Aldrich, "The Deciphered Heart: Conrad Aiken's Poetry and Prose Fiction," *SR*, LXXXV (1967), 485–520; Louis Untermeyer, "Conrad Aiken: Our Best Known Unread Poet," *SatR*, L (Nov. 25, 1967), 28–29, 76–77; and Robert E. Carlile, "*Great Circle*: Conrad Aiken's Musico-Literary Technique," *GaR*, XXII (1968), 27–36.

Bibliographical listings are in the Hoffman and Denney volumes cited above.

# AMOS BRONSON ALCOTT

**381.** COLLECTED WORKS

*The Letters of A. Bronson Alcott*, edited by Richard L. Herrnstadt, Ames, Iowa, 1970, publishes over 1,000, chiefly from the Alcott-Pratt Collection at Harvard University.

**382.** BIOGRAPHY AND CRITICISM

Of general interest is Kenneth Walter Cameron's *Transcendentalists and Minerva: Cultural Backgrounds of the American Renaissance with Fresh Discoveries in the Intellectual Climate of Emerson, Alcott and Thoreau,* Hartford, Conn., 1958. More specialized are the following: John C. Deedy, Jr., "The Fruit of Fruitlands," *CathW*, CLXXXIV (1957), 260–265; John C. Broderick, "Emerson, Alcott, and the American Institute of Instruction," *ESQ*, No. 13 (1958), pp. 27–29; Elizabeth Bancroft Schlesinger, "The Philosopher's Wife and the Wolf at the Door," *AH*, VIII (Aug., 1957), 32–35, 99–101; and George M. Harper, "Toward the Holy Land: Platonism in the Middle West," *SAB*, XXXII (1967), 1–6.

# LOUISA MAY ALCOTT

**383.** COLLECTED WORKS

*Glimpses of Louisa: A Centennial Sampling of the Best Short Stories* was selected, with an introduction, by Cornelia Meigs, Boston, 1968. John L. Cooley edited, with an introductory note, *A Sprig of Andromeda: A Letter on the Death of Henry David Thoreau,* New York, 1962. Other gleanings are E. B. Schlesinger, "The Alcotts through Thirty Years: Letters to Alfred Whitman," *HLB*, XI (1957), 363–385; and Nan Cooke Carpenter, "Louisa May Alcott and 'Thoreau's Flute': Two Letters," *HLQ*, XXIV (1960), 71–74.

# THOMAS BAILEY ALDRICH

**384.** BIOGRAPHY AND CRITICISM

Charles E. Samuels, *Thomas Bailey Aldrich*, New York, 1966, is the first attempt since 1908 to treat the author's whole career. Donald Tanasoca reconsiders one of the novels in *"The Stillwater Tragedy*: A Socio-Detective Novel," *AN&Q*, I (1963), 148–150.

# JAMES LANE ALLEN

### 386. COLLECTED WORKS

William K. Bottorff edited, "for the modern reader," *A Kentucky Cardinal, Aftermath, and Other Selected Works*, New Haven, Conn., 1967.

### BIOGRAPHY AND CRITICISM

William K. Bottorff also published a general study, *James Lane Allen*, New York, 1964.

# MAXWELL ANDERSON
## d. 1959

### 387. COLLECTED WORKS

*Four Verse Plays* [*Elizabeth the Queen, Mary of Scotland, Winterset, High Tor*] appeared in New York, 1959.

### BIOGRAPHY AND CRITICISM

Brief studies are Henry W. Knepler, "Maxwell Anderson: A Historical Parallel," *QQ*, LXIV (1957), 250–263; Henry G. Lee, "Maxwell Anderson's Impact on the Theatre," *NDQ*, XXV (1957), 49–52; Howard D. Pearce, "Job in Anderson's *Winterset*," *MD*, VI (1963), 32–41; Francis E. Abernathy, "*Winterset*: A Modern Revenge Tragedy," *MD*, VII (1964), 185–189; Laurence G. Avery, "The Conclusion of *Night over Taos*," *AL*, XXXVII (1965), 318–321; J. T. McCullen, Jr., "Two Quests for Truth: *King Oedipus* and *Winterset*," *LauR*, V (1965), 28–35; Angela Belli, "Lenormand's *Asie* and Anderson's *The Wingless Victory*," *CL*, XIX (1967), 226–239; Jordan Y. Miller, "Maxwell Anderson: Gifted Technician," *The Thirties: Fiction, Poetry, Drama*, ed. Warren French, Deland, Fla., 1967; Laurence G. Avery, "Maxwell Anderson: A Changing Attitude toward Love," *MD*, X (1967), 241–248; and William E. Taylor, "Maxwell Anderson: Traditionalists in a Theatre of Change," *Modern American Drama: Essays in Criticism*, ed. William E. Taylor, Deland, Fla., 1968.

Martha Cox's *Maxwell Anderson Bibliography*, Charlottesville, Va., 1958, includes work by the playwright, reviews of his plays, and critical discussions. A useful addendum is Vedder M. Gilbert, "The Career of Maxwell Anderson: A Checklist of Books and Articles," *MD*, II (1960), 386–394. See also Laurence G. Avery, *A Catalogue of the Maxwell Anderson Collection at the University of Texas*, Austin, Tex., 1968.

# SHERWOOD ANDERSON

388. REPRINTS

Ray Lewis White has completely retranscribed from the original manuscripts *Sherwood Anderson's Memoirs* in a fully annotated edition, Chapel Hill, N.C., 1969. White has also prepared critical texts of *A Story Teller's Story*, Cleveland, Ohio, 1968, based on the Newberry Library's typescript, and of *Tar: A Midwest Childhood*, Cleveland, Ohio, 1969. John H. Ferres edited a teaching edition of *Winesburg, Ohio: Text and Criticism*, New York, 1966. *Return to Winesburg*, ed. Ray Lewis White, Chapel Hill, N.C., 1967, is "a selection from four years of writing for a country newspaper."

CORRESPONDENCE

Gleanings are in G. Thomas Tanselle, "Realist or Dreamer: Letters of Sherwood Anderson and Floyd Dell," *MLR*, LVIII (1963), 532–537; and *idem*, "The Letters of Sherwood Anderson and August Derleth," *N&Q*, XII (1965), 266–273.

BIOGRAPHY AND CRITICISM

Three useful introductory studies are Rex Burbank, *Sherwood Anderson*, New York, 1964; David D. Anderson, *Sherwood Anderson: An Introduction and Interpretation*, New York, 1967; and Brom Weber's pamphlet, *Sherwood Anderson*, Minneapolis, Minn., 1964. William A. Sutton's *Exit to Elsinore*, Muncie, Ind., 1967, is a 45-page pamphlet on Anderson in Elyria, 1907–1913. Ray Lewis White edited *The Achievement of Sherwood Anderson: Essays in Criticism*, Chapel Hill, N.C., 1966, reviews and critical studies by 16 scholars.

Briefer estimates are Roger Asselineau, "Réalisme, rêve et expressionnisme dans Winesburg, Ohio," *Archives des Lettres Modernes,* No. 2 (1957), pp. 1–32; Walter B. Rideout, "Why Sherwood Anderson Employed Buck Fever," *GaR*, XIII (1959), 76–85; Louis J. Budd, "The Grotesques of Anderson and Wolfe," *MFS*, V (1959), 304–310; John H. Sullivan, "Winesburg Revisited," *AR*, XX (1960), 213–221; Edwin Fussell, "*Winesburg, Ohio*: Art and Isolation," *MFS*, VI (1960), 106–114; Floyd Dell, "On Being Sherwood Anderson's Literary Father," *NLB*, V (1961), 315–321; James K. Feibleman, "Memories of Sherwood Anderson," *Shen*, XIII (1962), 32–45; Frederick J. Hoffman, "The Voices of Sherwood Anderson." *Shen*, XIII (1962), 5–19; Valentina Poggi, "Il linguaggio narrativo de Sherwood Anderson," *SA*, VIII (1962), 93–109; Jon S. Lawry, "The Artist in America: The Case of Sherwood Anderson," *BSUF*, VII (1966), 15–26; Tsuneo Miyake, "Sherwood Anderson: *Dark*

Laughter," *KAL*, No. 9 (1966), pp. 34–40; George D. Murphy, "The Theme of Sublimation in Anderson's *Winesburg, Ohio*," *MFS*, XIII (1967), 237–246; Rosemary Laughlin, " 'Godliness' and the American Dream in *Winesburg, Ohio*," *TCL* (1967), 97–103; Thomas M. Lorch, "The Choreographic Structure of *Winesburg, Ohio*," *CLAJ*, XII (1968), 56–65; Chris Browning, "Kate Swift: Sherwood Anderson's Creative Eros," *TSL*, XIII (1968), 141–148; and James M. Mellard, "Narrative Forms in *Winesburg, Ohio*, *PMLA*, LXXXIII (1968), 1304–1312.

*Shenandoah*, XIII (Spring, 1962), is a special Anderson issue.

### 389. BIBLIOGRAPHY

Eugene P. Sheehy and Kenneth A. Lohf, *Sherwood Anderson: A Bibliography*, Los Gatos, Calif., 1960, is a "preliminary checklist of works by and about Sherwood Anderson." More recent is *The Merrill Checklist of Sherwood Anderson*, comp. Ray Lewis White, Columbus, Ohio, 1969. Walter B. Rideout prepared an interpretive bibliographical essay, "Sherwood Anderson," for *Fifteen Modern American Authors*, ed. Jackson R. Bryer, Durham, N.C., 1969, pp. 3–22. See also G. Thomas Tanselle, "Additional Reviews of Sherwood Anderson's Work," *PBSA*, LVI (1962), 358–365.

## SHOLEM ASCH

### 390. COLLECTED WORKS

*From Many Countries: The Collected Short Stories of Sholem Asch* appeared in London, 1958.

### BIOGRAPHY AND CRITICISM

See Charles A. Madison, "Notes on Sholem Asch, Novelist," *CJF*, XVI (1958), 174–179.

Of bibliographical interest is Libby Okun Cohen, "Sholem Asch in English Translation: A Bibliography," *BB*, XXII (1958), 109–111.

## JOHN JAMES AUDUBON

### 390. SEPARATE WORKS

Alice Ford edited, for the first time, *The 1826 Journal of John James Audubon*, Norman, Okla., 1967, covering a critical portion of his career. *Audubon in the West*, ed. John Francis McDermott, Norman, Okla., 1966, is the first publication of 20 letters written during Audubon's search for specimens for his *Viviparous Quadrupeds of North America*.

### 391. EDITED TEXTS AND REPRINTS

Edwin Way Teale edited *Audubon's Wildlife*, New York, 1964, with selections from his writing. *The Imperial Collection of Audubon Animals*, Maplewood, N.J., 1967, reprints *The Quadrupeds of North America* with the addition of a new text by Victor H. Cahalane.

### BIOGRAPHY AND CRITICISM

Alice Ford published a biography, *John James Audubon*, Norman, Okla., 1964, largely from untapped sources; it probably replaces the work of Francis H. Herrick. Alexander B. Adams's commendable *John James Audubon: A Biography*, New York, 1966, is aimed at a more popular audience. See also *Audubon by Himself: A Profile of John Audubon*, ed. Alice Ford, New York, 1969. A briefer work is Edward H. Dwight, "The Autobiographical Writings of John James Audubon," *MHSB*, XIX (1962), 26–35.

The *Princeton University Library Chronicle*, XXI (Autumn, 1959–Winter, 1960), is an issue devoted to two articles on Audubon and a 78-page catalog of an Audubon exhibition.

## IRVING BABBITT

### 392. BIOGRAPHY AND CRITICISM

Harry Levin, *Irving Babbitt and the Teaching of Literature*, Cambridge, Mass., 1961, is a 28-page pamphlet. Other studies are Helmut Papajewski, "Die Dualismuslehre der amerikanischen Humanisten," *Anglia*, LXXV (1957), 77–109; Robert Bloom, "Irving Babbitt's Emerson," *NEQ*, XXX (1957), 448–473; Chang Hsin-Hai, "Irving Babbitt and Oriental Thought," *MQR*, IV (1965), 234–244; and René Wellek, "Irving Babbitt, Paul More, and Transcendentalism," *Transcendentalism and Its Legacy*, ed. Myron Simon and Thornton H. Parsons, Ann Arbor, Mich., 1966, pp. 185–203.

## GEORGE BANCROFT

### 394. BIOGRAPHY AND CRITICISM

The major study is David Levin, *History as Romantic Art: Bancroft, Prescott, Motley, and Parkman*, Stanford, Calif., 1959. See also Richard C.

Vitzthum, "Theme and Method in Bancroft's *History of the United States*," *NEQ*, XLI (1968), 362–380.

# JOEL BARLOW

### 396. WORKS

For a discussion of correspondence, see Milton Cantor, "A Connecticut Yankee in a Barbary Court: Joel Barlow's Algerian Letters to His Wife," *WMQ*, XIX (1962), 86–109.

### BIOGRAPHY AND CRITICISM

Critical studies are Irving Brant, "Joel Barlow, Madison's Stubborn Minister," *WMQ*, XV (1958), 438–451; Milton Cantor, "Joel Barlow: Lawyer and Legal Philosopher," *AQ*, X (1958), 165–174; *idem*, "Joel Barlow's Mission to Algiers," *Historian*, XXV (1963), 172–194; and Helen Loschky, "The 'Columbiad' Tradition: Joel Barlow and Others," *BBr*, XXI (1967), 197–206.

### 397. PRIMARY SOURCES

See Dorothy W. Bridgwater, "The Joel Barlow Manuscripts in the Yale Library," *YULG*, XXXIV (1959), 57–63.

# PHILIP BARRY

### 398. BIOGRAPHY AND CRITICISM

The first full-length study is Joseph Roppolo, *Philip Barry*, New York, 1965. See also James M. Salem, "Philip Barry and the Spirituality of Love," *Ren*, XIX (1967), 101–109.

# JOHN AND WILLIAM BARTRAM

### 398. COLLECTED WORKS

Helen Gere Cruickshank edited *John and William Bartram's America: Selections from the Writings of the Philadelphia Naturalists*, New York, 1957.

### 399. BIOGRAPHY AND CRITICISM

Brief studies are J. M. Edelstein, "America's First Native Botanists," *QJCA*, XV (1958), 51–59; Francis D. West, "John Bartram: Geologist,"

*BFHA*, XLVII (1958), 35–38; and Whitfield J. Bell, Jr., and Ralph L. Ketcham, "A Tribute to John Bartram, with a Note on Jacob Engelbrecht," *PMHB*, LXXXIII (1959), 446–451.

## S(AMUEL) N(ATHANIEL) BEHRMAN
### *d. 1973*

**401.** SEPARATE WORKS*

*The Cold Wind and the Warm*, 1959; *Lord Pengo* (1962), 1963; *But for Whom Charlie*, 1964.

*The Burning Glass*, 1968, is a novel; *The Suspended Drawing Room*, 1965, a collection of essays. *Portrait of Max: An Intimate Memoir of Sir Max Beerbohm*, 1960, appeared in London as *Conversation with Max*.

## EDWARD BELLAMY

**401.** SEPARATE WORKS

See Joseph Schiffman, "Mutual Indebtedness: Unpublished Letters of Edward Bellamy to William Dean Howells," *HLB*, XII (1958), 363–374.

**402.** BIOGRAPHY AND CRITICISM

Sylvia E. Bowman and others contributed to *Edward Bellamy Abroad: An American Prophet's Influence*, New York, 1962. Briefer studies are W. Arthur Boggs, "Looking Backward at the Utopian Novel, 1888–1900," *BNYPL*, LXIV (1960), 329–336; and David Bleich, "Eros and Bellamy," *AQ*, XVI (1964), 445–459.

*Edward Bellamy, Novelist and Reformer*, Schenectady, N.Y., 1968, prints two essays, Daniel Aaron, "Bellamy—Utopian Conservative," and Harry Levin, "Some Paradoxes of Utopia," plus a four-page selected bibliography.

## STEPHEN VINCENT BENÉT

**403.** COLLECTED WORKS

Basil Davenport edited *Selected Poetry and Prose*, New York, 1960. *Selected Letters of Stephen Vincent Benét*, ed. Charles A. Fenton, appeared in New Haven, Conn., 1960. George Abbe edited *Stephen Vincent Benét*

* Dates in parentheses are of production when it differs from publication.

*on Writing: A Great Writer's Letters of Advice to a Young Beginner,* Brattleboro, Vt., 1964.

BIOGRAPHY AND CRITICISM

The first full-length critical study is Parry Stroud's *Stephen Vincent Benét,* New York, 1962. See also Mary Lynn Richardson, "The Historical Authenticity of John Brown's Raid in Stephen Vincent Benét's *John Brown's Body,*" *WVH,* XXIV (1963), 168–175; and John T. Flanagan, "Folk Elements in *John Brown's Body,*" *NYFQ,* XX (1964), 243–256.

## AMBROSE (GWINNETT) BIERCE

404. COLLECTED WORKS

The 1909–1912 edition of *Collected Works* was reprinted in New York, 1966, in 12 volumes; the 1922 edition of *The Letters* was reprinted in New York, 1967. For newly discovered letters, see M. E. Grenander, "Ambrose Bierce and Charles Warren Stoddard: Some Unpublished Correspondence," *HLQ,* XXIII (1960), 261–292.

EDITED TEXTS AND REPRINTS

Ernest Jerome Hopkins edited *The Enlarged Devil's Dictionary, with 851 Newly Discovered Words and Definitions . . . ,* Garden City, N.Y., 1967; and *The Ambrose Bierce Satanic Reader: Selections from the Invective Journalism of the Great Satirist,* Garden City, N.Y., 1968.

405. BIOGRAPHY AND CRITICISM

Carey McWilliams's *Ambrose Bierce: A Biography* (1929) was reissued in Hamden, Conn., 1967, with a new bibliographical introduction. Richard O'Connor writes a more popular version of the life in *Ambrose Bierce,* Boston, 1967.

Robert A. Wiggins, *Ambrose Bierce,* Minneapolis, Minn., 1964, is a pamphlet. Stuart C. Woodruff's *The Short Stories of Ambrose Bierce: A Study in Polarity,* Pittsburgh, Pa., 1965, should be used with some caution. For briefer work see David R. Weimer, "Ambrose Bierce and the Art of War," *Essays in Literary History,* ed. R. Kirk and C. F. Main, New Brunswick, N.J., 1960; Eugene E. Reed, "Ambrose Bierce's *Chickamauga*: An Identity Restored," *RLV,* XXVIII (1962), 49–53; Howard W. Bahr, "Ambrose Bierce and Realism," *SoQ,* I (1963), 309–331; Gisela Pira, "Ambrose Bierce," *NS* (1963), pp. 425–430; Eric Solomon, "The Bitterness of Battle: Ambrose Bierce's War Fiction," *MQ,* V (1964), 147–165; and M. E. Grenander, "Ambrose Bierce, John Camden Hotten, *The Friend's Delight* and *Nuggets and Dust,*" *HLQ,* XXVIII (1965), 353–371.

# ROBERT MONTGOMERY BIRD

407. BIOGRAPHY AND CRITICISM

The first full-length study since 1919 is Curtis Dahl, *Robert Montgomery Bird*, New York, 1963.

# GEORGE HENRY BOKER

408. BIOGRAPHY AND CRITICISM

See R. Baird Shuman, "A Note on George Boker's *Francesca da Rimini*," *AL*, XXXI (1960), 480–482; and Paul C. Sherr, "George Henry Boker's *Francesca da Rimini*, a Justification for the Literary Historian," *PH*, XXXIV (1967), 361–371.

# RANDOLPH (SILLIMAN) BOURNE

410. COLLECTED WORKS

*War and the Intellectuals: Essays by Randolph S. Bourne, 1915–1919*, edited by Carl Resek, New York, 1964, reprints almost all of *Untimely Papers*. *The World of Randolph Bourne* is an anthology edited, with an introduction, by Lillian Schlissel, New York, 1965.

BIOGRAPHY AND CRITICISM

John Adam Moreau, *Randolph Bourne: Legend and Reality*, Washington, D.C., 1966, is the first full-length biography; Sherman Paul, *Randolph Bourne*, Minneapolis, Minn., 1966, a useful pamphlet. Shorter critical studies are A. F. Beringause, "The Double Martyrdom of Randolph Bourne," *JHI*, XVIII (1957), 594–603; Van Wyck Brooks, "Randolph Bourne," *Fenollosa and His Circle*, New York, 1962; Edward Dahlberg, "Randolph Bourne," *Alms for Oblivion*, Minneapolis, Minn., 1964; Christopher Lasch, "Randolph Bourne and the Experimental Life," *The New Radicalism in America (1889–1963)*, New York, 1965; and Michael D. True, "Randolph Bourne—Fifty Years Later," *PLL*, III (1967), 86–95.

BIBLIOGRAPHY

Recent listings are in the Moreau and the Schlissel volumes cited above as well as Michael D. True, "The Achievement of an American Literary Radical: A Bibliography of the Writings of Randolph Silliman Bourne

(1886–1918)," *BNYPL*, LXIX (1965), 523–536; G. Thomas Tanselle, "Randolph Bourne: A Supplementary Note," *BNYPL*, LXX (1966), 327–330; and Michael D. True, "Writings about Randolph Bourne," *BNYPL*, LXX (1966), 331–337.

## HJALMAR HJORTH BOYESEN

**410.** BIOGRAPHY AND CRITICISM

Clarence A. Glasrud's biography, *Hjalmar Hjorth Boyesen*, appeared in Northfield, Minnesota, 1963. Of special interest are Marc Ratner, "The Iron Madonna: H. H. Boyesen's American Girl," *JA*, IX (1964), 166–172; Per E. Seyersted, "Hjalmar Hjorth Boyesen: Outer Success, Inner Failure," *Americana Norvegica: Norwegian Contributions to American Studies*, I, ed. Sigmund Skard and Henry H. Wasser, Oslo and Philadelphia, 1966, pp. 206–238; and Marc L. Ratner, "The Spencerian Romantic," *NAS*, XXIII (1967), 204–219.

## HUGH HENRY BRACKENRIDGE

**411.** SEPARATE WORKS

Daniel Marder edited *A Hugh Henry Brackenridge Reader, 1770–1815*, Pittsburgh, Pa., 1970.

BIOGRAPHY AND CRITICISM

A recent full-length study is Daniel Marder's *Hugh Henry Brackenridge*, New York, 1967. See also J. C. Greene, "Science and the Public in the Age of Jefferson," *Isis*, XLIX (1958), 13–28; Alfred Weber, "Hugh Henry Brackenridges Epistel an Sir Walter Scott," *JA*, VIII (1963), 267–269; J. F. S. Smeall, "The Evidence that Hugh Brackenridge Wrote 'The Cornwalliad,'" *PMLA*, LXXX (1965), 542–548; and William L. Nance, "Satiric Elements in Brackenridge's *Modern Chivalry*," *TSLL*, IX (1967), 381–389.

## ANNE BRADSTREET

**415.** EDITED TEXTS AND REPRINTS

*The Tenth Muse (1650) and, from the Manuscripts, Meditations Divine and Morall Together with Letters and Occasional Pieces*, ed. Josephine K.

Piercy, Gainesville, Fla., 1965, is a facsimile reproduction. *The Works of Anne Bradstreet*, ed. Jeannine Hensley, with a foreword by Adrienne Rich, Cambridge, Mass., 1967, "reproduces the second edition, *Several Poems*, published in 1678 by John Foster in Boston."

BIOGRAPHY AND CRITICISM

A much-needed study of the poet is Josephine K. Piercy's *Anne Bradstreet*, New York, 1965. See also Biancamaria Tedeschini Lalli, "Anne Bradstreet," *SA*, No. 3 (1957), pp. 9–27; Cecil D. Eby, Jr., "Anne Bradstreet and Thomas Gray: A Note on Influence," *EIHC*, XCVII (1961), 292–293; Ann Stanford, "Anne Bradstreet: Dogmatist and Rebel," *NEQ*, XXXIX (1966), 373–389; Helen McMahon, "Anne Bradstreet, Jean Bertault, and Dr. Crooke," *EAL*, III (1968), 118–123; and Abigail A. Hamblen, "Anne Bradstreet: Portrait of a Puritan Lady," *Cresset* (Valparaiso University), XXXII (1968), 11–13.

# VAN WYCK BROOKS
## d. 1963

**415.** SEPARATE WORKS

*Howells: His Life and World*, 1959; *From the Shadow of the Mountain: My Post-Meridian Years*, 1961; *Fenollosa and His Circle, with Other Essays in Biography*, 1962; *A New England Reader*, 1962.

**416.** CORRESPONDENCE

Robert E. Spiller edited *The Van Wyck Brooks-Lewis Mumford Letters: The Record of a Friendship, 1921–1963*, New York, 1970. Other unpublished letters appear in William Wasserstrom, *The Legacy of Van Wyck Brooks: A Study of Maladies and Motives*, Carbondale, Ill., 1971.

**416.** REPRINTS

*An Autobiography*, New York, 1965, is a one-volume edition of *Scenes and Portraits, Days of the Phoenix*, and *From the Shadow of the Mountain*, with an introduction by Malcolm Cowley and a foreword by John Hall Wheelock. Claire Sprague edited *Van Wyck Brooks: The Early Years: A Selection from His Works, 1908–1921*, New York, 1968.

BIOGRAPHY AND CRITICISM

The first full-length study is James R. Vitelli, *Van Wyck Brooks*, New York, 1969. William Wasserstrom, *Van Wyck Brooks*, Minneapolis,

Minn., 1968, is a recent pamphlet. See also his study listed under Correspondence, above. Gladys Brooks, *If Strangers Meet: A Memory*, New York, 1967, is a reminiscence by Brooks's wife. For briefer estimates, see Charles Angoff, "Van Wyck Brooks and Our Critical Tradition," *LitR*, VII (1963), 27-35; Malcolm Cowley, "A Career in Retrospect," *SatR*, XLVI (May 25, 1963), 17-18, 38; Charles A. Madison, "The Pilgrimage of Van Wyck Brooks," *CJF*, XXIV (1965), 43-46; and John Hall Wheelock, "Van Wyck Brooks: A Man in Quest of the Truth," *LC*, XXXI (1965), 1-6.

**417. BIBLIOGRAPHY**

Brief listings are in Vitelli and Wasserstrom, cited above.

# CHARLES BROCKDEN BROWN

**417. BIOGRAPHY AND CRITICISM**

Donald A. Ringe's *Charles Brockden Brown*, New York, 1966, is a serviceable study with little new material. Brief studies are numerous: W. B. Berthoff, "'A Lesson on Concealment': Brockden Brown's Method in Fiction," *PQ*, XXXVII (1958), 45-57; Larzer Ziff, "A Reading of *Wieland*," *PMLA*, LXXVII (1962), 51-57; Alfred Weber, "Eine neue entdeckte Kurzgeschichte C. B. Browns," *JA*, VIII (1963), 280-296; David H. Hirsh, "Charles Brockden Brown as a Novelist of Ideas," *BBr*, XX (1965), 165-184; Kenneth Bernard, "*Arthur Mervyn*: The Ordeal of Innocence," *TSLL*, VI (1965), 441-459; Paul Levine, "The American Novel Begins," *ASch*, XXXV (1965), 134-148; A. Owen Aldridge, "Charles Brockden Brown's Poem on Benjamin Franklin," *AL*, XXXVIII (1966), 230-235; Paul Witherington, "Image and Idea in *Wieland* and *Edgar Huntly*," *Serif*, III (1966), 19-26; Arthur G. Kimball, "Savages and Savagism: Brockden Brown's Dramatic Irony," *SIR*, VI (1967), 214-225; Robert E. Hemenway, "Charles Brockden Brown's Law Study: Some New Documents," *AL*, XXXIX (1967), 199-204; and *idem*, "Brockden Brown's Twice-Told Insanity Tale," *AL*, XL (1968), 211-215.

**419. BIBLIOGRAPHY**

See Robert E. Hemenway and Dean H. Keller, "Charles Brockden Brown: America's First Important Novelist: A Checklist of Biography and Criticism," *PBSA*, LX (1966), 349-362; Sydney J. Krause, assisted by Jane Nieset, "A Census of the Works of Charles Brockden Brown," *Serif*, III (1966), 27-55; and Krause's survey of available editions and manuscripts, "Charles Brockden Brown," *CEAAN*, I (1968), 13-14.

## CHARLES FARRAR BROWNE
## ("ARTEMUS WARD")

**419.** WORKS

*Artemus Ward: His Book*, Santa Barbara, Calif., 1964, is a facsimile of
the 1862 edition, with an introduction by Robert M. Hutchins.

BIOGRAPHY AND CRITICISM

The most recent full-length study is James C. Austin, *Artemus Ward*,
New York, 1964. Briefer studies are John Q. Reed, "Artemus Ward as
Satirist," *BCMVASA*, I (Spring, 1958), 14–20; *idem*, "Artemus Ward on
Reform and Reformers," *EL*, XXII (1958), 20–26; Curtis Dahl, "Artemus
Ward: Comic Panoramist," *NEQ*, XXXII (1959), 476–485; Paul Fatout,
"Artemus Ward among the Mormons," *WHR*, XIV (1960), 193–199;
John Q. Reed, "Artemus Ward's First Lecture Tour," *AL*, XXXIV
(1963), 571–573; Bryson L. Jaynes, "Artemus Ward on the Negro," *RS*,
XXXIII (1965), 178–180; John Q. Reed, "Artemus Ward: The Minor
Writer in American Studies," *MQ*, VII (1966), 241–251; and Robert W.
Richmond, "Humorist on Tour: Artemus Ward in Mid-America, 1864,"
*Kansas Historical Quarterly*, XXXIII (1967), 470–480.

A brief bibliographical listing is in Austin, cited above.

## ORESTES (AUGUSTUS) BROWNSON

**421.** BIOGRAPHY AND CRITICISM

The most recent study is Americo D. Lapati, *Orestes A. Brownson*, New
York, 1965. Briefer estimates are Edwin Fussell, "*Leaves of Grass* and
Brownson," *AL*, XXXI (1959), 77–78; Vincent F. Holden, "The Yankee
Paul," *CathW*, CLXXXVIII (1958), 24–30; Alvan S. Ryan, "The Critique
of Transcendentalism," *American Classics Reconsidered*, ed. Harold C.
Gardiner, New York, 1958, pp. 98–120; Thomas T. McAvoy, C.S.C.,
"Orestes A. Brownson and Archbishop John Hughes in 1860," *RPol*,
XXIV (1962), 19–47; Edward J. Power, "The State and Catholic Educa-
tion: Brownson, Spalding, and Ireland," *Cithara*, I (1962), 24–36; James
P. Hanigan, S.J., "Orestes Brownson and the Election of 1840," *RACHSP*,
LXXIII (1962), 45–50; Per Sveino, "Orestes A. Brownson's *New Views*,"
*Americana Norvegica: Norwegian Contributions to American Studies*, I,
ed. Sigmund Skard and Henry H. Wasser, Oslo and Philadelphia, 1966, pp.
97–109; C. Carroll Hollis, "Brownson on Native New England," *NEQ*, XL

(1967), 212–226; and Daniel R. Barnes, "Brownson and Newman: The Controversy Re-Examined," *ESQ*, L (1968), 9–20.

## WILLIAM CULLEN BRYANT

### 423. COLLECTED WORKS AND CORRESPONDENCE

Gleaning of letters and unpublished works are Seymour L. Gross, "An Uncollected Bryant Poem," *N&Q*, IV (1957), 358–359; Robert H. Woodward, "Bryant and Elizabeth Oakes Smith: An Unpublished Bryant Letter," *CLQ*, Ser. 5 (1959), pp. 69–74; Peter B. Morrill, "Unpublished Letters of William Cullen Bryant," *ESQ*, No. 27 (1962), pp. 47–48; Paul Crapo, "Bryant on Slavery, Copyright, and Capital Punishment," *ESQ*, No. 47 (1967), pp. 139–140; Joseph G. Ornato, "Bryant and the *United States Literary Gazette*," *ESQ*, No. 48 (1967), pp. 135–139; Richard E. Peck, "Two Lost Bryant Poems: Evidence of Thomson's Influence," *AL*, XXXIX (1967), 88–94; and David R. Rebmann, "Unpublished Letters of William Cullen Bryant," *ESQ*, No. 48 (1967), pp. 131–135.

### 424. BIOGRAPHY AND CRITICISM

Two American book-length studies are Curtiss S. Johnson, *Politics and a Belly-Full: The Journalistic Career of William Cullen Bryant, Civil War Editor of the New York Evening Post*, New York, 1962; and Albert F. McLean, Jr., *William Cullen Bryant*, New York, 1964. Anna Maria Crinò's *Echi, temi et motivi della poesia di William Cullen Bryant* was published in Verona, 1963. Briefer estimates are Donald M. Murray, "Dr. Peter Bryant: Preceptor in Poetry to William Cullen Bryant," *NEQ*, XXXIII (1960), 513–522; Curtis Dahl, "Mound-Builders, Mormons, and William Cullen Bryant," *NEQ*, XXXIV (1961), 178–190; Herman E. Spivey, "Bryant Cautions and Counsels Lincoln," *TSL*, VI (1961), 1–13; Evans Harrington, "Sensuousness in the Poetry of William Cullen Bryant," *UMSE*, VII (1965), 25–42; Benjamin T. Spencer, "Bryant: The Melancholy Progressive," *ESQ*, No. 43 (1966), pp. 99–103; and Edward K. Spann, "Bryant and Verplanck: The Yankee and the Yorker, 1821–1870," *NYH*, XLIX (1968), 11–28.

### 426. BIBLIOGRAPHY

See Earle E. Coleman, "The Exhibition in the Palace: A Bibliographical Essay," *BNYPL*, LXIV (1960), 459–477; and Thomas H. Voss, *William Cullen Bryant: An Annotated Checklist of the Exhibit in the Mullen Library of the Catholic University of America . . .* , Washington, D.C., 1967.

## JOHN BURROUGHS

**427.** COLLECTED WORKS AND BIOGRAPHY

Elizabeth Burroughs Kelley, *John Burroughs: Naturalist: The Story of His Work and Family by His Granddaughter*, New York, 1959, does little more than show the need for a thoroughgoing study of the author. For more specialized studies see Broadus F. Farrar, "John Burroughs, Theodore Roosevelt, and the Nature Fakers," *TSL*, IV (1959), 121–130; Harriet B. Shatraw, "A Child's View of a Naturalist," *UKCR*, XXVIII (1962), 178–182; Gregory Lansing Paine, "John Burroughs and the Cooperstown Seminary," *NYH*, XLIV (1963), 60–77; and Ben Harris McClary, "Burroughs to Whitman on Emerson: An Unpublished Letter," *ESQ*, No. 43 (1966), pp. 67–68.

## (HAROLD) WITTER BYNNER
### *d. 1968*

**428.** SEPARATE WORKS

*New Poems*, 1960.

*The Jade Mountain: A Chinese Anthology* (1929) was reprinted in New York, 1964.

**429.** BIOGRAPHY AND CRITICISM

See Horatio Colony, "Witter Bynner—Poet of Today," *LitR*, III (1960), 339–361; and Douglas Day, "The New Old Poetry of Witter Bynner," *Shen*, XII (1961), 3–11. William Jay Smith, *The Spectra Hoax*, Middletown, Conn., 1961, describes the 1916 poetry hoax of Witter Bynner and Arthur Davison Ficke under the names "Emanuel Morgan" and "Anne Knish."

Robert O. Lindsay, *Witter Bynner: A Bibliography*, appeared in Albuquerque, N.M., 1967.

## WILLIAM BYRD II

**429.** SEPARATE WORKS

Louis B. Wright edited with a lengthy introduction *The Prose Works of William Byrd of Westover: Narrative of a Colonial Virginian*, Cambridge, Mass., 1966, the four major works collated with the original Westover Manuscripts and printed together for the first time. With Marion Tinling he also edited *The Great American Gentleman: William Byrd of Westover in Virginia: His Secret Diary for the Years 1709–1712*, New York, 1963, a selection concentrating "upon the earliest of the three sections of Byrd's diary in print."

**430. BIOGRAPHY AND CRITICISM**

Special studies are Marshall Fishwick, "The Pepys of the Old Dominion," *AH*, XI (1959), 5–7, 117–119; Edd Winfield Parks, "William Byrd as Man of Letters," *GaR*, XIV (1960), 172–176; Ulrich Troubtezkoy, "Enough to Keep a Byrd Alive," *VC*, XI (1961), 36–41; and Richard Mott Gummere, "Byrd and Sewall: Two Colonial Classicists," *Transactions of the Colonial Society of Massachusetts*, XLII (1964), 156–173.

Of bibliographical interest is Edwin Wolf, II, "The Dispersal of the Library of William Byrd of Westover," *PAAS*, LXVIII (1958), 19–106.

# (JAMES) BRANCH CABELL

**431. SEPARATE WORKS**

*Between Friends: Letters of James Branch Cabell and Others*, New York, 1962, was edited by Padraic Colum and Margaret Freeman Cabell, with an introduction by Carl Van Vechten.

**BIOGRAPHY AND CRITICISM**

Three full-length studies have appeared in recent years: Joe Lee Davis, *James Branch Cabell*, New York, 1962; Arvin R. Wells, *Jesting Moses: A Study in Cabellian Comedy*, Gainesville, Fla., 1962; and Desmond Tarrant, *James Branch Cabell: The Dream and the Reality*, Norman, Okla., 1967. Louis D. Rubin, Jr., *No Place on Earth: Ellen Glasgow, James Branch Cabell, and Richmond-in-Virginia*, Austin, Tex., 1959, is "an informal, even personal commentary on the work of two Virginia authors, in terms of the place from which they came." *James Branch Cabell: Three Essays* by Carl Van Doren, H. L. Mencken, and Hugh Walpole, Port Washington, N.Y., 1967, is a valuable reprinting of three seminal studies of Cabell's work dated 1932, 1927, and 1920, respectively.

For briefer estimates, see Luigi Berti, "Lo Strano Caso di James Branch Cabell," *Inventario*, VIII (1956), 248–266; Marshall W. Fishwick, "Cabell and Glasgow: Tradition in Search of Meaning," *Shen*, VIII (1957), 24–35; Raymond Himelick, "Cabell and the Modern Temper," *SAQ*, LVIII (1959), 176–184; Dorothy B. Schlegel, "Cabell and His Critics," *The Dilemma of the Southern Writer*, ed. Richard K. Meeker, Farm-ville, Va., 1961, pp. 119–142; and Robert H. Canary, "Cabell's Dark Comedies," *MissQ*, XXI (1968), 83–92.

The Cabell•Society published its inaugural issue of *The Cabellian: A Journal of the Second American Renaissance* in Lynbrook, New York, 1968.

# GEORGE (WASHINGTON) CABLE

### 433. CORRESPONDENCE

Arlin Turner, ed., *Mark Twain* [and] *G. W. Cable: The Record of a Literary Friendship*, East Lansing, Mich., 1960, contains chiefly Cable's letters during his lecture tour with Twain.

### REPRINTS

*The Works of George Washington Cable*, under the editorship of Arlin Turner, has been announced for publication in New York by the Garrett Press in 19 volumes.

### BIOGRAPHY AND CRITICISM

Philip Butcher's *George W. Cable: The Northampton Years*, New York, 1959, studies his life in the North (1885–1922) and his fight for civil rights for Negroes. Butcher's *George W. Cable*, New York, 1962, is a survey of the whole career; as in Louis D. Rubin. Jr., *George W. Cable: The Life and Times of a Southern Heretic*, New York, 1969. Briefer studies are James B. Whipple, "Southern Rebel," *Phylon*, XX (1959), 345–357; Griffin T. Pugh, "George W. Cable's Theory and Use of Folk Speech," *SFQ*, XXIV (1960), 287–293; and *idem*, "George Washington Cable," *MissQ*, XX (1967), 69–76.

For more bibliography see Philip Butcher, "George Washington Cable (1844–1925)," *ALR*, I (1967), 20–25.

# ERSKINE (PRESTON) CALDWELL

### 434. SEPARATE WORKS

*Claudelle Inglish*, 1958; *When You Think of Me*, 1959; *Jenny by Nature*, 1961; *Close to Home*, 1962; *The Last Night of Summer*, 1963; *Around About America*, 1964; *In Search of Bisco*, 1965; *The Deer at Our House*, 1966; *Miss Mamma Aimee*, 1967; *In the Shadow of the Steeple* (London), 1967; *Deep South: Memory and Observation* (including *In the*

*Shadow of the Steeple*), 1968; *Writing in America*, 1968; *Summertime Island*, 1968; *The Weather Shelter*, 1969.

Reprints and translations are numerous and worldwide. *Men and Women*, Boston, 1961, is a collection of 22 stories with an introduction by Carvel Collins. *Three*, Boston, 1960, reprints *Tobacco Road, Georgia Boy*, and *The Sure Hand of God* in one volume.

### BIOGRAPHY AND CRITICISM

Caldwell talks about his life and art in "How to Live like an Author," *New World Writing*, No. 15 (1959), pp. 152–158; and "My Twenty-Five Years of Censorship," *Esquire*, L (Oct., 1958), 176–178. Alan Lelchuk and Robin White report an interview in "Erskine Caldwell," *Per/Se*, II (1967), 11–20.

The first lengthy critical essay is James Korges's pamphlet, *Erskine Caldwell*, Minneapolis, Minn., 1969. For briefer estimates see Robert Cantwell, "Caldwell's Characters: Why Don't They Leave?" *GaR*, XI (1957), 252–264; Carvel Collins, "Erskine Caldwell at Work," *Atl*, CCII (July, 1958), 21–27; Louise Y. Gossett, *Violence in Recent Southern Fiction*, Durham, N.C., 1965; and Kenneth Burke, *The Philosophy of Literary Form*, 2nd ed., Baton Rouge, La., 1967.

## JOHN CALDWELL CALHOUN

### 435. SEPARATE WORKS AND CORRESPONDENCE

Publication of *The Papers of John C. Calhoun* (Columbia, S.C.) has begun with Volume I (1801–1817), ed. Robert L. Meriwether, 1959; Volume II (1817–1818), ed. W. Edwin Hemphill, 1963; and Volume III (1818–1819), ed. W. Edwin Hemphill, 1967. Richard K. Crallé's six-volume edition of *The Works of John C. Calhoun (1851–1856)* has been reprinted, New York, 1968.

### BIOGRAPHY AND CRITICISM

A short critical biography is Gerald Capers, *John C. Calhoun, Opportunist: A Reappraisal*, Gainesville, Fla., 1960. Richard Current's *John C. Calhoun*, New York, 1966, has been described as "not so much a biography as an analysis and critique of Calhoun's philosophy." *John C. Calhoun: A Profile*, ed. John L. Thomas, New York, 1968, reprints 12 essays from the nineteenth and twentieth centuries. *John C. Calhoun*, ed. Margaret L. Coit, Englewood Cliffs, N.J., 1970, collects extracts from Calhoun's speeches and letters, excerpts from contemporaneous opinions, and portions of twentieth-century essays.

Brief bibliographical essays are appended to the Thomas and Coit volumes cited above.

## WILLA (SIBERT) CATHER

### 436. COLLECTED WORKS AND EDITED REPRINTS

The University of Nebraska Press has published in several volumes the previously unavailable early writings: *Willa Cather's Collected Short Fiction, 1892–1912*, ed. Mildred R. Bennett, 1965, rev. ed. by Bernice Slote, 1970; *The Kingdom of Art: Willa Cather's First Principles and Citical Statements, 1893–1896*, ed. Bernice Slote with two essays and a commentary by the editor, 1966; *April Twilights (1903): Poems by Willa Cather*, ed. Bernice Slote, 1968; *The World and the Parish: Willa Cather's Articles and Reviews, 1893–1902*, 2 vols., ed. William M. Curtin, 1970.

### 437. BIOGRAPHY AND CRITICISM

The major critical studies in the last decade are John H. Randall, *The Landscape and the Looking Glass: Willa Cather's Search for Value*, Boston, 1960; Edward A. Bloom and Lillian D. Bloom, *Willa Cather's Gift of Sympathy*, Carbondale, Ill., 1962; and James Woodress, *Willa Cather: Her Life and Art*, New York, 1970. A more specialized study is Richard Giannone's *Music in Willa Cather's Fiction*, Lincoln, Neb., 1968. Dorothy Van Ghent, *Willa Cather*, Minneapolis, Minn., 1964, is a brief pamphlet. James Schroeter reprints representative criticism in *Willa Cather and Her Critics*, Ithaca, N.Y., 1967.

Briefer estimates are George Greene, "*Death Comes for the Archbishop*," NMQ, XXVII (1957), 69–82; James E. Miller, Jr., "*My Ántonia*: A Frontier Drama of Time," AQ, X (1958), 476–484; Robert L. Gale, "Willa Cather and the Past," SA, IV (1958), 209–222; Leon Edel, *Willa Cather, The Paradox of Success*, Washington, D.C. (Library of Congress Lecture), 1960; L. V. Jacks, "The Classics and Willa Cather," PrS, XXXV (1961), 289–296; Clinton Keeler, "Narrative without Accent: Willa Cather and Puvis de Chavannes," AQ, XVII (1965), 119–126; Raymond Thorberg, "Willa Cather: From *Alexander's Bridge* to *My Ántonia*," TCL VII (1962), 147–158; Stanley Cooperman, "Willa Cather and the Bright Face of Death," L&P, XIII (1963), 81–87; Sister Colette Toler, S.C., "Willa Cather's Vision of the Artist," Person, XLV (1964), 503–523; Sister Peter Damian Charles, O.P., "Love and Death in Willa Cather's *O Pioneers!*," CLAJ, IX (1965), 140–150; Don D. Walker, "The Western Humanism of Willa Cather," WAL, I (1966), 75–90; D. H. Stewart, "Cather's Mortal Comedy," QQ, LXXIII (1966), 244–259; Lavon M.

Jobes, "Willa Cather's Last Novel," *UR*, XXXIV (1967), 77–80; Sister Lucy Schneider, C.S.J., "Willa Cather's Early Stories in the Light of Her 'Land-Philosophy,'" *MQ*, IX (1967), 75–94; William M. Curtin, "Willa Cather: Individualism and Style," *CLQ*, VIII (1968), 37–55; and J. Russell Reaver, "Mythic Motivation in Willa Cather's *O Pioneers!*," *WF*, XXXVII (1968), 19–25.

## 438. BIBLIOGRAPHY

A comprehensive bibliography is being compiled by John March for the University of Nebraska Press. Useful general listings are appended to the Schroeter and Giannone volumes, cited above. *The Kingdom of Art* includes a full checklist of Cather's critical and personal writing, 1891–1896; the *Collected Short Fiction* includes three bibliographical appendixes. Bernice Slote prepared an interpretive bibliographical essay, "Willa Cather," for *Fifteen Modern American Authors*, ed. Jackson R. Bryer, Durham, N.C., 1969, pp. 23–62. See also Richard Cary, "A Willa Cather Collection," *CLQ*, VIII (1968), 82–95.

## WILLIAM ELLERY CHANNING

### 438. SEPARATE WORKS

*Slavery* (1836) and *Emancipation* (1841) were reprinted in one volume, New York, 1968. Irving H. Bartlett edited *Unitarian Christianity and Other Essays*, New York, 1957.

### 439. BIOGRAPHY AND CRITICISM

The most recent biography is Madeleine Hook Rice, *Federal Street Pastor: The Life of William Ellery Channing*, New York, 1961. Arthur W. Brown's *William Ellery Channing*, New York, 1961, is an attempt "to continue the redefinition of William Ellery Channing's life and work that has been going on during the past decade." Of specialized interest is Hester Hastings, *William Ellery Channing and L'Académie des Sciences Morales et Politiques, 1870: "L'Étude sur Channing" and The "Lost" Prize Essay*, Providence, R.I., 1959. Briefer studies are Bernhard Fabian, "The Channing Revival: Remarks on Recent Publications," *JA*, II (1957), 197–212; Siegfried B. Puknat, "Auerbach and Channing," *PMLA*, LXXII (1957), 962–976; *idem*, "Channing and German Thought," *PAPS*, CI (1957), 195–203; Abe C. Ravitz, "The Return of William Ellery Channing," *AQ*, XIII (1961), 67–76; Robert S. Ward, "The American System in Literature," *NEQ*, XXXVIII (1965), 363–374; and Thomas F. Harwood, "Prejudice and Antislavery: The Colloquy between William Ellery Channing and Edward Strutt Abdy, 1834," *AQ*, XVIII (1966), 697–700.

# CHARLES W(ADDELL) CHESNUTT

**440. SEPARATE WORKS**

Four of Chesnutt's six volumes are back in print: *The Conjure Woman*, Upper Saddle River, N.J., 1968; *The Wife of His Youth and Other Stories of the Color Line*, Ann Arbor, Mich., 1968; *The House behind the Cedars*, Ridgewood, N.J., 1968; and *The Colonel's Dream*, New York, 1970.

**BIOGRAPHY AND CRITICISM**

Brief estimates are Robert A. Smith, "A Note on the Folktales of Charles W. Chesnutt," *CLAJ*, V (1962), 229–232; Sylvia Lyons Render, "Tar Heelia in Chesnutt," *CLAJ*, IX (1965), 39–50; Julian D. Mason, Jr., "Charles W. Chesnutt as Southern Author," *MissQ*, XX (1967), 77–89; and Carol B. Gartner, "Charles W. Chesnutt: Novelist of a Cause," *Markham Review*, III (1968), 5–12.

A bibliographical listing is in Dean H. Keller, "Charles Waddell Chesnutt (1858–1932)," *ALR*, III (1968), 1–4.

# THOMAS HOLLEY CHIVERS

**440. SEPARATE WORKS**

Brown University Press has begun the publication of *The Complete Works of Thomas Holley Chivers* with Volume I, *The Correspondence, 1838–1858*, ed. Emma Lester Chase and Lois Ferry Parks, 1957. The general editors are S. Foster Damon and Charles H. Watts, II. See also John Olin Eidson, "The Letters of Thomas Holley Chivers," *GaR*, XVIII (1964), 143–149.

**BIOGRAPHY AND CRITICISM**

Of special interest is "Thomas Holley Chivers: Mystic" in Edd Winfield Parks's *Ante-Bellum Southern Criticism*, Athens, Ga., 1962.

# HENRY CLAY

**441. COLLECTED WORKS AND CORRESPONDENCE**

The University of Kentucky Press has begun the publication of *The Papers of Henry Clay*, under the direction of James F. Hopkins: Volume I, *The Rising Statesman, 1797–1814* (1959); Volume II, *The Rising Statesman, 1815–1820* (1961); Volume III, *Presidential Candidate, 1821–1824* (1963).

Glyndon G. Van Deusen's *The Life of Henry Clay* (1937) was reprinted in Boston, 1963; George R. Poage's *Henry Clay and the Whig Party* (1936) in Gloucester, Mass., 1965; Bernard Mayo's *Henry Clay, Spokesman of the New West* (1937) in Hamden, Conn., 1966.

# SAMUEL L(ANGHORNE) CLEMENS
## ("MARK TWAIN")

### 442. SEPARATE WORKS

Bernard DeVoto prepared *Letters from the Earth* for publication in 1939, but Mark Twain's daughter, Clara Clemens Samossoud, objected to the "shocking" character of some of the pieces. The miscellany has now been issued, with an introduction by Henry Nash Smith, New York, 1962. Franklin R. Rogers edited the unfinished novel, *Simon Wheeler, Detective*, New York, 1963. Frederick Anderson edited, from an amanuensis copy, *Ah Sin: A Dramatic Work by Mark Twain and Bret Harte*, San Francisco, 1961. See also Charles Neider, "Reflections on Religion," *HudR*, XVI (1963), 329–352, for the first printing of five 1906 dictations, part of the autobiography hitherto suppressed.

### 443. COLLECTED WORKS, REPRINTS, AND CORRESPONDENCE

The University of California Press has begun the publication of a projected 14 volumes from The Mark Twain Papers in the General Library at the University of California at Berkeley. The first to appear, both in 1967, are *Mark Twain's Which Was the Dream? and Other Symbolic Writings of the Later Years*, ed. John S. Tuckey; and *Mark Twain's Satires and Burlesques*, ed. Franklin R. Rogers; followed in 1969 by *Mark Twain's Hannibal, Huck & Tom*, ed. Walter Blair; and *Mark Twain's Mysterious Stranger Manuscripts*, ed. William M. Gibson. Two volumes of letters in this series are noted below.

*The Iowa–California Edition of the Works of Mark Twain* will be published in 24 volumes by the University of California Press, concentrating on "those works that were published during the author's lifetime." John C. Gerber is Chairman of the Editorial Board; Frederick Anderson is Series Editor.

Charles Neider's editorial work on Mark Twain spans a decade, beginning with *The Complete Short Stories*, New York, 1957; and continuing with *The Autobiography of Mark Twain*, New York, 1959, selections arranged chonologically for the general reader, not the scholar; *Life as I Find It: Essays, Sketches, Tales, and Other Material*, Garden City, N.Y.,

1961; *The Complete Humorous Sketches and Tales*, Garden City, N.Y., 1961; *The Travels of Mark Twain*, Garden City, N.Y., 1961, selections from all the travel books arranged according to place; *The Complete Essays*, Garden City, N.Y., 1963; *The Complete Novels*, 2 vols., Garden City, N.Y., 1964; *The Adventures of Colonel Sellers, Being Mark Twain's Share of The Gilded Age*, Garden City, N.Y., 1965; and *The Complete Travel Books*, 2 vols., Garden City, N.Y., 1967.

Previously uncollected journalistic writings can be found in *Contributions to The Galaxy, 1868–1871, by Mark Twain (Samuel Langhorne Clemens)*, ed. Bruce R. McElderry, Jr., Gainesville, Fla., 1961; *Mark Twain on the Art of Writing*, Buffalo, 1961, three essays from the Buffalo *Express, 1869–1870*, edited by Martin B. Fried; *Mark Twain's San Francisco*, New York, 1963, 83 pieces written for Nevada and California newspapers, 1863–1866, edited by Bernard Taper; and *Clemens of the "Call": Mark Twain in San Francisco*, Berkeley, Calif., 1969, covering June to October, 1864, edited by Edgar M. Branch. *The Forgotten Writings of Mark Twain*, New York, 1963, contributions to the Buffalo *Express* 1868–1871, edited by Henry Duskus, must be used with caution since the Duskus commentary and the Mark Twain texts are not always clearly separated.

Four miscellaneous collections are of use to both general reader and student: *The Art, Humor, and Humanity of Mark Twain*, ed. Minnie M. Brashear and Robert M. Rodney, Norman, Okla., 1959; *Mark Twain and the Government*, ed. Svend Petersen, Caldwell, Idaho, 1960; *Mark Twain and the Damned Human Race*, ed. Janet Smith, New York, 1962; and *Selected Shorter Writings of Mark Twain*, ed. Walter Blair, Boston, 1962. Of more specialized interest are: *On the Poetry of Mark Twain: With Selections from His Verse*, ed. Arthur L. Scott, Urbana, Ill., 1966; and Mark Twain's 1887 speech, *General Grant by Matthew Arnold: With a Rejoinder by Mark Twain*, ed. John Y. Simon, Carbondale, Ill., 1966.

Among the volumes of collected correspondence, two are in the University of California edition of The Mark Twain Papers: Hamlin Hill's edition of *Mark Twain's Letters to His Publishers, 1867–1894*, Berkeley, Calif., 1967; and Lewis Leary's edition of *Mark Twain's Correspondence with Henry Huttleston Rogers, 1893–1909*, Berkeley, Calif., 1969. Of equal importance are Henry Nash Smith and William M. Gibson, eds., *The Correspondence of Samuel L. Clemens and William Dean Howells, 1872–1910*, 2 vols., Cambridge, Mass., 1960 (*Selected Mark Twain–Howells Letters*, Cambridge Mass., 1967, is a one-volume redaction); and Lewis Leary, ed., *Mark Twain's Letters to Mary* [Mrs. H. H. Rogers], New York, 1961. Previously unpublished letters appear in Dorothy Quick, *Enchantment: A Little Girl's Friendship with Mark Twain*, Norman, Okla., 1961. Franklin R. Rogers edited seven letters in *The Pattern for Mark*

*Twain's "Roughing It": Letters from Nevada by Samuel and Orion Clemens, 1861–1862*, Berkeley, Calif., 1961. Twenty-five letters written for the Sacramento *Union* in 1866 have been published in *Mark Twain's Letters from Hawaii*, ed. A. Grove Day, New York, 1966; and 58 letters for various newspapers appear in Daniel Morley McKeithan, ed., *Traveling with Innocents Abroad: Mark Twain's Original Reports from Europe and the Holy Land*, Norman, Okla., 1958.

### 446. BIOGRAPHY AND CRITICISM

Without doubt, the major work for the general reader is Justin Kaplan's *Mr. Clemens and Mark Twain*, New York, 1966, an eminently readable biography that begins with the author at age 30 and recreates his public as well as private life. Edward Wagenknecht revised his biography, *Mark Twain: The Man and His Work*, Norman, Okla., 1935, for a third edition in 1967. Paul Fatout's *Mark Twain in Virginia City*, Bloomington, Ind., 1964, concentrates on the period September, 1862–May, 1864; Dewey Ganzel's *Mark Twain Abroad: The Cruise of the "Quaker City,"* Chicago, 1968, on the year 1871, June to November. Milton Meltzer's, *Mark Twain Himself: A Pictorial Biography*, New York, 1960, reproduces 600 pictures of Clemens and his surroundings from 1835–1910, a remarkable collection. Family, friends, business partners, and rivals are illuminated in Arlin Turner, *Mark Twain and George W. Cable: The Record of a Literary Friendship*, East Lansing, Mich., 1960; Paul Fatout, *Mark Twain on the Lecture Circuit*, Bloomington, Ind., 1960; Caroline Thomas Harnsberger, *Mark Twain: Family Man*, New York, 1960, chiefly Clara Clemens Gabrilowitsch's reminiscences; Margaret Duckett, *Mark Twain and Bret Harte*, Norman, Okla., 1964; Hamlin Hill, *Mark Twain and Elisha Bliss*, Columbia, Mo., 1964; Leah A. Strong, *Joseph Hopkins Twichell: Mark Twain's Friend and Pastor*, Athens, Ga., 1966; Edith Colgate Salsbury, ed., *Susy and Mark Twain: Family Dialogues*, New York, 1965, a pastiche from books, letters, reminiscences, arranged in dialogue form; and Fred W. Lorch, *The Trouble Begins at Eight: Mark Twain's Lecture Tours*, Ames, Iowa, 1968. See also James M. Cox, "The Muse of Samuel Clemens," *MassR*, V (1963), 127–141, for important insights into Olivia Clemens's influence on her husband.

Of the scores of books of general criticism, Henry Nash Smith's *Mark Twain: The Development of a Writer*, Cambridge, Mass., 1962, is the best treatment of the whole career and the dilemmas the author faced. Frank Baldanza attempts the same scope in briefer and more simplified form in *Mark Twain: An Introduction and Interpretation*, New York, 1961. Louis J. Budd, *Mark Twain: Social Philosopher*, Bloomington, Ind., 1962; and Philip S. Foner, *Mark Twain: Social Critic*, New York, 1958, see the author's political ideas from wholly different points of view. Maxwell Geismar's *Mark Twain: An American Prophet*, Boston, 1970, is a highly individualized reading of the work, unorthodox and acerbic. Two valuable insights into Mark Twain's imagination are James M. Cox, *Mark Twain: The Fate of Humor*, Princeton, N.J., 1966; Pascal Covici, Jr., *Mark Twain's Humor: The Image of a World*, Dallas, Tex., 1962. Somewhat more specialized books, but still surveys of the whole canon, are Franklin R. Rogers, *Mark Twain's Burlesque Patterns as Seen in the Novels and Narratives, 1855–1885*, Dallas, Tex., 1960; Albert E. Stone, *The Innocent Eye: Childhood in Mark Twain's Imagination*, New Haven, Conn., 1961; Roger B. Salomon, *Twain and the Image of History*, New Haven, Conn., 1961; William C. Spengemann, *Mark Twain and the Backwoods Angel: The Matter of Innocence in the Works of Samuel L. Clemens*, Kent, Ohio, 1966; and Robert Regan, *Unpromising Heroes: Mark Twain and His Characters*, Berkeley, Calif., 1966. An attempt to portray Twain as amateur improviser rather than professional craftsman is Robert A. Wiggins's *Mark Twain, Jackleg Novelist*, Seattle, Wash., 1964. Howard G. Baetzhold's *Mark Twain and John Bull*, Bloomington, Ind., 1970, investigates "the British connection." Lewis Leary, *Mark Twain*, Minneapolis, Minn., 1960 is a brief pamphlet. General studies from European scholars include Giovanni Freddi, *Mark Twain*, Brescia, 1958; Karl-Heinz Schönfelder, *Mark Twain: Leben, Persönlichkeit, und Werk*, Salle, 1961; Douglas Grant, *Mark Twain*, Edinburgh, 1962; and Piero Mirizzi, *Mark Twain*, Rome, 1965.

Among recent studies of individual novels, Walter Blair's *Mark Twain and Huck Finn*, Berkeley, Calif., 1960, is supreme, as close to a definitive work as any critical analysis can be. *The True Adventures of Huckleberry Finn*, as told by John Seelye, Evanston, Ill., 1970, is delightful rewriting, "leaving in all the cuss words and the sex and the sadness" on the theory that "Mark Twain's book is for children and such, whilst this one here is for crickits." Also important are John S. Tuckey, *Mark Twain and Little Satan: The Writing of The Mysterious Stranger*, West Lafayette, Ind., 1963; Henry Nash Smith, *Mark Twain's Fable of Progress: Political and Economic Ideas in A Connecticut Yankee*, New Brunswick, N.J., 1964; and Bryant Morley French, *Mark Twain and The Gilded Age: The Book That Names an Era*, Dallas, Tex., 1965. Sydney J. Krause tries to substantiate William Dean Howells's praise of his friend in *Mark Twain as Critic*, Baltimore, Md., 1967; Allison Ensor examines Twain's theological beliefs in *Mark Twain and the Bible*, Lexington, Ky., 1969.

In recent years five volumes of collected essays on Mark Twain's work have appeared. Lewis Leary, ed., *A Casebook on Mark Twain's Wound*, New York, 1962, reprints criticism centering on the Brooks–DeVoto controversy. Henry Nash Smith, ed., *Mark Twain: A Collection of Critical Essays*, Englewood Cliffs, N.J., 1963, is chiefly twentieth-century criticism. Arthur L. Scott, ed., *Mark Twain: Selected Criticism*, Dallas, Tex., 1967, is a revised edition of a 1955 publication. Justin Kaplan selected 12 essays for *Mark Twain: A Profile*, New York, 1967; and Claude M. Simpson edited *Twentieth-Century Interpretations of The Adventures of Huckleberry Finn*, Englewood Cliffs, N.J., 1968. The Winter, 1964, issue of *American Quarterly* is devoted entirely to Mark Twain criticism, as is *Modern Fiction Studies*, Spring, 1968.

Of the more than 500 articles on Twain published in the last decade, the following is only a brief sampling: Fred W. Lorch, "Hawaiian Feudalism and Mark Twain's *A Connecticut Yankee in King Arthur's Court*," *AL*, XXX (1958), 50–66; Kenneth S. Lynn, "Huck and Jim," *YR*, XLVII (1958), 421–431; Lynn Altenbernd, "Huck Finn, Emancipator," *Criticism*, I (1959), 298–307; Herbert E. Klingelhofer, "Mark Twain, Edited and Bowdlerized," *MSS*, XI (1959), 2–12; John C. Gerber, "The Relation between Point of View and Style in the Works of Mark Twain," *Style in Prose Fiction*, ed. Harold C. Martin, New York, 1959; Robert Ornstein, "The Ending of *Huckleberry Finn*," *MLN*, LXXIV (1959), 698–702; Daniel G. Hoffman, "Jim's Magic: Black or White?" *AL*, XXXII (1960), 47–54; Dwight Macdonald, "Mark Twain: An Unsentimental Journey," *NY*, XXXVI (April 9, 1960), 160–196; Paul Schmidt, "River vs. Town: Mark Twain's *Old Times on the Mississippi*," *NCF*, XV (1960), 95–111; Charles Neider, *Mark Twain and the Russians: An Exchange of Views*, New York, 1960, a brief pamphlet; Arvin R. Wells, "Huck Finn and Holden Caulfield: The Situation of the Hero," *OUR*, II (1960), 31–42; Howard G. Baetzhold, " 'The Autobiography of Sir Robert Smith of Camelot': Mark Twain's Original Plan for *A Connecticut Yankee*," *AL*, XXXII (1961), 456–461; Clinton S. Burhans, Jr., "The Sober Affirmation of Mark Twain's Hadleyburg," *AL*, XXXIV (1962), 375–384; Tony Tanner, "Samuel Clemens and the Progress of a Stylistic Rebel," *BAASB*, No. 3 (1961), pp. 31–42; E. Hudson Long, "Twain's Ordeal in Retrospect," *SWR*, XLVIII (1963), 338–348; William C. Havard, "Mark Twain and the Political Ambivalence of Southwestern Humor," *MissQ*, XVII (1964), 95–106; Lawrence E. Mobley, "Mark Twain and the *Golden Era*," *PBSA*, LVIII (1964), 8–23; Franklin L. Jensen, "Mark Twain's Comments on Books and Authors," *ESRS*, XII (1964), 5–53; Philip Butcher, "Mark Twain Sells Roxy Down the River," *CLAJ*, VIII (1965), 225–233; Sherwood Cummings, "*What Is Man?* The Scientific Sources," *Essays on Determinism in American Literature*, ed. Sydney J. Krause, Kent, Ohio, 1965, pp. 108–116; Paul Baender, "Alias Macfarlane: A Revision of Mark Twain Biography," *AL*, XXXVIII (1966), 187–197; Eugene McNamara,

"Huck Lights Out for the Territory: Mark Twain's Unpublished Sequel," *UWR*, II (1966), 68–74; Leslie Fiedler, "An American Abroad," *PR*, XXXIII (1966), 77–91; Clyde L. Grimm, "*The American Claimant: Reclamation of a Farce*," *AQ*, XIX (1967), 86–103; Roger B. Salomon, "Mark Twain and Victorian Nostalgia," *Patterns of Commitment in American Literature*, ed. Marston LaFrance, Toronto, 1967, pp. 73–91; Bryant N. Wyatt, "Huckleberry Finn and the Art of Ernest Hemingway," *MTJ*, XIII (1967), 1–8; Hamlin Hill, "Mark Twain and His Enemies," *SoR*, IV (1968), 520–529; and Milton Rickels, "Samuel Clemens and the Conscience of Comedy," *SoR*, IV (1968), 558–568.

#### 450. BIBLIOGRAPHY

The third edition of Edward Wagenknecht's *Mark Twain: The Man and His Work*, Norman, Okla., 1967, reprints the original bibliography chapter as well as a valuable 30-page "Commentary on Mark Twain Criticism and Scholarship since 1960." A fuller bibliography, but without commentary, is Maurice Beebe and John Feaster, "Criticism of Mark Twain: A Selected Checklist," *MFS*, XIV (1968), 93–139. See also the two periodicals devoted to Twain studies, *The Mark Twain Journal* and *The Twainian*.

## JAMES FENIMORE COOPER

#### 451. COLLECTED WORKS AND CORRESPONDENCE

*The Works of James Fenimore Cooper*, an edition in 48 volumes, sponsored by Clark University and the American Antiquarian Society, will be published by the State University of New York. James Franklin Beard is Chairman of the Editorial Board.

Harvard University Press has completed publication of *The Letters and Journals of James Fenimore Cooper* in six volumes, edited by James Franklin Beard, Cambridge, Mass., 1960–1968.

#### EDITED TEXTS AND REPRINTS

Important facsimiles of otherwise uncollected material are *Early Critical Essays*, with an introduction by James F. Beard, Gainesville, Fla., 1955; and *Tales for Fifteen*, with an introduction by James F. Beard, Gainesville, Fla., 1959. *Notions of the Americans, Picked Up by a Travelling Bachelor* (1828), was reprinted in New York, 1963, with an introduction by Robert E. Spiller. Reprints of the novels are too numerous to list separately.

#### 452. BIOGRAPHY AND CRITICISM

Two general studies are Donald A. Ringe, *James Fenimore Cooper*, New York, 1962; and Warren S. Walker, *James Fenimore Cooper: An Introduc-*

*tion and Interpretation*, New York, 1962. The first full-length British study is George Dekker, *James Fenimore Cooper: The Novelist*, London, 1967 (published in New York, 1967, under the title *James Fenimore Cooper: The American Scott*). Thomas Philbrick makes a case for Cooper as "the true father of the sea novel" in *James Fenimore Cooper and the Development of American Sea Fiction*, Cambridge, Mass., 1961. Kay Seymour House concentrates on Cooper's characters and American cultural groups in *Cooper's Americans*, Columbus, Ohio, 1965. Robert E. Spiller, *James Fenimore Cooper*, Minneapolis, Minn., 1965, is a brief pamphlet. Warren S. Walker edited a useful collection of essays, *Leather-stocking and the Critics*, Chicago, 1965.

Other critical estimates are Gerhard Haeuptner, "Der Jäger Natty Bumppo: Das Bild des Menschen in den Lederstrumpferzählungen James Fenimore Coopers," *JA*, II (1957), 181–196; Charles A. Brady, "Mythmaker and Christian Romancer," *American Classics Reconsidered*, ed. Harold C. Gardiner, New York, 1958, pp. 59–97; David Brion Davis, "The Deerslayer, a Democratic Knight of the Wilderness," *Twelve Original Essays on Great American Novels*, ed. Charles Shapiro, Detroit, Mich., 1960, pp. 1–22; Gordon Mills, "The Symbolic Wilderness: James Fenimore Cooper and Jack London," *NCF*, XIII (1959), 329–340; William Wasserstrom, "The Origins of Culture: Cooper and Freud," *Psychoanalytic Study of Society*, ed. W. Muensterberger and Sidney Axelrad, New York, 1960, pp. 272–283; Harry Hayden Clark, "Fenimore Cooper and Science," *TWA*. XLVIII (1959), 179–204, and XLIX (1960), 249–282; Charles O'Donnell, "Progress and Property: The Later Cooper," *AQ*, XIII (1961), 402–409; Marcel Clavel, "Le 'Cooper Revival' aux États-Unis," *EA*, XV (1962), 36–45; John J. McAleer, "Biblical Analogy in the Leatherstocking Tales," *NCF*, XVII (1962), 217–235; David W. Noble, "Cooper, Leatherstocking and the Death of the American Adam," *AQ*, XVI (1964), 419–431; Richard Abcarian, "Cooper's Critics and the Realistic Novel," *TSLL*, VIII (1965), 33–41.

More recent are Frank M. Collins, "Cooper and the American Dream," *PMLA*, LXXXI (1966), 79–94; Kenneth Kurtz, "Emerson and Cooper: American Versions of the Heroic," *ESQ*, No. 42 (1965), pp. 1–8; James Woodress, "The Fortunes of Cooper in Italy," *SA*, XI (1967), 53–76; Jesse Bier, "The Bisection of Cooper: *Satanstoe* as Prime Example," *TSLL*, IX (1968), 511–521; and James H. Pickering, "New York in the Revolution: Cooper's *Wyandotté*," *NYH*, XLIX (1968), 121–141. See also discussions of Cooper's work in Howard Mumford Jones, *The Frontier in American Fiction*, Jerusalem, 1956; Marius Bewley, *The Eccentric Design: Form in the Classic American Novel*, New York, 1959; Klaus Lanzinger, *Die Epik im Amerikanischen Roman*, Frankfurt am Main,

1965; Edwin Fussell, *Frontier: American Literature and the West*, Princeton, N.J., 1965; and Joel Porte, *The Romance in America*, Middletown, Conn., 1969.

## JOHN COTTON

### 456. EDITED TEXTS AND REPRINTS

Everett H. Emerson edited a facsimile reprint of *God's Mercie Mixed with His Justice; or His Peoples Deliverance in Times of Danger* (1641), Gainesville, Fla., 1958. Larzer Ziff, ed., *John Cotton on the Churches of New England*, Cambridge, Mass., 1968, reprints, with modernized text, *A Sermon Preached by The Reverend Mr. Cotton Deliver'd at Salem 1636* (Boston, 1713), *The Keyes of the Kingdom of Heaven* (London, 1644), and *The Way of Congregational Churches* (London, 1648). See also the edited documents in *Roger Williams, John Cotton, and Religious Freedom*, ed. Irwin H. Polishook, Englewood Cliffs, N.J., 1967.

### BIOGRAPHY AND CRITICISM

Larzer Ziff's *The Career of John Cotton: Puritanism and the American Experience*, Princeton, N.J. 1962, is basically an intellectual history of the New England theocracy. Everett H. Emerson's *John Cotton*, New York, 1965, focuses entirely on the work, not the life.

Briefer studies are Richard Etulian, "John Cotton and the Anne Hutchinson Controversy," *Rendezvous*, II (1967), 9–18; Norman S. Grabo, "John Cotton's Aesthetic: A Sketch," *EALN*, III (1968), 4–10; and Jesper Rosenmeier, "The Teacher and the Witness: John Cotton and Roger Williams," *WMQ*, XXV (1968), 408–431.

## (HAROLD) HART CRANE

### 457. COLLECTED WORKS AND CORRESPONDENCE

Waldo Frank edited *The Complete Poems of Hart Crane*, New York, 1958. Brom Weber's edition of *The Letters of Hart Crane, 1916–1932* (1952) was reissued in Berkeley, Calif., 1965; followed by *The Complete Poems and Selected Letters and Prose of Hart Crane*, ed. Brom Weber, New York, 1966.

Susan Jenkins Brown's *Robber Rocks: Letters and Memories of Hart Crane, 1923–1932*, Middletown, Conn., 1969, combines Crane's letters to the Browns and their friends with a delightful memoir of the man. See also Joseph Katz *et al.*, eds., *Twenty-one Letters from Hart Crane to George*

*Bryan*, Columbus, Ohio, 1968; and William Burford and Christopher Middleton, eds., *The Poet's Vocation: Selections from Letters of Hölderlin, Rimbaud, and Hart Crane*, Austin, Tex., 1967.

BIOGRAPHY AND CRITICISM

The major biography in recent years is a lengthy work by John Unterecker, *Voyager: A Life of Hart Crane*, New York, 1969, which adds much detail to the previous accounts of the poet's life. See also Malcolm Cowley, "Two Winters with Hart Crane," *SR*, LXVII (1959), 547–556; *idem*, "The Leopard in Hart Crane's Brow," *Esquire*, L (Oct., 1958), 257–258 ff.; and the Susan Brown volume described above.

Of the many critical studies of the poet in the last decade, the most important are Herbert A. Leibowitz, *Hart Crane: An Introduction to the Poetry*, New York, 1968, concentrating almost wholly upon the short poems; R. W. B. Lewis, *The Poetry of Hart Crane*, Princeton, N.J., 1967, a comprehensive explication of the whole canon; and L. S. Dembo, *Hart Crane's Sanskrit Charge: A Study of The Bridge*, Ithaca, N.Y., 1960. General introductions for the beginning student are Samuel Hazo, *Hart Crane: An Introduction and Interpretation*, New York, 1963; Vincent G. Quinn, *Hart Crane*, New York, 1963; and Monroe K. Spears's pamphlet, *Hart Crane*, Minneapolis, Minn., 1965. Hunce Voelcker's *The Hart Crane Voyages*, New York, 1967, is an ambitious attempt to recreate "the genetic essence and spirituality" of the six poems. The first full-length European studies are Jean Guiguet, *L'Univers poétique de Hart Crane*, Paris, 1965; and Pietro Spinucci, *Il ponte di Brooklyn: "The Bridge" di Hart Crane e la poesia americana degli anni venti*, Milan, 1966. See also the chapter on Crane in James E. Miller, Jr., Karl Shapiro, and Bernice Slote, *Start with the Sun: Studies in Cosmic Poetry*, Lincoln, Neb., 1960.

Brief estimates are Marius Bewley. "Hart Crane's Last Poem," *Accent*, XIX (1959), 75–85; Henry Braun, "Hart Crane's *The Broken Tower*," *BUSE*, V (1961), 167–177; Sidney Richman, "Hart Crane's 'Voyages II': An Experiment in Redemption," *WSCL*, III (1962), 65–78; Albert Van Nostrand, " 'The Bridge' and Hart Crane's 'Span of Consciousness,' " *Aspects of American Poetry*, ed. Richard M. Ludwig, Columbus, Ohio, 1962, pp. 171–202; David R. Clark, "Hart Crane's Technique," *TSLL*, V (1963), 389–397; John Baker, "Commercial Sources for Hart Crane's *The River*," *WSCL*, VI (1965), 45–55; Maurice Kramer, "Six Voyages of a Derelict Seer," *SR*, LXXIII (1965), 410–423; Thomas A. Vogler, "A New View of Hart Crane's Bridge," *SR*, LXXIII (1965), 381–408; Joseph Riddel, "Hart Crane's Poetics of Failure," *ELH*, XXXIII (1966), 473–496; Patricia McClintock, "A Reading of Hart Crane's 'For the Marriage of Faustus and Helen,' " *MSE*, I (1967), 39–43; and Philip R. Yannella,

"Toward Apotheosis: Hart Crane's Visionary Lyrics," *Criticism*, X (1968), 313–333.

### 458. BIBLIOGRAPHY

Joseph Schwartz's *Hart Crane: An Annotated Critical Bibliography*, New York, 1970, is concerned exclusively with work about Crane. *Hart Crane: A Descriptive Bibliography*, ed. Joseph Schwartz and Robert C. Schweik, Pittsburgh, 1972, is a book-length guide to his printed work. See also Brom Weber's bibliographical essay "Hart Crane" in *Fifteen Modern American Authors*, ed. Jackson R. Bryer, Durham, N.C., 1969, pp. 63–100.

Kenneth A. Lohf compiled *The Literary Manuscripts of Hart Crane*, Columbus, Ohio, 1967, a calendar describing and locating in 16 American libraries all known manuscripts (both prose and poetry) and letters to and from Crane. See also William White, "Hart Crane: Bibliographical Addenda," *BB*, XXIV (1964), 35.


## STEPHEN CRANE

### 458. COLLECTED WORKS AND CORRESPONDENCE

*The University of Virginia Edition of the Works of Stephen Crane*, under the editorship of Fredson Bowers, inaugurated publication with *Bowery Tales: Maggie* [and] *George's Mother*, Charlottesville, Va., 1969, followed by *Tales of Whilomville* (1969), *Tales of Adventure* (1970), and *Tales of War* (1970). The ten volumes will contain "every known piece of Crane's writing and journalism" but will "exclude his letters and memoranda."

Thomas A. Gullason edited, with a particularly informative introduction, *The Complete Novels of Stephen Crane*, Garden City, N.Y., 1967. *The Poems of Stephen Crane: A Critical Edition*, New York, 1966, was prepared by Joseph Katz; *The Complete Short Stories and Sketches of Stephen Crane*, Garden City, N.Y., 1963, by Thomas A. Gullason.

*Stephen Crane: Uncollected Writings*, ed. Olov W. Fryckstedt, appeared in Upsala, Sweden, 1963. It was supplemented by *The War Dispatches of Stephen Crane*, ed. R. W. Stallman and E. R. Hagemann, New York, 1964; and the same editors' collection entitled *The New York City Sketches of Stephen Crane and Related Pieces*, New York, 1966. Thomas A. Gullason printed "A Stephen Crane Find: Nine Newspaper Sketches," *SHR*, II (Winter, 1968), 1–37, six of which were collected along with other material by R. W. Stallman in *Stephen Crane: Sullivan County Tales and Sketches*, Ames, Iowa, 1968. Of specialized interest is *The Notebook of Stephen Crane*, ed. Donald J. Greiner and Ellen B. Greiner, Charlottesville, Va., 1969, covering the years 1892–1894.

R. W. Stallman and Lillian Gilkes edited *Stephen Crane: Letters*, New York, 1960. For additional findings since that date, see Thomas A. Gullason, "The Letters of Stephen Crane: Additions and Corrections," *AL*, XLI (1969), 104-106; and the *Stephen Crane Newsletter*, ed. Joseph Katz, a quarterly publication from the Department of English, University of South Carolina, begun in 1966.

**459. EDITED TEXTS AND REPRINTS**

Reprintings of the fiction including facsimile editions are, of course, numerous. A good general introduction is *The Portable Stephen Crane*, ed. Joseph Katz, New York, 1969. The student will find these editions of special help: *Stephen Crane's Maggie: Text and Context*, ed. Maurice Bassan, Belmont, Calif., 1966; and *Stephen Crane's The Red Badge of Courage: Text and Criticism*, ed. Richard Lettis, Robert F. McDonnell, and William E. Morris, New York, 1959.

**BIOGRAPHY AND CRITICISM**

The most ambitious work to date is R. W. Stallman's *Stephen Crane: A Biography*, New York, 1968; but it is short on critical judgments and long on irrelevant details. In the first half of his lengthy Sorbonne dissertation, *Stephen Crane: Ecrivain-journaliste, 1871-1900*, Paris, 1969, Jean Cazemajou tries to prove Crane's failure as a man; the second, and more valuable half, discusses the work, especially its reception here and abroad. Lillian Gilkes's *Cora Crane: A Biography of Mrs. Stephen Crane*, Bloomington, Ind., 1960, is a beguiling and invaluable account of Crane's last years.

Two general critical surveys are Edwin H. Cady, *Stephen Crane*, New York, 1962; and Donald B. Gibson, *The Fiction of Stephen Crane*, Carbondale, Ill., 1968. See also Jean Cazemajou's pamphlet, *Stephen Crane*, Minneapolis, Minn., 1969. Eric Solomon's *Stephen Crane in England: A Portrait of the Artist*, Columbus, Ohio, 1965, concentrates on Wells, Conrad, Ford, and Henry James; his next study, *Stephen Crane: From Parody to Realism*, Cambridge, Mass., 1966, places Crane's creative work in its American cultural context. Maurice Bassan has compiled *Stephen Crane: A Collection of Critical Essays*, Englewood Cliffs, N.J., 1967.

Of the hundreds of shorter essays, these are a sampling: Donald A. Pizer, "Romantic Individualism in Garland, Norris, and Crane," *AQ*, X (1958), 463-475; Stanley B. Greenfield, "The Unmistakable Stephen Crane," *PMLA*, LXXIII (1958), 562-572; James B. Colvert, "Style and Meaning in Stephen Crane: 'The Open Boat,'" *TxSE*, XXXVII (1958), 34-45; William Bysshe Stein, "Stephen Crane's *Homo Absurdus*," *BuR*, VIII (1959), 168-188; Max Westbrook, "Stephen Crane: The Pattern of

Affirmation," *NCF*, XIV (1959), 219–229; Daniel G. Hoffman, "Stephen Crane's First Story," *BNYPL*, LXIV (1960), 273–278; Joseph X. Brennan, "The Imagery and Art of *George's Mother, CLAJ*, IV (1960), 106–115; Donald Pizer, "The Garland–Crane Relationship," *HLQ*, XXIV (1960), 75–82; A. J. Liebling, "The Dollars Damned Him," *NY*, XXXVII (Aug. 5, 1961), 48–60, 63–66, 69–72; O. W. Fryckstedt, "Stephen Crane in the Tenderloin," *SN*, XXXIV (1962), 135–163; Charles R. Metzger, "Realistic Devices in Stephen Crane's 'The Open Boat,'" *MQ*, IV (1962), 47–54; James B. Stronks, "Stephen Crane's English Years: The Legend Corrected," *PBSA*, LVII (1963), 340–349; David Fitelson, "Stephen Crane's *Maggie* and Darwinism," *AQ*, XVI (1964), 182–194; William L. Howarth, "*The Red Badge of Courage* Manuscript: New Evidence for a Critical Edition," *SB*, XVIII (1965), 229–247; Overton Philip James, "The 'Game' in 'The Bride Comes to Yellow Sky,'" *XUS*, IV (1965), 3–11; Donald Pizer, "Stephen Crane's *Maggie* and American Naturalism," *Criticism*, VII (1965), 168–175; Clark Griffith, "Stephen Crane and the Ironic Last Word," *PQ*, XLVII (1968), 83–91; and Ruth Miller, "Regions of Snow: The Poetic Style of Stephen Crane," *BNYPL*, LXXII (1968), 328–349.

### 460. BIBLIOGRAPHY

Two full descriptive bibliographies are in preparation. Until they appear an adequate substitute is *The Merrill Checklist of Stephen Crane*, compiled by Joseph Katz, Columbus, Ohio, 1969. See also Maurice Beebe and Thomas A. Gullason, "Criticism of Stephen Crane: A Selected Checklist with an Index to Studies of Separate Works," *MFS*, V (1959), 282–291; and the continuing bibliographies by Robert N. Hudspeth in *Thoth* (Syracuse University, Department of English) and by Joseph Katz in *Stephen Crane Newsletter* (University of South Carolina, Department of English).

## (MICHEL-GUILLAUME JEAN) ST. JEAN DE CRÈVECOEUR

### 461. SEPARATE WORKS

*Eighteenth-Century Travels in Pennsylvania and New York*, trans. and ed. Percy G. Adams, Lexington, Ky., 1961, is the first appearance in English of Crèvecoeur's last book. *Journey into Northern Pennsylvania and the State of New York* was newly translated by Clarissa Spencer Bostelmann, Ann Arbor, Mich., 1964.

### BIOGRAPHY AND CRITICISM

Special studies are Marius Bewley, "The Cage and the Prairie: Two Notes on Symbolism" *HudR*, X (1957), 403–414; Albert E. Stone, "Crèvecoeur's *Letters* and the Beginnings of an American Literature," *EUQ*, XVIII (1962), 197–213; Stanley F. Chyet, "Lewisohn and Crèvecoeur," *CJF*, XXII (1963), 130–136; Norman A. Plotkin, "Saint-John de Crèvecoeur Rediscovered: Critic or Panegyrist?" *FHS*, III (1964), 390–404; and Elayne A. Rapping, "Theory and Experience in Crèvecoeur's America," *AQ*, XIX (1967), 707–718.

# E(DWARD) E(STLIN) CUMMINGS
*d. 1962*

## 462. SEPARATE WORKS

*100 Selected Poems*, 1959; *Selected Poems 1923–1958* (London), 1960; *73 Poems*, 1963.

*Adventures in Value*, New York, 1962, contains 50 photographs by Marion Morehouse with a text by Cummings. *Fairy Tales*, a posthumous collection for children, appeared in New York, 1965.

*E. E. Cummings: A Miscellany Revised*, edited with an introduction by George J. Firmage, New York, 1965, corrects the 1958 text of this book and adds seven new pieces. Firmage also edited *Three Plays and a Ballet*, New York, 1967, which reprints *Him; Anthropos: or The Future of Art; Santa Claus, A Morality*; and *Tom, A Ballet*.

F. W. Dupee and George Stade edited *Selected Letters of E. E. Cummings*, New York, 1969.

### BIOGRAPHY AND CRITICISM

The only biography, Charles Norman's *The Magic-Maker: E. E. Cummings* (1958), was revised with a new last chapter, New York, 1964. See also Richard S. Kennedy, "Edward Cummings, the Father of the Poet," *BNYPL*, LXX (1966), 437–449.

The major critical work on Cummings has been done by Norman Friedman. His first book, *E. E. Cummings: The Art of His Poetry*, Baltimore, Md., 1960, was "conceived primarily as a formal study of the poetry, and hence its main topics are technical." In *E. E. Cummings: The Growth of a Poet*, Carbondale, Ill., 1964, "vision and development are the primary concerns, and hence technical matters are treated mainly as they illuminate these concerns." Considerably more elementary is Barry Marks's *E. E. Cummings*, New York, 1964. Robert E. Wegner's *The Poetry and Prose of E. E. Cummings*, New York, 1965, makes Cummings sound unbelievably bland. Eve Triem, *E. E. Cummings*, Minneapolis, Minn., 1969, is a pamphlet. A useful collection of critical essays, edited by Stanley V. Baum, is Σετί: *e e c; E. E. Cummings and the Critics*, East Lansing, Mich., 1962.

Other critical estimates are Philip Green, "an unessay on ee cumMingS," *NR*, CXXXVIII (May 19, 1958), 24–26; Ralph J. Mills, Jr., "The Poetry of Innocence: Notes on E. E. Cummings," *EJ*, XLVIII (1959), 433–442; Marcello Pagnini, "E. E. Cummings: Poetà dell'impressione e dell'analisi," *SA*, IV (1958), 343–361; Michael L. Lasser, "The Agony of E. E. Cummings," *LitR*, V (1961), 133–141; David Ray, "The Irony of E. E. Cummings," *CE*, XXIII (1962), 282–300; John Clendenning, "Cummings, Comedy, and Criticism," *ColQ*, XII (1963), 44–52; Fred E. H. Schroeder, "Obscenity and Its Function in the Poetry of E. E. Cummings," *SR*, LXXIII (1965), 469–478; David E. Smith, "*The Enormous Room* and *Pilgrim's Progress*," *TCL*, XI (1965), 67–75; Cirilo Bautista, "The Bright Monolith: A Note on the Poetry of E. E. Cummings," *SLQ*, III (1965), 517–554; Patricia B. Tal-Mason, "The Whole of E. E. Cummings," *TCL*, XIV (1968), 90–97; and James P. Dougherty, "Language as a Reality in E. E. Cummings," *BuR*, XVI (1968), 112–122.

### 463. BIBLIOGRAPHY

George J. Firmage compiled *E. E. Cummings: A Bibliography*, Middletown, Conn., 1960. For supplements see Norman Friedman, "E. E. Cummings and His Critics," *Criticism*, VI (1964), 114–133.

# JOHN W(ILLIAM) DE FOREST

### 463. SEPARATE WORKS

More than 40 reprints of De Forest's work are available. Under the direction of Joseph Jay Rubin, the Bald Eagle Press is publishing a "Monument Edition" beginning with *Honest John Vane, Playing Mischief*, and *Kate Beaumont* (State College, Pa., 1960, 1961, 1963). The Garrett Press in New York has begun a 17-volume edition under the direction of James F. Light.

### BIOGRAPHY AND CRITICISM

The first "comprehensive study of De Forest's life, mind, and art" is James F. Light's *John William De Forest*, New York, 1965. Edmund Wilson includes a 72-page essay on De Forest in his study of American Civil War literature, *Patriotic Gore*, New York, 1962.

Briefer estimates are James W. Gargano, "A De Forest Interview," *AL*, XXIX (1957), 320–322; Umberto Mariani, "Il realismo di John W. De Forest," *SA*, VII (1961), 77–103; Albert E. Stone, Jr., "Reading, Writing, and History: Best Novel [*Miss Ravenel's Conversion*] of the Civil War," *AH*, XIII (June, 1962), 84–88; Cecil Moffitt, "*Miss Ravenel's Conversion* and *Pilgrim's Progress*," *CE*, XXIII (1962), 352–357; Leo B. Levy, "Naturalism in the Making: De Forest's Honest John Vane," *NEQ*, XXXVII (1964), 89–98; Claude M. Simpson, Jr., "John W. De Forest, *Miss Ravenel's Conversion*," *The American Novel*, ed. Wallace Stegner, New York, 1965, pp. 35–46; James W. Gargano, "John W. De Forest and the Critics," *ALR*, IV (1968), 57–64; Chadwick Hansen, "Salem Witchcraft and De Forest's *Witching Time*," *EIHC*, CIV (1968), 89–108; and E. R. Hagemann, "John William De Forest Faces *The Nation*," *ALR*, IV (1968), 65–75.

Bibliographical guides are James F. Light, "John William De Forest (1826–1906)," *ALR*, I (1967), 32–35; Clayton L. Eichelberger *et al.*, "John William De Forest (1826–1906): A Critical Bibliography of Secondary Criticism," *ALR*, IV (1968), 1–56; and E. R. Hagemann, "A Checklist of Critical Comments in *The Nation* on John William De Forest, 1866–1879," *ALR*, IV (1968), 76–79.

See also Douglas Robillard, "De Forest Literary Manuscripts in the Yale Library," *ALR*, IV (1968), 81–83.

## JOHN DEWEY

### 465. EDITED TEXTS AND REPRINTS

The Southern Illinois University Press has begun publication of *The Early Works of John Dewey: 1882–1898* with Volume I, *1882–1888 Early Essays and Leibniz's New Essays Concerning the Human Understanding* (1969); Volume II, *1887: Psychology* (1967); Volume III, *1889–1892: Early Essays and Outlines of a Critical Theory of Ethics* (1969). Lewis E. Hahn is Chairman of the Editorial Advisory Board. Five volumes are planned.

Reginald D. Archambault edited, for the first time, *Lectures in the Philosophy of Education: 1899*, New York, 1966.

Important Dewey letters (1946–1950) are included in Hadley Cantril's edition of *The Morning Notes of Adelbert Ames, Jr.*, New Brunswick, N.J., 1960. Sidney Ratner and Jules Altman edited *John Dewey and Arthur F. Bentley: A Philosophical Correspondence, 1932–1951*, New Brunswick, N.J., 1964. See also Corinne C. Frost, "John Dewey's Letters to Corinne Chisholm Frost," *CLC*, IX (1960), 34–36; and James Gutmann, "A Note on the Dewey-Frost Correspondence," *CLC*, IX (1960), 32–33. Robert L. McCaul compiled "A Preliminary Listing of Dewey Letters, 1894–1904," *S&S*, LXXXVII (Oct. 10, 1959), 395–399.

Selections from Dewey's work can be found in *Dewey on Education*, ed. Martin S. Dworkin, New York, 1959; *On Experience, Nature, and Free-*

*dom: Representative Selections*, ed. Richard J. Bernstein, Indianapolis, Ind., 1960; *Philosophy, Psychology, and Social Practice*, ed. Joseph Ratner, New York, 1963; *Seleced Educational Writings*, ed. F. W. Garforth, London, 1966; and *John Dewey on Education: Appraisals*, ed. Reginald D. Archambault, New York, 1966.

## 466. BIOGRAPHY AND CRITICISM

Dewey's centennial year, 1959, stimulaed publication of a wide variety of critical volumes. George R. Geiger's *John Dewey in Perspective*, New York, 1958, is a valuable general introduction with "emphasis on the consummatory and esthetic aspects of Dewey's philosophy of experience." More specialized studies are Oscar Handlin, *John Dewey's Challenge to Education: Historical Perspectives on the Cultural Context*, New York, 1959; Robert J. Roth, *John Dewey and Self-Realization*, New York, 1963; Richard J. Bernstein, *John Dewey*, New York, 1966; Arthur G. Wirth, *John Dewey as Educator: His Design for Work in Education, 1894-1904*, New York, 1966; and A. H. Somjee, *The Political Theory of John Dewey*, New York, 1968.

Collections of essays and lectures are William Brickman and Stanley Lehrer, eds., *John Dewey: Master Educator*, New York, 1959; Charles W. Hendel, ed., *John Dewey and the Experimental Spirit in Philosophy*, New York, 1959; John Blewett, S.J., ed., *John Dewey: His Thought and Influence*, New York, 1960; and Douglas E. Lawson and Arthur E. Lean, eds., *John Dewey and the World View*, Carbondale, Ill., 1964. Corliss Lamont edited *Dialogue on John Dewey*, New York, 1959, a transcript of an evening of reminiscences and personal impressions of Dewey by 11 friends and colleagues.

European scholarship includes Adriano Bausola, *L'etica di John Dewey*, Milan, 1960; Tina Manferdini, *L'io e l'esperienza religiosa in John Dewey*, Bologna, 1963; Anselmo Mataix, *Le norma moral en John Dewey*, Madrid, 1964; Saverio Guglielmi, *Individuo e società in John Dewey*, Bologna, 1964; Hart Hendrik, *Communal Certainty and Authorized Truth: An Examination of John Dewey's Philosophy of Verification*, Amsterdam, 1966; and Gérard Deledalle, *L'idée d'expérience dans la philosophie de John Dewey*, Paris, 1967.

See also Morton Levitt, *Freud and Dewey on the Nature of Man*, New York, 1960; Edward Carter Moore, *American Pragmatism: Peirce, James, and Dewey*, New York, 1961; Thomas R. Martland, *The Metaphysics of William James and John Dewey*, New York, 1963; and W. K. Frankena, *Three Historical Philosophies of Education: Aristotle, Kant, Dewey*, Chicago, 1965.

Briefer studies are Robert M. Barry and John Fearon, O.P., "John

Dewey and American Thomism," *ABR*, X (1959), 219–228; Henry David Aiken, "American Pragmatism Reconsidered III: John Dewey," *Com*, XXXIV (1962), 334–344; Max Black, "Dewey's Philosophy of Language," *JP*, LIX (1962), 505–523; and George Dykhuizen, "John Dewey and the University of Michigan," *JHI*, XXIII (1962), 514–544.

Jo Ann Boydston and Robert L. Andresen compiled *John Dewey: A Checklist of Translations, 1900–1967*, Carbondale, Ill., 1969. *Guide to the Works of John Dewey*, ed. Jo Ann Boydston, Carbondale, Ill., 1970, is "a comprehensive bibliography of Dewey's works arranged in 12 categories, each introduced by a Dewey specialist."

# EMILY DICKINSON

### 467. COLLECTED WORKS

*The Complete Poems of Emily Dickinson*, ed. Thomas H. Johnson, Boston, 1960, prints a single version of all known poems. *Final Harvest: Emily Dickinson's Poems*, ed. Thomas H. Johnson, Boston, 1961, is a selection of 575 poems. Both volumes are based on Johnson's three-volume variorum edition of 1955, an addendum to which is David M. Higgins, ed., "Twenty-five Poems by Emily Dickinson: Unpublished Variant Versions," *AL*, XXXVIII (1966), 1–21, taken from Millicent Todd Bingham's papers at Amherst and the Library of Congress. George Monteiro edited a facsimile reproduction of *Poems (1890–1896)*, three volumes in one, Gainesville, Fla., 1967.

The best of the smaller collections are James Reeves, ed., *Selected Poems of Emily Dickinson*, New York, 1959, with an unusually perceptive introduction, and John Malcolm Brinnin, ed., *Emily Dickinson*, New York, 1960.

Stanford P. Rosenbaum edited *A Concordance to the Poems of Emily Dickinson*, Ithaca, N.Y., 1964, more than 100,000 words compiled by electronic computer.

### 468. LETTERS

Thomas H. Johnson edited *Emily Dickinson: Selected Letters*, Cambridge, Mass., 1971, derived from his three-volume edition of the complete *Letters* (1958).

### 469. BIOGRAPHY AND CRITICISM

The raw material for a biography and aids for further research have been gathered by Jay Leyda in *The Years and Hours of Emily Dickinson*, 2 vols., New Haven, Conn., 1960. Theodora Ward's *The Capsule of the*

*Mind*, Cambridge, Mass., 1961, is subtitled *Chapters in the Life of Emily Dickinson*; not a formal biography, it is nevertheless full of essentially original insights, with emphasis on T. W. Higginson and Samuel Bowles. David Higgins draws chiefly on the letters for his *Portrait of Emily Dickinson: The Poet and Her Prose*, New Brunswick, N.J., 1967, a charmingly written book that argues for Bowles as the poet's "master." Of peripheral but important biographical interest are Richard B. Sewall, *The Lyman Letters: New Light on Emily Dickinson and Her Family*, Amherst, Mass., 1965; and Tilden G. Edelstein, *Strange Enthusiasm: A Life of Thomas Wentworth Higginson*, New Haven, Conn., 1968.

Since the appearance of the Johnson texts of the poems and letters, Dickinson scholarship has flourished. Charles R. Anderson's *Emily Dickinson's Poetry: Stairway of Surprise*, New York, 1960, was the first of a growing body of criticism. Of the 15 volumes in the last decade, these are invaluable: Ruth Miller's impressively documented, ambitious work, *The Poetry of Emily Dickinson*, Middletown, Conn., 1968; Albert J. Gelpi's "internal biography" which places the Dickinson canon in the history of American poetry, *Emily Dickinson: The Mind of the Poet*, Cambridge, Mass., 1965; David T. Porter's close reading of the first three hundred poems with much attention to the prosody, *The Art of Emily Dickinson's Early Poetry*, Cambridge, Mass., 1966; Clark Griffith's *The Long Shadow: Emily Dickinson's Tragic Poetry*, Princeton, N.J., 1964, the most romantic and Freudian readings of the poems; and Brita Lindberg-Seyersted's comprehensive linguistic study, *The Voice of the Poet: Aspects of Style in the Poetry of Emily Dickinson*, Cambridge, Mass., 1968.

More specialized studies are Jack L. Capps, *Emily Dickinson's Reading, 1836–1886*, Cambridge, Mass., 1966; R. W. Franklin, *The Editing of Emily Dickinson: A Reconstruction*, Madison, Wis., 1967; and Klaus Lubbers, *Emily Dickinson: The Critical Revolution*, Ann Arbor, Mich., 1968, a survey of the reception of the poet's work over the past century. Thomas W. Ford's *Heaven Beguiles the Tired: Death in the Poetry of Emily Dickinson*, University, Ala., 1966, is overorganized and inconclusively argued. Bio-critical studies are John B. Pickard, *Emily Dickinson: An Introduction and Interpretation*, New York, 1967; Douglas Duncan, *Emily Dickinson*, Edinburgh, 1965; and Denis Donoghue's pamphlet, *Emily Dickinson*, Minneapolis, Minn., 1969, all excellent introductions for the student.

Richard B. Sewall edited *Emily Dickinson: A Collection of Critical Essays*, Englewood Cliffs, N.J., 1963. Caesar R. Blake and Carlton F. Wells assembled a more comprehensive collection, *The Recognition of Emily Dickinson: Selected Criticism since 1890*, Ann Arbor, Mich., 1964. Three papers on Dickinson delivered in Amherst are published in Archibald Mac-

Leish, Louise Bogan, and Richard Wilbur, *Emily Dickinson: Three Views*, Amherst, Mass., 1960. Other brief studies are Sergio Baldi, "La poesia di Emily Dickinson," *SA*, No. 2 (1956), pp. 45–66; Jack Garlington, "Emily Dickinson's Curious Biographers," *ColQ*, VI (1957), 170–177; Richard P. Adams, "Pure Poetry: Emily Dickinson," *TSE*, VII (1957), 133–152; Rebecca Patterson, "Emily Dickinson's Hummingbird," *EL*, XXII (1958), 12–19; Kurt Oppens, "Emily Dickinson: Überlieferung und Prophetie," *Merkur*, XIV (1960), 17–40; Glauco Cambon, "Violence and Abstraction in Emily Dickinson," *SR*, LXVIII (1960), 450–464; Judith Banzer, "'Compound Manner': Emily Dickinson and the Metaphysical Poets," *AL*, XXXII (1961), 415–433; Dennis S. R. Welland, "Emily Dickinson and Her 'Letter to the World,'" *The Great Experiment in American Literature*, ed. Carl Bode, London, 1961, pp. 53–78; Richard Bridgman, "Emily Dickinson: A Winter Poet in a Spring Land," *MSpr*, LVI (1962), 1–8; John Wheatcroft, "Emily Dickinson's Poetry and Jonathan Edwards on the Will," *BuR*, X (1961), 102–127; James E. Miller, Jr., "Emily Dickinson: The Thunder's Tongue," *MinnR*, II (1962), 289–304; Hans Galinsky, "Wege in die dichterische Welt Emily Dickinsons," *Geist einer freien Gesellschaft*, Lewis Hammond *et al.*, eds., Heidelberg, 1962, pp. 221–294; Teut Andreas Riese, "Emily Dickinson und der Sprachgeist amerikanischer Lyrik," *NS*, No. 3 (1963), pp. 145–159; Edith Perry Stamm, "Emily Dickinson: Poetry and Punctuation," *SatR*, XLVI (Mar. 30, 1963), 26–27, 74 [for rebuttal see Theodora Ward's Letter to the Editor, *SatR*, Apr. 27, 1963, and Lindberg-Seyersted's book cited above].

More recent are Suzanne M. Wilson, "Emily Dickinson and Twentieth-Century Poetry of Sensibility," *AL*, XXXVI (1964), 349–358; Jared R. Curtis, "Edward Taylor and Emily Dickinson: Voices and Visions," *SUS*, VII (1964), 159–167; Biancamaria Tedeschini Lalli, "Sul vocabolario poetico di Emily Dickinson," *SA*, X (1964), 181–200; Martha Winburn England, "Emily Dickinson and Isaac Watts: Puritan Hymnodists," *BNYPL*, LXIX (1965), 83–116; Hyatt H. Waggoner, "Emily Dickinson: The Transcendent Self," *Criticism*, VII (1965), 297–334; Paul W. Anderson, "The Metaphysical Mirth of Emily Dickinson," *GaR*, XX (1966), 72–83; John F. Lynen, "Three Uses of the Present: The Historian's, the Critic's, and Emily Dickinson's," *CE*, XXVIII (1966), 126–136; Rebecca Patterson, "Emily Dickinson's Debt to *Günderode*," *MQ*, VIII (1967), 331–354; and Ernest Sandeen, "Delight Deferred by Retrospect: Emily Dickinson's Late-Summer Poems," *NEQ*, XL (1967), 483–500.

### 470. BIBLIOGRAPHY

The major reference is Willis J. Buckingham's *Emily Dickinson, An Annotated Bibliography: Writings, Scholarship, Criticism, and Ana, 1850–*

*1968*, Bloomington, Ind., 1970. Sheila T. Clendenning, *Emily Dickinson, A Bibliography: 1850–1966*, Kent, Ohio, 1968, and the listings by Millicent Todd Bingham in her revision (1967) of *Ancestor's Brocades: The Literary Debut of Emily Dickinson* (New York, 1945) are also useful. Blake and Wells provide full listings of criticism in their volume cited above. See also Paola Guidetta, "La fortuna di Emily Dickinson in Italia (1931–1962)," *SA*, IX (1964), 121–172.

*The Emily Dickinson Bulletin*, ed. Frederick L. Morey, began publication in 1968 in Brentwood, Maryland.


## JOHN DICKINSON

### 471. BIOGRAPHY AND CRITICISM

The most recent full-length study is David L. Jacobson's *John Dickinson and the Revolution in Pennsylvania, 1764–1776*, Berkeley, Calif., 1965. See also H. Trevor Colburn, "John Dickinson: Historical Revolutionary," *PMHB*, LXXXIII (1959), 271–292; *idem*, "A Pennsylvania Farmer at the Court of King George: John Dickinson's London Letters, 1754–1756," *PMHB*, LXXXVI (1962), 241–286; and Bernhard Knollenberg, "John Dickinson vs. John Adams: 1774–1776," *PAPS*, CVII (1963), 138–144.


## HILDA DOOLITTLE (ALDINGTON)
## ("H. D.")
### *d. 1961*

### 472. SEPARATE WORKS

*Selected Poems of H. D.*, 1957; *Bid Me to Live*, 1960; *Helen in Egypt*, 1961.

### BIOGRAPHY AND CRITICISM

Important biographical information is in *The Heart of Artemis*, New York, 1962, the autobiography of Bryher, H. D.'s closest friend and benefactor; and in *D. H. Lawrence: A Composite Biography*, 3 vols., ed. Edward Nehls, Madison, Wis., 1957–1959.

The best introduction to her whole career is Vincent Quinn's *Hilda Doolittle (H. D.)*, New York, 1967. An earlier study, Thomas Burnett Swann's *The Classical World of H. D.*, Lincoln, Neb., 1962, is concerned only with her work on classical subjects.

For briefer estimates see Kathryn Gibbs Gibbons, "The Art of H. D.," *MissQ*, XV (1962), 152–160; and Ruggero Bianchi, "Saffo in America:

Hilda Doolittle," *SA*, XI (1965), 197–211. *Contemporary Literature*, X (1969), is a special issue devoted to H. D., containing critical articles, selected letters and poems, and a preliminary checklist.

## JOHN (RODERIGO) DOS PASSOS
### d. 1970

**473. SEPARATE WORKS**

*Prospects of a Golden Age*, 1959; *Midcentury*, 1961; *Mr. Wilson's War*, 1962; *Brazil on the Move*, 1963; *Occasions and Protests*, 1964; *Thomas Jefferson: The Making of a President*, 1964; *The Best Times: An Informal Memoir*, 1966; *The Shackles of Power: Three Jeffersonian Decades*, 1966; *The Portugal Story: Three Centuries of Exploration and Discovery*, 1969; *Easter Island: Island of Enigmas*, 1971.

**REPRINTS**

Kenneth S. Lynn edited *World in a Glass: A View of Our Century Selected from the Novels of John Dos Passos*, Boston, 1966.

**BIOGRAPHY AND CRITICISM**

The best critical studies are John H. Wrenn, *John Dos Passos*, New York, 1961; and Robert Gorham Davis's pamphlet, *John Dos Passos*, Minneapolis, Minn., 1962. George A. Knox and Herbert M. Stahl treat the New Playwrights Theatre experiment of the 1920's in *Dos Possos and "The Revolting Playwrights,"* Upsala, Sweden, 1964. See also Frederick Feied, *No Pie in the Sky: The Hobo as American Cultural Hero in the Works of Jack London, John Dos Passos, and Jack Kerouac*, New York, 1964; and Renate Schmidt-von Bardeleben, *Das Bild New Yorks im Erzählwerk von Dreiser und Dos Passos*, Munich, 1967.

Briefer estimates are James S. Smith, "The Novelist of Discomfort: A Reconsideration of John Dos Passos," *CE*, XIX (1958) 332–338; Richard Chase, "The Chronicles of Dos Passos," *Com*, XXXI (1961), 395–400; Blanche Gelfant, "The Search for Identity in the Novels of John Dos Passos," *PMLA*, LXXVI (1961), 133–149; David Sanders, "The 'Anarchism' of John Dos Passos," *SAQ*, LX (1961), 44–55; Daniel Aaron, "The Riddle of John Dos Passos," *Harpers*, CCXXIV (Mar., 1962), 55–60; John P. Diggins, "Dos Passos and Veblen's Villains," *AR*, XXIII (1963–1964), 485–500; E. A. Lowry, *"Manhattan Transfer*: Dos Passos' Wasteland," *UR*, XXX (1963), 47–52; David Sanders, "Interview with John Dos Passos," *ClareQ*, XI (1964), 89–100; *idem*, "'Lies' and the System: Enduring Themes from Dos Passos' Early Novels," *SAQ*, LXV (1966),

215–228; and Kenneth Ledbetter, "The Journey of John Dos Passos," *HAB*, XVIII (1967), 36–48.

A supplement to the Potter bibliography is in Virginia S. Reinhart, "John Dos Passos Bibliography: 1950–1966," *TCL*, XIII (1967), 167–178.

# THEODORE (HERMAN ALBERT) DREISER

### 474. SEPARATE WORKS

*Selected Poems by Theodore Dreiser* was edited by Robert Palmer Saalbach, New York, 1969.

From the Dreiser Papers at the University of Pennsylvania, Robert H. Elias edited a three-volume edition of *Letters of Theodore Dreiser*, Philadelphia, 1959. Louise Campbell, literary assistant and confidante of Dreiser from 1917 to 1945, edited with commentary *Letters to Louise*, Philadelphia, 1959, but the scholarship is seriously defective and the volume must be used with caution.

### 475. BIOGRAPHY AND CRITICISM

W. A. Swanberg's biography, *Dreiser*, New York, 1965, is a massive accumulation of familiar and previously unpublished material, a lively, full treatment of Dreiser's career. Ellen Moers's *Two Dreisers*, New York, 1969, is "a journey into the mind" of the novelist and the story of how *Sister Carrie* and *An American Tragedy* got written, but it is also partly a biographical account. A complement to both books is Marguerite Tjader, *Theodore Dreiser: A New Dimension*, Norwalk, Conn., 1965, a personal reminiscence, particularly well informed on his last years. Ruth Epperson Kennell, *Theodore Dreiser and the Soviet Union, 1927–1945: A First-Hand Chronicle*, New York, 1969, recounts in detail Dreiser's Russian tour, November, 1927–January, 1928, and its influence on his late work. It prints many previously unpublished letters.

Two bio-critical studies for the reader new to Dreiser's work are Philip L. Gerber, *Theodore Dreiser*, New York, 1964; and John J. McAleer, *Theodore Dreiser: An Introduction and Interpretation*, New York, 1968. Charles Shapiro *Theodore Dreiser: Our Bitter Patriot*, Carbondale, Ill., 1962; and Richard Lehan, *Theodore Dreiser: His World and His Novels*, Carbondale, Ill., 1969, concentrate on the fiction. European studies include Karl-Heinz Wirzberger, *Die Romane Theodore Dreisers*, Berlin, 1955; Cyrille Arnavon, *Theodore Dreiser: romancier américain*, Paris, 1956; and Renate Schmidt-von Bardeleben, *Das Bild New Yorks in Erzählwerk von Dreiser und Dos Passos*, Munich, 1967.

Briefer estimates are Randall Stewart, "Dreiser and the Naturalistic

Heresy," *VQR*, XXXIV (1958), 100–116; William J. Handy, "A Re-examination of Dreiser's *Sister Carrie*," *TSLL*, I (1959), 380–393; J. D. Thomas, "The Supernatural Naturalism of Dreiser's Novels," *RIP*, XLVI (1959), 53–69; Kenneth Bernard, "The Flight of Theodore Dreiser," *UKCR*, XXVI (1960), 251–259; Julian Markels, "Dreiser and the Plotting of Inarticulate Experience," *MR*, II (1961), 431–448; Sidney Richman, "Theodore Dreiser's *The Bulwark*: A Final Resolution," *AL*, XXXIV (1962), 229–245; Robert Penn Warren, *"An American Tragedy,"* *YR*, LII (1962), 1–15; Sheldon Norman Grebstein, "Dreiser's Victorian Vamp," *MASJ*, IV (1963), 3–12; William L. Phillips, "The Imagery of Dreiser's Novels," *PMLA*, LXXVIII (1963), 572–585; Charles Thomas Samuels, "Mr. Trilling, Mr. Warren, and *An American Tragedy*," *YR*, LIII (1964), 629–640; Yoshinobu Hakutani, "Dreiser and French Realism," *TSLL*, VI (1964), 200–212; Vern Wagner, "The Maligned Style of Theodore Dreiser," *WHR*, XIX (1965), 175–184; Claude M. Simpson, Jr., "Theodore Dreiser, *Sister Carrie*," *The American Novel*, ed. Wallace Stegner, New York, 1965, pp. 106–116; Lauriat Lane, Jr., "The Double in *An American Tragedy*," *MFS*, XII (1966), 213–220; Donald R. Stoddard, "Mencken and Dreiser: An Exchange of Roles," *LC*, XXXII (1966), 117–136; Strother B. Purdy, *"An American Tragedy* and *L'Etranger*," *CL*, XIX (1967), 252–268; Jack Salzman, "The Publication of *Sister Carrie*: Fact and Fiction," *LC*, XXXIII (1967), 119–133; and Walter Blackstock, "The Fall and Rise of Eugene Witla: Dramatic Vision of Artistic Integrity in *The 'Genius,'* " *LangQ*, V (1967), 15–18.

See also the sections on Dreiser in H. Wayne Morgan, *American Writers in Rebellion from Mark Twain to Dreiser*, New York, 1965; and Larzer Ziff, *The American 1890's: Life and Times of a Lost Generation*, New York, 1966.

### 477. BIBLIOGRAPHY

A much-needed compilation is Hugh C. Atkinson, *Theodore Dreiser: A Checklist*, Kent, Ohio, 1970. An important bibliographical essay by the editor of the Dreiser letters is Robert H. Elias, "Theodore Dreiser," *Fifteen Modern American Authors*, ed. Jackson R. Bryer, Durham N.C., 1969, pp. 101–138.

## PAUL LAURENCE DUNBAR

### 477. COLLECTED WORKS AND REPRINTS

*The Complete Poems of Paul Laurence Dunbar* (1913) was reprinted in New York, 1962; *Lyrics of Lowly Life* (1896) in New York, 1969.

Recent studies are James B. Stronk, "Paul Laurence Dunbar and William Dean Howells," *OHQ*, LXVII (1958), 95–108; and Darwin T. Turner, "Paul Laurence Dunbar: The Rejected Symbol," *JNH*, LII (1967), 1–13.

# WILLIAM DUNLAP

### 478. SEPARATE WORKS

Alexander Wyckoff edited an enlarged and revised edition of *A History of the Rise and Progress of the Arts of Design in the United States*, New York, 1965.

### 479. BIOGRAPHY AND CRITICISM

The chief work on Dunlap in recent years is Harold E. Dickson's *Arts of the Young Republic: The Age of William Dunlap*, Chapel Hill, N.C., 1968, spanning the years 1780–1834. See also Robert H. Canary, "William Dunlap and the Search for an American Audience," *MASJ*, IV (1963), 45–51; and Oral S. Coad, "William Dunlap: New Jersey Artist," *PNJHS*, LXXXIII (1965), 238–263.

# TIMOTHY DWIGHT

### 480. SEPARATE WORKS

*Travels in New-England and New-York (1821–1822)* has been recently edited by Barbara Miller Soloman in four volumes, Cambridge, Mass., 1969. *The Major Poems of Timothy Dwight*, ed. William J. McTaggart and William K. Bottoroff, Gainesville, Fla., 1969, is a facsimile reprinting of *America*, *The Conquest of Canaan*, *The Triumph of Infidelity*, and *Greenfield Hill*.

### BIOGRAPHY AND CRITICISM

The first full-length critical study is Kenneth Silverman, *Timothy Dwight*, New York, 1969. Briefer studies are Abe C. Ravitz, "Timothy Dwight's Decisions," *NEQ*, XXXI (1959), 514–519; Robert Edson Lee, "Timothy Dwight and the Boston *Palladium*," *NEQ*, XXXV (1962), 229–239; Jack Stillinger, "Dwight's *Triumph of Infidelity*: Text and Interpretation," *SB*, XV (1962), 259–266; Edmund S. Morgan, "Ezra Stiles and Timothy Dwight," *PMHS*, LXXII (1963), 101–117; Vincent Freimarck, "Rhetoric at Yale in 1807," *PAPS*, CX (1966), 235–255; and Kathryn Whitford, "Excursions into Romanticism: Timothy Dwight's *Travels*," *PLL*, II (1966), 225–233.

# JONATHAN EDWARDS

### 482. COLLECTED WORKS AND LETTERS

The Yale University Press edition of *The Works of Jonathan Edwards* proceeds with *A Treatise Concerning Religious Affections*, ed. John E. Smith, 1959; and *The Great Christian Doctrine of Original Sin Defended*, ed. Clyde A. Holbrook, 1970.

### 483. EDITED TEXTS AND REPRINTS

*"The Mind" of Jonathan Edwards: A Reconstructed Text*, ed. Leon Howard, Berkeley, Calif., 1963, is based on Edwards's youthful notebooks, first published in 1830.

### BIOGRAPHY AND CRITICISM

Seven critical studies in the last decade investigate all sides of Edwards's thought. Alfred O. Aldridge's *Jonathan Edwards*, New York, 1964, is a brief bio-critical study, a concise but unorthodox introduction. Edward H. Davidson's *Jonathan Edwards: The Narrative of a Puritan Mind*, Boston, 1966 (reissued Cambridge, Mass., 1968), is an intellectual biography, concentrating on Edwards's spiritual pilgrimage. Conrad Cherry's *The Theology of Jonathan Edwards: A Reappraisal*, Garden City, N.Y., 1966, is written from the perspective of Edwards's theory of faith, as is James Carse's *Jonathan Edwards and the Visibility of God*, New York, 1967. John H. Gerstner calls his work a highly restricted monograph, its emphasis indicated in the subtitle: *Steps to Salvation: The Evangelistic Message of Jonathan Edwards*, Philadelphia, 1960. Interpretation of Edwards's ontology and theology is at the heart of Douglas J. Elwood's *The Philosophical Theology of Jonathan Edwards*, New York, 1960. Still another approach to the essence of Edwards's thought is Roland André Delattre's *Beauty and Sensibility in the Thought of Jonathan Edwards: An Essay in Aesthetics and Theological Ethics*, New Haven, Conn., 1968.

Briefer estimates are gathered in *Jonathan Edwards: A Profile*, ed., David Levin, New York, 1969. See also William S. Morris, "The Reappraisal of Edwards," *NEQ*, XXX (1957), 515–525; C. C. Goen, "Jonathan Edwards: A New Departure in Eschatology," *CH*, XXVIII (Mar. 1959), 25–40; Arthur E. Murphy, "Jonathan Edwards on Free Will and Moral Agency," *PhR*, LXVIII (1959), 181–202; Wallace E. Anderson, "Immaterialism in Jonathan Edwards' Early Philosophical Notes," *JHI*,

XXV (1964), 181–200; Daniel B. Shea, Jr., "The Art and Instruction of Jonathan Edwards' *Personal Narrative*," *AL*, XXXVII (1964), 17–32; Claude A. Smith, "Jonathan Edwards and 'The Way of Ideas,'" *HTR*, LIX (1966), 153–173; Clyde A Holbrook, "Edwards and the Ethical Question," *HTR*, LX (1967), 163–175; Gail T. Parker, "Jonathan Edwards and Melancholy," *NEQ*, XLI (1968), 193–212; David C. Pierce, "Jonathan Edwards and the 'New Sense' of Glory," *NEQ*, XLI (1968), 82–95; and George Rupp, "The 'Idealism' of Jonathan Edwards," *HTR*, LXII (1969), 209–226.

## EDWARD EGGLESTON

**485.** SEPARATE WORKS

An 11-volume edition of *The Works of Edward Eggleston* is being prepared by William Peirce Randel for the Garrett Press of New York.

BIOGRAPHY AND CRITICISM

William Peirce Randel has followed his full-length biography (1946) with a briefer critical survey, *Edward Eggleston*, New York, 1963. See also Anne Beard, "Games and Recreations in the Novels of Edward Eggleston," *MF*, XI (1961), 85–104; Clarence A. Brown, "Edward Eggleston as a Social Historian," *ISHSJ*, LIV (1962), 405–418; and Thorp L. Wolford, "Edward Eggleston: Evolution of a Historian," *Indiana Magazine of History*, LXIII (1967), 17–48.

Bibliographical listings are in Jacob Blanck, *Bibliography of American Literature*, III, New Haven, Conn., 1959, 1–15; and William Peirce Randel, "Edward Eggleston (1837–1902)," *ALR*, I (1967), 36–38.

## JOHN ELIOT

**487.** BIOGRAPHY AND CRITICISM

The much-needed biography has at last been published, Ola Elizabeth Winslow's *John Eliot, "Apostle to the Indians,"* Boston, 1968.

## T(HOMAS) S(TEARNS) ELIOT
### *d. 1965*

**488.** SEPARATE WORKS

*Geoffrey Faber: 1889–1961*, 1961; *George Herbert*, 1962; *Knowledge and Experience in the Philosophy of F. H. Bradley*, 1964; *To Criticize the Critic, and Other Writings*, 1965.

489. COLLECTIONS AND REPRINTS

*Collected Poems, 1909–1962* appeared in New York and London, 1963. *The Complete Plays*, New York, 1969, was followed by *The Complete Poems and Plays*, London, 1969. *Poems Written in Early Youth*, compiled by John Hayward and formerly available only in a private edition, was reissued in New York and London, 1967. *The Waste Land: A Facsimile and Transcript of the Original Drafts*, edited by Valerie Eliot, was published simultaneously in London and New York, 1971. Reprintings of other volumes are too numerous to list separately.

BIOGRAPHY AND CRITICISM

The first critical biography is Bernard Bergonzi's *T. S. Eliot*, New York, 1971. Robert Sencourt's *T. S. Eliot: A Memoir*, New York, 1971, is an intimate record of a long friendship, edited by Donald Adamson and published two years after Sencourt's death. What might be called an intellectual biography is Herbert Howarth's portrait of Eliot and his age, *Notes on Some Figures behind T. S. Eliot*, Boston, 1964. Over 70 letters by Eliot are quoted from in William Turner Levy and Victor Scherle, *Affectionately, T. S. Eliot: The Story of a Friendship: 1947–1965*, Philadelphia, 1968. See also Donald Hall's *Paris Review* interview, No. 21 (1959); Leslie Paul, "A Conversation with T. S. Eliot," *KR* (Spring, 1964); Allesandro Pelligrini's "London Conversation with T. S. Eliot," *SR* (Spring, 1949); and the personal reminiscences included in Allen Tate, ed., *T. S. Eliot: The Man and His Work*, New York, 1966.

Of the more than 60 books on Eliot's work that have appeared in the last 12 years, five are indispensable: Hugh Kenner's comprehensive elucidation of the poet's career, *The Invisible Poet: T. S. Eliot*, New York, 1959; Northrop Frye's 100-page essay, not designed for beginners, *T. S. Eliot*, London, 1963; Leonard Unger's gathering of seven of his essays, *T. S. Eliot: Moments and Patterns*, Minneapolis, Minn., 1966; David E. Jones's *The Plays of T. S. Eliot*, London, 1960; and Marion Montgomery's *T. S. Eliot: An Essay on the American Magus*, Athens, Ga., 1969. To this group must also be added the revised edition (New York, 1961) of Kristian Smidt's *Poetry and Belief in the Work of T. S. Eliot*, first published in Oslo, 1949.

Three general introductions will serve the student well: Philip R. Headings, *T. S. Eliot*, New York, 1964; T. S. Pearce, *T. S. Eliot*, London, 1967; and Neville Braybrooke, *T. S. Eliot: A Critical Essay*, Grand Rapids, Mich., 1967. Genesius Jones's *Approach to the Purpose*, London, 1964, is devoted exclusively to the poetry; Seán Lucy's *T. S. Eliot and the Idea of Tradition*, London, 1960, chiefly to the critical writing. E. Martin Browne's genetic study, *The Making of T. S. Eliot's Plays*, Cambridge, Eng., 1969, benefits from his having directed all of the major plays. Carol H. Smith concentrates on *T. S. Eliot's Dramatic Theory and Practice: From Sweeney Agonistes to The Elder Statesman*, Princeton, N. J., 1963. The best introduction to Eliot's critical prose is Fei-Pai Lu's *T. S. Eliot: The Dialectical Structure of His Theory of Poetry*, Chicago, 1966. Eric Thompson gives a full treatment of F. H. Bradley's relation to Eliot's criticism and of the philosophical background of "Burnt Norton" in *T. S. Eliot: The Metaphysical Perspective*, Carbondale, Ill., 1963. Of the exegeses of *Four Quartets*, the earliest is C. A. Bodelsen, *T. S. Eliot's Four Quartets: A Commentary*, Copenhagen, 1958, 2nd ed., 1966; but see also Staffan Bergsten, *Time and Eternity: A Study of the Structure and Symbolism of T. S. Eliot's Four Quartets*, Stockholm, 1960; and Harry Blamires, *Word Unheard: A Guide through Eliot's Four Quartets*, London, 1969. Robert E. Knoll's *Storm over the Waste Land*, Chicago, 1964, is a source book for college classes; more ambitious and inclusive is Jay Martin's *A Collection of Critical Essays on "The Waste Land,"* Englewood Cliffs, N.J., 1968. Among the best foreign-language studies are Rudolf Germer, *T. S. Eliots Anfänge als Lyriker (1905–1915)*, Heidelberg, 1966; Karl Schlüter, *Der Mensch als Schauspieler: Studien zur Deutung von T. S. Eliots Gesellschaftsdramen*, Bonn, 1962; Laura Caretti, *T. S. Eliot in Italia*, Bari, 1968; Sunil Kanti Sen, *Metaphysical Tradition and T. S. Eliot*, Calcutta, 1965; and Vikramaditya Rai, *The Waste Land: A Critical Study*, Varanasi, 1965. See also four essays on Eliot collected in *Amerika: Vision und Wirklichkeit*, ed. Franz H. Link, Frankfurt am Main, 1968.

In the last decade, several valuable collections of essays on Eliot have appeared. Neville Braybrooke edited *T. S. Eliot: A Symposium for His Seventieth Birthday*, New York, 1958. Hugh Kenner reprints 19 pieces (1931–1959) in *T. S. Eliot: A Collection of Critical Essays*, Englewood Cliffs, N.J., 1962; P. Lal edited 55 essays and elegies in *T. S. Eliot: Homage from India*, Calcutta, 1965; Masao Hirai and E. W. F. Tomlin gathered 12 essays in *T. S. Eliot: A Tribute from Japan*, Tokyo, 1966; and Graham Martin edited 15 essays for *Eliot in Perspective*, London, 1970. The special issue of *Sewanee Review* (Jan.–Mar., 1966), edited by Allen Tate, reprinted under the title *T. S. Eliot: The Man and His Work*, New York, 1966, is the richest and most varied of all these collections. See also the chapters devoted to Eliot in A. Alvarez, *The Shaping Spirit*, London, 1961 (published in New York under the title *Stewards of Excellence*); J. Hillis Miller, *Poets of Reality*, Cambridge, Mass., 1965; and John F. Lynen, *The Design of the Present*, New Haven, Conn., 1969.

Other brief studies are C. L. Wrenn, "T. S. Eliot and the Language of Poetry," *Thought*, XXXII (1957), 239–254; E. P. Bollier, "T. S. Eliot and John Milton: A Problem in Criticism," *TSE*, VIII (1958), 165–192; Harvey Gross, "*Gerontion* and the Meaning of History," *PMLA*, LXXIII (1958), 299–304; F. R. Leavis, "T. S. Eliot's Stature as a Critic," *Com*, XXVI (1958), 399–410; John Wain, "A Walk in the Sacred Wood," *LonM*, V (1958), 45–53; Edmund Wilson, "'Miss Buttle' and 'Mr. Eliot,'" *NY*, XXXIV (May 24, 1958), 112–142; Sister Mary Gerard, "Eliot of the Circle and John of the Cross," *Thought*, XXXIV (1959), 107–127; Allen Austin, "T. S. Eliot's Objective Correlative," *UKCR*, XXVI (1959), 133–140; Denis Donoghue, "Eliot in the Sibyl's Leaves," *SR*, LXVIII (1960), 138–143; Grover Smith, Jr., "Getting Used to T. S. Eliot," *EJ*, XLIX (1960), 1–9, 15; Merrell D. Clubb, Jr., "The Heraclitean Element in Eliot's *Four Quartets*," *PQ*, XL (1961), 19–33; Katherine Anne Porter, "On First Meeting Mr. Eliot," *Shen*, XII (1961), 25–26; Carl Wooton, "The Mass: 'Ash Wednesday's' Objective Correlative," *ArQ*, XVII (1961), 31–42; William Wasserstrom, "T. S. Eliot and *The Dial*," *SR*, LXX (1962), 81–92; E. P. Bollier, "T. S. Eliot and F. H. Bradley: A Question of Influence," *TSE*, XII (1962), 87–111; Everett A. Gillis, "Religion in a Sweeney World," *ArQ*, XX (1964), 55–63; Austin Warren, "Continuity in T. S. Eliot's Criticism," *EWR*, I (1964), 1–12; Kenneth J. Reckford, "Heracles and Mr. Eliot," *CL*, XVI (1964), 1–18; William V. Spanos, "T. S. Eliot's *The Family Reunion*: The Strategy of Sacramental Transfiguration," *DramS*, IV (1965), 3–27; Stephen Spender, "Remembering Eliot," *Encounter*, XXIV (1965), 3–14; and Elizabeth K. Hewitt, "Structure and Meaning in T. S. Eliot's *Ash Wednesday*," *Anglia*, LXXXIII (1965), 426–450.

More recent studies are Helen Gardner, "The Comedies of T. S. Eliot," *EDH*, XXXIV (1966), 55–73; Hugh Kenner, "Eliot and the Tradition of the Anonymous," *CE*, XXVIII (1967), 558–564; Ronald Tamplin, "*The Tempest* and *The Waste Land*," *AL*, XXXIX (1967), 352–372; Philip LeBrun, "T. S. Eliot and Henry Bergson," *RES*, XVIII (1967), 149–161, 274–286; F. W. Bateson, "T. S. Eliot: The Poetry of Pseudo-Learning," *JGE*, XX (1968), 13–27; John Halverson, "Prufrock, Freud, and Others," *SR*, LXXVI (1968), 571–588; John Crowe Ransom, "A Postscript," *SoR*, IV (1968), 579–597; Richard Wasson, "The Rhetoric of Theatre: The Contemporaneity of T. S. Eliot," *DramS*, VI (1968), 231–243; Donald Gallup, "The 'Lost' Manuscripts of T. S. Eliot," *TLS* (Nov. 7, 1968), pp. 1238–1240; F. W. Bateson, "Editorial Commentary," *EIC*, XIX (1969), 1–5; Murray Krieger, "The Critical Legacy of Matthew Arnold: Or the Strange Brotherhood of T. S. Eliot, I. A. Richards, and Northrop Frye," *SoR*, V (1969), 457–474; Harold H. Watts, "The Tragic Hero in Eliot and Yeats," *CentR*, XIII (1969), 84–100; F. R. Leavis, "T. S. Eliot and the Life of English Literature: Opening Address at the Cheltenham Festival of Literature, October 1968," *MR*, X (1969), 9–34; and Donald Gallup, "T.

S. Eliot and Ezra Pound: Collaborators in Letters," *Atl*, CCXXV (Jan., 1970), 48–62.

### 492. BIBLIOGRAPHY

The essential work of reference for all students of Eliot is Donald Gallup, *T. S. Eliot: A Bibliography*, New York, 1969, a thorough revision of the 1953 volume. Translations are surveyed in Hans W. Bentz, *Thomas Stearns Eliot in Übersetzungen*, Frankfurt am Main, 1963; and Laura Caretti devotes the second half of *T. S. Eliot in Italia*, Bari, 1968, to a listing of Eliot translations and criticism.

Mildred Martin's *A Half-Century of Eliot Criticism, 1916–1965*, Cranbury, N.J., 1971, is an annotated bibliography of criticism in English, arranged chronologically and cross-indexed by subject, author, and title. Richard M. Ludwig, "T. S. Eliot," *Fifteen Modern American Authors*, ed. Jackson R. Bryer, Durham, N.C., 1969, pp. 139–174 is a bibliographical essay and survey of Eliot's critical reception. Bradley Gunter compiled *The Merrill Checklist of T. S. Eliot*, Columbus, Ohio, 1970. Additional listings of critical studies of Eliot can be found in the books by David E. Jones and Fei-Pai Lu, discussed above.

# RALPH WALDO EMERSON

### 492. COLLECTED WORKS AND CORRESPONDENCE

*Nature, Addresses, and Lectures*, ed. Robert E. Spiller, will inaugurate a new edition of *The Collected Works of Ralph Waldo Emerson* by Harvard University Press, under the general editorship of Alfred R. Ferguson.

Harvard University Press is publishing *The Journals and Miscellaneous Notebooks of Ralph Waldo Emerson* in 16 volumes, of which these have appeared: Volume I (1819–1822), ed. William H. Gilman, Alfred Ferguson, George P. Clark, Merrell R. Davis, 1960; Volume II (1822–1826), ed. William H. Gilman, Alfred R. Ferguson, Merrell R. Davis, 1961; Volume III (1826–1832), ed. William H. Gilman and Alfred R. Ferguson, 1963; Volume IV (1832–1834), ed. Alfred R. Ferguson; Volume V (1835–1838), ed. Merton M. Sealts, Jr., 1965; Volume VI (1824–1838) [notebooks only], ed. Ralph H. Orth, 1966; Volume VII (1838–1842), ed. A. W. Plumstead and Harrison Hayford, 1969; Volume VIII (1841–1843), ed. William H. Gilman and J. E. Parsons, 1971. William H. Gilman is Chief Editor of the series.

The three-volume edition of *The Early Lectures* is now complete, also from Harvard University Press: Volume I (1833–1836), ed. Stephen E. Whicher and Robert E. Spiller, 1959; Volume II (1836–1838), ed. Stephen E. Whicher, Robert E. Spiller, and Wallace E. Williams, 1964; Volume III (1838–1842), ed. Robert E. Spiller and Wallace E. Williams, 1972.

Joseph Slater's new edition of *The Correspondence of Emerson and Carlyle*, New York, 1964, re-edits the 1883 Norton edition. Edith W. Gregg edited *One First Love: The Letters of Ellen Louisa Tucker to Ralph Waldo Emerson*, Cambridge, Mass., 1962. See also gleanings published intermittently in the *Emerson Society Quarterly* (1955–current), ed. Kenneth W. Cameron.

### 493. EDITED TEXTS

Of the many reprints and collections of Emerson's work in recent years, these are notable: Stephen E. Whicher, ed., *Selections from Ralph Waldo Emerson*, Boston, 1957, an "organic anthology"; Alfred Kazin and Daniel Aaron, eds., *Emerson: A Modern Anthology*, Boston, 1959, for a topical arrangement; Robert E. Spiller, ed., *Selected Essays, Lectures and Poems of Ralph Waldo Emerson*, New York, 1965; Howard Mumford Jones, ed., *Emerson on Education: Selections*, New York, 1966; Lewis Mumford, ed., *Ralph Waldo Emerson: Essays and Journals*, New York, 1968; and Merton M. Sealts, Jr., and Alfred R. Ferguson, eds., *Emerson's 'Nature': Origin, Growth, Meaning*, New York, 1969.

### 494. BIOGRAPHY AND CRITICISM

The only addendum to the Ralph Rusk biography (1949) is Henry F. Pommer, *Emerson's First Marriage*, Carbondale, Ill., 1967.

The two major critical studies in the last decade are Jonathan Bishop's *Emerson on the Soul*, Cambridge, Mass., 1964; and Joel Porte's *Emerson and Thoreau: Transcendentalists in Conflict*, Middletown, Conn., 1966. Several others are equally acute but more specialized. Philip L. Nicoloff examines the production of *English Traits*, its principal ideas, and Emerson's racial theories in *Emerson on Race and History*, New York, 1961. Michael H. Cowan treats Emerson's literary fusion of several mythic themes in *City of the West: Emerson, America, and Urban Metaphor*, New Haven, Conn., 1967. Edmund G. Berry, *Emerson's Plutarch*, Cambridge, Mass., 1961, stresses the influence of Plutarch's moral essays rather than Neo-Platonic and Oriental reading on Emerson's thought. In *Emerson's Impact on the British Isles and Canada*, Charlottesville, Va., 1966, William J. Sowder traces the rise and fall of Emerson's reputation during the years 1840–1903. Two European studies are Edith Mettke, *Der Dichter Ralph*

*Waldo Emerson: Mystisches Denken und Poetischer Ausdruck,* Heidelberg, 1963, concentrating on the early poetry; and Maurice Gonnaud, *Individu et société dans l'oeuvre de Ralph Waldo Emerson,* Paris, 1964, a *biographie spirituelle.* A Japanese study is Yukio Irie, *Emerson and Quakerism,* Tokyo, 1967. Josephine Miles, *Ralph Waldo Emerson,* Minneapolis, Minn., 1964, is a perceptive brief survey of the whole career.

Briefer estimates have been edited by Milton R. Konvitz and Stephen E. Whicher in *Emerson: A Collection of Critical Essays,* Englewood Cliffs, N.J., 1962. Carl Bode's *Ralph Waldo Emerson: A Profile,* New York, 1968, is a general introduction via 11 diverse essays by Oliver Wendell Holmes, Ralph L. Rusk, Daniel Aaron, and others. For other essays see also, in addition to the *Emerson Society Quarterly,* Roland F. Lee, "Emerson through Kierkegaard: Toward a Definition of Emerson's Theory of Communication," *ELH,* XXIV (1957), 229–248; Randall Stewart, "Emerson, Asset or Liability," *TSL,* II (1957), 33–40; Carl F. Strauch, "The Importance of Emerson's Skeptical Mood," *HLB,* XI (1957), 117–139; Rolando Anzilotti, "Emerson in Italia," *RLMC,* XI (1958), 70–80; Maria Luisa Bolgeri, "Riflessione su Emerson," *HumB,* XIII (1958), 467–472; Vivian C. Hopkins, "Emerson and Bacon," *AL,* XXIX (1958), 408–430; C. Grant Loomis, "Emerson's Proverbs," *WF,* XVII (1958), 257–262; Nathalia Wright, "Ralph Waldo Emerson and Horatio Greenough," *HLB,* XII (1958) 91–116; Newton Arvin, "The House of Pain: Emerson and the Tragic Sense," *HudR,* XII (1959), 37–53; Robert Frost, "On Emerson," *Daedalus,* LXXXVIII (1959), 712–718; Saul K. Padover, "Ralph Waldo Emerson: The Moral Voice in Politics," *PSQ,* LXXIV (1959), 334–350; Paul Lauter, "Truth and Nature: Emerson's Use of Two Complex Words," *ELH,* XXVII (1960), 66–85; Clark Griffith, "'Emersonianism' and 'Poeism': Some Versions of the Romantic Sensibility," *MLQ,* XXII (1961), 125–134; René Wellek, "Emerson's Literary Theory and Criticism," *Worte und Werte,* ed. Gustav Erdman and Alfons Eichstaedt, Berlin, 1961, pp. 444–456; Edwin R. Clapp, "Emerson Revisited: The American Scholar, New Style," *WHR,* XVI (1962), 339–348; Robert E. Spiller, "From Lecture into Essay: Emerson's Method of Composition," *LCrit,* V (1962), 28–38; Ray Benoit, "Emerson on Plato: The Fire's Center," *AL,* XXXIV (1963), 487–498; John Clendenning, "Emerson and Bayle," *PQ,* XLIII (1964), 79–86; Therman B. O'Daniel, "Emerson as a Literary Critic," *CLAJ,* VIII (1964), 21–43, 157–189, 246–276; Adrian H. Jaffe, "Emerson and Sartre: Two Parallel Theories of Responsibility," *CLS,* I (1964), 113–117.

More recent studies are Harold Bloom, "The Central Man: Emerson, Whitman, Wallace Stevens," *MR,* VIII (1966), 23–42; John H. Sloan,

" 'The Miraculous Uplifting': Emerson's Relationship with His Audience," *QJS*, LII (1966), 10–15; Kenneth Burke, "I, Eye, Ay—Emerson's Early Essay on 'Nature': Thoughts on the Machinery of Transcendence," *SR*, LXXIV (1966), 875–895; Michel Gresset, "Le 'Dieu Libérateur' ou le poète selon Emerson," *LanM*, LX (1966), 271–280; Richard L. Francis, "Archangel in the Pleached Garden: Emerson's Poetry," *ELH*, XXXIII (1966), 461–472; Albert Gilman and Roger Brown, "Personality and Style in Concord," *Transcendentalism and Its Legacy*, ed., Myron Simon and Thornton H. Parsons, Ann Arbor, Mich., 1966, pp. 87–122; Epifanio San Juan, Jr., "Symbolic Significance in the Poems of Emerson," *SLQ*, IV (1966), 37–54; S. P. Das, "Emerson's Concept of Man," *LCrit*, VIII (1967), 13–20, Sheldon W. Liebman, "Emerson's Transformation in the 1820's," *AL*, XL (1968), 133–154; and Lawrence L. Buell, "Unitarian Aesthetics and Emerson's Poet-Priest," *AQ*, XX (1968), 3–20.

### 500. BIBLIOGRAPHY

In addition to the continuing bibliographies in the *Emerson Society Quarterly* (1955–current), see Jackson R. Bryer and Robert A. Rees, *A Checklist of Emerson Criticism, 1951–1961*, Hartford, Conn., 1964; and William J. Sowder, *Emerson's Reviewers and Commentators: A Biographical and Bibliographical Analysis of Nineteenth-Century Periodical Criticism with a Detailed Index*, Hartford, Conn., 1968. Robert A. Rees and R. D. Rust have compiled an index to the first decade (1955–1965) of the *Emerson Society Quarterly* (Hartford, Conn., 1966).

William Charvat prepared *Emerson's American Lecture Engagements: A Chronological List*, New York, 1961. As a companion volume to *Thoreau's Library*, Walter Harding compiled *Emerson's Library*, Charlottesville, Va., 1967.

In the last decade, Kenneth Walter Cameron has published in Hartford, Connecticut, a growing list of source books for Emerson scholars: *Emerson, Thoreau, and Concord in Early Newspapers* (1958), *Emerson and Thoreau as Readers* (1958); *An Emerson Index: Names, Exempla, Sententiae, Symbols, Words, and Motifs in Selected Notebooks* (1958); *A Commentary on Emerson's Early Lectures (1833–1836)*, 2 vols. (1961); *Ralph Waldo Emerson's Reading: A Corrected Edition* (1962); *Index-Concordance to Emerson's Sermons*, 2 vols. (1963); *Transcendental Climate: New Resources for the Study of Emerson, Thoreau, and Their Contemporaries*, 3 vols. (1963); *Emerson's Workshop: An Analysis of His Reading in Periodicals through 1836*, 2 vols. (1964); and *Emerson among His Contemporaries* (1967).

## JAMES T(HOMAS) FARRELL

**501. SEPARATE WORKS**

*Side Street and Other Stories*, 1961; *Boarding House Blues*, 1961; *Sound of a City*, 1962; *The Silence of History*, 1963; *What Time Collects*, 1964; *Collected Poems*, 1965; *When Time Was Born*, 1966; *Lonely for the Future*, 1966; *New Year's Eve, 1929,* 1967; *A Brand New Life*, 1968; *Childhood Is Not Forever*, 1969.

Luna Wolf edited *Selected Essays*, New York, 1964.

**BIOGRAPHY AND CRITICISM**

A good introduction to Farrell's career is Edgar M. Branch's pamphlet, *James T. Farrell*, Minneapolis, Minn., 1963. Briefer studies are Jack Kligerman, "The Quest for Self: James T. Farrell's Character Bernard Clare," *UKCR*, XXIX (1962), 9–16; Richard Mitchell, "*Studs Lonigan*: Research in Morality," *CRAS*, VI (1962), 202–214; Richard Schickel, "James T. Farrell: Another Time, Another Place," *Esquire*, LVIII (1962), 157, 272–275; T. G. Rosenthal, "Studs Lonigan and the Search for an American Tragedy," *BAASB*, No. 7 (1963), pp. 46–54; Wallace Douglas, "The Case of James T. Farrell," *TriQ*, No. 2 (1965), pp. 105–123; and Irving Halpern, "Studs Lonigan Revisited," *ABC*, XIX (1968), 10–12.

Edgar M. Branch prepared *A Bibliography of James T. Farrell's Writings, 1921–1957*, Philadelphia, 1959; followed by "A Supplement to the Bibliography of James T. Farrell's Writings," *ABC*, XI (1961), 42–48; and "Bibliography of James T. Farrell: A Supplement," *ABC*, XVII (1967), 9–19. See also Neda M. Westlake, "The James T. Farrell Collection at the University of Pennsylvania," *ABC*, XI (1961), 21–23.

## WILLIAM FAULKNER
### d. 1962

**502. SEPARATE WORKS**

*Requiem for a Nun: A Play from the Novel* (with Ruth Ford), 1959; *The Mansion*, 1959; *The Reivers*, 1962.

Carvel Collins collected Faulkner's apprentice writings in *Early Prose and Poetry*, Boston, 1962. James B. Meriwether edited *Essays, Speeches, and Public Letters*, New York, 1966. *The Faulkner-Cowley File: Letters and Memories 1944–1962*, ed. Malcolm Cowley, New York, 1966, is a revealing correspondence which began with Cowley's editing of the Viking *Portable Faulkner*.

Three collections of interviews, lectures, and conferences are *Faulkner in the University: Class Conferences at the University of Virginia 1957–1958*, ed. Frederick L. Gwynn and Joseph L. Blotner, Charlottesville, Va., 1959; *Faulkner at West Point*, ed. Joseph L. Fant and Robert P. Ashley, New York, 1964; and *Lion in the Garden: Interviews of William Faulkner, 1926–1962*, ed. James B. Meriwether and Michael Millgate, New York, 1968.

BIOGRAPHY AND CRITICISM

The "authorized" biography, by Joseph Blotner, is still in preparation. Meanwhile, the long opening chapter of Michael Millgate's *The Achievement of William Faulkner*, New York, 1966, serves to set the biographical record straight. Family history is available in two volumes of reminiscence: John Faulkner, *My Brother Bill*, New York, 1963; and Murry C. Falkner, *The Falkners of Mississippi*, Baton Rouge, La., 1967. *William Faulkner of Oxford*, Baton Rouge, La., 1965, is a gathering of reminiscences by more than 40 friends of the author, edited by James W. Webb and A. Wigfall Green. *Old Times in the Faulkner Country*, Chapel Hill, N.C., 1961, is a collaboration between John B. Cullen, who hunted with Faulkner, and Floyd C. Watkins, who assembled the book. H. Edward Richardson concentrates on the years 1913–1929 in *William Faulkner: The Journey to Self-Discovery*, Columbia, Mo., 1969. Martin J. Dain, *Faulkner's County: Yoknapatawpha*, New York, 1964, prints photographs taken in and around Oxford.

Of the more than 20 books on Faulkner's work in the last decade, four are generally considered invaluable: Cleanth Brooks, *William Faulkner: The Yoknapatawpha Country*, New Haven, Conn., 1963, and Olga W. Vickery, *The Novels of William Faulkner*, Baton Rouge, La., 1959, rev. ed., 1964, for comprehensive surveys; Michael Millgate, *The Achievement of William Faulkner*, New York, 1966, for source studies and textual criticism; and Hyatt H. Waggoner, *William Faulkner: From Jefferson to the World*, Lexington, Ky., 1959, for Faulkner's artistic development, with an emphasis on Christian elements in the work. Two briefer surveys, Frederick J. Hoffman, *William Faulkner*, New York, 1961; and Lawrance R. Thompson, *William Faulkner: An Introduction and Interpretation*, New York, 1963, are designed for the student. More specialized studies include Warren Beck's brilliant discussion of the Snopes trilogy, *Man in Motion*, Madison, Wis., 1961; Charles H. Nilon, *Faulkner and the Negro*, Boulder, Colo., 1962; John L. Longley, Jr., *The Tragic Mask: A Study of Faulkner's Heroes*, Chapel Hill, N.C., 1963; John W. Hunt, *William Faulkner: Art in Theological Tension*, Syracuse, N.Y., 1965; Richard P. Adams, *Faulkner: Myth and Motion*, Princeton, N.J., 1968; and Walter Brylowski, *Faulkner's*

*Olympian Laugh: Myth in the Novels*, Detroit, Mich., 1968. Of the European studies, the best are Heinrich Straumann, *William Faulkner*, Frankfurt/Bonn, 1968; R. N. Raimbault, *Faulkner*, Paris, 1963; Monique Nathan, *Faulkner par lui-méme*, Paris, 1963; Mario Materassi, *I romanzi di Faulkner*, Rome, 1968; and Jean Weisgerber, *Faulkner et Dostoïevski: confluences et influences*, Brussels, 1968.

Among the handbooks or guides to Faulkner, the most reliable is Robert W. Kirk and Marvin Klotz, *Faulkner's People: A Complete Guide and Index to the Characters in the Fiction of William Faulkner*, Berkeley, Calif., 1963. More ambitious, but burdened with too much synopsis is Edmond L. Volpe's *A Reader's Guide to William Faulkner*, New York, 1964. Miscellaneous collections of criticism began with the 1951 volume edited by Frederick J. Hoffman and Olga W. Vickery, now expanded into *William Faulkner: Three Decades of Criticism*: East Lansing, Mich.. 1960. Equally useful is *Faulkner: A Collection of Critical Essays*, ed. Robert Penn Warren, Englewood Cliffs, N.J., 1966. The Spring, 1967, issue of *Modern Fiction Studies* is a William Faulkner number containing nine critical essays. *The Mississippi Quarterly* (Summer, 1969) is a William Faulkner special issue of eight critical articles.

General critical studies are George P. Garrett, Jr., "An Examination of the Poetry of William Faulkner," *PULC*, XVIII (1957), 124–135; Alfred Kazin, "The Stillness of *Light in August*," *PR*, XXIV (1957), 519–538; C. Hugh Holman, "The Unity of Faulkner's *Light in August*," *PMLA*, LXXIII (1958), 155–166; George Monteiro, "Bankruptcy in Time: A Reading of William Faulkner's *Pylon*," *TCL*, IV (1958), 9–20; George Garrett, "Faulkner's Early Literary Criticism," *TSLL*, I (1959), 3–10; Cecil D. Eby, "Faulkner and the Southwestern Humorists," *Shen*, XI (1959), 13–21; Floyd C. Watkins, "The Gentle Reader and Mr. Faulkner's Morals," *GaR*, XIII (1959), 68–75; *idem*, "William Faulkner in His Own Country," *EUQ*, XV (1959), 228–239; Loic Bouvard, "Conversation with William Faulkner," *MFS*, V (1959), 361–364; Percy C. Adams, "The Franco-American Faulkner," *TSL*, V (1960), 1–13; Robert M. Slabey, "Myth and Ritual in *Light in August*," *TSLL*, II (1960), 328–349; Floyd C. Watkins, "William Faulkner, the Individual, and the World," *GaR*, XIV (1960), 238–247; George Sidney, "William Faulkner and Hollywood," *ColQ*, IX (1961), 367–377; Joseph Gold, "Delusion and Redemption in Faulkner's *A Fable*," *MFS*, VII (1961), 145–156; W. M. Frohock, "Faulkner and the *Roman Nouveau*: An Interim Report," *BuR*, X (1962), 186–193; W. R. Moses, "The Limits of Yoknapatawpha County," *GaR*, XVI (1962), 297–305; M. Thomas Inge, "William Faulkner and George Washington Harris: In the Tradition of Southwestern Humor," *TSL*, VII (1962), 47–59; Rudolf Haas, "Faulkner und die Humanität," *Univ.*, XVIII (1963), 347–362;

Vida Marcović, "Interview with Faulkner," *TSLL*, V (1964), 463–466; James B. Meriwether, "Early Notices of Faulkner by Phil Stone and Louis Cochran," *MissQ*, XVII (1964), 136–164; George Garrett, "The Influence of William Faulkner," *GaR*, XVIII (1964), 419–427; Otis B. Wheeler, "Some Uses of Folk Humor by Faulkner," *MissQ*, XVII (1964), 107–122.

More recent studies are Maurice Edgar Coindreau, "The Faulkner I Knew," *Shen*, XVI (1965), 27–35; Melvin Backman, "Sutpen and the South: A Study of *Absalom, Absalom!*," *PMLA*, LXXX (1965), 596–604; Gordon Price-Stephens, "The British Reception of William Faulkner—1929–1962," *MissQ*, XVIII (1965), 119–200; Richard G. Stern, "Faulkner at Home," *BA*, XXXIX (1965), 409–411; Robert Penn Warren, "Faulkner: The South and the Negro," *SoR*, I (1965), 501–529; Charles Doyle, "The Moral World of William Faulkner," *Ren*, XIX (1966), 3–12; Joseph Blotner, "William Faulkner, Roving Ambassador," *International Educational and Cultural Exchange* (Summer, 1966), pp. 1–22; Jessie A. Coffee, "Empty Steeples: Theme, Symbol, and Irony in Faulkner's Novels," *ArQ*, XXIII (1967), 197–206; Paul S. Walters, "Theory and Practice in Faulkner: *The Sound and the Fury*," *ESA*, X (1967), 22–39; Nancy D. Taylor, "The Dramatic Productions of *Requiem for a Nun*," *MissQ*, XX (1967), 123–134; Floyd C. Watkins, "Faulkner and His Critics," *TSLL*, X (1968), 317–329; Reynolds Price, "*Pylon*: The Posture of Worship," *Shen*, XIX (1968), 49–61; Cleanth Brooks, "Faulkner as Poet," *SLJ*, I (1968), 5–19; Leonard I. Kulseth, "Cincinnatus among the Snopses: The Role of Gavin Stevens," *BSUF*, X (1969), 28–34; James A. Winn, "Faulkner's Revisions—A Stylist at Work," *AL*, XLI (1969), 231–250; and William R. Ferris, Jr., "William Faulkner and Phil Stone: An Interview with Emily Stone," *SAQ*, LXVIII (1969), 536–542.

### 503. BIBLIOGRAPHY

Bibliographical study of Faulkner begins with James B. Meriwether's *The Literary Career of William Faulkner*, Princeton, N.J., 1961, a complement to his 1957 volume, *William Faulkner: A Check List*; and continues with Linton R. Massey's *William Faulkner, Man Working, 1919–1962*, Charlottesville, Va., 1968, a "catalogue of the William Faulkner Collections at the University of Virginia." Useful for sources is Joseph Blotner's *William Faulkner's Library: A Catalogue*, Charlottesville, Va., 1964. James B. Meriwether, "William Faulkner," *Fifteen Modern American Authors*, ed. Jackson R. Bryer, Durham, N.C., 1969, pp. 175–210, is an authoritative bibliographical essay.

The most comprehensive listing of work about Faulkner is Maurice Beebe's "Criticism of William Faulkner: A Selected Checklist," *MFS*, XIII (1967), 115–161. Still valuable is the more selective bibliography of criticism appended to Frederick J. Hoffman and Olga W. Vickery, eds., *William Faulkner: Three Decades of Criticism*, East Lansing, Mich., 1960, pp. 393–428. Bibliography on French editions and surveys can be found in Stanley D. Woodworth, *William Faulkner en France (1931–1952)*, Paris, 1959; and Monique Nathan, *Faulkner par lui-même*, Paris, 1963.

## JOHN FISKE

### 504. BIOGRAPHY AND CRITICISM

A well-received recent work is Milton Berman's *John Fiske: The Evolution of a Popularizer*, Cambridge, Mass., 1961. More specialized treatment of Fiske's philosophy is H. Burnell Pannill's *The Religious Faith of John Fiske*, Durham, N.C., 1957.

A bibliographical listing is in Jacob Blanck, *Bibliography of American Literature*, III, New Haven, Conn., 1959, 159–179.

## F(RANCIS) SCOTT (KEY) FITZGERALD

### 505. COLLECTED WORKS AND REPRINTS

John Kuehl edited *The Apprentice Fiction of F. Scott Fitzgerald, 1909–1917*, New Brunswick, N.J., 1965; and *Thoughtbook of Francis Scott Key Fitzgerald*, Princeton, N.J., 1965. *F. Scott Fitzgerald in His Own Time: A Miscellany*, edited by Matthew J. Bruccoli and Jackson R. Bryer, Kent, Ohio, 1971, collects materials by and about Fitzgerald that appeared in his lifetime but have never been reprinted. *The Fitzgerald Reader*, ed. Arthur Mizener, New York, 1963, includes *The Great Gatsby*, essays, short stories, and chapters from *Tender Is the Night* and *The Last Tycoon*. The six-volume Bodley Head Scott Fitzgerald, London, 1958–1963, is a close approximation to a collected edition.

Andrew Turnbull edited *The Letters of F. Scott Fitzgerald*, New York, 1963. Those addressed to his daughter in this volume were also published separately as *Letters to a Daughter*, New York, 1965, with an introduction by Frances Fitzgerald Lanahan.

### BIOGRAPHY AND CRITICISM

An important contribution to any investigation of the author's life is Andrew Turnbull's *Scott Fitzgerald*, New York, 1962, an intimate portrait, written from personal acquaintance with the author as well as extensive research. Fitzgerald's last years are finally revealed in Sheilah Graham's autobiography, *Beloved Infidel*, New York, 1958. His marriage to Zelda

Sayre is the focus of Nancy Milford's biography, *Zelda*, New York, 1970. To include the Fitzgerald-Graham story, Arthur Mizener revised his biography, *The Far Side of Paradise* (Boston, 1951, rev. ed., 1965). Students of the era will also want to see Morley Callaghan's *That Summer in Paris*, New York, 1963; and Ernest Hemingway's *A Moveable Feast*, New York, 1964.

The first full-length critical studies were published in Europe: James E. Miller's *The Fictional Technique of Scott Fitzgerald*, The Hague, 1957; and Sergio Perosa's *L'arte di F. Scott Fitzgerald*, Rome, 1961. Since then Miller has expanded his work to include sections on the last two novels, *F. Scott Fitzgerald: His Art and His Technique*, New York, 1964; and Perosa translated his work with the help of Charles Matz, *The Art of F. Scott Fitzgerald*, Ann Arbor, Mich., 1965. William F. Goldhurst concentrates on the men he thinks influenced Fitzgerald (Mencken, Hemingway, Lardner, Edmund Wilson) in *F. Scott Fitzgerald and His Contemporaries*, Cleveland, Ohio, 1963. Two more recent studies see Fitzgerald's work in the English Romantic tradition: Robert Sklar, *F. Scott Fitzgerald: The Last Laocoön*, New York, 1967; and Richard D. Lehan, *F. Scott Fitzgerald and the Craft of Fiction*, Carbondale, Ill., 1966. Milton Stern returns to a bio-critical reading in *The Golden Moment: The Novels of F. Scott Fitzgerald*, Urbana, Ill.; as does Henry Dan Piper in *F. Scott Fitzgerald: A Critical Portrait*, New York, 1965; and Aaron Latham in *Crazy Sundays: F. Scott Fitzgerald in Hollywood*, New York, 1971.

Of the four briefer introductions to the author's career, Kenneth Eble's *F. Scott Fitzgerald*, New York, 1963, is the most useful, with Milton Hindus's *F. Scott Fitzgerald: An Introduction and Interpretation*, New York, 1968, a close second. Charles E. Shain, *F. Scott Fitzgerald*, Minneapolis, Minn., 1961; and Edwin M. Moseley, *F. Scott Fitzgerald: A Critical Essay*, Grand Rapids, Mich., 1967, are pamphlets.

Recent gatherings of brief studies are Arthur Mizener's *F. Scott Fitzgerald: A Collection of Critical Essays*, Englewood Cliffs, N.J., 1963; Frederick J. Hoffman's *The Great Gatsby: A Study*, New York, 1962; Ernest Lockridge's *Twentieth-Century Interpretations of The Great Gatsby*, Englewood Cliffs, N.J., 1968; and Marvin J. LaHood's *Tender is the Night: Essays in Criticism*, Bloomington, Ind., 1969.

General critical studies are Arthur Mizener, "The Maturity of Scott Fitzgerald," *SR*, LXVII (1959), 658–675; John Kuehl, "Scott Fitzgerald: Romantic and Realist," *TSLL*, I (1959), 412–426; Edmund Wilson, "Sheilah Graham and Scott Fitzgerald," *NY*, XXXIV (Jan. 24, 1959), 115–124; Otto Friedrich, "F. Scott Fitzgerald: Money, Money, Money," *ASch*, XXIX (1960), 392–405; Budd Schulberg, "Old Scott: The Mask, the Myth, the Man," *Esquire*, LV (1961), 97–101; William F. Hall, "Dialogue and Theme in *Tender Is the Night*," *MLN*, LXXVI (1961), 616–622; Michael Millgate, "Scott Fitzgerald as Social Novelist: Statement and Technique in *The Last Tycoon*," *ES*, XLIII (1962), 29–34; Guy A. Cardwell, "The Lyric World of Scott Fitzgerald," *VQR*, XXXVIII (1962), 299–323; Kenneth E. Eble, "I've Been Reading Scott Fitzgerald, Seriously," *CUF*, V (1962), 38–41; Howard S. Babb, "*The Great Gatsby* and the Grotesque," *Criticism*, V (1963), 336–348; Philip Hobsbaum, "Scott Fitzgerald and His Critics: The Appreciation of Minor Art," *BAASB*, No. 6 (1963), pp. 31–41; G. Thomas Tanselle and Jackson R. Bryer, "*The Great Gatsby*: A Study in Literary Reputation," *NMQ*, XXXIII (1964), 409–425; Philip Young, "Fitzgerald's *Waste Land*," *FeL*, X (1964), 113–120; Laura Guthrie Hearn, "A Summer with F. Scott Fitzgerald," *Esquire*, LXII (1964), 160–165, 232 ff.; Kermit Vanderbilt, "James, Fitzgerald, and the American Self-Image," *MR*, VI (1965), 289–304.

More recent are Robert Emmet Long, "The Great Gatsby and the Tradition of Joseph Conrad," *TSLL*, VIII (1966), 257–276; 407–422; Sy Kahn, "*This Side of Paradise*: The Pageantry of Disillusion," *MQ*, VII (1966), 177–194; Gary J. Scrimgeour, "Against *The Great Gatsby*," *Criticism*, VIII (1966), 75–86; Joseph N. Riddel, "F. Scott Fitzgerald, the Jamesian Inheritance, and the Morality of Fiction," *MFS*, XI (1966), 331–350; Victor A. Doyno, "Patterns in *The Great Gatsby*," *MFS*, XII (1966), 415–426; Richard Foster, "Fitzgerald's Imagination: A Parable for Criticism" *MinnR*, VII (1967), 144–156; Benjamin T. Spencer, "Fitzgerald and the American Ambivalence," *SAQ*, LXVI (1967), 367–381; Richard A. Koenigsberg, "F. Scott Fitzgerald: Literature and the Work of Mourning," *AI*, XXIV (1967), 248–270; Barry Gross, "Newman to Gatsby: This Side of Innocence," *PMASAL*, LIII (1968), 279–289; *idem*, "The Dark Side of Twenty-five: Fitzgerald and *The Beautiful and Damned*," *BuR*, XVI (1968), 40–52; Harold Hurwitz, "*The Great Gatsby* and *Heart of Darkness*: The Confrontation Scenes," *FHA* (1969), pp. 27–34; and R. L. Samsell, "Hollywood—It Wasn't All That Bad," *FHA*, (1969), pp. 15–19.

*Modern Fiction Studies* devoted its Spring, 1961, issue to Fitzgerald. *The Fitzgerald/Hemingway Annual*, ed. Matthew J. Bruccoli, made its first appearance in Washington, D.C., in 1969. The *Fitzgerald Newsletter* (1957–1968) is discontinued.

## 506. BIBLIOGRAPHY

Until Matthew J. Bruccoli's descriptive bibliography appears, the following will serve: Bernard H. Porter, "The First Publications of F. Scott Fitzgerald," *TCL*, V (1959), 176–182; Matthew J. Bruccoli, *F. Scott Fitzgerald*:

*Collector's Handlist*, Columbus, Ohio, 1964; and all issues of *The Fitz-gerald Newsletter*. *The Fitzgerald/Hemingway Annual* should continue to print bibliography as well as critical essays.

In *The Critical Reputation of F. Scott Fitzgerald: A Bibliographical Study*, Hamden, Conn., 1967, Jackson R. Bryer has annotated over 2,100 items about Fitzgerald. He has also provided an important bibliographical essay in *Fifteen Modern American Authors*, ed. Jackson R. Bryer, Durham, N.C., 1969, pp. 211–238. See also Maurice Beebe and Jackson Bryer, "Criticism of F. Scott Fitzgerald: A Selected Checklist," *MFS*, VII (1961), 82–94.

Matthew J. Bruccoli's *The Composition of Tender Is the Night: A Study of the Manuscripts*, Pittsburgh, Pa., 1963, analyzes 17 drafts and three printed versions of the novel.

## JOHN GOULD FLETCHER

### 506. BIOGRAPHY AND CRITICISM

The first full-length critical study is Edna B. Stephens, *John Gould Fletcher*, New York, 1967. Briefer estimates are Mary Graham Lund, "The Love Songs of John Gould Fletcher," *MQ*, VII (1961), 83–91; and *idem*, "John Gould Fletcher: An Anachronism," *SWR*, LI (1966), 37–45.

## BENJAMIN FRANKLIN

### 508. COLLECTED WORKS AND CORRESPONDENCE

Of the projected 25, 14 volumes of *The Papers of Benjamin Franklin* have appeared under the editorship of Leonard W. Labaree, New Haven, Conn., 1959–1970. Now retired, Labaree will be succeeded by William B. Willcox.

### 510. EDITED TEXTS AND REPRINTS

For the first time, *The Autobiography of Benjamin Franklin* has been printed from the original manuscript and thoroughly edited for the general reader, by Leonard W. Labaree, Ralph L. Ketcham, Helen C. Boatfield, and Helene H. Fineman, New Haven, Conn., 1964. *The Bagatelles from Passy . . . Text and Facsimile* [of the Yale University Library copy] was edited by Claude-Anne Lopez and Willard R. Trask, New York, 1967. Ralph L. Ketcham compiled *The Political Thought of Benjamin Franklin*, Indianapolis, Ind., 1965. The serviceable *Benjamin Franklin: Representa-*

*tive Selections,* ed. Chester E. Jorgenson and Frank Luther Mott (1936) has been reprinted with an updated bibliography, New York, 1962. Reprintings of the *Autobiography* are too numerous to list separately.

511. BIOGRAPHY AND CRITICISM

In *Benjamin Franklin, Philosopher and Man,* Philadelphia, 1965, Alfred Owen Aldridge has attempted to "bring up to date all essential aspects of the story of Franklin's life while emphasizing the man himself." Thomas Fleming's *The Man Who Dared the Lightning,* New York, 1971, a lengthy study stressing the liberal aspects of his career, is subtitled *A New Look at Benjamin Franklin.* Ralph L. Ketcham's *Benjamin Franklin,* New York, 1966, is "an analytic study of Franklin's thought with a special awareness of the impact of Franklin's acts." Bruce Ingham Granger, *Benjamin Franklin: An American Man of Letters,* Ithaca, N.Y., 1964, makes a case for Franklin as master rhetorician. Briefer general surveys are Richard E. Amacher's *Benjamin Franklin,* New York, 1962; and Theodore Hornberger's pamphlet, *Benjamin Franklin,* Minneapolis, Minn., 1962.

Of the many specialized studies, two seem vital to any study of Franklin: Paul W. Conner's *Poor Richard's Politicks: Benjamin Franklin and His New American Order,* New York, 1965; and the first significant book on his religious credo, Alfred Owen Aldridge's *Benjamin Franklin and Nature's God,* Durham, N.C., 1967. New views of Franklin's pre-Revolutionary career are Cecil B. Currey's *Road to Revolution: Benjamin Franklin in England, 1765-1775,* Garden City, N.Y., 1968; and William S. Hanna's *Benjamin Franklin and Pennsylvania Politics,* Stanford, Calif., 1964. Roger Burlinghame concentrates on the public aspects of the decade spent in Europe in *Benjamin Franklin: Envoy Extraordinary,* New York, 1967; and Claude-Anne Lopez on the private in *Mon Cher Papa: Franklin and the Ladies of Paris,* New Haven, Conn., 1966. Antonio Pace overworks a thesis in an otherwise useful book, *Benjamin Franklin and Italy,* Philadelphia, 1958. Three recent items of Frankliniana are Max Hall, *Benjamin Franklin and Polly Baker: The History of a Literary Deception,* Chapel Hill, N.C., 1960; Charles Coleman Sellers, *Benjamin Franklin in Portraiture,* New Haven, Conn., 1962; and Margaret B. Korty, *Benjamin Franklin and Eighteenth-Century Libraries,* Philadelphia, 1965. Robert F. Sayre's study of three autobiographies, *The Examined Self,* Princeton, N.J., 1964, groups Franklin with Henry Adams and Henry James.

Briefer estimates are John J. Zimmerman, "Benjamin Franklin and *The Pennsylvania Chronicle,*" *PMHB,* LXXXI (1957), 351-364; Verner W. Crane, "Franklin's 'The Internal State of America' (1786)," *WMQ,* XV (1958), 214-227; Jesse Bier, "Franklin's *Autobiography:* Benchmark of

American Literature," *WHR*, XII (1958), 57–65; Robert Newcomb, "Franklin and Richardson," *JEGP*, LVII (1958), 27–35; Leonard W. Labaree, "In Search of 'B. Franklin,'" *WMQ*, XVI (1959), 188–197; Gilbert Chinard, "Random Notes on Two 'Bagatelles,'" *PAPS*, CIII (1959), 727–760; Hannah Benner Roach, "Benjamin Franklin Slept Here," *PMHB*, LXXXIV (1960), 127–174; Max Hall, "Hoax upon Hoax; or, Too Many Inventions for Ben," *EUQ*, XVI (1960), 221–228; Leonard W. Labaree, "The Bookish Mr. Franklin," *BuR*, X (1961), 46–56; Glen M. Rodgers, "Benjamin Franklin and the Universality of Science," *PMHB*, LXXXV (1961), 50–69; Walter Shear, "Franklin's Self-Portrait," *MQ*, IV (1962), 71–86; Robert Freeman Sayre, "The Worldly Franklin and the Provincial Critics," *TSLL*, IV (1963), 512–524; John William Ward, "'Who Was Benjamin Franklin?'" *ASch*, XXXII (1963), 541–553; David Levin, *"The Autobiography of Benjamin Franklin*: The Puritan Experimenter in Life and Art," *YR*, LIII (1964), 258–275; Julian Smith, "Coming of Age in America: Young Ben Franklin and Robin Molineux," *AQ*, XVII (1965), 550–558; and J. A. Leo Lemay, "Franklin and the *Autobiography*: An Essay on Recent Scholarship," *ECS*, I (1967), 185–211.

## HAROLD FREDERIC

### 515. SEPARATE WORKS

Thomas F. O'Donnell is editing a 14-volume edition of *The Works of Harold Frederic* for the Garrett Press of New York. He has also edited *Harold Frederic's Stories of York State*, Syracuse, N.Y., 1966, with an introduction by Edmund Wilson.

### 516. BIOGRAPHY AND CRITICISM

The last decade has produced a remarkable increase in Frederic scholarship. Thomas F. O'Donnell and Hoyt C. Franchere published a general introduction to his career, *Harold Frederic*, New York, 1961; and Austin Briggs, Jr., a comprehensive critical discussion of *The Novels of Harold Frederic*, Ithaca, N.Y., 1969. In addition to Stanton Garner's pamphlet, *Harold Frederic*, Minneapolis, Minn., 1969, briefer estimates are Abe C. Ravitz, "Harold Frederic's Venerable Copperhead," *NYH*, XLI (1960), 35–48; Robert H. Woodward, "Some Sources of Harold Frederic's *The Damnation of Theron Ware*," *AL*, XXXII (1961), 46–51; George W. Johnson, "Harold Frederic's Young Goodman Ware: The Ambiguities of a Realistic Romance," *MFS*, VIII (1963), 361–374; Heinz Wüstenhagen, "Harold Frederics *The Lawton Girl*," *ZAA*, XII (1964), 32–53; Charles

V. Genthe, *"The Damnation of Theron Ware* and *Elmer Gantry,"* RS, XXXII (1964), 334–343; Tom H. Towers, "The Problem of Determinism in Frederic's First Novel," *CE*, XXVI (1965), 361–366; J. R. K. Kantor, "Autobiography and Journalism: Sources for Harold Frederic's Fiction," *Serif*, IV (1967), 19–27; Elmer F. Suderman, *"The Damnation of Theron Ware* as a Criticism of American Religious Thought," *HLQ*, XXXIII (1969), 61–75.

The major bibliographical listings are Jacob Blanck, *Bibliography of American Literature*, III, New Haven, Conn., 1959, 217–223; and Thomas F. O'Donnell, *Checklist of Harold Frederic*, Columbus, Ohio, 1969. Additional bibliographical items are in two new journals, *American Literary Realism, 1870–1910* (1967-current) and *The Frederic Herald* (1967-current).

## MARY E(LEANOR) WILKINS FREEMAN

### 517. BIOGRAPHY AND CRITICISM

The first full-length critical study is Percy D. Westbrook's *Mary Wilkins Freeman*, New York, 1967.

A bibliographical listing is in Jacob Blanck, *Bibliography of American Literature*, III, New Haven, Conn., 1959, 224–243.

## PHILIP (MORIN) FRENEAU

### 517. COLLECTED WORKS AND EDITED REPRINTS

Philip M. Marsh edited *A Freneau Sampler*, New York, 1963.

### 518. BIOGRAPHY AND CRITICISM

The newest biography is Jacob Axelrod, *Philip Freneau, Champion of Democracy*, Austin, Tex., 1967, more a literary study than its subtitle suggests. Philip Marsh adds little to a reassessment of Freneau's career in *Philip Freneau: Poet and Journalist*, Minneapolis, Minn., 1967; and *The Works of Philip Freneau: A Critical Study*, Metuchen, N.J., 1968. See also Laurence B. Holland, "Philip Freneau: Poet in the New Nation," *The Literary Heritage of New Jersey*, Princeton, N.J., 1964, pp. 3–41; J. M. Santraud, "Un poète de la révolution américaine: Philip Freneau," *EA*, XVIII (1965), 337–353; and G. Ferris Cronkhite, "Freneau's 'The House of Night,'" *CLJ*, VIII (1969), 3–19.

The latest bibliographical listings are in Jacob Blanck, *Bibliography of American Literature*, III, New Haven, Conn., 1959, 244–256; and Philip Marsh, *Freneau's Published Prose: A Bibliography*, Metuchen, N.J., 1970.

# ROBERT (LEE) FROST
*d. 1962*

### 520. SEPARATE WORKS

*In the Clearing*, 1962.

### COLLECTED WORKS

*The Poetry of Robert Frost*, ed. Edward Connery Lathem, New York, 1969, is a handsomely printed comprehensive edition (all 11 books complete), to be followed in time by a definitive or variorum edition. Two volumes of prose have appeared since the poet's death: *Robert Frost: Farm Poultryman*, ed. Edward Connery Lathem and Lawrance Thompson, Hanover, N.H., 1963, 11 uncollected prose pieces from New England poultry journals; and *Selected Prose of Robert Frost*, ed. Hyde Cox and Edward Connery Lathem, New York, 1966. Lathem and Thompson also edited *Robert Frost and the Lawrence, Massachusetts, 'High School Bulletin': The Beginning of a Literary Career*, New York, 1966.

The major collection of letters was made by Lawrance Thompson who chose 466 from approximately 1,500 available for *Selected Letters*, New York, 1964. Also of major importance is a gathering edited by Louis Untermeyer, *The Letters of Robert Frost to Louis Untermeyer*, New York, 1963. *Robert Frost and John Bartlett: The Record of a Friendship*, ed. Margaret Bartlett Anderson, New York, 1963, contains Frost's letters augmented by narrative by the Bartletts' daughter. Frost's conversation is also recorded in *Interviews with Robert Frost*, ed. Edward Connery Lathem, New York, 1966; Louis Mertins, *Robert Frost: Life and Talks—Walking*, Norman, Okla., 1965; and Daniel Smythe, *Robert Frost Speaks*, New York, 1964 (taken from lectures and conversations, 1915–1962).

### REPRINTS

*Selected Poems*, with an introduction by Robert Graves, New York, 1963, was prepared by Frost and prints slightly revised versions of some poems.

### BIOGRAPHY AND CRITICISM

The major biography, by Lawrance Thompson, is planned to be in three volumes: the first two are *Robert Frost: The Early Years, 1874–1915*, New York, 1966; and *Robert Frost: The Years of Triumph, 1915–1938*, New York, 1970. Elizabeth S. Sergeant's *Robert Frost: The Trial by Existence*, New York, 1960, is an earlier attempt to capture the poet's life, written from long personal acquaintance. Frost's 1962 trip to the Soviet

Union is recorded in Franklin D. Reeve, *Robert Frost in Russia*, Boston, 1964; and Frederick B. Adams, Jr., *To Russia with Frost*, Boston, 1963. C. P. Snow offers fascinating sidelights and impressions of Frost in *Variety of Men*, New York, 1967. See also *New Hampshire's Child: The Derry Journals of Lesley Frost*, ed. Lawrance Thompson and Arnold Grade, Albany, N.Y., 1969.

Of the eight critical volumes in the last decade, two are vital to any study of the poet: Radcliffe Squires, *The Major Themes of Robert Frost*, Ann Arbor, Mich., 1963; and Reuben Brower, *The Poetry of Robert Frost: Constellations of Intention*, New York, 1963. Equally analytical in their approach, but also somewhat thesis-burdened, are John F. Lynen, *The Pastoral Art of Robert Frost*, New Haven, Conn., 1960; and George W. Nitchie, *Human Values in the Poetry of Robert Frost: A Study of a Poet's Convictions*, Durham, N.C., 1960. Of the briefer studies, Elizabeth Jennings's *Frost*, Edinburgh, 1964, is the most acute. Philip L. Gerber's *Robert Frost*, New York, 1966, is an adequate summary of the major themes; as is Elizabeth Isaacs's *An Introduction to Robert Frost*, Denver, Colo., 1962. Lawrance Thompson, *Robert Frost*, Minneapolis, Minn., 1959, rev. ed., 1967, is an introductory pamphlet.

Briefer estimates are assembled in two useful volumes: James M. Cox, ed., *Robert Frost: A Collection of Critical Essays*, Englewood Cliffs, N.J., 1962; and Robert A. Greenberg and James G. Hepburn, eds., *Robert Frost: An Introduction*, New York, 1961, a "controlled research" volume. Other general studies are John Ciardi, "Robert Frost: Master Conversationalist at Work," *SatR*, XLII (Mar. 21, 1959), 17–20, 54; Michael L. Lasser, "The Loneliness of Robert Frost," *LitR*, III (1959), 287–297; Denis Donoghue, "The Limitations of Robert Frost," *TC*, CLXVI (1959), 13–22; James M. Cox, "Robert Frost and the Edge of the Clearing," *VQR*, XXXV (1959), 73–88; Lionel Trilling, "A Speech on Robert Frost: A Cultural Episode," *PR*, XXVI (1959), 445–452; M. L. Rosenthal, "The Robert Frost Controversy [reactions to the Trilling speech]," *Nation*, CLXXXVIII (1959), 559–561; Richard Poirier, "The Art of Poetry II: Robert Frost [an interview]," *ParR*, No. 6 (1960), pp. 89–120; Vivian C. Hopkins, "Robert Frost: Out Far and In Deep," *WHR*, XIV (1960), 247–263; W. R. Irwin, "The Unity of Frost's Masques," *AL*, XXXII (1960), 302–312; Ely Stock, "*A Masque of Reason* and *J. B.*: Two Treatments of the Book of Job," *MD*, III (1961), 378–386; Roy Harvey Pearce, "Frost's Momentary Stay," *KR*, XXIII (1961), 258–273; John Ciardi, "Robert Frost: American Bard," *SatR*, XLV (Mar. 24, 1962), 15–17, 52–54; Arnold Whitridge, "Robert Frost and Carl Sandburg: The Two Elder Statesmen of American Poetry," *BNYPL*, LXVI (1962), 164–177; Jerome M. Irving, "A Parting Visit with Robert Frost," *HudR*, XVI (1963), 54–60; Alfred Kazin, "The Strength of Robert Frost," *Com*,

XXXVIII (1964), 49–52; Gordon S. Haight, "Robert Frost at Yale," *YULG*, XL (1965), 12–17; George Knox, "A Backward Motion toward the Source," *Person*, XLVII (1966), 365–381; James Dickey, "Robert Frost, Man and Myth," *Atl*, CCXVIII (Nov., 1966), 53–56; Richard Tillinghast, "Blueberries Sprinkled with Salt: Frost's Letters," *SR*, LXXIV (1966), 554–565; Andrei Sinyavsky, "On Robert Frost's Poems," *MR*, VII (1966), 431–441; Arthur M. Sampley, "The Tensions of Robert Frost," *SAQ*, LXV (1966), 431–437; Reginald L. Cook, "Frost the Diversionist," *NEQ*, XL (1967), 323–338; Clark Griffith, "Frost and the American View of Nature," *AQ*, XX (1968), 21–37; Harry Berger, Jr., "Poetry as Revision: Interpreting Robert Frost," *Criticism*, X (1968), 1–22; Wilbert Snow, "The Frost I Knew," *TQ*, XI (1968), 9–48; and Laurence J. Sasso, Jr., "Robert Frost: Love's Question," *NEQ*, XLII (1969), 95–107.

The Autumn, 1966, issue of *Southern Review* prints 14 articles in a section called "Robert Frost: Critical Views and Reminiscences."

**522. BIBLIOGRAPHY**

A full descriptive bibliography is still very much needed. In *The Poetry of Robert Frost* (1969), cited above, Edward Connery Lathem's "Bibliographical and Textual Notes" (pp. [523]–582) contain valuable information on each poem: the first appearance, all subsequent appearances in Frost's major selected and collected editions, and line-by-line specification of such textual variance as may exist in any of these printed sources.

Reginald L. Cook's bibliographical essay, "Robert Frost," is in *Fifteen Modern American Authors*, ed. Jackson R. Bryer, Durham, N.C., 1969, pp. 239–273. Donald J. Greiner prepared *The Merrill Checklist of Robert Frost*, Columbus, Ohio, 1969. John F. Lynen also appends a useful checklist and selective bibliography to his *Pastoral Art of Robert Frost*, cited above. Uma Parameswaran prepared "Robert Frost: A Bibliography of Articles and Books, 1958–1964," *BB*, XXV (1967), 46–48, 58, 69, 72. The Frost materials in the Library of Congress are listed in the printing of Louis Untermeyer's lecture, *Robert Frost: A Backward Look*, Washington, D.C., 1964.

Edward Connery Lathem edited *A Concordance to the Poetry of Robert Frost*, New York, 1971.

# (SARAH) MARGARET FULLER (OSSOLI)

**523. COLLECTED WORKS AND CORRESPONDENCE**

Perry Miller edited *Margaret Fuller, American Romantic: A Selection from Her Writings and Correspondence*, Garden City, N.Y., 1963.

*The Letters of James Freeman Clarke to Margaret Fuller*, ed. John Wesley Thomas, Hamburg, 1957, covers the years 1829–1848.

BIOGRAPHY AND CRITICISM

The most recent biography is Joseph J. Deiss, *The Roman Years of Margaret Fuller*, New York, 1969. Bio-critical studies are Arthur W. Brown, *Margaret Fuller*, New York, 1964; and Russell E. Durning, *Margaret Fuller: Citizen of the World*, Heidelberg, 1969.

Briefer estimates are Derek Colville, "The Transcendental Friends: Clarke and Margaret Fuller," *NEQ*, XXX (1957), 378–382; John Brown, "Margaret Fuller," *Palestra*, I (1962), 178–187; Francis E. Kearns, "Margaret Fuller and the Abolition Movement," *JHI*, XXV (1964), 120–127; and Helen Barolini, "A Study in Contrast: Effie in Venice and the Roman Spring of Margaret Fuller," *AR*, XXVIII (1969), 461–476.

A full bibliographical listing is in Jacob Blanck, *Bibliography in America*, III, New Haven, Conn., 1959, 262–269.


## ZONA GALE

**525.** BIOGRAPHY AND CRITICISM

The first full-length critical study is Harold P. Simonson, *Zona Gale*, New York, 1962. Simonson has also prepared a useful bibliography, "Zona Gale (1874–1938)," *ALR*, III (1968), 14–17.


## HAMLIN GARLAND

**526.** SEPARATE WORKS

Donald Pizer is editing a 44-volume edition of *The Works of Hamlin Garland* for the Garrett Press of New York. He has also edited *Hamlin Garland's Diaries*, San Marino, Calif., 1968, selections from 43 volumes of journals in the Huntington Library.

**527.** BIOGRAPHY AND CRITICISM

The first biography is Jean Holloway's *Hamlin Garland*, Austin, Tex., 1960. Donald Pizer's *Hamlin Garland's Early Work and Career*, Berkeley, Calif., 1960, covering the years 1884–1895, publishes a considerable amount of new material but it is chiefly for the specialist. The most comprehensive critical biography is Robert Mane's *Hamlin Garland: L'Homme et l'oeuvre (1860–1940)*, Paris, 1968.

Briefer estimates are B. R. McElderry, Jr., "Boy Life on the Prairie:

Hamlin Garland's Best Reminiscence," *EL*, XXII (1959), 5–16; Donald Pizer, "The Garland-Crane Relationship," *HLQ*, XXIV (1960), 75–82; Kathryn Whitford, "Patterns of Observation: A Study of Hamlin Garland's Middle Border Landscape," *TWA*, L (1961), 331–338; John E. Higgins, "A Man from the Middle Border: Hamlin Garland's Diaries," *WMH*, XLVI (1963), 294–302; Walter Lazenby, "Idealistic Realist on the Platform: Hamlin Garland," *QJS*, XLIX (1963), 138–145; James B. Stronks, "A Realist Experiments with Impressionism: Hamlin Garland's 'Chicago Studies,'" *AL*, XXXVI (1964), 38–52; Robert Mane, "Une recontre littéraire: Hamlin Garland et Stephen Crane," *EA*, XVII (1964), 30–46; Kathryn Whitford, "Crusader without a Cause: An Examination of Hamlin Garland's Middle Border," *MASJ*, VI (1965), 61–72; Charles T. Miller, "Hamlin Garland's Retreat from Realism," *WAL*, I (1966), 119–129; and Stanley R. Harrison, "Hamlin Garland and the Double Vision of Naturalism," *SSF*, VI (1969), 548–556.

The most recent bibliography is Donald Pizer, "Hamlin Garland (1860–1940)," *ALR*, I (1967), 45–51. See also Lloyd Arvidson, ed., *Centennial Tributes and a Checklist of the Hamlin Garland Papers in the University of Southern California Library*, Los Angeles, 1962; and the Robert Mane volume cited above.

# HENRY GEORGE

### 531. BIOGRAPHY AND CRITICISM

Two general studies are Steven B. Cord, *Henry George: Dreamer or Realist?*, Philadelphia, 1965; and Edward J. Rose, *Henry George*, New York, 1968. Elwood P. Lawrence's *Henry George in the British Isles*, East Lansing, Mich., 1957, treats George's five barnstorming visits to Great Britain in the 1880's.

# ELLEN (ANDERSON GHOLSON) GLASGOW

### 532. SEPARATE WORKS

*Beyond Defeat: An Epilogue to an Era*, ed. Luther Y. Gore, Charlottesville, Va., 1966, the previously unpublished sequel to *In This Our Life*.

Additional new material: Luther Y. Gore, ed., "'Literary Realism or Nominalism' by Ellen Glasgow: An Unpublished Essay," *AL*, XXXIV (1962), 72–79; and William W. Kelly, "'The Professional Instinct': An Unpublished Short Story by Ellen Glasgow," *WHR*, XVI (1962), 301–317.

COLLECTED WORKS AND CORRESPONDENCE

Richard K. Meeker edited *The Collected Stories of Ellen Glasgow*, Baton Rouge, La., 1963.

Additional correspondence can be found in James B. Colvert, "Agent and Author: Ellen Glasgow's Letters to Paul Revere Reynolds," *SB*, XIV (1961), 177–196; and Douglas Day, "Ellen Glasgow's Letters to the Saxtons," *AL*, XXXV (1963), 230–236.

BIOGRAPHY AND CRITICISM

The soundest critical study and the most lucidly written is Frederick P. W. McDowell, *Ellen Glasgow and the Ironic Art of Fiction*, Madison, Wis., 1960. Joan Foster Santas, *Ellen Glasgow's American Dream*, Charlottesville, Va., 1966, concentrates on the Southern social values and Ellen Glasgow's vision. Briefer general surveys are Blair Rouse, *Ellen Glasgow*, New York, 1962; Monique Parent, *Ellen Glasgow, Romancière*, Paris, 1962; and a pamphlet by Louis Auchincloss, *Ellen Glasgow*, Minneapolis, Minn., 1964. More specialized studies are Louis D. Rubin, Jr., *No Place on Earth: Ellen Glasgow, James Branch Cabell and Richmond-in-Virginia*, Austin, Tex., 1959; and C. Hugh Holman, *Three Modes of Modern Southern Fiction: Ellen Glasgow, William Faulkner, and Thomas Wolfe*, Athens, Ga., 1966.

Other critical estimates are Allen W. Becker, "Ellen Glasgow and the Southern Literary Tradition," *MFS*, V (1959), 295–303; Joan Curlee, "Ellen Glasgow's South," *BSTCF*, II (1961), 53–59; and Edgar E. Macdonald, "The Glasgow-Cabell Entente," *AL*, XLI (1969), 76–91.

533. BIBLIOGRAPHY

William W. Kelley, *Ellen Glasgow: A Bibliography*, ed. Oliver L. Steele, Charlottesville, Va., 1964, is both analytical and enumerative; it should remain standard for many years.

# JAMES HALL

535. BIOGRAPHY AND CRITICISM

A major critical biography is Randolph C. Randall's *James Hall, Spokesman of the New West*, Columbus, Ohio, 1964. See also Edgeley W. Todd, "The Authorship of 'The Missouri Trapper,'" *MHSB*, XV (1959), 194–200.

A listing of Hall's works is in Jacob Blanck, *Bibliography of American Literature*, III, New Haven, Conn., 1959, 344–355.

# ALEXANDER HAMILTON

### 537. COLLECTED WORKS

Columbia University Press has begun publication of *The Papers of Alexander Hamilton*, ed. Harold C. Syrett, assoc. ed., Jacob E. Cooke, New York, 1961 and continuing.

### EDITED TEXTS AND REPRINTS

Julius Goebel, Jr., *et al.* edited *The Law Practice of Alexander Hamilton: Documents and Commentary*, I, New York, 1964. Jacob E. Cooke edited *The Reports of Alexander Hamilton*, New York, 1964. *Alexander Hamilton's Pay Book* was edited by E. P. Panagopolous, Detroit, Mich., 1961. Harold C. Syrett and Jean G. Cooke edited *Interview in Weehawken: The Burr-Hamilton Duel as Told in Original Documents*, Middletown, Conn., 1960.

### BIOGRAPHY AND CRITICISM

Broadus Mitchell completed his biography with *Alexander Hamilton: The National Adventure, 1788-1804*, New York, 1962. John C. Miller's *Alexander Hamilton: Portrait in Paradox*, New York, 1959, is a biography with a strong emphasis on Hamilton's political career. The 1964 edition is retitled *Alexander Hamilton and the Growth of the New Nation*. Hamilton's philosophy and career are reassessed in Gilbert L. Lycan's *Alexander Hamilton and American Foreign Policy: A Design for Greatness*, Norman, Okla., 1969. Important specialized studies are Clinton Rossiter, *Alexander Hamilton and the Constitution*, New York, 1964; Samuel J. Konefsky, *John Marshall and Alexander Hamilton: Architects of the American Constitution*, New York, 1964; and Julian P. Boyd, *Number 7: Alexander Hamilton's Secret Attempts to Control American Foreign Policy, with Supporting Documents*, Princeton, N.J., 1964. Two useful introductions to Hamilton and his age are Richard B. Morris, *The Basic Ideas of Alexander Hamilton*, New York, 1957; and Jacob E. Cooke, ed., *Alexander Hamilton: A Profile*, New York, 1967. See also, *passim*, John C. Miller, *The Federalist Era*, New York, 1960; and Felix Gilbert, *To the Farewell Address: Ideas of Early American Foreign Policy*, Princeton, N.J., 1961.

Briefer estimates are Adrienne Koch, "Hamilton and Power," *YR*, XLVII (1958), 537-551; Stanley A. Rose, "Alexander Hamilton and the Historians," *Vanderbilt Law Review*, XI (1958), 853-886; Dumas Malone, "Hamilton on Balance," *PAPS*, CII (1958), 132-135; Cecelia M. Kenyon, "Alexander Hamilton: Rousseau of the Right," *PSQ*, LXXIII

(1958), 161–178; and Broadus Mitchell, "Alexander Hamilton as Finance Minister," *PAPS*, CII (1958), 117–123.

# JOEL CHANDLER HARRIS

### 540. EDITED TEXTS AND CORRESPONDENCE

David Bonnell Green edited "A New Joel Chandler Harris Letter," *GHQ*, XLII (1958), 106–109.

### 541. BIOGRAPHY AND CRITICISM

The most recent full-length study is Paul M. Cousins, *Joel Chandler Harris: A Biography*, Baton Rouge, La., 1968. Briefer estimates are M. Thomas Inge, "Sut Lovingood: An Examination of the Nature of a 'Nat'ral Born Durn'd Fool,'" *THQ*, XIX (1960), 231–251; Hamlin L. Hill, "Archy and Uncle Remus: Don Marquis's Debt to Joel Chandler Harris," *GaR*, XV (1961), 78–87; Herbert F. Smith, "Joel Chandler Harris's Contributions to *Scribner's Monthly* and *Century Magazine,* 1880–1887," *GHQ*, XLVII (1963), 169–179; David A. Walton, "Joel Chandler Harris as Folklorist: A Reassessment," *KFQ*, XI (1966), 21–26; Thomas H. English, "The Other Uncle Remus," *GaR*, XXI (1967), 210–217; and Darwin T. Turner, "Daddy Joel Harris and His Old Time Darkies," *SLJ*, I (1968), 20–41.

The most recent listings are Jacob Blanck, *Bibliography of American Literature*, III, New Haven, Conn., 1959, 387–401; *idem*, "BAL Addendum," *PBSA*, LXI (1967), 266; and Arlin Turner, "Joel Chandler Harris (1848–1908)," *ALR*, III (1968), 18–23.

# (FRANCIS) BRET(T) HARTE

### 543. BIOGRAPHY AND CRITICISM

Richard O'Connor's *Bret Harte: A Biography*, Boston, 1966, adds little in the way of new material or critical judgments, but it is a lively retelling. Margaret Duckett's *Mark Twain and Bret Harte*, Norman, Okla., 1964, though obviously biased in favor of Harte, is nevertheless a shattering revelation of the enmity behind this relationship. Briefer estimates are Margaret Duckett, "The 'Crusade' of a Nineteenth-Century Liberal," *TSL*, IV (1959), 109–120; Gustave O. Arlt, "Bret Harte: The Argonaut," *Southern California Quarterly*, XLIV (1962), 17–30; W. B. Gates, "Bret Harte and Shakespeare," *SCB*, XX (1960), 29–33; Eugene F. Timpe, "Bret Harte's

German Public," *JA*, X (1965), 215–220; Lynwood Carranco, "Bret Harte in Union (1857–1860)," *CHSQ*, XLV (1966), 99–112; Roy F. Hudson, "The Contributions of Bret Harte to American Oratory," *WAL*, II (1967), 213–222; J. R. Boggan, "The Regeneration of 'Roaring Camp,'" *NCF*, II (1967), 271–280; and D. M. McKeithan, "Bret Harte's Yuba Bill Meets the Ingenue," *MTJ*, XIV (1969), 1–7.

A listing of Harte's works is in Jacob Blanck, *Bibliography of American Literature*, III, New Haven, Conn., 1959, 412–478.

# NATHANIEL HAWTHORNE

## 545. COLLECTED WORKS

The French and Italian notebooks are still unedited, as is the complete collection of Hawthorne's letters. Gleanings of correspondence are in Edward C. Sampson, "Three Unpublished Letters by Hawthorne to Epes Sargent," *AL*, XXXIV (1962), 102–105; George Monteiro, "First Printing for a Hawthorne Letter," *AL*, XXXVI (1964), 346; and Benjamin Lease, "Hawthorne and *Blackwood's* in 1849: Two Unpublished Letters," *JA*, XIV (1969), 152–154.

## 546. EDITED TEXTS

The Ohio State University Press has begun publication of *The Centenary Edition of the Works of Nathaniel Hawthorne*, William Charvat, Claude M. Simpson, and Roy Harvey Pearce, general editors; Fredson Bowers, textual editor, with *The Scarlet Letter* (1963), *The Blithedale Romance* and *Fanshawe* (1964), *The House of the Seven Gables* (1965), *The Marble Faun* (1968), and *Our Old Home* (1970). Hyatt H. Waggoner and George Monteiro edited a facsimile edition of *The Scarlet Letter*, San Francisco, 1968. *The House of the Seven Gables*, ed. Hyatt H. Waggoner, Boston, 1964, is a newly edited text produced by a collation of the manuscript and the first edition. Richard E. Peck edited *Nathaniel Hawthorne, Poems*, [Charlottesville, Va.], 1967. *Hawthorne in England*, ed., Cushing Strout, Ithaca, N.Y., 1965, is a volume of selections from *Our Old Home* and *The English Note-Books*. Other reprintings of the novels are too numerous to list separately.

## 547. BIOGRAPHY AND CRITICISM

Hubert H. Hoeltje's *Inward Sky: The Mind and Heart of Nathaniel Hawthorne*, Durham, N.C., 1962, is a good attempt "to disclose . . . the whole man," but this biography is marred by the author's irritating habit of

not using quotation marks to indicate where Hawthorne leaves off and
Hoeltje begins. Edward Wagenknecht calls his *Nathaniel Hawthorne: Man
and Writer*, New York, 1961, "neither a chronological biography nor a
critical study," but "simply a study of Hawthorne's character and personality." Millicent Bell claims her *Hawthorne's View of the Artist*, New York,
1962, is "a book about Hawthorne rather than about a 'theme,'" but its
emphasis is chiefly aesthetic.

Of the numerous critical studies in the last decade, four are primary.
Richard Harter Fogle published a "supplement" to his 1952 critical study,
*Hawthorne's Fiction: The Light and the Dark* (rev. ed., 1964), under the
title *Hawthorne's Imagery: The "Proper Light and Shadow" in the Major
Romances*, Norman Okla., 1969, its scope being "confined largely to the
four major romances." Frederick C. Crews's *The Sins of the Fathers: Hawthorne's Psychological Themes*, New York, 1966, is a dogmatically Freudian but illuminating reading of the work. In *Hawthorne as Myth-Maker*,
Toronto, 1969, Hugo McPherson attempts to define "the nature of Hawthorne's 'cryptic preoccupation,' that inward vision or drama of which his
works are the particular if partial formulations." Terence Martin's *Nathaniel Hawthorne* New York, 1965, less ambitious than either the McPherson
or the Crews volumes, is a readable and intelligent introduction to Hawthorne.

The student will also want to consult James K. Folsom, *Man's Accidents
and God's Purposes: Multiplicity in Hawthorne's Fiction*, New Haven,
Conn., 1963; Marjorie J. Elder, *Nathaniel Hawthorne: Transcendental
Symbolist*, Athens, Ohio, 1969; John Caldwell Stubbs, *The Pursuit of
Form: A Study of Hawthorne and the Romance*, Urbana, Ill., 1970; and
Michael Davitt Bell, *Hawthorne and the Historical Romance of New Eng-
land*, Princeton, N.J., 1971. Less concerned with Hawthorne's fiction as
works of art are Arlin Turner, *Nathaniel Hawthorne: An Introduction and
Interpretation*, New York, 1961; and Henry G. Fairbanks, *The Lasting
Loneliness of Nathaniel Hawthorne: A Study of the Sources of Alienation
in Modern Man*, Albany, N.Y., 1965. For a brief survey see Hyatt H.
Waggoner's pamphlet, *Nathaniel Hawthorne*, Minneapolis, Minn., 1962.
Richard J. Jacobson, *Hawthorne's Conception of the Creative Process*,
Cambridge, Mass., 1965, is an honors prize essay.

Two European studies are Franz H. Link, *Die Erzählkunst Nathaniel
Hawthornes*, Heidelberg, 1962; and Jean Normand, *Nathaniel Hawthorne:
Esquisse d'une analyse de la création artistique*, Paris, 1964, trans. Derek
Coltman, Cleveland, Ohio, 1970.

Robert L. Gale compiled a useful reference work in *Plots and Characters
in the Fiction and Sketches of Nathaniel Hawthorne*, Hamden, Conn.,

1968. Evangeline M. O'Connor's *Analytical Index to the Works of Nathaniel Hawthorne* (1882) was reprinted in Detroit, Michigan, 1967.

See also chapters on Hawthorne in the following volumes: Harry Levin, *The Power of Blackness*, New York, 1958; Marius Bewley, *The Eccentric Design: Form in the Classic American Novel*, New York, 1959; Martin Green, *Re-appraisals: Some Commonsense Readings in American Literature*, New York, 1965 (an attack on Hawthorne's reputation); David Levin, *In Defense of Historical Literature*, New York, 1967; Joel Porte, *The Romance in America*, Middletown, Conn., 1961; and Daniel G. Hoffman, *Form and Fable in American Fiction*, New York, 1961.

Collections of brief critical studies are numerous: Roy Harvey Pearce, ed., *Hawthorne Centenary Essays*, Columbus, Ohio, 1964; A. N. Kaul, ed., *Hawthorne: A Collection of Critical Essays*, Englewood Cliffs, N.J., 1966; B. Bernard Cohen, ed., *The Recognition of Nathaniel Hawthorne: Selected Criticism since 1828*, Ann Arbor, Mich., 1969; Agnes M. Donohue, ed., *A Casebook on the Hawthorne Question*, New York, 1963; John C. Gerber, ed., *Twentieth-Century Interpretations of The Scarlet Letter*, Englewood Cliffs, N.J., 1968; and Seymour L. Gross, *A "Scarlet Letter" Handbook*, San Francisco, 1960. Kenneth W. Cameron's *Hawthorne among His Contemporaries*, Hartford, Conn., 1968, is a photostatic gathering of Victorian criticism and anecdote.

Other critical estimates are Richard P. Adams, "Hawthorne: The Old Manse Period," *TSE*, VIII (1958), 115–151; Edwin Fussell, "Hawthorne, James, and 'The Common Doom,'" *AQ*, X (1958), 438–453; Norman Holmes Pearson, "Elizabeth Peabody on Hawthorne," *EIHC*, XCIV (1958), 256–276; Randall Stewart, "Editing the American Notebooks," *EIHC*, XCIV (1958), 275–281; Roy Harvey Pearce, "Robin Molineux on the Analyst's Couch: A Note on the Limits of Psychoanalytic Criticism," *Criticism*, I (1959), 83–90; Charles Ryskamp, "The New England Sources of *The Scarlet Letter*," *AL*, XXXI (1959), 257–272; Barry A. Marks, "The Origin of Original Sin in Hawthorne's Fiction," *NCF*, XIV (1960), 359–362; Maurice Charney, "Hawthorne and the Gothic Style," *NEQ*, XXXIV (1961), 36–49; M. L. Allen, "Hawthorne's Art in His Short Stories," *SA*, VII (1961), 9–41; Alfred H. Marks, "Hawthorne's Daguerreotypist: Scientist, Artist, Reformer," *BSTCF*, III (1962), 61–74; Edward H. Davidson, "Dimmesdale's Fall," *NEQ*, XXXVI (1963), 358–370; Joseph Schwartz, "Three Aspects of Hawthorne's Puritanism," *NEQ*, XXXVI (1963), 192–208; William G. Carleton, "Hawthorne Discovers the English," *YR*, LIII (1964), 395–414; Sidney P. Moss, "The Problem of Theme in *The Marble Faun*," *NCF*, XVIII (1964), 393–399; William L. Vance, "The Comic Element in Hawthorne's Sketches," *SIR*, III (1964),

144–160; Gary J. Scrimgeour, "*The Marble Faun*: Hawthorne's Faery Land," *AL*, XXXVI (1964), 271–287; Roger Asselineau, "Hawthorne Abroad," *LanM*, LIX (1965), 156–163; Francis E. Kearns, "Margaret Fuller as a Model for Hester Prynne," *JA*, X (1965), 161–197; Austin Warren, "*The Scarlet Letter*: A Literary Exercise in Moral Theology," *SoR*, I (1965), 22–45.

More recent studies are Paul J. Hurley, "Young Goodman Brown's 'Heart of Darkness,'" *AL*, XXXVII (1966), 410–419; H. Bruce Franklin, "Hawthorne and Science Fiction," *CentR*, X (1966), 112–130; Neal F. Doubleday, "Hawthorne's Estimate of His Early Works," *AL*, XXXVII (1966), 403–409; Alfred J. Kloeckner, "The Flower and the Fountain: Hawthorne's Chief Symbols in 'Rappaccini's Daughter,'" *AL*, XXXVIII (1966), 323–336; Herbert W. Schneider, "The Democracy of Hawthorne," *EUQ*, XXII (1966), 123–132; Ernest W. Baughman, "Public Confession and *The Scarlet Letter*," *NEQ*, XL (1967), 532–550; Francis L. Battaglia, "*The House of the Seven Gables*: New Light on Old Problems," *PMLA*, LXXXII (1967), 579–590; Nina Baym, "The Head, the Heart, and the Unpardonable Sin," *NEQ*, XL (1967), 31–47; *idem*, "*The Blithedale Romance*: A Radical Reading," *JEGP*, LXVII (1968), 545–569; James E. Rocks, "Hawthorne and France: In Search of American Literary Nationalism," *TSE*, XVII (1969), 145–157; and Joe Davis, "The Myth of the Garden: Nathaniel Hawthorne's 'Rappaccini's Daughter,'" *SLitI*, II (1969), 3–12.

Special Hawthorne issues can be found in *The Emerson Society Quarterly*, No. 25 (1961); *Nineteenth-Century Fiction*, XIX (Sept., 1964); *Studies in the Novel*, II (Winter, 1970); and *Essex Institute Historical Collections*, C (Oct., 1964). *The Nathaniel Hawthorne Journal*, a projected annual edited by C. E. Frazer Clark, Jr., and first published in 1971 in Washington, D.C., contains among other items a census of Hawthorne letters (1813–1849) and a checklist of recent Hawthorne scholarship.

## 552. BIBLIOGRAPHY

The Nouvart Tashjian-Dwight Eckerman bibliography, long promised, has not yet appeared. A major listing is in Jacob Blanck, *Bibliography of American Literature*, IV, New Haven, Conn., 1963, 1–36.

Buford Jones compiled *A Checklist of Hawthorne Criticism 1951–1966: With a Detailed Index*, Hartford, Conn., 1967. An addendum to Jones is Kenneth W. Cameron's *Hawthorne Index*, Hartford, Conn., 1968. Useful bibliographies are appended to the Terence Martin, Bernard Cohen, and Seymour Gross volumes cited above. See also Robert Phillips *et al.*, "Nathaniel Hawthorne: Criticism of the Four Major Romances: A Selected Bibliography," *Thoth*, III (1962), 39–50.

Hawthorne manuscripts are discussed in *A Descriptive Guide to the Exhibition* [at The Grolier Club] *Commemorating the Death of Nathaniel Hawthorne 1804-1864*, New York, 1964; Richard Harwell, *Hawthorne and Longfellow: A Guide to an Exhibit* [at Bowdoin College], Brunswick, Me., 1966; Seymour L. Gross and Alfred J. Levy, "Some Remarks on the Extant Manuscripts of Hawthorne's Short Stories," *SB*, XIV (1961), 254–257; Kenneth Walter Cameron, "Inventory of Hawthorne's Manuscripts," *ESQ*, No. 29 (1962), pp. 5–20; and Oliver L. Steele, "On the Imposition of the First Edition of Hawthorne's *The Scarlet Letter*," *Library*, XVII (1962), 250–255.

# JOHN (MILTON) HAY

**553. COLLECTED WORKS AND CORRESPONDENCE**

See George Monteiro, "Letters to a 'Countryman': John Hay to Henry James," *BBr*, XIX (1963), 105–112.

**554. BIBLIOGRAPHY**

*The Life and Works of John Hay 1838-1905: A Commemorative Catalogue of the Exhibition Shown at the John Hay Library of Brown University*, Providence, R.I., 1961, is a useful gathering of information on manuscripts, books, articles by and about Hay. See also the listing in Jacob Blanck, *Bibliography of American Literature*, IV, New Haven, Conn., 1963, 37–63.

# PAUL HAMILTON HAYNE

**554. COLLECTED WORKS AND CORRESPONDENCE**

Gleanings of correspondence are Herbert F. Smith, "Some Unpublished Letters of Paul Hamilton Hayne," *JRUL*, XXV (1961), 24–27; and Eugene Nolte, ed., "Two Unpublished Letters from Paul Hamilton Hayne," *GHQ*, L (1966), 105–109.

Previously unpublished texts are in Richard Walser, "Seven 'Lost' Sonnets of Paul Hamilton Hayne," *BNYPL*, LXX (1966), 533–537.

**555. *Biography and Criticism***

A biographical sketch is Rayburn S. Moore, "Paul Hamilton Hayne," *GaR*, XXII (1968), 106–124. For critical estimates, see Edd W. Parks, "Paul Hamilton Hayne: Eclectic Critic of Poetry," *MissQ*, X (1957), 155–176; *idem*, "Paul Hamilton Hayne on Novels and Novelists," *GaR*,

XII (1958), 305–315; Claude R. Flory, "Paul Hamilton Hayne and the New South," *GHQ*, XLVI (1962), 388–394; John Archer Carter, "Paul Hayne's Sonnet 'To the New South,'" *GHQ*, XLVIII (1964), 192–195; and John Williams, "Hayne's 'The Prostrate South to the Radical North,'" *GHQ*, XLIX (1965), 98–101.

A listing of Hayne's works is in Jacob Blanck, *Bibliography of American Literature*, IV, New Haven, Conn., 1963, 64–74.

## LAFCADIO HEARN

### 556. COLLECTED WORKS

Makoto Sangu edited *Lafcadio Hearn: Editorials from The Kobe Chronicle*, Tokyo, 1960, dated October-December, 1894.

Gleanings of correspondence are in Ichiro Nishizaki, "Newly Discovered Letters from Lafcadio Hearn to Dr. Rudolph Matas," *Ochanomizu Joshi Daigaku Jimbun kagaku kiyō*, VIII (1956), 85–118.

### 558. BIOGRAPHY AND CRITICISM

The major biography, concentrating on the life rather than Hearn as critic or thinker, is Elizabeth Stevenson, *Lafcadio Hearn*, New York, 1961. O. W. Frost's *Young Hearn*, Tokyo, 1958, illuminates the obscure early years.

The major critical studies are Marcel Robert, *Lafcadio Hearn*, 2 vols., Tokyo, 1950–1951, Hearn's career to 1897; Beongcheon Yu's *An Ape of Gods: The Art and Thought of Lafcadio Hearn*, Detroit, Mich., 1964, chiefly concerned with the philosophical essays; and Arthur E. Kunst's treatment of Hearn "as a creative writer from his earliest days in Cincinnati to his last days in Japan," *Lafcadio Hearn*, New York, 1969. Albert Mordell's collection, *Discoveries: Essays on Lafcadio Hearn*, Tokyo, 1964, includes information on uncollected Hearn pieces. Other brief estimates are Edward Stokes, "Lafcadio Hearn's *Chita*," *AUMLA*, No. 5 (1957), pp. 1–9; Albert Mordell, " 'The Lady's' Unrequited Love for Hearn," *OW*, VI (1961), 51–60; *idem*, "Lafcadio Hearn and Dr. Rudolph Matas," *TJ*, VI (1961), 61–68; Edwin Jahn, "Lafcadio Hearn's Image of Japan," *OW*, VIII (1963), 33–40; Siegfried Mandel, "Lafcadio Hearn and the Jikininkis," *IEY*, No. 8 (1963), pp. 67–72; Arthur E. Kunst, "Lafcadio Hearn's Use of Japanese Sources," *LE&W*, X (1966), 245–263; and Katherine Bridges, "Lafcadio Hearn and Leona Queyrouse," *LaS*, VII (1968), 173–178. *Today's Japan*, IV (Jan., 1959), contains seven articles on Hearn. See also, *passim*, Earl Miner, *Japanese Tradition in British and American Literature*, Princeton, N.J., 1958.

**559.** BIBLIOGRAPHY

The Perkins bibliography (1934) was reprinted in New York, 1968. More recent listings are in Jacob Blanck, *Bibliography of American Literature*, IV, New Haven, Conn., 1963, 75–106; and Beongcheon Yu, "Lafcadio Hearn (or Koizumi Yakumo) (1850–1904)," *ALR*, I (1967), 52–55. See also *Descriptive Catalogue of the Hearniana in the Hearn Library of the Toyama University*, Toyama, Japan, 1959, a companion to Perkins.


## ERNEST (MILLER) HEMINGWAY
*d. 1961*

**559.** SEPARATE WORKS

*A Moveable Feast*, 1964; *"The Fifth Column" and Four Stories of the Spanish Civil War*, 1969; *Islands in the Stream*, 1970.

**560.** COLLECTIONS

William White reprints newspaper and magazine pieces, 1920–1956, in *By-Line: Ernest Hemingway: Selected Articles and Dispatches of Four Decades*, New York, 1967. *The Wild Years: Ernest Hemingway*, ed. Gene Z. Hanrahan, New York, 1962, is a selection of 73 Toronto *Star* articles, 1920–1924. Three high school stories are reprinted in Constance Cappel Montgomery's *Hemingway in Michigan*, New York, 1966. Matthew J. Bruccoli edited *Ernest Hemingway, Cub Reporter*, Pittsburgh, Pa., 1970, reprinting Hemingway's contributions to the Kansas City *Star*, 1917–1918.

BIOGRAPHY AND CRITICISM

The most valuable major biography is Carlos Baker's *Ernest Hemingway: A Life Story*, New York, 1969. An informal biographical sketch is Alfred G. Aronowitz and Peter Hamill's *Ernest Hemingway: The Life and Death of a Man*, New York, 1961. Family reminiscences include Leicester Hemingway's *My Brother, Ernest Hemingway*, Cleveland, Ohio, 1962; and Marcelline Hemingway Sanford's *At the Hemingways*, Boston, 1962. Morley Callaghan's *That Summer in Paris*, New York, 1963, is subtitled *Memories of Tangled Friendships with Hemingway, Fitzgerald, and Some Others*. Harold Loeb tells his version of the Paris and Pamplona days in *The Way It Was*, New York, 1959. Leo Lania (pseudonym Lazar Herrmann) combines well-chosen pictures with an inaccurate running biographical account in *Hemingway: A Pictorial Biography*, New York, 1961. Lloyd R. Arnold's *High on the Wild with Hemingway*, Caldwell, Idaho, 1968, documents the Idaho years 1939–1961 with pictures and prose. A. E. Hotch-ner's *Papa Hemingway*, New York 1966, which Mary Hemingway tried unsuccessfully to keep out of print, is a somewhat inaccurate account of Hemingway's last years by a former friend and business associate. See also, *passim*, Max Eastman, *Great Companions*, New York 1959; John Dos Passos, *The Best Times*, New York, 1966; Malcolm Cowley, *The Faulkner-Cowley File*, New York, 1966; Robert E. Knoll, ed., *McAlmon and the Lost Generation*, Lincoln, Neb., 1962; and George Plimpton's interview, "The Art of Fiction XXI: Ernest Hemingway," *ParR*, No. 18 (Spring, 1958).

Two of Hemingway's early critics have revised their major work: Carlos Baker enlarged his *Hemingway: The Writer as Artist* for a third edition, Princeton, N.J., 1963; Philip Young enlarged his *Ernest Hemingway* (New York, 1952) and retitled it *Ernest Hemingway: A Reconsideration*, University Park, Pa., 1966. Of the more recent critical studies, the surveys by Sheridan Baker, *Ernest Hemingway: An Introduction and Interpretation*, New York, 1967; and Leo Gurko, *Ernest Hemingway and the Pursuit of Heroism*, New York, 1968, are of primary importance. Richard B. Hovey's *Hemingway: The Inward Terrain*, Seattle, Wash., 1968, is a perceptive psychoanalytic study of the fiction. Other general studies are Earl N. Rovit, *Ernest Hemingway*, New York, 1963; Joseph De Falco, *The Hero in Hemingway's Short Stories*, Pittsburgh, Pa., 1963; Jackson J. Benson, *Hemingway: The Writer's Art of Self-Defense*, Minneapolis, Minn., 1969; and Delbert E. Wylder, *Hemingway's Heroes*, Albuquerque, N.M., 1969. More specialized are John Killinger, *Hemingway and the Dead Gods*, Lexington, Ky., 1960; Robert O. Stephens, *Hemingway's Nonfiction: The Public Voice*, Chapel Hill, N.C., 1968; Nicholas Joost, *Ernest Hemingway and the Little Magazines: The Paris Years*, Barre, Mass., 1968; and Robert W. Lewis, Jr., *Hemingway on Love*, Austin, Tex., 1965. Brief introductions for the student are Philip Young's pamphlet, *Ernest Hemingway*, Minneapolis, Minn., 1959; and Stewart Sanderson, *Hemingway*, Edinburgh, 1961.

Georges-Albert Astre's *Hemingway par lui-même*, Paris, 1961, has been translated into German by Kurt Kusenberg, *Ernest Hemingway in Selbstzeugnissen und Bilddokumenten*, Hamburg, 1961. Hanspeter Doerfel, *Hemingways Erzählperspektiven*, Saarbrücken, 1964, is a substantial study; as is Jerzy R. Krzyzanowski's *Ernest Hemingway*, Warsaw, 1963. See also Hans Jürgen Baden, *Literatur und Selbstmord*, Stuttgart, 1965; and Josette Smetana, *La philosophie de l'action chez Hemingway et Saint-Exupéry*, Paris, 1965.

Collections of critical essays are numerous: Carlos Baker, ed., *Hemingway and His Critics: An International Anthology*, New York, 1961, and

*Ernest Hemingway: Critiques of Four Major Novels*, New York, 1962; Robert P. Weeks, ed., *Hemingway: A Collection of Critical Essays*, Englewood Cliffs, N.J., 1962; Roger Asselineau, ed., *The Literary Reputation of Hemingway in Europe*, Paris, 1965; John Brown *et al., Hemingway*, Paris, 1961; Katharine T. Jobes, ed., *Twentieth-Century Interpretations of The Old Man and the Sea*, Englewood Cliffs, N.J., 1968; and John M. Howell, ed., *Hemingway's African Stories*, New York, 1969.

Other brief studies are William Forrest Dawson, "Ernest Hemingway: Petoskey Interview," *MAQR*, LXIV (1958), 114-123; Robert O. Stephens, "Hemingway's *Across the River and into the Trees*: A Reprise," *TxSE*, XXXVII (1958), 92-101; Max Eastman, "The Great and Small in Ernest Hemingway," *SatR*, XLII (Apr. 4, 1959), 13-15; 50-51; John A. Jones, "Hemingway: The Critics and the Public Legend," *WHR*, XIII (1959), 387-400; Richard Freedman, "Hemingway's Spanish Civil War Dispatches," *TSLL*, I (1959), 171-180; Annette T. Rubinstein, "Brave and Baffled Hunter," *Mainstream*, XIII (1960), 1-23; Allen Guttmann, "Mechanized Doom: Ernest Hemingway and the Spanish Civil War," *MR*, I (1960), 541-561; John Graham, "Ernest Hemingway: The Meaning of Style," *MFS*, VI (1960), 298-313; Harold Loeb, "The Young Writer in Paris and Pamplona," *SatR*, XLIV (July 29, 1961), 25-26; William Bysshe Stein, "Love and Lust in Hemingway's Short Stories," *TSLL*, III (1961), 234-242; Nancy Hale, "Hemingway and the Courage to Be," *VQR*, XXXVIII (1962), 620-639; S. L. A. Marshall, "How Papa Liberated Paris," *AH*, XIII (Apr., 1962), 5-7, 92-101; Barney Childs, "Hemingway and the Leopard of Kilimanjaro," *AN&Q*, II (1963), 3; Edmund Wilson, "That Summer in Paris," *NY*, XXXIX (Feb. 23, 1963), 139-148, and the rebuttal by Mary Hemingway, "Department of Amplification," *NY*, XXXIX (Mar. 16, 1963), 160-163; Alex Page, "Pakistan's Hemingway," *AR*, XXIII (1963), 202-211; Paul Lauter, "Plato's Stepchildren, Gatsby and Cohn," *MFS*, IX (1964), 338-346; Stephen Jan Parker, "Hemingway's Revival in the Soviet Union: 1955-1962," *AL*, XXV (1964), 485-501; Louis Broussard, "Hemingway as a Literary Critic," *ArQ*, XX (1964), 197-204.

Later estimates are Daniel Fuchs, "Ernest Hemingway, Literary Critic," *AL*, XXXVI (1965), 431-451; Philip Young, "On Disremembering Hemingway," *Atl*, CCXVIII (1966), 45-49; Robert Evans, "Hemingway and the Pale Cast of Thought," *AL*, XXXVIII (1966), 161-176; Cecil D. Eby, "The Real Robert Jordan," *AL*, XXXVIII (1966), 380-386; Peter Lisca, "The Structure of Hemingway's *Across The River and into the Trees*," *MFS*, XII (1966), 232-250; William White, "Hemingway as Reporter: An Unknown News Story," *JQ*, XLIII (1966), 538-542; Harold Loeb, "Hemingway's Bitterness," *ConnR*, I (1967), 7-24; Dave Marin, "Seven Hours with Papa," *SWR*, LIII (1968), 167-177; Donald St.

John, "Interview with Hemingway's 'Bill Gorton,'" *ConnR*, I (1968), 5–12; III (1969), 5–23; Bertram D. Sarason, "Hemingway in Havana: Two Interviews," *ConnR*, III (1969), 24–31; and Julian Smith, "Christ Times Four: Hemingway's Unknown Spanish Civil War Stories," *ArQ*, XXV (1969), 5–17.

Special Hemingway issues are *La Revue des Lettres Modernes*, Nos. 31–34 (1958); *Saturday Review*, XLIV (July 29, 1961); *Mark Twain Journal*, XI (1962); *Modern Fiction Studies*, XIV (1968); and *Journal of Arts and Letters* (Idaho State University), V (1970). The first issue of the *Fitzgerald/Hemingway Annual*, ed. Matthew J. Bruccoli, appeared in Washington, D.C., 1969.

**561.** BIBLIOGRAPHY

The major work is Audre Hanneman's *Ernest Hemingway: A Comprehensive Bibliography*, Princeton, N.J., 1967. It is the starting point for all bibliographical study of Hemingway. An interpretive bibliographical essay is Frederick J. Hoffman, "Ernest Hemingway," *Fifteen Modern American Authors*, ed. Jackson R. Bryer, Durham, N.C., 1969, pp. 275–300. For lists of critical studies, see Maurice Beebe and John Feaster, "Criticism of Ernest Hemingway: A Selected Checklist," *MFS*, XIV (1968), 337–369; and William White, *Merrill Guide to Ernest Hemingway*, Columbus, Ohio, 1969. A register of translations in European and Eastern languages is Hans W. Bentz, *Ernest Hemingway in Übersetzungen*, Frankfurt, 1963.

Philip Young and Charles W. Mann compiled *The Hemingway Manuscripts: An Inventory*, University Park, Pa., 1969. See also Max Westbrook, "Necessary Performance: The Hemingway Collection at Texas," *LCUT*, VII (1964), 27–31. James B. Meriwether discusses problems in and the need for an edition of Hemingway in "The Text of Ernest Hemingway," *PBSA*, LVII (1963), 403–421.

# JOSEPH HERGESHEIMER
*d. 1954*

**562.** BIBLIOGRAPHY AND CRITICISM

The first full-length critical study is Ronald E. Martin, *The Fiction of Joseph Hergesheimer*, Philadelphia, 1965. See also Gerald Langford, ed., *Ingenue among the Lions: The Letters of Emily Clark to Joseph Hergesheimer*, Austin, Tex., 1965.

**563.** BIBLIOGRAPHY

James J. Napier compiled "Joseph Hergesheimer: A Selected Bibliogra-

phy, 1913–1945," *BB*, XXIV (1963–1964), 46–48, 52, 69–70. See also Joseph
Evans Slate, "The Joseph Hergesheimer Collection," *LCUT*, VII (1961),
24–31.


# OLIVER WENDELL HOLMES

### 565. COLLECTED WORK AND CORRESPONDENCE

Albert Mordell edited *The Autocrat's Miscellanies*, New York, 1959, 30
uncollected essays.

### 566. BIOGRAPHY AND CRITICISM

The most recent survey of the career is Miriam R. Small's *Oliver Wen-
dell Holmes*, New York, 1963. Other evaluations are J. Chesley Mathews,
"Dr. Oliver Wendell Holmes and Dante," *Ital*, XXXIV (1957), 127–136;
Francisco Yndurain, "Unamuno y Oliver Wendell Holmes," *Atlántico*, No.
4 (1957), pp. 5–28; Charles Boewe, "A Medicated Poem by Oliver Wen-
dell Holmes," *NEQ*, XXXI (1958), 392–401; Jay B. Hubbell, "Oliver
Wendell Holmes, Rev. Joseph Cook, and the *University Quarterly*," *NEQ*,
XXXI (1958), 401–410; Oscar Kraines, "The Holmes Family and the
Jews," *CJF*, XVII (1958), 28–34; Karl P. Wentersdorf, "The Under-
ground workshop of Oliver Wendell Holmes," *AL*, XXXV (1963), 1–12;
Eleanor M. Tilton, "Holmes and His Critic Motley," *AL*, XXXVI (1965),
463–474; and J. Stanley Mattson, "Oliver Wendell Holmes and 'The
Deacon's Masterpiece': A Logical Story?" *NEQ*, XLI (1968), 104–114.

### 568. BIBLIOGRAPHY

The first major listing since the Ives bibliography (1907) is in Jacob
Blanck, *Bibliography of American Literature*, IV, New Haven, Conn.,
1963, 233–339. Eleanor M. Tilton offered "'Literary Bantlings': Addenda
to the Holmes Bibliography," *PBSA*, LI (1957), 1–18. See also *Oliver
Wendell Holmes: A Checklist of Printed and Manuscript Works . . . in the
Library of the University of Virginia*, comp. Anita Putnam, Lucy Clark,
and Marjorie Carver, Charlottesville, Va., 1960.


# WILLIAM DEAN HOWELLS

### 572. REPRINTS

The Indiana University Press began publication of its 41-volume *Selected Edition of W. D. Howells* (under the general editorship of Ronald
Gottesman) with *Their Wedding Journey* (1968), *The Altrurian Ro-*

*mances* (1968), *Literary Friends and Acquaintance* (1968), *The Shadow of a Dream* and *An Imperative Duty* (1969), *The Son of Royal Langbrith* (1969), *The Rise of Silas Lapham* (1970), and *A Chance Acquaintance* (1971).

*Letters of an Altrurian Traveller (1893–1894)*, ed. Clara M. Kirk and Rudolf Kirk, Gainesville, Fla., 1961, is a facsimile edition of the series as published in *Cosmopolitan Magazine*, 11 letters being reprinted for the first time. The Kirks also edited *"Criticism and Fiction" and Other Essays* by W. D. Howells, New York, 1959, making many fugitive pieces available as well as the central document (first published in 1891). Marilyn Baldwin edited *My Mark Twain: Reminiscences and Criticisms*, Baton Rouge, La., 1967. *The Complete Plays of W. D. Howells*, ed. Walter D. Meserve, New York, 1960, has a valuable introduction and an annotated bibliography.

LETTERS AND OTHER COLLECTED ITEMS

Henry Nash Smith and William M. Gibson, with the assistance of Frederick Anderson, edited *Mark Twain–Howells Letters: The Correspondence of Samuel L. Clemens and William D. Howells, 1872–1910*, 2 vols., Cambridge, Mass., 1960.

Further gleanings are in Richard Crowder, "American Nestor: Six Unpublished Letters from Howells to Ade," *BuR*, VII (1958), 144–149; Clara M. Kirk and Rudolf Kirk, "Letters to an 'Enchanted Guest': W. D. Howells to Edmund Gosse," *JRUL*, XXII (1959), 1–25; R. Baird Schuman, "The Howells-Lowell Correspondence: A New Item," *AL*, XXXI (1959), 338–340; James B. Stronks, "An Early Autobiographical Letter by William Dean Howells," *NEQ*, XXXIII (1960), 240–242; Jean Downey, "Three Unpublished Letters: Howells-Cooke," *AL*, XXXII (1961), 463–465; Howard A. Wilson, "William Dean Howells' Unpublished Letters about the Haymarket Affair," *ISHSJ*, LVI (1963), 5–19; and Richard Cary, "William Dean Howells to Thomas Sargeant Perry," *CLQ*, VII (1968), 157–215.

573· BIOGRAPHY AND CRITICISM

Edwin H. Cady completed his two-volume biography with *The Realist at War: The Mature Years, 1885–1920, of William Dean Howells*, Syracuse, N.Y., 1958. Van Wyck Brooks's *Howells: His Life and World*, New York, 1959, is an impressionistic reminiscence written from wide reading in his subject. Edward Wagenknecht's *William Dean Howells: The Friendly Eye*, New York, 1969, is a character portrait or "psychograph." Kenneth S. Lynn's *William Dean Howells: An American Life*, New York, 1971, is the most recent major biographical study.

The growth of critical interest in Howells's fiction has led to the publication of more than a dozen books. Clara M. Kirk and Rudolf Kirk focus on the primary texts in a concise survey of the whole career, *William Dean Howells*, New York, 1962. Kermit Vanderbilt, *The Achievement of William Dean Howells*, Princeton, N.J., 1968; and George N. Bennett, *William Dean Howells: The Development of a Novelist*, Norman, Okla., 1959, concentrate on close critical readings of certain novels. Clara M. Kirk followed her political study, *W. D. Howells, Traveler from Altruria, 1889–1894*, New Brunswick, N.J., 1962, with an investigation of Howells as art critic, *W. D. Howells and Art in His Time*, New Brunswick, N.J., 1965. Olov W. Fryckstedt, *In Quest of America: A Study of Howells' Early Development as a Novelist*, Cambridge, Mass., 1958, traces the author's intellectual growth and his knowledge of European writers. George C. Carrington, Jr., attempts a new critical approach, seeking the "real Howells" in *The Immense Complex Drama: The World and Art of the Howells Novel*, Columbus, Ohio, 1966. James L. Dean confines himself to a study of the travel literature in *Howells' Travels toward Art*, Albuquerque, N.M., 1969. Two special studies are William McMurray's *The Literary Realism of William Dean Howells*, Carbondale, Ill., 1967 (with emphasis on William James's pragmatism); and Robert L. Hough, *The Quiet Rebel: William Dean Howells as Social Commentator*, Lincoln, Neb., 1959 (chiefly non-literary opinions). William M. Gibson's pamphlet, *William Dean Howells*, Minneapolis, Minn., 1967, is a wholly adequate summary of Howells's achievement. See also chapters on Howells in Nathalia Wright, *American Novelists in Italy*, Philadelphia, 1965; Robert W. Schneider, *Five Novelists of the Progressive Era*, New York, 1965; Donald Pizer, *Realism and Naturalism in Nineteenth-Century American Literature*, Carbondale, Ill., 1966; Larzer Ziff, *The American 1890's*, New York, 1966; and Jay Martin, *Harvests of Change: American Literature 1865–1914*, Englewood Cliffs, N.J., 1967.

Kenneth E. Eble reprints 28 essays in *Howells: A Century of Criticism*, Dallas, Tex., 1962. Edwin H. Cady and David L. Frazier, eds., *The War of the Critics over William Dean Howells*, Evanston, Ill., 1962, spans the years 1860–1960 with 60 pieces by major American and British critics. Other brief estimates are George J. Becker, "William Dean Howells: The Awakening of Conscience," *CE*, XIX (1958), 283–291; Louis J. Budd, "Twain, Howells, and the Boston Nihilists," *NEQ*, XXXII (1959), 351–371; John Lydenberg and Edwin H. Cady, "The Howells Revival: Rounds Two and Three," *NEQ*, XXXII (1959), 394–407; James Woodress, "Four Decades of Howells Scholarship," *TSLL*, II (1960), 115–123; James W. Gargano, "*A Modern Instance*: The Twin Evils of Society," *TSLL*, IV (1962), 399–407; John E. Hart, "The Commonplace as Heroic in *The*

*Rise of Silas Lapham,*" *MFS*, VIII (1963), 375-383; Alma J. Payne, "William Dean Howells and the Independent Woman," *MidR*, V (1963), 44-52; David H. Hirsch, "William Dean Howells and Daisy Miller," *ELN*, I (1963), 123-128; Robert W. Walts, "Howells's Plans for Two Travel Books," *PBSA*, LVII (1964), 453-459.

More recent studies are Edwin H. Cady, "The Howells Nobody Knows," *MRR*, I (1965), 3-25; William Wasserstrom, "Howells' Mansion and Thoreau's Cabin," *CE*, XXVI (1965), 366-372; G. Thomas Tanselle, "The Architecture of *The Rise of Silas Lapham*," *AL*, XXXVII (1966), 430-457; Clare R. Goldfarb, "From Complicity to Altruria: The Use of Tolstoy in Howells," *UR*, XXXII (1966), 311-317; Arthur Boardman, "Social Point of View in the Novels of William Dean Howells," *AL*, XXXIX (1967), 42-59; Eric Solomon, "Howells, Houses, and Realism," *ALR*, IV (1968), 89-93; and Clara M. Kirk and Rudolf Kirk, "William Dean Howells, George William Curtis, and the Anarchist Affair," *AL*, XL (1969), 487-498.

### 576. BIBLIOGRAPHY

Since publication of the Gibson-Arms bibliography (1948), the major listing is in Jacob Blanck, *Bibliography of American Literature*, IV, New Haven, Conn., 1963, 384-448. John K. Reeves prepared "The Literary Manuscripts of W. D. Howells: A Descriptive Finding List," *BNYPL*, LXII (1958), 267-278, 350-363; LXV (1961), 465-476.

Useful bibliographies are included in Edward Wagenknecht's *William Dean Howells: The Friendly Eye*, New York, 1969; and Clara M. Kirk's and Rudolf Kirk's *William Dean Howells: Representative Selections*, rev. ed., New York, 1961. James Woodress and Stanley P. Anderson prepared "A Bibliography of Writing about William Dean Howells" for a special number (1969) of *American Literary Realism, 1879-1910*. See also intermittent issues of *The Howells Sentinel*, New Brunswick, N.J., a mimeographed bulletin for the Howells Group of MLA.

## (JAMES) LANGSTON HUGHES
### *d. 1967*

### 576. SEPARATE WORKS

Poems: *Selected Poems*, 1959; *Ask Your Mama: 12 Moods for Jazz*, 1961; *The Panther and the Lash: Poems of Our Times*, 1967.

Fiction: *The Best of Simple*, 1961; *Something in Common, and Other Stories*, 1964; *Simple's Uncle Sam*, 1965.

Miscellaneous: *Famous Negro Heroes of America*, 1958; *The First Book of Africa*, 1960 (rev. ed., 1964); *Fight for Freedom: The Story of the NAACP*, 1962; *Black Magic: A Pictorial History of the Negro in American Entertainment* (with Milton Meltzer), 1967.

Editions: *The Book of Negro Folklore* (coedited with Arna Bontemps), 1958; *An African Treasury: Articles, Essays, Stories, Poems by Black Africans*, 1960; *Poems from Black Africa*, 1963; *New Negro Poets: U.S.A.*, 1964; *The Book of Negro Humor*, 1966; *La Poésie Négro-Américaine*, 1966; *The Best Short Stories by Negro Writers: An Anthology from 1899 to the Present*, 1967.

*Five Plays by Langston Hughes*, ed. Webster Smalley, Bloomington, Ind., 1963, reprints *Mulatto, Soul Gone Home, Little Ham, Simply Heavenly, Tambourines to Glory*.

BIOGRAPHY AND CRITICISM

Milton Meltzer's *Langston Hughes: A Biography*, New York, 1968, is written out of a long personal relationship and two collaborations. The first full-length critical study is James A. Emmanuel, *Langston Hughes*, New York, 1967. Two European critiques are also useful: Raymond Quinot's *Langston Hughes, ou l'étoile noire*, Brussels, 1964, is biography combined with analyses of more than 20 poems; Jean Wagner, *Les poètes nègres des États-Unis*, Paris, 1963, treats Hughes's role in the Harlem Renascence. For briefer evaluations see Harold R. Isaacs, "Five Writers and Their African Ancestors," *Phylon*, XXI (1960), 243–265, 317–336; James A. Emmanuel, "Langston Hughes' First Short Story: 'Mary Winosky,'" *Phylon*, XXII (1961), 267–272; James Presley, "The American Dream of Langston Hughes," *SWR*, XLVIII (1963), 380–386; Therman B. O'Daniel, "Lincoln's Man of Letters," *Lincoln University Bulletin*, LXVII (July, 1964), 9–12; T. J. Spencer and Clarence Rivers, "Langston Hughes: His Style and Optimism," *Drama Critique*, VII (Spring, 1964), 99–102; Richard Rive, "Taos in Harlem: An Interview with Langston Hughes," *Contrast*, XIV (1967), 33–39; Aaron Kramer, "Robert Burns and Langston Hughes," *Freedomways*, VIII (1968), 159–166; Woodie King, Jr., "Remembering Langston: A Poet of the Black Theater, *NegroD*, XVIII (1969), 27–32, 95–96; and Wilfred Cartey, "Four Shadows of Harlem," *NegroD*, XVIII (1969), 22–25, 83–92. *College Language Association Journal*, XI (1968), is a special Langston Hughes number.

A critically annotated and well-organized bibliography is Donald C. Dickinson, *A Bio-Bibliography of Langston Hughes: 1902–1967*, Hamden, Conn., 1967. See also Therman B. O'Daniel, "Langston Hughes: A Selected Classified Bibliography," *CLAJ*, XI (1968), 349–366.

## JAMES GIBBONS HUNEKER

### 578. BIOGRAPHY AND CRITICISM

Arnold T. Schwab's *James Gibbons Huneker: Critic of the Seven Arts*, Stanford, Calif., 1963, is not only the first biography but also an authoritative study of the cultural life of the United States, 1880–1920. See also Annette T. Rottenberg, "Aesthete in America: The Short Stories of James Gibbons Huneker," *SSF*, II (1965), 358–366.

A listing of Huneker's works is in Jacob Blanck, *Bibliography of American Literature*, IV, New Haven, Conn., 1963, 449–458.

## WASHINGTON IRVING

### 579. COLLECTED WORKS

The University of Wisconsin Press has begun publication of a 28-volume edition of *The Complete Works of Washington Irving*, under the general editorship of Henry A. Pochmann, with *Journals and Notebooks, 1803–06* (1969), *Journals and Notebooks, 1819–27* (1970), and *Mahomet and His Successors* (1970).

### PRINTED LETTERS

Gleanings are in Ben W. Griffith, "An Experiment on the American Bookseller: Two Letters from Irving to Godwin," *NCF*, XII (1957), 237–239; Andrew Breen Meyers, ed., "Washington Irving's Madrid Journal 1827–1828 and Related Letters," *BNYPL*, LXII (1958), 217–227, 300–311, 407–419, 463–471; Clara L. Penney, "Washington Irving in Spain: Unpublished Letters Chiefly to Mrs. Henry O'Shea, 1844–1854," *BNYPL*, LXII (1958), 615–631, LXIII (1959), 23–39; Everett H. Emerson and Katherine T. Emerson, "Some Letters of Washington Irving: 1833–1843," *AL*, XXXV (1963), 156–172; Ben Harris McClary, "Washington Irving to Walter Scott: Two Unpublished Letters," *SSL*, III (1965), 114–118; *idem*, "Washington Irving's Admirable Scotch Friends: Three Unpublished Letters to the John Gibson Lockharts, *SSL*, IV (1966), 101–104; and *idem*, "Irving's Literary Midwifery: Five Unpublished Letters from British Repositories," *PQ*, XLVI (1967), 277–283.

### 580. EDITED TEXTS AND REPRINTS

Edgeley W. Todd prepared the first annotated edition of *The Adventures of Captain Bonneville, U.S.A., in the Rocky Mountains and the Far West, Digested from His Journal by Washington Irving*, Norman, Okla., 1961.

Irving published this book in 1837 under the title *The Rocky Mountains* and later renamed it. *Astoria, or Anecdotes of an Enterprise beyond the Rocky Mountains*, has had two important reprintings: William H. Goetzmann edited a two-volume edition of the 1836 *Astoria* unabridged, Philadelphia, 1961; Edgeley W. Todd edited a one-volume reprint of the 1860–1861 Author's Revised Edition, Norman, Okla., 1964. *Washington Irving's Contributions to The Corrector*, introduction and attribution by Martin Roth, appeared in Minneapolis, Minn., 1968. Other reprints are too numerous to list separately.

For discussions of Irving manuscript material, see Andrew B. Myers, "Washington Irving's Moorish Manuscript: A Columbia Rediscovery," *CLC*, VIII (Nov., 1958), 22–29; John Francis McDermott, "An Unpublished Washington Irving Manuscript," *PELL*, I (1965), 369–373; Daniel R. Barnes, "Washington Irving: An Unrecorded Periodical Publication," *SB*, XX (1967), 260–261; and Richard E. Peck, "An Unpublished Poem by Washington Irving," *AL*, XXXIX (1967), 204–207.

### 581. BIOGRAPHY AND CRITICISM

William L. Hedges's admirable *Washington Irving: An American Study, 1802–1832*, Baltimore, Md., 1965, focuses on Irving's relation to his intellectual environment and his influence on other writers. Edward Wagenknecht's *Washington Irving: Moderation Displayed*, New York, 1962, is a three-part study: the life, the man, the work. Lewis Leary's pamphlet, *Washington Irving*, Minneapolis Minn., 1963, is a general introduction to Irving's career. Irving's British publisher, John Murray, is the subject of *Washington Irving and the House of Murray: Geoffrey Crayon Charms the British, 1817–1856*, ed. Ben Harris McClary, Knoxville, Tenn., 1969. Readers interested in Irving's tour of the prairies in 1832 will want to see the recently discovered diary of one of the party, George F. Spaulding, ed., *On the Western Tour with Washington Irving: The Journal and Letters of Count de Pourtalès*, Norman, Okla., 1968.

Other special studies are Harold Dean Cater, "Washington Irving and Sunnyside," *NYH*, XXXVIII (1957), 123–166; Walter A. Reichart, "Washington Irving's Interest in German Folklore," *NYFQ*, XIII (1957), 181–192; Edgeley W. Todd, "Washington Irving Discovers the Frontier," *WHR*, XI (1957), 29–39; Marcel Heiman, "Rip Van Winkle: A Psychoanalytic Note on the Story and Its Author," *AI*, XVI (1959), 3–47; Philip Young, "Fallen from Time: The Mythic Rip Van Winkle," *KR*, XXII (1960), 547–573; James W. Webb, "Irving and His 'Favorite Author' [Goldsmith]," *UMSE*, III (1962), 61–74; Robert A. Bone, "Irving's Headless Hessian: Prosperity and the Inner Life," *AQ*, XV (1963), 167–175; Barbara D. Simison, "Some Autobiographical Notes of Washington

Irving," *YULG*, XXXVIII (1963), 3–13; John Clendenning, "Washington Irving and the Gothic Tradition," *BuR*, XII (1964), 90–98; Donald A. Ringe, "New York and New England: Irving's Criticism of American Society," *AL*, XXXVIII (1967), 455–467; Wayne R. Kime, "Washington Irving & Frontier Speech," *AS*, XLII (1967), 5–18; Andrew Myers, "Washington Irving and the Astor Library," *BNYPL*, LXXII (1968), 378–399; Carl R. Proffer, "Washington Irving in Russia: Pushkin, Gogol, Marlinsky," *CL*, XX (1968), 329–342; Walter A. Reichart, "Washington Irving and the Theatre," *MuK*, XIV (1968), 341–350; Charles G. Zug, III, "The Construction of 'The Devil and Tom Walker': A Study of Irving's Later Use of Folklore," *NYFQ*, XXIV (1968), 243–260; and Martin Roth, "The Final Chapter of Knickerbocker's *New York*," *MP*, LXVI (1969), 248–255.

### 583. BIBLIOGRAPHY

A recent full listing is in Jacob Blanck's *Bibliography of American Literature*, V, New Haven, Conn., 1969, 1–96. See also Walter A. Reichart, "The Earliest German Translations of Washington Irving's Writings: A Bibliography," *BNYPL*, LXI (1957), 491–498; Edwin T. Bowden, "American First Editions at TxU: XII. Washington Irving (1783–1859)," *LCUT*, VI (1959), 20–23; and H. L. Kleinfield, "A Census of Washington Irving Manuscripts," *BNYPL*, LXVIII (1964), 13–32.

## HENRY JAMES

### 584. COLLECTED WORKS AND CORRESPONDENCE

"The New York Edition" of *The Novels and Tales of Henry James*, 26 vols., 1907–1917, has been reissued, New York, 1962–1965. Leon Edel edited *The Complete Tales of Henry James*, 12 vols., London, 1962–1964, Philadelphia, 1962–1965. The first volume of the Bodley Head Henry James appeared in London in 1967.

Leon Edel's complete edition of the letters is still in preparation. Two recent volumes printing James letters are George Monteiro, *Henry James and John Hay: The Record of a Friendship*, Providence, R.I., 1965; and Jörg Hasler, *Switzerland in the Life and Work of Henry James: The Clare Benedict Collection of Letters from Henry James*, Bern, 1966. Gleanings can be found in Henry Brewster, "Henry James and the Gallo-American," *Botteghe Oscure*, XIX (1957), 170–194; John Nova Phillips, "A Twaddle of Graciousness," *Botteghe Oscure*, XIX (1957), 195–202; Geoffrey Keynes, "Henry James in Cambridge," *LonM*, VI (1959), 50–61; S. P. Rosenbaum, "Letters to the Pell-Clarkes from Their 'Old Cousin and

Friend' Henry James," *AL*, XXXI (1959), 46–58; *idem*, "Two Henry James Letters on *The American* and *Watch and Ward*," *AL*, XXX (1959), 533–537; Robert K. Gale, ed., "A Letter from Henry James to Francis Marion Crawford," *SA*, IV (1958), 415–419; George Monteiro, "An Unpublished Henry James Letter," *N&Q*, X (1963), 143–144; Fred L. Standley, "Henry James to Stopford Brooke: An Unpublished Letter," *VN*, No. 27 (1965), p. 29; Ben Harris McClary, " 'In Abject Terror of Rising': An Unpublished Henry James Letter," *ELN*, III (1966), 208–211; and Jean Bruneau, "Une lettre inédite de Henry James à Gustave Flaubert: Autour de Monckton Milnes, Lord Houghton," *RLC*, XLII (1968), 520–533. See also Leon Edel on the futility of hoping to find caches of letters, "Henry James Letters," *TLS* (June 17, 1965), p. 523.

### 585. EDITED TEXTS AND REPRINTS

Morris Shapira edited *Selected Literary Criticism*, London, 1963, covering the years 1865–1914. Leon Edel selected material for *The Henry James Reader*, New York, 1965. Two useful older anthologies have fortunately been reissued: Morton Dauwen Zabel's *Portable Henry James* (1951) has been revised by Lyall H. Powers, New York, 1968; Lyon N. Richardson's *Henry James: Representative Selections* (1941) was revised by the editor, Urbana, Ill., 1966. Other collections and reprints of single novels are too numerous to list separately.

### 586. BIOGRAPHY AND CRITICISM

The first volume (1953) of Leon Edel's admirable biography was followed by *The Conquest of London, 1870–1881* (Philadelphia, 1962); *The Middle Years, 1882–1895* (Philadelphia, 1962); *The Treacherous Years, 1895–1901* (Philadelphia, 1969). One more volume is promised. Drawing on the James family papers and his own collection of unpublished James letters, H. Montgomery Hyde in *Henry James at Home*, London, 1969, traces a portrait of "the Master" against the background of his homes in London and Sussex. Hyde has also published a little volume on *The Story of Lamb House, Rye: The Home of Henry James*, Rye, Sussex, 1966. Millicent Bell recounts in full "the story of a friendship," *Edith Wharton and Henry James*, New York, 1965. See also Gay Wilson Allen's *William James: A Biography*, New York, 1967; and *The Diary of Alice James*, ed. Leon Edel, New York, 1964.

James does not want for critics. From the more than 40 books written about his work in the last decade, it is difficult to compose a standard list. A good beginning might be Oscar Cargill's *The Novels of Henry James*, New York, 1961, since, in addition to much source-hunting and valuable commentary, he reviews Jamesian scholarship and criticism. S. Gorley

Putt's *Henry James: A Reader's Guide,* Ithaca, N.Y., 1966 (seemingly mistitled since it is commentary for scholars, not beginners), is challenging criticism as well as "a systematic survey of all of James' novels and tales." Dorothea Krook's *The Ordeal of Consciousness in Henry James,* New York, 1962, should be consulted by anyone seeking perceptive commentary on the later novels, as should Richard Poirier's *The Comic Sense of Henry James,* New York, 1960, for criticism of the early work, 1875–1882. Two books by Joseph A. Ward are criticism for the devotee: *The Imagination of Disaster: Evil in the Fiction of Henry James,* Lincoln, Neb., 1961; and *The Search for Form: Studies in the Structure of James's Fiction,* Chapel Hill, N.C., 1967. Fresh insights are found in Sallie Sears's *The Negative Imagination: Form and Perspective in the Novels of Henry James,* Ithaca, N.Y., 1969 (emphasis on the late novels); and Naomi Lebowitz's *The Imagination of Loving: Henry James's Legacy to the Novel,* Detroit, Mich., 1965 (emphasis on comparative literature). Laurence B. Holland's *The Expense of Vision: Essays on the Craft of Henry James,* Princeton, N.J., 1964, provides elaborate analyses of the major novels. Admirable for coverage in brief space are Bruce R. McElderry, Jr., *Henry James,* New York, 1965; Lyall H. Powers, *Henry James,* New York, 1970; and Leon Edel's pamphlet, *Henry James,* Minneapolis, Minn., 1960.

Several specialized studies are important additions to the growing body of Jamesian criticism: Christof Wegelin, *The Image of Europe in Henry James,* Dallas, Tex., 1968; Krishna Baldev Vaid, *Technique in the Tales of Henry James,* Cambridge, Mass., 1964; James Kraft, *The Early Tales of Henry James,* Carbondale, Ill., 1969; Peter Buitenhuis, *The Grasping Imagination: The American Writings of Henry James,* Toronto, 1970; Muriel G. Shine, *The Fictional Children of Henry James,* Chapel Hill, N.C., 1969; Jean Frantz Blackall, *Jamesian Ambiguity and "The Sacred Fount,"* Ithaca, N.Y., 1966; Leo B. Levy, *Versions of Melodrama: A Study of the Fiction and Drama of Henry James, 1865–1897,* Berkeley, Calif., 1957; Rudolf R. Kossmann, *Henry James: Dramatist,* Groningen, 1969; Ora Segal, *The Lucid Reflector: The Observer in Henry James' Fiction,* New Haven, Conn., 1969; and Viola Hopkins Winner, *Henry James and the Visual Arts,* Charlottesville, Va., 1970. The most violent and prolonged attack on James is Maxwell Geismar's *Henry James and the Jacobites,* Boston, 1963, answered by Edward Stone in the opening essays of his *The Battle and the Books: Some Aspects of Henry James,* Athens, Ohio, 1964. Robert L. Gale, *Plots and Characters in the Fiction of Henry James,* Hamden, Conn., 1965, is a useful reference volume for students and experts alike.

For criticism of James on a larger canvas, see Tony Tanner, *The Reign of Wonder,* New York, 1965; R. W. B. Lewis, *Trials of the Word,* New

Haven, Conn., 1965; Louis Auchincloss, *Reflections of a Jacobite*, Boston, 1961; Marius Bewley, *The Eccentric Design*, New York, 1959; Alan Holder, *Three Voyagers in Search of Europe*, Philadelphia, 1966; Nathalia Wright, *American Novelists in Italy*, Philadelphia, 1965; Charles L. Sanford, *The Quest for Paradise*, Urbana, Ill., 1961; Barbara Hardy, *The Appropriate Form: An Essay on the Novel*, London, 1964; Jay R. Martin, *Harvests of Change: American Literature, 1865-1914*, Englewood Cliffs, N.J., 1967; and Peter K. Garrett, *Scene and Symbol from George Eliot to James Joyce*, New Haven, Conn., 1969. European studies include Georges Markow-Totevy, *Henry James*, Paris, 1958; D. W. Jefferson, *Henry James*, Edinburgh, 1960; Tony Tanner, *Henry James*, London, 1968; Bruce Lowery, *Marcel Proust et Henry James*, Paris, 1964; Alberta Fabris, *Henry James e la Francia*, Rome, 1969; Christina Giorcelli, *Henry James e l'Italia*, Rome, 1969; and Frieder Busch, *Erzähler-, Figuren-, und Leserperspektive in Henry James' Roman "The Ambassadors,"* Munich, 1967.

Collections of critical comments and reviews are Roger Gard, ed., *Henry James: The Critical Heritage*, New York, 1968; Leon Edel, *Henry James: A Collection of Critical Essays*, New York, 1963; Tony Tanner, ed., *Henry James: Modern Judgements*, London, 1968; Gerald Willen, ed. *A Casebook on Henry James' Turn of the Screw*, New York, 1960; William T. Stafford, ed., *James's Daisy Miller: The Story, the Play, the Critics*, New York, 1963; *idem, Perspectives on James's The Portrait of a Lady: A Collection of Critical Essays*, New York, 1966; and Albert E. Stone, Jr., *Twentieth-Century Interpretations of The Ambassadors*, Englewood Cliffs, N.J., 1969.

Other brief studies, among the hundreds published, are Harold C. Goddard, "A Pre-Freudian Reading of *The Turn of the Screw*," *NCF*, XII (1957), 1-36; Arnold L. Goldsmith, "Henry James's Reconciliation of Free Will and Fatalism," *NCF*, XIII (1958), 109-126; R. W. Stallman, "The Houses that James Built—*The Portrait of a Lady*," *TQ*, I (1958), 176-196; Wright Morris, "Henry James's *The American Scene*," *TQ*, I (1958), 27-42; John E. Tilford, Jr., "James the Old Intruder," *MFS*, IV (1958), 157-164; René Wellek, "Henry James's Literary Theory and Criticism," *AL*, XXX (1958), 293-321; Gerhard Baumgaertel, "The Reception of Henry James in Germany," *Sym*, XIII (1959), 19-31; Peter Buitenhuis, "Henry James on Hawthorne," *NEQ*, XXXII (1959), 207-225; Howells Daniels, "Henry James and *An International Episode*," *BAASB*, n.s., I (1960), 3-35; Donald Emerson, "Henry James and the American Language," *TWA*, XLIX (1960), 237-247; Richard Gilman, "Americans Abroad," *AH*, XII (Oct., 1961), 9-27, 89-93; Frederick J. Hoffman, "Freedom and Conscious Form: Henry James and the American Self," *VQR*, XXXVII (1961), 269-285; Henry L. Terrie, Jr., "Henry

James and the 'Explosive Principle,'" *NCF*, XV (1961), 283–299; Robert E. Garis, "The Two Lambert Strethers: A New Reading of *The Ambassadors*," *MFS*, VII (1961), 305–316; Alwyn Berland, "Henry James and the Aesthetic Tradition," *JHI*, XXIII (1962), 407–419; Austin Warren, "The New England Conscience, Henry James, and Ambassador Strether," *MinnR*, II (1962), 149–161; C. F. Burgess, "The Seeds of Art: Henry James's *Donnée*," *L&P*, XIII (1963), 67–73; Mark Spilka, "Turning the Freudian Screw: How Not to Do It," *L&P*, XIII (1963), 105–111.

Later studies are Umberto Mariani, "The Italian Experience of Henry James," *NCF*, XIX (1964), 237–254; Louis D. Rubin, Jr., "One More Turn of the Screw," *MFS*, IX (1964), 314–328; Robert C. McLean, "The Subjective Adventure of Fleda Vetch," *AL*, XXXVI (1964), 12–30; John C. McCloskey, "What Maisie Knows: A Study of Childhood and Adolescence," *AL*, XXXVI (1965), 485–513; Richard Bridgman, "Henry James and Mark Twain," *The Colloquial Style in America*, New York, 1966, pp. 78–130; Charles Fish, "Form and Revision: The Example of *Watch and Ward*," *NCF*, XXII (1967), 173–190; John Felstiner, "Max Beerbohm and the Wings of Henry James," *KR*, XXXIX (1967), 449–471; Kimball King, "Theory and Practice in the Plays of Henry James," *MD*, X (1967), 24–33; Robert J. Reilly, "Henry James and the Morality of Fiction," *AL*, XXXIX (1967), 1–30; Maurita Willett, "Henry James's Indebtedness to Balzac," *RLC*, XLI (1967), 204–227; Tony Tanner, "Henry James and Henry Adams," *TriQ*, XI (1968), 91–108; Ernest R. Labrie, "Henry James's Idea of Consciousness," *AL*, XXXIX (1968), 517–529; Manfred Mackenzie, "Obscure Hurt in Henry James," *SoRA*, III (1968), 107–131; P. R. Grover, "Mérimée's Influence on Henry James," *MLR*, LXIII (1968), 810–817; and William Hoffa, "The Final Preface: Henry James's Autobiography," *SR*, LXXVII (1969), 277–293.

The Spring, 1966, issue of *Modern Fiction Studies* is a Henry James number.

589. BIBLIOGRAPHY

The chief bibliographical guide is Leon Edel and Dan H. Laurence: *A Bibliography of Henry James*, London, 1957, 2nd rev. ed., 1961. Jacob Blanck gives full listings in *Bibliography of American Literature*, V, New Haven, Conn., 1969, 117–181. See also Brian Birch, "Henry James: Some Bibliographical and Textual Matters," *Library*, XX (1965), 108–123.

The major listing of criticism about the author is Maurice Beebe and William T. Stafford, "Criticism of Henry James: A Selected Checklist," *MFS*, XII (1966), 117–177. Hajime Okita, *A Bibliography of Henry James in Japan*, Kyoto, 1965, is published in Japanese.

# WILLIAM JAMES

**590.** WORKS

*The Writings of William James: A Comprehensive Edition* was edited by John J. McDermott, New York, 1967. John K. Roth edited *The Moral Philosophy of William James*, New York, 1969. *William James on Psychical Research* was compiled and edited by Gardner Murphy and Robert O. Ballou, New York, 1960. Andrew J. Reck's *Introduction to William James,* Bloomington, Ind., 1967, is a selection of texts preceded by a long introductory essay.

Elizabeth Hardwick edited with an introduction *The Selected Letters of William James*, New York, 1961. See also Robert C. LeClair, ed., *The Letters of William James and Théodore Flournoy*, Madison, Wis., 1966, J. C. Kenna assembled "Ten Unpublished Letters from William James, 1842–1910, to Francis Herbert Bradley, 1846–1924," *Mind*, LXXV (1965), 309–331.

**591.** BIOGRAPHY AND CRITICISM

The newest biographical study is Gay Wilson Allen's *William James: A Biography*, New York, 1967. Leon Edel has much to say about the whole family in his multivolume (and still unfinished) biography of Henry James, Philadelphia, beginning 1953. Edel has also edited *The Diary of Alice James*, New York, 1964. Bernard P. Brennan adds a brief biographical sketch to his *William James*, New York, 1968, a volume designed "to convey to a beginner the principal angles of James's philosophical vision."

In addition to the volume cited above, Brennan concentrated on "a systematic formulation of James's moral philosophy" in *The Ethics of William James*, New York, 1961. More recent specialized studies are Bruce Wilshire, *William James and Phenomenology: A Study of the "Principles of Psychology,"* Bloomington, Ind., 1968; Hans Linschoten, *On the Way toward a Phenomenological Psychology: The Psychology of William James*, Pittsburgh, Pa., 1968; John K. Roth, *Freedom and the Moral Life: The Ethics of William James*, Philadelphia, 1969; and John Wild, *The Radical Empiricism of William James*, New York, 1969. Edward C. Moore's brief study, *William James*, New York, 1965, attempts to give "appropriate emphasis to various elements of James's thought so that the more notorious ones do not take an undue share of the spotlight." Gay Wilson Allen's *William James*, Minneapolis, Minn., 1970, is a pamphlet. Additional essays are in Edward C. Moore, *American Pragmatism: Peirce, James, and Dewey*, New York, 1961; Thomas R. Martland, Jr., *The Meta-*

*physics of William James and John Dewey: Process and Structure in Philosophy and Religion*, New York, 1963; and A. J. Ayer, *The Origins of Pragmatism: Studies in the Philosophy of Charles Sanders Peirce and William James*, San Francisco, 1968.

For more specialized studies see Truman G. Madsen, "William James: Philosopher-Educator," *BYUS*, IV (1961), 81–105; Henry David Aiken, "American Pragmatism Reconsidered II: William James," *Com*, XXXIV (1962), 238–246; Frederick J. Hoffman, "William James and the Modern Literary Consciousness," *Criticism*, IV (1962), 1–13; David A. Remley, "William James: The Meaning and Function of Art," *MASJ*, IV (1963), 39–48; Robert J. Roth, "The Religious Philosophy of William James," *Thought*, XLI (1965), 249–281; William J. MacLeod, "James's 'Will to Believe' Revisited," *Person*, XLVIII (1967), 149–166; and W. Richard Comstock, "William James and the Logic of Religious Belief," *JR*, XLVII (1967), 187–209.

593. BIBLIOGRAPHY

Ralph Barton Perry's 1920 bibliography is reprinted with additions by John J. McDermott in *The Writings of William James* cited above.

# (JOHN) ROBINSON JEFFERS
### *d. 1962*

593. SEPARATE WORKS

*The Beginning and the End and Other Poems*, 1963.

BIOGRAPHY AND CRITICISM

The first biography is Melba Berry Bennett's *The Stone Mason of Tor House: The Life and Work of Robinson Jeffers*, Los Angeles, 1966. Ann N. Ridgeway edited *The Selected Letters of Robinson Jeffers, 1897–1962*, Baltimore, Md., 1968, an unusually handsome volume illustrated with photographs by Leigh Wiener.

Frederic I. Carpenter's *Robinson Jeffers*, New York, 1962, is a brief survey of the life and a critical assessment of the major work. Mercedes C. Monjian defines Jeffers's philosophy as well as reviews the scholarship and criticism in *Robinson Jeffers: A Study in Inhumanism*, Pittsburgh, Pa., 1958. Arthur B. Coffin's *Robinson Jeffers: Poet of Inhumanism*, Madison, Wis., 1970, concentrates on the influence of Lucretius, Nietzsche, and the "cyclical" historicists (Vico, Spengler, Flinders Petrie) on Jeffers's thinking. Brother Antoninus assembled seven of his essays and an elegy to the poet in *Robinson Jeffers: Fragments of an Older Fury*, Berkeley, Calif.,

1968. Briefer studies are Oskar Seidlin, "The Oresteia Today: A Myth Dehumanized," *Thought*, XXXIV (1959), 434–452; Richard Gustafson, "The Other Side of Robinson Jeffers," *IEY*, No. 9 (1964), pp. 75–80; Hale Chatfield, "Robinson Jeffers: His Philosophy and His Major Themes," *LauR*, VI (1966), 56–71; and William H. Nolte, "Robinson Jeffers as Didactic Poet," *VQR*, XLII (1966), 257–271.

**595.** BIBLIOGRAPHY

The Alberts bibliography (1933) was reprinted in 1968. Addenda are in Hensley C. Woodbridge, "A Bibliographical Note on Jeffers," *ABC*, X (1959), 15–18; and William White, "Robinson Jeffers: A Checklist, 1959–1965," *Serif*, III (1966), 36–39. See also Anita Rutman, Lucy Clark, and Marjorie Carver, *Robinson Jeffers: A Checklist of Printed and Mansucript Works of Robinson Jeffers in the Library of the University of Virginia*, Charlottesville, Va., 1960.

# THOMAS JEFFERSON

**595.** COLLECTED WORKS

Volumes XVI–XVIII of *The Papers of Thomas Jefferson* have appeared under the editorship of Julian P. Boyd, Princeton, N.J., 1961–1971.

**596.** CORRESPONDENCE

The most important recent collection is *The Adams-Jefferson Letters: The Complete Correspondence between Thomas Jefferson and Abigail and John Adams*, 2 vols., ed. Lester J. Cappon, Chapel Hill, N.C., 1959. *The Family Letters of Thomas Jefferson*, ed. Edwin Morris Betts and James Adam Bear, Jr., Columbia, Mo., 1966, prints all extant letters to and from Jefferson and his children and grandchildren. A selection of these letters with commentary was made by Edward Boykin, *To the Girls and Boys*, New York, 1964. *The Jefferson-Dunglison Letters*, ed. John M. Dorsey, Charlottesville, Va., 1960, is correspondence with his doctor. See also *Thomas Jefferson on Science and Freedom: The Letter to the Student William Greene Munford, June 18, 1799*, ed. Julian P. Boyd, Worcester, Mass., 1964; and *Thomas Jefferson's Letter of May 20, 1826, to James Heaton on the Abolition of Slavery*, ed. Walter Muir Whitehill, Washington, D.C., 1967.

**597.** EDITED TEXTS AND REPRINTS

*The Autobiography* was reprinted with an introduction by Dumas Malone, New York, 1959. *Thomas Jefferson's Architectural Drawings* was compiled with commentary and checklist by Frederick Doveton Nichols,

Boston, 1961, supplementing and updating Fiske Kimball's work (1916).

Three volumes useful as introductions to Jefferson's writings are *The Essential Jefferson*, ed. Albert Fried, New York, 1963; *Thomas Jefferson and the Foundations of American Freedom*, ed. Saul K. Padover, New York, 1965; and *Crusade against Ignorance: Thomas Jefferson on Education*, ed. Gordon C. Lee, New York, 1961.

### 598. BIOGRAPHY AND CRITICISM

Dumas Malone has published two more volumes of his projected five-volume study called *Jefferson and His Time*: Volume III, *Jefferson and the Ordeal of Liberty*, Boston, 1962; Volume IV, *Jefferson the President: First Term, 1801–1805*, Boston, 1970. Merrill D. Peterson's long-awaited biography, a major work, is *Thomas Jefferson and the New Nation*, New York, 1970. Two other biographical studies are Stuart G. Brown, *Thomas Jefferson*, New York, 1963; and Thomas J. Fleming, *The Man from Monticello: An Intimate Life of Thomas Jefferson*, New York, 1969.

Life at Monticello and in the Jefferson family is recorded in William H. Gaines, Jr., *Thomas Mann Randolph: Jefferson's Son-in-law*, Baton Rouge, La., 1966; and Gordon Langley Hall, *Mr. Jefferson's Ladies*, Boston, 1966. Sarah N. Randolph's *The Domestic Life of Thomas Jefferson* (1871) was reprinted, with an introduction by Dumas Malone, New York, 1958. James A. Bear, Jr., edited *Jefferson at Monticello*, Charlottesville, Va., 1967, a reprinting of *Memoirs of a Monticello Slave, as Dictated to Charles Campbell by Isaac* (1951, ed. Rayford W. Logan), and *Jefferson at Monticello: The Private Life of Thomas Jefferson*, by Rev. Hamilton Wilcox Pierson (1862).

Among the many critical studies of the past decade, one of the most ambitious and indispensable is Merrill D. Peterson's *The Jefferson Image in the American Mind*, New York, 1960, "a book on what history made of Thomas Jefferson." Three volumes focused on the presidency are Dumas Malone, *Thomas Jefferson as Political Leader*, Berkeley, Calif., 1963; John Dos Passos, *Thomas Jefferson: The Making of a President*, Boston, 1964; and Frank Van der Linden, *The Turning Point: Jefferson's Battle for the Presidency*, Washington, D.C., 1962. More specialized studies are Lawrence S. Kaplan, *Jefferson and France: An Essay on Politics and Political Ideas*, New Haven, Conn., 1967; Robert M. Healey, *Jefferson on Religion in Public Education*, New Haven, Conn., 1962; James B. Conant, *Thomas Jefferson and the Development of American Public Education*, Berkeley, Calif., 1962; Leonard W. Levy, *Jefferson and Civil Liberties: The Darker Side*, Cambridge, Mass., 1963; John Murray Allison, *Adams and Jefferson: The Story of a Friendship*, Norman, Okla., 1966; and John Ord Tipple, *A. Hamilton/Th. Jefferson: The New Order*, Cleveland, Ohio, 1961.

Students of the period will find these volumes especially helpful: John C. Miller, *The Federalist Era, 1789–1801*, New York, 1960; Richard Beale Davis, *Intellectual Life in Jefferson's Virginia, 1790–1830*, Chapel Hill, N.C., 1964; John Dos Passos, *The Shackles of Power: Three Jeffersonian Decades*, New York, 1966; Robert M. McColley, *Slavery and Jeffersonian Virginia*, Urbana, Ill., 1964; and N. E. Cunningham, *The Jeffersonian Republicans in Power: Party Operations 1801–1809*, Chapel Hill, N.C., 1963.

E. Millicent Sowerby completed the fifth and last volume of her monumental undertaking, *Catalogue of the Library of Thomas Jefferson*, Washington, D.C., 1952–1959.

Merrill D. Peterson edited a collection of critical essays, *Thomas Jefferson: A Profile*, New York, 1967. Other brief studies are Dwight Boehm and Edward Schwartz, "Jefferson and the Theory of Degeneracy," *AQ*, IX (1957), 448–453; Henry Steele Commager, "Jefferson and the Book-Burners," *AH*, IX (Aug., 1958), 65–68; Helmut De Terra, "Alexander von Humboldt's Correspondence with Jefferson, Madison, and Gallatin," *PAPS*, CIII (1959), 783–806; Gloria Jahoda, "John Beckley: Jefferson's Campaign Manager," *BNYPL*, LXIV (1960), 247–260; Wilbur Samuel Howell, "The Declaration of Independence and Eighteenth-Century Logic," *WMQ*, XVIII (1961), 463–484; Marvin Fisher, "An Answer to Jefferson on Manufactures," *SAQ*, LXI (1962), 345–353; Stuart Gerry Brown, "The Mind of Thomas Jefferson," *Ethics*, LXXIII (1963), 79–99; David A. Randall, " 'Dukedom Large Enough': III. Thomas Jefferson and The Declaration of Independence," *PBSA*, LVI (1963), 472–480; George B. Watts, "Thomas Jefferson, the *Encyclopédie*, and the *Encyclopédie méthodique*," *FR*, XXXVIII (1965), 318–325; John Krnacik, "Thomas Jefferson's Interest in Italian Life, Language, and Art," *KFLQ*, XIII (1966), 130–137; M. J. Kehta, "The Religion of Thomas Jefferson," *IAC*, XVI (1967), 95–103; Susan Ford, "Thomas Jefferson and John Adams on the Classics," *Arion*, VI (1967), 116–132; Robert Brent, "Puncturing Some Jeffersonian Mythology," *SoQ*, VI (1968), 175–190; and Bernard W. Sheehan, "Paradise and the Noble Savage in Jeffersonian Thought," *WMQ*, XXVI (1969), 327–359.

## 602. BIBLIOGRAPHY

No complete bibliography of writings about Jefferson exists. The best substitute is the 63-page "Guide to Sources" Merrill D. Peterson appended to *The Jefferson Image in the American Mind*, New York, 1960. William Bainter O'Neal has prepared *A Checklist of Writings on Thomas Jefferson as an Architect*, Charlottesville, Va., 1957.

## SARAH ORNE JEWETT

**603.** COLLECTED WORKS AND CORRESPONDENCE

Kenneth S. Lynn is editing a 14-volume edition of *The Works of Sarah Orne Jewett* for the Garrett Press of New York.

*The World of Dunnet Landing: A Sarah Orne Jewett Collection*, ed. David Bonnell Green, Lincoln, Neb., 1962, reprints *The Country of the Pointed Firs* along with four stories and five critical essays on her work.

Richard Cary's *Sarah Orne Jewett Letters* (1956) has been revised and enlarged, Waterville, Me., 1967. See also John Eldridge Frost, "The Letters of Sarah Orne Jewett," *CLQ*, V (1959), 38-45; and C. Carroll Hollis, "Letters of Sarah Orne Jewett to Anna Laurens Davis," *CLQ*, VIII (1968), 97-138.

BIOGRAPHY AND CRITICISM

John Eldridge Frost's biography *Sarah Orne Jewett*, Kittery Point, Me., 1960, is an attempt to supply the data and documentation lacking in F. O. Matthiessen's life of Jewett (1929).

The first full-length critical study is Richard Cary's *Sarah Orne Jewett*, New York, 1962, followed by Margaret Farrand Thorp's pamphlet, *Sarah Orne Jewett*, Minneapolis, Minn., 1966. Other brief studies are Warner Berthoff, "The Art of Jewett's *Pointed Firs, NEQ*, XXXII (1959), 31-53; Hyatt H. Waggoner, "The Unity of *The Country of the Pointed Firs*," *TCL*, V (1959), 67-73; Mary Ellen Chase, "Sarah Orne Jewett as a Social Historian, *PrS*, XXXVI (1962), 231-237; Robin Macgowan, "Pastoral and the Art of Landscape in *The Country of the Pointed Firs*," *NEQ*, XXXVI (1963), 229-240; Jean Boggio-Sola, "The Poetic Realism of Sarah Orne Jewett," *CLQ*, VII (1965), 74-81; Paul J. Eakin, "Sarah Orne Jewett and the Meaning of Country Life," *AL*, XXXVIII (1967), 508-531; Eugene H. Pool, "The Child in Sarah Orne Jewett," *CLQ*, VII (1967), 503-509; Robert D. Rhode, "Sarah Orne Jewett and 'The Palpable Present Intimate,'" *CLQ*, VIII (1968), 146-155; and Richard Cary, "The Other Face of Jewett's Coin," *ALR*, II (1969), 263-270. The June, 1964, issue of the *Colby Library Quarterly* is a Jewett issue.

A full listing of her work is in Jacob Blanck, *Bibliography of American Literature*, V, New Haven, Conn., 1969, 189-205. See also David Bonnell Green, "The Sarah Orne Jewett Canon: Additions and a Correction," *PBSA*, LV (1961), 141-142; John E. Frost, "Sarah Orne Jewett Bibilography, 1949-1963," *CLQ*, VI (1964), 405-417; Richard Cary, "Sarah Orne Jewett (1849-1909)," *ALR*, I (1967), 61-66; *idem*, "Some Bibliographic Ghosts of Sarah Orne Jewett," *CLQ*, VIII (1968), 139-145; and

Clayton L. Eichelberger, "Sarah Orne Jewett (1849–1909): A Critical Bibliography of Secondary Comment," *ALR*, II (1969), 189–262.

## JOHN PENDLETON KENNEDY

**604.** BIOGRAPHY AND CRITICISM

The first full-length biography since 1871 is Charles H. Bohner, *John Pendleton Kennedy: Gentleman from Baltimore*, Baltimore, Md., 1961, especially informative on Kennedy as politician and political theorist as well as man of letters. Joseph V. Ridgely's *John Pendleton Kennedy*, New York, 1966, while also a survey of the career, focuses on Kennedy's novels.

Brief studies are William S. Osborne, "'The Swiss Traveller' Essays: Earliest Writings of John Pendleton Kennedy," *AL*, XXX (1958), 228–233; Rhoda Coleman Ellison, "An Interview with Horse-Shoe Robinson," *AL*, XXXI (1959), 329–332; Paul C. Wermuth, "*Swallow Barn*: A Virginia Idyll," *VC*, IX (1959), 30–34; William R. Taylor, "A Squire of Change Alley," *Cavalier and Yankee*, New York, 1963, pp. 156–181; and William S. Osborne, "John Pendleton Kennedy's *Horse Shoe Robinson*: A Novel with 'the Utmost Historical Accuracy,'" *MHM*, LIX (1964), 286–296.

The most recent listing of Kennedy's work is in Jacob Blanck, *Bibliography of American Literature*, V, New Haven, Conn., 1969, 228–242.

## SIDNEY LANIER

**606.** BIOGRAPHY AND CRITICISM

A recent critical biography is Edd Winfield Parks, *Sidney Lanier: The Man, the Poet, the Critic*, Athens, Ga., 1968. More specialized studies are Philip Graham, "Sidney Lanier and the Pattern of Contrast," *AQ*, XI (1959), 503–508; Joseph W. Hendren, "Time and Stress in English Verse with Special Reference to Lanier's Theory of Rhythm," *RIP*, XLVI (1959), 1–72; William White, "Sidney Lanier as a Critic," *TJ*, IV (Mar., 1959), 41–44; Roy Harvey Pearce, *The Continuity of American Poetry*, Princeton, N.J., 1961, pp. 236–246; Robert H. Ross, "'The Marshes of Glynn': A Study in Symbolic Obscurity," *AL*, XXXII (1961), 403–416; Cecil Abernathy, "Lanier in Alabama," *AlaR*, XVII (1964), 5–21; Harry R. Warfel, "Mystic Vision in 'The Marshes of Glynn,'" *MissQ*, XIX (1965), 34–40; John S. Edwards, "Sidney Lanier: Musical Pioneer," *GaR*, XXII (1968), 473–481; and Jack de Bellis, "Sidney Lanier and German Romance: An Important Qualification," *CLS*, V (1968), 145–155.

A bibliographical listing is in Jacob Blanck, *Bibliography of American Literature*, V, New Haven, Conn., 1969, 280–298.


# RING (RINGGOLD WILMER) LARDNER

### 609. REPRINTS AND COLLECTIONS

Collections of Lardner are plentiful. Alan Ross introduced *The Best Short Stories of Ring Lardner*, London, 1959. Babette Rosmond and Henry Morgan edited *Shut Up, He Explained*, New York, 1962; it reprints *The Young Immigrunts, The Big Town*, and a wide variety of shorter pieces. Maxwell Geismar edited *The Ring Lardner Reader*, New York, 1963; and Josephine Herbst provided a new introduction to a reprinting of *Gullible's Travels, Etc.*, Chicago, 1965.

### BIOGRAPHY AND CRITICISM

The first full-length critical study is Walton R. Patrick's *Ring Lardner*, New York, 1963; followed by Otto Friedrich's pamphlet, *Ring Lardner*, Minneapolis, Minn., 1965. Briefer estimates are Howard W. Webb, Jr., "The Meaning of Ring Lardner's Fiction: A Re-evaluation," *AL*, XXXI (1960), 434–445; and *idem*, "The Development of a Style: The Lardner Idiom," *AQ*, XII (1960), 482–492.

### BIOGRAPHY

See Matthew J. Bruccoli, "Ring Lardner's First Book," *PBSA*, LVIII (1964), 34–35; and *idem*, "Five Notes on Ring Lardner," *PBSA*, LVIII (1964), 297–298.


# (HARRY) SINCLAIR LEWIS

### 609. SEPARATE WORKS

*Storm in the West* (with Dore Schary), 1963, an unproduced screenplay.

### 610. BIOGRAPHY AND CRITICISM

The major critical biography is Mark Schorer's *Sinclair Lewis: An American Life*, New York, 1961. Vincent Sheean recounts "the tangled romance of Dorothy Thompson and Sinclair Lewis" in *Dorothy and Red*, New York, 1963. The story is elaborated in Dorothy Thompson, "The Boy and Man from Sauk Center," *Atl*, CCVI (Nov., 1960), 39–48; and Charles Angoff, "A Kansan in Westchester," *UR*, XXXI (1965), 283–288. Paul de Kruif talks at length about Lewis in *The Sweeping Wind: A Memoir*, New

York, 1962. Other recollections are Grace Hegger Lewis, "When Lewis Walked down Main Street," *NYTM* (July 3, 1960), pp. 10, 28–29; Allen Austin, "An Interview with Sinclair Lewis," *UKCR*, XXIV (1958), 199–210; and Budd Schulberg, "Lewis: Big Wind from Sauk Center," *Esquire*, LIV (1961), 110–114.

Lewis correspondence has been printed in James J. Napier, "Letters of Sinclair Lewis to Joseph Hergesheimer, 1915–1922," *AL*, XXXVIII (1966), 236–246; and Charles Duffy, "A Sinclair Lewis Letter," *AN&Q*, V (1967), 118–119. Mark Schorer edited excerpts from Lewis's journal, "A Minnesota Diary," *Esquire*, L (Oct., 1958), 160–162. *Letters from Jack London*, ed. King Hendricks and Irving Shepard, New York, 1965, contain unpublished correspondence between London and Lewis.

Two full-length critical studies are Sheldon Norman Grebstein, *Sinclair Lewis*, New York, 1962; and D. J. Dooley, *The Art of Sinclair Lewis*, Lincoln, Neb., 1967. Mark Schorer's *Sinclair Lewis*, Minneapolis, Minn., 1963, is a useful introductory pamphlet. Carl L. Anderson discusses Lewis's European reputation in *The Swedish Acceptance of American Literature*, Philadelphia, 1957. A specialized German study is Wilfried Edener's *Die Religionskritik in den Romanen von Sinclair Lewis*, Heidelberg, 1963.

Brief studies are growing in number. Mark Schorer edited *Sinclair Lewis: A Collection of Critical Essays*, Englewood Cliffs, N.J., 1962; and Robert J. Griffin compiled *Twentieth-Century Interpretations of Arrowsmith*, Englewood Cliffs, N.J., 1968. See also Geoffrey Moore, "Sinclair Lewis: A Lost Romantic," *The Young Rebel in American Literature*, ed. Carl Bode, London, 1959, pp. 51–76; Martin R. Ausmus, "Sinclair Lewis, *Dodsworth*, and the Fallacy of Reputation," *BA*, XXXIV (1960), 349–355; Charles Fenton, Jr., "The American Academy of Art and Letters vs. All Comers: Literary Rags and Riches in the 1920's," *SAQ*, LVIII (1959), 572–586; John T. Flanagan, "The Minnesota Backgrounds to Sinclair Lewis' Fiction," *MH*, XXXVII (1960), 1–13; J. D. Thomas, "Three American Tragedies: Notes on the Responsibilities of Fiction," *SCB*, XX (1960), 11–15; Michael Millgate, "Sinclair Lewis and the Obscure Hero," *SA*, VIII (1962), 111–127; G. Thomas Tanselle, "Sinclair Lewis and Floyd Dell: Two Views of the Midwest," *TCL*, IX (1964), 175–184.

More recent studies are Daniel R. Brown, "Lewis's Satire—A Negative Emphasis," *Ren*, XVIII (1966), 63–72; Philip Allan Friedman, "*Babbitt*: Satiric Realism in Form and Content," *SNL*, IV (1966), 20–29; Martin Light, "Lewis's 'Scarlet Sign': Accommodating to the Popular Market," *JPC*, I (1967), 106–113; Martin Bucco, "The Serialized Novels of Sinclair Lewis," *WAL*, IV (1969), 29–37; and James D. Barry, "*Dodsworth*: Sinclair Lewis' Novel of Character," *BSUF*, X (1969), 8–14.

*Sinclair Lewis Newsletter* began publication in 1969 at St. Cloud State College, St. Cloud, Minnesota.

James Lundquist prepared *A Sinclair Lewis Checklist*, Columbus, Ohio, 1970. A checklist of Lewis's publications is appended to Schorer's *Sinclair Lewis: An American Life*. See also the bibliographies in the books by Dooley and Grebstein cited above. A compilation of Russian items on Lewis is B. A. Gilenson and I. M. Levidovoi, *Sinkler L'ius: Bio-bibliograficheskii ukazatel' k 75-letiiu so dnia rozhdeniia*, Moscow, 1959.

## LUDWIG LEWISOHN

### 612. REPRINTS

*The Case of Mr. Crump*, New York, 1965, is the first American edition. Martin Buber, *For the Sake of Heaven*, New York, 1958, was translated from the German by Lewisohn.

### BIOGRAPHY AND CRITICISM

See Norton Mezvinsky, "The Jewish Thought of Ludwig Lewisohn," *CJF*, XVI (1957), 77–82; and Stanley F. Chyet, "Ludwig Lewisohn: The Years of Becoming," *AJA*, XI (1959), 125–147.

## ABRAHAM LINCOLN

### 613. LETTERS AND ADDRESSES

*Abraham Lincoln: Selected Speeches, Messages, and Letters*, ed. T. Harry Williams, New York, 1957, covers the years 1836–1865, omitting the longer speeches and the Douglas debates. Don E. Fehrenbacher edited *Abraham Lincoln: A Documentary Portrait through His Speeches and Writing*, New York, 1964. A more specialized volume, *In the Name of the People: Speeches and Writings of Lincoln and Douglas in the Ohio Campaign of 1859*, ed. Harry V. Jaffa and Robert W. Johannsen, Columbus, Ohio, 1959, prints seven documents, five of which were previously difficult to obtain.

### SELECTIONS AND REPRINTS

*The Essential Lincoln*, ed. Gerald E. Stearn and Albert Fried, New York, 1962, is a useful introduction for students. Richard N. Current's edition of *The Political Thought of Abraham Lincoln*, Indianapolis, Ind., 1967, is a gathering of excerpts under four major rubrics. *A Concise Lin-*

*coln Dictionary* was compiled by Ralph B. Winn, New York, 1959. Fred Kerner assembled *A Treasury of Lincoln Quotations*, Garden City, N.Y., 1965.

### 614. BIOGRAPHY AND CRITICISM

*Lincoln Day by Day: A Chronology, 1809–1865*, 3 vols., Washington, D.C., 1960, has been in preparation since 1924 and has been appearing piecemeal since then. Over 1,000 pages, it has finally been completed under the direction of Earl Schenck Miers and the Lincoln Sesquicentennial Commission, published by the U.S. Government Printing Office.

Lincoln's life and times have been so closely studied that what follows can be only a partial listing. The early years are covered by Louis A. Warren, *Lincoln's Youth: Indiana Years, Seven to Twenty-One*, New York, 1959; Francis Van Natter, *Lincoln's Boyhood*, Washington, D.C., 1963; and Paul Horgan, *Citizen of New Salem*, New York, 1961. Details of the legal career are available in John J. Duff, *A. Lincoln, Prairie Lawyer*, New York, 1960; John P. Frank, *Lincoln as a Lawyer*, Urbana, Ill., 1961; and Paul Simon, *Lincoln's Preparation for Greatness: The Illinois Legislative Years*, Norman, Okla., 1966. The presidential years are the burden of Courtlandt Canby's *Lincoln and the Civil War: A Profile and a History*, New York, 1960, edited from primary and secondary sources. The assassination has had continuous attention, the best studies being Theodore Roscoe's *The Web of Conspiracy*, Englewood Cliffs, N.J., 1960; and Emmett McLoughlin's *An Inquiry into the Assassination of Abraham Lincoln*, New York, 1963. But they should be supplemented by two remarkable photographic albums: Ralph Borreson, *When Lincoln Died*, New York, 1965; and Dorothy Meserve Kunhardt and Philip B. Kunhardt, Jr., *Twenty Days*, New York, 1965. Victor Searcher describes the funeral procession and burial in *The Farewell to Lincoln*, New York, 1965.

One-volume biographies are available in David Flowden's *Lincoln and His America, 1809–1865*, New York, 1969; and two brief volumes, J. R. Pole's *Abraham Lincoln*, London, 1964 (for the British audience); and Roy P. Basler's *Lincoln*, New York, 1962 (for the paperback market). David C. Mearns, long a Lincoln authority, gathered 14 of his essays into a kind of biographical study he calls *Largely Lincoln*, New York, 1961. Edward J. Kempf's massive *Abraham Lincoln's Philosophy of Common Sense*, 3 vols., New York, 1965, is a psychiatrist's examination of the biographical evidence. William J. Wolf's *The Religion of Abraham Lincoln*, New York, 1963, is a revised edition of his earlier volume, *The Almost Chosen People* (1959). To all of this must be added three impressive pictorial biographies: Stefan Lorant, *Lincoln: A Picture Story of His Life,*

New York, 1969, a third revised edition of over 700 pictures; Charles Hamilton and Lloyd Ostendorf, *Lincoln in Photographs*, Norman, Okla., 1963, with 108 new photographs; and Richard Hanser and Donald B. Hyatt, *Meet Mr. Lincoln*, New York, 1960, text and photographs from the N.B.C. television essay. Adin Baber has finally clarified a confused genealogy in his *Nancy Hanks: The Destined Mother of a President*, Glendale, Calif., 1963.

If the sesquicentennial birthdate (1959) produced a rash of biographies, the Civil War Centennial produced even more historical-political studies of Lincoln's public life and administrations. The Lincoln–Douglas debates are discussed in Harry V. Jaffa, *Crisis of the House Divided*, Garden City, N.Y., 1959; and Richard A. Heckman, *Lincoln versus Douglas*, Washington, D.C., 1967. Dan E. Fehrenbacher's *Prelude to Greatness: Lincoln in the 1850's*, Stanford, Calif., 1962, contains seven essays on the rising young politician. The war years are thoroughly studied in Richard N. Current, *Lincoln and the First Shot*, Philadelphia, 1963; William Catton and Bruce Catton, *Two Roads to Sumter*, New York, 1963; Dean Sprague, *Freedom under Lincoln*, Boston, 1965; Irving Werstein, *Abraham Lincoln versus Jefferson Davis*, New York, 1959; Thamar E. Dufwa, *Lincoln and Secession*, New York, 1965; and Philip V. Stern, *An End to Valor: The Last Days of the Civil War*, Boston, 1958. Postwar problems are the subject of William B. Hesseltine, *Lincoln's Plan of Reconstruction*, Tuscaloosa, Ala., 1960; Benjamin Quarles, *Lincoln and the Negro*, New York, 1962 (the first book on the subject); and William O. Douglas, *Mr. Lincoln and the Negroes: The Long Road to Equality*, New York, 1963. International relations during the war are treated in A. R. Tyrner-Tyrnauer, *Lincoln and the Emperors*, New York, 1962. Willard L. King writes of *Lincoln's Manager, David Davis*, Cambridge, Mass., 1960; and Winifred E. Wise reveals all the facts and some suppositions about *Lincoln's Secret Weapon* [i.e., Anna Ella Carroll], Philadelphia, 1961.

Collections of essays, speeches, and commemorative papers are equally plentiful: the best include *Lincoln: A Contemporary Portrait*, ed. Allan Nevins and Irving Stone, Garden City, N.Y., 1962; *Lincoln Images*, ed. O. F. Ander, Rock Island, Ill., 1960; *The Enduring Lincoln*, ed. Norman Graebner, Urbana, Ill., 1959; and, for the general reader rather than the scholar, *Lincoln for the Ages*, ed. Ralph G. Newman, Garden City, N.Y., 1960 (76 broadcasts for the sesquicentennial).

Literary scholars will want to inspect Herbert J. Edward and John E. Hankins, *Lincoln the Writer: The Development of His Style*, Orono, Me., 1962; and William W. Betts, ed., *Lincoln and the Poets: An Anthology with a Commentary*, Pittsburgh, Pa., 1965.

**615.** BIBLIOGRAPHY

Victor Searcher's *Lincoln Today: An Introduction to Modern Lincolniana*, New York, 1969, is a descriptive bibliography of "all books on Lincoln now in print; and all those published during and after 1955 even if not now in print," including fiction, poetry, and juvenile books. In addition, see the files of the *Lincoln Herald*, the *Journal of the Illinois State Historical Society*, the *Abraham Lincoln Quarterly*, and *Lincoln Lore*.

## (NICHOLAS) VACHEL LINDSAY

**616.** COLLECTIONS AND SELECTED WORKS

Mark Harris edited *Selected Poems*, New York, 1963. Gleanings of correspondence are in Doris M. Reed, "Letters of Vachel Lindsay in the Lilly Library at Indiana University," *IUB*, No. 5 (1960), pp. 21–63; and G. Thomas Tanselle, "Vachel Lindsay Writes to Floyd Dell," *JISHS*, LVII (1964), 366–379.

BIOGRAPHY AND CRITICISM

Eleanor Ruggles's *The West-Going Heart: A Life of Vachel Lindsay*, New York, 1959, is a "romantic biography," a factual, not critical account. Frederic G. Melcher adds more details in "Vachel Lindsay: An Account of a Friendship Recorded from Memory, August, 1957," *IUB*, No. 5 (1960), pp. 12–20.

Ann Massa's *Vachel Lindsay: Fieldworker for the American Dream*, Bloomington, Ind., 1970, is the work of an English scholar interested chiefly in Lindsay's ideas. Briefer critical evaluations are Harold Orey, "Lindsay and the Blood of the Lamb," *UKCR*, XXV (1958), 13–17; Alfred Kreymborg, "Exit Vachel Lindsay—Enter Ernest Hemingway," *LitR*, I (1957–58), 208–219; Peter Viereck, "The Crack-Up of American Optimism: Vachel Lindsay, the Dante of the Fundamentalists," *ModA*, IV (1960), 269–284; Edwin H. Cady, "Vachel Lindsay across the Chasm," *IUB*, No. 4 (1960), pp. 5–11; Albert Edmund Trombly, "Listeners and Readers: The Unforgetting of Vachel Lindsay," *SWR*, XLVII (1962), 294–302; and Ann Massa, "The Artistic Conscience of Vachel Lindsay," *JAmS*, II (1968), 239–253. See also Michael Yatron's study of Masters, Sandburg, and Lindsay, *America's Literary Revolt*, New York, 1959.

**618.** BIBLIOGRAPHY

The most recent listing is Cecil K. Byrd, "Check List of the Melcher Lindsay Collection," *IUB*, No. 5 (1960), pp. 64–106.

# JACK (JOHN GRIFFITH) LONDON

**619.** SEPARATE WORKS

An unfinished novel, *The Assassination Bureau Ltd.*, was completed by Robert L. Fish from notes left by London, New York, 1963.

The multivolume Bodley Head Jack London (London, 1963–current) is edited by Arthur Calder-Marshall. An eight-volume Russian edition appeared in 1956 and another in fourteen volumes in 1961. American reprintings of individual novels and collections of stories are too numerous to list separately.

*Letters from Jack London*, ed. King Hendricks and Irving Shepard, New York, 1965, prints nearly 400 letters from a collection of over 2,000. See also Warren I. Titus, ed., "Two Unpublished Letters of Jack London [to the novelist Winston Churchill]," *CHSQ*, XXXIX (1960), 309–310.

**620.** BIOGRAPHY AND CRITICISM

Richard O'Connor's *Jack London: A Biography*, Boston, 1964, is a popularized and familiar version of the story. The reprinting of Joan London's 1939 biography of her father, *Jack London and His Times*, Seattle, Wash., 1968, not only attests to the revival of interest in London but also publishes an informative new introduction.

Franklin Walker's *Jack London and the Klondike: The Genesis of an American Writer*, San Marino, Calif., 1966, is the first book-length study by an American critic. King Hendricks adds two pamphlets to the growing London literature: *Creator and Critic: A Controversy between Jack London and Philo M. Buck, Jr.*, Logan, Utah, 1961; and *Jack London: Master Craftsman of the Short Story*, Logan, Utah, 1966. Charles C. Walcutt's pamphlet, *Jack London*, Minneapolis, Minn., 1966, covers the whole career. V. M. Bykov, *Dzhek London*, Moscow, 1964, rev. ed., 1968, is less useful as criticism than explanation of London's colossal popularity in the USSR. See also Frederick J. Feied, *No Pie in the Sky: The Hobo as American Cultural Hero in the Works of Jack London, John Dos Passos, and Jack Kerouac*, New York, 1964.

Brief estimates are Sam S. Baskett, "Jack London's Heart of Darkness," *AQ*, X (1958), 66–77; Gordon Mills, "The Symbolic Wilderness: James Fenimore Cooper and Jack London," *NCF*, XIII (1959), 329–340; Clell T. Peterson, "Jack London's Alaskan Stories," *ABC*, IX (1959), 15–22; Samuel A. Shivers, "The Demoniacs in Jack London," *ABC*, XII (1961), 11–14; Earle Labor, "Jack London's Symbolic Wilderness: Four Versions," *NCF*, XVII (1962), 149–161; Donald R. Glancy, "Socialist with a Valet: Jack London's 'First, Last, and Only' Lecture Tour," *QJS*, XLIX

(1963), 31–39; Alfred S. Shivers, "Jack London's Mate-Women," *ABC*, XV (1964), 17–21; Richard H. Warner, "A Contemporary Sketch of Jack London," *AL*, XXXVIII (1966), 376–380; James Ellis, "A New Reading of *The Sea Wolf*," *WAL*, II (1967), 127–134; Richard Van Der Beets, "Nietzsche of the North: Heredity and Race in London's *The Son of the Wolf*," *WAL*, II (1967), 229–233; Alfred S. Shivers, "Jack London: Not a Suicide," *DR*, XLIX (1969), 43–57; and Paul Deane, "Jack London: Mirror of His Time," *LHR*, XI (1969), 45–50. See also the files of the *Jack London Newsletter*, Carbondale, Ill., 1967 and continuing; and the Jack London special number, *American Book Collector*, XVII (Nov., 1966).

### 621. BIBLIOGRAPHY

Two full listings are Hensley C. Woodbridge, John London, and George H. Tweney, comps., *Jack London: A Bibliography*, Georgetown, Calif., 1966; and Jacob Blanck, *Bibliography of American Literature*, V, New Haven, Conn., 1969, 431–467. Addenda are in the *American Book Collector* and the *Jack London Newsletter* cited above. For German bibliography see Renate Schubert, "Eine Jack London Auswahlbibliographie," *ZAA*, XII (1964), 94–108.

## HENRY WADSWORTH LONGFELLOW

### 622. COLLECTED WORKS

The first two of six projected volumes of *The Letters of Henry Wadsworth Longfellow* have been edited by Andrew Hilen, Cambridge, Mass., 1966. Barbara A. Melchiori adds "Longfellow in Italy, with Unpublished Letters of Longfellow and Howells," *SA*, XII (1966), 125–135.

### 623. EDITED TEXTS AND REPRINTS

A serviceable edition of "sixty poems and translations that reveal the poet at his best" is *The Essential Longfellow*, ed. Lewis Leary, New York, 1963. Other reprintings are too numerous to list separately.

### BIOGRAPHY AND CRITICISM

The most satisfactory biography is Newton Arvin, *Longfellow: His Life and Work*, Boston, 1963. Edward Wagenknecht's *Henry Wadsworth Longfellow: Portrait of an American Humorist*, New York, 1966, is basically an abridgement and revision of his *Longfellow: A Full-Length Portrait* (1959).

Cecil B. Williams's concise bio-critical study, *Henry Wadsworth Longfellow*, New York, 1964, is a good introduction for the student. Edward L.

Hirsch covers the same ground in his pamphlet, *Henry Wadsworth Longfellow*, Minneapolis, Minn., 1964. A more specialized treatment is Ernest J. Moyne, *Hiawatha and Kalevala: A Study of the Relationship between Longfellow's "Indian Edda" and the Finnish Epic*, Helsinki, 1963. Brief estimates are Rose M. Davis, "How Indian Is Hiawatha?" *MF*, VII (1957), 5–25; James M. Cox, "Longfellow and His Cross of Snow," *PMLA*, LXXV (1960), 97–100; Andrew Hilen, "Charley Longfellow Goes to War," *HLB*, XIV (1960), 59–81, 283–303; Robert S. Ward, "Longfellow and Melville: The Ship and the Whale," *ESQ*, No. 22 (1961), pp. 57–63; Ely Stock, "Longfellow's 'The Jewish Cemetery at Newport,'" *RIH*, XX (1961), 81–87; Alice M. Longfellow, "My Father," *Carrell*, I (1960), 1–14; Marius Bewley, "The Poetry of Longfellow," *HudR*, XVI (1963), 297–304; Loring E. Hart, "The Beginning of Longfellow's Fame," *NEQ*, XXXVI (1963), 63–76; John T. Krumpelmann, "Longfellow's Shakespeare Studies in Heidelberg," *NS*, XIII (1964), 405–413; Richard Ruland, "Longfellow and the Modern Reader," *EJ*, LV (1966), 661–668; Michael Zimmerman, "War and Peace: Longfellow's 'The Occultation of Orion,'" *AL*, XXXVIII (1967), 504–546; Robert S. Ward, "Longfellow's Roots in Yankee Soil," *NEQ*, XLI (1968), 180–192; and Janez Stanonik, "Longfellow and Smolnikar," *AN*, I (1968), 3–40.

## 626. BIBLIOGRAPHY

A full listing is in Jacob Blanck, *Bibliography of American Literature*, V, New Haven, Conn., 1969, 468–640. See also Richard B. Harwell, *Hawthorne and Longfellow: A Guide to an Exhibit* [at Bowdoin College], Brunswick, Me., 1966.

## AMY LOWELL

### 627. BIOGRAPHY AND CRITICISM

Brief studies are Margaret Widdemer, "The Legend of Amy Lowell," *TQ*, VI (1963), 193–200; and Ruggero Bianchi, "La poetica del secondo imagismo: A. Lowell e J. G. Fletcher," *RdE*, IX (1964), 214–247.

## JAMES RUSSELL LOWELL

### 629. COLLECTED WORKS

*Literary Criticism of James Russell Lowell* was edited by Herbert F. Smith, Lincoln, Neb., 1969.

Gleanings of letters are in R. Baird Shuman, "The Howells–Lowell Correspondence: A New Item," *AL*, XXXI (1959), 338–340; Philip Graham, ed., "Some Lowell Letters," *TSLL*, III (1962), 557–582; Charles J. Rooney, Jr., "A New Letter by Lowell," *AL*, XXXVI (1964), 214–215; and Robert A. Rees, "James Russell Lowell in Spain and England: New Letters," *ESQ*, XLVII (1967), 7–13.

### 630. BIOGRAPHY AND CRITICISM

The major biography, updating Scudder and concentrating on Lowell the man, is Martin B. Duberman, *James Russell Lowell*, Boston, 1966. Claire McGlinchee's *James Russell Lowell*, New York, 1967, is a concise survey of the whole career. Of peripheral interest is Lawrence H. Klibbe, *James Russell Lowell's Residence in Spain (1877–1880)*, Newark, N.J., 1964.

Briefer studies are Howard M. Munford, "The Disciple Proves Independent: Howells and Lowell," *PMLA*, LXXIV (1959), 484–487; J. Chesley Mathews, "James Russell Lowell's Interest in Dante," *Ital*, XXXVI (1959), 77–100; John C. Broderick, "Lowell's 'Sunthin' in the Pastoral Line,'" *AL*, XXXI (1959), 163–172; Leon Howard, "The Case of the Sanded Signature," *MSS*, XIII (1961), 13–17; Martin B. Duberman, "Twenty-Seven Poems by James Russell Lowell," *AL*, XXXV (1963), 322–351; G. Thomas Tanselle, "The Craftsmanship of Lowell: Revisions in *The Cathedral*," *BNYPL*, LXX (1966), 50–63; and Heyward Ehrlich, "Charles Frederick Briggs and Lowell's *Fable for Critics*," *MLQ*, XXVIII (1967), 329–341.

## ARCHIBALD MacLEISH

### 634. SEPARATE WORKS

*Poetry and Experience*, 1961; *The Eleanor Roosevelt Story*, 1965; *Herakles: A Play in Verse*, 1967; *The Wild Old Wicked Man and Other Poems*, 1968; *A Continuing Journey*, 1968; *Scratch: A Play*, 1971.

Editions: Felix Frankfurter, *Law and Politics: Occasional Papers, 1913–1938* (with E. F. Pritchard, Jr.), 1962.

### 635. COLLECTED WORKS

Warren V. Bush edited *The Dialogues of Archibald MacLeish and Mark Van Doren*, New York, 1964, conversations recorded in 1962.

### BIOGRAPHY AND CRITICISM

The first full-length critical study is Signi Lenea Falk, *Archibald MacLeish*, New York, 1966. Briefer estimates are Richard Eberhart, "Outer and Inner Verse Drama," *VQR*, XXXIV (1958), 618–623; Martin C.

D'Arcy, "*J. B.*, Wrong Answer to the Problem of Evil," *CathW*, CXC (1959), 81–85; Andrew MacLeish, "The Poet's Three Comforters: *J. B.* and the Critics," *MD*, II (1959), 224–230; Marion Montgomery, "On First Looking into Archibald MacLeish's Play in Verse, *J. B.*," *MD*, II (1959), 231–242; Charles M. Bond, "*J. B.* Is Not Job," *BuR*, IX (1961), 272–280; Sheldon Norman Grebstein, "*J. B.* and the Problem of Evil," *UKCR*, XXIX (1963), 253–261; Eleanor M. Sickels, "MacLeish and the Fortunate Fall," *AL*, XXXV (1963), 205–217; Lillian Gottesman, "*The Hamlet of A. MacLeish,*" *CLAJ*, XI (1967), 157–162; Gustav H. Blanke, "Archibald MacLeish: 'Ars Poetica,'" *JA*, XIII (1968), 236–245; and Eva Goldschmidt, "Archibald MacLeish, Librarian of Congress," *CRL*, XXX (1969), 12–24.

## 636. BIBLIOGRAPHY

The most recent listing is in Signi Falk's book, cited above.

# JAMES MADISON

## 636. COLLECTED WORKS AND REPRINTS

The University of Chicago has begun publication of *The Papers of James Madison*, ed. William T. Hutchinson and William M. E. Rachal, Chicago, 1962 and continuing.

*Notes of Debates in the Federal Convention of 1787, Reported by James Madison* has been republished with an introduction by Adrienne Koch, Athens, Ohio, 1966. Of the many editions of *The Federalist*, the best is that edited by Benjamin Wright, Cambridge, Mass., 1961. A single-volume edition of Madison's writings is Saul Padover's *The Forging of American Federalism: Selected Writings of James Madison*, New York, 1966.

## 637. BIOGRAPHY AND CRITICISM

Irving Brant has completed his monumental six-volume biography with *James Madison: Commander-in-Chief, 1812–1836*, Indianapolis, Ind., 1961. *The Fourth President: A Life of James Madison*, Indianapolis, Ind., 1970, is a one-volume redaction. His *James Madison and American Nationalism*, Princeton, N.J., 1968, defines Madison's role in the formation of American institutions and the early attitude toward state and national sovereignty. A one-volume popularized biography is Alfred Steinberg's *James Madison*, New York, 1965.

Two volumes that illuminate Madison's political philosophy are Neal Riemer's *James Madison*, New York, 1968; and Adrienne Koch's *Madi-*

son's *"Advice to My Country,"* Princeton, N.J., 1966. For background to the political theories of the period, see also Adrienne Koch, *Powers, Morals and the Founding Fathers*, Ithaca, N.Y., 1961; and Gottfried Dietze, *The Federalist: A Classic on Federalism and Free Government*, Baltimore, Md., 1960.

Briefer studies are Ralph L. Ketcham, "James Madison and the Nature of Man," *JHI*, XIX (1958), 62–76; Donald O. Dewey, "Madison's Response to Jackson's Foes," *THQ*, XX (1961), 167–176; Merrill Jensen, "The Papers of Madison and Franklin: A Review Article," *WMH*, XLVII (1964), 175–177; and Ralph Ketcham, "James Madison at Princeton," *PULC*, XXVIII (1966), 24–54.

A useful bibliographical essay is appended to Neal Riemer's study, cited above.

## EDGAR LEE MASTERS

### 639. BIOGRAPHY AND CRITICISM

Lois Hartley, *Spoon River Revisited*, Muncie, Ind., 1963, is a 30-page monograph. Michael Yatron treats the poet in conjunction with Vachel Lindsay and Carl Sandburg in *America's Literary Revolt*, New York, 1959.

Briefer estimates are August Derleth, "Masters and the Revolt from the Village," *ColQ*, VIII (1959), 164–167; Max Putzel, "Masters's 'Maltravers': Ernest McGaffey," *AL*, XXXI (1960), 491–493; Lois Hartley, "Edgar Lee Masters: Biographer and Historian," *ISHSJ*, LIV (1961), 56–83; *idem*, "Edgar Lee Masters, Political Essayist," *JISHS*, LVII (1964), 249–260; *idem*, "The Plays of Edgar Lee Masters," *BSUF*, VII (1966), 26–38; and Ernest Earnest, "Spoon River Revisited," *WHR*, XXI (1967), 59–65.

## COTTON MATHER

### 641. EDITED TEXTS AND REPRINTS

William R. Manierre, II, edited a diary which had been lost for 200 years, *The Diary of Cotton Mather, D.D., F.R.S., For the Year 1712*, Charlottesville, Va., 1964. David Levin's introduction corrects misinterpretations of Mather's work in his reprinting of *Bonifacius: An Essay upon the Good*, Cambridge, Mass., 1966. Facsimile reproductions of *Bonifacius* (1710) and *The Christian Philosopher* (1721), with introductions by Josephine K. Piercy, were published in Gainesville, Florida, 1967 and 1968, respectively. *Magnalia Christi Americana* was reprinted in New York, 1967.

Brief studies are William R. Manierre, II, "Some Characteristic Mather Redactions," *NEQ*, XXXI (1958), 496–505; Otho T. Beall, "Cotton Mather's Early 'Curiosa Americana' and the Boston Philosophical Society of 1683," *WMQ*, XVIII (1961), 360–372; William R. Manierre, II, "Cotton Mather and the Biographical Parallel," *AQ*, XIII (1961), 153–160; *idem*, "Verbal Patterns in Cotton Mather's *Magnalia*," *QJS*, XLVII (1961), 403–413; David Levin, "The Hazing of Cotton Mather," *NEQ*, XXXVI (1963), 147–171; Peter H. Smith, "Politics and Sainthood: Biography by Cotton Mather," *WMQ*, XX (1963), 186–206; Eugene E. White, "Cotton Mather's *Manuductio ad Ministerium*," *QJS*, XLIX (1963), 308–319; Austin Warren, "Grandfather Mather and His Wonder Book," *SR*, LXXII (1964), 96–116; Sacvan Bercovitch, "New England Epic: Cotton Mather's *Magnalia Christi Americana*," *ELH*, XXXIII (1965), 337–350; William R. Manierre, II, "A Description of 'Paterna': The Unpublished Autobiography of Cotton Mather," *SB*, XVIII (1965), 183–205; Hanna-Beate Schilling, "Cotton Mather's 'Politics and Sainthood,'" *JA*, XI (1966), 251–255; Thomas E. Johnston, "A Translation of Cotton Mather's Spanish Works: *La Fe del Christiano* and *La Religion Pura*," *EALN*, II (1967), 7–21; John P. Duffy, "Cotton Mather Revisited," *MSE*, I (1967), 30–38; William M. Richardson, "Cotton Mather: The Man and the Myth," *ArlQ*, I (1967), 281–294; and Mason I. Lowance, Jr., "Typology and the New England Way: Cotton Mather and the Exegesis of Biblical Types," *EAL*, IV (1969), 15–37.

## INCREASE MATHER

**644.** EDITED TEXTS AND REPRINTS

M. G. Hall edited "The Autobiography of Increase Mather," *PAAS*, LXXI (1963), 271–360. A facsimile reprint of *The Life and Death of . . . Richard Mather* was published with an introduction by Benjamin Franklin V. Bottorff and William K. Bottorff, Athens, Ohio, 1966. See also Ladislas Országh, "A Seventeenth-Century Hungarian Translation of a Work by Increase Mather," *AL*, XXXIV (1962), 94–96.

## HERMAN MELVILLE

**647.** COLLECTED WORKS

The Northwestern University Press–Newberry Library edition of *The Writings of Herman Melville*, in 15 volumes, under the general editorship of Harrison Hayford, Hershel Parker, and G. Thomas Tanselle, began publication with *Typee* (1968), *Omoo* (1968), *Redburn* (1969), *Mardi* (1970), and *White-Jacket* (1970).

A sixth volume in the projected *Complete Works* (Hendricks House) appeared in 1960: *Clarel*, edited by Walter E. Bezanson.

Merrell R. Davis and William H. Gilman edited *The Letters of Herman Melville*, New Haven, Conn., 1960, including 42 published for the first time. See also Hennig Cohen, "New Melville Letters," *AL*, XXXVIII (1967), 556–559.

## 648. EDITED TEXTS

Notable among the many reprintings of Melville's work are *Billy Budd, Sailor (An Inside Narrative): Reading Text and Genetic Text*, ed. from the manuscript by Harrison Hayford and Merton M. Sealts, Jr., Chicago, 1962; *The Battle-Pieces of Herman Melville*, ed. Hennig Cohen, New York, 1963; *Moby-Dick, or, The Whale*, ed. Charles Feidelson, Jr., Indianapolis, Ind., 1964; and *Moby-Dick: An Authoritative Text: Reviews and Letters by Melville: Analogues and Sources: Criticism*, ed. Harrison Hayford and Hershel Parker, New York, 1967.

*Moby-Dick—Rehearsed: A Drama in Two Acts* by Orson Welles was published in New York, 1965.

### BIOGRAPHY AND CRITICISM

Among the 30 recent books on Melville, several aim at being general introductions. The most useful of the group is Warner Berthoff's *The Example of Melville*, Princeton, N.J., 1962, a survey of Melville "first of all as a writer, a master of expression." Tyrus Hillway's *Herman Melville*, New York, 1963; Leon Howard's pamphlet, *Herman Melville*, Minneapolis, Minn., 1961; and Howard Vincent's *Guide to Herman Melville*, Columbus, Ohio, 1969, are intended for the same general audience. James E. Miller's *A Reader's Guide to Herman Melville*, New York, 1962, is somewhat mistitled since it is a specialist's, not a general reader's, approach. Lewis Mumford's *Herman Melville: A Study of His Life and Vision* (1929) was republished in a slightly revised edition, New York, 1962.

More specialized studies include Merlin Bowen, *The Long Encounter: Self and Experience in the Writings of Herman Melville*, Chicago, 1960; H. Bruce Franklin, *The Wake of the Gods: Melville's Mythology*, Stanford, Calif., 1963; Paul Brodtkorb, Jr., *Ishmael's White World: A Phenomenological Reading of Moby Dick*, New Haven, Conn., 1965; and Howard P. Vincent, *The Tailoring of Melville's White-Jacket*, Evanston, Ill., 1970. Edgar Dryden focuses on "the internal morphology of Melville's fictional world" in *Melville's Thematics of Form: The Great Art of Telling the*

*Truth*, Baltimore, Md., 1968. Like Brodtkorb's acute study, John D. Seelye's *Melville: The Ironic Diagram*, Evanston, Ill., 1970, is concerned with the predilections of form. Richard H. Fogle discusses *Melville's Shorter Tales*, Norman, Okla., 1960; Hugh W. Hetherington analyses *Melville's Reviewers, British and American, 1846–1891*, Chapel Hill, N.C., 1961; William Bysshe Stein concentrates on *The Poetry of Melville's Late Years: Time, History, Myth, and Religion*, Albany, N.Y., 1970. Melville's knowledge and use of the Near East are illuminated in Dorothee M. Finkelstein, *Melville's Orienda*, New Haven, Conn., 1961. Merton M. Sealts, Jr., revised and expanded his 1948–1952 *Harvard Library Bulletin* articles in *Melville's Reading: A Check-List of Books Owned and Borrowed*, Madison, Wis., 1966.

European studies include two brief introductions, Arthur R. Humphreys, *Herman Melville*, Edinburgh, 1962; and Jean-Jacques Mayoux, *Melville par lui-même*, Paris, 1958 (trans. John Ashbery, New York, 1960). More specialized work is Janez Stanonik, *Moby-Dick: The Myth and the Symbol: A Study in Folklore and Literature*, Ljubljana, 1962; Klaus Ensslen, *Melvilles Erzählungen: Stil- und Strukturanalysische Untersuchungen*, Heidelberg, 1966; Max Frank, *Die Farb- und Lichtsymbolik in Prosawerk Herman Melvilles*, Heidelberg, 1967; Klaus Lanzinger, *Primitivismus und Naturalismus im Prosaschaffen Herman Melvilles*, Innsbruck, 1959; and Heinz Kosok, *Die Bedeutung der Gothic Novel für das Erzählwerk Herman Melvilles*, Hamburg, 1963.

See also the following works, *passim*: Harry Levin, *The Power of Blackness*, New York, 1958; Marius Bewley, *The Eccentric Design*, New York, 1959; Daniel Hoffman, *Form and Fable in American Fiction*, New York, 1961; Leo Marx, *The Machine in the Garden*, New York, 1964; Loren Baritz, *City on a Hill: A History of Ideas and Myths in America*, New York, 1964, Edwin Fussell, *Frontier: American Literature and the American West*, Princeton, N.J., 1965; and James Guetti: *The Limits of Metaphor: A Study of Melville, Conrad, and Faulkner*, Ithaca, N.Y., 1967.

Collections of shorter critical studies are varied. General gatherings are Hershel Parker, ed., *The Recognition of Herman Melville: Selected Criticism since 1846*, Ann Arbor, Mich., 1967; and Richard Chase, ed., *Melville: A Collection of Critical Essays*, Englewood Cliffs, N.J., 1962. Hershel Parker and Harrison Hayford edited *Moby-Dick as Doubloon: Essays and Extracts (1851–1970)*, New York, 1970; Howard P. Vincent selected *Studies in Moby-Dick*, Columbus, Ohio, 1969. Seymour L. Gross edited *A Benito Cereno Handbook*, Belmont, Calif., 1965; John P. Runden edited *Melville's Benito Cereno: A Text for Guided Research*, Boston, 1965. William T. Stafford edited a "controlled research volume," *Melville's*

*Billy Budd and the Critics*, San Francisco, 1961, 2nd ed., 1968. The first two Melville Society annuals are symposia: *Bartleby the Scrivener*, ed. Howard P. Vincent, Kent, Ohio, 1966; and *Melville and Hawthorne in the Berkshires*, ed. Howard P. Vincent, Kent, Ohio, 1968.

Other brief studies are Richard H. Fogle, "*Billy Budd*—Acceptance of Irony?" *TSE*, VIII (1958), 107–113; Agostino Lombardo, "Introduzione a Melville," *SA*, No. 3 (1957), pp. 29–61; Guy A. Cardwell, "Melville's Gray Story: Symbols and Meaning in 'Benito Cereno,'" *BuR*, VIII (1958), 154–167; Leland R. Phelps, "*Moby-Dick* in Germany," *CL*, X (1958), 349–355; William Charvat, "Melville and the Common Reader," *SB*, XII (1959), 41–57; Edward Dahlberg, "*Moby Dick*—An Hamitic Dream," *LitR*, IV (1960), 87–118; Thomas Philbrick, "Melville's 'Best Authorities,'" *NCF*, XV (1960), 171–179; Nathalia Wright, "*Pierre*: Herman Melville's *Inferno*," *AL*, XXXII (1960), 167–181; Howard H. Schless, "*Moby Dick* and Dante: A Critique and Time Scheme," *BNYPL*, LXV (1961), 289–312; Paul Smith: *The Confidence-Man* and the Literary World of New York," *NCF*, XVI (1962), 329–337; Jack Jay Boies, "*The Whale* without Epilogue," *MLQ*, XXIV (1963), 172–176; John Halverson, "The Shadow of *Moby-Dick*," *AQ*, XV (1963), 436–446; Alan Heimart, "*Moby-Dick* and American Political Symbolism," *AQ*, XV (1963), 498–534; Neal F. Doubleday, "Jack Easy and Billy Budd," *ELN*, II (1964), 39–42; Valentina Poggi, "*Pierre*: Il 'Kraken' di Melville," *SA*, X (1964), 71–100; Victor H. Strandberg, "God and the Critics of Melville," *TSLL*, VI (1964), 322–333; E. F. Carlisle, "Captain Amasa Delano: Melville's American Fool," *Criticism*, VII (1965), 349–362; Phillip Drew, "Appearance and Reality in Melville's *The Confidence Man*," *ELH*, XXXI (1964), 418–442; Edward H. Rosenberry, "The Problem of *Billy Budd*," *PMLA*, LXXX (1965), 489–498; John T. Flanagan, "*The Spirit of the Times* Reviews Melville," *JEGP*, LXIV (1965), 57–64; John W. Rathbun, "*Billy Budd* and the Limits of Perception," *NCF*, XX (1965), 19–34.

More recent studies are Fred E. H. Schroeder, "'Enter Ahab, Then All': Theatrical Elements in Melville's Fiction," *DR*, XLVI (1966), 223–232; Priscilla Allen Zirker, "Evidence of the Slavery Dilemma in *White-Jacket*," *AQ*, XVIII (1966), 477–492; Sacvan Bercovitch, "Melville's Search for National Identity: Son and Father in *Redburn, Pierre*, and *Billy Budd*," *CLAJ*, X (1967), 217–228; Herbert G. Eldridge, "'Careful Disorder': The Structure of *Moby-Dick*," *AL*, XXXIX (1967), 145–162; S. A. Cowan, "In Praise of Self-Reliance: The Role of Bulkington in *Moby-Dick*," *AL*, XXXVIII (1967), 547–556; Leon F. Seltzer, "Camus's Absurd and the World of Melville's *Confidence-Man*," *PMLA*, LXXXII

(1967), 14–27; James Schroeter, "*Redburn* and the Failure of Mythic Criticism," *AL*, XXXIX (1967), 279–297; G. R. Wilson, Jr., "*Billy Budd* and Melville's Use of Dramatic Technique," *SSF*, IV (1967), 105–111; Richard B. Sewall, "Ahab's Quenchless Feud: The Tragic Vision in Shakespeare and Melville," *CompD*, I (1967), 207–218; Kingsley Widmer, "The Perplexity of Melville, 'Benito Cereno,'" *SSF*, V (1968), 225–238; T. Walter Herbert, Jr., "Calvinism and Cosmic Evil in *Moby-Dick*," *PMLA*, LXXXIV (1969), 1613–1619; Hans-Joachim Lang, "Melvilles Dialog mit Captain Ringbolt," *JA*, XIV (1969), 124–139; Eleanor E. Simpson, "Melville and the Negro: From *Typee* to 'Benito Cereno,'" *AL*, XLI (1969), 19–38; and G. Thomas Tanselle, "The Sales of Melville's Books," *HLB*, XVII (1969), 195–215.

Special Melville numbers can be found in *Modern Fiction Studies*, VIII (1962), the *Emerson Society Quarterly*, No. 28 (1962), and *Studies in the Novel*, I (Winter, 1969).

### 654. BIBLIOGRAPHY

There is still no full bibliography of Melville's work. The Bibliography Committee of the Melville Society provided *Melville Bibliography, 1952–1957*, Providence, R.I., 1959. An extensive bibliography by Maurice Beebe, Harrison Hayford, and Gordon Roper, "Criticism of Herman Melville: A Selected Checklist," appeared in *MFS*, VIII (1962), 312–346; followed by Michael Zimmerman, "Herman Melville in the 1920's: An Annotated Bibliography," *BB*, XXIV (1964), 117–120, 106 [*sic*], 139–144; J. Don Vann, "A Checklist of Melville Criticism, 1958–1968," *SNNTS*, I (1969), 507–530; and Howard P. Vincent, *The Merrill Checklist of Herman Melville*, Columbus, Ohio, 1969. A lengthy annotated bibliography on *Moby-Dick* is appended to Parker and Hayford's *Moby-Dick as Doubloon*, cited above. Leland R. Phelps prepared *A Preliminary Checklist of Foreign Materials on the Life and Works of Herman Melville*, Evanston, Ill., 1961. See also Tyrus Hillway and Hershel Parker, *Directory of Melville Dissertations*, Evanston, Ill., 1962.

## H(ENRY) L(OUIS) MENCKEN

### 655. REPRINTS AND COLLECTIONS

Raven I. McDavid, Jr., with the assistance of David W. Maurer, abridged the fourth edition of *The American Language* (1936) and its two supplements into one volume, New York, 1963. *H. L. Mencken, The American Scene: A Reader*, New York, 1965, was selected and edited with introduction and commentary by Huntington Cairns. William H. Nolte compiled in *H. L. Mencken's Smart Set Criticism*, Ithaca, N.Y., 1968, about a sixth of what Mencken wrote for the magazine. Louis Cheslock assembled *H. L. Mencken on Music: A Selection of His Writings on Music, together with an Account of H. L. Mencken's Musical Life and a History of the Saturday Night Club*, New York, 1961.

Mencken's letters have only begun to appear. An estimated 100,000 are extant. A lively collection, chiefly of literary interest, covering the years 1900–1956, is *Letters of H. L. Mencken*, selected and annotated by Guy Jean Forgue, New York, 1961. See also Mencken replies in *Letters of Theodore Dreiser*, ed. Robert H. Elias, 3 vols., Philadelphia, 1959; Upton Sinclair, *My Lifetime in Letters*, Columbia, Mo., 1960; and Edwin Castagna, "Some of H. L. Mencken's Friendly Correspondence," *MSS*, XX (1968), 3–12. Betty Adler compiled *Man of Letters: A Census of the Correspondence of H. L. Mencken*, Baltimore, Md., 1969.

BIOGRAPHY AND CRITICISM

The most recent biography is Carl Bode, *Mencken*, Carbondale, Ill., 1969. Biographical reminiscence by a friend for 30 years is informally told in Sara Mayfield's *The Constant Circle: H. L. Mencken and His Friends*, New York, 1968. Some of Alfred A. Knopf's memories are recorded in "For Henry, with Love: My Friendship with Mencken," *Atl*, CCIII (May, 1959), 50–54. See also James Walt, "Morning, Noon, and Night," *MAQR*, LXVI (1960), 138–145; *idem*, "Shadows at Noon: Mencken in the Twenties," *MAQR*, LXVI (1960), 220–229; Philip M. Wagner, "Mencken Remembered," *ASch*, XXXII (1963), 256–274; and Charles Angoff, "H. L. Mencken: A Postscript," *SAQ*, LXIII (1964), 227–239.

Guy Jean Forgue's *H. L. Mencken: L'Homme, l'oeuvre, l'influence*, Paris, 1967, filled with detailed information and acute critical judgments, deserves translation into English. M. K. Singleton, *H. L. Mencken and the American Mercury Adventure*, Durham, N.C., 1962, documents the editor's achievements and general policies. Carl R. Dolmetsch, *The Smart Set*, New York, 1966, is both a history and an anthology. William H. Nolte, *H. L. Mencken: Literary Critic*, Middletown, Conn., 1966, attempts to define the author's critical principles. Philip Wagner, *H. L. Mencken*, Minneapolis, Minn., 1966, is a pamphlet surveying the whole career.

Brief studies are Robert Allen Durr, "The Last Days of H. L. Mencken," *YR*, LVIII (1958), 58–77; Cedric B. Cowing, "H. L. Mencken: The Case of the 'Curdled' Progressive," *Ethics*, LXIX (1959), 255–267; Lewis Leary, "Changless Critic in Changing Times," *The Young Rebel in American Literature*, ed. Carl Bode, London, 1959, pp. 97–117; Stanley Wein-traub, "Apostate Apostle: H. L. Mencken as Shavophile and Shavophobe," *ETJ*, XII (1960), 184–190; Raven I. McDavid, "A New Look at Mencken's Vulgate," *BSTCF*, I (1960), 39–42; Peter Buitenhuis, "The Value of Mencken," *WHR*, XIV (1960), 19–28; E. A. Martin, "The Ordeal of H. L. Mencken," *SAQ*, LXI (1962), 326–338; H. Alan Wycherley, "Mencken and Knopf: The Editor and His Publisher," *AQ*, XVI (1964), 460–472; Paul F. Boller, Jr., "Purlings and Platitudes: Mencken's Americana," *SWR*, L (1965), 357–371; Douglas C. Stenerson, "Mencken's Early Newspaper Experience: The Genesis of a Style," *AL*, XXXVII (1965), 153–166; Henry Bosley Woolf, "Mencken Revisited," *ES*, XLVII (1966), 102–118; Douglas C. Stenerson, "The 'Forgotten Man' of H. L. Mencken," *AQ*, XVIII (1966), 686–696; Donald R. Stoddard, "Mencken and Dreiser: An Exchange of Roles," *LC*, XXXII (1966), 117–136; and C. Merton Babcock, "Mencken's Shortest Way with Academic Nondissenters," *UCQ*, XII (1967), 28–32.

*Menckeniana*, a current quarterly journal, first appeared in Baltimore, Maryland, in April, 1962.

## 656. PRIMARY SOURCES

Since Mencken's death in 1956, his books and papers have been distributed in a number of libraries. Chief storehouse is the Mencken Room of the Enoch Pratt Library, in Baltimore, Maryland, where more than 100 volumes of personal clippings, books and family scrapbooks, numerous letters, copies of all his printed works, and 2,000 books from his personal library can be consulted. An immense collection of literary and editorial correspondence, willed to the New York Public Library, was opened in 1971. A five-volume diary and four other volumes titled "Letters and Documents Relating to the Baltimore Sunpapers," deposited in the Enoch Pratt Library, are not to be opened until 1981. Four volumes of an unpublished work, "My Life as Author and Editor" and three volumes of an unpublished "Thirty-Five Years of Newspaper Work" are in the New York Public Library (with copies in Enoch Pratt and in Dartmouth College Library), but none of this material can be seen until 1991.

### BIBLIOGRAPHY

The major bibliography was compiled by Betty Adler with the assistance of Jane Wilhelm, *H. L. Mencken: The Bibliography*, Baltimore, Md., 1961. A continuing bibliographical checklist of current Mencken items appears in *Menckeniana*, cited above. See also the valuable appendix to Sara Mayfield's *The Constant Circle*, cited above.

# EDNA ST. VINCENT MILLAY

**657. BIOGRAPHY AND CRITICISM**

Two biographies follow Vincent Sheean's memoir (1951): Miriam Gurko, *Restless Spirit: The Life of Edna St. Vincent Millay*, New York, 1962; and Jean Gould, *The Poet and Her Book: A Biography of Edna St. Vincent Millay*, New York, 1969. Norman A. Brittin combines biography and criticism in *Edna St. Vincent Millay*, New York, 1967. James Gray's pamphlet *Edna St. Vincent Millay*, Minneapolis, Minn., 1967, covers the same ground.

Brief studies include Carl J. Weber, "A Poet's Memory," *CLQ*, IV (1958), 265–274; G. Thomas Tanselle, "Millay, Dell, and 'Recuerdo,'" *CLQ*, VI (1963), 202–205; Floyd Dell, "My Friend Edna St. Vincent Millay," *MTJ*, XII (1964), 1–3; and Mary J. McKee, "Millay's *Aria da Capo*: Form and Meaning," *MD*, IX (1966), 165–169.

**658. BIBLIOGRAPHY**

Recent listings are Vito J. Brenni and John E. James, "Edna St. Vincent Millay: Selected Criticism," *BB*, XXIII (1962), 177–178; and John J. Patton, "A Comprehensive Bibliography of Criticism of Edna St. Vincent Millay," *Serif*, V (1968), 10–32.

# JOAQUIN (CINCINNATUS HEINE [HINER]) MILLER

**659. BIOGRAPHY**

The latest critical biography is O. W. Frost's *Joaquin Miller*, New York, 1967. Special studies are Norman Talbot, "Joaquin Miller's Reception in English Periodicals," *REL*, IV (1963), 63–79; and Lewis E. Buchanan, "Joaquin Miller on the Passing of the Old West," *RS*, XXXII (1964), 326–333.

# WILLIAM VAUGHN MOODY

**BIOGRAPHY AND CRITICISM**

The most recent study is Martin Halpern's *William Vaughn Moody*, New York, 1964, a survey of the whole body of Moody's work. More specialized essays are Frederick Eckman, "Moody's Ode: The Collapse of the Heroic," *UTSE*, XXXVI (1957), 80–92; Maurice F. Brown, "Moody and Robinson," *CLQ*, V (1960), 185–194; and Richard Cary, "Robinson on Moody," *CLQ*, VI (1962), 176–183.


# MARIANNE (CRAIG) MOORE

**662. SEPARATE WORKS**

*O to Be a Dragon*, 1959; *A Marianne Moore Reader*, 1961; *Tell Me, Tell Me: Granite, Steel, and Other Topics*, 1966; *The Complete Poems*, 1967.

Prose works include *The Absentee: A Comedy in Four Acts, Based on Maria Edgeworth's Novel of the Same Name*, 1962; *Puss in Boots, The Sleeping Beauty, and Cinderella: A Retelling of Three Classic Fairy Tales Based on the French of Charles Perrault*, 1963; and *Poetry and Criticism* (an essay written in response to questions by Howard Nemerov), 1965.


**BIOGRAPHY AND CRITICISM**

Bio-critical studies are Donald Hall's *Marianne Moore: The Cage and the Animal*, New York, 1970; and Bernard F. Engel, *Marianne Moore*, New York, 1964. Tambimuttu edited *Festschrift for Marianne Moore's Seventy-Seventh Birthday by Various Hands*, New York, 1964. See also Wallace Fowlie, "Jorge Guillén, Marianne Moore, T. S. Eliot: Some Recollections," *Poetry*, XC (1957), 103–109; Marianne Moore, "Marianne Moore: A Self-Portrait," *Esquire*, LVIII (1962), 99; and George Plimpton, "The World Series with Marianne Moore: Letter from an October Afternoon," *Harpers*, CCXXIX (Oct., 1964), 50–58 (followed by her reply in the November issue).

Three recent critical volumes are George W. Nitchie's *Marianne Moore: An Introduction to the Poetry*, New York, 1969; Sister M. Thérèse's brief critical essay, *Marianne Moore*, Grand Rapids, Mich., 1969; and a pamphlet by a fellow poet, Jean Garrigue's *Marianne Moore*, Minneapolis, Minn., 1965. Charles Tomlinson edited *Marianne Moore: A Collection of Critical Essays*, Englewood Cliffs, N.J., 1969. A large section of A. Kingsley Weatherhead's *The Edge of the Image*, Seattle, Wash., 1967, is devoted to Miss Moore. See also, *passim*, W. H. Auden, *The Dyer's Hand*, New York, 1962; G. S. Fraser, *Vision and Rhetoric*, New York, 1960; Roy Harvey Pearce, *The Continuity of American Poetry*, Princeton, N.J., 1961; and William Wasserstrom, *The Time of The Dial*, Syracuse, N.Y., 1963.

Other brief studies are Elder Olson, "The Poetry of Marianne Moore," *ChiR*, XI (1957), 100–104; Charles Tomlinson, "Abundance, Not Too Much: The Poetry of Marianne Moore," *SR*, LXV (1957), 677–687; Robert Beloof, "Prosody and Tone: The 'Mathematics' of Marianne

Moore," *KR*, XX (1958), 116–123; Laurence Stapleton, "Marianne Moore and the Element of Prose," *SAQ*, LVII (1958), 366–374; Marie Boroff, "Dramatic Structure in the Poetry of Marianne Moore," *LitR*, II (1958), 112–123; Thomas B. Brumbaugh, "In Pursuit of Miss Moore," *MissQ*, XV (1962), 74–80; X. J. Kennedy, "Marianne Moore," *MinnR*, II (1962), 369–376; Sister Mary Cecilia, "The Poetry of Marianne Moore," *Thought*, XXXVIII (1963), 354–374; Mildred E. Hartsock, "Marianne Moore: A 'Salvo of Barks,'" *BuR*, XI (1962), 14–37; Lina Unali, "Marianne Moore," *SA*, IX (1963), 377–424; Hugh Kenner, "The Experience of the Eye: Marianne Moore's Tradition," *SoR*, I (1965), 754–769; Rebecca Price Parkin, "Certain Difficulties in Reading Marianne Moore: Poems; Exemplified in Her 'Apparition of Splendor,'" *PMLA*, LXXXI (1966), 167–172; *idem*, "Some Characteristics of Marianne Moore's Humor," *CE*, XXVII (1966), 403–408; Charles Tomlinson, "Marianne Moore; Her Poetry and Her Critics," *Agenda*, VI (1968), 137–142; and William T. Going, "Marianne Moore's 'Dream': Academic By-Path to Xanadu," *Studies in American Literature . . .* , ed. Robert Partlow, *PLL*, V (Summer Suppl., 1969), 145–153.

## PAUL ELMER MORE

**663.** REPRINTS

*The Skeptical Approach to Religion* (1934) was reprinted in Princeton, New Jersey, 1958, *On Being Human* (1936) in 1968. Daniel Aaron selected and edited *Shelburne Essays on American Literature*, New York, 1963. The collected *Shelburne Essays* (1904–1921) were reprinted in 11 volumes, New York, 1967.

BIOGRAPHY AND CRITICISM

The first biography, stressing his religious and philosophical thought, is Arthur Hazard Dakin, *Paul Elmer More*, Princeton, N.J., 1960. Two critical studies are Robert M. Davies, *The Humanism of Paul Elmer More*, New York, 1958; and Francis X. Duggan, *Paul Elmer More*, New York, 1967. See also James Holly Hanford, "The Paul Elmer More Papers," *PULC*, XXII (1961), 163–168; and Barrows Dunham, "Paul Elmer More," *MR*, VII (1966), 157–164.

## JOHN LOTHROP MOTLEY

**665.** BIOGRAPHY AND CRITICISM

The major study is David Levin, *History as Romantic Art: Bancroft, Prescott, Motley, and Parkman*, Stanford, Calif., 1959.

# JOHN MUIR

**666.** COLLECTED WORKS

Three works were recently reprinted: *The Mountains of California* (1894) in Garden City, New York, 1961; *The Yosemite* (1912) in Garden City, New York, 1962; and *The Story of My Boyhood and Youth* (1913) in Madison, Wisconsin, 1965. Frederic R. Gunsky edited *South of Yosemite: Sketches by John Muir*, Garden City, N.Y., 1968.

**667.** BIOGRAPHY AND CRITICISM

A critical biography is Herbert F. Smith, *John Muir*, New York, 1965. Holway Roy Jones concentrates on *John Muir and the Sierra Club: The Battle for Yosemite*, San Francisco, 1965.

# MARY NOAILLES MURFREE
## ("CHARLES EGBERT CRADDOCK")

**667.** SEPARATE WORKS

See William B. Dillingham, " 'When Old Baldy Spoke,' by Charles Egbert Craddock: Edited and with an Introduction," *EUQ*, XVIII (1962), 93–106.

BIOGRAPHY AND CRITICISM

A recent critical biography is Richard Cary's *Mary N. Murfree*, New York, 1967. More specialized studies are Archer Taylor, "Proverbs and Proverbial Phrases in the Writings of Mary N. Murfree (Charles Egbert Craddock)," *TFSB*, XXIV (1958), 11–50; and R. Baird Shuman, "Mary Murfree's Battle," *TSL*, VI (1961), 33–37.

The most recent bibliographical listing is Richard Cary, "Mary Noailles Murfree (1850–1922)," *ALR*, I (1967), 79–83.

# (BENJAMIN) FRANK(LIN) NORRIS

**668.** SEPARATE WORKS

James D. Hart edited *A Novelist in the Making: A Collection of Student Themes and the Novels* Blix *and* Vandover and the Brute, Cambridge, Mass., 1971. It "combines 44 of Norris' newly discovered and never before published student themes with their direct descendants, the early novels *Blix* and *Vandover and the Brute*."

COLLECTED WORKS AND REPRINTS

Donald Pizer edited *The Literary Criticism of Frank Norris*, Austin, Tex., 1964, uncollected pieces from 1895–1903. See also Franklin Walker, ed., "An Early Frank Norris Item," *QNL*, XXV (1960), 83–86; Richard Allan Davison, "Frank Norris's Thirteen Uncollected Newsletters," *N&Q*, XI (1964), 71–73; and *idem*, "The Remaining Seven of Frank Norris's 'Weekly Letters,'" *ALR*, III (1968), 47–65. Donald Pizer edited "Ten Letters by Frank Norris," *QNL*, XXVII (1962), 51–61.

Reprints of the novels are too numerous to list separately.

BIOGRAPHY AND CRITICISM

Warren French's *Frank Norris*, New York, 1962, is a survey of the whole career. Donald Pizer, in *The Novels of Frank Norris*, Bloomington, Ind., 1966, concentrates especially on the influence of Joseph LeComte's "evolutionary theism" on Norris's views. A more specialized study is William B. Dillingham, *Frank Norris: Instinct and Art*, Boston, 1969. The chief foreign re-evaluation is Klaus Lanzinger's *Die Epik im amerikanischen Roman: Eine Studie zu James F. Cooper, Herman Melville, Frank Norris und Thomas Wolfe*, Frankfurt am Main, 1965.

Briefer studies are Donald Pizer, "Individualism in Garland, Norris, and Crane," *AQ*, X (1958), 463–475; Stanley Cooperman, "Frank Norris and the Werewolf of Guilt," *MLQ*, XX (1959), 252–258; Herbert E. Francis, Jr., "A Reconsideration of Frank Norris," *EUQ*, XV (1959), 110–118; John C. Sherwood, "Norris and the *Jeannette*," *PQ*, XXXVII (1958), 245–252; Edgeley W. Todd, "The Frontier Epic: Frank Norris and John G. Neihardt," *WHR*, XIII (1959), 40–45; George W. Johnson, "Frank Norris and Romance," *AL*, XXXIII (1961), 52–63; *idem*, "The Frontier behind Frank Norris' *McTeague*," *HLQ*, XXVI (1962), 91–104; Robert W. Schneider, "Frank Norris: The Naturalist as Victorian," *MASJ*, III (1962), 13–27; James K. Folsom, "Social Darwinism or Social Protest? The 'Philosophy' of *The Octopus*," *MFS*, VIII (1963), 393–400; James Childs, "The First Draft of *McTeague*: 1893," *AN&Q*, III (1964), 37–38; Donald Pizer, "Nineteenth-Century American Naturalism: An Essay in Definition," *BuR*, XIII (1965), 1–18; Don D. Walker, "The Western Naturalism of Frank Norris," *WAL*, II (1967), 14–29; Robert H. Woodward, "Frank Norris and Frederic: A Source for *McTeague*," *Frederic Herald*, II (1968), 2; and Rodrigue E. Labrie, "The Howells–Norris Relationship and the Growth of Naturalism," *Discourse*, XI (1968), 363–371.

**669.** BIBLIOGRAPHY

The major listing is Kenneth A. Lohf and Eugene P. Sheehy, comps., *Frank Norris: A Bibliography*, Los Gatos, Calif., 1959. See also William

White, "Frank Norris: Bibliographical Addenda," *BB*, XXII (1959), 227–228; and Warren French, "Frank Norris (1870–1902)," *ALR*, I (1967), 84–89.

# CLIFFORD ODETS
*d. 1963*

**670.** BIOGRAPHY AND CRITICISM

A monologue by Odets, adapted from a 1961 interview with Arthur Wagner, was published as "How a Playwright Triumphs," *Harper's*, CCXXXII (Sept., 1966), 64–70, 73–74.

The first critical biographies are R. Baird Shuman, *Clifford Odets*, New York, 1963; and Gerald Weales, *Clifford Odets: Playwright*, New York, 1971. Edward Murray argues that Odets was "one of the very few dramatic poets" of the modern theater in his discussion of eight plays, *Clifford Odets: The Thirties and After*, New York, 1968. Michael J. Mendelsohn tries to prove that "Odets was a humanitarian by inclination and a radical by accident" in *Clifford Odets: Humane Dramatist*, Deland, Fla., 1969. See also, *passim*, Harold Clurman, *The Fervent Years*, New York, 1957; John Howard Lawson, *Theory and Technique of Playwrighting*, New York, 1960; and Winifred L. Dusenbury, *The Theme of Loneliness in Modern American Drama*, Gainesville, Fla., 1960.

Briefer estimates are Robert Brustein, "America's New Culture-Hero: Feeling without Words," *Com*, XXV (1958), 123–129; N. B. Fagin, "In Search of an American *Cherry Orchard*," *TQ*, I (1958), 132–141; Paola Chiesa Lasorsa, "Il teato di Clifford Odets," *SA*, VII (1961), 363–409; Catharine Hughes, "Odets: The Price of Success," *Cweal*, LXXVIII (1963), 558–560; Charles Kaplan, "Two Depression Plays and Broadway's Popular Idealism," *AQ*, XV (1963), 579–585; Rodolfo Usigli, "Mis encuentros con Clifford Odets," *Hispania*, XLVI (1963), 689–692; and Gerald W. Haslam, "Odets' Use of Yiddish-English in *Awake and Sing*," *RS*, XXXIV (1965), 161–164.

# EUGENE (GLADSTONE) O'NEILL

**670.** SEPARATE WORKS

*Hughie*, 1959.

Donald Gallup edited Karl Ragnar-Gierow's shortened version of a partly revised O'Neill manuscript, *More Stately Mansions*, New Haven, Conn., 1964. *Ten "Lost" Plays*, New York, 1964, with a foreword by Bennett Cerf, is offered by Random House as the "standard official edition," intended as a replacement for the "unauthorized version" of these plays first published in 1950 (*Lost Plays*, ed. Lawrence Gellert).

## 671. BIOGRAPHY AND CRITICISM

The first comprehensive biography is Arthur Gelb and Barbara Gelb, *O'Neill*, New York, 1962 (abridged version, 1965). The first volumes of what promise to be two-volume biographies are Louis Sheaffer, *O'Neill: Son and Playwright*, New York, 1968; and Doris Alexander, *The Tempering of Eugene O'Neill*, New York, 1962. Both books take the story of O'Neill's life to 1920. Croswell Bowen, *The Curse of the Misbegotten: A Tale of the House of O'Neill*, New York, 1959, is a popular account written with the assistance of Shane O'Neill, the playwright's son.

The best study of O'Neill as literary artist, the influences on his work, and his place in American letters is John Henry Raleigh's *The Plays of Eugene O'Neill*, Carbondale, Ill., 1965. Brief general surveys of the whole career are Frederic I. Carpenter, *Eugene O'Neill*, New York, 1964; and John Gassner's pamphlet, *Eugene O'Neill*, Minneapolis, Minn., 1965. More specialized are Egil Törnqvist, *A Drama of Souls: Studies in O'Neill's Super-naturalistic Techniques*, New Haven, Conn., 1969; and Timo Tiusanen, *O'Neill's Scenic Images*, Princeton, N. J., 1968, a discussion of all 49 plays in relation to the physical stage by the director of the Helsinki City Theatre. Sophus Keith Winther's *Eugene O'Neill: A Critical Study* (1934) was reprinted with a new chapter on the last four plays, New York, 1961. See also the discussions of O'Neill in Kenneth Tynan, *Curtains*, New York, 1961; Elder Olson, *Tragedy and the Theory of Drama*, Detroit, Mich., 1961; Robert Brustein, *The Theater of Revolt*, Boston, 1962; and Raymond Williams, *Modern Tragedy*, London, 1966.

Foreign studies include Karl Ragnar-Gierow, *Introduktioner Till Eugene O'Neills Dramatik*, Stockholm, 1958; Clifford Leech, *Eugene O'Neill*, Edinburgh, 1963; Horst Frenz, *Eugene O'Neill*, Berlin, 1965; D. V. K. Raghavacharyulu, *Eugene O'Neill: A Study*, Bombay, 1965; Franz H. Link, *Eugene O'Neill und die Wiedergeburt der Tragödie aus dem Unbewuszten*, Frankfurt am Main, 1967; and Knut Dorn, *Die Erlösungsthematik bei Eugene O'Neill: Eine Analyse der Strukturen im Spätwerk*, Heidelberg, 1968.

Collections of brief studies are plentiful and well edited: Oscar Cargill *et al.*, eds., *O'Neill and His Plays: Four Decades of Criticism*, New York, 1961; John Gassner, ed., *O'Neill: A Collection of Critical Essays*, Englewood Cliffs, N.J., 1964; Jordan Y. Miller, *Playwright's Progress: O'Neill and the Critics*, Chicago, 1965; and John Henry Raleigh, ed., *Twentieth-Century Interpretations of The Iceman Cometh*, Englewood Cliffs, N.J., 1968. Other brief estimates are Drew B. Pallette, "O'Neill's *A Touch of the Poet* and His Other Last Plays," *ArQ*, XIII (1957), 308–319; Walter Cerf, "Psychoanalysis and the Realistic Drama," *JAAC*, XVI (1958), 328–336; Robert F. Whitman, "O'Neill's Search for 'A Language of the Theatre,'" *QJS*, XLVI (1960), 153–170; Eugene M. Waith, "Eugene O'Neill: An Exercise in Unmasking," *ETJ*, XIII (1961), 182–191; Brigitte Sterne, "The Critical Reception of American Drama in Sweden," *MD*, IV (1962), 71–82; William H. Davenport, "The Published and Unpublished Poems of Eugene O'Neill," *YULG*, XXXVIII (1963), 51–66; Joseph P. O'Neill, S.J., "The Tragic Theory of Eugene O'Neill," *TSLL*, IV (1963), 481–498; Mordecai Marcus, "Eugene O'Neill's Debt to Thoreau in *A Touch of the Poet*," *JEGP*, LXII (1963), 270–279; Charles Fish, "Beginnings: O'Neill's *The Web*," *PULC*, XXVII (1965), 3–20; Robert C. Wright, "O'Neill's Universalizing Technique in *The Iceman Cometh*," *MD*, VIII (1965), 1–11.

More recent studies are Henry F. Pommer, "The Mysticism of Eugene O'Neill," *MD*, IX (1966), 26–39; A. Richard Sogliuzzo, "The Uses of the Mask in *The Great God Brown* and *Six Characters in Search of an Author*," *ETJ*, XVIII (1966), 224–229; James M. Salem, "Eugene O'Neill and the Sacrament of Marriage," *Serif*, III (1966), 23–35; John J. Fitzgerald, "The Bitter Harvest of O'Neill's Projected Cycle," *NEQ*, XL (1967), 364–374; Mardi Valgemae, "O'Neill and German Expressionism," *MD*, X (1967), 111–123; William R. Reardon, "O'Neill since World War II: Critical Reception in New York," *MD*, X (1967), 289–299; and Robert C. Lee, "Eugene O'Neill's Remembrance: The Past is the Present," *ArQ*, XXIII (1967), 293–305.

*Modern Drama*, III (1960), is a special Eugene O'Neill issue.

### 672. BIBLIOGRAPHY

The major critical bibliography is Jordan Y. Miller's *Eugene O'Neill and the American Critic*, Hamden, Conn., 1962. See also Jackson R. Bryer, "Forty Years of O'Neill Criticism: A Selected Bibliography," *MD*, IV (1961), 196–216; and John Henry Raleigh, "Eugene O'Neill," *Fifteen Modern American Authors*, ed. Jackson R. Bryer, Durham, N.C., 1969, pp. 301–322.

J. Russell Reaver published *An O'Neill Concordance*, 3 vols., Detroit, Mich., 1969.

# THOMAS NELSON PAGE

**673. SEPARATE WORKS**

*In Ole Virginia; or, Marse Chan and Other Stories* (1887), was reprinted with an introduction by Kimball King, Chapel Hill, N.C., 1969. See also Harriet R. Holman, ed., "Thomas Nelson Page's Account of Tennessee Hospitality," *THQ*, XXVIII (1969), 269–272.

**674. BIOGRAPHY AND CRITICISM**

The first full-length study is Theodore L. Gross, *Thomas Nelson Page*, New York, 1967. Briefer estimates are William J. Sowder, "Gerald W. Johnson, Thomas Nelson Page, and the South," *MissQ*, XIV (1961), 197–203; Kimball King, "Satirical Portraits by Thomas Nelson Page," *MissQ*, XVIII (1965), 74–81; and *idem*, "Regionalism in the Three Souths," *TWA*, LIV (1965), 37–50.

A recent bibliographical listing is Theodore L. Gross, "Thomas Nelson Page (1853–1922)," *ALR*, I (1967), 90–92.

# THOMAS PAINE

**675. COLLECTED WORKS**

Harry Hayden Clark's *Thomas Paine: Representative Selections* (1944), has been reprinted in a revised edition with updated bibliography, New York, 1961.

**676. BIOGRAPHY AND CRITICISM**

The major study in recent years is Alfred Owen Aldridge, *Man of Reason: The Life of Thomas Paine*, Philadelphia, 1959, with an emphasis on new French documents and information. A more specialized volume is R. R. Fennessy, *Burke, Paine, and The Rights of Man: A Difference of Political Opinions*, The Hague, 1963.

Briefer studies are Leo A. Bressler, "Peter Porcupine and the Bones of Thomas Paine," *PMHB*, LXXXII (1958), 176–185; Hans Arnold, "Die Aufnahme von Thomas Paines Schriften in Deutschland," *PMLA*, LXXIV (1959), 365–386; Donald Connolly, C.S.P., ed., "The Death of Thomas Paine," *RACHSP*, LXIX (1958), 119–123; Richard Gimbel, "The Resurgence of Thomas Paine," *PAAS*, LXIX (1959), 97–111; James T. Boulton, "Literature and Politics, I: Tom Paine and the Vulgar Style," *EIC*, XII (1962), 18–33; Matthew Hodgart, "Politics and Prose Style in the Late Eighteenth Century: *The Radicals*," *BNYPL*, LXVI (1962), 464–469; Mark O. Kistler, "German-American Liberalism and Thomas Paine," *AQ*, XIV (1962), 81–91; Horst Ihde, "Thomas Paine und die Französische Revolution," *ZAA*, XV (1967), 5–31; Strother B. Purdy, "A Note on the Burke–Paine Controversy," *AL*, XXXIX (1967), 373–375; Alfred Owen Aldridge, "Thomas Paine and the Classics," *ECS*, I (1968), 370–380; and Jerry W. Knudson, "The Rage around Tom Paine: Newspaper Reaction to His Homecoming in 1802," *New-York Historical Society Quarterly*, LIII (1969), 34–63.

### 678. BIBLIOGRAPHY

See Richard Gimbel's catalogue of a memorial exhibition, "Thomas Paine Fights for Freedom in Three Worlds: The New, the Old, the Next," *PAAS*, LXX (1961), 397–492.


## THEODORE PARKER

### 678. COLLECTED WORKS

Henry Steele Commager edited, with an introduction, *Theodore Parker: An Anthology*, Boston, 1960.

### 679. BIOGRAPHY AND CRITICISM

John Weiss's two-volume *Life and Correspondence of Theodore Parker* (1864) has been reprinted in New York, 1969. Recent brief studies are Perry Miller, "Theodore Parker: Apostasy with Liberalism," *HTR*, LIV (1961), 275–295; John C. Broderick, "Problems of the Literary Executor: The Case of Theodore Parker," *QJLC*, XXIII (1966), 261–273; and Charles J. Beirne, "The Theology of Theodore Parker and the War with Mexico," *EIHC*, CIV (1968), 130–137.


## FRANCIS PARKMAN

### 681. EDITED TEXTS AND REPRINTS

E. N. Feltskog's edition of *The Oregon Trail*, Madison, Wis., 1969, is an authoritative text "based on scholarly collation of all editions published in Parkman's lifetime." Other reprints of Parkman's work are too numerous to list separately.

Wilbur R. Jacobs edited *Letters of Francis Parkman*, 2 vols., Norman, Okla., 1960, a collection of over 400.

BIOGRAPHY AND CRITICISM

Howard Doughty's critical biography, *Francis Parkman*, New York, 1962, is also a close study of Parkman's style. See also David Levin's *History as Romantic Art: Bancroft, Prescott, Motley, and Parkman*, Stanford, Calif., 1959. Some briefer studies are Wilbur R. Jacobs, "Some of Parkman's Literary Devices," *NEQ*, XXXI (1958), 244–252; *idem*, "Highlights of Parkman's Formative Period," *PHR*, XXVII (1958), 149–158; Richard A. Thompson, "Francis Parkman on the Nature of Man," *M-A*, XLII (1960), 3–17; W. J. Eccles, "The History of New France According to Francis Parkman," *WMQ*, XVIII (1961), 163–175; William R. Taylor, "A Journey into the Human Mind: Motivation in Francis Parkman's *La Salle*," *WMQ*, XIX (1962), 230–237; John T. Hubbell, "Francis Parkman, Historian," *MQ*, VIII (1966), 29–39; Russel B. Nye, "Parkman, Red Fate, and White Civilization," *Essays on American Literature*, ed. Clarence Gohdes, Durham, N.C., 1967, pp. 152–163; Richard Vitzthum, "The Historian as Editor: Francis Parkman's Reconstruction of Sources in *Montcalm and Wolfe*," *JAH*, LIII (1966), 471–486; and David Levin, "Francis Parkman: *The Oregon Trail*," *Landmarks of American Writing*, ed. Hennig Cohen, New York, 1969, pp. 79–89.

# JAMES KIRKE PAULDING

**684.** SEPARATE WORKS

Ralph L. Ketcham edited "An Unpublished Sketch of James Madison by James K. Paulding," *VMHB*, LXVII (1959), 432–437.

**685.** COLLECTED WORKS AND CORRESPONDENCE

Ralph M. Aderman edited *The Letters of James Kirke Paulding*, Madison, Wis., 1962.

BIOGRAPHY AND CRITICISM

Brief studies are Ralph M. Aderman, "James Kirke Paulding's Literary Income," *BNYPL*, LXIV (1960), 117–129; Paton Yoder, "Private Hospitality in the South, 1775–1850," *MVHR*, XLVII (1960), 419–433; Amos L. Herold, "Paulding's Literary Theories," *BNYPL*, LXVI (1962), 236–243; Ralph M. Aderman, "James Kirke Paulding as Social Critic," *PELL*, I (1965), 217–229; and Joseph J. Arpad, "John Wesley Jarvis, James Kirke Paulding, and Colonel Nimrod Wildfire," *NYFQ*, XXI (1965), 92–106.

## JOHN HOWARD PAYNE

**686.** SEPARATE WORKS

Clemens de Baillou edited *John Howard Payne to His Countrymen,* Athens, Ga., 1961, the story of his arrest by the Georgia Guard and his plea for the Cherokee Indians in 1835.

BIOGRAPHY AND CRITICISM

Brief studies are E. Merton Coulter, "John Howard Payne's Visit to Georgia," *GHQ,* XLVI (1962), 333-376; Carl R. Woodring, "New Light on Byron, Trelawny, and Lady Hester Stanhope," *CLC,* XI (1962), 9-18; Grace Overmyer, "The Baltimore Mobs and John Howard Payne," *MHM,* LVIII (1963), 54-61; Thurman Wilkins, "John Howard Payne: Friend of the Cherokees," *CLC,* XII (1962), 3-11; and Robert Skloot, "John Howard Payne: The Early Years," *Sym,* V (Summer, 1966), 12-15.

## WILLIAM PENN

**687.** COLLECTED WORKS AND EDITED TEXTS

See Roger Thomas, "Letters of William Penn and Richard Baxter," *Journal of Friends' Historical Society,* XLVIII (1958), 204-207.

**688.** BIOGRAPHY AND CRITICISM

The most recent biography is Catherine Owens Peare's *William Penn,* Philadelphia, 1957. Penn's political career rather than "his association with the Society of Friends and his prominent role in the cause of religious toleration" is the subject of Joseph E. Illick's *William Penn, the Politician: His Relations with the English Government,* Ithaca, N.Y., 1965. Mary Maples Dunn concentrates on Penn as active politician in *William Penn: Politics and Conscience,* Princeton, N.J., 1967. More specialized studies are Edwin B. Bronner, *William Penn's Holy Experiment: The Founding of Pennsylvania, 1681-1701,* Philadelphia, 1962; and Vincent Buranelli, *The King and the Quaker: A Study of William Penn and James II,* Philadelphia, 1962.

Briefer essays are Alison Gilbert Olson, "William Penn, Parliament, and Proprietary Government," *WMQ,* XVIII (1961), 176-195; Marion Balderston, "The Real *Welcome* Passengers," *HLQ,* XXVI (1962), 31-56; and Nicholas B. Wainwright, "The Penn Collection," *PMHB,* LXXXVI (1963), 393-419.

# EDGAR ALLAN POE

### 689. COLLECTED WORKS

Harvard University Press has begun publication of *Collected Works of Edgar Allan Poe*, ed. Thomas O. Mabbott, with Volume I, *Poems*, Cambridge, Mass., 1969. An unusually handsome edition of *The Poems of Edgar Allan Poe* has been edited with an introduction, variant readings, and textual notes by Floyd Stovall, Charlottesville, Va., 1965. Robert L. Hough assembled a collection of *Literary Criticism of Edgar Allan Poe*, Lincoln, Neb., 1965.

Reprintings are now available of the 17-volume Virginia edition (1902) of *The Complete Works*, ed. James A. Harrison; and of Margaret Alterton and Hardin Craig's *Edgar Allan Poe: Representative Selections* (1935) with an updated bibliography, New York, 1962.

John W. Ostrom's *Letters of Edgar Allan Poe* (1948) has been reissued with a 56-page supplement, New York, 1966.

### 691. BIOGRAPHY AND CRITICISM

Two recent biographical studies are William Bittner, *Poe: A Biography*, Boston, 1962; and Edward Wagenknecht, *Edgar Allan Poe: The Man behind the Legend*, New York, 1963. Frances Winwar's *The Haunted Palace: A Life of Edgar Allan Poe*, New York, 1959, aims at a popular audience.

Among the critical volumes, two are general introductions in relatively brief space: Vincent Buranelli, *Edgar Allan Poe*, New York, 1961; and Geoffrey Rans, *Edgar Allan Poe*, Edinburgh, 1965. In *The Measure of Poe*, Norman, Okla., 1969, Louis Broussard sees Poe as "an artist of ideas" ahead of his time in scientific theory. Floyd Stovall concentrates on the poetry in *Edgar Poe the Poet: Essays New and Old on the Man and His Work*, Charlottesville, Va., 1959. Burton R. Pollin devotes 12 essays chiefly to sources and influences in *Discoveries in Poe*, Notre Dame, Ind., 1970. Poe's debt to the British quarterlies is acutely observed in Michael Allen's *Poe and the British Magazine Tradition*, New York, 1969. Poe's criticism is studied in three recent volumes: Edd Winfield Parks, *Edgar Allan Poe as Literary Critic*, Athens, Ga., 1964, the best introduction to the subject; Robert D. Jacobs, *Poe, Journalist and Critic*, Baton Rouge, La., 1969; and Sidney P. Moss, *Poe's Literary Battles: The Critic in the Context of His Literary Milieu*, Durham, N.C., 1963. Moss continued his study with *Poe's Major Crisis: His Libel Suit and New York's Literary World*, Durham, N.C., 1970. John Walsh re-examines the murder of Mary

Rogers in a fascinating study, *Poe the Detective: The Curious Circumstances behind "The Mystery of Marie Rogêt,"* New Brunswick, N.J., 1967. David M. Rein's *Edgar A. Poe: The Inner Pattern*, New York, 1960, is rather shaky psychological criticism, to be read with more perspective than the author achieves in his arguments.

Three studies from Germany are Walter Lennig, ed., *Edgar Allan Poe: In Selbstzeugnissen und Bilddokumenten*, Hamburg, 1959; and Klaus Lubbers, *Die Todesszene und Ihre Funktion im Kurzgeschichtenwerk von Edgar Allan Poe*, Munich, 1961; and especially important for his scope and acute analyses, Franz H. Link, *Edgar Allan Poe: Ein Dichter zwischen Romantik und Moderne*, Frankfurt am Main, 1968. See also the chapters on Poe in Harry Levin, *The Power of Blackness*, New York, 1958; Leslie A. Fiedler, *Love and Death in the American Novel*, New York, 1960; Edwin Fussell, *Frontier: American Literature and the American West*, Princeton, N.J., 1965; and Maria Elisabeth Kronegger, *James Joyce and Associated Image Makers*, New Haven, Conn., 1968.

Eric W. Carlson compiled 30 articles tracing the development of Poe's reputation in *The Recognition of Edgar Allan Poe: Selected Criticism since 1829*, Ann Arbor, Mich., 1966. A companion volume is Robert Regan, ed., *Poe: A Collection of Critical Essays*, Englewood Cliffs, N.J., 1967. Other brief studies are Clarke Olney, "Edgar Allan Poe: Science-Fiction Pioneer," *GaR*, XII (1958), 416–421; Willem Van Doorn, "Edgar Poe's 'Ulalume,'" *RLV*, XXIV (1958), 395–404; Robert D. Jacobs, "Poe among the Virginians," *VMHB*, LXVII (1959), 30–48; Dorothy J. Samuel, "Poe and Baudelaire: Parallels in Form and Symbol," *CLAJ*, III (1959), 88–105; James Southall Wilson, "The Personality of Poe," *VMHB*, LXVII (1959), 131–142; Jay B. Hubbell, "Poe and the Southern Literary Tradition," *TSLL*, II (1960), 151–171; Richard Cary, "Poe and the Great Debate," *TSLL*, III (1961), 223–233; Emerson R. Marks, "Poe as Literary Theorist: A Reappraisal," *AL*, XXXIII (1961), 296–306; James Schroeter, "A Misreading of Poe's 'Ligeia,'" *PMLA*, LXXVI (1961), 397–406; S. Gerald Sandler, "Poe's Indebtedness to Locke's *An Essay Concerning Human Understanding*," *BUSE*, V (1961), 107–121; Stephen L. Mooney, "The Comic in Poe's Fiction," *AL*, XXXIII (1962), 433–441; L. Moffitt Cecil, "The Two Narratives of Arthur Gordon Pym," *TSLL*, V (1963), 232–241; Edward Stone, "Poe In and Out of His Time," *ESQ*, No. 31 (1963), pp. 14–17; Eric W. Stockton, "Celestial Inferno: Poe's 'The City in the Sea,'" *TSL*, VIII (1963), 99–106; James M. Kiehl, "The Valley of Unrest: A Major Metaphor in the Poetry of Edgar Allan Poe," *Thoth*, V (1964), 42–52.

More recent studies are J. Lasley Dameron, "Poe's Reading of the British Periodicals," *MissQ*, XVIII (1965), 19–25; Michael J. Hoffman, "The House of Usher and Negative Romanticism," *SIR*, IV (1965), 158–168; Lewis A. Lawson, "Poe's Conception of the Grotesque," *MissQ*, XIX (1966), 200–205; Terence Martin, "The Imagination at Play: Edgar Allan Poe," *KR*, XXVIII (1966), 194–209; Joseph V. Ridgely and Iola S. Haverstick, "Chartless Voyage: The Many Narratives of Arthur Gordon Pym," *TSLL*, VIII (1966), 63–80; I. M. Walker, "The 'Legitimate Sources' of Terror in 'The Fall of the House of Usher,'" *MLR*, LXI (1966), 585–592; John H. Stroupe, "Poe's Imaginary Voyage: Pym as Hero," *SSF*, IV (1967), 315–321; Herbert F. Smith, "Usher's Madness and Poe's Organization: A Source," *AL*, XXXIX (1967), 379–389; Charles L. Sanford, "Edgar Allan Poe: A Blight Upon the Landscape," *AQ*, XX (1968), 54–66; Kermit Vanderbilt, "Art and Nature in 'The Masque of the Red Death,'" *NCF*, XXII (1968), 379–389; Allan Tate, "The Poetry of Edgar Allan Poe," *SR*, LXXVI (1968), 214–225; and Richard P. Benton, "'The Mystery of Marie Roget'—A Defense," *SSF*, VI (1969), 144–151.

The *Poe Newsletter* began publication in 1968 at Washington State University, Pullman, Washington.

### 696. BIBLIOGRAPHY

Listings of critical work on Poe are J. Lasley Dameron, *Edgar Allan Poe: A Checklist of Criticism, 1942–1960*, Charlottesville, Va., 1966; and J. Albert Robbins, *The Merrill Checklist of Edgar Allan Poe*, Columbus, Ohio, 1969. See also J. Lasley Dameron, "Poe at Mid-Century: Anglo-American Criticism, 1928–1960," *BSUF*, VIII (1967), 36–44; Richard P. Benton, "Current Bibliography on Edgar Allan Poe," *ESQ*, No. 38 (1965), pp. 144–147; and *idem*, "Current Bibliography on Edgar Allan Poe," *ESQ*, No. 47 (1967), pp. 84–87. The *Poe Newsletter* will continue publishing "Current Bibliography."

Burton R. Pollin compiled a *Dictionary of Names and Titles in Poe's Collected Works*, New York, 1968, based on Harrison's edition of Poe. J. Lasley Dameron and Louis Charles Stagg edited *An Index to Poe's Critical Vocabulary*, Hartford, Conn., 1966.

David A. Randall, *The J. K. Lilly Collection of Edgar Allan Poe: An Account of Its Formation*, Bloomington, Ind., 1964; and John Carl Miller, *John Henry Ingram's Poe Collection at the University of Virginia*, Charlottesville, Va., 1960, are the primary descriptive volumes on Poe material. See also Richard Gimbel, "'Quoth the Raven': A Catalogue of the Exhibition [at Yale University]," *YULG*, XXXIII (1959), 139–189.

# WILLIAM SYDNEY (SIDNEY) PORTER
## ("O. HENRY")

**697.** BIOGRAPHY AND CRITICISM

The most recent biography is Ethel Stephens Arnett's narrative of Porter's early life (1862–1892) *O. Henry from Polecat Creek*, Greensboro, N.C., 1962. A rewarding bio-critical study is Eugene Current-Garcia's *O. Henry (William Sydney Porter)*, New York, 1965. See also E. Hudson Long, *O. Henry: American Regionalist*, Austin, Tex., 1969.

Briefer studies are Gilbert Millstein, "O. Henry's New Yorkers—and Today's," *NYTM* (Sept. 9, 1962), 36–37, 132, 134–135; Donald F. Peel, "A Critical Study of the Short Stories of O. Henry," *NwMSCS*, XXV (1961), 3–24; Gisela Pira, "O. Henry," *NS*, (1962), 374–379; E. Hudson Long, "O. Henry as a Regional Artist," *Essays on American Literature*, ed. Clarence Gohdes, Durham, N.C., 1967, pp. 229–240; William Saroyan, "O What a Man Was O. Henry," *KR*, XXIX (1967), 671–675; and Malcolm D. McLean, "O. Henry in Honduras," *ALR*, III (1968), 39–46.

**698.** BIBLIOGRAPHY

The most recent listing is E. Hudson Long, "O. Henry (William Sydney Porter) (1862–1910)," *ALR*, (1967), 93–99.

# EZRA (LOOMIS) POUND
## *d. 1972*

**699.** SEPARATE WORKS

Poetry: *Thrones: 96–109 de los cantares*, 1959; *The Cantos [1–109]*, 1964; *Drafts and Fragments of Cantos CX–CXVII*, 1969; *Selected Cantos*, 1970.

Prose: *Impact: Essays on Ignorance and the Decline of American Civilization* (ed. Noel Stock), 1960.

Translations: *Love Poems of Ancient Egypt* (with Noel Stock), 1962.

Editions: *Confucius to Cummings: An Anthology of Poetry* (with Marcella Spann) 1964.

Among the numerous reprints of Pound's early work and translations, *A Lume Spento and Other Early Poems*, New York, 1965, is most important.

CORRESPONDENCE

*The Letters of Ezra Pound, 1907–1941*, ed. D. D. Paige, New York, 1950, is the major collection of a portion of Pound's extensive correspondence. Supplements are *Pound/Joyce: Letters and Essays,* edited with commentary by Forrest Read, New York, 1967; *EP to LU: Nine Letters Written to Louis Untermeyer by Ezra Pound,* ed. J. Albert Robbins, Bloomington, Ind., 1963; and 53 letters in Harry M. Meacham, *The Caged Panther: Ezra Pound at St. Elizabeths,* New York, 1967. Further gleanings are Carlo Izzo, ed., "23 lettere e cartoline inedite," *NC,* Nos. 5–6 (1956), pp. 123–154; Patricia Hutchins, "Letters from Ezra Pound," *TC,* CLXIV (1958), 355–363; Lino Curci, "Alcune lettere," *SA,* IV (1958), 421–430; Noel Stock, "Verse Is a Sword: Unpublished Letters of Ezra Pound, *XR,* I (1960), 258–265; G. Thomas Tanselle, "Two Early Letters of Ezra Pound," *AL,* XXXIV (1962), 114–119; and David Farmer, "An Unpublished Letter by Ezra Pound," *TQ,* X (1967), 95–104.

BIOGRAPHY AND CRITICISM

The first attempt at a comprehensive biography is Charles Norman's *Ezra Pound,* New York, 1960, rev. ed., 1969, a book all future biographers will have to acknowledge. A more balanced and critically more acute biography is Noel Stock's *The Life of Ezra Pound,* New York, 1970. Stock corresponded with Pound for five years before moving to Italy to work with him in Tirolo and Venice. The early years are treated in Patricia Hutchins, *Ezra Pound's Kensington: An Exploration, 1885–1913,* Chicago, 1965; the 1940's are the focus of Charles Norman, *The Case of Ezra Pound,* New York, 1948, rev. ed., 1968; and Julien Cornell, *The Trial of Ezra Pound: A Documented Account of the Treason Case by the Defendant's Lawyer,* New York, 1966. The years in St. Elizabeths Hospital are recorded by Michael Reck in *Ezra Pound: A Close-Up,* New York, 1967; and Harry M. Meacham in *The Caged Panther: Ezra Pound at St. Elizabeths,* New York, 1967. Eustace Mullins's *This Difficult Individual: Ezra Pound,* New York, 1961, is an unbridled impressionistic account of these same years and must be used with caution. Further biographical notes are in David Rattray, "A Weekend with Ezra Pound," *Nation,* CLXXXV (Nov. 16, 1957), 343–349; Kōjirō Yoshikawa, "An Interview with Ezra Pound," *EWR,* I (1964), 212–217; Patricia Hutchins, "Ezra Pound's Pisa," *SoR,* II (1966), 77–93; Mary de Rachewiltz [Pound's daughter], "Ezra Pound at Eighty," *Esquire,* LXV (1966), 114–116, 178–180; and Daniel Cory, "Ezra Pound: A Memoir," *Encounter,* XXX (1968), 30–39. See also Ernest Hemingway, *A Moveable Feast,* New York, 1964; B. L. Reid, *The Man from New York: John Quinn and His Friends,* New York, 1968; and Mary de Rachewiltz, *Discretions,* Boston, 1971, a memoir.

Critical studies of Pound have burgeoned in the last decade. For the student new to the poet's work, M. L. Rosenthal's *A Primer of Ezra Pound,* New York, 1960, is a concise, perceptive introduction. Donald Davie's

*Ezra Pound: Poet as Sculptor*, New York, 1964, concentrates on the poetry, treated chronologically and in detail, with much attention to both sound and shape. Noel Stock, *Poet in Exile: Ezra Pound*, New York, 1964, stresses Pound's learning, its use in his poetry, and his development and decline as thinker and poet.

The early years are treated in N. Christoph de Nagy, *The Poetry of Ezra Pound: The Pre-Imagist Stage*, Bern, 1960, rev. ed., 1968; Hugh Witemeyer, *The Poetry of Ezra Pound: Forms and Renewal, 1908–1920*, Berkeley, Calif., 1969; Thomas H. Jackson, *The Early Poetry of Ezra Pound*, Cambridge, Mass., 1968; and Herbert N. Schneidau, *Ezra Pound: The Image and the Real*, Baton Rouge, La., 1969. A "set of annotations" for the general reader of *The Collected Shorter Poems* is provided by K. K. Ruthven in *A Guide to Ezra Pound's "Personae" (1926)*, Berkeley, Calif., 1969. Pound as translator-transmogrifier is the subject of Wai-lim Yip, *Ezra Pound's Cathay*, Princeton, N.J., 1969; L. S. Dembo, *The Confucian Odes of Ezra Pound: A Critical Appraisal*, Berkeley, Calif., 1963; and J. P. Sullivan, *Ezra Pound and Sextus Propertius: A Study in Creative Translation*, Austin, Tex., 1964. See also chapters on Pound in Earl Miner, *The Japanese Tradition in British and American Literature*, Princeton, N.J., 1958; Lawrence W. Chisolm, *Fenollosa: The Far East and American Culture*, New Haven, Conn., 1963; and Richard Ellmann, *Eminent Domain: Yeats among Wilde, Joyce, Pound, Eliot, and Auden*, New York, 1967.

Readers of *The Cantos* will find much assistance in Clark Emery's survey of basic themes in *Ideas into Action: A Study of Pound's Cantos*, Coral Gables, Fla., 1958. George Dekker concentrates on "the theme of Eros" in *The Cantos of Ezra Pound: A Critical Study*, New York, 1963 (published in London as *Sailing after Knowledge: The Cantos of Ezra Pound*). Walter Baumann interprets chiefly Cantos IV and LXXXII in *The Rose in the Steel Dust: An Examination of the Cantos of Ezra Pound*, Bern, 1967, Coral Gables, Fla., 1970. A surprisingly strong attack on the flaws and disunity of the poem is Noel Stock's *Reading the Cantos: A Study of Meaning in Ezra Pound*, London, 1967. Daniel D. Pearlman attempts to reverse this judgment in *The Barb of Time: On the Unity of Ezra Pound's Cantos*, New York, 1970.

A perceptive guide to Pound's critical principles is N. Christoph de Nagy, *Ezra Pound's Poetics and Literary Tradition: The Critical Decade*, Bern, 1966. An introduction, but no more, to the influence of Douglas, Gesell, and del Mar on Pound is Earle Davis, *Vision Fugitive: Ezra Pound and Economics*, Lawrence, Kan., 1968. Less successful, in reversing direction, is K. L. Goodwin, *The Influence of Ezra Pound*, New York, 1966. Two critics try the difficult task of combining biography and criticism in too limited a space: William Van O'Connor, *Ezra Pound*, Minneapolis, Minn., 1963; and G. S. Fraser, *Ezra Pound*, Edinburgh, 1960.

Studies of Pound by foreign scholars include Nemi D'Agostino, *Ezra Pound*, Rome, 1960; Armando Uribe Arce, *Pound*, Santiago, Chile, 1963; Lore Lenberg, *Rosen aus Feilstaub: Studien zu den Cantos von Ezra Pound*, Wiesbaden, 1966; and Jeannette Lander, *Ezra Pound*, Berlin, 1968.

Collections of brief studies are *Ezra Pound: A Collection of Critical Essays*, ed. Walter E. Sutton, Englewood Cliffs, N.J., 1963; *Ezra Pound Perspectives: Essays in Honor of His Eightieth Birthday*, ed. Noel Stock, Chicago, 1965; and *New Approaches to Ezra Pound: A Co-ordinated Investigation of Pound's Poetry and Ideas,* ed. Eva Hesse, Berkeley, Calif., 1970 (a longer German version first appeared in Frankfurt am Main, 1967).

Other critical estimates are Achilles Fang, "Fenollosa and Pound," *HJAS*, XX (1957), 213–238; Charles B. Willard, "Ezra Pound's Debt to Walt Whitman," *SP*, LIV (1957), 573–581; W. M. Frohock, "The Revolt of Ezra Pound," *SWR*, XLIV (1959), 190–199; Paul A. Olson, "The Bollingen Controversy Ten Years after: Criticism and Content," *PrS*, XXXIII (1959), 225–229; Edith Sitwell, "Preface to Ezra Pound," *YLM*, CXXVI (1958), 42–44; Harvey Gross, "Pound's *Cantos* and the Idea of History," *BuR*, IX (1960), 14–31; Paul A. Olson, "Pound and the Poetry of Perception," *Thought*, XXXV (1960), 331–348; Richard G. Landini, "Vorticism and *The Cantos* of Ezra Pound," *WHR*, XIV (1960), 173–181; Alfredo Rizzardi, "The Mask of Experience: A Chapter upon Ezra Pound's Pisan Canto," *SUS*, XXXV (1960), 135–159; Christine Brooke-Rose, "Ezra Pound: Piers Plowman in the Modern Waste Land," *REL*, II (1961), 74–88.

More recent studies are William McNaughton, "Ezra Pound's Meters and Rhythms," *PMLA*, LXXXVIII (1963), 136–146; Harold M. Hurwitz, "Ezra Pound and Rabindranath Tagore," *AL*, XXXVI (1964), 53–63; A. L. French, "'Olympian Apathein': Pound's *Hugh Selwyn Mauberley* and Modern Poetry," *EIC*, XV (1965), 428–445; Hugh Kenner, "Ezra Pound and Chinese," *Agenda*, IV (1965), 38–41; William V. Spanos, "The Modulating Voice of *Hugh Selwyn Mauberley*," *WSCL*, VI (1965), 73–96; John C. Wang, "Ezra Pound as a Translator of Classical Chinese Poetry," *SR*, LXXIII (1965), 345–357; Thomas H. Jackson, "The Adventures of Messire Wrong-Head," *ELH*, XXXII (1965), 238–255; Benjamin T. Spencer, "Pound: The American Strain," *PMLA*, LXXXI (1966), 457–466; Mary de Rachewiltz, "Tempus Loquendi," *TQ*, X (1967), 36–39; Hugh Kenner, "The Invention of China," *Spectrum*, IX (1967), 21–52; *idem*, "Blood for Ghosts," *TQ*, X (1967), 67–79; W. K. Rose, "Ezra

Pound and Wyndham Lewis: The Crucial Years," *SoR*, IV (1968), 72–89; Walter Sutton, *"Mauberley, The Waste Land,* and the Problem of Unified Form," *WSCL*, IX (1968), 15–35; Hugh Kenner, "The Rope in the Knot," *KyR*, II (1968), 10–29; and Tom Scott, "The Poet as Scapegoat," *Agenda*, VII (1969), 49–58.

The December, 1958, issue of *Yale Literary Magazine*, the October–November, 1965, issue of *Agenda*, and the Winter, 1967, issue of *Texas Quarterly* are special Ezra Pound numbers.

### 700. BIBLIOGRAPHY

The indispensable work is Donald Gallup's *A Bibliography of Ezra Pound*, London, 1963, second impression, corrected, 1969. A useful descriptive bibliographical essay is John Espey, "Ezra Pound," *Fifteen Modern American Authors*, ed. Jackson R. Bryer, Durham, N.C., 1969, pp. 323–344. See also Donald Gallup, " 'Boobliography' and Ezra Pound," *TQ*, X (1967), 80–92.

The major collection of Pound material is now in the Beinecke Library, Yale University, but it is "sealed, pending agreement on satisfactory conditions for its use." Other important pieces are in the Houghton Library of Harvard University and the Lockwood Collection at the State University of New York at Buffalo.

# WILLIAM HICKLING PRESCOTT

### 701. COLLECTED WORKS

*The Papers of William Hickling Prescott*, a selection from letters, memoranda, and commonplace books was edited by C. Harvey Gardiner, Urbana, Ill., 1964. Gardiner also edited *The Literary Memoranda of William Hickling Prescott*, 2 vols., Norman, Okla., 1961. Reprintings of individual volumes are too numerous to list separately.

Gleanings of correspondence are in Edith A. Wright, "Letters and Manuscripts of William H. Prescott," *BPLQ*, XI (1959), 115–130.

### BIOGRAPHY AND CRITICISM

The first biographical study of Prescott in more than 60 years is C. Harvey Gardiner's *William Hickling Prescott: A Biography*, Austin, Tex., 1969. A more specialized study is Gardiner's *Prescott and His Publishers*, Carbondale, Ill., 1959. A gathering of articles and reviews is *William Hickling Prescott: A Memorial*, ed. Howard F. Cline, C. Harvey Gardiner, and Charles Gibson, Durham, N.C., 1959. See also, *passim*, David Levin, *History as Romantic Art: Bancroft, Prescott, Motley, and Parkman*, Stanford, Calif., 1959.

Briefer studies are Thomas F. McGann, "Prescott's Conquests," *AH*, VIII (1957), 4–9, 109–111; Vittorio Gabrieli, "William H. Prescott (1796–1859) e la storia come arte," *SA*, IV (1958), 9–56; Frank Goodwyn, "The Literary Style of William Hickling Prescott," *RIB*, IX (1959), 16–39; Guillermo Lohmann Villena, "Notes on Prescott's Interpretation of the Conquest of Peru," *HAHR*, XXXIX (1959), 46–80; Samuel Eliot Morison, "Robert Carter's Recollections of William H. Prescott," *NEQ*, XXXII (1959), 372–388; Hensley C. Woodbridge, "Prescott's Latin American Reputation," *ABC*, IX (1959), 7–12; and Hans Rudolf Guggisberg, "William Hickling Prescott und das Geschichtsbewusstsein der amerikanischen Romantik," *JA*, XI (1966), 176–193.

### 702. BIBLIOGRAPHY

See Jerry E. Patterson, "A Checklist of Prescott Manuscripts," *HAHR*, XXXIX (1959), 116–128; and Hensley C. Woodbridge, "William Hickling Prescott: A Bibliography," *RIB*, IX (1959), 48–77.

## ELMER (L.) RICE
### d. 1967

### 702. SEPARATE WORKS*

*Cue for Passion* (1958), 1959; *The Living Theatre*, 1959; *Minority Report: An Autobiography*, 1963; *Love among the Ruins*, 1963.

### 703. BIOGRAPHY AND CRITICISM

The first full-length critical study is Robert Hogan, *The Independence of Elmer Rice*, Carbondale, Ill., 1965. Frank Durham, *Elmer Rice*, New York, 1970, is a critical biography. See also Ward Morehouse, "Playwriting's Old Pro," *TArts*, XLIII (Apr., 1957), 17–20; and William R. Elwood, "An Interview with Elmer Rice on Expressionism," *ETJ*, XX (1968), 1–7.

The most recent bibliographical listings are in the volumes by Hogan and Durham cited above.

## JAMES WHITCOMB RILEY

### 704. BIOGRAPHY AND CRITICISM

Brief estimates are Seymour L. Gross, "Eugene Debs and James Whitcomb Riley," *BuR*, VIII (1959), 105–112; Dale B. J. Randall, "Dialect in the Verse of 'The Hoosier Poet,'" *AS*, XXXV (1960), 36–50; and Wil-

---

* Dates in parentheses are of production when it differs from publication.

liam R. Cagle, "James Whitcomb Riley: Notes on the Early Years," *MSS*, XVII (1965), 3–11.

## EDWIN ARLINGTON ROBINSON

### 705. COLLECTED WORKS

Two badly needed "selected" volumes have helped to bring Robinson back into circulation: Charles T. Davis, ed., *Edwin Arlington Robinson: Selected Early Poems and Letters*, New York, 1960; and Morton Dauwen Zabel, ed., *Selected Poems of Edwin Arlington Robinson*, New York, 1965.

### LETTERS

Richard Cary edited 189 previously unpublished letters (1897–1930) in *Edwin Arlington Robinson's Letters to Edith Brower*, Cambridge, Mass., 1968. Gleanings of correspondence are available in Robert Liddell Lowe, "Edwin Arlington Robinson to Harriet Monroe: Some Unpublished Letters," *MP*, LX (1962), 31–40; and *idem*, "A Letter of Edwin Arlington Robinson to James Barstow," *NEQ*, XXXVII (1964), 390–392.

### 706. BIOGRAPHY AND CRITICISM

The most recent full-length biography is Chard Powers Smith, *Where the Light Falls: A Portrait of Edwin Arlington Robinson*, New York, 1965, a personal reminiscence, a brief discussion of Robinson's ideas, and a somewhat shaky argument that Emma Shepherd Robinson (wife of the poet's brother Herman) was the dominant force in Robinson's life. Wallace L. Anderson's *Edwin Arlington Robinson: A Critical Introduction*, Boston, 1967, is revealing of Robinson's early years as well as critically perceptive. See also Mabel Daniels, "Edwin Arlington Robinson: A Musical Memoir," *CLQ*, VI (1963), 219–233; and Conrad Aiken, "Three Meetings with Robinson," *CLQ*, VIII (1969), 345–346.

The most stimulating evaluation of the poetry is Louis Coxe's critical biography, *Edwin Arlington Robinson: The Life of Poetry*, New York, 1968. Hoyt C. Franchere covers the same ground in *Edwin Arlington Robinson*, New York, 1968. W. R. Robinson's *Edwin Arlington Robinson: A Poetry of the Act*, Cleveland, Ohio, 1967, concentrates on the philosophical aspect of the poetry and its relationship to such contemporaneous philosophers as Santayana, Whitehead, and William James. See also chapters on Robinson in Roy Harvey Pearce, *The Continuity of American Poetry*, Princeton, N.J., 1961; and Glauco Cambon, *The Inclusive Flame*, Bloomington, Ind., 1963.

Two collections of brief studies are tributes for the centennial year.

Richard Cary reprints 28 interpretive essays from the years 1930–1969 in *Appreciation of Edwin Arlington Robinson*, Waterville, Me., 1969. Ellsworth Barnard edited a volume especially assembled for the occasion, *Edwin Arlington Robinson: Centenary Essays*, Athens, Ga., 1969. Other critical evaluations not available in these two collections are Richard P. Adams, "The Failure of Edwin Arlington Robinson," *TSE*, XI (1961), 97–151; Robert N. Hertz, "Two Voices of the American Village: Robinson and Masters," *MinnR*, II (1962), 345–358; Laurence Perrine, "Contemporary Reference of Robinson's Arthurian Poems," *TCL*, VIII (1962), 74–82; Richard Cary, "E. A. Robinson as Soothsayer," *CLQ*, VI (1963), 233–245; William J. Free, "E. A. Robinson's Use of Emerson," *AL*, XXXVIII (1966), 69–84; Scott Donaldson, "The Alien Pity: A Study of Character in E. A. Robinson's Poetry," *AL*, XXXVIII (1966), 219–266; Gertrude M. White, "Robinson's 'Captain Craig': A Reinterpretation," *ES*, XLVII (1966), 432–439; Sigmund Skard, "E. A. Robinson: 'Eros Turannos,' a Critical Survey," *Americana Norvegica*, I (1966), ed. Sigmund Skard and Henry H. Wasser, 286–330.

More recent studies are Barton L. St. Armand, "The Power of Sympathy in the Poetry of Robinson and Frost: The 'Inside' vs. the 'Outside' Narrative," *AQ*, XIX (1967), 564–574; Ronald Moran, "Meaning and Value in 'Luke Havergal,'" *CLQ*, VII (1967), 385–392; Paul Zietlow, "The Meaning of Tilbury Town: Robinson as a Regional Poet," *NEQ*, XL (1967), 188–211; David H. Burton, "Theodore Roosevelt and Edwin Arlington Robinson: A Common Vision," *Person*, XLIX (1968), 331–349; Richard Crowder, "Robinson's Reputation: Six Observations," *CLQ*, VIII (1969), 220–238; and J. C. Levenson, "Robinson's Modernity," *VQR*, XLIV (1969), 590–610.

The *Colby Library Quarterly*, VIII (1969), is a Robinson centennial issue.

### 708. BIBLIOGRAPHY

Supplements to the Lillian Lippincott (1937) bibliography are William White, "A Bibliography of Edwin Arlington Robinson, 1941–1963," *CLQ*, VII (1965), 1–26; and *idem*, "A Bibliography of Edwin Arlington Robinson, 1964–1969," *CLQ*, VIII (1969), 448–462. Ellsworth Barnard prepared a bibliographical survey, "Edwin Arlington Robinson," for *Fifteen Modern American Authors*, ed. Jackson R. Bryer, Durham, N.C., 1969, pp. 345–367. See also Richard Cary, "The Library of Edwin Arlington Robinson: Addenda," *CLQ*, VII (1967), 398–415; *idem*, "Robinson's Books and Periodicals: I–III," *CLQ*, VIII (1969), 266–277, 334–343; 399–413; and *idem*, "Robinson's Manuscripts and Letters," *CLQ*, VIII (1969), 479–487.

## O. E. (OLE EDVART) RÖLVAAG

**708.** BIOGRAPHY AND CRITICISM

The most recent analysis of Rölvaag's Norwegian background is Gudrun Hovde Gvåle, *O. E. Rølvaag, Nordmann og Amerikanar*, Oslo, 1962. Briefer studies are Charles Boewe, "Rölvaag's America: An Immigrant Novelist's Views," *WHR*, XI (1957), 3–12; Robert Steensma, "Rölvaag and Turner's Frontier Thesis," *NDQ*, XXVII (1959), 100–104; Maynard Fox, "The Bearded Face Set toward the Sun," *BSTCF*, I (1961), 62–84; and Sigmund Skard, Ingrid Semmingsen, and Dorothy B. Skårdal, "Gundrun Hovde Gvåle: O. E. Rølvaag, nordmann og amerikaner," *Edda*, LIII (1966), 361–402.

## EDGAR (EVERTSON) SALTUS

**710.** BIOGRAPHY AND CRITICISM

The first full-length critical study is Claire Sprague's *Edgar Saltus*, New York, 1968.

The largest gathering of Saltus material is described by Claire Sprague in "The Edgar Saltus Collection," *YULG*, XLII (Oct., 1967), 102–106.

## CARL (CHARLES AUGUST) SANDBURG
### *d. 1967*

**711.** SEPARATE WORKS

*Wind Song*, 1960; *Honey and Salt*, 1963.

COLLECTIONS AND REPRINTS

Mark Van Doren edited, with an introduction, *Harvest Poems, 1910–1960*, New York, 1960. Herbert Mitgang edited *The Letters of Carl Sandburg*, New York, 1968, a collection of 640, covering the years 1898–1967. *The World of Carl Sandburg* is a "stage presentation" conceived by Norman Corwin from 10 of Sandburg's published volumes and 18 new items previously unpublished.

BIOGRAPHY AND CRITICISM

North Callahan, *Carl Sandburg: Lincoln of Our Literature*, New York, 1969, is the first biography since the poet's death, "written with the full cooperation of the Sandburg family." Harry Golden's *Carl Sandburg*, Cleveland, Ohio, 1961, is an impressionistic portrait of an old friend. Paula Steichen's *My Connemara*, New York, 1969, is a "lyrical account of an idyllic childhood" spent on her grandfather Sandburg's farm in North Carolina. Joseph Haas and Gene Lovitz assembled *Carl Sandburg: A Pictorial Biography*, New York, 1967. Edward Steichen, the poet's brother-in-law, edited *Sandburg: Photographers View Carl Sandburg*, New York, 1966. See also the poet's own reminiscences in "A Visit with Carl Sandburg," *ClareQ*, VIII (1960), 17–25.

Richard Crowder's critical biography, *Carl Sandburg*, New York, 1964, is the best brief introduction to the poet's work. A more ambitious assessment of Sandburg's place in American literature is Hazel Durnell's *The America of Carl Sandburg*, Washington, D.C., 1965. Michael Yatron groups Sandburg with Masters and Lindsay in his critical study, *America's Literary Revolt*, New York, 1959. Briefer studies are John T. Flanagan, "Carl Sandburg at Eighty," *ISHSJ*, LI (1958), 191–198; Gay Wilson Allen, "Carl Sandburg: Fire and Smoke," *SAQ*, LIX (1960), 315–331; Renaud de Jouvenel, "Carl Sandburg: Éléments d'une biographie," *Europe*, XXXVII (Feb.–Mar., 1959), 70–78; Henry E. Kolbe, "Christ and Carl Sandburg," *Religion in Life*, XXVIII (1959), 248–261; Alan Jenkins, "Portraits of Carl Sandburg," *LH*, LXIII (1961), 77–84; Reuben W. Borough, "The Sandburg I Remember," *JISHS*, LIX (1966), 229–251; Eleanor G. Vance, "Glimpses of Carl Sandburg," *NAR*, IV (1967), 9–10; Archibald MacLeish, "A Memorial Tribute to Carl Sandburg," *MR*, IX (1968), 41–44; and Anna Martynova, "Carl Sandburg and the Soviet Reader," *SovL*, I (1968), 192–193.

The *Lincoln Herald*, LXX (1968), is a Sandburg memorial issue with articles by Allan Nevins, Edward Steichen, and others.

Mark Van Doren's Library of Congress lecture, *Carl Sandburg*, Washington, D.C., 1969, is published with a 64-page bibliography of Sandburg materials in the collections of the Library of Congress. See also John T. Flanagan, "Presentation Copies in the Sandburg Library [at the University of Illinois]," *CRL*, XXIV (1963), 47–52.

## GEORGE SANTAYANA

**712.** SEPARATE WORKS

*Animal Faith and Spiritual Life*, ed. John Lachs, New York, 1967, gathers "previously unpublished and uncollected writings . . . with critical essays on his thought." Daniel Cory edited *The Birth of Reason and Other Essays*, New York, 1968, a "final collection" by Santayana's literary executor of 22 essays and one poem, all previously unpublished. In the next year, however, John Lachs and Shirley Lachs edited *Physical Order and Moral Liberty: Previously Unpublished Essays of George Santayana*, Nashville, Tenn.

COLLECTED WORKS, REPRINTS, AND CORRESPONDENCE

Norman Henfrey edited *George Santayana: Selected Critical Writings*, 2 vols., Cambridge, Eng., 1968, concentrating on material published from 1895–1918. Two companion volumes are *George Santayana's America: Essays on Literature and Culture*, ed. James Ballowe, Urbana, Ill., 1967; and *Santayana on America: Essays, Notes, and Letters on American Life, Literature, and Philosophy*, ed. Richard Colton Lyon, New York, 1968. *The Genteel Tradition: Nine Essays by George Santayana*, ed. Douglas Wilson, Cambridge, Mass., 1967, collects scattered essays on this topic.

713. BIOGRAPHY AND CRITICISM

Daniel Cory published "a portrait with letters" in *Santayana: The Later Years*, New York, 1963. A brief survey of the whole career is Richard Butler's *The Life and World of George Santayana*, Chicago, 1960. Bruno Lind's *Vagabond Scholar: A Venture into the Privacy of George Santayana*, New York, 1962, is based on letters and dialogues between Santayana and the author.

Three general critical studies are Thomas N. Munson, S.J., *The Essential Wisdom of George Santayana*, New York, 1962; M. M. Kirkwood, *Santayana: Saint of the Imagination*, Toronto, 1961; and Willard E. Arnett, *George Santayana*, New York, 1968. Jerome Ashmore makes a close, but more limited, inspection of the philosopher's theories in *Santayana, Art, and Aesthetics*, Cleveland, Ohio, 1966. See also *Dialogue on Santayana* [by James Gutmann *et al.*], ed. Corliss Lamont and Mary Redmer, New York, 1959. Two recent European studies are Jana Novozámská, *G. Santayana a americká filosofie*, Prague, 1968; and V. D. Endovitskii, *Kritika filosofii amerikanskogo kriticheskogo realizma*, Moscow, 1968.

Briefer studies are William F. Goodwin, "Santayana's Naturalistic Reading of Indian Ontology and Axiology," *PPR*, XVIII (1957), 147–168; Horace K. Kallen *et al.*, "Conversation on Santayana," *AR*, XIX (1959), 237–270; Maurice F. Brown, "Santayana's American Roots," *NEQ*, XXXIII (1960), 147–163; John M. Major, "Santayana on Shakespeare," *SQ*, X (1959), 469–479; Joel Porte, "Santayana at the 'Gas House,'" *NEQ*, XXXV (1962), 337–346; George Boas, "The Legacy of Santayana," *RIPh*, XVII (1963), 37–49; Louise Nisbet Roberts, "In Defense of Santayana's Theories of Expression," *Tulane Studies in Philosophy*, XII (1963), 84–90; Carl H. Hamburg, "Symbolic Forms: Cassirer and Santayana," *Tulane Studies in Philosophy*, XII (1963), 76–83; Van Meter Ames, "Santayana at One Hundred," *JAAC*, XXII (1964), 243–247; William Walsh, "Santayana as a Critic," *REL*, V (1964), 69–77; W. Richard Comstock, "Dewey and Santayana in Conflict: Religious Dimensions of Naturalism," *JR*, XLV (1965), 119–136; Maurice Cohen, "Santayana on Romanticism and Egotism," *JR*, XLVI (1966), 264–281; Newton P. Stallknecht, "George Santayana and the Uses of Literature," *YCGL*, XV (1966), 5–18; A. G. Woodward, "George Santayana: 1863–1952," *ESA*, XII (1969), 107–131; A. Eliot Youman, "Santayana's Attachments," *NEQ*, XLII (1969), 373–387; and James Ballowe, "Santayana on Autobiography," *AL*, XLI (1969), 219–230.

The *Journal of Philosophy*, LXI (1964), contains four articles on Santayana.

# WILLIAM SAROYAN

**714. SHORT STORIES AND NOVELS**

*Boys and Girls Together*, 1963; *One Day in the Afternoon of the World*, 1964.

**715. PLAYS\***

*Sam, the Highest Jumper of Them All; or, The London Comedy* (1960), 1961; *Settled Out of Court* (with Henry Cecil) (1960), 1962; *High Time along the Wabash* (1961).

**MEMOIRS**

*Here Comes There Goes You Know Who*, 1961; *Not Dying*, 1963; *Short Drive, Sweet Chariot*, 1966; *I Used to Believe I Had Forever Now I'm Not So Sure*, 1968.

**MISCELLANEOUS**

*Look At Us/ Let's See/ Here We Are/ Look Hard, Speak Soft/ I See, You See, We All See/ Stop, Look, Listen/ Beholder's Eye/ Don't Look Now, But Isn't That You? (Us? U.S.?)* (with photographs by Arthur Rothstein), 1967; *Letters from Seventy-Four Rue Taitbout: or, Don't Go, But If You Must, Say Hello to Everybody*, 1969.

**REPRINTS**

*After Thirty Years: The Daring Young Man on the Flying Trapeze*, New York, 1964, is a reprinting of Saroyan's first volume of short stories preceded by a series of reflective essays on his art.

\* Dates in parentheses are of production when it differs from publication.

BIOGRAPHY AND CRITICISM

The first full-length bio-critical study is Howard R. Floan, *William Saroyan*, New York, 1966. Budd Schulberg recounts his associations with the author in "Saroyan: Ease and Unease on the Flying Trapeze," *Esquire*, LIV (Oct., 1960), 85–91. See also, *passim*, Harold Clurman, *Lies Like Truth*, New York, 1958; and George Jean Nathan, *The Magic Mirror*, ed. Thomas Quinn Curtiss, New York, 1960.

The first bibliography is David Kherdian, *A Bibliography of William Saroyan 1934–1964*, San Francisco, 1965.

## SAMUEL SEWALL

**717. SEPARATE WORKS**

Harvey Wish edited an abridged version, with an introduction, of *The Diary of Samuel Sewall*, New York, 1967. Sidney Kaplan edited with notes and commentary *The Selling of Joseph: A Memorial*, Amherst, Mass., 1969.

BIOGRAPHY AND CRITICISM

Two recent biographies are Ola Elizabeth Winslow, *Samuel Sewall of Boston*, New York, 1964; and T. B. Strandness, *Samuel Sewall: A Puritan Portrait*, Lansing, Mich., 1967.

## WILLIAM GILMORE SIMMS

**722. COLLECTED WORKS AND REPRINTS**

John C. Guilds is general editor of *The Centennial Edition of the Writings of William Gilmore Simms*, to be published in 15 volumes by the University of South Carolina Press. *Voltmeier; or, The Mountain Men*, "a post-war serial never before published in book-form," is the first volume to appear (Columbia, S.C., 1969).

*Cavalier of Old South Carolina: William Gilmore Simms's Captain Porgy*, ed. Hugh W. Hetherington, Chapel Hill, N.C., 1966, is an anthology of excerpts from seven of Simms's works plus a long introductory essay by the editor. Other reprints are too numerous to list separately.

BIOGRAPHY AND CRITICISM

A concise treatment of Simms's whole career is Joseph V. Ridgely, *William Gilmore Simms*, New York, 1962. Edd Winfield Parks concentrates on *William Gilmore Simms as Literary Critic*, Athens, Ga., 1961. Briefer studies are C. Hugh Holman, "The Status of Simms," *AQ*, X (1958), 181–185; W. B. Gates, "William Gilmore Simms and the Kentucky Tragedy," *AL*, XXXII (1960), 158–166; John R. Welsh, "William Gilmore Simms: Critic of the South," *Journal of Southern History*, XXVI (1960), 201–214; Maurice R. Cullen, Jr., "William Gilmore Simms, Southern Journalist," *JQ*, XXXVIII (1961), 298–302, 412; C. Hugh Holman, "William Gilmore Simms and the *American Renaissance*," *MissQ*, XV (1962), 126–137; William Stanley Hoole, "Alabama and W. Gilmore Simms," *AlaR*, XVI (1963), 83–107, 185–199; L. Moffit Cecil, "Symbolic Pattern in *The Yemassee*," *AL*, XXXV (1964), 510–514; Austin J. Shelton, "African Realistic Commentary on Culture Hierarchy and Racistic Sentimentalism in *The Yemassee*," *Phylon*, XXV (1964), 72–78; Mary A. Wimsatt, "Simms and Irving," *MissQ*, XX (1967), 25–37; Francesca C. Gozzini, "W. G. Simms e *The Yemassee*," *SA*, XIII (1967), 101–127; John C. Guilds, "William Gilmore Simms and the Southern Literary Gazette," *SB*, XXI (1968), 59–92; and *idem*, "The 'Lost' Number of the Southern Literary Gazette," *SB*, XXII (1969), 266–273.

John R. Welsh describes the Simms material at the University of South Carolina in "The Charles Carroll Simms Collection," *SAB*, XXXI (1960), 1–3.

## UPTON SINCLAIR
### *d. 1968*

**723. SEPARATE WORKS**

Novels: *Affectionately, Eve*, 1961.

Political and social studies: A new edition of *The Cry for Justice: An Anthology of the Literature of Social Protest* (1915) was prepared with the cooperation of Edward Sagarin and Albert Teichner, New York, 1964.

Letters and autobiography: *My Lifetime in Letters*, Columbia, Mo., 1960, prints 300 letters to Sinclair from a wide variety of literary and political figures. *The Autobiography of Upton Sinclair*, New York, 1962, reprints the major portion of *American Outpost: A Book of Reminiscences* (1932) and adds 12 more chapters to bring the narrative up to date. *Southern Belle*, New York, 1957, is the autobiography of Sinclair's wife, Mary Craig Sinclair.

Reprints: *Theirs Be the Guilt: A Novel of the War Between the States*, New York, 1959, is a reprinting of *Manassas* (1904). Other reprints and translations are too numerous to list separately.

**724.** BIOGRAPHY AND CRITICISM

Special studies are George J. Becker, "Upton Sinclair: Quixote in a Flivver," *CE*, XXI (1959), 133–140; Ronald Gottesman, "Louis Adamic and Upton Sinclair: The Record of a Friendship," *AN*, I (1968), 41–65; Don M. Wolfe, "An Evening with Upton Sinclair," *JHS*, I (1968), 265–267; and Judson A. Grenier, "Upton Sinclair: A Remembrance," *CHSQ*, XLVIII (1969), 165–169.

The Sinclair archive is deposited in the Lilly Library of Indiana University. For an exhibition there, Ronald Gottesman prepared *A Catalogue of Books, Manuscripts and Other Materials from the Upton Sinclair Archives*, Bloomington, Ind., 1963.

# JOHN SMITH

**726.** EDITED TEXTS AND REPRINTS

*The Generall Historie of Virginia, New England, and the Summer Isles* (1624) was most recently reprinted in Ann Arbor, Mich., 1966. The best collection of Smith's writing, *Travels and Works of Captain John Smith*, edited by Edward Arber in 1884, was reprinted in New York, 1967, with the introduction written by Arthur G. Bradley for the 1910 Edinburgh reprinting.

BIOGRAPHY AND CRITICISM

A major biographical study is Philip L. Barbour's *The Three Worlds of Captain John Smith*, Boston, 1964. Laura Polanyi Striker translated, from the Latin manuscript, Henry Wharton's *The Life of John Smith, English Soldier* (1685) and published it with an essay on "Captain John Smith in Seventeenth-Century Literature," Chapel Hill, N.C., 1957.

Briefer studies are Marshall Fishwick, "Was John Smith a Liar?" *AH*, IX (Oct., 1958), 29–33, 110–111; Laura Polanyi Striker, "The Hungarian Historian, Lewis L. Kropf, on Captain John Smith's *True Travels*: A Reappraisal," *VMHB*, LXVI (1958), 22–43; Edwin C. Rozwenc, "Captain John Smith's Image of America," *WMQ*, XVI (1959), 27–36; Philip L. Barbour, ed., "Two 'Unknown' Poems by Captain John Smith," *VMHB*, LXXV (1967), 157–158; Everett H. Emerson, "Captain John Smith, Autobiographer," *EALN*, II (1967), 18–23; *idem*, "Captain John Smith as Editor: *The Generall Historie*," *VMHB*, LXXV (1967), 143–156; and William G. Belser, Jr., "John Smith, Admiral of New England," *Nassau Review*, I (1969), 1–7.

# GERTRUDE STEIN

## 729. SEPARATE WORKS

Carl Van Vechten edited, with an introduction and notes, and with an essay on the author by F. W. Dupee, *Selected Writings*, New York, 1962. *Gertrude Stein's America*, ed. Gilbert A. Harrison, Washington, D.C., 1965, is a collection of excerpts from Stein's essays, novels, plays, poems, and lectures. *Gertrude Stein: Writings and Lectures, 1911–1945*, London, 1967, was edited by Patricia Meyerowitz with an introduction by Elizabeth Sprigge. *Gertrude Stein on Picasso*, ed. Edward Burns, appeared in New York, 1970.

Reprints of individual volumes are too numerous to list separately.

## BIOGRAPHY AND CRITICISM

The most recent biography is John Malcolm Brinnin's *The Third Rose: Gertrude Stein and Her World*, Boston, 1959, designed to "document the life and show the development of an artist." Alice B. Toklas's own account of her life with Gertrude Stein is called *What Is Remembered*, New York, 1963, published four years before Toklas's death.

Critical studies are numerous. The most comprehensive is Richard Bridgman's *Gertrude Stein in Pieces*, New York, 1970, "a descriptive reading of her entire work." In *Gertrude Stein and the Present*, Cambridge, Mass., 1967, Allegra Stewart focuses "upon [Stein's] underlying experience of contemplation and creative dissociation" with a heavy and persuasive emphasis on Jungian psychology and metaphysics. Michael J. Hoffman's *The Development of Abstractionism in the Writings of Gertrude Stein*, Philadelphia, 1965, limits discussion to the first ten years of Stein's works, ending with *Tender Buttons*. Frederick J. Hoffman surveys the whole career briefly in his pamphlet, *Gertrude Stein*, Minneapolis, Minn., 1961. On the other hand, B. L. Reid's *Art by Subtraction: A Dissenting Opinion of Gertrude Stein*, Norman, Okla., 1958, was "born of gradual disenchantment" and ends by being "an essay in decapitation—without acrimony, but with conviction." He objects chiefly to her aesthetic system for its subtraction of "beauty, instruction, and passion." See also Francis Russell, *Three Studies in Twentieth Century Obscurity*, Aldington, Kent, Eng., 1954, and Sir Francis Cyril Rose, *Gertrude Stein and Painting*, London, 1968.

Briefer studies are W. H. Gass, "Gertrude Stein: Her Escape from Protective Language," *Accent*, XVIII (1958), 233–244; Aline B. Saarinen, "The Steins in Paris," *ASch*, XXVII (1958), 437–448; Richard Bridgman,

"'Melanctha,'" *AL*, XXXIII (1961), 350–359; Hilary Corke, "Reflections on a Great Stone Face: The Achievement of Gertrude Stein," *KR*, XXIII (1961), 367–389; Daniel-Henry Kahnweiler, "Erinnerungen an Gertrude Stein," *Augenblick*, V (1961), 1–10; Frank Baldanza, "Faulkner and Stein: A Study in Stylistic Intransigence," *GaR*, XIII (1959), 274–286; George T. Wright, "Gertrude Stein and Her Ethic of Self-Containment," *TSL*, VIII (1963), 17–23; Kemp Malone, "Observations on *Paris France*," *PLL*, III (1967), 159–178; Virginia J. Tufte, "Gertrude Stein's Prothalamium: A Unique Poem in a Classical Mode," *YULG*, XLIII (1968), 17–23; and Donald Shults, "Gertrude Stein and the Problems of Time," *KAL*, XI (1968), 59–71.

# JOHN (ERNST) STEINBECK
## *d. 1968*

### 730. SEPARATE WORKS

*Travels with Charley in Search of America*, 1962; *America and Americans*, 1966; *Journal of a Novel: The East of Eden Letters*, 1969.

### 731. BIOGRAPHY AND CRITICISM

There is no full-length biography nor has one been announced since Steinbeck's death. The major critical study is Warren French, *John Steinbeck*, New York, 1961. F. W. Watt's *John Steinbeck*, Edinburgh, 1962; and Joseph Eddy Fontenrose's *John Steinbeck: An Introduction and Interpretation*, New York, 1964, are good general surveys, with some biographical background. Harry T. Moore's 1938 study, *The Novels of John Steinbeck*, has been reissued in a second edition with a "contemporary epilogue," New York, 1968. Helmut Liedloff's *Steinbeck in German Translation: A Study of Translational Practices*, Carbondale, Ill., 1965, is devoted to selected works. Two European studies are Hildegard Schumann, *Zum Problem des Kritischen Realismus bei John Steinbeck*, Halle, 1958; and Walter Rahn, *Die Funktionen der Kalifornischen Landschaft im Epischen Frühwerk John Steinbecks*, Munich, 1962. See also chapters on Steinbeck in R. W. B. Lewis, *The Picaresque Saint*, Philadelphia, 1959; Edwin Bowdoin, *The Dungeon of the Heart*, New York, 1961; W. J. Stuckey, *The Pulitzer Prize Novels: A Critical Backward Look*, Norman, Okla., 1966; Warren French, *The Social Novel at the End of an Era*, Carbondale, Ill., 1966; and Pascal Covici, Jr., *The Thirties* (ed. Warren French), DeLand, Fla., 1967.

Collections of briefer estimates are Warren French, ed., *A Companion to*

*The Grapes of Wrath*, New York, 1963; and Agnes M. Donohue, ed., *A Casebook on The Grapes of Wrath*, New York, 1968. Other brief studies are Fernand Corin, "Steinbeck and Hemingway: A Study in Literary Economy," *RLV*, XXIV (1958), 60–75; 153–160; Walter Fuller Taylor, "The Grapes of Wrath Reconsidered," *MissQ*, XII (1959), 136–144; Charles R. Metzger, "Steinbeck's Version of the Pastoral," *MFS*, VI (1960), 115–124; Robert J. Griffin and William A. Freedman, "Machines and Animals: Pervasive Motifs in *The Grapes of Wrath*," *JEGP*, LXII (1963), 569–580; Harry Morris, "*The Pearl*: Realism and Allegory," *EJ*, LII (1963), 487–495, 505; James Woodress, "John Steinbeck: Hostage to Fortune," *SAQ*, LXIII (1964), 385–398; Wilfred Paul Dvorak, "Notes toward the Education of the Heart," *IEY*, No. 10 (1965), pp. 46–49; Arnold L. Goldsmith, "Thematic Rhythm in *The Red Pony*," *CE*, XXVI (1965), 391–394; Ernest E. Karsten, Jr., "Thematic Structure in *The Pearl*," *EJ*, LIV (1965), 1–7; Horace P. Taylor, Jr., "John Steinbeck—The Quest," *McNR*, XVI (1965), 33–45; D. Russell Brown, "The Natural Man in John Steinbeck's Non-Teleological Tales," *BSUF*, VII (1965), 47–52.

More recent judgments are Charles A. Madison, "The Friendship of Covici and Steinbeck," *CJF*, XXIV (1966), 293–296; Harland S. Nelson, "Steinbeck's Politics Then and Now," *AR*, XXVII (1967), 118–133; Elroy Bode, "The World on Its Own Terms: A Brief for Steinbeck, Miller, and Simenon," *SWR*, LIII (1968), 406–416; Stanley Alexander, "*Cannery Row*: Steinbeck's Pastoral Poem," *WAL*, II (1968), 281–295; *idem*, "The Conflict of Form in *Tortilla Flat*," *AL*, XL (1968), 58–66; Elizabeth E. McMahan, "'The Crysanthemums': Study of a Woman's Sexuality," *MFS*, XIV (1968), 453–458; Henry L. Golemba, "Steinbeck's Attempt to Escape the Literary Fallacy," *MFS*, XV (1969), 231–239; and Bryant N. Wyatt, "Experimentation as Technique: The Protest Novels of John Steinbeck," *Discourse*, XII (1969), 143–153.

The Spring, 1965, issue of *Modern Fiction Studies* is a John Steinbeck special number. The *Steinbeck Newsletter* began publication in 1968. It is now the *Steinbeck Quarterly*, published in Muncie, Indiana.

The major bibliography is Tetsumaro Hayashi, *John Steinbeck: A Concise Bibliography (1930–1965)*, Metuchen, N.J., 1967. See also Warren French's bibliographical essay, "John Steinbeck," *Fifteen Modern American Authors*, ed. Jackson R. Bryer, Durham, N.C., 1969, pp. 369–387; Maurice Beebe and Jackson R. Bryer, "Criticism of John Steinbeck: A Selected Checklist," *MFS*, XI (1965), 90–103; Joan Steele, "John Steinbeck: A Checklist of Biographical, Critical, and Bibliographical Material," *BB*, XXIV (1965), 149–152, 162–163; and *John Steinbeck: An Exhibition of American and Foreign Editions*, with an introduction by William B. Todd,

## GEORGE STERLING

**732. BIOGRAPHY AND CRITICISM**

Gleanings of correspondence are in John R. Dunbar, ed., "Some Letters of George Sterling," *CHSQ*, XL (1961), 137–155; and *idem*, "Letters of George Sterling to Carey McWilliams," *CHSQ*, XLVI (1967), 235–252. See also Stanton Coblentz, "George Sterling: Western Phenomenon," *ArQ*, XIII (1957), 54–60; and Joseph W. Slade, "George Sterling: 'Prophet of the Suns,'" *Markham Review*, II (1968), 4–10.

## WALLACE STEVENS

**732. SEPARATE WORKS**

*Poems of Wallace Stevens*, selected and introduced by Samuel French Morse, New York, 1959, is a useful paperback volume. *Collected Poems* (1954) and *Opus Posthumous* (1957) are still in print; *The Necessary Angel: Essays on Reality and the Imagination* (1951) was reprinted in paperback, New York, 1965.

Holly Stevens, the poet's daughter, edited a major source book on Stevens's life and poetry, *Letters of Wallace Stevens*, New York, 1966, with nearly 1,000 entries as well as parts of a journal kept between 1898–1912. See also F[rank] K[ermode], "Some Stevens Letters," *Encounter*, XXVI (1966), 25–37.

A previously unpublished play, *Bowl, Cat and Broomstick* [1917], was introduced by A. Walton Litz, *Quarterly Review of Literature*, XVI (1969), 230–247.

**733. BIOGRAPHY AND CRITICISM**

The first critical biography is Samuel French Morse, *Wallace Stevens: Life as Poetry*, New York, 1970. Details of Stevens's early life in Pennsylvania are recorded in Michael Lafferty, "Wallace Stevens: Man of Two Worlds," *Historical Review of Berks County*, XXIV (Fall, 1959), 109–113, 130–132.

Critical attention to Stevens in recent years has been growing rapidly. Four books serve as introductions for the reader new to the poetry: Frank Kermode's close readings and general background, *Wallace Stevens*, Edinburgh, 1960, New York, 1961; Henry Wells's survey of "the intracacies of Stevens' style and thought," *Introduction to Wallace Stevens*, Bloomington, Ind., 1964; William Burney's coverage of the same ground, *Wallace Stevens*, New York, 1968; and Richard Allen Blessing, *Wallace Stevens'*

*"Whole Harmonium,"* Syracuse, N.Y., 1970. Three volumes attempt to cover all the major work in various directions: Joseph N. Riddel's *The Clairvoyant Eye: The Poetry and Poetics of Wallace Stevens*, Baton Rouge, La., 1965, is close and imaginative analysis; Frank Doggett's *Stevens' Poetry of Thought*, Baltimore, Md., 1966, concentrates on whence and how the poet absorbed ideas; James Baird's *The Dome and the Rock: Structure in the Poetry of Wallace Stevens*, Baltimore, Md., 1968, "traces the process of the Grand Poem [a dome upon the rock of being] and the total structure that it accomplished in language."

More specialized studies include Helen Hennessy Vendler's brilliant explications in *On Extended Wings: Wallace Stevens' Longer Poems*, Cambridge, Mass., 1969; Robert Buttel's indispensable coverage of the Harvard years and the evolution of Stevens's early style, *Wallace Stevens: The Making of Harmonium*, Princeton, N.J., 1967; and Daniel Fuchs's interpretive study of *The Comic Spirit of Wallace Stevens*, Durham, N.C., 1963. Eugene Paul Nassar, *Wallace Stevens: An Anatomy of Figuration*, Philadelphia, 1965, is rigorous classification of Stevens's imagery. Herbert J. Stern, *Wallace Stevens: Art of Uncertainty*, Ann Arbor, Mich., 1966, focuses on the early poems, Stevens's contemporaries, and religion. Ronald Sukenick, *Wallace Stevens: Musing the Obscure*, New York, 1967, is a "reader's guide" to 47 poems. See also chapters on Stevens in Roy Harvey Pearce, *The Continuity of American Poetry*, Princeton, N.J., 1961; Glauco Cambon, *The Inclusive Flame*, Bloomington, Ind., 1963; Frederick J. Hoffman, *The Mortal No: Death and the Modern Imagination*, Princeton, N.J., 1964; Denis Donoghue, *Connoisseurs of Chaos*, New York, 1965; J. Hillis Miller, *Poets of Reality*, Cambridge, Mass., 1966; and Frank Lentricchia, *The Gaiety of Language: An Essay on the Radical Poetics of W. B. Yeats and Wallace Stevens*, Berkeley, Calif., 1968.

Three collections of shorter critical articles are available: Ashley Brown and Robert S. Haller, eds., *The Achievement of Wallace Stevens*, Philadelphia, 1962; Marie Borroff, ed., *Wallace Stevens: A Collection of Critical Essays*, Englewood Cliffs, N.J., 1963; and Roy Harvey Pearce and J. Hillis Miller, eds., *The Act of the Mind: Essays on the Poetry of Wallace Stevens*, Baltimore, Md., 1965. Other brief estimates are Louis L. Martz, "Wallace Stevens: The World as Meditation," *YR*, XLVII (1958), 517–536; Ralph J. Mills, Jr., "Wallace Stevens: The Image of the Rock," *Accent*, XVIII (1958), 75–89; Michel Benamou, "Wallace Stevens: Some Relations between Poetry and Painting," *CL*, XI (1959), 47–60; Newton P. Stallknecht, "Absence in Reality," *KR*, XXI (1959), 545–562; Richard M. Gollin, "Wallace Stevens: The Poet of Society," *ColQ*, IX (1960), 47–58; George McFadden, "Probings for an Integration: Color Symbolism in Wallace Stevens," *MP*, LVIII (1961), 189–193; Merle E. Brown, "Concordia

Discors in the Poetry of Wallace Stevens," *AL*, XXXIV (1962), 246–269; Francis Murphy, "The Comedian as the Letter C," *WSCL*, III (1962), 79–99; Richard Eberhart, "Emerson and Wallace Stevens," *LitR*, VII (1963), 51–71; Carl Van Vechten, "Rogue Elephant in Porcelain," *YULG*, XXXVIII (1963), 41–50; Thomas Whitbread, "Wallace Stevens' 'Highest Candle,'" *TSLL*, IV (1963), 465–480; Michel Benamou, "Wallace Stevens and the Symbolist Imagination," *ELH*, XXXI (1964), 35–63; John Crowe Ransom, "The Planetary Poet," *KR*, XXVI (1964), 233–264.

More recent studies are D. A. Shankar, "Wallace Stevens: An Ontological Poet," *LCrit*, VI (1965), 78–82; Marjorie Buhr, "The Impossible Philosopher's Man: Wallace Stevens," *Carrell*, VI (1965), 7–13; Justus George Lawler, "The Poet, the Metaphysician, and the Desire for God," *DownR*, LXXXIV (1966), 288–304; J. V. Cunningham, "The Styles and Procedures of Wallace Stevens," *UDQ*, I (1966), 8–28; Michel Benamou, "Wallace Stevens and Apollinaire," *CL*, XX (1968), 289–300; Karl P. Wentersdorf, "Wallace Stevens, Dante Alighieri, and the Emperor," *TCL*, XIII (1968), 197–204; Joseph N. Riddel, "Blue Voyager," *Salmagundi*, II (1968), 61–74; and Isabel MacCaffrey, "The Other Side of Silence: 'Credences of Summer' as an Example," *MLQ*, XXX (1969), 417–438.

The Spring, 1964, issue of *Journal of English Literary History* is a special Wallace Stevens number. *The Wallace Stevens Newsletter*, ed. W. T. Ford, began publication in Chicago in 1969.

### 734. BIBLIOGRAPHY

The most recent bibliographical listing is Samuel F. Morse, Jackson R. Bryer, and Joseph N. Riddel, *Wallace Stevens Checklist and Bibliography of Stevens Criticism*, Denver, Colo., 1963. Joseph N. Riddel provided an interpretive bibliographical essay, "Wallace Stevens," for *Fifteen Modern American Authors*, ed. Jackson R. Bryer, Durham, N.C., 1969, pp. 389–423. See also Doris L. Eder, "A Review of Stevens Criticism to Date," *TCL*, XV (1969), 3–18.

Thomas F. Walsh compiled *Concordance to the Poetry of Wallace Stevens*, University Park, Pa., 1963.


## HARRIET (ELIZABETH) BEECHER STOWE

### 736. COLLECTED WORKS AND REPRINTS

Two important scholarly reprints, both with valuable introductions, are *Uncle Tom's Cabin*, ed. Kenneth S. Lynn, Cambridge, Mass., 1962; and *Oldtown Folks*, ed. Henry F. May, Cambridge, Mass., 1966. John Michael

Moran, Jr.. edited *Collected Poems*, Hartford, Conn., 1967. Other reprintings are too numerous to list separately.

BIOGRAPHY AND CRITICISM

Charles Edward Stowe's biography of his mother, *Life of Harriet Beecher Stowe: Compiled from Her Journals and Letters* (1889) was reprinted in Detroit, Michigan, 1967. The most recent popular biography is Johanna Johnston's *Runaway to Heaven: The Story of Harriet Beecher Stowe*, Garden City, N.Y., 1963. A more concise and better documented portrait is Edward Wagenknecht's "psychographic" study *Harriet Beecher Stowe: The Known and the Unknown*, New York, 1965.

John R. Adams's *Harriet Beecher Stowe*, New York, 1963, is a survey, chiefly critical, of Mrs. Stowe's whole career. In *The Novels of Harriet Beecher Stowe*, New York, 1969, Alice C. Crozier concentrates on the two slavery novels, but gives a critical reassessment of all her work. Edmund Wilson's discussion of Mrs. Stowe and her husband is in *Patriotic Gore: Studies in the Literature of the American Civil War*, New York, 1962.

Briefer assessments are Joseph P. Roppolo, "Harriet Beecher Stowe and New Orleans: A Study in Hate," *NEQ*, XXX (1957), 346–362; William H. Pease and Jane H. Pease, "Uncle Tom and Clayton: Fact, Fiction, and Mystery," *Ontario History*, L (1958), 61–73; Edward G. Fletcher, "Illustrations for Uncle Tom," *TQ*, I (1958), 166–180; Nancy Hale, "What God Was Writing," *TQ*, I (1958), 35–40; Charles Nichols, "The Origins of *Uncle Tom's Cabin*," *Phylon*, XIX (1958), 328–334; Joseph V. Ridgely, "*Woodcraft*: Simms's First Answer to *Uncle Tom's Cabin*," *AL*, XXXI (1960), 421–433; William R. Manierre, "A Southern Response to Mrs. Stowe: Two Letters of John R. Thompson," *VMHB*, LXIX (1961), 83–92; Severn Duvall, "*Uncle Tom's Cabin*: The Sinister Side of the Patriarchy," *NEQ*, XXXVI (1963), 3–22; Janet A. Emig, "The Flower in the Cleft: The Writings of Harriet Beecher Stowe," *BHPSO*, XXI (1963), 223–238; Benjamin F. Hudson, "Another View of 'Uncle Tom,'" *Phylon*, XXIV (1963), 79–87; Herbert Hill, "'Uncle Tom,' An Enduring American Myth," *Crisis*, LXXII (1965), 289–295, 325; Frank Lentricchia, Jr., "Harriet Beecher Stowe and the Byron Whirlwind," *BNYPL*, LXX (1966), 218–228; John William Ward, "*Uncle Tom's Cabin*, As a Matter of Historical Fact," *CUF*, IX (1966), 42–47; James Woodress, "Uncle Tom's Cabin in Italy," *Essays in American Literature*, ed. Clarence Gohdes, Durham, N.C., 1967, pp. 126–140; Cushing Strout, "*Uncle Tom's Cabin* and the Portent of Millennium," *YR*, LVII (1968), 375–385; and Donald K. Pickens, "Uncle Tom Becomes Nat Turner: A Commentary on Two American Heroes," *NALF*, III (1969), 45–48.

The most recent bibliographical study is John R. Adams, "Harriet Beecher Stowe (1811–1896)," *ALR*, II (1969), 160–164.

## BAYARD TAYLOR

### 738. COLLECTED WORKS AND REPRINTS

*Eldorado; or, Adventures in the Path of Empire* (1850), was reprinted in facsimile, with a biographical introduction by Richard H. Dillon, in Palo Alto, California, 1968. Stuart Atkins revised and edited Taylor's 1870–1871 translation of Goethe's *Faust*, New York, 1962.

### 739. BIOGRAPHY AND CRITICISM

John T. Krumplemann treats Taylor as "the foremost literary intermediary between America and Germany" in the second half of the nineteenth century in *Bayard Taylor and German Letters*, (Britannica et Americana, Band 4), Hamburg, 1959. See also William Hannan, "Bayard Taylor's Portrait of Pennsylvania Quakerism," *PF*, XVI (1966), 8–14; and Philip Allison Shelley, "Bayard Taylor and Schiller's *Don Carlos*," *Anglo-German and American-German Crosscurrents*, II, eds. Philip Allison Shelley and Arthur O. Lewis, Jr., Chapel Hill, N.C., 1962, pp. 33–96.

## EDWARD TAYLOR

### 740. EDITED TEXTS

*The Poems of Edward Taylor* was edited by Donald E. Stanford, with a foreword by Louis L. Martz, New Haven, Conn., 1960. An abridged, paperbound edition with a new introduction appeared in 1963.

Norman Grabo edited *Christographia*, New Haven, Conn., 1962, Taylor's sermons, 1701–1703, each with a poetic meditation; and *Treatise Concerning the Lord's Supper*, East Lansing, Mich., 1966, eight sermons preached in 1694.

*A Transcript of Edward Taylor's Metrical History of Christianity,* ed. Donald E. Stanford, Cleveland, Ohio, 1962, is the first publication (a photocopy of the typescript) of an untitled manuscript poem attributed to Taylor.

Francis Murphy edited *The Diary of Edward Taylor*, Springfield, Mass., 1964.

### BIOGRAPHY AND CRITICISM

The first full-length introduction to Taylor's poetry is Norman S. Grabo's *Edward Taylor*, New York, 1961. Donald E. Stanford's *Edward Taylor*,

Minneapolis, Minn., 1965, is a pamphlet surveying the whole career. Peter Nicolaisen concentrates on the metaphysical aspects of the poetry in *Die Bildlichkeit in der Dichtung Edward Taylors*, Neumünster, 1966.

Briefer studies are William R. Manierre, II, "Verbal Patterns in the Poetry of Edward Taylor," *CE*, XXIII (1962), 296–299; Alexander Medlicott, Jr., "Notes on Edward Taylor from the Diaries of Stephen Williams," *AL*, XXXIV (1962), 270–274; Francis Murphy, "Edward Taylor's Attitude toward Publication: A Question Concerning Authority," *AL*, XXXIV (1962), 393–394; John Clendenning, "Piety and Imagery in Edward Taylor's 'The Reflexion,'" *AQ*, XVI (1964), 203–210; Donald Junkins, "Edward Taylor's Revisions," *AL*, XXXVII (1965), 135–152; Charles W. Mignon, "Some Notes on the History of the Edward Taylor Manuscripts, *YULG*, XXXIX (1965), 168–173; Jean L. Thomas, "Drama and Doctrine in *Gods Determinations*," *AL*, XXXVI (1965), 452–462; Peter Thorpe, "Edward Taylor as Poet," *NEQ*, XXXIX (1966), 356–372; Clark Griffith, "Edward Taylor and the Momentum of Metaphor," *ELH*, XXXIII (1966), 448–460; Charles W. Mignon, "Diction in Edward Taylor's *Preparatory Meditations*," *AS*, XLI (1966), 243–253; Ursula Brumm, "Der 'Baum des Lebens' in den Meditationen Edward Taylors," *JA*, XII (1967), 109–123; Evan Prosser, "Edward Taylor's Poetry," *NEQ*, XL (1967), 375–398; Robert M. Benton, "Edward Taylor's Use of His Text," *AL*, XXXIX (1967), 31–41; E. F. Carlisle, "The Puritan Structure of Edward Taylor's Poetry," *AQ*, XX (1968), 147–163; Donald Junkins, "'Should Stars Wooe Lobster Claws?': A Study of Edward Taylor's Poetic Practice and Theory," *EAL*, III (1968), 88–117; Charles W. Mignon, "Edward Taylor's *Preparatory Meditations*: A Decorum of Imperfections," *PMLA*, LXXXIII (1968), 1423–1428; and M. G. Krishnamurthi, "Edward Taylor: A Note on the American Literary Tradition," *Indian Essays in American Literature*, ed. Sujit Mukherjee and D. V. K. Raghavacharyulu, Bombay, 1969, pp. 27–39.

The most recent bibliography is Constance J. Gefvert, *Edward Taylor: An Annotated Bibliography, 1668–1970*, Kent, Ohio, 1971. See also Carol Ann Hoffmann, "Edward Taylor: A Selected Bibliography," *BB*, XXIII (1960), 85–87.

## SARA TEASDALE

### 742. BIOGRAPHY AND CRITICISM

The first full-length study of her life is Margaret Haley Carpenter's *Sara Teasdale: A Biography*, New York, 1960. See also George Brandon Saul,

"A Delicate Fabric of Bird Song: The Verse of Sara Teasdale," *ArQ*, XIII (1957), 62–66.

The most recent bibliographical listing is Vivian Buchan "Sara Teasdale, 1884–1933," *BB*, XXV (1967), 94–97, 120–123.


# HENRY DAVID THOREAU

### 742. COLLECTED WORKS

*The Writings of Henry D. Thoreau* will be published in approximately 25 volumes by Princeton University Press under the general editorship of William Howarth. *Walden*, ed. J. Lyndon Shanley, Princeton, N.J., 1971, is the first to appear.

The Torrey-Allen edition of the *Journals* (1949), has been reissued with a foreword by Walter Harding, 14 volumes in two double-column folios, New York, 1963. An enlarged edition of *Collected Poems* (1943), ed. Carl Bode, appeared in Baltimore, Maryland, 1964.

### 743. EDITED TEXTS AND CORRESPONDENCE

Kenneth Walter Cameron edited *Thoreau's Literary Notebook in the Library of Congress*, Hartford, Conn., 1964; *Thoreau's Fact Book in the Harry Elkins Widener Collection in the Harvard College Library*, 2 vols., Hartford, Conn., 1966; and *Thoreau's Canadian Notebook; and, Record of Surveys*, Hartford, Conn., 1967. Leo Max Kaiser edited *Thoreau's Translation of The Seven against Thebes* (1843), Hartford, Conn., 1960, from a manuscript in the Huntington Library.

Additions to Thoreau correspondence are *Over Thoreau's Desk: New Correspondence 1838–1861*, ed. Kenneth Walter Cameron, Hartford, Conn., 1965; Kenneth Walter Cameron, "Annotations on Thoreau's *Correspondence*," *ESQ*, No. 24 (1961), pp. 6–105; William White, "Three Unpublished Thoreau Letters," *NEQ*, XXXIII (1960), 372–374; Joseph J. Moldenhauer, "Thoreau to Blake: Four Letters Re-Edited," *TSLL*, VIII (1966), 43–62; and Albert F. McLean, Jr., "Addenda to the Thoreau Correspondence," *BNYPL*, LXXI (1967), 265–267.

Recent editions of *A Week* and *Walden* and selections from the *Journals* are too numerous to list separately.

### 744. BIOGRAPHY AND CRITICISM

The most ambitious venture into Thoreau biography is Walter Harding, *The Days of Henry Thoreau*, New York, 1965, "a meticulously accurate chronicle" of Thoreau's life. A fascinating "supplement" is the profusely illustrated *Thoreau Profile* by Milton Meltzer and Walter Harding, the first attempt "to portray his life graphically" with a text "derived for the most part from Thoreau's autobiographical writings" as well as commentary by friends and contemporaries. William L. Howarth prepared a new and enlarged edition of Robert F. Stowell's *A Thoreau Gazetteer*, Princeton, N.J., 1970. Kenneth Walter Cameron edited *Thoreau and His Harvard Classmates* . . . , Hartford, Conn., 1965; and *Thoreau's Harvard Years* . . . , Hartford, Conn., 1966.

The best introduction to a study of Thoreau's life, ideas, reputation, and significant scholarship on these subjects is Walter Harding's *A Thoreau Handbook*, New York, 1959. Charles R. Anderson's *The Magic Circle of Walden*, New York, 1968, is "a close inspection of the structure and prose-texture of *Walden*." David Mason Greene concentrates on three chapters in *The Frail Duration: A Key to Symbolic Structure in Walden*, San Diego, Calif., 1966. Allen Beecher Hovey's *The Hidden Thoreau*, Beirut, 1966, is a brief but perceptive study of symbolism in Thoreau's work. John A. Christie treats Thoreau's reading of travel books in *Thoreau as World Traveler*, New York, 1965.

Two studies of Thoreau and his contemporaries are Joel M. Porte, *Emerson and Thoreau: Transcendentalists in Conflict*, Middletown, Conn., 1966; and Charles R. Metzger, *Thoreau and Whitman: A Study of Their Esthetics*, Seattle, Wash., 1961.

The centenary of Thoreau's death and increasing interest in his work generally have led to eight collections of brief critical essays on Thoreau. Chief among them are Sherman Paul, ed., *Thoreau: A Collection of Critical Essays*, Englewood Cliffs, N.J., 1962; and Wendell Glick, ed., *The Recognition of Henry David Thoreau: Selected Criticism since 1848*, Ann Arbor, Mich., 1969. But see also Walter R. Harding, ed., *Thoreau: Man of Concord*, New York, 1960; *idem, The Thoreau Centennial: Papers Marking the Observance* . . . , Albany, N.Y., 1964; John Harland Hicks, ed., *Thoreau in Our Season*, Amherst, Mass., 1966; J. Golden Taylor, ed., *The Western Thoreau Centenary: Selected Papers*, Logan, Utah, 1963; Richard Ruland, ed., *Twentieth-Century Interpretations of Walden*, Englewood Cliffs, N.J., 1968; and Lauriat Lane, Jr., ed., *Approaches to Walden*, San Francisco, 1961. Also vital are chapters on Thoreau in Alfred Kazin, *Contemporaries*, Boston, 1962; Tony Tanner, *The Reign of Wonder*, Cambridge, Eng., 1965; Edwin Fussell, *Frontier: American Literature and the American West*, Princeton, N.J., 1965; and Richard Poirier, *A World Elsewhere*, New York, 1966.

Other brief estimates are William Bysshe Stein, "*Walden*: The Wisdom of the Centaur," *ELH*, XXV (1958), 194–215; Carl Bode, "Thoreau: The Double Negative," *The Young Rebel in American Literature*, ed. Carl Bode, London, 1959, pp. 3–22; Lewis Leary, "Walden Goes Wandering:

The Transit of Good Intentions," *NEQ*, XXXII (1959), 3–30; Don W. Kleine, "Civil Disobedience: The Way to *Walden*," *MLN*, LXXV (1960), 297–304; Robert C. Albrecht, "Thoreau and His Audience: 'A Plea for Captain John Brown,'" *AL*, XXXII (1961), 393–402; John C. Broderick, "The Movement of Thoreau's Prose," *AL*, XXXIII (1961), 133–142; Perry Miller, "Thoreau in the Context of International Romanticism," *NEQ*, XXXIV (1961), 147–159; Howard Mumford Jones, "Thoreau as Moralist," *Atl*, CCX (Sept., 1962), 56–61; Leo Marx, "Thoreau's Excursions," *YR*, LI (1962), 363–369; H. M. Sweetland, "The Significance of Thoreau's Trip to the Upper Mississippi in 1861," *TWA*, LI (1962), 267–286; Louise B. Salomon, "The Straight-Cut Ditch: Thoreau on Education," *AQ*, XIV (1962), 19–36; Willard H. Bonner, "Mariners and Terreners: Some Aspects of Nautical Imagery in Thoreau," *AL*, XXXIV (1963), 507–519; D. Gordon Rohman, "*Walden I* and *Walden II*," *PMASAL*, XLVIII (1963), 639–648; Paul Schwaber, "Thoreau's Development in *Walden*," *Criticism*, V (1963), 64–77; Paul O. Williams, "The Concept of Inspiration in Thoreau's Poetry," *PMLA*, LXXIX (1964), 466–472; William Bysshe Stein, "Thoreau's First Book, A Spoor of Yoga: The Orient in *A Week on the Concord and Merrimack Rivers*," *ESQ*, No. 41 (1965), pp. 3–25.

More recent studies are Jonathan Bishop, "The Experience of the Sacred in Thoreau's *Week*," *ELH*, XXXIII (1966), 66–91; Alex C. Kern, "American Studies and American Literature: Approaches to a Study of Thoreau," *CE*, XXVII (1966), 480–486; Melvin E. Lyon, "Walden Pond as Symbol," *PMLA*, LXXXII (1967), 289–300; Thomas Woodson, "The Two Beginnings of *Walden*: A Distinction of Styles," *ELH*, XXXV (1968), 440–473; Berel Lang, "Thoreau and the Body Impolitic," *ColQ*, XVIII (1969), 51–57; and Charles R. Anderson, "Thoreau's Monastic Vows," *EA*, XXII (1969), 11–20.

All students of Thoreau will want to consult the continuing files of the *Thoreau Society Bulletin*, the *Thoreau Society Booklets*, and the *Emerson Society Quarterly*.

### 746. BIBLIOGRAPHY

Since 1941 Walter Harding has been contributing "Additions to the Thoreau Bibliography," to each issue of the *Thoreau Society Bulletin*. J. Stephen Sherwin and Richard C. Reynolds compiled *A Word Index to Walden: With Textual Notes*, Charlottesville, Va., 1960.

Kenneth Walter Cameron has published in Hartford, Connecticut, a series of valuable source books for Thoreau scholars: *Emerson and Thoreau as Readers* (1958), *Emerson, Thoreau, and Concord in Early Newspapers* (1958); *Transcendental Climate: New Resources for the Study of*

*Emerson, Thoreau, and Their Contemporaries,* 3 vols. (1963); and *Transcendental Epilogue: Primary Materials for Research in Emerson, Thoreau* ... (1965).

## HENRY TIMROD

**747. SEPARATE AND COLLECTED WORKS**

*The Collected Poems of Henry Timrod: A Variorum Edition,* Athens, Ga., 1965, was edited with an introduction by Edd Winfield Parks and Aileen Wells Parks.

D. J. Robillard edited "Two Timrod Letters [to Richard Henry Stoddard]," *NCHR,* XXXIX (1962), 549–553.

**BIOGRAPHY AND CRITICISM**

The first critical biography is Edd Winfield Parks's *Henry Timrod,* New York, 1964. See also Louis D. Rubin, Jr., "Henry Timrod and the Dying of the Light," *MissQ,* XI (1958), 101–111; and Edd Winfield Parks, "Timrod and Simms," *SAB,* XXXII (1967), 6–7.

## JOHN TRUMBULL

**748. COLLECTED WORKS**

*The Works of Colonel John Trumbull, Artist of the American Revolution,* was edited by Theodore Sizer, New Haven, Conn., 1950. In 1953, Sizer edited *The Autobiography of Colonel John Trumbull* as a supplement to the *Works.* The volume includes important appendixes and a supplement to the checklist first published in 1950.

Edwin T. Bowden edited *The Satiric Poems of John Trumbull: The Progress of Dulness and M'Fingal,* Austin, Tex., 1962. *The Poetical Works of John Trumbull,* 2 vols., was reprinted in Grosse Pointe, Mich., 1968.

**BIOGRAPHY AND CRITICISM**

See Max F. Schultz, "John Trumbull and Satirical Criticism of Literature," *MLN,* LXXIII (1958), 85–90.

## ROYALL TYLER

**749. WORKS**

*The Algerine Captive* (1797) was reprinted in a facsimile reproduction of the 1802 London edition, two volumes in one, with an introduction by Jack B. Moore, Gainesville, Fla., 1967.

Marius B. Péladeau's edition of *The Verse of Royall Tyler*, Charlottesville, Va., 1968, must be used with caution. The text is undependable.

### 750. BIOGRAPHY AND CRITICISM

A much-needed study of Tyler's life and works, based on unpublished letters and meticulous documentation, is G. Thomas Tanselle's *Royall Tyler*, Cambridge, Mass., 1967. Briefer studies are Roger B. Stein, "Royall Tyler and the Question of Our Speech," *NEQ*, XXXVIII (1965), 454–474; and Marius B. Péladeau, "Royall Tyler's *Other* Plays," *NEQ*, XL (1967), 48–60.


# JONES VERY

### 750. WORKS

Kenneth W. Cameron edited *Poems of Jones Very: James Freeman Clarke's Enlarged Collection of 1886 Re-edited with a Thematic and Topical Index*, Hartford, Conn., 1965. *Jones Very: Selected Poems* was edited by Nathan Lyons, New Brunswick, N.J., 1966. See also Kenneth W. Cameron, ed., "Two Harvard Essays by Jones Very," *ESQ*, No. 29 (1962), pp. 32–40; and Harry L. Jones, "The Very Madness: A New Manuscript," *CLAJ*, X (1967), 196–200.

### BIOGRAPHY AND CRITICISM

The most recent full-length study is Edwin Gittleman's *Jones Very: The Effective Years, 1833–1840*, New York, 1967. See also Anthony Herbold, "Nature as Concept and Technique in the Poetry of Jones Very," *NEQ*, XL (1967), 244–259; Paschal Reeves, "The Making of a Mystic: A Reconsideration of the Life of Jones Very," *EIHC*, CIII (1967), 3–30; and *idem*, "Jones Very as Preacher: The Extant Sermons," *ESQ*, No. 57 (1969), pp. 16–22.

Byrne R. S. Fone adds "A Note on the Jones Very Editions," *AN&Q*, VI (1968), 67–69, 88–89.


# NATHANIEL WARD

### 751. EDITED TEXTS AND REPRINTS

The most recent scholarly edition of *The Simple Cobler of Aggawam in America* (1647) was edited by P. M. Zall, Lincoln, Neb., 1969.

### BIOGRAPHY AND CRITICISM

The first full-length bio-critical study is by a French scholar, written in French: Jean Béranger, *Nathaniel Ward (ca. 1578–1652)*, Bordeaux, 1969.

See also Janette Bohi, "Nathaniel Ward, A Sage of Old Ipswich," *EIHC*, XCIX (1963), 3–32.

# GEORGE WASHINGTON

**752. COLLECTED WORKS**

The University of Virginia has announced plans for a 75-volume edition of the papers of George Washington, to be completed in 1988, under the general editorship of Donald Jackson.

Frank Donovan selected, edited, and interpreted *The George Washington Papers*, New York, 1964, a 300-page redaction, designed for the general reader, of the many editions of Washington papers, from Jared Sparks's to John Fitzpatrick's. Thomas J. Fleming edited *Affectionately Yours, George Washington: A Self-Portrait in Letters of Friendship*, New York, 1967, with a helpful running commentary.

**753. BIOGRAPHY AND CRITICISM**

The seven-volume edition of Douglas Southall Freeman's *George Washington: A Biography* (1948–1957) has been abridged by Richard Harwell into one volume, *Washington*, New York, 1968. James Flexner has published the first three volumes of a projected four-volume life: *George Washington: The Forge of Experience (1732–1775)*, Boston, 1965; *George Washington, in the American Revolution (1775–1783)*, Boston, 1968; and *George Washington, and the New Nation (1783–1793)*, Boston, 1970. A study of Washington's early life, based solely on contemporary evidence, is Bernhard Knollenberg, *George Washington: The Virginia Period, 1732–1775*, Durham, N.C., 1964, especially valuable for the generous notes and appendixes. Esmond Wright's *Washington and the American Revolution*, New York, 1957, is a concise biography for the reader new to the subject. More specialized treatments are Bliss Isely's *The Horseman of the Shenandoah: A Biographical Account of the Early Days of George Washington*, Milwaukee, Wis., 1962; and Clark Kinnaird's *George Washington: The Pictorial Biography*, New York, 1967. Marcus Cunliffe edited reprints of Mason Weems's *Life of Washington* (1800), Cambridge, Mass., 1962; and Woodrow Wilson's *George Washington* (1896), New York, 1963.

Political-historical studies have been numerous in recent years: Louis M. Sears, *George Washington and the French Revolution*, Detroit, Mich., 1960; William Bell Clark, *George Washington's Navy*, Baton Rouge, La., 1960; Paul F. Boller, *George Washington and Religion*, Dallas, Tex., 1963; and Marvin Kitman, *General Washington's Expense Account*, New York, 1970. See also Bernard Mayo, *Myths and Men: Patrick Henry, George*

*Washington, and Thomas Jefferson*, Athens, Ga., 1959; and Felix Gilbert, *To the Farewell Address: Ideas of Early American Foreign Policy*, Princeton, N.J., 1961.

Collections of briefer essays, by various hands, include *George Washington: A Profile*, ed. James Morton Smith, New York, 1969; and *George Washington*, comp. Morton Borden, Englewood Cliffs, N.J., 1969. G. A. Billias edited a gathering of 12 essays on Washington's staff: *George Washington's Generals*, New York, 1964, followed by a volume of 10 essays: *George Washington's Opponents: British Generals and Admirals in the American Revolution*, New York, 1969.

A useful addition to bibliographical study is *George Washington, 1732–1799: Chronology, Documents, and Bibliographical Aids*, ed. Howard F. Bremer, Dobbs Ferry, N.Y., 1967.

## DANIEL WEBSTER

### 755. COLLECTED WORKS

Bertha M. Rothe edited a *Daniel Webster Reader*, New York, 1956, a slim collection of excerpts from the collected writings and speeches. More recently Walker Lewis edited and arranged a more ambitious volume which he admits is "not critical, or even impartial. In essence it is an autobiography": *Speak for Yourself, Daniel: A Life of Webster in His Own Words*, Boston, 1969.

### BIOGRAPHY AND CRITICISM

Two special studies are Maurice G. Baxter, *Daniel Webster and the Supreme Court*, Amherst, Mass., 1966; and Norman D. Brown, *Daniel Webster and the Politics of Availability*, Athens, Ga., 1969, a study of Webster's presidential ambitions, 1834–1836.

See also Peter J. Parish, "Daniel Webster, New England, and the West," *JAH*, LIV (1967), 524–549.

## EDITH (NEWBOLD JONES) WHARTON

### 757. EDITED TEXTS AND REPRINTS

Louis Auchincloss edited *The Edith Wharton Reader*, New York, 1965, and R. W. B. Lewis edited *The Collected Short Stories of Edith Wharton*, 2 vols., New York, 1968. Other reprintings of individual novels and short stories are too numerous to list separately.

Since the opening in 1968 of the Wharton manuscripts at Yale University Library, R. W. B. Lewis has been at work on a definitive biography. Grace Kellogg's *The Two Lives of Edith Wharton: The Woman and Her Work*, New York, 1965, must be used with great caution since it documents few of its assumptions. On the other hand, Millicent Bell's *Edith Wharton and Henry James: The Story of Their Friendship*, New York, 1965, is an invaluable account of the years 1902–1916.

The most recent critical studies are Marilyn Jones Lyde, *Edith Wharton: Convention and Morality in the Work of a Novelist*, Norman, Okla., 1959; and Louis Auchincloss, *Edith Wharton*, Minneapolis, Minn., 1961. Irving Howe edited *Edith Wharton: A Collection of Critical Essays*, Englewood Cliffs, N.J., 1962. For other brief estimates see Viola Hopkins, "The Ordering Style of *The Age of Innocence*," *AL*, XXX (1958), 345–357; Kenneth Bernard, "Imagery and Symbolism in *Ethan Frome*," *CE*, XXIII (1961), 178–184; Patricia R. Plante, "Edith Wharton as a Short Story Writer," *MQ*, IV (1963), 363–379; Diana Trilling, "*The House of Mirth* Revisited," *ASch*, XXXII (1963), 113–128; Alexander M. Buchan, "Edith Wharton and 'The Elusive Bright-Winged Thing,'" *NEQ*, XXXVII (1964), 343–362; Vittoria Sanna, "I romanzi di Edith Wharton e la narrativa jamesiana," *SA*, X (1964), 229–291; John J. Murphy, "Edith Wharton's Italian Triptych, *The Valley of Decision*," *XUS*, IV (1965), 85–94; Richard Poirier, "Edith Wharton, *The House of Mirth*," *The American Novel from James Fenimore Cooper to William Faulkner*, ed. Wallace Stegner, New York, 1965, pp. 117–132; James W. Tuttleton, "The President and the Lady: Edith Wharton and Theodore Roosevelt," *BNYPL*, LXIX (1965), 49–57; Peter Buitenhuis, "Edith Wharton and the First World War," *AQ*, XVIII (1966), 493–505; James W. Tuttleton, "Leisure, Wealth, and Luxury: Edith Wharton's Old New York," *MQ*, VII (1966), 337–352; Richard H. Lawson, "The Influence of Gottfried Keller on Edith Wharton," *RLC*, XLII (1968), 366–379; Hilton Anderson, "Edith Wharton and the Vulgar American," *SoQ*, VII (1968), 17–22; and Christof Wegelin, "Edith Wharton and the Twilight of the International Novel," *SoR*, V (1969), 398–418.

### 759. BIBLIOGRAPHY

The most recent addition to Wharton bibliographies is Vito J. Brenni, *Edith Wharton: A Bibliography*, Morgantown, W. Va., 1966. See also Matthew J. Bruccoli, "Hidden Printings in Edith Wharton's *The Children*," *SB*, XV (1962), 269–273.

# WALT(ER) WHITMAN

### 760. COLLECTED WORKS AND CORRESPONDENCE

New York University Press has begun the publication, in 18 projected volumes, of *The Collected Writings of Walt Whitman* under the general editorship of Gay Wilson Allen and Sculley Bradley. The first to appear are *The Correspondence 1842–1892*, ed. Edwin Haviland Miller, 5 vols., 1961–1969; *The Early Poems and the Fiction*, ed. Thomas L. Brasher, 1963; *Prose Works 1892*, ed. Floyd Stovall, 2 vols., 1963–1964. *Leaves of Grass: Comprehensive Reader's Edition*, ed. Harold W. Blodgett and Sculley Bradley, 1965, is a preliminary publication of the authorized text for the variorum edition still in preparation, in four volumes.

### 761. EDITED TEXTS

Among the numerous reprintings of *Leaves of Grass*, these are the most important for the scholar: *Leaves of Grass: A Facsimile of the First Edition*, ed. Richard Bridgman, San Francisco, 1968; *Leaves of Grass: Facsimile Edition of the 1860 Text*, ed. Roy Harvey Pearce, Ithaca, N.Y., 1961; and the Blodgett–Bradley volume cited above, based on the 1891–1892 edition. *Song of Myself: Origin, Growth, Meaning*, ed. James E. Miller, Jr., New York, 1964, prints the 1855 and 1892 texts on facing pages.

*Walt Whitman's New York: From Manhattan to Montauk*, ed. Henry M. Christman, New York, 1963, is a collection of Whitman's articles published in the Brooklyn *Standard*, 1861–1862. Two volumes vital to a study of the genesis of *Leaves of Grass* are *An 1855-56 Notebook toward the Second Edition of Leaves of Grass*, introduction by Harold W. Blodgett, Carbondale, Ill., 1959; and *Walt Whitman's "Blue Book": The 1860-61 Leaves of Grass Containing His Manuscript Additions and Revisions*, ed. Arthur Golden, 2 vols., New York, 1968. Walter Loewenfels, with the assistance of Nan Braymer, edited *Walt Whitman's Civil War*, New York, 1960, compiled "from notebooks, newspaper dispatches, letters, published and unpublished works." *Walt Whitman's Memoranda During the War [&] Death of Abraham Lincoln*, ed. Roy P. Basler, Bloomington, Ind., 1962, is a reproduction of the two works in facsimile. Edwin Haviland Miller edited the Maggin Manuscript of R. M. Bucke's *Walt Whitman* (1883) under the title *Whitman on Whitman*, New York, 1969.

### 763. BIOGRAPHY AND CRITICISM

Gay Wilson Allen reissued his major critical biography, *The Solitary Singer* (1955), in a third edition with revisions and corrections, New York,

1967. Allen's *Walt Whitman*, New York, 1961, a brief life in pictures and words (many of them Whitman's), was reprinted (Detroit, Mich., 1969) with "new illustrations, revisions, updated bibliography, and a new section on criticism." Roger Asselineau's *L'Evolution de Walt Whitman* (Paris, 1954) was translated in two volumes: *The Evolution of Walt Whitman: The Creation of a Personality*, Cambridge, Mass., 1960, and *The Evolution of Walt Whitman: The Creation of a Book*, Cambridge, Mass., 1962. Horace L. Traubel's record of conversations, *With Walt Whitman in Camden* (3 vols., 1906–1914), has been continued in a fourth volume, ed. Sculley Bradley, Carbondale, Ill., 1953, and a fifth, ed. Gertrude Traubel, Carbondale, Ill., 1964. There is material for one more. Emory Holloway's *Free and Lonesome Heart: The Secret of Walt Whitman*, New York, 1960, tries to prove that Whitman was "bisexual in nature" and the father of John Whitman Wilder. It is an unverified account and must be used with caution. Thomas L. Brasher's study, *Whitman as Editor of the Brooklyn "Daily Eagle,"* Detroit, Mich., 1970, treats "a highly germinal" but until now neglected portion of Whitman's career.

Three volumes combine biography and criticism for the general reader new to the subject: James E. Miller, Jr., *Walt Whitman*, New York, 1962; Geoffrey Dutton, *Whitman*, Edinburgh, 1961; and Richard Chase, *Walt Whitman*, Minneapolis, Minn., 1961. Gay Wilson Allen collected a group of his essays in *Walt Whitman as Man, Poet, and Legend*, Carbondale, Ill., 1961, particularly helpful on Whitman's audience in this century; and he has superseded his own *Walt Whitman Handbook* (1946) with *A Reader's Guide to Walt Whitman*, New York, 1970. In *Walt Whitman's Poetry: A Psychological Journey*, Boston, 1968, Edwin Haviland Miller is concerned "with latent and manifest content, compulsive repetitions of words and situations, psychic dynamics, narcissism, orgiastic rhythms, and the like." Howard J. Waskow seeks to "define Whitman's formal range by demonstrating how each of his forms works" in *Whitman: Explorations in Form*, Chicago, 1966. Thomas Edwards Crawley, in *The Structure of Leaves of Grass*, Austin, Tex., 1970, defends the book as a unified work.

More specialized criticism includes Charles R. Metzger, *Thoreau and Whitman: A Study of Their Esthetics*, Seattle, Wash., 1961; C. N. Stavrou, *Whitman and Nietzsche: A Comparative Study of Their Thought*, Chapel Hill, N.C., 1964; O. K. Nambiar, *Walt Whitman and Yoga*, Bangalore, 1966; V. K. Chari, *Whitman in the Light of Vedantic Mysticism*, Lincoln, Neb., 1964; and Alan L. McLeod, ed., *Walt Whitman in Australia and New Zealand: A Record of His Reception*, Sydney, 1964. The Whitman tradition seen in the work of D. H. Lawrence, Hart Crane, and Dylan Thomas is discussed in *Start with the Sun: Studies in Cosmic Poetry*, Lincoln, Neb., 1960, by James E. Miller, Jr., Karl Shapiro, and Bernice Slote.

See also chapters on Whitman in Roy Harvey Pearce, *The Continuity of American Poetry*, Princeton, N.J., 1961; Wright Morris, *The Territory Ahead*, New York, 1963; R. W. B. Lewis, *Trials of the Word*, New Haven, Conn., 1965; Edwin Fussell, *Frontier: American Literature and the American West*, Princeton, N.J., 1965; Denis Donoghue, *Connoisseurs of Chaos*, New York, 1965; Douglas Grant, *Person and Place*, London, 1965; and Arnold Smithline, *Natural Religion in American Literature*, New Haven, Conn., 1966.

Gatherings of brief studies are Roy Harvey Pearce ed., *Whitman: A Collection of Critical Essays*, Englewood Cliffs, N.J., 1962; R. W. B. Lewis, *The Presence of Walt Whitman: Selected Papers from the English Institute*, New York, 1962; and Edwin Haviland Miller, ed., *A Century of Whitman Criticism* [1855-1955], Bloomington, Ind., 1969. Other estimates are C. Carroll Hollis, "Whitman and the American Idiom," *QJS*, XLIII (1957), 408-420; Edd Winfield Parks, "The Public and the Private Poet," *SAQ*, LVI (1957), 480-485; Charles E. Feinberg, "A Whitman Collector Destroys a Whitman Myth," *PBSA*, LII (1958), 73-92; John Kinnaird, "The Paradox of an American 'Identity,'" *PR*, XXV (1958), 380-405; David Daiches, "Walt Whitman as Innovator," *The Young Rebel in American Literature*, ed. Carl Bode, London, 1959, pp. 25-48; Walter Sutton, "The Analysis of Free Verse Form, Illustrated by a Reading of Whitman," *JAAC*, XVIII (1959), 241-254; Clark Griffith, "Sex and Death: The Significance of Whitman's *Calamus* Themes," *PQ*, XXXIX (1960), 18-38; Joseph Jones, "Carlyle, Whitman, and the Democratic Dilemma," *ESA*, III (1960), 179-197; William Randel, "Walt Whitman and American Myths," *SAQ*, LIX (1960), 103-113; Robert E. Cory, "The Prosody of Walt Whitman," *NDQ*, XXVIII (1960), 74-79; Clarence A. Brown, "Walt Whitman and the 'New Poetry,'" *AL*, XXXIII (1961), 33-45; Charles T. Davis, "Walt Whitman and the Problem of an American Culture," *CLAJ*, V (1961), 1-16; Roy Harvey Pearce, "Whitman Justified: The Poet in 1860," *MinnR*, I (1961), 261-294; Jorge Luis Borges, "The Achievements of Walt Whitman," *TQ*, V (1962), 43-48; Mordecai Marcus, "Walt Whitman and Emily Dickinson," *Person*, XLIII (1962), 497-514; Joseph N. Riddel, "Walt Whitman and Wallace Stevens: Functions of a 'Literatus,'" *SAQ*, LXI (1962), 506-520; Gene Bluestein, "The Advantages of Barbarism: Herder and Whitman's Nationalism," *JHI*, XXIV (1963), 115-126; Pierre Michel, "Whitman Revisited," *RLV*, XXIX (1963), 79-83; Edmund Reiss, "Whitman's Debt to Animal Magnetism," *PMLA*, LXXVIII (1963), 80-88; Steven Foster, "Bergson's 'Intuition' and Whitman's 'Song of Myself,'" *TSLL*, VI (1964), 376-387; Sydney J. Krause, "Whitman's Yawping Bird as Comic Defense," *BNYPL*, LXVIII (1964), 347-360.

More recent studies are Harold Aspiz, "Educating the Kosmos: 'There Was a Child Went Forth,'" *AQ*, XVIII (1966), 655–666; Harold Bloom, "The Central Man: Emerson, Whitman, Wallace Stevens," *MR*, VII (1966), 23–42; Arnold T. Schwab, "James Huneker on Whitman: A Newly Discovered Essay," *AL*, XXXVIII (1966), 208–218; Edward F. Grier, "Walt Whitman's Earliest Known Notebook," *PMLA*, LXXXIII (1968), 1453–1456; Lawrence Buell, "Transcendentalist Catalogue Rhetoric: Vision versus Form," *AL*, XL (1968), 325–339; Boris Gilenson, "Whitman in Russia," *SovL*, V (1969), 176–181; Roger Asselineau, "Walt Whitman: From Paumanok to More Than America," *PLL*, V (Summer Suppl., 1969), 18–39; and Philip Y. Coleman, "Walt Whitman's Ambiguities of 'I,'" *PLL*, V (Summer Suppl., 1969), 40–59.

## 767. PRIMARY SOURCES

In addition to the depositories already described in this volume, one must now add the Clifton Waller Barrett Collection at the University of Virginia; the Henry W. and Albert A. Berg Collection and the Oscar Lion Collection at the New York Public Library; the Hanley Collection at the University of Texas; and the Pierpont Morgan Library. The most notable private holdings are in the Charles E. Feinberg Collection, Detroit, Michigan, to be gradually acquired by the Library of Congress.

## 768. BIBLIOGRAPHY

William White is preparing the *Bibliography* volume of the New York University Press edition of Whitman. Until it appears, the following are invaluable: Evie Allison Allen, "A Checklist of Whitman Publications, 1945–1960," in Gay Wilson Allen, *Walt Whitman as Man, Poet, and Legend*, Carbondale, Ill., 1961; James T. F. Tanner, *Walt Whitman: A Supplementary Bibliography: 1961–1967*, Kent, Ohio, 1968; and William White, ed., *Walt Whitman's Journalism: A Bibliography*, Detroit, Mich., 1969. William White also contributes current bibliographies to the quarterly issues of *Walt Whitman Review* (1959–current). The *Walt Whitman Newsletter* (New York, 1955; Detroit, Mich., 1956–1959) became the *Walt Whitman Review* in March, 1959.

## JOHN GREENLEAF WHITTIER

### 769. COLLECTED WORKS AND CORRESPONDENCE

For gleanings of letters, see Roland H. Woodwell, ed., "Whittier on Abolition: A Letter to Emerson," *EIHC*, XCIII (1957), 254–259; Lewis E. Weeks, Jr., ed., "John Greenleaf Whittier to Harriet McEwen Kimball:

Eight Letters," *EIHC*, XCV (1959), 41–51; and Jean Downey, ed., "Whittier and Cooke: Unpublished Letters," *QH*, LII (1963), 33–36. John C. Hepler edited an unpublished poem: " 'Gordon': A New Whittier Poem," *NEQ*, XXXIV (1961), 93–95.

#### 770. EDITED TEXTS AND REPRINTS

John B. Pickard provided an introduction to a facsimile reproduction of *Legends of New England* (1831), Gainesville, Fla., 1965. Edward Wagenknecht edited, with an introduction, *The Supernaturalism of New England* (1847), Norman, Okla., 1969.

The most recent selection of the poems is *Whittier*, edited by Donald Hall, with an introduction, New York, 1960. For the Emerson Society, John B. Pickard prepared *Memorabilia of John Greenleaf Whittier*, Hartford, Conn., 1968.

#### BIOGRAPHY AND CRITICISM

Edward Wagenknecht's *John Greenleaf Whittier: A Portrait in Paradox*, New York, 1967, is the most recent attempt at biography. Two critical studies are valuable reassessments: Lewis G. Leary, *John Greenleaf Whittier*, New York, 1961; and John P. Pickard, *John Greenleaf Whittier: An Introduction and Interpretation*, New York, 1961.

For briefer estimates, see J. Welfred Holmes, "Whittier and Sumner: A Political Friendship," *NEQ*, XXX (1957), 58–72; Howard Mumford Jones, "Whittier Reconsidered," *EIHC*, XCIII (1957), 231–246; Hyatt H. Waggoner, "What I Had I Gave: Another Look at Whittier," *EIHC*, XCV (1959), 32–40; Edward D. Snyder, "Whittier and the Unitarians," *BFHA*, XLIX (1960), 111–116; Perry Miller, "John Greenleaf Whittier: the Conscience in Poetry," *Harvard Review*, II (1964), 8–24; Lewis E. Weeks, Jr., "Whittier Criticism over the Years," *EIHC*, C (1964), 159–182; George C. Carey, "Whittier Roots in a Folk Culture," *EIHC*, CIV (1968), 3–18; and Donald A. Ringe, "Sound Imagery in Whittier's *Snowbound*," *PLL*, V (1969), 139–144.

#### 772. BIBLIOGRAPHY

For continuing bibliographical listings, see all issues of the *Whittier Newsletter*.

## MICHAEL WIGGLESWORTH

#### 773. EDITED TEXTS AND REPRINTS

Edmund S. Morgan's edition of *The Diary of Michael Wigglesworth*, originally published in *Publications of the Colonial Society of Massachusetts*

*(Transactions 1942–1946)*, XXXV (1951), 311–344, is now available in paperback, New York, 1965.

BIOGRAPHY AND CRITICISM

The most recent biography is Richard Crowder's *No Featherbed to Heaven: A Biography of Michael Wigglesworth, 1631–1705*, East Lansing, Mich., 1962. See also Arthur Strange, "Michael Wigglesworth Reads the Poets," *AL*, XXXI (1959), 325–326; and Richard M. Gummere, "Michael Wigglesworth: From Kill-Joy to Comforter," *CJ*, LXII (1966), 1–8.

**774.** BIBLIOGRAPHY

See Frederick R. Goff, "Rare Books: Americana," *QJCA*, XVI (1959), 155–159.

## ROGER WILLIAMS

**774.** COLLECTED WORKS

*The Complete Writings of Roger Williams*, New York, 1963, reprints the Narragansett Edition (6 vols., 1866–1874) and adds a seventh volume of "new matter," edited by Perry Miller with "an essay in interpretation."

**775.** BIOGRAPHY AND CRITICISM

The most recent biography is Cyclone Covey's *The Gentle Radical: A Biography of Roger Williams*, New York, 1966. A brief summary of the whole career is Henry Chupack's *Roger Williams*, New York, 1969.

Two recent sociotheological studies are Edmund S. Morgan, *Roger Williams: The Church and the State*, New York, 1967; and John Garrett, *Roger Williams: Witness beyond Christendom, 1603–1683*, New York, 1970. See also Irwin H. Polishook, *Roger Williams, John Cotton, and Religious Freedom: A Controversy in New and Old England*, Englewood Cliffs, N.J., 1967; Robert J. Lowenherz, "Roger Williams and the Great Quaker Debate," *AQ*, XI (1959), 157–165; and Jesper Rosenmeier, "The Teacher and the Witness: John Cotton and Roger Williams," *WMQ*, XXV (1968), 408–431.

## WILLIAM CARLOS WILLIAMS
### *d. 1963*

**776.** SEPARATE WORKS

*Yes, Mrs. Williams: A Personal Record of My Mother*, 1959; *Many Loves and Other Plays*, 1961; *Pictures from Brueghel and Other Poems*, 1962; *Paterson, Books I–V*, 1963.

777. COLLECTED WORKS AND CORRESPONDENCE

*The Farmer's Daughters: The Collected Stories* appeared in Norfolk, Conn., 1961, with an introduction by Van Wyck Brooks. Randall Jarrell introduced *Selected Poems*, New York, 1963, 1969. Webster Schott edited *Imaginations: Collected Early Prose*, New York, 1970. M. L. Rosenthal edited *The William Carlos Williams Reader*, New York, 1966.

Gleanings of correspondence are in Edith Heal, "A Poet's Integrity: Letters from William Carlos Williams," *LitR*, IX (1965), 115–119.

BIOGRAPHY AND CRITICISM

The first bio-critical study is Thomas R. Whitaker, *William Carlos Williams*, New York, 1968. See also Walter Sutton, "A Visit with William Carlos Williams," *MinnR*, I (1961), 309–324; and Charles Angoff, "A Williams Memoir." *PrS*, XXXVIII (1964), 299–305.

The major critical studies, spanning the whole career, are James Guimond's *The Art of William Carlos Williams: A Discovery and Possession of America*, Urbana, Ill., 1968; and James E. Breslin's *William Carlos Williams: An American Artist*, New York, 1970. Two earlier studies of the poetry are Linda W. Wagner, *The Poems of William Carlos Williams*, Middletown, Conn., 1964; and Alan Ostrom, *The Poetic World of William Carlos Williams*, Carbondale, Ill., 1966. Mrs. Wagner followed her volume with *The Prose of William Carlos Williams*, Middletown, Conn., 1970. Much briefer but critically acute readings are John Malcolm Brinnin, *William Carlos Williams*, Minneapolis, Minn., 1963; and A. Walton Litz, "William Carlos Williams," *The Literary Heritage of New Jersey*, Princeton, N.J., 1964, pp. 83–130.

More specialized studies are Walter Scott Peterson, *An Approach to "Paterson,"* New Haven, Conn., 1967; Sherman Paul, *The Music of Survival: The Biography of a Poem by William Carlos Williams*, Urbana, Ill., 1968; Bram Dijkstra, *The Hieroglyphics of a New Speech: Cubism, Stieglitz, and the Early Poetry of William Carlos Williams*, Princeton, N.J., 1970; and Hélène Dupeyron-Marchessou, *William Carlos Williams et le renouveau du lyrisme*, Paris, 1967. See also chapters on Williams in J. Hillis Miller, *Poets of Reality*, Cambridge, Mass., 1966; and A. Kingsley Weatherhead, *The Edge of the Image*, Seattle, Wash., 1967.

J. Hillis Miller edited *William Carlos Williams: A Collection of Critical Essays*, Englewood Cliffs, N.J., 1966. Other brief estimates are Denis Donoghue, "For a Redeeming Language," TC, CLXIII (1958), 532–542; John C. Thirlwall, "The Genesis of the Epic 'Paterson,'" *TJ*, IV (Mar., 1959), 65–70; Hugh Kenner, "To Measure Is All We Know," *Poetry*, XCIV (1959), 127–132; Louis L. Martz, "The Unicorn in *Paterson*: William Carlos Williams," *Thought*, XXXV (1960), 537–554; Walter Sutton,

"Dr. Williams' *Paterson* and the Quest for Form," *Criticism*, II (1960), 242–259; Mary Ellen Solt, "William Carlos Williams: Poems in the American Idiom," *Folio*, XXV (1960), 3–28; Glauco Cambon, "William Carlos Williams and Ezra Pound: Two Examples of Open Poetry," *CE*, XXII (1961), 387–389; Robert Lowell, "William Carlos Williams," *HudR*, XIV (1961), 530–536; Harry R. Garvin, "William Carlos Williams' Journey to Marriage," *AION-SG*, IV (1961), 203–214; Gordon K. Grigsby, "The Genesis of *Paterson*," *CE*, XXIII (1962), 277–281; Bernard F. Engel, "Dr. Williams as Exhorter: The Meaning of Americanism," *PMASAL*, XLVII (1962), 579–586; Benjamin T. Spencer, "Doctor Williams' American Grain," *TSL*, VIII (1963), 1–16; M. L. Rosenthal, "Williams Carlos Williams and Some Young Germans," *MR*, IV (1963), 337–341; Peter Whigham, "William Carlos Williams," *Agenda*, III (1963), 25–32; Richard W. Noland, "A Failure of Contact: William Carlos Williams on America," *EUQ*, XX (1964), 248–260; Vittorio Sereni, "W.C.W.: An Italian View," *PrS*, XXXVIII (1964), 307–316.

More recent studies are Thom Gunn, "William Carlos Williams," *Encounter*, XXV (1965), 67–74; Roger Seamon, "The Bottle in the Fire: Resistance as Creation in William Carlos Williams's *Paterson*," *TCL*, XI (1965), 16–24; Joseph Evans Slate, "William Carlos Williams, Hart Crane, and 'the Virtue of History,'" *TSLL*, VI (1965), 486–511; Hans Galinsky, "William Carlos Williams: Eine vergleichende Studie zur Aufnahme seines Werkes in Deutschland, England und Italien (1912–1965). Teil I: Deutschland," *JA*, XI (1966), 96–175; *idem*, ". . . Teil II: England und Italien," JA, XII (1967), 167–205; James E. Breslin, "Whitman and the Early Development of William Carlos Williams," *PMLA*, LXXXII (1967), 613–621; Nancy Willard, "Testimony of the Invisible Man," *Shen*, XIX (1967), 42–49; J. E. Slate, "William Carlos Williams and the Modern Short Story," *SoR*, IV (1968), 647–664; Linda W. Wagner, "Williams' 'Nude': *Kora in Hell*," *SDR*, VII (1969), 3–18; Joel O. Conarroe, "The 'Preface' to *Paterson*," *ConL*, X (1969), 39–53; and Jeffrey Youdelman, "Pictures for a Sunday Afternoon: The Camera Eye in *Paterson*," *CP*, II (1969), 37–42.

Issues of periodicals devoted to Williams include the *Literary Review,* I (Autumn, 1957); the *Massachusetts Review*, III (Winter, 1962); the *Beloit Poetry Journal*, XIV (Fall, 1963); and *Journal of Modern Literature*, I (May, 1971).

BIBLIOGRAPHY

The major work is Emily Mitchell Wallace's exhaustive *Bibliography of William Carlos Williams*, Middletown, Conn., 1968. See also William White, "William Carlos Williams: Bibliography Review with Addenda,"

*ABC*, XIX (1969), 9–12; *The Merrill Checklist of William Carlos Williams*, comp. John Engels, Columbus, Ohio, 1969; and Jack Hardie, "'A Celebration of Light': Selected Checklist of Writings about William Carlos Williams," *JML*, I (1971), 593–642.

## (THOMAS) WOODROW WILSON

### 779. COLLECTED WORKS AND REPRINTS

Princeton University Press has begun publication of the projected 40-volume edition of *The Papers of Woodrow Wilson* (Vols. I–XI, 1966–1971) under the general editorship of Arthur S. Link.

Albert Fried edited *A Day of Dedication: The Essential Writings and Speeches of Woodrow Wilson*, New York, 1965. E. David Cronon compiled *The Political Thought of Woodrow Wilson*, Indianapolis, Ind., 1965. In recent years, a number of works by Wilson have come back into print: *Constitutional Government in the United States*, New York, 1961; *The New Freedom*, Englewood Cliffs, N.J., 1961; *Division and Reunion, 1829–1889*, New York, 1962; *George Washington*, New York, 1963; and *Mere Literature, and Other Essays*, New York, 1965.

Eleanor Wilson McAdoo edited *The Priceless Gift: The Love Letters of Woodrow Wilson and Ellen Louise Wilson*, New York, 1962.

### 780. BIOGRAPHY AND CRITICISM

Arthur S. Link began his multivolume biography in 1947. A second volume appeared in 1956, followed by *Wilson: The Struggle for Neutrality, 1914–1915*, Princeton, N.J., 1960; *Wilson: Confusions and Crises, 1915–1916*, Princeton, N.J., 1964; and *Wilson: Campaigns for Progressivism and Peace, 1916–1917*, Princeton, N.J., 1965. Link also published *Woodrow Wilson: A Brief Biography*, Cleveland, Ohio, 1963; and edited *Woodrow Wilson: A Profile*, New York, 1968, designed to introduce readers to Woodrow Wilson the man with "both partial chronological coverage and, at the end, some historical perspective on Wilson's contribution to modern history." These designs are also served by seven other recent volumes. Henry Wilkinson Bragdon concentrates on *Woodrow Wilson: The Academic Years*, Cambridge, Mass., 1967; as does George Coleman Osborn in *Woodrow Wilson: The Early Years*, Baton Rouge, La., 1968. Hardin Craig remembers *Woodrow Wilson at Princeton*, Norman, Okla., 1960. David W. Hirst produced "a documentary narrative" in *Woodrow Wilson, Reform Governor*, Princeton, N.J., 1965. A journalist's version of "the last years" is Gene Smith's *When the Cheering Stopped*, New York, 1964. Rear Admiral Cary T. Grayson, the President's physician, published *Woodrow*

*Wilson: An Intimate Memoir*, New York, 1960. Sigmund Freud and William C. Bullitt collaborated on *Thomas Woodrow Wilson, Twenty-Eighth President of the United States: A Psychological Study*, Boston, 1967, a dogmatic book without documentation. Arthur C. Walworth's important two-volume study, *Woodrow Wilson* (1958) has had a revised edition, Boston, 1965.

Specialized studies abound. Domestic affairs are analyzed in Seward W. Livermore, *Politics Is Adjourned: Woodrow Wilson and the War Congress, 1916-1918*, Middletown, Conn., 1966; and George C. Rapport, *The Statesman and the Boss: A Study of American Political Leadership Exemplified by Woodrow Wilson and Frank Hague*, New York, 1961. International affairs are the focus of N. Gordon Levin, *Woodrow Wilson and World Politics: America's Response to War and Revolution*, New York, 1968; Laurence W. Martin, *Peace without Victory: Woodrow Wilson and the British Liberals*, New Haven, Conn., 1958; Robert E. Quirk, *An Affair of Honor: Woodrow Wilson and the Occupation of Vera Cruz*, Lexington, Ky., 1962; Roy Watson Curry, *Woodrow Wilson and Far Eastern Policy, 1913-1921*, New York, 1957; and Harvey A. DeWeerd, *President Wilson Fights His War: World War I and the American Intervention*, New York, 1968.

See also, *passim*, Robert E. Quirk, *The Mexican Revolution, 1914-1915: The Convention of Aquascalientes*, Bloomington, Ind., 1960; Frank K. Kelly, *The Fight for the White House: The Story of 1912*, New York, 1961; Ernest May, *The World War and American Isolation*, Cambridge, Mass., 1959; Arno J. Mayer, *The Political Origins of the New Diplomacy, 1917-1918*, New Haven, Conn., 1959; Wesley M. Bagby, *The Road to Normalcy: The Presidential Campaign and Election of 1920*, Baltimore, Md., 1962; Arno J. Mayer, *The Politics and Diplomacy of Peacemaking: Containment and Counter-revolution at Versailles, 1918-1919*, New York, 1967; Edward M. Coffman, *The War to End All Wars: Military Experience in World War I*, New York, 1968; and Ralph Stone, *The Irreconcilables: The Fight against the League of Nations*, Lexington, Ky., 1970.

Sixteen essays about Wilson are gathered in *The Philosophy and Policies of Woodrow Wilson,* ed. Earl Latham, Chicago, 1958. Other brief studies are John Wells Davidson, "Wilson as Presidential Leader," *Current History*, XXXIX (1960), 198-202; Laurence W. Martin, "Necessity and Principle: Woodrow Wilson's Views," *RPol*, XXII (1960), 96-114; R. Balfour Daniels, "The Common Touch, *ForumH*, III (1960), 35-39; John S. Smith, "Organized Labor and Government in the Wilson Era: 1913-1921: Some Conclusions," *Labor History*, III (1962), 265-286; George Osborn, "The Romance of Woodrow Wilson and Ellen Axson," *NCHR*, XXXIX (1962), 32-57; Laurence R. Veysey, "The Academic

Mind of Woodrow Wilson," *MVHR*, LXIX (1963), 613–634; George Baker, "The Wilson Administration and Cuba, 1913–1921," *M-A*, XLVI (1964), 49–63; and Milton Katz, "Woodrow Wilson and the Twentieth Century," *Confluence*, V (1965), 229–238.

### 781. BIBLIOGRAPHY

A new Wilson bibliography is badly needed. Some recent material is listed in the generally inadequate *Woodrow Wilson, 1856–1924: Chronology-Documents-Bibliographical Aids*, ed. Robert I. Vexler, Dobbs Ferry, N.Y., 1969. For bibliography of the whole age, see Arthur S. Link and William M. Leary, Jr., *The Progressive Era and the Great War, 1896–1920*, New York, 1969.

## JOHN WISE

### 784. EDITED TEXTS AND REPRINTS

*A Vindication of the Government of New-England Churches* (1717) was reprinted in facsimile with an introduction by Perry Miller, Gainesville, Fla., 1958; *The Churches Quarrel Espoused* (1713) with an introduction by George A. Cook, Gainesville, Fla., 1966.

## THOMAS (CLAYTON) WOLFE

### 784. SEPARATE WORKS

*Thomas Wolfe's Purdue Speech, "Writing and Living"* (ed. William Braswell and Leslie A. Field, 1964); *The Notebooks of Thomas Wolfe* (ed. Richard S. Kennedy and Paschal Reeves), 2 vols., 1970; *The Mountains* (ed. Pat M. Ryan), 1970.

### 785. COLLECTED WORKS, CORRESPONDENCE, AND REPRINTS

C. Hugh Holman edited *The Short Novels of Thomas Wolfe*, New York, 1961, a reprinting of the magazine version of four novels ("A Portrait of Bascom Hawke," "The Web of Earth," "I Have a Thing to Tell You," and "The Party at Jack's") plus the newly assembled short novel version of "No Door." *The Thomas Wolfe Reader*, ed. C. Hugh Holman, New York, 1962, includes *The Story of a Novel* and integrated units from all six volumes of Wolfe's work.

C. Hugh Holman and Sue Fields Ross compiled *The Letters of Thomas Wolfe to His Mother: Newly Edited from the Original Manuscripts*, Chapel Hill, N.C., 1968. See also Mary Lindsay Thornton, "'Dear Mabel': Letters of Thomas Wolfe to His Sister Mabel Wolfe Wheaton," *SAQ*, LX (1961), 469–483; and Abe Capek, "The Development of Thomas Wolfe in the Light of His Letters," *ZAA*, X (1962), 162–178.

BIOGRAPHY AND CRITICISM

The facts of Wolfe's life are still being sifted and, where possible, separated from the legend. Two notable attempts at biography are Elizabeth Nowell's detailed *Thomas Wolfe*, Garden City, N.Y., 1960; and Andrew Turnbull, *Thomas Wolfe*, New York, 1967. Miss Nowell was a Scribner editor and for five years Wolfe's agent. Turnbull assembled an intimate, vital portrait by means of countless interviews with Wolfe's contemporaries. Mabel Wolfe Wheaton and LeGette Blythe, *Thomas Wolfe and His Family*, Garden City, N.Y., 1961, is a rambling chronicle, especially informative on Wolfe's early years in Asheville. Shorter reminiscences are V. L. O. Chittick, "Tom Wolfe's Farthest West," *SWR*, XLVIII (1963), 93–110; and Clement Eaton, "Student Days with Thomas Wolfe," *GaR*, XVII (1963), 146–155.

Richard S. Kennedy's *The Window of Memory: The Literary Career of Thomas Wolfe*, Chapel Hill, N.C., 1962, is indispensable as both biography and criticism, being a close examination of the manuscripts, how the novels were made from them, and the elusive details of Wolfe's literary career. Of the three general introductions to Wolfe's life and work, the most satisfactory is Bruce R. McElderry's *Thomas Wolfe*, New York, 1964. Richard Walser, *Thomas Wolfe*, New York, 1961; and C. Hugh Holman, *Thomas Wolfe*, Indianapolis, Ind., 1960, cover the same ground. Paschal Reeves studies one side of Wolfe's work in *Thomas Wolfe's Albatross: Race and Nationality in America*, Athens, Ga., 1969. Vardis Fisher, a fellow novelist, collected his impressions in *Thomas Wolfe As I Knew Him and Other Essays*, Denver, Colo., 1963. Three foreign studies are Walter Voigt, *Die Bildersprache Thomas Wolfes*, Munich, 1960; Guido Botta, *Thomas Wolfe o della solitudine*, Naples, 1964; and Hans Helmcke, *Die Familie im Romanwerk von Thomas Wolfe*, Heidelberg, 1967.

Two collections of brief critical assessments are *The World of Thomas Wolfe*, ed. C. Hugh Holman, New York, 1962; and *Thomas Wolfe: Three Decades of Criticism*, New York, 1968. Other studies are Philip W. Barber, "Tom Wolfe Writes a Play," *Harper's*, CCXVI (May, 1958), 71–76; Virginia Stevens, "Thomas Wolfe's America," *Mainstream*, XI (1958), 1–24; Joseph Katz, "Balzac and Wolfe: A Study of Self-Destructive Overproductivity," *Psychoanalysis*, V (1957), 3–19; Paschal Reeves, "The Humor of Thomas Wolfe," *SFQ*, XXIV (1960), 109–120; Frank Kearns, ed., "Tom Wolfe on the Drama," *CaQ*, XI (1960), 5–10; J. Russell Reaver and Robert I. Strozier, "Thomas Wolfe and Death," *GaR*, XVI (1962),

330–350; Francis E. Skipp, "The Editing of *Look Homeward, Angel,*" *PBSA,* LVII (1963), 1–13; Edward Stone, "A Rose for Thomas Wolfe," *OUR,* V (1963), 17–24; Louis D. Rubin, Jr., "The Self Recaptured," *KR,* XXV (1963), 393–415; Anthony Channell Hilfer, "Wolfe's Altamont: The Mimesis of Being," *GaR,* XVIII (1964), 451–456.

More recent estimates are Elmer D. Johnson, "Thomas Wolfe as a Literary Critic," *Radford Review,* XX (1966), 107–117; Albert W. Vogel, "The Education of Eugene Gant," *NMQ,* XXXVI (1966), 278–292; Heinz Ludwig, "Ein Beitrag zum Verständnis von Thomas Wolfes 'Death the Proud Brother,'" *NS,* XV (1966), 173–182; Clayton L. Eichelberger, "Wolfe's 'No Door' and the Brink of Discovery," *GaR,* XXI (1967), 319–327; Werner Bräunig, "Auf der Strasse Leben: Thomas Wolfe," *SuF,* XIX (1967), 983–998; William Styron, "The Shade of Thomas Wolfe," *Harper's,* CCXXXVI (Apr., 1968), 96–104; C. Hugh Holman, "Europe as Catalyst for Thomas Wolfe," *Essays in American and English Literature,* ed. Max F. Schulz, Athens, Ohio, 1968, 122–137; and Duane Schneider, "Thomas Wolfe and the Quest for Language," *OUR,* XI (1969), 5–18.

The Autumn, 1965, issue of *Modern Fiction Studies* is devoted solely to Thomas Wolfe.

Elmer D. Johnson compiled *Of Time and Thomas Wolfe: A Bibliography with a Character Index of His Works,* New York, 1959, and *Thomas Wolfe: A Checklist,* Kent, Ohio, 1970. See also Maurice Beebe and Leslie A. Field, "Criticism of Thomas Wolfe: A Selected Checklist," *MFS,* XI (1965), 315–328; C. Hugh Holman's interpretive bibliographical essay, "Thomas Wolfe," *Fifteen Modern American Authors,* ed. Jackson R. Bryer, Durham, N.C., 1969, pp. 425–456; and Hans Helmcke, "Die 'Thomas-Wolfe-Renaissance' in den Vereinigten Staaten," *JA,* IX (1964), 181–195.

# JOHN WOOLMAN

787. COLLECTED WORKS AND REPRINTS

The 1774 edition of *The Works of John Woolman* was reprinted with a new foreword by William A. Beardslee, New York, 1970. Frederick B. Tolles provided a valuable introduction to an inexpensive volume which reprints *The Journal of John Woolman* (from the "standard" Whittier edition) and *A Plea for the Poor,* New York, 1961.

See also Ormerod Greenwood, ed., "John Woolman and Susanna Lightfoot: His Unpublished Letter to Her," *Journal of Friends' Historical Society,* XLVIII (1958), 147–156; and Henry J. Cadbury, "A Woolman Manuscript," *QH,* LVII (1968), 35–41.

**788.** BIOGRAPHY AND CRITICISM

Edwin H. Cady's *John Woolman*, New York, 1965, explicates Woolman's social and religious ideas and their relevance to our own age. Paul Rosenblatt's *John Woolman*, New York, 1969, surveys the whole career with heavy emphasis on the *Journal* and on Woolman's contemporaries, Benjamin Franklin and Jonathan Edwards. *The Quakers in the American Colonies* by Rufus M. Jones, Isaac Sharpless, and Amelia M. Gummere, New York, 1962, has been called "essential for understanding Woolman's position in Quaker history."

Briefer studies are W. Forrest Altman, "John Woolman's Reading of the Mystics," *BFHA*, XLVIII (1959), 103–115; Phillips Moulton, "John Woolman: Exemplar of Ethics," *QH*, LIV (1965), 81–93; and Marianna W. Davis, "The Connatural Ground of John Woolman's Triangle," *CLAJ*, IX (1965), 132–139; and Henry J. Cadbury, "Sailing to England with John Woolman," *QH*, LV (1966), 88–103.

# RICHARD WRIGHT
*d. 1960*

**789.** WRITINGS

*Eight Men* (short stories), 1961; *Lawd Today* (novel), 1963.

Thomas Knipp edited, with an introduction, *Richard Wright: Letters to Joe C. Brown*, Kent, Ohio, 1968.

BIOGRAPHY AND CRITICISM

The definitive biography of Wright is yet to be written. Two recent attempts are Constance Webb, *Richard Wright: A Biography*, New York, 1968; and John A. Williams, *The Most Native of Sons: A Biography of Richard Wright*, Garden City, N.Y., 1970.

Three recent full-length critical studies are Dan McCall, *The Example of Richard Wright*, New York, 1969; Edward Margolies, *The Art of Richard Wright*, Carbondale, Ill., 1969; and Russell Carl Brignano, *Richard Wright: An Introduction to the Man and His Works*, Pittsburgh, Pa., 1970. Robert A. Bone's pamphlet, *Richard Wright*, Minneapolis, Minn., 1969, is a concise introduction.

Briefer estimates are Raymond Las Vergnas, "Richard Wright," *RdP* (Aug., 1958), pp. 124–131; Kingsley Widmer, "The Existential Darkness: Richard Wright's *The Outsider*," *WSCL*, I (1960), 13–21; James Baldwin, "Richard Wright," *Encounter*, XVI (1961), 58–60; Albert Gerard, "Vie et vocation de Richard Wright," *RGB*, XCVII (1961), 65–78; James Baldwin, "The Survival of Richard Wright," *Reporter*, XXIV (Mar. 16, 1961), 52–55; Nick Aaron Ford, "Richard Wright, a Profile," *CJF*, XXI (1962),

26–30; Gaetano Bisol, "Richard Wright: Drama razziale e narrativa negra di protesta," *Letture*, XX (1965), 259–276; Monika Plessner, "Richard Wright, Vorkämpfer der zweiten amerikanischen Revolution," *FH*, XX (1965), 840–852; Herbert Hill *et al.*, "Reflections on Richard Wright: A Symposium on an Exiled Native Son," *Anger and Beyond: The Negro Writer in the United States*, ed. Herbert Hill, New York, 1966, pp. 196–212; Richard Kostelanetz, "The Politics of Unresolved Quests in the Novels of Richard Wright," *XUS*, VIII (1969), 31–64; Raman K. Singh, "Some Basic Ideas and Ideals in Richard Wright's Fiction," *CLAJ*, XIII (1969), 78–84; and James Nagel, "Images of 'Vision' in *Native Son*," *UR*, XXXV (1969), 109–115, and Donald B. Gibson, ed., *Five Black Writers: Essays on Wright, Ellison, Baldwin, Hughes, and LeRoi Jones*, New York, 1970.

*Negro Digest*, XVIII (1968), and *College Language Association Journal*, XII (1969), published special Richard Wright issues.

Bibliographical listings can be found in Jackson R. Bryer, "Richard Wright (1908–1960): A Selected Check List of Criticism," *WSCL*, I (1960), 22–33; Michel Fabre and Edward Margolies, "Richard Wright (1908–1960): A Bibliography," *BB*, XXIV (1965), 131–133, 137; and Constance Webb, "Richard Wright: A Bibliography," *NegroD*, XVIII (1969), 86–92. See also Kenneth Kinnamon, "Richard Wright Items in the Fales Collection," *Bulletin of the Society for the Libraries of New York University*, No. 66 (1965), p. 4.

## ELINOR (HOYT) WYLIE

### 790. BIOGRAPHY AND CRITICISM

The most recent bio-critical study is Thomas A. Gray's *Elinor Wylie*, New York, 1969. See also Thomas A. Gray, "Elinor Wylie: The Puritan Marrow and the Silver Filigree," *ArQ*, XIX (1963), 343–357; Thomas J. Wertenbaker, Jr., "Into the Poet's Shoes," *EJ*, LIII (1964), 370–372; George Brandon Saul, " 'Icy Song': The Verse of Elinor Wylie," *BNYPL*, LXIX (1965), 618–622; and Evelyn T. Helmick, "Elinor Wylie's Novels, Allegories of Love," *Carrell*, IX (1968), 17–28.

# BIBLIOGRAPHIES: ADDITIONAL INDIVIDUAL AUTHORS

John Peale Bishop
R. P. Blackmur
Kenneth Burke
James Gould Cozzens
Caroline Gordon
J. P. Marquand
John O'Hara
John Crowe Ransom
Robert E. Sherwood
Booth Tarkington
Allen Tate
Albion W. Tourgée
Carl Van Vechten
Robert Penn Warren
Thornton Wilder
Edmund Wilson

# JOHN PEALE BISHOP

**1013.** SEPARATE WORKS

See Robert L. White, "Some Unpublished Poems of John Peale Bishop," *SR*, LXXI (1963), 527–537.

COLLECTIONS

Allen Tate edited, with an introduction, *Selected Poems*, London, 1960.

BIOGRAPHY AND CRITICISM

The first full-length study is Robert L. White, *John Peale Bishop*, New York, 1966. Shorter work can be found in Cecil D. Eby, Jr., "The Fiction of John Peale Bishop," *TCL*, VII (1962), 3–9; Joseph Frank, "The Achievement of John Peale Bishop," *MinnR*, II (1962), 325–344; Eugene Haun, "John Peale Bishop: A Celebration," *Reality and Myth*, ed. William E. Walker and Robert L. Welker, Nashville, Tenn., 1964, pp. 80–97; S. C. Moore, "The Criticism of John Peale Bishop," *TCL*, XII (1966), 66–77; and Leslie A. Fiedler, "John Peale Bishop and the Other Thirties," *Com*, XLIII (1967), 74–82.

# R(ICHARD) P(ALMER) BLACKMUR
## *d. 1965*

**1014.** SEPARATE WORKS

Essays: *Eleven Essays in the European Novel*, 1964; *A Primer of Ignorance* (ed. Joseph Frank), 1967.

Editions: *The Wings of the Dove* by Henry James, 1958; *Washington Square* by Henry James, 1959; *American Short Novels*, 1960; *The American* by Henry James, 1960; *The Portrait of a Lady* by Henry James, 1961; *The Tragic Muse* by Henry James, 1961; *The Celestial Railroad and Other Stories* by Nathaniel Hawthorne, 1963.

BIOGRAPHY AND CRITICISM

Critical estimates are Denis Donoghue, "Poetic in the Common Enterprise," *TC*, CLXI (1957), 537–546; Richard Foster, "R. P. Blackmur: The Technical Critic as Romantic Agonist," *WR*, XXIII (1959), 259–270;

and Maurice Kramer, "A Critic's Obscurity: R. P. Blackmur," *CE*, XXII (1961), 553–555.

## KENNETH (DUVA) BURKE

**1015. SEPARATE WORKS**

Fiction: *The Complete White Oxen: Collected Short Fiction*, 1968.

Non-fiction: *The Rhetoric of Religion: Studies in Logology*, 1961; *Language as Symbolic Action: Essays on Life, Literature, and Method*, 1966.

Poetry: *Collected Poems, 1915–1967*, 1968.

**COLLECTED WORKS**

*Perspectives by Incongruity* and *Terms for Order*, both volumes edited by Stanley Edgar Hyman with the assistance of Barbara Karmiller, Bloomington, Ind., 1964, now bound together in one volume, are selections of Burke's poetry, fiction, and essays plus excerpts from previously published books.

**BIOGRAPHY AND CRITICISM**

Two early studies attempt to explain Burke's position in American letters: George Knox, *Critical Moments: Kenneth Burke's Categories and Critiques*, Seattle, Wash., 1957; and L. Virginia Holland, *Counterpoint: Kenneth Burke and Aristotle's Theories of Rhetoric*, New York, 1959. A far more ambitious analysis of Burke's whole development is William H. Rueckert, *Kenneth Burke and the Drama of Human Relations*, Minneapolis, Minn., 1963. Merle E. Brown, *Kenneth Burke*, Minneapolis, Minn., 1969, is an introductory pamphlet.

An invaluable volume for surveying Burke's reception is *Critical Responses to Kenneth Burke, 1924–1966*, ed. William H. Rueckert, Minneapolis, Minn., 1969. Additional brief studies are Luciano Gallino, "Kenneth Burke e la critica americana," *SA*, No. 3 (1957), pp. 315–346; Marie Hochmuth Nichols, "Kenneth Burke: Rhetorical and Critical Theory," *Rhetoric and Criticism*, Baton Rouge, La., 1963; Joseph Schwartz, "Kenneth Burke, Aristotle, and the Future of Rhetoric," *CCC*, XVII (1966), 210–216; Denis Donoghue, "Kenneth Burke's Dangling Novel," *Encounter*, XXIX (1967), 78–84; and Neal J. Osborn, "Toward the Quintessential Burke," *HudR*, XXI (1968), 308–321.

**BIBLIOGRAPHY**

Rueckert's *Critical Responses to Kenneth Burke* contains "The Writings of Kenneth Burke," a checklist prepared by Armin Paul Frank and

Mechthild Frank, pp. 495–512, and Rueckert's own "Works about Kenneth Burke," pp. 515–522.

# JAMES GOULD COZZENS

**1016.** SEPARATE WORKS

*Children and Others*, 1964; *Morning, Noon, and Night*, 1968.

BIOGRAPHY AND CRITICISM

The first study of the entire range of Cozzens's work is Frederick Bracher, *The Novels of James Gould Cozzens*, New York, 1959. Harry John Mooney, Jr., *James Gould Cozzens: Novelist of Intellect*, Pittsburgh, Pa., 1963, examines the major themes and traces them through eight novels. Granville Hicks, *James Gould Cozzens*, Minneapolis, Minn., 1965, is a brief pamphlet. The first British study is D. E. S. Maxwell, *Cozzens*, Edinburgh, 1964.

Brief estimates are Louis McKernan, "Profile of an Aristocrat: James Gould Cozzens," *CathW*, CLXXXVI (1957), 114–119; Francis X. Duggan, "Facts and All Man's Fictions," *Thought*, XXXIII (1959), 604–616; Richard H. Powers, "Praise the Mighty: Cozzens and the Critics," *SWR*, XLIII (1958), 263–270; Harold H. Watts, "James Gould Cozzens and the Genteel Tradition," *ColQ*, VI (1958), 257–273; John Lydenberg, "Cozzens' Man of Responsibility," *Shen*, X (1959), 11–18; Heinrich Straumann, "The Quarrel about Cozzens: or, The Vagaries of Book Reviewing," *ES*, XL (1959), 251–265; Robert E. Scholes, "The Commitment of James Gould Cozzens," *ArQ*, XVI (1960), 129–144; Michael Millgate, "The Judgements of James Gould Cozzens," *CritQ*, IV (1962), 87–91; Chester E. Eisinger, "The Voice of Aggressive Aristocracy," *Midway*, No. 18 (1964), pp. 100–128; Abigail Ann Hamblen, "The Paradox of James Gould Cozzens," *WHR*, XIX (1965), 355–361; and Arthur Mizener, "The Undistorting Mirror," *KR*, XXVIII (1966), 595–611.

Bibliographical listings with commentary are in Richard M. Ludwig, "James Gould Cozzens: A Review of Research and Criticism," *TSLL*, I (1959), 123–136; and James B. Meriwether, "The English Editions of James Gould Cozzens," *SB*, XV (1963), 207–217.

# CAROLINE GORDON

**1016.** SEPARATE WORKS

Criticism: *A Good Soldier: A Key to the Novels of Ford Madox Ford*, 1963.

**1017.** BIOGRAPHY AND CRITICISM

The first lengthy essay is Frederick P. W. McDowell's pamphlet, *Caroline Gordon*, Minneapolis, Minn., 1966. Briefer estimates are William Van O'Connor, "Art and Miss Gordon," *South*, ed. Louis D. Rubin, Jr., and Robert D. Jacobs, Garden City, N.Y., 1961, pp. 314–322; Brainard Cheney, "Caroline Gordon's Ontological Quest," *Ren,* XVI (1963), 3–12; Ashley Brown, "The Novel as Christian Comedy," *Reality and Myth*, ed. William E. Walker and Robert L. Welker, Nashville, Tenn., 1964, pp. 161–178; Marie Fletcher, "The Fate of Woman in the Changing South: A Persistent Theme in the Fiction of Caroline Gordon," *MissQ*, XXI (1968), 17–28; James E. Rocks, "The Mind and Art of Caroline Gordon," *MissQ*, XXI (1968), 1–16; *idem*, "The Christian Myth as Salvation: Caroline Gordon's *The Strange Children*," *TSE*, XVI (1968), 149–160; Ashley Brown, "The Achievement of Caroline Gordon," *SHR*, II (1968), 279–290; and Larry Rubin, "Christian Allegory in Caroline Gordon's 'The Captive,'" *SSF*, V (1968), 283–289.

The *Southern Review*, VII, n.s. (April, 1971) published five essays on the author and her work along with an interview and an excerpt from her latest novel.

## J(OHN) P(HILLIPS) MARQUAND
*d. 1960*

**1017.** SEPARATE WORKS

*Timothy Dexter, Revisited*, 1960, a rewriting of *Lord Timothy Dexter of Newburyport, Mass.* (1925).

**1018.** BIOGRAPHY AND CRITICISM

There is no biography, but valuable background material is available in Frederick Houghton and Richard Whitman, "J. P. Marquand Speaking," *Cosmopolitan*, CXLVII (Aug., 1959), 46–50; and John J. Gross, "The Late John P. Marquand: An Essay in Biography," *English Record*, XIX (1968), 2–12.

The first book-length critical study is John J. Gross, *John P. Marquand*, New York, 1963. C. Hugh Holman's pamphlet, *John P. Marquand*, Minneapolis, Minn., 1965, combines biography with concise critical judgments. Other critical evaluations are Alfred Kazin, "John P. Marquand and the American Failure," *Atl*, CCII (Nov., 1958), 152–156; Franz M. Oppenheimer, "Lament for Unbought Grace: The Novels of John P. Marquand," *AR*, XVIII (1958), 41–61; Louis Auchincloss, "Marquand and

O'Hara: The Novel of Manners," *Nation*, CLXCI (Nov. 19, 1960), 383–384; George Goodwin, Jr., "The Last Hurrahs: George Apley and Frank Skeffington," *MR*, I (1960), 461–471; Chester F. Eisinger, *Fiction of the Forties*, Chicago, 1963, pp. 289–294; Robert O. Johnson, "Mr. Marquand and Lord Tennyson," *RS*, XXXII (1964), 28–38; and George Greene, "A Tunnel from Persepolis: The Legacy of John Marquand," *QQ*, LXXIII (1966), 345–356.

Bibliographical listings are in the books by Gross and Holman cited above. See also William White, "More Marquandiana, 1956–1968," *Serif*, VI (1969), 33–36.

## JOHN (HENRY) O'HARA
### d. 1970

**1019.** SEPARATE WORKS

Novels: *Ourselves to Know*, 1960; *Sermons and Soda Water: A Trilogy*, 1960; *The Big Laugh*, 1962; *Elizabeth Appleton*, 1963; *The Lockwood Concern*, 1965; *The Instrument*, 1967; *Lovey Childs: A Philadelphian's Story*, 1969.

Short Stories: *Assembly*, 1961; *The Cape Cod Lighter*, 1962; *The Hat on the Bed*, 1963; *The Horse Knows the Way*, 1964; *Waiting for Winter*, 1966; *And Other Stories*, 1968.

Plays: *Five Plays*, including *The Farmer's Hotel, The Searching Sun, The Champagne Pool, Veronique*, and *The Way It Was*, 1961.

Essays: *Three Views of the Novel* (with Irving Stone and MacKinlay Kantor), 1957; *My Turn*, 1966.

COLLECTIONS

*Selected Short Stories* is a Modern Library volume with an introduction by Lionel Trilling, New York, 1957. *49 Stories*, New York, 1963, is a selection from *Assembly* (1961) and *The Cape Cod Lighter* (1962). *The O'Hara Generation*, New York, 1969, reprints 22 stories from the nine volumes of O'Hara's short stories published between 1935 and 1966.

BIOGRAPHY AND CRITICISM

The first full-length study is Sheldon Norman Grebstein's *John O'Hara*, New York, 1966. A more recent survey of the whole career is Charles Child Walcutt's pamphlet, *John O'Hara*, Minneapolis, Minn., 1969. See also, *passim*, Albert Van Nostrand, *The Denatured Novel*, Indianapolis, Ind., 1960; Louis Auchincloss, *Reflections of a Jacobite*, Boston, 1961;

Alfred Kazin, *Contemporaries*, Boston, 1962; Albert William Levi, *Literature, Philosophy, and the Imagination*, Bloomington, Ind., 1962; John Mason Brown, *As They Appear*, New York, 1962; and William V. Shannon, *The American Irish*, New York, 1963.

Brief evaluations are Delmore Schwartz, "Smile and Grin, Relax and Collapse," *PR*, XVII (1950), 292-296; Norman Podhoretz, "Gibbsville and New Leeds: The America of John O'Hara and Mary McCarthy," *Com*, XXI (1956), 269-273; Robert Weaver, "Twilight Area of Fiction: The Novels of John O'Hara," *QQ*, LXVI (1959), 320-325; Jack Keating, "John O'Hara's World of Yale, Society, and Sex," *Cosmopolitan*, CXLIX (Sept., 1960), 59-63; Jesse Bier, "O'Hara's *Appointment in Samarra*: His First and Only Real Novel," *CE*, XXV (1963), 135-141; John Aldridge, "Highbrow Authors and Middlebrow Books," *Playboy*, XI (Apr., 1964), 166-174; Scott Donaldson, "Appointment with the Dentist: O'Hara's Naturalistic Novel," *MFS*, XIV (1968), 435-442; and Don A. Schanche, "John O'Hara Is Alive and Well in the First Half of the Twentieth Century," *Esquire*, LXXII (Aug., 1969), 84-86, 142-149.

The best bibliography is the listing appended to Grebstein's book, cited above.

## JOHN CROWE RANSOM

**1019. SEPARATE WORKS**

Poetry: *Selected Poems*, rev. and enl., 1963.

Essays: *God without Thunder* (1930) was reprinted in 1965, *The World's Body* (1938) in 1964.

**1020. BIOGRAPHY AND CRITICISM**

The first full-length studies of Ransom's work are Karl F. Knight, *The Poetry of John Crowe Ransom: A Study of Diction, Metaphor, and Symbol*, The Hague, 1964; Robert Buffington, *The Equilibrist: A Study of John Crowe Ransom's Poems, 1916-1963*, Nashville, Tenn., 1967; and Thornton H. Parsons, *John Crowe Ransom*, New York, 1969. Thomas Daniel Young edited an important collection of reprinted articles, *John Crowe Ransom: Critical Essays and a Bibliography*, Baton Rouge, La., 1968. See also John L. Stewart's pamphlet, *John Crowe Ransom*, Minneapolis, Minn., 1962; and *passim*, Louis Cowan, *The Fugitive Group: A Literary History*, Baton Rouge, La., 1959; and John L. Stewart, *The Burden of Time: The Fugitives and Agrarians*, Princeton, N.J., 1965.

Briefer estimates are Louis D. Rubin, Jr., "John Ransom's Cruell Battle," *Shen*, IX (1958), 23–35; Bernard Bergonzi, "A Poem about the History of Love," *CritQ*, IV (1962), 127–137; Robert Beloof, "Strength in the Exquisite: A Study of John Crowe Ransom's Prosody," *AION-SG*, IV (1961), 215–222; Graham Hough, "John Crowe Ransom: The Poet and the Critic," *SoR*, I (1965), 1–21; F. P. Jarvis, "F. H. Bradley's *Appearance and Reality* and the Critical Theory of John Crowe Ransom," *PELL*, I (1965), 187–191; Samuel H. Woods, Jr., " 'Philomela': John Crowe Ransom's *Ars Poetica*," *CE*, XXVII (1966), 408–413; Robert Penn Warren, "Notes on the Poetry of John Crowe Ransom at His Eightieth Birthday," *KR*, XXX (1968), 319–349; Allen Tate, "Gentleman in a Dustcoat: Honors Day Address at Kenyon College in Celebration of John Crowe Ransom's Eightieth Birthday, April 30, 1968," *SR*, CXXVI (1968), 375–381; Colin Partridge, " 'Aesthetic Distance' in the Poetry of John Crowe Ransom," *SoRA*, III (1968), 159–167; David Mann and Samuel H. Woods, Jr., "John Crowe Ransom's Poetic Revisions," *PMLA*, CXXXIII (1968), 15–21; and Miller Williams, "Color as Symbol and the Two-Way Metaphor in the Poetry of John Crowe Ransom," *MissQ*, XXII (1969), 29–37.

*Shenandoah*, XIV (Spring, 1963), is a John Crowe Ransom special issue.

Mildred Brook Peters prepared an exhaustive bibliography of the works by and about Ransom for the Thomas Daniel Young volume cited above.

## ROBERT E(MMET) SHERWOOD

**1021.** BIOGRAPHY AND CRITICISM

John Mason Brown published before his death the first volume of what was to have been the definitive biography: *The Worlds of Robert E. Sherwood: Mirror to His Times, 1896–1939*, New York, 1965. It was followed by *The Ordeal of a Playwright: Robert E. Sherwood and the Challenge of War*, ed. Norman Cousins, New York, 1970, one completed section of the projected second volume. Briefer bio-critical studies are R. Baird Shuman, *Robert E. Sherwood*, New York, 1964, and Walter J. Meserve, *Robert E. Sherwood, Reluctant Moralist*, New York, 1970. See also, *passim*, John Gassner, *Theatre at the Crossroads*, New York, 1960; and Winifred L. Dusenbury, *The Theme of Loneliness in Modern American Drama*, Gainesville, Fla., 1960.

Other brief estimates are James Nardin, "The Plays of Robert E. Sherwood," *Chrysalis*, X (1957), 3–14; Anne N. Lausch, "The Road to Rome by Way of Alexandria and Tavazzano," *ShawR*, VI (1963), 2–12; *idem*,

"Robert Sherwood's 'Heartbreak Houses,'" *ShawR*, VI (1963), 42–50; and R. Baird Shuman, "The Shifting Pacifism of Robert E. Sherwood," *SAQ*, LXV (1966), 382–389.

# BOOTH TARKINGTON

**1023.** COLLECTED WORKS

Alan S. Downer edited *On Plays, Playwrights, and Playgoers: Selections from the Letters of Booth Tarkington to George C. Tyler and John Peter Tooley, 1918–1925*, Princeton, N.J., 1959.

*Monsieur Beaucaire* (1900) was reprinted with a preface by J. Donald Adams, New York, 1963; *Seventeen* (1916) with an introduction by Bernard J. Weiss, New York, 1964; and *Alice Adams* (1921) with an afterword by Gerard P. Meyer, New York, 1961.

BIOGRAPHY AND CRITICISM

Brief critical studies are John D. Seeyle, "That Marvelous Boy—Penrod Once Again," *VQR*, XXXVII (1961), 591–604; James Woodress, "Popular Taste in 1899: Booth Tarkington's First Novel [*The Gentleman from Indiana*]," *Essays in American and English Literature*, ed. Max F. Schultz *et al.*, Athens, Ohio, 1968, pp. 108–121; and Abigail A. Hamblen, "Booth Tarkington's Classic of Adolescence [*Seventeen*]," *SHR*, III (1969), 225–231.

# (JOHN ORLEY) ALLEN TATE

**1024.** SEPARATE WORKS

Poetry: *Poems*, 1960.

Essays: *Collected Essays*, 1959; *Essays of Four Decades*, 1968.

Miscellaneous: *Modern Verse in English: 1900–1950* (edited with David Cecil), 1958; *Selected Poems of John Peale Bishop* (edited, with an introduction, by Tate), 1960; *The Arts of Learning* (edited with Ralph Ross and John Berryman), 1960; *Selected Poems of Denis Devlin* (edited with Robert Penn Warren), 1963; *T. S. Eliot: The Man and His Work: A Critical Evaluation by Twenty-Six Distinguished Writers* (edited by Tate), 1966; *The Complete Poems and Selected Criticism of Edgar Allan Poe* (edited by Tate), 1968.

Reprints: *The Fathers* (1938) was reprinted in Denver, Colo., 1960. *Reactionary Essays on Poetry and Ideas* (1936), *Reason in Madness: Critical Essays* (1941), and *The Hovering Fly and Other Essays* (1949) were reprinted in Freeport, N.Y., 1968. *Jefferson Davis* (1929) was reprinted in New York, 1969.

**1025.** BIOGRAPHY AND CRITICISM

The first biographical study is Radcliffe Squires's *Allen Tate: A Literary Biography*, New York, 1971.

Roger K. Meiners's *The Last Alternatives: A Study of the Works of Allen Tate*, Denver, Colo., 1963, is the first full-length critical treatment. It was followed by George Hemphill's pamphlet, *Allen Tate*, Minneapolis, Minn., 1964; Ferman Bishop's explication of "some of the most representative works of the various periods of Tate's career," *Allen Tate*, New York, 1967; and M. E. Bradford's pamphlet, *Rumors of Mortality: An Introduction to Allen Tate,* Dallas, Tex., 1969. See also, *passim,* John M. Bradbury, *The Fugitives: A Critical Account,* Chapel Hill, N.C., 1958; Louise Cowan, *The Fugitive Group: A Literary History*, Baton Rouge, La., 1959; John L. Stewart, *The Burden of Time: The Fugitives and Agrarians,* Princeton, N.J., 1965; and Rob Roy Purdy, ed., *Fugitives' Reunion: Conversations at Vanderbilt May 3–5, 1956,* Nashville, Tenn., 1959.

Briefer estimates are C. A. Ward, "Myths: Further Vanderbilt Agrarian Views," *UKCR*, XXV (1958), 53–56; Lillian Feder, "Allen Tate's Use of Classical Literature," *CRAS*, IV (1960), 89–114; Frank Kermode, "Old Orders Changing," *Encounter*, XV (1960), 72–76; Michael Millgate, "An Interview with Allen Tate," *Shen*, XII (1961), 27–34; Louis D. Rubin, Jr., "Allen Tate: The Arrogant Circumstance," *South: Modern Southern Literature in Its Cultural Setting*, ed. Louis D. Rubin, Jr., and Robert D. Jacobs, Garden City, N.Y., 1961, pp. 221–247; Carol Johnson, "The Heroism of the Rational: The Poetry of Allen Tate," *Ren*, XVII (1964), 89–96; Donald Davidson, "The Meaning of War: A Note on Allen Tate's 'To the Lacedemonians,'" *SoR*, I (1965), 720–730; Richard J. O'Dea, "The Poetry of Allen Tate," *Nine Essays in Modern Literature*, ed. Donald E. Stanford, Baton Rouge, La., 1965, pp. 145–158; *idem, "The Fathers*, a Revaluation," *TCL*, XII (1966), 87–95; *idem,* "Allen Tate's 'The Cross,'" *Ren*, XVIII (1966), 156–160; Ashley Brown, "Allen Tate as Satirist," *Shen,* XIX (1968), 44–54; Martin Newitz, "Tradition, Time, and Allen Tate," *MissQ*, XXI (1968), 37–42; Patricia Kane, "An Irrepressible Conflict: Allen Tate's *The Fathers*," *Crit*, X (1968), 9–16; and Frederick K. Sanders, "Theme and Structure in *The Fathers*," *ArlQ*, I (1967–68), 244–256.

*Sewanee Review*, LXVII (Autumn, 1959), is an "Homage to Allen Tate" issue. *Critique: Studies in Modern Fiction* published "an issue for Allen Tate," Vol. X, No. 2 (1968). It reprints Willard Thorp's 1942 checklist and follows it with James Korges's addendum to 1968, listing work by and about Tate. Marshall Fallwell, Jr. (with the assistance of Martha Cook and Francis Immler) edited *Allen Tate: A Bibliography*, New York, 1969, a checklist of "all of Tate's important writings and the most significant commentary about him through 1967."

## ALBION W(INEGAR) TOURGÉE

**1026. SEPARATE WORKS**

John Hope Franklin edited a new printing, with introduction, of *A Fool's Errand*, Cambridge, Mass., 1961.

**1027. BIOGRAPHY AND CRITICISM**

Two recent full-length studies are Theodore L. Gross's bio-critical *Albion W. Tourgée*, New York, 1963; and Otto H. Olsen's *Carpetbagger's Crusade: The Life of Albion Tourgée*, Baltimore, Md., 1965. See also Ted N. Weissbuch, "Albion W. Tourgée: Propagandist and Critic of Reconstruction," *OHQ*, LXX (1961), 27–44; Monte M. Olenick, "Albion W. Tourgée: Radical Republican Spokesman of the Civil War Crusade," *Phylon*, XXIII (1962), 332–345; Sidney Kaplan, "Albion W. Tourgée: Attorney for the Segregated," *JNH*, XLIX (1964), 128–133; and Dean H. Keller, ed., "A Civil War Diary of Albion W. Tourgée," *Ohio History*, LXXIV (1965), 99–131.

Dean H. Keller prepared "A Checklist of the Writings of Albion W. Tourgée (1838–1905)," *SB*, XVIII (1965), 269–279. See also *An Index to the Albion W. Tourgée Papers in the Chautauqua County Historical Society, Westfield, New York*, ed. Dean H. Keller (*Kent State University Bulletin*, LII, No. 5, May, 1964).

## CARL VAN VECHTEN
### *d. 1964*

**1027. SEPARATE WORKS**

Editions: *Gertrude Stein: Selected Writings*, 1962.

**BIOGRAPHY AND CRITICISM**

Edward Leuders followed his *Carl Van Vechten and the Twenties* (1955) with a concise critical biography, *Carl Van Vechten*, New York, 1965. A more ambitious study, in terms of full perspective, is Bruce Kellner's *Carl Van Vechten and the Irreverent Decades*, Norman, Okla., 1968.

Klaus W. Jones followed his 1955 bibliography with "Additions to the Bibliography of Carl Van Vechten," *PBSA*, LV (1961), 42–45.

# ROBERT PENN WARREN

**1028.** SEPARATE WORKS

Fiction: *The Cave*, 1959; *Wilderness: A Tale of the Civil War*, 1961; *Flood: A Romance of Our Time*, 1964; *Meet Me in the Green Glen*, 1971.

Poetry: *You, Emperors, and Others: Poems, 1957–1960*, 1960; *Selected Poems, New and Old, 1923–1966*, 1966; *Incarnations: Poems, 1966–1968*, 1968; *Audubon, A Vision*, 1969.

Plays: *All the King's Men*, 1960.

Essays: *The Legacy of the Civil War: Meditations on the Centennial*, 1961; *Who Speaks for the Negro?* 1965.

Miscellaneous: *The Scope of Fiction* (with Cleanth Brooks), 1960; *Faulkner: A Collection of Critical Essays* (edited by Warren), 1966; *Randall Jarrell, 1914–1965* (edited with Robert Lowell and Peter Taylor), 1967; *John Greenleaf Whittier's Poetry: An Appraisal and Selection*, 1971.

BIOGRAPHY AND CRITICISM

The first full-length study is Charles Bohner's *Robert Penn Warren*, New York, 1964. Paul West covers the whole career briefly in *Robert Penn Warren*, Minneapolis, Minn., 1964. Victor H. Strandberg concentrates on the development of major themes in *A Colder Fire: The Poetry of Robert Penn Warren*, Lexington, Ky., 1965. The most recent assessments of all of Warren's work are Leonard Casper, *Robert Penn Warren: The Dark and Bloody Ground*, Seattle, Wash., 1960; and John Lewis Longley, Jr., *Robert Penn Warren*, Austin, Tex., 1969. A study of the philosophical and social backgrounds of Warren's work is Klaus Poenicke, *Robert Penn Warren: Kunstwerk und Kritische Theorie*, Heidelberg, 1959.

Briefer essays are assembled by John Lewis Longley, Jr., ed., *Robert Penn Warren: A Collection of Critical Essays*, New York, 1965; and A. Fred Sochatoff *et al., All the King's Men: A Symposium* (Carnegie Series in English, No. 3), Pittsburgh, Pa., 1957. Maurice Beebe and L. A. Field edited *Robert Penn Warren's All the King's Men: A Critical Handbook*, Belmont, Calif., 1966. See also, *passim*, Rob Roy Purdy, ed., *Fugitives' Reunion: Conversations at Vanderbilt, May 3–5, 1956*, Nashville, Tenn., 1959; John M. Bradbury, *The Fugitives: A Critical Account*, Chapel Hill, N.C., 1958; Louise Cowan, *The Fugitive Group: A Literary History*,

Baton Rouge, La., 1959; Cleanth Brooks, *The Hidden God*, New Haven, Conn., 1963; and Chester E. Eisinger, *Fiction of the Forties*, Chicago, 1963.

Additional brief studies are Frederick P. W. McDowell, "The Romantic Tragedy of Self in *World Enough and Time*," *Crit*, I (1957), 34–48; Ralph Ellison and Eugene Walter, "The Art of Fiction: XVIII: Robert Penn Warren," *ParR*, IV (Spring–Summer, 1957), 112–140; Malcolm O. Sillars, "Warren's *All the King's Men*: A Study in Populism," *AQ*, IX (1957), 345–353; Floyd C. Watkins, "Billie Potts at the Fall of Time," *MissQ*, XI (1958), 19–28; Morgan Blum, "*Promises* as Fulfillment," *KR*, XXI (1959), 97–120; Alfred Kazin, "The Seriousness of Robert Penn Warren," *PR*, XXVI (1959), 312–316; John L. Stewart, "Robert Penn Warren and the Knot of History," *ELH*, XXVI (1959), 102–136; John Edward Hardy, "Robert Penn Warren's Double-Hero," *VQR*, XXXVI (1960), 583–597; Charles Kaplan, "Jack Burden: Modern Ishmael," *CE*, XXII (1960), 19–24; Roger Sale, "Having It Both Ways in *All the King's Men*," *HudR*, XIV (1961), 68–76; Alvan S. Ryan, "Robert Penn Warren's *Night Rider*: The Nihilism of the Isolated Temperament," *MFS*, VII (1961), 338–346; John Hicks, "Exploration of Value: Warren's Criticism," *SAQ*, LXII (1963), 508–515; M. L. Rosenthal, "Robert Penn Warren's Poetry," *SAQ*, LXII (1963), 499–507; John R. Strugnell, "Robert Penn Warren and the Uses of the Past," *REL*, IV (1963), 93–102; and especially Robert Penn Warren, "*All the King's Men*: The Matrix of Experience," *YR*, LIII (1964), 161–167.

More recent studies are James H. Justus, "The Use of Gesture in Warren's *The Cave*," *MLQ*, XXVI (1965), 448–461; *idem*, "The Mariner and Robert Penn Warren," *TSLL*, VIII (1966), 117–128; Arthur Mizener, "Robert Penn Warren: *All the King's Men*," *SoR*, III (1967), 874–894; John R. Moore, "Robert Penn Warren: You Must Go Home Again," *SoR*, IV (1968), 320–332; Victor Strandberg, "Warren's Osmosis," *Criticism*, X (1968), 23–40; L. Hugh Moore, Jr., "Robert Penn Warren and the Terror of Answered Prayer," *MissQ*, XXI (1968), 29–36; and Ladell Payne, "Willie Stark and Huey Long: Atmosphere, Myth, or Suggestion?," *AQ*, XX (1968), 580–595.

*Modern Fiction Studies*, VI (Spring, 1960) is a Robert Penn Warren issue, devoted to seven critical studies and Maurice Beebe and Erin Marcus's "Criticism of Robert Penn Warren: A Selected Checklist."

Mary Nance Huff compiled *Robert Penn Warren: A Bibliography*, New York, 1968, listing all of his work, collected and uncollected, through 1967, and 50 pages of books and articles about Warren.

# THORNTON (NIVEN) WILDER

**1030.** SEPARATE WORKS

Novels: *The Eighth Day*, 1967.

*Plays: *Someone from Assisi* (1962); *Infancy* (1962); *Childhood* (1962).

BIOGRAPHY AND CRITICISM

The first full-length study is Rex Burbank's *Thornton Wilder*, New York, 1961. It was followed by Malcolm Goldstein's *The Art of Thornton Wilder*, Lincoln, Neb., 1965; and Donald Haberman's *The Plays of Thornton Wilder: A Critical Study*, Middletown, Conn., 1967. Bernard Grebanier's *Thornton Wilder*, Minneapolis, Minn., 1964, is a pamphlet. The best German study is Helmut Papajewski, *Thornton Wilder*, Frankfurt am Main, 1961 (trans. John Conway, New York, 1968). Heinz Beckmann, *Thornton Wilder*, Velber bei Hannover, 1966, is concerned chiefly with the plays; Hermann Stresau, *Thornton Wilder*, Berlin, 1963, is a brief survey of the whole career.

Briefer estimates are Henry Morton Robinson, "The Curious Case of Thornton Wilder," *Esquire*, XLVII (Mar., 1957), 70–71, 124–126; Cyrille Arnavon, "La vogue de Thornton Wilder," *EA*, X (1957), 421–430; H. Wayne Morgan, "The Early Thornton Wilder," *SWR*, XLIII (1958), 245–253; Gerald Weales, "Unfashionable Optimist," *Cweal*, LXVII (1958), 486–488; Edmund Fuller, "Thornton Wilder: The Notation of the Heart," *ASch*, XXVIII (1959), 210–217; George D. Stephens, *"Our Town*—Great American Tragedy?," *MD*, I (1959), 258–264; Horst Frenz, "The Reception of Thornton Wilder's Plays in Germany," *MD*, III (1960), 123–137; John Modic, "The Eclectic Mr. Wilder," *BSTCF*, I (1961), 55–61; Flora Lewis, "Thornton Wilder at 65 Looks Ahead—and Back," *NYTM* (Apr. 15, 1962), pp. 28–29, 54, 56, 58; George Greene, "The World of Thornton Wilder," *Thought*, XXXVII (1962), 563–584; Heinz Kosok, "Thornton Wilder, Ein Literaturbericht," *JA*, IX (1964), 196–227; Hermine I. Popper, "The Universe of Thornton Wilder," *Harper's*, CCXXX (June, 1965), 72–78, 81; Franz H. Link, "Das Theater Thornton Wilders," *NS*, XIV (1965), 305–318; and Gerald Rabkin, *"The Skin of Our Teeth* and the Theatre of Thornton Wilder," *The Forties: Fiction, Poetry, Drama*, ed. Warren French, Deland, Fla., 1969.

For bibliographical listings see J. M. Edelstein, comp., *A Bibliographical Checklist of the Writings of Thornton Wilder*, New Haven, Conn., 1959; Heinz Kosok, "Thornton Wilder: A Bibliography of Criticism," *TCL*, IX

---

* Dates in parentheses are of production when publication has not occurred.

(1963), 93–100; and Jackson R. Bryer, "Thornton Wilder and the Reviewers," *PBSA*, LVIII (1964), 34–49.

# EDMUND WILSON
*d. 1973*

**1032. SEPARATE WORKS**

Autobiography: *A Prelude: Landscapes, Characters and Conversations from the Earlier Years of My Life*, 1967.

Criticism: *The Bit Between My Teeth: A Literary Chronicle of 1950–1965*, 1965; *The Fruits of the MLA*, 1968.

Plays and Dialogues: *The Duke of Palermo and Other Plays*, 1969.

Essays and Poems: *Night Thoughts*, 1961.

Essays: History and Travel: *Apologies to the Iroquois*, 1960; *Patriotic Gore: Studies in the Literature of the American Civil War*, 1962; *The Cold War and the Income Tax: A Protest*, 1963; *O Canada: An American's Notes on Canadian Culture*, 1965; *The Dead Sea Scrolls, 1947–1969*, 1969; *Upstate: Records and Recollections of Northern New York*, 1971.

## BIOGRAPHY AND CRITICISM

Sherman Paul's *Edmund Wilson: A Study of Literary Vocation in Our Time*, Urbana, Ill., 1965, is an intellectual biography with emphasis on Wilson's cultural role. Charles P. Frank, *Edmund Wilson*, New York, 1970, is an assessment of the author's whole work, a task Warner Berthoff tries to encompass in even briefer space in *Edmund Wilson*, Minneapolis, Minn., 1968.

.Other estimates are Robert E. Spiller, "The Influence of Edmund Wilson," *Nation*, CLXXXVI (1958), 159–161; Richard Chase, "Wilson as Critic," *Nation*, CLXXXVI (1958), 161, 164, 166; Alfred Kazin, "The Historian as Reporter: Edmund Wilson and the 1930's," *Reporter*, XVIII (Mar. 20, 1958), 43–46; Norman Podhoretz, "Edmund Wilson, the Last Patrician," *Reporter*, XIX (Dec. 25, 1958), 25–28; XX (Jan. 8, 1959), 32–35; R. J. Kaufmann, "The Critic as Custodian of Sanity: Edmund Wilson," *CritQ*, I (1959), 85–98; Lewis M. Dabney, "Edmund Wilson and *Patriotic Gore*," *CUF*, V (1962), 20–26; Keith Botsford, "The American Plutarch, the Last Roman, or Plain Mr. Wilson," *TQ*, VI (1963), 129–140; Allesandro Pellegrini, "L'opera critica di Edmund Wilson," *OPL*, XI (1965), 69–96; Frank Kermode, "Edmund Wilson's Achievement," *Encounter*, XXVI (1966), 61–70.

Richard David Ramsey's *Edmund Wilson: A Bibliography*, New York, 1971, is "a comprehensive list of his writings as well as the most important commentary about them."

# BIBLIOGRAPHIES: ADDITIONAL INDIVIDUAL AUTHORS

Edward Albee
W. H. Auden
Saul Bellow
Lillian Hellman
Randall Jarrell
Robert Lowell
Norman Mailer
F. O. Matthiessen
Arthur Miller
Flannery O'Connor
Katherine Anne Porter
Theodore Roethke
John Updike
Eudora Welty
Richard Wilbur
Tennessee Williams

# EDWARD ALBEE
*b. 1928*

SEPARATE WORKS

*Plays: *The Zoo Story* (1959), 1960; *The Death of Bessie Smith*, 1960;
*The Sandbox*, 1960; *The American Dream* (1960), 1961; *Fam and Yam*
(1960); *Who's Afraid of Virginia Woolf?*, 1962; *Tiny Alice* (1964),
1965; *A Delicate Balance*, 1966; *Box* (1968), 1969; *Quotations from
Chairman Mao Tse-tung* (1968), 1969; *All Over*, 1971.

Adaptations: *Bartleby* (iibretto with James Hinton, Jr., from the story
by Herman Melville) (1961); *The Ballad of the Sad Café* (from the novel
by Carson McCullers), 1963; *Malcolm* (from the novel by James Purdy),
1966; *Everything in the Garden* (from the play by Giles Cooper) (1967),
1968.

BIOGRAPHY AND CRITICISM

Biographical gleanings can be found in the volumes by Richard E.
Amacher and C. W. E. Bigsby cited below. Two lengthy conversations with
the author are recorded in Digby Diehl, "Edward Albee Interviewed,"
*TransR*, No. 13 (1963), pp. 57–72; and William Flanagan, "The Art of
the Theatre: IV: Edward Albee, An Interview," *ParR*, XXXIX (1966),
92–121. See also the last chapter of the volume by Michael E. Rutenberg
cited below; and R. S. Stewart, ed., "John Gielgud and Edward Albee Talk
about the Theatre," *Atl*, CCXV (1965), 61–68.

The first full-length study is Gilbert Debusscher's *Edward Albee: Tradi-
tion and Renewal* (translated from the French by Anne D. Williams),
Brussels, 1967. Richard E. Amacher surveys the whole career in *Edward
Albee*, New York, 1969, as does Michael E. Rutenberg in *Edward Albee:
Playwright in Protest*, New York, 1969. Ruby Cohn's *Edward Albee*, Minneapolis, Minn., 1969, is a pamphlet. Two European studies, both concentrating on *Virginia Woolf* and *Tiny Alice*, are C. W. E. Bigsby, *Albee*,
Edinburgh, 1969; and Ruth Eva Schulz-Seitz, *Edward Albee, der Dich-
terphilosoph der Bühne*, Frankfurt am Main, 1966. See also, *passim*,
Martin Esslin, *The Theatre of the Absurd*, Garden City, N.Y., 1961; Walter Kerr, *The Theater in Spite of Itself*, New York, 1963; and Robert

---

* Dates in parentheses are of production when it differs from publication or when publication has not occurred.

Brustein, *The Theatre of Revolt: An Approach to Modern Drama*, Boston, 1964.

Earlier criticism can be found in Tom Prideaux, "The Albee Attitude, Both Sweet and Sour," *Life*, LIII (Dec. 14, 1962), 110; Rose A. Zimbardo, "Symbolism and Naturalism in Edward Albee's *The Zoo Story*," *TCL*, VIII (1962), 10–17; Marya Mannes, "The Half World of American Drama," *Rep,* XXVIII (Apr. 25, 1963), 48; Diana Trilling, "Who's Afraid of the Culture Elite?," *Esquire*, LX (1963), 69–88; Alfred Chester, "Edward Albee: Red Herrings and White Whales," *Com*, XXXV (1963), 296–301; Richard Schechner, "Who's Afraid of Edward Albee?," *TDR*, VII (1963), 7–10; and Alan Schneider, "Why So Afraid?," *TDR*, VII (1963), 10–13; Rubem Rocha Filho, "Albee: Processo e tentativa," *Tempo Brasileiro*, No. 3 (1963), pp. 161–172; Diana Trilling, "The Riddle of Albee's *Who's Afraid of Virginia Woolf?*," *Claremont Essays*, New York, 1964, pp. 203–227; Tom F. Driver, "What's the Matter with Edward Albee?," *Rep*, XXX (Jan. 2, 1964), 38–39; Wendell V. Harris, "Morality, Absurdity, and Albee," *SWR*, XLIX (1964), 249–256; Allan Lewis, "The Fun and Games of Edward Albee," *ETJ*, XVI (1964), 29–39; Walter C. Daniel, "Absurdity in *The Death of Bessie Smith*," *CLAJ*, VIII (1964), 76–80; Karl O. Paetel, "Edward Albee und das 'Theater des Absurden,'" *NSammlung,* IV (1964), 282–287; Mario Corona, "Edward Albee," *SA*, X (1964), 369–394; Robert Brustein, *Seasons of Discontent*, New York, 1965, pp. 28–29 ff.; Lee Baxandall, "The Theatre of Edward Albee," *TDR*, IX (1965), 19–40; Thomas B. Markus, "*Tiny Alice* and Tragic Catharsis," *ETJ*, XVII (1965), 225–233; Emil Roy, "*Who's Afraid of Virginia Woolf?* and the Tradition," *BuR*, XIII (1965), 27–36; Peter Wolfe, "The Social Theatre of Edward Albee," *PrS*, XXXIX (1965), 248–262; Melvin L. Plotinsky, "The Transformations of Understanding: Edward Albee in the Theatre of the Irresolute," *DramS*, IV (1965), 220–232; Peter Spielberg, "The Albatross in Albee's Zoo," *CE*, XXVII (1966), 562–565; F. Anthony Macklin, "The Flagrant Albatross," *CE*, XXVIII (1966), 58–59; and Peter Spielberg, "Reply: The Albatross Strikes Again!," *CE*, XXVIII (1966), 59.

More recent estimates are Leighton M. Ballew, "Who's Afraid of Tiny Alice?," *GaR*, XX (1966), 292–299; Bernard F. Dukore, "Tiny Albee," *DramS*, V (1966), 60–66; John W. Markson, "*Tiny Alice*: Edward Albee's Negative Oedipal Enigma," *AI*, XXIII (1966), 3–21; Arthur K. Oberg, "Edward Albee: His Language and Imagination," *PrS*, XL (1966), 139–146; Sharon D. Spencer, "Edward Albee: The Anger Artist," *ForumH*, IV (1967), 25–30; Arthur Evans, "Love, History and Edward Albee," *Ren*, XIX (1967), 115–118, 131; Paul Witherington, "Language of Movement in Albee's *The Death of Bessie Smith*," *TCL*, XIII (1967), 84–88; Jean Gould, "Pauvre petit garçon riche," *CRB*, LXIII (1967), 11–17; Louis Paul, "A Game Analysis of Albee's *Who's Afraid of Virginia Woolf?*: The Core of Grief," *L&P*, XVII (1967), 47–51; Randolph Goodman, "Playwatching with a Third Eye," *CUF*, X (1967), 18–22; Henry Knepler, "Edward Albee: Conflict of Tradition," *MD*, X (1967), 274–279; Linda L. Woods, "Isolation and the Barrier of Language in *The Zoo Story*," *RS*, XXXVI (1968), 224–231; Richard A. Davidson, "Edward Albee's *Tiny Alice*: A Note of Re-examination," *MD*, XI (1968), 54–60; and C. W. Bigsby, "The Strategy of Madness: An Analysis of Edward Albee's *A Delicate Balance*," *WSCL*, IX (1968), 223–235.

BIBLIOGRAPHY

Margaret W. Rule has assembled "An Edward Albee Bibliography," *TCL*, XIV (1968), 35–44.

# W(YSTAN) H(UGH) AUDEN
## *1907–1973*

SEPARATE WORKS

Poetry: *Poems*, 1930; *The Orators: An English Study*, 1932 (revised in 1966); *Poems* (second edition), 1933; *Look, Stranger!*, 1936 (American edition titled *On This Island*, 1937); *Letters from Iceland* (with Louis MacNeice), 1937 (revised in 1967); *Journey to a War* (with Christopher Isherwood), 1939; *Another Time*, 1940; *The Double Man*, 1941 (English edition titled *New Year Letter*, 1941); *For the Time Being: A Christmas Oratorio*, 1944; *The Collected Poetry*, 1945; *The Age of Anxiety: A Baroque Eclogue*, 1947; *Collected Shorter Poems 1930–1944*, 1950; *Nones*, 1951; *The Shield of Achilles*, 1955; *Homage to Clio*, 1960; *About the House*, 1965; *Collected Shorter Poems 1927–1957*, 1966; *Collected Longer Poems*, 1968; *City without Walls*, 1969.

*Poems*, 1934 is the first American edition of Auden's work and contains *The Orators, The Dance of Death*, and *Poems*, 1933. *Selected Poems*, 1938, were not chosen by Auden, nor were *Some Poems*, 1940; both volumes are reprintings of earlier verse. *Selected Poetry*, 1958, selected and edited by Auden, was published by Penguin Books in England and by Random House in New York. *W. H. Auden: A Selection* (London, 1965) was edited, with notes and a critical essay, by Richard Hoggart.

Prose: *Education, Today and Tomorrow* (with T. C. Worsley), 1939; *The Enchaféd Flood, or, The Romantic Iconography of the Sea*, 1950;

*Making, Knowing, and Judging* [Inaugural Lecture, Oxford University], 1956; *The Dyer's Hand and Other Essays*, 1962; *Selected Essays*, 1964; *Secondary Worlds* [Eliot Memorial Lectures], 1968; *A Certain World: A Commonplace Book*, 1970.

Plays: *The Dance of Death*, 1933; *The Dog Beneath the Skin* (with Christopher Isherwood), 1935; *The Ascent of F6* (with Christopher Isherwood), 1936; *On the Frontier* (with Christopher Isherwood), 1938.

Libretti: *Paul Bunyan* (unpublished; performed 1941); *The Rake's Progress* (with Chester Kallman), 1951; *Delia, or a Masque of Night* (with Chester Kallman), 1953; *Elegy for Young Lovers* (with Chester Kallman), 1961; *The Bassarids* (with Chester Kallman), 1966.

Translations: *No More Peace!* by Ernst Toller (lyrics translated and adapted by Auden, text translated by Edward Crankshaw), 1937; *The Magic Flute* (with Chester Kallman), 1956; *Don Giovanni* (with Chester Kallman), 1961; *Italian Journey: 1786-1788* by Johann Wolfgang von Goethe (with Elizabeth Mayer), 1962; *Markings* by Dag Hammarskjöld (with Leif Sjöberg), 1964; *Two Addresses* by St. John Perse (with Robert Fitzgerald), 1966; *Antiworlds* by Andrei Voznesensky (with others), 1966.

Editions: *Oxford Poetry 1926* (with Charles Plumb), 1926; *Oxford Poetry 1927* (with Cecil Day Lewis), 1927; *The Poet's Tongue: An Anthology* (with John Garrett), 1935; *The Oxford Book of Light Verse*, 1938; *A Selection from the Poems of Alfred, Lord Tennyson*, 1944; *The American Scene* by Henry James, 1946; *Slick But Not Streamlined: Poems and Short Pieces* by John Betjeman, 1947; *The Portable Greek Reader*, 1948; *Poets of the English Language* (with Norman Holmes Pearson), 5 vols., 1950; *Edgar Allan Poe: Selected Poetry and Prose*, 1950; *The Living Thoughts of Kierkegaard*, 1952; *An Elizabethan Song Book* (with Chester Kallman and Noah Greenberg), 1955; *Selected Writings of Sydney Smith*, 1956; *The Faber Book of Modern American Verse* (American edition titled *The Criterion Book of Modern American Verse*), 1956; *Van Gogh: A Self-Portrait*, 1961; *The Viking Book of Aphorisms* (with Louis Kronenberger; English edition titled *The Faber Book of Aphorisms*), 1962; *A Choice of De la Mare's Verse*, 1963; *Nineteenth-Century British Minor Poets* (with George R. Creeger), 1966; *To Nevill Coghill from Friends* (with John Lawlor), 1966.

Between 1947-1957, Auden was editor of the Yale Series of Younger Poets.

Miscellaneous: *Ballad of Heroes*, for tenor or soprano solo, chorus, and orchestra (with Randall Swingler; music by Benjamin Britten), 1939; *The Duchess of Malfi* by John Webster (adapted with Bertolt Brecht and H. R. Hays), 1941; *The Play of Daniel* (narration by Auden, edited by Noah Greenberg, translation by Jean Misrahi), 1959.

BIOGRAPHY AND CRITICISM

In lieu of a biography, these autobiographical volumes by friends of Auden are useful: Christopher Isherwood, *Lions and Shadows: An Education in the Twenties,* London, 1937; Cyril Connolly, *Enemies of Promise,* London, 1938; John Lehmann, *The Whispering Gallery,* New York, 1955; Cecil Day Lewis, *The Buried Day,* New York, 1960; and Stephen Spender, *World within World,* London, 1951.

Three brief studies serve as introductions for the reader new to Auden's work: Francis Scarfe, *W. H. Auden,* Monaco, 1949; Richard Hoggart, *W. H. Auden,* London, 1957; Barbara Everett, *Auden,* Edinburgh, 1964; and George T. Wright, *W. H. Auden,* New York, 1969. The first full-scale treatment is Richard Hoggart's admirable book, *Auden: An Introductory Essay,* London, 1951, which he modestly calls "middleman's work," aimed at sending the reader back to the poetry better informed, no longer needing the critic. The most comprehensive study, invaluable in every respect, is Monroe K. Spears, *The Poetry of W. H. Auden: The Disenchanted Island,* New York, 1963. Spears had the poet's cooperation in preparing this survey of a whole career—his operas, plays, songs, and criticism as well as his poetry. Three more recent studies, all commendable, are John G. Blair, *The Poetic Art of W. H. Auden,* Princeton, N.J., 1965; Herbert Greenberg, *The Quest for the Necessary: W. H. Auden and the Dilemma of Divided Consciousness,* Cambridge, Mass., 1968; and Justin Replogle, *Auden's Poetry,* Seattle, Wash., 1969. Two volumes concentrating on Auden's work since 1945 are George W. Bahlke, *The Later Auden,* New Brunswick, N.J., 1970; and Gerald Nelson, *Changes of Heart: A Study of the Poetry of W. H. Auden,* Berkeley, Calif., 1969. John Fuller's *A Reader's Guide to W. H. Auden,* New York, 1970, is a chronological survey of Auden's poetry and drama designed "to help the reader with difficult passages and to trace some of the sources and allusions."

*The Making of the Auden Canon* by Joseph Warren Beach (Minneapolis, Minn., 1957), a highly specialized textual study, is "meant to be a record of the facts in regard to W. H. Auden's procedure in making up the texts of the *Collected Poetry* (Random House, 1945) and the *Collected Shorter Poems* (Faber and Faber, 1950)." It is also a strangely biased interpretation of Auden's career, almost hostile in tone.

Monroe Spears argues that "most good criticism of Auden is recent" and as illustration reprints the work of 13 critics plus a valuable introduction in *Auden: A Collection of Critical Essays* (Englewood Cliffs, N.J., 1964). His selection concentrates on the last two decades. Among early critical estimates are Morton Dauwen Zabel, "A Dawn in Britain," *Poetry,* XXXVIII (1931), 101–104; Malcolm Cowley, "Spender and Auden," *NR,* LXXX (Sept. 26, 1934), 189–190; Edith Sitwell, *Aspects of Modern*

*Poetry*, London, 1934, pp. 227–264; A. J. M. Smith, "Old Game, New Rules," *Poetry*, XLVII (1935), 43–46; the "English Number" of *Poetry* (Jan., 1937) and the "Auden Double Number" of *New Verse* (Nov., 1937); James J. Southworth, "Wystan Hugh Auden," *SR*, XLVI (1938), 189–205; Stephen Spender, "The Poetic Dramas of W. H. Auden and Christopher Isherwood," *New Writings*, n.s., I (1938), 102–108; Delmore Schwartz, "The Two Audens," *KR*, I (1939), 34–45; J. Symons, "Auden and Poetic Drama," *Life and Letters Today*, XX (1939), 70–79; David Daiches, "W. H. Auden: The Search for a Public," *Poetry*, LIV (1939), 148–156; and Cleanth Brooks, *Modern Poetry and the Tradition*, Chapel Hill, NC., 1939, pp. 110–135.

Throughout the 1930's, F. R. Leavis attacked Auden in the pages of *Scrutiny* and in both editions of his *New Bearings in English Poetry*. On this side of the Atlantic, fellow-poet Randall Jarrell continued the assault in "Changes of Attitude and Rhetoric in Auden's Poetry," *SoR*, VII (1941), 326–349; and "Freud to Paul: The Stages of Auden's Ideology," *PR*, XII (1945), 437–457. Other views are D. S. Savage, "The Poet's Perspectives," *Poetry*, LXIV (1944), 148–158; Dan S. Norton, "Auden's Poetry," *VQR*, XXI (1945), 434–441; Ruth Lechlitner, "The Odyssey of Auden," *Poetry*, LXVI (1945), 204–215; Donald A. Stauffer, " 'Which Side Am I Supposed to Be On?': The Search for Beliefs in W. H. Auden's Poetry," *VQR*, XXII (1946), 570–580; John Bradbury, "Auden and the Tradition," *WR*, XII (1948), 223–229; D. M. Anderson, "Aspects of Auden," *Landfall*, III (1949), 270–279; Robert Fitzgerald, "An Heir and His Inheritance," *HudR*, IV (1951), 309–314; Robert Roth, "The Sophistication of W. H. Auden: A Sketch in Longinian Method," *MP*, XLVIII (1951), 193–204; Jacques Vallette, "W. H. Auden: Aspectes d'un inquiétude," *LanM*, XLV (1951), 153–165; Howard Griffin, "Conversation on Cornelia Street: A Dialog with W. H. Auden," *Poetry*, LXXXIII (1953), 96–106; Morton Seif, "The Impact of T. S. Eliot on Auden and Spender," *SAQ*, LIII (1954), 61–69; Jean Weisgerber, "W. H. Auden as a Critic," *RLV*, X (1955), 116–125; W. W. Robson, "Mr. Auden's Profession," *TC*, CLXI (1957), 255–263; Edward Callan, "The Development of Auden's Poetic Theory since 1940," *TCL*, IV (1958), 79–91; Nathan A. Scott, Jr., "The Poetry of Auden," *ChiR*, XIII (1959), 53–75; and Gerhard Stebner, "W. H. Auden *The Ascent of F6*: Interpretation eines Dramas," *NS* (1961), 397–413.

More recent estimates are F. W. Cook, "Primordial Auden," *EIC*, XII (1962), 402–412; Donna Gerstenberger, "Poetry and Politics: The Verse Drama of Auden and Isherwood," *MD*, V (1962), 123–132; Chris Wallace-Crabbe," Auden's *New Year Letter* and the Fate of Long Poems,"

*MCR* (1962), 128–136; John Bayley, "Our Northern Manichee," *Encounter*, XXI (1963), 74–81; Frederick P. W. McDowell, " 'Subtle, Various, Ornamental, Clever': Auden in His Recent Poetry," *WSCL*, III (1962), 29–44: Cleanth Brooks, "W. H. Auden as a Critic," *KR*, XXVI (1964), 173–189; G. S. Fraser, "Auden: The Composite Giant," *Shen*, XV (1964), 46–59; George T. Wright, "A General View of Auden's Poetry," *TSL*, X (1965), 43–64; Robert Bloom, "W. H. Auden's Bestiary of the Human," *VQR*, XLII (1966), 207–233; Edward Callan, "Auden's Ironic Masquerade: Criticism as Morality Play," *UTQ*, XXXV (1966), 133–143; Philip Toynbee, "Ou est-on mieux que chez soi? A propos de *About the House*, par W. H. Auden," *TR*, No. 220 (1966), pp. 143–146; Lee M. Whitehead, "Art as Communion: Auden's 'The Sea and the Mirror,' " *Per*, XIV (1966), 171–178; W. H. Sellers, "New Light on Auden's *The Orators*," *PMLA*, LXXII (1967), 455–464; Polly Pratt, "W. H. Auden [Interview]," *ASch*, XXXVI (1967), 266–270; Kenneth Lewars, "Auden's Swarthmore Chart," *ConnR*, I (1968), 44–56; Edward Mendelsohn, "The Coherence of Auden's *The Orators*," *ELH*, XXXV (1968), 114–133; Robert Bloom, "The Humanization of Auden's Early Style," *PMLA*, LXXXIII (1968), 443–454; Paul Goetsch, "W. H. Auden und Amerika," *JA*, XIII (1968), 215–227; and Barbara Hardy, "W. H. Auden, *Thirties to Sixties: A Face and a Map*," *SoR*, V (1969), 655–672.

*Shenandoah*, XVIII (1967), devoted to the work of Auden, includes essays by Anne Freemantle, Bonamy Dobrée, Carl Izzo, Julian Symons, and Monroe K. Spears, among others.

### BIBLIOGRAPHY

Perhaps the earliest bibliographical listing is "Writings by W. H. Auden," in *New Verse*, Nos. 26–27 (Nov., 1937), pp. 32–46. Joseph P. Clancy provided "A W. H. Auden Bibliography, 1924–1955" in *Thought*," XXX (Summer, 1955), 260–270.

Edward Callan's *An Annotated Check List of the Works of W. H. Auden*, Denver, Colo., 1958, first appeared in *Twentieth Century Literature*, IV (Apr., 1958), 30–50. It does not list the appearance of Auden's poems in periodicals, a deficiency compensated for in Monroe K. Spears's *The Poetry of W. H. Auden*, which also includes a first-line index to and a printing history of each poem.

B. C. Bloomfield, a British scholar, has published the full-scale bibliographical treatment of Auden's work: *W. H. Auden: A Bibliography: The Early Years through 1955*, Charlottesville, Va., 1964. It includes a listing of selected reviews and criticism as well as all the standard information.

## SAUL BELLOW
### b. 1915

SEPARATE WORKS

Novels: *Dangling Man*, 1944; *The Victim*, 1947; *The Adventures of Augie March*, 1953; *Seize the Day,* 1956; *Henderson the Rain King*, 1959; *Herzog*, 1964; *Mr. Sammler's Planet*, 1970.

Short Stories: *Mosby's Memoirs and Other Stories*, 1968.

Plays: *The Wrecker* (1954) was collected in *Seize the Day. The Last Analysis* was produced in 1964, revised and published in 1965.

BIOGRAPHY AND CRITICISM

Three brief introductions to Bellow's work are Tony Tanner, *Saul Bellow*, New York, 1965; Earl Rovit, *Saul Bellow*, Minneapolis, Minn., 1967; and Robert Detweiler, *Saul Bellow: A Critical Essay*, Grand Rapids, Mich., 1967. The first full-length studies are Keith Michael Opdahl, *The Novels of Saul Bellow: An Introduction*, University Park, Pa., 1967; and Pierre Dommergues, *Saul Bellow*, Paris, 1967. More recent books are John Jacob Clayton, *Saul Bellow: In Defense of Man*, Bloomington, Ind., 1968, and Irving Malin, *Saul Bellow's Fiction*, Carbondale, Ill., 1969. Malin has also edited a collection of 12 essays, *Saul Bellow and the Critics*, New York, 1967.

Early estimates are Malcolm Cowley, "Naturalism: No Teacup Tragedies," *The Literary Situation*, New York, 1954, pp. 74-95; Reuben Frank, "Saul Bellow: The Evolution of a Contemporary Novelist," *WR*, XVIII (1954), 101-112; John W. Aldridge, "The Society of Three Novels," *In Search of Heresy*, New York, 1956, 126-148; Piero Sanavio, "Il romanzo di Saul Bellow," *SA* No. 2 (1956), pp. 261-284; Leslie Fielder, "Saul Bellow," *PrS*, XXXI (1957), 103-110; Edmund Bergler, "Writers of Half-Talent," *AI*, XIV (1957), 155-164; Leslie Fiedler, "The Breakthrough: The American Jewish Novelist and the Fictional Image of the Jew," *Mid*, IV (1958), 15-35; Chester E. Eisinger, "Saul Bellow: Love and Identity," *Accent*, XVIII (1958), 179-203; Maxwell Geismar, "Saul Bellow: Novelist of the Intellectuals," *American Moderns*, New York, 1958, pp. 210-224; Richard Chase, "The Adventures of Saul Bellow: Progress of a Novelist," *Com*, XXVII (1959), 323-330; Herbert Gold, "Fiction of the Fifties," *HR*, XII (1959), 192-201; Paul Levine, "Saul Bellow: The Affirmation of the Philosophical Fool," *Per*, X (1959), 163-176; Alfred Kazin, "The Alone Generation," *Harper's*, CCXIX (Oct., 1959), 127-131; Anthony Quinton, "The Adventures of Saul Bellow, *LonM*, VI (1959), 55-59; Theodore Ross, "Notes on Saul Bellow," *CJF*, XVIII (1959),

21-27; Irving Howe, "Mass Society and Post-Modern Fiction," *A World More Attractive*, New York, 1963, pp. 77-97; Ralph Freedman, "Saul Bellow: The Illusion of Environment," *WSCL*, I (1960), 50-65; Ihab Hassan, "Saul Bellow: Five Faces of a Hero," *Crit*, III (1960), 28-36; J. C. Levenson, "Bellow's Dangling Man," *Crit*, III (1960), 3-14; Cyrille Arnavon, "Le roman africain de Saul Bellow: *Henderson the Rain King*," *EA*, XIV (1961), 25-35; Daniel Hughes, "Reality and the Hero: *Lolita* and *Henderson the Rain King*," *MFS*, VI (1960-1961), 345-364; Alfred Kazin, "The World of Saul Bellow," *Contemporaries*, Boston, 1962, pp. 217-233; Marcus Klein, "A Discipline of Nobility: Saul Bellow's Fiction," *KR*, XXIV (1962), 203-226; Jack Ludwig, *Recent American Novelists*, Minneapolis, Minn., 1962, pp. 7-18; Daniel Weiss, "Caliban on Prospero: A Psychoanalytic Study of the Novel 'Seize the Day' by Saul Bellow," *AI*, XIX (1962), 277-306; Malcolm Bradbury, "Saul Bellow and the Naturalist Tradition," *REL*, IV (1963), 80-92; and Robert G. Davis, "The American Individualist Tradition: Bellow and Styron," *The Creative Present*, ed. N. Balakian and C. Simmons, New York, 1963, pp. 111-141.

More recent estimates are Denis Donoghue, "Commitment and the Dangling Man," *Studies: An Irish Quarterly Review*, LIII (1964), 174-187; Frederick J. Hoffman, "The Fool of Experience: Saul Bellow's Fiction," *Contemporary American Novelists*, Carbondale, Ill., 1964, pp. 80-94; Norman Podhoretz, "The Adventures of Saul Bellow," *Doings and Undoings*, New York, 1964, pp. 205-227; Brian Way, "Character and Society in *The Adventures of Augie March*," *BAASB*, No. 8 (1964), pp. 36-44; George Garrett, "To Do Right in a Bad World: Saul Bellow's Herzog," *HC*, II (1965), 1-12; Jonathan Baumbach, "The Double Vision: *The Victim* by Saul Bellow," *The Landscape of Nightmare*, New York, 1965, pp. 35-54; Richard Poirier, "Bellows to Herzog," *PR*, XXXII (1965), 264-271; Agostino Lombardo, "La narrativa di Saul Bellow," *SA*, XI (1965), 309-344; Francesco Binni, "Percorso narrativo di Saul Bellow," *Ponte*, XXII (1966), 831-842; Robert H. Fossum, "The Devil and Saul Bellow," *CLS*, III (1966), 197-206; Norman Mailer, "Some Children of the Goddess," *Cannibals and Christians*, New York, 1966, pp. 104-130; Maurice Samuels, "My Friend, the Late Moses Herzog," *Mid*, XII (1966), 3-25; Monique Nathan, "Saul Bellow," *Esprit*, XXXIV (1966), 363-370; David Galloway, *The Absurd Hero in American Fiction*, Austin, Tex., 1966, pp. 82-139; Sheridan Baker, "Saul Bellow's Bout with Chivalry," *Criticism*, IX (1967), 109-122; Abraham Chapman, "The Image of Man as Portrayed by Saul Bellow," *CLAJ*, X (1967), 285-298; Gordon L. Harper, "Saul Bellow," *Writers at Work: The Paris Review Interviews*: 3rd ser., New York, 1967, pp. 175-196; Hélène Cixous, "Situation de Saul Bellow," *LetN* (1967), 130-145; Patrick Morrow, "Threat and Accommodation: The Novels of Saul Bellow," *MQ*, VIII (1967), 389–411; Irvin Stock, "The Novels of Saul Bellow," *SoR*, III (1967), 13–42; Stanley Trachtenberg, "Saul Bellow's *Luftmenschen*: The Compromise with Reality," *Criticism*, IX (1967), 37–61; W. M. Frohock, "Saul Bellow and His Penitent Picaro," *SWR*, LIV (1968), 36–44; Robert Shulman, "The Style of Bellow's Comedy," *PMLA*, LXXXIII (1968), 109–117; and Nathan A. Scott, Jr., "*Sola Gratia*: The Principle of Bellow's Fiction," *Adversity and Grace: Studies in Recent American Literature*, Chicago, 1968, pp. 27–57.

BIBLIOGRAPHY

The first published listing is Harold W. Schneider, "Two Bibliographies: Saul Bellow and William Styron," *Crit*, III (Summer, 1960), 71–91. Fuller listings are in David Galloway, *The Absurd Hero in American Fiction*, Austin, 1966, pp. 210–226; Keith Michael Opdahl, *The Novels of Saul Bellow*, University Park, Pa., 1967, pp. 181–193; and Pierre Dommergues, *Saul Bellow*, Paris, 1967, pp. 235–241.

# LILLIAN HELLMAN
*b. 1905*

SEPARATE WORKS

*Plays: *The Children's Hour*, 1934; *Days to Come* (1936), 1937; *The Little Foxes*, 1939; *Watch on the Rhine*, 1941; *The Searching Wind*, 1944; *Another Part of the Forest* (1946), 1947; *The Autumn Garden*, 1951; *Toys in the Attic*, 1960.

Screenplays: *The Dark Angel* (with Mordaunt Shairp), 1935; *These Three*, 1936; *Dead End*, 1937; *The Little Foxes*, 1941; *The North Star*, 1943; *The Searching Wind*, 1946; *The Chase*, 1966.

Adaptations: *Montserrat* (from the French play by Emmanuel Roblès) (1949), 1950; *The Lark* (from the French play by Jean Anouilh) (1955), 1956; *Candide* (a comic operetta with Richard Wilbur and Leonard Bernstein, from the French tale by Voltaire) (1956), 1957; *My Mother, My Father and Me* (from the novel *How Much?* by Burt Blechman) (1963).

Autobiography: *An Unfinished Woman: A Memoir*, 1969.

Editions: *The Selected Letters of Anton Chekhov*, 1955; *The Big Knockover: Selected Stories and Short Novels* by Dashiell Hammett, 1966.

* Dates in parentheses are of production when it differs from publication or when publication has not occurred.

BIOGRAPHY AND CRITICISM

The first critical biography is Richard Moody, *Lillian Hellman: Playwright*, Indianapolis, Ind., 1971.

Critical studies include George Jean Nathan, "Playwrights in Petticoats," *AmMerc*, LII (1941), 750–752; Charlotte Hughes, "Women Playmakers," *NYTM*, XXVII (May 4, 1941), 10–11 ff.; Margaret Case Harriman, "Miss Lily of New Orleans," *NY*, XVII (Nov. 8, 1941), 22–26; Edith J. R. Isaacs, "Lillian Hellman, a Playwright on the March," *TArts*, XXVIII (1944), 19–24; John Mason Brown, "A New Miss Hellman," *SRL*, XXXIV (Mar. 31, 1951), 27–29; Richard G. Stern, "Lillian Hellman on Her Plays," *Contact*, No. 3 (1959), pp. 113–119; Marvin Felheim, "*The Autumn Garden*: Mechanics and Dialectics," *MD*, III (1960), 191–195; Thomas Meehan, "Q: Miss Hellman, What's Wrong with Broadway; A: It's a Bore," *Esquire*, LVIII (1962), 140–142 ff.; Jacob Adler, II, "Miss Hellman's Two Sisters," *ETJ*, XV (1963), 112–117; and John Phillips and Anne Hollander, "Lillian Hellman," *Writers at Work; The Paris Review Interviews*: 3rd ser., New York, 1967.

BIBLIOGRAPHY

Manfred Triesch, *The Lillian Hellman Collection at the University of Texas*, Austin, Tex., 1966, is the beginning of bibliographical work on the playwright, a descriptive catalogue of typescripts of plays, of motion picture scripts, and of adaptations.

# RANDALL JARRELL
## *1914–1965*

SEPARATE WORKS

Poetry: *Blood for a Stranger*, 1942; *Little Friend, Little Friend*, 1945; *Losses*, 1948; *The Seven-League Crutches*, 1951; *Selected Poems*, 1955; *The Woman at the Washington Zoo: Poems and Translations*, 1960; *The Lost World*, 1965; *The Complete Poems*, 1969.

Fiction: *Pictures from an Institution*, 1954.

Criticism: *Poetry and the Age*, 1953; *A Sad Heart at the Supermarket: Essays and Fables*, 1962; *The Third Book of Criticism*, 1969.

For Children: *The Gingerbread Rabbit*, 1964; *The Bat-Poet*, 1964; *The Animal Family*, 1965.

Translations: *The Ghetto and the Jews of Rome* by Ferdinand Adolf Gregorovius (with Moses Hadas), 1948; *The Golden Bird and Other Fairy Tales of the Brothers Grimm*, 1962; *The Rabbit Catcher and Other Fairy Tales of Ludwig Bechstein*, 1962.

Editions: *The Anchor Book of Stories*, 1958; *The Best Short Stories of Rudyard Kipling*, 1961; *Six Russian Short Novels*, 1963; *The English in England: Short Stories* by Rudyard Kipling, 1963; *In the Vernacular: The English in India: Short Stories* by Rudyard Kipling, 1963.

BIOGRAPHY AND CRITICISM

Invaluable as an introduction to the character and talents of the poet is a memorial volume edited by Robert Lowell, Peter Taylor, and Robert Penn Warren, *Randall Jarrell, 1914–1965*, New York, 1967. It is a collection of tributes, reminiscences, and reprinted reviews by 28 friends and fellow-poets, including Karl Shapiro's Library of Congress lecture, "The Death of Randall Jarrell." This lecture is also published separately, with a bibliographical list of Jarrell material in the Library, as *Randall Jarrell: A Lecture*, Washington, D.C., 1967.

Earlier estimates are W. S. Graham and Hayden Carruth, "Jarrell's Losses: A Controversy," *Poetry*, LXXII (1948), 302–311; Parker Tyler, "The Dramatic Lyricism of Randall Jarrell," *Poetry*, LXXIX (1952), 335–346; John Ciardi, "Over the Edge of Bathos," *Nation*, CLXXXI (July 30, 1955), 100; J. F. Kobler, "Randall Jarrell Seeks Truth in Fantasy," *ForumH*, III (1961), 17–20; David Ray, "The Lightning of Randall Jarrell," *PrS*, XXXV (1961), 45–52; Walter B. Rideout, " 'To Change, To Change!': The Poetry of Randall Jarrell," *Poets in Progress*, ed. Edward Hungerford, Evanston, Ill., 1962, pp. 156–178; Donald Hall, "Nightmares and Irresponsibilities," *NR*, CXLIII (Dec. 26, 1960), 18–19; John Logan, "Rilkean Sense," *SatR*, XLIV (Jan. 28, 1961), 29–30; Samuel Moon, "Finding the Lost World," *Poetry*, CVI (1965), 425–426; R. W. Flint, "On Randall Jarrell," *Com*, XLI (1966), 79–81; H. Russell Hill, "Poetry and Experience," *EJ*, LV (1966), 162–168 ff.; Alfred Kazin, "Prince of Reviewers," *Rep*, XXXV (Sept. 8, 1966), 45–46 ff.; Richard J. Calhoun, "Randall Jarrell: Towards a Reassessment," *SAB*, IV (1967), 1–4; and John Crowe Ransom, "The Rugged Way of Genius: A Tribute to Randall Jarrell," *SoR*, III (1967), 263–281.

*Analects* (Woman's College, University of North Carolina), I (Spring, 1961), is a Randall Jarrell issue.

BIBLIOGRAPHY

Charles Marshall Adams published *Randall Jarrell: A Bibliography*, Chapel Hill, N.C., 1958, to which he added a supplement in *Analects*, I (1961), 49–56.

# ROBERT (TRAILL SPENCE) LOWELL (JR.)
*b. 1917*

## SEPARATE WORKS

Poetry: *Land of Unlikeness*; 1944; *Lord Weary's Castle*, 1946; *Poems 1938–1949*, 1950; *The Mills of the Kavanaughs*, 1951; *Life Studies*, 1959; *Imitations*, 1961; *For the Union Dead*, 1964; *Selected Poems*, 1965; *Near the Ocean*, 1967; *Notebook 1967–1968*, 1969; *Notebook*, 1970.

Plays: *The Old Glory* [three plays based on two stories, "My Kinsman, Major Molineux" and "Endecott and the Red Cross," by Nathaniel Hawthorne and a novella, "Benito Cereno," by Herman Melville], 1965, rev. ed., 1968.

Translations: *Phaedra* [a verse rendering of Racine's *Phèdre*], 1961; *The Voyage and Other Versions of Poems by Baudelaire*, 1968; *Prometheus Bound* [a free adaptation of the play by Aeschylus], 1969.

Editions: *Randall Jarrell 1914–1965* (with Peter Taylor and Robert Penn Warren), 1967.

## BIOGRAPHY AND CRITICISM

Lowell is his own best biographer in *Life Studies*, New York, 1959. *Robert Lowell: A Portrait of the Artist in His Time*, ed. Michael London and Robert Boyers, New York, 1970, contains general appraisals, a long interview, and essays on separate works by 25 writers, including Allen Tate, Randall Jarrell, Leslie Fiedler, and Hayden Carruth. See also John Ciardi, "Letter," *Poetry*, LXXII (1948), 263; John McCormick, "Falling Asleep over Grillparzer: An Interview with Robert Lowell," *Poetry*, LXXXI (1953), 269–279; Frederick Seidel, "Robert Lowell [An Interview]," *ParR* No. 25 (Winter–Spring, 1961), pp. 56–95; Stanley Kunitz, "Talk with Robert Lowell," *NYTBR* (Oct. 4, 1964), pp. 34–38; and A. Alvarez, "A Talk with Robert Lowell," *Encounter*, XXIV (1956), 39–43.

The first book-length study is Hugh B. Staples, *Robert Lowell, The First Twenty Years*, New York, 1962, and it is still a major work on Lowell. Philip Cooper, *The Autobiographical Myth of Robert Lowell*, Chapel Hill, N.C., 1970, concentrates mainly on the poems published since *Life Studies*. Jerome Mazzaro, *The Poetic Themes of Robert Lowell*, Ann Arbor, Mich., 1965, is useful for further explication of the poems and commentary on Lowell's spiritual career. Jay Martin's pamphlet, *Robert Lowell*, Minneapolis, Minn., 1970, covers the whole career concisely. William J. Martz has assembled a valuable book for the classroom in *The Achievement of Robert Lowell: A Comprehensive Selection of His Poems with a Critical Intro-*

*duction*, Glenview, Ill., 1966. Thomas Parkinson edited *Robert Lowell: A Collection of Critical Essays*, Englewood Cliffs, N.J., 1968.

Early criticism is available in Conrad Aiken, "Varieties of Poetic Statement," *NR*, CXI (Oct. 23, 1944), 528–530; John Frederick Nims, "Two Catholic Poets," *Poetry*, LXV (1945), 264–268; Randall Jarrell, "From the Kingdom of Necessity," *Nation*, CLXIV (Jan. 18, 1947), 74–77; Austin Warren, "A Double Discipline," *Poetry*, LXX (1947), 262–265; William Elton, "A Note on Robert Lowell," *Poetry*, LXXI (1947), 138–140; Frank O'Malley, "The Blood of Robert Lowell," *Ren*, II (1949), 3–9; Paul Engle, "Five Years of Pulitzer Poets," *CE*, X (1949), 237–244; Anthony Harrigan, "American Formalists," *SAQ*, XLIX (1950), 483–489; F. Cudworth Flint, "Let the Snake Wait," *VQR*, XXVII (1951), 471–480; Randall Jarrell, "A View of Three Poets," *PR*, XVIII (1951), 691–700; Donald Hall, "American Poets since the War: II," *WoR*, n.s., XLVII (1953), 48–54; T. H. Jones, "The Poetry of Robert Lowell," *Month* (London), IX (1953), 133–143; DeSales Standerwick, "Notes on Robert Lowell," *Ren*, VIII (1955–1956), 75–84; Will C. Jumper, "Whom Seek Ye? A Note on Robert Lowell's Poetry," *HudR*, IX (1956), 117–125; Alfredo Rizzardi, "Poesia di Robert Lowell," *SA*, II (1956), 219–230; and Joseph Bennett, "Two Americans, a Brahmin and the Bourgeoisie," *HudR*, XII (1959), 431–439.

Later estimates are Thom Gunn, "Excellences and Variety," *YR*, XLIX (1960), 295–305; Glauco Cambon, "Dea Roma and Robert Lowell," *Accent*, XX (1960), 51–61; DeSales Standerwick, "Pieces Too Personal," *Ren*, XIII (1960), 53–56; Alfredo Rizzardi, "Leopardi tradotto da Robert Lowell," *SA*, VII (1961), 443–463; Morris Bishop and Hayden Carruth, "Lowell's Translations," *Poetry*, C (1962), 41–47; Dallas E. Wiebe, "Mr. Lowell and Mr. Edwards," *WSCL*, III (1962), 21–31; O. B. Hardison, "Robert Lowell: The Poet and the World's Body," *Shen*, XIV (1963), 24–32; Neville Braybrooke, "The Poetry of Robert Lowell," *CathW*, CXCVIII (1964), 230–237, and "Robert Lowell and the Unjust Steward: A Study of His Poetry," *DR*, XLIV (1964), 28–34; John Wain, "The New Robert Lowell," *NR*, CLI (Oct. 17, 1964), 21–23; A. Kingsley Weatherhead, "Imagination and Fancy: Robert Lowell and Marianne Moore," *TSLL* (1964), 188–199; Richard Fein, "The Trying-Out of Robert Lowell," *SR*, LXXXII (1964), 131–139; Richard Howard, "Voice of a Survivor," *Nation*, CXCIX (Oct. 26, 1964), 278–280; Glauco Cambon, "Lowell e Roethke: poesia in extremis," *SA*, X (1964), 429–435; Irvin Ehrenpreis, "The Age of Lowell," *American Poetry*, ed. Irvin Ehrenpreis, New York, 1965, pp. 68–95; Richard Fein, "Mary and Bellona: The War Poetry of Robert Lowell," *SoR*, I (1965), 820–834; Richard J. Calhoun, "The Poetic Metamorphosis of Robert Lowell," *FurmS*, XIII (1965),

7–17; and A. R. Jones, "Necessity and Freedom: The Poetry of Robert Lowell, Sylvia Plath, and Anne Sexton," *CritQ*, VII (1965), 11–30.

More recent estimates are Samuel Moon, "Master as Servant," *Poetry*, CVIII (1966), 189–190; Baruch Hochman, "Robert Lowell's *The Old Glory*," *TDR*, (1967), 127–138; Daniel Hoffman, "Robert Lowell's *Near the Ocean*: The Greatness and Horror of Empire," *HC* (1967), 1–16; Thomas Woodson, "Robert Lowell's 'Hawthorne,' Yvor Winters, and the American Literary Tradition," *AQ*, XIX (1967), 575–582; Sister Mary Terese Rink, B.V.M., "The Sea in Lowell's 'Quaker Graveyard in Nantucket,'" *Ren*, XX (1967), 39–43; Marjorie Perloff, "Death by Water: The Winslow Elegies of Robert Lowell," *ELH*, XXXIV (1967), 116–140; Paul Zweig, "A Murderous Solvent," *Nation*, CCIV (Apr. 24, 1967), 536–538; Victor Doyno, "Poetic Language and Transformation," *Style*, I (1967), 151–157; John Holloway, "Robert Lowell and the Public Dimension," *Encounter*, XXX (1968), 73–79; Terry Miller, "The Prosodies of Robert Lowell," *SM*, XXV (1968), 425–434; Susan Yankowitz, "Lowell's *Benito Cereno*: An Investigation of American Innocence," *Yale/Theatre*, II (1968), 81–90; and Robin Fulton, "Lowell and Ungaretti," *Agenda*, VI (1968), 118–123.

In November, 1961, the *Harvard Advocate* devoted a whole issue to Lowell; *Salmagundi*, I (1967), is a Robert Lowell issue containing articles by Stanley Kunitz, Jerome Mazzaro, Robert Ilson, Ben Belitt, Thomas Parkinson, and Herbert Leibowitz.

BIBLIOGRAPHY

Jerome Mazzaro, *The Achievement of Robert Lowell: 1939–1959*, Detroit, Mich., 1960, is a preliminary checklist of books and individual poems by, and works about, Lowell. See also Hugh B. Staples, "Robert Lowell: Bibliography 1939–1959, with an Illustrative Critique," *HLB*, XIII (1959), 292–318, especially helpful on early reviews; and Jerome Mazzaro, "Checklist: 1939–1968" in *Robert Lowell: A Portrait of the Artist in His Time*, cited above.

# NORMAN MAILER
### b. 1923

SEPARATE WORKS

Novels: *The Naked and the Dead*, 1948; *Barbary Shore*, 1951; *The Deer Park*, 1955; *An American Dream*, 1965; *Why Are We in Vietnam?* 1967.

Essays, Poems, Lectures, and Stories: *The White Negro*, 1957; *Adver-*

*tisements for Myself,* 1959; *Death for the Ladies and Other Disasters,* 1962; *The Presidential Papers,* 1963; *Cannibals and Christians,* 1966; *The Short Fiction of Norman Mailer,* 1967; *The Bullfight: A Photographic Narrative with Text by Norman Mailer,* 1967; *The Idol and the Octopus: Political Writings in the Kennedy and Johnson Administrations,* 1968; *The Armies of the Night: History as a Novel, The Novel as History,* 1968; *Miami and the Siege of Chicago: An Informal History of the Republican and Democratic Conventions of 1968,* 1968; *Of a Fire on the Moon,* 1971; *The Prisoner of Sex,* 1971.

Plays: *The Deer Park,* 1967.

BIOGRAPHY AND CRITICISM

The first survey of Mailer's career is Richard J. Foster's pamphlet, *Norman Mailer,* Minneapolis, Minn., 1968. The first full-length study, tracing Mailer's development from *The Naked and the Dead* to *Armies of the Night* is Barry H. Leeds's *The Structured Vision of Norman Mailer,* New York, 1969. Joe Flaherty describes Mailer's 1969 New York City campaign for public office in *Managing Mailer,* New York, 1970. *Running against the Machine,* ed. Peter Manso, New York, 1969, is a compilation of documents from that campaign.

Earlier estimates and reviews are Richard Chase, "Novelist Going Places," *Com,* XX (1955), 581–583; Dudley Nichols, "Secret Places of the Groin," *Nation,* CLXXXI (Nov. 5, 1955), 393–395; William Pfaff, "Writer as Vengeful Moralist," *Cweal,* LXII (1955), 230; S. Alexander, "Not Even Good Pornography," *Rep,* XIII (Oct. 20, 1955), 46–48; Robert E. Fitch, "Mystique de la merde," *NR,* CXXXV (Sept. 3, 1956), 17–18; Herbert Goldstone, "The Novels of Norman Mailer," *EJ,* XLV (1957), 113–121; Eugene Burdick, "Innocent Nihilists Adrift in Squaresville," *Rep,* XVIII (Apr. 3, 1958), 30–33; Alfred Kazin, "How Good is Norman Mailer?" *Rep,* XXI (Nov. 26, 1959), 40–41; Harvey Swados, "Must Writers Be Characters?" *SatR,* XLIII (Oct. 1, 1960), 12–14; Norman Podhoretz, "Norman Mailer: The Embattled Vision," *PR,* XXVI (1959), 371–391; Richard◆ G. Stern, "Hip, Hell, and the Navigator: An Interview with Norman Mailer," *WR,* XXIII (1959), 101–109; Gore Vidal, "The Norman Mailer Snydrome," *Nation,* CLXC (1959), 13–16; F. W. Dupee, "The American Norman Mailer," *Com,* XXIX (1960), 128–132; Charles I. Glicksberg, "Norman Mailer: The Angry Young Novelist in America," *WSCL,* I (1960), 25–34; Dwight Macdonald, "Massachusetts vs. Mailer," *NY,* XXXVI (Oct. 8, 1960), 154–166; James Baldwin, "The Black Boy Looks at the White Boy: Norman Mailer," *Esquire,* LV (1961), 102–106; George Steiner, "Naked But Not Dead," *Encounter,* XVII (1961), 67–70; Bruce A. Cook, "Norman Mailer: The Temptation to Power," *Ren*, XIV (1962), 206–215; Diana Trilling, "Norman Mailer," *Encounter*, XIX (1962), 45–56; Marvin Mudrick, "Mailer and Styron: Guests of the Establishment," *HudR*, XVII (1964), 346–366; Brom Weber, "A Fear of Dying: Norman Mailer's *An American Dream*," *HC*, II (1965), 1–6, 8–11; and Leo Bersani, "The Interpretation of Dreams," *PR*, XXXII (1965), 603–608.

More recent studies are James Jones, "Small Comment from a Penitent Novelist," *Esquire*, LX (Dec., 1963), 40 ff.; Brock Brower, "Always the Challenger," *Life*, LIX (Sept. 24, 1965), 94–117; Richard Poirier, "Morbimindedness," *Com*, XXIX (1965), 91–94; Paul Pickrel, "Thing of Darkness," *Harper's*, CCXXX (Apr., 1965), 116–117; John Wain, "Mailer's America," *NR*, CLV (Oct. 1, 1966), 19–20; John W. Aldridge, "Victim and Analyst," *Com*, XLII (1966), 131–133; Mario Corona, "Norman Mailer," *SA*, XI (1965), 359–407; James Toback, "Norman Mailer Today," *Com*, (1967), 68–76; Paul B. Newman, "Mailer: The Jew as Existentialist," *NAR*, II (1965), 49–55; Robert Solotaroff, "Down Mailer's Way," *ChiR*, XIX (1967), 11–25; William H. Pritchard, "Norman Mailer's Extravagances," *MR*, VIII (1967), 562–568; Allan J. Wagenheim, "Square's Progress: *An American Dream*," *Crit*, X (1968), 45–68; Samuel Hux, "Mailer's Dream of Violence," *MinnR*, VIII (1968), 152–157; Steven Marcus, "Norman Mailer," *Writers at Work: The Paris Review Interviews*: 3rd ser., New York, 1967; Max F. Schultz, "Mailer's Divine Comedy," *WSCL*, IX (1968), 36–57; and David Helsa, "The Two Roles of Norman Mailer," *Adversity and Grace: Studies in Recent American Literature*, ed. Nathan A. Scott, Jr., Chicago, 1968, pp. 211–238.

See also the pages devoted to Mailer in Ihab Hassan, *Radical Innocence: Studies in the Contemporary American Novel*, Princeton, N.J., 1961; Norman Podhoretz, *Doings and Undoings: The Fifties and After in American Writing*, New York, 1964; John W. Aldridge, *Time to Murder and Create: The Contemporary Novel in Crisis*, New York, 1966; Ronald Berman, *America in the Sixties: An Intellectual History*, New York, 1968; and Richard Gilman, *The Confusion of Realms*, New York, 1970.

# F(RANCIS) O(TTO) MATTHIESSEN
## *1902–1950*

### SEPARATE WORKS

Criticism: *Sarah Orne Jewett*, 1929; *Translation: An Elizabethan Art*, 1931; *The Achievement of T. S. Eliot: An Essay on the Nature of Poetry*, 1935 (enlarged edition, 1947, posthumous edition with a chapter by C. L. Barber on Eliot's later work, 1958); *American Renaissance: Art and*

*Experience in the Age of Emerson and Whitman*, 1941; *Henry James: The Major Phase*, 1944; *The James Family: Including Selections from the Writings of Henry James Senior, William, Henry, and Alice James*, 1947; *Russell Cheney, 1881–1945: A Record of His Work*, 1947; *From the Heart of Europe*, 1948; *Theodore Dreiser*, 1951; *Responsibilities of the Critic: Essays and Reviews* (selected and edited by Jack Rackliffe), 1952.

Editions: *Stories of Writers and Artists* by Henry James, 1944; *Herman Melville: Selected Poems*, 1944; *The Notebooks of Henry James* (with Kenneth B. Murdock),1947; *The American Novels and Stories of Henry James*, 1947; *The Oxford Book of American Verse*, 1950.

BIOGRAPHY AND CRITICISM

The most important discussion of Matthiessen's work is a volume edited by Paul M. Sweezy and Leo Huberman, *F. O. Matthiessen (1902–1950): A Collective Portrait*, New York, 1950. See also George Mayberry, "The Achievement of F. O. Matthiessen," *NR*, CXXII (June 19, 1950), 17–18; Robert Peel, "A Collective Portrait, a Challenging Reminder," *Christian Science Monitor Magazine* (Dec. 9, 1950), p. 7; Hubert N. Hart, "Francis Otto Matthiessen," *CathW*, CLXXI (1950), 448–451; Malcolm Cowley, "Matty for One," *NR*, CXXII (Apr. 24, 1950), 21, Willard Thorp, "Part of a Monument," *NR*, CXXVII (Oct. 27, 1952), 19–20; Nobushige Tadokoro, "F. O. Matthiessen and His Expatriation," *KAL*, No. 1 (June, 1958), pp. 26–39; and Walter Sutton, *Modern American Criticism*, Englewood Cliffs, N.J., 1963, pp. 92–97.

# ARTHUR MILLER
## *b. 1915*

SEPARATE WORKS

*Plays: That They May Win (1943), 1945; The Man Who Had All the Luck (1944), 1945; All My Sons, 1947; Death of a Salesman, 1949; The Crucible, 1953; A Memory of Two Mondays, 1955; A View from the Bridge, 1955; Collected Plays, 1957; After the Fall, 1964; Incident at Vichy (1964), 1965; The Price, (1967), 1968.

Screenplay: *The Misfits*, 1961.

Fiction: *Focus*, 1945; *I Don't Need You Any More*, 1967.

Prose Journal: *Situation Normal*, 1944; *In Russia* (with Inge Morath), 1969.

* Dates in parentheses are of production when it differs from publication.

Adaptations: *An Enemy of the People* by Henrik Ibsen (1950), 1951.

For Children: *Jane's Blanket*, 1963.

For a listing of Miller's short stories, radio plays, essays, and interviews, see Leonard Moss, *Arthur Miller*, New York, 1967, pp. 136–142.

### BIOGRAPHY AND CRITICISM

There is no biography. Five critical studies of Miller's work incorporate varying amounts of biographical data: Dennis Welland, *Arthur Miller*, New York, 1961; Sheila Huftel, *Arthur Miller: The Burning Glass*, New York, 1965; Leonard Moss, *Arthur Miller,* New York, 1967; Edward Murray, *Arthur Miller, Dramatist*, New York, 1967; and Benjamin Nelson, *Arthur Miller: Portrait of a Playwright*, New York, 1970. Robert Hogan's *Arthur Miller*, Minneapolis, Minn., 1964, is a much too rapid survey of Miller's career. Rainer Lubbren's *Arthur Miller*, Velber bei Hannover, 1966, is the first study in German.

Robert W. Corrigan, ed., *Arthur Miller: A Collection of Critical Essays*, Englewood Cliffs, N.J., 1969, spans Miller's career from *All My Sons* to *The Price*. Two earlier collections are John D. Hurrell, ed., *Two Modern American Tragedies: Reviews and Criticism of Death of a Salesman and A Streetcar Named Desire*, New York, 1961; and Gerald Weales, *Death of a Salesman: Text and Criticism*, New York, 1967. James Goode's *The Story of the Misfits*, Indianapolis, Ind., 1963, is a description of the making of the film.

Early critical estimates begin with Alan S. Downer, "Mr. Williams and Mr. Miller," *Furioso*, IV (Summer, 1949), 66–70; Eleanor Clark, "Old Glamour, New Gloom," *PR*, XVI (1949), 631–636; Sighle Kennedy, "Who Killed the Salesman?," *CathW*, CLXX (1951), 110–116; Eric Bentley, "Miller's Innocence," *NR*, CXXVIII (Feb. 16, 1953), 22–23; Henry Hewes, "Arthur Miller and How He Went to the Devil," *SR*, XXXVI (Jan. 31, 1953), 24–26; Robert Warshow, "The Liberal Conscience in *The Crucible*," *Com*, XV (Mar., 1953), 265–271; Kenneth Tynan, "American Blues: The Plays of Arthur Miller and Tennessee Williams," *Encounter*, II (May, 1954), 13–19; Jacques Lemarchand, "Les Sorcières de Salem," *NRF*, III (1955), 309–313; Thierry Maulnier, "Les Socières de Salem," *RdP*, LXII (1955), 137–140; Gordon W. Couchman, "Arthur Miller's Tragedy of Babbitt," *ETJ*, VII (1955), 206–211; Paul N. Siegel, "Willy Loman and King Lear," *CE*, XVII (1956), 341–345; Walter Goodman, "How Not to Produce a Film," *NR*, CXXXIII (Dec. 26, 1955), 12–13; William Wiegand, "Arthur Miller and the Man who Knows," *WR*, XXI (1956), 85–103; R. H. Rovere, "Arthur Miller's Conscience," *NR*, CXXXVI

(June 17, 1957), 13–15; Harry Kalven, Jr., "A View from the Law," *NR*, CXXXVI (May 27, 1957), 8–13; Mary McCarthy, "Naming Names: The Arthur Miller Case," *Encounter*, VIII (May, 1957), 23–25; Richard Findlater, "No Time for Tragedy?," *TC*, CLXI (1957), 56–62; Arthur Miller, Gore Vidal *et al.*, *"Death of a Salesman*, a Symposium," *TDR*, II (May, 1958), 63–69; Grazia Caluimi, "Lineamenti del teatre di Arthur Miller," *SA*, IV (1958), 295–316; Allan Seager, "The Creative Agony of Arthur Miller," *Esquire*, LII (Oct., 1959), 123–126; Raymond Williams, "The Realism of Arthur Miller," *CritQ*, I (1959), 140–149; Samuel A. Yorks, "Joe Keller and His Sons," *WHR*, XIII (1959), 401–407; M. W. Steinberg, "Arthur Miller and the Idea of Modern Tragedy," *DR*, XL (1960), 329–340; William B. Dillingham, "Arthur Miller and the Loss of Conscience," *EUQ*, XVI (1960), 40–50; Henry Brandon, "The State of the Theatre: A Conversation with Arthur Miller," *Harper's*, CCXXI (Nov., 1960), 63–69; Tom F. Driver, "Strength and Weakness in Arthur Miller," *TDR*, IV (1960), 45–52; Henry Popkin, "Arthur Miller: The Strange Encounter," *SR*, LXVIII (1960), 34–60; and George De Schweinitz, *"Death of a Salesman*: A Note on Epic and Tragedy," *WHR*, XIV (1960), 91–96.

More recent studies are Henry Popkin, "Arthur Miller Out West," *Com*, XXXI (1961), 433–436; Gerald Weales, "Arthur Miller: Man and His Image," *TDR*, VII (1962), 165–180; John A. Hagopian, "Arthur Miller: The *Salesman*'s Two Cases," *MD*, VI (1963), 117–125; Joseph A. Hynes, "Arthur Miller and the Impasse of Naturalism," *SAQ*, LXII (1963), 327–334; Paul West, "Arthur Miller and the Human Mice," *HJ*, LXI (1963), 84–86; Arthur Ganz, "The Silence of Arthur Miller," *DramS*, III (1963), 224–237; Robert Brustein, "Muddy Track at Lincoln Center," *NR*, CL (Dec. 26, 1964), 26–27; Arvin R. Wells, "The Living and the Dead in *All My Sons*," *MD*, VII (May, 1964), 46–51; Harold Clurman, "Director's Notes: *Incident at Vichy*," *TDR*, IX (1965), 77–90; Arthur D. Epstein, "A Look at *A View from the Bridge*," *TSLL*, VII (1965), 109–122; William R. Brashear, "The Empty Bench: Morality, Tragedy, and Arthur Miller," *MQR*, (1966), 270–278; Martin Roth, "Sept-d'un-coup," *ChiR*, XIX (1966), 108–111; C. W. Bigsby, "The Fall and After: Arthur Miller's Confession," *MD*, X (1967), 124–136; Clinton W. Trowbridge, "Arthur Miller: Between Pathos and Tragedy," *MD*, X (1967), 221–232; Philip G. Hill, *"The Crucible*: A Structural View," *MD*, X (1967), 312–317; Robert W. Corrigan, "The Achievement of Arthur Miller," *CompD*, II (1968), 141–160; Barclay W. Bates, "The Lost Path in *Death of a Salesman*," *MD*, XI (1968), 164–172; and D. S. Maini, "The Moral Vision of Arthur Miller," *Indian Essays in American Literature*, ed., S. Mukherjee and D. K. V. Raghavacharyulu, Bombay, 1969, pp. 85–96.

BIBLIOGRAPHY

See Martha Turnquist Eissenstat, "Arthur Miller: A Bibliography," *MD*, V (1962), 93–106; and Tetsumaro Hayashi, *Arthur Miller Criticism (1930–1967)*, Metuchen, N.J., 1969. A useful bibliography is appended to Leonard Moss's book, cited above.

## FLANNERY O'CONNOR

### *1925–1965*

SEPARATE WORKS

Novels: *Wise Blood*, 1952; *The Violent Bear It Away*, 1960.

Short Stories: *A Good Man Is Hard to Find and Other Stories*, 1955; *Everything That Rises Must Converge*, 1965.

Essays and Lectures: *Mystery and Manners: Occasional Prose* (selected and edited by Sally and Robert Fitzgerald), 1969.

COLLECTED WORKS

*Flannery O'Connor: The Complete Stories*, New York, 1971, with an introduction by Robert Giroux, prints 31 stories, 12 of them previously uncollected.

BIOGRAPHY AND CRITICISM

The first full-length critical study is Carter W. Martin's *The True Country: Themes in the Fiction of Flannery O'Connor*, Nashville, Tenn., 1969; the emphasis is on O'Connor's Roman Catholicism and its effect on her fiction. Stanley Edgar Hyman, *Flannery O'Connor*, Minneapolis, Minn., 1966; and Robert Drake, *Flannery O'Connor*, Grand Rapids, Mich., 1966, are brief pamphlets. Melvin J. Friedman and Lewis A. Lawson have edited an important collection of ten critical essays, *The Added Dimension: The Art and Mind of Flannery O'Connor*, New York, 1966, divided between those who share O'Connor's religious perspective and those who do not.

Briefer estimates begin with Carl Hartman, "Jesus without Christ," *WR*, XVII (1952), 76–81; William Esty, "In America, Intellectual Bomb Shelters," *Cweal*, LXVII (Mar. 7, 1958), 586–588; Louis D. Rubin, Jr., "Flannery O'Connor: A Note on Literary Fashions," *Crit.*, II (Fall, 1958), 11–18; Jane Hart, "Strange Earth: The Stories of Flannery O'Connor," *GaR*, XII (Summer, 1958), 215–222; Robert M. McCown, "Flannery O'Connor and the Reality of Sin," *CathW*, CLXXXVIII (1959), 285–291; P. Albert Duhamel, "Flannery O'Connor's Violent View of Reality," *CathW*, CXC (1960), 280–285; Willard Thorp, "Suggs and Sut in Modern Dress," *MissQ*, XIII (1960), 169–175; Robert O. Bowen, "Hope vs. Despair in the New Gothic Novel," *Ren*, XIII (1961), 147–152; James F.

Farnham, "The Grotesque in Flannery O'Connor," *America*, CV (May 13, 1961), 277, 280–281; Margaret Inman Meaders, "Flannery O'Connor: Literary Witch," *ColQ*, X (1962), 377–386; Melvin J. Friedman, "Flannery O'Connor: Another Legend in Southern Fiction," *EJ*, LI (1962), 233–243; Sister Bertrande Meyers, D.C., "Four Stories of Flannery O'Connor," *Thought*, XXXVII (1962), 410–426; Robert Fitzgerald, "The Countryside and the True Country," *SR*, LXX (1962), 380–394; John Hawkes, "Flannery O'Connor's Devil," *SR*, LXX (1962), 395–407; Jonathan Baumbach, "The Acid of God's Grace: The Fiction of Flannery O'Connor," *GaR*, XVII (1963), 334–346; Maurice Bassan, "Flannery O'Connor's Way: Shock with Moral Intent," *Ren*, XV (1963), 195–199, 211; Rainulf Stelzmann, "Shock and Orthodoxy: An Interpretation of Flannery O'Connor's Novels and Short Stories," *XUS*, II (Mar., 1963), 4–20; Gerard E. Sherry, "An Interview with Flannery O'Connor," *The Critic*, XXI (June–July, 1963), 29–31; Michel Gresset, "Le petit monde de Flannery O'Connor," *MdF*, No. 1203 (Jan., 1964), pp. 141–143; and Thomas Merton, "Flannery O'Connor," *Jubilee*, XII (Nov., 1964), 49–53.

More recent studies are J. M. G. Le Clézio, "L'univers de Flannery O'Connor," *NRF*, XIII (1965), 488–493; Bob Dowell, "The Moment of Grace in the Fiction of Flannery O'Connor," *CE*, XXVII (1965), 235–239; Warren Coffey, "Flannery O'Connor," *Com*, XL (1965), 93–99; Lewis A. Lawson, "Flannery O'Connor and the Grotesque: *Wise Blood*," *Ren*, XVII (Spring, 1965), 137–147, 156; Robert M. Rechnitz, "Passionate Pilgrim: Flannery O'Connor's *Wise Blood*," *GaR*, XIX (1965), 310–316; Ollye Tine Snow, "The Functional Gothic of Flannery O'Connor," *SWR*, L (1965), 286–299; Richard Stern, "Flannery O'Connor: A Remembrance and Some Letters," *Shen*, XVI (Winter, 1965), 5–10; Richard Coleman, "Flannery O'Connor: A Scrutiny of Two Forms of Her Many-Leveled Art," *Phoenix*, No. 1 (1966), pp. 30–66; John J. Burke, S.J., "Convergence of Flannery O'Connor and Chardin," *Ren*, XIX (1966), 41–47, 52; John F. McCarthy, "Human Intelligence versus Divine Truth: the Intellectual in Flannery O'Connor's Works," *EJ*, LV (1966), 1143–1148; Thomas F. Walsh, "The Devils of Hawthorne and Flannery O'Connor," *XUS*, V (1966), 117–122; Hugh Rank, "O'Connor's Image of the Priest," *NEQ*, XLI (1968), 3–29; Martha Stephens, "Flannery O'Connor and the Sanctified-Sinner Tradition," *ArQ*, XXIV (1968), 223–239; Peter L. Hays, "Dante, Tobit, and 'The Artificial Nigger,'" *SSF*, V (1968), 263–268; and Thomas M. Lorch, "Flannery O'Connor: Christian Allegorist," *Crit*, X (1968), 69–80.

Three journals have devoted all or part of one issue to Flannery O'Connor's work: *Critique: Studies in Modern Fiction*, II (Fall, 1958); *Esprit*, VIII (Winter, 1964); and *Sewanee Review*, LXXVI (Spring, 1968).

BIBLIOGRAPHY

The best bibliographies are Joan T. Brittain, "Flannery O'Connor: A Bibliography," *BB*, XXV (1967–1968), 98–100, 123–124, 142; and Lewis A. Lawson, "Bibliography," in *The Added Dimension: The Art and Mind of Flannery O'Connor*, ed. Melvin J. Friedman and Lewis A. Lawson, New York, 1966, pp. 281–302.

## KATHERINE ANNE PORTER
*b. 1894*

•

SEPARATE WORKS

Short Stories: *Flowering Judas and Other Stories*, 1930; *The Leaning Tower and Other Stories*, 1944.

Novels: *Pale Horse, Pale Rider: Three Short Novels*, 1939; *Ship of Fools*, 1962.

Essays: *The Days Before*, 1952.

Translations: *The Itching Parrot* by José Joaquin Fernandez de Lizárdi, 1942.

COLLECTED WORKS AND CORRESPONDENCE

*Selected Short Stories*, 1945, was an Overseas Edition for the Armed Forces and not for sale. *The Old Order: Stories of the South*, New York, 1955, is a collection from *Flowering Judas, The Leaning Tower*, and *Pale Horse, Pale Rider*. *The Collected Stories* ["Every story I ever finished and published is here"] appeared first in London, 1964, then New York, 1965. *The Collected Essays and Occasional Writings*, New York, 1970, includes all of *The Days Before*, reviews, poems, and previously uncollected essays.

For gleanings of letters see Donald Sutherland, "Ole Woman River: A Correspondence with Katherine Anne Porter," *SR*, LXXIV (1966), 754–767.

BIOGRAPHY AND CRITICISM

There is no biography, but Barbara Thompson's *Paris Review* interview (No. 29, 1963) and Glenway Wescott's "Katherine Anne Porter Personally" in *Images of Truth: Remembrances and Criticism* (New York, 1962) are especially illuminating. See also James Ruoff, "Katherine Anne Porter Comes to Kansas," *MQ*, IV (1963), 205–234.

The most comprehensive critical study is William L. Nance, S.M., *Katherine Anne Porter and the Art of Rejection*, Chapel Hill, N.C., 1964, "based on one unifying theory: that an oppression-rejection pattern of human relations is crucial to all her work." An equally acute study is

George Hendrick's *Katherine Anne Porter*, New York, 1965. Three useful pamphlets are Harry John Mooney, Jr., *The Fiction and Criticism of Katherine Anne Porter*, Pittsburgh, Pa., 1957, rev. ed. 1962; Ray B. West, Jr., *Katherine Anne Porter*, Minneapolis, Minn., 1963; and Winifred S. Emmons, *Katherine Anne Porter: The Regional Stories*, Austin, Tex., 1967.

*Katherine Anne Porter: A Critical Symposium*, ed. Lodwick Hartley and George Core, Athens, Ga., 1969, is an impressive collection of 16 essays by Robert Penn Warren, Eudora Welty, Cleanth Brooks, and others, plus the Thompson interview and the Wescott biographical reminiscence cited above.

Other estimates are Margaret Marshall, "Writers in the Wilderness: Katherine Anne Porter," *Nation*, CL (Apr. 13, 1940), 473–475; Charles A. Allen, "Katherine Anne Porter: Psychology as Art," *SWR*, XLI (1956), 223–230; Marjorie Ryan, "*Dubliners* and the Stories of Katherine Anne Porter," *AL*, XXXI (1960), 464–473; Marvin Pierce, "Point of View: Katherine Anne Porter's *Noon Wine*," *OUR*, III (1961), 95–113; Theodore Solotaroff, "*Ship of Fools* and the Critics," *Com*, XXXIV (1962), 277–286; Daniel Curley, "Katherine Anne Porter: The Larger Plan," *KR*, XXV (1963), 671–695; Robert Neil Hertz, "Sebastian Brant and Porter's *Ship of Fools*," *MQ*, VI (1965), 389–401; Paul W. Miller, "Katherine Anne Porter's *Ship of Fools*, A Masterpiece Manqué," *UR*, XXXII (1965), 151–157; Robert L. Perry, "Porter's 'Hacienda' and the Theme of Change," *MQ*, VI (1965), 403–415; Stephen Donadio, "The Collected Miss Porter," *PR*, XXXIII (1966), 278–284; M. Liberman, "The Responsibility of the Novelist: The Critical Reception of *Ship of Fools*," *Criticism*, VIII (1966), 377–388; John Van Zyl, "Surface Elegance, Grotesque Content: A Note on the Short Stories of Katherine Anne Porter," *ESA*, IX (1966), 168–175; Robert Penn Warren, "Uncorrupted Consciousness: The Short Stories of Katherine Anne Porter," *YR*, LV (1966), 280–290; Howard Baker, "The Upward Path: Notes on the Work of Katherine Anne Porter," *SoR*, IV (1968), 1–19; and Thomas F. Walsh, "The 'Noon Wine' Devils," *GaR*, XXII (1968), 90–96.

BIBLIOGRAPHY

*A Bibliography of the Works of Katherine Anne Porter and a Bibliography of the Criticism of the Works of Katherine Anne Porter* is an unwieldy title but a useful full-length checklist, prepared by Louise Waldrip and Shirley Ann Bauer and published by the Scarecrow Press, Metuchen, New Jersey, 1969. A good selective bibliography is appended to *Katherine Anne Porter: A Critical Symposium*, cited above. Both lists owe a debt to William A. Sylvester, "Selected and Critical Bibliography of the Uncollected

Works of Katherine Anne Porter," *BB*, XIX (1947), 36; and Edward Schwartz, "Katherine Anne Porter: A Critical Bibliography," *BNYPL*, LVII (1953), 211–247.

# THEODORE ROETHKE
## *1908–1963*

SEPARATE WORKS

Poetry: *Open House*, 1941; *The Lost Son and Other Poems*, 1948; *Praise to the End!* 1951; *The Waking: Poems 1933–1953*; 1953; *Words for the Wind: the Collected Verse of Theodore Roethke*, 1958; *I Am! Says the Lamb*, 1961; *Sequence, Sometimes Metaphysical*, 1963; *The Far Field*, 1964.

For Children: *Party at the Zoo*, 1963.

COLLECTED WORKS AND CORRESPONDENCE

*The Collected Poems of Theodore Roethke*, a complete edition, appeared in New York, 1966. Ralph J. Mills, Jr., has edited two volumes that are valuable companions to the poems: *On the Poet and His Craft: Selected Prose of Theodore Roethke*, Seattle, Wash., 1965, and (with considerable help from Beatrice Roethke, the poet's widow) *Selected Letters of Theodore Roethke*, Seattle, Wash., 1968. *The Achievement of Theodore Roethke*, Glenview, Ill., 1966, is "a comprehensive selection of his poems with a critical introduction" by William J. Martz.

BIOGRAPHY AND CRITICISM

The first full-length biography is *The Glass House: The Life of Theodore Roethke*, New York, 1968, by Allan Seager.

Arnold Stein edited *Theodore Roethke: Essays on the Poetry*, Seattle, Wash., 1965, a collection of nine tributes and explications by Stephen Spender, William Meredith, Roy Harvey Pearce, and others. Ralph J. Mills, Jr., *Theodore Roethke*, is a Minnesota pamphlet published a few months after the poet's death. The first comprehensive survey of the poet's work is Karl Malkoff, *Theodore Roethke: An Introduction to the Poetry*, New York, 1966.

Earlier critical estimates are Stanley Kunitz, "News of the Root," *Poetry*, LXXIII (1949), 222–225; M. L. Rosenthal, "Closing in on the Self," *Nation*, CLXXXVIII (Mar. 21, 1959), 258–260; Stanley Kunitz, "Roethke: Poet of Transformations," *NR*, CLII (Jan. 23, 1965), 23–29; Hugh B. Staples, "The Rose in the Sea-Wind: A Reading of Theodore Roethke's

'North American Sequence,'" *AL*, XXXVI (1964), 189–203; Richard Eberhart, "On Theodore Roethke's Poetry," *SoR*, I (1965), 612–620; Denis Donoghue, "Theodore Roethke," *Connoisseurs of Chaos*, New York, 1965, pp. 216–245; and Richard Gustafson, "In Roethkeland," *MQ*, VII (1966), 167–174.

BIBLIOGRAPHY

The most ambitious work to date is James Richard McLeod's *Theodore Roethke: A Manuscript Checklist*, Kent, Ohio, 1971, and a University of Washington Master of Librarianship thesis by John Matheson, "Theodore Roethke: A Bibliography" (1958). Useful shorter listings are in Karl Malkoff's *Theodore Roethke*, cited above, and Susan W. Hollenberg's "Theodore Roethke: Bibliography," *TCL*, XII (1967), 216–222.

## JOHN UPDIKE
### b. 1932

SEPARATE WORKS

Novels: *The Poorhouse Fair*, 1959; *Rabbit, Run*, 1960; *The Centaur*, 1963; *Of the Farm*, 1965; *Couples*, 1968; *Bech: A Book*, 1970; *Rabbit Redux*, 1971.

Short Stories: *The Same Door*, 1959; *Pigeon Feathers and Other Stories*, 1962; *Olinger Stories: A Selection*, 1964; *The Music School*, 1966.

Poetry: *The Carpentered Hen and Other Tame Creatures* (English edition titled *Hoping for a Hoopee*), 1958; *Telephone Poles and Other Poems*, 1963; *Midpoint and Other Poems*, 1969.

Essays: *Assorted Prose*, 1965.

For Children: *The Magic Flute* by Wolfgang Amadeus Mozart (with Warren Chappell), 1962; *The Ring* by Richard Wagner (with Warren Chappell), 1964; *A Child's Calendar*, 1965; *Bottom's Dream: Adapted from William Shakespeare's A Midsummer Night's Dream*, 1969.

BIOGRAPHY AND CRITICISM

Until a biographer appears, the profile by Jane Howard, "Can a Nice Novelist Finish First?," *Life*, LXI, (Nov. 4, 1966), 74–82; and the *Time* cover-story, "View from the Catacombs," XCI (Apr. 26, 1968) 73–75, are useful substitutes. See also the *Paris Review* interview by Charles Thomas Samuels, No. 45 (Winter, 1968).

Two recent pamphlets are Charles Thomas Samuels, *John Updike*, Minneapolis, Minn., 1969; and Alice Hamilton and Kenneth Hamilton, *John Updike: A Critical Essay*, Grand Rapids, Mich., 1967. The Hamiltons enlarged their work into the first full-length study (with selected bibliography), *The Elements of John Updike*, Grand Rapids, Mich., 1970. It concentrates on the Christian elements in his work. It was followed by Larry E. Taylor, *Pastoral and Anti-pastoral Patterns in John Updike's Fiction*, Carbondale, Ill., 1971; and Rachael C. Burchard, *John Updike: Yea Sayings*, Carbondale, Ill., 1971. There are chapters on Updike in the following books: Arthur Mizener, *The Sense of Life in the Modern Novel*, Boston, 1964; Robert Detweiler, *Four Spiritual Crises in Mid-Century American Fiction*, Gainesville, Fla., 1963; Howard M. Harper, Jr., *Desperate Faith*, Chapel Hill, N.C., 1967; and David D. Galloway, *The Absurd Hero in American Fiction*, Austin, Tex., 1966.

Among early critical estimates are Dean Doner, "Rabbit Angstrom's Unseen World," *New World Writing*, XX (1962), 58–75; Stanley Edgar Hyman, "The Artist as a Young Man," *NL*, XLV (Mar. 19, 1962), 22–23; J. A. Ward, "John Updike's Fiction," *Crit*, V (Spring–Summer, 1962), 27–40; Michael Novak, "Updike's Quest for Liturgy," *Cweal*, LXXVIII (1963), 192–195; William Van O'Connor, "John Updike and William Styron: The Burden of Talent," *Contemporary American Novelists*, ed. Harry T. Moore, Carbondale, Ill., 1964; and Norman Podhoretz, "Dissent on Updike," *Doings and Undoings*, New York, 1964.

More recent studies are D. J. Enright, "Updike's Ups and Downs," *Holiday*, XXXVIII (Nov., 1965), 162, 164–166; Norris W. Yates, "The Doubt and Faith of John Updike," *CE*, XXVI (1965), 469–474; Cyrille Arnavon, "Les romans de John Updike," *Europe*, No. 446 (June, 1966), 193–213; Gerry Brenner, "*Rabbit, Run*: John Updike's Criticism of the 'Return to Nature,'" *TCL*, XII (1966), 3–14; Rudolf Haas, "Griechischer Mythos in modernen Roman: John Updikes *The Centaur*," *Lebende Antike: Symposium für Rudolf Sühnel*, ed. Horst Meller and Hans-Joachim Zimmerman, Berlin, 1967; Elizabeth Matson, "A Chinese Paradox, But Not Much of One: John Updike in His Poetry," *MinnR*, VII (1967), 157–167; Richard H. Rupp, "Style in Search of a Center," *SR*, LXXV (1967), 693–709; Bryant N. Wyatt, "John Updike: The Psychological Novel in Search of Structure," *TCL*, XIII (1967), 89–96; and John C. Stubbs, "The Search for Perfection in *Rabbit, Run*," *Crit*, X (1968), 94–101.

BIBLIOGRAPHY

Checklists are appended to both of the pamphlets listed above. The best work, however, is C. Clarke Taylor, *John Updike: A Bibliography*, Kent, Ohio, 1968.

# EUDORA WELTY
*b. 1909*

SEPARATE WORKS

Novels: *The Robber Bridegroom*, 1942; *Delta Wedding*, 1946; *The Ponder Heart*, 1954; *Losing Battles*, 1970.

Short Stories: *A Curtain of Green and Other Stories*, 1941; *The Wide Net and Other Stories*, 1943; *The Golden Apples*, 1949; *The Bride of the Innisfallen and Other Stories*, 1955.

Miscellaneous: *Place in Fiction*, 1957; *Three Papers on Fiction*, 1962; *The Shoe Bird*, 1964.

COLLECTIONS

*Selected Stories of Eudora Welty*, New York, 1954, reprints *A Curtain of Green* and *The Wide Net* with an excellent introduction by Katherine Anne Porter. *Thirteen Stories*, New York, 1965, was compiled, with an introduction, by Ruth M. Vande Kieft.

CRITICISM

The first full-length study is Ruth M. Vande Kieft, *Eudora Welty*, New York, 1962. Alfred Appel, Jr., enlarges the critical scope in *A Season of Dreams: The Fiction of Eudora Welty*, Baton Rouge, La., 1965, concentrating on her humor, the use of the grotesque, and the themes of isolation and loneliness. J. A. Bryant, Jr., *Eudora Welty*, Minneapolis, Minn., 1968, is a brief survey of her whole career.

Early critical estimates are Robert Penn Warren, "The Love and Separateness in Miss Welty," *KR*, VI (1944), 246–259; John Crowe Ransom, "Delta Fiction," *KR*, VIII (1946), 503–507; Eunice Glenn, "Fantasy in the Fiction of Eudora Welty," *A Southern Vanguard*, ed. Allen Tate, New York, 1947; John E. Hardy, "*Delta Wedding* as Region and Symbol," *SR*, LX (1952), 397–417; Granville Hicks, "Eudora Welty," *CE*, XIV (Nov., 1952), 69–76; Harry C. Morris, "Eudora Welty's Use of Mythology," *Shen*, VI (Spring, 1955), 34–40; William M. Jones, "Name and Symbol in the Prose of Eudora Welty," *SFQ*, XXII (1958), 173–185; Lorenza Galli, "La narrativa di Eudora Welty," *SA*, V (1959), 281–300; and Robert W. Daniel, "Eudora Welty: The Sense of Place," *South*, ed. Louis D. Rubin, Jr., and Robert D. Jacobs, New York, 1961.

More recent studies are Louis D. Rubin, Jr., "The Golden Apples of the Sun," *The Faraway Country: Writers of the Modern South*, Seattle, Wash., 1963; Marvin Felheim, "Eudora Welty and Carson McCullers," *Contemporary American Novelists*, ed. Harry T. Moore, Carbondale, Ill.,

1964; Kurt Opitz, "Eudora Welty: The Order of a Captive Soul," *Crit*, VII (1965), 79–91; William M. Jones, "The Plot as Search," *SSF*, V (1967), 37–43; Daniel Curley, "Eudora Welty and the Quondam Obstruction," *SSF*, V (1968), 209–224; and John E. Hardy, "The Achievement of Eudora Welty," *SHR*, II (1968), 269–278.

The Spring, 1969, issue of *Shenandoah* is a "Tribute to Eudora Welty" with essays by R. B. Heilman, Joyce Carol Oates, Reynolds Price, Malcolm Cowley, Walker Percy, Allen Tate, and others.

BIBLIOGRAPHY

There is no comprehensive bibliography, but the following works are varied and useful: Katherine H. Smythe, "Eudora Welty: A Checklist," *BB*, XXI (1956), 207–208; Leona Jordan, "Eudora Welty: Selected Criticism," *BB*, XXIII (1960), 14–15; Seymour L. Gross, "Eudora Welty: A Bibliography of Criticism and Comment," *Secretary's News Sheet*, Bibliographical Society, University of Virginia, No. 45 (Apr., 1960), pp. 1–32; McKelva Cole, "Book Reviews of Eudora Welty: A Check-list," *BB*, XXIII (1963), 240; and W. U. McDonald, Jr., "Eudora Welty Manuscripts: An Annotated Finding List," *BB*, XXIV (1963), 44–46.

# RICHARD (PURDY) WILBUR
## *b. 1921*

SEPARATE WORKS

Poetry: *The Beautiful Changes and Other Poems*, 1947; *Ceremony and Other Poems*, 1950; *Things of This World*, 1956; *Poems 1943–1956* (London), 1957; *Advice to a Prophet and Other Poems*, 1961; *Walking to Sleep*, 1969.

For Children: *Loudmouse*, 1963.

Translations: *The Misanthrope* by Molière, 1955; *Tartuffe* by Molière, 1963.

Miscellaneous: *A Bestiary* (edited by Wilbur, illustrated by Alexander Calder), 1955; *Candide* (a comic operetta with Lillian Hellman and Leonard Bernstein, from the tale by Voltaire), 1957; *Poe: Complete Poems* (edited with an introduction by Wilbur), 1959; *Poems* by William Shakespeare (edited by Alfred Harbage), 1966.

COLLECTIONS

*The Poems of Richard Wilbur*, New York, 1963, is a paperback volume which reprints *The Beautiful Changes, Ceremony, Things of This World*, and *Advice to a Prophet*.

CRITICISM

The only book-length study is Donald L. Hill's *Richard Wilbur*, New York, 1967. Briefer estimates are F. C. Golffing, "A Remarkable New Talent," *Poetry*, LXXI (Jan., 1948), 221–223; Thomas Cole, "Wilbur's Second Volume," *Poetry*, LXXXII (Apr., 1953), 37–39; Donald Hall, "Claims on the Poet," *Poetry*, LXXXVIII (Sept., 1956), 398–403; R. W. Flint, "The Foolproof Style of American Poets," *Audience*, II (Nov. 18, 1955), 1–5; Theodore Holmes and William Meredith, "Wilbur's New Book: Two Views," *Poetry*, C (Apr., 1962), 37–40; Oscar Cargill, "Poetry since the Deluge," *EJ*, XLIII (Feb., 1954), 57–64; Francis W. Warlow, "Richard Wilbur," *BuR*, VII (1958), 217–233; Roger Asselineau, "Les fleurs de verre de Richard Wilbur," *Crit*, No. 161 (1961), pp. 843–848; Frederic E. Faverty, "Well-Open Eyes; or, The Poetry of Richard Wilbur," *Poets in Progress*, ed. Edward B. Hungerford, Evanston, Ill., 1962; John A. Myers, Jr., "Death in the Suburbs," *EJ*, LII (1963), 377–379; Richard Crowder, "Richard Wilbur and France," *Rives* (Paris), No. 25 (Spring, 1964), pp. 2–8; Richard Gustafson. "Richard Wilbur and the Beasts," *IEY*, No. 11 (1966), pp. 59–63; and Arthur E. McGuinness, "A Question of Consciousness: Richard Wilbur's *Things of This World*," *ArQ*, XXIII (1967), 313–326.

Wilbur talks about his own poetry in "On My Own Work," *Shen*, XVII (1965), 57–67. John P. Field compiled *Richard Wilbur: A Bibliographical Checklist*, Kent, Ohio, 1971.

# TENNESSEE (THOMAS LANIER) WILLIAMS
## *b. 1914*

SEPARATE WORKS

*Long Plays: *Battle of Angels* (1940), 1945; *The Glass Menagerie*, 1945; *You Touched Me!* (with Donald Windham) (1945), 1947; *A Streetcar Named Desire*, 1947; *Summer and Smoke*, 1948; *The Rose Tattoo*, 1951; *Camino Real*, 1953; *Cat on a Hot Tin Roof*, 1955; *Orpheus Descending* (1957), 1958; *Garden District: Something Unspoken* and *Suddenly Last Summer* (1958), London, 1959; *Sweet Bird of Youth*, 1959; *Period of Adjustment*, 1960; *The Night of the Iguana* (1961), 1962; *The Milk Train Doesn't Stop Here Anymore* (1963), 1964; *Slapstick Tragedy: The Mutilated and The Gnädiges Fräulein* (1966), 1967; *Kingdom on Earth (The Seven Descents of Myrtle)*, 1968; *In a Bar of a Tokyo Hotel*, 1969.

Short Plays: 27 *Wagons Full of Cotton and Other One-Act Plays*, 1946;

---

* Dates in parentheses are of the New York production when it differs from publication.

*American Blues: Five Short Plays*, 1948; *I Rise in Flames, Cried the Phoenix*, 1951; *Lord Byron's Love Letter* (libretto for a one-act opera by Raffaello de Banfield), 1955.

Screenplays: *The Glass Menagerie* (with Peter Berneis), 1950; *A Streetcar Named Desire* (with Oscar Saul), 1951; *The Rose Tattoo*, 1955; *Baby Doll*, 1956; *Suddenly Last Summer* (with Gore Vidal), 1959; *The Fugitive Kind* (with Meade Roberts), 1960.

Fiction: *One Arm and Other Stories*, 1948; *The Roman Spring of Mrs. Stone*, 1950; *Hard Candy: A Book of Stories*, 1954; *Three Players of a Summer Game and Other Stories*, London, 1960; *The Knightly Quest: A Novella and Four Short Stories*, 1967.

Poetry: *In the Winter of Cities*, 1956.

COLLECTIONS

New Directions published *Three Plays (The Rose Tattoo, Camino Real, and Sweet Bird of Youth)* in 1964. Secker and Warburg published, in London, *Four Plays (The Glass Menagerie, A Streetcar Named Desire, Summer and Smoke,* and *Camino Real)* in 1956, followed by *Five Plays (Cat on a Hot Tin Roof, The Rose Tattoo, Orpheus Descending, Garden District: Something Unspoken,* and *Suddenly Last Summer)*, 1962. *Dragon Country*, New York, 1970, is a collection of eight plays: *In the Bar of a Tokyo Hotel; I Rise in Flame, Cried the Phoenix; The Mutilated; I Can't Imagine Tomorrow; Confessional; The Frosted Glass Coffin; The Gnädiges Fräulein; A Perfect Analysis Given by a Parrot.*

*The Theatre of Tennessee Williams*, 3 vols., New York, 1971, is the first in a new series which will, in time, reprint Williams's plays.

BIOGRAPHY AND CRITICISM

In lieu of a full biography these volumes will have to serve: a family portrait by the playwright's mother, Edwina Dakin Williams (as told to Lucy Freeman), *Remember Me to Tom*, New York, 1963; a series of recollections by a Southern poet, Gilbert Maxwell, *Tennessee Williams and Friends*, Cleveland, Ohio, 1965; and a transcript of 24 interviews of actors, actresses, and directors who worked with Williams: Mike Steen, *A Look at Tennessee Williams*, New York, 1969. Supplementary biographical data can be found in Lincoln Barnett, "Tennessee Williams," *Life*, XXIV (Feb. 16, 1948), 113–114; John Gassner, "Tennessee Williams: Dramatist of Frustration," *CE*, X (Oct., 1948), 1–7; Paul Moor, "A Mississippian Named Tennessee," *Harper's*, CXCVII (July, 1948), 63–71; and R. C. Lewis, "A Playwright Named Tennessee," *NYTM* (Dec. 7, 1947), pp. 19, 67–70.

The best general introduction to Williams's work is Signi Lenea Falk, *Tennessee Williams*, New York, 1961. Nancy M. Trischler views Williams as a neo-Romantic and thus stresses biographical elements in *Tennessee Williams: Rebellious Puritan*, New York, 1961. Francis Donahue attempts "an interweaving of Williams' life and works" and the critical reaction to his plays in *The Dramatic World of Tennessee Williams*, New York, 1964. Esther M. Jackson, *The Broken World of Tennessee Williams*, Madison, Wis., 1965 is a critical exploration of form and ideas in the plays; Benjamin Nelson, *Tennessee Williams: The Man and His Work*, New York, 1961, is more comprehensive in scope. An early European estimate is Willy H. Thiem, *Tennessee Williams*, Düsseldorf, 1956. Gerald Weales, *Tennessee Williams*, Minneapolis, Minn., 1965, is a pamphlet. *Two Modern American Tragedies*, ed. John D. Hurrell, New York, 1961, is a collection of reviews and criticisms of *Death of a Salesman* and *A Streetcar Named Desire*.

Little serious criticism appeared before the mid-1950's. For early estimates see Irwin Shaw, "Theatre: Masterpiece," *NR*, CXVII (Dec. 22, 1947), 34–35; Alan S. Downer, "Mr. Williams and Mr. Miller," *Furioso*, IV (Summer, 1949), 66–70; Harry Taylor, "The Dilemma of Tennessee Williams," *MM*, I (Apr. 1948), 51–56; Kenneth Tynan, "American Blues: The Plays of Arthur Miller and Tennessee Williams," *Encounter* (London), II (May, 1954), 13–19; Robert Roth, "Tennessee Williams in Search of a Form," *ChiR*, IX (Summer, 1955), 86–94; C. N. Stavrou, "The Neurotic Heroine in Tennessee Williams," *L&P*, V (1955), 26–34; Arthur B. Waters, "Tennessee Williams: 10 Years Later," *TArts*, XXXIX (July, 1955), 72–73, 96; and Albert Gérard, "The Eagle and the Star, Symbolic Motifs in 'The Roman Spring of Mrs. Stone,'" *ES*, XXXVI (1955), 145–153.

Samplings from the next decade include Roger Asselineau, "Tennessee Williams ou la nostalgie de la pureté," *EA*, X (Oct.–Dec., 1957), 431–443; Peter Hall, "Tennessee Williams: Notes on the Moralist," *Encore*, IV (Sept.–Oct., 1957), 16–19; Richard B. Vowles, "Tennessee Williams: The World of His Imagery," *TDR*, III (Dec., 1958), 51–56; Charles Brooks, "The Comic Tennessee Williams," *QJS*, XLIV (1958), 275–281; Robert Brustein, "Williams' Nebulous Nightmare," *HudR*, XII (1959), 255–260; Paul G. Buchloh, "Verweisende Zeichen in Tennessee Williams: *Camino Real*," *Anglia*, LXXVII (1959), 173–203; Robert Emmet Jones, "Tennessee Williams' Early Heroines," *MD*, II (1959), 221–219; Horst Frenz and Ulrich Weisstein, "Tennessee Williams and His German Critics," *Sym*, XIV (1960), 258–275; Henry Popkin, "The Plays of Tennessee Williams," *TDR*, IV (1960), 45–64; K. M. Sagar, "What Mr. Williams Has Made of D. H. Lawrence," *TC*, CLXVIII (1960), 143–153; Arthur Ganz, "The

Desperate Morality of the Plays of Tennessee Williams," *ASch*, XXXI (1961), 278–294; William Sharp, "An Unfashionable View of Tennessee Williams," *TDR*, VI (1962), 160–171; John Buell, "The Evil Imagery of Tennessee Williams," *Thought*, XXXVIII (1963), 167–189; Joseph N. Riddel, "*A Streetcar Named Desire*—Nietzsche Descending," *MD*, V (1963), 421–430; William H. Peden, "Mad Pilgrimage: The Short Stories of Tennessee Williams," *SSF*, I (1964), 243–250; William M. Roulet, "*Sweet Bird of Youth*: Williams' Redemptive Ethic," *Cithera*, III (1964), 31–36; Roger B. Stein, "*The Glass Menagerie* Revisited: Catastrophe without Violence," *WHR*, XVIII (1964), 141–153; and Gastone Toschi, "La morbida e diabolica magia di Tennessee Williams," *Letture*, XIX (1964), 563–582.

More recent studies are Durant Da Ponte, "Tennessee Williams' Gallery of Feminine Characters," *TSL*, X (1965), 7–26; Robert B. Heilman, "Tennessee Williams: Approaches to Tragedy," *SoR*, I (1965), 770–790; Paul J. Hurley, "Tennessee Williams: The Playwright as Social Critic," *TA*, XXI (1964), 40–56; Marvin Spevack, "Tennessee Williams: The Idea of the Theater," *JA*, X (1965), 221–231; Gerald Weales, "Tennessee Williams's 'Lost' Play [*At Liberty*, pub. 1941]," *AL*, XXXVII (1965), 321–323; Gordon Rogoff, "The Restless Intelligence of Tennessee Williams," *TDR*, X (1966), 78–92; John Von Szeliski, "Tennessee Williams and the Tragedy of Sensitivity," *WHR*, XX (1966), 203–211; Paul J. Hurley, "*Suddenly Last Summer* as 'Morality Play,'" *MD*, VIII (1966), 392–402; William Sacksteder, "The Three Cats: A Study in Dramatic Structure," *DramS*, V (1967), 252–266; J. D. Hainsworth, "Tennessee Williams: Playwright on a Hot Tin Roof?" *EA*, XX (1968), 225–232; James L. Rowland, "Tennessee's Two Amandas," *RS*, XXXV (1968), 331–340; Leonard Quirino, "Tennessee Williams' Persistent *Battle of Angels*," *MD*, XI (1968), 27–39; Ferdinand Leon, "Time, Fantasy, and Reality in *Night of the Iguana*," *MD*, XI (1968), 87–96; and Tom S. Reck, "The First *Cat on a Hot Tin Roof*: Williams' 'Three Players,'" *UR*, XXXIV (1968), 187–192.

BIBLIOGRAPHY

In addition to the descriptive bibliography appended to Signi Falk's *Tennessee Williams*, cited above, see Nadine Dony, "Tennessee Williams: A Selected Bibliography," *MD*, I (1958), 181–191; and Charles A. Carpenter, Jr., and Elizabeth Cook, "Addenda to 'Tennessee Williams: A Selected Bibliography,'" *MD*, II (1959), 220–223. The Dony–Carpenter–Cook listings are invaluable for reviews of individual plays.

# INDEX

This index includes names of authors and editors of books; titles of journals, collections, and vital compilations; and numerous general entries such as "Radio," "Censorship," "Transcendentalism," and "Negro culture." Because of their great number, the names of authors of articles have had to be omitted.

For each author who is given an individual bibliography, the main entry is italicized. These authors are indicated by an asterisk before the surname.

Cox, Palmer, 227
Cox, Ross, 265
Cox, Sidney, 521, 921
Coxe, Louis O., 959, 1284
Coyle, Lee, 1140
Coyner, David H., 267
Cozzens, Frederick Swartwout, 206, 536
*Cozzens, James Gould, *1016, 1329*
Cracker-box philosophers, 205–208, 842
*"Craddock, Charles Egbert" (Mary Noailles
    Murfree), 312, *667–668, 1266*
Craig, Hardin, 691, 1275, 1318
Craigie, Pearl ("John Oliver Hobbes"), 136
Craigie, Sir William, 188, 189
Craigie House, 129
Crallé, Richard K., 343, 434, 1159
Cranch, Christopher Pearse, 113, 226, 346
*Crane, Hart, 53, 65, 66, 156, 170, *457–458,
    893–894,* 1045, 1075, *1170–1172,* 1311
Crane, R. S., 807
*Crane, Stephen, 62, 65, 131, 134, 322, 329,
    458–459, 894–896,* 1070, *1172–1174*
Crane, Verner W., 260, 280, 511, 723, 917,
    918
Crankshaw, Edward, 1346
Crapsey, Adelaide, 155
Craven, Avery O., 600, 816, 1068
Craven, Wayne, 1103
Craven, Wesley Frank, 813, 814, 1063
Crawford, Bartholow V., 68, 743, 746
Crawford, Francis Marion, 332, 361–362
Crawford, William Rex, 370
Crawley, Thomas Edwards, 1311
Creeger, George R., 1346
Creel, George, 780
Creighton, Thomas H., 835
Cremin, Lawrence A., 1095
Creoles in literature, 294–296, 314–315
Crerar Library, John (Chicago), 11
Cresmer Collection (University of Southern
    California), 621
Cresson, Margaret, 835
*Crèvecoeur, St. Jean de, 87, 339, *461–462,
    896,* 1063, *1174–1175*
Crews, Frederick C., 940, 1216
Cribbs, George A., 276
Crichton, Kyle, 297
Crick, Bernard R., 1041
*Crick Bottom Plays,* 317
Cridge, Alfred D., 351
Crinò, Anna Maria, 1155
*Critical Dictionary of English Literature,* 27–
    28
Critical movements, twentieth century, 52–
    69, 807–810, 1053–1061
*Critical Quarterly,* 1058
*Criticism,* 1058
Criticism, magazines of, 62–64, 809–810,
    1058–1059
*Critique: Studies in Modern Fiction,* 1335,
    1364
Crittenden, Christopher, 16

*Croakers,* 109
Croce, Benedetto, 57
Croce, George C., 1102
Crocker, Hannah Mather, 122
Crocker, Lionel G., 400
Crockett, David, 193, 202, 203, 240, 841
Croly, David G., 328
Croly, Herbert, 62
Cronau, Rudolf, 287, 293
Crone, G. R., 1063
Cronin, Thomas E., 1086
Cronon, E. David, 1318
Cronyn, George W., 214
Crosby, Fanny Jane, 233
Cross, Arthur L., 76
Cross, Harold L., 822
Cross, Marion E., 250
Cross, Robert D., 829, 1094
Cross, Tom P., 16, 798
Cross, Wilbur L., 62
Crosser, Paul K., 898
Crothers, Rachel, 160
Crothers, Samuel McChord, 165
Croushore, James H., 897
Crowder, Richard, 978, 1287, 1315
Crowe, Charles, 1131
Crowther, Bosley, 836
Crozer Theological Seminary, 7
Crozier, Alice C., 1299
Crozier, Eric, 959
Cruickshank, Helen Gere, 1147
Crum, Mason, 198
Cruse, Amy, 367
Cruse, Harold, 1091
Cubberley, Ellwood P., 180
Culbertson, William S., 538
Cullen, Countee, 156
Cullen, John B., 1197
Cultural centers, 112, 124–125, 154, 172,
    304–325 *passim*
Cultural history. *See* Literary and cultural
    history
Cultural islands. *See* Mingling of tongues
*Cummings, E. E., 66, 149, 156, *462–463,
    896–897, 1175–1176*
Cummings, Paul, 1103
Cummins, Maria Susanna, 220
Cummins, Sarah J., 263
*Cumulative Book Index,* 22, 797
*Cumulative Catalog of Books Represented by
    Library of Congress Printed Cards,* 4
Cuney-Hare, Maude, 183
Cunliffe, Marcus, 809, 995, 1065, 1307
Cunningham, Charles E., 480
Cunningham, N. E., 1241
Cunningham, Scott, 1028
Cunningham, Virginia, 904
Cunz, Dieter, 853
Curme, George O., 190
Current, Richard N., 951, 996, 1159, 1246,
    1248
*Current Biography,* 27